D1270733

WORLD LITERATURE

An Anthology of Human Experience

World Literature

AN ANTHOLOGY OF HUMAN EXPERIENCE

EDITED BY

ARTHUR E. CHRISTY, late of University of Illinois

HENRY W. WELLS, Columbia University

NEW YORK AMERICAN BOOK COMPANY CHICAGO

BOSTON ATLANTA DALLAS CINCINNATI SAN FRANCISCO

E. P. 1

CHRISTY AND WELLS: WORLD LITERATURE

MADE IN U. S. A.

Introduction

Our world today presents urgent problems in living which every thinking man must recognize. The earth shrinks, because of our scientific conquest of distance; but the individual's world is paradoxically thereby enlarged. The vastness of our new environment bewilders us. All parts of the world, human and geographical, have been brought together. As never before, consequently, life demands that education shall prepare men to understand that they are members of the human race. We urgently need maps of the mind to supplement and interpret our maps of the globe, if ever we are to orient ourselves and feel at home in the new environment in which our generation must live and work out its destiny.

In the new world outlook which has been forced upon us the old virtues of patriotism and love of country have in no way been weakened. The lesson of American history demonstrates indeed that catholicity of mind may be the chief source of cultural health in our commonwealth. The founders of the nation were themselves among the most cosmopolitan men of their time. Franklin was truly a citizen of the world. And Jefferson drew from overseas suggestions for the American constitutional system and ideas for the conduct of our national life which he turned to such account that the entire world of our day is his heir. Indeed the author of the Declaration of Independence possessed perhaps the most cosmopolitan mind that our country had yet produced. It was wide knowledge of the world which enabled him to serve his generation well. The subsequent nineteenth century saw the rise of nationalisms which laid the foundations of world wars. It is now the task of the twentieth century to realize anew the common bonds of humanity. The nations most cosmopolitan in spirit and in knowledge will be the leaders of the new age.

Really to understand the peoples of other lands it is necessary to know their past as well as their present, their traditions as well as their aspirations. We must understand wherein their values are grounded. Over four hundred years ago a great materialistic movement, personified by Columbus, Magellan and da Gama, opened up the whole world to the white races. Today a far greater civilizing movement must open up the nations of the world to one another, binding together those whom brutal conquest and greed once contracted chiefly to make foes. We are clearly destined to a greatly accelerated era of internationalism in trade, art and literature. We shall come to realize more clearly than ever before that our civilization has always been composite—a growth fertilized from many lands and races—and that in future it is certain by greatly accelerated degrees to become even more a synthesis

These conditions, the common and elementary knowledge of our own day, hav strong significance for all branches of thought and education, and nowhere m clearly than in the humanities. They mean that we must seriously revise our p of view, our school and college courses, and the text books on which they are b

The first and inevitable conclusion is that every citizen, no matter how private and humble a life he may lead, should be better informed about foreign lands and peoples. Thus far only advanced students of foreign languages have attained intimate contacts with foreign cultures. But not all our students have studied languages and few students indeed have really mastered more than two or three, one of which is likely enough to be an obsolete language. A smattering of French or German certainly does not make a man a citizen of the world. Moreover the study of languages in recent years has often been conducted in a spirit more favorable to the growth of a narrow nationalism than a catholic world outlook, since our language texts have commonly been treated as veiled propaganda for their respective lands. Much of the material presented under the heading of philosophy remains so abstract that it possesses little value for interpreting neighboring cultures, while elementary history and geography, though more concrete, can hardly give us the intimate knowledge of a people's mind which literature affords. More and more the study of World Literature is being called upon to afford the needed aid.

These facts are not entirely new to educators. For more than a decade American scholars and teachers have slowly but steadily explored the problem and prepared useful texts. Their intentions have been admirable. Occasionally, however, their techniques have been distinctly awkward, for they were based on traditional approaches to literature and nationalistic outlooks which are manifestly inadequate for the task of interpreting today's world to the student and of integrating its life. The result has been the wide-spread impression that all surveys of world literature are necessarily superficial and that there can be in it no discipline which will develop the desired sharpness of intellectual analysis and sympathetic insight. It becomes increasingly apparent, however, that the dangers of superficiality are not inherent in the material, but in the handling and focus of attention. There is enough in the subject, when properly pursued, to hold the interest of the best students and to test both the mettle and scholarship of the most competent teachers.

In the republic of letters there is happily room for honest differences of opinion. Statements containing forthright and challenging views should be regarded purely as sincere efforts to develop an educational program so urgently needed rather than invidious reflections on the methods of anthologists who blazed the first trails. To this end, then, the editors of this book may appropriately state that in their view the organization of materials for the study of world literature according to nationalistic and linguistic classifications disunites mankind. Indeed the nationalistic emphasis clearly leads to partiality and invidious comparisons. Furthermore, no scholar or well-informed teacher would today presume to suggest that samples can ever hope to represent adequately a national literature. For the student to read in one section a mere handful of Italian or French or German authors, with the selections representing all manner of subject matter and historical periods, is to bewilder him and to arouse a deeper conviction of the inexplicability of the world. The significance of nationalism itself is grossly exaggerated, while its secrets remain unexplored. Such an arrangement of materials vitiates the essential purpose of the study of world literature. That it is mainly the result of traditional nationalistic self-glorification and criticism of one's own art and history is manifest. That it can continue to serve the purpose of true education, except in very intensive study of a single literature, may be honestly doubted.

A second method of organizing materials for study is that of arrangement on a chronological basis. To the average student nothing is likely to be more wholly artificial than the concept of historical time, inevitably remote from his personal experience. The young reader is generally first introduced to the Greeks. He then marches bravely on Rome, digresses briefly to the East, stumbles through the Dark Ages, is led through the forbidding abstractions of, say, the Renaissance, the Enlightenment, the Romantic Age, and the so-called Age of Realism. The historical implications are presumably as superficial to the teacher as they are wholly unreal to the student. Both have met Frenchmen, Germans, Italians, and Japanese. They have never seen on the street "The Medieval Man," "The Renaissance Man," or "The Realistic Man," nor any other allegorical personification of our ingenious social philosophers. While one may argue that Plato, Buddha, and Christ, Wordsworth, Keats, and Emerson were all romantics, it can readily be seen that conventional chronological labels are often inapplicable to their work and thought. Great spirits and books cannot be confined in pigeonholes. The truth is that all literary movements result from states of mind, and that except for differences of idiom made by time and place these states of mind are shared by countless writers representing all great literatures. Idealists and realists, naturalists and romanticists, in their essential character, have not been restricted chronologically or geographically in human history.

Thirdly, an organization which focuses the student's attention upon literary types and forms results in emphasis upon the mere techniques of literature. Few students are literary craftsmen or artisans. They may of course with great profit study the sonnet, the ballade, the essay, and the short story, if they are interested in literary *genres* for their own sake. But great books viewed in such a fashion very rarely reveal to the student the true world of thought and human experience of which they are a part. The veil of literary artifice conceals. The specialist in Comparative Literature whose interest is mainly in literary genealogy will discover significance in the relation between *genres,* but such meanings are recherché and almost certainly obscure to the average teacher. In any event, the prestige which the study of literary *genres* enjoyed shortly before the beginning of the present century has steadily diminished since a generation ago it was undermined by the trenchant criticism of the wise and democratic thinker, Benedetto Croce.

If a new approach to the study of World Literature is thus needed, it may be discovered through a constructively meaningful account of humanity. The approaches of the past have resulted in anthologies which contain a series of little masterpieces, each independent of the other and each truly worthy of admiration, but in which the underlying ideas remain unrelated to the context of human experience, and consequently isolated or superficial. It is profitable no doubt to allow a series of masterpieces to pass before the eye of the student. But when coals are scattered they never really take fire. In a scientific sense the study of Comparative Literature may simply be defined as the study of the innovation, continuity, and interrelations of literary thought. Nevertheless, however scientific may occasionally be its methods, Comparative Literature is also the most humane of all the studies which reveal what men all instinctively feel. At its best the emphasis will be on our common humanity.

The aims of the present anthology may therefore be briefly stated as follows. Earlier books in any way resembling it are best described as collections of World Literature. Although the principles of Comparative Literature may occasionally have been approached in these compilations, the editors of the present book believe it to be the first volume of the sort firmly grounded in the basic conceptions of Comparative Literature. The originality of the book is to be seen in its arrangement, which is in turn the direct consequence of the feeling and the ideal which lies behind it.

The sections into which our book is divided present, then, in rapid outline the literary record of some of the most persistent aspects of man's life. We see in turn how successive peoples, from the earliest to the latest times, and in Asia no less than in Europe and America, have grappled with their common problems. Similarities in aspirations and difficulties are emphasized rather than dissimilarities; and the general purpose of the selections is to bring all issues clearly to the door of present-day America. They show definitely and specifically how the present is impelled by the past, how the past pours itself into the present, how all lands and ages experience life as one joy and sorrow, and how America is in our modern, sharply contracted world a part of the tragically precarious brotherhood of mankind. In short, we present not only specimens of art but clear currents of life. The masterpieces are clarified by their settings, each in a vital relation to its neighbors. We offer not a ponderous miscellany but a text that invites continuous reading and lively discussion on the part of either student or teacher. Each section contains a fairly large number of items from a number of languages. Each begins as far back as reasonably possible: often in Asia, sometimes well before Christ; each comes forward as far as it can practicably go, usually to the twentieth century and to both modern England and, in particular, modern America. Here in close proximity and to much the same purpose may be read utterances by Chinese, Japanese, Hindus, Persians, Arabians, Greeks, Romans, Spaniards, Italians, Frenchmen, Germans, Dutchmen, Norwegians, Swedes, Russians, South Americans, Australians, Englishmen and North Americans. The book does not divide these many voices; it unites them. They speak again and again of the same themes, even while they also bear instructive marks of their race and time. So their voices are translated not only into a language but into a meaning which the student can understand. The tendency of the themes to repeat themselves, as in a musical composition, makes the whole more interesting and intelligible. The reader perceives the authors and races as learning from one another and laboring towards the solution of the same problems of living. Although he reads works from approximately forty nations and thirty different languages, — an exceptionally wide scope to be represented in any anthology, — he is at the same time examining the roots of our American civilization, derived from all parts of the globe. The general plan prevents confusion, even amidst the multiplicity of riches.

Furthermore, not only is each section systematically ordered, but the arrangement of the sections in relation to one another is carefully planned. The first few sections deal with man's physical, intellectual and spiritual relations to nature and with his religions. Following these sections on cosmology, science and religion, are those on national or public life. These in turn are succeeded by groups of selections illustrating various phases of his more personal or intimate spiritual life, as well as his relations to family and friends and his enjoyment of the fine arts and homely pleasures. Finally, an epilogue deals with his far visions into the future of human society and that confident hope of human betterment by which alone we are buoyed up and inspired to our best endeavors and accomplishments. In keeping with the spirit of the book, both verse and prose are represented. Even though poetry loses most in translation, it wins an important claim upon any anthology because of its superior succinctness of expression. The poetry and prose are not, however, made two separate parts of the book, since this division would violate the humanistic purpose which the book aims to serve. To avoid harshness of contrast and aid in the smooth enjoyment of the whole, the sections themselves have for the most part been separately arranged and devoted wholly to either poetry or prose. The two forms are thus carefully interspersed throughout all parts, affording a balanced ration. Moreover, as will readily be seen, there are certain themes and attitudes presented more naturally in verse and others in prose.

The book is of course not designed to do anyone's thinking for him; it is intended to offer every legitimate aid which within one cover can be gathered towards a rational and sympathetic understanding of the community of mankind. With selections from hundreds of books and authors, it opens before the reader the panorama of world literature in explanatory perspective. Each group of selections is preceded by a commentary noting the lines of continuity between the individual selections; extended exploratory reading is suggested in the Index of Authors. In one sense the book is ambitious, for it undertakes a survey seldom equalled in scope. In another it is offered in all modesty, for it is clearly only a preface or introduction to the world we inhabit: a beginning wherein every reader may find sharp stimulus for more detailed explorations. It affords a map of the world, necessarily drawn on a small scale. Its careful reader may, however, truthfully say not only, "Much have I travelled in the realms of gold," but, "In relatively small compass I have perceived the bases of the civilization of America, some outstanding characteristics of the varied civilizations of the globe, and, above all, good evidence of their unity and our common humanity." The editors of this book claim it to be the first anthology systematically grounded on the principles of Comparative Literature. We offer a text which, we believe, is conceived from a very practical and realistic point of view as a useful tool for a kind of education in the humanities so urgently required at the present time.

II

A book of this nature inevitably calls to mind certain possible objections as to the choice of particular selections, translations and subject matter. Both the working out of details and the precise nature of the general scope and plan are subject to much debate, and the editors may fairly be expected to offer some brief argument in favor of the decisions which they have made. Even granting the aim and philosophy of such a book to be sound, there is always the question of its execution.

Any anthology must, of course, always anticipate the charge of presumption. It has been said that choosing what one likes is as personal as poking one's fire; no one else can do it so well. To criticism based on individual preference instead of a judicious consideration of the purpose of a book there is no answer. We are confident, however, that careful consideration of the titles grouped in the individual sections which follow and recognition of the stern limitations of available space will indicate that neither whimsical arbitrariness nor a desire to inject writing which we personally like has determined the content of this book. Some readers may feel that their favorite authors have been left out of the pages which follow, or that inferior pieces have been included which would not deserve space in a book ten times as extensive.

We would remind them simply that our purpose has been to present a source book of readings which will be useful to all serious individuals who would discover for themselves the basic ideas in many of the world's greatest cultural heritages, and also to introduce them to their neighbors' ancestral gods, the things which they admire or which provoke them to scorn and laughter, their love of beauty and justice, their social ideals and moral values, their bent toward intellectual adventure and imaginative creation, and their courage in handling good fortune and tragic reverses. To suggest man's best traits is, we believe, to arouse in the reader a sense of kinship in human experience with other peoples. Manifestly such a purpose is quite different from presuming to say that our selections represent all that is best and timeless in the world's treasure-house of literature. We are confident that our selections will nevertheless disclose to readers many of the great classics and writers of foreign literatures who in future years may be a joy to them.

The problem of the use of translations is a vexing one. The world is full of great books which are best read in entirety and in the original languages. This fact is freely acknowledged. But few readers command the languages required, and fewer still have resources from which to select the great classics of the world's literature for study and comparison. Furthermore to select judiciously and to read both widely and wisely is a task hardly accomplished without introductory guidance and aid. It is folly to argue that a translation is as good as the original. But a needed perspective on the usefulness of translations will be obtained if one considers the centuries-old debt of western civilization to translations of the Bible, of Homer and Virgil, of Dante and Plutarch. However one may argue for the need of studying original texts (and the editors of this book heartily agree upon the ultimate necessity), those who are generous will not deprive the uninitiated or the unlearned in many languages of the pleasure that comes from reading for the first time in translations the Arabian Nights or Don Quixote, Omar Khayyám or Froissart, the Odyssey, Plato, the New Testament, Confucius, or Goethe, to mention but a few. Consider also the list of major writers in English and American literature alone who have drawn inspiration from great foreign books in translation. Chaucer, Spenser, and Shakespeare were among them, as also were Thomas Gray, and William Morris, Whitman and Thoreau and Emerson, and John Keats, who revelled in Chapman's Homer and enriched the literature of his own times as a result. No true scholar, we repeat, would fail to encourage in a reader respect for foreign languages. On the other hand, there are translations which although not technically flawless, are matchless pieces of literature. The Authorized Version of the Bible is an excellent example. Learned revisers have spent years of labor in correcting its errors, but they have yet to improve on it as a masterpiece of literature. Many translations may be mere approximations of the original, but they are entirely adequate to the task of conveying from one generation to another, and from one people to another, the essential experiences of the race.

The principle of selection which the editors have used can best be suggested in the words of Jean Jaurés: "Take from the altar of the past the fire, not the ashes." There are certain books upon which whole literatures have been based. There are systems of thought and religion which have conditioned the attitudes of men toward life and experience common to all men, and others which seem alien to us but which appear timeless to other peoples. All these we have sought to represent in this book.

In the academic world, departmental isolationism and narrowly technical training have only too clearly bred their own peculiar evils. A happy balance must be sought between the training which produces "uneducated specialists" and the universal survey of knowledge which leads to superficiality and ineffectualness. Whatever may be the discipline ultimately agreed upon, its essential trait must be the realization that provincialism is not determined by geography alone. As we have already seen, the leaders of our country at the birth of the Republic eloquently illustrate this truth. All scholars will agree that a little knowledge is a dangerous thing. But it may quite as appropriately be said that in the education of Americans for cultural intercourse with other peoples in the world a little knowledge is preferable to none at all. It can manifestly be increased among serious readers who have discovered for the first time that there are relations and parallels between their own heritage and the heritages of their foreign neighbors. The interdependence of all departments of individual and social life at home should lead to honest recognition of the interdependence of all branches of the human family.

For these reasons this book is not limited to *belles lettres*. No intelligent person would deny his debt to the scientific developments which provide him with creature comforts or to the medical knowledge which assuages pain and saves life. Similarly, to realize that both individual and national security depend on the smooth ordering of international life is to recognize that social scientists are partners in laying the foundations of the world in which the human spirit may most effectively achieve its fullest creative possibilities. We have therefore included in this book a number of the classics of scientific and social literature which reveal man's fortitude in the extension of knowledge about his world and his courage in the search for the good life. These, no less than fiction or poetry, represent man's creative instinct.

Emerson reminded his generation in *The American Scholar* that one must "take the whole society to find the whole man;" that man is not only "a farmer, a professor, or an engineer," but also "priest, and scholar, and statesman, and soldier." More recently the field of human learning has been likened by a contemporary American scholar to three concentric circles. The outer circle may represent the natural and physical sciences, both pure and applied. The intermediate circle may represent the social sciences; and the innermost the humanities, with all that they involve of the most highly personal aspects of human life. Man, within the triple circle of his life, is affected by them all; and he in turn should comprehend all. A too specialized knowledge may not only wither but fester and become poisonous to itself and to all surrounding itself. As a man shares the good of his fellows, whether in science, politics or the arts, he also shares their evil. The interdependence of all sorts and conditions of men, both at home and abroad, becomes increasingly apparent. The admonition of Isaiah to extend the cords of one's tent and to strengthen one's stakes contains no inherent contradiction when applied to humanistic education.

III

Having stated what we sincerely believe to be the need for our book, summarized its general plan, and defended some of the editorial policies followed in its pages, it remains to reemphasize in a few words its educational philosophy. The book has been compiled in the earnest conviction that one of the chief tasks of modern education is the development of an appreciative understanding of the common denominators of human experiences in all parts of the world. Under insistent pressure of international politics and the havoc of war, men have come to realize the economic interdependence of disparate and hitherto widely separated peoples. They are slower, however, to learn that the world is in truth round and to discover that their sympathies are flat. They rarely bend their thought to the human problems of peoples on the other side of the earth. And yet only so will they find peace in which to discover fully "the things that are not Caesar's" and the beauties and insights preserved in the great civilizing heritages of humankind.

It is imperative that in our day renewed and conscious effort be directed toward the development of intercultural understanding. If, in the words of an eminent statesman, our world soon "will be a village street from Edinburgh to Chungking," the task becomes a moral responsibility. Whatever else democracy may be, it is ultimately a way of living for mature and civilized men based on respect for others and a conception of human experience rooted deep in the yearnings of many races and peoples. No truly democratic education can therefore hope to meet the needs of our time if limited to a single cultural tradition. Such an education is obsolete.

Indeed the development of genuinely catholic human sympathies and of an international outlook are ultimately inseparable in any plan for democratic education. On every hand there is recognition that the educational tasks confronting us are complex and difficult. Difficulties, however, are never an excuse for shirking tasks which must be undertaken. They are, rather, challenges to educational statesmanship and to all men whose minds are not dulled by the dust of routine. "It is provided in the very essence of things," wrote Walt Whitman, "that from any fruition of success, no matter what, shall come forth something to make a greater struggle necessary." The advances made in the development of the democratic spirit among individual peoples must now be extended into the society of nations.

Many of the social evils of our times arise from prejudice. This prejudice is largely based on ignorance. And it is clear that ignorance itself must first be removed before trouble-making prejudices can be erased. To urge a broader understanding of the humanity of our fellow men is not to urge indiscriminate appropriation or a forsaking of ancestral heritages for a vague eclecticism. In any comprehensive consideration of the evils of economic jealousy among nations of the world, it is well to remember other allied sources of misunderstanding and conflict. Statesmen attempt to create an international economy through which all men may secure the needed bread that the earth provides. In the long view, however, men need even more the spirit of generosity and forgiveness which earth's seasons seldom fail to show. Without it no bread is sweet and all statecraft impotent.

Through the wide door of world literature we may approach an understanding of the unity of the human spirit which transcends boundaries of geography and race. A lifetime is, of course, all too short for exploring and mastering all that is worth knowing about the world's great literatures, the dignity of the human spirit which they reveal, and the rich heritage in which all men may share. It is our hope that this book will start some readers on their way. The study which may begin in a classroom should lead in after years to rich worlds of private thought and pleasure. But no less will it be a preparation for that generosity of mind and magnanimity of spirit which are the foundations of democracy itself, of international goodwill and of the hope of human progress.

A. E. C. and H. W. W.

Contents

INTRODUCTION v

PART ONE: MAN AND HIS CULTURAL HERITAGES 3

On Books . . . . *Kaibara Ekken* 5
Japanese Poetry . . . . *Ki no Tsurayuki* 5
Books Which Have Influenced Me . . . *Robert Louis Stevenson* 8
Literature as Revelation . . . . . . *Gilbert Murray* 11
The Provinces of the Several Arts . . . . *John Addington Symonds* . . . 17
The History of Literature . . . . . . *Hippolyte Taine* 23
Future and Past . . . . *José Enrique Rodó* 30

PART TWO: GENESES: THE ORIGINS OF MAN AND LIFE 35

The Protagoras Myth . . . . *Plato* 36
The Universal Self . . . . *from the Upanishads* 37
Genesis: The Creation . . . . *from the Old Testament* 39
The Prose Edda . . . . *Snorri Sturluson* 42
The Walam Olum . . . . *a Lenape Legend* 48
The Sun Goddess and the Mikado . . . . *Japanese* 52

PART THREE: THE PEOPLE'S STORY 57

Gilgamesh . . . . *from Babylonian tablets* 60
The Quarrel . . . . *from Homer's Iliad* 63
The Death of Turnus . . . . *from Virgil's Aeneid* 68
The Death of Roland . . . . *from the Song of Roland* 71
The Fall of Siegfried . . . . *from the Song of the Nibelungs* . . 74
Passage to India . . . . *from the Lusiad, Luis Vaz de Camoëns* 77
The Fallen Angels . . . . *from Paradise Lost, John Milton* . . 80
John Brown . . . . *from John Brown's Body, Stephen Vincent Benét* 84

PART FOUR: MYTHS, FABLES, AND ALLIED FORMS 91

The Ass in the Lion's Skin . . . . . *from the Jātaka Collections* . . . 92
The Dove and the Crow . . . . . . *from the Panchatantra* 92
The Jackal . . . . *from the Hitopadesa* 94
The Country Mouse and the Town Mouse . *Aesop* 95
The Shipwreck of Simonides . . . . . *Phædrus* 95
The Star Family, or Celestial Sisters . . . *a Shawnee legend* 96
Brother Rabbit's Money Mint . . . . . *Joel Chandler Harris* 97
The Just Hare . . . . *Adolf Dygasiński* 99
Chinese Cinderella . . . . *(legendary)* 10

Title	Author	Page
The Young Ravens That Call upon Him	*Charles G. D. Roberts*	104
Mujo the Drunkard	*Vuk Karadžić*	105
The Father	*Björnstjerne Björnson*	106
Children and Old People	*Ivan Cankar*	108
The Quest Begins	*Frederik Willem van Eeden*	109
PART FIVE: SCRIPTURES OF SOME LIVING RELIGIONS		115
1. BRAHMANISM AND BUDDHISM		
The Story of Svetaketu	*Chandogya Upanishad*	116
The Eternal Self	*Bhagavad Gita*	119
The Great Retirement	*Jātaka*	124
The Attainment of Buddhaship	*Jātaka*	126
Questions Which Tend Not to Edification	*Buddha*	129
The Middle Doctrine	*Samyutta-Nikāya*	131
2. CONFUCIANISM AND TAOISM		
The Doctrine of the Mean	*Confucius*	132
The Philosophy of Chuang-Tze: The Infinite	*Chuang-Tze*	138
3. JUDAISM AND CHRISTIANITY		
Psalms of David	*Old Testament*	142
Isaiah	*Old Testament*	145
Some Sayings and Discourses of Jesus	*New Testament*	146
Spiritual Gifts	*St. Paul, New Testament*	153
4. MOHAMMEDANISM		
The Teaching of Mohammed	*from the Koran*	154
The Forty-Two Traditions	*An-Nawawi*	159
PART SIX: CREATIVE IMAGINATION		165
Facing Death	*Chih Ming*	168
The Morning Bell of Fang T'a	*Hsi P'ei Lan*	168
Three with the Moon and His Shadow	*Li Po*	168
Business Men	*Ch'ēn Tzu-ang*	168
The Wake	*Tsurayuki*	168
The Bewildered Arab	*Jami*	168
Hymn to the Sun	*Ikhnaton*	169
Canticle of the Sun	*St. Francis of Assisi*	170
The Night Serene	*Luis De León*	170
"What Becomes of a Strain of Music"	*Juan Ramón Jiménez*	171
Domestic Scenes	*Miguel de Unamuno*	172
Twelve by the Clock	*Jorge Guillen*	172
The Perfect Life	*Jorge Carrera Andrade*	172
The Infinite	*Giacomo Leopardi*	173
Prometheus	*Johann Wolfgang von Goethe*	173
Song of Fate	*Friedrich Hölderlin*	173
[illegible]lent Hour	*Rainer Maria Rilke*	174
[illegible]his Station	*Johannes V. Jensen*	174
[illegible]	*Joachim du Bellay*	175
[illegible]	*Charles Baudelaire*	175
[illegible]	*Emile Verhaeren*	176
[illegible]	*Fyodor Tyutchev*	177
[illegible]angueo	*Anon., English*	177

A Hymn to Christ at the Author's Last Going into Germany . . . . *John Donne* 178
The World . . . . *Henry Vaughan* 178
A Drop of Dew . . . . *Andrew Marvell* . . . 179
A Song to David . . . . *Christopher Smart* 180
The Tiger . . . . *William Blake* 182
Song from Milton . . . . *Blake* 182
Auguries of Innocence . . . . . . *Blake* 182
Intimations of Immortality from Recollections of Early Childhood . . . . . . *William Wordsworth* . . . 184
The Child in Our Soul . . . . . . *Björnstjerne Björnson* . . . 186
The Kingdom of God . . . . . . *Francis Thompson* 186
The Starlit Night . . . . *Gerard Manley Hopkins* . . . 187
Stella Flammarum (To Halley's Comet) . . *William Wilfred Campbell* . . . 187
When I Heard the Learn'd Astronomer . . *Walt Whitman* 188
Brahma . . . . *Ralph Waldo Emerson* . . . 188
Hamatreya . . . . *Emerson* 188
"All Things Are Current Found" . . . . *Henry David Thoreau* . . . 189
"Behind Me Dips Eternity" . . . . . *Emily Dickinson* 189
You, Andrew Marvell . . . . . . *Archibald MacLeish* . . . 189
Morning Song from "Senlin" . . . . *Conrad Aiken* 190
Peter Quince at the Clavier . . . . . *Wallace Stevens* 191

PART SEVEN: THE UNFOLDING UNIVERSE 193

The Medieval Christian World . . . . *Cosmas Indicopleustes* . . . 195
The Revolutions of the Celestial Spheres . *Copernicus* 200
The Method of Inductive Science . . . . *Francis Bacon* 208
Observations of Animalculae . . . . *Anthony Van Leeuwenhoek* . . 210
The Sex of Plants . . . . *Linnaeus* 214
The Theory of Evolution . . . . . . *Charles Darwin* 217
Inoculation for Hydrophobia . . . . *Louis Pasteur* 224
The Exploration of Space . . . . . *Edwin Hubble* 229

PART EIGHT: TRAVEL AND EXPLORATION 235

The Travels of Marco Polo 236
Diary of a Pilgrim to Ise . . . . . *Saka* 248
The Spaniards in Mexico . . . . . *Bernal Díaz del Castillo* . . 251
A Tour in Lapland . . . . *Linnaeus* 256
Around the Horn . . . . *Richard Henry Dana, Jr.* . . . 260
The Last March . . . . *Robert Falcon Scott* . . . 266
The Road to the West . . . . . . *Langdon Warner* 272
On the Way to Myself . . . . . . *Marcus Ehrenpreis* . . . 276

PART NINE: SOCIAL SATIRE 279

Satire on Paying Calls . . . . . . *Ch'eng Hsiao* 282
Woman . . . . *Fu Hsüan* 283
The Syracusan Women . . . . . . *Theocritus* 283
Journey to Brundusium . . . . . . *Horace* 285
The Bold Satirist . . . . *Horace* 287
The Town and the Country Mouse . . . *Horace* 288
Unchanged . . . . *Martial* 290
The Tenth Satire . . . . *Juvenal* 290

The Romance of the Rose . . . . *Jean de Meun* 293
The Lesser Testament . . . . . . *Villon* 294
Two Confessions . . . . *William Langland* 296
Prologue to the Canterbury Tales . . . . *Geoffrey Chaucer* 297
Avarice . . . . *Luis de León* 300
Babylon and Sion (Goa and Lisbon) . . . *Luis Vaz de Camoëns* . . . 300
Letrilla: the Lord of Dollars . . . . . *Francisco de Quevedo y Villegas* 301
The Departed Friend . . . . *Salvador Novo* 301
Relations . . . . *Alessandro Tassoni* 302
Friar Lubin . . . . *Clément Marot* 302
The Boy and the Schoolmaster . . . . . *Jean de La Fontaine* . . . 302
The Oyster and the Litigants . . . . . *La Fontaine* 303
The Cockerel, the Cat, and the Young Mouse *La Fontaine* 303
Dawn . . . . *Charles Baudelaire* 304
Waifs and Strays . . . . *Arthur Rimbaud* 304
The Fishermen . . . . *Emile Verhaeren* 305
Anno 1829 . . . . *Heinrich Heine* 306
A Thought . . . . *Mikhail Yuryevich Lermontov* 306
Russia . . . . *Alexander Blok* 306
The Lie . . . . *Sir Walter Raleigh* 307
Epistle to Dr. Arbuthnot . . . . . . *Alexander Pope* 307
On the Death of Dr. Swift . . . . . . *Jonathan Swift* 310
A Journey to Exeter . . . . *John Gay* 311
London . . . . *William Blake* 312
To a Louse . . . . *Robert Burns* 313
Up at a Villa — Down in the City . . . *Robert Browning* 313
Recitation and Song . . . . *from "Patience," W. S. Gilbert* 315
Sabbath-Day Chace . . . . *Philip Freneau* 315
Ode to Channing . . . . *Ralph Waldo Emerson* . . . 317
Joe Greene . . . . *Merrill Moore* 318
Tract . . . . *William Carlos Williams* . . 318
Clean Curtains . . . . *Carl Sandburg* 319

PART TEN: FOUNDATIONS OF THE STATE 321

Government by Philosophers . . . . . *Plato* 322
The Nature of Democracy . . . . . . *Aristotle* 327
Duties of the Individual to the State . . . *Cicero* 331
Benevolence . . . . *Mencius* 335
The Conduct of a Successful Ruler . . . *Niccolò Machiavelli* 337
The Illustrious Grand Vezir . . . . . . *Sari Mehmed Pasha* 344
The Origin of Government and the Source and Limits of Its Authority . . . . . . *John Milton* 347
The English Bill of Rights (1689) 351
The Social Contract . . . . *Jean Jacques Rousseau* . . . 352
The Rights of Man and Republicanism . . . *Thomas Paine* 357
Declaration of the Rights of Man and of Citizens (1789) . . . . *(French)* 363
Declaration of Rights . . . . *Percy B. Shelley and W. Godwin* 364
Communist Manifesto . . . . *Karl Heinrich Marx* 366
The Order of Rank . . . . *Friedrich Nietzsche* 376

PART ELEVEN: POLITICAL SATIRE 381

The Nefarious War . . . . *Li Po* 382
On the Birth of His Son . . . . . . *Su Tung-p'o* 383

PART EIGHTEEN: THE CONDUCT OF LIFE . . . 655

Summum Bonum . . . *Aristotle* . . . 656
Ecclesiastes . . . *Old Testament* . . . 663
Buddhist Aphorisms . . . *Dhammapada* . . . 668
The Encheiridion . . . *Epictetus* . . . 671
Meditations . . . *Marcus Aurelius* . . . 675
The Gulistan . . . *Sa'di* . . . 683
Notes on Human Life . . . *Leonardo da Vinci* . . . 690
Social Intercourse . . . *Kaibara Ekken* . . . 692
Resolutions . . . *Jonathan Edwards* . . . 694
The Way to Wealth . . . *Benjamin Franklin* . . . 697
The Evening Hours of a Hermit . . . *Johann Heinrich Pestalozzi* . . . 701
Thoughts . . . *Joseph Joubert* . . . 705
Reflections and Maxims . . . *Goethe* . . . 708
Panegyric of Birds . . . *Giacomo Leopardi* . . . 710
Self-Reliance . . . *Ralph Waldo Emerson* . . . 713
Labour . . . *Thomas Carlyle* . . . 719
A Talk Among Leisured People . . . *Leo Tolstoy* . . . 721

PART NINETEEN: WIT AND EPIGRAM . . . 725

On a Quiet Night . . . *Li Po* . . . 728
Burial Song . . . *Anon., Chinese* . . . 728
Lao-Tzu . . . *Po Chü-i* . . . 728
Five Japanese Haiku:
  The Afterglow . . . *Basho* . . . 728
  Dusk . . . *Basho* . . . 728
  Winter . . . *Joso* . . . 728
  Quiet . . . *Yaha* . . . 728
  Loneliness . . . *Hanshin* . . . 728
Alas! . . . *Sa'di* . . . 728
Sparta . . . *Terpander* . . . 728
Evening . . . *Sappho* . . . 728
A Small City on a Rock . . . *Phocylides* . . . 729
Lais' Mirror . . . *Plato* . . . 729
On a Seal . . . *Plato* . . . 729
A Swallow . . . *Evenus* . . . 729
Passing Away . . . *Lucian* . . . 729
Reading Hesiod . . . *Marcus Argentarius* . . . 729
Leave a Kiss Within the Cup . . . *Agathias Scholasticus* . . . 729
At Thermopylæ . . . *Simonides* . . . 729
The Athenian Dead . . . *Simonides* . . . 729
Lost at Sea . . . *Simonides* . . . 730
A Hound . . . *Simonides* . . . 730
Star . . . *Plato* . . . 730
Heraclitus . . . *Callimachus* . . . 730
Pass On . . . *Theodorides* . . . 730
A Dead Song-Writer . . . *Lucilius* . . . 730
A Bride . . . *Meleager* . . . 730
Persian Fopperies . . . *Horace* . . . 731
Bought Locks . . . *Martial* . . . 731
On the Soul . . . *Hadrian* . . . 731
To Anne . . . *Clément Marot* . . . 731
At My Father's Grave . . . *Matthais Claudius* . . . 731

Wanderer's Night-Songs . . . . *Johann Wolfgang von Goethe* 731
With Inky Sails . . . . *Heinrich Heine* 732
Song of Autumn . . . . *Paul Verlaine* 732
Earth to Earth . . . . *Anon., English* 732
Even Such Is Time . . . . *Sir Walter Raleigh* 732
Sealed in Vain . . . . *William Shakespeare* . . . 732
On the Countess of Pembroke . . . . . *Ben Jonson and William Browne* 732
On My First Son . . . . *Jonson* 732
Upon the Death of Sir Albert Morton's Wife . *Sir Henry Wotton* 733
To Dianeme . . . . *Robert Herrick* 733
Anacreontic . . . . *Herrick* 733
On the Hon. Simon Harcourt . . . . . *Alexander Pope* 733
Rose Aylmer . . . . *Walter Savage Landor* . . . 733
With Rue My Heart Is Laden . . . . . *Alfred Edward Housman* . . . 733
Concord Hymn . . . . *Ralph Waldo Emerson* . . . 733
A Farm Picture . . . . *Walt Whitman* 734
Epitaph for Lincoln . . . . *Whitman* 734
To Make a Prairie . . . . *Emily Dickinson* 734
Fog . . . . *Carl Sandburg* 734
Fire and Ice . . . . *Robert Frost* 734

PART TWENTY: Worlds of the Mind and Spirit 735

The Image of the Cave . . . . *Plato* 736
On the God Within Us . . . . *Seneca* 739
True Happiness, and The Intellectual Beauty *Plotinus* 741
Of the Greatest Good . . . . *Boethius* 745
Of the Royal Way of the Holy Cross . . . *Thomas à Kempis* 748
Discourse on Method . . . . *René Descartes* 750
Thoughts . . . . *Blaise Pascal* 756
The Savoyard Vicar's Creed . . . . . . *Jean Jacques Rousseau* . . . 760
On the Feeling of Immortality in Youth . . *William Hazlitt* 764
Where I Lived, and What I Lived For . . . *Henry D. Thoreau* 768
Solitude . . . . *Miguel de Unamuno* 773
Infallibility . . . . *John Henry Newman* 775
The Realization of the Infinite . . . . *Rabindranath Tagore* 779
Retrospect . . . . *"Æ" (George William Russell)* 784
Preface to a New Philosophy . . . . . *George Santayana* 787
Gorgias' Farewell . . . . *José Enrique Rodó* 789

PART TWENTY-ONE: Man in Love 793

The Wife . . . . *Anon., Chinese* 795
The Night of Sorrow . . . . *Li Po* 795
The Beautiful Woman . . . . *Tu Fu* 796
Plucking the Rushes . . . . *Anon., Chinese* 796
Crossing the Mountain Alone . . . . . *Princess Daihaku* 796
Pretext . . . . *Yakamochi* 796
A Bright Night . . . . *Anon., Japanese* 796
Love's Terror . . . . *Anon., Japanese* 796
Whirlpool . . . . *Anon., Japanese* 797
The Song of Songs . . . . *Old Testament* 797
I Cease Not from Desire . . . . *Hafiz* 797
To a Bride . . . . *Sappho* 798
Wormwood . . . . *Sapphic Fragment* 798
At the Mid Hour of Night . . . . . . *Anacreon* 798

Love . . . . *Euripides* 799
Love the Vagrant . . . . *Meleager* 799
Love Sleeping . . . . *Plato* 799
Bridal Hymn . . . . *Catullus* 800
Slowly, Slowly . . . . *Ovid* 802
Revenge . . . . *Horace* 803
The Vigil of Venus . . . . *Anon., Latin* 803
I Serve . . . . *Sir Meinloh von Sevelingen* . . 806
Matin-Song . . . . *Anon., German* 806
"There Is a Lady Conquering" . . . *Walther von der Vogelweide* . 806
His Own True Wife . . . . *Sir Wolfram von Eschenbach* . 806
"Fair Is Her Body" . . . . *Anon., French* 807
The Complaint of the Fair Armoress . . *François Villon* 807
Of the Gentle Heart . . . . *Guido Guinicelli* 808
"Ladies That Have Intelligence in Love" . . *Dante* 809
Who Wishes to Behold . . . . . . *Petrarch* 810
A Deathless Flower . . . . *Michelangelo* 810
A Supplication . . . . *Sir Thomas Wyatt* 810
Song . . . . *Sir Philip Sidney* 810
Epithalamion . . . . *Edmund Spenser* 811
Five Sonnets . . . . *William Shakespeare* 816
Song from Amphitryon . . . . . . *John Dryden* 817
Farewell to Nancy . . . . *Robert Burns* 817
La Belle Dame Sans Merci . . . . . *John Keats* 818
She Walks in Beauty . . . . *George Gordon, Lord Byron* . 818
Sonatina . . . . *Rubén Darío* 818
Beauty Rohtraut . . . . *Eduard Mörike* 819
Two Songs . . . . *Heinrich Heine* 820
The Dance by the Roadside . . . . . *Gustaf Fröding* 820
All, All . . . . *Charles Baudelaire* 821
The Lake . . . . *Alphonse Marie Louis Lamartine* . 821
Woman and Cat . . . . *Paul Verlaine* 822
Cortège . . . . *Verlaine* 822
The Young Reaper . . . . *Alexis B. Koltsov* 823
Elysium . . . . *Emily Dickinson* 823
Steelhead . . . . *Robinson Jeffers* 823
To Earthward . . . . *Robert Frost* 825

PART TWENTY–TWO: THE STREAM OF STORY TELLING 827

Anpu and Bata: The Tale of the Two Brothers . . . . *(Egyptian)* 828
A Fickle Widow . . . . *(Chinese)* 833
Cupid and Psyche . . . . *Apuleius* 837
The Story of Malchus . . . . *St. Jerome* 846
The Story of Griselda . . . . *Giovanni Boccaccio* 849
How Guzmán Excited the Compassion of My Lord Cardinal . . . . *Mateo Alemán* 855
The Casting of the Perseus . . . . . *Benvenuto Cellini* 857
Don Quixote . . . . *Miguel de Cervantes Saavedra* . 862
Memnon the Philosopher, or Human Wisdom *Voltaire* 874
The Latin Boy: A Tale from Montenegro . . *Simo Matavulj* 876
The Pope's Mule . . . . *Alphonse Daudet* 881
The Christmas Tree and the Wedding . . *Feodor Dostoievsky* 885
The Taking of Lungtungpen . . . . . *Rudyard Kipling* 889
The Hero . . . . *Gabriele d'Annunzio* 891

Chivalry . . . . *Ricardo Fernández-Guardia* . . . 893
A New-Year's Eve Confession . . . . . *Hermann Sudermann* 897
The Eclipse . . . . *Selma Lagerlöf* 899
Banasiowa . . . . *Maria Konopnicka* 902

PART TWENTY-THREE: THE HAPPY LIFE 907

"From Break of Day" . . . . *Anon., Chinese* 909
Success . . . . *Wang Chi* 909
The Arrival of a Guest . . . . *Tu Fu* 909
"Shady, Shady" . . . . *T'ao Ch'ien* 909
Rubáiyát . . . . *Omar Khayyám* 909
Children . . . . *Euripides* 913
Baucis and Philemon . . . . *Ovid* 914
Revery of a Business Man . . . . . . *Horace* 916
The Means to Attain Happy Life . . . . *Martial* 917
The Old Man of Verona . . . . *Claudius Claudianus* 917
Gaudeamus Igitur . . . . *Anon., Medieval Latin* 918
Winter-Time . . . . *Sir Neidhart von Reuental* . . . 918
The Life Removed . . . . *Luis de León* 918
Let Me Go Warm . . . . *Luis de Gongora* 919
Youth Is Sweet and Well . . . . *Lorenzo de' Medici* 920
With Dreams of Wealth and Fame . . . . *Giuseppe Parini* 920
Content . . . . *Robert Greene* 921
Under the Greenwood Tree . . . . . . *William Shakespeare* 921
The Happy Heart . . . . *Thomas Dekker* 922
"Now Winter Nights . . ." . . . . . . *Thomas Campion* 922
A Thanksgiving to God, for His House . . *Robert Herrick* 922
L'Allegro . . . . *John Milton* 923
Nurse's Song . . . . *William Blake* 924
Leisure . . . . *William Henry Davies* 925
A Prayer for My Daughter . . . . . . *William Butler Yeats* 925
The Happy Ulysses . . . . *Joachim du Bellay* 925
The Summer's Revel . . . . *Pierre de Ronsard* 926
The King of Yvetot . . . . *Pierre Jean de Béranger* 926
Ballad of the Bells . . . . *Paul Fort* 927
Evening in May . . . . *Gabriele d'Annunzio* 927
The Laborer . . . . *Richard Dehmel* 927
Winter Evening (To His Old Nurse) . . . *Alexander Pushkin* 928
Country Girl, Don't Stay Away . . . . . *Luis Carlos López* 928
There Was a Child Went Forth . . . . . *Walt Whitman* 929
The Picnic Boat . . . . *Carl Sandburg* 930
Happiness . . . . *Sandburg* 930
Fish Crier . . . . *Sandburg* 930

PART TWENTY-FOUR: VOICES OF THE FORUM 931

The Hebrew Prophets
Jeremiah . . . . *Old Testament* 932
Ezekiel . . . . *Old Testament* 934
The Funeral Oration of Pericles . . . . *Thucydides* 935
Why Another Crusade? . . . . *St. Bernard* 939
Address to the Diet at Worms . . . . . *Martin Luther* 939
Speech in the Virginia Convention of Delegates . . . . *Patrick Henry* 941
Address to the French National Assembly . *Alphonse Marie L. Lamartine* . . . 943

Inaugural Address . . . . *Jefferson Davis* 946
Address at Gettysburg . . . . . . *Abraham Lincoln* 949
Second Inaugural Address . . . . . *Lincoln* 949
To the Italian Working-Men . . . . . *Giuseppe Mazzini* 950
Fascism and the Corporations . . . . *Benito Mussolini* 956
In the Name of the People . . . . . *Franklin Delano Roosevelt* . . . 961
Dunkirk . . . . *Winston Churchill* 964

PART TWENTY-FIVE: MAN AT WORK 969

Works and Days . . . . *Hesiod* 972
Of Human Progress . . . . *Lucretius* 975
The Honey-Farm . . . . *Virgil* 980
Ballad of Poor Chimney Sweeps . . . . *François Villon* 983
Hymn to the Winds . . . . *Joachim du Bellay* 983
Harvest Song . . . . *Ludwig Hölty* 983
The Ox . . . . *Giosuè Carducci* 984
Brazil . . . . *Ronald de Carvalho* 984
Reaping the Barley . . . . *Jorge Carrera Andrade* 985
The Cocooning . . . . *Frédéric Mistral* 985
The Mill . . . . *Emile Verhaeren* 985
We Grow Out of Iron . . . . . . *Alexey Gastev* 986
The Charcoal-Burner's Son . . . . . *Eric Gustaf Geijer* 986
Factory Street in Daylight . . . . . *Paul Zech* 987
The Worked-Out Mine . . . . . . *Edward Dyson* 987
The Man and the Machine . . . . . *Edwin John Pratt* 988
The Sleepers . . . . *William Henry Davies* 988
Let Us Be Off! . . . . *Cecil Day Lewis* 988
The Landscape Near an Aerodrome . . . *Stephen Spender* 988
The Lumbermen . . . . *John Greenleaf Whittier* 989
Song of the Broad-Axe . . . . . . *Walt Whitman* 990
The Man With the Hoe . . . . . . *Edwin Markham* 996
After Apple-Picking . . . . *Robert Frost* 996
Cape Hatteras . . . . *Hart Crane* 997
Classic Scene . . . . *William Carlos Williams* 998
Five Towns on the B. and O. . . . . . *Carl Sandburg* 998

PART TWENTY-SIX: THE UTOPIAN DREAM 999

Earth's Holocaust . . . . *Nathaniel Hawthorne* 1000
The Moral Equivalent of War . . . . *William James* 1009
Earth, Air and Mind . . . . *H. G. Wells* 1015

APPENDIX

Topics for Discussion 1025
Index of Authors 1045
Nationalities Represented 1097
Acknowledgments 1099
General Index 1105

WORLD LITERATURE

PART ONE

Man and His Cultural Heritages

THROUGH THE universal leveling of civilizations – to which modern scientific achievements, trade, and wars have given such tremendous impetus – there has grown an ever expanding network of communication among the peoples of the earth. All sections of humanity in all parts of the world, irrespective of their historical detachment and development, are now face to face with the problems of mutual understanding and cosmopolitanism. The need for surveys of both past and present is great. An appreciation of the cultural heritages of the past lends perspective to life.

Despite all that has been written by primitivists on the charms of the golden ages of the past and the unspoiled children of nature, it is the good fortune of modern man not to be among the first human beings. A great heritage of cultural values has been bequeathed to us by past generations. It will have come down to us in vain if it does not emancipate us from the zeal for petty things and from intolerance. We are marked as men by qualities which distinguish us from savages and beasts. "The use of letters," said the historian Gibbon, "is the principal circumstance that distinguishes a civilized people from a herd of savages incapable of knowledge or reflection." Whatever may be said of man's inhumanity to man and the tragic errors of our kind, we do not willingly make use of what is worst in us as the distinguishing trait of what is human. We find inspiration in great souls whom cruelty could not discourage, in minds which sought to dispel the ignorance of their day, and in spirits which were pathfinders to the good life, uncowed by adversity.

It is an old saying that Rome had a greater civilization and Greece a higher culture. However one may choose to define Civilization and Culture, there are many practical problems in human life and the conduct of man's affairs which must be considered. Civilization and Culture will ultimately be found operative in interlocked yet distinct areas of life. There are the contrasting objectives of the life of animality and humanity, of activity and contemplation, of the inner and outer worlds in which all men live. Man belongs to nature, but he also has trans-natural or spiritual gods. He is civilized as he efficiently organizes the material world for the provision of creative wants; improves the conditions in which he houses himself and the means of transportation through which he distributes food, fuel, and clothing; progresses in the sciences which alleviate pain and conquer disease; implements all the agencies of social justice with the authority of law and its enforcement; and learns to live at peace with his fellows. Whatever other elements in civilization might be mentioned, its place in man's life is always clearly recognized. The chief problems of civilization involve inescapable and urgent demands in the economy of man's material life. Cultural values, on the other hand, embrace the satisfactions of his mind and spirit.

There is ample warrant for recording that not until the Industrial Revolution was the supremacy of intellectual values called in question, and the problems of cultural *versus* utilitarian ends raised in discussions of general education. Ancient Greece looked to the intellect to give man happiness. Ancient India postulated enlightenment of the mind as the means of salvation. Ancient Israel stressed the moral culture of the spirit and will. Ancient China sought in its own past for ethical foundations needed to support a stable and just society. And the Scholastic philosophers of medieval Christendom rested their beliefs on conceptual doctrines. The most essential element in culture is the relation of its values to the intellect and the will, with the accompanying implicit contrasts between the life of the mind and spirit, and the life of material activity. It is only recently in the life of humanity that there has been direct repudiation of its faith in the supremacy of the intellectual life. "Art," wrote Tolstoi, "should unite men with God and with one another." The interior or contemplative life of man is ignored under grave penalties, since he lives in two worlds – an inner and an outer. Neglect of either one means decline in the fullest enjoyment of all that life offers.

Books are not an artificial substitute for life. Anybody who has been lifted above himself by great books, music, or art, knows in his moments of exaltation that he was in contact with the essence of life at its best. Such hours of transcendence give direction, purpose, and value to living – indeed, it is in them that we most truly live. To say that we are all better for them is an understatement. Instead of being synthetic substitutes for life, books are distillations of life itself and preserve what is best in man's experiences in all realms of being, his insights into the mysterious world about him, his great hours of physical courage and moral fortitude, his apperceptions of all beauty and goodness and truth wherever found, and his utopian dreams.

In books are found, furthermore, a record of all that man has believed and done, the results of his conceiving imagination and creative thought, wholesome laughter and scorn of his own folly, quiet insight, and unsleeping interest in the affairs of his fellows. Man is of course at all times a creature of his age, conditioned by his environment; and in books are also accounts of how he has sought to manipulate his world and to understand or control the forces which shape his destiny. What he chooses to learn from his cultural heritage, what meaning he derives from the past, it is not extravagant to say, will determine both the temper and the quality of life in every generation. Emerson remarked that man has seen but half of life if he has never been shown the house of pain. The truth of the observation is instinctively recognized. But Emerson would also have been the first to add many other mansions of the mind and spirit which are part and parcel of man's lot and heritage. They can be entered through the literature of the world, become private possessions, and remain without restrictions of time a never ending delight.

On Books

KAIBARA EKKEN

The pleasure to be found in reading books is profound. They make the heart calm and tranquil, even though it may be far removed from either mountains or trees. They make you rich without necessity of acquiring this world's goods. No pleasure is a fit substitute for the pleasure to be derived from reading.

Books enable one to become familiar with the laws of Nature, that is, to acquaint oneself with the positive and negative laws of Heaven and Earth. They recall the days of the remotest past, enabling us to roam freely over the entire world. Great is the power of books!

The books that give us the greatest pleasure are those of the Sages; next to them come books of history. It is 2,370 years since the time of Jimmutenno, the first Mikado, and it is 4,400 years since the reign of Ko, Emperor of China; yet all the events which transpired during these long periods are recorded in books, and in the perusal of them one feels as if one had lived many thousands of years. Great is the pleasure of books!

"The man who is not well versed in the history of ancient and modern times," said Kantaishi, "is but an animal clothed in man's robe." The hearts of those whose knowledge is limited only to the present and things around them are narrow and dark. They are like that of a man who has never been awakened from sleep. Unfortunate are they who know not the pleasure of books.

Those who read books concerning both ancient and modern times have broad minds, and their understandings are clear.

Whenever we, who are wedded to the pursuit of learning, open a book, a great happiness wells in our hearts — this happiness is the gift of Heaven. As a rule, flowers which have many beautiful petals bear no fruit; consequently, learned men seldom leave behind them any wealth. Heaven sends poverty to men of learning, in order to make their genius shine; therefore let them not seek after riches.

To possess clear windows, a clear table, a good writing-brush, ink-slab and ink-stick, in addition to a light to burn, is one of the great joys of life; as Sotoba said, there are many poor students who cannot afford to get these materials. In the olden days there were men who read by the light of the snow and even by the glow of fireflies.

In making the books of the Sages your teachers, brush, ink, paper and ink-slab your friends, you will receive great happiness and much benefit. The light, also, is a treasure greatly to be prized.

In the reading of books, don't grudge time; nevertheless, the hot, noon-day hours are not suitable, and reading then will profit you but little. The quiet hours of night afford the best opportunity in which to think and enjoy the ancient writings.

To sing or recite the old songs and poems of both our country, Yamato, and China, according to the different sceneries and different seasons — is to give oneself much joy. Doing this is much to be preferred to composing poems ourselves. Even the most gifted poets of the olden days expressed their sentiments before their guests, not by their own verses, but by reciting the ballads of an older age again. This example should be followed. We may fancy our own verses good; but others will think them ridiculous. Let the specially-gifted compose poems; for us such labour is best left alone.

Most things cannot be enjoyed without friends — but reading can. While sitting alone in our rooms we may traverse the entire world, understanding the reason for thousands of things. Living in this age, we can discourse with those who lived thousands of years ago. Unworthy as we are, we can become the friends of the Sages. These pleasures, books only can bestow upon us. Those who cannot enjoy them are poor men indeed; those who most enjoy them obtain the most happiness.

— From The Way of Contentment by Kaibara Ekken, Japanese (1629–1713), translated by Ken Hoshino.

~ ✿ ~

Japanese Poetry

KI NO TSURAYUKI

Our native poetry springs from the heart of man as its seed, producing the countless leaves of language. Multitudinous are the affairs of men in this world, what their minds think, what their eyes see, what their ears hear they must find words to express. Listening to the nightingale singing amid the blossoms of spring, or to the murmur of frogs among the marshes in autumn, we know that every living thing that liveth hath its part in the mingled music of Nature. Our poetry, with effortless ease, moveth heaven and earth, draweth sympathy from invisible demons and deities, softens the relations between men and women, and refresheth the heart of the warrior; from the time of the manifestation of heaven and earth it hath its origin, but its transmission to our day began in relation to sunbright heaven with the work of Shitateruhime and in relation to the earth, mother of metals, with that of Susanowo no Mikoto.

Thus the heart of man came to find expression in the various modes of speech for its joy in the beauty of flowers, its wonder at the song of birds, its tender welcome of the spring mists, its mournful sympathy with the evanescence of the morning dew. As step by step from the first movement of the foot, distant journeys are achieved in the course of time, as grain by grain high mountains are piled up from the mere dust at their base until their peaks are lost in the drifting clouds of heaven, so hath the verse of our land, little by little, become rich and abundant. The quintain opening with the line *Naniha tsu* is the first example of poetry composed by royal command. In the stanza beginning with *Asaka Yama* we have an instance of a maid's banter; these two pieces are the father and mother of our poetry and still guide the earliest steps of the young student of verse.

Now Japanese poetry may be arranged under six categories, just as of Chinese poetry there are six categories. The categories are these: *sohe*, or satirical or *innuendo* verse; *kazohe*, or descriptive pieces; *nazorahe*, figurative pieces; *tatohe*, allusive songs; *tagadoto*, lyrical poems; and *ihahi*, congratulatory odes.

In these days men are lost in sensuality, their aim is mere decoration, therefore, their verse is vain and trivial. In those circles where luxury only is cultivated, true poetry is as hidden from knowledge as a log of fossil wood buried deep in the ground; in more elegant coteries verse is known, indeed, but is little better than the bloom of the so-called flower-reed that never produceth an ear of grain.

When we remember how poetry arose we see that such ought not to be its condition.

In ancient days the mikados themselves, on blossomy spring mornings and moonlit autumn nights, called together their courtiers, and bade them compose verses on various subjects. Some would celebrate their wanderings in difficult places after the blossomy sprays of spring, others their unguided rambles in the darkness of night to gaze upon the orb of the rising moon of autumn. These productions the Sovran would himself examine, and determine which were excellent and which were poor.

Nor were such the only themes. The tiny pebble and the vast mass of Tsukuba's hill were used as similes wherewith to honour the Sovran; when the heart was overflowing with the happiness of existence and the pleasure of life, when love of one's fellowmen could be compared with the eternal fumes of Fuji, when the murmur of the cicada recalled sadly the memory of an absent friend, the pines of Takasago and Suminoye, the pleasures of life-long wedded love, Wotoko's hill, the vigour of past manhood, and when in the *ominameshi* flower was seen the symbol of the briefness of the season of girlish bloom, it was in verse they found relief.

Again to verse were they moved when they saw the ground white with snowy showers of fallen cherry blossoms on spring mornings; or heard on autumn evenings the rustle of falling leaves; or year after year gazed upon the mirror's reflection of the doleful ravages of time, shown by grey hairs and wavy wrinkles; or trembled as they watched the passing dewdrop quivering on the beaded grass, or the river's flow flecked with perishing bubbles – symbols of their own fleeting lives; or noted the leaves in all their glory today perishing on the morrow, or what one had admired yesterday regarded with indifference today.

Then, too, their subjects might be the sound of the waves beating on the base of the pine hills, the solitary drawer of water at the fount in mid-moorland, the contemplation of the fall of the *hagi* leaf in autumn, the count of the times the woodcock preens his feathers in the red dawn, the comparison of man's existence to a *kure* bamboo joint floating down a river, the flood of Yóshino as symbol of man's varied fortunes in the world, dismay at tidings of the disappearance of Fuji's fumes or of the mending of Nagara's bridge – in regard to all these subjects the making of verses composed their minds.

Thus from antiquity was poetry cultivated, but it was in the Nara period that the art flourished. Of that age Kakinomoto no Hitómaro was the very prince of poets. Then appeared Yamabe no Akáhito, and of the two it were hard to say which was the greater, which the lesser genius. In addition to these great poets, a number of men of talent distinguished themselves in the succeeding ages; the line was maintained, and did not come to an end.

Long before the present compilation was made, the Anthology known as the *Manyôshiu* appeared. Since that time more than ten reigns, more than a hundred years, have passed. At the present day in City-Royal those who are versed in the learning of antiquity or sympathize with the spirit of its verse are very few – they may be counted by twos and threes. Nevertheless, there exist some poets still; here and there men of merit are to be found, with many who do not get beyond mediocrity.

I cannot, of course, here speak of men of rank and office, but among others who have produced verse some may be mentioned.

There is, first of all, Sôjô Henjo, whose manner is successful, but his work is deficient in truth, like the picture of a beautiful woman, which excites emotion, but to no avail. Then we have Arihara Narihira, very full of feeling but poor in diction; his poetry reminds one of a faded flower that yet preserves some of its perfume. Bunya no Yasuhide, on the other hand, is an artist in words; with him form is better than substance. He is like a pedlar dressed up in fine silks. The priest of Mt. Uji, Kisen, is obscure, and his beginnings and endings do not chime; he is like an autumnal moon, bright at even, dim at dawn.

As to Ononokomachi, she has pathos but lacks power, like a fair but feeble woman. Ohotomo no Kuronushi, lastly, has a pretty turn for verse, but his form is poor; he is like a faggot-bearing boor resting under a blossomy cherry-tree.

Besides the above, many other versifiers are more or less known, the list of their names, indeed, would be as endless as a coil of *kazura* on a moorside; they are as multitudinous as the leaves of a forest of thick-foliaged trees, but they intend poetry rather than accomplish it.

Now in this His Majesty's gracious reign, when already ninefold had become the return of the four seasons, and the waves of His universal benevolence rippled beyond the Eight Islands, while the protective shadow of His broad and large favour had grown more spacious than that cast by vast Tsukubane's hill, amid the myriad cares of government He, our Sovran, yet found leisure, nor neglected the multitude of matters. Therefore he forgot not antiquity, nor willed that the great past should be clean lost, but desired that the memory thereof should be handed on to future generations. And so it came about that on the eighteenth day of the fourth month of the fifth year of Yengi [25 May, 905] He charged the Dainaiki, Ki no Tomonori, and the Privy Secretary, Ki no Tsurayuki [with others], to make a selection of ancient poems not contained in the Anthology, with permission to add to these a few of their own composition. Some thousand poems were accordingly arranged in twenty books, to which we have given the title *Kokinwakashiu* – a Garner or Anthology of Japanese Verse, Old and New. Various are the themes dealt with; from the gathering of plum-blossoms in early spring for chaplets, and the summer song of the cuckoo; and the plucking of the ruddy sprays of autumn, to the contemplation of winter's snow; the crane and the tortoise, as presages of long reign to His Majesty and long life to His subjects; the bush-clover and summer herbs, symbols of spousal love; Afusaka hill, where the prayers of travellers to and from the Capital are offered to the god of Támuke; lastly, divers themes not drawn from the four seasons of spring and summer and autumn and winter.

So is our task ended, and an Anthology compiled plentiful as the floods fed by the unfailing waters of the hills, rich in examples as the seashore in grains of sand; may its reception meet with none of the obstructions that bar the stream of Asuka, and the joys it shall afford accumulate, as dust and pebbles gather together to form a high mountain, into a boulder of delight.

Lastly, as to our own style, any charm it may possess is but as the passing perfume of a spring blossom, and to claim for our work the durability of an autumnal night would expose us to criticism as to form, while as to substance we are filled with shame; yet, whether like a drifting cloud we move or rest, whether like a belling stag we stand up or lie down, we rejoice to have been born in an age when such a task as that we have sought to achieve has been imposed upon us by royal command.

Hitomaro has passed away — but shall the poetic art stand still? Things change with change of times, joys and sorrows come and go — but shall not the letter of these poems be preserved? For ever the willows shoot forth their thready branches, the leaves of the pine-tree never fail, the coils of the creepers wander endlessly over the moorsides, the sea-fowl cease not to imprint their tracts upon the sands of the shore; and for ever, we trust, shall men, taking pleasure in the form and profiting by the content of these poems, revere the verse of ancient days as the moon in high heaven, and applaud the age which saw the production of this Anthology.

— *From the Japanese of Ki no Tsurayuki (d. 946), translated by F. V. Dickins.*

Books Which Have Influenced Me

ROBERT LOUIS STEVENSON

THE EDITOR has somewhat insidiously laid a trap for his correspondents, the question put appearing at first so innocent, truly cutting so deep. It is not, indeed, until after some reconnaissance and review that the writer awakes to find himself engaged upon something in the nature of autobiography, or, perhaps worse, upon a chapter in the life of that little beautiful brother whom we once all had, and whom we have all lost and mourned, the man we ought to have been, the man we hoped to be. But when word has been passed (even to an editor), it should, if possible, be kept; and if sometimes I am wise and say too little, and sometimes weak and say too much, the blame must lie at the door of the person who entrapped me. The most influential books, and the truest in their influence, are works of fiction. They do not pin the reader to a dogma, which he must afterward discover to be inexact; they do not teach him a lesson, which he must afterward unlearn. They repeat, they rearrange, they clarify the lessons of life; they disengage us from ourselves, they constrain us to the acquaintance of others; and they show us the web of experience, not as we can see it for ourselves, but with a singular change — that monstrous, consuming *ego* of ours being, for the nonce, struck out. To be so, they must be reasonably true to the human comedy; and any work that is so serves the turn of instruction. But the course of our education is answered best by those poems and romances where we breathe a magnanimous atmosphere of thought and meet generous and pious characters. Shakespeare has served me best. Few living friends have had upon me an influence so strong for good as Hamlet or Rosalind. The last character, already well beloved in the reading, I had the good fortune to see, I must think, in an impressionable hour, played by Mrs. Scott Siddons. Nothing has ever more moved, more delighted, more refreshed me; nor has the influence quite passed away. Kent's brief speech over the dying Lear had a great effect upon my mind, and was the burthen of my reflections for long, so profoundly, so touchingly generous did it appear in sense, so overpowering in expression. Perhaps my dearest and best friend outside of Shakespeare is D'Artagnan — the elderly D'Artagnan of the "Vicomte de Bragelonne." I know not a more human soul, nor, in his way, a finer; I shall be very sorry for the man who is so much of a pedant in morals that he cannot learn from the Captain of Musketeers. Lastly, I must name the "Pilgrim's Progress," a book that breathes of every beautiful and valuable emotion.

But of works of art little can be said; their influence is profound and silent, like the influence of nature; they mould by contact; we drink them up like water, and are bettered, yet know not how. It is in books more specifically didactic that we can follow out the effect, and distinguish and weigh and compare. A book which has been very influential upon me fell early into my hands, and so may stand first, though I think its influence was only sensible later on, and perhaps still keeps growing, for it is a book not easily outlived — The "Essays" of Montaigne. That temperate and genial picture of life is a great gift to place in the hands of persons of to-day; they will find in these smiling pages a magazine of heroism and wisdom, all of an antique strain; they will have their "linen decencies" and excited orthodoxies fluttered, and will (if they have any gift of reading) perceive that these have not been fluttered without some excuse and ground of reason; and (again if they have any gift of reading) they will end by seeing that this old gentleman was in a dozen ways a finer fellow, and held in a dozen ways a nobler view of life, than they or their contemporaries.

The next book, in order of time, to influence me, was the New Testament, and in particular the Gospel according to St. Matthew. I believe it would startle and move any one if they could make a certain effort of imagination and read it freshly like a book, not droningly and dully like a portion of the Bible. Any one would then be able to see in it those truths which we are all courteously supposed to know and all modestly refrain from applying. But upon this subject it is perhaps better to be silent.

I come next to Whitman's "Leaves of Grass," a book of singular service, a book which tumbled the world upside down for me, blew into space a thousand cobwebs of genteel and ethical illusion, and, having thus shaken my tabernacle of lies, set me back again upon a strong foundation of all the original and manly virtues. But it is, once more, only a book for those who have the gift of reading. I will be very frank — I believe it is so with all good books, except perhaps, fiction. The average man lives, and must live, so wholly in convention, that gunpowder charges of the truth are more apt to discompose than to invigorate his creed. Either he cries out upon blasphemy and indecency, and crouches the closer round that little idol of part-truths and part-conveniences which is the contemporary deity, or he is convinced by what is new, forgets what is old, and becomes truly blasphemous and indecent himself. New truth is only useful to supplement the old; rough truth is only wanted to expand, not to destroy, our civil and often elegant conventions. He who cannot judge had better stick to fiction and the daily papers. There he will get little harm, and, in the first at least, some good.

Close upon the back of my discovery of Whitman, I came under the influence of Herbert Spencer. No more persuasive rabbi exists, and few better. How much of his vast structure will bear the touch of time, how much is clay and how much brass, it were too curious to inquire. But his words, if dry, are always manly and honest; there dwells in his pages a spirit of highly abstract joy, plucked naked like an algebraic symbol, but still joyful; and the reader will find there a *caput-mortuum* (dry bones) of piety, with little indeed of its loveliness but with most of its essentials; and these two qualities make him a wholesome, as his intellectual vigour makes him a bracing, writer. I should be much of a hound if I lost my gratitude to Herbert Spencer.

"Goethe's Life," by Lewes, had a great importance for me when it first fell into my hands — a strange instance of the partiality of man's good and man's evil. I know no one whom I less admire than Goethe; he seems a very epitome of the sins of genius, breaking open the doors of private life, and wantonly wounding friends, in that crowning offence of "Werther," and in his own character a mere pen-and-ink Napoleon, conscious of the rights and duties of superior talents as a Spanish inquisitor was conscious of the rights and duties of his office. And yet in his fine devotion to his art, in his honest and serviceable friendship for Schiller, what lessons are contained! Biography, usually so false to its office, does here for once perform for us some of the work of fiction, reminding us, that is, of the truly mingled tissue of man's nature, and how huge faults and shining virtues cohabit and persevere in the same character. History serves us well to this effect, but in the originals, not in the pages of the popular epitomiser, who is bound, by the very nature of his task, to make us feel the difference of epochs instead of the essential identity of man, and even in the originals only to those who can recognise their own human virtues and defects in strange forms, often inverted and under strange names, often interchanged. Martial is a poet of no good repute, and it gives a man new thoughts to read his works dispassionately, and find in this unseemly jester's serious passages the image of a kind, wise, and self-respecting gentleman. It is customary, I suppose, in reading Martial, to leave out these pleasant verses; I never heard of them, at least, until I found them for myself; and this partiality is one among a thousand things that help to build up our distorted and hysterical conception of the great Roman empire.

This brings us by a natural transition to a very noble book — the "Meditations" of Marcus Aurelius. The dispassionate gravity, the noble forgetfulness of self, the tenderness of others, that are there expressed and were practised on so great a scale in the life of its writer, make this book a book quite by itself. No one can read it and not be moved. Yet it scarcely or rarely appeals to the feelings — those very mobile, those not very trusty parts of man. Its address lies farther back; its lesson comes more deeply home; when you have read, you carry away with you a memory of the man himself; it is as though you had touched a loyal hand, looked into brave eyes, and made a noble friend; there is another bond on you thenceforward, binding you to life and to the love of virtue.

Wordsworth should perhaps come next. Every one has been influenced by Wordsworth, and it is hard to tell precisely how. A certain innocence, a rugged austerity of joy, a sight of the stars, "the silence that there is among the hills," something of the cold thrill of dawn, cling to his work and give it a particular address to what is best in us. I do not know that you learn a lesson; you need not — Mill did not — agree with any one of his beliefs; and yet the spell is cast. Such are the best teachers: a dogma learned is only a new error — the old one was perhaps as good; but a spirit communicated is a perpetual possession. These best teachers climb beyond teaching to the plane of art; it is themselves, and what is best in themselves that they communicate.

I should never forgive myself if I forgot "The Egoist." It is art, if you like, but it belongs purely to didactic art, and from all the novels I have read (and I have read thousands) stands in a place by itself. Here is a Nathan for the modern David; here is a book to send the blood into men's faces. Satire, the angry picture of human faults, is not great art; we can all be angry with our neighbour; what we want is to be shown not his defects, of which we are too conscious, but his merits, to which we are too blind. And "The Egoist" is a satire; so much must be allowed; but it is a satire of a singular quality, which tells you nothing of that obvious mote which is engaged from first to last with that invisible beam. It is yourself that is hunted down; these are your own faults that are dragged into the day and numbered, with lingering relish, with cruel cunning and precision. A young friend of Mr. Meredith's (as I have the story) came to him in an agony. "This is too bad of you," he cried. "Willoughby is me!" "No, my dear fellow," said the author, "he is all of us." I have read "The Egoist" five or six times myself, and I mean to read it again; for I am like the young friend of the anecdote — I think Willoughby an unmanly but a very serviceable exposure of myself.

I suppose, when I am done, I shall find that I have forgotten much that was most influential, as I see already I have forgotten Thoreau, and Hazlitt, whose paper "On the Spirit of Obligations" was a turning point in my life, and Penn, whose little book of aphorisms had a brief but strong effect on me, and Mitford's "Tales of Old Japan," wherein I learned for the first time the proper attitude of any rational man to his country's laws — a secret found, and kept, in the Asiatic islands. That I should commemorate all is more than I can hope or the editor could ask. It will be more to the point, after having said so much upon improving books, to say a word or two about the improvable reader. The gift of reading, as I have called it, is not very common, nor very generally understood. It consists, first of all, in a vast intellectual endowment — a free grace, I find I must call it — by which a man rises to understand that he is not punctually right, nor those from whom he differs absolutely wrong. He may hold dogmas; he may hold them passionately; and he may know that others hold them but coldly, or hold them differently, or hold them not at all. Well, if he has the gift of reading, these others will be full of meat for him. They will see the other side of propositions and the other side of virtues. He need not change his dogma for that, but he may change his reading of that dogma, and he must supplement and correct his deductions from it. A human truth, which is always very much a lie, hides as much of life as it displays. It is men who hold another truth, or, as it seems to us, perhaps, a dangerous lie, who can extend our restricted field of knowledge, and rouse our drowsy consciences. Something that seems quite new, or that seems insolently false or very dangerous, is the test of a reader. If he tries to see what it means, what truth excuses it, he has the gift, and let him read. If he is merely hurt, or offended, or exclaims upon his author's folly, he had better take to the daily papers; he will never be a reader.

And here, with the aptest illustrative force, after I have laid down my part-truth, I must step in with its opposite. For, after all, we are vessels of a very limited content. Not all men can read all books; it is only in a chosen few that any man will find his appointed food; and the fittest lessons are the most palatable, and make themselves welcome to the mind. A writer learns this early, and it is his chief support; he goes on unafraid, laying down the law; and he is sure at heart that most of what he says is demonstrably false, and much of a mingled strain, and some hurtful, and very little good for service; but he is sure besides that when his words fall into the hands of any genuine reader, they will be weighed and winnowed, and only that which suits will be assimilated; and when they fall into the hands of one who cannot intelligently read, they come quite silent and inarticulate, falling upon deaf ears, and his secret is kept as if he had not written.

— *Robert Louis Stevenson, English (1850–1894). From the British Weekly, 1887.*

~ ❁ ~

Literature as Revelation

GILBERT MURRAY

MOST PEOPLE of culture, I believe, like literature because they like to be amused, or because the technique of expression interests them and rouses their strongest faculties, or because a book stands to them for society and conversation, or because they just happen to like the smell and feel of a book and the gentle exercise of cutting pages with a paper-knife. Or they like to study the varieties of human nature as shown in books, and to amass the curious information that is to be found there. Those are the really cultured people. You will find that they like Lamb's *Essays,* and *Lavengro,* and Burton's *Anatomy,* and Evelyn's *Diary,* and the *Religio Medici,* and the *Literary Supplement.* And the other class — to which I certainly belonged all through my youth and perhaps on the whole still belong — does not really much like the process of reading, but reads because it wants to get somewhere, to discover something, to find a light which will somehow illumine for them either some question of the moment or the great riddles of existence. I believe this is the spirit in which most people in their youth read books; and, considering their disappointments, it is remarkable, and perhaps not altogether discreditable, how often they cling to this hope far on into the region of grey hairs or worse than grey hairs.

Now, in putting before you the case for these over-sanguine or over-youthful people, I believe, as I have said, that I shall have the persons of culture and the connoisseurs against me; but the artists and writers themselves will be really on my side. Almost all the writers — and they are pretty numerous — whom I have known intimately are, I believe, subject to a secret sadness when they are praised for being amusing or entertaining or readable or the like. What really delights them, especially the novelists and writers of light comedy, is to be treated as teachers and profound thinkers. Nobody is quite content to think that the serious business of his own life makes merely the fringe and pastime of other people's. There is a well-known story of an essay written on the poet Keats by a stern young Nonconformist at a certain university, in which he said that after all the important question to ask was whether Keats had ever saved a soul. He answered it, I regret to say, in the negative, and condemned Keats accordingly. Now this essayist is generally ridiculed by persons of culture for having set up for the poor poet a perfectly absurd and irrelevant test. "Keats," says the man of culture, "was no more trying to save souls than to improve railway locomotives. He was simply trying to write beautiful poetry, which is an entirely different thing."

Now I do not believe that the man of culture is right. I suspect that the young Nonconformist was perfectly correct in the test he applied; that a really great poet ought to save souls and does save souls; and, furthermore, that he will not be at all grateful to you if you tell him that souls are not his business, and he can leave them to the parson. I think, if the essayist went wrong — and if he concluded that Keats was a bad poet I take it as certain that he did go wrong — it was partly that he took the saving of a soul in too narrow and theological a sense, and partly that he had not really sunk himself deep enough into Keats's thought to know whether he could save a soul or not. That is, in the first place I would have asked him to consider whether it is not in some sense "saving a soul" to enable a living man to rise up above himself and his personal desires, and to see beauty and wonder in places where hitherto he had seen nothing; in the second place, I would have asked him whether, before condemning Keats, he had really considered and really understood what Keats meant when, for example, in the climax of one of his greatest poems, he sums up the message to mankind of the Grecian Urn:

"Beauty is truth, truth beauty," — that is all
Ye know on earth, and all ye need to know.

I do not say that that message is true. I do not myself fully understand what Keats meant by it. But I am sure that to him, and to many people who learnt it from him, that thought has come as a revelation.

Let me speak of another case in my own experience. I remember when I was a boy of fifteen in Paris, sitting down on a bench in the garden of the Tuileries with a copy of Rousseau's book on the *Contrat Social,* which I had just bought for twopence-halfpenny. I knew it was a celebrated book, and sat down in a sober mood to read it, partly from a sense of duty. And the first sentence of the first chapter ran: "Man was born free, and he is everywhere in chains."

"Man was born free, and he is everywhere in chains." I remember the thrill with which I read and re-read those words. As a matter of fact, I quite misunderstood their place in Rousseau's argument. But so did other people, and I can realize now the thrill with which, when they were first published, they ran through Europe, awakening, unforgettable, stirring the seeds of fire that blazed out in the Great Revolution.

Take a third instance, the passage in Milton's great pamphlet pleading for the freedom of the Press, where Milton seems gradually, with increasing intensity, to realize what a book really at its best is, something greater than a living man. Now to kill a man is, of course a sin. It is to slay God's image; but to kill a good book is to kill the very essence of a man's thought, "to slay God's image, as it were, in the eye." For the particular man is but human and will in any case die before long; "but a good book is the precious life-blood of a master-spirit, treasured up for a life beyond life." When you take in your hand some of the great immortal books of the past, how that sentence comes back to your mind and illumines them! My thoughts turn naturally to some of those Greek tragedies on which I especially work; the *Agamemnon* of Aeschylus, say, or the *Trojan Women* of Euripides. What is it, that one should read it and re-read it now, two thousand odd years after it was written? What is it, that it should still have the power to stir one's whole being? That is the answer: it is simply what Milton has said, nothing more and nothing less, "the precious life-blood of a master-spirit, treasured up for a life beyond life."

I have taken three instances of the kind of writing that has an element of what I venture to call "revelation," but before going further I will stop to answer some criticisms about them. In the first place, the person of culture, to whom we were a little disagreeable at the beginning of this lecture, will interpose. "You appear," he will say, "to be basing your admiration of Keats on the truth of one exceedingly obscure and questionable proposition about Beauty being the same as Truth. Personally, I do not care a straw whether it is true or not; I only care whether it is suitable in its place in the poem; but even supposing it is true, it is only a tiny fragment of Keats's work. What about all the rest of his work, which, to his credit be it said, contains hardly any of these dogmatic sentences which you choose to describe as revelation? Is Keats's greatness to rest on the very few apothegms about life which his work contains — they are far more numerous and probably more true in Martin Tupper or Ella Wheeler Wilcox — or is it to rest frankly on the sheer beauty of the mass of his work? You know quite well it must rest on the latter."

How are we to answer this? Well, in the first place we must explain that I only chose those isolated sentences for convenience sake. It was easier to explain what I meant by revelation if I could find it expressed in a single sentence. But as a rule the writers who have most of the element of revelation about them do not crystallize their revelation into formulae. It is something that radiates from all their work, as in practical life there is generally far more inspiration radiating from the example of a man's whole activity than from the moral precepts that he happens to utter. Shelley is simply bursting with this power of revelation. To a man who has once read himself into Shelley, the world never looks the same again. The same is true of Goethe, the same is emphatically true of certain Greek poets, like Aeschylus and Euripides. But it would be hard to select any particular sentences from their works as summing up the essence of their doctrine. Even Tolstoy, who has this power of revelation to an extraordinary degree, and who was always trying, trying consciously and intensely, to put into clear words the message that was burning inside him, even Tolstoy never really gets it expressed. He lays down, in his religious books, lots and lots of rules, some of them sensible, some of them less so, some of them hopelessly dogmatic and inhuman, many of them thrilling and magnificent, but never, never getting near to the full expression of the main truth he had discovered about the world and was trying to teach. The message of Keats, whatever it is, lies in all Keats, though by accident a great part of it may be summed up in a particular sentence. The message of Plato is in all Plato, the message of Tolstoy in all Tolstoy. There is a beautiful passage in Renan's *Life of Jesus* where he points out that when Jesus Himself was asked what His doctrine was, what exact new dogmatic truth He had to declare, He could give no direct answer. He certainly could not produce a series of doctrinal texts; He could only say "Follow me." The message a man has to give radiates from him; it is never summed up in a sentence or two.

So, if we go back to Keats and the person of culture, we will say to him not in the least that the greatness of Keats depends on the truth or importance of one or two statements he made; but that it does depend very greatly on a certain intense power of vision and feeling which runs through the whole of his work and which happens to express itself almost in the form of a religious dogma in one or two places — say in the opening passage of *Endymion* and the last stanza of the *Ode on a Grecian Urn*.

Now let me notice another curious thing about these revelations in literature. They are never statements of fact. They are never accurately measured. I am not sure that you might not safely go further and say they are never really discoveries; they are nearly all of them as old as the hills, or at least as old as the Greek philosophers and the Book of Job. Their value is not in conveying a new piece of information; their value lies in their power of suddenly directing your attention, and the whole focus of your will and imagination, towards a particular part of life. "Man was born free, and he is everywhere in chains." That is only true to a limited extent; and so far as it is true it is not in the least new. But Rousseau expressed it more vividly, perhaps felt it more keenly, believed it to be more important, than other people had. What is more, he meant to draw conclusions from it; and I think what thrills one especially in reading or thinking of the words is the thought of those conclusions that are to be drawn. They are not defined; they are left vague; that makes them all the more tremendous.

Think of life as a vast picture gallery, or museum; or better, perhaps, as a vast engineering workshop. It is all those things, among others. Then think of oneself walking through it. You know how the average man walks through a museum or a workshop when he knows nothing particular about it. You try hard to be intelligent; failing in that, you try to conceal your lack of intelligence. You would like to be interested, but you do not know what is interesting and what is not. Some of the specimens strike you as pretty; some of the engines seem to you very powerful; you are dazzled and amused by the blaze of the fires, you are secretly interested in the men and wish you could talk to them. But in the main you come out at the other end tired and rather dispirited and having got remarkably little out of it. That is the way a stupid and uneducated man, with no one to help him, goes through life.

Next, suppose you go through the same museum, or the same workshop, with a thoroughly competent guide. In the museum he knows what all the specimens are, which are rare and which ordinary, and why they are interesting; he makes you look at things; makes you understand things; makes you see a hundred details, every one of them significant, that you would never have noticed by yourself. In the workshop, he shows how the various machines work, tells how they were invented and what difference their invention made; he takes you to see a particularly skilled workman and makes you realize where his skill comes in; he makes you feel the cleverness and the beauty of the machinery. That is like going through life with the help and guidance of a proper average educator, what one calls a person of culture.

Now thirdly, suppose on the day of your visit the ordinary guide is not available. Instead you are taken by a man who is not a regular guide to the institution but is working, so they tell you, at certain parts of it. And you find very likely as you go with him that there are large parts that he does not know or at least has nothing to say about, but when you get to his particular subject he tells you not only what the other guide told, but also various things which the other guide thought not worth mentioning, but which, as now explained to you, seem searching and deep and new; and you gradually realize that you are talking to a man who has made, or is on the point of making, a great discovery. In the museum he takes specimens that seemed to have nothing to do with each other and shows that when you put them together there comes a sudden flood of suggestion, a stream of questions never yet asked, but when once asked sure to find an answer. And you go away not so much filled with knowledge, but all alive with interest and the sense of movement; feeling that your feet have been set on a road into the future. You have seen some one thing or set of things with an intensity that has revealed what was before unsuspected and made, as it were, an illumination in one part of life. That, I think, is like going through under the guidance of the sort of literature that gives inspiration.

The great difference, intellectually speaking, between one man and another is simply the number of things they can see in a given cubic yard of world. Do you remember Huxley's famous lecture on *A Piece of Chalk*, delivered to the working men of Norwich in 1868, and how the piece of chalk told him secrets of the infinite past, secrets of the unfathomed depths of the sea? The same thing happens with a book. I remember once picking up a copy of *Macbeth* belonging to the great Shakespearian scholar, Andrew Bradley, and reading casually his pencilled notes in the margin. The scene was one which I knew by heart and thought I understood; but his notes showed me that I had missed about half a dozen points on every page. It seems to me that the writers who have the power of revelation are just those who, in some particular part of life, have seen or felt considerably more than the average run of intelligent human beings. It is this specific power of seeing or feeling more things to the cubic yard in some part of the world that makes a writer's work really inspiring.

To have felt and seen more than other people in some particular region of life: does that give us any sort of guarantee that the judgments which a man passes are likely to be true? Not in the least. Suppose a man has seen and experienced some particular corner of, say, the Battle of the Somme and can give you a thrilling and terrific account of it, that is no particular reason for expecting that his views about the war as a whole will be true. It is on the whole likely that he will see things in a wrong proportion. The point in his favour is only that he does really know *something*, and, whatever his general views are, he can help you to know something. I will confess my own private belief, which I do not wish anyone to share, that of all the books and all the famous sayings that have come as a revelation to human beings, not one is strictly true or has any chance of being true. Nor, if you press me, do I really think it is their business to be strictly true. They are not meant to be statements of fact. They are cries of distress, calls of encouragement, signals flashing in the darkness; they seem to be statements in the indicative mood, but they are really in the imperative or the optative – the moods of command or prayer or longing; they often make their effect not by what they say but by the tone in which they say it, or even by the things they leave unsaid.

Do you remember Garibaldi's speech to his men when his defence of Rome had proved fruitless, and the question was whether to make terms with the Austrians or to follow him? "Let those who wish to continue the War against the stranger come with me. I offer neither pay nor quarters nor provisions. I offer hunger, thirst, forced marches, battles and death." The force of that appeal was in what he did not say. He obviously offered them something else too; something so glorious that as a matter of fact most of them followed him; but he did not mention it.

Sometimes the word of revelation is a metaphor; the speaker knows he cannot attain exact truth, he can only, as it were, signal in the direction of it. There is a wonderful story in a little-read Saxon historian, who wrote in Latin, the Venerable Bede, about the conversion of the Saxons to Christianity. The King was debating whether or no to accept the new religion, and consulted his counsellors. And one old Pagan warrior said:

"Do you remember how last midwinter King Edwin held festival in the great hall, with brands burning and two huge fires on the hearths, while outside there was storm and utter darkness? And the windows by the roof being open, a bird flew suddenly from the darkness outside into the warm and lighted place and out on the other side into the outer darkness. Like that bird is the life of man."

Or what again shall we say of the following? A message sent many years ago by the famous Russian revolutionary, Katherine Breshkovsky — the grandmother of the Revolution as she is called; a message smuggled out of prison and sent to her friends and followers bidding them not to despair or to think that nothing was being accomplished. "Day and night we labour; instead of meat, drink and sleep, we have dreams of Freedom. It is youth calling to youth through prison walls and across the world." It seems like a series of statements which it is hard to describe as either true or not true. Yet I doubt if it is really a statement; it is more like a call in the night.

Or take the saying of one of the ancient rabbis after the fall of Jerusalem, when the heathen had conquered the holy places and to a pious Jew the very roots of life seemed to be cut: "Zion is taken from us; nothing is left save the Holy One and His Law." Nothing is left save the Holy One and His Law. Does it not seem at the same time to say two things: that nothing is left, and that everything is left that really matters? All is lost, and nothing that matters is lost. The message has just that quality of self-contradiction which shows that it is not saying all it means, that it is pointing to something beyond itself, calling the hearer's attention not to a fact but to a mystery.

Or take one of the greatest and simplest of all these burning words, the word of a Greek philosopher of a late and decadent period, who has nevertheless made a great stir in the world: "Though I speak with the tongues of men and of angels, and have not charity, I am but a sounding brass or a tinkling cymbal. Though I give my body to be burned, and have not charity, it profiteth me nothing." Who can analyse that into a statement of fact?

By now, I think, we have reached a point where we can formulate a further conclusion about these words of inspiration or revelation. They never are concerned with direct scientific fact or even with that part of experience which is capable of being expressed in exact statement. They are concerned not with that part of our voyage which is already down in the Admiralty charts. They are concerned with the part that is uncharted; the part that is beyond the mist, whither no one has travelled, or at least whence no one has brought back a clear account. They are all in the nature of the guess that goes before scientific knowledge; the impassioned counsel of one who feels strongly but cannot, in the nature of things, prove his case. This fact explains three things about them: their emotional value, their importance, and their weakness. Their weakness is that they are never exactly true, because they are never based on exact knowledge. Their importance is that they are dealing with the part of the journey that is just ahead of us, the hidden ground beyond the next ridge which matters to us now more than all the rest of the road. Their emotional value is intense just because they are speaking of the thing we most long to know, and in which the edge of the emotion is not dulled by exact calculations. A good Moslem believes in Mohammed far more passionately than any one believes in the multiplication table. That is just because in the case of the multiplication table he *knows* and is done with it; in the case of Mohammed he does not *know*, and makes up for his lack of knowledge by passionate feeling.

The same consideration explains why young people in each generation are so specially fond of the writers who have this quality of revelation about them. Young people, if they are normally ambitious and full of vitality, as one expects them to be, are always on the look out for a revelation. For purely physical or biological reasons, they are hopeful; they expect that the time coming, which will be their own time, is sure to be much better than the present, in which they hardly count, or the past, in which they did not count at all. (It is amusing to note in passing that, when there is a difference of opinion between young and old, each tends to reject the other for the same reason — because he seems to represent the superseded past. The young man listens impatiently to the old, thinking: Yes, of course; that is what they thought when people wore whiskers, in the time of Queen Victoria. And the old man listens impatiently to the young, thinking: Yes, of course; that is just the sort of nonsense I used to talk when my whiskers were just sprouting, in the reign of Queen Victoria.) I am inclined to think in general that the typical attitude of a young man — a fairly modest and reasonable young man — towards his elders is to feel that they evidently know a great deal and have read a surprising quantity of books, but how strangely they have contrived to miss the one thing that matters! And the one thing that matters, where will he find it? Clearly in some teacher whom his elders have not heard, or have not listened to. It may be a personal acquaintance whose conversation inspires him. It may be a new writer with a message, or an older writer whom his elders might have read but did not. It may be some quite ancient writer, in whom a new message has been discovered. There are two requirements only for the prophet — or rather for entrance to the competition for rank as a prophet. You must have been neglected by the last generation, and you must have the prophetic style. You must have some strong conviction, however vague and however disproportionate, about those parts of life which are imperfectly charted and immediately interesting, and you must represent something unknown or at least untaught by our uncles and our schoolmasters. . . .

When I am disposed, as I suppose all of us sometimes are, to despair of modern civilization and to think that the world has gone mad, I always counteract the impression in one way. I turn from contemplating vast masses of life, which one cannot fully survey and cannot possibly divide into elements and add up into totals, and take some one particular branch of human activity. Ask the various specialists and they will generally tell you that, though the world as a whole is very likely going to the dogs, the particular part they know about has improved. Ask the engineer; he will tell you of the enormous advance made in engineering; the schoolmaster, he may complain that education does not advance faster, but he has no doubt that it is advancing; the doctor, he thinks the world is in a very poor state because it does not attend sufficiently to medical men, but medicine itself is improving hand over hand; the sociologist or social reformer, he will denounce the present state of things as heartily as any one could wish, but he will generally admit that in detail everything that has been worked at has been made rather better.

And after all, if most of our pilots in these strange waters sooner or later turn out mistaken and have to be left behind or even thrown overboard, why should any reasonable person be surprised at that? It is all in the bargain. It is all in the ordinary bargain that man perforce makes with life. There is no finality. There is no full and exact statement, even about those parts of experience which are already reduced to order and marked down on the charts. And meantime Man is moving always, every hour, forth into the uncharted; into the region, not of knowledge and certainty, but of experiment, and guesswork, and daring and wisdom. I believe with all my heart in human progress. But progress is not an advance along a straight path; it is the groping of people with darkness ahead of them and light behind; the questing this way and that of men climbing an unknown precipice; the search for good paths through an unexplored bog, where the best way of advance is no doubt generally discovered by guides who have studied the ways and habits of bogs but may sometimes be hit upon by a child. And the popular prophets, the speakers of burning words, are generally those who at least believe that they have seen some path, and cry to us some advice that seems to them the one thing most needed at the moment.

At the moment their words seem to be of extreme importance; and when the moment has passed, as a rule, their advice has passed too. Only there still remain — and this is perhaps the greatest difference, next to differences in sincerity, between the various breeds of prophet — that there still remain some whose words seem to apply not only to the moment for which they spoke them but to the permanent or constantly recurrent needs of humanity. These are the men for whom we scholars seek in the literature of diverse and widely removed ages. They are the people who have felt most profoundly and expressed most poignantly those facts about life which are always important and always easily overlooked, those visions and aspirations in which the human race is always afresh finding its calm in the midst of storm, its "deliverance from the body of this death"; and their words stay with us as something more than literature, more than mere art of writing or pleasant help for the passing of leisure hours: "the precious life-blood of a master-spirit, treasured up for a life beyond life."

—*From Essays and Addresses by Gilbert Murray, English (1866–).*

The Provinces of the Several Arts

JOHN ADDINGTON SYMONDS

I

"ART," said Goethe, "is but form-giving." We might vary this definition, and say, "Art is a method of expression or presentation." Then comes the question: If art gives form, if it is a method of expression or presentation, to what does it give its form, what does it express or present? The answer certainly must be: Art gives form to human consciousness; expresses or presents the feeling or the thought of man. Whatever else art may do by the way, in the communication of innocent pleasures, in the adornment of life and the softening of manners, in the creation of beautiful shapes and sounds, this, at all events, is its prime function.

While investing thought and sentiment, the spiritual subject-matter of all art, with form, or finding for it proper modes of presentation, each of the arts employs a special medium obeying the laws of beauty proper to that medium. The vehicles of the arts, roughly speaking, are solid substances (like ivory, stone, wood, metal), pigments, sounds, and words. The masterly handling of these vehicles and the realization of their characteristic types of beauty have come to be regarded as the craftsman's paramount concern. And in a certain sense this is a right conclusion; for dexterity in the manipulation of the chosen vehicle, and power to create a beautiful object, distinguish the successful artist from the man who may have had like thoughts and feelings. This dexterity, this power, are the properties of the artist *qua* artist. Yet we must not forget that the form created by the artist for the expression of a thought or feeling is not the final end of art itself. That form, after all, is but the mode of presentation through which the spiritual content must be made. It is the business of art to create an ideal world, in which perception, emotion, understanding, action, and all elements of human life sublimed by thought, shall reappear in concrete forms as beauty. This being so, the logical criticism of art demands that we should not only estimate the technical skill of an artist and his faculty for presenting beauty to the æsthetic sense, but that we should also ask ourselves what portion of the human spirit he has chosen to invest with form, and how he has conceived his subject. It is not necessary that the ideas embodied in a work of art should be the artist's own. They may be common to the race and age; as, for instance, the conception of sovereign deity expressed in the "Olympian Zeus" of Pheidias, or the expression of divine maternity expressed in Raphael's "Madonna di San Sisto." Still the personality of the artist, his own intellectual and moral nature, his peculiar way of thinking and feeling, his individual attitude toward the material given to him in ideas of human consciousness, will modify his choice of subject and of form, and will determine his specific type of beauty. To take an example: supposing that an idea, common to his race and age, is given to the artist for treatment; this will be the final end of the work of art which he produces. But his personal qualities and technical performance determine the degree of success or failure to which he attains in seizing that idea and in presenting it with beauty. Signorelli fails where Perugino excels, in giving adequate and lovely form to the religious sentiment. Michel Angelo is sure of the sublime, and Raphael of the beautiful.

Art is thus the expression of the human spirit by the artist to his fellow-men. The subject-matter of the arts is commensurate with what man thinks and feels and does. It is as deep as religion, as wide as life. But what distinguishes art from religion or from life is, that this subject-matter must assume beautiful form, and must be presented directly or indirectly to the senses. Art is not the school or the cathedral, but the playground, the paradise of humanity. It does not teach, it does not preach. Nothing abstract enters into art's domain. Truth and goodness are transmuted into beauty there, just as in science beauty and goodness assume the shape of truth, and in religion truth and beauty become goodness. The rigid definitions, the unmistakable laws of science, are not to be found in art. Whatever art has touched acquires a concrete sensuous embodiment, and thus ideas presented to the mind in art have lost a portion of their pure thought-essence. It is on this account that the religious conceptions of the Greeks were so admirably fitted for the art of sculpture, and certain portions of the mediæval Christian mythology lent themselves so well to painting. For the same reason the metaphysics of ecclesiastical dogma defy the artist's plastic faculty. Art, in a word, is a middle term between reason and the senses. Its secondary aim, after the prime end of manifesting the human spirit in beautiful form has been accomplished, is to give tranquil and innocent enjoyment.

II

From what has gone before, it will be seen that no human being can make or mold a beautiful form without incorporating in that form some portion of the human mind, however crude, however elementary. In other words, there is no work of art without a theme, without a motive, without a subject. The presentation of that theme, that motive, that subject, is the final end of art. The art is good or bad according as the subject has been well or ill presented, consistently with the laws of beauty special to the art itself. Thus we obtain two standards for æsthetic criticism. We judge a statue, for example, both by the sculptor's intellectual grasp upon his subject, and also by his technical skill and sense of beauty. In a picture of the "Last Judgment" by Fra Angelico we say that the bliss of the righteous has been more successfully treated than the torments of the wicked, because the former has been better understood, although the painter's skill in each is equal. In the Perseus of Cellini we admire the sculptor's spirit, finish of execution, and originality of design, while we deplore that want of sympathy with the heroic character which makes his type of physical beauty slightly vulgar and his facial expression vacuous.

If the phrase "Art for art's sake" has any meaning, this meaning is simply that the artist, having chosen a theme, thinks exclusively in working at it of technical dexterity or the quality of beauty. There are many inducements for the artist thus to narrow his function, and for the critic to assist him by applying the canons of a soulless connoisseurship to his work; for the conception of the subject is but the starting-point in art-production, and the artist's difficulties and triumphs as a craftsman lie in the region of technicalities. He knows, moreover, that however deep or noble his idea may be, his work of art will be worthless if it fail in skill or be devoid of beauty. What converts a thought into a statue or picture, is the form found for it; and so the form itself seems all-important. The artist, therefore, too easily imagines that he may neglect his theme; that a fine piece of coloring, a well-balanced composition, or, as Cellini put it, *"un bel corpo ignudo,"* is enough. And this is especially easy in an age which reflects much upon the arts, and pursues them with enthusiasm, while its deeper thoughts and sentiments are not of the kind which translate themselves readily into artistic form. But, after all, a fine piece of coloring, a well-balanced composition, a sonorous stanza, a learned essay in counterpoint, are not enough. They are all excellent good things, yielding delight to the artistic sense and instruction to the student. Yet when we think of the really great statues, pictures, poems, music of the world, we find that these are really great because of something more – and that more is their theme, their presentation of a noble portion of the human soul. Artists and art students may be satisfied with perfect specimens of a craftsman's skill, independent of his theme; but the mass of men will not be satisfied; and it is as wrong to suppose that art exists for artists and art students, as to talk of art for art's sake. Art exists for humanity. Art transmutes thought and feeling into terms of beautiful form. Art is great and lasting in proportion as it appeals to the human consciousness at large, presenting to it portions of itself in adequate and lovely form.

III

It was necessary in the first place firmly to apprehend the truth that the final end of all art is the presentation of a spiritual content; it is necessary in the next place to remove confusions by considering the special circumstances of the several arts.

Each art has its own vehicle of expression. What it can present and how it can present it, depends upon the nature of this vehicle. Thus, though architecture, sculpture, painting, music, poetry, meet upon the common ground of spiritualized experience – though the works of art produced by the architect, sculptor, painter, musician, poet, emanate from the spiritual nature of the race, are colored by the spiritual nature of the men who make them, and express what is spiritual in humanity under concrete form invented for them by the artist – yet it is certain that all of these arts do not deal exactly with the same portions of this common material in the same way or with the same results. Each has its own department. Each exhibits qualities of strength and weakness special to itself. To define these several departments, to explain the relation of these several vehicles of presentation to the common subject-matter, is the next step in criticism.

IV

Of the fine arts, architecture alone subserves utility. We build for use. But the geometrical proportions which the architect observes, contain the element of beauty and powerfully influence the soul. Into the language of arch and aisle and colonnade, of cupola and façade and pediment, of spire and vault, the architect translates emotion, vague perhaps but deep, mute but unmistakable. When we say that a building is sublime or graceful, frivolous or stern, we mean that sublimity or grace, frivolity or sternness, is inherent in it. The emotions connected with these qualities are inspired in us when we contemplate it, and are presented to us by its form. Whether the architect deliberately aimed at the sublime or graceful – whether the dignified serenity of the Athenian genius sought to express itself in the Parthenon, and the mysticism of mediæval Christianity in the gloom of Chartres Cathedral – whether it was Renaissance paganism which gave its mundane pomp and glory to St. Peter's, and the refined selfishness of royalty its specious splendor to the palace of Versailles – need not be curiously questioned. The fact that we are impelled to raise these points, that architecture more almost than any other art connects itself indissolubly with the life, the character, the moral being of a nation and an epoch, proves that we are justified in bringing it beneath our general definition of the arts. In a great measure because it subserves utility, and is therefore dependent upon the necessities of life, does architecture present to us through form the human spirit. Comparing the palace built by Giulio Romano for the Dukes of Mantua with the contemporary castle of a German prince, we cannot fail at once to comprehend the difference of spiritual conditions, as these displayed themselves in daily life, which then separated Italy from the Teutonic nations. But this is not all. Spiritual quality in the architect himself finds clear expression in his work. Coldness combined with violence marks Brunelleschi's churches; a certain suavity and well-bred taste the work of Bramante; while Michelangelo exhibits wayward energy in his Library of S. Lorenzo, and Amadeo self-abandonment to fancy in his Lombard chapels. I have chosen examples from one nation and one epoch in order that the point I seek to make, the demonstration of a spiritual quality in buildings, may be fairly stated.

V

Sculpture and painting distinguish themselves from the other fine arts by the imitation of concrete existences in nature. They copy the bodies of men and animals, the aspects of the world around us, and the handiwork of mankind. Yet, in so far as they are rightly arts, they do not make imitation an object in itself. The grapes of Zeuxis at which birds pecked, the painted dog at which a cat's hair bristles – if such grapes or such a dog were ever put upon canvas – are but evidences of the artist's skill, not of his faculty as artist. These two plastic, or, as I prefer to call them, figurative arts, use their imitation of the external world for the expression, the presentation of internal, spiritual things. The human form is for them the outward symbol of the inner human spirit, and their power of presenting spirit is limited by the means at their disposal.

Sculpture employs stone, wood, clay, the precious metals to model forms, detached and independent, or raised upon a flat surface in relief. Its domain is the whole range of human character and consciousness, in so far as these can be indicated by fixed facial expression, by physical type, and by attitude. If we dwell for an instant on the greatest historical epoch of sculpture, we shall understand the domain of this art in its range and limitation. At a certain point of Greek development the Hellenic Pantheon began to be translated by the sculptors into statues; and when the genius of the Greeks expired in Rome, the cycle of their psychological conceptions had been exhaustively presented through this medium. During that long period of time, the most delicate gradations of human personality, divinized, idealized, were submitted to the contemplation of the consciousness which gave them being, in appropriate types. Strength and swiftness, massive force and airy lightness, contemplative repose and active energy, voluptuous softness and refined grace, intellectual sublimity and lascivious seductiveness – the whole rhythm of qualities which can be typified by bodily form – were analyzed, selected, combined in various degrees, to incarnate the religious conceptions of Zeus, Aphrodite, Herakles, Dionysus, Pallas, Fauns and Satyrs, Nymphs of woods and waves, Tritons, the genius of Death, heroes and hunters, lawgivers and poets, presiding deities of minor functions, man's lustful appetites and sensual needs. All that men think, or do, or are, or wish for, or imagine in this world, had found exact corporeal equivalents. Not physiognomy alone, but all the portions of the body upon which the habits of the animating soul are wont to stamp themselves, were studied and employed as symbolism. Uranian Aphrodite was distinguished from her Pandemic sister by chastened, lust-repelling loveliness. The muscles of Herakles were more ponderous than the tense sinews of Achilles. The Hermes of the palæstra bore a torso of majestic depth; the Hermes who carried messages from heaven had limbs alert for movement. The brows of Zeus inspired awe; the breasts of Dionysus breathed delight.

A race accustomed, as the Greeks were, to read this symbolism, accustomed, as the Greeks were, to note the individuality of naked form, had no difficulty in interpreting the language of sculpture. Nor is there even now much difficulty in the task. Our surest guide to the subject of a bas-relief or statue is study of the physical type considered as symbolical of spiritual quality. From the fragment of a torso the true critic can say whether it belongs to the athletic or the erotic species. A limb of Bacchus differs from a limb of Poseidon. The whole psychological conception of Aphrodite Pandemos enters into every muscle, every point, no less than into her physiognomy, her hair, her attitude.

There is, however, a limit to the domain of sculpture. This art deals most successfully with personified generalities. It is also strong in the presentation of incarnate character. But when it attempts to tell a story, we often seek in vain its meaning. Battles of Amazons or Centaurs upon bas-reliefs, indeed, are unmistakable. The subject is indicated here by some external sign. The group Laocoön appeals at once to a reader of Virgil, and the divine vengeance of Leto's children upon Niobe is manifest in the Uffizzi marbles. But who are the several heroes of the Æginetan pediment, and what was the subject of the Pheidian statues on the Parthenon? Do the three graceful figures of a bas-relief which exists at Naples and in the Villa Albani, represent Orpheus, Hermes, and Eurydice, or Antiope and her two sons? Was the winged and sworded genius upon the Ephesus column meant for a genius of Death or a genius of Love?

This dimness of significance indicates the limitations of sculpture, and inclines some of those who feel its charm to assert that the sculptor seeks to convey no intellectual meaning, that he is satisfied with the creation of beautiful form. There is an element of good sense in this revolt against the faith which holds that art is nothing but a mode of spiritual presentation. Truly the artist aims at producing beauty, is satisfied if he conveys delight. But it is impossible to escape from the certainty that, while he is creating forms of beauty, he means something, feels something; and that something, that theme for which he finds the form, is part of the world's spiritual heritage. Only the crudest works of figurative art, capricci and arabesques, have no intellectual content; and even these are good in so far as they convey the playfulness of fancy.

VI

Painting employs colors upon surfaces – walls, panels, canvas. What has been said about sculpture will apply in a great measure to this art. The human form, the world around us, the works of man's hands, are represented in paintings, not for their own sake merely, but with the view of bringing thought, feeling, action, home to the consciousness of the spectator from the artist's consciousness on which they have been impressed. Painting can tell a story better than sculpture, can represent more complicated feelings, can suggest thoughts of a subtler intricacy. Through color, it can play, like music, directly on powerful but vague emotion. It is deficient in the fullness and roundness of concrete reality. A statue stands before us, the soul incarnate in palpable form, fixed and frozen for eternity. The picture is a reflection cast upon a magic glass; not less permanent, but reduced to shadow of palpable reality. To follow these distinctions farther would be alien from the present purpose. It is enough to repeat that, within their several spheres, according to their several strengths and weaknesses, both sculpture and painting present the spirit to us only as the spirit shows itself immersed in things of sense. The light of a lamp enclosed within an alabaster vase is still lamplight, though shorn of luster and toned to colored softness. Even thus the spirit, immersed in things of sense presented to us by the figurative arts, is still spirit, though diminished in its intellectual clearness and invested with hues not its own. To fashion that alabaster form of art with utmost skill, to make it beautiful, to render it transparent, is the artist's function. But he will have failed of the highest if the light within burns dim, or if he gives the world a lamp in which no spiritual flame is lighted.

VII

Music transports us to a different region. Like architecture, it imitates nothing. It uses pure sound, and sound of the most wholly artificial kind — so artificial that the musical sounds of one race are unmusical, and therefore unintelligible, to another. Like architecture, music relies upon mathematical proportions. Unlike architecture, music serves no utility. It is the purest art of pleasure — the truest paradise and playground of the spirit. It has less power than painting, even less power than sculpture, to tell a story or to communicate an idea. For we must remember that when music is married to words, the words, and not the music, reach our thinking faculty. And yet, in spite of all this, music presents man's spirit to itself through form. The domain of the spirit over which music reigns, is emotion — not defined emotion, not feeling even so generally defined as jealousy or anger — but those broad bases of man's being out of which emotions spring, defining themselves through action into this or that set type of feeling. Architecture, we have noticed, is so connected with specific modes of human existence, that from its main examples we can reconstruct the life of men who used it. Sculpture and painting, by limiting their presentation to the imitation of external things, have all the help which experience and association render. The mere artificiality of music's vehicle separates it from life and makes its message untranslatable. Nevertheless, this very disability under which it labors is the secret of its extraordinary potency.

To expect clear definition from music — the definition which belongs to poetry — would be absurd. The sphere of music is in sensuous perception; the sphere of poetry is in intelligence. Music, dealing with pure sound, must always be vaguer in significance than poetry, which deals with words. Nevertheless its effect upon the sentient subject may be more intense and penetrating for this very reason. We cannot fail to understand what words are intended to convey; we may very easily interpret in a hundred different ways the message of sound. But this is not because words are wider in their reach and more alive; rather because they are more limited, more stereotyped, more dead. They symbolize something precise and unmistakable; but this precision is itself attenuation of the something symbolized. The exact value of the counter is better understood when it is a word than when it is a chord, because all that a word conveys has already become a thought, while all that musical sounds convey remains within the region of emotion which has not been intellectualized. Poetry touches emotion through the thinking faculty. If music reaches the thinking faculty at all, it is through fibers of emotion. But emotion, when it has become thought, has already lost a portion of its force, and has taken to itself a something alien to its nature. Therefore the message of music can never rightly be translated into words. It is the very largeness and vividness of the sphere of simple feeling which makes its symbolical counterpart in sound so seeming vague. But in spite of this incontestable defect of seeming vagueness, an emotion expressed by music is nearer to our sentient self, if we have ears to take it in, than the same emotion limited by language. It is intenser, it is more immediate, as compensation for being less intelligible, less unmistakable in meaning. It is an infinite, an indistinct realm, where each consciousness defines and sets a limitary form.

Nothing intervenes between the musical work of art and the fibers of the sentient being it immediately thrills. We do not seek to say what music means. We feel the music. And if a man should pretend that the music has not passed beyond his ears, has communicated nothing but a musical delight, he simply tells us that he has not felt music. The ancients on this point were wiser than some moderns when, without pretending to assign an intellectual significance to music, they held it for an axiom that one type of music bred one type of character, another type another. A change in the music of a state, wrote Plato, will be followed by changes in its constitution. It is of the utmost importance, said Aristotle, to provide in education for the use of the ennobling and the fortifying moods. These philosophers knew that music creates a spiritual world, in which the spirit cannot live and move without contracting habits of emotion. In this vagueness of significance but intensity of feeling lies the magic of music. A melody occurs to the composer, which he certainly connects with no act of the reason, which he is probably unconscious of connecting with any movement of his feeling, but which nevertheless is the form in sound of an emotional mood. When he reflects upon the melody secreted thus impromptu, he is aware, as we learn from his own lips, that this work has correspondence with emotion. Beethoven calls one symphony Heroic, another Pastoral; of the opening of another he says, "Fate knocks at the door." Mozart sets comic words to the mass-music of a friend, in order to make his sense of its inaptitude for religious sentiment. All composers use phrases like Maestoso, Pomposo, Allegro, Lagrimoso, Con Fuoco, to express the general complexion of the mood their music ought to represent.

VIII

Before passing to poetry, it may be well to turn aside and consider two subordinate arts, which deserve a place in any system of æsthetics. These are dancing and acting. Dancing uses the living human form, and presents feeling or action; the passions and the deeds of men, in artificially educated movements of the body. The element of beauty it possesses, independently of the beauty of the dancer, is rhythm. Acting or the art of mimicry presents the same subject-matter, no longer under the conditions of fixed rhythm, but as an ideal reproduction of reality. The actor is what he represents, and the element of beauty in his art is perfection of realization. It is his duty as an artist to show us Orestes or Othello, not perhaps exactly as Othello and Orestes were, but as the essence of their tragedies, ideally incorporate in action, ought to be. The actor can do this in dumb show. Some of the greatest actors of the ancient world were mimes. But he usually interprets a poet's thought, and attempts to present an artistic conception in a secondary form of art, which has for its advantage his own personality in play.

IX

The last of the fine arts is literature; or, in the narrower sphere of which it will be well to speak here only, is poetry. Poetry employs words in fixed rhythms, which we call metres. Only a small portion of its effect is derived from the beauty of its sound. It appeals to the sense of hearing far less immediately than music does. It makes no appeal to the eyesight, and takes no help from the beauty of color. It produces no palpable, tangible object. But language being the storehouse of all human experience, language being the medium whereby spirit communicates with spirit in affairs of life, the vehicle which transmits to us the thoughts and feelings of the past, and on which we rely for continuing our present to the future, it follows that, of all the arts, poetry soars highest, flies widest, and is most at home in the region of the spirit. What poetry lacks of sensuous fullness, it more than balances by intellectual intensity. Its significance is unmistakable, because it employs the very material men use in their exchange of thoughts and correspondence of emotions. To the bounds of its empire there is no end. It embraces in its own more abstract being all the arts. By words it does the work in turn of architecture, sculpture, painting, music. It is the metaphysic of the fine arts. Philosophy finds place in poetry; and life itself, refined to its last utterance, hangs trembling on this thread which joins our earth to heaven, this bridge between experience and the realms where unattainable and imperceptible will have no meaning.

If we are right in defining art as the manifestation of the human spirit to man by man in beautiful form, poetry, more incontestably than any other art, fulfills this definition and enables us to gauge its accuracy. For words are the spirit, manifested to itself in symbols with no sensual alloy. Poetry is therefore the presentation, through words, of life and all that life implies. Perception, emotion, thought, action, find in descriptive, lyrical, reflective, dramatic, and epical poetry their immediate apocalypse. In poetry we are no longer puzzled with problems as to whether art has or has not of necessity a spiritual content. There cannot be any poetry whatsoever without a spiritual meaning of some sort: good or bad, moral, immoral, or non-moral, obscure or lucid, noble or ignoble, slight or weighty – such distinctions do not signify. In poetry we are not met by questions whether the poet intended to convey a meaning when he made it. Quite meaningless poetry (as some critics would fain find melody quite meaningless, or a statue meaningless, or a Venetian picture meaningless) is a contradiction in terms. In poetry, life, or a portion of life, lives again, resuscitated and presented to our mental faculty through art. The best poetry is that which reproduces the most of life, or its intensest moments. Therefore the extensive species of the drama and the epic, the intensive species of the lyric, have been ever held in highest esteem. Only a paradoxical critic maintains the thesis that poetry is excellent in so far as it assimilates the vagueness of music, or estimates a poet by his power of translating sense upon the border-land of nonsense into melodious words. Where poetry falls short in the comparison with other arts, is in the quality of form giving, in the quality of sensuous concreteness. Poetry can only present forms to the mental eye and to the intellectual sense, stimulate the physical senses by indirect suggestion. Therefore dramatic poetry, the most complicated kind of poetry, relies upon the actor; and lyrical poetry, the intensest kind of poetry, seeks the aid of music. But these comparative deficiencies are overbalanced, for all the highest purposes of art, by the width and depth, the intelligibility and power, the flexibility and multitudinous associations of language. The other arts are limited in what they utter. There is nothing which has entered into the life of man which poetry cannot express. Poetry says everything in man's own language to the mind. The other arts appeal imperatively, each in its own region, to man's senses; and the mind receives art's message by the help of symbols from the world of sense. Poetry lacks this immediate appeal to sense. But the elixir which it offers to the mind, its quintessence extracted from all things of sense, reacts through intellectual perception upon all the faculties that make men what they are.

X

I used a metaphor in one of the foregoing paragraphs to indicate the presence of the vital spirit, the essential element of thought or feeling, in the work of art. I said it radiated through the form, as lamplight through an alabaster vase. Now the skill of the artist is displayed in modelling that vase, in giving it shape, rich and rare, and fashioning its curves with subtlest workmanship. In so far as he is a craftsman, the artist's pains must be bestowed upon this precious vessel of the animating theme. In so far as he has power over beauty, he must exert it in this plastic act. It is here that he displays dexterity; here that he creates; here that he separates himself from other men who think and feel. The poet, more perhaps than any other artist, needs to keep this steadily in view; for words being our daily vehicle of utterance, it may well chance that the alabaster vase of language should be hastily or trivially modelled. This is the true reason why "neither gods nor men nor the columns either suffer mediocrity in singers." Upon the poet it is specially incumbent to see that he has something rare to say and some rich mode of saying it. The figurative arts need hardly be so cautioned. They run their risk in quite a different direction. For sculptor and for painter, the danger is lest he should think that alabaster vase his final task. He may too easily be satisfied with molding a beautiful but empty form.

— *From Essays Speculative and Suggestive, by John Addington Symonds, English (1840–1893).*

The History of Literature

HIPPOLYTE TAINE

I

THERE IS then a system in human sentiments and ideas; and this system has for its motive power certain general traits, certain marks of the intellect and the heart common to men of one race, age, or country. . . .

What is really the mental structure of

man? Images or representations of things, which float within him, exist for a time, are effaced, and return again, after he has been looking upon a tree, an animal, any visible object. This is the subject-matter, the development whereof is double, either speculative or practical, according as the representations resolve themselves into a *general conception* or an *active resolution*. Here we have the whole of man in an abridgment; and in this limited circle human diversities meet, sometimes in the womb of the primordial matter, sometimes in the twofold primordial development. However minute in their elements, they are enormous in the aggregate, and the least alteration in the factors produces vast alteration in the results. According as the representation is clear and as it were punched out or confused and faintly defined, according as it embraces a great or small number of the characteristics of the object, according as it is violent and accompanied by impulses, or quiet and surrounded by calm, all the operations and processes of the human machine are transformed. So, again, according as the ulterior development of the representation varies, the whole human development varies. If the general conception in which it results is a mere dry notation (in Chinese fashion), language becomes a sort of algebra, religion and poetry dwindle, philosophy is reduced to a kind of moral and practical common sense, science to a collection of utilitarian formulas, classifications, mnemonics, and the whole intellect takes a positive bent. If, on the contrary, the general representation in which the conception results is a poetical and figurative creation, a living symbol, as among the Aryan races, language becomes a sort of delicately-shaded and colored epic poem, in which every word is a person, poetry and religion assume a magnificent and inexhaustible grandeur, metaphysics are widely and subtly developed, without regard to positive applications; the whole intellect, in spite of the inevitable deviations and shortcomings of its effort, is smitten with the beautiful and the sublime, and conceives an ideal capable by its nobleness and its harmony of rallying round it the tenderness and enthusiasm of the human race. If, again, the general conception in which the representation results is poetical but not graduated; if man arrives at it not by an uninterrupted gradation, but by a quick intuition; if the original operation is not a regular development, but a violent explosion — then, as with the Semitic races, metaphysics are absent, religion conceives God only as a king solitary and devouring, science cannot grow, the intellect is too rigid and unbending to reproduce the delicate operations of nature, poetry can give birth only to vehement and grandiose exclamations, language cannot unfold the web of argument and of eloquence, man is reduced to a lyric enthusiasm, and unchecked passion, a fanatical and limited action. In this interval between the particular representation and the universal conception are found the germs of the greatest human differences. Some races, as the classical, pass from the first to the second by a graduated scale of ideas, regularly arranged, and general by degrees; others, as the Germanic, traverse the same ground by leaps, without uniformity, after vague and prolonged groping. Some, like the Romans and English, halt at the first steps; others, like the Hindoos and Germans, mount to the last. If, again, after considering the passage from the representation to the idea, we consider that from the representation to the resolution, we find elementary differences of the like importance and the like order, according as the impression is sharp, as in southern climates, or dull, as in northern; according as it results in instant action, as among barbarians, or slowly, as in civilized nations; as it is capable or not of growth, inequality, persistence, and relations. The whole network of human passions, the chances of peace and public security, the sources of labor and action, spring from hence. Such is the case with all primordial differences: their issues embrace an entire civilization; and we may compare them to those algebraical formulas which, in a narrow limit, contain in advance the whole curve of which they form the law. Not that this law is always developed to its issue; there are perturbing forces; but when it is so, it is not that the law was false, but that it was not single. New elements become mingled with the old; great forces from without counteract the primitive. The race emigrates, like the Aryan, and the change of climate has altered in its case the whole economy, intelligence, and organization of society. The people has been conquered, like the Saxon nation, and a new political structure has imposed on it customs, capacities, and inclinations which it had not. The nation has installed itself in the midst of a conquered people, downtrodden and threatening, like the ancient Spartans; and the necessity of living like troops in the field has violently distorted in an unique direction the whole moral and social constitution. In each case, the mechanism of human history is the same. We continually find, as the original mainspring, some very general disposition of mind and soul, innate and appended by nature to the race, or acquired and produced by some circumstance acting upon the race. These mainsprings, once admitted, produced their effect gradually: I mean that after some centuries they bring the nation into a new condition, religious, literary, social, economic; a new condition which, combined with their renewed effort, produces another condition, sometimes good, sometimes bad, sometimes slowly, sometimes quickly, and so forth; so that we may regard the whole progress of each distinct civilization as the effect of a permanent force which, at every stage, varies its operation by modifying the circumstances of its action.

II

Three different sources contribute to produce this elementary moral state — *race, surroundings,* and *epoch*. What we call the race are the innate and hereditary dispositions which man brings with him into the world, and which, as a rule, are united with the marked differences in the temperament and structure of the body. They vary with various peoples. There is a natural variety of men, as of oxen and horses, some brave and intelligent, some timid and dependent, some capable of superior conceptions and creations, some reduced to rudimentary ideas and inventions, some more specially fitted to special works, and gifted more richly with particular instincts, as we meet with species of dogs better favored than others — these for coursing, those for fighting, these for the chase, those again for house-dogs or shepherds' dogs. We have here a distinct force — so distinct, that amid the vast deviations which the other two motive forces produce in him, one can recognize it still; and a race, like the old Aryans, scattered from the Ganges as far as the Hebrides, settled in every clime, spread over every stage of civilization, transformed by thirty centuries of revolutions, nevertheless manifests in its languages, religions, literatures, philosophies, the community of blood and of intellect which to this day binds its offshoots together. Different as they are, their parentage is not obliterated; barbarism, culture and grafting, differences of sky and soil, fortunes good and bad, have labored in vain: the great marks of the original model have remained, and we find again the two or three principal lineaments of the primitive stamp underneath the secondary imprints which time has laid upon them. There is nothing astonishing in this extraordinary tenacity. Although the vastness of the distance lets us but half perceive — and by a doubtful light — the origin of species, the events of history sufficiently illumine the events anterior to history, to explain the almost immovable steadfastness of the primordial marks. When we meet with them, fifteen, twenty, thirty centuries before our era, in an Aryan, an Egyptian, a Chinese, they represent the work of several myriads of centuries. For as soon as an animal begins to exist, it has to reconcile itself with its surroundings; it breathes and renews itself, is differently affected according to the variations in air, food, temperature. Different climate and situation bring it various needs, and consequently a different course of activity; and this, again, a different set of habits; and still again, a different set of aptitudes and instincts. Man, forced to accommodate himself to circumstances, contracts a temperament and a character corresponding to them; and his character, like his temperament, is so much more stable, as the external impression is made upon him by more numerous repetitions, and is transmitted to his progeny by a more ancient descent. So that at any moment we may consider the character of a people as an abridgment of all its preceding actions and sensations; that is, as a quantity and as a weight, not infinite, since everything in nature is finite, but disproportioned to the rest, and almost impossible to lift, since every moment of an almost infinite past has contributed to increase it, and because, in order to raise the scale, one must place in the opposite scale a still greater number of actions and sensations. Such is the first and richest source of these master faculties from which historical events take their rise; and one sees at the outset that if it be powerful, it is because this is no simple spring, but a kind of lake, a deep reservoir wherein other springs have, for a multitude of centuries, discharged their several streams.

Having thus outlined the interior structure of a race, we must consider the surroundings in which it exists. For man is not alone in the world; nature surrounds him, and his fellow-men surround him; accidental and secondary tendencies overlay his primitive tendencies, and physical or social circumstances disturb or confirm the character committed to their charge. Sometimes the climate has had its effect. Though we can follow but obscurely the Aryan peoples from their common fatherland to their final settlements, we can yet assert that the profound differences which are manifest between the German races on the one side, and the Greek and Latin on the other, arise for the most part from the difference between the countries in which they are settled: some in cold moist lands, deep in black marshy forests or on the shores of a wild ocean, beset by melancholy or violent sensations, prone to drunkenness and gluttony, bent on a fighting, blood-spilling life; others, again, within loveliest landscapes, on a bright and pleasant sea-coast, enticed to navigation and commerce, exempt from gross cravings of the stomach, inclined from the beginning to social ways, to a settled organization of the state, to feelings and dispositions such as develop the art of oratory, the talent for enjoyment, the inventions of science, letters, arts. Sometimes the state policy has been at work, as in the two Italian civilizations: the first wholly turned to action, conquest, government, legislation, on account of the original site of its city of refuge, its borderland emporium, its armed aristocracy, who, by importing and drilling strangers and conquered, created two hostile armies, having no escape from its internal discords and its greedy instincts but in systematic warfare; the other, shut out from unity and any great political ambition by the stability of its municipal character, the cosmopolitan position of its pope, and the military intervention of neighboring nations, directed by the whole bent of its magnificent and harmonious genius towards the worship of pleasure and beauty. Sometimes the social conditions have impressed their mark, as eighteen centuries ago by Christianity, and twenty-five centuries ago by Buddhism, when around the Mediterranean, as well as in Hindostan, the extreme results of Aryan conquest and civilization induced intolerable oppression, the subjugation of the individual, utter despair, the thought that the world was cursed, with the development of metaphysics and myth, so that man in this dungeon of misery, feeling his heart softened, begot the idea of abnegation, charity, tender love, gentleness, humility, brotherly love — there, in a notion of universal nothingness, here under the Fatherhood of God. Look around you upon the regulating instincts and faculties implanted in a race — in short, the mood of intelligence in which it thinks and acts at the present time: you will discover most often the work of some one of these prolonged situations, these surrounding circumstances, persistent and gigantic pressures, brought to bear upon an aggregate of men who, singly and together, from generation to generation, are continually molded and modeled by their action; in Spain, a crusade against the Mussulmans which lasted eight centuries, protracted even beyond and until the exhaustion of the nation by the expulsion of the Moors, the spoliation of the Jews, the establishment of the Inquisition, the Catholic wars; in England, a political establishment of eight centuries, which keeps a man erect and respectful, in independence and obedience, and accustoms him to strive unitedly, under the authority of the law; in France, a Latin organization, which, imposed first upon docile barbarians, then shattered in the universal crash, was reformed from within under a lurking conspiracy of the national instinct, was developed under hereditary kings, ends in a sort of leveling republic, centralized, administrative, under dynasties exposed to revolution. These are the most efficacious of the visible causes which mold the primitive man: they are to nations what education, career, condition, abode, are to individuals; and they seem to comprehend everything, since they comprehend all external powers which shape human matter, and by which the external acts on the internal.

There is yet a third rank of causes; for, with the forces within and without, there is the work which they have already produced together, and this work itself contributes to produce that which follows. Beside the permanent impulse and the given surroundings, there is the acquired momentum. When the national character and surrounding circumstances operate, it is not upon a *tabula rasa,* but on a ground on which marks are already impressed. According as one takes the ground at one moment or another, the imprint is different; and this is the cause that the total effect is different. Consider, for instance, two epochs of a literature or art — French tragedy under Corneille and under Voltaire, the Greek drama under Æschylus and under Euripides, Italian painting under Da Vinci and under Guido. Truly, at either of these two extreme points the general idea has not changed; it is always the same human type which is its subject of representation or painting; the mold of verse, the structure of the drama, the form of body has endured. But among several differences there is this, that the one artist is the precursor, the other the successor; the first has no model, the second has; the first sees objects face to face, the second sees them through the first; that many great branches of art are lost, many details are perfected, that simplicity and grandeur of impression have diminished, pleasing and refined forms have increased — in short, that the first work has influenced the second. Thus it is with a people as with a plant; the same sap, under the same temperature, and in the same soil, produces, at different steps of its progressive development, different formations, buds, flowers, fruits, seed-vessels, in such a manner that the one which follows has always the first for its condition, and grows from its death. And if now you consider no longer a brief epoch, as our own time, but one of those wide intervals which embrace one or more centuries, like the middle ages, or our last classic age, the conclusion will be similar. A certain dominant idea has had sway; men, for two, for five hundred years, have taken to themselves a certain ideal model of man: in the middle ages, the knight and the monk; in our classic age, the courtier, the man who speaks well. This creative and universal idea is displayed over the whole field of action and thought; and after covering the world with its works, involuntarily systematic, it has faded, it has died away, and lo, a new idea springs up, destined to a like domination, and the like number of creations. And here remember that the second depends in part upon the first, and that the first, uniting its effect with those of national genius and surrounding circumstances, imposes on each new creation its bent and direction. The great historical currents are formed after this law — the long dominations of one intellectual pattern, or a master idea, such as the period of spontaneous creations called the Renaissance, or the period of oratorical models called the Classical Age, or the series of mystical compositions called the Alexandrian and Christian eras, or the series of mythological efflorescences which we meet with in the infancy of the German people, of the Indian and the Greek. Here as elsewhere we have but a mechanical problem; the total effect is a result, depending entirely on the magnitude and direction of the producing causes. The only difference which separates these moral problems from physical ones is, that the magnitude and direction cannot be valued or computed in the first as in the second. If a need or a faculty is a quantity, capable of degrees, like a pressure or a weight, this quantity is not measurable like the pressure or the weight. We cannot define it in an exact or approximative formula; we cannot have more, or give more, in respect of it, than a literary impression; we are limited to marking and quoting the salient points by which it is manifested, and which indicate approximately and roughly the part of the scale which is its position. But though the means of notation are not the same in the moral and physical sciences, yet as in both the matter is the same, equally made up of forces, magnitudes, and directions, we may say that in both the final result is produced after the same method. It is great or small, as the fundamental forces are great or small and act more or less exactly in the same sense, according as the distinct effects of race, circumstance, and epoch combine to add the one to the other, or to annul one another. Thus are explained the long impotences and the brilliant triumphs which make their appearance irregularly and without visible cause in the life of a people; they are caused by internal concords or contrarieties. There was such a concord when in the seventeenth century the sociable character and the conversational aptitude, innate in France, encountered the drawing-room manners and the epoch of oratorical analysis; when in the nineteenth century the profound and elastic genius of Germany encountered the age of philosophical compositions and of cosmopolitan criticism. There was such a contrariety when in the seventeenth century the rude and lonely English genius tried blunderingly to adopt a novel politeness; when in the sixteenth century the lucid and prosaic French spirit tried vainly to cradle a living poetry. That hidden concord of creative forces produced the finished urbanity and the noble and regular literature under Louis XIV and Bossuet, the grand metaphysics and broad critical sympathy of Hegel and Goethe. That hidden contrariety of creative forces produced the imperfect literature, the scandalous comedy, the abortive drama under Dryden and Wycherley, the vile Greek importations, the groping elaborate efforts, the scant half-graces under Ronsard and the Pleiad. So much we can say with confidence, that the unknown creations toward which the current of the centuries conducts us, will be raised up and regulated altogether by the three primordial forces; that if these forces could be measured and computed, one might deduce from them as from a formula the specialties of future civilization; and that if, in spite of the evident crudeness of our notations, and the fundamental inexactness of our measures, we try now to form some idea of our general destiny, it is upon an examination of these forces that we must ground our prophecy. For in enumerating them, we traverse the complete circle of the agencies; and when we have considered race, circumstance, and epoch, which are the internal mainsprings, the external pressure, and the acquired momentum, we have exhausted not only the whole of the actual causes, but also the whole of the possible causes of motion.

III

It remains for us to examine how these causes, when applied to a nation or an age, produce their results. As a rivulet falling from a height spreads its streams, according to the depth of the descent, stage after stage, until it reaches the lowest level of the soil, so the disposition of intellect or soul impressed on a people by race, circumstance, or epoch, spreads in different proportions and by regular descents, down the diverse orders of facts which make up its civilization. If we arrange the map of a country, starting from the watershed, we find that below this common point the streams are divided into five or six principal basins, then each of these into several secondary basins, and so on, until the whole country with its thousand details is included in the ramifications of this network. So, if we arrange the psychological map of the events and sensations of a human civilization, we find first of all five or six well-defined provinces — religion, art, philosophy, the state, the family, the industries; then in each of these provinces natural departments; and in each of these, smaller territories, until we arrive at the numberless details of life such as may be observed within and around us every day. If now we examine and compare these diverse groups of facts, we find first of all that they are made up of parts, and that all have parts in common. Let us take first the three chief works of human intelligence — religion, art, philosophy. What is a philosophy but a conception of nature and its primordial causes, under the form of abstractions and formularies? What is there at the bottom of a religion or of an art but a conception of this same nature and of these same causes, under form of symbols more or less concise, and personages more or less marked; with this difference, that in the first we believe that they exist, in the second we believe that they do not exist? Let the reader consider a few of the great creations of the intelligence in India, Scandinavia, Persia, Rome, Greece, and he will see that, throughout, art is a kind of philosophy made sensible, religion a poem taken for true, philosophy an art and a religion dried up, and reduced to simple ideas. There is, therefore, at the core of each of these three groups, a common element, the conception of the world and its principles; and if they differ among themselves, it is because each combines with the common, a distinct element: now the power of abstraction, again the power to personify and to believe, and finally the power to personify and not believe. Let us now take the two chief works of human association, the family and the state. What forms the state but a sentiment of obedience by which the many unite under the authority of a chief? And what forms the family but the sentiment of obedience, by which wife and children act under the direction of a father and husband? The family is a natural state, primitive and restrained, as the state is an artificial family, ulterior and expanded; and among the differences arising from the number, origin, and condition of its members, we discover in the small society as in the great, a like disposition of the fundamental intelligence which assimilates and unites them. Now suppose that this element receives from circumstance, race or epoch certain special marks, it is clear that all the groups into which it enters, will be modified proportionately. If the sentiment of obedience is merely fear, you will find, as in most Oriental states, a brutal despotism, exaggerated punishment, oppression of the subject, servility of manners, insecurity of property, an impoverished production, the slavery of women, and the customs of the harem. If the sentiment of obedience has its root in the instinct of order, sociality, and honor, you will find, as in France, a perfect military organization, a fine administrative hierarchy, a want of public spirit with occasional jerks of patriotism, ready docility of the subject with a revolutionary impatience, the cringing courtier with the counter-efforts of the genuine man, the refined sympathy between conversation and society on the one hand, and the worry at the fireside and among the family on the other, the equality of the married with the incompleteness of the married state, under the necessary constraint of the law. If, again, the sentiment of obedience has its root in the instinct of subordination and the idea of duty, you will find, as among the Germans, security and happiness in the household, a solid basis of domestic life, a tardy and incomplete development of society, an innate respect for established dignities, a superstitious reverence for the past, the keeping up of social inequalities, natural and habitual regard for the law. So in a race, according as the aptitude for general ideas varies, religion, art, and philosophy vary. If man is naturally inclined to the widest universal conceptions, and apt to disturb them at the same time by the nervous delicacy of his over-sensitive organization you will find, as in India, an astonishing abundance of gigantic religious creations, a glowing outgrowth of vast and transparent epic poems, a strange tangle of subtle and imaginative philosophies, all so well interwoven, and so penetrated with a common essence, as to be instantly recognized, by their breadth, their coloring, and their want of order, as the products of the same climate and the same intelligence. If, on the other hand, a man naturally staid and balanced in mind limits of his own accord the scope of his ideas, in order the better to define their form, you will find, as in Greece, a theology of artists and tale-tellers; distinctive gods, soon considered distinct from things, and transformed, almost at the outset, into recognized personages; the sentiment of universal unity all but effaced, and barely preserved in the vague notion of Destiny; a philosophy rather close and delicate than grand and systematic, confined to a lofty metaphysics, but incomparable for logic, sophistry, and morals; poetry and arts superior for clearness, spirits, scope, truth, and beauty to all that have ever been known. If, once more, man, reduced to narrow conceptions, and deprived of all speculative refinement, is at the same time altogether absorbed and straitened by practical occupations, you will find, as in Rome, rudimentary deities, mere hollow names, serving to designate the trivial details of agriculture, generation, household concerns, etiquettes, in fact of marriage, of the farm, producing a mythology, a philosophy, a poetry, either worth nothing or borrowed. Here, as everywhere, the law of mutual dependence comes into play. A civilization forms a body, and its parts are connected with each other like the parts of an organic body. As in an animal, instincts, teeth, limbs, osseous structure, muscular envelope, are mutually connected, so that a change in one produces a corresponding change in the rest, and a clever naturalist can by a process of reasoning reconstruct out of a few fragments almost the whole body; even so in a civilization, religion, philosophy, the organization of the family, literature, the arts, make up a system in which every local change induces a general change, so that an experienced historian, studying some particular part of it, sees in advance and half predicts the character of the rest. There is nothing vague in this interdependence. In the living body the regulator is, first, its tendency to manifest a certain primary type; then its necessity for organs whereby to satisfy its wants, and for harmony with itself in order that it may live. In a civilization, the regulator is the presence, in every great human creation, of a productive element, present also in other surrounding creations — to wit, some faculty, aptitude, disposition, effective and discernable, which, being possessed of its proper character, introduces it into all the operations in which it assists, and, according to its variations, causes all the works in which it co-operates to vary also.

IV

At this point we can obtain a glimpse of the principal features of human transformations, and begin to search for the general laws which regulate, not events only, but classes of events, not such and such religion or literature, but a group of literatures or religions. If, for instance, it were admitted that a religion is a metaphysical poem, accompanied by a belief; and remarking at the same time that there are certain epochs, races, and circumstances in which belief, the poetical and metaphysical faculty, are combined with an unwonted vigor; if we consider that Christianity and Buddhism were produced at periods of grand productions, and amid such miseries as raised up the fanatics of the Cévennes; if we recognize, on the other hand, that primitive religions are born at the awakening of human reason, during the richest blossoming of human imagination, at a time of the fairest artlessness and the greatest credulity; if we consider, also, that Mohammedanism appeared with the dawning of poetic prose, and the conception of national unity, among a people destitute of science, at a period of sudden development of the intellect—we might then conclude that a religion is born, declines, is reformed and transformed according as circumstances confirm and combine with more or less exactitude and force its three generative instincts; and we should understand why it is endemic in India, amid imaginative, philosophic, eminently fanatic brains; why it blossomed forth so strangely and grandly in the middle ages, amid an oppressive organization, new tongues and literatures; why it was aroused in the sixteenth century with a new character and heroic enthusiasm, amid universal regeneration, and during the awakening of the German races; why it breaks out into eccentric sects amid the rude American democracy, and under the bureaucratic Russian despotism; why, in fine, it is spread, at the present day, over Europe in such different dimensions and such various characteristics, according to the differences of race and civilization. And so far every kind of human production—for literature, music, the fine arts, philosophy, science, statecraft, industries, and the rest. Each of these has for its direct cause a moral disposition, or a combination of moral dispositions: the cause given, they appear; the cause withdrawn, they vanish: the weakness or intensity of the cause measures their weakness or intensity. They are bound up with their causes, as a physical phenomenon with its condition, as the dew with the fall of the variable temperature, as dilatation with heat. There are such dualities in the moral as in the physical world, as rigorously bound together, and as universally extended in the one as in the other. Whatever in the one case produces, alters, suppresses the first term, produces, alters, suppresses the second as a necessary consequence. Whatever lowers the temperature, deposits the dew. Whatever develops credulity side by side with poetical thoughts, engenders religion. Thus phenomena have been produced; thus they will be produced. As soon as we know the sufficient and necessary condition of one of these vast occurrences, our understanding grasps the future as well as the past. We can say with confidence in what circumstances it will reappear, foresee without rashness many portions of its future history, and sketch with care some features of its ulterior development.

—*From the Introduction to The History of English Literature, by Hippolyte Taine, French (1828–1893), translated by Henri Van Laun.*

~ ✿ ~

Future and Past

JOSÉ ENRIQUE RODÓ

Near this statue where you have seen me preside each day over our talks as friends—talks which I hope have succeeded in dispelling from the work of teaching any touch of austerity—I have once more to speak to you, that our parting hour may be like the seal stamped upon our agreement both in feeling and in ideas. So I invoke Ariel as my divinity, and I could wish to-day for my lecture the most gentle and persuasive force that ever it has had, for I think that to speak to youth of noble motives, of lofty ideas, whatever they are, is as a kind of sacred oratory. I also think that the spirit of youth is as a generous soil, where the seed of an opportune word may in a short time return the fruits of an immortal harvest. I earnestly wish to coöperate with you in a page of that programme which, in preparing yourselves for the free air of action, you have doubtless formed in your inner thought for the end of your efforts, the object to which each personality shall devote his life. For that intimate, personal programme — which rarely is formulated or written out, but more usually stays within the breast until it is revealed in outer action — fails never in the spirit of those peoples or those persons who are something above the rabble. If, with relation to individual liberty, Goethe could say so profoundly that only he is worthy of liberty and life who can conquer it for himself each day; with much more reason might I say that the honour of every human generation requires that it shall conquer for itself, by the persevering activity of its own thinking, by the effort of its own will, its faith in the determined, the persistent manifestation of the ideal, and the place of the ideal in the evolution of all ideas. And in conquering your own you should begin by recognizing as the first object of faith your own selves. The youth which you love is a power whose application you must work yourselves, and a treasury for the use of which yourselves are responsible. Prize that treasure and that power; see that the lofty consciousness of its possession stay radiant and effective in yourselves. I say to you with Renan: "Youth is the discovery of that immense horizon which is life." And the discovery which reveals unknown lands must be made complete with the virile force which shall rule them. No spectacle can be imagined more fit to captivate at once the interest of the thinker and the enthusiasm of the artist, than that which a human generation presents when it goes to meet a future all vibrant with the impatience of action, of lofty front, with a smiling and high disdain for deceit, the soul purified by sweet and distant mirages which wake in it mysterious impulses, like the visions of Cipango and Eldorado in the heroical chronicles of the Conquistadores.

. . . . .

Before posterity, before history, every great people ought to appear as a growth whose harmonious development has produced a fruit whose fine essence offers to the future the fragrance of its ideality and a fecund seed. Without this durable, human result, raised above the transitory end of the immediately useful, the power and grandeur of empires are but as dreams of a night in the existence of man, to be unheeded, uncounted in the doings of the day which weave the world's destiny. A great civilization, a great people, in the eye of history, is that which after its time has passed still leaves the chords of its memory vibrating, its spirit a lasting legacy to posterity, a new and divine portion of the sum of things. So Carlyle said of the souls of his heroes. So when Helena, in Goethe's poem, called from the realms of night, returns again to the shades, she leaves to Faust her tunic and her veil; the vestments are not herself, but as she has worn them, they breathe of her divineness and possess ever a spell to elevate the soul of him who keeps them above all vulgar things.

An organized society which limits its idea of civilization to the accumulation of material abundance, and of justice to their equitable distribution among its members, will never make of its great cities any thing that differs essentially from the heaping-up of anthills. Populous, opulent cities do not suffice to make a civilization immutable, intensive; they are, indeed, necessary for the highest culture, are its natural atmosphere; the soul of the great man can rarely grow from amid the petty interests of small towns; but this quantitative side of a nation's greatness, like the size of its armies, is but means, not results. Of the stones of Carthage not one remains to bear any message of light, and all the immensity of Babylon or Nineveh does not fill in human memory the hollow of man's hand as compared with the few furlongs that lie between the Acropolis and and the Piraeus. In the perspective of the ideal no city appears great, though it occupy all the space around the towers of Nimrod, nor strong because it can build again those Babylonian walls which carried six chariots abreast; nor beautiful because it was paved with flagstones of alabaster and girt with the gardens of Semiramis. . . . No. In this view that city only is great whose spirit's barriers extend far beyond the mountains or the seas, whose very name pronounced illuminates for posterity an epoch of human thought, a horizon of history. It is strong and lovely when its days are something more than the invariable repetition of the same echo, repeated in never-ending circle; when in it there is something which floats above the faces of the crowd; when amid its night lights there are the lamps which light the solitude of vigils devoted only to thought; thoughts whence germinate ideas which are to come to the sunlight of the coming day with a cry to humanity, a force that shall compel men's souls.

Then only may the extent and material greatness of the city measure the intensity of its civilization. Royal capitals, avenues of proud palaces, are a narrower home than the desert for man's thinking when it is not thought that overlords them. In Tennyson's "Maud" there is a symbol of this torturing of the soul when man's society leaves it still in solitude; where the hero in his madness dreams himself to be dead and buried but a few feet underground, beneath a London pavement; and his consciousness remains, despite his death, attached to the poor remains of his body; the confused clamour of the street makes a dull rumbling that shakes his narrow tomb and impedes his every dream of peace; the weight of an indifferent multitude weighs heavily above his grave, the heavy tread of horses seems to trample on it with disdain; the days succeed days with inexorable tedium. And Maud would wish her grave still farther, farther down, deeper yet within the earth; the dim noises of its surface serve but to keep alive the consciousness that she is dead.

Already there exist, in our Latin America, cities whose material grandeur and apparent civilization place them in the first rank; but one may fear lest a touch of thought upon their exterior, so sumptuous, may make the shining vessel ring hollow within; lest our cities too — though they had their Moreno, their Rivadavia, their Sarmiento, cities which gave initiative to an immortal revolution that, like a stone cast on water, spread the glory of their heroes and the words of their tribunes in ever-widening circles over a vast continent — may end like Tyre or Sidon, or as Carthage ended.

It is your generation that must prevent this; the youth which is of to-day, blood and muscle and nerve of the future. I speak to you, seeing in you those who are destined to guide the others in coming battles for a spiritual cause. The perseverance of your strength must be in you as your certainty of victory. Be not afraid to preach the evangel of refinement to the Scythians, of intelligence to the Boeotians, of disinterest to the Phoenicians. It is enough that thought insists on being, on showing that it exists, as Diogenes proved of movement, to make its spread irresistible and its ultimate triumph secure. Palm by palm, of its own impulse, it will win what space it needs to establish its kingdom among all the other manifestations of life. In its physical organization it will elevate and augment the hollow of the very skull it works in, by its own activity: the thinking races in their physiological growth reveal this power of the unseen workman within. In his social organization also will the thinker well know how to broaden the stage for his drama without the intervention of any power alien to his own. But that conviction, which should preserve from a discouragement whose one utility is to make us rid ourselves of the mean and mediocre, should also keep us from the impatience which demands from time any alteration of its majestic rhythm.

Every one who devotes himself to propagate and preserve in contemporary America a disinterested ideal of the soul — art, science, ethics, religious belief, a political policy of ideals — should educate his belief in the persevering preparation for the future. The past belonged entirely to the sword arm; the present seems well-nigh given over to the horny hand that clears away and builds; the future — a future that seems all the nearer as the thinking and willing of those who look forward to it grow more earnest — shall offer the stability, the scenario, the right atmosphere, to make the higher evolution of man's soul.

Can you not picture to yourselves the America we others dream of? Hospitable to things of the spirit, and not only to the immigrant throngs; thoughtful, without sacrificing its energy of action; serene and strong and withal full of generous enthusiasm; resplendent with the charm of morning calm like the smile of a waking infant, yet with the light of awakening thought. Think on her at least; the honour of your future history depends on your keeping constantly before your eyes the vision of that America, radiant above the realities of the present like the rose window above the dark nave of a cathedral. . . . You may not be its founders; but you will at all events be its forerunners. In the glories of the future there be also palms for such. To prepare the advent of a new human type, a new social unity, a profound student of history, Edgar Quinet, has observed that there always precedes, long before, a scattered group, premature, whose rôle in the evolution of society is like that of the prophetic species in biology discovered by Heer. The new type begins by barely signalizing individualities; these later get organized into varieties, and finally these last, encountering a favouring medium, attain the rank of a species; then, says Quinet, the "group" becomes the multitude, and rules.

This is why your moral philosophy, in labour or in combat, should be the reverse of the Horatian *carpe diem;* treat the present moment only as the first step in the stairway you are to tread, or as a breach in the enemy wall you are to enter by. Ask not at once for the final victory, but for bettering your conditions for the conflict. Thus will your energy have the greater stimulus, since the dramatic interest is greater in the continual renewal and advance, fit school to purify the forces of an heroic generation, than in the serene and Olympic attitude in which a golden age might infest the acolytes of its glory. "It is not the possession of good things, but their attainment which gives to man delight and glory in his power," said Taine, speaking of the happy times of the Renaissance.

Perhaps it were an audacious and ingenuous hope to believe in so rapid and fortunate an evolution, so efficacious an employment of your powers, as to expect that the span of your own generation will suffice to bring in America the conditions of intellectual life; from our now primitive surroundings a true social interest; from our present dead level a summit which shall really be supreme. But where there may not be entire transformation there may be progress; and even though you know that the first fruits of the soil you labour may not be yours, they will if you are generous and brave be a new stimulus to action. The best work is that which places the goal beyond the visible horizon, and the purest abnegation that which renounces for the present, not indeed the laurel of men's applause, but the bliss of seeing one's labour consummate and its goal attained.

Antiquity had altars "for the unknown Gods." Consecrate a part of your soul to the unknown future. As societies develop, thought for the future becomes more and more a factor in their growth and an inspiration to their labours. From the blind improvidence of the savage, who only sees in it that time which shall bring him to the setting of the day's sun and conceives not how his lot in other days may be determined by his present action, up to our anxious preoccupation with the future and provision for our posterity, there is an immense distance; yet even this may seem little enough some day. We are only capable of progress in so far as we can adapt our actions every day to the conditions of a more distant future, to countries farther and farther away. Assurance of our part in bringing about a work which shall survive us, fruitful in times to come, exalts our human dignity and gives us triumph even over the limitations of our nature. If unhappily humanity had to despair definitely of the immortality of the individual consciousness, the most religious sentiment that it could substitute would be that which comes of the thought that even after our dissolution into the heart of things there would outlast, as part of all human inheritance, the very best of all that we had felt or thought, our deepest and our purest essence — just as the beams of a long-extinguished star go on indefinitely and still cheer us mortals, albeit with a melancholy light.

The future is, in the life of human societies, the one inspiring thought. From pious veneration of the past and the cult of tradition, on the one hand, and, on the other, a daring impulse toward the future, comes the noble force which, uplifting the common thought above the present limitations, imparts to its collective agitations and sentiments a sense for some ideal. Men and peoples work under the inspiration of ideas, as the beasts by instinct; and that society which labours and struggles, even unconsciously, to impose an idea upon actualities, acts as does the bird who, building its nest at the prompting of some inner imagination, obeys at once an unconscious memory of the past and a mysterious presentiment of the future.

A preoccupation for the ulterior destiny of our life, by eliminating any suggestion of self-interest, purifies and tranquillizes it and also ennobles; and it is a proud honour of this century that the impelling force of this thought for the future, this sense of what is due the dignity of a rational being, should have shown itself so clearly. Even in the depths of the most utter pessimism, in the bosom of that bitter metaphysic which brought from the East the love of dissolution and nonentity, even Hartmann, the apostle for the return to the Unconscious, has preached, and with some appearance of logic, the austere duty of going on with the work of improvement, labouring for the good of the future, so that human effort, aiding evolution, may bring about a more rapid impulse to the final end – which is the termination of all sorrow, and likewise of all life.

But not, as did Hartmann, in the name of death, but in that of life and hope do I ask of you a portion of your soul for the labour for the future; and it is to ask this of you that I have sought inspiration in the gentle and lovely image of my Ariel. The bountiful Spirit whom Shakespeare hit upon to clothe with so high a symbolism, perhaps with that divine unconsciousness of all it meant which is common to great geniuses, shows clearly, even in this statuette, its ideal significance, admirably expressed in the sculptor's lines. Ariel is reason, and the higher truth. Ariel is that sublime sentiment of the perfectibility of man through whose virtue human clay is magnified and transformed in the realm of things for each one who lives by his light – even that miserable clay of which Ahriman spoke to Manfred. . . . Ariel is, to nature, that crowning of its work which ends the ascending process of organic life with the call of the spirit. Ariel triumphant signifies ideality and order in life, noble inspiration in thought, unselfishness in conduct, high taste in art, heroism of action, delicacy and refinement in manners and usages. He is the eponymous hero in the épopée of man, the immortal protagonist, since first his presence inspired the feeble struggles of reason in primitive man, when he first knitted his brow in the effort to shape the flint, or to scratch rude drawings on a reindeer's bones; since first with his arms he fanned the sacred fire which the ancient Aryan, progenitor of the peoples we call civilized, lit, by what mystery we know not, on the banks of the Ganges, and forged from the divine flame the sceptre of man's mastery. Ariel accompanies him still, and onward, breeding races ever higher, until at the end he hovers radiant above those souls which have over-passed the natural limit of humanity; the same for Plato on the Sunium Promontory as for Francis of Assisi on the solitude of the Albern Mont. His invincible power has as its impulse every uplifting moment of a human life. Though overcome a thousand and one times by the untamable rebellion of Caliban, proscribed by the victorious barbarian, smothered in the clouds of battle, his bright wings spotted by trailing in "the eternal dunghill of Job," Ariel ever rises again, immortally renews his beauty and his youth. Ariel runs nimbly as at the call of Prospero to all who really care for him and seek to find him. His kindly power goes even out at times to those who would deny him. He guides the blind forces of evil and ignorance often to aid, and unwittingly, in works of good. He crosses human history with a song, as in the "Tempest," to inspire those who labour and those who fight until he brings about the fulfilment of that divine plan to them unknown – and he is permitted, as in Shakespeare's play, to snap his bonds in twain and soar forever into his circle of diviner light.

And more than for these words of mine I would have you ever remember tenderly this little figure of Ariel. I would that the image, light and graceful, of this bronze, impress itself upon your inmost spirit. . . . Once I saw, in a museum, an old coin; worn and effaced I could still read its device, in the thin gold, the one word *Esperanza.* I pondered on the influence that simple inscription might have had on the many generations through whose hands the coin had passed; how many fainting spirits it had cheered, how many generous impulses it had fostered, how many desperate resolutions it had prevented. So may the figure of this bronze, graven in your hearts, fulfil in your lives this invisible yet determining part. In dark hours of discouragement may it rekindle in your conscience the warmth of the ideal, return to your hearts the glow of a perishing hope. And Ariel, first enthroned behind the bastion of your inner life, may sally thence to the attack and conquering of other souls. I see the bright spirit smiling back upon you in future times, even though your own still works in shadow. I have faith in your will and in your strength, even more in those to whom you shall transfer your life, transmit your work. I dream in rapture of that day when realities shall convince the world that the Cordillera which soars above the continent of the Americas has been carved to be the pedestal of this statue, the altar of the cult of Ariel.

—*From Ariel by José Enrique Rodó, Uruguayan (1872–1917), translated by F. J. Stimson (J. S. of Dale).*

PART TWO

Geneses: The Origins of Man and Life

THE SEARCH for the First Cause and Guardian of the world has been a continuous experience in the history of all peoples, and the conclusions reached are an element in the common consciousness of many generations. Desire for knowledge of the origin and nature of things has prompted the questions of children, savages, and philosophers. Whether because of eager wonder merely, the religious instinct, or the philosopher's thirst for knowledge, the desire for an adequate explanation of the world and life appears inborn; and the great literature of the past reveals its various manifestations.

Primitive man is philosophical when he refuses to take the world about him as a matter of course, seeks to discover how it came about, and makes it an object of reflection. He may be mentally a child, filled with little more than a child's love of tales which explain objects that have attracted his interest. He may be an adult, filled with vague fears of the unknown and a readiness to believe any explanation however grotesque or absurd. As he matures in experience, he may find himself standing helpless in a universe governed by forces he does not understand and living a life whose destiny he cannot discern. The explanations he works out for the riddle of his existence in a mysterious world may be defective in logic and riotous in fancy. But at all stages his task is in varying degrees none other than that of the modern scientist, theologian, and philosopher, who are likewise seeking for an adequate explanation of the constitution of the universe.

The background of all myths, all religions, and all philosophies reveals the fact that man has a religious and a speculative instinct. As he first invents tales that will satisfy children, he later invents theories, some gay or grave, some clever or absurd, some prosaic or poetical, which will satisfy himself in his changing moods, spiritual needs, and varying stages of intellectual development. The beliefs and conduct of modern man are still conditioned by elemental instinct and the heritage of myths, beliefs, and insights handed down from the past. These he puts to use as he finds them suited to his purposes. On them he founds his religion, as did the ancient Hebrews and the branches of Christendom which are their heirs. Like the modern Japanese, he may use a myth as the foundation of the state and of government. The mythology of the Hindu reveals clearly the philosophic idealism of the race, even in its earliest manifestations, and the faith that from the unseen world of infinite spirit have mysteriously come the phenomena of our finite world. And the Greeks' myths of creation clearly suggest how inextricably involved are man's relations with his gods and his experience of good and evil.

That the theories of creation which may be found in the literatures of the world must be interpreted anew in the light of modern discoveries in geology, biology, and astronomy on the one hand, and in terms of researches in a people's myths and folklore on the other, will be granted by all informed students of comparative cultures. That these theories contain much of interest for the historian of the speculative and religious life of man will be apparent to all who read them. Religion is one of man's native vital forces. Though it may be distorted or exploited, it is not manufactured. In the face of elemental cosmic forces, it continues a constant force in human life. However changed may be the beliefs of modern men from those of their primitive ancestors, the race still seeks the Maker of all things, and would believe him the guardian of the moral life and the upholder of natural law. The accounts of the origins of man and life which have been inherited from the past continue to serve multitudes of our fellow men today.

The Protagoras Myth

PLATO

Time was when there were Gods, but mortal creatures after their kind were not. Now when the appointed time came unto these also that they should be born, the gods fashioned them under the Earth, compounding them of earth, and of fire, and of whatsoever is made by the mingling of fire and earth. Now when they were ready to bring them to light, they gave commandment unto Prometheus and Epimetheus to adorn them and distribute unto each the powers that were meet. But Epimetheus entreated of Prometheus to let him distribute. "When I have distributed," quoth he, "do thou see whether it is done well."

So he prevailed with him, and distributed: and unto some he gave strength without swiftness, but the weaker he adorned with swiftness; unto others he gave weapons; and for those unto whom he gave not weapons he contrived other means of safety; to wit, unto those of them which he clothed with smallness he appointed winged escape, or habitation under ground; and unto those which he increased with bigness, the safety which cometh therefrom. After this fashion, then, did he distribute, ever making one gift equal unto another. These things he contrived, lest perchance any race should be cut off. But when he had furnished them with means for escaping destruction from one another, he contrived for them convenient defence against the seasons of the year, clothing them with thick hairs and stout hides sufficient to keep off the cold of winter and the burning heat; the which might also be for couches proper and native unto each one of them, when they went to their lairs. Moreover, he shod some of them with hoofs, and others with hairs and thick skin without blood. After that he appointed unto them different kinds of food: unto some the herbs of the earth, unto others the fruits of the trees, unto others roots; and some there were unto which he appointed for food the flesh of other beasts. And he ordained that they should bring forth young, some few, and others, which were devoured of these, many, that their race might be preserved.

Now, inasmuch as Epimetheus was not very wise, he unwittingly spent all the qualities he had upon the brutes; and lo! mankind was still left unto him unadorned, and he knew not what he should do concerning them.

While he yet doubteth, Prometheus cometh unto him to look into his distribution; and perceiveth that all other creatures are duly furnished in all things, but that man is naked and without shoes or bed or weapons: and now was come the appointed day on the which man also should go forth from the earth into the light.

Wherefore Prometheus, being brought to his wits' end to devise any means of safety for man, stealeth the cunning workman's wisdom of Hephaestus and Athena, together with fire – for without fire none can get this wisdom or use it; and this he giveth as a gift unto man.

Thus did man get the mechanic wisdom needful for his bare life; but the wisdom which is needful for the life political he had not, for it was with Zeus; and unto Prometheus it was no longer permitted to enter into the citadel, the dwelling-place of Zeus; moreover, the guards of Zeus were terrible; but into the common dwelling of Athena and Hephaestus, wherein they plied their craft, he secretly entered, and stole the fiery art of Hephaestus, and also Athena's art, and gave them unto man. Whence came convenient living unto man; but as for Prometheus, he was afterwards arraigned for theft because of Epimetheus, as the story telleth.

Now man, having been made a partaker of the divine lot, by reason of his kinship with the Godhead, alone among living creatures believed in Gods, and began to take it in hand to set up altars unto them and make graven images of them. Then soon with cunning device did he frame articulate speech and names, and invented houses to dwell in, and raiment and shoes to put on, and beds for rest, and food from the fruits of the earth.

Thus furnished, men at first dwelt scattered abroad, and there were no cities. Wherefore men were continually devoured by wild beasts, for they were altogether weaker than the beasts, and their craftsman's art could help them to get food enough, but was not sufficient for their war with the wild beasts; for they had not yet the art political, whereof the art of warfare is a part.

Wherefore they sought to assemble themselves together, and save themselves by building cities.

Now when they were assembled together, they wronged one another, because they had not the art political; so they were again scattered abroad, and were like to be destroyed.

But Zeus, fearing lest our race should perish utterly, commandeth Hermes to go unto men bearing modesty and justice, for the ordering of cities, and to be bonds joining men together in friendship. Hermes inquireth of Zeus how he shall give justice and modesty unto men. "Are these," quoth he, "to be distributed as the arts are distributed, the which are distributed after this wise – one man hath the art of physic, or some other art, and is sufficient unto many who have it not? Shall I distribute justice and modesty among men thus, or give them unto all?" "Unto all," said Zeus, "and let all be partakers of them. For if few were partakers as of the arts, cities would not arise. Also make it a law from me, that he who cannot partake of modesty and justice shall be put to death, for he bringeth plague into the city."

For this reason, O Socrates, the Athenians and others, when they consult about things which need the skill of the carpenter or other handicraftsman, think that few advisers are enough, and if any one who is not of those thrust himself forward to advise, they will have none of him. Thus do they, thou sayest. And I say 'tis but reasonable they should do this. But when they enter into counsel concerning those things that pertain unto virtue political, which must needs walk alway in the path of righteousness and temperance, then with reason do they bear with any man as a counsellor, considering that all men must partake of this virtue, else there could be no city.

– From The Myths of Plato, Greek (427?–347 B.C.), translated by J. A. Stewart.

The Universal Self

FROM THE UPANISHADS

IN THE BEGINNING this was Self alone, in the shape of a person. He looking around saw nothing but his Self. He first said, "This is I"; therefore he became I by name. Therefore even now, if a man is asked, he first says, "This is I," and then pronounces the other name which he may have. And because before all this, he (the Self) burnt down all evils, therefore he was a person. Verily he who knows this, burns down every one who tries to be before him.

He feared, and therefore any one who is lonely fears. He thought, "As there is nothing but myself, why should I fear?" Thence his fear passed away. For what should he have feared? Verily fear arises from a second only.

But he felt no delight. Therefore a man who is lonely feels no delight. He wished for a second. He was as large as man and wife together. He then made this his Self to fall in two, and thence arose husband and wife. Therefore Yagnavalkya said: "We two are thus, each of us, like half a shell." Therefore the void which was there is filled by the wife. He embraced her, and men were born.

She thought, "How can he embrace me, after having produced me from himself? I shall hide myself."

She then became a cow, the other became a bull and embraced her, and hence cows were born. The one became a mare, the other a stallion; the one a male ass, the other a female ass. He embraced her, and hence one-hoofed animals were born. The one became a she-goat, the other a he-goat; the one became a ewe, the other a ram. He embraced her, and hence goats and sheep were born. And thus he created everything that exists in pairs, down to the ants.

He knew, "I indeed am this creation, for I created all this." Hence he became the creation, and he who knows this lives in this his creation.

Next he thus produced fire by rubbing. From the mouth, as from the fire-hole, and from the hands he created fire. Therefore both the mouth and the hands are inside without hair, for the fire-hole is inside without hair.

And when they say, "Sacrifice to this or sacrifice to that god," each god is but his manifestation, for he is all gods.

Now, whatever there is moist, that he created from seed; this is Soma. So far verily is this universe either food or eater. Soma indeed is food, Agni eater. This is the highest creation of Brahman, when he created the gods from his better part, and when he, who was then mortal, created the immortals. Therefore it was the highest creation. And he who knows this lives in this his highest creation.

Now all this was then undeveloped. It became developed by form and name, so that one could say, "He, called so and so, is such a one." Therefore at present also all this is developed by name and form, so that one can say, "He, called so and so, is such a one."

He (Brahman or the Self) entered thither, to the very tips of the fingernails, as a razor might be fitted in a razor-case, or as fire in a fireplace.

He cannot be seen, for, in part only, when breathing, he is breath by name; when speaking, speech by name; when seeing, eye by name; when hearing, ear by name; when thinking, mind by name. All these are but the names of his acts. And he who worships (regards) him as the one or the other, does not know him, for he is apart from this when qualified by the one or the other. Let men worship him as Self, for in the Self all these are one. This Self is the footstep of everything, for through it one knows everything. And as one can find again by footsteps what was lost, thus he who knows this finds glory and praise.

This, which is nearer to us than anything, this Self, is dearer than a son, dearer than wealth, dearer than all else.

And if one were to say to one who declares another than the Self dear, that he will lose what is dear to him, very likely it would be so. Let him worship the Self alone as dear. He who worships the Self alone as dear, the object of his love will never perish.

Here they say: "If men think that by knowledge of Brahman they will become everything, what then did that Brahman know, whence all this sprang?"

Verily in the beginning this was Brahman, that Brahman knew its Self only, saying, "I am Brahman." From it all this sprang. Thus, whatever Deva was awakened (so as to know Brahman), he indeed became that Brahman; and the same with Rishis and men. The Rishi Vamadeva saw and understood it, singing, "I was Manu (moon), I was the sun." Therefore now also he who thus knows that he is Brahman, becomes all this, and even the Devas cannot prevent it, for he himself is their Self.

Now if a man worships another deity, thinking the deity is one and he another, he does not know. He is like a beast for the Devas. For verily, as many beasts nourish a man, thus does every man nourish the Devas. If only one beast is taken away, it is not pleasant; how much more when many are taken! Therefore it is not pleasant to the Devas that men should know this.

Verily in the beginning this was Brahman, one only. That being one, was not strong enough. It created still further the most excellent Kshatra (power), viz. those Kshatras (powers) among the Devas – Indra, Varuna, Soma, Rudra, Parjanya, Yama, Mrityu, Isana. Therefore there is nothing beyond the Kshatra, and therefore at the Rajasuya sacrifice the Brahmana sits down below the

Kshatriya. He confers that glory on the Kshatra alone. But Brahman is nevertheless the birthplace of the Kshatra. Therefore though a king is exalted, he sits down at the end of the sacrifice below the Brahmana, as his birthplace. He who injures him, injures his own birthplace. He becomes worse, because he has injured one better than himself.

He was not strong enough. He created the Vis (people), the classes of Devas which in their different orders are called Vasus, Rudras, Adityas, Visve Devas, Maruts.

He was not strong enough. He created the Sudra colour (caste), as Pushan (as nourisher). This earth verily is Pushan (the nourisher); for the earth nourishes all this whatsoever.

He was not strong enough. He created still further the most excellent Law (dharma). Law is Kshatra (power) of the Kshatra, therefore there is nothing higher than the law. Thenceforth even a weak man rules a stronger with the help of the Law, as with the help of a king. Thus the Law is what is called the true. And if a man declares what is true, they say he declares the Law; and if he declares the Law, they say he declares what is true. Thus both are the same. . . .

In the beginning this was Self alone, one only. He desired, "Let there be a wife for me that I may have offspring, and let there be wealth for me that I may offer sacrifices." Verily this is the whole desire, and, even if wishing for more, he would not find it. Therefore now also a lonely person desires, "Let there be a wife for me that I may have offspring, and let there be wealth for me that I may offer sacrifices." And so long as he does not obtain either of these things, he thinks he is incomplete. Now his completeness is made up as follows: mind is his Self (husband); speech the wife; breath the child; the eye all worldly wealth, for he finds it with the eye; the ear his divine wealth, for he hears it with the ear. The body (atman) is his work, for with the body he works. This is the fivefold sacrifice, for fivefold is the animal, fivefold man, fivefold all this whatsoever. He who knows this, obtains all this.

—*From the Brihadaranyaka Upanishad, translated by F. Max Müller.*

~ ✿ ~

Genesis: The Creation

In the beginning God created the heaven and the earth. And the earth was without form, and void; and darkness was upon the face of the deep. And the Spirit of God moved upon the face of the waters.

And God said, Let there be light: and there was light. And God saw the light, that it was good: and God divided the light from the darkness. And God called the light Day, and the darkness he called Night. And the evening and the morning were the first day.

And God said, Let there be a firmament in the midst of the waters, and let it divide the waters from the waters. And God made the firmament, and divided the waters which were under the firmament from the waters which were above the firmament: and it was so. And God called the firmament Heaven. And the evening and the morning were the second day.

And God said, Let the waters under the heaven be gathered together unto one place, and let the dry land appear: and it was so. And God called the dry land Earth; and the gathering together of the waters called he Seas: and God saw that it was good.

And God said, Let the earth bring forth grass, the herb yielding seed, and the fruit-tree yielding fruit after his kind, whose seed is in itself, upon the earth: and it was so. And the earth brought forth grass, and herb yielding seed after his kind, and the tree yielding fruit, whose seed was in itself, after his kind: and God saw that it was good.

And the evening and the morning were the third day.

And God said, Let there be lights in the firmament of the heaven, to divide the day from the night; and let them be for signs, and for seasons, and for days, and years. And let there be for lights in the firmament of the heaven to give light upon the earth: and it was so. And God made two great lights; the greater light to rule the day, and the lesser light to rule the night: he made the stars also. And God set them in the firmament of the heaven to give light upon the earth, and to rule over the day, and over the night, and to divide the light from the darkness: and God saw that it was good.

And the evening and the morning were the fourth day.

And God said, Let the waters bring forth

abundantly the moving creature that hath life, and fowl that may fly above the earth in the open firmament of heaven. And God created great whales, and every living creature that moveth, which the waters brought forth abundantly, after their kind, and every winged fowl after his kind: and God saw that it was good. And God blessed them, saying, Be fruitful and multiply, and fill the waters in the seas, and let fowl multiply in the earth.

And the evening and the morning were the fifth day.

And God said, Let the earth bring forth the living creature after his kind, cattle, and creeping thing, and beast of the earth after his kind: and it was so. And God made the beast of the earth after his kind, and cattle after their kind, and every thing that creepeth upon the earth after his kind: and God saw that it was good.

And God said, Let us make man in our image, after our likeness: and let them have dominion over the fish of the sea, and over the fowl of the air, and over the cattle, and over all the earth, and over every creeping thing that creepeth upon the earth. So God created man in his own image, in the image of God created he him; male and female created he them. And God blessed them, and God said unto them, Be fruitful, and multiply, and replenish the earth, and subdue it: and have dominion over the fish of the sea, and over the fowl of the air, and over every living thing that moveth upon the earth.

And God said, Behold, I have given you every herb bearing seed, which is upon the face of all the earth, and every tree, in the which is the fruit of a tree yielding seed; to you it shall be for meat. And to every beast of the earth, and to every fowl of the air, and to every thing that creepeth upon the earth, wherein there is life, I have given every green herb for meat: and it was so.

And God saw every thing that he had made, and behold, it was very good. And the evening and the morning were the sixth day.

II

Thus the heavens and the earth were finished, and all the host of them. And on the seventh day God ended his work which he had made; and he rested on the seventh day from all his work which he had made. And God blessed the seventh day, and sanctified it: because that in it he had rested from all his work which God created and made.

These are the generations of the heavens and of the earth when they were created, in the day that the Lord God made the earth and the heavens, and every plant of the field before it was in the earth, and every herb of the field before it grew: for the Lord God had not caused it to rain upon the earth, and there was not a man to till the ground. But there went up a mist from the earth, and watered the whole face of the ground. And the Lord God formed man of the dust of the ground, and breathed into his nostrils the breath of life; and man became a living soul.

And the Lord God planted a garden eastward in Eden; and there he put the man whom he had formed. And out of the ground made the Lord God to grow every tree that is pleasant to the sight, and good for food; the tree of life also in the midst of the garden, and the tree of knowledge of good and evil.

And a river went out of Eden to water the garden: and from thence it was parted, and became into four heads. The name of the first is Pison: that is it which compasseth the whole land of Havilah, where there is gold; and the gold of that land is good: there is bdellium and the onyx-stone. And the name of the second river is Bihon: the same is it that compasseth the whole land of Ethiopia. And the name of the third river is Hiddekel: that is it which goeth toward the east of Assyria. And the fourth river is Euphrates.

And the Lord God took the man, and put him into the garden of Eden to dress it and to keep it.

And the Lord God commanded the man, saying, Of every tree of the garden thou mayest freely eat: but of the tree of the knowledge of good and evil, thou shalt not eat of it: for in the day that thou eatest thereof thou shalt surely die.

And the Lord God said, It is not good that the man should be alone: I will make him an help meet for him.

And out of the ground the Lord God formed every beast of the field, and every fowl of the air, and brought them unto Adam to see what he would call them; and whatsoever Adam called every living creature, that was the name thereof. And Adam gave names to all cattle, and to the fowl of the air, and to every beast of the field: but for Adam there was not found an help meet for him.

And the Lord God caused a deep sleep to fall upon Adam, and he slept; and he took one of his ribs, and closed up the flesh instead thereof: and the rib, which the Lord God had taken from man, made he a woman, and brought her unto the man.

And Adam said, This is now bone of my bones, and flesh of my flesh: she shall be called Woman, because she was taken out of Man. Therefore shall a man leave his father and his mother, and shall cleave unto his wife: and they shall be one flesh. And they were both naked, the man and his wife, and were not ashamed.

III

Now the serpent was more subtile than any beast of the field which the Lord God had made. And he said unto the woman, Yea, hath God said, Ye shall not eat of every tree of the garden?

And the woman said unto the serpent, We may eat of the fruit of the trees of the garden: but of the fruit of the tree which is in the midst of the garden, God hath said, Ye shall not eat of it, neither shall ye touch it, lest ye die.

And the serpent said unto the woman, Ye shall not surely die: for God doth know, that in the day ye eat thereof, then your eyes shall be opened; and ye shall be as gods, knowing good and evil.

And when the woman saw that the tree was good for food, and that it was pleasant to the eyes, and a tree to be desired to make one wise, she took of the fruit thereof, and did eat, and gave also unto her husband with her; and he did eat. And the eyes of them both were opened, and they knew that they were naked; and they sewed fig-leaves together, and made themselves aprons.

And they heard the voice of the Lord God walking in the garden in the cool of the day: and Adam and his wife hid themselves from the presence of the Lord God amongst the trees of the garden.

And the Lord God called unto Adam, and said unto him, Where art thou?

And he said, I heard thy voice in the garden: and I was afraid, because I was naked; and I hid myself.

And he said, Who told thee that thou wast naked? Hast thou eaten of the tree, whereof I commanded thee that thou shouldest not eat?

And the man said, The woman whom thou gavest to be with me, she gave me of the tree, and I did eat.

And the Lord God said unto the woman, What is this that thou hast done? And the woman said, The serpent beguiled me, and I did eat.

And the Lord God said unto the serpent, Because thou hast done this, thou art cursed above all cattle, and above every beast of the field; upon thy belly shalt thou go, and dust shalt thou eat all the days of thy life: and I will put enmity between thee and the woman, and between thy seed and her seed; it shall bruise thy head, and thou shalt bruise his heel.

Unto the woman he said, I will greatly multiply thy sorrow and thy conception; in sorrow thou shalt bring forth children; and thy desire shall be to thy husband, and he shall rule over thee.

And unto Adam he said, Because thou has hearkened unto the voice of thy wife, and hast eaten of the tree of which I commanded thee, saying, Thou shalt not eat of it: cursed is the ground for thy sake; in sorrow shalt thou eat of it all the days of thy life; thorns also and thistles shall it bring forth to thee; and thou shalt eat the herb of the field; in the sweat of thy face shalt thou eat bread, till thou return unto the ground; for out of it wast thou taken: for dust thou art, and unto dust shalt thou return.

And Adam called his wife's name Eve, because she was the mother of all living.

Unto Adam also and to his wife did the Lord God make coats of skins, and clothed them.

And the Lord God said, Behold, the man is become as one of us, to know good and evil: and now, lest he put forth his hand, and take also of the tree of life, and eat, and live for ever: therefore the Lord God sent him forth from the garden of Eden, to till the ground from whence he was taken.

So he drove out the man; and he placed at the east of the garden of Eden Cherubims, and a flaming sword which turned every way, to keep the way of the tree of life.

—From the First Book of Moses, called Genesis. Hebrew, the Authorized (King James) version.

The Prose Edda

SNORRI STURLUSON

Prologue

IN THE BEGINNING God created heaven and earth and all those things which are in them; and last of all, two of human kind, Adam and Eve, from whom the races are descended. And their offspring multiplied among themselves and were scattered throughout the earth. But as time passed, the races of men became unlike in nature: some were good and believed on the right; but many more turned after the lusts of the world and slighted God's command. Wherefore, God drowned the world in a swelling of the sea, and all living things, save them alone that were in the ark with Noah. After Noah's flood eight of mankind remained alive, who peopled the earth; and the races descended from them. And it was even as before: when the earth was full of folk and inhabited of many, then all the multitude of mankind began to love greed, wealth, and worldly honor, but neglected the worship of God. Now accordingly it came to so evil a pass that they would not name God; and who then could tell their sons of God's mighty wonders? Thus it happened that they lost the name of God; and throughout the wideness of the world the man was not found who could distinguish in aught the trace of his Creator. But not the less did God bestow upon them the gifts of the earth: wealth and happiness, for their enjoyment in the world; He increased also their wisdom, so that they knew all earthly matters, and every phase of whatsoever they might see in the air and on the earth.

One thing they wondered and pondered over: what it might mean, that the earth and the beasts and the birds had one nature in some ways, and yet were unlike in manner of life. In this was their nature one: that the earth was cleft into lofty mountain-peaks, wherein water spurted up, and it was not needful to dig longer for water there than in the deep valleys; so it is also with beasts and birds: it is equally far to the blood in the head and the feet. Another quality of the earth is, that in each year grass and flowers grow upon the earth, and in the same year all that growth falls away and withers; it is even so with beasts and birds: hair and feathers grow and fall away each year. This is the third nature of the earth, that when it is opened and dug up, the grass grows straightway on the soil which is uppermost on the earth. Boulders and stones they likened to the teeth and bones of living beings. Thus they recognized that the earth was quick, and had life with some manner of nature of its own; and they understood that she was wondrous old in years and mighty in kind: she nourished all that lived, and she took to herself all that died. Therefore they gave her a name, and traced the number of their generations from her. The same thing, moreover, they learned from their aged kinsmen: that many hundreds of years have been numbered since the same earth yet was, and the same sun and stars of the heavens; but the courses of these were unequal, some having a longer course, and some a shorter.

From things like these the thought stirred within them that there might be some governor of the stars of heaven: one who might order their courses after his will; and that he must be very strong and full of might. This also they held to be true: that if he swayed the chief things of creation, he must have been before the stars of heaven; and they saw that if he ruled the courses of the heavenly bodies, he must also govern the shining of the sun, and the dews of the air, and the fruits of the earth, whatsoever grows upon it; and in like manner the winds of the air and the storms of the sea. They knew not yet where his kingdom was; but this they believed: that he ruled all things on earth and in the sky, the great stars also of the heaven, and the winds of the sea. Wherefore, not only to tell of this fittingly, but also that they might fasten it in memory, they gave names out of their own minds to all things. This belief of theirs has changed in many ways, according as the peoples drifted asunder and their tongues became severed one from another. But all things they discerned with the wisdom of the earth, for the understanding of the spirit was not given to them; this they perceived, that all things were fashioned of some essence.

The world was divided into three parts: from the south, extending into the west and bordering on the Mediterranean Sea, — all this part was called Africa, the southern quarter of which is hot, so that it is parched with the sun. The second part, from west to north and bordering on the ocean, is called

Europa or Enea; its northern part is so cold that no grass grows upon it, and no man dwells there. From the north and all down over the eastern part, even to the south, is called Asia. In that region of the world is all fairness and pride, and the fruits of the earth's increase, gold and jewels. There also is the centre of the earth; and even as the land there is lovelier and better in every way than in other places, so also were the sons of men there most favored with all goodly gifts: wisdom, and strength of the body, beauty, and all manner of knowledge.

Near the earth's centre was made that goodliest of homes and haunts that ever have been, which is called Troy, even that which we call Turkland. This abode was much more gloriously made than others, and fashioned with more skill of craftsmanship in manifold wise, both in luxury and in the wealth which was there in abundance. There were twelve kingdoms and one High King, and many sovereignties belonged to each kingdom; in the stronghold were twelve chieftains. These chieftains were in every manly part greatly above other men that have ever been in the world. One king among them was called Múnón or Mennón; and he was wedded to the daughter of the High King Priam, her who was called Tróán; they had a child named Trór, whom we call Thor. He was fostered in Thrace by a certain war-duke called Lóríkus; but when he was ten winters old he took unto him the weapons of his father. He was as goodly to look upon, when he came among other men, as the ivory that is inlaid in oak; his hair was fairer than gold. When he was twelve winters old he had his full measure of strength; then he lifted clear of the earth ten bear-skins all at one time; and then he slew Duke Lóríkus, his foster-father, and with him his wife Lórá, or Glórá, and took into his own hands the realm of Thrace, which we call Thrúdheim. Then he went forth far and wide over the lands, and sought out every quarter of the earth, overcoming alone all berserks and giants, and one dragon, greatest of all dragons, and many beasts. In the northern half of his kingdom he found the prophetess that is called Síbil, whom we call Sif, and wedded her. The lineage of Sif I cannot tell; she was fairest of all women, and her hair was like gold. Their son was Lóridi, who resembled his father; his son was Einride, his son Vingethor, his son Vingener, his son Móda, his son Magi, his son Seskef, his son Bedvig, his son Athra (whom we call Annarr), his son Itermann, his son Heremód, his son Skjaldun (whom we call Skjöld), his son Bjáf (whom we call Bjárr), his son Ját, his son Gudólfr, his son Finn, his son Fríallaf (whom we call Fridleifr); his son was he who is named Vóden, whom we call Odin: he was a man far-famed for wisdom and every accomplishment. His wife was Frígídá, whom we call Frigg.

Odin had second sight, and his wife also; and from their foreknowledge he found that his name should be exalted in the northern part of the world and glorified above the fame of all other kings. Therefore, he made ready to journey out of Turkland, and was accompanied by a great multitude of people, young folk and old, men and women; and they had with them much goods of great price. And wherever they went over the lands of the earth, many glorious things were spoken of them, so that they were held more like gods than men. They made no end to their journeying till they were come north into the land that is now called Saxland; there Odin tarried for a long space, and took the land into his own hand, far and wide.

In that land Odin set up three of his sons for land-wardens. One was named Vegdeg: he was a mighty king and ruled over East Saxland; his son was Vitgils; his sons were Vitta, Heingistr's father, and Sigarr, father of Svedbeg, whom we call Svipdagr. The second son of Odin was Beldeg, whom we call Baldr: he had the land which is now called Westphalia. His son was Brandr, his son Frjódigar (whom we call Fródi), his son Freóvin, his son Uvigg, his son Gevis (whom we call Gave). Odin's third son is named Sigi, his son Rerir. These the forefathers ruled over what is now called Frankland; and thence is descended the house known as Völsungs. From all these are sprung many and great houses.

Then Odin began his way northward, and came into the land which they called Reidgothland; and in that land he took possession of all that pleased him. He set up over the land that son of his called Skjöldr, whose son was Fridleifr,—and thence descends the house of Skjöldungs: these are the kings of the Danes. And what was then called Reidgothland is now called Jutland.

After that he went northward, where the land is called Sweden; the king there was named Gylfi. When the king learned of the coming of those men of Asia, who were called Aesir, he went to meet them, and made offer to them that Odin should have such power in his realm as he himself wielded. And such well-being followed ever upon their footsteps, that in whatsoever lands they dwelt were good seasons and peace; and all believed that they caused these things, for the lords of the land perceived that they were unlike other men whom they had seen, both in fairness and also in wisdom.

The fields and the choice lands in that place seemed fair to Odin, and he chose for himself the site of a city which is now called Sigtun. There he established chieftains in the fashion which had prevailed in Troy; he set up also twelve head-men to be doomsmen over the people and to judge the laws of the land; and he ordained also all laws as there had been before in Troy, and according to the customs of the Turks. After that he went into the north, until he was stopped by the sea, which men thought lay around all the lands of the earth; and there he set his son over this kingdom, which is now called Norway. This king was Saemingr; the kings of Norway trace their lineage from him, and so do also the jarls and the other mighty men, as is said in the *Háleyjatal*. Odin had with him one of his sons called Yngvi, who was king in Sweden after him; and those houses come from him that are named Ynglings. The Aesir took wives of the land for themselves, and some also for their sons, and these kindreds became many in number, so that throughout Saxland, and thence all over the region of the north, they spread out until their tongue, even the speech of the men of Asia, was the native tongue over all these lands. Therefore men think that they can perceive, from their forefathers' names which are written down, that those names belonged to this tongue, and that the Aesir brought the tongue hither into the northern region, into Norway and into Sweden, into Denmark and into Saxland. But in England there are ancient lists of land-names and place-names which show that these names came from another tongue than this.

THE BEGUILING OF GYLFI

King Gylfi ruled the land that men now call Sweden. It is told of him that he gave to a wandering woman, in return for her merry-making, a plow-land in his realm, as much as four oxen might turn up in a day and a night. But this woman was of the kin of the Aesir; she was named Gefjun. She took from the north, out of Jötunheim, four oxen which were the sons of a certain giant and herself, and set them before the plow. And the plow cut so wide and so deep that it loosened up the land; and the oxen drew the land out into the sea and to the westward, and stopped in a certain sound. There Gefjun set the land, and gave it a name, calling it Selund. And from that time on, the spot whence the land had been torn up is water: it is now called the Lögr in Sweden; and bays lie in that lake even as the headlands in Selund. Thus says Bragi, the ancient skald:

Gefjun drew from Gylfi gladly the wave-trove's freehold,
Till from the running beasts sweat reeked, to Denmark's increase;
The oxen bore, moreover, eight eyes, gleaming brow-lights,
O'er the field's wide booty, and four heads in their plowing.

King Gylfi was a wise man and skilled in magic; he was much troubled that the Aesir-people were so cunning that all things went according to their will. He pondered whether this might proceed from their own nature, or whether the divine powers which they worshipped might ordain such things. He set out on his way to Asgard, going secretly, and clad himself in the likeness of an old man, with which he dissembled. But the Aesir were wiser in this matter, having second sight; and they saw his journeying before ever he came, and prepared against him deceptions of the eye. When he came into the town, he saw there a hall so high that he could not easily make out the top of it: its thatching was laid with golden shields after the fashion of a shingled roof. So also says Thjódólfr of Hvin, that Valhall was thatched with shields:

On their backs they let beam, sore battered with stones,
Odin's hall-shingles, the shrewd sea-farers.

In the hall-doorway Gylfi saw a man juggling with anlaces, having seven in the air at one time. This man asked of him his name. He called himself Gangleri, and said he had come by the paths of the serpent, and prayed for lodging for the night, asking: "Who owns the hall?" The other replied that it was their king; "and I will attend thee to see him; then shalt thou thyself ask him concerning his name;" and the man wheeled about before him into the hall, and he went after, and straightway the door closed itself on his heels. There he saw a great room and much people, some with games, some drinking; and some had weapons and were fighting. Then he looked about him, and thought unbelievable many things which he saw; and he said:

All the gateways ere one goes out
Should one scan:
For 't is uncertain where sit the unfriendly
On the bench before thee.

He saw three high-seats, each above the other, and three men sat thereon, one on each. And he asked what might be the name of those lords. He who had conducted him in answered that the one who sat on the nethermost high-seat was a king, "and his name is Hárr; but the next is named Jafnhárr; and he who is uppermost is called Thridi." Then Hárr asked the newcomer whether his errand were more than for the meat and drink which were always at his command, as for every one there in the Hall of the High One. He answered that he first desired to learn whether there were any wise man there within. Hárr said, that he should not escape whole from thence unless he were wiser.

And stand thou forth who speirest;
Who answers, he shall sit.

Gangleri began his questioning thus: "Who is foremost, or oldest, of all the gods?" Hárr answered: "He is called in our speech Allfather, but in the Elder Asgard he had twelve names: one is Allfather; the second is Lord, or Lord of Hosts; the third is Nikarr, or Spear-Lord; the fourth is Nikudr, or Striker; the fifth is Knower of Many Things; the sixth, Fulfiller of Wishes; the seventh, Far-Speaking One; the eighth, The Shaker, or He that Putteth the Armies to Flight; the ninth, The Burner; the tenth, The Destroyer; the eleventh, The Protector; the twelfth, Gelding."

Then asked Gangleri: "Where is this god, or what power hath he, or what hath he wrought that is a glorious deed?" Hárr made answer: "He lives throughout all ages and governs all his realm, and directs all things, great and small." Then said Jafnhárr: "He fashioned heaven and earth and air, and all things which are in them." Then spake Thridi: "The greatest of all is this: that he made man, and gave him the spirit, which shall live and never perish, though the flesh-frame rot to mould, or burn to ashes; and all men shall live, such as are just in action, and be with himself in the place called Gimlé. But evil men go to Hel and thence down to the Misty Hel; and that is down in the ninth world." Then said Gangleri: "What did he before heaven and earth were made?" And Hárr answered: "He was then with the Rime-Giants."

Gangleri said: "What was the beginning, or how began it, or what was before it?" Hárr answered: "As is told in *Völuspá:*

Erst was the age when nothing was:
Nor sand nor sea, nor chilling stream-waves;
Earth was not found, nor Ether-Heaven, —
A Yawning Gap, but grass was none."

Then said Jafnhárr: "It was many ages before the earth was shaped that the Mist-World was made; and midmost within it lies the well that is called Hvergelmir, from which spring the rivers called Svöl, Gunnthrá, Fjörm, Fimbulthul, Slídr and Hríd, Sylgr and Ylgr, Vid, Leiptr; Gjöll is hard by Hel-gates." And Thridi said: "Yet first was the world in the southern region, which was named Múspell; it is light and hot; that region is glowing and burning, and impassable to such as are outlanders and have not their holdings there. He who sits there at the land's-end, to defend the land, is called Surtr; he brandishes a flaming sword, and at the end of the world he shall go forth and harry, and overcome all the gods, and burn all the world with fire; thus is said in *Völuspá:*

Surtr fares from the south with switch-eating flame, —
On his sword shimmers the sun of the War-Gods;
The rock-crags crash; the fiends are reeling;
Heroes tread Hel-way; Heaven is cloven."

Gangleri asked: "How were things wrought, ere the races were and the tribes of men increased?" Then said Hárr: "The streams called Ice-waves, those which were so long come from the fountain-heads that the yeasty venom upon them had hardened like the slag that runs out of the fire, — these then became ice; and when the ice halted and ceased to run, then it froze over above. But the drizzling rain that rose from the venom congealed to rime, and the rime increased, frost over frost, each over the other, even into Ginnungagap, the Yawning Void." Then spake Jafnhárr: "Ginnungagap, which faced toward the northern quarter, became filled with heaviness, and masses of ice and rime, and from within, drizzling rain and gusts; but the southern part of the Yawning Void was lighted by those sparks and glowing masses which flew out of Múspellheim." And Thridi said: "Just as cold arose out of Niflheim, and all terrible things, so also all that looked toward Múspellheim became hot and glowing; but Ginnungagap was as mild as windless air, and when the breath of heat met the rime, so that it melted and dripped, life was quickened from the yeast-drops, by the power of that which sent the heat, and became a man's form. And that man is named Ymir, but the Rime-Giants call him Aurgelmir; and thence are come the races of the Rime-Giants, as it says in *Völuspá the Less:*

All the witches spring from Witolf,
All the warlocks are of Willharm,
And the spell-singers spring from Swarthead;
All the ogres of Ymir come.

But concerning this says Vafthrúdnir the giant:

Out of the Ice-waves issued venom-drops,
Waxing until a giant was;
Thence are our kindred come all together, —
So it is they are savage forever."

Then said Gangleri: "How did the races grow thence, or after what fashion was it brought to pass that more men came into being? Or do ye hold him God, of whom ye but now spake?" And Jafnhárr answered: "By no means do we acknowledge him God; he was evil and all his kindred: we call them Rime-Giants. Now it is said that when he slept, a sweat came upon him, and there grew under his left hand a man and a woman, and one of his feet begat a son with the other; and thus the races are come; these are the Rime-Giants. The old Rime-Giant, him we call Ymir."

Then said Gangleri: "Where dwelt Ymir, or wherein did he find sustenance?" Hárr answered: "Straightway after the rime dripped, there sprang from it the cow called Audumla; four streams of milk ran from her udders, and she nourished Ymir." Then asked Gangleri: "Wherewithal was the cow nourished?" And Hárr made answer: "She licked the ice-blocks, which were salty; and the first day that she licked the blocks, there came forth from the blocks in the evening a man's hair; the second day, a man's head; the third day the whole man was there. He is named Buri: he was fair of feature, great and mighty. He begat a son called Borr, who wedded the woman named Bestla, daughter of Bölthorn the giant; and they had three sons: one was Odin, the second Vili, the third Vé. And this is my belief, that he, Odin, with his brothers, must be ruler of heaven and earth; we hold that he must be so called; so is that man called whom we know to be mightiest and most worthy of honor, and ye do well to let him be so called."

Then said Gangleri: "What covenant was between them, or which was the stronger?" And Hárr answered: "The sons of Borr slew Ymir the giant; lo, where he fell there gushed forth so much blood out of his wounds that with it they drowned all the race of the Rime-Giants, save that one, whom giants call Bergelmir, escaped with his household; he went upon his ship, and his wife with him, and they were safe there. And from them are come the races of the Rime-Giants, as is said here:

Untold ages ere earth was shapen,
  Then was Bergelmir born;
That first I recall, how the famous wise giant
  On the deck of the ship was laid down."

Then said Gangleri: "What was done then by Borr's sons, if thou believe that they be gods?" Hárr replied: "In this matter there is no little to be said. They took Ymir and bore him into the middle of the Yawning Void, and made of him the earth: of his blood the sea and the waters; the land was made of his flesh, and the crags of his bones; gravel and stones they fashioned from his teeth and his grinders and from those bones that were broken." And Jafnhárr said: "Of the blood, which ran and welled forth freely out of his wounds, they made the sea, when they had formed and made firm the earth together, and laid the sea in a ring round about her; and it may well seem a hard thing to most men to cross over it." Then said Thridi: "They took his skull also, and made of it the heaven, and set it up over the earth with four corners; and under each corner they set a dwarf: the names of these are East, West, North, and South. Then they took the glowing embers and sparks that burst forth and had been cast out of Muspellheim, and set them in the midst of the Yawning Void, in the heaven, both above and below, to illumine heaven and earth. They assigned places to all fires: to some in heaven; some wandered free under the heavens; nevertheless, to these also they gave a place, and shaped them courses. It is said in old songs, that from these the days were reckoned, and the tale of years told, as is said in *Völuspá:*

The sun knew not where she had housing;
The moon knew not what might he had;
The stars knew not where stood their places.
Thus was it ere the earth was fashioned."

Then said Gangleri: "These are great tidings which I now hear; that is a wondrous great piece of craftsmanship, and cunningly made. How was the earth contrived?" And Hárr answered: "She is ring-shaped without, and round about her without lieth the deep sea; and along the strand of that sea they gave lands to the races of giants for habitation. But on the inner earth they made a citadel round about the world against the hostility of the giants, and for their citadel they raised up the brows of Ymir the giant, and called that place Midgard. They took also his brain and cast it in the air, and made from it the clouds, as is here said:

Of Ymir's flesh the earth was fashioned,
And of his sweat the sea;
Crags of his bones, trees of his hair,
And of his skull the sky.
Then of his brows the blithe gods made
Midgard for sons of men;
And of his brain the bitter-mooded
Clouds were all created."

Then said Gangleri: "Much indeed they had accomplished then, methinks, when earth and heaven were made, and the sun and the constellations of heaven were fixed, and division was made of days; now whence come the men that people the world?" And Hárr answered: "When the sons of Borr were walking along the sea-strand, they found two trees, and took up the trees and shaped men of them: the first gave them spirit and life; the second, wit and feeling; the third, form, speech, hearing, and sight. They gave them clothing and names: the male was called Askr, and the female Embla, and of them was mankind begotten, which received a dwelling-place under Midgard. Next they made for themselves in the middle of the world a city which is called Ásgard; men call it Troy. There dwelt the gods and their kindred; and many tidings and tales of it have come to pass both on earth and aloft. There is one abode called Hlidskjálf, and when Allfather sat in the high-seat there, he looked out over the whole world and saw every man's acts, and knew all things which he saw. His wife was called Frigg daughter of Fjörgvinn; and of their blood is come that kindred which we call the races of the Aesir, that have peopled the Elder Ásgard, and those kingdoms which pertain to it; and that is a divine race. For this reason must he be called Allfather: because he is father of all the gods and of men, and of all that was fulfilled of him and of his might. The Earth was his daughter and his wife; on her he begot the first son, which is Ása-Thor: strength and prowess attend him, wherewith he overcometh all living things.

"Nörfi or Narfi is the name of a giant that dwelt in Jötunheim: he had a daughter called Night; she was swarthy and dark, as befitted her race. She was given to the man named Naglfari; their son was Audr. Afterward she was wedded to him that was called Annarr; Jörd was their daughter. Last of all Dayspring had her, and he was of the race of Aesir; their son was Day: he was radiant and fair after his father. Then Allfather took Night, and Day her son, and gave to them two horses and two chariots, and sent them up into the heavens, to ride round about the earth every two half-days. Night rides before with the horse named Frosty-Mane, and on each morning he bedews the earth with the foam from his bit. The horse that Day has is called Sheen-Mane, and he illumines all the air and the earth from his mane."

Then said Gangleri: "How does he govern the course of the sun or of the moon?" Hárr answered: "A certain man was named Mundilfari, who had two children; they were so fair and comely that he called his son Moon, and his daughter Sun, and wedded her to the man called Glenr. But the gods were incensed at that insolence, and took the brother and sister, and set them up in the heavens; they caused Sun to drive those horses that drew the chariot of the sun, which the gods had fashioned, for the world's illumination, from that glowing stuff which flew out of Múspellheim. Those horses are called thus: Early-Wake and All-Strong; and under the shoulders of the horses the gods set two wind-bags to cool them, but in some records that is called 'iron-coolness.' Moon steers the course of the moon, and determines its waxing and waning. He took from the earth two children, called Bil and Hjúki, they that went from the well called Byrgir, bearing on their shoulders the cask called Saegr, and the pole Simul. Their father is named Vidfinnr. These children follow Moon, as may be seen from the earth."

Then said Gangleri: "The sun fares swiftly, and almost as if she were afraid: she could not hasten her course any more if she feared her destruction." Then Hárr made answer: "It is no marvel that she hastens furiously: close cometh he that seeks her, and she has no escape save to run away." Then said Gangleri: "Who is he that causes her this disquiet?" Hárr replied: "It is two wolves; and he that runs after her is called Skoll; she fears him, and he shall take her. But he that leaps before her is called Hati Hródvitnisson. He is eager to seize the moon; and so it must be." Then said Gangleri: "What is the race of the wolves?" Hárr answered: "A witch dwells to the east of Midgard, in the forest called Ironwood: in that wood dwell the troll-women, who are known as Ironwood-Women. The old witch bears many giants for sons, and all in the shape of wolves; and from this source are these wolves sprung. The saying runs thus: from this race shall come one that shall be mightiest of all, he that is named Moon-Hound; he shall be filled with the flesh of all those men that die, and he shall swallow the moon, and sprinkle with blood the heavens and all the air; thereof shall the sun lose shining, and the winds in that day shall be unquiet and roar on every side. So it says in *Völuspá:*

Eastward dwells the Old One in Ironwood,
And there gives birth to Fenrir's brethren;
There shall spring of them all a certain one,
The moon's taker in troll's likeness.

He is filled with flesh of fey men.
Reddens the gods' seats with ruddy blood-
gouts;
Swart becomes sunshine in summers after,
The weather all shifty. Wit ye yet, or what?"

Then said Gangleri: "What is the way to heaven from earth?" Then Hárr answered, and laughed aloud: "Now, that is not wisely asked; has it not been told thee, that the gods made a bridge from earth to heaven, called Bifröst? Thou must have seen it; it may be that ye call it 'rainbow.' It is of three colors, and very strong, and made with cunning and with more magic art than other works of craftsmanship. But strong as it is, yet must it be broken, when the sons of Múspell shall go forth harrying and ride it, and swim their horses over great rivers; thus they shall proceed." Then said Gangleri: "To my thinking the gods did not build the bridge honestly, seeing that it could be broken, and they able to make it as they would." Then Hárr replied: "The gods are not deserving of reproof because of this work of skill: a good bridge is Bifröst, but nothing in this world is of such nature that it may be relied on when the sons of Múspell go a-harrying."

—*From the Prose Edda of Snorri Sturluson, Icelander (1178–1241), translated by Arthur Gilchrist Brodeur.*

The Walam Olum

A LENAPE LEGEND

I

At first, in that place, at all times, above the
earth,
On the earth, was an extended fog, and there
great Manito was.
At first, forever, lost in space, everywhere,
the great Manito was.
He made the extended land and the sky.
He made the sun, the moon, the stars.
He made them all to move evenly.
Then the wind blew violently, and it cleared,
and the water flowed off far and strong.
And groups of islands grew newly, and there
remained.
Anew spoke the great Manito, a manito to
manitos,
To beings, mortals, souls and all,
And ever after he was a manito to men, and
their grandfather.
He gave the first mother, the mother of be-
ings,

He gave the fish, he gave the turtles, he gave the beasts, he gave the birds.
But an evil Manito made evil beings only, monsters,
He made the flies, he made the gnats.
All beings were then friendly.
Truly the manitos were active and kindly
To those very first men, and to those first mothers; fetched them wives,
And fetched them food, when first they desired it.
All had cheerful knowledge, all had leisure, all thought in gladness.
But very secretly an evil being, a mighty magician, came on earth,
And with him brought badness, quarreling, unhappiness,
Brought bad weather, brought sickness, brought death.
All this took place of old on the earth, beyond the great tide-water, at the first.

II

Long ago there was a mighty snake and beings evil to men.
This mighty snake hated those who were there and greatly disquieted those whom he hated.
They both did harm, they both injured each other, both were not in peace.
Driven from their homes they fought with this murderer.
The mighty snake firmly resolved to harm the men.
He brought three persons, he brought a monster, he brought a rushing water.
Between the hills the water rushed and rushed, dashing through and through, destroying much.
Nanabush, the Strong White One, grandfather of beings, grandfather of men, was on the Turtle Island.
There he was walking and creating, as he passed by and created the turtle.
Beings and men all go forth, they walk in the floods and shallow waters, down stream thither to the Turtle Island.
There were many monster fishes, which ate some of them.
The Manito daughter, coming, helped with her canoe, helped all, as they came and came.
And also Nanabush, Nanabush, the grandfather of all, the grandfather of beings, the grandfather of men, the grandfather of the turtle.
The men then were together on the turtle, like to turtles.
Frightened on the turtle, they prayed on the turtle that what was spoiled should be restored.
The water ran off, the earth dried, the lakes were at rest, all was silent, and the mighty snake departed.

III

After the rushing waters had subsided the Lenape of the turtle were close together, in hollow houses, living together there.
It freezes where they abode, it snows where they abode, it storms where they abode, it is cold where they abode.
At this northern place they speak favorably of mild, cool lands, with many deer and buffaloes.
As they journeyed, some being strong, some rich, they separated into house-builders and hunters;
The strongest, the most united, the purest, were the hunters.
The hunters showed themselves at the north, at the east, at the south, at the west.
In that ancient country, in that northern country, in that turtle country, the best of the Lenape were the Turtle men.
All the cabin fires of that land were disquieted, and all said to their priest, "Let us go."
To the Snake land to the east they went forth, going away, earnestly grieving.
Split asunder, weak, trembling, their land burned, they went, torn and broken, to the Snake Island.
Those from the north being free, without care, went forth from the land of snow, in different directions.
The fathers of the Bald Eagle and the White Wolf remain along the sea, rich in fish and mussels.
Floating up the streams in their canoes, our fathers were rich, they were in the light, when they were at those islands.
Head Beaver and Big Bird said, "Let us go to Snake Island," they said.
All say they will go along to destroy all the land.
Those of the north agreed,
Those of the east agreed.
Over the water, the frozen sea,
They went to enjoy it.
On the wonderful, slippery water,

On the stone-hard water all went,
On the great Tidal Sea, the mussel-bearing sea.
Ten thousand at night,
All in one night,
To the Snake Island, to the east, at night,
They walk and walk, all of them.
The men from the north, the east, the south,
The Eagle clan, the Beaver clan, the Wolf clan,
The best men, the rich men, the head men,
Those with wives, those with daughters, those with dogs,
They all come, they tarry at the land of the spruce pines;
Those from the west come with hesitation,
Esteeming highly their old home at the Turtle land.

IV

Long ago the fathers of the Lenape were at the land of spruce pines.
Hitherto the Bald Eagle band had been the pipe bearer,
While they were searching for the Snake Island, that great and fine land.
They having died, the hunters, about to depart, met together,
All say to Beautiful Head, "Be thou chief.
Coming to the Snakes, slaughter at that Snake hill, that they leave it."
All of the Snake tribe were weak, and hid themselves in the Swampy Vales.
After Beautiful Head, White Owl was chief at Spruce Pine land.
After him, Keeping-Guard was chief of that people.
After him, Snow Bird was chief; he spoke of the south,
That our fathers should possess it by scattering abroad.
Snow Bird went south, White Beaver went east.
The Snake land was at the south, the great Spruce Pine land was toward the shore;
To the east was the Fish land, toward the lakes was the Buffalo land.
After Snow Bird, the Seizer was chief, and all were killed,
The robbers, the snakes, the evil men, the stone men.

. .

After the Seizer there were ten chiefs, and there was much warfare south and east.
After them, the Peaceable was chief at Snake land.
After him, Not-Black was chief, who was a straight man.
After him, Much-Loved was chief, a good man.
After him, No-Blood was chief, who walked in cleanliness.
After him, Snow-Father was chief, he of the big teeth.
After him, Tally-maker was chief, who made records.
After him, Shiverer-with-Cold was chief, who went south to the corn land.
After him, Corn-Breaker was chief, who brought about the planting of corn.
After him, the Strong-Man was chief, who was useful to the chieftains.
After him, the Salt-Man was chief; after him the Little-One was chief.
There was no rain, and no corn, so they moved further seaward.
At the place of caves, in the Buffalo land, they at last had food, on a pleasant plain.
After the Little-One came the Fatigued; after him, the Stiff-One.
After him, the Reprover; disliking him, and unwilling to remain,
Being angry, some went off secretly, moving east.

. .

The wise ones who remained made the Loving-One chief.
They settled again on the Yellow river, and had much corn on stoneless soil.
All being friendly, the Affable was chief, the first of that name.
He was very good, this Affable, and came as a friend to all the Lenape.
After this good one, Strong-Buffalo was chief and pipe-bearer.
Big-Owl was chief; White-Bird was chief.
The Willing-One was chief and priest; he made festivals.
Rich-Again was chief; the Painted-One was chief.
White-Fowl was chief; again there was war, north and south.
The Wolf-wise-in-Counsel was chief.
He knew how to make war on all; he slew Strong-Stone.
The Always-Ready-One was chief; he fought against the Snakes.
The Strong-Good-One was chief; he fought against the northerners.
The Lean-One was chief; he fought against the Tawa people.

The Opossum-Like was chief; he fought in sadness,
And said, "They are many; let us go together to the east, to the sunrise."

. . . . .

They separated at Fish river; the lazy ones remained there.
Cabin-Man was chief; the Talligewi possessed the east.
Strong-Friend was chief; he desired the eastern land.
Some passed on east; the Talega ruler killed some of them.
All say, in unison, "War, war."
The Talamatan, friends from the north, come, and all go together.
The Sharp-One was chief; he was the pipe-bearer beyond the river.
They rejoiced greatly that they should fight and slay the Talega towns.
The Stirrer was chief; the Talega towns were too strong.
The Fire-Builder was chief; they all gave to him many towns.
The Breaker-in-Pieces was chief; all the Talega go south.
He-has-Pleasure was chief; all the people rejoice.
They stay south of the lakes; the Talamatan friends north of the lakes.
When Long-and-Mild was chief, those who were not his friends conspired.
Truthful-Man was chief; the Talamatans made war.
Just-and-True was chief; the Talamatans trembled.

V

All were peaceful, long ago, there at the Talega land.
The Pipe-Bearer was chief at the White river.
White-Lynx was chief; much corn was planted.
Good-and-Strong was chief; the people were many.
The Recorder was chief; he painted the records.
Pretty-Blue-Bird was chief; there was much fruit.
Always-There was chief; the towns were many.
Paddler-up-Stream was chief; he was much on the rivers.
Little-Cloud was chief; many departed,
The Nanticokes and the Shawnees going to the south.
Big-Beaver was chief, at the White Salt Lick.
The Seer, the praised one, went to the west.
He went to the west, to the southwest, to the western villages.
The Rich-Down-River-Man was chief, at Talega river.
The Walker was chief; there was much war.
Again with the Tawa people, again with the Stone people, again with the northern people.
Grandfather-of-Boats was chief; he went to lands in boats.
Snow-Hunter was chief; he went to the north land.
Look-About was chief; he went to the Talega mountains.
East-Villager was chief; he was east of Talega.

. . . . .

A great land and a wide land was the east land,
A land without snakes, a rich land, a pleasant land.
Great Fighter was chief, toward the north.
At the Straight river, River-Loving was chief.
Becoming-Fat was chief at Sassafras land.
All the hunters made wampum again at the great sea.
Red-Arrow was chief at the stream again.
The Painted-Man was chief at the Mighty Water.
The Easterners and the Wolves go northeast.
Good-Fighter was chief, and went to the north.
The Mengwe, the Lynxes, all trembled.
Again an Affable was chief, and made peace with all,
All were friends, all were united, under this great chief.
Great-Beaver was chief, remaining in Sassafras land.
White-Body was chief on the sea shore.
Peace-Maker was chief, friendly to all.
He-Makes-Mistakes was chief, hurriedly coming.
At this time whites came on the Eastern sea.

. . . . .

At this time, from north and south, the whites came.

They are peaceful; they have great things;
who are they?

—*From Daniel G. Brinton, The Lenâpé and Their Legends, North American Indian.*

~ ⚙ ~

The Sun Goddess and the Mikado

THE FIRST GODS who came into being in the Plain of Heaven when heaven and earth first began, were three, solitary and invisible, and they had no active part in the creation. After a time they again disappeared, leaving no offspring or any effects of their presence. After these three came two other gods, who however were born from primitive reed-like shoots that sprouted from an earth which was without form, like floating oil. These gods were also solitary and invisible.

Then came five generations of gods, of which the first generation were solitary and invisible, and then five successive generations of pairs of gods, male and female, ending with Izanagi and Izanami, the male and female deities of desire. These last two were commanded by the gods of heaven to make and give birth to the drifting land, which up to this time had remained formless and shifting. They were given a magic spear, and as they stood upon the bridge which united heaven and earth they reached down and stirred the primordial sea with the point of the spear. Drops of the brine that dripped off the point gradually condensed and became an island, to which was given the name of Onogoro.

Izanagi and Izanami then came down from heaven and took up their abode upon Onogoro, upon which they erected a pillar to show that it was the central place of the future land, and they also built for themselves a palace. After this they gave birth to a number of islands and divinities, beginning with the "eight great islands" of Japan. Finally, Izanami gave birth to the god of fire, but died as a result. From her scorched and disintegrating body were born other gods and goddesses or ore and clay and food, while from the tears of her husband was born the goddess of weeping. Izanagi then drew his sword and slew the god of fire, and from the blood that issued forth came other gods with names that suggest violent action, while from the remains of the god of fire were born various mountain gods.

Izanagi grieved for his departed wife, and made his way underground to the Land of Yomi (Hades) to seek her and bring her back. He found and told her that their creative task was as yet unfinished, but she replied that she had already eaten some of the food of the nether-world, and that special permission would thus have to be obtained before she could return with him. She promised to seek this permission, and begged him not to try to look at her, but Izanagi became impatient, and, breaking off the large tooth at the end of his comb, he lit a light and looked. To his horror he saw that her body was swarming with maggots, and that in the putrified remains gods of thunder were dwelling. He fled, but Izanami, in a rage, sent the Hag of Hades to pursue him. Izanagi flung down his head-dress, which miraculously turned into a cluster of grapes, which the hag was constrained to devour before she resumed the pursuit. Izanagi again saved himself by throwing down his comb, which turned into a thicket of bamboo-sprouts, and again she was delayed. Then Izanami sent the Gods of Thunder and an army of fifteen hundred warriors of Hades to pursue him. Izanagi tried to keep them back by flourishing his sword behind him as he fled, and when he found three peaches at the border-line between Hades and the world of the living he turned upon his tormentors and made them flee in turn as he pelted them with these miraculous peaches. Finally, Izanami herself came, but Izanagi blocked the road with a boulder which a thousand men could scarcely have lifted, and from opposite sides of this barrier the two took their final leave of each other. Izanami threatened to destroy a thousand people of Japan each day, and to this Izanagi defiantly replied that in that case he would cause fifteen hundred to be born.[1]

Izanagi now took steps to cleanse himself of the pollution of Hades, and bathed himself in a river. Divinities were born from each garment as he threw it down, and many others as he washed himself. At last, however, as he washed his face, the Sun Goddess (Amaterasu) was born from his left eye, the Moon God from his right eye,

---

[1] This is the first mention of human beings in the *Kojiki*. Japanese explain their origin by saying that most of the gods born in their land gradually lost their divine characteristics and became entirely human. The Japanese race thus claims divine origin.

and the God of Force (Susanoo) from his nose. Izanagi was much pleased, and, giving his necklace to the Sun Goddess, he told her to rule the Plain of Heaven. He commanded the Moon God to rule the night, and Susanoo to rule over the Sea-Plain. The first two were amenable, and left at once to perform their duties, but the God of Force spent his time in weeping and lamenting. When his father asked the reason, Susanoo replied that he would rather be dead with Izanami in Hades, so Izanagi, in wrath, banished him to a distant part of Japan.

Susanoo, however, wished to take leave of his sister Amaterasu, and as he journeyed to meet her mountains and plains quivered and in every land there were earthquakes. Amaterasu, fearing that he was come to take the Plain of Heaven away from her, armed herself, and stamped, as Japanese wrestlers do, although her strength was such that she kicked away the earth like snow. She asked him his reason for coming. Susanoo replied that he had only come to say goodbye, and when she challenged the sincerity of his intentions, he agreed to submit to a contest in producing children. She thereupon took his sword, and breaking it into three pieces, chewed it into splinters and blew them away, whereupon they became three goddesses. Susanoo then took her long necklace, and after crunching it and blowing away the pieces, they became five gods. Amaterasu insisted that she had won the victory, because male deities had been born from her necklace, and only female deities from his sword, but Susanoo refused to accept such a decision. He proceeded to break down the divisions between her rice-fields, and strew filth in the rooms of her palace. Finally he threw the flayed carcass of a horse down through the roof of the palace. This so frightened the Goddess that she forsook her palace and took refuge in a deep cave, with the result that the world and heaven were plunged into darkness.

When they realized that the darkness threatened to be permanent, the eight hundred myriads of gods and goddesses assembled in the bed of the River of Heaven (the Milky Way) to consult as to what they should do, and were advised by a god who had a reputation for wisdom. Under his direction they brought out barndoor fowls and made them crow; they dug iron from mountain mines and made a polished mirror, and a string of curved jewels, eight feet long; and they performed divination with cherry bark from a sacred mountain, and with a shoulder blade taken from a stag. Then they hung the mirror and the jewels from a sacred *sakaki* tree that had been pulled up by the roots, and one of the gods recited a liturgy. The God of Strength hid himself beside the door of the cave, and the goddess Uzume decked herself with clubmoss and bamboo grass, and danced upon an upturned wooden tub, while the eight hundred myriads of gods laughed together at her indecent antics. Hearing the laughter, the Sun Goddess opened the door of the cave and peeped out; whereupon two of the gods took the polished iron mirror and held it before her, and as Amaterasu gazed at it in astonishment and came a little further out from the cave, the God of Strength seized her by the hand and drew her out, while the god Futotama drew across the entrance of the cave behind her a magic rope made of straw pulled up by the roots, to prevent her from re-entering. And both the Plain of Heaven and the Central-Land-of-Reed-Plains (Japan) were once more flooded with sunlight.

Susanoo was now punished by the gods for his misdeeds. They imposed on him an immense fine, cut off his beard, and pulled out the nails of his fingers and toes, and banished him from heaven. He came down to the headwaters of a river in the province of Izumo. There he saw some chopsticks floating down the current, and went in search of the people he concluded were living upstream. He found an aged couple with a girl between them, and they were weeping. When Susanoo asked why they wept, the old man replied that he originally had eight daughters, but that an eight-headed dragon had come down from the mountains of Koshi every year to devour one of his daughters, until now only one was left, and the time for the dragon to come again being now at hand, they could not help but weep. This dragon had eyes like the winter-cherry, a body with eight heads and eight tails, and on its back grew moss and forests of trees. It was so large that its length stretched over a number of hills and valleys. Susanoo asked the old man if he would bestow his daughter's hand upon him if he slew the dragon, and having received the promise, he changed her into a comb and put her into his hair, and instructed the old man to distill some powerful rice-wine, and to pour this into eight tubs. When the dragon came it dipped a head into each tub, and drank up the wine, after which it became intoxicated and slept. Then Susanoo drew his great sword and hewed the dragon into pieces, until the nearby river turned to the color of blood. While he was hewing at the middle tail, his sword was nicked by something within, which he found to be a wonderful sharp sword, which he took and presented to the Sun Goddess. This sword was afterwards called the "Herb Queller," and it became one of the Three Imperial Treasures.[1] Susanoo wedded the daughter of the old couple, and his descendants ruled for a long time in Izumo.

Meanwhile the Sun Goddess thought it was time that her son (one of those born from her necklace) should go down to Japan to rule it, but he told her that he now had a son of his own, whose name was Ninigi, and who was ready to go. He was given the divine "Herb Quelling Sword," as well as the jewels and the mirror used when the Sun Goddess had been lured from her cave. A number of gods and goddesses offered him their aid, and promised to accompany him. Ninigi came down from heaven and landed on a mountain peak in the island of Tsukushi (Kyūshū). Here he built his palace and began his rule.

Ninigi happened one day to meet a beautiful maiden near the place where he had chosen to live, and asked her father for her hand. The father sent both of his daughters, but the elder one was so homely that Ninigi refused to have her. He sent her home and wedded only the younger daughter. The father was filled with shame and resentment, and told Ninigi that if he had married both daughters, the older one would have brought his descendants long life and the younger would have brought them great prosperity and renown, but that now they would be frail and short-lived. This is the reason why the Emperors of Japan do not live to a great age.

Ninigi's wife bore him the sons Hosuseri and Hohodemi. The former became a fisherman and the latter a hunter. One day Hohodemi, a little bored, persuaded his elder brother to exchange fishhook for hunting bow. However, Hosuseri came back from the mountains in ill humor, not having taken a single head of game. Hohodemi had not caught any fish, and he had besides been so unfortunate as to lose his brother's fishhook. Hosuseri was inconsolable, and even though Hohodemi broke up his sword and forged five hundred fishhooks for him, he stubbornly insisted upon the return of the original fishhook. Hohodemi, while lamenting his ill-luck on the seashore, was approached by the God of Salt, to whom he told his story. The god gave him a boat, and advised him to go to the palace of the God of the Sea, there to climb a cassia-tree by the well near the gate of the palace and wait for the Sea-God's daughter, who could help him. Hohodemi followed these directions, and when the maidens of this princess came to the well to draw water, they saw Hohodemi's reflection in the water, and carried word of him to their mistress. When Hohodemi was taken into the presence of the God of the Sea he found such favor that the hand of the princess was given him in marriage. He lived there for three years, when he chanced to remember his brother Hosuseri, and told his story, and why he had come. Upon this all the fishes of the sea were summoned, and they reported that the sea-bream was complaining of something sticking in its throat. Examination revealed the missing fishhook, which Hohodemi prepared to take to his brother. The God of the Sea gave him two magic jewels which could control the tides, and these saved his life, for, when he met Hosuseri, the latter tried to kill him. Hohodemi first raised the tide-flowing jewel, and inrushing currents of great violence swept in from the sea and overwhelmed Hosuseri. In great fear he shouted for help and promised to serve his brother forever, so Hohodemi raised the tide-ebbing jewel, with the result that the salt water receded and left the contrite and grateful Hosuseri at his feet. From that time on, Hosuseri and his

---

[1] The Three Imperial Treasures comprise the Sword, the Mirror, and the Jewel. They correspond to the crown of a European sovereign, and their possession is evidence of the right to rule. The giving by Susanoo of this divine sword to the Sun Goddess is an indication in the story that his Izumo Clan acknowledged the overlordship of the Imperial Clan from Kyūshū. Historical evidence has revealed that the culture of Izumo had strong Korean affinities, and that at one time it was a serious rival of the Imperial Clan. One can see why the compilers of the *Kojiki* were thus so careful to point out the crimes of Susanoo, and to emphasize his inferiority to Amaterasu.

descendants acted as guards for Hohodemi and his imperial progeny.

Hohodemi had a son by the Sea-God's daughter, and this son was the father of Prince Yamato-Iware, who was afterwards known as Jimmu, and who became the first Emperor of Japan.

It was while Jimmu and his elder brother Itsuse dwelt in the palace Ninigi had built at Takachiho, that the two decided to attempt the subjugation of the insubordinate tribes to the east. They journeyed through the Inland Sea to what is now Osaka, but when they attempted a landing they were beaten off, and Itsuse was wounded by an arrow. He then said that the children of the Sun should not attack in the direction of the Rising Sun, but should have the Sun behind them, as an ally, when they attacked, so they rounded the promontory of Kii in boats, and attacked from that direction. But Itsuse died of his wound while the results of the campaign were still in doubt. Jimmu received a sword from heaven, with which he cut an army of his enemies to pieces, and his journey inland to Yamato was guided by an immense crow, which had a wingspread of eight feet. Jimmu also dealt with a tribe of cave-dwelling robbers, whom he lured from their caves by the promise of a great banquet, and had them cut down when they were drunk. After he fought his way to Yamato, he built for himself a palace at Kashiwabara near Mount Unebi, wedded the daughter of a local chief, and established his dynasty. He was fifty-two when he ascended the throne in 660 B.C.,[1] and he reigned until 585 B.C., when he died at the age of 127 years, and his son, known to history as the Emperor Suizei, reigned in his stead.

— *Adapted from Japanese sources for this book by George S. Noss.*

---

[1] Historians place the probable date of Jimmu as sometime near the beginning of the Christian Era. The name of Jimmu was not given to him until after the Japanese began to use the Chinese system of writing, or more than twelve centuries after his reputed death. A number of the Emperors who are supposed to have succeeded him are nothing more than names. Japanese history does not begin to be really reliable until after the fifth century of the Christian Era. The Japanese have their own Imperial Era, which begins in 660 B.C.

PART THREE

The People's Story

~ ✿ ~

ALTHOUGH WE too easily overlook the foundations upon which our social structure rests, in our more serious moments we must reflect upon them. When we do this, we commonly think of these fundamentals as basic ideals. And when poets, as they are fond of doing, grapple imaginatively with the expression of such ideals, they occasionally produce epics. An epic, then, is a long, serious poem, celebrating in heroic terms the ideals underlying a society. Usually epics are strongly nationalistic; frequently they are also religious; and often, too, mythological. Considered from a more technical point of view, the epic is a species of narrative poetry. It tells at length the best loved stories of a people. Thus in writing *Paradise Lost,* Milton turned to the Old Testament, since this part of the Bible most fully expressed the Puritan culture. In the present day American poets have turned to Abraham Lincoln or John Brown as heroes significant in terms of the typical American view of life. The histories of these men become epic material.

Such poetry flourishes most luxuriously among a people who, with a considerable degree of culture, still live close to nature. A primitive epic may be handed down largely by oral tradition. Often it much resembles sacred literature, or the sacred books themselves may assume an epic character. The epic commonly celebrates the father or founder of a people. Sometimes a single epic, as the Finnish *Kalevala,* stands out above all others in the same tongue, being beyond dispute the major poem of a nation. On other occasions, as in the instance of the Norse Sagas, a number of epics cluster about a single theme, forming one mass of epic material comparable to the numerous "books" of the Christian Bible. Other kinds of poetry share in the epic spirit while in important respects diverging from the epic form. Thus the Homeric Hymns, the odes of Pindar, or the dramas of Aeschylus – all of which deal at times with characters familiar in the Homeric epics, the *Iliad* and *Odyssey* – differ from the epic chiefly because of their less ambitious forms and scope and not because of a fundamental dissimilarity in spirit. A prose novel of great scope and vision, as Tolstoy's *War and Peace,* or James Joyce's *Ulysses,* occasionally achieves epic proportions.

Because force always underlies our social structures, heroism in arms is almost always a national ideal, and epic poetry commonly deals in greater or less degree with bravery in battle. Epics in this respect range from the *Iliad,* largely a story of war, to Milton's *Paradise Lost,* where, in part as concession to literary tradition, Milton devotes one book out of twelve to fighting – here in heaven instead, as more usual, upon earth.

The epic world is above all a spacious one: its canvas presents an entire people and as a rule displays their history, reaching back to an heroic and largely legendary past. Many epics enhance this spaciousness by including both known and unknown worlds. Classical epics, for example, contain episodes on Olympus, on earth and in Hades, while several Christian epics present scenes in heaven, on earth, and in hell.

It is customary to distinguish between the folk epic, the product of a long evolution through many hands and many mouths, and the literary epic, the writing of a single man. Thus the *Iliad* has often been declared a folk epic, while the *Aeneid* or *Paradise Lost* best exhibit the literary type. But since the history of alleged folk epics is generally obscure, less than we would like can be said definitely on this topic. Still more involved, though in more open daylight, are discussions of the rival provinces of epic and romance. Some epics, as *The Song of Roland,* may also be called romances, and some romances, as Thomas Malory's *Le Morte D'Arthur,* undoubtedly share epic qualities. *The Song of Roland* captures the patriotic heart and social consciousness of its public more fully than *Le Morte D'Arthur.* The chief medieval epics are, as a rule, of pre-feudal and Germanic origin, as the Norse Sagas, best represented in Iceland; *Beowulf,* of Scandinavian origin though existing only in the Anglo Saxon tongue; and the German *Nibelungenlied,* from which a specimen is given here.

Because of the great prestige of a few epics, readers sometimes forget that thousands of such poems have actually been produced, or at least attempted. As no type of poem, if successful, brings its author greater fame, so none admits such dismal failure. The phrase "epic dullness," accordingly, does not refer, as some persons superciliously suppose, to dull passages in great poems but to the great dullness of poor ones. Many score of inferior works in the epic manner were written in England during the eighteenth century and a large number in France during the nineteenth. A misguided Englishman, Sir Richard Blackmore, acquired a negative fame by the many tedious epics which he had written. Much as we emphatically say that a bad play is no play at all, so it might fairly be urged that a poor poem with epic pretensions really achieves neither epic proportions nor epic qualities. In few instances is the gulf so vast between intention and achievement. The true epic demands virtues making it acceptable through many generations of national life.

China is relatively poor in epic materials, due perhaps to her advanced philosophical culture and pacifist traditions. But typical epics of a religious or a military temper are to be found in Persia, India and Japan. The Oriental epic from which a selection is made here, the tale of Gilgamesh, is chosen because of the peculiar position which it occupies in cultural transition between East and West. Far older than any known poetry of Europe, and probably the oldest of all known epics, it already exhibits the major features of poems later to arise on that continent. Moreover it presumably played some part in their actual development. The history of *Gilgamesh* as it appears here is briefly as follows. During the last century massive clay tablets were discovered in what was ancient Babylonia and brought to the British Museum in London. Here they were in time deciphered; and the present free translation was made by the American poet and scholar, W. E. Leonard. As the translator in his Introduction observes, the poem anticipates the semi-historical European epic wherein a hero founds a great nation by strength of arm and wisdom of soul. The narrative recounts his wars and loves, and the aid and enmity encountered in both from supernatural beings. Expression is cast in the most heroic and exalted tone. The tale, says the American historian, J. H. Breasted, "tells how the gigantic hero, after many mighty deeds and strange adventures, failed to gain immortal life. . . . The story was known throughout the whole of Asia Minor and he passed from there to Greece under the new name of 'Heracles,' later 'Hercules.'" The story is also related to the Biblical account of the flood. Although many of the tablets are lost, enough remains for us to trace with considerable certainty the roots of our own literary tradition. The relationship is the closer since Oriental civilization reached Italy by way of the ancient Etruscans, who in certain marks of culture anticipated the Greeks and unquestionably left an impress upon their Roman neighbors.

The Homeric poems have always been regarded as expressions of the essence of Greek civilization. They were among the chief unifying factors in the numerous city states constituting ancient Greece. Their simplicity and directness of statement, vigor of feeling, humanity of character delineation, and strength and nobility of conception remain unsurpassed and have set the key for a great number of subsequent epics composed in the Western World. Homer's gods have the weaknesses of his men while his men share the nobility of his gods. Nothing certain is known of Homer himself, who remains virtually a god of epic poetry, and even the assumption of a unitary composition for the poems has been seriously questioned. The *Iliad* depicts events during the siege laid by the Greeks to Troy. It is the sterner and apparently the more primitive of Homer's two epics and may have originated as early as the eighth century B.C. The *Odyssey*, with definitely romantic tendencies, describes the arduous return of Ulysses from the successful siege to his wife Penelope, who remained in Ithaca. It may be the work either of the chief poet of the *Iliad* or of a later hand skilled in a more graceful though less powerful art. Both poems were admired throughout the civilized Europe of the classical period, lost track of during the Middle Ages, and restored to popularity with the increased study of Greek beginning in the fourteenth century.

Virgil's *Aeneid* combines qualities from both the *Iliad* and *Odyssey* with a gain in the ripening influences of Roman taste and culture of the Augustan period but a loss in the imaginative intensity characteristic of the Greeks. From the *Aeneid* is given the account of Aeneas's victory over his enemy, Turnus, with which the epic ends. All parts of the poem are inspired by Virgil's reverence for Rome and Roman traditions.

Among the more notable of the epics of continental Europe during the Christian period are the French *Song of Roland*, the German *Nibelungenlied* (Song of the Nibelungs), and the Portuguese epic, The *Lusiad*, by Luis Vaz de Camoëns, represented in turn in our selections. The two earlier poems are anonymous. The first celebrates with a robust simplicity the wars of Charlemagne, aided by his knights, Roland and Oliver, against the Saracens from Spain. Similarly, the German epic, with its picture of the national hero, Siegfried, contains reminiscences of the struggles of the Germanic Burgundians with the Huns. Unlike the *Song of Roland*, it abounds in memories of pagan mythology. The *Lusiad* describes the conquests of the Portuguese under their leader, Vasco Da Gama, who, in the year 1498, greatly aided, as he piously believed, by God's grace, sailed around the southern extremity of Africa to introduce European domination in India.

Milton's *Paradise Lost*, published in 1667, expresses in unmistakably epic terms the more spiritualized ideals of Puritanism, which had envisaged the rise of a theocracy, or religiously dominated state. Milton wrote primarily for that large body of Englishmen who believed in a Protestant theology and a neo-classical education. In short, he champions both Calvinistic doctrine and a classical conception of culture.

As a specimen of the epic or heroic poetry in America, we have chosen a passage from Stephen Vincent Benét's *John Brown's Body.* Benét's epic celebrates a democratic enthusiast for equality among the races, the liberator, John Brown. It also contrasts the dissimilar traditions of the American North and South, brought into high relief by the overwhelming disaster of civil war.

As contemporary poets grow less and less dependent upon Greek and Latin literature they neglect, to be sure, some of the superficial features of the epic form as prescribed by the critics of Homer and Virgil. But while the letter of the form is neglected, the epic spirit burns as powerfully as ever, entering even into relatively brief poems, such as Hart Crane's *The Bridge,* from which a selection will later be given, or actually producing long ones, such as that presented in this section. Heroism, patriotism, and the basic forces in our life will always demand expression and receive it in essentially epic poetry.

Gilgamesh

All things he saw, even to the ends of the earth,
He underwent all, learned to know all,
He peered through all secrets,
Through wisdom's mantle that veileth all.
What was hidden he saw,
What was covered he undid;
Of times before the stormflood he brought report.
He went on a long far way,
Giving himself toil and distress;
Wrote then on a stone-tablet the whole of his labour.
He built the walls of ramparted Uruk,
He laid the foundations, steadfast as bronze,
Of holy Eanna, the pure temple . . .

Two thirds of him is god,
One third of him is man,
There's none can match the form of his body . . .

(*The inhabitants of Uruk call upon the gods for help:*)

"Gilgamesh keeps the son from the father,
Building the walls through the day, through the night.
He is herdsman of ramparted Uruk,
He is herdsman and lord of his folk,
Strong and splendid, knowing wisdom.
Gilgamesh keeps the lover from the maiden,
The daughter of a hero,
The chosen of a noble!"
The great gods heard their outcries.
The gods of heaven called the lord Anu:
"Was he not of thy making, this almighty wild bull,
This hero Gilgamesh?
He hath not his like in the whole land . . .
Gilgamesh keeps the son from the father,
Building the walls through the day, through the night,
He is herdsman of ramparted Uruk,
He is herdsman and lord of his folk,
Strong and splendid,
Knowing wisdom.
Gilgamesh keeps the lover from the maiden,
The daughter of a hero,
The chosen of a noble!"

The great god Anu lent ear to their cries.
Aruru was summoned, she the great goddess:
"Thou, Aruru, madest Gilgamesh;
Now make another like unto him.
So long as he pleases
Let him come at Gilgamesh.
Let them contend together,
That Uruk may have peace."

As Aruru heard this,
She shaped in her heart a warrior of Anu.

Aruru washed her hands,
She pinched up some clay and spat on it.
She moulded Engidu,
Fashioned a hero, a glorious scion,
A fighter of Ninurta's.
His whole body was shaggy with hair,
Hair he bore on his head like a woman,
The plenty of his hair sprouted like grain.
He knew naught of land and people,
He was clothed like the god of the herds.
With the gazelles he eats the plants,
With the wild beasts he drinks at the watering-place,
With the throng at the water he makes glad his heart.

He walked to the watering-place
Toward a hunter, a stalker of wild beasts;
On one day, on a second, and a third,
Toward the hunter he walked to the watering-place.
The hunter saw him, the hunter's face grew troubled.
Without his quarry he turned back to his house.
He was down-cast, troubled; he shrieked.
His heart was afraid and his face was dark.
Grief made way into his heart,
And he looked like a wanderer of far ways.

The hunter opened his mouth,
Speaks, and says to his father:
"My father, a man that came from the hills
Hath become strong indeed in the land,
Mighty in power like a fighter of Anu's.
Ever he goeth along on the hills,
He is ever beside the wild beasts,
Ever are his feet at the watering-place.
I am afraid, I cannot go near to him.
He hath filled my pits which I dug;
My traps which I laid
He hath destroyed.
So from my hands he let my quarry get away,
The throngs of the fields;
No catch he allows me."

The father opened his mouth,
Speaks, and says to the hunter:
"Seek out Gilgamesh, the lord of Uruk . . .
Beg for a priestess and lead her back with thee . . .
When the wild beasts come to the watering-place,
Then let her cast her garment off,
That he may take his fill of her.
When he sees her, he will draw near;
Then will he become a stranger to his wild beasts,
Who on his own steppes grew up with him."

The hunter heard the counsel of his father . . .
He started on the way, he entered into Uruk.
He goes to Gilgamesh, and to him he says:
"A man that came from the hills
Hath become strong indeed in the land.
Mighty in power like a fighter of Anu's.
Ever he goeth along on the hills,
He is ever beside the wild beasts,
Ever are his feet at the watering-place.
I am afraid, I cannot go near to him.
He hath filled my pits which I dug;
My traps which I laid
He hath destroyed.
So from my hands he let my quarry get away,
The throngs of the fields;
No catch he allows me."

Gilgamesh says to him, to the hunter:
"Go my hunter, and get thee a priestess.
When the wild beasts come to the watering-place,
Then let her cast her garment off,
That he may take his fill of her.
When he sees her, he will draw near;
Then will he become a stranger to his wild beasts,
Who on his own steppes grew up with him."

The hunter went yonder and got him a priestess.
They made themselves ready, went forth straight on.
On the third day they came to their goal:
The hunter and the priestess sat themselves down.
One day, a second day, they sat by the watering-place.
The wild beasts come along and drink at the watering-place.

Glad is the throng of the flood.
So too comes he, Engidu . . .
With the gazelles he eats the plants,
With the beasts he drinks at the watering-place,
His heart is happy with the throng of the flood.
Then the priestess saw him, the great strong one,
The wild fellow, the man of the steppes:
"There he is, woman!
Loosen thy buckle,

Unveil thy delight,
That he may take his fill of thee!
Hang not back, take up his lust!
When he sees thee, he will draw near.
Open thy robe that he rest upon thee!
Arouse in him rapture, the work of woman.
Then will he become a stranger to his wild beasts,
Who on his own steppes grew up with him.
His bosom will press against thee."
Then the priestess loosened her buckle,
Unveiled her delight,
For him to take his fill of her.
She hung not back, she took up his lust,
She opened her robe that he rest upon her.
She aroused in him rapture, the work of woman.
His bosom pressed against her.
Engidu forgot where he was born.
For six days and seven nights
Was Engidu given over to love with the priestess.

When he had sated himself with the fill of her,
He raised up his face to his wild ones:
At sight of Engidu, the gazelles flee away,
The wild of the fields shrink back before him.
Then Engidu marvelled,
His body stood as in a spell,
His knees quivered, because his wild ran off . . .
The speed of his onset is not what it was.
He hearkens and opens his ear:
He turns about and sits down at the feet of the priestess.
He looks the priestess in the face,
And to what the priestess now speaks
His ears give heed.

The priestess says to him, to Engidu:
"Engidu, how beautiful thou, how like a god!
Why must thou rush with animals over the steppes?
Come, I will lead thee into ramparted Uruk,
To a pure house, the dwelling of Anu and Ishtar,
Where Gilgamesh lives, matchless in might,
And like a wild bull lords it over the folk." . . .
She talks to him, till he likes her words.
Knowing his own heart, he seeketh a friend.
Engidu says to her, to the priestess:
"Woman, go to! Lead me to the pure, the holy house,
The dwelling of Anu and Ishtar,
Where Gilgamesh lives, matchless in might,
And like a wild bull lords it over the folk.
I will challenge him to a fight.
I will call the strong one.
I will call out in Uruk:
'I too am a strong one!'
I alone can alter fate,
I, born on the steppes, matchless in might.
O Gilgamesh, may I behold thy face!
Well I know what the outcome will be."
Then she stripped off the one of her robes,
And clothed him therewith;
In the other robe she herself remained clad.
She took him by the hand
And led him like a bridegroom
To a festal meal at a pinfold,
And the shepherds foregathered around him.
But Engidu, born in the steppes,
Was wont to eat only plants with the gazelles,
Only to drink water with the wild,
Only to be glad with the throng of the flood,
Only to suck the milk of the wild creatures.
Then they set bread before him.
He was bewildered, and looked on it, and marvelled.
Engidu understood not how to eat bread,
To drink wine he had not learned.
Then the priestess opens her mouth and says to Engidu:
"Eat bread, Engidu, the glory of life,
Drink wine, Engidu, the custom of the land."
Then Engidu ate bread till he was full,
Then he drank wine, seven beakers.
His spirit loosed itself, he grew merry,
His heart rejoiced and his face glowed . . .
He anointed himself with oil, and became like a noble,
He put on a robe and was then as a bridegroom.
He took his weapon, he attacked lions,
So that the great shepherds found rest at night,
For Engidu was their safeguard . . .
Engidu and the priestess
Arrived at ramparted Uruk.
They found the people adorned with fillets,
Day and night they were keeping a feast . . .
The priestess says to him, to Engidu:
"Engidu . . . I will show thee Gilgamesh . . .
Thou shalt look upon him and behold his face.
His whole body is filled with strength,

His power is greater than thine.
He goes not to rest by day and by night . . .
Shamash loves Gilgamesh,
Anu, Ellil, and Ea made him wise.
Ere thou camest hither from the hills,
Did Gilgamesh in Uruk behold thee in dreams.
Gilgamesh rose up, and told his dreams,
And says to his mother:
'My mother, this night I saw a dream:
The stars stood in heaven,
Then there fell from on high
An image as of Anu upon me.
I sought to lift it up, it was too heavy for me;
I sought to shake it off,
I could not shake it off.
The folk of Uruk assembled before it . . .
And the warriors kissed its feet.
I gathered it close in my arms like a woman,
And threw it at thy feet,
And thou didst liken it to me.'

"The lady Ninsun, who knows all things,
Says to her lord,
The lady Ninsun, who knows all, says to Gilgamesh:
'Gilgamesh, if the stars stood in heaven,
And there fell upon thee an image as of Anu,
And thou soughtest to lift it up, but it was too heavy for thee,
And thou soughtest to shake it off,
And thou threwest it at my feet,
And I did liken it to thee . . .
Verily, that is one as thou, Gilgamesh,
Who was born in the steppes,
And whom the hills reared.
Thou wilt see him and fight with him.
The warriors will kiss his feet.
Thou wilt spare him and lead him to me.'

"Gilgamesh lay down and saw a second dream,
And told it to his mother:
'My mother, I saw a second dream:
I walked on the street of Uruk,
An axe lay there, and the people assembled around it.
The axe, strange was its shape.
Upon it I looked and was glad.
I gathered it close in my arms like a woman,
And threw it at thy feet,
And thou didst liken it to me.'

"The lady Ninsun, who knows all things,
Says to her son,
The lady Ninsun, who knows all, says to Gilgamesh:
'Gilgamesh, if thou saw'st an axe,
If thou gather'dst it close in thine arms like a woman,
And I likened it unto thee,
That meaneth a strong man,
A comrade, who rescues his friend.
His power will be strong in the land,
And mighty as an axe will be his strength' . . .
These, Engidu, were the dreams of Gilgamesh."

Thuswise the priestess talks to Engidu.
They go together to seek out Gilgamesh.

— *From Gilgamesh: An Epic of Old Babylonia, by William Ellery Leonard (ultimate source, ancient Babylonian tablets).*

The Quarrel

HOMER'S ILIAD

Sing, Goddess, of Achilles, Peleus' son,
In his stark wrath, which brought upon the Greeks
Infinite troubles, and shot on to Death
Many strong souls of heroes, whom it made
A prey to dogs and all the birds that came;
In the accomplishing of Zeus' design,
From when at first they quarrelled and they parted,
Atrides king of men, and bright Achilles.
Who of the gods set on those two to strife?
The son of Zeus and Leto. He was angered
Against the king and stirred an evil plague
Upon the army, and the people perished,
Because Atrides had disdained his priest
Chryses: for he had come to the quick ships
Of the Achæans to redeem his daughter,
Uncounted ransom bringing; and he carried
The fillets of the Archer-god Apollo
Upon a golden sceptre, and made prayer
To all the Achæans, but in chiefest place
To both the Atridæ, marshals of the host:
'Atridæ, and ye other armed Achæans,
Now may the gods in their Olympian houses
Grant you to ravage Priam's town and come
In honour home! But give me back my child
And take her ransom, showing deference
To Phœbus son of Zeus, who smites afar.'
Then all the other Achæans shouted 'Ay!
Respect the priest: and take the noble price.'

Only Atrides Agamemnon's heart
Disliked it, and he sent the priest away
Rudely, and laid on him a harsh command:
'Let not me find thee by the hollow ships
Or loitering now, or coming back anon,
Old man, lest possibly thou have no profit
From either wand or chaplet of thy god!
Her will I not let go; not till old age
Comes on her in my house in Argos, far
From home, where she shall ply the loom and share
My bed. No, get thee hence: provoke me not,
That thou mayst go the safer.'
So said he, and the terrified old man
Obeyed his order: and he walked in silence
Along the beach of the loud-sounding sea;
Where in a lone place he made earnest prayer
To King Apollo, fair-haired Leto's son:
'Lord of the silver bow, give ear! that hast
Chryse and holy Cilla in thy keeping
And guardest Tenedos with thy strong arm;
O God of Mice, if ever I have roofed
One temple to thy heart, if ever I have
Burned unto thee fat thighs of bulls or goats;
Fulfil this prayer for me, and let the Danai
Pay by thine arrows for these tears of mine.'
So said he praying, and Apollo heard.
Down from Olympus' peaks he came, enraged
At heart; and from his shoulders hung his bow
And lidded quiver, and upon his shoulders
The arrows rattled as he walked in wrath;
And like the night he came. Then down he sat
Far off the ships and let an arrow fly;
And a grim clang came from the silver bow.
At first he reached the mules and the quick dogs,
And then he turned and loosed his pointed bolt
Upon the troops; and all the time the pyres
Of dead were burning thickly.
Nine days along the camp Apollo's shafts
Went forth; and on the tenth Achilles called
The people to the assembly: for the thought
Was put in him by Here, white-armed goddess,
Who sorrowed for the Greeks to see them dying.
Now when they all were gathered and had come
Together, in their midst arose and said
Achilles swift of foot:
'Atrides, 'tis high time for us to turn
And wander home — unless we die here first,
If war and plague conspire to beat the Achæans!
Come, let us ask some priest or soothsayer,
Ay, or a dream-expounder, since of Zeus
Come also dreams, if he can tell us why
Phœbus Apollo is so greatly angered,
And if he censures us because of vow
Or hecatomb; in hopes he may be pleased
To take the savour of a sacrifice
Of lambs or spotless goats, and turn the plague
Away from us.'
So said he and sat down: and unto them
Rose Calchas son of Thestor, far the best
Of augurs, one who knew the things that are
And shall be and have been: 'twas he who guided
The galleys of the Achæans unto Troy
By divination which Apollo gave him.
And with good-will he spoke to them and said:
'Achilles, dear to Zeus, thou biddest me
Expound Apollo's wrath, the Archer-lord:
Then will I speak; but do thou heed and swear
To back me stoutly with thy word and arm;
For I do think to anger one who rules
The Argives all with power, and the Achæans
Obey him. For a king when he is hot
Against a humbler man is much too strong:
And though he may digest his spite today,
Yet will he nurse a grievance in his bosom
Until such time as he has worked it out.
Consider then, if thou wilt hold me safe.'
Then swift Achilles answered him and said:
'Ay, ay, be bold, and tell us what thou canst
Of heaven's will. For by Apollo whom
Zeus loveth and to whom thou prayest, Calchas,
When thou interpretest the will of heaven
Unto the Danai, there is never a man
While yet I live and see the light on earth,
Of all the Danai by the hollow ships,
Shall lay a heavy hand on thee, not though
'Twere Agamemnon that thou namedst, who
Now boasts himself far best of all the Achæans.'
Then taking courage said the blameless seer:
'No, not for any vow or hecatomb
He censures us, but for his servant's sake

Whom Agamemnon slighted, and refused
To free his child or take her price: therefore
The Archer sent these pains, and yet will send;
Nor from the Danai will he turn this shame
And havoc, till we give the bright-eyed girl
Back to her father without pay or price,
And send a solemn hecatomb to Chryse.
Then might we soften him to hear our prayer.'

So saying down he sat, and unto them
Wide-ruling Agamemnon, Atreus' son,
Arose in anger. His dark heart was near
To burst with rage, and his two eyes were like
A flame of fire; and with an ominous look
At Calchas first he spoke:

'Prophet of evil, never hast thou said
One word to cheer me; 'tis thy constant joy
To preach thine evil things, but one good word
Thou never yet hast uttered nor fulfilled!
And now art thou expounding to the Danai
That for this reason is the Archer working
Distress for them, because I would not take
Chryseis' noble ransom – since so much
I wish to keep the girl herself at home.
Yea, I prefer her to my wedded wife,
For Clytemnestra is no way her better,
In face or form or wit or works. And yet
E'en so, if 'tis the better plan, I am willing
To give her up: I want to have my people
Saved, not destroyed. But make ye ready straight
Some prize for me, so that I may not go
Without a prize alone of all the Argives,
As were indeed improper. For ye see
Ay, all of you, my honour going elsewhere.'

Then swift Achilles answered him and said:
'Most glorious son of Atreus, and of all men
Most grasping! how then shall the generous Greeks
Give thee a prize? We know of no reserve
Of common treasure; we have always shared
The loot of towns we sacked; nor were it decent
To re-collect it from the host afresh.
No: now let go thy girl unto the god,
And threefold, fourfold we Achæans will
Repay thee, soon as ever Zeus allows us
To sack the strong-walled citadel of Troy.'

But royal Agamemnon made him answer:
'Not so, good as thou art, godlike Achilles,
Think to befool me! thou shalt not elude
Nor overbear me. Dost thou hope that thou
Shouldst keep thy prize, while I sit lacking one,
That thou dost bid me yield her? Very well;
If the great-heart Achæans offer me
A prize I like, that I be compensated;
But if they will not, then I will come myself,
And take one – thine, or Aias' or Odysseus';
And bitter shall he be to whom I come!
Well, let us take thought of these things afterwards;
But launch a black ship on the bright sea now;
Muster the complement of oars; embark
A hecatomb, and ship this girl aboard,
Fair-cheeked Chryseis. In command of her
Let some one chosen from the council go,
Aias, Idomeneus, or great Odysseus,
Or thou, most violent of all mankind,
Pelides, to make sacrifice for us
And so propitiate the Archer-god.'

Then swift Achilles answered with a scowl:
'O shameless-mannered, selfish-minded man!
How canst thou look for hearty loyalty
From any of the Achæans, on the march
Or in hot battle? Hither came not I
To fight by reason of the Trojan spearmen:
Me had they done no wrong; they never drove
My cows nor horses off; they never spoiled
My harvest in rich Phthia, nurse of men,
Since in between lay many a barrier
Of shadowy mountains and resounding sea.
And yet we followed thee, most shameless man,
To gladden thee by winning recompense
For thee and Menelaus from the Trojans,
Thou hound! Thou thinkest nothing of our service:
Thou dost ignore it. And thou threatenest now
Thyself to take away my prize, for which
I toiled so hard, and which was given me by
The sons of the Achæans! For I never
Have equal prize with thee, each time the Achæans
Ransack a thriving city of the Trojans.
My hands do most of the wild work of war,
But when the sharing comes, then thy reward
Is much the bigger, and I go my way
Fatigued with fighting to the ships, and take
Some morsel, yet mine own. But now enough,
I am for Phthia: better far go home,
I, and my curving ships! I have no fancy,

Remaining here despised, to fill thee up
With wealth and riches.'
Then Agamemnon king of men replied:
'Desert by all means, if thy soul desires.
I will not beg thee tarry for my sake.
No, I have others by me, who will hold me
In honour, and above all Zeus most wise.
Of all the heaven-born kings I hate thee most,
For thy delight is always in dissension
And war and fightings. If thou art so brave,
That must have been a gift to thee from God.
Home with thy ships and troops, and discipline
Thy Myrmidons! I do not value thee
Nor mind thy rage: and thus I give thee warning.
Whereas Apollo doth exact from me
Chryseis, her with mine own ship and men
I will send back – and then I will myself
Come to thy hut and bring away Briseis
Fair-cheeked, that prize of thine, to prove to thee
How much am I above thee, that another
May be afraid to boast himself my peer
And match me to my face.'
So said he; but Peleion was aggrieved,
And in his shaggy breast his heart was swayed
Two ways at once; to draw the sharp-edged sword
That hung beside him, break the assembly up,
And kill Atrides, or to stay his anger
And curb his spirit. And as in heart and mind
He pondered this, and was in act to pull
His great sword from its sheath, Athene came
From heaven, for Here, white-armed goddess, sent her,
Who loved and cared for both the chiefs alike.
She stood behind and by his golden hair
She caught Peleion, seen of him alone;
None of the rest beheld her; and Achilles
Marvelled, and turned and recognized at once
Athene with a fierce light in her eyes.
And thus to her in winged words he said:
'Why art thou come again, O child of Zeus
Who bears the aegis? is it to behold
Atrides Agamemnon's insolence?
Well, I will tell thee, and I think my words
Shall be fulfilled: soon his high-handed ways
Are like to cost him life.'
Athene, grey-eyed goddess, answered him:
'I come to stay thy wrath, if thou wilt listen,
From heaven, for Here, white-armed goddess, sent me,
Who loves and cares for both you two alike.
Leave off this quarrel; do not draw thy sword;
But cast the consequences in his teeth.
For this I tell thee, and the thing shall be
Fulfilled, that thou shalt have for his affront
Hereafter recompense three times as rich;
But hold thy hand and hearken unto us.'
Then the swift-foot Achilles answered her:
'Bound am I, goddess, to observe your order,
Though I am much in rage – and better so!
The gods give readier hearing to the man
Who does their bidding.'
He spoke, and on the silver haft he laid
His heavy hand and drove the great sword home
Within its sheath, and made himself obey
Athene's word. And toward Olympus she
Was gone, to join the other gods among
The palaces of aegis-bearing Zeus.
But Peleus' son, his anger unabated,
Again assailed Atrides savagely:
'Wine-sodden, dog in eye and doe at heart,
Thou never yet hast dared to arm thyself
And lead the host to battle, nor to share
The risks of ambush with our bravest men:
That seems like death to thee! Much pleasanter
To range the wide cantonment of the Greeks
And sequestrate the prize of any man
Who dare oppose thee – folk-devouring king,
That rulest feeble people! Otherwise
This outrage, son of Atreus, were thy last.
Lo, I will say my say, and swear thereto
A solemn oath. Yea, by this staff of mine,
Which never more shall put out leaf or shoot
Since first it left its stem upon the hills,
Nor yet grow green again, because the axe
Has stripped its leaves and bark – and now the sons
Of the Achæans, those who sit in judgment
And guard traditions by command of Zeus,
They bear it in their hands – so shall it be
A potent oath to thee: the day shall come
When all the sons of the Achæans will
Long for Achilles: and in that day thou
In thy distress shalt have no strength to help,
When multitudes fall dying at the hands

Of slaughtering Hector. Thou shalt eat thy heart
Within thee, for remorse that thou didst slight
The noblest of the Achæans.'
Pelides spoke, and dashed to earth his staff
Studded with golden nails, and sat him down,
While on his side Atrides glared with rage.
Among them sprang up Nestor, sweet of speech,
Pylos' clear orator, from whose tongue flowed
Discourse more sweet than honey: he had seen
Two generations wane of mortal men,
Of those who had been born and bred with him
In sacred Pylos, and among the third
Now was he king; and with good thoughts to them
He made harangue and said:
'Ay me! here comes a great calamity
Upon the Achæan land. 'Twould gladden Priam
And Priam's sons and give the other Trojans
Exceeding joyful hearts, if they could hear
Of all this broil between you two, who are
Best of the Danai in debate or battle.
Hearken to me: you both are younger men
Than I: there was a time when I consorted
With better men than you, and never they
Made light of me. I have never seen nor shall
I see such men as those — Peirithous,
Cæneus and Dryas, shepherd of the host,
Exadius and the godlike Polyphemus,
And Theseus, son of Ægeus, peer of gods.
They were the strongest of men reared on earth;
Strongest they were, and with the strongest fought,
The Centaurs of the fells, and horribly
Destroyed them. And to serve with these came I
From Pylos, from a distant land afar,
For they invited me; and so I played
Mine own part in the war; but of the men
On earth today could no man fight with them.
I say they listened to my counsels; they
Gave heed unto my words; so do ye two
Heed likewise, for 'tis better to give heed.
Neither do thou, for all thy rank, exact
The girl from him; but let her be, e'en as
The sons of the Achæans gave her first
To him for prize: nor, Peleus' son, do thou
Seek to oppose a king by force, because
A sceptred king with glory given of Zeus
Enjoys no common honour. Though thou art
Brave, and a goddess bore thee, yet his place
Is higher, since he rules more men than thou.
And thou, Atrides, curb thy rage, and slack
Thy wrath, I do beseech thee, with Achilles,
A man whom all the Achæans feel to be
A mighty bulwark against evil war.'
Then royal Agamemnon answered him:
'Ay, ay, old sir, all that thou sayst is right
But this man wishes to o'ertop all others;
He would be lord of all and king of all
And give commands to all — but I know one
Who will not suffer that! Well, if the gods
Who live for ever made a warrior of him,
Do they enjoin him therefore to insult me?'
Then answered great Achilles, breaking in:
'Coward and abject I might well be called
If on each point, whate'er thou sayst, I should
Give way to thee. Go and dictate to others;
Give me no orders, for I tell thee, I
Will none of it! And hear, and lay to heart
This one word more. Upon the girl's account
I will not come to blows — because you gave
That which you take — with thee, nor any other:
But of all else beside my swift black ship
That I possess, thou shalt not carry off
One whit without my leave. Ay, come and try,
That all the host may know: and on the spot
Shall thy black blood go spurting round my spear.'
So from the clash of bitter words they rose,
And broke up the assembly by the ships.
Achilles towards his huts and level ships
Went with Menœtius' son and his own men;
But Agamemnon had a light ship dragged
To sea, and picked and shipped a score of rowers
And stowed in her a hetacomb for the god,
And led and set on board Chryseis fair;
And as commander deep Odysseus went.
So they embarked and sailed the watery ways.
Meanwhile the son of Atreus urged the people
To cleanse themselves; whereon they cleansed themselves
And cast off their uncleanness in the sea;
And by the shore of the unfruitful sea
Offered to Phœbus perfect hecatombs

Of bulls and goats, and on the spires of
smoke
The savour went to heaven.
Thus was the camp employed: but Agamemnon
Pursued the quarrel which he had already
Threatened against Achilles: and he called
Talthybius and Eurybates, the pair
That were his pursuivants and active squires:
'Go to Achilles' hut, the son of Peleus,
And take fair-cheeked Briseis by the hand,
And bring her here. And if he will not give
her,
Then I myself will come with a large force
And take her, which will be the worse for
him.'
With that he sent them forth and laid on
them
His harsh command. Unwillingly they two
Walked by the shore of the unvintaged sea,
And to the Myrmidonian huts and ships
They came. And him they found beside his
hut
And black ship, seated; and at sight of them
Achilles was not glad: and they, afraid
And awed before the king stood still, and
had
No word to say or ask him; but he knew
Their errand in his mind and said to them:
'Hail, heralds, messengers of Zeus and men!
Come nearer. 'Tis not you I hold to blame,
But Agamemnon who has sent you here
About the girl Briseis. Go thou then,
High-born Patroclus, bring the maiden out
And give her to their charge. But let these
two
Be witnesses before the blessed gods
And mortal men, and that perverted king,
Against the day to come, when there is need
Of me to save them all from shame and ruin.
The king in truth is mad, and, blind with
rage,
He cannot look ahead nor look behind,
Nor see how his Achæans might be safe
In battle by the ships.'

— *From the Greek of Homer's Iliad (c. 800 B.C.), translated by Sir William Marris.*

∽ ۞ ∼

The Death of Turnus

VIRGIL'S AENEID

Now Turnus rolls aloof o'er empty plains,
And here and there some straggling foes he
gleans,
His flying coursers please him less and less,
Ashamed of easy fight, and cheap success.
Thus half-contented, anxious in his mind,
The distant cries come driving in the wind —
Shouts from the walls, but shouts in murmurs drowned;
A jarring mixture, and a boding sound.
"Alas!" said he, "what mean these dismal
cries?
What doleful clamours from the town
arise?"
Confused, he stops, and backward pulls the
reins.
She, who the driver's office now sustains,
Replies: — "Neglect, my lord, these new
alarms:
Here fight, and urge the fortune of your
arms:
There want not others to defend the wall.
If by your rival's hand the Italians fall,
So shall your fatal sword his friends oppress,
In honour equal, equal in success."
To this, the prince: — "O sister! — for I
knew,
The peace infringed proceeded first from
you:
I knew you, when you mingled first in fight:
And now in vain you would deceive my
sight —
Why, goddess, this unprofitable care?
Who sent you down from heaven, involved
in air,
Your share of mortal sorrows to sustain,
And see your brother bleeding on the plain?
For to what power can Turnus have recourse,
Or to resist his fate's prevailing force? . . .
Is death so hard to bear? — Ye gods below!
(Since those above so small compassion
show),
Receive a soul unsullied yet with shame,
Which not belies my great forefathers'
name."
He said; and while he spoke, with flying
speed
Came Saces urging on his foamy steed:
Fixed on his wounded face a shaft he bore,
And, seeking Turnus, sent his voice before:
"Turnus! on you, on you alone, depends
Our last relief: — compassionate your
friends!
Like lightning, fierce Aeneas, rolling on,
With arms invests, with flames invades, the
town:
The brands are tossed on high; the winds
conspire
To drive along the deluge of the fire.

All eyes are fixed on you: your foes rejoice
Even the king staggers, and suspends his choice —
Doubts to deliver or defend the town,
Whom to reject, or whom to call his son.
The queen, on whom your utmost hopes were placed,
Herself suborning death, has breathed her last.
'Tis true, Messapus, fearless of his fate,
With fierce Atinas' aid, defends the gate:
On every side surrounded by the foe,
The more they kill, the greater numbers grow;
An iron harvest mounts, and still remains to mow.
You, far aloof from your forsaken bands,
Your rolling chariot drive o'er empty sands."
Stupid he sate, his eyes on earth declined,
And various cares revolving in his mind:
Rage, boiling from the bottom of his breast,
And sorrow mixed with shame, his soul oppressed;
And conscious worth lay labouring in his thought,
And love by jealousy to madness wrought.
By slow degrees his reason drove away
The mists of passion, and resumed her sway.
Then, rising on his car, he turned his look,
And saw the town involved in fire and smoke.
A wooden tower with flames already blazed,
Which his own hands on beams and rafters raised.
And bridges laid above to join the space,
And wheels below to roll from place to place.
"Sister! the Fates have vanquished: let me go
The way which Heaven and my hard fortune show.
The fight is fixed; nor shall the branded name
Of a base coward blot your brother's fame.
Death is my choice; but suffer me to try
My force, and vent my rage before I die."
He said; and leaping down without delay,
Through crowds of scattered foes he freed his way.
Striding he passed, impetuous as the wind,
And left the grieving goddess far behind.
As, when a fragment, from a mountain torn
By raging tempests, or by torrents borne,
Or sapped by time, or loosened from the roots —
Prone through the void the rocky ruin shoots,
Rolling from crag to crag, from steep to steep;
Down sink, at once, the shepherds and their sheep:
Involved alike, they rush to nether ground;
Stunned with the shock they fall, and stunned from earth rebound:
So Turnus, hasting headlong to the town,
Shouldering and shoving, bore the squadrons down.
Still pressing onward, to the walls he drew,
Where shafts and spears and darts promiscuous flew,
And sanguine streams the slippery ground embrue.
First stretching out his arm, in sign of peace,
He cries aloud, to make the combat cease: —
"Rutulians, hold! and Latin troops, retire!
The fight is mine; and me the gods require.
'Tis just that I should vindicate alone
The broken truce, or for the breach atone.
This day shall free from wars the Ausonian state,
Or finish my misfortunes in my fate."
Both armies from their bloody work desist,
And, bearing backward, form a spacious list.
The Trojan hero, who received from fame
The welcome sound, and heard the champion's name,
Soon leaves the taken works and mounted walls:
Greedy of war where greater glory calls,
He springs to fight, exulting in his force;
His jointed armour rattles in the course.
Like Eryx, or like Athos, great he shows,
Or father Appennine, when white with snows,
His head divine obscure in clouds he hides,
And shakes the sounding forest on his sides.
The nations, overawed, surcease the fight;
Immovable their bodies, fixed their sight.
Even death stands still; nor from above they throw
Their darts, nor drive their battering-rams below.
In silent order either army stands,
And drop their swords, unknowing, from their hands.
The Ausonian king beholds, with wondering sight,
Two mighty champions matched in single fight,
Born under climes remote, and brought by fate,
With swords to try their titles to the state.
Now, in closed field, each other from afar

They view; and, rushing on, begin the war.
They launch their spears; then hand to hand they meet,
The trembling soil resounds beneath their feet:
Their bucklers clash; thick blows descend from high,
And flakes of fire from their hard helmets fly.
Courage conspires with chance; and both engage
With equal fortune and with mutual rage.
As, when two bulls for their fair female fight
In Sila's shades, or on Taburnus' height,
With horns adverse they meet; the keeper flies;
Mute stands the herd; the heifers roll their eyes,
And wait the event — which victor they shall bear,
And who shall be the lord, to rule the lusty year:
With rage of love the jealous rivals burn,
And push for push, and wound for wound, return;
Their dewlaps gored, their sides are laved in blood;
Loud cries and roaring sounds rebellow through the wood:
Such was the combat in the listed ground;
So clash their swords, and so their shields resound.
Jove sets the beam: in either scale he lays
The champions' fate, and each exactly weighs.
On this side, life, and lucky chance ascends;
Loaded with death, that other scale descends.
Raised on the stretch, young Turnus aims a blow
Full on the helm of his unguarded foe:
Shrill shouts and clamours ring on either side,
As hopes and fears their panting hearts divide.
But all in pieces flies the traitor sword,
And, in the middle stroke, deserts his lord.
Now 'tis but death or flight; disarmed he flies,
When in his hand an unknown hilt he spies.
Fame says that Turnus, when his steeds he joined,
Hurrying to war, disordered in his mind,
Snatched the first weapon which his haste could find.
'Twas not the fated sword his father bore,
But that his charioteer Metiscus wore.
This, while the Trojans fled, the toughness held:
But, vain against the great Vulcanian shield,
The mortal-tempered steel deceived his hand:
The shivered fragments shone amid the sand.

. . . . .

Now stern Aeneas waves his weighty spear
Against his foe, and thus upbraids his fear: —
"What farther subterfuge can Turnus find?
What empty hopes are harboured in his mind?
'Tis not thy swiftness can secure thy flight;
Nor with their feet, but hands, the valiant fight.
Vary thy shape in thousand forms, and dare
What skill and courage can attempt in war;
Wish for the wings of winds, to mount the sky;
Or hid within the hollow earth to lie!"
The champion shook his head, and made this short reply: —
"No threats of thine my manly mind can move;
'Tis hostile Heaven I dread, and partial Jove."
He said no more, but, with a sigh, repressed
The mighty sorrow in his swelling breast.
Then, as he rolled his troubled eyes around,
An antique stone he saw, the common bound
Of neighbouring fields, and barrier of the ground —
So vast, that twelve strong men of modern days
The enormous weight from earth could hardly raise.
He heaved it at a lift, and, poised on high,
Ran staggering on against his enemy,
But so disordered, that he scarcely knew
His way, or what unwieldy weight he threw.
His knocking knees are bent beneath the load,
And shivering cold congeals his vital blood.
The stone drops from his arms, and, falling short
For want of vigour, mocks his vain effort.
And as, when heavy sleep has closed the sight,
The sickly fancy labours in the night;
We seem to run; and, destitute of force,
Our sinking limbs forsake us in the course:
In vain we heave for breath; in vain we cry;

The nerves, unbraced, their usual strength
deny;
And on the tongue the faltering accents die;
So Turnus fared; whatever means he tried,
All force of arms, and points of art employed,
The Fury flew athwart, and made the endeavour void.
A thousand various thoughts his soul confound;
He stared about, nor aid nor issue found;
His own men stop the pass, and his own
walls surround.
Once more he pauses, and looks out again,
And seeks the goddess charioteer in vain.
Trembling he views the thundering chief
advance,
And brandishing aloft the deadly lance:
Amazed he cowers beneath his conquering
foe,
Forgets to ward, and waits the coming blow
Astonished while he stands, and fixed with
fear,
Aimed at his shield he sees the impending
spear.
The hero measured first, with narrow
view,
The destined mark; and, rising as he threw,
With its full swing the fatal weapon flew.
Not with less rage the rattling thunder falls,
Or stones from battering-engines break the
walls:
Swift as a whirlwind, from an arm so strong,
The lance drove on, and bore the death
along.
Nought could his sevenfold shield the prince
avail,
Nor aught, beneath his arms, the coat of
mail:
It pierced through all, and with a grisly
wound
Transfixed his thigh, and doubled him to
ground.
With groans the Latins rend the vaulted
sky:
Woods, hills, and valleys, to the voice reply.
Now low on earth the lofty chief is laid,
With eyes cast upwards, and with arms displayed,
And recreant, thus to the proud victor
prayed: —
"I know my death deserved, nor hope to
live:
Use what the gods and thy good fortune give.
Yet think, oh! think, if mercy may be shown
(Thou hadst a father once, and hast a son),
Pity my sire, now sinking to the grave;
And for Anchises' sake, old Daunus save!
Or, if thy vowed revenge pursue my death,
Give to my friends my body void of breath!
Thine is the conquest, thine the royal wife:
Against a yielded man, 'tis mean ignoble
strife."
In deep suspense the Trojan seemed to
stand,
And, just prepared to strike, repressed his
hand.
He rolled his eyes, and every moment felt
His manly soul with more compassion melt;
When, casting down a casual glance, he
spied
The golden belt that glittered on his side,
The fatal spoil which haughty Turnus tore
From dying Pallas, and in triumph wore.
Then, roused anew to wrath, he loudly cries
(Flames, while he spoke, came flashing from
his eyes),
"Traitor! dost thou, dost thou to grace pretend,
Clad, as thou art, in trophies of my friend?
To his sad soul a grateful offering go!
'Tis Pallas, Pallas gives this deadly blow."
He raised his arm aloft, and, at the word,
Deep in his bosom drove the shining sword.
The streaming blood distained his arms
around,
And the disdainful soul came rushing
through the wound.

—*From the Latin of Virgil (70 B.C.–19 B.C.), translated by John Dryden (abridged).*

~ ✿ ~

The Death of Roland

FROM THE SONG OF ROLAND

THE PAGANS RUN, wild and angry. They hurry towards Spain. Count Roland has not the strength to chase them. He has lost his horse Veillantif, and he must be left there on foot. He went to help archbishop Turpin. He unlaced his gilded helmet from his head and took off his white coat of light mail. He has cut away his shirt and stuffed the folds of it into his great wounds. Then he has held him in his arms against his breast, and then he has laid him down softly on the green grass. Roland has asked him very sweetly, 'E! gentle man, now give me your leave to go. Our companions whom we held so dear are dead, and we should not leave them there. I will go and look for them and know them, and bring them together and set them in order before you.' The archbishop said, 'Go, and come back. This field is yours by God's mercy, and mine.'

Roland turns away from him. He goes all alone through the field. He looks in the valleys and he looks on the hills. There he found Gerin and his companion Gerer, and he found Berenger and Otun. There he found Anseis and Sansun. He found Gerard, the old man of Russillun. The baron has taken them one by one and has come with them all to the archbishop; then he put them in line before his knees. The archbishop cannot hold himself from weeping. He lifts up his hand and makes his blessing. Afterwards he has said, 'Lords, you were set for sorrow. May God the glorious have all your souls and set them in holy flowers in Paradise. My own death tears me with great pain. I shall not see the strong emperor.'

Roland turns from him and goes again to search through the field. He has found his companion Oliver. He has held him close in his arms against his breast, and comes back as well as he can to the archbishop. He has laid him on a shield by the others, and the archbishop has absolved and blessed them. And then their sorrow and their pity become greater. Roland says, 'Oliver, my lovely companion, you were the son of duke Reiner, who held the border in the valley of Runers. To break a shaft and to pierce shields, to overcome the proud and make them fear, and to uphold good men and give them counsel, there is no better knight in any country.'

When count Roland sees his peers dead and Oliver, whom he could love so much, he had tenderness for them and he begins to weep. He had no colour in his face, and he had such sorrow that he could not stand. He cannot help himself, he faints on the ground. The archbishop said, 'Baron, you were set for sorrow.'

When the archbishop saw that Roland faints, then he had such sorrow that he never had greater. He put out his hand and has taken the olifant. There is a running stream at Rencesvals. He wants to go to it, and will give Roland some water. He leaves him, stumbling in short steps. He is so weak that he cannot go forward. He has no strength, he has lost so much blood. Before a man could take fifty paces in the field, his heart fails him and he has fallen forward; his death comes on him in great anguish.

Count Roland comes back from his faint. He lifts himself up on his feet, but his suffering is great. He looks down to the valley and up to the hill. He sees the noble baron lying on the green grass beyond his companions. It is the archbishop, whom God set up in his name. He confesses his sins and looks up, he has joined both his hands and lifted them up to heaven, and he prays to God that he may give him Paradise. Turpin is dead, the soldier of Charles. In great battles and in fine sermons he has always been his champion against the pagans. May God give him his holy blessing.

Count Roland sees the archbishop on the ground. He sees his bowels lying outside of his body; his brain boils out through his forehead. He has crossed his white hands which are beautiful on his breast between the two collar-bones. He makes his deep lament for him in the way of his country. 'E! gentle man, knight of good blood, today I give you to the glorious of heaven. There will never be a man who serves him with greater will. Since the apostles, no man has been such a prophet to hold up the law and to bring men to it. Let your soul have no suffering, may the gate of Paradise be open to you.'

Roland feels that death is near to him. His brain is bursting out of his ears. He prays to God for his peers that he may call them to him. And then he prays for himself to the angel Gabriel. He took the olifant, that no one may make it a reproach to him, and in his other hand his sword Durendal. He walks towards Spain to a waste field, further than a crossbow can throw a bolt. He climbs on a hill. There are four stones made of marble, under a fine tree. He falls on his back on the green grass; there he has fainted, for death is near to him.

The hills are high, and the trees are very high. There are four shining stones there, of marble. Count Roland faints on the green grass. All the time a saracen is watching him. He pretended that he was dead and lay among the others. He smeared his face and body with blood. He sets himself on his feet and is quick to run. He was fine and strong and a good soldier. In his pride he begins his mortal madness. He seized Roland's body and his sword, and said a word to him. 'Charles's nephew is beaten. I shall wear this sword in Arabia.' As he pulled it from him, the count began to come to himself.

Roland feels that he is taking his sword. He opened his eyes and has said a word to him. 'As I know it, you are not of our men.' He takes the olifant, for he will not lose it, and strikes him on his helmet, which was jewelled in gold. He breaks the steel and his head and his bones, he has dashed both his eyes out of his head, and thrown him over dead, down at his feet. Afterwards he says, 'Low pagan, how were you so daring as to take hold of me, either in right or wrong? No man will hear it who will not think you mad. The mouth of my horn is broken, the crystal and the gold of it are on the ground.'

Roland feels that he has lost his sight. He sets himself on his feet, he calls up all the strength he has. He has lost the colour of his face. There is a brown stone in front of him. In sorrow and bitterness he strikes ten blows on the stone. The steel grates, it does not break nor splinter. 'E!' said the count, 'help me, St. Mary. E! good Durendal, you were set for sorrow. Now I am lost, and I am your keeper no more. I have won so many battles on the field with you and fought down so many great countries which Charles holds, whose beard is grey. Let no man have you who would run before another. A good soldier has held you for a long time. There will never be such a one again in holy France.'

Roland struck on the stone of sardonie. The steel grates, it does not break nor splinter. When he sees that he cannot break it at all, he begins to lament his sword to himself. 'E! Durendal, how beautiful you are and bright and white; how you shine and flame again in the sun. Charles was in the valley of Moriane when God sent to him from heaven by his angel that he should give you to a captain of his counts. Then the gentle king, the great, set the sword on me. And with it I conquered Anjou and Bretagne, with it I conquered Poitou and Maine, I conquered Normandy the free, and I conquered Provence and Equitaigne, and Lombardy and all the country of Rome. With it I conquered Bavaria and all Flanders, and Burgundy and all Poland and Constantinople whose faith he held; and in Saxony his will was done. With it I conquered Scotland and England which he held as his own place. I have conquered with it so many countries which Charles holds, whose beard is white. Now I have sorrow and heaviness for this sword. I would rather die than that it should stay among the pagans. God our Father, do not let France be shamed in it.'

Roland struck on a brown stone. He beats down a greater piece of it than I could tell you. The steel grates, it does not fly apart nor break; it has bounded up again to the sky. When the count saw that he could not break it at all, he lamented it very sweetly to himself. 'E! Durendal, how beautiful you are and very sacred. In your golden hilt there are many relics, the tooth of St. Peter, and of the blood of St. Basil and hairs of my lord St. Denis and the dress of St. Mary. It is not right that the pagans should have you in their power, you should be served by Christian men. Let no man have you who does cowardice. I have conquered many great countries with you which Charles holds, whose beard is white, and the emperor is strong and grand in them.'

Roland feels that death is taking him. It is coming down from his head to his heart. He has run under a pine tree, he has lain down on his face on the green grass; he puts the sword and the olifant under his body. He turned his head towards the pagan people, and he has done this because he would have Charles and all his people say, 'The gentle count, he died unbeaten.' He confesses his sins feebly and often. He raised his glove to God in offering for his sins.

Roland feels that his time is no more. He is on a steep hill that looks towards Spain. He has beaten his breast with one hand. 'God, *mea culpa* for my sins against your grace, the great ones and the small ones, which I have done from the hour in which I was born until this day in which I am overtaken.' He has held up his right glove to God; the angels of heaven come down to him.

Count Roland lay under a pine tree. He has turned his face towards Spain. He began to bring many things into his mind; the many countries which the baron overcame, sweet France, the men of his line, and Charlemagne his lord who nourished him; and he cannot hold himself from weeping and sighing. But he will not be forgetful of himself. He confesses his sin and prays to God for mercy. 'True Father who have never lied, who raised Lazarus from the dead and saved Daniel from the lions, save my soul from every danger of the sins I did in my life.' He raised his right glove to God, and St. Gabriel has taken it from his hand. He held his head bowed on his arm, he joined his hands, and he has gone to his end. God sent his angel Cherubim and St. Michael of the Peril, and with them St. Gabriel came to him. They take the soul of the count to Paradise.

—From the French of The Song of Roland, anon. (12th Cent.), translated by René Hague.

The Fall of Siegfried

FROM THE SONG OF THE NIBELUNGS

Hagen of Trony went to Kriemhild, to take his leave of her, for they would away.

"Well for me," said Kriemhild, "that ever I won to husband a man that standeth so true by his friends, as doth Siegfried by my kinsmen. Right proud am I. Bethink thee now, Hagen, dear friend, how that in all things I am at thy service, and have ever willed thee well. Requite me through my husband, that I love, and avenge not on him what I did to Brunhild. Already it repenteth me sore. My body hath smarted for it, that ever I troubled her with my words. Siegfried, the good knight, hath seen to that."

Whereto Hagen answered, "Ye will shortly be at one again. But Kriemhild, prithee tell me wherein I can serve thee with Siegfried, thy husband, and I will do it, for I love none better."

"I should fear naught for his life in battle, but that he is foolhardy, and of too proud a courage. Save for that, he were safe enow."

Then said Hagen, "Lady, if thou fearest hurt for him in battle, tell me now by what device I may hinder it, and I will guard him afoot and on horse."

She answered, "Thou art my cousin, and I thine. To thy faith I commend my dear husband, that thou mayst watch and keep him."

Then she told him what she had better have left unsaid.

"My husband is stark and bold. When that he slew the dragon on the mountain, he bathed him in its blood; wherefore no weapon can pierce him. Nevertheless, when he rideth in battle, and spears fly from the hands of heroes, I tremble lest I lose him. Alack! for Siegfried's sake how oft have I been heavy of my cheer! And now, dear cousin, I will trust thee with the secret, and tell thee, that thou mayst prove thy faith, where my husband may be wounded. For that I know thee honourable, I do this. When the hot blood flowed from the wound of the dragon, and Siegfried bathed therein, there fell atween his shoulders the broad leaf of a lime tree. There one might stab him, and thence is my care and dole."

Then answered Hagen of Trony, "Sew, with thine own hand, a small sign upon his outer garment, that I may know where to defend him when we stand in battle."

She did it to profit the knight, and worked his doom thereby. She said, "I will sew secretly, with fine silk, a little cross upon his garment, and there, O knight, shalt thou guard to me my husband when ye ride in the thick of the strife, and he withstandeth his foeman in the fierce onset."

"That will I do, dear lady," answered Hagen.

Kriemhild thought to serve Siegfried; so was the hero betrayed.

Then Hagen took his leave and went forth glad; and his king bade him say what he had learned.

"If thou wouldst turn from the journey, let us go hunting instead; for I have learned the secret, and have him in my hand. Wilt thou contrive this?"

"That will I," said the king.

And the king's men rejoiced. Never more, I ween, will knight do so foully as did Hagen, when he brake his faith with the queen.

The next morning Siegfried, with his thousand knights, rode merrily forth; for he thought to avenge his friends. And Hagen rode nigh him, and spied at his vesture. When he saw the mark, he sent forward two of his men secretly, to ride back to them with another message: that Ludger bade tell the king his land might remain at peace.

Loth was Siegfried to turn his rein or he

had done battle for his friends. Gunther's vassals scarce held him back. Then he rode to the king, that thanked him.

"Now, God reward thee, Siegfried, my kinsman, that thou didst grant my prayer so readily. Even so will I do by thee, and that justly. I hold thee trustiest of all my friends. Seeing we be quit of this war, let us ride a hunting to the Odenwald after the bear and the boar, as I have often done."

Hagen, the false man, had counselled this.

. . . . .

Gunther and Hagen, the fierce warriors, went hunting with false intent in the forest, to chase the boar, the bear, and the wild bull, with their sharp spears. What fitter sport for brave men?

Siegfried rode with them in kingly pomp. They took with them good store of meats. By a cool stream he lost his life, as Brunhild, King Gunther's wife, had devised it.

But or he set out, and when the hunting-gear was laid ready on the sumpters that they were to take across the Rhine, he went to Kriemhild, that was right doleful of her cheer. He kissed his lady on the mouth. "God grant I may see thee safe and well again, and thou me. Bide here merry among thy kinsfolk, for I must forth."

Then she thought on the secret she had betrayed to Hagen, but durst not tell him. The queen wept sore that ever she was born, and made measureless dole.

She said, "Go not hunting. Last night I dreamed an evil dream: how that two wild boars chased thee over the heath; and the flowers were red with blood. Have pity on my tears, for I fear some treachery. There be haply some offended, that pursue us with deadly hate. Go not, dear lord; in good faith I counsel it."

But he answered, "Dear love, I go but for a few days. I know not any that beareth me hate. Thy kinsmen will me well, nor have I deserved otherwise at their hand."

"Nay, Siegfried, I fear some mischance. Last night I dreamed an evil dream: how that two mountains fell on thee, and I saw thee no more. If thou goest, thou wilt grieve me bitterly."

But he caught his dear one in his arms and kissed her close; then he took leave of her and rode off.

She never saw him alive again.

They rode thence into a deep forest to seek sport. The king had many bold knights with him, and rich meats, that they had need of for the journey. Sumpters passed laden before them over the Rhine, carrying bread and wine, and flesh and fish, and meats of all sorts, as was fitting for a rich king.

. . . . .

Hastily, with their bows and spears, the warriors, swift of foot, chased the bear, but there were so many dogs that none durst shoot among them, and the forest rang with the din. Then the bear fled before the dogs, and none could keep pace with him save Kriemhild's husband, that ran up to him and pierced him dead with his sword, and carried the carcase back with him to the fire. They that saw it said he was a mighty man.

. . . . .

Then they bade the sportsmen to the table, and they sat down, a goodly company enow, on a fair meadow. Ha! what dishes, meet for heroes, were set before them. But the cup-bearers were tardy, that should have brought the wine. Save for that, knights were never better served. If there had not been false-hearted men among them, they had been without reproach. The doomed man had no suspicion that might have warned him, for his own heart was pure of all deceit. Many that his death profited not at all had to pay for it bitterly.

Then said Sir Siegfried, "I marvel, since they bring us so much from the kitchen, that they bring not the wine. If good hunters be entreated so, I will hunt no more. Certes, I have deserved better at your hands."

Whereto the king at the table answered falsely, "What lacketh to-day we will make good another time. The blame is Hagen's, that would have us perish of thirst."

Then said Hagen of Trony, "Dear master, methought we were to hunt to-day at Spessart, and I sent the wine thither. For the present we must go thirsty; another time I will take better care."

But Siegfried cried, "Small thank to him. Seven sumpters with meat and spiced wines should he have sent here at the least, or, if that might not be, we should have gone nigher to the Rhine."

Hagen of Trony answered, "I know of a cool spring close at hand. Be not wroth with me, but take my counsel, and go thither." The which was done, to the hurt of many warriors. Siegfried was sore athirst and bade push back the table, that he might go to the spring at the foot of the mountain. Falsely had the knights contrived it. The wild beasts that Siegfried's hand had slain they let pile on a waggon and take home, and all they that saw it praised him.

Foully did Hagen break faith with Siegfried. He said, when they were starting for the broad lime tree, "I hear from all sides that none can keep pace with Kriemhild's husband when he runneth. Let us see now."

Bold Siegfried of the Netherland answered, "Thou mayst easily prove it, if thou wilt run with me to the brook for a wager. The praise shall be to him that winneth there first."

"Let us see then," said Hagen the knight.

And stark Siegfried answered, "If I lose, I will lay me at thy feet in the grass."

A glad man was King Gunther when he heard that!

Said Siegfried further, "Nay, I will undertake more. I will carry on me all that I wear — spear, shield, and hunting gear." Whereupon he girded on his sword and his quiver in haste. Then the others did off their clothes, till they stood in their white shirts, and they ran through the clover like two wild panthers; but bold Siegfried was seen there the first. Before all men he won the prize in everything. He loosed his sword straightway, and laid down his quiver. His good spear he leaned against the lime tree; then the noble guest stood and waited, for his courtesy was great. He laid down his shield by the stream. Albeit he was sore athirst, he drank not till that the king had finished, who gave him evil thanks.

The stream was cool, pure, and good. Gunther bent down to the water, and rose again when he had drunk. Siegfried had gladly done the like, but he suffered for his courtesy. Hagen carried his bow and his sword out of his reach, and sprang back and gripped the spear. Then he spied for the secret mark on his vesture; and while Siegfried drank from the stream, Hagen stabbed him where the cross was, that his heart's blood spurted out on the traitor's clothes. Never since hath knight done so wickedly. He left the spear sticking deep in his heart, and fled in grimmer haste than ever he had done from any man on this earth afore.

When stark Siegfried felt the deep wound, he sprang up maddened from the water, for the long boar spear stuck out from his heart. He thought to find bow or sword; if he had, Hagen had got his due. But the sore-wounded man saw no sword, and had nothing save his shield. He picked it up from the water's edge and ran at Hagen. King Gunther's man could not escape him. For all that he was wounded to the death, he smote so mightily that the shield well-nigh brake, and the precious stones flew out. The noble guest had fain taken vengeance.

Hagen fell beneath his stroke. The meadow rang loud with the noise of the blow. If he had had his sword to hand, Hagen had been a dead man. But the anguish of his wound constrained him. His colour was wan; he could not stand upright; and the strength of his body failed him, for he bare death's mark on his white cheek. Fair women enow made dole for him.

Then Kriemhild's husband fell among the flowers. The blood flowed fast from his wound, and in his great anguish he began to upbraid them that had falsely contrived his death. "False cowards!" cried the dying knight. "What availeth all my service to you, since ye have slain me? I was true to you, and pay the price for it. Ye have done ill by your friends. Cursed by this deed are your sons yet unborn. Ye have avenged your spite on my body all too bitterly. For your crime ye shall be shunned by good knights."

All the warriors ran where he lay stabbed. To many among them it was a woeful day. They that were true mourned for him, the which the hero had well deserved of all men.

The King of Burgundy, also, wept for his death, but the dying man said, "He needeth not to weep for the evil, by whom the evil cometh. Better had he left it undone, for mickle is his blame."

Then said grim Hagen, "I know not what ye rue. All is ended for us — care and trouble. Few are they now that will withstand us. Glad am I that, through me, his might is fallen."

"Lightly mayst thou boast now," said Siegfried; "if I had known thy murderous hate, it had been an easy thing to guard my body from thee. My bitterest dole is for Kriemhild, my wife. God pity me that ever I had a son. For all men will reproach him that he hath murderers to his kinsmen. I would grieve for that, had I the time."

He said to the king, "Never in this world was so foul a murder as thou hast done on me. In thy sore need I saved thy life and thine honour. Dear have I paid for that I did well by thee." With a groan the wounded man said further, "Yet if thou canst show truth to any on this earth, O King, show it to my dear wife, that I commend to thee. Let it advantage her to be thy sister. By all princely honour stand by her. Long must my father and my knights wait for my coming. Never hath woman won such woe through a dear one."

He writhed in his bitter anguish, and spake painfully, "Ye shall rue this foul deed in the days to come. Know this of a truth, that in slaying me ye have slain yourselves."

The flowers were all wet with blood. He strove with death, but not for long, for the weapon of death cut too deep. And the bold knight and good spake no more.

When the warriors saw that the hero was dead, they laid him on a shield of ruddy gold, and took counsel how they should conceal that Hagen had done it. Many of them said, "Evil hath befallen us. Ye shall all hide it, and hold to one tale — when Kriemhild's husband was riding alone in the forest, robbers slew him."

But Hagen of Trony said, "I will take him back to Burgundy. If she that hath troubled Brunhild know it, I care not. It concerneth me little if she weep."

— *From the German of The Song of the Nibelungs, anon. (c. 1200), translated by Margaret Armour (abridged).*

Passage to India

FROM THE LUSIAD

Arms and the heroes signalised in fame,
Who from the western Lusitanian shore
Beyond e'en Taprobana sailing came
O'er seas that ne'er had traversed been before,
Dauntless in wars and dangers without name,
Achieving all of human force and more,
And midst a race remote in distant clime
New kingdom raised to future so sublime;

And all the glorious memories that grace
Those Kings who sallied forth to propagate
The Faith, the empire; and the countries base,
Asian and African, did devastate;
And those who hold by valorous deeds such place
That from death's law their names they liberate,
Through all the world in song will I rehearse,
If art and genius so inspire my verse.

Cease now those mighty voyages to proclaim,
The Trojan and the learned Greek sustained;
Boast not of victories and all their fame,
That Trajan and great Alexander gained;
I sing a daring Lusitanian name,
O'er Neptune and o'er Mars to rule ordained;
Cease all the Ancient Muse resounds, for lo!
Another valour bolder front doth show,

And ye, my nymphs of Tagus, since my rhyme
With ardent genius new ye now inspire,
If I was wont, well pleased, in former time
To celebrate your stream with humble lyre,
Oh grant me now a lofty note sublime,
A grand and glowing line of poet's fire,
That of your waters Phoebus may ordain
They shall not envy those of Hippocrene.

Grant me a daring and sonorous tone,
Not as from flute or shepherd's reed might flow,
But from harmonious martial trumpet blown,
That fires the breast and flushes all the brow;
Grant me such Song your famous race would own,
Worthy their feats whose aid e'en Mars doth know,
That through the world I may resound the strain,
If verse can valour so sublime contain.

And thou, the best-born fortress and the stay
Of ancient Lusitanian liberty,
Nor less, of hope the most assured ray
For growth of nascent Christianity;
Thou, the avenging marvel of our day,
New terror of the Moorish lance to be,
Given to the world by God, to rule it all,
That of the world great part to God may fall:

Thou flourishing young branch of a green tree
By Christ more well-beloved as His own
Than any born in Occident that be,
Or as Cesarian or most Christian known;
Behold this on thy shield, where thou dost see
A victory long past here present shown,

Wherein He gave thee for thy arms displayed
Those that upon the Cross His own He made.

Thou mighty Monarch, o'er whose high domain
Sol when he riseth earliest ray doth cast,
Beholds it in mid hemisphere again,
And at his setting moment leaves it last;
Thou, the foreshadowed conqueror, scourge and bane,
Who the vile Ishmaelitish knight shalt blast,
And Oriental Turk and Heathen tribe,
Who still their sacred river's stream imbibe:

Incline thy majesty awhile, I pray —
For that same gentle mood, methinks, in thee
Smiles now as shall smile in thy latter day,
When thou art rising to Eternity —
Bend down thy gaze in earth; a new display
The royal and benignant eye shall see
Of love for patriot deeds of valour bold,
Spread far and wide in verses manifold.

The love of country thou shalt see, not moved
By vile reward, e'en half eternal, grand;
For 'tis not vile reward to be approved
By an acclaim of my paternal land;
Hark: thou shalt blazoned see the name beloved
Of those whom, lord supreme, thou dost command:
And thou shalt judge which yields the nobler grace,
King of the world to be, or such a race.

Hark; thou shalt not behold with empty deeds,
Fantastical, fictitious, and untrue,
Thy people praised, as boastful Muse must needs,
Seeking to shine with glory more than due:
So great thy true deeds are, their fame exceeds
E'en all of fabulous and dreamy hue,
Of Rodamonte and Rugeiro vain,
Orlando too, could all as true be ta'en.

. . . . .

On thee the shivering Moor keeps eye, as one
From whom his fear forebodes the fatal stroke;
The barbarous heathen at thy sight alone
Already bends the neck to take the yoke;
Tethys, in dower, the whole cerulean throne
For thy command prepares, and hath bespoke
Thy purchase as her son-in-law to be,
Charmed by thy gentle grace and majesty.

. . . . .

But at this moment while they ready stand
Behold the master, watching o'er the sky,
The whistle blows; the sailors, every hand,
Starting awaken; and on deck they fly.
And as the wind increased he gave command,
In lowering foresails all their strength to ply;
'Look sharp, my lads, from yon black cloud,' he cries,
'That hangs above, the winds increasing rise.'

Or ere the foresails are well gathered in
A vast and sudden storm around them roar'd;
'Strike sail!' the Master shouts amidst the din,
'Strike, strike the mainsail, lend all hands a'board!'
But the indignant winds the fight begin,
And, joined in fury ere it could be lower'd,
With blustering noise the sail in pieces rend
As if the world were coming to an end.

With this the sailors wound the heaven with cries,
By sudden terror and confusion blind;
For, sails all torn, the vessel over lies,
And ships a mass of water in the wind;
'Cast overboard,' the master's order flies;
'Cast overboard, together, with a mind!
Go others work the pumps! stick to the last!
The pumps, and quick! for we are foundering fast.'

The soldiers, all alive, now hasten fast
To work the pumps, but scarcely had essayed
When the dread seas in which the ship was cast
So tossed her that they all were prostrate laid:
Three hardy powerful sailors, to the last,
To guide the wheel but fruitless efforts made;
With cords on either side it must be bound,
For force and art of man but vain are found.

The winds were such, that scarcely could they show
More force of cruel impetus around,

Than if it were their purpose, then, to blow
The mighty tower of Babel to the ground.
On the high cresting seas which higher grow
Like a small boat the mighty ship doth bound,
Exciting wonder that on such a main
She can her labouring course so long sustain.

The powerful ship with Gama's brother Paul,
With mast asunder snapped by wind and wave,
Half under water lies; the sailors call
On Him Who once appeared the world to save;
Nor less, vain cries from Coelho's vessel all
Pour on the air, fearing a watery grave,
Although the master had such caution shown
That ere the wind arose the sails were down.

Now rising to the clouds they seem to go,
O'er the wild waves of Neptune borne on end;
Now to the bowels of the depths below
It seems to all their senses they descend;
Notus and Auster, Boreas, Aquilo,
The very world's machinery would rend;
While flashings fire the black and ugly night
And shed from pole to pole a blazing light.

. . . . .

Vasco da Gama, seeing that so near
The end of his desire he stood to die,
That now to hell the waves to gape appear,
Now with new fury mount into the sky;
Of life uncertain, all confused with fear,
With nought of aid whereon he could rely,
Calls upon that all-powerful sacred Aid,
Who can the impossible; and thus he prayed:

'Divine, Angelic, Heavenly Guard and Friend!
Whom Heavens and Earth and Ocean all obey,
Thou Who all Israel didst succour lend
Through Erythraean sea to take their way;
Thou Who deliveredst Paul, and didst defend
'Gainst ugly flood and quicksand, many a day,
Him with his sons who were, by Thy decree,
New parents of the drown'd void world to be;

'If I new dangerous fears have dared to oppose,
Have other Scylla and Charybdis passed,
And sandy shoals where shallow water flows,
'Midst foul Acroceraunian rocks been cast;
With such laborious works about to close,
Why dost Thou now forsake us at the last,
If this our labour do not Thee offend,
But rather only to Thy service tend?

'O blest! to whom the privilege remained
On the sharp point of Afric's lance to die,
While they with power the Sacred Faith maintained
In Moorish lands of infidelity;
Whose deeds, illustrious, reputation gained,
Who must survive supreme in memory,
Who gained their life e'en when they laid it down,
Death being sweetened by its own renown!'

. . . . .

Now, o'er the hills broke forth the morning bright,
Where Ganges' stream is murmuring heard to flow,
When from the lofty top the sailors sight
High land, which was descried upon the prow.
Free from the storm and from the first seas' fight,
Vain terror from their hearts is banished now;
Melinde's pilot cries with jocund tongue,
''Tis land of Calecut, if I'm not wrong;

'This is, indeed, the land that thou hast sought,
This the true India which doth now appear;
If in the world thou hast no farther thought,
Then thy long labour is all ended here!'
Gama can bear no more; all over-wrought
With joy to find the land now known and near,
With knees upon the ground and hands toward Heaven,
For this, God's mercy great, his thanks are given.

He rendered thanks to God, with heart and mind,
For He not only had the country shown,
Which midst such terror he had come to find,
For which such labours he had undergone:
But that he had so shortly left behind
Death, which upon the seas the winds had blown,
So hard and wild and dread, it made him seem
Like one just wakened from a horrid dream!

Upon these dreadful dangers it depends,
These heavy labours and anxieties,
That they acquire, who are of fame the friends,
Immortal honours and advanced degrees:
Not leaning on the trunks, wherefrom descends
The ancient glory of their ancestries,
Nor laid on gilded couches, wrapt within
The Russian sable's fine luxurious skin;

Not with choice viands new and exquisite,
Not in the soft and lazy paths of joy,
Not with delights, varied and infinite,
Which generous breasts enfeeble and destroy;
Not with the never governed appetite,
Wherewith is Fortune everwont to toy,
Who suffers none his footsteps to retrace
For any deed of valour or of grace;

But by an effort with strong arm to seal
The honours which he thus his own has made,
Watchful and putting on his polished steel,
Enduring storms, by cruel waves o'erlaid;
Victorious where the far South's colds congeal,
In regions tossed, all destitute of aid,
Reduced to feed upon corrupted fare,
Mingled with arduous suffering and despair;

By force of spirit, when the brow grows pale,
To wear a look possessed, collected, gay,
When the hot whistling cannon balls assail,
Tearing his comrades' arms or legs away;
Thus, noble hardness will at heart prevail,
Of wealth and honours scorning the display,
Of wealth and honours but by fortune gained,
And not by virtue, righteous and sustained.

'Tis thus the understanding becomes bright,
Which by experience mature doth grow,
And looks, as from exalted moral height,
On the base crooked human course below;
Such man, where rule shall own the force of right
And doth not leaning of affection know,
Shall rise to high command, as rise he ought,
Against his own desire and all unsought.

—*From the Portuguese of The Lusiad, by Louis de Camoëns (1524?–1579?), translated by J. J. Aubertin (abridged).*

The Fallen Angels

FROM PARADISE LOST

Of Man's first disobedience, and the fruit
Of that forbidden tree whose mortal taste
Brought death into the World, and all our woe,
With loss of Eden, till one greater Man
Restore us, and regain the blissful seat,
Sing, Heavenly Muse, that, on the secret top
Of Oreb, or of Sinai, didst inspire
That shepherd who first taught the chosen seed
In the beginning how the heavens and earth
Rose out of Chaos: or, if Sion hill
Delight thee more, and Siloa's brook that flowed
Fast by the oracle of God, I thence
Invoke thy aid to my adventurous song,
That with no middle flight intends to soar
Above the Aonian mount, while it pursues
Things unattempted yet in prose or rhyme.
And chiefly Thou, O Spirit, that dost prefer
Before all temples the upright heart and pure,
Instruct me, for Thou know'st; Thou from the first
Wast present, and, with mighty wings outspread,
Dove-like sat'st brooding on the vast Abyss,
And mad'st it pregnant: what in me is dark
Illumine, what is low raise and support;
That, to the highth of this great argument,
I may assert Eternal Providence,
And justify the ways of God to men.
  Say first — for Heaven hides nothing from thy view,
Nor the deep tract of Hell — say first what cause
Moved our grand Parents, in that happy state,
Favoured of Heaven so highly, to fall off
From their Creator, and transgress his will
For one restraint, lords of the World besides.
Who first seduced them to that foul revolt?
  The infernal Serpent; he it was whose guile,
Stirred up with envy and revenge, deceived
The mother of mankind, what time his pride
Had cast him out from Heaven, with all his host
Of rebel Angels, by whose aid, aspiring
To set himself in glory above his peers,
He trusted to have equalled the Most High,
If he opposed, and, with ambitious aim

Against the throne and monarchy of God,
Raised impious war in Heaven and battle proud,
With vain attempt. Him the Almighty Power
Hurled headlong flaming from the ethereal sky,
With hideous ruin and combustion, down
To bottomless perdition, there to dwell
In adamantine chains and penal fire,
Who durst defy the Omnipotent to arms.
Nine times the space that measures day and night
To mortal men, he, with his horrid crew,
Lay vanquished, rolling in the fiery gulf,
Confounded, though immortal. But his doom
Reserved him to more wrath; for now the thought
Both of lost happiness and lasting pain
Torments him: round he throws his baleful eyes,
That witnessed huge affliction and dismay,
Mixed with obdurate pride and steadfast hate.
At once, as far as Angel's ken, he views
The dismal situation waste and wild.
A dungeon horrible, on all sides round,
As one great furnace flamed; yet from those flames
No light; but rather darkness visible
Served only to discover sights of woe,
Regions of sorrow, doleful shades, where peace
And rest can never dwell, hope never comes
That comes to all, but torture without end
Still urges, and a fiery deluge, fed
With ever-burning sulphur unconsumed.
Such place Eternal Justice had prepared
For those rebellious; here their prison ordained
In utter darkness, and their portion set,
As far removed from God and light of Heaven
As from the centre thrice to the utmost pole.
Oh how unlike the place from whence they fell!
There the companions of his fall, o'erwhelmed
With floods and whirlwinds of tempestuous fire,
He soon discerns; and, weltering by his side,
One next himself in power, and next in crime,
Long after known in Palestine, and named
BEËLZEBUB. To whom the Arch-Enemy,
And thence in Heaven called SATAN, with bold words
Breaking the horrid silence, thus began: —
"If thou beest he — but Oh how fallen! how changed
From him! — who, in the happy realms of light,
Clothed with transcendent brightness, didst outshine
Myriads, though bright — if he whom mutual league,
United thoughts and counsels, equal hope
And hazard in the glorious enterprise,
Joined with me once, now misery hath joined
In equal ruin; into what pit thou seest
From what highth fallen: so much the stronger proved
He with his thunder: and till then who knew
The force of those dire arms? Yet not for those,
Nor what the potent Victor in his rage
Can else inflict, do I repent, or change,
Though changed in outward lustre, that fixed mind,
And high disdain from sense of injured merit,
That with the Mightiest raised me to contend,
And to the fierce contention brought along
Innumerable force of Spirits armed,
That durst dislike his reign, and, me preferring,
His utmost power with adverse power opposed
In dubious battle on the plains of Heaven,
And shook his throne. What though the field be lost?
All is not lost — the unconquerable will,
And study of revenge, immortal hate,
And courage never to submit or yield:
And what is else not to be overcome.
That glory never shall his wrath or might
Extort from me. To bow and sue for grace
With suppliant knee, and deify his power
Who, from the terror of this arm, so late
Doubted his empire — that were low indeed;
That were an ignominy and shame beneath
This downfall; since, by fate, the strength of Gods,
And this empyreal substance, cannot fail;
Since, through experience of this great event,
In arms not worse, in foresight much advanced,
We may with more successful hope resolve
To wage by force or guile eternal war,
Irreconcilable to our grand Foe,
Who now triumphs, and in the excess of joy
Sole reigning holds the tyranny of Heaven."
So spake the apostate Angel, though in pain,

Vaunting aloud, but racked with deep despair;
And him thus answered soon his bold compeer: —
"O Prince, O Chief of many thronèd Powers
That led the embattled Seraphim to war
Under thy conduct, and, in dreadful deeds
Fearless, endangered Heaven's perpetual King,
And put to proof his high supremacy,
Whether upheld by strength, or chance, or fate!
Too well I see and rue the dire event
That, with sad overthrow and foul defeat,
Hath lost us Heaven, and all this mighty host
In horrible destruction laid thus low,
As far as Gods and Heavenly Essences
Can perish: for the mind and spirit remains
Invincible, and vigour soon returns,
Though all our glory extinct, and happy state
Here swallowed up in endless misery.
But what if He our Conqueror (whom I now
Of force believe almighty, since no less
Than such could have o'erpowered such force as ours)
Have left us this our spirit and strength entire,
Strongly to suffer and support our pains,
That we may so suffice his vengeful ire,
Or do him mightier service as his thralls
By right of war, whate'er his business be,
Here in the heart of Hell to work in fire,
Or do his errands in the gloomy Deep?
What can it then avail though yet we feel
Strength undiminished, or eternal being
To undergo eternal punishment?"
Whereto with speedy words the Arch-Fiend replied: —
"Fallen Cherub, to be weak is miserable,
Doing or suffering: but of this be sure —
To do aught good never will be our task,
But ever to do ill our sole delight,
As being the contrary to His high will
Whom we resist. If then his providence
Out of our evil seek to bring forth good,
Our labour must be to pervert that end,
And out of good still to find means of evil;
Which ofttimes may succeed so as perhaps
Shall grieve him, if I fail not, and disturb
His inmost counsels from their destined aim.
But see! the angry Victor hath recalled
His ministers of vengeance and pursuit
Back to the gates of Heaven: the sulphurous hail,
Shot after us in storm, o'erblown hath laid
The fiery surge that from the precipice
Of Heaven received us falling; and the thunder,
Winged with red lightning and impetuous rage,
Perhaps hath spent his shafts, and ceases now
To bellow through the vast and boundless Deep.
Let us not slip the occasion, whether scorn
Or satiate fury yield it from our Foe.
Seest thou yon dreary plain, forlorn and wild,
The seat of desolation, void of light,
Save what the glimmering of these livid flames
Casts pale and dreadful? Thither let us tend
From off the tossing of these fiery waves;
There rest, if any rest can harbour there;
And, re-assembling our afflicted powers,
Consult how we may henceforth most offend
Our enemy, our own loss how repair,
How overcome this dire calamity,
What reinforcement we may gain from hope,
If not what resolution from despair."
Thus Satan, talking to his nearest mate,
With head uplift above the wave, and eyes
That sparkling blazed; his other parts besides
Prone on the flood, extended long and large,
Lay floating many a rood, in bulk as huge
As whom the fables name of monstrous size,
Titanian or Earth-born, that warred on Jove,
Briareos or Typhon, whom the den
By ancient Tarsus held, or that sea-beast
Leviathan, which God of all his works
Created hugest that swim the ocean-stream.
Him, haply slumbering on the Norway foam,
The pilot of some small night-foundered skiff,
Deeming some island, oft, as seamen tell,
With fixèd anchor in his scaly rind,
Moors by his side under the lee, while night
Invests the sea, and wishèd morn delays.
So stretched out huge in length the Arch-Fiend lay,
Chained on the burning lake; nor ever thence
Had risen, or heaved his head, but that the will
And high permission of all-ruling Heaven
Left him at large to his own dark designs,
That with reiterated crimes he might
Heap on himself damnation, while he sought
Evil to others, and enraged might see
How all his malice served but to bring forth

Infinite goodness, grace, and mercy, shewn
On Man by him seduced, but on himself
Treble confusion, wrath, and vengeance poured.
Forthwith upright he rears from off the pool
His mighty stature; on each hand the flames
Driven backward slope their pointing spires, and, rolled
In billows, leave i' the midst a horrid vale.
Then with expanded wings he steers his flight
Aloft, incumbent on the dusky air,
That felt unusual weight; till on dry land
He lights – if it were land that ever burned
With solid, as the lake with liquid fire,
And such appeared in hue as when the force
Of subterranean wind transports a hill
Torn from Pelorus, or the shattered side
Of thundering Ætna, whose combustible
And fuelled entrails, thence conceiving fire,
Sublimed with mineral fury, aid the winds,
And leave a singèd bottom all involved
With stench and smoke. Such resting found the sole
Of unblest feet. Him followed his next mate;
Both glorying to have scaped the Stygian flood
As gods, and by their own recovered strength,
Not by the sufferance of supernal power.
"Is this the region, this the soil, the clime,"
Said then the lost Archangel, "this the seat
That we must change for Heaven? – this mournful gloom
For that celestial light? Be it so, since He
Who now is sovran can dispose and bid
What shall be right: farthest from Him is best,
Whom reason hath equalled, force hath made supreme
Above his equals. Farewell, happy fields,
Where joy for ever dwells! Hail, horrors! hail,
Infernal World! and thou, profoundest Hell,
Receive thy new possessor – one who brings
A mind not to be changed by place or time.
The mind is its own place, and in itself
Can make a Heaven of Hell, a Hell of Heaven.
What matter where, if I be still the same,
And what I should be, all but less than he
Whom thunder hath made greater? Here at least
We shall be free; the Almighty hath not built
Here for his envy, will not drive us hence:
Here we may reign secure; and, in my choice,
To reign is worth ambition, though in Hell:
Better to reign in Hell than serve in Heaven.
But wherefore let we then our faithful friends,
The associates and co-partners of our loss,
Lie thus astonished on the oblivious pool,
And call them not to share with us their part
In this unhappy mansion, or once more
With rallied arms to try what may be yet
Regained in Heaven, or what more lost in Hell?"
So Satan spake; and him Beëlzebub
Thus answered: – "Leader of those armies bright
Which, but the Omnipotent, none could have foiled!
If once they hear that voice, their liveliest pledge
Of hope in fears and dangers – heard so oft
In worst extremes, and on the perilous edge
Of battle, when it raged, in all assaults
Their surest signal – they will soon resume
New courage and revive, though now they lie
Grovelling and prostrate on yon lake of fire,
As we erewhile, astounded and amazed;
No wonder, fallen such a pernicious highth!"
He scarce had ceased when the superior Fiend
Was moving toward the shore; his ponderous shield,
Ethereal temper, massy, large, and round,
Behind him cast. The broad circumference
Hung on his shoulders like the moon, whose orb
Through optic glass the Tuscan artist views
At evening, from the top of Fesolè,
Or in Valdarno, to descry new lands,
Rivers, or mountains, in her spotty globe.
His spear – to equal which the tallest pine
Hewn on Norwegian hills, to be the mast
Of some great ammiral, were but a wand –
He walked with, to support uneasy steps
Over the burning marle, not like those steps
On Heaven's azure; and the torrid clime
Smote on him sore besides, vaulted with fire.
Nathless he so endured, till on the beach
Of that inflamèd sea he stood, and called
His legions – Angel Forms, who lay entranced
Thick as autumnal leaves that strow the brooks
In Vallombrosa, where the Etrurian shades
High over-arched embower; or scattered sedge
Afloat, when with fierce winds Orion armed

Hath vexed the Red-Sea coast, whose waves o'erthrew
Busiris and his Memphian chivalry,
While with perfidious hatred they pursued
The sojourners of Goshen, who beheld
From the safe shore their floating carcases
And broken chariot-wheels. So thick bestrown,
Abject and lost, lay these, covering the flood,
Under amazement of their hideous change.
He called so loud that all the hollow deep
Of Hell resounded: — "Princes, Potentates,
Warriors, the Flower of Heaven — once yours; now lost,
If such astonishment as this can seize
Eternal Spirits! Or have ye chosen this place
After the toil of battle to repose
Your wearied virtue, for the ease you find
To slumber here, as in the vales of Heaven?
Or in this abject posture have ye sworn
To adore the Conqueror, who now beholds
Cherub and Seraph rolling in the flood
With scattered arms and ensigns, till anon
His swift pursuers from Heaven-gates discern
The advantage, and, descending, tread us down
Thus drooping, or with linkèd thunderbolts
Transfix us to the bottom of this gulf? —
Awake, arise, or be for ever fallen!"
They heard, and were abashed, and up they sprung
Upon the wing, as when men wont to watch,
On duty sleeping found by whom they dread,
Rouse and bestir themselves ere well awake.
Nor did they not perceive the evil plight
In which they were, or the fierce pains not feel;
Yet to their General's voice they soon obeyed
Innumerable. As when the potent rod
Of Amram's son, in Egypt's evil day,
Waved round the coast, up-called a pitchy cloud
Of locusts, warping on the eastern wind,
That o'er the realm of impious Pharaoh hung
Like Night, and darkened all the land of Nile;
So numberless were those bad Angels seen
Hovering on wing under the cope of Hell,
'Twixt upper, nether, and surrounding fires;
Till, as a signal given, the uplifted spear
Of their great Sultan waving to direct
Their course, in even balance down they light
On the firm brimstone, and fill all the plain:
A multitude like which the populous North
Poured never from her frozen loins to pass
Rhene or the Danaw, when her barbarous sons
Came like a deluge on the South, and spread
Beneath Gibraltar to the Libyan sands.
Forthwith, from every squadron and each band,
The heads and leaders thither haste where stood
Their great Commander — godlike Shapes, and Forms
Excelling human; princely Dignities;
And Powers that erst in Heaven sat on thrones,
Though of their names in Heavenly records now
Be no memorial, blotted out and rased
By their rebellion from the Books of Life.

— From Paradise Lost by John Milton, English (1608–1674).

John Brown

STEPHEN VINCENT BENÉT

They reached the Maryland bridge of Harper's Ferry
That Sunday night. There were twenty-two in all,
Nineteen were under thirty, three not twenty-one,
Kagi, the self-taught scholar, quiet and cool,
Stevens, the cashiered soldier, Puritan-fathered,
A singing giant, gunpowder-tempered and rash.
Dauphin Thompson, the pippin-cheeked country-boy,
More like a girl than a warrior; Oliver Brown,
Married last year when he was barely nineteen;
Dangerfield Newby, colored and born a slave,
Freeman now, but married to one not free
Who, with their seven children, waited him South,
The youngest baby just beginning to crawl;
Watson Brown, the steady lieutenant, who wrote
Back to his wife,
"Oh, Bell, I want to see you
And the little fellow very much but must wait.

There was a slave near here whose wife was sold South.
They found him hanging in Kennedy's orchard next morning.
I cannot come home as long as such things are done here.
I sometimes think that we shall not meet again."

These were some of the band. For better or worse
They were all strong men.
The bearded faces look strange
In the old daguerreotypes: they should be the faces
Of prosperous, small-town people, good sons and fathers,
Good horse-shoe pitchers, good at plowing a field,
Good at swapping stories and good at praying.
American wheat, firm-rooted, good in the ear.
There is only one whose air seems out of the common,
Oliver Brown. That face has a masculine beauty
Somewhat like the face of Keats.
They were all strong men.

They tied up the watchman and took the rifle-works.
Then John Brown sent a raiding party away
To fetch in Colonel Washington from his farm.
The Colonel was George Washington's great-grand-nephew,
Slave-owner, gentleman-farmer, but, more than these,
Possessor of a certain fabulous sword
Given to Washington by Frederick the Great.
They captured him and his sword and brought them along
Processionally.
The act has a touch of drama,
Half costume-romance, half unmerited farce.
On the way, they told the Washington slaves they were free,
Or free to fight for their freedom.
The slaves heard the news
With dazed, scared eyes of cattle before a storm.
A few came back with the band and were given pikes,
And, when John Brown was watching, pretended to mount
A slipshod guard over the prisoners.
But, when he had walked away, they put down their pikes
And huddled together, talking in mourning voices.
It didn't seem right to play at guarding the Colonel
But they were afraid of the bearded patriarch
With the Old Testament eyes.
A little later
It was Patrick Higgins' turn. He was the night-watchman
Of the Maryland bridge, a tough little Irishman
With a canny, humorous face, and a twist in his speech.
He came humming his way to his job.
"Halt!" ordered a voice.
He stopped a minute, perplexed. As he told men later,
"Now I didn't know what 'Halt!' mint, any more
Than a hog knows about a holiday."
There was a scuffle.
He got away with a bullet-crease in his scalp
And warned the incoming train. It was half-past-one.
A moment later, a man named Shepherd Heyward,
Free negro, baggage-master of the small station,
Well-known in the town, hardworking, thrifty and fated,
Came looking for Higgins.
"Halt!" called the voice again,
But he kept on, not hearing or understanding,
Whichever it may have been.
A rifle cracked.
He fell by the station-platform, gripping his belly,
And lay for twelve hours of torment, asking for water
Until he was able to die.
There is no stone,
No image of bronze or marble green with the rain
To Shepherd Heyward, free negro of Harper's Ferry,
And even the books, the careful, ponderous histories,
That turn live men into dummies with smiles of wax
Thoughtfully posed against a photographer's background

In the act of signing a treaty or drawing a sword,
Tell little of what he was.
And yet his face
Grey with pain and puzzled at sudden death
Stares out at us through the bookworm-dust of the years
With an uncomprehending wonder, a blind surprise.
"I was getting along," it says, "I was doing well.
I had six thousand dollars saved in the bank.
It was a good town, a nice town, I liked the folks
And they liked me. I had a good job there, too.
On Sundays I used to dress myself up slick enough
To pass the plate in church, but I wasn't proud
Not even when trashy niggers called me Mister,
Though I could hear the old grannies over their snuff
Mumbling along, 'Look, chile, there goes Shepherd Heyward.
Ain't him fine in he Sunday clo'es — ain't him sassy and fine?
You grow up decent and don't play ball in the street,
And maybe you'll get like him, with a gold watch and chain.'
And then, suddenly — and what was it all about?
Why should anyone want to kill me? Why was it done?"

So the grey lips. And so the hurt in the eyes.
A hurt like a child's, at punishment unexplained
That makes the whole child-universe fall to pieces.
At the time of death, most men turn back toward the child.

Brown did not know at first that the first man dead
By the sword he thought of so often as Gideon's sword
Was one of the race he had drawn that sword to free.
It had been dark on the bridge. A man had come
And had not halted when ordered. Then the shot
And the scrape of the hurt man dragging himself away.
That was all. The next man ordered to halt would halt.
His mind was too full of the burning judgments of God
To wonder who it had been. He was cool and at peace.
He dreamt of a lamb, lying down by a rushing stream.

So the night wore away, indecisive and strange.
The raiders stuck by the arsenal, waiting perhaps
For a great bell of jubilation to toll in the sky,
And the slaves to rush from the hills with pikes in their hands,
A host redeemed, black rescue-armies of God.
It did not happen.
Meanwhile, there was casual firing.
A townsman named Boerley was killed.
Meanwhile, the train
Passed over the bridge to carry its wild news
Of abolition-devils sprung from the ground
A hundred and fifty, three hundred, a thousand strong
To pillage Harper's Ferry, with fire and sword.
Meanwhile the whole countryside was springing to arms.
The alarm-bell in Charlestown clanged "Nat Turner has come!
Nat Turner has come again, all smoky from Hell,
Setting the slave to murder and massacre!"
The Jefferson Guards fell in. There were boys and men.
They had no uniforms but they had weapons.
Old squirrel-rifles, taken down from the wall,
Shot guns loaded with spikes and scraps of iron.
A boy dragged a blunderbuss as big as himself.
They started for the Ferry.
In a dozen
A score of other sleepy, neighboring towns
The same bell clanged, the same militia assembled.

The Ferry itself was roused and stirring with dawn.

And the firing began again.
A queer, harsh sound
In the ordinary streets of that clean, small town,
A desultory, vapid, meaningless sound.

God knows why John Brown lingered! Kagi, the scholar,
Who, with two others, held the rifle-works,
All morning sent him messages urging retreat.
They had the inexorable weight of common sense
Behind them, but John Brown neither replied
Nor heeded, brooding in the patriarch-calm
Of a lean, solitary pine that hangs
On the cliff's edge, and sees the world below
A tiny pattern of toy fields and trees,
And only feels its roots gripping the rock
And the almighty wind that shakes its boughs,
Blowing from eagle-heaven.

Of course they were cut off. The whole attempt
Was fated from the first.
Just about noon
The Jefferson Guards took the Potomac Bridge
And drove away the men Brown posted there.

There were three doors of possible escape
Open to Brown. With this the first slammed shut.
The second followed it a little later
With the recapture of the other bridge
That cut Brown off from Kagi and the arsenal
And penned the larger body of the raiders
In the armory.
Again the firing rolled,
And now the first of the raiders fell and died,
Dangerfield Newby, the freed Scotch-mulatto
Whose wife and seven children, slaves in Virginia,
Waited for him to bring them incredible freedom.
They were sold South instead, after the raid.
His body lay where the townspeople could reach it.
They cut off his ears for trophies.
If there are souls,
As many think that there are or wish that there might be,
Crystalline things that rise on light wings exulting
Out of the spoilt and broken cocoon of the body,
Knowing no sorrow or pain but only deliverance,
And yet with the flame of speech, the patterns of memory,
One wonders what the soul of Dangerfield Newby
Said, in what terms, to the soul of Shepherd Heyward,
Both born slave, both freed, both dead the same day.
What do the souls that bleed from the corpse of battle
Say to the tattered night?
Perhaps it is better
We have no power to visage what they might say.

The firing now was constant, like the heavy
And drumming rains of summer. Twice Brown sent
Asking a truce. The second time there went
Stevens and Watson Brown with a white flag.
But things had gone beyond the symbol of flags.
Stevens, shot from a window, fell in the gutter
Horribly wounded. Watson Brown crawled back
To the engine house that was the final fort
Of Brown's last stand, torn through and through with slugs.

A Mr. Brua, one of Brown's prisoners,
Strolled out from the unguarded prison-room
Into the bullets, lifted Stevens up,
Carried him over to the old hotel
They called the Wager House, got a doctor for him,
And then strolled back to take his prisoner's place
With Colonel Washington and the scared rest.
I know no more than this of Mr. Brua
But he seems curiously American,
And I imagine him a tall, stooped man
A little yellow with the Southern sun,
With slow, brown eyes and a slow way of talking,

Shifting the quid of tobacco in his cheek
Mechanically, as he lifted up
The dirty, bloody body of the man
Who stood for everything he most detested
And slowly carrying him through casual wasps
Of death to the flyspecked but sunny room
In the old hotel, wiping the blood and grime
Mechanically from his Sunday coat,
Settling his black string-tie with big, tanned hands,
And, then, incredibly, going back to jail.
He did not think much about what he'd done
But sat himself as comfortably as might be
On the cold bricks of that dejected guard-room
And slowly started cutting another quid
With a worn knife that had a brown bone-handle.

He lived all through the war and died long after,
This Mr. Brua I see. His last advice
To numerous nephews was "Keep out of trouble,
But if you're in it, chew and don't be hasty,
Just do whatever's likeliest at hand."

I like your way of talking, Mr. Brua,
And if there still are people interested
In cutting literary clothes for heroes
They might do worse than mention your string-tie.

There were other killings that day. On the one side, this,
Leeman, a boy of eighteen and the youngest raider,
Trying to flee from the death-trap of the engine-house
And caught and killed on an inlet in the Potomac.
The boy lay on a tiny shelf of rock
For hours, a sack of clothes still stung by bullets.

On the other side—Fontaine Beckham, mayor of the town,
Went to look at Heyward's body with Patrick Higgins.
The slow tears crept to his eyes. He was getting old.
He had thought a lot of Heyward. He had no gun
But he had been mayor of the town for a dozen years,
A peaceful, orderly place full of decent people,
And now they were killing people, here in his town,
He had to do something to stop it, somehow or other.

He wandered out on the railroad, half-distraught
And peeped from behind a water-tank at the raiders.
"Squire, don't go any farther," said Higgins, "It ain't safe."
He hardly heard him, he had to look out again.
Who were these devils with horns who were shooting his people?
They didn't look like devils. One was a boy
Smooth-cheeked, with a bright half-dreamy face, a little
Like Sally's eldest.
Suddenly, the air struck him
A stiff, breath-taking blow. "Oh," he said, astonished.
Took a step and fell on his face, shot through the heart.
Higgins watched him for twenty minutes, wanting to lift him
But not quite daring. Then he turned away
And went back to the town.
The bars had been open all day,
Never to better business.
When the news of Beckham's death spread from bar to bar,
It was like putting loco-weed in the whiskey,
The mob came together at once, the American mob,
They mightn't be able to take Brown's last little fort
But there were two prisoners penned in the Wager House.
One was hurt already, Stevens, no fun killing him.
But the other was William Thompson, whole and unwounded,
Caught when Brown tried to send his first flag of truce.

They stormed the hotel and dragged him out to the bridge,
Where two men shot him, unarmed, then threw the body
Over the trestle. It splashed in the shallow water,
But the slayers kept on firing at the dead face.

The carcass was there for days, a riven target,
Barbarously misused.
Meanwhile the armory yard
Was taken by a new band of Beckham's avengers,
The most of Brown's prisoners freed and his last escape cut off.

What need to tell of the killing of Kagi the scholar,
The wounding of Oliver Brown and the other deaths?
Only this remains to be told. When the drunken day
Reeled into night, there were left in the engine-house
Five men, alive and unwounded, of all the raiders.

Watson and Oliver Brown
Both of them hurt to the death, were stretched on the floor
Beside the corpse of Taylor, the young Canadian.
There was no light, there. It was bitterly cold.
A cold chain of lightless hours that slowly fell
In leaden beads between two fingers of stone.
Outside, the fools and the drunkards yelled in the streets,
And, now and then, there were shots. The prisoners talked
And tried to sleep.
John Brown did not try to sleep.
The live coals of his eyes severed the darkness;
Now and then he heard his young son Oliver calling
In the thirsty agony of his wounds, "Oh, kill me!
Kill me and put me out of this suffering!"
John Brown's jaw tightened. "If you must die," he said,
"Die like a man." Toward morning the crying ceased.
John Brown called out to the boy but he did not answer.
"I guess he's dead," said John Brown.
If his soul wept
They were the incredible tears of the squeezed stone.
He had not slept for two days, but he would not sleep.

The night was a chained, black leopard that he stared down,
Erect on his feet. One wonders what sights he saw
In the cloudy mirror of his most cloudy heart,
Perhaps God clothed in a glory, perhaps himself
The little boy who had stolen three brass pins
And been well whipped for it.
When he was six years old
An Indian boy had given him a great wonder,
A yellow marble, the first he had ever seen.
He treasured it for months but lost it at last,
Boylike. The hurt of the loss took years to heal.
He never quite forgot.
He could see it now,
Smooth, hard and lovely, a yellow, glistening ball,
But it kept rolling away through cracks of darkness
Whenever he tried to catch it and hold it fast.
If he could only touch it, he would be safe,
But it trickled away and away, just out of reach,
There by the wall . . .
Outside the blackened East
Began to tarnish with a faint, grey stain
That caught on the fixed bayonets of the marines.
Lee of Virginia, Light Horse Harry's son,
Observed it broaden, thinking of many things,
But chiefly wanting to get his business done,
A curious, wry, distasteful piece of work
For regular soldiers.
Therefore to be finished
As swiftly and summarily as possible
Before this yelling mob of drunk civilians
And green militia once got out of hand.
His mouth set. Once already he had offered
The honor of the attack to the militia,
Such honor as it was.
Their Colonel had
Declined with a bright nervousness of haste.
"Your men are paid for doing this kind of work.
Mine have their wives and children." Lee smiled briefly,
Remembering that. The smile had a sharp edge.
Well, it was time.
The whooping crowd fell silent
And scattered, as a single man walked out

Toward the engine-house, a letter in his hand.
Lee watched him musingly. A good man, Stuart.
Now he was by the door and calling out.
The door opened a crack.
Brown's eyes were there
Over the cold muzzle of a cocked carbine.
The parleying began, went on and on,
While the crowd shivered and Lee watched it all
With the strict commonsense of a Greek sword
And with the same sure readiness.
Unperceived,
The dawn ran down the valleys of the wind,
Coral-footed dove, tracking the sky with coral . . .
Then, sudden as powder flashing in a pan,
The parleying was done.
The door slammed shut.
The little figure of Stuart jumped aside
Waving its cap.
And the marines came on.
Brown watched them come. One hand was on his carbine.
The other felt the pulse of his dying son.
"Sell your lives dear," he said. The rifle-shots
Rattled within the bricked-in engine-room
Like firecrackers set off in a stone jug,
And there was a harsh stink of sweat and powder.
There was a moment when the door held firm.
Then it was cracked with sun.
Brown fired and missed.
A shadow with a sword leaped through the sun.
"That's Ossawattomie," said the tired voice
Of Colonel Washington.
The shadow lunged
And Brown fell to his knees.
The sword bent double,
A light sword, better for parades than fighting,
The shadow had to take it in both hands
And fairly rain his blows with it on Brown
Before he sank.
Now two marines were down,
The rest rushed in over their comrades' bodies,
Pinning one man of Brown's against the wall
With bayonets, another to the floor.

Lee, on his rise of ground, shut up his watch.
It had been just a quarter of an hour
Since Stuart gave the signal for the storm,
And now it was over.
All but the long dying.

—*From John Brown's Body, by Stephen Vincent Benét, American (1898–1943).*

PART FOUR

Myths, Fables, and Allied Forms

DOCTOR SAMUEL JOHNSON once wrote in the *Rambler:*

> The cheerful sage, when solemn dictates fail,
> Conceals the moral counsel in a tale.

In these lines he stated clearly the basic purpose of a large body of the world's literature. No great standard literature is without samples of tales which reflect the experience and wisdom of the people who created it; and from the stories of the nursery to the parables of the great scriptures such tales are told and retold with infinite variations.

In the hands of sophisticated writers of our day the art continues. Its long history is marked by many changes and the overlapping of forms. There are also differences in emphases. But the common purpose and character of the didactic tale is apparent in most of its manifestations. A brief suggestion of the main forms and their traits will make this fact clear.

Fables may be described as short tales in prose or verse told to point a moral. Most frequently the characters are animals; sometimes they are people or inanimate objects. The fables of Aesop and La Fontaine are probably the best known and most popular. In their earliest forms the subject matter may reflect primitive man's concept of the supernatural forces of the world, or his desire to narrate unusual incidents in his experience and to draw moral conclusions from them. Myths, which are generally anonymous, are like fables in that they have their roots in the primitive beliefs and folk-experiences of races or nations, and often present supernatural explanations for natural events. They differ from fables chiefly in the fact that they are less concerned with moral didacticism and are the product of a social group rather than an individual. But they take shape around common ideas or themes, and attempt to account for such facts as creation and death, or explain the meaning of life and the origin of evil. They also chronicle the adventures of racial heroes and stress the lessons of courage or fortitude. Legends, similarly, are narratives handed down from the past. They are distinguished from myth and fable in that they have more historical truth and lay less stress on the supernatural. But like myths and fables they reflect the lore of peoples and serve as expressions of the racial or national spirit. As such they are often told to inspire a people to moral vigor or to point a lesson in a tribe's experience.

There are other forms of the narrator's art which may be loosely allied, with qualifications, to myths, fables, and legends. Parables, for example, are illustrative stories which may either answer a question or point a moral; and in this sense their purpose is to instruct. Allegories, of which fables and parables are frequent forms, may be called extended metaphors. The allegorical treatment of a subject usually consists of presenting incidents, people, or objects through personification or symbolism; and in this loose usage meanings beyond the bare details of the story are intended. The bestiary, a type of literature popular during the medieval centuries of Christendom, used the real or imagined traits and habits of beasts and birds as the text for allegorical and mystical teaching. Human attributes were ascribed to animals, and as in the fables of ancient Greece and the Orient were treated so as to present moral values or to expound doctrine.

Whatever distinctions may be drawn between these types, especially in their nicer uses by later writers whose art is sophisticated, myths and fables and their allied forms have in common the element of a "moral counsel in a tale." In perhaps no other form of narrative literature is the debt of the Occident to the ancient Orient more clearly apparent and recognized.

The Ass in the Lion's Skin

FROM THE JATAKA COLLECTIONS

ONCE UPON A TIME, while Brahma-datta was reigning in Benares, the future Buddha was born one of a peasant family; and when he grew up, he gained his living by tilling the ground.

At that time a hawker used to go from place to place, trafficking in goods carried by an ass. Now at each place he came to, when he took the pack down from the ass's back he used to clothe him in a lion's skin, and turn him loose in the rice and barley-fields, and when the watchmen in the fields saw the ass, they dared not go near him, taking him for a lion. So one day the hawker stopped in a village; and while he was getting his own breakfast cooked, he dressed the ass in a lion's skin and turned him loose in a barley-field. The watchmen in the field dared not go up to him; but going home, they published the news. Then all the villagers came out with weapons in their hands; and blowing chanks, and beating drums, they went near the field and shouted. Terrified with the fear of death, the ass uttered a cry — the cry of an ass!

And when he knew him then to be an ass, the future Buddha pronounced the first stanza:

"This is not a lion's roaring,
Nor a tiger's, nor a panther's;
Dressed in a lion's skin,
'Tis a wretched ass that roars!"

But when the villagers knew the creature to be an ass, they beat him till his bones broke; and, carrying off the lion's skin, went away. Then the hawker came, and seeing the ass fallen into so bad a plight, pronounced the second stanza:

"Long might the ass,
Clad in a lion's skin,
Have fed on barley green,
But he brayed,
And that moment he came to ruin."

And even while he was yet speaking the ass died on the spot!

— *Translated from the Pāli by T. W. Rhys Davids, in Buddhist Birth Stories.*

~ ✿ ~

The Dove and the Crow

FROM THE PANCHATANTRA

WHEN VISHNU SARMA had finished telling and expounding these fables, his pupils were lost in admiration of their teacher, whose wisdom had been so clearly marked by his dexterous mingling of amusement with instruction. They rose and all three fell at his feet, thanking him for the wise lessons he had given them; they assured him that henceforth they would regard him as their guru and that they hoped with his help and advice to rise from the state of ignorance in which they had hitherto been. They prayed him to continue the work so happily begun and to give them more of his interesting lessons.

Vishnu Sarma was charmed to see that his pupils were well disposed and noticed with satisfaction that his plan had so far succeeded. He continued his task with enthusiasm and proceeded to tell them fresh fables.

"Now," said Vishnu Sarma, "listen, my young princes, to the fable I am going to tell you. In the complex nature of this life we must all help one another. It is by this mutual help that the weak escape the dangers to which they are exposed from the strong, as you shall now hear."

A certain dove, by name Chitrani, had built her nest on the top of the mountain Kanakachala and was living there comfortably with her family. At the foot of the mountain dwelt a crow. One day Vega-Varma (such was the crow's name) was flying round in search of food when he noticed a fowler spreading his nets in the way. He was frightened at sight of the danger and at once returned home.

The dove Chitrani passed by the same place with her family, but being off their guard, they all flew into the net and were captured. What was to be done? How could they escape from certain death? There was in fact no escape, no hope of obtaining their liberty. Already the fowler was running up to seize his prey, when all at once under the impulse of danger they took to flight together, carrying with them the net that enclosed them. So they succeeded in escaping, and the fowler, who had reckoned upon his capture, was not a little surprised when he saw them fly away with his nets. But they reached their home in safety still entangled in the nets into which they had flown.

When the crow saw them coming in this strange chariot, he hastened to meet them; and as soon as Chitrani saw him, she told him of their adventures and asked him to help them by disentangling the nets. The crow replied that he could not free them, but suggested a rat of the name of Hiranya Varma who lived close by and who could help them. Accordingly Chitrani called the rat, who came up at once, and when he saw the captives he began to scold Chitrani for her imprudence and folly which had brought them to this pass. Chitrani defended herself and quoted the maxim: "No one, be he never so wise or prudent, can escape his destiny." Then the rat, pitying the poor doves, called his fellows, and they all set to work to gnaw the knots of the nets, so that very soon they had freed Chitrani and her family.

The crow, who had seen the signal service performed by the rat for the doves, was anxious to make friends with him; he hoped also to obtain a useful ally should occasion arise. He accordingly made overtures to him; but the rat replied that they were of totally different species, the one living in the air and the other in the earth; he did not see the use of the close friendship of two creatures between whom Nature had fixed such a wide gulf.

But the crow insisted. Matters of personal interest and friendship, he said, are decided by our inclination. We do not consider distance or the difference of condition. So the rat yielded and they swore a close friendship. One day when they were out together they happened to meet a deer; they stopped him and asked his name and where he was going. The deer said he was called Chitranga, told them his story, and asked if he might join them. They readily consented, and so the three struck up a lasting friendship.

One day while they were out together and were very thirsty, in their search for water they found a well into which a tortoise had fallen. As soon as she saw the three friends she begged them to take her out of her prison and to put her somewhere where she could live in comfort. Pitying her plight, they rescued her and took her to a spring of clear water; and she, mindful of this service, also became their friend.

For a long time the four lived happily together, but one day when the deer had gone away to graze he fell into the snare of a hunter. But when the rat saw that his friend the deer was so long in returning, he guessed that he had met with an accident. So he called the crow and told him what he feared and advised him to fly up and try to discover their friend. This the crow did, and after looking about for some time, at last saw poor Chitranga in the snare struggling hard to get out, but in vain.

The crow at once told Hiranya Varma what had happened to their friend, and he, calling his fellow-rats, sallied out to help him. They soon set him free. Chitranga went home with his friends and the accident was soon forgotten. But later on, when the four friends were resting quietly in the shade of a tree, they were suddenly disturbed by the unexpected sight of a crowd of hunters. This alarmed them. The crow and the deer could easily avoid pursuit, but not so the rat, and least of all the tortoise. The other two would not leave them to the mercy of the hunters, who were coming on quickly, and so the deer undertook to attract attention to himself in order to save the life of his friends. He pretended to be lame. The hunters, seeing him limp and apparently hardly able to hold himself up, all ran to capture the easy prey. But the deer led them a long dance, sometimes quickening his pace, sometimes slowing down, until at last, having made them follow for a long time, he fairly used his four legs and was soon out of sight. Meanwhile the tortoise and the rat had found a place of safety out of reach of the hunters.

Once more the four friends were united and lived quietly together; these dangers had taught them the value of true unity and of sincere friendship, and by experience they learned how the weak need to support one another.

—*Indian (traditional; collected by the fourth century). From Ancient Indian Fables and Stories, by Stanley P. Rice.*

The Jackal

FROM THE HITOPADESA

A CERTAIN JACKAL, as he was roaming about the borders of a town, just as his inclinations led him, fell into a dyer's vat; but being unable to get out, in the morning he feigned himself dead. At length, the master of the vat, which was filled with indigo, came, and seeing a jackal lying with his legs uppermost, his eyes closed, and his teeth bare, concluded that he was dead, and so, taking him out, he carried him a good way from the town, and there left him. The sly animal instantly got up, and ran into the woods; when, observing that his coat was turned blue, he meditated in this manner: "I am now of the finest color! what great exaltation may I not bring about for myself?" Saying this, he called a number of jackals together, and addressed them in the following words: "Know that I have lately been sprinkled king of the forests, by the hands of the goddess herself who presides over these woods, with a water drawn from a variety of choice herbs. Observe my color, and henceforward let every business be transacted according to my orders." The rest of the jackals, seeing him of such a fine complexion, prostrated themselves before him, and said: "According as Your Highness commands!" By this step he made himself honored by his own relations, and so gained the supreme power over those of his own species, as well as all the other inhabitants of the forests. But after a while, finding himself surrounded by a levee of the first quality, such as the tiger and the like, he began to look down upon his relations; and, at length, he kept them at a distance. A certain old jackal, perceiving that his brethren were very much cast down at this behavior, cried: "Do not despair! If it continue thus, this imprudent friend of ours will force us to be revenged. Let me alone to contrive his downfall. The lion, and the rest who pay him court, are taken by his outward appearance; and they obey him as their king, because they are not aware that he is nothing but a jackal: do something then by which he may be found out. Let this plan be pursued: Assemble all of you in a body about the close of the evening, and set up one general howl in his hearing; and I'll warrant you, the natural disposition of his species will incline him to join in the cry; for,

Whatever may be the natural propensity of anyone is very hard to be overcome. If a dog were made king, would he not gnaw his shoe straps?

And thus the tiger, discovering that he is nothing but a jackal, will presently put him to death." The plan was executed, and the event was just as it had been foretold.

—*Translated from the Sanskrit (fourteenth century?), by Charles Wilkins.*

The Country Mouse and the Town Mouse

AESOP

ONCE UPON A TIME a Country Mouse who had a friend in town invited him, for old acquaintance' sake, to pay him a visit in the country. The invitation being accepted in due form, the Country Mouse, though plain and rough and somewhat frugal in his nature, opened his heart and store, in honor of hospitality and an old friend. There was not a carefully stored-up morsel that he did not bring forth out of his larder, peas and barley, cheese-parings and nuts, hoping by quantity to make up what he feared was wanting in quality, to suit the palate of his dainty guest. The Town Mouse, condescending to pick a bit here and a bit there, while the host sat nibbling a blade of barley-straw, at length exclaimed, "How is it, my good friend, that you can endure the dullness of this unpolished life? You are living like a toad in a hole. You can't really prefer these solitary rocks and woods to streets teeming with carriages and men. On my honor, you are wasting your time miserably here. We must make the most of life while it lasts. A mouse, you know, does not live forever. So come with me and I'll show you life and the town." Overpowered with such fine words and so polished a manner, the Country Mouse assented; and they set out together on their journey to town. It was late in the evening when they crept stealthily into the city, and midnight ere they reached the great house, where the Town Mouse took up his quarters. Here were couches of crimson velvet, carvings in ivory, everything in short that denoted wealth and luxury. On the table were the remains of a splendid banquet, to procure which all the choicest shops in the town had been ransacked the day before. It was now the turn of the courtier to play the host; he places his country friend on purple, runs to and fro to supply all his wants, presses dish upon dish and dainty upon dainty, and as though he were waiting on a king, tastes every course ere he ventures to place it before his rustic cousin. The Country Mouse, for his part, affects to make himself quite at home, and blesses the good fortune that had wrought such a change in his way of life; when, in the midst of his enjoyment, as he is thinking with contempt of the poor fare he has forsaken, on a sudden the door flies open, and a party of revellers returning from a late entertainment, bursts into the room. The affrighted friends jump from the table in the greatest consternation and hide themselves in the first corner they can reach. No sooner do they venture to creep out again than the barking of dogs drives them back in still greater terror than before. At length, when things seemed quiet, the Country Mouse stole out from his hiding place, and bidding his friend good-bye, whispered in his ear, "Oh, my good sir, this fine mode of living may do for those who like it; but give me my barley-bread in peace and security before the daintiest feast where Fear and Care are in waiting."

—By Aesop, Greek (sixth century B.C.?), translated by Thomas James.

The Shipwreck of Simonides

PHÆDRUS

A LEARNED MAN has always a fund of riches in himself.

Simonides, who wrote such excellent lyric poems, the more easily to support his poverty, began to make a tour of the celebrated cities of Asia, singing the praises of victors for such reward as he might receive. After he had become enriched by this kind of gain, he resolved to return to his native land by sea (for he was born, it is said, in the island of Ceos). Accordingly he embarked in a ship, which a dreadful tempest, together with its own rottenness, caused to founder at sea. Some gathered together their girdles, others their precious effects, which formed the support of their existence. One who was over inquisitive, remarked: "Are you going to save none of your property, Simonides?" He made reply: "All my possessions are about me." A few only made their escape by swimming, for the majority, being weighed down by their burdens, perished. Some thieves too made their appearance, and seized what each person had saved, leaving him naked. Clazomenæ, an ancient city, chanced to be near; to which the shipwrecked persons repaired. Here a person devoted to the pursuits of literature, who had often read the lines of Simonides, and was a very great admirer of him though he had never seen him, knowing from his very language who he was, received him with the greatest pleasure into his house, and furnished him with clothes, money, and attendants. The others meanwhile were carrying about their pictures, begging for victuals. Simonides chanced to meet them; and, as soon as he saw them, remarked: "I told you that all my property was about me; what you have endeavored to save is lost."

—From the Latin of Phædrus, Roman (15 B.C.?–55 A.D.?), translated by H. T. Riley.

The Star Family, or Celestial Sisters

A SHAWNEE LEGEND

WAUPEE, or the White Hawk, lived in a remote part of the forest, where animals and birds were abundant. Every day he returned from the chase with the reward of his toil, for he was one of the most skilful and celebrated hunters of his tribe. With a tall, manly form, and the fire of youth beaming from his eye, there was no forest too gloomy for him to penetrate, and no track made by the numerous kinds of birds and beasts which he could not follow.

One day he penetrated beyond any point which he had before visited. He travelled through an open forest, which enabled him to see a great distance. At length he beheld a light breaking through the foliage, which made him sure that he was on the borders of a prairie. It was a wide plain covered with grass and flowers. After walking some time without a path, he suddenly came to a ring worn through the sod, as if it had been made by footsteps following a circle. But what excited his surprise was, that there was no path leading to or from it. Not the least trace of footsteps could be found, even in a crushed leaf or broken twig. He thought he would hide himself, and lie in wait to see what this circle meant. Presently he heard the faint sounds of music in the air. He looked up in the direction they came from, and saw a small object descending from above. At first it looked like a mere speck, but rapidly increased, and, as it came down, the music became plainer and sweeter. It assumed the form of a basket, and was filled with twelve sisters of the most lovely forms and enchanting beauty. As soon as the basket touched the ground, they leaped out, and began to dance round the magic ring, striking, as they did so, a shining ball as we strike the drum. Waupee gazed upon their graceful forms and motions from his place of concealment. He admired them all, but was most pleased with the youngest. Unable longer to restrain his admiration, he rushed out and endeavored to seize her. But the sisters, with the quickness of birds, the moment they descried the form of a man, leaped back into the basket and were drawn up into the sky.

Regretting his ill luck and indiscretion, he gazed till he saw them disappear, and then said, "They are gone, and I shall see them no more." He returned to his solitary lodge, but found no relief to his mind. Next day he went back to the prairie, and took his station near the ring; but in order to deceive the sisters, he assumed the form of an opossum. He had not waited long, when he saw the wicker car descend, and heard the same sweet music. They commenced the same sportive dance, and seemed even more beautiful and graceful than before. He crept slowly towards the ring, but the instant the sisters saw him they were startled, and sprang into their car. It rose but a short distance, when one of the elder sisters spoke. "Perhaps," said she, "it is come to show us how the game is played by mortals." "Oh no!" the youngest replied; "quick, let us ascend." And all joining in a chant, they rose out of sight.

Waupee returned to his own form again, and walked sorrowfully back to his lodge. But the night seemed a very long one, and he went back betimes the next day. He reflected upon the sort of plan to follow to secure success. He found an old stump near by, in which there were a number of mice. He thought their small form would not create alarm, and accordingly assumed it. He brought the stump and sat it up near the ring. The sisters came down and resumed their sport. "But see," cried the younger sister, "that stump was not there before." She ran affrighted towards the car. They only smiled, and gathering round the stump, struck it in jest, when out ran the mice, and Waupee among the rest. They killed them all but one, which was pursued by the youngest sister; but just as she had raised her stick to kill it, the form of Waupee arose, and he clasped his prize in his arms. The other eleven sprang to their basket and were drawn up to the skies.

He exerted all his skill to please his bride

and win her affections. He wiped the tears from her eyes. He related his adventures in the chase. He dwelt upon the charms of life on the earth. He was incessant in his attentions, and picked out the way for her to walk as he led her gently towards his lodge. He felt his heart glow with joy as she entered it, and from that moment he was one of the happiest of men. Winter and summer passed rapidly away, and their happiness was increased by the addition of a beautiful boy to their lodge. She was a daughter of one of the stars, and as the scenes of earth began to pall her sight, she sighed to revisit her father. But she was obliged to hide these feelings from her husband. She remembered the charm that would carry her up, and took occasion, while Waupee was engaged in the chase, to construct a wicker basket, which she kept concealed. In the mean time she collected such rarities from the earth as she thought would please her father, as well as the most dainty kinds of food. When all was in readiness, she went out one day, while Waupee was absent, to the charmed ring, taking her little son with her. As soon as they got into the car, she commenced her song and the basket rose. As the song was wafted by the wind, it caught her husband's ear. It was a voice which he well knew, and he instantly ran to the prairie. But he could not reach the ring before he saw his wife and child ascend. He lifted up his voice in loud appeals, but they were unavailing. The basket still went up. He watched it till it became a small speck, and finally it vanished in the sky. He then bent his head down to the ground, and was miserable.

Waupee bewailed his loss through a long winter and a long summer. But he found no relief. He mourned his wife's loss sorely, but his son's still more. In the meantime his wife had reached her home in the stars, and almost forgot, in the blissful employments there, that she had left a husband on the earth. She was reminded of this by the presence of her son, who, as he grew up, became anxious to visit the scene of his birth. His grandfather said to his daughter one day, "Go, my child, and take your son down to his father, and ask him to come up and live with us. But tell him to bring along a specimen of each kind of bird and animal he kills in the chase." She accordingly took the boy and descended. Waupee, who was ever near the enchanted spot, heard her voice as she came down the sky. His heart beat with impatience as he saw her form and that of his son, and they were soon clasped in his arms.

He heard the message of the Star, and began to hunt with the greatest activity, that he might collect the present. He spent whole nights, as well as days, in searching for every curious and beautiful bird or animal. He only preserved a tail, foot, or wing of each, to identify the species; and, when all was ready, they went to the circle and were carried up.

Great joy was manifested on their arrival at the starry plains. The Star Chief invited all his people to a feast, and, when they had assembled, he proclaimed aloud, that each one might take of the earthly gifts such as he liked best. A very strange confusion immediately arose. Some chose a foot, some a wing, some a tail, and some a claw. Those who selected tails or claws were changed into animals, and ran off; the others assumed the form of birds, and flew away. Waupee chose a white hawk's feather. His wife and son followed his example, when each one became a white hawk. Pleased with his transformation, and new vitality, the chief spread out gracefully his white wings, and followed by his wife and son, descended to the earth, where the species are still to be found.

—*From The Myth of Hiawatha, and Other Oral Legends of the North American Indians, by Henry Rowe Schoolcraft, American (1793–1864).*

Brother Rabbit's Money Mint

JOEL CHANDLER HARRIS

ONE DAY the little boy was telling Uncle Remus about how much money one of his mother's brothers was going to make. Oh, it was ever so much — fifty, a hundred, maybe a thousand bales of cotton in one season. Uncle Remus groaned a little during this recital.

"Wharbouts he gwine ter make it?" the old man inquired with some asperity.

"Oh, in Mississippi," said the little boy. "Uncle James told papa that the cotton out there grows so high that a man sitting on his horse could hide in it."

"Did Marse Jeems see dat cotton hisse'f?" asked Uncle Remus.

"Yes, he did. He's been out there, and he

saw it with his own eyes. He says he can make ever so many hundred dollars in Mississippi where he makes one here."

"Marse John ain't gwine, is he?"

"No; I heard papa tell mamma that Uncle James was drawing his long bow, and then mamma said she reckoned that her kinfolks were as truthful as anybody else's."

Immediately Uncle Remus's features lost their severity, and he lay back in his chair to laugh.

"Dat Miss Sally, up en down. Hit her kinnery en you got ter hit her. But yo' pa know Marse Jeems, en I been knowin' 'm sence he wuz in his teens; en when he git ter talkin' he'll stretch his blanket spite er de worl'. He allers would do dat, en he allers will. Now, dat des de long en de short un it. I don't keer ef he is kin ter Miss Sally, he'll talk wil'.

"Bless yo' soul, honey. I done hear talk er Massasip long 'fo' you wuz bornded. I done seed um go dar, en I done seed um come back, en eve'y time I hear folks talk 'bout makin' mo' money off dar dan dey kin anywhars nigher home, it put me in min' er de time when Brer Fox went huntin' de place whar dey make money."

"Is it a story, Uncle Remus?" asked the little boy.

"Well, 't ain't ez you may say one er deze yer reg'lar up en down tales, what runs crossways. Dish yer tale goes right straight. Brer Fox meet up wid Brer Rabbit in de big road, en dey pass de time er day, en ax one er nudder how der fambly connection is. Brer Fox say he sorter middlin' peart, en Brer Rabbit say he sorter betwix *'My gracious!'* en *'Thank gracious!'* Whiles dey er runnin' on en confabbin', Brer Fox hear sump'n rattlin' in Brer Rabbit's pocket.

"He 'low, 'Ef I ain't mighty much mistaken, Brer Rabbit, I hear money rattlin'.'

"Brer Rabbit sorter grin slow en hol' his head keerless.

"He say, ''T ain't nothin' much — des some small change what I bleedz ter take wid me in de case er needcessity.'

"Wid dat he drawed out a big han'ful er speeshy-dollars, en quarters, en sev'mpunces, en thrips, en all right spang-bang new. Hit shined in de sun twel it fair blin' yo' eyes.

"Brer Fox 'low, 'Laws a massy, Brer Rabbit! I ain't seed so much money sence I sol' my watermilions las' year. Ain't you skeerd some un'll fling you down en take it 'way fum you?'

"Brer Rabbit say, 'Dem what man 'nuff ter take it kin have it'; en he des strut 'long de road dar mo' samer dan one er deze yer milliumterry mens what got yaller stripes on der britches.

"Brer Fox 'low, 'Whar de name er goodness you git so much new speeshy, Brer Rabbit?'

"Brer Rabbit say, 'I git it whar dey make it at; dat whar I git it.'

"Brer Fox stop by de side er de road, en look 'stonish. He 'low, 'Wharbouts does dey make dish yer speeshy at?'

"Brer Rabbit say, 'Fust in one place en den in anudder. You got ter do like me, Brer Fox; you got ter keep yo' eye wide open.'

"Brer Fox 'low, 'Fer massy sake, Brer Rabbit, tell me how I gwine ter fine de place.'

"He beg en he beg, Brer Fox did, en Brer Rabbit look at 'im hard, like he got some doubts on his min'. Den Brer Rabbit sot down by de side er de road en mark in de san 'wid his walkin' cane.

"Bimeby he say, 'Well, spozen I tell you, you'll go blabbin' it 'roun' de whole neighborhoods, en den dey'll git it all, en we won't git none 't all.'

"But Brer Fox des vow en declar' ter gracious dat he won't tell a livin' soul, en den ole Brer Rabbit sorter bent hisse'f back en cle'r up his th'oat.

"He say, ''T ain't much atter you fine it out, Brer Fox; all you got ter do is ter watch de road twel you see a waggin come 'long. Ef you'll look right close, you'll see dat de waggin', ef hit's de right kind er waggin, is got two front wheels en two behime wheels; en you'll see fuddermo' dat de front wheels is lots littler dan de behime wheels. Now, when you see dat, what is you bleedz ter b'lieve?'

"Brer Fox study little while, en den shuck his head. He 'low, 'You too much fer me, Brer Rabbit.'

"Brer Rabbit look like he feel sorry kaze Brer Fox sech a numbskull. He say, 'When you see dat, you bleedz ter b'lieve dat atter so long a time de big wheel gwine ter ketch de little one. Yo' common sense ought ter tell you dat.'

"Brer Fox 'low, 'Hit sholy look so.'

"Brer Rabbit say, 'Ef you know dat de big wheel gwine ter ketch de little wheel, en dat bran new money gwine ter drap fum betwixt um when dey grind up 'ginst one anudder, what you gwine do den?'

"Still Brer Fox study, en shake his head. Brer Rabbit look like he gittin' sick.

"He say, 'You kin set down en let de waggin go on by, ef you don't want no bran new money. Den agin, ef you want de money, you kin foller 'long en keep watch, en see when de behime wheels overtake de front uns en be on han' when de money starts ter drappin'.'

"Brer Fox look like he got de idee. He sorter laugh.

"Brer Rabbit say, 'Nex' time you see a waggin gwine by, Brer Fox, des holler for me ef you don't want ter take no chances. Des bawl out! I ain't got 'nuff speeshy, en I ain't gwine ter have 'nuff.'

"Brer Fox, he broke off a broom straw en 'gun ter chaw on it, en des' 'bout dat time, dey hear a waggin comin' 'cross de hill.

"Brer Rabbit 'low, 'Des say de word, Brer Fox, en ef you ain't gwine 'long atter de waggin, I'll go myse'f!'

"Brer Fox say, 'Maybe de wheels done grinded tergedder back yonder a piece.'

"Brer Rabbit 'low, 'I ain't got time ter 'spute, Brer Fox. Ef you ain't gwine, des say de word!'

"Brer Fox sorter laugh like he shame. He say, 'I b'lieve I'll go a little piece er de way en see how de wheels run.'

"Wid dat," said Uncle Remus, looking up at the ceiling with a peculiar smile, "Brer Rabbit wish Brer Fox good luck, en went on 'bout his business. Yit he ain't go so fur dat he can't watch Brer Fox's motions. At de rise er de nex' hill he look back, en dar he see Brer Fox trottin' 'long atter de waggin. When he see dat, Brer Rabbit des lay down in de grass en kick up his heels en holler."

Uncle Remus laughed, and the little boy laughed. The old negro's merriment was as keen as that of the youngster, for his humor swept over a wide field of human experience. The little boy laughed at the transparent trick; Uncle Remus no doubt beheld in his imagination a long procession of human Brer Foxes "polin' 'long," up hill and down hill, waiting for the hind wheels to overtake the front ones. After a while the little boy asked what became of Brother Fox.

"Well, honey," said Uncle Remus, "he des foller 'long, trottin' en gallopin', waitin' fer de wheels ter ketch up wid one anudder. Ef he ain't in Massasip by dis time, I'm mighty much mistaken. I boun' yo' Unc' Jeems'll see 'im when he go out dar! Brer Fox had ter take his foot in his han', en git dar de bes' way he kin; yo' Unc' Jeems gwine by conveyance."

—From Uncle Remus and His Friends by Joel Chandler Harris, American (1848–1908).

The Just Hare

ADOLF DYGASIŃSKI

ONCE UPON A TIME there lived in a certain village a peasant called Matthias, who was a very good man. One day he went to the forest. There he collected dry wood, lopped off dead knots of wood and twigs, and was making them into a pile. Then he caught a sound – something was groaning near by, as if begging for mercy. Matthias felt afraid, he hesitated. Should he go and look, or not? Finally he went forward cautiously to see whatever it could be.

And behold, an enormous spruce tree had fallen, and crushed a bear so cruelly that his eyeballs were sticking out of his head.

"Have pity on me, mortal, save my life," said the poor bear pitifully.

The peasant was seized with compassion and set to work. Very carefully he shoved under the tree trunk first one pole and then another. He put out all his strength, and each time he raised a pole he immediately put a little block under it, to prop it up. He had to wipe the sweat from his brow, but he saved the bear and went off home.

Some time passed. Matthias had forgotten all about his exploit when he went again to the forest for firewood. There the first thing he saw was the bear, who at once asked him: "Was it you, peasant, who once saved my life?"

"Yes, it was me. What of it?"

"You see, my friend, I feel I absolutely must give you a reward for I am horribly worried because I owe you a debt of gratitude."

"What sort of reward, might I ask?"

"My dear fellow, I must eat you up. There's nothing else for it."

"Would you dare, you shaggy monster, to kill your benefactor?"

"Why, everybody in this world pays back good with evil, so I cannot show my gratitude to you in any other way."

"Nonsense, only skunks act like that. Justice and gratitude have existed, exist, and will go on existing in the world."

At that the bear burst out laughing. "I have never seen such another fool in the whole course of my life," he said. "But listen, I will admit that you are right, if you can find a judge who will decide the case between us as you think it should be decided."

"I will find him," cried Matthias and went off to look for a judge.

He met a peasant. "Come with me," he said to the peasant, "and pronounce judgment between me and a bear."

The peasant came, made a show of listening to the issue in question, then nudged Matthias with his elbow, winked at him and whispered in his ear: "Tell me first how much you will pay me, if I decide the case to your advantage. If not, you lose."

The bear at once remarked this exchange of words and growled: "Justice cannot be bought or sold. You won't throw dust in my eyes in that way."

Matthias scratched his head. "It's a bad thing for a man to be that kind of judge."

He hastened off to look for another.

He fell in with an ox whom he knew, and invited him to give judgment.

"Do you take me for a complete fool?" replied the ox. "I see before me two butchers, and I should be glad if the devil would take at least one of you. . . . It would be the end of me if I were to pronounce judgment on people like you," he bellowed, then turned up his eyes and fled.

Matthias almost burst into tears. He had thought that justice and gratitude were ordinary things, created at the same time as the world.

He went off again to look for a judge, and over there a swallow was sitting on a bough. She chirped: "Don't take anything either too big or too little, Matthias."

H'm, reflected the peasant, I must take a ram.

He found a ram, brought him along and asked: "What is your opinion?"

The ram bleated and burst out with a curse: "I tell you I know nothing of justice or injustice, gratitude or ingratitude! I can bleat for you and that's the end of it. If you want agreement, our sheep dog – now he's an expert judge. One ram by the throat, another by the head, and then we, a thousand sheep, have to live in agreement. Oh yes, our doggie is a great judge."

The bear's eyes sparkled with joy. "My good fellow," he said to Matthias, "gratitude to you is consuming me, and poisons my life more and more. I absolutely must eat you in order to pay my debt to you."

"Wait a little," said the peasant. "This ram is stupid. For that matter, since the world began, no ram has ever been a judge. But I shall bring along a proper one."

Matthias hurried away and summoned a dog. "You are a faithful animal," he said. "Assuredly you have gratitude and justice in you."

The dog reflected and then said: "Last night robbers attacked my master. I warned him in time and saved his life and his property; but today, out of gratitude and justice, he beat me so hard that, as you can see, I am scarcely able to crawl."

Matthias fell into despair and thought to himself: "I was a fool to listen to the swallow. Neither too big nor too little – foolish words. I shall summon a horse – that is a proper animal."

The horse came and said: "I know gratitude and justice excellently, since I drive and carry my master and work for him in the plough."

"Well, what then?" asked Matthias, cheering up.

"In return my master starves me, and rewards me cruelly with the whip."

"Great God," cried Matthias, aghast. "Have gratitude and justice perished from Thy fair world?"

But the swallow chirped: "Your judge, Matthias, should be neither too big nor too little, but he must be of the wilds."

"It's clearly the clever old fox that I must summon," he said to himself, and fetched the fox.

Reynard swished his tail from side to side, looked slyly round, listened to the case and finally said: "It seems frightfully odd to me, Bruin, that you have not yet crunched up this stupid Matthias. Your conscience must be gnawing you terribly, for it is the worst thing possible to have a debt of gratitude and not to pay it back with ingratitude. Eat up the fellow with no more fuss. If you don't, I'll say that you too are a fool."

At this the bear lay down and rolled with laughter and said: "The fox is a good counsellor, Matthias, for you are getting too thin for me in your search for justice, and I don't like eating a thin man."

Matthias shuddered as he saw the brute of a bear licking his chops, and he went off to invite the wolf to be judge, although he had by now very little faith in his searches.

The wolf gave his muzzle a shake and looked at the bear's belly, but Matthias thought to himself: "He is plainly meditating on justice."

Meanwhile the wolf addressed them in these words: "Clearly, Bruin, hunger is not troubling you, seeing that you allow a fellow like this to play at lawsuits. If you like, I'll settle him and we can go shares in eating him."

But the bear snorted and growled: "I don't want any partnership with wolves."

He turned to Matthias and said: "One way or the other, it's my affair and I must eat you, in order once for all to repay my debt of gratitude."

The peasant begged as a favour to be allowed to bring one more judge.

He went away, said a prayer or two and commended himself to God, but the swallow dropped down on the path and chirped: "Matthias, Matthias, only those know justice who are harried by injustice day and night, who never do the slightest harm to anyone, and who have to hide in order to live."

"Where can a poor unfortunate like me find such a one?"

"He has dodged under a bush not far away, he hides from man, dog, wolf, fox. . . . Approach him very carefully, so that he may not think that you want to kill him and take to flight."

"How shall I talk to him?"

"Go and repeat these words: 'I praise the Lord God, I do no harm to anyone, I have gratitude and justice in my heart!'"

Matthias started, walked along and repeated what the swallow had told him. Suddenly the hare tumbled out from under the bush, squeaked and said: "I have heard about your adventure with the bear, and I was thinking of how to help you."

"Oh, hare, may God inspire you with a good idea! For the bear is trying to prove to me that there is neither gratitude nor justice in the world."

"Often there is no gratitude," said the hare, "for it must proceed from created beings, and they are often ungrateful. But justice proceeds from God Himself and it will never pass away."

The hearing began. The bear said: "It is my duty to eat him, but I want first to convince him that there is neither gratitude nor justice in the world."

Matthias also stated his case.

"What you two say is good," said the hare, "only I absolutely must see how it all was before I decide your case."

"I was lying under a tree trunk," said the bear, "and this stupid peasant prised up the trunk and set me free. Let him have his reward for it."

"I must see how you looked," repeated the hare.

So they went and found the place where the trunk had pinned down the bear. The poles and logs were still supporting the trunk.

The hare said: "Crawl in, Bruin, and show me how you were lying."

When the bear had lain down, the hare winked to the peasant: "Pull the poles and logs out quickly, one by one."

The peasant did this, and the bear at once began to sigh, and groan, and plead: "Do release me. The trunk is crushing me."

But the hare replied: "Now things are as they were in the beginning. Neither of you owes anything to the other. There is no gratitude in the world, but justice has overtaken you."

Then he turned to Matthias and said: "Fly home swiftly. Praise God, do no ill to any one, and have gratitude and justice in your heart, although you may be the only man in the world who has them!"

—*Adolf Dygasiński, Polish (?–1903), translated for the Slavonic Review by D. F. Tait.*

Chinese Cinderella

THERE WERE once two sisters; the eldest was very beautiful and everyone called her 'Beauty'; but the younger had a face covered with pock marks, and everyone called her 'Pock Face.' She was the daughter of the second wife, and was very spoilt, and had a bad character. Beauty's mother had died when her daughter was very small, and after her death she had turned into a yellow cow, which lived in the garden. Beauty adored the yellow cow, but it had a miserable existence, because the step-mother treated it so badly.

One day, the step-mother took the ugly daughter to the theatre and left the elder one at home. She wanted to accompany them, but her step-mother said: 'I will take you to-morrow, if you tidy the hemp in my room.'

Beauty went off and sat down in front of the stack of hemp, but after a long time she had only divided half. Bursting into tears, she took it off to the yellow cow, who swallowed the whole mass and then spat it out again all clearly arranged bit by bit. Beauty dried her tears, and gave the hemp to her mother on her return home: 'Mother, here is the hemp. I can go to the theatre to-morrow, can't I?'

But when the next day came, her step-mother again refused to take her, saying: 'You can go when you have separated the sesame seeds from the beans.' The poor girl had to divide them seed by seed, until the exhausting task made her eyes ache. Again she went to the yellow cow, who said to her: 'You stupid girl, you must separate them with a fan.' Now she understood, and the sesame and beans were soon divided. When she brought the seeds all nicely separated, her step-mother knew that she could no longer prevent her going to the theatre, but she asked her: 'How can a servant girl be so clever? Who helped you?' And Beauty had to admit that the yellow cow had advised her, which made the step-mother very angry. Without, therefore, saying a word, she killed and ate the cow, but Beauty had loved the cow so dearly that she could not eat its flesh. Instead, she put the bones in an earthenware pot and hid them in her bedroom.

Day after day, the step-mother did not take her to the theatre, and one evening, when she had gone there herself with Pock Face, Beauty was so cross that she smashed everything in the house, including the earthenware pot. Whereupon there was a crack, and a white horse, a new dress, and a pair of embroidered shoes came out. The sudden appearance of these things gave her a terrible fright, but she soon saw that they were real objects and, quickly pulling on the new dress and the shoes, she jumped on to the horse and rode out of the gate.

While riding along, one of her shoes slipped off into the ditch. She wanted to dismount and fetch it, but could not do so; at the same time she did not want to leave it lying there. She was in a real quandary, when a fishmonger appeared. 'Brother fishmonger! Please pick up my shoe,' she said to him. He answered with a grin: 'With great pleasure, if you will marry me.' 'Who would marry you?' she said crossly. 'Fishmongers always stink.' And seeing that he had no chance, the fishmonger went on his way. Next, an assistant of a rice shop went by, and she said to him: 'Brother rice broker, please give me my shoe.' 'Certainly, if you will marry me,' said the young man. 'Marry a rice broker! Their bodies are all covered with dust.' The rice broker departed, and soon an oil merchant came by, whom she also asked to pick up her shoe. 'I will pick it up if you consent to marry me,' he replied. 'Who could want to marry you?' Beauty said with a sigh. 'Oil merchants are always so greasy.' Shortly after a scholar came by, whom she also asked to pick up her shoe. The scholar turned to look at her, and then said: 'I will do so at once if you promise to marry me.' The scholar was very handsome, so she nodded her head in agreement, and he picked up the shoe and put it on her foot. Then he took her back to his house and made her his wife.

Three days later, Beauty went with her husband to pay the necessary respects to her parents. Her step-mother and sister had quite changed their manner and treated them both in the most friendly and attentive fashion. In the evening, they wanted to keep Beauty at home, and she, thinking they meant it kindly, agreed to stay and to follow her husband in a few days. The next morning her sister took her by the hand and said to her with a laugh: 'Sister, come and look into the well. We will see which of us is the more beautiful.' Suspecting nothing, Beauty went to the well and leant over to look down, but at this moment her sister gave her a shove and pushed her into the well, which she quickly covered up with a basket. Poor Beauty lost consciousness and was drowned.

After ten days, the scholar began to wonder why his wife had still not returned. He sent a messenger to enquire, and the step-mother sent back a message that his wife was suffering from a bad attack of smallpox and was not well enough to return for the moment. The scholar believed this, and every day he sent over salted eggs and other sickbed delicacies, all of which found their way into the stomach of the ugly sister.

After two months, the step-mother was irritated by the continual messages from the scholar and made up her mind to practise a deception, and to send back her own daughter as his wife. The scholar was horrified when he saw her and said: 'Goodness! How changed you are! Surely you are not Beauty. My wife was never such a monster. Good Heavens!' Pock Face replied seriously: 'If I am not Beauty, whom do you think I am then? You know perfectly well I was very ill with smallpox, and now you want to disown me. I shall die! I shall die!' And she began to howl. The tender-hearted scholar could not bear to see her weeping, and although he still had some doubts, he begged her forgiveness and tried to console her, so that gradually she stopped weeping.

Beauty, however, had been transformed into a sparrow, and she used to come and call out when Pock Face was combing her hair: 'Comb once, peep; comb twice, peep; comb thrice, up to the spine of Pock Face.' And the wicked wife answered: 'Comb once, comb twice, comb thrice, to the spine of Beauty.' The scholar was very mystified by this conversation, and he said to the sparrow: 'Why do you sing like that? Are you by any chance my wife? If you are, call three times, and I will put you in a golden cage and keep you as a pet.' The sparrow called out three times, and the scholar bought a golden cage to keep it in. The ugly sister was very angry when she saw that her husband kept the sparrow in a cage, and she secretly killed it and threw it into the garden, where it was once more transformed into a bamboo with many shoots. When Pock Face ate them, an ulcer formed on her tongue, but the scholar found them excellent. The wicked woman became suspicious again and had the bamboo cut down and made into a bed, but when she lay on it, innumerable needles pricked her, while the scholar found it extremely comfortable. Again she became very cross and threw the bed away.

Next door to the scholar lived an old woman who sold money-bags. One day, on her way home, she saw the bed and thought to herself: 'No one has died here, why have they thrown the bed away? I shall take it,' and she took the bed into her house and passed a very comfortable night. The next day, she saw that the food in the kitchen was ready cooked. She ate it up, but naturally she felt a little nervous, not having any idea who could have prepared it. Thus for several days she found she could have dinner the moment she came home, but finally, being no longer able to contain her anxiety, she came back early one afternoon and went into the kitchen, where she saw a dark shadow washing rice. She ran up quickly and clasped the shadow round the waist. 'Who are you?' she asked, 'and why do you cook food for me?' The shadow replied: 'I will tell you everything. I am the wife of your neighbour the scholar and am called "Beauty." My sister threw me into the well and I was drowned, but my soul was not dispersed. Please give me a rice-pot as head, a stick as hand, a dish-cloth as entrails, firehooks as feet, and then I can assume my former shape again.' The old woman gave her what she asked for, and in a moment a beautiful girl appeared, and the old woman was so delighted at seeing such a charming girl, that she questioned her very closely. She told the old woman everything, and then said: 'Old woman, I have got a bag, which you must offer for sale outside the scholar's house. If he comes out, you must sell it to him.' And she gave her an embroidered bag.

The next day the old woman stood outside the scholar's house and shouted that she had a bag for sale. Maddened by the noise, he came out to ask what kind of bags she sold, and she showed him Beauty's embroidered bag. 'Where did you get this bag?' he asked. 'I gave it to my wife.' The old woman then told the whole story to the scholar, who was overjoyed to hear that his wife was still alive. He arranged everything with the old woman, laid down a red cloth on the ground, and brought Beauty back to his house.

When Pock Face saw her sister return, she gave her no peace. She began to grumble and say that the woman was only pretending to be Beauty, and that in point of fact she was a spirit. She wanted to have a trial to see which was the genuine wife. Beauty, also, would not admit herself in the wrong, and said: 'Good. We will have a test.' Pock Face suggested that they should walk on eggs, and whoever broke the shells would be the loser, but although she broke all the eggs, and Beauty none, she refused to admit her loss and insisted on another trial. This time they were to walk up a ladder made of knives. Beauty went up and down first without receiving the tiniest scratch, but before Pock Face had gone two steps, her feet were cut to the bone. Although she had lost again, she insisted on another test, that of jumping into a cauldron of hot oil. She hoped that Beauty, who would have to jump in first, would be burnt. Beauty, however, was quite unharmed by the boiling oil, but the wicked sister fell into it and did not appear again.

Beauty put the roasted bones of the wicked sister into a box and sent them over to her step-mother by a stuttering old servant woman, who was told to say: 'Your daughter's flesh.' But the step-mother loved carp and understood 'carp flesh' instead of 'your daughter's flesh.' She thought her daughter had sent her over some carp and opened the box in a state of great excitement; but when she saw the charred bones of her daughter lying inside, she let out a piercing scream and fell down dead.

— Translated from the Chinese by Wolfram Eberhard.

The Young Ravens That Call upon Him

CHARLES G. D. ROBERTS

IT WAS just before dawn, and a grayness was beginning to trouble the dark about the top of the mountain.

Even at that cold height there was no wind. The veil of cloud that hid the stars hung but a handbreadth above the naked summit. To eastward the peak broke away sheer, beetling in a perpetual menace to the valleys and the lower hills. Just under the brow, on a splintered and creviced ledge, was the nest of the eagles.

As the thick dark shrank down the steep like a receding tide, and the grayness reached the ragged heap of branches forming the nest, the young eagles stirred uneasily under the loose droop of the mother's wings. She raised her head and peered about her, slightly lifting her wings as she did so; and the nestlings, complaining at the chill air that came in upon their unfledged bodies, thrust themselves up amid the warm feathers of her thighs. The male bird, perched on a jutting fragment beside the nest, did not move. But he was awake. His white, narrow, flat-crowned head was turned to one side, and his yellow eye, under its straight, fierce lid, watched the pale streak that was growing along the distant eastern sea-line.

The great birds were racked with hunger. Even the nestlings, to meet the petitions of whose gaping beaks they stinted themselves without mercy, felt meager and uncomforted. Day after day the parent birds had fished almost in vain; day after day their wide and tireless hunting had brought them scant reward. The schools of alewives, mackerel, and herring seemed to shun their shores that spring. The rabbits seemed to have fled from all the coverts about their mountain.

The mother eagle, larger and of mightier wing than her mate, looked as if she had met with misadventure. Her plumage was disordered. Her eyes, fiercely and restlessly anxious, at moments grew dull as if with exhaustion. On the day before, while circling at her viewless height above a lake far inland, she had marked a huge lake-trout, basking near the surface of the water. Dropping upon it with half-closed, hissing wings, she had fixed her talons in its back. But the fish had proved too powerful for her. Again and again it had dragged her under water, and she had been almost drowned before she could unloose the terrible grip of her claws. Hardly, and late, had she beaten her way back to the mountain-top.

And now the pale streak in the east grew ruddy. Rust-red stains and purple, crawling fissures began to show on the rocky face of the peak. A piece of scarlet cloth, woven among the fagots of the nest, glowed like new blood in the increasing light. And presently a wave of rose appeared to break and wash down over the summit, as the rim of the sun came above the horizon.

The male eagle stretched his head far out over the depth, lifted his wings and screamed harshly, as if in greeting of the day. He paused a moment in that position, rolling his eye upon the nest. Then his head went lower, his wings spread wider, and he launched himself smoothly and swiftly into the abyss of air as a swimmer glides into the sea. The female watched him, a faint wraith of a bird darting through the gloom, till presently, completing his mighty arc, he rose again into the full light of the morning. Then on level, all but moveless wing, he sailed away toward the horizon.

As the sun rose higher and higher, the darkness began to melt on the tops of the lower hills and to diminish on the slopes of the upland pastures, lingering in the valleys as the snow delays there in spring. As point by point the landscape uncovered itself to his view, the eagle shaped his flight into a vast circle, or rather into a series of stupendous loops. His neck was stretched towards the earth, in the intensity of his search for something to ease the bitter hunger of his nestlings and his mate.

Not far from the sea, and still in darkness, stood a low, round hill, or swelling upland. Bleak and shelterless, whipped by every wind that the heavens could let loose, it bore no bush but an occasional juniper scrub. It was covered with mossy hillocks, and with a short grass, meager but sweet. There in the chilly gloom, straining her ears to catch the lightest footfall of approaching peril, but hearing only the hushed thunder of the surf, stood a lonely ewe over the lamb to which she had given birth in the night.

Having lost the flock when the pangs of travail came upon her, the unwonted solitude filled her with apprehension. But as soon as the first feeble bleating of the lamb fell upon her ear, everything was changed. Her terrors all at once increased tenfold—but they were for her young, not for herself; and with them came a strange boldness such as her heart had never known before. As the little weakling shivered against her side, she uttered low, short bleats and murmurs of tenderness. When an owl hooted in the woods across the valley, she raised her head angrily and faced the sound, suspecting a menace to her young. When a mouse scurried past her, with a small, rustling noise amid the withered mosses of the hillock, she stamped fiercely, and would have charged had the intruder been a lion.

When the first gray of the dawn descended over the pasture, the ewe feasted her eyes with the sight of the trembling little creature, as it lay on the wet grass. With gentle nose she coaxed and caressed it, till presently it struggled to its feet, and, with its pathetically awkward legs spread wide apart to preserve its balance, it began to nurse. Turning her head as far around as she could, the ewe watched its every motion with soft murmurings of delight.

And now that wave of rose, which had long ago washed the mountain and waked the eagles, spread tenderly across the open pasture. The lamb stopped nursing; and the ewe, moving forward two or three steps, tried to persuade it to follow her. She was anxious that it should as soon as possible learn to walk freely, so they might together rejoin the flock. She felt that the open pasture was full of dangers.

The lamb seemed afraid to take so many steps. It shook its ears and bleated piteously. The mother returned to its side, caressed it anew, pushed it with her nose, and again moved away a few feet, urging it to go with her. Again the feeble little creature refused, bleating loudly. At this moment there came a terrible hissing rush out of the sky, and a great form fell upon the lamb. The ewe wheeled and charged madly; but at the same instant the eagle, with two mighty buffetings of his wings, rose beyond her reach and soared away toward the mountain. The lamb hung limp from his talons; and with piteous cries the ewe ran beneath, gazing upward, and stumbling over the hillocks and juniper bushes.

In the nest of the eagles there was content. The pain of their hunger appeased, the nestlings lay dozing in the sun, the neck of one resting across the back of the other. The triumphant male sat erect upon his perch, staring out over the splendid world that displayed itself beneath him. Now and again he half lifted his wings and screamed joyously at the sun. The mother bird, perched upon a limb on the edge of the nest, busily rearranged her plumage. At times she stooped her head into the nest to utter over her sleeping eaglets a soft chuckling noise, which seemed to come from the bottom of her throat.

But hither and thither over the round bleak hill wandered the ewe, calling for her lamb, unmindful of the flock, which had been moved to other pastures.

—*From Earth's Enigmas by Charles G. D. Roberts, Canadian (1860–1943).*

~ ❁ ~

Mujo the Drunkard

VUK KARADŽIĆ

THE STORY GOES that once upon a time there lived in Constantinople a Turk named Bekri Mujo (Mujo the Drunkard), who had inherited from his father untold riches which he squandered in drinking and wild living and at last had no clothes left save a friese blanket to walk the street in, and an old cap with a hole in it, through which his pigtail fell. One day the Sultan met him in the street drunk and began to upbraid him for having run through so much riches and come to so shameful a plight; but Mujo surlily turned on him, saying: "What concern is it of yours if I drink? If I drink it is on my own money that I drink; and if you think that I have no money, for what price will you give me Stambul?" Although the Sultan knew that he had not even a penny, he thought that someone else with money might have set him on, and so, being unable to draw back from his promise, he answered: "I will not give you, Mujo, the whole of Stambul for any price, but I will give you half of it for such and such a sum, and then we can, if need be, rule there together." To this Mujo answered: "Good. I shall bring you the money tomorrow morning." And so they parted. When Mujo did not come with the money at the appointed time next day, the Sultan sent men to fetch him; but the now sober Mujo confessed that he had not even a penny, to say nothing of being able to buy Constantinople or the half of it. So the Sultan immediately ordered him to be beheaded for having lied and talked nonsense. Mujo began to beg for mercy; but when he saw that it was of no avail, he said to the Sultan: "Since you have made up your mind about it, you can easily kill me; but I beg you to grant me a favour before you kill me. Find in your empire three men: a poor man who possesses nothing in the world, a blind man who sees nothing, and a lame man who has no legs but only a trunk; bring them here, give them plenty of meat and drink, and let us both see what they will do." The Sultan agreed to this, and at once gave his orders. Three such men were found and brought; and when they were seated side by side, food and drink were set before them and they began to feast. When they had eaten and drunk well, the blind man said: "Thanks be to God and our honoured Sultan, who has given us white bread to eat and red wine to drink." On this the cripple, as quick as lightning, said: "One-eyed whoreson that you are, how do you know that the bread is white and the wine red if you cannot see? I'll kick your tail for you." Thereupon the poor man shouted: "Beat him on my account and charge the bill to me." Then Bekri Mujo said to the Sultan: "You see, honoured Sultan, what drink does. The blind man has no eyes, nor the cripple legs, nor the poor man money; but now that they have drunk, the blind man acquires eyes, and the poor man money; in the same way I acquired money yesterday, and would have bought Stambul from you." On seeing and hearing all that had passed, the Sultan pardoned Bekri Mujo and granted him his life.

The Sultan amazed at the strength wine has and seeing how it was the undoing of drunkards, determined to taste it for once himself; he therefore ordered one evening some of the finest coast wine to be brought to him, and he drank deeply of it. When he awoke next morning, he was ill and his head ached so that he could not raise it from the pillow. When this news spread about the court, all the doctors quickly gathered together to cure the Sultan; but the Sultan said that Bekri Mujo would be able to cure him of his illness better than all the doctors, and so they were to summon him at once. When Bekri Mujo came, the Sultan told him of his illness and the reason for it, and asked him what he was to do now. Bekri Mujo answered that he was to drink again what he had drunk the night before and then his headache would at once leave him. Then the Sultan asked him: "But what shall I do if my head again begins to ache when I become sober?" And Mujo answered: "Drink once again." "And how long will that last?" asked the Sultan. "Until you come to be wrapped in a friese blanket just as I am," answered Mujo.

—*Vuk Karadžić, Serb (1787–1864), translated from the Serbian by N. B. Jopson.*

~ ⚙ ~

The Father

BJÖRNSTJERNE BJÖRNSON

THE MAN whose story is here to be told was the wealthiest and most influential person in his parish; his name was Thord Overaas. He appeared in the priest's study one day, tall and earnest.

"I have gotten a son," said he, "and I wish to present him for baptism."

"What shall his name be?"

"Finn—after my father."

"And the sponsors?"

They were mentioned, and proved to be the best men and women of Thord's relations in the parish.

"Is there anything else?" inquired the priest, and looked up.

The peasant hesitated a little.

"I should like very much to have him baptized by himself," said he, finally.

"That is to say on a week-day?"

"Next Saturday, at twelve o'clock noon."

"Is there anything else?" inquired the priest.

"There is nothing else"; and the peasant twirled his cap, as though he were about to go.

Then the priest rose. "There is yet this, however," said he, and walking toward Thord, he took him by the hand and looked gravely into his eyes: "God grant that the child may become a blessing to you!"

One day sixteen years later, Thord stood once more in the priest's study.

"Really, you carry your age astonishingly well, Thord," said the priest; for he saw no change whatever in the man.

"That is because I have no troubles," replied Thord.

To this the priest said nothing, but after a while he asked: "What is your pleasure this evening?"

"I have come this evening about that son of mine who is to be confirmed to-morrow."

"He is a bright boy."

"I did not wish to pay the priest until I heard what number the boy would have when he takes his place in church to-morrow."

"He will stand number one."

"So I have heard; and here are ten dollars for the priest."

"Is there anything else I can do for you?" inquired the priest, fixing his eyes on Thord.

"There is nothing else."

Thord went out.

Eight years more rolled by, and then one day a noise was heard outside of the priest's study, for many men were approaching, and at their head was Thord, who entered first.

The priest looked up and recognized him.

"You come well attended this evening, Thord," said he.

"I am here to request that the banns may be published for my son; he is about to marry Karen Storliden, daughter of Gudmund, who stands here beside me."

"Why, that is the richest girl in the parish."

"So they say," replied the peasant, stroking back his hair with one hand.

The priest sat awhile as if in deep thought, then entered the names in his book, without making any comments, and the men wrote their signatures underneath. Thord laid three dollars on the table.

"One is all I am to have," said the priest.

"I know that very well; but he is my only child, I want to do it handsomely."

The priest took the money.

"This is now the third time, Thord, that you have come here on your son's account."

"But now I am through with him," said Thord, and folding up his pocket-book he said farewell and walked away.

The men slowly followed him.

A fortnight later, the father and son were rowing across the lake, one calm, still day, to Storliden to make arrangements for the wedding.

"This thwart is not secure," said the son, and stood up to straighten the seat on which he was sitting.

At the same moment the board he was standing on slipped from under him; he threw out his arms, uttered a shriek, and fell overboard.

"Take hold of the oar!" shouted the father, springing to his feet and holding out the oar.

But when the son had made a couple of efforts he grew stiff.

"Wait a moment!" cried the father, and began to row toward his son. Then the son rolled over on his back, gave his father one long look, and sank.

Thord could scarcely believe it; he held the boat still, and stared at the spot where his son had gone down, as though he must surely come to the surface again. There rose some bubbles, then some more, and finally one large one that burst; and the lake lay there as smooth and bright as a mirror again.

For three days and three nights people saw the father rowing round and round the spot, without taking either food or sleep; he was dragging the lake for the body of his son. And toward morning of the third day he found it, and carried it in his arms up over the hills to his gard.

It might have been about a year from that day, when the priest, late one autumn evening, heard someone in the passage outside of the door, carefully trying to find the latch. The priest opened the door, and in walked a tall, thin man, with bowed form and white hair. The priest looked long at him before he recognized him. It was Thord.

"Are you out walking so late?" said the priest, and stood still in front of him.

"Ah yes! it is late," said Thord, and took a seat.

The priest sat down also, as though waiting. A long, long silence followed. At last Thord said:

"I have something with me and I should like to give to the poor; I want it to be invested as a legacy in my son's name."

He rose, laid some money on the table, and sat down again. The priest counted it.

"It is a great deal of money," said he.

"It is half the price of my gard. I sold it to-day."

The priest sat long in silence. At last he asked, but gently:

"What do you propose to do now, Thord?"

"Something better."

They sat there for a while, Thord with downcast eyes, the priest with his eyes fixed on Thord. Presently the priest said, slowly and softly:

"I think your son has at last brought you a true blessing."

"Yes, I think so myself," said Thord, looking up, while two big tears coursed slowly down his cheeks.

—*By Björnstjerne Björnson, Norwegian (1832–1910), translated by R. B. Anderson.*

Children and Old People

IVAN CANKAR

THE CHILDREN were in the habit of talking together before they went to sleep. They sat for awhile on a broad, flat stove and told one another whatever happened to occur to them. The evening dusk peered into the room through dim windows, with its eyes full of dreams; the silent shadows writhed upward from every corner and carried away with them their marvellous fairy tales.

The children related whatever entered their minds, but their thoughts were only of beautiful stories spun from the sun and its warmth, from love and hope woven of dreams. All their future was just one long, glorious holiday; between their Christmas and Easter came no Ash Wednesday. Somewhere behind variegated curtains all life silently overflowed, twinkling and flashing from light to light. Their words were half-understood whispers; no story had either a beginning or distinct images; no fairy tale had an end. Sometimes all four children spoke at once, yet no one of them disturbed another; they all gazed fascinated at that wondrously beautiful celestial light, and in that setting every word rang true, every tale had its splendid end.

The children so much resembled one another that in the twilight one could not distinguish the countenance of Tonček, the youngest, a boy of four, from that of Lojzka, the oldest, a girl of ten. All had small, tiny faces and big, wide-open visionary eyes.

That evening something unknown, something from a foreign land, reached out with a violent hand into the celestial light and struck ruthlessly among the holidays, stories and fairy tales. The post had brought notice that father "had fallen" in Italy. "He had fallen." Something unknown, new, strange, totally unintelligible stepped in front of them; stood there, high and large; and had neither face, nor eyes, nor mouth. It could fit nowhere, neither into that noisy life before the church and on the street, nor into that warm twilight on the stove, nor even into their fairy tales. It was nothing happy, nor yet anything particularly sad, for it was dead; it had no eyes that could reveal with a look, no mouth that could tell them in a word why and whence it came. Thought stood helpless and timid before this enormous vision—as if in front of a mighty black wall—and could advance nowhere. The phantom approached the wall; it stared there and stood mute.

"Well, when will he return now?" asked Tonček pensively.

Lojzka lashed him with an angry glance. "How can he return if he has fallen?"

All were silent; all four stood before the mighty black wall and could not look over it.

"I shall go to war, too!" suddenly spoke up Matija, seven years old, as if he had seized with his quick hand upon the right idea, and knew just what he must say.

"You're too little," Tonček, the four-year-old who still wore smocks, admonished him in a deep voice.

Milka, the tiniest and the sickliest among them, who was wrapped up in her mother's spacious shawl, so that she looked like a wayfarer's bundle, asked in a soft, quiet voice that sounded as if it came from somewhere under the shadows:

"Tell us what war is like, Matija. . . . Tell us a story!"

Matija explained: "Well, war means that people kill other people with knives, strike with swords and shoot with guns. The more you kill and strike, the better; nobody says anything to you because it must be so. That is war."

"But why do they kill and strike?" asked sickly Milka.

"For the Emperor!" said Matija, and they became hushed. In the far distance there appeared before their veiled eyes something awe-inspiring, radiating light from beneath a brilliant aureole. They did not stir; their breath scarcely ventured from their lips—they seemed to be in church at high benediction.

Upon this Matija again gesticulated with his nervous hand and seized upon his idea, perhaps in order to dispel the quiet that lay gloomily all around them.

"I shall go to war, too. . . . Down with the enemy!"

"What's the enemy like? . . . Does he have horns?" asked Milka unexpectedly, in a feeble voice.

"Of course he has . . . how could he be an enemy if he didn't?" affirmed Tonček gravely, almost angrily.

Even Matija himself did not know how to answer.

"I don't think he has," he said slowly but he stopped, inarticulate.

"How can he have horns? He's a human being just like us!" Lojzka spoke up indignantly, and then she became lost in thought and continued: "Only he hasn't a soul!"

After long consideration Tonček asked: "What's it like if a man falls in the war—backward like this?"

He showed them how a man falls backward.

"They hurt him . . . to death!" Matija explained calmly.

"Father promised me he would bring back his gun with him!"

"How can he bring it if he has fallen?" Lojzka retorted crossly.

"Then they have hurt him . . . to death?"

"To death!"

Eight young, wide-open eyes stared timidly and tearfully into the twilight . . . stared at something unknown, incomprehensible to the heart and brain.

Meanwhile their grandfather and grandmother sat on a bench in front of the house. The last red rays of the sunset shone through the dark foliage in the garden. The evening was a tranquil one; only heart-rending, choking and breaking sobs could be heard coming from the stable; their young mother, who had gone out to tend the cattle, was probably still there.

The two people sat very close together, bent low; and they held each other's hands as they had once held them long years ago; they gazed at the dying sunset with tearless eyes and said nothing.

—*Ivan Cankar, Slovenian (1876–1918), translated from the Slovene by A. J. Klančar and George R. Noyes.*

~ ❁ ~

The Quest Begins

FREDERIK W. VAN EEDEN

I WILL TELL YOU something about Little Johannes and his quest. My story is very like a fairy tale, but everything in it really happened. As soon as you lose faith in it, read no farther, for then it was not written for you. And, should you chance to meet Little Johannes, you must never speak to him about it, for that would grieve him and make him sorry I had told you all this.

Johannes lived in an old house with a big garden. It was hard to find the way about them, for in the house were many dark halls, flights of stairs, chambers, and spacious garrets; and in the garden everywhere were fencings and hot-houses. To Johannes it was the whole world in itself. He could make far journeys in it, and he gave names to everything he discovered. For the house he chose names from the animal kingdom; the caterpillar loft, because there he fed the caterpillars and watched them change their state; the chicken room, because he had once found a hen there. This had not come of itself, but had been put there by Johannes' mother, to brood. For things in the garden, preferring those products of which he was most fond, he chose names from the vegetable kingdom, such as Raspberry Mountain, Gooseberry Woods, and Strawberry Valley.

Behind all was a little spot he named Paradise; and there, of course, it was exceedingly delightful. A great sheet of water lay there — a pond where white water-lilies were floating, and where the reeds held long, whispered conversations with the wind. On the opposite side lay the dunes. Paradise itself was a little grass-plot on the near shore, encircled by shrubbery. From the midst of this shot up the tall nightingale-plant. There, in the thick grass, Johannes often lay gazing through the swaying stalks to the gentle hilltops beyond the water. He used to go every warm summer evening and lie looking for hours, without ever growing weary of it. He thought about the still depths of the clear water before him — how cozy it must be down amid the water plants, in that strange half-light. And then again, he thought of the faraway, gloriously-tinted clouds which hovered above the dunes — wondering what might be behind them, and if it would not be fine to be able to fly thither. Just as the sun was sinking, the clouds piled up upon one another till they seemed to form the entrance to a grotto; and from the depths of that grotto glowed a soft, red light. Then Johannes would feel a longing to be there. Could I only fly into it! he thought. What would really be beyond? Shall I some time — some time be able to get there?

But often as he made this wish, the grotto always fell apart in ashen, dusky flecks, and he never was able to get nearer to it. Then it would grow cold and damp by the pond, and again he would seek his dark little bedroom in the old house.

He lived there not entirely alone. He had a father who took good care of him, a dog named Presto, and a cat named Simon. Of course, he thought most of his father, but he by no means considered Presto and Simon so very much beneath him, as a big man would have. He confided even more secrets to Presto than to his father, and for Simon he felt a devout respect. That was not strange, for Simon was a big cat with glossy, black fur, and a thick tail. By merely looking at him one could see that he was perfectly convinced of his own greatness and wisdom. He always remained dignified and proper, even when he condescended to play with a rolling spool, or while gnawing a waste herring-head behind a tree. At the extreme demonstrativeness of Presto he closed his green eyes disdainfully, and thought: "Well — dogs know no better!"

Can you realize now, that Johannes had great awe of him? He held much more intimate relations with the little brown dog. Presto was neither beautiful nor superior, but an unusually good and sagacious dog, never farther than two steps away from Johannes, and patiently listening to whatever his master told him. I do not need to tell you how much Johannes thought of Presto. But he still had room in his heart for other things. Does it seem strange that his little dark bedroom, with the diamond window-panes, held also a large place? He liked the wall hangings, with the big flowers in which he saw faces — faces he had so often studied when he was ill, or while he lay awake mornings. He liked the one small picture that hung there. It represented stiff figures walking in a still stiffer garden beside a smooth lake, where sky-high fountains were spouting, and coquetting swans were swimming. He liked best, however, the hanging clock. He always wound it up carefully and seriously, and considered it a necessary courtesy to watch it while it was striking. At least that was the way unless he happened to be asleep. If, through neglect, the clock ran down, Johannes felt very guilty and begged pardon a thousand times. You would have laughed, perhaps, if you had heard him in conversation with his room. But confess how often you talk to your own self. It does not appear to you in the least ridiculous. Besides, Johannes was convinced that his hearers understood him perfectly, and he had no need of an answer. Secretly, however, he expected an answer some day from the clock or the wallpaper.

Johannes certainly had schoolmates, but they were not properly friends. He played with them, invented plots in school, and formed robber bands with them out-of-doors; but he only felt really at home when he was alone with Presto. Then he never longed for the boys, but felt himself at ease and secure.

His father was a wise and serious man, who often took Johannes with him on long expeditions through the woods and over the dunes. They talked but little — and Johannes followed ten steps behind his father, greeting the flowers he met. And the old trees, which must always remain in the selfsame place, he stroked along their rough bark with his friendly little hand. Then the good-natured giants rustled their thanks.

Sometimes his father wrote letters in the sand, one by one, and Johannes spelled the words which they formed. Again, the father stopped and taught Johannes the name of some plant or animal.

And Johannes often asked questions, for he saw and heard many perplexing things. He often asked silly questions. He wanted to know why the world was just as it is, why plants and animals must die, and if miracles could take place. But Johannes' father was a wise man, and did not tell all he knew. That was well for Johannes.

Evenings, before he went to sleep, Johannes always made a long prayer. His nurse had taught him. He prayed for his father and for Presto. Simon, he thought, did not need to be prayed for. He prayed a good deal for himself, too, and almost always ended with the wish that some day there might be a miracle. And when he had said *Amen,* he peeped expectantly around the darkening room, at the faces on the wall hangings, which looked still stranger in the faint twilight; and at the door-knob, and the clock, where the miracle ought now to begin. But the clock always kept on ticking in the very same way – the door-knob did not stir – it grew quite dark, and Johannes fell asleep without having seen the miracle.

But some day it would happen. He knew it would.

II

It was warm by the pool and utterly still. The sun, flushed and tired with his daily work, seemed to rest a moment on the rim of the dunes, for a breathing spell before diving under. The smooth water reflected, almost perfectly, the flaming face of the sun. The leaves of the birch tree which hung over the pond took advantage of the stillness to look at themselves attentively, in the mirror-like water. The solitary heron, standing on one foot between the broad leaves of a water-lily, forgot that he had come out to catch frogs, and, deep in thought, was gazing along his nose.

Then came Johannes to the grass plot, to see the cloud-grotto. Plump! plump! sprang the frogs from the bank. The mirror was all rippled, the image of the sun was broken up into broad bands, and the beech leaves rustled angrily, for they had not yet viewed themselves long enough.

Fastened to the bare roots of a beech tree lay a little old boat. Johannes had been strictly forbidden to get into it; but oh! how strong the temptation was this evening! The clouds had already taken the semblance of a wondrous portal, behind which the sun would soon sink to rest. Glittering ranks of clouds ranged themselves at the sides, like a golden-armored life-guard. The face of the water reflected the glow, and red rays darted through the reeds like arrows.

Slowly, Johannes loosened the boat-rope from the roots. He would drift there, in the midst of the splendor. Presto had already sprung into the boat, and before his master intended it the reeds moved apart, and away they both drifted towards the evening sun.

Johannes lay in the bow, and gazed into the depths of the light-grotto. Wings! thought he. Wings now, and away I would fly!

The sun had disappeared, but the clouds were all aglow. In the east the sky was deep blue. A row of willows stood along the bank, their small, pale leaves thrust motionlessly out into the still air. They looked like exquisite, pale-green lace against the somber background.

Hark! What was that? It darted and whizzed like a gust of wind cutting a sharp furrow in the face of the water. It came from the dunes – from the grotto in the clouds!

When Johannes looked round, a big, blue dragon-fly sat on the edge of the boat. He had never seen one so large. It rested there, but its wings kept quivering in a wide circle. It seemed to Johannes that the tips of its wings made a luminous ring.

That must be a dragon-fly, he thought – a rare thing.

The ring grew larger and larger, and the wings whirled so fast that Johannes could see nothing but a haze. And little by little, from out this haze, he saw the shining of two dark eyes; and a light, frail form in a garment of delicate blue sat in the place of the dragon-fly. A wreath of white wind-flowers rested upon the fair hair, and at the shoulders were gauzy wings which shimmered in a thousand hues, like a soap bubble.

A thrill of happiness coursed through Johannes. *This* was a miracle!

"Will you be my friend?" he whispered.

This was a queer way of speaking to a stranger. But this was not an everyday case, and he felt as if he had always known this little blue being.

"Yes, Johannes," came the reply, and the voice sounded like the rustling of the reeds in the night wind, or the pattering of raindrops on the forest leaves.

"What is your name?" asked Johannes.

"I was born in the cup of a wind-flower. Call me Windekind."

Windekind laughed, and looked in Johannes' eyes so merrily that his heart was blissfully cheered.

"Today is my birthday," said Windekind. "I was born not far away, of the first rays of the moon and the last rays of the sun. They say the sun is feminine. It is not true. The sun is my father."

Johannes determined forthwith to speak of the sun as masculine, the next morning, in school.

"Look! There comes up the round, fair face of my mother. Good evening, Mother! Oh! Oh! But she looks both good-natured and distressed!"

He pointed to the eastern horizon. There, in the dusky heavens, behind the willow lacework which looked black against the silver disk, rose the great shining moon. Her face wore a pained expression.

"Come, come, Mother! Do not be troubled. Indeed, I can trust him!"

The beautiful creature fluttered its gauzy wings frolicsomely and touched Johannes on the cheek with the iris in its hand.

"She does not like it that I am with you. You are the first one. But I trust you, Johannes. You must never, never speak my name nor talk about me to a human being. Do you promise?"

"Yes, Windekind," said Johannes. It was still so strange to him. He felt inexpressibly happy, yet fearful of losing his happiness. Was he dreaming? Near him, Presto lay calmly sleeping on the seat. The warm breath of his dog put him at rest. The gnats swarmed over the face of the water, and danced in the sultry air, just as usual. Everything was quite clear and plain about him. It must be true! And all the time he felt resting upon him the trustful glance of Windekind. Then again he heard the sweet, quavering voice:

"I have often seen you here, Johannes. Do you know where I was? Sometimes I sat on the sandy bottom of the pond, among the thick water plants, and looked up at you as you leaned over to drink, or to peep at the water beetles, or the newts. But you never saw me. And many times I peeped at you from the thick reeds. I am often there. When it is warm I sleep in an empty reed-bird's nest. And, oh! it is so soft!"

Windekind rocked contentedly on the edge of the boat, and struck at the gnats with his flower.

"I have come now to give you a little society. Your life will be too dreary, otherwise. We shall be good friends, and I will tell you many things — far better things than the schoolmaster palms off upon you. He knows absolutely nothing about them. And when you do not believe me, I shall let you see and hear for yourself. I will take you with me."

"Oh, Windekind! dear Windekind! Can you take me there?" cried Johannes, pointing to the sky, where the crimson light of the setting sun had just been streaming out of the golden cloud-gates. That glorious arch was already melting away in dull, gray mist, yet from the farthest depths a faint, rosy light was still shining.

Windekind gazed at the light which was gilding his delicate features and his fair locks, and he gently shook his head.

"Not yet, Johannes, not yet. You must not ask too much just now. Even I have not yet been at my father's home."

"I am always with my father," said Johannes.

"No! That is not your father. We are brothers, and my father is your father, too. But the earth is your mother, and for that reason we are very different. Besides, you were born in a house, with human beings, and I in a wind-flower. The latter is surely better. But it will be all the same to us."

Then Windekind sprang lightly upon the side of the boat, which did not even stir beneath his weight, and kissed Johannes' forehead.

That was a strange sensation for Johannes. Everything about him was changed.

He saw everything now, he thought, much better and more exactly. The moon looked more friendly, too, and he saw that the water-lilies had faces, and were gazing at him pensively.

Suddenly he understood why the gnats

were all the time dancing so merrily around one another, back and forth and up and down, till their long legs touched the water. Once he had thought a good deal about it, but now he understood perfectly.

He knew, also, what the reeds were whispering, and he heard the trees on the bank softly complaining because the sun had set.

"Oh, Windekind, I thank you! This is delightful. Yes, indeed, we will have nice times together!"

"Give me your hand," said Windekind, spreading his many-colored wings. Then he drew Johannes in the boat, over the water, through the lily leaves which were glistening in the moonlight.

—*From The Quest by Frederik Willem van Eeden, Dutch (1860–1932), translated by Laura W. Cole.*

PART FIVE

Scriptures of Some Living Religions

~ ❁ ~

To think of religions solely in terms of dogma or creed, of ecclesiastical institutions and dour priests, is a mistake. Few of the founders of the world's greatest systems of religious and ethical thought came from monasteries. It was a Chinese school teacher, Confucius, who half a millennium before the Christian era became moral preceptor of one quarter of the human race. His thought is still essential even in the worldly Chinese outlook on life. It was an Indian prince, blessed with the wealth of great palaces and skilled in arms and youthful sports, who sought release for mortals from the bondage of material things and human passions. It was a Palestinian carpenter, founder of the nominal religion of the most highly industrialized nations of the western world, who taught and lived the principle that the lasting riches of life are not those which thieves may steal or moth and rust corrupt. The great religions grew out of human experience and need. It is an error to think of them as originally conceived for purposes of policing unruly man, or as devices for maintaining the rights of privileged classes, or as systematized views of misanthropes upon the world and its inhabitants.

The wise reader of the world's bibles will not allow his personal disbelief in religion, or his preference for a particular communion, to blind him to the insights contained in the great scriptures of mankind. Disbelief in religion, if it is complete, involves more than a disbelief in a particular creed or dogma; it involves eventual disbelief in the ultimate meaning and purpose of life itself, and the truly religious would doubtless add, in its spiritual source and eternal value. What is truth no editor of a book like this anthology would venture or presume to say. The selections which follow offer to students passages from the scriptures of the most prominent religions of the world which will serve as a basis for understanding the great differences between them. The distinctions must be inferred by the student. Thoreau called the bibles of the world a "literature *par excellence,*" and they may be read as mere literature. For many readers the world's bibles will offer revelations of fundamental psychological needs in man and his slow discovery of universal moral laws on which psychological health depends. Still others may find in them great affirmations about life, and such affirmations epitomize human experience.

Modern psychology has of course thrown much light on all the factors which determine the religious experiences of men. The following words from C. G. Jung's *Modern Man in Search of a Soul* contain an impartial explanation of the tremendous rôle which religion plays in the life of man and the reasons for its persisting force, despite all changes in belief and taste and economic condition: "During the past thirty years, people from all the civilized countries of the earth have consulted me. I have treated many hundreds of patients, the larger number being Protestants, a smaller number Jews, and not more than five or six believing Catholics. Among all my patients in the second half of life – that is to say, over thirty-five – there has not been one whose problem in the last resort was not that of finding a religious outlook on life. It is safe to say that every one of them fell ill because he had lost that which the living religions of every age have given to their fellows, and none of them has been really healed who did not regain his religious outlook."

Even in psychiatric clinics, therefore, religion appears to have a place. The reason is doubtless to be found in a revealing summary by the American philosopher, Professor William Ernest Hocking: "The great religions have all spoken ill of original human nature; but they have never despaired of its possibilities." The selections which follow have been selected from the bibles of Hinduism, Buddhism, Confucianism, Judaism, Christianity, and Mohammedanism. They are intended to suggest the basic outlook on life of the adherents of these religions.

---

1. BRAHMANISM AND BUDDHISM

The Story of Svetaketu

FROM THE CHANDOGYA UPANISHAD

I

THERE LIVED ONCE Svetaketu Aruneya, the grandson of Aruna. To him his father, Uddalaka, the son of Aruna, said: "Svetaketu, go to school; for there is none belonging to our race, darling, who, not having studied the Veda, is, as it were, a Brahmana by birth only."

Having begun his apprenticeship with a teacher when he was twelve years of age, Svetaketu returned to his father when he was twenty-four, having then studied all the Vedas – conceited, considering himself well-read, and stern.

His father said to him: "Svetaketu, as you are so conceited, considering yourself so well-read, and so stern, my dear, have you ever asked for that instruction by which we hear what cannot be heard, by which we perceive what cannot be perceived, by which we know what cannot be known?"

"What is that instruction, Sir?" he asked.

The father replied: "My dear, as by one clod of clay all that is made of clay is known, the difference being only a name, arising from speech, but the truth being that all is clay; and as, my dear, by one nugget of gold all that is made of gold is known, the difference being only a name, arising from speech, but the truth being that all is gold; and as, my dear, by one pair of nail-scissors all that is made of iron is known, the difference being only a name, arising from speech, but the truth being that all is iron – thus, my dear, is that instruction."

The son said: "Surely those venerable men, my teachers, did not know that. For if they had known it, why should they not have told it me? Do you, Sir, therefore tell me that." "Be it so," said the father.

II

"In the beginning, my dear, there was that only which is, one only, without a second. Others say, in the beginning there was that only which is not, one only, without a second; and from that which is not, that which is was born.

"But how could it be thus, my dear?" the father continued. "How could that which is, be born of that which is not? No, my dear, only that which is, was in the beginning, one only, without a second.

"It thought, May I be many, may I grow forth. It sent forth fire. That fire thought,

May I be many, may I grow forth. It sent forth water. And therefore whenever anybody anywhere is hot and perspires, water is produced on him from fire alone.

"Water thought, May I be many, may I grow forth. It sent forth earth (food). Therefore whenever it rains anywhere, most food is then produced. From water alone is eatable food produced.

III

"Of all living things there are indeed three origins only, that which springs from an egg, that which springs from a living being, and that which springs from a germ.

"That Being (i.e. that which had produced fire, water, and earth) thought, Let me now enter those three beings (fire, water, earth) with this living Self, and let me then develop names and forms.

"Then that Being having said, Let me make each of these three tripartite, so that fire, water, and earth should each have itself for its principal ingredient, besides an admixture of the other two, entered into those three beings with this living Self only, and revealed names and forms. He made each of these tripartite; and how these three beings become each of them tripartite, that learn from me now, my friend!

IV

"The red colour of burning fire (agni) is the colour of fire, the white colour of fire is the colour of water, the black colour of fire the colour of earth. Thus vanishes what we call fire, as a mere variety, being a name, arising from speech. What is true is the three colours (or forms). The red colour of the sun (aditya) is the colour of fire, the white of water, the black of earth. Thus vanishes what we call the sun, as a mere variety, being a name, arising from speech. What is true is the three colours. The red colour of the moon is the colour of fire, the white of water, the black of earth. Thus vanishes what we call the moon, as a mere variety, being a name, arising from speech. What is true is the three colours. The red colour of the lightning is the colour of fire, the white of water, the black of earth. Thus vanishes what we call the lightning, as a mere variety, being a name, arising from speech. What is true is the three colours.

"Great householders and great theologians of olden times who knew this have declared the same, saying, 'No one can henceforth mention to us anything which we have not heard, perceived, or known.' Out of these (three colours or forms) they knew all. Whatever they thought looked red, they knew was the colour of fire. Whatever they thought looked white, they knew was the colour of water. Whatever they thought looked black, they knew was the colour of earth. Whatever they thought was altogether unknown, they knew was some combination of those three beings (devata).

"Now learn from me, my friend, how those three beings, when they reach man, become each of them tripartite.

V

"The earth (food) when eaten becomes threefold; its grossest portion becomes fæces, its middle portion flesh, its subtilest portion mind. Water when drunk becomes threefold; its grossest portion becomes water, its middle portion blood, its subtilest portion breath. Fire (i.e. in oil, butter, etc.) when eaten becomes threefold; its grossest portion becomes bone, its middle portion marrow, its subtilest portion speech.

"For truly, my child, mind comes of earth, breath of water, speech of fire."

"Please, Sir, inform me still more," said the son.

"Be it so, my child," the father replied.

VI

"That which is the subtile portion of curds, when churned, rises upwards, and becomes butter. In the same manner, my child, the subtile portion of earth (food), when eaten, rises upwards, and becomes mind. That which is the subtile portion of water, when drunk, rises upwards, and becomes breath. That which is the subtile portion of fire, when consumed, rises upwards, and becomes speech. For mind, my child, comes of earth, breath of water, speech of fire."

"Please, Sir, inform me still more," said the son.

"Be it so, my child," the father replied.

VII

"Man (purusha), my son, consists of sixteen parts. Abstain from food for fifteen days, but drink as much water as you like, for breath comes from water, and will not be cut off, if you drink water."

Svetaketu abstained from food for fifteen

days. Then he came to his father and said: "What shall I say?" The father said: "Repeat the Rik, Yagus and Saman verses." He replied: "They do not occur to me, Sir."

The father said to him: "As of a great lighted fire one coal only of the size of a firefly may be left, which would not burn much more than this (i.e. very little), thus, my dear son, one part only of the sixteen parts of you is left, and therefore with that one part you do not remember the Vedas. Go and eat! Then wilt thou understand me."

Then Svetaketu ate, and afterwards approached his father. And whatever his father asked him, he knew it all by heart. Then his father said to him:

"As of a great lighted fire one coal of the size of a firefly, if left, may be made to blaze up again by putting grass upon it, and will thus burn more than this, thus, my dear son, there was one part of the sixteen parts left to you, and that, lighted up with food, burnt up, and by it you remember now the Vedas." After that, he understood what his father meant when he said: "Mind, my son, comes from food, breath from water, speech from fire." He understood what he said, yea, he understood it. . . .

"Please, Sir, inform me still more," said the son.

"Be it so, my child," the father replied.

IX

"As the bees, my son, make honey by collecting the juices of distant trees, and reduce the juice into one form, and as these juices have no discrimination, so that they might say, I am the juice of this tree or that, in the same manner, my son, all these creatures, when they have become merged in the True (either in deep sleep or in death), know not that they are merged in the True. Whatever these creatures are here, whether a lion, or a wolf, or a boar, or a worm, or a midge, or a gnat, or a mosquito, that they become again and again. Now that which is that subtile essence, in it all that exists has its self. It is the True. It is the Self, and thou, O Svetaketu, art it."

"Please, Sir, inform me still more," said the son.

"Be it so, my child," the father replied.

X

"These rivers, my son, run, the eastern like the Ganga, toward the east, the western like the Sindhu, toward the west. They go from sea to sea (i.e. the clouds lift up the water from the sea to the sky, and send it back as rain to the sea). They become indeed sea. And as those rivers, when they are in the sea, do not know, I am this or that river, in the same manner, my son, all these creatures, when they have come back from the True, know not that they have come back from the True. Whatever these creatures are here, whether a lion, or a wolf, or a boar, or a worm, or a midge, or a gnat, or a mosquito, that they become again and again.

"That which is that subtile essence, in it all that exists has its self. It is the True. It is the Self, and thou, O Svetaketu, art it."

"Please, Sir, inform me still more," said the son.

"Be it so, my child," the father replied.

XI

"If someone were to strike at the root of this large tree here, it would bleed, but live. If he were to strike at its stem, it would bleed, but live. If he were to strike at its top, it would bleed, but live. Pervaded by the living Self that tree stands firm, drinking in its nourishment and rejoicing; but if the life (the living Self) leaves one of its branches, that branch withers; if it leaves a second, that branch withers; if it leaves a third, that branch withers. If it leaves the whole tree, the whole tree withers.

"In exactly the same manner, my son, know this." Thus he spoke: "This body indeed withers and dies when the living Self has left it; the living Self dies not.

"That which is that subtile essence, in it all that exists has its self. It is the True. It is the Self, and thou, O Svetaketu, art it."

"Please, Sir, inform me still more," said the son.

"Be it so, my child," the father replied.

XII

"Fetch me thence a fruit of the Nyagrodha tree."

"Here is one, Sir."

"Break it."

"It is broken, Sir."

"What do you see there?"

"These seeds, almost infinitesimal."

"Break one of them."

"It is broken, Sir."

"What do you see there?"

"Not anything, Sir."

The father said: "My son, that subtile essence which you do not perceive there, of that very essence this great Nyagrodha tree exists.

"Believe it, my son. That which is the subtile essence, in it all that exists has its self. It is the True. It is the Self, and thou, O Svetaketu, art it."

"Please, Sir, inform me still more," said the son.

"Be it so, my child," the father replied.

XIII

"Place this salt in water, and then wait on me in the morning."

The son did as he was commanded.

The father said to him: "Bring me the salt which you placed in the water last night."

The son having looked for it, found it not, for, of course, it was melted.

The father said: "Taste it from the surface of the water. How is it?"

The son replied: "It is salt."

"Taste it from the middle. How is it?"

The son replied: "It is salt."

"Taste it from the bottom. How is it?"

The son replied: "It is salt."

The father said: "Throw it away and then wait on me."

He did so; but salt exists for ever.

Then the father said: "Here also, in this body, forsooth, you do not pereceive the True, my son; but there indeed it is.

"That which is the subtile essence, in it all that exists has its self. It is the True. It is the Self, and thou, O Svetaketu, art it."

"Please, Sir, inform me still more," said the son.

"Be it so, my child," the father replied.

XVI

"My child, they bring a man hither whom they have taken by the hand, and they say: 'He has taken something, he has committed a theft.' When he denies, they say, 'Heat the hatchet for him.' If he committed the theft, then he makes himself to be what he is not. Then the false-minded, having covered his true Self by a falsehood, grasps the heated hatchet — he is burnt, and he is killed.

"But if he did not commit the theft, then he makes himself to be what he is. Then the true-minded, having covered his true Self by truth, grasps the heated hatchet — he is not burnt, and he is delivered.

"As that truthful man is not burnt, thus has all that exists its self in that. It is the True. It is the Self, and thou, O Svetaketu, art it." He understood what he said, yea, he understood it.

— *Translated from the Sanskrit by F. Max Müller, in Sacred Books of the East, Vol. I.*

~ ☼ ~

The Eternal Self

FROM THE BHAGAVAD GITA

I

Arjuna Said:

What is the Eternal? What is the highest Self? What is the Work, O best of men? What is called the highest Being, and what is declared to be the highest Divinity?

What and in what manner is the highest Sacrifice, here, in the body, O Slayer of Madhu? And how art thou to be known at the time of going forth in death, by those who are self-ruled?

The Master Said:

Unchanging is the supreme Eternal. Self-conscious Life is called the highest Self. The emanating Power which causes the form and forthcoming of all beings, is called Karma, the great Work.

The highest Being is existence subject to change. Individual Spirit is the highest Divinity. The highest Sacrifice am I, here in the body, O best of embodied creatures!

And he who goes forth, putting off the body, and at the time of the end remembering Me, such a one goes to My Being; of this there is no doubt.

Whatever Being one remembers, when putting off the body at death, to that verily he goes, O Son of Kunti, ever formed in the likeness of that Being.

Therefore at every instant remember Me, and fight on; with heart and soul-vision fixed on Me, thou shalt assuredly come to Me.

Such a one with thought assiduously held in union with Me, and wandering in no other way, goes to the supreme Spirit, the Divine, ever thinking thereon, O son of Pritha.

He who holds in his heart that Seer, the Ancient, the Giver of commands, who is smaller than small; who is the Disposer of the All, of form unthinkable, in color like the sun, beyond the darkness;

At the time of the end united in love, with heart unwavering, and with the power of union, gathering the life-power between the brows, he enters straightway into the supreme Spirit, the Divine.

That which knowers of the Vedas call the Unchanging, to which saints, freed from passion, enter in, that which they seek, who vow service to the Eternal, that resting place shall I briefly tell to thee.

Firmly holding all the doors of the senses, and holding emotion within the heart, drawing the life-breath together in the brow, steadfastly set on the practice of union;

Sounding the syllable Om, for the Eternal, with heart set upon Me, who goes forth thus, putting off the body, he enters on the highest Way.

He who ever rests his heart on Me, with no other thought, for him I am easy to find, for the seeker of union, thus holding ever to union.

Entering into Me, the Mighty-souled return not to rebirth, to this unenduring house of pain; they have reached supreme attainment.

All beings, Creator and worlds alike, return again and again, O Arjuna; but, son of Kunti, entering into Me, there is no more rebirth.

They who know the Day of the Creator, as completed in a thousand ages, and the Night of the Creator as ending in a thousand ages, they are knowers of day and night.

All manifest things spring forth from the Unmanifest, at the coming of the Day; and at the coming of the Night, they melt away into the Unmanifest again.

The whole host of beings, coming into being again and again, melts away at the coming of the Night, and comes forth inevitably at the coming of the Day, O son of Pritha.

But beyond this manifest Being, there is another Being, unmanifest, everlasting, which does not pass away, even when all beings perish.

That Unmanifest is called the Everlasting, and this they call the Supreme Way, gaining which they return not again; this is My highest home.

This supreme Spirit, O son of Pritha, is to be found by undivided love; in This all beings dwell, by This was the universe stretched forth.

But at what time going forth, seekers of union return not, or return, that time I shall declare to thee, O bull of the Bharatas.

They who go forth at death in the flame, the light, the day, the moonlit weeks, the summer, they, knowers of the Eternal, enter the Eternal.

But the seeker of union who goes forth in the smoke, the night, the moonless weeks, the winter, he, entering into the lunar light, returns again.

These are deemed the world's immemorial ways of light and darkness; by the one he goes to return no more, by the other he returns again.

Knowing these two paths, O son of Pritha, the seeker of union goes not astray. Therefore at all times be thou united in union, O Arjuna.

The holy reward that is pointed out in the Vedas, sacrifices, penances and gifts, that perfect reward the seeker of union, who knows all this, passes beyond, entering into the supreme home, the source of all.

II

The Master Said:

This most secret wisdom I will declare to thee, since thou dost not cavil, and with it knowledge, knowing which thou shalt be freed from darkness.

This is the royal science, the royal secret, this is the most excellent purifier; it is to be understood by intuition, it is righteous, it is happiness to follow, it passes not away.

Men without faith in this law, O consumer of the foe, failing to reach Me, turn back again along the way of the circle of death.

By Me, whose form is unmanifest, was this whole world stretched forth; all beings are set in Me, but I am not contained in them.

Yet do not beings dwell in Me; behold My lordly power! I am the supporter of all beings, though I dwell not in beings; My Soul causes beings to be.

As the mighty wind, that goes everywhere, rests ever in space, so do all beings dwell in Me; thus understand!

All beings, O son of Kunti, go to My nature at the end of the age; and I put them all forth again at the beginning of the world-period.

Establishing My own nature, again and again I put forth this host of beings inevitably, by the power of Nature.

Nor do all these works bind Me down, O winner of wealth; seated in lordship above them, unattached to all these works.

Under My supervision Nature engenders beings moving and motionless; through this motive power, O son of Kunti, the world circles on its way.

The deluded contemn Me, thus entered into a human form, not knowing My supreme nature, as mighty Lord of beings.

Vain their hopes, vain their works, vain their wisdom, of little knowledge; they have entered into savage and demoniac natures, full of delusions.

But the Mighty-souled, O son of Pritha, who draw near My divine nature, love Me with undivided heart, knowing Me the source of beings, that passes not away.

Ever doing honor to Me, striving, firm in their vows, they bow down to Me in love, drawing near to Me in perpetual union.

And others, offering the sacrifice of wisdom, draw near to Me, as in unity or diversity, or manifold, appearing in all things.

I am the offering, I am the sacrifice, I am the oblation, I am the libation; I am the chant, I am the holy oil, I am the fire, I am what is offered.

I am the father of this world, the mother, the guardian, the father's father; I am the end of knowledge, the purifier, the sacred syllable, the hymn, the chant, the sacred sentence.

I am the way, the supporter, the lord, the witness, the home, the refuge, the beloved; the forthcoming and withdrawing, the place, the treasure, the everlasting seed.

I give warmth, I withhold the rain and send it forth; I am immortality and death, existent and non-existent, O Arjuna.

The men of the Three Vedas, Soma-drinkers, pure from sin, offering sacrifices, seek from Me the way of heaven; they, gaining Lord Indra's paradise, eat divine feasts of the gods in heaven.

They, having enjoyed that wide heavenly world, on the waning of their merit enter the mortal world. Thus putting their trust in the threefold Vedic law, and full of desires, they gain as reward their going and return.

But those who think on Me with undivided heart, drawing near to Me in worship, for them ever joined to Me in union, I bring a sure reward.

Even they who worship other deities with love, filled with faith, they also, O son of Kunti, even though irregularly, worship Me;

For I am the enjoyer and lord of all sacrifices; yet they know Me not truly, and so they fall.

Those who vow to the gods, go to the gods; those who vow to the Fathers, go to the Fathers; those who sacrifice to the departed, go to the departed, and those who sacrifice to Me go to Me.

He who with love gives Me a leaf, a flower, a fruit, or water, this gift of love I accept from him who is self-conquered.

Whatever thou doest, whatever thou eatest, whatever thou offerest, whatever thou givest, whatever penance thou doest, O son of Kunti, do it as an offering to Me.

Thus shalt thou be set free from the bonds of works, fruits of deeds fair or foul; thy soul united through renunciation and union, liberated, thou shalt come to Me.

I am equal toward all beings; nor is any hated or favored of Me; but they who love Me with dear love, they are in Me and I in them.

Should even a chief of sinners love Me with undivided love, he is to be held a saint, for he has decided wisely.

Soon he becomes altogether righteous, entering ever into peace; and know certainly, O son of Kunti, my beloved will not perish.

Whosoever they be, O son of Pritha, who take refuge in Me, even though they be born of sin, women or merchants or serfs, they also go on the highest way.

How much more holy priests and royal sages, full of love! Therefore, as thou dwellest in this unlasting, sorrowing world, do thou love Me.

Set thy heart on Me, thy love on Me, sacrifice to Me, bow down to Me, thus joining thyself to Me in union, and bent on Me, thou shalt come to Me.

III

The Master Said:

Further, verily, O mighty-armed one, hear thou My supreme word, which I shall declare to thee because thou lovest it, desiring what is dear to thee.

The hosts of the gods know not My birth, nor the mighty Seers; for I am the source of all the gods, and all the mighty Seers.

Who knows Me unborn, beginningless,

mighty Lord of the world, he undeluded among mortals, is freed from all sin.

Soul-vision, wisdom, victory over delusion, patience, truth, control and peace, happiness, sorrow, birth and death, fear and valor;

Gentleness, equity, joy, fervor, charity, honor, dishonor, such are the natures of beings, proceeding from Me in their varied forms.

The seven mighty Seers, and the four Lords of mankind are mind-born from My being, of whom these worlds are the offspring.

Who rightly knows this My splendor and power, he is united in unwavering union; this is altogether sure.

I am the source of all, from Me the universe comes forth; the Awakened, thinking thus, love Me, following after love.

Their hearts set on Me, their lives given to Me, they joy and rejoice forever.

To them, ever joined in union, and full of love, I give soul-vision, whereby they may enter into Me.

Bending down to them, yet retaining My own nature, I drive away their darkness born of unwisdom, with the flaming lamp of wisdom.

Arjuna Said:

The supreme Eternal, the supreme home, the supreme purifier art Thou, the everlasting Spirit, the divine; source of the gods, the unborn Lord;

Thus have all the Seers declared Thee, and the divine Seer Narada also; and Asita, Devala and Vyasa, and Thou also sayest so to me.

All this I hold to be true which Thou speakest, O long-haired one; for neither the gods nor the spirits of darkness know Thy forthcoming, Lord!

Thou Thyself, through Thyself, knowest Thyself, most excellent Spirit, Creator of beings, Lord of beings, God of gods, Ruler of the world!

Thou alone art worthy to declare Thy forms, for divine are the manifold forms of Thyself, whereby permeating these worlds, Thou dwellest in them.

How may I know Thee, O Lord of union, ever meditating on Thee? and in what forms art Thou to be thought of, Lord, by me?

Declare again in order Thy power and glory, O arouser of the people! for I can never be sated with hearing this immortal tale.

The Master Said:

Verily I shall declare to thee the divine forms whereby I manifest Myself, naming the chiefest, O best of the children of Kuru, for My forms are endless.

I am the Self, O thou of crested locks, dwelling inwardly in all beings; Verily I am the beginning, and the middle, and the end also of beings.

Of the sons of the Mother, I am Vishnu; among lights, I am the rayed sun; of the storm lords I am Marichi; in the mansions of the night, I am the moon.

Of the Vedas, I am the Veda of chants; among the gods, I am Indra; of perceiving powers, I am the heart; I am the consciousness of beings.

Among devourers, I am Shiva; among gnomes and sprites, I am the Lord of treasures; among fire-powers, I am the Fire-Lord; among peaks, I am mount Meru.

Among priests, O son of Pritha, know Me to be their chief, Vrihaspati; among leaders of hosts, I am the War-god; among waters, I am the ocean.

Among mighty Seers, I am Bhrigu; among words, I am the sacred syllable; among sacrifices, I am unuttered prayer; among hills, I am the Himalayas.

Among trees, I am the tree of life; and Narada among divine Seers: among seraphs, I am he of the painted car; and Kapila the silent, among those who have attained.

Among horses, know Me as the divine steed, born of ambrosia; among elephants, I am Indra's elephant; among men, I am the king.

Among weapons, I am the thunderbolt; among cattle, I am the cow of desires; I am the love-god, the engenderer; among serpents, I am the serpent-king.

Among snakes, I am the snake of eternity; among the water-born, I am the ocean-lord; among the fathers, I am Aryaman; and the Lord of the dead, among constrainers.

I am Prahlada among demons; I am time, among measurers; among beasts, I am the king of beasts; and Garuda among winged creatures.

Among purifiers, I am the wind; I am Rama among warriors; among fish, I am the sacred crocodile; among rivers, I am the Ganges.

Of all that comes forth, I am the beginning and middle and end, O Arjuna; among sciences, I am the science of the divine soul; I am the word of those that speak.

Among letters, I am A; I am the dual among compounds; I am unwaning Time; I am the Ruler, appearing through all things.

I am all-consuming Death; I am the birth of things that shall be; I am honor, grace, voice, among things feminine; and memory and wisdom, firmness, patience.

Among chants, I am the great Chant; among hymns, I am the Gayatri; among months, I am the month of the deer-head; I am flower-bringing spring among the seasons.

I am the dice among uncertain things; the fire of the fiery; I am victory and decision; I am the goodness of the good.

Among the children of Vrishni, I am Vasudeva; among the sons of Pandu, I am Arjuna, conqueror of wealth; among silent seers, I am Vyasa; among poets, I am Ushanas the poet.

I am the scepter of the dominant; I am the rule of those seeking victory; I am the silence of things secret; I am the wisdom of the wise.

And whatever is the seed among all beings, that am I, O Arjuna; nothing that is could be without Me, among things moving or unmoving.

Nor is there any end of My divine forms, O consumer of the foe; this I have told thee for thy instruction, as an enumeration of My manifold forms.

Whatever being is glorious, gracious or powerful, thou shalt recognize that as sprung from a fragment of My fire.

But what need hast Thou of this manifold wisdom, O Arjuna? With one part of My being I stand establishing this whole world.

IV

Arjuna Said:

They who thus ever united and full of love draw near to Thee, and they who worship the unmanifest Eternal, — which of these are the best knowers of union?

The Master Said:

They who, resting their hearts in Me, ever united, draw near to Me, full of supreme faith, these I hold to be most perfect in union.

But they who worship the Eternal, undefined, unmanifest, omnipresent, unthinkable, the basis of things, immovable and firm,

Restraining the bodily powers, everywhere equal-minded, they come to Me, verily, who thus rejoice in the weal of all beings.

But the toil of those whose minds are set on the Unmanifest is greater, for the way of the Unmanifest is hard for mortals to attain.

But they who in Me renouncing all works, are bent on Me, draw near to Me, meditating with single-hearted union,

I am become their Savior from the ocean of death and rebirth after no long time, O son of Pritha, because they have set their hearts on Me.

Therefore set thy heart on Me, enter into Me, with thy soul! Thou shalt verily dwell in Me in the world above! Of this, there is no doubt.

But if thou art not able to concentrate thy imagination steadily on Me, then seek to reach Me by union through assiduous practice, O conqueror of wealth!

And if thou art incapable of assiduous practice, then dedicate all thy works to Me; and doing all works for My sake thou shalt reach mystic power.

But if thou art unable even to do this, taking refuge in union with Me, then self-controlled, make the renunciation of the fruit of all works.

For wisdom is better than assiduous practice, but soul-vision is better than wisdom. From soul-vision comes renunciation of the fruit of works. From renunciation, peace swiftly comes.

Putting away hate for any being, friendly, pitiful, without desire of possessions, without vanity, equal in weal and woe, patient,

Content, ever following union, self-ruled, firmly determined, with heart and soul centered in Me, who thus loves Me is beloved of Me.

He whom the world fears not, who fears not the world, free from exaltation, anguish, fear, disquiet, such a one is beloved of Me.

Unconcerned, pure, direct, impartial, unperturbed, renouncing all personal initiatives, who thus loves Me is beloved of Me.

Who exults not nor hates nor grieves nor longs, renouncing fortune and misfortune, who is thus full of love is beloved of Me.

Equal to foe and friend, equal in honor and dishonor, equal in cold and heat, weal and woe, from attachment altogether free,

Balanced in blame or praise, full of silence, content with whatever may befall, seeking no home here, steadfast-minded, full of love, this man is beloved of Me.

And they who draw near to the righteous Immortal thus declared, full of faith, resting in Me, full of love, they are beyond all beloved of Me.

—*Translated from the Sanskrit of the Bhagavad Gita, Books VIII, IX, X, and XII, by Charles Johnston.*

The Great Retirement

FROM THE JĀTAKA

Now on a certain day the Future Buddha wished to go to the park, and told his charioteer to make ready the chariot. Accordingly the man brought out a sumptuous and elegant chariot, and adorning it richly, he harnessed to it four state-horses of the Sindhava breed, as white as the petals of the white lotus, and announced to the Future Buddha that everything was ready. And the Future Buddha mounted the chariot, which was like to a palace of the gods, and proceeded towards the park.

"The time for the enlightenment of prince Siddhattha draweth nigh," thought the gods; "we must show him a sign:" and they changed one of their number into a decrepit old man, broken-toothed, gray-haired, crooked and bent of body, leaning on a staff, and trembling, and showed him to the Future Buddha, but so that only he and the charioteer saw him.

Then said the Future Buddha to the charioteer, in the manner related in the Mahāpadāna, —

"Friend, pray, who is this man? Even his hair is not like that of other men." And when he heard the answer, he said, "Shame on birth, since to every one that is born old age must come." And agitated in heart, he thereupon returned and ascended his palace.

"Why has my son returned so quickly?" asked the king.

"Sire, he has seen an old man," was the reply; "and because he has seen an old man, he is about to retire from the world."

"So you want to kill me, that you say such things? Quickly get ready some plays to be performed before my son. If we can but get him to enjoying pleasure, he will cease to think of retiring from the world." Then the king extended the guard to half a league in each direction.

Again, on a certain day, as the Future Buddha was going to the park, he saw a diseased man whom the gods had fashioned; and having again made inquiry, he returned, agitated in heart, and ascended his palace.

And the king made the same inquiry and gave the same orders as before; and again extending the guard, placed them for three quarters of a league around.

And again on a certain day, as the Future Buddha was going to the park, he saw a dead man whom the gods had fashioned; and having again made inquiry, he returned, agitated in heart, and ascended his palace.

And the king made the same inquiry and gave the same orders as before; and again extending the guard, placed them for a league around.

And again on a certain day, as the Future Buddha was going to the park, he saw a monk, carefully and decently clad, whom the gods had fashioned; and he asked his charioteer, "Pray, who is this man?"

Now although there was no Buddha in the world, and the charioteer had no knowledge of either monks or their good qualities, yet by the power of the gods he was inspired to say, "Sire, this is one who has retired from the world;" and he thereupon proceeded to sound the praises of retirement from the world. The thought of retiring from the world was a pleasing one to the Future Buddha, and this day he went on until he came to the park. The repeaters of the Dīgha, however, say that he went to the park after having seen all the Four Signs on one and the same day.

When he had disported himself there throughout the day, and had bathed in the royal pleasure-tank, he went at sunset and sat down on the royal resting-stone with the intention of adorning himself. Then gathered around him his attendants with diverse-colored cloths, many kinds and styles of ornaments, and with garlands, perfumes and ointments. At that instant the throne on which Sakka was sitting grew hot. And Sakka, considering who it could be that was desirous of dislodging him, perceived that it was the time of the adornment of a Future Buddha. And addressing Vissakamma, he said, —

"My good Vissakamma, to-night, in the

middle watch, prince Sidhattha will go forth on the Great Retirement, and this is his last adorning of himself."

. . . . .

And having adorned himself with great richness, — while adepts in different kinds of tabors and tom-toms were showing their skill, and Brahmans with cries of victory and joy, and bards and poets with propitious words and shouts of praise saluted him, — he mounted his superbly decorated chariot.

At this juncture, Suddhodana the king, having heard that the mother of Rāhula had brought forth a son, sent a messenger, saying, "Announce the glad news to my son."

On hearing the message, the Future Buddha said, "An impediment (rāhula) has been born; a fetter has been born."

"What did my son say?" questioned the king; and when he had heard the answer, he said, "My grandson's name shall be prince Rāhula from this very day."

But the Future Buddha in his splendid chariot entered the city with a pomp and magnificence of glory that enraptured all minds. At the same moment Kisā Gotamī, a virgin of the warrior caste, ascended to the roof of her palace, and beheld the beauty and majesty of the Future Buddha, as he circumambulated the city; and in her pleasure and satisfaction at the sight, she burst forth into this song of joy: —

> Full happy now that mother is,
> Full happy now that father is,
> Full happy now that woman is,
> Who owns this lord so glorious!

On hearing this, the Future Buddha thought, "In beholding a handsome figure the heart of a mother attains Nirvana, the heart of a father attains Nirvana, the heart of a wife attains Nirvana. This is what she says. But wherein does Nirvana consist?" And to him, whose mind was already averse to passion, the answer came: "When the fire of lust is extinct, that is Nirvana; when the fires of hatred and infatuation are extinct, that is Nirvana; when pride, false belief, and all other passions and torments are extinct, that is Nirvana. She has taught me a good lesson. Certainly, Nirvana is what I am looking for. It behooves me this very day to quit the household life, and to retire from the world in quest of Nirvana. I will send this lady a teacher's fee." And loosening from his neck a pearl necklace worth a hundred thousand pieces of money, he sent it to Kisā Gotamī. And great was her satisfaction at this, for she thought, "Prince Siddhattha has fallen in love with me, and has sent me a present."

And the Future Buddha entered his palace in great splendor, and lay on his couch of state. And straightway richly dressed women, skilled in all manner of dance and song, and beautiful as celestial nymphs, gathered about him with all kinds of musical instruments, and with dance, song, and music they endeavored to please him. But the Future Buddha's aversion to passion did not allow him to take pleasure in the spectacle, and he fell into a brief slumber. And the women, exclaiming, "He for whose sake we should perform has fallen asleep. Of what use is it to weary ourselves any longer?" threw their various instruments on the ground, and lay down. And the lamps fed with sweet-smelling oil continued to burn. And the Future Buddha awoke, and seating himself cross-legged on his couch, perceived these women lying alseep, with their musical instruments scattered about them on the floor, — some with their bodies wet with trickling phlegm and spittle; some grinding their teeth, and muttering and talking in their sleep; some with their mouths open; and some with their dress fallen apart so as plainly to disclose their loathsome nakedness. This great alteration in their appearance still further increased his aversion for sensual pleasures. To him that magnificent apartment, as splendid as the palace of Sakka, began to seem like a cemetery filled with dead bodies impaled and left to rot; and the three modes of existence appeared like houses all ablaze. And breathing forth the solemn utterance, "How oppressive and stifling is it all!" his mind turned ardently to retiring from the world. "It behooves me to go forth in the Great Retirement this very day," said he; and he arose from his couch, and coming near the door, called out, —

"Who's there?"

"Master, it is I, Channa," replied the courtier who had been sleeping with his head on the threshold.

"I wish to go forth on the Great Retirement to-day. Saddle a horse for me."

"Yes, sire." And taking saddle and bridle with him, the courtier started for the stable. There, by the light of lamps fed with sweet-smelling oils, he perceived the mighty steed

Kanthaka in his pleasant quarters, under a canopy of cloth beautified with a pattern of jasmine flowers. "This is the one for me to saddle to-day," thought he; and he saddled Kanthaka.

"He is drawing the girth very tight," thought Kanthaka, whilst he was being saddled; "it is not at all as on other days, when I am saddled for rides in the park and the like. It must be that today my master wishes to issue forth on the Great Retirement." And in his delight he neighed a loud neigh. And that neigh would have spread through the whole town, had not the gods stopped the sound, and suffered no one to hear it.

Now the Future Buddha, after he had sent Channa on his errand, thought to himself, "I will take just one look at my son;" and, rising from the couch on which he was sitting, he went to the suite of apartments occupied by the mother of Rāhula, and opened the door of her chamber. Within the chamber was burning a lamp fed with sweet-smelling oil, and the mother of Rāhula lay sleeping on a couch strewn deep with jasmine and other flowers, her hand resting on the head of her son. When the Future Buddha reached the threshold, he paused, and gazed at the two from where he stood.

"If I were to raise my wife's hand from off the child's head, and take him up, she would awake, and thus prevent my departure. I will first become a Buddha, and then come back and see my son." So saying, he descended from the palace.

—From the Introduction to the Jātaka, translated from the Pāli by Henry Clarke Warren.

The Attainment of Buddhaship

FROM THE JĀTAKA

THEN THE Future Buddha took his noonday rest on the banks of the river, in a grove of sal-trees in full bloom. And at nightfall, at the time the flowers droop on their stalks, he rose up, like a lion when he bestirs himself, and went towards the Bo-tree, along a road which the gods had decked, and which was eight usabhas wide.

The snakes, the fairies, the birds, and other classes of beings did him homage with celestial perfumes, flowers, and other offerings, and celestial choruses poured forth heavenly music; so that the ten thousand worlds were filled with these perfumes, garlands, and shouts of acclaim.

Just then there came from the opposite direction a grass-cutter named Sotthiya, and he was carrying grass. And when he saw the Great Being, that he was a holy man, he gave him eight handfuls of grass. The Future Buddha took the grass, and ascending the throne of wisdom, stood on the southern side and faced the north. Instantly the southern half of the world sank, until it seemed to touch the Avīci hell, while the northern half rose to the highest of the heavens.

"Methinks," said the Future Buddha, "this cannot be the place for the attainment of the supreme wisdom;" and walking round the tree with his right side towards it, he came to the western side and faced the east. Then the western half of the world sank, until it seemed to touch the heavens. Wherever, indeed, he stood, the broad earth rose and fell, as though it had been a huge cart-wheel lying on its hub, and some one were treading on the rim.

"Methinks," said the Future Buddha, "this also cannot be the place for the attainment of supreme wisdom;" and walking round the tree with his right side towards it, he came to the northern side and faced the south. Then the northern half of the world sank, until it seemed to touch the Avīci hell, while the southern half rose to the highest of the heavens.

"Methinks," said the Future Buddha, "this also cannot be the place for the attainment of supreme wisdom;" and walking round the tree with his right side towards it, he came to the eastern side and faced the west. Now it is on the eastern side of their Bo-trees that all the Buddhas have sat cross-legged and that side neither trembles nor quakes.

Then the Great Being, saying to himself, "This is the immovable spot on which all the Buddhas have planted themselves! This is the place for destroying passion's net!" took hold of his handful of grass by one end, and shook it out there. And straightway the blades of grass formed themselves into a seat fourteen cubits long, of such symmetry of shape as not even the most skilful painter or carver could design.

Then the Future Buddha turned his back to the trunk of the Bo-tree and faced the east. And making the mighty resolution, "Let my skin, and sinews, and bones become dry, and welcome! and let all the flesh and blood in my body dry up; but never from this seat will I stir, until I have attained the supreme and absolute wisdom!" he sat himself down cross-legged in an unconquerable position, from which not even the descent of a hundred thunder-bolts at once could have dislodged him.

At this point the god Māra, exclaiming, "Prince Siddhattha is desirous of passing beyond my control, but I will never allow it!" went and announced the news to his army, and sounding the Māra war-cry, drew out for battle. Now Māra's army extended in front of him for twelve leagues, and to the right and to the left for twelve leagues, and in the rear as far as to the confines of the world, and it was nine leagues high. And when it shouted, it made an earthquake-like roaring and rumbling over a space of a thousand leagues. And the god Māra, mounting his elephant, which was a hundred and fifty leagues high, and had the name "Girded-with-mountains," caused a thousand arms to appear on his body, and with these he grasped a variety of weapons. Also in the remainder of that army, no two persons carried the same weapon; and diverse also in their appearances and countenances, the host swept on like a flood to overwhelm the Great Being.

Now deities throughout the thousand worlds were busy singing the praises of the Great Being. Sakka, the king of the gods, was blowing the conch-shell Vijayuttara. (This conch, they say, was a hundred and twenty cubits long, and when once it had been filled with wind, it would sound for four months before it stopped.) The great black snake-king sang more than a hundred laudatory verses. And Mahā-Brahma stood holding aloft the white umbrella. But as Māra's army gradually drew near to the throne of wisdom, not one of these gods was able to stand his ground, but each fled straight before him. The black snake-king dived into the ground, and coming to the snake-abode, Mañjerika, which was five hundred leagues in extent, he covered his face with both hands and lay down. Sakka slung his conch-shell Vijayuttara over his back, and took up his position on the rim of the world. Mahā-Brahma left the white umbrella at the end of the world, and fled to his Brahma-abode. Not a single deity was able to stand his ground, and the Great Being was left sitting alone.

Then said Māra to his followers, —

"My friends, Siddhattha, the son of Suddhodana, is far greater than any other man, and we shall never be able to fight him in front. We will attack him from behind."

All the gods had now disappeared, and the Great Being looked around on three sides, and said to himself, "There is no one here." Then looking to the north, he perceived Māra's army coming on like a flood, and said, —

"Here is this multitude exerting all their strength and power against me alone. My mother and father are not here, nor my brother, nor any other relative. But I have these Ten Perfections, like old retainers long cherished at my board. It therefore behooves me to make the Ten Perfections my shield and my sword, and to strike a blow with them that shall destroy this strong array." And he remained sitting, and reflected on the Ten Perfections.

Thereupon the god Māra caused a whirlwind, thinking, "By this will I drive away Siddhattha." Straightway the east wind and all the other different winds began to blow; but although these winds could have torn their way through mountain-peaks half a league, or two leagues, or three leagues high, or have uprooted forest-shrubs and trees, or have reduced to powder and scattered in all directions, villages and towns, yet when they reached the Future Buddha, such was the energy of the Great Being's merit, they lost all power and were not able to cause so much as a fluttering of the edge of his priestly robe.

Then he caused a great rain-storm, saying, "With water will I overwhelm and drown him." And through his mighty power, clouds of a hundred strata, and clouds of a thousand strata arose, and also the other different kinds. And these rained down, until the earth became gullied by the torrents of water which fell, and until the floods had risen over the tops of every forest-tree. But on coming to the Great Being, this mighty inundation was not able to wet his priestly robes as much as a dew-drop would have done.

Then he caused a shower of rocks, in which immense mountain-peaks flew smoking and flaming through the sky. But on reaching the Future Buddha they became celestial bouquets of flowers.

Then he caused a shower of weapons,

in which single-edged, and double-edged swords, spears, and arrows flew smoking and flaming through the sky. But on reaching the Future Buddha they became celestial flowers.

Then he caused a shower of live coals, in which live coals as red as kimsuka flowers flew through the sky. But they scattered themselves at the Future Buddha's feet as a shower of celestial flowers.

Then he caused a shower of hot ashes, in which ashes that glowed like fire flew through the sky. But they fell at the Future Buddha's feet as sandal-wood powder.

Then he caused a shower of sand, in which very fine sand flew smoking and flaming through the sky. But it fell at the Future Buddha's feet as celestial flowers.

Then he caused a shower of mud, in which mud flew smoking and flaming through the sky. But it fell at the Future Buddha's feet as celestial ointment.

Then he caused a darkness, thinking, "By this will I frighten Siddhattha, and drive him away." And the darkness became fourfold, and very dense. But on reaching the Future Buddha it disappeared like darkness before the light of the sun.

Māra, being thus unable with these nine storms of wind, rain, rocks, weapons, live coals, hot ashes, sand, mud, and darkness, to drive away the Future Buddha, gave command to his followers, "Look ye now! Why stand ye still? Seize, kill, drive away this prince!" And arming himself with a discus, and seated upon the shoulders of the elephant "Girded-with-mountains," he drew near the Future Buddha, and said, —

"Siddhattha, arise from this seat! It does not belong to you, but to me."

When the Great Being heard this he said, —

"Māra, you have not fulfilled the Ten Perfections in any of their three grades; nor have you made the five great donations; nor have you striven for knowledge, nor for the welfare of the world, nor for enlightenment. This seat does not belong to you, but to me."

Unable to restrain his fury, the enraged Māra now hurled his discus. But the Great Being reflected on the Ten Perfections, and the discus changed into a canopy of flowers, and remained suspended over his head. Yet they say that this keen-edged discus, when at other times Māra hurled it in anger, would cut through solid stone pillars as if they had been the tips of bamboo shoots. But on this occasion it became a canopy of flowers. Then the followers of Māra began hurling immense mountain-crags, saying, "This will make him get up from his seat and flee." But the Great Being kept his thoughts on the Ten Perfections, and the crags also became wreaths of flowers, and then fell to the ground.

. . . . .

It was before the sun had set that the Great Being thus vanquished the army of Māra. And then, while the Bo-tree in homage rained red, coral-like sprigs upon his priestly robes, he acquired in the first watch of the night the knowledge of previous existences; in the middle watch of the night, the divine eye; and in the last watch of the night his intellect fathomed Dependent Origination.

Now while he was musing on the twelve terms of Dependent Origination, forwards and backwards, round and back again, the ten thousand worlds quaked twelve times, as far as to their ocean boundaries. And when the Great Being, at the dawning of the day, had thus made the ten thousand worlds thunder with his attainment of omniscience, all these worlds became most gloriously adorned. Flags and banners erected on the eastern rim of the world let their streamers fly to the western rim of the world; likewise those erected on the western rim of the world, to the eastern rim of the world; those erected on the northern rim of the world, to the southern rim of the world; and those erected on the southern rim of the world, to the northern rim of the world; while those erected on the level of the earth let theirs fly until they beat against the Brahma-world; and those of the Brahma-world let theirs hang down to the level of the earth. Throughout the ten thousand worlds the flowering trees bloomed; the fruit trees were weighted down by their burden of fruit; trunk-lotuses bloomed on the trunks of trees; branch-lotuses on the branches of trees; vine-lotuses on the vines; hanging-lotuses in the sky; and stalk-lotuses burst through the rocks and came up by sevens. The system of ten thousand worlds was like a bouquet of flowers sent whirling through the air, or like a thick carpet of flowers; in the intermundane spaces the eight-thousand-league-long hells, which not even the light of seven suns had formerly been able to illumine, were now flooded with radiance; the eighty-four-thousand-league-deep ocean became sweet to the taste; the rivers checked their flowing; the blind from birth received their sight; the deaf from birth their hearing; the cripples from birth the use of their limbs; and the bonds and fetters of captives broke and fell off.

When thus he had attained to omniscience, and was the centre of such unparalleled glory and homage, and so many prodigies were happening about him, he breathed forth that solemn utterance which has never been omitted by any of the Buddhas: —

Through birth and rebirth's endless round,
Seeking in vain, I hastened on,
To find who framed this edifice.
What misery! — birth incessantly!

O builder! I've discovered thee!
This fabric thou shalt ne'er rebuild!
Thy rafters all are broken now,
And pointed roof demolished lies!
This mind has demolition reached,
And seen the last of all desire!

— *From the Introduction to the Jātaka, translated from the Pāli by Henry Clarke Warren.*

Questions Which Tend Not to Edification

A SERMON BY BUDDHA

ON A certain occasion The Blessed One was dwelling at Sāvatthi in Jetavana monastery in Anāthapindika's Park. Now it happened to the venerable Māluñkyāputta, being in seclusion and plunged in meditation, that a consideration presented itself to his mind, as follows: —

"These theories which The Blessed One has left unelucidated, has set aside and rejected, — that the world is eternal, that the world is not eternal, that the world is finite, that the world is infinite, that the soul and the body are identical, that the soul is one thing and the body another, that the saint exists after death, that the saint does not exist after death, that the saint both exists and does not exist after death, that the saint neither exists nor does not exist after death, — these The Blessed One does not elucidate to me. And the fact that The Blessed One does not elucidate them to me does not please me nor suit me. Therefore I will draw near to The Blessed One and inquire of him concerning this matter. If The Blessed One will elucidate to me, either that the world is eternal, or that the world is not eternal, or that the world is finite, or that the world is infinite, or that the soul and the body are identical, or that the soul is one thing and the body another, or that the saint exists after death, or that the saint does not exist after death, or that the saint both exists and does not exist after death, or that the saint neither exists nor does not exist after death, in that case will I lead the religious life under The Blessed One. If The Blessed One will not elucidate to me, either that the world is eternal, or that the world is not eternal, . . . or that the saint neither exists nor does not exist after death, in that case will I abandon religious training and return to the lower life of a layman."

Then the venerable Māluñkyāputta arose at eventide from his seclusion, and drew near to where The Blessed One was; and having drawn near and greeted The Blessed One, he sat down respectfully at one side. And seated respectfully at one side, the venerable Māluñkyāputta spoke to The Blessed One as follows: —

"Reverend Sir, it happened to me, as I was just now in seclusion and plunged in meditation, that a consideration presented itself to my mind, as follows: 'These theories which The Blessed One has left unelucidated, has set aside and rejected, — that the world is eternal, that the world is not eternal, . . . that the saint neither exists nor does not exist after death, — these The Blessed One does not elucidate to me. And the fact that The Blessed One does not elucidate them to me does not please me nor suit me. I will draw near to The Blessed One and inquire of him concerning this matter. If The Blessed One will elucidate to me, either that the world is eternal, or that the world is not eternal, . . . or that the saint neither exists nor does not exist after death, in that case will I lead the religious life under The Blessed One. If The Blessed One will not elucidate to me, either that the world is eternal, or that the world is not eternal, . . . or that the saint neither exists nor does not exist after death, in that case will I abandon religious training and return to the lower life of a layman.'

"If The Blessed One knows that the world is eternal, let The Blessed One elucidate to me that the world is eternal; if The Blessed One knows that the world is not eternal, let

The Blessed One elucidate to me that the world is not eternal. If The Blessed One does not know either that the world is eternal or that the world is not eternal, the only upright thing for one who does not know, or who has not that insight, is to say, 'I do not know; I have not that insight.' "

. . . . .

"Pray, Mālunkyāputta, did I ever say to you, 'Come, Mālunkyāputta, lead the religious life under me, and I will elucidate to you either that the world is eternal, or that the world is not eternal, . . . or that the saint neither exists nor does not exist after death'?"

"Nay, verily, Reverend Sir."

"Or did you ever say to me, 'Reverend Sir, I will lead the religious life under The Blessed One, on condition that The Blessed One, elucidate to me either that the world is eternal, or that the world is not eternal, . . . or that the saint neither exists nor does not exist after death'?"

"Nay, verily, Reverend Sir."

"So you acknowledge, Mālunkyāputta, that I have not said to you, 'Come, Mālunkyāputta, lead the religious life under me and I will elucidate to you either that the world is eternal, or that the world is not eternal, . . . or that the saint neither exists nor does not exist after death;' and again that you have not said to me, 'Reverend Sir, I will lead the religious life under The Blessed One, on condition that The Blessed One elucidate to me either that the world is eternal, or that the world is not eternal, . . . or that the saint neither exists nor does not exist after death.' That being the case, vain man, whom are you so angrily denouncing?

"Mālunkyāputta, any one who should say, 'I will not lead the religious life under The Blessed One until The Blessed One shall elucidate to me either that the world is eternal, or that the world is not eternal, . . . or that the saint neither exists nor does not exist after death;' — that person would die, Mālunkyāputta, before The Tathāgata had ever elucidated this to him.

"It is as if, Mālunkyāputta, a man had been wounded by an arrow thickly smeared with poison, and his friends and companions, his relatives and kinsfolk, were to procure for him a physician or surgeon; and the sick man were to say, 'I will not have this arrow taken out until I have learnt whether the man who wounded me belonged to the warrior caste, or to the Brahman caste, or to the agricultural caste, or to the menial caste.'

"Or again he were to say, 'I will not have this arrow taken out until I have learnt the name of the man who wounded me, and to what clan he belongs.'

"Or again he were to say, 'I will not have this arrow taken out until I have learnt whether the man who wounded me was tall, or short, or of the middle height.'

"Or again he were to say, 'I will not have this arrow taken out until I have learnt whether the man who wounded me was black, or dusky, or of a yellow skin.'

"Or again he were to say, 'I will not have this arrow taken out until I have learnt whether the bow which wounded me was a cāpa, or a kodaṇḍa.'

"Or again he were to say, 'I will not have this arrow taken out until I have learnt whether the bow-string which wounded me was made from swallow-wort, or bamboo, or sinew, or maruva, or from milk-weed.'

"Or again he were to say, 'I will not have this arrow taken out until I have learnt whether the shaft which wounded me was a kaccha or a ropima.'

"Or again he were to say, 'I will not have this arrow taken out until I have learnt whether the shaft which wounded me was feathered from the wings of a vulture, or of a heron, or of a falcon, or of a peacock, or of a sithilahanu.'

"Or again he were to say, 'I will not have this arrow taken out until I have learnt whether the shaft which wounded me was wound round with the sinews of an ox, or of a buffalo, or of a ruru deer, or of a monkey.'

"Or again he were to say, 'I will not have this arrow taken out until I have learnt whether the arrow which wounded me was an ordinary arrow, or a claw-headed arrow, or a vekanda, or an iron arrow, or a calf-tooth arrow, or a karavīrāpatta.' That man would die, Mālunkyāputta, without ever having learnt this.

"In exactly the same way, Mālunkyāputta, any one who should say, 'I will not lead the religious life under The Blessed One until The Blessed One shall elucidate to me either that the world is eternal, or that the world is not eternal, . . . or that the saint neither exists nor does not exist after death;' — that person would die, Mālunkyāputta, before The Tathāgata had ever elucidated this to him.

"The religious life, Māluṅkyāputta, does not depend on the dogma that the world is eternal; nor does the religious life, Māluṅkyāputta, depend on the dogma that the world is not eternal. Whether the dogma obtain, Māluṅkyāputta, that the world is eternal, or that the world is not eternal, there still remain birth, old age, death, sorrow, lamentation, misery, grief, and despair, for the extinction of which in the present life I am prescribing.

"The religious life, Māluṅkyāputta, does not depend on the dogma that the world is finite; . . .

"The religious life, Māluṅkyāputta, does not depend on the dogma that the soul and the body are identical; . . .

"The religious life, Māluṅkyāputta, does not depend on the dogma that the saint exists after death; . . .

"The religious life, Māluṅkyāputta, does not depend on the dogma that the saint both exists and does not exist after death; nor does the religious life, Māluṅkyāputta, depend on the dogma that the saint neither exists nor does not exist after death. Whether the dogma obtain, Māluṅkyāputta, that the saint both exists and does not exist after death, or that the saint neither exists nor does not exist after death, there still remain birth, old age, death, sorrow, lamentation, misery, grief, and despair, for the extinction of which in the present life I am prescribing.

"Accordingly, Māluṅkyāputta, bear always in mind what it is that I have not elucidated, and what it is that I have elucidated. And what, Māluṅkyāputta, have I not elucidated? I have not elucidated, Māluṅkyāputta, that the world is eternal; I have not elucidated that the world is not eternal; I have not elucidated that the world is finite; I have not elucidated that the world is infinite; I have not elucidated that the soul and the body are identical; I have not elucidated that the soul is one thing and the body another; I have not elucidated that the saint exists after death; I have not elucidated that the saint does not exist after death; I have not elucidated that the saint both exists and does not exist after death; I have not elucidated that the saint neither exists nor does not exist after death. And why, Māluṅkyāputta, have I not elucidated this? Because, Māluṅkyāputta, this profits not, nor has to do with the fundamentals of religion, nor tends to aversion, absence of passion, cessation, quiescence, the supernatural faculties, supreme wisdom, and Nirvana; therefore have I not elucidated it.

"And what, Māluṅkyāputta, have I elucidated? Misery, Māluṅkyāputta, have I elucidated; the origin of misery have I elucidated; the cessation of misery have I elucidated; and the path leading to the cessation of misery have I elucidated. And why, Māluṅkyāputta, have I elucidated this? Because, Māluṅkyāputta, this does profit, has to do with the fundamentals of religion, and tends to aversion, absence or passion, cessation, quiescence, knowledge, supreme wisdom, and Nirvana; therefore have I elucidated it. Accordingly, Māluṅkyāputta, bear always in mind what it is that I have not elucidated, and what it is that I have elucidated."

Thus spake The Blessed One; and, delighted, the venerable Māluṅkyāputta applauded the speech of The Blessed One.

—*From the Majjhima-Nikāya (Sutta 63), translated from the Pāli by Henry Clarke Warren.*

The Middle Doctrine

THE WORLD, for the most part, O Kaccāna, holds either to a belief in being or to a belief in non-being. But for one who in the light of the highest knowledge, O Kaccāna, considers how the world arises, belief in the non-being of the world passes away. And for one who in the light of the highest knowledge, O Kaccāna, considers how the world ceases, belief in the being of the world passes away. The world, O Kaccāna, is for the most part bound up in a seeking, attachment, and proclivity (for the groups), but a priest does not sympathize with this seeking and attachment, nor with the mental affirmation, proclivity, and prejudice which affirms an Ego. He does not doubt or question that it is only evil that springs into existence, and only evil that ceases from existence, and his conviction of this fact is dependent on no one besides himself. This, O Kaccāna, is what constitutes Right Belief.

That things have being, O Kaccāna, constitutes one extreme of doctrine; that things have no being is the other extreme. These extremes, O Kaccāna, have been avoided by The Tathāgata, and it is a middle doctrine he teaches: —

On ignorance depends karma;
On karma depends consciousness;
On consciousness depend name and form;
On name and form depend the six organs of sense;
On the six organs of sense depends contact;
On contact depends sensation;
On sensation depends desire;
On desire depends attachment;
On attachment depends existence;
On existence depends birth;
On birth depend old age and death, sorrow, lamentation, misery, grief, and despair. Thus does this entire aggregation of misery arise.

But on the complete fading out and cessation of ignorance ceases karma;

On the cessation of karma ceases consciousness;
On the cessation of consciousness cease name and form;
On the cessation of name and form cease the six organs of sense;
On the cessation of the six organs of sense ceases contact;
On the cessation of contact ceases sensation;
On the cessation of sensation ceases desire;
On the cessation of desire ceases attachment;
On the cessation of attachment ceases existence;
On the cessation of existence ceases birth;
On the cessation of birth cease old age and death, sorrow, lamentation, misery, grief, and despair. Thus does this entire aggregation of misery cease.

—*From the Samyutta-Nikāya, translated from the Pāli by Henry Clarke Warren.*

2. CONFUCIANISM AND TAOISM

The Doctrine of the Mean

CONFUCIUS

WHAT HEAVEN has conferred is called The Nature; an accordance with nature is called The Path of duty; the regulation of this path is called Instruction.

The path may not be left for an instant. If it could be left, it would not be the path. On this account, the superior man does not wait till he sees things, to be cautious, nor till he hears things, to be apprehensive.

There is nothing more visible than what is secret, and nothing more manifest than what is minute. Therefore, the superior man is watchful over himself, when he is alone.

While there are no stirrings of pleasure, anger, sorrow, or joy, the mind may be said to be in the state of Equilibrium. When those feelings have been stirred, and they act in their due degree, there ensues what may be called the state of Harmony. This Equilibrium is the great root from which grow all the human actings in the world, and this Harmony is the universal path which they all should pursue.

Let the states of equilibrium and harmony exist in perfection, and a happy order will prevail throughout heaven and earth, and all things will be nourished and flourish.

Chung-ne said, "The superior man embodies the course of the Mean; the mean man acts contrary to the course of the Mean.

"The superior man's embodying the course of the Mean is because he is a superior man, and so always maintains the Mean. The mean man's acting contrary to the course of the Mean is because he is a mean man, and has no caution."

The Master said, "Perfect is the virtue which is according to the Mean! Rare have they long been among the people, who could practise it!"

The Master said, "I know how it is that the path of the Mean is not walked in:—The knowing go beyond it, and the stupid do not come up to it. I know how it is that the path of the Mean is not understood:—The men of talents and virtue go beyond it, and the worthless do not come up to it.

"There is nobody but eats and drinks. But they are few who can distinguish flavours."

The Master said, "Alas! How is the path of the Mean untrodden!"

The Master said, "There was Shun:—He indeed was greatly wise! Shun loved to question others, and to study their words, though they might be shallow. He concealed what was bad in them, and displayed what was good. He took hold of their two extremes, determined the Mean, and employed it in his government of the people. It was by this that he was Shun!"

The Master said, "Men all say, 'We are wise;' but being driven forward and taken in a net, a trap, or a pitfall, they know not how to escape. Men all say, 'We are wise;' but happening to choose the course of the Mean, they are not able to keep it for a round month."

The Master said, "This was the manner of Hwuy:—he made choice of the Mean, and whenever he got hold of what was good, he clasped it firmly, as if wearing it on his breast, and did not lose it."

The Master said, "The empire, its States, and its families may be perfectly ruled; dignities and emoluments may be declined; naked weapons may be trampled under the feet; but the course of the Mean cannot be attained to."

Tsze-loo asked about forcefulness.

The Master said, "Do you mean the forcefulness of the South, the forcefulness of the North, or the forcefulness which you should cultivate yourself?

"To show forbearance and gentleness in teaching others; and not to revenge unreasonable conduct: — This is the forcefulness of Southern regions, and the good man makes it his study.

"To lie under arms; and meet death without regret; — this is the forcefulness of Northern regions, and the forceful make it their study.

"Therefore, the superior man cultivates a friendly harmony, without being weak. How firm is he in his forcefulness! He stands erect in the middle, without inclining to either side. — How firm is he in his forcefulness! When good principles prevail in the government of his country, he does not change from what he was in retirement. — How firm is he in his forcefulness! When bad principles prevail in the country, he maintains his course to death without changing. — How firm is he in his forcefulness!"

The Master said, "To live in obscurity, and yet practise wonders, in order to be mentioned with honour in future ages; — This is what I do not do.

"The good man tries to proceed according to the right path, but when he has gone half-way, he abandons it; — I am not able so to stop.

"The superior man accords with the course of the Mean. Though he may be all unknown, unregarded by the world, he feels no regret. — It is only the sage who is able for this.

"The way which the superior man pursues, reaches wide and far, and yet is secret.

"Common men and women, however ignorant, may intermeddle with the knowledge of it; yet in its utmost reaches, there is that which even the sage does not know. Common men and women, however much below the ordinary standard of character, can carry it into practice; yet in its utmost reaches, there is that which even the sage is not able to carry into practice. Great as heaven and earth are, men still find some things in them with which to be dissatisfied. Thus it is, that were the superior man to speak of it in its minuteness, nothing in the world would be found able to split it."

It is said in the Book of Poetry, "The hawk flies up to heaven; the fishes leap in the deep." This expresses how this way is seen above and below.

The way of the superior man may be found, in its simple elements, in the intercourse of common men and women; but in its utmost reaches, it shines brightly through heaven and earth.

The Master said, "The path is not far from man. When men try to pursue a course, which is far from the common indications of consciousness, this of course cannot be considered The Path.

"In the Book of Poetry, it is said, 'In hewing an axe-handle, the pattern is not far off.' We grasp one axe-handle to hew the other, and yet, if we look askance from the one to the other, we may consider them as apart. Therefore, the superior man governs men, according to their nature, with what is proper to them, and as soon as they change what is wrong, he stops.

"In a high situation, he does not treat with contempt his inferiors. In a low situation, he does not court the favour of his superiors. He rectifies himself, and seeks for nothing from others, so that he has no dissatisfactions. He does not murmur against heaven, nor grumble against men.

"The way of the superior man may be compared to what takes place in travelling, when to go to a distance we must first traverse the space that is near, and in ascending a height, when we must begin from the lower ground."

It is said in the Book of Poetry, "Happy union with wife and children is like the music of lutes and harps. When there is concord among brethren, the harmony is delightful and enduring. Thus may you regulate your family, and enjoy the pleasure of your wife and children."

The Master said, "In such a state of things, parents have entire complacence!"

The Master said, "How abundantly do spiritual beings display the powers that belong to them!

"We look for them, but do not see them; we listen to, but do not hear them; yet they enter into all things, and there is nothing without them.

"They cause all the people in the empire to fast and purify themselves, and array themselves in their richest dresses, in order to attend at their sacrifices. Then, like overflowing water, they seem to be over the heads, and on the right and left of their worslippers."

It is said in the Book of Poetry, "The approaches of the spirits, you cannot surmise; — and can you treat them with indifference?

"Such is the manifestness of what is minute! Such is the impossibility of repressing the outgoings of sincerity!"

The Master said, "How greatly filial was Shun! His virtue was that of a sage; his dignity was the imperial throne; his riches were all within the four seas. He offered his sacrifices in his ancestral temple, and his descendants preserved the sacrifices to himself.

"Therefore having such great virtue, it could not but be that he should obtain the throne, that he should obtain those riches, that he should obtain his fame, that he should attain to his long life.

"Thus it is that Heaven, in the production of things, is surely bountiful to them, according to their qualities. Hence the tree is flourishing, it nourishes, while that which is ready to fall, it overthrows.

"In the Book of Poetry, it is said, 'The admirable, amiable, prince displayed conspicuously his excelling virtue, adjusting his people, and adjusting his officers. Therefore, he received from Heaven the emoluments of dignity. It protected him, assisted him, decreed him the throne; sending from heaven these favours, as it were repeatedly.'

"We may say therefore that he who is greatly virtuous will be sure to receive the appointment of Heaven."

The Master said, "It is only king Wăn of whom it can be said that he had no cause for grief! His father was king Ke, and his son was king Woo. His father laid the foundations of his dignity, and his son transmitted it.

"King Woo continued the enterprise of king T'ae, king Ke, and king Wăn. He only once buckled on his armour, and got possession of the empire. He did not lose the distinguished personal reputation which he had throughout the empire. His dignity was the imperial throne. His riches were the possession of all within the four seas. He offered his sacrifices in his ancestral temple, and his descendants maintained the sacrifices to himself."

The Master said, "How far extending was the filial piety of king Woo and the duke of Chow!

"Now filial piety is seen in the skilful carrying out of the wishes of our forefathers, and the skilful carrying forward of their undertakings.

"In spring and autumn, they repaired and beautified the temple-halls of their fathers, set forth their ancestral vessels, displayed their various robes, and presented the offerings of the several seasons.

"By means of the ceremonies of the ancestral temple, they distinguished the imperial kindred according to their order of descent. By ordering the parties present according to their rank, they distinguished the more noble and the less. By the arrangement of the services, they made a distinction of talents and worth. In the ceremony of general pledging, the inferiors presented the cup to their superiors, and thus something was given the lowest to do. At the concluding feast, places were given according to the hair, and thus was made the distinction of years.

"They occupied the places of their forefathers, practised their ceremonies, and performed their music. They reverenced those whom they honoured, and loved those whom they regarded with affection. Thus they served the dead as they would have served them alive; they served the departed as they would have served them had they been continued among them.

"By the ceremonies of the sacrifices to Heaven and Earth they served God, and by the ceremonies of the ancestral temple they sacrificed to their ancestors. He who understands the ceremonies of the sacrifices to Heaven and Earth, and the meaning of the several sacrifices to ancestors, would find the government of a kingdom as easy as to look into his palm!"

The duke Gae asked about government.

The Master said, "The government of Wăn and Woo is displayed in the records, — the tablets of wood and bamboo. Let there be the men, and the government will flourish; but without the men, the government decays and ceases.

"With the right men the growth of government is rapid, just as vegetation is rapid in the earth; and moreover their government might be called an easily-growing rush.

"Therefore the administration of government lies in getting proper men. Such men are to be got by means of the ruler's own character. That character is to be cultivated by his treading in the ways of duty. And the treading those ways of duty is to be cultivated by the cherishing of benevolence.

"Benevolence is the characteristic element of humanity, and the great exercise of it is in loving relatives. Righteousness is the accordance of actions with what is right, and the great exercise of it is in honouring the worthy. The decreasing measures of the love due to relatives, and the steps in the honour due to the worthy, are produced by the principle of propriety.

"When those in inferior situations do not possess the confidence of their superiors, they cannot retain the government of the people.

"Hence the sovereign may not neglect the cultivation of his own character. Wishing to cultivate his character, he may not neglect to serve his parents. In order to serve his parents, he may not neglect to acquire a knowledge of men. In order to know men, he may not dispense with a knowledge of Heaven.

"The duties of universal obligation are five, and the virtues wherewith they are practised are three. The duties are those between sovereign and minister, between father and son, between husband and wife, between elder brother and younger, and those belonging to the intercourse of friends. Those five are the duties of universal obligation. Knowledge, magnanimity, and energy, these three, are the virtues universally binding. And the means by which they carry the duties into practice is singleness.

"Some are born with the knowledge of those duties; some know them by study; and some acquire the knowledge after a painful feeling of their ignorance. But the knowledge being possessed, it comes to the same thing. Some practise them with a natural ease; some from a desire for their advantages; and some by strenuous effort. But the achievement being made, it comes to the same thing."

The Master said, "To be fond of learning is to be near to knowledge. To practise with vigour is to be near to magnanimity. To possess the feeling of shame is to be near to energy.

"He who knows these three things knows how to cultivate his own character. Knowing how to cultivate his own character, he knows how to govern other men. Knowing how to govern other men, he knows how to govern the empire with all its States and families.

"All who have the government of the empire with its States and families have nine standard rules to follow; – viz. the cultivation of their own characters; the honouring of men of virtue and talents; affection towards their relatives; respect towards the great ministers; kind and considerate treatment of the whole body of officers; dealing with the mass of the people as children; encouraging the resort of all classes of artisans; indulgent treatment of men from a distance; and the kindly cherishing of the princes of the States.

"By the ruler's cultivation of his own character, the duties of universal obligation are set up. By honouring men of virtue and talents, he is preserved from errors of judgment. By showing affection to his relatives, there is no grumbling nor resentment among his uncles and brethren. By respecting the great ministers, he is kept from errors in the practice of government. By kind and considerate treatment of the whole body of officers, they are led to make the most grateful return for his courtesies. By dealing with the mass of the people as his children, they are led to exhort one another to what is good. By encouraging the resort of all classes of artisans, his resources for expenditure are rendered ample. By indulgent treatment of men from a distance, they are brought to resort to him from all quarters. And by kindly cherishing the princes of the States, the whole empire is brought to revere him.

"Let a man proceed in this way, and, though dull, he will surely become intelligent; though weak, he will surely become strong.

"When we have intelligence resulting from sincerity, this condition is to be ascribed to nature; when we have sincerity resulting from intelligence, this condition is to be ascribed to instruction. But given the sincerity, and there shall be the intelligence, given the intelligence, and there shall be the sincerity.

"It is only he who is possessed of the most

complete sincerity that can exist under heaven, who can give its full development to his nature. Able to give its full development to his own nature, he can do the same to the nature of other men. Able to give its full development to the nature of other men, he can give their full development to the natures of animals and things. Able to give their full development to the natures of creatures and things, he can assist the transforming and nourishing powers of Heaven and Earth. Able to assist the transforming and nourishing powers of Heaven and Earth, he may with Heaven and Earth form a ternion.

"Next to the above is he who cultivates to the utmost the shoots of goodness in him. From those he can attain to the possession of sincerity. This sincerity becomes apparent. From being apparent, it becomes manifest. From being manifest, it becomes brilliant. Brilliant, it affects others. Affecting others, they are changed by it. Changed by it, they are transformed. It is only he who is possessed of the most complete sincerity that can exist under heaven, who can transform.

"It is characteristic of the most entire sincerity to be able to foreknow. When a nation or family is about to flourish, there are sure to be happy omens; and when it is about to perish, there are sure to be unlucky omens. Such events are seen in the milfoil and tortoise, and affect the movements of the four limbs. When calamity or happiness is about to come, the good shall certainly be foreknown by him, and the evil also. Therefore the individual possessed of the most complete sincerity is like a spirit.

"Sincerity is that whereby self-completion is effected, and its way is that by which man must direct himself.

"Sincerity is the end and beginning of things; without sincerity there would be nothing. On this account, the superior man regards the attainment of sincerity as the most excellent thing.

"The possessor of sincerity does not merely accomplish the self-completion of himself. With this quality he completes other men and things also. The completing himself shows his perfect virtue. The completing other men and things shows his knowledge. Both these are virtues belonging to the na[illegible] and this is the way by which a union is [illegible] the external and internal. There[illegible]er he — the entirely sincere man — employs them, — that is, these virtues, — their action will be right.

"Hence to entire sincerity there belongs ceaselessness.

"Not ceasing, it continues long. Continuing long, it evidences itself.

"Evidencing itself, it reaches far. Reaching far, it becomes large and substantial. Large and substantial, it becomes high and brilliant.

"Large and substantial; — this is how it contains all things. High and brilliant; — this is how it overspreads all things. Reaching far and continuing long; — this is how it perfects all things.

"So large and substantial, the individual possessing it is the co-equal of Earth. So high and brilliant, it makes him the co-equal of Heaven. So far-reaching and long-continuing, it makes him infinite.

"Such being its nature, without any display, it becomes manifested; without any movement, it produces changes; and without any effort, it accomplishes its ends.

"The way of Heaven and Earth may be completely declared on one sentence. — They are without any doubleness, and so they produce things in a manner that is unfathomable.

"How great is the path proper to the sage!

"Like overflowing water, it sends forth and nourishes all things, and rises up to the height of heaven.

"All complete is its greatness! It embraces the three hundred rules of ceremony, and the three thousand rules of demeanour.

"It waits for the proper man, and then it is trodden.

"Hence it is said, 'Only by perfect virtue can the perfect path, in all its course, be made a fact.'

"Therefore, the superior man honours his virtuous nature, and maintains constant inquiry and study, seeking to carry it out to its breadth and greatness, so as to omit none of the more exquisite and minute points which it embraces, and to raise it to its greatest height and brilliancy, so as to pursue the course of the Mean. He cherishes his old knowledge, and is continually acquiring new. He exerts an honest, generous earnestness, in the esteem and practice of all propriety.

"Thus, when occupying a high situation, he is not proud, and in a low situation, he is not insubordinate. When the kingdom is well-governed, he is sure by his words to rise;

and when it is ill-governed, he is sure by his silence to command forbearance to himself. Is not this what we find in the Book of Poetry, — 'Intelligent is he and prudent, and so preserves his person?' "

The Master said, "Let a man who is ignorant be fond of using his own judgment; let a man without rank be fond of assuming a directing power to himself; let a man who is living in the present age go back to the ways of antiquity; — on the persons of all who act thus calamities will be sure to come.

"To no one but the emperor does it belong to order ceremonies, to fix the measures, and to determine the characters.

"He who attains to the sovereignty of the empire, having those three important things, shall be able to effect that there shall be few errors under his government.

"However excellent may have been the regulations of those of former times, they cannot be attested. Not being attested, they cannot command credence, and not being credited, the people would not follow them. However excellent might be the regulations made by one in an inferior situation, he is not in a position to be honoured. Unhonoured, he cannot command credence, and not being credited, the people would not follow his rules.

"Therefore, the institutions of the Ruler are rooted in his own character and conduct, and sufficient attestation of them is given by the masses of the people. He examines them by comparison with those of the three kings, and finds them without mistake. He sets them up before heaven and earth, and finds nothing in them contrary to their mode of operation. He presents himself with them before spiritual beings, and no doubts about them arise. He is prepared to wait for the rise of a sage, a hundred ages after, and has no misgivings.

"His presenting himself with his institutions before spiritual beings, without any doubts about them arising, shows that he knows Heaven. His being prepared, without any misgivings, to wait for the rise of a sage a hundred ages after, shows that he knows men.

"Such being the case, the movements of such a ruler, illustrating his institutions, constitute an example to the empire for ages. His acts are for ages a law to the empire. His words are for ages a lesson to the empire. Those who are far from him, look longingly for him; and those who are near him, are never wearied with him.

"Chung-ne handed down the doctrines of Yaou and Shun, as if they had been his ancestors, and elegantly displayed the regulations of Wăn and Woo, taking them as his model. Above, he harmonized with the times of heaven, and below, he was conformed to the water and land.

"He may be compared to heaven and earth, in their supporting and containing, their overshadowing and curtaining, all things. He may be compared to the four seasons in their alternating progress, and to the sun and moon in their successive shining.

"It is only he, possessed of all sagely qualities that can exist under heaven, who shows himself quick in apprehension, clear in discernment, of far-reaching intelligence and all-embracing knowledge, fitted to exercise rule; magnanimous, generous, benign, and mild, fitted to exercise forbearance; impulsive, energetic, firm, and enduring, fitted to maintain a firm hold; self-adjusted, grave, never swerving from the Mean, and correct, fitted to command reverence; accomplished, distinctive, concentrative, and searching, fitted to exercise discrimination.

"All-embracing is he and vast, deep and active as a fountain, sending forth in their due seasons his virtues.

"All-embracing and vast, he is like heaven. Deep and active as a fountain, he is like the abyss. He is seen, and the people all reverence him; he speaks, and the people all believe him; he acts, and the people are all pleased with him.

"Therefore, his fame overspreads the Middle kingdom, and extends to all barbarous tribes. Wherever ships and carriages reach; wherever the strength of man penetrates; wherever the heavens overshadow and the earth sustains; wherever the sun and moon shine; wherever frosts and dews fall: — all who have blood and breath unfeignedly honour and love him. Hence it is said, — 'He is the equal of Heaven.'

"It is only the individual possessed of the most entire sincerity that can exist under heaven, who can adjust the great invariable relations of mankind, establish the great fundamental virtues of humanity, and know the transforming and nurturing operations of Heaven and Earth; — shall this individual have any being or anything beyond himself on which he depends?

"Call him man in his ideal, how earnest is he! Call him an abyss, how deep is he! Call him Heaven, how vast is he!

"Who can know him, but he who is indeed quick in apprehension, clear in discernment, of far-reaching intelligence, and all-embracing knowledge, possessing all heavenly virtue?"

It is said in the Book of Poetry, "Over her embroidered robe she puts a plain, single garment," intimating a dislike to the display of the elegance of the former. Just so, it is the way of the inferior man to seek notoriety, while he daily goes more and more to ruin. It is characteristic of the superior man, appearing insipid, yet never to produce satiety; while showing a simple negligence, yet to have his accomplishments recognized; while seemingly plain, yet to be discriminating. He knows how what is distant lies in what is near. He knows where the wind proceeds from. He knows how what is minute becomes manifested. Such an one, we may be sure, will enter into virtue.

It is said in the Book of Poetry, "Although the fish sinks and lies at the bottom, it is still quite clearly seen." Therefore, the superior man examines his heart, that there may be nothing wrong there, and that he may have no cause for dissatisfaction with himself. That wherein the superior man cannot be equalled is simply this, — his work which other men cannot see.

It is said in the Book of Poetry, "Looked at in your apartment, be there free from shame, where you are exposed to the light of heaven." Therefore, the superior man, even when he is not moving, has a feeling of reverence, and while he speaks not, he has the feeling of truthfulness.

It is said in the Book of Poetry, "In silence is the offering presented, and the spirit approached to; there is not the slightest contention." Therefore, the superior man does not use rewards, and the people are stimulated to virtue. He does not show anger, and the people are awed more than by hatchets and battle-axes.

It is said in the Book of Poetry, "What needs no display is virtue. All the princes imitate it. Therefore, the superior man being sincere and reverential, the whole world is conducted to a state of happy tranquillity."

It is said in the Book of Poetry, "I regard with pleasure your brilliant virtue, making no great display of itself in sounds and appearances." The Master said, "Among the appliances to transform the people, sounds and appearances are but trivial influences. It is said in another ode, 'Virtue is light as a hair.' Still, a hair will admit of comparison as to its size. 'The doings of the supreme Heaven have neither sound nor smell.' — That is perfect virtue."

— From Confucius, Chinese (B.C. 551–478), translated by James Legge.

~ ⚙ ~

The Philosophy of Chuang-Tze

THE INFINITE

THE MASTER SAID, "How profound in its repose, how infinite in its purity, is Tao!

"If metal and stone were without Tao, they would not be capable of emitting sound. And just as they possess the property of sound but will not emit sound unless struck, so surely is the same principle applicable to all creation.

"The man of complete virtue remains blankly passive as regards what goes on around him. He is as originally by nature, and his knowledge extends to the supernatural. Thus, his virtue expands his heart, which goes forth to all who come to take refuge therein.

"Without Tao, form cannot be endued with life. Without virtue, life cannot be endued with intelligence. To preserve one's form, live out one's life, establish one's virtue, and realize Tao, — is not this complete virtue?

"Issuing forth spontaneously, moving without premeditation, all things following in his wake, — such is the man of complete virtue!

"He can see where all is dark. He can hear where all is still. In the darkness he alone can see light. In the stillness he alone can detect harmony. He can sink to the lowest depths of materialism. To the highest heights of spirituality he can soar. This because he stands in due relation to all things. Though a mere abstraction, he can minister to their wants, and ever and anon receive them into rest, — the great, the small, the long, the short, for ever without end."

GARDENER

WHEN TZE KUNG went south to the Ch'u State on his way back to the Chin State, he passed through Han-yin. There he saw an old man engaged in making a ditch to connect his vegetable garden with a well. He had a pitcher in his hand, with which he was bringing up water and pouring it into the ditch, – great labour with very little result.

"If you had a machine here," cried Tze Kung, "in a day you could irrigate a hundred times your present area. The labour required is trifling as compared with the work done. Would you not like to have one?"

"What is it?" asked the gardener.

"It is a contrivance made of wood," replied Tze Kung, "heavy behind and light in front. It draws up water as you do with your hands, but in a constantly overflowing stream. It is called a well-sweep."

Thereupon the gardener flushed up and said, "I have heard from my teacher that those who have cunning implements are cunning in their dealings, and that those who are cunning in their dealings have cunning in their hearts, and that those who have cunning in their hearts cannot be pure and incorrupt, and that those who are not pure and incorrupt are restless in spirit, and that those who are restless in spirit are not fit vehicles for Tao. It is not that I do not know of these things. I should be ashamed to use them."

At this Tze Kung was much abashed, and said nothing. Then the gardener asked him who he was, to which Tze Kung replied that he was a disciple of Confucius.

"Are you not one who extends his learning with a view to being a sage; who talks big in order to put himself above the rest of mankind; who plays in a key to which no one can sing so as to spread his reputation abroad? Rather become unconscious of self and shake off the trammels of the flesh, – and you will be near. But if you cannot govern your own self, what leisure have you for governing the empire? Begone! Do not interrupt my work."

Tze Kung changed colour and slunk away, being not at all pleased with this rebuff; and it was not before he had travelled some thirty li that he recovered his usual appearance.

"What did the man we met do," asked a disciple, "that you should change colour and not recover for such a long time?"

"I used to think there was only one man in all the world," replied Tze Kung. "I did not know that there was also this man. I have heard the Master say that the test of a scheme is its practicability, and that success must be certain. The minimum of effort with the maximum of success, – such is the way of the Sage.

"Not so this manner of man. Aiming at Tao, he perfects his virtue. By perfecting his virtue he perfects his body, and by perfecting his body he perfects his spiritual part. And the perfection of the spiritual part is the Tao of the sage. Coming into life he is as one of the people, knowing not whither he is bound. How complete is his purity? Success, profit, skill, – these have no place in his heart. Such a man, if he does not will it, he does not stir; if he does not wish it, he does not act. If all the world praises him, he does not heed. If all the world blames him, he does not repine. The praise and the blame of the world neither advantage him nor otherwise. He may be called a man of perfect virtue. As for me, I am but a mere creature of impulse."

THE NATURE OF GOD

The Tao of God operates ceaselessly; and all things are produced. The Tao of the sovereign operates ceaselessly; and the empire rallies around him. The Tao of the sage operates ceaselessly; and all within the limit of surrounding ocean acknowledge his sway. He who apprehends God, who is in relation with the sage, and who recognizes the radiating virtue of the sovereign, – his actions will be to him unconscious, the actions of repose.

The repose of the sage is not what the world calls repose. His repose is the result of his mental attitude. All creation could not disturb his equilibrium: hence his repose.

When water is still, it is like a mirror, reflecting the beard and the eyebrows. It gives the accuracy of the water-level, and the philosopher makes it his model. And if water thus derives lucidity from stillness, how much more the faculties of the mind? The mind of the sage being in repose becomes the mirror of the universe, the speculum of all creation.

Repose, tranquillity, stillness, inaction, – these were the levels of the universe, the ultimate perfection of Tao. Therefore wise rulers and sages rest therein. Resting therein they reach the unconditioned, from which springs the conditioned; and with the conditioned comes order. Again, from the unconditioned comes repose, and from repose comes movement, and from movement comes attainment. Further, from repose comes inaction, and from inaction comes potentiality of action. And inaction is happiness; and where there is happiness no cares can abide, and life is long.

Repose, tranquillity, stillness, inaction,—these were the source of all things. Due perception of this was the secret of Yao's success as a ruler, and of Shun's success as his minister. Due perception of this constitutes the virtue of sovereigns on the throne, the Tao of the inspired sage and of the uncrowned king below. Keep to this in retirement, and the lettered denizens of sea and dale will recognize your power. Keep to this when coming forward to pacify a troubled world, and your merit shall be great and your name illustrious, and the empire united into one. In your repose you will be wise; in your movements, powerful. By inaction you will gain honour; and by confining yourself to the pure and simple, you will hinder the whole world from struggling with you for show.

To fully apprehend the scheme of the universe, this is called the great secret of being in accord with God, whereby the empire is so administered that the result is in accord with man. To be in accord with man is human happiness; to be in accord with God is the happiness of God.

Appeal to arms is the lowest form of virtue. Rewards and punishments are the lowest form of education. Ceremonies and laws are the lowest form of government. Music and fine clothes are the lowest form of happiness. Weeping and mourning are the lowest form of grief. These five should follow the movements of the mind.

The ancients indeed cultivated the study of accidentals, but they did not allow it to precede that of essentials. The prince precedes, the minister follows. The father precedes, the son follows. The elder brother precedes, the younger follows. Seniors precede, juniors follow. Men precede, women follow. Husbands precede, wives follow. Distinctions of rank and precedence are part of the scheme of the universe, and the sage adopts them accordingly. In point of spir[illegible]ality, heaven is honourable, earth is lowly. [illegible] and summer precede autumn and [illegible] is the order of the seasons. In [illegible] production of all things, there are phases of existence. There are the extremes of maturity and decay, the perpetual tide of change. And if heaven and earth, divinest of all, admit of rank and precedence, how much more man?

In the ancestral temple, parents rank before all; at court, the most honourable; in the village, the elders; in matters to be accomplished, the most trustworthy. Such is the order which appertains to Tao. He who in considering Tao disregards this order, thereby disregards Tao; and he who in considering Tao disregards Tao,—whence will he secure Tao?

Therefore, those of old who apprehended Tao, first apprehended God. Tao came next, and then charity and duty to one's neighbour, and then the functions of public life, and then forms and names, and then employment according to capacity, and then distinctions of good and bad, and then discrimination between right and wrong, and then rewards and punishments. Thus wise men and fools met with their dues; the exalted and the humble occupied their proper places. And the virtuous and the worthless being each guided by their own natural instincts, it was necessary to distinguish capabilities, and to adopt a corresponding nomenclature, in order to serve the ruler, nourish the ruled, administer things generally, and elevate self. Where knowledge and plans are of no avail, one must fall back upon the natural. This is perfect peace, the acme of good government.

Of old, Shun asked Yao, saying, "How does your Majesty employ your faculties?"

"I am not arrogant towards the defenceless," replied Yao. "I do not neglect the poor. I grieve for those who die. I pity the orphan. I sympathize with the widow. Beyond this, nothing."

"Good indeed!" cried Shun, "but yet not great."

"How so?" inquired Yao.

"Be passive," said Shun, "like the virtue of God. The sun and moon shine; the four seasons revolve; day and night alternate; clouds come and rain falls."

"Alas!" cried Yao, "what a muddle I have been making. You are in accord with God; I am in accord with man."

Of old, heaven and earth were considered great; and the Yellow Emperior and Yao and Shun all thought them perfection. Consequently, what did those do who ruled the empire of old? They did what heaven and earth do; no more.

Lao Tze said, "Tao is not too small for the greatest, nor too great for the smallest. Thus all things are embosomed therein; wide indeed its boundless capacity, unfathomable its depth.

"Form, and virtue, and charity, and duty to one's neighbour, these are the accidentals of the spiritual. Except he be a perfect man, who shall determine their place? The world of the perfect man, is not that vast? And yet it is not able to involve him in trouble. All struggle for power, but he does not join. Though discovering nothing false, he is not tempted astray. In spite of the utmost genuineness, he still confines himself to essentials.

"He thus places himself outside the universe, beyond all creation, where his soul is free from care. Apprehending Tao, he is in accord with virtue. He leaves charity and duty to one's neighbour alone. He treats ceremonies and music as adventitious. And so the mind of the perfect man is at peace.

"Books are what the world values as representing Tao. But books are only words, and the valuable part of words is the thought therein contained. That thought has a certain bias which cannot be conveyed in words, yet the world values words as being the essence of books. But though the world values them, they are not of value; as that sense in which the world values them is not the sense in which they are valuable.

"That which can be seen with the eye is form and colour; that which can be heard with the ear is sound and noise. But alas! the people of this generation think that form, and colour, and sound, and noise, are means by which they can come to understand the essence of Tao. This is not so. And as those who know do not speak, while those who speak do not know, whence should the world derive its knowledge?"

CONFUCIUS AND LAO TZE

CONFUCIUS HAD LIVED to the age of fifty-one without hearing Tao, when he went south to P'ei, to see Lao Tze.

Lao Tze said, "So you have come, sir, have you? I hear you are considered a wise man up north. Have you got Tao?"

"Not yet," answered Confucius.

"In what direction," asked Lao Tze, "have you sought for it?"

"I sought it for five years," replied Confucius, "in the science of numbers, but did not succeed."

"And then? . . ." continued Lao Tze.

"Then," said Confucius, "I spent twelve years seeking for it in the doctrine of the Yin and Yang, also without success."

"Just so," rejoined Lao Tze. "Were Tao something which could be presented, there is no man but would present it to his sovereign, or to his parents. Could it be imparted or given, there is no man but would impart it to his brother or give it to his child. But this is impossible, for the following reason. Unless there is a suitable endowment within, Tao will not abide. Unless there is outward correctness, Tao will not operate. The external being unfitted for the impression of the internal, the true sage does not seek to imprint. The internal being unfitted for the reception of the external, the true sage does not seek to receive.

"Reputation is public property; you may not appropriate it in excess. Charity and duty to one's neighbour are as caravanserais established by wise rulers of old; you may stop there one night, but not for long, or you will incur reproach.

"The perfect men of old took their road through charity, stopping a night with duty to their neighbour, on their way to ramble in transcendental space. Feeding on the produce of non-cultivation, and establishing themselves in the domain of no obligations, they enjoyed their transcendental inaction. Their food was ready to hand; and being under no obligations to others, they did not put any one under obligation to themselves. The ancients called this the outward visible sign of an inward and spiritual grace.

"Those who make wealth their all in all, cannot bear loss of money. Those who make distinction their all in all, cannot bear loss of fame. Those who affect power will not place authority in the hands of others. Anxious while holding, distressed if losing, yet never taking warning from the past and seeing the folly of their pursuit, – such men are the accursed of God.

"Resentment, gratitude, taking, giving, censure of self, instruction of others, power of life and death, – these eight are the instruments of right; but only he who can adapt himself to the vicissitudes of fortune, without being carried away, is fit to use them. Such a one is an upright man among the upright. And he whose heart is not so constituted, — the door of divine intelligence is not yet opened for him."

Confucius visited Lao Tze, and spoke of charity and duty to one's neighbour.

Lao Tze said, "The chaff from winnowing will blind a man's eyes so that he cannot tell the points of the compass. Mosquitoes will keep a man awake all night with their biting. And just in the same way this talk of charity and duty to one's neighbour drives me nearly crazy. Sir! strive to keep the world to its own original simplicity. And as the wind bloweth where it listeth, so let virtue establish itself. Wherefore such undue energy, as though searching for a fugitive with a big drum?

"The snow-goose is white without a daily bath. The raven is black without daily colouring itself. The original simplicity of black and of white is beyond the reach of argument. The vista of fame and reputation is not worthy of enlargement. When the pond dries up and the fishes are left upon dry ground, to moisten them with the breath or to damp them with a little spittle is not to be compared with leaving them in the first instance in their native rivers and lakes."

On returning from this visit to Lao Tze, Confucius did not speak for three days. A disciple asked him, saying, "Master, when you saw Lao Tze, in what direction did you admonish him?"

"I saw a dragon," replied Confucius, " — a dragon which by convergence showed a body, by radiation became colour, and riding upon the clouds of heaven, nourished the two principles of creation. My mouth was agape: I could not shut it. How then do you think I was going to admonish Lao Tze?"

— *From the Works of Chuang Tze, Chinese (fourth century B.C.), translated by Herbert A. Giles.*

~ ✿ ~

3. JUDAISM AND CHRISTIANITY

Psalms of David

THE FIRST PSALM

BLESSED IS THE MAN that walketh not in the [illegible]sel of the ungodly, nor standeth in the [illegible]nners, nor sitteth in the seat of [illegible]

But his delight is in the law of the Lord; and in his law doth he meditate day and night.

And he shall be like a tree planted by the rivers of water, that bringeth forth his fruit in his season; his leaf also shall not wither; and whatsoever he doeth shall prosper.

The ungodly are not so: but are like the chaff which the wind driveth away.

Therefore the ungodly shall not stand in the judgment, nor sinners in the congregation of the righteous.

For the Lord knoweth the way of the righteous: but the way of the ungodly shall perish.

THE NINETEENTH PSALM

THE HEAVENS declare the glory of God; and the firmament sheweth his handywork.

Day unto day uttereth speech, and night unto night sheweth knowledge.

There is no speech nor language, where their voice is not heard.

Their line is gone out through all the earth, and their words to the end of the world. In them hath he set a tabernacle for the sun,

Which is as a bridegroom coming out of his chamber, and rejoiceth as a strong man to run a race.

His going forth is from the end of the heaven, and his circuit unto the ends of it: and there is nothing hid from the heat thereof.

The law of the Lord is perfect, converting the soul: the testimony of the Lord is sure, making wise the simple.

The statutes of the Lord are right, rejoicing the heart: the commandment of the Lord is pure, enlightening the eyes.

The fear of the Lord is clean, enduring for ever: the judgments of the Lord are true and righteous altogether.

More to be desired are they than gold, yea, than much fine gold: sweeter also than honey and the honeycomb.

Moreover, by them is thy servant warned: and in keeping of them there is great reward.

Who can understand his errors? cleanse thou me from secret faults.

Keep back thy servant also from presumptuous sins; let them not have dominion over me: then shall I be upright, and I shall be innocent from the great transgression.

Let the words of my mouth, and the meditation of my heart, be acceptable in thy sight, O Lord, my strength, and my redeemer.

THE TWENTY-THIRD PSALM

THE LORD IS MY SHEPHERD; I shall not want.

He maketh me to lie down in green pastures: he leadeth me beside the still waters.

He restoreth my soul: he leadeth me in the paths of righteousness for his name's sake.

Yea, though I walk through the valley of the shadow of death, I will fear no evil: for thou art with me; thy rod and thy staff they comfort me.

Thou preparest a table before me in the presence of mine enemies: thou anointest my head with oil; my cup runneth over.

Surely goodness and mercy shall follow me all the days of my life: and I will dwell in the house of the Lord for ever.

THE TWENTY-FOURTH PSALM

THE EARTH is the Lord's and the fulness thereof; the world, and they that dwell therein.

For he hath founded it upon the seas, and established it upon the floods.

Who shall ascend into the hill of the Lord? and who shall stand in his holy place?

He that hath clean hands, and a pure heart; who hath not lifted up his soul unto vanity, nor sworn deceitfully.

He shall receive the blessing from the Lord, and righteousness from the God of his salvation.

This is the generation of them that seek him, that seek thy face, O Jacob.

Lift up your heads, O ye gates; and be ye lift up, ye everlasting doors; and the King of glory shall come in.

Who is this King of glory? the Lord strong and mighty, the Lord mighty in battle.

Lift up your heads, O ye gates; even lift them up, ye everlasting doors; and the King of glory shall come in.

Who is this King of glory? the Lord of hosts, he is the King of glory.

THE THIRTY-SEVENTH PSALM

FRET NOT THYSELF because of evil doers, neither be thou envious against the workers of iniquity.

For they shall soon be cut down like the grass, and wither as the green herb.

Trust in the Lord, and do good; so shalt thou dwell in the land, and verily thou shalt be fed.

Delight thyself also in the Lord; and he shall give thee the desires of thine heart.

Commit thy way unto the Lord; trust also in him; and he shall bring it to pass.

And he shall bring forth thy righteousness as the light, and thy judgment as the noonday.

Rest in the Lord, and wait patiently for him: fret not thyself because of him who prospereth in his way, because of the man who bringeth wicked devices to pass.

Cease from anger, and forsake wrath: fret not thyself in any wise to do evil.

For evil doers shall be cut off: but those that wait upon the Lord, they shall inherit the earth.

For yet a little while, and the wicked shall not be: yea, thou shalt diligently consider his place, and it shall not be.

But the meek shall inherit the earth; and shall delight themselves in the abundance of peace.

The wicked plotteth against the just, and gnasheth upon him with his teeth.

The Lord shall laugh at him: for he seeth that his day is coming.

The wicked have drawn out the sword, and have bent their bow, to cast down the poor and needy, and to slay such as be of upright conversation.

Their sword shall enter into their own heart, and their bows shall be broken.

A little that a righteous man hath is better than the riches of many wicked.

For the arms of the wicked shall be broken: but the Lord upholdeth the righteous.

The Lord knoweth the days of the upright: and their inheritance shall be for ever.

They shall not be ashamed in the evil time: and in the days of famine they shall be satisfied.

But the wicked shall perish, and the enemies of the Lord shall be as the fat of lambs: they shall consume; into smoke shall they consume away.

The wicked borroweth, and payeth not again: but the righteous sheweth mercy, and giveth.

For such as be blessed of him shall inherit the earth; and they that be cursed of him shall be cut off.

The steps of a good man are ordered by the Lord: and he delighteth in his way.

Though he fall, he shall not be utterly cast

down: for the Lord upholdeth him with his hand.

I have been young, and now am old; yet have I not seen the righteous forsaken, nor his seed begging bread.

He is ever merciful, and lendeth; and his seed is blessed.

Depart from evil, and do good; and dwell for evermore.

For the Lord loveth judgment, and forsaketh not his saints; they are preserved for ever: but the seed of the wicked shall be cut off.

The righteous shall inherit the land, and dwell therein for ever.

The mouth of the righteous speaketh wisdom, and his tongue talketh of judgment.

The law of his God is in his heart; none of his steps shall slide.

The wicked watcheth the righteous, and seeketh to slay him.

The Lord will not leave him in his hand, nor condemn him when he is judged.

Wait on the Lord, and keep his way, and he shall exalt thee to inherit the land: when the wicked are cut off, thou shalt see it.

I have seen the wicked in great power, and spreading himself like a green bay tree.

Yet he passed away, and lo, he was not: yea, I sought him, but he could not be found.

Mark the perfect man, and behold the upright: for the end of that man is peace.

But the transgressors shall be destroyed together: the end of the wicked shall be cut off.

But the salvation of the righteous is of the Lord: he is their strength in the time of trouble.

And the Lord shall help them, and deliver them: he shall deliver them from the wicked, and save them, because they trust in him.

THE FORTY-SECOND PSALM

As the hart panteth after the water-brooks, so panteth my soul after thee, O God.

My soul thirsteth for God, for the living God: when shall I come and appear before God?

My tears have been my meat day and night, while they continually say unto me, Where is thy God?

When I remember these things, I pour out [illegible]y soul in me: for I had gone with the mul-[illegible] I went with them to the house of [illegible] the voice of joy and praise, with [illegible]hat kept holy-day.

Why art thou cast down, O my soul? and why art thou disquieted in me? hope thou in God: for I shall yet praise him for the help of his countenance.

O my God, my soul is cast down within me: therefore will I remember thee from the land of Jordan, and of the Hermonites, from the hill Mizar.

Deep calleth unto deep at the noise of thy water-spouts: all thy waves and thy billows are gone over me.

Yet the Lord will command his loving-kindness in the day-time, and in the night his song shall be with me, and my prayer unto the God of my life.

I will say unto God my rock, Why hast thou forgotten me? why go I mourning because of the oppression of the enemy?

As with a sword in my bones, mine enemies reproach me; while they say daily unto me, Where is thy God?

Why art thou cast down, O my soul? and why art thou disquieted within me? hope thou in God: for I shall yet praise him, who is the health of my countenance, and my God.

THE NINETY-FIRST PSALM

He that dwelleth in the secret place of the Most High shall abide under the shadow of the Almighty.

I will say of the Lord, He is my refuge and my fortress: my God; in him will I trust.

Surely he shall deliver thee from the snare of the fowler, and from the noisome pestilence.

He shall cover thee with his feathers, and under his wings shalt thou trust: his truth shall be thy shield and buckler.

Thou shalt not be afraid of the terror by night; nor for the arrow that flieth by day;

Nor for the pestilence that walketh in darkness; nor for the destruction that wasteth at noon-day.

A thousand shall fall at thy side, and ten thousand at thy right hand; but it shall not come nigh thee.

Only with thine eyes shalt thou behold and see the reward of the wicked.

Because thou hast made the Lord which is my refuge, even the Most High, thy habitation;

There shall no evil befall thee, neither shall any plague come nigh thy dwelling.

For he shall give his angels charge over thee, to keep thee in all thy ways.

They shall bear thee up in their hands, lest thou dash thy foot against a stone.

Thou shalt tread upon the lion and adder: the young lion and the dragon shalt thou trample under feet.

Because he hath set his love upon me, therefore will I deliver him: I will set him on high, because he hath known my name.

He shall call upon me, and I will answer him: I will be with him in trouble; I will deliver him, and honour him.

With long life will I satisfy him, and shew him my salvation.

— *From the Old Testament, Authorized (King James) Version.*

Isaiah

I

[GOD AND HIS PROMISES]

COMFORT YE, comfort ye my people, saith your God. Speak ye comfortably to Jerusalem, and cry unto her, that her warfare is accomplished, that her iniquity is pardoned: for she hath received of the Lord's hand double for all her sins.

The voice of him that crieth in the wilderness, Prepare ye the way of the Lord, make straight in the desert a highway for our God. Every valley shall be exalted, and every mountain and hill shall be made low: and the crooked shall be made straight, and the rough places plain: And the glory of the Lord shall be revealed, and all flesh shall see it together: for the mouth of the Lord hath spoken it.

The voice said, Cry.

And he said, What shall I cry? All flesh is grass, and all the goodliness thereof is as the flower of the field. The grass withereth, the flower fadeth: because the spirit of the Lord bloweth upon it: surely the people is grass. The grass withereth, the flower fadeth: but the word of our God shall stand for ever.

O Zion, that bringest good tidings, get thee up into the high mountain; O Jerusalem, that bringest good tidings, lift up thy voice with strength; lift it up, be not afraid; say unto the cities of Judah, Behold your God! Behold the Lord God will come with strong hand, and his arm shall rule for him: behold, his reward is with him, and his work before him. He shall feed his flock like a shepherd: he shall gather the lambs with his arm, and carry them in his bosom, and shall gently lead those that are with young.

Who hath measured the waters in the hollow of his hand, and meted out heaven with the span, and comprehended the dust of the earth in a measure, and weighed the mountains in scales, and the hills in a balance? Who hath directed the Spirit of the Lord, or being his counsellor hath taught him? With whom took he counsel, and who instructed him, and taught him in the path of judgment, and taught him knowledge, and shewed to him the way of understanding?

Behold, the nations are as a drop of a bucket, and are counted as the small dust of the balance: behold, he taketh up the isles as a very little thing. And Lebanon is not sufficient to burn, nor the beasts thereof sufficient for a burnt-offering. All nations before him are as nothing; and they are counted to him less than nothing, and vanity.

To whom then will ye liken God? or what likeness will ye compare unto him?

The workman melteth a graven image, and the goldsmith spreadeth it over with gold, and casteth silver chains. He that is so impoverished that he hath no oblation chooseth a tree that will not rot; he seeketh unto him a cunning workman to prepare a graven image, that shall not be moved.

Have ye not known? have ye not heard? hath it not been told you from the beginning? have ye not understood from the foundations of the earth?

It is he that sitteth upon the circle of the earth, and the inhabitants thereof are as grasshoppers; that stretcheth out the heavens as a curtain, and spreadeth them out as a tent to dwell in: that bringeth the princes to nothing; he maketh the judges of the earth as vanity.

Yea, they shall not be planted; yea, they shall not be sown; yea, their stock shall not take root in the earth: and he shall also blow upon them, and they shall wither, and the whirlwind shall take them away as stubble.

To whom then will ye liken me, or shall I be equal? saith the Holy One.

Lift up your eyes on high, and behold who hath created these things, that bringeth out their host by number: he calleth them all by names, by the greatness of his might, for that he is strong in power; not one faileth.

Why sayest thou, O Jacob, and speakest,

O Israel, My way is hid from the Lord, and my judgment is passed over from my God?

Hast thou not known? hast thou not heard, that the everlasting God, the Lord, the Creator of the ends of the earth, fainteth not, neither is weary? there is no searching of his understanding. He giveth power to the faint; and to them that have no might he increaseth strength. Even the youths shall faint and be weary, and the young men shall utterly fall: But they that wait upon the Lord shall renew their strength; they shall mount up with wings as eagles; they shall run, and not be weary; and they shall walk, and not faint.

II

[A PROMISE OF JOY AND PEACE]

HO, EVERY ONE that thirsteth, come ye to the waters, and he that hath no money; come ye, buy, and eat; yea, come, buy wine and milk without money and without price.

Wherefore do ye spend money for that which is not bread? and your labour for that which satisfieth not? hearken diligently unto me, and eat ye that which is good, and let your soul delight itself in fatness.

Incline your ear, and come unto me: hear, and your soul shall live; and I will make an everlasting covenant with you, even the sure mercies of David. Behold, I have given him for a witness to the people, a leader and commander to the people. Behold, thou shalt call a nation that thou knowest not, and nations that knew not thee shall run unto thee because of the Lord thy God, and for the Holy One of Israel; for he hath glorified thee.

Seek ye the Lord while he may be found, call ye upon him while he is near: Let the wicked forsake his way, and the unrighteous man his thoughts: and let him return unto the Lord, and he will have mercy upon him; and to our God, for he will abundantly pardon.

For my thoughts are not your thoughts, neither are your ways my ways, saith the Lord. For as the heavens are higher than the earth, so are my ways higher than your ways, and my thoughts than your thoughts.

For as the rain cometh down, and the snow from heaven, and returneth not thither, but watereth the earth, and maketh it bring forth and bud, that it may give seed to the ... and bread to the eater: so shall my ...hat goeth forth out of my mouth: ...urn unto me void, but it shall accomplish that which I please, and it shall prosper in the thing whereto I sent it.

For ye shall go out with joy, and be led forth with peace: the mountains and the hills shall break forth before you into singing, and all the trees of the field shall clap their hands. Instead of the thorn shall come up the fir-tree, and instead of the brier shall come up the myrtle tree: and it shall be to the Lord for a name, for an everlasting sign that shall not be cut off.

—*From the Old Testament: Isaiah, Chapters 40 and 55. The Authorized (King James) Version.*

Some Sayings and Discourses of Jesus

THE SERMON ON THE MOUNT

And seeing the multitudes, he went up into a mountain: and when he was set, his disciples came unto him:

And he opened his mouth, and taught them, saying,

Blessed are the poor in spirit: for theirs is the kingdom of heaven.

Blessed are they that mourn: for they shall be comforted.

Blessed are the meek: for they shall inherit the earth.

Blessed are they which do hunger and thirst after righteousness: for they shall be filled.

Blessed are the merciful: for they shall obtain mercy.

Blessed are the pure in heart: for they shall see God.

Blessed are the peacemakers: for they shall be called the children of God.

Blessed are they which are persecuted for righteousness' sake: for theirs is the kingdom of heaven.

Blessed are ye, when men shall revile you, and persecute you, and shall say all manner of evil against you falsely, for my sake. Rejoice, and be exceeding glad: for great is your reward in heaven: for so persecuted they the prophets which were before you.

Ye are the salt of the earth: but if the salt have lost his savour, wherewith shall it be salted? it is thenceforth good for nothing, but to be cast out, and to be trodden under foot of men.

Ye are the light of the world. A city that

is set on a hill cannot be hid. Neither do men light a candle, and put it under a bushel, but on a candlestick; and it giveth light unto all that are in the house. Let your light so shine before men, that they may see your good works, and glorify your Father which is in heaven.

Think not that I am come to destroy the law, or the prophets: I am not come to destroy, but to fulfil. For verily I say unto you, Till heaven and earth pass, one jot or one tittle shall in no wise pass from the law, till all be fulfilled. Whosoever therefore shall break one of these least commandments, and shall teach men so, he shall be called the least in the kingdom of heaven: but whosoever shall do and teach them, the same shall be called great in the kingdom of heaven. For I say unto you, That except your righteousness shall exceed the righteousness of the scribes and Pharisees, ye shall in no case enter into the kingdom of heaven.

Ye have heard that it was said by them of old time, Thou shalt not kill; and whosoever shall kill shall be in danger of the judgment. But I say unto you, That whosoever is angry with his brother without a cause shall be in danger of the judgment: and whosoever shall say to his brother, Raca, shall be in danger of the council: but whosoever shall say, Thou fool, shall be in danger of hell fire. Therefore if thou bring thy gift to the altar, and there rememberest that thy brother hath aught against thee, leave there thy gift before the altar, and go thy way; first be reconciled to thy brother, and then come and offer thy gift.

Agree with thine adversary quickly, while thou art in the way with him; lest at any time the adversary deliver thee to the judge, and the judge deliver thee to the officer, and thou be cast into prison. Verily I say unto thee, Thou shalt by no means come out thence, till thou hast paid the uttermost farthing.

Ye have heard that it was said by them of old time, Thou shalt not commit adultery. But I say unto you, That whosoever looketh on a woman to lust after her hath committed adultery with her already in his heart.

And if thy right eye offend thee, pluck it out, and cast it from thee: for it is profitable for thee that one of thy members should perish, and not that thy whole body should be cast into hell. And if thy right hand offend thee, cut it off, and cast it from thee: for it is profitable for thee that one of thy members should perish, and not that thy whole body should be cast into hell.

It hath been said, Whosoever shall put away his wife, let him give her a writing of divorcement: But I say unto you, That whosoever shall put away his wife, saving for the cause of fornication, causeth her to commit adultery: and whosoever shall marry her that is divorced committeth adultery.

Again, ye have heard that it hath been said by them of old time, Thou shalt not forswear thyself, but shalt perform unto the Lord thine oaths: But I say unto you, Swear not at all; neither by heaven; for it is God's throne: nor by the earth; for it is his footstool: neither by Jerusalem; for it is the city of the great King. Neither shalt thou swear by thy head, because thou canst not make one hair white or black. But let your communication be, Yea, yea; Nay, nay: for whatsoever is more than these cometh of evil.

Ye have heard that it hath been said, An eye for an eye, and a tooth for a tooth: But I say unto you, That ye resist not evil: but whosoever shall smite thee on thy right cheek, turn to him the other also. And if any man will sue thee at the law, and take away thy coat, let him have thy cloak also. And whosoever shall compel thee to go a mile, go with him twain. Give to him that asketh thee, and from him that would borrow of thee turn not thou away.

Ye have heard that it hath been said, Thou shalt love thy neighbour, and hate thine enemy. But I say unto you, Love your enemies, bless them that curse you, do good to them that hate you, and pray for them which despitefully use you, and persecute you; that ye may be the children of your Father which is in heaven: for he maketh his sun to rise on the evil and on the good, and sendeth rain on the just and on the unjust.

For if ye love them which love you, what reward have ye? do not even the publicans the same? And if ye salute your brethren only, what do ye more than others? do not even the publicans so?

Be ye therefore perfect, even as your Father which is in heaven is perfect.

Take heed that ye do not your alms before men, to be seen of them: otherwise ye have no reward of your Father which is in heaven. Therefore when thou doest thine alms, do not sound a trumpet before thee, as the hypocrites do in the synagogues and in the streets, that they may have glory of men. Verily I say unto you, They have their reward. But when thou doest alms, let not thy left hand know what thy right hand doeth: that thine alms may be in secret: and thy Father which seeth in secret himself shall reward thee openly.

And when thou prayest, thou shalt not be as the hypocrites are: for they love to pray standing in the synagogues and in the corners of the streets, that they may be seen of men. Verily I say unto you, They have their reward. But thou, when thou prayest, enter into thy closet, and when thou hast shut thy door, pray to thy Father which is in secret; and thy Father which seeth in secret shall reward thee openly. But when ye pray, use not vain repetitions, as the heathen do: for they think that they shall be heard for their much speaking. Be not ye therefore like unto them, for your Father knoweth what things ye have need of, before ye ask him.

After this manner therefore pray ye:

Our Father which art in heaven, Hallowed be thy name. Thy kingdom come. Thy will be done in earth, as it is in heaven. Give us this day our daily bread. And forgive us our debts, as we forgive our debtors. And lead us not into temptation, but deliver us from evil: For thine is the kingdom, and the power, and the glory, for ever. Amen.

For if ye forgive men their trespasses, your heavenly Father will also forgive you. But if ye forgive not men their trespasses, neither will your Father forgive your trespasses.

Moreover when ye fast, be not, as the hypocrites, of a sad countenance: for they disfigure their faces, that they may appear unto men to fast. Verily I say unto you, They have their reward. But thou, when thou fastest, anoint thine head, and wash thy face; that thou appear not unto men to fast, but unto thy Father which is in secret: and thy Father which seeth in secret, shall reward thee openly.

Lay not up for yourselves treasures upon earth, where moth and rust doth corrupt, and where thieves break through and steal: But lay up for yourselves treasures in heaven, where neither moth nor rust doth corrupt, and where thieves do not break through nor steal: For where your treasure is, there will your heart be also.

The light of the body is the eye: if therefore thine eye be single, thy whole body shall be full of light. But if thine eye be evil, thy whole body shall be full of darkness. If therefore the light that is in thee be darkness, how great is that darkness!

No man can serve two masters: for either he will hate the one, and love the other; or else he will hold to the one, and despise the other. Ye cannot serve God and mammon.

Therefore I say unto you, Take no thought for your life, what ye shall eat, or what ye shall drink; nor yet for your body, what ye shall put on. Is not the life more than meat, and the body than raiment? Behold the fowls of the air: for they sow not, neither do they reap, nor gather into barns; yet your heavenly Father feedeth them. Are ye not much better than they? Which of you by taking thought can add one cubit unto his stature? And why take ye thought for raiment? Consider the lilies of the field, how they grow; they toil not, neither do they spin: and yet I say unto you, That even Solomon in all his glory was not arrayed like one of these. Wherefore, if God so clothe the grass of the field, which to-day is, and to-morrow is cast into the oven, shall he not much more clothe you, O ye of little faith?

Therefore take no thought, saying, What shall we eat? or, What shall we drink? or, Wherewithal shall we be clothed? (For after all these things do the Gentiles seek:) for your heavenly Father knoweth that ye have need of all these things. But seek ye first the kingdom of God, and his righteousness; and all these things shall be added unto you. Take therefore no thought for the morrow: for the morrow shall take thought for the things of itself. Sufficient unto the day is the evil thereof.

Judge not, that ye be not judged. For with what judgment ye judge, ye shall be judged: and with what measure ye mete, it shall be measured to you again. And why beholdest thou the mote that is in thy brother's eye, but considerest not the beam that is in thine own eye? Or how wilt thou say to thy brother, Let me pull out the mote out of thine eye; and, behold, a beam is in thine own eye? Thou hypocrite, first cast out the beam out of thine own eye; and then shalt thou see clearly to cast out the mote out of thy brother's eye.

Give not that which is holy unto the dogs, neither cast ye your pearls before swine, lest they trample them under their feet, and turn again and rend you.

Ask, and it shall be given you; seek, and ye shall find; knock, and it shall be opened unto you. For every one that asketh receiveth; and he that seeketh findeth; and to him that knocketh it shall be opened. Or what man is there of you, whom if his son ask bread, will he give him a stone? Or if he ask a fish, will he give him a serpent? If ye then, being evil, know how to give good gifts unto your children, how much more shall your Father which is in heaven give good things to them that ask him?

Therefore all things whatsoever ye would that men should do to you, do ye even so to them: for this is the law and the prophets.

Enter ye in at the strait gate: for wide is the gate, and broad is the way, that leadeth to destruction, and many there be which go in thereat: because strait is the gate, and narrow is the way, which leadeth unto life, and few there be that find it.

Beware of false prophets, which come to you in sheep's clothing, but inwardly they are ravening wolves. Ye shall know them by their fruits. Do men gather grapes of thorns, or figs of thistles? Even so every good tree bringeth forth good fruit; but a corrupt tree bringeth forth evil fruit. A good tree cannot bring forth evil fruit, neither can a corrupt tree bring forth good fruit. Every tree that bringeth not forth good fruit is hewn down, and cast into the fire. Wherefore by their fruits ye shall know them.

Not every one that saith unto me, Lord, Lord, shall enter into the kingdom of heaven; but he that doeth the will of my Father which is in heaven. Many will say to me in that day, Lord, Lord, have we not prophesied in thy name? and in thy name have cast out devils? and in thy name done many wonderful works? And then will I profess unto them, I never knew you: depart from me, ye that work iniquity.

Therefore whosoever heareth these sayings of mine, and doeth them, I will liken him unto a wise man, which built his house upon a rock: and the rain descended, and the floods came, and the winds blew, and beat upon that house; and it fell not: for it was founded upon a rock.

And every one that heareth these sayings of mine, and doeth them not, shall be likened unto a foolish man, which built his house upon the sand: and the rain descended, and the floods came, and the winds blew, and beat upon that house; and it fell: and great was the fall of it.

And it came to pass, when Jesus had ended these sayings, the people were astonished at his doctrine, for he taught them as one having authority, and not as the scribes.

—*From the Gospel According to Matthew, Chapters 5, 6 and 7.*

THE GOOD SHEPHERD

Verily, verily, I say unto you, He that entereth not by the door into the sheepfold, but climbeth up some other way, the same is a thief and a robber. But he that entereth in by the door is the shepherd of the sheep. To him the porter openeth; and the sheep hear his voice: and he calleth his own sheep by name, and leadeth them out. And when he putteth forth his own sheep, he goeth before them, and the sheep follow him: for they know his voice. And a stranger will they not follow, but will flee from him: for they know not the voice of strangers.

This parable spake Jesus unto them; but they understood not what things they were which he spake unto them.

Then said Jesus unto them again, Verily, verily, I say unto you, I am the door of the sheep. All that ever came before me are thieves and robbers: but the sheep did not hear them. I am the door: by me if any man enter in, he shall be saved, and shall go in and out, and find pasture.

The thief cometh not, but for to steal, and to kill, and to destroy: I am come that they might have life, and that they might have it more abundantly. I am the good shepherd: the good shepherd giveth his life for the sheep. But he that is an hireling, and not the shepherd, whose own the sheep are not, seeth the wolf coming, and leaveth the sheep, and fleeth: and the wolf catcheth them, and scattereth the sheep. The hireling fleeth, because he is an hireling, and careth not for the sheep.

I am the good shepherd, and know my sheep, and am known of mine. As the Father knoweth me, even so know I the Father: and I lay down my life for the sheep. And other sheep I have, which are not of this fold: them also I must bring, and they shall hear my voice; and there shall be one fold, and one shepherd.

Therefore doth my Father love me, because I lay down my life, that I might take it again. No man taketh it from me, but I lay it down of myself. I have power to lay it down, and I have power to take it again. This commandment have I received of my Father.

There was a division therefore again among the Jews for these sayings, and many of them said, He hath a devil, and is mad; why hear ye him? Others said, These are not the words of him that hath a devil. Can a devil open the eyes of the blind?

And it was at Jerusalem the feast of the dedication, and it was winter. And Jesus walked in the temple in Solomon's porch. Then came the Jews round about him, and said unto him, How long dost thou make us to doubt? If thou be the Christ, tell us plainly.

Jesus answered them, I told you, and ye believed not: the works that I do in my Father's name, they bear witness of me. But ye believe not, because ye are not of my sheep, as I said unto you. My sheep hear my voice, and I know them, and they follow me: and I give unto them eternal life; and they shall never perish, neither shall any man pluck them out of my hand.

My Father, which gave them me, is greater than all; and no man is able to pluck them out of my Father's hand. I and my Father are one.

—*From the Gospel According to John, Chapter 10.*

CHILDREN OF THE LIGHT

And Jesus answered them, saying, The hour is come, that the Son of man should be glorified.

Verily, verily, I say unto you, Except a corn of wheat fall into the ground and die, it abideth alone: but if it die, it bringeth forth much fruit. He that loveth his life shall lose it; and he that hateth his life in this world shall keep it unto life eternal. If any man serve me, let him follow me; and where I am, there shall also my servant be: if any man serve me, him will my Father honour.

Now is my soul troubled; and what shall I say? Father, save me from this hour: but for this cause came I unto this hour. Father, glorify thy name.

Then came there a voice from heaven, saying, I have both glorified it, and will glorify it again. The people therefore that stood by, and heard it, said that it thundered: others said, An angel spake to him.

Jesus answered and said, This voice came not because of me, but for your sakes. Now is the judgment of this world; now shall the prince of this world be cast out. And I, if I be lifted up from the earth, will draw all men unto me.

This he said, signifying what death he should die. The people answered him, We have heard out of the law that Christ abideth for ever: and how sayest thou, The Son of man must be lifted up? who is this Son of man?

Then Jesus said unto them, Yet a little while is the light with you. Walk while ye have the light, lest darkness come upon you: for he that walketh in darkness knoweth not whither he goeth. While ye have light, believe in the light, that ye may be the children of light.

These things spake Jesus, and departed, and did hide himself from them.

—*From the Gospel According to John, Chapter 12.*

THE LIGHT OF THE WORLD

He that believeth on me, believeth not on me, but on him that sent me. And he that seeth me seeth him that sent me.

I am come a light into the world, that whosoever believeth on me should not abide in darkness.

And if any man hear my words, and believe not, I judge him not: for I came not to judge the world, but to save the world. He that rejecteth me, and receiveth not my words, hath one that judgeth him: the word that I have spoken, the same shall judge him in the last day.

For I have not spoken of myself; but the Father which sent me, he gave me a commandment, what I should say, and what I should speak. And I know that his commandment is life everlasting: whatsoever I speak therefore, even as the Father said unto me, so I speak.

—*From the Gospel According to John, Chapter 12.*

MY PEACE I GIVE UNTO YOU

Let not your heart be troubled: ye believe in God, believe also in me. In my Father's house are many mansions: if it were not so, I would have told you. I go to prepare a place for you. And if I go and prepare a place for you, I will come again, and receive you unto myself; that where I am, there ye may be also. And whither I go ye know, and the way ye know.

Thomas saith unto him, Lord, we know not whither thou goest; and how can we know the way?

Jesus saith unto him, I am the way, the truth, and the life: no man cometh unto the Father, but by me. If ye had known me, ye should have known my Father also: and from henceforth ye know him, and have seen him.

Philip saith unto him, Lord, shew us the Father, and it sufficeth us.

Jesus saith unto him, Have I been so long time with you, and yet hast thou not known me, Philip? he that hath seen me hath seen the Father; and how sayest thou then, Shew us the Father? Believest thou not that I am in the Father, and the Father in me? the words that I speak unto you I speak not of myself: but the Father that dwelleth in me, he doeth the works. Believe me that I am in the Father, and the Father in me: or else believe me for the very works' sake.

Verily, verily, I say unto you, He that believeth on me, the works that I do shall he do also; and greater works than these shall he do; because I go unto my Father.

And whatsoever ye shall ask in my name, that will I do, that the Father may be glorified in the Son. If ye shall ask any thing in my name, I will do it.

If ye love me, keep my commandments. And I will pray the Father, and he shall give you another Comforter, that he may abide with you for ever, even the Spirit of truth; whom the world cannot receive, because it seeth him not, neither knoweth him: but ye know him; for he dwelleth with you, and shall be in you.

I will not leave you comfortless: I will come to you. Yet a little while, and the world seeth me no more; but ye see me: because I live, ye shall live also. At that day ye shall know that I am in my Father, and ye in me, and I in you.

He that hath my commandments, and keepeth them, he it is that loveth me; and he that loveth me shall be loved of my Father, and I will love him, and will manifest myself to him.

Judas saith unto him, not Iscariot, Lord, how is it that thou wilt manifest thyself unto us, and not unto the world?

Jesus answered and said unto him, If a man love me, he will keep my words: and my Father will love him, and we will come unto him, and make our abode with him. He that loveth me not keepeth not my sayings: and the word which ye hear is not mine, but the Father's which sent me.

These things have I spoken unto you, being yet present with you. But the Comforter, which is the Holy Ghost, whom the Father will send in my name, he shall teach you all things, and bring all things to your remembrance, whatsoever I have said unto you.

Peace I leave with you, my peace I give unto you: not as the world giveth, give I unto you. Let not your heart be troubled, neither let it be afraid. Ye have heard how I said unto you, I go away, and come again unto you. If ye loved me, ye would rejoice, because I said, I go unto the Father: for my Father is greater than I.

And now I have told you before it come to pass, that, when it is come to pass, ye might believe. Hereafter I will not talk much with you: for the prince of this world cometh, and hath nothing in me. But that the world may know that I love the Father; and as the Father gave me commandment, even so I do. Arise, let us go hence.

—*From the Gospel According to John, Chapter 14.*

THE TRUE VINE

I am the true vine, and my Father is the husbandman. Every branch in me that beareth not fruit he taketh away: and every branch that beareth fruit, he purgeth it, that it may bring forth more fruit.

Now ye are clean through the word which I have spoken unto you.

Abide in me, and I in you. As the branch cannot bear fruit of itself, except it abide in the vine; no more can ye, except ye abide in me. I am the vine, ye are the branches. He that abideth in me, and I in him, the same bringeth forth much fruit: for without me ye can do nothing. If a man abide not in me, he is cast forth as a branch, and is withered; and men gather them, and cast them into the fire, and they are burned. If ye abide in me, and my words abide in you, ye shall ask what ye will, and it shall be done unto you.

Herein is my Father glorified, that ye bear much fruit; so shall ye be my disciples. As the Father hath loved me, so have I loved you: continue ye in my love. If ye keep my commandments, ye shall abide in my love; even as I have kept my Father's commandments, and abide in his love. These things have I spoken unto you, that my joy might remain in you, and that your joy might be full.

This is my commandment, That ye love one another, as I have loved you. Greater love hath no man than this, that a man lay down his life for his friends.

Ye are my friends, if ye do whatsoever I command you. Henceforth I call you not servants; for the servant knoweth not what his lord doeth: but I have called you friends; for all things that I have heard of my Father I have made known unto you. Ye have not chosen me, but I have chosen you, and ordained you, that ye should go and bring forth fruit, and that your fruit should remain; that whatsoever ye shall ask of the Father in my name, he may give it you.

These things I command you, that ye love one another.

If the world hate you, ye know that it hated me before it hated you. If ye were of the world, the world would love his own; but because ye are not of the world, but I have chosen you out of the world, therefore the world hateth you.

Remember the word that I said unto you, The servant is not greater than his lord. If they have persecuted me, they will also persecute you; if they have kept my saying, they will keep yours also. But all these things will they do unto you for my name's sake, because they know not him that sent me.

If I had not come and spoken unto them, they had not had sin; but now they have no cloak for their sin.

He that hateth me hateth my Father also.

If I had not done among them the works which none other man did, they had not had sin: but now have they both seen and hated both me and my Father. But this cometh to pass, that the word might be fulfilled that is written in their law, They hated me without a cause.

But when the Comforter is come, whom I will send unto you from the Father, even the Spirit of truth, which proceedeth from the Father, he shall testify of me. And ye also shall bear witness, because ye have been with me from the beginning.

—*From the Gospel According to John, Chapter 15.*

BE OF GOOD CHEER

These things have I spoken unto you, that ye should not be offended.

They shall put you out of the synagogues: yea, the time cometh, that whosoever killeth you will think that he doeth God service. And these things will they do unto you, because they have not known the Father, nor me.

But these things have I told you, that when the time shall come, ye may remember that I told you of them. And these things I said not unto you at the beginning, because I was with you. But now I go my way to him that sent me; and none of you asketh me, Whither goest thou? But because I have said these things unto you, sorrow hath filled your heart.

Nevertheless I tell you the truth; It is expedient for you that I go away, for if I go not away, the Comforter will not come unto you; but if I depart, I will send him unto you. And when he is come, he will reprove the world of sin, and of righteousness, and of judgment; of sin, because they believe not on me; of righteousness because I go to my Father, and ye see me no more; of judgment, because the prince of this world is judged.

I have yet many things to say unto you, but ye cannot bear them now. Howbeit when he, the Spirit of truth, is come, he will guide you into all truth: for he shall not speak of himself; but whatsoever he shall hear, that shall he speak, and he will shew you things to come. He shall glorify me, for he shall receive of mine, and shall shew it unto you.

All things that the Father hath are mine: therefore said I, that he shall take of mine, and shall shew it unto you.

A little while, and ye shall not see me: and again, a little while, and ye shall see me, because I go to the Father.

Then said some of his disciples among themselves, What is this that he saith unto us, A little while, and ye shall not see me: and again, a little while, and ye shall see me: and, Because I go to the Father? They said therefore, What is this that he saith, A little while? we cannot tell what he saith.

Now Jesus knew that they were desirous to ask him, and said unto them, Do ye inquire among yourselves of that I said, A little while, and ye shall not see me: and again, a little while, and ye shall see me? Verily, verily, I say unto you, That ye shall weep and lament, but the world shall rejoice; and ye shall be sorrowful, but your sorrow shall be turned into joy.

A woman when she is in travail hath sorrow, because her hour is come; but as soon as she is delivered of the child, she remembereth no more the anguish, for joy that a man is born into the world. And ye now therefore have sorrow, but I will see you again, and your heart shall rejoice, and your joy no man taketh from you.

And in that day ye shall ask me nothing. Verily, verily, I say unto you, Whatsoever ye shall ask the Father in my name, he will give it you. Hitherto have ye asked nothing in my name: ask, and ye shall receive, that your joy may be full.

These things have I spoken unto you in proverbs: but the time cometh, when I shall no more speak unto you in proverbs, but I shall show you plainly of the Father. At that day ye shall ask in my name: and I say not unto you, that I will pray the Father for you: for the Father himself loveth you, because ye have loved me, and have believed that I came out from God.

I came forth from the Father, and am come into the world: again, I leave the world, and go to the Father.

His disciples said unto him, Lo, now speakest thou plainly, and speakest no proverb. Now are we sure that thou knowest all things, and needest not that any man should ask thee: by this we believe that thou camest forth from God.

Jesus answered them, Do you now believe? Behold, the hour cometh, yea, is now come, that ye shall be scattered, every man to his own, and shall leave me alone: and yet I am not alone, because the Father is with me.

These things I have spoken unto you, that in me ye might have peace. In the world ye shall have tribulation: but be of good cheer; I have overcome the world.

—From the Gospel According to John, Chapter 16.

SPIRITUAL GIFTS

ST. PAUL

Now concerning spiritual gifts, brethren, I would not have you ignorant. Ye know that ye were Gentiles, carried away unto these dumb idols, even as ye were led. Wherefore I give you to understand, that no man speaking by the Spirit of God calleth Jesus accursed: and that no man can say that Jesus is the Lord, but by the Holy Ghost.

Now there are diversities of gifts, but the same Spirit. And there are differences of administrations, but the same Lord. And there are diversities of operations, but it is the same God which worketh all in all. But the manifestation of the Spirit is given to every man to profit withal.

For to one is given by the Spirit the word of wisdom; to another, the word of knowledge by the same Spirit; to another, faith by the same Spirit; to another, the gifts of healing by the same Spirit; to another, the working of miracles; to another, prophecy; to another, discerning of spirits; to another, divers kinds of tongues; to another, the interpretation of tongues: but all these worketh that one and the self-same Spirit, dividing to every man severally as he will.

For as the body is one, and hath many members, and all the members of that one body, being many, are one body: so also is Christ. For by one Spirit are we all baptized into one body, whether we be Jews or Gentiles, whether we be bond or free; and have been all made to drink into one Spirit.

For the body is not one member, but many. If the foot shall say, Because I am not the hand, I am not of the body; is it therefore not of the body? And if the ear shall say, Because I am not the eye, I am not of the body; is it therefore not of the body? If the whole body were an eye, where were the hearing? If the whole were hearing, where were the smelling? But now hath God set the members every one of them in the body, as it hath pleased him.

And if they were all one member, where were the body? But now are they many members, yet but one body. And the eye cannot say unto the hand, I have no need of thee: nor again the head to the feet, I have no need of you.

Nay, much more those members of the body, which seem to be more feeble, are necessary: and those members of the body, which we think to be less honourable, upon these we bestow more abundant honour; and our uncomely parts have more abundant comeliness. For our comely parts have no need: but God hath tempered the body together, having given more abundant honour to that part which lacked: that there should be no schism in the body; but that the members should have the same care one for another. And whether one member suffer, all the members suffer with it; or one member be honoured, all the members rejoice with it.

Now ye are the body of Christ, and members in particular. And God hath set some in the church, first apostles, secondarily prophets, thirdly teachers, after that miracles, then gifts of healings, helps, governments, diversities of tongues.

Are all apostles? are all prophets? are all teachers? are all workers of miracles? have all the gifts of healing? do all speak with tongues? do all interpret?

But covet earnestly the best gifts. And yet shew I unto you a more excellent way.

Though I speak with the tongues of men and of angels, and have not charity, I am become as sounding brass, or a tinkling cymbal. And though I have the gift of prophecy, and understand all mysteries, and all knowledge; and though I have all faith, so that I could remove mountains, and have not charity, I am nothing. And though I bestow all my goods to feed the poor, and though I give my body to be burned, and have not charity, it profiteth me nothing.

Charity suffereth long, and is kind; charity envieth not; charity vaunteth not itself, is not puffed up, doth not behave itself unseemly, seeketh not her own, is not easily provoked, thinketh no evil; rejoiceth not in iniquity, but rejoiceth in the truth; beareth all things, believeth all things, hopeth all things, endureth all things.

Charity never faileth: but whether there be prophecies, they shall fail; whether there be tongues, they shall cease; whether there be knowledge, it shall vanish away.

For we know in part, and we prophesy in part. But when that which is perfect is come, then that which is in part shall be done away.

When I was a child, I spake as a child, I understood as a child, I thought as a child: but when I became a man, I put away childish things. For now we see through a glass, darkly; but then face to face: now I know in part; but then shall I know even as also I am known.

And now abideth faith, hope, charity, these three; but the greatest of these is charity.

—From the First Epistle to the Corinthians, New Testament, Chapters 12 and 13.

∽ ✿ ∼

4. MOHAMMEDANISM

The Teaching of Mohammed

BLOOD CLOTS

In the Name of God, the Compassionate, the Merciful.[1]
Read! in the name of thy Lord who created; —
Created man from clots of blood: —
Read! For thy Lord is the most beneficent,
Who hath taught the use of the pen; —
Hath taught man that which he knew not.

Nay, verily, man is most extravagant in wickedness
Because he seeth himself possessed of wealth.
Verily unto the Lord is the return of all.
What thinkest thou of him who forbiddeth
A servant of God when he prayeth?
What thinkest thou? that he hath followed the true guidance or enjoined piety?
What thinkest thou, if he hath treated the truth as a lie and turned his back?
Doth he not know that God seeth?
Nay, verily, if he desist not, we will assuredly seize him by the forelock,
The lying sinful forelock!
Then let him summon his associates;
We too will summon the guards of hell:
Nay! obey him not; but adore, and draw nigh to God.

JUDGMENT

When the sun shall be folded up,
And when the stars shall shoot downwards,
And when the mountains shall be set in motion,
And when the camels ten months gone with foal shall be abandoned,
And when the wild beasts shall be gathered together,
And when the seas shall be swollen,
And when souls shall be paired with their bodies,
And when the damsel that had been buried alive shall be asked
For what crime she was put to death,
And when the leaves of the Book shall be unrolled,
And when the heaven shall be stripped away,
And when hell shall be made to blaze,
And when paradise shall be brought near,
Every soul shall know what it hath produced.

[1] This formula is prefixed to each "Sura," or Revelation of the *Koran.*

And I swear by the stars of retrograde motion,
Which move swiftly and hide themselves away,
And by the night when it cometh darkening on,
And by the dawn when it clears away the darkness by its breath,
That verily this is the word of an illustrious messenger,
Powerful with the Lord of the throne, of established rank,
Obeyed by angels, faithful also to his trust,
And your compatriot is not one possessed by djinn;
For he saw him in the clear horizon:
Nor doth he keep back heaven's secrets,
Nor doth he teach the doctrine of a cursed Satan.
Whither then are ye going?
Verily this Koran is no other than a warning to all creatures;
To him among you who willeth to walk in a straight path:
But will it ye shall not, unless as God willeth it, Lord of the worlds.

THE RESPLENDENT

By the noon-day brightness,
And by the night when it darkeneth!
Thy Lord hath not forsaken thee, neither hath he hated thee,
And surely the future shall be better for thee than the present,
And thy Lord shall assuredly be bounteous to thee and thou be satisfied.
Did he not find thee an orphan and provide thee a home?
And he found thee erring and guided thee,
And found thee needy and enriched thee.
As to the orphan therefore wrong him not;
And as to him that asketh of thee, chide him not away;
And as for the favours of thy Lord, tell them then abroad.

WOE TO THE STINTER

Woe to those who stint the measure:
Who when they take by measure from others, exact the full;
But when they mete to them or weigh to them,. minish —
Have they no thought that they shall be raised again
For a great day,
A day when mankind shall stand before the Lord of the worlds?

Nay, verily, the register of the wicked is in Sidjin;
And what shall make thee understand what Sidjin is?
It is a book distinctly written.
Woe, on that day, to those who treated our signs as lies,
Who treated the day of judgment as a lie!
But none treat it as a lie, save the transgressor, the criminal,
Who, when our signs are rehearsed to him, saith, "Tales of the ancients!"
Nay, but their own works have got the mastery over their hearts:
Yes; they shall surely be shut out as by a veil from their Lord on that day;
Then shall they be surely burned in hell-fire:
Then shall it be said to them, "This is what ye deemed a lie."

Nay, verily the register of the righteous is in Illiyoun;
And what shall make thee understand what Illiyoun is?
A book distinctly written;
The angels who draw nigh unto God attest it.
Surely among delights shall the righteous dwell!
Seated on bridal couches they will gaze around;
Thou shalt mark in their faces the brightness of delight;
Choice sealed wine shall be given them to quaff, —
The seal of musk. — For this let those pant who pant for bliss —
Mingled therewith shall be the waters of Tasnim —
Fount whereof they who draw nigh to God shall drink.
The sinners indeed laugh the faithful to scorn:
And when they pass by them they wink at one another, —
And when they return to their own people, they return jesting,
And when they see them they say, "Verily these are the erring ones."
And yet they have no mission to be their guardians.
Therefore, on that day the faithful shall laugh the infidels to scorn,

As reclining on bridal couches they behold them.
Is there a repayment to the unbelievers in accordance with their deeds?

THE DAY

By the mountain,
And by the Book written
On an outspread scroll,
And by the frequented fane,
And by heaven's lofty roof,
And by the swollen sea,
Verily, a chastisement from thy Lord is most imminent,
And none shall put it back.
With reeling on that day the heaven shall reel,
And with moving shall the mountains move,
And woe, on that day, to those who called the apostles liars,
Who plunged for pastime into vain disputes —
On that day shall they be thrust with thrusting to the fire of hell: —
"This is the fire which ye treated as a lie!
Is it magic, then? or, do ye not see it?
Burn ye therein: and bear it patiently or impatiently it will be the same to you: ye only receive the reward of your doings."

But 'mid gardens and delights shall they dwell who have feared God,
Rejoicing in what their Lord hath given them; and that from the pain of hell-fire hath their Lord preserved them.
"Eat and drink with healthy enjoyment, in recompense for your deeds."
On couches ranged in rows shall they recline; and to the damsels with large dark eyes will we wed them.
And to those who have believed, whose offspring have followed them in the faith, will we again unite their offspring; nor of the meed of their works will we in the least defraud them. Pledged to God is every man for his actions.
And fruits in abundance will we bestow on them, and such flesh as they shall desire;
Therein shall they present to one another the cup which shall engender no light discourse, no motive to sin:
And youths shall go round unto them beautiful as imbedded pearls:
And they shall accost one another and ask mutual questions.
"A time indeed there was," will they say, "when we were full of care as to the future lot of our families;
But kind hath God been to us, and from the pestilential torment of the scorching wind hath he preserved us;
Verily, heretofore we called upon him — and he of a truth, he is the Beneficent, the Merciful."
Warn thou, then. For thou by the favour of thy Lord art neither soothsayer nor possessed.

Or will they say, "A poet! let us await some adverse turn of his fortune"?
Say, wait ye, and in sooth I too will wait with you.
Or is it their dreams which inspire them with this? or is it that they are a perverse people?
Or say they, "He hath forged it (the Koran) himself"? Nay rather, they will not believe.
Let them then produce a discourse like it, if they speak the truth.
Or were they created of nothing? or were they the creators of themselves?
Or created they the heavens and earth? Nay rather, they have no faith.
Or hold they thy Lord's treasures? or bear they the rule supreme?
Or have they a ladder for hearing the angels? Then let any one who hath heard them bring a clear proof of it.
Or hath God the daughters, and ye the sons?
Or askest thou pay of them? But they are themselves weighed down with debts.
Or have they a knowledge of the secret things? Then let them write them down.
Or desire they to lay snares for thee? But the snared ones are they who do not believe.
Or have they any god beside God? Glory be to God above what they join with him.
And should they see a fragment of the heaven falling down, they would say, "It is only a dense cloud."
Leave them then until they come face to face with their day wherein they shall swoon away;
A day in which their snares shall not at all avail them, neither shall they be helped.
And verily, beside this is there a punishment for the evil-doers: but most of them know it not.
But wait thou patiently the judgment of thy Lord, for verily thou art in our eye; and

celebrate the praise of thy Lord when thou risest up,
And in the night-season: and praise him at the waning of the stars.

GOD OF MERCY

The God of mercy hath taught the Koran,
Hath created man,
Hath taught him articulate speech.
The sun and the moon have each their times,
And the plants and the trees bend in adoration.
And the heaven, he hath reared it on high; and he hath appointed the balance,
That in the balance ye should not transgress;
Weigh therefore with fairness, and scant not the balance.
And the earth, he hath prepared it for the living tribes:
Therein are fruits, and the palms with sheathed clusters,
And the grain with its husk, and the supports of life.
Which then of the bounties of your Lord will ye twain deny?
He created man of clay like an earthen vessel,
And he created the djinn of pure fire:
Which then of the bounties of your Lord will ye twain deny?
He is Lord of the East,
And He is Lord of the West:
Which then of the bounties of your Lord will ye twain deny?
He hath let loose the two seas which meet each other:
Yet between them is a barrier which they overpass not:
Which then of the bounties of your Lord will ye twain deny?
From each he bringeth up the pearls both great and small:
Which then of the bounties of your Lord will ye twain deny?
And his are the ships towering up at sea like the tall mountains:
Which then of the bounties of your Lord will ye twain deny?
All on the earth passeth away,
But the face of thy Lord abideth in its majesty and glory:
Which then of the bounties of your Lord will ye twain deny?
To him maketh suit all that is in the heaven and the earth; every day doth he work:
Which then of the bounties of your Lord will ye twain deny?
We will settle accounts with you, O ye men and djinn:
Which then of the bounties of your Lord will ye twain deny?

THE END

And when the doom shall light upon them, we will cause a monster to come forth to them out of the earth, and cry to them, that "mankind have not firmly believed our signs" (revelations).
And on that day will we gather out of every nation a company of those who have gainsaid our signs, and they shall be kept marching in ranks
Till they come before God, who will say, "Treated ye my signs as impostures, although ye embraced them not in your knowledge? What is it that ye have done?"
And doom shall light upon them for their evil deeds, and nought shall they have to plead.
See they not that we have ordained the night that they may rest in it, and the day with its gift of light? Of a truth herein are signs to people who believe.
On that day there shall be a blast on the trumpet, and all that are in the heavens, and all that are on the earth, shall be terror-stricken, save him whom God pleaseth to deliver; and all shall come to him in humble guise.
And thou shalt see the mountains, which thou thinkest so firmly fixed, pass away with the passing of a cloud! 'Tis the work of God, who ordereth all things! Lo! He is well aware of your actions.
He who shall present himself with good works, shall reap the benefit therefrom, and they shall be secure from terror on that day;
And they who shall present themselves with evil shall therefore be flung face downwards into the fire. Shall ye be recompensed but as ye have wrought?

Say: Specially am I commanded to worship the Lord of this land, which he hath sanctified. And all things are his: and I am commanded to be one of those who surrender themselves to God (a Muslim),
And to recite the Koran: and whoever is rightly guided, will be rightly guided only

to his own behoof; and as to him who erreth, then say, I truly am a warner only.

And say, Praise be to God! He will show you his signs, and ye shall acknowledge them: and of what ye do, thy Lord is not regardless.

RITUALISTIC AND MORAL PRESCRIPTIONS

There is no piety in turning your faces toward the east or the west, but he is pious who believeth in God and the last day and the angels and the scriptures and the prophets; who for the love of God disburseth his wealth to his kindred, and to the orphans, and the needy, and the wayfarer, and those who ask, and for ransoming; who observeth prayer, and payeth the legal alms, and who is one of those who are faithful to their engagements when they have engaged in them, and patient under ills and hardships and in time of trouble: these are they who are just, and these are they who fear God.

O believers! retaliation for bloodshedding is prescribed to you: the free man for the free, and the slave for the slave, and the woman for the woman: but he to whom his brother shall make any remission is to be dealt with equitably; and a payment should be made to him with liberality.

This is a relaxation from your Lord and a mercy. For him therefore who after this shall transgress, a sore punishment!

But in this law of retaliation is your security for life, O men of understanding! Haply ye will fear God.

It is prescribed to you when any one of you is at the point of death, that if he leave goods, he bequeath equitably to his parents and kindred; this is binding on those who fear God: —

Whoso then after he hath heard what a bequest is shall change it, the guilt of this shall be on those only who alter it; verily, God heareth, knoweth:

But he who feareth from the testator any mistake or wrong, and shall make a settlement between the parties — that then shall be no guilt in him; verily, God is forgiving, merciful.

O believers! a fast is prescribed to you, as it was prescribed to those before you, that ye may fear God,

For certain days. But he among you who shall be sick, or on a journey, shall fast that same number of other days: and for those who are able to keep it and yet break it, there shall be as an expiation the maintenance of a poor man. And he who of his own accord performeth a good work, shall derive good from it: and that ye fast is good for you — if ye but knew it.

As to the month Ramadhan in which the Koran was sent down to be man's guidance, and an explanation of that guidance, and an illumination, as soon as any one of you observeth the moon, let him set about the fast; but he who is sick, or upon a journey, shall fast a like number of other days. God wishes you ease and wisheth not your discomfort, and that you fulfil the numbers of days, and that you glorify God for his guidance: and haply you will be thankful.

And when my servants ask thee concerning me, then verily will I be nigh unto them — will answer the cry of him that crieth, when he crieth unto me: but let them hearken unto me, and believe in me. Haply they will proceed aright.

You are allowed on the night of the fast to approach your wives: they are your garment and ye are their garment. God knoweth that ye have mutually defrauded yourselves therein; so he turneth unto you and remitteth unto you. Now, therefore, go in unto them with full desire for that which God hath ordained for you; and eat and drink until ye can discern a white thread from a black thread by the daybreak: afterwards fast strictly till night, and go not in unto them, but pass the time in the Mosques. These are the bounds set up by God: therefore come not near to transgress them. Thus God maketh his signs clear to men: haply they will fear him.

Consume not your wealth among yourselves in vain things; nor offer it to judges as a bribe that ye may consume a part of men's wealth unjustly, while ye know the sin which ye commit.

They will ask thee of the new moons. Say: They are periods fixed for man's service and for the pilgrimage. But there is no piety in entering your houses at the back, but piety consists in the fear of God. Enter your houses then by their doors; and fear God: haply ye shall be prosperous.

HOLY WAR

And fight for the cause of God against those who fight against you: but commit not the injustice of attacking them first: verily God loveth not the unjust:

And kill them wherever ye shall find them, and eject them from whatever place they have ejected you; for seduction from the truth is worse than slaughter: yet attack them not at the sacred Mosque, until they attack you therein; but if they attack you, then slay them — Such the recompense of the infidels! —

But if they desist, then verily God is gracious, merciful —

And do battle against them until there be no more seduction from the truth and the only worship be that of God: but if they desist, then let there be no hostility, save against wrong-doers.

War is prescribed to you; but to this ye have a repugnance:

Yet haply ye are averse from a thing, though it be good for you, and haply ye love a thing though it be bad for you: And God knoweth; but ye, ye know not.

They will ask thee concerning war in the sacred month. Say: The act of fighting therein is a grave crime: but the act of turning others aside from the path of God, and unbelief in him, and to prevent access to the sacred Mosque, and to drive out his people, is worse in the sight of God; and civil strife is worse than bloodshed. But they will not cease to war against you until they turn you from your religion, if they be able; but whoever of you shall turn from his religion and die an infidel, their works shall be fruitless in this world and in the next: and they shall be consigned to the fire: therein to abide for aye.

But they who believe, and who fly their country, and fight in the cause of God, may hope for God's mercy: and God is gracious, merciful.

PRAISE TO GOD

God! There is no god but he; the Living, the Self-subsisting; neither slumber seizeth him, nor sleep; his, whatsoever is in the heavens and whatsoever is in the earth! Who is he that can intercede with him but by his own permission? He knoweth what is present with his creatures, and what is yet to befall them; yet nought of his knowledge do they comprehend, save what he willeth. His throne reacheth over the heavens and the earth, and the upholding of both burdeneth him not; and he is the High, the Great!

Let there be no compulsion in religion. Now is the right way made distinct from error; whoever therefore denieth Taghoot and believeth in God hath taken hold on a strong handle that hath no flaw therein: and God is he who heareth, knoweth.

God is the patron of believers: he bringeth them out of darkness into light:

As to those who believe not, their patrons are Taghoot: they bring them out of light into darkness: they shall be inmates of hell-fire: they shall abide therein for ever.

— *Translated from the Koran, Arabic (Seventh Century) by J. M. Rodwell.*

~ ⚙ ~

The Forty-Two Traditions of An-Nawawi

1. Actions are to be judged only in accordance with intentions; and every one gets only what he intended; hence he whose emigration is for the sake of Allah and his apostle, his emigration is for the sake of Allah and his apostle; and he who emigrates for a worldly thing, to get it; or for a wife, to marry her; so his emigration is for that for which he emigrated.

2. It was one day when we were sitting with the apostle of Allah, that a man came towards us with very white clothes and very black hair. The traces of travel were not seen on him, and not one of us recognized him. He sat down by the prophet and propped his knees up against his knees, and placed the palms of his hands on his thighs, and said, "Oh Mohammed, tell me about Islam." And the apostle of Allah said to him, "Islam is that you should give witness that there is no deity except Allah, and that Mohammed is the apostle of Allah; and you should perform the prayer ceremony, and give alms, and fast in Ramadhan; and pilgrimage to the house, if you can manage it." He said, "You are right." We were surprised at his asking, and saying he was right. He said, "Tell me about faith." He said, "You should believe in Allah and his angels and his books and his apostles and in the last day and in predesti-

nation (both good and evil)." He said, "You are right; tell me about *ihsan.*" He said, "You should worship Allah, as if you saw him; for although you do not see him, he sees you." He said, "Tell me about the hour." He said, "The one who is questioned does not know more about it than the questioner." He said, "Tell me about its indications." He said, "It is that a female slave will give birth to her master, or mistress; and that thou wilt see the barefoot and the naked and the destitute and the shepherds going so far as to build." Then off he went and I waited a long time. Then he said, "Do you know, 'Umar, who the questioner was?" I said, "Allah and his apostle know better." He said, "It was Gabriel. He came to teach you your religion."

3. Islam is built on five points: — the witness of there being no deity except Allah, and of Mohammed being the apostle of Allah; the performing of prayer; the giving of alms; the pilgrimage to the house; and the fast of Ramadhan.

4. The creation of any one of you is when he is compressed in his mother's womb for forty days as a speck; then he becomes a clot in the same way; then he becomes a coagulation in the same way; then the angel is sent to him, so he breathes the spirit into him: and the angel is bidden to write up his sustenance, the allotted span of his life, his works, and whether he will be wretched or happy after death; and by Allah (than whom there is no deity) indeed any one of you will work the work of the people of paradise, so that there is only a yard between him and it, and then that which is written overtakes him, and he works the work of the people of the fire and enters it; and indeed any one of you works the work of the people of the fire, so that there is but a yard between him and it, and then that which is written overtakes him, and he works the work of the people of paradise and enters it.

5. The one who introduces (as from himself) into our affair that which has nothing to do with it is a reprobate.

6. What is lawful is obvious, and what is unlawful is obvious; and between them are matters which are ambiguous and of which many people are ignorant. Hence, he who is careful in regard to the ambiguous has justified himself in regard to his religion and his honour; but he who stumbles in the ambiguous has stumbled in the forbidden, as the shepherd pasturing around the forbidden land is on the verge of pasturing in it: is it not that every king of the Arabs has protected land, and is not the protected land of Allah that which he has forbidden? Is it not the fact that there is in the body a clot of blood; if it is in good condition, the whole body is too; and if it is in rotten condition, so too is the whole body; is not this the heart?

7. Religion is good advice. We said, "Whose?" He, the prophet, said, "Allah's and His Book's and His apostle's, and the Imams of the Muslims, and the generality of them."

8. I have been commanded to wage war upon people until they witness that there is no deity except Allah, and that Mohammed is the apostle of Allah; and that they perform the prayer and give alms. Then if they do that, so far as I am concerned, their lives and property will be protected, unless in conflict with the rights of Islam; and their account is with Allah Ta'ala.

9. What I have forbidden you, avoid; and what I have ordered you, comply with to the utmost of your ability; for what destroyed those who were before you was only the quantity of their questions, and their differences over the matter of their prophets.

10. Allah Ta'ala is good; he accepteth only what is good; and Allah gave to the believers the same command that he gave to those whom he sent. For the Almighty said, "O apostles, eat of the good things and do that which is good." And the Almighty said, "O ye who believe, eat of the good things that we have granted to you." Then he remembered the man on the long journey, dusty and with dishevelled hair, stretching out his hands to heaven and saying, O Lord, O Lord; while his food was forbidden and his drink was forbidden and his raiment was forbidden; and he was fed on that which was forbidden — then how should answer be afforded him?

11. Let go the things in which you are in doubt for the things in which there is no doubt.

12. Leaving alone things which do not concern him is one of the good things in a man's Islam.

13. No one of you is a believer until he loves for his brother what he loves for himself.

14. The blood of a Muslim man is not lawful but for one of three reasons: — an adulterous married person; an avenger of

blood; and the one who leaves his religion, that is, splits the community.

15. He that believes in Allah and the last day, let him speak good or hold his peace; and he who believes in Allah and the last day, let him honour his neighbour; and he who believes in Allah and the last day, let him honour his guest.

16. A man said to the prophet, "Give me a command." He said, "Do not get angry." The man repeated the question several times, and he said, "Do not get angry."

17. Allah has prescribed *Ihsan* for everything; hence, if you kill, do it well; and if you slaughter, do it well; and let each one of you sharpen his knife and let his victim die at once.

18. Fear Allah, wherever thou art; and follow up bad actions with good, so as to wipe them out; and behave in a decent way to people.

19. I was behind the prophet one day, and he said, "Young man, I will teach you a lesson; keep hold on Allah and he will keep hold on you; keep hold on Allah, and you will find him in front of you; if you ask anything, ask it from Allah; if ye seek help, seek it from Allah. And know that the nation, if it has agreed in benefiting you in anything, will not benefit you in anything, save in what Allah has written for you; and if it has agreed on harming you in anything, will not harm you in anything, save in a thing Allah has written against you; — the pens are discarded and the pages are dry."

20. Among the things which people comprehended from the material of the first prophecy was, If you are not ashamed, then do whatever you wish.

21. I said, "O apostle of Allah, tell me something about Islam, which I could not ask of any one except you." He said, "Say, I believe in Allah; and then go straight."

22. A man asked the apostle of Allah and said, "Is it your opinion, that, if I pray the prescribed prayers; and fast in Ramadhan; and believe firmly in what is allowable; and shun what is forbidden, and do not do anything more than that, I shall enter the garden?" He said, "Yes."

23. Purification is part of religion; and "Praise be to Allah" fills the scales; and "Allah be exalted" and "Praise be to Allah" fill what is between heaven and earth; and prayer is light; and almsgiving is a proof; and patience is brightness; and the Koran is an argument in your favour or against you; and every one goes about his business at the beginning of the day and sells his soul: he either frees it or causes it to perish.

24. It was when he was relating things about his Lord, that he said:

"O my servants, I have forbidden myself wickedness, and have made it a forbidden thing in the midst of you, so do not do injustice to one another.

"O my servants, every one of you is in error, except the one I have guided, so ask guidance from me and I will guide you.

"O my servants, every one of you is hungry, except him whom I have fed; so ask food of me and I will feed you.

"O my servants, every one of you is naked except him whom I have clothed; so ask clothing of me and I will clothe you.

"O my servants, you sin day and night; and I pardon your sins; so ask pardon of me and I will pardon you.

"O my servants, you will never reach harming me, so as to harm me; and you will never reach benefiting me, so as to benefit me.

"O my servants, were the first of you and last of you, both of men and *djinn* — were they in accord once with the most godly heart of a single man amongst you — that would not add aught to my kingdom.

"O my servants, were the first of you and the last of you, both of men and *djinn* — were they according to the dissipated heart of any single man amongst you — that would not diminish aught from my kingdom.

"O my servants, were the first of you and the last of you, both of men and *djinn* — were they to rise up in a single spot on the surface of the earth and to ask me something and I gave to each one what he asked, that would not diminish aught from me, except as the needle does not diminish anything from the sea, when it is thrown in.

"O my servants, it is only your works that I take account of for you; then I recompense you for them; and he who finds good, let him praise Allah; and he who finds otherwise, let him blame himself alone."

25. Some of the companions of the prophet said to him: "The people of wealth brought rewards, praying as we pray and fasting as we fast, and giving alms from the superabundance of their properties." He said: "Has not Allah appointed for you of what you should give alms? Surely in every

act of adoration there is almsgiving; and in every *takbir* there is almsgiving; and in every *al hamdu lillah*, there is almsgiving; and in every *Hallelujah* there is almsgiving; and in every bidding to do what is right there is almsgiving; and in every prohibition of what is forbidden there is almsgiving; and in the marriage of any one of you there is almsgiving." They said, "O apostle of Allah, will any one of us reach his desire, and there be in it a reward for him?" He said, "Do you think that, were he to put it among the forbidden things, it would be a sin for him; and likewise if he put it among the allowable things, there would be a reward?"

26. Almsgiving is incumbent upon every "bone" of people each day that the sun rises; it is almsgiving if you make adjustment between a couple; and if you help a man in the matter of his riding-animal and mount him upon her or lift his baggage for him upon her. A good word is almsgiving; and in every step you walk towards prayer there is an act of almsgiving; and it is almsgiving when you ward danger off the road.

27. Righteousness is goodness of character; and sinfulness is what is woven in the soul, and you hate that people should ascertain the matter.

I went to the apostle of Allah, and he said: "You have come to ask about righteousness." I said, "Yes." He said, "Ask your heart to decide; righteousness is what the soul and the heart feel tranquil about; and sinfulness is what is fixed in the soul, and roams about in the breast, even if people give their decision in your favour over and over again."

28. The apostle of Allah exhorted us with an exhortation, by which our hearts were distressed and our eyes flowed down with tears; and we said, "O apostle of Allah, it is as if it were a farewell exhortation; give us a 'last will and testament.'" He said, "My behest is your being piously disposed towards Allah (may he be praised and exalted), listening and obeying, even if a 'slave' is invested with authority over you. Indeed the one who lives from you will notice a big 'discord'; and it is for you to keep my *sunna* and the *sunna* of the rightly-guided Khalifas; cling to them as with your molar teeth; and beware of novel affairs, for surely all innovation is error."

29. I, Mu'adh, said, "O apostle of Allah, inform me of a work which will bring me into the garden and keep me far from the fire." He said, "You have indeed made inquiry about something great; but indeed it is easy for one for whom Allah facilitates things; you should worship Allah without joining aught with him; you should perform prayer, give alms, and fast in Ramadhan; and make pilgrimage to the house." Then he said, "Shall I not indicate to you the doors to good. Fasting is a protection, and almsgiving quenches sin as water quenches fire, and the prayer of a man at the dead of night."

Then he said, "Shall I not tell you about the 'pith' of the matter, and its base and the apex of its prominence?" I said, "Of course, O apostle of Allah." He said, "The 'pith' is Islam; and its base is prayer, and apex of its prominence is holy war." Then he said, "Shall I tell you how to get all this?" I said, "Of course, O apostle of Allah." So he took hold of his tongue, and said, "Control this." I said, "O prophet of Allah, we are indeed to blame for what we speak with it." So he said, "Your mother is bereft of you; will people be toppled into the fire on their faces except for the harvest of their tongues?"

30. Allah Ta'ala has enjoined ordinances, and you must not neglect them; and has laid down limits, and you must not transgress them; and has forbidden certain things which you must not violate; and has been silent over certain things as an act of mercy towards you, not out of forgetfulness, so do not investigate these.

31. A man came to the apostle of Allah and said, "O apostle of Allah, indicate me a work, which, were I to do it, Allah would love me for it, and people would love me too." And he said, "Be abstemious in the world, and Allah will love you; and be abstemious in what belongs to people, and people will love you."

32. Let there be no injury in the world and no requital.

33. If people were granted their claims, then men might claim the possessions and blood of any group of people, but the burden of proof is on the one who stakes the claim; and the oath on the one who denies.

34. Whoever of you sees something of which Allah disapproves, then let him change it with his hand; and if that is impossible, then with his tongue; and if that is impossible, then with his heart; and that is faith of the weakest kind.

35. Do not be envious of each other; and

do not outbid each other; and do not hate each other; do not oppose each other; and do not undersell each other; and be, O slaves of Allah, as brothers. A Muslim is a brother to a Muslim, not oppressing him and not forsaking him; not lying to him and not despising him. Here is true piety (and he, Mohammed, would point to his breast three times) — it's quite bad enough for a man to despise his brother Muslim. A Muslim's life, property and honour are inviolate to a Muslim.

36. He who dispels from a believer one of the griefs of the world, Allah will dispel for him a grief on the day of resurrection; he who cheers up a person in difficulties, Allah will cheer him in this world and the next; he who shields a Muslim, Allah will shield him in this world and the next. Allah is there to help his slave, so long as he is out to help his brother, and he who walks a path seeking therein knowledge, Allah will make easy for him a path to paradise through it. And when a company meets together in one of the houses of Allah to pore over the book of Allah and to study it together amongst themselves, the Shechinah comes down to them and mercy overshadows them; and the angels surround them; and Allah remembers them among them that are his; and the one whose work makes him procrastinate will not be hastened along by the nobility of his ancestry.

37. Surely Allah has written down good deeds and evil ones; then he made that clear, so that he who is concerned about a good deed, but does not perform it, Allah has written it down with himself as a perfect good deed; and if he is concerned about it and fulfils it, then Allah has written it down with himself for ten good deeds up to seven hundredfold — exceeding manifold; and if he is concerned about a bad deed and does not fulfil it, then Allah has written it down with himself as one good, perfect deed; and if he is concerned about it and fulfilled it, then Allah has written it down as a single bad deed.

38. Allah Ta'ala said: Whoever is hostile to a supporter of mine, on him will I declare war; and my slave will not approach me with anything dearer than that which I put on him as an obligation; and he continues presenting me with matters of supererogation, that I may love him. And when I love him, I am his hearing by which he hears; and his sight by which he sees; and his hand by which he strikes for me; and his foot by which he walks. And if he asks me for anything, I will certainly give it to him; and if he takes refuge in me, I will certainly give him refuge.

39. Surely Allah for my sake has overlooked the error of my nation and its forgetfulness, and its being forced to do a thing it does not like.

40. Be in the world as if you were a stranger or a traveller: when evening time comes, expect not the morning; and when morning time comes expect not the evening; and prepare as long as you are in good health for sickness, and so long as you are alive for death.

41. Not one of you is a believer until his passion becomes in line with that which I have brought.

42. Allah Ta'ala said: So long as you call upon me and hope in me, I forgive you all that originates from you; and I will not heed, O son of man, should your sins reach the horizon of the heavens, and then you asked my pardon and I would pardon you. O son of man, were you to come to me with almost an earth-ful of sins, and then you met me without joining anything with me in the godhead, then would I come to you with an earth-ful of forgiveness.

— *Translated by Eric F. F. Bishop for The Moslem World, April, 1939.*

PART SIX

Creative Imagination

In a memorable line of metaphysical poetry, Hamlet declares: "there is nothing either good or bad, but thinking makes it so." Shakespeare's Hamlet is very much of a poet, resembling the dramatist himself and all deeply imaginative persons in knowing the power of the human mind to create realms of thought in greater or less degree independent of the ruts wherein we are thrown by daily experience. The business man who sees only his practical affairs or the man or woman who feels only the pressure of daily drudgery fails to realize that the mind is potentially gifted not only to crawl as a grub but to soar on wings. From time immemorial it has been one of the leading quests of the human mind and heart to search these freer spaces of the imagination. Art not merely photographic and religion not merely ethical represent two notable excursions into these impalpable domains. Child and poet are alike visionaries, creating worlds, or seeing gleams, undiscovered on land or sea by the prosaic eye. The free creation of fantastic objects and events gives us merely the literature of fancy, revealing only a naive and trivial aspect of the imaginative world. When, however, the mature mind explores with keen intelligence its own spiritual potentialities, we have genuinely metaphysical thought. Science and philosophy, with their methods of psychology and argument, investigate these realms rationally. No men, however, prove more truly at home in them or return to us with richer treasures than the poets themselves. Some critics have even rashly, or at least boldly, described the metaphysical element as the very heart of poetry itself. Be this as it may, it is certain that no more precious body of verse exists than that properly termed metaphysical. Although the practice is as old as literary records themselves, only recently have critics seriously grappled with it as a literary phenomenon. The rediscovery of oriental poetry by the Western World, the rise of our own science of psychology, and the strongly metaphysical quality in modern literature as a whole, have, with much besides, formulated and fortified this highly rewarding point of view.

By a practical device, metaphysical verse can be distinguished from religious poetry, with which it is often obviously allied. It must be clear at a glance that not all metaphysical verse is religious; and since most religious verse is ethical, ceremonial or even semi-historical, certainly not all religious verse is metaphysical. The latter type is best described as the voice of spiritual exploration. To a people with strong religious belief, worlds of heaven and hell may seem virtually as real as this world, and the supernatural become no more a realm to explore than one's own backyard. A traditional discrimination of the Christian Church between its own essential creed and the various outcroppings of mystical thought within the larger circumference of the Church aids our own distinction. Restatements in verse of familiar orthodox belief, as in the usual Church hymns, are not generally regarded as metaphysical poetry; while much, though not all, of the verse inspired by the more spiritual of the cults may properly be so called. Metaphysical poetry is first of all poetry and only in a secondary sense theology or philosophy. Its imagination must body forth experience in art. For poetry, it is insufficient to give, as may theology or philosophy, a mere graph or map of the world to be explored. The intellectual approach alone will not suffice. Poetry affords a personal record of men who have witnessed and felt the things of which they speak.

Much of the purest and greatest of metaphysical verse has arisen in the East, especially during those earlier centuries in which the East was itself most spiritually creative and dynamic. Leading metaphysical philosophies of the Orient, as Taoism, Buddhism and Sufiism, have inspired superb mystical poetry in China, India and Persia. Such verse was composed from the dawn of oriental history, many centuries before Christ, to the close of our own Middle Ages. While much of this poetry in its most comprehensive and epic forms tends to escape the understanding of the Occidental reader, many of the shorter pieces are as fresh and clear as if written today and by our own neighbors. Above all, the metaphysical lyric of the East challenges our admiration, and accordingly it is from this body of verse that the first selections for this section of our book are drawn.

One of the notable features in the history of metaphysical poetry is the virtually complete gulf created by the classical and neo-classical poetic traditions. It is true that the Greek Pindar in a few almost casual phrases makes such statements as the declaration that life is a dream; but this becomes for Pindar a sad and even a tragic confession, and proves largely barren for his poetry as a whole, which celebrates the glory of the Greek city states and their champions in the Greek athletic festivals. The golden age of Latin poetry proves even less attracted to the metaphysical. All the weight of the classical poetic tradition in the West has, therefore, been thrown in the direction of a practical, ethical, social, and materialistic view of life. Christianity, with an Eastern home, carried within its austere theological system the only promising seeds of metaphysical thought for Europe, and these too seldom germinated into significant verse of a genuinely metaphysical quality. Our selections here include but one specimen of explorative and vital mysticism in the continental literature of medieval Europe, that by Saint Francis.

It is no less obvious than paradoxical that the all-accomplished Greeks possessed keen powers of metaphysical speculation which, although inspiring Plato and his followers, failed to find adequate expression in their poetry. Homer, not Plato, dominated ancient verse. The platonic outlook, with its tradition of vague idealism and generalization, unquestionably has its limitations as a stimulant to a humane literature. Yet with the new vogue of Platonism in the Renaissance came a brilliant emergence of metaphysical verse, well exhibited, for example, in the noble sonnets of the artist, Michelangelo.

The Spanish have a long and a profound tradition of mysticism, by no means in all cases dependent upon the Spanish devotion to the Church. From their lyric poets and their lyrical dramatists come many of the finest examples of metaphysical poetry produced by the Western World, the tradition extending from the age of Fray Luis de León, Saint Teresa and Calderon in the sixteenth century to such writers in our own times as Miguel de Unamuno and the poet, Jorge Guillen.

The German mind has produced much of our greatest metaphysical literature both in philosophic prose and soaring verse, from the poems by Goethe composed a century and a half ago to the work of Rainer Maria Rilke, written only a few years past. Since Rilke is perhaps the greatest poet of the twentieth century, and since as a poet he devoted himself almost exclusively to brief metaphysical lyrics which have been many times adequately translated into English, a close study of his work becomes here of particular importance.

Metaphysical verse has a richer and more varied history in English than in French. As usual, the English prove centrifugal, throwing off their sparks of inspiration in all directions while failing to concentrate in a central glow. Some admirable mystical poetry was composed during the later English Middle Ages, of which a specimen is here included. More powerful, however, was the vogue of metaphysical poetry begun about 1600 by the great though dark genius, John Donne, and ardently pursued for a period of some sixty years. That a mystical poetry of note existed even in the rationalistic eighteenth century may be seen in Christopher Smart's *Song of David.* The spiritual revival in the nineteenth century fostered a mystical poetry with a Catholic background.

American poets have also made many contributions to the metaphysical lyric, partly through the subjectivity of the Puritan mind, partly through the prolonged devotion in this country to British thought of the seventeenth century, and partly through material and spiritual contacts with the Far East. The chief intellectual ferment in America prior to the twentieth century was, beyond a doubt, the transcendental movement originating in New England, directly or indirectly the inspiration of the most valuable writings of Emerson, Thoreau, Melville, Emily Dickinson, and Walt Whitman. These authors are at least potentially among the great masters of the metaphysical style. With such valiant pioneers behind them, American poets of our own day have continued to cultivate fruitful fields in the literature of the spirit. The considerable popularity of Rilke in the United States indicates paths which much of our finest lyrical verse must in all probability traverse within the immediate future.

Facing Death

Unreal!
Unreal are both creation
And destruction,
And man's body
Is illusion and a dream.

It is the house
Where for a space
Sojourn his heart and mind;
But seek not there
For man's real self —
It does not dwell therein.

—*From the Chinese of Chih Ming (Sui Dynasty, 589–618), translated by Henry H. Hart.*

The Morning Bell of Fang T'a

In the east of the city,
Near my home,
Stands the great, square, stone pagoda.

I lie on my pillow
And hear its chimes
Riding the winds of night.

And when, each morning,
Through my curtain
I see the glow of dawn,
I know not if the world is real,
Or a vision and a dream.

—*From the Chinese of Hsi P'ei Lan (Ch'ing Dynasty, 1644–1911), translated by Henry H. Hart.*

Three with the Moon and His Shadow

With a jar of wine I sit by the flowering trees.
I drink alone, and where are my friends?
Ah, the moon above looks down on me;
I call and lift my cup to his brightness.
And see, there goes my shadow before me.
Hoo! We're a party of three, I say, —
Though the poor moon can't drink,
And my shadow but dances around me,
We're all friends to-night,
The drinker, the moon and the shadow.
Let our revelry be meet for the spring time!

I sing, the wild moon wanders the sky.
I dance, my shadow goes tumbling about.
While we're awake, let us join in carousal;
Only sweet drunkeness shall ever part us.
Let us pledge a friendship no mortals know,
And often hail each other at evening
Far across the vast and vaporous space!

—*From the Chinese of Li Po (701–762), translated by Shigeyoshi Obata.*

Business Men

Business men boast of their skill and cunning
But in philosophy they are like little children.
Bragging to each other of successful depredations
They neglect to consider the ultimate fate of the body.
What should they know of the Master of Dark Truth
Who saw the wide world in a jade cup,
By illumined conception got clear of Heaven and Earth:
On the chariot of Mutation entered the Gate of Immutability?

—*From the Chinese of Ch'ēn Tzu-ang (656–698), translated by Arthur Waley.*

The Wake

My existence in the world has been
As transitory as the reflection of the moon
Which lodges in water
Gathered in the palm of the hand,
About which one doubts whether it is there or not!

—*From the Japanese of Tsurayuki, translated by Arthur Waley.*

The Bewildered Arab

From the solitary desert
Up to Baghdad came a simple
Arab; there amid the rout
Grew bewildered of the countless
People, hither, thither, running,
Coming, going, meeting, parting,
Clamor, clatter, and confusion,
All about him and about.

Travel-wearied, hubbub-dizzy,
Would the simple Arab fain

Get to sleep — "But then, on waking,
How," quoth he, "amid so many
Waking, know myself again?"

So, to make the matter certain,
Strung a gourd about his ankle,
And, into a corner creeping,
Baghdad and himself and people
Soon were blotted from his brain.

But one that heard him and divined
His purpose, slyly crept behind;
From the sleeper's ankle clipping,
Round his own the pumpkin tied,
And laid him down to sleep beside.

By and by the Arab, waking,
Looks directly for his signal —
Sees it on another's ankle —
Cries aloud, "Oh, good-for-nothing,
Rascal to perplex me so!
That by you I am bewildered,
Whether I be I or no!
If I — the pumpkin why on you?
If you — then where am I, and who?"

— *From the Persian of Jami (1414–1492), translated by Edward FitzGerald.*

~ ✣ ~

Hymn to the Sun

THE SPLENDOUR OF ATON

Thy dawning is beautiful in the horizon of heaven,
O living Aton, Beginning of life!
When thou risest in the eastern horizon of heaven,
Thou fillest every land with thy beauty;
For thou art beautiful, great, glittering, high over the earth;
Thy rays, they encompass the lands, even all thou hast made.
Thou art Re, and thou hast carried them all away captive;
Thou bindest them by thy love.
Though thou art afar, thy rays are on earth;
Though thou art on high, thy footprints are the day.

NIGHT

When thou settest in the western horizon of heaven,
The world is in darkness like the dead.
They sleep in their chambers,
Their heads are wrapt up,
Their nostrils stopped, and none seeth the other.
Stolen are all their things, that are under their heads,
While they know it not.
Every lion cometh forth from his den,
All serpents, they sting.
Darkness reigns,
The world is in silence,
He that made them has gone to rest in his horizon.

DAY AND MAN

Bright is the earth,
When thou risest in the horizon,
When thou shinest as Aton by day.
The darkness is banished,
When thou sendest forth thy rays,
The Two Lands of Egypt are in daily festivity,
Awake and standing upon their feet,
For thou hast raised them up.
Their limbs bathed, they take their clothing;
Their arms uplifted in adoration to thy dawning.
Then in all the world, they do their work.

DAY AND THE ANIMALS AND PLANTS

All cattle rest upon their herbage,
All trees and plants flourish,
The birds flutter in their marshes,
Their wings uplifted in adoration to thee.
All the sheep dance upon their feet,
All winged things fly,
They live when thou hast shone upon them.

DAY AND THE WATERS

The barques sail up-stream and down-stream alike.
Every highway is open because thou hast dawned.
The fish in the river leap up before thee,
And thy rays are in the midst of the great sea.

CREATION OF MAN

Thou art he who createst the man-child in woman,
Who makest seed in man,
Who givest life to the son in the body of his mother,
Who soothest him that he may not weep,
A nurse even in the womb.

Who giveth breath to animate every one
 that he maketh.
When he cometh forth from the body,
On the day of his birth,
Thou openest his mouth in speech,
Thou suppliest his necessities.

CREATION OF ANIMALS

When the chicklet crieth in the egg-shell,
Thou givest him breath therein, to preserve
 him alive.
When thou hast perfected him
That he may pierce the egg,
He cometh forth from the egg,
To chirp with all his might;
He runneth about upon his two feet,
When he hath come forth therefrom.

THE WHOLE CREATION

How manifold are all thy works!
They are hidden from before us,
O thou sole god, whose powers no other possesseth.
Thou didst create the earth according to thy
 desire,
While thou wast alone:
Men, all cattle large and small,
All that are upon the earth,
That go about upon their feet;
All that are on high,
That fly with their wings;
The countries of Syria and Nubia,
The land of Egypt;
Thou settest every man in his place,
Thou suppliest their necessities.
Every one has his possessions,
And his days are reckoned.
Their tongues are divers in speech,
Their forms likewise and their skins,
For thou divider, hast divided the peoples.

—*From the Egyptian of Ikhnaton (Amenhotep IV) (1375?–1358? B.C.), translated by James Henry Breasted.*

~❁~

Canticle of the Sun

O Most High, Omnipotent, Good Lord; Thine be the praise, the glory and the honor; to Thee be every blessing. To Thee alone, Most Highest, are they due, and there is no man worthy to speak of Thee.

Be praised, O Lord, with all Thy creatures, especially my lord Brother Sun, who gives the day, and by whom Thou showest light. He is beautiful and shining with great splendor; of Thee, Most Highest, he is the symbol.

Be praised, O Lord, for Sister Moon and the stars; Thou hast formed them in the heavens, clear, precious and beautiful.

Be praised, O Lord, for Brother Wind and for air and cloud, for fair and for all weather by which Thou givest Thy creatures sustenance.

Be praised, O Lord, for Sister Water, the which is so useful, humble, precious and chaste.

Be praised, O Lord, for Brother Fire, by which Thou lightest up the night. He is beautiful and gay, vigorous and strong.

Be praised, O Lord, for our Sister Mother Earth, the which supports and nourishes us and produces diverse fruits, with brilliant flowers and grass.

Be praised, O Lord, for those, who for love of Thee forgive, who bear sickness and tribulation; blessed those who in peace shall endure, for by Thee, Most High, they shall be crowned.

Be praised, O Lord, for our Sister Death of the Body, from the which no man living may escape; woe to them who shall die in mortal sin and blessed those who shall be found in Thy most holy will, for the second death shall work them no harm.

Give praises and blessing and render thanks to my Lord, and serve Him with great humility.

—*From the Italian of St. Francis of Assisi (1182–1226), translated by Eleanor L. Turnbull.*

~❁~

The Night Serene

When I contemplate o'er me
 The heaven of stars profound,
And mark the earth before me
 In darkness swathed around,—
 In careless slumber and oblivion bound;

Then love and longing waken
The anguish of my soul;
Mine eyes with tears are taken
Like founts beyond control,
My voice sighs forth at last its voice of dole: —

O Temple-Seat of Glory,
Of Beauteousness and Light,
To thy calm promontory
My soul was born! What blight
Holds it endungeoned here from such a height?

What mortal aberration
Hath so estranged mankind
That from God's destination
He turns, abandoned, blind,
To follow mocking shade and empty rind?

No thought amid his slumber
He grants impending fate,
While nights and dawns keep number
In step apportionate,
And life is filched away — his poor estate.

Alas! — arise, weak mortals,
And measure all your loss!
Begirt for deathless portals,
Can souls their birthright toss
Aside, and live on shadows vain and dross?

Oh, let your eyes beholding
Yon pure celestial sphere,
Unmask the wiles enfolding
The life that flatters here —
The little day of mingled hope and fear!

What more can base earth render
Than one poor moment's pause,
Compared with that far splendor
Where in its primal cause
Lives all that is — that shall be — and that was!

Who on yon constellation
Eternal can set gaze, —
Its silvery gradation,
Its majesty of ways,
The concord and proportion it displays, —

In argent wonder turning
The moon doth nightly rove,
Squired by the Star of Learning
And melting Star of Love,
She trails with gentle retinue above —

And lo! through outer spaces
Where Mars is rolled aflame!
Where Jupiter retraces
The calmed horizon's frame
And all the heavens his ray beloved acclaim!

Beyond swings Saturn, father
Of the fabled age of gold;
And o'er his shoulders gather
Night's chantries manifold,
In their proportioned grade and lustre stoled! —

Who can behold such vision
And still earth's baubles prize?
Nor sob the last decision
To rend the bond that ties
His soul a captive from such blissful skies?

For there Content hath dwelling;
And Peace, her realm; and there
'Mid joys and glories swelling
Lifts up the dais fair
With Sacred Love enthroned beyond compare.

Immensurable Beauty
Shows cloudless to that light;
And there a Sun doth duty
That knows no stain of night;
There Spring Eternal blossoms without blight.

O fields of Truth-Abiding
Green pasturelands and rills!
And mines of treasures hiding!
O joyous-breasted hills!
Re-echoing vales where every balm distils!

— *From the Spanish of Fray Luis De León (1527–1591), translated by Thomas Walsh.*

~ ❂ ~

"What Becomes of a Strain of Music"

What becomes of a strain of music
When it ceases to sound; what
To a breath of air that ceases
To stir, and what
To a light blown out?

Speak, Death, and what art thou but silence,
Stillness and shadow?

— From the Spanish of Juan Ramón Jiménez (1881–), translated by John Crow.

Domestic Scenes

When shades of night have come
And all my house is sleeping,
The silent peace of home
Its arms about them keeping,
And the only sound I hear
Is my children's measured breathing, —
Then my dream sees life appear
Toward a larger meaning wreathing;
Then their breathing seems a prayer
Through their voice of dream repeating,
While their consciousness is bare
In their God the Father meeting.
Dream, O Dream, thou art the sign
Of the life that knows no ending,
Of that stainless life divine
On this present life attending!

Look not upon me with such eyes, my son;
I would not have thee read my secret clear,
Nor would I so deceive my little one
That poison through thy fragile veins should sear.
Never, O never, may thy father's gloom
Obstruct thee from the joy and glow of day —
To speak of joy does voice presume? —
I do not wish thee joy,
For on this earth
To live in mirth
One must be saint or fool; —
And fool, — God save thee, boy! —
And saint — I know not of the school.

Go, stir the brazier coals, my child;
The fire is growing cold.
How brief today the sun has smiled!
To think the orb that you behold
One day shall cinder turn,
And God's great brow, the heavens, enfold
Its ashes like an urn.

— From the Spanish of Miguel de Unamuno (1864–1936), translated by Thomas Walsh.

Twelve by the Clock

I said: All now complete!
A poplar vibrated.
The silvered leaves
Sounded with love.
The greens were grey,
Love was sun.
Then, mid-day,
A bird lifted
Its song in the wind
With such adoration
That the flower growing
Among the tallest wheat
Felt itself sung. It was I,
Center in that instant
Of so much around,
Who saw it all
Complete for a God.
I said: All, complete.
Twelve by the clock!

— From the Spanish of Jorge Guillen (1893–), translated by Frances Avery Pleak.

The Perfect Life

Rabbit: timid brother! My teacher and philosopher!
Your life has taught me the lesson of silence.
For since in solitude you find your mine of gold,
the world's eternal onward march means nothing to you.

Tiny seeker after wisdom,
you leaf, as through a book, the good and humble cabbage;
and like Saint Simeon, from your hole
you watch the evolutions of the swallows.

Ask your good God for a garden in Heaven,
a garden with crystal cabbages in glory,
a spring of fresh water for your tender nose,
and a flight of doves above your head.

You live in the odour of perfect sanctity.
The cincture of Father Saint Francis will touch you
on the day of your death. And in Heaven
the souls of children will play with your long ears!

— From the Spanish of the Ecuadorian Jorge Carrera Andrade (1903–), translated by Dudley Fitts.

The Infinite

Dear to me always was this lonely hill,
And this hedge that excludes so large a part
Of the ultimate horizon from my view,
But as I sit and gaze, my thought conceives
Interminable vastnesses of space
Beyond it, and unearthly silences,
And profoundest calm; whereat my heart almost
Becomes dismayed. And I hear the wind
Blustering through these branches, I find myself
Comparing with this sound that infinite silence;
And then I call to mind eternity,
And the ages that are dead, and this that now
Is living, and the noise of it. And so
In this immensity my thought sinks drowned:
And sweet it seems to shipwreck in this sea.

—*From the Italian of Giacomo Leopardi (1798–1837), translated by R. C. Trevelyan.*

Prometheus

Blacken thy heavens, Jove,
With thunder-clouds,
And exercise thee, like a boy
Who thistles crops,
With smiting oaks and mountain-tops!
Yet must leave me standing
My own firm Earth;
Must leave my cottage, which thou didst not build,
And my warm hearth,
Whose cheerful glow
Thou enviest me.

I know naught more pitiful
Under the sun than you, Gods!
Ye nourish scantily,
With altar-taxes
And with cold lip-service;—
This your majesty
Would perish, were not
Children and beggars
Credulous fools.

When I was a child,
And knew not whence or whither,
I would turn my wildered eye
To the sun, as if up yonder were
An ear to hear to my complaining,—
A heart, like mine,
On the oppressed to feel compassion.

Who helped me,
When I braved the Titans' insolence?
Who rescued me from death,
From slavery?
Hast thou not all thyself accomplished,
Holy-glowing heart?
And, glowing young and good,
Most ignorantly thanked
The slumberer above there?

I honor thee? For what?
Hast thou the miseries lightened
Of the down-trodden?
Hast thou the tears ever banished
From the afflicted?
Have I not to manhood been molded
By omnipotent Time,
And by Fate everlasting,—
My lords and thine?

Dreamedst thou ever
I should grow weary of living,
And fly to the desert,
Since not all our
Pretty dream-buds ripen?
Here sit I, fashion men
In mine own image,—
A race to be like me,
To weep and to suffer,
To be happy and to enjoy themselves,—
All careless of *thee* too,
As I!

—*From the German of Johann Wolfgang von Goethe (1749–1832), translated by John S. Dwight.*

Song of Fate

You walk up there in the light
On yielding ground, holy Deities!
Divine bright breezes
Touch you softly,
As the artist's fingers
Holy chords.

Fateless, like the sleeping
Infant, breathe the Divinities,
Chastely preserved
In modest budding
Blossoms ever their spirit,
And their holy eyes
Gaze with quiet
Eternal clearness.

But for us is appointed
No place of abiding,
We dwindle, we drop down,
Suffering mortals,
Blindly from one hour
Into another,
Like water from cliff
To cliff thrown
Yearlong down into the abyss.

—*From the German of Friedrich Hölderlin (1770–1843), translated by Emery Neff.*

~ ❁ ~

Silent Hour

Whoever weeps somewhere out in the world
Weeps without cause in the world
Weeps over me.

Whoever laughs somewhere out in the night
Laughs without cause in the night
Laughs at me.

Whoever wanders somewhere in the world
Wanders in vain in the world
Wanders to me.

Whoever dies somewhere in the world
Dies without cause in the world
Looks at me.

—*From the German of Rainer Maria Rilke (1875–1926), translated by Jessie Lemont.*

~ ❁ ~

At Memphis Station

Half-awake and half-dozing,
in an inward seawind of Danaid dreams,
I stand and gnash my teeth
At Memphis Station, Tennessee.
It is raining.

The night is so barren, extinguished,
and the rain scourges the earth
with a dark, idiotic energy.
Everything is soggy and impassable.

Why are we held up, hour upon hour?
Why should my destiny be stopped here?
Have I fled rain and soul-corrosion
In Denmark, India, and Japan,
to be rain-bound, to rot, in Memphis,
Tennessee, U. S. A.?

And now it dawns. Drearily light oozes
down over this damp jail.
The day uncovers mercilessly
the frigid rails and all the black mud,
the waiting-room with the slot-machine,
orange peels, cigar- and match-stumps.
The day grins through with spewing roof-gutters,
and the infinite palings of rain,
rain, say I, from heaven and to earth.

How deaf the world is, and immovable!
How banal the Creator!
And why do I go on paying dues
at this plebeian sanatorium of an existence!

Stillness. See how the engine,
the enormous machine, stands calmly and seethes;
shrouding itself in smoke, it is patient.
Light your pipe on a fasting heart,
damn God, and swallow your sorrow!

Yet go and stay in Memphis!
Your life, after all, is nothing but
a sickening drift of rain, and your fate
was always to be belated
in some miserable waiting-room or other—
Stay in Memphis, Tennessee!

For within one of these bill-shouting houses,
happiness awaits you, happiness,
if you can only gulp down your impatience—
and here there is sleeping a buxom young girl
with one ear lost in her hair;
she will come to encounter you
some fine day on the street,
like a wave of fragrance,
looking as though she knew you.

Is it not spring?
Does the rain not fall richly?
Is there not the sound of an amorous murmur,
a long, subdued conversation of love
mouth to mouth
between the rain and the earth?
The day began so sadly,
but now, see the rainfall brighten!
Do you not allow the day its right of battle?
So now it is light. And there is a smell of mould
from between the rusted underpinning of the platform

mingled with the rain-dust's rank breath—
a suggestion of spring—
is there no consolation?

And now see, see how the Mississippi
in its bed of flooded forest
wakes against the day!
See how the titanic river revels in its twisting!
How royally it dashes through its bends, and swings the rafts
Of trees and torn planks in its whirls!
See how it twirls a huge stern-wheeler
in its deluge-arms
like a dancer, master of the floor!
See the sunken headland—oh, what immense, primeval peace
over the landscape of drowned forests!
Do you not see how the current's dawn-waters
clothe themselves mile-broad in the day's cheap light,
and wander healthily under the teeming clouds!

Pull yourself together, irreconcilable man!
Will you never forget that you have been promised Eternity?
Will you grudge the earth its due, your poor gratitude?
What would you do, with your heart of love?

Pull yourself together, and stay in Memphis;
announce yourself in the market as a citizen;
go in and insure yourself among the others;
pay your premium of vulgarity,
so that they can know they are safe, as regards you,
and you will not be fired out of the club.
Court the damosel with roses and gold rings,
and begin your saw-mill, like other people.
Yank on your rubbers regularly . . .
Look about you, smoke your sapient pipe
in sphinx-deserted Memphis . . .

Ah! there comes that miserable freight-train
which has kept us waiting six hours.
It rolls in slowly—with smashed sides;
it pipes weakly; the cars limp on three wheels;
and the broken roof drips with clay and slime.
But in the tender, among the coals,
lie four still forms
covered with bloody coats.

Then our huge express-locomotive snorts;
advances a little; stops, sighing deeply;
and stands crouched for the leap. The track is clear.

And we travel onward
through the flooded forest
under the rain's gaping sluices.

—*From the Danish of Johannes V. Jensen (1873–), translated by S. Foster Damon.*

Sonnet

If of our life the span be not a day
Within eternity, if time his flight
Stay not, revolving hopeless, day and night,
If all things living be of death the prey,
O my imprisoned soul, where lies thy way,
Wherefore in darkness dost thou so delight?
Thy wings were formed to bear thee in thy flight
To shining regions of eternal day.
There is the good to which all men aspire,
There is the peace which is our hearts' desire,
There, too, is love and there is pleasure's store.
There, O my soul, guided to heaven's height,
Thou mayest learn to know the ideal light;
The beauty that in this world I adore.

—*From the French of Joachim du Bellay (1525–1560), translated by Eleanor L. Turnbull.*

The Albatross

Sometimes, to entertain themselves, the men of the crew
Lure upon the deck an unlucky albatross, one of those vast
Birds of the sea that follow unwearied the voyage through,
Flying in slow and elegant circles above the mast.

No sooner have they disentangled him from their nets
Than this aërial colossus, shorn of his pride,
Goes hobbling pitiably across the planks and lets
His great wings hang like heavy, useless oars at his side.

How droll is the poor floundering creature, how limp and weak —
He, but a moment past so lordly, flying in state!
They tease him: One of them tries to stick a pipe in his beak;
Another mimics with laughter his odd lurching gait.

The Poet is like that wild inheritor of the cloud,
A rider of storms, above the range of arrows and slings;
Exiled on earth, at bay amid the jeering crowd,
He cannot walk for his unmanageable wings.

—From the French of Charles Baudelaire (1821–1867), translated by George Dillon.

∽ ❂ ∼

November

The highways run in figure of the rood
Infinitely beyond the wood.
And far away beyond the plains cross-wise
They run into the infinite skies.
Crosses they trace even as they fare
On through the cold and livid air
Where wildly streaming the wind voyages
To the infinite beyond the trees.

The trees and winds like unto pilgrims are,
Sad trees and mad through which the tempests roll,
Trees like long lines of saints coming from far,
Like the long lines of all the dead
For whom the dark bells toll.

O northern trees astrain for life,
And winds shattering the earth they sweep,
O keen remorse, O human sobs, O bitter strife
Writhing in mortal hearts and ever burrowing deep!

November crouches by the feeble hearth,
And warms his bony fingers at the flame;
O hidden dead without a home or name,
O winds battering the stubborn walls of earth,
Ever hurled back from them and thrown
Out into vastnesses unknown.

O all saints' names scattered in litanies,
O all ye trees below —
O names of saints whose vague monotony is
Infinitely drawn out in memory;
O praying arms that be
Madly as riven branches outstretched wide
To some strange Christ on the horizon crucified.

November here in greyish cloak doth hide
His stricken terror by the ingleside,
And turns his sombre, sudden glance
Across the transept's broken panes of glass
To the tormented trees and winds that pass
Over the blind and terrible expanse.

The saints, the dead, the trees and the wild wind,
The identical and dread processions go
Turning and turning in long nights of snow;
The saints, the dead, the trees and the wild wind,
Blended forever in our memoried hours
When the great hammer blows
That in the echoing bells resonant are
Fling forth their grief to the horizon far
From heights of imprecatory towers.

And near the hearth the dark November lights
With trembling hands of hope for winter nights
The lamp that shall burn for us dim and high;
And full of tears suppliant November prays
To move the dull hearts of the sullen days.

And ever, in the woods without, the iron-coloured sky,
Ever the winds, the saints, the dead,
And the processions long and deep
Of trees with tortured boughs outspread
That from the world's end onward sweep.
Across the plains the high roads like the rood
Onward unto the infinite stray,
The highways and their crosses far away
Infinitely beyond the valley and wood.

—From the French of the Belgian poet Emile Verhaeren (1855–1916), translated by Ludwig Lewisohn.

∽ ❂ ∼

Silentium

Be silent, hidden, and conceal
Whate'er you dream, whate'er you feel.
Oh, let your visions rise and die
Within your heart's unfathomed sky,
Like stars that take night's darkened route.
Admire and scan them and be mute.

The heart was born dumb; who can sense
Its tremors, recondite and tense?
And who can hear its silent cry?
A thought when spoken is a lie.
Uncovered springs men will pollute,—
Drink hidden waters, and be mute.

Your art shall inner living be.
The world within your fantasy
A kingdom is that waits its Saul.
The outer din will still its call,
Day's glare its secret suns confute.
Drink in its music, and be mute.

—*From the Russian of Fyodor Tyutchev (1803–1873), translated by Babette Deutsch and Avrahm Yarmolinsky.*

~ ❁ ~

Quia Amore Langueo
(*Since I Am Faint with Love*)

In a valley of this restless mind
I sought in mountain and in mead,
Trusting a true love to find.
Upon a hill then took I heed;
A voice I heard (and near I speed)
In great sorrow complaining so:
"See, dear soul, how my sides bleed
Quia amore langueo."

Upon this hill I found a tree,
Under a tree a Man sitting;
From head to foot wounded was He;
His heart blood I saw bleeding;
A seemly Man to be a king,
A gracious face to look unto.
I asked why He had paining;
"*Quia amore langueo.*

"I am true Love that false was never;
My sister, man's soul, I loved her thus.
Because we would in no wise dissever
I left my kingdom glorious,
I purveyed her a palace full precious;
She fled, I followed, I loved her so
That I suffered this pain piteous
Quia amore langueo.

"My fair love and my spouse bright!
I saved her from beating, and she hath Me beat;
I clothed her in grace and heavenly light;
This bloody shirt she hath on Me set;
From longing of love yet would I not let;
Sweet strokes are these, lo!
I promised love and love her yet,
Quia amore langueo.

"I crowned her with bliss and she Me with thorn;
I led her to chamber and she Me to die;
I brought her to honor and she Me to scorn;
I gave her reverence and she Me villany;
To love one who loveth is no mastery;
Her hate made never My love her foe;
Ask Me then no question why—
Quia amore langueo.

"Look unto My hands, man!
These gloves were given Me when I her sought;
They are not white, but red and wan;
Embroidered with love My spouse them brought.
They will not off; I loose them nought;
I woo her with them wherever she go.
These hands for her so friendly fought
Quia amore langueo.

"Marvel not, man, though I sit still.
See, love hath shod Me wondrous strait;
Buckled My feet, as was her will,
With sharp nails (well thou may'st wait!)
In My love was never deceit;
All My members I have opened her to;
My body made her heart-pangs abate
Quia amore langueo.

"In My side I have made her nest;
Look in, how wet a wound is here!
This is her chamber, here shall she rest,
That she may sleep with Me so dear,
Here may she wash, if any filth were;
Here is salve for all her woe;
Come when she will, she shall have cheer
Quia amore langueo.

"I will abide till she be ready,
I will sue her if she say nay;
If she be heedless, I will be greedy,
If she be haughty, I will her pray;
If she weep, then I cannot stay;
My arms are spread to clasp her so;
Cry once, I come: now, soul, assay
Quia amore langueo.

"Fair love, let us go play;
Apples are ripe in my garden;
I shall clothe thee in a new array,
Thy meat shall be milk, honey and wine.
Fair love, let us go dine;
Thy sustenance is in my scrip, lo!
Tarry thou not, My fair spouse mine,
Quia amore langueo.

"If thou be foul, I shall make thee clean;
If thou be sick, I shall thee heal;
If thou mourn ought, I shall thee screen;
Why wilt thou not, fair love, with Me deal?
Foundest thou ever love so leal?
What wilt thou, soul, that I should do?
I may not unkindly 'gainst thee appeal
Quia amore langueo.

"What shall I do now with My spouse
But await her with my gentleness,
Until she looks out of her house
Of fleshly affection? My love she is;
Her bed is made, her bolster of bliss,
Her chamber is chosen; there is no mo'.
Look out on Me at the window of kindness
Quia amore langueo.

"My love is in her chamber; hold your peace!
Make you no noise, but let her sleep.
My babe I would noways ill at ease;
I may not hear My dear child weep.
With My pap I shall her keep;
Nor marvel you not though I tend her true;
This wound in My side had ne'er been so deep
But *Quia amore langueo.*

"Long thou for love never so high,
My love is more than thine may be.
Thou weepest, thou gladdest; I sit thee by;
Yet wouldst thou once, love, look unto Me!
Should I always feed thee
With children's food? Nay, love, not so!
I will prove thy love with adversity
Quia amore langueo.

"Wax not weary, mine own wife!
What praise is aye to live in comfort?
In tribulation I reign more rife
More often times than in fair sport.
In weal and in woe I am ever support;
Mine own wife, leave Me not so!
Thy mead is marked when thou art amort:
Quia amore langueo."

—*Anon., English (c. 1400), slightly modernized.*

~ ⚙ ~

A Hymn to Christ at the Author's Last Going into Germany

In what torn ship soever I embark,
That ship shall be my emblem of Thy Ark;
What sea soever swallow me, that flood
Shall be to me an emblem of Thy blood;
Though Thou with clouds of anger do disguise
Thy face, yet through that mask I know those eyes,
Which, though they turn away sometimes,
They never will despise.

I sacrifice this Island unto Thee,
And all whom I loved there and who loved me;
When I have put our seas 'twixt them and me,
Put Thou Thy sea betwixt my sins and Thee.
As the tree's sap doth seek the root below
In winter, in my winter now I go,
Where none but Thee, th'Eternal root
Of true Love, I may know.

Nor Thou nor Thy religion dost control
The amorousness of an harmonious soul,
But Thou would'st have that love Thyself; as Thou
Art jealous, Lord, so I am jealous now,
Thou lov'st not till from loving more Thou free
My soul; who ever gives, takes liberty.
O, if Thou car'st not whom I love,
Alas, Thou lov'st not me.

Seal then this bill of my Divorce to All,
On whom those fainter beams of love did fall;
Marry those loves, which in youth scattered be
On Fame, Wit, Hopes (false mistresses) to Thee.
Churches are best for prayer that have least light;
To see God only I go out of sight.
And to 'scape stormy days, I choose
An everlasting night.

—*John Donne, English (1573–1631).*

~ ⚙ ~

The World

I saw eternity, the other night,
Like a great ring of pure and endless light,
All calm as it was bright;

And round beneath it time in hours, days, years,
Driven by the spheres,
Like a vast shadow moved, in which the world
And all her train were hurled.
The doting lover in his quaintest strain
Did there complain;
Near him, his lute, his fancy, and his flights,
Wit's sour delights,
With gloves and knots, the silly snares of pleasure,
Yet his dear treasure,
All scattered lay, while he his eyes did pour
Upon a flower.

The darksome statesman, hung with weights and woe,
Like a thick midnight-fog, moved there so slow
He did not stay nor go;
Condemning thoughts, like sad eclipses, scowl
Upon his soul,
And clouds of crying witnesses without
Pursued him with one shout.
Yet digged the mole, and, lest his ways be found,
Worked under ground,
Where he did clutch his prey. But one did see
That policy:
Churches and altars fed him; perjuries
Were gnats and flies;
It rained about him blood and tears; but he
Drank them as free.

The fearful miser on a heap of rust
Sat pining all his life there, did scarce trust
His own hands with the dust;
Yet would not place one piece above, but lives
In fear of thieves.
Thousands there were as frantic as himself,
And hugged each one his pelf:
The downright epicure placed heaven in sense,
And scorned pretense;
While others, slipped into a wide excess,
Said little less;
The weaker sort slight, trivial wares enslave,
Who think them brave;
And poor, despisèd Truth sat counting by
Their victory.

Yet some, who all this while did weep and sing,
And sing and weep, soared up into the ring.
But most would use no wing.
"O fools!" said I, "thus to prefer dark night
Before true light!
To live in grots and caves, and hate the day
Because it shows the way,
The way which from this dead and dark abode
Leads up to God;
A way where you might tread the sun and be
More bright than he!"
But as I did their madness so discuss,
One whispered thus:
"This ring the Bridegroom did for none provide
But for His bride."

—*Henry Vaughan, English (1622–1695).*

A Drop of Dew

See how the orient dew,
Shed from the bosom of the morn
Into the blowing roses,
Yet careless of its mansion new,
For the clear region where 'twas born
Round in itself incloses,
And in its little globe's extent
Frames as it can its native element;
How it the purple flower does slight,
Scarce touching where it lies,
But gazing back upon the skies,
Shines with a mournful light
Like its own tear,
Because so long divided from the sphere.
Restless it rolls and unsecure,
Trembling lest it grow impure,
Till the warm sun pity its pain,
And to the skies exhale it back again.
So the soul, that drop, that ray
Of the clear fountain of eternal day,
Could it within the human flower be seen,
Rememb'ring still its former height,
Shuns the sweet leaves and blossoms green;
And recollecting its own light,
Does, in its pure and circling thoughts, express
The greater heaven in an heaven less.
In how coy a figure wound,
Every way it turns away;
So the world excluding round,
Yet receiving in the day;
Dark beneath but bright above,
Here disdaining, there in love;

How loose and easy hence to go,
How girt and ready to ascend;
Moving but on a point below,
It all about does upwards bend.
Such did the manna's sacred dew distil,
White and entire, though congealed and chill;
Congealed on earth, but does, dissolving, run
Into the glories of th' almighty sun.

—*Andrew Marvell, English (1621–1678)*

A Song to David

O servant of God's holiest charge,
The minister of praise at large,
Which thou mayst now receive;
From thy blest mansion hail and hear,
From topmost eminence appear
To this the wreath I weave.

His muse, bright angel of his verse,
Gives balm for all the thorns that pierce,
For all the pangs that rage;
Blest light, still gaining on the gloom,
The more than Michal of his bloom,
The Abishag of his age.

He sang of God — the mighty source
Of all things — the stupendous force
On which all strength depends;
From whose right arm, beneath whose eyes,
All period, power and enterprise
Commences, reigns and ends.

The world — the clustering spheres he made,
The glorious light, the soothing shade,
Dale, champaign, grove, and hill;
The multitudinous abyss,
Whose secrecy remains in bliss,
And wisdom hides her skill.

O David, scholar of the Lord!
Such is thy science, whence reward,
And infinite degree;
O strength, O sweetness, lasting ripe!
God's harp thy symbol, and thy type
The lion and the bee!

For Adoration all the ranks
Of angels yield eternal thanks,
And David in the midst;
With God's good poor, which, last and least,
In man's esteem, thou to thy feast,
O blessed bridegroom, bidst.

For Adoration seasons change,
And order, truth, and beauty range,
Adjust, attract, and fill:
The grass the polyanthus checks;
And polished porphyry reflects,
By the descending rill.

Rich almonds colour to the prime
For Adoration; tendrils climb,
And fruit-trees pledge their gems;
And Ivis, with her gorgeous vest,
Builds for her eggs her cunning nest,
And bell-flowers bow their stems.

The spotted ounce and playsome cubs
Run rustling 'mongst the flowering shrubs,
And lizards feed the moss;
For Adoration beasts embark,
While waves upholding halcyon's ark
No longer roar and toss.

While Israel sits beneath his fig,
With coral root and amber sprig
The weaned adventurer sports;
Where to the palm the jasmine cleaves,
For Adoration 'mong the leaves
The gale his peace reports.

The wealthy crop of whitening rice
'Mongst thyine woods and groves of spice,
For Adoration grow;
And, marshalled in the fencéd land,
The peaches and pomegranates stand,
Where wild carnations blow.

The laurels with the winter strive;
The crocus burnishes alive
Upon the snow-clad earth;
For Adoration myrtles stay
To keep the garden from dismay,
And bless the sight from dearth.

The pheasant shows his pompous neck;
And ermine, jealous of a speck,
With fear eludes offence;
The sable, with his glossy pride,
For Adoration is descried,
Where frosts and waves condense.

For Adoration, beyond match,
The scholar bullfinch aims to catch
The soft flute's ivory touch;
And careless, on the hazel spray
The daring redbreast keeps at bay
The damsel's greedy clutch.

For Adoration, in the skies,
The Lord's philosopher espies
  The dog, the ram, the rose;
The planets' ring, Orion's sword;
Nor is his greatness less adored
  In the vile worm that glows.

For Adoration, on the strings
The western breezes work their wings,
  The captive ear to soothe –
Hark! 'tis a voice – how still, and small –
That makes the cataracts to fall,
  Or bids the sea be smooth!

For Adoration, incense comes
From bezoar, and Arabian gums,
  And from the civet's fur;
But as for prayer, or e'er it faints,
Far better is the breath of saints
  Than galbanum or myrrh.

For Adoration, in the dome
Of Christ, the sparrows find a home,
  And on his olives perch:
The swallow also dwells with thee,
O man of God's humility,
  Within his Saviour's church.

Sweet is the dew that falls betimes,
And drops upon the leafy limes;
  Sweet Hermon's fragrant air:
Sweet is the lily's silver bell,
And sweet the wakeful tapers' smell
  That watch for early prayer.

Sweet the young Nurse, with love intense,
Which smiles o'er sleeping innocence;
  Sweet when the lost arrive:
Sweet the musician's ardour beats,
While his vague mind's in quest of sweets,
  The choicest flowers to hive.

Sweeter, in all the strains of love,
The language of thy turtle-dove,
  Paired to thy swelling chord;
Sweeter, with every grace endued,
The glory of thy gratitude,
  Respired unto the Lord.

Strong is the horse upon his speed;
Strong in pursuit the rapid glede,
  Which makes at once his game:
Strong the tall ostrich on the ground;
Strong through the turbulent profound
  Shoots xiphias to his aim.

Strong is the lion – like a coal
His eyeball – like a bastion's mole
  His chest against the foes:
Strong the gier-eagle on his sail,
Strong against tide the enormous whale
  Emerges as he goes.

But stronger still in earth and air,
And in the sea the man of prayer,
  And far beneath the tide:
And in the seat to faith assigned,
Where ask is have, where seek is find,
  Where knock is open wide.

Beauteous the fleet before the gale;
Beauteous the multitudes in mail,
  Ranked arms, and crested heads;
Beauteous the garden's umbrage mild,
Walk, water, meditated wild,
  And all the bloomy beds.

Beauteous the moon full on the lawn;
And beauteous, when the veil's withdrawn,
  The virgin to her spouse:
Beauteous the temple, decked and filled,
When to the heaven of heavens they build
  Their heart-directed vows.

Beauteous, yea beauteous more than these,
The Shepherd King upon his knees,
  For his momentous trust;
With wish of infinite conceit,
For man, beast, mute, the small and great,
  And prostrate dust to dust.

Precious, the bounteous widow's mite;
And precious, for extreme delight,
  The largess from the churl:
Precious the ruby's blushing blaze,
And alba's blest imperial rays,
  And pure cerulean pearl.

Precious the penitential tear;
And precious is the sigh sincere;
  Acceptable to God:
And precious are the winning flowers,
In gladsome Israel's feast of bowers,
  Bound on the hallowed sod.

More precious that diviner part
Of David, even the Lord's own heart,
  Great, beautiful, and new:
In all things, where it was intent,
In all extremes, in each event,
  Proof – answering true to true.

Glorious the sun in mid career;
Glorious the assembled fires appear;
Glorious the comet's train:
Glorious the trumpet and alarm;
Glorious the Almighty's stretched-out arm;
Glorious the enraptured main:

Glorious the northern lights astream;
Glorious the song, when God's the theme;
Glorious the thunder's roar:
Glorious hosannah from the den;
Glorious the catholic amen;
Glorious the martyr's gore:

Glorious — more glorious is the crown
Of Him that brought salvation down,
By meekness called thy Son;
Thou that stupendous truth believed,
And now the matchless deed's achieved,
Determined, Dared, and Done.

— *Christopher Smart, English (1722–72) (abridged).*

∽ ❂ ∼

The Tiger

Tyger, tyger: burning bright
In the forests of the night,
What immortal hand or eye
Could frame thy fearful symmetry?

In what distant deeps or skies
Burnt the fire of thine eyes?
On what wings dare he aspire?
What the hand dare seize the fire?

And what shoulder, and what art,
Could twist the sinews of thy heart?
And, when thy heart began to beat,
What dread hand, and what dread feet?

What the hammer? what the chain?
In what furnace was thy brain?
What the anvil? what dread grasp
Dare its deadly terrors clasp?

When the stars threw down their spears,
And watered heaven with their tears,
Did he smile his work to see?
Did he who made the Lamb make thee?

Tyger, tyger: burning bright
In the forests of the night,
What immortal hand or eye,
Dare frame thy fearful symmetry?

— *William Blake, English (1757–1827).*

∽ ❂ ∼

Song from Milton

And did those feet in ancient time
Walk upon England's mountains green?
And was the holy Lamb of God
On England's pleasant pastures seen?

And did the Countenance Divine
Shine forth upon our clouded hills?
And was Jerusalem builded here
Among these dark Satanic Mills?

Bring me my Bow of burning gold!
Bring me my Arrows of desire!
Bring me my Spear! O clouds, unfold!
Bring me my Chariot of fire!

I will not cease from Mental Fight,
Nor shall my Sword sleep in my hand,
Till we have built Jerusalem
In England's green and pleasant Land.

— *William Blake, English (1757–1827).*

∽ ❂ ∼

Auguries of Innocence

To see a World in a Grain of Sand
And a Heaven in a Wild Flower,
Hold Infinity in the palm of your hand
And Eternity in an hour.

A Robin Redbreast in a Cage
Puts all Heaven in a Rage.
A dove house fill'd with doves & pigeons
Shudders Hell thro' all its regions.
A dog starv'd at his Master's Gate
Predicts the ruin of the State.
A Horse misus'd upon the Road
Calls to Heaven for Human blood.
Each outcry of the hunted Hare
A fibre from the Brain does tear.
A Skylark wounded in the wing,
A Cherubim does cease to sing.
The Game Cock clip'd & arm'd for fight
Does the Rising Sun affright.
Every Wolf's & Lion's howl
Raises from Hell a Human Soul.
The wild deer, wand'ring here & there,
Keeps the Human Soul from Care.
The Lamb misus'd breeds Public strife
And yet forgives the Butcher's Knife.
The Bat that flits at close of Eve
Has left the Brain that won't Believe.
The Owl that calls upon the Night
Speaks the Unbeliever's fright.

He who shall hurt the little Wren
Shall never be belov'd by Men.
He who the Ox to wrath has mov'd
Shall never be by Woman lov'd.
The wanton Boy that kills the Fly
Shall feel the Spider's enmity.
He who torments the Chafer's sprite
Weaves a Bower in endless Night.
The Catterpiller on the Leaf
Repeats to thee thy Mother's grief.
Kill not the Moth nor Butterfly,
For the Last Judgment draweth nigh.
He who shall train the Horse to War
Shall never pass the Polar Bar.
The Begger's Dog & Widow's Cat,
Feed them & thou will grow fat.
The gnat that sings his Summer's song
Poison gets from Slander's tongue.
The poison of the Snake & Newt
Is the sweat of Envy's Foot.
The poison of the Honey Bee
Is the Artist's Jealousy.
The Prince's Robes & Beggar's Rags
Are Toadstools on the Miser's Bags.
A truth that's told with bad intent
Beats all the Lies you can invent.
It is right it should be so;
Man was made for Joy & Woe;
And when this we rightly know
Thro' the World we safely go.
Joy & Woe are woven fine,
A Clothing for the Soul divine;
Under every grief & pine
Runs a joy with silken twine.
The Babe is more than swadling Bands;
Throughout all these Human Lands
Tools were made, & Born were hands,
Every Farmer Understands.
Every Tear from Every Eye
Becomes a Babe in Eternity;
This is caught by Females bright
And return'd to its own delight.
The Bleat, the Bark, Bellow & Roar
Are Waves that Beat on Heaven's Shore.
The Babe that weeps the Rod beneath
Writes Revenge in realms of death.
The Beggar's Rags, fluttering in Air,
Does to Rags the Heavens tear.
The Soldier, arm'd with Sword & Gun,
Palsied strikes the Summer's Sun.
The poor Man's Farthing is worth more
Than all the Gold on Afric's Shore.
One Mite wrung from the Labrer's hands
Shall buy & sell the Miser's Lands:
Or, if protected from on high,
Does that while Nation sell & buy.
He who mocks the Infant's Faith
Shall be mock'd in Age & Death.
He who shall teach the Child to Doubt
The rotting Grave shall ne'er get out.
He who respects the Infant's faith
Triumphs over Hell & Death.
The Child's Toys & the Old Man's Reasons
Are the Fruits of the Two seasons.
The Questioner, who sits so sly,
Shall never know how to Reply.
He who replies to words of Doubt
Doth put the Light of Knowledge out.
The strongest Poison ever known
Came from Caesar's Laurel Crown.
Nought can deform the Human Race
Like to the Armour's iron brace.
When Gold & Gems adorn the Plow
To peaceful Arts shall Envy Bow.
A Riddle or the Cricket's Cry
Is to Doubt a fit Reply.
The Emmet's Inch & Eagle's Mile
Make Lame Philosophy to smile.
He who Doubts from what he sees
Will ne'er Believe, do what you Please
If the Sun & Moon should doubt,
They'd immediately Go out.
To be in a Passion you Good may do,
But no Good if a Passion is in you.
The Whore & Gambler, by the State
Licenc'd, build that Nation's Fate.
The Harlot's cry from Street to Street
Shall weave Old England's winding Sheet.
The Winner's Shout, the Loser's Curse,
Dance before dead England's Hearse.
Every Night & every Morn
Some to Misery are Born.
Every Morn & every Night
Some are Born to sweet delight.
Some are Born to sweet delight,
Some are Born to Endless Night.
We are led to Believe a Lie
When we see not Thro' the Eye
Which was Born in a Night to perish in a Night
When the Soul Slept in Beams of Light.
God Appears & God is Light
To those poor Souls who dwell in Night,
But does a Human Form Display
To those who Dwell in Realms of day.

— *William Blake, English (1757–1827).*

Intimations of Immortality from Recollections of Early Childhood

I

There was a time when meadow, grove and stream,
The earth, and every common sight,
To me did seem
Appareled in celestial light,
The glory and the freshness of a dream.
It is not now as it hath been of yore; —
Turn wheresoe'er I may,
By night or day,
The things which I have seen I now can see no more.

II

The Rainbow comes and goes,
And lovely is the Rose;
The Moon doth with delight
Look round her when the heavens are bare;
Waters on a starry night
Are beautiful and fair;
The sunshine is a glorious birth;
But yet I know, where'er I go,
That there hath passed away a glory from the earth.

III

Now, while the birds thus sing a joyous song,
And while the young lambs bound
As to the tabor's sound,
To me alone there came a thought of grief:
A timely utterance gave that thought relief,
And I again am strong.
The cataracts blow their trumpets from the steep;
No more shall grief of mine the season wrong;
I hear the Echoes through the mountains throng,
The Winds come to me from the fields of sleep,
And all the earth is gay;
Land and sea
Give themselves up to jollity,
And with the heart of May
Doth every Beast keep holiday; —
Thou Child of Joy,
Shout round me, let me hear thy shouts, thou happy Shepherd-boy!

IV

Ye blessèd Creatures, I have heard the call
Ye to each other make; I see
The heavens laugh with you in your jubilee;
My heart is at your festival,
My head hath its coronal,
The fullness of your bliss, I feel — I feel it all.
Oh evil day! if I were sullen
While Earth herself is adorning,
This sweet May-morning,
And the Children are culling
On every side,
In a thousand valleys far and wide,
Fresh flowers; while the sun shines warm,
And the Babe leaps up on his Mother's arm: —
I hear, I hear, with joy I hear!
— But there's a Tree, of many, one,
A single Field which I have looked upon,
Both of them speak of something that is gone:
The Pansy at my feet
Doth the same tale repeat:
Whither is fled the visionary gleam?
Where is it now, the glory and the dream?

V

Our birth is but a sleep and a forgetting:
The Soul that rises with us, our life's Star,
Hath had elsewhere its setting,
And cometh from afar:
Not in entire forgetfulness,
And not in utter nakedness,
But trailing clouds of glory do we come
From God, who is our home:
Heaven lies about us in our infancy!
Shades of the prison-house begin to close
Upon the growing Boy,
But he beholds the light, and whence it flows,
He sees it in his joy;
The Youth, who daily farther from the east
Must travel, still is Nature's Priest,
And by the vision splendid
Is on his way attended;
At length the Man perceives it die away,
And fade into the light of common day.

VI

Earth fills her lap with pleasures of her own;
Yearnings she hath in her own natural kind.
And, even with something of a Mother's mind,
And no unworthy aim,

The homely Nurse doth all she can
To make her Foster-child, her Inmate Man,
Forget the glories he hath known,
And that imperial palace whence he came.

VII

Behold the Child among his new-born blisses,
A six years' Darling of a pigmy size!
See, where 'mid work of his own hand he lies,
Fretted by sallies of his mother's kisses,
With light upon him from his father's eyes!
See, at his feet, some little plan or chart,
Some fragment from his dream of human life,
Shaped by himself with newly-learnèd art;
A wedding or a festival,
A mourning or a funeral;
And this hath now his heart,
And unto this he frames his song:
Then will he fit his tongue
To dialogues of business, love, or strife;
But it will not be long
Ere this be thrown aside,
And with new joy and pride
The little Actor cons another part;
Filling from time to time his "humorous stage"
With all the Persons, down to palsied Age,
That Life brings with her in her equipage;
As if his whole vocation
Were endless imitation.

VIII

Thou, whose exterior semblance doth belie
Thy Soul's immensity;
Thou best Philosopher, who yet dost keep
Thy heritage, thou Eye among the blind,
That, deaf and silent, read'st the eternal deep,
Haunted for ever by the eternal mind, —
Mighty Prophet! Seer blest!
On whom those truths do rest,
Which we are toiling all our lives to find,
In darkness lost, the darkness of the grave;
Thou, over whom thy Immortality
Broods like the Day, a Master o'er a Slave,
A Presence which is not to be put by;
Thou little Child, yet glorious in the might
Of heaven-born freedom on thy being's height,
Why with such earnest pains dost thou provoke
The years to bring the inevitable yoke,
Thus blindly with thy blessedness at strife?
Full soon thy Soul shall have her earthly freight,
And custom lie upon thee with a weight,
Heavy as frost, and deep almost as life!

IX

O joy! that in our embers
Is something that doth live,
That nature yet remembers
What was so fugitive!
The thought of our past years in me doth breed
Perpetual benediction: not indeed
For that which is most worthy to be blest —
Delight and liberty, the simple creed
Of Childhood, whether busy or at rest,
With new-fledged hope still fluttering in his breast: —
Not for these I raise
The song of thanks and praise;
But for those obstinate questionings
Of sense and outward things,
Fallings from us, vanishings;
Blank misgivings of a Creature
Moving about in worlds not realized,
High instincts before which our mortal nature
Did tremble like a guilty Thing surprised:
But for those first affections,
Those shadowy recollections,
Which, be they what they may,
Are yet the fountain-light of all our day,
Are yet a master-light of all our seeing;
Uphold us, cherish, and have power to make
Our noisy years seem moments in the being
Of the eternal Silence: truths that wake,
To perish never:
Which neither listlessness, nor mad endeavor,
Nor Man nor Boy,
Nor all that is at enmity with joy,
Can utterly abolish or destroy!
Hence in a season of calm weather
Though inland far we be,
Our Souls have sight of that immortal sea
Which brought us hither,
Can in a moment travel thither,
And see the Children sport upon the shore,
And hear the mighty waters rolling evermore.

X

Then sing, ye Birds, sing, sing a joyous song!
And let the young Lambs bound
As to the tabor's sound!
We in thought will join your throng,
Ye that pipe and ye that play,
Ye that through your hearts to-day
Feel the gladness of the May!

What though the radiance which was once so bright
Be now for ever taken from my sight,
 Though nothing can bring back the hour
Of splendor in the grass, of glory in the flower;
  We will grieve not, rather find
  Strength in what remains behind;
  In the primal sympathy
  Which having been must ever be;
  In the soothing thoughts that spring
  Out of human suffering;
  In the faith that looks through death,
In years that bring the philosophic mind.

XI

And O, ye Fountains, Meadows, Hills, and Groves,
Forebode not any severing of our loves!
Yet in my heart of hearts I feel your might;
I only have relinquished one delight
To live beneath your more habitual sway.
I love the Brooks which down their channels fret,
Even more than when I tripped lightly as they;
The innocent brightness of a new-born Day
  Is lovely yet;
The Clouds that gather round the setting sun
Do take a sober coloring from an eye
That hath kept watch o'er man's mortality;
Another race hath been, and other palms are won.
Thanks to the human heart by which we live,
Thanks to its tenderness, its joys, and fears,
To me the meanest flower that blows can give
Thoughts that do often lie too deep for tears.

— *William Wordsworth, English (1770–1850).*

The Child in Our Soul

 Toward God in heaven spacious
With artless faith a boy looks free,
 As toward his mother gracious,
And top of Christmas-tree.
But early in the storm of youth
There wounds him deep the serpent's tooth;
 His childhood's faith is doubted
  And flouted.

 Soon stands in radiant splendor
With bridal wreath his boyhood's dream;
 Her loving eyes and tender
The light of heaven's faith stream.
As by his mother's knee of yore
God's name he stammers yet once more,
 The rue of tears now paying
  And praying.

 When now life's conflict stirring
Leads him along through doubtings wild,
 Then upward points unerring
Close by his side his child.
With children he a child is still
And whatsoe'er his heart may chill,
 Prayer for his son is warming,
  Transforming.

 The greatest man in wonder
Must ward the child within his breast,
 And list 'mid loudest thunder
Its whisperings unrepressed.
Where oft a hero fell with shame,
The child it was restored his name,
 His better self revealing,
  And healing.

 All great things thought created
In child-like joy sprang forth and grew;
 All strength and goodness mated,
Obeyed the child's voice true.
When beauty in the soul held sway,
The child gave it in artless play; —
 All wisdom worldly-minded
  Is blinded.

 Hail him, who forward presses
So far that he a home is worth!
 For there alone possesses
The child-life peace on earth.
Though worn we grieve and hardened grow,
What solace 't is our home to know
 With children's laughter ringing
  And singing.

— *From the Norwegian of Björnstjerne Björnson (1832–1910), translated by Arthur Hubbell Palmer.*

The Kingdom of God

"IN NO STRANGE LAND"

O world invisible, we view thee,
O world intangible, we touch thee,
O world unknowable, we know thee.
Inapprehensible, we clutch thee.

Does the fish soar to find the ocean,
The eagle plunge to find the air —

That we ask of the stars in motion
If they have rumour of thee there?

Not where the wheeling systems darken,
And our benumbed conceiving soars! —
The drift of pinions, would we harken,
Beats at our own clay-shuttered doors.

The angels keep their ancient places; —
Turn but a stone and start a wing!
'Tis ye, 'tis your estranged faces,
That miss the many-splendoured thing.

But when so sad thou canst not sadder,
Cry; and upon thy so sore loss
Shall shine the traffic of Jacob's ladder
Pitched betwixt Heaven and Charing Cross.

Yea, in the night, my Soul, my daughter,
Cry, — clinging Heaven by the hems:
And lo, Christ walking on the water
Not of Gennesareth, but Thames!

— *Francis Thompson, English (1859–1907).*

∽ ❁ ∼

The Starlight Night

Look at the stars! look, look up at the skies!
  O look at all the fire-folk sitting in the air!
  The bright boroughs, the circle-citadels there!
Down in dim woods the diamond delves! the elves'-eyes!
The grey lawns cold where gold, where quickgold lies!
  Wind-beat whitebeam! airy abeles set on a flare!
  Flake-doves sent floating forth at a farm-yard scare! —
Ah well! it is all a purchase, all is a prize.

Buy then! bid then! — What? — Prayer, patience, alms, vows.
Look, look: a May-mess, like on orchard boughs!
  Look! March-bloom, like on mealed-with-yellow sallows!
These are indeed the barn; withindoors house
The shocks. This piece-bright paling shuts the spouse
  Christ home, Christ and his mother and all his hallows.

— *Gerard Manley Hopkins, English (1844–1889).*

∽ ❁ ∼

Stella Flammarum

(TO HALLEY'S COMET)

Strange wanderer out of the deeps,
  Whence, journeying, come you?
From what far, unsunned sleeps
  Did fate foredoom you,
Returning for ever again,
  Through the surgings of man,
A flaming, awesome portent of dread
  Down the centuries' span?

Riddle! from the dark unwrung
  By all earth's sages; —
God's fiery torch from His hand outflung,
  To flame through the ages;
Thou Satan of planets eterne,
  'Mid angry path,
Chained, in circlings vast, to burn
  Out ancient wrath.

By what dread hand first loosed
  From fires eternal?
With majesties dire infused
  Of force supernal,
Takest thy headlong way
  O'er the highways of space?
O wonderful, blossoming flower of fear
  On the sky's far face!

What secret of destiny's will
  In thy wild burning?
What portent dire of humanity's ill
  In thy returning?
Or art thou brand of love
  In masking of bale?
And bringest thou ever some mystical surcease
  For all who wail?

Perchance, O Visitor dread,
  Thou hast thine appointed
Task, thou bolt of the vast outsped!
  With God's anointed,
Performest some endless toil
  In the universe wide,
Feeding or curing some infinite need
  Where the vast worlds ride.

Once, only once, thy face
  Will I view in this breathing;
Just for a space thy majesty trace
  'Mid earth's mad seething;
Ere I go hence to my place,
  As thou to thy deeps,
Thou flambent core of a universe dread,
  Where all else sleeps.

But thou and man's spirit are one,
Thou poet! thou flaming
Soul of the dauntless sun,
Past all reclaiming!
One in that red unrest,
That yearning, that surge,
That mounting surf of the infinite dream,
O'er eternity's verge.

—*William Wilfred Campbell, Canadian (1861–1919).*

When I Heard the Learn'd Astronomer

When I heard the learn'd astronomer,
When the proofs, the figures, were ranged in columns before me,
When I was shown the charts and diagrams, to add, divide, and measure them,
When I sitting heard the astronomer where he lectured with much applause in the lecture-room,
How soon unaccountable I became tired and sick,
Till rising and gliding out I wander'd off by myself,
In the mystical moist night-air, and from time to time,
Look'd up in perfect silence at the stars.

—*Walt Whitman, American (1819–1892).*

Brahma

If the red slayer think he slays,
Or if the slain think he is slain,
They know not well the subtle ways
I keep, and pass, and turn again.

Far or forgot to me is near;
Shadow and sunlight are the same;
The vanished gods to me appear;
And one to me are shame and fame.

They reckon ill who leave me out;
When me they fly, I am the wings;
I am the doubter and the doubt,
And I the hymn the Brahmin sings.

The strong gods pine for my abode,
And pine in vain the sacred Seven;
But thou, meek lover of the good!
Find me, and turn thy back on heaven.

—*Ralph Waldo Emerson, American (1803–1882).*

Hamatreya

Bulkeley, Hunt, Willard, Hosmer, Meriam, Flint
Possessed the land which rendered to their toil
Hay, corn, roots, hemp, flax, apples, wool and wood.
Each of these landlords walked amidst his farm,
Saying, ''Tis mine, my children's and my name's.
How sweet the west wind sounds in my own trees.
How graceful climb those shadows on my hill!
I fancy these pure waters and the flags
Know me, as does my dog: we sympathize;
And, I affirm, my actions smack of the soil.'
Where are these men? Asleep beneath their grounds:
And strangers, fond as they, their furrows plough.
Earth laughs in flowers, to see her boastful boys
Earth-proud, proud of the earth which is not theirs;
Who steer the plough, but cannot steer their feet
Clear of the grave.
They added ridge to valley, brook to pond,
And sighed for all that bounded their domain;
'This suits me for a pasture; that's my park;
We must have clay, lime, gravel, granite-ledge,
And misty lowland, where to go for peat.
The land is well, — lies fairly to the south.
'Tis good, when you have crossed the sea and back,
To find the sitfast acres where you left them.'
Ah! the hot owner sees not Death, who adds
Him to his land, a lump of mould the more.
Hear what the Earth says: —

EARTH-SONG

'Mine and yours;
Mine, not yours.
Earth endures;
Stars abide —

Shine down in the old sea;
Old are the shores;
But where are old men?
I who have seen much,
Such have I never seen.

'The lawyer's deed
Ran sure,
In tail,
To them, and to their heirs
Who shall succeed,
Without fail,
Forevermore.

'Here is the land,
Shaggy with wood,
With its old valley,
Mound and flood.
But the heritors? —
Fled like the flood's foam.
The lawyer, and the laws,
And the kingdom,
Clean swept herefrom.

'They called me theirs,
Who so controlled me;
Yet every one
Wished to stay, and is gone,
How am I theirs,
If they cannot hold me,
But I hold them?'

When I heard the Earth-song
I was no longer brave;
My avarice cooled
Like lust in the chill of the grave.

—*Ralph Waldo Emerson, American (1803–1882).*

"All Things Are Current Found"

All things are current found
On earthly ground,
Spirits, and elements
Have their descents.

Night and day, year on year,
High and low, far and near,
These are our own aspects,
These are our own regrets.

Ye gods of the shore,
Who abide evermore,
I see your far headland,
Stretching on either hand;

I hear the sweet evening sounds
From your undecaying grounds;
Cheat me no more with time,
Take me to your clime.

—*Henry David Thoreau, American (1817–1862).*

"Behind Me Dips Eternity"

Behind me dips Eternity,
Before me Immortality,
Myself the term between —
Death but a drift of Eastern gray
Dissolving into dawn away
Before the West begins.

'Tis Kingdom — afterwards — they say,
In perfect pauseless monarchy,
Whose Prince is son of none —
Himself His dateless dynasty,
Himself Himself diversify
In duplicate divine.

'Tis Miracle before me then,
Then miracle behind, between, —
A crescent is the sea
With midnight to the north of her
And midnight to the south of her,
And maelstrom in the sky.

—*Emily Dickinson, American (1830–1886).*

You, Andrew Marvell

And here face down beneath the sun
And here upon earth's noonward height
To feel the always coming on
The always rising of the night

To feel creep up the curving east
The earthly chill of dusk and slow
Upon those under lands the vast
And ever-climbing shadow grow

And strange at Ecbatan the trees
Take leaf by leaf the evening strange
The flooding dark about their knees
The mountains over Persia change

And now at Kermanshah the gate
Dark, empty, and the withered grass
And through the twilight now the late
Few travelers in the westward pass

And Baghdad darken and the bridge
Across the silent river gone,
And through Arabia the edge
Of evening widen and steal on

And deepen on Palmyra's street
The wheel rut in the ruined stone
And Lebanon fade out and Crete
High through the clouds and overblown

And over Sicily the air
Still flashing with the landward gulls
And loom and slowly disappear
The sails above the shadowy hulls

And Spain go under and the shore
Of Africa, the gilded sand
And evening vanish and no more
The low pale light across that land

Nor now the long light on the sea—

And here face downward in the sun
To feel how swift, how secretly
The shadow of the night comes on. . . .

—*Archibald MacLeish, American (1892–).*

Morning Song from "Senlin"

It is morning, Senlin says, and in the morning
When the light drips through the shutters like the dew,
I arise, I face the sunrise,
And do the things my fathers learned to do.
Stars in the purple dusk above the rooftops
Pale in a saffron mist and seem to die,
And I myself on a swiftly tilting planet
Stand before a glass and tie my tie.

Vine-leaves tap my window,
Dew-drops sing to the garden stones,
The robin chirps in the chinaberry tree
Repeating three clear tones.

It is morning. I stand by the mirror
And tie my tie once more.
While waves far off in a pale rose twilight
Crash on a white sand shore.
I stand by a mirror and comb my hair:
How small and white my face!—
The green earth tilts through a sphere of air
And bathes in a flame of space.
There are houses hanging above the stars
And stars hung under a sea . . .
And a sun far off in a shell of silence
Dapples my walls for me. . . .

It is morning, Senlin says, and in the morning
Should I not pause in the light to remember God?
Upright and firm I stand on a star unstable,
He is immense and lonely as a cloud.
I will dedicate this moment before my mirror
To him alone, for him I will comb my hair.
Accept these humble offerings, clouds of silence!
I will think of you as I descend the stair.

Vine-leaves tap my window,
The snail-track shines on the stones;
Dew-drops flash from the chinaberry tree
Repeating two clear tones.

It is morning, I awake from a bed of silence,
Shining I rise from the starless waters of sleep.
The walls are about me still as in the evening,
I am the same, and the same name still I keep.
The earth revolves with me, yet makes no motion,
The stars pale silently in a coral sky.
In a whistling void I stand before my mirror,
Unconcerned, and tie my tie.

There are horses neighing on far-off hills
Tossing their long white manes,
And mountains flash in the rose-white dusk,
Their shoulders black with rains. . . .
It is morning, I stand by the mirror
And surprise my soul once more;
The blue air rushes above my ceiling,
There are suns beneath my floor. . . .

. . . It is morning, Senlin says, I ascend from darkness
And depart on the winds of space for I know not where;
My watch is wound, a key is in my pocket,
And the sky is darkened as I descend the stair.
There are shadows across the windows, clouds in heaven,
And a god among the stars; and I will go
Thinking of him as I might think of daybreak
And humming a tune I know. . . .

Vine-leaves tap at the window,
Dew-drops sing to the garden stones,
The robin chirps in the chinaberry tree
Repeating three clear tones.

— Conrad Aiken, American (1889–).

~ ❁ ~

Peter Quince at the Clavier

I

Just as my fingers on these keys
Make music, so the self-same sounds
On my spirit make a music, too.

Music is feeling, then, not sound;
And thus it is that what I feel,
Here in this room, desiring you,

Thinking of your blue-shadowed silk,
Is music. It is like the strain
Waked in the elders by Susanna:

Of a green evening, clear and warm,
She bathed in her still garden, while
The red-eyed elders, watching, felt

The basses of their being throb
In witching chords, and their thin blood
Pulse pizzicati of Hosanna.

II

In the green-evening, clear and warm,
Susanna lay.
She searched
The touch of springs,
And found
Concealed imaginings.
She sighed
For so much melody.

Upon the bank she stood
In the cool
Of spent emotions.
She felt, among the leaves,
The dew
Of old devotions.

She walked upon the grass,
Still quavering.
The winds were like her maids
On timid feet,
Fetching her woven scarves,
Yet wavering.

A breath upon her hand
Muted the night.
She turned —
A cymbal crashed,
And roaring horns.

III

Soon, with a noise like tambourines,
Came her attendant Byzantines.

They wondered why Susanna cried
Against the elders by her side:

And as they whispered, the refrain
Was like a willow swept by rain.

Anon their lamps' uplifted flame
Revealed Susanna and her shame.

And then the simpering Byzantines
Fled, with a noise like tambourines.

IV

Beauty is momentary in the mind —
The fitful tracing of a portal;
But in the flesh it is immortal.

The body dies; the body's beauty lives.
So evenings die, in their green going,
A wave, interminably flowing.
So gardens die, their meek breath scenting
The cowl of Winter, done repenting.
So maidens die to the auroral
Celebration of a maiden's choral.

Susanna's music touched the bawdy strings
Of those white elders; but, escaping,
Left only Death's ironic scraping.
Now in its immortality, it plays
On the clear viol of her memory,
And makes a constant sacrament of praise.

— Wallace Stevens, American (1879–).

PART SEVEN

The Unfolding Universe

THE COMPANY of the world's peers comprises scientists, no less than saints and sages, or prophets and creative artists. The scientific knowledge of the world is an indispensable part of man's heritage from the past. The human race has outgrown some of its heroes in knowledge, but it will never outgrow them in spirit. Save for the persistence of the scientist in seeking the control of disease, and his courage in the quest of universal knowledge, many men would still be shackled by superstition or would be living in want, deprived of opportunities for the spirit to flourish or the mind to create. Science has exorcised many a demon, healed many a disease, provided the leisure in which the arts might thrive, extended the span of our lives, and demonstrated that we move in a universe which staggers the imagination with its orderliness and immensity. Despite the jealousies which underlie nationalistic rivalries in all departments of cultural life and the economic tensions which lead to hatred and wars, the world has grown kinder because science has ignored the distinctions of race and bequeathed its blessings upon all men without respect to creed or color.

To discerning minds there is no quarrel between the values of science and of religion and literature. At their best, all have a moral basis: they seek and express the truth essential in the economy of man's life and of the universe. There is warrant for remarking that a test of one's adulthood is the extent to which one does or does not cling with childish tenacity to foibles and fancies, ignoring or accepting the achievements of great minds in unfamiliar fields of work, discounting or utilizing their contribution to man's common wealth. The heroic spirits of the past challenge both the standards of our modern life and our intellectual honesty.

The scientific literature of the world is therefore an indispensable part of the record of man's long efforts to master his environment, to ascertain its nature and meaning, and to put the discovered laws of the universe to use. Indeed it is man's experience and capacity for such work that mark his superiority to other forms of animal life. Much has been written about the inhumanity of science and the destructive ends to which scientific knowledge has been devoted. In interesting contrast, however, to the pessimism inherent in some religions and the conclusion of many writers that life is essentially "a tale told by an idiot" and nature is "red in tooth and claw," Darwin's conclusion may profitably be noted: "According to my judgment happiness decidedly prevails." Both scientists and religious seers agree that the generative forces of the universe are kind and that its laws harmoniously uphold an order that cannot be violated without penalties. If man has suffered at the hand of science, his pain has come chiefly from his misuse of scientific knowledge and from ignorance.

The view of the universe presented in the extracts taken from the writings of Cosmas Indicopleustes and Edwin Hubble which follow offer excellent illustrations of the apparent conflicts between science and religion. It cannot be denied that the progress of scientific discovery has often brought sharp challenge to many traditional systems of belief. Controversy over the new astronomy of the Renaissance is an excellent case in point. Both Galileo and his persecutors were sincere: the former selflessly sought scientific truth about the solar system, the latter sought to protect man's central place in a religious conception of the universe. The men who opposed the new astronomy, which made the earth a mere satellite of the sun, honestly believed that if this astronomical fact were admitted man would lose his special dignity on earth, there would be no centrality to the human drama, and grounds for the belief in the infinite value of each human soul would be lost. The scholastics who scorned and persecuted the first modern scientists thus sought no selfish ends – they sincerely believed they were serving truth and conscience. The scientists who similarly persevered in their work often suffered cruelly from misunderstanding and persecution; and it was for later generations to recognize their contributions and to honor them. In any period of intellectual change or revaluation, the individual who rests in the confidence that truth cannot contradict truth will be able to view the movements about him with objectivity and poise.

Poets have pointed out that man is of imagination all compact. Curiosity and credulity are characteristics of the human mind. Both in the historical records of our race's childhood and in the contemporary literatures which reflect the presumptive maturity of modern man, there is evidence of a desire in all departments of life to retain outmoded ideas because they are comfortable and to respond to facts emotionally rather than rationally. Man's conception of the process of creation and of the universe has gradually modified through the centuries in the light of advancing knowledge in geology and astronomy, biology and paleontology. The early visions of the making of this world, and the entire universe with it at a given time, have grown into a grander vision of worlds formed progressively by action of universal laws, a universe in which countless new worlds are being created today, just as our own satellite of the sun was formed ages past. The idea of a primeval chaos which found expression in the cosmogonies of the ancients has now given place to the conviction that, as far back as man may go on the wings of the imagination into the past, this universe, however different in aspect, was still a cosmos. Whether this study of the unfolding universe is *extensive* or *intensive,* as suggested in some of the extracts which follow, one fact is apparent: the universe is not capricious and its laws are dependable.

For the humanist, in addition to all the boons of modern physics and medicine, science brings the assurance that in the mysterious world about us an astronomer's first surmises, a seer's vision of moral grandeur, a poet's dream of beauty, and a botanist's study of the minutest forms of life, may all contribute in ways we cannot now know to the well being of man.

The Medieval Christian World

COSMAS INDICOPLEUSTES

As many as ardently desire true knowledge and are lovers of the true light, and earnestly endeavour to become fellow-citizens of the saints in the age to come, who regard the Old and New Testament as in reality divine scripture, who are obedient to Moses and the Christ, who follow out to the end the principles they have adopted, who acknowledge that the world was produced by God out of mere nothing, and who believe that there is a resurrection of men and a judgment, and the righteous shall inherit the Kingdom of Heaven; all these carefully examine the divine scriptures all throughout, to see whether in Moses, who wrote the account of the Creation, and in the other Prophets, they contain descriptions of the places and figures of the whole creation, among which is indicated also the position of the Kingdom of Heaven, which the Lord Christ promises God will give to righteous men. And when they find the Old and New Testaments to be in mutual harmony, they abide therein firmly grounded and immovable, in nothing confounded by their adversaries. But those on the other hand who prank themselves out in the wisdom of this world, and are self-confident that by scholastic reasonings they can comprehend its figure and position, scoff at all divine scripture as a mass of fables, stigmatising Moses and the prophets, the Lord and the Apostles as idle babblers, and given over to vain decisions; while with supercilious airs, as if they far surpassed in wisdom the rest of mankind, they attribute to the heavens a spherical figure and a circular motion, and by geometrical methods and calculations applied to the heavenly bodies, as well as by the abuse of words and by worldly craft, endeavour to grasp the position and figure of the world by means of the solar and lunar eclipses, leading others into error while they are in error themselves in maintaining that such phenomena could not present themselves if the figure was other than spherical. But concerning these matters we shall not enter into any discussion just at present, since those persons sufficiently confute the one the other. But those who wish to profess Christianity, while wishing at the same time to bedeck themselves with the principles, the wisdom, and the diversity of the errors of this world, and contend that one thing and another should be accepted, seem to differ nothing from a shadow which exists while the intermediate body from which it is projected is in light, but which cannot exist when that body is not in light, nay, is even obliterated by the light when the body is illuminated all round.

It is against such men my words are directed, for divine scripture denounces them, as of old it denounced the strangers sojourning in Samaria, because they feared God and burned incense and offered worship on the high places. Were one to call such men double-faced, he would not be wrong, for, look you, they wish both to be with us and with those that are against us, thus making void their renunciation of Satan whom they renounced in baptism, and again running back to him. Now, such men cannot be with us at all; but they occupy a middle position, like empty houses standing high up in the air, without having either foundations in the earth below, or anything from above to hold them fast. For while they have as yet scarcely come by their principles, they set about destroying them; and before they have yet destroyed them, they show that their end is unaccomplished, as they stand firm neither on the one side nor the other, but rather laugh at every one, and are themselves laughed at by all. In the first place, then, when arguing with them about the spherical figure, we showed that this figure was not possible, and was indeed quite inconsistent with the nature of things. Certain of them say that the heaven is a body consisting of four elements, but some later on superciliously reconstructed it with an additional fifth new element, though formerly its essential constitution comprised only four elements, for they saw at a glance that the heaven could not revolve if it was composed of these. But herein again they are found to be blind even when they think that those who are sharp-sighted do not see. For since the heaven is seen to be of sundry and diverse colours, whence a power to produce heat and cold seems to be inherent in them, they say that the eyes of all are deceived by reason of their immense distance. Well, then, let any one of them who so wishes come forward and tell us: Why do the stars which, according to you are evidently fixed in an immovable sphere, not apparently differ in colour and size, though their distances from us are seen to be unequal, if the centre of the earth be the point from which our eyes are directed towards them? And how is it that many of the fixed stars are equal and like to the planet we call Mars, to which a lower sphere has been assigned, and how do we in like manner see not a few of them to be like the planet Jupiter? But further, we do not even see the heaven itself to be of one and the same colour, for, if it were asked from whence can we surmise that the cloud-like concretions which you have named the galaxy, and which you have so designated simply because of the difference of their colour, have derived their peculiar appearance, while the surface on which the ray of vision strikes is uniform? And if I replied that these were proofs of the composition and mixture of different elements, no one, I apprehend, would dare to contradict me, even though he were a lover of falsehood, and much less if one of those who always assign the foremost place to truth. Now if the heaven has been constituted not of one single element endowed with a circular motion of its own, but of the mixture of the four elements, then it cannot well revolve. For it has been said that it must either be moved downward if the heavy element preponderate, or be carried upward if the opposite light one prevail, or must be stationary when no element is preponderant. This is certainly obvious to everybody. For no one would admit that he has ever seen the heaven move either upwards or downwards. It must be allowed therefore that it is firmly fixed. But should they ask: Whence are these motions that differ from the rest in an element that is simple and without qualities? since they say, and not untruly, that those bodies which they call planets revolve oppositely to the universe; and if in like manner they say that their revolution is accomplished in certain times which the Creator has fixed, it is evident that they do not even deny that the planets advance from the East.

Then being mazed with perplexing doubts, as usually happens to those who shrink from the truth, they say, on finding no way of escape, that the stars make retrogressions and pauses. But tell me, ye souls that are so ingenious in tying and untying knots, if from their very nature they have motion, how comes it that they stand still? For nothing that can thwart them enters as an element into their natural constitution. And tell me this besides, what is the force or what the necessity which imposes on them the contrary motion? And here let no one tell me that it is an ocular deception; for it is no minute distance to which they advance, seeing that they are often observed to shift their place from a sign of the zodiac that is in the rear to one in front. But what must we say of our opponents when passing on to the operations of the stars themselves, they reach the very height of absurdity, all unconscious that they themselves stand still or move backward, and are but a sorry set of good-for-nothing rascals? Now anyone would say that the star previously seen in Aries, but at present appearing in Pisces, was not in the house of Mars, but in that of Jupiter, and that it makes *movements,* not such as they babble about when it is in Aries, but those which they ascribe to it in its transit through Pisces. But if they do not admit the retrograde motion of the *planets* which is apparent, whence then or wherefore is their course in both directions? They will perhaps in reply assign as the cause those invisible epicycles which they have assumed as vehicles on which, as they will insist, the planets are borne along. But they will be in no better case from this invention, for we shall ask: Why have they need of vehicles? Is it because they are incapable of motion? Then, if so, why should you assert them to be animated, and that too even with souls more than usually divine? Or is it that they are capable? The very idea is, methinks, ridiculous. And why have not the moon and the sun their epicycles? Is it that they are not worthy on account of their inferiority? But this could not be said by men in their sober senses. Was it then from the scarcity of suitable material the Creator could not construct vehicles for them? On your own head let the blasphemy of such a thought recoil.

Cease, O ye wiseacres! prating worthless nonsense, and learn at last though late to follow the divine oracles and not your own baseless fancies. For, tell us, how ye think that the fixed stars move in an opposite direction to the universe? Is such a motion theirs only or that of the sphere in which they are placed? Then, if it is theirs, how do they traverse unequal orbits in equal time? And how comes it that of the stars in the galaxy not one has ever gone outside of it, nor any of those outside is seen nearer it or within it? But if one should say that it is the sphere which moves in the opposite direction, then it will be found that at the same time it moves oppositely to itself. But who can imagine a greater absurdity than this? Thus they do their best to prevent any one surpassing them in their effrontery — or rather, let me say, in impiety, since they do not blush to affirm that there are people who live on the under surface of the earth. What then, should some one question them and say: Is the sun to no purpose carried under the earth? these absurd persons will, on the spur of the moment, without thinking, reply that the people of the Antipodes are there — men carrying their heads downwards, and rivers having a position opposite to the rivers here! thus taking in hand to turn everything upside down rather than to follow the doctrines of the truth, in which there are no futile sophisms, but which are plain and easy and full of godliness, while they procure salvation for those who reverently consult them.

But you will most effectually rebuke them if you say: Why does that sphere of yours not revolve from the north to the south, or from some other quarter to its opposite? And do not tell me, in answer, that such seemed better to the Maker of the world. But how can you deem that you speak consistently with the nature of things in supposing that the whole heaven is in motion and describes a circle, without also supposing that outside of it there is either some other space or body, even though it were imaginary. For it is impossible any thing can move apart from the four elements, but must move either in earth, or in water, or in air, or in fire, whether it is transferred from place to place into the infinite, or whether it always revolves in the same place. But if the heaven as it revolves passes into the infinity of space, we must suppose that beyond it there is an infinite earth into which it rolls, when noiselessly leaving what is behind it; but if one of the other three elements be supposed, in not one of them is the sphere adapted to roll and rotate; nay, were it to be shot into any of them, a whizzing noise would attend the transition. But if, again, it rolls and rotates always in the same spot without moving from place to place, then it must be upheld by supports like a turner's lathe, or an artificial globe, or on an axis like a machine or a waggon. And if so, then we must again inquire by what the supports and axles are themselves upheld, and so *ad infinitum*. And tell me, pray, how are we to suppose the axis passes through the middle of the earth, and of what material it consists.

When these problems then concerning the nature of things are discussed, there remains the conclusion, as we said before, that the heaven is fixed and does not revolve. But even in supposing that the earth is in the middle of the universe, as its centre, you immediately give the death-blow to your own theory when you repeat that the middle is below, for it is impossible that the same thing can at once both be in the middle and below, for the middle is the middle between up and down, or between right and left, or between before and behind. Why do you then, when beleaguered with difficulties, utter absurdities contrary to nature, in opposition to scripture? For being in terror lest any one should pose you with this question: How can this unspeakable weight of the earth be held suspended by the air and not fall down? you invented stories of things that are not true, but strange; and, reversing the order of things, give out that the middle is below; so that if any should suppose that instead of the earth, fire was the middle, you would then say that the middle was above instead of below, seeing that the tendency of fire is upward. To me, therefore, they seem to subvert the first by means of the second, and the second by means of the first. But if they say that the air because it surrounds the earth equally on all sides, is pushed on by the universe, and that the earth remains immovable, and swerves neither to the one side nor the other, why do men and the irrational animals that live on land or fly in the air not move along with it, while all of them cleave the air in walking and in traversing it, and in going on high. And not only is it incapable of resisting these, but it cannot even sustain the weight of feathers and the smallest of straws, but all of them cut it, it is so attenuated and so rare, and they outstrip it according to the force with which they are propelled. How then can we receive such theories?

But should one wish to examine more elaborately the question of the Antipodes, he would easily find them to be old wives' fables. For if two men on opposite sides placed the soles of their feet each against each, whether they chose to stand on earth, or water, or air, or fire, or any other kind of body, how could both be found standing upright? The one would assuredly be found in the natural upright position, and the other, contrary to nature, head downward. Such notions are opposed to reason, and alien to our nature and condition. And how, again, when it rains upon both of them, is it possible to say that the rain falls down upon the two, and not that it falls down to the one and falls up to the other, or falls against them, or towards them, or away from them. For to think that there are Antipodes compels us to think also that rain falls on them from an opposite direction to ours; and any one will, with good reason, deride these ludicrous theories, which set forth principles incongruous, ill-adjusted, and contrary to nature.

And if one should examine that other sophism of theirs, namely, that the earth is inflated with air, and that earthquakes occur when the pent-up air shakes the earth violently, he would be amazed at the imposture and the contradiction in their statements. For if the earth when equally pressed by the whole air stands unshaken and unswerving, then, when inflated it ought to be all the heavier in that quarter, and to swerve to a side, after the example of man which they adduce. For not only does a man shake and tremble when attacked with flatulency, but he trembles when seized with terror, and when overcome with wine, and pinched with cold, and when his blood boils with anger, and when he is old and imbecile, but when he reels under the effects of flatulency death results. Why then does not the earth also, which according to them is inflated with air, not collapse and lose its proper place? And why, again, do they further say that Egypt, because its soil is porous and its furrows allow the air to escape without violent shocks, is not subject to earthquakes, while in point of fact earthquakes have been of frequent occurrence in that country, and so violent as to overthrow cities and level them with the ground: and not only so, but even in the times of the Greeks, when Alexander, and Seleucus, and Antiochus, and Ptolemy ruled and reigned, they had recourse to the assistance of philosophers – Aristotle and his like – and frequently gave practical effect to what they advised? And when Antioch was being founded by Seleucus and Antiochus, how was it that the philosophers were not able to point out that the country there was not safe from earthquakes, but on the contrary exposed to their frequent visitations? And this we say from having seen that this city has been repeatedly overthrown by earthquakes; and not Antioch only but Corinth also, which has close at her hand the mob of the philosophers.

But if we should care to examine yet another of their opinions – that in which they say and try to prove by illustrations – that rain is produced from vapour drawn up by heat into the atmosphere, in the same way, say they, as the bath draws up vapour from the heat, and lets it fall in drops; and just as a cupping-glass draws up moisture by means of tow and fire, so too does the sun draw up vapour, and in course of time lets it fall in drops, whence rain is produced. One cannot but marvel at such wisdom as this, imposing, as it does by its speciousness, upon the multitude. For since the bath derives its heat not from above but from below, how can it be said to draw up, and not rather to push up? So too in the case of a caldron: it receives its heat not from above but from below, and in both instances the vapours are pushed up by the heat, and in the rebound, due in the one case to the roof and in the other to the lid, they fall in drops. Similar is the case of the cupping-glass, which, did not this instrument itself constrain nature and suck up moisture, would never have sucked it up at all, no, not even if fire and tow had been applied ten thousand times over. But further, when one thrusts a damp faggot into the fire, moisture is to such a degree pushed by the heat that both moisture and smoke are expelled from the other end of the faggot. And when one has kindled a fire on the ground he sees the moisture in the faggots conveyed upwards by the smoke, not drawn up by what is above but pushed up by the heat of the fire. Nay, more, if one washes a garment and spreads it on the ground, and if, when it has been dried by the sun, he lifts it up, he will find the moisture which has been expelled from it by the heat impressed on the ground in the very shape of the garment. In like manner, if one places a hot piece of meat on a trencher, he will see the moisture discharged in both directions, both upwards and downwards, the heat being intermediate, for above he sees the steam mounting upwards, and below he sees the trencher bathed in moisture on which the meat has impressed its own shape; whence it appears that heat does not draw up, as these sages tell us, but rather pushes up.

But when we propose a new question to them: Why is it that in the Thebaïd, where the ground is parched up by the heat, the moisture is not drawn up and turned into rain for that country? they defend themselves by saying that it is a moderate and not an excessive heat that causes the drawing up. To this we shall give a very summary reply: And how happens it, we shall ask, that beyond the Thebaïd, in Ethiopia, where the heat is far greater, there are copious downfalls of rain? And how can they say, those many and tip-top wise men, that the sun has the power of drawing upwards, and assert also quite confidently that in the course of his revolution he becomes heated by friction, while they will not entertain the supposition that the heat is in him by nature. But more: when they allow that the air is moist and hot, what need have those wiseacres to resort to sophistry and say that the moisture is drawn up from elsewhere, when up above they have the heat and moisture at the same spot? But if one should ask them about one particular element as it is in itself, that is, should ask them to show its distinctive quality, they immediately find themselves at a loss, and attribute two qualities to one single element and say: Earth is *dry and cold;* water, *cold and moist;* air, *moist and warm;* fire, *warm and dry;* so that, being beleaguered with difficulties, they assign eight qualities to the four elements. But at times they say that all the qualities exist in each of the elements. Once more, therefore, they contradict their own words, by ascribing not four but only two qualities to each of the four elements. I marvel accordingly at those most excellent men when they attribute to water *coldness and humidity,* and to the air *humidity and heat.* How do they say that water, that is, the *cold and moist,* congeals and becomes ice in wintertime? Wherefrom comes that extreme cold which converts it into ice? For if they shall say that the departure of the sun naturally produces this effect, why does it not produce the same effect on the air, which is naturally *warm,* and at the same time *moist,* but makes it, on the contrary, extremely *cold?* And how does *the cold* itself – that is, water – not make the air – that is, *the moist* – freeze, but, on the contrary, it is the latter which makes the former freeze, as we actually see? Now though I have many things more to say about this question and the examples which they erroneously adduce in favour of their view of it, I curb myself, for I feel ashamed of the foolishness of what is said by them, and consider what has already been said on this subject sufficient.

There is, however, another sophism held by these wise men which I am especially anxious to deal with, and will forthwith proceed to discuss. They say that the heaven which they call a body contains the whole world, and stoutly maintain that outside of it nothing whatever exists; and yet they define angels and demons and souls, which are parts of the world as uncircumscribed, neither containing the heaven, nor contained by the heaven, not understanding what they say, since that which neither contains nor is contained is never by any possibility seen among things that are. If then these things be as they say, let them tell us with respect to their own soul whether it is, or is not. And if they say it is not, then to their own shame and disgrace they assume themselves to be soulless. But if they say that it exists, let them tell us whether it is in them or not in them. If they reply that it is not in them, they answer not less shamelessly and foolishly than they did before. But if they reply that the soul is in them, we must ask them a further question: As the body is circumscribed by the heaven, why is not the soul also circumscribed? And if, as they say, it illuminates the body without being circumscribed along with it, the question arises, where is it when it illuminates the body? since it is impossible that, being a created thing, it should not exist with things created. And if they say it exists somewhere within the heaven, then it is again circumscribed by the body itself of the heaven, although it was represented by them as uncircumscribed. But if they make it exist outside the heaven, they, in the first place, confute themselves; in the next place, it will either be in a part of the heaven and occupy but a small part of it, or it will be in the whole of it, in which case it will circumscribe the heaven and will be found having form like a bodily substance; and this a spherical form embracing and limiting the sphere. But if, again, they say that as being uncircumscribed it pervades all things both within and without, let them not blind themselves to the fact that they are both introducing polytheism and imagining an equality with God. For this property pertains to none except the uncreated Deity who created and fashioned the universe. So then, professing themselves to be wise, they become fools, as says the blessed Paul the Apostle, having changed the glory of the uncircumscribed Deity to their own created souls, thus appropriating to themselves the glory due to God. They must therefore in every way be avoided. For, saith the Apostle, from those turn away who hold an outward form of godliness but deny the power thereof.

—*From Book III of Christian Topography, of Cosmas Indicopleustes, Egyptian (sixth century A.D.), translated from the Greek by J. W. McCrindle, published by the Hakluyt Society, London.*

The Revolutions of the Celestial Spheres

COPERNICUS

Preface and Dedication to Pope Paul III

I can reckon easily enough, Most Holy Father, that as soon as certain people learn that in these books of mine which I have written about the revolutions of the spheres of the world I attribute certain motions to the terrestrial globe, they will immediately shout to have me and my opinion hooted off the stage. For my own works do not please me so much that I do not weigh what judgments others will pronounce concerning them. And although I realize that the thoughts of a philosopher are beyond the judgment of the crowd, because it is his office to seek the truth in all things, insofar as God has granted that to human reason; nevertheless, I think we should avoid becoming the subject of opinions utterly foreign to rightness. And when I considered that those who know that the opinion that the earth rests unmoving in the middle of the heavens as if it were the center of the heavens has been confirmed by the judgments of many ages would hold this ἀκροάμα absurd if I were to assert to the contrary that the earth moves; for a long time I was in great difficulty as to whether I should bring to light my commentaries written to show forth the earth's movement, or whether it would not be better to follow the example of the Pythagoreans and certain others who used to hand down the mysteries of their philosophy not in writing but by word of mouth and only to their colleagues and friends, witness the letter of Lysis to Hipparchus. And it seems to me that they did that not, as some suppose, because they were jealous of sharing their doctrines with people but in order that things of very great beauty which have been zealously investigated by great men should not be despised by those who find it a bother to expend any great energy on letters—except on the money-making variety—or who are provoked by the exhortations and example of others to the liberal study of philosophy but on account of their natural stupidity hold the position among philosophers that drones hold among bees. Therefore when I weighed these things in my mind, the scorn which I had to fear on account of the newness and absurdity of my opinion almost drove me to destroy a work already undertaken.

But my friends made me change my course in spite of my hesitation and resistance. First among them was Nicholas Schonberg, Cardinal of Capua, famous in all branches of learning; next to him was my devoted friend Tiedeman Giese, Bishop of Culm, a man filled with great zeal for the divine and liberal arts: for he in particular urged me frequently and even spurred me on by reproaches into publishing this book and letting come to light a work which I had kept hidden among my things for not merely nine years, but for almost four times nine years. Not a few other learned and distinguished men demanded the same thing of me, urging me to refuse no longer—on account of the fear which I felt—to contribute my work to the common utility of those who are really interested in mathematics: they said that perhaps to the extent that my teaching about the movement of the earth now seems to very many persons to be absurd, to that extent will be the more an object of admirations and gratitude, when after the publication of my commentaries the same persons see the fog of absurdity dissipated by my luminous demonstrations. Accordingly I was led by such persuasion and by hope finally to permit my friends to undertake the publication of a work which they had long sought from me.

But perhaps Your Holiness will not be so much surprised at my giving the results of my nocturnal study to the light, — after having taken such care in working them out that I did not hesitate to put in writing my thoughts on the movement of the earth — as you will be eager to learn from me what came into my mind that in opposition to the general opinion of mathematicians and almost in opposition to common sense I should dare to imagine some movement of the earth. And so I am unwilling to hide from Your Holiness that nothing except my knowledge that mathematicians have not agreed with one another in their researches moved me to think out a different rational way of drawing up the movements of the spheres of the world. For in the first place mathematicians are so uncertain about the movements of the sun and moon that they can neither demonstrate nor observe the unchanging magnitude of the revolving year. Then in setting up the solar and lunar movements and those of the other five wandering stars, they do not employ the same principles, assumptions or demonstrations for the revolutions and apparent movements. For some make use only of homocentric circles, others of eccentric circles and epicycles, by means of which however they do not fully attain what they seek. For although those who have put their trust in homocentric circles have demonstrated that various different movements can be composed of such circles, nevertheless they have not been able to establish anything for certain that would fully correspond to the appearances. But even if those who have thought up eccentric circles seem to have been able for the most part to explain the apparent movements by fitting calculations, they have nevertheless admitted a great deal which seems to contradict the first principles of regularity of movement. Finally, they have not been able to discover or to infer the thing which is chief of all, i.e., the form of the world and the certain symmetry of its parts. But they are in exactly the same fix as some one taking from different places hands, feet, head and the other limbs — very fine in themselves but not formed with reference to one body and having no correspondence with one another, so that such parts made up a monster and not a man. And so in the process of demonstration which we call "method" they are found either to have omitted something necessary or to have admitted something foreign which by no means pertains to the matter; and they would by no means have been in this fix, if they had followed sure principles. For if the hypotheses they assumed were not untrustworthy, everything which followed from the hypotheses would have been verified beyond a shadow of a doubt; and though what I am saying may be obscure right now, nevertheless it will become clearer in the proper place.

Accordingly when I had meditated upon this lack of certitude in the traditional mathematics concerning the composition of movements of the spheres of the world, I began to be annoyed that the philosophers, who in other respects had made a very careful scrutiny of the least details of the world, had discovered no rational certitude in the movements of the world-machine, which has been built for us by the best and most orderly workman of all. Wherefore I took the trouble to read all the books by philosophers which I could get hold of, to see if any of them even supposed that the movements of the spheres of the world were different from those laid down by those who taught mathematics in the schools. And as a matter of fact I found first in Cicero that Nicetus thought the earth moved. And afterwards I found in Plutarch that there were some others who were of the same opinion: I shall copy out his words here, so that they may be known to all:

"Some think that the earth is at rest; but Philolaus the Pythagorean says that it moves around the fire with an obliquely circular motion, like the sun and moon. Herakleides of Pontus and Ekphantus the Pythagorean do not give the earth any movements of translation, but rather a limited movement of rising and setting around its center, like a wheel."

Therefore I also, having been given occasions, began to meditate upon the mobility of the earth. And although the opinion seemed absurd, nevertheless because I knew that others before me had been allowed the liberty to imagine special circles in order to show forth astral phenomena, I thought I too would be readily permitted to make an experiment as to whether or not by laying down that the earth had some movement I could find demonstrations less shaky than those of my predecessors for the revolutions of the celestial spheres.

And so, having postulated the movements which I attribute to the earth further on in the work, I finally discovered by the help of long and numerous observations that if the movements of the other wandering stars were correlated with the circular movement of the earth, and if the movements were computed in accordance with the revolution of each star, not only would all the phenomena follow from that but also the order and magnitudes of all the planets and of their spheres or orbital circles; and it would bind the heavens together so closely that nothing could be transposed in any part of them without disrupting the remaining parts and the universe as a whole. Accordingly in composing my work I adopted the following order: in the first book I describe all the locations of the spheres or orbital circles together with the movements which I attribute to the earth, so that this book contains as it were the general set-up of the universe. But afterwards in the remaining books I correlate all the movements of the other stars and their spheres or orbital circles with the mobility of the earth, so that it can be gathered from that how far the phenomena of movement of the remaining stars and their orbital circles can be saved by being correlated with the movements of the earth. And I have no doubt that talented and learned mathematicians will agree with me, if – as philosophy demands in the first place – they are willing to give not superficial but profound thought and effort to what I bring forward in this work in showing forth these things. And in order that the unlearned as well as the learned might see that I was not seeking to avoid the judgment of any man, I preferred to dedicate these results of my nocturnal study to Your Holiness rather than to anyone else; because, even in this remote corner of the earth where I live, you are held to be most eminent both in the dignity of your order and in your love of letters and even of mathematics; so that by the authority of your judgment, you can easily provide a guard against the bites of slanderers, despite the proverb that there is no medicine for the bite of a sycophant.

But if however there are certain idle talkers who take it upon themselves to pronounce judgment, although wholly ignorant of mathematics, and if by shamelessly distorting the sense of some passage in Holy Writ to suit their purpose, they dare to reprehend and to attack my work; they worry me so little that I shall even despise their judgments as hybridic. For it is well known that Lectantius, otherwise a distinguished writer but hardly a mathematician, spoke in an utterly puerile fashion concerning the form of the earth and laughed at those who affirmed that the earth had the form of a globe. And so the studious need not be surprised if people like that laugh at us. Mathematics is written for mathematicians; and among them, if I am not mistaken, my labors will be seen to contribute something to the ecclesiastical republic, the principate of which Your Holiness now holds. For not many years ago under Leo X when the Lateran Council was considering the question of reforming the Ecclesiastical Calendar, no decision was reached, for the sole reason that the magnitude of the year and the months and the movements of the sun and moon had not yet been measured with sufficient accuracy. From that time on I gave attention to making more exact observations of these things and was encouraged to do so by that most distinguished man, Paul, Bishop of Fossombrone, who had been present at those deliberations. But what I have established in this matter I leave to the judgment of Your Holiness in particular and to that of all other learned mathematicians. And so not to appear to Your Holiness to make more promises concerning the utility of this work than I can fulfill, I now pass on to the body of the work.

Book I

Among the many and varied literary and artistic studies upon which the natural talent of man is nourished, I think that those above all should be embraced and pursued with the greatest zeal which have to do with things that are very beautiful and very worthy of knowledge. Such studies are those which deal with the godlike circular movements of the world, the course of the stars, their magnitudes, distances, risings and settings, and the causes of the other celestial phenomena; and which finally explicate the whole form. For what could be more beautiful than the heavens which contain all beautiful things? Their very names make this clear: *Caelum* (heavens) by naming that which is beautifully carved; and *Mundus* (world) purity and elegance. Many philosophers have called the world a visible god on account of its extraordinary excellence. So if the worth of the arts were measured by the subject-matter with which they deal, this art — which some call astronomy, others astrology, and many of the ancients the consummation of mathematics — would be by far the most outstanding. This art which is as it were the head of all the arts and the one most worthy of a free man has nearly all the other branches of mathematics to support it. Arithmetic, geometry, optics, geodesy, mechanics, and whatever others, all assist it. And since a property of all good arts is to draw the mind of man away from vice and direct it to better things, these arts can do that more plentifully on account of the unbelievable pleasure of mind which they furnish. For who, after applying himself to things which he sees established in the best order and directed by divine ruling would not through contemplation of them and through a certain habituation be awakened to that which is best and would not admire the artificer of all things, in whom is all happiness and every good? For the divine psalmist surely did not say gratuitously that he took pleasure in the workings of God and rejoiced in the works of his hands, unless by means of these things as by some sort of vehicle we are transported to the contemplation of the highest good?

Now as regards the utility and ornament which they confer upon a commonwealth, — to pass over the innumerable advantages they give to private citizens — Plato calls our attention to the right things, for in the seventh book of the *Laws* he says that this study should be pursued especially in order that through it the divisions of time into days, months, and years and the determination of solemnities and sacrifices should keep the state alive and watchful; and he says that if anyone denies that this study is necessary for a man who is going to take up any of the highest branches of learning, then such a person is thinking foolishly; and he thinks that it is impossible for anyone to become godlike or be called so who has no necessary knowledge of the sun, moon, and the other stars.

However this more divine than human science, which inquires into the highest things, is not lacking in difficulties. And in particular we see that as regards its principles and postulates, which the Greeks call hypotheses, many of those who undertook to deal with them were not in accord and hence did not support themselves with the same reasons. In addition, the courses of the planets and the revolution of the stars cannot be determined by exact calculations and reduced to perfect knowledge except through the passage of time and with the help of many prior observations, transmitted so to speak by hand to posterity. For even if Claud Ptolemy of Alexandria, who stands far in front of all the others on account of his admirable care and industry, with the help of more than forty years of observations brought this art to such a high point that there seemed to be nothing left which he had not touched upon; nevertheless we see that very many things are not in accord with the movements which should follow from his doctrine but rather with movements which were discovered later and were unknown to him. Whence even Plutarch in speaking of the revolving solar year says, "So far the movement of the stars has overcome the ingenuity of the mathematicians." Now to take the year itself as my example, I believe it is well known how many different opinions there are about it, so that many people have given up hope of making an exact determination of it. Similarly, in the case of the other stars I shall try — with the help of God, without whom we can do nothing — to make a more detailed inquiry concerning them since the greater the interval of time between us and the founding fathers of this art — whose discoveries we can compare with the new ones made by us — the more means we have of supporting our own theory. Furthermore I confess that I shall expound many things differently from my predecessors — although with their aid, for it was they who first opened the road of inquiry into these things.

The World Is Spherical

In the beginning we should remark that the world is like a globe; whether because this form is the most perfect of all, as it is an integral whole and needs no joints; or because it is the figure having the greatest volume and so would be especially suitable for comprehending and conserving all things; or even because the separate parts of the world, i.e., the sun, moon, and stars are seen under such a form; or because all things seek to be delimited by such a form, as is apparent in the case of drops of water and other liquid bodies, when they become delimited through themselves. And so no one would hesitate to say that this form belongs to the heavenly bodies.

The Earth Is Spherical Too

The earth is like a globe too, since on every side it rests upon its center. But that it is a perfect sphere is not seen right away on account of the great height of its mountains and the lowness of its valleys, though they modify its universal roundness to only a very small extent. That is made clear in this way. For when people journey northward from any region, the northern vertex of the axis of daily revolution gradually moves overhead, and the other moves downward to the same extent; and many stars situated in the north do not seem to set and many in the south do not seem to rise any more. So Italy does not see Canopus, which is visible in Egypt. And Italy sees the last star of Fluvius which is not visible in this region situated in a more frigid zone. Conversely for people who travel southward, the second group of stars become higher in the sky; while others become lower, which to us seem high up. Moreover the inclinations of the poles have everywhere the same ratio with the measured spaces of the earth, and that happens in no other figure except the spherical. Whence it is manifest that the earth itself is contained between the vertices and is therefore a globe. Add to this the fact that the inhabitants of the East do not perceive the eclipses of the sun and moon when they occur in the evening; and the inhabitants of the West, when they occur in the morning; while of those who live in the middle region – some see them earlier and some later. The navigators have perceived that the waters too are fixed within this figure: for example, when land is not visible from the deck of a ship, it may be seen from the top of the mast, and conversely, if something shining is attached to the top of the mast, it appears to those remaining on the shore to come down gradually, as the ship moves from land, until finally it disappears, as if setting. Moreover it is admitted that water, which by its nature flows, always seeks lower places – the same way as earth – and does not climb up the shore any farther than the convexity of the shore allows. That is why the land is so much higher where it rises up from the ocean.

Does the Earth Have a Circular Movement?

It has been shown that the earth has the form of a globe. I think we must see whether or not a movement follows from its form and what the place of the earth is in the universe. For without doing that it will not be possible to find a sure reason for the celestial phenomena. Although there are so many authorities for saying that the earth rests in the center of the world that people think the contrary supposition is ridiculous and inopinable; if however we consider the thing attentively, we will see that the question has not yet been decided and is by no means to be scorned. For every apparent change in place occurs on account of either the movement of the thing seen or of the seer or on account of the unequal movement of both. For the motion of things moved equally in the same respects – I mean that of the thing seen and the seer – is not perceptible. Now it is from the earth that the celestial circuit is beheld and presented to our sight. Therefore if some movement should belong to the earth it will appear, in the parts of the universe which are outside, as the same movement but in the opposite direction, as though the things outside were passing over; and the daily revolution in especial is such a movement. For the daily revolution appears to carry the whole universe along, with the exception of the earth and the things around it. And if you admit that the heavens possess none of this movement but that the earth turns from west to east, you will find – if you make a serious examination – that as regards the apparent rising and setting of the sun, moon, and stars the case is so. And since it is the heavens which contain and embrace all things as the place common to the universe, it will not be clear at once why movement should not be attributed to the contained rather than to the container, to the thing placed rather than to the thing providing the place.

As a matter of fact the Pythagoreans Herakleides and Ekphantus were of this opinion and so was Nicetas the Syracusan in Cicero: they made the earth to revolve at the midpoint of the world. For they believed that the stars set by reason of the interposition of the earth and that with cessation of that they rose again. Now with this assumption there follows other things, and a no lesser difficulty concerning the place of the earth, though it is taken for granted and believed by nearly all that the earth is the midpoint of the world. For if any one denied that the earth is located at the midpoint or center of the world and did not admit that the distance (between the two) was great enough to be compared with (the distance to) the sphere of the fixed stars but was considerable and quite apparent in relation to the spheres of the sun and the planets; and if for that reason he thought that their movements appeared irregular because they were organized around a different center from the center of the earth, he might perhaps be able to give a perfectly sound reason for irregular apparent movement. For the fact that the wandering stars are seen to be sometimes nearer the earth and at other times farther away necessarily argues that the center of the earth is not the center of their circles. It is not yet clear whether the earth draws near to them and moves away or they draw near to the earth and move away.

And so it would not be very surprising if some one attributed some other movement to the earth in addition to the daily revolution. As a matter of fact Philolaus the Pythagorean — a mathematician of no ordinary ability, whom Plato's biographers say Plato went to Italy for the sake of seeing – is supposed to have held that the earth moved in a circle and wandered in some other movements and was one of the stars.

Many however have believed that they could show by geometrical reasoning that the earth is in the midpoint of the world; that it has the proportionality of a point in relation to the immensity of the heavens, occupies the central position, and for this reason is immovable because, when the universe moves, the center remains unmoved and the things which are closest to the center are moved the most slowly.

Why the Ancients Thought the Earth Was at Rest at the Middle of the World as Its Center

Wherefore for other reasons the ancient philosophers tried to force the earth to remain at rest at the midpoint of the world and as principal cause they put forward heaviness and lightness. For earth is the heaviest element; and all things of any weight are borne towards it and strive to move towards the very center of it.

For since the earth is a globe towards which from every direction heavy things by their own nature are borne along lines making right angles with its surface, the heavy things would fall on one another at the center if they were not held back at the surface: for a straight line making right angles with a plane surface where it touches a sphere leads to the center. And those things which are borne toward the center seem to follow along in order to be at rest at the center. All the more then will the earth be at rest at the center and, being the receptacle for falling bodies, will remain immobile because of its weight.

They strive similarly to prove this by reason of movement and its nature. For Aristotle says that the movement of a body which is one and simple, is simple; and the simple movements are the rectilineal and the circular. And of rectilineal movements, one is upward, and the other is downward. As a consequence every simple movement is either toward the center, i.e., downward, or away from the center, i.e., upward, or around the center, i.e., is circular. It is a property of earth and water only, which are heavy, to be borne downward, i.e., to seek the center: for air and fire, which possess lightness, move upward, i.e., away from the center. It seems fitting to attribute rectilineal movement to the four elements and to give the heavenly bodies a circular movement around the center. So Aristotle. Therefore, said Ptolemy of Alexandria, if the earth moved, even if only by its daily rotation, the contrary of what was said above would necessarily take place. For this movement which would traverse the total circuit of the earth in twenty-four hours would necessarily be very headlong and of an unsurpassable velocity. Now things which are suddenly and violently whirled around are seen to be utterly unfitted for reuniting, and the more unified are seen to become dispersed, unless some constant force constrains them to stick together. And a long time ago, he says, the scattered earth would have passed beyond the heavens, as is certainly ridiculous; and *a fortori* so would all the living creatures and all the other separate masses which could by no means remain unshaken. Moreover, freely falling bodies would not arrive at their destination, and certainly not along the perpendicular line which they assume so quickly. And we would see clouds and other things floating in the air always borne toward the west.

Answer to the Aforesaid Reasons and Their Inadequacy

For these and similar reasons they say that the earth remains at rest at the midpoint of the world and that there is no doubt about this. But if some one opines that the earth moves, he will also say that the movement is natural and not violent. Now things which take place naturally produce effects contrary to those which take place violently. For things which are moved by force or vehemence necessarily get broken up and are unable to subsist for a long time. But things which are caused by nature are in a right condition and are kept in their best organization. Therefore Ptolemy had no reason to fear that the earth and all things on the earth would be scattered in a revolution caused by the efficacy of nature, which is greatly different from that of art or from that which can result from the genius of man. But why didn't he feel anxiety about the world instead, whose movement must necessarily be of greater velocity, the greater the heavens are than the earth? or have the heavens become so immense, because an unspeakably vehement motion has pulled the heavens away from the center, and because the heavens would fall if they came to rest anywhere else?

Surely if this reasoning were tenable, the magnitude of the heavens would extend infinitely. For the farther the movement is borne upward by the vehement force, the greater will be the velocity of the movement, on account of the increasing circumference which must be traversed every twenty-four hours: and conversely, the immensity of the sky would increase with the increase in movement. In this way the velocity would make the magnitude increase infinitely. And in accordance with the axiom of physics that "that which is infinite cannot be traversed or moved in any way," then the heavens will necessarily come to rest.

But they say that beyond the heavens there isn't any body or place or void or anything at all, and accordingly it is not possible for the heavens to move outward: in that case it is rather surprising that something can be held together by nothing. But if the heavens were infinite and were finite only with respect to a hollow space inside, then it will be said with more truth that there is nothing outside the heavens, since anything which occupied any space would be in them; but the heavens will remain immobile. For movement is the most powerful reason wherewith they try to conclude that the universe is finite.

But let us leave to the philosophers of nature the dispute as to whether the world is finite or infinite, and let us hold as certain that the earth held together between its two poles terminates in a spherical surface. Why therefore should we hesitate any longer to grant to it the movement which accords naturally with its form, rather than put the whole world in a commotion – the world whose limits we do not and cannot know? And why not admit that the appearance of diurnal revolution belongs to the heavens but the reality belongs to the earth? And things are as when Aeneas said in Virgil: "We sail out of the harbor, the land and cities move away." As a matter of fact, when a ship floats on over a tranquil sea, all the things outside seem to the voyagers to be moving in a movement which is the image of their own, and they think on the contrary that they themselves and all the things with them are at rest. So it can easily happen in the case of the movement of the earth that the whole world should be believed to be moving in a circle. Then what will we say about the clouds and the other things floating in the air or falling or rising up, except that not only the earth and the watery element with which it is conjoined are moved in this way but also no small part of the air and whatever other things have a similar connection with the earth? whether because the air close by, which is mixed with earthy and watery matter, shares in the same nature as the earth or because the movement of the air is an acquired one, in which it participates without resistance on account of the contiguity and perpetual rotation of the earth. Conversely, it is no less astonishing for them to say that the highest region of the air follows the celestial movement, as is shown by those stars which appear suddenly – I mean those called comets or bearded stars by the Greeks. For that place is assigned for their generation; and like all the other stars they rise and set. We can say that that part of the air is deprived of terrestrial motion on account of its great distance from the earth. Hence the air which is nearest to the earth and the things floating in it will appear tranquil, unless they are driven to and fro by the wind or some other force, as happens. For how is the wind in the air different from a current in the sea? But we must confess that in comparison with the world the movement of falling and of rising bodies is twofold and is in general compounded of the rectilineal and the circular. As regards things which move downward on account of their weight, because they have very much earth in them, doubtlessly their parts possess the same nature as the whole, and it is for the same reason that fiery bodies are drawn upward with force. For even this earthly fire feeds principally on earthly matter; and they define flame as burning smoke. Now it is a property of fire to make that which it invades to expand; and it does this with such force that it can be stopped by no means or contrivance from breaking prison and completing its job. Now expanding movement moves away from the center to the circumference; and so if some part of earth were set on fire, it would be borne away from the center upward. Accordingly, as they say, a simple body possesses a simple movement – this is first verified in the case of circular movement – as long as the simple body remains in its unity in its natural place. In this place, in fact, its movement is none other than the circular, which remains entirely in itself, as though at rest. Rectilineal movement however belongs to those which journey away from their natural place or are shoved out of it or are outside it somehow. But nothing is more repugnant to the order of the whole and to the form of the world than for anything to be outside of its place. Therefore rectilineal movement belongs only to things which are not in the right condition and are not perfectly conformed to their nature – when they are separated from their whole and abandon its unity. Furthermore, bodies which are moved upward or downward do not possess a simple, uniform and regular movement – even without taking into account circular movement. For they cannot be in conformity with their lightness or their force of weight. And those which fall possess a slow movement at the beginning but increase their velocity as they fall. And conversely we note that this earthly fire – and we see no other – when carried high up immediately dies down, as though manifesting the violence of earthly matter.

Now circular movement always goes on regularly, for it has an unfailing cause; but (in rectilineal movement) the acceleration stops, because, when the bodies have reached their place, they are no longer heavy or light, and so the motion ends. Therefore since circular movement belongs to wholes and rectilineal to parts, we can say that the circular movement abides with the rectilineal, as animal with sick. And the fact that Aristotle divided simple movement into three genera: away from the center, toward the center, and around the center, should be considered merely as an act of reason, just as we distinguish between line, point, and surface, though none of them can subsist without the others or without body. In addition there is the fact that the state of immobility is regarded as more noble and godlike than that of change and instability, which for that reason should belong to the earth rather than to the world. I will add that it seems rather absurd to attribute movement to the container or to that which provides the place and not rather to that which is contained and has a place, i.e., the earth; and lastly, since it is clear that the wandering stars are sometimes nearer and sometimes farther away from the earth, then the movement of one and the same body around the center – and they mean the center of the earth – will be both away from the center and toward the center. Therefore it is necessary that movement around the center should be taken more generally; and it should be enough if each movement is in accord with its own center. You see therefore that for all these reasons it is more probable that the earth moves than that it is at rest – especially in the case of the diurnal revolution, as it is most proper to the earth. And I think that is enough as regards the first part of the question.

Whether Many Movements Can Be Attributed to the Earth, and Concerning the Center of the World

Therefore since nothing hinders the mobility of the earth, I think we should now see whether more than one movement belongs to it, so that it could be regarded as one of the wandering stars. For the apparently irregular movement of the planets and their variable distances from the earth — which cannot be understood as occurring in circles which are homocentric with the earth — show that the earth is not the center of their circular movements. Therefore since there are many centers, it does not require audacity to doubt whether the center of gravity of the earth rather than some other is the center of the world. I myself think that gravity or heaviness is nothing except a certain natural appetency implanted in the parts by the divine providence of the universal artisan, in order that they should unite in their oneness and wholeness, coming together in the form of a globe. It is believable that this effect is present in the sun, moon, and the other bright planets and that through its efficacy they remain in the spherical figure in which they are visible, though they nevertheless accomplish their circular movements in many different ways. Therefore if the earth too possesses movements different from the one around its center, then they will necessarily be movements which similarly appear on the outside and in many things; and we find the annual revolution among these movements. For if the annual revolution were changed from being solar to being terrestrial, and immobility were granted to the sun, the risings and setting of the signs and of the fixed stars — by reason of which the stars are matutinal or vespertine — will appear in the same way; and it will be seen that the stoppings, retrogressions and progressions of the wandering stars are not theirs, but are a movement of the earth and that they borrow the appearances of this movement. Lastly, the sun will be regarded as occupying the mid-point of the world. The reason for the order in which all these things succeed one another and the harmony of the whole world teaches us their truth, if only — as they say — we would look at the thing with both eyes.

— *From On the Revolution of the Celestial Spheres, by Nicolaus Copernicus, Polish (1473–1543), translated by Charles Glenn Wallis.*

The Method of Inductive Science

FRANCIS BACON

THEY WHO HAVE presumed to dogmatize on nature, as on some well investigated subject, either from self-conceit or arrogance, and in the professorial style, have inflicted the greatest injury on philosophy and learning. For they have tended to stifle and interrupt inquiry exactly in proportion as they have prevailed in bringing others to their opinion: and their own activity has not counterbalanced the mischief they have occasioned by corrupting and destroying that of others. They again who have entered upon a contrary course, and asserted that nothing whatever can be known, whether they have fallen into this opinion from their hatred of the ancient sophists, or from the hesitation of their minds, or from an exuberance of learning, have certainly adduced reasons for it which are by no means contemptible. They have not, however, derived their opinion from true sources, and, hurried on by their zeal and some affectation, have certainly exceeded due moderation. But the more ancient Greeks (whose writings have perished), held a more prudent mean, between the arrogance of dogmatism, and the despair of scepticism; and though too frequently intermingling complaints and indignation at the difficulty of inquiry, and the obscurity of things, and champing, as it were, the bit, have still persisted in pressing their point, and pursuing their intercourse with nature; thinking, as it seems, that the better method was not to dispute upon the very point of the possibility of anything being known, but to put it to the test of experience. Yet they themselves, by only employing the power of the understanding, have not adopted a fixed rule, but have laid their whole stress upon intense meditation, and a continual exercise and perpetual agitation of the mind.

Our method, though difficult in its operation, is easily explained. It consists in determining the degrees of certainty, whilst we, as it were, restore the senses to their former rank, but generally reject that operation of the mind which follows close upon the senses, and open and establish a new and certain course for the mind from the first actual perceptions of the senses themselves. This, no doubt, was the view taken by those who have assigned so much to logic; showing clearly thereby that they sought some support for the mind, and suspected its natural and spontaneous mode of action. But this is now employed too late as a remedy, when all is clearly lost, and after the mind, by the daily habit and intercourse of life, has come prepossessed with corrupted doctrines, and filled with the vainest idols. The art of logic, therefore, being (as we have mentioned) too late a precaution and in no way remedying the matter, has tended more to confirm errors, than to disclose truth. Our only remaining hope and salvation is to begin the whole labor of the mind again; not leaving it to itself, but directing it perpetually from the very first, and attaining our end as it were by mechanical aid. If men, for instance, had attempted mechanical labors with their hands alone, and without the power and aid of instruments, as they have not hesitated to carry on the labors of their understanding with the unaided efforts of their mind, they would have been able to move and overcome but little, though they had exerted their utmost and united powers. And just to pause awhile on this comparison, and look into it as a mirror; let us ask, if any obelisk of a remarkable size were perchance required to be moved, for the purpose of gracing a triumph or any similar pageant, and men were to attempt it with their bare hands, would not any sober spectator avow it to be an act of the greatest madness? And if they should increase the number of workmen, and imagine that they could thus succeed, would he not think so still more? But if they chose to make a selection, and to remove the weak, and only employ the strong and vigorous, thinking by this means, at any rate, to achieve their object, would he not say that they were more fondly deranged? Nay, if not content with this, they were to determine on consulting the athletic art, and were to give orders for all to appear with their hands, arms, and muscles regularly oiled and prepared, would he not exclaim that they were taking pains to rave by method and design? Yet men are hurried on with the same senseless energy and useless combination in intellectual matters, as long as they expect great results either from the number and agreement, or the excellence and acuteness of their wits; or even strengthen their minds with logic, which may be considered as an athletic preparation, but yet do not desist (if we rightly consider the matter) from applying their own understandings merely with all this zeal and effort. Whilst nothing is more clear, than that in every great work executed by the hand of man without machines or implements, it is impossible for the strength of individuals to be increased, or that of the multitude to combine.

Having premised so much, we lay down two points on which we would admonish mankind lest they should fail to see or to observe them. The first of these is, that it is our good fortune (as we consider it), for the sake of extinguishing and removing contradiction and irritation of mind, to leave the honor and reverence due to the ancients untouched and undiminished, so that we can perform our intended work, and yet enjoy the benefit of our respectful moderation. For if we profess to offer something better than the ancients, and yet should pursue the same course as they have done, we could never, by any artifice, contrive to avoid the imputation of having engaged in a contest or rivalry as to our respective wits, excellencies, or talents; which, though neither inadmissible nor new (for why should we not blame and point out anything that is imperfectly discovered or laid down by them, of our own right, a right common to all?), yet however just and allowable, would perhaps be scarcely an equal match, on account of the disproportion of our strength. But since our present plan leads us to open an entirely different course to the understanding, and one unattempted and unknown to them, the case is altered. There is an end to party zeal, and we only take upon ourselves the character of a guide, which requires a moderate share of authority and good fortune, rather than talents and excellence. The first admonition relates to persons, the next to things.

We make no attempt to disturb the system of philosophy that now prevails, or any other which may or will exist, either more correct or more complete. For we deny not that the received system of philosophy, and others of a similar nature, encourage discussion, embellish harangues, are employed, and are of service in the duties of the professor, and the affairs of civil life. Nay, we openly express and declare that the philosophy we offer will not be very useful in such respects. It is not obvious, or to be understood in a cursory view, nor does it flatter the mind in its preconceived notions, nor will it descend to the level of the generality of mankind unless by its advantages and effects.

Let there exist, then (and may it be of advantage to both), two sources, and two distributions of learning, and in like manner two tribes, and as it were kindred families of contemplators or philosophers, without any hostility or alienation between them; but rather allied and united by mutual assistance. Let there be, in short, one method of cultivating the sciences, and another in discovering them. And as for those who prefer and more readily receive the former, on account of their haste or from motives arising from their ordinary life, or because they are unable from weakness of mind to comprehend and embrace the other (which must necessarily be the case with by far the greater number), let us wish that they may prosper as they desire in their undertaking, and attain what they pursue. But if any individual desire, and is anxious not merely to adhere to, and make use of present discoveries, but to penetrate still further, and not to overcome his adversaries in disputes, but nature by labor, not in short to give elegant and specious opinions, but to know to a certainty and demonstration, let him, as a true son of science (if such be his wish), join with us; that when he has left the antechambers of nature trodden by the multitude, an entrance may at last be discovered to her inner apartments. And in order to be better understood, and to render our meaning more familiar by assigning determinate names, we have accustomed ourselves to call the one method the anticipation of the mind, and the other the interpretation of nature.

We have still one request left. We have at least reflected and taken pains, in order to render our propositions not only true, but of easy and familiar access to men's minds, however wonderfully prepossessed and limited. Yet it is but just that we should obtain this favor from mankind (especially in so great a restoration of learning and the sciences), that whosoever may be desirous of forming any determination upon an opinion of this our work either from his own perceptions, or the crowd of authorities, or the forms of demonstrations, he will not expect to be able to do so in a cursory manner, and whilst attending to other matters; but in order to have a thorough knowledge of the subject, will himself, by degrees, attempt the course which we describe and maintain; will be accustomed to the subtlety of things which is manifested by experience; and will correct the depraved and deeply-rooted habits of his mind by a seasonable, and, as it were, just hesitation: and then, finally (if he will), use his judgment when he has begun to be master of himself.

—*From the Preface to the Novum Organum of Francis Bacon, English (1561–1626), translated from the Latin by Joseph Devey.*

~ ✿ ~

Observations of Animalculae

ANTHONY VAN LEEUWENHOEK

In the year 1675, I discovered living creatures in rain water, which had stood but a few days in a new earthen pot, glazed blue within. This invited me to view this water with great attention, especially those little animals appearing to me ten thousand times less than those represented by Mons. Swammerdam, and by him called Water-fleas or Water-lice, which may be perceived in the water with the naked eye.

The first sort by me discovered in the said water, I divers times observed to consist of 5, 6, 7, or 8 clear globules, without being able to discern any film that held them together, or contained them. When these *animalcula* or living atoms did move, they put forth two little horns, continually moving themselves: the place between these two horns was flat, though the rest of the body was roundish, sharpening a little towards the end, where they had a tail, near four times the length of the whole body, of the thickness (by my microscope) of a spider's web; at the end of which appeared a globule, of the bigness of one of those which made up the body; which tail I could not perceive, even in very clear water, to be moved by them. These little creatures, if they chanced to light upon the least filament or string, or other such particle, of which there are many in water, especially after it has stood some days, they stuck entangled therein, extending their body in a long round, and striving to disentangle their tail; whereby it came to pass, that their whole body leapt back towards the globule of the tail, which then rolled together serpent-like, and after the manner of copper or iron wire that having been wound about a stick, and unwound again, retains those windings and turnings. This motion of extension and contraction continued a while; and I have seen several hundreds of these poor little creatures, within the space of a grain of gross sand, lie fast clustered together in a few filaments.

I also discovered a second sort, the figure of which was oval; and I imagined their head to stand on the sharp end. These were a little bigger than the former. The inferior part of their body is flat, furnished with divers incredibly thin feet, which moved very nimbly, and which I was not able to discern till after several observations. The upper part of the body was round, and had within 8, 10, or 12 globules, where they were very clear. These little animals did sometimes change their figure into a perfect round, especially when they came to lie on any dry place. Their body was also very flexible; for as soon as they hit against any the smallest fibre or string, their body was bent in, which bending presently also yerked out again. When I put any of them on a dry place, I observed, that changing themselves into a round, their body was raised pyramidal-wise with an extant point in the middle, and having lain thus a little while with a motion of their feet, they burst asunder, and the globules were presently diffused and dissipated, so that I could not discern the least thing of any film, in which the globules had doubtless been enclosed: and at the time of their bursting asunder I was able to discover more globules than when they were alive.

But then I observed a third sort of little animals, that were twice as long as broad, and to my eye yet eight times smaller than the first. Yet for all this, I thought I discerned little feet, whereby they moved very briskly, both in a round and straight line.

There was, further, a fourth sort, which were so small that I was not able to give them any figure at all. These were a thousand times smaller than the eye of a big louse: for I judge, the axis of the eyes of such a louse to be more than ten times as long as the axis of any of the said little creatures. These exceeded all the former in celerity. I have often observed them to stand still as it were upon a point, and then turn themselves about with that swiftness, as we see a top turn round, the circumference they made being no bigger than that of a small grain of sand; and then extending themselves straight forward, and by and by lying in a bending posture.

I discovered also several other forms of animals, but these were very big respectively; of which I intend not to speak here; only this, that they were generally made up of such soft parts, as the former, they bursting asunder as soon as they came to want water.

OBSERVATION II.

The 26 May, it rained hard; the rain growing less, I caused some of that rain water, running down from the house top, to be gathered in a clean glass, after it had been washed two or three times with the water. And in this I observed some few very little living creatures, and seeing them, I thought they might have been produced in the leaden gutters in some water that had there remained before.

OBSERVATION III.

On the same day, the rain continuing, I took a great porcelain dish, and exposed it to the free air upon a wooden vessel, about a foot and a half high, that so no earthy parts, from the falling of the rain water upon that place, might be spattered or dashed into the said dish. With the first water that fell into the dish, I washed it very clean, and then flung the water away, and received fresh into it, but could discern no living creatures therein; only I saw many irregular terrestrial parts in the same. The 30 of May, after I had, ever since the 26th, observed every day twice or thrice the same rain water, I now discovered some, yet very few, exceeding little animals, which were very clear.

The 31st of May, I perceived in the same water more of those animals, as also some that were somewhat bigger. And I imagine, that many thousands of these little creatures do not equal an ordinary grain of sand in bigness: and comparing them with a cheese mite (which may be seen to move with the naked eye) I make the proportion of one of these small water creatures to a cheese mite, to be like that of a bee to a horse: for the circumference of one of these little animals in water, is not so big as the thickness of a hair in a cheese mite.

OBSERVATION IV.

June 9th, having received, early in the morning, some rain water in a dish, as before, and poured it into a very clean wine glass, and exposed it about 8 of the clock in the morning to the air, about the height of the third story of my house, to find whether the little animals would appear the sooner in the water, thus standing in the air.

Observing the same accordingly the 10th of June, I imagined I saw some living creatures therein; but because they seemed to be but very few in number, nor were plainly discernible, I had no mind to trust this observation.

The 11th of the same month, seeing this water move in the glass from a stiff gale of wind (which had blown for 36 hours without intermission, accompanied with a cold, that I could very well endure my winter clothes) I did not think I should then perceive any living creatures therein; yet viewing it attentively, I did, with admiration, observe a thousand of them in one drop of water, which were of the smallest sort that I had seen hitherto.

The 12th of June, the wind being at west, the sun shining with interloping clouds, I viewed the same rain water, and found the forementioned little animals so plentifully in the water which I took up from the surface, that one or two thousand in one single drop did not make up their number.

The 13th of the same month, viewing the same water again, I found, besides the animals already noted, a sort of creatures, that were eight times as big as they, of almost a round figure: and as those very small *animalcula* did swim gently among one another, moving like as gnats do in the air; so did these bigger ones move far more swiftly, tumbling round as 'twere, and then making a sudden downfall.

The 14th of June I did find these very little creatures in no smaller number. The 16th, I saw them as before; and this water, which had been, in all, $\frac{1}{6}$ of a pint, being now more than half dried up, I flung it away.

OBSERVATION V.

The 9th of June, I put of the same rain water in a very clean wine glass in my counter or study, and viewing the same, I perceived no living creatures in it.

Note, that my study stands toward the northeast, in my antechamber, and is very close, joined together with wainscoat, having no other opening than one hole of an inch and a half broad, and 8 inches long, towards the street furnished with 4 windows, of which the two lowermost open inwards, and by night are closed with two wooden shutters; so that there comes in but little air from without, unless it be that I use a candle in making my observations, in which case I lift up a little casement, that the steam of my candle may not offend me; but yet drawing a curtain at that time over almost all the windows.

The 10th of June, observing the mentioned rain water, which now had stood 24 hours in my study, I noted some few very small living creatures, in which, by reason of their extreme minuteness, I could see no figure, and among the rest I discovered one that was somewhat greater, of an oval figure.

Note, that when I say I have viewed the water, I mean that I have viewed only 3, 4, or 5 drops of the water, which I also flung away.

The 11th of June, looking upon this water afresh, I saw the said little creatures again, but there were then but very few of them.

The 12th, I saw them as the day before; besides, I took notice of one figured like a mussel shell, with its hollow side downwards, and it was of a length equal to the eye of a louse.

The 13th, early, I discovered the extreme small creatures in greater number, and among them I saw a bigger one, as I did before. In the evening of the same day I saw the same very small insects again in no less number, taking notice, that the same had a transparent part standing out behind: I discovered also some little animals which were somewhat longer than an oval, and these were about six times as big as the extreme small creatures: Their head, which run out somewhat in length, they often drew in, and then appeared to be almost round. I perceived also some that were altogether round, and the axis of these was twice as long as that of the smallest creatures. These two greater sorts were very flexile, so that their body did bend at the touch of the least and finest filament.

The 14th of June I perceived the oval insects in greater plenty.

The 16, I saw them in yet greater numbers; and they were flat beneath, and round above; and besides, I noted very small creatures, that were three times as long as they were broad: And divers other sorts, too long to describe here. And in the evening of the same day, I discovered little feet in the small oval creatures, which were many in number; as also a much bigger creature of the same figure, which was likewise furnished with legs. And here I gave over my observations as to this water.

OBSERVATION VI.

The 17th of this month of June it rained very hard; and I catched some of that rain water in a new porcelain dish, which had never been used before, but found no living creatures at all in it, but many terrestrial particles, and, among others, such as I thought came from the smoke of smiths' coals, and some thin strids, thinner than the thrid of a silkworm, which seemed to be made up of globules; and where they lay thick upon one another, they had a green colour.

The 26th, having been eight days out of town, and kept my study shut up close, when I was come home and did view the said water, I perceived several *animalcula,* that were very small. And herewith I desisted from making at this time any further observations of rain water.

Meantime, this Town of Delft being very rich in water, and we receiving from the River of Maase fresh water, which maketh our water very good; I viewed this water divers times, and saw extreme small creatures in it, of different kinds and colours; and even so small, that I could very hardly discern their figures: But some were much bigger, the describing of whose motion and shape would be too tedious: This only I must mention here, that the number of them in this water was far less than that of those found in rain water; for if I saw a matter of 25 of them in one drop of this Town water, that was much.

In the open court of my house I have a well, which is about 15 foot deep, before one comes to the water. It is encompassed with high walls, so that the sun, though in *Cancer,* yet can hardly shine much upon it. This water comes out of the ground, which is sandy, with such a power, that when I have laboured to empty the well, I could not so do it but there remained ever a foot's depth of water in it. This water is in summer time so cold, that you cannot possibly endure your hand in it for any reasonable time. Not thinking at all to meet with any living creatures in it, (it being of a good taste and clear), looking upon it in *Sept.* of the last year, I discovered in it a great number of living animals very small, that were exceeding clear, and a little bigger than the smallest of all I ever saw; and I think, that in a grain weight of this water there was above 500 of those creatures, which were very quiet and without motion.

In the Winter I perceived none of these little animals, nor have I seen any of them this year before the month of *July,* and then they appeared not very numerous, but in the month of *August* I saw them in great plenty.

July 27. 1676. I went to the sea-side, at *Schevelingen,* the wind coming from the sea with a very warm sunshine; and viewing some of the sea water very attentively, I discovered divers living animals therein. I gave to a man, that went into the sea to wash himself, a new glass bottle, bought on purpose for that end, entreating him, that being on the sea, he would first wash it well twice or thrice, and then fill it full of the sea water; which desire of mine having been complied with, I tied the bottle close with a clean bladder, and coming home, and viewing it, I saw in it a little animal that was blackish, looking as if it had been made up of two globules. This creature had a peculiar motion, after the manner as when we see a very little flea leaping upon a white paper; so that it might very well be called a water-flea; but it was by far not so great as the eye of that little animal, which Dr. *Swammerdam* calls the water-flea. I also discovered little creatures therein, that were clear, of the same size with the former animal which I first observed in this water, but of an oval figure, whose motion was serpent-like. I took further notice of a third sort, which were very slow in their motion: Their body was of a mouse colour, clear toward the oval point; and before the head, and behind the body there stood out a sharp little point angle-wise. This sort was a little bigger. But there was yet a fourth sort somewhat longer than oval. Yet of all these I could see sometimes but three or four, sometimes but one.

July 31. After I had from the 27. of this month viewed this water every day, but perceived no little animals in it, looking upon it now, I saw an 100, where before I had seen but one; but these were of another figure, and not only lesser, but they were also very clear, and of an oblong oval figure, only with this difference, that methought their heads ended sharper: And although they were a thousand times smaller than a small grain of sand, yet I discerned, that when they lay out of the water in a dry place, that they burst in pieces and spread out into 3 or 4 very little globules, and into some aqueous matter, without my being able to discern any other parts in them.

The 2d and 4th of *August* I saw many of the aforesaid small animals: but the 6th and 8th, I did not by far perceive so many of them as before. And those few ones I saw the 8th, were so very small, that even by my microscope they were hardly discernible.

—*From Observations . . . Concerning Little Animals by Him Observed in Rain- Well- Sea- and Snow Water, by Anthony van Leeuwenhoek, Dutch (1632–1723). Philosophical Transactions of the Royal Society of London, Vol. XII, No. 133.*

The Sex of Plants

LINNAEUS

THE ORGANS common in general to all plants are: 1st. The root, with its capillary vessels, extracting nourishment from the ground. 2nd. The leaves, which may be called the limbs, and which, like the feet and wings of animals, are organs of motion; for being themselves shaken by the external air, they shake and exercise the plant. 3rd. The trunk, containing the medullary substance, which is nourished by the bark, and for the most part multiplied into several compound plants. 4th. The fructification, which is the true body of the plant, set at liberty by a metamorphosis, and consists only of the organs of generation; it is often defended by a calyx, and furnished with petals, by means of which it in a manner flutters in the air.

Many flowers have no calyx, as several of the lily tribe, the Hippuris, etc., many want the corolla, as grasses, and the plants called apetalous; but there are none more destitute of stamina and pistilla, those important organs destined to the formation of fruit. We therefore infer from experience that the stamina are the male organs of generation, and the pistilla of the female; and as many flowers are furnished with both at once, it follows that such flowers are hermaphrodites. Nor is this so wonderful, as that there should be any plants in which the different sexes are distinct individuals; for plants being immovably fixed to one spot, cannot like animals, travel in search of a mate. There exists, however, in some plants a real difference of sex. From seeds of the same mother, some individuals shall be produced, whose flowers exhibit stamina without pistilla, and may therefore properly be called male; while the rest being furnished with pistilla without stamina are therefore denominated females; and so uniformly does this take place, that no vegetable was ever found to produce female flowers without flowers furnished with stamina being produced, either on the same individual or on another plant of the same species, and *vice versa.*

As all seed vessels are destined to produce seeds, so are the stamina to bear the pollen, or fecundating powder. All seeds contain within their membranes a certain medullary substance, which swells when dipped into warm water. All pollen, likewise, contains in its membrane an elastic substance, which, although very subtle, and almost invisible, by means of warm water often explodes with great vehemence. While plants are in flower, the pollen falls from their antheræ, and is dispersed abroad, as seeds are dislodged from their situation when the fruit is ripe. At the same time that the pollen is scattered, the pistillum presents its stigma, which is then in its highest vigour, and, for a portion of the day at least, is moistened with a fine dew. The stamina either surround this stigma, or if the flowers are of the drooping kind, they are bent towards one side, so that the pollen can easily find access to the stigma, where it not only adheres by means of the dew of that part, but the moisture occasions its bursting, by which means its contents are discharged. That issued from it being mixed with the fluid of the stigma, is conveyed to rudiments of the seed. Many evident instances of this present themselves to our notice; but I have nowhere seen it more manifest than in the Jacobean Lily (*Amaryllis formosissima*), the pistillum of which, when sufficient heat is given the plant to make it flower in perfection, is bent downwards and from its stigma issues a drop of limpid fluid, so large that one would think it in danger of falling to the ground. It is, however, gradually reabsorbed into the style about three or four o'clock and becomes invisible until about ten the next morning, when it appears again; by noon it attains its largest dimensions; and in the afternoon, by a gentle and scarcely perceptible decrease it returns to its source. If we shake the antheræ over the stigma, so that the pollen may fall on this limpid drop, we see the fluid soon after become turbid and assume a yellow color; and we perceive little rivulets, or opaque streaks running from the stigma towards the rudiments of the seed. Some time afterwards, when the drop has totally disappeared, the pollen may be observed adhering to the stigma, but of an irregular figure, having lost its original form. No one, therefore, can assent to what Morland and others have asserted, that the pollen passes into the stigma, pervades the style and enters the tender rudiments of the seed, as Leeuwenhoek supposed his worms to enter the ova. A most evident proof of the falsehood of this opinion may be obtained from any species of *Mirabilis* (Marvel of Peru), whose pollen is so very large that it almost exceeds the style itself in thickness, and, falling on the stigma, adheres firmly to it; that organ sucking and exhausting the pollen, as a cuttle fish devours everything that comes within its grasp. One evening in the month of August, I removed all the stamina from three flowers of the *Mirabilis Longiflora,* at the same time destroying all the rest of the flowers which were expanded; I sprinkled these three flowers with the pollen of *Mirabilis Jalappa;* the seed-buds swelled, but did not ripen. Another evening I performed a similar experiment, only sprinkling the flowers with the pollen of the same species; all these flowers produced ripe seeds.

Some writers have believed that the stamina are parts of the fructification, which serve only to discharge an impure or excrementitious matter, and by no means formed for so important a work as generation. But it is very evident that these authors have not sufficiently examined the subject; for, as in many vegetables, some flowers are furnished with stamina only, and others only with pistilla; it is altogether impossible that stamina situated at so very great a distance from the fruit, as on a different branch, or perhaps on a separate plant, should serve to convey any impurities from the embryo.

No physiologist could demonstrate, *a priori,* the necessity of the masculine fluid to the rendering the eggs of animals prolific, but experience has established it beyond a doubt. We therefore judge *a posteriori* principally, of the same effect in plants.

In the month of January, 1760, the *Antholyza Cunonia* flowered in a pot in my parlour, but produced no fruit, the air of the room not being sufficiently agitated to waft the pollen to the stigma. One day, about noon, feeling the stigma very moist, I plucked off one of the antheræ, by means of a fine pair of forceps, and gently rubbed it on one part of the expanded stigmata. The spike of flowers remained eight or ten days longer; when I observed, in gathering the branch for my herbarium, that the fruit of that flower only on which the experiment had been made, had swelled to the size of a bean. I then dissected this fruit and discovered that one of the three cells contained seeds in considerable number, the other two being entirely withered.

In the month of April I sowed the seeds of hemp (*Cannabis*) in two different pots. The young plants came up so plentifully, that each pot contained thirty or forty. I placed each by the light of a window, but in different and remote apartments. The hemp grew extremely well in both pots. In one of them I permitted the male and female plants to remain together, to flower and bear fruit, which ripened in July, being macerated in water, and committed to the earth, sprung up in twelve days. From the other, however, I removed all the male plants, as soon as they were old enough for me to distinguish them from the females. The remaining females grew very well, and presented their long pistilla in great abundance, these flowers continuing a very long time, as if in expectation of their mates; while the plants in the other pot had already ripened their fruit, their pistilla having, quite in a different manner, faded as soon as the males had discharged all their pollen. It was truly a beautiful and truly admirable spectacle to see the unimpregnated females preserve their pistilla so long green and flourishing, not permitting them to begin to fade till they had been for a very considerable time exposed in vain, to the access of the male pollen.

Afterwards, when these virgin plants began to decay through age, I examined all their calyces in the presence of several botanists and found them large and flourishing, although every one of the seed-buds was brown, compressed, membranaceous, and dry, not exhibiting any appearance of cotyledons or pulp. Hence I am perfectly convinced that the circumstance which authors have recorded, of the female hemp having produced seeds, although deprived of the male, could only have happened by means of pollen brought by the wind from some distant place. No experiment can be more easily performed than the above; none more satisfactory in demonstrating the generation of plants.

The *Clutia tenella* was in like manner kept growing in my window during the months of June and July. The male plant was in one pot, the female in another. The latter abounded with fruit, not one of its flowers proving abortive. I removed the two pots into different windows of the same apartment; still all the female flowers continued to become fruitful. At length I took away the male entirely, leaving the female alone, and cutting off all the flowers which it had already borne. Every day new ones appeared from the axilla of every leaf; each remained eight or ten days, after which their foot stalks turning yellow, they fell barren to the ground. A botanical friend, who had amused himself with observing this phenomenon with me, persuaded me to bring, from the stove in the garden, a single male flower, which he placed over one of the female ones, then in perfection, tying a piece of red silk around its pistillum. The next day the male flower was taken away, and this single seed-bud remained, and bore fruit. Afterwards I took another male flower out of the same stove, and with a pair of slender forceps pinched off one of its antheræ, which I afterwards gently scratched with a feather, so that a very small portion of its pollen was discharged upon one of the three stigmata of a female flower, the other two stigmata being covered with paper. This fruit likewise attained its due size, and on being cut transversely, exhibited one cell filled with a large seed, and the other two empty. The rest of the flowers, being unimpregnated, faded and fell off. This experiment may be performed with as little trouble as the former.

The *Datisca cannabina* came up in my garden from seed ten years ago, and has every year been plentifully increased by means of its perennial root. Flowers in great number have been produced by it; but, being all female, they proved abortive. Being desirous of producing male plants, I obtained more seeds from Paris. Some more plants were raised; but these likewise to my great mortification, all proved females, and bore flowers, but no fruit. In the year 1757 I received another parcel of seeds. From these I obtained a few male plants, which flowered in 1758. These were planted at a great distance from the females; and when their flowers were just ready to emit their pollen, holding a paper under them, I gently shook the spike of panicle with my finger, till the paper was almost covered with the yellow powder. I carried this to the females, which were flowering in another part of the garden, and placed it over them. The cold nights of the year in which this experiment was made, destroyed these Datiscas, with many other plants, much earlier than usual. Nevertheless, when I examined the flowers of those plants, which I had sprinkled with the fertilizing powder, I found the seeds of their due magnitude; while in the more remote Datiscas, which had not been impregnated with pollen, no traces of seeds were visible.

Several species of Momordica, cultivated by us, like other Indian vegetables, in close stoves, have frequently borne female flowers; which, although at first very vigorous, after a short time have constantly faded and turned yellow, without perfecting any seed, till I instructed the gardener, as soon as he observed a female flower, to gather a male one, and place it above the female. By this contrivance we are so certain of obtaining fruit that we dare pledge ourselves to make any female flowers fertile that shall be fixed on.

The *Jatropha urens* has flowered every year in my hot-house; but the female flowers coming before the males, in a week's time dropped their petals and faded before the latter were opened; from which cause no fruit has been produced, but the *germina* themselves have fallen off. We have therefore never had any fruit of the Jatropha till the year 1752, when the male flowers were in vigour on a tall tree, at the same time that the females began to appear on a small Jatropha which was growing in a garden-pot. I placed this pot under the other tree, by which means the female flowers bore seeds, which grew on being sown. I frequently amused myself with taking the male flowers from one plant, and scattering them over the female flowers of another, and have always found the seeds of the latter impregnated by it.

Two years ago I placed a piece of paper under some of these male flowers and afterwards folded up the pollen which had fallen upon it, preserving it so folded up, if I remember right, four or six weeks, at the end of which time another branch of the same Jatropha was in flower. I then took the pollen, which I had so long preserved in paper, and strewed it over three female flowers, the only ones at that time expanded. The three females proved fruitful, while all the rest, which grew in the same bunch, fell off abortive.

The interior petals of the *Ornithogalum,* commonly but improperly called *Canadense,* cohere so closely together that they only just admit the air to the germen and will scarcely permit the pollen of another flower to pass; this plant produced every day new flowers and fruit, the fructification never failing in any instance; I therefore, with the utmost care, extracted the antheræ from one of the flowers with a hooked needle, and as I hoped, this single flower proved barren. This experiment was repeated about a week after with the same success.

I removed all of the antheræ out of a flower of *Chelidonium corniculatum* (scarlet-horned poppy), which was growing in a remote part of the garden, upon the first opening of its petals, and stripped off all the rest of the flowers; another day I treated another flower of the same plant in a similar manner, but sprinkled the pistillum of this with the pollen borrowed from another plant of the same species; the result was, that the first flower produced no fruit, but the second afforded very perfect seed. My design in this experiment was to prove that the mere removal of the antheræ from a flower is not in itself sufficient to render the germen abortive.

Having the *Nicotiana fruticosa* growing in a garden-pot, and producing plenty of flowers and seed, I extracted the antheræ from the newly expanded flowers before they had burst, at the same time cutting away all the other flowers; this germen produced no fruit, nor did it even swell.

I removed an urn, in which the *Asphodelus fistulosus* was growing, to one corner of the garden, and from one of the flowers which had lately opened, I extracted its antheræ; this caused the impregnation to fail. Another day I treated another flower in the same manner; but, bringing a flower from a plant in a different part of the garden, with which I sprinkled the pistillum of the mutilated one, its germen became by that means fruitful.

Ixia chinensis, flowering in my stove, the windows of which were shut, all its flowers proved abortive. I therefore took one of its antheræ in a pair of pincers, and with them sprinkled the stigmata of two flowers, and the next day one stigma only of a third flower; the seed-buds of these flowers remained, grew to a large size and bore seed, the fruit of the third, however, contained ripe seed only in one of its cells.

To relate more experiments would only be to fatigue the reader unnecessarily. All nature proclaims the truth I have endeavored to inculcate, and every flower bears witness to it. Any person may make the experiment for himself with any plant he pleases, only taking care to place the pot in which it is growing, in the window of a room sufficiently out of reach of other flowers; and I will venture to promise him that he will obtain no perfect fruit unless pollen has access to the pistillum.

— *From Reflections on the Study of Nature; and a Dissertation on the Sexes of Plants, by Linnaeus (Carl von Linné), Swedish (1707–1778), translated from the Latin by Sir James E. Smith.*

The Theory of Evolution

CHARLES DARWIN

SEVERAL WRITERS have misapprehended or objected to the term Natural Selection. Some have even imagined that Natural Selection induces variability, whereas it implies only the preservation of such variations as arise and are beneficial to the being under its conditions of life. No one objects to agriculturists speaking of the potent effects of man's selection; and in this case the individual differences given by nature, which man for some object selects, must of necessity first occur. Others have objected that the term selection implies conscious choice in the animals which become modified; and it has even been urged that as plants have no volition, Natural Selection is not applicable to them! In the literal sense of the word, no doubt, Natural Selection is a false term; but whoever objected to chemists speaking of the elective affinities of the various elements?—and yet an acid cannot strictly be said to elect the base with which it in preference combines. It has been said that I speak of Natural Selection as an active power or Deity; but who objects to an author speaking of the attraction of gravity as ruling the movements of the planets? Everyone knows what is meant and is implied by such metaphorical expressions; and they are almost necessary for brevity. So again it is difficult to avoid personifying the word Nature; but I mean by nature only the aggregate action and product of many natural laws, and by laws the sequence of events as ascertained by us. With a little familiarity such superficial objections will be forgotten.

We shall best understand the probable course of Natural Selection by taking the case of a country undergoing some slight physical change; for instance, of climate. The proportional numbers of its inhabitants will almost immediately undergo a change, and some species will probably become extinct. We may conclude, from what we have seen of the intimate and complex manner in which the inhabitants of each country are bound together, that any change in the numerical proportions of the inhabitants, independently of the change of climate itself, would seriously affect the others. If the country were open on its borders, new forms would certainly immigrate, and this would likewise seriously disturb the relations of some of the former inhabitants. Let it be remembered how powerful the influence of a single introduced tree or mammal has been shown to be. But in the case of an island, or of a country partly surrounded by barriers, into which new and better adapted forms could not freely enter, we should then have places in the economy of nature which would assuredly be better filled up if some of the original inhabitants were in some manner modified; for had the area been open to immigration, these same places would have been seized on by intruders. In such cases, slight modifications which in any way favored the individuals of any species by better adapting them to their altered conditions, would tend to be preserved; and Natural Selection would have free scope for the work of improvement.

We have good reason to believe, as shown in the first chapter, that changes in the conditions of life give a tendency to increased variability; and in the foregoing cases the conditions have changed, and this would manifestly be favorable to Natural Selection by affording a better chance of the occurrence of profitable variations. Unless such occur, Natural Selection can do nothing. Under the term of "variations," it must never be forgotten that mere individual differences are included. As man can produce a great result with his domestic animals and plants by adding up in any given direction individual differences, so could Natural Selection, but far more easily from having incomparably longer time for action. Nor do I believe that any great physical change, as of climate, or any unusual degree of isolation to check immigration, is necessary in order that new and unoccupied places should be left, for Natural Selection to fill up by improving some of the varying inhabitants. For as all the inhabitants of each country are struggling together with nicely balanced forces, extremely slight modifications in the structure or habits of one species would often give it an advantage over others; and still further modifications of the same kind would often still further increase the advantage, as long as the species continued under the same conditions of life and profited by similar means of subsistence and defense. No country can be named, in which all the native inhabitants are now so perfectly adapted to each other and to the physical conditions under which they live, that none of them could be still better adapted or improved; for in all countries the natives have been so far conquered by naturalized productions that they have allowed some foreigners to take firm possession of the land. And as foreigners have thus in every country beaten some of the natives, we may safely conclude that the natives might have been modified with advantage, so as to have better resisted the intruders.

As man can produce, and certainly has produced, a great result by his methodical and unconscious means of selection, what may not Natural Selection effect? Man can act only on external and visible characters; Nature, if I may be allowed to personify the natural preservation or survival of the fittest, cares nothing for appearances, except in so far as they are useful to any being. She can act on every internal organ, on every shade of constitutional difference, on the whole machinery of life. Man selects only for his own good; Nature only for that of the being which she tends. Every selected character is fully exercised by her, as is implied by the fact of their selection. Man keeps the natives of many climates in the same country: he seldom exercises each selected character in some peculiar and fitting manner; he feeds a long and a short-beaked pigeon on the same food; he does not exercise a long-backed or long-legged quadruped in any peculiar manner; he exposes sheep with long and short wool to the same climate. He does not allow the most vigorous males to struggle for the females. He does not rigidly destroy all inferior animals, but protects during each varying season, as far as lies in his power, all his productions. He often begins his selection by some half-monstrous form; or at least by some modification prominent enough to catch the eye or to be plainly useful to him. Under Nature, the slightest differences of structure or constitution may well turn the nicely balanced scale in the struggle for life, and so be preserved. How fleeting are the wishes and efforts of man! How short his time, and consequently how poor will be his results, compared with those accumulated by Nature during whole geological periods! Can we wonder then that Nature's productions should be far "truer" in character than man's productions; that they should be infinitely better adapted to the most complex conditions of life, and should plainly bear the stamp of far higher workmanship?

It may metaphorically be said that Natural Selection is daily and hourly scrutinizing, throughout the world, the slightest variations; rejecting those that are bad, preserving and adding up all that is good; silently and insensibly working, *whenever and wherever opportunity offers,* at the improvement of each organic being in relation to its organic and inorganic conditions of life. We see nothing of these slow changes in progress until the hand of time has marked the lapse of ages, and then so imperfect is our view into long-past geological ages, that we see only that the forms of life are now different from what they formerly were.

In order that any great amount of modification should be effected in a species, a variety when once formed must again, perhaps after a long interval of time, vary or present individual differences of the same favorable nature as before; and these must be again preserved, and so onward step by step. Seeing that individual differences of the same kind perpetually recur, this can hardly be considered as an unwarrantable assumption. But whether it is true, we can judge only by seeing how far the hypothesis accords with and explains the general phenomena of nature. On the other hand, the ordinary belief that the amount of possible variation is a strictly limited quantity, is likewise a simple assumption.

Although Natural Selection can act only through and for the good of each being, yet characters and structures, which we are apt to consider as of very trifling importance, may thus be acted on. When we see leaf-eating insects green, and bark-feeders mottled gray; the Alpine ptarmigan white in winter, the red grouse the color of heather — we must believe that these tints are of service to these birds and insects in preserving them from danger. Grouse, if not destroyed at some period of their lives, would increase in countless numbers; they are known to suffer largely from birds of prey; and hawks are guided by eyesight to their prey — so much so, that on parts of the Continent persons are warned not to keep white pigeons, as being the most liable to destruction. Hence Natural Selection might be effective in giving the proper color to each kind of grouse and in keeping that color, when once acquired, true and constant. Nor ought we to think that the occasional destruction of an animal of any particular color would produce little effect: we should remember how essential it is in a flock of white sheep to destroy a lamb with the faintest trace of black. We have seen how the color of hogs which feed on the "paint-root" in Virginia, determines whether they should live or die. In plants, the down on the fruit and the color of the flesh are considered by botanists as characters of the most trifling importance; we hear from an excellent horticulturist, Downing, that in the United States smooth-skinned fruits suffer far more from a beetle, a curculio, than those with down; that purple plums suffer far more from a certain disease than yellow plums; whereas another disease attacks yellow-fleshed peaches far more than those with other colored flesh. If with all the aids of art, these slight differences make a great difference in cultivating the several varieties, assuredly, in a state of nature, where the trees would have to struggle with other trees and with a host of enemies, such differences would effectually settle which variety, whether a smooth or downy, a yellow or a purple-fleshed fruit, should succeed.

In looking at many small points of difference between species, which, as far as our ignorance permits us to judge, seem quite unimportant, we must not forget that climate, food, etc., have no doubt produced some direct effect. It is also necessary to bear in mind that owing to the law of correlation, when one part varies, and the variations are accumulated through Natural Selection, other modifications, often of the most unexpected nature, will ensue.

As we see that those variations which under domestication appear at any particular period of life, tend to reappear in the offspring at the same period; — for instance, in the shape, size, and flavor of the seeds of the many varieties of our culinary and agricultural plants; in the caterpillar and cocoon stages of the varieties of the silkworm; in the eggs of poultry, and in the color of the down of their chickens; in the horns of our sheep and cattle when nearly adult; so in a state of nature Natural Selection will be enabled to act on and modify organic beings at any age, by the accumulation of variations profitable at that age, and by their inheritance at a corresponding age. If it profit a plant to have its seeds more and more widely disseminated by the wind, I can see no greater difficulty in this being effected through Natural Selection, than in the cotton-planter increasing and improving by selection the down in the pods on his cotton-trees. Natural Selection may modify and adapt the larva of an insect to a score of contingencies wholly different from those which concern the mature insect; and these modifications may effect, through correlation, the structure of the adult. So, conversely, modifications in the adult may affect the structure of the larva; but in all cases Natural Selection will insure that they shall not be injurious: for if they were so, the species would become extinct.

Natural Selection will modify the structure of the young in relation to the parent, and of the parent in relation to the young. In social animals it will adapt the structure of each individual for the benefit of the whole community, if the community profits by the selected change. What Natural Selection cannot do, is to modify the structure of one species, without giving it any advantage, for the good of another species; and though statements to this effect may be found in works of natural history, I cannot find one case which will bear investigation. A structure used only once in an animal's life, if of high importance to it, might be modified to any extent by Natural Selection; for instance, the great jaws possessed by certain insects, used exclusively for opening the cocoon, or the hard tip to the beak of unhatched birds, used for breaking the eggs. It has been asserted that of the best short-beaked tumbler-pigeons a greater number perish in the egg than are able to get out of it; so that fanciers assist in the act of hatching. Now if Nature had to make the beak of a full-grown pigeon very short for the bird's own advantage, the process of modification would be very slow, and there would be simultaneously the most rigorous selection of all the young birds within the egg, which had the most powerful and hardest beaks, for all with weak beaks would inevitably perish; or more delicate and more easily broken shells might be selected, the thickness of shell being known to vary like every other structure.

It may be well here to remark that with all beings there must be much fortuitous destruction, which can have little or no influence on the course of Natural Selection. For instance, a vast number of eggs or seeds are annually devoured, and these could be modified through Natural Selection only if they varied in some manner which protected them from their enemies. Yet many of these eggs or seeds would perhaps, if not destroyed, have yielded individuals better adapted to their conditions of life than any of those which happened to survive. So again a vast number of mature animals and plants, whether or not they be the best adapted to their conditions, must be annually destroyed by accidental causes, which would not be in the least degree mitigated by certain changes of structure or constitution which would in other ways be beneficial to the species. But let the destruction of the adults be ever so heavy, if the number which can exist in any district be not wholly kept down by such causes — or again, let the destruction of eggs or seeds be so great that only a hundredth or a thousandth part are developed — yet of those which do survive, the best adapted individuals, supposing that there is any variability in a favorable direction, will tend to propagate their kind in larger numbers than the less well adapted. If the numbers be wholly kept down by the causes just indicated, as will often have been the case, Natural Selection will be powerless in certain beneficial directions; but this is no valid objection to its efficiency at other times and in other ways; for we are far from having any reason to suppose that many species ever undergo modification and improvement at the same time in the same area.

—*From the Origin of Species, by Charles Robert Darwin, English (1809–1882).*

EVOLUTION COMPARED WITH SPECIAL CREATION

Authors of the highest eminence seem to be fully satisfied with the view that each species has been independently created. To my mind it accords better with what we know of the laws impressed on matter by the Creator, that the production and extinction of the past and present inhabitants of the world should have been due to secondary causes, like those determining the birth and death of an individual. When I view all beings not as special creations, but as the lineal descendants of some few beings which lived long before the first bed of the Cambrian system was deposited, they seem to me to become ennobled. Judging from the past, we may safely infer that not one living species will transmit its unaltered likeness to a distant futurity. And of the species now living, very few will transmit progeny of any kind to a far distant futurity; for the manner in which all organic beings are grouped shows that the greater number of species in each genus, and all the species in many genera, have left no descendants, but have become utterly extinct. We can so far take a prophetic glance into futurity as to foretell that it will be the common and widely spread species, belonging to the larger and dominant groups within each class, which will ultimately prevail and procreate new and dominant species. As all the living forms of life are the lineal descendants of those which lived long before the Cambrian epoch, we may feel certain that the ordinary succession by generation has never once been broken, and that no cataclysm has desolated the whole world. Hence we may look with some confidence to a secure future of great length. And as natural selection works solely by and for the good of each being, all corporeal and mental endowments will tend to progress towards perfection.

It is interesting to contemplate a tangled bank, clothed with many plants of many kinds, with birds singing on the bushes, with various insects flitting about, and with worms crawling through the damp earth, and to reflect that these elaborately constructed forms, so different from each other, and dependent upon each other in so complex a manner, have all been produced by laws acting around us. These laws, taken in the largest sense, being Growth with Reproduction; Inheritance, which is almost implied by reproduction; Variability from the indirect and direct action of the conditions of life, and from use and disuse: a Ratio of Increase so high as to lead to a Struggle for Life, and as a consequence to Natural Selection, entailing Divergence of Character and the Extinction of less-improved forms. Thus from the war of nature, from famine and death, the most exalted object which we are capable of conceiving—namely, the production of the higher animals—directly follows. There is grandeur in this view of life, with its several powers, having been originally breathed by the Creator into a few forms or into one; and that whilst this planet has gone cycling on according to the fixed law of gravity, from so simple a beginning endless forms most beautiful and most wonderful have been and are being evolved.

—*From the Origin of Species, by Charles Robert Darwin, English (1809–1882).*

CREATIVE DESIGN

During these two years I was led to think much about religion. Whilst on board the *Beagle* I was quite orthodox, and I remember being heartily laughed at by several of the officers (though themselves orthodox) for quoting the Bible as an unanswerable authority on some point of morality. I suppose it was the novelty of the argument that amused them. But I had gradually come by this time, *i.e.* 1836 to 1839, to see that the

Old Testament was no more to be trusted than the sacred books of the Hindoos. The question then continually rose before my mind and would not be banished – is it credible that if God were now to make a revelation to the Hindoos, he would permit it to be connected with the belief in Vishnu, Siva, &c., as Christianity is connected with the Old Testament? This appeared to me utterly incredible.

By further reflecting that the clearest evidence would be requisite to make any sane man believe in the miracles by which Christianity is supported, – and that the more we know of the fixed laws of nature the more incredible do miracles become, – that the men of that time were ignorant and credulous to a degree almost incomprehensible to us, – that the Gospels cannot be proved to have been written simultaneously with the events, – that they differ in many important details, far too important, as it seemed to me, to be admitted as the usual inaccuracies of eyewitnesses; – by such reflections as these, which I give not as having the least novelty or value, but as they influenced me – I gradually came to disbelieve in Christianity as a divine revelation. The fact that many false religions have spread over large portions of the earth like wild-fire had some weight with me.

But I was very unwilling to give up my belief; I feel sure of this, for I can well remember often and often inventing daydreams of old letters between distinguished Romans, and manuscripts being discovered at Pompeii or elsewhere, which confirmed in the most striking manner all that was written in the Gospels. But I found it more and more difficult, with free scope given to my imagination, to invent evidence which would suffice to convince me. Thus disbelief crept over me at a very slow rate, but was at last complete. The rate was so slow that I felt no distress.

Although I did not think much about the existence of a personal God until a considerably later period of my life, I will here give the vague conclusions to which I have been driven. The old argument from design in Nature, as given by Paley, which formerly seemed to me so conclusive, fails, now that the law of natural selection has been discovered. We can no longer argue that for instance the beautiful hinge of a bivalve shell must have been made by an intelligent being, like the hinge of a door by man. There seems to be no more design in the variability of organic beings, and in the action of natural selection, than in the course which the wind blows. But I have discussed this subject at the end of my book on the 'Variations of Domesticated Animals and Plants'; and the argument there given has never, as far as I can see, been answered.

But passing over the endless beautiful adaptations which we everywhere meet with, it may be asked, How can the generally beneficent arrangement of the world be accounted for? Some writers indeed are so much impressed with the amount of suffering in the world, that they doubt, if we look to all sentient beings, whether there is more of misery or of happiness; whether the world as a whole is a good or bad one. According to my judgment happiness decidedly prevails, though this would be very difficult to prove. If the truth of this conclusion be granted, it harmonizes well with the effects which we might expect from natural selection. If all the individuals of any species were habitually to suffer to an extreme degree, they would neglect to propagate their kind; but we have no reason to believe that this has ever, or at least often, occurred. Some other considerations moreover lead to the belief that all sentient beings have been formed so as to enjoy, as a general rule, happiness.

Everyone who believes as I do, that all the corporeal and mental organs (excepting those which are neither advantageous nor disadvantageous to the possessor) of all beings have been developed through natural selection, or the survival of the fittest, together with use or habit, will admit that these organs have been formed so that their possessors may compete successfully with other beings, and thus increase in number. Now an animal may be led to pursue that course of action which is most beneficial to the species by suffering, such as pain, hunger, thirst, and fear; or by pleasure, as in eating and drinking, and in the propagation of the species, etc., or by both means combined, as in the search for food. But pain or suffering of any kind, if long continued, causes depression and lessens the power of action, yet is well adapted to make a creature guard itself against any great or sudden evil. Pleasurable sensations, on the other hand, may be long continued without any depressing effect; on the contrary, they stimulate the whole system to increased action. Hence it has come to pass that most or all sentient beings have been developed in such a manner, through natural selection, that pleasurable sensations serve as their habitual guides. We see this in the pleasure from exertion, even occasionally from great exertion of the body or mind — in the pleasure of our daily meals, and especially in the pleasure derived from sociability, and from loving our families. The sum of such pleasures as these, which are habitual or frequently recurrent, give, as I can hardly doubt, to most sentient beings an excess of happiness over misery, although many occasionally suffer much. Such suffering is quite compatible with the belief in natural selection, which is not perfect in its action, but tends only to render each species as successful as possible in the battle for life with other species, in wonderfully complex and changing circumstances.

That there is much suffering in the world, no one disputes. Some have attempted to explain this with reference to man by imagining that it serves for his moral improvement. But the number of men in the world is as nothing compared with that of all other sentient beings, and they often suffer greatly without any moral improvement. This very old argument from the existence of suffering against the existence of an intelligent First Cause seems to me a strong one; whereas, as just remarked, the presence of much suffering agrees well with the view that all organic beings have been developed through variation and natural selection.

At the present day, the most usual argument for the existence of an intelligent God is drawn from the deep inward conviction and feelings which are experienced by most persons.

Formerly I was led by feelings such as those just referred to (although I do not think that the religious sentiment was ever strongly developed in me), to the firm conviction of the existence of God and of the immortality of the soul. In my Journal I wrote that whilst standing in the midst of the grandeur of a Brazilian forest, "it is not possible to give an adequate idea of the higher feelings of wonder, admiration, and devotion, which fill and elevate the mind." I well remember my conviction that there is more in man than the mere breath of his body. But now the grandest scenes would not cause any such convictions and feelings to rise in my mind. It may be truly said that I am like a man who has become color-blind, and the universal belief by men of the existence of redness makes my present loss of perception of not the least value as evidence. This argument would be a valid one if all men of all races had the same inward conviction of the existence of one God; but we know that this is very far from being the case. Therefore I cannot see that such inward convictions and feelings are of any weight as evidence of what really exists. The state of mind which grand scenes formerly excited in me, and which was intimately connected with a belief in God, did not essentially differ from that which is often called the sense of sublimity; and however difficult it may be to explain the genesis of this sense, it can hardly be advanced as an argument for the existence of God, any more than the powerful though vague and similar feelings excited by music.

With respect to immortality, nothing shows me [so clearly] how strong and almost instinctive a belief it is, as the consideration of the view now held by most physicists, namely, that the sun with all the planets will in time grow too cold for life, unless indeed some great body dashes into the sun, and thus gives it fresh life. Believing as I do that man in the distant future will be a far more perfect creature than he now is, it is an intolerable thought that he and all other sentient beings are doomed to complete annihilation after such long-continued slow progress. To those who fully admit the immortality of the human soul, the destruction of our world will not appear so dreadful.

Another source of conviction in the existence of God, connected with the reason, and not with the feelings, impresses me as having much more weight. This follows from the extreme difficulty or rather impossibility of conceiving this immense and wonderful universe, including man, with his capacity of looking far backward and far into futurity, as the result of blind chance or necessity. When thus reflecting I feel compelled to look to a First Cause, having an intelligent mind in some degree analogous to that of man; and I deserve to be called a Theist. This conclusion was strong in my mind about the time, as far as I can remember, when I wrote the 'Origin of Species'; and it is since that time that it has very gradually, with many fluctuations, become weaker. But then arises the doubt: Can the mind of man, which has, as I fully believe, been developed from a mind as low as that possessed by the lowest animals, be trusted when it draws such grand conclusions?

I cannot pretend to throw the least light on such abstruse problems. The mystery of the beginning of all things is insoluble by us; and I for one must be content to remain an Agnostic.

— *From the Life and Letters of Charles Darwin, edited by his Son, Francis Darwin.*

Inoculation for Hydrophobia

LOUIS PASTEUR

GENTLEMEN: — Your Congress meetings are the place for the discussion of the gravest problems of medicine; they serve also to point out the great landmarks of the future. Three years ago, on the eve of the London Congress, the doctrine of micro-organisms, the ætiological cause of transmissible maladies, was still the subject of sharp criticisms. Certain refractory minds continued to uphold the idea that "disease is in us, from us, by us."

It was expected that the decided supporters of the theory of the spontaneity of diseases would make a bold stand in London; but no opposition was made to the doctrine of "exteriority," or external causes, the first cause of contagious diseases, and those questions were not discussed at all.

It was there seen, once again, that when all is ready for the final triumph of truth, the united conscience of a great assembly feels it instinctively and recognises it.

All clear-sighted minds had already foreseen that the theory of the spontaneity of diseases received its death-blow on the day when it became possible reasonably to consider the spontaneous generation of microscopic organisms as a myth, and when, on the other hand, the life-activity of those same beings was shown to be the main cause of organic decomposition and of all fermentation.

From the London Congress, also, dates the recognition of another very hopeful progress; we refer to the attenuation of different viruses, to the production of varying degrees of virulence for each virus, and their preservation by suitable methods of cultivation; to the practical application, finally, of those new facts in animal medicine.

New microbic prophylactic viruses have been added to those of fowl-cholera and of splenic fever. The animals saved from death by contagious diseases are now counted by hundreds of thousands, and the sharp opposition which those scientific novelties met with at the beginning was soon swept away by the rapidity of their onward progress.

Will the circle of practical applications of those new notions be limited in future to the prophylaxis of animal distempers? We must never think little of a new discovery, nor despair of its fecundity; but more than that, in the present instance, it may be asserted that the question is already solved in principle. Thus, splenic fever is common to animals and man, and we make bold to declare that, were it necessary to do so, nothing could be easier than to render man also proof against that affection. The process which is employed for animals might, almost without a change, be applied to him also. It would simply become advisable to act with an amount of prudence which the value of the life of an ox or a sheep does not call for. Thus, we should use three or four vaccine-viruses instead of two, of progressive intensity of virulence, and choose the first ones so weak that the patient should never be exposed to the slightest morbid complication, however susceptible to the disease he might be by his constitution.

The difficulty, then, in the case of human diseases, does not lie in the application of the new method of prophylaxis, but rather in the knowledge of the physiological properties of their viruses. All our experiments must tend to discover the proper degree of attenuation for each virus. But experimentation, if allowable on animals, is criminal on man. Such is the principal cause of the complication of researches bearing on diseases exclusively human. Let us keep in mind, nevertheless, that the studies of which we are speaking were born yesterday only, that they have already yielded valuable results, and that new ones may be fairly expected when we shall have gone deeper into the knowledge of animal maladies, and of those in particular which affect animals in common with man.

The desire to penetrate farther forward in that double study led me to choose rabies as the subject of my researches, in spite of the darkness in which it was veiled.

The study of rabies was begun in my laboratory four years ago, and pursued since then without other interruption than what was inherent to the nature of the researches themselves, which present certain unfavourable conditions. The incubation of the disease is always protracted, the space disposed of is never sufficient, and it thus becomes impossible at a given moment to multiply the experiments as one would like. Notwithstanding those material obstacles, lessened by the interest taken by the French Government in all questions of great scientific interest, we now no longer count the experiments which we have made, my fellow workers and myself. I shall limit myself to-day to an exposition of our latest acquisitions.

The name alone of a disease, and of rabies above all others, at once suggests to the mind the notion of a remedy.

But it will, in the majority of cases, be labour lost to aim in the first instance at discovering a mode of cure. It is, in a manner, leaving all progress to chance. Far better to endeavour to acquaint oneself, first of all, with the nature, the cause, and the evolution of the disease, with a glimmering hope, perhaps, of finally arriving at its prophylaxis.

To this last method we are indebted for the result that rabies is no longer to-day to be considered as an insoluble riddle.

We have found that the virus of rabies develops itself invariably in the nervous system, brain, and spinal cord, in the nerves, and in the salivary glands; but it is not present at the same moment in every one of those parts. It may, for example, develop itself at the lower extremity of the spinal cord, and only after a time reach the brain. It may be met with at one or at several points of the encephalon whilst being absent at certain other points of the same region.

If an animal is killed whilst in the power of rabies, it may require a pretty long search to discover the presence here or there in the nervous system, or in the glands, of the virus of rabies. We have been fortunate enough to ascertain that in all cases, when death has been allowed to supervene naturally, the swelled-out portion, or bulb, of the medulla oblongata nearest to the brain, and uniting the spinal cord with it, is always rabid. When an animal has died of rabies (and the disease always ends in death), rabid matter can with certainty be obtained from its bulb, capable of reproducing the disease in other animals when inoculated into them, after trephining, in the arachnoid space of the cerebral meninges.

Any street dog whatsoever, inoculated in the manner described with portions of the bulb of an animal which has died of rabies, will certainly develop the same disease. We have thus inoculated several hundreds of dogs brought without any choice from the pound. Never once was the inoculation a failure. Similarly also, with uniform success, several hundred guinea-pigs, and rabbits more numerous still.

Those two great results, the constant presence of the virus in the bulb at the time of death, and the certainty of the reproduction of the disease by inoculation into the arachnoid space, stand out like experimental axioms, and their importance is paramount. Thanks to the precision of their application, and to the well-known daily repetition of those two criteria of our experiments, we have been able to move forward steadily and surely in that arduous study. But, however solid those experimental bases, they were, nevertheless, incapable in themselves of giving us the faintest notion as to some method of vaccination against rabies. In the present state of science the discovery of a method of vaccination against some virulent malady presupposes:

1. That we have to deal with a virus capable of assuming diverse intensities, of which the weaker ones can be put to vaccinal or protective uses.

2. That we are in possession of a method enabling us to reproduce those diverse degrees of virulence at will.

At the present time, however, science is acquainted with one sort of rabies only — viz., dog rabies.

Rabies, whether in dog, man, horse, ox, wolf, fox, etc., comes originally from the bite of a mad dog. It is never spontaneous, neither in the dog nor in any other animal. There are none seriously authenticated among the alleged cases of so-called spontaneous rabies, and I add that it is idle to argue that the first case of rabies of all must have been spontaneous. Such an argument does not solve the difficulty, and wantonly calls into question the as yet inscrutable problem of the origin of life. It would be quite as well, against the assertion that an oak tree always proceeded from another oak tree, to argue that the first of all oak trees that ever grew must have been produced spontaneously. Science, which knows itself, is well aware that it would be useless for her to discuss about the origin of things; she is aware that, for the present at any rate, that origin is placed beyond the ken of her investigations.

In fine, then, the first question to be solved on our way towards the prophylaxis of rabies is that of knowing whether the virus of that malady is susceptible of taking on varying intensities, after the manner of the virus of fowl-cholera or of splenic fever.

But in what way shall we ascertain the possible existence of varying intensities in the virus of rabies? By what standard shall we measure the strength of a virus which either fails completely or kills? Shall we have recourse to the visible symptoms of rabies? But those symptoms are extremely variable, and depend essentially on the particular point of the encephalon or of the spinal cord where the virus has in the first instance fixed and developed itself. The most caressing rabies, for such do exist, when inoculated into another animal of the same species, give rise to furious rabies of the intensest type.

Might we then perhaps make use of the duration of incubation as a means of estimating the intensity of our virus? But what can be more changeful than the incubative period? Suppose a mad dog were to bite several sound dogs: one of them will take rabies in one month or six weeks, another after two or three months or more. Nothing, too, is more changeful than the length of incubation according to the different modes of inoculation. Thus, other circumstances the same, after bites or hypodermic inoculation rabies occasionally develops itself, and at other times aborts completely; but inoculations on the brain are never sterile, and give the disease after a relatively short incubation.

It is possible, nevertheless, to gauge with sufficient accuracy the degree of intensity of our virus by means of the time of incubation, on condition that we make use exclusively of the intra-cranial mode of inoculation; and secondly, that we do away with one of the great disturbing influences inherent to the results of inoculation made by bites, under the skin or in the veins, by injecting the right proportion of material.

The duration of incubation, as a matter of fact, may depend largely on the quantity of efficient virus — that is to say, on the quantity of virus which reaches the nervous system without diminution or modification. Although the quantity of virus capable of giving rabies may be, so to speak, infinitely small, as seen in the common fact of the disease developing itself after rabid bites which, as a rule, introduce into the system a barely appreciable weight of virus, it is easy to double the length of incubation by simply changing the proportion of those very small quantities of inoculated matter. I may quote the following examples: —

On May 10, 1882, we injected into the popliteal vein of a dog ten drops of a liquid prepared by crushing a portion of the bulb of a dog, which had died of ordinary canine madness, in three or four times its volume of sterilised broth.

Into a second dog we injected $\frac{1}{100}$th of that quantity, into a third $\frac{1}{200}$th. Rabies showed itself in the first dog on the eighteenth day after the injection, on the thirty-fifth day in the second dog, whilst the third one did not take the disease at all, which means that, for the last animal, with the particular mode of inoculation employed, the quantity of virus injected was not sufficient to give rabies. And yet that dog, like all dogs, was susceptible of taking the disease, for it actually took it twenty-two days after a second inoculation, performed on September 3, 1882.

I now take another example bearing on rabbits, and by a different mode of inoculation. This time, after trephining, the bulb of a rabbit which had died of rabies after inoculation of an extremely powerful virus is triturated and mixed with two or three times its volume of sterilised broth. The mixture is allowed to stand a little, and then two drops of the supernatant liquid are injected after terphining into a first rabbit, into a second rabbit one-fourth of that quantity, and in succession into other rabbits, $\frac{1}{16}$th, $\frac{1}{64}$th, $\frac{1}{128}$th, and $\frac{1}{152}$nd of that same quantity. All those rabbits died of rabies, the incubation having been eight days, nine and ten days for the third and fourth, twelve and sixteen days for the last ones.

Those variations in the length of incubation were not the result of any weakening or diminution of the intrinsic virulence of the virus brought on possibly by its dilution, for the incubation of eight days was at once recovered when the nervous matter of all those rabbits was inoculated into new animals.

Those examples show that, whenever rabies follows upon bites or hypodermic inoculations, the differences in respect of length of incubation must be chiefly ascribed to the variations, at times within considerable limits, of the ever-undeterminate proportions of the inoculated viruses which reach the central nervous system.

If, therefore, we desire to make use of the length of incubation as a measure of the intensity of the virulence, it will be indispensable to have recourse to inoculation on the surface of the brain, after trephining, a process the action of which is absolutely certain, coupled with the use of a larger quantity of virus than what is strictly sufficient to give rise to rabies. By those means the irregularities in the length of incubation for the same virus tend to disappear completely, because we always have the maximum effect which that virus can produce; that maximum coincides with a minimum length of incubation.

We have thus, finally, become possessed of a method enabling us to investigate the possible existence of different degrees of virulence, and to compare them with one another. The whole secret of the method, I repeat, consists in inoculating on the brain, after trephining, a quantity of virus which, although small in itself, is still greater than what is simply necessary to reproduce rabies. We thus disengage the incubation from all disturbing influences and render its duration dependent exclusively on the activity of the particular virus used, that activity being in each case estimated by the minimum incubation determined by it.

This method was applied in the first instance to the study of canine madness, and in particular to the question of knowing whether dog-madness was always one and the same, with perhaps the slight variations which might be due to the differences of race in diverse dogs.

We accordingly got hold of a number of dogs affected with ordinary street rabies, at all times of the year, at all seasons of the same year or of different years, and belonging to the most dissimilar canine races. In each case the bulbar portion of the medulla oblongata was taken out from the recently dead animal, triturated and suspended in two or three times its volume of sterilised liquid, making use all along of every precaution to keep our materials pure, and two drops of this liquid injected after trephining into one or two rabbits. The inoculation is made with a Pravaz syringe, the needle of which, slightly curved at its extremity, is inserted through the dura-mater into the arachnoid space. The results were as follows: all the rabbits, from whatever sort of dog inoculated, showed a period of incubation which ranged between twelve and fifteen days, without almost a single exception. Never did they show an incubation of eleven, ten, nine, or eight days, never an incubation of several weeks or of several months.

Dog-rabies, the ordinary rabies, the only known rabies, is thus sensibly one in its virulence, and its modifications, which are very limited, appear to depend solely on the varying aptitude for rabies of the different known races. But we are going now to witness a deep change in the virulence of dog-rabies.

Let us take one, any one, of our numerous rabbits, inoculated with the virus of an ordinary mad dog, and, after it has died, extract its bulb, prepare it just as described, and inject two drops of the bulb-emulsion into the arachnoid space of a second rabbit, whose bulb will in turn and in time be injected into a third rabbit, the bulb of which again will serve for a fourth rabbit, and so on.

There will be evidence, even from the first few passages, of a marked tendency towards a lessening of the period of incubation in the succeeding rabbits. Just one example:

Towards the end of the year 1882 fifteen cows and one bull died of rabies on a farm situated in the neighbourhood of the town of Melun. They had been bitten on October 2 by the farm dog, which had become mad. The head of one of the cows, which had died on November 15, was sent to my laboratory by M. Rossignol, a veterinary surgeon in Melun. A number of experiments were made on dogs and rabbits, and showed that the following parts, the only encephalic (or those pertaining to the brain) ones tested, were rabid: the bulb, the cerebellum, the frontal lobe, the sphenoidal lobe. The rabbits trephined and inoculated with those different parts showed the first symptoms of rabies on the seventeenth and eighteenth days after inoculation. With the bulb of one of those rabbits two more were inoculated, of which one took rabies on the fifteenth day, the other on the twenty-third day.

We may notice, once for all, that when rabies is transferred from one animal to another of a different species, the period of incubation is always very irregular at first in the individuals of the second species if the virus had not yet become fixed in its maximum virulence for the first species. We have just seen an example of that phenomenon, since one of the rabbits had an incubation of fifteen days, the other of twenty-three days, both having received the same virus and all other circumstances remaining apparently the same for them.

The bulb of the first one of those last rabbits which died was injected into two more rabbits, still after trephining. One of them took rabies on the tenth day, the other on the fourteenth day. The bulb of the first one that died was again injected into a couple of new rabbits, which developed the disease in ten days and twelve days respectively. A fifth time two new animals were inoculated from the first one that died, and they both took the disease on the eleventh day after inoculation: similarly, a sixth passage was made, and gave an incubation of eleven days, twelve days for the seventh passage, ten and eleven for the eighth, ten days for the ninth and tenth passages, nine days for the eleventh, eight and nine days for the twelfth, and so on, with differences of twenty-four hours at the most, until we got to the twenty-first passage, when rabies declared itself in eight days, and subsequently to that always in eight days up to the fiftieth passage, which was only effected a few days ago. That long experimental series which is still going on was begun on November 15, 1882, and will be kept up for the purpose of preserving in our rabies virus that maximum virulence which it has come to now for some considerable time, as it is easy to calculate.

Allow me to call your attention to the ease and safety of the operations for trephining and then inoculating the virus. Throughout the last twenty months we have been able without a single interruption in the course of the series to carry the one initial virus through a succession of rabbits which were all trephined and inoculated every twelfth day or so.

Guinea-pigs reach more rapidly the maximum virulence of which they are susceptible. The period of incubation is in them also variable and irregular at the beginning of the series of successive passages, but it soon enough fixes itself at a minimum of five days. The maximum virulence in guinea-pigs is reached after seven or eight passages only. It is worth noting that the number of passages required before reaching the maximum virulence, both in guinea-pigs and in rabbits, varies with the origin of the first virus with which the series is begun.

If now this rabies with maximum virulence be transferred again into the dog from guinea-pig or rabbit, there is produced a dog-virus which in point of virulence goes far beyond that of ordinary canine madness.

But, a natural query – of what use can be that discovery as to the existence and artificial production of diverse varieties of rabies, every one of them more violent and more rapidly fatal than the habitual madness of the dog? The man of science is thankful for the smallest find he can make in the field of pure science, but the many, terrified at the very name of hydrophobia, claim something more than mere scientific curiosities. How much more interesting it would be to become acquainted with a set of rabies viruses which should, on the contrary, be possessed of attenuated degrees of virulence! Then, indeed, might there be some hope of creating a number of vaccinal rabies viruses such as we have done for the virus of fowl-cholera, of the microbe of saliva, of the red evil of swine (swine-plague), and even of acute septicæmia. Unfortunately, however, the methods which had served for those different viruses showed themselves to be either inapplicable or inefficient in the case of rabies. It therefore became necessary to find out new and independent methods, such, for example, as the cultivation *in vitro* of the mortal rabies virus.

Jenner was the first to introduce into current science the opinion that the virus which he called the grease of the horse, and which we call now more exactly horse-pox, probably softened its virulence, so to speak, in passing through the cow and before it could be transferred to man without danger. It was therefore natural to think of a possible diminution of the virulence of rabies by a number of passages through the organisms of some animal or other, and the experiment was worth trying. A large number of attempts were made, but the majority of the animal species experimented on exalted the virulence after the manner of rabbits and guinea-pigs; fortunately, however, it was not so with monkeys.

On December 6, 1883, a monkey was trephined and inoculated with the bulb of a dog, which had itself been similarly inoculated from a child who had died of rabies. The monkey took rabies eleven days later, and when dead served for inoculation into a second monkey, which also took the disease on the eleventh day. A third monkey, similarly inoculated from the second one, showed the first symptoms on the twenty-third day, etc. The bulb of each one of the monkeys was inoculated, after trephining, into two rabbits each time. The rabbits inoculated from the first monkey developed rabies between thirteen and sixteen days, those from the second monkey between fourteen and twenty days, those from the third monkey between twenty-six and thirty days, those from the fourth monkey both of them after the twenty-eighth day, those from the fifth monkey after twenty-seven days, those from the sixth monkey after thirty days.

It cannot be doubted after that, that successive passages through monkeys, and from the several monkeys to rabbits, do diminish the virulence of the virus for the latter animals; they diminish it for dogs also. The dog inoculated with the bulb of the fifth monkey gave an incubation of no less than fifty-eight days, although it had been inoculated in the arachnoid space.

The experiments were renewed with fresh sets of monkeys and led to similar results. We were therefore actually in possession of a method by means of which we could attenuate the virulence of rabies. Successive inoculations from monkey to monkey elaborate viruses which, when transferred to rabbits, reproduce rabies in them, but with a progressively lengthening period of incubation. Nevertheless, if one of those rabbits be taken as the first for inoculations through a series of rabbits, the rabies thus cultivated obeys the law which we have seen before, and has its virulence increased at each passage.

The practical application of those facts gives us a method for the vaccination of dogs against rabies. As a starting point, make use of one of the rabbits inoculated from a monkey sufficiently removed from the first animal of the monkey series for the inoculation — hypodermic or intra-venous — of that rabbit's bulb not to be mortal for a new rabbit. The next vaccinal inoculations are made with the bulbs of rabbits derived by successive passages from that first rabbit.

In the course of our experiments we made use, as a rule, for inoculation, of the virus of rabbits which had died after an incubation of four weeks, repeating three or four times each the vaccinal inoculations made with the bulbs of rabbits derived in succession from one another and from the first one of the series, itself coming directly from the monkey. I abstain from giving more details, because certain experiments which are actually going on allow me to expect that the process will be greatly simplified.

— *From an Address delivered August 10, 1884, at the Copenhagen meeting of the International Medical Congress by Louis Pasteur, French (1822–1895).*

The Exploration of Space

EDWIN HUBBLE

THE EXPLORATION of space has penetrated only recently into the realm of the nebulae. The advance into regions hitherto unknown has been made during the last dozen years with the aid of great telescopes. The observable region of the universe is now defined and a preliminary reconnaissance has been completed. The chapters which follow are reports on various phases of the reconnaissance.

The earth we inhabit is a member of the solar system — a minor satellite of the sun. The sun is a star among the many millions which form the stellar system. The stellar system is a swarm of stars isolated in space. It drifts through the universe as a swarm of bees drifts through the summer air. From our position somewhere within the system, we look out through the swarm of stars, past the borders, into the universe beyond.

The universe is empty, for the most part, but here and there, separated by immense intervals, we find other stellar systems, comparable with our own. They are so remote that, except in the nearest systems, we do not see the individual stars of which they are composed. These huge stellar systems appear as dim patches of light. Long ago they were named "nebulae" or "clouds" — mysterious bodies whose nature was a favorite subject for speculation.

But now, thanks to great telescopes, we know something of their nature, something of their real size and brightness, and their mere appearance indicates the general order of their distances. They are scattered through space as far as telescopes can penetrate. We see a few that appear large and bright. These are the nearer nebulae. Then we find them smaller and fainter, in constantly increasing numbers, and we know that we are reaching out into space, farther and ever farther, until, with the faintest nebulae that can be detected with the greatest telescope, we arrive at the frontiers of the known universe.

This last horizon defines the observable region of space. It is a vast sphere, perhaps a thousand million light-years in diameter. Throughout the sphere are scattered a hundred million nebulae – stellar systems – in various stages of their evolutionary history. The nebulae are distributed singly, in groups, and occasionally in great clusters, but when large volumes of space are compared, the tendency to cluster averages out. To the very limits of the telescope, the large-scale distribution of nebulae is approximately uniform.

One other general characteristic of the observable region has been found. Light which reaches us from the nebulae is reddened in proportion to the distance it has traveled. This phenomenon is known as the velocity-distance relation, for it is often interpreted, in theory, as evidence that the nebulae are all rushing away from our stellar system, with velocities that increase directly with distances.

RECEDING HORIZONS

This sketch roughly indicates the current conception of the realm of the nebulae. It is the culmination of a line of research that began long ago. The history of astronomy is a history of receding horizons. Knowledge has spread in successive waves, each wave representing the exploitation of some new clew to the interpretation of observational data.

The exploration of space presents three such phases. At first the explorations were confined to the realm of the planets, then they spread through the realm of the stars, and finally they penetrated into the realm of the nebulae.

The successive phases were separated by long intervals of time. Although the distance of the moon was well known to the Greeks, the order of the distance of the sun and the scale of planetary distances was not established until the latter part of the seventeenth century. Distances of stars were first determined almost exactly a century ago, and distances of nebulae, in our own generation. The distances were the essential data. Until they were found, no progress was possible.

The early explorations halted at the edge of the solar system, facing a great void that stretched away to the nearer stars. The stars were unknown quantities. They might be little bodies, relatively near, or they might be gigantic bodies, vastly remote. Only when the gap was bridged, only when the distances of a small, sample collection of stars had been actually measured, was the nature determined of the inhabitants of the realm beyond the solar system. Then the explorations, operating from an established base among the now familiar stars, swept rapidly through the whole of the stellar system.

Again there was a halt, in the face of an even greater void, but again, when instruments and technique had sufficiently developed, the gap was bridged by the determination of the distances of a few of the nearer nebulae. Once more, with the nature of the inhabitants known, the explorations swept even more rapidly through the realm of the nebulae and halted only at the limits of the greatest telescope.

THE THEORY OF THE ISLAND UNIVERSES

This is the story of the explorations. They were made with measuring rods, and they enlarged the body of factual knowledge. They were always preceded by speculations. Speculations once ranged through the entire field, but they have been pushed steadily back by the explorations until now they lay undisputed claim only to the territory beyond the telescopes, to the dark unexplored regions of the universe at large.

The speculations took many forms and most of them have long since been forgotten. The few that survived the test of the measuring rod were based on the principle of the uniformity of nature – the assumption that any large sample of the universe is much like any other. The principle was applied to stars long before distances were determined. Since the stars were too far away for the measuring instruments, they must necessarily be very bright. The brightest object known was the sun. Therefore, the stars were assumed to be like the sun, and distances could be estimated from their apparent faintness. In this way, the conception of a stellar system, isolated in space, was formulated as early as 1750. The author was Thomas Wright (1711–86) an English instrument maker and private tutor.

But Wright's speculations went beyond the Milky Way. A single stellar system, isolated in the universe, did not satisfy his philosophic mind. He imagined other, similar systems and, as visible evidence of their existence, referred to the mysterious clouds called "nebulae."

Five years later, Immanuel Kant (1724–1804) developed Wright's conception in a form that endured, essentially unchanged, for the following century and a half. Some of Kant's remarks concerning the theory furnish an excellent example of reasonable speculation based on the principle of uniformity. A rather free translation runs as follows:

I come now to another part of my system, and because it suggests a lofty idea of the plan of creation, it appears to me as the most seductive. The sequence of ideas that led us to it is very simple and natural. They are as follows: let us imagine a system of stars gathered together in a common plane, like those of the Milky Way, but situated so far away from us that even with the telescope we cannot distinguish the stars composing it; let us assume that its distance, compared to that separating us from the stars of the Milky Way, is in the same proportion as the distance of the Milky Way is to the distance from the earth to the sun; such a stellar world will appear to the observer, who contemplates it at so enormous a distance, only as a little spot feebly illumined and subtending a very small angle; its shape will be circular, if its plane is perpendicular to the line of sight, elliptical, if it is seen obliquely. The faintness of its light, its form, and its appreciable diameter will obviously distinguish such a phenomenon from the isolated stars around it.

We do not need to seek far in the observations of astronomers to meet with such phenomena. They have been seen by various observers, who have wondered at their strange appearance, have speculated about them, and have suggested sometimes the most amazing explanations, sometimes theories which were more rational, but which had no more foundation than the former. We refer to the nebulae, or, more precisely, to a particular kind of celestial body which M. de Maupertius describes as follows:

"These are small luminous patches, only slightly more brilliant than the dark background of the sky; they have this in common, that their shapes are more or less open ellipses; and their light is far more feeble than that of any other objects to be perceived in the heavens."

Kant then mentions and rejects the views of Derham that the patches are openings in the firmament, through which the fiery Empyrean is seen, and of Maupertius that the nebulae are enormous single bodies, flattened by rapid rotation. Kant then continues:

It is much more natural and reasonable to assume that a nebula is not a unique and solitary sun, but a system of numerous suns, which appear crowded, because of their distance, into a space so limited that their light, which would be imperceptible were each of them isolated, suffices, owing to their enormous numbers, to give a pale and uniform luster. Their analogy with our own system of stars; their form, which is precisely what it should be according to our theory; the faintness of their light, which denotes an infinite distance; all are in admirable accord and lead us to consider these elliptical spots as systems of the same order as our own – in a word, to be Milky Ways similar to the one whose constitution we have explained. And if these hypotheses, in which analogy and observation consistently lend mutual support, have the same merit as formal demonstrations, we must consider the existence of such systems as demonstrated. . . .

We see that scattered through space out to infinite distances, there exist similar systems of stars (nebulous stars, nebulae), and that creation, in the whole extent of its infinite grandeur, is everywhere organized into systems whose members are in relation with one another. . . . A vast field lies open to discoveries, and observation alone will give the key.

The theory, which came to be called the theory of island universes, found a permanent place in the body of philosophical speculation. The astronomers themselves took little part in the discussions: they studied the nebulae. Toward the end of the nineteenth century, however, the accumulation of observational data brought into prominence the problem of the status of the nebulae and, with it, the theory of island universes as a possible solution.

THE NATURE OF THE NEBULAE

(a) *The Formulation of the Problem*

A few nebulae had been known to the naked-eye observers and, with the development of telescopes, the numbers grew, slowly at first, then more and more rapidly. At the time Sir William Herschel (1738–1822), the first outstanding leader in nebular research, began his surveys, the most extensive published lists were those by Messier, the last of which (1784) contained 103 of the most conspicuous nebulae and clusters. These objects are still known by the Messier numbers – for example, the great spiral in Andromeda is M31. Sir William Herschel catalogued 2,500 objects, and his son, Sir John (1792–1871), transporting the telescopes to the southern hemisphere (near Capetown in South Africa) added many more. Positions of about 20,000 nebulae are now available, and perhaps ten times that number have been identified on photographic plates. The mere size of catalogues has long since ceased to be important. Now the desirable data are the numbers of nebulae brighter than successive limits of apparent faintness, in sample areas widely distributed over the sky.

Galileo, with his first telescopes, resolved a typical "cloud" – Praesepe – into a cluster of stars. With larger telescopes and continued study, many of the more conspicuous nebulae met the same fate. Sir William Herschel concluded that all nebulae could be resolved into star-clusters, if only sufficient telescopic power were available. In his later days, however, he revised his position and admitted the existence, in certain cases, of a lumious "fluid" which was inherently unresolvable. Ingenious attempts were made to explain away these exceptional cases until Sir William Huggins (1824–1910), equipped with a spectograph, fully demonstrated in 1864 that some of the nebulae were masses of luminous gas.

Huggins' results clearly indicated that nebulae were not all members of a single, homogeneous group and that some kind of classification would be necessary before they could be reduced to order. The nebulae actually resolved into stars – the star-clusters – were weeded out of the lists to form a separate department of research. They were recognized as component parts of the galactic system, and thus had no bearing on the theory of island universes.

Among unresolved nebulae, two entirely different types were eventually differentiated. One type consisted of the relatively few nebulae definitely known to be unresolvable – clouds of dust and gas mingled among, and intimately associated with, the stars in the galactic system. They were usually found within the belt of the Milky Way and were obviously, like the star-clusters, members of the galactic system. For this reason, they have since been called "galactic" nebulae. They are further subdivided into two groups, "planetary" nebulae and "diffuse" nebulae, frequently shortened to "planetaries" and "nebulosities."

The other type consisted of the great numbers of small, symmetrical objects found everywhere in the sky except in the Milky Way. A spiral structure was found in most, although not in all, of the conspicuous objects. They had many features in common and appeared to form a single family. They were given various names but, to anticipate, they are now known as "extragalactic" nebulae and will be called simply "nebulae."

The status of the nebulae, as the group is now defined, was undetermined because the distances were wholly unknown. They were definitely beyond the limits of direct measurement, and the scanty, indirect evidence bearing on the problem could be interpreted in various ways. The nebulae might be relatively nearby objects and hence members of the stellar system, or they might be very remote and hence inhabitants of outer space. At this point, the development of nebular research came into immediate contact with the philosophical theory of island universes. The theory represented, in principle, one of the alternative solutions of the problem of nebular distances. The question of distances was frequently put in the form: Are nebulae island universes?

(b) *The Solution of the Problem*

The situation developed during the years between 1885 and 1914; from the appearance of the bright nova in the spiral M31, which stimulated a new interest in the question of distances, to the publication of Slipher's first extensive list of radial velocities of nebulae, which furnished data of a new kind and encouraged serious attempts to find a solution of the problem.

The solution came ten years later, largely with the help of a great telescope, the 100-inch reflector, that had been completed in the interim. Several of the most conspicuous nebulae were found to be far beyond the limits of the galactic system — they were independent, stellar systems in extragalactic space. Further investigations demonstrated that the other, fainter nebulae were similar systems at greater distances, and the theory of island universes was confirmed.

The 100-inch reflector partially resolved a few of the nearest, neighboring nebulae into swarms of stars. Among these stars various types were recognized which were well known among the brighter stars in the galactic system. The intrinsic luminosities (candle powers) were known, accurately in some cases, approximately in others. Therefore, the apparent faintness of the stars in the nebulae indicated the distances of the nebulae.

The most reliable results were furnished by Cepheid variables, but other types of stars furnished estimates of orders of distance, which were consistent with the Cepheids. Even the brightest stars, whose intrinsic luminosities appear to be nearly constant in certain types of nebulae, have been used as statistical criteria to estimate mean distances for groups of systems.

THE INHABITANTS OF SPACE

The nebulae whose distances were known from the stars involved furnished a sample collection from which new criteria, derived from the nebulae and not from their contents, were formulated. It is now known that the nebulae are all of the same order of intrinsic luminosity. Some are brighter than others, but at least half of them are within the narrow range from one half to twice the mean value, which is 85 million times the luminosity of the sun. Thus, for statistical purposes, the apparent faintness of the nebulae indicates their distances.

With the nature of the nebulae known and the scale of nebular distances established, the investigations proceeded along two lines. In the first place the general features of the individual nebulae were studied; in the second, the characteristics of the observable region as a whole were investigated.

The detailed classification of nebular forms has led to an ordered sequence ranging from globular nebulae, through flattening, ellipsoidal figures, to a series of unwinding spirals. The fundamental pattern of rotational symmetry changes smoothly through the sequence in a manner that suggests increasing speed of rotation. Many features are found which vary systematically along the sequence, and the early impression that the nebulae were members of a single family appears to be confirmed. The luminosities remain fairly constant through the sequence (mean value, 8.5×10^7 suns, as previously mentioned), but the diameters steadily increase from about 1,800 light-years for the globular nebulae to about 10,000 light-years for the most open spirals. The masses are uncertain, the estimates ranging from 2×10^9 to 2×10^{11} times the mass of the sun.

. . . . .

Thus the explorations of space end on a note of uncertainty. And necessarily so. We are, by definition, in the very center of the observable region. We know our immediate neighbourhood rather intimately. With increasing distance, our knowledge fades, and fades rapidly. Eventually, we reach the dim boundary — the utmost limits of our telescopes. There, we measure shadows, and we search among ghostly errors of measurement for landmarks that are scarcely more substantial.

The search will continue. Not until the empirical resources are exhausted, need we pass on to the dreamy realms of speculation.

— *From the Realm of the Nebulae, by Edwin P. Hubble, American (1889–   ).*

PART EIGHT

Travel and Exploration

THE SPIRIT OF WANDERLUST, so often associated with the gypsy, is in reality international. It knows no bounds of place or race, just as travelers refuse to be deterred by them. The knitting of the world into that sense of comradeship which is found "on the road" will in the end require more than a romantic willingness to accept all that fortune may bring, with the cheer which old wine and old tales give to the fatigues at the end of a dusty day. It will demand the perseverance of the scientist in his search for truth, the courage which makes light of all hardships, and the fortitude which rises above frustration. In the end the travelers of the world, whatever their motive in going abroad, will contribute generously to the building of the commonwealth of man.

From the beginning of time, when men first left their native valleys to climb the hedging mountains and view the world beyond, inquiring minds among travelers have asked countless questions. A passage from Philostratus's *The Life of Apollonius of Tyana* is a classic illustration:

"And as they were passing over the summit of the mountain, going on fast, for it was very steep, Apollonius asked of Damis the following question: 'Tell me,' he said, 'where we were yesterday.' And he replied: 'On the plain.' 'And today, O Damis, where are we?' 'In the Caucasus,' said he, 'if I mistake not.' 'Then when were you lower down than you are now?' he asked again, and Damis replied: 'That's a question hardly worth asking. For yesterday we were traveling through the valley below, while today we are close up to heaven.' 'Then you think,' said the other, 'O Damis, that our road yesterday lay low down, whereas our road today lies high up?' 'Yes, by Zeus,' he replied, 'unless at least I'm mad.' 'In what respect then,' said Apollonius, 'do you suppose that our roads differ from one another, and what advantage has today's path for you over that of yesterday?' 'Because,' said Damis, 'yesterday I was walking along where a great many people go, but today, where are very few.' 'Well,' said the other, 'O Damis, can you not also in a city turn out of the main street and walk where you will find very few people?' 'I did not say that,' replied Damis, 'but that yesterday we were passing through villages and populations, whereas today we are ascending through an untrodden and divine region: for you heard our guide say that the barbarians declare this tract to be the home of the gods.' And with that he glanced up to the summit of the mountain. But Apollonius recalled his attention to the original question by asking: 'Can you tell me then, O Damis, what understanding of divine mystery you get by walking so near the heavens?' 'None whatever,' he replied. 'And yet you ought,' said Apollonius. 'When your feet are placed on a platform so divine and vast as this, you ought at once to utter thoughts of the clearest kind about the heaven and about the sun and moon, which you probably think you could touch from a vantage ground so close to heaven.' 'Whatever,' said he, 'I knew about God's nature yesterday, I equally know today, and so far no fresh idea has occurred to me concerning him.' 'So then,' replied the other, 'you are, O Damis, still below, and have won nothing from being high up, and you are as far from heaven as you were yesterday. And my question which I asked you to begin with was a fair one, although you thought I asked it in order to make fun of you.' "

Especially since the days of Marco Polo, the literature of travel has illustrated the varied motives which have impelled men to go abroad. Some travel for mere wanderlust. Some restless souls impressed by uncertainties of life make pilgrimages to the shrines of their faith. With zeal for religious proselyting or love of glory and gold, some seek to extend religious or economic empires, as did the *conquistadores* of Spain. Others, like the scientist Linnaeus, seek only for useful knowledge, cheerfully enduring physical hardship and scorning personal danger. The equipment of the modern archaeologists who, like Warner, seek for "the little objects which mean so much to us in reconstructing the life of the past," is a far cry from that of scientists two centuries ago; but there is no diminishing in their thirst for knowledge or in their fortitude. At times bitter adversity and death frustrate even such heroes as Robert Falcon Scott. The rewards of travel and exploration are varied; but though they may at times be tragic, they do not deter men who range from mere vagabonds to the noblest spirits of the race.

In the literature of travel the reader of world literature discovers gay comrades, richly stored minds, men whose eyes are open to the beauties of the world which ordinary people pass lightly by, and magnanimous spirits who defy all hardship and scorn self-pity. It represents an autobiographical literature revealing the true character of individuals with crystal clarity, no less than one of the chief means of mutual understanding among the races of mankind.

From The Travels of Marco Polo

PROLOGUE

Ye Emperors, Kings, Dukes, Marquises, Earls, and Knights, and all other people desirous of knowing the diversities of the races of mankind, as well as the diversities of kingdoms, provinces, and regions of all parts of the East, read through this book, and ye will find in it the greatest and most marvellous characteristics of the peoples especially of Armenia, Persia, India, and Tartary, as they are severally related in the present work by Marco Polo, a wise and learned citizen of Venice, who states distinctly what things he saw and what things he heard from others. For this book will be a truthful one.

It must be known, then, that from the creation of Adam to the present day, no man, whether Pagan, or Saracen, or Christian, or other, of whatever progeny or generation he may have been, ever saw or inquired into so many and such great things as Marco Polo above mentioned. Who, wishing in his secret thoughts that the things he had seen and heard should be made public by the present work, for the benefit of those who could not see them with their own eyes, he himself being in the year of our Lord 1298 in prison at Genoa, caused the things which are contained in the present work to be written by master Rustigielo, a citizen of Pisa, who was with him in the same prison at Genoa; and he divided it into three parts.

HOW THE TWO BROTHERS POLO SET FORTH FROM CONSTANTINOPLE

It should be known to the reader that, at the time when Baldwin II. was emperor of Constantinople where a magistrate representing the doge of Venice then resided, and in the year of our Lord 1260, Nicolo Polo, the father of the said Marco, and Maffeo, the brother of Nicolo, respectable and well-informed men, embarked in a ship of their own, with a rich and varied cargo of merchandise, and reached Constantinople in safety. After mature deliberation on the subject of their proceedings, it was determined, as the measure most likely to improve their trading capital, that they should prosecute their voyage into the Euxine or Black Sea. With this view they made purchases of many fine and costly jewels, and taking their departure from Constantinople, navigated that sea to a port named Soldaia, from whence they travelled on horseback many days until they reached the court of a powerful chief of the Western Tartars, named Barka, who dwelt in the cities of Bolgara and Sarra, and had the reputation of being one of the most liberal and civilized princes hitherto known amongst the tribes of Tartary. He expressed much satisfaction at the arrival of these travellers, and received them with marks of distinction. In return for which courtesy, when they had laid before him the jewels they brought with them, and perceived that their beauty pleased him, they presented them for his acceptance. The liberality of this conduct on the part of the two brothers struck him with admiration; and being unwilling that they should surpass him in generosity, he not only directed double the value of the jewels to be paid to them, but made them in addition several rich presents.

The brothers having resided a year in the dominions of this prince, they became desirous of revisiting their native country, but were impeded by the sudden breaking out of a war between him and another chief, named Alaù, who ruled over the Eastern Tartars. In a fierce and very sanguinary battle that ensued between their respective armies, Alaù was victorious, in consequence of which, the roads being rendered unsafe for travellers, the brothers could not attempt to return by the way they came; and it was recommended to them, as the only practicable mode of reaching Constantinople, to proceed in an easterly direction, by an unfrequented route, so as to skirt the limits of Barka's territories. Accordingly they made their way to a town named Oukaka, situated on the confines of the kingdom of the Western Tartars. Leaving that place, and advancing still further, they crossed the Tigris [Volga], one of the four rivers of Paradise, and came to a desert, the extent of which was seventeen days' journey, wherein they found neither town, castle, nor any substantial building, but only Tartars with their herds, dwelling in tents on the plain. Having passed this tract they arrived at length at a well-built city called Bokhara, in a province of that name, belonging to the dominions of Persia, and the noblest city of that kingdom, but governed by a prince whose name was Barak. Here, from inability to proceed further, they remained three years.

It happened while these brothers were in Bokhara, that a person of consequence and gifted with eminent talents made his appearance there. He was proceeding as ambassador from Alaù before mentioned, to the Great Khan supreme chief of all the Tartars, named Kublai, whose residence was at the extremity of the continent, in a direction between north-east and east. Not having ever before had an opportunity, although he wished it, of seeing any natives of Italy, he was gratified in a high degree at meeting and conversing with these brothers, who had now become proficients in the Tartar language; and after associating with them for several days, and finding their manners agreeable to him, he proposed to them that they should accompany him to the presence of the Great Khan, who would be pleased by their appearance at his court, which had not hitherto been visited by any person from their country; adding assurances that they would be honourably received, and recompensed with many gifts. Convinced as they were that their endeavours to return homeward would expose them to the most imminent risks, they agreed to this proposal, and recommending themselves to the protection of the Almighty, they set out on their journey in the suite of the ambassador, attended by several Christian servants whom they had brought with them from Venice.

The course they took at first was between

the north-east and north, and an entire year was consumed before they were enabled to reach the imperial residence, in consequence of the extraordinary delays occasioned by the snows and the swelling of the rivers, which obliged them to halt until the former had melted and the floods had subsided. Many things worthy of admiration were observed by them in the progress of their journey, but which are here omitted. . . .

HOW THE GREAT KHAN SENT THE TWO BROTHERS AS HIS ENVOYS TO THE POPE

Being introduced to the presence of the Great Khan, Kublai, the travellers were received by him with the condescension and affability that belonged to his character, and as they were the first Latins who had made their appearance in that country, they were entertained with feasts and honoured with other marks of distinction. Entering graciously into conversation with them, he made earnest inquiries on the subject of the western parts of the world, of the Emperor of the Romans, and of other Christian kings and princes. He wished to be informed of their relative consequence, the extent of their possessions, the manner in which justice was administered in their several kingdoms and principalities, how they conducted themselves in warfare, and above all he questioned them particularly respecting the Pope, the affairs of the Church, and the religious worship and doctrine of the Christians. Being well instructed and discreet men, they gave appropriate answers upon all these points, and as they were perfectly acquainted with the Tartar language, they expressed themselves always in becoming terms; insomuch that the Great Khan, holding them in high estimation, frequently commanded their attendance.

When he had obtained all the information that the two brothers communicated with so much good sense, he expressed himself well satisfied, and having formed in his mind the design of employing them as his ambassadors to the Pope, after consulting with his ministers on the subject, he proposed to them, with many kind entreaties, that they should accompany one of his Barons, named Khogatal, on a mission to the See of Rome.

His object, he told them, was to make a request to his Holiness that he would send to him a hundred men of learning, thoroughly acquainted with the principles of the Christian religion, as well as with the seven arts, and qualified to prove to the learned of his dominions by just and fair argument, that the faith professed by Christians is superior to, and founded upon more evident truth than, any other; that the gods of the Tartars and the idols worshipped in their houses were only evil spirits, and that they and the people of the East in general were under an error in reverencing them as divinities. He, moreover, signified his pleasure that upon their return they should bring with them, from Jerusalem, some of the Holy Oil from the lamp which is kept burning over the Sepulchre of our Lord Jesus Christ, whom he professed to hold in veneration and to consider as the true God. Having heard these commands addressed to them by the Great Khan they humbly prostrated themselves before him, declaring their willingness and instant readiness to perform, to the utmost of their ability, whatever might be the royal will. Upon which he caused letters, in the Tartarian language, to be written in his name to the Pope of Rome, and these he delivered into their hands.

He likewise gave orders that they should be furnished with a golden tablet displaying the imperial cipher, according to the usage established by his majesty; in virtue of which the person bearing it, together with his whole suite, are safely conveyed and escorted from station to station by the governors of all places within the imperial dominions, and are entitled, during the time of their residing in any city, castle, town, or village, to a supply of provisions and everything necessary for their accommodation.

Being thus honourably commissioned they took their leave of the Great Khan, and set out on their journey, but had not proceeded more than twenty days when the officer, named Khogatal, their companion, fell dangerously ill, and unable to proceed further, he halted at a certain city. In this dilemma it was determined, upon consulting all who were present, and with the approbation of the man himself, that they should leave him behind. In the prosecution of their journey they derived essential benefit from being provided with the royal tablet, which procured them attention in every place through which they passed. Their expenses were defrayed, and escorts were furnished. But notwithstanding these advantages, so great were the natural difficulties they had to encounter, from the extreme cold, the snow, the ice, and the flooding of the rivers, that their progress was unavoidably tedious, and three years elapsed before they were enabled to reach a sea-port town in the lesser Armenia, named Laiassus.

Departing from thence by sea, they arrived at Acre in the month of April, 1269. . . .

OF THE PROVINCE OF MOSUL AND ITS DIFFERENT INHABITANTS, OF THE PEOPLE NAMED KURDS, AND OF THE TRADE OF THIS COUNTRY

Mosul is a large province inhabited by various descriptions of people, one class of whom pay reverence to Mahomet, and are called Arabians. The others profess the Christian faith, but not according to the Canons of the Church, which they depart from in many instances, and are denominated Nestorians, Jacobites, and Armenians. They have a patriarch whom they call Jacolit, and by him Archbishops, Bishops, and Abbots are consecrated and sent to all parts of India, to Baudas, or to Cathay, just as the Pope of Rome does in the Latin countries.

All those cloths of gold and of silk which we call muslins are of the manufacture of Mosul, and all the great merchants termed Mossulini, who convey spices and drugs, in large quantities, from one country to another, are from this province.

In the mountainous parts there is a race of people named Kurds, some of whom are Christians and others Mahometans. They are all an unprincipled people, whose occupation it is to rob the merchants. In the vicinity of this province there are places named Mus and Maredin, where cotton is produced in great abundance, of which they prepare the cloths called boccasini, and many other fabrics. The inhabitants are manufacturers and traders, and are all subjects of the king of the Tartars. We shall now speak of the city of Baudas.

OF THE GREAT CITY OF BAUDAS ANCIENTLY CALLED BABYLON AND OF THE VARIOUS SCIENCES STUDIED IN THAT CITY AND HOW IT WAS TAKEN

Baudas (Baghdad) is a large city, heretofore the residence of the Calif or Pontiff of all the Saracens, as the Pope is of all Christians. A great river flows through the midst of it, by means of which the merchants transport their goods to and from the Sea of India; the distance being computed at seventeen days' navigation, in consequence of the windings of its course. Those who undertake the voyage, after leaving the river, touch at a place named Kisi, from whence they proceed to sea: but previously to their reaching this anchorage they pass a city named Balsara, in the vicinity of which are groves of palm-trees producing the best dates in the world.

In Baudas there is a manufacture of silks wrought with gold, and also of damasks, as well as of velvets ornamented with the figures of birds and beasts. Almost all the pearls brought to Europe from India have undergone the process of boring, at this place. The Mahometan law is here regularly studied, as are also magic, physics, astronomy, geomancy, and physiognomy. It is the noblest and most extensive city to be found in this part of the world. . . .

OF THE JOURNEY FROM KOBIAM TO THE PROVINCE OF TIMOCHAIN ON THE NORTHERN CONFINES OF PERSIA AND OF A PARTICULAR SPECIES OF TREE

Leaving Kobiam you proceed over a desert of eight days' journey exposed to great drought; neither fruits nor any kind of trees are met with, and what water is found has a bitter taste. Travellers are therefore obliged to carry with them so much as may be necessary for their sustenance. Their cattle are constrained by thirst to drink such as the desert affords, which their owners endeavour to render palatable to them by mixing it with flour.

At the end of eight days you reach the province of Timochain, situated towards the north, on the borders of Persia, in which are many towns and strong places. There is here an extensive plain remarkable for the production of a species of tree called the tree of the sun, and by Christians *Arbre Sec*, the dry or fruitless tree. Its nature and qualities are these: — It is lofty, with a large stem, having its leaves green on the upper surface, but white or bluish on the under. It produces husks or capsules like those in which the chestnut is enclosed, but these contain no fruit. The wood is solid and strong, and of a yellow colour resembling the box. There is no other species of tree near it for the space of a hundred miles, excepting in one quarter, where trees are found within the distance of about ten miles. It is reported by the inhabitants of this district that a battle was fought there between Alexander, king of Macedonia, and Darius.

The towns are well supplied with every necessary and convenience of life, the climate being temperate and not subject to extremes either of heat or cold. The people are of the Mahometan religion. They are in general a handsome race, especially the women, who, in my opinion, are the most beautiful in the world.

OF THE OLD MAN OF THE MOUNTAIN OF HIS PALACE AND GARDENS

Having spoken of this country, mention shall now be made of the old man of the mountain. The district in which his residence lay obtained the name of Mulehet, signifying in the language of the Saracens, the place of heretics, and his people that of Mulehetites, or holders of heretical tenets; as we apply the term of Patharini to certain heretics amongst Christians. The following account of this chief, Marco Polo testifies to having heard from sundry persons.

He was named Aloadin, and his religion was that of Mahomet. In a beautiful valley enclosed between two lofty mountains, he had formed a luxurious garden, stored with every delicious fruit and every fragrant shrub that could be procured. Palaces of various sizes and forms were erected in different parts of the grounds, ornamented with works in gold, with paintings, and with furniture of rich silks. By means of small conduits contrived in these buildings, streams of wine, milk, honey, and some of pure water, were seen to flow in every direction.

The inhabitants of these palaces were elegant and beautiful damsels, accomplished in the arts of singing, playing upon all sorts of musical instruments, dancing, and especially those of dalliance and amorous allurement. Clothed in rich dresses they were seen continually sporting and amusing themselves in the garden and pavilions, their female guardians being confined within doors and never suffered to appear. The object which the chief had in view in forming a garden of this fascinating kind, was this: that Mahomet having promised to those who should obey his will the enjoyments of Paradise, where every species of sensual gratification should be found, in the society of beautiful nymphs, he was desirous of its being understood by his followers that he also was a prophet and the compeer of Mahomet, and had the power of admitting to Paradise such as he should choose to favour.

In order that none without his licence might find their way into this delicious valley, he caused a strong and inexpugnable castle to be erected at the opening of it, through which the entry was by a secret passage. At his court, likewise, this chief entertained a number of youths, from the age of twelve to twenty years, selected from the inhabitants of the surrounding mountains, who showed a disposition for martial exercises, and appeared to possess the quality of daring courage. To them he was in the daily practice of discoursing on the subject of the paradise announced by the prophet, and of his own power of granting admission. And at certain times he caused opium to be administered to ten or a dozen of the youths; and when half dead with sleep he had them conveyed to the several apartments of the palaces in the garden.

HOW THE OLD MAN USED TO TRAIN HIS ASSASSINS

Upon awakening from the state of stupor, their senses were struck with all the delightful objects that have been described, and each perceived himself surrounded by lovely damsels, singing, playing, and attracting his regards by the most fascinating caresses, serving him also with delicate foods and exquisite wines; until intoxicated with excess of enjoyment amidst actual rivulets of milk and wine, he believed himself assuredly in Paradise, and felt an unwillingness to relinquish its delights.

When four or five days had thus been passed, they were thrown once more into a drugged state, and carried out of the garden. Upon their being introduced to his presence, and questioned by him as to where they had been, their answer was, "In Paradise, through the favour of your highness": and then before the whole court, who listened to them with eager curiosity and astonishment, they gave a circumstantial account of the scenes to which they had been witnesses.

The chief thereupon addressing them, said: "We have the assurances of our prophet that he who defends his lord shall inherit Paradise, and if you show yourselves devoted to the obedience of my orders, that happy lot awaits you." Animated to enthusiasm by words of this nature, all deemed themselves happy to receive the commands of their master, and were forward to die in his service.

The consequence of this system was, that when any of the neighbouring princes, or others, gave offence to this chief, they were put to death by these his disciplined assassins; none of whom felt terror at the risk of losing their own lives, which they held in little estimation, provided they could execute their master's will. On this account his tyranny became the subject of dread in all the surrounding countries.

He had also constituted two deputies or representatives of himself, of whom one had his residence in the vicinity of Damascus, and the other in Kurdistan; and these pursued the plan he had established for training their young dependents. Thus there was no person, however powerful, who, having become exposed to the enmity of the Old Man of the Mountain, could escape assassination.

HOW THE OLD MAN CAME BY HIS END

His territory being situated within the dominions of Alaù, the brother of the Great Khan Mangu, that prince had information of his atrocious practices, as above related, as well as of his employing people to rob travellers in their passage through his country, and in the year 1252 sent one of his armies to besiege this chief in his castle. It proved, however, so capable of defence, that for three years no impression could be made upon it; until at length he was forced to surrender from the want of provisions, and being made prisoner was put to death. His castle was dismantled, and his garden of Paradise destroyed. And from that time there has been no Old Man of the Mountain.

OF THE KIND OF PAPER MONEY ISSUED BY THE GREAT KHAN AND MADE TO PASS CURRENT THROUGHOUT HIS DOMINIONS

In this city of Kanbalu is the mint of the Great Khan, who may truly be said to possess the secret of the alchemists, as he has the art of producing money by the following process.

He causes the bark to be stripped from those mulberry-trees the leaves of which are used for feeding silk-worms, and takes from it that thin inner rind which lies between the coarser bark and the wood of the tree. This being steeped, and afterwards pounded in a mortar, until reduced to a pulp, is made into paper, resembling, in substance, that which is manufactured from cotton, but quite black. When ready for use, he has it cut into pieces of money of different sizes, nearly square, but somewhat longer than they are wide. Of these, the smallest pass for a half tournois; the next size for a Venetian silver groat; others for two, five, and ten groats; others for one, two, three, and as far as ten bezants of gold. The coinage of this paper money is authenticated with as much form and ceremony as if it were actually of pure gold or silver; for to each note a number of officers, specially appointed, not only subscribe their names, but affix their seals also. When this has been regularly done by the whole of them, the principal officer, appointed by his Majesty, having dipped into vermilion the royal seal committed to his custody, stamps with it the piece of paper, so that the form of the seal tinged with the vermilion remains impressed upon it. In this way it receives full authenticity as current money, and the act of counterfeiting it is punished as a capital offence.

When thus coined in large quantities, this paper currency is circulated in every part of the Great Khan's dominions; nor dares any person, at the peril of his life, refuse to accept it in payment. All his subjects receive it without hesitation, because, wherever their business may call them, they can dispose of it again in the purchase of merchandise they may require; such as pearls, jewels, gold, or silver. With it, in short, every article may be procured.

Several times in the course of the year, large caravans of merchants arrive with such articles as have just been mentioned, together with gold tissues, which they lay before the Great Khan. He thereupon calls together twelve experienced and skilful persons, selected for this purpose, whom he commands to examine the articles with great care, and to fix the value at which they should be purchased. Upon the sum at which they have been thus conscientiously appraised he allows a reasonable profit, and immediately pays for them with his paper. To this the owners can have no objection, because, as has been observed, it answers the purpose of their own disbursements; and even though they should be inhabitants of a country where this kind of money is not current, they invest the amount in other articles of merchandise suited to their own markets.

When any persons happen to be possessed of paper money which from long use has become damaged, they carry it to the mint, where, upon the payment of only three per cent, they receive fresh notes in exchange. Should any be desirous of procuring gold or silver for the purposes of manufacture, such as of drinking-cups, girdles, or other articles wrought of these metals, they in like manner apply to the mint, and for their paper obtain the bullion they require.

All his Majesty's armies are paid with this currency, which is to them of the same value as if it were gold or silver. Upon these grounds, it may certainly be affirmed that the Great Khan has a more extensive command of treasure than any other sovereign in the universe.

OF THE NOBLE AND MAGNIFICENT CITY OF KIN-SAI

Upon leaving Va-giu you pass, in the course of three days' journey, many towns, castles, and villages, all of them well inhabited and opulent. The people have abundance of provisions. At the end of three days you reach the noble and magnificent city of Kin-sai [= capital; Hang-chau], a name that signifies "The Celestial City," and which it merits from its pre-eminence to all others in the world, in point of grandeur and beauty, as well as from its abundant delights, which might lead an inhabitant to imagine himself in paradise.

This city was frequently visited by Marco Polo, who carefully and diligently observed and inquired into every circumstance respecting it, all of which he recorded in his notes, from whence the following particulars are briefly stated. According to common estimation, this city is an hundred miles in circuit. Its streets and canals are extensive, and there are squares, or market-places, which being necessarily proportioned in size to the prodigious concourse of people by whom they are frequented, are exceedingly spacious. It is situated between a lake of fresh and very clear water on the one side, and a river of great magnitude on the other, the waters of which, by a number of canals, large and small, are made to run through every quarter of the city, carrying with them all the filth into the lake, and ultimately to the sea. This furnishes a communication by water, in addition to that by land, to all parts of the town. The canals and the streets being of sufficient width to allow of boats on the one, and carriages in the other, to pass easily with articles necessary for the inhabitants.

It is commonly said that the number of bridges, of all sizes, amounts to twelve thousand. Those which are thrown over the principal canals and are connected with the main streets, have arches so high, and built with so much skill, that vessels with their masts can pass under them. At the same time, carts and horses can pass over, so well is the slope from the street graded to the height of the arch. If they were not so numerous, there would be no way of crossing from one place to another.

Beyond the city, and enclosing it on that side, there is a ditch about forty miles in length, very wide, and full of water that comes from the river before mentioned. This was excavated by the ancient kings of the province, in order that when the river should overflow its banks, the superfluous water might be diverted into this channel. This serves at the same time as a measure of defence. The earth dug out from thence was thrown to the inner side, and has the appearance of many hillocks, surrounding the place.

There are within the city ten principal squares or market-places, besides innumerable shops along the streets. Each side of these squares is half a mile in length, and in front of them is the main street, forty paces in width, and running in a direct line from one extremity of the city to the other. It is crossed by many low and convenient bridges. These market-squares are at the distance of four miles from each other. In a direction parallel to that of the main street, but on the opposite side of the squares, runs a very large canal, on the nearer bank of which capacious warehouses are built of stone, for the accommodation of the merchants who arrive from India and other parts with their goods and effects. They are thus conveniently situated with respect to the market-places. In each of these, upon three days in every week, there is an assemblage of from forty to fifty thousand persons, who attend the markets and supply them with every article of provision that can be desired.

There is an abundant quantity of game of all kinds, such as roebucks, stags, fallow deer, hares, and rabbits, together with partridges, pheasants, francolins, quails, common fowls, capons, and such numbers of ducks and geese as can scarcely be expressed; for so easily are they bred and reared on the lake, that, for the value of a Venetian silver groat, you may purchase a couple of geese and two couple of ducks.

There, also, are the shambles, where they slaughter cattle for food, such as oxen, calves, kids, and lambs, to furnish the tables of rich persons and of the great magistrates. As to the people of the lower classes, they eat every kind of meat, without any discrimination.

At all seasons there is in the markets a great variety of herbs and fruits, and especially pears of an extraordinary size, weighing ten pounds each, that are white in the inside, like paste, and have a very fragrant smell. There are peaches also, in their season, both of the yellow and white kind, and of a delicious flavour. Grapes are not produced there, but are brought in a dried state, and very good, from other parts. This applies also to wine, which the natives do not hold in estimation, being accustomed to their own liquor prepared from rice and spices. From the sea, which is fifteen miles distant, there is daily brought up the river, to the city, a vast quantity of fish; and in the lake also there is abundance, which gives employment at all times to persons whose sole occupation it is to catch them. The sorts are various according to the season of the year. At the sight of such an importation of fish, you would think it impossible that it could be sold; and yet, in the course of a few hours, it is all taken off, so great is the number of inhabitants, even of those classes which can afford to indulge in such luxuries, for fish and flesh are eaten at the same meal.

Each of the ten market-squares is surrounded with high dwelling-houses, in the lower part of which are shops, where every kind of manufacture is carried on, and every article of trade is sold; such, amongst others, as spices, drugs, trinkets, and pearls. In certain shops nothing is vended but the wine of the country, which they are continually brewing, and serve out fresh to their customers at a moderate price. The streets connected with the market-squares are numerous, and in some of them are many cold baths, attended by servants of both sexes. The men and women who frequent them, have from their childhood been accustomed at all times to wash in cold water, which they reckon highly conducive to health. At these bathing places, however, they have apartments provided with warm water, for the use of strangers, who cannot bear the shock of the cold. All are in the daily practice of washing their persons, and especially before their meals. . . .

In other streets are the dwellings of the physicians and the astrologers, who also give instructions in reading and writing, as well as in many other arts. They have apartments also amongst those which surround the market-squares. On opposite sides of each of these squares there are two large edifices, where officers appointed by the Great Khan are stationed, to take immediate notice of any differences that may happen to arise between the foreign merchants, or amongst the inhabitants of the place. It is their duty likewise to see that the guards upon the several bridges in their respective vicinities are duly placed, and in cases of neglect, to punish the offenders at their discretion.

On each side of the principal street, already mentioned as extending from one end of the city to the other, there are houses and mansions of great size, with their gardens, and near to these, the dwellings of the artisans, who work in shops, at their several trades; and at all hours you see such multitudes of people passing and repassing, on their various avocations, that the providing food in sufficiency for their maintenance might be deemed an impossibility. It is observed, however, that on every market-day, the squares are crowded with tradespeople, who cover the whole space with the articles brought by carts and boats, for all of which they find sale. From the single article of pepper, some notion may be formed of the whole quantity of provisions, meat, wine, groceries, and the like, required for the consumption of the inhabitants of Kin-sai. Marco Polo learned from an officer employed in the Great Khan's customs, the daily amount of pepper bought was forty-three loads, each load being two hundred and forty-three pounds.

The inhabitants of the city are idolaters, and they use paper money as currency. The men as well as the women have fair complexions, and are handsome. The greater part of them are always clothed in silk, in consequence of the vast quantity of that material produced in the territory of Kin-sai, exclusively of what the merchants import from other provinces.

Amongst the handicraft trades exercised in the place, there are twelve considered to be superior to the rest, as being more generally useful. There are a thousand workshops for each craft, and each shop furnishes employment for ten, fifteen, or twenty workmen, and in a few instances as many as forty, under their respective masters. The opulent masters in these shops do not labour with their own hands, but, on the contrary, assume airs of gentility and affect parade. Their wives equally abstain from work. They have much beauty, as has been remarked, and are brought up with delicate and languid habits. The costliness of their dresses, in silks and jewelry, can scarcely be imagined. Although the laws of their ancient kings ordained that each citizen should exercise the profession of his father, yet they were allowed, when they acquired wealth, to avoid manual labour, provided they kept up the establishment, and employ persons to work at their paternal trades.

Their houses are well built and richly adorned with carved work. So much do they delight in ornaments of this kind, in paintings, and fancy buildings, that the sums they lavish on such objects are enormous.

The natural disposition of the native inhabitants of Kin-sai is peaceful, and by the example of their former kings, who were themselves unwarlike, they have been accustomed to habits of tranquillity. The management of arms is unknown to them, nor do they keep any in their houses. They conduct their mercantile and manufacturing concerns with perfect candour and honesty. They are friendly towards each other, and persons who inhabit the same street, both men and women, from the mere circumstance of neighbourhood, appear like one family.

In their domestic manners they are free from jealousy or suspicion of their wives, to whom great respect is shown, and any man would be accounted infamous who should presume to use indecent expressions to a married woman. To strangers also, who visit their city in the way of commerce, they give proofs of cordiality, inviting them freely to their houses, showing them friendly attention, and furnishing them with the best advice and assistance in their mercantile transactions. On the other hand, they dislike the sight of soldiery, not excepting the guards of the Great Khan, for they remind them that they were deprived of the government of their native kings and rulers.

On the borders of the lake are many handsome and spacious edifices belonging to men of rank and great magistrates. There are likewise many idol temples, with their monasteries, occupied by a number of monks, who perform the service of the idols. Near the central part are two islands, upon each of which stands a superb building, with an incredible number of apartments and separate pavilions. When the inhabitants of the city have occasion to celebrate a wedding, or to give a sumptuous entertainment, they resort to one of these islands, where they find ready for their purpose every article that can be required, such as vessels, napkins, table linen, and the like, which are provided and kept there at the common expense of the citizens, by whom also the buildings were erected. It may happen that at one time there are a hundred parties assembled there, at wedding or other feasts, all of whom, notwithstanding, are accommodated with separate rooms or pavilions, so judiciously arranged that they do not interfere with each other.

In addition to this, there are upon the lake a great number of pleasure vessels or barges, calculated for holding ten, fifteen, to twenty persons, being from fifteen to twenty paces in length, with a wide and flat flooring, and not liable to heel to either side in passing through the water. Such persons as take delight in the amusement, and mean to enjoy it, either in the company of their women or that of their male companions, engage one of these barges, which are always kept in the nicest order, with proper seats and tables, together with every other kind of furniture necessary for giving an entertainment. The cabins have a flat roof or upper deck, where the boatmen take their place, and by means of long poles, which they thrust to the bottom of the lake, which is not more than one or two fathoms in depth, they shove the barges along, until they reach the desired spot. These cabins are painted inside with various colours and with a variety of figures; all parts of the vessel are likewise adorned with painting. There are windows on each side, which may either be kept shut, or opened, to give an opportunity to the company, as they sit at table, of looking out in every direction and feasting their eyes on the variety and beauty of the scenes as they pass them. And truly the gratification afforded in this manner, upon the water, exceeds any that can be derived from the amusements on the land; for as the lake extends the whole length of the city, on one side, you have a view, as you stand in the boat, at a certain distance from the shore, of all its grandeur and beauty, its palaces, temples, convents, and gardens, with trees of the largest size growing down to the water's edge, whilst at the same time you enjoy the sight of other boats of the same description, continually passing you, filled in like manner with parties in pursuit of amusement. In fact, the inhabitants of this place, as soon as the labours of the day have ceased, or their mercantile transactions are closed, think of nothing else than of passing the remaining hours in parties of pleasure, with their wives or their mistresses, either in these barges, or about the city in carriages, of which it will here be proper to give some account, as constituting one of the amusements of these people.

FURTHER PARTICULARS CONCERNING THE GREAT CITY OF KIN-SAI

It must be observed, in the first place, that the streets of Kin-sai are all paved with stone and bricks, and so likewise are all the principal roads extending from thence through the province of Manji, by means of which passengers can travel to every part without soiling their feet. But as the couriers of his Majesty, who go on horseback with great speed, cannot make use of the pavement, a part of the road, on one side, is on their account left unpaved.

The main street of the city is paved with stone and brick to the width of ten paces on each side, the intermediate part being filled up with small gravel, and provided with arched drains for carrying off the rain-water that falls, into the neighbouring canals, so that it remains always dry. On this gravel carriages continually pass and repass. They are of a long shape, covered at top, have curtains and cushions of silk, and are capable of holding six persons. Both men and women who feel disposed to take their pleasure, are in the daily practice of hiring them for that purpose, and accordingly at every hour you may see vast numbers of them driven along the middle part of the street. Some of them proceed to visit certain gardens, where the company are introduced, by those who have the management of the place, to shady recesses contrived by the gardeners for that purpose. Here the men indulge themselves all day in the society of their women, returning home, when it becomes late, in the manner they came.

It is the custom of the people of Kin-sai, upon the birth of a child, for the parents to make a note, immediately, of the day, hour, and minute at which the delivery took place. They then inquire of an astrologer under what sign or aspect of the heavens the child was born; and his answer is likewise committed carefully to writing. When therefore he is grown up, and is about to engage in any mercantile adventure, voyage, or treaty of marriage, this document is carried to the astrologer, who, having examined it, and weighed all the circumstances, pronounces certain oracular words, in which these people, who sometimes find them justified by the event, place great confidence. Of these astrologers, or rather magicians, great numbers are to be met with in every market-place, and no marriage is ever celebrated until an opinion has been pronounced upon it by one of that profession.

It is also their custom, upon the death of any great and rich personage, to observe the following ceremonies. The relations, male and female, clothe themselves in coarse dresses, and accompany the body to the place appointed for burning it. The procession is likewise attended by performers on various musical instruments, which are sounded as it moves along, and prayers to their idols are chanted in a loud voice. When arrived at the spot, they throw into the flame many pieces of cotton-paper, upon which are painted representations of male and female servants, horses, camels, silk wrought with gold, as well as of gold and silver money. This is done, in the belief that the deceased will possess in the other world all these conveniences, in their natural state of flesh and bones, together with the money and the silks. As soon as the pile has been consumed, they sound all the instruments of music at the same time, producing a loud and long-continued noise. They imagine that by these ceremonies their idols are induced to receive the soul of the man whose corpse has been reduced to ashes.

In every street of this city there are stone

buildings or towers. In case of a fire breaking out in any quarter, an accident by no means unusual, as the houses are mostly constructed of wood, the inhabitants may remove their effects to these towers for security.

By a regulation which his Majesty has established, there is a guard of ten watchmen stationed, under cover, upon all the principal bridges, of whom five do duty by day and five by night. Each of these guards is provided with a sonorous wooden instrument as well as one of metal, together with a water device, by means of which the hours of the day and night are ascertained. As soon as the first hour of the night is expired, one of the watchmen gives a single stroke upon the wooden instrument, and also upon the metal gong, which announces to the people of the neighbouring streets that it is the first hour. At the expiration of the second, two strokes are given; and so on progressively, increasing the number of strokes as the hours advance. The guard is not allowed to sleep, and must be always on the alert. In the morning, as soon as the sun begins to appear, a single stroke is again struck, as in the evening, and so onwards from hour to hour.

Some of these watchmen patrol the streets, to observe whether any person has a light or fire burning after the hour appointed for extinguishing them. Upon making the discovery, they affix a mark to the door, and in the morning the owner of the house is taken before the magistrates, by whom, if he cannot assign a legitimate excuse for his offence, he is punished. Should they find any person abroad at an unseasonable hour, they arrest and confine him, and in the morning he is carried before the same tribunal. If they notice any person who from lameness or other infirmity is unable to work, they place him in one of the hospitals, of which there are several in every part of the city, founded by the ancient kings, and liberally endowed. When cured, he is obliged to work at some trade. . . .

For the purposes of nightly watch, there are mounds of earth thrown up, at the distance of above a mile from each other, on the top of which a wooden frame is constructed, with a sounding board, which being struck with a mallet by the guard stationed there, the noise is heard to a great distance. If precautions of this nature were not taken upon occasions of fire, there would be danger of half the city being consumed; and their use is obvious also in the event of popular commotion, as, upon the signal being given, the guards at the several bridges arm themselves, and repair to the spot where their presence is required. . . .

Marco Polo, happening to be in the city of Kin-sai at the time of making the annual report to his Majesty's commissioners of the amount of revenue and the number of inhabitants, had an opportunity of observing that the latter were registered at one hundred and sixty tomans of fire-places, that is to say, of families dwelling under the same roof; and as a toman is ten thousand, it follows that the whole city must have contained one million six hundred thousand families.

Every father of a family, or housekeeper, is required to affix a writing to the door of his house, specifying the name of each individual of his family, whether male or female, as well as the number of his horses. When any person dies, or leaves the dwelling, the name is struck out, and upon the occasion of a birth, it is added to the list. By these means the great officers of the province and governors of the cities are at all times acquainted with the exact number of the inhabitants. The same regulation is observed throughout the province of Cathay as well as of Manji. In like manner, all the keepers of inns and public hotels inscribe in a book the names of those who take up their occasional abode with them, marking the day and the hour of their arrival and departure; a copy of which is transmitted daily to those magistrates who have been spoken of as stationed in the market-squares. It is a custom in the province of Manji, with the indigent class of the people, who are unable to support their families, to sell their children to the rich, in order that they may be fed and brought up in a better manner than their own poverty would admit.

OF THE REVENUES OF THE GREAT KHAN

We shall now speak of the revenue which the Great Khan draws from the city of Kin-sai and the places within its jurisdiction, constituting the ninth division or kingdom of Manji. In the first place, upon salt, the most productive article, he levies a yearly duty of eighty tomans of gold, each toman being eighty thousand saggi, and each saggio fully equal to a gold florin, and consequently amounting to six million four hundred thousand ducats. This vast produce is occasioned by the distance of the province to the sea, and the number of salt lakes or marshes, in which, during the heat of summer, the water becomes crystallized, and from whence a quantity of salt is taken, sufficient for the supply of five of the other divisions of the province.

There is here cultivated and manufactured a large quantity of sugar, which pays, as do all other groceries, three and one-third per cent. The same is also levied upon the wine, or fermented liquor, made of rice. The twelve classes of artisans, of whom we have already spoken, as having each a thousand shops, and also the merchants, as well those who import the goods into the city, in the first instance, as those who carry them from thence to the interior, or who export them by sea, pay, in like manner, a duty of three and one-third per cent. But goods coming by sea from distant countries and regions, such as from India, pay ten per cent. So likewise all native articles of the country, as cattle, the vegetable produce of the soil, and silk, pay a tax to the king.

The account being made up in the presence of Marco Polo, he had an opportunity of seeing that the revenue of his Majesty, exclusively of that arising from salt, already stated, amounted in the year to the sum of two hundred and ten tomans, or sixteen million eight hundred thousand ducats.

OF THE PLACE WHERE LIETH THE HOLY BODY OF ST. THOMAS AND THE MIRACLES THEREOF

In this province of Maabar is the body of the glorious martyr, Saint Thomas the Apostle, who there suffered martyrdom. It rests in a small city [near Madras] not frequented by many merchants, because it is a place not very accessible. A vast number both of Christians and Saracens resort thither. The latter regard him as a great Saint, and name him Ananias, signifying a "Holy Man."

The Christians who perform this pilgrimage collect earth from the spot where he was slain, which is of a red colour, and reverentially carry it away with them; often employing it afterwards in the performance of miracles, and giving it, when diluted with water, to the sick, by which many disorders are cured.

In the year of our Lord 1288, a powerful baron of the country, who at the time of gathering the harvest had accumulated a very great quantity of rice, and not having granaries sufficient to deposit it all, thought proper to make use of the religious house belonging to the church of Saint Thomas. This being against the will of those who had charge of it, they beseeched him not to occupy this building given over to the accommodation of pilgrims who came to visit the tomb. But the pagan baron refused to remove the grain. On the following night the Saint appeared to him in a vision, holding in his hand a fork, which he pointed at the throat of the baron, saying to him: "If thou dost not immediately leave my house which thou hast occupied, I shall put thee to a miserable death." Awaking in a violent alarm, the baron instantly gave orders for doing what was required of him, declaring publicly that he had seen the Saint in a vision. A variety of miracles are daily performed there, such as the healing of those who are sick or deformed.

The Christians who have the care of the church possess groves of those trees which produce the Indian nuts, and from these they get their living; paying, as a tax to one of the royal brothers, a groat monthly for each tree.

It is related that the death of this most holy Saint took place in the following manner. Having retired to a hermitage, where he was engaged in prayer, and being surrounded by a number of pea-fowls, with which bird the country abounds, an idolater of the tribe of the Gaui, before described, who happened to be passing that way, and did not perceive the holy man, shot an arrow at a peacock, which struck the Saint in the side. Finding himself wounded, he had time only to thank the Lord for all his mercies, and into His hands he resigned his spirit.

In this province the natives, although black, are not born of so deep a dye as they afterwards attain by artificial means, esteeming blackness the perfection of beauty. For this purpose, three times every day, they rub the children over with oil of sesame. The images of their deities they represent black, but the devil they paint white, and assert that all the demons are of that colour. Those amongst them who pay adoration to the ox, take with them, when they go to battle, some of the hair of a wild bull, which they attach to the manes of their horses, believing its virtue to be such, that every one who carries it about with him is secure from all kind of danger. On this account the hair of the wild bull sells for a high price in these countries.

CONCLUSION

And now ye have heard all that I can tell you about the Tartars and the Saracens and their customs, and likewise about the other countries of the world as far as my travels and knowledge extend. Only we have said nothing whatever about the Greater Sea and the provinces that lie round it, although we know it thoroughly. But it seems to me a needless task to speak about places which are visited by people every day. For there are so many who sail all about the sea constantly.

Of the manner in which we took our departure from the Court of the Great Khan you have heard at the beginning of the book, in that chapter where we told you of the difficulty that Messer Maffeo and Messer Nicolo and Messer Marco had about getting the Great Khan's leave to go; and in the same chapter is related the lucky chance that led to our departure. And you may be sure that but for that chance, we should never have got away in spite of all our trouble, and never have got back to our country again.

I believe it was God's pleasure that we should get back in order that people might learn about the things that the world contains.

—*From The Travels of Marco Polo, Venetian (1254–1324), Sir Henry Yule's version.*

~ ✿ ~

Diary of a Pilgrim to Ise

SAKA

ABOUT the tenth day of the tenth month of the first year of the era Kōei I arrived at the port of Anonotsu in Ise with the intention of making a pilgrimage to the Great Shrines. I stayed here for some three days with someone I had once met at home in order to beguile myself and stimulate my interest in the further journey. This port is rather far up a winding inlet away from the shore, and the sound of the oars as the sailor rowed up by moonlight rang in my ears with the dawning, and the roar of the waves and the howling of the wind had made it difficult to sleep, so I wrote:

Bitter blows the wind
In my lodging by the sea,
Sleep is difficult;
If my sleeve is wet with dew,
That is due to other spray.

As I left Anonotsu and passed by Akogi Beach the smoke of the salt-burners had a dreary look and rose to the sky overhead and it too made me feel restless, as the cry of the solitary sea-bird falling on my ear reminded me how uncertain and full of vicissitudes is this life of ours. And a sudden shower blew over the water. We braved the swift billows of the Kumozu River and passed by the well-known ferry of Ono-no-furue, and I thought that if I could see these places with a companion from the Capital the unknown ways would not be so lonesome.

The wind whistled chilly in the pines as we came to Miwatari Beach. When I saw a traveller seated taking a rest facing the long inlet and I asked him what he was doing there, I was told that he was waiting for the tide to go out so as not to take the long way round. So I sat down to while away the time and give vent to just what chanced to come into my mind.

As there is no ferry I sit down under a tree.
The smoke of the fishing hamlet is dark
against the setting sun,
The chill waters ebb and the way seems not
so far,
But the roar of the wind in the pines sounds
strange in the traveller's ear.

And the sinking of the sun in the west naturally reminds us of our latter end that it too is not far off, while the ebbing and flowing of the tide suggests that there is, as it were, a life and death even in the waters, . . .

When on the way to these Shrines one does not feel like an ordinary person any longer but as though reborn in another world. How solemn is the unearthly shadow of the huge groves of ancient pines and chamaecyparis, and there is a delicate pathos in the few rare flowers that have withstood the winter frosts so gaily. The cross-beams of the Torii or Shintō Gate Way is without any curve, symbolizing by its straightness the sincerity of the direct beam of the Divine promise. The shrine-fence is not painted red nor is the Shrine itself roofed with cedar shingles. The eaves, with their rough reed-thatch, recall memories of the ancient days when the roofs were not trimmed. So did they spare expense out of compassion for the hardships of the people. Within the Shrine there are many buildings where the festival rites are performed, constructed just like those in the Imperial Palace. Buddhist monks may go only as far as the Sacred Tree known as the Cryptomeria of the Five Hundred Branches (Ioe-no-sugi). They may not go to the Shrine. This, too, is a ceremonial rule of the Imperial Court.

. . . .

To the south-east of the Shrine beyond the sacred pool on a high hill there is a shrine called Taka-no-miya. In the ancient style it was called Taga-no-gozen, and if, when praying to the Shrine, one first informs the Deity here of it, he will forward the petition to the Great Shrine, he being as it were Regent to the Son of Heaven. And there is no example of this indirect communication in any other shrine.

Moreover, behind this Shrine is a wondrous great crag where all the deities assemble and here supernatural visitants are always present, it is said. It is believed too that there are forty-eight caves, and there are some places on the stones that are quite warm, so that it is evident that someone has just been sitting on them. And sometimes people meet a strange unearthly old man there. Chinese scholars speak of the thirty-six heavenly caves. These are the ancient ones where the Taoist magicians perform their rites, but in this mountain there are forty-eight of them, and hallowed resorts and fairy confines where the deities and spirits hold their revels.

And those who go to view the flowers and autumn tints at times see houses of no ordinary kind that belong to a hamlet hidden from mortal eyes, while sounds of music and merrymaking fall on their ears and their eyes are dazzled by stately equipages and rich apparel. At dusk they return home and tell their friends what delightful things they have experienced and the next day a number of them go together to that place, but there is nothing at all to be seen. Without doubt this is a fairy village. They are not like Liu-Yuan in China who came back after such an experience to find that seven generations had passed, for they can tell their tale to their friends, but rather like a fisherman at Wu-ling, who found a certain path one day, but when he went back, could not find the village. And so these miraculous events go on one after another.

When I went to worship at the Shrine of the Moon-Deity Tsukiyomi the fallen leaves in the grove covered my traces and the winter powdered the foliage in the court. And the name of Tsukiyomi recalled so vividly the age of the deities that I was inspired to write:

How many long years
Has this ancient shrine-fence stood
Wet with countless dews,
And the Moon of the Gods' Age
Is this selfsame autumn moon.

I fear that my clumsy pen can hardly do justice to the road from Yamada to the Inner Shrine. Sometimes the spray over the hills seems to reflect their reversed silhouettes, sometimes the way is shrouded in cloud so that the countless peaks of the hills are hidden. As we approach the village of Uji the name is welcome to us with its suggestion of nearness to the Capital, and as it lies under the hills at the south-west of the Outer Shrine it is a place where you might imagine people would make cottages to live in retirement. As we went on deep in the shade of the chamaecyparis groves there was not even the smoke of any habitation to be seen, and we felt as though we had suddenly transcended the bounds of this painful world, while the hills with their cloud-capped mystery transported us to the world of Taoist fairyland.

When I entered the second Torii or Shintō Gate Way to worship it was dark under the pines at the foot of the hill and the branches were so thick-matted that one could hardly discern "the Pine of one hundred branches." The cryptomerias within the Shrine precincts were so dense that even the oblique projecting roof-beams could hardly be made out. When I come to reflect on my condition my mind is full of the Ten Evils and I felt shame at so long forsaking the will of Buddha, yet as I wear one of the three monkish robes I must feel some chagrin at my estrangement from the Way of the Deities.

And particularly is it the deeply-rooted custom of this Shrine that we should bring no Buddhist rosary or offering, or any special petition in our hearts and this is called "Inner Purity." Washing in sea water and keeping the body free from all defilement is called "Outer Purity." And when both these Purities are attained there is then no barrier between our mind and that of the Deity. And if we feel to become thus one with the Divine, what more do we need and what is there to pray for? When I heard that this was the true way of worshipping at the Shrine, I could not refrain from shedding tears of gratitude.

. . . . .

The wind is blowing intermittently from the hills and the rain falls in showers while the waves are breaking noisily on the river banks, but the pilgrims to the Shrine pour the water over themselves in the ceremonial ablutions without seeming to feel the cold at all. The poor peasant women in their hempen dresses look quite merry as they purify themselves, while those of high degree, whose long patterned sleeves are so sweetly perfumed, seem not at all disconcerted as they bare their bodies. The all-embracing water does not discriminate between the dirt of the righteous and the unrighteous, and the saving stream reflects the shadow of high and low alike. The waters of the Mimosuso River run out into the Sea of Ise, and there is no distinction between those of the small stream and of the mighty ocean. The one becomes part of the great whole, the sea as it were of one and the same doctrine. And that reminds me that we do not lave our bodies in the waters of the grace of the Buddha Amida, but rather choose to wallow in the turbid mud of evil, while our minds do not seek the vast sea of the favour of the deities, and it is only by chance that we light on these purifying streams. And these reflections bring tears to my eyes as I leave the sacred precincts.

. . . . .

As for the scenery, what I had heard in Kyōto was nothing to the reality. The far-off coast stretches out into the distance with the pine groves melting into the haze and here and there are islands dotted about, rising steeply some hundred feet or so high and standing out sharply in the moonlight.

On this beach there is an ancient deity called Samimyōjin. It is said that she was here before the Daijingū was inaugurated. In this province, involved in the civil wars, the gales blow hard from the mountain peaks and the waves off shore are always heavy, so the path to this Shrine is buried deep in fallen pineneedles giving it an air of mellow impressiveness. Wondering what mysterious cause led this Deity to manifest herself here I felt full of gratitude in Providence. This place is commonly called Tateishi or the Standing Stones or Rocks. It is not far from Ōyodo (Oizu) Beach and the outlines of Isles of Ise may be seen in the distance.

Going along toward the south the sand is as white as snow and well deserves its fame as Kiyoki-nagisa or the Spotless Beach. The great green combers fall with a deafening roar on the rugged coast.

We find our way along an inlet that goes into the hills and pay a visit to a temple of Kwannon (Avalokiteśvara) called Edera. As we cross a mossy stone bridge and go up a winding slope, the chuckle of the stream in the valley comes faintly to our ears. We had to brush away the yellow leaves to find the ancient track while with the help of the bamboos we reached the far-off peak. There had been some monks living here till recently, we heard, but in the present disturbed state of the country there is no place where these contemplatives can find a lodging for long. There are four or five buildings tenanted only by fishermen. There were no lamps at cold night and the torches of the fishing boats, flickering fitfully over the waves, were all the lights to be seen. The frosted temple bell was mute and there was nought but the distant ring of the woodman's axe to be heard. There was no offering of flowers or incense and we felt as though the saving promise of the All-seeing Goddess of the Thousand Hands was made of no effect. Tears stood in our eyes as we journeyed on oppressed with the thought of the wretched state of society and the degeneracy of the people that resulted in the neglect of Buddhism. As we descended from this temple to the beach at the foot of the hills, the curving shore with the line of breakers beyond and the groves of pine trees here and there was like a picture. This I thought ought to be the place called Makie-no-matsu or the "Pine Encompassed Bay," but I could not find anyone who knew anything about it. I asked a fisher maiden who was gathering sea-weed on the beach but she made no reply. There was a stout-looking fellow hauling up a boat, and I questioned him too as to whether this inlet was not called Makie. He said he did not know but told me that the haven here was at the mouth of the Mimosuso River. I became more and more entranced by the scenery of the place so that I set down my sentiments in my clumsy Chinese verse, though I fear that it may call for only a laughter from posterity:

The pines on the shore are like a picture,
With the evening sunset behind them,
Rubbing my old eyes, the time passes,
As I labour long at my stanzas.
The waters grow to a small stream
And become a tributary of the great sea.
The waves roll across in countless numbers,
Stretching out into the far away sky.
When the mist thins, the hills loom vast;
Then thick clouds dwarf their height.
The tide flows and then ebbs:
With the moon it is high or low.
I have drifted hither and thither
For sixty years and more,
But never before have I seen
A seascape as fine as this.

As I am unable to control my feelings of admiration, I put them down on paper, in this way, such as it is, for posterity.

The shore rimed with hoar frost, the rustle of the lespedeza in the breeze, the wild geese alighting on the sand, flying on the surface of the waves, all made an ideal seascape. Far away to the east can be seen the sails of the ships as they go out of the straits ever farther into the boundless ocean, while the sound of the oars of the boats that go from island to island echoes sharply against the steep cliffs.

Now the haze has cleared away and the confines of the sky and sea can be seen, and I fancy I can get a faint glimpse of what I think to be the isle of Irako and Narumi Beach. The Ama-no-takigawa also runs into this sea and mingles with its waves. The mighty bulk of a lofty peak rises over the distant hills, and at first one takes it for a great cloud bank, but only as it does not move in the wind do you realize that it is Mount Fuji. It is as though a thousand miles of famous views were concentrated in one supreme scene. That is the wonder of this coast. "If I live, yes, certainly once more," I think to myself, but the old can never be sure of anything.

Since the waves of time
Never roll back again,
I may not return,
So there is no sound of hope
In this "Twice Seen" Beach's name.

. . . .

Some autumn tints still lingered on the hills, but the wind blew harshly up to the brocade curtains of the sanctuary. The stream gurgled in the valley as of old but the rain soaked through the thatch of the rustic cells. The time-worn fence of the garden was only held together by the ivy, and the tiles of the mouldering eaves seemed falling on the pines that overhung them. Long had it been in this perilous state and its future survival seemed doubtful. It gave me a melancholy feeling when I reflected how typical it all was of the uncertainty of life.

—*By Saka, Japanese (fourteenth century), translated by A. L. Sadler.*

~ ✿ ~

The Spaniards in Mexico

BERNAL DÍAZ

SOME studious readers in Spain may have heard that Mexico was a very great city built in the water like Venice, and that it was governed by a great prince called Montezuma. Now it appears that Montezuma had received news of our arrival when we came first, with Francisco Hernández de Córdova, and of what had happened at the battle of Catoche and at Champoton, and also what had happened at the battle of this same Champoton during this voyage, and he knew that we soldiers being few in number had defeated the warriors of that town and their very numerous allies, and he knew as well that we had entered the Rio Tabasco and what had taken place between us and the caciques of that town, moreover he understood that our object was to seek for gold, in exchange for the things we had brought with us. All this news had been brought to him painted on a cloth made of *hennequen* which is like linen, and as he knew that we were coasting along towards his provinces he sent orders to his governors that if we should arrive in their neighbourhood with our ships that they should barter gold for our beads, especially the green beads, which are something like their *chalchihuites,* which they value as highly as emeralds; he also ordered them to find out more about our persons and our plans.

It is a fact, as we now know, that their Indian ancestors had foretold that men with beards would come from the direction of the sunrise and would rule over them. Whatever the reason may have been, many Indians sent by the Great Montezuma were watching for us at the river I have mentioned with long poles, and on every pole a banner of white cotton cloth, which they waved and called to us, as though making signals of peace, to come to them.

When from the ships we saw such an unusual sight, we were fairly astonished and the General and most of the Captains were agreed that to find out what it meant we should lower two of the boats, and that all those who carried guns or crossbows and twenty of the most daring and active soldiers should go in them, and that Francisco de Montejo should accompany us, and that if we should discover that the men who were waving the banners were warriors that we should at once bring news of it and of anything else that we could find out.

Thank God at that time we had fine weather, which is rare enough on this coast. When we got on shore we found three Caciques, one of them the governor appointed by Montezuma, who had many of the Indians of his household with him. They brought many of the fowls of the country and maize bread such as they always eat, and fruits such as pineapples and zapotes, which in other parts are called mameies, and they were seated under the shade of the trees, and had spread mats on the ground, and they invited us to be seated, all by signs, for Julianillo, the man from Cape Catoche, did not understand their language which is Mexican. Then they brought pottery braziers with live coals, and fumigated us with a sort of resin.

As soon as the Captain Montejo had reported all that had taken place, the General determined to anchor his ships and go ashore with all his captains and soldiers. When the Caciques and governors saw him on land and knew that he was the Captain General of us all, according to their custom, they paid him the greatest respect. In return he treated them in a most caressing manner and ordered them to be given blue and green glass beads and by signs he made them understand that they should bring gold to barter with us. Then the Governor sent orders to all the neighbouring towns to bring jewels to exchange with us, and during the six days that we remained there they brought more than sixteen thousand dollars worth of jewelry of low grade gold, worked into various forms.

When the General saw that the Indians were not bringing any more gold to barter, and as we had already been there six days and the ships ran risk of danger from the North and North East wind, he thought it was time to embark.

So we took formal possession of the land in the name of His Majesty, and as soon as this had been done the General spoke to the Indians and told them that we wished to return to our ships and he gave them presents of some shirts from Spain. We took one of the Indians from this place on board ship with us, and after he had learnt our language he became a Christian and was named Francisco, and later on I met him living with his Indian wife.

. . . .

On Holy Thursday, in the year 1519, we arrived with all the fleet at the Port of San Juan de Ulúa, and as the Pilot Alaminos knew the place well from having come there with Juan de Grijalva he at once ordered the vessels to drop anchor where they would be safe from the northerly gales. The flagship hoisted her royal standards and pennants, and within half an hour of anchoring, two large canoes came out to us, full of Mexican Indians. Seeing the big ship with the standards flying they knew that it was there they must go to speak with the captain; so they went direct to the flagship and going on board asked who was the Tatuan, which in their language means the chief. Doña Marina, who understood the language well, pointed him out. Then the Indians paid many marks of respect to Cortés, according to their usage, and bade him welcome, and said that their lord, a servant of the great Montezuma, had sent them to ask what kind of men we were, and of what we were in search, and added that if we were in need of anything for ourselves or the ships, that we should tell them and they would supply it. Our Cortés thanked them through the two interpreters, Aguilar and Doña Marina, and ordered food and wine to be given them and some blue beads, and after they had drunk he told them that we came to see them and to trade with them and that our arrival in their country should cause them no uneasiness but be looked on by them as fortunate. The messengers returned on shore well content, and the next day, which was Good Friday, we disembarked with the horses and guns, on some sand hills which rise to a considerable height, for there was no level land, nothing but sand dunes; and the artilleryman Mesa placed the guns in position to the best of his judgment. Then we set up an altar where Mass was said and we made huts and shelters for Cortés and the captains, and three hundred of the soldiers brought wood and made huts for themselves and we placed the horses where they would be safe and in this way was Good Friday passed.

The next day, Saturday, Easter Eve, many Indians arrived sent by a chief who was a governor under Montezuma, named Pitalpitoque (whom we afterwards called Ovandillo), and they brought axes and dressed wood for the huts of the Captain Cortés and the other ranchos near to it, and covered them with large cloths on account of the strength of the sun, for the heat was very great—and they brought fowls, and maize cakes and plums, which were then in season, and I think that they brought some gold jewels, and they presented all these things to Cortés; and said that the next day a governor would come and would bring more food. Cortés thanked them heartily and ordered them to be given certain articles in exchange with which they went away well content. The next day, Easter Sunday, the governor whom they spoke of arrived. His name was Tendile, a man of affairs, and he brought with him Pitalpitoque, who was also a man of importance amongst the natives and there followed them many Indians with presents of fowls and vegetables. Tendile ordered these people to stand aside on a hillock and with much humility he made three obeisances to Cortés according to their custom, and then to all the soldiers who were standing around. Cortés bade them welcome through our interpreters and embraced them and asked them to wait, as he wished presently to speak to them. Meanwhile he ordered an altar to be made as well as it could be done in the time, and Fray Bartolomé de Olmedo, who was a fine singer, chanted Mass, and Padre Juan Diaz assisted, and the two governors and the other chiefs who were with them looked on. When Mass was over, Cortés and some of our captains and the two Indian officers of the great Montezuma dined together. When the tables had been cleared away, Cortés went aside with the two Caciques and our two interpreters and explained to them that we were Christians and vassals of the greatest lord on earth, who had many great princes as his vassals and servants, and that we had come to this country, because for many years he had heard rumours about the country and the great prince who ruled it. That he wished to be friends with this prince and to tell him many things in the name of the Emperor, which things, when he knew and understood them, would please him greatly. Moreover, he wished to trade with their prince and his Indians in good friendship, and he wanted to know where this prince would wish that they should meet so that they might confer together. Tendile replied somewhat proudly, and said:—"You have only just now arrived and you already ask to speak with our prince; accept now this present which we give you in his name, and afterwards you will tell me what you think fitting." With that he took out of a *petaca,* which is a sort of chest, articles of gold beautifully and richly worked, and ordered ten loads of white cloth made of cotton and feathers to be brought, wonderful things to see, besides quantities of food. Cortés received it all with smiles in a gracious manner and gave in return beads of twisted glass and other small beads from Spain, and he begged them to send them to their towns to ask the people to come and trade with us as he had brought many beads to exchange for gold, and they replied that they would do as he asked. Cortés then ordered his servants to bring an arm-chair, richly carved and inlaid, and some *margaritas,* stones with many intricate designs in them, and a string of twisted glass beads packed in cotton scented with musk and a crimson cap with a golden medal engraved with a figure of St. George on horseback, lance in hand, slaying the dragon, and he told Tendile that he should send the chair to his prince Montezuma, so that he could be seated in it when he, Cortés, came to see and speak with him, and that he should place the cap on his head, and that the stones and all the other things were presents from our lord the King, as a sign of his friendship, for he was aware that Montezuma was a great prince, and Cortés asked that a day and a place might be named where he could go to see Montezuma. Tendile received the presents and said that his lord Montezuma was such a great prince that it would please him to know our great King, and that he would carry the presents to him at once and bring back a reply.

. . . .

As we had already been four days in Mexico and neither the Captain nor any of us had left our lodgings except to go to the houses and gardens, Cortés said to us that it would be well to go to the great Plaza of Tlaltelolco and see the great Temple of Huichilobos, and that he wished to consult the Great Montezuma and have his approval. For this purpose he sent Jerónimo de Aguilar and the Doña Marina as messengers, and with them went our Captain's small page named Orteguilla, who already understood something of the language. When Montezuma knew his wishes he sent to say that we were welcome to go; on the other hand, as he was afraid that we might do some dishonour to his Idols, he determined to go with us himself with many of his chieftains. He came out from his Palace in his rich litter, but when half the distance had been traversed and he was near some oratories, he stepped out of the litter, for he thought it a great affront to his idols to go to their house and temple in that manner. Some of the great chieftains supported him with their arms, and the tribal lords went in front of him carrying two staves like sceptres held on high, which was the sign that the Great Montezuma was coming. (When he went in his litter he carried a wand half of gold and half of wood, which was held up like a wand of justice.) So he went on and ascended the great Cue accompanied by many priests, and he began to burn incense and perform other ceremonies to Huichilobos.

Our Captain and all of those who had horses went to Tlaltelolco on horseback, and nearly all of us soldiers were fully equipped, and many Caciques whom Montezuma had sent for that purpose went in our company. When we arrived at the great market place called Tlaltelolco, we were astounded at the number of people and the quantity of merchandise that it contained, and at the good order and control that was maintained, for we had never seen such a thing before. The chieftains who accompanied us acted as guides.

When we arrived near the Great Cue and before we had ascended a single step of it, the Great Montezuma sent down from above, where he was making his sacrifices, six priests and two chieftains to accompany our Captain. On ascending the steps, which are one hundred and fourteen in number, they attempted to take him by the arms so as to help him to ascend, (thinking that he would get tired,) as they were accustomed to assist their Lord Montezuma, but Cortés would not allow them to come near him. When we got to the top of the great Cue, on a small plaza which has been made on the top where there was a space like a platform with some large stones placed on it, on which they put the poor Indians for sacrifice; there was a bulky image like a dragon and other evil figures and much blood shed that very day.

Montezuma came out of an oratory where his cursed idols were, at the summit of the great Cue, and two priests came with him, and after paying great reverence to Cortés, and to all of us he said: "You must be tired, Señor Malinche, from ascending this our great Cue," and Cortés replied through our interpreters who were with us that he and his companions were never tired by anything. Then Montezuma took him by the hand and told him to look at this great city and all the other cities that were standing in the water, and the many other towns on the land round the lake, and that if he had not seen the great market place well, that from where they were they could see it better.

So we stood looking about us, for that huge and cursed temple stood so high that from it one could see over everything very well; and we saw the three causeways which led into Mexico, that is the causeway of Iztapalapa by which we had entered four days before, and that of Tepeaquilla; and we saw the fresh water that comes from Chapultepec which supplies the city; and we saw the bridges on the three causeways which were built at certain distances apart through which the water of the lake flowed in and out from one side to the other; and we beheld on that great lake a great multitude of canoes, some coming with supplies of food and others returning loaded with cargoes of merchandise; and we saw that from every house of that great city and of all the other cities that were built in the water it was impossible to pass from house to house, except by drawbridges which were made of wood or in canoes; and we saw in those cities Cues and oratories like towers and fortresses and all gleaming white, and it was a wonderful thing to behold; then the houses with flat roofs, and on the causeways other small towers and oratories which were like fortresses.

After having examined and considered all that we had seen we turned to look at the great market place and the crowds of people that were in it, some buying and others selling, so that the murmur and hum of their voices and words that they used could be heard more than a league off. Some of the soldiers among us who had been in many parts of the world, in Constantinople, and all over Italy, and in Rome, said that so large a market place and so full of people, and so well regulated and arranged, they had never beheld before.

Let us leave this, and return to our Captain, who said to Fray Bartolomé de Olmedo, who happened to be near him: "It seems to me, Señor Padre, that it would be a good thing to throw out a feeler to Montezuma, as to whether he would allow us to build our church here"; and the Padre replied that it would be a good thing if it were successful, but it seemed to him that it was not quite a suitable time to speak about it, for Montezuma did not appear to be inclined to do such a thing.

Then our Cortés said to Montezuma: "Your Highness is indeed a very great prince and worthy of even greater things. We are rejoiced to see your cities, and as we are here in your temple, what I now beg as a favour is that you will show us your gods and Teules." Montezuma replied that he must first speak with his high priests, and when he had spoken to them he said that we might enter into a small tower and apartment, a sort of hall, where there were two altars, with very richly carved boardings on the top of the roof. On each altar were two figures, like giants with very tall bodies and very fat, and the first which stood on the right hand they said was the figure of Huichilobos their god of War; it had a very broad face and monstrous and terrible eyes, and the whole of his body was covered with precious stones, and gold and pearls, and with seed pearls stuck on with a paste that they make in this country out of a sort of root, and all the body and head was covered with it, and the body was girdled by great snakes made of gold and precious stones, and in one hand he held a bow and in the other some arrows. And another small idol that stood by him, they said was his page, and he held a short lance and a shield richly decorated with gold and stones. Huichilobos had round his neck some Indians' faces and other things like hearts of Indians, the former made of gold and the latter of silver, with many precious blue stones.

There were some braziers with incense which they call copal, and in them they were burning the hearts of the three Indians whom they had sacrificed that day, and they had made the sacrifice with smoke and copal. All the walls of the oratory were so splashed and encrusted with blood that they were black, the floor was the same and the whole place stank vilely. Then we saw on the other side on the left hand there stood the other great image the same height as Huichilobos, and it had a face like a bear and eyes that shone, made of their mirrors which they call *Tezcat*, and the body plastered with precious stones like that of Huichilobos, for they say that the two are brothers; and this Tezcatepuca was the god of Hell and had charge of the souls of the Mexicans, and his body was girt with figures like little devils with snakes' tails. The walls were so clotted with blood and the soil so bathed with it that in the slaughter houses of Spain there is not such another stench.

They had offered to this Idol five hearts from the day's sacrifices. In the highest part of the Cue there was a recess of which the woodwork was very richly worked, and in it was another image half man and half lizard, with precious stones all over it, and half the body was covered with a mantle. They say that the body of this figure is full of the seeds that there are in the world, and they say that it is the god of seed time and harvest, but I do not remember its name, and everything was covered with blood, both walls and altar, and the stench was such that we could hardly wait the moment to get out of it.

They had an exceedingly large drum there, and when they beat it the sound of it was so dismal and like, so to say, an instrument of the infernal regions, that one could hear it a distance of two leagues, and they said that the skins it was covered with were those of great snakes. In that small place there were many diabolical things to be seen, bugles and trumpets and knives, and many hearts of Indians that they had burned in fumigating their idols, and everything was so clotted with blood, and there was so much of it, that I curse the whole of it, and as it stank like a slaughter house we hastened to clear out of such a bad stench and worse sight. Our Captain said to Montezuma through our interpreter, half laughing: "Señor Montezuma, I do not understand how such a great Prince and wise man as you are has not come to the conclusion, in your mind, that these idols of yours are not gods, but evil things that are called devils, and so that you may know it and all your priests may see it clearly, do me the favour to approve of my placing a cross here on the top of this tower, and that in one part of these oratories where your Huichilobos and Tezcatepuca stand we may divide off a space where we can set up an image of Our Lady (an image which Montezuma had already seen) and you will see by the fear in which these Idols hold it that they are deceiving you."

Montezuma replied half angrily (and the two priests who were with him showed great annoyance), and said: "Señor Malinche, if I had known that you would have said such defamatory things I would not have shown you my gods; we consider them to be very good, for they give us health and rains and good seed times and seasons, and many victories as we desire, and we are obliged to worship them and make sacrifices, and I pray you not to say another word to their dishonour."

When our Captain heard that and noted the angry looks he did not refer again to the subject, but said with a cheerful manner: "It is time for your Excellency and for us to return," and Montezuma replied that it was well, but that he had to pray and offer certain sacrifices on account of the *tatacul,* that is to say sin, which he had committed in allowing us to ascend his great Cue, and being the cause of our being permitted to see his gods, and of our dishonouring them by speaking evil of them, so that before he left he must pray and worship.

Then Cortés said: "I ask your pardon if it be so," and then we went down the steps, and as they numbered one hundred and fourteen, and as some of our soldiers were suffering from tumours and abscesses, their legs were tired by the descent.

—*From The Discovery and Conquest of Mexico, 1517–1521, by Bernal Díaz del Castillo, Spanish (1492–1581?), translated by A. P. Maudslay.*

~ ❁ ~

A Tour in Lapland

LINNAEUS

VERY EARLY IN THE MORNING I quitted Genom in a hacep or small boat, such as shall be hereafter described, proceeding along the western branch of the river of Umoea; for the river which takes its name from that place divides into two branches near Gresele, two miles from Umoea. One branch comes from Lycksele, the other, as I was told, from Sorsele. By the western branch, as I have just mentioned, we proceeded to Lycksele. When the sun rose, nothing could be more pleasant than the view of this clear unruffled stream, neither contaminated by floods, nor disturbed by the breath of Æolus. All along its translucent margin the forests which clothed its banks were reflected like another landscape in the water. On both sides were several large level heaths, guarded by steep ramparts towards the river, and these were embellished with plants and bushes, the whole reversed in the water appearing to great advantage. The huge pines, which had hitherto braved Neptune's power, smiled with a fictitious shadow in the stream. Neptune however, in alliance with his brother Æolus, had already triumphed over many of their companions, the former by attacking their roots, while the latter had demolished their branches.

We passed several small islets separated from the main land by the action of the current, as *Calnäsholm* (the isle of Calnäs), &c. Close to the shore were many *Charadrii hiaticulæ* (ringed plovers) and *Tringæ* (sandpipers). One of the latter my companions shot, but destroyed it so completely that we obtained only a wing and a leg entire, the remaining parts being so torn that I could not make out the species. The foot consisted of four toes, of which the hinder one was very small, and the two external ones joined by a web at their base.

A little further on a couple of young owls were suspended on a tree. On my inquiring what these birds had done to be so served, the rower made me remark, on the most lofty of the fir trees, concave cylinders of wood, closed at top and bottom, and having an aperture on one side. These cylinders are placed on the highest part of the trees, in order to tempt wild ducks to lay their eggs in them, and they are afterwards plundered by the country people. In one of these nests a brood of young owls had been hatched instead of young ducks.

. . . . .

The river along which we had rowed for the space of almost three miles, and which had hitherto been easily navigable, now threatened us occasionally with interruption, from small shelves forming cascades, and at length we came to three of these, very near each other, which were absolutely impassable. One of them is called the waterfall of Tuken. My companion, after committing all my property to my own care, laid his knapsack on his back, and turning the boat bottom upwards, placed the two oars longitudinally, so as to cross the seats. These rested on his arms as he carried the boat over his head, and thus he scampered away over hills and valleys, so that the devil himself could not have come up with him.

. . . . .

The forest here was full of the noblest pine trees, growing to no purpose with respect to the inhabitants, as the wood is not used even for building huts, nor the bark for food, as it is in some other parts. I wonder they have not contrived to turn these trees to some account, by burning them for tar or pitch.

The colonists who reside among the Laplanders are beloved by them, and treated with great kindness. These good people willingly point out to the strangers where they may fix their abode so as to have access to moist meadows affording good hay, which they themselves do not want, their herds of reindeer preferring the driest pastures. They expect in return that the colonists should supply them with milk and flour.

Ovid's description of the silver age is still applicable to the native inhabitants of Lapland. Their soil is not wounded by the plough, nor is the iron din of arms to be heard; neither have mankind found their way to the bowels of the earth, nor do they engage in wars to define its boundaries. They perpetually change their abode, live in tents, and follow a pastoral life, just like the patriarchs of old.

Among these people the men are employed in the business of cookery, so that the master of a family has no occasion to speak a good word to his wife, when he wishes to give a hospitable entertainment to his guests.

. . . . .

At length we came to a sort of bay or creek of the river, which we were under the necessity of wading through. The water reached above our waists, and was very cold. In the midst of this creek was so deep a hole that the longest pole could scarcely fathom it. We had no resource but to lay a pole across it, on which we passed over at the hazard of our lives; and indeed when I reached the other side, I congratulated myself on having had a very narrow escape. A neighbouring mountain affords grey slate, but of a loose and brittle kind.

We had next to pass a marshy tract, almost under water, for the course of a mile, nor is it easy to conceive the difficulties of the undertaking. At every step we were knee-deep in water; and if we thought to find a sure footing on some grassy tuft, it proved treacherous, and only sunk us lower. Sometimes we came where no bottom was to be felt, and were obliged to measure back our weary steps. Our half boots were filled with the coldest water, as the frost, in some places, still remained in the ground. Had our sufferings been inflicted as a capital punishment, they would, even in that case, have been cruel; what then had we to complain of? I wished I had never undertaken my journey, for all the elements seemed adverse. It rained and blowed hard upon us. I wondered that I escaped with life, though certainly not without excessive fatigue and loss of strength.

After having thus for a long time gone in pursuit of my new Lapland guide, we reposed ourselves about six o'clock in the morning, wrung the water out of our clothes, and dried our weary limbs, while the cold north wind parched us as much on one side as the fire scorched us on the other, and the gnats kept inflicting their stings. I had now my fill of travelling.

. . . . .

We waited till about two o'clock in the afternoon for the Laplander I had sent on the expedition above mentioned, who at length returned quite spent with fatigue. He had made the requisite inquiries at many of the huts, but in vain. He was accompanied by a person whose appearance was such that at first I did not know whether I beheld a man or a woman. I scarcely believe that any poetical description of a fury could come up to the idea, which this Lapland fair-one excited. It might well be imagined that she was truly of Stygian origin. Her stature was very diminutive. Her face of the darkest brown from the effects of smoke. Her eyes dark and sparkling. Her eyebrows black. Her pitchy-coloured hair hung loose about her head, and on it she wore a flat red cap. She had a grey petticoat; and from her neck, which resembled the skin of a frog, were suspended a pair of large loose breasts of the same brown complexion, but encompassed, by way of ornament, with brass rings. Round her waist she wore a girdle, and on her feet a pair of half-boots.

Her first aspect really struck me with dread; but though a fury in appearance, she addressed me, with mingled pity and reserve, in the following terms:

"O thou poor man! what hard destiny can have brought thee hither, to a place never visited by any one before? This is the first time I ever beheld a stranger. Thou miserable creature! how didst thou come, and whither wilt thou go? Dost thou not perceive what houses and habitations we have, and with how much difficulty we go to church?"

I entreated her to point out some way by which I might continue my journey in any direction, so as not to be forced to return the way I came.

"Nay, man," said she, "thou hast only to go the same way back again; for the river overflows so much, it is not possible for thee to proceed further in this direction. From us thou hast no assistance to expect in the prosecution of thy journey, as my husband, who might have helped thee, is ill. Thou mayest inquire for our next neighbour, who lives about a mile off, and perhaps, if thou shouldst meet with him, he may give thee some assistance, but I really believe it will scarcely be in his power."

I inquired how far it was to Sorsele. "That we do not know," replied she; "but in the present state of the roads it is at least seven days journey from hence, as my husband has told me."

My health and strength being by this time materially impaired by wading through such an extent of marshes, laden with my apparel and luggage, for the Laplander had enough to do to carry the boat; by walking for whole nights together; by not having for a long time tasted any boiled meat; by drinking a great quantity of water, as nothing else was to be had; and by eating nothing but fish, unsalted and crawling with vermin, I must have perished but for a piece of dried and salted reindeer's flesh, given me by my kind hostess the clergyman's wife at Lycksele. This food, however, without bread, proved unwholesome and indigestible. How I longed once more to meet with people who feed on spoon-meat! I inquired of this woman whether she could give me any thing to eat. She replied, "Nothing but fish." I looked at the fresh fish, as it was called, but perceiving its mouth to be full of maggots, I had no appetite to touch it; but though it thus abated my hunger, it did not recruit my strength. I asked if I could have any reindeer tongues, which are commonly dried for sale, and served up even at the tables of the great; but was answered in the negative. "Have you no cheese made of reindeer's milk?" said I. "Yes," replied she, "but it is a mile off." "If it were here, would you allow me to buy some?" "I have no desire," answered the good woman, "that thou shouldst die in my country for want of food."

On arriving at her hut, I perceived three cheeses lying under a shed without walls, and took the smallest of them, which she, after some consultation, allowed me to purchase.

. . . . .

I took my departure very early in the morning. The weather was so hazy I could not see the distance of half a gun-shot before me. I wandered along in a perpetual mist, which made the grass as wet as if it had rained. The sun appeared quite dim, wading as it were through the clouds. By nine o'clock the mists began to disperse, and the sun shone forth. The spruce fir (*Pinus abies*), hitherto of an uniform dark green, now began to put forth its lighter-coloured buds, a welcome sign of advancing summer.

Chamaedaphne of Buxbaum (*Andromeda polifolia*) was at this time in its highest beauty, decorating the marshy grounds in a most agreeable manner. The flowers are quite blood-red before they expand, but when full-grown the corolla is of a flesh-colour. Scarcely any painter's art can so happily imitate the beauty of a fine female complexion; still less could any artificial colour upon the face itself bear a comparison with this lovely blossom. As I contemplated it I could not help thinking of Andromeda as described by the poets; and the more I meditated upon their descriptions, the more applicable they seemed to the little plant before me, so that if these writers had had it in view, they could scarcely have contrived a more apposite fable. Andromeda is represented by them as a virgin of most exquisite and unrivalled charms; but these charms remain in perfection only so long as she retains her virgin purity, which is also applicable to the plant, now preparing to celebrate its nuptials. This plant is always fixed on some little turfy hillock in the midst of the swamps, as Andromeda herself was chained to a rock in the sea, which bathed her feet, as the fresh water does the roots of the plant. Dragons and venomous serpents surrounded her, as toads and other reptiles frequent the abode of her vegetable prototype, and, when they pair in the spring, throw mud and water over its leaves and branches. As the distressed virgin cast down her blushing face through excessive affliction, so does the rosy-coloured flower hang its head, growing paler and paler till it withers away. Hence, as this plant forms a new genus, I have chosen for it the name of *Andromeda.*

. . . . .

All the little woods and copses by the road side abounded with butterflies of the fritillary tribe, without silver spots. The great dragon fly with two flat lobes at its tail (*Libellula forcipata*), and another species with blue wings (*L. virgo*), were also common.

Various modes of rocking children in cradles are adopted in different places. In Smoland the cradle is suspended by an elastic pole, on which it swings up and down perpendicularly. The poorer Laplanders rock their infants on branches of trees, but those of superior rank have cradles that commonly roll from side to side. In the part of the country where I was now travelling, the cradles rock vertically, or from head to foot.

Close to the road hung the under-jaw of a horse, having six fore teeth, much worn and blunted, two canine teeth, and at a distance from the latter twelve grinders, six on each side. If I knew how many teeth and of what peculiar form, as well as how many udders, and where situated, each animal has, I should perhaps be able to contrive a most natural methodical arrangement of quadrupeds.

I could not help remarking that the very best fields of this part of the country, in which from six to ten barns commonly stood, were almost entirely occupied with turfy hillocks producing nothing but hair-moss, *Polytrichum,* and that quite dried up. Some of the barns were evidently in a decayed state; which made me suspect this condition of the land to be an increasing evil, and that it had formerly been more productive than at present. Indeed some of these tumps were so close together that no grass had room to grow between them. If the cause of this evil, and a cure for it, could be discovered, the husbandman would have reason to rejoice. Wherever these hillocks abounded, the earth seemed to be of a loose texture, consisting of either mud or clay. When I stepped upon them they gave way, and when cut open they appeared all hollow and unsound. I conceive the frost to have a great share in their formation, which when it leaves the ground causes a vacuity, and the turf, loosened from the soil, is raised up.

. . . . .

In the afternoon I took leave of Hyttan, and, at the distance of a mile from thence, arrived at the mountain of Wallavari (*or Hwallawari*), a quarter of a mile in height. When I reached this mountain, I seemed entering on a new world; and when I had ascended it, I scarcely knew whether I was in Asia or Africa, the soil, situation, and every one of the plants, being equally strange to me. Indeed I was now, for the first time, upon the Alps! Snowy mountains encompassed me on every side. I walked in snow, as if it had been the severest winter. All the rare plants that I had previously met with, and which had from time to time afforded me so much pleasure, were here as in miniature, and new ones in such profusion, that I was overcome with astonishment, thinking I had now found more than I should know what to do with.

. . . . .

The lofty mountains, piled one upon another, showed no signs of volcanic fire, but were covered with stones, all of a fissile kind, and by that means easily distinguishable. From the snow, which lay so plentifully on these mountains as to cover half the ground, water was continually running down in streams like so many springs, or like rivers cut through the deep snow, for the refreshment of travellers. We found it very good.

The little alpine variety of the ptarmigan (*Tetrao lagopus*) was now accompanied by its young. I caught one of these, upon which the hen ran so close to me, that I could easily have taken her also. She kept continually jumping round and round me; but I thought it a pity to deprive the tender brood of their mother, neither would my compassion for the mother allow me long to detain her offspring, which I restored to her in safety.

After having walked four or five miles in the course of the night, I went to sleep in the morning in one of the cottages of the country.

The inhabitants, sixteen in number, lay there all naked. They washed themselves by rubbing the body downwards, not upwards. They washed their dishes with their fingers, squirting water out of their mouths upon the spoon, and then poured into them boiled reindeer's milk, which was as thick as common milk mixed with eggs, and had a strong flavour. Some thousands of reindeer came home in the morning, which were milked by the men as well as the women, who kneeled down on one knee.

From the top of the head of some of these reindeer I took out the maggots which trouble them so much. I observed here in plenty the large fly with a yellow neck, and yellow segments of the body (*Oestrus tarandi*), which probably is the insect (in a perfect state), as I judge by the length of the legs.

My hosts gave me *missen* to eat; that is, whey, after the curd is separated from it, coagulated by boiling, which renders it very firm. Its flavour was good, but the washing of the spoon took away my appetite, as the master of the house wiped it dry with his fingers, whilst his wife cleaned the bowl, in which milk had been, in a similar manner, licking her finger after every stroke.

I also tasted some *jumo,* which they mixed with reindeer's milk, but it did not please me.

. . . . .

We rose early this morning, and after walking a quarter of a mile arrived at the lofty icy mountain. This is indeed of a very great elevation, and covered with perpetual snow, the surface of which was, for the most part, frozen quite hard. Sometimes we walked firmly over it, but it occasionally gave way, crumbling under our feet like sand. Every now and then we came to a river taking its course under the snowy crust, which in some parts had yielded to the force of the currents, and the sides of each chasm exhibited many snowy strata one above another. Here the mountain streams began to take their course westward, a sign of our having reached Norwegian Lapland. The delightful tracts of vegetation, which had hitherto been so agreeably interspersed among the alpine snows, were now no longer to be seen. No charming flowers were here scattered under our feet. The whole country was one dazzling snowy waste. The cold east wind quickened our steps, and obliged us to protect our hands that we might escape chilblains. I was glad to put on an additional coat. As we proceeded across the north side of this mountain, we were often so violently driven along by the force of the wind, that we were taken off our feet, and rolled a considerable way down the hill. This once happened to me in so dangerous a place, that, after rolling to the distance of a gun-shot, I arrived near the brink of a precipice, and thus my part in the drama had very nearly come to an end.

—*From A Tour in Lapland, by Linnaeus (Carl von Linné), Swede (1707–1778), translated by James Edward Smith.*

∽ ✲ ∼

Around the Horn

RICHARD HENRY DANA, JR.

IN OUR FIRST ATTEMPT to double the Cape, when we came up to the latitude of it, we were nearly seventeen hundred miles to the westward, but, in running for the Straits of Magellan, we stood so far to the eastward that we made our second attempt at a distance of not more than four or five hundred miles; and we had great hopes, by this means, to run clear of the ice; thinking that the easterly gales, which had prevailed for a long time, would have driven it to the westward. With the wind about two points free, the yards braced in a little, and two close-reefed topsails and a reefed foresail on the ship, we made great way toward the southward; and almost every watch, when we came on deck, the air seemed to grow colder, and the sea to run higher. Still we saw no ice, and had great hopes of going clear of it altogether, when, one afternoon, about three o'clock, while we were taking a *siesta* during our watch below, "All hands!" was called in a loud and fearful voice. "Tumble up here, men! — tumble up! — don't stop for your clothes — before we're upon it!" We sprang out of our berths and hurried upon deck. The loud, sharp voice of the captain was heard giving orders, as though for life or death, and we ran aft to the braces, not waiting to look ahead, for not a moment was to be lost. The helm was hard up, the after yards shaking, and the ship in the act of wearing. Slowly, with the stiff ropes and iced rigging, we swung the yards round, everything coming hard and with a creaking and rending sound, like pulling up a plank which has been frozen into the ice. The ship wore round fairly, the yards were steadied, and we stood off on the other tack, leaving behind us, directly under our larboard quarter, a large ice island, peering out of the mist, and reaching high above our tops; while astern, and on either side of the island, large tracts of field-ice were dimly seen, heaving and rolling in the sea. We were now safe, and standing to the northward; but, in a few minutes more, had it not been for the sharp lookout of the watch, we should have been fairly upon the ice, and left our ship's old bones adrift in the Southern Ocean. After standing to the northward a few hours, we wore ship, and, the wind having hauled, we stood to the southward and eastward. All night long a bright lookout was kept from every part of the deck; and whenever ice was seen on the one bow or the other the helm was shifted and the yards braced, and, by quick working of the ship, she was kept clear. The accustomed cry of "Ice ahead!" — "Ice on the lee bow!" — "Another island!" in the same tones, and with the same orders following them, seemed to bring us directly back to our old position of the week before. During our watch on deck, which was from twelve to four, the wind came out ahead, with a pelting storm of hail and sleet, and we lay hove-to, under a close-reefed fore topsail, the whole watch. During the next watch it fell calm with a drenching rain until day-break, when the wind came out to the westward, and the weather cleared up, and showed us the whole ocean, in the course which we should have steered, had it not been for the head wind and calm, completely blocked up with ice. Here, then, our progress was stopped, and we wore ship, and once more stood to the northward and eastward; not for the Straits of Magellan, but to make another attempt to double the Cape, still farther to the eastward; for the captain was determined to get round if perseverance could do it, and the third time, he said, never failed.

With a fair wind we soon ran clear of the field-ice, and by noon had only the stray islands floating far and near upon the ocean. The sun was out bright, the sea of a deep blue, fringed with the white foam of the waves, which ran high before a strong southwester; our solitary ship tore on through the open water as though glad to be out of her confinement; and the ice islands lay scattered here and there, of various sizes and shapes, reflecting the bright rays of the sun, and drifting slowly northward before the gale. It was a contrast to much that we had lately seen, and a spectacle not only of beauty, but of life; for it required but little fancy to imagine these islands to be animate masses which had broken loose from the "thrilling regions of thick-ribbed ice," and were working their way, by wind and current, some alone, and some in fleets, to milder climes. No pencil has ever yet given anything like the true effect of an iceberg. In a picture, they are huge, uncouth masses, stuck in the sea, while their chief beauty and grandeur — their slow, stately motion, the whirling of the snow about their summits, and the fearful groaning and cracking of their parts — the picture cannot give. This is the large iceberg — while the small and distant islands, floating on the smooth sea, in the light of a clear day, look like little floating fairy isles of sapphire.

From a northeast course we gradually hauled to the eastward, and after sailing about two hundred miles, which brought us as near to the western coast of Terra del Fuego as was safe, and having lost sight of the ice altogether — for the third time we put the ship's head to the southward, to try the passage of the Cape. The weather continued clear and cold, with a strong gale from the westward, and we were fast getting up with the latitude of the Cape, with a prospect of soon being round. One fine afternoon, a man who had gone into the fore-top to shift the rolling tackles sung out at the top of his voice, and with evident glee, "Sail ho!" Neither land nor sail had we seen since leaving San Diego; and only those who have traversed the length of a whole ocean alone can imagine what an excitement such an announcement produced on board. "Sail ho!" shouted the cook, jumping out of his galley; "Sail ho!" shouted a man, throwing back the slide of the scuttle, to the watch below, who were soon out of their berths and on deck; and "Sail ho!" shouted the captain down the companion-way to the passenger in the cabin. Beside the pleasure of seeing a ship and human beings in so desolate a place, it was important for us to speak a vessel, to learn whether there was ice to eastward, and to ascertain the longitude; for we had no chronometer, and had been drifting about so long that we had nearly lost our reckoning; and opportunities for lunar observations are not frequent or sure in such a place as Cape Horn. For these various reasons the excitement in our little community was running high, and conjectures were made, and everything thought of for which the captain would hail, when the man aloft sung out: "Another sail, large on the weather bow!" This was a little odd, but so much the better, and did not shake our faith in their being sails. At length the man in the top hailed, and said he believed it was land, after all. "Land in your eye!" said the mate, who was looking through the telescope; "they are ice islands, if I can see a hole through a ladder"; and a few moments showed the mate to be right; and all our expectations fled; and instead of what we most wished to see we had what we most dreaded, and what we hoped we had seen the last of. We soon, however, left these astern, having passed within about two miles of them, and at sundown the horizon was clear in all directions.

Having a fine wind, we were soon up with and passed the latitude of the Cape, and, having stood far enough to the southward to give it a wide berth, we began to stand to the eastward, with a good prospect of being round and steering to the northward, on the other side, in a very few days. But ill luck seemed to have lighted upon us. Not four hours had we been standing on in this course before it fell dead calm, and in half an hour it clouded up, a few straggling blasts, with spits of snow and sleet, came from the eastward, and in an hour more we lay hove-to under a close-reefed main topsail, drifting bodily off to leeward before the fiercest storm that we had yet felt, blowing dead ahead, from the eastward. It seemed as though the genius of the place had been roused at finding that we had nearly slipped through his fingers, and had come down upon us with tenfold fury. The sailors said that every blast, as it shook the shrouds, and whistled through the rigging, said to the old ship; "No, you don't! – No, you don't!"

For eight days we lay drifting about in this manner. Sometimes – generally towards noon – it fell calm; once or twice a round copper ball showed itself for a few moments in the place where the sun ought to have been, and a puff or two came from the westward, giving some hope that a fair wind had come at last. During the first two days we made sail for these puffs, shaking the reefs out of the topsails and boarding the tacks of the courses; but finding that it only made work for us when the gale set in again, it was soon given up, and we lay-to under our close-reefs. We had less snow and hail than when we were farther to the westward, but we had an abundance of what is worse to a sailor in cold weather, – drenching rain. Snow is blinding, and very bad when coming upon a coast, but, for genuine discomfort, give me rain with freezing weather. A snow-storm is exciting, and it does not wet through the clothes (a fact important to a sailor); but a constant rain there is no escaping from. It wets to the skin, and makes all protection vain. We had long ago run through all our dry clothes, and as sailors have no other way of drying them than by the sun, we had nothing to do but to put on those which were the least wet. At the end of each watch, when we came below, we took off our clothes and wrung them out; two taking hold of a pair of trousers, one at each end – and jackets in the same way. Stockings, mittens, and all, were wrung out also, and then hung up to drain and chafe dry against the bulkheads. Then, feeling of all our clothes, we picked out those which were the least wet, and put them on, so as to be ready for a call, and turned-in, covered ourselves up with blankets, and slept until three knocks on the scuttle and the dismal sound of "All Starbowlines ahoy! Eight bells, there below! Do you hear the news?" drawled out from on deck, and the sulky answer of "Aye, aye!" from below, sent us up again.

On deck all was dark, and either a dead calm, with the rain pouring steadily down, or, more generally, a violent gale dead ahead, with rain pelting horizontally, and occasional variations of hail and sleet; decks afloat with water swashing from side to side, and constantly wet feet, for boots could not be wrung out like drawers, and no composition could stand the constant soaking. In fact, wet and cold feet are inevitable in such weather, and are not the least of those items which go to make up the grand total of the discomforts of a winter passage round Cape Horn. Few words were spoken between the watches as they shifted; the wheel was relieved, the mate took his place on the quarter-deck, and lookouts in the bows; and each man had his narrow space to walk fore and aft in, or rather to swing himself forward and back in, from one belaying-pin to another, for the decks were too slippery with ice and water to allow of much walking. To make a walk, which is absolutely necessary to pass away the time, one of us hit upon the expedient of sanding the decks; and afterwards, whenever the rain was not so violent as to wash it off, the weather-side of the quarter-deck and a part of the waist and forecastle were sprinkled with the sand which we had on board for holystoning, and thus we made a good promenade, where we walked fore and aft, two and two, hour after hour, in our long, dull, and comfortless watches. The bells seemed to be an hour or two apart, instead of half an hour, and an age to elapse before the welcome sound of eight bells. The sole object was to make the time pass on. Any change was sought for which would break the monotony of the time; and even the two hours' trick at the wheel, which came round to us in turn, once in every other watch, was looked upon as a relief. The never-failing resource of long yarns, which eke out many a watch, seemed to have failed us now; for we had been so long together that we had heard each other's stories told over and over again till we had them by heart; each one knew the whole history of each of the others, and we were fairly and literally talked out. Singing and joking we were in no humor for; and, in fact, any sound of mirth or laughter would have struck strangely upon our ears, and would not have been tolerated any more than whistling or a wind instrument. The last resort, that of speculating upon the future, seemed now to fail us; for our discouraging situation, and the danger we were really in (as we expected every day to find ourselves drifted back among the ice), "clapped a stopper" upon all that. From saying "*when* we get home," we began insensibly to alter it to "*if* we get home," and at last the subject was dropped by a tacit consent.

In this state of things, a new light was struck out, and a new field opened, by a change in the watch. One of our watch was laid up for two or three days by a bad hand (for in cold weather the least cut or bruise ripens into a sore), and his place was supplied by the carpenter. This was a windfall, and there was a contest who should have the carpenter to walk with him. As "Chips" was a man of some little education, and he and I had had a good deal of intercourse with each other, he fell in with me in my walk. He was a Finn, but spoke English well, and gave me long accounts of his country – the customs, the trade, the towns, what little he knew of the government (I found he was no friend of Russia), his voyages, his first arrival in America, his marriage and courtship; he had married a country-woman of his, a dress-maker, whom he met with in Boston. I had very little to tell him of my quiet, sedentary life at home; and in spite of our best efforts, which had protracted these yarns through five or six watches, we fairly talked each other out, and I turned him over to another man in the watch, and put myself upon my own resources.

I commenced a deliberate system of time-killing, which united some profit with a cheering up of the heavy hours. As soon as I came on deck, and took my place and regular walk, I began with repeating over to myself in regular order a string of matters which I had in my memory – the multiplication table and the tables of weights and measures; the Kanaka numerals; then the States of the Union, with their capitals; the counties of England, with their shire towns, and the kings of England in their order, and other things. This carried me through my facts, and, being repeated deliberately, with long intervals, often eked out the first two bells. Then came the Ten Commandments, the thirty-ninth chapter of Job, and a few other passages from Scripture. The next in the order, which I seldom varied from, came

Cowper's Castaway, which was a great favorite with me; its solemn measure and gloomy character, as well as the incident it was founded upon, making it well suited to a lonely watch at sea. Then his lines to Mary, his address to the Jackdaw, and a short extract from Table Talk (I abounded in Cowper, for I happened to have a volume of his poems in my chest); "Ille et nefasto" from Horace, and Goethe's Erl König. After I had got through these, I allowed myself a more general range among everything that I could remember, both in prose and verse. In this way, with an occasional break by relieving the wheel, heaving the log, and going to the scuttle-butt for a drink of water, the longest watch was passed away; and I was so regular in my silent recitations that, if there was no interruption by ship's duty, I could tell very nearly the number of bells by my progress.

Our watches below were no more varied than the watch on deck. All washing, sewing, and reading was given up, and we did nothing but eat, sleep, and stand our watch, leading what might be called a Cape Horn life. The forecastle was too uncomfortable to sit up in; and whenever we were below, we were in our berths. To prevent the rain and the sea-water which broke over the bows from washing down, we were obliged to keep the scuttle closed, so that the forecastle was nearly air-tight. In this little, wet, leaky hole, we were all quartered, in an atmosphere so bad that our lamp, which swung in the middle from the beams, sometimes actually burned blue, with a large circle of foul air about it. Still, I was never in better health than after three weeks of this life. I gained a great deal of flesh, and we all ate like horses. At every watch when we came below, before turning in, the bread barge and beef kid were overhauled. Each man drank his quart of hot tea night and morning, and glad enough we were to get it; for no nectar and ambrosia were sweeter to the lazy immortals than was a pot of hot tea, a hard biscuit, and a slice of cold salt beef to us after a watch on deck. To be sure, we were mere animals, and, had this life lasted a year instead of a month, we should have been little better than the ropes in the ship. Not a razor, nor a brush, nor a drop of water, except the rain and the spray, had come near us all the time; for we were on an allowance of fresh water; and who would strip and wash himself in salt water on deck, in the snow and ice, with the thermometer at zero?

After about eight days of constant easterly gales, the wind hauled occasionally a little to the southward, and blew hard, which, as we were well to the southward, allowed us to brace in a little, and stand on under all the sail we could carry. These turns lasted but a short while, and sooner or later it set in again from the old quarter; yet at each time we made something, and were gradually edging along to the eastward. One night, after one of these shifts of the wind, and when all hands had been up a great part of the time, our watch was left on deck, with the mainsail hanging in the buntlines, ready to be set if necessary. It came on to blow worse and worse, with hail and snow beating like so many furies upon the ship, it being as dark and thick as night could make it. The mainsail was blowing and slatting with a noise like thunder, when the captain came on deck and ordered it to be furled. The mate was about to call all hands, when the captain stopped him, and said that the men would be beaten out if they were called up so often; that, as our watch must stay on deck, it might as well be doing that as anything else. Accordingly, we went upon the yard; and never shall I forget that piece of work. Our watch had been so reduced by sickness, and by some having been left in California, that, with one man at the wheel, we had only the third mate and three beside myself to go aloft; so that at most we could only attempt to furl one yard-arm at a time. We manned the weather yard-arm, and set to work to make a furl of it. Our lower masts being short, and our yards very square, the sail had a head of nearly fifty feet, and a short leech, made still shorter by the deep reef which was in it, which brought the clew away out on the quarters of the yard, and made a bunt nearly as square as the mizzen royal yard. Beside this difficulty, the yard over which we lay was cased with ice, the gaskets and rope of the foot and leech of the sail as stiff and hard as a piece of leather hose, and the sail itself about as pliable as though it had been made of sheets of sheathing copper. It blew a perfect hurricane, with alternate blasts of snow, hail, and rain. We had to *fist* the sail with bare hands. No one could trust himself to mittens, for if he slipped he was a gone man. All the boats were hoisted in on deck, and there was nothing to be lowered for him. We had need of every finger God had given us. Several times we got the sail upon the yard, but it blew away again before we could secure it. It required men to lie over the yard to pass each turn of the gaskets, and when they were passed it was almost impossible to knot them so that they would hold. Frequently we were obliged to leave off altogether and take to beating our hands upon the sail to keep them from freezing. After some time — which seemed forever — we got the weather side stowed after a fashion, and went over to leeward for another trial. This was still worse, for the body of the sail had been blown over to leeward, and, as the yard was a-cock-bill by the lying over of the vessel, we had to light it all up to windward. When the yard-arms were furled, the bunt was all adrift again, which made more work for us. We got all secure at last, but we had been nearly an hour and a half upon the yard, and it seemed an age. It had just struck five bells when we went up, and eight were struck soon after we came down. This may seem slow work; but considering the state of everything, and that we had only five men to a sail with just half as many square yards of canvas in it as the mainsail of the Independence, sixty-gun ship, which musters seven hundred men at her quarters, it is not wonderful that we were no quicker about it. We were glad enough to get on deck, and still more to go below. The oldest sailor in the watch said, as he went down: "I shall never forget that main yard; it beats all my going a-fishing. Fun is fun, but furling one yard-arm of a course at a time, off Cape Horn, is no better than man-killing."

During the greater part of the next two days, the wind was pretty steady from the southward. We had evidently made great progress, and had good hope of being soon up with the Cape, if we were not there already. We could put but little confidence in our reckoning, as there had been no opportunities for an observation, and we had drifted too much to allow of our dead reckoning being anywhere near the mark. If it would clear off enough to give a chance for an observation, or if we could make land, we should know where we were; and upon these, and the chances of falling in with a sail from the eastward, we depended almost entirely.

Friday, July 22d. This day we had a steady gale from the southward, and stood on under close sail, with the yards eased a little by the weather braces, the clouds lifting a little, and showing signs of breaking away. In the afternoon, I was below with Mr. Hatch, the third mate, and two others, filling the bread locker in the steerage from the casks, when a bright gleam of sunshine broke out and shone down the companion-way, and through the skylight, lighting up everything below, and sending a warm glow through the hearts of all. It was a sight we had not seen for weeks — an omen, a god-send. Even the roughest and hardest face acknowledged its influence. Just at that moment we heard a loud shout from all parts of the deck, and the mate called out down the companion-way to the captain, who was sitting in the cabin. What he said we could not distinguish, but the captain kicked over his chair, and was on deck at one jump. We could not tell what it was; and, anxious as we were to know, the discipline of the ship would not allow of our leaving our places. Yet, as we were not called, we knew there was no danger. We hurried to get through with our job, when, seeing the steward's black face peering out of the pantry, Mr. Hatch hailed him to know what was the matter. "Lan' o, to be sure, sir! No you hear 'em sing out, 'Lan' o?' De cap'em say 'im Cape Horn!"

This gave us a new start, and we were soon through our work and on deck; and there lay the land, fair upon the larboard beam, and slowly edging away upon the quarter. All hands were busy looking at it — the captain and mates from the quarter-deck, the cook from his galley, and the sailors from the forecastle; and even Mr. Nuttall, the passenger, who had kept in his shell for nearly a month, and hardly been seen by anybody, and who we had almost forgotten was on board, came out like a butterfly, and was hopping round as bright as a bird.

The land was the island of Staten Land, just to the eastward of Cape Horn; and a more desolate-looking spot I never wish to set eyes upon — bare, broken, and girt with rocks and ice, with here and there, between the rocks and broken hillocks, a little stunted vegetation of shrubs. It was a place well suited to stand at the junction of the two oceans, beyond the reach of human cultivation, and encounter the blasts and snows of a perpetual winter. Yet, dismal as it was, it was a pleasant sight to us; not only as being the first land we had seen, but because it told us that we had passed the Cape — were in the Atlantic — and that, with twenty-four hours of this breeze, we might bid defiance to the Southern Ocean. It told us, too, our latitude and longitude better than any observation; and the captain now knew where we were, as well as if we were off the end of Long Wharf.

In the general joy, Mr. Nuttall said he should like to go ashore upon the island and examine a spot which probably no human being had ever set foot upon; but the captain intimated that he would see the island, specimens and all, in — another place, before he would get out a boat or delay the ship one moment for him.

We left the land gradually astern; and at sundown had the Atlantic Ocean clear before us.

— *From Two Years Before the Mast, by Richard Henry Dana, Jr., American (1815–1882).*

The Last March

ROBERT F. SCOTT

Sunday, February 18. — R.32. Temp. —5·5°. At Shambles Camp. We gave ourselves 5 hours' sleep at the lower glacier depôt after the horrible night, and came on at about 3 to-day to this camp, coming fairly easily over the divide. Here with plenty of horsemeat we have had a fine supper, to be followed by others such, and so continue a more plentiful era if we can keep good marches up. New life seems to come with greater food almost immediately, but I am anxious about the Barrier surfaces.

Monday, February 19. — Lunch T. —16°. It was late (past noon) before we got away to-day, as I gave nearly 8 hours' sleep, and much camp work was done shifting sledges and fitting up new one with mast, &c., packing horsemeat and personal effects. The surface was every bit as bad as I expected, the sun shining brightly on it and its covering of soft loose sandy snow. We have come out about 2′ on the old tracks. Perhaps lucky to have a fine day for this and our camp work, but we shall want wind or change of sliding conditions to do anything on such a surface as we have got. I fear there will not be much change for the next 3 or 4 days.

R.33. Temp. —17°. We have struggled out 4·6 miles in a short day over a really terrible surface — it has been like pulling over desert sand, not the least glide in the world. If this goes on we shall have a bad time, but I sincerely trust it is only the result of this windless area close to the coast and that, as we are making steadily outwards, we shall shortly escape it. It is perhaps premature to be anxious about covering distance. In all other respects things are improving. We have our sleeping-bags spread on the sledge and they are drying, but, above all, we have our full measure of food again. To-night we had a sort of stew fry of pemmican and horseflesh, and voted it the best hoosh we had ever had on a sledge journey. The absence of poor Evans is a help to the commissariat, but if he had been here in a fit state we might have got along faster. I wonder what is in store for us, with some little alarm at the lateness of the season.

Tuesday, February 21. — R.35. Lunch Temp. —9½°; Supper Temp. —11°. Gloomy and overcast when we started; a good deal warmer. The marching almost as bad as yesterday. Heavy toiling all day, inspiring gloomiest thoughts at times. Rays of comfort when we picked up tracks and cairns. At lunch we seemed to have missed the way, but an hour or two after we passed the last pony walls, and since, we struck a tent ring, ending the march actually on our old pony-tracks. There is a critical spot here with a long stretch between cairns. If we can tide that over we get on the regular cairn route, and with luck should stick to it; but everything depends on the weather. We never won a march of 8½ miles with greater difficulty, but we can't go on like this. We are drawing away from the land and perhaps may get better things in a day or two. I devoutly hope so.

Wednesday, February 22. — R.36. Supper Temp. —2°. There is little doubt we are in for a rotten critical time going home, and the lateness of the season may make it really serious. Shortly after starting to-day the wind grew very fresh from the S.E. with strong surface drift. We lost the faint track immediately, though covering fairly rapidly. Lunch came without sight of the cairn we had hoped to pass. In the afternoon, Bowers being sure we were too far to the west, steered out. Result, we have passed another pony camp without seeing it. Looking at the map to-night there is no doubt we are too far to the east. With clear weather we ought to be able to correct the mistake, but will the weather clear? It's a gloomy position, more especially as one sees the same difficulty returning even when we have corrected the error. The wind is dying down to-night and the sky clearing in the south, which is hopeful. Meanwhile it is satisfactory to note that such untoward events fail to damp the spirit of the party. To-night we had a pony hoosh so excellent and filling that one feels really strong and vigorous again.

Thursday, February 23.—R.37. Lunch Temp. −9·8°; Supper Temp. −12°. Started in sunshine, wind almost dropped. Luckily Bowers took a round of angles and with help of the chart we fogged out that we must be inside rather than outside tracks. The data were so meagre that it seemed a great responsibility to march out and we were none of us happy about it. But just as we decided to lunch, Bowers' wonderful sharp eyes detected an old double lunch cairn, the theodolite telescope confirmed it, and our spirits rose accordingly. This afternoon we marched on and picked up another cairn; then on and camped only 2½ miles from the depôt. We cannot see it, but, given fine weather, we cannot miss it. We are, therefore, extraordinarily relieved. Covered 8·2 miles in 7 hours, showing we can do 10 to 12 on this surface. Things are again looking up, as we are on the regular line of cairns, with no gaps right home, I hope.

Friday, February 24.—Lunch. Beautiful day—too beautiful—an hour after starting loose ice crystals spoiling surface. Saw depôt and reached it middle forenoon. Found store in order except shortage oil—shall have to be *very* saving with fuel—otherwise have ten full days' provision from to-night and shall have less than 70 miles to go. Note from Meares who passed through December 15, saying surface bad; from Atkinson, after the fine marching (2¼ days from pony depôt), reporting Keohane better after sickness. Short note from Evans, not very cheerful, saying surface bad, temperature high. Think he must have been a little anxious. It is an immense relief to have picked up this depôt and, for the time, anxieties are thrust aside. There is no doubt we have been rising steadily since leaving the Shambles Camp. The coastal Barrier descends except where glaciers press out. Undulation still but flattening out. Surface soft on top, curiously hard below. Great difference now between night and day temperatures. Quite warm as I write in tent. We are on tracks with half-march cairn ahead; have covered 4½ miles. Poor Wilson has a fearful attack snow-blindness consequent on yesterday's efforts. Wish we had more fuel.

Night camp R.38. Temp. −17°. A little despondent again. We had a really terrible surface this afternoon and only covered 4 miles. We are on the track just beyond a lunch cairn. It really will be a bad business if we are to have this pulling all through. I don't know what to think, but the rapid closing of the season is ominous. It is great luck having horsemeat to add to our ration. To-night we had a real fine "hoosh." It is a race between the season and hard conditions and our fitness and good food.

Saturday, February 25.—Lunch Temp. −13°. Managed just 6 miles this morning. Started somewhat despondent; not relieved when pulling seemed to show no improvement. Bit by bit surface grew better, less sastrugi, more glide, slight following wind for a time. Then we began to travel a little faster. But the pulling is still *very* hard; undulations disappearing but inequalities remain.

Twenty-six Camp walls about 2 miles ahead, all tracks in sight—Evans' track very conspicuous. This is something in favour, but the pulling is tiring us, though we are getting into better ski drawing again. Bowers hasn't quite the trick and is a little hurt at my criticisms, but I never doubted his heart. Very much easier—write diary at lunch—excellent meal—now one pannikin very strong tea—four biscuits and butter.

Hope for better things this afternoon, but no improvement apparent. Oh! for a little wind—E. Evans evidently had plenty.

R.39. Temp. −30°. Better march in afternoon. Day yields 11·4 miles—the first double figure of steady dragging for a long time, but it meant and will mean hard work if we can't get a wind to help us. Evans evidently had a strong wind here, S.E. I should think. The temperature goes very low at night now when the sky is clear as at present. As a matter of fact this is wonderfully fair weather—the only drawback the spoiling of the surface and absence of wind. We see all tracks very plain, but the pony-walls have evidently been badly drifted up. Some kind people had substituted a cairn at last Camp 27. The old cairns do not seem to have suffered much.

Sunday, February 26. – Lunch Temp. −17°. Sky overcast at start, but able see tracks and cairn distinct at long distance. Did a little better, 6½ miles to date. Bowers and Wilson now in front. Find great relief pulling behind with no necessity to keep attention on track. Very cold nights now and cold feet starting march, as day footgear doesn't dry at all. We are doing well on our food, but we ought to have yet more. I hope the next depôt, now only 50 miles, will find us with enough surplus to open out. The fuel shortage still an anxiety.

R.40. Temp. −21°. Nine hours' solid marching has given us 11½ miles. Only 43 miles from the next depôt. Wonderfully fine weather but cold, very cold. Nothing dries and we get our feet cold too often. We want more food yet and especially more fat. Fuel woefully short. We can scarcely hope to get a better surface at this season, but I wish we could have some help from the wind, though it might shake us badly if the temp. didn't rise.

Monday, February 27. – Desperately cold last night: −33° when we got up, with −37° minimum. Some suffering from cold feet, but all got good rest. We *must* open out on food soon. But we have done 7 miles this morning and hope for some 5 this afternoon. Overcast sky and good surface till now, when sun shows again. It is good to be marching the cairns up, but there is still much to be anxious about. We talk of little but food, except after meals. Land disappearing in satisfactory manner. Pray God we have no further set-backs. We are naturally always discussing possibility of meeting dogs, where and when, &. It is a critical position. We may find ourselves in safety at next depôt, but there is a horrid element of doubt.

Camp R.41. Temp. −32°. Still fine clear weather but very cold – absolutely calm to-night. We have got off an excellent march for these days (12·2) and are much earlier than usual in our bags. 31 miles to depôt, 3 days' fuel at a pinch, and 6 days' food. Things begin to look a little better; we can open out a little on food from to-morrow night, I think.

Very curious surface – soft recent sastrugi which sink underfoot, and between, a sort of flaky crust with large crystals beneath.

Tuesday, February 28. – Lunch. Thermometer went below −40° last night; it was desperately cold for us, but we had a fair night. I decided to slightly increase food; the effect is undoubtedly good. Started marching in −32° with a slight north-westerly breeze – blighting. Many cold feet this morning; long time over foot gear, but we are earlier. Shall camp earlier and get the chance of a good night, if not the reality. Things must be critical till we reach the depôt, and the more I think of matter, the more I anticipate their remaining so after that event. Only 24½ miles from the depôt. The sun shines brightly, but there is little warmth in it. There is no doubt the middle of the Barrier is a pretty awful locality.

Camp 42. Splendid pony hoosh sent us to bed and sleep happily after a horrid day, wind continuing; did 11½ miles. Temp. not quite so low, but expect we are in for cold night (Temp. −27°).

Wednesday, February 29. – Lunch. Cold night. Minimum Temp. −37·5°; −30° with north-west wind, force 4, when we got up. Frightfully cold starting; luckily Bowers and Oates in their last new finesko; keeping my old ones for present. Expected awful march and for first hour got it. Then things improved and we camped after 5½ hours marching close to lunch camp −22½°. Next camp is our depôt and it is exactly 13 miles. It ought not to take more than 1½ days; we pray for another fine one. The oil will just about spin out in that event, and we arrive 3 clear days' food in hand. The increase of ration has had an enormously beneficial result. Mountains now looking small. Wind still very light from west – cannot understand this wind.

Thursday, March 1. – Lunch. Very cold last night – minimum −41·5°. Cold start to march, too, as usual now. Got away at 8 and have marched within sight of depôt; flag something under 3 miles away. We did 11½ yesterday and marched 6 this morning. Heavy dragging yesterday and *very* heavy this morning. Apart from sledging considerations the weather is wonderful. Cloudless days and nights and the wind trifling. Worse luck, the light airs come from the north and keep us horribly cold. For this lunch hour the exception has come. There is a bright and comparatively warm sun. All our gear is out drying.

Friday, March 2. – Lunch. Misfortunes rarely come singly. We marched to the

(Middle Barrier) depôt fairly easily yesterday afternoon, and since that have suffered three distinct blows which have placed us in a bad position. First we found a shortage of oil; with most rigid economy it can scarce carry us to the next depôt on this surface (71 miles away). Second, Titus Oates disclosed his feet, the toes showing very bad indeed, evidently bitten by the late temperatures. The third blow came in the night, when the wind, which we had hailed with some joy, brought dark overcast weather. It fell below —40° in the night, and this morning it took 1½ hours to get our foot gear on, but we got away before eight. We lost cairn and tracks together and made as steady as we could N. by W., but have seen nothing. Worse was to come — the surface is simply awful. In spite of strong wind and full sail we have only done 5½ miles. We are in a *very* queer street since there is no doubt we cannot do the extra marches and feel the cold horribly.

Saturday, March 3. — Lunch. We picked up the track again yesterday, finding ourselves to the eastward. Did close on 10 miles and things looked a trifle better; but this morning the outlook is blacker than ever. Started well and with good breeze; for an hour made good headway; then the surface grew awful beyond words. The wind drew forward; every circumstance was against us. After 4¼ hours things so bad that we camped, having covered 4½ miles. (R.46). One cannot consider this a fault of our own — certainly we were pulling hard this morning — it was more than three parts surface which held us back — the wind at strongest, powerless to move the sledge. When the light is good it is easy to see the reason. The surface, lately a very good hard one, is coated with a thin layer of woolly crystals, formed by radiation no doubt. These are too firmly fixed to be removed by the wind and cause impossible friction on the runners. God help us, we can't keep up this pulling, that is certain. Amongst ourselves we are unendingly cheerful, but what each man feels in his heart I can only guess. Pulling on footgear in the morning is getting slower and slower, therefore every day more dangerous.

Sunday, March 4. Lunch. Things looking *very* black indeed. As usual we forgot our trouble last night, got into our bags, slept splendidly on good hoosh, woke and had another, and started marching. Sun shining brightly, tracks clear, but surface covered with sandy frostrime. All the morning we had to pull with all our strength, and in 4½ hours we covered 3½ miles. Last night it was overcast and thick, surface bad; this morning sun shining and surface as bad as ever. One has little to hope for except perhaps strong dry wind — an unlikely contingency at this time of year. Under the immediate surface crystals is a hard sastrugi surface, which must have been excellent for pulling a week or two ago. We are about 42 miles from the next depôt and have a week's food, but only about 3 or 4 days' fuel — we are as economical of the latter as one can possibly be, and we cannot afford to have food and pull as we are pulling. We are in a very tight place indeed, but none of us despondent *yet*, or at least we preserve every semblance of good cheer, but one's heart sinks as the sledge stops dead at some sastrugi behind which the surface sand lies thickly heaped. For the moment the temperature is on the —20° — an improvement which makes us much more comfortable, but a colder snap is bound to come again soon. I fear that Oates at least will weather such an event very poorly. Providence to our aid! We can expect little from man now except the possibility of extra food at the next depôt. It will be real bad if we get there and find the same shortage of oil. Shall we get there? Such a short distance it would have appeared to us on the summit! I don't know what I should do if Wilson and Bowers weren't so determinedly cheerful over things.

Monday, March 5. — Lunch. Regret to say going from bad to worse. We got a slant of wind yesterday afternoon, and going on 5 hours we converted our wretched morning run of 3½ miles into something over 9. We went to bed on a cup of cocoa and pemmican solid with the chill off. (R.47). The result is telling on all, but mainly on Oates, whose feet are in a wretched condition. One swelled up tremendously last night and he is very lame this morning. We started march on tea and pemmican as last night — we pretend to prefer the pemmican this way. Marched for 5 hours this morning over a slightly better surface covered with high moundy sastrugi. Sledge capsized twice; we pulled on foot, covering about 5½ miles. We are two pony marches and 4 miles about from our depôt. Our fuel dreadfully low and the poor Soldier nearly done. It is pathetic enough because we can do nothing for him;

more hot food might do a little, but only a little, I fear. We none of us expected these terribly low temperatures, and of the rest of us Wilson is feeling them most; mainly, I fear, from his self-sacrificing devotion in doctoring Oates' feet. We cannot help each other, each has enough to do to take care of himself. We get cold on the march when the trudging is heavy, and the wind pierces our warm garments. The others, all of them, are unendingly cheerful when in the tent. We mean to see the game through with a proper spirit, but it's tough work to be pulling harder than we ever pulled in our lives for long hours, and to feel that the progress is so slow. One can only say "God help us!" and plod on our weary way, cold and very miserable, though outwardly cheerful. We talk of all sorts of subjects in the tent, not much of food now, since we decided to take the risk of running a full ration. We simply couldn't go hungry at this time.

Tuesday, March 6. – Lunch. We did a little better with help of wind yesterday afternoon, finishing 9½ miles for the day, and 27 miles from depôt. (R.48). But this morning things have been awful. It was warm in the night and for the first time during the journey I overslept myself by more than an hour; then we were slow with foot gear; then, pulling with all our might (for our lives) we could scarcely advance at rate of a mile an hour; then it grew thick and three times we had to get out of harness to search for tracks. The result is something less than 3½ miles for the forenoon. The sun is shining now and the wind gone. Poor Oates is unable to pull, sits on the sledge when we are track-searching – he is wonderfully plucky, as his feet must be giving him great pain. He makes no complaint, but his spirits only come up in spurts now, and he grows more silent in the tent. We are making a spirit lamp to try and replace the primus when our oil is exhausted. It will be a very poor substitute and we've not got much spirit. If we could have kept up our 9-mile days we might have got within reasonable distance of the depôt before running out, but nothing but a strong wind and good surface can help us now, and though we had quite a good breeze this morning, the sledge came as heavy as lead. If we were all fit I should have hopes of getting through, but the poor Soldier has become a terrible hindrance, though he does his utmost and suffers much I fear.

Wednesday, March 7. – a little worse I fear. One of Oates' feet *very* bad this morning; he is wonderfully brave. We still talk of what we will do together at home.

We only made 6½ miles yesterday. (R.49). This morning in 4½ hours we did just over 4 miles. We are 16 from our depôt. If we only find the correct proportion of food there and this surface continues, we may get to the next depôt (Mt. Hooper, 72 miles farther) but not to One Ton Camp. We hope against hope that the dogs have been to Mt. Hooper; then we might pull through. If there is a shortage of oil again we can have little hope. One feels that for poor Oates the crisis is near, but none of us are improving, though we are wonderfully fit considering the really excessive work we are doing. We are only kept going by good food. No wind this morning till a chill northerly air came ahead. Sun bright and cairns showing up well. I should like to keep the track to the end.

Thursday, March 8. – Lunch. Worse and worse in morning; poor Oates' left foot can never last out, and time over foot gear something awful. Have to wait in night foot gear for nearly an hour before I start changing, and then am generally first to be ready. Wilson's feet giving trouble now, but this mainly because he gives so much help to others. We did 4½ miles this morning and are now 8½ miles from the depôt – a ridiculously small distance to feel in difficulties, yet on this surface we know we cannot equal half our old marches, and that for that effort we expend nearly double the energy. The great question is, what shall we find at the depôt? If the dogs have visited it we may get along a good distance, but if there is another short allowance of fuel, God help us indeed. We are in a very bad way, I fear, in any case.

Saturday, March 10. – Things steadily downhill. Oates' foot worse. He has rare pluck and must know that he can never get through. He asked Wilson if he had a chance this morning, and of course Bill had to say he didn't know. In point of fact he had none. Apart from him, if he went under now, I doubt whether we could get through. With great care we might have a dog's chance, but no more. The weather conditions are awful, and our gear gets steadily more icy and difficult to manage. At the same time of course poor Titus is the greatest handicap. He keeps us waiting in the morning until we have partly lost the warming effect of our good breakfast, when the only wise policy is to be up and away at once; again at lunch. Poor chap! it is too pathetic to watch him; one cannot but try to cheer him up.

Yesterday we marched up the depôt, Mt. Hooper. Cold comfort. Shortage on our allowance all round. I don't know that anyone is to blame. The dogs which would have been our salvation have evidently failed. Meares had a bad trip home I suppose.

This morning it was calm when we breakfasted, but the wind came from W.N.W. as we broke camp. It rapidly grew in strength. After travelling for half an hour I saw that none of us could go on facing such conditions. We were forced to camp and are spending the rest of the day in a comfortless blizzard camp, wind quite foul. (R.52.)

Sunday, March 11. — Titus Oates is very near the end, one feels. What we or he will do, God only knows. We discussed the matter after breakfast; he is a brave fine fellow and understands the situation, but he practically asked for advice. Nothing could be said but to urge him to march as long as he could. One satisfactory result to the discussion; I practically ordered Wilson to hand over the means of ending our troubles to us, so that anyone of us may know how to do so. Wilson had no choice between doing so and our ransacking the medicine case. We have 30 opium tabloids apiece and he is left with a tube of morphine. So far the tragical side of our story. (R.53.) . . . .

The sky completely overcast when we started this morning. We could see nothing, lost the tracks, and doubtless have been swaying a good deal since — 3·1 miles for the forenoon — terribly heavy dragging — expected it. Know that 6 miles is about the limit of our endurance now, if we get no help from wind or surfaces. We have 7 days' food and should be about 55 miles from One Ton Camp to-night, $6 \times 7 = 42$. We shall be 47 miles from the depôt. I doubt if we can possibly do it. The surface remains awful, the cold intense, and our physical condition running down. God help us! Not a breath of favourable wind for more than a week, and apparently liable to head winds at any moment.

Wednesday, March 14. — No doubt about the going downhill, but everything going wrong with us. Yesterday we woke to a strong northerly wind with temp. —37°. Couldn't face it, so remained in camp (R.54) till 2, then did 5¼ miles. Wanted to march later, but party feeling the cold badly as the breeze (N.) never took off entirely, and as the sun sank the temp. fell. Long time getting supper in dark. (R.55).

This morning started with southerly breeze, set sail and passed another cairn at good speed; half-way, however, the wind shifted to W. by S. or W.S.W., blew through our wind clothes and into our mits. Poor Wilson horribly cold, could not get off ski for some time. Bowers and I practically made camp, and when we got into the tent at last we were all deadly cold. Then temp. now midday down —43° and the wind strong. We *must* go on, but now the making of every camp must be more difficult and dangerous. It must be near the end, but a pretty merciful end. Poor Oates got it again in the foot. I shudder to think what it will be like to-morrow. It is only with greatest pains rest of us keep off frostbites. No idea there could be temperatures like this at this time of year with such winds. Truly awful outside the tent. Must fight it out to the last biscuit, but can't reduce rations.

Friday, March 16 *or Saturday* 17. — Lost track of dates, but think the last correct. Tragedy all along the line. At lunch, the day before yesterday, poor Titus Oates said he couldn't go on; he proposed we should leave him in his sleeping-bag. That we could not do, and induced him to come on, on the afternoon march. In spite of its awful nature for him he struggled on and we made a few miles. At night he was worse and we knew the end had come.

Should this be found I want these facts recorded. Oates' last thoughts were of his Mother, but immediately before he took pride in thinking that his regiment would be pleased with the bold way in which he met his death. We can testify to his bravery. He has borne intense suffering for weeks without complaint, and to the very last was able and willing to discuss outside subjects. He did not — would not — give up hope to the very end. He was a brave soul. This was the end. He slept through the night before last, hoping not to wake; but he woke in the morning — yesterday. It was blowing a blizzard. He said, "I am just going outside and may be some time." He went out into the blizzard and we have not seen him since.

I take this opportunity of saying that we have stuck to our sick companions to the last. In case of Edgar Evans, when absolutely out of food and he lay insensible, the safety of the remainder seemed to demand his abandonment, but Providence mercifully removed him at this critical moment. He died a natural death, and we did not leave him till two hours after his death. We knew that poor Oates was walking to his death, but though we tried to dissuade him, we knew it was the act of a brave man and an English gentleman. We all hope to meet the end with a similar spirit, and assuredly the end is not far. I can only write at lunch and then only occasionally. The cold is intense, −40° at midday. My companions are unendingly cheerful, but though we constantly talk of fetching through I don't think any one of us believes it in his heart.

We are cold on the march now, and at all times except meals. Yesterday we had to lay up for a blizzard and to-day we move dreadfully slowly. We are at No. 14 pony camp, only two pony marches from One Ton Depôt. We leave here our theodolite, a camera, and Oates' sleeping-bags. Diaries, &., and geological specimens carried at Wilson's special request, will be found with us or on our sledge.

Sunday, March 18. — Today, lunch, we are 21 miles from the depôt. Ill fortune presses, but better may come. We have had more wind and drift from ahead yesterday; had to stop marching; wind N.W., force 4, temp. −35°. No human being could face it, and we are worn out *nearly*.

My right foot has gone, nearly all the toes — two days ago I was proud possessor of best feet. These are the steps of my downfall. Like an ass I mixed a small spoonful of curry powder with my melted pemmican — it gave me violent indigestion. I lay awake and in pain all night; woke and felt done on the march; foot went and I didn't know it. A very small measure of neglect and have a foot which is not pleasant to contemplate. Bowers takes first place in condition, but there is not much to choose after all. The others are still confident of getting through — or pretend to be — I don't know! We have the last *half* fill of oil in our primus and a very small quantity of spirit — this alone between us and thirst. The wind is fair for the moment, and that is perhaps a fact to help. The mileage would have seemed ridiculously small on our outward journey.

Monday, March 19. — Lunch. We camped with difficulty last night, and were dreadfully cold till after our supper of cold pemmican and biscuit and a half a pannikin of cocoa cooked over the spirit. Then, contrary to expectation, we got warm and all slept well. To-day we started in the usual dragging manner. Sledge dreadfully heavy. We are 15½ miles from the depôt and ought to get there in three days. What progress! We have two days' food but barely a day's fuel. All our feet are getting bad — Wilson's best, my right foot worst, left all right. There is no chance to nurse one's feet till we can get hot food into us. Amputation is the least I can hope for now, but will the trouble spread? That is the serious question. The weather doesn't give us a chance — the wind from N. to N.W. and −40° temp. to-day.

Wednesday, March 21. — Got within 11 miles of depôt Monday night; had to lay up all yesterday in severe blizzard. To-day forlorn hope, Wilson and Bowers going to depôt for fuel.

Thursday, March 22 *and* 23. — Blizzard bad as ever — Wilson and Bowers unable to start — to-morrow last chance — no fuel and only one or two of food left — must be near the end. Have decided it shall be natural — we shall march for the depôt with or without our effects and die in our tracks.

Thursday, March 29. — Since the 21st we have had a continuous gale from W.S.W. and S.W. We had fuel to make two cups of tea apiece and bare food for two days on the 21th. Every day we have been ready to start for our depôt *11 miles* away, but outside the door of the tent it remains a scene of whirling drift. I do not think we can hope for any better things now. We shall stick it out to the end, but we are getting weaker, of course, and the end cannot be far.

It seems a pity, but I do not think I can write more.

R. Scott.

For God's sake look after our people.

— *From Scott's Last Expedition, the Personal Journals of Captain Robert Falcon Scott, R.N., English (1868–1912).*

The Road to the West

LANGDON WARNER

THE WAYFARER who leaves Sianfu to take up the trail to the west will never forget that first fifteen miles outside the city wall. Every step was holy ground for, as the cart track threaded its way among the standing crops, there rose on every side of us mounds and earthen pyramids, grassed over but spared from the plough. They hide the tombs of early emperors and kings and concubines who made China when it was really the Middle Kingdom. So holy are they that no man to-day can dig near them and no one can guess what treasure they contain.

In mediaeval times, and earlier no doubt, they were largely looted of their gold and precious things, but the archaeologist of today knows how careless such looting was. The robber doubtless scorned pottery which nowadays would be set in a glass case as the pride of any museum; he pitched aside lovely bronzes, and he failed to find the little objects which mean so much to us in reconstructing the life of the past.

Before many years are gone, either the grave robbers will have ploughed their clumsy way through these mounds again, to recover for the foreign market what their predecessors left; or scientists, by special permit, will be allowed to come with their measuring tapes and their cameras to open in all reverence those kingly tombs by the river Wei. Then and not till then shall we know how royalty was buried and with what splendid companionship of delicate bronze and jade and of models of ceremonial ox carts and prancing war horses. To pass among these mounds, scattered as far as the eye could reach, big and little, near and far, was an experience in self-restraint for the digger.

Some fifteen miles of such temptation were slowly passed and we found ourselves on the sandy bank of the turgid river Wei, halting till one of the huge square scows should pole us across. There was a miniature fair by the river bank. Dozens of cooking booths had been set up and under them dough balls were bobbing in cauldrons of grease and gray macaroni strings were being draped about boards by filthy hands. Carters squatted about, noisily sucking at steaming bowls while their mules slept with drooping ears and dislocated haunches.

While we watched and spat out watermelon seeds, a scow shaped like a mammoth packing box was poled and chanteyed alongside the beach in most unsailorlike fashion. A gangway of rotting planks was set against the gunwales and our carts manhandled to the deck followed by the mules. It was obvious that mules may be divided into two schools of thought when it comes to ferry boats; one must be prodded from behind and dragged from the front and incited with hideous yells and cracking whips; the other sights the deck from afar off and charges as if it were a redoubt. To the latter sort men are attached as drags, on the ears and tail and such other outlying portions as seem safe. It is evidently hoped that in this way the mule can be stopped on deck before he plops into the water on the other side. As our party was made up of both types of mules it was a relief when they were all aboard and wedged between the carts. No accident happened except to one animal, which went through the deck of the scow and thrummed excitedly on the bottom till I feared he would open a seam in her planks. But he merely stayed in the attitude of one chinning himself on parallel bars till the other shore was reached and we could concentrate enough coolies on his ears and nose to lift him bodily through the hole and on deck again.

With a chant we sagged across the fast river, making two lengths down stream to one across, and each of us landed astraddle the sweating back of a coolie who dumped him on the dry sand and dashed back to prod the mules overboard and drag the laden carts down creaking planks. It was under the city wall of Sien Yang that we found ourselves, and a zigzag track leading up through the bastioned gate above our heads.

For all its bold front on the bluff above the rushing river the town itself was dejected enough. It did not need ten minutes in the streets to tell the reason, for everywhere the little clay opium pipes were for sale and in the shade of the temple enclosures lay bundles of rags which were men with their heads on bricks, forgetting in merciful sleep that they were doomed to be Chinese and in misery. One big tumble-down temple compound must have had twenty such forms, each one with a tattered quilt of patches over its bones and a brick on edge beneath its head. Beside every one was the telltale lamp and pin and pipe, with a smear of dried poppy juice on a chip or a piece of paper near by. Something sewn on the coat of one of these figures attracted Wang's attention and he turned him over with his foot. A white label attached to the man's breast, and set forth with an official seal, read that he was empowered to "detect and arrest all persons using or selling opium within the city limits." He was half awake but sodden with the drug, and never resented the intruding foot which rolled him over. Disgusted, we strolled to the city gate and watched the ferry boats, jammed with carts and mules and little laden donkeys as they grounded on the shoals below us and spilled their deck loads to splash ashore and up the bluff to the town.

Next morning, through a drizzle which became a steady hard rain, we plodded past five more miles of mounds, set even closer together than those on the other bank of the river, and associated with names as great and as legendary. Wet as we were, it was pleasant to reach shelter and to notice that the rain stopped with sundown. But at five o'clock next morning it was less pleasant when we partook of coffee and rolled up our beds to be stuffed in the carts.

Here was rain indeed, the sort of rain we had been dreading, rapidly sloughing the roads and damping through the cart hoods to the depths of our luggage. It was no time for walking, even in raincoats, and we stolidly set ourselves to sit in the stifling jostling dampness of the carts by the hour together. By noon, however, we knew other forms of discomfort. For we stuck fast, mired in the ruts hub deep, and the mules were down almost as often as they were up. Generally they scrambled to their feet soon enough, but when a wheeler went down and the mud was deep, the heavy shafts wedged him deeper till it took all our efforts to pry him loose.

The night closed in and we knew that we were on the road only because our mules were nearly belly deep in it. Stops grew more frequent till the poor animals had less and less pluck to pull their foundered feet out of the clinging stuff. No one knew how far we were from the village of Feng Zse where the inn lay, and none of us believed that the next mule who fell could be persuaded to rise. The next mule did fall, and an hour's work in the deluge failed to stir him. The paper round our candle lamp had long ago been reduced to pulp and the candle was doused by squalls. We toiled desperately in the pitchy black till Jayne and I, by means of threats and impassioned shouts, were able to dispatch a man with orders to plough on ahead till he came to the village and to come back as fast as possible with fresh mules and more men.

Such a message is all very well in China, but it is given with a sinking heart. One knows that the messenger will not hurry, that when he gets there he will think first of his own comfort and that his efforts to send help will be feeble at best. The man had been gone for three quarters of an hour when Jayne and I decided to make a sally to hurry things up. We were drenched, of course, and muddied to the thighs—nothing that lay ahead in the driving rain and dark could make us more miserable. In fact, it was all so thorough and complete a misfortune that it seemed inexpressibly humorous when I, walking delicately as Agag, stepped clear off the road and landed sprawling full length in mud of such consistency that Jayne had to present a leg to haul me up by and then we must stop while I scraped clay from between my glued-up fingers. We rocked and shouted and clung together, weak with laughter, thankful that the storm was so furious that our carters, standing ten feet off, could not hear us and know that we were mad.

The humour passed and we bent chuckling to the business of walking, expecting hours of inching progress. Barely ten minutes of floundering and slipping up a slope, and we found ourselves before a glimmer of light. Never was any smoky wick in a cracked saucer of rancid oil so welcome. Our carter had of course reached it long before and no doubt would soon have begun to think of the plight of his comrades, but we cut him short and sent three men back to the rescue while another went for mules. Half an hour later as we were scraping ourselves, preparatory to undressing and going to bed supperless, it proved that the men whom we had sent were not yet even started. Threats and promises in broken Chinese sent them on their way after they had finished their opium pipes, and in another two hours the supplies came up and a meal was cooked which we ate from our bedsteads set in a miry shed but removed from the sheets of water that were still falling. We did not know till next morning that the fifth carter was deserted by his friends and did not reach the inn, two hundred yards from the slough, till three o'clock. We had been fourteen hours and a half on the march and made fifteen English miles.

Anxious as we were to get ahead, it was almost a relief next morning to find that there could be no question of struggling on over semi-passable or quite impassable roads. The rain was falling as hard as ever, the tracks were deep rivers of mud, and the mules were not fit to move after their experience of the day before. The letters which were written during that long day of confinement in the shed gave people at home an idea that China was a sea of mud and that we were constantly marooned for days together on the few islands that were left. As a matter of fact, in eight months of travel we were only once more delayed by rain for a full day.

For days now we travelled high in the autumn weather, which never for a moment could be thought dull, no matter how tired or how homesick we might feel. It was a country of deep gorges and of terraced hills with buckwheat in flower all about us in pink bloom. When the road sank in a narrow trench we walked a hundred feet above it on a cliff path and could see miles ahead where the flat tongue on which we travelled sloped up a mountain's side. On either side of our plateau were chasms which split us off from other table lands where farms were and clustered hamlets; near by, but a good half day's scramble to visit. Clouds came at evening to gather in the west and in the east just where a reddened sun could make the most glorious play on their shoulders. The heat was gone except at noontime, when a man walking likes best to sweat and know that there is cool twilight ahead and a night beneath a blanket. One walked free and for very pleasure there, as seldom happens in China. Our feet had hardened till we thought no more of a long day than of a short one, and our legs and lungs were in tune with the weather.

The third day, outside Pinshow, where we had hopes of a find of sculpture, we stopped to examine the cave chapels of Suei Lien Tung which had been reported by Rockhill and others. But the crumbling sandstone had preserved only little holes in the cliff and we marched on disappointed. Three miles on, however, our hopes were again raised at the sight of modern temples built against the mountain side and entrances in the rock above and below.

We climbed the steps of the wooden temple and, leaning through the rock window into the cliff at the back, looked full into the huge visage of a seated Buddha which we guessed to be sixty feet high. On either side stood his attendants erect, and about their heads circled a thousand pigeons which nested in the crannies of their hair and crowns. The central fat face itself and the gross form showed no hint of an elder grandeur. Pious restorations had weakened every clean-cut line and made heavy the folds of antique drapery. But behind the head, untouched since the 9th Century, ran the concentric circles of the flat halo. The inner ring was of crisp lotus petals, the next of vine tendrils, then a circlet of little Buddhas seated in bliss, and beyond angels floated with swinging scarfs. This halo was proof positive of antiquity, but we searched in vain for an inscribed stone which should carry an exact date. Cut in the rock wall of the south side in the chapel we saw niches in which were left some worn remains of trinities of the same period. The three figures of each group stood apart, each on a branch of a high lotus joined below like the branches of a candlestick. They were graceful enough, even in their decay, and they seemed like the sculptor's sketch still to be finished from the stone.

But I would have given much to see them when every jewel on the roughened headdresses was cut and coloured and when the drapery was scarlet and the holy faces gold. In those days, in the twilight, brocaded monks made stately circumambulation behind the huge figure through the little tunnel against the cave wall and out again, with candles and with torches and song to the high altar below the giant knees. No doubt paintings and tapestries hung from the walls and lights were drawn high on pulleys to cast their rays mysteriously on a benign face above. But now pigeons slanted about, and their droppings gave out an acrid lonely stench as they fouled the garments and the hands that were raised in blessing. It was China again, the China that we were growing familiar with, not the long-ago country that we were in search of.

Before we left we climbed profanely high on the Buddha's lap and saw how well the ancients had understood to deceive us. From that height the standing Bodhisattva which was on each side of the seated figure, and of precisely the same height, was seen to be absurdly short from the knees down to the feet. But from a proper and respectful position on the floor of the chapel the upper body was foreshortened till it seemed in scale with the legs. This was no accident; the sculptors had deliberately met the problem of a distorted vision in a workmanlike manner. One would give much to know when this technique was developed and whether it came with the religion from India brought by the priestly artists and teachers.

—*From The Long Old Road in China, by Langdon Warner, American (1881–).*

On the Way to Myself

MARCUS EHRENPREIS

EVERY TIME I am bound East I have the sensation of journeying towards myself. The feeling is at bottom a humble one, quite unlike the usual self-sufficiency of the western tourist who proceeds condescendingly to the backward Orient to behold things exotic. It arises from the feeling that the East, where least Europeanized, has preserved more that is intrinsically human than the West and stands closer to the sources of our being.

I make my way through Eastern cities, bazaars, mosques, along highways and across deserts and, unwittingly and unresistingly, become one with a strange new atmosphere. The atmosphere of home evaporates at an increasing rate and recedes into the remote and fanciful. The significance that attaches to the habitual daily doings dwindles to nothing. Our sensations, excitements, and struggles decrease in importance; our certainties seem more and more doubtful. I have a revelation of something grander and profounder. The sky is higher, the air clearer, and the range of vision greater. I am encompassed by the quietude of profound loneliness. I become more distinctly aware of myself, as the walker through empty chambers hears the reverberations of each footstep. I apprehend, so to speak, the beating of my own soul. To give oneself up willingly and unreservedly to such a new mood is to make, unexpectedly, a valuable discovery: one finds oneself. One sometimes has a sensation as of passing before a large mirror and being amazed to observe that one is wearing one's clothes inside out. Here, more than when at home, I am oppressed by the inescapable feeling that we Westerners in most instances take hold of life the wrong way, we grasp it from without instead of seizing it from within. We occupy ourselves with all that concerns the outer conditions of life (as well as with much that has nothing to do with it) but totally neglect our selves, our inner being. We listen to all kinds of voices, true and false, but remain deaf to the call of our own inner voice. Quiet intercourse with ourselves is all-important, but for that we never have time. Our real or imagined interests, needs, duties and responsibilities seem to encoat us, but we rarely or never heed our paramount obligation, that to our own nature. As Tagore says of the Westerners: "With much mending of nets they have no time to fish." We convert means into final ends, rights into duties. We are slaves under our liberties.

All of this becomes clearer while travelling in the Orient than at home. In this backward Orient one feels closer to the truth and farther from illusion. In this world of simple realities one learns to think essentially, not only formally, and the distinction between kernel and shell issues more sharply.

With every day that passes my humility and shame increase. The muezzin calling to prayer, the black-bearded and dome-browed picture post-card vender, prompt me to self-searching. My pride in the consciousness of culture suffers a jolt. Whatever I encounter on my way seems to say to me: You Westerners constitute but half of civilized mankind, and not precisely the better half. The Oriental seems not to cherish an exaggerated respect for us Europeans. If we, perhaps, can claim a greater measure of civilization, those about me here have more culture. I recall the enlightened words of Empress Elizabeth to Christomanos, her Greek reader: "I feel thoroughly at home in Cairo; even in the thickest pack of donkeys and carriers I am less hemmed in than at a court ball and am almost as happy as in a forest. . . . Culture resides also in the Arabian desert that has not yet been penetrated by civilization. The throttling of culture connotes civilization. The latter makes its home in the West. It is a misplacement and counterfeit of the aim of life. Civilization is trolley cars, culture is the beautiful, free forest. Civilization is to be well read, culture means thinking. Civilization calls to us, singly and collectively, as if we were fledglings; culture is intrinsic to each individual, a heritage from the entire past."

Facing these Orientals, untouched as they are by civilization, the artificiality and unnaturalness of our western civilization becomes unusually apparent. Here I understand well the utterance of Ecclesiastes as the Oriental's condemnation of the artificiality of the West: "Lo, this only have I found, that God hath made man simple; but they have sought out many inventions." We go through life as if masked, clad in alien garb and strait-jacketed. For the greater part of the day we are members of professions, exports, partisans, society folk, but only rarely human beings without special category. The ego vanishes behind the changing make-up. Man, whom God "made simple," has disfigured himself with his "many inventions" to the point of being unrecognizable. In the East I meet, with increasing frequency, human beings without inventions, without fancy dress, without labels. A life of amusement and social gaiety, in the European sense, is unknown to them. Their being is not centred in the chosen profession as with us. They do not live to work. A minimum of toil suffices to satisfy their incredibly small needs. The Oriental hardly knows poverty in our sense because he is fully contented. This contentment is the Oriental's great virtue, perhaps his great fortune as well. Even in this day he needs naught — like the patriarch Jacob — but, literally, "bread to eat and clothes to clothe himself in." He has plenty of time in which to sit at ease, to devote himself to his family, to withdraw within himself, to meditate on life's puzzles or to listen to words of eternal truth. He belongs to himself! Here the lowest wretch seems to me to be less of a slave than the freest of Westerners. In his book on India, Waldemar Bonsels tells of buying from a pedlar near Mangalore a native shawl to hang in his room. "This little transaction yielded sufficient to enable the man to retire to privacy for several weeks." I meet like characters here. The ascetic fruit-vender in front of my hotel at Mount Carmel spends most of his day in contemplation. He begins down in Haifa with prayers and reading the Koran. After that he brings his basket of fruits to us "unbelievers." This modest commerce is but an interlude in his mental occupation. Towards evening he returns to the mosque with its cool and elevated atmosphere. In his own way this poor hawker is a nobleman, intellectual and inspired. Whatever is coarse and brutal seems foreign to him. His mind is pure and uncomplicated, he lives at peace with himself and with his God. In my intercourse with this folk I sometimes find it difficult to maintain faith in my western superiority, and I desire to possess as my own something of their spiritual reserve and poise.

I carry with me the Bible and the Koran, and sometimes also Lâo-Tsze's *Tao-Teh King;* I have no use for other books. Here the Bible becomes newly intelligible to me, here the holy words become imbued with living life. This sky and this air gave form and colour to the scriptural word; in this landscape its flaming pathos radiated. Besides, the Bible is the best guide to the East, it leads me to a better understanding of what is new and unfamiliar here. The sacred scrolls of old reveal to me the same spiritual atmosphere, the same common chords of life, the same primitive earthliness, and the same immediate feeling of God's nearness that pervade this place today. Not much has changed since primeval times, essentially all is as it has been. The process of Europeanization has touched only the outer edge. The prospect, the people, and their habits remain virtually what they were. Wherever I turn I seem to meet animated quotations from the holy texts. The sacred books of the great religions reveal themselves in an aspect that generally receives little attention. I come to perceive the high degree in which these religious writings are books of the Orient, unsurpassed and by no means antiquated expressions of Orientalism as a way of life. Breathing this air of Asia we live in the world of the Bible; the sun glows hotly above our heads, the expanse reaching into the infinite creates something like a physical perception of God's presence. The world of our childhood recurs to consciousness. Are we not once more in the nursery? These primitive, introspective people are our first acquaintances; these place names are the first we heard of; these heights, deserts, valleys and sacred lakes awoke our childish imaginations and near them we dreamt our azure dreams. Is this not, in a sense, our home, the spiritual home of all of us? Have we not all refreshed ourselves at the fountains of the East?

The soil whereon I stand is sacred to all mankind. Age-old memories are aglow amidst the weathered ruins. A silence that is almost unreal engulfs me. The absoluteness of the quiet wakes me as the halting of a train rouses one in a railway carriage. "*La musique ne commence que là, où le bruit a cessé,*" says Claudel. The lulling beats of the engine stop and I wake to consciousness of myself. It is a different sky that arches over me than the pale, cold heaven that is pinched between grey walls at home. This heaven is the one of the Old Testament, the one "declaring the glory of God," and this is the firmament which "showeth His handiwork." The people of the Bible surround me here, well-known personalities which, seemingly, emerge living from the pages of Genesis.

The approach of evening finds me seated on a lonely hill near Tiberias, my eyes drinking in the divine beauty of Gennesaret. The landscape is covered with an everlasting peace, the air charged with eternal secrets. Shepherds and shepherdesses are on their way home with their flocks and I affect to recognize Jacob and Rachel amongst them. An aged Moslem is sitting alone on a rock, gazing into the infinite. It may be that he experiences God in this silently articulate Nature as the Psalmist once experienced Him: "There is no speech nor language, no sound to be heard, and yet their line is gone out through all the earth and their words to the end of the world." A reverent mood envelops us and each for himself turns to his devotions. Imperceptibly man and landscape have coalesced, and the meekness of the Psalmist comes over us: "When I consider the heavens, the work of thy hands, the moon and the stars, which thou hast ordained; What is man, that thou art mindful of him?"

Wonderingly I observe the old Moslem seated nearby, his soul awake, lost in the endless. Is he an interpreter of the Koran, a seer, a saint? Perhaps he cultivates figs as did Amos of Tekoa, or sells Oriental rugs one day a week at the European hotels. His emaciated body, his threadbare clothes, his fiery eyes, his whole being, cry to me that this man has but one important concern in life: his soul. Everything about him seems to confirm Tagore's "I am more than I appear to be." And I surmise that this Moslem accepts the profound and literal reality of the early Christian (thus truly Oriental) word: "For what is a man profited, if he shall gain the whole world, and lose his own soul?"

—*From The Soul of the East, by Marcus Ehrenpreis, Swedish (1869–), translated from the Swedish by Alfhild Huebsch.*

PART NINE

Social Satire

~ ⚙ ~

WHILE SCIENCE CONTRIBUTES its explanations of nature, the humanities offer their appraisals of mankind. From the dawn of civilization the human mind has turned inward upon itself. Man has found man to be his chief source of amusement and object of affection. His broadest smiles and hottest anger have been directed upon himself. But even in the warmest praise bestowed upon a social institution, there is almost sure to lurk some adverse criticism, either of a rival institution or of weakness within the very establishment which is commended. Thus when the literary mind turns to social criticism, it is extremely likely to lean also to satire. Indeed the entire literature of the criticism of manners falls, broadly speaking, under the general term satire. Man looking upon himself is prone either to smile at his follies or to storm against his crimes. A later and less extensive section of this book deals with literary pictures of the happy life. Many of these are brief, resembling vignettes. It would seem that unbroken sunshine is the exception in the human climate; and literature as a rule reports the presence of some clouds in the sky.

What may fairly be called satire exists, then, wherever mankind has reached a reasonably high level of civilization. Looking about us, we find selfishness, vanity, stupidity, and incompetence to exist, if not to reign, on every hand. The objects of satire are almost monotonously the same, since human nature seems never to outgrow its inveterate defects. And the more intelligent we become, the more we are likely to perceive our shortcomings. It is therefore natural that the early Chinese, unsurpassed in moral discernment, social intelligence, and a traditional urbanity, should have developed a poetical literature rich in social and political comment. Even from a few selections such as those supplied here, it is clear that the chief trends in Western satire were paralleled or anticipated in the Orient. The Chinese prove equally skilled in a gracious and polite satire and in a vigorous and vituperative invective, in a word, equally suave or indignant. The field of satire stretches so broadly that in the present section the selections bear definitely upon the general domain of social satire or criticism of manners, while the section thereafter deals with the limited but extremely vital domain of political satire. Although the two are not entirely separable, they stand sufficiently apart to be distinguishable.

Many of the satirical poems in Chinese are almost wholly intelligible to a Western reader. Nevertheless the contours of the subject first become clear where the literature as a whole is more thoroughly known to us. The ancient Mediterranean culture laid the foundations upon which the Western mind has ever since been building. Most of the satirical poetry of Greece has been lost to us, due in part to the shadows which rapidly fall upon local allusions, always a bar to the universal significance of a literature of manners. The best of Greek satire is contained in the astringent comedies of Aristophanes, from which specimens will later be examined. In the later Greek world a gentle criticism of manners arose, best exhibited in the delightfuly urbane picture of idle, pleasure-loving women in the idyls of Theocritus. Here lay the basis for the urbane type of Latin satire. The Roman literature is more fully preserved for us than the Greek, and was even more addicted than the imaginative Greek to satirical subject matter. In Rome for the first time satire was developed as a specific form of poetry. As defined by the comic dramatist, Terence, the criticism of life flows naturally in two channels. There is the light satire attuned to amusement and good nature, and the savage satire attuned to anger and indignation. Horace practiced both forms, but the more genial form he used both more often and more successfully. His three "Satires" here given are all of the urbane type. The only deeply serious poem of his which we have produced is one of his "Odes." The master of the graver Roman satire is Juvenal, whose slashing language and moral wrath have proved an inspiration for nearly a score of centuries. The satirical poems of Martial, Petronius, Catullus and others seem of minor weight beside Juvenal's mighty lines; and Horace and Juvenal have therefore been deemed largely sufficient to represent here the scope and essence of the Latin art.

The most striking and characteristic forms of medieval satire spring directly from the Christian consciousness. A few medieval poets knew Juvenal, and such lines as the speech of Sordello, in Dante's *Divine Comedy,* still retain the essentials of classical invective. This passage will be included under our heading of political satire. With the majority of medieval authors, however, such genuine classicism is unknown. The medieval mind is more complex, more ironic and more paradoxical than the ancient. The satirical temper of the former is colored by an heightened consciousness of sin and by the presence of an evasiveness almost inevitable in a society which diligently preaches as its highest ideal an austere morality beyond the possibility of general practice. Medieval satire flourishes especially on the strength of the ascetic code. The two favorite butts of the satirist are the sensual woman and the hypocritical priest, the first being the fiction of an ascetic priesthood, the second, the rejoinder of an irrepressible laity.

This paradoxical medieval mind is more disposed than the classical both to assault evil and to discover it a jest; both to condemn and to pity. After Aristophanes the classical world perforce sobered down; and both Aristotle and Horace, strange to say, affected to deplore laughter. The people of the Middle Ages, however, are ever willing to laugh, even at the saints and devils themselves. They love strange antitheses. There is a "gothic wildness" in both medieval satire and humor never found in the more logical Romans.

Our selections from the Middle Ages exhibit these ambiguities. Villon's *Lesser Testament* contains topical allusions that are shadowy to the most ingenious scholars, yet its general intention is clear enough, and the work has been imitated even in our own times. Villon's entire poem is both macabre and ironical. Cleverness, gaiety and animal spirits keep this insatiable jester from being entirely sober even in the face of death. Again, the passage by Jean de Meung selected as representative of the satirical part of *The Romance of the Rose* shows another author caught in typical contradictions: the more genial side of his character leads him to honor both Nature and her masterpiece, woman, while the other and more orthodox side induces him to distrust both.

The contradictions in the French satirists are paralleled in the English. Chaucer's most brilliant passage, his Prologue to the *Canterbury Tales,* is singularly rich in irony, affecting to praise such characters as the Monk, the Friar, and the Prioress, when in fact it condemns them. Finally, William Langland's picture of persons personifying the seven deadly sins is largely serious; yet the ambiguity of the medieval mind does not desert even this most ardent of reformers. Not only does he hate his sinners. He also loves them; first, because a good Christian should both love and pity his enemies; and second, because he simply cannot resist finding them amusing. Villon, Jean de Meung, Chaucer and Langland share alike in the medieval consciousness, which is largely a riddle of its own.

National or racial differences are, naturally, nowhere more apparent than in the literature of manners. From the Renaissance in the sixteenth century to the Romantic Age at the beginning of the nineteenth, French satire is at its best in the polite, urbane and Horatian mood. It may be seen to much advantage in the plays of Molière. It is here happily represented in the poetry of La Fontaine. Although his fables are for the most part stories reaching back to the ancient Orient, his spirit is of the essence of France. The satirical spirit of Russian, Spanish and German literature proves on the whole more serious, more moral and more Juvenalian. Conduct is viewed less as a matter of manners or etiquette and more as a grave, ethical affair. Poems from the Spanish of Quevedo and from the Portuguese of Camoëns indicate the traditional severity and pitiless realism with which intelligent men of the Iberian world have long viewed their society. Mercurial as was Heine's temperament, he was no easy critic of German society. And the poem here given from the Russian of Lermontov illustrates the remorseless character of sociological criticism common in Russia, where men have turned with unexampled savagery upon the roots of an entire civilization.

The French Revolution and the romantic movement in literature, two intimate allies, deeply affected the course of modern French satire. Most notable in nineteenth-century France is the return to Juvenalian satire in Hugo and the emergence of a largely new, though somewhat medieval, satire in Baudelaire. Hugo's most typical effusions, to be represented in the section on political satire, are his *Chatiments,* wherein he taunts "Napoleon the Little" with a vituperative power scarcely heard since Dante and Juvenal, both of whom, as the reader will note, Hugo invokes as his masters. Baudelaire deals in Christian ambiguities. Although he has little but scorn for the upper classes, he looks with a great pity and almost a great love upon the social outcasts. His poems on the underworld of Paris are compounded of morbidity and nobility. However interpreted, they rank among the most poetic arraignments that man has ever made of man.

The long course of satirical or "manners painting" verse in England is hardly to be rivalled in the Western World. Some of this verse is, of course, political; the larger part is social. Among the notable medieval satirists are not only Chaucer and Langland but such poets as William Dunbar and John Skelton. Space forbids us adequately to represent the Elizabethan satire, which culminates in the work of Donne and in Shakespeare's *King Lear.* Sir Walter Raleigh's remarkable poem, *The Lie,* gives, however, in epitome the harsher tones of the Elizabethan spirit. Space also prevents quotation from what is today one of the most commonly neglected of English masterpieces, though the object of much imitation from Swift to W. H. Auden, namely *Hudibras,* Samuel Butler's humorous taunt at the Puritans. The eighteenth century gives us a group of masterful satirists largely neo-classical in their art. Thus we shall see Alexander Pope in his *Epistle to Dr. Arbutnot* successfully emulating the first satire of the second book of Horace, and John Gay in his *Ride to Exeter* following in the footsteps of the fifth satire of Horace's first book. Swift has his own sardonic interpretation of the scenes of the talkative women so charitably presented by Theocritus. Later we shall find Browning in his *Up at a Villa – Down in the City* following the familiar track of Horace's country and city mice (*Satires,* II, 6). The Revolutionary period yields the incomparable glint of the satires of Burns, the superb scope of Byron (recapitulating Aristophanes, Horace, Quevedo and La Fontaine) and the tragic earnestness of William Blake. Romanticism, however, in time dulled the edge of verse satire in England. The satires too often become heavy and inartful. Tennyson, Arnold and Swinburne in their most typical verse do not excel in humor. The British genius found a happier outlet in the operas of W. S. Gilbert. But in our own day British literary satire has emphatically revived.

Social satire in both verse and prose has already enjoyed in the United States a brilliant, if relatively brief, career. This satirical literature is one of the most enviable monuments of our traditional love for freedom of speech and of the press. We have by no means neglected our privilege of self criticism. Evidence is here afforded by Philip Freneau's most legitimate quarrels with the New England Puritans, by Emerson's profound arraignment of our materialistic civilization, by the sharp anti-clerical wit of the minor poet, William Carlos Williams, and by Carl Sandburg's discerning but tolerant criticism of our national psychology, which he knows so well. In Emerson we find an heir to the savage anger of Juvenal, though Emerson has a far larger grasp of life than did the Latin poet. Juvenal seems almost provincial beside the New England sage, to whom Confucius was as familiar a companion as Shakespeare. The three other poets exhibit a democratic good humor which, one likes to feel, is the chief flower of American manners, just as an aristocratic suavity flowered best in La Fontaine's France and the unfettered imagination in the Athens of Aristophanes.

Satire on Paying Calls

When I was young, throughout the hot season
There were no carriages driving about the roads,
People shut their doors and lay down in the cool:
Or if they went out, it was not to pay calls.
Nowadays – ill-bred, ignorant fellows,
When they feel the heat, make for a friend's house.
The unfortunate host, when he hears some-one coming
Scowls and frowns, but can think of no escape.
"There's nothing for it but to rise and go to the door,"
And in his comfortable seat he groans and sighs.

The conversation does not end quickly:
Prattling and babbling, what a lot he says!
Only when one is almost dead with fatigue

He asks at last if one isn't finding him tiring.
(One's arm is almost in half with continual fanning:
The sweat is pouring down one's neck in streams.)
Do not say that this is a small matter:
I consider the practice a blot on our social life.
I therefore caution all wise men
That August visitors should not be admitted.

—From the Chinese of Ch'eng Hsiao (c. 250), translated by Arthur Waley.

Woman

How sad it is to be a woman!
Nothing on earth is held so cheap,
Boys stand leaning at the door
Like Gods fallen out of Heaven.
Their hearts brave the Four Oceans,
The wind and dust of a thousand miles.
No one is glad when a girl is born:
By *her* the family sets no store.
When she grows up, she hides in her room
Afraid to look a man in the face.
No one cries when she leaves her home—
Sudden as clouds when the rain stops.
She bows her head and composes her face,
Her teeth are pressed on her red lips:
She bows and kneels countless times.
She must humble herself even to the servants.
His love is distant as the stars in Heaven,
Yet the sunflower bends toward the sun.
Their hearts more sundered than water and fire—
A hundred evils are heaped upon her.
Her face will follow the years' changes:
Her lord will find new pleasures.
They that were once like substance and shadow
Are now as far as Hu from Ch'in.[1]
Yet Hu and Ch'in shall sooner meet
Than they whose parting is like Ts'an and Ch'en.[2]

—From the Chinese of Fu Hsüan (d. 278), translated by Arthur Waley.

[1] Two lands. [2] Two stars.

The Syracusan Women

Characters

Gorgo. Praxinoa. Old Woman. First stranger. Second stranger.

GORGO

Is Praxinoa at home?

PRAXINOA

Dear Gorgo, yes!
How late you are! I wonder, I confess,
That you are come e'en now. Quick, brazen-front!

(*To Eunoa*)

A chair there—stupid! lay a cushion on't.

GORGO

Thank you, 'tis very well.

PRAXINOA

Be seated, pray.

GORGO

My untamed soul! what dangers on the way!
I scarce could get alive here: such a crowd!
So many soldiers with their trappings proud!
A weary way it is—you live so far.

PRAXINOA

The man, whose wits with sense are aye at war,
Bought at the world's end but to vex my soul
This dwelling—no! this serpent's lurking-hole,
That we might not be neighbours: plague o' my life,
His only joy is quarrelling and strife.

GORGO

Talk not of Dinon so before the boy;
See! how he looks at you!

PRAXINOA

My honey-joy!
My pretty dear! 'tis not papa I mean.

GORGO

Handsome papa! the urchin, by the Queen,
Knows every word you say.

PRAXINOA

The other day—
For this in sooth of every thing we say—
The mighty man of inches went and brought me
Salt—which for nitre and ceruse he bought me.

GORGO

And so my Diocleide—a brother wit,
A money-waster, lately thought it fit
To give seven goodly drachms for fleeces five—
Mere rottenness, but dog's hair, as I live,

The plucking of old scrips — a work to make.
But come, your cloak and gold-claspt kirtle take,
And let us speed to Ptolemy's rich hall,
To see the fine Adonian festival.
The queen will make the show most grand, I hear.

PRAXINOA

All things most rich in rich men's halls appear.
To those who have not seen it, one can tell
What one has seen.

GORGO

'Tis time to go — 'tis well
For those who all the year have holidays.

PRAXINOA

Eunoa! my cloak — you wanton! quickly raise,
And place it near me — cats would softly sleep;
And haste for water — how the jade does creep!
The water first — now, did you ever see?
She brings the cloak first: well, then, give it me.
You wasteful slut, not too much — pour the water!
What! have you wet my kirtle! sorrow's daughter!
Stop, now: I'm washed — gods love me: where's the key
Of the great chest? be quick, and bring it me.

GORGO

The gold-claspt and full-skirted gown you wear
Becomes you vastly. May I ask, my dear,
How much in all it cost you from the loom?

PRAXINOA

Don't mention it: I'm sure I did consume
More than two minae on it: and I held on
The work with heart and soul.

GORGO

Bur when done, well done!

PRAXINOA

Truly — you're right. My parasol and cloak —
Arrange it nicely. Cry until you choke,
I will not take you, child; horse bites, you know —
Boo! Boo! no use to have you lame. Let's go.
Play with the little man, my Phrygian! call
The hound in; lock the street-door of the hall.

Gods, what a crowd: they swarm like ants, how ever
Shall we work through them with our best endeavour?
From when thy sire was numbered with the blest,
Many fine things, and this among the rest,
Hast thou done, Ptolemy! No villain walks
The street, and picks your pocket, as he talks
On some pretence with you, in Egypt's fashion:
As once complete in every style, mood, passion,
Resembling one another, rogues in grain,
Would mock and pilfer, and then — mock again.
What will become of us, dear Gorgo? see!
The king's war-horses! Pray, don't trample me,
Good sir! the bay-horse rears! how fierce a one!
Eunoa, stand from him: dog-heart! won't you run?
He'll kill his leader! what a thought of joy,
That safe at home remains my precious boy!

GORGO

Courage! they're as they were — and we behind them.

PRAXINOA

I nearly lost my senses; now I find them,
And am myself again. Two things I hold
In mortal dread — a horse and serpent cold,
And have done from a child. Let us keep moving;
O! what a crowd is on us, bustling, shoving.

GORGO

(*To an old woman*)

Good mother, from the palace?

OLD WOMAN

Yes, my dear.

GORGO

Is it an easy thing to get in there?

OLD WOMAN

Th' Achaeans got to Troy, there's no denying;
All things are done, as they did that — by trying.

GORGO

The old dame spoke oracles.

PRAXINOA

Our sex, as you know,
Know all things — e'en how Zeus espoused his Juno.

GORGO

Praxinoa! what a crowd about the gates!

PRAXINOA

Immense! your hand; and, Eunoa, hold your mate's;
Do you keep close, I say, to Eutychis,
And close to us, for fear the way you miss.
Let us, together all, the entrance gain:
Ah me! my summer-cloak is rent in twain.
Pray, spare my cloak, heaven bless you, gentleman!

STRANGER

'Tis not with me — I will do what I can.

PRAXINOA

The crowd, like pigs, are thrusting.

STRANGER

Cheer thy heart,
'Tis well with us.

PRAXINOA

And for your friendly part,
This year and ever be it well with you!
A kind and tender man as e'er I knew.
See! how our Eunoa is prest — push through —
Well done! all in — as the gay bridegroom cried,
And turned the key upon himself and bride.

GORGO

What rich, rare tapestry! Look, and you'll swear
The fingers of the goddesses were here.

PRAXINOA

August Athene! who such work could do?
Who spun the tissue, who the figures drew?
How life-like are they, and they seem to move!
True living shapes they are, and not inwove!
How wise is man! and there he lies outspread
In all his beauty on his silver bed,
Thrice-loved Adonis! in his youth's fresh glow,
Loved even where the rueful stream doth flow.

A STRANGER

Cease ye like turtles idly thus to babble:
They'll torture all of us with brogue and gabble.

GORGO

Who's you? what's it to you our tongues we use?
Rule your own roost, not dames of Syracuse.
And this too know we were in times foregone
Corinthians, sir, as was Bellerophon.
We speak the good old Greek of Pelop's isle:
Dorians, I guess, may Dorian talk the while.

PRAXINOA

Nymph! grant we be at none but one man's pleasure;
A rush for you — don't wipe my empty measure.

GORGO

Praxinoa, hush! behold the Argive's daughter,
The girl who sings as though the Muses taught her,
That won the prize for singing Sperchis' ditty,
Prepares to chaunt Adonis; something pretty
I'm sure she'll sing: with motion, voice, and eye,
She now preludes — how sweetly, gracefully! . . .

— *From the Greek of Theocritus (c. 316–c. 260 B.C.), translated by J. M. Chapman.*

Journey to Brundusium

'Twas a long journey lay before us,
When I and honest Heliodorus,
(Who far in point of rhetoric
Surpasses every living Greek,)
Each leaving our respective home
Together sallied forth from Rome.
First at Aricia we alight,
And there refresh and pass the night,
Our entertainment rather coarse
Than sumptuous, but I've met with worse.
Thence o'er the causeway soft and fair
To Appii-forum we repair.
But as this road is well supplied
(Temptation strong!) on either side
With inns commodious, snug, and warm,
We split the journey, and perform
In two days' time what's often done
By brisker travellers in one.
Here rather choosing not to sup
Than with bad water mix my cup,
After a warm debate in spite
Of a provoking appetite,
I sturdily resolved at last
To balk it, and pronounce a fast,
And in a moody humour wait,
While my less dainty comrades bait.
Now o'er the spangled hemisphere
Diffused the starry train appear,
When there arose a desperate brawl;
The slaves and bargemen, one and all,
Rending their throats (have mercy on us!)
As if they were resolved to stun us.

"Steer the barge this way to the shore!
I tell you we'll admit no more!
Plague! will you never be content?"
Thus a whole hour at least is spent,
While they receive the several fares,
And kick the mule into his gears.
Happy, these difficulties past,
Could we have fallen asleep at last!
But, what with humming, croaking, biting,
Gnats, frogs, and all their plagues uniting,
These tuneful natives of the lake
Conspired to keep us broad awake.
Besides, to make the concert full,
Two maudlin wights, exceeding dull,
The bargeman and a passenger,
Each in his turn, essayed an air
In honour of his absent fair.
At length the passenger, oppressed
With wine, left off, and snored the rest.
The weary bargeman too gave o'er,
And hearing his companion snore,
Seized the occasion, fixed the barge,
Turned out his mule to graze at large,
And slept forgetful of his charge.
And now the sun o'er eastern hill,
Discovered that our barge stood still;
When one, whose anger vexed him sore,
With malice fraught, leaps quick on shore,
Plucks up a stake, with many a thwack
Assails the mule and driver's back.

. . . . .

With smiles the rising morn we greet,
At Sinuessa pleased to meet
With Plotius, Varius, and the bard
Whom Mantua first with wonder heard.
The world no purer spirits knows;
For none my heart more warmly glows.
Oh! what embraces we bestowed,
And with what joy our breasts o'erflowed!
Sure while my sense is sound and clear,
Long as I live, I shall prefer
A gay, good-natured, easy friend,
To every blessing Heaven can send.
At a small village, the next night,
Near the Volturnus we alight;
Where, as employed on state affairs,
We were supplied by the purveyors
Frankly at once, and without hire,
With food for man and horse, and fire.
Capua next day betimes we reach,
Where Virgil and myself, who each
Laboured with different maladies,
His such a stomach, — mine such eyes, —
As would not bear strong exercise,
In drowsy mood to sleep resort;
Maecenas to the tennis-court.
Next at Cocceius's farm we're treated,
Above the Caudian tavern seated;
His kind and hospitable board
With choice of wholesome food was stored.

. . . . .

To Beneventum next we steer;
Where our good host, by over care
In roasting thrushes lean as mice,
Had almost fallen a sacrifice.
The kitchen soon was all on fire,
And to the roof the flames aspire.
There might you see each man and master
Striving, amidst this sad disaster,
To save the supper. Then they came
With speed enough to quench the flame.
From hence we first at distance see
The Apulian hills, well known to me,
Parched by the sultry western blast;
And which we never should have passed,
Had not Trivicus by the way
Received us at the close of day.
But each was forced at entering here
To pay the tribute of a tear,
No more of smoke than fire was seen;
The hearth was piled with logs so green.
From hence in chaises we were carried
Miles twenty-four, and gladly tarried
At a small town, whose name my verse
(So barbarous is it) can't rehearse.
Know it you may by many a sign,
Water is dearer far than wine.
There bread is deemed such dainty fare,
That every prudent traveller
His wallet loads with many a crust;
For at Canusium, you might just
As well attempt to gnaw a stone
As think to get a morsel down.

. . . . .

At Rubi we arrived that day,
Well jaded by the length of way,
And sure poor mortals ne'er were wetter.
Next day no weather could be better;
No roads so bad; we scarce could crawl
Along to fishy Barium's wall.
The Egnations next, who by the rules
Of common sense are knaves or fools,
Made all our sides with laughter heave,
Since we with them must needs believe
That incense in their temples burns,
And without fire to ashes turns.
To circumcision's bigots tell
Such tales! for me, I know full well,
That in high heaven, unmoved by care,

The gods eternal quiet share;
Nor can I deem their spleen the cause
Why fickle Nature breaks her laws.
Brundusium last we reach; and there
Stop short the muse and traveller.

—*From the Latin of Horace (65–8 B.C.), translated by William Cowper (abridged).*

~ ۞ ~

The Bold Satirist

Horace. There are, to whom too poignant I appear;
Beyond the laws of satire too severe.
My lines are weak, unsinewed, others say,
'A man might spin a thousand such a day.'
What shall I do, Trebatius?
Trebatius. Write no more.
H. What! Give the dear delight of scribbling o'er?
T. Yes.
H. Let me die but your advice were best.
But sir, I cannot sleep; I cannot rest.
T. Swim o'er the Tiber, if you want to sleep,
Or the dull sense in t'other bottle steep:
If you must write, to Caesar tune your lays,
Indulge your genius, and your fortune raise.
H. Oh! were I equal to the glorious theme,
Bristled with spears his iron war should gleam:
A thousand darts should pierce the hardy Gaul,
And from his horse the wounded Parthian fall.
T. Then give his peaceful virtues forth to fame;
His fortitude and justice be your theme.
H. Yes. I will hold the daring theme in view,
Perhaps hereafter your advice pursue.
But Caesar never will your Flaccus hear;
A languid panegyric hurts his ear.
Too strongly guarded from the poet's lays,
He spurns the flatterer, and his saucy praise.
T. Better even this, than cruelly defame,
And point buffoons and villains out by name,
Sure to be hated even by those you spare,
Who hate in just proportion as they fear.
H. Tell me, Trebatius, are not all mankind
To different pleasures, different whims inclined?
Millonius dances when his head grows light,
And the dim lamp shines double to his sight.
The twin-born brothers in their sports divide;
Pollux loves boxing; Castor joys to ride.
Indulge me then in this my sole delight,
Like great and good Lucilius let me write.
Behold him frankly to his book impart,
As to a friend, the secrets of his heart:
To write was all his aim; too heedless bard,
And well or ill, unworthy his regard.
Hence the old man stands open to your view,
Though with a careless hand the piece he drew.

. . . . .

Let this digression, as it may, succeed—
No honest man shall by my satire bleed;
It guards me like a sword, and safe it lies
Within the sheath, till villains round me rise.
Dread king and father of the mortal race,
Behold me, harmless bard, how fond of peace!
And may all kinds of mischief-making steel
In rust, eternal rust, thy vengeance feel!
But who provokes me, or attacks my fame,
"Better not touch me, friend," I loud exclaim;
His eyes shall weep the folly of his tongue,
By laughing crowds in rueful ballad sung.
Th' informer Cervius threatens with the laws;
Turius your judge, you surely lose your cause:
Are you the object of Canidia's hate?
Drugs, poisons, incantations, are your fate:
For powerful Nature to her creatures shows
With various arms to terrify their foes.
The wolf with teeth, the bull with horns can fight;
Whence, but from instinct, and an inward light?
His long-lived mother trust to Scaeva's care—
T. No deed of blood his pious hand could dare.
H. Wondrous indeed! that bulls ne'er strive to bite,
Nor wolves, with desperate horns engage in fight;
No mother's blood the gentle Scaeva spills,
But with a draught of honeyed poison kills.
Then, whether age my peaceful hours attend,
Or death his sable pinions round me bend;
Or rich, or poor; at Rome; to exile driven;
Whatever lot by powerful fate is given,
Yet write I will.

T. O boy, thy fate is sped,
And short thy days. Some lord shall strike thee dead
With freezing look —
H. What! in his honest page,
When good Lucilius lashed a vicious age,
From conscious villains tore the mask away,
And stripped them naked to the glare of day.
. . . .

What though with great Lucilius I disclaim
All saucy rivalship of birth or fame,
Spite of herself even Envy must confess
That I the friendship of the great possess,
And, if she dare attempt my honest fame,
Shall break her teeth against my solid name.
This is my plea; on this I rest my cause —
What say my counsel, learned in the laws?
T. Your case is clearer; yet let me advise;
For sad mishaps from ignorance arise.
Behold the pains and penalties decreed
To libellers —
H. To libellers indeed!
But, if with truth his characters he draws,
Even Caesar shall support the poet's cause;
The formal process shall be turned to sport,
And you dismissed with honour by the court.

— *From the Latin of Horace (65–8 B.C.), translated by Philip Francis (abridged).*

The Town and the Country Mouse

This was of old my wishes' utmost bound; —
A snug estate with house and garden ground,
Where a small grove might wave its foliage near
And a pure spring run bubbling all the year.
Indulgent Heaven has granted this, and more:
'Tis well; no further blessings I implore.
Great son of Maia, make but to endure
The boons I have, and stamp their tenure sure!
If to no fraud I owe what I possess,
If by no fault or folly make it less, —
If from my lips no idle vows escape,
As, "Oh for yonder nook that mars the shape
Of my domain!" or, "Oh would chance unfold
To these blest eyes some secret hoard of gold!"
(As he that ploughing found a treasured store
And bought the land he tilled for hire before)
If pleased with what is given thy votary lives,
Nor indisposed to bless the hand that gives: —
Thus I entreat thee: still vouchsafe to shed
Thy tutelary influence o'er my head;
Increase my cattle, to my flocks be kind,
And fatten all I have — except my mind!
Fled from the city and the city's care
To breathe on Sabine hills a purer air,
(Welcome, sweet theme! than which I ne'er can chuse
One more congenial to my slip-shod muse)
Ambition's burthen from my mind I cast,
And shun the pressure of the noxious blast;
Autumn's grim form, that loads the frequent bier
And gluts the grave, remits his terrors here.
Thou whom the morning's busy crowd adore!
Or Janus! — if that title please thee more —
Great Sire, since all mankind, by Heaven's decree,
Ere they commence their labours, bow to thee, —
With thee begins my song. — From peaceful home
To offer bail thou summon'st me to Rome.
"Arise," I hear thee cry — "Begone with speed;
Let none anticipate the friendly deed.
What though the withering north wind scour the plain?
What though bleak winter, fraught with snow and rain,
Bid the swift day in narrower circles run?
'Tis business calls, and business must be done."
Suppose me then at Rome, in forms express
Bound to what soon may plunge me in distress:
Next I've to push my passage through the throng,
Elbow the slow, and irritate the strong.
"Madman!" cries one among the saucy rout,
"What brings you here, and what are you about?
With such officious zeal you rush to greet
Maecenas, that you jostle all you meet!"
This, I must own, is music to my ear:
Reproach like this I feel a pride to hear.
Entering at last Esquilia's shady gloom,
Scarce am I ushered to the Levee-room,
When — Oh, what swarms of dull requests invade,
Buzz at my ear and thicken round my head!

"Roscius to-morrow ere the hour of eight
Begs your attendance as his advocate."—
"Your brother clerks hope you'll return to-day
On business which admits of no delay."—
Another brings me parchments: "Sir, you'll please
To let Maecenas fix his seal to these."
Should one with hesitating air reply,
"Whate'er, Sir, the result may be, I'll try;"
"Nay," he rejoins, enforcing his request,
"Try but in earnest—none can doubt the rest."

. . . . .

'Mid such distractions doomed to waste the day,
How often, how devoutly do I pray—
Dear rural shades, where peace and silence reign,
Ah, when shall I behold you once again!
When studious there the paths of science tread,
And hold high converse with the mighty dead?
Or, indolently sunk in sloth serene,
Quaff sweet oblivion of the world's dull scene?
When shall the beans, by Samian sage adored,
With savoury pork and pottage grace my board?
O halcyon nights! O feasts that never cloy!—
Feasts that the gods themselves might taste with joy!
When I and mine beside my own loved hearth,
Seasoning our simple meal with sober mirth,
Regale on viands plentiful though plain,
And leave the remnants to the saucy train!
There free from foolish rules, the guests at ease
Carouse from goblets of what size they please:
This sips the cup, and that without control
Draws deep potations from the ampler bowl.
Nor is it long ere subjects of debate
Are started—not of this or that estate—
Not of the mansions where the great may dwell,
Nor whether Lepos dances ill or well;—
But other topics of more near concern,
And things which it were misery not to learn.

. . . . .

'Mid such debates friend Servius oft lets fall
Some pithy tale in point that charms us all:
Thus, if one chanced to praise the dear bought bliss
Of rich Arellius, straight his tale was this:—
Once on a time (as ancient legends tell)
A field-mouse welcomed to his humble cell
A mouse from town, old cronies both. Our host,
Though of economy he made much boast,
Yet, when occasion offered, could unbend,
And knew with open heart to greet a friend.
In one word mustering now his choicest fare,
Wild oats he brought, with many a hoarded tare,
Scraps of half-nibbled pork, and raisins sweet;
In hopes at least by varying thus the treat
To tempt the squeamish palate of the cit,
Who sneered contempt and scarcely touched a bit.
Not so the master of the mansion; he,
Stretched on a stubble couch, devoured with glee
Coarse chaff and darnel, leaving all the best
With due politeness to his daintier guest.
At last the cit, unable to refrain,
Broke forth,—"I vow, my friend, it gives me pain
To see you thus put up with vulgar food,
Cooped in the covert of a shaggy wood.
Do take my counsel; quit this hideous den,
Run up to Town with me, and live with men.
And, since in every creature upon earth
Lurks seeds of dissolution from its birth,—
Since soon or late, however great or small,
Inexorable Death awaits us all,—
Be wise, be happy; revel while you may,
And lengthen by enjoyment life's short day."
Such cogent reasoning who could long oppose?
Light bounding out of doors to Town he goes:
And side by side they trip, resolved to creep
Up the town walls when all were fast asleep.
Now pitchy night had wrapt the world in gloom,
When chance conducts them to a lordly dome,
Where broidered cushions stained with Tyrian dye
On ivory couches struck the dazzled eye,
And fragments of the feast of yesterday
Piled up aloft in tempting baskets lay.
Placing the peasant on a sumptuous seat,
Himself officiates and prolongs the treat;
With busy speed from fish to pastry springs,

Brings all the best, and tastes it ere he brings.
The clown exulting in his altered fate
Lolls like a prince upon his bed of state,
Thinks of his former fare with high disdain,
Roves o'er the feast, and stuffs and swills again.
When suddenly the doors with thundering noise
Burst open and at once dispel their joys:
Off in a trice each bounces from his chair,
And scampers round the hall he scarce knows where:
Anon, to add to their alarm, rush in
Fierce hounds, the wide roof echoing to their din.
Then thus the rustic: "Friend, excuse my haste;
Farewell! this life may suit a town-bred taste:
Remote from danger rather let me dwell
Cheered with an acorn in my wild-wood cell!"

—*From the Latin of Horace (65–8 B.C.), translated by Francis Howes (abridged).*

Unchanged

For hours without stopping
Mamurra goes shopping
Where golden Rome's grand bazaar lies:
Comely slaves he inspects,
Pointing out their defects
As he quite eats them up with his eyes.
His taste far surpasses
The taste of the masses:
Their best girls he tells them to show,
And upstairs in the mart
Studies slaves set apart,
Unprofaned by the gaze of the low.

He then, satiated,
Has tables uncrated;
Iv'ry stands from top shelves bids them get:
A tortoise shell chair,
Thrice measured with care,
He groans is too small for his set.
He appeared to be telling
Corinthian by smelling;
In Myron's art flaws he descried;
Sighed on finding a spot
In a crystalline pot;
Ordered ten agate jars laid aside.
Over old bowls he lingered;
Their chasing he fingered;
Then asked to see cups Mentor wrought.
After counting the gems
On their handles he hems —
And would like to see ear-rings, he thought.
Then the jewel shops he haunted,
Real sardonyx wanted,
And priced one as big as a dome.
Now the day being spent,
He bought two cups — one cent —
Tucked them under his arm and walked home.

—*From the Latin of Martial (c. 40–c. 104), translated by Paul Nixon.*

The Tenth Satire of Juvenal

THE ARGUMENT

THE POET'S DESIGN, in this divine satire, is to represent the various wishes and desires of mankind; and to set out the folly of them. He runs through all the several heads of riches, honours, eloquence, fame for martial achievements, long life, and beauty; and gives instances, in each, how frequently they have proved the ruin of those that owned them. He concludes therefore, that since we generally choose so ill for ourselves, we should do better to leave it to the gods, to make the choice for us. All we can safely ask of heaven lies within a very small compass. 'Tis but health of body and mind. And if we have these, it is not much matter what we want besides; for we have already enough to make us happy.

Look round the habitable world, how few
Know their own good; or knowing it, pursue.
How void of reason are our hopes and fears!
What in the conduct of our life appears
So well design'd, so luckily begun,
But, when we have our wish, we wish undone?
Whole houses, of their whole desires possest,
Are often ruin'd, at their own request.
In wars, and peace, things hurtful we require,
When made obnoxious to our own desire.
With laurels some have fatally been crown'd;

Some, who the depths of eloquence have found,
In that unnavigable stream were drown'd.
The brawny fool, who did his vigour boast,
In that presuming confidence was lost:
But more have been by avarice opprest,
And heaps of money crowded in the chest:
Unwieldy sums of wealth, which higher mount
Than files of marshall'd figures can account.
To which the stores of Crœsus, in the scale,
Would look like little dolphins, when they sail
In the vast shadow of the British whale.
For this, in Nero's arbitrary time,
When virtue was a guilt, and wealth a crime,
A troop of cut-throat guards were sent to seize
The rich men's goods, and gut their palaces:
The mob, commission'd by the government,
Are seldom to an empty garret sent.
The fearful passenger, who travels late,
Charg'd with the carriage of a paltry plate,
Shakes at the moonshine shadow of a rush;
And sees a red-coat rise from every bush:
The beggar sings, e'en when he sees the place
Beset with thieves, and never mends his pace.
Of all the vows, the first and chief request
Of each is, to be richer than the rest:
And yet no doubts the poor man's draught control,
He dreads no poison in his homely bowl,
Then fear the deadly drug, when gems divine
Enchase the cup, and sparkle in the wine.

. . . . . .

Some ask for envied pow'r; which public hate
Pursues, and hurries headlong to their fate:
Down go the titles; and the statue crown'd,
Is by base hands in the next river drown'd.
The guiltless horses, and the chariot wheel,
The same effects of vulgar fury feel:
The smith prepares his hammer for the stroke,
While the lung'd bellows hissing fire provoke;
Sejanus, almost first of Roman names,
The great Sejanus crackles in the flames.

. . . . . .

Now tell me truly, wouldst thou change thy fate
To be, like him, first minister of state?
To have thy levees crowded with resort,
Of a depending, gaping, servile court:
Dispose all honours of the sword and gown,
Grace with a nod, and ruin with a frown:
To hold thy prince in pupil-age, and sway
That monarch, whom the master'd world obey?
While he, intent on secret lusts alone,
Lives to himself, abandoning the throne;
Coop'd in a narrow isle, observing dreams
With flattering wizards, and erecting schemes!
I well believe, thou wouldst be great as he;
For every man's a fool to that degree;
All wish the dire prerogative to kill;
E'en they would have the power, who want the will:
But wouldst thou have thy wishes understood,
To take the bad together with the good,
Wouldst thou not rather choose a small renown,
To be the mayor of some poor paltry town,
Bigly to look, and barbarously to speak;
To pound false weights, and scanty measures break?
Then, grant we that Sejanus went astray
In ev'ry wish, and knew not how to pray:
For he who grasp'd the world's exhausted store,
Yet never had enough, but wish'd for more,
Rais'd a top-heavy tower, of monstrous height,
Which mould'ring, crush'd him underneath the weight.

. . . . . .

So much the thirst of honour fires the blood;
So many would be great, so few be good.
For who would Virtue for herself regard,
Or wed, without the portion of reward?
Yet this mad chase of fame, by few pursu'd,
Has drawn destruction on the multitude:
This avarice of praise in times to come,
Those long inscriptions, crowded on the tomb,
Should some wild fig-tree take her native bent,
And heave below the gaudy monument,
Would crack the marble titles, and disperse
The characters of all the lying verse.
For sepulchres themselves must crumbling fall

In time's abyss, the common grave of all.
  Great Hannibal within the balance lay;
And tell how many pounds his ashes weigh;

. . . . .

Spain first he won, the Pyrenæans past,
And steepy Alps, the mounds that Nature cast:
And with corroding juices, as he went,
A passage through the living rocks he rent.
Then, like a torrent, rolling from on high,
He pours his headlong rage on Italy;
In three victorious battles over-run;
Yet still uneasy, cries, There's nothing done,
Till level with the ground their gates are laid;
And Punic flags on Roman towers display'd.
  Ask what a face belong'd to his high fame:
His picture scarcely would deserve a frame:
A signpost dauber would disdain to paint
The one-ey'd hero on his elephant.
Now what's his end, O charming Glory! say,
What rare fifth act to crown this huffing play?
In one deciding battle overcome,
He flies, is banish'd from his native home:
Begs refuge in a foreign court, and there
Attends, his mean petition to prefer;
Repuls'd by surly grooms, who wait before
The sleeping tyrant's interdicted door.
  What wondrous sort of death has heaven design'd,
Distinguish'd from the herd of human kind,
For so untam'd, so turbulent a mind!
Nor swords at hand, nor hissing darts afar,
Are doom'd to avenge the tedious bloody war;
But poison, drawn through a ring's hollow plate,
Must finish him; a sucking infant's fate.
Go, climb the rugged Alps, ambitious fool,
To please the boys, and be a theme at school.

. . . . .

Jove, grant me length of life and years good store
Heap on my bending back, I ask no more.
Both sick and healthful, old and young, conspire
In this one silly mischievous desire.
Mistaken blessing, which old age they call,
'Tis a long, nasty, darksome hospital,
A ropy chain of rheums; a visage rough,
Deform'd, unfeatur'd, and a skin of buff.
A stitch-fall'n cheek, that hangs below the jaw;
Such wrinkles, as a skilful hand would draw
For an old grandam ape, when, with a grace,
She sits at squat, and scrubs her leathern face. . . .
  To Venus, the fond mother makes a prayer,
That all her sons and daughters may be fair:
True, for the boys a mumbling vow she sends;
But, for the girls, the vaulted temple rends. . . .
  And yet Lucretia's fate would bar that vow:
And fair Virginia would her fate bestow
On Rutila; and change her faultless make
For the foul rumple of her camel back. . . .
  Now Silius wants thy counsel, give advice;
Wed Cæsar's wife, or die; the choice is nice.
Her comet-eyes she darts on ev'ry grace;
And takes a fatal liking to his face. . . .
The genial bed is in the garden drest:
The portion paid, and ev'ry rite express'd,
Which in a Roman marriage is profest.
'Tis no stol'n wedding this, rejecting awe,
She scorns to marry, but in form of law:
In this moot case, your judgment: to refuse
Is present death, besides the night you lose:
If you consent, 'tis hardly worth your pain;
A day or two of anxious life you gain:
Till loud reports through all the town have past,
And reach the prince: for cuckolds hear the last.
Indulge thy pleasure, youth, and take thy swing;
For not to take is but the selfsame thing;
Inevitable death before thee lies;
But looks more kindly through a lady's eyes.
  What then remains? Are we depriv'd of will,
Must we not wish, for fear of wishing ill?
Receive my counsel, and securely move;
Intrust thy fortune to the Powers above.
Leave them to manage for thee, and to grant
What their unerring wisdom sees thee want:
In goodness as in greatness they excel;
Ah that we lov'd ourselves but half so well!
We, blindly by our headstrong passions led,
Are hot for action, and desire to wed;
Then wish for heirs: but to the gods alone
Our future offspring, and our wives are known;
Th' audacious strumpet, and ungracious son.
  Yet not to rob the priests of pious gain,
That altars be not wholly built in vain;
Forgive the gods the rest, and stand confin'd
To health of body, and content of mind:

A soul, that can securely death defy,
And count it nature's privilege, to die;
Serene and manly, harden'd to sustain
The load of life, and exercis'd in pain:
Guiltless of hate, and proof against desire;
That all things weighs, and nothing can admire.
That dares prefer the toils of Hercules
To dalliance, banquet, and ignoble ease.
The path to peace is virtue: what I show,
Thyself may freely on thyself bestow:
Fortune was never worshipp'd by the wise;
But, set aloft by fools, usurps the skies.

—*From the Latin of Juvenal (c. 60–c. 140), translated by John Dryden (abridged).*

From the Romance of the Rose

(SECTIONS 92–93)

Zeuxis, the painter, strove in vain,
That he might Nature's skill attain. . . .
Zeuxis, nor any other who
Hath e'er been born could reach thereto,
How well soe'er they understood
All Nature's loveliness, and would
Employ their hands to imitate
Her works — thereof enamorate.
For God alone it is who can
Such glories work, not puny man.
Most gladly would I, dared I hope,
Such matters stood within my scope,
Describe all Nature unto you,
But power of words would lack thereto,
Though to that task, surhuman I,
Addressed my spirit earnestly
A hundred times: nay, nay, far more
Than I shall e'er gain credit for;
Presumption were it most extreme
That I should ever dare to dream
That such a mighty work could be
Achieved by my capacity. . . .
When God, whose glory is above
All measurement, in bounteous love
Created Nature, he did make
Of her a fountain (whence should break
Unceasingly a thousand rills)
Of beauty, which the whole world fills.
This fount wells ever and cannot
By time be wasted as I wot,
More high than heaven, and than the sea
More deep, 'tis called immensity.
How then describe that body or
That countenance, that hath far more
Of beauty than the fleur-de-lis,
Which we new blown in May-tide see?
The rose is not more red, more white
Nor snow which clads the mountain height,
But 'tis a folly to compare
That which beyond all thought is fair,
And Nature's beauty doth o'ergo
All that man's heart or mind can know.

When Nature heard the Barons swear
Their solemn oath, it brought to her
Great solace for the woe that weighed
Her heart down, yet scarce unafraid
She cried:

NATURE

Alas! what have I done?
On me returns, unhappy one!
The memory of a fault that I
Committed in days long gone by
When first this beauteous world was made,
And justly had by penance paid
Therefor, since fain am I to win
Pardon for my unwitting sin.
Alas! how many a thousand time
Must I repent me of my crime!
How have I then my pains employed?
Am I of wit so far devoid,
That I who thought my friends to serve,
And thence their praise and thanks deserve,
Must yet acknowledge in the end
That 'tis my foes whom I befriend?
My kindness brings me but distress.

THE AUTHOR

Then to her priest doth she confess,
Who in her chapel hastes to say
The mass, although in no new way,
For alway had he service due
Performed, since he was priest thereto. . . .
Genius, quoth she, my gentle priest,
Master o'er greatest as o'er least
Of all created things, and who
Directs and charges them to do
Such works as are to them assigned,
Each one according to his kind,
Now do I feel remorse oppress
My spirit, and would fain confess
A folly that my heart hath riven,
And yet remaineth unforgiven. . . .

GENIUS

Before all else I counsel this,
Dear mistress, that you dry your tears,
Then if your heart confession cheers,
Tell me at full whatever thing
It is that doth thy spirit wring.

Great must your grief be, as I trow,
For noble hearts will ne'er allow
Slight woes to wear them, vile must be
The wretch who works you misery.
But oft a woman's heart will fire
For smallest cause with bitterest ire.

To Virgil I the case refer,
Who well knew woman's character.
A woman's heart is nowise stable,
Saith he, but ever variable,
Capricious, and by anger led.
And Solomon declares her head
Is than an angry serpent's worse,
Which merited God's primal curse. . . .
And Titus Livius, (who well knew
The modes and manners through and through
Of women, and their minds perverse,)
In language vigorous and terse
Declares, he best succeeds who tries
To warp their minds with japes and lies;
So foolish are they and unstable,
That truth they hate, but cling to fable.
And in the Holy Scripture we
This judgment plainly writ may see:
That at the bottom of all vice
In women is foul avarice.

The man who trusteth to his wife
His secrets, risks both fame and life,
For never man of woman born,
But sot, or one of wit forlorn,
Would to a woman e'er reveal
A thing 'twere prudent to conceal,
Lest he should hear it back again.
Much better had one flee to Spain
Than trust unto a woman's care
A secret, e'en though debonair
And loyal she be. Nor any act
That best were hid, if he have tact,
Will any man perform and do
In woman's presence, or he'll rue.
For though it peril his estate
Or life, she will or soon or late,
However long she may delay,
His secret counselling betray
And tell, though no one should demand
Or seek the matter at her hand.

—From the French of Jean de Meun (c. 1250–c. 1305), translated by F. S. Ellis (abridged).

From the Lesser Testament

This fourteen six and fiftieth year,
I, François Villon, clerk that be,
Considering, with senses clear,
Bit betwixt teeth and collar-free,
That one must needs look orderly
Unto his works (as counselleth
Vegetius, wise Roman he),
Or else amiss one reckoneth, —

In this year, as before I said,
Hard by the dead of Christmas-time,
When upon wind the wolves are fed
And for the rigour of the rime
One hugs the hearth from none to prime,
Wish came to me to break the stress
Of that most dolorous prison-clime
Wherein Love held me in duresse. . . .

She that hath bound me with her eyes
(Alack, how fierce and fell to me!),
Without my fault in any wise,
Wills and ordains that I should dree
Death and leave life and liberty.
Help see I none, save flight alone:
She breaks the bonds betwixt her and me
Nor hearkens to my piteous moan.

To 'scape the ills that hem me round,
It were the wiser to depart.
Adieu! To Angers I am bound,
Since she I love will nor impart
Her grace nor any of her heart.
I die — with body whole enough —
For her; a martyr to Love's smart,
Enrolled among the saints thereof. . . .

And since (need being on me laid)
I go and haply never may
Again return, (not being made
Of steel or bronze or other way
Than other men: life but a day
Lasteth and death knows no relent);
For me, I journey far away;
Wherefore I make this Testament.

First, in the name of God the Lord,
The Son and eke the Holy Spright,
And in her name by whose accord
No creature perisheth outright,
To Master Villon, Guillaume hight,
My fame I leave, that still doth swell
In his name's honour day and night,
And eke my tents and pennoncel.

Item, to her, who, as I've said,
So dourly banished me her sight
That all my gladness she forbade
And ousted me of all delight,
I leave my heart in deposite,
Piteous and pale and numb and dead.
She brought me to this sorry plight:
May God not wreak it on her head!

Item, my trenchant sword of steel
I leave to Master Ythier
Merchant — to whom myself I feel
No little bounden, — that he may,
According to my will, defray
The scot for which in pawn it lies
(Six sols), and then the sword convey
To Jehan le Cornu, free of price.

To Master Robert Vallee (who,
Poor clerkling to the Parliament,
Owns valley neither hill,) I do
Will first, by this my Testament,
My hose be giv'n incontinent,
Which on the clothes-pegs hang, that he
May tire withal, 'tis my intent,
His mistress Jehanne more decently. . . .

Item, my gloves and silken hood
My friend Jacques Cardon, I declare,
Shall have in fair free gift for good;
Also the acorns willows bear
And every day a capon fair
Or goose; likewise a tenfold vat
Of chalk-white wine, besides a pair
Or lawsuits, lest he wax too fat. . . .

Item, my right of nomination
Holden of the University,
I leave, by way of resignation,
To rescue from adversity
Poor clerks that of this city be, —
Hereunder named, for very ruth
That thereunto incited me,
Seeing them naked all as Truth. . . .

Item, I leave the hospitals
My curtains spun the spiders by;
And to the lodgers 'neath the stalls
Each one a buffet on the eye
And leave to tremble, as they lie,
Bruised, frozen, drenched, unshorn and lean,
With hose shrunk half way up the thigh,
Gowns all to-clipt and woeful mien.

Unto my barber I devise
The ends and clippings of my hair;
Item, on charitable wise,
I leave my old boots, every pair,
Unto the cobbler and declare
My clothes the broker's, so these two
May when I'm dead my leavings share,
For less than what they cost when new. . . .

Item, to Mairebeuf, as well
As Nicholas de Louvieux,
Each one I leave a whole eggshell
Full of old crowns and francs, and to
The seneschal of Gouvieux,
Peter de Ronseville, no less;
Such crowns I mean, to tell you true,
As the prince giveth for largesse.

Finally, being here alone
To-night and in good trim to write,
I heard the clock of the Sorbonne,
That aye at nine o'clock of night
Is wont the Angelus to smite:
Then I my task did intermit,
That to our Lady mild I might
Do suit and service, as is fit.

This done, I half forgot myself,
What while I felt Dame Memory
Take in and lay upon her shelf
(The wit, as 'twere, being bound in me,
Though not for wind-bibbing, perdie,)
Her faculties collateral,
Th' opinative in each degree
And others intellectual. . . .

Then, when my senses in due course
Grew calm and understanding clear,
I thought to finish my discourse,
But found my inkpot frozen sheer
And candle out, nor far nor near
Fire might I find, so must of need,
All muffled up for warmer cheer,
Get me to sleep and end my rede.

Done at the season aforesaid
Of the right well-renowned Villon,
Who eats nor white nor oaten bread,
Black as a malkin, shrunk and wan.
Tents and pavilions every one
He's left to one or t'other friend;
All but a little pewter's gone,
That will, ere long, come to an end.

— *From the French of François Villon (1431–1463?), translated by John Payne (abridged).*

~ ✿ ~

Two Confessions

ENVY

With an heavy heart Envy asked pardon,
And commenced sorrowfully to say his prayer.
He was pale as a pebble, as if palsy shook him,
And clothed in a coarse suit — I cannot describe it,
Short coat and curtle, with a cutlass beside him.
The foresleeves of his frock were of friar's clothing.
His cheeks lowered and looked as foully
As a leek that has long lain in sunshine.
His body was bursting with wrath; he bit lips fiercely,
And clenched hands hard, as if he hoped finally
In words or works to wreck his anger.
The words that he wrung forth were tongued as adders,
Backbiting and besmearing, bearing false witness,
Chiding and challenging were his chief diet.
And this was all his courtesy wherever he wandered.

"I would shrive myself," said this shrew, "and for shame I dare not.
I would be more glad, by God, that Gyb had misfortune
Than to win this week a wey of the cheese of Essex.
I have a neighbour near me whom I annoy often
And belie him to lords to make him lose silver,
And to make his friends foes through my false speaking.
His gain and his good luck grieve me sorely.
Between house and house I sow hatred,
So that life and limb are lost through my whispers.
When I meet at market the man whom I envy
I greet him graciously or with friendly manners
And fear to offend him, for he is the stronger.
If I had might and mastery, God knows my wishes!

When I should come before the cross kneeling in the churches,
And pray for the people as the priest teaches,
For pilgrims and for palmers and all people after them —
Then I cry on my knees, 'Christ give them sorrow,
Who took off my tankard and tore my linen!'

Then my eyes wander away from the altar
And note how Elene has a new jacket.
I wish it were mine and all its web with it.
I laugh when men lose for it delights my humour;
I wail when men win, and weep in misery.
I declare they do ill when I do worse,
And mortally hate the man who reminds me of my offences.
I wish that everyone were my own servant,
For he who has more than I angers me sorely.
So I live without love, like a low mongrel,
And all my body bursts from the bitterness of my anger.

Many years I might not eat as a man normally,
For envy and an evil will sit evilly on the stomach.
May no sugar nor sweet food assuage my swelling,
Nor shrift, nor shame, without scraping my palate?"
"Yes, readily," said Repentance, and addressed him wisely,
"Sorrow for sin is the soul's salvation."

"I am sorry," he said; "I am seldom otherwise.
And this makes me so meagre, that I miss vengeance!
I have been with burgesses who dwell in London,
And made backbiting a broker to blame merchandise.
When he sold and I not, I was always ready
To lie and to lower and to libel my neighbours,
Their words, their works, and whatever I imagined.
Now conscience grips me that I committed such evil.
Lord, before I leave life, for the love of thyself,
Grant me, good Lord, some grace for amendment!"

WRATH

Now Wrath awoke with white eyes staring,
Snivelling through his nose, and with his neck hanging.

"I am Wrath," he said, "I was once a friar,
Grafting and grubbing in the garden of our convent.
Also on lectors and on limitours my lies were grafted;
And bore leaves of lowly speech for lords and ladies;
And later blossomed abroad in bowers of confession;
And now the fruit is fallen; and the folk more willing
To show their shrifts to them than to shrive them to their parsons.
Now that parsons have perceived that friars part the winnings,
Possessioners preach and deprave the friars,
And friars find them in fault, as the folk witness;
And when both preach to the people in places without number,
I, Wrath, walk beside them, and win them with my teaching.
So these spirituals speak, each despising the other,
Until they are both beggars and live by my spirituality,
Or else are rich and ride through the country.
I, Wrath, never rest from roving forever
After these false folk, for such is my pleasure.

My aunt is a nun; yea, and an abbess;
She would sooner swoon and die than suffer discomfort.
I have been cook in her kitchen and the convent's servant
Many a long month, and served monks also.
I was pottage-maker to the prioress and to other poor ladies;
And made them junkets of jangling that dame Joan was a bastard,
That dame Clarice was a knight's daughter, but her father was a cuckold,
That dame Pernel was a priest's wench,— prioress will she be never,
For she had a child in cherry time; all our chapter knew it.

I, Wrath, made their warts of wicked speeches,
Till "you lie" and "you lie" leapt out together,
And each hit the other under the cheekbone.
Had they knives, by Christ, they would have killed each other!
I am wont to worship with wives and widows,
Imparked in pews; and the parson may tell you
How little I loved Lettice-at-the-Hedge-Row,
For when she had holy bread before me my heart began to alter.
I might go among monks, but many times I shun them,
For they have many sturdy spirits to spy into my doings,
As the prior and the subprior and our own pater abbas.
If I tell any tales, they take them to the council,
And make me fast Fridays on bread and water.
I am chastened like a child in the chapter chamber,
And beaten on the bare back and no breech to save me.
So I have no liking to live among them.
I dine there on dry fish and drink ale that is feeble,
And if wine comes once, and I drink wine at even,
I have the flux of a foul mouth five days after.
All the wickedness that I hear of any of our brethren
I carry to our cloister, and all our convent knows it."

"Now repent," said Repentance, "and repeat no longer
Any news that you may know of, naturally or by connivance.
And do not drink over delicately, nor too deep neither,
Lest will and wrath be worse than ever.
Be sober," he said, and assoiled me afterwards,
And bade me weep for my wickedness and wish amendment.

— *William Langland, English (14th century), modernized by Henry W. Wells.*

From the Prologue to the Canterbury Tales of Geoffrey Chaucer

When that sweet April showers with downward shoot
The drought of March have pierc'd into the root,

And bathéd every vein with liquid power,
Whose virtue rare engendereth the flower;
When Zephyrus also with his fragrant breath
Inspiréd hath in every grove and heath
The tender shoots of green, and the young sun
Hath in the Ram one half his journey run,
And small birds in the trees make melody,
That sleep and dream all night with open eye;
So nature stirs all energies and ages
That folks are bent to go on pilgrimages,
And palmers for to wander thro' strange strands,
To sing the holy mass in sundry lands:
And more especially, from each shire's end
Of England, they to Canterbury wend,
The holy blissful martyr for to seek,
Who hath upheld them when that they were weak.

It fell, within that season on a day
In Southwark, at the Tabard as I lay,
Ready to wend upon my pilgrim route
To Canterbury, with a heart devout,
At night was come into that hostelry
Well nine-and-twenty in a company,
Of sundry folk who thus had chanced to fall
In fellowship, and pilgrims were they all,
That now to Canterbury town would ride.
The chambers and the stables they were wide,
And all of us refresh'd, and of the best.

And shortly when the sun was gone to rest,
So had I spoken with them every one,
That I was of their fellowship anon,
And made them promise early for to rise
To take our way there, as we did advise.
But ne'ertheless, while I have time and space,
Ere that I further in this story pace,
Methinks it were accordant with good sense
To tell you the condition and pretence
Of each of them, so as it seem'd to me;
And which they were — of what kind, and degree. . . .

A Monk there was, of skill and mastery proved;
A bold hand at a leap, who hunting loved:
A manly man, to be an abbot able.
Full many a dainty horse had he in stable,
And when he rode, men might his bridle hear,
Gingling in a whistling wind as clear
And eke as loud, as doth the chapel bell
Where reign'd he lord o'er many a holy cell.
The rules of Saint Maurs and Saint Benedict,
Because that they were old and something strict,
This sturdy monk let old things backward pace,
And of the new world follow'd close the trace.
He rated not the text at a pluck'd hen,
Which saith that hunting fits not holy men,
Or that a monk beyond his bricks and mortar
Is like a fish without a drop of water —
That is to say, a monk out of his cloister: —
Now this same text he held not worth an oyster!
And I say his opinion was not bad.
Why should he study and make himself half mad
Upon a book in cloister ever to pore,
Or labour with his hands, and dig and bore
As Austin bids? How shall the world be served?
Let the world's work for Austin be reserved.
Therefore our monk spurr'd on, a jolly wight.
Greyhounds he kept, as swift as bird of flight:
In riding hard and hunting for the hare,
Was all his joy; for no cost would he spare.

I saw his large sleeves trimm'd above the hand
With fur, and that the finest of the land;
And for to keep his hood beneath his chin,
He had of beaten gold a curious pin:
A love-knot at the greater end there was.
His head was bald, and shone like any glass;
And eke his face, as it had been anoint.
He was a lord full fat, and in good point.
His eyes were deep and rolling in his head,
Which steam'd as doth a furnace melting lead.
His boots were supple, his horse right proud to see;
Now certainly a prelate fair was he:
He was not pale as a poor pining ghost.
A fat swan loved he best of any roast.
His palfrey was as brown as is a berry.

A Friar there was, a wanton and a merry;
Licensed to beg, a wondrous solemn man.
In all the orders four there's none that can
So much of dalliance wrap in language fair.
Full many a marriage had he brought to bear
For women young, and paid the cost with sport.
Unto his order he was rare support.
Right well beloved, in fellowship was he
With jolly franklins all, and yeomanry;

And eke with women, of each town the flower,
For in confession he possess'd a power
More than a curate, as himself could state,
Being of his order a licentiate.
Full sweetly would he hear confession made;
Pleasantly was his absolution said.
He was an easy man in penance naming,
And knew that alms fell heavy from light blaming;
Since to an order poor when much is given,
It proves the culprit has been rightly shriven;
For if a sinner pay dear for his bent,
He knew the man must certainly repent;
And many a man so hard is of his heart,
He will not weep, although his soul should smart;
Therefore, instead of prayers and groans and tears,
Men must give money to the poor fryeres.
His tippet always was stuff'd full of knives,
And pins, as presents meant for handsome wives.
And certainly his note was blithe and gay;
Well could he sing, and on the psaltery play.
In songs and tales the prize o'er all bore he.
His neck was white as is the fleur de lis.
Strong was he also, as a champion,
And knew the taverns well in every town,
And every ostler there, and tapster gay,
Much more than he knew beggars by the way.
For unto such a worthy man as he,
Nothing is gain'd from his good faculty
By giving to such lazars countenance:
It is not right — no interest can advance —
To deal with knaves and scrubs who have so little;
But all with rich, and those who sell good victual.
Therefore 'bove all where profit might arise,
Courteous he was, and full of service wise.
There was no man one half so virtuous:
He was the cleverest beggar in all his house;
And farm'd a certain district, as in grant.
None of his brethren came within his haunt.
And though a widow scarcely had a shoe,
So pleasant was his "*In principio*,"
He still would have a farthing ere he went.
His harvest was far better than his rent.
And rage he could, as it had been a whelp,
In love-days; yet he often gave great help:
For there was he, not like a cloisterer frore,
With threadbare cape, as suits a scholar poor,
But he was like a bishop or a pope.
Of double worsted was his semi-cope,
Round as a new bell from the moulder's press.
Somewhat he lispèd for his wantonness,
To make his English sweet upon his tongue.
And in his harping, when that he had sung,
His eyes they twinkled in his head aright,
As do the stars upon a frosty night.
And Hubert was this worthy friar's name.

There was from Bath a good Wife and a witty;
But she was somewhat deaf, and that was pity.
In the cloth trade such crowds unto her went,
She beat the looms of Ypres and of Ghent.
In all the parish good wife none was there
That to mass-offering step before her dare;
And if they did, certain so wrath was she
That she at once forgot all charity.
Her folded head-cloths were of finest ground;
I durst swear almost that they weigh'd a pound,
Which on the Sunday were upon her head.
Her stockings fine were of a scarlet red,
Full straightly tied, and shone right moist and new.
Bold was her face, and fair and red of hue.
She was a worthy woman to the core;
Five husbands had she brought from the church door,
Not reckoning other company in youth:
But there's no need to tell this now, in sooth.
And thrice had she been at Jerusalem;
She had pass'd over many a strange stream.
Cologne she knew; Bologna, Rome, had seen;
And in Galicia, at the shrine, had been.
She had known much of journeying by the way.
Her teeth had gaps between them, sooth to say.
Upon an ambler easily she sat,
With wimple large, and on her head an hat,
As broad as is a buckler or a targe.
A riding-skirt about her round hips large
Was tied, and sharp spurs were on both her feet.
In fellowship well could she laugh, and treat
Of remedies of love she learnt by chance,
For of that art she well knew the old dance.

. . . . .

With him there rode a courteous Pardoner
Of Rounceval, his friend and his compeer,
Who had arrived straight from the Roman See.

Full loud he sung 'Come hither, love, to me!'
Our Sompnour's voice bore a stiff burden round;
No trombone ever had so great a sound.
This Pardoner had hair as yellow as wax,
But smooth it hung as doth a strike of flax:
By ounces hung the long locks that he had,
And he therewith his shoulders overspread.
Full thin it lay, in single shreds adown,
But hood, for jollity, he would wear none;
For it was truss'd up in his wallet close.
He thought he rode all in new-fashion'd gloss:
Dishevell'd, save his cap, he rode all bare.
Such glaring eyes he had, as hath an hare.
A picture of our Lord was sew'd on 's cap.
His wallet lay before him in his lap,
Brim full of pardons, come from Rome all hot.
A voice he had as small as hath a goat.
No beard had he, and none could ever have;
As smooth it was as from the finest shave;
He fitly rode a gelding or a mare.
But of his craft, from Berwick unto Ware,
You could not such another Pardoner trace;
For in his pack he had a pillow-case,
Which, as he said, was once our Lady's veil.
He said he had a fragment of the sail
Saint Peter held, when, as his heart misgave him
Upon the sea, he pray'd our Lord to save him.
He had a cross of mixt ore, set with stones,
And in a glass-case treasured up pigs' bones.
But with these relics rare, when that he found
A parson poor, dwelling on rustic ground.
He in a single day more money got
Than the poor parson in two months, I wot.
And thus with flattery, feints, and knavish japes,
He made the parson and the people his apes.
But truly for to tell you all at last,
He was in church a noble ecclesiast.
Well would he read a lesson or a story,
Yet best of all he sang an offertory,
For well he knew when he that song had sung,
That he must preach and polish up his tongue,
To win the silver, as he right well could;
Therefore he sang the merrier and loud.

—*Geoffrey Chaucer, English (1340–1400) (modernized).*

Avarice

Portugal's ships in vain
Plough the wide seas; for not Moluccas' spice
Nor gold of Persian main
Can with false lure entice
Whom sweet content without riches doth suffice.

For India brings no rest
Unto man's heart, nor can the emerald rare,
Philip, our woes arrest,
But wrinkled with more care
Is he who holds of wealth a larger share.

The Persian treasure left
The Roman's thirst unsatisfied, nay first
Him of his life bereft,
And Tantalus, immersed
In waters deep, is ever more athirst.

Such thirst and even worse
Befalls the miser everlastingly
Toiling, who fast his purse
Keeps closed, to cross the sea
Most bold, not bold in generosity.

For what avails for me
The hoarded gold that murders gentle sleep,
If 'tis but slavery
And clouded still doth keep
Its owner's brow, poor though he treasure heap?

—*From the Spanish of Luis de León (1527?–1592), translated by Audrey F. G. Bell.*

Babylon and Sion (Goa and Lisbon)

Here, where fecundity of Babel frames
Stuff for all ills wherewith the world doth teem,
Where loyal Love is slurred with disesteem,
For Venus all controls, and all defames;
Where vice's vaunts are counted, virtue's shames;
Where Tyranny o'er Honor lords supreme;
Where blind and erring sovereignty doth deem
That God for deeds will be content with names;

Here in this world where whatso is, is wrong,
Where Birth and Worth and Wisdom begging go

To doors of Avarice and Villainy, —
Trammeled in the foul chaos, I prolong
My days, because I must. Woe to me! Woe!
Sion, had I not memory of thee!

— *From the Portuguese of Luis Vaz de Camoëns 1524–1580), translated by Richard Garnett.*

Letrilla: The Lord of Dollars

Over kings and priests and scholars
Rules the mighty Lord of Dollars.

Mother, into gold I yield me,
He and I are ardent lovers;
Pure affection now discovers
How his sunny rays shall shield me!
For a trifle more or less
All his power will confess, —
Over kings and priests and scholars
Rules the mighty Lord of Dollars.

In the Indies did they nurse him,
While the world stood round admiring;
And in Spain was his expiring;
And in Genoa did they hearse him;
And the ugliest at his side
Shines with all of beauty's pride;
Over kings and priests and scholars
Rules the mighty Lord of Dollars.

He's a gallant, he's a winner,
Black or white be his complexion;
He is brave without correction
As a Moor or Christian sinner.
He makes cross and medal bright,
And he smashes laws of right, —
Over kings and priests and scholars
Rules the mighty Lord of Dollars.

Noble are his proud ancestors
For his blood-veins are patrician;
Royalties make the position
Of his Orient investors;
So they find themselves preferred
To the duke or country herd, —
Over kings and priests and scholars
Rules the mighty Lord of Dollars.

Of his standing who can question
When there yields unto his rank, a
Hight-Castillian Dona Blanca,
If you follow the suggestion? —
He that crowns the lowest stool,
And to hero turns the fool, —
Over kings and priests and scholars
Rules the mighty Lord of Dollars. . . .

Never meets he dames ungracious
To his smiles or his attention,
How they glow but at the mention
Of his promises capacious!
And how bare-faced they become
To the coin beneath his thumb! —
Over kings and priests and scholars
Rules the mighty Lord of Dollars.

Mightier in peaceful season
(And in this his wisdom showeth)
Are his standards, than when bloweth
War his haughty blasts and breeze on;
In all foreign lands at home,
Equal e'en in pauper's loam, —
Over kings and priests and scholars
Rules the mighty Lord of Dollars.

— *From the Spanish of Francisco de Quevedo y Villegas (1580–1645), translated by Thomas Walsh (abridged).*

The Departed Friend

Napoleon writes me:
"The School is very big
we get up very early
we speak nothing but English,
I'm sending you a picture of the building . . ."

We won't steal candy together any more
from the cupboards, or run
off to the river to half drown ourselves,
or snitch the bloodstained watermelons.

I'm ready now for my sixth-year exams;
afterwards, as far as I can make out,
I'll learn everything you ought to learn,
I'll be a doctor,
I'll have ambitions, a beard, long pants . . .

But if I have a son
I'll see that no one ever teaches him anything.
I want him to be lazy and happy —
the way I never could be because of my parents,
nor my parents because of my grandparents,
nor my grandparents because of God.

— *From the Spanish of the Mexican Salvador Novo (1904–), translated by Muna Lee.*

Relations

Relations mine (if any still remain),
May God preserve you in good health and cheer:
The Devil take you for my part again,
And may no word of you e'er reach my ear!
Who doth believe you should be flogged right sore!
Let me be taken by fierce Turkish bands,
Or infidels, or even priests before
I chance to fall into relations' hands!
If we should see each other in the street,
We'll take our hats off if you will, and say:
Good-morrow, Master; but if interests wait
For settlement, then better 'twere to treat
Each for himself and each in his own way.
Relations? To the gallows with them straight,
This frankly let me state:
And if there be who blame my perorations,
Let them relate themselves with my relations!

—*From the Italian of Alessandro Tassoni (1565–1635), translated by Lorna de' Lucchi.*

Friar Lubin

To gallop off to town post-haste,
So oft, the times I cannot tell;
To do vile deed, nor feel disgraced, —
Friar Lubin will do it well.
But a sober life to lead,
To honor virtue, and pursue it,
That's a pious, Christian deed, —
Friar Lubin cannot do it.

To mingle, with a knowing smile,
The goods of others with his own,
And leave you without cross or pile,
Friar Lubin stands alone.
To say 'tis yours is all in vain,
If once he lays his finger to it;
For as to giving back again,
Friar Lubin cannot do it.

With flattering words and gentle tone,
To woo and win some guileless maid,
Cunning pander need you none, —
Friar Lubin knows the trade,
Loud preacheth he sobriety,
But as for water, doth eschew it;
Your dog may drink it, — but not he;
Friar Lubin cannot do it.

ENVOY

When an evil deed's to do,
Friar Lubin is stout and true;
Glimmers a ray of goodness through it,
Friar Lubin cannot do it.

—*From the French of Clément Marot (1495–1544), translated by H. W. Longfellow.*

The Boy and the Schoolmaster

Wise counsel is not always wise,
As this my tale exemplifies.
A boy, that frolick'd on the banks of Seine
Fell in, and would have found a watery grave,
Had not that hand that planteth ne'er in vain
A willow planted there, his life to save.
While hanging by its branches as he might,
A certain sage preceptor came in sight;
To whom the urchin cried, 'Save, or I'm drown'd!'
The master, turning gravely at the sound,
Thought proper for a while to stand aloof,
And give the boy some seasonable reproof.
"You little wretch! this comes of foolish playing,
Commands and precepts disobeying.
A naughty rogue, no doubt, you are,
Who thus requite your parents' care.
Alas! their lot I pity much,
Whom fate condemns to watch o'er such."
This having coolly said, and more,
He pull'd the drowning lad ashore.

This story hits more marks than you suppose.
All critics, pedants, men of endless prose, —
Three sorts, so richly bless'd with progeny,
The house is bless'd that doth not lodge any, —
May in it see themselves from head to toes.
No matter what the task,
Their precious tongues must teach;
Their help in need you ask,
You first must hear them preach.

—*From the French of Jean de La Fontaine (1621–1695), translated by Elizur Wright.*

The Oyster and the Litigants

Two pilgrims on the sand espied
An oyster thrown up by the tide.
In hope, both swallow'd ocean's fruit;
But ere the fact there came dispute.
While one stoop'd down to take the prey,
The other push'd him quite away.
Said he, " 'Twere rather meet
To settle which shall eat.
Why, he who first the oyster saw
Should be its eater, by the law;
The other should but see him do it."
Replied his mate, "If thus you view it,
Thank God the lucky eye is mine."
"But I've an eye not worse than thine,"
The other cried, "and will be cursed,
If, too, I didn't see it first."
"You saw it, did you? Grant it true,
I saw it then, and felt it too,"
Amidst this sweet affair,
Arrived a person very big,
Ycleped Sir Nincom Periwig.
They made him judge, — to set the matter square.
Sir Nincom, with a solemn face,
Took up the oyster and the case:
In opening both, the first he swallow'd,
And, in due time, his judgment follow'd.
"Attend: the court awards you each a shell
Cost free; depart in peace, and use them well."
Foot up the cost of suits at law,
The leavings reckon and awards,
The cash you'll see Sir Nincom draw,
And leave the parties — purse and cards.

— *From the French of Jean de La Fontaine (1621–1695), translated by Elizur Wright.*

The Cockerel, the Cat, and the Young Mouse

A youthful mouse, not up to trap,
Had almost met a sad mishap.
The story hear him thus relate,
With great importance, to his mother: —
"I pass'd the mountain bounds of this estate,
And off was trotting on another,
Like some young rat with nought to do
But see things wonderful and new,
When two strange creatures came in view.
The one was mild, benign, and gracious;
The other, turbulent, rapacious,
With voice terrific, shrill, and rough,
And on his head a bit of stuff
That look'd like raw and bloody meat,
Raised up a sort of arms, and beat
The air, as if he meant to fly,
And bore his plumy tail on high."

A cock, that just began to crow,
As if some nondescript,
From far New Holland shipp'd,
Was what our mousling pictures so.
"He beat his arms," said he, "and raised his voice,
And made so terrible a noise,
That I, who, thanks to Heaven, may justly boast
Myself as bold as any mouse,
Scud off, (his voice would even scare a ghost!)
And cursed himself and all his house;
For, but for him, I should have staid,
And doubtless an acquaintance made
With her who seem'd so mild and good.
Like us, in velvet cloak and hood,
She wears a tail that's full of grace,
A very sweet and humble face, —
No mouse more kindness could desire, —
And yet her eye is full of fire.
I do believe the lovely creature
A friend of rats and mice by nature.
Her ears, though, like herself, they're bigger,
Are just like ours in form and figure.
To her I was approaching, when,
Aloft on what appear'd his den,
The other scream'd, — and off I fled."
"My son," his cautious mother said,
"That sweet one was the cat,
The mortal foe of mouse and rat,
Who seeks by smooth deceit,
Her appetite to treat.
So far the other is from that,
We yet may eat
His dainty meat;
Whereas the cruel cat,
Whene'er she can, devours
No other meat than ours."
Remember while you live,
It is by looks that men deceive.

— *From the French of Jean de La Fontaine (1621–1695), translated by Elizur Wright.*

Dawn

Outside the barracks now the bugle called, and woke
The morning wind, which rose, making the lanterns smoke.

It was that hour when tortured dreams of stealthy joys
Twist in their beds the thin brown bodies of growing boys;
When, like a blood-shot eye that blinks and looks away,
The lamp still burns, and casts a red stain on the day;
When the soul, pinned beneath the body's weight and brawn,
Strives, as the lamplight strives to overcome the dawn;
The air, like a sad face whose tears the breezes dry,
Is tremulous with countless things about to die;
And men grow tired of writing, and women of making love.

Blue smoke was curling now from the cold chimneys of
A house or two; with heavy lids, mouths open wide,
Prostitutes slept their slumber dull and stupefied;
While labourers' wives got up, with sucked-out breasts, and stood
Blowing first on their hands, then on the flickering wood.
It was that hour when cold, and lack of things they need,
Combine, and women in childbirth have it hard indeed.

Like a sob choked by frothy hemorrhage, somewhere
Far-off a sudden cock-crow tore the misty air;
A sea of fog rolled in, effacing roofs and walls;
The dying, that all night in the bare hospitals
Had fought for life, grew weaker, rattled, and fell dead;
And gentlemen, debauched and drunk, swayed home to bed.

Aurora now in a thin dress of green and rose,
With chattering teeth advanced. Old sombre Paris rose,
Picked up its tools, and, over the deserted Seine,
Yawning, rubbing its eyes, slouched forth to work again.

—From the French of Charles Baudelaire (1821–1867), translated by Edna St. Vincent Millay.

~ ✿ ~

Waifs and Strays

Black in the fog and in the snow,
Where the great air-hole windows glow,
With rounded rumps,

Upon their knees five urchins squat,
Looking down where the baker, hot,
The thick dough thumps,

They watch his white arm turn the bread,
Ere through an opening flaming red
The loaf he flings.

They hear the good bread baking, while
The chubby baker with a smile
An old tune sings.

Breathing the warmth into their soul,
They squat around the red air-hole,
As a breast warm

And when, for feasters' midnight bout,
The ready bread is taken out,
In a cake's form;

And while beneath the blackened beams,
Sings every crust of golden gleams,
While the cricket brags,

The hole breathes warmth into the night,
And into them life and delight,
Under their rags,

And the urchins covered with hoar frost,
On billows of enchantment tossed
Their little souls,

Glue to the grate their rosy
Noses, singing through the cosy
Glowing holes,

But with low voices like a prayer,
Bending down to the light down there,
Where heaven gleams.

— So eager that they burst their breeches
And in the winter wind that screeches
  Their linen streams.

— From the French of Arthur Rimbaud (1854–1891), translated by Jethro Bithell.

~ ❁ ~

The Fishermen

Up from the sea a flaky, dank,
Thickening fog rolls up, and chokes
Windows and closed doors, and smokes
Upon the slippery river bank.

Drowned gleams of gas-lamps shake and fall
Where rolls the river's carrion;
The moon looks like a corpse, and on
The heaven's rim its burial.

But flickering lanterns now and then
Light up and magnify the backs,
Bent obstinately in their smacks,
Of the old river fishermen,
Who all the time, from last sunset,
For what night's fishing none can know,
Have cast their black and greedy net,
Where silent, evil waters flow.

Deep down beyond the reach of eye
Fates of Evil gathering throng,
Which lure the fishers where they lie
To fish for them with patience strong,
True to their task of simple toiling
In contradictory fogs embroiling.

And o'er them peal the minutes stark,
With heavy hammers peal their knells,
The minutes sound from belfry bells,
The minutes hard of autumn dark,
The minutes list.

And the black fishers in their ships,
In their cold ships, are clad in shreds;
Down their cold nape their old hat drips
And drop by drop in water sheds
All the mist.

Their villages are numb and freeze;
Their huts are all in ruin sunk,
And the willows and the walnut-trees
The winds of the west have whipped and
  shrunk;
And not a bark comes through the dark,
And never a cry through the void midnight,
That floated, humid ashes blight.

And never helping one another,
Never brother hailing brother,
Never doing what they ought,
For himself each fisher's thought:
And the first draws his net, and seizes
All the fry of his poverty;
And the next drags up, as keen as he,
The empty bottoms of diseases;
Another opens out his net
To griefs that on the surface swim;
And another to his vessel's rim
Pulls up the flotsam of regret.

The river churns, league after league,
Along the dikes, and runs away,
As it has done so many a day,
To the far horizon of fatigue;
Upon its bank skins of black clay
By night perspire a poison draught;
The fogs are fleeces far to waft,
And to men's houses journey they.

Never a lantern streaks the dark,
And nothing stirs in the fisher's bark,
Save, nimbusing with halos of blood,
The thick white felt of the clustering fogs,
Silent Death, who with madness clogs
The brains of the fishermen on the flood.

Lonely at the fog's cold heart,
Each sees not each, though side by side;
Their arms are tired, their vessels ride
By sandbanks marked on ruin's chart.

Why in the dark do they not hail each other?
Why does not a brother's voice console not
  brother?

No, numb and haggard they remain,
With vaulted back and heavy brain,
With, by their side, their little light
Rigid in the river's night.
Like blocks of shadow there they are,
And never pierce their eyes afar
Beyond the acid, spongy wet;
And they suspect not that above,
Luring them with a magnet's love,
Stars immense are shining yet.

These fishers in black torment tossed,
They are the men immensely lost
Among the knells and far aways
And far beyonds where none can gaze;

And in their souls' monotonous deeps
The humid autumn midnight weeps.

—From the French of the Belgian poet Emile Verhaeren (1855–1916), translated by Jethro Bithell.

Anno 1829

I crave an ampler, worthier sphere:
I'd liefer bleed at every vein
Than stifle 'mid these hucksters here,
These lying slaves of paltry gain.

They eat, they drink; they're every whit
As happy as their type, the mole;
Large are their bounties – as the slit
Through which they drop the poor man's dole.

With pipe in mouth they go their way,
With hands in pockets; they are blest
With grand digestions: only *they*
Are such hard morsels to digest!

The hand that's red with some dark deed,
Some giant crime, were white as wool
Compared with these sleek saints, whose creed
Is paying all their debts in full.

Ye clouds that sail to far-off lands,
O waft me to what clime ye will!
To Lapland's snows, to Lybia's sands,
To the world's end – but onward still!

Take me, O clouds! They ne'er look down;
But (proof of a discerning mind)
One moment hung o'er Hamburg town,
The next they leave it leagues behind.

—From the German of Heinrich Heine (1799–1856), translated by Charles Stuart Calverley.

A Thought

I gaze with grief upon our generation.
Its future black or vacant – and to-day,
Bent with a load of doubt and understanding,
In sloth and cold stagnation it grows old.
When scarcely from the cradle we were rich
In follies, in our fathers' tardy wits.
Life wearied us – a road without a goal,
A feast upon a foreign holiday.
Toward good and evil shamefully impassive,
In mid-career we fade without a fight.
Before a danger pusillanimous,
Before a power that scorns us we are slaves.
Precocious fruit, untimely ripe, we hang,
Rejoicing neither sight nor touch nor tongue,
A wrinkled orphan runt among the blossoms,
Their beauty's hour the hour of its decay.

The hues of poetry, the shapes of art,
Wake in our minds no lovely ecstasy.
We hoard the dregs of feelings that are dead,
Misers, we dig and hide a debased coin.
We hate by chance, we love by accident;
We make no sacrifice to hate or love.
Within our minds presides a secret chill
Even while the flame is burning in our blood.
A bore to us our fathers' gorgeous sporting,
Their conscientious childish vast debauch.
We hasten tomb-wards without joy or glory,
With but a glance of ridicule thrown back.
A surly-hearted crowd and soon forgotten,
We pass in silence, trackless from the world,
Tossing no fruit of dreaming to the ages,
No deed of genius even half begun.
Our dust the justice of the citizen
In future time will judge in songs of venom. . . .
Will celebrate the weak and squandering father
In bitter mockery the cheated son.

—From the Russian of Mikhail Yuryevich Lermontov (1814–1841), translated by Max Eastman.

Russia

To sin, unshamed, to lose, unthinking,
The count of careless nights and days,
And then, while the head aches with drinking,
Steal to God's house, with eyes that glaze;

Thrice to bow down to earth, and seven
Times cross oneself beside the door,
With the hot brow, in hope of heaven,
Touching the spittle-covered floor;

With a brass farthing's gift dismissing
The offering, the holy Name
To mutter with loose lips, in kissing
The ancient, kiss-worn icon-frame;

And coming home, then, to be tricking
Some wretch out of the same small coin,

And with an angry hiccup, kicking
A lean cur in his trembling groin;

And where the icon's flame is quaking
Drink tea, and reckon loss and gain,
From the fat chest of drawers taking
The coupons wet with spittle-stain;

And sunk in feather-beds to smother
In slumber, such as bears may know, —
Dearer to me than every other
Are you, my Russia, even so.

— *From the Russian of Alexander Blok (1880–1921), translated by Babette Deutsch and Avrahm Yarmolinsky.*

The Lie

Go, Soul, the body's guest,
  Upon a thankless arrant;
Fear not to touch the best;
  The truth shall be thy warrant:
Go, since I needs must die,
And give the world the lie.

Say to the Court, it glows
  And shines like rotten wood;
Say to the Church, it shows
  What's good, and doth no good:
If Church and Court reply,
Then give them both the lie.

. . . . .

Tell zeal it wants devotion;
  Tell love it is but lust;
Tell time it is but motion;
  Tell flesh it is but dust:
And wish them not reply,
For thou must give the lie.

Tell age it daily wasteth;
  Tell honour how it alters;
Tell beauty how she blasteth;
  Tell favour how it falters:
And as they shall reply,
Give every one the lie.

Tell wit how much it wrangles
  In tickle points of niceness;
Tell wisdom she entangles
  Herself in over-wiseness:
And when they do reply,
Straight give them both the lie.

Tell physic of her boldness;
  Tell skill it is pretention;
Tell charity of coldness;
  Tell law it is contention:
And as they do reply,
So give them still the lie.

Tell Fortune of her blindness;
  Tell Nature of decay;
Tell friendship of unkindness;
  Tell justice of delay;
And if they will reply,
Then give them all the lie.

Tell arts they have no soundness,
  But vary by esteeming;
Tell schools they want profoundness,
  And stand too much on seeming:
If arts and schools reply,
Give arts and schools the lie.

Tell faith it's fled the city;
  Tell how the country erreth;
Tell manhood shakes off pity;
  Tell virtue least preferreth:
And if they do reply,
Spare not to give the lie.

So when thou hast, as I
  Commanded thee, done blabbing —
Although to give the lie
  Deserves no less than stabbing —
Stab at thee he that will,
No stab the soul can kill.

— *Sir Walter Raleigh, English (1552–1618) (abridged).*

Epistle to Dr. Arbuthnot

POPE ARBUTHNOT

P. Shut, shut the door, good John! fatigued, I said;
Tie up the knocker, say I'm sick, I'm dead.
The Dog-star rages! nay, 'tis past a doubt
All Bedlam or Parnassus is let out:
Fire in each eye, and papers in each hand,
They rave, recite, and madden round the land.
What walls can guard me, or what shades can hide?
They pierce my thickets, thro' my grot they glide,

By land, by water, they renew the charge,
They stop the chariot, and they board the
barge.
No place is sacred, not the church is free,
Ev'n Sunday shines no Sabbath-day to me:
Then from the Mint walks forth the man of
rhyme,
Happy to catch me just at dinner time.
Is there a Parson much bemused in beer,
A maudlin Poetess, a rhyming Peer,
A clerk foredoom'd his father's soul to cross,
Who pens a stanza when he should engross?
Is there who, lock'd from ink and paper,
scrawls
With desp'rate charcoal round his darken'd
walls?
All fly to Twit'nam, and in humble strain
Apply to me to keep them mad or vain,
Arthur, whose giddy son neglects the laws,
Imputes to me and my damn'd works the
cause:
Poor Cornus sees his frantic wife elope,
And curses Wit and Poetry, and Pope.
Friend to my life (which did not you pro-
long,
The world had wanted many an idle song)!
What Drop or Nostrum can this plague re-
move?
Or which must end me, a fool's wrath or
love?
A dire dilemma! either way I'm sped;
If foes, they write, if friends, they read me
dead.
Seiz'd and tied down to judge, how wretched
I!
Who can't be silent, and who will not lie.
To laugh were want of goodness and of
grace,
And to be grave exceeds all power of face.
I sit with sad civility, I read
With honest anguish and an aching head,
And drop at last, but in unwilling ears,
This saving counsel, 'Keep your piece nine
years.'
'Nine years!' cries he, who high in Drury-
lane,
Lull'd by soft zephyrs thro' the broken pane,
Rhymes ere he wakes, and prints before
Term ends,
Obliged by hunger and request of friends:
'The piece, you think, is incorrect? why, take
it!
I'm all submission: what you'd have it—
make it.'
Three things another's modest wishes
bound,
'My friendship, and a Prologue, and ten
pound.'

. . . . .

'Tis sung, when Midas' ears began to
spring
(Midas, a sacred person and a king),
His very Minister who spied them first
(Some say his Queen) was forc'd to speak
or burst.
And is not mine, my friend, a sorer case,
When ev'ry coxcomb perks them in my face?

A. Good friend, forbear! you deal in dan-
gerous things;
I'd never name Queens, Ministers, or Kings;
Keep close to ears, and those let asses prick,
'Tis nothing— P. Nothing! if they bite and
kick?
Out with it, Dunciad! let the secret pass,
That secret to each fool, that he's an ass:
The truth once told (and wherefore should
we lie?)
The Queen of Midas slept, and so may I.
You think this cruel? take it for a rule,
No creature smarts so little as a fool.
Let peals of laughter, Codrus! round thee
break,
Thou unconcern'd canst hear the mighty
crack;
Pit, Box, and Gall'ry in convulsions hurl'd,
Thou stand'st unshook amidst a bursting
world.
Who shames a Scribbler? break one cobweb
thro',
He spins the slight self-pleasing thread anew:
Destroy his fib, or sophistry—in vain!
The creature's at his dirty work again,
Throned in the centre of his thin designs,
Proud of a vast extent of flimsy lines.
Whom have I hurt? has Poet yet or Peer
Lost the arch'd eyebrow or Parnassian sneer?
And has not Colley still his lord and whore?
His butchers Henley? his freemasons Moore?
Does not one table Bavius still admit?
Still to one Bishop Philips seem a wit?
Still Sappho— A. Hold! For God's sake—
you'll offend.
No names—be calm—learn prudence of a
friend.
I too could write, and I am twice as tall;
But foes like these— P. One flatt'rer's
worse than all.
Of all mad creatures, if the learn'd are
right,
It is the slaver kills, and not the bite.

A fool quite angry is quite innocent:
Alas! 'tis ten times worse when they repent.

. . . . .

Why did I write? what sin to me unknown
Dipp'd me in ink, my parents' or my own?
As yet a child, nor yet a fool to fame,
I lisp'd in numbers, for the numbers came:
I left no calling for this idle trade,
No duty broke, no father disobey'd:
The Muse but serv'd to ease some friend, not wife,
To help me thro' this long disease my life,
To second, Arbuthnot! thy art and care,
And teach the being you preserv'd, to bear.

. . . . .

Did some more sober critic come abroad,
If wrong, I smiled, if right, I kiss'd the rod.
Pains, reading, study, are their just pretence,
And all they want is spirit, taste, and sense.
Commas and points they set exactly right,
And 'twere a sin to rob them of their mite.
Yet ne'er one sprig of laurel graced these ribalds,
From slashing Bentleys down to piddling Tibbalds.
Each wight who reads not, and but scans and spells,
Each word-catcher that lives on syllables,
Ev'n such small critics some regard may claim,
Preserv'd in Milton's or in Shakspeare's name.
Pretty! in amber to observe the forms
Of hairs, or straws, or dirt, or grubs, or worms!
The things, we know, are neither rich nor rare,
But wonder how the devil they got there.
Were others angry: I excused them too;
Well might they rage, I gave them but their due.
A man's true merit 'tis not hard to find;
But each man's secret standard in his mind,
That casting-weight Pride adds to emptiness,
This, who can gratify? for who can guess?
The bard whom pilfer'd pastorals renown,
Who turns a Persian tale for half-a-crown,
Just writes to make his barrenness appear,
And strains from hard-bound brains eight lines a year;
He who still wanting, tho' he lives on theft,
Steals much, spends little, yet has nothing left;
And he who now to sense, now nonsense, leaning,
Means not, but blunders round about a meaning:
And he whose fustian's so sublimely bad,
It is not poetry, but prose run mad:
All these my modest satire bade translate,
And own'd that nine such poets made a Tate.
How did they fume, and stamp, and roar, and chafe!
And swear not Addison himself was safe.
Peace to all such! but were there one whose fires
True Genius kindles, and fair Fame inspires,
Bless'd with each talent and each art to please,
And born to write, converse, and live with ease;
Should such a man, too fond to rule alone,
Bear, like the Turk, no brother near the throne;
View him with scornful, yet with jealous eyes,
And hate for arts that caus'd himself to rise;
Damn with faint praise, assent with civil leer,
And without sneering teach the rest to sneer;
Willing to wound, and yet afraid to strike,
Just hint a fault, and hesitate dislike;
Alike reserv'd to blame or to commend,
A tim'rous foe, and a suspicious friend;
Dreading ev'n fools; by flatterers besieg'd,
And so obliging that he ne'er oblig'd;
Like Cato, give his little Senate laws,
And sit attentive to his own applause:
While Wits and Templars ev'ry sentence raise,
And wonder with a foolish face of praise —
Who but must laugh if such a man there be?
Who would not weep, if Atticus were he?

. . . . .

Oh let me live my own, and die so too
(To live and die is all I have to do)!
Maintain a poet's dignity and ease,
And see what friends, and read what books I please;
Above a Patron, tho' I condescend
Sometimes to call a minister my Friend.
I was not born for courts or great affairs;
I pay my debts, believe, and say my pray'rs;
Can sleep without a poem in my head,
Nor know if Dennis be alive or dead.

. . . . .

Curst be the verse, how well soe'er it flow,
That tends to make one worthy man my foe,
Give Virtue scandal, Innocence a fear,

Or from the soft-eyed virgin steal a tear!
But he who hurts a harmless neighbour's
peace,
Insults fall'n Worth, or Beauty in distress,
Who loves a lie, lame slander helps about,
Who writes a libel, or who copies out;
That fop whose pride affects a patron's name,
Yet absent, wounds an author's honest fame;
Who can your merit selfishly approve,
And show the sense of it without the love;
Who has the vanity to call you friend,
Yet wants the honour, injured, to defend;
Who tells whate'er you think, whate'er you
say,
And, if he lie not, must at least betray; . . .
Who reads but with a lust to misapply,
Make satire a lampoon, and fiction, lie:
A lash like mine no honest man shall dread,
But all such babbling blockheads in his stead.
Let Sporus tremble — A. What? that
thing of silk,
Sporus, that mere white curd of Ass's milk?
Satire or sense, alas! can Sporus feel?
Who breaks a butterfly upon a wheel?
P. Yet let me flap this bug with gilded
wings,
This painted child of dirt, that stinks and
stings;
Whose buzz the witty and the fair annoys,
Yet Wit ne'er tastes, and Beauty ne'er en-
joys;
So well-bred spaniels civilly delight
In mumbling of the game they dare not bite.
Eternal smiles his emptiness betray,
As shallow streams run dimpling all the way,
Whether in florid impotence he speaks,
And, as the prompter breathes, the puppet
squeaks,
Or at the ear of Eve, familiar toad,
Half froth, half venom, spits himself abroad,
In puns, or politics, or tales, or lies,
Or spite, or smut, or rhymes, or blasphemies;
His wit all see-saw between *that* and *this*,
Now high, now low, now master up, now
miss,
And he himself one vile Antithesis.
Amphibious thing! that acting either part,
The trifling head, or the corrupted heart;
Fop at the toilet, flatt'rer at the board,
Now trips a lady, and now struts a lord.
Eve's tempter thus the Rabbins have exprest,
A cherub's face, a reptile all the rest;
Beauty that shocks you, Parts that none will
trust,
Wit that can creep, and Pride that licks the
dust.
Not Fortune's worshipper, nor Fashion's
fool,
Not Lucre's madman, nor Ambition's tool,
Not proud nor servile; — be one poet's praise,
That if he pleas'd, he pleas'd by manly ways:
That flatt'ry ev'n to Kings, he held a shame,
And thought a lie in verse or prose the same;
That not in fancy's maze he wander'd long,
But stoop'd to truth, and moralized his song;
That not for Fame, but Virtue's better end,
He stood the furious foe, the timid friend,
The damning critic, half approving wit,
The coxcomb hit, or fearing to be hit;
Laugh'd at the loss of friends he never had,
The dull, the proud, the wicked, and the
mad;
The distant threats of vengeance on his
head,
The blow unfelt, the tear he never shed;
The tale revived, the lie so oft o'erthrown,
The imputed trash and dulness not his own;
The morals blacken'd when the writings
'scape,
The libell'd person, and the pictured shape;
Abuse on all he lov'd, or lov'd him, spread,
A friend in exile, or a father dead;
The whisper, that, to greatness still too near,
Perhaps yet vibrates on his Sov'reign's ear —
Welcome for thee, fair Virtue! all the past;
For thee, fair Virtue! welcome ev'n the last!

— *Alexander Pope, English (1688–1744) (abridged).*

On the Death of Doctor Swift

The time is not remote when I
Must by the course of nature die;
When I foresee, my special friends
Will try to find their private ends:
And, though 'tis hardly understood
Which way my death can do them good,
Yet thus, methinks, I hear them speak:
"See, how the dean begins to break!
Poor gentleman, he droops apace!
You plainly find it in his face.
That old vertigo in his head
Will never leave him till he's dead.
Besides, his memory decays;
He recollects not what he says;
He cannot call his friends to mind;
Forgets the place where last he dined;
Plies you with stories o'er and o'er;
He told them fifty times before.
How does he fancy we can sit
To hear his out-of-fashion wit?

But he takes up with younger folks,
Who for his wine will bear his jokes.
Faith! he must make his stories shorter,
Or change his comrades once a quarter;
In half the time he talks them round,
There must another set be found.
For poetry he's past his prime;
He takes an hour to find a rhyme;
His fire is out, his wit decayed,
His fancy sunk, his Muse a jade.
I'd have them throw away his pen —
But there's no talking to some men."
And then their tenderness appears
By adding largely to my years:
"He's older than he would be reckoned,
And well remembers Charles the Second.
He hardly drinks a pint of wine;
And that, I doubt, is no good sign.
His stomach too begins to fail;
Last year we thought him strong and hale;
But now he's quite another thing;
I wish he may hold out till spring!"
They hug themselves, and reason thus:
"It is not yet so bad with us!"

Behold the fatal day arrive!
"How is the dean?" "He's just alive."
Now the departing prayer is read.
"He hardly breathes." "The dean is dead."
Before the passing bell begun,
The news through half the town is run.
"O! may we all for death prepare!
What has he left? and who's his heir?"
"I know no more than what the news is;
'Tis all bequeathed to public uses."
"To public uses! There's a whim!
What had the public done for him?
Mere envy, avarice, and pride;
He gave it all — but first he died.
And had the dean in all the nation
No worthy friend, no poor relation?
So ready to do strangers good,
Forgetting his own flesh and blood!"

. . . . .

My female friends, whose tender hearts
Have better learned to act their parts,
Receive the news in doleful dumps:
"The dean is dead — pray what is trumps? —
The Lord have mercy on his soul!
— Ladies, I'll venture for the vole. —
Six deans, they say, must bear the pall —
I wish I knew what king to call. —
Madam, your husband will attend
The funeral of so good a friend?
No, madam, 'tis a shocking sight,
And he's engaged to-morrow night;
My Lady Club will take it ill
If he should fail her at quadrille.
He loved the dean — I lead a heart —
But dearest friends, they say, must part.
His time was come, he ran his race;
We hope he's in a better place."

"He gave the little wealth he had
To build a house for fools and mad;
And showed by one satiric touch
No nation wanted it so much.
That kingdom he had left his debtor,
I wish it soon may have a better."

— *Jonathan Swift, English (1667–1745) (abridged).*

~ ✿ ~

A Journey to Exeter

(*An Epistle to the Right Honorable the Earl of Burlington*)

While you, my Lord, bid stately piles ascend,
Or in your Chiswick bow'rs enjoy your friend;
Where Pope unloads the boughs within his reach,
Of purple vine, blue plum, and blushing peach;
I journey far — You knew fat Bards might tire,
And, mounted, sent me forth your trusty Squire.
'Twas on the day that city dames repair
To take their weekly dose of Hyde-Park air;
When forth we trot: no carts the road infest,
For still on Sundays country horses rest.
Thy gardens, Kensington, we leave unseen;
Through Hammersmith jog on to Turnham-green:
Then Turnham-green, which dainty pigeons fed,
But feeds no more: for Solomon is dead.
Three dusty miles reach Brandford's tedious town,
For dirty streets, and white-leg'd chickens known. . . .
At Hartley-Row the foaming bit we prest,
While the fat landlord welcom'd ev'ry guest.
Supper was ended, healths the glasses drown'd,
Our host extoll'd his wine at ev'ry round,
Relates the Justices late meeting there,
How many bottles drank, and what their cheer;

What lords had been his guests in days of yore,
And prais'd their wisdom much, their drinking more.
Let travellers the morning vigils keep:
The morning rose; but we lay fast asleep.
Twice tedious miles we bore the sultry sun,
And Popham-Lane was scarce in sight by one:
The straggling village harbour'd thieves of old,
'Twas here the stage-coach'd lass resign'd her gold;
That gold which had in London purchas'd gowns,
And sent her home a Belle to country towns.
But robbers haunt no more the neighbouring wood:
Here unown'd infants find their daily food;
For should the maiden mother nurse her son,
'Twould spoil her match when her good name is gone.
Our jolly hostess nineteen children bore,
Nor fail'd her breast to suckle nineteen more.
Be just, ye Prudes, wipe off the long arrear;
Be virgins still in town, but mothers here. . . .
Now the steep hill fair Dorchester o'erlooks,
Border'd by meads, and wash'd by silver brooks.
Here sleep my two companions, eyes supprest,
And propt in elbow chairs they snoring rest:
I wakeful sit, and with my pencil trace
Their painful postures, and their eyeless face;
Then dedicate each glass to some fair name,
And on the sash the diamond scrawls my flame.
Now o'er true Roman way our horses sound,
Gracious would kneel, and kiss the sacred ground.
On either side low fertile valleys lie,
The distant prospects tire the trav'ling eye.
Through Bridport's stony lanes our route we take,
And the proud steep descend to Morcombe's lake.
As hearses pass'd our landlord robb'd the pall,
And with the mournful scutcheon hung his hall.
On unadulterate wine we here regale,
And strip the lobster of his scarlet mail.
We climb'd the hills, when starry night arose,
And Axminster affords a kind repose.
The maid, subdued by fees, her trunk unlocks,
And gives the cleanly aid of dowlas smocks.
We rise; our beards demand the barber's art;
A female enters, and performs the part.
The weighty golden chain adorns her neck,
And three gold rings her skilful hand bedeck:
Smooth o'er our chin her easy fingers move,
Soft as when Venus strok'd the beard of Jove.
Now from the steep, midst scatter'd farms and groves,
Our eye through Honiton's fair valley roves.
Behind us soon the busy town we leave,
Where finest lace industrious lasses weave.
Now swelling clouds roll'd on; the rainy load
Stream'd down our hats, and smoked along the road;
When (O blest sight!) a friendly sign we spy'd,
Our spurs are slacken'd from the horse's side;
For sure a civil host the house commands,
Upon whose sign this courteous motto stands,
This is the ancient hand, and eke the pen;
Here is for horses hay, and meat for men.
But now the driving gales suspend the rain,
We mount our steeds, and Devon's city gain.
Hail, happy native land! – but I forbear,
What other counties must with envy hear.

—*John Gay, English (1685–1732) (abridged).*

London

I wander through each chartered street,
Near where the chartered Thames does flow,
And mark in every face I meet
Marks of weakness, marks of woe.

In every cry of every man,
In every infant's cry of fear,
In every voice, in every ban,
The mind-forged manacles I hear.

How the chimney-sweeper's cry
Every blackening church appals;
And the hapless soldier's sigh
Runs in blood down palace walls.

But most through midnight streets I hear
How the youthful harlot's curse
Blasts the new-born infant's tear,

And blights with plagues the marriage
    hearse.

— *William Blake, English (1757–1827).*

~ ❁ ~

To a Louse on Seeing One on a Lady's Bonnet at Church

Ha! whaur ye gaun, ye crowlin ferlie?
Your impudence protects you sairly;
I canna say but ye strunt rarely,
    Owre gauze and lace;
Tho', faith! I fear ye dine but sparely
    On sic a place.

Ye ugly, creepin, blastit wonner,
Detested, shunn'd by saunt an' sinner,
How daur ye set your fit upon her —
    Sae fine a lady?
Gae somewhere else and seek your dinner
    On some poor body.

Swith! in some beggar's haffet squattle;
There ye may creep, and sprawl, and sprattle,
Wi' ither kindred, jumping cattle,
    In shoals and nations;
Whaur horn nor bane ne'er daur unsettle
    Your thick plantations.

Now haud you there, ye're out o' sight,
Below the fatt'rels, snug and tight;
Na, faith ye yet; ye'll no be right,
    Till ye've got on it —
The verra tapmost, tow'rin height
    O' Miss's bonnet.

My sooth! right bauld ye set your nose out,
As plump and grey as ony groset:
O for some rank, mercurial rozet,
    Or fell, red smeddum,
I'd gie you sic a hearty dose o't,
    Wad dress your droddum.

I wad na be surpris'd to spy
You on an auld wife's flainen toy;
Or aiblins some bit duddie boy,
    On's wyliecoat;
But Miss's fine Lunardi! fye!
    How daur ye do't?

O Jeany, dinna toss your head,
An' set your beauties a' abread!
Ye little ken what cursed speed
    The blastie's makin:
Thae winks an' finger-ends, I dread,
    Are notice takin.

O wad some Power the giftie gie us
To see oursels as ithers see us!
It wad frae mony a blunder free us,
    An' foolish notion:
What airs in dress an' gait wad lea'e us,
    An' ev'n devotion!

— *Robert Burns, Scottish (1759–1796).*

Crowlin ferlie, *crawling wonder.* Strunt, *strut.* Fit, *feet.* Haffet, *temple.* Squattle, *sprawl.* Sprattle, *struggle.* Fatt'rels, *trimmings.* Bauld, *bold.* Groset, *gooseberry.* Rozet, *red pigment.* Smeddum, *powder.* Droddum, *breech.* Flainen, flannel. Aiblins, *perhaps.* Duddie, *ragged.* Wyliecoat, *vest.* Lunardi, *balloon-bonnet.*

Abread, *abroad.*

~ ❁ ~

Up at a Villa — Down in the City

(*As distinguished by an Italian person of quality*)

Had I but plenty of money, money enough
    and to spare,
The house for me, no doubt, were a house in
    the city-square.
Ah, such a life, such a life, as one leads at the
    window there!

Something to see, by Bacchus, something to
    hear, at least!
There, the whole day long, one's life is a perfect feast;
While up at a villa one lives, I maintain it,
    no more than a beast.

Well now, look at our villa! stuck like the
    horn of a bull
Just on a mountain's edge as bare as the
    creature's skull,
Save a mere shag of a bush with hardly a
    leaf to pull!
— I scratch my own, sometimes, to see if the
    hair's turned wool.

But the city, oh the city — the square with
    the houses! Why?
They are stone-faced, white as a curd, there's
    something to take the eye!
Houses in four straight lines, not a single
    front awry!

You watch who crosses and gossips, who saunters, who hurries by:
Green blinds, as a matter of course, to draw when the sun gets high;
And the shops with fanciful signs which are painted properly.

What of a villa? Though winter be over in March by rights,
'Tis May perhaps ere the snow shall have withered well off the heights:
You've the brown ploughed land before, where the oxen steam and wheeze,
And the hills over-smoked behind by the faint grey olive trees.

Is it better in May, I ask you? you've summer all at once;
In a day he leaps complete with a few strong April suns!
'Mid the sharp short emerald wheat, scarce risen three fingers well,
The wild tulip, at end of its tube, blows out its great red bell,
Like a thin clear bubble of blood, for the children to pick and sell.

Is it ever hot in the square? There's a fountain to spout and splash!
In the shade it sings and springs; in the shine such foam-bows flash
On the horses with curling fish-tails, that prance and paddle and pash
Round the lady atop in the conch — fifty gazers do not abash,
Though all that she wears is some weeds round her waist in a sort of sash!

All the year long at the villa, nothing's to see though you linger,
Except yon cypress that points like Death's lean lifted forefinger.
Some think fireflies pretty, when they mix in the corn and mingle,
Or thrid the stinking hemp till the stalks of it seem a-tingle.
Late August or early September, the stunning cicala is shrill
And the bees keep their tiresome whine round the resinous firs on the hill.
Enough of the seasons, — I spare you the months of the fever and chill.

Ere opening your eyes in the city, the blessed church-bells begin:
No sooner the bells leave off, than the diligence rattles in:
You get the pick of the news, and it costs you never a pin.
By and by there's the travelling doctor gives pills, lets blood, draws teeth;
Or the Pulcinello-trumpet breaks up the market beneath.
At the post-office such a scene-picture — the new play, piping hot!
And a notice how, only this morning, three liberal thieves were shot.
Above it, behold the archbishop's most fatherly of rebukes,
And beneath, with his crown and his lion, some little new law of the Duke's!
Or a sonnet with flowery marge, to the Reverend Don So-and-So,
Who is Dante, Boccaccio, Petrarca, Saint Jerome, and Cicero,
"And moveover," (the sonnet goes rhyming,) "the skirts of St. Paul has reached,
Having preached us those six Lent-lectures more unctuous than ever he preached."
Noon strikes, — here sweeps the procession! our Lady borne smiling and smart
With a pink gauze gown all spangles, and seven swords stuck in her heart!
Bang-whang-whang, goes the drum, *tootle-te-tootle* the fife;
No keeping one's haunches still: it's the greatest pleasure in life.

But bless you, it's dear — it's dear! fowls, wine, at double the rate.
They have clapped a new tax upon salt, and what oil pays passing the gate
It's a horror to think of. And so, the villa for me, not the city!
Beggars can scarcely be choosers — but still — ah, the pity, the pity!
Look, two and two go the priests, then the monks with cowls and sandals,
And the penitents dressed in white shirts, a-holding the yellow candles.
One, he carries a flag up straight, and another a cross with handles,
And the Duke's guard brings up the rear, for the better prevention of scandals.
Bang-whang-whang, goes the drum, *tootle-te-tootle* the fife.
Oh, a day in the city-square, there is no such pleasure in life!

— *Robert Browning, English (1812–1889).*

Recitation and Song

from "Patience"

BUNTHORNE

Am I alone,
And unobserved? I am!
Then let me own
I'm an esthetic sham!
This air severe
Is but a mere
Veneer!
This cynic smile
Is but a wile
Of guile!
This costume chaste
Is but good taste
Misplaced!
Let me confess
A languid love for lilies does *not* blight me!
Lank limbs and haggard cheeks do *not* delight me!
I do *not* care for dirty greens
By any means.
I do *not* long for all one sees
That's Japanese.
I am *not* fond of uttering platitudes
In stained-glass attitudes.
In short, my medievalism's affectation,
Born of a morbid love of admiration!

SONG

If you're anxious for to shine in the high esthetic line as a man of culture rare,
You must get up all the germs of the transcendental terms, and plant them everywhere.
You must lie upon the daisies and discourse in novel phrases of your complicated state of mind,
The meaning doesn't matter if it's only idle chatter of a transcendental kind.
And everyone will say
As you walk your mystic way,
"If this young man expresses himself in terms too deep for *me*,
Why, what a very singularly deep young man this deep young man must be!"

Be eloquent in praise of the very dull old days which have long since passed away,
And convince 'em, if you can, that the reign of good Queen Anne was Culture's palmiest day.
Of course you will pooh-pooh whatever's fresh and new, and declare it's crude and mean;
For art stopped short in the cultivated court of the Empress Josephine.
And everyone will say
As you walk your mystic way,
"If that's not good enough for him which is good enough for *me*,
Why, what a very cultivated kind of youth this kind of youth must be!"

Then a sentimental passion of a vegetable fashion must excite your languid spleen,
An attachment *à la* Plato for a bashful young potato, or a not-too-French French bean!
Though the Philistines may jostle, you will rank as an apostle in the high esthetic band,
If you walk down Piccadilly, with a poppy or a lily in your medieval hand.
And everyone will say,
As you walk your flowery way,
"If he's content with a vegetable love which would certainly not suit *me*,
Why, what a particularly pure young man this pure young man must be!"

— *W. S. Gilbert, English (1836–1911).*

Sabbath-Day Chace

(*Written Under the Character of Hezekiah Salem.*)

On a fine Sunday morning I mounted my steed
And southward from *Hartford* had meant to proceed;
My baggage was stow'd in a cart very snug,
Which *Ranger*, the gelding, was destined to lug;
With his harness and buckles, he loom'd very grand,
And was drove by young *Darby*, a lad of the land —
On land, or on water, most handy was he,
A jockey on shore, and a sailor at sea,
He knew all the roads, he was so very keen
And the *Bible* by heart, at the age of fifteen.
As thus I jogg'd on, to my saddle confined.
With *Ranger* and *Darby* a distance behind;
At last in full view of a steeple we came
With a *cock* on the spire (I suppose he was game;

A dove in the pulpit may suit your grave people,
But always remember – a cock on the steeple).
Cries Darby – "Dear master, I beg you to stay;
Believe me, there's danger in driving this way;
Our deacons on Sundays have power to arrest
And lead us to church – if your honour thinks best –
Though still I must do them the justice to tell,
They would choose you should pay them the fine full as well."
The fine (said I) Darby, how much may it be –
A shilling or sixpence? – why, now let me see,
Three shillings are all the small pence that remain
And to change a half joe would be rather *profane.*
Is it more than three shillings, the fine that you speak on;
What say you good Darby – will that serve the deacon?
"Three shillings (cried Darby) why, master, you're jesting!
Let us *luff* while we can and make sure of our *westing* –
Forty shillings, excuse me, is too much to pay
It would take my month's wages – that's all I've to say.
By taking *this road* that inclines to the right
The squire and the sexton may bid us good night,
If once to old Ranger I give up the rein
The parson himself may pursue us in vain."
"Not I, my good Darby (I answer'd the lad)
Leave the church on the left! they would think we were mad;
I would sooner rely on the heels of my steed,
And pass by them all like a *Jehu* indeed: –
As long as I'm able to lead in the race
Old Ranger, the gelding, will go a good pace,
As the deacon pursues, he will fly like a swallow,
And you in the cart must, undoubtedly, follow."
Then approaching the church, as we pass'd by the door
The sexton peep'd out, with a saint or two more,
A deacon came forward and waved us his hat,
A signal to drop him some money – mind that! –
"Now, Darby, (I halloo'd) be ready to skip,
Ease off the curb bridle – give Ranger the whip:
While you have the rear, and myself lead the way,
No doctor or deacon shall catch us this day."
By this time the deacon had mounted his poney
And chaced for the sake of our souls and – our money:
The saint, as he followed, cried – "Stop them, halloo!"
As swift as he followed, as swiftly we flew –
"Ah master! (said Darby), I very much fear
We must drop him some money to check his career,
He is gaining upon us and waves with his hat
There's nothing, dear master, will stop him but that.
Remember the Beaver (you well know the fable)
Who flying the hunters as long as he's able,
When he finds that his efforts can nothing avail
But death and the puppies are close to his tail,
Instead of desponding at such a dead lift
He bites off *their object*, and makes a free gift –
Since fortune all hope of escaping denies
Better give them a little, than lose the whole prize."
But scarce had he spoke, when we came to a place
Whose muddy condition concluded the chace,
Down settled the cart – and old Ranger stuck fast
Aha! (said the Saint) have I catch'd ye at last?

"the rest is missing"

— *Philip Freneau, American (1752–1832).*

Ode

INSCRIBED TO W. H. CHANNING

Though loath to grieve
The evil time's sole patriot,
I cannot leave
My honeyed thought
For the priest's cant,
Or statesman's rant.

If I refuse
My study for their politique,
Which at the best is trick,
The angry Muse
Puts confusion in my brain.

But who is he that prates
Of the culture of mankind,
Of better arts and life?
Go, blindworm, go,
Behold the famous States
Harrying Mexico
With rifle and with knife!

Or who, with accent bolder,
Dare praise the freedom-loving mountaineer?
I found by thee, O rushing Contoocook!
And in thy valleys, Agiochook!
The jackals of the negro-holder.

The God who made New Hampshire
Taunted the lofty land
With little men; —
Small bat and wren
House in the oak: —

If earth-fire cleave
The upheaved land, and bury the folk,
The southern crocodile would grieve.
Virtue palters; Right is hence;
Freedom praised, but hid;
Funeral eloquence
Rattles the coffin-lid.

What boots thy zeal,
O glowing friend,
That would indignant rend
The northland from the south?
Wherefore? to what good end?
Boston Bay and Bunker Hill
Would serve things still; —
Things are of the snake.

The horseman serves the horse,
The neatherd serves the neat,
The merchant serves the purse,
The eater serves his meat;
'Tis the day of the chattel,
Web to weave, and corn to grind;
Things are in the saddle,
And ride mankind.

There are two laws discrete,
Not reconciled, —
Law for man, and law for thing;
The last builds town and fleet,
But it runs wild,
And doth the man unking.

'Tis fit the forest fall,
The steep be graded,
The mountain tunnelled,
The sand shaded,
The orchard planted,
The glebe tilled,
The prairie granted,
The steamer built.

Let man serve law for man;
Live for friendship, live for love,
For truth's and harmony's behoof;
The state may follow how it can,
As Olympus follows Jove.

Yet do not I implore
The wrinkled shopman to my sounding woods,
Nor bid the unwilling senator
Ask votes of thrushes in the solitudes.
Every one to his chosen work; —
Foolish hands may mix and mar;
Wise and sure the issues are.
Round they roll till dark is light,
Sex to sex, and even to odd; —
The over-god
Who marries Right to Might,
Who peoples, unpeoples, —
He who exterminates
Races by stronger races,
Black by white faces, —
Knows to bring honey
Out of the lion;
Grafts gentlest scion
On pirate and Turk.
The Cossack eats Poland,
Like stolen fruit;
Her last noble is ruined,
Her last poet mute:
Straight, into double band
The victors divide;

Half for freedom strike and stand; —
The astonished Muse finds the thousands at her side.

— Ralph Waldo Emerson, American (1803–1882).

∽ ۞ ∼

Joe Greene

Joe Greene was a tom-cat, he had learned his manners
Watching tom-cats, although his people were tanners
Who first had a pit in the backyard in the earth.
After ten years, and after Joe's timely birth,
They acquired a factory and employed a dozen men.
Then a little later, along about 1910,
They expanded the business to take in half the block
And installed a night watchman and a time-punch clock.

When Joe was ready for Andover he went there:
It slid off his mind like water off the famed duck's back.
At Harvard also Joe proceeded to lack
What some call taste and other savoir faire,
So now in his motor, with its chromium shiny bright,
He purrs through the day at the factory and yowls through the night.

— Merrill Moore, American (1903–).

∽ ۞ ∼

Tract

I will teach you   my townspeople
how to perform   a funeral —
for you have it   over a troop
of artists —
unless one should   scour the world —
you have the ground sense   necessary.

See!   the hearse leads.
I begin with   a design for a hearse.
For Christ's sake   not black —
nor white either —   and not polished!
Let it be weathered —   like a farm wagon —
with gilt wheels   (this could be
applied fresh   at small expense)
or no wheels at all:
a rough dray to   drag over the ground.

Knock the glass out!
My God — glass,   my townspeople!
For what purpose?   Is it for the dead
to look out or   for us to see
how well he is housed   or to see
the flowers or   the lack of them —
or what?
To keep the rain   and snow from him?
He will have a   heavier rain soon:
pebbles and dirt   and what not.
Let there be no glass —
and no upholstery   phew!
and no little   brass rollers
and small easy wheels   on the bottom —
my townspeople   what are you thinking of?

A rough   plain hearse then
with gilt wheels   and no top at all.
On this   the coffin lies
by its own weight.
No wreathes please —
especially no   hot house flowers.
Some common memento   is better,
something he prized   and is known by:
his old clothes —   a few books perhaps —
God knows what!   You realize
how we are   about these things
my townspeople —
something will be found —   anything
even flowers   if he had come to that.

So much for   the hearse.
For heaven's sake though   see to the driver!
Take off   the silk hat!   In fact
that's no place   at all for him —
up there   unceremoniously
dragging our friend out   to his own dignity!
Bring him down —   bring him down!
Low and inconspicuous!   I'd not have him ride
on the wagon at all —   damn him —
the undertaker's   understrapper!
Let him hold   the reins
and walk   at the side
and inconspicuously   too!

Then briefly   as to yourselves:
Walk behind —   as they do in France,
seventh class, or   if you ride
Hell take curtains!   Go with some show
of inconvenience;   sit openly —
to the weather   as to grief.
Or do you think   you can shut grief in?
What — from us?   We who have perhaps
nothing to lose?   Share with us
share with us —   it will be money

in your pockets.
Go now
I think you are ready.

— William Carlos Williams, American (1883–)

∽ ❂ ∼

Clean Curtains

New neighbors came to the corner house at Congress and Green Streets.

The look of their clean white curtains was the same as the rim of a nun's bonnet.

One way was an oyster pail factory, one way they made candy, one way paper boxes, strawboard cartons.

The warehouse trucks shook the dust of the ways loose and the wheels whirled dust — there was dust of hoof and wagon wheel and rubber tire — dust of police and fire wagons — dust of the winds that circled at midnights and noon listening to no prayers.

"O mother, I know the heart of you," I sang passing the rim of a nun's bonnet — O white curtains — and people clean as the prayers of Jesus here in the faded ramshackle at Congress and Green.

Dust and the thundering trucks won — the barrages of the street wheels and the lawless wind took their way — was it five weeks or six the little mother, the new neighbors, battled and then took away the white prayers in the windows?

— Carl Sandburg, American (1878–)

PART TEN

Foundations of the State

~ ⚙ ~

THE LITERATURE of political theory is a rewarding study. It offers answers to numerous questions which all men ask in the course of their lives regarding the conditions under which they live, and it gives them a basis for comparing their experience, their successes and failures in the ordering of social estates, with those of other peoples or generations. Political theory is of course as old as organized society. Even among primitive peoples chieftains rely on some kind of general justification or explanation for the demands they make upon the allegiance of their followers. In general it may be said that Oriental writers commonly assumed that existing forms of government were sanctioned by religion or tradition. Oriental writers who discussed political topics were therefore chiefly concerned with the virtues and vices of governors, or with the precedents established in some golden age of the past. It is chiefly in Occidental societies that men have asked disquieting questions which led to revolutions or reforms. Why do we have government at all? What do we owe to it? What are its best forms? From what spheres of our personal and social life should it be excluded? Who should control it? What does it owe to its subjects? Upon what precedents or moral grounds can the relinquishing of personal liberty be demanded by the state? The answers to these and many other related questions represent a branch of literature which is one of our greatest heritages. It contains the record of our social progress and the various ways through which our commonwealths were formed.

Since Plato's time and beginning with his *Republic*, some of the best minds of Europe and America have devoted themselves to the development and exposition of their points of view. Whether they look philosophically on man's social life, draw up a "bill of rights" or "social contract," or publish a manifesto calling for revolution, their writings present the historical background of our political thought and offer valuable aid in examining the meaning and tendency of our political environments. These environments are the results of the political experience and sagacity of our ancestors. Rooted in a long past, there is in man an impulse to construct better schemes for the conduct of social life. Philosophers have drawn the plans and statesmen have put them into operation. There is warrant for observing that the maturity of individuals is to be found in their handling of social relations, and of nations in their management of political affairs. In few areas of life will a knowledge of human experience serve more useful ends.

Government by Philosophers

PLATO

WE WERE enquiring into the nature of absolute justice and into the character of the perfectly just, and into injustice and the perfectly unjust, that we might have an ideal. We were to look at these in order that we might judge of our own happiness and unhappiness according to the standard which they exhibited and the degree in which we resembled them, but not with any view of showing that they could exist in fact.

True, he said.

Would a painter be any the worse because, after having delineated with consummate art an ideal of a perfectly beautiful man, he was unable to show that any such man could ever have existed?

He would be none the worse.

Well, and were we not creating an ideal of a perfect State?

To be sure.

And is our theory a worse theory because we are unable to prove the possibility of a city being ordered in the manner described?

Surely not, he replied.

That is the truth, I said. But if, at your request, I am to try and show how and under what conditions the possibility is highest, I must ask you, having this in view, to repeat your former admissions.

What admissions?

I want to know whether ideals are ever fully realized in language? Does not the word express more than the fact, and must not the actual, whatever a man may think, always, in the nature of things, fall short of the truth? What do you say?

I agree.

Then you must not insist on my proving that the actual State will in every respect coincide with the ideal: if we are only able to discover how a city may be governed nearly as we proposed, you will admit that we have discovered the possibility which you demand; and will be contented. I am sure that I should be contented — will not you?

Yes, I will.

Let me next endeavor to show what is that fault in States which is the cause of their present maladministration, and what is the least change which will enable a State to pass into the truer form; and let the change, if possible, be of one thnig only, or, if not, of two; at any rate, let the changes be as few and slight as possible.

Certainly, he replied.

I think, I said, that there might be a reform of the State if only one change were made, which is not a slight or easy though still a possible one.

What is it? he said.

Now then, I said, I go to meet that which I liken to the greatest of the waves; yet shall the word be spoken, even though the wave break and drown me in laughter and dishonor; and do you mark my words.

Proceed.

I said: *Until philosophers are kings, or the kings and princes of this world have the spirit and power of philosophy, and political greatness and wisdom meet in one, and those commoner natures who pursue either to the exclusion of the other are compelled to stand aside, cities will never have rest from their evils, — no, nor the human race, as I believe, — and then only will this our State have a possibility of life and behold the light of day.* Such was the thought, my dear Glaucon, which I would fain have uttered if it had not seemed too extravagant; for to be convinced that in no other State can there be happiness private or public is indeed a hard thing.

. . . . .

And thus, Glaucon, after the argument has gone a weary way, the true and the false philosophers have at length appeared in view.

I do not think, he said, that the way could have been shortened.

I suppose not, I said; and yet I believe that we might have had a better view of both of them if the discussion could have been confined to this one subject and if there were not many other questions awaiting us, which he who desires to see in what respect the life of the just differs from that of the unjust must consider.

And what is the next question? he asked.

Surely, I said, the one which follows next in order. Inasmuch as philosophers only are able to grasp the eternal and unchangeable, and those who wander in the region of the many and variable are not philosophers, I must ask you which of the two classes should be the rulers of our State?

And how can we rightly answer that question?

Whichever of the two are best able to guard the laws and institutions of our State — let them be our guardians.

Very good.

Neither, I said, can there be any question that the guardian who is to keep anything should have eyes rather than no eyes?

There can be no question of that.

And are not those who are verily and indeed wanting in the knowledge of the true being of each thing, and who have in their souls no clear pattern, and are unable as with a painter's eye to look at the absolute truth and to that original to repair, and having perfect vision of the other world to order the laws about beauty, goodness, justice in this, if not already ordered, and to guard and preserve the order of them — are not such persons, I ask, simply blind?

Truly, he replied, they are much in that condition.

And shall they be our guardians when there are others who, besides being their equals in experience and falling short of them in no particular of virtue, also know the very truth of each thing?

There can be no reason, he said, for rejecting those who have this greatest of all great qualities; they must always have the first place unless they fail in some other respect.

Suppose then, I said, that we determine how far they can unite this and the other excellences.

By all means.

In the first place, as we began by observing, the nature of the philosopher has to be ascertained. We must come to an understanding about him, and, when we have done so, then, if I am not mistaken, we shall also acknowledge that such a union of qualities is possible, and that those in whom they are united, and those only, should be rulers in the State.

What do you mean?

Let us suppose that philosophical minds always love knowledge of a sort which shows them the eternal nature not varying from generation and corruption.

Agreed.

And further, I said, let us agree that they are lovers of all true being; there is no part whether greater or less, or more or less honorable, which they are willing to renounce; as we said before of the lover and the man of ambition.

True.

And if they are to be what we were describing, is there not another quality which they should also possess?

What quality?

Truthfulness: they will never intentionally receive into their mind falsehood, which is their detestation, and they will love the truth.

Yes, that may be safely affirmed of them.

"May be," my friend, I replied, is not the word; say rather, "must be affirmed": for he whose nature is amorous of anything cannot help loving all that belongs or is akin to the object of his affections.

Right, he said.

And is there anything more akin to wisdom than truth?

How can there be?

Can the same nature be a lover of wisdom and a lover of falsehood?

Never.

The true lover of learning then must from his earliest youth, as far as in him lies, desire all truth?

Assuredly.

But then again, as we know by experience, he whose desires are strong in one direction will have them weaker in others; they will be like a stream which has been drawn off into another channel.

True.

He whose desires are drawn towards knowledge in every form will be absorbed in the pleasures of the soul, and will hardly feel bodily pleasure — I mean, if he be a true philosopher and not a sham one.

That is most certain.

Such an one is sure to be temperate and the reverse of covetous; for the motives which make another man desirous of having and spending, have no place in his character.

Very true.

Another criterion of the philosophical nature has also to be considered.

What is that?

There should be no secret corner of illiberality; nothing can be more antagonistic than meanness to a soul which is ever longing after the whole of things both divine and human.

Most true, he replied.

Then how can he who has magnificence of mind and is the spectator of all time and all existence, think much of human life?

He cannot.

Or can such a one account death fearful?

No indeed.

Then the cowardly and mean nature has no part in true philosophy?

Certainly not.

Or again: can he who is harmoniously constituted, who is not covetous or mean, or a boaster, or a coward — can he, I say, ever be unjust or hard in his dealings?

Impossible.

Then you will soon observe whether a man is just and gentle, or rude and unsociable; these are the signs which distinguish even in youth the philosophical nature from the unphilosophical.

True.

There is another point which should be remarked.

What point?

Whether he has or has not a pleasure in learning; for no one will love that which gives him pain, and in which after much toil he makes little progress.

Certainly not.

And again, if he is forgetful and retains nothing of what he learns, will he not be an empty vessel?

That is certain.

Laboring in vain, he must end in hating himself and his fruitless occupation?

Yes.

Then a soul which forgets cannot be ranked among genuine philosophic natures; we must insist that the philosopher should have a good memory?

Certainly.

And once more, the inharmonious and unseemly nature can only tend to disproportion?

Undoubtedly.

And do you consider truth to be akin to proportion or to disproportion?

To proportion.

Then, besides other qualities, we must try to find a naturally well-proportioned and gracious mind, which will move spontaneously towards the true being of everything.

Certainly.

Well, and do not all these qualities, which we have been enumerating, go together, and are they not, in a manner, necessary to a soul, which is to have a full and perfect participation of being?

They are absolutely necessary, he replied.

And must not that be a blameless study which he only can pursue who has the gift of a good memory, and is quick to learn, — noble, gracious, the friend of truth, justice, courage, temperance, who are his kindred?

The god of jealousy himself, he said, could find no fault with such a study.

And to men like him, I said, when perfected by years and education, and to these only you will intrust the State.

Here Adeimantus interposed and said: To these statements, Socrates, no one can offer a reply; but when you talk in this way, a strange feeling passes over the minds of your hearers: They fancy that they are led astray a little at each step in the argument, owing to their own want of skill in asking and answering questions; these littles accumulate, and at the end of the discussion they are found to have sustained a mighty overthrow and all their former notions appear to be turned upside down. And as unskilful players of draughts are at last shut up by their more skilful adversaries and have no piece to move, so they too find themselves shut up at last; for they have nothing to say in this new game of which words are the counters; and yet all the time they are in the right. The observation is suggested to me by what is now occurring. For any one of us might say, that although in words he is not able to meet you at each step of the argument, he sees as a fact that the votaries of philosophy, when they carry on the study, not only in youth as a part of education, but as the pursuit of their maturer years, most of them become strange monsters, not to say utter rogues, and that those who may be considered the best of them are made useless to the world by the very study which you extol.

Well, and do you think that those who say so are wrong?

I cannot tell, he replied; but I should like to know what is your opinion.

Hear my answer; I am of opinion that they are quite right.

Then how can you be justified in saying that cities will not cease from evil until philosophers rule in them, when philosophers are acknowledged by us to be of no use to them?

You ask a question, I said, to which a reply can only be given in a parable.

Yes, Socrates; and that is a way of speaking to which you are not at all accustomed, I suppose.

I perceive, I said, that you are vastly amused at having plunged me into such a hopeless discussion; but now hear the parable, and then you will be still more amused at the meagerness of my imagination: for the manner in which the best men are treated in their own States is so grievous that no single thing on earth is comparable to it; and therefore, if I am to plead their cause, I must have recourse to fiction, and put together a figure made up of many things, like the fabulous unions of goats and stags which are found in pictures. Imagine then a fleet or a ship in which there is a captain who is taller and stronger than any of the crew, but he is a little deaf and has a similar infirmity in sight, and his knowledge of navigation is not much better. The sailors are quarreling with one another about the steering — every one is of opinion that he has a right to steer, though he has never learned the art of navigation and cannot tell who taught him or when he learned, and will further assert that it cannot be taught, and they are ready to cut in pieces any one who says the contrary. They throng about the captain, begging and praying him to commit the helm to them; and if at any time they do not prevail, but others are preferred to them, they kill the others or throw them overboard, and having first chained up the noble captain's senses with drink or some narcotic drug, they mutiny and take possession of the ship and make free with the stores; thus, eating and drinking, they proceed on their voyage in such manner as might be expected of them. Him who is their partisan and cleverly aids them in their plot for getting the ship out of the captain's hands into their own whether by force or persuasion, they compliment with the name of sailor, pilot, able seaman, and abuse the other sort of man, whom they call a good-for-nothing; but that the true pilot must pay attention to the year and seasons and sky and stars and winds, and whatever else belongs to his art, if he intends to be really qualified for the command of a ship, and that he must and will be the steerer, whether other people like or not — the possibility of this union of authority with the steerer's art has never seriously entered into their thoughts or been made part of their calling. Now in vessels which are in a state of mutiny and by sailors who are mutineers, how will the true pilot be regarded? Will he not be called by them a prater, a star-gazer, a good-for-nothing?

Of course, said Adeimantus.

Then you will hardly need, I said, to hear the interpretation of the figure, which describes the true philosopher in his relation to the State; for you understand already.

Certainly.

Then suppose you now take this parable to the gentleman who is surprised at finding that philosophers have no honor in their cities; explain it to him and try to convince him that their having honor would be far more extraordinary.

I will.

Say to him, that, in deeming the best votaries of philosophy to be useless to the rest of the world, he is right; but also tell him to attribute their uselessness to the fault of those who will not use them, and not to themselves. The pilot should not humbly beg the sailors to be commanded by him — that is not the order of nature; neither are "the wise to go to the doors of the rich" — the ingenious author of this saying told a lie — but the truth is, that, when a man is ill, whether he be rich or poor, to the physician he must go, and he who wants to be governed, to him who is able to govern. The ruler who is good for anything ought not to beg his subjects to be ruled by him; although the present governors of mankind are of a different stamp; they may be justly compared to the mutinous sailors, and the true helmsmen to those who are called by them good-for-nothings and star-gazers.

Precisely so, he said.

For these reasons, and among men like these, philosophy, the noblest pursuit of all, is not likely to be much esteemed by those of the opposite faction; not that the greatest and most lasting injury is done to her by her opponents, but by her own professing followers, the same of whom you suppose the accuser to say, that the greater number of them are arrant rogues, and the best are useless; in which opinion I agreed.

Yes.

And the reason why the good are useless has now been explained?

True.

Then shall we proceed to show that the corruption of the majority is also unavoidable, and that this is not to be laid to the charge of philosophy any more than the other?

By all means.

And let us ask and answer in turn, first going back to the description of the gentle and noble nature. Truth, as you will remember, was his leader, whom he followed always and in all things; failing in this, he was an impostor, and had no part or lot in true philosophy.

Yes, that was said.

Well, and is not this one quality, to mention no others, greatly at variance with present notions of him?

Certainly, he said.

And have we not a right to say in his defence, that the true lover of knowledge is always striving after being — that is his nature; he will not rest in the multiplicity of individuals which is an appearance only, but will go on — the keen edge will not be blunted, nor the force of his desire abate until he have attained the knowledge of the true nature of every essence by a sympathetic and kindred power in the soul, and by that power drawing near and mingling and becoming incorporate with very being, having begotten mind and truth, he will have knowledge and will live and grow truly, and then, and not till then, will he cease from his travail.

Nothing, he said, can be more just than such a description of him.

And will the love of a lie be any part of a philosopher's nature? Will he not utterly hate a lie?

He will.

And when truth is the captain, we cannot suspect any evil of the band which he leads?

Impossible.

Justice and health of mind will be of the company, and temperance will follow after?

True, he replied.

. . . . .

Observe, Glaucon, that there will be no injustice in compelling our philosophers to have a care and providence of others; we shall explain to them that in other States, men of their class are not obliged to share in the toils of politics: and this is reasonable, for they grow up at their own sweet will, and the government would rather not have them. Being self-taught, they cannot be expected to show any gratitude for a culture which they have never received. But we have brought you into the world to be rulers of the hive, kings of yourselves and of the other citizens, and have educated you far better and more perfectly than they have been educated, and you are better able to share in the double duty. Wherefore each of you, when his turn comes, must go down to the general underground abode, and get the habit of seeing in the dark. When you have acquired the habit, you will see ten thousand times better than the inhabitants of the den, and you will know what the several images are, and what they represent, because you have seen the beautiful and just and good in their truth. And thus our State, which is also yours, will be a reality, and not a dream only, and will be administered in a spirit unlike that of other States, in which men fight with one another about shadows only and are distracted in the struggle for power, which in their eyes is a great good. Whereas the truth is that the State in which the rulers are most reluctant to govern is always the best and most quietly governed, and the State in which they are most eager, the worst.

Quite true, he replied.

And will our pupils, when they hear this, refuse to take their turn at the toils of State, when they are allowed to spend the greater part of their time with one another in the heavenly light?

Impossible, he answered; for they are just men, and the commands which we impose upon them are just; there can be no doubt that every one of them will take office as a stern necessity, and not after the fashion of our present rulers of State.

Yes, my friend, I said; and there lies the point. You must contrive for your future rulers another and a better life than that of a ruler, and then you may have a well-ordered State; for only in the State which offers this, will they rule who are truly rich, not in silver and gold, but in virtue and wisdom, which are the true blessings of life. Whereas if they go to the administration of public affairs, poor and hungering after their own private advantage, thinking that hence they are to snatch the chief good, order there can never be; for they will be fighting about office, and the civil and domestic broils which thus arise will be the ruin of the rulers themselves and of the whole State.

Most true, he replied.

And the only life which looks down upon the life of political ambition is that of true philosophy. Do you know of any other?

Indeed, I do not, he said.

And those who govern ought not to be lovers of the task? For, if they are, there will be rival lovers, and they will fight.

No question.

Who then are those whom we shall compel to be guardians? Surely they will be the men who are wisest about affairs of state, and by whom the State is administered, and who at the same time have other honors and another and better life than that of politics?

They are the men, and I will choose them, he replied.

—From The Republic of Plato, Greek (429–347 B.C.), translated by Benjamin Jowett.

The Nature of Democracy

ARISTOTLE

First of all let us speak of democracy, which will also bring to light the opposite form of government commonly called oligarchy. For the purposes of this enquiry we need to ascertain all the elements and characteristics of democracy, since from the combinations of these the varieties of democratic government arise. There are several of these differing from each other, and the difference is due to two causes. One has been already mentioned, — differences of population; for the popular element may consist of husbandmen, or of mechanics, or of labourers, and if the first of these be added to the second, or the third to the two others, not only does the democracy become better or worse, but its very nature is changed. A second cause remains to be mentioned: the various properties and characteristics of democracy, when variously combined make a difference. For one democracy will have less and another will have more, and another will have all of these characteristics. There is an advantage in knowing them all, whether a man wishes to establish some new form of democracy, or only to remodel an existing one. Founders of States try to bring together all the elements which accord with the ideas of the several constitutions; but this is a mistake of theirs, as I have already remarked when speaking of the destruction and preservation of States. We will now set forth the principles, characteristics, and aims of such States.

The basis of a democratic State is liberty; which, according to the common opinion of men, can only be enjoyed in such a State; — this they affirm to be the great end of every democracy. One principle of liberty is for all to rule and be ruled in turn, and indeed democratic justice is the application of numerical not proportionate equality; whence it follows that the majority must be supreme, and that whatever the majority approve must be the end and the just. Every citizen, it is said, must have equality, and therefore in a democracy the poor have more power than the rich, because there are more of them, and the will of the majority is supreme. This, then, is one note of liberty which all democrats affirm to be the principle of their State. Another is that a man should live as he likes. This, they say, is the privilege of a free man, and, on the other hand, not to live as a man likes is the mark of a slave. This is the second characteristic of democracy, whence has arisen the claim of men to be ruled by none, if possible, or, if this is impossible, to rule and be ruled in turns; and so it coincides with the freedom based upon equality.

Such being our foundation and such the nature of democracy, its characteristics are as follows: — the election of officers by all out of all; and that all should rule over each, and each in his turn over all; that the appointment to all offices, or to all but those which require experience and skill, should be made by lot; that no property qualification should be required for offices, or only a very low one; that no one should hold the same office twice, or not often, except in the case of military offices; that the tenure of all offices, or of as many as possible, should be brief; that all men should sit in judgment, or that judges selected out of all should judge in all matters, or in most, or in the greatest and most important, — such as the scrutiny of accounts, the constitution and private contracts; that the assembly should be supreme over all causes, or at any rate over the most important, and the magistrates over none or only over a very few. Of all institutions, a council is the most democratic when there is not the means of paying all the citizens, but when they are paid even this is robbed of its power; for the people then draw all cases to themselves, as I said in the previous discussion. The next characteristic of democracy is payment for services; assembly law-courts, magistrates, everybody receives pay, when it is to be had; or when it is not to be had for all, then it is given to the law-courts and to the stated assemblies, to the council and to the magistrates, or at least to any of them who are compelled to have their meals together. And whereas oligarchy is characterized by birth, wealth, and education, the notes of democracy appear to be the opposite of these, — low birth, poverty, mean employment. Another note is that no magistracy is perpetual, but if any such have survived some ancient change in the constitution it should be stripped of its power, and the holders should be elected by lot and no longer by vote. These are points common to all democracies; but democracy and demos in their truest form are based upon the recognized principle of democratic justice, that all should count equally; for equality implies that the rich should have no more share in the government than the poor, and should not be the only rulers, but that all should rule equally according to their numbers. And in this way men think that they will secure equality and freedom in their State.

Next comes the question, how is this equality to be obtained? Is the qualification to be so distributed that five hundred rich shall be equal to a thousand poor? and shall we give the thousand a power equal to that of the five hundred? or, if this is not to be the mode, ought we, still retaining the same ratio, to take equal numbers from each and give them the control of the elections and of the courts? — Which, according to the democratical notion, is the juster form of the constitution, — this or one based on numbers only? Democrats say that justice is that to which the majority agree, oligarchs that to which the wealthier class; in their opinion the decision should be given according to the amount of property. In both principles there is some inequality and injustice. For if justice is the will of the few, any one person who has more wealth than all the rest of his class put together, ought, upon the oligarchical principle, to have the sole power — but this would be tyranny; or if justice is the will of the majority, as I was before saying, they will unjustly confiscate the property of the wealthy minority. To find a principle of equality in which they both agree we must enquire into their respective ideas of justice.

Now they agree in saying that whatever is decided by the majority of the citizens is to be deemed law. Granted: — but not without some reserve; since there are two classes out of which a State is composed, — the poor and the rich, — that is to be deemed law, on which both or the greater part of both agree; and if they disagree, that which is approved by the greater number, and by those who have the higher qualification. For example, suppose that there are ten rich and twenty poor, and some measure is approved by six of the rich and disapproved by fifteen of the poor, and the remaining four of the rich join with the party of the poor, and the remaining five of the poor with that of the rich; in such a case the will of those whose qualifications, when both sides are added up, are the greatest, should prevail. If they turn out to be equal, there is no greater difficulty than at present, when, if the assembly or the courts are divided, recourse is had to the lot, or to some similar expedient. But, although it may be difficult in theory to know what is just and equal, the practical difficulty of inducing those to forbear who can, if they like, encroach, is far greater, for the weaker are always asking for equality and justice, but the stronger care for none of these things.

Of the four kinds of democracy, as was said in the previous discussion, the best is that which comes first in order; it is also the oldest of them all. I am speaking of them according to the natural classification of their inhabitants. For the best material of democracy is an agricultural population; there is no difficulty in forming a democracy where the mass of the people live by agriculture or tending of cattle. Being poor, they have no leisure, and therefore do not often attend the assembly, and not having the necessaries of life they are always at work, and do not covet the property of others. Indeed, they find their employment pleasanter than the cares of government or office where no great gains can be made out of them, for the many are more desirous of gain than of honour. A proof is that even the ancient tyrannies were patiently endured by them, as they still endure oligarchies, if they are allowed to work and are not deprived of their property; for some of them grow quickly rich and the others are well enough off. Moreover they have the power of electing the magistrates and calling them to account; their ambition, if they have any, is thus satisfied; and in some democracies, although they do not all share in the appointment of officers, except through representatives elected in turn out of the whole people, as at Mantinea; – yet, if they have the power of deliberating, the many are contented. Even this form of government may be regarded as a democracy, and was such at Mantinea. Hence it is both expedient and customary in such a democracy that all should elect to offices, and conduct scrutinies, and sit in the law-courts, but that the great offices should be filled up by election and from persons having a qualification; the greater requiring a greater qualification, or, if there be no offices for which a qualification is required, then those who are marked out by special ability should be appointed. Under such a form of government the citizens are sure to be governed well, (for the offices will always be held by the best persons; the people are willing enough to elect them and are not jealous of the good). The good and the notables will then be satisfied, for they will not be governed by men who are their inferiors, and the persons elected will rule justly, because others will call them to account. Every man should be responsible to others, nor should any one be allowed to do just as he pleases; for where absolute freedom is allowed there is nothing to restrain the evil which is inherent in every man. But the principle of responsibility secures that which is the greatest good in States; the right persons rule and are prevented from doing wrong, and the people have their due. It is evident that this is the best kind of democracy, and why? because the people are drawn from a certain class. The ancient laws of many States which aimed at making the people husbandmen are excellent. They provided either that no one should possess more than a certain quantity of land, or that, if he did, the land should not be within a certain distance from the town or the acropolis. Formerly in many States there was law forbidding any one to sell his original allotment of land. There is a similar law attributed to Oxylus, which is to the effect that there should be a certain portion of every man's property on which he could not borrow money. A useful corrective to the evil of which I am speaking would be the law of the Aphytæans, who, although they are numerous, and do not possess much land, are all of them husbandmen. For their properties are reckoned in the census, not entire, but only in such small portions that even the poor may have more than the amount required.

Next best to an agricultural, and in many respects similar, are a pastoral people, who live by their flocks; they are the best trained of any for war, robust in body and able to camp out. The people of whom other democracies consist are far inferior to them, for their life is inferior; there is no room for moral excellence in any of their employments, whether they be mechanics or traders or labourers. Besides, people of this class can readily come to the assembly, because they are continually moving about in the city and in the agora; whereas husbandmen are scattered over the country and do not meet, or equally feel the want of assembling together. Where the territory extends to a distance from the city, there is no difficulty in making an excellent democracy or constitutional government; for the people are compelled to settle in the country, and even if there is a town population the assembly ought not to meet when the country people cannot come. We have thus explained how the first and best form of democracy should be constituted; it is clear that the other or inferior sorts will deviate in a regular order, and the population which is excluded will at each stage be of a lower kind.

The last form of democracy, that in which all share alike, is one which cannot be borne by all States, and will not last long unless well regulated by laws and customs. The more general causes which tend to destroy this or other kinds of government have now been pretty fully considered. In order to constitute such a democracy and strengthen the people, the leaders have been in the habit of including as many as they can, and making citizens not only of those who are legitimate, but even of the illegitimate, and of those who have only one parent a citizen, whether father or mother; for nothing of this sort comes amiss to such a democracy. This is the way in which demagogues proceed. Whereas the right thing would be to make no more additions when the number of the commonalty exceeds that of the notables or of the middle class, – beyond this not to go. When in excess of this point the State becomes disorderly, and the notables grow excited and impatient of the democracy, as in the insurrection at Cyrene; for no notice is taken of a little evil, but when it increases it strikes the eye. Measures like those which

Cleisthenes passed when he wanted to increase the power of the democracy at Athens, or such as were taken by the founders of popular government at Cyrene, are useful in the extreme form of democracy. Fresh tribes and brotherhoods should be established; the private rights of families should be restricted and converted into public ones; in short, every contrivance should be adopted which will mingle the citizens with one another and get rid of old connections. Again, the measures which are taken by tyrants appear all of them to be democratic; such, for instance, as the license permitted to slaves (which may be to a certain extent advantageous) and also that of women and children, and the allowing everybody to live as he likes. Such a government will have many supporters, for most persons would rather live in a disorderly than in a sober manner.

The mere establishment of a democracy is not the only or principal business of a legislator, or of those who wish to create such a State, for any State, however badly constituted, may last one, two, or three days; a far greater difficulty is the preservation of it. The legislator should therefore endeavour to have a firm foundation according to the principles already laid down concerning the preservation and destruction of States; he should guard against the destructive elements, and should make laws, whether written or unwritten, which will contain all the preservatives of States. He must not think the truly democratical or oligarchical measure to be that which will give the greatest amount of democracy or oligarchy, but that which will make them last longest. The demagogues of our own day often get property confiscated in the law-courts in order to please the people. But those who have the welfare of the State at heart should counteract them, and make a law that the property of the condemned which goes into the treasury should not be public but sacred. Thus offenders will be as much afraid, for they will be punished all the same, and the people, having nothing to gain, will not be so ready to condemn the accused. Care should also be taken that State trials are as few as possible, and heavy penalties should be inflicted on those who bring groundless accusations; for it is the practice to indict, not members of the popular party, but the notables, although the citizens ought to be all equally attached to the State, or at any rate should not regard their rulers as enemies.

Now, since in the last and worst form of democracy the citizens are very numerous, and can hardly be made to assemble unless they are paid, and to pay them when there are no revenues presses hardly upon the notables (for the money must be obtained by a property-tax and confiscations and corrupt practices of the courts, things which have before now overthrown many democracies); where, I say, there are no revenues, the government should hold few assemblies, and the law-courts should consist of many persons, but sit for a few days only. This system has two advantages: first, the rich do not fear the expense, even although they are unpaid themselves when the poor are paid; and secondly, causes are better tried, for wealthy persons, although they do not like to be long absent from their own affairs, do not mind going for a few days to the law-courts. Where there are revenues the demagogues should not be allowed after their manner to distribute the surplus; the poor are always receiving and always wanting more and more, for such help is like water poured into a leaky cask. Yet the true friend of the people should see that they be not too poor, for extreme poverty lowers the character of the democracy; measures also should be taken which will give them lasting prosperity; and as this is equally the interest of all classes, the proceeds of the public revenues should be accumulated and distributed among them, if possible, in such quantities as may enable them to purchase a little farm, or, at any rate, make a beginning in trade and husbandry. And if this benevolence cannot be extended to all, money should be distributed in turn according to tribes or other divisions, and in the meantime the rich should pay the fee for the attendance of the poor at the necessary assemblies; and should in turn be excused from useless public services. By administering the State in this spirit the Carthaginians retain the affections of the people; their policy is from time to time to send some of them into their dependent towns, where they grow rich. It is also worthy of a generous and sensible nobility to divide the poor amongst them, and give them the means of going to work. The example of the people of Tarentum is also well deserving of imitation, for, by sharing the use of their own property with the poor, they gain their good will. Moreover, they divide all their offices into two classes, one-half of them being elected by vote, the other by lot; the latter that the people may participate in them, and the former, that the State may be better administered. A like result may be gained by dividing the same offices, so as to have two classes of magistrates, one chosen by vote, the other by lot.

—*From Book VI of the Politics of Aristotle, Greek (384–322 B.C.), translated by Benjamin Jowett.*

Duties of the Individual to the State

CICERO

THOSE WHOM Nature has endowed with the capacity for administering public affairs should put aside all hesitation, enter the race for public office, and take a hand in directing the government; for in no other way can a government be administered or greatness of spirit be made manifest. Statesmen, too, no less than philosophers — perhaps even more so — should carry with them that greatness of spirit and indifference to outward circumstances to which I so often refer, together with calm of soul and freedom from care, if they are to be free from worries and lead a dignified and self-consistent life. This is easier for the philosophers; as their life is less exposed to the assaults of fortune, their wants are fewer; and if any misfortune overtakes them, their fall is not so disastrous. Not without reason, therefore, are stronger emotions aroused in those who engage in public life than in those who live in retirement, and greater is their ambition for success; the more, therefore, do they need to enjoy greatness of spirit and freedom from annoying cares.

If anyone is entering public life, let him beware of thinking only of the honour it brings; but let him be sure also that he has the ability to succeed. At the same time, let him take care not to lose heart too readily through discouragement nor yet to be over-confident through ambition. In a word, before undertaking any enterprise, careful preparation must be made.

Most people think that the achievements of war are more important than those of peace; but this opinion needs to be corrected. For many men have sought occasions for war from the mere ambition for fame. This is notably the case with men of great spirit and natural ability, if they are adapted to a soldier's life and fond of warfare. But if we will face the facts, we shall find that there have been many instances of achievement in peace more important and no less renowned than in war.

However highly Themistocles, for example, may be extolled — and deservedly — and however much more illustrious his name may be than Solon's, and however much Salamis may be cited as witness of his most glorious victory — a victory glorified above Solon's statesmanship in instituting the Areopagus — yet Solon's achievement is not to be accounted less illustrious than his. For Themistocles's victory served the State once and only once; while Solon's work will be of service for ever. For through his legislation the laws of the Athenians and the institutions of their fathers are maintained. And while Themistocles could not readily point to any instance in which he himself had rendered assistance to the Areopagus, the Areopagus might with justice assert that Themistocles had received assistance from it; for the war was directed by the counsels of that senate which Solon had created. . . .

There are, therefore, instances of civic courage that are not inferior to the courage of the soldier. Nay, the former calls for even greater energy and greater devotion than the latter.

That moral goodness which we look for in a lofty, high-minded spirit is secured, of course, by moral, not by physical, strength. And yet the body must be trained and so disciplined that it can obey the dictates of judgment and reason in attending to business and in enduring toil. But that moral goodness which is our theme depends wholly upon the thought and attention given to it by the mind. And in this way, the men who in a civil capacity direct the affairs of a nation render no less important service than they who conduct its wars: by their statesmanship oftentimes wars are either averted or terminated; sometimes also they are declared. Upon Marcus Cato's counsel, for example, the Third Punic War was undertaken, and in its conduct his influence was dominant, even after he was dead. And so diplomacy in the friendly settlement is more desirable than courage in settling them on the battlefield; but we must be careful not to take that course merely for the sake of avoiding war rather than for the sake of public expediency. War, however, should be undertaken in such a way as to make it evident that it has no other object than to secure peace.

But it takes a brave and resolute spirit not to be disconcerted in times of difficulty or ruffled and thrown off one's feet, as the saying is, but to keep one's presence of mind and one's self-possession and not to swerve from the path of reason.

Now all this requires great personal courage; but it calls also for great intellectual ability by reflection to anticipate the future, to discover some time in advance what may happen whether for good or for ill, and what must be done in any possible event, and never to be reduced to having to say: "I had not thought of that."

These are the activities that mark a spirit, strong, high, and self-reliant in its prudence and wisdom. But to mix rashly in the fray and to fight hand to hand with the enemy is but a barbarous and brutish kind of business. Yet when the stress of circumstances demands it, we must gird on the sword and prefer death to slavery and disgrace.

As to destroying and plundering cities, let me say that great care should be taken that nothing be done in reckless cruelty or wantonness. And it is a great man's duty in troublous times to single out the guilty for punishment, to spare the many, and in every turn of fortune to hold to a true and honourable course. For whereas there are many, as I have said before, who place the achievements of war above those of peace, so one may find many to whom adventurous, hot-headed counsels seem more brilliant and impressive than calm and well-considered measures.

We must, of course, never be guilty of seeming cowardly and craven in our avoidance of danger; but we must also beware of exposing ourselves to danger needlessly. Nothing can be more foolhardy than that. Accordingly, in encountering danger we should do as doctors do in their practice: in light cases of illness they give mild treatment; in cases of dangerous sickness they are compelled to apply hazardous and even desperate remedies. It is, therefore, only a madman who, in a calm, would pray for storm; a wise man's way is, when the storm does come, to withstand it with all the means at his command, and especially, when the advantages to be expected in case of a successful issue are greater than the hazards of the struggle.

The dangers attending great affairs of state fall sometimes upon those who undertake them, sometimes upon the State. In carrying out such enterprises, some run the risk of losing their lives, others their reputation and the good-will of their fellow-citizens. It is our duty, then, to be more ready to endanger our own than the public welfare and to hazard honour and glory more readily than other advantages.

Many, on the other hand, have been found who were ready to pour out not only their money but their lives for their country and yet would not consent to make even the slightest sacrifice of personal glory — even though the interests of their country demanded it. For example, when Callicratidas, as Spartan admiral in the Peloponnesian War, had won many signal successes, he spoiled everything at the end by refusing to listen to the proposal of those who thought he ought to withdraw his fleet from the Arginusæ and not to risk an engagement with the Athenians. His answer to them was that "the Spartans could build another fleet, if they lost that one, but he could not retreat without dishonour to himself." And yet what he did dealt only a slight blow to Sparta; there was another which proved disastrous, when Cleombrotus in fear of criticism recklessly went into battle against Epaminondas. In consequence of that the Spartan power fell.

How much better was the conduct of Quintus Maximus! Of him Ennius says:

"One man — and he alone — restored our
  state by delaying.
Not in the least did fame with him take precedence of safety;
Therefore now does his glory shine bright,
  and it grows ever brighter."

This sort of offence must be avoided no less in political life. For there are men who for fear of giving offence do not dare to express their honest opinion, no matter how excellent.

Those who propose to take charge of the affairs of government, should not fail to remember two of Plato's rules: first, to keep the good of the people so clearly in view that regardless of their own interests they will make their every action conform to that; second, to care for the welfare of the whole body politic and not in serving the interests of some one party to betray the rest. For the administration of the government, like the office of a trustee, must be conducted for the benefit of those entrusted to one's care, not of those to whom it is entrusted. Now, those who care for the interests of a part of the citizens and neglect another part, introduce into the civil service a dangerous element — dissension and party strife. The result is that some are found to be loyal supporters of the democratic, others of the aristocratic party, and few of the nation as a whole.

As a result of this party spirit bitter strife arose at Athens, and in our own country not only dissensions but also disastrous civil wars broke out. All this the citizen who is patriotic, brave, and worthy of a leading place in the state will shun with abhorrence; he will dedicate himself unreservedly to his country, without aiming at influence or power for himself; and he will devote himself to the State in its entirety in such a way as to further the interests of all. Besides, he will not expose anyone to hatred or disrepute by groundless charges, but he will surely cleave to justice and honour so closely that he will submit to any loss, however heavy, rather than be untrue to them, and will face death itself rather than renounce them.

A most wretched custom, assuredly, is our electioneering and scrambling for office. Concerning this also we find a fine thought in Plato: "Those who compete against one another," he says, "to see which of two candidates shall administer the government, are like sailors quarrelling as to which one of them shall do the steering." And he likewise lays down the rule that we should regard only those as adversaries who take up arms against the State, not those who strive to have the government administered according to their convictions. This was the spirit of the disagreement between Publius Africanus and Quintus Metellus: there was in it no trace of rancour.

Neither must we listen to those who think that one should indulge in violent anger against one's political enemies and imagine that such is the attitude of a great-spirited, brave man. For nothing is more commendable, nothing more becoming in a pre-eminently great man than courtesy and forbearance. Indeed, in a free people, where all enjoy equal rights before the law, we must school ourselves to affability and what is called "mental poise;" for if we are irritated when people intrude upon us at unseasonable hours or make unreasonable requests, we shall develop a sour, churlish temper, prejudicial to ourselves and offensive to others. And yet gentleness of spirit and forbearance are to be commended only with the understanding that strictness may be exercised for the good of the State; for without that, the government cannot be well administered. On the other hand, if punishment or correction must be administered, it need not be insulting; it ought to have regard to the welfare of the State, not to the personal satisfaction of the man who administers the punishment or reproof.

We should take care also that the punishment shall not be out of proportion to the offence, and that some shall not be chastised for the same fault for which others are not even called to account. In administering punishment it is above all necessary to allow no trace of anger. For if anyone proceeds in a passion to inflict punishment, he will never observe that happy mean which lies between excess and defect. This doctrine of the mean is approved by the Peripatetics — and wisely approved, if only they did not speak in praise of anger and tell us that it is a gift bestowed on us by Nature for a good purpose. But in reality, anger is in every circumstance to be eradicated; and it is to be desired that they who administer the government should be like the laws, which are led to inflict punishment not by wrath but by justice. . . .

Of these public services, some are of such a nature that they concern the whole body of citizens; others, that they affect individuals only. And these latter are the more productive of gratitude. If possible, we should by all means attend to both kinds of service; but we must take care in protecting the interests of individuals that what we do for them shall be beneficial, or at least not prejudicial, to the State. Gaius Gracchus inaugurated largesses of grain on an extensive scale; this had a tendency to exhaust the exchequer. Marcus Octavius inaugurated a moderate dole; this was both practicable for the State and necessary for the commons; it was, therefore, a blessing both to the citizens and to the State.

The man in an administrative office, however, must make it his first care that every one shall have what belongs to him and that private citizens suffer no invasion of their property rights by act of the State. It was a ruinous policy that Philippus proposed when in his tribuneship he introduced his agrarian bill. However, when his law was rejected, he took his defeat with good grace and displayed extraordinary moderation. But in his public speeches on the measure he often played the demagogue, and that time viciously, when he said that "there were not in the State two thousand people who owned any property." That speech deserves unqualified condemnation, for it favoured an equal distribution of property; and what more ruinous policy than that could be conceived? For the chief purpose in the establishment of constitutional States and municipal governments was that individual property rights might be secured. For although it was by Nature's guidance that men were drawn together into communities, it was in the hope of safeguarding their possessions that they sought the protection of cities.

The administration should also put forth every effort to prevent the levying of a property tax, and to this end precautions should be taken long in advance. Such a tax was often levied in the times of our forefathers on account of the depleted state of their treasury and their incessant wars. But if any State (I say "any," for I would rather speak in general terms than forbode evils to our own; however, I am not discussing our own State but States in general) – if any State ever has to face a crisis requiring the imposition of such a burden, every effort must be made to let all the people realize that they must bow to the inevitable, if they wish to be saved. And it will also be the duty of those who direct the affairs of the State to take measures that there shall be an abundance of the necessities of life. It is needless to discuss the ordinary ways and means; for the duty is self-evident; it is necessary only to mention the matter.

But the chief thing in all public administration and public service is to avoid even the slightest suspicion of self-seeking. "I would," says Gaius Pontius, the Samnite, "that fortune had withheld my appearance until a time when the Romans began to accept bribes, and that I had been born in those days! I should then have suffered them to hold their supremacy no longer." Aye, but he would have had many generations to wait; for this plague has only recently infected our nation. And so I rejoice that Pontius lived then instead of now, seeing that he was so mighty a man! It is not yet a hundred and ten years since the enactment of Lucius Piso's bill to punish extortion; there had been no such law before. But afterward came so many laws, each more stringent than the other, so many men were accused and so many were convicted, so horrible a war was stirred up on account of the fear of what our courts would do to still others, so frightful was the pillaging and plundering of the allies when the laws and courts were suppressed, that now we find ourselves strong not in our own strength but in the weakness of others.

Panætius praises Africanus for his integrity in public life. Why should he not? But Africanus had other and greater virtues. The boast of official integrity belongs not to that man alone but to his times. When Paulus got possession of all the wealth of Macedon – and it was enormous – he brought into our treasury so much money that the spoils of a single general did away with the need for a tax on property in Rome for all time to come. But to his own house he brought nothing save the glory of an immortal name. Africanus emulated his father's example and was none the richer for his overthrow of Carthage. And what shall we say of Lucius Mummius, his colleague in the censorship? Was he one penny the richer when he had destroyed to its foundations the richest of cities? He preferred to adorn Italy rather than his own house. And yet by the adornment of Italy his own house was, as it seems to me, still more splendidly adorned.

There is, then, to bring the discussion back to the point from which it digressed, no vice more offensive than avarice, especially in men who stand foremost and hold the helm of state. For to exploit the State for selfish profit is not only immoral; it is criminal, infamous. And so the oracle, which the Pythian Apollo uttered, that "Sparta should not fall from any other cause than avarice," seems to be a prophecy not to the Lacedæmonians alone, but to all wealthy nations as well. They who direct the affairs of state, then, can win the good-will of the masses by no other means more easily than by self-restraint, and self-denial.

But they who pose as friends of the people, and who for that reason either attempt to have agrarian laws passed, in order that the occupants may be driven out of their homes, or propose that money loaned should be remitted to the borrowers, are undermining the foundations of the commonwealth: first of all, they are destroying harmony, which cannot exist when money is taken away from one party and bestowed upon another; and second, they do away with equity, which is utterly subverted, if the rights of property are not respected. For, as I said above, it is the peculiar function of the state and the city to guarantee to every man the free and undisturbed control of his own particular property. And yet, when it comes to measures so ruinous to public welfare, they do not gain even that popularity which they anticipate. For he who has been robbed of his property is their enemy; he to whom it has been turned over actually pretends that he had no wish to take it; and most of all, when his debts are cancelled, the debtor conceals his joy, for fear that he may be thought to have been insolvent; whereas the victim of the wrong both remembers it and shows his resentment openly. Thus even though they to whom property has been wrongly awarded be more in number than they from whom it has been unjustly taken, they do not for that reason have more influence; for in such matters influence is measured not by numbers but by weight. And how is it fair that a man who never had any property should take possession of lands that had been occupied for many years or even generations, and that he who had them before should lose possession of them? . . .

We must, therefore, take measures that there shall be no indebtedness of a nature to endanger the public safety. It is a menace that can be averted in many ways; but should a serious debt be incurred, we are not to allow the rich to lose their property, while the debtors profit by what is their neighbour's. For there is nothing that upholds a government more powerfully than its credit; and it can have no credit, unless the payment of debts is enforced by law. Never were measures for the repudiation of debts more strenuously agitated than in my consulship. Men of every sort and rank attempted with arms and armies to force the project through. But I opposed them with such energy that this plague was wholly eradicated from the body politic. Indebtedness was never greater; debts were never liquidated more easily or more fully; for the hope of defrauding the creditor was cut off and payment was enforced by law. But the present victor, though vanquished then, still carried out his old design, when it was no longer of any personal advantage to him. So great was his passion for wrong-doing that the very doing of wrong was a joy to him for its own sake, even when there was no motive for it.

Those, then, whose office it is to look after the interests of the State will refrain from that form of liberality which robs one man to enrich another. Above all, they will use their best endeavours that every one shall be protected in the possession of his own property by the fair administration of the law and the courts, that the poorer classes shall not be oppressed because of their helplessness, and that envy shall not stand in the way of the rich, to prevent them from keeping or recovering possession of what justly belongs to them; they must strive, too, by whatever means they can, in peace or in war, to advance the State in power, in territory, and in revenues.

Such service calls for great men; it was commonly rendered in the days of our ancestors; if men will perform duties such as these, they will win popularity and glory for themselves and at the same time render eminent service to the State.

— From the Offices, Book II, of Cicero, Roman (106–43 B.C.), translated by Walter Miller.

⁂

Benevolence

MENCIUS

MENCIUS SAID: "Benevolence brings glory to a prince, and the opposite of it brings disgrace. For the princes of the present day to hate disgrace and yet live complacently doing what is not benevolent, is like hating moisture and yet living in a low situation.

"If a prince hates disgrace, the best course

for him to pursue is to esteem virtue and honor virtuous scholars, giving the worthiest among them places of dignity, and the able offices of trust. When throughout his kingdom there are leisure and rest from external troubles, taking advantage of such a season, let him clearly digest the principles of his government with its legal sanctions, and then even great kingdoms will be constrained to stand in awe of him.

"It is said in the Book of Poetry:

'Before the heavens were dark with rain,
I gathered the bark from the roots of the mulberry-trees,
And wove it closely to form the window and door of my nest;
Now, I thought, ye people below,
Perhaps ye will not dare to insult me.'

Confucius said: 'Did not he who made this ode understand the way of governing?' If a prince is able rightly to govern his kingdom, who will dare to insult him?

"But now the princes take advantage of the time, when throughout their kingdoms there are leisure and rest from external troubles, to abandon themselves to pleasure and indolent indifference; they, in fact, seek for calamities for themselves.

"Calamity and happiness in all cases are men's own seeking. This is illustrated by what is said in the Book of Poetry:

'Be always studious to be in harmony with the ordinances of God,
So you will certainly get for yourself much happiness;'

and by the passage of the Tai Chia: 'When Heaven sends down calamities, it is still possible to escape from them; when we occasion the calamities ourselves, it is not possible any longer to live.'"

Mencius said: "If a ruler give honor to men of talents and virtue and employ the able, so that the offices shall all be filled by individuals of distinction and mark — then all the scholars of the empire will be pleased, and wish to stand in his court.

"If, in the market-place of his capital, he levy a ground rent on the shops but do not tax the goods, or enforce the proper regulations without levying ground rent, then all the traders of the empire will be pleased, and wish to store their goods in his market-place.

"If, at his frontier-passes, there be an inspection of persons, but no taxes charged on goods or other articles, then all the travelers of the empire will be pleased, and wish to make their tours on his roads.

"If he require that the husbandmen give their mutual aid to cultivate the public field, and exact no other taxes from them, then all the husbandmen of the empire will be pleased, and wish to plow in his fields.

"If from the occupiers of the shops in his market-place he do not exact the fine of the individual idler, or of the hamlet's quota of cloth, then all the people of the empire will be pleased, and wish to come and be his people.

"If a ruler can truly practise these five things, then the people in the neighboring kingdoms will look up to him as a parent. From the first birth of mankind till now, never has any one led children to attack their parent, and succeeded in his design. Thus, such a ruler will not have an enemy in all the empire, and he who has no enemy in the empire is the minister of Heaven. Never has there been a ruler in such a case who did not attain to the imperial dignity."

Mencius said: "All men have a mind which can not bear to see the sufferings of others.

"The ancient kings had this commiserating mind, and they, as a matter of course, had likewise a commiserating government. When with a commiserating mind was practised a commiserating government, the government of the empire was as easy a matter as the making anything go round in the palm.

"When I say that all men have a mind which can not bear to see the sufferings of others, my meaning may be illustrated thus: even nowadays, if men suddenly see a child about to fall into a well, they will without exception experience a feeling of alarm and distress. They will feel so, not as a ground on which they may gain the favor of the child's parents, nor as a ground on which they may seek the praise of their neighbors and friends, nor from a dislike to the reputation of having been unmoved by such a thing.

"From this case we may perceive that the feeling of commiseration is essential to man, that the feeling of shame and dislike is essential to man, that the feeling of modesty and complaisance is essential to man, and that the feeling of approving and disapproving is essential to man.

"The feeling of commiseration is the principle of benevolence. The feeling of shame and dislike is the principle of righteousness. The feeling of modesty and complaisance is the principle of propriety. The feeling of approving and disapproving is the principle of knowledge.

"Men have these four principles just as they have their four limbs. When men, having these four principles, yet say of themselves that they can not develop them, they play the thief with themselves, and he who says of his prince that he can not develop them, plays the thief with his prince.

"Since all men have these four principles in themselves, let them know to give them all their development and completion, and the issue will be like that of fire which has begun to burn, or that of a spring which has begun to find vent. Let them have their complete development, and they will suffice to love and protect all within the four seas. Let them be denied that development, and they will not suffice for a man to serve his parent with."

Mencius said: "Is the arrow-maker less benevolent than the maker of armor of defense? And yet, the arrow-maker's only fear is lest men should not be hurt. So it is with the priest and the coffin-maker. The choice of a profession, therefore, is a thing in which great caution is required.

"Confucius said: 'It is virtuous manners which constitute the excellence of a neighborhood. If a man, in selecting a residence, do not fix on one where such prevail, how can he be wise?'

"Now, benevolence is the most honorable dignity conferred by Heaven, and the quiet home in which man should dwell. Since no one can hinder us from being so, if yet we are not benevolent — this is being not wise.

"From the want of benevolence and the want of wisdom will ensue the entire absence of propriety and righteousness — he who is in such a case must be the servant of other men. To be the servant of men and yet ashamed of such servitude is like a bow-maker's being ashamed to make bows, or an arrow-maker's being ashamed to make arrows.

"If he be ashamed of his case, his best course is to practise benevolence.

"The man who would be benevolent is like the archer. The archer adjusts himself and then shoots. If he misses, he does not murmur against those who surpass himself. He simply turns round and seeks the cause of his failure in himself."

—By Mencius (Mang-Tse), Chinese (371–288 B.C.), translated by James Legge.

~ ❂ ~

The Conduct of a Successful Ruler

NICCOLÒ MACHIAVELLI

I

Of Such Things as Render Men (especially Princes) Worthy of Blame or Applause.

It remains now that we see in what manner a prince ought to comport with his subjects and friends; and because many have written of this subject before, it may perhaps seem arrogant in me, especially considering that in my discourse I shall deviate from the opinion of other men. But my intention being to write for the benefit and advantage of him who understands, I thought it more convenient to respect the essential verity, rather than an imaginary view, of the subject; for many have framed imaginary commonwealths and governments to themselves which never were seen nor had any real existence. And the present manner of living is so different from the way that ought to be taken, that he who neglects what is done to follow what ought to be done, will sooner learn how to ruin than how to preserve himself; for a tender man, and one that desires to be honest in everything, must needs run a great hazard among so many of a contrary principle. Wherefore it is necessary for a prince who is willing to subsist to harden himself, and learn to be good or otherwise according to the exigence of his affairs. Laying aside, therefore, all imaginable notions of a prince, and discoursing of nothing but what is actually true, I say that all men when they are spoken of, especially princes, who are in a higher and more eminent station, are remarkable for some quality or other that makes them either honorable or contemptible. Hence it is that some are counted liberal, others (according to the propriety of the Tuscan word *Misero*, for *Quaro* in our language is one that desires to acquire by rapine or any other way; *Misero* is he that abstains too much from making use of his own) miserable; some munificent, others rapacious; some cruel, others merciful; some faithless, others precise; one poor-spirited and effeminate, another fierce and ambitious; one courteous, another haughty; one modest, another libidinous; one sincere, another cunning; one rugged and morose, another accessible and easy; one grave, another giddy; one devout, another an atheist. No man, I am sure, will deny but that it would be an admirable thing and highly to be commended to have a prince endued with all the good qualities aforesaid; but because it is impossible to have, much less to exercise, them all by reason of the frailty and grossness of our nature, it is convenient that he be so well instructed as to know how to avoid the scandal of those vices which may deprive him of his state, and be very cautious of the rest, though their consequence be not so pernicious but that where they are unavoidable he need trouble himself the less. Again, he is not to concern himself if he run under the infamy of those vices without which his dominion is not to be preserved; for if we consider things impartially we shall find some things in appearance are virtuous, and yet, if pursued, would bring certain destruction; while others, on the contrary, that are seemingly bad, which, if followed by a prince, procure his peace and security.

II

Of Liberality and Parsimony.

To begin, then, with the first of the abovementioned qualities, I say, it would be advantageous to be accounted liberal; nevertheless, liberality so used as not to render you formidable does but injure you; for if it be used virtuously and as it ought to be, it will not be known, nor secure you from the imputation of its contrary. To keep up, therefore, the name of liberal amongst men, it is necessary that no kind of luxury be omitted, so that a prince of that disposition will consume his revenue in that kind of expenses, and be obliged at last, if he would preserve that reputation, to become grievous, and a great exactor upon the people, and do whatever is practicable for the getting of money, which will cause him to be hated of his subjects and despised by everybody else when he once comes to be poor, so that offending many with his liberality and rewarding but few, he becomes sensible of the first disaster, and runs great hazard of being ruined the first time he is in danger; which, when afterward he discovers, and desires to remedy, he runs into the other extreme, and grows as odious for his avarice. So, then, if a prince cannot exercise this virtue of liberality so as to be publicly known, without detriment to himself, he ought, if he be wise, not to dread the imputation of being covetous, for in time he shall be esteemed liberal when it is discovered that by his parsimony he has increased his revenue to a condition of defending himself against invasion and of engaging in enterprises upon other people without oppressing of them; so that he shall be accounted noble to all from whom he takes nothing away, which are an infinite number, and near and parsimonious only to such few as he gives nothing to.

In our days we have seen no great action done but by those who were accounted miserable; the other have been always undone. Pope Julius II made use of his bounty to get into the Chair, but to enable himself to make war with the King of France he never practised it after, and by his frugality he maintained several wars without any tax or imposition upon the people, his long parsimony having furnished him for his extraordinary expenses. The present King of Spain, if he had affected to be thought liberal, could never have undertaken so many great designs nor obtained so many great victories. A prince, therefore, ought not so much to concern himself (so he exacts not upon his subjects, so he be able to defend himself, so he becomes not poor and despicable, nor commits rapine upon his people) though he be accounted covetous, for that is one of those vices which fortify his dominion. If any one objects that Cæsar by his liberality made his way to the empire, and many others upon the same score of reputation have made themselves great, I answer, that you are actually a prince, or are in a fair way to be made one. In the first case, liberality is hurtful; in the second, it is necessary, and Cæsar was one of those who designed upon the empire. But when he was arrived at that dignity, if he had lived, and had not retrenched his expenses, he would have ruined that empire. If any replies, many have been princes, and with their armies performed great matters, who have been reputed liberal, I rejoin that a prince spends either of his own, or his subjects', or other people's. In the first case he is to be frugal;

in the second, he may be as profuse as he pleases, and baulk no point of liberality. But that prince whose army is to be maintained with free quarter and plunder and exactions from other people, is obliged to be liberal, or his army will desert him; and well he may be prodigal of what neither belongs to him nor his subjects, as was the case with Cæsar, and Cyrus, and Alexander; for to spend upon another's stock rather adds to than subtracts from his reputation; it is spending of his own that is so mortal and pernicious. Nor is there anything that destroys itself like liberality; for in taking away the faculty of using it, thou becomest poor and contemptible, or, to avoid that poverty, thou makest thyself odious and a tyrant; and there is nothing of so much importance to a prince to avoid as to be either contemptible or odious, both of which depend much upon the prudent exercise of your liberality. Upon these considerations it is more wisdom to lie under the scandal of being miserable, which is an imputation rather infamous than odious, than to be thought liberal and run yourself into a necessity of playing the tyrant, which is infamous and odious both.

III

Of Cruelty and Clemency, and whether it is best for a Prince to be beloved or feared.

To come now to the other qualities proposed, I say every prince is to desire to be esteemed rather merciful than cruel, but with great caution that his mercy be not abused; Cæsar Borgia was counted cruel, yet that cruelty reduced Romagna, united it, settled it in peace, and rendered it faithful: so that if well considered, he will appear much more merciful than the Florentines, who rather than be thought cruel suffered Pistoia to be destroyed. A prince, therefore, is not to regard the scandal of being cruel, if thereby he keeps his subjects in their allegiance and united, seeing that by some few examples of justice you may be more merciful than they who by a universal exercise of pity permit several disorders to follow, which occasion rapine and murder; and the reason is, because that exorbitant mercy has an ill effect upon the whole universality, whereas particular executions extend only to particular persons. But among all princes a new prince has the hardest task to avoid the scandal of being cruel by reason of the newness of his government, and the dangers which attend it: hence Virgil in the person of Dido excused the inhospitality of her government.

Res dura, et regni novitas, me talia cogunt
Moliri, et late fines Custode tueri.

My new dominion and my harder fate
Constrains me to't, and I must guard my
State.

Nevertheless, he is not to be too credulous of reports, too hasty in his motions, nor create fears and jealousies to himself, but so to temper his administrations with prudence and humanity that neither too much confidence may make him careless, nor too much diffidence intolerable. And hence arises a new question, Whether it be better to be beloved than feared, or feared than beloved? It is answered, both would be convenient, but because that is hard to attain, it is better and more secure, if one must be wanting, to be feared than beloved; for in general men are ungrateful, inconstant, hypocritical, fearful of danger, and covetous of gain; while they receive any benefit by you, and the danger is at a distance, they are absolutely yours, and their blood, their estates, their lives and their children, as I said before, are all at your service; but when mischief is at hand, and you have present need of their help, they make no scruple to revolt; and that prince who leaves himself naked of other preparations, and relies wholly upon their professions, is sure to be ruined; for amity contracted by price, and not by the greatness and generosity of the mind, may seem a good pennyworth; yet when you have occasion to make use of it, you will find no such thing. Moreover, men do with less remorse offend against those who desire to be beloved than against those who are ambitious of being feared; the reason is that love is fastened only by a ligament of obligation, which the ill-nature of mankind breaks upon every occasion that is presented to his profit; but fear depends upon an apprehension of punishment, which is never to be dispelled. Yet a prince is to render himself awful in such sort that, if he gains not his subjects' love, he may eschew their hatred; for to be feared and not hated are compatible enough, and he may be always in that condition if he offers no violence to their estates, nor attempts anything upon the honor of their wives, as also when he has occasion to take away any man's life, if he takes his time when the cause is manifest, and he has good matter for his justification; but above all things he is to have a care for intrenching upon their estates, for men do sooner forget the death of their father than the loss of their patrimony; besides, occasions of confiscation never fail, and he that once gives way to that humor of rapine shall never want temptation to ruin his neighbor. But, on the contrary, provocations to blood are more rare, and do sooner evaporate, but when a prince is at the head of his army, and has a multitude of soldiers to govern, then it is absolutely necessary not to value the epithet of cruel, for without that no army can be kept in unity, nor in disposition for any great act.

Among the several instances of Hannibal's great conduct, it is one that, having a vast army constituted out of several nations, and conducted to make war in an enemy's country, there never happened any sedition among them, or any mutiny against their general, either in his adversity or prosperity. This can only be attributed to his great cruelty, which, added to his infinite virtues, rendered him both awful and terrible to his soldiers; without that all his virtues would have signified nothing. Some writers there are, but of little consideration, who admire his great exploits and condemn the true causes of them. But to prove that his other virtues would never have carried him through, let us reflect upon Scipio, a person honorable not only in his own time, but in all history whatever; nevertheless his army mutinied in Spain, and the true cause of it was his too much gentleness and lenity, which gave his soldiers more liberty than was suitable or consistent with military discipline. Fabius Maximus upbraided him by it in the Senate, and called him corrupter of the Roman Militia; the inhabitants of Locris having been plundered and destroyed by one of Scipio's lieutenants, they were never redressed, nor the legate's insolence corrected, all proceeding from the mildness of Scipio's nature, which was so eminent in him, that a person undertaking to excuse him in the Senate declared that there were many who knew better how to avoid doing ill themselves than to punish it in other people; which temper would doubtless in time have eclipsed the glory and reputation of Scipio, had that authority been continued in him; but receiving orders and living under the direction of the Senate, that ill quality was not only not discovered in him, but turned to his renown. I conclude, therefore, according to what I have said about being feared or beloved, that forasmuch as men do love at their own discretion, but fear at their prince's, a wise prince is obliged to lay his foundation upon that which is in his own power, not that which depends on other people, but, as I said before, with great caution that he does not make himself odious.

IV

How far a Prince is obliged by his Promise.

How honorable it is for a prince to keep his word, and act rather with integrity than collusion, I suppose everybody understands: nevertheless, experience has shown in our times that those princes who have not pinned themselves up to that punctuality and preciseness have done great things, and by their cunning and subtilty have not only circumvented those with whom they had to deal, but have overcome and been too hard for those who have been so superstitiously exact. For further explanation you must understand there are two ways of contending, by law and by force: the first is proper to men; the second to beasts; but because many times the first is insufficient, recourse must be had to the second. It belongs, therefore, to a prince to understand both, when to make use of the rational and when of the brutal way; and this is recommended to princes, though abstrusely, by ancient writers, who tell them how Achilles and several other princes were committed for education to Chiron the Centaur, who was to keep them under his discipline, choosing them a master, half man and half beast, for no other reason but to show how necessary it is for a prince to be acquainted with both, for that one without the other will be of little duration. Seeing, therefore, it is of such importance to a prince to take upon him the nature and disposition of a beast, of all the whole flock he ought to imitate the lion and the fox; for the lion is in danger of toils and snares, and the fox of the wolf; so that he must be a fox to find out the snares, and a lion to fright away the wolves, but they who keep wholly to the lion have no true notion of themselves. A prince, therefore, who is wise and prudent, cannot or ought not to keep his parole, when the keeping of it is to his prejudice, and the causes for which he promised removed. Were men all good this doctrine was not to be taught, but because they are wicked and not likely to be punctual with you, you are not obliged to any such strictness with them; nor was there ever any prince that lacked lawful pretence to justify his breach of promise. I might instance in many modern examples, and show how many confederations, and peaces, and promises have been broken by the infidelity of princes, and how he that best personated the fox had the better success. Nevertheless, it is of great consequence to disguise your inclination, and to play the hypocrite well; and men are so simple in their temper and so submissive to their present necessities, that he that is neat and cleanly in his collusions shall never want people to practise them upon. I cannot forbear one example which is still fresh in our memory. Alexander VI never did, nor thought of, anything but cheating, and never wanted matter to work upon; and though no man promised a thing with greater asseveration, nor confirmed it with more oaths and imprecations, and observed them less, yet understanding the world well he never miscarried.

A prince, therefore, is not obliged to have all the forementioned good qualities in reality, but it is necessary to have them in appearance; nay, I will be bold to affirm that, having them actually, and employing them upon all occasions, they are extremely prejudicial, whereas, having them only in appearance, they turn to better account; it is honorable to seem mild, and merciful, and courteous, and religious, and sincere, and indeed to be so, provided your mind be so rectified and prepared that you can act quite contrary upon occasion. And this must be premised, that a prince, especially if come but lately to the throne, cannot observe all those things exactly which cause men to be esteemed virtuous, being oftentimes necessitated, for the preservation of his state, to do things inhuman, uncharitable, and irreligious; and, therefore, it is convenient for his mind to be at his command, and flexible to all the puffs and variations of fortune; not forbearing to be good while it is in his choice, but knowing how to be evil when there is a necessity. A prince, then, is to have particular care that nothing falls from his mouth but what is full of the five qualities aforesaid, and that to see and hear him he appears all goodness, integrity, humanity, and religion, which last he ought to pretend to more than ordinarily, because more men do judge by the eye than by the touch; for everybody sees but few understand; everybody sees how you appear, but few know what in reality you are, and those few dare not oppose the opinion of the multitude, who have the majesty of their prince to defend them; and in the actions of all men, especially princes, where no man has power to judge, everyone looks to the end. Let a prince, therefore, do what he can to preserve his life, and continue his supremacy, the means which he uses shall be thought honorable, and be commended by everybody; because the people are always taken with the appearance and event of things, and the greatest part of the world consists of the people; those few who are wise taking place when the multitude has nothing else to rely upon. There is a prince at this time in being (but his name I shall conceal) who has nothing in his mouth but fidelity and peace; and yet had he exercised either the one or the other, they had robbed him before this both of his power and reputation.

V

That Princes ought to be cautious of becoming either odious or contemptible.

And because in our discourse of the qualifications of a prince we have hitherto spoken only of those which are of greatest importance, we shall now speak briefly of the rest. That a prince make it his business (as is partly hinted before) to avoid such things as may make him odious or contemptible, and that as often as he does that he plays his part very well, and shall meet no danger or inconveniences by the rest of his vices. Nothing, as I said before, makes a prince so insufferably odious as usurping his subjects' estates and debauching their wives, which are two things he ought studiously to forbear; for while the generality of the world live quietly upon their estates and unprejudiced in their honor, they live peaceably enough, and all his contention is only with the pride and ambition of some few persons who are in many ways and with great ease restrained. But a prince is contemptible when he is counted effeminate, light, inconstant, pusillanimous, and irresolute; and of this he ought to be as careful as of a rock in the sea, and strive that in all his actions there may appear magnanimity, courage, gravity, and fortitude, desiring that in the private affairs of his subjects his sentence and determination may be irrevocable, and himself to stand so in their opinion that none may think it possible either to delude or divert him. The prince who causes himself to be esteemed in that manner shall be highly redoubted, and if he be feared, people will not easily conspire against him, nor readily invade him, because he is known to be an excellent person and formidable to his subjects; for a prince ought to be terrible in two places — at home to his subjects, and abroad to his equals, from whom he defends himself by good arms and good allies; for, if his power be good, his friends will not be wanting, and while his affairs are fixed at home, there will be no danger from abroad, unless they be disturbed by some former conspiracy; and upon any commotion *ab extra*, if he be composed at home, has lived as I prescribe, and not deserted himself, he will be able to bear up against any impression, according to the example of Nabis the Spartan.

When things are well abroad his affairs at home will be safe enough, unless they be perplexed by some secret conspiracy, against which the prince sufficiently provides if he keeps himself from being hated or despised, and the people remain satisfied of him, which is a thing very necessary, as I have largely inculcated before. And one of the best remedies a prince can use against conspiracy is to keep himself from being hated or despised by the multitude; for nobody plots but expects by the death of the prince to gratify the people, and the thought of offending them will deter him from any such enterprise, because in conspiracies the difficulties are infinite. By experience we find that many conjurations have been on foot, but few have succeeded, because no man can conspire alone, nor choose a confederate but out of those who are discontented; and no sooner shall you impart your mind to a malcontent but you give him opportunity to reconcile himself, because there is nothing he proposes to himself but he may expect from the discovery. So that the gain being certain on that side, and hazardous and uncertain on the other, he must be either an extraordinary friend to you or an implacable enemy to the prince if he does not betray you; in short, on the side of the conspirators there is nothing but fear and jealousy, and apprehension of punishment; but, on the prince's side, there is the majesty of the Government, the laws, the assistance of his friends and State, which defend him so effectually that, if the affections of the people be added to them, no man can be so rash and precipitate as to conspire; for if, before the execution of his design, the conspirator has reason to be afraid, in this case he has much more afterwards, having offended the people in the execution and left himself no refuge to fly to. Of this many examples may be produced. . . .

And it has been the constant care of all wise princes and all well-governed States not to reduce the nobility to despair nor the people to discontent, which is one of the most material things a prince is to prevent. Among the best-ordered monarchies of our times France is one, in which there are many good laws and constitutions tending to the liberty and preservation of the king. The first of them is the Parliament and the authority wherewith it is vested; for he who was the founder of that monarchy, being sensible of the ambition and insolence of the nobles, and judging it convenient to have them bridled and restrained; and knowing on the other side, the hatred of the people against the nobility, and that it proceeded from fear, being willing to secure them, to exempt the king from the displeasure of the nobles if he sided with the Commons, or from the malice of the Commons if he inclined to the nobles, he erected a third judge, who, without any reflection upon the king, should keep the nobility under, and protect the people; nor could there be a better order, wiser, nor of greater security to the king and the kingdom, whence we may deduce another observation — That princes are to leave things of injustice and envy to the ministry and execution of others, but acts of favor and grace are to be performed by themselves. . . .

VI

How a Prince is to demean himself to gain reputation.

Nothing recommends a prince so highly to the world as great enterprises and noble expressions of his own valor and conduct. We have in our days Ferdinand, King of Aragon — the present King of Spain — who may, and not improperly, be called a new prince, since from a small and weak king become for fame and renown the greatest monarch in Christendom; and if his exploits be considered you will find them all brave, but some of them extraordinary. In the beginning of his reign he invaded the kingdom of Granada, and that enterprise was the foundation of his grandeur. He began it leisurely, and without suspicion of impediment, holding the barons of Castile employed in that service, and so intent upon that war that they dreamt not of any innovation, while in the meantime, before they were aware, he got reputation and authority over them. He found out a way of maintaining his army at the expense of the Church and the people; and by the length of that war to establish such order and discipline among his soldiers, that afterwards they gained him many honorable victories. Besides this, to adapt him for greater enterprises (always making religion his pretence), by a kind of devout cruelty he destroyed and exterminated the Jews called Marrani, than which nothing could be more strange or deplorable. Under the same cloak of religion he invaded Africa, made his expedition into Italy, assaulted France, and began many great things which always kept the minds of his subjects in admiration and suspense, wondering what the event of his machinations would be. And these enterprises had so sudden a spring and result one from the other that they gave no leisure to any man to be at quiet, or to continue anything against him. It is likewise of great advantage to a prince to give some rare example of his own administration at home (such is reported of Monsieur Bernardo da Milano), when there is occasion for somebody to perform anything extraordinary in the civil government whether it be good or bad, and to find out such a way either to reward or punish him as may make him much talked of in the world. Above all, a prince is to have a care in all his actions to behave himself so as may give him the reputation of being excellent as well as great.

A prince is likewise much esteemed when he shows himself a sincere friend or a generous enemy — that is, when without any hesitation he declares himself in favor of one against another, which, as it is more frank and princely, so it is more profitable than to stand neutral; for if two of your potent neighbors be at war, they are either of such condition that you are to be afraid of the victor or not; in either of which cases it will be always more for your benefit to discover yourself freely, and make a fair war. For in the first case, if you do not declare, you shall be a prey to him who overcomes, and it will be a pleasure and satisfaction to him that is conquered to see you his fellow-sufferer; nor will anybody either defend or receive you, and the reason is because the conqueror will never understand them to be his friends who would not assist him in his distress; and he that is worsted will not receive you because you neglected to run his fortune with your arms in your hands. . . . And those princes who are ill-advised, to avoid some present danger follow the neutral way, are most commonly ruined; but when a prince discovers himself courageously in favor of one party, if he with whom you join overcome, though he be very powerful, and you seem to remain at his discretion, yet he is obliged to you, and must needs have a respect for you, and men are not so wicked with such signal and exemplary ingratitude as to oppress you. Besides, victories are never so clear and complete as to leave the conqueror without all sparks of reflection, and especially upon what is just. But if your confederate comes by the worst, you are received by him, and assisted while he is able, and becomest a companion of his fortune, which may possibly restore thee. In the second place, if they who contend be of such condition that they have no occasion to fear, let which will overcome, you are in prudence to declare yourself the sooner, because by assisting the one you contribute to the ruin of the other, whom, if your confederate had been wise, he ought rather to have preserved; so that he overcoming remains wholly at your discretion, and by your assistance he must of necessity overcome. And here it is to be noted, if he can avoid it, a prince is never to league himself with another more powerful than himself in an offensive war; because in that case if he overcomes you remain at his mercy, and princes ought to be as cautious as possible of falling under the discretion of other people. The Venetians, when there was no necessity for it, associated with France against the Duke of Milan, and that association was the cause of their ruin. But where it is not to be avoided, as happened to the Florentines when the Pope and the Spaniard sent their armies against Lombardy, there a prince is to adhere for the reasons aforesaid. Nor is any prince or government to imagine that in those cases any certain counsel can be taken, because the affairs of this world are so ordered, that in avoiding one mischief we fall commonly into another. But a man's wisdom is most conspicuous where he is able to distinguish of dangers and make choice of the least.

Moreover, it is a prince's wisdom to show himself a virtuoso, and honorer of all that is excellent in any art whatsoever. He is likewise to encourage and assure his subjects that they may live quietly in peace, and exercise themselves in their several vocations, whether merchandise, agriculture, or any other employment whatever, to the end that no one may forbear improving or embellishing his estate for fear it should be taken from him, or forbear advancing his trade in apprehension of taxes; but the prince is rather to excite them by propositions of reward and immunities to all such as shall any way amplify his territory or power. He is obliged, likewise, at convenient times in the year to entertain the people by feastings and plays, and spectacles of recreation; and, because all cities are divided into companies or wards, he ought to have respect to those societies, be merry with them sometimes, and give them some instance of his humanity and magnificence, but always retaining the majesty of his degree, which is never to be debased in any case whatever.

—*From The Prince, Chapters XV–XIX, and XXI, by Niccolò Machiavelli, Italian (1469–1527), anonymous translation.*

The Illustrious Grand Vezir

SARI MEHMED PASHA

SINCE THE LORD without Equal, who showers down abundant gifts (may His Glory be exalted beyond the reach of imagination!), has made that firmly founded dynasty, the surpassing Ottoman Sultanate, to be the refuge of the rulers of the times, and has made their court, which pours on every hand favors from the ocean of abundance, to be distributor of the sustenance decreed by Providence to the people of the world, it has consequently become a necessary responsibility and obvious obligation of the pādishāh to fulfil the incumbent gratitude due for this Divine Grace in accordance with the precept "Every one of you is a shepherd and every one of you is responsible for his flock." Therefore he should make affluent the condition of the governed and establish good order in the affairs of the citizens and carry out the injunctions of the illustrious Holy Law and protect the boundaries of the territories and coasts of the Moslems. As he obeys and executes continuously this essential and indispensably important command by protecting good order according to the rule: "There is no state save with men of substance and no men of substance save with wealth," he must certainly show his brilliance through the management of fortunate vezirs and the assembling of armies experienced in wars of the Faith. In consequence of this, it is more manifest than the sun and more clear than yesterday, most necessary of needs for both country and government, among the most essential of essentials of the practice of the sultanate that he should appoint a religious and upright minister, one like Aristotle in sagacity, an unrestricted representative, one who will obtain the products of labor and lay up stores of provisions and wealth and make the state treasures as abundant as the sea, one who will strive for the protection and preservation of secure tranquillity and good order among the poor subjects entrusted to him by the Creator of Mankind, as well as for that of all the servants of God. The whole of the regulating and ordering of the affairs of the country and of the ameliorating of the condition of the subjects should be committed to his responsibility, in accordance with the maxim: "Give back the trust to its owner." He should be granted complete freedom in the business of the vezirate and requests which he presents to the Imperial Presence should not be denied. The unrestrained grand vezir must have the favor of his patron and must seek after the highest virtues. As partaker in the freshness of one who shares the harvest of both noble and peasant, let him make laudable efforts and abundant endeavors utterly to destroy illegal practices and injustice, to remove the weeds and thorns of tyranny and corruption, and to drive out the torments of oppression and obstinacy by the benefactions of justice and equity.

First among the obligations of lofty endeavor and essential measures of the sublime sultanate is the support in affluence of the inhabitants of the most honored cities and districts, the most blessed habitations and regions, Mekka the Noble and Medina the Illuminated (may God – exalted is He – glorify them until the Day of Judgment!), through the complete shipment from Cairo of their customary yearly rents in grain. Before all else the produce of their properties must be properly loaded on ships, in order that it may be kept clean and pure. And to the *vāli* of Egypt repeated orders must be sent to make him extremely vigilant and insistent upon gathering everyone together at the proper time and place. Reliable men must be appointed to protect the rights of the poor during the course of the journey.

Throughout their period of authority let them treat with equality the humble and the noble, the wealthy and the poor, the learned and the unlearned, the one from afar and the one from nearby, the visitor and the neighbor. Let them not make use of their power until the evidence is complete. In short, let them treat all alike in executing the holy law, making no distinction between great and small, rich and poor, subject and prince.

To the glorious pādishāh let them speak the word of truth without veiling or concealment. And let them never conceal the truth, which is necessary to every one, nor neglect to speak it where it is needed. For the Prophet of God (on whom be the commendation and salutation of God) has said: "Words of truth are the best alms."

Though a man give a thousand aspers of
alms a day, he gains not this reward.
Speak the truth in its place; be not silent,
for the word of truth is the finest alms.

One must not restrain one's self from speaking words of truth whatever the place may be. . . .

The grand vezir and all mankind should pray for His Majesty the Pādishāh of Islam and not fail in blessing him. For the Prophet (on whom be the commendation and salutation of God) has said: "Curse not the sultan, for behold! he is the shadow of God on earth." Let everyone always and with sincere heart bless and praise the pādishāh of mankind and hold not to the contrary course, for God who is Great in Majesty has made him caliph. He is the shadow of God on the face of the earth. Prayer for him is the duty of everyone:

Bless the pādishāh; never curse him, for God
has made him caliph.
Imagine not vain thoughts of that noble personage,
for he is God's shadow on earth.

Let thy heart be filled with love for the glorious pādishāh; let his praise and eulogy be perpetually on thy tongue. With all thy being strive and persevere in his service. Strive assiduously to veil his defects. Perform with truth and sincerity whatever his service and praise may require. Do it not with duplicity or with self-comfort as goal. Let no weariness of serving be shown to the pādishāh, nor any appearance of being self-satisfied and independent.

The grand vezir especially must not be a time-server, thinking of the benefits of money. Let him shun the hope of gathering wealth and treasure and spend his ability in preparing a remedy for the weakness and languidness which prevent the good health of the country. For his rejoicing and glorying in the simple service of the pādishāh's court will gain for him felicity in this world and that to come. Let him always expend without stint persistent endeavors, that his actions may be successful in the manner desired. And let him not employ the special costumes and effects of sultans, approaching the circle of partnership with them. Let him not fail in his duty to know his proper degree of modesty and humility when the pādishāh shows him honor and respect, granting him the favor of proximity, nor let him become puffed up with his greatness and exhibit to the people an appearance of haughtiness and disdain. . . . Let him not make haste or hurry in any task, for lack of patience and hastiness cause errors in the affairs of country and nation and disorder in the conditions of the faith and government. Speaking generally, it is fitting that habits of patience and firmness in affairs, deliberateness, and the resolution of one who makes precedents, should be practised. And one should hope for the attainment of a good end, awaiting expectantly the gaining of joy and health through the Glorious and Exalted Lord God. God – exalted is He – (may He be magnified and glorified!) has said: "Only the patient will be paid back their reward in full without measure."

The grand vezir should perform the five obligatory prayers in his dwelling together with the company there. His door should be open and consultation with him should be easy. It has been said: "If any person to whom a single affair of the believers is entrusted shut his door so that the oppressed and needy cannot reach him, to that man the Gate of Mercy will be closed in the time of his great need, and he will be deprived of the universal compassion and perfect kindness of the Exalted and Lofty God."

The purpose of government and dominion in this passing world is not the obtaining of pleasures nor the satisfying of desires. Peradventure it is the laying up a store in the world to come and the gaining through good deeds of an eternal good name and eternal fame. It is not fitting that the important time of rulers should be spent in music and song and love of pleasure. When one has reached such a station, the essentials are calmness, piety, justice, and contentment with what one has. As far as he can, one should seek goodness for himself and strive for the betterment of the world. In the meetings of the lofty council no permission should be given to any one for playing the fool, nor for meaningless jesting and joking, nor for the loud laughter of the low-bred, nor for backbiting and calumny and evil deeds. Mimicry and juggling and senseless gestures of diversion and amusement should not be allowed. Conversations should always be confined to consultation regarding religion and government and to plans for the preservation of the country. For it has been said: "The gold of dignity is better than jesting." Let him always be in fear and awe of the God of Glory (Glorious is His divine Majesty!), and let him not deviate from the truth nor turn aside from the highroad of integrity. Let him strive to carry out the pure law of the faith. For it has been said: "Everything fears him who fears God."

. . . . .

It is no way fitting to destroy the honor of a man, but rather to protect his integrity as far as possible and without spite or recompense to strive with goodness to make happy spirits and to console hearts. Let him not seek with a spirit of spite to rend the curtain of honor or demolish the structure of existence of any one. Let him control himself in time of wrath and bind his heart with the cord of patience and quiet. If, according to the law, he must chastise any one, let the blows not exceed the canonical number. Let him be especially vigiiant against breaking hearts. For it has been said: "The heart of the believer is the throne of God."

O thou who hast crushed hearts,
Thou hast not known at all the secret of the heart:
The perfect heart is the abode of God and his firm throne.
The believer's heart is the spacious throne of God.
Breaking of hearts is the greatest of sins:
It is the most presumptuous of disobediences.
Make haste to repair hearts;
Destroy not the throne of God.

It is fitting also not to be heedless of the weak and poor and to know that the investigation of their condition is a duty. For the requirement of gaining for one's self the affections of mankind is the means of obtaining the approval of the Creator. It is most fitting to treat every one with sympathy and not to view any one with contempt and insult. As it has been said:

Look not with contempt upon the dervish clad in tatters;
He also in his own way passes as ruler of this transient world.

And let him take no pleasure in the calamity of any created beings even though they be enemies. Let him spend freely of the treasure of endeavor in protecting the subjects who are under his power and in establishing duly the rights of the people. In executing the firmly founded Sacred Law let him take care with seemly efforts and abundant endeavors. Let him exert himself for the repression of brigands, the guarding and protecting of the subjects, the preservation of the country, the destruction of innovations in law, the repelling and suppressing of the wrongs of believers, and the eradicating and expelling of the foundations of disorder. . . .

Love of good fame is the foundation of all virtues. It has been said: "From virtue and goodness come respect for the good and a pleasant face for the people, and forgiveness for the blunders of the ignorant." One must guard one's self against having evil designs against others. For if thou designest evil against another, that evil ought first to be received by thyself. Harm no one behind his back. Thou shouldst support those who have fallen and not be found in opposition to any one, and shouldst avoid causing the ruin of any one. Prefer not slander and calumny and impute not guilt to any one by reporting untruth. For it is certain that ere long such things will be requited. As it has been said: "He who digs a pit for his brother has fallen into it himself." That is to say, if a person dig a well for his brother to fall into, that well has been dug for himself. One must ever be thankful for the benefactions which are the goodness and kindness of the Lord of the Two Worlds, and must be patient and long-suffering in calamity and resigned to God's design. Overwhelmed with the bountiful gifts of the Lord God (may He be extolled and His lauds recited!), let thanks be given always to Him and let hearts be disinclined to any other end. Let him put entire trust in the True One and commit all his affairs to the charge of God the Creator, exalted is He. When calamities befall him, let him be patient and long-suffering, not complaining. The Prophet (on whom be the commendation and salutation of God—exalted is He!) has said: "God compensates him who is patient in calamity."

Whoever in this world of change may meet
with sudden calamity,
If he be patient with it and make no complaint, God will reward him.

Let him be resigned to the decree of God and assiduous in renouncing sin and in begging forgiveness.

For if the arrow of Providence be sped by
the bow of Fate
There is no shield against it save resignation.

Let him desire no other helper than the Most High and Supreme God and His universal beneficence and let him have recourse to the Prophet of God and have fellowship with him. Let him associate with persons of good habits and wisdom. Let him not be sorrowful over what is past, nor let him suffer the hardship and care which are in the future. Let him strive diligently to do good. Let him seek both in public and in private to be disciplined in mind. For it has been said: "Culture is better than gold." . . .

Cling not to office and attach not thy heart so much to a thing that thou mayest through lack of it remain in the whirlpool of sorrow and affliction. Always strive to be small in fame. . . . When worldly position falls to thy lot, grow not proud, trusting in good fortune because of that position. Suffer no concern or care when thou hast it not. The sages have said: "The beginning of rank in this world is bestowing favors and its end is pouring forth sweat." That is to say, it is spending thyself and pouring thine honor to the earth. The greatest of sages have likened the situation of rulers to a hot bath. He who is inside wishes to be out and he who is outside wishes to be in. The person who is in the service of the Lofty Government should be patient and long-suffering in trouble and hardship. He should not consider his employment as due to his own aptitude, nor should he pay attention to reproaches. Always he should give thanks to the Lord Creator (exalted is His name!) and commit his affairs to the charge of the True God. He should surely associate himself with the favor of God and never cease from prayer. It is certain that servitors at one time receive kindness and at another time reproach from their master. Such being the case, they should give thanks when they receive kindness and be patient and long-suffering when they receive reproach, nor should they exhibit their weakness by complaining. . . .

Let them not spend the priceless term of life on trifling things. While they have the opportunity of being alive and have a respite from the appointed day of death, let them expend their time in worship and dedicate their hours to good works.

If they are rulers, let them confine themselves to giving peace to the servants of God, without rewards or personal aims. Reverencing in word and deed the conditions recorded above, let them strive and endeavor to act as they ought under all circumstances.

—*From The Book of Counsel for Vezirs and Governors by Sari Mehmed Pasha, Turk (end of the sixteenth and beginning of the seventeenth century), translated by Walter Livingston Wright, Jr.*

~ ✿ ~

The Origin of Government and the Source and Limits of Its Authority

JOHN MILTON

NO MAN, who knows aught, can be so stupid to deny that all men naturally were born free, being the image and resemblance of God himself, and were by privilege above all the creatures, born to command and not to obey. And that they lived so, till from the root of Adam's transgression falling among themselves to do wrong and violence, and foreseeing that such courses must needs tend to the destruction of them all, they agreed by common league to bind each other from mutual injury, and jointly to defend themselves against any that gave disturbance or opposition to such agreement. Hence came cities, towns, and commonwealths. And because no faith in all was found sufficiently binding, they saw it needful to ordain some authority that might restrain by force and punishment what was violated against peace and common right.

This authority and power of self-defence and preservation being originally and naturally in every one of them, and unitedly in them all; for ease, for order, and lest each man should be his own partial judge, they communicated and derived either to one whom for the eminence of his wisdom and integrity they chose above the rest, or to more than one, whom they thought of equal deserving: the first was called a king; the other magistrates: not to be their lords and masters – though afterwards those names in some places were given voluntarily to such as had been authors of inestimable good to the people – but to be their deputies and commissioners, to execute, by virtue of their intrusted power, that justice, which else every man by the bond of nature and of covenant must have executed for himself, and for one another. And to him that shall consider well why among free persons one man by civil right should bear authority and jurisdiction over another, no other end or reason can be imaginable.

These for a while governed well, and with much equity decided all things at their own arbitrament; till the temptation of such a power left absolute in their hands, perverted them at length to injustice and partiality. Then did they who now by trial had found the danger and inconveniences of committing arbitrary power to any, invent laws, either framed or consented to by all, that should confine and limit the authority of whom they chose to govern them: that so Man, of whose failing they had proof, might no more rule over them, but Law and Reason, abstracted as much as might be from personal errors and frailties. "While, as the magistrate was set above the people, so the law was set above the magistrate." When this would not serve, but that the law was either not executed, or misapplied, they were constrained from that time, the only remedy left them, to put conditions and take oaths from all kings and magistrates at their first installment, to do impartial justice by law: who, upon these terms and no other, received allegiance from the people, that is to say, bond or covenant to obey them in execution of those laws, which they, the people, had themselves made or assented to. And this ofttimes with express warning, that if the king or magistrate proved unfaithful to his trust, the people would be disengaged. They added also counsellors and parliaments, not to be only at his beck, but, with him or without him, at set times, or at all times, when any danger threatened, to have care of the public safety. Therefore saith Claudius Sesell, a French statesman, "The Parliament was set as a bridle to the king;" which I instance rather, not because our English lawyers have not said the same long before, but because that French monarchy is granted by all to be a far more absolute one than ours. That this and the rest of what hath hitherto been spoken is most true, might be copiously made appear through all stories, heathen and Christian; even of those nations where kings and emperors have sought means to abolish all ancient memory of the people's right by their encroachments and usurpations. But I spare long insertions, appealing to the German, French, Italian, Arragonian, English, and not least the Scottish histories; not forgetting this only by the way, that William the Norman, though a conqueror, and not unsworn at his coronation, was compelled a second time to take oath at St. Alban's ere the people would be brought to yield obedience.

It being thus manifest that the power of Kings and Magistrates is nothing else but what is only derivative, transferred, and committed to them in trust from the People to the common good of them all, in whom the power yet remains fundamentally and cannot be taken from them without a violation of their natural birthright; and seeing that from hence Aristotle and the best of political writers have defined a king, "him who governs to the good and profit of his people, and not for his own ends;" it follows from necessary causes, that the titles of sovereign lord, natural lord and the like are either arrogancies or flatteries, not admitted by emperors and kings of best note, and disliked by the church both of Jews (Isa. xxvi. 13) and ancient Christians, as appears by Tertullian and others. Although generally the people of Asia, and with them the Jews also, especially since the time they chose a king against the advice and counsel of God, are noted by wise authors much inclinable to slavery.

Secondly, that to say, as is usual, the king hath as good right to his crown and dignity as any man to his inheritance, is to make the subject no better than the king's slave, his chattel, or his possession that may be bought and sold: and doubtless, if hereditary title were sufficiently inquired, the best foundation of it would be found but either in courtesy or convenience. But suppose it to be of right hereditary, what can be more just and legal, if a subject for certain crimes be to forfeit by law from himself and posterity all his inheritance to the king, than that a king, for crimes proportional, should forfeit all his title and inheritance to the people? Unless the people must be thought created all for him, he not for them, and they all in one body inferior to him single; which were a kind of treason against the dignity of mankind to affirm.

Thirdly, it follows, that to say kings are accountable to none but God, is the overcoming of all law and government. For if they may refuse to give account, then all covenants made with them at coronation, all oaths are in vain, and mere mockeries; all laws which they swear to keep, made to no purpose: for if the king fear not God — as how many of them do not — we hold then our lives and estates by the tenure of his mere grace and mercy, as from a god, not a mortal magistrate; a position that none but court parasites or men besotted would maintain. Aristotle, therefore, whom we commonly allow for one of the best interpreters of nature and morality, writes in the fourth of his *Politics*, chap. x, that "monarchy unaccountable is the worst sort of tyranny, and least of all to be endured by free-born men."

And surely no Christian prince, not drunk with high mind and prouder than those pagan Cæsars that deified themselves, would arrogate so unreasonably above human condition, or derogate so basely from a whole nation of men, his brethren, as if for him only subsisting and to serve his glory, valuing them in comparison of his own brute will and pleasure no more than so many beasts, or vermin under his feet not to be reasoned with but to be trod on; among whom there might be found so many thousand men for wisdom, virtue, nobleness of mind, and all other respects but the fortune of his dignity, far above him. Yet some would persuade us that this absurd opinion was King David's, because in the 51st Psalm he cries out to God, "Against thee only have I sinned;" as if David had imagined, that to murder Uriah and adulterate his wife had been no sin against his neighbor, whenas that law of Moses was to the king expressly (Deut. xvii) not to think so highly of himself above his brethren. David, therefore, by those words, could mean no other, than either that the depth of his guiltiness was known to God only, or to so few as had not the will and power to question him, or that the sin against God was greater beyond compare than against Uriah. Whatever his meaning were, any wise man will see, that the pathetical words of a psalm can be no certain decision to a point that hath abundantly more certain rules to go by.

How much more rationally spake the heathen king Demophoön, in a tragedy of Euripides, than these interpreters would put upon King David! "I rule not my people by tyranny, as if they were barbarians; but am myself liable, if I do unjustly, to suffer justly." Not unlike was the speech of Trajan, the worthy emperor, to one whom he made general of his prætorian forces: "Take this drawn sword," saith he, "to use for me if I reign well; if not, to use against me." Thus Dion relates. And not Trajan only, but Theodosius, the younger, a Christian emperor, and one of the best, caused it to be enacted as a rule undeniable and fit to be acknowledged by all kings and emperors, that a prince is bound to the laws; that on the authority of the law the authority of a prince depends, and to the laws ought to submit. Which edict of his remains yet unrepealed in the code of Justinian (1. i. tit. 24), as a sacred constitution to all the succeeding emperors. How can any king in Europe maintain and write himself accountable to none but God, when emperors in their own imperial statutes have written and decreed themselves accountable to law? And indeed where such account is not feared, he that bids a man reign over him above law, may bid as well as savage beast.

It follows, lastly, that since the King or Magistrate holds his authority of the People, both originally and naturally for their good, in the first place, and not his own, then may the people, as oft as they shall judge it for the best, either choose him or reject him, retain him or depose him, though no tyrant, merely by the liberty and right of free-born men to be governed as seems to them best. . . .

Thus far hath been considered chiefly the power of Kings and Magistrates; how it was and is originally the people's, and by them conferred in trust only to be employed to the common peace and benefit; with liberty therefore and right remaining in them, to reassume it to themselves, if by kings or magistrates it be abused; or to dispose of it by any alteration, as they shall judge most conducing to the public good.

We may from hence with more ease and force of argument determine what a tyrant is, and what the people may do against him. A tyrant, whether by wrong or by right coming to the crown, is he who, regarding neither law nor the common good, reigns only for himself and his factions: thus St. Basil, among others, defines him. And because his power is great, his will boundless and exorbitant, the fulfilling whereof is for the most part accompanied with innumerable wrongs and oppressions of the people, murders, massacres, rapes, adulteries, desolation, and subversion of cities and whole provinces; look how great a good and happiness a just king is, so great a mischief is a tyrant; as he the public father of his country, so this the common enemy against whom what people lawfully may do, as against a common pest and destroyer of mankind, I suppose no man of clear judgment need go further to be guided than by the very principles of nature in him. . . .

For as to this question in hand, what the people by their just right may do in change of government, or of governor, we see it cleared sufficiently, besides other ample authority, even from the mouths of princes themselves. And surely they that shall boast, as we do, to be a free nation, and not have in themselves the power to remove or to abolish any governor, supreme or subordinate, with the government itself, upon urgent causes, may please their fancy with a ridiculous and painted freedom, fit to cozen babies; but they are indeed under tyranny and servitude, as wanting that power which is the root and source of all liberty, to dispose and economize in the land which God hath given them, as masters of family in their own house and free inheritance. Without which natural and essential power of a free nation, though bearing high their heads, they can in due esteem be thought no better than slaves and vassals born in the tenure and occupation of another inheriting lord, whose government, though not illegal, or intolerable, hangs over them as a lordly scourge, not as a free government; and therefore to be abrogated.

How much more justly then may they fling off tyranny, or tyrants, who being once deposed can be no more than private men, as subject to the reach of justice and arraignment as any other transgressors? And certainly if men, not to speak of heathen both wise and religious, have done justice upon tyrants what way they could soonest, how much more mild and humane then is it, to give them fair and open trial; to teach lawless kings, and all who so much adore them, that not mortal man nor his imperious will, but Justice, is the only true sovereign and supreme majesty upon earth? Let men cease therefore, out of faction and hypocrisy, to make outcries and horrid things of things so just and honorable, though perhaps till now no Protestant state or kingdom can be alleged to have openly put to death their king, which lately some have written, and imputed to their great glory; much mistaking the matter. It is not, neither ought it to be, the glory of a Protestant state never to have put their king to death; it is the glory of a Protestant king never to have deserved death. And if the Parliament and military council do what they do without precedent, if it appear their duty, it argues the more wisdom, virtue and maganimity, that they know themselves able to be a precedent to others; who perhaps in future ages, if they prove not too degenerate, will look up with honor, and aspire toward these exemplary and matchless deeds of their ancestors, as to the highest top of their civil glory and emulation; which heretofore, in the pursuance of fame and foreign dominion, spent itself vaingloriously abroad; but henceforth may learn a better fortitude, to dare execute highest justice on them that shall by force of arms endeavor the oppressing and bereaving of religion and their liberty at home. That no unbridled potentate or tyrant, but to his sorrow, for the future may presume such high and irresponsible licence over mankind, to havoc and turn upside down whole kingdoms of men, as though they were no more in respect of his perverse will than a nation of pismires.

—*From The Tenure of Kings and Magistrates, by John Milton, English (1608–1674).*

The English Bill of Rights

(1689)

WHEREAS the Lords Spiritual and Temporal, and Commons, assembled at Westminster, lawfully, fully, and freely representing all the estates of the people of this realm, did, upon the thirteenth day of February, in the year of our Lord one thousand six hundred eighty-eight, present unto their Majesties, then called and known by the names and style of William and Mary, Prince and Princess of Orange, being present in their proper persons, a certain declaration in writing, made by the said Lords and Commons, in the words following; viz.: —

Whereas the late King James II., by the assistance of divers evil counsellors, judges, and ministers employed by him, did endeavour to subvert and extirpate the Protestant religion, and the laws and liberties of this kingdom: —

1. By assuming and exercising a power of dispensing with and suspending of laws, and the execution of laws, without consent of Parliament.

2. By committing and prosecuting divers worthy prelates, for humbly petitioning to be excused from concurring to the same assumed power.

3. By issuing and causing to be executed a commission under the Great Seal for erecting a court, called the Court of Commissioners for Ecclesiastical Causes.

4. By levying money for and to the use of the Crown, by pretence of prerogative, for other time, and in other manner than the same was granted by Parliament.

5. By raising and keeping a standing army within this kingdom in time of peace, without consent of Parliament, and quartering soldiers contrary to law.

6. By causing several good subjects, being Protestants, to be disarmed, at the same time when Papists were both armed and employed contrary to law.

7. By violating the freedom of election of members to serve in Parliament.

8. By prosecutions in the Court of King's Bench, for matters and causes cognizable only in Parliament; and by diverse other arbitrary and illegal courses.

9. And whereas of late years, partial, corrupt, and unqualified persons, have been returned and served on juries in trials, and particularly divers jurors in trials for high treason, which were not freeholders.

10. And excessive bail hath been required of persons committed in criminal cases, to elude the benefit of the laws made for the liberty of the subjects.

11. And excessive fines have been imposed; and illegal and cruel punishments inflicted.

12. And several grants and promises made of fines and forfeitures, before any conviction of judgment against the persons upon whom the same were to be levied —

All which are utterly and directly contrary to the known laws and statutes, and freedom of this realm:

And whereas the said late King James II. having abdicated the government, and the throne being thereby vacant, his Highness the Prince of Orange (whom it hath pleased Almighty God to make the glorious instrument of delivering this kingdom from popery and arbitrary power) did (by the advice of the Lords Spiritual and Temporal, and divers principal persons of the Commons) cause letters to be written to the Lords Spiritual and Temporal, being Protestants, and other letters to the several counties, cities, universities, boroughs, and Cinque Ports, for the choosing of such persons as represent them, as were of right to be sent to Parliament, to meet and sit at Westminster upon the two-and-twentieth day of January, in this year one thousand six hundred eighty and eight, in order to such an establishment, as that their religion, laws, and liberties might not again be in danger of being subverted; upon which letters, elections have been accordingly made:

And thereupon the said Lords Spiritual and Temporal, and Commons, pursuant to their respective letters and elections, being now assembled in a full and free representation of this nation, taking into their most serious consideration the best means for attaining the ends aforesaid, do in the first place (as their ancestors in like case have usually done), for the vindicating and asserting their ancient rights and liberties, declare: —

1. That the pretended power of suspending of laws, or the execution of laws, by regal authority, without consent of Parliament, is illegal.

2. That the pretended power of dispensing with laws, or the execution of laws, by regal authority, as it hath been assumed and exercised of late, is illegal.

3. That the commission for erecting the late Court of Commissioners for Ecclesiastical Causes, and all others commissions and courts of like nature, are illegal and pernicious.

4. That levying money for or to the use of the Crown, by pretence of prerogative, without grant of Parliament, for longer time or in other manner than the same is or shall be granted, is illegal.

5. That it is the right of the subject to petition the king, and all commandments and prosecutions for such petitioning are illegal.

6. That the raising or keeping a standing army within the kingdom in time of peace, unless it be with consent of Parliament, is against law.

7. That the subjects which are Protestants may have arms for their defence suitable to their conditions, and as allowed by law.

8. That election of members of Parliament ought to be free.

9. That the freedom of speech, and debates or proceedings in Parliament, ought not to be impeached or questioned in any court or place out of Parliament.

10. That excessive bail ought not to be required, nor excessive fines imposed, nor cruel and unusual punishment inflicted.

11. That jurors ought to be duly impanelled and returned, and jurors which pass upon men in trials for high treason ought to be freeholders.

12. That all grants and promises of fine and forfeitures of particular persons before conviction, are illegal and void.

13. And that for redress of all grievances, and for the amending, strengthening and preserving of the laws, Parliaments ought to be held frequently.

And they do claim, demand, and insist upon all and singular the premises, as their undoubted rights and liberties; and that no declarations, judgments, doings or proceedings, to the prejudice of the people in any of the said premises, ought in any wise to be drawn hereafter into consequence or example. . . .

—*From The Bill of Rights, drawn up by a committee of the Convention Parliament in February, 1689, and read before William and Mary on the 13th of that month.*

~ ⚙ ~

The Social Contract

JEAN JACQUES ROUSSEAU

Introductory Note

I wish to enquire whether, taking men as they are and laws as they can be made, it is possible to establish some just and certain rule of administration in civil affairs. In this investigation I shall always strive to reconcile what right permits with what interest prescribes, so that justice and utility may not be severed.

I enter upon this inquiry without demonstrating the importance of my subject. I shall be asked whether I am a prince or a legislator that I write on politics. I reply that I am not; and that it is for this very reason that I write on politics. If I were a prince or a legislator, I should not waste my time in saying what ought to be done; I should do it or remain silent.

Having been born a citizen of a free State, and a member of the sovereign body, however feeble an influence my voice may have in public affairs, the right to vote upon them is sufficient to impose on me the duty of informing myself about them; and I feel happy, whenever I meditate on governments, always to discover in my researches new reasons for loving that of my own country.

Subject of the First Book

Man is born free, and everywhere he is in chains. Many a one believes himself the master of others, and yet he is a greater slave than they. How has this change come about? I do not know. What can render it legitimate? I believe that I can settle this question.

If I considered only force and the results that proceed from it, I should say that so long as a people is compelled to obey and does obey, it does well; but that, so soon as it can shake off the yoke and does shake it off, it does better; for, if men recover their freedom by virtue of the same right by which it was taken away, either they are justified in resuming it, or there was no justification for depriving them of it. But the social order is a sacred right which serves as a foundation for all others. This right, however, does not come from nature. It is therefore based on conventions. The question is to know what these conventions are. Before coming to that, I must establish what I have just laid down.

Primitive Societies

The earliest of all societies, and the only natural one, is the family; yet children remain attached to their father only so long as they have need of him for their own preservation. As soon as this need ceases, the natural bond is dissolved. The children being freed from the obedience which they owed to their father, and the father from the cares which he owed to his children, become equally independent. If they remain united, it is no longer naturally but voluntarily; and the family itself is kept together only by convention.

This common liberty is a consequence of man's nature. His first law is to attend to his own preservation, his first cares are those which he owes to himself; and as soon as he comes to years of discretion, being sole judge of the means adapted for his own preservation, he becomes his own master.

The family is, then, if you will, the primitive model of political societies; the chief is the analogue of the father, while the people represent the children; and all, being born free and equal, alienate their liberty only for their own advantage. The whole difference is that in the family the father's love for his children repays him for the care that he bestows upon them; while in the state the pleasure of ruling makes up for the chief's lack of love for his people.

Grotius denies that all human authority is established for the benefit of the governed, and he cites slavery as an instance. His invariable mode of reasoning is to establish right by fact. A juster method might be employed, but none more favorable to tyrants.

It is doubtful, then, according to Grotius, whether the human race belongs to a hundred men, or whether these hundred men belong to the human race; and he appears throughout his book to incline to the former opinion, which is also that of Hobbes. In this way we have mankind divided like herds of cattle, each of which has a master, who looks after it in order to devour it.

Just as a herdsman is superior in nature to his herd, so chiefs, who are the herdsmen of men, are superior in nature to their people. Thus, according to Philo's account, the Emperor Caligula reasoned, inferring truly enough from this analogy that kings are gods, or that men are brutes.

The reasoning of Caligula is tantamount to that of Hobbes and Grotius. Aristotle, before them all, had likewise said that men are not naturally equal, but that some are born for slavery and others for dominion.

Aristotle was right, but he mistook the effect for the cause. Every man born in slavery is born for slavery; nothing is more certain. Slaves lose everything in their bonds, even the desire to escape from them; they love their servitude as the companions of Ulysses loved their brutishness. If, then, there are slaves by nature, it is because there have been slaves contrary to nature. The first slaves were made such by force; their cowardice kept them in bondage.

I have said nothing about King Adam nor about Emperor Noah, the father of three great monarchs who shared the universe, like the children of Saturn with whom they are supposed to be identical. I hope that my moderation will give satisfaction; for, as I am a direct descendant of one of these princes, and perhaps of the eldest branch, how do I know whether, by examination of titles, I might not find myself the lawful king of the human race? Be that as it may, it cannot be denied that Adam was sovereign of the world, as Robinson was of his island, so long as he was its sole inhabitant; and it was an agreeable feature of that empire that the monarch, secure on his throne, had nothing to fear from rebellions, or wars, or conspirators.

The Right of the Strongest

The strongest man is never strong enough to be always master, unless he transforms his power into right, and obedience into duty. Hence the right of the strongest — a right apparently assumed in irony, and really established in principle. But will this phrase never be explained to us? Force is a physical power; I do not see what morality can result from its effects. To yield to force is an act of necessity, not of will; it is at most an act of prudence. In what sense can it be a duty?

Let us assume for a moment this pretended right. I say that nothing results from it but inexplicable nonsense; for if force constitutes right, the effect changes with the cause, and any force which overcomes the first succeeds to its rights. As soon as men can disobey with impunity, they may do so legitimately; and since the strongest is always in the right, the only thing is to act in such a way that one may be the strongest. But what sort of a right is it that perishes when force ceases? If it is necessary to obey by compulsion, there is no need to obey from duty; and if men are no longer forced to obey, obligation is at an end. We see, then, that this word *right* adds nothing to force; it here means nothing at all.

Obey the powers that be. If that means, Yield to force, the precept is good but superfluous; I reply that it will never be violated. All power comes from God, I admit; but every disease comes from him too; does it follow that we are prohibited from calling in a physician? If a brigand should surprise me in the recesses of a wood, am I bound not only to give up my purse when forced, but am I also morally bound to do so when I might conceal it? For, in effect, the pistol which he holds is a superior force.

Let us agree, then, that might does not make right, and that we are bound to obey none but lawful authorities. Thus my original question ever recurs.

Slavery

Since no man has any natural authority over his fellow-men, and since force is not the source of right, conventions remain as the basis of all lawful authority among men.

If an individual, says Grotius, can alienate his liberty and become the slave of a master, why should not a whole people be able to alienate theirs, and become subject to a king? In this there are many equivocal terms requiring explanation; but let us confine ourselves to the word *alienate*. To alienate is to give or sell. Now, a man who becomes another's slave does not give himself; he sells himself at the very least for his subsistence. But why does a nation sell itself? So far from a king supplying his subjects with their subsistence, he draws his from them; and, according to Rabelais, a king does not live on a little. Do subjects, then, give up their persons on condition that their property also shall be taken? I do not see what is left for them to keep.

It will be said that the despot secures to his subjects civil peace. Be it so; but what do they gain by that, if the wars which his ambition brings upon them, together with his insatiable greed and the vexations of his administration, harass them more than their own dissensions would? What do they gain by it if this tranquillity is itself one of their miseries? Men live tranquilly also in dungeons; is that enough to make them contented there? The Greeks confined in the cave of the Cyclops lived peacefully until their turn came to be devoured.

To say that a man gives himself for nothing is to say what is absurd and inconceivable; such an act is illegitimate and invalid, for the simple reason that he who performs it is not in his right mind. To say the same thing of the whole nation is to suppose a nation of fools; and madness does not confer rights.

Even if each person could alienate himself, he could not alienate his children; they are born free men; their liberty belongs to them, and no one has a right to dispose of it except themselves. Before they have come to years of discretion, the father can, in their name, stipulate conditions for their preservation and welfare, but not surrender them irrevocably and unconditionally; for such a gift is contrary to the ends of nature, and exceeds the rights of paternity. In order, then, that an arbitrary government might be legitimate, it would be necessary that the people in each generation should have the option of accepting or rejecting it; but in that case such a government would no longer be arbitrary.

To renounce one's liberty is to renounce one's quality as a man, the rights and also the duties of humanity. For him who renounces everything there is no possible compensation. Such a renunciation is incompatible with man's nature, for to take away all freedom from his will is to take away all morality from his actions. In short, a convention which stipulates absolute authority on the one side and unlimited obedience on the other is vain and contradictory. Is it not clear that we are under no obligations whatsoever towards a man from whom we have a right to demand everything? And does not this single condition, without equivalent, without exchange, involve the nullity of the act? For what right would my slave have against me, since all that he has belongs to me? His rights being mine, this right of me against myself is a meaningless phrase.

. . . . .

That it is Always Necessary to go Back to a First Convention

If I should concede all that I have so far refuted, those who favor despotism would be no farther advanced. There will always be a great difference between subduing a multitude and ruling a society. When isolated men, however numerous they may be, are subjected one after another to a single person, this seems to me only a case of master and slaves, not of a nation and its chief; they form, if you will, an aggregation, but not an association, for they have neither public property nor a body politic. Such a man, had he enslaved half the world, is never anything but an individual; his interest, separated from that of the rest, is never anything but a private interest. If he dies, his empire after him is left disconnected and disunited, as an oak dissolves and becomes a heap of ashes after the fire has consumed it.

A nation, says Grotius, can give itself to a king. According to Grotius, then, a nation is a nation before it gives itself to a king. This gift itself is a civil act, and presupposes a public resolution. Consequently, before examining the act by which a nation elects a king, it would be proper to examine the act by which a nation becomes a nation; for this act, being necessarily anterior to the other, is the real foundation of the society.

In fact, if there were no anterior convention, where, unless the election were unanimous, would be the obligation upon the minority to submit to the decision of the majority? And whence do the hundred who desire a master derive the right to vote on behalf of ten who do not desire one? The law of the plurality of votes is itself established by convention, and presupposes unanimity once at least.

The Social Pact

I assume that men have reached a point at which the obstacles that endanger their preservation in the state of nature overcome by their resistance the forces which each individual can exert with a view to maintaining himself in that state. Then this primitive condition can no longer subsist, and the human race would perish unless it changed its mode of existence.

Now, as men cannot create any new forces, but only combine and direct those that exist, they have no other means of self-preservation than to form by aggregation a sum of forces which may overcome the resistance, to put them in action by a single motive power, and to make them work in concert.

This sum of forces can be produced only by the combination of many; but the strength and freedom of each man being the chief instruments of his preservation, how can he pledge them without injuring himself, and without neglecting the cares which he owes to himself? This difficulty, applied to my subject, may be expressed in these terms: —

"To find a form of association which may defend and protect with the whole force of the community the person and property of every associate, and by means of which each, coalescing with all, may nevertheless obey only himself, and remain as free as before." Such is the fundamental problem, of which the social contract furnishes the solution.

The clauses of this contract are so determined by the nature of the act that the slightest modification would render them vain and ineffectual; so that, although they have never perhaps been formally enunciated, they are everywhere the same, everywhere tacitly admitted and recognized, until, the social pact being violated, each man regains his original rights and recovers his natural liberty, while losing the conventional liberty for which he renounced it.

These clauses, rightly understood, are reducible to one only, viz. the total alienation to the whole community of each associate with all his rights; for, in the first place, since each gives himself up entirely, the conditions are equal for all; and, the conditions being equal for all, no one has any interest in making them burdensome to others.

Further, the alienation being made without reserve, the union is as perfect as it can be, and an individual associate can no longer claim anything; for, if any rights were left to individuals, since there would be no common superior who could judge between them and the public, each, being on some point his own judge, would soon claim to be so on all; the state of nature would still subsist, and the association would necessarily become tyrannical or useless.

In short, each giving himself to all, gives himself to nobody; and as there is not one associate over whom we do not acquire the same rights which we concede to him over ourselves, we gain the equivalent of all that we lose, and more power to preserve what we have.

If, then, we set aside what is not of the essence of the social contract, we shall find that it is reducible to the following terms: "Each of us puts in common his person and his whole power under the supreme direction of the general will; and in return we receive every member as an indivisible part of the whole."

Forthwith, instead of the individual personalities of all the contracting parties, this act of the association produces a moral and collective body, which is composed of as many members as the assembly has voices, and which receives from this same act its unity, its common self (*moi*), its life, and its will. This public person, which is thus formed by the union of all the individual members, formerly took the name of *city,* and now takes that of *republic* or *body politic,* which is called by its members *state* when it is passive, *sovereign* when it is active, *power* when it is compared to similar bodies. With regard to the associates, they take collectively the name of *people,* and are called individually *citizens,* as participating in the sovereign power, and *subjects,* as subjected to the laws of the state. But these terms are often confused and are mistaken one for another; it is sufficient to know how to distinguish them when they are used with complete precision.

The Sovereign

We see from this formula that the act of association contains a reciprocal engagement between the public and individuals, and that every individual, contracting so to speak with himself, is engaged in a double relation, viz. as a member of the sovereign towards individuals, and as a member of the state towards the sovereign. But we cannot apply here the maxim of civil law that no one is bound by engagements made with himself; for there is a great difference between being bound to oneself and to a whole of which one forms part.

We must further observe that the public resolution which can bind all subjects to the sovereign in consequence of the two different relations under which each of them is regarded cannot, for a contrary reason, bind the sovereign to itself; and that accordingly it is contrary to the nature of the body politic for the sovereign to impose on itself a law which it cannot transgress. As it can only be considered under one and the same relation, it is in the position of an individual contracting with himself; whence we see that there is not, nor can be, any kind of fundamental law binding upon the body of the people, not even the social contract. This does not imply that such a body cannot perfectly well enter into engagements with others in what does not derogate from this contract; for, with regard to foreigners, it becomes a simple being, an individual.

But the body politic or sovereign, deriving its existence only from the sanctity of the contract, can never bind itself, even to others, in anything that derogates from the original act, such as alienation of some portion of itself, or submission to another sovereign. To violate the act by which it exists would be to annihilate itself; and what is nothing produces nothing.

So soon as the multitude is thus united in one body, it is impossible to injure one of the members without attacking the body, still less to injure the body without the members feeling the effects. Thus duty and interest alike oblige the two contracting parties to give mutual assistance; and the men themselves should seek to combine in this twofold relationship all the advantages which are attendant on it.

Now, the sovereign, being formed only of the individuals that compose it, neither has nor can have any interest contrary to theirs; consequently the sovereign power needs no guarantee towards its subjects, because it is impossible that the body should wish to injure all its members; and we shall see hereafter that it can injure no one as an individual. The sovereign, for the simple reason that it is so, is always everything that it ought to be.

But this is not the case as regards the relation of subjects to the sovereign, which, notwithstanding the common interest, would have no security for the performance of their engagements, unless it found means to insure their fidelity.

Indeed, every individual may, as a man, have a particular will contrary to, or divergent from, the general will which he has as a citizen; his private interest may prompt him quite differently from the common interest; his absolute and naturally independent existence may make him regard what he owes to the common cause as a gratuitous contribution, the loss of which will be less harmful to others than the payment of it will be burdensome to him; and, regarding the moral person that constitutes the state as an imaginary being because it is not a man, he would be willing to enjoy the rights of a citizen without being willing to fulfill the duties of a subject. The progress of such injustice would bring about the ruin of the body politic.

In order, then, that the social pact may not be a vain formulary, it tacitly includes this engagement, which can alone give force to the others, — that whoever refuses to obey the general will shall be constrained to do so by the whole body; which means nothing else than that he shall be forced to be free; for such is the condition which, uniting every citizen to his native land, guarantees him from all personal dependence; a condition that insures the control and working of the political machine, and alone renders legitimate civil engagements, which, without it, would be absurd and tyrannical, and subject to the most enormous abuses.

— From The Social Contract, by Jean Jacques Rousseau, French (1712–1778), translated by Henry J. Tozer.

The Rights of Man and Republicanism

THOMAS PAINE

1. On the Origin and Design of Government

Some writers have so confounded society with government, as to leave little or no distinction between them; whereas they are not only different, but have different origins. Society is produced by our wants, and government by our wickedness; the former promotes our happiness *positively* by uniting our affections, the latter *negatively* by restraining our vices. The one encourages intercourse, the other creates distinctions. The first is a patron, the last a punisher.

Society in every state is a blessing, but government, even in its best state, is but a necessary evil; in its worst state an intolerable one: for when we suffer, or are exposed to the same miseries *by a government*, which we might expect in a country *without government*, our calamity is heightened by reflecting that we furnish the means by which we suffer. Government, like dress, is the badge of lost innocence; the palaces of kings are built upon the ruins of the bowers of paradise. For were the impulses of conscience clear, uniform and irresistibly obeyed, man would need no other lawgiver; but that not being the case, he finds it necessary to surrender up a part of his property to furnish means for the protection of the rest; and this he is induced to do by the same prudence which in every other case advises him, out of two evils to choose the least. *Wherefore*, security being the true design and end of government, it unanswerably follows that whatever *form* thereof appears most likely to insure it to us, with the least expense and greatest benefit, is preferable to all others.

In order to gain a clear and just idea of the design and end of government, let us suppose a small number of persons settled in some sequestered part of the earth, unconnected with the rest; they will then represent the first peopling of any country, or of the world. In this state of natural liberty, society will be their first thought. A thousand motives will excite them thereto; the strength of one man is so unequal to his wants, and his mind so unfitted for perpetual solitude, that he is soon obliged to seek assistance and relief of another, who in his turn requires the same. Four or five united would be able to raise a tolerable dwelling in the midst of a wilderness, but one man might labor out the common period of life without accomplishing anything; when he had felled his timber he could not remove it, nor erect it after it was removed; hunger in the meantime would urge him to quit his work, and every different want would call him a different way. Disease, nay even misfortune, would be death; for though neither might be mortal, yet either would disable him from living, and reduce him to a state in which he might rather be said to perish than to die.

Thus necessity, like a gravitating power, would soon form our newly arrived emigrants into society, the reciprocal blessings of which would supersede, and render the obligations of law and government unnecessary while they remained perfectly just to each other; but as nothing but Heaven is impregnable to vice, it will unavoidably happen that in proportion as they surmount the first difficulties of emigration, which bound them together in a common cause, they will begin to relax in their duty and attachment to each other: and this remissness will point out the necessity of establishing some form of government to supply the defect of moral virtue.

Some convenient tree will afford them a state house, under the branches of which the whole colony may assemble to deliberate on public matters. It is more than probable that their first laws will have the title only of REGULATIONS and be enforced by no other penalty than public disesteem. In this first parliament every man by natural right will have a seat.

But as the colony increases, the public concerns will increase likewise, and the distance at which the members may be separated will render it too inconvenient for all of them to meet on every occasion as at first, when their number was small, their habitations near, and the public concerns few and trifling. This will point out the convenience of their consenting to leave the legislative part to be managed by a select number chosen from the whole body, who are supposed to have the same concerns at stake which those have who appointed them, and who will act in the same manner as the whole body would act were they present. If the colony continue increasing, it will become necessary to augment the number of representatives, and that the interest of every part of the colony may be attended to, it will be found best to divide the whole into convenient parts, each part sending its proper number: and that the *elected* might never form to themselves an interest separate from the *electors,* prudence will point out the propriety of having elections often: because as the *elected* might by that means return and mix again with the general body of the *electors* in a few months, their fidelity to the public will be secured by the prudent reflection of not making a rod for themselves. And as this frequent interchange will establish a common interest with every part of the community, they will mutually and naturally support each other, and on this (not on the unmeaning name of king) depends the *strength of government, and the happiness of the governed.*

Here then is the origin and rise of government; namely, a mode rendered necessary by the inability of moral virtue to govern the world; here too is the design and end of government, viz., freedom and security. And however our eyes may be dazzled with show, or our ears deceived by sound; however prejudice may warp our wills, or interest darken our understanding, the simple voice of nature and reason will say, it is right. . . .

2. *On the Nature and Origin of Rights*

The error of those who reason by precedents drawn from antiquity, respecting the rights of man, is that they do not go far enough into antiquity. They do not go the whole way. They stop in some of the intermediate stages of an hundred or a thousand years, and produce what was then done, as a rule for the present day. This is no authority at all. If we travel still farther into antiquity, we shall find a direct contrary opinion and practice prevailing; and if antiquity is to be authority, a thousand such authorities may be produced, successively contradicting each other; but if we proceed on, we shall at last come out right; we shall come to the time when man came from the hand of his Maker. What was he then? Man. Man was his high and only title, and a higher cannot be given him. But of titles I shall speak hereafter.

We have now arrived at the origin of man, and at the origin of his rights. As to the manner in which the world has been governed from that day to this, it is no further any concern of ours than to make a proper use of the errors or the improvements which the history of it presents. Those who lived an hundred or a thousand years ago, were then moderns, as we are now. They had *their* ancients, and those ancients had others, and we also shall be ancients in our turn. If the mere name of antiquity is to govern in the affairs of life, the people who are to live an hundred or a thousand years hence, may as well take us for a precedent, as we make a precedent of those who lived an hundred or a thousand years ago. The fact is, that portions of antiquity, by proving everything, establish nothing. It is authority against authority all the way, till we come to the divine origin of the rights of man at the creation. Here our inquiries find a resting-place, and our reason finds a home. If a dispute about the rights of man had arisen at the distance of an hundred years from the creation, it is to this source of authority they must have referred, and it is to this same source of authority that we must now refer.

Though I mean not to touch upon any sectarian principle of religion, yet it may be worth observing, that the genealogy of Christ is traced to Adam. Why then not trace the rights of man to the creation of man? I will answer the question. Because there have been upstart governments, thrusting themselves between, and presumptuously working to *un-make* man.

If any generation of men ever possessed the right of dictating the mode by which the world should be governed forever, it was the first generation that existed; and if that generation did it not, no succeeding generation can show any authority for doing it, nor can set any up. The illuminating and divine principle of the equal rights of man (for it has its origin from the maker of man) relates, not only to the living individuals, but to generations of men succeeding each other. Every generation is equal in rights to generations which preceded it, by the same rule that every individual is born equal in rights with his contemporary.

Every history of the creation, and every traditionary account, whether from the lettered or unlettered world, however they may vary in their opinion or belief of certain particulars, all agree in establishing one point, *the unity of man;* by which I mean that men are all of *one degree,* and consequently that all men are born equal, and with equal natural right, in the same manner as if posterity had been continued by *creation* instead of *generation,* the latter being the only mode by which the former is carried forward; and consequently every child born into the world must be considered as deriving its existence from God. The world is as new to him as it was to the first man that existed, and his natural right in it is of the same kind.

The Mosaic account of the creation, whether taken as divine authority or merely historical, is full to this point, *the unity or equality of man.* The expression admits of no controversy. "And God said, Let us make man in our own image. In the image of God created he him; male and female created he them." The distinction of sexes is pointed out, but no other distinction is even implied. If this be not divine authority, it is at least historical authority, and shows that the equality of man, so far from being a modern doctrine, is the oldest upon record.

It is also to be observed that all the religions known in the world are founded, so far as they relate to man, on the *unity of man,* as being all of one degree. Whether in heaven or in hell, or in whatever state man may be supposed to exist hereafter, the good and the bad are the only distinctions. Nay, even the laws of governments are obliged to slide into this principle, by making degrees to consist in crimes and not in persons.

It is one of the greatest of all truths, and of the highest advantage to cultivate. By considering man in this light, and by instructing him to consider himself in this light, it places him in a close connection with all his duties, whether to his Creator or to the creation, of which he is a part; and it is only when he forgets his origin, or, to use a more fashionable phrase, his *birth and family,* that he becomes dissolute. It is not among the least of the evils of the present existing governments in all parts of Europe that man, considered as man, is thrown back to a vast distance from his maker, and the artificial chasm filled up with a succession of barriers, or sort of turnpike gates, through which he has to pass. I will quote Mr. Burke's catalogue of barriers that he has set up between man and his maker. Putting himself in the character of a herald, he says: "We fear God — we look with *awe* to kings — with affection to Parliaments — with duty to magistrates — with reverence to priests, and with respect to nobility." Mr. Burke has forgotten to put in "*chivalry.*" He has also forgotten to put in Peter.

The duty of man is not a wilderness of turnpike gates, through which he is to pass by tickets from one to the other. It is plain and simple, and consists but of two points. His duty to God, which every man must feel; and with respect to his neighbor, to do as he would be done by. If those to whom power is delegated do well, they will be respected: if not, they will be despised; and with regard to those to whom no power is delegated, but who assume it, the rational world can know nothing of them.

Hitherto we have spoken only (and that but in part) of the natural rights of man. We have now to consider the civil rights of man, and to show how the one originates from the other. Man did not enter into society to become *worse* than he was before, nor to have fewer rights than he had before, but to have those rights better secured. His natural rights are the foundation of all his civil rights. But in order to pursue this distinction with more precision, it will be necessary to mark the different qualities of natural and civil rights.

A few words will explain this. Natural rights are those which appertain to man in right of his existence. Of this kind are all the intellectual rights, or rights of the mind, and also all those rights of acting as an individual for his own comfort and happiness, which are not injurious to the natural rights of others. Civil rights are those which appertain to man in right of his being a member of society. Every civil right has for its foundation some natural right preëxisting in the individual, but to the enjoyment of which his individual power is not, in all cases, sufficiently competent. Of this kind are all those which relate to security and protection.

From this short review it will be easy to distinguish between that class of natural rights which man retains after entering into society and those which he throws into the common stock as a member of society.

The natural rights which he retains are all those in which the power to execute is as perfect in the individual as the right itself. Among this class, as is before mentioned, are all the intellectual rights, or rights of the mind; consequently religion is one of those rights. The natural rights which are not retained are those in which, though the right is perfect in the individual, the power to execute them is defective. They answer not his purpose. A man, by natural right, has a right to judge in his own cause; and so far as the right of the mind is concerned, he never surrenders it. But what availeth it him to judge, if he has not power to redress? He therefore deposits this right in the common stock of society, and takes the arm of society, of which he is a part, in preference and in addition to his own. Society *grants* him nothing. Every man is a proprietor in society, and draws on the capital as a matter of right.

From these premises two or three certain conclusions will follow:

1st, That every civil right grows out of a natural right; or, in other words, is a natural right exchanged.

2d, That civil power properly considered as such is made up of the aggregate of that class of the natural rights of man, which becomes defective in the individual in point of power, and answers not his purpose, but when collected to a focus becomes competent to the purpose of everyone.

3d, That the power produced from the aggregate of natural rights, imperfect in power in the individual, cannot be applied to invade the natural rights which are retained in the individual, and in which the power to execute is as perfect as the right itself. . . .

3. *The Two Modes of Government*

Reason and ignorance, the opposites of each other, influence the great bulk of mankind. If either of these can be rendered sufficiently extensive in a country, the machinery of government goes easily on. Reason shows itself, and ignorance submits to whatever is dictated to it.

The two modes of the government which prevail in the world are, 1st, government by election and representation; 2nd, government by hereditary succession. The former is generally known by the name of republic; the latter by that of monarchy and aristocracy.

Those two distinct and opposite forms erect themselves on the two distinct and opposite bases of reason and ignorance. As the exercise of government requires talents and abilities, and as talents and abilities cannot have hereditary descent, it is evident that hereditary succession requires a belief from man to which his reason cannot subscribe, and which can only be established upon his ignorance; and the more ignorant any country is, the better it is fitted for this species of government.

On the contrary, government in a well-constituted republic, requires no belief from man beyond what his reason authorizes. He sees the *rationale* of the whole system, its origin and its operation; and as it is best supported when best understood, the human faculties act with boldness, and acquire, under this form of government, a gigantic manliness.

As, therefore, each of those forms acts on a different basis, the one moving freely by the aid of reason, the other by ignorance; we have next to consider what it is that gives motion to that species of government which is called mixed government, or, as it is sometimes styled, a government of *this, that and t'other.*

The moving power in this species of government is, of necessity, corruption. However imperfect election and representation may be in mixed governments, they still give exercise to a greater portion of reason than is convenient to the hereditary part; and therefore it becomes necessary to buy the reason up. A mixed government is an imperfect everything, cementing and soldering the discordant parts together by corruption, to act as a whole. Mr. Burke appears highly disgusted that France, since she had resolved on a revolution, did not adopt what he calls "A British constitution"; and the regretful manner in which he expresses himself on this occasion implies a suspicion that the British constitution needed something to keep its defects in countenance.

In mixed governments there is no responsibility; the parts cover each other till responsibility is lost; and the corruption which moves the machine contrives at the same time its own escape. When it is laid down as a maxim that *a king can do no wrong,* it places him in a state of similar security with that of idiots and persons insane, and responsibility is out of the question with respect to himself. It then descends upon the minister who shelters himself under a majority in parliament which, by places, pensions, and corruption, he can always command; and that majority justifies itself by the same authority with which it protects the minister. In this rotatory motion, responsibility is thrown off from the parts and from the whole.

. . . .

What is government more than the management of the affairs of a nation? It is not, and from its nature cannot be, the property of any particular man or family, but of the whole community at whose expense it is supported; and though by force and contrivance it has been usurped into an inheritance, the usurpation cannot alter the right of things. Sovereignty, as a matter of right, appertains to the nation only and not to any individual; and a nation has at all times an inherent, indefeasible right to abolish any form of government it finds inconvenient, and to establish such as accords with its interest, disposition, and happiness. The romantic and barbarous distinctions of men into kings and subjects, though it may suit the condition of courtiers cannot that of citizens; and is exploded by the principle upon which governments are now founded. Every citizen is a member of the sovereignty, and, as such can acknowledge no personal subjection; and his obedience can be only to the laws.

4. *Of Society and Civilization*

A great part of that order which reigns among mankind is not the effect of government. It has its origin in the principles of society and the natural constitution of man. It existed prior to government, and would exist if the formality of government was abolished. The mutual dependence and reciprocal interest which man has upon man, and all the parts of civilized community upon each other, create that great chain of connection which holds it together. The landholder, the farmer, the manufacturer, the merchant, the tradesman, and every occupation, prospers by the aid which each receives from the other, and from the whole. Common interest regulates their concerns, and forms their law; and the laws which common usage ordains have a greater influence than the laws of government. In fine society performs for itself almost everything which is ascribed to government.

To understand the nature and quantity of government proper for man, it is necessary to attend to his character. As Nature created him for social life, she fitted him for the station she intended. In all cases she made his natural wants greater than his individual powers. No one man is capable, without the aid of society, of supplying his own wants; and those wants, acting upon every individual, impel the whole of them into society, as naturally as gravitation acts to a center.

But she has gone further. She has not only forced man into society by a diversity of wants which the reciprocal aid of each other can supply, but she has implanted in him a system of social affections, which, though not necessary to his existence, are essential to his happiness. There is no period in life when this love for society ceases to act. It begins and ends with our being.

If we examine with attention into the composition and constitution of man, the diversity of his wants, and the diversity of talents in different men for reciprocally accommodating the wants of each other, his propensity to society, and consequently, to preserve the advantages resulting from it, we shall easily discover that a great part of what is called government is mere imposition.

Government is no further necessary than to supply the few cases to which society and civilization are not conveniently competent; and instances are not wanting to show, that everything which government can usefully add thereto, has been performed by the common consent of society, without government.

For upwards of two years from the commencement of the American War, and to a longer period in several of the American states, there were no established forms of government. The old governments had been abolished, and the country was too much occupied in defense to employ its attention in establishing new governments; yet during this interval order and harmony were preserved as inviolate as in any country in Europe. There is a natural aptness in man, and more so in society, because it embraces a greater variety of abilities and resource, to accommodate itself to whatever situation it is in. The instant formal government is abolished, society begins to act: a general association takes place, and common interest produces common security.

So far is it from being true, as has been pretended, that the abolition of any formal government is the dissolution of society, that it acts by a contrary impulse, and brings the latter the closer together. All that part of its organization which it has committed to its government devolves again upon itself, and acts through its medium. When men, as well from natural instinct as from reciprocal benefits, have habituated themselves to social and civilized life, there is always enough of its principles in practice to carry them through any changes they may find necessary or convenient to make in their government. In short, man is so naturally a creature of society that it is almost impossible to put him out of it.

Formal government makes but a small part of civilized life; and when even the best that human wisdom can devise is established, it is a thing more in name and idea than in fact. It is to the great and fundamental principles of society and civilization — to the common usage universally consented to, and mutually and reciprocally maintained — to the unceasing circulation of interest, which, passing through its million channels, invigorates the whole mass of civilized man — it is to these things, infinitely more than to anything which even the best instituted government can perform, that the safety and prosperity of the individual and of the whole depends.

The more perfect civilization is, the less occasion has it for government, because the more does it regulate its own affairs, and govern itself; but so contrary is the practice of old governments to the reason of the case, that the expenses of them increase in the proportion they ought to diminish. It is but few general laws that civilized life requires, and those of such common usefulness, that whether they are enforced by the forms of government or not, the effect will be nearly the same. If we consider what the principles are that first condense men into society, and what are the motives that regulate their mutual intercourse afterwards, we shall find, by the time we arrive at what is called government, that nearly the whole of the business is performed by the natural operation of the parts upon each other.

Man, with respect to all those matters, is more a creature of consistency than he is aware, or than governments would wish him to believe. All the great laws of society are laws of nature. Those of trade and commerce, whether with respect to the intercourse of individuals or of nations, are laws of mutual and reciprocal interest. They are followed and obeyed, because it is the interest of the parties to do so, and not on account of any formal laws their governments may impose or interpose.

But how often is the natural propensity to society disturbed or destroyed by the operations of government! When the latter, instead of being ingrafted on the principles of the former, assumes to exist for itself, and acts by partialities of favor and oppression, it becomes the cause of the mischiefs it ought to prevent . . .

When men think of what government is, they must necessarily suppose it to possess a knowledge of all the objects and matters upon which its authority is to be exercised. In this view of government, the republican system, as established by America and France, operates to embrace the whole of a nation; and the knowledge necessary to the interest of all the parts is to be found in the center, which the parts by representation form: but the old governments are on a construction that excludes knowledge as well as happiness; government by monks, who know nothing of the world beyond the walls of a convent, is as consistent as government by kings.

What were formerly called revolutions, were little more than a change of persons or an alteration of local circumstances. They rose and fell like things of course, and had nothing in their existence or their fate that could influence beyond the spot that produced them. But what we now see in the world, from the revolutions of America and France, are a renovation of the natural order of things, a system of principles as universal as truth and the existence of man, and combining moral with political happiness and national prosperity.

"I. Men are born, and always continue free and equal in respect to their rights. Civil distinctions, therefore, can be founded only on public utility.

"II. The end of all political associations is the preservation of the natural and imprescriptible rights of man and these rights are liberty, property, security and resistance of oppression.

"III. The nation is essentially the source of all sovereignty; nor can any individual, or any body of men, be entitled to any authority which is not expressly derived from it."

5. *Republicanism*

It has always been the political craft of courtiers and court-governments to abuse something which they called republicanism; but what republicanism was, or is, they never attempt to explain. Let us examine a little into this case.

The only forms of government are, the democratical, the aristocratical, the monarchical, and what is now called the representative.

What is called a *republic* is not any *particular form* of government. It is wholly characteristical of the purport, matter, or object for which government ought to be instituted, and on which it is to be employed, *res-publica,* the public affairs, or the public good; or, literally translated, the *public thing*. It is a word of a good original, referring to what ought to be the character and business of government; and in this sense it is naturally opposed to the word *monarchy,* which has a base original signification. It means arbitrary power in an individual person; in the exercise of which, *himself,* and not the *res-publica,* is the object.

Every government that does not act on the principle of a republic, or, in other words, that does not make the *res-publica* its whole and sole object, is not a good government. Republican government is no other than government established and conducted for the interest of the public, as well individually as collectively. It is not necessarily connected with any particular form, but it most naturally associates with the representative form, as being best calculated to secure the end for which a nation is at the expense of supporting it.

—*From The Rights of Man and Common Sense, by Thomas Paine, English (1737–1809).*

Declaration of the Rights of Man and of Citizens

(1789)

The representatives of the people of France, formed into a national assembly, considering that ignorance, neglect, or contempt of human rights, are the sole causes of public misfortunes and corruptions of government, have resolved to set forth in a solemn declaration these natural, imprescriptible, and inalienable rights: that this declaration being constantly present to the minds of the members of the body social, they may be ever kept attentive to their rights and their duties: that the acts of the legislative and executive powers of government, being capable of being every moment compared with the end of political institutions, may be more respected: and also, that the future claims of the citizens, being directed by simple and incontestable principles, may always tend to the maintenance of the constitution and the general happiness.

For these reasons the national assembly doth recognize and declare, in the presence of the supreme being, and with the hope of his blessing and favor, the following *sacred* rights of men and of citizens:

I. Men are born and always continue free and equal in respect of their rights. Civil distinctions, therefore, can be founded only on public utility.

II. The end of all political associations is the preservation of the natural and imprescriptible rights of man; and these rights are liberty, property, security, and resistance of oppression.

III. The nation is essentially the source of all sovereignty; nor can any *individual,* or *any body of men,* be entitled to any authority which is not expressly derived from it.

IV. Political liberty consists in the power of doing whatever does not injure another. The exercise of the natural rights of every man has no other limits than those which are necessary to secure to every *other* man the free exercise of the same rights; and these limits are determinable only by the law.

V. The law ought to prohibit only actions hurtful to society. What is not prohibited by the law should not be hindered; nor should anyone be compelled to that which the law does not require.

VI. The law is an expression of the will of the community. All citizens have a right to concur, either personally, or by their representatives, in its formation. It should be the same to all, whether it protects or punishes; and all being equal in its sight, are equally eligible to all honors, places, and employments, according to their different abilities, without any other distinction than that created by their virtues and talents.

VII. No man should be accused, arrested, or held in confinement, except in cases determined by the law, and according to the forms which it has prescribed. All who promote, solicit, execute, or cause to be executed, arbitrary orders, ought to be punished; and every citizen called upon or apprehended by virtue of the law, ought immediately to obey, and renders himself culpable by resistance.

VIII. The law ought to impose no other penalties but such as are absolutely and evidently necessary: and no one ought to be punished, but in virtue of a law promulgated before the offense, and legally applied.

IX. Every man being presumed innocent till he has been convicted, whenever his detention becomes indispensable, all rigor to him, more than is necessary to secure his person, ought to be provided against by the law.

X. No man ought to be molested on account of his opinions, not even on account of his religious opinions, provided his avowal of them does not disturb the public order established by the law.

XI. The unrestrained communication of thoughts and opinions being one of the most precious rights of man, every citizen may speak, write, and publish freeely, provided he is responsible for the abuse of this liberty in cases determined by the law.

XII. A public force being necessary to give security to the rights of men and of citizens, that force is instituted for the benefit of the community, and not for the particular benefit of the persons with whom it is entrusted.

XIII. A common contribution being necessary for the support of the public force, and for defraying the other expenses of government, it ought to be divided equally among the members of the community, according to their abilities.

XIV. Every citizen has a right, either by himself or his representative, to a free voice in determining the necessity of public contributions, the appropriation of them, and their amount, mode of assessment, and duration.

XV. Every community has a right to demand of all its agents, an account of their conduct.

XVI. Every community in which a separation of powers and a security of rights is not provided for, wants a constitution.

XVII. The right to property being inviolable and sacred, no one ought to be deprived of it, except in cases of evident public necessity legally ascertained, and on condition of a previous just indemnity.

Declaration of Rights

PERCY BYSSHE SHELLEY
AND
WILLIAM GODWIN

1. Government has no rights; it is a delegation from several individuals for the purpose of securing their own. It is therefore

just, only so far as it exists by their consent, useful only so far as it operates to their well-being.

2. If these individuals think that the form of government which they or their forefathers constituted is ill adapted to produce their happiness, they have a right to change it.

3. Government is devised for the security of Rights. The rights of man are liberty, and an equal participation of the commonage of Nature.

4. As the benefit of the governed is, or ought to be, the origin of government, no man can have any authority that does not expressly emanate from *their* will.

5. Though all governments are not so bad as that of Turkey, yet none are so good as they might be. The majority of every country have a right to perfect their government. The minority should not disturb them; they ought to secede, and form their own system in their own way.

6. All have a right to an equal share in the benefits and burdens of Government. Any disabilities for opinion imply, by their existence, barefaced tyranny on the side of Government, ignorant slavishness on the side of the governed.

7. The rights of men, in the present state of society, are only to be secured by some degree of coercion to be exercised on their violator. The sufferer has a right that the degree of coercion employed be as slight as possible.

8. It may be considered as a plain proof of the hollowness of any proposition if power be used to enforce instead of reason to persuade its admission. Government is never supported by fraud until it cannot be supported by reason.

9. No man has a right to disturb the public peace by personally resisting the execution of a law, however bad. He ought to acquiesce, using at the same time the utmost powers of his reason to promote its repeal.

10. A man must have a right to act in a certain manner, before it can be his duty. He may, before he ought.

11. A man has a right to think as his reason directs; it is a duty he owes to himself to think with freedom, that he may act from conviction.

12. A man has a right to unrestricted liberty of discussion. Falsehood is a scorpion that will sting itself to death.

13. A man has not only a right to express his thoughts, but it is his duty to do so.

14. No law has a right to discourage the practice of truth. A man ought to speak the truth on every occasion. A duty can never be criminal; what is not criminal cannot be injurious.

15. Law cannot make what is in its nature virtuous or innocent to be criminal, any more than it can make what is criminal to be innocent. Government cannot make a law; it can only pronounce that which was the law before its organization; viz., the moral result of the imperishable relations of things.

16. The present generation cannot bind their posterity: the few cannot promise for the many.

17. No man has a right to do an evil thing that good may come.

18. Expediency is inadmissible in morals. Politics are only sound when conducted on principles of morality: they are, in fact, the morals of nations.

19. Man has no right to kill his brother. It is no excuse that he does so in uniform: he only adds the infamy of servitude to the crime of murder.

20. Man, whatever be his country, has the same rights in one place as another—the rights of universal citizenship.

21. The government of a country ought to be perfectly indifferent to every opinion. Religious differences, the bloodiest and most rancorous of all, spring from partiality.

22. A delegation of individuals, for the purpose of securing their rights, can have no undelegated power of restraining the expression of their opinion.

23. Belief is involuntary; nothing involuntary is meritorious or reprehensible. A man ought not to be considered worse or better for his belief.

24. A Christian, a Deist, a Turk, and a Jew, have equal rights: they are men and brethren.

25. If a person's religious ideas correspond not with your own, love him nevertheless. How different would yours have been had the chance of birth placed you in Tartary or India!

26. Those who believe that Heaven is, what earth has been, a monopoly in the hands of a favoured few, would do well to reconsider their opinion; if they find that it came from their priest or their grandmother, they could not do better than reject it.

27. No man has a right to be respected for any other possessions but those of virtue and talents. Titles are tinsel, power a corruptor, glory a bubble, and excessive wealth a libel on its possessor.

28. No man has a right to monopolize more than he can enjoy; what the rich give to the poor, whilst millions are starving, is not a perfect favour, but an imperfect right.

29. Every man has a right to a certain degree of leisure and liberty, because it is his duty to attain a certain degree of knowledge. He may before he ought.

30. Sobriety of body and mind is necessary to those who would be free; because, without sobriety, a high sense of philanthropy cannot actuate the heart, nor cool and determined courage execute its dictates.

31. The only use of government is to repress the vices of man. If man were today sinless, tomorrow he would have a right to demand that government and all its evils should cease.

Man! thou whose rights are here declared, be no longer forgetful of the loftiness of thy destination. Think of thy rights, of those possessions which will give thee virtue and wisdom, by which thou mayest arrive at happiness and freedom. They are declared to thee by one who knows thy dignity, for every hour does his heart swell with honorable pride in the contemplation of what thou mayest attain – by one who is not forgetful of thy degeneracy, for every moment brings home to him the bitter conviction of what thou art.

Awake! – arise! – or be for ever fallen.

— From the Declaration of Rights, English, by Percy Bysshe Shelley (1792–1822) and William Godwin (1756–1836).

~ ۞ ~

Communist Manifesto

KARL HEINRICH MARX

BOURGEOISIE AND PROLETARIAT

The history of all hitherto existing society is the history of class struggles. Freeman and slave, patrician and plebeian, lord and serf, guild-master and journeyman – in a word, oppressor and oppressed – stood in constant opposition to one another, carried on an uninterrupted, now hidden, now open fight, a fight that each time ended either in a revolutionary re-constitution of society at large or in the common ruin of the contending classes.

In the earlier epochs of history, we find almost everywhere a complicated arrangement of society into various orders, a manifold gradation of social rank. In ancient Rome we have patricians, knights, plebeians, slaves; in the Middle Ages, feudal lords, vassals, guild-masters, journeymen, apprentices, serfs; in almost all of these classes, again, subordinate gradations.

The modern bourgeois society, that has sprouted from the ruins of feudal society, has not done away with class antagonisms. It has but established new classes, new conditions of oppression, new forms of struggle, in place of the old ones. Our epoch, the epoch of the bourgeoisie, possesses, however, this distinctive feature: it has simplified the class antagonisms. Society as a whole is more and more splitting up into two great hostile camps, into two great classes directly facing each other: Bourgeoisie and Proletariat.

From the serfs of the Middle Ages sprang the chartered burghers of the earliest towns. From these burgesses the first elements of the bourgeoisie were developed. The discovery of America, the rounding of the Cape, opened up fresh ground for the rising bourgeoisie. The East-Indian and Chinese markets, the colonization of America, trade with the colonies, the increase in the means of exchange and in commodities generally, gave to commerce, to navigation, to industry, an impulse never before known, and thereby, to the revolutionary element in the tottering feudal society, a rapid development.

The feudal system of industry, under which industrial production was monopolized by closed guilds, now no longer sufficed for the growing wants of the new markets. The manufacturing system took its place. The guild-masters were pushed on one side by the manufacturing middle-class; division of labor between the different corporate guilds vanished in the face of division of labor in each single workshop.

Meantime the markets kept ever growing; the demand, ever rising. Even manufacture no longer sufficed. Thereupon, steam and machinery revolutionized industrial production. The place of manufacture was taken by the giant, Modern Industry, the place of the industrial middle-class, by industrial millionaires, the leaders of whole industrial armies, the modern bourgeois.

Modern industry has established the world-market, for which the discovery of America paved the way. This market has given an immense development to commerce, to navigation, to communication by land. This development has, in its turn, reacted on the extension of industry; and in proportion as industry, commerce, navigation, railways extended, in the same proportion the bourgeoisie developed, increased its capital, and pushed into the background every class handed down from the Middle Ages. We see, therefore, how the modern bourgeoisie is itself the product of a long course of development, of a series of revolutions in the modes of production and of exchange.

Each step in the development of the bourgeoisie was accompanied by a corresponding political advance of that class. An oppressed class under the sway of the feudal nobility, an armed and self-governing association in the medieval commune, here independent urban republic (as in Italy and Germany), there taxable "third estate" of the monarchy (as in France), afterwards, in the period of manufacture proper, serving either the semi-feudal of the absolute monarchy as a counterpoise against the nobility, and, in fact, corner stone of the great monarchies in general, the bourgeoisie has at last, since the establishment of modern industry and of the world-market, conquered for itself, in the modern representative state, exclusive political sway. The executive of the modern state is but a committee for managing the common affairs of the whole bourgeoisie.

The bourgeoisie, historically, has played a most revolutionary part. The bourgeoisie, wherever it has got the upper hand, has put an end to all feudal, patriarchal, idyllic relations. It has pitilessly torn asunder the motley feudal ties that bound man to his "natural superiors," and has left remaining no other nexus between man and man than naked self-interest, than callous "cash payment." It has drowned the most heavenly ecstasies of religious fervor, of chivalrous enthusiasm, of philistine sentimentalism, in the icy water of egotistical calculation. It has resolved personal worth into exchange value, and in place of the numberless indefeasible chartered freedoms, has set up that single, unconscionable freedom – Free Trade. In one word, for exploitation veiled by religious and political illusions it has substituted naked, shameless, direct brutal exploitation.

The bourgeoisie has stripped of its halo every occupation hitherto honored and looked up to with reverent awe. It has converted the physician, the lawyer, the priest, the poet, the man of science, into its paid wage-laborers. The bourgeoisie has torn away from the family its sentimental veil, and has reduced the family relation to a mere money relation. The bourgeoisie has disclosed how it came to pass that the brutal display of vigor in the Middle Ages, which reactionists so much admire, found its fitting complement in the most slothful indolence. It has been the first to show what man's activity can bring about. It has accomplished wonders far surpassing Egyptian pyramids, Roman aqueducts, and Gothic cathedrals; it has conducted expeditions that put in the shade all former crusades and Exoduses of nations.

The bourgeoisie can not exist without constantly revolutionizing the instruments of production, and thereby the relations of production, and with them the whole relations of society. Conservation of the old modes of production in unaltered form was, on the contrary, the first condition of existence for all earlier industrial classes. Constant revolutionizing of production, uninterrupted disturbance of all social conditions, everlasting uncertainty and agitation distinguish the bourgeois epoch from all earlier ones. All fixed, fast-frozen relations, with their train of ancient and venerable prejudices and opinions, are swept away; all new-formed ones become antiquated before they can ossify; all that is solid melts into air; all that is holy is profaned; and man is at last compelled to face with sober senses his real conditions of life, and his relations with his kind.

The need of a constantly expanding market for its products chases the bourgeoisie over the whole surface of the globe; it must nestle everywhere, settle everywhere, establish connections everywhere. The bourgeoisie has, through its exploitation of the world-market, given a cosmopolitan character to production and consumption in every country. To the great chagrin of reactionists, it has drawn from under the feet of industry the national ground on which it stood. All old-established national industries have been destroyed or are daily being destroyed. They are dislodged by new industries, whose introduction becomes a life-and-death question for all civilized nations — by industries that no longer work up indigenous raw material, but raw material drawn from the remotest zones, industries whose products are consumed not only at home but in every quarter of the globe. In place of the old wants, satisfied by the productions of the country, we find new wants, requiring for their satisfaction the products of distant lands and climes. In place of the old local and national seclusion and self-sufficiency, we have intercourse in every direction, universal interdependence of nations; and as in material, so also in intellectual production. The intellectual creations of individual nations become common property. National one-sidedness and narrow-mindedness become more and more impossible, and from the numerous national and local literatures there arises a world-literature.

The bourgeoisie, by the rapid improvement of all instruments of production, by the immensely facilitated means of communication, draws all, even the most barbarian, nations into civilization. The cheap prices of its commodities are the heavy artillery with which it batters down all Chinese walls, with which it forces the barbarians' intensely obstinate hatred of foreigners to capitulate. It compels all nations, on pain of extinction, to adopt the bourgeois mode of production; it compels them to introduce what it calls civilization into their midst; *i.e.*, to become bourgeois themselves. In a word, it creates a world after its own image.

The bourgeoisie has subjected the country to the rule of the towns. It has created enormous cities, has greatly increased the urban population as compared with the rural, and has thus rescued a considerable part of the population from the idiocy of rural life. Just as it has made the country dependent on the towns, so it has made barbarian and semi-barbarian countries dependent on the civilized ones, nations of peasants on nations of bourgeois, the East on the West.

The bourgeoisie keeps more and more doing away with the scattered state of the population, of the means of production, and of property. It has agglomerated population, centralized means of production, and has concentrated property in a few hands. The necessary consequence of this was political centralization. Independent or but loosely connected provinces, with separate interests, laws, governments, and systems of taxation, become lumped together in one nation, with one government, one code of laws, one national class-interest, one frontier, and one customs-tariff.

The bourgeoisie, during its rule of scarce one hundred years, has created more massive and more colossal productive forces than had all preceding generations together. Subjection of nature's forces to man, machinery, application of chemistry to industry and agriculture, steam navigation, railways, electric telegraphs, clearing of whole continents for cultivation, canalization of rivers, whole populations conjured out of the ground — what earlier century had even a presentiment that such productive forces slumbered in the lap of social labor?

We see then — the means of production and of exchange, on whose foundation the bourgeoisie built itself up, were generated in feudal society. At a certain stage in the development of these means of production and exchange, the conditions under which feudal society produced and exchanged, the feudal organization of agriculture and manufacturing industry, in one word, the feudal relations of property, became no longer compatible with the already developed productive forces; they became so many fetters. They had to burst asunder; they were burst asunder. Into their places stepped free competition, accompanied by a social and political constitution adapted to it, and by the economical and political sway of the bourgeois class.

A similar movement is going on before our own eyes. Modern bourgeois society with its relations of production, of exchange, and of property, a society that has conjured up such gigantic means of production and of exchange, is like the sorcerer who is no longer able to control the powers of the nether world whom he has called up by his spells. For many a decade past the history of industry and commerce is but the history of the revolt of modern productive forces against modern conditions of production, against the property relations that are the conditions for the existence of the bourgeoisie and of its rule. It is enough to mention the commercial crises that by their periodical return put on its trial, each time more threateningly, the existence of the entire bourgeois society. In these crises a great part not only of the existing products, but also of the previously created productive forces, are periodically destroyed. In these crises there breaks out an epidemic that, in all earlier epochs would have seemed an absurdity — the epidemic of over-production. Society suddenly finds itself put back into a state of momentary barbarism; it appears as if a famine, a universal war of devastation, had cut off the supply of every means of subsistence; industry and commerce seem to be destroyed — and why? Because there is too much civilization, too much means of subsistence, too much industry, too much commerce. The productive forces at the disposal of society no longer tend to further the development of the condition of bourgeois property; on the contrary, they have become too powerful for these conditions, by which they are fettered, and so soon as they overcome these fetters, they bring disorder into the whole of bourgeois society, endanger the existence of bourgeois property. The conditions of bourgeois society are too narrow to comprise the wealth created by them. And how does the bourgeoisie get over these crises? On the one hand by enforced destruction of a mass of productive forces; on the other, by the conquest of new markets, and by the more thorough exploitation of the old ones — that is to say, by paving the way for more extensive and more destructive crises, and by diminishing the means whereby crises are prevented.

The weapons with which the bourgeoisie felled feudalism to the ground are now turned against the bourgeoisie itself. But not only has the bourgeoisie forged the weapons that bring death to itself; it has also called into existence the men who are to wield those weapons — the modern working-class — the proletarians. In proportion as the bourgeoisie, *i.e.*, capital, is developed, in the same proportion is the proletariat, the modern working-class, developed — a class of laborers who live only so long as they find work, and who find work only so long as their labor increases capital. These laborers, who must sell themselves piecemeal, are a commodity, like every other article of commerce, and are consequently exposed to all the vicissitudes of competition, to all the fluctuations of the market.

Owing to the extensive use of machinery and to division of labor, the work of the proletarians has lost all individual character, and, consequently, all charm for the workman. He becomes an appendage of the machine, and it is only the most simple, most monotonous, and most easily acquired knack that is required of him. Hence the cost of production of a workman is restricted almost entirely to the means of subsistence that he requires for his maintenance, and for the propagation of his race. But the price of a commodity, and also of labor, is equal to its cost of production. In proportion, therefore, as the repulsiveness of the work increases, the wage decreases. Nay more, in proportion as the use of machinery and division of labor increases, in the same proportion the burden of toil also increases, whether by prolongation of the working hours, by increase of the work exacted in a given time, or by increased speed of the machinery, *et cetera.*

Modern industry has converted the little workshop of the patriarchal master into the great factory of the industrial capitalist. Masses of laborers, crowded into the factories, are organized like soldiers. As privates of the industrial army they are placed under the command of a perfect hierarchy of officers and sergeants. Not only are they the slaves of the bourgeois class, and of the bourgeois state; they are daily and hourly enslaved by the machine, by the over-looker, and, above all, by the individual bourgeois manufacturer himself. The more openly this despotism proclaims gain to be its end and aim, the more petty, the more hateful, and the more embittering it is.

The less the skill and exertion of strength implied in manual labor — in other words, the more modern industry becomes developed — the more is the labor of men superseded by that of women. Differences of age and sex have no longer any distinctive social validity for the working class; all are instruments of labor, more or less expensive to use, according to their age and sex.

No sooner is the exploitation of the laborer by the manufacturer so far at an end that he receives his wages in cash, than he is set upon by the other portions of the bourgeoisie, the landlord, the shopkeeper, the pawnbroker, and others.

The lower strata of the middle class — the small tradespeople, shopkeepers and retired tradesmen generally, the handicraftsmen and peasants – all these sink gradually into the proletariat, partly because their diminutive capital does not suffice for the scale on which modern industry is carried on and is swamped in the competition with the large capitalists, partly because their specialized skill is rendered worthless by new methods of production. Thus the proletariat is recruited from all classes of the population.

The proletariat goes through various stages of development. With its birth begins its struggle with the bourgeoisie. At first the contest is carried on by individual laborers, then by the work-people of a factory, then by the operatives of one trade, in one locality, against the individual bourgeois who directly exploits them. They direct their attacks not against the bourgeois conditions of production, but against the instruments of production themselves. They destroy imported wares that compete with their labor; they smash to pieces machinery; they set factories ablaze; they seek to restore by force the vanished status of the workman of the Middle Ages.

At this stage the laborers still form an incoherent mass scattered over the whole country, and broken up by their mutual competition. If anywhere they unite to form more compact bodies, this is not yet the consequence of their own active union, but of the union of the bourgeoisie, which class, in order to attain its own political ends, is compelled to set the whole proletariat in motion, and is, moreover, yet for a time able to do so. At this stage, therefore, the proletarians do not fight their enemies, but the enemies of their enemies, the remnants of absolute monarchy, the landowners, the non-industrial bourgeois, the petty bourgeois. Thus the whole historical movement is concentrated in the hands of the bourgeoisie; every victory so obtained is a victory for the bourgeoisie.

But with the development of industry the proletariat not only increases in number; it becomes concentrated in greater masses, its strength grows, and it feels that strength more. The various interests and conditions of life within the ranks of the proletariat are more and more equalized, in proportion as machinery obliterates all distinctions of labor, and nearly everywhere reduces wages to the same low level. The growing competition among the bourgeois, and the resulting commercial crises, make the wages of the workers ever more fluctuating. The unceasing improvement of machinery, ever more rapidly developing, makes their livelihood more and more precarious; the collisions between individual workmen and individual bourgeois take more and more the character of collisions between two classes. Thereupon the workers begin to form combinations (trades-unions) against the bourgeois; they club together in order to keep up the rate of wages; they found permanent associations in order to make provision beforehand for these occasional revolts. Here and there the contest breaks out into riots. Now and then the workers are victorious, but only for a time. The real fruit of their battles lies, not in the immediate result, but in the ever-expanding union of the workers. This union is helped on by the improved means of communication that are created by modern industry, and that place the workers of different localities in contact with one another. It was just this contact that was needed to centralize the numerous local struggles, all of the same character, into one national struggle between classes. But every class struggle is a political struggle. And that union, to attain which the burghers of the Middle Ages, with their miserable highways, required centuries, the modern proletarians, thanks to railways, achieve in a few years.

This organization of the proletarians into a class, and consequently into a political party, is continually being upset again by the competition between the workers themselves. But it ever rises up again, stronger, firmer, mightier. It compels legislative recognition of particular interests of the workers, by taking advantage of the divisions among the bourgeoisie itself. Thus the ten-hours bill in England was carried.

Altogether collisions between the classes of the old society further, in many ways, the course of development of the proletariat. The bourgeoisie finds itself involved in a constant battle – at first with the aristocracy; later on with those portions of the bourgeoisie itself whose interests have become antagonistic to the progress of industry; at all times with the bourgeoisie of foreign countries. In all these battles it sees itself compelled to appeal to the proletariat, to ask for its help, and thus to drag it into the political arena. The bourgeoisie itself, therefore, supplies the proletariat with its own elements of political and general education; in other words, it furnishes the proletariat with weapons for fighting the bourgeoisie.

Further, as we have already seen, entire sections of the ruling classes are, by the advance of industry, precipitated into the proletariat, or are at least threatened in their conditions of existence. These also supply the proletariat with fresh elements of enlightenment and progress.

Finally, in times when the class-struggle nears the decisive hour, the process of dissolution going on within the ruling class, in fact, within the whole range of old society, assumes such a violent, glaring character, that a small section of the ruling class cuts itself adrift, and joins the revolutionary class, the class that holds the future in its hands. Just as, therefore, at an earlier period, a section of the nobility went over to the bourgeoisie, so now a portion of the bourgeoisie goes over to the proletariat, and in particular, a portion of the bourgeois ideologists, who have raised themselves to the level of comprehending theoretically the historical movements as a whole.

Of all the classes that stand face to face with the bourgeoisie today, the proletariat alone is a really revolutionary class. The other classes decay and finally disappear in the face of modern industry; the proletariat is its special and essential product.

The lower middle class, the small manufacturer, the shopkeeper, the artisan, the peasant, all these fight against the bourgeoisie, to save from extinction their existence as fractions of the middle class. They are, therefore, not revolutionary, but conservative. Nay more, they are reactionary; for they try to roll back the wheel of history. If by chance they are revolutionary, they are so only in view of their impending transfer into the proletariat; they thus defend not their present, but their future interests; they desert their own standpoint to place themselves at that of the proletariat.

The "dangerous class," the social scum, that passively rotting mass thrown off by the lowest layers of old society, may, here and there, be swept into the movement by a proletarian revolution; its conditions of life, however, prepare it far more for the part of a bribed tool of reactionary intrigue.

In the conditions of the proletariat, those of old society at large are already virtually swamped. The proletarian is without property; his relation to his wife and children has no longer anything in common with the bourgeois family-relations; modern industrial labor, modern subjection to capital, the same in England as in France, in America as in Germany, has stripped him of every trace of national character. Law, morality, religion, are to him so many bourgeois prejudices, behind which lurk in ambush just as many bourgeois interests.

All the preceding classes that got the upper hand, sought to fortify their already acquired status by subjecting society at large to their conditions of appropriation. The proletarians can not become masters of the productive forces of society, except by abolishing their own previous mode of appropriation, and thereby also every other previous mode of appropriation. They have nothing of their own to secure and to fortify; their mission is to destroy all previous securities for, and insurances of, individual property.

All previous historical movements were movements of minorities, or in the interests of minorities. The proletarian movement is the self-conscious, independent movement of the immense majority. The proletariat, the lowest stratum of our present society, can not stir, can not raise itself up without the whole superincumbent strata of official society being sprung into the air.

Though not in substance, yet in form, the struggle of the proletariat with the bourgeoisie is at first a national struggle. The proletariat of each country must, of course, first of all settle matters with its own bourgeoisie.

In depicting the most general phases of the development of the proletariat, we traced the more or less veiled civil war, raging within existing society, up to the point where that war breaks out into open revolution, and where the violent overthrow of the bourgeoisie lays the foundations for the sway of the proletariat.

Hitherto every form of society has been based, as we have already seen, on the antagonism of oppressing and oppressed classes. But in order to oppress a class, certain conditions must be assured to it under which it can at least continue its slavish existence. The serf, in the period of serfdom, raised himself to membership in the commune, just as the petty bourgeois, under the yoke of feudal absolutism, managed to develop into a bourgeois. The modern laborer, on the contrary, instead of rising with the progress of industry, sinks deeper and deeper below the conditions of existence of his own class. He becomes a pauper, and pauperism develops more rapidly than population and wealth; and here it becomes evident that the bourgeoisie is unfit any longer to be the ruling class in society, and to impose its conditions of existence upon society as an overriding law. It is unfit to rule, because it is incompetent to assure an existence to its slave within his slavery, because it can not help letting him sink into such a state that it has to feed him, instead of being fed by him. Society can no longer live under this bourgeoisie; in other words, its existence is no longer compatible with society.

The essential condition for the existence and for the sway of the bourgeois class is the formation and augmentation of capital; the condition for capital is wage-labor. Wage-labor rests exclusively on competition between the laborers. The advance of industry, whose involuntary promoter is the bourgeoisie, replaces the isolation of the laborers, due to competition, by their involuntary combination, due to association. The development of modern industry, therefore, cuts from under its feet the very foundation on which the bourgeoisie produces and appropriates products. What the bourgeoisie therefore produces, above all, is its own grave-diggers. Its fall and the victory of the proletariat are equally inevitable.

PROLETARIANS AND COMMUNISTS

In what relation do the Communists stand to the proletarians as a whole? The Communists do not form a separate party opposed to other working-class parties. They have no interests separate and apart from those of the proletariat as a whole. They do not set up any sectarian principles of their own, by which to shape and mold the proletarian movement. The Communists are distinguished from the other working-class parties by this only: (1) in the national struggles of the proletarians of the different countries, they point out and bring to the front the common interests of the entire proletariat, independently of all nationality; (2) in the various stages of development which the struggle of the working class against the bourgeoisie has to pass through, they always and everywhere represent the interests of the movement as a whole.

The Communists, therefore, are on the one hand practically the most advanced and resolute section of the working-class parties of every country, that section which pushes forward all others; on the other hand, theoretically, they have over the great mass of the proletariat the advantage of clearly understanding the line of march, the conditions, and the ultimate general results of the proletarian movement.

The immediate aim of the Communists is the same as that of all the other proletarian parties: formation of the proletariat into a class, overthrow of the bourgeois supremacy, conquest of political power by the proletariat.

The theoretical conclusions of the Communists are in no way based on ideas or principles that have been invented, or discovered, by this or that would-be universal reformer. They merely express, in general terms, actual relations springing from an existing class struggle, from a historical movement going on under our very eyes. The abolition of existing property relations is not at all a distinctive feature of Communism. All property relations in the past have continually been subject to historical change consequent upon the change in historical conditions. The French Revolution, for example, abolished feudal property in favor of bourgeois property.

The distinguishing feature of Communism is not the abolition of property generally, but the abolition of bourgeois property. But modern bourgeois private property is the final and most complete expression of the system of producing and appropriating products that is based on class antagonism, on the exploitation of the many by the few. In this sense, the theory of the Communists may be summed up in the single sentence: Abolition of private property.

We Communists have been reproached with the desire of abolishing the right of personally acquiring property as the fruit of a man's own labor, which property is alleged to be the ground work of all personal freedom, activity, and independence.

Hard-won, self-acquired, self-earned property! Do you mean the property of the petty artisan and of the small peasant, a form of property that preceded the bourgeois form? There is no need to abolish that; the development of industry has to a great extent already destroyed it, and is still destroying it daily.

Or do you mean modern bourgeois private property?

But does wage-labor create any property for the laborer? Not a bit. It creates capital, *i.e.,* that kind of property which exploits wage-labor, and which can not increase except upon condition of getting a new supply of wage-labor for fresh exploitation. Property, in its present form, is based on the antagonism of capital and wage-labor.

Let us examine both sides of this antagonism.

To be a capitalist is to have not only a purely personal, but a social status in production. Capital is a collective product, and only by the united action of many members, nay, in the last resort, only by the united action of all members of society, can it be set in motion. Capital is therefore not a personal, it is a social power. When, therefore, capital is converted into common property, into the property of all members of society, personal property is not thereby transformed into social property. It is only the social character of the property that is changed. It loses its class-character.

Let us now take wage-labor.

The average price of wage-labor is the minimum wage, *i.e.,* that quantum of the means of subsistence which is absolutely requisite to keep the laborer in bare existence as a laborer. What, therefore, the wage-laborer appropriates by means of his labor, merely suffices to prolong and reproduce a bare existence. We by no means intend to abolish this personal appropriation of the products of labor, an appropriation that is made for the maintenance and reproduction of human life, and that leaves no surplus wherewith to command the labor of others. All that we want to do away with is the miserable character of this appropriation, under which the laborer lives merely to increase capital, and is allowed to live only in so far as the interests of the ruling class require it.

In bourgeois society, living labor is but a means to increase accumulated labor. In communist society, accumulated labor is but a means to widen, to enrich, to promote the existence of the laborer. In bourgeois society, therefore, the past dominates the present; in communist society, the present dominates the past. In bourgeois society capital is independent and has individuality, while the living persons is dependent and has no individuality.

And the abolition of this state of things is called by the bourgeois, abolition of individuality and freedom! And rightly so. The abolition of bourgeois individuality, bourgeois independence, and bourgeois freedom is undoubtedly aimed at.

By freedom is meant, under the present bourgeois conditions of production: free trade, free selling and buying. But if selling and buying disappears, free selling and buying disappears also. This talk about free selling and buying, and all the other "brave words" of our bourgeoisie about freedom in general, have a meaning, if any, only in contrast with restricted selling and buying, with the fettered traders of the Middle Ages, but have no meaning when opposed to the communistic abolition of buying and selling, of the bourgeois conditions of production, and of the bourgeoisie itself.

You are horrified at our intending to do away with private property. But in your own existing society private property is already done away with for nine-tenths of the population; its existence for the few is solely due to its non-existence in the hands of those nine-tenths. You reproach us, therefore, with intending to do away with a form of property the necessary condition for whose existence is the non-existence of any property for the immense majority of society. In one word, you reproach us with intending to do away with *your* property. Precisely so; that is just what we intend.

From the moment when labor can no longer be converted into capital, money, or rent, into a social power capable of being monopolized – *i.e.,* from the moment when individual property can no longer be transformed into bourgeois property, into capital – from that moment, you say, individuality vanishes. You must, therefore, confess that by "individual" you mean no other person than the bourgeois, than the middle-class owner of property. This person must, indeed, be swept out of the way and made impossible.

Communism deprives no man of the power to appropriate the products of society; all that it does is to deprive him of the power to subjugate the labor of others by means of such appropriation.

It has been objected that upon the abolition of private property all work will cease, and universal laziness will overtake us. According to this, bourgeois society ought long ago to have gone to the dogs through sheer idleness; for those of its members who work acquire nothing, and those who acquire anything do not work. The whole of this objection is but another expression of the tautology that there can no longer be any wage-labor when there is no longer any capital.

All objections urged against the communistic mode of producing and appropriating material products have, in the same way, been urged against the communistic modes of producing and appropriating intellectual products. Just as, to the bourgeois, the disappearance of class property is the disappearance of production itself, so the disappearance of class culture is to him identical with the disappearance of all culture. That culture, the loss of which he laments, is, for the enormous majority, a mere training to act as a machine.

But don't wrangle with us so long as you apply to our intended abolition of bourgeois property the standard of your bourgeois notions of freedom, culture, law, *et cetera.* Your very ideas are but the outgrowth of the conditions of your bourgeois production and bourgeois property, just as your jurisprudence is but the will of your class made into a law for all, a will whose essential character and direction are determined by the economic conditions of existence of your class. The selfish misconception that induces you to transform into eternal laws of nature and of reason the social forms springing from your present mode of production and form of property – historical relations that rise and disappear in the progress of production – this misconception you share with every ruling class that has preceded you. What you see clearly in the case of ancient property, what you admit in the case of feudal property, you are of course forbidden to admit in the case of your own bourgeois form of property.

Abolition of the family! Even the most radical flare up at this infamous proposal of the Communists. On what foundation is the present family, the bourgeois family, based? On capital, on private gain! In its completely developed form this family exists only among the bourgeoisie. But this state of things finds its complement in the practical absence of the family among the proletarians, and in public prostitution. The bourgeois family will vanish as a matter of course when its complement vanishes, and both will vanish with the vanishing of capital.

Do you charge us with wanting to stop the exploitation of children by their parents? To this crime we plead guilty.

But, you will say, we destroy the most hallowed of relations, when we replace home education by social. And your education! Is not that also social, and determined by the social conditions under which you educate, by the intervention, direct or indirect, of society by means of schools, *et cetera*? The Communists have not invented the intervention of society in education; they do but seek to alter the character of that intervention, and to rescue education from the influence of the ruling class.

The bourgeois clap-trap about the family and education, about the hallowed correlation of parent and child, becomes all the more disgusting, the more, by the action of modern industry; all family ties among the proletarians are torn asunder, and their children transformed into simple articles of commerce and instruments of labor.

"But you Communists would introduce community of women," screams the whole bourgeois chorus.

The bourgeois sees in his wife a mere instrument of production. He hears that the instruments of production are to be exploited in common, and, naturally, can come to no other conclusion than that the lot of being common to all will likewise fall to the women. He has not even a suspicion that the real point aimed at is to do away with the status of women as mere instruments of production.

For the rest, nothing is more ridiculous than the virtuous indignation of our bourgeois at the community of women which, they pretend, is to be openly and officially established by the Communists. The Communists have no need to introduce community of women; it has existed almost from time immemorial. Our bourgeois, not content with having the wives and daughters of their proletarians at their disposal, not to speak of common prostitutes, take the greatest pleasure in seducing each others' wives. Bourgeois marriage is in reality a system of wives in common and thus, at the most, what the Communists might possibly be reproached with, is that they desire to introduce, in substitution for a hypocritically concealed, an openly legalized community of women. For the rest, it is self-evident, that the abolition of the present system of production must bring with it the abolition of the community of women springing from that system, *i.e.*, of prostitution both public and private.

The Communists are further reproached with desiring to abolish countries and nationalities. The working men have no country. We can not take from them what they do not possess. Since the proletariat must first of all acquire political supremacy, must rise to be the leading class of the nation, must constitute itself the nation, it is, so far, itself national, though not in the bourgeois sense of the word. National differences, and antagonisms between peoples, are daily more and more vanishing, owing to the development of the bourgeoisie, to freedom of commerce, to the world-market, to uniformity in the mode of production and in the conditions of life corresponding thereto. The supremacy of the proletariat will cause them to vanish still faster. United action, of the leading civilized countries at least, is one of the first conditions for the emancipation of the proletariat. In proportion as the exploitation of one individual by another is put an end to, the exploitation of one nation by another will also be put an end to. In proportion as the antagonism between classes within the nation vanishes, the hostility of one nation to another will come to an end.

The charges against Communism made from a religious, a philosophical, and generally, from an idealogical standpoint, are not deserving of serious examination.

Does it require deep intuition to comprehend that man's ideas, views, and conceptions, in one word, man's consciousness, changing with every change in the conditions of his material existence, in his social relations, and in his social life? What else does the history of ideas prove, than that intellectual production changes in character in proportion as material production is changed? The ruling ideas of each age have ever been the ideas of its ruling class. When people speak of ideas that revolutionize society, they do but express the fact that within the old society the elements of a new one have been created, and that the dissolution of the old ideas keeps even pace with the dissolution of the old conditions of existence.

When the ancient world was in its last throes, the ancient religions were overcome by Christianity. When Christian ideas succumbed in the eighteenth century to rationalist ideas, feudal society fought its death-battle with the then revolutionary bourgeoisie. The ideas of religious liberty and freedom of conscience, merely gave expression to the sway of free competition within the domain of knowledge.

"Undoubtedly," it will be said, "religious, moral, philosophical, and juridical ideas have been modified in the course of historical development. But religion, morality, philosophy, political science, and law constantly survived this change. There are, besides, eternal truths, such as freedom, justice, *et cetera,* that are common to all states of society. But Communism abolishes eternal truths, it abolishes all religion, and all morality, instead of constituting them on a new basis; it therefore acts in contradiction to all past historical experience."

What does this accusation reduce itself to? The history of all past society has consisted in the development of class antagonisms that assumed different forms at different epochs. But whatever form they may have taken, one fact is common to all past ages, *viz.*, the exploitation of one part of society by the other. No wonder, then, that the social consciousness of past ages, despite all the multiplicity and variety it displays, moves within certain common forms, or general ideas, which can not completely vanish except with the total disappearance of class antagonisms. The communist revolution is the most radical rupture with traditional property-relations; no wonder that its development involves the most radical rupture with traditional ideas.

But let us have done with the bourgeois objections to Communism.

We have seen above, that the first step in the revolution by the working class, is to raise the proletariat to the position of ruling class, to win the battle of democracy. The proletariat will use its political supremacy, to wrest, by degrees, all capital from the bourgeoisie, to centralize all instruments of production in the hands of the state, *i.e.*, of the proletariat organized as the ruling class; and to increase the total of productive forces as rapidly as possible. Of course, in the beginning, this can not be effected except by means of despotic inroads on the rights of property, and on the conditions of bourgeois production; by means of measures, therefore, which appear economically insufficient and untenable, but which, in the course of the movement, outstrip themselves, necessitate further inroads upon the old social order, and are unavoidable as a means of entirely revolutionizing the mode of production.

These measures will of course be different in different countries. Nevertheless, in the most advanced countries the following will be pretty generally applicable:

1. Abolition of property in land and application of all rents of land to public purposes.
2. A heavy progressive or graduated income tax.
3. Abolition of all right of inheritance.
4. Confiscation of the property of all emigrants and rebels.
5. Centralization of credit in the hands of the state, by means of a national bank with state capital and an exclusive monopoly.
6. Centralization of the means of communication and transport in the hands of the state.
7. Extension of factories and instruments of production owned by the state; the bringing into cultivation of waste lands, and the improvement of the soil generally in accordance with a common plan.
8. Equal liability of all to labor; establishment of industrial armies, especially for agriculture.
9. Combination of agriculture with manufacturing industries; gradual abolition of the distinction between town and country, by a more equable distribution of population over the country.
10. Free education for all children in public schools; abolition of children's factory labor in its present form; combination of education with industrial production, *etc., etc.*

When, in the course of development, class distinctions have disappeared, and all production has been concentrated in the hands of a vast association of the whole nation, the public power will lose its political character. Political power, properly so called, is merely the organized power of one class for oppressing another. If the proletariat during its contest with the bourgeoisie is compelled by the force of circumstances to organize itself as a class, if, by means of a revolution, it makes itself the ruling class, and, as such, sweeps away by force the old conditions of production, then it will, along with these conditions, have swept away the conditions for the existence of class antagonism, and of classes generally, and will thereby have abolished its own supremacy as a class. In place of the old bourgeois society, with its classes and class antagonisms, we shall have an association in which the free development of each is the condition for the free development of all. . . .

—From The Communist Manifesto, by Karl Heinrich Marx, German (1818–1883) and Friedrich Engels, German (1820–1895), translated by Samuel Moore.

The Order of Rank

FRIEDRICH NIETZSCHE

I

In this age of universal suffrage, in which everybody is allowed to sit in judgment upon everything and everybody, I feel compelled to re-establish the order of rank.

II

Quanta of power alone determine rank and distinguish rank: nothing else.

III

The will to power. — How must those men be constituted who would undertake this transvaluation? The order of rank is the order of power: war and danger are the prerequisites which allow of a rank maintaining its conditions. The prodigious example: man in Nature — the weakest and shrewdest creature making himself master, and putting a yoke upon all less intelligent forces.

IV

I distinguish between the type which represents ascending life and that which represents decay, decomposition and weakness. Ought one to suppose that the question of rank between these two types can be at all doubtful? . . .

V

The modicum of power which you represent decides your rank; all the rest is cowardice.

VI

The advantages of standing detached from one's age. — Detached from the two movements, that of individualism and that of collectivist morality; for even the first does not recognize the order of rank, and would give one individual the same freedom as another. My thoughts are not concerned with the degree of freedom which should be granted to the one or to the other or to all, but with the degree of power which the one or the other should exercise over his neighbour or over all, and more especially with the question to what extent a sacrifice of freedom, or even enslavement, may afford the basis for the cultivation of a *superior* type. In plain words: *how could one sacrifice the development of mankind* in order to assist a higher species than man to come into being?

VII

Concerning rank. — The terrible consequences of "freedom" — in the end everybody thinks he has the right to every problem. The order of rank has vanished.

VIII

It is necessary for *higher* men to declare war upon the masses! In all directions mediocre people are joining hands in order to make themselves masters. Everything that pampers, that softens, and that brings the "people" or "woman" to the front, operates in favour of universal suffrage — that is to say, the dominion of *inferior* men. But we must make reprisals, and draw the whole state of affairs (which commenced in Europe with Christianity) to the light of day and to judgment.

IX

A teaching is needed which is strong enough to work in a *disciplinary* manner; it should operate in such a way as to strengthen the strong and to paralyse and smash up the world-weary.

The annihilation of declining races. The decay of Europe. The annihilation of slave-tainted valuations. The dominion of the world as a means to the rearing of a higher type. The annihilation of the humbug which is called morality (Christianity as a hysterical kind of honesty in this regard: Augustine, Bunyan). The annihilation of universal suffrage — that is to say, that system by means of which the lowest natures prescribe themselves as a law for higher natures. The annihilation of mediocrity and its prevalence. (The one-sided, the individuals — peoples; constitutional plenitude should be aimed at by means of the coupling of opposites; to this end race-combinations should be tried.) The new kind of courage — no *a priori* truths (those who were accustomed to believe in something sought such truths!), but free submission to a ruling thought, which has its time; for instance, time conceived as the quality of space, etc.

X

The root of all evil: that the slave morality of modesty, chastity, selfishness, and absolute obedience should have triumphed. Dominating natures were thus condemned (1) to hypocrisy, (2) to qualms of conscience, — creative natures regarded themselves as rebels against God, uncertain and hemmed in by eternal values. . . .

XI

The rights which a man arrogates to himself are relative to the duties which he sets himself, and to the tasks which he feels *capable of performing.* The great majority of men have no right to life, and are only a misfortune to their higher fellows.

XII

The degeneration of the ruler and of the ruling classes has been the cause of all the great disorders in history! Without the Roman Caesars and Roman society, Christianity would never have prevailed.

When it occurs to inferior men to doubt whether higher men exist, then the danger is great! It is then that men finally discover that there are virtues even among inferior, suppressed, and poor-spirited men, and that everybody is equal before God: which is the *non plus ultra* of all confounded nonsense that has ever appeared on earth! For in the end higher men begin to measure themselves according to the standard of virtues upheld by the slaves — and discover that they are "proud," etc., and that all their *higher* qualities should be condemned.

When Nero and Caracalla stood at the helm, it was then that the paradox arose: "The lowest man is of more value than that one on the throne!" And thus the path was prepared for an *image of God* which was as remote as possible from the image of the mightiest, — God on the Cross!

XIII

To be obsessed by moral considerations presupposes a very low grade of intellect:

it shows that the instinct for special rights, for standing apart, the feeling of freedom in creative natures, in "children of God" (or of the devil), is lacking. And irrespective of whether he *preaches* a ruling morality or *criticises* the prevailing ethical code from the point of view of his own ideal: by doing these things a man shows that he belongs to the herd — even though he may be what it is most in need of — that is to say, a "shepherd."

XIV

. . . The majority of people are only piecemeal and fragmentary examples of man: only when all these creatures are jumbled together does one man arise. Whole ages and whole peoples, in this sense, have a fragmentary character about them; it may perhaps be part of the economy of human development that man should develop himself only piecemeal. But, for this reason, one should not forget that the only important consideration is the rise of the synthetic man; that inferior men, and by far the great majority of people, are but rehearsals and exercises out of which here and there *a whole man* may arise; a man who is a human milestone, and who indicates how far mankind has advanced up to a certain point. Mankind does not advance in a straight line; often a type is attained which is again lost (for instance, with all the efforts of three hundred years, we have not reached the *men of the Renaissance* again, and in addition to this we must not forget that the man of the Renaissance was already behind his brother of classical antiquity).

XV

Of this I am convinced, that if the rise of great and rare men had been made dependent upon the voices of the multitude (taking for granted, of course, that the latter knew the qualities which belong to greatness, and also the price that all greatness pays for its self-development), then there would never have been any such thing as a great man!

The fact that things pursue their course *independently* of the voice of the many, is the reason why a few astonishing things have taken place on earth.

XVI

I am attempting an *economic* justification of virtue. The object is to make man as useful as possible, and to make him approximate as nearly as one can to an infallible machine: to this end he must be equipped with *machine-like virtues* (he must learn to value those states in which he works in a most mechanically useful way, as the highest of all: to this end it is necessary to make him as disgusted as possible with the other states, and to represent them as very dangerous and despicable).

Here is the first stumbling-block: the tediousness and monotony which all mechanical activity brings with it. To learn to endure *this* — and not only to endure it, but to see tedium enveloped in a ray of exceeding charm: this hitherto has been the task of all higher schools. To learn something which you don't care a fig about, and to find precisely your "duty" in this "objective" activity; to learn to value happiness and duty as things apart; this is the invaluable task and performance of higher schools. . . . Such an existence may perhaps require a philosophical glorification and justification more than any other: pleasurable feelings must be valued by some sort of infallible tribunal, as altogether of inferior rank; "duty *per se*," perhaps even the pathos of reverence in regard to everything unpleasant, — must be demanded imperatively as that which is above all useful, delightful, and practical things. . . . A mechanical form of existence regarded as the highest and most respectable form of existence, worshipping itself. . . .

XVII

The economic valuation of all the ideals that have existed hitherto — that is to say, the selection and rearing of definite passions and states at the cost of other passions and states. The law-giver (or the instinct of the community) selects a number of states and passions the existence of which guarantees the performance of regular actions (mechanical actions would thus be the result of the regular requirements of those passions and states).

In the event of these states and passions containing ingredients which were painful, a means would have to be found for overcoming this painfulness by means of a valuation; pain would have to be interpreted as something valuable, as something pleasurable in a higher sense. Conceived in a formula: *"How does something unpleasant be-*

come pleasant?" For instance, when our obedience and our submission to the law become honoured, thanks to the energy, power, and self-control they entail. The same holds good of our public spirit, of our neighbourliness, of our patriotism, our "humanisation," our "altruism," and our "heroism." The *object of all idealism* should be to induce people to do unpleasant things cheerfully.

XVIII

The *belittlement* of man must be held as the chief aim for a long while: because what is needed in the first place is a broad basis from which a stronger species of man may arise (to what extent hitherto has *every stronger* species of man arisen from a *substratum of inferior people?*).

XIX

He who thinks over the question of how the type man may be elevated to its highest glory and power, will realise from the start that he must place himself beyond morality; for morality was directed in its essentials at the opposite goal — that is to say, its aim was to arrest and to annihilate that glorious development wherever it was in process of accomplishment. For, as a matter of fact, development of that sort implies that such an enormous number of men must be subservient to it, that a *counter*-movement is only too natural: the weaker, more delicate, more mediocre existences, find it necessary to take up sides *against* that glory of life and power; and for that purpose they must get a new valuation of themselves by means of which they are able to condemn, and if possible to destroy, life in this high degree of plenitude. Morality is therefore essentially the expression of hostility to life, in so far as it would overcome vital types.

Our psychologists, whose glance dwells involuntarily upon the symptoms of decadence, lead us to mistrust intellect ever more and more. People persist in seeing only the weakening, pampering, and sickening effects of intellect, but there are now going to appear: —

New barbarians	Cynics Experimentalists Conquerors	The union of intellectual superiority and of an overflow of strength.

XXI

I point to something new: certainly for such a democratic community there is a danger of barbarians; but these are sought only down below. There is also *another kind of barbarians* who come from the heights: a kind of conquering and ruling natures, which are in search of material that they can mould. Prometheus was a barbarian of this stamp.

XXII

Concerning the ruling types. — The shepherd as opposed to the "lord" (the former is only a means to the maintenance of the herd; the latter, the *purpose* for which the herd exists).

XXIII

A healthy and vigorous little boy will look up sarcastically if he be asked: "Wilt thou become virtuous?" — but he immediately becomes eager if he be asked: "Wilt thou become stronger than thy comrades?"

How does one become stronger? — By deciding slowly; and by holding firmly to the decision once it is made. Everything else follows of itself. Spontaneous and changeable natures: both species of the weak. We must not confound ourselves with them; we must feel distance — betimes!

Beware of good-natured people! Dealings with them make one torpid. All environment is good which makes one exercise those defensive and aggressive powers which are instinctive in man. All one's inventiveness should apply itself to putting one's power of will to the test. . . . *Here* the determining factor must be recognised as something which is not knowledge, astuteness, or wit.

One must learn to command betimes, — likewise to obey. A man must learn modesty and tact in modesty: he must learn to distinguish and to honour where modesty is displayed; he must likewise distinguish and honour wherever he bestows his confidence.

What does one repent most? One's modesty; the fact that one has not lent an ear to one's most individual needs; the fact that one has mistaken one's self; the fact that one has esteemed one's self low; the fact that one has lost all delicacy of hearing in regard to one's instincts. — This want of reverence in regard to one's self is avenged by all sorts of losses: in health, friendship, well-being, pride, cheerfulness, freedom, determination, courage. A man never forgives himself, later on, for this want of genuine egoism: he regards it as an objection and as a cause of doubt concerning his real ego.

XXIV

Against John Stuart Mill. – I abhor the man's vulgarity when he says: "What is right for one man is right for another"; "Do not to others that which you would not that they should do unto you." Such principles would fain establish the whole of human traffic *upon mutual services,* so that every action would appear to be a cash payment for something done to us. The hypothesis here is ignoble to the last degree: it is taken for granted that there is some sort of *equivalence in value between my actions and thine;* the most personal value of an action is simply cancelled in this manner (that part of an action which has no equivalent and which cannot be remunerated). "Reciprocity" is a piece of egregious vulgarity; the mere fact that what I do *cannot* and *may* not be done by another, that there is *no such thing* as *equivalence* (except in those very *select circles* where one actually has one's equal, *inter pares*), that in a really profound sense a man never requites because he is something *unique* in himself and can only do *unique* things, – this fundamental conviction contains the cause of *aristocratic aloofness from the mob,* because the latter believes in equality, and *consequently* in the feasibility of equivalence and "reciprocity."

XXV

The only nobility is that of birth and blood. Wherever people speak of the "aristocracy of intellect," reasons are generally not lacking for concealing something; it is known to be a password among ambitious Jews. Intellect alone does not ennoble; on the contrary, something is always needed *to ennoble intellect.* – What then is needed? – Blood.

XXVI

I teach that there are higher and lower men, and that a single individual may under certain circumstances justify whole millenniums – that is to say, a wealthier, more gifted, greater, and more complete man, as compared with innumerable imperfect and fragmentary men.

XXVII

Away from rulers and rid of all bonds, live the highest men: and in the rulers they have their instruments.

XXVIII

The order of rank: he who *determines* values and leads the will of millenniums, and does this by leading the highest natures – he *is the highest man.*

XXIX

I fancy I have divined some of the things that lie hidden in the soul of the highest man; perhaps every man who has divined so much must go to ruin: but he who has seen the highest man must do all he can to make him *possible.*

Fundamental thought: we must make the future the standard of all our valuations – and not seek the laws for our conduct behind us.

XXX

Not "mankind," but *Superman* is the goal!

— *From The Will To Power by Friedrich Wilhelm Nietzsche, German (1844–1900), translated by Anthony M. Ludovici.*

PART ELEVEN

Political Satire

POLITICAL satire, being only a branch, though probably the most flourishing branch, of satire in general, requires little independent introduction. The cardinal fact stands out only too clearly: that in no respect has human thought preserved greater continuity throughout the ages than in the inveterate disposition of mankind to be critical of government. English literary criticism and biography have, perhaps, too seldom observed that a life of public affairs has in the case of many of the world's chief poets shared important room with their purely literary activity. Almost all the leading Greek poets were men of action as well as men of letters. In the Orient, literary and official classes tended to become identical. Virgil was spokesman for Augustus, Dante a political exile, Chaucer a valued servant of the state, and Milton a foreign secretary. Despite Goethe's romantic fallacy to the contrary, that poetry and politics do not agree, one notes the repeated harmony of the two in the poets themselves and in their outstanding works.

The surprising modernity and intelligibility of the Chinese is never clearer than in their political satires. Amused jests at the dullness of a bureaucratic class mingle with serious assaults upon the inhumanity of predatory wars and the arrogance of an aristocracy that grinds the poor into dust. One can read a translation of a political poem by Po Chü-i or Su Tung-p'o and easily fancy it an original work by Carl Sandburg. Horace's sixteenth epode on the horrors of civil war reads much like a poem by Tu Fu or Li Po, or, for that matter, like passages of solemn warning and regret in Dante's *Divine Comedy*.

Where the subject matter throughout the entire world presents so much repetition, it becomes of most value merely to observe the nations or times which have called forth political satire at its best. While the Spaniards have for ten centuries been suffering the gravest political disasters in Europe and some of the saddest miscarriages of political wisdom and justice, their poets have given the world much of its finest political invective. The traditions of Gómez Manrique and Quevedo have in some measure passed even into the New World, as evidenced in the politically conscious verse of Rubén Darío.

Avowedly suffering almost as grave ills of misgovernment from the times of Dante to those of Leopardi, Italy has been a land of continual political theorizing and critical complaint. The speech given by Dante to Sordello is paralleled by a famous ode six centuries later by Leopardi. Of special interest and beauty are the brief pieces here given by Campanella and Filecaja, the latter freely but superbly rendered in the English of Byron.

Political satire in French verse claims no works more celebrated than the chastisements meted in scorn by Victor Hugo to Napoleon "le petit." More profound in thought and poetry, however, are the quieter comments on our society sounded in the minor key by the great Belgian poet, Emile Verhaeren. Like Verhaeren in being spokesman for the political rights of all laboring classes in an industrial society, Richard Dehmel ranks among the more powerful and humane of German lyricists. The most consistent body of political protest against alleged injustice issues, of course, from Russia. Of the earlier poets to voice the claims of the Russian masses, Pushkin and Lermontov stand out most conspicuously. In the recent period of the Soviet regime the work of Alexander Blok has attracted widest attention. His chief poem, *The Twelve,* too long for inclusion in this volume, is based upon events of the Soviet Revolution in the winter of 1918, in the midst of which its stirring lines were written.

Among the masterpieces in the English poetry of political satire are the protests of Milton against intolerance and brutality, the burning hymns of the humanitarian, Shelley, the flights of Byron's fiery indignation, and the deeply sincere expressions of Irish patriotism by William Butler Yeats. Byron's *Don Juan* contains some of the most vigorous satire against the persistent madness of European wars. Yeats, like other of his Irish contemporaries, as James Joyce and George Russell (Æ), was almost by instinct a devoted reader and emulator of foreign literatures. In turn he looked to the Celtic Middle Ages, to England's rich literary heritage, to Greece and to the Orient.

Much vigorous political satire has been composed in America, as, for example, by Freneau and Trumbull during the Revolutionary period, by Lowell and Whitman during the years of anti-slavery agitation, and by champions of our new renaissance of democracy, such as Stephen Vincent Benét and Carl Sandburg. Two figures who are among the most representative are emphasized here: Whittier for the period of the Civil War, and Archibald MacLeish for recent years.

The Nefarious War

Last year we fought by the head-stream of the So-kan,
This year we are fighting on the Tsung-ho road.
We have washed our armor in the waves of the Chiao-chi lake,
We have pastured our horses on Tien-shan's snowy slopes.
The long, long war goes on ten thousand miles from home,
Our three armies are worn and grown old.

The barbarian does man-slaughter for plowing;
On his yellow sand-plains nothing has been seen but blanched skulls and bones.
Where the Chin emperor built the walls against the Tartars,
There the defenders of Han are burning beacon fires.
The beacon fires burn and never go out,
There is no end to war! —

In the battlefield men grapple each other and die;
The horses of the vanquished utter lamentable cries to heaven,
While ravens and kites peck at human entrails,

Carry them up in their flight, and hang them on the branches of dead trees.
So, men are scattered and smeared over the desert grass,
And the generals have accomplished nothing.

Oh, nefarious war! I see why arms
Were so seldom used by the benign sovereigns.

—From the Chinese of Li Po (701–762), translated by Shigeyoshi Obata.

~ ❁ ~

On the Birth of His Son

Families, when a child is born
Want it to be intelligent.
I, through intelligence,
Having wrecked my whole life,
Only hope the baby will prove
Ignorant and stupid.
Then he will crown a tranquil life
By becoming a Cabinet Minister.

—From the Chinese of Su Tung-p'o (1036–1101), translated by Arthur Waley.

~ ❁ ~

The Flower Market

In the Royal City spring is almost over:
Tinkle, tinkle—the coaches and horsemen pass.
We tell each other "This is the peony season":
And follow with the crowd that goes to the Flower Market.
"Cheap and dear—no uniform price:
The cost of the plant depends on the number of blossoms.
For the fine flower,—five bits of silk.
Above is spread an awning to protect them:
Around is woven a wattle-fence to screen them.
If you sprinkle water and cover the roots with mud,
When they are transplanted, they will not lose their beauty."
Each household thoughtlessly follows the custom,
Man by man, no one realizing.
There happened to be an old farm labourer
Who came by chance that way.
He bowed his head and sighed a deep sigh:
But this sigh nobody understood.
He was thinking, "A cluster of deep-red flowers
Would pay the taxes of ten poor houses."

—From the Chinese of Po Chü-i (772–846), translated by Arthur Waley.

~ ❁ ~

The Charcoal-Seller

An old charcoal-seller
Cutting wood and burning charcoal in the forest of the Southern Mountain.
His face, stained with dust and ashes, has turned to the colour of smoke.
The hair on his temples is streaked with gray: his ten fingers are black.
The money he gets by selling charcoal, how far does it go?
It is just enough to clothe his limbs and put food in his mouth.
Although, alas, the coat on his back is a coat without lining,
He hopes for the coming of cold weather, to send up the price of coal!
Last night, outside the city,—a whole foot of snow;
At dawn he drives the charcoal wagon along the frozen ruts.
Oxen,—weary; man,—hungry; the sun, already high;
Outside the Gate, to the south of the Market, at last they stop in the mud.
Suddenly, a pair of prancing horsemen. Who can it be coming?
A public official in a yellow coat and a boy in a white shirt.
In their hands they hold a written warrant: on their tongues—the words of an order;
They turn back the wagon and curse the oxen, leading them off to the north.
A whole wagon of charcoal,
More than a thousand pieces!
If officials choose to take it away, the woodman may not complain.
Half a piece of red silk and a single yard of damask,
The Courtiers have tied to the oxen's collar, as the price of a wagon of coal!

—Po Chü-i, translated by Arthur Waley.

~ ❁ ~

The Horrors of Civil War

Another age ground down by civil strife!
Rome by her children impious and accurst,
Down-trampled out of life!
Great Rome, our Rome, our mother, she that erst
Rolled back the Marsian, scattered the array
Of old Etruria's monarch, Porsena;
Humbled the pride of Capua, braved the sword
Of Spartacus; the blue-eyed German horde;
The craft and fury of the Gaul;
And him abhorred by mothers, Hannibal.

Amid her streets, her temples nigh,
The mountain wolf shall unmolested lie.
O'er her cold ashes the Barbarian ride;
The war-horse spurn the tomb
Of Romulus, and from earth's sacred womb
Scatter the dust which storms and suns defied.

How meet this ruin! Swear as swore
The doomed Phocaeans' race of yore,
To leave their fields, their loved abodes,
The altars of their household gods,
To tempt new seas and stretch their sail
Full-blown before the driving gale.
Be yours, submissive still to Fate,
Like them self-sentenced yet elate,
Fearless o'er ocean's trackless waste to fly
To lands unshamed and liberty.
Romans, is this your will? Then from the shore
Launch forth your ships; the gods approve. Obey
Yon bird of Fate that points the way;
But first make oath: swear to return no more.

Sooner shall rocks rise from their ocean grave
And float upheaved upon the wave;
Sooner shall Padus lave
Matinus' summit crowned with pine;
Sooner shall crown-capped Apennine
Rush to the Tyrrhene sea; tigers unite
With hinds, the ring-dove with the kite,
Than we return. Such, Romans, be your oath!
Let cowards press their beds of sloth.
Forth, manly spirits, womanish tears disdain;
Forsake the Etruscan shores and dare the boundless main!

Hence self-devoted go,
Ye who love honor best!
Visions of glory rush upon my eyes;
Prophetic voices rise:
See, see before us distant glow
Through the thin dawn-mists of the West
Rich sunlit plains and hilltops gemmed with snow,
The Islands of the Blest!

There the grey olive year by year
Yields its unfailing fruitage; there the vine
Ripens, unpruned, its clusters into wine.
There figs, ungraffed, their russet harvest grow,
And fields unplowed their wealth on man bestow.
There from the caverned ilex sere
Wells the wild honey trickling slow;
There herds and flocks unbidden bring
At eve their milky offering;
There from the crags' embattled steep
The laughing waters leap.
No wolf around the sheepfold striding
With mighty howl the sleeping lamb affrights;
No venomed snakes obscenely gliding
Sway the tall herbage; no destroying blights,
Nor storm, nor flood, nor scorching suns despoil,
(Such is the will of Jove) the teeming soil.

Blest summer shores untrod
By Jason or the Colchian sorceress,
By Tyrian rover, or the wearied crew
Of sage Ulysses in their dire distress.

Merciful gift of a relenting god,
Home of the homeless, preordained for you.
Last vestige of the age of gold;
Last refuge of the good and bold;
From stars malign, from plague and tempests free,
Far mid the western waves a secret sanctuary.

—*From the Latin of Horace (65–8 B.C.), translated by Stephen Edward De Vere.*

~ ❁ ~

Political Chaos in Italy

"Yonder there behold! a soul that stationed
All, all alone is looking hitherward;
It will point out to us the quickest way."
We came up unto it; O Lombard soul,
How lofty and disdainful thou didst bear thee,

And grand and slow in moving of thine eyes!
Nothing whatever did it say to us,
But let us go our way, eyeing us only
After the manner of a couchant lion;
Still near to it Virgilius drew, entreating
That it would point us out the best ascent;
And it replied not unto his demand,
But of our native land and of our life
It questioned us; and the sweet Guide began;
"Mantua," — and the shade, all in itself recluse,
Rose tow'rds him from the place where first it was,
Saying: "O Mantuan, I am Sordello
Of thine own land!" and one embraced the other.
Ah! servile Italy, grief's hostelry!
A ship without a pilot in great tempest!
No Lady thou of Provinces, but brothel!
That noble soul was so impatient, only
At the sweet sound of his own native land,
To make its citizen glad welcome there;
And now within thee are not without war
Thy living ones, and one doth gnaw the other
Of those whom one wall and one fosse shut in!
Search, wretched one, all round about the shores
Thy seaboard, and then look within thy bosom,
If any part of thee enjoyeth peace!
What boots it, that for thee Justinian
The bridle mend, if empty be the saddle?
Withouten this the shame would be the less.
Ah! people, thou that oughtest to be devout,
And to let Caesar sit upon the saddle,
If well thou hearest what God teachest thee,
Behold how fell this wild beast has become,
Being no longer by the spur corrected,
Since thou hast laid thy hand upon the bridle.
O German Albert! who abandonest
Her that has grown recalcitrant and savage,
And oughtest to bestride her saddle-bow,
May a just judgment from the stars down fall
Upon thy blood, and be it new and open,
That thy successor may have fear thereof;
Because thy father and thyself have suffered,
By greed of those transalpine lands distrained,
The garden of the empire to be waste.
Come and behold Montecchi and Cappelletti,
Monaldi and Fillippeschi, careless man!
Those sad already, and these doubt-depressed!
Come, cruel one; come and behold the oppression
Of thy nobility, and cure their wounds,
And thou shalt see how safe is Santafiore!
Come and behold thy Rome, that is lamenting,
Widowed, alone, and day and night exclaims,
"My Caesar, why hast thou forsaken me?"
Come and behold how loving are the people;
And if for us no pity moveth thee,
Come and be made ashamed of thy renown!
And if it lawful be, O Jove Supreme!
Who upon earth for us wast crucified,
Are thy just eyes averted otherwhere?
Or preparation is 't, that, in the abyss
Of thy own counsel, for some good thou makest
From our perception utterly cut off?
For all the towns of Italy are full
Of tyrants, and becometh a Marcellus
Each peasant churl who plays the partisan!
My Florence! well mayst thou contented be
With this digression, which concerns thee not,
Thanks to thy people who such forethought take!
Many at heart have justice, but shoot slowly,
That unadvised they come not to the bow,
But on their very lips thy people have it!
Many refuse to bear the common burden;
But thy solicitous people answereth
Without being asked, and crieth: "I submit."
Now be thou joyful, for thou hast good reason;
Thou affluent, thou in peace, thou full of wisdom;
If I speak true, the event conceals it not.
Athens and Lacedaemon, they who made
The ancient laws, and were so civilized,
Made towards living well a little sign
Compared with thee, who makest such fine-spun
Provisions, that to middle of November

Reaches not what thou in October spinnest.
How oft, within the time of thy remembrance,
Laws, money, offices, and usages
Hast thou remodelled, and renewed thy members?
And if thou mind thee well, and see the light,
Thou shalt behold thyself like a sick woman,
Who cannot find repose upon her down,
But by her tossing wardeth off her pain.

—*From the Italian of Dante Alighieri (1265–1321), translated by Henry Wadsworth Longfellow.*

"Awake! The Day Is Coming Now"

Awake! The day is coming now
That brings the sweat of anguish to the brow
Of Christians, Jews, and Pagans all!
Many a token in the sky
And on the earth shows it is nigh:
The sun no longer shows
His face; and treason sows
His secret seeds that no man can detect;
Fathers by their children are undone;
The brother would the brother cheat;
And the cowled monk is a deceit,
Who should the way to Heaven direct;
Might is right, and justice there is none.
Arise! we slept, nor of the peril recked.

—*From the German of Walther von der Vogelweide (c. 1170–c. 1230), translated by Jethro Bithell.*

Italy

Italia! Oh Italia! thou who hast
The fatal gift of beauty, which became
A funeral dower of present woes and past,
On thy sweet brow is sorrow plow'd by shame,
And annals graved in characters of flame.
Oh, God! that thou wert in thy nakedness
Less lovely or more powerful, and couldst claim
Thy right, and awe the robbers back, who press
To shed thy blood, and drink the tears of thy distress;
Then might'st thou more appal, or less desired,
Be homely and be peaceful, undeplored
For thy destructive charms; then, still untired,
Would not be seen the armed torrents pour'd
Down the steep Alps; nor would the hostile horde
Of many-nation'd spoilers from the Po
Quaff blood and water; nor the stranger's sword
Be thy sad weapon of defense, and so
Victor or vanquished, thou the slave of friend or foe.

—*From the Italian of Vincenzo da Filicaja (1642–1707), translated by Lord Byron.*

The People

The people is a beast of muddy brain
That knows not its own force, and therefore stands
Loaded with wood and stone; the powerless hands
Of a mere child guide it with bit and rein;
One kick would be enough to break the chain;
But the beast fears, and what the child demands,
It does; nor its own terror understands,
Confused and stupefied by bugbears vain.
Most wonderful! with its own hand it ties
And gags itself—gives itself death and war
For pence doled out by kings from its own store.
Its own are all things between earth and heaven;
But this it knows not; and if one arise
To tell this truth, it kills him unforgiven.

—*From the Italian Tomasso Campenella (1568–1639), translated by John Addington Symonds.*

To Italy

O Italy, I see the lonely towers,
The arches and the columns and the walls
Of bygone days. The glory and the steel
That girt our fathers I behold not. Now
Unarmed, thou show'st a naked breast, a brow
Undiademed. Ah me, what wounds, what blood!

How art thou fallen, O most beautiful!
I cry to heaven, unto earth I cry:
Say, say, who brought her to so dire a pass?
Her arms are bound in chains; with scattered locks
And face unveiled, she sits disconsolate,
Forgotten, and her head between her knees
Hiding, she weeps. Ah, weep, my Italy,
Thou hast good cause, thou who wert born to rule,
Now fallen on so dark a destiny.

Were thy dim eyes two gushing founts of tears
They ne'er could quench thy sorrow and thy shame,
Who wert a queen, and art become a slave.
Who now doth speak of thee, remembering
Thy vaunted past, but saith: She once was great,
She is no more? Why? Why? Where is thy might,
Thine ancient valor, arms, and constancy?
Who hath unclasped thy sword? Who thee betrayed?
What subtle craft, what labor, or what power
Despoiled thee of thy mantle and thy crown?
How, when didst fall from majesty so low?
Will none defend thee, will none fight for thee
Among thy children? Arms, to arms! Alone
I'll fight for thee, I'll fall for thee alone,
And be my blood a brand to fire cold hearts.

Where are thy children? Noise of arms I hear,
Of chariots and of shouting and of drums:
In foreign lands thy sons are combating.
Attend, O Italy. I see afar
A swaying throng of horses and of men,
Whirling of smoke and dust, and in the midst,
As lightning streaks the cloud, a flash of blades.
Art thou not comforted? Thy tear-dimmed eyes
Upon th' uncertain battle canst not bend?
What moves thy youth to fight upon those fields?
Ye gods, for alien lands Italian steel
Is bared. Unhappy he who fighting falls,
Not for his native shores and children dear,
But for the stranger, slain by others' foe,
And dying cannot say: O sacred soil,
I give thee back the life thou gavest me.

Oh fortunate and blest those days of old
When for their country peoples thronged to die.
Be ye for ever honored and most praised,
O Thessalonian passes, where dark fate
To Persian arms allied proved powerless
Against a handful of intrepid souls.
Methinks your waves and plants, your very stones
And watching mountains with incessant voice
Proclaim how all that coast was covered thick
With those undaunted hosts that fell for Greece.
Then, wild with fear, Xerxes o'er Hellespont
Fled, for all time a spectacle and scorn.
Simonides with failing steps did climb
Anthela's mount, where that heroic band
Dying were freed from death, and all about
Gazing with streaming eyes at hills and sea,
Took up his lyre and sang: O blessed ye
Who bared your breasts unto the foe's sharp steel
For love of her who gave you to the light,
Whom Greece hath tested, and the world reveres.
What mighty love your youthful spirits moved
To face 'mid clash of arms such bitter doom?
O children, with what shining countenance
Was Death to you revealed, that smiling thus
Ye ran to him 'mid pain and wounds so sore?
It seemed ye went to dance and feasting gay,
Yet night awaited you, and Tartarus;
Nor child nor spouse stood by when on that shore,
Without a kiss, without a tear, ye died.

But for the Persian 'twas dread chastisement,
Undying anguish. For as 'mid a drove
Of bulls a lion plunging, now on one
Now on another leaps, with claws and teeth
Tearing their flesh, so 'mid the Persian hordes
Raged the heroic fury of the Greeks.
See horses prone and men; see broken tents
And chariots trip the vanquished in their flight.
And see among the foremost, wild-eyed, pale,
The tyrant. See how with barbaric blood
Encrimsoned, the pursuing heroes fall,
One after one, by wounds o'ercome at last.
Live, live, most blessed ones, while yet the world

Hath tongue and hand to blaze your glorious deed!

The stars, uprooted, shall be hurled from heaven
Into the deep, and their majestic fires
'Mid hissing ruin quenched, ere memory
Your image shall unclasp, or spurn your love.
Your tomb an altar is, whereto shall come
Mothers, unto their children showing there
The shining traces of your blood. Behold,
O glorious ones, bowed on this hallowed ground,
I kiss these stones, this sod; may they be blest
And praised eternally from pole to pole.
Ah would that I were buried here with you,
And that this soil were sodden with my blood.
But since fate wills not that my dying eyes
Should close in battle for a land oppressed,
May the gods grant your poet's humble fame
Mingled with yours shall through the ages last.

— *From the Italian of Leopardi (1798–1837), translated by Romilda Rendel.*

Your Excellency

Your Excellency, who eyes me with disfavour
Because of a few insolent tricks once played,
Who deems me lacking in Teutonic savour
When certain brutes I'd have in stocks displayed,
Would really do me a considerable favour
By hearing an experience lately made
One morning in Saint Ambrose's, way back
Of Milan, somewhat off the beaten track. . . .
The church I found crammed full of soldiery,
From northern regions for the better part,
Croatians and Bohemians, forced to be
Sticks planted in our vineyards! Bless my heart,
They were indeed like very sticks to see,
Under their General's nose, stiff as a dart,
With whiskers made of tow and, Lord, what faces,
Before their God as nailed into their places!
I shrank back for an instant, entering there
Among that mob I really must confess
To a sense of disgust which you, through the office you bear,
Could hardly be expected even to guess;
An offensive smell, a paucity of air
Within that haven of pure loveliness!
Pardon me, Excellency, even the tapers that
Stood on the altar reeked of suet fat!
But when the priest uplifted in his hand
The sacred viands unto consecration,
Beside the altar suddenly a band
Awoke my soul to a sweet exultation;
Trumpets I heard, like voices near at hand
Lamenting for the passion of a nation
Mourning aloud, by waves of anguish tossed,
Remembering the blessings that were lost.
'Twas one of Verdi's hymns, that one beginning,
"O God, from my native roof-tree," you will know
It, from the "Lombards"; in the waste they're singing
Their plaint to God; the hymn that has moved so
Many a heart to ecstasy. Here flinging
My old self hence among the crowd, as though
Those creatures had been people of my race,
Involuntarily I took my place.
How could I help myself, the piece was fine
And ours, your Excellency, played as it should be?
When it's a question of art and a temperament like mine
Vowed unto art, then prejudices flee!
But, when the music ceased, back into line
I came, the fellow you are used to see!
Then from the mouths of those dormice there fell
A sound that worked upon me like a spell;
A German chant that slowly rose on high
Unto God's heaven from the sacred fane;
I will remember it until I die!
It was a prayer, but seemed a wail of pain!
So grave, so simple in its beauty, I
Was filled with sheer amazement that a strain
Of such exquisite harmony ever could
Be harboured in those foreign skulls of wood.
My soul was flooded with the bitter-sweet
Of childhood's melodies culled long ago
From dear, familiar lips; those we repeat
For consolation in our times of woe;
Thoughts that a well-beloved mother greet,
Yearnings for love and peace, and with these, Oh!
Such fear of exile and of loneliness,
I almost swooned, so poignant my distress!
Ended the strains, I fell to pondering,

My thoughts grown gentler, kinder, and
more clear:
After all, I said, the self-same despot king
It is who holds Slavs and Italians here,
Far from their homes, as slaves that they
may bring
Us slavery; sheeplike, driven forth through
fear
From Bohemia and Croatia, to grass
Throughout the winter in a strange morass.
Stern discipline and a hard life indeed,
Mute and derided, often lonely too,
Blind instruments of an ever-watchful greed
By which they profit nothing, have no clue
To for the most part. How that lusty seed
Of hate, constraining Lombards to eschew
What's German, has been fostered by whose
throne
Stands fast through discord and dreads peace
alone!

Poor fellows, far away from home, amid
A hostile people! Which of us can say
What hatred deep down in their souls lies
hid
For the oppressor? I could wager they
Scorn him no less than we do! Let me rid
Them of my presence quickly; if I stay
I'm sure to kiss that corporal there, the tall
One stuck up like a ladder by the wall!

— From the Italian of Giuseppe Giusti (1809–1850), translated by Lorna de' Lucchi.

On the Bad Government of Toledo

When mighty Rome was conqueror,
'Twas Scipio led the van of fighting;
Old Fabius was her counselor;
And Titus Livius did her writing.

And not a maid or wife but came
And stripped the ornaments from off her,
To offer them for warlike fame
And save her country from dishonor.

Where none there be to rule the town
How soon its triumph will be ended!
How soon the roof-tree tumble down
Where not a dweller is attended!

When pigs without the dogs to herd
Will straggle quick to their perdition,
Can troops without a captain's word
Be long maintained in war-condition?

For sheep without a shepherd's rod
Will lay in waste both field and garden;
And monks that know no prior's nod
Will fall to sins beyond a pardon.

The vineyards left unwatched to grow
Unto each passer-by will yield them;
The courts where gallants never show
Are hands that have no gloves to shield
them.

The shoe that fares without a sole
Can ill preserve the foot that wears it;
The strings escaped the lute's control
Will make a sound – if you can bear it –

The church that boasts no lettered throng,
Like palace without walls, must tremble;
Who looks for fish both big and strong
Save where the firmest nets dissemble?

In faith, that blow me-seemeth light
Of which a swordless hand is giver; –
But a sword without a hand of might,
Full little thrust will it deliver!

— From the Spanish of Gómez Manrique (1415–1491), translated by Thomas Walsh.

Sonnet: Death Warnings

I saw the ramparts of my native land,
One time so strong, now dropping in de-
cay,
Their strength destroyed by this new age's
way
That has worn out and rotted what was
grand.
I went into the fields; there I could see
The sun drink up the waters newly
thawed;
And on the hills the moaning cattle
pawed,
Their miseries robbed the light of day for
me.

I went into my house; I saw how spotted,
Decaying things made that old home their
prize;
My withered walking-staff had come to
bend.
I felt the age had won; my sword was rotted;

And there was nothing on which to set my eyes
That was not a reminder of the end.

— *From the Spanish of Quevedo y Villegas (1580–1645), translated by John Masefield.*

~ ⚙ ~

To Roosevelt

'Tis only with the Bible or with Walt Whitman's verse,
That you, the mighty hunter, are reached by other men.
You're primitive and modern, you're simple and complex, —
A veritable Nimrod with naught of Washington.
You are the United States;
You are the future foe
Of free America that keeps its Indian blood,
That prays to Jesus Christ, and speaks in Spanish still.
You are a fine example of a strong and haughty race;
You're learned and you're clever; to Tolstoy you're opposed;
And whether taming horses or slaying savage beasts,
You seem an Alexander and Nebuchadnezzar too.
(As madmen today are wont to say,
You're a great professor of energy.)
You seem to be persuaded
That life is but combustion,
That progress is eruption,
And where you send the bullet
You bring the future.

The United States are rich, they're powerful and great
(They join the cult of Mammon to that of Hercules),
And when they stir and roar, the very Andes shake. . . .

But our America, which since the ancient times . . .
Has had its native poets; which lives on fire and light,
On perfumes and on love; our vast America,
The land of Montezuma, the Inca's mighty realm,
Of Christopher Columbus the fair America,
America the Spanish, the Roman Catholic, . . .
O men of Saxon eyes and fierce, barbaric soul,
This land still lives and dreams, and loves and stirs!
Take care!
The daughter of the Sun, the Spanish land, doth live!
And from the Spanish lion a thousand whelps have sprung!
'Tis need, O Roosevelt, that you be God himself . . .
Before you hold us fast in your grasping, iron claws.

And though you count on all, one thing is lacking: God!

— *From the Spanish of the Nicaraguan poet, Rubén Darío (1867–1916), translated by Elijah Clarence Hills.*

~ ⚙ ~

Tropic Siesta

Sultry Sunday, noon
of shimmering
sun. A policeman
as if embedded in the curb,
profoundly asleep. A dog's
filth smeared on a fence. An abbot's
indigestion, the muffled
cacophony of a locust. . . .

Solitude of the grave, complete
and sullen silence. But
suddenly in the ugly town

the dominical hush is broken,
for a raving drunkard screams:
Hooray for the Liberal Party!

— *From the Spanish of the Colombian Luis Carlos López (1880–), translated by Donald Devenish Walsh.*

~ ⚙ ~

Pamphlet

I have broken the rainbow
against my heart
as one breaks a useless sword against the knee.
I have blown the clouds of rose colour and blood colour
beyond the farthest horizons.
I have drowned my dreams

in order to glut the dreams that sleep for me
in the veins
of men who sweated and wept and raged
to season my coffee. . . .

The dream that sleeps in breasts stifled by tuberculosis
(A little air, a little sunshine!);
the dream that dreams in stomachs strangled by hunger
(A bit of bread, a bit of white bread!);
the dream of bare feet
(Fewer stones on the road, Lord, fewer broken bottles!);
the dream of calloused hands
(Moss . . . clean cambric . . . things smooth, soft, soothing!);
The dream of trampled hearts
(Love . . . Life . . . Life! . . .)

I am the pamphleteer of God,
God's agitator,
and I go with the mob of stars and hungry men
toward the great dawn. . . .

—*From the Spanish of the Puerto Rican Luis Muñoz Marín (1898–), translated by Muna Lee de Muñoz Marín.*

A Warning for Abraham Lincoln

Captain, I have seen
how from the hollow of your wound
the bees emerge contented
to settle upon the eyes of Walt Whitman
and rock his rustling beard.

Captain, I am seeking you,
for I have heard that they are trying to murder you again.
And this time we know it.

Listen to his footsteps
who conspires behind the door among the locusts,
loosing the swarm and gloating at the thought of their feast of green.

Beware, Captain, beware!
For the ears of grain are trembling and the sky is sombre.
Elytrons and pincers and mandibles
are telling you: Beware!

There, in your theatre box.
I know it, and I tell you:
for over the most beautiful fields hovers the eclipse,
and no stone will remain on stone,
for already your city is crying through its crevices.

If they kill you again,
who will gather the honey from your beehives,
or guide the trains
of your milk of peace toward your ants?

If they kill you again,
who will look after your black ants?
If they kill again,
never more will it be possible,
not even in the laurel of dream,
for your ant-hills to swarm
from dawn to dusk.

Captain, I am seeking you
to tell you they are after you
with the muzzle of the gun
which already would open the new wound
without bees:
ah, for in that hollow of your bloodless death
all the beehives would perish.

And where then
could we bury you,
those of us who follow after your bee's voice
and drink of your sad eyes?

Where,
if you were not living, but dead?

—*From the Spanish of the Venezuelan Jacinto Fombona-Pachano (1901–), translated by Angel Flores.*

Crossroads

We were shut off from the street
by the rainblurred window.
I was far from the world,
lost in the pools of her eyes.

She was small and soft,
and she made herself smaller in my arms
and softer beneath my gaze.
Between us and the street
the rain and the windowpane
were two chasms of silver.

Life was there, shipwrecked in her eyes.
Beauty lay asleep in her perfumed breasts.
Light – all the light – was mine upon her lips.
Humanity – my humanity – was she.
Beyond the window,
beyond the rain,
they passed by. . . .
I raised my eyes from hers
to watch them pass.
Onward plodded the bare feet
splashing in the mud.
And faces passed, shadowed by hunger,
and hands worn hard by wretchedness,
and hearts bowed by injustice,
and the dawning voices of hate.
The bare feet passed.

There was the mother, child on hip,
and the old man mumbling his sorrow,
and the young man waving a banner.
They were marching face forward toward life
in harmonious rebellion.

I do not know if they cried it out to me,
or I to myself:
but in the ranks of those marchers-by
were my place, my banner, and my cry.

The rainblurred window
shut me off from the street
along which my people were passing,
I turned my eyes back to her
so closely merged with me between my arms,
and said:
They are calling me, those who pass by.

Her blurred eyes
shut me away from her soul
as the rainy windowpane
shut me off from the street.
She answered slowly:
Don't go away.
And she made herself even smaller in my arms
and offered me her trembling mouth,
and pressed close to me I felt her throbbing breasts.

I listened to the bare feet
splashing in the mud,
and I sensed the faces shadowed by hunger.

My heart was a pendulum between her and the street. . . .
And I do not know with what strength I freed myself from her eyes,
tore myself from her arms.

I left her clouding her anguish with her tears
behind the rain and the windowpane,
but incapable of crying out to me: *Wait!*
I am going with you!

— *From the Spanish of the Venezuelan Miguel Otero Silva (1908–), translated by Donald Devenish Walsh.*

The Trumpets of the Mind

Sound, sound forever, clarions of thought!

When Joshua 'gainst the high-walled city fought,
He marched around it with his banner high,
His troops in serried order following nigh,
But not a sword was drawn, no shaft out-sprang;
Only the trumpets the shrill onset rang.
At the first blast, smiled scornfully the king,
And at the second sneered, half-wondering:
"Hop'st thou with noise my stronghold to break down?"
— At the third round the ark of old renown
Swept forward, still the trumpets sounding loud,
And then the troops with ensigns waving proud.
Stepped out upon the old walls children dark,
With horns to mock the notes and hoot the ark.
At the fourth turn, braving the Israelites,
Women appeared upon the crenelated heights –
Those battlements embrowned with age and rust –
And hurled upon the Hebrews stones and dust,
And spun and sang when weary of the game.
At the fifth circuit came the blind and lame,
And with wild uproar clamorous and high
Railed at the clarion ringing to the sky.
At the sixth time, upon a tower's tall crest,
So high that there the eagle built his nest,
So hard that on it lightning lit in vain,
Appeared in merriment the king again:
"These Hebrew Jews musicians are, me-seems!"
He scoffed, loud laughing, "but they live on dreams."

The princes laughed submissive to the king,
Laughed all the courtiers in their glittering ring,
And thence the laughter spread through all the town.

And at the seventh blast the city walls fell down.

— From the French of Victor Hugo (1802–1885), anonymous translation.

Indignation

Thou who loved Juvenal, and filed
His style so sharp to scar imperial brows,
And lent the lustre lightening
The gloom in Dante's murky verse that flows, —
Muse Indignation! haste, and help
My building up before this roseate realm
And its fruitless victories,
Whence transient shame Right's prophets overwhelm,
So many pillories deserved,
That eyes to come will pry without avail
Upon the wood impenetrant,
And glean no glitter of its tarnished tale.

— From the French of Victor Hugo (1802–1885), anonymous translation.

The King of the Rainy Country

A rainy country this, that I am monarch of, —
A rich but powerless king, worn-out while yet a boy;
For whom in vain the falcon falls upon the dove;
Not even his starving people's groans can give him joy;
Scorning his tutors, loathing his spaniels, finding stale
His favourite jester's quips, yawning at the droll tale.
His bed, for all its *fleur de lis,* looks like a tomb;
The ladies of the court, attending him, to whom
He, being a prince, is handsome, see him lying there
Cold as a corpse, and lift their shoulders in despair:
— No garment they take off, no garter they leave on
Excites the gloomy eye of this young skeleton.
The royal alchemist, who makes him gold from lead,
The baser element from out the royal head
Cannot extract; nor can those Roman baths of blood,
For some so efficacious, cure the hebetude
Of him, along whose veins, where flows no blood at all,
For ever the slow waters of green Lethe crawl.

— From the French of Charles Baudelaire (1821–1867), translated by Edna St. Vincent Millay.

The Poor

With hearts of poor men it is so:
That they are full of tears that flow.
That they are pale as head-stones white
In the moon light.

And so with poor men's backs it is —
More bent with heavy miseries
Than sagging roofs of brown huts be
Beside the sea.

And it is so with poor men's hands,
Like leaves along autumnal lands,
Leaves that lie sere and dead and late
Beside the gate.

And it is so with poor men's eyes,
Humble and in all sorrow wise,
And like the cattle's, sad and dumb,
When the storms come.

Oh, it is so with the poor folk
That under misery's iron yoke
Have gestures weary and resigned
On earth's far plains of sun and wind.

— From the French of the Belgian poet Emile Verhaeren (1855–1916), translated by Ludwig Lewisohn.

Congress 1878

They sit at the green baize table
With puckered brows and pondering eyes;
The happiness of Europe lies

And the balance of power, on the green table.

And greedily, greedily we must snatch
All the crumbs from the table falling . . .
"Peace! Peace! Peace!" the nations are calling,
And anxiously our breaths we catch.

Now our race shall prosper well.
Harken! Wild cries of joy are resounding!
. . . But what of the hearts in hope abounding
That under the blue and green banner fell?

O many, many tears are shed!
Childless now is many a mother;
And bitter hearts mourn husband, brother . . .
Alas! The dead are dead.

And now the diplomats have met,
For of the long war they are tired;
And the last cannon has been fired. . . .
"A talk may end our quarrel yet!

"Enough of bloodshed! Either side
Gave proof of courage quite heroic!
And every statesman was a stoic!
Honor was saved by them that died!

"And if between our realms a grim
Bottomless chasm kept us sundered,
Our furious cannon as they thundered
Filled it with corpses to the brim.

"Fraternity now bids us cease
From all this laying waste and killing;
And Christian love should make us willing
To join our weary hands in peace."

At this, warm tears flow from their eyes . . .
And every generous heart refuses
To trust the slander that accuses
These great men of deceit and lies. . . .

Peace, peace again! Wave, wave your hats!
Let the bells ring from every steeple!
Now better days dawn for our people!
A triumph for the diplomats!

And we have learned this one great lesson:
A Congress ends the bloodiest war. . . .
As soon as honest Krupps of Essen
Have — what the states were fighting for. . . .

— From the Flemish of Victor Alexis de la Montagne, translated by Jethro Bithell.

Enfant Perdu

In Freedom's War, of "Thirty Years" and more,
A lonely outpost have I held — in vain!
With no triumphant hope or prize in store,
Without a thought to see my home again.

I watched both day and night: I could not sleep
Like my well-tented comrades far behind,
Though near enough to let their snoring keep
A friend awake, if e'er to doze inclined.

And thus, when solitude my spirits shook,
Or fear — for all but fools know fear sometimes, —
To rouse myself and them, I piped and took
A gay revenge in all my wanton rhymes.

Yes! there I stood, my musket always ready,
And when some sneaking rascal showed his head,
My eye was vigilant, my aim was steady,
And gave his brains an extra dose of lead.

But war and justice have far different laws,
And worthless acts are often done right well;
The rascals' shots were better than their cause,
And I was hit — and hit again, and fell!

That outpost is abandoned: while the one
Lies in the dust, the rest in troops depart;
Unconquered — I have done what could be done,
With sword unbroken, and with broken heart.

— From the German of Heinrich Heine (1797–1856), translated by Lord Houghton.

The Soldier Boy

My father was a soldier young, the finest you might see;
Took arms at fifteen, in two years he came to man's degree.
The field of honor he could hold,
He kept his station, gay and bold,
In blood, in fire, in hunger, cold, —
Ay, such a man was he.

I was a boy when peace was broke and he went forth to fight,
But still I mind his splendid stride, I mind him day and night;
His hat, his plume, his sunburnt hue,
The shadow of his eyebrows too,
His gallant form, so grand to view,
Will never leave my sight.

Then from our army in the north right soon were tidings brought
How fearless and how strong he was, how in each fight he fought.
He had a medal now to wear,
By next report he had a pair:
Ah me, how glorious to be there!
Within my heart I thought.

The winter passed, the snow was gone, the spring was blithe and brave,
When came the news: "Your father's dead, his life he nobly gave."
Just how I felt I hardly ken,
Was now distressed, now glad again;
But mother wept three days, and then
Was carried to her grave.

Close to the banner he was killed that day on Lappo plain,
They said he never blenched in fight but there when he was slain.
At Uttismalm, for Gustav's land,
My grandsire died with sword in hand,
His father fell at Willmanstrand,
That was in Charles's reign.

'T was so it went, 't was so they bled, their course was clear and straight;
How glorious in their life they lived, and in their death how great!
Oh, who would plod on sluggishly?
Nay, hot with youth in battle-glee
Die for your king and country, see
How manlier such a fate!

I'm but a beggar boy myself, who eats of others' bread,
I've neither home nor shelter now, with both my parents dead;
But I've no wish to go and cry,
For taller every day am I,
To be a soldier boy I try,
And have no care or dread.

And if I live till I am big and reach fifteen some day,
To that same hunger, war, and death I'll go without dismay.
When whizzing bullets fill the air,
Whoever seeks may find me there,
For I in turn would follow where
My fathers led the way.

— From the Swedish of Johan Ludvig Runeberg (1804–1877), translated by Charles Wharton Stork.

~ ⚙ ~

A Sail

A far sail shimmers, white and lonely,
Through the blue haze above the foam.
What does it seek in foreign harbors?
What has it left behind at home?

The billows romp, and the wind whistles.
The rigging swings, the tall mast creaks.
It is not happiness he flees from,
Alas, it is not joy he seeks.

Below, the sea, like blue light flowing,
Above, the sun shines without cease,
But it is storm the rebel asks for,
As though in storms were peace.

— From the Russian of Mikhail Yuryevich Lermontov (1814–1841), translated by Babette Deutsch and Avrahm Yarmolinsky.

~ ⚙ ~

"With Freedom's Seed"

With freedom's seed the desert sowing,
I walked before the morning star;
With pure and guiltless fingers throwing —
Where slavish plows had left a scar —
The living seed that should have quickened,
But hope, at last grown weary, sickened,
I learn how sad lost labors are . . .
Graze if you will, you peaceful nations,
Who never rouse at honor's horn!
Should flocks heed freedom's invocations?

Their part is to be slain or shorn,
And wear the bells tame sires have worn
Through whipped and sheeplike generations.

—From the Russian of Alexander Pushkin (1799–1837), translated by Babette Deutsch and Avrahm Yarmolinsky.

Message to Siberia

Deep in the Siberian mine,
Keep your patience proud;
The bitter toil shall not be lost,
The rebel thought unbowed.

The sister of misfortune, Hope,
In the under-darkness dumb
Speaks joyful courage to your heart:
The day desired will come.

And love and friendship pour to you
Across the darkened doors,
Even as round your galley-beds
My free music pours.

The heavy-hanging chains will fall,
The walls will crumble at a word;
And Freedom greet you in the light,
And brothers give you back the sword.

—From the Russian of Alexander Pushkin (1799–1837), translated by Max Eastman.

On the Late Massacre in Piedmont

Avenge, O Lord, thy slaughtered saints, whose bones
Lie scattered on the Alpine mountains cold;
Even them who kept thy truth so pure of old,
When all our fathers worshiped stocks and stones,
Forget not: in thy book record their groans
Who were thy sheep, and in their ancient fold
Slain by the bloody Piedmontese, that rolled
Mother with infant down the rocks. Their moans
The vales redoubled to the hills, and they
To heaven. Their martyred blood and ashes sow
O'er all the Italian fields, where still doth sway
The triple Tyrant; that from these may grow
A hundredfold, who, having learnt thy way,
Early may fly the Babylonian woe.

—John Milton, English (1698–1674).

A Man's a Man for A' That

Is there for honest poverty
That hangs his head, an' a' that?
The coward slave, we pass him by,
We dare be poor for a' that!
For a' that, an' a' that,
Our toils obscure an' a' that,
The rank is but the guinea stamp;
The man's the gowd for a' that.

What though on hamely fare we dine,
Wear hodden-grey, an' a' that?
Gie fools their silks, and knaves their wine,
A man's a man's for a' that.
For a' that, an' a' that,
Their tinsel show an' a' that;
The honest man, tho' e'er sae poor,
Is King o' men for a' that.

Ye see yon birkie, ca'd a lord,
Wha struts, an' stares, an' a' that;
Tho' hundreds worship at his word,
He's but a coof for a' that.
For a' that, an' a' that,
His ribband, star, an' a' that,
The man o' independent mind
He looks an' laughs at a' that.

A prince can mak a belted knight,
A marquis, duke, an' a' that;
But an honest man's aboon his might,
Gude faith, he mauna fa' that!
For a' that, an' a' that,
Their dignities an' a' that,
The pith o' sense, an' pride o' worth,
Are higher rank than a' that.

Then let us pray that come it may,
As come it will for a' that,
That sense and worth, o'er a' the earth,
Shall bear the gree, an' a' that.
For a' that, an' a' that,
It's coming yet for a' that,
That man to man, the warld o'er,
Shall brothers be for a' that.

—Robert Burns, Scottish (1759–1796).

The Siege of Ismail

FROM "DON JUAN"

O Love! O Glory! what are ye who fly
Around us ever, rarely to alight?
There's not a meteor in the polar sky
Of such transcendent and more fleeting flight.
Chill, and chain'd to cold earth, we lift on high
Our eyes in search of either lovely light;
A thousand and a thousand colours they
Assume, then leave us on our freezing way.

And such as they are, such my present tale is,
A non-descript and ever-varying rhyme,
A versified Aurora Borealis,
Which flashes o'er a waste and icy clime.
When we know what all are, we must bewail us,
But ne'ertheless I hope it is no crime
To laugh at *all* things — for I wish to know
What, after *all,* are *all* things — but a *show*?

They accuse me — *Me* — the present writer of
The present poem — of — I know not what —
A tendency to under-rate and scoff
At human power and virtue, and all that;
And this they say in language rather rough.
Good God! I wonder what they would be at!
I say no more than hath been said in Danté's
Verse, and by Solomon and by Cervantes;

By Swift, by Machiavel, by Rochefoucault,
By Fénelon, by Luther, and by Plato;
By Tillotson, and Wesley, and Rousseau,
Who knew this life was not worth a potato.
'Tis not their fault, nor mine, if this be so —
For my part, I pretend not to be Cato,
Nor even Diogenes. — We live and die,
But which is best, you know no more than I.

Socrates said, our only knowledge was
'To know that nothing could be known;' a pleasant
Science enough, which levels to an ass
Each man of wisdom, future, past, or present.
Newton (that proverb of the mind), alas!
Declared, with all his grand discoveries recent,
That he himself felt only "like a youth
Picking up shells by the great ocean — Truth."

Ecclesiastes said, "that all is vanity" —
Most modern preachers say the same, or show it
By their examples of true Christianity:
In short, all know, or very soon may know it;
And in this scene of all-confess'd inanity,
By saint, by sage, by preacher, and by poet,
Must I restrain me, through the fear of strife,
From holding up the nothingness of life?

Dogs, or men! — for I flatter you in saying
That ye are dogs — your betters far — ye may
Read, or read not, what I am now essaying
To show ye what ye are in every way.
As little as the moon stops for the baying
Of wolves, will the bright muse withdraw one ray
From out her skies — then howl your idle wrath!
While she still silvers o'er your gloomy path.

"Fierce loves and faithless wars" — I am not sure
If this be the right reading — 'tis no matter;
The fact's about the same, I am secure;
I sing them both, and am about to batter
A town which did a famous siege endure,
And was beleaguer'd both by land and water
By Souvaroff, or Anglicè Suwarrow,
Who loved blood as an alderman loves marrow.

The fortress is call'd Ismail, and is placed
Upon the Danube's left branch and left bank,
With buildings in the Oriental taste,
But still a fortress of the foremost rank,
Or was at least, unless 'tis since defaced,
Which with your conquerors is a common prank:
It stands some eighty versts from the high sea,
And measures round of toises thousands three.

The Russians now were ready to attack:
But oh, ye goddesses of war and glory!

How shall I spell the name of each Cossacque
  Who were immortal, could one tell their story?
Alas! what to their memory can lack?
  Achilles' self was not more grim and gory
Than thousands of this new and polish'd nation,
Whose names want nothing but — pronunciation.

Still I'll record a few, if but to increase
  Our euphony: there was Strongenoff, and Strokonoff,
Meknop, Serge Lwow, Arsniew of modern Greece,
  And Tschitsshakoff, and Roguenoff, and Chokenoff,
And others of twelve consonants apiece;
  And more might be found out, if I could poke enough
Into gazettes; but Fame (capricious strumpet),
It seems, has got an ear as well as trumpet.

I wonder (although Mars no doubt's a god I
  Praise) if a man's name in a *bulletin*
May make up for a *bullet in* his body?
  I hope this little question is no sin,
Because, though I am but a simple noddy,
  I think one Shakespeare puts the same thought in
The mouth of some one in his plays so doting,
Which many people pass for wits by quoting.

"Let there be light! said God, and there was light!"
  "Let there be blood!" says man, and there's a sea!
The fiat of this spoil'd child of the Night
  (For Day ne'er saw his merits) could decree
More evil in an hour, than thirty bright
  Summers could renovate, though they should be
Lovely as those which ripen'd Eden's fruit;
For war cuts up not only branch, but root.

Oh, thou eternal Homer! who couldst charm
  All ears, though long; all ages, though so short,
By merely wielding with poetic arm
  Arms to which men will never more resort,
Unless gunpowder should be found to harm
  Much less than is the hope of every court,
Which now is leagued young Freedom to annoy;
But they will not find Liberty a Troy: —

Oh, thou eternal Homer! I have now
  To paint a siege, wherein more men were slain,
With deadlier engines and a speedier blow,
  Than in thy Greek gazette of that campaign;
And yet, like all men else, I must allow,
  To vie with thee would be about as vain
As for a brook to cope with ocean's flood;
But still we moderns equal you in blood;

If not in poetry, at least in fact;
  And fact is truth, the grand desideratum!
Of which, howe'er the Muse describes each act,
  There should be ne'ertheless a slight substratum.
But now the town is going to be attack'd;
  Great deeds are doing — how shall I relate 'em?
Souls of immortal generals! Phœbus watches.
To colour up his rays from your despatches.

Oh, ye great bulletins of Bonaparte!
  Oh, ye less grand long lists of kill'd and wounded!
Shade of Leonidas, who fought so hearty,
  When my poor Greece was once, as now, surrounded!
Oh, Cæsar's Commentaries! now impart, ye
  Shadows of glory! (lest I be confounded)
A portion of your fading twilight hues,
So beautiful, so fleeting, to the Muse.

When I call "fading" martial immortality,
  I mean, that every age and every year,
And almost every day, in sad reality,
  Some sucking hero is compell'd to rear,
Who, when we come to sum up the totality
  Of deeds to human happiness most dear,
Turns out to be a butcher in great business,
Afflicting young folks with a sort of dizziness.

Medals, rank, ribands, lace, embroidery, scarlet,
  Are things immortal to immortal man,
As purple to the Babylonian harlot:
  An uniform to boys is like a fan
To women; there is scarce a crimson varlet

But deems himself the first in Glory's van.
But Glory's glory; and if you would find
What that is — ask the pig who sees the wind!

All was prepared — the fire, the sword, the men
To wield them in their terrible array.
The army, like a lion from his den,
Marched forth with nerve and sinews bent to slay, —
A human Hydra, issuing from its fen
To breathe destruction on its winding way,
Whose heads were heroes, which cut off in vain
Immediately in others grew again.

History can only take things in the gross;
But could we know them in detail, perchance
In balancing the profit and the loss,
War's merit it by no means might enhance,
To waste so much gold for a little dross,
As hath been done, mere conquest to advance.
The drying up a single tear has more
Of honest fame, than shedding seas of gore.

And why? — because it brings self-approbation;
Whereas the other, after all its glare,
Shouts, bridges, arches, pensions from a nation,
Which (it may be) has not much left to spare,
A higher title, or a loftier station,
Though they may make Corruption gape or stare,
Yet, in the end, except in Freedom's battles,
Are nothing but a child of Murder's rattles.

And such they are — and such they will be found:
Not so Leonidas and Washington,
Whose every battle-field is holy ground,
Which breathes of nations saved, not worlds undone.
How sweetly on the ear such echoes sound!
While the mere victor's may appal or stun
The servile and the vain, such names will be
A watchword till the future shall be free.

But never mind; — "God save the king!" and kings!
For if *he* don't, I doubt if *men* will longer —
I think I hear a little bird, who sings
The people by and by will be the stronger:
The veriest jade will wince whose harness wrings
So much into the raw as quite to wrong her
Beyond the rules of posting, — and the mob
At last fall sick of imitating Job.

At first it grumbles, then it swears, and then,
Like David, flings smooth pebbles 'gainst a giant;
At last it takes to weapons such as men
Snatch when despair makes human hearts less pliant.
Then comes "the tug of war;" — 'twill come again,
I rather doubt; and I would fain say "fie on 't,"
If I had not perceived that revolution
Alone can save the earth from hell's pollution.

All that the mind would shrink from of excesses;
All that the body perpetrates of bad;
All that we read, hear, dream, of man's distresses;
All that the devil would do if run stark mad;
All that defies the worst which pen expresses;
All by which hell is peopled, or as sad
As hell — mere mortals who their power abuse —
Was here (as heretofore and since) let loose.

If here and there some transient trait of pity
Was shown, and some more noble heart broke through
Its bloody bond, and saved perhaps some pretty
Child, or an aged, helpless man or two —
What's this in one annihilated city,
Where thousand loves, and ties, and duties grew?
Cockneys of London! Muscadins of Paris!
Just ponder what a pious pastime war is.

— *From Cantos VII and VIII of Don Juan (abridged), by George Gordon, Lord Byron, English (1788–1924).*

Song to the Men of England

I

Men of England, wherefore plough
For the lords who lay ye low?
Wherefore weave with toil and care
The rich robes your tyrants wear?

II

Wherefore feed, and clothe, and save,
From the cradle to the grave,
Those ungrateful drones who would
Drain your sweat – nay, drink your blood?

III

Wherefore, Bees of England, forge
Many a weapon, chain, and scourge,
That these stingless drones may spoil
The forced produce of your toil?

IV

Have ye leisure, comfort, calm,
Shelter, food, love's gentle balm?
Or what is it ye buy so dear
With your pain and with your fear?

V

The seed ye sow, another reaps;
The wealth ye find, another keeps;
The robes ye weave, another wears;
The arms ye forge, another bears.

VI

Sow seed, – but let no tyrant reap;
Find wealth, – let no impostor heap;
Weave robes, – let not the idle wear;
Forge arms, – in your defence to bear.

VII

Shrink to your cellars, holes, and cells;
In halls ye deck another dwells.
Why shake the chains ye wrought? Ye see
The steel ye tempered glance on ye.

VIII

With plough and spade, and hoe and loom,
Trace your grave, and build your tomb,
And weave your winding-sheet, till fair
England be your sepulchre.

— *Percy Bysshe Shelley, English (1792–1822).*

An Irish Airman Foresees His Death

I know that I shall meet my fate
Somewhere among the clouds above;
Those that I fight I do not hate.
Those that I guard I do not love;
My country is Kiltartan Cross,
My countrymen Kiltartan's poor,
No likely end could bring them loss
Or leave them happier than before.
Nor law, nor duty bade me fight,
Nor public men, nor cheering crowds,
A lonely impulse of delight
Drove to this tumult in the clouds;
I balanced all, brought all to mind,
The years to come seemed waste of breath,
A waste of breath the years behind
In balance with this life, this death.

— *William Butler Yeats, Irish (1865–1939).*

Discovery

Six thousand years in these dull regions pass'd
'Tis time, you'll say, we knew their bounds at last,
Knew to what skies our setting suns retire,
And where the wintry suns expend their fire;
What land to land protracts the varied scene,
And what extended oceans roll between;
What worlds exist beneath *antarctic skies,*
And from *Pacific* waves what verdant islands rise.
In vain did Nature shore from shore divide:
Art formed a passage and her waves defied:
When his bold plan the master pilot drew
Dissevered worlds stept forward at the view,
And lessening still the intervening space,
Disclosed new millions of the human race.
Proud even of toil, succeeding ages joined
New seas to vanquish, and new worlds to find;
Age following age still farther from the shore,
Found some new wonder that was hid before,
'Till launched at length, with avarice doubly bold,
Their hearts expanding as the world grew old,
Some to be rich, and some to be renowned,
The earth they rifled, and explored it round.
Ambitious Europe! polished in thy pride,
Thine was the art that toil to toil allied

Thine was the gift, to trace each heavenly sphere,
And seize its beams, to serve ambition here:
Hence fierce *Pizarro* stock'd a world with graves,
Hence *Montezuma* left a race of slaves—
Which project suited best with heaven's decree
To force new doctrines, or to leave them free?—
Religion only feigned to claim a share,
Their riches, not their souls, employed your care.—
Alas! how few of all that daring train
That seek new worlds embosomed in the main,
How few have sailed on virtues nobler plan,
How few with motives worthy of a man!—
While through the deep-sea waves we saw them go
Where'er they found a *man* they made a foe;
Superior only by superior art,
Forgot the social virtues of the heart,
Forgetting still, where'er they madly ran,
That sacred friendship binds mankind to man,
Fond of exerting power untimely shewn,
The momentary triumph all their own!
Met on the wrecks and ravages of time,
They left no native master of their clime,
His trees, his towns, with hardened front they claimed,
Seized every region that a despot named
And forced the oath that bound him to obey
Some prince unknown, ten thousand miles away.
Slaves to their passions, man's imperious race,
Born for contention, find no resting place,
And the vain mind, bewildered and perplext,
Makes this world wretched to enjoy the next.
Tired of the scenes that Nature made their own,
They rove to conquer what remains unknown:
Avarice, undaunted, claims whate'er she sees,
Surmounts earth's circle, and foregoes all ease;
Religion, bolder, sends some *sacred* chief
To bend the nations to her own belief.
To their vain standard Europe's sons invite,
Who hold no other *world* can think aright.
Behold their varied tribes, with self applause,
First in religion, liberty, and laws,
And while they bow to cruelty and blood,
Condemn the Indian with his milder god—
Ah, race to justice, truth, and honour blind,
Are thy convictions to convert mankind!
Vain price—convince them that your own are just,
Or leave them happy, as you found them first.
What charm is seen through Europe's realms of strife
That adds new blessings to the savage life?—
On them warm suns with equal splendour shine,
Their each domestic pleasure equals thine,
Their native groves as soft a bloom display,
As self-contented roll their lives away,
And the gay soul, in fancy's visions blest,
Leaves to the care of chance her heaven of rest.—
What are the arts that rise on Europe's plan
But arts destructive to the bliss of man?
What are all wars, where'er the marks you trace,
But the sad records of our world's disgrace?
Reason degraded from her tottering throne,
And precepts, called divine, observed by none.
Blest in their distance from that bloody scene,
Why spread the sail to pass the gulphs between?—
If winds can waft to ocean's utmost verge,
And there new islands and new worlds emerge—
If wealth, or war, or science bid thee roam,
Ah, leave religion and thy laws at home.
Leave the free native to enjoy his store,
Nor teach destructive arts, unknown before—
Woes of their own those new found worlds invade,
There, too, fierce passions the weak soul degrade,
Invention there has winged the unerring dart,
There the swift arrow vibrates to the heart,
Revenge and death contending bosoms share,
And pining envy claims her subjects there.—
Are these too few?—then see despotic power
Spends on a throne of logs her busy hour.
Hard by, and half ambitious to ascend,
Priests, interceding with the gods, attend—
Atoning victims at their shrines they lay,

Their crimson knives tremendous rites display,
Or the proud despot's gore remorseless shed,
Through life detested, or adored when dead.
Born to be wretched, search this globe around,
Dupes to a few the race of man is found!
Seek some new world in some new climate plac'd,
Some gay *Ta-ia* on the watery waste,
Though Nature clothes in all her bright array,
Some proud tormentor steals her charms away:
Howe'er she smiles beneath those milder skies,
Though men decay the monarch never dies!
Howe'er the groves, howe'er the gardens bloom,
A *monarch* and a *priest* is still their doom!

—*Philip Freneau, American (1752–1832).*

~ ☼ ~

Massachusetts to Virginia

The blast from Freedom's Northern hills, upon its Southern way,
Bears greeting to Virginia from Massachusetts Bay:
No word of haughty challenging, nor battle bugle's peal,
Nor steady tread of marching files, nor clang of horsemen's steel.

No trains of deep-mouthed cannon along our highways go;
Around our silent arsenals untrodden lies the snow;
And to the land-breeze of our ports, upon their errands far,
A thousand sails of commerce swell, but none are spread for war.

We hear thy threats, Virginia! thy stormy words and high
Swell harshly on the Southern winds which melt along our sky;
Yet not one brown, hard hand foregoes its honest labor here,
No hewer of our mountain oaks suspends his axe in fear.

Wild are the waves which lash the reefs along St. George's bank;
Cold on the shores of Labrador the fog lies white and dank;
Through storm, and wave, and blinding mist, stout are the hearts which man
The fishing-smacks of Marblehead, the sea-boats of Cape Ann.

The cold north light and wintry sun glare on their icy forms,
Bent grimly o'er their straining lines or wrestling with the storms;
Free as the winds they drive before, rough as the waves they roam,
They laugh to scorn the slaver's threat against their rocky home.

What means the Old Dominion? Hath she forgot the day
When o'er her conquered valleys swept the Briton's steel array?
How, side by side with sons of hers, the Massachusetts men
Encountered Tarleton's charge of fire, and stout Cornwallis, then?

Forgets she how the Bay State, in answer to the call
Of her old House of Burgesses, spoke out from Faneuil Hall?
When, echoing back her Henry's cry, came pulsing on each breath
Of Northern winds the thrilling sounds of "Liberty or Death!"

What asks the Old Dominion? If now her sons have proved
False to their fathers' memory, false to the faith they loved;
If she can scoff at Freedom, and its great charter spurn,
Must we of Massachusetts from truth and duty turn?

We hunt your bondmen, flying from Slavery's hateful hell;
Our voices, at your bidding, take up the bloodhound's yell;
We gather, at your summons, above our fathers' graves,
From Freedom's holy altar-horns to tear your wretched slaves!

Thank God! not yet so vilely can Massachusetts bow;
The spirit of her early time is with her even now;
Dream not because her Pilgrim blood moves slow and calm and cool,

She thus can stoop her chainless neck, a sister's slave and tool!

All that a sister State should do, all that a free State may,
Heart, hand, and purse we proffer, as in our early day;
But that one dark loathsome burden ye must stagger with alone,
And reap the bitter harvest which ye yourselves have sown!

Hold, while ye may, your struggling slaves, and burden God's free air
With woman's shriek beneath the lash, and manhood's wild despair;
Cling closer to the "cleaving curse" that writes upon your plains
The blasting of Almighty wrath against a land of chains.

Still shame your gallant ancestry, the cavaliers of old,
By watching round the shambles where human flesh is sold;
Gloat o'er the new-born child, and count his market value, when
The maddened mother's cry of woe shall pierce the slaver's den!

Lower than plummet soundeth, sink the Virginia name;
Plant, if ye will, your fathers' graves with rankest weeds of shame;
Be, if ye will, the scandal of God's fair universe;
We wash our hands forever of your sin and shame and curse.

A voice from lips whereon the coal from Freedom's shrine hath been,
Thrilled, as but yesterday, the hearts of Berkshire's mountain men:
The echoes of that solemn voice are sadly lingering still
In all our sunny valleys, on every wind-swept hill.

And when the prowling man-thief came hunting for his prey
Beneath the very shadow of Bunker's shaft of gray,
How, through the free lips of the son, the father's warning spoke;
How, from its bonds of trade and sect, the Pilgrim city broke!

A hundred thousand right arms were lifted up on high,
A hundred thousand voices sent back their loud reply;
Through the thronged towns of Essex the startling summons rang,
And up from bench and loom and wheel her young mechanics sprang!

The voice of free, broad Middlesex, of thousands as of one,
The shaft of Bunker calling to that of Lexington;
From Norfolk's ancient villages, from Plymouth's rocky bound
To where Nantucket feels the arms of ocean close her round;

From rich and rural Worcester, where through the calm repose
Of cultured vales and fringing woods the gentle Nashua flows,
To where Wachuset's wintry blasts the mountain larches stir,
Swelled up to Heaven the thrilling cry of "God save Latimer!"

And sandy Barnstable rose up, wet with the salt sea spray;
And Bristol sent her answering shout down Narragansett Bay!
Along the broad Connecticut old Hampden felt the thrill,
And the cheer of Hampshire's woodmen swept down from Holyoke Hill.

The voice of Massachusetts! Of her free sons and daughters,
Deep calling unto deep aloud, the sound of many waters!
Against the burden of that voice what tyrant power shall stand?
No fetters in the Bay State! No slave upon her land!

Look to it well, Virginians! In calmness we have borne,
In answer to our faith and trust, your insult and your scorn;
You've spurned our kindest counsels; you've hunted for our lives;
And shaken round our hearths and homes your manacles and gyves!

We wage no war, we lift no arm, we fling no torch within

The fire-damps of the quaking mine beneath your soil of sin;
We leave ye with your bondmen, to wrestle, while ye can,
With the strong upward tendencies and god-like soul of man!

But for us and for our children, the vow which we have given
For freedom and humanity is registered in heaven;
No slave-hunt in our borders, — no pirate on our strand!
No fetters in the Bay State, — no slave upon our land!

—*John Greenleaf Whittier, American (1807–1892).*

Burying Ground by the Ties

Ayee! Ai! This is heavy earth on our shoulders:
There were none of us born to be buried in this earth:
Niggers we were Portuguese Magyars Polacks:

We were born to another look of the sky certainly:
Now we lie here in the river pastures:
We lie in the mowings under the thick turf:

We hear the earth and the all-day rasp of the grasshoppers:
It was we laid the steel on this land from ocean to ocean:
It was we (if you know) put the U. P. through the passes

Bringing her down into Laramie full load
Eighteen mile on the granite anticlinal
Forty-three foot to the mile and the grade holding:

It was we did it: hunkies of our kind:
It was we dug the caved-in holes for the cold water:
It was we built the gully spurs and the freight sidings:

Who would do it but we and the Irishmen bossing us?
It was all foreign-born men there were in this country:
It was Scotsmen Englishmen Chinese Squareheads Austrians. . . .

Ayee! but there's weight to the earth under it:
Not for this did we come out — to be lying here
Nameless under the ties in the clay cuts:

There's nothing good in the world but the rich will buy it:
Everything sticks to the grease of a gold note —
Even a continent — even a new sky!

Do not pity us much for the strange grass over us:
We laid the steel to the stone stock of these mountains:
The place of our graves is marked by the telegraph poles!

It was not to lie in the bottoms we came out
And the trains going over us here in the dry hollows. . . .

—*Archibald MacLeish, American (1892–).*

PART TWELVE

The Critical Intellect

FIRMLY grounded in the traditions of Western culture lies an analytical and intellectual approach to life, which has colored all our thinking and strongly influenced certain phases of our poetry. The poets have given expression to this persistent but elusive tendency of man in a manner which early assumed a conventional style called the Ode. Whereas the Ode can be strictly formulated only by the insistence of pedants, the poetic tradition which it represents has exhibited itself consistently in many tongues, from that of the earliest Greek poetry to the most modern American speech. Many lyrics have at times been called odes which share little or nothing in these tendencies, and others never termed odes participate in them, nevertheless a little study of Comparative Literature shows a continuous evolution of thought and form that entitles us to speak of the spirit and reality of the genre.

The Ode is best identified by a formality of expression for which an underlying intellectual element proves the basis. It is, then, a lyric that most clearly fulfills Matthew Arnold's description of literature itself as a criticism of life. At first a highly conscious literary form defined by the theory and practice of the Greeks and Romans, it has become an almost instinctive manner of poetical composition. What began as an adjunct of ritual, in time passed into neo-classical learning and has largely issued again into a new phase of the civilized consciousness. That the Ode began as a liturgical rather than a popular form of verse, has doubtless been of subtle aid in preserving it as an intellectual and an aristocratic form of composition. Furthermore, its two chief stems, the Greek and the Latin, account for many later inconsistencies in its seemingly confused history. Analogues in other literatures than that of the Western World exist; but it is best to regard so indigenous a practice as remaining within the framework of Western culture. The witty and impassioned "odes" of Hafiz, for example, may for our present purposes be regarded as odes only by courtesy.

In the earliest known stages of Greek civilization the epic was chanted to the lyre, the elegy was accompanied on the flute, the popular lyric sung informally, usually by a single voice, and the Ode sung, as later the Christian hymns, in chorus, and, quite unlike the Christian hymns, often during the performance of a sacred dance. There was a leader of the chorus who later grew increasingly important, affording the clue to the evolution of both the drama and the personal lyric. For while the Ode began and largely remained a poetical form of public address, it came in time also to admit a distinctly personal address to its public. In Greece it remained as a rule associated with religious and political subjects, of interest to the entire community; but it became also "occasional verse." Odes were sung on public occasions as well as in public places, to celebrate important events, such as festivals of gods or men. The extant poems of Pindar, the first great writer of odes now known to us, celebrate victors in Greek athletic games, usually by way of linking their ancestry or the traditions of their cities with the myths of gods and heroes. In these odes even the austere Pindar occasionally speaks in his own person. The Greek drama developed out of the singing and dancing of ritualistic odes, and the lyrical element in Aeschylus, the first of the great tragic poets known to us, surpasses the more purely dramatic. Sophocles' odes are less prominent in his plays, and those of Euripides still less conspicuous and much more romantic and casual. Aristophanes in his comedies uses brilliant odes, wherein, according to a traditional right, at least once in each play he digresses to address the audience in an amusingly personal vein. But since his personal references are today often hard to comprehend, his odes of this nature are excluded from this anthology. The important thing to note is that the Ode, in addition to its communal, stately and impersonal qualities, was also developing a personal though hardly a subjective note.

Latin poets, learning their craft largely from the Greek, invariably stamp their works with the powerful genius of Roman culture. At their hands the Ode loses much of its pure lyricism, its religious enthusiasm, and epic or tragic splendor, but retains full critical or intellectual vigor and wins new provinces for personal expression, urbanity and lightness. In short, the intellectual element loses something of its original gravity, and no Roman poet equals the supreme humor and gusto of Aristophanes. The clear and translucent odes of Horace become models of stylized and restrained art, the perfect expressions of a gracious culture. Where Greek odes often possessed a complex structure so subtle as to appear chaotic, the odes of Horace are composed in plainer and more obvious verse forms.

Odes by Horace or poems outwardly similar to his were readily imitated throughout the greater part of the Middle Ages, and, indeed, have never ceased to be models for poets. But in the later part of the Renaissance – in Italy of the sixteenth and England of the seventeenth century – the elusive odes of Pindar were imitated and mistakenly supposed by many authors to be "irregular," or "free." Hence arose the two opposed traditions of the "regular" Horatian ode and the more romantic and loose-reined "Pindarique." Such distinctions are more in form than in matter.

The Horatian ode has been especially agreeable to the French spirit, as our poem by Gautier evinces. A fine dramatic ode expressive of the Dutch temper is here given from Vondel. In the German odes – as in so many others – the formality and intellectuality of the genre often induces stiffness and want of poetic imagination. The homeland of the Ode is among the Latin races. Leopardi, the great poet and scholar of Italy, excels all moderns in the writing of odes. Both in their dramas and their more occasional poetry the Spanish often realize the nobility and dignity of the form. The sound discipline of the classical tradition fusing with the romantic spirit produced admirable work, also, in the typically English and eclectic poetry of Coleridge, Keats and Shelley. Occasionally in closet dramas, from Shelley's *Hellas* and *Prometheus Unbound* to Hardy's *Dynasts* and the literary plays of the American, Robinson Jeffers, notable odes appear, native and vigorous but still reminiscent of the Greeks. Shelley in particular possessed an imagination supplying at least some equivalent for the dance rhythms of the ancients.

The last two poems in this section exhibit the spirit rather than the letter of this long-lived Western tradition. Neither of the two American authors in question calls his poem an ode, though one uses the similar word, "hymn." Yet each poem obviously owes a large part of its strength to a literary temper now, after long centuries, thoroughly inherent in our artistic consciousness. Whatever these poems may be called, they are not lyrics in a merely modern or even a medieval tradition. They are rendered so much the firmer, more critical and more forceful by the stream that rises in Pindar's inspired paeans of victory and Horace's gracious and formal monuments to civilized living. Pedantic and over-literary odes will doubtless continue to be written, though one hopes in decreasing numbers. But, with undiminished vigor and firmness, the essential spirit of the Ode still marches forward.

The First Pythian Ode of Pindar

O Golden Lyre, who art Phoebus' treasure
Which he shares with the dusk-haired Song-queens aye,
The light feet hear thee beating the measure
As the revellers marshal their dance-array.
O Lyre, thy signals the singers obey
When in preludes of choral song low-dreaming
O'er thy strings quick-throbbing the harmonies glide.
Thou quenchest the thunderbolt's self red-gleaming
Javelined with flame-jets aye outstreaming.
On the sceptre of Zeus the slumber-tide
O'er his eagle ripples, on either side

Of the king of birds as his pinions are trailing:
O'er his bowing head doth a dark mist flow
Sweet-sealing his eyes; 'neath sleep's prevailing
His back heaves wave-like soft and slow,
Spell-bound by thy melodies pulsing low.
Yea, the soul of the wild War-god lies sleeping
Hushed, warm-cradled in slumber's nest,
And his keen spear slips from his strong hand's keeping.
Gods' hearts are thy shafts in enchantment steeping
By the inspiration of Phoebus to rest
Lulled, and by the deep-bosomed Muses' behest.

But creatures beloved not of Zeus, things haunting
Earth's crypts, and the sea's gulfs storm-uprolled,
Flee panic-struck, hearing the Pierids chanting,
As was Typhon, whom Tartarus' dread depths hold,
The hundred-headed, the hate undying
Of the Gods, in Cilician caverns of old
Nursed. Sicily now and her sea-defying
Cliffs above Kyme are heavily lying
On his shag-haired breast, and the cloud-kissing height
Of a crag-column crusheth him – Etna, white
Through the livelong year with snows that bite
With ice-fangs cold.

Upbelched from his deep-hidden crypts is a fountain
Of pure white fire none dare draw nigh.
In the day from the lava-flood rifting the mountain
Is the lurid smoke uptossed to the sky;
In the darkness a red-rolling flame flares high
As it sweepeth the rocks with thunderous crashing
To the sea that afar below doth lie.
'Tis the monster upspurting through anguish-gnashing
Jaws that fire-fountain fearfully flashing –
A wondrous portent appalling the eye,
A marvel to hear when men pass by;

Such horror is prisoned through years unending
'Neath the heights dark-leaved in the earth's embrace,
While his back is furrowed with gory rending
By the flints of his restless resting-place!
O Zeus, may we in thy sight find grace
Who dost make this mountain thine habitation,
This rich land's forefront, whose name-sake-town
Her founder ennobled, what time his nation
Was 'of Etna' published by proclamation
Of the Pythian herald who spake the renown
Of Hiero's car-won victory-crown.

As seafarers hail as the first boon of Heaven
That their sails by a fair-speeding wind be fanned
When the anchor is weighed, as an earnest given
Of yet fairer return to the home-land's strand,
So reason enkindleth the expectation
That with this fair fortune linked hand in hand
Shall the fame be of this thy new creation
For athletes and horses and glad celebration
Of her name by the singers. O Lycian King
And Delian, who lovest Castaly's spring,
Of thy goodwill vouchsafe it, and stablish the thing
For this hero-land.

'Tis the Gods that ope all paths unto mortals
Whereby unto excellence toilers attain;
For poesy's, prowess's, eloquence' portals
They unbar. Albeit to praise I am fain
This hero, I trust I shall hurl not in vain
Wide of the lists my javelin, winging
From the hand that hath poised it its quivering flight,
Beyond all rivals my shaft far-flinging.
May the days through his life-tide be alway bringing
Wealth, bliss, in a course ever steered aright,
With oblivion of fortune's past despite.

He shall surely recall the old wars' story —
He whose steadfast soul was their battle-stay —
When his folk at the Gods' hands reaped for them glory
Such as none other Hellenes have borne away
From a stricken field, nor such goodly prey.
For, a new Philoktetes, with help all-availing
Battleward fared he, when came to implore
Humbly his friendship the proud ones, quailing
From foes over-strong — as the heroes went sailing
To Lemnos, to bring him to Troyland's shore
Whom the wound snake-venomed tormented sore,

The archer, Poias' son, and he wended
Troyward, though sickness-worn was his frame,
And he ravaged the city of Priam, and ended
The Danaans' toil; for of Fate this came.
So by Hiero's side may a God go guiding
His steps, as in years past ever the same,
The desire of his heart in its season providing.
By Deinomenes' side, O my Muse, abiding
Chant thou the meed by the chariot won
Of the father whose triumph is joy for the son.
This king, then, whose reign is in Etna begun,
Sing we his fame,

For whom, with freedom on God's rock grounded,
The statutes of Hyllus pledged to maintain,
That city hath been by Hiero founded;
For the sons of Pamphylus are ever fain —
Yea, so is the line of the Herakleid strain
'Neath the beetling crags of Taÿgetus dwelling —
By Aegimus' Dorian laws to abide.
They gat them Amyklae, and prospered past telling
Who from Pindus down-swooping in glory excelling
By the Tyndarids dwelt, who on white steeds ride,
And their spear-fame as flower-studded meads blossomed wide.

Zeus All-accomplisher, grant that never
May the tale of the fortunes of burgher and king
Be worser than now; may they prosper ever

Where Amenas' waters are murmuring!
By thy grace may the old chief's counsels bring
To his son and his folk, with all honour, fruition
In their borders ever of concord and peace.
May the war-cry of Tuscan no more nor Phoenician
Be heard on our shores since battle's decision
By Cumae brought woe for lost ships upon these
Who in insolence claimed to be lords of the seas;

When the captain of Sicily's fleet on-leading
The might of Syracuse, hurled to the sea
Their warrior youths from their ships light-speeding,
And set you thereby, ye Hellenes, free
From thralldom's yoke hanging heavily o'er ye.
Yea, Athens and Sparta shall guerdon me
With thanks for my Salamis-lay, for the story
Of the battle before Kithairon, the glory
Won when the Medes of the curved bow fell:
And by Himera's bank shall the song-flood swell
To Deinomenes' sons' battle-prowess, and tell
Of their victory.

If in season due by thy speech, if blended
Into close-knit order thy thoughts be, as when
A weaver upgathers his threads, attended
Shall thy words be with scantier cavil of men.
For if speech be tedious and long-drawn, then
Thine hearers' eager expectancy dieth.
And when burghers the praise of their fellows hear,
On their hearts a weight of jealousy lieth.
Yet better is envy than pity, which sigheth
Over failure. In justice thy folk do thou steer,
And in truth's forge fashion thy tongue's keen spear.

How light soe'er be the word that hath flitted
From thy lips, it is weighty, as coming from thee.
To thy keeping a nation's weal is committed:
Of thy deeds, good or ill, many watchers there be.
Be thy spirit a flower of chivalry.
If thou wilt that report true-royal declare thee,
No niggard be thou: like a wise timoneer
Thy sails spread wide, that the breeze may bear thee
Onward. Let time-serving guile not ensnare thee
By flattery, friend! Nought save the sincere
Praise that, when mortals are no more here,

Lives on after death, to the world revealeth
What their true life was whose days are sped,
And in chronicles shines and in lays outpealeth.
Blooms Croesus' kindness with petals unshed;
But Phalaris, ruthlessly joying in rending
Men's lives from the tortured in brass glowing red,
He is compassed with infamy's hate unending,
Nor lutes nor young voices in harmony blending
In the hall of the feasters his name shall greet.
Best of all is fair fortune; yet fame is sweet.
Who wins both, life's chief crowns all meet
To engarland his head.

—From the Greek of Pindar (522–448 B.C.?), translated by Arthur S. Way.

~ ✿ ~

Chorus of the Furies

Voice 1. Look, sisters, look!
Voice 2. On the right, on the left, and round about,
Search every nook!
Voice 3. Warily watch him,
The blood-guilty ranger,
That Fraud may not snatch him,
From me, the Avenger!
Voice 1. At the shrine of the goddess,
He bendeth him lowly,
Embracing her image,
The ancient, the holy.
Voice 2. With hands crimson-reeking,

He clingeth profanely,
A free pardon seeking
From Pallas — how vainly!
Voice 3. For blood, when it floweth,
For once and for ever
It sinks, and it knoweth
To mount again never.
Voice 1. Thou shalt pay me with pain;
From thy heart, from thy liver
I will suck, I will drain
Thy life's crimson river.
Voice 2. The cup from thy veins
I will quaff it, how rarely!
I will wither thy brains,
Thou shalt pine late and early.
Voice 3. I will drag thee alive,
For thy guilt matricidal,
To the dens of the damned,
For thy lasting abidal.

— From the Greek of Aeschylus (525–456 B.C.), chorus from The Eumenides, translated by John Stuart Blackie.

The Grove of Colônus

CHORUS

Stranger, where thy feet now rest
In this land of horse and rider,
Here is earth all earth excelling,
White Colônus here doth shine!
Oftenest here and homing best
Where the close green coverts hide her,
Warbling her sweet mournful tale
Sings the melodious nightingale,
Myriad-berried woods her dwelling,
And the wine-hued ivy, where
Through the sacred leafage lonely
No sun pierces, or rude air
Stirs from outer storm, and only
Those divine feet walk the region —
Thine, O Reveller, thine,
Bacchus, following still that legion
Dear, thy nursing Nymphs divine.

Fresh with heavenly dews, and crowned
With earliest white in shining cluster,
Each new morn the young narcissus
Blooms, that antique use of old
Bids the Great Queens bind around
Their twain brows; in golden lustre
Here the crocus beams; and here
Spring, nor minish all the year,
Cool deep wells that feed Cephissus:
Rich with balm of speedy birth
Day by day the sleepless river
Issuing o'er the breasted Earth
Wandereth in pure streams to give her
Ease and life. Nor frown the Muses
Or their quires withhold;
Nay, nor sweet Love's Queen refuses
Her bright chariot-reins of gold.

And a marvellous herb of the soil grows here,
Whose match I never have heard it sung
In the Dorian isle of Pelops near
Or in Asia far hath sprung.
'Tis a plant that flourishes unsubdued,
Self-engendering, self-renewed,
To her armed foes' dismay:
That never so fair but in this land bloomed, —
With the grey-blue silvery leaf soft-plumed,
Her nurturing Olive-spray.
No force, no ravaging hand shall raze it,
In youth so rash, or in age so wise,
For the orb of Zeus in heaven surveys it,
And blue-grey light of Athêna's eyes.

Yet again my song shall arise and tell
Of the proudest jewel the region wears;
To her Mother's portion of old it fell,
And the Child her birth-right shares: —
Blest in gift of the horse is she,
Gift of the young horse, gift of the sea,
Twice-blest in a two-fold dower:
Thy gift, O Lord of the waves, her throne,
For in her streets first upon earth was shown
Thy chastening bridle's power;
And here most wonderful over the waters
Slender and shapely the trimmed oar fleet
In the sea-dance following Nêreus' daughters
Leaps to the foam of a hundred feet.

— From the Greek of Sophocles (495–406 B.C.), translated by Walter Headlam.

Troy

CHORUS

In Salamis, filled with the foaming
Of billows and murmur of bees,
Old Télamon stayed from his roaming,
Long ago, on a throne of the seas;
Looking out on the hills olive-laden,
Enchanted, where first from the earth
The grey-gleaming fruit of the Maiden
Athêna had birth;
A soft grey crown for a city

Belovèd, a City of Light:
Yet he rested not there, nor had pity,
But went forth in his might,
Where Hêraclês wandered, the lonely
Bow-bearer, and lent him his hands
For the wrecking of one land only,
Of Îlion, Îlion only,
Most hated of lands!

Of the bravest of Hellas he made him
A ship-folk, in wrath for the Steeds,
And sailed the wide waters, and stayed him
At last amid Símoïs reeds;
And the oars beat slow in the river,
And the long ropes held in the strand,
And he felt for his bow and his quiver,
The wrath of his hand.
And the old king died; and the towers
That Phœbus had builded did fall,
And his wrath, as a flame that devours,
Ran red over all;
And the fields and the woodlands lay blasted,
Long ago. Yea, twice hath the Sire
Uplifted his hand and downcast it
On the wall of the Dardan, downcast it
As a sword and as fire.

In vain, all in vain,
O thou 'mid the wine-jars golden
That movest in delicate joy,
Ganymêdês, child of Troy,
The lips of the Highest drain
The cup in thine hand upholden:
And thy mother, thy mother that bore thee,
Is wasted with fire and torn;
And the voice of her shores is heard,
Wild, as the voice of a bird,
For lovers and children before thee
Crying, and mothers outworn.
And the pools of thy bathing are perished,
And the wind-strewn ways of thy feet:
Yet thy face as aforetime is cherished
Of Zeus, and the breath of it sweet;
Yea, the beauty of Calm is upon it
In houses at rest and afar.
But thy land, He hath wrecked and o'erthrown it
In the wailing of war.

O Love, ancient Love,
Of old to the Dardan given;
Love of the Lords of the Sky;
How didst thou lift us high
In Îlion, yea, and above
All cities, as wed with heaven!
For Zeus — O leave it unspoken:
But alas for the love of the Morn;
Morn of the milk-white wing,
The gentle, the earth-loving,
That shineth on battlements broken
In Troy, and a people forlorn!
And, lo, in her bowers Tîthônus,
Our brother, yet sleeps as of old:
O, she too hath loved us and known us,
And the Steeds of her star, flashing gold,
Stooped hither and bore him above us;
Then blessed we the Gods in our joy.
But all that made them to love us
Hath perished from Troy.

— From the Greek of Euripides (480–406 B.C.), translated by Gilbert Murray.

~ ❁ ~

Chorus of Birds

Ye men who are dimly existing below,
who perish and fade as the leaf,
Pale, woebegone, shadowlike, spiritless folk,
life feeble and wingless and brief,
Frail castings in clay, who are gone in a day,
like a dream full of sorrow and sighing,
Come listen with care to the Birds of the air,
the ageless, the deathless, who flying
In the joy and the freshness of Ether, are wont
to muse upon wisdom undying.
We will tell you of things transcendental; of Springs
and of Rivers the mighty upheaval;
The nature of Birds; and the birth of the Gods:
and of Chaos and Darkness primeval.
When this ye shall know, let old Prodicus[1] go,
and be hanged without hope of reprieval.
There was Chaos at first, and Darkness, and Night,
and Tartarus vasty and dismal;
But the Earth was not there, not the Sky, nor the Air,
till at length in the bosom abysmal
Of Darkness an egg, from the whirlwind conceived,
was laid by the sable-plumed Night.
And out of that egg, as the Seasons revolved,
sprang Love, the entrancing, the bright,
Love brilliant and bold with his pinions of gold,

[1] A famous philosopher.

like a whirlwind, refulgent and sparkling!
Love hatched us, commingling in Tartarus wide,
with Chaos, the murky, the darkling,
And brought us above, as the firstlings of love,
and first to the light we ascended.
There was never a race of Immortals at all
till Love had the universe blended;
Then all things commingling together in love,
there arose the fair Earth, and the Sky,
And the limitless Sea; and the race of the Gods,
the Blessed, who never shall die.
So we than the Blessed are older by far;
and abundance of proof is existing
That we are the children of Love, for we fly,
unfortunate lovers assisting.
And many a man who has found, to his cost,
that his powers of persuasion have failed,
And his loves have abjured him for ever, again
by the power of the Birds has prevailed;
For the gift of a quail, or a Porphyry rail,
or a Persian, or goose, will regain them.
And the chiefest of blessings ye mortals enjoy,
by the help of the Birds ye obtain them.
'Tis from us that the signs of the Seasons in turn,
Spring, Winter, and Autumn are known.
When to Libya the crane flies clanging again,
it is time for the seed to be sown,
And the skipper may hang up his rudder awhile,
and sleep after all his exertions,
And Orestes may weave him a wrap to be warm
when he's out on his thieving excursions.
Then cometh the kite, with its hovering flight,
of the advent of Spring to tell,
And the Spring sheep-shearing begins; and next,
your woollen attire you sell,
And buy you a lighter and daintier garb,
when you note the return of the swallow.
Thus your Ammon, Dodona, and Delphi are we;
we are also your Phoebus Apollo.
For whatever you do, if a trade you pursue,
or goods in the market are buying,
Or the wedding attend of a neighbour and friend,
first you look to the Birds and their flying.

—*From the Greek of Aristophanes (448–380? B.C.), translated by Benjamin Bickley Rogers.*

Vanity of Riches

My ceiling shows not brave
With gold or ivories;
No marble architrave
On quarried pillars lies,
Which utmost Libya gave.

No despot did devise
On me, a stranger heir,
His royal treasuries;
No dames of birth prepare
For me Laconian dyes.

Pure faith is all my store,
Faith, and so rich a vein
Of poet power and lore
That wealth itself is fain
To seek this humble door.

I ask not Heaven to send
Aught else; I never pressed
For more, my puissant friend,
Who am entirely blessed
One Sabine farm to tend.

To-morrow ousts to-day;
Young moons grow large and less;
Death dogs thy steps; but aye
On marble palaces,
O fool, thy fancies stray,

Who, reckless of the tomb,
Dost build, and 'mid the roar
Of Baian surf presume
On the great sea, whose shore
Yields not ambition room.

What, shall this lust of gain
Not even the landmarks keep
Which that is thine contain?
This avarice o'er-leap
Thy client's scant domain?

Thence the poor exiles fare,
Husband and wife; and, strained
To their sad bosoms, bear
Young babes all squalor-stained,
And gods, their father's care.

Natheless no other hall
 More surely shalt thou find,
Thou gilded prodigal,
 Than that by Death designed,
The greediest of us all.

What would'st thou? Earth's embrace
 Impartial shall enfold
King's son and peasant base; —
 Prometheus' guile and gold
From Charon gained no grace.

Proud Tantalus, he wears,
 He and his race, the chains
Of Death, who needs no prayers
 To lighten of their pains
The world's worn laborers.

—From the Latin of Horace (65–8 B.C.), translated by T. Rutherford Clark.

∽ ❂ ∼

The Golden Age

O lovely age of gold!
Not that the rivers rolled
With milk, or that the woods wept honey-dew;
Not that the ready ground
Produced without a wound,
Or the mild serpent had no tooth that slew;
Not that a cloudless blue
For ever was in sight,
Or that the heaven, which burns
And now is cold by turns,
Looked out in glad and everlasting light;
No, nor that even the insolent ships from far
Brought war to no new lands nor riches worse than war:

But solely that that vain
And breath-invented pain,
That idol of mistake, that worshiped cheat,
That Honor, — since so called
By vulgar minds appalled, —
Played not the tyrant with our nature yet.
It had not come to fret
The sweet and happy fold
Of gentle human-kind;
Nor did its hard law bind
Souls nursed in freedom; but that law of gold,
That glad and golden law, all free, all fitted,
Which Nature's own hand wrote, — What pleases is permitted.

Then among streams and flowers
The little winged powers
Went singing carols without torch or bow;
The nymphs and shepherds sat
Mingling with innocent chat
Sports and low whispers; and with whispers low,
Kisses that would not go.
The maiden, budding o'er,
Kept not her bloom uneyed,
Which now a veil must hide,
Nor the crisp apples which her bosom bore;
And oftentimes, in river or in lake,
The lover and his love their merry bath would take.

'Twas thou, thou, Honor, first
That didst deny our thirst
Its drink, and on the fount thy covering set;
Thou bad'st kind eyes withdraw
Into constrained awe,
And keep the secret for their tears to wet;
Thou gather'dst in a net
The tresses from the air,
And mad'st the sports and plays
Turn all to sullen ways,
And putt'st on speech a rein, in steps a care.
Thy work it is, — thou shade, that wilt not move, —
That which was once the gift is now the theft of Love.

Our sorrows and our pains,
These are thy noble gains.
But, O, thou Love's and Nature's masterer,
Thou conqueror of the crowned,
What dost thou on this ground,
Too small a circle for thy mighty sphere?
Go, and make slumber dear
To the renowned and high;
We here, a lowly race,
Can live without thy grace,
After the use of mild antiquity.
Go, let us love; since years
No truce allow, and life soon disappears;
Go, let us love; the daylight dies, is born;
But unto us the light
Dies once for all; and sleep brings on eternal night.

—From the Italian of Torquato Tasso (1544–1595), translated by Leigh Hunt.

∽ ❂ ∼

The Broom

Here on the arid shoulder
Of this terrible mountain,
Vesuvius the destroyer,
Which no tree and no flower gladdens but thine,
Sweet-scented broom, thou scatterest here and there
Thy solitary shrubs,
Contented with the desert. So I have seen
Thy tufts adorn with beauty those lone plains
That compass round the city
Which on a time was mistress of mankind,
Those plains that seem with stern
And silent aspect to remind the traveller
Of her lost empire, which they witnessed once.
Now on this soil once more I find thee, lover
Of desolate regions by mankind abandoned,
Faithful companion of afflicted fortunes.
These lands that now are strewn
With sterile cinders, and buried under streams
Of lava turned to stone,
That resounds to the footstep of the pilgrim;
Where the snake nestles, and writhes in the sun,
And where into some cleft
In cavernous rocks the rabbit hurries home —
Here once were happy homesteads,
And tilth, and yellowing harvests, and the sound
Of lowing herds; here too
Gardens and palaces,
Retreats dear to the leisure
Of powerful lords; and here were famous towns,
Which once the lofty mountain, thundering forth
Molten streams from its fiery mouth, destroyed
With all their habitants. Now the whole region
One ruin overwhelms,
Amid which thou art rooted, gentle flower,
And as though pitying others' misery
Fillest the air with a sweet scent, whose breath
Comforts the wilderness. To these bare slopes
Let him come who is wont to exalt with praise
Our human state; and here let him behold
How kindly our race is cared for
By loving Nature. Here too shall he learn
At a just rate to value
The might and grandeur of the seed of man,
Whom his hard nurse, when he forbodes it least,
By a slight shock in a moment may destroy
In part, and can with shocks
Only a little less slight as suddenly
Wholly annihilate.
Charactered in these shores
We may behold mankind's
Magnificent and progressive destinies.

Here gaze as in a mirror,
Thou Age so proud and foolish,
That didst forsake the path
Which till then Thought re-arisen had marked out
For thy advance, and now with back-turned footsteps
Thou boastest thy retreat,
Misnaming it thy progress.
All those fine intellects, whom evil fate
Has made thy sons, welcome thy childish babbling
With flattery, though often
Scornfully within themselves
They think of thee. Such shame
Never will I take with me to my grave.
First rather that contempt of thee, which lies
Locked fast within my heart,
Openly as I have strength will I proclaim;
Though oblivion must entomb
Him who has pleased too little his own time.
That evil fate, which I
With thee shall share, even now moves me to laughter.
Of liberty thou dreamest, yet wouldst prison
Thought in new bondage, Thought
That alone lifted us
In part from savagery, through which alone
We grow more civilized, and to a nobler fate
Our commonwealth is guided.
And so the truth displeased thee
Which told of this harsh lot, this lowly station
That Nature gave us. Therefore like a coward
Thou hast turned thy back upon the light, whereby
Truth was revealed; and recreant, callest those
Who seek truth base, and him
Alone great-souled who mocking

Himself or others, be he knave or madman,
Exalts our mortal state above the stars.

A man of poor estate and feeble of body,
Yet of a generous and lofty soul,
Will neither boast nor deem
That he is wealthy or strong,
Nor will provoke men's ridicule by a vain
Display of splendid living,
Or of brave strength and courage;
But without shame letting himself be seen
Beggared of health and riches, makes a frank
Avowal, and according to the truth
Judges of his condition.
Great-souled I cannot deem
That creature, but a fool,
Who born to perish, reared in misery, cries,
"For joy was I created,"
And with his fetid pride
Fills whole books, promising here on earth
high destinies
And marvellous felicity (unknown
Not only in this world, but even in heaven)
To peoples, whom one wave
From a quaking sea, one blast
Of noxious air, one subterranean shock
Destroys so utterly
That scarcely may their memory survive.
But of a noble nature
Is he who dares lift up
Against our common doom
His mortal eyes, and frankly, from the truth
Subtracting naught, confesses
Those ills that are our portion, and how
lowly
And frail is our condition;
He who in suffering
Shows himself great and strong; who will not
add
Fraternal hate and wrath,
Of all evils the worst,
To his own woes, by blaming Man as cause
Of his unhappiness, but lays the blame
On her who in truth is guilty, her who of
mortals
Mother by birth, by choice is their stepdame.
Her he calls foe; and since in the beginning
Mankind's whole family,
As with truth he believes, was linked and
banded
Against her, he imagines
All men to be confederate together,
And with a love sincere
Embraces all alike,
Bestowing and expecting succour prompt
And valiant in the perils and the anguish
Of their joint warfare. But with armed hand
to assail
Another man, and for his neighbour's feet
Set snares and stumbling-blocks,
Seems to him folly as great as his would be
Who, when the foe surrounds him and the
assault
Threatens most furiously,
Forgets the enemy, and against his friends
Raises a bitter feud,
And scatters panic and havoc with his sword
Mid his own warriors.
When to the common folk
Such thoughts shall grow familiar once
again,
When that primitive dread,
Which against cruel Nature
United mankind once in social bonds,
Shall in part be renewed
By truth and wisdom, then shall honesty
And righteous intercourse,
Justice and charity, in far other soil
Be rooted than are those arrogant fancies,
Founded whereon the morals of the crowd
Are wont to stand as firmly
As aught can stand that has its seat in error.

Oft on these desolate shores,
Which in dark funeral hues
The hardened waves have clothed, and still
seem surging,
I sit by night; and looking up I watch
Over the mournful waste
The stars in purest azure blazing bright,
Mirrored in the far sea,
And the serene depths of the firmament
Gleaming all round with scintillating fires.
And when I fix my eyes upon those lights,
Which to me seem mere points,
But are indeed so vast
That land and sea compared with them are
verily
A mere point; and to which
Not only Man, but even
This globe, where Man is nothing,
Is utterly unknown; and when I gaze
Upon those infinitely more remote
Clusters of stars, that seem
To us like mist, to which not alone Man
And this our earth, but all these stars of ours
Infinite both in number and in size,
All these, together with the golden sun,
Are either unknown, or appear as small
As they to the earth, a point
Of nebulous radiance; what to my thought
Do you seem then, O race

Of Man? And so, remembering
Your state on earth, whereof the soil I tread
Bears witness; nevertheless that you believe
Yourself the lord, the end
Assigned to all things; and how many times
You were pleased to fable that to this obscure
Grain of sand called the earth, on your account
The authors of the universe descended
And with your fathers oft familiarly
Held converse; and how even this present age
(That seems in knowledge and civility
The most advanced of all), giving new life
To those derided dreams,
Insults wise-minded men — what feelings then,
O unhappy race of mortals, and what thoughts
Concerning you assail my heart in the end?
Laughter or pity, I know not which prevails.

As a small apple falling from a tree,
Which in the lingering autumn
Ripeness and no force else to the earth has dropped,
Crushes the loved halls of a people of ants,
Caverned laboriously
In the soft soil, their works,
And all the wealth which that industrious tribe
With long and zealous toil has garnered in
So providently through all the days of summer —
Crushes, devastates, buries
In a moment; ev'n so from that thundering womb
Hurled to the heights of heaven,
There swooped down from above
A blackness like the night, a destroying cloud
Of cinders, pumice, rocks,
With boiling torrents mingled;
Or down the mountain's flank
Raging through fields and meadows,
Onward, in molten masses
Of incandescent sand and metals blent,
Came sweeping a vast flood,
And thus in a few moments wrecked and shattered
And buried deep those cities
Once washed by the sea's waves
On yonder shore. Therefore above them now
Browses the goat; new towns
Rise yonder, based upon the sepulchres
Of those dead cities, while the lofty mountain
Seems to spurn with its foot the prostrate walls.
No more esteem or care
Has Nature for Man's seed
Than for the ant: and if the one is slaughtered
More rarely than the other,
For this there seems no cause
Save that Man is less fertile in his breed.

Full eighteen hundred years
Have passed, since whelmed beneath the force of fire
Vanished those populous villages and towns;
And the poor husbandman
Tending his vine, whom hardly in these fields
The dead incinerated soil can nourish,
Still with suspicious glance
Peers at the fatal summit,
Which grown no whit more kindly than of old
Still stands there terribly, still menaces
Destruction against himself, against his sons,
And their starved fields. And often
As sleepless all night long
Beneath the wandering breeze the poor wretch lies
Upon his rustic hovel's roof, in panic
He starts up many a time, marking the course
Of the all-dreaded lava that boils up
From the inexhaustible womb
Over the sandy ridge, while Capri's shores
From far reflect the glow,
And the harbour of Naples, and Mergellina.
And if he sees it nearing, or if deep down
Within the household well he hears the water
Seething and bubbling, he awakes his children,
Awakes his wife in haste, and snatching up
What of their gear they can, away they fly;
The nest he has loved so long,
His small field, which alone
Saved him from famine, from afar he sees
A prey to the burning flood,
Which arrives, crackling, then inexorably
Spreads itself over them for ever more.
Back to the light of day
After age-long oblivion, dead Pompeii

Returns, like a skeleton
Which from beneath the soil
Avarice or reverence has disinterred;
And from the lonely forum,
Standing among the ranks
Of broken pillars, the traveller far off
May contemplate the cloven mountain-top
And smoking crest, that still
Threatens the ruins scattered round its base.
And in the horror of the secret night,
Through the empty theatres,
Through mutilated shrines and shattered walls
Of houses, where the rearmouse hides its young,
Like an ill-omened torch
Flickering balefully through deserted halls,
The gleam of the funereal lava runs,
From afar through the darkness,
Tingeing all places with its reddening glow,
So, knowing naught of Man, nor of those ages
He calls antique, nor of his long descent
From distant ancestry,
Nature stays ever green and young; or rather,
So long is her slow course,
That she seems to stand still. Meantime realms fall,
Nations and tongues pass; of that naught she sees.
And Man presumes to boast himself eternal.

And thou, O tender broom,
Whose fragrant brushwood lends
Adornment to these desolated fields,
Thou too, like them, shalt yield soon to the power
And cruelty of that subterranean fire,
Which to its former channel
Returning shall spread out its greedy hem
Over thy delicate boscage. And thou then
Wilt unresisting bow thine innocent head
Under the deadly weight:
But till then neither wilt thou hold it bowed
In cowardly supplication all in vain
Before the coming doom; nor towards the stars
Lift it erect in overweening pride;
Nor wilt thou scorn this waste,
Where chance, not thine own choice,
Allotted thee a birthplace and a home;
Wiser so, and less weak
Than Man in this, that ne'er hast thou believed
Thy fragile stock endowed
By fate or by thyself with immortality.

— From the Italian of Giacomo Leopardi (1798–1837), translated by R. C. Trevelyan.

~ ❂ ~

Sylvan Ode

Woods of my fathers, sovereign deity,
To whom the Incas and the Aztecs bowed,
I stand and greet you from the trembling sea
That like some white-haired slave before a queen,
With all its shining foam, fawns at your feet.
I greet you from the sea above whose combers
Your heavy perfumes break upon the wind;
Behind them tower your mutilated trunks
And beckon me to the Americas.
I greet you from the sea that woos you still,
Like some wild chieftain with disheveled locks,
Knowing that from your undeciphered heart
Is born the hollow ship that scars its face
And mocks its depths with straining keel and sail.
Woods of my fathers, sovereign deity,
To whom the Incas and the Aztecs bowed,
I stand and greet you from the shining sea.

I turn to you and feel my soul set free:
Forgotten is the stress of modern ways.
I have become for very sight of you,
Like one of your wise tribal patriarchs,
Who slept of old upon your tender grass,
And drank the milk of goats and ate their bread
Sweetened with honey of the forest bee.
I look on you and I am comforted,
For the thick ranks of all your tufted trees
Recall to me how centuries ago
With twice ten thousand archers at my heels,
I led the way to where the mountains smoke
And lift their craters from the shores of lakes;
And how, at length, I wandered to the realm
Of the great Inca, Yupanqui, and went,
Following him upon the mountain tops,
Down to Arauco and its peaceful slopes,
And rested in a tent of condors' wings.
I look on you and I am comforted,

Because the centuries have marked me out
To be your poet, and to raise the hymns
Of joy and grief, that in heroic dawns
The Cuzco smote upon his lyre of stone —
Legends of Aztec Emperors and songs
Of bold Palenkes and Tahuantisuyos,
Vanished like Babylon from off this earth.

Here in your presence, with your savage spell
Leaping in all my veins, the centuries
Lift like a vision from the abyss of time
And pass before me in unfading youth.
So I evoke the ages still unformed
That saw your first tree burst its bonds of stone,
And all the others headlong on its track,
With the ordained disorder of the stars.
So I evoke the endless chain of time,
Of creeping growth and slow montony,
That passed before your roots were fired with sap,
And all your trunks took form beneath their bark;
And all the knots of every branch were loosed,
To join the hymn of your primeval Spring.
And now your flowering branches are a cage
For singing birds — fantastic orchestra —,
Above whose din the fickle mocking-bird
Pours its strange song; and only one is mute:
The solemn *quetzal,* that in silence flaunts
His rainbow plumage with heraldic pomp
Above the tombs of a departed race.

Your countless blue and rosy butterflies
Flutter and fan themselves coquettishly;
Your buzzing insects glitter in the sun,
Glimmer and glow like gems and talismans
Encrusted in the hilts of ancient swords.
Your crickets scold, and when the day is spent,
And fireflies light your depths, where beasts of prey
Stalk in the gloom, as through a nightmare gleam
The sulphurous pupils of satanic eyes.

Yours is the tapir, that in mountain pools
Mirrors the shape of his deformity,
And rends the jungle with his monstrous head;
Yours the lithe jaguar, nimble acrobat,
That from the branches darts upon his prey;
And yours the tiger-cat, sly strategist,
With gums of plush and alabaster fang.
The crocodile is yours, that venerable
Amphibious guardian of crops and streams,
Whose emerald eyes peer from the oozy caves;
And yours the boa, that seems a mighty arm
Hewn from the shadow by a giant axe.

But like a sponge, into your labyrinth
Of tropic growth, you suck each living thing —
The strength of muscles and the blood of veins —
There to beget in your exuberance
The warlike plumes of your imperial palms,
Whose milky fruits refreshed in by-gone day
The tribes grown weary with long pilgrimage.
And there the patriarchal *ceiba* tree
Offered its canopy to pondering chiefs
Counciling war or peace beneath its boughs.
And there is Pindar's oak, and there the tree
Of Lebanon, and the mahogany,
Whose fragrant wood in European courts
The cunning craftsman polishes and shapes
To thrones of kings and marriage-beds of queens.

Woods of my fathers, sovereign deity,
To whom the Incas and the Aztecs bowed,
I greet you from the sea, and breathe this prayer:
That with the night, the close approaching night,
You may entomb me in your sacred dusk
Like some dim spectre of forgotten cults,
And that, to fire my eyes with savage light
And wild reflection of your revelry,
To burn upon the tip of every tree
That points into the night, you set a star.

— From the Spanish of the Peruvian poet José Santos Chocano (1875–1934), translated by John Pierrepont Rice.

~ ❂ ~

Chorus of Batavian Women

Ours was a happy lot,
Ere foreign tyrants brought
The servile iron yoke, which bound
Our necks with humbling slavery to the ground.

Once all was confidence and peace; — the just
Might to his neighbour trust.
The common plough turned up the common land,
And Nature scattered joy with liberal hand.
The humble cot of clay
Kept the thick shower, the wind, and hail away.
Upon the frugal board
No luxuries were stored;
But 'neath a forest-tree the table stood, —
A simple plank, — unpolished and rude:
Our feasts, the wild game of the wood;
And curds and cheese our daily food.
Man, in his early virtues blest,
Slept satisfied on woman's breast,
Who, modest and confiding, saw
In him her lord, and love, and law.
Then was the stranger and the neighbour, each,
Welcomed with cordial thoughts and honest speech;
And days flowed cheerful on, as days should flow, —
Unmoved by distant or domestic woe.

Then was no value set on silver things,
Nor golden stores, nor coin, nor dazzling rings;
They bartered what they had for what they wanted; —
And sought no foreign shores, — but planted
Their own low dwellings in their motherland;
Raised all by their own hand,
And furnished with whatever man requires
For his moderate desires.
They had no proud adornings, — were not gilt
Nor sculptured, — nor in crowded cities built;
But in wide-scattered villages they spread,
Where stand no friendly lamps above the head:
Rough and undecked the simple cot,
With the rich show of pomp encumbered not.
As when in decorated piles are seen
The bright fruits peeping through the foliage green;
Bark of the trees and hides of cattle cover
The lowly hut, when storms rage fiercely over:
Man had not learned the use of stone;
Tiles and cement were all unknown;
Some place of shelter dug, — dark, dreary, far, —
For the dread hour of danger or of war,
When the stray pirate broke on the serene
And cheerful quiet of that early scene.

No usurer, then, with avarice's burning thirst,
His fellow-men had cursed.
The coarse-wove flax, the unwrought fleece, alone,
On the half-naked, sturdy limbs were thrown.
The daughters married late
To a laborious fate;
And to their husbands bore a healthy race,
To take their fathers' place.
If e'er dispute or discord dared intrude,
'T was soon, by wisdom's voice, subdued;
The wisest then was called to reign,
The bravest did the victory gain:
The proud were made to feel
They must submit them to the general weal;
For to the proud and high a given way
Was marked, that thence they might not stray: —
And thus was freedom kept alive.
Rulers were taught to strive
For subjects' happiness, — and subjects brought
The cheerful tribute of obedient thought;
And 't was indeed a glorious sight,
To see them wave their weapons bright:
No venal bands, the murderous hordes of fame;
But freedom's sons, — all armed in freedom's name.

No judge outdealing justice in his hate,
Nor in his favor. Wisdom's train sedate
Of books, and proud philosophy,
And stately speech, could never needed be,
While they for virtue's counsellings might look
On Nature's open book,
Where bright and free the Godhead's glory falls; —
Not on the imprisoning walls
Of temples, — for their temple was the wood, —
The heavens its arch, — its aisles were solitude.

And then they sang the praise
Of heroes, and the seers of older days.
They never dared to pry
Into the mysteries of the Deity;
They never weighed his schemes, nor judged his will, —
But saw his works, and loved and praised him still;
Obeyed in awe, — kept pure their hearts within;
For this they knew, — God hates and scourges sin.
Some dreams of future bliss were theirs,
And thus they dwelt, and thus they died,
The happy tenants of a happy soil, —
Till came the cruel stranger to despoil.

But, O, that blessed time is past!
The strangers now possess our land;
Batavia is subdued, at last, —
Batavia fettered, ruined, banned!
Yes, — honor, truth have taken flight
To seats sublimer, thrones more pure.
Look, Julius, from thy throne of light, —
See what thy Holland's sons endure!
Thy children still are proud to claim
Their Roman blood, their source, from thee;
Friends, brothers, comrades bear the name; —
Desert them not in misery!
Terror and power and cruel wrong
Have a free people's bliss undone;
Too harsh their sway, — their rule too long!
Arouse thee from thy cloudy throne;
And if thou hate disgrace and crime,
Recall, recall departed time!

— *From the Dutch of Joost van den Vondel (1587–1679), translated by Sir John Bowring.*

The Unrealities

And dost thou faithlessly abandon me?
Must thy cameleon phantasies depart?
Thy griefs, thy gladnesses, take wing and flee
The bower they builded in this lonely heart?
O, Summer of Existence, golden, glowing!
Can nought avail to curb thine onward motion?
In vain! The river of my years is flowing,
And soon shall mingle with the eternal ocean.

Extinguished in dead darkness lies the sun
That lighted up my shriveled world of wonder;
Those fairy bands Imagination spun
Around my heart have long been rent asunder.
Gone, gone forever is the fine belief,
The all-too-generous trust in the Ideal:
All my Divinities have died of grief,
And left me welded to the Rude and Real.

As clasped the enthusiastic Prince of old
The lovely statue, stricken by its charms,
Until the marble, late so dead and cold,
Glowed into throbbing life beneath his arms,
So fondly round enchanting Nature's form,
I too entwined my passionate arms, till, pressed
In my embraces, she began to warm
And breathe and revel in my bounding breast.

And, sympathizing with my virgin bliss,
The speechless things of Earth received a tongue,
They gave me back Affection's burning kiss,
And loved the Melody my bosom sung:
Then sparkled hues of Life on tree and flower,
Sweet music from the silver fountain flowed;
All soulless images in that brief hour
The Echo of my Life divinely glowed!

How struggled all my feelings to extend
Themselves afar beyond their prisoning bounds!
O, how I longed to enter Life and blend
Me with its words and deeds, its shapes and sounds.
This human theater, how fair it beamed
While yet the curtain hung before the scene!
Uprolled, how little then the arena seemed!
That little how contemptible and mean!

How roamed, imparadised in blest illusion,
With soul to which the upsoaring Hope lent pinions,
And heart as yet unchilled by Care's intrusion,

How roamed the stripling-lord through
his dominions!
Then Fancy bore him to the palest star
Pinnacled in the lofty æther dim:
Was nought so elevated, nought too far,
But thither the Enchantress guided him!

With what rich reveries his brain was rife!
What adversary might withstand him
long?
How glanced and danced before the Czar of
Life
The visions of his thought, a dazzling
throng!
For there was FORTUNE with her golden
crown,
There flitted LOVE with heart-bewitching
boon,
There glittered starry-diademed RENOWN,
And TRUTH, with radiance like the sun of
noon!

But ah! ere half the journey yet was over,
That gorgeous escort wended separate
ways;
All faithlessly forsook the pilgrim-rover,
And one by one evanished from his gaze.
Away inconstant-handed FORTUNE flew;
And, while the thirst of Knowledge
burned alway
The dreary mists of Doubt arose and threw
Their shadow over TRUTH's resplendent
ray.

I saw the sacred garland-crown of FAME
Around the common brow its glory shed:
The rapid Summer died, the Autumn came,
And LOVE, with all his necromancies, fled,
And ever lonelier and silenter
Grew the dark images of Life's poor
dream,
Till scarcely o'er the dusky scenery there
The lamp of HOPE itself could cast a
gleam.

And now, of all, Who, in my day of dolor,
Alone survives to clasp my willing hand?
Who stands beside me still, my best consoler,
And lights my pathway to the Phantom-
strand?
Thou, FRIENDSHIP! stancher of our wounds
and sorrows,
From whom this lifelong pilgrimage of
pain
A balsam for its worst afflictions borrows;
Thou whom I early sought, nor sought in
vain!

And thou whose labors by her light are
wrought,
Soother and soberer of the spirit's fever,
Who, shaping all things, ne'er destroyest
aught,
Calm OCCUPATION! thou that weariest
never!
Whose efforts rear at last the mighty Mount
Of Life, though merely grain on grain
they lay,
And, slowly toiling, from the vast Account
Of Time strike minutes, days, and years
away.

— *From the German of Friedrich von Schiller (1759–1805), translated by James Clarence Mangan.*

Art

All things are doubly fair
If patience fashion them
And care —
Verse, enamel, marble, gem

No idle chains endure:
Yet, Muse, to walk aright
Lace tight
Thy buskin proud and sure.

Fie on facile measure,
A shoe where every lout
At pleasure
Slip his foot in and out!

Sculptor lay by the clay
On which thy nerveless finger
May linger,
Thy thoughts flown far away.

Keep to Carrara rare,
Struggle with Paros cold,
That hold
The subtle line and fair.

Lest haply nature lose
That proud, that perfect line,
Make thine
The bronze of Syracuse.

And with a tender dread
Upon an agate's face
Retrace
Apollo's golden head.

Despise a watery hue
And tints that soon expire.
With fire
Burn thine enamel true.

Twine, twine in artful wise
The blue-green mermaid's arms,
Mid charms
Of thousand heraldries.

Show in their triple lobe
Virgin and Child, that hold
Their globe,
Cross crowned and aureoled.

— All things return to dust
Save beauties fashioned well;
The bust
Outlasts the citadel.

Oft doth the plowman's heel,
Breaking an ancient clod,
Reveal
A Cæsar or a god.

The gods, too, die, alas!
But deathless and more strong
Than brass
Remains the sovereign song.

Chisel and carve and file,
Till thy vague dream imprint
Its smile
On the unyielding flint.

— *From the French of Théophile Gautier (1811–1872), translated by George Santayana.*

Ode to a Nightingale

My heart aches, and a drowsy numbness pains
My sense, as though of hemlock I had drunk,
Or emptied some dull opiate to the drains
One minute past, and Lethe-wards had sunk:
'Tis not through envy of thy happy lot,
But being too happy in thine happiness, —
That thou, light-wingèd Dryad of the trees,
In some melodious plot
Of beechen green, and shadows numberless,
Singest of summer in full-throated ease.

O for a draught of vintage! that hath been
Cooled a long age in the deep delvèd earth,
Tasting of Flora and the country green,
Dance, and Provençal song, and sunburnt mirth!
O for a beaker full of the warm South,
Full of the true, the blushful Hippocrene,
With beaded bubbles winking at the brim,
And purple-stainèd mouth;
That I might drink, and leave the world unseen,
And with thee fade away into the forest dim:

Fade far away, dissolve, and quite forget
What thou among the leaves hast never known,
The weariness, the fever, and the fret
Here, where men sit and hear each other groan;
Where palsy shakes a few, sad, last gray hairs,
Where youth grows pale, and specter-thin, and dies;
Where but to think is to be full of sorrow
And leaden-eyed despairs,
Where Beauty cannot keep her lustrous eyes,
Or new Love pine at them beyond tomorrow.

Away! away! for I will fly to thee,
Not charioted by Bacchus and his pards,
But on the viewless wings of Poesy,
Though the dull brain perplexes and retards:
Already with thee! tender is the night,
And haply the Queen-Moon is on her throne,
Clustered around by all her starry Fays;
But here there is no light,
Save what from heaven is with the breezes blown
Through verdurous glooms and winding mossy ways.

I cannot see what flowers are at my feet,
Nor what soft incense hangs upon the boughs,
But, in embalmèd darkness, guess each sweet
Wherewith the seasonable month endows
The grass, the thicket, and the fruit-tree wild;
White hawthorn, and the pastoral eglantine;

Fast-fading violets covered up in leaves;
And mid-May's eldest child,
The coming musk-rose, full of dewy wine,
The murmurous haunt of flies on summer eves.

Darkling I listen; and for many a time
I have been half in love with easeful Death,
Called him soft names in many a musèd rhyme,
To take into the air my quiet breath;
Now more than ever seems it rich to die,
To cease upon the midnight with no pain,
While thou art pouring forth thy soul abroad
In such an ecstasy!
Still wouldst thou sing, and I have ears in vain —
To thy high requiem become a sod.

Thou wast not born for death, immortal Bird!
No hungry generations tread thee down;
The voice I hear this passing night was heard
In ancient days by emperor and clown:
Perhaps the self-same song that found a path
Through the sad heart of Ruth, when, sick for home,
She stood in tears amid the alien corn;
The same that oft-times hath
Charmed magic casements, opening on the foam
Of perilous seas, in faery lands forlorn.

Forlorn! the very word is like a bell
To toll me back from thee to my sole self!
Adieu! the fancy cannot cheat so well
As she is famed to do, deceiving elf.
Adieu! adieu! thy plaintive anthem fades
Past the near meadows, over the still stream,
Up the hill-side; and now 'tis buried deep
In the next valley-glades:
Was it a vision, or a waking dream?
Fled is that music: — Do I wake or sleep?

— *John Keats, English (1795–1821).*

Chorus from Hellas

The world's great age begins anew,
The golden years return,
The earth doth like a snake renew
Her winter weeds outworn:
Heaven smiles, and faiths and empires gleam,
Like wrecks of a dissolving dream.

A brighter Hellas rears its mountains
From waves serener far;
A new Peneus rolls his fountains
Against the morning star.
Where fairer Tempes bloom, there sleep
Young Cyclads on a sunnier deep.

A loftier Argo cleaves the main,
Fraught with a later prize;
Another Orpheus sings again,
And loves, and weeps, and dies.
A new Ulysses leaves once more
Calypso for his native shore.

Oh, write no more the tale of Troy,
If earth Death's scroll must be!
Nor mix with Laian rage the joy
Which dawns upon the free:
Although a subtler Sphinx renew
Riddles of death Thebes never knew.

Another Athens shall arise,
And to remoter time
Bequeath, like sunset to the skies,
The splendor of its prime;
And leave, if naught so bright may live,
All earth can take or Heaven can give.

Saturn and Love their long repose
Shall burst, more bright and good
Than all who fell, than One who rose,
Than many unsubdued:
Not gold, not blood, their altar dowers,
But votive tears and symbol flowers.

Oh, cease! must hate and death return?
Cease! must men kill and die?
Cease! drain not to its dregs the urn
Of bitter prophecy.
The world is weary of the past,
Oh, might it die or rest at last!

— *Percy Bysshe Shelley, English (1792–1822).*

The Overworld

Enter the Spirit and Chorus of the Years, the Spirit and Chorus of the Pities, the Shade of the Earth, the Spirits Sinister and Ironic with their Choruses, Rumours, Spirit-messengers and Recording Angels.

Europe has now sunk netherward to its far-off position as in the Fore Scene, and it is beheld again as a prone and emaciated figure of which the Alps form the vertebræ, and the branching mountain-chains the ribs, the Spanish Peninsula shaping the head of the écorché. The lowlands look like a grey-green garment half-thrown off, and the sea around like a disturbed bed on which the figure lies.

SPIRIT OF THE YEARS

Thus doth the Great Foresightless mechanize
In blank entrancement now as evermore
Its ceaseless artistries in Circumstance
Of curious stuff and braid, as just forthshown.
  Yet but one flimsy riband of Its web
Have we here watched in weaving — web Enorm,
Whose furthest hem and selvage may extend
To where the roars and plashings of the flames
Of earth-invisible suns swell noisily,
And onwards into ghastly gulfs of sky,
Where hideous presences churn through the dark —
Monsters of magnitude without a shape,
Hanging amid deep wells of nothingness.

Yet seems this vast and singular confection
Wherein our scenery glints of scantest size,
Inutile all — so far as reasonings tell.

SPIRIT OF THE PITIES

Thou arguest still the Inadvertent Mind. —
But, even so, shall blankness be for aye?
Men gained cognition with the flux of time,
And wherefore not the Force informing them,
When far-ranged aions past all fathoming
Shall have swung by, and stand as backward years?

SPIRIT OF THE YEARS

What wouldst have hoped and had the Will to be? —
How wouldst have pæaned It, if what hadst dreamed
Thereof were truth, and all my showings dream?

SPIRIT OF THE PITIES

The Will that fed my hope was far from thine,
One I would thus have hymned eternally: —

SEMICHORUS I OF THE PITIES (aerial music)

To Thee whose eye all Nature owns,
Who hurlest Dynasts from their thrones,[1]
And liftest those of low estate
We sing, with Her men consecrate!

SEMICHORUS II

Yea, Great and Good, Thee, Thee we hail,
Who shak'st the strong, Who shield'st the frail,
Who hadst not shaped such souls as we
If tender mercy lacked in Thee!

SEMICHORUS I

Though times be when the mortal moan
Seems unascending to Thy throne,
Though seers do not as yet explain
Why Suffering sobs to Thee in vain;

SEMICHORUS II

We hold that Thy unscanted scope
Affords a food for final Hope,
That mild-eyed Prescience ponders nigh
Life's loom, to lull it by-and-by.

SEMICHORUS I

Therefore we quire to highest height
The Wellwiller, the kindly Might
That balances the Vast for weal,
That purges as by wounds to heal.

SEMICHORUS II

The systemed suns the skies enscroll
Obey Thee in their rhythmic roll,
Ride radiantly at Thy command,
Are darkened by Thy Masterhand!

SEMICHORUS I

And these pale panting multitudes
Seen surging here, their moils, their moods,
All shall "fulfil their joy" in Thee
In Thee abide eternally!

SEMICHORUS II

Exultant adoration give
The Alone, through Whom all living live,
The Alone, in Whom all dying die,
Whose means the End shall justify! Amen.

SPIRIT OF THE PITIES

So did we evermore sublimely sing;
So would we now, despite thy forthshowing!

---

[1] *καθεῖλε* ΔΥΝΑΣΤΑΣ *ἀπὸ θρόνων*. — Magnificat.

SPIRIT OF THE YEARS

Something of difference animates your quir-
ing,
O half-convinced Compassionate and fond,
From chords consistent with our spectacle!
You almost charm my long philosophy
Out of my strong-built thought, and bear me
back
To when I thanksgave thus. . . . Ay, start
not, Shades;
In the Foregone I knew what dreaming was,
And could let raptures rule! But not so now.
Yea, I psalmed thus and thus. . . . But not
so now.

SEMICHORUS I OF THE YEARS (aerial music)

O Immanence, That reasonest not
In putting forth all things begot,
Thou build'st Thy house in space — for
what?

SEMICHORUS II

O Loveless, Hateless! — past the sense
Of kindly eyed benevolence,
To what tune danceth this Immense?

SPIRIT IRONIC

For one I cannot answer. But I know
'Tis handsome of our Pities so to sing
The praises of the dreaming, dark, dumb
Thing
That turns the handle of this idle Show!

As once a Greek asked I would fain ask too,
Who knows if all the Spectacle be true,
Or an illusion of the gods (the Will,
To wit) some hocus-pocus to fulfil?

SEMICHORUS I OF THE YEARS (aerial music)

Last as first the question rings
Of the Will's long travailings;
Why the All-mover,
Why the All-prover
Ever urges on and measures out the chord-
less chime of Things.[1]

SEMICHORUS II

Heaving dumbly
As we deem,
Moulding numbly
As in dream,
Apprehending not how fare the sentient sub-
jects of Its scheme.

[1] Hor. *Epis.* i. 12.

SEMICHORUS I OF THE PITIES

Nay; — shall not Its blindness break?
Yea, must not Its heart awake,
Promptly tending
To Its mending
In a genial germing purpose, and for loving-
kindness' sake?

SEMICHORUS II

Should It never
Curb or cure
Aught whatever
Those endure
Whom It quickens, let them darkle to extinc-
tion swift and sure.

CHORUS

But — a stirring thrills the air
Like to sounds of joyance there
That the rages
Of the ages
Shall be cancelled, and deliverance offered
from the darts that were,
Consciousness the Will informing, till It fash-
ion all things fair!

— *From The Dynasts, An Epic Drama of the War With Napoleon, by Thomas Hardy, English (1840–1928).*

Hymn to Chance

How shall we summon you?
The tiny names of gods will not serve us
now,
Nor the magic names of the various sons of
gods,
Nor the names of their mothers murmured
tenderly,
Nor the masks of creatures which you have
assumed.
Gray hands enfolding all our lives,
Gray hands, caress the stumbling of our
tongues.

Lord Gardener, you have made our lives
arise,
Thin shoots of green articulated bone,
Growing and bending and falling under
your breath.
You have grafted on these stems our nervy
flesh
Enriched with blood and our slow-blooming
brains;

You have made our fingers wise with restlessness.
You have laid the earth out and the sea and the lower skies,
You have set us on loose feet beside the earth
That your many colored garden may run wild.
And now from these garnished jaws your garden sings,
Lord Chance,
And your flowers coruscate with blossoming.

You are munificent, how shall we count your gifts?
We enumerate like groping babyhood,
For our thoughts are bound and packaged in your hands,
The world is formed and furled in your ceaseless hands,
The hours and days drip from your fingertips,
The ages and our lives fall clustering
And the seasons fall unjustly from your hands.

Lord Prince of Hell, you have given us thought, the worm
Which coils insistently through our too sensate dust.
It is this disease, Lord Death, which corrupts us all,
For we lie to animate our meagreness,
To make us to ourselves less mean
And our companions less like mangled fools.

Lord Costumer, the cabinets of our blood
Have been hung with robes to clothe our nakedness;
You have given us the burning skin of joy,
You have turned our feet from circling slavery
With the brilliance of a dollar thrown in the air.
You have given the close bitter gown of grief,
The acid lining of our joyousness.
You have given us spirit, Lord, we are not abashed,
And we have known quietude when our muscles moved
Smoothly in laboring or in love
And our nerves made harmony of their clamoring.
We have raised ourselves immense memorials,
And our laughter, like your own, has lapped the world.

You have given us the variable one, the infinite and the small,
Which we have repaid with stiff ingratitude.
We have insulted you as Lady Luck;
We have made our lives a foolishness
Because your eyes were neither cool nor kind.
We are the victims of unfounded lust,
We have discovered laws, forgive us, Lord;
Forgive us, Lord, we are neither fine nor swift,
We have not known our proper elegance.
We have said tomorrow comes and the twinkling sun
Will not refuse to flatter us with heat;
We have hid ourselves in minuscules of time.
We have made ourselves low beds in an empty room;
But our beds drift in the dark and our lies dissolve
And there is your face shimmering and your hands
Weaving the chaos where we come and go.

Grand Anarch, there is disrepute for us,
But our words are not disreputable nor mean;
We have spoken for ourselves and our dignity,
Tearing our cheapness from us for a while.
At this moment now, conceive us once again
More suitable to the curving of your hands;
Make us tough and mystical,
Give us such eyes as will penetrate your eyes
And lungs to draw the breath you give to us.
Hear us for we do not beg;
We only pray you heal our idiot ways
And the kind of lonely madness which we have
Of bleeding one another on the road.
We travel in the belly of the wind;
It is you, Lord, who will make us lame or swift.

— *Phelps Putnam, American (1894–   ).*

Antique Harvesters

(*Scene: Of the Mississippi the bank sinister, and of the Ohio the bank sinister*)

Tawny are the leaves turned, but they still hold.

It is the harvest; what shall this land produce?
A meager hill of kernels, a runnel of juice.
Declension looks from our land, it is old.
Therefore let us assemble, dry, gray, spare,
And mild as yellow air.

"I hear the creak of a raven's funeral wing."
The young men would be joying in the song
Of passionate birds; their memories are not long.
What is it thus rehearsed in sable? "Nothing."
Trust not but the old endure, and shall be older
Than the scornful beholder.

We pluck the spindling ears and gather the corn.
One spot has special yield? "On this spot stood
Heroes and drenched it with their only blood."
And talk meets talk, as echoes from the horn
Of the hunter – echoes are the old men's arts,
Ample are the chambers of their hearts.

Here come the hunters, keepers of a rite.
The horn, the hounds, the lank mares coursing by
Under quaint archetypes of chivalry;
And the fox, lovely ritualist, in flight
Offering his unearthly ghost to quarry;
And the fields, themselves to harry.

Resume, harvesters. The treasure is full bronze
Which you will garner for the Lady, and the moon
Could tinge it no yellower than does this noon;
But the gray will quench it shortly – the fields, men, stones.
Pluck fast, dreamers; prove as you rumble slowly
Not less than men, not wholly.

Bare the arm too, dainty youths, bend the knees
Under bronze burdens. And by an autumn tone
As by a gray, as by a green, you will have known
Your famous Lady's image; for so have these.
And if one say that easily will your hands
More prosper in other lands,

Angry as wasp-music be your cry then:
"Forsake the Proud Lady, of the heart of fire,
The look of snow, to the praise of a dwindled choir,
Song of degenerate specters that were men?
The sons of the fathers shall keep her, worthy of
What these have done in love."

True, it is said of our Lady, she ageth.
But see, if you peep shrewdly, she hath not stooped;
Take no thought of her servitors that have drooped,
For we are nothing; and if one talk of death –
Why, the ribs of the earth subsist frail as a breath
If but God wearieth.

— *John Crowe Ransom, American (1888–).*

PART THIRTEEN

Great Episodes and Characters of History

THE BEGINNING of wisdom and all serious goodness is to be found in man's ability to imagine himself in the place of others. Among all the values of history or the lessons it might teach, none is greater than a power to take hold of the imagination and to inspire. There may appear many chapters in the records of humanity which seem dry and useless. But studied aright, they tell the story of man on this earth; and their ultimate worth will depend on one's view of man himself. The world has seen many knaves and despots. On the whole it has also been blessed with great conjunct personalities in whom the best souls of the human race and its highest achievements of mind and spirit can be found. In Bolingbroke's *Letters on the Study and Use of History,* published in 1752, appears an observation that has been tested by many generations: "History is the ancient author: experience is the modern language. We form our taste on the first; we translate the sense and reason, we transfuse the spirit and force: but we imitate only the particular graces of the original; we imitate them according to the idiom of our own tongue, that is, we substitute often equivalents in lieu of them, and are far from affecting to copy them servilely."

There are of course numerous definitions of the object of historical studies. In the technical literature of the subject one may find such phrases as the following: "The science of history is that science which investigates and presents, in their context in psychophysical causality, the facts, determined by space and time, of the evaluation of men in their individual as well as typical and collective activity as social beings." For the general reader such definitions may suggest few literary or aesthetic satisfactions. If man himself is worthy of study, however, all records he has left of himself are indispensable and must be critically examined. There are also styles and theories of how history should be written – indeed, scholars have studied the "history of history," and philosophers have sought with various formulae to explain the broad social movements of the past. These also offer fascinating problems and engaging studies. But for the general student who approaches history through popular or semi-popular literature, the following selections will suggest the fact that annals and chronicles are more than guideposts to memory; they also reveal man's hours of spiritual greatness and highest achievements.

Thermopylæ

HERODOTUS

KING XERXES pitched his camp in the region of Malis called Trachinia, while on their side the Greeks occupied the straits. These straits the Greeks in general call Thermopylæ (the Hot Gates); but the natives and those who dwell in the neighbourhood call them Pylæ (the Gates). Here then the two armies took their stand; the one master of all the region lying north of Trachis, the other of the country extending southward of that place to the verge of the continent.

The Greeks who at this spot awaited the coming of Xerxes were the following: — From Sparta, three hundred men-at-arms: from Arcadia, a thousand Tegeans and Mantineans, five hundred of each people; a hundred and twenty Orchomenians, from the Arcadian Orchomenus; and a thousand from other cities; from Corinth, four hundred men: from Phlius, two hundred: and from Mycenæ, eighty. Such was the number from the Peloponnese. There were also present, from Bœotia, seven hundred Thespians and four hundred Thebans.

Besides these troops, the Locrians of Opus and the Phocians had obeyed the call of their countrymen, and sent, the former all the force they had, the latter a thousand men. For envoys had gone from the Greeks at Thermopylæ among the Locrians and Phocians, to call on them for assistance, and to say — "They were themselves but the vanguard of the host, sent to precede the main body, which might every day be expected to follow them. The sea was in good keeping, watched by the Athenians, the Eginetans, and the rest of the fleet. There was no cause why they should fear; for after all the invader was not a god but a man; and there never had been, and never would be, a man who was not liable to misfortunes from the very day of his birth, and those greater in proportion to his own greatness. The assailant, therefore, being only a mortal, must needs fall from his glory." Thus urged, the Locrians and the Phocians had come with their troops to Trachis.

The various nations had each captains of their own under whom they served; but the one to whom all especially looked up, and who had the command of the entire force, was the Lacedæmonian, Leonidas. Now Leonidas was the son of Anaxandridas, who was the son of Leo, who was the son of Eurycratidas, who was the son of Anaxander, who was the son of Eurycrates, who was the son of Polydorus, who was the son of Alcamenes, who was the son of Telecles, who was the son of Archelaus, who was the son of Agesilaus, who was the son of Doryssus, who was the son of Labotas, who was the son of Echestratus, who was the son of Agis, who was the son of Eurysthenes, who was the son of Aristodemus, who was the son of Aristomachus, who was the son of Cleodæus, who was the son of Hyllus, who was the son of Hercules.

Leonidas had come to be king of Sparta quite unexpectedly. Having two elder brothers, Cleomenes and Dorieus, he had no thought of ever mounting the throne. However when Cleomenes died without male offspring, as Dorieus was likewise deceased, having perished in Sicily, the crown fell to Leonidas, who was older than Cleombrotus, the youngest of the sons of Anaxandridas, and, moreover, was married to the daughter of Cleomenes. He had now come to Thermopylæ, accompanied by the three hundred men which the law assigned him, whom he had himself chosen from among the citizens, and who were all of them fathers with sons living. On his way he had taken the troops from Thebes, whose number I have already mentioned, and who were under the command of Leontiades the son of Eurymachus. The reason why he made a point of taking troops from Thebes and Thebes only was, that the Thebans were strongly suspected of being well inclined to the Medes. Leonidas therefore called on them to come with him to the war, wishing to see whether they would comply with his demand, or openly refuse, and disclaim the Greek alliance. They, however, though their wishes leant the other way, nevertheless sent the men.

The force with Leonidas was sent forward by the Spartans in advance of their main body, that the sight of them might encourage the allies to fight, and hinder them from going over to the Medes, as it was likely that they might have done had they seen Sparta backward. They intended presently, when they had celebrated the Carneian festival, which was what now kept them at home, to leave a garrison in Sparta, and hasten in full force to join the army. The rest of the allies also intended to act similarly; for it happened that the Olympic festival fell exactly at this same period. None of them looked to see the contest at Thermopylæ decided so speedily; wherefore they were content to send forward a mere advanced guard. Such accordingly were the intentions of the allies.

The Greek forces at Thermopylæ, when the Persian army drew near to the entrance of the pass, were seized with fear, and a council was held to consider about a retreat. It was the wish of the Peloponnesians generally that the army should fall back upon the Peloponnese, and there guard the Isthmus. But Leonidas, who saw with what indignation the Phocians and Locrians heard of this plan, gave his voice for remaining where they were, while they sent envoys to the several cities to ask for help, since they were too few to make a stand against an army like that of the Medes.

While this debate was going on, Xerxes sent a mounted spy to observe the Greeks, and note how many they were, and what they were doing. He had heard, before he came out of Thessaly, that a few men were assembled at this place, and that at their head were certain Lacedæmonians, under Leonidas, a descendant of Hercules. The horseman rode up to the camp, and looked about him, but did not see the whole army; for such as were on the further side of the wall (which had been rebuilt and now was carefully guarded) it was not possible for him to behold; but he observed those on the outside, who were encamped in front of the rampart. It chanced that at this time the Lacedæmonians held the outer guard, and were seen by the spy, some of them engaged in gymnastic exercises, others combing their long hair. At this the spy greatly marvelled, but he counted their number, and when he had taken accurate note of everything, he rode back quietly; for no one pursued after him, or paid any heed to his visit. So he returned and told Xerxes all that he had seen.

Upon this, Xerxes, who had no means of surmising the truth — namely, that the Spartans were preparing to do or die manfully — but thought it laughable that they should be engaged in such employments, sent and called to his presence Demaratus the son of Ariston, who still remained with the army. When he appeared, Xerxes told him all that he had heard, and questioned him concerning the news, since he was anxious to understand the meaning of such behaviour on the part of the Spartans. Then Demaratus said —

"I spake to thee, O king, concerning these men long since, when we had but just begun our march upon Greece; thou, however, didst only laugh at my words, when I told thee of all this, which I saw would come to pass. Earnestly do I struggle at all times to speak the truth to thee, sire; and now listen to it once more. These men have come to dispute the pass with us, and it is for this that they are now making ready. 'Tis their custom, when they are about to hazard their lives, to adorn their heads with care. Be assured, however, that if thou canst subdue the men who are here and the Lacedæmonians who remain in Sparta, there is no other nation in all the world which will venture to lift a hand in their defence. Thou hast now to deal with the first kingdom and town in Greece, and with the bravest men."

Then Xerxes, to whom what Demaratus said seemed altogether to surpass belief, asked further, "how it was possible for so small an army to contend with his?"

"O king," Demaratus answered, "let me be treated as a liar, if matters fall not out as I say."

But Xerxes was not persuaded any the more. Four whole days he suffered to go by, expecting that the Greeks would run away. When, however, he found on the fifth that they were not gone, thinking that their firm stand was mere imprudence and recklessness, he grew wroth, and sent against them the Medes and Cissians, with orders to take them alive and bring them into his presence. Then the Medes rushed forward and charged the Greeks, but fell in vast numbers: others however took the places of the slain, and would not be beaten off, though they suffered terrible losses. In this way it became clear to all, and especially to the king, that though he had plenty of combatants, he had but very few warriors. The struggle, however, continued during the whole day.

Then the Medes, having met so rough a reception, withdrew from the fight; and their place was taken by the band of Persians under Hydarnes, whom the king called his "Immortals": they, it was thought, would soon finish the business. But when they joined battle with the Greeks, 'twas with no better success than the Median detachment — things went much as before — the two armies fighting in a narrow space, and the barbarians using shorter spears than the Greeks, and having no advantage from their numbers. The Lacedæmonians fought in a way worthy of note, and showed themselves far more skillful in fight than their adversaries, often turning their backs, and making as though they were all flying away, on which the barbarians would rush after them with much noise and shouting, when the Spartans at their approach would wheel round and face their pursuers, in this way destroying vast numbers of the enemy. Some Spartans likewise fell in these encounters, but only a very few. At last the Persians, finding that all their efforts to gain the pass availed nothing, and that whether they attacked by divisions or in any other way, it was to no purpose, withdrew to their own quarters.

During these assaults, it is said that Xerxes, who was watching the battle, thrice leaped from the throne on which he sate, in terror for his army.

Next day the combat was renewed, but with no better success on the part of the barbarians. The Greeks were so few that the barbarians hoped to find them disabled, by reason of their wounds, from offering any further resistance; and so they once more attacked them. But the Greeks were drawn up in detachments according to their cities, and bore the brunt of the battle in turns, — all except the Phocians, who had been stationed on the mountain to guard the pathway. So when the Persians found no difference between that day and the preceding, they again retired to their quarters.

Now, as the king was in a great strait, and knew not how he should deal with the emergency, Ephialtes, the son of Eurydemus, a man of Malis, came to him and was admitted to a conference. Stirred by the hope of receiving a rich reward at the king's hands, he had come to tell him of the pathway which led across the mountain to Thermopylæ; by which disclosure he brought destruction on the band of Greeks who had there withstood the barbarians. This Ephialtes afterwards, from fear of the Lacedæmonians, fled into Thessaly; and during his exile, in an assembly of the Amphictyons held at Pylæ, a price was set upon his head by the Pylagoræ. When some time had gone by, he returned from exile, and went to Anticyra, where he was slain by Athenades, a native of Trachis. Athenades did not slay him for his treachery, but for another reason, which I shall mention in a later part of my history: yet still the Lacedæmonians honoured him none the less. Thus then did Ephialtes perish a long time afterwards.

Besides this there is another story told, which I do not at all believe — to wit, that Onetas the son of Phanagoras, a native of Carystus, and Corydallus, a man of Anticyra, were the persons who spoke on this matter to the king, and took the Persians across the mountain. One may guess which story is true, from the fact that the deputies from the Greeks, the Pylagoræ, who must have had the best means of ascertaining the truth, did not offer the reward for the heads of Onetas and Corydallus, but for that of Ephialtes of Trachis; and again from the flight of Ephialtes, which we know to have been on this account. Onetas, I allow, although he was not a Malian, might have been acquainted with the path, if he had lived much in that part of the country; but as Ephialtes was the person who actually led the Persians round the mountain by the pathway, I leave his name on record as that of the man who did the deed.

Great was the joy of Xerxes on this occasion; and as he approved highly of the enterprise which Ephialtes undertook to accomplish, he forthwith sent upon the errand Hydarnes, and the Persians under him. The troops left the camp about the time of the lighting of the lamps. The pathway along which they went was first discovered by the Malians of these parts, who soon afterwards led the Thessalians by it to attack the Phocians, at the time when the Phocians fortified the pass with a wall, and so put themselves under covert from danger. And ever since the path has always been put to an ill use by the Malians.

The course which it takes is the following: — Beginning at the Asopus, where that stream flows through the cleft in the hills, it runs along the ridge of the mountain (which is called, like the pathway over it, Anopæa), and ends at the city of Alpenus — the first Locrian town as you come from Malis — by the stone called Melampygus and the seats of the Cercopians. Here is it as narrow as at any other point.

The Persians took this path, and crossing the Asopus, continued their march through the whole of the night, having the mountains of Œta on their right hand, and on their left those of Trachis. At dawn of day they found themselves close to the summit. Now the hill was guarded, as I have already said, by a thousand Phocian men-at-arms, who were placed there to defend the pathway, and at the same time to secure their own country. They had been given the guard of the mountain path, while the other Greeks defended the pass below, because they had volunteered for the service, and had pledged themselves to Leonidas to maintain the post.

The ascent of the Persians became known to the Phocians in the following manner: — During all the time that they were making their way up, the Greeks remained unconscious of it, inasmuch as the whole mountain was covered with groves of oak; but it happened that the air was very still, and the leaves which the Persians stirred with their feet made, as it was likely they would, a loud rustling, whereupon the Phocians jumped up and flew to seize their arms. In a moment the barbarians came in sight, and perceiving men arming themselves, were greatly amazed; for they had fallen in with an enemy when they had expected no opposition. Hydarnes, alarmed at the sight, and fearing lest the Phocians might be Lacedæmonians, enquired of Ephialtes to what nation these troops belonged. Ephialtes told him the exact truth, whereupon he arrayed his Persians for battle. The Phocians, galled by the showers of arrows to which they were exposed, and imagining themselves the special object of the Persian attack, fled hastily to the crest of the mountain, and there made ready to meet death; but while their mistake continued, the Persians, with Ephialtes and Hydarnes, not thinking it worth their while to delay on account of Phocians, passed on and descended the mountain with all possible speed.

The Greeks at Thermopylæ received the first warning of the destruction which the dawn would bring on them from the seer Megistias, who read their fate in the victims as he was sacrificing. After this deserters came in, and brought the news that the Persians were marching round by the hills: it was still night when these men arrived. Last of all, the scouts came running down from the heights, and brought in the same accounts, when the day was just beginning to break. Then the Greeks held a council to consider what they should do, and here opinions were divided: some were strong against quitting their post, while others contended to the contrary. So when the council had broken up, part of the troops departed and went their ways homeward to their several states; part however resolved to remain, and to stand by Leonidas to the last.

It is said that Leonidas himself sent away the troops who departed, because he tendered their safety, but thought it unseemly that either he or his Spartans should quit the post which they had been especially sent to guard. For my own part, I incline to think that Leonidas gave the order, because he perceived the allies to be out of heart and unwilling to encounter the danger to which his own mind was made up. He therefore commanded them to retreat, but said that he himself could not draw back with honour; knowing that, if he stayed, glory awaited him, and that Sparta in that case would not lose her prosperity. For when the Spartans, at the very beginning of the war sent to consult the oracle concerning it, the answer which they received from the Pythoness was, "that either Sparta must be overthrown by the barbarians, or one of her kings must perish." The prophecy was delivered in hexameter verse, and ran thus: —

"Oh! ye men who dwell in the streets of broad Lacedæmon,
Either your glorious town shall be sacked by the children of Perseus,
Or, in exchange, must all through the whole Laconian country
Mourn for the loss of a king, descendant of great Heracles.
He cannot be withstood by the courage of bulls or of lions,
Strive as they may; he is mighty as Jove; there is nought that shall stay him,
Till he have got for his prey your king, or your glorious city."

The remembrance of this answer, I think, and the wish to secure the whole glory for the Spartans, caused Leonidas to send the allies away. This is more likely than that they quarrelled with him, and took their departure in such unruly fashion.

To me it seems no small argument in favour of this view, that the seer also who accompanied the army, Megistias, the Acarnanian, — said to have been of the blood of Melampus, and the same who was led by the appearance of the victims to warn the Greeks of the danger which threatened them, – received orders to retire (as it is certain he did) from Leonidas, that he might escape the coming destruction. Megistias, however, though bidden to depart, refused, and stayed with the army; but he had an only son present with the expedition, whom he now sent away.

So the allies, when Leonidas ordered them to retire, obeyed him and forthwith departed. Only the Thespians and the Thebans remained with the Spartans; and of these the Thebans were kept back by Leonidas as hostages, very much against their will. The Thespians, on the contrary, stayed entirely on their own accord, refusing to retreat, and declaring that they would not forsake Leonidas and his followers. So they abode with the Spartans, and died with them. Their leader was Demophilus, the son of Diadromes.

At sunrise Xerxes made libations, after which he waited until the time when the forum is wont to fill, and then began his advance. Ephialtes had instructed him thus, as the descent of the mountain is much quicker, and the distance much shorter, than the way round the hills, and the ascent. So the barbarians under Xerxes began to draw nigh; and the Greeks under Leonidas, as they now went forth determined to die, advanced much further than on previous days, until they reached the more open portion of the pass. Hitherto they had held their station within the wall, and from this had gone forth to fight at the point where the pass was the narrowest. Now they joined battle beyond the defile, and carried slaughter among the barbarians, who fell in heaps. Behind them the captains of the squadrons, armed with whips, urged their men forward with continual blows. Many were thrust into the sea, and there perished; a still greater number were trampled to death by their own soldiers; no one heeded the dying. For the Greeks, reckless of their own safety and desperate, since they knew that, as the mountains had been crossed, their destruction was nigh at hand, exerted themselves with the most furious valour against the barbarians.

By this time the spears of the greater number were all shivered, and with their swords they hewed down the ranks of the Persians; and here, as they strove, Leonidas fell fighting bravely, together with many other famous Spartans, whose names I have taken care to learn on account of their great worthiness, as indeed I have those of all the three hundred. There fell too at the same time very many famous Persians: among them, two sons of Darius, Abrocomes and Hyperanthes, his children by Phratagune, the daughter of Artanes. Artanes was brother of King Darius, being a son of Hystaspes, the son of Arsames; and when he gave his daughter to the king, he made him heir likewise of all his substance; for she was his only child.

Thus two brothers of Xerxes here fought and fell. And now there arose a fierce struggle between the Persians and the Lacedæmonians over the body of Leonidas, in which the Greeks four times drove back the enemy, and at last by their great bravery succeeded in bearing off the body. This combat was scarcely ended when the Persians with Ephialtes approached; and the Greeks, informed that they drew nigh, made a change in the manner of their fighting. Drawing back into the narrowest part of the pass, and retreating even behind the cross wall, they posted themselves upon a hillock, where they stood all drawn up together in one close body, except only the Thebans. The hillock whereof I speak is at the entrance of the straits, where the stone lion stands which was set up in honour of Leonidas. Here they defended themselves to the last, such as still had swords using them, and the others resisting with their hands and teeth; till the barbarians who in part had pulled down the wall and attacked them in front, in part had gone round and now encircled them upon every side, overwhelmed them and buried the remnant left beneath showers of missile weapons.

Thus nobly did the whole body of Lacedæmonians and Thespians behave, but nevertheless one man is said to have distinguished himself above all the rest, to wit, Dieneces the Spartan. A speech which he made before the Greeks engaged the Medes, remains on record. One of the Trachinians told him, "such was the number of the barbarians, that when they shot forth their arrows the sun would be darkened by their multitude." Dieneces, not at all frightened at these words, but making light of the Median numbers, answered, "Our Trachinian friend brings us excellent tidings. If the Medes darken the sun, we shall have our fight in the shade." Other sayings too of a like nature are said to have been left on record by this same person.

Next to him two brothers, Lacedæmonians, are reputed to have made themselves conspicuous: they were named Alpheus and Maro, and were the sons of Orsiphantus. There was also a Thespian who gained greater glory than any of his countrymen: he was a man called Dithyrambus, the son of Harmatidas.

The slain were buried where they fell; and in their honour, nor less in honour of those who died before Leonidas sent the allies away, an inscription was set up, which said, —

"Here did four thousand men from Pelops' land
Against three hundred myriads bravely stand."

This was in honour of all. Another was for the Spartans alone: —

"Go, stranger, and to Lacedæmon tell
That here, obeying her behest, we fell."

This was for the Lacedæmonians. The seer had the following: —

"The great Megistias' tomb you here may view,
Whom slew the Medes, fresh from Spercheius' fords.
Well the wise seer the coming death foreknew,
Yet scorned he to forsake his Spartan lords."

These inscriptions, and the pillars likewise, were all set up by the Amphictyons, except that in honour of Megistias, which was inscribed to him (on account of their sworn friendship) by Simonides, the son of Leoprepes.

— By Herodotus, Greek (fifth century B.C.), translated by George Rawlinson.

The Apology and Death of Socrates

PLATO

How you have felt, O men of Athens, at hearing the speeches of my accusers, I cannot tell; but I know that their persuasive words almost made me forget who I was; — such was the effect of them; and yet they have hardly spoken a word of truth. But many as their falsehoods were, there was one of them which quite amazed me; — I mean when they told you to be upon your guard, and not to let yourself be deceived by the force of my eloquence. They ought to have been ashamed of saying this, because they were sure to be detected as soon as I opened my lips and displayed my deficiency; they certainly did appear to be most shameless in saying this, unless by the force of eloquence they mean the force of truth: for then I do indeed admit that I am eloquent. But in how different a way from theirs! Well, as I was saying, they have hardly uttered a word, or not more than a word, of truth; but you shall hear from me the whole truth: not, however, delivered after their manner, in a set oration duly ornamented with words and phrases. No, indeed! but I shall use the words and arguments which occur to me at the moment; for I am certain that this is right, and that at my time of life I ought not to be appearing before you, O men of Athens, in the character of a juvenile orator — let no one expect this of me. And I must beg of you to grant me one favor, which is this — If you hear me using the same words in my defense which I have been in the habit of using, and which most of you may have heard in the agora, and at the tables of the money-changers, or anywhere else, I would ask you not to be surprised at this, and not to interrupt me. For I am more than seventy years of age, and this is the first time that I have ever appeared in a court of law, and I am quite a stranger to the ways of the place; and therefore I would have you regard me as if I were really a stranger, whom you would excuse if he spoke in his native tongue, and after the fashion of his country; — that I think is not an unfair request. Never mind the manner, which may or may not be good; but think only of the justice of my cause, and give heed to that: let the judge decide justly and the speaker speak truly.

And first, I have to reply to the older charges and to my first accusers, and then I will go to the later ones. For I have had many accusers, who accused me of old, and their false charges have continued during many years; and I am more afraid of them than of Anytus and his associates, who are dangerous, too, in their own way. But far more dangerous are these, who began when you were children, and took possession of your minds with their falsehoods, telling of one Socrates, a wise man, who speculated about the heaven above, and searched into the earth beneath, and made the worse appear the better cause. These are the accusers whom I dread; for they are the circulators of this rumor, and their hearers are too apt to fancy that speculators of this sort do not believe in the gods. And they are many, and their charges against me are of ancient date, and they made them in days when you were impressible — in childhood, or perhaps in youth — and the cause when heard went by default, for there was none to answer. And, hardest of all, their names I do not know and cannot tell; unless in the chance case of a comic poet. But the main body of these slanderers who from envy and malice have wrought upon you — and there are some of them who are convinced themselves, and impart their convictions to others — all these, I say, are most difficult to deal with; for I cannot have them up here, and examine them, and therefore I must simply fight with shadows in my own defense, and examine when there is no one who answers. I will ask you then to assume with me, as I was saying, that my opponents are of two kinds; one recent, the other ancient: and I hope that you will see the propriety of my answering the latter first, for these accusations you heard long before the others, and much oftener.

Well, then, I will make my defense, and I will endeavor in the short time which is allowed to do away with this evil opinion of me which you have held for such a long time; and I hope I may succeed, if this be well for you and me, and that my words may find favor with you. But I know that to accomplish this is not easy — I quite see the nature of the task. Let the event be as God wills: in obedience to the law I make my defense.

I will begin at the beginning, and ask what the accusation is which has given rise to this slander of me, and which has encouraged Meletus to proceed against me. What do the slanderers say? They shall be my prosecutors, and I will sum up their words in an affidavit. "Socrates is an evil-doer, and a curious person, who searches into things under the earth and in heaven, and he makes the worse appear the better cause; and he teaches the aforesaid doctrines to others." That is the nature of the accusation, and that is what you have seen yourselves in the comedy of Aristophanes, who has introduced a man whom he calls Socrates, going about and saying that he can walk in the air, and talking a deal of nonsense concerning matters of which I do not pretend to know either much or little — not that I mean to say anything disparaging of anyone who is a student of natural philosophy. I should be very sorry if Meletus could lay that to my charge. But the simple truth is, O Athenians, that I have nothing to do with these studies. Very many of those here present are witnesses to the truth of this, and to them I appeal. Speak then, you who have heard me, and tell your neighbors whether any of you have ever known me hold forth in few words or in many upon matters of this sort. . . . You hear their answer. And from what they say of this you will be able to judge of the truth of the rest.

As little foundation is there for the report that I am a teacher, and take money; that is no more true than the other. Although, if a man is able to teach, I honor him for being paid. There is Gorgias of Leontium, and Prodicus of Ceos, and Hippias of Elis, who go the round of the cities, and are able to persuade the young men to leave their own citizens, by whom they might be taught for nothing, and come to them, whom they not only pay, but are thankful if they may be allowed to pay them. There is actually a Parian philosopher residing in Athens, of whom I have heard; and I came to hear of him in this way: — I met a man who has spent a world of money on the Sophists, Callias the son of Hipponicus, and knowing that he had sons, I asked him: "Callias," I said, "if your two sons were foals or calves, there would be no difficulty in finding someone to put over them; we should hire a trainer of horses or a farmer probably who would improve and perfect them in their own proper virtue and excellence; but as they are human beings, whom are you thinking of placing over them? Is there anyone who understands human and political virtue? You must have thought about this as you have sons; is there anyone?" "There is," he said. "Who is he?" said I, "and of what country? and what does he charge?" "Evenus the Parian," he replied; "he is the man, and his charge is five minæ." Happy is Evenus, I said to myself, if he really has this wisdom, and teaches at such a modest charge. Had I the same, I should have been very proud and conceited; but the truth is that I have no knowledge of the kind, O Athenians.

I dare say that someone will ask the question, "Why is this, Socrates, and what is the origin of these accusations of you: for there must have been something strange which you have been doing? All this great fame and talk about you would never have arisen if you had been like other men: tell us, then, why this is, as we should be sorry to judge hastily of you." Now I regard this as a fair challenge, and I will endeavor to explain to you the origin of this name of "wise," and of this evil fame. Please to attend them. And although some of you may think I am joking, I declare that I will tell you the entire truth. Men of Athens, this reputation of mine has come of a certain sort of wisdom which I possess. If you ask me what kind of wisdom, I reply, such wisdom as is attainable by man, for to that extent I am inclined to believe that I am wise; whereas the persons of whom I was speaking have a superhuman wisdom, which I may fail to describe, because I have it not myself; and he who says that I have, speaks falsely, and is taking away my character. And here, O men of Athens, I must beg you not to interrupt me, even if I seem to say something extravagant. For the word which I will speak is not mine. I will refer you to a witness who is worthy of credit, and will tell you about my wisdom — whether I have any, and of what sort — and that witness shall be the god of Delphi. You must have known Chærephon; he was early a friend of mine, and also a friend of yours, for he shared in the exile of the people, and returned with you. Well, Chærephon, as you know, was very impetuous in all his doings, and he went to Delphi and boldly asked the oracle to tell him whether — as I was saying, I must beg you not to interrupt — he asked the oracle to tell him whether there was anyone wiser than I was, and the Pythian prophetess answered that there was no man wiser. Chærephon is dead himself, but his brother, who is in court, will confirm the truth of this story.

Why do I mention this? Because I am going to explain to you why I have such an evil name. When I heard the answer, I said to myself, What can the god mean? and what is the interpretation of this riddle? for I know that I have no wisdom, small or great. What can he mean when he says that I am the wisest of men? And yet he is a god and cannot lie; that would be against his nature. After a long consideration, I at last thought of a method of trying the question. I reflected that if I could only find a man wiser than myself, then I might go to the god with a refutation in my hand. I should say to him, "Here is a man who is wiser than I am; but you said that I was the wisest." Accordingly I went to one who had the reputation of wisdom, and observed to him — his name I need not mention; he was a politician whom I selected for examination — and the result was as follows: When I began to talk with him, I could not help thinking that he was not really wise, although he was thought wise by many, and wiser still by himself; and I went and tried to explain to him that he thought himself wise, but was not really wise; and the consequence was that he hated me, and his enmity was shared by several who were present and heard me. So I left him, saying to myself, as I went away: Well, although I do not suppose that either of us knows anything really beautiful and good, I am better off than he is — for he knows nothing, and thinks that he knows. I neither know nor think that I know. In this latter particular, then, I seem to have slightly the advantage of him. Then I went to another, who had still higher philosophical pretensions, and my conclusion was exactly the same. I made another enemy of him, and of many others besides him.

After this I went to one man after another, being not unconscious of the enmity which I provoked, and I lamented and feared this: but necessity was laid upon me — the word of God, I thought, ought to be considered first. And I said to myself, Go I must to all who appear to know, and find out the meaning of the oracle. And I swear to you, Athenians, by the dog I swear! — for I must tell you the truth — the result of my mission was just this: I found that the men most in repute were all but the most foolish; and that some inferior men were really wiser and better. I will tell you the tale of my wanderings and of the "Herculean" labors, as I may call them, which I endured only to find at last the oracle irrefutable. When I left the politicians, I went to the poets; tragic, dithyrambic, and all sorts. And there, I said to myself, you will be detected; now you will find out that you are more ignorant than they are. Accordingly, I took them some of the most elaborate passages in their own writings, and asked what was the meaning of them—thinking that they would teach me something. Will you believe me? I am almost ashamed to speak of this, but still I must say that there is hardly a person present who would not have talked better about their poetry than they did themselves. That showed me in an instant that not by wisdom do poets write poetry, but by a sort of genius and inspiration; they are like diviners or soothsayers who also say many fine things, but do not understand the meaning of them. And the poets appeared to me to be much in the same case; and I further observed that upon the strength of their poetry they believed themselves to be the wisest of men in other things in which they were not wise. So I departed, conceiving myself to be superior to them for the same reason that I was superior to the politicians.

At last I went to the artisans, for I was conscious that I knew nothing at all, as I may say, and I was sure that they knew many fine things; and in this I was not mistaken, for they did know many things of which I was ignorant, and in this they certainly were wiser than I was. But I observed that even the good artisans fell into the same error as the poets; because they were good workmen they thought that they also knew all sorts of high matters, and this defect in them overshadowed their wisdom — therefore I asked myself on behalf of the oracle, whether I would like to be as I was, neither having their knowledge nor their ignorance, or like them in both; and I made answer to myself and the oracle that I was better off as I was.

This investigation has led to my having many enemies of the worst and most dangerous kind, and has given occasion also to many calumnies, and I am called wise, for my hearers always imagine that I myself possess the wisdom which I find wanting in others: but the truth is, O men of Athens, that God only is wise; and in this oracle he means to say that the wisdom of men is little or nothing; he is not speaking of Socrates, he is only using my name as an illustration, as if he said, He, O men, is the wisest, who, like Socrates, knows that his wisdom is in truth worth nothing. And so I go my way, obedient to the god, and make inquisition into the wisdom of anyone, whether citizen or stranger, who appears to be wise; and if he is not wise, then in vindication of the oracle I show him that he is not wise; and this occupation quite absorbs me, and I have no time to give either to any public matter of interest or to any concern of my own, but I am in utter poverty by reason of my devotion to the god.

There is another thing: — young men of the richer classes, who have not much to do, come about me of their own accord; they like to hear the pretenders examined, and they often imitate me, and examine others themselves; there are plenty of persons, as they soon enough discover, who think that they know something, but really know little or nothing: and then those who are examined by them instead of being angry with themselves are angry with me: This confounded Socrates, they say; this villainous misleader of youth! — and then if somebody asks them, Why, what evil does he practice or teach? they do not know, and cannot tell; but in order that they may not appear to be at a loss, they repeat the ready-made charges which are used against all philosophers about teaching things up in the clouds and under the earth, and having no gods, and making the worse appear the better cause; for they do not like to confess that their pretense of knowledge has been detected — which is the truth: and as they are numerous and ambitious and energetic, and are all in battle array and have persuasive tongues, they have filled your ears with their loud and inveterate calumnies. And this is the reason why my three accusers, Meletus and Anytus and Lycon, have set upon me: Meletus, who has a quarrel with me on behalf of the poets; Anytus, on behalf of the craftsmen; Lycon, on behalf of the rhetoricians; and as I said at the beginning, I cannot expect to get rid of this mass of calumny all in a moment. And this, O men of Athens, is the truth and the whole truth; I have concealed nothing, I have dissembled nothing. And yet I know that this plainness of speech makes them hate me, and what is their hatred but a proof that I am speaking the truth? — this is the occasion and reason of their slander of me, as you will find out either in this or in any future inquiry.

I have said enough in my defense against the first class of my accusers; I turn to the second class, who are headed by Meletus, that good and patriotic man, as he calls himself. And now I will try to defend myself against them: these new accusers must also have their affidavit read. What do they say?

Something of this sort: That Socrates is a doer of evil, and corrupter of the youth, and he does not believe in the gods of the state, and has other new divinities of his own. That is the sort of charge; and now let us examine the particular counts. He says that I am a doer of evil, who corrupts the youth; but I say, O men of Athens, that Meletus is a doer of evil, and the evil is that he makes a joke of a serious matter, and is too ready at bringing other men to trial from a pretended zeal and interest about matters in which he really never had the smallest interest. And the truth of this I will endeavor to prove.

Come hither, Meletus, and let me ask a question of you. You think a great deal about the improvement of youth?

Yes, I do.

Tell the judges, then, who is their improver; for you must know, as you have taken the pains to discover their corrupter, and are citing and accusing me before them. Speak, then, and tell the judges who their improver is. Observe, Meletus, that you are silent, and have nothing to say. But is not this rather disgraceful, and a very considerable proof of what I was saying, that you have no interest in the matter? Speak up, friend, and tell us who their improver is.

The laws.

But that, my good sir, is not my meaning. I want to know who the person is, who, in the first place, knows the laws.

The judges, Socrates, who are present in court.

What do you mean to say, Meletus, that they are able to instruct and improve youth?

Certainly they are.

What, all of them, or some only and not others?

All of them.

By the goddess Here, that is good news! There are plenty of improvers, then. And what do you say of the audience – do they improve them?

Yes, they do.

And the Senators?

Yes, the Senators improve them.

But perhaps the ecclesiasts corrupt them? – or do they too improve them?

They improve them.

Then every Athenian improves and elevates them; all with the exception of myself; and I alone am their corrupter? Is that what you affirm?

That is what I stoutly affirm.

I am very unfortunate if that is true. But suppose I ask you a question: Would you say that this also holds true in the case of horses? Does one man do them harm and all the world good? Is not the exact opposite of this true? One man is able to do them good, or at least not many; the trainer of horses, that is to say, does them good, and others who have to do with them rather injure them? Is not that true, Meletus, of horses, or any other animals? Yes, certainly. Whether you and Anytus say yes or no, that is no matter. Happy indeed would be the condition of youth if they had one corrupter only, and all the rest of the world were their improvers. And you, Meletus, have sufficiently shown that you never had a thought about the young: your carelessness is seen in your not caring about matters spoken of in this very indictment.

And now, Meletus, I must ask you another question: Which is better, to live among bad citizens, or among good ones? Answer, friend, I say; for that is a question which may be easily answered. Do not the good do their neighbors good, and the bad do them evil?

Certainly.

And is there anyone who would rather be injured than benefited by those who live with him? Answer, my good friend; the law requires you to answer – does anyone like to be injured?

Certainly not.

And when you accuse me of corrupting and deteriorating the youth, do you allege that I corrupt them intentionally or unintentionally?

Intentionally, I say.

But you have just admitted that the good do their neighbors good, and the evil do them evil. Now is that a truth which your superior wisdom has recognized thus early in life, and am I, at my age, in such darkness and ignorance as not to know that if a man with whom I have to live is corrupted by me, I am very likely to be harmed by him, and yet I corrupt him, and intentionally, too? that is what you are saying, and of that you will never persuade me or any other human being. But either I do not corrupt them, or I corrupt them unintentionally, so that on either view of the case you lie. If my offense is unintentional, the law has no cognizance of unintentional offenses: you ought to have taken me privately, and warned and admonished me; for if I had been better advised, I should have left off doing what I only did unintentionally—no doubt I should; whereas you hated to converse with me or teach me, but you indicted me in this court, which is a place not of instruction, but of punishment.

I have shown, Athenians, as I was saying, that Meletus has no care at all, great or small, about the matter. But still I should like to know, Meletus, in what I am affirmed to corrupt the young. I suppose you mean, as I infer from your indictment, that I teach them not to acknowledge the gods which the state acknowledges, but some other new divinities or spiritual agencies in their stead. These are the lessons which corrupt the youth, as you say.

Yes, that I say emphatically.

Then, by the gods, Meletus, of whom we are speaking, tell me and the court, in somewhat plainer terms, what you mean! for I do not as yet understand whether you affirm that I teach others to acknowledge some gods, and therefore do believe in gods and am not an entire atheist—this you do not lay to my charge; but only that they are not the same gods which the city recognizes—the charge is that they are different gods. Or, do you mean to say that I am an atheist simply, and a teacher of atheism?

I mean the latter—that you are a complete atheist.

That is an extraordinary statement, Meletus. Why do you say that? Do you mean that I do not believe in the godhead of the sun or moon, which is the common creed of all men?

I assure you, judges, that he does not believe in them; for he says that the sun is stone, and the moon earth.

Friend Meletus, you think that you are accusing Anaxagoras; and you have but a bad opinion of the judges, if you fancy them ignorant to such a degree as not to know that these doctrines are found in the books of Anaxagoras the Clazomenian, who is full of them. And these are the doctrines which the youth are said to learn of Socrates, when there are not unfrequently exhibitions of them at the theater (price of admission one drachma at the most); and they might cheaply purchase them, and laugh at Socrates if he pretends to father such eccentricities. And so, Meletus, you really think that I do not believe in any god?

I swear by Zeus that you believe absolutely in none at all.

You are a liar, Meletus, not believed even by yourself. For I cannot help thinking, O men of Athens, that Meletus is reckless and impudent, and that he has written this indictment in a spirit of mere wantonness and youthful bravado. Has he not compounded a riddle, thinking to try me? He said to himself:—I shall see whether this wise Socrates will discover my ingenious contradiction, or whether I shall be able to deceive him and the rest of them. For he certainly does appear to me to contradict himself in the indictment as much as if he said that Socrates is guilty of not believing in the gods, and yet of believing in them—but this surely is a piece of fun.

I should like you, O men of Athens, to join me in examining what I conceive to be his inconsistency; and do you, Meletus, answer. And I must remind you that you are not to interrupt me if I speak in my accustomed manner.

Did ever man, Meletus, believe in the existence of human things, and not of human beings? . . . I wish, men of Athens, that he would answer, and not be always trying to get up an interruption. Did ever any man believe in horsemanship, and not in horses? or in flute-playing and not in flute-players? No, my friend; I will answer to you and to the court, as you refuse to answer for yourself. There is no man who ever did. But now please to answer the next question: Can a man believe in spiritual and divine agencies, and not in spirits or demigods?

He cannot.

I am glad that I have extracted that answer, by the assistance of the court; nevertheless you swear in the indictment that I teach and believe in divine or spiritual agencies (new or old, no matter for that); at any rate, I believe in spiritual agencies, as you say and swear in the affidavit; but if I believe in divine beings, I must believe in spirits or demigods; is not that true? Yes, that is true, for I may assume that your silence gives assent to that. Now what are spirits or demigods? are they not either gods or the sons of gods? Is that true?

Yes, that is true.

But this is just the ingenious riddle of which I was speaking: the demigods or spirits are gods, and you say first that I don't believe in gods, and then again that I do believe in gods; that is, if I believe in demigods. For if the demigods are the illegitimate sons of gods, whether by the nymphs or by any other mothers, as is thought, that, as all men will allow, necessarily implies the existence of their parents. You might as well affirm the existence of mules, and deny that of horses and asses. Such nonsense, Meletus, could only have been intended by you as a trial of me. You have put this into the indictment because you had nothing real of which to accuse me. But no one who has a particle of understanding will ever be convinced by you that the same man can believe in divine and superhuman things, and yet not believe that there are gods and demigods and heroes.

I have said enough in answer to the charge of Meletus: any elaborate defense is unnecessary; but as I was saying before, I certainly have many enemies, and this is what will be my destruction if I am destroyed; of that I am certain; not Meletus, nor yet Anytus, but the envy and detraction of the world, which has been the death of many good men, and will probably be the death of many more; there is no danger of my being the last of them.

Someone will say: And are you not ashamed, Socrates, of a course of life which is likely to bring you to an untimely end? To him I may fairly answer: There you are mistaken: a man who is good for anything ought not to calculate the chance of living or dying; he ought only to consider whether in doing anything he is doing right or wrong — acting the part of a good man or of a bad. Whereas, according to your view, the heroes who fell at Troy were not good for much, and the son of Thetis above all, who altogether despised danger in comparison with disgrace; and when his goddess mother said to him, in his eagerness to slay Hector, that if he avenged his companion Patroclus, and slew Hector, he would die himself — "Fate," as she said, "waits upon you next after Hector"; he, hearing this, utterly despised danger and death, and instead of fearing them, feared rather to live in dishonor, and not to avenge his friend. "Let me die next," he replies, "and be avenged of my enemy, rather than abide here by the beaked ships, a scorn and a burden of the earth." Had Achilles any thought of death and danger? For wherever a man's place is, whether the place which he has chosen or that in which he has been placed by a commander, there he ought to remain in the hour of danger; he should not think of death or of anything, but of disgrace. And this, O men of Athens, is a true saying.

Strange, indeed, would be my conduct, O men of Athens, if I who, when I was ordered by the generals whom you chose to command me at Potidæa and Amphipolis and Delium, remained where they placed me, like any other man, facing death — if, I say, now, when, as I conceive and imagine, God orders me to fulfill the philosopher's mission of searching into myself and other men, I were to desert my post through fear of death, or any other fear; that would indeed be strange, and I might justly be arraigned in court for denying the existence of the gods, if I disobeyed the oracle because I was afraid of death: then I should be fancying that I was wise when I was not wise. For this fear of death is indeed the pretense of wisdom, and not real wisdom, being the appearance of knowing the unknown; since no one knows whether death, which they in their fear apprehend to be the greatest evil, may not be the greatest good. Is there not here conceit of knowledge, which is a disgraceful sort of ignorance? And this is the point in which, as I think, I am superior to men in general, and in which I might perhaps fancy myself wiser than other men — that whereas I know but little of the world below, I do not suppose that I know: but I do know that injustice and disobedience to a better, whether God or man, is evil and dishonorable, and I will never fear or avoid a possible good rather than a certain evil. And therefore if you let me go now, and reject the counsels of Anytus, who said that if I were not put to death I ought not to have been prosecuted, and that if I escape now, your sons will all be utterly ruined by listening to my words — if you say to me, Socrates, this time we will not mind Anytus, and will let you off, but upon one condition, that you are not to inquire and speculate in this way any more, and that if you are caught doing this again you shall die — if this was the condition on which you let me go, I should reply: Men of Athens, I honor and love you; but I shall obey God rather than you, and while I have life and strength I shall never cease from the practice and teaching of philosophy, exhorting anyone whom I meet after my manner, and convincing him, saying: O my friend, why do you who are a citizen of the great and mighty and wise city of Athens, care so much about laying up the greatest amount of money and honor and reputation, and so little about wisdom and truth and the greatest improvement of the soul, which you never regard or heed at all? Are you not ashamed of this? And if the person with whom I am arguing says: Yes, but I do care; I do not depart or let him go at once; I interrogate and examine and cross-examine him, and if I think that he has no virtue, but only says that he has, I reproach him with undervaluing the greater, and overvaluing the less. And this I should say to everyone whom I meet, young and old, citizen and alien, but especially to the citizens, inasmuch as they are my brethren. For this is the command of God, as I would have you know; and I believe that to this day no greater good has ever happened in the state than my service to the God. For I do nothing but go about persuading you all, old and young alike, not to take thought for your persons and your properties, but first and chiefly to care about the greatest improvement of the soul. I tell you that virtue is not given by money, but that from virtue come money and every other good of man, public as well as private. This is my teaching, and if this is the doctrine which corrupts the youth, my influence is ruinous indeed. But if anyone says that this is not my teaching, he is speaking an untruth. Wherefore, O men of Athens, I say to you, do as Anytus bids or not as Anytus bids, and either acquit me or not; but whatever you do, know that I shall never alter my ways, not even if I have to die many times.

Men of Athens, do not interrupt, but hear me; there was an agreement between us that you should hear me out. And I think that what I am going to say will do you good: for I have something more to say, at which you may be inclined to cry out; but I beg that you will not do this. I would have you know that, if you kill such an one as I am, you will injure yourselves more than you will injure me. Meletus and Anytus will not injure me: they cannot; for it is not in the nature of things that a bad man should injure a better than himself. I do not deny that he may, perhaps, kill him, or drive him into exile, or deprive him of civil rights; and he may imagine, and others may imagine, that he is doing him a great injury: but in that I do not agree with him; for the evil of doing as Anytus is doing — of unjustly taking away another man's life — is greater far. And now, Athenians, I am not going to argue for my own sake, as you may think, but for yours, that you may not sin against the God, or lightly reject his boon by condemning me. For if you kill me you will not easily find another like me, who, if I may use such a ludicrous figure of speech, am a sort of gadfly, given to the state by the God; and the state is like a great and noble steed who is tardy in his motions owing to his very size, and requires to be stirred into life. I am that gadfly which God has given the state and all day long and in all places am always fastening upon you, arousing and persuading and reproaching you. And as you will not easily find another like me, I would advise you to spare me. I dare say that you may feel irritated at being suddenly awakened when you are caught napping; and you may think that if you were to strike me dead, as Anytus advises, which you easily might, then you would sleep on for the remainder of your lives, unless God in his care of you gives you another gadfly. And that I am given to you by God is proved by this: that if I had been like other men, I should not have neglected all my own concerns, or patiently seen the neglect of them during all these years, and have been doing yours, coming to you individually, like a father or elder brother, exhorting you to regard virtue; this, I say, would not be like human nature. And had I gained anything, or if my exhortations had been paid, there would have been some sense in that: but now, as you will perceive, not even the impudence of my accusers dares to say that I have ever exacted or sought pay of anyone; they have no witness of that. And I have a witness of the truth of what I say; my poverty is a sufficient witness.

Someone may wonder why I go about in private, giving advice and busying myself with the concerns of others, but do not venture to come forward in public and advise the state. I will tell you the reason of this. You have often heard me speak of an oracle or sign which comes to me, and is the divinity which Meletus ridicules in the indictment. This sign I have had ever since I was a child. The sign is a voice which comes to me and always forbids me to do something which I am going to do, but never commands me to do anything, and this is what stands in the way of my being a politician. And rightly, as I think. For I am certain, O men of Athens, that if I had engaged in politics, I should have perished long ago and done no good either to you or to myself. And don't be offended at my telling you the truth: for the truth is that no man who goes to war with you or any other multitude, honestly struggling against the commission of unrighteousness and wrong in the state, will save his life; he who will really fight for the right, if he would live even for a little while, must have a private station and not a public one.

I can give you as proofs of this, not words only, but deeds, which you value more than words. Let me tell you a passage of my own life, which will prove to you that I should never have yielded to injustice from any fear of death, and that if I had not yielded I should have died at once. I will tell you a story — tasteless, perhaps, and commonplace, but nevertheless true. The only office of state which I ever held, O men of Athens, was that of senator; the tribe of Antiochis, which is my tribe, had the presidency at the trial of the generals who had not taken up the bodies of the slain after the battle of Arginusæ; and you proposed to try them all together, which was illegal, as you all thought afterwards; but at the time I was the only one of the Prytanes who was opposed to the illegality, and I gave my vote against you; and when the orators threatened to impeach and arrest me, and have me taken away, and you called and shouted, I made up my mind that I would run the risk, having law and justice with me, rather than take part in your injustice because I feared imprisonment and death. This happened in the days of the democracy. But when the oligarchy of the Thirty was in power, they sent for me and four others into the rotunda, and bade us bring Leon the Salaminian from Salamis, as they wanted to execute him. This was a specimen of the sort of commands which they were always giving with the view of implicating as many as possible in their crimes; and then I showed, not in words only, but in deed, that, if I may be allowed to use such an expression, I cared not a straw for death, and that my only fear was the fear of doing an unrighteous or unholy thing. For the strong arm of that oppressive power did not frighten me into doing wrong; and when we came out of the rotunda the other four went to Salamis and fetched Leon, but I went quietly home. For which I might have lost my life, had not the power of the Thirty shortly afterwards come to an end. And to this many will witness.

Now do you really imagine that I could have survived all these years, if I had led a public life, supposing that like a good man I had always supported the right and had made justice, as I ought, the first thing? No, indeed, men of Athens, neither I nor any other. But if I have been always the same in all my actions, public as well as private, and never have I yielded any base compliance to those who are slanderously termed my disciples or to any other. For the truth is that I have no regular disciples: but if anyone likes to come and hear me while I am pursuing my mission, whether he be young or old, he may freely come. Nor do I converse with those who pay only, and not with those who do not pay; but anyone, whether he be rich or poor, may ask and answer me and listen to my words; and whether he turns out to be a bad man or a good one; that cannot be justly laid to my charge, as I never taught him anything. And if anyone says that he has ever learned or heard anything from me in private which all the world has not heard, I should like you to know that he is speaking an untruth.

But I shall be asked, Why do people delight in continually conversing with you? I have told you already, Athenians, the whole truth about this: they like to hear the cross examination of the pretenders to wisdom; there is amusement in this. And this is a duty which the God has imposed upon me, as I am assured by oracles, visions, and in every sort of way in which the will of divine power was ever signified to anyone. This is true, O Athenians; or, if not true, would be soon refuted. For if I am really corrupting the youth, and have corrupted some of them already, those of them who have grown up and have become sensible that I gave them bad advice in the days of their youth should come forward as accusers and take their revenge; and if they do not like to come themselves, some of their relatives, fathers, brothers, or other kinsmen, should say what evil their families suffered at my hands. Now is their time. Many of them I see in the court. There is Crito, who is of the same age and of the same *deme* with myself; and there is Critobulus his son, whom I also see. Then again there is Lysanias of Sphettus, who is the father of Æschines — he is present; and also there is Antiphon of Cephisus, who is the father of Epignes; and there are the brothers of several who have associated with me. There is Nicostratus the son of Theosdotides, and the brother of Theodotus (now Theodotus himself is dead, and therefore he, at any rate, will not seek to stop him); and there is Paralus the son of Demodocus, who had a brother Theages; and Adeimantus the son of Ariston, whose brother Plato is present; and Æantodorus, who is the brother of Apollodorus, whom I also see. I might mention a great many others, any of whom Meletus should have produced as witnesses in the course of his speech; and let him still produce them, if he has forgotten; I will make way for him. And let him say, if he has any testimony of the sort which he can produce. Nay, Athenians, the very opposite is the truth. For all these are ready to witness on behalf of the corrupter, of the destroyer of their kindred, as Meletus and Anytus call me; not the corrupted youth only – there might have been a motive for that – but their uncorrupted elder relatives. Why should they too support me with their testimony? Why, indeed, except for the sake of truth and justice, and because they know that I am speaking the truth, and that Meletus is lying.

Well, Athenians, this and the like of this is nearly all the defense which I have to offer. Yet a word more. Perhaps there may be someone who is offended at me, when he calls to mind how he himself, on a similar or even less serious occasion, had recourse to prayers and supplications with many tears, and how he produced his children in court, which was a moving spectacle, together with a posse of his relations and friends; whereas I, who am probably in danger of my life, will do none of these things. Perhaps this may come into his mind, and he may be set against me, and vote in anger because he is displeased at this. Now if there be such a person among you, which I am far from affirming, I may fairly reply to him: My friend, I am a man, and like other men, a creature of flesh and blood, and not of wood or stone, as Homer says; and I have a family, yes, and sons, O Athenians, three in number, one of whom is growing up, and the two others are still young; and yet I will not bring any of them hither in order to petition you for an acquittal. And why not? Not from any self-will or disregard of you. Whether I am or am not afraid of death is another question, of which I will not now speak. But my reason simply is that I feel such conduct to be discreditable to myself, and you, and the whole state. One who has reached my years, and who has a name for wisdom, whether deserved or not, ought not to debase himself. At any rate, the world has decided that Socrates is in some way superior to other men. And if those among you who are said to be superior in wisdom and courage, and any other virtue, demean themselves in this way, how shameful is their conduct! I have seen men of reputation, when they have been condemned, behaving in the strangest manner: they seemed to fancy that they were going to suffer something dreadful if they died, and that they could be immortal if you only allowed them to live; and I think that they were a dishonor to the state, and that any stranger coming in would say of them that the most eminent men of Athens, to whom the Athenians themselves give honor and command, are no better than women. And I say that these things ought not to be done by those of us who are of reputation; and if they are done, you ought not to permit them; you ought rather to show that you are more inclined to condemn, not the man who is quiet, but the man who gets up a doleful scene, and makes the city ridiculous.

But, setting aside the question of dishonor, there seems to be something wrong in petitioning a judge, and thus procuring an acquittal instead of informing and convincing him. For his duty is, not to make a present of justice, but to give judgment; and he has sworn that he will judge according to the laws, and not according to his own good pleasure; and neither he nor we should get into the habit of perjuring ourselves – there can be no piety in that. Do not then require me to do what I consider dishonorable and impious and wrong, especially now, when I am being tried for impiety on the indictment of Meletus. For if, O men of Athens, by force of persuasion and entreaty, I could overpower your oaths, then I should be teaching you to believe that there are no gods, and convict myself, in my own defense, of not believing in them. But that is not the case; for I do believe that there are gods, and in a far higher sense than that in which any of my accusers believe in them. And to you and to God I commit my cause, to be determined by you as is best for you and me.

There are many reasons why I am not grieved, O men of Athens, at the vote of condemnation. I expected this, and am only surprised that the votes are so nearly equal; for I had thought that the majority against me would have been far larger; but now, had thirty votes gone over to the other side, I should have been acquitted. And I may say that I have escaped Meletus. And I may say more; for without the assistance of Anytus and Lycon, he would not have had a fifth part of the votes, as the law requires, in which case he would have incurred a fine of a thousand drachmæ, as is evident.

And so he proposes death as the penalty. And what shall I propose on my part, O men of Athens? Clearly that which is my due. And what is that which I ought to pay or to receive? What shall be done to the man who has never had the wit to be idle during his whole life; but has been careless of what the many care about — wealth and family interests, and military offices, and speaking in the assembly, and magistracies, and plots, and parties. Reflecting that I was really too honest a man to follow in this way and live, I did not go where I could do no good to you or to myself; but where I could do the greatest good privately to every one of you, thither I went, and sought to persuade every man among you that he must look to himself, and seek virtue and wisdom before he looks to his private interests, and look to the state before he looks to the interests of the state; and that this should be the order which he observes in all his actions. What shall be done to such a one? Doubtless some good thing, O men of Athens, if he has his reward; and the good should be of a kind suitable to him. What would be a reward suitable to a poor man who is your benefactor, who desires leisure that he may instruct you? There can be no more fitting reward than maintenance in the Prytaneum, O men of Athens, a reward which he deserves far more than the citizen who has won the prize at Olympia in the horse or chariot race, whether the chariots were drawn by two horses or by many. For I am in want, and he has enough; and he only gives you the appearance of happiness, and I give you the reality. And if I am to estimate the penalty justly, I say that maintenance in the Prytaneum is the just return.

Perhaps you may think that I am braving you in saying this, as in what I said before about the tears and prayers. But that is not the case. I speak rather because I am convinced that I never intentionally wronged anyone, although I cannot convince you of that — for we have had a short conversation only; but if there were a law at Athens, such as there is in other cities, that a capital cause should not be decided in one day, then I believe that I should have convinced you; but now the time is too short. I cannot in a moment refute great slanders; and, as I am convinced that I never wronged another, I will assuredly not wrong myself. I will not say of myself that I deserve any evil, or propose any penalty. Why should I? Because I am afraid of the penalty of death which Meletus proposes? When I do not know whether death is a good or an evil, why should I propose a penalty which would certainly be an evil? Shall I say imprisonment? And why should I live in prison, and be the slave of the magistrates of the year — of the Eleven? Or shall the penalty be a fine, and imprisonment until the fine is paid? There is the same objection. I should have to lie in prison, for money I have none, and I cannot pay. And if I say exile (and this may possibly be the penalty which you will affix), I must indeed be blinded by the love of life if I were to consider that when you, who are my own citizens, cannot endure my discourses and words, and have found them so grievous and odious that you would fain have done with them, others are likely to endure me. No, indeed, men of Athens, that is not very likely. And what a life should I lead, at my age, wandering from city to city, living in ever-changing exile, and always being driven out! For I am quite sure that into whatever place I go, as here so also there, the young men will come to me; and if I drive them away, their elders will drive me out at their desire: and if I let them come, their fathers and friends will drive me out for their sakes.

Someone will say: Yes, Socrates, but cannot you hold your tongue, and then you may go into a foreign city, and no one will interfere with you? Now I have great difficulty in making you understand my answer to this. For if I tell you that this would be a disobedience to a divine command, and therefore that I cannot hold my tongue, you will not believe that I am serious; and if I say again that the greatest good of man is daily to converse about virtue, and all that concerning which you hear me examining myself and others, and that the life which is unexamined is not worth living – that you are still less likely to believe. And yet what I say is true, although a thing of which it is hard for me to persuade you. Moreover, I am not accustomed to think that I deserve any punishment. Had I money I might have proposed to give you what I had, and have been none the worse. But you see that I have none, and can only ask you to proportion the fine to my means. However, I think that I could afford a mina, and therefore, I propose that penalty: Plato, Crito, Critobulus, and Appolodorus, my friends here, bid me say thirty minæ, and they will be the sureties. Well then, say thirty minæ, let that be the penalty; for that they will be ample security to you.

Not much time will be gained, O Athenians, in return for the evil name which you will get from the detractors of the city, who will say that you killed Socrates, a wise man; for they will call me wise even although I am not wise when they want to reproach you. If you had waited a little while, your desire would have been fulfilled in the course of nature. For I am far advanced in years, as you may perceive and not far from death. I am speaking now only to those of you who have condemned me to death. And I have another thing to say to them: You think that I was convinced through deficiency of words – I mean, that if I had thought fit to leave nothing undone, nothing unsaid, I might have gained an acquittal. Not so; the deficiency which led to my conviction was not of words – certainly not. But I had not the boldness or impudence or inclination to address you, weeping and wailing and lamenting, and saying and doing many things which you have been accustomed to hear from others, and which, as I say, are unworthy of me. But I thought that I ought not to do anything common or mean in the hour of danger: nor do I now repent of the manner of my defense, and I would rather die having spoken after my manner, than speak in your manner and live. For neither in war nor yet at law ought any man to use every way of escaping death. For often in battle there is no doubt that if a man will throw away his arms, and fall on his knees before his pursuers, he may escape death; and in other dangers there are other ways of escaping death, if a man is willing to say and do anything. The difficulty, my friends, is not in avoiding death, but in avoiding unrighteousness; for that runs faster than death. I am old and move slowly, and the slower runner has overtaken me, and my accusers are keen and quick, and the faster runner, who is unrighteousness, has overtaken them. And now I depart hence condemned by you to suffer the penalty of death, and they, too, go their ways condemned by the truth to suffer the penalty of villainy and wrong; and I must abide by my award – let them abide by theirs. I suppose that these things may be regarded as fated – and I think that they are well.

And now, O men who have condemned me, I would fain prophesy to you; for I am about to die, and that is the hour in which men are gifted with prophetic power. And I prophesy to you who are my murderers, that immediately after my death punishment far heavier than you have inflicted on me will surely await you. Me you have killed because you wanted to escape the accuser, and not to give an account of your lives. But that will not be as you suppose: far otherwise. For I say that there will be more accusers of you than there are now; accusers whom hitherto I have restrained: and as they are younger they will be more severe with you, and you will be more offended at them. For if you think that by killing men you can avoid the accuser censuring your lives, you are mistaken; that is not a way of escape which is either possible or honorable; the easiest and noblest way is not to be crushing others, but to be improving yourselves. This is the prophecy which I utter before my departure, to the judges who have condemned me.

Friends, who would have acquitted me, I would like also to talk with you about this thing which has happened, while the magistrates are busy, and before I go to the place at which I must die. Stay then awhile, for we may as well talk with one another while there is time. You are my friends, and I should like to show you the meaning of this event which has happened to me. O my judges – for you I may truly call judges – I should like to tell you of a wonderful circumstance. Hitherto the familiar oracle within me has constantly been in the habit of opposing me even about trifles, if I was going to make a slip or error about anything; and now as you see there has come upon me that which may be thought, and is generally believed to be, the last and worst evil. But the oracle made no sign of opposition, either as I was leaving my house and going out in the morning, or when I was going up into this court, or while I was speaking, at anything which I was going to say; and yet I have often been stopped in the middle of a speech; but now in nothing I either said or did touching this matter has the oracle opposed me. What do I take to be the explanation of this? I will tell you. I regard this as a proof that what has happened to me is a good, and that those of us who think that death is an evil are in error. This is a great proof to me of what I am saying, for the customary sign would surely have opposed me had I been going to evil and not to good.

Let us reflect in another way, and we shall see that there is great reason to hope that death is a good, for one of two things: either death is a state of nothingness and utter unconsciousness, or, as men say, there is a change and migration of the soul from this world to another. Now if you suppose that there is no consciousness, but a sleep like the sleep of him who is undisturbed even by the sight of dreams, death will be an unspeakable gain. For if a person were to select the night in which his sleep was undisturbed even by dreams, and were to compare with this the other days and nights of his life, and then were to tell us how many days and nights he had passed in the course of his life better and more pleasantly than this one, I think that any man, I will not say a private man, but even the great king, will not find many such days or nights, when compared with the others. Now if death is like this, I say that to die, is gain; for eternity is then only a single night. But if death is the journey to another place, and there, as men say, all the dead are, what good, O my friends and judges, can be greater than this? If indeed when the pilgrim arrives in the world below, he is delivered from the professors of justice in this world, and finds the true judges who are said to give judgment there, Minos and Rhadamanthus and Æacus and Triptolemus, and other sons of God who were righteous in their own life, that pilgrimage will be worth making. What would not a man give if he might converse with Orpheus and Musæus and Hesiod and Homer? Nay, if this be true, let me die again and again. I, too, shall have a wonderful interest in a place where I can converse with Palamedes, and Ajax the son of Telamon, and other heroes of old, who have suffered death through an unjust judgment; and there will be no small pleasure, as I think, in comparing my own sufferings with theirs. Above all, I shall be able to continue my search into true and false knowledge; as in this world, so also in that; I shall find out who is wise, and who pretends to be wise, and is not. What would not a man give, O judges, to be able to examine the leader of the great Trojan expedition; or Odysseus or Sisyphus, or numberless others, men and women too! What infinite delight would there be in conversing with them and asking them questions! For in that world they do not put a man to death for this; certainly not. For besides being happier in that world than in this, they will be immortal, if what is said is true.

Wherefore, O judges, be of good cheer about death, and know this of a truth — that no evil can happen to a good man, either in life or after death. He and his are not neglected by the gods; nor has my own approaching end happened by mere chance. But I see clearly that to die and be released was better for me; and therefore the oracle gave no sign. For which reason also, I am not angry with my accusers, or my condemners; they have done me no harm, although neither of them meant to do me any good; and for this I may gently blame them.

Still I have a favor to ask of them. When my sons are grown up, I would ask you, O my friends, to punish them; and I would have you trouble them, as I have troubled you, if they seem to care about riches, or anything, more than about virtue; or if they pretend to be something when they are really nothing — then reprove them, as I have reproved you, for not caring about that for which they ought to care, and thinking that they are something when they are really nothing. And if you do this, I and my sons will have received justice at your hands.

The hour of departure has arrived, and we go our ways — I to die, and you to live. Which is better, God only knows.

FROM THE PHÆDO

When he had done speaking, Crito said: And have you any commands for us, Socrates — anything to say about your children, or any other matter in which we can serve you?

Nothing particular, Crito, he replied: only, as I have always told you, take care of yourselves; that is a service which you may be ever rendering to me and mine and to all of us, whether you promise to do so or not. But if you have no thought for yourselves, and care not to walk according to the rule which I have prescribed for you, not now for the first time, however much you may profess or promise at the moment, it will be of no avail.

We will do our best, said Crito: And in what way shall we bury you?

In any way that you like; but you must get hold of me, and take care that I do not run away from you. Then he turned to us, and added with a smile: — I cannot make Crito believe that I am the same Socrates who have been talking and conducting the argument; he fancies that I am the other Socrates whom he will soon see, a dead body — and he asks, How shall he bury me? And though I have spoken many words in the endeavor to show that when I have drunk the poison I shall leave you and go to the joys of the blessed, — these words of mine, with which I was comforting you and myself, have had, as I perceive, no effect upon Crito. And therefore I want you to be surety for me to him now, as at the trial he was surety to the judges for me; but let the promise be of another sort; for he was surety for me to the judges that I would remain, and you must be my surety to him that I shall not remain, but go away and depart; and then he will suffer less at my death, and not be grieved when he sees my body being burned or buried. I would not have him sorrow at my hard lot, or say at the burial, Thus we lay out Socrates, or, Thus we follow him to the grave or bury him; for false words are not only evil in themselves, but they infect the soul with evil. Be of good cheer then, my dear Crito, and say that you are burying my body only, and do with that whatever is usual, and what you think best.

When he had spoken these words, he arose and went into a chamber to bathe; Crito followed him and told us to wait. So we remained behind, talking and thinking of the subject of discourse, and also of the greatness of our sorrow; he was like a father of whom we were being bereaved, and we were about to pass the rest of our lives as orphans. When he had taken the bath his children were brought to him — (he had two young sons and an elder one); and the women of his family also came, and he talked to them and gave them a few directions in the presence of Crito; then he dismissed them and returned to us.

Now the hour of sunset was near, for a good deal of time had passed while he was within. When he came out, he sat down with us again after his bath, but not much was said. Soon the jailer, who was the servant of the Eleven, entered and stood by him, saying: — To you, Socrates, whom I know to be the noblest and gentlest and best of all who ever came to this place, I will not impute the angry feelings of other men, who rage and swear at me, when, in obedience to the authorities, I bid them drink the poison — indeed, I am sure that you will not be angry with me; for others, as you are aware, and not I, are to blame. And so fare you well, and try to bear lightly what must needs be — you know my errand. Then bursting into tears he turned away and went out.

Socrates looked at him and said: I return your good wishes, and will do as you bid. Then turning to us, he said, How charming the man is: since I have been in prison he has always been coming to see me, and at times he would talk to me, and was as good to me as could be, and now see how generously he sorrows on my account. We must do as he says, Crito; and therefore let the cup be brought, if the poison is prepared: if not, let the attendant prepare some.

Yet, said Crito, the sun is still upon the hill-tops, and I know that many a one has taken the draught late, and after the announcement has been made to him, he has eaten and drunk, and enjoyed the society of his beloved; do not hurry— there is time enough.

Socrates said: Yes, Crito, and they of whom you speak are right in so acting, for they think that they will be gainers by the delay; but I am right in not following their example, for I do not think that I should gain anything by drinking the poison a little later; I should only be ridiculous in my own eyes for sparing and saving a life which is already forfeit. Please then to do as I say, and not to refuse me.

Crito made a sign to the servant, who was standing by; and he went out, and having been absent for some time, returned with the jailer carrying the cup of poison. Socrates said: You, my good friend, who are experienced in these matters, shall give me directions how I am to proceed. The man answered: You have only to walk about until your legs are heavy, and then to lie down, and the poison will act. At the same time he handed the cup to Socrates, who in the easiest and gentlest manner, without the least fear or change of color or feature, looking at the man with all his eyes, Echecrates, as his manner was, took the cup and said: What do you say about making a libation out of this cup to any god? May I, or not? The man answered: We only prepare, Socrates, just so much as we deem enough. I understand, he said: but I may and must ask the gods to prosper my journey from this to the other world — even so — and so be it according to my prayer. Then raising the cup to his lips, quite readily and cheerfully he drank off the poison. And hitherto most of us had been able to control our sorrow; but now when we saw him drinking, and saw too that he had finished the draught, we could no longer forbear, and in spite of myself my own tears were flowing fast; so that I covered my face and wept, not for him, but at the thought of my own calamity in having to part from such a friend. Nor was I the first; for Crito, when he found himself unable to restrain his tears, had got up, and I followed; and at that moment, Apollodorus, who had been weeping all the time, broke out in a loud and passionate cry which made cowards of us all. Socrates alone retained his calmness: What is this strange outcry? he said. I sent away the women mainly in order that they might not misbehave in this way, for I have been told that a man should die in peace. Be quiet then, and have patience. When we heard his words we were ashamed, and refrained our tears; and he walked about until, as he said, his legs began to fail, and then he lay on his back, according to the directions, and the man who gave him the poison now and then looked at his feet and legs; and after a while he pressed his foot hard, and asked him if he could feel; and he said, No; and then his leg, and so upwards and upwards, and showed us that he was cold and stiff. And he felt them himself, and said: When the poison reaches the heart, that will be the end. He was beginning to grow cold about the groin, when he uncovered his face, for he had covered himself up, and said — they were his last words — he said: Crito, I owe a cock to Asclepius; will you remember to pay the debt? The debt shall be paid, said Crito; is there anything else? There was no answer to this question; but in a minute or two a movement was heard, and the attendants uncovered him; his eyes were set, and Crito closed his eyes and mouth.

Such was the end, Echecrates, of our friend; concerning whom I may truly say, that of all the men of his time whom I have known, he was the wisest and justest and best.

— From the Apology of Socrates and Phædo by Plato, Greek (c. 429–347 B.C.), translated by Benjamin Jowett.

~ ❂ ~

The Trial of Jesus

FROM THE APOCHRYPHAL NEW TESTAMENT

I

ANNAS AND CAIAPHAS, and Summas, and Datam, Gamaliel, Judas, Levi, Nephthalim, Alexander, Cyrus, and other Jews, went to Pilate about Jesus, accusing him with many bad crimes. And said, We are assured that Jesus is the son of Joseph the carpenter, and born of Mary, and that he declares himself the Son of God, and a king; and not only so, but attempts the dissolution of the Sabbath, and the laws of our fathers.

Pilate replied: What is it which he declares? and what is it which he attempts dissolving?

The Jews told him, We have a law which forbids doing cures on the sabbath day; but he cures both the lame and the deaf, those afflicted with the palsy, the blind, and lepers, and demoniacs, on that day by wicked methods.

Pilate replied, How can he do this by wicked methods? They answered, He is a conjuror, and casts out devils by the prince of devils; and so all things become subject to him.

Then said Pilate, Casting out devils seems not to be the work of an unclean spirit, but to proceed from the power of God.

The Jews replied to Pilate, We entreat your highness to summon him before your tribunal, and hear him yourself. Then Pilate called a messenger, and said to him, By what means will Christ be brought hither?

Then the messenger went forth, and knowing Christ, worshipped him; and having spread the cloak which he had in his hand upon the ground, he said, Lord, walk upon this, and go in, for the governor calls thee.

When the Jews perceived what the messenger had done, they exclaimed against him to Pilate, and said, Why did you not give him his summons by a beadle, and not by a messenger? – For the messenger, when he saw him, worshipped him, and spread the cloak which he had in his hand upon the ground before him, and said unto him, Lord, the governor calls thee.

Then Pilate called the messenger, and said, Why hast thou done thus? The messenger replied, When thou sentest me from Jerusalem to Alexander, I saw Jesus sitting in a mean figure upon a she-ass, and the children of the Hebrews cried out, Hosannah, holding boughs of trees in their hands. Others spread their garments in the way, and said Save us, thou who art in heaven; blessed is he who cometh in the name of the Lord. Then the Jews cried out against the messenger. . . .

Pilate then said to them, Why do you yourselves testify to the words spoken by the children, namely, by your silence? In what hath the messenger done amiss? And they were silent. Then the governor said unto the messenger, Go forth and endeavour by any means to bring him in. But the messenger went forth and did as before; and said, Lord, come in, for the governor calleth thee.

And as Jesus was going in by the ensigns, who carried the standards, the tops of them bowed down and worshipped Jesus. Whereupon the Jews exclaimed more vehemently against the ensigns. But Pilate said to the Jews, I know it is not pleasing to you that the tops of the standards did of themselves bow and worship Jesus; but why do ye exclaim against the ensigns, as if they had bowed and worshipped? They replied to Pilate, We saw the ensigns themselves bowing and worshipping Jesus. Then the governor called the ensigns and said unto them, Why did you do thus? The ensigns said to Pilate, We are all Pagans and worship the gods in temples; and how should we think anything about worshipping him? We only held the standards in our hands and they bowed themselves and worshipped him.

Then said Pilate to the rulers of the synagogue, Do ye yourselves choose some strong men, and let them hold the standards, and we shall see whether they will then bend of themselves. So the elders of the Jews sought out twelve of the most strong and able old men, and made them hold the standards and they stood in the presence of the governor.

Then Pilate said to the messenger, Take Jesus out, and by some means bring him in again. And Jesus and the messenger went out of the hall. . . .

Then the governor commanded Jesus to come in again . . . And when Jesus went in, the standards bowed themselves as before, and worshipped him.

II

Now when Pilate saw this, he was afraid, and was about to rise from his seat.

But while he thought to rise, his own wife who stood at a distance, sent to him, saying, Have thou nothing to do with that just man; for I have suffered much concerning him in a vision this night. When the Jews heard this they said to Pilate, Did we not say unto thee, he is a conjuror? Behold, he hath caused thy wife to dream.

Pilate then calling Jesus, said, thou hast heard what they testify against thee, and makest no answer? Jesus replied, If they had not a power of speaking, they could not have spoke; but because every one has the command of his own tongue, to speak both good and bad, let him look to it.

But the elders of the Jews answered, and said unto Jesus, What shall we look to? In the first place, we know concerning thee that thou wast born through fornication; secondly, that upon the account of thy birth the infants were slain in Bethlehem; thirdly, that thy father and mother fled into Egypt, because they could not trust their own people.

Some of the Jews who stood by spake more favourably, We cannot say that he was born of fornication; but we know that his mother Mary was betrothed to Joseph, and so he was not born through fornication . . .

Then said Anna and Caiaphas to Pilate, Those twelve men will not believe that we know him to be basely born, and to be a conjuror, although he pretends that he is the Son of God, and a king: which we are so far from believing, that we tremble to hear.

Then Pilate commanded every one to go out except the twelve men who said that he was not born through fornication, and Jesus to withdraw to a distance, and said to them, Why have the Jews a mind to kill Jesus?

They answered him, They are angry because he wrought cures on the sabbath day. Pilate said, Will they kill him for a good work? They said unto him, Yes, Sir.

III

Then Pilate, filled with anger, went out of the hall, and said to the Jews, I call the whole world to witness that I find no fault in this man. The Jews replied to Pilate, If he had not been a wicked person, we had not brought him before thee. Pilate said to them, Do ye take him and try him by your law. Then the Jews said, It is not lawful for us to put anyone to death. Pilate said to the Jews, The command, therefore, thou shalt not kill, belongs to you, but not to me.

And he went again into the hall, and called Jesus by himself, and said to him, Art thou the king of the Jews? And Jesus answering, said to Pilate, Dost thou speak this of thyself, or did the Jews tell it thee concerning me? Pilate answering, said to Jesus, Am I a Jew? The whole nation and rulers of the Jews have delivered thee up to me. What hast thou done? Jesus answering, said, My kingdom is not of this world: if my kingdom were of this world, then would my servants fight, and I should not have been delivered to the Jews; but now my kingdom is not from hence. Pilate said, Art thou a king then? Jesus answered, Thou sayest that I am a king: to this end was I born, and for this end came I into the world; for this purpose I came, that I should bear witness to the truth; and every one who is of the truth, heareth my voice.

Pilate saith to him, What is truth? Jesus said, Truth is from heaven. Pilate said, Therefore truth is not on earth. Jesus said to Pilate, Believe that truth is on earth among those who when they have the power of judgment, are governed by truth, and form right judgment.

IV

Then Pilate left Jesus in the hall, and went out to the Jews, and said, I find not any one fault in Jesus.

The Jews say unto him, But he said, I can destroy the temple of God, and in three days build it up again.

Pilate saith unto them, What sort of temple is that of which he speaketh? Then the Jews say unto him, That which Solomon was forty-six years in building, he said he would destroy, and in three days build up. Pilate said to them again, I am innocent from the blood of that man; do ye look to it. The Jews say to him, His blood be upon us and our children.

Then Pilate calling together the elders and scribes, priests and Levites, saith to them privately, Do not act thus; I have found nothing in your charge against him concerning his curing sick persons and breaking the sabbath, worthy of death.

The priests and Levites replied to Pilate, By the life of Caesar, if anyone be a blasphemer, he is worthy of death; but this man hath blasphemed against the Lord.

Then the governor again commanded the Jews to depart out of the hall; and calling Jesus, said to him, What shall I do with thee? Jesus answered him, Do according as it is written. Pilate said to him, How is it written? Jesus saith to him, Moses and the prophets have prophesied concerning my suffering and resurrection. The Jews hearing this, were provoked, and said to Pilate, Why wilt thou hear any longer the blasphemy of that man? Pilate saith to them, If these words seem to you blasphemy, do you take him, bring him to your court, and try him according to your law. The Jews reply to Pilate, Our law saith, he shall be obliged to receive nine and thirty stripes, but if after this manner he shall blaspheme against the Lord, he shall be stoned.

Pilate saith unto them, If that speech of his was blasphemy, destroy him according to your law. The Jews say unto Pilate, our law commands us not to put any one to death: we desire that he may be crucified, because he deserves the death of the cross. Pilate saith to them, It is not fit he should be crucified: let him only be whipped and sent away.

But when the governor looked upon the people that were present and the Jews, he saw many of the Jews in tears, and said to the chief priests of the Jews, All the people do not desire his death. The elders of the Jews answered to Pilate, We and all the people came hither for this very purpose, that he should die. Pilate saith to them, Why should he die? They said to him, Because he declares himself to be the Son of God, and a King.

V

But Nicodemus, a certain Jew, stood before the governor, and said, I entreat thee,

O righteous judge, that thou wouldst favour me with the liberty of speaking a few words. Pilate saith to him, Speak on.

Nicodemus said, I spake to the elders of the Jews, and the scribes, and priests, and Levites, and all the multitude of the Jews, in their assembly: What is it ye would do with this man? He is a man who hath wrought many useful and glorious miracles, such as no man on earth ever wrought before, nor will ever work. Let him go, and do him no harm; if he cometh from God, his miracles will continue; but if from men, they will come to nought. Thus Moses, when he was sent by God into Egypt, wrought the miracles which God commanded him, before Pharaoh king of Egypt; and though the magicians of that country, Jannes and Jambres, wrought by their magic the same miracles which Moses did, yet they could not work all which he did; and the miracles the magicians wrought, were not of God, as ye know, O scribes and Pharisees; but they who wrought them perished, and all who believed them. And now let this man go; because the very miracles for which ye accuse him, are from God; and he is not worthy of death.

The Jews then said to Nicodemus, Art thou become his disciple, and making speeches in his favour?

Nicodemus said to them, Is the governor become his disciple also, and does he make speeches for him? Did not Caesar place him in that high post?

When the Jews heard this they trembled, and gnashed their teeth at Nicodemus, and said to him, Mayest thou receive his doctrine for truth, and have thy lot with Christ! Nicodemus replied, Amen; I will receive his doctrine, and my lot with him, as ye have said.

Then another certain Jew rose up, and desired leave of the governor to hear him a few words. And the governor said Speak what thou hast a mind.

And he said, I lay for thirty-eight years by the sheep-pool at Jerusalem, labouring under a great infirmity, and waiting for a cure which should be wrought by the coming of an angel, who at a certain time troubled the water; and whosoever first after the troubling of the water stepped in, was made whole of whatsoever disease he had. And when Jesus saw me languishing there, he said to me, Wilt thou be made whole? And I answered, Sir, I have no man, when the water is troubled, to put me into the pool. And he said unto me, Rise, take up thy bed and walk. And I was immediately made whole, and took up my bed, and walked.

The Jews then said to Pilate, Our Lord Governor, pray ask him what day it was on which he was cured of his infirmity. The infirm person replied, It was on the sabbath. The Jews said to Pilate, Did we not say that he wrought his cures on the sabbath, and cast out devils by the prince of devils?

Then another Jew came forth, and said, I was born blind, could hear sounds, but could not see anyone; and as Jesus was going along, I heard the multitude passing by, and I asked what was there? They told me that Jesus was passing by: then I cried out saying, Jesus, Son of David, have mercy on me. And he stood still, and commanded that I should be brought to him, and said to me, What wilt thou? I said, Lord, that I may receive my sight. He said to me, receive thy sight: and presently I saw, and followed him, rejoicing and giving thanks.

Another Jew also came forth, and said, I was a leper, and he cured me by his word only, saying, I will, be thou clean; and presently I was cleansed from my leprosy. And another Jew came forth, and said, I was crooked, and he made me straight by his word.

And a certain woman named Veronica, said, I was afflicted with an issue of blood twelve years, and I touched the hem of his garment, and presently the issue of my blood stopped.

The Jews then said, We have a law that a woman shall not be allowed as an evidence. . . .

Besides these, also many others of the Jews, both men and women, cried out, and said, He is truly the Son of God, who cures all diseases only by his word, and to whom the devils are altogether subject. Some of them farther said, This power can proceed from none but God.

Pilate said to the Jews, Why are not the devils subject to your doctors? Some of them said, The power of subjecting devils cannot proceed but from God. But others said to Pilate, that he hath raised Lazarus from the dead, after he had been four days in the grave. The governor hearing this, trembling said to the multitude of the Jews, What will it profit you to shed innocent blood?

VI

Then Pilate having called together Nicodemus, and the fifteen men who said that Jesus was not born through fornication, said to them, What shall I do, seeing there is like to be a tumult among the people. They said unto him, we know not; let them look to it who raise the tumult. Pilate then called the multitude again, and said to them, Ye know that ye have a custom, that I should release to you one prisoner at the feast of the passover; I have a noted prisoner, a murderer, who is called Barabbas, and Jesus who is called Christ, in whom I find nothing that deserves death; which of them therefore have you in mind that I should release to you? They all cry out, and say, Release to us Barabbas.

Pilate saith to them, What then shall I do with Jesus who is called Christ? They all answer, Let him be crucified. Again they cry out and say to Pilate, You are not the friend of Caesar, if you release this man; for he hath declared that he is the Son of God, and a king. But are you inclined that he should be king, and not Caesar?

Then Pilate filled with anger said to them, Your nation hath always been seditious, and you are always against those who have been serviceable to you.

The Jews replied, Who are those who have been serviceable to us? Pilate answered them, Your God who delivered you from the hard bondage of the Egyptians, and brought you over the Red Sea as though it had been dry land, and fed you in the wilderness with manna and the flesh of quails, and brought water out of the rock, and gave you a law from heaven: ye provoked him all ways, and desired for yourselves a molten calf, and worshipped it, and sacrificed to it, and said, These are thy Gods, O Israel, which brought thee out of the land of Egypt! On account of which your God was inclined to destroy you; but Moses interceded for you, and your God heard him, and forgave your iniquity. Afterwards ye were enraged against, and would have killed, your prophets, Moses and Aaron, when they fled to the temple, and ye were always murmuring against God and his prophets.

And arising from his judgment seat, he would have gone out; but the Jews all cried out, We acknowledge Caesar to be king, and not Jesus. Whereas this person, as soon as he was born, the wise men came and offered gifts unto him; which when Herod heard, he was exceedingly troubled, and would have killed him. When his father knew this, he fled with him and his mother Mary into Egypt. Herod, when he heard that he was born, would have slain him; and accordingly sent and slew all the children which were in Bethlehem, and in all the coasts thereof, from two years old and under.

When Pilate heard this account, he was afraid; and commanding silence among the people who made a noise, he said to Jesus, Art thou therefore a king? And all the Jews replied to Pilate, he is the very person whom Herod sought to have slain.

Then Pilate, taking water, washed his hands before the people and said, I am innocent of the blood of this just person; look ye to it. Then Pilate, commanded Jesus to be brought before him, and spake to him in the following words:

Thy own nation hath charged thee as making thyself a king; wherefore I, Pilate, sentence thee to be whipped according to the laws of former governors; and that thou be first bound, then hanged upon a cross in that place where thou art now a prisoner; and also two criminals with thee, whose names are Dimas and Gestas.

. . .

(The omitted chapters describe the death of Jesus on the cross, the harrowing of Hell, and the resurrection.)

XXII

After these things Pilate went to the temple of the Jews, and called together all the rulers and scribes, and doctors of the law, and went with them into a chapter of the temple. And commanding that all the gates should be shut, said to them, I have heard that ye have a certain large book in this temple; I desire you, therefore, that it may be brought before me.

And when the great book, carried by four ministers of the temple, and adorned with gold and precious stones, was brought, Pilate said to them all, I adjure you by the God of your Fathers, who made and commanded this temple to be built, that ye conceal not the truth from me. Ye know all things which are written in that book; tell me therefore now, if ye in the Scriptures have found any thing of that Jesus whom ye have crucified, and at what time of the world he ought to have come: shew it to me.

Then having sworn Annas and Caiaphas, they commanded all the rest who were with them to go out of the chapel. And they shut the gates of the temple and of the chapel, and said to Pilate, Thou hast made us to swear, O judge, by the building of this temple, to declare to thee that which is true and right. After we had crucified Jesus, not knowing that he was the Son of God, but supposing that he wrought his miracles by some magical arts, we summoned a large assembly in this temple.

And when we were deliberating among one another about the miracles which Jesus had wrought, we found many witnesses of our own country, who declared that they had seen him alive after his death, and that they had heard him discoursing with his disciples, and saw him ascending unto the height of the heavens, and entering into them; and we saw two witnesses, whose bodies Jesus raised from the dead, who told us of many strange things which Jesus did among the dead, of which we have a written account in our hands.

And it is our custom annually to open this holy book before an assembly, and to search there for the counsel of God. And we found in the first of the seventy books, where Michael the archangel is speaking to the third son of Adam the first man, an account that after five thousand five hundred years, Christ the most beloved Son of God was to come on earth, and we further considered that perhaps he was the very God of Israel who spoke to Moses, Thou shalt make the ark of the testimony; two cubits and a half shall be the length thereof, and a cubit and a half the breadth thereof, and a cubit and a half the height thereof. By these five cubits and a half for the building of the ark of the Old Testament, we perceived and knew that in five thousand years and a half thousand years, Jesus Christ was to come in the ark or tabernacle of the body; and so our Scriptures testify that he is the Son of God, and the Lord and King of Israel.

And because after his suffering, our chief priests were surprised at the signs which were wrought by his means, we opened that book to search all the generations down to the generation of Joseph and Mary the mother of Jesus, supposing him to be of the seed of David; and we found the account of the creation, and at what time he made the heaven and the earth and the first man Adam, and that from thence to the flood, were two thousand, two hundred and twelve years. And from the flood to Abraham, nine hundred and twelve. And from Abraham to Moses, four hundred and thirty. And from Moses to David the king, five hundred and ten. And from David to the Babylonish captivity five hundred years. And from the Babylonish captivity to the incarnation of Christ, four hundred years. The sum of all which amounts to five and a half thousand.

And so it appears, that Jesus whom we crucified, is Jesus Christ the Son of God, and true and Almighty God. Amen.

— *From the Apocryphal Gospel of Nicodemus (circ. third century?), translated by William Hone.*

The Character of Caesar

THEODOR MOMMSEN

THE NEW monarch of Rome, the first ruler of the whole domain of Romano-Hellenic civilization, Gaius Julius Caesar, was in his fifty-sixth year (born 12th July, 652 A.U.C.) when the battle of Thapsus, the last link in a long chain of momentous victories, placed the decision of the future of the world in his hands. Few men have had their elasticity so thoroughly put to the proof as Caesar—the sole creative genius produced by Rome, and the last produced by the ancient world, which accordingly moved on in the track that he marked out for it until its sun had set. Sprung from one of the oldest noble families of Latium, which traced back its lineage to the heroes of the Iliad and the kings of Rome, and in fact to the Venus-Aphrodite common to both nations, he spent the years of his boyhood and early manhood as the genteel youth of that epoch were wont to spend them. He had tasted the sweetness as well as the bitterness of the cup of fashionable life, had recited and declaimed, had practiced literature and made verses in his idle hours, had prosecuted love intrigues of every sort, and got himself initiated into all the mysteries of shaving, curls, and ruffles pertaining to the toilette wisdom of the day, as well as into the far more mysterious art of always borrowing and never paying.

But the flexible steel of that nature was

proof against even these dissipated and flighty courses; Caesar retained both his bodily vigor and his elasticity of mind and heart unimpaired. In fencing and in riding he was a match for any of his soldiers, and at Alexandria his swimming saved his life; the incredible rapidity of his journeys, which usually were performed by night for the sake of gaining time — a thorough contrast to the procession-like slowness with which Pompeius moved from one place to another — was the astonishment of his contemporaries and not the least among the causes of his success. The mind was like the body. His remarkable power of intuition revealed itself in the precision and practicability of all his arrangements, even where he gave orders without having seen with his own eyes. His memory was matchless; and it was easy for him to carry on several occupations simultaneously with equal self-possession. Although a gentleman, a man of genius, and a monarch, he had still a heart. So long as he lived, he cherished the purest veneration for his worthy mother, Aurelia (his father having died early). To his wives, and above all to his daughter Julia, he devoted an honorable affection, which was not without reflex influence even on political affairs. With the ablest and most excellent men of his time, of high and of humble rank, he maintained noble relations of mutual fidelity, with each after his kind. As he himself never abandoned any of his partisans after the pusillanimous and unfeeling manner of Pompeius, but adhered to his friends — and that not merely from calculation — through good and bad times without wavering, several of these, such as Aulus Hirtius and Gaius Matius, even after his death gave noble testimonies of their attachment to him.

If in a nature so harmoniously organized there is any one trait to be singled out as characteristic, it is this: that he stood aloof from all ideology and everything fanciful. As a matter of course Caesar was a man of passion, for without passion there is no genius; but his passion was never stronger than he could control. He had had his season of youth, and song, love, and wine had taken joyous possession of his mind; but with him they did not penetrate to the inmost core of his nature. Literature occupied him long and earnestly; but while Alexander could not sleep for thinking of the Homeric Achilles, Caesar in his sleepless hours mused on the inflections of the Latin nouns and verbs. He made verses as everybody then did, but they were weak; on the other hand he was interested in subjects of astronomy and natural science. While wine was and continued to be with Alexander the destroyer of care, the temperate Roman, after the revels of his youth were over, avoided it entirely. Around him, as around all those whom the full luster of woman's love has dazzled in youth, fainter gleams of it continued imperishably to linger; even in later years he had his love adventures and successes with women, and he retained a certain foppishness in his outward appearance, or to speak more correctly, a pleasing consciousness of his own manly beauty. He carefully covered the baldness which he keenly felt with the laurel chaplet that he wore in public in his later years; and he would doubtless have surrendered some of his victories if he could thereby have brought back his youthful locks. But however much, even when monarch, he enjoyed the society of women, he only amused himself with them, and allowed them no manner of influence over him. Even his much-censured relation to Queen Cleopatra was only contrived to mask a weak point in his political position.

Caesar was thoroughly a realist and a man of sense; and whatever he undertook and achieved was pervaded, penetrated and guided by the cool sobriety which constitutes the most marked peculiarity of his genius. To this he owed the power of living energetically in the present, undisturbed either by recollection or by expectation; to this he owed the capacity of acting at any moment with collected vigor, and applying his whole genius even to the smallest and most incidental enterprise; to this he owed the many-sided power with which he grasped and mastered whatever understanding can comprehend and will can compel; to this he owed the self-possessed ease with which he arranged his periods as well as projected his campaigns; to this he owed the "marvelous serenity" which remained steadily with him through good and evil days; to this he owed the complete independence which admitted of no control by favorite or by mistress, or even by friend. It resulted, moreover, from this clearness of judgment that Caesar never formed to himself illusions regarding the power of fate and the ability of man; in his case the friendly veil was lifted up which conceals from man the inadequacy of his working. However prudently he planned and contemplated all possibilities, the feeling was never absent from his heart that in all things, fortune, that is to say accident, must bestow success; and with this may be connected the circumstance that he so often played a desperate game with destiny, and in particular again and again hazarded his person with daring indifference. As indeed occasionally men of predominant sagacity betake themselves to a pure game of hazard, so there was in Caesar's rationalism a point at which it came in some measure into contact with mysticism.

Gifts such as these could not fail to produce a statesman. From early youth, accordingly, Caesar was a statesman in the deepest sense of the term; and his aim was the highest which man is allowed to propose to himself— the political, military, intellectual, and moral regeneration of his own deeply decayed nation, and of the still more deeply decayed Hellenic nation intimately akin to his own. The hard school of thirty years' experience changed his views as to the means by which this aim was to be reached; his aim itself remained the same in the times of his hopeless humiliation and of his unlimited plenitude of power, in the times when as demagogue and conspirator he stole towards it by paths of darkness, and in those when, as joint possessor of the supreme power and then as monarch, he worked at his task in the full light of day before the eyes of the world. All the measures of a permanent kind that proceeded from him at the most various times assume their appropriate places in the great building-plan. We cannot therefore properly speak of isolated achievements of Caesar; nothing he did was isolated.

With justice men.commend Caesar the orator for his masculine eloquence, which, scorning all the arts of the advocate, like a clear flame at once enlightened and warmed. With justice men admire in Caesar the author the inimitable simplicity of the composition, the unique purity and beauty of the language. With justice the greatest masters of war of all times have praised Caesar the general, who, in a singular degree disregarding routine and tradition, knew always how to find out the mode of warfare by which in the given case the enemy was conquered, and which was consequently in the given case the right one; who, with the certainty of divination, found the proper means for every end; who after defeat stood ready for battle like William of Orange, and ended the campaign invariably with victory; who managed that element of warfare, the treatment of which serves to distinguish military genius from the mere ordinary ability of an officer — the rapid movement of masses — with unsurpassed perfection, and found the guarantee of victory not in the massiveness of his forces but in the celerity of their movements, not in long preparation but in rapid and bold action even with inadequate means. But all these were with Caesar mere secondary matters: he was no doubt a great orator, author, and general, but he became each of these merely because he was a consummate statesman.

The soldier more especially played in him altogether an accessory part; and it is one of the principal peculiarities by which he is distinguished from Alexander, Hannibal, and Napoleon, that he began his political activity not as an officer but as a demagogue. According to his original plan he had purposed to reach his object, like Pericles and Gaius Gracchus, without force of arms; and throughout eighteen years, as leader of the popular party, he had moved exclusively amid political plans and intrigues: until, reluctantly convinced of the necessity for a military support, he headed an army when he was already forty years of age. It was natural that even afterwards he should remain still more statesman than general; like Cromwell, who also transformed himself from a leader of opposition into a military chief and democratic king, and who, in general, little as the Puritan hero seems to resemble the dissolute Roman, is yet in his development, as well as in the objects which he aimed at and the results which he achieved, of all statesmen perhaps the most akin to Caesar. Even in his mode of warfare this improvised generalship may still be recognized; the enterprises of Napoleon against Egypt and against England do not more clearly exhibit the artillery lieutenant who had risen by service to command, than the similar enterprises of Caesar exhibit the demagogue metamorphosed into a general. A regularly trained officer would hardly have been prepared, through political considerations of a not altogether stringent nature, to set aside the best-founded military scruples in the way in which Caesar did on several occasions, most strikingly in the case of his landing in Epirus.

Several of his acts are therefore censurable from a military point of view; but what the general loses, the statesman gains. The task of the statesman is universal in its nature, like Caesar's genius; if he undertook things the most varied and most remote one from another, they had all, without exception, a bearing on the one great object to which with infinite fidelity and consistency he devoted himself; and he never preferred one to another of the manifold aspects and directions of his great activity. Although a master of the art of war, he yet from statesmanly considerations did his utmost to avert the civil strife and, when it nevertheless began, to keep his laurels from the stain of blood. Although the founder of a military monarchy, yet with an energy unexampled in history, he allowed no hierarchy of marshals or government of pretorians to come into existence. If he had a preference for any one form of services rendered to the state, it was for the sciences and arts of peace rather than for those of war.

The most remarkable peculiarity of his action as a statesman was its perfect harmony. In reality all the conditions for this most difficult of all human functions were united in Caesar. A thorough realist, he never allowed the images of the past or venerable tradition to disturb him; with him nothing was of value in politics but the living present and the law of reason; just as in grammar he set aside historical and antquarian research, and recognized nothing but on the one hand the living *usus loquendi* and on the other hand the rule of symmetry. A born ruler, he governed the minds of men as the wind drives the clouds, and compelled the most heterogeneous natures to place themselves at his service — the smooth citizen and the rough subaltern, the noble matrons of Rome, and the fair princesses of Egypt and Mauritania, the brilliant cavalry officer and the calculating banker. His talent for organization was marvelous. No statesman has ever compelled alliances, no general has ever collected an army out of unyielding and refractory elements, with such decision, and kept them together with such firmness, as Caesar displayed in constraining and upholding his coalitions and his legions. Never did regent judge his instruments and assign each to the place appropriate for him with so acute an eye.

He was monarch; but he never played the king. Even when absolute lord of Rome, he retained the deportment of the party leader; perfectly pliant and smooth, easy and charming in conversation, complaisant towards everyone, it seemed as if he wished to be nothing but the first among his peers.

Caesar entirely avoided the blunder of so many men otherwise on an equality with him, who have carried into politics the tone of military command; however much occasion his disagreeable relations with the Senate gave for it, he never resorted to outrages such as that of the eighteenth Brumaire. Caesar was monarch; but he was never seized with the giddiness of the tyrant. He is perhaps the only one among the mighty men of the earth who in great matters and little never acted according to inclination or caprice, but always without exception according to his duty as ruler; and who, when he looked back on his life, found doubtless erroneous calculations to deplore, but no false step of passion to regret. There is nothing in the history of Caesar's life which even on a small scale can be compared with those poetico-sensual ebullitions — such as the murder of Kleitos or the burning of Persepolis — which the history of his great predecessor in the East records. He is, in fine, perhaps the only one of those mighty men who has preserved to the end of his career the statesman's tact of discriminating between the possible and the impossible, and has not broken down in the task which for nobly gifted natures is the most difficult of all — the task of recognizing, when on the pinnacle of success, its natural limits. What was possible he performed; and never left the possible good undone for the sake of the impossible better, never disdained at least to mitigate by palliatives evils that were incurable. But where he recognized that fate had spoken, he always obeyed. Alexander on the Hyphasis, Napoleon at Moscow, turned back because they were compelled to do so, and were indignant at destiny for bestowing even on its favorites merely limited successes: Caesar turned back voluntarily on the Thames and on the Rhine; and at the Danube and the Euphrates thought not of unbounded plans of world-conquest, but merely of carrying into effect a well-considered regulation of the frontiers.

Such was this unique man, whom it seems so easy and yet is so infinitely difficult to describe. His whole nature is transparent clearness; and tradition preserves more copious and more vivid information regarding him than regarding any of his peers in the ancient world. Of such a person our conceptions may well vary in point of shallowness or depth, but strictly speaking they cannot be different; to every inquirer not utterly perverted, the grand figure has exhibited the same essential features and yet no one has succeeded in reproducing it to the life. The secret lies in its perfection. In his character as a man as well as in his place in history, Caesar occupies a position where the great contrasts of existence meet and balance each other. Of the mightiest creative power and yet at the same time of the most penetrating judgment; no longer a youth and not yet an old man; of the highest energy of will and the highest capacity of execution; filled with republican ideals and at the same time born to be a king; a Roman in the deepest essence of his nature, and yet called to reconcile and combine in himself as well as in the outer world the Roman and the Hellenic types of culture – Caesar was the entire and perfect man. Accordingly we miss in him more than in any other historical personage what are called characteristic features, which are in reality nothing else than deviations from the natural course of human development. What in Caesar passes for such at the first superficial glance is, when more closely observed, seen to be the peculiarity not of the individual but of the epoch of culture or of the nation: his youthful adventures, for instance, were common to him as to all his more gifted contemporaries of like position; his unpoetical but strongly logical temperament was the temperament of Romans in general.

It formed part also of Caesar's full humanity that he was in the highest degree influenced by the conditions of time and place; for there is no abstract humanity – the living man cannot but occupy a place in a given nationality and in a definite line of culture. Caesar was a perfect man just because more than any other he placed himself amidst the currents of his time, and because more than any other he possessed the essential peculiarity of the Roman nation – practical aptitude as a citizen – in perfection; for his Hellenism in fact was only the Hellenism which had been long intimately blended with the Italian nationality. But in this very circumstance lies the difficulty, we may perhaps say the impossibility, of depicting Caesar to the life. As the artist can paint everything save only consummate beauty, so the historian, when once in a thousand years he encounters the perfect, can only be silent regarding it. For normality admits doubtless of being expressed, but it gives us only the negative notion of the absence of defect; the secret of nature, whereby in her most finished manifestations normality and individuality are combined, is beyond expression.

Nothing is left us but to deem those fortunate who beheld this perfection, and to gain some faint conception of it from the reflected luster which rests imperishably on the works that were the creation of this great nature. These also, it is true, bear the stamp of the time. The Roman hero himself stood by the side of his youthful Greek predecessor, not merely as an equal but as a superior; but the world had meanwhile become old and its youthful luster had faded. The action of Caesar was no longer, like that of Alexander, a joyous marching onward towards a goal indefinitely remote: he built on and out of ruins, and was content to establish himself as tolerably and as securely as possible within the ample but yet definite bounds once assigned to him. With reason, therefore, the delicate poetic tact of the nations has not troubled itself about the unpoetical Roman, and has invested the son of Philip alone with all the golden luster of poetry, with all the rainbow hues of legend. But with equal reason the political life of nations has during thousands of years again and again reverted to the lines which Caesar drew; and the fact that the people to whom the world belongs still at the present day designate the highest of their monarchs by his name, conveys a warning deeply significant and, unhappily, fraught with shame.

—*From The History of Rome by Theodor Mommsen, German (1817–1903), translated by W. P. Dickson.*

The Defeat of the Armada

JAMES ANTHONY FROUDE

IN THE GALLERY at Madrid there is a picture, painted by Titian, representing the Genius of Spain coming to the delivery of the afflicted of Christ. Titian was dead, but the temper of the age survived, and in the study of that great picture you will see the spirit in which the Spanish nation had set out for the conquest of England. The scene is the seashore. The Church a naked Andromeda, with dishevelled hair, fastened to the trunk of an ancient disbranched tree. The cross lies at her feet, the cup overturned, the serpents of heresy biting at her from behind with uplifted crests. Coming on before a leading breeze is the sea monster, the Moslem fleet, eager for their prey; while in front is Perseus, the Genius of Spain, banner in hand, with the legions of the faithful laying not raiment before him, but shield and helmet, the apparel of war for the Lady of Nations to clothe herself with strength and smite her foes.

In the Armada the crusading enthusiasm had reached its point and focus. England was the stake to which the Virgin, the daughter of Sion, was bound in captivity. Perseus had come at last in the person of the Duke of Medina Sidonia, and with him all that was best and brightest in the countrymen of Cervantes, to break her bonds and replace her on her throne. They had sailed into the Channel in pious hope, with the blessed banner waving over their heads.

To be the executor of the decrees of Providence is a lofty ambition, but men in a state of high emotion overlook the precautions which are not to be dispensed with even on the sublimest of errands. Don Quixote, when he set out to redress the wrongs of humanity, forgot that a change of linen might be necessary, and that he must take money with him to pay his hotel bills. Philip II, in sending the Armada to England, and confident in supernatural protection, imagined an unresisted triumphal procession. He forgot that contractors might be rascals, that water four months in the casks in a hot climate turned putrid, and that putrid water would poison his ships' companies, though his crews were companies of angels. He forgot that the servants of the evil one might fight for their mistress after all, and that he must send adequate supplies of powder, and, worst forgetfulness of all, that a great naval expedition required a leader who understood his business. Perseus, in the shape of the Duke of Medina Sidonia, after a week of disastrous battles, found himself at the end of it in an exposed roadstead, where he ought never to have been, nine-tenths of his provisions thrown overboard as unfit for food, his ammunition exhausted by the unforeseen demands upon it, the seamen and soldiers harassed and dispirited, officers the whole week without sleep, and the enemy, who had hunted him from Plymouth to Calais, anchored within half a league of him.

Still, after all his misadventures, he had brought the fleet, if not to the North Foreland, yet within a few miles of it, and to outward appearance not materially injured. Two of the galleons had been taken; a third, the *Santa Aña,* had strayed; and his galleys had left him, being found too weak for the Channel sea; but the great armament had reached its destination substantially uninjured so far as English eyes could see. Hundreds of men had been killed and hundreds more wounded, and the spirit of the rest had been shaken. But the loss of life could only be conjectured on board the English fleet. The English admiral could only see that the Duke was now in touch with Parma. Parma, they knew, had an army at Dunkirk with him, which was to cross to England. He had been collecting men, barges, and transports all the winter and spring, and the backward state of Parma's preparations could not be anticipated, still less relied upon. The Calais anchorage was unsafe; but at that season of the year, especially after a wet summer, the weather usually settled; and to attack the Spaniards in a French port might be dangerous for many reasons. It was uncertain after the day of the Barricades whether the Duke of Guise or Henry of Valois was master of France, and a violation of the neutrality laws might easily at that moment bring Guise and France into the field on the Spaniards' side. It was, no doubt, with some such expectation that the Duke and his advisers had chosen Calais as the point at which to bring up. It was now Saturday, the 7th of August. The governor of the town came off in the evening to the *San Martin.* He expressed surprise to see the Spanish fleet in so exposed a position, but he was profuse in his offers of service. Anything which the

Duke required should be provided, especially every facility for communicating with Dunkirk and Parma. The Duke thanked him, said that he supposed Parma to be already embarked with his troops, ready for the passage, and that his own stay in the roads would be but brief. On Monday morning at latest he expected that the attempt to cross would be made. The governor took his leave, and the Duke, relieved from his anxieties, was left to a peaceful night. He was disturbed on the Sunday morning by an express from Parma informing him that, so far from being embarked, the army could not be ready for a fortnight. The barges were not in condition for sea. The troops were in camp. The arms and stores were on the quays at Dunkirk. As for the fly-boats and ammunition which the Duke had asked for, he had none to spare. He had himself looked to be supplied from the Armada. He promised to use his best expedition, but the Duke, meanwhile, must see to the safety of the fleet.

Unwelcome news to a harassed landsman thrust into the position of an admiral and eager to be rid of his responsibilities. If by evil fortune the northwester should come down upon him, with the shoals and sandbanks close under his lee, he would be in a bad way. Nor was the view behind him calculated for comfort. There lay the enemy almost within gunshot, who, though scarcely more than half his numbers, had hunted him like a pack of blood-hounds, and, worse than all, in double strength; for the Thames squadron — three Queen's ships and thirty London adventurers — under Lord H. Seymour and Sir John Hawkins, had crossed in the night. There they were between him and Cape Grisnez, and the reinforcements meant plainly enough that mischief was in the wind.

After a week so trying the Spanish crews would have been glad of a Sunday's rest if they could have had it; but the rough handling which they had gone through had thrown everything into disorder. The sick and wounded had to be cared for, torn rigging looked to, splintered timbers mended, decks scoured, and guns and arms cleaned up and put to rights. And so it was that no rest could be allowed; so much had to be done, and so busy was everyone, that the usual rations were not served out and the Sunday was kept as a fast. In the afternoon the stewards went ashore for fresh meat and vegetables. They came back with their boats loaded, and the prospect seemed a little less gloomy. Suddenly, as the Duke and a group of officers were watching the English fleet from the *San Martin's* poop deck, a small smart pinnace, carrying a gun in her bow, shot out from Howard's lines, bore down on the *San Martin,* sailed round her, sending in a shot or two as she passed, and went off unhurt. The Spanish officers could not help admiring such airy impertinence. Hugh de Monçada sent a ball after the pinnace, which went through her mainsail, but did no damage, and the pinnace again disappeared behind the English ships.

So a Spanish officer describes the scene. The English story says nothing of the pinnace; but she doubtless came and went as the Spaniard says, and for sufficient purpose. The English, too, were in straits, though the Duke did not dream of it. You will remember that the last supplies which the Queen had allowed to the fleet had been issued in the middle of June. They were to serve for a month, and the contractors were forbidden to prepare more. The Queen had clung to her hope that her differences with Philip were to be settled by the Commission at Ostend; and she feared that if Drake and Howard were too well furnished they would venture some fresh rash stroke on the coast of Spain, which might mar the negotiations. Their month's provisions had been stretched to serve for six weeks, and when the Armada appeared but two full days' rations remained. On these they had fought their way up Channel. Something had been brought out by private exertion on the Dorsetshire coast, and Seymour had, perhaps, brought a little more. But they were still in extremity. The contractors had warned the Government that they could provide nothing without notice, and notice had not been given. The adventurers were in better state, having been equipped by private owners. But the Queen's ships in a day or two more must either go home or their crews would be starving. They had been on reduced rations for near two months. Worse than that, they were still poisoned by the sour beer. The Queen had changed her mind so often, now ordering the fleet to prepare for sea, then recalling her instructions and paying off the men, that those whom Howard had with him had been enlisted in haste, had come on board as they were, and their clothes were hanging in rags on them. The fighting and the sight of the flying Spaniards were meat and drink, and clothing too, and had made them careless of all else. There was no fear of mutiny; but there was a limit to the toughest endurance. If the Armada was left undisturbed a long struggle might be still before them. The enemy would recover from its flurry, and Parma would come out from Dunkirk. To attack them directly in French waters might lead to perilous complications, while delay meant famine. The Spanish fleet had to be started from the roads in some way. Done it must be, and done immediately.

Then, on that same Sunday afternoon a memorable council of war was held in the *Ark's* main cabin. Howard, Drake, Seymour, Hawkins, Martin Frobisher, and two or three others met to consult, knowing that on them at that moment the liberties of England were depending. Their resolution was taken promptly. There was no time for talk. After nightfall a strong flood tide would be setting up along shore to the Spanish anchorage. They would try what could be done with fire ships, and the excursion of the pinnace, which was taken for bravado, was probably for a survey of the Armada's exact position. Meantime eight useless vessels were coated with pitch — hulls, spars, and rigging. Pitch was poured on the decks and over the sides, and parties were told off to steer them to their destination and then fire and leave them.

The hours stole on, and twilight passed into dark. The night was without a moon. The Duke paced his deck late with uneasy sense of danger. He observed lights moving up and down the English lines, and imagining that the *endemoniada gente* — the infernal devils — might be up to mischief, ordered a sharp look-out. A faint westerly air was curling the water, and towards midnight the watchers on board the galleons made out dimly several ships which seemed to be drifting down upon them. Their experience since the action off Plymouth had been so strange and unlooked for that anything unintelligible which the English did was alarming.

The phantom forms drew nearer, and were almost among them when they broke into a blaze from water-line to truck, and the two fleets were seen by the lurid light of the conflagration; the anchorage, the walls and windows of Calais, and the sea shining red far as eye could reach, as if the ocean itself was burning. Among the dangers which they might have to encounter, English fireworks had been especially dreaded by the Spaniards. Fire ships — a fit device of heretics — had worked havoc among the Spanish troops, when the bridge was blown up, at Antwerp. They imagined that similar infernal machines were approaching the Armada. A capable commander would have sent a few launches to grapple the burning hulks, which of course were now deserted, and tow them out of harm's way. Spanish sailors were not cowards, and would not have flinched from duty because it might be dangerous; but the Duke and Diego Florez lost their heads again. A signal gun from the *San Martin* ordered the whole fleet to slip their cables and stand out to sea.

Orders given in panic are doubly unwise, for they spread the terror in which they originate. The danger from the fire ships was chiefly from the effect on the imagination, for they appear to have drifted by and done no real injury. And it speaks well for the seamanship and courage of the Spaniards that they were able, crowded together as they were, at midnight and in sudden alarm to set their canvas and clear out without running into one another. They buoyed their cables, expecting to return for them at daylight, and with only a single accident, to be mentioned directly, they executed successfully a really difficult manoeuvre.

The Duke was delighted with himself. The fire ships burned harmlessly out. He had baffled the inventions of the *endemoniada gente*. He brought up a league outside the harbour, and supposed that the whole Armada had done the same. Unluckily for himself, he found it at daylight divided into two bodies. The *San Martin* with forty of the best appointed of the galleons were riding together at their anchors. The rest, two-thirds of the whole, having no second anchors ready, and inexperienced in Channel tides and currents, had been lying to. The west wind was blowing up. Without seeing where they were going they had drifted to leeward, and were two leagues off, towards Gravelines, dangerously near the shore. The Duke was too ignorant to realise the full peril of the situation. He signalled to them to return and rejoin him. As the wind and tide stood it was impossible. He proposed to follow them. The pilots told him that if he did the whole fleet might be lost on the banks. Towards the land the look of things was not more encouraging.

One accident only had happened the night before. The *Capitana* galleass, with Don Hugo de Monçada and eight hundred men on board, had fouled her helm in a cable in getting under way and had become unmanageable. The galley slaves disobeyed orders, or else Don Hugo was as incompetent as his commander-in-chief. The galleass had gone on the sands, and as the tide ebbed had fallen over on her side. Howard, seeing her condition, had followed her in the *Ark* with four or five other of the Queen's ships, and was furiously attacking her with his boats, careless of neutrality laws. Howard's theory was, as he said, to pluck the feathers one by one from the Spaniard's wing, and here was a feather worth picking up. The galleass was the most splendid vessel of her kind afloat, Don Hugo one of the greatest of Spanish grandees.

Howard was making a double mistake. He took the galleass at last, after three hours' fighting. Don Hugo was killed by a musket ball. The vessel was plundered, and Howard's men took possession, meaning to carry her away when the tide rose. The French authorities ordered him off, threatening to fire upon him; and after wasting the forenoon, he was obliged at last to leave her where she lay. Worse than this, he had lost three precious hours, and had lost along with them, in the opinion of the Prince of Parma, the honours of the great day.

Drake and Hawkins knew better than to waste time plucking single feathers. The fire ships had been more effective than they could have dared to hope. The enemy was broken up. The Duke was shorn of half his strength, and the Lord had delivered him into their hand. He had got under way, still signaling wildly, and uncertain in which direction to turn. His uncertainties were ended for him by seeing Drake bearing down upon him with the whole English fleet, save those which were loitering about the galleass. The English had now the advantage of numbers. The superiority of their guns he knew already, and their greater speed allowed him no hope to escape a battle. Forty ships alone were left to him to defend the banner of the crusade and the honour of Castile; but those forty were the largest and the most powerfully armed and manned that he had, and on board them were Oquendo, De Leyva, Recalde, and Bretandona, the best officers in the Spanish navy next to the lost Don Pedro.

It was now or never for England. The scene of the action which was to decide the future of Europe was between Calais and Dunkirk, a few miles off shore, and within sight of Parma's camp. There was no more manoeuvring for the weather-gage, no more fighting at long range. Drake dashed straight upon his prey as the falcon stoops upon its quarry. A chance had fallen to him which might never return; not for the vain distinction of carrying prizes into English ports, not for the ray of honour which would fall on him if he could carry off the sacred banner itself and hang it in the Abbey at Westminster, but a chance so to handle the Armada that it should never be seen again in English waters, and deal such a blow on Philip that the Spanish Empire should reel with it. The English ships had the same superiority over the galleons which steamers have now over sailing vessels. They had twice the speed; they could lie two points nearer to the wind. Sweeping round them at cable's length, crowding them in one upon the other, yet never once giving them a chance to grapple, they hurled in their cataracts of round shot. Short as was the powder supply, there was no sparing it that morning. The hours went on, and still the battle raged, if battle it could be called where the blows were all dealt on one side and the suffering was all on the other. Never on sea or land did the Spaniards show themselves worthier of their great name than on that day. But from the first they could do nothing. It was said afterwards in Spain that the Duke showed the white feather, that he charged his pilot to keep him out of harm's way, that he shut himself up in his cabin, buried in woolpacks, and so on. The Duke had faults enough, but poltroonery was not one of them. He, who till he entered the English Channel had never been in action on sea or land, found himself, as he said, in the midst of the most furious engagement recorded in the history of the world. As to being out of harm's way, the standard at his masthead drew the hottest of the fire upon him. The *San Martin's* timbers were of oak and a foot thick, but the shot, he said, went through them enough to shatter a rock. Her deck was a slaughterhouse; half his company were killed or wounded, and no more would have been heard or seen of the *San Martin* or her commander had not Oquendo and De Leyva pushed in to the rescue and enabled him to creep away under their cover. He himself saw nothing, even from his masthead. But all round it was but a repetition of the same scene. The Spanish shot flew high, as before, above the low English hulls, and they were themselves helpless butts to the English guns. And it is noticeable and supremely creditable to them that not a single galleon struck her colours. One of them, after a long duel with an Englishman, was on the point of sinking. An English officer, admiring the courage which the Spaniards had shown, ran out upon his bowsprit, told them that they had done all which became men, and urged them to surrender and save their lives. For answer they cursed the English as cowards and chickens because they refused to close. The officer was shot. His fall brought a last broadside on them, which finished the work. They went down, and the water closed over them. Rather death to the soldiers of the Cross than surrender to a heretic.

The deadly hail rained on. In some ships blood was seen streaming out of the scupper-holes. Yet there was no yielding; all ranks showed equal heroism. The priests went up and down in the midst of the carnage, holding the crucifix before the eyes of the dying. Towards the afternoon the Spanish fire slackened. Their powder was gone, and they could make no return to the cannonade which was still overwhelming them. They admitted freely afterwards that if the attack had been continued but two hours more they must all have struck or gone ashore. But the English magazines were empty also; the last cartridge was shot away, and the battle ended from mere inability to keep it up. It had been fought on both sides with peculiar determination. In the English there was the accumulated resentment of thirty years of menace to their country and their creed, with the enemy in tangible shape at last to be caught and grappled with; in the Spanish, the sense that if their cause had not brought them the help they looked for from above, the honour and faith of Castile should not suffer in their hands.

It was over. The English drew off, regretting that their thrifty mistress had limited their means of fighting for her, and so obliged them to leave their work half done. When the cannon ceased the wind rose, the smoke rolled away, and in the level light of the sunset they could see the results of the action.

A galleon in Recalde's squadron was sinking with all hands. The *San Philip* and the *San Matteo* were drifting dismasted towards the Dutch coast, where they were afterwards wrecked. Those which were left with canvas still showing were crawling slowly after their comrades who had not been engaged, the spars and rigging so cut up that they could scarce bear their sails. The loss of life could only be conjectured, but it had been obviously terrible. The nor'-wester was blowing up and was pressing the wounded ships upon the shoals, from which, if it held, it seemed impossible in their crippled state they would be able to work off.

In this condition Drake left them for the night, not to rest, but from any quarter to collect, if he could, more food and powder. The snake had been scotched, but not killed. More than half the great fleet were far away, untouched by shot, perhaps able to fight a second battle if they recovered heart. To follow, to drive them on the banks if the wind held, or into the North Sea, anywhere so that he left them no chance of joining hands with Parma again, and to use the time before they had rallied from his blows, that was the present necessity. His own poor fellows were famished and in rags; but neither he nor they had leisure to think of themselves. There was but one thought in the whole of them, to be again in chase of the flying foe. Howard was resolute as Drake. All that was possible was swiftly done. Seymour and the Thames squadron were to stay in the Straits and watch Parma. From every attainable source food and powder were collected for the rest – far short in both ways of what ought to have been, but, as Drake said, 'we were resolved to put on a brag and go on as if we needed nothing.' Before dawn the admiral and he were again off on the chase.

The brag was unneeded. What man could do had been done, and the rest was left to the elements. Never again could Spanish seamen be brought to face the English with Medina Sidonia to lead them. They had a fool at their head. The Invisible Powers in whom they had been taught to trust had deserted them. Their confidence was gone and their spirit broken. Drearily the morning broke on the Duke and his consorts the day after the battle. The Armada had collected in the night. The nor'-wester had freshened to a gale, and they were labouring heavily along, making fatal leeway towards the shoals.

It was St. Lawrence's Day, Philip's patron saint, whose shoulder-bone he had lately added to the treasures of the Escurial; but St. Lawrence was as heedless as St. Dominic. The *San Martin* had but six fathoms under her. Those nearer to the land signalled five, and right before them they could see the brown foam of the breakers curling over the sands, while on their weather-beam, a mile distant and clinging to them like the shadow of death, were the English ships which had pursued them from Plymouth like the dogs of the Furies. The Spanish sailors and soldiers had been without food since the evening when they anchored at Calais. All Sunday they had been at work, no rest allowed them to eat. On the Sunday night they had been stirred out of their sleep by the fire ships. Monday they had been fighting, and Monday night committing their dead to the sea. Now they seemed advancing directly upon inevitable destruction. As the wind stood there was still room for them to wear and thus escape the banks, but they would then have to face the enemy, who seemed only refraining from attacking them because while they continued on their present course the winds and waves would finish the work without help from man. Recalde, De Leyva, Oquendo, and other officers were sent for to the *San Martin* to consult. Oquendo came last, 'Ah, Señor Oquendo,' said the Duke as the heroic Biscayan stepped on board, 'que haremos?' (what shall we do?) 'Let your Excellency bid load the guns again,' was Oquendo's gallant answer. It could not be. De Leyva himself said that the men would not fight the English again. Florez advised surrender. The Duke wavered. It was said that a boat was actually lowered to go off to Howard and make terms, and that Oquendo swore that if the boat left the *San Martin* on such an errand he would fling Florez into the sea. Oquendo's advice would have, perhaps, been the safest if the Duke could have taken it. There were still seventy ships in the Armada little hurt. The English were 'bragging,' as Drake said, and in no condition themselves for another serious engagement. But the temper of the entire fleet made a courageous course impossible. There was but one Oquendo. Discipline was gone. The soldiers in their desperation had taken the command out of the hands of the seamen. Officers and men alike abandoned hope, and, with no human prospect of salvation left to them, they flung themselves on their knees upon the decks and prayed the Almighty to have pity on them. But two weeks were gone since they had knelt on those same decks on the first sight of the English shore to thank Him for having brought them so far on an enterprise so glorious. Two weeks; and what weeks! Wrecked, torn by cannon shot, ten thousand of them dead or dying — for this was the estimated loss by battle — the survivors could now but pray to be delivered from a miserable death by the elements. In cyclones the wind often changes suddenly back from north-west to west, from west to south. At that moment, as if in answer to their petition, one of these sudden shifts of wind saved them from the immediate peril. The gale backed round to S.S.W., and ceased to press them on the shoals. They could ease their sheets, draw off into open water, and steer a course up the middle of the North Sea.

So only that they went north, Drake was content to leave them unmolested. Once away into the high latitudes they might go where they would. Neither Howard nor he, in the low state of their own magazines, desired any unnecessary fighting. If the Armada turned back they must close with it. If it held its present course they must follow it till they could be assured it would communicate no more for that summer with the Prince of Parma. Drake thought they would perhaps make for the Baltic or some port in Norway. They would meet no hospitable reception from either Swedes or Danes, but they would probably try. One only imminent danger remained to be provided against. If they turned into the Forth, it was still possible for the Spaniards to redeem their defeat, and even yet shake Elizabeth's throne. Among the many plans which had been formed for the invasion of England, a landing in Scotland had long been the favourite. Guise had always preferred Scotland when it was intended that Guise should be the leader. Santa Cruz had been in close correspondence with Guise on this very subject, and many officers in the Armada must have been acquainted with Santa Cruz's views. The Scotch Catholic nobles were still savage at Mary Stuart's execution, and had the

Armada anchored in Leith Roads with twenty thousand men, half a million ducats, and a Santa Cruz at its head, it might have kindled a blaze at that moment from John o' Groat's Land to the Border.

But no such purpose occurred to the Duke of Medina Sidonia. He probably knew nothing at all of Scotland or its parties. Among the many deficiencies which he had pleaded to Philip as unfitting him for the command, he had said that Santa Cruz had acquaintances among the English and Scotch peers. He had himself none. The small information which he had of anything did not go beyond his orange gardens and his tunny fishing. His chief merit was that he was conscious of his incapacity; and, detesting a service into which he had been fooled by a hysterical nun, his only anxiety was to carry home the still considerable fleet which had been trusted to him without further loss. Beyond Scotland and the Scotch isles there was the open ocean, and in the open ocean there were no sandbanks and no English guns. Thus, with all sail set he went on before the wind. Drake and Howard attended him till they had seen him past the Forth, and knew then that there was no more to fear. It was time to see to the wants of their own poor fellows, who had endured so patiently and fought so magnificently. On the 13th of August they saw the last of the Armada, turned back, and made their way to the Thames.

—From English Seamen in the Sixteenth Century, by James Anthony Froude, English (1818–1894).

Columbus Sets Sail

WILLIAM H. PRESCOTT

CERTAIN ADVENTURERS from the northern provinces of Biscay and Guipuscoa, in 1393, had made themselves masters of one of the smallest of the group of islands supposed to be the Fortunate Isles of the ancients, since known as the Canaries. Other private adventurers from Seville extended their conquests over these islands in the beginning of the following century. These were completed in behalf of the crown under Ferdinand and Isabella, who equipped several fleets for their reduction, which at length terminated in 1495 with that of Teneriffe. From the commencement of their reign, Ferdinand and Isabella had shown an earnest solicitude for the encouragement of commerce and nautical science, as is evinced by a variety of regulations, which, however imperfect from the misconception of the true principles of trade in that day, are sufficiently indicative of the dispositions of the government. Under them, and indeed under their predecessors as far back as Henry the Third, a considerable traffic had been carried on with the western coast of Africa, from which gold-dust and slaves were imported into the city of Seville. The annalist of that city notices the repeated interference of Isabella in behalf of these unfortunate beings, by ordinances tending to secure them a more equal protection of the laws, or opening such social indulgences as might mitigate the hardships of their condition. A misunderstanding gradually arose between the subjects of Castile and Portugal, in relation to their respective rights of discovery and commerce on the African coast, which promised a fruitful source of collision between the two crowns, but which was happily adjusted by an article in the treaty of 1479, that terminated the war of succession. By this it was settled that the right of traffic and of discovery on the western coast of Africa should be exclusively reserved to the Portuguese, who in their turn should resign all claims on the Canaries to the crown of Castile. The Spaniards, thus excluded from further progress to the south, seemed to have no other opening left for naval adventure than the hitherto untravelled regions of the great western ocean. Fortunately, at this juncture an individual appeared among them, in the person of Christopher Columbus, endowed with capacity for stimulating them to this heroic enterprise and conducting it to a glorious issue.

This extraordinary man was a native of Genoa, of humble parentage, though perhaps honorable descent. He was instructed in his early youth at Pavia, where he acquired a strong relish for the mathematical sciences, in which he subsequently excelled. At the age of fourteen he engaged in a seafaring life, which he followed with little intermission till 1470; when, probably little more than thirty years of age, he landed in Portugal, the country to which adventurous spirits from all parts of the world then resorted, as the great theatre of maritime enterprise. After his arrival, he continued to make voyages to the then known parts of the world, and, when on shore, occupied himself with the construction and sale of charts and maps; while his geographical researches were considerably aided by the possession of papers belonging to an eminent Portuguese navigator, a deceased relative of his wife. Thus stored with all that nautical science in that day could supply, and fortified by large practical experience, the reflecting mind of Columbus was naturally led to speculate on the existence of some other land beyond the western waters; and he conceived the possibility of reaching the eastern shores of Asia, whose provinces of Zipango and Cathay were emblazoned in such gorgeous colors in the narratives of Mandeville and the Poli, by a more direct and commodious route than that which traversed the Eastern continent.

The existence of land beyond the Atlantic, which was not discredited by some of the most enlightened ancients, had become matter of common speculation at the close of the fifteenth century, when maritime adventure was daily disclosing the mysteries of the deep, and bringing to light new regions, that had hitherto existed only in fancy. A proof of this popular belief occurs in a curious passage of the "Morgante Maggiore" of the Florentine poet Pulci, a man of letters, but not distinguished for scientific attainments beyond his day. The passage is remarkable, independently of the cosmographical knowledge it implies, for its allusion to phenomena in physical science not established till more than a century later. The Devil, alluding to the vulgar superstition respecting the Pillars of Hercules, thus addresses his companion Rinaldo:

"Know that this theory is false; his bark
The daring mariner shall urge far o'er
The western wave, a smooth and level plain,
Albeit the earth is fashioned like a wheel.
Man was in ancient days of grosser mould,
And Hercules might blush to learn how far
Beyond the limits he had vainly set,
The dullest sea-boat soon shall wing her way.
Man shall descry another hemisphere.
Since to one common centre all things tend,
So earth, by curious mystery divine
Well balanced, hangs amid the starry spheres.
At our Antipodes are cities, states,
And thronged empires, ne'er divined of yore.
But see, the Sun speeds on his western path
To glad the nations with expected light."

Columbus's hypothesis rested on much stronger ground than mere popular belief. What indeed was credulity with the vulgar, and speculation with the learned, amounted in his mind to a settled practical conviction, that made him ready to peril life and fortune on the result of the experiment. He was fortified still further in his conclusions by a correspondence with the learned Italian Toscanelli, who furnished him with a map of his own projection, in which the eastern coast of Asia was delineated opposite to the western frontier of Europe.

Filled with lofty anticipations of achieving a discovery which would settle a question of such moment, so long involved in obscurity, Columbus submitted the theory on which he had founded his belief in the existence of a western route to King John the Second of Portugal. Here he was doomed to encounter for the first time the embarrassments and mortifications which so often obstruct the conceptions of genius, too sublime for the age in which they are formed. After a long and fruitless negotiation, and a dishonorable attempt on the part of the Portuguese to avail themselves clandestinely of his information, he quitted Lisbon in disgust, determined to submit his proposals to the Spanish sovereigns, relying on their reputed character for wisdom and enterprise.

The period of his arrival in Spain, being the latter part of 1484, would seem to have been the most unpropitious possible to his design. The nation was then in the heat of the Moorish war, and the sovereigns were unintermittingly engaged, as we have seen, in prosecuting their campaigns, or in active preparation for them. The large expenditure incident to this exhausted all their resources; and indeed the engrossing character of this domestic conquest left them little leisure for indulging in dreams of distant and doubtful discovery. Columbus, moreover, was unfortunate in his first channel of communication with the court. He was furnished by Fray Juan Perez de Marchena, guardian of the convent of La Rabida in Andalusia, who had early taken a deep interest in his plans, with an introduction to Fernando de Talavera. prior of Prado, and confessor of the queen, a person high in the royal confidence, and gradually raised through a succession of ecclesiastical dignities to the archiepiscopal see of Granada. He was a man of irreproachable morals, and of comprehensive benevolence for that day, as is shown in his subsequent treatment of the unfortunate Moriscos. He was also learned; although his learning was that of the cloister, deeply tinctured with pedantry and superstition, and debased by such servile deference even to the errors of antiquity as at once led him to discountenance every thing like innovation or enterprise.

With these timid and exclusive views, Talavera was so far from comprehending the vast conceptions of Columbus, that he seems to have regarded him as a mere visionary, and his hypothesis as involving principles not altogether orthodox. Ferdinand and Isabella, desirous of obtaining the opinion of the most competent judges on the merits of Columbus's theory, referred him to a council selected by Talavera from the most eminent scholars of the kingdom, chiefly ecclesiastics, whose profession embodied most of the science of that day. Such was the apathy exhibited by this learned conclave, and so numerous were the impediments suggested by dulness, prejudice, or skepticism, that years glided away before it came to a decision. During this time, Columbus appears to have remained in attendance on the court, bearing arms occasionally in the campaigns, and experiencing from the sovereigns an unusual degree of deference and personal attention; an evidence of which is afforded in the disbursements repeatedly made by the royal order for his private expenses, and in the instructions issued to the municipalities of the different towns in Andalusia to supply him gratuitously with lodging and other personal accommodations.

At length, however, Columbus, wearied out by this painful procrastination, pressed the court for a definite answer to his propositions; when he was informed that the council of Salamanca pronounced his scheme to be "vain, impracticable, and resting on grounds too weak to merit the support of the government." Many in the council, however, were too enlightened to acquiesce in this sentence of the majority. Some of the most considerable persons of the court, indeed, moved by the cogency of Columbus's arguments and affected by the elevation and grandeur of his views, not only cordially embraced his scheme, but extended their personal intimacy and friendship to him. Such, among others, were the grand cardinal Mendoza, a man whose enlarged capacity, and acquaintance with affairs, raised him above many of the narrow prejudices of his order, and Deza, archbishop of Seville, a Dominican friar, whose commanding talents were afterwards unhappily perverted in the service of the Holy Office, over which he presided as successor to Torquemada. The authority of these individuals had undoubtedly great weight with the sovereigns, who softened the verdict of the junto by an assurance to Columbus that, "although they were too much occupied at present to embark in his undertaking, yet at the conclusion of the war they should find both time and inclination to treat with him." Such was the ineffectual result of Columbus's long and painful solicitation; and, far from receiving the qualified assurance of the sovereigns in mitigation of their refusal, he seems to have considered it as peremptory and final. In great dejection of mind, therefore, but without further delay, he quitted the court, and bent his way to the south, with the apparently almost desperate intent of seeking out some other patron to his undertaking.

Columbus had already visited his native city of Genoa, for the purpose of interesting it in his scheme of discovery; but the attempt proved unsuccessful. He now made application, it would seem, to the dukes of Medina Sidonia and Medina Celi, successively, from the latter of whom he experienced much kindness and hospitality; but neither of these nobles, whose large estates lying along the sea-shore had often invited them to maritime adventure, was disposed to assume one which seemed too hazardous for the resources of the crown. Without wasting time in further solicitation, Columbus prepared with a heavy heart to bid adieu to Spain (1491) and carry his proposals to the king of France, from whom he had received a letter of encouragement while detained in Andalusia.

His progress, however, was arrested at the convent of La Rabida, which he visited previous to his departure, by his friend the guardian, who prevailed on him to postpone his journey till another effort had been made to move the Spanish court in his favor. For this purpose the worthy ecclesiastic undertook an expedition in person to the newly-erected city of Santa Fe, where the sovereigns lay encamped before Granada. Juan Perez had formerly been confessor of Isabella, and was held in great consideration by her for his excellent qualities. On arriving at the camp, he was readily admitted to an audience, when he pressed the suit of Columbus with all the earnestness and reasoning of which he was capable. The friar's eloquence was supported by that of several eminent persons whom Columbus during his long residence in the country had interested in his project, and who viewed with sincere regret the prospect of its abandonment. Among these individuals are particularly mentioned Alonso de Quintanilla, comptroller-general of Castile, Louis de St. Angel, a fiscal officer of the crown of Aragon, and the marchioness of Moya, the personal friend of Isabella, all of whom exercised considerable influence over her counsels. Their representations, combined with the opportune season of the application, occurring at the moment when the approaching termination of the Moorish war allowed room for interest in other objects, wrought so favorable a change in the dispositions of the sovereigns that they consented to resume the negotiation with Columbus. An invitation was accordingly sent to him to repair to Santa Fe, and a considerable sum provided for his suitable equipment and his expenses on the road.

Columbus, who lost no time in availing himself of this welcome intelligence, arrived at the camp in season to witness the surrender of Granada, when every heart, swelling with exultation at the triumphant termination of the war, was naturally disposed to enter with greater confidence on a new career of adventure. In his interview with the king and queen, he once more exhibited the arguments on which his hypothesis was founded. He then endeavored to stimulate the cupidity of his audience by picturing the realms of Mangi and Cathay, which he confidently expected to reach by this western route, in all the barbaric splendors which had been shed over them by the lively fancy of Marco Polo and other travellers of the Middle Ages; and he concluded with appealing to a higher principle, by holding out the prospect of extending the empire of the Cross over nations of benighted heathen, while he proposed to devote the profits of his enterprise to the recovery of the Holy Sepulchre. This last ebullition, which might well have passed for fanaticism in a later day, and given a visionary tinge to his whole project, was not quite so preposterous in an age in which the spirit of the crusades might be said still to linger, and the romance of religion had not yet been dispelled by sober reason. The more temperate suggestion of the diffusion of the gospel was well suited to affect Isabella, in whose heart the principle of devotion was deeply seated, and who, in all her undertakings, seems to have been far less sensible to the vulgar impulses of avarice or ambition than to any argument connected, however remotely, with the interests of religion.

Amidst all these propitious demonstrations towards Columbus, an obstacle unexpectedly arose in the nature of his demands, which stipulated for himself and heirs the title and authority of Admiral and Viceroy over all lands discovered by him, with one-tenth of the profits. This was deemed wholly inadmissible. Ferdinand, who had looked with cold distrust on the expedition from the first, was supported by the remonstrances of Talavera, the new archbishop of Granada, who declared that "such demands savored of the highest degree of arrogance, and would be unbecoming in their Highnesses to grant to a needy foreign adventurer." Columbus, however, steadily resisted every attempt to induce him to modify his propositions. On this ground the conferences were abruptly broken off, and he once more turned his back upon the Spanish court, resolved rather to forego his splendid anticipations of discovery, at the very moment when the career so long sought was thrown open to him, than surrender one of the honorable distinctions due to his services. This last act is perhaps the most remarkable exhibition in his whole life, of that proud, unyielding spirit which sustained him through so many years of trial, and enabled him at length to achieve his great enterprise, in the face of every obstacle which man and nature had opposed to it.

The misunderstanding was not suffered to be of long duration. Columbus's friends, and especially Louis de St. Angel, remonstrated with the queen on these proceedings in the most earnest manner. He frankly told her that Columbus's demands, if high, were at least contingent on success, when they would be well deserved, while, if he failed, he required nothing. St. Angel expatiated on his qualifications for the undertaking, so signal as to insure in all probability the patronage of some other monarch, who would reap the fruits of his discoveries; and he ventured to remind the queen that her present policy was not in accordance with the magnanimous spirit which had hitherto made her the ready patron of great and heroic enterprise. Far from being displeased, Isabella was moved by his honest eloquence. She contemplated the proposals of Columbus in their true light; and, refusing to hearken any longer to the suggestions of cold and timid counsellors, she gave way to the natural impulses of her own noble and generous heart. "I will assume the undertaking," said she, "for my own crown of Castile, and am ready to pawn my jewels to defray the expenses of it, if the funds in the treasury shall be found inadequate." The treasury had been reduced to the lowest ebb by the late war; but the receiver, St. Angel, advanced the sums required, from the Aragonese revenues deposited in his hands. Aragon, however, was not considered as adventuring in the expedition, the charges and emoluments of which were reserved exclusively for Castile.

Columbus, who was overtaken by the royal messenger at a few leagues distance only from Granada, experienced the most courteous reception on his return to Santa Fe, where a definitive arrangement was concluded with the Spanish sovereigns, April 17th, 1492. By the terms of the capitulation, Ferdinand and Isabella, as lords of the ocean-seas, constituted Christopher Columbus their admiral, viceroy, and governor-general of all such islands and continents as he should discover in the western ocean, with the privilege of nominating three candidates, for the selection of one by the crown, for the government of each of these territories. He was to be vested with exclusive right of jurisdiction over all commercial transactions within his admiralty. He was to be entitled to one-tenth of all the products and profits within the limits of his discoveries, and an additional eighth, provided he should contribute one eighth part of the expense. By a subsequent ordinance, the official dignities above enumerated were settled on him and his heirs forever, with the privilege of prefixing to their names the title of Don, which had not then degenerated into an appellation of mere courtesy.

No sooner were the arrangements completed, than Isabella prepared, with her characteristic promptness, to forward the expedition by the most efficient measures. Orders were sent to Seville and the other ports of Andalusia, to furnish stores and other articles requisite for the voyage, free of duty, and at as low rates as possible. The fleet, consisting of three vessels, was to sail from the little port of Palos in Andalusia, which had been condemned for some delinquency to maintain two caravels for a twelvemonth for the public service. The third vessel was furnished by the admiral, aided, as it would seem, in defraying the charges by his friend the guardian of La Rabida, and the Pinzons, a family in Palos long distinguished for its enterprise among the mariners of that active community. With their assistance, Columbus was enabled to surmount the disinclination, and indeed open opposition, manifested by the Andalusian mariners to his perilous voyage; so that in less than three months his little squadron was equipped for sea. A sufficient evidence of the extreme unpopularity of the expedition is afforded by a royal ordinance of the 30th of April, promising protection to all persons who should embark in it from criminal prosecution of whatever kind, until two months after their return. The armament consisted of two caravels, or light vessels without decks, and a third of larger burden. The total number of persons who embarked amounted to one hundred and twenty; and the whole charges of the crown for the expedition did not exceed seventeen thousand florins. The fleet was instructed to keep clear of the African coast, and other maritime possessions of Portugal. At length, all things being in readiness, Columbus and his whole crew partook of the sacrament, and confessed themselves after the devout manner of the ancient Spanish voyagers when engaged in any important enterprise; and on the morning of the 3d of August, 1492, the intrepid navigator, bidding adieu to the old world, launched forth on that unfathomed waste of waters where no sail had been ever spread before.

—*From Ferdinand and Isabella by William H. Prescott, American (1796–1859).*

The Fall of the Bastile

JEAN FRANÇOIS MARMONTEL

IN EVERY PLACE where parties of the people usually assemble on festivals the fermentation was extreme. The *Palais-Royal* was filled with a tumultuous crowd, agitated like the waves of the sea in a violent storm. At first a mournful and long murmur dwelt on the ear, and soon a threatening rumour more fearfully spread. The people took the green cockade; leaves of trees were substituted for it; and, as a signal for insurrection, the populace, having entered the shop of a maker of wax models, took the busts of Necker and the Duke d'Orleans, and carried them about Paris.

Another crowd assembled in the square of Louis XV, and the tumult continued to increase. To dissipate it, some troops were ordered to advance. Their commander, the Baron de Bezenval, had repaired thither with a company of grenadiers of the Swiss guards. The Prince de Lambesc came and joined him at the head of fifty dragoons of the Royal-German Corps. The presence of the troops completed the irritation of the people. All began to insult them. The troops were careless of these clamours; but, assailed with stones, by which some of them were wounded, the dragoons were losing all patience, when Bezenval gave orders to the Prince de Lambesc to advance in order to force the people to fall back into the Tuileries. This order was executed with so much caution, that not a man of the people was either beaten down or bruised. It was not till the moment when the dragoons were retiring, that a madman, who obstinately persisted in shutting the Pont-Tournant against the prince, was slightly wounded by him.

Throughout Paris the report was instantly spread of a massacre of the citizens in the garden of the Tuileries, where, it was said, the dragoons of Lambesc were riding in among the crowd with drawn swords, and the colonel at their head, murdering old men, crushing children, beating down pregnant women, or making them miscarry with affright.

At the same time, on the false report that their regiment was insulted, the grenadiers of the French guards forced the Duke du Châtelet, their colonel, to let them escape from the garden of the hotel de Richelieu, where he kept them confined. From that time the regiment of guards was entirely devoted to the people; and that was what the factious most ardently desired.

Thus Paris, without courts of justice, without police, without a guard, at the mercy of one hundred thousand men wandering wildly in the middle of the night, and for the most part wanting bread, believed itself on the point of being besieged from without, and pillaged from within. Twenty-five thousand soldiers were posted round its walls, at Saint Denis, at Courbevoye, at Charenton, at Sèves, at La Muette, in the Champ de Mars; and while they should blockade it, and cut off all supplies of provisions, it would be a prey to a starving people. Such was the terrible picture which, in the night between the 12th and 13th of July, was present to every fancy.

But the insurgents themselves, seized with the common terror, committed no pillage. The armourers' shops were the only ones they forced, and they there took only arms. As soon as it was day, the city was filled with a tumultuous populace, that, knocking at every door, asked with loud cries for arms and bread, and that, believing there was a magazine of muskets and swords under the town-hall, flocked thither in order to force it. . . .

In the mean time the alarm bell was rung in every church, and the districts assembled to decide on the means of providing for the safety of the city both within and without; for it was not less urgent to defend it against the villains with which it swarmed than against the troops that encircled it. From this moment the citizens formed bands of volunteers, who came and drew up by common consent in the squares and public gardens. But arms were still wanted, and still incessantly demanded at the town-hall. The mayor, the unfortunate Flesselles, is sent for; he arrives there through the crowd, calls himself the father of the people, and is applauded on that very spot where to-morrow his bleeding body will be dragged and torn.

The electors appoint a permanent committee at the town-hall, to be there accessible night and day to this people so tortured with affright. Flesselles, at the head of the committee, imprudently announces that he expects ten thousand muskets from Charleville, and thirty thousand soon afterward. He had even, as it is said, the fatal levity to trifle with the most impatient, by sending them here and there to places where he made them believe they would find arms. They hastened to the search, saw they were deceived, and returned to denounce him to the people as an impostor, who, in betraying, insulted them.

The committee of the electors, in order to hearten the people, resolved that a Parisian army should be immediately formed, to the number of forty-eight thousand men. All the districts came to offer themselves to compose it on the same day. The green cockade was laid aside, and the red and blue took its place; (green was the colour of a prince who was not a republican.)

In the mean time the people had gone to to the *garde-meuble*, and had carried away the precious arms that were preserved there as curiosities, either for beauty of the workmanship with which they were enriched, or for their antiquity, and out of respect for the heroes whose glory they recalled. The sword of Henry the Fourth was the booty of a vagabond.

But for so many thousand men this small number of arms was a feeble resource. They returned furious to the town-hall, still demanding arms, saying that there were some, and accusing the electors of conniving with the enemies of the people, in order to leave Paris without defence. Pressed by these reproaches, which were accompanied by threats, the committee conceived the idea of authorizing all the districts to get pikes and other arms of that kind made, and the people were satisfied.

But a better expedient, which the districts themselves conceived and adopted, was to send, in the evening, to Les Invalides, and summon the governor, Sombreuil, to deliver to them the arms which they knew were deposited in the hôtel. The commander-general of the troops, who had a camp very near there, and to whom Sombreuil addressed them, demanded time to send to Versailles for the king's orders; and that time was granted him.

The terror of the following night, more deep and more pensive, took a mournful character; the gates of the city were shut and guarded; patrols, already formed, kept the vagabonds in awe. Fires kindled in the streets inspired fear, intimidated crime, and showed everywhere knots of the people wandering like spectres. This stern and dismal silence was only broken by the stifled and terrible voice of those who, from door to door, cried out, "Arms and bread!"

In the Faubourg Saint Laurent, the house of the monks of Saint Lazare was set on fire and sacked. The incendiaries expected to find there a magazine of corn.

In the mean time the *Palais-Royal* was full of those mercenary conspirators, who were employed to stir up the fire of sedition; and the night passed there in accusations, and in atrocious motions, not only against Flesselles, but against the committee of the electors, who were denounced as traitors to the country.

On the day before, five thousand weight of powder, which was leaving Paris, had been seized at the gates, and deposited at the town-hall, under the chamber of the electors. In the middle of the night the few persons who remained on watch in this chamber are informed that, from the side of the Faubourg Saint Antoine, fifteen thousand men, the confidential band of the leaders of the Palais-Royal, are coming to force the town-hall. Among the number on watch was a citizen, Le Grand de SaintRéné, a man of a feeble and sickly constitution, but of a strong and firm courage. "Let them come and attack us," said he, "we'll be blown up together." He immediately ordered the guards of the hall to bring six barrels of powder into the adjoining room. His resolution was known. The first barrel that was brought made the most intrepid turn pale, and the people withdrew. Thus by one single man the town-hall was preserved. The kingdom, too, would have been saved in the same manner, if the king had had such men at the head of his councils and his camps. But he himself recommended to all to spare the people, and he never could consent to any act of vigour and severity against his subjects; a virtuous weakness, that has brought his head under the axe of the executioner.

During this frightful night the citizens kept themselves locked in their houses, each trembling at home, for himself and for those that were dearest to him. But on the 14th, in the morning, these personal fears yielding to public alarm, the whole city was but one and the same people: Paris had an army; this army, spontaneously assembled in haste, was yet ill acquainted with the rules of discipline; but public spirit supplied them. Single, it commanded every thing like an invisible power. What gave this great character to public spirit, was the address that had been employed to fascinate opinion. The best citizens, seeing in the troops that came to protect Paris only enemies, who would carry fire and sword within its walls, all imagined that they had to combat for their homes, for their wives and children. The necessity, the peril, the care of the common safety and defence, the resolution of perishing, or of saving what they had most dear on earth, alone occupied every mind; and formed of all tempers and all wills that surprising accord which, of an immense and violently agitated city, made an army obedient to the intention of all, without receiving an order from any one; so that every one could at once obey, where no one commanded.

Fire-arms and powder were still wanting to this army; and the committee of the city having protested anew that none had been found even at the arsenal, the people returned to Les Invalides. The order that Sombreuil expected from Versailles did not arrive. The people prepared to employ force; and such was the irresolution of the court, or rather such was the repugnance of the king to every species of violence, that in the Champ-de-Mars, at a few paces from the hôtel which they came to force open, the troops received no orders to defend it. Without choosing to yield anything, the government abandoned everything; a sure way of losing all with disgrace.

It was then under the eyes of six Swiss battalions, and of eight hundred horse, as well dragoons as hussars, all motionless in their camp, that the Hôtel des Invalides was opened to the people; a very positive proof, as Bezenval has since affirmed it to be, that the troops were forbidden to fire on the citizens; and here was the great advantage of the people, that the king would only suffer them to be curbed, without ever consenting that they should either be treated as enemies or as rebels. This same order was observed throughout Paris, at the barriers, on the ramparts, in the square of Louis XV. This, too, was what, in every post around, rendered the troops accessible to corruption, by the facility with which they were allowed to mix with people.

This people, men and women, accosted the soldier, and with the glass in their hand, presented to him the lures of joyous licentiousness. "What!" said they, "do you come to make war upon us? Do you come to spill our blood? Would you have the courage to draw your sword against your brothers, to fire upon your friends? Are you not Frenchmen and citizens like ourselves? Are you not, like us, the children of the people that ask only to be free, and to be no longer oppressed? You serve the king, you love him; and we too love our good king and are ready to serve him. He is not the enemy of his people; but he is deceived, and you are commanded, in his name, to do what he does not approve. You serve, not him, but that unjust nobility, that nobility that dishonours you by treating you like slaves. Come, brave soldiers, come and revenge yourselves for a servitude that disgraces you. The king and liberty! down with the aristocrats, our oppressors and your tyrants!"

The soldier, naturally the friend of the people, was not deaf to this language. He saw but one step to take from poverty to abundance, from constraint to liberty. A great number deserted, and being so near Paris, it was impossible that they should not be corrupted.

The people then, in the presence of the troops of the Champ-de-Mars, ransacked with full license the Hôtel des Invalides. Twenty-eight thousand muskets were found there in the vaults of the dome; and with this booty, and the cannon of the esplanade drawn through Paris in triumph, the conquerors returned to the town-hall. There they learned that the governor of the Bastile, the Marquis de Launay, summoned in his turn to furnish arms and ammunition, had answered that he had none. A general cry was instantly heard from every corner of the square, "Let's go and attack the Bastile."

This resolution appeared to be sudden and unexpected among the people. But it was premeditated in the council of the chiefs of the revolution. The Bastile, as a state prison, had always been odious, on account of the iniquitous use to which the despotism of ministers had applied it under preceding reigns; and, as a fortress, it was formidable, particularly to those populous and mutinous faubourgs which its walls commanded, and which, in their riots, saw themselves under the fire of the cannon of its towers. To agitate these multitudes at its will, and make them act boldly, the republican faction then ardently desired that they might be rid of this overawing object. Honest men, even the most peaceful and most enlightened, wished too that the Bastile might be destroyed, because they hated the despotism of which it was the bulwark; and in this wish they consulted their personal security more than their real safety; for the despotism of license is a thousand times more dreadful than that of authority, and the unbridled populace is the most cruel of tyrants. The Bastile then should not have been destroyed, but its keys should have been deposited in the sanctuary of the laws.

The court thought it impregnable; it would have been so, or its attack and siege would have cost rivers of blood, if it had been defended; but the man to whom the guard of it was confided, the Marquis de Launay, would not, or dared not, or could not, use the means he had of rendering its resistance murderous; and this populace, that so vilely assassinated him, owed him thanks and praises.

De Launay had expected to intimidate the crowd; but it is evident that he wished to spare them. He had fifteen pieces of cannon on the towers; and, whatever calumny may have said to palliate the crime of his assassination, not one single cannon-shot was fired from these towers. There were besides, in the interior of the castle, three cannon loaded with canister shot, pointed in front of the drawbridge. These would have made great slaughter at the moment when the people came pouring in crowds into the first court; he fired but one, and that but once. He was provided with firearms of every kind, with six hundred musketoons, twelve rampart muskets carrying balls of a pound and a half, and four hundred "biscaïens." He had procured from the arsenal abundance of ammunition, bullets, fifteen thousand cartridges, and twenty thousand pounds of powder. In fine, he had collected on the two towers of the drawbridge a mass of stones and broken iron, in order to crush the besiegers if they should advance to the foot of the walls. But, in all these preparations to sustain a siege, he had forgotten provisions; and shut up in his castle with eighty invalids, thirty-two Swiss soldiers and his staff, all the store he had on the day of the attack consisted of two sacks of flour and a little rice; a proof that all the rest was only to inspire terror.

The small number of Swiss soldiers that had been sent to him were sure men, and well disposed to defend themselves; the invalids were not so, and he must have known that; but at least he ought not to have exposed them to the fear of dying for hunger. Unequal to his situation, and in that stupor with which the presence of danger strikes a weak mind, he looked on it with a steadfast but troubled eye; and rather motionless with astonishment than resolution. Unhappily, not a man in the council supplied the foresight he wanted.

To intoxicate the people with this first success, the attack and capture of the Bastile have been extravagantly extolled as an exploit. The following is the account of this conquest, which I have learned from the very mouth of him who was proclaimed and borne in triumph as the conductor of the enterprise, and as its hero.

"This Bastile," said the brave Elie to me, "was not forcibly taken. It surrendered even before it was attacked. It surrendered on the promise that I gave, upon the honour of a French officer, and on the part of the people, that not a man should be hurt if the fortress surrendered." This is the simple fact, and such as Elie attests it to me. The following details of it are written as he dictates.

The fore-courts of the Bastile had been abandoned. Some determined men having dared to break the drawbridge which barred the entrance into the first court, the people rushed in there in crowds; and, deaf to the voice of the soldiers, who from the tops of the towers forbore to fire on them, and cried out to them to retire, they persisted in advancing toward the walls of the castle. It was then that they were fired upon by the soldiers; and being put to flight, they saved themselves under the covert of the fore-courts. One killed, and a few wounded, spread terror even to the town-hall; multitudes came to demand urgently in the name of the people that deputations might be resorted to, in order to stop the carnage. Two of these deputations arrived, one by the arsenal, and the other by the side of the Faubourg Saint Antoine. "Advance," cried the invalids to them from the tops of the towers, "we will not fire on you; advance with your flag. The governor is going down, the castle bridge will be let down, in order to introduce you, and we will give hostages." The white flag was already hoisted on the towers, and the soldiers held their arms inverted in sign of peace. But neither of the deputations dared to advance so far as the last fore-court. At the same time, the crowd was pressing toward the drawbridge, and firing from all sides. The besieged then had reason to think that these appearances of deputation were but a trick to surprise them; and after having cried in vain to the people not to advance, they found themselves obliged to fire in their turn.

The people, repulsed a second time, and furious at seeing some of their own body fall under the fire of the fortress, took that revenge in which it usually indulges. The barracks and shops of the fore-court were pillaged; the house of the governor was delivered to the flames. The firing of one cannon, loaded with case shot, and a discharge of musketry, had driven back this crowd of robbers and incendiaries; when, at the head of a dozen brave citizens, Elie, advancing to the very edge of the ditch, cried out to the besieged to surrender, promising that not a man should be hurt. He then perceived a hand extended through an opening in a part of the drawbridge and presenting to him a note. This note was received by means of a plank that was held over the ditch; it was written in these words: "We have twenty thousand pounds of powder. We will blow up the castle if you do not accept our capitulation. *Signed* De Launay."

Elie, after having read the note, cried out that he accepted it; and, on the part of the fort, all hostilities ceased. However, De Launay, before he gave himself up to the people, wished that the capitulation should be ratified and signed at the town-hall, and that, to secure his own safety and that of the soldiers, an imposing guard should receive and protect them. But the unfortunate invalids, thinking to hasten their deliverance, did violence to the governor, by crying out from the court, "The Bastile surrenders."

It was then that De Launay, seizing the match of a cannon, threatened to go and set fire to the powder magazine; and perhaps he was firmly resolved to do it. The sentinels who guarded that magazine presented their bayonets; and in spite of himself, without further precaution or delay, he saw himself forced to surrender.

The little drawbridge of the fort being first opened, Elie entered with his companions, all brave and honorable men, and fully determined to keep his word. On seeing him, the governor went up to him, embraced him, and presented him his sword, with the keys of the Bastile.

"I refused his sword," said Elie to me, "and took only the keys." His companions received the staff and the officers of the garrison with the same cordiality, swearing to serve them as a guard and defence; but they swore in vain.

As soon as the great bridge was let down (and it is not known by what hand that was done) the people rushed into the court of the castle, and, full of fury, seized on the troop of invalids. The Swiss, who were dressed in linen frocks, escaped among the crowd, all the rest were arrested. Elie, and the honest men who had entered first with him, exerted all their efforts to tear from the hands of the people the victims which they themselves had delivered to them. But ferocity was obstinately attached to its prey. Several of these soldiers, whose lives had been promised them, were assassinated; others were dragged like slaves through the streets of Paris. Twenty-two were brought to the Grêve, and, after humiliations and inhuman treatment, they had the affliction of seeing two of their comrades hanged. When they were presented at the town-hall, a furious madman said to them: "You have fired on your fellow-citizens; you deserve to be hanged; and you shall be so presently." Fortunately, the French guards interceded for their pardon; the people suffered itself to be persuaded. But it was without pity for the officers of the garrison. De Launay, torn from the arms of those who wished to save him, had his head cut off under the walls of the town-hall. In the midst of his assassins, he defended his life with the bravery of despair; but he fell under their number. Delorme Salbray, his major, was murdered in the same manner. The adjutant Mirai had been so, near the Bastile. Pernon, an old lieutenant of the Invalids, was assassinated on the wharf Saint-Paul, as he was going to the hall. Another lieutenant, Caron, was covered with wounds. The head of the Marquis de Launay was carried about Paris by this same populace that he might have crushed, had he not been moved to pity.

Such were the exploits of those who have since been called the heroes and conquerors of the Bastile. On the 14th of July 1789, about eleven o'clock in the morning, the people had assembled before it; at forty minutes after four it had surrendered. At half an hour after six the head of the governor was carried in triumph to the *Palais-Royal*. Among the number of conquerors, which were said to amount to eight hundred, many people have been mentioned who had not even approached the castle.

—*From the Memoirs of Marmontel, French (1723–1799), translated by William Dean Howells.*

The Victory of the Americans over Burgoyne at Saratoga, 1777

SIR EDWARD S. CREASY

THE WAR which rent away the North American colonies of England is, of all subjects in history, the most painful for an Englishman to dwell on. It was commenced and carried on by the British Ministry in iniquity and folly, and it was concluded in disaster and shame. But the contemplation of it cannot be evaded by the historian, however much it may be abhorred. Nor can any military event be said to have exercised more important influence on the future fortune of mankind, than the complete defeat of Burgoyne's expedition in 1777; a defeat which rescued the revolted colonists from certain subjection; and which, by inducing the courts of France and Spain to attack England in their behalf, ensured the independence of the United States, and the formation of that transatlantic power which, not only America, but both Europe and Asia now see and feel.

Still, in proceeding to describe this "decisive battle of the world," a very brief recapitulation of the earlier events of the war may be sufficient; nor shall I linger unnecessarily on a painful theme.

The five northern colonies of Massachusetts, Connecticut, Rhode Island, New Hampshire, and Vermont, usually classed together as the New England colonies, were the strongholds of the insurrection against the mother-country. The feeling of resistance was less vehement and general in the central settlement of New York; and still less so in Pennsylvania, Maryland, and the other colonies of the south, although everywhere it was formidably active. Virginia should, perhaps, be particularized for the zeal which its leading men displayed in the American cause; but it was among the descendants of the stern Puritans that the spirit of Cromwell and Vane breathed in all its fervour; it was from the New Englanders that the first armed opposition to the British crown had been offered; and it was by them that the most stubborn determination to fight to the last, rather than waive a single right or privilege, had been displayed. In 1775, they had succeeded in forcing the British troops to evacuate Boston; and the events of 1776 had made New York (which the royalists captured in that year) the principal basis of operations for the armies of the mother-country.

A glance at the map will show that the Hudson River, which falls into the Atlantic at New York, runs down from the north at the back of the New England States, forming an angle of about forty-five degrees with the line of the coast of the Atlantic, along which the New England States are situated. Northward of the Hudson, we see a small chain of lakes communicating with the Canadian frontier. It is necessary to attend closely to these geographical points, in order to understand the plan of the operations which the English attempted in 1777, and which the battle of Saratoga defeated.

The English had a considerable force in Canada; and in 1776 had completely repulsed an attack which the Americans had made upon that province. The British Ministry resolved to avail themselves, in the next year, of the advantage which the occupation of Canada gave them, not merely for the purpose of defence, but for the purpose of striking a vigorous and crushing blow against the revolted colonies. With this view, the army in Canada was largely reinforced. Several thousand veteran troops were sent out from England, with a corps of artillery abundantly supplied, and led by select and experienced officers. Large quantities of military stores were also furnished for the equipment of the Canadian volunteers, who were expected to join the expedition. It was intended that the force thus collected should march southward by the line of the lakes, and thence along the banks of the Hudson River. The British army in New York (or a large detachment of it) was to make a simultaneous movement northward, up the line of the Hudson, and the two expeditions were to unite at Albany, a town on that river. By these operations all communication between the northern colonies and those of the centre and south would be cut off. An irresistible force would be concentrated, so as to crush all further opposition in New England; and when this was done, it was believed that the other colonies would speedily submit. The Americans had no troops in the field that seemed able to baffle these movements. Their principal army, under Washington, was occupied in watching over Pennsylvania and the south. At any rate it was believed that, in order to oppose the plan intended for the new campaign, the insurgents must risk a pitched battle, in which the superiority of the royalists, in numbers, in discipline, and in equipment, seemed to promise to the latter a crowning victory. Without question the plan was ably formed; and had the success of the execution been equal to the ingenuity of the design, the re-conquest or submission of the thirteen United States must, in all human probability, have followed; and the independence which they proclaimed in 1776 would have been extinguished before it existed a second year. No European power had as yet come forward to aid America. It is true that England was generally regarded with jealousy and ill-will, and was thought to have acquired, at the treaty of Paris, a preponderance of dominion which was perilous to the balance of power; but though many were willing to wound, none had yet ventured to strike; and America, if defeated in 1777, would have been suffered to fall unaided.

Burgoyne had gained celebrity by some bold and dashing exploits in Portugal during the last war; he was personally as brave an officer as ever headed British troops; he had considerable skill as a tactician; and his general intellectual abilities and acquirements were of a high order. He had several very able and experienced officers under him, among whom were Major-General Phillips and Brigadier-General Frazer. His regular troops amounted exclusively of the corps of artillery, to about seven thousand two hundred men, rank and file. Nearly half of these were Germans. He had also an auxiliary force of from two to three thousand Canadians. He summoned the warriors of several tribes of the Red Indians near the western lakes to join his army. Much eloquence was poured forth, both in America and in England, in denouncing the use of these savage auxiliaries. Yet Burgoyne seems to have done no more than Montcalm, Wolfe, and other French, American, and English generals had done before him. But, in truth, the lawless ferocity of the Indians, their unskilfulness in regular action, and the utter impossibility of bringing them under any discipline, made their services of little or no value in times of difficulty: while the indignation which their outrages inspired, went far to rouse the whole population of the invaded districts into active hostilities against Burgoyne's force.

Burgoyne assembled his troops and confederates near the river Bouquet, on the west side of Lake Champlain. He then, on the 21st of June 1777, gave his Red Allies a war-feast, and harangued them on the necessity of abstaining from their usual cruel practices against unarmed people and prisoners. At the same time he published a pompous manifesto to the Americans, in which he threatened the refractory with all the horrors of war, Indian as well as European. The army proceeded by water to Crown Point, a fortification which the Americans held at the northern extremity of the inlet by which the water from Lake George is conveyed to Lake Champlain. He landed here without opposition; but the reduction of Ticonderoga, a fortification about twelve miles to the south of Crown Point, was a more serious matter, and was supposed to be the critical part of the expedition. Ticonderoga commanded the passage along the lakes, and was considered to be the key to the route which Burgoyne wished to follow. The English had been repulsed in an attack on it in the war with the French in 1758 with severe loss. But Burgoyne now invested it with great skill; and the American General, St. Clair, who had only an ill-equipped army of about three thousand men, evacuated it on the 5th of July. It seems evident that a different course would have caused the destruction or capture of his whole army; which, weak as it was, was the chief force then in the field for the protection of the New England States. When censured by some of his countrymen for abandoning Ticonderoga, St. Clair truly replied, "that he had lost a post, but saved a province." Burgoyne's troops pursued the retiring Americans, gained several advantages over them, and took a large part of their artillery and military stores.

The loss of the British in these engagements was trifling. The army moved southward along Lake George to Skenesborough; and thence, slowly, and with great difficulty, across a broken country, full of creeks and marshes, and clogged by the enemy with felled trees and other obstacles, to Fort Edward, on the Hudson River, the American troops continuing to retire before them.

Burgoyne reached the left bank of the Hudson River on the 30th of July. Hitherto he had overcome every difficulty which the enemy and the nature of the country had placed in his way. His army was in excellent order and in the highest spirits; and the peril of the expedition seemed over, when they were once on the bank of the river which was to be the channel of communication between them and the British army in the south. But their feelings, and those of the English nation in general when their successes were announced, may best be learned from a contemporary writer. Burke, in the "Annual Register" for 1777, describes them thus:

"Such was the rapid torrent of success, which swept everything away before the northern army in its onset. It is not to be wondered at, if both officers and private men were highly elated with their good fortune, and deemed that and their prowess to be irresistible; if they regarded their enemy with the greatest contempt; considered their own toils to be nearly at an end; Albany to be already in their hands; and the reduction of the northern provinces to be rather a matter of some time, than an arduous task full of difficulty and danger.

"At home the joy and exultation was extreme; not only at court but with all those who hoped or wished the unqualified subjugation, and unconditional submission, of the colonies. The loss in reputation was greater to the Americans, and capable of more fatal consequences, than even that of ground, of posts, of artillery, or of men. All the contemptuous and most degrading charges which had been made by their enemies, of their wanting the resolution and abilities of men, even in their defense of whatever was dear to them, were now repeated and believed. Those who still regarded them as men, and who had not yet lost all affection to them as brethren, who also retained hopes that a happy reconciliation upon constitutional principles, and without sacrificing the dignity or the just authority of government on the one side, or a dereliction of the rights of freemen on the other, was not even now impossible, notwithstanding their favorable dispositions in general, could not help feeling upon this occasion that the Americans sunk not a little in their estimation. It was not difficult to diffuse an opinion that the war in effect was over; and that any further resistance could only serve to render the terms of their submission the worse. Such were some of the immediate effects of the loss of those grand keys of North America, Ticonderoga and the lakes."

The astonishment and alarm which these events produced among the Americans were naturally great; but in the midst of their disasters none of the colonists showed any disposition to submit. The local governments of the New England States, as well as the Congress, acted with vigour and firmness in their efforts to repel the enemy. General Gates was sent to take the command of the army at Saratoga; and Arnold, a favourite leader of the Americans, was despatched by Washington to act under him, with reinforcements of troops and guns from the main American army. Burgoyne's employment of the Indians now produced the worst possible effects. Though he laboured hard to check the atrocities which they were accustomed to commit, he could not prevent the occurrence of many barbarous outrages, repugnant both to the feelings of humanity and to the laws of civilised warfare. The American commanders took care that the reports of these excesses should be circulated far and wide, well knowing that they would make the stern New Englanders not droop, but rage. Such was their effect; and though, when each man looked upon his wife, his children, his sisters, or his aged parents, the thought of the merciless Indian "thirsting for the blood of man, woman, and child," of "the cannibal savage torturing, murdering, roasting, and eating the mangled victims of his barbarous battles," might raise terror in the bravest breasts; this very terror produced a directly contrary effect to causing submission to the royal army. It was seen that the few friends of the royal cause, as well as its enemies, were liable to be the victims of the indiscriminate rage of the savages; and thus "the inhabitants of the open and frontier countries had no choice of acting: they had no means of security left, but by abandoning their habitations and taking up arms. Every man saw the necessity of becoming a temporary soldier, not only for his own security, but for the protection and defence of those connections which are dearer than life itself. Thus an army was poured forth by the woods, mountains, and marshes, which in this part were thickly sown with plantations and villages. The Americans recalled their courage; and when their regular army seemed to be entirely wasted, the spirit of the country produced a much greater and more formidable force."

While resolute recruits, accustomed to the use of firearms, and all partially trained by service in the provincial militias, were thus flocking to the standard of Gates and Arnold at Saratoga; and while Burgoyne was engaged at Fort Edward in providing the means for the further advance of his army through the intricate and hostile country that still lay before him, two events occurred, in each of which the British sustained loss, and the Americans obtained advantage, the moral effects of which were even more important than the immediate result of the encounters. When Burgoyne left Canada, General St. Leger was detached from that province with a mixed force of about one thousand men, and some light field-pieces, across Lake Ontario against Fort Stanwix, which the Americans held. After capturing this, he was to march along the Mohawk River to its confluence with the Hudson, between Saratoga and Albany, where his force and that of Burgoyne were to unite. But, after some successes, St. Leger was obliged to retreat, and to abandon his tents and large quantities of stores to the garrison. At the very time that General Burgoyne heard of this disaster, he experienced one still more severe in the defeat of Colonel Baum with a large detachment of German troops at Bennington, whither Burgoyne had sent them for the purpose of capturing some magazines of provisions, of which the British army stood greatly in need. The Americans, augmented by continual accessions of strength, succeeded, after many attacks, in breaking this corps, which fled into the woods, and left its commander mortally wounded on the field: they then marched against a force of five hundred grenadiers and light infantry, which was advancing to Colonel Baum's assistance, under Lieutenant-Colonel Breyman; who, after a gallant resistance, was obliged to retreat on the main army. The British loss in these two actions exceeded six hundred men: and a party of American loyalists, on their way to join the army, having attached themselves to Colonel Baum's corps, were destroyed with it.

Notwithstanding these reverses, which added greatly to the spirit and numbers of the American forces, Burgoyne determined to advance. It was impossible any longer to keep up his communications with Canada by way of the lakes, so as to supply his army on his southward march; but having by unremitting exertions collected provisions for thirty days, he crossed the Hudson by means of a bridge of rafts, and, marching a short distance along its western bank, he encamped on the 14th of September on the heights of Saratoga, about sixteen miles from Albany. The Americans had fallen back from Saratoga, and were now strongly posted near Stillwater, about half-way between Saratoga and Albany, and showed a determination to recede no farther.

Meanwhile Lord Howe, with the bulk of the British army that had lain at New York, had sailed away to the Delaware, and there commenced a campaign against Washington, in which the English general took Philadelphia, and gained other showy, but unprofitable successes. But Sir Henry Clinton, a brave and skilful officer, was left with a considerable force at New York; and he undertook the task of moving up the Hudson to cooperate with Burgoyne. Clinton was obliged for this purpose to wait for reinforcements which had been promised from England, and these did not arrive till September. As soon as he received them, Clinton embarked about 3000 of his men on a flotilla, convoyed by some ships of war under Commander Hotham, and proceeded to force his way up the river, but it was long before he was able to open any communication with Burgoyne.

The country between Burgoyne's position at Saratoga and that of the Americans at Stillwater was rugged, and seamed with creeks and watercourses; but after great labour in making bridges and temporary causeways, the British army moved forward. About four miles from Saratoga, on the afternoon of the 19th of September, a sharp encounter took place between part of the

English right wing, under Burgoyne himself, and a strong body of the enemy, under Gates and Arnold. The conflict lasted till sunset. The British remained masters of the field; but the loss on each side was nearly equal (from five hundred to six hundred men); and the spirits of the Americans were greatly raised by having withstood the best regular troops of the English army. Burgoyne now halted again, and strengthened his position by field-works and redoubts; and the Americans also improved their defences. The two armies remained nearly within cannon-shot of each other for a considerable time, during which Burgoyne was anxiously looking for intelligence of the promised expedition from New York, which, according to the original plan, ought by this time to have been approaching Albany from the south. At last, a messenger from Clinton made his way, with great difficulty, to Burgoyne's camp, and brought the information that Clinton was on his way up the Hudson to attack the American forts which barred the passage up that river to Albany. Burgoyne, in reply, on the 30th of September, urged Clinton to attack the forts as speedily as possible, stating that the effect of such an attack, or even the semblance of it, would be to move the American army from its position before his own troops. By another messenger, who reached Clinton on the 5th of October, Burgoyne informed his brother general that he had lost his communications with Canada, but had provisions which would last him till the 20th. Burgoyne described himself as strongly posted, and stated that though the Americans in front of him were strongly posted also, he made no doubt of being able to force them, and making his way to Albany; but that he doubted whether he could subsist there, as the country was drained of provisions. He wished Clinton to meet him there, and to keep open a communication with New York.

Burgoyne had over-estimated his resources, and in the very beginning of October found difficulty and distress pressing him hard.

The Indians and Canadians began to desert him; while, on the other hand, Gates's army was continually reinforced by fresh bodies of the militia. An expeditionary force was detached by the Americans, which made a bold, though unsuccessful, attempt to retake Ticonderoga. And finding the number and spirit of the enemy to increase daily, and his own stores of provision to diminish, Burgoyne determined on attacking the Americans in front of him, and by dislodging them from their position, to gain the means of moving upon Albany, or at least of relieving his troops from the straitened position in which they were cooped up.

Burgoyne's force was now reduced to less than 6000 men. The right of his camp was on some high ground a little to the west of the river; thence his entrenchments extended along the lower ground to the bank of the Hudson, the line of their front being nearly at a right angle with the course of the stream. The lines were fortified with redoubts and fieldworks, and on a height on the flank of the extreme right a strong redoubt was reared, and intrenchments, in a horse-shoe form, thrown up. The Hessians, under Colonel Breyman, were stationed here, forming a flank defence to Burgoyne's main army. The numerical force of the Americans was now greater than the British, even in regular troops, and the numbers of the militia and volunteers which had joined Gates and Arnold were greater still.

General Lincoln, with 2000 New England troops, had reached the American camp on the 29th of September. Gates gave him the command of the right wing, and took in person the command of the left wing, which was composed of two brigades under Generals Poor and Leonard, of Colonel Morgan's rifle corps, and part of the fresh New England militia. The whole of the American lines had been ably fortified under the direction of the celebrated Polish General, Kosciusko, who was now serving as a volunteer in Gates's army. The right of the American position, that is to say, the part of it nearest to the river, was too strong to be assailed with any prospect of success: and Burgoyne therefore determined to endeavour to force their left. For this purpose he formed a column of 150 regular troops, with two twelve-pounders, two howitzers, and six six-pounders. He headed this in person, having Generals Phillips, Reidesel, and Frazer under him. The enemy's force immediately in front of his lines was so strong that he dared not weaken the troops who guarded them, by detaching any more to strengthen his column of attack.

It was on the 7th of October that Burgoyne led his column forward; and on the preceding day, the 6th, Clinton had successfully executed a brilliant enterprise against two American forts which barred his progress up the Hudson. He had captured them both, with severe loss to the American forces opposed to him; he had destroyed the fleet which the Americans had been forming on the Hudson, under the protection of their forts; and the upward river was laid open to his squadron. He had also, with admirable skill and industry, collected in small vessels, such as could float within a few miles of Albany, provisions sufficient to supply Burgoyne's army for six months. He was now only a hundred and fifty-six miles distant from Burgoyne; and a detachment of 1700 men actually advanced within forty miles of Albany. Unfortunately Burgoyne and Clinton were each ignorant of the other's movements; but if Burgoyne had won his battle on the 7th, he must on advancing have soon learned the tidings of Clinton's success, and Clinton would have heard of his. A junction would soon have been made of the two victorious armies, and the great objects of the campaign might yet have been accomplished. All depended on the fortune of the column with which Burgoyne, on the eventful 7th of October 1777, advanced against the American position. There were brave men, both English and German, in its ranks; and in particular it comprised one of the best bodies of grenadiers in the British service.

Burgoyne pushed forward some bodies of irregular troops to distract the enemy's attention; and led his column to within three quarters of a mile from the left of Gates's camp, and then deployed his men into line. Three grenadiers under Major Ackland, and the artillery under Major Williams, were drawn up on the left; a corps of Germans, under General Reidesel, and some British troops under General Phillips, were in the centre; and the English Light Infantry, and the 24th regiment, under Lord Balcarres and General Frazer, were on the right. But Gates did not wait to be attacked; and directly the British line was formed and began to advance, the American general, with admirable skill, caused General Poor's brigade of New York and New Hampshire troops, and part of General Leonard's brigade, to make a sudden and vehement rush against its left, and at the same time sent Colonel Morgan, with his rifle corps and other troops, amounting to 1500, to turn the right of the English. The grenadiers under Ackland sustained the charge of superior numbers nobly. But Gates sent more Americans forward, and in a few minutes the action became general along the centre, so as to prevent the Germans from detaching any help to the grenadiers. Morgan, with his riflemen, was now pressing Lord Balcarres and General Frazer hard, and fresh masses of the enemy were observed advancing from their extreme left, with the evident intention of forcing the British right, and cutting off its retreat. The English light infantry and the 24th now fell back, and formed an oblique second line, which enabled them to baffle this manoeuvre, and also to succour their comrades in the left wing, the gallant grenadiers, who were overpowered by superior numbers, and, but for this aid, must have been cut to pieces.

The contest now was fiercely maintained on both sides. The English cannon were repeatedly taken and retaken; but when the grenadiers near them were forced back by the weight of superior numbers, one of the guns was permanently captured by the Americans, and turned upon the English. Major Williams and Major Ackland were both made prisoners, and in this part of the field the advantage of the Americans was decided. The British centre still held its ground; but now it was that the American general Arnold appeared upon the scene, and did more for his countrymen than whole battalions could have effected. Arnold, when the decisive engagement of the 7th of October commenced, had been deprived of his command by Gates, in consequence of a quarrel between them about the action of the 19th of September. He had listened for a short time in the American camp to the thunder of the battle, in which he had no military right to take part, either as commander or as combatant. But his excited spirit could not long endure such a state of inaction. He called for his horse, a powerful brown charger, and springing on it, galloped furiously to where the fight seemed to be the thickest. Gates saw him, and sent an aide-de-camp to recall him; but Arnold spurred far in advance, and placed himself at the head of three regiments which had formerly been under him, and which welcomed their old commander with joyous cheers. He led them instantly upon the British centre; and then galloping along the American line, he issued orders for a renewed and a closer attack which were obeyed with alacrity, Arnold himself setting the example of the most daring personal bravery, and charging more than once, sword in hand, into the English ranks. On the British side the officers did their duty nobly; but General Frazer was the most eminent of them all, restoring order wherever the line began to waver, and infusing fresh courage into his men by voice and example. Mounted on an iron-grey charger, and dressed in the full uniform of a general officer, he was conspicuous to foes as well as to friends. The American Colonel Morgan thought that the fate of the battle rested on this gallant man's life, and calling several of his best marksmen round him, pointed Frazer out, and said: "That officer is General Frazer; I admire him, but he must die. Our victory depends on it. Take your stations in that clump of bushes, and do your duty." Within five minutes, Frazer fell mortally wounded, and was carried to the British camp by two grenadiers. Just previously to his being struck by the fatal bullet, one rifle-ball had cut the crupper of his saddle, and another had passed through his horse's mane close behind the ears. His aide-de-camp had noticed this, and said: "It is evident that you are marked out for particular aim; would it not be prudent for you to retire from this place?" Frazer replied: "My duty forbids me to fly from danger;" and the next moment he fell.

Burgoyne's whole force was now compelled to retreat towards their camp; the left and centre were in complete disorder, but the light infantry and the 24th checked the fury of the assailants, and the remains of the column with great difficulty effected their return to their camp; leaving six of their cannons in the possession of the enemy, and great numbers of killed and wounded on the field; and especially a large proportion of the artillerymen, who had stood to their guns until shot down or bayoneted beside them by the advancing Americans.

Burgoyne's column had been defeated, but the action was not yet over. The English had scarcely entered the camp, when the Americans, pursuing their success, assaulted it in several places with remarkable impetuosity, rushing in upon the intrenchments and redoubts through a severe fire of grape-shot and musketry. Arnold especially, who on this day appeared maddened with the thirst of combat and carnage, urged on the attack against a part of the intrenchments which was occupied by the light infantry under Lord Balcarres. But the English received him with vigour and spirit. The struggle here was obstinate and sanguinary. At length, as it grew towards evening, Arnold, having forced all obstacles, entered the works with some of the most fearless of his followers. But in this critical moment of glory and danger, he received a painful wound in the same leg which had already been injured at the assault on Quebec. To his bitter regret he was obliged to be carried back. His party still continued the attack, but the English also continued their obstinate resistance, and at last night fell, and the assailants withdrew from this quarter of the British intrenchments. But in another part the attack had been more successful. A body of the Americans, under Colonel Brooke, forced their way in through a part of the horseshoe intrenchments on the extreme right, which was defended by the Hessian reserve under Colonel Breyman. The Germans resisted well, and Breyman died in defence of his post; but the Americans made good the ground which they had won, and captured baggage, tents, artillery, and a store of ammunition, which they were greatly in need of. They had, by establishing themselves on this point, acquired the means of completely turning the right flank of the British, and gaining their rear. To prevent this calamity, Burgoyne effected during the night an entire change of position. With great skill he removed his whole army to some heights near the river, a little northward of the former camp, and he there drew up his men, expecting to be attacked on the following day. But Gates was resolved not to risk the certain triumph which his success had already secured for him. He harassed the English with skirmishes, but attempted no regular attack. Meanwhile he detached bodies of troops on both sides of the Hudson to prevent the British from recrossing that river, and to bar their retreat. When night fell, it became absolutely necessary for Burgoyne to retire again, and, accordingly, the troops were marched through a stormy and rainy night towards Saratoga, abandoning their sick and wounded, and the greater part of their baggage, to the enemy.

Before the rear-guard quitted the camp, the last sad honours were paid to the brave

General Frazer, who expired on the day after the action.

He had, almost with his last breath, expressed a wish to be buried in the redoubt which had formed the part of the British lines where he had been stationed, but which had now been abandoned by the English, and was within full range of the cannon which the advancing Americans were rapidly placing in position to bear upon Burgoyne's force. Burgoyne resolved, nevertheless, to comply with the dying wish of his comrade; and the interment took place under circumstances the most affecting that have ever marked a soldier's funeral. Still more interesting is the narrative of Lady Ackland's passage from the British to the American camp, after the battle, to share the captivity and alleviate the sufferings of her husband, who had been severely wounded, and left in the enemy's power. The American historian, Lossing, has described both these touching episodes of the campaign, in a spirit that does honour to the writer as well as to his subject. After narrating the death of General Frazer on the 8th of October, he says that "It was just at sunset, on that calm October evening, that the corpse of General Frazer was carried up the hill to the place of burial within the 'great redoubt.' It was attended only by the military members of his family and Mr. Brudenell, the chaplain; yet the eyes of hundreds of both armies followed the solemn procession, while the Americans, ignorant of its true character, kept up a constant cannonade upon the redoubt. The chaplain, unawed by the danger to which he was exposed, as the cannon-balls that struck the hill threw the loose soil over him, pronounced the impressive funeral service of the Church of England with an unfaltering voice. The growing darkness added solemnity to the scene. Suddenly the irregular firing ceased, and the solemn voice of a single cannon, at measured intervals, boomed along the valley, and awakened the responses of the hills. It was a minute gun fired by the Americans in honour of the gallant dead. The moment the information was given that the gathering at the redoubt was a funeral company, fulfilling, at imminent peril, the last-breathed wishes of the noble Frazer, orders were issued to withhold the cannonade with balls, and to render military homage to the fallen brave.

"The case of Major Ackland and his heroic wife present kindred features. He belonged to the grenadiers, and was an accomplished soldier. His wife accompanied him to Canada in 1776; and during the whole campaign of that year, and until his return to England after the surrender of Burgoyne, in the autumn of 1777, endured all the hardships, dangers, and privations of an active campaign in an enemy's country. At Chambly, on the Sorel, she attended him in illness, in a miserable hut; and when he was wounded in the battle of Hubbardton, Vermont, she hastened to him at Henesborough from Montreal, where she had been persuaded to remain, and resolved to follow the army hereafter. Just before crossing the Hudson, she and her husband had had a narrow escape from losing their lives in consequence of their tent accidentally taking fire.

"During the terrible engagement of the 7th October, she heard all the tumult and dreadful thunder of the battle in which her husband was engaged; and when, on the morning of the 8th, the British fell back in confusion to their new position, she, with the other women, was obliged to take refuge among the dead and dying; for the tents were all struck, and hardly a shed was left standing. Her husband was wounded, and a prisoner in the American camp. That gallant officer was shot through both legs. When Poor and Leonard's troops assaulted the grenadiers and artillery on the British left, on the afternoon of the 7th, Wilkinson, Gates's adjutant-general, while pursuing the flying enemy when they abandoned their battery, heard a feeble voice exclaim, 'Protect me, sir, against that boy.' He turned and saw a lad with a musket taking deliberate aim at a wounded British officer, lying in a corner of a low fence. Wilkinson ordered the boy to desist, and discovered the wounded man to be Major Ackland. He had him conveyed to the quarters of General Poor on the heights, where every attention was paid to his wants.

"When the intelligence that he was wounded and a prisoner reached his wife, she was greatly distressed, and, by the advice of her friend, Baroness Reidesel, resolved to visit the American camp, and implore the favour of a personal attendance upon her husband. On the 9th she sent a message to Burgoyne by Lord Petersham, his aide-de-camp, asking permission to depart.

'Though I was ready to believe,' says Burgoyne, 'that patience and fortitude, in a supreme degree, were to be found, as well as every other virtue, under the most tender forms, I was astonished at this proposal. After so long an agitation of spirits, exhausted not only for want of rest, but absolutely want of food, drenched in rains for twelve hours together, that a woman should be capable of such an undertaking as delivering herself to an enemy, probably in the night, and uncertain of what hands she might fall into, appeared an effort above human nature. The assistance I was able to give was small indeed. I had not even a cup of wine to offer. All I could furnish her with was an open boat, and a few lines, written upon dirty wet paper, to General Gates, recommending her to his protection.' The following is a copy of the note sent by Burgoyne to General Gates: — 'Sir, — Lady Harriet Ackland, a lady of the first distinction of family, rank, and personal virtues, is under such concern on account of Major Ackland, her husband, wounded and a prisoner in your hands, that I cannot refuse her request to commit her to your protection. Whatever general impropriety there may be in persons of my situation and yours to solicit favours, I cannot see the uncommon perseverance in every female grace, and the exaltation of character of this lady, and her very hard fortune, without testifying that your attentions to her will lay me under obligations. I am, sir, your most obedient servant, J. Burgoyne.' She set out in an open boat upon the Hudson, accompanied by Mr. Brudenell, the chaplain, Sarah Pollard, her waiting-maid, and her husband's valet, who had been severely wounded, while searching for his master upon the battle-field. It was about sunset when they started, and a violent storm of rain and wind, which had been increasing since the morning, rendered the voyage tedious and perilous in the extreme. It was long after dark when they reached the American outposts; the sentinel heard their oars, and hailed them. Lady Harriet returned the answer herself. The clear, silvery tones of a woman's voice amid the darkness, filled the soldier on duty with superstitious fear, and he called a comrade to accompany him to the river bank. The errand of the voyagers was made known, but the faithful guard, apprehensive of treachery, would not allow them to land until they sent for Major Dearborn. They were invited by that officer to his quarters, where every attention was paid to them, and Lady Harriet was comforted by the joyful tidings that her husband was safe. In the morning she experienced parental tenderness from General Gates, who sent her to her husband, at Poor's quarters, under a suitable escort. There she remained until he was removed to Albany."

Burgoyne now took up his last position on the heights near Saratoga; and hemmed in by the enemy, who refused any encounter, and baffled in all his attempts at finding a path of escape, he there lingered until famine compelled him to capitulate. The fortitude of the British army during this melancholy period has been justly eulogized by many historians, but I prefer quoting the testimony of a writer, as free from all possibility of partiality. Botta says:

"It exceeds the power of words to describe the pitiable condition to which the British army was now reduced. The troops were worn down by a series of toil, privation, sickness, and desperate fighting. They were abandoned by the Indians and Canadians; and the effective force of the whole army was now diminished by repeated and heavy losses, which had principally fallen on the best soldiers and the most distinguished officers, from ten thousand combatants to less than one half that number. Of this remnant, little more than three thousand were English.

"In these circumstances, and thus weakened, they were invested by an army of four times their own number, whose position extended three parts of a circle round them; who refused to fight them, as knowing their weakness, and who from the nature of the ground, could not be attacked in any part. In this helpless condition, obliged to be constantly under arms, while the enemy's cannon played on every part of their camp, and even the American rifle-balls whistled in many parts of the lines, the troops of Burgoyne maintained their customary firmness, and while sinking under a hard necessity, they showed themselves worthy of a better fate. They could not be reproached with an action or a word which betrayed a want of temper or of fortitude."

At length the 13th of October arrived, and as no prospect of assistance appeared and the provisions were nearly exhausted, Burgoyne, by the unanimous advice of a council of war, sent a messenger to the American camp to treat for a convention.

General Gates in the first instance demanded that the royal army should surrender prisoners of war. He also proposed that the British should ground their arms. Burgoyne replied, "This article is inadmissible in every extremity; sooner than this army will consent to ground their arms in their encampment, they will rush on the enemy, determined to take no quarter." After various messages, a convention for the surrender of the army was settled, which provided that "The troops under General Burgoyne were to march out of their camp with the honours of war, and the artillery of the intrenchments, to the verge of the river, where the arms and artillery were to be left. The arms to be piled by word of command from their own officers. A free passage was to be granted to the army under Lieutenant-General Burgoyne to Great Britain, upon condition of not serving again in North America during the present contest."

The articles of capitulation were settled on the 15th of October; and on that very evening a messenger arrived from Clinton with an account of his successes, and with the tidings that part of his force had penetrated as far as Esopus, within fifty miles of Burgoyne's camp. But it was too late. The public faith was pledged; and the army was, indeed, too debilitated by fatigue and hunger to resist an attack if made; and Gates certainly would have made it, if the convention had been broken off. Accordingly, on the 17th, the convention of Saratoga was carried into effect. By this convention 5790 men surrendered themselves as prisoners. The sick and wounded left in the camp when the British retreated to Saratoga, together with the numbers of the British, German, and Canadian troops, who were killed, wounded, or taken, and who had deserted in the preceding part of the expedition, were reckoned to be 4689.

The British sick and wounded who had fallen into the hands of the Americans after the battle of the 7th, were treated with exemplary humanity; and when the convention was executed, General Gates showed a noble delicacy of feeling, which deserves the highest degree of honour. Every circumstance was avoided which could give the appearance of triumph. The American troops remained within their lines until the British had piled their arms; and when this was done, the vanquished officers and soldiers were received with friendly kindness by their victors, and their immediate wants were promptly and liberally supplied. Discussions and disputes afterwards arose as to some of the terms of the convention; and the American Congress refused for a long time to carry into effect the article which provided for the return of Burgoyne's men to Europe; but no blame was imputable to General Gates or his army, who showed themselves to be generous as they had proved themselves to be brave.

Gates, after the victory, immediately despatched Colonel Wilkinson to carry the happy tidings to Congress. On being introduced into the hall, he said, "The whole British army has laid down its arms at Saratoga; our own, full of vigour and courage, expect your order. It is for your wisdom to decide where the country may still have need for their service." Honours and rewards were liberally voted by the Congress to their conquering general and his men; "and it would be difficult (says the Italian historian, Botta) to describe the transports of joy which the news of this event excited among the Americans. They began to flatter themselves with a still more happy future. No one any longer felt any doubt about their achieving their independence. All hoped, and with good reason, that a success of this importance would at length determine France, and the other European powers that waited for her example, to declare themselves in favour of America. *There could no longer be any question respecting the future; since there was no longer the risk of espousing the cause of a people too feeble to defend themselves.*"

The truth of this was soon displayed in the conduct of France. When the news arrived at Paris of the capture of Ticonderoga, and of the victorious march of Burgoyne towards Albany, events which seemed decisive in favour of the English, instructions had been immediately despatched to Nantz, and the other ports of the kingdom, that no American privateers should be suffered to enter them, except from indispensable necessity, as to repair their vessels, to obtain provisions, or to escape the perils of the sea. The American commissioners at Paris, in their disgust and despair, had almost broken off all negotiations with the French Government; and they even endeavoured to open communications with the British Ministry. But the British government, elated with the first successes of Burgoyne, refused to listen to any overtures for accommodation. But when the news of Saratoga reached Paris, the whole scene was changed. Franklin and his brother commissioners found all their difficulties with the French government vanish. The time seemed to have arrived for the House of Bourbon to take a full revenge for all its humiliations and losses in previous wars. In December a treaty was arranged, and formally signed in the February following, by which France acknowledged *the Independent United States of America.* This was, of course, tantamount to a declaration of war with England. Spain soon followed France; and before long Holland took the same course. Largely aided by French fleets and troops, the Americans vigorously maintained the war against the armies which England, in spite of her European foes, continued to send across the Atlantic. But the struggle was too unequal to be maintained by this country for many years: and when the treaties of 1783 restored peace to the world, the independence of the United States was reluctantly recognized by their ancient parent and recent enemy, England.

—From The Fifteen Decisive Battles of the World: From Marathon to Waterloo, by Sir Edward Shepherd Creasy, English (1812–1878) [first eleven pages omitted].

∽ ❂ ∼

The Discovery of Radium

EVE CURIE

I

WHILE a young wife kept house, washed her baby daughter and put pans on the fire, in a wretched laboratory at the School of Physics a woman physicist was making the most important discovery of modern science.

At the end of 1897 the balance sheet of Marie Curie's activity showed two university degrees, a fellowship and a monograph on the magnetization of tempered steel. No sooner had she recovered from childbirth than she was back again at the laboratory.

The next stage in the logical development of her career was the doctor's degree. Several weeks of indecision came in here. She had to choose a subject of research which would furnish fertile and original material. Like a writer who hesitates and asks himself questions before settling the subject of his next novel, Marie, reviewing the most recent work in physics with Pierre, was in search of a subject for a thesis.

At this critical moment Pierre's advice had an importance which cannot be neglected. With respect to her husband, the young woman regarded herself as an apprentice: he was an older physicist, much more experienced than she. He was even, to put it exactly, her chief, her "boss."

But without a doubt Marie's character, her intimate nature, had a great part in this all-important choice. From childhood the Polish girl had carried the curiosity and daring of an explorer within her. This was the instinct that had driven her to leave Warsaw for Paris and the Sorbonne, and had made her prefer a solitary room in the Latin Quarter to the Dluskis' downy nest. In her walks in the woods she always chose the wild trail or the unfrequented road.

At this moment she was like a traveler musing on a long voyage. Bent over the globe and pointing out, in some far country, a strange name that excites his imagination, the traveler suddenly decides to go there and nowhere else: so Marie, going through the reports of the latest experimental studies, was attracted by the publication of the French scientist Henri Becquerel of the preceding year. She and Pierre already knew this work; she read it over again and studied it with her usual care.

After Roentgen's discovery of X rays, Henri Poincaré conceived the idea of determining whether rays like the X ray were emitted by "fluorescent" bodies under the action of light. Attracted by the same problem, Henri Becquerel examined the salts of a "rare metal," uranium. Instead of finding the phenomenon he had expected, he observed another, altogether different and incomprehensible: he found that uranium salts *spontaneously* emitted, without exposure to light, some rays of unknown nature. A compound of uranium, placed on a photographic plate surrounded by black paper, made an impression on the plate through the paper. And, like the X ray, these astonishing "uranic" salts discharged an electroscope by rendering the surrounding air a conductor.

Henri Becquerel made sure that these surprising properties were not caused by a preliminary exposure to the sun and that they persisted when the uranium compound had been maintained in darkness for several months. For the first time, a physicist had observed the phenomenon to which Marie was later to give the name of *radioactivtiy*. But the nature of the radiation and its origin remained an enigma.

Becquerel's discovery fascinated the Curies. They asked themselves whence came the energy – tiny, to be sure – which uranium compounds constantly disengaged in the form of radiation. And what was the nature of this radiation? Here was an engrossing subject of research, a doctor's thesis! The subject tempted Marie most because it was a virgin field: Becquerel's work was very recent and so far as she knew nobody in the laboratories of Europe had yet attempted to make a fundamental study of uranium rays. As a point of departure, and as the only bibliography, there existed some communications presented by Henri Becquerel at the Academy of Science during the year 1896. It was a leap into great adventure, into an unknown realm.

There remained the question of where she was to make her experiments – and here the difficulties began. Pierre made several approaches to the director of the School of Physics with practically no results: Marie was given the free use of a little glassed-in studio on the ground floor of the school. It was a kind of storeroom, sweating with damp, where unused machines and lumber were put away. Its technical equipment was rudimentary and its comfort nil.

Deprived of an adequate electrical installation and of everything that forms material for the beginning of scientific research, she kept her patience, sought and found a means of making her apparatus work in this hole. . . .

The candidate for the doctor's degree set her first task to be the measurement of the "power of ionization" of uranium rays – that is to say, their power to render the air a conductor of electricity and so to discharge an electroscope. The excellent method she used, which was to be the key to the success of her experiments, had been invented for the study of other phenomena by two physicists well known to her: Pierre and Jacques Curie. Her technical installation consisted of an "ionization chamber," a Curie electrometer and a piezoelectric quartz.

At the end of several weeks the first result appeared: Marie acquired the certainty that the intensity of this surprising radiation was proportional to the quantity of uranium contained in the samples under examination, and that this radiation, which could be measured with precision, was not affected either by the chemical state of combination of the uranium or by external factors such as lighting or temperature.

These observations were perhaps not very sensational to the uninitiated, but they were of passionate interest to the scientist. It often happens in physics that an inexplicable phenomenon can be subjected, after some investigation, to laws already known, and by this very fact loses its interest for the research worker. Thus, in a badly constructed detective story, if we are told in the third chapter that the woman of sinister appearance who might have committed the crime is in reality only an honest little housewife who leads a life without secrets, we feel discouraged and cease to read.

Nothing of the kind happened here. The more Marie penetrated into intimacy with uranium rays, the more they seemed without precedent, essentially unknown. They were like nothing else. Nothing affected them. In spite of their very feeble power, they had an extraordinary individuality.

Turning this mystery over and over in her head, and pointing toward the truth, Marie felt and could soon affirm that the incomprehensible radiation was an *atomic* property. She questioned: Even though the phenomenon had only been observed with uranium, nothing proved that uranium was the only chemical element capable of emitting such radiation. Why should not other bodies possess the same power? Perhaps it was only by chance that this radiation had been observed in uranium first, and had remained attached to uranium in the minds of physicists. Now it must be sought for elsewhere. . . .

No sooner said than done. Abandoning the study of uranium, Marie undertook to examine *all known chemical bodies*, either in the pure state or in compounds. And the result was not long in appearing: compounds of another element, thorium, also emitted spontaneous rays like those of uranium and of similar intensity. The physicist had been right: the surprising phenomenon was by no means the property of uranium alone, and it became necessary to give it a distinct name. Mme. Curie suggested the name of *radioactivity*. Chemical substances like uranium and thorium, endowed with this particular "radiance," were called *radio elements*.

Radioactivity so fascinated the young scientist that she never tired of examining the most diverse forms of matter, always by the same method. Curiosity, a marvelous feminine curiosity, the first virtue of a scientist, was developed in Marie to the highest degree. Instead of limiting her observation to simple compounds, salts and oxides, she had the desire to assemble samples of minerals from the collection at the School of Physics, and of making them undergo almost at hazard, for her own amusement, a kind of customs inspection which is an electrometer test. Pierre approved, and chose with her the veined fragments, hard or crumbly, oddly shaped, which she wanted to examine.

Marie's idea was simple — simple as the stroke of genius. At the crossroads where Marie now stood, hundreds of research workers might have remained, nonplussed, for months or even years. After examining all known chemical substances, and discovering — as Marie had done — the radiation of thorium, they would have continued to ask themselves in vain whence came this mysterious radioactivity. Marie, too, questioned and wondered. But her surprise was translated into fruitful acts. She had used up all evident possibilities. Now she turned toward the unplumbed and the unknown.

She knew in advance what she would learn from an examination of the minerals, or rather she thought she knew. The specimens which contained neither uranium nor thorium would be revealed as totally "inactive." The others, containing uranium or thorium, would be radioactive.

Experiment confirmed this prevision. Rejecting the inactive minerals, Marie applied herself to the others and measured their radioactivity. Then came a dramatic revelation: the radioactivity was a *great deal stronger* than could have been normally foreseen by the quantity of uranium or thorium contained in the products examined!

"It must be an error in experiment," the young woman thought; for doubt is the scientist's first response to an unexpected phenomenon.

She started her measurements over again, unmoved, using the same products. She started over again ten times, twenty times. And she was forced to yield to the evidence: the quantities of uranium and of thorium found in these minerals were by no means sufficient to justify the exceptional intensity of the radiation she observed.

Where did this excessive and abnormal radiation come from? Only one explanation was possible: the minerals must contain, in small quantity, a *much more powerfully radioactive substance* than uranium and thorium.

But what substance? In her preceding experiments, Marie had already examined *all known chemical elements*.

The scientist replied to the question with the sure logic and the magnificent audaciousness of a great mind: The minerals certainly contained a radioactive substance, which was at the same time a chemical element unknown until this day: *a new element*.

A new element! It was a fascinating and alluring hypothesis — but still a hypothesis. For the moment this powerfully radioactive substance existed only in the imagination of Marie and of Pierre. But it did exist there. . . .

By the force of her own intuition the physicist had shown to herself that the wonderful substance must exist. She decreed its existence. But its incognito still had to be broken. Now she would have to verify hypothesis by experiment, isolate this material and see it. She must be able to announce with certainty: "It is there."

Pierre Curie had followed the rapid progress of his wife's experiments with passionate interest. Without directly taking part in Marie's work, he had frequently helped her by his remarks and advice. In view of the stupefying character of her results, he did not hesitate to abandon his study of crystals for the time being in order to join his efforts to hers in the search for the new substance.

Thus, when the immensity of a pressing task suggested and exacted collaboration, a great physicist was at Marie's side — a physicist who was the companion of her life. Three years earlier, love had joined this exceptional man and woman together — love, and perhaps some mysterious foreknowledge, some sublime instinct for the work in common.

The available force was now doubled. Two brains, four hands, now sought the unknown element in the damp little workroom in the Rue Lhomond. From this moment onward it is impossible to distinguish each one's part in the work of the Curies. We know that Marie, having chosen to study the radiation of uranium as the subject of her thesis, discovered that other substances were also radioactive. We know that after the examination of minerals she was able to announce the existence of a new chemical element, powerfully radioactive, and that it was the capital importance of this result which decided Pierre Curie to interrupt his very different research in order to try to isolate this element with his wife. At that time — May or June 1898 — a collaboration began which was to last for eight years, until it was destroyed by a fatal accident.

We cannot and must not attempt to find out what should be credited to Marie and what to Pierre during these eight years. It would be exactly what the husband and wife did not want. The personal genius of Pierre Curie is known to us by the original work he had accomplished before this collaboration. His wife's genius appears to us in the first intuition of discovery, the brilliant start; and it was to reappear to us again, solitary, when Marie Curie the widow unflinchingly carried the weight of a new science and conducted it, through research, step by step, to its harmonious expansion. We therefore have formal proof that in the fusion of their two efforts, in this superior alliance of man and woman, the exchange was equal. . . .

Marie and Pierre looked for this "very active" substance in an ore of uranium called pitchblende, which in the crude state had shown itself to be four times more radioactive than the pure oxide of uranium that could be extracted from it. But the composition of this ore had been known for a long time with considerable precision. The new element must therefore be present in very small quantity or it would not have escaped the notice of scientists and their chemical analysis.

According to their calculations — "pessimistic" calculations, like those of true physicists, who always take the less attractive of two probabilities — the collaborators thought the ore should contain the new element to a maximum quantity of one per cent. They decided that this was very little. They would have been in consternation if they had known that the radioactive element they were hunting down did not count for more than a millionth part of pitchblende ore.

They began their prospecting patiently, using a method of chemical research invented by themselves, based on radioactivity, they separated all the elements in pitchblende by ordinary chemical analysis and then measured the radioactivity of each of the bodies thus obtained. By successive eliminations they saw the "abnormal" radioactivity take refuge in certain parts of the ore. As they went on, the field of investigation was narrowed. It was exactly the technique used by the police when they search the houses of a neighborhood, one by one, to isolate and arrest a malefactor.

But there was more than one malefactor here: the radioactivity was concentrated principally in two different chemical fractions of the pitchblende. For M. and Mme. Curie it indicated the existence of two new elements instead of one. By July 1898 they were able to announce the discovery of one of these substances with certainty.

"You will have to name it," Pierre said to his young wife, in the same tone as if it were a question of choosing a name for little Irène.

The one-time Mlle. Sklodovska reflected in silence for a moment. Then, her heart turning toward her own country which had been erased from the map of the world, she wondered vaguely if the scientific event would be published in Russia, Germany and Austria — the oppressor countries — and answered timidly:

"Could we call it 'polonium'?"

In the *Proceedings of the Academy* for July 1898 we read:

> We believe the substance we have extracted from pitchblende contains a metal not yet observed, related to bismuth by its analytical properties. If the existence of this new metal is confirmed we propose to call it *polonium,* from the name of the original country of one of us. . . .

Life was unchanged in the little flat in the little flat in the Rue de la Glacière. Marie and Pierre worked even more than usual; that was all. When the heat of summer came, the young wife found time to buy some baskets of fruit in the markets and, as usual, she cooked and put away preserves for the winter, according to the recipes used in the Curie family. Then she locked the shutters on her windows, which gave on burned leaves;

she registered their two bicycles at the Orleans station, and, like thousands of other young women in Paris, went off on holiday with her husband and her child.

This year the couple had rented a peasant's house at Auroux, in Auvergne. Happy to breathe good air after the noxious atmosphere of the Rue Lhomond, the Curies made excursions to Mende, Puy, Clermont, Mont-Dore. They climbed hills, visited grottoes, bathed in rivers. Every day, alone in the country, they spoke of what they called their new metals," polonium and "the other"—the one that remained to be found. In September they would go back to the damp workroom and the dull minerals; with freshened ardor they would take up their search again. . . .

In spite of their prosaic character—or perhaps because of it—some notes written by Mme. Curie in that memorable year 1898 seem to us worth quoting. Some are to be found in the margins of a book called *Family Cooking*, with respect to a recipe for gooseberry jelly:

> I took eight pounds of fruit and the same weight in crystallized sugar. After an ebullition of ten minutes, I passed the mixture through a rather fine sieve. I obtained fourteen pots of very good jelly, not transparent, which "took" perfectly.

In a school notebook covered with gray linen, in which the young mother had written little Irène's weight day by day, her diet and the appearance of her first teeth, we read under the date of July 20, 1898, some days after the publication of the discovery of polonium:

> Irène says "thanks" with her hand. She can walk very well now on all fours. She says "Gogli, gogli, go." She stays in the garden all day at Sceaux on a carpet. She can roll, pick herself up, and sit down.

On August 15, at Auroux:

> Irène has cut her seventh tooth, on the lower left. She can stand for half a minute alone. For the past three days we have bathed her in the river. She cries, but today (fourth bath) she stopped crying and played with her hands in the water.
>
> She plays with the cat and chases him with war cries. She is not afraid of strangers any more. She sings a great deal. She gets up on the table when she is in her chair.

Three months later, on October 17, Marie noted with pride:

> Irène can walk very well, and no longer goes on all fours.

On January 5, 1899:

> Irène has fifteen teeth!

Between these two notes—that of October 17, 1898, in which Irène no longer goes on all fours, and that of January 5 in which Irène has fifteen teeth—and a few months after the note on the gooseberry preserve, we find another note worthy of remark.

It was drawn up by Marie and Pierre and a collaborator called G. Bémont. Intended for the Academy of Science, and published in the *Proceedings* of the session of December 26, 1898, it announced the existence of a second new chemical element in pitchblende.

Some lines of this communication read as follows:

> *The various reasons we have just enumerated lead us to believe that the new radioactive substance contains a new element to which we propose to give the name of RADIUM.*
>
> *The new radioactive substance certainly contains a very strong proportion of barium; in spite of that its radioactivity is considerable. The radioactivity of radium therefore must be enormous.*

II

A man chosen at random from a crowd to read an account of the discovery of radium would not have doubted for one moment that radium existed: beings whose critical sense has not been sharpened and simultaneously deformed by specialized culture keep their imaginations fresh. They are ready to accept an unexpected fact, however extraordinary it may appear, and to wonder at it.

The physicist colleagues of the Curies received the news in slightly different fashion. The special properties of polonium and radium upset fundamental theories in which scientists had believed for centuries. How was one to explain the spontaneous radiation of the radioactive bodies? The discovery upset a world of acquired knowledge and contradicted the most firmly established ideas on the composition of matter. Thus the physicist kept on the reserve. He was violently interested in Pierre and Marie's work, he could perceive its infinite developments, but before being convinced he awaited the acquisition of decisive results.

The attitude of the chemist was even more downright. By definition, a chemist only believes in the existence of a new substance when he has seen the substance, touched it, weighed and examined it, confronted it with acids, bottled it, and when he has determined its "atomic weight."

Now, up to the present, nobody had "seen" radium. Nobody knew the atomic weight of radium. And the chemists, faithful to their principles, concluded: "No atomic weight, no radium. Show us some radium and we will believe you."

To show polonium and radium to the incredulous, to prove to the world the existence of their "children," and to complete their own conviction, M. and Mme. Curie were now to labor for four years.

The aim was to obtain pure radium and polonium. In the most strongly radioactive products the scientists had prepared, these substances figured only in imperceptible traces. Pierre and Marie already knew the method by which they could hope to isolate the new metals, but the separation could not be made except by treating very large quantities of crude material.

Here arose three agonizing questions:

How were they to get a sufficient quantity of ore? What premises could they use to effect their treatment? What money was there to pay the inevitable cost of the work?

Pitchblende, in which polonium and radium were hidden, was a costly ore, treated at the St. Joachimsthal mines in Bohemia for the extraction of uranium salts used in the manufacture of glass. Tons of pitchblende would cost a great deal: a great deal too much for the Curie household.

Ingenuity was to make up for wealth. According to the expectation of the two scientists, the extraction of uranium should leave, intact in the ore, such traces of polonium and radium as the ore contains. There was no reason why these traces should not be found in the residue. And, whereas crude pitchblende was costly, its residue after treatment had very slight value. By asking an Austrian colleague for a recommendation to the directors of the mines of St. Joachimsthal would it not be possible to obtain a considerable quantity of such residue for a reasonable price?

It was simple enough: but somebody had to think of it.

It was necessary, of course, to buy this crude material and pay for its transportation to Paris. Pierre and Marie appropriated the required sum from their very slight savings. They were not so foolish as to ask for official credits. . . . If two physicists on the scent of an immense discovery had asked the University of Paris or the French government for a grant to buy pitchblende residue they would have been lost in the files of some office, and they would have had to wait months for a reply, probably unfavorable in the end. Out of the traditions and principles of the French Revolution, which had created the metric system, founded the Normal School, and encouraged science in many circumstances, the State seemed to have retained, after more than a century, only the deplorable words pronounced by Fouquier-Tinville at the trial in which Lavoisier was condemned to the guillotine: "The Republic has no need for scientists."

But at least could there not be found, in the numerous buildings attached to the Sorbonne, some kind of suitable workroom to lend to the Curie couple? Apparently not. After vain attempts, Pierre and Marie staggered back to their point of departure, which is to say to the School of Physics where Pierre taught, to the little room where Marie had done her first experiments. The room gave on a courtyard, and on the other side of the yard there was a wooden shack, an abandoned shed, with a skylight roof in such bad condition that it admitted the rain. The Faculty of Medicine had formerly used the place as a dissecting room, but for a long time now it had not even been considered fit to house the cadavers. No floor: an uncertain layer of bitumen covered the earth. It was furnished with some worn kitchen tables, a blackboard which had landed there for no known reason, and an old cast-iron stove with a rusty pipe.

A workman would not willingly have worked in such a place; Marie and Pierre, nevertheless, resigned themselves to it. The shed had one advantage: it was so untempting, so miserable, that nobody thought of refusing them the use of it. Schutzenberger, the director of the school, had always been very kind to Pierre Curie and no doubt regretted that he had nothing better to offer. However that may be, he offered nothing else; and the couple, very pleased at not being put out into the street with their material, thanked him, saying that "this would do" and that they would "make the best of it."

As they were taking possession of the shed, a reply arrived from Austria. Good news! By extraordinary luck, the residue of recent extractions of uranium had not been scattered. The useless material had been piled up in a no-man's-land planted with pine trees, near the mine of St. Joachimsthal. Thanks to the intercession of Professor Suess and the Academy of Science of Vienna, the Austrian government, which was the proprietor of the State factory there, decided to present a ton of residue to the two French lunatics who thought they needed it. If, later on, they wished to be sent a greater quantity of the material, they could obtain it at the mine on the best terms. For the moment the Curies had to pay only the transportation charges on a ton of ore.

One morning a heavy wagon, like those which deliver coal, drew up in the Rue Lhomond before the School of Physics. Pierre and Marie were notified. They hurried bareheaded into the street in their laboratory gowns. Pierre, who was never agitated, kept his calm; but the more exuberant Marie could not contain her joy at the sight of the sacks that were being unloaded. It was pitchblende, *her* pitchblende, for which she had received a notice some days before from the freight station. Full of curiosity and impatience, she wanted to open one of the sacks and contemplate her treasure without further waiting. She cut the strings, undid the coarse sackcloth and plunged her two hands into the dull brown ore, still mixed with pine needles from Bohemia.

There was where radium was hidden. It was from there that Marie must extract it, even if she had to treat a mountain of this inert stuff like dust on the road.

Marya Sklodovska had lived through the most intoxicating moments of her student life in a garret; Marie Curie was to know wonderful joys again in a dilapidated shed. It was a strange sort of beginning over again, in which a sharp subtle happiness (which probably no woman before Marie had ever experienced) twice elected the most miserable setting.

The shed in the Rue Lhomond surpassed the most pessimistic expectations of discomfort. In summer, because of its skylights, it was as stifling as a hothouse. In winter one did not know whether to wish for rain or frost; if it rained, the water fell drop by drop, with a soft, nerve-racking noise, on the ground or on the worktables, in places which the physicists had to mark in order to avoid putting apparatus there. If it froze, one froze. There was no recourse. The stove, even when it was stoked white, was a complete disappointment. If one went near enough to touch it one received a little heat, but two steps away and one was back in the zone of ice.

It was almost better for Marie and Pierre to get used to the cruelty of the outside temperature, since their technical installation – hardly existent – possessed no chimneys to carry off noxious gases, and the greater part of their treatment had to be made in the open air, in the courtyard. When a shower came the physicists hastily moved their apparatus inside: to keep on working without being suffocated they set up draughts between the opened door and windows. . . .

In such conditions M. and Mme. Curie worked for four years from 1898 to 1902.

During the first year they busied themselves with the chemical separation of radium and polonium and they studied the radiation of the products (more and more active) thus obtained. Before long they considered it more practical to separate their efforts. Pierre Curie tried to determine the properties of radium, and to know the new metal better. Marie continued those chemical treatments which would permit her to obtain salts of pure radium.

In this division of labor Marie had chosen the "man's job." She accomplished the toil of a day laborer. Inside the shed her husband was absorbed by delicate experiments. In the courtyard, dressed in her old dust-covered and acid-stained smock, her hair blown by the wind, surrounded by smoke which stung her eyes and throat, Marie was a sort of factory all by herself.

> I came to treat as many as twenty kilograms of matter at a time, she writes, which had the effect of filling the shed

with great jars full of precipitates and liquids. It was killing work to carry the receivers, to pour off the liquids and to stir, for hours at a stretch, the boiling matter in a smelting basin.

Radium showed no intention of allowing itself to be known by human creatures. Where were the days when Marie naïvely expected the radium content of pitchblende to be *one per cent?* The radiation of the new substance was so powerful that a tiny quantity of radium, disseminated through the ore, was the source of striking phenomena which could be easily observed and measured. The difficult, the impossible thing, was to isolate this minute quantity, to separate it from the gangue in which it was so intimately mixed.

The days of work became months and years: Pierre and Marie were not discouraged. This material which resisted them, which defended its secrets, fascinated them. United by their tenderness, united by their intellectual passions, they had, in a wooden shack, the "anti-natural" existence for which they had both been made, she as well as he. . . .

Whenever Pierre and Marie, alone in this poor place, left their apparatus for a moment and quietly let their tongues run on, their talk about their beloved radium passed from the transcendent to the childish.

"I wonder what *It* will be like, what *It* will look like," Marie said one day with the feverish curiosity of a child who has been promised a toy. "Pierre, what form do you imagine *It* will take?"

"I don't know," the physicist answered gently. "I should like it to have a very beautiful color. . . ."

Marie continued to treat, kilogram by kilogram, the tons of pitchblende residue which were sent her on several occasions from St. Joachimsthal. With her terrible patience, she was able to be, every day for four years, a physicist, a chemist, a specialized worker, an engineer and a laboring man all at once. Thanks to her brain and muscle, the old tables in the shed held more and more concentrated products — products more and more rich in radium. Mme. Curie was approaching the end: she no longer stood in the courtyard, enveloped in bitter smoke, to watch the heavy basins of material in fusion. She was now at the stage of purification and of the "fractional crystallization" of strongly radioactive solutions. But the poverty of her haphazard equipment hindered her work more than ever. It was now that she needed a spotlessly clean workroom and apparatus perfectly protected against cold, heat and dirt. In this shed, open to every wind, iron and coal dust was afloat which, to Marie's despair, mixed itself into the products purified with so much care. Her heart sometimes constricted before these little daily accidents, which took so much of her time and her strength.

Pierre was so tired of the interminable struggle that he would have been quite ready to abandon it. Of course, he did not dream of dropping the study of radium and of radioactivity. But he would have willingly have renounced, for the time being, the special operation of preparing pure radium. The obstacles seemed insurmountable. Could they not resume this work later on, under better conditions? More attached to the meaning of natural phenomena than to their material reality, Pierre Curie was exasperated to see the paltry results to which Marie's exhausting effort had led. He advised an armistice.

He counted without his wife's character. Marie wanted to isolate radium and she would isolate it. She scorned fatigue and difficulties, and even the gaps in her own knowledge which complicated her task. After all, she was only a very young scientist: she still had not the certainty and great culture Pierre had acquired by twenty years' work, and sometimes she stumbled across phenomena or methods of calculation which she knew very little, and for which she had to make hasty studies.

So much the worse! With stubborn eyes under her great brow, she clung to her apparatus and her test tubes.

In 1902, forty-five months after the day on which the Curies announced the probable existence of radium, Marie finally carried off the victory in this war of attrition: she succeeded in preparing a decigram of pure radium, and made a first determination of the atomic weight of the new substance, which was 225.

The incredulous chemists — of whom there were still a few — could only bow before the facts, before the superhuman obstinacy of a woman.

Radium officially existed.

It was nine o'clock at night. Pierre and

Marie Curie were in their little house at 108 Boulevard Kellermann, where they had been living since 1900. The house suited them well. From the boulevard, where three rows of trees half hid the fortifications, could be seen only a dull wall and a tiny door. But behind the one-story house, hidden from all eyes, there was a narrow provincial garden, rather pretty and very quiet. And from the "barrier" of Gentilly they could escape on their bicycles toward the suburbs and the woods. . . .

Old Dr. Curie, who lived with the couple, had retired to his room. Marie had bathed her child and put it to bed, and had stayed for a long time beside the cot. This was a rite. When Irène did not feel her mother near her at night she would call out for her incessantly, with that "Mé!" which was to be our substitute for "Mamma" always. And Marie, yielding to the implacability of the four-year-old baby, climbed the stairs, seated herself beside the child and stayed there in the darkness until the young voice gave way to light, regular breathing. Only then would she go down again to Pierre, who was growing impatient. In spite of his kindness, he was the most possessive and jealous of husbands. He was so used to the constant presence of his wife that her least eclipse kept him from thinking freely. If Marie delayed too long near her daughter, he received her on her return with a reproach so unjust as to be comic:

"You never think of anything but that child!"

Pierre walked slowly about the room. Marie sat down and made some stitches on the hem of Irène's new apron. One of her principles was never to buy ready-made clothes for the child: she thought them too fancy and impractical. In the days when Bronya was in Paris the two sisters cut out their children's dresses together, according to patterns of their own invention. These patterns still served for Marie.

But this evening she could not fix her attention. Nervous, she got up; then, suddenly:

"Suppose we go down there for a moment?"

There was a note of supplication in her voice – altogether superfluous, for Pierre, like herself, longed to go back to the shed they had left two hours before. Radium, fanciful as a living creature, endearing as a love, called them back to its dwelling, to the wretched laboratory.

The day's work had been hard, and it would have been more reasonable for the couple to rest. But Pierre and Marie were not always reasonable. As soon as they had put on their coats and told Dr. Curie of their flight, they were in the street. They went on foot, arm in arm, exchanging few words. After the crowded streets of this queer district, with its factory buildings, wastelands and poor tenements, they arrived in the Rue Lhomond and crossed the little courtyard. Pierre put the key in the lock. The door squeaked, as it had squeaked thousands of times, and admitted them to their realm, to their dream.

"Don't light the lamps!" Marie said in the darkness. Then she added with a little laugh:

"Do you remember the day when you said to me 'I should like radium to have a beautiful color'?"

The reality was more entrancing than the simple wish of long ago. Radium had something better than "a beautiful color": it was spontaneously luminous. And in the somber shed where, in the absence of cupboards, the precious particles in their tiny glass receivers were placed on tables or on shelves nailed to the wall, their phosphorescent bluish outlines gleamed, suspended in the night.

"Look . . . Look!" the young woman murmured.

She went forward cautiously, looked for and found a straw-bottomed chair. She sat down in the darkness and silence. Their two faces turned toward the pale glimmering, the mysterious sources of radiation, toward radium – their radium. Her body leaning forward, her head eager, Marie took up again the attitude which had been hers an hour earlier at the bedside of her sleeping child.

Her companion's hand lightly touched her hair.

She was to remember forever this evening of glowworms, this magic.

— *From Madame Curie, a Biography, by Eve Curie, French (1904–), translated by Vincent Sheean.*

PART FOURTEEN

Contacts of Races

~ ❁ ~

THE TRUE HUMANITARIANS of the world are those who, in the words of Shelley, become the

> . . . nerve, o'er which do creep
> The else unfelt oppressions of this earth.

Time will come when men will learn that what befalls others will inevitably touch them. Once life was simpler and the world was smaller; and it was easy to realize the truth of old maxims. Today we live in a world of haste, preoccupation with machines, and both international and interracial conflicts which confuse our sense of human values. Some poets and tellers of tales, however, enable us to see clearly the human traits which have made life endurable.

In the literature which they have created is reflected a world which man himself has made; in which characters clearly demonstrate that as their life and thought are narrow, their sympathies shrink to a like scale. It is also a most pleasant and humane world — as men seek goodness and beauty about them; or it is cruel and intolerant — as they shut themselves up with their petty selves and few magnanimous sentiments. And some of the greatest chapters of this literature deal with the experiences of men and women who have come to love individuals of foreign blood, who have struggled with the poignant problems of social adjustment arising from mixed blood, who know intimately the pathos of separation from beloved kindred by vast oceans, who are beneficiaries of unexpected acts of generosity from other nationals who expect no return. This literature is as old as the first meeting of Noah's descendants. In all the centuries since his sons, according to the old tale, founded the various branches of the human family, its members have loved or hated, constructively admired or jealously exploited the best in each other.

"I believe in the ultimate decency of things," wrote Robert Louis Stevenson in a letter to a friend, "ay, and if I woke in hell I should still believe it." Such optimism may be difficult to maintain in the world we know. But the dreams of poets have proved truer and more enduring than the views of realistic observers. As men keep eyes alert and ears open, they may discover with the delight of pathfinders the reaches of the human spirit and the sympathetic kinship with all mankind which is the chief trait of the citizen of the world.

The Book of Ruth

I

Now it came to pass in the days when the judges ruled, that there was a famine in the land. And a certain man of Beth-lehem-judah went to sojourn in the country of Moab, he, and his wife, and his two sons. And the name of the man was Elimelech, and the name of his wife Naomi, and the name of his two sons Mahlon and Chilion, Ephrathites of Beth-lehem-judah. And they came into the country of Moab, and continued there. And Elimelech Naomi's husband died; and she was left, and her two sons. And they took them wives of the women of Moab; the name of the one was Orpah, and the name of the other Ruth: and they dwelt there about ten years. And Mahlon and Chilion died also both of them; and the woman was left of her two sons and her husband.

Then she arose with her daughters in law, that she might return from the country of Moab: for she had heard in the country of Moab how that the Lord had visited his people in giving them bread. Wherefore she went forth out of the place where she was, and her two daughters in law with her; and they went on the way to return unto the land of Judah.

And Naomi said unto her two daughters in law, Go, return each to her mother's house: the Lord deal kindly with you, as ye have dealt with the dead, and with me. The Lord grant you that ye may find rest, each of you in the house of her husband. Then she kissed them; and they lifted up their voice, and wept.

And they said unto her, Surely we will return with thee unto thy people.

And Naomi said, Turn again, my daughters: why will ye go with me? are there yet any more sons in my womb, that they may be your husbands? Turn again, my daughters, go your way; for I am too old to have an husband. If I should say, I have hope, if I should have an husband also tonight, and should also bear sons; would ye tarry for them till they were grown? would ye stay for them from having husbands? nay, my daughters; for it grieveth me much for your sakes, that the hand of the Lord is gone out against me.

And they lifted up their voice, and wept again: and Orpah kissed her mother in law; but Ruth clave unto her.

And she said, Behold, thy sister in law is gone back unto her people, and unto her gods: return thou after thy sister in law.

And Ruth said, Intreat me not to leave thee, or to return from following after thee: for whither thou goest, I will go; and where thou lodgest, I will lodge; thy people shall be my people, and thy God my God: where thou diest, will I die, and there will I be buried: the Lord do so to me, and more also, if aught but death part thee and me.

When she saw that she was steadfastly minded to go with her, then she left speaking unto her. So they two went until they came to Beth-lehem. And it came to pass, when they were come to Beth-lehem, that all the city was moved about them, and they said, Is this Naomi?

And she said unto them, Call me not Naomi, call me Mara: for the Almighty hath dealt very bitterly with me. I went out full, and the Lord hath brought me home again empty: why then call ye me Naomi, seeing the Lord hath testified against me, and the Almighty hath afflicted me?

So Naomi returned, and Ruth the Moabitess, her daughter in law, with her, which returned out of the country of Moab: and they came to Bethlehem in the beginning of barley harvest.

II

And Naomi had a kinsman of her husband's, a mighty man of wealth, of the family of Elimelech; and his name was Boaz.

And Ruth the Moabitess said unto Naomi, Let me now go to the field, and glean ears of corn after him in whose sight I shall find grace. And she said unto her, Go, my daughter.

And she went, and came, and gleaned in the field after the reapers; and her hap was to light on a part of the field belonging unto Boaz, who was of the kindred of Elimelech.

And behold, Boaz came from Beth-lehem, and said unto the reapers, The Lord be with you. And they answered him, The Lord bless thee. Then said Boaz unto his servant that was set over the reapers, Whose damsel is this? And the servant that was set over the reapers answered and said, It is the Moabitish damsel that came back with Naomi out of the country of Moab: and she said, I pray you, let me glean and gather after the reapers among the sheaves: so she came, and hath continued even from the morning until now, that she tarried a little in the house.

Then said Boaz unto Ruth, Hearest thou not, my daughter? Go not to glean in another field, neither go from hence, but abide here fast by my maidens: let thine eyes be on the field that they do reap, and go thou after them: have I not charged the young men that they shall not touch thee? and when thou art athirst, go unto the vessels, and drink of that which the young men have drawn.

Then she fell on her face, and bowed herself to the ground, and said unto him, Why have I found grace in thine eyes, that thou shouldest take knowledge of me, seeing I am a stranger?

And Boaz answered and said unto her, It hath fully been shewed me, all that thou hast done unto thy mother in law since the death of thine husband: and how thou hast left thy father and thy mother, and the land of thy nativity, and art come unto a people which thou knewest not heretofore. The Lord recompense thy work, and a full reward be given thee of the Lord God of Israel, under whose wings thou art come to trust.

Then she said, Let me find favour in thy sight, my lord; for that thou hast comforted me, and for that thou hast spoken friendly unto thine handmaid, though I be not like unto one of thy handmaidens.

And Boaz said unto her, At meal time come thou hither, and eat of the bread, and dip thy morsel in the vinegar. And she sat beside the reapers: and he reached her parched corn, and she did eat, and was sufficed, and left.

And when she was risen up to glean, Boaz commanded his young men, saying, Let her glean even among the sheaves, and reproach her not: and let fall also some of the handfuls of purpose for her, and leave them, that she may glean them, and rebuke her not.

So she gleaned in the field until even, and beat out that she had gleaned: and it was about an ephah of barley. And she took it up, and went into the city: and her mother in law saw what she had gleaned: and she brought forth, and gave to her that she had reserved after she was sufficed.

And her mother in law said unto her, Where hast thou gleaned today? and where wroughtest thou? blessed be he that did take knowledge of thee. And she shewed her mother in law with whom she had wrought, and said, The man's name with whom I wrought today is Boaz.

And Naomi said unto her daughter in law, Blessed be he of the Lord, who hath not left off his kindness to the living and to the dead. And Naomi said unto her, The man is near of kin unto us, one of our next kinsmen.

And Ruth the Moabitess said, He said unto me also, Thou shalt keep fast by my young men, until they have ended all my harvest.

And Naomi said unto Ruth her daughter in law, It is good, my daughter, that thou go out with his maidens, that they meet thee not in any other field.

So she kept fast by the maidens of Boaz to glean unto the end of barley harvest and of wheat harvest; and dwelt with her mother in law.

III

Then Naomi her mother in law said unto her, My daughter, shall I not seek rest for thee, that it may be well with thee? And now is not Boaz of our kindred, with whose maidens thou wast? Behold, he winnoweth barley tonight in the threshing floor. Wash thyself therefore, and anoint thee, and put thy raiment upon thee, and get thee down to the floor: but make not thyself known unto the man, until he shall have done eating and drinking. And it shall be when he lieth down, that thou shalt mark the place where he shall lie, and thou shalt go in, and uncover his feet, and lay thee down; and he will tell thee what thou shalt do.

And she said unto her, All that thou sayest unto me I will do.

And she went down unto the floor, and did according to all that her mother in law bade her. And when Boaz had eaten and drunk, and his heart was merry, he went to lie down at the end of the heap of corn: and she came softly, and uncovered his feet, and laid her down.

And it came to pass at midnight, that the man was afraid, and turned himself: and behold, a woman lay at his feet.

And he said, Who are thou? And she answered, I am Ruth thine handmaid: spread therefore thy skirt over thine handmaid; for thou art a near kinsman.

And he said, Blessed be thou of the Lord, my daughter: for thou hast shewed more kindness in the latter end than at the beginning, inasmuch as thou followedst not young men, whether poor or rich. And now, my daughter, fear not; I will do to thee all that thou requirest: for all the city of my people doth know that thou art a virtuous woman. And now it is true that I am thy near kinsman: howbeit there is a kinsman nearer than I. Tarry this night, and it shall be in the morning, that if he will perform unto thee the part of a kinsman, well; let him do the kinsman's part: but if he will not do the part of a kinsman to thee, then will I do the part of a kinsman to thee, as the Lord liveth: lie down until the morning.

And she lay at his feet until the morning: and she rose up before one could know another. And he said, Let it not be known that a woman came into the floor. Also he said, Bring the veil that thou hast upon thee, and hold it. And when she held it, he measured six measures of barley, and laid it on her: and she went into the city.

And when she came to her mother in law, she said, Who are thou, my daughter? and she told her all that the man had done to her. And she said, These six measures of barley gave he me; for he said to me, Go not empty unto thy mother in law.

Then said she, Sit still, my daughter, until thou know how the matter will fall: for the man will not be in rest, until he have finished the thing this day.

IV

Then went Boaz up to the gate, and sat him down there: and behold, the kinsman of whom Boaz spake came by; unto whom he said, Ho, such a one! turn aside, sit down here. And he turned aside, and sat down. And he took ten men of the elders of the city, and said, Sit ye down here. And they sat down.

And he said unto the kinsman, Naomi, that is come again out of the country of Moab, selleth a parcel of land, which was our brother Elimelech's: and I thought to advertise thee, saying, Buy it before the inhabitants, and before the elders of my people. If thou wilt redeem it, redeem it: but if thou wilt not redeem it, then tell me, that I may know: for there is none to redeem it besides thee; and I am after thee. And he said, I will redeem it.

Then said Boaz, What day thou buyest the field of the hand of Naomi, thou must buy it also of Ruth the Moabitess, the wife of the dead, to raise up the name of the dead upon his inheritance.

And the kinsman said, I cannot redeem it for myself, lest I mar mine own inheritance: redeem thou my right to thyself; for I cannot redeem it.

Now this was the manner in former time in Israel concerning redeeming and concerning changing, for to confirm all things; a man plucked off his shoe, and gave it to his neighbour: and this was a testimony in Israel. Therefore the kinsman said unto Boaz, Buy it for thee. So he drew off his shoe.

And Boaz said unto the elders, and unto all the people, Ye are witnesses this day, that I have bought all that was Elimelech's, and all that was Chilion's and Mahlon's, of the hand of Naomi. Moreover, Ruth the Moabitess, the wife of Mahlon, have I purchased to be my wife, to raise up the name of the dead upon his inheritance, that the name of the dead be not cut off from among his brethren, and from the gate of his place: ye are witnesses this day.

And all the people that were in the gate, and the elders, said, We are witnesses. The Lord make the woman that is come into thine house like Rachel and like Leah, which two did build the house of Israel: and do thou worthily in Ephratah and be famous in Beth-lehem: and let thine house be like the house of Pharez, whom Tamar bare unto Judah, of the seed which the Lord shall give thee of this young woman.

So Boaz took Ruth, and she was his wife: and when he went in unto her, the Lord gave her conception, and she bare a son.

And the women said unto Naomi, Blessed be the Lord, which hath not left thee this day without a kinsman, that his name may be famous in Israel. And he shall be unto thee a restorer of thy life, and a nourisher of thine old age: for thy daughter in law, which loveth thee, which is better to thee than seven sons, hath borne him.

And Naomi took the child, and laid it in her bosom, and became nurse unto it. And the women her neighbours gave it a name, saying, There is a son born to Naomi; and they called his name Obed: he is the father of Jesse, the father of David.

—From the Book of Ruth, in the Old Testament (Hebrew), the Authorized (King James) version.

The Procurator of Judea

ANATOLE FRANCE

LAELIUS LAMIA, born in Italy of illustrious parents, had not yet discarded the *toga prætexta* when he set out for the schools of Athens to study philosophy. Subsequently he took up his residence at Rome, and in his house on the Esquiline, amid a circle of youthful wastrels, abandoned himself to licentious courses. But being accused of engaging in criminal relations with Lepida, the wife of Sulpicius Quirinus, a man of consular rank, and being found guilty, he was exiled by Tiberius Cæsar. At that time he was just entering his twenty-fourth year. During the eighteen years that his exile lasted he traversed Syria, Palestine, Cappadocia, and Armenia, and made prolonged visits to Antioch, Cæsarea, and Jerusalem. When, after the death of Tiberius, Caius was raised to the purple, Lamia obtained permission to return to Rome. He even regained a portion of his possessions. Adversity had taught him wisdom.

He avoided all intercourse with the wives and daughters of Roman citizens, made no efforts toward obtaining office, held aloof from public honours, and lived a secluded life in his house on the Esquiline. Occupying himself with the task of recording all the remarkable things he had seen during his distant travels, he turned, as he said, the vicissitudes of his years of expiation into a diversion for his hours of rest. In the midst of these calm enjoyments, alternating with assiduous study of the works of Epicurus, he recognized with a mixture of surprise and vexation that age was stealing upon him. In his sixty-second year, being afflicted with an illness which proved in no slight degree troublesome, he decided to have recourse to the waters of Baiæ. The coast at that point, once frequented by the halcyon, was at this date the resort of the wealthy Roman, greedy of pleasure. For a week Lamia lived alone, without a friend in the brilliant crowd. Then one day, after dinner, an inclination to which he yielded urged him to ascend the inclines, which, covered with vines that resembled bacchantes, looked out upon the waves.

Having reached the summit he seated himself by the side of a path beneath a terebinth, and let his glances wander over the lovely landscape. To his left, livid and bare, the Phlegræan plain stretched out towards the ruins of Cumæ. On his right, Cape Misenum plunged its abrupt spur beneath the Tyrrhenian sea. Beneath his feet luxurious Baiæ, following the graceful outline of the coast, displayed its gardens, its villas thronged with statues, its porticos, its marble terraces along the shores of the blue ocean where the dolphins sported. Before him, on the other side of the bay, on the Campanian coast, gilded by the already sinking sun, gleamed the temples which far away rose above the laurels of Posilippo, whilst on the extreme horizon Vesuvius looked forth smiling.

Lamia drew from a fold of his toga a scroll containing the *Treatise upon Nature*, extended himself upon the ground, and began to read. But the warning cries of a slave necessitated his rising to allow of the passage of a litter which was being carried along the narrow pathway through the vineyards. The litter being uncurtained, permitted Lamia to see stretched upon the cushions as it was borne nearer to him the figure of an elderly man of immense bulk, who, supporting his head on his hand, gazed out with a gloomy and disdainful expression. His nose, which was aquiline, and his chin, which was prominent, seemed desirous of meeting across his lips, and his jaws were powerful.

From the first moment Lamia was convinced that the face was familiar to him. He hesitated a moment before the name came to him. Then suddenly hastening towards the litter with a display of surprise and delight —

"Pontius Pilate!" he cried. "The gods be praised who have permitted me to see you once again!"

The old man gave a signal to the slaves to stop, and cast a keen glance upon the stranger who had addressed him.

"Pontius, my dear host," resumed the latter, "have twenty years so far whitened my hair and hollowed my cheeks that you no longer recognise your friend Lælius Lamia?"

At this name Pontius Pilate dismounted from the litter as actively as the weight of his years and the heaviness of his gait permitted him, and embraced Lælius Lamia again and again.

"Gods! what a treat it is to me to see you once more! But, alas, you call up memories of those long-vanished days when I was Procurator of Judæa, in the province of Syria.

Why, it must be thirty years ago that I first met you. It was at Cæsarea, whither you came to drag out your weary term of exile. I was fortunate enough to alleviate it a little, and out of friendship, Lamia, you followed me to that depressing place Jerusalem, where the Jews filled me with bitterness and disgust. You remained for more than ten years my guest and my companion, and in converse about Rome and things Roman we both of us managed to find consolation – you for your misfortunes, and I for my burdens of State."

Lamia embraced him afresh.

"You forget two things, Pontius; you are overlooking the facts that you used your influence on my behalf with Herod Antipas, and that your purse was freely open to me."

"Let us not talk of that," replied Pontius, "since after your return to Rome you sent me by one of your freedmen a sum of money which repaid me with usury."

"Pontius, I could never consider myself out of your debt by the mere payment of money. But tell me, have the gods fulfilled your desires? Are you in the enjoyment of all the happiness you deserve? Tell me about your family, your fortunes, your health."

"I have withdrawn to Sicily, where I possess estates, and where I cultivate wheat for the market. My eldest daughter, my best-beloved Pontia, who has been left a widow, lives with me, and directs my household. The gods be praised, I have preserved my mental vigour; my memory is not in the least degree enfeebled. But old age always brings in its train a long procession of griefs and infirmities. I am cruelly tormented with gout. And at this very moment you find me on my way to the Phlegræan plain in search of a remedy for my sufferings. From that burning soil, whence at night flames burst forth, proceed acrid exhalations of sulphur, which, so they say, ease the pains and restore suppleness to the stiffened joints. At least, the physicians assure me that it is so."

"May you find it so in your case, Pontius! But, despite the gout and its burning torments, you scarcely look as old as myself, although in reality you must be my senior by ten years. Unmistakably you have retained a greater degree of vigour than I ever possessed, and I am overjoyed to find you looking so hale. Why, dear friend, did you retire from the public service before the customary age? Why, on resigning your governorship in Judæa, did you withdraw to a voluntary exile on your Sicilian estates? Give me an account of your doings from the moment that I ceased to be a witness of them. You were preparing to suppress a Samaritan rising when I set out for Cappadocia, where I hoped to draw some profit from the breeding of horses and mules. I have not seen you since then. How did that expedition succeed? Pray tell me. Everything interests me that concerns you in any way."

Pontius Pilate sadly shook his head.

"My natural disposition," he said, "as well as a sense of duty, impelled me to fulfil my public responsibilities, not merely with diligence, but even with ardour. But I was pursued by unrelenting hatred. Intrigues and calumnies cut short my career in its prime, and the fruit it should have looked to bear has withered away. You ask me about the Samaritan insurrection. Let us sit down on this hillock. I shall be able to give you an answer in few words. These occurrences are as vividly present to me as if they had happened yesterday.

"A man of the people, of persuasive speech – there are many such to be met with in Syria – induced the Samaritans to gather together in arms on Mount Gerizim (which in that country is looked upon as a holy place) under the promise that he would disclose to their sight the sacred vessels which in the ancient days of Evander and our father, Æneas, had been hidden away by an eponymous hero, or rather a tribal deity, named Moses. Upon this assurance the Samaritans rose in rebellion; but having been warned in time to forestall them, I dispatched detachments of infantry to occupy the mountain, and stationed cavalry to keep the approaches to it under observation.

"These measures of prudence were urgent. The rebels were already laying siege to the town of Tyrathaba, situated at the foot of Mount Gerizim. I easily dispersed them, and stifled the as yet scarcely organized revolt. Then, in order to give a forcible example with as few victims as possible, I handed over to execution the leaders of the rebellion. But you are aware, Lamia, in what straight dependence I was kept by the proconsul Vitellius, who governed Syria not in, but against the interests of Rome, and looked upon the provinces of the empire as territories which could be farmed out to tetrarchs. The head men among the Samaritans, in their resentment against me, came and fell at his feet lamenting. To listen to them, nothing had been further from their thoughts than to disobey Cæsar. It was I who had provoked the rising, and it was purely in order to withstand my violence that they had gathered together around Tyrathaba. Vitellius listened to their complaints, and handing over the affairs of Judæa to his friend Marcellus, commanded me to go and justify my proceedings before the Emperor himself. With a heart overflowing with grief and resentment I took ship. Just as I approached the shores of Italy, Tiberius, worn out with age and the cares of empire, died suddenly on the self-same Cape Misenum, whose peak we see from this very spot magnified in the mists of evening. I demanded justice of Caius, his successor, whose perception was naturally acute, and who was acquainted with Syrian affairs. But marvel with me, Lamia, at the maliciousness of fortune, resolved on my discomfiture. Caius then had in his suite at Rome the Jew Agrippa, his companion, the friend of his childhood, whom he cherished as his own eyes. Now Agrippa favoured Vitellius, inasmuch as Vitellius was the enemy of Antipas, whom Agrippa pursued with his hatred. The Emperor adopted the prejudices of his beloved Asiatic, and refused even to listen to me. There was nothing for me to do but bow beneath the stroke of unmerited misfortune. With tears for my meat and gall for my portion, I withdrew to my estates in Sicily, where I should have died of grief if my sweet Pontia had not come to console her father. I have cultivated wheat, and succeeded in producing the fullest ears in the whole province. But now my life is ended; the future will judge between Vitellius and me."

"Pontius," replied Lamia, "I am persuaded that you acted towards the Samaritans according to the rectitude of your character, and solely in the interests of Rome. But were you not perchance on that occasion a trifle too much influenced by that impetuous courage which has always swayed you? You will remember that in Judæa it often happened that I who, younger than you, should naturally have been more impetuous than you, was obliged to urge you to clemency and suavity."

"Suavity towards the Jews!" cried Pontius Pilate. "Although you have lived amongst them, it seems clear that you ill understand those enemies of the human race. Haughty and at the same time base, combining an invincible obstinacy with a despicably mean spirit, they weary alike your love and your hatred. My character, Lamia, was formed upon the maxims of the divine Augustus. When I was appointed Procurator of Judæa, the world was already penetrated with the majestic ideal of the *pax romana.* No longer, as in the days of our internecine strife, were we witnesses to the sack of our province for the aggrandizement of a proconsul. I knew where my duty lay. I was careful that my actions should be governed by prudence and moderation. The gods are my witnesses that I was resolved upon mildness, and upon mildness only. Yet what did my benevolent intentions avail me? You were at my side, Lamia, when, at the outset of my career as ruler, the first rebellion came to a head. Is there any need for me to recall the details to you? The garrison had been transferred from Cæsarea to take up its winter quarters at Jerusalem. Upon the ensigns of the legionaries appeared the presentment of Cæsar. The inhabitants of Jerusalem, who did not recognize the indwelling divinity of the Emperor, were scandalized at this, as though, when obedience is compulsory, it were not less abject to obey a god than a man. The priests of their nation appeared before my tribunal imploring me with supercilious humility to have the ensigns removed from within the holy city. Out of reverence for the divine nature of Cæsar and the majesty of the empire, I refused to comply. Then the rabble made common cause with the priests, and all around the pretorium portentous cries of supplication arose. I ordered the soldiers to stack their spears in front of the tower of Antonia, and to proceed, armed only with sticks like lictors, to disperse the insolent crowd. But, heedless of blows, the Jews continued their entreaties, and the more obstinate amongst them threw themselves on the ground and, exposing their throats to the rods, deliberately courted death. You were a witness of my humiliation on that occasion, Lamia. By the order of Vitellius I was forced to send the insignia back to Cæsarea. That disgrace I had certainly not merited. Before the immortal gods I swear that never once during my term of office did I flout justice and the laws. But I am grown old. My enemies and detractors are dead. I shall die unavenged. Who will retrieve my character?"

He moaned and lapsed into silence. Lamia replied:

"That man is prudent who neither hopes nor fears anything from the uncertain events of the future. Does it matter in the least what estimate men may form of us hereafter? We ourselves are after all our own witnesses, and our own judges. You must rely, Pontius Pilate, on the testimony you yourself bear to your own rectitude. Be content with your own personal respect and that of your friends. For the rest, we know that mildness by itself will not suffice for the work of government. There is but little room in the actions of public men for that indulgence of human frailty which the philosophers recommend."

"We'll say no more at present," said Pontius. "The sulphurous fumes which rise from the Phlegræan plain are more powerful when the ground which exhales them is still warm beneath the sun's rays. I must hasten on. Adieu! But now that I have rediscovered a friend, I should wish to take advantage of my good fortune. Do me the favour, Lælius Lamia, to give me your company at supper at my house to-morrow. My house stands on the seashore, at the extreme end of the town in the direction of Misenum. You will easily recognize it by the porch, which bears a painting representing Orpheus surrounded by tigers and lions, whom he is charming with the strains from his lyre.

"Till to-morrow, Lamia," he repeated, as he climbed once more into his litter. "To-morrow we will talk about Judæa."

The following day at the supper hour Lamia presented himself at the house of Pontius Pilate. Two couches only were in readiness for occupants. Creditably but simply equipped, the table held a silver service in which were set out beccaficos in honey, thrushes, oysters from the Lucrine lake, and lampreys from Sicily. As they proceeded with their repast, Pontius and Lamia interchanged inquiries with one another about their ailments, the symptoms of which they described at considerable length, mutually emulous of communicating the various remedies which had been recommended to them. Then, congratulating themselves on being thrown together once more at Baiæ, they vied with one another in praise of the beauty of that enchanting coast and the mildness of the climate they enjoyed. Lamia was enthusiastic about the charms of the courtesans who frequented the seashore laden with golden ornaments and trailing draperies of barbaric broidery. But the aged Procurator deplored the ostentation with which by means of trumpery jewels and filmy garments foreigners and even enemies of the empire beguiled the Romans of their gold. After a time they turned to the subject of the great engineering feats that had been accomplished in the country; the prodigious bridge constructed by Caius between Puteoli and Baiæ, and the canals which Augustus excavated to convey the waters of the ocean to Lake Avernus and the Lucrine lake.

"I also," said Pontius, with a sigh, "I also wished to set afoot public works of great utility. When, for my sins, I was appointed Governor of Judæa, I conceived the idea of furnishing Jerusalem with an abundant supply of pure water by means of an aqueduct. The elevation of the levels, the proportionate capacity of the various parts, the gradiant for the brazen reservoirs to which the distribution pipes were to be fixed — I had gone into every detail, and decided everything for myself with the assistance of mechanical experts. I had drawn up regulations for the superintendents so as to prevent individuals from making unauthorized depredations. The architects and the workmen had their instructions. I gave orders for the commencement of operations. But far from viewing with satisfaction the construction of that conduit, which was intended to carry to their town upon its massive arches not only water but health, the inhabitants of Jerusalem gave vent to lamentable outcries. They gathered tumultuously together exclaiming against the sacrilege and impiousness, and hurling themselves upon the workmen, scattered the very foundation stones. Can you picture to yourself, Lamia, a filthier set of barbarians? Nevertheless, Vitellius decided in their favour, and I received orders to put a stop to the work."

"It is a knotty point," said Lamia, "how far one is justified in devising things for the commonwealth against the will of the populace."

Pontius Pilate continued as though he had not heard this interruption.

"Refuse an aqueduct! What madness! But whatever is of Roman origin is distasteful to the Jews. In their eyes we are an unclean race, and our very presence appears a profanation to them. You will remember that they would never venture to enter the pretorium for fear of defiling themselves, and that I was consequently obliged to discharge my magisterial functions in an open-air tribunal on that marble pavement your feet so often trod.

"They fear us and they despise us. Yet is not Rome the mother and warden of all these peoples who nestle smiling upon her venerable bosom? With her eagles in the van, peace and liberty have been carried to the very confines of the universe. Those whom we have subdued we look on as our friends, and we leave those conquered races, nay, we secure to them the permanence of their customs and their laws. Did Syria, aforetime rent asunder by its rabble of petty kings, ever even begin to taste of peace and prosperity until it submitted to the armies of Pompey? And when Rome might have reaped a golden harvest as the price of her goodwill, did she lay hands on the hoards that swell the treasuries of barbaric temples? Did she despoil the shrine of Cybele at Pessinus, or the Morimene and Cilician sanctuaries of Jupiter, or the temple of the Jewish god at Jerusalem? Antioch, Palmyra, and Apamea, secure despite their wealth, and no longer in dread of the wandering Arab of the desert, have erected temples to the genius of Rome and the divine Cæsar. The Jews alone hate and withstand us. They withhold their tribute till it is wrested from them, and obstinately rebel against military service."

"The Jews," replied Lamia, "are profoundly attached to their ancient customs. They suspected you, unreasonably I admit, of a desire to abolish their laws and change their usages. Do not resent it, Pontius, if I say that you did not always act in such a way as to disperse their unfortunate illusion. It gratified you, despite your habitual self-restraint, to play upon their fears, and more than once have I seen you betray in their presence the contempt with which their beliefs and religious ceremonies inspired you. You irritated them particularly by giving instructions for the sacerdotal garments and ornaments of their high priest to be kept in ward by your legionaries in the Antonine tower. One must admit that though they have never risen like us to an appreciation of things divine, the Jews celebrate rites which their very antiquity renders venerable."

Pontius Pilate shrugged his shoulders.

"They have very little exact knowledge of the nature of the gods," he said. "They worship Jupiter, yet they abstain from naming him or erecting a statue of him. They do not even adore him under the semblance of a rude stone, as certain of the Asiatic peoples are wont to do. They know nothing of Apollo, of Neptune, of Mars, nor of Pluto, nor of any goddess. At the same time, I am convinced that in days gone by they worshipped Venus. For even to this day their women bring doves to the altar as victims; and you know as well as I that the dealers who trade beneath the arcades of their temple supply those birds in couples for sacrifice. I have even been told that on one occasion some madman proceeded to overturn the stalls bearing these offerings, and their owners with them. The priests raised an outcry about it, and looked on it as a case of sacrilege. I am of opinion that their custom of sacrificing turtle-doves was instituted in honour of Venus. Why are you laughing, Lamia?"

"I was laughing," said Lamia, "at an amusing idea which, I hardly know how, just occurred to me. I was thinking that perchance some day the Jupiter of the Jews might come to Rome and vent his fury upon you. Why should he not? Asia and Africa have already enriched us with a considerable number of gods. We have seen temples in honour of Isis and the dog-faced Anubis erected in Rome. In the public squares, and even on the racecourses, you may run across the Bona Dea of the Syrians mounted on an ass. And did you never hear how, in the reign of Tiberius, a young patrician passed himself off as the horned Jupiter of the Egyptians, Jupiter Ammon, and in this disguise procured the favours of an illustrious lady who was too virtuous to deny anything to a god? Beware, Pontius, lest the invisible Jupiter of the Jews disembark some day on the quay at Ostia!"

At the idea of a god coming out of Judæa, a fleeting smile played over the severe countenance of the Procurator. Then he replied gravely:

"How would the Jews manage to impose their sacred law on outside peoples when they are in a perpetual state of tumult amongst themselves as to the interpretation of that law? You have seen them yourself, Lamia, in the public squares, split up into twenty rival parties, with staves in their hands, abusing each other and clutching one another by the beard. You have seen them on the steps of the temple, tearing their filthy garments as a symbol of lamentation, with some wretched creature in a frenzy of prophetic exaltation in their midst. They have never realized that it is possible to discuss peacefully and with an even mind those matters concerning the divine which yet are hidden from the profane and wrapped in uncertainty. For the nature of the immortal gods remains hidden from us, and we cannot arrive at a knowledge of it. Though I am of opinion, none the less, that it is a prudent thing to believe in the providence of the gods. But the Jews are devoid of philosophy, and cannot tolerate any diversity of opinions. On the contrary, they judge worthy of the extreme penalty all those who on divine subjects profess opinions opposed to their law. And as since the genius of Rome has towered over them, capital sentences pronounced by their own tribunals can only be carried out with the sanction of the proconsul or the procurator, they harry the Roman magistrate at any hour to procure his signature to their baleful decrees, they besiege the pretorium with their cries of 'Death!' A hundred times, at least, have I known them, mustered, rich and poor together, all united under their priests, make a furious onslaught on my ivory chair, seizing me by the skirts of my robe, by the thongs of my sandals, and all to demand of me — nay, to exact from me — the death sentence on some unfortunate whose guilt I failed to perceive, and as to whom I could only pronounce that he was as mad as his accusers. A hundred times, do I say! Not a hundred, but every day and all day. Yet it was my duty to execute their law as if it were ours, since I was appointed by Rome not for the destruction, but for the upholding of their customs, and over them I had the power of the rod and the axe. At the outset of my term of office I endeavoured to persuade them to hear reason. I attempted to snatch their miserable victims from death. But this show of mildness only irritated them the more; they demanded their prey, fighting around me like a horde of vultures with wing and beak. Their priests reported to Cæsar that I was violating their law, and their appeals, supported by Vitellius, drew down upon me a severe reprimand. How many times did I long, as the Greeks used to say, to dispatch accusers and accused in one convoy to the crows!

"Do not imagine, Lamia, that I nourish the rancour of the discomfited, the wrath of the superannuated, against a people which in my person has prevailed against both Rome and tranquillity. But I foresee the extremity to which sooner or later they will reduce us. Since we cannot govern them, we shall be driven to destroy them. Never doubt it. Always in a state of insubordination, brewing rebellion in their inflammatory minds, they will one day burst forth upon us with a fury beside which the wrath of the Numidians and the mutterings of the Parthians are mere child's play. They are secretly nourishing preposterous hopes, and madly premeditating our ruin. How can it be otherwise, when, on the strength of an oracle, they are living in expectation of the coming of a prince of their own blood whose kingdom shall extend over the whole earth. There are no half measures with such a people. They must be exterminated. Jerusalem must be laid waste to the very foundation. Perchance, old as I am, it may be granted me to behold the day when her walls shall fall and the flames shall envelop her houses, when her inhabitants shall pass under the edge of the sword, when salt shall be strewn on the place where once the temple stood. And in that day I shall at length be justified."

Lamia exerted himself to lead the conversation back to a less acrimonious note.

"Pontius," he said, "it is not difficult for me to understand both your long-standing resentment and your sinister forebodings. Truly, what you have experienced of the character of the Jews is nothing to their advantage. But I lived in Jerusalem as an interested onlooker, and mingled freely with the people, and I succeeded in detecting certain obscure virtues in these rude folk which were altogether hidden from you. I have met Jews who were all mildness, whose simple manners and faithfulness of heart recalled to me what our poets have related concerning the Spartan lawgiver. And you yourself, Pontius, have seen perish beneath the cudgels of your legionaries simple-minded men who have died for a cause they believed to be just without revealing their names. Such men do not deserve our contempt. I am saying this because it is desirable in all things to preserve moderation and an even mind. But I own that I never experienced any lively sympathy for the Jews. The Jewess, on the contrary, I found extremely pleasing. I was young, then, and the Syrian women stirred all my senses to response. Their ruddy lips, their liquid eyes that shone in the shade, their sleepy gaze pierced me to the very marrow. Painted and stained, smelling of nard and myrrh, steeped in odours, their physical attractions are both rare and delightful."

Pontius listened impatiently to these praises.

"I was not the kind of man to fall into the snares of the Jewish women," he said; "and since you have opened the subject yourself, Lamia, I was never able to approve of your laxity. If I did not express with sufficient emphasis formerly how culpable I held you for having intrigued at Rome with the wife of a man of consular rank, it was because you were then enduring heavy penance for your misdoings. Marriage from the patrician point of view is a sacred tie; it is one of the institutions which are the support of Rome. As to foreign women and slaves, such relations as one may enter into with them would be of little account were it not that they habituate the body to a humiliating effeminacy. Let me tell you that you have been too liberal in your offerings to the Venus of the Marketplace; and what, above all, I blame in you is that you have not married in compliance with the law and given children to the Republic, as every good citizen is bound to do."

But the man who had suffered exile under Tiberius was no longer listening to the venerable magistrate. Having tossed off his cup of Falernian, he was smiling at some image visible to his eye alone.

After a moment's silence he resumed in a very deep voice, which rose in pitch by little and little:

"With what languorous grace they dance, those Syrian women! I knew a Jewess at Jerusalem who used to dance in a poky little room, on a threadbare carpet, by the light of one smoky little lamp, waving her arms as she clanged her cymbals. Her loins arched, her head thrown back, and, as it were, dragged down by the weight of her heavy red hair, her eyes swimming with voluptuousness, eager, languishing, compliant, she would have made Cleopatra herself grow pale with envy. I was in love with her barbaric dances, her voice — a little raucous and yet so sweet — her atmosphere of incense, the semi-somnolescent state in which she seemed to live. I followed her everywhere. I mixed with the vile rabble of soldiers, conjurers, and extortioners with which she was surrounded. One day, however, she disappeared, and I saw her no more. Long did I seek her in disreputable alleys and taverns. It was more difficult to learn to do without her than to lose the taste for Greek wine. Some months after I lost sight of her, I learned by chance that she had attached herself to a small company of men and women who were followers of a young Galilean thaumaturgist. His name was Jesus; he came from Nazareth, and he was crucified for some crime, I don't quite know what. Pontius, do you remember anything about the man?"

Pontius Pilate contracted his brows, and his hand rose to his forehead in the attitude of one who probes the deeps of memory. Then after a silence of some seconds:

"Jesus?" he murmured, "Jesus — of Nazareth? I cannot call him to mind."

— *From Mother of Pearl, by Anatole France (Jacques Anatole François Thibault), French, (1844–1924); translated by Frederick Chapman.*

~ ✲ ~

Aucassin and Nicolete

'Tis of Aucassin and Nicolete.
Who would list to the good lay
Gladness of the captive gray?
'Tis how two young lovers met,
Aucassin and Nicolete,
Of the pains the lover bore
And the sorrows he outwore,
For the goodness and the grace,
Of his love, so fair of face.

Sweet the song, the story sweet,
There is no man hearkens it,
No man living 'neath the sun,
So outwearied, so foredone,
Sick and woeful, worn and sad,
But is healed, but is glad,
'Tis so sweet.

So SAY THEY, speak they, tell they the Tale:

How the Count Bougars de Valence made war on Count Garin de Biaucaire, war so great, and so marvelous, and so mortal that never a day dawned but alway he was there, by the gates and walls, and barriers of the town with a hundred knights, and ten thousand men at arms, horsemen and footmen: so burned he the Count's land, and spoiled his country, and slew his men. Now the Count Garin de Biaucaire was old and frail, and his good days were gone over. No heir had he, neither son nor daughter, save one young man only; such an one as I shall tell you. Aucassin was the name of the damoiseau: fair was he, goodly, and great, and featly fashioned of his body, and limbs. His hair was yellow, in little curls, his eyes blue and laughing, his face beautiful and shapely, his nose high and well set, and so richly seen was he in all things good, that in him was none evil at all. But so suddenly overtaken was he of Love, who is a great master, that he would not, of his will, be dubbed knight, nor take arms, nor follow tourneys, nor do whatsoever him beseemed. Therefore his father and mother said to him:

"Son, go take thine arms, mount thy horse, and hold thy land, and help thy men, for if they see thee among them, more stoutly will they keep in battle their lives, and lands, and thine, and mine."

"Father," said Aucassin, "I marvel that you will be speaking. Never may God give me aught of my desire if I be made knight, or mount my horse, or face stour and battle wherein knights smite and are smitten again, unless thou give me Nicolete, my true love, that I love so well."

"Son," said the father, "this may not be. Let Nicolete go, a slave girl she is, out of a strange land, and the captain of this town bought her of the Saracens, and carried her hither, and hath reared her and let christen the maid, and took her for his daughter in God, and one day will find a young man for her, to win her bread honorably. Herein hast thou nought to make or mend, but if a wife thou wilt have, I will give thee the daughter of a King, or a Count. There is no man so rich in France, but if thou desire his daughter, thou shalt have her."

"Faith! my father," said Aucassin, "tell me where is the place so high in all the world, that Nicolete, my sweet lady and love, would not grace it well? If she were Empress of Constantinople or of Germany, or Queen of France or England, it were little enough for her; so gentle is she and courteous, and debonaire, and compact of all good qualities."

Here singeth one:

Aucassin was of Biaucaire
Of a goodly castle there,
But from Nicolete the fair
None might win his heart away
Though his father, many a day,
And his mother said him nay,
"Ha! fond child, what wouldest thou?
Nicolete is glad enow!
Was from Carthage cast away,
Paynims sold her on a day!
Wouldst thou win a lady fair
Choose a maid of high degree
Such an one is meet for thee."
"Nay of these I have no care,
Nicolete is debonaire,
Her body sweet and the face of her
Take my heart as in a snare,
Loyal love is but her share
That is so sweet."

Then speak they, say they, tell they the Tale:

When the Count Garin de Biaucaire knew that he would avail not to withdraw Aucassin his son from the love of Nicolete, he went to the Captain of the city, who was his man, and spake to him saying:

"Sir Count; away with Nicolete thy daughter in God; cursed be the land whence she was brought into this country, for by reason of her do I lose Aucassin, that will neither be dubbed knight, nor do aught of the things that fall to him to be done. And wit ye well," he said, "that if I might have her at my will, I would burn her in a fire, and yourself might well be sore adread."

"Sir," said the Captain, "this is grievous to me that he comes and goes and hath speech with her. I had bought the maiden at mine own charges, and nourished her, and baptized, and made her my daughter in God. Yea, I would have given her to a young man that should win her bread honorably. With this had Aucassin thy son nought to make or mend. But, sith it is thy will and thy pleasure, I will send her into that land and that country where never will he see her with his eyes."

"Have a heed to thyself," said the Count Garin, "thence might great evil come on thee."

So parted they from each other. Now the Captain was a right rich man: so had he a rich palace with a garden in face of it; in an upper chamber thereof he let place Nicolete with one old woman to keep her company, and in that chamber put bread and meat and wine and such things as were needful. Then he let seal the door, that none might come in or go forth, save that there was one window, over against the garden, and strait enough, where through came to them a little air.

Here singeth one:

Nicolete as ye heard tell
Prisoned is within a cell
That is painted wondrously
With colors of a far countrie,
And the window of marble wrought,
There the maiden stood in thought,
With straight brows and yellow hair
Never saw ye fairer fair!
On the wood she gazed below,
And she saw the roses blow,
Heard the birds sing loud and low,
Therefore spoke she woefully:
"Ah me, wherefore do I lie
Here in prison wrongfully:
Aucassin, my love, my knight,
Am I not thy heart's delight,
Thou that lovest me aright!
'Tis for thee that I must dwell
In the vaulted chamber cell,
Hard beset and all alone!
By our Lady Mary's Son
Here no longer will I wonn,
If I may flee!"

Then speak they, say they, tell they the Tale:

Nicolete was in prison, as ye have heard soothly, in the chamber. And the noise and bruit of it went through all the country and all the land, how that Nicolete was lost. Some said she had fled the country, and some that the Count Garin de Biaucaire had let slay her. Whosoever had joy thereof, Aucassin had none, so he went to the Captain of the town and spoke to him, saying:

"Sir Captain, what hast thou made of Nicolete, my sweet lady and love, the thing that best I love in all the world? Hast thou carried her off or ravished her away from me? Know well that if I die of it, the price shall be demanded of thee, and that will be well done, for it shall be even as if thou hadst slain me with thy two hands, for thou hast taken from me the thing that in this world I loved the best."

"Fair Sir," said the Captain, "let these things be. Nicolete is a captive that I did bring from a strange country. Yea, I bought her at my own charges of the Saracens, and I bred her up and baptized her, and made her my daughter in God. And I have cherished her, and one of these days I would have given her a young man, to win her bread honorably. With this thou hast naught to make, but do thou take the daughter of a King or a Count. Nay more, what wouldst thou deem thee to have gained, hadst thou made her thy leman, and taken her to thy bed? Plentiful lack of comfort hadst thou got thereby, for in Hell would thy soul have lain while the world endures, and into Paradise wouldst thou have entered never."

"In Paradise what have I to win? Therein I seek not to enter, but only to have Nicolete, my sweet lady that I love so well. For into Paradise go none but such folk as I shall tell thee now. Thither go these same old priests, and halt old men and maimed, who all day and night cower continually before the altars, and in the crypts; and such folk as wear old amices and old clouted frocks, and naked folk and shoeless, and covered with sores, perishing of hunger and thirst, and of cold, and of little ease. These be they that go into Paradise, with them have I naught to make. But into Hell would I fain go; for into Hell fare the goodly clerks, and goodly knights that fall in tourneys and great wars, and stout men at arms, and all men noble. With these would I liefly go. And thither pass the sweet ladies and courteous that have two lovers, or three, and their lords also thereto. Thither goes the gold, and the silver, and cloth of vair, and cloth of gris, and harpers, and makers, and the princes of this world. With these I would gladly go, let me but have with me Nicolete, my sweetest lady."

"Certes," quoth the Captain, "in vain wilt thou speak thereof, for never shalt thou see her; and if thou hadst word with her, and thy father knew it, he would let burn in a fire both her and me, and thyself might well be sore adread."

"That is even what irketh me," quoth Aucassin. So he went from the Captain sorrowing.

Here singeth one:

Aucassin did so depart
Much in dole and heavy at heart
For his love so bright and dear,
None might bring him any cheer,

None might give good words to hear.
To the palace doth he fare
Climbeth up the palace-stair,
Passeth to a chamber there,
Thus great sorrow doth he bear,
For his lady and love so fair.
"Nicolete how fair art thou,
Sweet thy foot-fall, sweet thine eyes,
Sweet the mirth of thy replies,
Sweet thy laughter, sweet thy face,
Sweet thy lips and sweet thy brow,
And the touch of thine embrace,
All for thee I sorrow now,
Captive in an evil place,
Whence I ne'er may go my ways
Sister, sweet friend!"

So say they, speak they, tell they the Tale:

While Aucassin was in the chamber sorrowing for Nicolete his love, even then the Count Bougars de Valence, that had his war to wage, forgat it no wit, but had called up his horsemen and his footmen, so made he for the castle to storm it. And the cry of battle arose, and the din, and knights and men at arms busked them, and ran to walls and gates to hold the keep. And the townsfolk mounted to the battlements, and cast down bolts and pikes. Then while the assault was great and even at its height, the Count Garin de Biaucaire came into the chamber where Aucassin was making lament, sorrowing for Nicolete, his sweet lady that he loved so well.

"Ha! son," quoth he, "how caitiff art thou, and cowardly, that canst see men assail thy goodliest castle and strongest. Know thou that if thou lose it, thou losest all. Son, go to, take arms, and mount thy horse, and defend thy land, and help thy men and fare into the stour. Thou needst not smite nor be smitten. If they do but see thee among them, better will they guard their substance, and their lives, and thy land and mine. And thou art so great, and hardy of thy hands, that well mightst thou do this thing, and to do it is thy devoir."

"Father," said Aucassin, "what is this thou sayest now? God grant me never aught of my desire, if I be dubbed knight, or mount steed, or go into the stour where knights do smite and are smitten, if thou givest me not Nicolete, my sweet lady, whom I love so well."

"Son," quoth his father, "this may never be: rather would I be quite disinherited and lose all that is mine, than that thou shouldst have her to thy wife, or to love *par amours*."

So he turned him about. But when Aucassin saw him going he called to him again saying,

"Father, go to now, I will make with thee fair covenant."

"What covenant, fair son?"

"I will take up arms, and go into the stour, on this covenant, that, if God bring me back sound and safe, thou wilt let me see Nicolete my sweet lady, even so long that I may have of her two words or three, and one kiss."

"That will I grant," said his father.

At this was Aucassin glad.

Here one singeth:

Of the kiss heard Aucassin
That returning he shall win.
None so glad would he have been
Of a myriad marks of gold
Of a hundred thousand told.
Called for raiment brave of steel,
Then they clad him, head to heel,
Twyfold hauberk doth he don,
Firmly braced the helmet on.
Girt the sword with hilt of gold,
Horse doth mount, and lance doth wield,
Looks to stirrups and to shield,
Wondrous brave he rode to field.
Dreaming of his lady dear
Setteth spurs to the destrere,
Rideth forward without fear,
Through the gate and forth away
To the fray.

So speak they, say they, tell they the Tale:

Aucassin was armed and mounted as ye have heard tell. God! how goodly sat the shield on his shoulder, the helm on his head, and the baldric on his left haunch! And the damoiseau was tall, fair, featly fashioned, and hardy of his hands, and the horse whereon he rode swift and keen, and straight had he spurred him forth of the gate. Now believe ye not that his mind was on kine, nor cattle of the booty, nor thought he how he might strike a knight, nor be stricken again: nor no such thing. Nay, no memory had Aucassin of aught of these; rather he so dreamed of Nicolete, his sweet lady, that he dropped his reins, forgetting all there was to do, and his horse that had felt the spur, bore him into the press and hurled among the foe, and they laid hands on him all about, and took him captive, and seized away his spear and shield, and straightway they led him off a prisoner, and were even now discoursing of what death he should die.

And when Aucassin heard them,

"Ha! God," said he, "sweet Savior. Be these my deadly enemies that have taken me, and will soon cut off my head? And once my head is off, no more shall I speak with Nicolete, my sweet lady, that I love so well. Natheless have I here a good sword, and sit a good horse unwearied. If now I keep not my head for her sake, God help her never, if she love me more!"

The damoiseau was tall and strong, and the horse whereon he sat was right eager. And he laid hand to sword, and fell a-smiting to right and left, and smote through helm and *nasal*, and arm and clenched hand, making a murder about him, like a wild boar when hounds fall on him in the forest, even till he struck down ten knights, and seven he hurt, and straightway he hurled out of the press, and rode back again at full speed, sword in hand. The Count Bougars de Valence heard say they were about hanging Aucassin, his enemy, so he came into that place and Aucassin was ware of him, and gat his sword into his hand, and lashed at his helm with such a stroke that he drave it down on his head, and he being stunned, fell groveling. And Aucassin laid hands on him, and caught him by the *nasal* of his helmet, and gave him to his father.

"Father," quoth Aucassin, "lo here is your mortal foe, who hath so warred on you with all malengin. Full twenty years did this war endure, and might not be ended by man."

"Fair son," said his father, "thy feats of youth shouldst thou do, and not seek after folly."

"Father," said Aucassin, "sermon me no sermons, but fulfill my covenant."

"Ha! what covenant, fair son?"

"What, father, hast thou forgotten it? By mine own head, whosoever forgets, will I not forget it, so much it hath me at heart. Didst thou not covenant with me when I took up arms, and went into the stour, that if God brought me back safe and sound, thou wouldst let me see Nicolete, my sweet lady, even so long that I may have of her two words or three, and one kiss? So didst thou covenant, and my mind is that thou keep thy word."

"I!" quoth the father, "God forsake me when I keep this covenant! Nay, if she were here I would let her burn in the fire, and thyself shouldst be sore adread."

"Is this thy last word?" quoth Aucassin.

"So help me God," quoth his father, "yea!"

"Certes," quoth Aucassin, "this is a sorry thing meseems, when a man of thine age lies!"

"Count of Valence," quoth Aucassin, "I took thee?"

"In sooth, Sir, didst thou," saith the Count.

"Give me thy hand," saith Aucassin.

"Sir, with good will."

So he set his hand in the other's.

"Now givest thou me thy word," saith Aucassin, "that never whiles thou art living man wilt thou avail to do my father dishonor, or harm him in body, or in goods, but do it thou wilt?"

"Sir, in God's name," saith he, "mock me not, but put me to my ransom; ye cannot ask of me gold nor silver, horses nor palfreys, *vair* nor *gris,* hawks nor hounds, but I will give you them."

"What?" quoth Aucassin. "Ha, knowest thou not it was I that took thee?"

"Yea, sir," quoth the Count Bougars.

"God help me never, but I will make thy head fly from thy shoulders, if thou makest not truth," said Aucassin.

"In God's name," said he, "I make what promise thou wilt."

So they did the oath, and Aucassin let mount him on a horse, and took another and so led him back till he was all in safety.

Here one singeth:

When the Count Garin doth know
That his child would ne'er forego
Love of her that loved him so,
Nicolete, the bright of brow,
In a dungeon deep below
Childe Aucassin did he throw.
Even there the Childe must dwell
In a dun-walled marble cell.
There he waileth in his woe
Crying thus as ye shall know.
"Nicolete, thou lily white,
My sweet lady, bright of brow,
Sweeter than the grape art thou,
Sweeter than sack posset good
In a cup of maple wood!
Was it not but yesterday
That a palmer came this way,
Out of Limousin came he,

And at ease he might not be,
For a passion him possessed
That upon his bed he lay,
Lay, and tossed, and knew not rest
In his pain discomforted.
But thou camest by the bed,
Where he tossed amid his pain,
Holding high thy sweeping train,
And thy kirtle of ermine,
And thy smock of linen fine,
Then these fair white limbs of thine,
Did he look on, and it fell
That the palmer straight was well,
Straight was hale – and comforted,
And he rose up from his bed,
And went back to his own place,
Sound and strong, and full of face!
My sweet lady, lily white,
Sweet thy footfall, sweet thine eyes,
And the mirth of thy replies.
Sweet thy laughter, sweet thy face,
Sweet thy lips and sweet thy brow,
And the touch of thine embrace.
Who but doth in thee delight?
I for love of thee am bound
In this dungeon underground,
All for loving thee must lie
Here where loud on thee I cry,
Here for loving thee must die
For thee, my love."

Then say they, speak they, tell they the Tale:

Aucassin was cast into prison as ye have heard tell, and Nicolete, of her part, was in the chamber. Now it was summer time, the month of May, when days are warm, and long, and clear, and the night still and serene. Nicolete lay one night on her bed and saw the moon shine clear through a window, yea, and heard the nightingale sing in the garden, so she minded her of Aucassin her lover whom she loved so well. Then fell she to thoughts of Count Garin de Biaucaire, that hated her to the death; therefore deemed she that there she would no longer abide, for that, if she were told of, and the Count knew whereas she lay, an ill death would he make her die. Now she knew that the old woman slept who held her company. Then she arose, and clad her in a mantle of silk she had by her, very goodly, and took napkins, and sheets of the bed, and knotted one to the other, and made therewith a cord as long as she might, so knitted it to a pillar in the window, and let herself slip down into the garden, then caught up her raiment in both hands, behind and before, and kilted up her kirtle, because of dew that she saw lying deep on the grass, and so went her way down through the garden.

Her locks were yellow and curled, her eyes blue and smiling, her face featly fashioned, the nose high and fairly set, the lips more red than cherry or rose in time of summer, her teeth white and small; her breasts so firm that they bore up the folds of her bodice as they had been two apples; so slim she was in the waist that your two hands might have clipped her, and the daisy flowers that brake beneath her as she went tiptoe, and that bent above her instep, seemed black against her feet, so white was the maiden. She came to the postern gate, and unbarred it, and went out through the streets of Biaucaire, keeping always on the shadowy side, for the moon was shining right clear, and so wandered she till she came to the tower where her lover lay. The tower was flanked with buttresses, and she cowered under one of them, wrapped in her mantle. Then thrust she her head through a crevice of the tower that was old and worn, and so heard she Aucassin wailing within, and making dole and lament for the sweet lady he loved so well. And when she had listened to him she began to say:

Here one singeth:

Nicolete the bright of brow
On a pillar leanest thou,
All Aucassin's wail dost hear
For his love that is so dear,
Then thou spakest, shrill and clear,
"Gentle knight withouten fear
Little good befalleth thee,
Little help of sigh or tear,
Ne'er shalt thou have joy of me.
Never shalt thou win me; still
Am I held in evil will
Of thy father and thy kin,
Therefore must I cross the sea,
And another land must win."
Then she cut her curls of gold,
Cast them in the dungeon hold,
Aucassin doth clasp them there,
Kissed the curls that were so fair,
Them doth in his bosom bear,
Then he wept, even as of old,
All for his love!

Then say they, speak they, tell they the Tale:

When Aucassin heard Nicolete say that she would pass into a far country, he was all in wrath.

"Fair sweet friend," quoth he, "thou shalt not go, for then wouldst thou be my death. And the first man that saw thee and had the might withal, would take thee straightway into his bed to be his leman. And once thou camest into a man's bed and that bed not mine, wit ye well that I would not tarry till I had found a knife to pierce my heart and slay myself. Nay, verily, wait so long I would not; but would hurl myself on it so soon as I could find a wall, or a black stone, thereon would I dash my head so mightily, that the eyes would start, and my brain burst. Rather would I die even such a death, than know thou hadst lain in a man's bed, and that bed not mine."

"Aucassin," she said, "I trow thou lovest me not as much as thou sayest, but I love thee more than thou lovest me."

"Ah, fair sweet friend," said Aucassin, "it may not be that thou shouldst love me even as I love thee. Woman may not love man as man loves woman, for a woman's love lies in the glance of her eye, and the bud of her breast, and her foot's tip-toe, but the love of man is in his heart planted, whence it can never issue forth and pass away."

Now while Aucassin and Nicolete held this parley together, the town's guards came down a street, with swords drawn beneath their cloaks, for the Count Garin had charged them that if they could take her they should slay her. But the sentinel that was on the tower saw them coming, and heard them speaking of Nicolete as they went, and threatening to slay her.

"God!" quoth he, "this were great pity to slay so fair a maid! Right great charity it were if I could say aught to her, and they perceive it not, and she should be on her guard against them, for if they slay her, then were Aucassin, my damoiseau, dead, and that were great pity."

Here one singeth:

Valiant was the sentinel,
Courteous, kind, and practiced well,
So a song did sing and tell
Of the peril that befell.
"Maiden fair that lingerest here,
Gentle maid of merry cheer,
Hair of gold, and eyes as clear
As the water in a mere,
Thou, meseems, hast spoken word
To thy lover and thy lord,
That would die for thee, his dear;
Now beware the ill accord,
Of the cloaked men of the sword,
These have sworn and keep their word,
They will put thee to the sword
Save thou take heed!"

Then speak they, say they, tell they the Tale:

"Ha!" quoth Nicolete, "be the soul of thy father and the soul of thy mother in the rest of Paradise, so fairly and so courteously hast thou spoken me! Please God, I will be right ware of them, God keep me out of their hands."

So she shrank under her mantle into the shadow of the pillar till they had passed by, and then took she farewell of Aucassin, and so fared till she came unto the castle wall. Now that wall was wasted and broken, and some deal mended, so she clomb thereon till she came between wall and fosse, and so looked down, and saw that the fosse was deep and steep, whereat she was sore adread.

"Ah, God," saith she, "sweet Savior! If I let myself fall hence, I shall break my neck, and if here I abide, tomorrow they will take me and burn me in a fire. Yet liefer would I perish here than that tomorrow the folk should stare on me for a gazing-stock."

Then she crossed herself, and so let herself slip into the fosse, and when she had come to the bottom, her fair feet, and fair hands that had not custom thereof, were bruised and frayed, and the blood springing from a dozen places, yet felt she no pain nor hurt, by reason of the great dread wherein she went. But if she were in cumber to win there, in worse was she to win out. But she deemed that there to abide was of none avail, and she found a pike sharpened, that they of the city had thrown out to keep the hold. Therewith made she one stepping place after another, till, with much travail, she climbed the wall. Now the forest lay within two crossbow shots, and the forest was of thirty leagues this way and that. Therein also were wild beasts, and beasts serpentine, and she feared that if she entered there they would slay her. But anon she deemed that if men found her there they would hale her back into the town to burn her.

Here one singeth:

Nicolete, the fair of face,
Climbed upon the coping stone,
There made she lament and moan
Calling on our Lord alone
For his mercy and his grace.
"Father, king of Majesty,
Listen, for I nothing know
Where to flee or whither go.
If within the wood I fare,
Lo, the wolves will slay me there,
Boars and lions terrible,
Many in the wild wood dwell,
But if I abide the day,
Surely worse will come of it,
Surely will the fire be lit
That shall burn my body away,
Jesus, lord of Majesty,
Better seemeth it to me,
That within the wood I fare,
Though the wolves devour me there
Than within the town to go,
Ne'er be it so!"

Then speak they, say they, tell they the Tale:

Nicolete made great moan, as ye have heard; then commended she herself to God, and anon fared till she came unto the forest. But to go deep in it she dared not, by reason of the wild beasts, and beasts serpentine. Anon crept she into a little thicket, where sleep came upon her, and she slept till prime next day, when the shepherds issued forth from the town and drove their bestial between wood and water. Anon came they all into one place by a fair fountain which was on the fringe of the forest, thereby spread they a mantle, and thereon set bread. So while they were eating, Nicolete wakened, with the sound of the singing birds, and the shepherds, and she went unto them, saying, "Fair boys, our Lord keep you!"

"God bless thee," quoth he that had more words to his tongue than the rest.

"Fair boys," quoth she, "know ye Aucassin, the son of Count Garin de Biaucaire?"

"Yea, well we know him."

"So may God help you, fair boys," quoth she, "tell him there is a beast in this forest, and bid him come chase it, and if he can take it, he would not give one limb thereof for a hundred marks of gold, nay, nor for five hundred, nor for any ransom."

Then looked they on her, and saw her so fair that they were all astonished.

"Will I tell him thereof?" quoth he that had more words to his tongue than the rest; "foul fall him who speaks of the thing or tells him the tidings. These are but visions ye tell of, for there is no beast so great in this forest, stag, nor lion, nor boar, that one of his limbs is worth more than two deniers, or three at the most, and ye speak of such great ransom. Foul fall him that believes your word, and him that telleth Aucassin. Ye be a Fairy, and we have none liking for your company, nay, hold on your road."

"Nay, fair boys," quoth she, "nay, ye will do my bidding. For this beast is so mighty of medicine that thereby will Aucassin be healed of his torment. And lo! I have five sols in my purse, take them, and tell him: for within three days must he come hunting it hither, and if within three days he find it not, never will he be healed of his torment."

"My faith," quoth he, "the money will we take, and if he come hither we will tell him, but seek him we will not."

"In God's name," quoth she; and so took farewell of the shepherds, and went her way.

Here one singeth:

Nicolete the bright of brow
From the shepherds doth she pass
All below the blossomed bough
Where an ancient way there was,
Overgrown and choked with grass,
Till she found the cross-roads where
Seven paths do all way fare,
Then she deemeth she will try,
Should her lover pass thereby,
If he love her loyally.
So she gathered white lilies,
Oak-leaf, that in green wood is,
Leaves of many a branch I wis,
Therewith built a lodge of green,
Goodlier was never seen,
Swore by God who may not lie,
"If my love the lodge should spy,
He will rest awhile thereby
If he love me loyally."
Thus his faith she deemed to try,
"Or I love him not, not I,
Nor he loves me!"

Then speak they, say they, tell they the Tale:

Nicolete built her lodge, of boughs, as ye have heard, right fair and featously, and wove it well, within and without, of flowers and leaves. So lay she hard by the lodge in a deep coppice to know what Aucassin will do. And the cry and the bruit went abroad through all the country and all the land, that Nicolete was lost. Some told that she had fled, and some that the Count Garin had let slay her. Whosoever had joy thereof, no joy had Aucassin. And the Count Garin, his father, had taken him out of prison, and had sent for the knights of that land, and the ladies, and let make a right great feast, for the comforting of Aucassin his son. Now at the high time of the feast, was Aucassin leaning from the gallery, all woeful and discomforted. Whatsoever men might devise of mirth, Aucassin had no joy thereof, nor no desire, for he saw not her that he loved. Then a knight looked on him, and came to him, and said:

"Aucassin, of that sickness of thine have I been sick, and good counsel will I give thee, if thou wilt hearken to me — "

"Sir," said Aucassin, "gramercy, good counsel would I fain hear."

"Mount thy horse," quoth he, "and go take thy pastime in yonder forest, there wilt thou see the good flowers and grass, and hear the sweet birds sing. Perchance thou shalt hear some word, whereby thou shalt be the better."

"Sir," quoth Aucassin, "gramercy, that will I do."

He passed out of the hall, and went down the stairs, and came to the stable where his horse was. He let saddle and bridle him, and mounted, and rode forth from the castle, and wandered till he came to the forest, so rode till he came to the fountain and found the shepherds at point of noon. And they had a mantle stretched on the grass, and were eating bread, and making great joy.

Here singeth one:

There were gathered shepherds all,
Martin, Esmeric, and Hal,
Aubrey, Robin, great and small.
Saith the one, "Good fellows all,
God keep Aucassin the fair,
And the maid with yellow hair,
Bright of brow and eyes of vair.
She that gave us gold to ware.
Cakes therewith to buy ye know,
Goodly knives and sheaths also.
Flutes to play, and pipes to blow,
May God him heal!"

Here speak they, say they, tell they the Tale:

When Aucassin heard the shepherds, anon he bethought him of Nicolete, his sweet lady he loved so well, and he deemed that she had passed thereby; then set he spurs to his horse, and so came to the shepherds.

"Fair boys, God be with you."

"God bless you," quoth he that had more words to his tongue than the rest.

"Fair boys," quoth Aucassin, "say the song again that anon ye sang."

"Say it we will not," quoth he that had more words to his tongue than the rest, "foul fall him who will sing it again for you, fair sir!"

"Fair boys," quoth Aucassin, "know ye me not?"

"Yea, we know well that you are Aucassin, our damoiseau, natheless we be not your men, but the Count's."

"Fair boys, yet sing it again, I pray you."

"Hearken! by the Holy Heart," quoth he, "wherefore should I sing for you, if it likes me not? Lo, there is no such rich man in this country, saving the body of Garin the Count, that dare drive forth my oxen, or my cows, or my sheep, if he finds them in his fields, or his corn, lest he lose his eyes for it, and wherefore should I sing for you, if it likes me not?"

"God be your aid, fair boys, sing it ye will, and take ye these ten sols I have here in a purse."

"Sir, the money will we take, but never a note will I sing, for I have given my oath, but I will tell thee a plain tale, if thou wilt."

"By God," saith Aucassin, "I love a plain tale better than naught."

"Sir, we were in this place, a little time agone, between prime and tierce, and were eating our bread by this fountain, even as now we do, and a maid came past, the fairest thing in the world, whereby we deemed that she should be a fay, and all the wood shone round about her. Anon she gave us of that she had, whereby we made covenant with her, that if ye came hither we would bid you hunt in this forest, wherein is such a beast that, an ye might take him, ye would not give one limb of him for five hundred marks of silver, nor for no ransom; for this beast is so mighty of medicine, that, an ye could take him, ye should be healed of your torment, and within three days must ye take him, and if ye take him not then, never will ye look on him. So chase ye the beast, an ye will, or an ye will let be, for my promise have I kept with her."

"Fair boys," quoth Aucassin, "ye have said enough. God grant me to find this quarry."

Here singeth one:

Aucassin when he had heard,
Sore within his heart was stirred,
Left the shepherds on that word,
Far into the forest spurred
Rode into the wood; and fleet
Fled his horse through paths of it,
Three words spake he of his sweet,
"Nicolete the fair, the dear,
'Tis for thee I follow here
Track of boar, nor slot of deer,
But thy sweet body and eyes so clear,
All thy mirth and merry cheer,
That my very heart have slain,
So please God to me maintain
I shall see my love again,
Sweet sister, friend!"

Then speak they, say they, tell they the Tale:

Aucassin fared through the forest from path to path after Nicolete, and his horse bare him furiously. Think ye not that the thorns him spared, nor the briars, nay, not so, but tare his raiment, that scarce a knot might be tied with the soundest part thereof, and the blood sprang from his arms, and flanks, and legs, in forty places, or thirty, so that behind the Childe men might follow on the track of his blood in the grass. But so much he went in thoughts of Nicolete, his lady sweet, that he felt no pain nor torment, and all the day hurled through the forest in this fashion nor heard no word of her. And when he saw Vespers draw nigh, he began to weep for that he found her not. All down an old road, and grassgrown he fared, when anon, looking along the way before him, he saw such an one as I shall tell you. Tall was he, and great of growth, laidly and marvelous to look upon: his head huge, and black as charcoal, and more than the breadth of a hand between his two eyes, and great cheeks, and a big nose and broad big nostrils and ugly, and thick lips redder than a collop, and great teeth yellow and ugly, and he was shod with hosen and shoon of bull's hide, bound with cords of bark over the knee, and all about him a great cloak twyfold, and he leaned on a grievous cudgel, and Aucassin came unto him, and was afraid when he beheld him.

"Fair brother, God aid thee."

"God bless you," quoth he.

"As God he helpeth thee, what makest thou here?"

"What is that to thee?"

"Nay, naught, naught," saith Aucassin, "I ask but out of courtesy."

"But for whom weepest thou," quoth he, "and makest such heavy lament? Certes, were I as rich a man as thou, the whole world should not make me weep."

"Ha! know ye me?" saith Aucassin.

"Yea, I know well that ye be Aucassin, the son of the Count, and if ye tell me for why ye weep, then will I tell you what I make here."

"Certes," quoth Aucassin, "I will tell you right gladly. Hither came I this morning to hunt in this forest; and with me a white hound, the fairest in the world; him have I lost, and for him I weep."

"By the Heart our Lord bare in his breast," quoth he, "are ye weeping for a stinking hound? Foul fall him that holds thee high henceforth! for there is no such rich man in the land, but if thy father asked it of him, he would give thee ten, or fifteen, or twenty, and be the gladder for it. But I have cause to weep and make dole."

"Wherefore so, brother?"

"Sir, I will tell thee. I was hireling to a rich villain, and drove his plow; four oxen had he. But three days since came on me great misadventure, whereby I lost the best of mine oxen, Roger, the best of my team. Him go I seeking, and have neither eaten nor drunken these three days, nor may I go to the town, lest they cast me into prison, seeing that I have not wherewithal to pay. Out of all the wealth of the world have I no more than ye see on my body. A poor mother bare me, that had no more but one wretched bed; this have they taken from under her, and she lies in the very straw. This ails me more than mine own case, for wealth comes and goes; if now I have lost, another tide will I gain, and will pay for mine ox whenas I may; never for that will I weep. But you weep for a stinking hound. Foul fall whoso thinks well of thee!"

"Certes thou art a good comforter, brother, blessed be thou! And of what price was thine ox?"

"Sir, they ask me twenty sols for him, whereof I cannot abate one doit."

"Nay, then," quoth Aucassin, "take these twenty sols I have in my purse, and pay for thine ox."

"Sir," saith he, "gramercy. And God give thee to find that thou seekest."

So they parted each from other, and Aucassin rode on: the night was fair and still, and so long he went that he came to the lodge of boughs, that Nicolete had builded and woven within and without, over and under, with flowers, and it was the fairest lodge that might be seen. When Aucassin was ware of it, he stopped suddenly, and the light of the moon fell therein.

"God!" quoth Aucassin, "here was Nicolete, my sweet lady, and this lodge builded she with her fair hands. For the sweetness of it, and for love of her, will I alight, and rest here this night long."

He drew forth his foot from the stirrup to alight, and the steed was great and tall. He dreamed so much on Nicolete his right sweet lady, that he slipped on a stone, and drave his shoulder out of its place. Then knew he that he was hurt sore, natheless he bore him with what force he might, and fastened with the other hand the mare's son to a thorn. Then turned he on his side, and crept backwise into the lodge of boughs. And he looked through a gap in the lodge and saw the stars in heaven, and one that was brighter than the rest; so began he to say:

Here one singeth:

"Star, that I from far behold,
Star, the Moon calls to her fold,
Nicolete with thee doth dwell,
My sweet love with locks of gold,
God would have her dwell afar,
Dwell with him for evening star,
Would to God, whate'er befell,
Would that with her I might dwell.
I would clip her close and strait,
Nay, were I of much estate,
Some king's son desirable,
Worthy she to be my mate,
Me to kiss and clip me well,
Sister, sweet friend!"

So speak they, say they, tell they the Tale:

When Nicolete heard Aucassin, right so came she unto him, for she was not far away. She passed within the lodge, and threw her arms about his neck, and clipped and kissed him.

"Fair sweet friend, welcome be thou."

"And thou, fair sweet love, be thou welcome."

So either kissed and clipped the other, and fair joy was them between.

"Ha! sweet love," quoth Aucassin, "but now was I sore hurt, and my shoulder wried, but I take no force of it, nor have no hurt therefrom since I have thee."

Right so felt she his shoulder and found it was wried from its place. And she so handled it with her white hands, and so wrought in her surgery, that by God's will who loveth lovers, it went back into its place. Then took she flowers, and fresh grass, and leaves green, and bound these herbs on the hurt with a strip of her smock, and he was all healed.

"Aucassin," saith she, "fair sweet love, take counsel what thou wilt do. If thy father let search this forest tomorrow, and men find me here, they will slay me, come to thee what will."

"Certes, fair sweet love, therefore should I sorrow heavily, but, an if I may, never shall they take thee."

Anon gat he on his horse, and his lady before him, kissing and clipping her, and so rode they at adventure.

Here one singeth:

Aucassin the frank, the fair,
Aucassin of the yellow hair,
Gentle knight, and true lover,
From the forest doth he fare,
Holds his love before him there,
Kissing cheek, and chin, and eyes,
But she spake in sober wise,
"Aucassin, true love and fair,
To what land do we repair?"
"Sweet my love, I take no care,
Thou art with me everywhere!"
So they pass the woods and downs,
Pass the villages and towns,
Hills and dales and open land,
Came at dawn to the sea sand,
Lighted down upon the strand,
Beside the sea.

Then say they, speak they, tell they the Tale:

Aucassin lighted down and his love, as ye have heard sing. He held his horse by the bridle, and his lady by the hands; so went they along the sea shore, and on the sea they saw a ship, and he called unto the sailors, and they came to him. Then held he such speech with them, that he and his lady were brought aboard that ship, and when they were on the high sea, behold a mighty wind and tyrannous arose, marvelous and great, and drave them from land to land, till they came unto a strange country, and won the haven of the castle of Torelore. Then asked they what this land might be, and men told them that it was the country of the King of Torelore. Then he asked what manner of man was he, and was there war afoot, and men said,

"Yea, and mighty!"

Therewith took he farewell of the merchants, and they commended him to God. Anon Aucassin mounted his horse, with his sword girt, and his lady before him, and rode at adventure till he was come to the castle. Then asked he where the King was, and they said that he was in childbed.

"Then where is his wife?"

And they told him she was with the host, and had led with her all the force of that country.

Now when Aucassin heard that saying, he made great marvel, and came into the castle, and lighted down, he and his lady, and his lady held his horse. Right so went he up into the castle, with his sword girt, and fared hither and thither till he came to the chamber where the King was lying.

Here one singeth:

Aucassin the courteous knight
To the chamber went forthright,
To the bed with linen dight
Even where the King was laid.
There he stood by him and said:
"Fool, what makst thou here abed?"
Quoth the King: "I am brought to bed
Of a fair son, and anon
When my month is over and gone,
And my healing fairly done,
To the Minster will I fare
And will do my churching there,
As my father did repair.
Then will sally forth to war,
Then will drive my foes afar
From my countrie!"

Then speak they, say they, tell they the Tale:

When Aucassin heard the King speak on this wise, he took all the sheets that covered him, and threw them all abroad about the chamber. Then saw he behind him a cudgel, and caught it into his hand, and turned, and took the King, and beat him till he was well-nigh dead.

"Ha! fair sir," quoth the King, "what would you with me? Art thou beside thyself, that beatest me in mine own house?"

"By God's heart," quoth Aucassin, "thou ill son of an ill wench, I will slay thee if thou swear not that never shall any man in all thy land lie in of child henceforth for ever."

So he did that oath, and when he had done it,

"Sir," said Aucassin, "bring me now where thy wife is with the host."

"Sir, with good will," quoth the King.

He mounted his horse, and Aucassin gat on his own, and Nicolete abode in the Queen's chamber. Anon rode Aucassin and the King even till they came to that place where the Queen was, and lo! men were warring with baked apples, and with eggs, and with fresh cheeses, and Aucassin began to look on them, and made great marvel.

Here singeth one:

Aucassin his horse doth stay,
From the saddle watched the fray,
All the stour and fierce array;
Right fresh cheeses carried they,
Apples baked, and mushrooms gray,
Whoso splasheth most the ford
He is master called and lord.
Aucassin doth gaze awhile,
Then began to laugh and smile
And made game.

Then speak they, say they, tell they the Tale:

When Aucassin beheld these marvels, he came to the King, and said, "Sir, be these thine enemies?"

"Yea, Sir," quoth the King.

"And will ye that I should avenge you of them?"

"Yea," quoth he, "with all my heart."

Then Aucassin put hand to sword, and hurled among them, and began to smite to the right hand and the left, and slew many of them. And when the King saw that he slew them, he caught at his bridle and said,

"Ha! fair sir, slay them not in such wise."

"How," quoth Aucassin, "will ye not that I should avenge you of them?"

"Sir," quoth the King, "over-much already hast thou avenged me. It is nowise our custom to slay each other."

Anon turned they and fled. Then the King and Aucassin betook them again to the castle of Torelore, and the folk of that land counseled the King to put Aucassin forth, and keep Nicolete for his son's wife, for that she seemed a lady high of lineage. And Nicolete heard them and had no joy of it, so began to say:

Here singeth one:

Thus she spake the bright of brow:
"Lord of Torelore and king,
Thy folk deem me a light thing,
When my love doth me embrace,
Fair he finds me, in good case,
Then am I in such derray,
Neither harp, nor lyre, nor lay,
Dance nor game, nor rebeck play
Were so sweet."

Then speak they, say they, tell they the Tale:

Aucassin dwelt in the castle of Torelore, in great ease and great delight, for that he had with him Nicolete his sweet love, whom he loved so well. Now while he was in such pleasure and such delight, came a troop of Saracens by sea, and laid siege to the castle and took it by main strength. Anon took they the substance that was therein and carried off the men and maidens captives. They seized Nicolete and Aucassin, and bound Aucassin hand and foot, and cast him into one ship, and Nicolete into another. Then rose there a mighty wind over sea, and scattered the ships. Now that ship wherein was Aucassin, went wandering on the sea, till it came to the castle of Biaucaire, and the folk of the country ran together to wreck her, and there found they Aucassin, and they knew him again. So when they of Biaucaire saw their damoiseau, they made great joy of him, for Aucassin had dwelt full three years in the castle of Torelore, and his father and mother were dead. So the people took him to the castle of Biaucaire, and there were they all his men. And he held the land in peace.

. . . . .

Now leave we Aucassin, and speak we of Nicolete. The ship wherein she was cast pertained to the King of Carthage, and he was her father, and she had twelve brothers, all princes or kings. When they beheld Nicolete, how fair she was, they did her great worship, and made much joy of her, and many times asked her who she was, for surely seemed she a lady of noble line and high parentry. But she might not tell them of her lineage, for she was but a child when men stole her away. So sailed they till they won the City of Carthage, and when Nicolete saw the walls of the castle, and the country-side, she knew that there had she been nourished and thence stolen away, being but a child. Yet was she not so young a child but that well she knew she had been daughter of the King of Carthage; and of her nurture in that City.

Here one singeth:

Nicolete the good and true
To the land hath come anew,
Sees the palaces and walls,
And the houses and the halls!
Then she spake and said, "Alas!
That of birth so great I was,
Cousin of the Amiral
And the very child of him
Carthage counts King of Paynim,
Wild folk hold me here withal;
Nay, Aucassin, love of thee
Gentle knight, and true, and free
Burns and wastes the heart of me.
Ah, God grant it of his grace,
That thou hold me, and embrace,
That thou kiss me on the face
Love and lord!"

Then speak they, say they, tell they the Tale:

When the King of Cathage heard Nicolete speak in this wise, he cast his arms about her neck.

"Fair, sweet love," saith he, "tell me who thou art, and be not adread of me."

"Sir," said she, "I am daughter to the King of Carthage, and was taken, being then a little child, it is now fifteen years gone."

When all they of the court heard her speak thus, they knew well that she spake sooth: so made they great joy of her, and led her to the castle in great honor, as the King's daughter. And they would have given her to her lord a King of Paynim, but she had no mind to marry. There dwelt she three days or four. And she considered by that means she might seek for Aucassin. Then she got her a viol, and learned to play on it, till they would have married her on a day to a great King of Paynim, and she stole forth by night, and came to the seaport, and dwelt with a poor woman thereby. Then took she a certain herb, and therewith smeared her head and her face, till she was all brown and stained. And she let make coat, and mantle, and smock, and hose, and attired herself as if she had been a harper. So took she the viol and went to a mariner, and so wrought on him that he took her aboard his vessel. Then hoisted they sail, and fared on the high seas even till they came to the land of Provence. And Nicolete went forth and took the viol, and went playing through all that country, even till she came to the castle of Biaucaire, where Aucassin lay.

Here one singeth:

At Biaucaire below the tower
Sat Aucassin, on an hour,
Heard the bird, and watched the flower,
With his barons him beside,
Then came on him in that tide,
The sweet influence of love
And the memory thereof;
Thought of Nicolete the fair,
And the dainty face of her
He had loved so many years,
Then was he in dule and tears!
Even then came Nicolete
On the stair a foot she set,
And she drew the viol bow
Through the strings and chanted so;
"Listen, lords and knights, to me,
Lords of high or low degree,
To my story list will ye
All of Aucassin and her
That was Nicolete the fair?
And their love was long to tell
Deep woods through he sought her well,
Paynims took them on a day
In Torelore and bound they lay.
Of Aucassin naught know we,
But fair Nicolete the free
Now in Carthage doth she dwell,
There her father loves her well,
Who is king of that countrie.
Her a husband hath he found,
Paynim lord that serves Mahound!
Ne'er with him the maid will go,
For she loves a damoiseau,
Aucassin, that ye may know,
Swears to God that never mo
With a lover she will go
Save with him she loveth so
In long desire."

So speak they, say they, tell they the Tale:

When Aucassin heard Nicolete speak in this wise, he was right joyful, and drew her on one side, and spoke, saying:

"Sweet fair friend, know ye nothing of this Nicolete, of whom ye have thus sung?"

"Yea, Sir, I know her for the noblest creature, and the most gentle, and the best that ever was born on ground. She is daughter to the King of Carthage that took her there where Aucassin was taken, and brought her into the city of Carthage, till he knew that verily she was his own daughter, whereon he made right great mirth. Anon wished he to give her for her lord one of the greatest kings of all Spain, but she would rather let herself be hanged or burned, than take any lord, how great soever."

"Ha! fair sweet friend," quoth the Count Aucassin, "if thou wilt go into that land again, and bid her come and speak to me, I will give thee of my substance, more than thou wouldst dare to ask or take. And know ye, that for the sake of her, I have no will to take a wife, howsoever high her lineage. So wait I for her, and never will I have a wife, but her only. And if I knew where to find her, no need would I have to seek her."

"Sir," quoth she, "if ye promise me that, I will go in quest of her for your sake, and for hers, that I love much."

So he sware to her, and anon let give her twenty livres, and she departed from him, and he wept for the sweetness of Nicolete. And when she saw him weeping, she said:

"Sir, trouble not thyself so much withal. For in a little while shall I have brought her into this city, and ye shall see her."

When Aucassin heard that, he was right glad thereof. And she departed from him, and went into the city to the house of the Captain's wife, for the Captain her father in God was dead. So she dwelt there, and told all her tale; and the Captain's wife knew her, and knew well that she was Nicolete that she herself had nourished. Then she let wash and bathe her, and there rested she eight full days. Then took she an herb that was named *Eyebright* and anointed herself therewith, and was as fair as ever she had been all the days of her life. Then she clothed herself in rich robes of silk whereof the lady had great store, and then sat herself in the chamber on a silken coverlet, and called the lady and bade her go and bring Aucassin her love, and she did even so. And when she came to the Palace she found Aucassin weeping, and making lament for Nicolete his love, for that she delayed so long. And the lady spake unto him and said:

"Aucassin, sorrow no more, but come thou on with me, and I will shew thee the thing in the world that thou lovest best; even Nicolete thy dear love, who from far lands hath come to seek of thee." And Aucassin was right glad.

Here singeth one:

When Aucassin heareth now
That his lady bright of brow
Dwelleth in his own countrie,
Never man was glad as he.
To her castle doth he hie
With the lady speedily,
Passeth to the chamber high,
Findeth Nicolete thereby.
Of her true love found again
Never maid was half so fain.
Straight she leaped upon her feet;
When his love he saw at last,
Arms about her did he cast,
Kissed her often, kissed her sweet,
Kissed her lips and brows and eyes.
Thus all night do they devise,
Even till the morning white.
Then Aucassin wedded her,
Made her Lady of Biaucaire.
Many years abode they there,
Many years in shade or sun,
In great gladness and delight.
Ne'er hath Aucassin regret
Nor his lady Nicolete.
Now my story all is done,
Said and sung!

—*By an unknown French author (twelfth century), translated by Andrew Lang.*

Baba Meglena

CYRIL KRISTOV

THE LITTLE MACEDONIAN town of Prilep still lay in its first sweet sleep. Not a door had banged, not a sound had come from any kitchen, when some one knocked at the window of Baba Meglena.

Like all old people, Baba Meglena slept as lightly as a cat, and at once popped her dishevelled head out of the blankets and stretched her neck towards the window, which was right above her. Stars were still shining clearly, and by their light she saw a woman, clothed all in white, who had climbed on to the coping just below her window. The old woman started with fright, but quickly recognized a neighbour, the young Mitana, who had hurried to her in her night clothes straight from her bed. Mitana, too, was frightened when she saw Baba Meglena's tousled head and nearly fell off the coping; but she quickly caught hold of the two iron stanchions of the window and brought her face close to the pane.

"Baba Maglena," she said, "the child of the Corbadzi Mitaki has died in the night. Mother Gena was there all through the night: they kept her there by force and told her that she must let no one know. They want to bury the child this very morning."

"Really!" replied Baba Meglena from within, and got up at once. "Go and put your clothes on, and come back to me quickly." If Baba Meglena had been told that her house was on fire, she couldn't have dashed out of the door more quickly. Old and worn as she was, the news that the child of the only friend of the Greeks in all the little town, the universally detested Corbadzi Mitaki, had died, instantly transformed her. In the movements of her knotted hands as they ran through her dishevelled grey hair was something masculine, and when she clambered over the low hedge, in order to save going round by the road, she looked for all the world like a robber. Her warlike appearance was increased still further by a few pointed tufts of white hair which stuck out from under her torn head-dress. Her eyes, sunk deep in her head, had an unusual gleam in them; her toothless mouth wore an uncanny, malignant smile.

Like a cat she sprang over the hedge to Mitana's house, and, soon after, the two hastened through the court beyond, came into a narrow lane, and passed the neighbour's houses to see what was happening at Corbadzi Mitaki's. Even from a distance they saw the old Pope Vitan coming out of the house, so back they turned. There was no doubt that someone was dead at the Corbadzis.

Lest the Pope should see them, the women squeezed themselves in at the first courtyard gate that offered itself, and then found their way through hedges and across perhaps a couple of dozen neighbours' patches; so that, before the first pink of dawn was in the sky, the news was all over the little place as it awoke. Only then did Baba Meglena hurry home, caught up her distaff, and started back again.

. . . . .

Soon after, a long procession of women, with their distaffs in their belts, was seen wending its way between the bean-fields along the brook that divides the little town into two. They took the direction of the cemetery, which lies on a hill above the town. As the women climbed it others came from the outlying streets and swelled their ranks. Among them were many old and bent forms, then matrons and maidens, and even little girls. At their head walked Baba Meglena, pointed tufts of hair still sticking out from her torn cap, as though they were passing in stern review the women who followed her up the hill.

When the first part of the procession halted at the churchyard, the crowd formed into a solid mass, which tapered steadily away down the hill. Meanwhile the sun had risen and blazed down upon the women as they stood among the graves. There was a noise all round like that among women bathing. After a short discussion, they spread themselves all round the edge of the churchyard, where the hawthorns formed its edge. From below, late comers kept arriving and filled all the gaps.

. . . . .

At this time the household of the Corbadzi Mitaki was still in confusion at the death, and knew nothing of what had happened.

It was only when Mitaki, surprised at the long absence of the Pope, stepped out into the porch in order to fetch him, and when his eyes turned accidentally to the churchyard, that he saw the close ranks of the women sitting under the hawthorn bushes.

Suddenly, it was clear to him what was in the air. He went in again to the house, where the nearer relatives were consoling the mother in her prostration and grief, and asked them bluntly if they knew nothing about it, just as though it was their doing. Terrified, they all went out to the porch. The mother gave a cry and tore her hair. The dead boy was her only child, and how should she bear this disgrace? Mitaki bit his lips, picked up his hat and went down the steps.

He went to the market place. All the shops were open, as though nothing unusual had happened: but still Mitaki noticed that people looked at him somewhat mockingly.

He turned to a shopman, to whom he often lent money at interest.

"Friend Ivan," he said, "go and put sense into your wife's head, or else you'll smart for it."

Friend Ivan tried to pretend that he did not know what it was all about, but Mitaki went on, in still more threatening and surly tones, "That's all I have to say to you," he said, and turned away to another shopman.

Several men who were afraid of the friend of Greeks and Turks did actually go to the churchyard; but they were greeted in such a fashion as to lose all fancy for going a second time.

Mid-day had struck, and even the dusk began to come, yet the dead child still lay unburied at Mitaki's.

Many a time had the iron plate that served as bell been beaten and its notes grown silent. When once again the notes were struck, some of the women in the churchyard exclaimed bitterly: "Go on ringing, do, if you have nothing to do."

The mother was in a state of collapse from loud lamenting.

Towards evening the Corbadzi Miaki went to the Turkish authorities in the village; but, after a long conversation, he came home more sullen than ever.

. . . . .

It was already night when the women went to their houses. Some of them gave their bigger children a piece of bread, with instructions to keep an eye on the Pope's house, and as soon as they saw him coming out, to hurry home with the news. They were afraid that the dead child might, perhaps, be buried during the night, though such a thing as a night burial had never been heard or seen.

The Corbadzi Mitaki could no longer listen to the lamentations of his wife, and went out of the house. Once more he went to the Turk, Ahmed Aga, and talked to him at such length that he lost patience and said: "Forgive me, Corbadzi, but you have lost your reason. If they were men, I would drive them out myself; but to raise my hand against women, that's not laid down in any law."

Mitaki hung his head. When he saw that there was nothing to be done by force, he would have liked to try persuasion. During the night he sent some of his kinsfolk, and a few poor old women who were indebted to him, the round of the houses – telling them to try and persuade the excited women in presence of their husbands. The messengers came back as they had gone: a few of them had very nearly been beaten.

There was no way out. The Corbadzi had to put up with the unheard-of disgrace of burying his only child outside the churchyard. Of this he convinced himself as soon as it was day.

The churchyard was again invested by the women. Though some of them had been beaten that night by their husbands, who were afraid of the Corbadzi, they took their places next morning all the same.

As on the day before, they had their distaffs with them, and bundles containing bread and other eatables. Once more the iron bell was beaten several times. By midday the corpse could hardly be left in the house. It was a summer day of blazing heat.

There was only one thing to be done. Pope Vitan must go himself, in order to quiet the women down. He was a very worthy man, and an eloquent priest. How often had he made the women weep by his sermons about saints and martyrs! Mitaki started off to the old Pope.

"Dear Father, I will give you ten, no, twenty Turkish pounds, if you will rid me of this evil," he said gloomily. "Go and tell them something out of Holy Writ that will make them go away."

Although the Pope was secretly on the side of the women, he was tempted by the money that always appeals to slavish men. He got up and went. It's not a matter of a few pence, he thought to himself, there are twenty pounds to be made.

He went to the women and explained to them that it was a sin to act thus. Christ says that we should be merciful and must forgive even our enemies. But his voice lacked that solemn and convincing note that, from the pulpit, moved the women to tears. Finally, Baba Meglena could no longer keep quiet. She came forward and said to him:

"Father, hear what I have to say to you. If you bury the child of this heathen in the churchyard, we shall do something quite extraordinary. Beware you, too, will not come to lie among these Christian dead, at least so long as I live. Look at me well! Is it fitting for a priest to take the part of usurers?"

Pope Vitan muttered something, hung his head, and went back to the house.

What was to be done? The dead child could not be left there any longer. The mother was more dead than alive for grief and shame.

The relatives at last decided to carry the body to the churchyard, no matter what might come of it. They clung to the hope that, when the women saw the corpse, they would soften and give way.

Once more the bell sounded. A little group of people came from the house of the Corbadzi Mitaki, carrying the corpse, and made their way towards the churchyard.

. . . . .

"Look! They're bringing It! Here it comes! They're coming – they're coming!' called the women in the churchyard, and all eyes were turned towards the little town.

The funeral procession could be seen passing through the bean-fields. The mourning voice of the Pope could already be heard clearly. Among the five or six men who walked bareheaded, with downcast eyes, behind the women of the family, could be seen a couple of gipsies, carrying spade and shovel.

The defenders of the churchyard began to turn their distaffs busily; they pretended to take no notice of the approaching procession, but none of them could help taking a secret glance at it.

When the body was brought there, the place through which it had to be carried into the churchyard was closed as it were by a living wall. All the women had closed up in serried ranks, shoulder to shoulder, silent, almost as if turned to stone.

The bearers laid the body on the ground. The Pope, with trembling voice, recited a prayer. All were silent, with bent heads and beating hearts. This breathless silence, as before a storm, was broken by the priest himself.

"Make way, women, that we may bury a child of God!" he said in mild tones.

"Here only Christians are buried!" came the sharp voice of Baba Meglena.

Everyone started at its harsh note and at the meaning of the words.

"Don't act thus, good people! It is a sin before God! Since yesterday the dead lies unburied," said Pope Vitan, in a still softer and supplicating voice.

"Heathens have nothing to do with Christians, either in this world or in the next," called out Baba Meglena, more harshly than before.

"Are we not Christians, then?" came timidly from the Corbadzi Mitaki.

"If you are a Christian, what have you to do with heathens?" several voices called out.

"Go along; take your child to the market place, and let the Hodza bury it," broke in Baba Meglena in commanding tones, furious at the Corbadzi's intervention.

The mother screamed, as though a knife had gone to her heart. It was terrible and heart-breaking to hear her, and yet impressive. The vengeance of the people upon a heartless usurer was revealed in its most pitiless form. Some of the guardians of the churchyard began to soften, and to whisper to each other. Most of them were mothers, and understood the laments of the unhappy woman.

But Baba Meglena, the chance mouthpiece of the people's anger, had closed the door of her heart to forgiveness. She was resolved to check the rising tide of pity.

"Go and bury your dead out there!" she said, and pointed with her hand beyond the churchyard. "Are we such fools as to guard the churchyard since yesterday, and to let you bury him now beside our mothers and fathers?"

The simple but convincing words of Baba Meglena showed both sides that further bargaining was hopeless.

The bearers lifted the bier, and the procession again set in motion. Soon afterwards the two gipsies began to dig the grave outside the churchyard.

The mother sat, overcome with grief and pain, bending over the corpse. A few women who supported her tried in vain to calm her. Full of gloomy thoughts, Mitaki stood to one side.

The protectors of the churchyard had again distributed themselves along its edge. Their trembling fingers often broke off the thread from the distaff, or let the spindle run out. No one spoke a word.

At last the grave was ready. The priest read the last prayers. Two men lowered the corpse into the earth. The mother, with her last strength, screamed aloud and tore her hair. Clods of earth fell upon the rough sawn coffin, and the two gipsies used their shovels.

Then, suddenly, a horrible, fierce, unearthly scream struck terror into everyone. The Corbadzi Mitaki, the friend of Greek and Turk, the heartless usurer, who had flayed three skins off a single back, who looked on others' tears as on water, because his eyes did not know what tears were, now roared aloud in his agony, like a beast that is being slaughtered.

There was something in this inhuman sound that moved the hardest heart. The punishment of the oppressor, carried out so pitilessly by the oppressed themselves, was something so solemn that it filled even the most slavish souls. Boundless grief and pain at such deadly insult unloosed in this utterly withered heart a flood of tears, and now they flowed freely.

Even a few of the guardians of the churchyard wept silently to themselves, but not one moved from her place. They did not stand up and move homeward down the hill until the funeral was over.

—By Cyril Kristov, Bulgarian, translated anonymously.

Late

ABRAHAM RAISIN

It was in sad and hopeless mood that Antosh watched the autumn making its way into his peasant's hut. The days began to shorten and the evenings to lengthen, and there was no more petroleum in the hut to fill his humble lamp; his wife complained too—the store of salt was giving out; there was very little soap left, and in a few days he would finish his tobacco. And Antosh cleared his throat, spat, and muttered countless times a day:

"No salt, no soap, no tobacco; we haven't got anything. A bad business!"

Antosh had no prospect of earning anything in the village. The one village Jew was poor himself, and had no work to give. Antosh had only *one* hope left. Just before the Feast of Tabernacles he would drive a whole cart-load of fir-boughs into the little town and bring a tidy sum of money home in exchange.

He did this every year, since buying his thin horse in the market for six rubles.

"When shall you have Tabernacle?" he asked every day of the village Jew. "Not yet," was the Jew's daily reply. "But when *shall* you?" Antosh insisted one day.

"In a week," answered the Jew, not dreaming how very much Antosh needed to know precisely.

In reality there were only five more days to Tabernacles, and Antosh had calculated with business accuracy that it would be best to take the fir-boughs into the town two days before the festival. But this was really the first day of it.

He rose early, ate his dry, black bread dipped in salt, and drank a measure of water. Then he harnessed his thin, starved horse to the cart, took his hatchet, and drove into the nearest wood.

He cut down the branches greedily, seeking out the thickest and longest.

"Good ware is easier sold," he thought, and the cart filled, and the load grew higher and higher. He was calculating on a return of three gulden, and it seemed still too little, so that he went on cutting, and laid on a few more boughs. The cart could hold no more, and Antosh looked at it from all sides, and smiled contentedly.

"That will be enough," he muttered, and loosened the reins. But scarcely had he driven a few paces, when he stopped and looked the cart over again.

"Perhaps it's not enough, after all?" he questioned fearfully, cut down five more boughs, laid them onto the already full cart, and drove on.

He drove slowly, pace by pace, and his thoughts traveled slowly too, as though keeping step with the thin horse.

Antosh was calculating how much salt and how much soap, how much petroleum and how much tobacco he could buy for the return for his ware. At length the calculating tired him, and he resolved to put it off till he should have the cash. Then the calculating would be done much more easily.

But when he reached the town, and saw that the booths were already covered with fir-boughs, he felt a pang at his heart. The booths and the houses seemed to be twirling round him in a circle, and dancing. But he consoled himself with the thought that every year, when he drove into town, he found many booths already covered. Some cover earlier, some later. The latter paid the best.

"I shall ask higher prices," he resolved, and all the while fear tugged at his heart. He drove on. Two Jewish women were standing before a house; they pointed at the cart with their finger, and laughed aloud.

"Why do you laugh?" queried Antosh, excitedly.

"Because you are too soon with your fir-boughs," they answered, and laughed again.

"How too soon?" he asked, astonished.

"Too soon – too soon – " laughed the women.

"Pfui," Antosh spat, and drove on, thinking, "Berko said himself, 'In a week.' I am only two days ahead."

A cold sweat covered him, as he reflected he might have made a wrong calculation, founded on what Berko had told him. It was possible that he had counted the days badly – had come too late! There is no doubt: all the booths are covered with fir-boughs. He will have no salt, no tobacco, no soap, and no petroleum.

Sadly he followed the slow paces of his languid horse, which let his weary head droop as though out of sympathy for his master.

Meantime the Jews were crowding out of the synagogues in festal array, with their prayer-scarfs and prayer-books in their hands. When they perceived the peasant with the cart of fir-boughs, they looked questioningly one at the other: Had they made a mistake and begun the festival too early?

"What have you there?" some one inquired.

"What?" answered Antosh, taken aback. "Fir-boughs! Buy, my dear friend, I sell it cheap!" he begged in a piteous voice.

The Jews burst out laughing.

"What should we want it for now, fool?" "The festival has begun!" said another. Antosh was confused with his misfortune, he scratched the back of his head, and exclaimed, weeping:

"Buy! Buy! I want salt, soap! I want petroleum!"

The group of Jews, who had begun by laughing, were now deeply moved. They saw the poor, starving peasant standing there in his despair, and were filled with a lively compassion.

"A poor Gentile – it's pitiful!" said one, sympathetically. "He hoped to make a fortune out of his fir-boughs, and now!" observed another.

"It would be proper to buy up that bit of

fir," said a third, "else it might cause a Chillul ha-Shem." "On a festival?" objected some one else.

"It can always be used for firewood," said another, contemplating the cartful.

"Whether or no! It's a festival — "

"No salt, no soap, no petroleum — " It was the refrain of the bewildered peasant, who did not understand what the Jews were saying among themselves. He could only guess that they were talking about him. "Hold! he doesn't want *money!* He wants ware. Ware without money may be given on a festival," called out one.

The interest of the bystanders waxed more lively. Among them stood a storekeeper, whose shop was close by. "Give him, Chayyim, a few jars of salt and other things that he wants — even if it comes to a few gulden. We will contribute."

"All right, willingly!" said Chayyim. "A poor Gentile!"

"A precept, a precept! It would be carrying out a religious precept, as surely as I am a Jew!" chimed in every individual member of the crowd.

Chayyim called the peasant to him; all the rest followed. He gave him out of the stores two jars of salt, a bar of soap, a bottle of petroleum, and two packets of tobacco.

The peasant did not know what to do for joy. He could only stammer in a low voice, "Thank you! Thank you!"

"And there's a bit of Sabbath loaf," called out one, when he had packed the things away, "take that with you!"

"There's some more!" and a second hand held some out to him.

"More!"

"More!"

"And more!"

They brought Antosh bread and cake from all sides; his astonishment was such that he could scarcely articulate his thanks.

The people were pleased with themselves, and Yainkel Leives, a cheerful man, who was well supplied for the festival, because his daughter's "intended" was staying in his house, brought Antosh a glass of brandy:

"Drink, and drive home, in the name of God!"

Antosh drank the brandy with a quick gulp, bit off a piece of cake, and declared joyfully, "I shall never forget it!"

"Not at all a bad Gentile," remarked some one in the crowd.

"Well, what would you have? Did you expect him to beat you?" queried another, smiling.

The words "to beat" made a melancholy impression on the crowd, and it dispersed in silence.

— *From Yiddish Tales by Abraham Raisin, Russian, translated from the Yiddish by Helena Frank.*

∽ ⚙ ∼

His Chance in Life

RUDYARD KIPLING

If you go straight away from Levees and Government House Lists, past Trades' Balls — far beyond everything and everybody you ever knew in your respectable life — you cross, in time, the Borderline where the last drop of White blood ends and the full tide of Black sets in. It would be easier to talk to a new-made Duchess on the spur of the moment than to the Borderline folk without violating some of their conventions or hurting their feelings. The Black and the White mix very quaintly in their ways. Sometimes the White shows in spurts of fierce, childish pride — which is Pride of Race run crooked — and sometimes the Black and still fiercer abasement and humility, half-heathenish customs, and strange unaccountable impulses to crime. One of these days, this people — understand they are far lower than the class whence Derozio, the man who imitated Byron, sprung — will turn out a writer or a poet; and then we shall know how they live and what they feel. In the meantime, any stories about them cannot be absolutely correct in fact or inference.

Miss Vezzis came from across the Borderline to look after some children who belonged to a lady until a regularly ordained nurse could come out. The lady said Miss Vezzis was a bad, dirty nurse, and inattentive. It never struck her that Miss Vezzis had her own life to lead and her own affairs to worry over, and that these affairs were the most important things in the world to Miss Vezzis. Very few mistresses admit this sort of reasoning. Miss Vezzis was as black as a boot, and, to our standard of taste, hideously ugly. She wore cotton-print gowns and bulged shoes; and when she lost her temper with the children, she abused them in the language of the Borderline — which is part

English, part Portuguese, and part Native. She was not attractive; but she had her pride, and she preferred being called 'Miss Vezzis.'

Every Sunday, she dressed herself wonderfully and went to see her Mamma, who lived, for the most part, on an old cane chair in a greasy *tussar*-silk dressing-gown and a big rabbit-warren of a house full of Vezzises, Pereiras, Ribieras, Lisboas and Gonsalveses, and a floating population of loafers; besides fragments of the day's market, garlic, stale incense, clothes thrown on the floor, petticoats hung on strings for screens, old bottles, pewter crucifixes, dried *immortelles,* pariah puppies, plaster images of the Virgin, and hats without crowns. Miss Vezzis drew twenty rupees a month for acting as nurse, and she squabbled weekly with her Mamma as to the percentage to be given towards housekeeping. When the quarrel was over, Michele D'Cruze used to shamble across the low mud wall of the compound and make love to Miss Vezzis after the fashion of the Borderline, which is hedged about with much ceremony. Michele was a poor, sickly weed and very black; but he had his pride. He would not be seen smoking a *huqa* for anything; and he looked down on natives as only a man with seven-eighths native blood in his veins can. The Vezzis Family had their pride too. They traced their descent from a mythical platelayer who had worked on the Sone Bridge when railways were new in India, and they valued their English origin. Michele was a Telegraph Signaller on Rs. 35 a month. The fact that he was in Government employ made Mrs. Vezzis lenient to the shortcomings of his ancestors.

There was a compromising legend — Dom Anna the tailor brought it from Poonani — that a black Jew of Cochin had once married into the D'Cruze family; while it was an open secret that an uncle of Mrs. D'Cruze was, at that very time, doing menial work, connected with cooking, for a Club in Southern India! He sent Mrs. D'Cruze seven rupees eight annas a month; but she felt the disgrace to the family very keenly all the same.

However, in the course of a few Sundays, Mrs. Vezzis brought herself to overlook these blemishes and gave her consent to the marriage of her daughter with Michele, on condition that Michele should have at least fifty rupees a month to start married life upon. This wonderful prudence must have been a lingering touch of the mythical platelayer's Yorkshire blood; for across the Borderline people take a pride in marrying when they please — not when they can.

Having regard to his departmental prospects, Miss Vezzis might as well have asked Michele to go away and come back with the Moon in his pocket. But Michele was deeply in love with Miss Vezzis, and that helped him to endure. He accompanied Miss Vezzis to Mass one Sunday, and after Mass, walking home through the hot stale dust with her hand in his, he swore by several Saints whose names would not interest you, never to forget Miss Vezzis; and she swore by her Honour and the Saints — the oath runs rather curiously; *'In nomine Sanctissimæ —'* (whatever the name of the she-Saint is) and so forth, ending with a kiss on the forehead, a kiss on the left cheek, and a kiss on the mouth — never to forget Michele.

Next week Michele was transferred, and Miss Vezzis dropped tears upon the window-sash of the 'Intermediate' compartment as he left the Station.

If you look at the telegraph-map of India you will see a long line skirting the coast from Backergunge to Madras. Michele was ordered to Tibasu, a little Sub-office one-third down this line, to send messages on from Berhampur to Chicacola, and to think of Miss Vezzis and his chances of getting fifty rupees a month out of office-hours. He had the noise of the Bay of Bengal and a Bengali Babu for company; nothing more. He sent foolish letters, with crosses tucked inside the flaps of the envelopes, to Miss Vezzis.

When he had been at Tibasu for nearly three weeks his chance came.

Never forget that unless the outward and visible signs of Our Authority are always before a native he is as incapable as a child of understanding what authority means, or where is the danger of disobeying it. Tibasu was a forgotten little place with a few Orissa Mohammedans in it. These, hearing nothing of the Collector-*Sahib* for some time and heartily despising the Hindu Sub-Judge, arranged to start a little Mohurrum riot of their own. But the Hindus turned out and broke their heads; when, finding lawlessness pleasant, Hindus and Mohammedans together raised an aimless sort of Donnybrook just to see how far they could go. They looted each other's shops, and paid off private grudges in the regular way. It was a nasty little riot, but not worth putting in the newspapers.

Michele was working in his office when he heard the sound that a man never forgets all his life — the *'ah-yah'* of an angry crowd. (When that sound drops about three tones, and changes to a thick, droning *ut*, the man who hears it had better go away if he is alone.) The Native Police Inspector ran in and told Michele that the town was in an uproar and coming to wreck the Telegraph Office. The Babu put on his cap and quietly dropped out of the window; while the Police Inspector, afraid, but obeying the old race-instinct which recognizes a drop of White blood as far as it can be diluted, said, 'What orders does the *Sahib* give?'

The *'Sahib'* decided Michele. Though horribly frightened, he felt that, for the hour, he, the man with the Cochin Jew and the menial uncle in his pedigree, was the only representative of English authority in the place. Then he thought of Miss Vezzis and the fifty rupees, and took the situation on himself. There were seven native policemen in Tibasu, and four crazy smooth-bore muskets among them. All the men were gray with fear, but not beyond leading. Michele dropped the key of the telegraph instrument, and went out, at the head of his army, to meet the mob. As the shouting crew came round a corner of the road, he dropped and fired; the men behind him loosing instinctively at the same time.

The whole crowd — curs to the back-bone — yelled and ran; leaving one man dead, and another dying in the road. Michele was sweating with fear; but he kept his weakness under, and went down into the town, past the house where the Sub-Judge had barricaded himself. The streets were empty. Tibasu was more frightened than Michele, for the mob had been taken at the right time.

Michele returned to the Telegraph Office, and sent a message to Chicacola asking for help. Before an answer came, he received a deputation of the elders of Tibasu, telling him that the Sub-Judge said his actions generally were 'unconstitutional,' and trying to bully him. But the heart of Michele D'Cruze was big and white in his breast, because of his love for Miss Vezzis the nurse-girl, and because he had tasted for the first time Responsibility and Success. Those two make an intoxicating drink, and have ruined more men than ever has Whisky. Michele answered that the Sub-Judge might say what he pleased, but until the Assistant Collector came, the Telegrapher Signaller was the Government of India in Tibasu, and the elders of the town would be held accountable for further rioting. Then they bowed their heads and said, 'Show mercy!' or words to that effect, and went back in great fear; each accusing the other of having begun the rioting.

Early in the dawn, after a night's patrol with his seven policemen, Michele went down the road, musket in hand, to meet the Assistant Collector, who had ridden in to quell Tibasu. But, in the presence of his young Englishman, Michele felt himself slipping back more and more into the native; and the tale of the Tibasu Riots ended, with the strain on the teller, in an hysterical outburst of tears, bred by sorrow that he had killed a man, shame that he could not feel as uplifted as he had felt through the night, and childish anger that his tongue could not do justice to his great deeds. It was the White drop in Michele's veins dying out, though he did not know it.

But the Englishman understood; and, after he had schooled those men of Tibasu, and had conferred with the Sub-Judge till that excellent official turned green, he found time to draft an official letter describing the conduct of Michele. Which letter filtered through the Proper Channels, and ended in the transfer of Michele up-country once more, on the Imperial salary of sixty-six rupees a month.

So he and Miss Vezzis were married with great state and ancientry; and now there are several little D'Cruzes sprawling about the verandahs of the Central Telegraph Office.

But, if the whole revenue of the Department he serves were to be his reward, Michele could never, never repeat what he did at Tibasu for the sake of Miss Vezzis the nurse-girl.

Which proves that when a man does good work out of all proportion to his pay, in seven cases out of nine there is a woman at the back of the virtue.

The two exceptions must have suffered from sunstroke.

— From Plain Tales from the Hills by Rudyard Kipling, English (1865–1936).

Victory

PIERRE MILLE

After his last campaign in North Tonkin, Barnavaux was sent back to France. He had been shifted about from Toulon to Cherbourg, from Cherbourg to Rochefort, and then, as it seems essential that Paris should be turned into a military museum, where idlers can gaze their fill at specimens of every branch of the army, he was eventually quartered at the Cherche-Midi military prison. I found him there one Sunday, sitting on a stone bench in the yard. Barnavaux was not on duty, and yet he had not gone out. His sleeves were decorated with a sergeant's stripes and he caught me looking at them with considerable astonishment.

"Yes," he replied, to my mute question. "I made up my mind to get promotion. Do you know how old I am? Thirty-five! I am old, horribly old; I feel as if I had all the age of the world on my shoulders. It's all up! I'm no good as a soldier now, so I must turn sergeant."

"Barnavaux," I said, "when you have no respect for hierarchy even where it concerns yourself, I fear for your eternal salvation. That is the sin against the Holy Ghost, the only one that shall never be forgiven!"

"You don't understand what I mean," he returned. "I mean that I've been promoted and if I can manage to go ahead – for it isn't such an easy matter, it doesn't take much to reduce a man to the ranks – it is because of the pension, so that I can get a job somewhere and wear a livery instead of a uniform. I might usher in the millionaires who wait in a queue before the offices of the Minister of Finance. Or I might be a *huissier* in a black suit and silver chain seated behind a green table containing a red blotter and black inkstand. That is what they call 'becoming a modest servant of the State!' I have read that sort of thing in the papers."

"Well," I said, "I don't think you'll need pity!"

"I'm not saying that I shall! At any rate it will be better than the dog's life I've led for the last twelve years."

When Barnavaux runs down the soldier's life I know he is not himself. He went on:

"Look at the place we're in! They tell me it used to be the mansion of some *grand seigneur*. After that it became a barracks. Now they put prisoners here, poor devils! And soon they're going to pull the whole place down to make a boulevard. Nothing in the place of something. It's just the same with the Colonial infantry, it's a damned fraud nowadays. The *marsouins* used to be soldiers; now they are criminals. Not that you can't make a soldier out of a criminal, I'm not saying that. But you must teach them *l'honneur du corps*. That will take the place of any other honour. Why don't they learn that sort of thing now? Why are they not taught it?"

It was the middle of summer and the sun poured down on the pavements. There was also the horrible smell that comes in the hot weather from the dried-up drains.

"Do you remember the summer in Annam?" said Barnavaux again. It is much hotter than here, but it smells of jasmine and that other plant, you know, ylang, which leaves such a strong scent on your fingers if you only crush one little leaf, just one!"

Barnavaux worried me, for he was philosophizing, talking politics almost, and was home-sick for a country not his own. I felt it was necessary to change the drift of his thoughts, so I took him for a long walk, and we had lunch in an arbour on the banks of the Marne, surrounded by silent fishermen. When he rose from table he had recovered some of his usual serenity, and, as luck would have it, we directed our steps towards Champigny-la-Bataille, where is the Théâtre de la Nature.

The performances take place in a huge old garden, probably deserted since 1870. Very likely there was fighting there during the siege, for the walls are broken away, as though battlemented; and, when the actors fire off their guns, it gives you a little shiver as you think of those far-away, terrible days. But now, as I said before, it is only a garden, grand, peaceful and beautiful. The trees are covered with moss and make a more beautiful, more tragic background than any stage scenery. The plays are acted on a side stretch of grass backed by a hillock. The actors ascend and descend a real stairway cut out of the rock, and the only drawback is the painted canvas, representing a fortress.

That day they were playing a piece, taken, I think, from the terrible adventures of two officers sent on a mission to Nigeria who refused to obey an order to retreat, and killed the colonel in command of the retreating column. The scene, however, had been changed from Central Africa to the Sahara, and commencing as it did in the form of an anti-militarist drama, it abruptly changed into a piece that might have been written by Corneille.

The criminal officer, a brute who has ordered all the head-men of a village to be shot, after promising them freedom if they will lay down their arms, a monster maddened by blood and drink who makes light of all the murders he has committed, hearing that he is found out, says to himself:

"So they have declared that the law no longer protects me! Very well, I will remain here and found a kingdom of my own. I have taken this country and I intend to keep it."

Believing he can count on his native Spahis, he sends for the non-commissioned Bachir and expounds his plans.

"Sidi Lieutenant," replied Bachir, "we loved you. We looked upon you as made of something different to ourselves. Had you ordered me to kill myself I would have done so without a murmur. But now it is quite different. When my comrades see the corpses of those whom you have destroyed, the corpses of their brothers, they will kill you. Well, men in the pay of the French government may not kill a French officer — here is your revolver."

"Kill myself!" exclaims d'Epernon, "kill myself! you don't know me!"

And he begins to sing, the fool, to sing the old song:

> "Nous n'irons plus au bois,
> Les lauriers sont coupés."

Ah, yes! they were cut down for an assassin like himself! And just as he is in the act of refusing to kill himself it is evident that he feels that suicide is the only way out for him.

"And did you imagine that I needed you, my fine fellow, to tell me what I had to do? The fellow gives advice and forgets his place! Quartermaster Bachir, remember to whom you are speaking."

That was a good hit, you know. Barnavaux grunted approval as he heard it and saw the man draw himself up and stand at attention.

"Quartermaster Bachir, you take the command of the column."

"Good, *mon lieutenant!*"

"Return to In-Salah in short marches of twenty kilometres. It is useless to tire the horses."

"Good, *mon lieutenant!*"

"You will draw up a report on — on all that has taken place."

"Good, *mon lieutenant!*"

"Now I can rest. Farewell, Bachir."

And Bachir, bending nearly double, kisses his hand in Arab fashion. Then all that is heard is a revolver shot somewhere away in the bush.

. . . . .

The sun had gone down low in the west, and the wind was blowing gently through the green branches of the trees. The sky was the colour of clear gold. People may make fun of open-air theatres, because there are so many of them nowadays, but it is certain they fill you with a feeling different from that produced by the ordinary theatres where you have a roof to protect you and electric lamps to lighten your darkness. It is a deeper, more primitive feeling. Some of the words seem to strike against the trees before they come back to you, full of a stronger and more poignant meaning. For example, if you want to see wrestling in Paris, you have to go to some booth or café-concert, while in Switzerland the contest takes place in a green field at the foot of a mountain, and gives you the impression of some religious rite. It is the same in these theatres that have the sky for covering: the words spoken there are invested with an added majesty.

"Well?" I said to Barnavaux.

He is a simple soul and there was a lump in his throat. He blew his nose vigorously as he replied:

"The man who wrote that is no fool. He knows a thing or two about the desert, and he's not far out about the Touareg Hoggar, the Aydjer or the Aoullimidden. Then the end is fine and made a great impression on me. But when the men refuse to follow their chief — and I know what is alluded to, it didn't happen in the Sahara, but in the Soudan a few years ago, didn't it? — well, they haven't hit upon the right reason for the faithfulness of the Senegalese. They don't think as we do, and know nothing of devotion to the colours or of *esprit de corps*. But

I know what they were thinking – I was there myself."

"Well?" I inquired.

"It's a bit complicated. I'm not good at explaining things, it's not in my line. However, I will try and make it clear to you: as far as the Senegalese were concerned *there was a contract signed in Senegal.* That's what it was!"

"You are right, I don't follow," said I.

"There was a contract signed in Senegal," repeated Barnavaux. "And those niggers wanted to get back to Senegal to receive their share of the money. Then their wives and fields were there, their country, in fact. That was the chief reason why they would not stay in Nigeria, playing at being great chiefs. But that is not the only one. There was also *the might of the paper.*

"That's difficult to explain, too, however, I'll try. Suppose a marabout gives a charm to a Mahommedan Tirailleur in the shape of an amulet, to preserve him against bullets or to make him loved by women, it is the words written on the paper by the marabout that *compel* events, that force the guns not to harm and the women to love him. Now the contract they had made with France was on paper, a paper they considered as mysterious and powerful as any marabout's, and they believed that if they failed to carry out their share of the contract some great misfortune would overtake them in this world – perhaps they would be haunted by avenging spirits who would drag them along by the feet – I expect that in former days, when white men were as yet uncivilized, they were in the habit of making some such oath."

"And yet that is what they called honour, Barnavaux," I answered.

"Yes," said Barnavaux thoughtfully, "perhaps that is what they understood by honour."

He found these ideas rather difficult to follow, but went on, as though afraid of the thoughts he was discovering in himself.

"And so, nowadays, when people don't believe in magic and sorcery, when they don't realize the beauty and power of words, the only people who, I take it, are in the right are those who, in the present age, think only of themselves. Rich folk, for instance, revolutionaries and the new type of Colonial infantry recruit. And so they were right, those fellows in the Soudan who killed their comrades in order to be made chiefs. If so, I have been in the wrong all this time! I've been a fool! a fool!"

With an impatient foot he struck the rocky ground on which the grass was now triumphantly growing.

"They've made a fool of me! For twelve years I've been wandering round, and risking my life in countries I can't forget, and the only reward I have is to be able to say: 'I'm still alive! here's another day!' The only countries that remain for ever in a man's thoughts are those where he has feared and faced death. And they've returned me nothing, and I shall never see them again; they will be like the dreams I used to have when I was a little chap living with my father, a baker, at Choisy-le-Roi. I used to dream I was eating hot cakes and then to wake up with an empty stomach."

Ah, it was not easy to answer Barnavaux. In former days when the Gauls and Germans roamed the world over, they took with them their wives and little ones, and those who conquered in battle claimed for their own the land on which the struggle took place; they cultivated it, it was theirs. How different are things nowadays, from the migrations of those young warriors and their women. There were no old men, no shirkers, no useless people then! what fine races, what noble aristocracies they must have founded!

But Barnavaux was labouring under the impression that he had fought twelve years for nothing, or only for others, which, in his opinion, came to the same thing. For a century at least, Frenchmen have their own individual ambitions and will not work for any but themselves. Unless one keeps this fact well in mind it is impossible to understand anything that takes place in France to-day. The French lower classes are not ignorant enough to submit, like fine, well-trained horses, who win fortunes for their owners, and end their existence as cab-hacks; but they are not well-informed enough yet, not great enough to realize that they have an interest in the concern – in the beautiful and ancient land in which they live, the first country in the world – and they have lost the meaning of the word devotion. Barnavaux was now becoming imbued with the same idea that obsesses most Frenchmen and troubles the greater number of them, that he was unjustly treated, and that he had worked and struggled all his life in vain. Ah, how could I put him right? how could I explain things to him?

. . . . .

After dining in the same arbour where he had lunched in the morning I took him home with me. He knew where things were kept, and immediately reached up to the mantelpiece for a long pewter pipe from Annam, one of those that you smoke with a lighted coal on the bowl.

"Listen," I said, "I want to read you a story I have written, and I want to explain to you how it affects you—all of us in France and Europe."

"What is it about?" he asked.

"You will see. It happened long ago, in the days you know but little about; but you will see the point when I get to the end of the tale."

He put the glowing coal on the tobacco, drew in a deep mouthful of smoke, and composed himself to listen.

"Stachys," said Agabus in a whisper, "have you any more of those dried chestnuts that you got at Tarente? Give me a few. I will give you a quarter of an hour's sleep to-night in exchange."

Loosing his oar with one hand, Stachys attempted to reach the wallet hanging at his right side. The lash of a whip stung him on the shoulder, and he resumed his rowing without a murmur.

In the falling light the keel of the galley looked like the upturned corpse of some monstrous animal. It was a trireme. On the deck the Thranites, sheltered from the sun by a tent, rowed three abreast, with oars as long and thin as the legs of a water-fly. They were sturdy, fearless slaves, and able, during battle, to sit immovable at their oars under the rain of arrows shot at them by the archers fore and aft on the enemy's ships. The confidence placed in these men gave them certain privileges, and made of them the aristocracy of the galley-slaves. The rowers below envied them. The Zygites, two to each oar, could not even raise their heads without striking against the beams of the deck. Under them again, came the Thalamites, each manipulating a heavy oar that protruded from the round port-holes nearly level with the water.

Six feet above the hold was a long plank running the whole length of the boat, on which a man kept up a continual pacing backwards and forwards; it was Herodion, the *incitator*, the slave-keeper. He had formerly been a gladiator, and was condemned to the galleys for murder; like the others he had rowed, bent double under the lash, and panted in the sweltering heat. He himself could not imagine how it came to pass that he had been able to survive so many of his comrades who had never been unchained from their benches until they were thrown overboard. And as a reward for not having succumbed and because he was strong and savage they had made him *incitator*. With a whip made of Nile hippopotamus hide in his hand, he struck right and left, incessantly pacing up and down upon his plank like an imprisoned wild beast.

Stachys was in the third row of Thalamites, at the very bottom of the hold. His mind had become so weakened that he hardly felt the extent of his misery. The days in his sea-cellar, or in the hovels where the rowers were huddled pell-mell at the end of a campaign, were much the same as the nights; he hardly noticed them. And yet, after the midday repast, the blood beat more rapidly in his temples, and then he remembered the town of Joppa, his birthplace. There was a hill with palm and orange trees that unfurled their luxuriant foliage right down to the sea-shore, hiding from view the terraced houses and earthen huts with their wooden porticoes. He had lived with his mother in one of these huts when he was a little boy. Later he had learned to read Greek, and had become the steward of a kind master. But he had stolen money entrusted to him, and had been sold to a Roman pro-consul for the galleys. The monotony of his miserable existence dulled his thoughts for the most part, and life or death mattered little to him; only very trivial things interested him now: for instance, one day one of the Zygites above him had slipped and remained hanging from the chain fastened to his foot. Stachys still laughed when he thought of it.

As long as the rowers remained in the trireme, this chain was never removed; under them was a filthy pool of water, emptied daily by slaves carrying copper vessels. The rowers despised these unfortunates, and would secretly kick at them with their iron-bound feet. In the depth of their ignorant souls they were jealous of such ignoble work, because it was easy.

None of the Thalamites disliked Herodion; they had grown quite accustomed to blows and, like dogs, they felt the need of some one to command them. Their duty was to row, and the slave-keeper supplied the brains necessary to guide the perpetual movement of their arms; but they hated the Zygites, who would take advantage of their position immediately above them to give them sly kicks. They also hated the tent that covered them, and also the courage with which they faced danger; all these things filled them with fury.

And at night, also, the trireme continued her course, but more slowly. One row in three stopped work, and each man was thus able to get a few hours' sleep.

They had started from Ostia and were going towards the East. That was all Stachys had been able to make out, for he was in perpetual darkness, daylight only entering through the port-holes. One morning, however, a voice of command rang out.

Herodion's whip fell more frequently, and the trireme travelled at a greater pace. Now and again one or another of the men was ordered to cease rowing, and then the boat turned round so quickly that their heads swam and they experienced a feeling of intoxication, part pleasure and part pain, as one experiences when driving very quickly down a steep slope. On deck a great clamour was going on, the sound of clanking coats of mail and of shields falling with a clatter to the ground. Trumpets brayed out until the sound echoed again; further off other trumpets replied so that the air was full of sounds, like cattle calling to one another across the fields. The atmosphere was charged with terror and excitement.

"A great battle must be going on up there," said Stachys, "a great battle!"

And the supple thong bit into his back.

The whole ship was quivering, the galley-slaves breathing all together in great gasps, and Herodion, his eyes almost starting out of his head, bellowed commands. Suddenly Agabus turned livid and fell face downward, in the filthy pool at the bottom of the hold. He had broken a blood vessel. Herodion sprang forward, and lifted him so that he should not suffocate, and the slaves were touched at this proof of their master's care.

"Apollo!" murmured Stachys. "Oh, sun of Heliopolis!"

A great clamour arose from the sea, a clamour of Greek, Latin, Syrian and Egyptian words, together with the moans of drowning or mortally wounded men.

"It is a battle, a great battle!"

A sudden violent shock made itself felt in the hold. On one side of the vessel every oar was simultaneously broken. Another galley had tried to stave in their vessel and had failed in the attempt. Dreadful groans arose from the wretched slaves, who were precipitated upon one another as though they had been cut down with a scythe, limbs broken and chests crushed. Blood spurted on the walls and ran along the benches. Splinters of wood flew about like arrows amongst the writhing mass of men. One of Stachys' eyes was put out.

The tumult lasted a long time, but at length calmed down. Slaves descended into the hold to carry away the dead; the benches were washed down and they were all fed. But Stachys could not eat; he was feverish and in great pain. The sun, peeping in through the port-holes, told him that their course lay southwards, and for six days and nights they followed this direction.

On the morning of the seventh day they stopped. The Thalamites, who knew the Mediterranean well, and had the strange, divining faculty possessed by all draught beasts, knew without being told by Herodion that they had just entered the port of Alexandria.

They knew this because of the peculiar odour of the still water, which is never the same in any two ports. Evidently there was a large crowd of people on the jetty, for a great uproar could be heard away in the distance; the shrill tones of women, beginning very high up in the scale, slowly descending and then ascending before they finally died away, lost in the deeper voices of the men. The words "Oktabianos Kaisar," pronounced in the Greek fashion, could occasionally be heard.

The trireme was close to a high quay, and suddenly the galley-slaves saw something against the timbers of the vessel, something falling gently into the water; a rain of something much softer than real rain, a slow, light and pearly shower. Herodion, half on deck, and craning his neck through the hatchway, cried:

"Roses! Roses! The people of Alexandria are throwing us roses!"

And he pushed a heap of petals down on the slaves.

They fell gently, and lay on bare and bleeding shoulders. Their perfume mingled with the stench from the cesspool and the smell of blood.

Then, bewildered at the sight, the unfortunates cried as with one voice from the depths of their eternal darkness:

"Herodion! Herodion! why do the people of Alexandria throw us flowers?"

And in reply Herodion roared:

"Brutes! Beasts! It is because of the victory *we* have gained at Actium!"

"Yes," said Barnavaux, "I understand. They had gained the battle, those poor devils rowing in the hold among the vermin and the lashes. They won it! But what good did it do them? tell me that. They did not even know they had done it – no one ever did before you suggested it."

"Oh, yes," I replied, "people did know it. They knew it, because the battle of Actium was perhaps the greatest battle ever fought. It was necessary to decide who were to be the masters of the world, the Asiatics or Africans, or the white people, the people of Europe: ourselves, Barnavaux, ourselves! If those poor devils who were being flogged in the galleys had not conquered, we should have been working for the others to-day."

"The others?" exclaimed Barnavaux. "The blacks of the Nile, the Arabs and the men of Syria with their big, hooked noses? They would have been the masters? If we had not smashed them, they would have smashed us? Yes, it is true: when one nation is keeping quiet, another is advancing. What rot it is to speak of peace! arrant rot! People are fighting somewhere all the time, individuals, nations and races, even during so-called peace. People fight as to who shall make the most money, or have the most children. They fight with the customs officers. And war with lances, arrows, rifles, cannons, and ironclads is only the inevitable end of that universal war that we call peace. *Real* war only takes place because it is less dangerous, less loathsome, and less killing than the hypocritical wars of peace. That was the kind of fight waged by the rowers at Actium, and had they not conquered, they would not even have been able to earn their bread by rowing on merchant vessels. The others, the enemy, the Niggers, the Arabs, the Syrians, and the yellow people from Asia would have taken their place. Then fame and glory are only other words for daily bread!"

He stopped a moment, bewildered.

"Why don't they explain these things to us, here in France? Tell me: I – I, Barnavaux, have really done my share? I have earned my bread, helped on the cause of humanity, and added to the glory of the white race?"

"I think so," I said.

—*From Under the Tricolour by Pierre Mille, French (1864–1941), translated by Bérengère Drillien.*

~ ❂ ~

The Pier

MORI OGWAI

THE PIER IS LONG – LONG ——

The rails of four railroads cut straight and obliquely the beams of the iron bridge on which the long and short cross-beams are like the bars of a xylophone on which children play. Through the cracks of the cross-beams, that almost catch the heels of shoes and wooden clogs, here and there the black waves are shown, reflected on the white flashes of sunshine.

The sky has cleared into a deep blue. On the inside of the train where she was sitting with her husband starting to-day, she did not think the wind was blowing.

When leaving the jinrikisha, in which she rode from the station of Yokohama, and standing on this pier, she found that the wind of the fifth of March was still blowing as if to bite the skin, fluttering the skirts of the Azuma coat.

It is the Azuma coat in silver gray, which she loosely wears on her body, that carries the child of her husband, who is starting today, this day which is not far from the month of confinement.

She came with her hair in Sokuhatsu. Her boa is of white ostrich. Holding the light green umbrella with tassels, she walks along, surrounded by four or five maidservants.

The pier is long – long ——

The big ships are anchoring on the right and the left of the pier. Some are painted in black, some in white.

The anchored ships are making a fence

for the wind. Every time she leaves the place where are ships, a gust of wind blows and flutters the skirts of her Azuma coat.

Two years ago, immediately after he was graduated from the university of literature, the count, her husband, had married her. It was during the previous year that she gave birth to her first child, a princess like a jewel. At the end of the year the husband became a Master of Ceremonies at the Court. And, now, he is starting to London, charged with his official duty.

In his newly made gray overcoat, flinging the cane with crooked handle, her husband is walking rapidly along the pier. The viscount, who is going with him, and whose height is taller by a head than his, also walks rapidly beside him, clad in a suit of similar color.

The French ship, on which her husband is about to go abroad, is anchoring at the extreme end of the right side of the pier.

A stool, like that which is used to repair the wires of a trolley, is stationed on the pier, and from it a gangplank is laid across to the bulwark.

While walking slowly, she sees her husband and the viscount, his companion, crossing the gangplank and entering the ship.

The group of people looking after them are standing, here and there, on the pier. Almost all of them are those who came to bid adieu to her husband and the viscount. Perhaps there are no other passengers on this ship about to sail who are so important and are looked at by so many people.

Some of them are going to the foot of the stool on which the gangplank is laid, and stop there to wait for their companions. Some of them are standing at the place, a bit before the stool, where the blocks and ropes are laid down.

Among these people there must be some who are intimately known to her husband, and some who know him but slightly. But, standing under this clear sky, they all seem dejected; or is it only her fancy?

The pier is long – long ——

Following slowly after them, unconsciously she looks off to her right where there were many round windows on the side of the ship. The faces and chests of women are seen from one of those round windows. Three of them are from thirty to forty years of age; all with white aprons on their chests. They must be the waitresses of the ship. Supposing them to be the waitresses who wait on the passengers of the ship, on which her husband is on board, she feels envious of even those humble women.

There is also a woman at the bulwark, looking down on the pier, who wears a big bonnet with white cloth and carries a small leather bag in her hand. Two big eyes, as if painted with shadows, are shining on her wrinkled face above the large nose, like a hook. She looks like a Jewess. She also must be a traveler who is going on this ship. She is also envious of her.

The pier is long – long ——

At last she arrives at the foot of the gangplank. Cautiously she carries her body, which has the second infant of her husband under the Azuma coat, and descends on the deck of the big black-painted ship. She hands the umbrella to a maidservant.

Led by the people who have come to say farewell and were already on board, she goes back along the bulwark toward the prow. There are rooms for passengers at the end of the way, the numbers of which increase from twenty-seven to twenty-nine.

The viscount is standing at the entrance and addresses her.

"This is the room, madam."

Peeping into the room she finds two beds, under which the familiar packages and trunks are deposited. Her husband is standing before one of the beds.

"Look it through, madam. It is like this."

This is the room; she must look through it carefully. During the long, long voyage of her husband, this is the room where her dreams must come and go.

A man, who looks like the captain, comes, and, addressing her husband in French, guides him to the saloon of the ship. She follows her husband and the viscount and enters the room.

This is a spacious and beautiful saloon. Several tables are arranged, each bearing a flower basket. . . . Gradually the people who came to say farewell gather into the room.

By the order of this man, who looks like the captain, a waiter brings forth many cups in the shape of morning-glories, and, pouring champagne into them, he distributes them among the people. Another waiter brings cakes, like those which are brought with ice cream, piled on a plate in the form of the well crib, and distributes them among the people.

The people who received the cups go one after another, and stand before her husband and the viscount, wishing them a happy voyage, and drink from the cups.

Sitting on a small chair beside the table, she is waiting for the time when the congratulations are at an end. During his busy moments, now and then, her husband lifts his eyes to her.

However, there is no more to be said to her before many people. Also, there is no more to be said to him, before many people.

The bell rings. Having bidden farewell to her husband and to the viscount the people are going out, one after another. She also follows them, saluting her husband and the viscount.

Again crossing the dangerous gangplank, she descends to the pier. She receives the light green umbrella from the hand of her maidservant, and raises it.

Her husband and the viscount are standing on the bulwark, looking in her direction. She is looking up at them from under her umbrella. She feels that her eyes, as she looks up, are growing gradually larger and larger.

Again the bell rings. A few French sailors begin to untie the rope from the gangplank. A Japanese laborer in Hanten is standing on the stool like that which is used in repairing the trolley, preparing to draw down the gangplank. Hanging on the rope of the wheel, pulled by the man in Hanten, the gangplank at last leaves the bulwark.

The noon-gun of the city of Yokohama resounds. With this as a signal, the ship, from the hold of which for some time a noise has been issuing, silently begins to move.

The elderly Europeans, who seem to be a married couple, are standing at the bulwark. They are talking about something of a jolly nature with a white-haired old man who is standing on the pier, with one of his feet placed on an apparatus to roll the ropes, which looks like a big bobbin. They do not seem to regret the parting.

It looks as if the ship is moving. It looks as if the pier is moving. There seems to be the distance of a Pallaraxe [1] between the place where her husband and the viscount are standing and the place where she is standing. She feels her eyes growing larger and larger.

Some of the people who are looking after them are running to the end of the pier. She cannot do such an immodest thing. Suddenly something white waves at the bulwark. It was a handkerchief waved by the hand of a woman who wears a big bonnet decorated with a white cloth. A tall man stands at the end of the pier, in red waistcoat and tan shoes. A white handkerchief waves also from the hand of this man. This also must be a parting in human life.

These two persons set the fashion, and the handkerchiefs are waved here and there. White things are waving also from the people who are looking after the group surrounding the count. She also grasps the batiste handkerchief which she has brought in her sleeve, but she cannot do such an immodest thing.

When the ship seemed to have left the pier, it turned its prow a bit to the right. The place where her husband and the viscount were standing has disappeared at last.

Still she can see a boy about fifteen or sixteen, standing at the stern, in a blue, cold-looking garment like a blouse. What mother is waiting for him in France? Or has he no parents? What is he looking at, standing by the rail at the stern?

Slowly she turned her feet and walked among the maidservants surrounding her.

The pier is long — long ——

At the place where the black-painted ship was anchored, until a short time ago, the water is glittering like the scales of fish, as the small ripples are reflecting the pale sunshine.

— *By Mori Ogwai, Japanese (1860–1922), translated by Torao Taketomo.*

[1] There seems to be a parallax variation (*alternative translation, by courtesy of the Japanese Department, Columbia University*).

In the Twilight of the Gods

LAFCADIO HEARN

"Do you know anything about josses?"

"Josses?"

"Yes; idols, Japanese idols — josses."

"Something," I answered, "but not very much."

"Well, come and look at my collection, won't you? I've been collecting josses for twenty years, and I've got some worth seeing. They're not for sale, though — except to the British Museum."

I followed the curio dealer through the bric-à-brac of his shop, and across a paved yard into an unusually large go-down. Like all go-downs it was dark: I could barely discern a stairway sloping up through gloom. He paused at the foot.

"You'll be able to see better in a moment," he said. "I had this place built expressly for them; but now it is scarcely big enough. They're all in the second story. Go right up; only be careful — the steps are bad."

I climbed, and reached a sort of gloaming, under a very high roof, and found myself face to face with the gods.

In the dusk of the great go-down the spectacle was more than weird: it was apparitional. Arhats and Buddhas and Bodhisattvas, and the shapes of a mythology older than they, filled all the shadowy space; not ranked by hierarchies, as in a temple, but mingled without order, as in a silent panic. Out of the wilderness of multiple heads and broken aureoles and hands uplifted in menace or in prayer — a shimmering confusion of dusty gold half lighted by cobwebbed air-holes in the heavy walls — I could at first discern little; then, as the dimness cleared, I began to distinguish personalities. I saw Kwannon, of many forms; Jizō, of many names; Shaka, Yakushi, Amida, the Buddhas and their disciples. They were very old; and their art was not all of Japan, nor of any one place or time: there were shapes from Korea, China, India — treasures brought over sea in the rich days of the early Buddhist missions. Some were seated upon lotus-flowers, the lotus-flowers of the Apparitional Birth. Some rode leopards, tigers, lions, or monsters mystical — typifying lightning, typifying death. One, triple-headed and many-handed, sinister and splendid, seemed moving through the gloom on a throne of gold, uplifted by a phalanx of elephants. Fudō I saw, shrouded and shrined in fire, and Maya-Fujin, riding her celestial peacock; and strangely mingling with these Buddhist visions, as in the anachronism of a Limbo, armored effigies of daimyo and images of the Chinese sages. There were huge forms of wrath, grasping thunderbolts, and rising to the roof: the Deva-kings, like impersonations of hurricane power; the Ni-O, guardians of long-vanished temple gates. Also there were forms voluptuously feminine: the light grace of the limbs folded within their lotus-cups, the suppleness of the fingers numbering the numbers of the Good Law, were ideals possibly inspired in some forgotten time by the charm of an Indian dancing-girl. Shelved against the naked brickwork above, I could perceive multitudes of lesser shapes: demon figures with eyes of a black cat, and figures half man, half bird, winged and beaked like eagles — the Tengu of Japanese fancy.

"Well?" queried the curio dealer, with a chuckle of satisfaction at my evident surprise.

"It is a very great collection," I responded.

He clapped his hand on my shoulder, and exclaimed triumphantly in my ear, "Cost me fifty thousand dollars."

But the images themselves told me how much more was their cost to forgotten piety, notwithstanding the cheapness of artistic labor in the East. Also they told me of the dead millions whose pilgrim feet had worn hollow the steps leading to their shrines, of the buried mothers who used to suspend little baby-dresses before their altars, of the generations of children taught to murmur prayers to them, of the countless sorrows and hopes confided to them. Ghosts of the worship of centuries had followed them into exile; a thin, sweet odor of incense haunted the dusty place.

"What would you call that?" asked the voice of the curio dealer. "I've been told it's the best of the lot."

He pointed to a figure resting upon a triple golden lotus — Avalokitesvara: she

who looketh down about the sound of prayer. . . . Storms and hate give way to her name. Fire is quenched by her name. Demons vanish at the sound of her name. By her name one may stand firm in the sky, like a sun. . . .

The delicacy of the limbs, the tenderness of the smile, were dreams of the Indian paradise.

"It is a Kwannon," I made reply, "and very beautiful."

"Somebody will have to pay me a very beautiful price for it," he said, with a shrewd wink. "It cost me enough! As a rule, though, I get these things pretty cheap. There are few people who care to buy them, and they have to be sold privately, you know: that gives me an advantage. See that joss in the corner — the big black fellow? What is it?"

"Emmei-Jizō," I answered — "Jizō, the giver of long life. It must be very old."

"Well," he said, again taking me by the shoulder, "the man from whom I got that piece was put in prison for selling it to me."

Then he burst into a hearty laugh — whether at the recollection of his own cleverness in the transaction, or at the unfortunate simplicity of the person who had sold the statue contrary to law, I could not decide.

"Afterwards," he resumed, "they wanted to get it back again, and offered me more than I had given for it. But I held on. I don't know everything about josses, but I do know what they are worth. There isn't another idol like that in the whole country. The British Museum will be glad to get it."

"When do you intend to offer the collection to the British Museum?" I presumed to ask.

"Well, I first want to get up a show," he replied. "There's money to be made by a show of josses in London. London people never saw anything like this in their lives. Then the church folks help that sort of a show, if you manage them properly; it advertises the missions. 'Heathen idols from Japan! . . . How do you like the baby?"

I was looking at a small gold-colored image of a naked child, standing, one tiny hand pointing upward, and the other downward — representing the Buddha newly born.

Sparkling with light he came from the womb, as when the Sun first rises in the east. . . . Upright he took deliberately seven steps; and the prints of his feet upon the ground remained burning as seven stars. And he spake with clearest utterance, saying, "This birth is a Buddha birth. Re-birth is not for me. Only this last time am I born for the salvation of all on earth and in heaven."

"That is what they call a Tanjo-Shaka," I said. "It looks like bronze."

"Bronze it is," he responded, tapping it with his knuckles to make the metal ring. "The bronze alone is worth more than the price I paid."

I looked at the four Devas whose heads almost touched the roof, and thought of the story of their apparition told in the Mahavagga.

On a beautiful night the Four Great Kings entered the holy grove, filling all the place with light; and having respectfully saluted the Blessed One, they stood in the four directions, like four great firebrands.

"How did you ever manage to get those big figures upstairs?" I asked.

"Oh, hauled them up! We've got a hatchway. The real trouble was getting them here by train. It was the first railroad trip they ever made. . . . But look at these here: *they* will make the sensation of the show!"

I looked, and saw two small wooden images, about three feet high.

"Why do you think they will make a sensation?" I enquired innocently.

"Don't you see what they are? They date from the time of the persecutions. *Japanese devils trampling on the Cross!"*

They were small temple guardians only; but their feet rested upon X-shaped supports.

"Did any person tell you these were devils trampling on the Cross?" I made bold to ask.

"What else are they doing?" he answered evasively. "Look at the Crosses under their feet!"

"But they are not devils," I insisted; "and those cross-pieces were put under their feet simply to give equilibrium."

He said nothing, but looked disappointed; and I felt a little sorry for him. "Devils trampling on the Cross," as a display line in some London poster announcing the arrival of "josses from Japan," might certainly have been relied on to catch the public eye.

"This is more wonderful," I said, pointing to a beautiful group — Maya with the infant Buddha issuing from her side, according to tradition.

Painlessly the Bodhisattva was born from her right side. It was the eighth day of the fourth moon.

"That's bronze, too," he remarked, tapping it. "Bronze josses are rare. We used to buy them up and sell them for old metal. Wish I'd kept some of them! You ought to have seen the bronzes, in those days, coming in from the temples — bells and vases and josses! That was the time we tried to buy the Daibutsu at Kamakura."

"For old bronze?" I queried.

"Yes. We calculated the weight of the metal, and formed a syndicate. Our first offer was thirty thousand. We could have made a big profit, for there's a good deal of gold and silver in that work. The priests wanted to sell, but the people wouldn't let them."

"It's one of the world's wonders," I said. "Would you really have broken it up?"

"Certainly. Why not? What else could you do with it? . . . That one there looks just a Virgin Mary, doesn't it?"

He pointed to the gilded image of a female clasping a child to her breast.

"Yes," I replied; "but it is Kishibōjin, the goddess who loves little children."

"People talk about idolatry," he went on musingly. "I've seen things like many of these in Roman Catholic chapels. Seems to me religion is pretty much the same the world over."

"I think you are right," I said.

"Why, the story of Buddha is like the story of Christ, isn't?"

"To some degree," I assented.

"Only, he wasn't crucified."

I did not answer; thinking of the text, "In all the world there is not one spot even so large as a mustard-seed where he has not surrendered his body for the sake of creatures." Then it suddenly seemed to me that this was absolutely true. For the Buddha of the deeper Buddhism is not Gautama, nor yet any one Tathâgata, but simply the divine in man. Chrysalides of the infinite we all are: each contains a ghostly Buddha, and the millions are but one. All humanity is potentially the Buddha-to-come, dreaming through the ages in Illusion; and the teacher's smile will make beautiful the world again when selfishness shall die. Every noble sacrifice brings nearer the hour of his awakening; and who may justly doubt — remembering the myriads of the centuries of man — that even now there does not remain one place on earth where life has not been freely given for love or duty?

I felt the curio dealer's hand on my shoulder again.

"At all events," he cried in a cheery tone, "they'll be appreciated in the British Museum — eh?"

"I hope so. They ought to be."

Then I fancied them immured somewhere in that vast necropolis of dead gods, under the gloom of a pea-soup fog, chambered with forgotten divinities of Egypt or Babylon, and trembling faintly at the roar of London — all to what end? Perhaps to aid another Alma Tadema to paint the beauty of another vanished civilization; perhaps to assist the illustration of an English Dictionary of Buddhism; perhaps to inspire some future laureate with a metaphor startling as Tennyson's figure of the "oiled and curled Assyrian bull." Assuredly they would not be preserved in vain. The thinkers of a less conventional and selfish era would teach new reverence for them. Each eidolon shaped by human faith remains the shell of a truth eternally divine; and even the shell itself may hold a ghostly power. The soft serenity, the passionless tenderness, of these Buddha faces might yet give peace of soul to a West weary of creeds transformed into conventions, eager for the coming of another teacher to proclaim,

I have the same feeling for the high as for the low, for the moral as for the immoral, for the depraved as for the virtuous, for those holding sectarian views and false opinions as for those whose beliefs are good and true.

— Lafcadio Hearn, American of Irish and Greek parentage (1850–1904).

~ ✿ ~

Father Andrea

PEARL BUCK

FATHER ANDREA lived all day for the hours at night when he might study the stars. The days in his parish in the Chinese city were long and crowded, filled with people and voices crying and complaining and demanding, and the nights were short and radiant with the silent, peaceful stars, shining like torches out of the dark purple sky. He could never get enough of them. The hours with his telescope went so quickly that many times he remembered to sleep only when the dawn came up out of the east with such ruddy splendor that the stars faded. But he did not need sleep. He could return to the day refreshed and braced by those hours of study and observation of the golden stars, when the voices that clamored after him all day were asleep for a brief while. "Bless sleep!" he would say to himself, chuckling as he climbed the steps to the tiny observatory he had built on top of the schoolhouse.

He was a small, stout, smiling man, whose

exterior revealed nothing of his soft, mystic soul. If one saw only his apple cheeks and dark beard and red, smiling mouth, one would say that he was a lover of visible life. One needed to see his eyes to discover that he was a lover of things unseen. His lips went on smiling even when a leper came twisting and beseeching about his feet, or a wretched slave-girl ran in, cowering and crying, through the gates of the mission. But his eyes, deep set and dark, were often full of tears.

During the day he lifted up the lepers with his hands and washed them and fed them and soothed them and smeared oil upon their wounds. He stood between the slave-girl and her angry, cursing mistress, smiling, waiting, talking in that quiet, ceaseless, murmuring way he had. The woman's angry voice rose above it like a storm above a brook, but sooner or later his gentle, insistent speech won, and she would sit sulking, in answer to his invitation, in the seat of honor at the right of the square table in his little guest-hall, and sip the tea he had asked the servant to bring. And then, with his small, dark, tragic eyes grave above his smiling mouth, he would talk on, praising, suggesting, regretting, hinting gently of the necessity of better things, until in the end the slave went away with the mistress. He would never help people to break away from what held them fast. His great concern always was to help them bear more easily the inevitable yoke that life had placed upon each of them. That was the one thing he was sure of – that there was no getting away from the oppression that life itself brought.

Talking in the morning to the boys in his school, he said one day more earnestly than he had ever before said anything:

"My sons, I will tell you a thing. You think, when you are children, that you will break away from the bondage of your parents and that when you go to school you will be free of them. In school you dream of manhood, when there will be no more teachers for you to obey. But you can never be free! When your immortal souls took on flesh, they became even as the Son of Man was – bound. No man is free – we are not free of one another – we can never be free of God.

"The thing is, not to cry futilely after freedom, but to discover cheerfully how to bear the burden of bondage upon us. Even the stars in heaven are not free. They too must obey the paths of order in law, lest by their wantonness they wreck the universe. You have seen the shooting stars in the sky in summer. They seem beautiful in freedom, a burst of light and splendor against the clouds. But their end is destruction and darkness. It is the stars marching steadily on in their appointed ways which endure to the end."

The little blue-coated Chinese boys stared at him, wondering at the passion in his quiet voice and at the unwonted somberness of his round, smiling face. They did not understand him at all.

All day long he trotted hither and thither about his duty, beginning at dawn by saying mass for a few faithful old women who came decently garbed in their cotton coats and trousers, with black kerchiefs folded about their heads. It troubled him sometimes that they did not grasp much of what he said; his Chinese had never been perfect and it was spoken with a soft Italian elision that could never seize the gutturals firmly. But at last, seeing their patient faces as they fixed their eyes on the Virgin and her Son, he decided that it did not matter what he said so long as they looked at the sacred picture and struggled to think of its meaning.

Before noon he tried to teach a little in the boys' school, but it was a harried business, because at any moment he would be called without to settle some affair of the poor.

"Father, I sold this man tenpence of rice last night and trusted him until this morning for the money, and now, having eaten the rice, he tells me he has nothing."

Two men in coolie trousers, their backs bare and blackened with the sun, stood before him, one angry, one defiant.

"Now, then, was not my stomach empty? Am I to starve when you have food? The revolutionists are coming, and, when they come, all men like you who have rice must give to us who have not, and no talk of money, either!"

The two glared at each other as angry cocks will glare before attacking, and Father Andrea put a hand on each man's arm. His hands told the story begun by his eyes, small, brown, perfectly shaped hands that were broken and wrinkled with the washings and scrubbings he gave them. It was one of the agonies of his life that he could not subdue his flesh to the point of touching dark, unwashed bodies without some shrinking of his spirit. It was an obsession with him to wash his hands again and again, so that they were always scented faintly with carbolic soap. One of his private penances was to go without washing his hands, making himself endure the shuddering when he put them upon a child's head, crusted with the scale of disease. He had schooled himself to touch everything that made him recoil and, seeing his freely moving, kindly, expressive hands, no one dreamed of the inner withdrawal.

So now, one of his hands warm and persuasive upon the arm of each man, he said to the defiant one: "My friend, I know nothing of the revolutionists. But this I do know. My garden needs weeding today, and, if you will weed it, I will gladly pay you wages and, out of the wages, I who know your good heart am sure you will not withhold the tenpence to your neighbor. He is a poor man with children, and you have eaten his rice. It is written, 'If any would not work, neither should he eat.' It is one of the laws of life, which even the revolution cannot rightly change."

Instantly the tension on the two faces faded away, and the two men laughed and showed their white teeth, and Father Andrea laughed, wrinkling his round, rosy face, and went back to his boys. At the end of the day he paid the man double wages. "Take it," he said when the man made a feint of refusal. "Some day I will ask you to work for me again, and on that day I may not have the money by me."

In the afternoon, after his dish of rice and beans and macaroni, he put on his flat black hat and went out and visited the people and drank tea with them and ate the hard-boiled eggs the housewives would cook for him, although his soul loathed them, and listened, smiling, to all that was said. He knew no rich people. These scorned him as a Catholic priest and a foreigner, and he would not have forced his presence upon them even if he could. He went into the low, thatched houses of the poor and into the mat sheds of beggars, and he gave them his money as fast as it came into his hands. Of the great storm gathering without, the storm of the revolution, these people know nothing, and no more did Father Andrea know. He had read no newspapers for years, and he had no idea of anything that was happening beyond this round of days and splendid nights.

Once a week he allowed himself to remember his own country. On the evening of the seventh day he washed himself and trimmed his dark beard and put a little scent upon his hands, and then he went up into the tiny observatory and sat in an old easy chair he had there. On the other nights he sat upon a stool by the table and took out his pens and papers and his measuring instruments and in his small, accurate handwriting he made notes which he sent to his Superior in Siccawei. Through all these years of evenings he had gradually become one of the chief of a group of astronomers in the Far East, although he did not know it. To him his study of the heavens was the relaxation and exhilaration of a brain formed for meticulous observation and keen, hard thinking.

But on this seventh day he took no paper and pens. He sat down and opened the windows and fixed his eyes upon the stars and allowed his thoughts to take him back to Italy, his country, to which he had not returned for twenty-seven years and which he would never behold again. He had been a young man when he left, scarcely thirty, but even after all these years he remembered with passionate sharpness the agony of that parting. Even yet he could see the bay, rounding into a circle smaller and smaller as the ship drew out from the land. Every week he thought gravely and with a sense of guilt that above his sense of mission still was the memory of that parting, and that sharper than the parting of his body from his motherland, from his home and parents and his sister and his brother, was the parting of his spirit from his beloved, his Vitellia, who had loved his brother more than him.

He had done penance all these years for this sin, that he had come into the Church, not for devotion to God and Mary, but because Vitellia did not love him. Not that she or anyone else knew it. His brother was tall and handsome and grave, with beautiful, languishing brown eyes, and Vitellia was tall and pale and exquisite as an olive-tree in new leafage, her colors all soft and subdued and mistlike. She was head and shoulders above the little rosy man he always was. No one thought of him seriously. He was always laughing and joking and merry, his small, deep-set, black eyes crackling with humor.

Even after his brother's marriage he did not stop his joking. But he waited to see whether or not his brother was good to Vitellia. There was nothing to complain of there. His brother was a good man, although a little dull inside his beauty of body, and, when he found himself married and soon with a child coming, he settled down into his father's wine business and they were very happy. No, there was nothing to complain of there.

Then it was that Andrea became frightened at the power of his passion. He saw that nothing would keep him from revealing himself except entire submission to his fate. That took a year of fever and agony, and it was not complete until he saw that for him there was no renunciation wholly efficacious except priesthood in some far country. Then he fled to the fathers in his village.

His family had laughed at him — everyone laughed at him — and Vitellia had nearly ruined him by clinging to his hand and saying in that voice of hers that was more to him than music, "But brother mine, my Andrea, who will play with my children and be always in my house?" He had shaken his head, smiling and speechless, and she had looked at him in surprise and seen that his eyes were full of tears. "Must you, if you mind so much, Andrea?" And he had nodded.

Ah, well, it was all done, long, long ago. For many years he had not allowed himself to think of her because she was another man's wife, and he had come to the stars night after night and prayed passionately for peace. It seemed to him that he could never do penance enough for loving Vitellia more than anyone else always to the very end. That made him deny himself fiercely and force himself to every distasteful touch and duty. Once, when his flesh had burned after her, he had gone widely out into the streets and had brought in a beggar from the winter's night, a poor, shivering wretch, and had laid him in his bed and covered him with his blankets and had stretched himself out beside the creature all night long, his teeth clenched and his stomach sick. But in the morning he whispered triumphantly to his body, "Now will you be quiet and cease troubling me!" All this explained the smiling tragedy in his eyes and his constant preaching of bearing one's yoke.

When one day a black-bordered letter came, the first letter in many years, he opened it, and within was the news of Vitellia's death. Then it seemed that peace of a sort came upon him, and after a while he allowed himself his relaxation on the evening of seventh days and even at last permitted himself to think a little of her. Now that she was dead, he could imagine her up yonder, moving in that free, light way she had, among the stars. She was no one's wife now — she belonged to no one. She was a part of heaven, and he could think of her as of a star and be without sin.

He began to preach less vehemently and more patiently about bearing the yoke. When one of his schoolboys ran away to join the revolutionists, he went out with a sigh and sought him and talked with him gently, begging him to come back to his weeping mother.

"The good God puts us into life with a duty to perform," he said tenderly, smiling a little, with his arm about the boy's shoulders.

But the boy shook himself free and moved away. "In the revolution there is no God and there is no duty," he said imperiously. "We are all free, and we preach a gospel of freedom for everyone."

"Ah?" said Father Andrea softly.

For the first time a premonition fell upon him. He had up to this time paid no attention to the talk of revolution. His paths had not led him a mile from the congested quarter where he lived. It occurred to him that now he must look into such talk, especially if his boys were going off like this. He began to speak then of other things, but the boy was wary and obviously eager to have him gone. There were other lads about and an officer or two. The boy's answers grew shorter and shorter. He cast angry looks at his fellows. At last Father Andrea said kindly: "I see that you have other things on your mind. I will leave you now. Do not forget the prayers that you have been taught, my child."

He put his hand on the lad's head for an instant and turned away, but, before he left the barracks, a hoot of laughter arose, and he heard the lads shouting to their comrade, "Running-dog of a foreigner, are you?"

He had no idea what this meant, and he thought once of going back. He stopped to listen. Someone cried out, laughing like a whip's cut, "Ah, a Christian!" Then he heard the boy's voice raised angrily, half-sobbing: "I hate the priest — I know nothing of his religion. I am a revolutionist! Does anyone dare to question me?"

Father Andrea stood stricken. What words were these to come from his lad's mouth, his lad who had been in his school ever since he was five years old? He trembled a little, and a thought shot into his mind like a pang. "So did Peter deny his Lord!" And he went back into the little mission that was his home and shut himself up in his room and wept bitterly.

After that it seemed to him that he had been standing on the edge of a whirlpool and had not known it. He had said that he must investigate this revolution and see that his boys were not carried away. But there was no need of investigation. Knowledge and experience came pouring over him, and he was caught in a maze of difficulties.

There was so much he had not known. He had never heard of political differences between East and West. He had come only as one who wished to bury himself in his mission to a land where there was not his true Church. In this one spot in an immense crowded city he had lived day after day for twenty-seven years, and his small, black-robed figure had become as much a part of the street as an ancient temple or bridge. Children, as long as they could remember, were accustomed to the sight of him, trudging along in all weathers, his pockets bulging ridiculously with peanuts for them. No one thought of him. Women washing at the well looked up as he came by, knew that it must be an hour after noon and sighed to think of the hours before sunset. Men nodded at him carelessly from the counters of the little shops open to the streets and accepted with good humor his tracts and pictures of the Virgin.

Now this was changed. He was no longer Father Andreas, a harmless, aging priest. He became instead a foreigner.

One day a child refused to take the peanuts he held out to it. "My mother says they may be poisoned," the child said, looking up at Father Andrea with wide eyes.

"Poisoned?" said Father Andrea vaguely and in great surprise.

The next day he returned with his pockets as heavy as when he started, and after that he took no more peanuts. Once a woman spat after him as he passed the well. Then men shook their heads coldly when he smiled and proffered his tracts. He was completely bewildered.

At last one night his native assistant came to him. He was a good old man with a straggling, scanty white beard, honest and a little stupid, so that he never quite got his Aves right. Father Andrea had wondered sometimes if he should not find someone more able, but he could never bring himself to tell the old man that he was not perfect. Now he said to Father Andrea, "My Father, do not go out until this madness is past."

"What madness?" asked Father Andrea.

"This talk about foreigners and revolutions. The people are listening to these young men in long black gowns who come from the South, and they say that the foreigners are killing the people and stealing their hearts with new religions."

"New religions?" said Father Andrea mildly. "There is nothing new about mine. I have been here preaching and teaching for more than a quarter of a century."

"Even so, sir, you are a foreigner," replied the old man apologetically.

"Well," said Father Andrea at last, "this astonishes me very much!"

But he listened to the old man after the next day; for, when he stepped from the gate into the street, a great stone flung at him flew against his breast and broke into two pieces the ebony cross that hung there, and, when he put up his hand, aghast, another stone flew against him and cut his hand badly. He turned white and went into the mission house and shut the door and fell upon his knees and looked at the broken cross. For a long time he could say nothing, but at last words came to his lips and he prayed an old prayer. "Father, forgive them: for they know not what they do."

After that he stayed in the compound. Within a few days no one came any more, and he locked the door of the empty schoolroom sadly. It was as if he were in the quiet center of a storm. From outside the lonely compound where he and his old assistant pottered about the garden, strange sounds rose up in confusion from the streets. He locked the gate, opening it only once a day in the evening for the old man to creep out and buy a little food. At last one day the old man came back with his basket empty.

"They will not let me buy food for you," he said piteously. "To save your life I must pretend to leave you, and I must pretend to hate you. But every night I will throw food over the western corner of the garden. And every evening at the hour I will repeat the Ave. Our God must look after you beyond this."

Thereafter Father Andrea was quite alone. He spent a great deal of time in the observatory, and he allowed himself to think and remember every evening now. The days were long and solitary, and he missed even the lepers. There was no more need to wash his hands except of the clean garden earth that clung to them after he had been working among the vegetables. And, outside, the noise rose and mounted until he fancied that he was on some small island in the midst of a raging sea and that one day the waves would break over him even there.

He withdrew into his thoughts more and more, and he built little dreams of Italy and of the grape garden where he had played as a boy. He could smell the hot sun on the ripe grapes — incomparable fragrance! Sitting in the old easy chair night after night, he began to reconstruct from the beginning his life. It was May, and the stars were brilliant in a purple sky. But he no longer touched his note-books and pens. He had become indifferent to anything of the stars except their sheer unearthly beauty. Thank God for stars and sky everywhere! These Chinese skies in May were like the skies of Italy in summer, the stars hanging heavy and golden in the dark sky. Once on a night like this in Italy he had leaned from his window and gone suddenly mad with the beauty of the stars, and he had run blindly out of the house to Vitellia. His heart was beating like a great drum, shaking his body with every throb, and he had cried that he must tell her that he loved her. When he had got to his brother's house, his brother had opened the door and said kindly: "We were just about to sleep, Andrea. Is there anything we can do for you?"

Behind his brother he saw Vitellia, shadowy in the room, her face pale and indistinct as a flower in the twilight. She came forward and rested her hand lightly upon her husband's arm and leaned her head upon his shoulder. She was quite content. Passion went out of him.

"No, thank you," he stammered. "I thought — I did not know it was so late — I thought I might come in and talk a little while, perhaps."

"Yes, another day," said his brother gravely. And Vitellia had called, "Good night, brother Andrea!" And the door shut, and he was alone.

That was the night he had stayed in the garden the whole night through, and at dawn he had said at last that he would give himself to the poor, since Vitellia did not need him — the poor of a far country.

Ah, all that passion and pain and the youth he had had to wear down by sheer indomitable will to suffer! He would still never be free of it — never, so long as he lived, quite free. He wondered if there among the stars Vitellia knew — there where surely everything was known. He hoped so. That would mean that he need not tell her of all the pain. She would understand as she had never understood on earth, and they could start in at once on the new heavenly relationship.

He sighed and went down into the garden then, and there at the western end he found a small bundle of cold rice and meat wrapped in a lotus leaf and he ate it and then said his Aves, his fingers hovering over the broken cross on his breast.

From outside the wall, in the street, there came the sound of steady, marching feet, thousands upon thousands of feet. He listened awhile, wondering, and then, with a sigh, he went up again to his observatory and sat down, and, looking off into the clear spaces of heaven, he slept lightly.

In the morning he awoke with a start of premonition, as if he had been aroused suddenly by a noise. He could not for an instant collect himself. The stars were weak in the gray light of the dawn, and the roof of the church was dark and wet with dew. From without there came a sound of mad confusion, and shooting and shouts rent the air. He listened. There were several shots in quick succession. He sat up, trying to think what this could be. Was this what had waked him? There was no more marching. A huge blaze lighted up the distant eastern sky. Something was burning — that was the rich quarter of the city, where the streets were hung with the scarlet and yellow banners of the big grain-shops and silk-shops and sing-song houses. But it might be only the sun rising? No, there was no such splendor of sunrise out of this gray sky.

He dragged himself from the chair and went downstairs heavily, with vague alarm. He had not slept restfully, and his mind felt fogged. As he reached the foot of the steps and stood upon the grass, there came a terrific pounding at the gate, and he moved quickly to open it, rubbing his head a little to collect his thoughts. This was the noise he had heard in his sleep! He fumbled at the great wooden bar and withdrew it at last and opened the gate and stared out in amazement. Hundreds of men stood there in a mass – soldiers in gray uniform. Their faces were ferocious as he had not dreamed human faces could be, and he shrank from them as he had never shrunk from his lepers. They leveled their guns at him then with a tigerish shout. He was not afraid, only completely amazed.

"But what do you want, my friends?" he asked in surprise.

A young man, scarcely older than his schoolboy who had run away, stepped forward and tore the rosary from about his neck. The fragment of broken cross, all that was left of the cross he had worn for so many years, fell to the ground.

"We have come to rid the world of imperialists and capitalists!" the young man shouted.

"Imperialists and capitalists?" said Father Andrea, wondering. They were words he had never heard. It had been many years since he had read anything except the ancient Church fathers and his books of astronomy. He did not have the faintest idea what the lad meant.

But the boy cocked his gun and pointed it at Father Andrea. "We are the revolutionists!" he cried. His voice was rough and harsh as if he had been shouting for many hours, and his smooth, youthful face was blotched and red as if with drinking. "We come to set everyone free!"

"Set everyone free?" said Father Andrea slowly, smiling a little. He stooped to pick up his cross from the dust.

But before his hand could touch that cross, the boy's finger moved spasmodically upon the trigger and there was a sharp report, and Father Andrea fell upon the ground, dead.

—*By Pearl Buck (Pearl Sydenstricker Walsh), American (1892–).*

~ ✿ ~

The Dark Princess

W. E. B. DU BOIS

MATTHEW sat in the dining room of the Princess von Lützower Ufer. Looking about, his heart swelled. For the first time since he had left New York, he felt himself a man, one of those who could help build a world and guide it. He had no regrets. Medicine seemed a far-off, dry-as-dust thing.

The oak paneling of the room went to the ceiling and there broke softly with carven light against white flowers and into long lucent curves. The table below was sheer with lace and linen, sparkling with silver and crystal. The servants moved deftly, and all of them were white save one who stood behind the Princess' high and crimson chair. At her right sat Matthew himself, hardly realizing until long afterward the honor thus done an almost nameless guest.

Fortunately he had the dinner jacket of the year before last with him. It was not new, but it fitted his form perfectly, and his was a form worth fitting. He was a bit shocked to note that all the other men but two were in full evening dress. But he did not let this worry him much.

Ten of them sat at the table. On the Princess' left was a Japanese, faultless in dress and manner, evidently a man of importance, as the deference shown him and the orders on his breast indicated. He was quite yellow, short and stocky, with a face which was a delicately handled but perfect mask. There were two Indians, one a man grave, haughty, and old, dressed richly in turban and embroidered tunic, the other, in conventional dress and turban, a young man, handsome and alert, whose eyes were ever on the Princess. There were two Chinese, a young man and a young woman, he in a plain but becoming Chinese costume of heavy blue silk, she in a pretty dress, half Chinese, half European in effect. An Egyptian and his wife came next, he suave, talkative, and polite – just a shade too talkative and a bit too polite, Matthew thought; his wife a big, handsome, silent woman, elegantly jeweled and gowned, with much bare flesh. Beyond them was a cold and rather stiff Arab who spoke seldom, and then abruptly.

Of the food and wine of such dinners, Matthew had read often but never partaken;

and the conversation, now floating, now half submerged, gave baffling glimpses of unknown lands, spiritual and physical. It was all something quite new in his experience, the room, the table, the service, the company.

He could not keep his eyes from continually straying sidewise to his hostess. Never had he seen color in human flesh so regally set: the rich and flowing grace of the dress out of which rose so darkly splendid the jeweled flesh. The black and purple hair was heaped up on her little head, and in its depths gleamed a tiny coronet of gold. Her voice and her poise, her self-possession and air of quiet command, kept Matthew staring almost unmannerly, despite the fact that he somehow sensed a shade of resentment in the young and handsome Indian opposite.

They had eaten some delicious tidbits of meat and vegetables and then were served with a delicate soup when the Princess, turning slightly to her right, said:

"You will note, Mr. Towns, that we represent here much of the Darker World. Indeed, when all our circle is present we represent all of it, save your world of Black Folk."

"All the darker world except the darkest," said the Egyptian.

"A pretty large omission," said Matthew with a smile.

"I agree," said the Chinaman; but the Arab said something abruptly in French. Matthew had said that he knew "some" French. But his French was of the American variety which one excavates from dictionaries and cements with grammar, like bricks. He was astounded at the ease and the fluency with which most of this company used languages, so easily, without groping or hesitation and with light, sure shading. They talked art in French, literature in Italian, politics in German, and everything in clear English.

"M. Ben Ali suggests," said the Princess, "that even you are not black, Mr. Towns."

"My grandfather was, and my soul is. Black blood with us in America is a matter of spirit and not simply of flesh."

"Ah! mixed blood," said the Egyptian.

"Like all of us, especially me," laughed the Princess.

"But, your Royal Highness — not Negro," said the elder Indian in a tone that hinted a protest.

"Essentially," said the Princess lightly, "as our black and curly-haired Lord Buddha testifies in a hundred places. But" — a bit impetuously — "enough of that. Our point is that Pan-Africa belongs logically with Pan-Asia; and for that reason Mr. Towns is welcomed tonight by you, I am sure, and by me especially. He did me a service as I was returning from the New Palace."

They all looked interested, but the Egyptian broke out:

"Ah, Your Highness, the New Palace, and what is the fad today? What has followed expressionism, cubism, futurism, vorticism? I confess myself at sea. Picasso alarms me. Matisse sets me aflame. But I do not undertand them. I prefer the classics."

"The Congo," said the Princess, "is flooding the Acropolis. There is a beautiful Kandinsky on exhibit, and some lovely and startling things by unknown newcomers."

"*Mais,*" replied the Egyptian, dropping into French — and they were all off to the discussion, save the silent Egyptian woman and the taciturn Arab.

Here, again, Matthew was puzzled. These persons easily penetrated worlds where he was a stranger. Frankly, but for the context he would not have known whether Picasso was a man, a city, or a vegetable. He had never heard of Matisse. Lightly, almost carelessly, as he thought, his companions leaped to unknown subjects. Yet they knew. They knew art, books, and literature, politics of all nations, and not newspaper politics merely, but inner currents and whisperings, unpublished facts.

"Ah, pardon," said the Egyptian, returning to English, "I forgot Monsieur Towns speaks only English and does not interest himself in art."

Perhaps Matthew was sensitive and imagined that the Egyptian and the Indian rather often, if not purposely, strayed to French and subjects beyond him.

"Mr. Towns is a scientist?" asked the Japanese.

"He studies Medicine," answered the Princess.

"Ah — a high service," said the Japanese. "I was reading only today of the work on cancer by your Peyton Rous in Carrel's laboratory."

Towns was surprised. "What, has he discovered the etiological factor? I had not heard."

"No, not yet, but he's a step nearer."

For a few moments Matthew was talking eagerly, until a babble of unknown tongues interrupted him across the table.

"Proust is dead, that 'snob of humor'—yes, but his *Recherche du Temps Perdu* is finished and will be published in full. I have only glanced at parts of it. Do you know Gasquet's *Hymnes*?"

"Beraud gets the Prix Goncourt this year. Last year it was the Negro Maran—"

"I have been reading Croce's *Æsthetic* lately—"

"Yes, I saw the Meyerhold theater in Moscow—gaunt realism—*Howl China* was tremendous."

Then easily, after the crisp brown fowl, the Princess tactfully steered them back to the subject which some seemed willing to avoid.

"And so," she said, "the darker peoples who are dissatisfied—"

She looked at the Japanese and paused as though inviting comment. He bowed courteously.

"If I may presume, your Royal Highness, to suggest," he said slowly, "the two categories are not synonymous. We ourselves know no line of color. Some of us are white, some yellow, some black. Rather, is it not, Your Highness, that we have from time to time taken counsel with the oppressed peoples of the world, many of whom by chance are colored?"

"True, true," said the Princess.

"And yet," said the Chinese lady, "it is the dominating Europe which has flung this challenge of the color line, and we cannot avoid it."

"And on either count," said Matthew, "whether we be bound by oppression or by color, surely we Negroes belong in the foremost ranks."

There was a slight pause, a sort of hesitation, and it seemed to Matthew as though all, expected the Japanese to speak. He did, slowly and gravely:

"It would be unfair to our guest not to explain with some clarity and precision that the whole question of the Negro race both in Africa and in America is for us not simply a question of suffering and compassion. Need we say that for these peoples we have every human sympathy? But for us here and for the larger company we represent, there is a deeper question—that of the ability, qualifications, and real responsibilties of the black race in Africa or elsewhere."

Matthew left the piquant salad and laid down his fork slowly. Up to this moment he had been quite happy. Despite the feeling of being out of it now and then, he had assumed that this was his world, his people, from the high and beautiful lady whom he worshiped more and more, even to the Egyptians, Indians, and Arab who seemed slightly, but very slightly, aloof or misunderstanding.

Suddenly now there loomed plain and clear the shadow of a color line, a prejudice within prejudice, and he and his again the sacrifice. His eyes became somber and did not lighten even when the Princess spoke.

"I cannot see that it makes great difference what ability Negroes have. Oppression is oppression. It is our privilege to relieve it."

"Yes," answered the Japanese, "but who will do it? Who can do it but those superior races whose necks now bear the yoke of the inferior rabble of Europe?"

"This," said the Princess, "I have always believed; but as I have told your Excellency, I have received impressions in Moscow which have given me very serious thought—first as to our judgment of the ability of the Negro race, and second"—she paused in thought—"as to the relative ability of all classes and peoples."

Matthew stared at her, as she continued:

"You see, Moscow has reports—careful reports of the world's masses. And the report on the Negroes of America was astonishing. At the time, I doubted its truth: their education, their work, their property, their organizations; and the odds, the terrible, crushing odds against which, inch by inch, and heartbreak by heartbreak, they have forged their unfaltering way upward. If the report is true, they are a nation today, a modern nation worthy to stand beside any nation here."

"But can we put any faith in Moscow?" asked the Egyptian. "Are we not keeping dangerous company and leaning on broken reeds?"

"Well," said Matthew, "if they are as sound in everything as in this report from America, they'll bear listening to."

The young Indian spoke gently and evenly, but with bright eyes.

"Naturally," he said, "one can see Mr.

Towns needs must agree with the Bolshevik estimate of the lower classes."

Matthew felt the slight slur and winced. He thought he saw the lips of the Princess tighten ever so little. He started to answer quickly, with aplomb if not actual swagger.

"I reckon," he began – then something changed within him. It was as if he had faced and made a decision, as though some great voice, crying and reverberating within his soul, spoke for him and yet was him. He started to say, "I reckon there's as much high-born blood among American Negroes as among any people. We've had our kings, presidents, and judges – " He started to say this, but he did not finish. He found himself saying quite calmly and with slightly lifted chin:

"I reckon you're right. We American blacks are very common people. My grandfather was a whipped and driven slave; my father was never really free and died in jail. My mother plows and washes for a living. We come out of the depths – the blood and mud of battle. And from just such depths, I take it, came most of the worth while things in this old world. If they didn't – God help us."

The table was very still, save for the very faint clink of china as the servants brought in the creamed and iced fruit.

The Princess turned, and he could feel her dark eyes full upon him.

"I wonder – I wonder," she murmured, almost catching her breath.

The Indian frowned. The Japanese smiled, and the Egyptian whispered to the Arab.

"I believe that is true," said the Chinese lady thoughtfully, "and if it is, this world is glorious."

"And if it is not?" asked the Egyptian icily.

"It is perhaps both true and untrue," the Japanese suggested. "Certainly Mr. Towns has expressed a fine and human hope, although I fear that always blood must tell."

"No, it mustn't," cried Matthew, "unless it is allowed to talk. Its speech is accidental today. There is some weak, thin stuff called blood, which not even a crown can make speak intelligently; and at the same time some of the noblest blood God ever made is dumb with chains or poverty."

The elder Indian straightened, with blazing eyes.

"Surely," he said, slowly and calmly, "surely the gentleman does not mean to reflect on royal blood?"

Matthew started, flushed darkly, and glanced quickly at the Princess. She smiled and said lightly, "Certainly not," and then with a pause and a look straight across the table to the turban and tunic, "nor will royal blood offer insult to him." The Indian bowed to the tablecloth and was silent.

As they rose and sauntered out to coffee in the silk and golden drawing room, there was a discussion, started, of course, by the Egyptian, first of the style of the elaborate piano case and then of Schönberg's new and unobtrusive transcription of Bach's triumphant choral Prelude, "Komm, Gott, Schöpfer."

The Princess sat down. Matthew could not take his eyes from her. Her fingers idly caressed the keys as her tiny feet sought the pedals. From white, pearl-embroidered slippers, her young limbs, smooth in pale, dull silk, swept up in long, low lines. Even the delicate curving of her knees he saw as she drew aside her drapery and struck the first warm tones. She played the phrase in dispute – great chords of aspiration and vision that melted to soft melody. The Egyptian acknowledged his fault. "Yes – yes, that was the theme I had forgotten."

Again Matthew felt his lack of culture audible, and not simply of his own culture, but of all the culture in white America which he had unconsciously and foolishly, as he now realized, made his norm. Yet withal Matthew was not unhappy. If he was a bit out of it, if he sensed divided counsels and opposition, yet he still felt almost fiercely that this was his world. Here were culture, wealth, and beauty. Here was power, and here he had some recognized part. God! If he could just do his part, any part! And he waited impatiently for the real talk to begin again.

It began and lasted until after midnight. It started on lines so familiar to Matthew that he had to shut his eyes and stare again at their swarthy faces: Superior races – the right to rule – born to command – inferior breeds – the lower classes – the rabble. How the Egyptian rolled off his tongue his contempt for the "r-r-rabble!" How contemptuous was the young Indian of inferior races! But how humorous it was to Matthew to see all tables turned; the rabble now was the white workers of Europe; the inferior races were the ruling whites of Europe and America. The superior races were yellow and brown.

"You see," said the Japanese, "Mr. Towns, we here are all agreed and not agreed. We are agreed that the present white hegemony of the world is nonsense; that the darker peoples are the best — the natural aristocracy, the makers of art, religion, philosophy, life, everything except brazen machines."

"But why?"

"Because of the lônger rôle of natural aristocracy among us. We count our millenniums of history where Europe counts her centuries. We have our own carefully thought-out philosophy and civilization, while Europe has sought to adopt an ill-fitting mélange of the cultures of the world."

"But does this not all come out the same gate, with the majority of mankind serving the minority? And if this is the only ideal of civilization, does the tint of a skin matter in the question of who leads?" Thus Matthew summed it up.

"Not a whit — it is the natural inborn superiority that matters," said the Japanese, "and it is that which the present color bar of Europe is holding back."

"And what guarantees, in the future more than in the past and with colored more than with white, the wise rule of the gifted and powerful?"

"Self-interest and the inclusion in their ranks of all really superior men of all colors — the best of Asia together with the best of the British aristocracy, of the German Adel, of the French writers and financiers — of the rulers, artists, and poets of all peoples."

"And suppose we found that ability and talent and art is not entirely or even mainly among the reigning aristocrats of Asia and Europe, but buried among millions of men down in the great sodden masses of all men and even in Black Africa?"

"It would come forth."

"Would it?"

"Yes," said the Princess, "it would come forth, but when and how? In slow and tenderly nourished efflorescence, or in wild and bloody upheaval with all that bitter loss?"

"Pah!" blurted the Egyptian — "pardon, Royal Highness — but what art ever came from the canaille!"

The blood rushed to Matthew's face. He threw back his head and closed his eyes, and with the movement he heard again the Great Song. He saw his father in the old log church by the river, leading the moaning singers in the Great Song of Emancipation. Clearly, plainly he heard the mighty voice and saw the rhythmic swing and beat of the thick brown arm. Matthew swung his arm and beat the table; the silver tinkled. Silence dropped on all, and suddenly Matthew found himself singing. His voice full, untrained but mellow, quivered down the first plaintive bar.

"When Israel was in Egypt land — "

Then it gathered depth:

"Let my people go!"

He forgot his audience and saw only the shining river and the bowed and shouting throng:

"Oppressed so hard, they could not stand,"
Let my people go."

Then Matthew let go restraint and sang as his people sang in Virginia, twenty years ago. His great voice, gathered in one long deep breath, rolled the Call of God:

"Go down, Moses!
Way down into the Egypt land,
Tell Old Pharaoh
To let my people go!"

He stopped as quickly as he had begun, ashamed, and beads of sweat gathered on his forehead. Still there was silence — silence almost breathless. The voice of the Chinese woman broke it.

"It was an American slave song! I know it. How — how wonderful!"

A chorus of approval poured out, led by the Egyptian.

"That," said Matthew, "came out of the black rabble of America." And he trilled his "r." They all smiled as the tension broke.

"You assume then," said the Princess at last, "that the mass of the workers of the world can rule as well as be ruled?"

"Yes — or rather can work as well as be worked, can live as well as be kept alive. America is teaching the world one thing and only one thing of real value, and that is, that ability and capacity for culture is not the hereditary monopoly of a few, but the widespread possibility for the majority of mankind if they only have a decent chance in life."

The Chinaman spoke: "If Mr. Towns' assumption is true, and I believe it is, and recognized, as some time it must be, it will revolutionize the world."

"It will revolutionize the world," smiled the Japanese, "but not – today."

"Nor this *siècle,"* growled the Arab.

"Nor the next – and so *in sæcula sæculorum,"* laughed the Egyptian.

"Well," said the little Chinese lady, "the unexpected happens."

And Matthew added ruefully, "It's about all that does happen!"

He lapsed into blank silence, wondering how he had come to express the astonishing philosophy which had leapt unpremeditated from his lips. Did he himself believe it? As they arose from the table the Princess called him aside.

— From Dark Princess, a Romance, by W. E. Burghardt Du Bois, American (1868–).

PART FIFTEEN

Man Against Fate

~ ✿ ~

WHILE POETRY AND STORY TELLING have flourished at all times and among all peoples, drama, certainly one of the most powerful of the arts, has existed in only a limited number of civilizations, reaching its heights in but a few and there for brief periods. In short, man always has poems and stories, but can dispense with a developed stage. Some theatrical ceremony or ritual, dance spectacle or mimetic art, seems, to be sure, universal. But to have a mature dramatic art requires established theaters, town life, and a considerable degree and special kind of culture. An advanced literary sense must be combined with a lively instinct for acting. Theatrical life, being a collaborative effort, easily gains and loses momentum. Its very history is spectacular. Hence the great playwrights have appeared in constellations with voids between, as may be seen if we recall the names of Aeschylus, Sophocles, Euripides, and Aristophanes in Athens, Corneille, Racine and Molière in France, Shakespeare, Marlowe and Jonson in England, and Calderon and Lope de Vega in Spain.

Although drama has long existed in well developed forms among the chief peoples of the Far East, it has never been regarded there with the esteem or even reverence which it has enjoyed for considerable periods in Europe. Unfortunately it has remained in the eyes of Orientals largely a spectacular or an oral art but not conspicuously a literary one. Music has played a great part in theatrical entertainments in both China and Japan. The subjects of their largely operatic plays have usually been romantic tales symbolically treated and standing closer to our romantic comedy than to either our tragedy or our comedy of manners. In the Near East drama may hardly be said to have existed at all, and Mohammedanism has erected a prejudice against it. In Europe plays seem to have reached only the most rudimentary form shortly before the stage burst into its greatest flowering in the city of Athens during the fifth century B.C. While important inventions have, of course, since been made in the theater characteristic of later times and cultures, many of the chief features of the art as practiced most successfully today remain substantially the discoveries of the Attic stage.

The evolution of this theater from a religious ritual materially aided the weight and substance of its thought. The Greek religion, already rich in the materials of poetry, was a leading creative force in Greek life. A mythological or epic background lay behind the majority of the plays. Some dealt with the chief ethical and metaphysical beliefs of the people, others, directly with their imminent social problems. The plays were thus religious, patriotic and profoundly human, elucidating the life of both the state and the individual. As a civic and religious function the theater was attended freely by all citizens of Athens and regarded as a crowning glory of their national life. Its importance for the Athenians was probably greater than that of any other drama for its community. In whatever respects subsequent plays have been most vital, they have shared something with this extraordinary period of dramatic origins.

From the standpoint of technique, too, the Greeks laid foundations for much that was best in plays to come centuries thereafter. When the dramatists of the Renaissance created a secular theater to express the ideals of their new humanism, they went to the classics for much of their technical skill. Even today we are still learning from the Greek art of the theater, as plays by Eugene O'Neill have often shown. The earliest play preserved to us in full, *The Suppliants* of Aeschylus, shows, to be sure, a primitive theater hardly developed beyond an elaborate cantata performed by a chorus with occasional recitative by one or two actors. Aeschylus himself, however, made rapid progress, so that nothing can be more dramatic than his own *Agamemnon,* one of his latest works. Although here the chorus still remains prominent, it is skilfully worked into the action and idea of the play. Poetry is allied with spectacle and both with a high development of dramatic suspense and climax. Dramatic feeling is intensified by a clash of violently opposed wills. The audience is moved by a supreme concentration of action molded to lines as refined and economical as those of Greek sculpture or architecture. By alternate use of two types of poetry, the lyric style for both the choral parts and certain subjective passages, and the epic style for the more active portions, remarkable elasticity and strength were achieved. Aeschylus developed a vigorous and convincing technique of dramatic dialogue. Finding the stage in its infancy, he left it endowed with a perfection which has become the envy of centuries.

His two chief followers, Sophocles and Euripides, not less gifted than he, modified and enriched, though they could scarcely improve, the theater that he bequeathed to them. They reduced choral parts, increased the number of actors, and enlarged and humanized the subject matter. Sophocles advanced from Aeschylean austerity and grandeur to a wholly mellow and self-contained art; and, finally, Euripides perfected an almost decadent one. Euripides led the march from a largely religious world to a largely secular world and from an old faith through new beliefs to new doubts. His romantic sentimentality together with his intellectual irony and skepticism have helped to make him of the three Greek masters of tragedy the most imitated in the Christian era, though not always the most admired. Although the average aesthetic achievement attained by Sophocles is possibly the highest, the *Agamemnon* is generally considered today the most powerful single tragedy of the ancient world.

The Greeks, so far as we are aware, first created tragedy and attempted to define it. The question wherein the essential nature of tragedy lies has raised philosophical and psychological discussion carried on through many centuries since the times of Aristotle. The views have differed in detail but generally shared much in common. Few thinkers doubt the reality of the tragic experience, though a few recent skeptics – very questionably, we believe – have held that true tragedies are not now being written for the stage or screen. A tragedy, said Aristotle, through scenes of pain and horror stimulates the mind to pity and fear. Some later critics have seen in tragedy the heroic struggle of man against inescapable destiny. They have found it a tribute to the freedom of man's will at the same time that mankind lies victim of a cruel fate. Others, with only a slightly different interpretation, prefer to see it as the drama which induces fortitude and endurance conquering the most devastating ills. All critics agree that it promotes high seriousness in its spectators. It presents at the same time a disease and a purgation of the mind from the worst ravages of the disease. Its exposition of the emotions carries with it their own antitoxin. Modern scientific psychology strongly confirms the general attitude toward tragedy expressed by Aristotle. And, despite a few disparaging voices to the contrary, it is the common experience of the modern man that plays from almost all civilized countries have in the past answered this description and continue to do so at the present day.

The precarious course of the theater is well illustrated by the ancients. The Romans, with a strong genius for satire and the literature of manners, developed a comedy based upon the work of late Greek playwrights now largely lost, but never equalled the brilliance of Aristophanes and had no theater resembling the Greek tragic stage. Throughout the greater part of the Middle Ages drama was virtually unknown, although in the latter part of the era lively farces became popular and mammoth cycles of religious plays based on the Scriptures and depicting with considerable force the death and sorrows of Christ were presented annually in the chief towns. This medieval drama was admirably adjusted to the needs of medieval life. It never reached, however, a high literary level nor acquired qualities comparable to those which make the classical drama of universal interest.

During the Renaissance throughout all countries of Europe a new theater arose, partly as a new and indigenous growth, partly as a violent transformation of the medieval stage, but in large measure as consequence of the rediscovery of the classics. In Italy this stage remained even servile to classical models and in France it so remained in great part until comedy was wholly revivified in the latter part of the seventeenth century by the genius of the incisive Molière. Spanish drama was brilliant and poetic but lacked form. The fullest flowering of the sixteenth-century stage occurred, therefore, in England. London supported half a dozen theaters which regularly entertained a considerable portion of the population. Shakespeare's comedies remained largely romantic in sentiment and those of his friend, Ben Jonson, to a similar degree imitative of Latin models. So the outstanding contribution of the Elizabethan theater lies in the tragedies of Shakespeare. Although these supreme dramas possess a more fluid form than the Greek, they often produce remarkably similar emotional effects, fulfilling Aristotle's dictum that the mind is purged by tragedy through participation in pity and fear. Of all Renaissance plays that most often associated with the Greek is *Macbeth*, a tragedy in many respects Aeschylean. Pity and fear are most powerfully evoked; the play possesses poetic grandeur, a unity of purpose, a fine sense of brevity, a mood of devastating horror and awe, together with a tense atmosphere of national calamity. Its witch-scenes and several episodes with the secondary characters offer striking parallels to the Greek chorus. To read *Agamemnon* and *Macbeth* together gives notable evidence of the continuity of the human spirit active upon the austere heights of tragic feeling.

The ultra-romantic and religious drama of Spain and the chaste and beautiful neoclassical tragedy which culminated in the French dramas of Racine hold less attraction for the world today than the work of the great Greeks or Elizabethans. Modern drama in the customary sense of the term begins with the Norwegian, Ibsen, whose chief work lies in a series of tragedies written for the most part during the eighteen-eighties. Comparisons between Ibsen and all three of the Greek tragic masters have proved unescapable. In technique, temper and meaning his work resembles theirs and serves a like function. He suggests a Greek playwright thoroughly translated into the terms of a younger world. Like Euripides, Ibsen speaks for a radical minority on social and intellectual problems in a world perturbed by skepticism and rapid change. Like Euripides, too, he found his native country hostile to him and lived in a foreign land. Ibsen possessed a remarkably sure instinct for theatrical technique comparable to that of Sophocles. And the dark intensity of his tragic mood not infrequently proves Aeschylean. *Ghosts* is of all his plays the most often associated with Aeschylus. Its stark simplicity and its intensity of thought, its ironical and bitter realism, its haunting sense of an inherited family curse, and its merciless tragic catastrophe all link it with the first master of tragedy and his plays dealing with the doomed house of Mycenae.

Although by no means all our serious theatrical art clings so closely to classical formulas as this work by Ibsen, the mood and general form of our more serious drama remain essentially as they have been. The most moving playwrights tend to be those who most resemble in the spirit, though not always in the letter, the art of Aeschylus, Shakespeare and Ibsen. The already mentioned work of Eugene O'Neill in America, for example, bears out this observation. To sum up this long history in a sentence: the essence of great drama is a discovery of the Greeks; a new fluidity and liveliness is evinced by Shakespeare and the Elizabethans; while Ibsen and his school effectively pour the spirit of a new culture into the old vessels. The background for all our more sombre drama is sufficiently contained within these points of reference.

Because the plays of Shakespeare and Ibsen are as a rule easily accessible to readers, and moreover are of considerable length, they are not included in this book, although no student of the history of the tragic mood can overlook them. More fitting for the present purposes are two plays which, though brief, are still of the highest intrinsic merit. J. M. Synge's *Riders to the Sea* epitomizes the Aeschylean conception of man in his tragic struggles against fate. It is essentially a folk play, expressing stark and naked tragedy among the most primitive of European peoples, the inhabitants of the bare and storm-drenched Aran Islands off the west coast of Ireland. As a drama by an American to illustrate the continuity of the tragic tradition we have chosen *The Death of Eve* by William Vaughn Moody. This work consists of one act of a projected three act play left unfinished at Moody's early death, but it contains some of the finest tragic verse as yet written in America.

Agamemnon

AESCHYLUS

Persons

WATCHMAN.
CHORUS OF ARGIVE ELDERS.
CLYTEMNESTRA, *Wife of Agamemnon.*
HERALD.
AGAMEMNON, *King of Argos and Mycenæ.*
CASSANDRA, *a Trojan Prophetess, Daughter of Priam.*
ÆGISTHUS, *Son of Thyestes.*

SCENE — *The Royal Palace in Argos.*

WATCH. I pray the gods a respite from these toils,
This long year's watch that, dog-like, I have kept,
High on the Atridan's battlements, beholding
The nightly council of the stars, the circling
Of the celestial signs, and those bright regents,
High-swung in ether, that bring mortal men
Summer and winter. Here I watch the torch,
The appointed flame that wings a voice from Troy,
Telling of capture; thus I serve her hopes,
The masculine-minded who is sovereign here.
And when night-wandering shades encompass round
My dew-sprent dreamless couch (for fear doth sit
In slumber's chair, and holds my lids apart),
I chaunt some dolorous ditty, making song,
Sleep's substitute, surgeon my nightly care,
And the misfortunes of this house I weep,
Not now, as erst, by prudent counsels swayed.
Oh! soon may the wished for sign relieve my toils,
Thrice-welcome herald, gleaming through the night!

(*The beacon is seen shining.*)

All hail thou cresset of the dark! fair gleam
Of day through midnight shed, all hail! bright father
Of joy and dance, in Argos, hail! all hail!
Hillo! hilloa!
I will go tell the wife of Agamemnon
To shake dull sleep away, and lift high-voiced
The jubilant shout well-omened, to salute
This welcome beacon; if, indeed, old Troy
Hath fallen — as flames this courier torch to tell.
Myself will dance the prelude to this joy.
My master's house hath had a lucky throw,
And thrice six falls to me, thanks to the flame!
Soon may he see his home; and soon may I
Carry my dear-loved master's hand in mine!
The rest I whisper not, for on my tongue
Is laid a seal. These walls, if they could speak,
Would say strange things. Myself to those that know
Am free of speech, to whoso knows not dumb. (*Exit.*

Enter CHORUS *in procession. March time.*

Nine years have rolled, the tenth is rolling,
Since the strong Atridan pair,
Menelaus and Agamemnon,
Sceptered kings by Jove's high grace,
With a host of sworn alliance,
With a thousand triremes rare,
With a righteous strong defiance,
Sailed for Troy. From furious breast
Loud they clanged the peal of battle;
Like the cry of vultures wild
O'er the lone paths fitful-wheeling,
With their plumy oarage oaring
Over the nest by the spoiler spoiled,
The nest dispeopled now and bare,
Their long but fruitless care.
But the gods see it: some Apollo,
Pan or Jove, the wrong hath noted,
Heard the sharp and piercing cry
Of the startled birds, shrill-throated
Tenants of the sky;
And the late-chastising Fury
Sent from above to track the spoiler,
Hovers vengeful nigh.

Thus great Jove, the high protector
Of the hospitable laws,
'Gainst Alexander sends the Atridans,
Harnessed in a woman's cause,
The many-lorded fair.
Toils on toils shall come uncounted,
(Jove hath willed it so);
Limb-outwearying hard endeavour,
Where the strong knees press the dust,
Where the spear-shafts split and shiver,
Trojan and Greek shall know.
But things are as they are: the chain
Of Fate doth bind them; sighs are vain,
Tears, libations, fruitless flow,
To divert from purposed ire

The powers whose altars know no fire.
But we behind that martial train
 Inglorious left remain,
Old and frail, and feebly leaning
Strength as of childhood on a staff.
Yea! even as life's first unripe marrow
In the tender bones are we,
 From war's harsh service free.
For hoary Eld, life's leaf up-shrunken,
Totters, his three-footed way
Feebly feeling, weak as childhood,
Like a dream that walks by day.
But what is this? what wandering word,
Clytemnestra queen, hath reached thee?
What hast seen? or what hast heard
That from street to street swift flies
Thy word, commanding sacrifice?
All the altars of all the gods
That keep the city, gods supernal,
Gods Olympian, gods infernal,
Gods of the Forum, blaze with gifts;
Right and left the flame mounts high,
 Spiring to the sky,
With the gentle soothings cherished
Of the oil that knows no malice,
And the sacred cake that smokes
From the queen's chamber in the palace.
What thou canst and may'st, declare;
Be the healer of the care
That bodes black harm within me; change it
To the bright and hopeful ray,
Which from the altar riseth, chasing
From the heart the sateless sorrow
 That eats vexed life away.

The Chorus, *having now arranged themselves into a regular band in the middle of the Orchestra, sing the First* Choral Hymn.

STROPHE

I'll voice the strain. What though the arm be weak
 That once was strong,
The suasive breath of Heaven-sent memories stirs
 The old man's breast with song.
 My age hath virtue left
To sing what fateful omens strangely beckoned
 The twin kings to the fray,
What time to Troy concentuous marched
 The embattled Greek array.
Jove's swooping bird, king of all birds, led on
The kings of the fleet with spear and vengeful hand:
By the way-side from shining seats serene,
Close by the palace, on the spear-hand seen,
Two eagles flapped the air,
One black, the other silver-tipt behind,
And with keen talons seized a timorous hare,
Whose strength could run no more,
Itself, and the live burden which it bore.
Sing woe and well-a-day! But still
May the good omens shame the ill.

ANTISTROPHE

The wise diviner of the host beheld,
 And knew the sign;
The hare-devouring birds with diverse wings
 Typed the Atridan pair,
 The diverse-minded kings,
And thus the fate he chaunted: — Not in vain
 Ye march this march to-day;
 Old Troy shall surely fall, but not
 Till moons on moons away
Have lingering rolled. Rich stores by labour massed
Clean-sweeping Fate shall plunder. Grant the gods,
While this strong bit for Troy we forge with gladness,
No heavenly might in jealous wrath o'ercast
 Our mounting hope with sadness.
For the chaste Artemis a sore grudge nurses
Against the kings; Jove's winged hounds she curses,
 The fierce war-birds that tore
The fearful hare, with the young brood it bore.
 Sing woe and well-a-day! but still
 May the good omens shame the ill.

EPODE

The lion's fresh-dropt younglings, and each whelp
That sucks wild milk, and through the forest roves,
Live not unfriended; them the fair goddess loves,
 And lends her ready help.
The vision of the birds shall work its end
In bliss, but dashed not lightly with black bane;
I pray thee, Pæan, may she never send
Contrarious blasts dark-lowering, to detain
 The Argive fleet.
Ah! ne'er may she desire to feast her eyes
On an unblest unholy sacrifice,
From festal use abhorrent, mother of strife,
And sundering from her lawful lord the wife.

Stern-purposed waits the child-avenging wrath
  About the fore-doomed halls,
Weaving dark wiles, while with sure-memoried sting
  Fury to Fury calls.
Thus hymned the seer, the doom, in dubious chaunt
Bliss to the chiefs dark-mingling with the bane,
  From the way-haunting birds; and we
    Respondent to the strain,
  Sing woe and well-a-day! but still
  May the good omen shame the ill.

STROPHE I

Jove, or what other name
The god that reigns supreme delights to claim,
Him I invoke; him of all powers that be,
  Alone I find,
Who from this bootless load of doubt can free
  My labouring mind.

ANTISTROPHE I

Who was so great of yore,
With all-defiant valour brimming o'er,
Is mute; and who came next by a stronger arm
  Thrice-vanquished fell;
But thou hymn victor Jove: so in thy heart
  His truth shall dwell.

STROPHE II

For Jove doth teach men wisdom, sternly wins
To virtue by the tutoring of their sins;
Yea! drops of torturing recollection chill
The sleeper's heart; 'gainst man's rebellious will
  Jove works the wise remorse:
Dread Powers, on awful seats enthroned, compel
  Our hearts with gracious force.

ANTISTROPHE II

The elder chief, the leader of the ships,
Heard the dire doom, nor dared to ope his lips
Against the seer, and feared alone to stand
'Gainst buffeting fate, what time the Chalcian strand
  Saw the vexed Argive masts
In Aulis tides hoarse-refluent, idly chained
  By the fierce Borean blasts;

STROPHE III

Blasts from Strymon adverse braying,
Harbour-vexing, ship-delaying,
Snapping cables, shattering oars,
Wasting time, consuming stores,
With vain-wandering expectation,
And with long-drawn slow vexation
  Wasting Argive bloom.
At length the seer forth-clanged the doom,
A remedy strong to sway the breeze,
And direful Artemis to appease,
  But to the chiefs severe:
The Atridans with their sceptres struck the ground,
  Nor could restrain the tear.

ANTISTROPHE III

Then spake the elder. To deny,
How hard! still harder to comply!
My daughter dear, my joy, my life,
To slay with sacrificial knife,
And with life's purple-gushing tide,
Imbrue a father's hand, beside
  The altar of the gods.
This way or that is ill: for how
Shall I despise my federate vow?
How leave the ships? That all conspire
  Thus hotly to desire
The virgin's blood — wind-soothing sacrifice —
Is the gods' right. So be it.

STROPHE IV

Thus to necessity's harsh yoke he bared
His patient neck. Unblissful blew the gale
  That turned the father's heart
To horrid thoughts unholy, thoughts that dared
The extreme of daring. Sin from its primal spring
Mads the ill-counsell'd heart, and arms the hand
  With reckless strength. Thus he
Gave his own daughter's blood, his life, his joy,
To speed a woman's war, and consecrate
  His ships for Troy.

ANTISTROPHE IV

In vain with prayers, in vain she beats dull ears
With a father's name; the war-delighting chiefs
  Heed not her virgin years.
The father stood; and when the priests had prayed,

Take her, he said; in her loose robes enfolden,
Where prone and spent she lies, so lift the maid;
Even as a kid is laid,
So lay her on the altar; with dumb force
Her beauteous mouth gag, lest it breathe a voice
Of curse to Argos.

STROPHE V

And as they led the maid, her saffron robe
Sweeping the ground, with pity-moving dart
She smote each from her eye,
Even as a picture beautiful, fain to speak,
But could not. Well that voice they knew of yore;
Oft at her father's festive board,
With gallant banqueters ringed cheerly round,
The virgin strain they heard
That did so sweetly pour
Her father's praise, whom Heaven had richly crowned
With bounty brimming o'er.

ANTISTROPHE V

The rest I know not, nor will vainly pry;
But Calchas was a seer not wont to lie.
Justice doth wait to teach
Wisdom by suffering. Fate will have its way.
The quickest ear is pricked in vain to-day,
To catch to-morrow's note. What boots
To forecast woe, which, on no wavering wing,
The burthen'd hour shall bring.
But we, a chosen band,
Left here sole guardians of the Apian land,
Pray Heaven, all good betide!

Enter CLYTEMNESTRA

CHORUS. Hail Clytemnestra! honour to thy sceptre!
When her lord's throne is vacant, the wife claims
His honour meetly. Queen, if thou hast heard
Good news, or to the hope of good that shall be,
With festal sacrifice dost fill the city,
I fain would know; but nothing grudge thy silence.

CLYTEM. Bearing blithe tidings, saith the ancient saw,
Fair Morn be gendered from boon mother Night!
News thou shalt hear beyond thy topmost hope;
The Greeks have ta'en old Priam's city.

CHORUS. How!
Troy taken! the word drops from my faithless ear.

CLYTEM. The Greeks have taken Troy. Can I speak plainer?

CHORUS. Joy o'er my heart creeps, and provokes the tear.

CLYTEM. Thine eye accuses thee that thou art kind.

CHORUS. What warrant of such news? What certain sign?

CLYTEM. Both sign and seal, unless some god deceive me.

CHORUS. Dreams sometimes speak; did suasive visions move thee?

CLYTEM. Where the soul sleeps, and the sense slumbers, there
Shall the wise ask for reasons?

CHORUS. Ever swift
Though wingless, Fame, with tidings fair hath cheered thee.

CLYTEM. Thou speak'st as one who mocks a simple girl.

CHORUS. Old Troy is taken? how?—when did it fall?

CLYTEM. The self-same night that mothers this to-day.

CHORUS. But how? what stalwart herald ran so fleetly?

CLYTEM. Hephæstus. He from Ida shot the spark;
And flaming straightway leapt the courier fire
From height to height; to the Hermæan rock
Of Lemnos, first from Ida; from the isle
The Athóan steep of mighty Jove received
The beaming beacon; thence the forward strength
Of the far-travelling lamp strode gallantly
Athwart the broad sea's back. The flaming pine
Rayed out a golden glory like the sun,
And winged the message to Macistus' watchtower.
There the wise watchman, guiltless of delay,
Lent to the sleepless courier further speed;
And the Messapian station hailed the torch
Far-beaming o'er the floods of the Eurípus.
There the grey heath lit the responsive fire,
Speeding the portioned message; waxing strong,

And nothing dulled across Asopus' plain
The flame swift darted like the twinkling
moon,
And on Cithæron's rocky heights awaked
A new receiver of the wandering light.
The far-sent ray, by the faithful watch not
spurned,
With bright addition journeying, bounded
o'er
Gorgópus' lake and Ægiplanctus' mount,
Weaving the chain unbroken. Hence it
spread
Not scant in strength, a mighty beard of
flame,
Flaring across the headlands that look down
On the Saronic gulf. Speeding its march,
It reached the neighbour-station of our city,
Arachne's rocky steep; and thence the halls
Of the Atridæ recognised the signal,
Light not unfathered by Idæan fire.
Such the bright train of my torch-bearing
heralds,
Each from the other fired with happy news,
And last and first was victor in the race.
Such the fair tidings that my lord hath sent,
A sign that Troy hath fallen.
CHORUS. And for its fall
Our voice shall hymn the gods anon: mean-
while
I'm fain to drink more wonder from thy
words.
CLYTEM. This day Troy fell. Methinks I
see't; a host
Of jarring voices stirs the startled city,
Like oil and acid, sounds that will not
mingle,
By natural hatred sundered. Thou may'st
hear
Shouts of the victor, with the dying groan,
Battling, and captives' cry; upon the dead —
Fathers and mothers, brothers, sisters,
wives —
The living fall — the young upon the old;
And from enthrallèd necks wail out their
woe.
Fresh from the fight, through the dark night
the spoilers
Tumultuous rush where hunger spurs them
on,
To feast on banquets never spread for them.
The homes of captive Trojan chiefs they
share
As chance decides the lodgment; there se-
cure
From the cold night-dews and the biting
frosts,
Beneath the lordly roof, to their hearts' con-
tent
They live, and through the watchless night
prolong
Sound slumbers. Happy if the native gods
They reverence, and the captured altars
spare,
Themselves not captive led by their own
folly!
May no unbridled lust of unjust gain
Master their hearts, no reckless rash desire!
Much toil yet waits them. Having turned the
goal,
The course's other half they must mete out,
Ere home receive them safe. Their ships
must brook
The chances of the sea; and, these being
scaped,
If they have sinned the gods their own will
claim,
And vengeance wakes till blood shall be
atoned.
I am a woman; but mark thou well my
words;
I hint the harm; but with no wavering scale,
Prevail the good! I thank the gods who gave
me
Rich store of blessings, richly to enjoy.
CHORUS. Woman, thou speakest wisely as a
man,
And kindly as thyself. But having heard
The certain signs of Agamemnon's coming,
Prepare we now to hymn the gods; for surely
With their strong help we have not toiled in
vain.

A regal Jove! O blessed Night!
Thou hast won thee rich adornments,
Thou hast spread thy shrouding meshes
O'er the towers of Priam. Ruin
Whelms the young, the old. In vain
Shall they strive to o'erleap the snare,
And snap the bondsman's galling chain,
In woe retrieveless lost.
Jove, I fear thee, just protector
Of the wrong'd host's sacred rights;
Thou didst keep thy bow sure bent
'Gainst Alexander; not before
The fate-predestined hour, and not
Beyond the stars, with idle aim,
Thy cunning shaft was shot.

CHORAL HYMN

STROPHE I

The hand of Jove hath smote them; thou
May'st trace it plainly;

What the god willed, behold it now
Not purposed vainly!
The gods are blind, and little caring,
So one hath said, to mark the daring
Of men, whose graceless foot hath ridden
O'er things to human touch forbidden.
Godless who said so; sons shall rue
Their parents' folly,
Who flushed with wealth, with insolence flown,
The sober bliss of man outgrown,
The trump of Mars unchastened blew,
And stirred red strife without the hue
Of justice wholly.
Live wiselier thou; not waxing gross
With gain, thou shalt be free from loss.
Weak is his tower, with pampering wealth
In brief alliance
Who spurns great Justice' altar dread
With damned defiance;
Him the deep hell shall claim, and shame
His vain reliance.

ANTISTROPHE I

Self-will, fell Até's daughter, still
Fore-counselling ruin,
Shall spur him on resistless borne
To his undoing.
Fined with sharp loss beyond repairing,
His misery like a beacon flaring,
Shall shine to all. Like evil brass,
That tested shows a coarse black mass,
His deep distemper he shall show
By dints of trial.
Even as a boy in wanton sport,
Chasing a bird to his own hurt,
And to the state's redeemless loss,
Whom, when he prays, the gods shall cross
With sheer denial,
And sweep the lewd and lawless liver
From earth's fair memory for ever;
Thus to the Atridans' palace came
False Alexander,
And shared the hospitable board,
A bold offender,
Filching his host's fair wife away
To far Scamander.

STROPHE II

She went, and to the Argive city left
Squadrons shield-bearing,
Battle preparing,
Swords many-flashing,
Oars many-plashing;
She went, destruction for her dowry bearing,
To the Sigean shore;
Light with swift foot she brushed the door-stead, daring
A deed undared before.
The prophets of the house loud wailing,
Cried with sorrow unavailing,
"Woe to the Atridans! woe!
The lofty palaces fallen low!
The marriage and the marriage bed,
The steps once faithful, fond to follow
There where the faithful husband led!"
He silent stood in sadness, not in wrath,
His own eye scarce believing,
As he followed her flight beyond the path
Of the sea-wave broadly heaving.
And phantoms sway each haunt well known,
Which the lost loved one wont to own,
And the statued forms that look from their seats
With a cold smile serenely,
He loathes to look on; in his eye
Pines Aphrodité leanly.

ANTISTROPHE II

In vain he sleeps; for in the fretful night
Shapes of fair seeming
Flit through his dreaming,
Soothing him sweetly,
Leaving him fleetly
Of bliss all barren. The shape fond fancy weaves him
His eager grasp would keep,
In vain; it cheats the hand; and leaves him, sweeping
Swift o'er the paths of sleep.
These sorrows pierce the Atridan chiefs,
And, worse than these, their private griefs,
But general Greece that to the fray
Sent her thousands, mourns to-day;
And Grief stout-hearted at each door
Sits to bear the burden sore
Of deathful news from the Trojan shore.
Ah! many an Argive heart to-day
Is pricked with wail and mourning,
Knowing how many went to Troy,
From Troy how few returning!
The mothers of each house shall wait
To greet their sons at every gate;
But, alas! not men, but dust of men
Each sorrowing house receiveth,
The urn in which the fleshly case
Its cindered ruin leaveth.

STROPHE III

For Mars doth market bodies, and for gold
Gives dust, and in the battle of the bold
Holds the dread scales of Fate.
Burnt cinders, a light burden, but to friends
A heavy freight,
He sends from Troy; the beautiful vase he sends
With dust, for hearts, well lined, on which descends
The frequent tear.
And friends do wail their praise; this here
Expert to wield the pointed spear,
And this who cast his life away,
Nobly in ignoble fray,
For a strange woman's sake.
And in their silent hearts hate burns;
Against the kings
The moody-muttered grudge creeps forth,
And points its stings.
Others they mourn who 'neath Troy's wall
Entombed, dark sleep prolong,
Low pressed beneath the hostile sod,
The beautiful, the strong!

ANTISTROPHE III

O hard to bear, when evil murmurs fly,
Is a nation's hate; unblest on whom doth lie
A people's curse!
My heart is dark, in my fear-procreant brain
Bad begets worse.
For not from heaven the gods behold in vain
Hands red with slaughter. The black-mantled train
Who watch and wait,
In their own hour shall turn to bane
The bliss that grew from godless gain.
The mighty man with heart elate
Shall fall; even as the sightless shades,
The great man's glory fades.
Sweet to the ear is the popular cheer
Forth billowed loudly;
But the bolt from on high shall blast his eye
That looketh proudly.
Be mine the sober bliss, and far
From fortune's high-strung rapture;
Not capturing others, may I never
See my own city's capture!

EPODE

Swift-winged with thrilling note it came,
The blithe news from the courier-flame;
But whether true and witnessed well,
Or if some god hath forged a lie,
What tongue can tell?
Who is so young, so green of wit,
That his heart should blaze with a fever fit,
At a tale of this fire-courier's telling,
When a new rumour swiftly swelling,
May turn him back to dole? To lift the note
Of clamorous triumph ere the fight be fought,
Is a light chance may fitly fall,
Where women wield the spear.
A wandering word by woman's fond faith sped
Swells and increases,
But with dispersion swift a woman's tale
Is lost and ceases.

Enter CLYTEMNESTRA

Soon shall we know if the light-bearing lamps
And the bright signals of the fiery changes
Spake true or, dream-like, have deceived our sense
With smiling semblance. For, behold, where comes,
Beneath the outspread olive's branchy shade,
A herald from the beach; and thirsty dust,
Twin-sister of the clay, attests his speed.
Not voiceless he, nor with the smoking flame
Of mountain pine will bring uncertain news.
His heraldry gives increase to our joy,
Or – but to speak ill-omened words I shun; –
May fair addition fair beginning follow!

CHORUS. Whoso fears evil where no harm appears,
Reap first himself the fruit of his own fears.

Enter HERALD

Hail Argive land! dear fatherland, all hail!
This tenth year's light doth shine on my return!
And now this one heart's hope from countless wrecks
I save! Scarce hoped I e'er to lay my bones
Within the tomb where dearest dust is stored.
I greet thee, native land! thee, shining sun!
Thee, the land's Sovereign, Jove! thee, Pythian King,
Shooting no more thy swift-winged shafts against us.
Enough on red Scamander's banks we knew
Thee hostile; now our saviour-god be thou,

Apollo, and our healer from much harm!
And you, all gods that guide the chance of
fight,
I here invoke; and thee, my high protector,
Loved Hermes, of all heralds most revered.
And you, all heroes that sent forth our hosts,
Bring back, I pray, our remnant with good
omens.
O kingly halls! O venerated seats!
O dear-loved roofs, and ye sun-fronting gods,
If ever erst, now on this happy day,
With these bright-beaming eyes, duly re-
ceive
Your late returning king; for Agamemnon
Comes, like the sun, a common joy to all.
Greet him with triumph, as beseems the
man,
Who with the mattock of justice-bringing
Jove
Hath dug the roots of Troy, hath made its
altars
Things seen no more, its towering temples
razed,
And caused the seed of the whole land to
perish.
Such yoke on Ilium's haughty neck the elder
Atridan threw, a king whom gods have
blessed
And men revere, 'mongst mortals worthy
most
Of honour; now nor Paris, nor in the bond
Partner'd with him, old Troy more crime
may boast
Than penalty; duly in the court of fight,
In the just doom of rape and robbery
damned,
His pledge is forfeited; his hand hath reaped
Clean bare the harvest of all bliss from Troy.
Doubly they suffer for a double crime.

CHORUS. Hail soldier herald, how farest thou?

HERALD. Right well!
So well that I could bless the gods and die.

CHORUS. Doubtless thy love of country tried
thy heart?

HERALD. To see these shores I weep for very
joy.

CHORUS. And that soul-sickness sweetly held
thee?

HERALD. How?
Instruct my wit to comprehend thy words.

CHORUS. Smitten with love of them that
much loved thee.

HERALD. Say'st thou? loved Argos us as we
loved Argos?

CHORUS. Ofttimes we sorrowed from a sunless soul.

HERALD. How so? Why should the thought
of the host have clouded
Thy soul with sadness?

CHORUS. Sorrow not causeless came;
But I have learned to drug all woes by silence.

HERALD. Whom should'st thou quail before,
the chiefs away?

CHORUS. I could have used thy phrase, and
wished to die.

HERALD. Die now, an' thou wilt, for joy!
The rolling years
Have given all things a prosperous end,
though some
Were hard to bear; for who, not being a
god,
Can hope to live long years of bliss un-
broken?
A weary tale it were to tell the tithe
Of all our hardships; toils by day, by night,
Harsh harbourage, hard hammocks, and
scant sleep.
No sun without new troubles, and new
groans,
Shone on our voyage; and when at length
we landed,
Our woes were doubled; 'neath the hostile
walls,
On marshy meads night-sprinkled by the
dews,
We slept, our clothes rotted with drenching
rain,
And like wild beasts with shaggy-knotted
hair.
Why should I tell bird-killing winter's sor-
rows,
Long months of suffering from Idéan snows,
Then summer's scorching heat, when noon
beheld
The waveless sea beneath the windless air
In sleep diffused; these toils have run their
hour.
The dead care not to rise; their roll our
grief
Would muster o'er in vain; and we who live
Vainly shall fret at the cross strokes of fate.
Henceforth to each harsh memory of the
past
Farewell! we who survive this long-drawn
war
Have gains to count that far outweigh the
loss.
Well may we boast in the face of the shin-
ing sun,
O'er land and sea our winged tidings waft-
ing,

THE ACHÆAN HOST HATH CAPTURED TROY; and now
On the high temples of the gods we hang
These spoils, a shining grace, there to remain
An heritage for ever. These things to hear
Shall men rejoice, and with fair praises laud
The state and its great generals, laud the grace
Of Jove the Consummator. I have said.
CHORUS. I own thy speech the conqueror; for a man
Can never be too old to learn good news,
And though thy words touch Clytemnestra most,
Joy to the Atridan's halls is wealth to me.
CLYTEM. I lifted first the shout of jubilee,
Then when the midnight sign of the courier fire
Told the deep downfall of the captured Troy;
But one then mocked my faith, that I believed
The fire-sped message in so true a tale.
'Tis a light thing to buoy a woman's heart
With hopeful news, they cried; and with these words
They wildered my weak wit. And yet I sped
The sacrifice, and raised the welcoming shout
In woman's wise, and at a woman's word
Forthwith from street to street uprose to the gods
Well-omened salutations, and glad hymns,
Lulling the fragrant incense-feeding flame.
What needs there more? The event has proved me right,
Himself — my lord — with his own lips shall speak
The weighty tale; myself will go make ready
With well-earned honour to receive the honoured.
What brighter bliss on woman's lot may beam,
Than when a god gives back her spouse from war,
To ope the gates of welcome. Tell my husband,
To his loved home, desired of all, to haste.
A faithful wife, even as he left her, here
He'll find expectant, like a watch-dog gentle
To him and his, to all that hate him harsh.
The seals that knew his stamp, when hence he sailed,
Unharmed remain, untouched: and for myself
Nor praise nor blame from other man I know,
No more than dyer's art can tincture brass.
HERALD. A boast like this, instinct with very truth,
Comes from a noble lady without blame.
CHORUS. Wise words she spake, and words that need no comment
To ears that understand. But say, good Herald,
Comes Menelaus safe back from the wars,
His kindly sway in Argos to resume?
HERALD. I cannot gloss a lie with fair pretence;
The best told lie bears but a short-lived fruit.
CHORUS. Speak the truth plainly, if thou canst not pleasantly;
These twain be seldom wedded; and here, alas!
They stand out sundered with too clear a mark.
HERALD. The man is vanished from the Achæan host,
He and his vessel. Thou hast heard the truth.
CHORUS. Sailed he from Ilium separate from the fleet?
Or did the tempest part him from his friends!
HERALD. Like a good marksman thou hast hit the mark,
In one short sentence summing many sorrows.
CHORUS. Alive is he or dead? What word hath reached you?
What wandering rumour from sea-faring men?
HERALD. This none can tell, save yon bright sun aloft,
That cherishes all things with his friendly light.
CHORUS. How came the storm on the fleet? or how was ended
The wrath of the gods?
HERALD. Not well it suits to blot
With black rehearsal this auspicious day.
Far from the honors of the blissful gods
Be grief's recital. When with gloomy visage
An ugly tale the herald's voice unfolds,
At once a general wound, and private grief,
An army lost, the sons of countless houses
Death-doomed by the double scourge so dear to Ares,
A twin-speared harm, a yoke of crimson slaughter:
A herald saddled with such woes may sing
A pæan to the Erinnyes. But I,
Who to this city blithe and prosperous

Brought the fair news of Agamemnon's safety,
How shall I mingle bad with good, rehearsing
The wintry wrath sent by the gods to whelm us?
Fire and the sea, sworn enemies of old,
Made friendly league to sweep the Achæan host
With swift destruction pitiless. Forth rushed
The tyrannous Thracian blasts, and wave chased wave,
Fierce 'neath the starless night, and ship on ship
Struck clashing; beak on butting beak was driven;
The puffing blast, the beat of boiling billows,
The whirling gulph (an evil pilot) wrapt them
In sightless death. And when the shining sun
Shone forth again, we see the Ægean tide
Strewn with the purple blossoms of the dead,
And wrecks of shattered ships. Us and our bark
Some god, no man, the storm-tost hull directing,
Hath rescued scathless, stealing us from the fray,
Or with a prayer begging our life from Fate.
Kind Fortune helmed us further, safely kept
From yeasty ferment in the billowy bay,
Nor dashed on far-ledged rocks. Thus having 'scaped
That ocean hell, scarce trusting our fair fortune,
We hailed the lucid day; but could we hope,
The chance that saved ourselves had saved our friends?
Our fearful hearts with thoughts of them we fed,
Far-labouring o'er the loosely-driving main.
And doubtless they, if yet live breath they breathe,
Deem so of us, as we must fear of them,
That they have perished. But I hope the best.
And first and chief expect ye the return
Of Menelaus. If the sun's blest ray
Yet looks on him, where he beholds the day
By Jove's devising, not yet willing wholly
To uproot the race of Atreus, hope may be
He yet returns. Thou hast my tale; and I
Have told the truth untinctured with a lie.
(*Exit.*

CHORAL HYMN

STROPHE I

Who gave her a name
So true to her fame?
Does a Providence rule in the fate of a word?
Sways there in heaven a viewless power
O'er the chance of the tongue in the naming hour?
Who gave her a name,
This daughter of strife, this daughter of shame,
The spear-wooed maid of Greece?
Helen the taker! 'tis plain to see
A taker of ships, a taker of men,
A taker of cities is she.
From the soft-curtained chamber of Hymen she fled,
By the breath of giant Zephyr sped,
And shield-bearing throngs in marshalled array
Hounded her flight o'er the printless way,
Where the swift-plashing oar
The fair booty bore
To swirling Simois' leafy shore,
And stirred the crimson fray.

ANTISTROPHE I

For the gods sent a bride,
Kin but not kind,
Ripe with the counsel of wrath to Troy,
In the fulness of years, the offender to prove,
And assert the justice of Jove;
For great Jove is lord
Of the rights of the hearth and the festal board.
The sons of Priam sang
A song to the praise of the bride:
From jubilant throats they praised her then,
The bride from Hellas brought;
But now the ancient city hath changed
Her hymn to a doleful note.
She weeps bitter tears; she curses the head
Of the woe-wedded Paris; she curses the bed
Of the beautiful bride
That crossed the flood,
And filched the life of her sons, and washed
Her wide-paved streets with blood.

STROPHE II

Whoso nurseth the cub of a lion
Weaned from the dugs of its dam, where the draught
Of its mountain-milk was free,
Finds it gentle at first and tame.

It frisks with the children in innocent
game,
And the old man smiles to see;
It is dandled about like a babe in the arm,
It licketh the hand that fears no harm,
And when hunger pinches its fretful maw,
It fawns with an eager glee.

ANTISTROPHE II

But it grows with the years; and soon reveals
The fount of fierceness whence it came:
And, loathing the food of the tame,
It roams abroad, and feasts in the fold,
On feasts forbidden, and stains the floor
Of the house that nursed it with gore.
A curse they nursed for their own undoing,
A mouth by which their own friends shall
perish;
A servant of Até, a priest of Ruin,
Some god hath taught them to cherish.

STROPHE III

Thus to Troy came a bride of the Spartan
race,
With a beauty as bland as a windless calm,
Prosperity's gentlest grace;
And mild was love's blossom that rayed from
her eye,
The soft-winged dart that with pleasing pain
Thrills heart and brain.
But anon she changed: herself fulfilled
Her wedlock's bitter end;
A fatal sister, a fatal bride,
Her fateful head she rears;
Herself the Erinnys from Jove to avenge
The right of the injured host, and change
The bridal joy to tears.

ANTISTROPHE III

'Twas said of old, and 'tis said to-day,
That wealth to prosperous stature grown
Begets a birth of its own:
That a surfeit of evil by good is prepared,
And sons must bear what allotment of
woe
Their sires were spared.
But this I rebel to believe: I know
That impious deeds conspire
To beget an offspring of impious deeds
Too like their ugly sire.
But whoso is just, though his wealth like a
river
Flow down, shall be scathless: his house
shall rejoice
In an offspring of beauty for ever.

STROPHE IV

The heart of the haughty delights to beget
A haughty heart. From time to time
In children's children recurrent appears
The ancestral crime.
When the dark hour comes that the gods
have decreed,
And the Fury burns with wrathful fires,
A demon unholy, with ire unabated,
Lies like black night on the halls of the
fated:
And the recreant son plunges guiltily on
To perfect the guilt of his sires.

ANTISTROPHE IV

But Justice shines in a lowly cell;
In the homes of poverty, smoke-begrimed,
With the sober-minded she loves to dwell.
But she turns aside
From the rich man's house with averted eye,
The golden-fretted halls of pride
Where hands with lucre are foul, and the
praise
Of counterfeit goodness smoothly sways:
And wisely she guides in the strong man's
despite
All things to an issue of RIGHT.

CHORUS. But, hail the king! the city-taking
Seed of Atreus' race.
How shall I accost thee! How
With beseeming reverence greet thee?
Nor above the mark, nor sinking
Beneath the line of grace?
Many of mortal men there be,
'Gainst the rule of right preferring
Seeming to substance; tears are free
In the eye when woe its tale rehearseth,
But the sting of sorrow pierceth
No man's liver; many force
Lack-laughter faces to relax
Into the soft lines traced by joy.
But the shepherd true and wise
Knows the faithless man, whose eyes,
With a forward friendship twinkling,
Fawn with watery love.
For me, I nothing hide. O King,
In my fancy's picturing,
From the Muses far I deemed thee,
And thy soul not wisely helming
When thou drew'st the knife
For Helen's sake, a woman, whelming
Thousands in ruin, rushing rashly
On unwelcome strife.
But now all's well. No shallow smiles
We wear for thee, thy weary toils

All finished. Thou shalt know anon
What friends do serve thee truly,
And who in thy long absence used
Their stewardship unduly.

Enter AGAMEMNON *with attendants;* CASSANDRA *behind*

AGA. First Argos hail! and ye, my country's gods,
Who worked my safe return, and nerved my arm
With vengeance against Priam! for the gods,
Taught by no glozing tongue, but by the sight
Of their own eyes knew justice; voting ruin
And men-destroying death to ancient Troy,
Their fatal pebbles in the bloody urn
Not doubtingly they dropt; the other vase,
Unfed with hope of suffrage-bearing hand,
Stood empty. Now the captured city's smoke
Points where it fell. Raves Ruin's storm; the winds
With crumbled dust and dissipated gold
Float grossly laden. To the immortal gods
These thanks, fraught with rich memory of much good,
We pay; they taught our hands to spread the net
With anger-whetted wit; a woman's frailty
Laid bare old Ilium to the Argive bite,
And with the setting Pleiads outleapt a birth
Of strong shield-bearers from the fateful horse.
A fierce flesh-tearing lion leapt their walls,
And licked a surfeit of tyrannic blood.
This prelude to the gods. As for thy words
Of friendly welcome, I return thy greeting,
And as your thought, so mine; for few are gifted
With such rich store of love, to see a friend
Preferred and feel no envy; 'tis a disease
Possessing mortal men, a poison lodged
Close by the heart, eating all joy away
With double barb – his own mischance who suffers
And bliss of others sitting at his gate,
Which when he sees he groans. I know it well;
They who seemed most my friends, and many seemed,
Were but the mirrored show, the shadowy ghost
Of something like to friendship, substanceless.
Ulysses only, most averse to sail,
Was still most ready in the yoke with me
To bear the harness; living now or dead,
This praise I frankly give him. For the rest,
The city and the gods, we will take counsel
In full assembly freely. What is good
We will give heed that it be lasting; where
Disease the cutting or the caustic cure
Demands, we will apply it. I, meanwhile,
My hearth and home salute, and greet the gods,
Who, as they sent me to the distant fray,
Have brought me safely back. Fair victory,
Once mine, may she dwell with me evermore!

CLYTEM. Men! Citizens! ye reverend Argive seniors,
No shame feel I, even in your face, to tell
My husband-loving ways. Long converse lends
Boldness to bashfulness. No foreign griefs,
Mine own self-suffered woes I tell. While he
Was camping far at Ilium, I at home
Sat all forlorn, uncherished by the mate
Whom I had chosen; this was woe enough
Without enforcement; but, to try me further,
A host of jarring rumours stormed my doors,
Each fresh recital with a murkier hue
Than its precedent; and I must hear all.
If this my lord, had borne as many wounds
In battle as the bloody fame recounted,
He had been pierced throughout even as a net;
And had he died as oft as Rumour slew him,
He might have boasted of a triple coil
Like the three-bodied Geryon, while on earth
(Of him below I speak not), and like him
Been three times heaped with a cloak of funeral dust.
Thus fretted by cross-grained reports, ofttimes
The knotted rope high-swung had held my neck,
But that my friends with forceful aid prevented.
Add that my son, pledge of our mutual vows,
Orestes is not here; nor think it strange.
Thy Phocian spear-guest, the most trusty Strophius,
Took him in charge, a twofold danger urging,
First thine beneath the walls of Troy, and further
The evil likelihood that, should the Greeks
Be worsted in the strife, at home the voice
Of many-babbling anarchy might cast
The council down, and as man's baseness is,

At fallen greatness insolently spurn.
Moved by these thoughts I parted with my boy,
And for no other cause. Myself the while
So woe-worn lived, the fountains of my grief
To their last drop were with much weeping drained;
And far into the night my watch I've kept
With weary eyes, while in my lonely room
The night-torch faintly glimmered. In my dream
The buzzing gnat, with its light-brushing wing,
Startled the fretful sleeper; thou hast been
In waking hours, as in sleep's fitful turns
My only thought. But having bravely borne
This weight of woe, now with blithe heart I greet
Thee, my heart's lord, the watch-dog of the fold,
The ship's sure mainstay, pillared shaft whereon
Rests the high roof, fond parent's only child,
Land seen by sailors past all hope, a day
Lovely to look on when the storm hath broken,
And to the thirsty wayfarer the flow
Of gushing rill. O sweet it is, how sweet
To see an end of the harsh yoke that galled us!
These greetings to my lord; nor grudge me, friends,
This breadth of welcome; sorrows we have known
Ample enough. And now, thou precious head,
Come from thy car; nay, do not set thy foot,
The foot that trampled Troy, on common clay.
What ho! ye laggard maids! why lags your task
Behind the hour? Spread purple where he treads.
Fitly the broidered foot-cloth marks his path,
Whom Justice leadeth to his long-lost home
With unexpected train. What else remains
Our sleepless zeal, with favour of the gods,
Shall order as befits.

AGA. Daughter of Leda, guardian of my house!
Almost thou seem'st to have spun thy welcome out
To match my lengthened absence; but I pray thee
Praise with discretion, and let other mouths
Proclaim my pæans. For the rest, abstain
From delicate tendance that would turn my manhood
To woman's temper. Not in barbaric wise
With prostrate reverence base, kissing the ground,
Mouth sounding salutations; not with purple,
Breeder of envy, spread my path. Such honors
Suit the immortal gods; me, being mortal,
To tread on rich-flowered carpetings wise fear
Prohibits. As a man, not as a god,
Let me be honored. Not the less my fame
Shall be far blazoned, that on common earth
I tread untapestried. A sober heart
Is the best gift of God; call no man happy
Till death hath found him prosperous to the close.
For me, if what awaits me fall not worse
Than what hath fallen, I have good cause to look
Bravely on fate.

CLYTEM. Nay, but my good lord will not
In this gainsay my heart's most warm desire.

AGA. My wish and will thou shalt not lightly mar.

CLYTEM. Hast thou a vow belike, and fear'st the gods?

AGA. If e'er man knew, I know my will in this.

CLYTEM. Had Priam conquered, what had Priam done?

AGA. His feet had trod the purple; doubt it not.

CLYTEM. What Priam would, thou may'st, unless the fear
Of popular blame make Agamemnon quail.

AGA. But popular babble strengthens Envy's wing.

CLYTEM. Thou must be envied if thou wilt be great.

AGA. Is it a woman's part to hatch contention?

CLYTEM. For once be conquered; they who conquer may
Yield with a grace.

AGA. And thou in this vain strife
Must be perforce the conqueror; is it so?

CLYTEM. 'Tis even so: for once give me the reins.

AGA. Thou hast thy will. Come, boy, unbind these sandals,
That are the prostrate subjects to my feet,
When I do tread; for with shod feet I never

May leave my print on the sea-purple, lest
Some god with jealous eye look from afar
And mark me. Much I fear with insolent foot
To trample wealth, and rudely soil the web
Whose precious threads the pure-veined silver buys.
So much for this. As for this maid, receive
The stranger kindly: the far-seeing gods
Look down with love on him who mildly sways.
For never yet was yoke of slavery borne
By willing neck; of all the captive maids
The choicest flower she to my portion fell.
And now, since thou art victor o'er my will,
I tread the purple to my father's hall.

CLYTEM. The wide sea flows; and who shall dry it up?
The ocean flows, and in its vasty depths
Is brewed the purple's dye, as silver precious,
A tincture ever-fresh for countless robes.
But Agamemnon's house is not a beggar;
With this, and with much more the gods provide us;
And purple I had vowed enough to spread
The path of many triumphs, had a god
Given me such 'hest oracular to buy
The ransom of thy life. We have thee now,
Both root and trunk, a tree rich leafage spreading
To shade this mansion from the Sirian dog.
Welcome, thou double blessing! to this hearth
That bringest heat against keen winter's cold,
And coolness when the sweltering Jove prepares
Wine from the crudeness of the bitter grape;
Enter the house, made perfect by thy presence.
Jove, Jove, the perfecter! perfect thou my vow,
And thine own counsels quickly perfect thou!
(*Exeunt.*

CHORAL HYMN

STROPHE I

Whence these shapes of fear that haunt me?
These hovering portents why?
Is my heart a seer inspired,
To chaunt unbidden and unhired
Notes of dark prophecy?
Blithe confidence, my bosom's lord,
That swayed the doubtful theme,
Arise, and with thy clear command
Chase the vain-vexing dream!
Long years have rolled; and still I fear,
As when the Argive band
Unloosed their cables from the shore,
And eager plied the frequent oar
To the far Ilian strand.

ANTISTROPHE I

Now they return: my vouching eyes
To prop my faith conspire,
And yet my heart, in self-taught hymns,
As with a Fury's burden brims,
And will not own the lyre.
I fear, I fear: the bold-faced Hope
Hath left my heart all drear;
And my thought, not idly tossed within,
Feels evil creeping near.
For the heart hath scent of things to come,
And prophesies by fear;
And yet I pray, may all conspire
To prove by boding heart a liar,
And me a foolish seer.

STROPHE II

Full-blooded health, that in the veins
With lusty pulses hotly wells,
Shall soon have check. Disease beside it
Wall to wall, ill-sundered, dwells.
The proud trireme, with sudden shock,
In its mid career, on a sunken rock
Strikes, and all is lost.
Yet there is hope; the ship may rein
Its plunge, from whelming ruin free,
If with wise sling the merchant fling
Into the greedy sea
A part to save the whole. And thus
Jove, that two-handed stores for us,
In our mid woe may pause,
Heap gifts on gifts from yearly furrows,
And save the house from swamping sorrows,
And lean starvation's jaws.

ANTISTROPHE II

But, oh! when black blood stains the ground,
And the mortal mortal lies,
Shall the dead hear when thou chauntest?
To thy charming shall he rise?
Once there was a leech so wise
Could raise the dead, but, from the skies,
Struck by Jove, he ceased.
But cease my song. Were link with link
In the chain of things not bound together
That each event must wait its time,
Nor one dare trip the other,
My tongue had played the prophet's part,
And rolled the burden from my heart;

But now, to doubt resigned,
With smothered fears, all dumb I wait
The unravelling hour; while sparks of fate
Flit through my darksome mind.

Enter CLYTEMNESTRA

CLYTEM. Come thou, too, in; this maid, I mean; Cassandra!
For not in wrath Jove sent thee here to share
Our family lustrations, and to stand,
With many slaves, beside the household altar.
Step from this car, nor bear thy spirit proudly
Above thy fate, for even Alcmena's son,
To slavery sold, once bore the hated yoke.
What must be, must be; rather thank the chance
That gave thee to an old and wealthy house;
For they who reap an unexpected growth
Of wealth, are harsh to slaves beyond the line
Of a well-tempered rule. Here thou shalt find
The common use of bondage.
CHORUS. Plainly she speaks;
And thou within Fate's iron toils once caught
Wert wise to go — if go thou wilt — but, soothly,
Thou hast no willing look.
CLYTEM. Nay! an' she be not
Barbarian to the bone, and speaking nought
Save swallow jabber, she shall hear my voice.
I'll pierce her marrow with it.
CHORUS. Captive maid,
Obey! thou shouldst; 'tis best; be thou persuaded
To leave thy chariot-seat and follow her.
CLYTEM. No time have I to stand without the gate
Prating with her. Within, on the central hearth,
The fire burns bright, the sheep's fat slaughter waiting,
To furnish forth a banquet that transcends
The topmost of our hopes. Wilt thou obey,
Obey me quickly! If with stubborn sense
Thou hast nor ear to hear, nor voice to speak,
Answer my sign with thy barbarian hand.
CHORUS. A wise interpreter the maid demands;
Like a wild beast new caught, even so she stands.
CLYTEM. Ay! she is mad; her wit to sober counsels
Is deaf; she comes from the new-captured city,
Untaught to bear the Argive bit with patience,
But foams and dashes bloody froth. I will not
Make myself base by wasting words on her. (*Exit*.
CHORUS. Poor maid, I may not blame; I pity thee.
Come, leave thy seat; for, though the yoke be strange,
Necessity compels, and thou must bear it.

STROPHE I

CASS. Ah! ah! woes me! woe! woe!
Apollo! O Apollo!
CHORUS. Why dost thou wail to Loxias? is he
A gloomy god that he should list sad tales?

ANTISTROPHE I

CASS. Ah! ah! woes me! woe! woe!
Apollo! O Apollo!
CHORUS. Again with evil-omened voice she cries
Upon the god least fit to wait on woe.

STROPHE II

CASS. Apollo! Apollo!
My way-god, my leader Apollo!
Apollo the destroyer!
Thou with light labour hast destroyed me quite.
CHORUS. Strange oracles against herself she speaks;
Ev'n in the bondsman's bosom dwells the god.

ANTISTROPHE II

CASS. Apollo! Apollo!
Apollo, my leader, whither hast thou led me?
My way-god, Apollo?
What homes receive thy captive prophetess?
CHORUS. The Atridæ's homes. This, an' thou knowst it not,
I tell thee; and the words I speak are true.

STROPHE III

CASS. Ha! the house of the Atridæ!
Well the godless house I know,
With the dagger and the rope,
And the self-inflicted blow!
Where red blood is on the floor,
And black murder at the door —
This house — this house I know.
CHORUS. She scents out slaughter, mark me, like a hound,
And tracks the spot where she shall feast on blood.

ANTISTROPHE III

CASS. Ay! I scent a truthful scent,
And the thing I say I know.
See! see! these weeping children,
How they vouch the monstrous woe!
Their red wounds are bleeding fresh,
And their father eats their flesh,
This bloody house I know.
CHORUS. The fame of thy divinings far renowned
Have reached us, but we wish no prophets here.

STROPHE IV

CASS. Ha! ha! what plots she now!
A new sorrow, a new snare
To the house of the Atridæ,
And a burden none may bear!
A black harm to all and each,
A disease that none may leech,
And the evil plot to mar
All help and hope is far.
CHORUS. Nay now I'm lost and mazed in vain surmise.
What first she said I knew – the common rumour.

ANTISTROPHE IV

CASS. Ha! woman wilt thou dare?
Thy bed's partner and thy mate
In the warm refreshing bath
Shall he find his bloody fate?
How shall I dare to say
What comes and will not stay?
See, to do her heart's command
Where she stretches her red hand!
CHORUS. Not yet I understand: through riddles dark
And cloudy oracles my wits are wandering.

STROPHE V

CASS. Ha! what bloody sight is this!
'Tis a net of Hades spread –
'Tis a snare to snare her lord,
The fond sharer of her bed.
The black chorus of the place
Shout for vengeance o'er the race,
Whose offence cries for atoning,
With a heavy death of stoning!

STROPHE VI

CHORUS. What black Fury of the place
Shall shout vengeance o'er the race?
Such strange words I hate to hear.
The blithe blood, that crimson ran
In my veins, runs pale and wan
With the taint of yellow fear,
As when in the mortal anguish,
Life's last fitful glimpses languish
And Fate, as now, is near!

ANTISTROPHE V

CASS. Ha! ha! the work proceeds!
From the bull keep back the cow!
Lo! now she seizes him
By the strong black horn, and now
She hath wrapt him round with slaughter;
She strikes! and in the water
Of the bath he falls. Mark well,
In the bath doth murder dwell.

ANTISTROPHE VI

CHORUS. No prophetic gift is mine
The dark saying to divine,
But this sounds like evil quite;
For to mortal man was never
The diviner's voice the giver
Of a message of delight,
But in words of mazy mourning,
Comes the prophet's voice of warning,
With a lesson of affright.

STROPHE VII

CASS. Fill the cup, and brim the woe!
'Tis my own heart's blood must flow.
Me! miserable me!
From old Troy why didst thou bring me,
Poor captive maid, to sing thee
Thy dirge, and die with thee?

STROPHE VIII

CHORUS. By a god thou art possessed,
And he raveth in thy breast,
And he sings a song of thee
That hath music, but no glee.
Like a dun-plumed nightingale,
That, with never-sated wail,
Crieth Itys! Itys! aye,
As it scatters, in sweet flow,
The thick blossoms of its woe,
So singest thou to-day.

ANTISTROPHE VII

CASS. Ah! the clear-toned nightingale!
Mellow bird, thou dost not wail,
For the good gods gave to thee
A light shape of fleetest winging,
A bright life of sweetest singing,
But a sharp-edged death to me.

ANTISTROPHE VIII

CHORUS. By a god thou art possessed,
And he goads thee without rest,

And he racks thy throbbing brain
With a busy-beating pain,
And he presses from thy throat
The heavy struggling note,
And the cry that rends the air.
Who bade her tread this path,
With the prophecy of wrath,
And the burden of despair?

STROPHE IX

CASS. O the wedlock and the woe
Of the evil Alexander,
To his chiefest friends a foe!
O my native stream Scamander,
Where in youth I wont to wander,
And was nursed for future woes,
Where thy swirling current flows!
But now on sluggish shore
Of Cocytus I shall pour,
'Mid the Acherusian glades,
My divinings to the shades.

STROPHE X

CHORUS. Nothing doubtful is the token;
For the words the maid hath spoken
To a very child are clear.
She hath pierced me to the marrow;
And her cry of shrieking sorrow
Ah! it crushes me to hear.

ANTISTROPHE IX

CASS. The proud city lieth lowly,
Nevermore to rise again!
It is lost and ruined wholly;
And before the walls in vain
Hath my pious father slain
Many meadow-cropping kine,
To appease the wrath divine.
Where it lieth it shall lie,
Ancient Ilium: and I
On the ground, when all is past,
Soon my reeking heart shall cast.

ANTISTROPHE X

CHORUS. Ah! the mighty god, wrath-laden,
He hath smote the burdened maiden
With a weighty doom severe.
From her heart sharp cries he wringeth,
Dismal, deathful strains she singeth,
And I wait the end in fear.

CASS. No more my prophecy, like a young bride
Shall from a veil peep forth, but like a wind
Waves shall it dash from the west in the sun's face,
And curl high-crested surges of fierce woes,
That far outbillow mine. I'll speak no more
In dark enigmas. Ye my vouchers be,
While with keen scent I snuff the breath of the past,
And point the track of monstrous crimes of eld.
There is a choir, to destiny well-tuned,
Haunts these doomed halls, no mellow-throated choir,
And they of human blood have largely drunk:
And by that wine made bold, the Bacchanals
Cling to their place of revels. The sister'd Furies
Sit on these roofs, and hymn the prime offence
Of this crime-burthened race; the brother's sin
That trod the brother's bed. Speak! do I hit
The mark, a marksman true? or do I beat
Your doors, a babbling beggar prophesying
False dooms for hire? Be ye my witnesses,
And with an oath avouch, how well I know
The hoary sins that hang upon these walls.

CHORUS. Would oaths make whole our ills, though I should wedge them
As stark as ice? But I do marvel much
That thou, a stranger born, from distant seas,
Dost know our city as it were thine own.

CASS. Even this to know, Apollo stirred my breast.

CHORUS. Apollo! did'st thou strike the god with love?

CASS. Till now I was ashamed to hint the tale.

CHORUS. The dainty lips of nice prosperity
Misfortune opens.

CASS. Like a wrestler he
Strove for my love; he breathed his grace upon me.

CHORUS. And hast thou children from divine embrace?

CASS. I gave the word to Loxias, not the deed.

CHORUS. Hadst thou before received the gift divine?

CASS. I had foretold my countrymen all their woes.

CHORUS. Did not the anger of the god pursue thee?

CASS. It did; I warned, but none believed my warning.

CHORUS. To us thou seem'st to utter things that look
Only too like the truth.

CASS. Ah me! woe! woe

Again strong divination's troublous whirl
Seizes my soul, and stirs my labouring breast
With presages of doom. Lo! where they sit,
These pitiful young ones on the fated roof,
Like to the shapes of dreams! The innocent babes,
Butchered by friends that should have blessed them, and
In their own hands their proper bowels they bear,
Banquet abhorred, and their own father eats it.
This deed a lion, not a lion-hearted
Shall punish; wantonly in her bed, whose lord
Shall pay the heavy forfeit, he shall roll,
And snare my master – woe's me, even *my* master,
For slavery's yoke my neck must learn to own.
Ah! little weens the leader of the ships,
Troy's leveller, how a hateful bitch's tongue,
With long-drawn phrase, and broad-sown smile, doth weave
His secret ruin. This a woman dares;
The female mars the male. Where shall I find
A name to name such monster? dragon dire,
Rock-lurking Scylla, the vexed seaman's harm,
Mother of Hades, murder's Mænad, breathing
Implacable breath of curses on her kin.
All-daring woman! shouting in her heart,
As o'er the foe, when backward rolls the fight,
Yet hymning kindliest welcome with her tongue.
Ye look mistrustful; I am used to that.
That comes which is to come; and ye shall know
Full soon, with piteous witness in your eyes,
How true, and very true, Cassandra spake.

CHORUS. Thyestes' banquet, and his children's flesh
I know, and shudder; strange that she should know
The horrors of that tale; but for the rest
She runs beyond my following.

CASS. Thus I said;
Thine eyes shall witness Agamemnon's death.

CHORUS. Hush, wretched maiden! lull thy tongue to rest,
And cease from evil-boding words!

CASS. Alas!
The gods that heal all evil, heal not this.

CHORUS. If it must be; but may the gods forefend!

CASS. Pray thou, and they will have more time to kill.

CHORUS. What man will dare to do such bloody deed?

CASS. I spake not of a *man:* thy thoughts shoot wide.

CHORUS. The deed I heard, but not whose hand should do it.

CASS. And yet I spake good Greek with a good Greek tongue.

CHORUS. Thou speakest Apollo's words: true, but obscure.

CASS. Ah me! the god! like fire within my breast
Burns the Lycéan god. Ah me! pain! pain!
A lioness two-footed with a wolf
Is bedded, when the noble lion roamed
Far from his den; and she will murder me.
She crowns the cup of wrath; she whets the knife
Against the neck of the man, and he must pay
The price of capture, I of being captive.
Vain gauds, that do but mock my grief, farewell!
This laurel-rod, and this diviner's wreath
About my neck, should they outlive the wearer?
Away! As ye have paid me, I repay.
Make rich some other prophetess with woe!
Lo! where Apollo looks, and sees me now
Doff this diviner's garb, the self-same weeds
He tricked me erst withal, to live for him,
The public scorn, the scoff of friends and foes,
The mark of every ribald jester's tongue,
The homeless girl, the raving mountebank,
The beggar'd, wretched, starving maniac.
And now who made the prophetess unmakes her,
And leads me to my doom – ah! not beside
My father's altar doomed to die! the block
From my hot life shall drink the purple stain.
But we shall fall not unavenged: the gods
A mother-murdering shoot shall send from far
To avenge his sire; the wanderer shall return
To pile the cope-stone on these towering woes.
The gods in heaven a mighty oath have sworn,

To raise anew the father's prostrate fate
By the son's arm. — But why stand here, and beat
The air with cries, seeing what I have seen;
When Troy hath fallen, suffering what it suffered,
And they who took the city by the doom
Of righteous gods faring as they shall fare?
I will endure to die, and greet these gates
Of Hades gaping for me. Grant me, ye gods,
A mortal stroke well-aimed, and a light fall
From cramped convulsion free! Let the red blood
Flow smoothly from its fount, that I may close
These eyes in peaceful death.
CHORUS. O hapless maid!
And wise as hapless! thou hast spoken long!
But if thou see'st the harm, why rush on fate
Even as an ox, whom favouring gods inspire
To stand by the altar's steps, and woo the knife.
CASS. I'm in the net. Time will not break the meshes.
CHORUS. But the last moment of sweet life is honoured.
CASS. My hour is come; what should I gain by flight?
CHORUS. Thou with a stout heart bravely look'st on fate.
CASS. Bravely thou praisest: but the happy hear not
Such commendations.
CHORUS. Yet if death must come,
His fame is fair who nobly fronts the foe.
CASS. Woe's me, the father and his noble children!
CHORUS. Whither now? What father and what children? Speak.
CASS. (*Approaching and starting back from the house.*)
Woe! woe!
CHORUS. What means this WOE? What horrid fancy scares thee?
CASS. Blood-dripping murder reeks from yonder house.
CHORUS. How? 'Tis the scent of festal sacrifice.
CASS. The scent of death — a fragrance from the grave.
CHORUS. Soothly no breath of Syrian nard she names.
CASS. But now the time is come. I go within
To wail for Agamemnon and myself.
I've done with life. Farewell! My vouchers ye,
Not with vain screaming, like a fluttering bird,
Above the bush I cry. Yourselves shall know it
Then when, for me a woman, a woman dies,
And for a man ill-wived a man shall fall.
Trust me in this. Your honest faith is all
The Trojan guest, the dying woman, craves.
CHORUS. O wretched maid! O luckless prophetess!
CASS. Yet will I speak one other word, before
I leave this light. Hear thou my vows, bright sun,
And, though a slave's death be a little thing,
Send thou the avenging hand with full requital,
To pay my murderers back, as they have paid.
Alas! the fates of men! their brightest bloom
A shadow blights; and, in their evil day,
An oozy sponge blots out their fleeting prints,
And they are seen no more. From bad to worse
Our changes run, and with the worst we end.
(*Exit.*

CHORUS. Men crave increase of riches ever
With insatiate craving. Never
From the finger-pointed halls
Of envied wealth their owner calls,
"Enter no more! I have enough!"
This man the gods with honour crowned;
He hath levelled with the ground
Priam's city, and in triumph
Glorious home returns;
But if doomed the fine to pay
Of ancient guilt, and death with death
To guerdon in the end,
Who of mortals will not pray,
From high-perched Fortune's favour far,
A blameless life to spend.
AGA. (*From within.*) O I am struck! struck with a mortal blow!
CHORUS. Hush! what painful voice is speaking there of strokes and mortal blows?
AGA. O struck again! struck with a mortal blow!
CHORUS. 'Tis the king that groans; the work, the bloody work, I fear, is doing.
Weave we counsel now together, and concert a sure design.
1ST CHORUS. I give my voice to lift the loud alarm,
And rouse the city to besiege the doors.
2ND CHORUS. Rather forthwith go in ourselves, and prove

The murderer with the freshly-dripping blade.
3RD CHORUS. I add my pebble to thine. It is not well
That we delay. Fate hangs upon the moment.
4TH CHORUS. The event is plain, with this prelusive blood
They hang out signs of tyranny to Argos.
5TH CHORUS. Then why stay we? Procrastination they
Tramp underfoot; they sleep not with their hands.
6TH CHORUS. Not so. When all is dark, shall we unwisely
Rush blindfold on an unconsulted deed?
7TH CHORUS. Thou speakest well. If he indeed be dead,
Our words are vain to bring him back from Hades.
8TH CHORUS. Shall we submit to drag a weary life
Beneath the shameless tyrants of this house?
9TH CHORUS. Unbearable! and better far to die!
Death is a gentler lord than tyranny.
10TH CHORUS. First ask we this, if to have heard a groan
Gives a sure augury that the man is dead.
11TH CHORUS. Wisdom requires to probe the matter well:
To guess is one thing, to know another.
12TH CHORUS. So wisely spoken. With full-voiced assent
Inquire we first how Agamemnon fares.

(*The scene opens from behind, and discovers* CLYTEMNESTRA *standing over the dead bodies of* AGAMEMNON *and* CASSANDRA)

CLYTEM. I spoke to you before; and what I spoke
Suited the time; nor shames me now to speak
Mine own refutal. For how shall we entrap
Our foe, our seeming friend, in scapeless ruin,
Save that we fence him round with nets too high
For his o'erleaping? What I did, I did
Not with a random inconsiderate blow,
But from old Hate, and with maturing Time.
Here, where I struck, I take my rooted stand,
Upon the finished deed: the blow so given,
And with wise forethought so by me devised,
That flight was hopeless, and to ward it vain.
With many-folding net, as fish are caught,
I drew the lines about him, mantled round
With bountiful destruction; twice I struck him,
And twice he groaning fell with limbs diffused
Upon the ground; and as he fell, I gave
The third blow, sealing him a votive gift
To gloomy Hades, saviour of the dead.
And thus he spouted forth his angry soul,
Bubbling a bitter stream of frothy slaughter,
And with the dark drops of the gory dew
Bedashed me; I delighted nothing less
Than doth the flowery calix, full surcharged
With fruity promise, when Jove's welkin down
Distils the rainy blessing. Men of Argos,
Rejoice with me in this, or, if ye will not,
Then do I boast alone. If e'er 'twas meet
To pour libations to the dead, he hath them
In justest measure. By most righteous doom,
Who drugged the cup with curses to the brim,
Himself hath drunk damnation to the dregs.
CHORUS. Thou art a bold-mouthed woman. Much we marvel
To hear thee boast thy husband's murder thus.
CLYTEM. Ye tempt me as a woman, weak, unschooled.
But what I say, ye know, or ought to know,
I say with fearless heart. Your praise or blame
Is one to me. Here Agamemnon lies,
My husband, dead, the work of this right hand—
The hand of a true workman. Thus it stands.

STROPHE

CHORUS. Woman! what food on wide earth growing
Hast thou eaten of? What draught
From the briny ocean quaffed,
That for such deed the popular breath
Of Argos should with curses crown thee,
As a victim crowned for death?
Thou hast cast off: thou hast cut off
Thine own husband: thou shalt be
From the city of the free
Thyself a cast-off: justly hated
With staunch hatred unabated.

CLYTEM. My sentence thou hast spoken; shameful flight,
The citizens' hate, the people's vengeful curse:
For him thou hast no curse, the bloody man
Who, when the fleecy flocks innumerous pastured,
Passed the brute by, and sacrificed my child,
My best-beloved, fruit of my throes, to lull
The Thracian blasts asleep. Why did thy wrath,
In righteous guerdon of this foulest crime,
Not chase this man from Greece? A greedy ear
And a harsh tongue thou hast for me alone.
But mark my words, threats I repay with threats;
If that thou canst subdue me in fair fight,
Subdue me; but if Jove for me decide,
Thou shalt be wise, when wisdom comes too late.

ANTISTROPHE

CHORUS. Thou art high and haughty-hearted,
And from lofty thoughts within thee
Mighty words are brimming o'er:
For thy sober sense is madded
With the purple-dripping gore;
And thine eyes with fatness swell
From bloody feasts: but mark me well,
Time shall come, avenging Time,
And hunt thee out, and track thy crime:
Then thou, when friends are far, shalt know
Stroke for stroke, and blow for blow.

CLYTEM. Hear thou this oath, that seals my cause with right:
By sacred Justice, perfecting revenge,
By Até, and the Erinnys of my child,
To whom I slew this man, I shall not tread
The threshold of pale Fear, the while doth live
Ægisthus, now, as he hath been, my friend,
Stirring the flame that blazes on my hearth,
My shield of strong assurance. For the slain,
Here lieth he that wronged a much-wronged woman,
Sweet honey-lord of Trojan Chryseids.
And for this spear-won maid, this prophetess,
This wise diviner, well-beloved bed-fellow,
And trusty messmate of great Agamemnon,
She shares his fate, paying with him the fee
Of her own sin, and like a swan hath sung
Her mortal song beside him. She hath been
Rare seasoning added to my banquet rare.

STROPHE I

CHORUS. O would some stroke of Fate — no dull disease
Life's strings slow-rending,
No bed-bound pain — might bring, my smart to soothe,
The sleep unending!
For he, my gracious lord, my guide, is gone,
Beyond recalling;
Slain for a woman's cause, and by the hands
Of woman falling.

STROPHE II

O Helen! Helen! phrenzied Helen,
Many hearts of thee are telling!
Damned destruction thou hast done,
There where thousands fell for one
'Neath the walls of Troy!

ANTISTROPHE II

Bloomed from thee the blossom gory
Of famous Agamemnon's glory;
Thou hast roused the slumbering strife,
From age to age, with eager knife,
Watching to destroy.

STROPHE III

CLYTEM. Death invoke not to relieve thee
From the ills that vainly grieve thee!
Nor, with ire indignant swelling,
Blame the many-murdering Helen!
Damned destruction did she none,
There, where thousands fell for one,
'Neath the walls of Troy.

ANTISTROPHE I

O god that o'èr the doomed Atridan halls
With might prevailest,
Weak woman's breast to do thy headlong will
With murder mailest!
O'er his dead body, like a boding raven,
Thou tak'st thy station,
Piercing my marrow with thy savage hymn
Of exultation.

ANTISTROPHE III

CLYTEM. Nay, but now thou speakest wisely;
This thrice-potent god precisely
Works our woe, and weaves our sorrow.
He with madness stings the marrow,
And with greed that thirsts for blood;
Ere to-day's is dry, the flood
Flows afresh to-morrow.

STROPHE IV

CHORUS. Him, even him, this terrible god, to bear
These walls are fated;
From age to age he worketh wildly there
With wrath unsated.
Not without Jove, Jove cause and end of all,
Nor working vainly.
Comes no event but with high sway the gods
Have ruled it plainly.

STROPHE V.

CHORUS. O the king! the king! for thee
Tears in vain my cheek shall furrow,
Words in vain shall voice my sorrow!
As in a spider's web thou liest;
Godless meshes spread for thee,
An unworthy death thou diest!

STROPHE VI

CHORUS. There, even there thou liest, woe's me, outstretched
On couch inglorious;
O'er thee the knife prevailed, keen-edged, by damned
Deceit victorious.

STROPHE VII

CLYTEM. Nay, be wise, and understand;
Say not Agamemnon's wife
Wielded in this human hand
The fateful knife.
But a god, my spirit's master,
The unrelenting old Alastor
Chose this wife, his incarnation,
To avenge the desecration
Of foul-feasting Atreus; he
Gave, to work his wrath's completion,
To the babes this grown addition.

ANTISTROPHE IV

CHORUS. Thy crime is plain: bear thou what thou hast merited,
Guilt's heavy lading;
But that fell Spirit, from sire to son inherited,
Perchance was aiding.
Black-mantled Mars through consanguineous gore
Borne onwards blindly,
Old horrors to atone, fresh Murder's store
Upheaps unkindly.

ANTISTROPHE V

O the king! the king! for thee
Tears in vain my cheek shall furrow,
Words in vain shall voice my sorrow!
As in a spider's web thou liest;
Godless meshes spread for thee,
An unworthy death thou diest.

ANTISTROPHE VI

CHORUS. There, even there, thou liest, woe's me, outstretched
On couch inglorious!
O'er thee the knife prevailed, keen-edged, by damned
Deceit victorious.

ANTISTROPHE VII

CLYTEM. Say not thou that he did die
By unworthy death inglorious;
Erst himself prevailed by damned
Deceit victorious,
Then when he killed the deep-lamented
Iphigenía, nor relented
When for my body's fruit with weeping
I besought him. Springs his reaping
From what seed he sowed. Not he
In Hades housed shall boast to-day;
So slain by steel as he did slay.

STROPHE VIII

CHORUS. I'm tossed with doubt, on no sure counsel grounded,
With fear confounded.
No drizzling drops, a red ensanguined shower,
Upon the crazy house, that was my tower,
Comes wildly sweeping,
On a new whetstone whets her blade the Fate
With eyes unweeping.

STROPHE IX

CHORUS. O Earth, O Earth, would thou hadst yawned,
And in thy black pit whelmed me wholly,
Ere I had seen my dear-loved lord
In the silver bath thus bedded lowly!
Who will bury him? and for him
With salt tears what eyes shall brim?
Wilt thou do it — thou, the wife
That slew thy husband with the knife?
Wilt thou dare, with blushless face,
Thus to offer a graceless grace?
With false show of pious moaning,
Thine own damned deed atoning?

STROPHE X

CHORUS. What voice the praises of the godlike man
Shall publish clearly?

And o'er his tomb the tear from eyelids wan
Shall drop sincerely?

STROPHE XI

CLYTEM. In vain thy doubtful heart is tried
With many sorrows. By my hand
Falling he fell, and dying died.
I too will bury him; but no train
Of mourning men for him shall plain
In our Argive streets; but rather
In the land of sunless cheer
She shall be his convoy; she,
Iphigenía, his daughter dear.
By the stream of woes swift-flowing,
Round his neck her white arms throwing,
She shall meet her gentle father,
And greet him with a kiss.

ANTISTROPHE VIII

CHORUS. Crime quitting crime, and which, the more profanely
Were questioned vainly;
'Tis robber robbed, and slayer slain, for, though
Oft-times it lag, with measured blow for blow
Vengeance prevaileth,
While great Jove lives. Who breaks the close-linked woe
Which Heaven entaileth?

ANTISTROPHE IX

CHORUS. O Earth, O Earth, would thou hadst yawned,
And in thy black pit whelmed me wholly,
Ere I had seen my dear-loved lord
In the silver bath thus bedded lowly!
Who will bury him? and for him
With salt tears, what eyes shall brim?
Wilt thou do it? thou, the wife
That killed thy husband with the knife?
Wilt thou dare, with blushless face,
Thus to offer a graceless grace?
With false show of pious moaning
Thine own damned deed atoning?

ANTISTROPHE X

CHORUS. What voice the praises of the god-like man
Shall publish clearly?
And o'er his tomb the tear from eyelids wan
Shall drop sincerely?

ANTISTROPHE XI

CLYTEM. Cease thy cries. Where Heaven entaileth,
Thyself didst say, woe there prevaileth.
But for this tide enough hath been
Of bloody work. My score is clean.
Now to the ancient stern Alastor,
That crowns the Pleisthenids with disaster,
I vow, having reaped his crop of woe
From me, to others let him go,
And hold with them his bloody bridal,
Of horrid murders suicidal!
Myself, my little store amassed
Shall freely use, while it may last,
From murdering madness healed.

Enter ÆGISTHUS

ÆGIS. O blessed light! O happy day proclaiming
The justice of the gods! Now may I say
The Olympians look from heaven sublime, to note
Our woes, and right our wrongs, seeing as I see
In the close meshes of the Erinnyes tangled
This man — sweet sight to see! — prostrate before me,
Having paid the forfeit of his father's crime.
For Atreus, ruler of this Argive land,
This dead man's father — to be plain — contending
About the mastery, banished from the city
Thyestes, his own brother and my father.
In suppliant guise back to his hearth again
The unhappy prince returned, content if he
Might tread his native acres, not besprent
With his own blood. Him with a formal show
Of hospitality — not love — received
The father of this dead, the godless Atreus;
And to my father for the savoury use
Of festive viands gave his children's flesh
To feed on; in a separate dish concealed
Were legs and arms, and the fingers' pointed tips,
Broke from the body. These my father saw not;
But what remained, the undistinguished flesh,
He with unwitting greed devoured, and ate
A curse to Argos. Soon as known, his heart
Disowned the unholy feast, and with a groan
Back-falling he disgorged it. Then he vowed
Dark doom to the Pelopidae, and woes
Intolerable, while with his heel he spurned
The supper, and thus voiced the righteous curse:
THUS PERISH ALL THE RACE OF PLEISTHENES!
See here the cause why Agamemnon died,

And why his death most righteous was devised
By me; for I, Thyestes' thirteenth son,
While yet a swaddled babe, was driven away
To houseless exile with my hapless sire.
But me avenging Justice nursed, and taught me,
Safer by distance, with invisible hand
To reach this man, and weave the brooded plot,
That worked his sure destruction. Now 'tis done;
And gladly might I die, beholding him,
There as he lies where Vengeance trapped his crimes.

CHORUS. Ægisthus, that thou wantonest in the woe
Worked by thy crime I praise not. Thou alone
Didst slay this man, and planned the piteous slaughter
With willing heart. So say'st thou: but mark well,
Justice upon thy head the stony curse
Shall bring avoidless from the people's hand.

ÆGIS. How? Thou who sittest on the neathmost bench,
Speak'st thus to me who ply the upper oar?
'Tis a hard task to teach an old man wisdom,
And dullness at thy years is doubly dull;
But chains and hunger's pangs sure leeches are,
And no diviner vends more potent balms
To drug a doting wit. Have eyes, and see,
Kick not against the pricks, nor vainly beat
Thy head on rocks.

CHORUS. (*to* CLYTEMNESTRA). Woman how couldst thou dare,
On thine own hearth to plot thy husband's death;
First having shamed his bed, to welcome him
With murder from the wars?

ÆGIS. Speak on; each word shall be a fount of tears,
I'll make thy tongue old Orpheus' opposite.
He with sweet sounds led wild beasts where he would,
Thou where thou wilt not shalt be led, confounding
The woods with baby cries. Thou barkest now,
But, being bound, the old man shall be tame.

CHORUS. A comely king wert thou to rule the Argives!
Whose wit had wickedness to plan the deed,
But failed the nerve in thy weak hand to do it.

ÆGIS. 'Twas wisely schemed with woman's cunning wit
To snare him. I, from ancient date his foe,
Stood in most just suspicion. Now, 'tis done;
And I, succeeding to his wealth, shall know
To hold the reins full tightly. Who rebels
Shall not with corn be fatted for my traces,
But, stiffly haltered, he shall lodge secure
In darkness, with starvation for his mate.

CHORUS. Hear me yet once. Why did thy dastard hand
Shrink from the deed? But now his wife hath done it,
Tainting this land with murder most abhorred,
Polluting Argive gods. But still Orestes
Looks on the light; him favouring Fortune shall
Nerve with one stroke to smite this guilty pair.

ÆGIS. Nay, if thou for brawls art eager, and for battle, thou shalt know —

CHORUS. Ho! my gallant co-mates, rouse ye! 'tis an earnest business now!
Quick, each hand with sure embracement hold the dagger by the hilt!

ÆGIS. I can also hold a hilted dagger — not afraid to die.

CHORUS. DIE! — we catch the word thou droppest; lucky chance, if thou wert dead!

CLYTEM. Not so, best-beloved! there needeth no enlargement to our ills.
We have reaped a liberal harvest, gleaned a crop of fruitful woes,
Gained a loss in brimming measure: blood's been shed enough to-day.
Peacefully, ye hoary Elders, enter now your destined homes,
Ere mischance o'ertake you, deeming WHAT IS DONE HATH SO BEEN DONE,
AS IT BEHOVED TO BE; contented if the dread god add no more,
He that now the house of Pelops smiteth in his anger dire.
Thus a woman's word doth warn ye, if that ye have wit to hear.

ÆGIS. Babbling fools are they; and I forsooth must meekly bear the shower,
Flowers of contumely cast from doting drivellers, tempting fate!

O! if length of hoary winters brought discretion, ye should know
Where the power is; wisely subject you the weak to me the strong.

CHORUS. Ill beseems our Argive mettle to court a coward on a throne.

ÆGIS. Shielded now, be brave with words; my deeds expect some future day.

CHORUS. Ere that day belike some god shall bring Orestes to his home.

ÆGIS. Feed, for thou hast nothing better, thou and he, on empty hope.

CHORUS. Glut thy soul, a lusty sinner, with sin's fatness, while thou may'st.

ÆGIS. Thou shalt pay the forfeit, greybeard, of thy braggart tongue anon.

CHORUS. Oh, the cock beside its partlet now may crow right valiantly!

CLYTEM. Heed not thou these brainless barkings. While to folly folly calls,
Thou and I with wise command shall surely sway these Argive halls.

—*Translated from the Greek of Aeschylus (525–456 B.C.) by John Stuart Blackie.*

Riders to the Sea

JOHN MILLINGTON SYNGE

SCENE—*An island off the west of Ireland.*

Cottage kitchen, with nets, oilskins, spinning wheel, some new boards standing by the wall, etc. CATHLEEN, *a girl of about twenty, finishes kneading cake, and puts it down in the pot oven by the fire; then wipes her hands, and begins to spin at the wheel.* NORA, *a young girl, puts her head in at the door.*

NORA (*in a low voice*). Where is she?

CATHLEEN. She's lying down, God help her, and may be sleeping, if she's able.

(NORA *comes in softly, and takes a bundle from under her shawl.*)

CATHLEEN (*spinning the wheel rapidly*). What is it you have?

NORA. The young priest is after bringing them. It's a shirt and a plain stocking were got off a drowned man in Donegal.

(CATHLEEN *stops her wheel with a sudden movement, and leans out to listen.*)

NORA. We're to find out if it's Michael's they are, sometime herself will be down looking by the sea.

CATHLEEN. How would they be Michael's, Nora? How would he go the length of that way to the Far North?

NORA. The young priest says he's known the like of it. "If it's Michael's they are," says he, "you can tell herself he's got a clean burial by the grace of God, and if they're not his, let no one say a word about them, for she'll be getting her death," says he, "with crying and lamenting."

(*The door which* NORA *half-closed is blown open by a gust of wind.*)

CATHLEEN (*looking out anxiously*). Did you ask him would he stop Bartley going this day with the horses to the Galway fair?

NORA. "I won't stop him," says he, "but let you not be afraid. Herself does be saying prayers half through the night, and the Almighty God won't leave her destitute," says he, "with no son living."

CATHLEEN. Is the sea bad by the white rocks, Nora?

NORA. Middling bad, God help us. There's a great roaring in the west, and it's worse it'll be getting when the tide's turned to the wind. (*She goes over to the table with the bundle.*) Shall I open it now?

CATHLEEN. Maybe she'd wake up on us, and come in before we'd done. (*Coming to the table.*) It's a long time we'll be, and the two of us crying.

NORA (*goes to the inner door and listens*). She's moving about on the bed. She'll be coming in a minute.

CATHLEEN. Give me the ladder, and I'll put them up in the turf loft, the way she won't know of them at all, and maybe when the tide turns she'll be going down to see would he be floating from the east.

(*They put the ladder against the gable of the chimney;* CATHLEEN *goes up a few steps and hides the bundle in the turf loft.* MAURYA *comes from the inner room.*)

MAURYA (*looking up at* CATHLEEN *and speaking querulously*). Isn't it turf enough you have for this day and evening?

CATHLEEN. There's a cake baking at the fire for a short space (*throwing down the turf*) and Bartley will want it when the tide turns if he goes to Connemara.

(NORA *picks up the turf and puts it round the pot oven.*)

MAURYA (*sitting down on a stool at the fire*). He won't go this day with the wind rising from the south and west. He won't go this day, for the young priest will stop him surely.

NORA. He'll not stop him, Mother, and I heard Eamon Simon and Stephen Pheety and Colum Shawn saying he would go.

MAURYA. Where is he itself?

NORA. He went down to see would there be another boat sailing in the week, and I'm thinking it won't be long till he's here now, for the tide's turning at the green head, and the hooker's tacking from the east.

CATHLEEN. I hear someone passing the big stones.

NORA (*looking out*). He's coming now, and he in a hurry.

BARTLEY (*comes in and looks round the room; speaking sadly and quietly*). Where is the bit of new rope, Cathleen, was bought in Connemara?

CATHLEEN (*coming down*). Give it to him, Nora; it's on a nail by the white boards. I hung it up this morning, for the pig with the black feet was eating it.

NORA (*giving him a rope*). Is that it, Bartley?

MAURYA. You'd do right to leave that rope, Bartley, hanging by the boards. (BARTLEY *takes the rope.*) It will be wanting in this place, I'm telling you, if Michael is washed up tomorrow morning, or the next morning, or any morning in the week, for it's a deep grave we'll make him by the grace of God.

BARTLEY (*beginning to work with the rope*). I've no halter the way I can ride down on the mare, and I must go now quickly. This is the one boat going for two weeks or beyond it, and the fair will be a good fair for horses I heard them saying below.

MAURYA. It's a hard thing they'll be saying below if the body is washed up and there's no man in it to make the coffin, and I after giving a big price for the finest white boards you'd find in Connemara. (*She looks round at the boards.*)

BARTLEY. How would it be washed up, and we after looking each day for nine days, and a strong wind blowing a while back from the west and south?

MAURYA. If it wasn't found itself, that wind is raising the sea, and there was a star up against the moon, and it rising in the night. If it was a hundred horses, or a thousand horses you had itself, what is the price of a thousand horses against a son where there is one son only?

BARTLEY (*working at the halter, to* CATHLEEN). Let you go down each day, and see the sheep aren't jumping in on the rye, and if the jobber comes you can sell the pig with the black feet if there is a good price going.

MAURYA. How would the like of her get a good price for a pig?

BARTLEY (*to* CATHLEEN). If the west wind holds with the last bit of the moon, let you and Nora get up weed enough for another cock for the kelp. It's hard set we'll be from this day with no one in it but one man to work.

MAURYA. It's hard set we'll be surely the day you're drownd'd with the rest. What way will I live and the girls with me, and I an old woman looking for the grave?

(BARTLEY *lays down the halter, takes off his old coat, and puts on a newer one of the same flannel.*)

BARTLEY (*to* NORA). Is she coming to the pier?

NORA (*looking out*). She's passing the green head and letting fall her sails.

BARTLEY (*getting his purse and tobacco*). I'll have half an hour to go down, and you'll see me coming again in two days, or in three days, or maybe in four days if the wind is bad.

MAURYA (*turning round to the fire, and putting her shawl over her head*). Isn't it a hard and cruel man won't hear a word from an old woman, and she holding him from the sea?

CATHLEEN. It's the life of a young man to be going on the sea, and who would listen to an old woman with one thing and she saying it over?

BARTLEY (*taking the halter*). I must go now quickly. I'll ride down on the red mare, and the gray pony'll run behind me. . . . The blessing of God on you. (*He goes out.*)

MAURYA (*crying out as he is in the door*). He's gone now, God spare us, and we'll not see him again. He's gone now, and when the black night is falling I'll have no son left me in the world.

CATHLEEN. Why wouldn't you give him

your blessing and he looking round in the door? Isn't it sorrow enough is on everyone in this house without your sending him out with an unlucky word behind him, and a hard word in his ear?

(MAURYA *takes up the tongs and begins raking the fire aimlessly without looking round.*)

NORA (*turning toward her*). You're taking away the turf from the cake.

CATHLEEN (*crying out*). The Son of God forgive us, Nora, we're after forgetting his bit of bread. (*She comes over to the fire.*)

NORA. And it's destroyed he'll be going till dark night, and he after eating nothing since the sun went up.

CATHLEEN (*turning the cake out of the oven*). It's destroyed he'll be, surely. There's no sense left on any person in a house where an old woman will be talking forever.

(MAURYA *sways herself on her stool.*)

CATHLEEN (*cutting off some of the bread and rolling it in a cloth; to* MAURYA). Let you go down now to the spring well and give him this and he passing. You'll see him then and the dark word will be broken, and you can say "God speed you," the way he'll be easy in his mind.

MAURYA (*taking the bread*). Will I be in it as soon as himself?

CATHLEEN. If you go now quickly.

MAURYA (*standing up unsteadily*). It's hard set I am to walk.

CATHLEEN (*looking at her anxiously*). Give her the stick, Nora, or maybe she'll slip on the big stones.

NORA. What stick?

CATHLEEN. The stick Michael brought from Connemara.

MAURYA (*taking a stick* NORA *gives her*). In the big world the old people do be leaving things after them for their sons and children, but in this place it is the young men do be leaving things behind for them that do be old.

(*She goes out slowly.* NORA *goes over to the ladder.*)

CATHLEEN. Wait, Nora, maybe she'd turn back quickly. She's that sorry, God help her, you wouldn't know the thing she'd do.

NORA. Is she gone round by the bush?

CATHLEEN (*looking out*). She's gone now. Throw it down quickly, for the Lord knows when she'll be out of it again.

NORA (*getting the bundle from the loft*). The young priest said he'd be passing tomorrow, and we might go down and speak to him below if it's Michael's they are surely.

CATHLEEN (*taking the bundle*). Did he say what way they were found?

NORA (*coming down*). "There were two men," says he, "and they rowing round with poteen before the cocks crowed, and the oar of one of them caught the body, and they passing the black cliffs of the north."

CATHLEEN (*trying to open the bundle*). Give me a knife, Nora, the string's perished with the salt water, and there's a black knot on it you wouldn't loosen in a week.

NORA (*giving her a knife*). I've heard tell it was a long way to Donegal.

CATHLEEN (*cutting the string*). It is surely. There was a man in here a while ago — the man sold us that knife — and he said if you set off walking from the rocks beyond, it would be seven days you'd be in Donegal.

NORA. And what time would a man take, and he floating?

(CATHLEEN *opens the bundle and takes out a bit of a stocking. They look at them eagerly.*)

CATHLEEN (*in a low voice*). The Lord spare us, Nora! isn't it a queer hard thing to say if it's his they are surely?

NORA. I'll get his shirt off the hook the way we can put the one flannel on the other. (*She looks through some clothes hanging in the corner*) It's not with them, Cathleen, and where will it be?

CATHLEEN. I'm thinking Bartley put it on him in the morning, for his own shirt was heavy with the salt in it (*pointing to the corner*). There's a bit of a sleeve was of the same stuff. Give me that and it will do.

(NORA *brings it to her and they compare the flannel.*)

CATHLEEN. It's the same stuff, Nora; but if it is itself aren't there great rolls of it in the shops of Galway, and isn't it many another man may have a shirt of it as well as Michael himself?

NORA (*who has taken up the stocking and counted the stitches, crying out*). It's Michael, Cathleen, it's Michael; God spare his soul, and what will herself say when she hears this story, and Bartley on the sea?

CATHLEEN (*taking the stocking*). It's a plain stocking.

NORA. It's the second one of the third pair I knitted, and I put up threescore stitches, and I dropped four of them.

CATHLEEN (*counts the stitches*). It's that number is in it (*crying out*). Ah, Nora, isn't it a bitter thing to think of him floating that way to the Far North, and no one to keen him but the black hags that do be flying on the sea?

NORA (*swinging herself round, and throwing out her arms on the clothes*). And isn't it a pitiful thing when there is nothing left of a man who was a great rower and fisher, but a bit of an old shirt and a plain stocking?

CATHLEEN (*after an instant*). Tell me is herself coming, Nora? I hear a little sound on the path.

NORA (*looking out*). She is, Cathleen. She's coming up to the door.

CATHLEEN. Put these things away before she'll come in. Maybe it's easier she'll be after giving her blessing to Bartley, and we won't let on we've heard anything the time he's on the sea.

NORA (*helping* CATHLEEN *to close the bundle*). We'll put them here in the corner.

(*They put them into a hole in the chimney corner.* CATHLEEN *goes back to the spinning wheel.*)

NORA. Will she see it was crying I was?

CATHLEEN. Keep your back to the door the way the light'll not be on you.

(NORA *sits down at the chimney corner, with her back to the door.* MAURYA *comes in very slowly, without looking at the girls, and goes over to her stool at the other side of the fire. The cloth with the bread is still in her hand. The girls look at each other, and* NORA *points to the bundle of bread.*)

CATHLEEN (*after spinning for a moment*). You didn't give him his bit of bread?

(MAURYA *begins to keen softly, without turning round.*)

CATHLEEN. Did you see him riding down?

(MAURYA *goes on keening.*)

CATHLEEN (*a little impatiently*). God forgive you; isn't it a better thing to raise your voice and tell what you seen, than to be making lamentation for a thing that's done? Did you see Bartley, I'm saying to you.

MAURYA (*with a weak voice*). My heart's broken from this day.

CATHLEEN (*as before*). Did you see Bartley?

MAURYA. I seen the fearfulest thing.

CATHLEEN (*leaves her wheel and looks out*). God forgive you; he's riding the mare now over the green head, and the gray pony behind him.

MAURYA (*starts, so that her shawl falls back from her head and shows her white tossed hair. With a frightened voice*). The gray pony behind him.

CATHLEEN (*coming to the fire*). What is it ails you, at all?

MAURYA (*speaking very slowly*). I've seen the fearfulest thing any person has seen, since the day Bride Dara seen the dead man with a child in his arms.

CATHLEEN AND NORA. Uah. (*They crouch down in front of the old woman at the fire.*)

NORA. Tell us what it is you seen.

MAURYA. I went down to the spring well, and I stood there saying a prayer to myself. Then Bartley came along, and he riding on the red mare with the gray pony behind him. (*She puts up her hands, as if to hide something from her eyes.*) The Son of God spare us, Nora!

CATHLEEN. What is it you seen?

MAURYA. I seen Michael himself.

CATHLEEN (*speaking softly*). You did not, mother; it wasn't Michael you seen, for his body is after being found in the Far North, and he's got a clean burial by the grace of God.

MAURYA (*a little defiantly*). I'm after seeing him this day, and he riding and galloping. Bartley came first on the red mare; and I tried to say, "God speed you," but something choked the words in my throat. He went by quickly; and "the blessing of God on you," says he, and I could say nothing. I looked up then, and I crying, at the gray pony, and there was Michael upon it — with fine clothes on him, and new shoes on his feet.

CATHLEEN (*begins to keen*). It's destroyed we are from this day. It's destroyed, surely.

NORA. Didn't the young priest say the Almighty God wouldn't leave her destitute with no son living?

MAURYA (*in a low voice, but clearly*). It's little the like of him knows of the sea. . . .

Bartley will be lost now, and let you call in Eamon and make me a good coffin out of the white boards, for I won't live after them. I've had a husband, and a husband's father, and six sons in this house – six fine men, though it was a hard birth I had with every one of them and they coming to the world – and some of them were found and some of them were not found, but they're gone now the lot of them. . . . There were Stephen and Shawn, were lost in the great wind, and found after in the Bay of Gregory of the Golden Mouth, and carried up the two of them on the one plank, and in by that door.

(*She pauses for a moment, the girls start as if they heard something through the door that is half open behind them.*)

NORA (*in a whisper*). Did you hear that, Cathleen? Did you hear a noise in the north-east?

CATHLEEN (*in a whisper*). There's some-one after crying out by the seashore.

MAURYA (*continues without hearing any-thing*). There was Sheamus and his father, and his own father again, were lost in a dark night, and not a stick or sign was seen of them when the sun went up. There was Patch after was drowned out of a curagh that turned over. I was sitting here with Bartley, and he a baby, lying on my two knees, and I seen two women, and three women, and four women coming in, and they crossing themselves, and not saying a word. I looked out then, and there were men coming after them, and they holding a thing in the half of a red sail, and water dripping out of it – it was a dry day, Nora – and leav-ing a track to the door.

(*She pauses again with her hand stretched out toward the door. It opens softly and old women begin to come in, crossing themselves on the threshold, and kneeling down in front of the stage with red petticoats over their heads.*)

MAURYA (*half in a dream, to* CATHLEEN). Is it Patch, or Michael, or what is it at all?

CATHLEEN. Michael is after being found in the Far North, and when he is found there how could he be here in this place?

MAURYA. There does be a power of young men floating round in the sea, and what way would they know if it was Michael they had, or another man like him, for when a man is nine days in the sea, and the wind blowing, it's hard set his own mother would be to say what man was it.

CATHLEEN. It's Michael, God spare him, for they're after sending us a bit of his clothes from the Far North.

(*She reaches out and hands* MAURYA *the clothes that belonged to* MICHAEL. MAURYA *stands up slowly, and takes them in her hands.* NORA *looks out.*)

NORA. They're carrying a thing among them and there's water dripping out of it and leaving a track by the big stones.

CATHLEEN (*in a whisper to the women who have come in*). Is it Bartley it is?

ONE OF THE WOMEN. It is surely, God rest his soul.

(*Two younger women come in and pull out the table. Then men carry in the body of* BARTLEY, *laid on a plank, with a bit of a sail over it, and lay it on the table.*)

CATHLEEN (*to the women, as they are do-ing so*). What way was he drowned?

ONE OF THE WOMEN. The gray pony knocked him into the sea, and he was washed out where there is a great surf on the white rocks.

(MAURYA *has gone over and knelt down at the head of the table. The women are keening softly and swaying themselves with a slow movement.* CATHLEEN *and* NORA *kneel at the other end of the table. The men kneel near the door.*)

MAURYA (*raising her head and speaking as if she did not see the people around her*). They're all gone now, and there isn't any-thing more the sea can do to me. . . . I'll have no call now to be up crying and pray-ing when the wind breaks from the south, and you can hear the surf is in the east, and the surf is in the west, making a great stir with the two noises, and they hitting one on the other. I'll have no call now to be going down and getting holy water in the dark nights after Samhain, and I won't care what way the sea is when the other women will be keening. (*To* NORA.) Give me the holy water, Nora, there's a small sup still on the dresser.

(NORA *gives it to her.*)

MAURYA (*drops* MICHAEL'*s clothes across* BARTLEY'*s feet, and sprinkles the holy water over him*). It isn't that I haven't prayed for you, Bartley, to the Almighty God. It isn't that I haven't said prayers in the dark night till you wouldn't know what I'd be saying; but it's a great rest I'll have now, and it's time surely. It's a great rest I'll have now, and great sleeping in the long nights after Samhain, if it's only a bit of wet flour we do have to eat, and maybe a fish that would be stinking.

(*She kneels down again, crossing herself, and saying prayers under her breath.*)

CATHLEEN (*to an old man*). Maybe yourself and Eamon would make a coffin when the sun rises. We have fine white boards herself bought, God help her, thinking Michael would be found, and I have a new cake you can eat while you'll be working.

THE OLD MAN (*looking at the boards*). Are there nails with them?

CATHLEEN. There are not, Colum; we didn't think of the nails.

ANOTHER MAN. It's a great wonder she wouldn't think of the nails, and all the coffins she's seen made already.

CATHLEEN. It's getting old she is, and broken.

(MAURYA *stands up again very slowly and spreads out the pieces of* MICHAEL'S *clothes beside the body, sprinkling them with the last of the holy water.*)

NORA (*in a whisper to* CATHLEEN). She's quiet now and easy; but the day Michael was drowned you could hear her crying out from this to the spring well. It's fonder she was of Michael, and would anyone have thought that?

CATHLEEN (*slowly and clearly*). An old woman will be soon tired with anything she will do, and isn't it nine days herself is after crying and keening, and making great sorrow in the house?

MAURYA (*puts the empty cup mouth downwards on the table, and lays her hands together on* BARTLEY'S *feet*). They're all together this time, and the end is come. May the Almighty God have mercy on Bartley's soul, and on Michael's soul, and on the souls of Sheamus and Patch, and Stephen and Shawn (*bending her head*); and may He have mercy on my soul, Nora, and on the soul of everyone is left living in the world.

(*She pauses, and the keen rises a little more loudly from the women, then sinks away.*)

MAURYA (*continuing*). Michael has a clean burial in the Far North, by the grace of the Almighty God. Bartley will have a fine coffin out of the white boards, and a deep grave surely. What more can we want than that? No man at all can be living forever, and we must be satisfied.

(*She kneels down again and the curtain falls slowly.*)

—*John Millington Synge, Irish (1871–1909).*

~ ❂ ~

The Death of Eve

WILLIAM VAUGHN MOODY

ACT I

A rocky mountain slope rising on the left by rude stone stairs towards Cain's stronghold in Nod, dimly discerned above. On the right and toward the rear the scene falls away to a wide desert country. In the foreground, on the lowest level of a terraced plateau, is a rudely sculptured well-curb. Behind this, on a higher level, a stone seat, known as the Seat of Supplication, faces the Mercy-Seat, a throne of the same primitive type, carved from the living rock. The mountain stair, which rises behind the Mercy-Seat toward the distant city, is barred, at a higher elevation, by a stone gateway.

On the Seat of Supplication sits Eve, shrouded. Her hand rests on the shoulder of Jubal, who sits at her feet. As the scene progresses, the sky gradually fades, then flushes with the colors of a tropical sunset.

EVE. Yea, Jubal?
JUBAL. Nothing, mother.
EVE. Thy lips moved;
The hand upon thy knee rose as in question,
And fell as in reply.
JUBAL. I slept; I dreamed.
EVE. Sleep yet; the heat is strong.

(*Pause.*)

JUBAL. I dreamed he came
At sunset here unto the Strangers' well
To know us and our errand.
EVE. Soon or late,
They say, his custom.
JUBAL. Aye, they say it is.
But why should travelers seeking to great
Cain,

Wayfarers, weaponed only with their hands,
Or come, as now, in love and duty to him — ?
EVE. I know not. 'T is his pleasure.
JUBAL. And 't is thine,
Being, O mother, even what thou art
And hast been what thou hast been — 't is thy will
To hide thy name, to wait obscurely here,
Where at Cain's feet the desert suppliants
Kneel to unload their wrongs!
EVE. Question it not.
JUBAL. But I must wonder.
EVE. Wonder not either.
JUBAL. Nay,
I will not then.

(*Pause.*)

At home 't will be the hour
When the parched flocks climb faster as they feed,
Scenting the upper cisterns. Downward again
Toward folding time.
EVE. (*Gazing at the sky.*) I think the sun at home
Sits not in such a shoulder of the heavens.
We fetch him all about and overtake him.
JUBAL. So do we.

(*Pause.*)

Is it well that we do so?
EVE. We make our journey; if the lights of Heaven
Move from their ancient places as we move,
Let the Heavens look to it; it is none of ours!
JUBAL. Thou sayest; and Jubal rises to thy words. —
At home Eve never spake so.
EVE. Jubal, Jubal,
I know not what is in me! I am changed
From all I was. Or am I back-returned
Through life's deep changes to my changeless self?
Look in my face, and say.
JUBAL. Thy face is changed; —
And that behind the face, which looketh through,
Peers like a stranger.
EVE. Since our latest guide,
Standing upon the red cliffs yester dawn,
Pointed and said, "Cain's City!" —
JUBAL. Longer ago
The change came.
EVE. (*Murmurs.*) Know'st me.
JUBAL. O mother, since the night
When thy loud whisper startled me awake,
And following thee in wonder from the tents
I found our camels houseled for the start,
And the wide moonlit stretches calling us, —
Since then, through desert perils, famine, beasts,
More ravenous men, and thirst the crown of terrors,
Thou art Eve, not that bowed soul we knew,
Not that great worn and patient majesty;
But like an angel going on an errand
Not for his lord but for his longing self,
Who burns from morn to morn and deep to deep
Toward his place, so Eve is, since the time
She fled, by night and stealth, from Adam's tent,
And took the wilderness. — To what purpose took,
She keeps from me too long!
EVE. Have I not said?
To look upon my first-born's face again,
And know him what he grows to.
JUBAL. I am content.
EVE. Jubal believes I scant him?
JUBAL. I am content!
There is no scanting in thee. Silence, speech,
Giving, withholding, doing, and letting be,
Sit on thee lovely as a change of jewels
And bounteous as the River of the South:
Forget my lips that they were troublesome.
EVE. Why do you hold my words for less than truth?
JUBAL. Nay.
EVE. Say on.
JUBAL. Freely?
EVE. Say right freely on.
JUBAL. Eve knows ere Jubal speaks, yet he will speak.
At home lies bed-rid Adam in the tent,
With wasted hands and slow blank eyes agrope
To find the sole things they remember plain,
The hands and eyes of Eve, who never failed
To meet that need till now. And Eve sits here,
Within her eyes a high and thirsty light,
Brighter than burning Adam ever stilled
In that far storied morning of their loves;
Within her hands — Alas, I speak too near!
EVE. Speak on.
JUBAL. And in her hands — I know not how
To say my meaning.
EVE. Say, though.
JUBAL. On her hands,
That lie so quiet and so empty here,

A look as if they seized the hands of God,
And dragged Him with her through his holy mountain
Unwillingly to do her glorious will.
EVE. (*Draws him to her.*) Nearer. Bend back. Now by sweet Adah's pangs,
It is a goodly boy's face. Is it strong
As it is fresh and goodly?
JUBAL. It is his
Whom Eve chose out, a boy, and left unchosen
Others, firm men.
EVE. What if she tried them first,
The others, the firm men? Seth, Enoch, all?
Thy father Lamech, too, and Irad, too?
Firm men, firm men! I shook them from their firmness!
Sinews and blood and heart-strings, at a word
Melted to water! At a woman's word,
Touching far off her cloudy enterprise!

(*Pause.*)

One more is left to try!

(*Long pause.*)

JUBAL. Mother, I saw
When thou did'st speak with Seth.
EVE. (*Startled.*) Saw'st? Thou saw'st?
JUBAL. I saw but heard not. Am no eavesdropper,
No peep-thief neither, but mine eyes had looked
Before I knew 't was secret.
EVE. (*Low.*) When was this?
JUBAL. Early the third night ere we fled away
From Adam's tent-place. In the camel-close
I sat among the beasts, for one was big
And near her time. 'T was star-dusk, very still;
Only the beast groan'd low and human-like,
Or nosed my stroking hand and held her peace.
Thereby, over against, a voice, thy voice,
Never the words, only the naked voice,
Heavy and scant, as if a half-dead tongue
Fashioned its meaning stiffly. Then the moon
Stood all at once her height upon the hill
And showed thy form and Seth's within the gate.
Thy face I could not see, but saw thy hands
Raised unto Seth, pleading or threatening,
And saw the face of Seth, with mortal fear
Disfeatured,—updrawn forehead, loosened jaw,
And staring eyes gone empty.—Then, as one
Who shakes the night-witch Lilith from his breast,
He came into his manhood, took thy hands
And drew them down, kissed thee, and spoke thee small
As one bespeaks a trance-awakened child,
Softly and small, until it knows itself
And its familiar things. So went ye hence.
And next day and the next Seth's eyes were on thee,
Frightened and vague; but Eve walked straight her ways
Not heeding him.
EVE. Who heeds a broken staff?
—Nay, nay, that wrongs him! Broken not, but bent,
No more but bent a little.—A good son,
Tender and meek and patient with all men,
And most with me, child, most of all with me!
I blame not Seth. Let him look to it, then,
He blame me not. O would 't were by with blame!
When has the oak been proud against the willow?
Or the light aspen shook her jeweled hands
In scorn of the removeless mountain pine?
To every soul his stature, girth, and grain,
Each sovereign to its end: the use is all.—
And yet, and yet—Look you, he thought me crazed!
So did the others, or were ripe to think.
Some day they would have risen and stoned me forth,
To be like those banned women of the rocks,
Who haunt the savage summits of our land,
Aye, you have seen them! They were human once,
Daughters and sisters, mothers and right wives;
And now they sit there, high up in the sun
On noon-steeped crags, naked but for their hair,—
She-satyrs laughing with their satyr mates:
I might have sat aloft with them by now,
And thought not strange to be there.

(*Pause.*)

JUBAL. Eve must know
Another thing, ere I have cleared my life.
EVE. Clear thee!
JUBAL. I saw her speak with Abel too.
EVE. (*Looking fearfully about.*) Thou sunlight shelter us! Abel?
JUBAL. His ghost.
EVE. The night we fled away?

JUBAL. Thou know'st 't is so.
EVE. How know? Albeit I blench to hear it said,
Yet I do talk with Abel, my lost son,
By night and day, forever!
JUBAL. Day and night,
Life, death, the hid, the shown, are in thy knowledge.
In his simplicity hath Jubal spoke,
And now his heart is free.
EVE. Not yet! Not yet!
Abel? Thine eyes saw Abel? His risen ghost?
JUBAL. The thousand eyeballs of this flesh, they saw,
What time my crowding spirits, wild and pale,
Made all my curdled blood from head to heel
Their tower of outlook.
EVE. By the altar? Was it?
JUBAL. Yea, yea.
EVE. Cain's altar?
JUBAL. Abel's altar mound;
Though both be eat to nothing with the years.
EVE. Aye, aye, the eating years! At first I thought
I was mistook; 't would be the farther mound.
After these years they should let something grow there.
JUBAL. Though salt were sown not, nor the stones not flung,
No plant would spring within the awful vale
Where murder first was born. — I followed thee
Scarce hoping to come thence again alive,
And crouched apart while Eve did call on Abel;
Thrice did she cry on him.
EVE. Ere I cried once
I knew 't was vain. He would not let me go.
Living and dead they failed me!

(*Pause.*)

JUBAL. Lamech too!
EVE. Ah, for thy father Lamech, honor him!
Good father, and good husband to his wives!
They point him and he goes, what man would not?
Both fair, and one right good; Adah is good.
Loves not much farther outward than her door,
But that is well for women, — narrow love,
Narrow and deep.
JUBAL. Then 't is not well with Eve,
Who loves as wide as life, though deep as death.
EVE. Once, once! No longer now, these years of years!
They would not have me so. — Great years of years
Since Eve in anguish called her wild heart in
And taught it what to do. — Yet, yet, thou sayest —
What said'st thou of me?
JUBAL. What thyself said first,
O mighty Eve! Thy soul is back returned
Through life's sad changes to that joy it was
When first it soared into the new-made light.
EVE. Seemeth almost it is so. — Years of years!

(*Pause.*)

JUBAL. Hark! Heard'st thou?
EVE. Women coming to the well.
JUBAL. (*As the voices approach.*) Mother, beseech ye, be as if we slept!
For they will mock thee as before they did.
EVE. I care not for their mocking.
JUBAL. Be besought!
CHORUS OF WATER-BEARERS. (*Two groups, one of young, the other of old women, sing in alternation.*)
OLD WOMEN. *Like a hunter in his mountain walks the purpose of the Lord!*
YOUNG WOMEN. *O, the prey alert and little, be its littleness its ward!*
OLD WOMEN. *Like a linnet on the lime-twig sings the bow-string on the bow.*
YOUNG WOMEN. *O, the serpent when he sitteth on his coils singeth so!*
CHORUS. (*In unison.*) *Even though, even though!*
Be it ours to flee and double, be it His to bring us low.
Blessed she who tastes his arrow and lies broken in the wood.
She has fled, she has fallen: it is good.

(*They fill their jars at the well.*)

FIRST WOMAN. What makes the witch-wife hither? Have ye heard?
SECOND WOMAN. What make they all, who sit on yonder stone
To wait Cain's coming?
THIRD WOMAN. The old tale.
Some sons of jackals, loping sharp-set by,
Have sniffed her hut, and stopped unbid to meat;
Some neighbor hath put sheep's-bane in her well;
An idle whirlwind, rising up to play,

Has wantoned with her little patch of dates,
And left it bleeding.
SECOND WOMAN. Has none spoke with her?
FOURTH WOMAN. Aye, to much purpose! She is sullen dumb,
Sun-crazed, or hath a spirit. 'T was my son
Who found her in the gates. "Cain!" would she cry.
And "Cain!" again. By what she mumbled else
She will be outlandish.
FIFTH WOMAN. By raiment too.
And then the starveling camel, did you mark?
Longer in limb and muzzle than our breed,
The pelt more reddish.
FOURTH WOMAN. Let us stir her up!

(*Some go toward Eve and Jubal. Abdera, a young girl, puts herself in their path.*)

ABDERA. Ye shall not mock them!
FOURTH WOMAN. What! Weaned since, swaddling-clout?
SECOND WOMAN. The maid says well. They are all travel-spent.
They sit like souls foredone for weariness.
FOURTH WOMAN. They feign! They feign! Saw ye? The stripling peeps
And lowers beneath his arm!
SECOND WOMAN. And let them feign.
Take up your jars, and take your singing up.
(*All except Abdera mount the path behind.*)
FOURTH WOMAN. (*Looking back.*) Look yon! Look yon! The little harlotry
Stops for her hire.
THIRD WOMAN. 'T will be the lad that pays!
CHORUS OF WATER-BEARERS. (*As they ascend the slope behind, and pass through the gate.*)
Till the coming up of day,
Till the cool night flee away,
Till the Hunter rises up to pursue,
O my sisters, we will laugh, we will play!
Though He wake and walk anear us,
He is mused, He will not hear us;
Though He wanders lone and late,
He will never hear how mate whispereth to darkling mate.
Yea, and though He hear, and though!
Will He judge us, even so?
He is mused, He walketh harmless. In the shadowy mountain hid
We will lure our lovers to us, even as our mothers did!
When He cometh forth at dawn, and His anger burns anew,
As our hunted mothers did, even so we will do:
Flee and crouch and feint and double, leap the snare or gnaw it through!
EVE. Who art thou? Tell us.
ABDERA. Abdera.
EVE. Whose daughter?
ABDERA. Till now the daughter of captivity,
A leaf blown in by tempest of those wars
Which crushed the stem I grew to.
EVE. And from now?
ABDERA. (*Kneeling.*) If thou art earthly and hast need of love,
Thy servant and thy daughter. — O receive me!

(*Pause.*)

JUBAL. Mother, she waits. Wilt thou not speak to her?
Her countenance, that was so bright, is fallen.
(*Eve draws Abdera near and bends over her.*)
ABDERA. (*To Eve.*) Why weep'st thou?

(*Pause.*)

(*To Jubal.*) O why weeps she? At my words
She looked beyond, with thinking, sightless eyes,
As I have seen my father's gods to look
Out of the dreaming stone; and then — alas,
Tell me what 't is you weep for!
EVE. (*Lifting her head.*) Sweet my child,
My fair new daughter, 't is for thee I weep.
ABDERA. No cause. See, I am glad now; all is well.
EVE. Therefore I weep, that we all three are glad,
And all is well, thrice well.

(*She draws Jubal to her, also.*)

(*To Jubal.*) What say you, boy?
Hearts change! Here is a stranger in thy place.
— There is a wondrous vine called Jealousy;
It springs between this pulse-beat and the next,
And hangs the roofs of heaven with bitterness.
Does Jubal feel it growing?
JUBAL. Nay, — I know not.
EVE. (*To Abdera.*) He knows not. Then, alas, we know too well!
JUBAL. (*Touching his heart.*) Mother, the Vine! I felt it springing here
Even as thou spakest, and hanging as it were
The roofs of Heaven, but not with bitterness.

EVE. There may be other seeds I know not of,
That spring as fast, and load their trellises
With leaves of light and lovely fruits between.
ABDERA. Some I have seen with fairy vans outspread
Sail high, and yet no wind, or good as none.
And some have hands and fingers: they will cling
To sheep or goat or ass, all one to them
So they be carried where they long to be.
EVE. Aye, where they long to be! Winds of the world,
Blow as ye will and blow what seeds ye will
If this kind mingle in.
JUBAL. She wonders at us.
Speak to her.
EVE. Wonder'st thou? Are we so strange?
ABDERA. I was brought young to Cain's fierce citadel.
And since, day after day, season by season,
Now stark alone and now in bands of trouble,
The hurt and hungry people gather in,
To crouch upon this stone. Some I have feared,
Yea, hated for the wickedness in them,
Being myself made wicked by that hate;
Some seemed to fade to nothing where they sat,
Scarce there at all, and hardly gone, forgotten;
Of some I asked in wonder, "Who are ye?
What countrymen, what errand, and what cheer?"
My heart not beating till the answer fell,
And long, long wildly beating to remember.—
To-day I came, and lo, nothing to wonder,
Nothing to question of! Two trees of life
Planted from always unto everlasting
By the still waters; and my quiet soul,
With outspread hands and upturned countenance
In the bright shadow, saying, "Glory, glory!"
JUBAL. (*Low.*) One tree.
ABDERA. (*Low to Jubal.*) Thy parable?
JUBAL. (*Indicating Eve, who sits in reverie.*)
She is the tree;
And I with thee stand singing in her shadow.
EVE. (*Rousing.*) What think the people of their master Cain?
ABDERA. That he is master; that he is lord and king.
EVE. No more?
ABDERA. Some mutter darkly and apart.
EVE. What should they mutter of?
ABDERA. (*Looking about as in fear.*)
That Cain is old;
That as he grows more weak he grows more cruel.
JUBAL. Cruel? To thee?
ABDERA. The storm that breaks the tower
Roots not the little hyssop from the chink.
Nor do I hold him cruel of his will,
But in his withered blood a poison works,
Distilling wrath and panic.—Long ago,
In his hot youth, upon some jealousy
He slew his brother. Then the angry gods
Set on his brow a sign to know him by;
And since, in hopeless visions of his bed,
Or when the priestesses rave round his car,
Gashing themselves, and to their frothèd mouths
Setting the adder's mouth, or when he lairs,
His madness on, with demons of the waste—
The patient gods, the unwithdrawing gods,
Dropwise and piecemeal wean his soul from him.
EVE. Old? Madness? Withered? Girl, can'st thou not speak plain?
Mutter not thou, whate'er yon rebels do!
(*To Jubal.*) Did she say "old"?
JUBAL. What has she said amiss?
—She shrinks with fear.
EVE. Old!
JUBAL. Seth, though the later born,
Thou knowest, Seth too—
EVE. Seth too? And what of him?
Yes, yes, all's clear. Seth truly! That is well.
Children as ye two be! To the dropped lamb
The yearling from the father of the flock
Stands not a hair apart in reverend time.—
And cruel, say they? He was never so!
Hasty and hot, a blood where rage would run
As swift as sun-fire through dry prairie grass,
But cruel—never that.—Thy shoulder, Jubal.
A faintness is come on me. 'T will pass, 't is passing.
Old—old and cruel.

(*She rouses again.*)

Girl, girl! What else was't, then?
Weak? As he grows more weak? Why I have seen
The young oak shudder in his wrestling arms,
And its torn roots come groaning from the hill,
When for a sport he did but breathe himself.

– Ages of years! – Thrust from his gate like dogs!
Weak, weak, indeed, to be afeard of us.

(*Her head sinks on Jubal's shoulder; her eyes close. Abdera kisses the hem of Eve's garment, rises, and takes up her jar.*)

ABDERA. She set me in the garden of her love;
At first I grew, as ne'er by so sweet clime
A tree was told to prosper and put forth;
But at the last not so. – Sour were my fruits,
Apples of ignorance.

(*She turns to go.*)

JUBAL. Where wilt thou go?
Stay yet! I thought – O ye two spake such things!
I thought – and thou wilt leave us now again?
ABDERA. Let me not leave you! Whither should I go?
I know naught else. – I have been always here.
JUBAL. (*He draws Abdera to him.*)
O never leave us more!
ABDERA. (*Yielding to his embrace.*)
Fair, fair my brother.
JUBAL. – Know'st thou nor guessest nothing who she is?
ABDERA. She is the tree 'neath which we sing together,
Herself in all her boughs to Heaven singing.
JUBAL. She sings not to the Heavens, but to the earth;
Once hoarsely, like a look-out overwatched,
Now in a new voice, battle-songs and birth-songs.
ABDERA. When first I looked on her I seemed to sit
A child and sleepy in my father's tent;
The wandering prophet sang, and 'neath my lids
I saw great shapes rise out of elder time;
Beginning earth, with other beasts and birds;
Æonian forests where winged serpents flew;
Seasons not ours, and long since fallen gods.
JUBAL. She saw creation's morning; she will stay
To watch the everlasting twilight fall. –
ABDERA. Hush! –
JUBAL. (*Looking about.*) None to hear.
ABDERA. (*Pointing in fear.*)
Look where above the sand
The hot light dances. Should it dance for naught?
JUBAL. Know ye more gods but One?
ABDERA. My fathers knew;
And sometimes I – Hush! Bow thee! They walk, they hear!
JUBAL. (*Looking upward, toward the citadel.*)
Not gods, but men, come from the eyrie town,
Slow down the mountain stair! One walks between,
And two that stead him upon either hand;
And some before with singing, and yet some
Behind, with spears and banners.
ABDERA. (*Whispers to Eve.*) Cain, he comes!

(*All three rise and gaze upward. The procession descends. Cain, aged and broken, seats himself in the throne-seat surrounded by his armed men, while Eve, veiled but for the eyes, stands supported by Jubal and Abdera. The chief officer at Cain's side lifts his hand.*)

CHIEF OFFICER. The king is come into his judgment seat –
If any in this presence have a cause,
The time is gracious, and the king gives ear.
EVE. (*Gazing from Cain to one and another of his men.*)
Seek not to try me, who am overtried!
Is this the king, or sits one in his room?
CAIN. What says the woman?
OFFICER. If thou be the king.
CAIN. What should be answered?
OFFICER. Mock not thy servant, lord,
Nor thy great self.
CAIN. (*Mutters.*)
Still king, or not yet wakened
From dreaming such a matter.
(*To Eve.*) Unveil thy face.
Uncover thee and speak.

(*Eve drops her veil. Cain stares with slow gathering terror, then rises.*)

Thou hag of hell,
Glare not upon me with those caverned eyes!
(*To his officers.*)
Whoever has done this, his life shall pay.
Do ye spread out your nets among the dead,
And toll them here out of the earth and air
To daunt me, and to shake me from myself?
(*To the priests who advance.*)
Try her if she be human! Speak the word!
Make the dread sign!
EVE. Make not your sign on me!
For on your bloods and bodies ere the birth
Myself have made on you a mightier sign.
– Cain, Cain, dost thou not know me? Look again!

(*Cain, gazing at her stupefied, makes a sign to his men to leave him.*)

CAIN. (*As they linger.*)
Back to the city! Away! Go, every one!

(*They mount the steps, with backward looks. An aged warrior lingers. Jubal and Abdera, clinging together in awe and fear, slip away down the desert path behind.*)

WARRIOR. By one who in suspicion has grown grey,
And all to shield and warn thee, lord, be warned.
Many and subtle are thine enemies.
In many shapes they hunt thee for thy soul.

CAIN. Leave us alone! Go, go! Alone, alone.

(*The old man mounts the steps. Cain, with averted head, mutters to Eve.*)

God knows I know thee not.

EVE. (*Approaching nearer.*)
Cain, Cain, look up!
Grieve no more; pity my grief. Eve knows thou knowest.

(*He draws her to him, and sinks on the bench,—she at his feet, her head buried in his knees. Song above, distant.*)

CAIN. (*As the singing ceases.*)
The first that I remember of my life
Was such a place, such a still afternoon,
I sitting thus, thy bright head in my knees,
And such a bird above us as him yonder
Who dips and hushes, lifts and takes his note.
I know not what child's trespass I had done,
Nor why it drove the girl out of thy face,
Clutched at thy heart with panic, and in thine eyes
Set shuddering love.

EVE. O my first-born, my child!
O herald star in the wilderness appearing,
After the nine-fold moon of dubious speech,
Proclaiming silence soon to fall in Heaven—
The everlasting silence that soon did fall,
When by me lay thy little frame of breathing,
And blind and weak thou foundest out the breast!

CAIN. There was a day when winter held the hills
And all the lower places looking sunward
Knew that the spring was near. Until that day
I had but walked in a boy's dream and dazzle,
And in soft darkness folded on herself
My soul had spun her blind and silken house.
It was my birthday, for at earliest dawn
You had crept to me in the outer tent,
Kissed me with tears and laughter, whispering low
That I was born, and that the world was there,
A gift you had imagined and made for me.
Now, as I climbed the morning hills, behold,
Those words were true: the world at last was there;
At last 't was mine, and I was born at last.
I walked, and on my shoulders and my reins
Strength rang like armor; I sat, and in my belly
Strength gnawed like a new vinegar; I ran
And strength was on me like superfluous wings,
Even the six wings of the cherubim,
Twice twain to cover me and twain to fly.

EVE. O green tree! O the young man in the house!
A gold frontlet of pride, and a green cedar!

(*Pause.*)

CAIN. (*His voice changes.*)
I knew that you would come.

EVE. Lo, I am here.

CAIN. And knew 't would be too late.

EVE. In full good time.

CAIN. Look on me; look once. Is this crazed frame
The thing Eve bare in joy? Let us climb down
Unto the sheep-pools; I will sit apart,
And do thou lean thee out over the pool
And look and tell me if that face be hers
Who waited while yon silence fell in Heaven
And Cain came forth the doors.—Too late, too late!

EVE. Late, late,—but in fair time! Never too late.

(*Silence.*)

CAIN. They told me Eve was dead.

EVE. (*Startled.*) They told—alas,
Who told?

CAIN. Chance-comers, wanderers from the waste.

EVE. And do chance-wandering tongues still sound this name?

CAIN. Here one and there one, never aught aright,
But every man his tale, after his heart.

EVE. Even in the tent my people do me this.
Even in my face, almost! Yea, I have lain,
Bowed on thy father's breast, and heard them do it.

I feigned to sleep; I heard them. And look you, son,
Here is the worst. Their glozing tales once heard,
Once pored on through long watches of the night,
They rise before my soul like very truth,
As bright, as fair, as strange, — almost, almost!

CAIN. (*Darkly.*)
On Adam's breast? How long since?

EVE. The road is far,
And hard to find. Also, the second moon,
One camel sickened, and his pining mate
Went laggard. — Son, what ails thee?

CAIN. He lives?

EVE. Who lives?
— Aye, aye, he lives. Hast heard aught, child? He lives,
Surely thy father lives.

CAIN. And thou art here?

EVE. But most for his sake. — Listen while I tell!
— Why do you harshly thrust my hands away,
And lift your clenched hands trembling to the sky
With wild and smothered words?

CAIN. (*Pushing her from him.*)
I know you not,
Unclasp my knees. — I thought you were yourself
Yours, therefore mine at last. It is not so.
His, his, the same as when he cursed me forth
And Eve stood stockish, never one plea made,
One wail set up, one gesture of farewell,
No more than from a stone!

EVE. She was a stone;
As afterwards, long years, a frozen stone.
No seasons and no weather on the earth;
Sun, moon, and stars dead in a field of death;
And in her dead heart, nothing, nothing, nothing!
After long years, she wakened, knew herself,
Rose up to wring some profit from her days,
Conceived again, and once again brought forth;
Yea, saw the teeming race in circles kindle
Roaring to God, a flame of generation.
From out the tossing battle of that fire
Flashed seldom and again wild news of thee,
And one red instant, ere night drove between,
Thy form would stand gigantic in the glare,
Islanded huge among thine enemies, —
As when the ice-bear rears upon the floe
And swings her flailing paws against the pack,
Or when the sea-volcano from his loins
Shakes climbing cities.

CAIN. Better, better far
That Eve had never sought, nor Cain been found,
Than thus, being together, to be sundered
More than by ice-fields or the raving sea.

EVE. O Cain, how sundered? — Look on me! Kiss my lips,
And feel it is not so.

CAIN. (*Repulsing her.*) 'T is not so then.
There is no gateway shut between our souls,
No watchers stationed, and no lifted sword
Flaming forever!

EVE. Ere I fled to thee
I knelt in fear by Abel's altar-mound
And begged his leave to go. His spirit rose,
Or seemed to rise, and seemed to threaten me.
The same night on thy father's breast I bowed,
And spoke of this my journey. In his eyes,
If still they seemed to know me who I was,
Kindled none other knowledge. — Albeit I rose,
And fled away, and suffered much, and came,
Thy name among the nations my sole guide,
Desire of thee my strength and company.
— Be glad of me! O lovingly entreat me!
Make all my meanings good, till such a time
As these our wounds are healed. Then if, perchance,
Our hearts at ease, I something should unveil
My stranger will, my cloudier purposes —

CAIN. Yea, yea, I wondered what would lurk behind!
— Not for my sake, that were too mere a mother.
— Wills, purposes! Lo, am I taken in
Because your tongue veers off and skirts the quick?
Do I not hear the words you dare not speak
Thunder above your speech? Do not your eyes
Hover and flinch and crawl upon my brow,
Seeking, and shuddering off to turn again
In sick and deadly search? — Look then! 'T is here.

(*He pushes back the head-band, baring the sign.*)

It is not faded, though these hands have shed
Rivers of kindred blood to wash it off.
— 'T was this you came for: bring your errand full.
Look and begone!

(*Eve, staring at the Sign, has fainted. Her head drops on Cain's shoulder. He tries to lift her head.*)

Pitiful God not, this!
She could not come after the endless years,
To go so soon. — Mother, thou wilt not deal
Thus much unkindness to an unkind son,
As leave him when harsh words were on his lips.
Of old, when in our rage we thrust thee out,
Thou wouldst return again, unreconciled
To harshness and to wrath. O do it now,
In pity!
EVE. (*Waking.*) Where am I?
CAIN. Thou living Dread,
Whose fountains yet flow mercy!
EVE. What hath passed? —
A faintness overfell me. Often of late,
But never quite so deep, so heavy deep.
I am far come, child. Lead me to thy house.
Much must be said, but there is time for all.
Nothing in haste; nothing before its hour.
CAIN. Wait till I call my people.
EVE. (*Rising.*) I am strong.
We will go up together. — I have dreamed
Of this our going-in, and spite of all
'T is very like my dream, yea, very like. —
Thy people cursed me, stoned and thrust me down;
But now I walk under thy mighty shadow. —

(*She pauses in their ascent, and looks out over the desert.*)

Where will my children be?
CAIN. Thy children, mother?
EVE. Jubal, my travel-mate, a stripling boy
But great of heart; and Abdera, thy maid.
CAIN. Mine?
EVE. So: thou hast forgot or never knew.
Leave them; no matter where. They cannot stray.
The sun will shepherd them.
CAIN. The sun is set.
EVE. The stars, then, pouring influence. — Lead me on.
Art thou faint, also? Two can make a strength.

(*They begin to mount the steps. Above, Azrael, the Death Angel, appears, slowly descending, as from the city. With his left hand he clasps to his breast the hilt of a long sword; in his right he holds a stalk of flowering asphodel. Eve, seeing him, shrinks back, drawing Cain with her. Azrael, gazing at the pair, lifts the asphodel and descends to the left by a desert path, disappearing behind the Seat of Supplication. Eve gazes at the apparition in terrified silence, points at it as it disappears, then hides her head in Cain's breast.*)

CAIN. What ails thee, mother? Why dost thou point and peer
And shrink away — ?
EVE. (*Whispers.*) Saw'st nothing?
CAIN. Where?
EVE. (*Pointing.*) Yonder.
And there, and yonder.
CAIN. Nothing.
EVE. Look again!

(*Eve stands with face averted, while Cain peers over where the path behind the Seat of Supplication descends hidden to the plain.*)

CAIN. Two by the sheep-wells walking.
EVE. Two?
CAIN. Thine eyes!
Thy lips, mother!
EVE. How many did ye say?
CAIN. Twain, boy and girl.
EVE. Lord, Lord!
CAIN. Mother, thy face — ?
EVE. And this my son saw nothing!
CAIN. What should I see?
EVE. Nothing. — I praise Him. Long years yet for thee, —
Fair years, till then. — Nothing. I praise Him!
CAIN. Thou hast endured too much. If in her house
And throne of rule that sovereign mind be shaken,
Yet night and sleep and the new-risen day —
EVE. Nor night nor day can help me who have seen
The angel of the Lord, the summoner.
There, there he stood, and lifted slowly up
His pallid flower, and without speech said, "Come!"
As once before in Adam's tent he did,
And Eve, beholding, rose and fled away,

To look on thee ere darkness. Son, thou strength,
Spread thy strong hands o'er this rebellious head,
That our two strengths yet for a little while
May hold against Jehovah! My fierce son,
Thou burning flame from childhood, look on me
And say that thou wilt do it, though the skies
Open to warn us back! Thy promise, Cain!
CAIN. What would ye of me, that these opening skies
And that up-startled Wrath — ?
EVE. I had a son
Who questioned his own wrath, the skies thereof,
His own heart's wrathful skies, what they were prone to,
And seeing where his will went, followed it.
I came to find that son. And shall I find him
But as the rest, whose marrow in their bones
Curdles to hear Eve's whisper? Nay, thou Cain,
Whose soul is as a torch blown back for speed,
'T is thou shalt light me on that fearful way
That I must go, and that I haste to go
Ere darkness falls forever.
CAIN. Though Cain were still
That flame which once he was, how should he light thee,
Not knowing of thy way nor of thine errand?
Fearful? And be it so. My goings-out
And comings-in be fearful. Tell me plain.
EVE. Plain will I tell thee, son. — There was a place —
There was a place — and it will still be there,
For nightly I am told so — there is a place
That once —
CAIN. Mother!
EVE. That once I knew —
CAIN. O woman!
EVE. Thou sayest. — A place that Eve the woman knew,
Once, far off, long ago, when she was young —
With him —
CAIN. Hush!
EVE. Young with him —
CAIN. Wilt thou be still?
EVE. Adam the man —
CAIN. Woe on thee!
EVE. Him the man
And her the woman, in their ignorance —
And still it waits there, waits for her to come,
Now she has gathered up a little knowledge. —
Be patient, child. — See, I am very patient.
I tell thee quietly I would go thither;
Ere darkness falls, Eve must go back again.
She hath an errand.
CAIN. Will thy lips cease now,
Ere they bring doomsday down?
EVE. Hast ever — listen —
Hast ever, in thy desert wanderings,
Seen, or had news? Seen mayhap afar off — ?
CAIN. Once, once!
EVE. Far off? Or near to?
CAIN. Near enough.
EVE. Ye stood and saw?
CAIN. Yea, verily.
EVE. How near?
CAIN. Flesh goes not nearer than this flesh went near,
Yet 't was far off.
EVE. How far?
CAIN. Far as a hawk
Up-wind can keep his wings set.
EVE. Very near!
— Saw'st thou — ?
CAIN. O mother, hush on what I saw!
Hush, for thy life's sake, for thy reason's sake.
— Night falls. Lean on me; let me lead thee home.
EVE. Home thou must lead me, to that wondrous home
That was and is and shall be till I come.
— Turn not away so! — Touching this same journey,
I humbly do beseech thee, look thereon,
And be well pleased to lend thy royal favor,
Thereto the needed beasts and muniments
Proportioned to the distance and the time;
This only being besought, that my twain children,
Jubal and her, go up with me along
Into the gaze and silence of the Lord,
And that our starting be by dawn to-morrow. —
Unless, by favor, thy decreeing lips
Should breathe "To-night" and do it. Might it be?
'T is but an hour to moonrise, and the moon
Is at her full, or nearly. Say'st "To-night?"
Aye, aye, thy silence cries I have a son!
— Tonight! That is right royal.
CAIN. Neither to-night,
Nor yet to-morrow, nor the day to come,
Nor any day till Cain, Eve's bloody son,
Gone brain-sick as his dam — Call to him then

And haply he will hear thee where he raves
Above his moaning nation! But for now—
EVE. Now, even now. So, I beseech no more.
But lay on thee my still and high command.
CAIN. I will not hear thee; cannot, dare not hear!
EVE. Thou wilt not hear me? Yea, but thou wilt hear!
Thy ears be not thy ears. I moulded them.
Thy life is not thy life. I gave it thee,
And do require it back. Thy beating heart
Beats not unto itself, but unto me,
Whose voice did tell it when to beat and how.
Thy deeds are not thy deeds. Ye conned them here,
Under this breast, where lay great store of deeds
Undone, for thee to choose from.

(*She uncovers the Sign on his forehead.*)

'T is not thy head
Weareth this Sign. 'T is my most cruel head,
Whose cruel hand, whose swift and bloody hand
Smote in its rage my own fair man-child down.
Not thy hand, Cain, not thine; but my dark hand;
And my dark forehead wears the sign thereof,
As now I take it on me.

(*She kisses him on the Sign.*)

CAIN. (*With bowed head.*) Peace, at last.
After these struggles, peace.
EVE. At dawn, O Cain?
CAIN. Whenever and wherever.
EVE. My great son!

(*Cain and Eve mount toward the gate, and pass through, out of sight. Jubal and Abdera appear from the valley, behind the Seat of Supplication, and mount toward the city. Under the gate Jubal stops and looks over the desert.*)

JUBAL. O Abdera, the strangeness of the world.
ABDERA. Not strange.—Strange, strange before; no longer so.
JUBAL. Look where the star leans flaming from his throne
And viewless worlds are suppliant in his porches.

(*They pass through the gate and disappear, climbing upward.*)

—*William Vaughn Moody, American (1869–1910).*

PART SIXTEEN

The Comedy of Manners

THE ESSENTIAL CHARACTER OF A PLAY is to be judged more by its prevailing tone than by its conclusion. By a common though uncritical use of the words tragedy and comedy, the former is sometimes understood to be a type of play that ends sadly, usually with death, and the latter, as one that terminates happily. This distinction describes the conclusion but not the play. The Greeks, who formulated their arts strictly, understood such matters differently. A large proportion of their tragedies end without violence and even with a joyous reconciliation of the dramatic struggle. All their comedies, it is true, end happily, usually with a dance and feasting. But, clearly, tragedy is constituted not by the nature of its ending but by its high seriousness, and comedy by its pervasive mirth. One type of play arouses pity and fear, the other laughter. The extension of the word comedy to mean any work, dramatic or nondramatic, with a happy ending, and the use of the term tragedy in the converse sense, actually arose in the early Middle Ages, when the drama itself was in abeyance. This terminology is reflected in the title given to Dante's poem, *The Divine Comedy.* It is unfortunate that two words only have been so often called upon to do duty for the entire prolific output of the theater. During the Elizabethan age, as now, for example, any play with very little humor but a pleasant or a sentimental tone or happy ending was called a comedy. While no really satisfactory word in English is to be found for such a production, the phrase "dramatic romance" is, perhaps, most descriptive.

The contrast between pure comedy and the romantic variety of play is aided by the first work given in the present section. *Takasago* is an anonymous Japanese drama of medieval origin belonging to the type known in Japan as "Noh" plays. Like so many theatrical productions in ancient or modern Europe, it is a serious love story ending in a wedding. Ceremonial and mythological elements are conspicuous. An oriental *Midsummer-Night's Dream,* the play is full of magic and of the poetry of fancy. While deeply marked with primitive Japanese superstitions necessarily obscure to most if not all Western readers, its charm and humanity keep it perennially fresh and enjoyable.

In contrast with *Takasago,* the three other plays here reproduced are true comedies in the sense that they abound in laughter and maintain an unmistakably humorous view of life. They may further be described as comedies of manners, since each so clearly voices the spirit of the country and people from which it springs. They enjoy the rich vitality derived from a faithful expression of the native spirit. Each is indigenous, racy, abounding in local color. Yet precisely because each dramatist has his roots so firmly in the soil of his own locality, he seems so much the abler in expressing human experiences intelligible throughout the civilized world. Their plays are imaginative as well as realistic, and universal as well as nationalistic; wherever they are produced they have the power to entertain.

No art form provides a clearer picture of national characteristics than comedy. This holds equally true of comedies for the screen or stage. Hence in achieving a truly cosmopolitan vein an appetite for a wide variety of comedies and a good familiarity with them constitutes one of the happiest possessions of a liberally educated man. It has often been said that the soul of a nation may be discerned in its humor. National eccentricities, according to a common use of the word in Shakespeare's day, for example, were even designated as national "humors."

Three brief European comedies which follow are chosen to lend the strongest confirmation to the foregoing statements. To make contrasts sharper, they all belong to approximately the same historical period, namely, to the early part of the present century. They represent in turn the idealistic and morally perturbed Russian spirit, the sunny and pastoral spirit of the Italians of Sicily, and the gay and sophisticated Hungarian spirit. In *An Incident* Leonid Nikolaievich Andreyev writes a burlesque of the old, ethically distraught Russia of the age of Tolstoy, as seen by young realists and radicals of the succeeding century. At first glimpse his play may even appear tragic. But as the reader or spectator enters further into the humorous irony of the piece, he recognizes it to be a spoofing of the shallow, romantic, and self-conscious imitation of the morality of Tolstoy and Dostoevski. This is a somewhat grim and typically Russian humor, tart and remarkably robust. Although the poor man who fancies himself a criminal and insists on his own punishment is actually a sick soul, in the eyes of the playwright, his audience and his reader he becomes wholly ridiculous.

The Jar, by Luigi Pirandello, delightfully depicts the genial, laughter-loving soul of the common people of Southern Italy. Its story is really implausible, its spirit farcical. Its innocent humor, so free from any gravity or moral responsibility, breathes the true genius of the old Italian culture. The entire scene is fragrant with the scent of the grape vines and odor of wines. Historically the play has its roots also in Italian drama going back at least to the Middle Ages, when Italy was for all Europe the mother of farce, puppetry and song.

The little comedy by the Hungarian, Ferenc Molnár, on the contrary, expresses the light and genial sophistication of life in the art-loving towns of central Europe. For over a century the theatrical life and indeed the artistic life generally, arrived at some of its most genial fruits in such culturally important cities as Budapest, Vienna, Prague and Salzburg. These were not only great centers for music and the theater, but for a highly animated and pleasure-loving intellectual class. Vienna, for example, in the nineteenth century gave the world the waltz. In the twentieth century it gave us the sprightly comedies of Arthur Schnitzler, of which *Anatol* is the most widely known. But no playwright more admirably expresses the lighter spirit of this urbane world than the fanciful, sentimental, light-hearted and eloquent Ferenc Molnár, a large number of whose plays have in recent years enlivened both the stage and screen in the United States.

Takasago

MOTOKIYO

Dramatis Personae

TOMONARI, *Guardian of the Shinto shrine of Aso, in Kiushiu*
AN OLD MAN, *Really the spirit of the Sumiyoshi fir-tree*
AN OLD WOMAN, *Really the spirit of the Takasago fir-tree*
THE GOD OF SUMIYOSHI
CHORUS

CHORUS. Now for the first time he ties the lace of his travelling garb:
His goal is distant many a long day's journey.

TOMONARI. Now, this is I, Tomonari, guardian of the shrine of Aso, in the province of Higo, in Kiushiu. Never having seen the capital, I have now made up my mind, and am going up to the capital. Moreover, I wish to take this opportunity of viewing the bay of Takasago, in Harima.

CHORUS. To-day he has made up his mind, and has donned his travelling raiment for a journey to a distant goal — the capital. With waves that rise along the shore, and a genial wind of spring upon the ship-path, how many days pass without a trace of him we know not, until at length he has reached the longed-for bay of Takasago, on the coast of Harima.

OLD MAN *and* OLD WOMAN (*chant*). The wind of spring that blows through the fir-tree of Takasago has gone down with the sun; the vesper bell is heard from the Temple of Onoye.

OLD WOMAN. The waves are hidden from us by the mist-enshrouded rocks.

BOTH. There is naught but the sound to mark the rise and fall of the tide.

OLD MAN. Whom can I take to be my friend? Except the fir-tree of Takasago, my ancient comrade, there is none to converse with me of the bygone days on which are ever-gathering white snows of forgetfulness. I grow older and older, accustomed to hear nothing but the wind in the fir-tree either when I rise or go to sleep in my nest of an aged crane, where the night-long moon sheds its rays, and the spring sends down its hoar-frosts. So I make my own heart my companion, and thus give utterance to my thoughts.

BOTH. Let us sweep away the fir-needles that lie beneath the tree, sleeve touching sleeve of our garments, whereon rest fallen leaves shaken down by the shore-wind asking their news of the firs.

. . . . .

TOMONARI. While waiting for some of the villagers to appear, an old man and an old woman have come hither. I pray you, old people, permit me to ask you a question.

OLD MAN. It is I whom you address? What is it you desire to know?

TOMONARI. Which is the tree that is called the fir-tree of Takasago?

OLD MAN. The very tree whose shade we are cleansing is the fir-tree of Takasago.

TOMONARI. The phrase "growing old together" is used of the Takasago and Suminoye fir-trees. But this place and Sumiyoshi (the same as Suminoye) are in provinces distant from one another. How then can they be called the fir-trees which "grow old together"?

OLD MAN. As you have deigned to observe, it is stated in the preface to the *Kokinshiu* that the fir-trees of Takasago and Suminoye make us feel as if they were growing old together. However that may be, here am I, an old man, who belong to Sumiyoshi, in the province of Settsu, while the old woman here is of this place. Be pleased to tell me, if you can, how that may be.

TOMONARI. Strange! I see you old couple here together. What mean you then by saying that you dwell apart, one in distant Suminoye, the other in Takasago, divided from one another by seashore, hill, and province?

OLD WOMAN. What an odd speech! Though many a mile of mountain and river separate them, the way of a husband and wife whose hearts respond to one another with mutual care, is not far apart.

. . . . .

OLD WOMAN. There is Suminoye.
OLD MAN. And here is Takasago.
TOMONARI. The fir-trees blend their hues.
OLD MAN. And the spring air —
TOMONARI. Is genial, while —

(*Here the chorus strikes in with a canticle which is chanted as the indispensable accompaniment of every regular Japanese wedding, and is one of the best known passages in Japanese literature. Figures representing the two old folks under the fir-tree with brooms in their hands are, on such oc-*

casions, set out on a sort of tray. This is a favourite subject of the Japanese artist.)

CHORUS. On the four seas
Still are the waves;
The world is at peace.
Soft blow the time-winds,
Rustling not the branches.
In such an age
Blest are the very firs,
In that they meet
To grow old together.
Vain indeed
Are reverent upward looks;
Vain even are words to tell
Our thanks that we were born
In such an age,
Rich with the bounty
Of our sovereign lord.

. . . . .

OLD MAN. I hear the the sound of the bell of Onoye, in Takasago.

CHORUS. The dawn is near,
And the hoar-frost falls
On the fir-tree twigs;
But its leaves' dark green
Suffer no change.
Morning and evening
Beneath its shade
The leaves are swept away,
Yet they never fail.
True it is
That these fir-trees
Shed not all their leaves;
Their verdure remains fresh
For ages long,
As the Masaka trailing vine;
Even amongst evergreen trees —
The emblem of unchangeableness —
Exalted is their fame
As a symbol to the end of time —
The fame of the fir-trees that have grown old together.

TOMONARI. And ye who have made known the bygone story of these ancient firs whose branches have indeed earned fame — tell me. I pray you, by what names are ye called.

OLD MAN *and* OLD WOMAN. Why conceal it longer; We are the spirits of the fir-trees of Takasago and Suminoye that have grown old together, manifested under the form of a married pair.

CHORUS. Wonderful! A miracle wrought by the fir-trees of this famous place!

OLD MAN *and* OLD WOMAN. Plants and trees are without souls —

CHORUS. Yet in this august reign —

OLD MAN *and* OLD WOMAN. Even for plants and trees —

CHORUS. Good is it to live
For ever and ever
In this land
Of our great sovereign,
Under his rule.
To Sumiyoshi, therefore,
He would now take his way
And there wait upon the god.
He embarks in a fisher's boat
That lies by the beach,
Where the waves of evening roll,
And spreading his sail
To the favouring breeze,
Puts out into the deep,
Puts out into the deep.

TOMONARI. From Takasago I set sail
In this skiff that lies by the shore,
And put forth with the tide
That goes out with the moon.
I pass under the lee
Of Awaji's shore,
I leave far behind me Naruwo,
And now I have arrived
At Suminoye.

(*The god of Sumiyoshi appears, and enters into a poetical dialogue with the chorus.*)

CHORUS. We give thanks for this manifestation;
Ever anew we will worship
Thy spirit with sacred dance
By Sumiyoshi's pure moonlight.
And now, world without end,
The extended arms of the dancing maidens
In sacerdotal robes
Will expel noxious influences;
Their hands folded to rest in their bosoms
Will embrace all good fortune;
The hymn of a thousand autumns
Will draw down blessings on the people,
And the song of ten thousand years
Prolong our sovereign's life.
And all the while,
The voice of the breeze,
As it blows through the firs
That grow old together,
Will yield us delight.

— *From the Japanese of Motokiyo (d. 1455), translated by W. G. Aston.*

An Incident

LEONID ANDREYEV

Characters

KRASNOBRUHOV, *a merchant*
GAVRILENKO, *a policeman*
POLICE OFFICIAL

Two persons take part in the action: a merchant, Krasnobruhov, who confesses his crime, and a police official. There is also a policeman, Gavrilenko, who brings in the repenting merchant, and some other living automata who carry him out.

The room resembles an unfurnished factory. The official barks abruptly into the telephone; his voice expresses anger and astonishment. Gavrilenko leads in the merchant, holding him respectfully, with two fingers only. Krasnobruhov is a fat, healthy-looking old man, with a red beard. He appears to be very much excited. He wears no hat, and his clothes are in suspicious disorder.

THE OFFICIAL (*at the telephone*). Who? What? Why, of course, I can hear you if I am speaking to you — the murdered? Oh, yes! Yes, yes, two of them — Of course I can hear you. What is it? What *are* the motives? Well? I can't understand a thing. Who ran away? The wounded man ran away? Say, what are you talking about? Where did the wounded man run to?

GAVRILENKO. Your Honor, so I brought him —

THE OFFICIAL. Don't bother me! Oh, yes, so one ran away, and you're bringing over the other — and what about the murderers? What? Ran away also? Look here, don't you try to get me all muddled up with those motives of yours! What's that? I can't make out a blessed thing. Listen to me! If you want to make the report — Do you hear me? — Go ahead and make it! Don't whistle through your nose at me. I'm not a clarinet. What? What music? No, no, I say, I'm not a clarinet. Do you hear? Hello! Oh, damn you! Hello! (*Hangs up the receiver, throwing an angry side-glance at* KRASNOBRUHOV. *Then sits down.*) Well? What do you want?

GAVRILENKO. So your Honor, if you will permit me to report, he blocked the traffic and the wagons. He came out in the middle of the market-place, right in the middle of the traffic, and hollered out that he was a merchant and had killed a man, and so I took him along.

THE OFFICIAL. Drunk? You old goat, drunk as a pig?

GAVRILENKO. Not at all, your Honor, quite sober. Only he stopped in the middle of the market-place, right in the road, and started hollering out, so that, your Honor, not a wagon could pass, and a big crowd collected. He hollered out, "I killed a human being, brethren, I confess!" And so I brought him over. It's his conscience, your Honor.

THE OFFICIAL. Why didn't you say that at the beginning, you blockhead? Let him go, Gavrilenko, don't hold him like a dog. Who are you?

KRASNOBRUHOV. Prokofi Karpovich Krasnobruhov, a merchant. (*Kneels down and says in a repentant tone*) I confess, brethren! Take me, bind me! I killed a human being!

THE OFFICIAL (*rising to his feet*). Oh! So that's what you are!

KRASNOBRUHOV. I confess, brethren, I confess! Let me atone for my sins! I can't stand it any longer! Take me, bind me — I killed a human being! I'm an unconfessed scoundrel, a criminal against nature! I killed a human being!

(*Lowers his head to the ground.*)

GAVRILENKO. That's the way he was hollering out there, your Honor, right in the middle of the traffic —

THE OFFICIAL. Shut up! Stand up, now! Tell me all about it. Whom did you kill?

KRASNOBRUHOV (*getting up heavily and smiting himself on the chest*). I murdered a human being. I want to atone for my crime. I can't stand it any more. It's too much for me. My conscience won't let me live, brethren. Come on, shave me![1]

THE OFFICIAL. Shave you!

KRASNOBRUHOV. Shave my head, put me in irons! I want to atone for my crime. (*Sobs aloud.*) I killed a human being. Forgive me, brethren!

(*Falls on his knees again and bows to the ground.*)

THE OFFICIAL. Up with you! Now talk like a sane man, will you?

GAVRILENKO. That's just the way he did

[1] In Russia, half of the head of a convict is shaved just before he is deported to Siberia. — Translator's Note.

up there, your Honor, and started hollering —

THE OFFICIAL. Shut up! What's your name? Is this your trunk?

KRASNOBRUHOV (*gets up again and wipes his tears and perspiration*). What trunk? I don't know about any trunk. We deal in vegetables. Oh, Lord! In vegetables.

THE OFFICIAL. What trunk! Don't know anything about the trunk, hey? But when you stuffed him into the trunk, you knew all about it, eh? And when you shipped his body by freight, you knew it, eh?

KRASNOBRUHOV. I don't know about any trunks. Wish I could get a drink of water. (*To* GAVRILENKO) Give me a drink of water, boy, I'm all hoarse. (*Sighs heavily.*) O — oh.

THE OFFICIAL (*to* GAVRILENKO). Stay where you are. And you don't know which trunk it is? Gavrilenko, how many trunks have we here?

GAVRILENKO. Four trunks, your Honor, and one suit case. We've opened three, your Honor, and haven't had time for the fourth yet.

THE OFFICIAL (*to the merchant*). Did you hear that?

KRASNOBRUHOV (*sighing*). I don't know about any trunks.

THE OFFICIAL. Where is yours then?

KRASNOBRUHOV. My what?

THE OFFICIAL. How should I know whom you killed there, or cut, or strangled? Where's the body?

KRASNOBRUHOV. The body? Oh, I guess it's all rotted away now. (*Falls on his knees again.*) I confess, brethren, I killed a human being! And buried the body, brethren. I thought I could deceive the people, but I see now that I can't do it. My conscience won't let me. I can't sleep or rest at all now. Everything's dark before my eyes, and all I have now is my suffering. I want to atone for my sins. Strike me, beat me!

THE OFFICIAL. Up with you! Speak plainly now!

KRASNOBRUHOV (*gets up and mops his face*). I am speaking plain enough, I reckon. I thought that after some time I'd forget it, perhaps, and find joy in life, and burn candles to the poor soul. But no! My torment is unnatural. I haven't a minute of rest. And every year it gets worse and worse. I thought it might pass away. And now I confess, brethren! I was sorry for the property. We deal in vegetables and I was ashamed for my wife and children. How could it happen so suddenly? I was a good man all the time, and then, a scoundrel, a murderer, a criminal against nature!

THE OFFICIAL. Speak to the point, I tell you!

KRASNOBRUHOV. But I am speaking to the point. Every night I cry and cry. And my wife says to me, says she, "What's the use of crying here, Karpich, and shedding tears on the pillows? Better go to the people and bow down to the ground and accept the suffering. What difference does it make to you?" says she. "You're pretty old already; let them send you to Siberia; you can live there, too. And we'll pray for you here. Go on, Karpich, go on!" So we cried together, and cried; and couldn't decide it. It's hard, it's frightful, brethren! When I look around me — We deal in vegetables; you know, carrots, and cabbages and onions. (*Sobs.*) And she says to me, "Go on, Karpich, don't be afraid. Drink some tea, have a little fun, and then go and bear your cross!" — And I tried doing it once. She gave me a clean shirt, and treated me to tea with honey, and combed my hair with her white hand, — but I couldn't do it! I was too weak! Lost my courage! I got as far as the market-place, and came out into the middle of the street, and suddenly a car came up — So I turned into a saloon. I confess, my friends, instead of repentance, I spent three days and three nights in the saloon, polishing the bar and licking the floor. I don't know where all that drink went to. That's what conscience does to you!

THE OFFICIAL. Yes. That's conscience for you, all right! But I'm very glad, very glad. — Gavrilenko, did you hear?

GAVRILENKO. That's just the way he was hollering there, your Honor.

THE OFFICIAL. Shut up! But go ahead, my friend.

KRASNOBRUHOV. I'm no friend, I'm an enemy of mankind, a criminal against nature. Take me, bind me! I killed a human being! I'm a murderer! Come now, bind me! Shave me!

THE OFFICIAL. Yes, yes, I'm very glad to see you repenting. Gavrilenko, do you happen to remember this case? What cases have we?

GAVRILENKO. Don't remember, your Honor!

KRASNOBRUHOV. Bind me!

THE OFFICIAL. Yes, yes, I can understand your noble impatience, but — And when did it happen? Of course, we know everything, but there are so many cases, you know! Look how many trunks we have. It's like a freight station — Whom did you — when was it?

KRASNOBRUHOV. When? Oh, I guess it must be about twenty-one years. Twenty-one and a little extra, maybe. About twenty-two, you might say.

THE OFFICIAL. Twenty-two? What do you want then?

KRASNOBRUHOV. I thought I'd get over it. But no! It gets worse and worse every year, more and more bitter every day. In the beginning I didn't have any visions at least. And now visions come to me. I confess, brethren, I'm a murderer!

THE OFFICIAL. But allow me — Twenty-two years — What guild [1] do you belong to?

KRASNOBRUHOV. The first. We sell wholesale.

THE OFFICIAL. Yes, yes, Gavrilenko, a chair. Take a seat, please.

KRASNOBRUHOV. Wish I could get a drink, — I'm all hoarse.

THE OFFICIAL. And so you had tea with honey again?

KRASNOBRUHOV. Yes, of course.

THE OFFICIAL. Gavrilenko, two glasses of tea — make one weak — You take your tea weak, don't you? Your name, please?

KRASNOBRUHOV. Prokofi Karpovich Krasnobruhov. But when are you going to bind me, your Honor?

THE OFFICIAL. Take a seat, please. And, Prokofi Karpich, isn't that your store on the corner? A wonderful sign you have there! That's real art. You know, sometimes, I am astonished at the artistic beauty of our signs. Why, sometimes my friends ask me why I don't go to art galleries, the Hermitage, and so on, you know — And I say, "Why should I go there? Why, my whole district is an art gallery." Ye-es! (GAVRILENKO *returns with the tea.*) I'm sorry, but we have no honey here. The office, you know.

KRASNOBRUHOV. I'm not thinking about honey now. I left the business to my children. Let them have it now. But when are you going to bind me, your Honor? I wish you'd hurry it up.

THE OFFICIAL. Bind you? Gavrilenko, get out of here! And next time you see a dignified person on the market-place, treat him with more respect, do you hear? Where is his hat?

GAVRILENKO. It was lost there in the street. The people left nothing of it. So, your Honor, when he came out there, hollering and —

THE OFFICIAL. Get out! Yes, there's people for you. How can you ever make them understand the fundamentals of law and order, so to speak? I'm sick and tired of them. My friends sometimes ask me, "How is it, Pavel Petrovich, that we never hear a pleasant word from you?" And how can you expect anything like that? I'd be glad myself, you know; I'm just dying for society conversation. There are so many things in the world, you know! The war, the Cross of St. Sophia, and, — in general, — politics, you know!

KRASNOBRUHOV. I wish you'd bind me now.

THE OFFICIAL. Bind you? Why, that's a pure misunderstanding, Prokofi Karpich, a pure misunderstanding. But why don't you drink your tea? Your worthy feelings do you honor and, in general, I'm very glad, but — the time limitation. You must have forgotten about the limitation! I hope it wasn't your parents.

KRASNOBRUHOV. Oh, no, no, not my parents. It was a girl — in the woods — and I buried her there.

THE OFFICIAL. Now you see! I understood right away that it wasn't your parents. That's not the kind of man you are! Of course, if it were your parents, you know, — well, your father or mother, — then there's no time limitation. But for your girl, and in criminal cases generally, murders and so on, everything is covered by the ten years' limitation. So you didn't know that? Is that so? Of course, we'll have to make an investigation, a confirmation, but that's nothing. You shouldn't have excited yourself so. Go back home and sell your vegetables, and we'll be your customers. — What about the tea, though?

KRASNOBRUHOV. How can I think about the tea, when I feel as if there were hot coals under me?

THE OFFICIAL. You shouldn't have tor-

[1] Russian merchants belong to one of three "guilds," according to the size of their business. The first is the highest and requires the largest license-money. — Translator's Note.

mented yourself so, no indeed! Of course, you weren't acquainted with the Law. You should have gone to a lawyer, instead of to your wife.

KRASNOBRUHOV (*falls on his knees*). Bind me! Don't make me suffer!

THE OFFICIAL. Well, now, now, please get up! Why, we can't bind you. You're a queer fellow! Why, if we were to bind everyone like you, we shouldn't have enough rope to go round! Go home now and – We have your address.

KRASNOBRUHOV. But where shall I go to? I've come here. Why don't you bind me, instead of saying that? There is no rope, you say. What's the use of mocking me? I came to you in earnest and you make fun of me! (*Sighing.*) But, of course, I deserve it. I repent. Bind me! Beat me! Mock me, brethren! Strike this old face of mine; don't spare my beard! I'm a murderer!

(*Falls down on his knees.*)

THE OFFICIAL (*impatiently*). But look here, that's too much! Get up! I'm telling you to go home; I've no time to waste with you. Go home!

KRASNOBRUHOV (*without rising*). I've no home, brethren, no asylum except the prison! Bind me. (*Shouting.*) Shave me!

THE OFFICIAL (*also shouting*). What do you take me for? A barber? Get up!

KRASNOBRUHOV. I won't get up! I'm repenting before you, and you can't refuse me! My conscience torments me! I don't want your tea. Bind me! Tie my hands! Shave me!

THE OFFICIAL (*calling*). Gavrilenko! (*The policeman enters.*) Just listen to the way he shouts here! With that conscience of his, eh? As if I had time to bother with you. – Gavrilenko, raise him!

(GAVRILENKO *attempts to raise the merchant, who resists him.*)

GAVRILENKO (*muttering*). That's just the way he was hollering – I can't raise him, your Honor, he won't get up.

THE OFFICIAL. Ah, he won't? Petruchenko! Sidorenko! Youshchenko! Raise him! (*The policemen run in, and the four raise the merchant, while the official becomes even more angry.*) Just listen to this! He goes to the very market-place and blocks the traffic! Just wait, I'll teach you to block the traffic; I'll teach you to shout in a public place!

KRASNOBRUHOV. You don't dare! Bind me, or I'll send in a complaint. I don't care! I'll go to the minister himself! I killed a human being! My conscience won't let me live! I repent!

THE OFFICIAL. Your conscience? My goodness, he's happy about it! And where was your conscience before this? Why didn't you come sooner? Now you are ready enough to go into the market-place and create a disorder! Why didn't you come sooner?

KRASNOBRUHOV. Because I hadn't suffered enough before. And now I can't stand it any more; that's why I came! You daren't refuse me!

THE OFFICIAL. Hadn't suffered enough? Listen to that mockery. Here we are looking and searching for them; we've got five trunks here, and a special bloodhound, and he – He hid himself, the rascal, and not a sound. As though he weren't there. And then he gets out into the market-place and starts shouting, "My conscience. Bind me!" Here we are, breaking our heads over the new cases, and he comes around with that girl of his – Get out! Get out of here!

KRASNOBRUHOV. I won't go. You daren't drive me back! I've already said good-by to my wife. I won't go!

THE OFFICIAL. Then you'll say "Good-morning" to your wife again. My goodness, he said "Good-by" to his wife, and drank some tea with honey, and put a clean shirt on! I'll bet you had to pour twenty glasses down your throat, before you filled up. And now he comes around here! Get out!

KRASNOBRUHOV. And did you see me drink it? Maybe only half of it was tea and the other half my bitter tears! I won't go! Send me to Siberia! Put me in irons! Shave my head!

THE OFFICIAL. There's no prison for you. Go and hire a room in Siberia, if you want to. We've got no prison for you.

KRASNOBRUHOV. You'll send me to prison! I won't go anywhere else, do you hear me? Brethren, I want to suffer for my deed; I want to go to Siberia for twenty years. I'm a murderer. I killed a human being.

THE OFFICIAL. No Siberia for you, do you hear? Why didn't you come sooner? We can't send you to prison now. We haven't room enough for real ones. And he comes around here with his conscience! He suffers, the scoundrel! Go ahead and suffer. There is no prison for you.

KRASNOBRUHOV. So you won't send me?

THE OFFICIAL. No!

KRASNOBRUHOV. You'll shave my head, all right.

THE OFFICIAL. Go and shave yourself!

KRASNOBRUHOV. No! You shave me. (*Attempts to kneel down; bends his legs at the knees, but is held in the air by the four policemen.*) Brethren, have pity on me! Bind me! Haven't you got a piece of cord somewhere? Any old piece. I won't run away even if you tie me with a piece of twine. My conscience won't let me. Any old piece. Isn't there any room for me at all in prison, your Honor? I don't need much room, your Honor. Please bind me and shave off my gray hair! Please let me walk at least over the edge of the Vladimir [1] trail and get covered with its dust! Give me the shameful badge,[2] Cain's badge! Lead me to the hangman, let him torture me!

THE OFFICIAL. Gavrilenko! Take him out! Sidorenko! Help him!

KRASNOBRUHOV (*resists them*). I won't go! I won't go if you drag me! Shave my head!

THE OFFICIAL. Youshchenko! Give a hand! You'll go, all right.

KRASNOBRUHOV (*struggling*). Shave me! I'll complain. You have no right!

THE OFFICIAL. Gavrilenko, carry him out!

GAVRILENKO. Get him by the leg! Catch him under the arms!

KRASNOBRUHOV (*struggling*). You won't carry me out!

THE OFFICIAL. Go on, now! (*The merchant is carried out with care and respect. The official smooths out his moustache, and raises his glass of tea, which proves to be cold.*) Vasilenko! A glass of hot tea! Oh, the deuce – Hot tea! Yes – Is the wounded man here?

VASILENKO. He's dead now, your Honor, dead and cold.

THE OFFICIAL. Get out of here!

CURTAIN

— From the Russian of Leonid Andreyev (1871–1919), translated by Leo Pasvolsky.

∽ ✪ ∼

[1] The trail through Russia and western Siberia, over which gangs of convicts are led into the penal colonies. – Translator's Note.

[2] On the back of each convict's coat, there is a badge that resembles the ace of diamonds. – Translator's Note.

The Jar

LUIGI PIRANDELLO

Characters

DON LOLO ZIRAFA, *a Sicilian farmer (don, "mister")*

ZI' DIMA LICASI, *a tinker (zi' for zio, "uncle")*

SCIME, *a lawyer*

'MPARI PE, *boss farmer to Don Lolo ('mpari for compare, "godfather")*

TARARA, *an olive shaker*

FILLICO, *another olive shaker*

'GNA TANA, *an olive gatherer ('gna for signora)*

TRISUZZA, *another olive gatherer*

CARMINELLA, *a third olive gatherer*

A DRIVER (*of mules*)

NOCIARELLO, *a country lad*

A grass-grown yard in front of Don Lolo's farmhouse on the crest of a hill.

Left, the façade of the farmhouse, a rustic building, of two stories; in the middle, a door, red, but somewhat weatherbeaten; above the door a window opening on a little balcony; windows upstairs and down, the lower ones fitted with iron gratings. Right, an olive tree, huge, of great age, its trunk gnarled and twisted. A stone settee has been built in around the trunk, completely encircling it. Beyond the olive tree the yard drops off down the steep hill, showing the end of a rough mountain road. Rear, the tops of olive trees, following the descending slope.

It is October.

As the curtain rises 'mpari Pe is seated on the stone seat under the olive tree.

A rustic folk song. Peasant women, olive gatherers, are singing as they climb the hill along the road, Right. Their baskets are heaped high with olives. Two of the women have their baskets on their heads. The other is carrying hers in her arms.

As 'mpari Pe hears the song, he rises, leaps up on the settee to see better, and then calls:

'MPARI PE. Oh! Oooh! Hey you old pumps without pistons! And you there, drip nose! Look what you're doing, name of Satan! You're losing your load! (*The women come on stage up over the road, Right.* NOCIARELLO *is with them. They have ceased their song.*)

TRISUZZA. What's stuck in your gullet, 'mpari Pe?

LA 'GNA TANA. Lord bless us, if he isn't learning to curse and swear as bad as the boss!

CARMINELLA. Even a tree would learn to curse, just standing around this place!

'MPARI PE. You don't have to spread your olives all over the road, do you?

TRISUZZA. My olives? On the road? Not a one! Not a one did I drop!

'MPARI PE. Lord, pity you, if Don Lolo had been at the window and seen what you were doing!

LA 'GNA TANA. Let him sit at the window till his bottom aches! When a woman earns her day's pay, she isn't afraid of anyone.

'MPARI PE. Why didn't you look where you were going? Singing there with your nose in the air!

CARMINELLA. A woman can't even sing around here?

LA 'GNA TANA. Nosireesir! All you can do is curse and swear! He and the boss must be trying for a prize, to see which can spit the dirtiest words.

TRISUZZA. Why the good Lord hasn't struck this house with lightning is more than I know!

'MPARI PE. Hey, you old hens, stop your cackling, and get rid of your loads! What do you think you're paid for, screeching and gabbing?

CARMINELLA. What, another trip, today?

'MPARI PE. Leave it to you, and every day would be Saturday, so's you could knock off at noon! There's time aplenty for two more trips. Shake your squeaky bones, and get back to work! (*He shoos the women, with* NOCIARELLO, *around the corner of the house, Left. The women begin to sing again "a dispetto".*)

'MPARI PE (*turns and calls up toward the balcony*). Hey, Don Lolo.

DON LOLO (*inside*). Who wants me this time!

'MPARI PE. The mules have come, with the manure! (DON LOLO *storms out of the house. He is a powerful man, about forty, with shifting, suspicious eyes. He is in a temper most of the time. On his head a broad-brimmed straw hat that shows signs of wear; in his ears, two rings, gold. He is in his shirt sleeves, the cuffs rolled up to his elbows. The shirt of rough, checkerboard flannel, purple and white, is open in front so as to show the hair on his chest.*)

DON LOLO. The mules? At this time of day? Where are they? Which way did you steer them?

'MPARI PE. Don't lose your temper! There they are, over there! The driver wants to know where he is to unload.

DON LOLO. Unload, hey? So he wants to unload? And without my seeing what kind of stuff he has brought! And just now I can't. I'm busy with my lawyer!

'MPARI PE. And how about moving the big jar?

DON LOLO (*surveying him from head to foot*). Say, tell me: who's running this shebang, you or me . . . ?

'MPARI PE. Oh, I meant . . .

DON LOLO. Don't mean anything! Your job is to do what I tell you! Don't mean anything! Now I should like to know why in hell I should be talking to the lawyer about the jar?. . .

'MPARI PE. Well, you don't know how worried I am. That's a brand new jar. And it's standing there right in the open in the press room. (*He points, Left, toward the house.*) Take my advice, Don Lolo, stand it somewhere else!

DON LOLO. No! I've told you a hundred times — no! It stands where it is, and no one is going to lay a finger on it!

'MPARI PE. But right by the door, with women and youngsters running in and out . . . !

DON LOLO. Blood of Jehosophat! You're bound to have me crazy about that jar?

'MPARI PE. Well, so long as you don't mind if it's broken!

DON LOLO. God, here I am busy with a lawyer! And I don't want to bother with anything else! Where do you expect me to stand the jar? In the storeroom, no! There isn't any room there, till I get the old hogshead out! And now, I haven't got time, I haven't got time! (*The* MULE DRIVER *comes in, Right.*)

DRIVER. Well, how about it? Where do I dump that manure? It will be dark in no time!

DON LOLO. And now it's you! Saints Rhubarb and Calomel strain your eyes out — you and your mules with you! Is this the time of day to come?

DRIVER. I got here as soon as I could!

DON LOLO. Well, you can't sell me any

cats in a bag. I see what I pay for! And you spread it around the pasture as I tell you and where I tell you. And today – it's too late!

DRIVER. You don't say? Want to hear some news, Don Lolo? I dump my load right behind that wall, the first place I come to. Then I go home.

DON LOLO. Now I'd just like to see you do it!

DRIVER. Well you watch, and I'll show you something! (*He starts away in a rage.*)

'MPARI PE (*restraining him*). Oh come now, why all the fuss?

DON LOLO. Let him go – let him try it!

DRIVER. Is he the only one who has a right to get mad? I can get as mad as he can! What a man to work for! Every trip, a fight!

DON LOLO. Say, sonny, if you know anybody that wants an argument with me – look . . . (*he draws from his pocket a little red book*) – they've got this to reckon with! Know what this is? Prayer-book, perhaps you think, for some of the women folks to go to church with! Well sir, I'll tell you what it is – look, "C-i-v-i-l C-o-d-e" – "The Civil Code." My lawyer gave it to me – he's paying me a visit, you know. And I've learned how to use it, this little book; and no one, not even God Almighty, is going to play any tricks on me after this. It's all here – every thing foreseen, case by case. . . . Besides, I hire my lawyer by the year! . . .

'MPARI PE. Here he is now! (SCIME, *the lawyer, appears in the farmhouse door, an old straw hat on his head, a newspaper open in his hands.*)

SCIME. What's up now, Don Lolo?

DON LOLO. Look, signor Scime, this salamander here comes around at sundown with a load of manure for the pasture, and instead of excusing himself . . .

DRIVER (*trying to get in a word to the lawyer*). I told him I couldn't get here any sooner . . .

DON LOLO. . . . why, he threatens me . . .

DRIVER. No such thing! . . .

DON LOLO. . . . threatens to dump it down behind the wall . . .

DRIVER . . . because you said . . .

DON LOLO. . . . said what? I said I wanted it spread over the pasture in piles all of the same size!

DRIVER. Give us a rest! Why doesn't he come along then? There's still two hours of sun, signor Scime. Fact is, if you want to know the truth, fact is, he wants to paw the stuff over with his hands, saving your presence, turd by turd! You don't know him!

DON LOLO. Say, who hires this lawyer, you or me? Don't listen to him, signor Scime! Just walk along down the road there, same as you always do, and you'll find a nice cool place under the mulberry to read your paper in. I'll be down before long, and we'll go on with that matter of the jar. (*To the* DRIVER.) And you, come along with me! How many mules did you bring? (*He starts away with the* DRIVER, *Right.*)

DRIVER. We agreed on twelve! Twelve I brought! (*They disappear behind the farmhouse.*)

SCIME (*raising his hands in despair and shaking them toward the point where* DON LOLO *has disappeared*). Whew, whew, whew! This rural blessedness is too much for me! I get away from here tomorrow morning, headed for some nice quiet city! That man! He's driving me crazy!

'MPARI PE. He drives everybody crazy! And what an idea you had to go and give him that little red book! Before that, whenever anything went against the grain he used to say: "Hitch up the old gray mule!" . . .

SCIME. Yes, to ride into town and bother me with God knows what! That's why I gave him the little red book. I thought he would work off steam trying to decide the law for himself – it would give me a chance to breathe! What devil ever put it into my head to come out here to spend a week? The doctor, you see, thought I ought to take a little vacation in the country – rest, air! The minute this fellow found out about it – well, he would have it that I should come here. I say yes, finally, but on condition that we do no talking about business. And what does he do? For five days past he's been after me day and night, talking about a jar . . . what jar, in the name of God?

'MPARI PE. Oh, I know – the big jar, for the olive oil! It came in last week from the factory in Santo Stegano di Camestra. That's where they make them. Oooo! A beauty, big round as this, and high as this – fat, fat as a Mother Superior in a convent. But what's up? Dispute with the factory people there?

SCIME. Dispute? The devil's to pay! They charged him twenty-five for it, and he says he expected a bigger one!

'MPARI PE (*amazed*). A bigger one!

SCIME. Five days, five days of it! (*He starts down the road*). But tomorrow, tomorrow morning, before the chickens are up – I'm off! (*He disappears down the road. From far away across the field, behind the scenes, the cadenced call of the tinker,* ZI DIMA LICASI: *"Old plates to mend," "Old cups to mend," "Old jars to mend." Down the path from behind the farmhouse come* TARARA *and* FILLICO, *the one with a ladder on his shoulders, the other with two bamboo rods in his hand.*)

'MPARI PE (*as they appear*). How's this? Stopped work already?

FILICO. The boss told us to come in, as he went by with the mules . . .

'MPARI PE. . . . told you you could go home?

TARARA. Not him! He said we should wait here to help with some job or other in the storeroom.

FILLICO. Help get out the old hogshead!

'MPARI PE. Good for him! Glad he took my advice for once in his life! Come along, Tarara! (*He starts away, Left, but from behind the farmhouse, with empty baskets, come* TRISUZZA, LA 'GNA TANA *and* CARMINELLA.)

LA 'GNA TANA (*at sight of the two helpers*). What? Aren't you going to shake any more down for us?

'MPARI PE. Knocking off, for today.

TRISUZZA. If you don't shake them down, how are we going to pick them up?

'MPARI PE. Brains! Brains! . . . Wait till the boss gets back, and he'll tell you!

CARMINELLA. We just sit here, our hands in our laps?

'MPARI PE. What do I know about it? You might start picking over, in the barn.

LA 'GNA TANA. Me? Without orders from the boss? I won't do anything!

'MPARI PE. Well, send someone and get the orders. (*He goes off, Right, with* TARARA *and* FILLICO.)

CARMINELLA. You go, Nociarello.

LA 'GNA TANA. And tell him just what I say: the men have finished shaking, and the women want to know what they've got to do next . . .

TRISUZZA. . . . and whether he wants us to begin picking over – you tell him just what I say!

NOCIARELLO (*to* CARMINELLA). I'll tell him just what you say (*to* TRISUZZA). I'll tell him just what you say, I will.

CARMINELLA. Run, shoo! (NOCIARELLO *runs off full speed, by the path, Right. From the Left, thunderstruck, frightened, in evident dismay – they show this state of mind by gestures of arms and hands – come first* FILLICO, *then* TARARA, *and then* 'MPARI PE.)

FILLICO. Holy Virgin, Holy Virgin, help us!

TARARA. I wish I was somewhere else!

'MPARI PE. What did I tell him! What did I tell him! Serves him right!

THE WOMEN (*together crowding around*). What's the matter? What is it? What has happened?

'MPARI PE. The jar! The new jar!

TARARA (*with a gesture*). Like you would with a knife!

THE WOMEN (*together*). The jar? Oh! Holy Mother help us!

FILLICO. In two, you know – clean as a whistle!

LA 'GNA TANA. How did it happen?

TRISUZZA. No one touched it!

CARMINELLA. Don Lolo will say things no woman should hear!

TRISUZZA. He'll run wild!

FILLICO. This is no place for me! I'll leave my pay envelope and go look for another job!

TARARA. You're crazy! Then he'll blame us, and there'll be no getting it out of his head! No, everybody stays here (*to* 'MPARI PE). You go and call him. Or rather, no! Call him from here! Just give him a call!

'MPARI PE (*getting up on the seat around the tree*). Well, I'll try! (*He calls several times, using his hands for a megaphone.*) Don Lolo-o-o. Don Lolo-o-o-o! No use. He doesn't hear. He's swearing along there behind the mules! Don Lolo-o-o-o! No, better to go down and get him!

TARARA. But, in the name of God, don't let him get the idea we . . .

'MPARI PE. Don't worry! How could I blame you, honestly! (*He runs off, top speed, along the path*).

TARARA. And us people, we stand together, whatever he says, whatever he does – we all say the same thing: the jar broke all by itself!

LA 'GNA TANA. 'Twouldn't be the first time such a thing happened!

TRISUZZA. Everybody knows that: new jars always break by themselves!

FILLICO. Because – you know how it is – often times when they bake them in the furnace — a spark — you know — gets caught in the clay — and then, all of a sudden — crack! . . .

CARMINELLA. Just so! The way a gun goes off! (*Crossing herself.*) The Lord deliver us! (*From within, Right, the voices of* DON LOLO *and* 'MPARI PE.)

DON LOLO'S VOICE. I'm going to find out who did it, if I go to hell for it.

'MPARI PE'S VOICE. But no one did it— I can swear!

TRISUZZA. He's coming!

LA 'GNA TANA (*crossing herself*). Lord, help us! (DON LOLO *comes down the path, followed by* 'MPARI PE *and* NOCIARELLO. *He rushes first up to* TARARA, *then up to* FILLICO, *seizing them by their shirtfronts and shaking them.*)

DON LOLO. Was it you? Was it you? One of you it must have been, and you'll foot the bill, so help me God!

TARARA AND FILLICO (*together, meanwhile trying to tear loose*). Me? You're crazy! Let me go! Off me, those hands! I swear to God!

THE OTHERS (*all together,* 'MPARI PE *joining in*). It broke by itself! It broke by itself! Nobody's fault! We found it broken! I told you so, over and over again!

DON LOLO (*at his wits' end, insisting now at one, now at another*). Crazy, me crazy? Of course, all innocent little lambs! It broke by itself! Is that so! It broke by itself! Well, you'll all chip in, that's what you'll do! Each his share! Go and get it and bring it here! ('MPARI PE, TARARA, FILLICO, *hurry off to get the jar*). We'll have a look at it, in broad daylight! And if there's any sign of a kick, or a bump — I take you fools by the throat and choke the price out of you! You'll all chip in, that's what you'll do — men and women alike!

THE WOMEN (*all together*). Us? We will, eh? Us? What did we have to do with it? Never even looked at the thing!

DON LOLO. But you too were going in and out of the press room!

TRISUZZA. Yeah, and we broke the jar, brushing it with our skirts, this way! (*She gathers her skirt up in one hand and, to make fun of him, pretends to whip him across the legs with it. The three men return from the Left, bringing in the big broken jar.*)

LA 'GNA TANA. What a pity! Look at the poor thing!

DON LOLO (*raising his arms in despair, as though he were mourning for some dead relative*). The new one! Twenty-five gone up in smoke! And where do I put the new crop of oil? And what a beauty! Spite, or else plain deviltry! Twenty-five just thrown away! And there was a crop this year! What'll I do? What'll I do?

TARARA. No, no! Look!

FILLICO. It can be mended!

'MPARI PE. Only a piece off!

TARARA. Just one piece!

FILLICO. A clean break!

TARARA. May have been cracked when it came!

DON LOLO. Cracked, hell! It rang like a bell!

'MPARI PE. That's right! I tried it myself!

FILLICO. The right mender could make it good as new, so's you couldn't even see the crack!

TARARA. Zi' Dima Licasi! He can do it! And he must be in the neighborhood! I heard him calling!

LA 'GNA TANA. A fine workman, that — brains! He has a cement that, once it's set, you couldn't break it with a hammer! Run, Nociarello! He's somewhere near here! Oh, there he is, down by Mosca's fence! Run and tell him to come here at once. (NOCIARELLO *goes off, Left, on the dead run.*)

DON LOLO (*shouting*). Will you all shut up? I can't hear myself think! Licasi and his cement be damned! That jar is gone!

'MPARI PE. Well, I told you so, I told you so!

DON LOLO (*too angry to enunciate*). What did you tell me, belly of a jackass! What did you tell me! Weren't you saying she broke by herself? Well, suppose I'd have kept it with the Body of Christt . . . wouldn't she have broken just the same?

TARARA (*to* 'MPARI PE). You talk too much!

DON LOLO. That fool would damn a man's soul!

FILLICO. You'll see, you'll see! You can have it fixed good as new, for a few cents! And you know, a mended jar lasts longer than a brand new one!

DON LOLO. And, damn it, damn it, I have those mules on my hands, half way up the hill! (*To* 'MPARI PE.) What are you doing here, standing around staring like an idiot! Get to work! Get to work! Run up there and see what he's doing! ('MPARI PE *runs up the path.*) Ah! Oh! Uh (*wiping his fore-*

head)! Zi' Dima! Blast zi' Dima! This is a matter for the lawyer! If she broke by herself — well, there must have been something wrong with her! But she rang, though, she rang, like a bell! And I took her for all right! I signed the receipt my own self! Twenty-five lost, twenty-five! Kiss it goodbye, that money! (Zi' Dima Licasi *comes in down the path, Left, followed by* Nociarello.)

Fillico. Oh, zi' Dima, zi' Dima!

Tarara (*whispering to* Don Lolo). Notice, he never talks!

La 'gna Tana (*whispering to* Don Lolo, *mysteriously*). He never talks, never a word!

Don Lolo. Don't talk, eh? (*To* zi' Dima). No words, and no manners, eh? No manners! Don't you ever say howdydo, when you come to a man's house?

Zi' Dima Licasi. What do you want, my work or my manners? It's my work that earns my living! Tell me what you want done, and I do it!

Don Lolo. So you can talk, when you want to sass people! Haven't you got eyes in your head? Can't you see what I want done?

Fillico. Mend her up, this jar! You know, zi' Dima, some of your cement!

Don Lolo. They say it does wonders! Make it yourself? (Zi' Dima Licasi *looks at him sullenly, and makes no answer.*) Show us some of your cement.

Tarara (*whispering to* Don Lolo). You won't get anywhere with him in that tone of voice!

La 'gna Tana. He never lets nobody see it!

Don Lolo. What is the damn mud anyway — dust from the throne of God Almighty? (*To* zi' Dima Licasi). Well, tell me whether you can fix the damn thing.

Zi' Dima Licasi (*setting his tool box on the ground, and taking out a little bundle wrapped in a dirty blue handkerchief*). What's all the hurry, hey? Give me a chance to look at it! (*He sits flat on the ground, unrolls the handkerchief, slowly, cautiously. All crane their necks for a glimpse of the wonderful cement.*)

La 'gna Tana (*whispering to* Don Lolo). It's the cement!

Don Lolo. Looks to me more like vomit! (*Eventually* zi' Dima Licasi *gets the handkerchief unwound, and produces from it a pair of eyeglasses, the bows and the nose-piece broken and replaced with string.*)

Everybody (*laughing*). Eyeglasses! Who'd have thought? Is that his famous cement? Looks more like a halter for a donkey!

Zi' Dima Licasi (*very deliberately wiping the glasses with a corner of the dirty handkerchief, examining them carefully, and finally adjusting them to his nose. Then, just as deliberately, he examines the jar*). I can fix it.

Don Lolo. *Oyez, Oyez!* Boom-m-m! His Honor pronounces sentence! But I tell you one thing, I don't take any stock in that cement of yours! We'll have rivets, clinched on the inside! (Zi' Dima Licasi *looks up at him. Then he takes off the glasses, wraps them up in the handkerchief again, puts the handkerchief in the tool box, and the tool box on his shoulder, and starts away.*) Say, what's the idea? Where are you going?

Zi' Dima Licasi. About my business!

Don Lolo. Pig or Holy Ghost, you treat them all alike!

Fillico (*trying to pacify* zi' Dima Licasi). Oh say now, *zi'* Dima, don't mind him!

Tarara (*taking him on the other side*). Just do as he says, what's the difference?

Don Lolo. Who does he think he is, the Father of his country? Scab on a pig's hide, can't you see I've got to put oil in her? Well, it soaks through, the oil does. Split a mile long — and just a little cement? It's got to have rivets — rivets as well as cement! Who's paying for this job?

Zi' Dima Licasi. They're all like that! Just like them all! No brains! No brains! Pitcher, bowl, cup, mug, no matter how big, no matter how little, always rivets! False teeth in an old woman's face to tell the world: "I'm busted, and they fixed me up!" I offer a good job, and nobody wants it! They won't let a man do a clean job the way it ought to be done! (*He walks up to* Don Lolo.) Listen to me, if this jar don't ring like new when I get through — just with cement . . .

Don Lolo. I said no! I said no! Think I'm going to argue with that man? (*To* Tarara.) One good thing — you say he doesn't talk much! (*To* zi' Dima Licasi.) No use preaching to me! If they all want rivets, it's a sign that rivets is what they want. . . .

Zi' Dima Licasi. No it isn't! It's a sign they don't know anything!

La 'gna Tana. I know I don't know anything, but I like rivets too, zi' Dima!

Trisuzza. 'Course there ought to be rivets — they hold better!

Zi' Dima Licasi. But they make holes! Can't you see they make holes! Each pair of rivets, two holes: twenty pairs, forty holes! But with just cement . . .

Don Lolo. Balsam, what a head! Find me a mule as balky as that! Holes, very well! Holes! Holes is what I want, holes with rivets in them! And I'm paying here! (*To the* Women.) You, now, off to the barn, and start picking over! (*To the* Men.) And you, you go into the storeroom, and help get out the old hogshead. Lively now! (*He pushes them off toward the farmhouse.*)

Zi' Dima Licasi. Hold on there — not so fast!

Don Lolo. Oh, we'll see about the money when you get through — you don't waste any more of my time!

Zi' Dima Licasi. And you leave me here alone? Someone's got to hold up the broken piece. That's a big jar!

Don Lolo. Yes — hey there, Tarara — you help him! Fillico, you come with me! (*He goes out with* Fillico. *The* Women *with* Nociarello, *have already disappeared.* Zi' Dima Licasi *sets to work at once, in bad humor, however. He takes a bit and stock from his tool box, and begins making the holes for the rivets, first in the jar, then in the broken fragment. As he works* Tarara *engages him in conversation.*)

Tarara. Lucky it's no worse than it is. I don't see how we got off so easy! I thought my time had come! Don't let that man spoil your breakfast, zi' Dima. He wants rivets? Give him rivets! Twenty, thirty? (Zi' Dima Licasi *looks up at him.*) More than that? Thirty-five? (Zi' Dima Licasi *looks up at him.*) How many, you think?

Zi' Dima Licasi. See this bit I'm working with? Every time I make it go round? Ruh-ruh-ruh-ruh! Every sound is a grind at my heart!

Tarara. Is it true what they say — that you got your mixture for your cement in a dream?

Zi' Dima Licasi (*without stopping*). Yes, I dreamt it!

Tarara. Who was it came to you, in a dream?

Zi' Dima Licasi. My father!

Tarara. Oh, your father! So he came to you in a dream, and told you how to mix it?

Zi' Dima Licasi. Puddenhead!

Tarara. Me? Why?

Zi' Dima Licasi. Know who my father was?

Tarara. No, who was he?

Zi' Dima Licasi. The Devil that's going to get you!

Tarara. So the Devil was your father! And who was your mother?

Zi' Dima Licasi. The pitch all you know-nothings are going to boil in!

Tarara. Black pitch!

Zi' Dima Licasi. White pitch! The Old Man showed me how to make it white! You'll see how it works, when he begins to stew you, down there in Hell! There, however, you'll find it black! Bring your two fingers together and you never get them loose again! If I stick your upper lip to your nose, you stay Zulu the rest of your life!

Tarara. You get it on *your* fingers, and it doesn't seem to hurt *you!*

Zi' Dima Licasi. Puddenhead! Whoever heard of a dog biting his own master! (*He tosses the bit-stock aside and rises to his feet.*) Come here now! You just hold this up! (*He makes* Tarara *support the broken piece, while he draws a tin can from his tool box, opens it, and takes out a pinch of cement with his thumb and finger, holding it up.*) Look at this? Cement, eh? Just ordinary cement! Well, you watch! (*He spreads the cement over the broken edge of the jar, then on the edges of the fragment.*) Three or four pinches like this — just the least little! Don't let it fall! Now I get inside. . . .

Tarara. Oh, from the inside you work!

Zi' Dima Licasi. How else, puddenhead? If you're going to clinch the rivets, you have to do it on the inside, don't you? Wait a minute! (*He rummages around in his tool box.*) Wire, I need, and pincers! (*He finds what he wants, and gets inside the jar.*) You now, just wait till I get comfortable here . . . here we are . . . now just raise that piece, and fit it in — just a little higher, just a little higher — even all round? . . . easy now . . . oh, there . . . there we are . . . now hold her there, hold her! (*Tarara does as he is told, and* zi' Dima Licasi *is hidden within the jar. Shortly after, sticking his head out of the mouth of the jar.*) Now pull, damn you, pull! Not a rivet in her! Awh, pull, use your muscle! There you see? Could you move it? Could you move it? Not the fraction of an inch! Well, you couldn't stir it with ten pairs of oxen, either. Go! Go and tell your boss!

TARARA. All right zi' Dima, but are you sure you can get out now?

ZI' DIMA LICASI. Never had any trouble getting out before!

TARARA. But this jar . . . I don't know – the mouth seems to me a little tight for a man your size. Try, and let's see! ('MPARI PE *comes back up the road, Right.*)

'MPARI PE. What's that? Stuck? Stuck in the jar?

TARARA (*to* ZI' DIMA LICASI, *in the jar*). Not so hard! Wait, let me tip it!

'MPARI PE. One arm at a time now! Your arm! . . .

TARARA. No, your arm, your arm!

ZI' DIMA LICASI. What the devil! How's this? Can't I squeeze through there?

'MPARI PE. So small at the mouth, a jar that size?

TARARA (*laughing*). It would be a joke if he couldn't get out, now that he's got it all fixed.

ZI' DIMA LICASI. What are you laughing at, blood of Satan! Give me a hand! (*He leaps furiously up at the mouth of the jar.*)

'MPARI PE. Wait, that doesn't do any good! Let's try tipping it over!

ZI' DIMA LICASI. No, that's worse! I stick here, at the shoulders!

TARARA. It's a fact! You have a little too much shoulder on one side!

ZI' DIMA LICASI. Me, too much? You said yourself the jar was too narrow at the mouth!

'MPARI PE. And now what are we going to do about it?

TARARA. This, now, is something to talk about! Hah, hah (*laughing, and running toward the farmhouse, calling*). Hey, Fillico, 'gna Tana! Hey Trisuzza, Carminella, hey! Come quick! Zi' Dima is stuck in the jar! He can't get out! (FILLICO, LA 'GNA TANA, TRISUZZA, CARMINELLA, *and* NOCIARELLO *come running on, Right.*)

ALL OF THEM (*together*). Stuck in the jar? He is? Hah! Hah! How did it happen? He can't get out?

ZI' DIMA LICASI (*raising his voice over the hubbub, and snarling like an angry cat*). Hey, get me out of here! My hammer there, in the tool box!

'MPARI PE. Hammer nothing! Are you crazy? Think you're going to break that jar, now you've just got it mended? The boss must tell you to do that, himself!

FILLICO. Here he comes now! (DON LOLO *comes running on, Right.*)

THE WOMEN (*telling the glad tidings, running to meet him*). Stuck in the jar! Stuck in the jar! He can't get out!

DON LOLO. In the jar?

ZI' DIMA LICASI (*at the same time*). Help! Help! Help!

DON LOLO. How can I help you, dunce of an old rat, if you didn't have brains enough to measure the hump on your back (*general laughter*), before you went and stuck yourself in there!

LA 'GNA TANA. Look what a fix he's in, poor zi' Dima!

FILLICO. The funniest damn thing you ever saw in your life!

DON LOLO. Wait, man, wait! Not so fast! Try one arm first!

'MPARI PE. No use! We've tried that, and every other way!

ZI' DIMA LICASI (*getting one arm out at last, while the others pull on it*). Ouch! Ouch! Don't! Don't! You're pulling me in two!

DON LOLO. Don't get excited – just one more pull!

ZI' DIMA LICASI (*tearing loose*). No, let me alone! Let me alone!

DON LOLO. Well, what can I do then?

ZI' DIMA LICASI. Just hand me that hammer! . . .

DON LOLO. What, break it? After you've just mended it?

ZI' DIMA LICASI. Think I'm going to stay in here?

DON LOLO. Well, we've got to see what we can do about it!

ZI' DIMA LICASI. See, hell! I'm going to get out of here, see or no see!

THE WOMEN (*in chorus*). He's right! You can't keep him in there! We've got to break it!

DON LOLO. Did you ever see the like of this! Just a moment now, just a moment now, while I look in the little red book . . . this is something new! This case never came up before! (*To* NOCIARELLO.) Here, boy, you run. . . . No, it's better if you go, Fillico (*pointing toward the path, Right*). Down there, under the mulberry – the lawyer! And tell him to come here, quick! (*As* FIL-

LICO *goes off, Right, he turns to* ZI' DIMA LICASI *who is still struggling inside the jar.*) Quiet, in there, you! (*To the others.*) Keep him quiet, will you! First it breaks by itself, and now. . . . That's no jar – that's some contraption of the Devil! (*To* ZI' DIMA LICASI, *who is still making a noise.*) Easy, there, I tell you! Don't you dare break that jar!

ZI' DIMA LICASI. Either you break it, or I tip it over myself and roll it against one of those trees, if I break my neck doing it! Get me out! Get me out!

DON LOLO. The lawyer will be here in just a jiffy. He'll settle the rights and wrongs of this case! I stick to my claims on the jar, and I begin by doing my duty! All you people bear witness – I pay you a ten spot, a fair price for your job! (*He draws from a pocket a large leather pocketbook, tied around with twine, and takes from it a ten lira bill.*)

ZI' DIMA LICASI. I won't take it! I want to get out!

DON LOLO. You'll get out when the lawyer says you can! Meantime, I pay you! (*He lifts the bill, conspicuously, in one hand and lets it down inside the jar. Up the path, Right, comes the lawyer,* SCIME, *laughing, followed by* FILLICO, *also laughing.*)

DON LOLO (*observing his good humor*). What's there to laugh about? Of course, it's no concern of yours! The jar is mine!

SCIME (*holding his sides, while the others join in his mirth*). But do you think . . . do you think you can . . . can keep him in . . . in there . . . in there just because you . . . you don't . . . don't want to lose your jar?

DON LOLO. You think it all falls on me? I stand the loss, I do, as well as be made a fool of?

SCIME. You don't want to go to jail for kidnapping, do you? That's kidnapping!

DON LOLO. Kidnapping? Who's doing the kidnapping? He kidnapped himself! I'll prove it! (*To* ZI' DIMA LICASI.) Who is keeping you in there? Come out of that jar! Come out of that jar!

ZI' DIMA LICASI. You get me out, if you can see a way to do it!

DON LOLO. Oh, excuse me, it's not my job to get you out! You went in of your own accord! Come out, I say!

SCIME. Ladies and gentlemen, may I have the floor?

TARARA. Speak! Let's hear the lawyer! What's the law in the case?

SCIME. There are two points involved, gentlemen of the jury, and the two contestants must govern themselves accordingly! (*He first addresses* DON LOLO.) You, on the one hand, Don Lolo, are bound to liberate the man, Licasi! . . .

DON LOLO (*speaking up*). I am? I am? And how, by breaking the jar?

SCIME. Wait, let me finish! On the other hand – God's sake, let me finish, won't you? – you've got to – otherwise, kidnapping, kidnapping! (*Now to* ZI' DIMA LICASI.) On the other hand, you, zi' Dima Licasi, must answer for the damage you have caused by getting inside the jar without considering whether you would be able to get out! . . .

ZI' DIMA LICASI. But, if you please, signor Scime, I didn't pay any attention to that. I've been at this trade for years. I have mended a million jars, always from inside, to clinch the rivets, as you have to do. I never wasn't able to get out before. It's for him then to go and talk with the man who made this damn jar with such a small mouth! No fault of mine!

DON LOLO. But that hump on your back – did the man who made the jar make the hump on your back, just to keep you from getting out? If I sue on grounds of the narrow mouth, signor Scime, the minute he comes in with that hump, the judge begins to laugh – and I'm left with the costs! . . .

ZI' DIMA LICASI. That isn't so! I've had this hump many a year, I'd have you know, and this is the first jar I couldn't get out of! From the others, as easy as through the door of my house! . . .

SCIME. That doesn't excuse you, zi' Dima Licasi. You were bound to take the measure before you got in, to see whether you could get out . . .

DON LOLO. . . . so he's got to pay me for the jar!

ZI' DIMA LICASI. . . . Pay for your grandmother!

SCIME. Not so fast, now! Not so fast! . . . Pay for it as new?

DON LOLO. Of course, new! Why not?

SCIME. It was broken, man!

ZI' DIMA LICASI. And I fixed it!

DON LOLO. You fixed it! You fixed it! And you said yourself – as good as new! But if I break it again to get you out, I won't be able to mend it again, and I lose the whole jar, signor Scime!

SCIME. That's why I said — zi' Dima Licasi must stand his share of the loss! Let me do the talking, will you?

DON LOLO. Talk! Talk!

SCIME. My dear zi' Dima, take your choice: either your cement was good for something or else it wasn't . . .

DON LOLO (*delighted, addressing the crowd, confidentially*). Just listen to that! Oh I tell you, when he starts that way, you can't fool him! Some lawyer! . . . We've got him in a fix! . . .

SCIME. If your cement was good for nothing — well, in that case you're guilty of making false pretenses, like any other swindler. But if, on the other hand, it's good for something, why then, the jar, mended as it is, must have a certain value! What value? I leave it to you! How high would you put it?

ZI' DIMA LICASI. With me inside? (*General laughter.*)

SCIME. No joking — the way it is!

ZI' DIMA LICASI. I'll tell you what! If Don Lolo had let me fix it the way I wanted to, with just cement, in the first place, I wouldn't have had to get inside, because I could have done it from out there; and in the second place, the jar would have been as good as new, and would have been worth every cent he paid for it. But all patched up the way it is, with all those holes for those rivets, it's worth just about as much as my old woman's tin dishpan! It isn't worth a penny more than a third of what it cost!

DON LOLO. A third? A third?

SCIME (*quickly to* DON LOLO, *pretending to be parrying a blow*). A third, he said! Sh-h-h you, let him talk! A third? How much would a third be?

DON LOLO. It cost twenty-five: a third, eight thirty-three . . .

ZI' DIMA LICASI. Less perhaps! More, not a bit!

SCIME. We take you at your word — you pay Don Lolo eight thirty-three!

ZI' DIMA LICASI. To him! Me? I pay him eight thirty-three? . . .

SCIME. . . . so that he will break the jar and let you out! You pay the actual value you set on the jar yourself!

DON LOLO. Smooth as oil!

ZI' DIMA LICASI. Me pay? Me pay? You've gone crazy, signor Scime! The worms are going to get me, right in here! Say you, Tarara, my pipe, there in the tool-box!

TARARA (*obeying*). This one?

ZI' DIMA LICASI. Thanks, and now a light! (*Tarara strikes a match and lights the pipe.*) Thanks, and a good day to everybody! (*He disappears inside the jar, his pipe smoking.*)

DON LOLO (*dumbfounded*). And now what's to be done about it, if he won't come out?

SCIME (*scratching his head, laughing*). Yes, to tell the truth, so long as he was anxious to get out, we could do something; but now, with him refusing to come out . . .

DON LOLO (*going up to the jar and calling to* ZI' DIMA LICASI). Well, what's your idea? Going to stay there the rest of your life?

ZI' DIMA LICASI (*putting his head out*). More comfortable here than in my own house! Cool, cool as a cucumber! (*He disappears again, the smoke rising from the jar.*)

DON LOLO (*angry at the general laughter*). And you jackasses, shut up! You all bear witness that it's him that's refusing to come out, in order not to pay what he owes me, while I offer to break the jar! (*with an idea, to the lawyer*). Couldn't I sue him for rent?

SCIME (*laughing*). 'Course you could! But you have to have a constable to evict him first!

DON LOLO. But as long as he is in there I can't use the jar!

ZI' DIMA LICASI (*appearing at the mouth of the jar*). You're wrong! I'm not in here of choice. Let me out, and I go away, skidoo! But if it's money out of me, you're dreaming, man, you're dreaming! I don't budge!

DON LOLO (*seizing the jar by the edge of the mouth and shaking it furiously*). You don't budge, eh? You don't budge!

ZI' DIMA LICASI (*at the opening*). You see — it's my cement! There aren't any rivets!

DON LOLO. Well, then, who did the harm, pickpocket, me or you? And you think I'm going to pay?

SCIME (*dragging him away by an arm*). Don't do that! You make it worse! Let him spend a night in there, and you'll see that by morning he'll be glad enough to come out! When we get him in that state of mind, you . . . well, eight thirty-three or nothing! . . . So now, we go away, and leave him to stew in his own juice! (*He drags* Don Lolo *off toward the farmhouse.*)

Zi' Dima Licasi (*at the mouth of the jar*). Say, Don Lolo!

Scime (*to* Don Lolo, *without stopping*). Don't pay any attention! Come along, come along!

Zi' Dima Licasi (*before they get into the house*). Good night, Scime — but see what I got! (*He holds up the ten lira bill; then as the two disappear, to the others*). The rest of us, we celebrate — a housewarming for my new mansion! Say Tarara, take this, and down at Mosca's — wine, bread, fried fish, *peperoni!* And we celebrate!

All of Them (*clapping and cheering, as* Tarara *runs away to buy the things*). Good for zi' Dima! We celebrate! What fun!

Fillico. Couldn't have better weather. Look at that moon! Just coming up! (*Pointing to the left.*) It's as bright as day!

Zi' Dima Licasi. Oh-ay, I can't see the moon, I can't see the moon! I want to see the moon! Roll me over that way a little, so's I can see the moon! But be easy! (*All take a hand and roll the jar over toward the path, Right.*) Easy, easy! There we are! And I can see the moon! Oh what a moon! Bright as the sun! How about a little music? Who sings the first song?

La 'gna Tana. You, Trisuzza!

Trisuzza. No, I couldn't! Carminella!

Zi' Dima Licasi. Well, we all sing! You, Fillico, out with your harmonica! And we all join in! The women folks will dance a little! Hey, there, you old cows, shake a leg there! (Fillico *produces his harmonica and begins a tune; the others join hands and begin a dance, confusedly, round and round the jar, 'zi* Dima Licasi *shouting to mark time. Shortly, the door of the farmhouse swings open, and* Don Lolo *rushes out in a fury.*)

Don Lolo. What's this, blood of Satan, where do you think you are, in a bawdy house? Here, you lousy old camel, put this in your pipe and smoke it! (*He gives the jar a violent kick, and it goes rolling down the hill, amid the cries of the company. The jar is heard to crash against a tree.*)

La 'gna Tana (*screaming*). You killed him!

Fillico (*looking down the hill*). No, there he is! He's crawling out! Didn't hurt him! (*The company claps and cheers.*)

Everybody. Three cheers for zi' Dima Licasi! Hurrah! Hurrah! Hurrah! (*As* zi' Dima Licasi *appears up the hill, they lift him to their shoulders and carry him off in triumph, Left.*)

Zi' Dima Licasi. I win, I win, I win!

Curtain

— *From the Italian of Luigi Pirandello (1867–1936), translated by Arthur Livingston.*

∽ ⚙ ∼

Still Life

FERENC MOLNÁR

Characters

The Actor
The Actress
Lizzie, *her maid-of-all-work*

Scene: *The Actress' apartment.*

Actor (*entering*). Good evening!

Lizzie (*sorting some clean linen*). Good evening!

Actor. Isn't your mistress at home?

Lizzie (*almost gruffly*). No!

Actor. When do you expect her?

Lizzie. I don't know.

(*Pause.*)

Actor. Do you think I ought to wait for her?

Lizzie. I don't know.

Actor. How is it possible that she is not at home yet? She is not playing to-night, and on such days she usually dines at eight o'clock. Now it is already quarter past nine! Didn't she say when she would be home?

Lizzie. No.

Actor. Isn't she going to eat at home?

Lizzie. I do not know.

Actor. You don't know? What do you mean, you don't know? Have you prepared dinner or haven't you? You ought to know that.

Lizzie (*almost gruffly*). Leave me alone.

(*Starts to leave the room.*)

Actor. You vile creature, I'll murder you. I'll murder you yet! You'll shorten my life! You'll send me to the penitentiary yet — for I will murder you. Stay here.

LIZZIE. Let me go out.

ACTOR (*grabs her arm*). You'll stay here and confess.

LIZZIE. Since when have we been pals? Don't talk to me that way. Let me go.

ACTOR. You dare talk this way to Sovari? The famous Sovari? Is this the way to talk to me? To me, at whose sight managers tremble?

LIZZIE. Let me go.

ACTOR. No, you will confess. I don't care if you are uncouth. I know that you are, anyway. As a matter of fact I am glad you are nasty because I know that when your mistress comes home, she'll be nasty, too. Nevertheless, I will murder you if you lie and are silent and keep secrets and conspire and are false and help her to deceive me. You are to die, Lizzie. You won't even be conscious of it, and all of a sudden I will come in and you will be dead.

LIZZIE. Let me alone. What do you want of me?

ACTOR. Who was here this afternoon?

LIZZIE. I do not know. This afternoon? I was out to get some yeast.

ACTOR. You do not know? This afternoon you were out to fetch yeast? Very well. When did she leave the house?

LIZZIE. When I got back, she was gone.

ACTOR. When you got back she was gone. Very well. Whose cigar butt is this in the ash tray?

LIZZIE. You left that here yesterday.

ACTOR (*pointing to an ash tray*). And you have not emptied that ash tray since?

LIZZIE. No, neither will I empty it tomorrow.

ACTOR. Do you accept money?

LIZZIE. Oh, yes.

ACTOR (*takes some money out of his pocket*). How much do you want? What's the price of your confession?

LIZZIE. Put it back! I'll take no money from you.

ACTOR. Whom do you take money from?

LIZZIE. From my mistress.

ACTOR. And from Count Tibor, with whom you are in league, from whom you accept money, whom you aid against me, you villain, against me! I foresee that in the end I will go to jail on account of you. What's that perfume I smell in the linen? Where did you buy the new perfume? Don't bother to answer. You don't know. Very well, my child, very well. How it all will end I have already told you. What's this new perfume? Who bought it for her?

(*Doorbell rings.*)

LIZZIE. My mistress is coming! Don't worry, I'll tell her all about you. In just another minute you'll hold your peace.

ACTRESS (*enters with* LIZZIE. *Looks through the* ACTOR *as if he were not there at all*). How long has he been here?

LIZZIE. Not very long. Only about ten minutes.

ACTRESS (*very loud*). Did you tell him to wait for me?

LIZZIE. No.

ACTRESS. Then why is he waiting?

LIZZIE. I don't know.

ACTRESS. Did you tell him that I would not be home for dinner?

LIZZIE. No.

ACTRESS. Why didn't you tell him that I didn't say when I would be home? It is an accident that I am back so early. I have told you hundreds of times not to let anybody come into the house while I am out.

LIZZIE. What can I do against brute force?

ACTRESS. Very simple. Call a policeman! Understand?

LIZZIE. I understand, kiss your hand. Next time I will do that.

ACTOR (*after a pause*). Half past nine. Half past nine.

ACTRESS. Quarter past.

ACTOR. Half past.

ACTRESS (*nervous*). And if it is half past? And if it's quarter to ten? Or half past twenty-nine? What business of yours is it? Who are you? Are you my husband?

ACTOR. Where were you until half past nine in the night?

ACTRESS. Nowhere.

ACTOR. Bum! Bum! Where were you from two in the afternoon till half past nine? I'll murder you.

(*Picks up a chair.*)

ACTRESS. Now, now, now — no theatricals. Out, out!

ACTOR (*puts the chair down*). Where were you until half past nine? We shall die together, for it cannot go on like this any longer. We'll die in the Turkish bath. First I'll shoot you, then myself. My nerves can't stand this any longer, you faithless one, you deceiver, you good-for-nothing, you bum.

ACTRESS. Monkey. Give me a kiss.

(*Reads the paper.*)

ACTOR (*sighing*). Shocking!

ACTRESS (*reading the paper*). Sit by me, you monkey, and kiss me here.

(*Points to a spot on her neck.*)

ACTOR. Don't read the paper now.

(*He sobs.*)

ACTRESS. Now, now, now. There's no reason for you to start crying right away. Aren't you ashamed of yourself? The famous, the great, the *Sovari* cries like a baby.

ACTOR (*stifling his sobs*). God, how unhappy I am!

ACTRESS. That's enough. Quite enough. Behave. Will you do it again?

(*They kiss.*)

ACTOR. Where were you from two until half past nine?

ACTRESS. I did not leave the house until four.

ACTOR. That's not so, because I was here at half past two and you were no longer at home. Something is happening to you, Sciarelli. Something's stirring inside of you again — I feel it. For a while you behave, but now you are starting all over again. What is the matter with you? What do you want of me? Why do you torture me? Do you love another? What is the matter with you? Do you want to kill me? To ruin me? On days when you torture me like this, at night I play like a ham. You are ruining my talent. You are robbing me of my bread. What do you want? Where were you this afternoon? Answer me, otherwise I don't know what I'll do.

ACTRESS. I was at home. I just went over to the neighbors, to the Reiners'.

ACTOR. The Reiners weren't at home all day.

ACTRESS. That's why I came right back.

ACTOR. I sat here from half past two until half past three and you didn't come. Did it take you an hour to come back here from the neighboring house?

ACTRESS. I came back immediately. On the stairs I met the janitor who told me that his wife had just had a new baby boy. So I went right down with him and looked at the little boy. He was born early to-day.

ACTOR. Sciarelli, that is not true. The janitor's wife had a boy three months ago. I know because I gave her money then. If this is the same child, you are a liar, but if it is a new one and only three months after, it is a miracle.

ACTRESS. I saw immediately that it was an older child. They fooled me. They always think up things to make me give them tips.

ACTOR. And then? Where did you go after that?

ACTRESS. I stayed at home until seven.

ACTOR. That is not so.

ACTRESS. Oh, yes, it is so.

ACTOR. It is not so because at half past six I was here again and you were not at home. Besides, the match that I put into the keyhole was still untouched, so you were not home at all after I left here at half past three. You have lied again. You are overrun with lies.

ACTRESS. And if I did lie? What are you? Who are you? Are you my husband?

ACTOR. Starting again. Starting all over again.

ACTRESS. Yes, it is starting. But if you wish, it will stop. Everything will stop. I have had enough of this. Everybody is amazed that I still talk to you.

ACTOR. Who is amazed? Mrs. Froschel is amazed. Pia Putzi is amazed. And you give a darn about them? They are the ones who set the standard for you? Do you know what I'll do to them? Don't get me excited or I'll tell you what I'll do. And the manager's wife is amazed too, eh? The manager's wife who cannot count even on her hair the number of lovers she has had, because her hair falls out quicker than the number of her lovers increase.

ACTRESS. Yes, every one thinks it is ignoble of you not to want to marry me. If you do not respect me then do not come here, and if you do come here, make no scenes, because you have no right to. Why do you come here? I know — that's all you want me for.

ACTOR. For what?

ACTRESS. For *that*. That's what everybody says.

ACTOR. You are starting again.

ACTRESS. Yes, I am starting in again. Every day I am humiliated in some way. Up to now society did not know just where to place me, but here I have my exact position: in this lousy theatre I am just the least person, because not even Sovari wants to marry me.

ACTOR. "Not even Sovari." What kind of talk is that? Who is Sovari that they dare to speak of him in such manner? Who said that?

ACTRESS. I did.

ACTOR. And I repeat what I have already said a hundred times. Sovari is a respectable man who cannot swallow your past in one gulp.

ACTRESS. My past? How ungentlemanly! Even to say such a thing!

ACTOR. You force me to. "Not even Sovari!" Am I so unimportant that I must marry anybody at all in a hurry? May I not doubt, consider, hesitate? Have I no honor? I have a respectable, poor family; a poor but proud mother and a poor, respectable sister who is in despair because I and you – I and you . . . I . . . . and with you . . .

ACTRESS. Out! Out!

ACTOR. No wonder I lose my tact when you get me excited.

ACTRESS. My past. What do you know of my past?

ACTOR. Lieutenant Sterzhofer in Graz.

ACTRESS. I took French lessons from him, and I am grateful to him for them. Every day he gave me a lesson. He labored over me. Quite unselfishly!

ACTOR. Judge Pauli. What kind of lessons did he give you? For when the lieutenant was gone, he became the daily caller. You even went to Vienna with him!

ACTRESS. What should I have done? He happened to be going there at the same time.

ACTOR. Pharmacist Zeislhuber.

ACTRESS. In the first place he isn't a pharmacist. He owns a drug store. You are crazy.

ACTOR. Robert Stein.

ACTRESS. You are not normal.

ACTOR. Hugo Kaudersch.

ACTRESS. Kaudersch!!

ACTOR. Ahlfelder.

ACTRESS. Ahlfelder!!!

ACTOR. Lieutenant Sauerwein.

ACTRESS. Good God!

ACTOR. Dr. Stickerz.

ACTRESS. You're a pig!

ACTOR. Bela Kern.

ACTRESS. Idiot!

ACTOR. Wollmann, Pumpke, Rudolfi, Grassel, Stern.

ACTRESS. Stern!!!

ACTOR. Jodlebauer!

ACTRESS. Stern!!!!

ACTOR. Hambacher, Keller, Worzel.

ACTRESS. Stern!!!!!

ACTOR. That's interesting. Only Stern bothers her.

ACTRESS (*pointing to the door*). Out with you!

ACTOR. I forgave all, all of this, because I am mad; you are right in one thing – I love you like a madman.

ACTRESS. Get out of here!

ACTOR. I wouldn't say a word if you behaved decently now. But you are starting all over again. Now I feel, I know that you want to deceive me, that you are deceiving me.

ACTRESS (*goes to the door and shouts*). Lizzie! Call a policeman.

LIZZIE (*voice*). Yes, madame.

ACTOR. It is enough to drive one to despair, how a woman can drive one out of one's mind.

ACTRESS. Please do not exert yourself. A policeman will be here presently. The authorities will attend to the rest.

ACTOR. But it is revolting – all the things that I have said. I cannot even recognize myself any more. You can see even from how confused I am that I become quite mad when you torture me. It is clear . . . how much I love you.

ACTRESS. You can tell it to the authorities later. You wanted to murder me. That is a criminal offense.

ACTOR. Is that so? Now, if I had broken a plate, that would have been something. But things that one only says?

ACTRESS. You monkey. How can you be so nervous?

ACTOR. You deceived me. Do you love me? Say that you love me.

ACTRESS. As soon as you recover your sanity.

ACTOR. It's coming back now. Just one more thing, my dear. Permit me only this one single question, and after that it will be all over. It will be as beautiful as it is becoming to two artists, gentle and kind.

ACTRESS. What is it?

ACTOR. When you came home just now, you rang the bell.

ACTRESS. Yes. Well?

ACTOR. Why did you ring?

ACTRESS. I can't – I don't understand you.

ACTOR. You do not? My child, just think. Please don't misunderstand, but I know that usually you do not ring because you have a key. Lizzie has a key, too. Perhaps I am not indiscreet when I admit that even I have a key. Why did you have to ring? What did you do with your key?

ACTRESS. You want to ask to whom I gave my key.

ACTOR. I do not express myself so rudely.

ACTRESS. You are so funny . . . because Lizzie's key was in the lock from the inside.

ACTOR. That is not true, because ten minutes before you came I opened the door with my own key. The lock was empty and Lizzie has not moved out of this room since. Where is your key? Do not bring Lizzie's key here, for then she will have none.

ACTRESS. You see, everything is because of this.

ACTOR. Because of what, and what is?

ACTRESS. Everything is because of this, and this is why everything is. Because of this cross examination, because of this sickness, because of this jealousy. All unhappiness comes from that. That's why I dare not move, I dare not say anything, because to you everything is a lie and an excuse. One of the keys has been lost. Lizzie lost her key.

ACTOR. Why did you say then that it was in the lock from the inside?

ACTRESS. Because I do not dare to say anything any more. You are like a madman. You force me to lie even though you know there is nothing I hate so much as lies.

(*She weeps.*)

ACTOR. If you didn't cry now, then everything would be all right. But since you are shedding tears there must be something wrong about this key.

ACTRESS. How can you say such a thing?

ACTOR. Because you tell all sorts of lies. Because nothing is true. Neither the superintendent, nor the Reiners, nor going away, nor coming home, nor the losing of the key. Nothing is true. You were seen beyond the railroad with Count Tibor and the Count kissed your neck several times and finally put you into a cab and you drove away from there. You stopped in front of Tibor's mansion and you went inside with that man. Do not tell me that you went in for a minute only because you went in at three o'clock in the afternoon. Don't say that you came right out because you came away from him exactly at nine o'clock. I'll murder you, you . . . you! One more move and you will be on your knees in front of me.

(*Clutches her arm.*)

ACTRESS. Let go of my arm.

ACTOR. Never.

ACTRESS. I'll bite your hand.

ACTOR. I'd like to see you do that. (*She bites his hand.*) Very well, I'll let you go. Had you not bit me now you would have died. The beast protects herself cleverly. You will never see me again. Adieu.

ACTRESS (*rings the bell. To* LIZZIE *as she enters*). Lizzie, didn't I tell you to call a policeman? Why didn't you do as I told you?

LIZZIE. I thought you were just saying that.

ACTRESS. Run right out and get a policeman. One cannot even be sure of one's life.

(LIZZIE *exits.*)

ACTOR. You will die. I have been told about everything.

ACTRESS. So you work with spies?

ACTOR. I saw you, too. You are a revolting woman. One more word out of you and I'll tell you what you are.

ACTRESS. No, no, I could not survive that.

ACTOR. And yet . . . ah, there is still a spark of decency left in you. Don't cry.

ACTRESS (*sobs*). If you say that, I cannot survive.

ACTOR. Your poor mother out in the country in her little room . . . if she had seen. If she only knew what you have become.

ACTRESS. Leave my mother alone.

ACTOR. That good, fine, clean old woman. That saint, that martyr.

ACTRESS. Don't mix my mother up with it. Don't insult my mother.

ACTOR. I? Insult her? I am sorry for the poor woman. If she only knew what has become of her child.

ACTRESS. What do you want of me? Why do you embitter me? Why do you tear my heart out? You use my mother to stop me from deceiving you. Very well, you shall know — know what you do not know. Yes . . .

ACTOR. Well? What?

(*Pulls a revolver out of his pocket.*)

ACTRESS. You shall know it! Put that knife away.

ACTOR. It isn't a knife, it's a revolver.

ACTRESS. Well, then, put it away.

ACTOR. You will die.

ACTRESS. I could not survive it.

ACTOR. So you admit it. Briefly, you admit it. Say it, my child. Don't be afraid. You need not be sad over my broken heart. Say that you admit it.

ACTRESS. In the first place, this is my apartment. And in the second place, it is already half past ten.

ACTOR. Only quarter past.

ACTRESS. Half past. But it is all the same. A stranger has no right to create a disturbance at night. Go home. I never want to see you again. You have no right here.

ACTOR. I have no right. But Count Tibor has rights.

ACTRESS. He has just as much right as you have.

(*She rings for the maid.*)

ACTOR. That's fine. Thank you. Do you know what you are? I'll tell you what you are, you . . .

ACTRESS. What do I care? Say it. This isn't the first time you will have said it. (*To* LIZZIE *as she enters.*) Lizzie, have you prepared supper?

LIZZIE (*giving her a piece of bread and butter*). I did not know that you would be home.

ACTOR (*sitting sideways, to himself*). A man who sacrificed his name, his career, his everything for a woman . . .

ACTRESS (*to* LIZZIE). If there were only some cold cuts here at least. Is there none of the ham left?

ACTOR (*still talking to himself*). Aha, aha. And what for? Just to have his most beautiful and truest feeling insulted.

LIZZIE. You ate the last of the ham bone yesterday.

ACTRESS. That's right, I ate from the ham bone yesterday.

ACTOR (*still to himself*). A man who has only one single fault . . . the woman he loves . . .

ACTRESS. Is Blau's delicatessen closed?

LIZZIE. Oh, yes, at this time of the night.

ACTOR (*to himself*). Artists' fate! Ha, ha! Artists' fate!

LIZZIE. But I can get something cold from the saloon.

ACTOR (*to himself*). The fate of gullible man.

ACTRESS (*to* LIZZIE). That will be the best.

ACTOR (*to himself*). Faith, honor, reverence, a true and manly virile love — does that mean nothing to you? Answer, Sciarelli.

ACTRESS (*to* LIZZIE). What shall I eat? We had herring yesterday. Let it be . . . let it be . . .

ACTOR (*to her*). All of the values of the soul and of the body are accepted as gifts! The most important — the soul!

ACTRESS (*to* LIZZIE). A few slices of salami, some tongue, and some liverwurst.

ACTOR (*to her*). . . . with which one then becomes bored; for you are tired of my soul, are you not?

ACTRESS (*to* LIZZIE). And a dill pickle.

ACTOR (*to her*). And then I'm dragged in the mud! In the mud!

LIZZIE. Beer, too?

ACTRESS. Dark.

LIZZIE. We have apples here.

ACTOR (*to her*). And the demand that we forge an eternal bond! Do you think that is right?

ACTRESS (*to* LIZZIE). Have you money?

LIZZIE. Yes. But, madame, if you please, the dark beer . . .

ACTOR (*to her*). How do you reconcile that with the demand that I lead you to the altar?

LIZZIE. His dark beer is no good. I'd rather bring light beer.

ACTRESS. Very well. And if he has no salami, then bring some ham.

LIZZIE. I'll bring whatever is fresh.

ACTOR (*laughing bitterly*). Lizzie, you are well trained. When I have a lot of money I'm going to buy you.

LIZZIE (*to* ACTRESS). Please don't be angry with me for not preparing supper, but you said that you would not be home this evening.

ACTOR. Briefly, you had planned to dine *à separée.*

ACTRESS (*to him*). Yes, *à separée* . . .

(*She eats the bread and butter.*)

ACTOR. She eats serenely as a child — an innocent, hungry little girl. Briefly, a *separée* was planned.

ACTRESS. Yes, *separée.*

ACTOR. Then why are you still sitting here? Why are you eating here? A poor, cold actor's supper in this exquisite atmosphere?

ACTRESS. The *separée* was planned. Let's not forget that. I am a *separée* lady. Get out! I never want to see you any more.

ACTOR. I know, I know. I have known for the last half hour that you want to go away from home. Now you want to go away in the night. You are dressed.

ACTRESS. Why are you wearing full dress?

ACTOR. Because none of my other suits are any good.

ACTRESS. In a *separée.*

ACTOR. Something like that.

ACTRESS. Well then, my dear, go. But go now – really, quietly, and forever.

ACTOR. Very well. Very well, you'll see. Very well, my precious.

(*He goes out.* LIZZIE *enters with a tray on which is the supper.*)

ACTRESS. Is he gone?

LIZZIE. Yes.

ACTRESS. Did he say anything to you?

LIZZIE. He said that I would see, too.

ACTRESS. What did you answer?

LIZZIE. I? Nothing. I closed the door behind him.

ACTRESS (*looking at the food*). What did you bring?

LIZZIE. A nice ham bone and a bit of red wine.

(*There is a noise outside.*)

ACTRESS. Did you hear that?

LIZZIE. Did you hear that? He is gone, now.

ACTRESS. Look out the window.

LIZZIE (*looks out the window*). He is going away.

ACTRESS. In which direction?

LIZZIE. Toward Church Square. Now he has stopped. He is coming back.

ACTRESS (*sighing*). If only some day it would get to the point where he wouldn't come right back when he goes away forever.

LIZZIE. He didn't come in. He has passed the house door.

ACTRESS. I see him better from here than you can, looking at him. He is brandishing his cane in the air.

LIZZIE. Yes, ma'am.

ACTRESS. That is for Count Tibor.

LIZZIE. He is kicking the air with one foot.

ACTRESS. That's for you. Let him be, and come here.

LIZZIE (*comes to her*). He is a good man. He is like butter, like oleomargarine. He does whatever you want him to do.

ACTRESS. How do you know what I want? That is what you believe. I will be his wife as soon as I want to. Now the question is something else.

LIZZIE (*at the window*). He is coming, he is coming! He just rang the house doorbell.

ACTRESS. Lizzie!

LIZZIE. Yes, madame?

ACTRESS. Salt, pepper.

LIZZIE. My God, forgive me!

ACTRESS. This is your fourth year with me but never has it happened that nothing was missing.

(*The* ACTOR *enters. Silently paces the floor.*)

LIZZIE. Wouldn't you like to eat something?

ACTOR. Aha, you want to poison me!

LIZZIE. How well you guessed it.

(*She hurries out.*)

ACTOR. What's this? Lizzie is nice to me? It seems that you have forgiven me while I was not here.

ACTRESS. You were not here? I thought you were here.

ACTOR. I had gone.

ACTRESS. So? I didn't even notice. When you go away it is as when other people come in.

ACTOR. I went away and came back.

ACTRESS. Naturally. And I was so happy at last to be able to eat in peace.

ACTOR. But you haven't eaten a single bite since I left.

ACTRESS. Oh, yes I did.

ACTOR. You are just beginning to eat your dinner and the bread and butter . . . there were exactly three bites in it. Here they are: one, two, three, and you just bit for the fourth time. I observed that carefully.

ACTRESS. What do you want to prove by that?

ACTOR. That you stopped eating when I left. Don't make yourself worse than you are, you precious, you sweet. Now that I am watching you eat, I could cry again . . .

ACTRESS. Do I eat so beautifully?

ACTOR. No, when you eat, it touches me because you don't do that on the stage. Your eating is still mine, it is real, it is personal, it is you. Eat, sweetheart, eat . . . with this bread and butter in your hand all is right, is personal, personal, personal.

ACTRESS (*puts the bread and butter aside*). Wait a minute. I must put my bread and butter away, to embrace you. Do you love me?

ACTOR. I adore you.

ACTRESS. Much?

ACTOR. Madly. (*He kisses her.*) Personal; that, too, was personal!

(LIZZIE *enters bringing a pail with a bottle of champagne in it.*)

LIZZIE. Take care, please, the champagne is in it!

ACTOR. What did Lizzie say?

ACTRESS. Something about champagne. We should be careful.

ACTOR. Now sit down there, my sweet little kittykins, and eat, my precious. I will serve you. (*Looking at the champagne.*) Oh! It's French! Mumm's! Where did you get this Mumm's?

(*Pours some into a glass.*)

ACTRESS. I'll tell you, but don't get excited. Cout Tibor sent me two bottles of it. (*The* ACTOR *pours the champagne back into the bottle.*) What are you doing?

ACTOR. I refuse to drink any of it.

ACTRESS. Don't start again. When we get married everything will be mutual anyway. . . . We'll put our salaries together, and even the gifts will belong to both of us. . . . If you get anything from the public you will give me half, will you not?

ACTOR. All of it, precious.

ACTRESS. Then why don't you drink some of this?

ACTOR. Why did the Count send it?

ACTRESS. For me to drink it.

ACTOR. But how? What was the reason? He wanted to come here at night and drink champagne.

ACTRESS. But, please . . .

ACTOR. How did he suddenly get the idea of sending two bottles of champagne?

(*Again fills the glasses.*)

ACTRESS. They played some sort of an amateur performance and this Count Tibor played a Jew . . .

ACTOR. A Jew!

ACTRESS. He needed a big, black beard and came to me. I told Hanzs Scheller and he went and made up the Count Tibor as a Jew. He got ten marks for it, which were very welcome because the poor fellow has five children and the sixth one is on the way. There you are.

ACTOR. Six children? That's right. But what has that to do with the champagne?

(*He drinks.*)

ACTRESS. Oh, didn't I tell you about that? He sent these two bottles of champagne by Scheller because I recommended Scheller to him. Count Tibor scored a huge success in the piece. That's simple enough.

ACTOR. Because you told this story so quickly, it is far from being true. But now it doesn't make any difference. I have a principle: I do not drink of free champagne which desiring counts send my wife.

ACTRESS. And the gold cigarette case that was given you by the red-headed Mrs. Rado? Did you hesitate to give that to me? Did I ask you what you got that for?

ACTOR. But permit me, I gave her lessons!

(*He drinks.*)

ACTRESS. You gave her lessons!

ACTOR. I coached her movements for an amateur performance.

ACTRESS. Movements! See? That is the same.

ACTOR. Well, then, if it is the same! (*He drinks*). Phoey! I am a good-for-nothing because I drink this champagne! Phoey!

(*He drinks.*)

ACTRESS. Yes, now you are disgraced. You pighead, you genius, you ox!

ACTOR (*embracing her*). Can't we always talk to each other so nicely and pleasantly?

ACTRESS. You . . . you wonderful one! My God! Why am I not as talented as you are?

ACTOR. Well, you mustn't demand too much.

ACTRESS. All this aggravation is because I am not worthy of you. A second soubrette with a small voice . . . and the very best comic *bon vivant,* the very, very best . . . and what will you be when you have developed fully!

ACTOR. If I could live in quiet peace . . . if you didn't torture me, I could develop.

ACTRESS. You will develop, my sweet, you will develop.

ACTOR. And will you be true to me?

ACTRESS. I am true, you ninny, only I do not show it!

ACTOR. My angel, if only I knew what it is you want of me. Because you want something, I am certain. I hereby kiss away your tears and you will tell me what you want.

ACTRESS. Call me Emma.

ACTOR. Sciarelli, I am already used to this, your glorious name.

(*He drinks.*)

ACTRESS. Glorious! At other times you do not speak of me like this. At other times you look down on me. You do not consider me talented.

ACTOR. I? You? Chancellor, have you any other wish?

ACTRESS. Only one . . . just a single one . . .

ACTOR. Well?

ACTRESS. And that is the most important one. Seriously.

ACTOR. Aha, ha, ha!

ACTRESS. What do you mean?

ACTOR. Now I'll find out why I suffered so much this evening.

ACTRESS. Why do you stand directly in front of me at the end of the second finale in this new operetta?

ACTOR. I stand directly in front of you?

ACTRESS. Yes, you cover me. You hide me from the audience.

ACTOR. In the second finale?

ACTRESS. Yes. Once in a hundred years I have a small rôle in which I could stand out and even now you stand in front of me.

" Oh, you little, droll king's son,
Oh, you little, droll king's son,
You king's son, king's son, king's son,"

Then I, who play the Princess, lean over toward the table on the right and collapse on it because the king's son leaves me. And you come as the Premier and sing:

"That our hope, our salvation
Shall not desert us, desert us,"

And we sing:

"Desert us, desert us, desert us,
desert us, desert us,"

Isn't it so?

ACTOR. Yes, desert us, desert us, desert us. Well, and —

ACTRESS. So then. Now I have the opportunity to do a nice bit: I sob, wring my hands, look up to heaven, faint — all beautiful things, all effective — and what happens? You stand right in front of me.

ACTOR. Sciarelli? I stand in front of you?

ACTRESS. Yes. You see? You don't even notice it. In the beginning I didn't say a thing, because I tried to sob behind your back. I stuck my head out, but all in vain, because you jump around. When I stuck my head toward the right, you jumped toward the right. When I stuck it toward the left, you jumped toward the left, so the audience does not see me and my entire rôle is spoiled.

ACTOR. So that is why you tortured me so here all evening?

ACTRESS. What can I do so long as I have no other weapon?

ACTOR. So that is why I should marry you? That is why my sister should jump out of a fourth story window?

ACTRESS. This is the first time I hear about that. Very nice. You kept quiet about that until now.

ACTOR. I am not accustomed to threatening with the suicide of others.

ACTRESS. I am so unhappy, Sovari, I am so unhappy.

(*She sinks on the table.*)

ACTOR. Sciarelli, this is no time for jokes. One question. Pardon, but just a single question. What am I in that piece?

ACTRESS. You are the Premier.

ACTOR. Well, what do you think? That there is no acting to that part? The Premier simply sings that he is overthrown, that his career is done for? Do you know what kind of pain that is? It is one of the greatest blows in life and it is the duty of the actor to express that, to reproduce it. So when I say: "done for," I jump to the right and hold my head, and when I say "done for" again, I hold my head again and jump hither and thither with a bitter face, like every overthrown premier. Such a thing must be acted out. Right . . . left . . . done for . . . done for. . . .

ACTRESS. You see? You see? You see? This is how you cover me . . . this is exactly how you cover me . . .

ACTOR. But if there is no room elsewhere! At the left — here, there — stand the pages and the peasants in yellow. In the middle, sits the old King. Here — there — stand the Royal Guards and the opposition peasants in green. Where, then, can I jump around?

ACTRESS (*weeping*). Anywhere except in front of me. And still you dare to say that you love me?

Actor. Like the moon — the stars. Like the boatman of the sea, the rising sun on the shores of the Pamphiles.

Actress. Then why do you suppress me?

Actor. Sciarelli! I? Suppress you?

Actress. You yourself admit that you cover me. I covered Benutzky for two months in Linz, because she paddled my fiancé.

Actor. Why?

Actress. Because her husband was my fiancé. Helping to play, that is love. Not to marry one and to die for one. That is for the civilians. In the third act I would have the right to stand in front of you because by that time you are already an overthrown Premier, and I recover my rank as Princess. See! Yet I do not do it. That is love.

Actor. It is all the same. You may take my life, but I will not permit you to interfere with my art. If you don't like it, see the manager.

Actress. Very well. If I do go to see him, I will go as an artist and not as a woman.

Actor. We know that. You go into his office as an artist and come out as a woman. Go. See the manager.

Actress. I am going.

Actor. Threaten me.

Actress. Will you step aside in the finale?

Actor. No, I would rather marry you.

Actress. Will you not step aside for me?

Actor. No.

Actress. Then I will stand in front of you in the third act, when the King dismisses you.

Actor. I'd like to see you do that.

Actress. Very well, you'll see me do it.

Actor. Very well, I would like to see it — And this woman dares to say that she loves me!

Actress. See, you take it that way, too.

(*She weeps.*)

Actor. If the public only saw Sciarelli crying at home!

Actress. It is terrible how I suffer. Give me a swallow of champagne.

Actor. There is none left. The bottle is empty.

Actress. But my full glass was around here somewhere.

Actor. That's empty, too. Phew, this champagne!

Actress. What have you got against this champagne?

Actor. Don't be afraid, I'll pay for it. I'll pay for it on the first.

Actress. Why are you so cruel to me? You are killing me.

Actor. Or you, me.

Actress. Love me, Sovari . . . I will excuse you from marriage, I will excuse you from suicide. Don't forsake me in my career. Worship me just a little bit more. . . . You see how weak I am, compared to you. . . . I am nothing and you are the great, the powerful, the strong, the genius, the lion!

Actor. Will you ever interfere in my art again?

Actress. No.

Actor. Never?

Actress. Never again.

Actor. Well, then . . . I will never again stand in front of you in the finale. That's all right, that's all right. I am doing it of my own free will, however. It is my whim as a gentleman and I am not forced to it. You must solemnly acknowledge that.

Actress. I acknowledge it. You. . . . You . . . my lord . . . my master.

Actor. Say: My lion. I like that.

Actress. My lion, my desert! You . . . You, My Sunday! You . . . my King, you . . . my President!

Actor. President! That, perhaps, is still nicer than lion.

Actress. I adore you! If I weren't ashamed. . . .

Actor. What then?

Actress. No, no, I am embarrassed.

Actor. Tell me, my sweet. Say it, say what you have on your heart.

Actress. If I weren't ashamed . . . I would ask you for an autograph.

Actor. You precious. (Lizzie *fetches the other bottle of champagne.*) What is this?

Actress. It is the other bottle of champagne.

Actor. So you may see what kind of a gentleman you are dealing with, you will get some of this bottle, too!

(*Takes the bottle to open it.*)

Curtain

—*From the Hungarian of Ferenc Molnár (1878–), translated by Sanford J. Greenburger.*

PART SEVENTEEN

Man in Bereavement

THAT MEN THINK OF DEATH quite as deeply though perhaps less often than they think of love, is faithfully reflected by poetry. So has it been from the beginning of recorded time, among the more primitive as well as the more advanced peoples, in the Orient no less than in the Occident. Indeed so nearly universal is the never finished book of the dead that, for the sake of brevity and avoidance of mere repetition, the poems selected in the present group are confined to the Western World and to the longer and more formal type often called the threnody or lament. Such a method facilitates comparisons between the products of one nation and another, especially since half of the selections belong to a continuous tradition extending from the Age of Greece at least to the nineteenth century and consciously pursued by the authors themselves. The interesting contrasts become the more striking because of the common background.

The course is, broadly speaking, from the mythological and allegorical to the sociological and the realistic. We begin with a religious hymn, a lament by a deathless god for a mortal who is still a step beyond mortality, and conclude with poems that explore the bereavements of individuals mourning for their beloved and of nations lamenting for their lost children.

Poems such as these, dealing with the most elemental of human feelings, really need little commentary or explanation, save a few notes to place them more clearly in their historical settings. In outward appearance and even in name at times agreeing with the Ode, unlike the typical ode they have a core much more clearly emotional than intellectual. One notes that Bion's lament of Venus for Adonis, for example, is a highly emotional hymn to be sung in the festivals of Adonis. By the modern reader it should be remembered that Adonis's death was not the absolute death of a common mortal. The myth symbolized fertility, especially in the vegetable world. As the last verses of the poem casually remind us, Adonis descends annually to the lower world, and annually rises to live anew.

The lament for Bion, commonly ascribed to the poet Moschus, is obviously written in reference to Bion's own hymn for Adonis, thus beating a track familiar to countless authors of threnodies in both the classical and the Christian eras. Boccacio's beautiful elegy to Olympia, itself much imitated by subsequent authors, represents the fusion of the two rival traditions, one emphasizing the contrast of the seasonal resurgence of nature with the irrevocable death of the individual mortal, the other joining to the thought of natural resurgence a Christian faith in the resurrection of body and soul.

A glimpse into the more purely Christian attitude toward death is afforded by two remarkable lyrics, the first, a ballade written in the fifteenth century by François Villon. Unlike the classical poems, this is almost wholly subjective. The poet, who believes himself about to be hung, in the company of five other culprits, vividly imagines the physical horrors of death and disintegration upon the gibbet and fervently implores the prayers of the passers-by for the safety of their souls. No poem of universal meaning can well be at the same time more colored by the age of its origin or more aloof from alien traditions. The second poem, the noble *Coplas,* or ballad, by Jorge Manrique, expresses the Christian paradox of the dignity of man and the contempt of worldliness.

In passing to the two most splendid of English elegies, the reader advances along the main currents of the neo-classical tradition effectively blending the ancient with the Christian. By introducing into *Lycidas* references to the political struggles of his age, Milton deserts the more generalized conceptions of Boccaccio's elegy. Similarly, he has been more ingenious than Boccaccio in the use of a classical imagery to give poetic expression to events in the life of his departed friend. The procession of mourners envisaged by Bion and Moschus is again enacted in the highly ritualistic lines of the Puritan poet. But there is the same fusion of classical and Christian ideas, and the same colorful garment of nature-worship expressing a Christian faith in personal immortality.

Of all the great English elegies, Shelley's *Adonais* is the most faithful to its classical background. The reader with the threnodies of Bion and Moschus clearly in mind happily recognizes the passages in which Shelley utilizes the art and imagery of his predecessors to his own ends. As Moschus lamented the death of the pastoral poet, Bion, Shelley mourns the death of the pastoral poet, Keats. As the first Adonis was slain by a boar, so the second Adonis, according to Shelley's poetic legend, was slain by a boar symbolizing the hostility of literary critics and the obtuseness of the public. And finally, as Venus lyrically bewailed her dying love, so the Lyric Muse and all her train bewail the young poet to whom they have given their hearts. Shelley deserts the elegiac poets of Greece only to remember the Greek philosophers, for his concluding stanzas contain a hymn wholly inspired by the elements of Platonic doctrine. These poems are, of course, but two of the many English elegies molded by the classical tradition. Spenser, Arnold and Swinburne notably excel in the same form, traces of which are apparent as early as Chaucer's *Book of the Duchess.*

Life was meanwhile evolving forms less ritualistic and more appropriate to the expression of the moods and sympathies of a changing civilization. Thus behind Gray's famous elegy is the democratic sentiment of the romantic creed: the veneration not of the gods but of the common man. What more personal thoughts, if any, may have been in Gray's mind while writing are hidden from the reader. Gray's theme is death the democrat. Brooding over the democracy of the grave, he at the same time chastens the vaunt of the great and ennobles the life of the poor. Although few English poems are more classical in purity and simplicity of phrase, Gray's content belongs not so much to the Christian Middle Ages, so admirably illustrated in the ballade by Villon, as to a dawn of political and social democracy.

The highly subjective character of the best of modern French poetry appears in the famous lines, *Souvenir,* by Alfred de Musset. Here the thought, as in Gray's poem, is simple, while the experience is, to say the least, quite as profound. On exploring the depths of his own soul, torn between grief in the loss and rapture in the memory of the beloved, Musset finds the recollection of happiness in the end stronger than the pangs of bereavement. His stanzas betray an inner struggle not unknown wherever man is found, but seldom so powerfully envisaged as in the modern soul.

A strong realism, or preference for the concrete as against the abstract, which is a dominating characteristic of both Spanish art and literature, in all respects etches the poignant lines of José Asuncion Silva's elegy, *Nocturne.* Here is a poem quite as subjective and introspective as Musset's and yet strengthened by a biting realism not only in the thought and imagery but in the terse, colloquial and ineloquent language. Although written by a Venezuelan poet of the late nineteenth century, the lyric is as truly an elegy as any composed in the ancient world for the traditional accompaniment of the lamenting flute. But there is no ceremony in this threnody, and there is no more allegory than demanded by the symbolic character of all truly poetic thought.

In America the threnody has still more clearly compromised between old and new. Certain forms again and again repeated seem as inevitable as the subject matter. Almost invariably we discover in turn a description of the deceased, a picture of his mourners, and some apology for their consolation. So is it with Whitman's celebrated elegy, "When Lilacs Last in the Dooryard Bloomed." A loss that seems personal to the poet is magnified into a national grief when Whitman, in this threnody for Lincoln, laments not only the dead President but all who have fallen during the sad war where our national hero was the victorious commander-in-chief. Whitman uses subtle symbols: the tearful falling of the moon affords a natural image of his grief; the cedar is symbol of the memorial ceremonies; and the bird, of the solemn final consolation. Whitman's nature-imagery recapitulates that of Moschus; his picture of Lincoln's funeral cortege across the States, with the melancholy flags and the muffled music of grief, has analogues in the liturgical elements in Bion, Moschus, Milton, and Shelley. The complaint that Whitman's masterpiece in free verse was in fact too conventional was, we believe, a mistake in aesthetic judgment, but shows no small insight into historical criticism and comparative literature.

Lament for Adonis

Wail, wail, Ah for Adonis! He is lost to us, lovely Adonis!
Lost is lovely Adonis! The Loves respond with lamenting.

Nay, no longer in robes of purple recline, Aphrodite:
Wake from thy sleep, sad queen, black-stoled, rain blows on thy bosom;
Cry to the listening world, *He is lost to us, lovely Adonis!*
Wail, wail, Ah for Adonis! The Loves respond with lamenting.

Lovely Adonis is lying, sore hurt in his thigh, on the mountains,
Hurt in his thigh with the tusk, while grief consumes Aphrodite:
Slowly he drops toward death, and the black blood drips from his fair flesh,

Down from his snow-white skin; his eyes wax dull 'neath the eyelids,
Yea and the rose hath failed his lips, and around them the kisses
Die and wither, the kisses that Kupris will not relinquish:
Still, though he lives no longer, a kiss consoles Aphrodite;
But he knows not, Adonis, she kissed him while he was dying.
Wail, wail, Ah for Adonis! The Loves respond with lamenting.

Cruel, cruel the wound in the thigh that preys on Adonis:
But in her heart Cytherea hath yet worse wounds to afflict her.
Round him his dear hounds bay, they howl in their grief to the heavens;
Nymphs of the woodlands wail: but she, the Queen Aphrodite,
Loosing her locks to the air, roams far and wide through the forest,
Drowned in grief, disheveled, unsandaled, and as she flies onward,
Briars stab at her feet and cull the blood of the goddess.
She with shrill lamentation thro' glen and thro' glade is carried,
Calling her Syrian lord, demanding him back, and demanding.
But where he lies, dark blood wells up and encircles the navel;
Blood from the gushing thighs empurples the breast; and the snow-white
Flank that was once so fair, is now dyed red for Adonis.
Wail, wail, Ah, Cytherea! The Loves respond with lamenting.

She then hath lost her lord, and with him hath lost her celestial
Beauty; for fair was he, and fair, while he lived, Aphrodite:
Now in his death her beauty hath died. *Ah, Ah, Cytherea!*
All the mountains lament, and the oaks moan, *Ah for Adonis!*
Streams as they murmur and flow complain of thy griefs, Aphrodite:
Yea and the springs on the hills, in the woods, weep tears for Adonis:
Flowers of the field for woe flush crimson red; and Cythêra,
Thorough the dells and the glens, shrills loud the dirge of her anguish:
Woe, woe, Ah, Cytherea! He is lost to us, lovely Adonis!
Echo repeats the groan: *Lost, lost, is lovely Adonis!*
Kupris, who but bewailed thy pangs of a love overwhelming?

She, when she saw, when she knew the unstanchable wound of Adonis,
When she beheld the red blood on his pale thigh's withering blossom,
Spreading her arms full wide, she moaned out: "Stay, my Adonis!
Stay, ill-fated Adonis! that I once more may approach thee!
Clasp thee close to my breast, and these lips mingle with thy lips!
Rouse for a moment, Adonis, and kiss me again for the last time;
Kiss me as long as the kiss can live on the lips of a lover;
Till from thy inmost soul to my mouth and down to my marrow
Thy life-breath shall run, and I quaff the wine of thy philter,
Draining the draught of thy love: that kiss will I treasure, Adonis,
E'en as it were thyself; since thou, ill-starred, art departing,
Fleeing me far, O Adonis, to Acheron faring, the sad realm
Ruled by a stern savage king: while I, the unhappy, the luckless,
I live; goddess am I, and I may not follow or find thee.
Persephone, take thou my lord, my lover; I know thee
Stronger far than myself: all fair things drift to thy dwelling.
I meanwhile am accursed, possessed with insatiable sorrow,
Weeping my dead, my Adonis who died, and am shaken and shattered.
Diest thou then, my desired? and desire like a dream hath escaped me.
Widowed is now Cytherea; the Loves in her halls are abandoned;
Perished with thee is my girdle. Ah, why wouldst thou hunt, over-bold one?
Being so beautiful, why wast thou mad to fight with a wild beast?"
Thus then Kupris mourned; and the Loves respond with lamenting:
Wail, wail, Ah for Adonis! He is lost to us, lovely Adonis!

Tears the Paphian shed, drop by drop for the drops of Adonis'
Blood; and on earth each drop, as it fell, grew into a blossom:
Roses sprang from the blood, and the tears gave birth to the wind-flower.
  Wail, wail, Ah, Cytherea! He is lost to us, lovely Adonis!

  Wail, wail, Ah for Adonis! He is lost to us, lovely Adonis!
Now in the oak-woods cease to lament for thy lord, Aphrodite.
No proper couch is this which the wild leaves strew for Adonis.
Let him thy own bed share, Cytherea, the corpse of Adonis;
E'en as a corpse he is fair, fair corpse as fallen aslumber.
Now lay him soft to sleep, sleep well in the wool of the bedclothes,
Where with thee through the night in holy dreams he commingled,
Stretched on a couch all gold, that yearns for him stark though he now be.
Shower on him garlands, flowers: all fair things died in his dying;
Yea, as he faded away, so shrivel and wither the blossoms.
Syrian spikenard scatter, anoint him with myrrh and with unguents:
Perish perfumes all, since he, thy perfume, is perished.
  Wail, wail, Ah for Adonis! The Loves respond with lamenting.

Lapped in his purple robes is the delicate form of Adonis.
Round him weeping Loves complain and moan in their anguish,
Clipping their locks for Adonis: and one of them treads on his arrows,
One of them breaks his bow, and one sets heel on the quiver;
One hath loosed for Adonis the latchet of sandals, and some bring
Water to pour in an urn; one laves the wound in his white thigh;
One from behind with his wings keeps fanning dainty Adonis.
  Wail, wail, Ah for Adonis! The Loves respond with lamenting.

  Wail, wail, Ah, Cytherea! The Loves respond with lamenting.

Every torch at the doors hath been quenched by thy hand, Hymenæus;
Every bridal wreath hath been torn to shreds; and no longer,
Hymen, Hymen no more is the song, but a new song of sorrow,
Woe, woe! and *Ah for Adonis!* resounds in lieu of the bridesong.
This the Graces are shrilling, the son of Cinyras hymning,
Lost is lovely Adonis! in loud antiphonal accents.
Woe, woe! sharply repeat, far more than the praises of Paiôn,
Woe! and *Ah for Adonis!* the Muses who wail for Adonis,
Chaunt their charms to Adonis. — But he lists not to their singing;
Not that he wills not to hear, but the Maiden doth not release him.
Cease from moans, Cytherea, to-day refrain from the death-songs:
Thou must lament him again, and again shed tears in a new year.

— *From the Greek of Bion (c. 120 B.C.), translated by John Addington Symonds.*

Epitaph of Bion

Mournfully answer my groan, dark vales and Dorian water,
And with me, ye rivers, lament for our darling — for Bion!
Drop with tears, ye plants, and moan, ye groves of the woodland:
Flowers, O now breathe out your lives in sorrowful clusters.
Roses, blush with grief, and pale anemonies redden!
Hyacinth, babble thy letters, and plainer within thy petals
Wear the *alas! alas!* — A beautiful singer has perished!
  Now, Sicilian Muses, begin the song of your sorrow.

Utter it, nightingales, in tangled leafage bewailing,
Say to the full Sicilian fountains of Arethusa,
Bion, the herdsman, is dead! and say that melody with him,
Aye, and the Doric strain, are hushed in silence for ever.

Now, Sicilian Muses, begin the song of your sorrow.

Weep, ye swans of Strymôn, beside the waters forlornly,
And with piteous voices a sorrowful madrigal warble,
Such as his voice was wont to sing in your rites of mourning.
Tell Æagrian maidens and nymphs of Bistonian valleys,
Once more tell them all: *He is gone, the Dorian Orpheus!*

Now, Sicilian Muses, begin the song of your sorrow.

He that was dear to the herds no longer sings, and no longer
Carols, reclining beneath the lonely shade of the oak-trees,
But in Pluto's hall a Lethêan melody murmurs.
Mute are the hills henceforth, and ever the heifers bemoan him,
Roaming astray with the bulls, nor care to eat of the herbage.

Now, Sicilian Muses, begin the song of your sorrow.

Even Apollo bewept thy swift fate, Bion, and Satyrs
Mingled their sobs with those of the sable-vestured Priapi;
Pans are sighing to hear thy minstrelsy, while through the copses
Nymphs of the springs bewailed, and their tears descended in waters.
Echo, also, amid the rocks, deplores that in silence
Now no more thy lips can she mimic; and at thy dying
Trees have dropped their fruit, and all the flowers have withered;
Nor from the ewes has fair milk flowed,—nor trickles the honey
Still from hives but, grieved, has died in the wax: for it boots not,
Since thy honey has wasted, to gather the sweets of the clover.

Now, Sicilian Muses, begin the song of your sorrow.

Never so much by the bordering coasts lamented the dolphin,
Never so much on the rocks the nightingale sang, nor so sadly
Plained the swallow ever along the uplands, nor Ceyx
Over Alcyone's pains made ever such piteous clamor,
Never so much the cerylus sang in the live-green billows,
Neither so much in eastern vales did the bird of Memnôn,
Fluttering round the mound of the Son of Eôs, bemoan him,
As they have wailed for Bion — our Bion departed for ever!

Now, Sicilian Muses, begin the song of your sorrow.

Nightingales, grieving with all the swallows, — whom once he delighted,
Whom he was teaching to babble, — now perched on the opposite branches
Cried to each other in woe: and birds of the forest responded, —
Grieve, ye bereaved, and we — we also have part in your mourning!

Now, Sicilian Muses, begin the song of your sorrow.

Who henceforth shall sing to thy pipe, O thrice-desired?
Who shall put mouth to thy reeds? Who so bold? for thy inspiration
Even yet they breathe, and thy lips which filled them with music,
And in the rushes Echo is still devouring thy numbers.
Say, shall I bear to Pan the flute? perhaps to awake it
Even he would not dare, lest his prize to thine should be second.

Now, Sicilian Muses, begin the song of your sorrow.

She, too, weeps for thy lay, — Galatea, whom once thou delightedst
When by thy side she sat along the shores of the ocean.
Not like Cyclops sangst thou: him the fair Galatea
Used to flee, forsooth, but thee more sweetly regarded,
Oft, than the sea, and now, in the wearisome, sandy, stretches
Sits forgetting the wave, and still she pastures thy oxen.

Now, Sicilian Muses, begin the song of your sorrow.

With thee, herdsman, utterly perished the gifts of the Muses

Virginal kisses enchanting, the lips of the youths that caressed us;
All around thy tomb the sorrowful Loves are weeping.
More, far more than her dearest kiss doth Cypris adore thee,
More than the kiss with which she clung to dying Adonis.
Now, Sicilian Muses, begin the song of your sorrow.

This is thy second pang, Melês, thou tunefullest river:
This is a new distress. Calliope's mouth of sweetness,
Homer, left thee first, and thine illustrious offspring
Thou didst weep, they say, didst weep with passionate streamlets,
Sending thy voice throughout the length and breadth of the ocean;
Now thou sobbest anew, and another son art deploring.
Both were dear to the springs: and of the Pegásean fountain
One indeed would quaff, and the other of Arethusa.
That one verily sang of Tyndarus' beautiful daughter,
Thetis's mighty son, and Menelaos Atreides;
Not of wars, nor of tears, but of Pan would the other be chanting,
And would discourse of herdsmen and, singing, would pasture the cattle;
Shepherds'-pipes would he fashion, and milk the lovable heifer,
Aye, and would teach the kisses of youths, — and deep in his bosom
Nourish Erôs and wake the passion of Aphroditê.
Now, Sicilian Muses, begin the song of your sorrow.

All the towns lament thee, Bion, — each illustrious city.
Ascra, indeed, for thee far more than for Hesiod sorrows;
Not so much for Pindar yearn the Bœotian woodlands;
Pleasant Lesbos never so much wept over Alcæus:
Nor hath the Teian town shed tears so much for her minstrel.
More than Archilochus thee now Paros mourns; and as sadly
Mytilene repeats even yet thy song and not Sappho's.
All the makers of pastorals, all to whom from the Muses
Comes a melodious voice, bewail aloud thy departure:
Weeps the glory of Samos, Sicelidas; while now lamenting
He of Cydonians erst with his glad eye joyous to gaze on,
Lycidas, pours forth tears; and mourns amid folk Triopæan,
There on the banks of Hales, Philetas; Theocritus also
Grieves in his own Syracuse; but I, moreover, now sing thee
Strains of Ansonian woe, — myself to the art not unwonted,
But of the Dorian Muse, the bucolic, which thou to thy scholars
Taught betimes, an heir: thy riches only, to others
Thou didst leave, but me with the gift of thy minstrelsy honored!
Now, Sicilian Muses, begin the song of your sorrow.

Even the mallows, — alas! alas! — when once in the garden
They, or the pale-green parsley and crisp growing anise, have perished,
Afterwards they will live and flourish again at their season;
We, the great and brave, — or the wise, — when death has benumbed us,
Deaf in the hollow ground a silent, infinite slumber
Sleep: for ever we lie in the trance that knoweth no waking.
Verily thou no less shalt be sepulchred also in silence,
While it has pleased the nymphs that the croak of the frog shall be ceaseless.
Him, though, would I not envy: for no sweet music he utters.
Now, Sicilian Muses, begin the song of your sorrow.

Poison came to thy mouth: thou knewest poison, my Bion!
How, O how could it meet thy lips, nor change to their sweetness?
Who, while thou didst speak, so barbarous as to commingle
Poison, and pass to thee, nor flee the spell of thy numbers?
Now, Sicilian Muses, begin the song of your sorrow.

Justice o'erreaches all. And I, in tears at this anguish,
Also bewail thy fate. And knew I the byway they followed,
Downward to Tartarus groping, — Orpheus, and once Odysseus,
And Alcides erst, — I also haply would seek for
Pluto's mansion, that I might chance again to behold thee
And, if thou singest to Pluto, might hear thy lay. But to Cora
Something Sicilian warble and some sweet song of the meadows.
She is Sicilian also, and played in the valleys Ætnæan,
Aye, and the Dorian melody knew; and therefore unhonored
Shall not be thy strain, but, as before thee to Orpheus
Sweetly touching his lyre she gave Eurydice ransomed,
Bion, thee no less will she send to thy hills. And would Pluto
Yield anything to my piping, I also would sing to regain thee.

—*From the Greek by Moschus (fl. second century B.C.), translated by Edmund Clarence Stedman.*

Olympia

SILVIUS
CAMALUS
THERAPON
OLYMPIA

SILV. If I err not, the sylvan sprites rejoice.
List, boys! with song of birds the grove is filled.
With gentle whine Wolf scampers to and fro;
Something he sees; he wags as for a friend.
Bright day, long heralded, bestreaks the shades:
go, seek ye what it is, and what good Wolf
yonder has seen; and quickly bring me word.

CAM. Our master, when alack! he cannot lull
his aching heart to sleep, from downy bed
gives orders, and poor we, toil-weary boys,
what recketh he? — must forth and view dread night.

SILV. In Western Ocean when the Dawn's first streak
illumines Earth, when Delia westward leads
her brother's team, when hinds o'er lions vaunt,
a servant then perchance will do as bid.
But, Therapon, do thou unbar the door!
Fear not; see thou, I pray, what Wolf has seen. —

THER. Haste, sir, arise, come forth! Our ancient oaks
are all by fire possessed; light conquers night.
The grove is all a-glow; fierce flames now lap
the very gods within. Awed by the sight,
I hied me thence. The flames now lap the gods!

SILV. Pan, holy God of shepherds, be my help!
Go ye, my boys, with water face the flames.
Stay, Therapon! stay here awhile. — What is't?
What see I? Am I sane? Perchance I sleep:
Nay, yonder light, it is nor flame nor fire.
Seest not the branches fair, the hazels green
amid the glow, the beech-trees all about
inviolate? Here burns no evil heat.

THER. Look skyward! spangled stars betoken night.
Daylight the wood illumes. What wonder next?

SILV. So Nature marks her changes; day and night
commingled she displays. But here I see
nor Phoebe's beams nor Sol's. Rare fragrances
feel'st not, as if Dame Nature here had made
a grove of Araby? What flowers fresh
has Night brought forth? What strains hear I above?
God-haunted spots and pastures these things show —

(OLYMPIA *enters.*)

OLYM. Hail, chiefest glory, dearest father, hail!
Fear not, I am thy daughter. Why this look?

SILV. I' faith, I know not, do I wake or dream!
My child's voice hear I, and her image sweet
stands here before me. Fool! Too oft the gods
With shadows trick dull mortals. Let us home!

OLYM. Silvius, doubt not! think'st thou Olympia
would mock her father, or herself reveal
against God's will? To dry thy tears I come.

SILV. Now know I, 'tis no trick of love or dream.
O too beloved! thy father's dearest hope!
What god restrained thee, child? Me Fusca told
that, whilst I journey'd to Campania's hills,
Vesuvian pastures, thou from us was reft,
and, hid in sacred soil, was lost to sight.
Thinking 'twas so, in misery I mourn'd;
I wailed thee, daughter mine, on mountain heights,
in woods and far-off glades, and call'd thee oft.
But me, if I be worthy, tell what haunts
have held thee this long day. Who gave to thee
thy robe so white, entwined with yellow gold?
What light shines in thine eyes, ne'er seen before?
Thy comrades — who? Wondrous, how grown art thou
in so brief time! Thou seem'st for spousal fit.
OLYM. The vestments, sire, which thou to me didst give,
Great Mother Earth holds in her mighty lap.
These robes, this form, this glorious beauty, heavenly bright
The Virgin gave; with Her I was. But, lo,
My comrades hast ne'er seen before? Rejoice!
SILV. I call them not to mind. More beauteous sure
was not Narcissus, nor was Daphnis such,
the wood-nymphs' darling, nor Alexis fair!
OLYM. Know'st thou thy Marius not, thy Julus, too,
and these sweet sisters mine? Thy dear ones all!
SILV. The sight of cheeks down-shaded reft from me
the faces that I know. Now join we hands;
come ye to my embrace and kisses glad,
and let me sate my soul. Thy praises, Pan,
how shall I sing, and thine, Sylvanus? Boys,
Strip you for wrestling; lead our ancient games!
From sacred beeches hang the victor's meeds!
Let beakers foam; and jocund Bacchus laud!
With garlands deck the gods; with grassy turf
heap high their altars. To Diana slay
a heifer white; to Night a tawny beast!
Reeds for the lads, good youth; for lasses wreaths!
OLYM. Reeds, Silvius, have we here, and goodly wreaths;
and, if so please thee festal cheer to stir,
strains will we chant these woods have never known.
SILV. Hushed is the wood; Arno flows silently;
hush'd are the fields; and hushed be ye, my boys.

OLYM. *"Endless our life by Codrus' grace divine!*
He, sent of late from high Olympus down
into the Maid, the Golden Age recalled;
shepherds' vile scorn He bore, on cedar hung;
a triumph gave He Death, of His free will.
Endless our life by Codrus' grace divine!
So from the blemished sheep He washed old taints,
old maladies and sores, with His bright blood;
then sought He Pluto's dales, broke up his folds,
and brought to light the Father's flocks and herds.
Endless our life by Codrus' grace divine!
Death slain, Elysium's fragrant fields He oped;
to gardens honey-sweet His host He led,
Victor all-bright with laurel and with oak,
and gave us evermore the wish'd-for homes.
Endless our life by Codrus' grace divine.
At doomsday, when their slough all kinds resume,
He comes again, to part the lambs from goats, —
these to wild beasts, to Thrones eternal those:
anon a heaven new will compass them.
Endless our life by Codrus' grace divine."

. . . . .

SILV. Tell me, ye youths, caught ye the heavenly sense
of yon sweet strain? Ne'er Tityrus sang so,
nor aged Mopsus in his sunny wood.
Sacred it is, to be remembered aye!
Unto the maids, from me give snow-white doves;
unto the lads strong bows from Ischiros!
OLYM. Hold thou them! To the glorious climes we haunt
nought mortal comes. Immortals shun things frail.
SILV. What climes? oh, daughter mine, what climes, I pray?

Yon roof us all will cover; quiet sleep
green sward will give; a turf 'neath oak our board;
the crystal brook our fount of richest draughts;
and our wild woodlands chestnuts ripe will bring,
and apples fresh; our fruitful herd young kids
and cheese. What other climes, then, would ye seek?
  OLYM. Have I not told thee, father dear, that Earth
the trappings keeps that thou to me didst give?
I am not what I was, the child thou knewest;
now am I numbered with the god-like throng.
Me fair Olympus calls, my comrades too;
homeward we turn. Sweet father mine, farewell!
  SILV. Leav'st thou me wretched thus, I weep to death.
  OLYM. Away with grief! Think'st thou to burst thy fate
with tears? As many as created be,
we all are born for death. I have but done
what thou shalt do. Rate not with spleen, I pray,
the gods' eternal years. Believe peace is thine
hereafter; render praise to Heav'n for me,
that, dying, I 'scaped death and toils below.
Awhile apart, sure thou wilt see me soon,
and lead with me in bliss unending years.
  SILV. Mine eyes will waste with tears, mine age will pine.
After life's woes in what wood shall I seek
thee, fleeing hence, twice reft from these mine arms?
  OLYM. Elysium I seek, where thou wilt come.
  SILV. Elysium! The Mantuan bard, methinks,
sang once and piped thereof; was none more skilled.
Is thine the spot he sang? Fain would I learn.
  OLYM. His mighty mind, indeed, some glories grasped,
some beauties of the place; he sang but few
of all the many joys Elysium holds, —
home of the blest, our Gods' most fair abode!
  SILV. What mountains hath it? in what regions set?
what he saw not, or what he left unsung,
tell me! To hear was oft sweet balm for toil.
Perchance the soul will yearn those sights to see.
  OLYM. Remote, beyond the reach of sickly sheep,
bright with perpetual light, a mountain rears;
there Phoebus first, from Earth below, ascends;
on topmost peak a wood, with towering palms,
with festal laurels, cedars ever-green,
peace-loving olive-trees, to Pallas dear.
Who could describe the many flowers? the scents
the zephyrs waft? and who the silvery streams,
their wondrous waters sprinkling all about,
meandering here and there with murmur sweet,
and drawing in their course full many a bough?
Such golden fruit th' Hesperides ne'er saw;
gold-hued are birds there; and gold-horned goats,
and gentle deer; moreover, lambs are there
whose snowy fleeces gleam with brightest gold;
and oxen, too, and bulls, and fatted cows,
resplendent all with gold; yea, lions tame,
and griffins tame, their names with gold all bright.
Golden our sun, and silvern is our moon;
grander than yours the stars that shine on us.
'Tis ever Spring; no southern gale strikes there;
a joyous calm the place pervades. Earth's mists,
and Night, all things that jar, are banished thence.
Death comes not to the flocks, nor ailing Age;
and far are grievous cares, and want, and grief.
Things wished for freely come to all. What more?
The air, so soft, with sweet-toned song resounds.
  SILV. Marvels thou tell'st! Sure, sacred is that wood,
the Gods' abode! But who o'errules it, say;
who dwell therein, and what the usages?
  OLYM. High, on a grassy mound, in glory sits
Arcesilas, shepherding flocks and worlds.
But, verily, would'st thou His aspect know,
it were in vain; the mind this cannot grasp.
All life is He, too fair, wholly serene;

and in His bosom rests a Lamb, milk-white,
sweet sustenance for folk, whereby we live;
thence comes our weal, and life to those reborn.
And from Them both alike there flames a
fire,
wondrous to believe! To all things spreads
that light:
the sad it comforts, purges the mind's eye,
counsels the wretched, strengthens those that
fall,
with sweetest love informs the souls of men.
An aged band of Satyrs, suppliant,
their hoary locks with rosy chaplets crowned,
stand there; with lute and song the Lamb
they praise.
And then the Purple Order, well revered,
their temples all engirt with laurel green.
At cross-roads these with pipes the true God
sang,
and, strong of soul, they conquered cruel
toils.
Then come the Snow-white Host; lilies their
brows
enwreathe. To these is joined our little band,
thy children fair. The Saffron Order next,
illustrious, resplendent, with loud voice
sing praises of the Gods, and serve the King.

. . . .

SILV. 'Twere to be wished! But who, as
Daedalus,
will give me agile wings, and bind them on,
show me the easy way, and teach me flight?
OLYM. Thy brother feed, give to the weary
milk,
to prisoners alms; the naked clothe, the fallen
raise, whilst thou canst; take strangers to thy
home.
Such offices will give thee eagle's wings;
and, God thy guide, thou wilt to Heaven
fly. —
SILV. Whither, my daughter, whither
fleest thou,
leaving thy father tearful? — Ah, she passed
to upper air, and drew the scents she
brought.
With tears my life I'll dree, and fare to
death.
Boys, drive the calves afield! Lo, Phosphor
gleams,
and Sol emerges now from misty shades.

— *From the Latin of the Italian poet, Boccaccio (1313–1375), translated by Sir Israel Gollancz (slightly abridged).*

Ballade of the Gibbet

An epitaph in the form of a ballade that François Villon wrote of himself and his company, they expecting shortly to be hanged.

Brothers and men that shall after us be,
Let not your hearts be hard to us:
For pitying this our misery
Ye shall find God the more piteous.
Look on us six that are hanging thus,
And for the flesh that so much we cherished
How it is eaten of birds and perished,
And ashes and dust fill our bones' place,
Mock not at us that so feeble be,
But pray God pardon us out of His grace.

Listen we pray you, and look not in scorn,
Though justly, in sooth, we are cast to die;
Ye wot no man so wise is born
That keeps his wisdom constantly.
Be ye then merciful, and cry
To Mary's Son that is piteous,
That his mercy take no stain from us,
Saving us out of the fiery place.
We are but dead, let no soul deny
To pray God succor us of His grace.

The rain out of heaven has washed us clean;
The sun has scorched us black and bare;
Ravens and rooks have pecked at our eyne,
And feathered their nests with our beards
and hair.
Round are we tossed, and here and there,
This way and that, at the wild wind's will;
Never a moment my body is still;
Birds they are busy about my face.
Live not as we, not fare as we fare;
Pray God pardon us out of His grace.

Envoy

Prince Jesus, Master of all! to thee
We pray Hell gain no mastery,
That we come never anear that place;
And ye men, make no mockery,
Pray God, pardon us out of His grace.

— *From the French of François Villon (1431–1489), translated by Andrew Lang.*

Ode on the Death of His Father

O, let the soul her slumbers break!
Let thought be quickened, and awake, —
Awake and see
How soon this life is past and gone,

And death comes softly stealing on,
  How silently!

Swiftly our pleasures glide away:
Our hearts recall the distant day
  With many sighs;
The moments that are speeding fast
We heed not; but the past – the past –
  More highly prize.

Onward its course the present keeps,
Onward the constant current sweeps,
  Till life is done;
And did we judge of time aright,
The past and future in their flight
  Would be as one.

Let no one fondly dream again
That Hope and all her shadowy train
  Will not decay;
Fleeting as were the dreams of old,
Remembered like a tale that's told,
  They pass away.

Our lives are rivers, gliding free
To that unfathomed, boundless sea,
  The silent grave:
Thither all earthly pomp and boast
Roll, to be swallowed up and lost
  In one dark wave.

Thither the mighty torrents stray,
Thither the brook pursues its way,
  And tinkling rill.
There all are equal. Side by side,
The poor man and the son of pride
  Lie calm and still.

. . . . .

To one alone my thoughts arise, –
The eternal Truth, – the Good and Wise:
  To Him I cry,
Who shared on earth our common lot,
But the world comprehended not
  His deity.

This world is but the rugged road
Which leads us to the bright abode
  Of peace above;
So let us choose that narrow way
Which leads no traveller's foot astray
  From realms of love.

Our cradle is the starting-place;
In life we run the onward race,
  And reach the goal;
When, in the mansions of the blest,
Death leaves to its eternal rest
  The weary soul.

Did we but use it as we ought,
This world would school each wandering thought
  To its high state.
Faith wings the soul beyond the sky,
Up to that better world on high
  For which we wait.

. . . . .

Tell me, – the charms that lovers seek
In the clear eye and blushing cheek, –
  The hues that play
O'er rosy lip and brow of snow, –
When hoary age approaches slow,
  Ah, where are they?

The cunning skill, the curious arts,
The glorious strength that youth imparts
  In life's first stage, –
These shall become a heavy weight,
When Time swings wide his outward gate
  To weary age.

The noble blood of Gothic name,
Heroes emblazoned high to fame,
  In long array, –
How, in the onward course of time,
The landmarks of that race sublime
  Were swept away!

. . . .

These gifts in Fortune's hands are found;
Her swift-revolving wheel turns round,
  And they are gone!
No rest the inconstant goddess knows,
But changing, and without repose,
  Still hurries on.

Even could the hand of avarice save
Its gilded bawbles, till the grave
  Reclaimed its prey,
Let none on such poor hopes rely,
Life, like an empty dream, flits by,
  And where are they?

Earthly desires and sensual lust
Are passions springing from the dust, –
  They fade and die;
But, in the life beyond the tomb,
They seal the immortal spirit's doom
  Eternally!

. . . .

Who is the champion? who the strong?
Pontiff and priest, and sceptred throng?

On these shall fall
As heavily the hand of Death,
As when it stays the shepherd's breath
Beside his stall.

I speak not of the Trojan name, —
Neither its glory nor its shame
Has met our eyes;
Nor of Rome's great and glorious dead, —
Though we have heard so oft and read,
Their histories.

Little avails it now to know
Of ages past so long ago,
Nor how they rolled;
Our theme shall be of yesterday,
Which to oblivion sweeps away,
Like days of old.

Where is the king, Don Juan? where
Each royal prince and noble heir
Of Aragon?
Where are the courtly gallantries?
The deeds of love and high emprise,
In battle done?

Tourney and joust, that charmed the eye,
And scarf, and gorgeous panoply,
And nodding plume, —
What were they but a pageant scene?
What, but the garlands, gay and green,
That deck the tomb?

Where are the high-born dames, and where
Their gay attire, and jewelled hair,
And odors sweet?
Where are the gentle knights, that came
To kneel, and breathe love's ardent flame,
Low at their feet?

Where is the song of Troubadour?
Where are the lute and gay tambour
They loved of yore?
Where is the mazy dance of old, —
The flowing robes, inwrought with gold,
The dancers wore?

And he who next the sceptre swayed,
Henry, whose royal court displayed
Such power and pride, —
O, in what winning smiles arrayed,
The world its various pleasures laid
His throne beside!

. . . . . .

The noble steeds, and harness bright,
And gallant lord, and stalwart knight,
In rich array; —
Where shall we seek them now? Alas!
Like the bright dew-drops on the grass,
They passed away —

His brother, too, whose factious zeal
Usurped the sceptre of Castile,
Unskilled to reign, —
What a gay, brilliant court had he,
When all the flower of chivalry
Was in his train!

But he was mortal, and the breath
That flamed from the hot forge of Death
Blasted his years;
Judgment of God! that flame by thee,
When raging fierce and fearfully,
Was quenched in tears!

Spain's haughty Constable, — the true
And gallant Master, — whom we knew
Most loved of all, —
Breathe not a whisper of his pride;
He on the gloomy scaffold died, —
Ignoble fall!

. . .

O World! so few the years we live,
Would that the life which thou dost give
Were life indeed!
Alas! thy sorrows fall so fast,
Our happiest hour is when, at last,
The soul is free.

. . . . .

And he, the good man's shield and shade,
To whom all hearts their homage paid,
As Virtue's son, —
Roderick Manrique, — he whose name
Is written on the scroll of Fame,
Spain's champion;

His signal deeds and prowess high
Demand no pompous eulogy, —
Ye saw his deeds!
Why should their praise in verse be sung?
The name that dwells on every tongue
No minstrel needs.

To friends a friend; — how kind to all
The vassals of this ancient hall
And feudal fief!
To foes how stern a foe was he!
And to the valiant and the free
How brave a chief!

What prudence with the old and wise!
What grace in youthful gayeties!

In all how sage!
Benignant to the serf and slave,
He showed the base and falsely brave
A lion's rage.

. . . . .

He left no well filled treasury,
He heaped no pile of riches high,
Nor massive plate;
He fought the Moors, — and, in their fall,
City and tower and castled wall
Were his estate.

. . . . .

By his unrivalled skill, by great
And veteran service to the state,
By worth adored,
He stood, in his high dignity,
The proudest knight of chivalry, —
Knight of the Sword.

. . . . .

And when so oft, for weal or woe,
His life upon the fatal throw
Had been cast down, —
When he had served, with patriot zeal,
Beneath the banner of Castile,
His sovereign's crown, —

And done such deeds of valor strong,
That neither history nor song
Can count them all;
Then, on Ocana's castled rock,
Death at his portal came to knock,
With sudden call, —

Saying, "Good Cavalier, prepare
To leave this world of toil and care
With joyful mien;
Let thy strong heart of steel this day
Put on its armour for the fray, —
The closing scene.

. . . . .

"Think not the struggle that draws near
Too terrible for man, nor fear
To meet the foe;
Nor let thy noble spirit grieve,
Its life of glorious fame to leave
On earth below.

. . . . .

"The eternal life, beyond the sky,
Wealth cannot purchase, nor the high
And proud estate;
The soul in dalliance laid, — the spirit
Corrupt with sin, — shall not inherit
A joy so great.

"But the good monk, in cloistered cell,
Shall gain it by his book and bell,
His prayers and tears;
And the brave knight, whose arm endures
Fierce battle, and against the Moors
His standard rears.

"And thou, brave knight, whose hand has poured
The life-blood of the pagan horde
O'er all the land,
In heaven shalt thou receive, at length,
The guerdon of thine earthly strength
And dauntless hand."

. . . . .

"O Death, no more, no more delay!
My spirit longs to flee away
And be at rest: —
The will of Heaven my will shall be, —
I bow to the divine decree,
To God's behest.

. . . . .

"O thou, that for our sins didst take
A human form, and humbly make
Thy home on earth!
Thou, that to thy divinity
A human nature didst ally
By mortal birth, —

"And in that form didst suffer here
Torment, and agony, and fear,
So patiently!
By thy redeeming grace alone,
And not for merits of my own,
O, pardon me!"

As thus the dying warrior prayed,
Without one gathering mist or shade
Upon his mind, —
Encircled by his family,
Watched by affection's gentle eye,
So soft and kind, —

His soul to Him who gave it rose.
God lead it to its long repose
Its glorious rest!
And, though the warrior's sun has set,
Its light shall linger round us yet
Bright, radiant, blest.

— *From the Spanish of Jorge Manrique (fl. fifteenth century), translated by H. W. Longfellow (abridged).*

Lycidas

In this Monody the Author bewails a learned Friend, unfortunately drowned in his passage from Chester on the Irish Seas, 1637; and, by occasion, foretells the ruin of our corrupted Clergy, then in their height.

Yet once more, O ye laurels, and once more,
Ye myrtles brown, with ivy never sere,
I come to pluck your berries harsh and crude,
And with forced fingers rude
Shatter your leaves before the mellowing year.
Bitter constraint and sad occasion dear
Compels me to disturb your season due;
For Lycidas is dead, dead ere his prime,
Young Lycidas, and hath not left his peer.
Who would not sing for Lycidas? he knew
Himself to sing, and build the lofty rhyme.
He must not float upon his watery bier
Unwept, and welter to the parching wind,
Without the meed of some melodious tear.
Begin, then, Sisters of the sacred well
That from beneath the seat of Jove dóth spring;
Begin, and somewhat loudly sweep the string.
Hence with denial vain and coy excuse:
So may some gentle Muse
With lucky words favor *my* destined urn,
And as he passes turn,
And bid fair peace be to my sable shroud!
For we were nursed upon the self-same hill,
Fed the same flock, by fountain, shade, and rill;
Together both, ere the high lawns appeared
Under the opening eyelids of the Morn,
We drove a-field, and both together heard
What time the gray-fly winds her sultry horn,
Battening our flocks with the fresh dews of night,
Oft till the star that rose at evening bright
Toward heaven's descent had sloped his westering wheel.
Meanwhile the rural ditties were not mute;
Tempered to the oaten flute
Rough Satyrs danced, and Fauns with cloven heel
From the glad sound would not be absent long;
And old Damœtas loved to hear our song.
But, oh! the heavy change, now thou art gone,
Now thou art gone and never must return!
Thee, Shepherd, thee the woods and desert caves,
With wild thyme and the gadding vine o'ergrown,
And all their echoes, mourn.
The willows, and the hazel copses green,
Shall now no more be seen
Fanning their joyous leaves to thy soft lays.
As killing as the canker to the rose,
Or taint-worm to the weanling herds that graze,
Or frost to flowers that their gay wardrobe wear,
When first the white-thorn blows;
Such, Lycidas, thy loss to shepherd's ear.
Where were ye, Nymphs, when the remorseless deep
Closed o'er the head of your loved Lycidas?
For neither were ye playing on the steep
Where your old bards, the famous Druids, lie,
Nor on the shaggy top of Mona high,
Nor yet where Deva spreads her wizard stream.
Ay me! I fondly dream,
"Had ye been there," . . . for what could that have done ?
What could the Muse herself that Orpheus bore,
The Muse herself, for her enchanting son,
Whom universal nature did lament,
When, by the rout that made the hideous roar,
His gory visage down the stream was sent,
Down the swift Hebrus to the Lesbian shore?
Alas! what boots it with uncessant care
To tend the homely, slighted, shepherd's trade,
And strictly meditate the thankless Muse?
Were it not better done, as others use,
To sport with Amaryllis in the shade,
Or with the tangles of Neæra's hair?
Fame is the spur that the clear spirit doth raise
(That last infirmity of noble mind)
To scorn delights and live laborious days;
But the fair guerdon when we hope to find,
And think to burst out into sudden blaze,
Comes the blind Fury with the abhorrèd shears
And slits the thin-spun life. "But not the praise,"
Phœbus replied, and touched my trembling ears:
"Fame is no plant that grows on mortal soil,
Nor in the glistering foil

Set off to the world, nor in broad rumor lies,
But lives and spreads aloft by those pure eyes
And perfect witness of all-judging Jove;
As he pronounces lastly on each deed,
Of so much fame in heaven expect thy meed."
O fountain Arethuse, and thou honored flood,
Smooth-sliding Mincius, crowned with vocal reeds,
That strain I heard was of a higher mood.
But now my oat proceeds,
And listens to the Herald of the Sea
That came in Neptune's plea.
He asked the waves, and asked the felon winds,
What hard mishap hath doomed this gentle swain?
And questioned every gust of rugged wings,
That blows from off each beakèd promontory.
They knew not of his story;
And sage Hippotades their answer brings,
That not a blast was from his dungeon strayed;
The air was calm, and on the level brine
Sleek Panopé with all her sisters played.
It was that fatal and perfidious bark,
Built in the eclipse, and rigged with curses dark,
That sunk so low that sacred head of thine.
Next, Camus, reverend sire, went footing slow,
His mantle hairy, and his bonnet sedge,
Inwrought with figures dim, and on the edge
Like to that sanguine flower inscribed with woe.
"Ah! who hath reft," quoth he, "my dearest pledge?"
Last came, and last did go,
The Pilot of the Galilean Lake,
Two massy keys he bore of metals twain
(The golden opes, the iron shuts amain).
He shook his mitred locks, and stern bespake:—
"How well could I have spared for thee, young swain,
Enow of such as, for their bellies' sake,
Creep, and intrude, and climb into the fold!
Of other care they little reckoning make
Than how to scramble at the shearers' feast
And shove away the worthy bidden guest.
Blind mouths! that scarce themselves know how to hold
A sheep-hook, or have learned ought else the least
That to the faithful herdman's art belongs!
What recks it them? What need they? They are sped;
And, when they list, their lean and flashy songs
Grate on their scrannel pipes of wretched straw;
The hungry sheep look up, and are not fed,
But, swoln with wind and the rank mist they draw,
Rot inwardly, and foul contagion spread;
Besides what the grim wolf with privy paw
Daily devours apace, and nothing said.
But that two-handed engine at the door
Stands ready to smite once, and smite no more."
Return, Alphëus; the dread voice is past
That shrunk thy streams; return, Sicilian Muse,
And call the vales, and bid them hither cast
Their bells and flowerets of a thousand hues.
Ye valleys low, where the mild whispers use
Of shades, and wanton winds, and gushing brooks,
On whose fresh lap the swart star sparely looks,
Throw hither all your quaint enameled eyes
That on the green turf suck the honeyed showers,
And purple all the ground with vernal flowers.
Bring the rathe primrose that forsaken dies,
The tufted crow-toe, and pale jessamine,
The white pink, and the pansy freaked with jet,
The glowing violet,
The musk-rose, and the well-attired woodbine,
With cowslips wan that hang the pensive head,
And every flower that sad embroidery wears;
Bid amaranthus all his beauty shed,
And daffadillies fill their cups with tears,
To strew the laureate hearse where Lycid lies.
For so, to interpose a little ease,
Let our frail thoughts dally with false surmise.
Ay me! whilst thee the shores and sounding seas
Wash far away, where'er thy bones are hurled;
Whether beyond the stormy Hebrides,

Where thou perhaps under the whelming tide,
Visit'st the bottom of the monstrous world;
Or whether thou, to our moist vows denied,
Sleep'st by the fable of Bellerus old,
Where the great Vision of the guarded mount
Looks toward Namancos and Bayona's hold.
Look homeward, Angel, now, and melt with ruth:
And, O ye dolphins, waft the hapless youth.
Weep no more, woeful shepherds, weep no more,
For Lycidas, your sorrow, is not dead,
Sunk though he be beneath the watery floor.
So sinks the day-star in the ocean bed,
And yet anon repairs his drooping head,
And tricks his beams, and with new-spangled ore
Flames in the forehead of the morning sky:
So Lycidas sunk low, but mounted high,
Through the dear might of Him that walked the waves,
Where, other groves and other streams along,
With nectar pure his oozy locks he laves,
And hears the unexpressive nuptial song,
In the blest kingdoms meek of joy and love.
There entertain him all the Saints above,
In solemn troops, and sweet societies,
That sing, and singing in their glory move,
And wipe the tears for ever from his eyes.
Now, Lycidas, the shepherds weep no more;
Henceforth thou art the Genius of the shore,
In thy large recompense, and shalt be good
To all that wander in that perilous flood.

Thus sang the uncouth swain to the oaks and rills,
While the still morn went out with sandals gray;
He touched the tender stops of various quills,
With eager thought warbling his Doric lay:
And now the sun had stretched out all the hills,
And now was dropped into the western bay.
At last he rose, and twitched his mantle blue:
To-morrow to fresh woods, and pastures new.

— *John Milton, English (1608–1674).*

~ ❂ ~

Adonais

I

I weep for Adonais — he is dead!
Oh weep for Adonais! tho' our tears
Thaw not the frost which binds so dear a head!
And thou, sad Hour, selected from all years
To mourn our loss, rouse thy obscure compeers,
And teach them thine own sorrow! Say: "With me
Died Adonais; till the future dares
Forget the Past, his fate and fame shall be
An echo and a light unto eternity!"

II

Where wert thou mighty Mother, when he lay,
When thy Son lay, pierced by the shaft which flies
In darkness? where was lorn Urania
When Adonais died? With veilèd eyes,
Mid listening Echoes, in her Paradise
She sate, while one, with soft enamoured breath,
Rekindled all the fading melodies,
With which, like flowers that mock the corse beneath,
He had adorned and hid the coming bulk of death.

III

Oh weep for Adonais — he is dead!
Wake, melancholy Mother, wake and weep!
Yet wherefore? Quench within their burning bed
Thy fiery tears, and let thy loud heart keep
Like his, a mute and uncomplaining sleep;
For he is gone, where all things wise and fair
Descend; — oh, dream not that the amorous Deep
Will yet restore him to the vital air;
Death feeds on his mute voice, and laughs at our despair.

IV

Most musical of mourners, weep again!
Lament anew, Urania! — He died,
Who was the Sire of an immortal strain,
Blind, old, and lonely, when his country's pride,
The priest, the slave, and the liberticide,
Trampled and mockt with many a loathèd rite
Of lust and blood; he went, unterrified,
Into the gulf of death; but his clear Sprite

Yet reigns o'er earth; the third among the sons of light.

V

Most musical of mourners, weep anew!
Not all to that bright station dared to climb;
And happier they their happiness who knew,
Whose tapers yet burn thro' that night of time
In which suns perisht; others more sublime,
Struck by the envious wrath of man or God,
Have sunk, extinct in their refulgent prime;
And some yet live, treading the thorny road,
Which leads, thro' toil and hate, to Fame's serene abode.

VI

But now, thy youngest, dearest one has perisht,
The nursling of thy widowhood, who grew,
Like a pale flower by some sad maiden cherisht,
And fed with true-love tears, instead of dew;
Most musical of mourners, weep anew!
Thy extreme hope, the loveliest and the last,
The bloom, whose petals nipt before they blew
Died on the promise of the fruit, is waste;
The broken lily lies – the storm is overpast.

VII

To that high Capital, where kingly Death
Keeps his pale court in beauty and decay,
He came; and bought, with price of purest breath,
A grave among the eternal. – Come away!
Haste, while the vault of blue Italian day
Is yet his fitting charnel-roof! while still
He lies, as if in dewy sleep he lay;
Awake him not! surely he takes his fill
Of deep and liquid rest, forgetful of all ill.

VIII

He will awake no more, oh, never more! –
Within the twilight chamber spreads apace,
The shadow of white Death, and at the door
Invisible Corruption waits to trace
His extreme way to her dim dwelling-place;
The eternal Hunger sits, but pity and awe
Soothe her pale rage, nor dare she to deface
So fair a prey, till darkness, and the law
Of change shall o'er his sleep the mortal curtain draw.

IX

Oh weep for Adonais! – The quick Dreams,
The passion-wingèd Ministers of thought,
Who were his flocks, whom near the living streams
Of his young spirit he fed, and whom he taught
The love which was its music, wander not, –
Wander no more, from kindling brain to brain,
But droop there, whence they sprung; and mourn their lot
Round the cold heart, where, after their sweet pain,
They ne'er will gather strength, or find a home again.

X

And one with trembling hands clasps his cold head,
And fans him with her moonlight wings, and cries;
"Our love, our hope, our sorrow, is not dead;
See, on the silken fringe of his faint eyes,
Like dew upon a sleeping flower, there lies
A tear some Dream has loosened from his brain,"
Lost Angel of a ruined Paradise!
She knew not 't was her own; as with no stain
She faded, like a cloud which had outwept its rain.

XI

One from a lucid urn of starry dew
Washt his light limbs as if embalming them;
Another clipt her profuse locks, and threw
The wreath upon him, like an anadem,

Which frozen tears instead of pearls begem;
Another in her wilful grief would break
Her bow and wingèd reeds, as if to stem
A greater loss with one which was more weak;
And dull the barbèd fire against his frozen cheek.

XII

Another Splendor on his mouth alit,
That mouth, whence it was wont to draw the breath
Which gave it strength to pierce the guarded wit,
And pass into the panting heart beneath
With lightning and with music: the damp death
Quencht its caress upon his icy lips;
And, as a dying meteor stains a wreath
Of moonlight vapor, which the cold night clips,
It flusht thro' his pale limbs, and past to its eclipse.

XIII

And others came . . . Desires and Adorations,
Wingèd Persuasions and veiled Destinies,
Splendors, and Glooms, and glimmering Incarnations
Of hopes and fears, and twilight Fantasies;
And Sorrow, with her family of Sighs,
And Pleasure, blind with tears, led by the gleam
Of her own dying smile instead of eyes,
Came in slow pomp; — the moving pomp might seem
Like pageantry of mist on an autumnal stream.

XIV

All he had loved and moulded into thought,
From shape, and hue, and odor, and sweet sound,
Lamented Adonais. Morning sought
Her eastern watchtower, and her hair unbound,
Wet with the tears which should adorn the ground,
Dimmed the aerial eyes that kindle day;
Afar the melancholy thunder moaned,
Pale Ocean in unquiet slumber lay,
And the wild winds flew round, sobbing in their dismay.

XVIII

Ah woe is me! Winter is come and gone,
But grief returns with the revolving year;
The airs and streams renew their joyous tone;
The ants, the bees, the swallows reappear;
Fresh leaves and flowers deck the dead Seasons' bier;
The amorous birds now pair in every brake,
And build their mossy homes in field and brere;
And the green lizard, and the golden snake,
Like unimprisoned flames, out of their trance awake.

XIX

Thro' wood and stream and field and hill and Ocean
A quickening life from the Earth's heart has burst
As it has ever done, with change and motion,
From the great morning of the world when first
God dawned on Chaos; in its stream immerst
The lamps of Heaven flash with a softer light;
All baser things pant with life's sacred thirst;
Diffuse themselves; and spend in love's delight,
The beauty and the joy of their renewèd might.

XX

The leprous corpse toucht by this spirit tender
Exhales itself in flowers of gentle breath;
Like incarnations of the stars, when splendor
Is changed to fragrance, they illumine death
And mock the merry worm that wakes beneath;
Naught we know, dies. Shall that alone which knows
Be as a sword consumed before the sheath
By sightless lightning? — the intense atom glows

A moment, then is quencht in a most cold
repose.

XXI

Alas! that all we loved of him should be,
But for our grief, as if it had not been,
And grief itself be mortal! Woe is me!
Whence are we, and why are we? of what
scene
The actors or spectators? Great and mean
Meet massed in death, who lends what
life must borrow.
As long as skies are blue, and fields are
green,
Evening must usher night, night urge the
morrow,
Month follow month with woe, and year
wake year to sorrow.

XXII

He will awake no more, oh, never more!
"Wake thou," cried Misery, "childless
Mother, rise
Out of thy sleep, and slake, in thy heart's
core,
A wound more fierce than his with tears
and sighs."
And all the Dreams that watcht Urania's
eyes,
And all the Echoes whom their sister's
song
Had held in holy silence, cried: "Arise!"
Swift as a Thought by the snake Memory
stung,
From her ambrosial rest the fading Splen-
dor sprung.

XXIV

Out of her secret Paradise she sped,
Thro' camps and cities rough with stone,
and steel,
And human hearts, which to her airy
tread
Yielding not, wounded the invisible
Palms of her tender feet where'er they
fell:
And barbèd tongues, and thoughts more
sharp than they
Rent the soft Form they never could repel,
Whose sacred blood, like the young tears
of May,
Paved with eternal flowers that undeserving
way.

XXV

In the death chamber for a moment
Death,
Shamed by the presence of that living
Might,
Blusht to annihilation, and the breath
Revisited those lips, and life's pale light
Flasht thro' those limbs, so late her dear
delight.
"Leave me not wild and drear and com-
fortless,
As silent lightning leaves the starless night!
Leave me not!" cried Urania: her distress
Roused Death: Death rose and smiled, and
met her vain caress.

XXVII

"O gentle child, beautiful as thou wert,
Why didst thou leave the trodden paths
of men
Too soon, and with weak hands tho'
mighty heart
Dare the unpastured dragon in his den?
Defenceless as thou wert, oh where was
then
Wisdom the mirrored shield, or scorn the
spear?
Or hadst thou waited the full cycle, when
Thy spirit should have filled its crescent
sphere,
The monsters of life's waste had fled from
thee like deer.

XXIX

"The sun comes forth, and many reptiles
spawn;
He sets, and each ephemeral insect then
Is gathered into death without a dawn,
And the immortal stars awake again;
So is it in the world of living men:
A godlike mind soars forth, in its delight
Making earth bare and veiling heaven,
and when
It sinks, the swarms that dimmed or
shared its light
Leave to its kindred lamp the spirit's awful
night."

XXXVI

Our Adonais has drunk poison — oh!
What deaf and viperous murderer could
crown
Life's early cup with such a draught of
woe?
The nameless worm would now itself dis-
own:
It felt, yet could escape the magic tone
Whose prelude held all envy, hate, and
wrong,

But what was howling in one breast alone,
Silent with expectation of the song,
Whose master's hand is cold, whose silver lyre unstrung.

XXXVII

Live thou, whose infamy is not thy fame!
Live! fear no heavier chastisement from me,
Thou noteless blot on a remembered name!
But be thyself, and know thyself to be!
And ever at thy season be thou free
To spill the venom when thy fangs o'erflow:
Remorse and Self-contempt shall cling to thee;
Hot Shame shall burn upon thy secret brow,
And like a beaten hound tremble thou shalt — as now.

XXXVIII

Nor let us weep that our delight is fled
Far from these carrion kites that scream below;
He wakes or sleeps with the enduring dead;
Thou canst not soar where he is sitting now. —
Dust to the dust! but the pure spirit shall flow
Back to the burning fountain whence it came,
A portion of the Eternal, which must glow
Thro' time and change, unquenchably the same,
Whilst thy cold embers choke the sordid hearth of shame.

XXXIX

Peace, peace! he is not dead, he doth not sleep —
He hath awakened from the dream of life —
'T is we, who lost in stormy visions, keep
With phantoms an unprofitable strife,
And in mad trance, strike with our spirit's knife
Invulnerable nothings. — *We* decay
Like corpses in a charnel; fear and grief
Convulse us and consume us day by day,
And cold hopes swarm like worms within our living clay.

XL

He has outsoared the shadow of our night;
Envy and calumny and hate and pain,
And that unrest which men miscall delight,
Can touch him not and torture not again;
From the contagion of the world's slow stain
He is secure, and now can never mourn
A heart grown cold, a head grown gray in vain;
Nor, when the spirit's self has ceased to burn,
With sparkless ashes load an unlamented urn.

XLI

He lives, he wakes — 't is Death is dead, not he;
Mourn not for Adonais. — Thou young Dawn
Turn all thy dew to splendor, for from thee
The spirit thou lamentest is not gone;
Ye caverns and ye forests, cease to moan!
Cease ye faint flowers and fountains, and thou Air
Which like a mourning veil thy scarf hadst thrown
O'er the abandoned Earth, now leave it bare
Even to the joyous stars which smile on its despair!

XLII

He is made one with Nature: there is heard
His voice in all her music, from the moan
Of thunder to the song of night's sweet bird;
He is a presence to be felt and known
In darkness and in light, from herb and stone,
Spreading itself where'er that Power may move
Which has withdrawn his being to its own;
Which wields the world with never wearied love,
Sustains it from beneath, and kindles it above.

XLIII

He is a portion of the loveliness
Which once he made more lovely: he doth bear

His part, while the one Spirit's plastic stress
Sweeps thro' the dull dense world, compelling there
All new successions to the forms they wear;
Torturing the unwilling dross that checks its flight
To its own likeness, as each mass may bear;
And bursting in its beauty and its might
From trees and beasts and men into the Heaven's light.

XLIV

The splendors of the firmament of time
May be eclipst, but are extinguisht not;
Like stars to their appointed height they climb
And death is a low mist which can not blot
The brightness it may veil. When lofty thought
Lifts a young heart above its mortal lair,
And love and life contend in it, for what
Shall be its earthly doom, the dead live there
And move like winds of light on dark and stormy air.

XLV

The inheritors of unfulfilled renown
Rose from their thrones, built beyond mortal thought,
Far in the Unapparent. Chatterton
Rose pale, his solemn agony had not
Yet faded from him; Sidney, as he fought
And as he fell and as he lived and loved
Sublimely mild, a Spirit without spot,
Arose; and Lucan, by his death approved:
Oblivion as they rose shrank like a thing reproved.

XLVI

And many more, whose names on Earth are dark,
But whose transmitted effluence cannot die
So long as fire outlives the parent spark,
Rose, robed in dazzling immortality.
"Thou art become as one of us," they cry,
"It was for thee yon kingless sphere has long
Swung blind in unascended majesty,
Silent alone amid an Heaven of Song.
Assume thy wingèd throne, thou Vesper of our throng!"

XLVII

Who mourns for Adonais? Oh come forth
Fond wretch! and know thyself and him aright.
Clasp with thy panting soul the pendulous Earth;
As from a centre, dart thy spirit's light
Beyond all worlds, until its spacious might
Satiate the void circumference: then shrink
Even to a point within our day and night;
And keep thy heart light lest it make thee sink
When hope has kindled hope, and lured thee to the brink.

XLVIII

Or go to Rome, which is the sepulchre
Oh! not of him, but of our joy: 't is naught
That ages, empires, and religions there
Lie buried in the ravage they have wrought;
For such as he can lend, — they borrow not
Glory from those who made the world their prey;
And he is gathered to the kings of thought
Who waged contention with their time's decay,
And of the past are all that can not pass away.

XLIX

Go thou to Rome, — at once the Paradise,
The grave, the city, and the wilderness;
And where its wrecks like shattered mountains rise,
And flowering weeds, and fragrant copses dress
The bones of Desolation's nakedness
Pass, till the Spirit of the spot shall lead
Thy footsteps to a slope of green access
Where, like an infant's smile, over the dead
A light of laughing flowers along the grass is spread.

L

And gray walls moulder round, on which dull Time
Feeds, like slow fire upon a hoary brand;
And one keen pyramid with wedge sublime,

Pavilioning the dust of him who planned
This refuge for his memory, doth stand
Like flame transformed to marble; and beneath,
A field is spread, on which a newer band
Have pitcht in Heaven's smile their camp of death
Welcoming him we lose with scarce extinguisht breath.

LI

Here pause: these graves are all too young as yet
To have outgrown the sorrow which consigned
Its charge to each; and if the seal is set,
Here, on one fountain of a mourning mind,
Break it not thou! too surely shalt thou find
Thine own well full, if thou returnest home,
Of tears and gall. From the world's bitter wind
Seek shelter in the shadow of the tomb.
What Adonais is, why fear we to become?

LII

The One remains, the many change and pass;
Heaven's light forever shines, Earth's shadows fly;
Life, like a dome of many-colored glass,
Stains the white radiance of Eternity,
Until Death tramples it to fragments. — Die,
If thou wouldst be with that which thou dost seek!
Follow where all is fled! — Rome's azure sky,
Flowers, ruins, statues, music, words, are weak
The glory they transfuse with fitting truth to speak.

LIII

Why linger, why turn back, why shrink, my Heart?
Thy hopes are gone before: from all things here
They have departed; thou shouldst now depart!
A light is past from the revolving year,
And man, and woman; and what still is dear
Attracts to crush, repels to make thee wither.
The soft sky smiles, — the low wind whispers near;
'T is Adonais calls! oh, hasten thither,
No more let Life divide what Death can join together.

LIV

That Light whose smile kindles the Universe,
That Beauty in which all things work and move,
That Benediction which the eclipsing Curse
Of birth can quench not, that sustaining Love
Which thro' the web of being blindly wove
By man and beast and earth and air and sea,
Burns bright or dim, as each are mirrors of
The fire for which all thirst; now beams on me,
Consuming the last clouds of cold mortality.

LV

The breath whose might I have invoked in song
Descends on me; my spirit's bark is driven,
Far from the shore, far from the trembling throng
Whose sails were never to the tempest given;
The massy earth and spherèd skies are riven!
I am borne darkly, fearfully, afar;
Whilst burning thro' the inmost veil of Heaven,
The soul of Adonais, like a star,
Beacons from the abode where the Eternal are.

— *Percy Bysshe Shelley, English (1792–1822) (abridged).*

Elegy

WRITTEN IN A COUNTRY CHURCH-YARD

The Curfew tolls the knell of parting day,
The lowing herd wind slowly o'er the lea,
The plowman homeward plods his weary way,
And leaves the world to darkness and to me.

Now fades the glimmering landscape on the sight,
And all the air a solemn stillness holds,
Save where the beetle wheels his droning flight,
And drowsy tinklings lull the distant folds;

Save that from yonder ivy-mantled tower
The moping owl does to the moon complain
Of such as, wandering near her secret bower,
Molest her ancient solitary reign.

Beneath those rugged elms, that yew-tree's shade,
Where heaves the turf in many a moldering heap,
Each in his narrow cell for ever laid,
The rude Forefathers of the hamlet sleep.

The breezy call of incense-breathing Morn,
The swallow twittering from the straw-built shed,
The cock's shrill clarion, or the echoing horn,
No more shall rouse them from their lowly bed.

For them no more the blazing hearth shall burn,
Or busy housewife ply her evening care:
No children run to lisp their sire's return,
Or climb his knees the envied kiss to share.

Oft did the harvest to their sickle yield,
Their furrow oft the stubborn glebe has broke;
How jocund did they drive their team afield!
How bowed the woods beneath their sturdy stroke.

Let not Ambition mock their useful toil,
Their homely joys, and destiny obscure;
Nor Grandeur hear with a disdainful smile
The short and simple annals of the poor.

The boast of heraldry, the pomp of power,
And all that beauty, all that wealth e'er gave,
Await alike the inevitable hour.
The paths of glory lead but to the grave.

Nor you, ye Proud, impute to These the fault,
If Memory o'er their Tomb no Trophies raise,
Where through the long-drawn isle and fretted vault
The pealing anthem swells the note of praise.

Can storied urn or animated bust
Back to its mansion call the fleeting breath?
Can Honor's voice provoke the silent dust,
Or Flattery soothe the dull cold ear of Death?

Perhaps in this neglected spot is laid
Some heart once pregnant with celestial fire;
Hands, that the rod of empire might have swayed,
Or waked to ecstasy the living lyre.

But Knowledge to their eyes her ample page
Rich with the spoils of time did ne'er unroll;
Chill Penury repressed their noble rage,
And froze the genial current of the soul.

Full many a gem of purest ray serene,
The dark unfathomed caves of ocean bear:
Full many a flower is born to blush unseen,
And waste its sweetness on the desert air.

Some village Hampden, that with dauntless breast
The little tyrant of his fields withstood,
Some mute inglorious Milton here may rest,
Some Cromwell guiltless of his country's blood.

The applause of listening senates to command,
The threats of pain and ruin to despise,
To scatter plenty o'er a smiling land,
And read their history in a nation's eyes,

Their lot forbade: nor circumscribed alone
Their growing virtues, but their crimes confined;
Forbade to wade through slaughter to a throne,
And shut the gates of mercy on mankind,

The struggling pangs of conscious truth to hide,
To quench the blushes of ingenuous shame,
Or heap the shrine of Luxury and Pride
With incense kindled at the Muse's flame.

Far from the madding crowd's ignoble strife,
Their sober wishes never learned to stray;
Along the cool sequestered vale of life
They kept the noiseless tenor of their way.

Yet even these bones from insult to protect,
Some frail memorial still erected nigh,
With uncouth rhymes and shapeless sculpture decked,
Implores the passing tribute of a sigh.

Their name, their years, spelt by the unlettered muse,
The place of fame and elegy supply;
And many a holy text around she strews,
That teach the rustic moralist to die.

For who, to dumb Forgetfulness a prey,
This pleasing anxious being e'er resigned,
Left the warm precincts of the cheerful day,
Nor cast one longing lingering look behind?

On some fond breast the parting soul relies,
Some pious drops the closing eye requires;
Even from the tomb the voice of Nature cries,
Even in our ashes live their wonted fires.

For thee, who mindful of the unhonored dead
Dost in these lines their artless tale relate;
If chance, by lonely contemplation led,
Some kindred spirit shall inquire thy fate, —

Haply some hoary-headed swain may say,
"Oft have we seen him at the peep of dawn
Brushing with hasty steps the dews away
To meet the sun upon the upland lawn.

"There at the foot of yonder nodding beech
That wreathes its old fantastic roots so high,
His listless length at noontide would he stretch,
And pore upon the brook that babbles by.

"Hard by yon wood, now smiling as in scorn,
Muttering his wayward fancies he would rove,
Now drooping, woeful-wan, like one forlorn,
Or crazed with care, or crossed in hopeless love.

"One morn I missed him on the customed hill,
Along the heath, and near his favorite tree;
Another came; nor yet beside the rill,
Nor up the lawn, nor at the wood was he;

"The next, with dirges due in sad array
Slow through the church-way path we saw him borne. —
Approach and read (for thou canst read) the lay,
Graved on the stone beneath yon aged thorn."

THE EPITAPH

Here rests his head upon the lap of Earth
A Youth to Fortune and to Fame unknown.
Fair Science frowned not on his humble birth,
And Melancholy marked him for her own.

Large was his bounty, and his soul sincere,
Heaven did a recompense as largely send:
He gave to Misery all he had, a tear,
He gained from Heaven ('twas all he wished) a friend.

No farther seek his merits to disclose,
Or draw his frailties from their dread abode
(There they alike in trembling hope repose),
The bosom of his Father and his God.

— *Thomas Gray, English (1716–1771).*

Souvenir

I weep, but with no bitterness I weep,
To look again upon thee, hallowed spot,
O dearest grave, and most of men forgot,
Where buried love doth sleep.

What witchcraft think you that this desert hath,
Dear friends, who take my hand and bid me stay,
Now that the gentle wont of many a day
Would lead me down this path?

Here are the wooded slopes, the flowering heath,
The silver footprints on the silent sand,

The loitering lanes, alive with lovers' breath,
Where first I kissed her hand.

I know these fir-trees, and this mossy stone,
And this deep gorge, and all its winding ways;
These friendly giants, whose primeval moan
Hath rocked my happy days.

My footsteps' echo in this tangled tree
Gives back youth's music, like a singing bird;
Dear haunts, fair wilderness her presence stirred,
Did you not watch for me?

I will not dry these tear-drops: let them flow,
And soothe a bitterness that yet might last,
And o'er my waking-weary eyelids throw
The shadow of the past.

My useless plainings shall not make to cease
The happy echoes of the vows we vowed:
Proud is this forest in its noble peace,
And my heart too is proud.

Give o'er to hopeless grief the bitter hours
You kneel to pray upon a brother's tomb:
Here blows the breath of love, and graveyard flowers
Not in this garden bloom.

See! The moon rides athwart a bank of cloud.
Thy veils, fair Queen of Night, still cling to thee,
But soon thou loosenest thy virgin shroud
And smilest to be free.

As the rich earth, still dank with April rain,
Beneath thy rays exhales day's captive balm,
So from my purged soul, as pure, as calm,
The old love breathes again.

Where are they gone, those ghosts of sorrow pale,
Where fled the passion that my heart defiled?
Once in the bosom of this friendly vale
I am again a child.

O might of time, O changes of the year,
Ye undo sorrow and the tears we shed,
But, touched with pity, on our blossoms here
Your light feet never tread.

Heavenly solace, be for ever blest!
I had not thought a sword could pierce so far
Into the heart, and leave upon the breast
So sweet and dear a scar.

Far from me the sharp word, the thankless mind,
Of vulgar sorrow customary weed,
Shroud that about the corse of love they wind
Who never loved indeed.

Why, Dante, dost thou say the saddest curse
Is joy remembered in unhappy days?
What grief compelled thee to this bitter verse
In sorrow's harsh dispraise?

O'er all the worlds is light bereft of gladness
When sad eclipses cast their blight on us?
Did thy great soul, in its immortal sadness,
Speak to thee, Dante, thus?

No, by this sacred light upon me cast!
Not in thy heart this blasphemy had birth.
It is the truest happiness on earth
To have a happy past.

What! When the soul forlorn finds yet a spark
Mid the hot ashes of her stifled sighs,
And doth that flame, her only treasure, mark
With captivated eyes,

Bathing her wounds in the delicious past
That mirrors brokenly her loves again,
Thy cruel word her feeble joy would blast
And turn to bitter pain?

And couldst thou wrong thine own Francesca so,
Wrong thy bright angel with a word like this,
Her whose lips, parting to rehearse her woe,
Broke an eternal kiss?

What, righteous Heaven, is our human thought,
And to the love of truth who yet will cling,
If every pain or joy e'er shunned or sought
Turns to a doubtful thing?

How can you live, strange souls that nothing awes?

In midst of haste and passion, song and mirth,
Nor all the stars of heaven give you pause,
Nor all the sins of earth;

But when upon your fated way you meet
Some dumb memorial of a passion dead,
That little pebble stops you, and you dread
To bruise your tender feet.

You cry aloud that life is but a dream,
And, to the truth awaking, wring your hands,
And grieve your bubble but a moment stands
Upon time's foaming stream.

Poor fools! That moment when your soul could shake
The numbing fetters off that it enthrall,
That fleeting moment was your all in all—
Oh, mourn not for its sake!

But rather mourn your weight of early dross,
Your joyless toil, your stains of blood and mire,
Your sunless days, your nights without desire;
In these was utter loss.

What profit have you of your late lament,
And what from heaven do your murmurs crave,
The plaints you sow upon the barren grave
Of every pleasure spent?

Life is a dream, and all things pass, I know:
If some fair splendor we be charmed withal,
We pluck the flower, and at the breath we blow
Its withered petals fall.

Ay, the first kiss and the first virgin vow
That ever mortals upon earth did swear,
That whirlwind caught which strips the frozen bough
And stones to sand doth wear.

A witness to the lovers' troth was night,
With changeful skies, o'ercast with mystery,
And stars unnumbered, that an inward light
Devours unceasingly.

They saw death hush the song bird in the glade,
Blast the pale flower, and freeze the torpid worm,
And choke the fountain where the image played
Of their forgotten form.

Yet they joined hands above the moldering clod,
Blind with love's light that flashed across the sky,
Nor felt the cold eye of the changeless God
Who watches all things die.

Fools! says the sage: thrice blest! the poet says.
What wretched joy is to the faint heart dear
Whom noise of torrents fills with weak amaze
And the wind fills with fear?

I have seen beneath the sun more beauties fail
Than white sea foam or leaves of forest sere;
More than the swallows and the roses frail
Desert the widowed year.

Mine eyes have gazed on sights of deeper woe
Than Juliet dead within the gorged tomb,
And deadlier than the cup that Romeo
Drank to his love and doom.

I have seen my love, when all I loved had perished,
Who to a whited sepulcher is turned;
Seen the thin dust of all I ever cherished
In her cold heart inurned,—

Dust of that faith which, in our bosoms furled,
The gentle night had warded well from doubt.
More than a single life, alas! a world
Was that day blotted out.

Still young I found her, and, men said, more fair;
In heaven's light her eyes could still rejoice,
And her lips opened, and a smile was there,
And sound as of a voice.

But not that gentle voice, that tender grace,
Those eyes I worshiped when they looked their prayer:
My heart, still full of her, searched, searched her face
And could not find her there.

And still I could have gone to her, and cast
My arms about that chill and lifeless stone,
And cried, Where hast thou left it, faithless one,
Where hast thou left the past?

But no: it rather seemed as if by chance
Some unknown woman had that voice and eye;
I looked up into heaven; with cold glance
I passed that statue by.

Not without pangs of shame and bitterness
I watched her smiling shadow glide away;
But what of that? Immortal nature, say,
Have I loved therefore less?

On me the gods may now their lightnings fling,
They cannot undo truth, nor kill the past.
Like a wrecked sailor to a broken mast
To my dead love I cling.

I make no question of what flowers may bloom,
What virtue from the seasons man may borrow,
What heavenly lamp may flood with light to-morrow
The vault of this great tomb.

I only say: Here at this hour, one day,
I loved, and I was loved, and she was fair.
This treasure which no death can filch away
My soul to God shall bear.

—From the French of Alfred de Musset (1810–1857), translated by George Santayana.

Nocturne

One night,
One night all full of murmurs, of perfumes and the brush of wings,
Within whose mellow nuptial glooms there shone fantastic fireflies,
Meekly at my side, slender, hushed and pale,
As though with infinite presentiment of woe
Your very depths of being were troubled, —
By the path of flowers that led across the plain,
You came treading,
And the rounded moon
Through heaven's blue and infinite profound was shedding whiteness.
And your shadow
Languid, delicate;
And my shadow,
Sketched by the white moonlight's ray
Upon the solemn sands
Of the path, were joined together,
As one together,
As one together,
As one together in a great single shadow,
As one together in a great single shadow,
As one together in a great single shadow, —

Another night
Alone — all my soul
Suffused with infinite woes and agonies of death,
Parted from you, by time, by the tomb and estrangement,
By the infinite gloom
Through which our voices fail to pierce,
Silent and lonely,
Along that road I journeyed —

And the dogs were heard barking at the moon,
At the pale-faced moon,
And the croaking
Of the frogs —

I was pierced with cold, such cold as on your bed
Came over your cheeks, your breasts, your adorable hands,
Between the snowy whiteness
Of your mortuary sheets;
It was the cold of the sepulchre, the chill of death,
The frost of nothingness. —
And my shadow
Sketched by the white moonlight's ray,
Went on alone,
Went on alone,
Went on alone over the solitary wastes;
And your shadow, slender and light,
Languid, delicate,
As on that soft night of your springtime death,
As on that night filled with murmurs, with perfumes and the brush of wings,
Came near and walked with me,
Came near and walked with me,
Came near and walked with me — Oh, shadows interlaced! —
Oh, shadows of the bodies joining in shadow of the souls! —

Oh, shadows running each to each in the nights of woes and tears! —

— *From the Spanish of the Colombian poet, José Asunción Silva (1865–1896), translated by Thomas Walsh.*

∽ ❁ ∼

When Lilacs Last in the Dooryard Bloomed

I

When lilacs last in the dooryard bloomed,
And the great star early drooped in the western sky in the night,
I mourned, and yet shall mourn with ever-returning spring.

Ever-returning spring, trinity sure to me you bring,
Lilac blooming perennial and drooping star in the west,
And thought of him I love.

II

O powerful western fallen star!
O shades of night — O moody, tearful night!
O great star disappeared — O the black murk that hides the star!
O cruel hands that hold me powerless — O helpless soul of me!
O harsh surrounding cloud that will not free my soul.

III

In the dooryard fronting an old farmhouse near the white-washed palings,
Stands the lilac-bush tall-growing with heart-shaped leaves of rich green,
With many a pointed blossom rising delicate, with the perfume strong I love,
With every leaf a miracle — and from this bush in the dooryard,
With delicate-colored blossoms and heart-shaped leaves of rich green,
A sprig with its flower I break.

IV

In the swamp in secluded recesses,
A shy and hidden bird is warbling a song.
Solitary the thrush,
The hermit withdrawn to himself, avoiding the settlements,
Sings by himself a song.

Song of the bleeding throat,
Death's outlet song of life (for well dear brother I know,
If thou wast not granted to sing thou wouldst surely die.)

V

Over the breast of the spring, the land, amid cities,
Amid lanes and through old woods, where lately the violets peeped from the ground, spotting the gray débris,
Amid the grass in the fields each side of the lanes, passing the endless grass,
Passing the yellow-speared wheat, every grain from its shroud in the dark-brown fields uprisen,
Passing the apple-tree blows of white and pink in the orchards,
Carrying a corpse to where it shall rest in the grave,
Night and day journeys a coffin.

VI

Coffin that passes through lanes and streets,
Through day and night with the great cloud darkening the land,
With the pomp of the inlooped flags with the cities draped in black,
With the show of the States themselves as of crape-veiled women standing,
With processions long and winding and the flambeaus of the night,
With the countless torches lit, with the silent sea of faces and the unbared heads,
With the waiting depot, the arriving coffin, and the somber faces,
With dirges through the night, with the thousand voices rising strong and solemn,
With all the mournful voices of the dirges poured around the coffin,
The dim-lit churches and the shuddering organs — where amid these you journey,
With the tolling tolling bells' perpetual clang,
Here, coffin that slowly passes,
I give you my sprig of lilac.

VII

(Nor for you, for one alone,
Blossoms and branches green to coffins all I bring,
For fresh as the morning, thus would I chant a song for you, O sane and sacred death.

All over bouquets of roses,
O death, I cover you over with roses and early lilies,
But mostly and now the lilac that blooms the first,
Copious I break, I break the sprigs from the bushes,
With loaded arms I come, pouring for you,
For you, and the coffins all of you, O death.)

VIII

O western orb sailing the heaven,
Now I know what you must have meant as a month since I walked,
As I walked in silence the transparent shadowy night,
As I saw you had something to tell as you bent to me night after night,
As you drooped from the sky low down as if to my side (while the other stars all looked on),
As we wandered together the solemn night (for something, I know not what, kept me from sleep),
As the night advanced, and I saw on the rim of the west how full you were of woe,
As I stood on the rising ground in the breeze in the cool transparent night,
As I watched where you passed and was lost in the netherward black of the night,
As my soul in its trouble dissatisfied sank, as where you, sad orb,
Concluded, dropped in the night, and was gone.

IX

Sing on, there in the swamp,
O singer bashful and tender! I hear your notes, I hear your call,
I hear, I come presently, I understand you;
But a moment I linger, for the lustrous star has detained me,
The star, my departing comrade, holds and detains me.

X

O how shall I warble myself for the dead one there I loved?
And how shall I deck my song for the large sweet soul that has gone?
And what shall my perfume be for the grave of him I love?

Sea-winds blown from east and west,
Blown from the Eastern sea and blown from the Western sea, till there on the prairies meeting,
These, and with these, and the breath of my chant,
I'll perfume the grave of him I love.

XI

O what shall I hang on the chamber walls?
And what shall the pictures be that I hang on the walls,
To adorn the burial-house of him I love?

Pictures of growing spring and farms and homes,
With the Fourth-month eve at sundown, and the gray smoke lucid and bright,
With floods of the yellow gold of the gorgeous, indolent, sinking sun, burning, expanding the air,
With the fresh sweet herbage under foot, and the pale green leaves of the trees prolific,
In the distance the flowing glaze, the breast of the river, with a wind-dapple here and there,
With ranging hills on the banks, with many a line against the sky, and shadows,
And the city at hand with dwellings so dense, and stacks of chimneys,
And all the scenes of life and the workshops, and the workmen homeward returning.

XII

Lo, body and soul – this land,
My own Manhattan with spires, and the sparkling and hurrying tides, and the ships,
The varied and ample land, the South and the North in the light, Ohio's shores and flashing Missouri,
And ever the far-spreading prairies covered with grass and corn.

Lo, the most excellent sun so calm and haughty,
The violet and purple morn with just-felt breezes,
The gentle soft-born measureless light,
The miracle spreading, bathing all, the fulfilled noon,
The coming eve delicious, the welcome night and the stars,
Over my cities shining all, enveloping man and land.

XIII

Sing on, sing on you gray-brown bird,
Sing from the swamps, the recesses, pour your chant from the bushes,
Limitless out of the dusk, out of the cedars and pines.

Sing on dearest brother, warble your reedy song,
Loud human song, with voice of uttermost woe.

O liquid and free and tender!
O wild and loose to my soul — O wondrous singer!
You only I hear — yet the star holds me (but will soon depart),
Yet the lilac with mastering odor holds me.

XIV

Now while I sat in the day and looked forth,
In the close of the day with its light and the fields of spring, and the farmers preparing their crops,
In the large unconscious scenery of my land with its lakes and forests,
In the heavenly aerial beauty (after the perturbed winds and the storms),
Under the arching heavens of the afternoon swift passing, and the voices of children and women,
The many-moving sea-tides, and I saw the ships how they sailed,

And the summer approaching with richness, and the fields all busy with labor,
And the infinite separate houses, how they all went on, each with its meals and minutia of daily usages,
And the streets how their throbbings throbbed, and the cities pent — lo, then and there,
Falling upon them all and among them all, enveloping me with the rest,
Appeared the cloud, appeared the long black trail,
And I knew death, its thought, and the sacred knowledge of death.

Then with the knowledge of death as walking one side of me,
And the thought of death close-walking the other side of me,
And I in the middle as with companions, and as holding the hands of companions,
I fled forth to the hiding, receiving night that talks not,
Down to the shores of the water, the path by the swamp in the dimness.
To the solemn shadowy cedars and ghostly pines so still.

And the singer so shy to the rest received me,
The gray-brown bird I know received us comrades three,
And he sang the carol of death, and a verse for him I love.

From deep secluded recesses,
From the fragrant cedars and the ghostly pines so still,
Came the carol of the bird.

And the charm of the carol rapt me,
As I held as if by their hands my comrades in the night,
And the voice of my spirit tallied the song of the bird.

Come lovely and soothing death,
Undulate round the world, serenely arriving, arriving,
In the day, in the night, to all, to each,
Sooner or later delicate death.

Praised be the fathomless universe,
For life and joy, and for objects and knowledge curious,
And for love, sweet love — but praise! praise! praise!
For the sure-enwinding arms of cool-enfolding death.

Dark mother always gliding near with soft feet,
Have none chanted for thee a chant of fullest welcome?
Then I chant it for thee, I glorify thee above all,
I bring thee a song that when thou must indeed come, come unfalteringly.

Approach, strong deliveress!
When it is so, when thou hast taken them, I joyously sing the dead,
Lost in the loving floating ocean of thee,
Laved in the flood of thy bliss, O death.

From me to thee glad serenades,
Dances for thee I propose, saluting thee, adornments and feastings for thee,

And the sights of the open landscape and the high-spread sky are fitting,
And life and the fields, and the huge and thoughtful night.

The night in silence under many a star,
The ocean shore and the husky whispering wave whose voice I know,
And the soul turning to thee, O vast and well-veiled death,
And the body gratefully nestling close to thee.

Over the tree-tops I float thee a song,
Over the rising and sinking waves, over the myriad fields and the prairies wide,
Over the dense-packed cities all and the teeming wharves and ways,
I float this carol with joy, with joy to thee O death.

XV

To the tally of my soul,
Loud and strong kept up the gray-brown bird,
With pure deliberate notes, spreading, filling the night.

Loud in the pines and cedars dim,
Clear in the freshness moist and the swamp-perfume,
And I with my comrades there in the night.

While my sight that was bound in my eyes unclosed,
As to long panoramas of visions.

And I saw askant the armies,
I saw as in noiseless dreams hundreds of battle-flags,
Borne through the smoke of the battles and pierced with missiles I saw them,
And carried hither and yon through the smoke, and torn and bloody,
And at last but a few shreds left on the staffs (and all in silence),
And the staffs all splintered and broken.

I saw battle-corpses, myriads of them,
And the white skeletons of young men, I saw them,
I saw the debris and debris of all the slain soldiers of the war,
But I saw they were not as was thought,
They themselves were fully at rest, they suffered not,
The living remained and suffered, the mother suffered,
And the wife and the child and the musing comrade suffered,
And the armies that remained suffered.

XVI

Passing the visions, passing the night,
Passing, unloosing the hold of my comrades' hands,
Passing the song of the hermit bird and the tallying song of my soul,
Victorious song, death's outlet song, yet varying, ever-altering song,
As low and wailing, yet clear the notes, rising and falling, flooding the night,
Sadly sinking and fainting, as warning and warning, and yet again bursting with joy,
Covering the earth and filling the spread of the heaven,
As that powerful psalm in the night I heard from recesses,
Passing, I leave thee lilac with heart-shaped leaves,
I leave thee there in the door-yard, blooming, returning with spring.

I cease from my song for thee,
From my gaze on thee in the west, fronting the west, communing with thee,
O comrade lustrous with silver face in the night.

Yet each to keep and all, retrievements out of the night,
The song, the wondrous chant of the gray-brown bird,
And the tallying chant, the echo aroused in my soul,
With the lustrous and drooping star with the countenance full of woe,
With the holders holding my hand nearing the call of the bird,
Comrades mine, and I in the midst, and their memory ever to keep, for the dead I loved so well,
For the sweetest, wisest soul of all my days and lands — and this for his dear sake.
Lilac and star and bird twined with the chant of my soul,
There in the fragrant pines and the cedars dusk and dim.

— *Walt Whitman, American (1819–1892).*

PART EIGHTEEN

The Conduct of Life

Tragically, for many men life often consists of a wearisome round of birth, childhood, middle years, old age, and death. Through all their years, hard to say, they remain spiritually and intellectually almost in the state wherein they were born, thoughtless of life's possibilities, indifferent to its art, satisfied with creature comforts. Others attain the finest traits of youth and remain blissfully young, retaining the qualities which have often been sighed for in old age — scorn of difficulty and danger, vigor and freshness of will, and intense delight in the joys of keen-edged senses. At their best, such spirits find joy in contests hardly fought and honestly won. Others, however, look on life as a stupendous raffle; and the prize is to the unscrupulous, power and mastery over men and things being the chief end of living. Still others so invest themselves and become absorbed in their intellectual pursuits that, like the mathematician Archimedes, they plead when Death draws near: "Do not disturb my circles!" And, to cite but one more group, there are other-worldly minds who, like St. Augustine, conclude that men were made for communion with God and their spirits are ever restless till they find their rest in Him. These suggested types by no means embrace all the sorts and conditions of men, but they do indicate how great may be the varieties of mind and character even among our associates. Expressed in literature, their outlooks, attitudes, and conclusions about the conduct of life reveal that human nature's daily food is as varied as the temperaments of men.

The creative spirits of the past knew nothing of Freud or Einstein, but they had nevertheless observed the gamut of human experience and discovered the rules or disciplines which must be followed if man is to live more than an animal existence or to achieve more than do playboys of fashion. It was Michelangelo who said: "It is only well with me when I have a chisel in my hand." These words reflect one of the profoundest conclusions about the good life which can be found. It is that as truly as the body is dwarfed if it does not grow up, so the self is stunted if it does not escape from its self-absorption in work or in the discovery of loyalties beyond the self. The ancients did not write in the idioms of modern psychology, but in their writings will be found conclusions which are acute and insights which are profound.

Such writings have often been called Wisdom Literature. In its varied forms this literature has been derived from simple observations on conduct and experiences of faith in life, from tense sententious sayings known as proverbs, from the speculative literature of men who have followed the Socratic injunction "Know thyself," and from miscellaneous writings which presumably contain all that is "revealed unto babes" and is "hid from the wise and prudent." The art of proverb-making is universal. It flourishes among the rudest tribes as well as the most brilliantly endowed peoples. From the earliest times, proverbs and maxims have revealed the knowledge of life reached intuitively by unsophisticated men. In course they may become finely polished epigrams distinguished for literary grace and keenness of moral perception. Or, eventually evolving into the essay, whether formal or informal, this literature may contain the conclusions of philosophers or rustic wits on the business of living. Whatever the final mode of expression, there exists in world literature a significant type which might be called the secular scripture of mankind.

As indicated in the selections which follow, this literature has been enriched by some of the most eminent writers of the past, and ranges from advice on how to get rich to the assurance that the life of the universe depends on infinite resources.

Summum Bonum

ARISTOTLE

AND NOW, resuming the statement with which we commenced, since all knowledge and moral choice grasps at good of some kind or another, what good is that which we say πολιτική aims at? or, in other words, what is the highest of all the goods which are the objects of action?

So far as name goes, there is a pretty general agreement: for Happiness both the multitude and the refined few call it, and "living well" and "doing well" they conceive to be the same with "being happy;" but about the Nature of this Happiness, men dispute, and the multitude do not in their account of it agree with the wise. For some say it is some one of those things which are palpable and apparent, as pleasure or wealth or honour; in fact, some one thing, some another; nay, oftentimes the same man gives a different account of it; for when ill, he calls it health; when poor, wealth: and conscious of their own ignorance, men admire those who talk grandly and above their comprehension. Some again hold it to be something by itself, other than and beside these many good things, which is in fact to all these the cause of their being good.

Now to sift all the opinions would be perhaps rather a fruitless task; so it shall suffice to sift those which are most generally current, or are thought to have some reason in them.

And here we must not forget the difference between reasoning from principles, and reasoning to principles: for with good cause did Plato too doubt about this, and inquire whether the right road is from principles or to principles, just as in the racecourse from the judges to the further end, or *vice versâ*.

Of course, we must begin with what is known; but then this is of two kinds, what we *do* know, and what we *may* know: perhaps then as individuals we must begin with what we *do* know. Hence the necessity that he should have been well trained in habits, who is to study, with any tolerable chance of profit, the principles of nobleness and justice and moral philosophy generally. For a principle is a matter of fact, and if the fact is sufficiently clear to a man there will be no reason in addition of the reason for the fact. And he that has been thus trained either has principles already, or can receive them easily: as for him who neither has nor can receive them, let him hear his sentence from Hesiod:

"He is best of all who of himself conceiveth all things;
Good again is he too who can adopt a good suggestion;
But whoso neither of himself conceiveth nor hearing from another
Layeth it to heart;—he is a useless man."

But to return from this digression.

Now of the Chief Good (*i.e.* of Happiness) men seem to form their notions from the different modes of life, as we might naturally expect: the many and most low conceive it to be pleasure, and hence they are content with the life of sensual enjoyment. For there are three lines of life which stand out prominently to view: that just mentioned, and the life in society, and, thirdly, the life of contemplation.

Now the many are plainly quite slavish, choosing a life like that of brute animals; yet they obtain some consideration, because many of the great share the tastes of Sardanapalus. The refined and active again conceive it to be honour: yet it is plainly too superficial for the object of our search, because it is thought to rest with those who pay rather than with him who receives it, whereas the Chief Good we feel instinctively must be something which is our own, and not easily to be taken from us.

And besides, men seem to pursue honour, that they may believe themselves to be good: for instance, they seek to be honoured by the wise, and by those among whom they are known, and for virtue: clearly then, in the opinion at least of these men, virtue is higher than honour. In truth, one would be much more inclined to think this to be the end of the life in society; yet this itself is plainly not sufficiently final: for it is conceived possible, that a man possessed of virtue might sleep or be inactive all through his life, or, as a third case, suffer the greatest evils and misfortunes: and the man who should live thus no one would call happy, except for mere disputation's sake.

And for these let this much suffice, for they have been treated of at sufficient length in my Encyclia.

A third line of life is that of contemplation, concerning which we shall make our examination in the sequel.

As for the life of money-making, it is one of constraint, and wealth manifestly is not the good we are seeking, because it is for use, that is, for the sake of something further: and hence one would rather conceive the forementioned ends to be the right ones, for men rest content with them for their own sakes. Yet, clearly, they are not the objects of our search either, though many words have been wasted on them. So much then for these.

Again, the notion of one Universal Good (the same, that is, in all things), it is better perhaps we should examine, and discuss the meaning of it, though such an inquiry is unpleasant, because they are friends of ours who have introduced these εἴδη. Still perhaps it may appear better, nay to be our duty where the safety of truth is concerned, to upset if need be even our own theories, specially as we are lovers of wisdom: for since both are dear to us, we are bound to prefer the truth. Now they who invented this doctrine of εἴδη did not apply it to those things in which they spoke of priority and posteriority, and so they never made any δέα of numbers; but good is predicated in the categories of Substance, Quality, and Relation; now that which exists of itself, *i.e.* Substance, is prior in the nature of things to that which is relative, because this latter is an offshoot, as it were, and result of that which is; on their own principle then there cannot be a common ἰδέα in the case of these.

In the next place, since good is predicated in as many ways as there are modes of existence (for it is predicated in the category of Substance, as God, Intellect—and in that of Quality, as the Virtues—and in that of Quantity, as the Mean—and in that of Relation, as the Useful—and in that of time, as Opportunity—and in that of Place, as Abode; and other such like things), it manifestly cannot be something common and universal and one in all: else it would not have been predicated in all the categories, but in one only.

Thirdly, since those things which range under one ἰδέα are also under the cognisance of one science, there would have been, on their theory, only one science taking cognisance of all goods collectively: but in fact there are many even for those which range under one category: for instance, of Opportunity or Seasonableness (which I have before mentioned as being in the category of Time), the science is, in war, generalship; in disease, medical science, and of the Mean (which I quoted before as being in the category of Quantity), in food, the medical science; and in labour or exercise, the gymnastic science. A person might fairly doubt also what in the world they mean by very-this that or the other, since, as they would themselves allow, the account of the humanity is one and the same in the very-Man, and in any individual Man: for so far as the individual and the very-Man are both Man, they will not differ at all: and if so, then very-good and any particular good will not differ, in so far as both are good. Nor will it do to say, that the eternity of the very-good makes it to be more good; for what has lasted white ever so long, is no whiter than what lasts but for a day.

No. The Pythagoreans do seem to give a more credible account of the matter, who place "One" among the goods in their double list of goods and bads: which philosophers, in fact, Speusippus seems to have followed.

But of these matters let us speak at some other time. Now there is plainly a loophole to object to what has been advanced, on the plea that the theory I have attacked is not by its advocates applied to all goods: but those goods only are spoken of as being under one ἰδέα, which are pursued, and with which men rest content simply for their own sakes: whereas those things which have a tendency to produce or preserve them in any way, or to hinder their contraries, are called good because of these other goods, and after another fashion. It is manifest then that the goods may be so called in two senses, the one class for their own sakes, the other because of these.

Very well then, let us separate the independent goods from the instrumental, and see whether they are spoken of under one ἰδέα. But the question next arises, what kind of goods are we to call independent? All such as are pursued even when separated from other goods, as, for instance, being wise, seeing, and certain pleasures and honours (for these, though we do pursue them with some further end in view, one would still place among the independent goods)? or does it come in fact to this, that we can call nothing independent good except the ἰδέα and so the concrete of it will be nought?

If, on the other hand, these are independent goods, then we shall require that the account of the goodness be the same clearly in all, just as that of the whiteness is in snow and white lead. But how stands the fact? Why of honour and wisdom and pleasure the accounts are distinct and different in so far as they are good. The Chief Good then is not something common, and after one ἰδέα.

But then, how does the name come to be common (for it is not seemingly a case of fortuitous equivocation)? Are different individual things called good by virtue of being from one source, or all conducing to one end, or rather by way of analogy, for that intellect is to the soul as sight is to the body, and so on? However, perhaps we ought to leave these questions now, for an accurate investigation of them is more properly the business of a different philosophy. And likewise respecting the ἰδέα: for even if there is some one good predicated in common of all things that are good, or separable and capable of existing independently, manifestly it cannot be the object of human action or attainable by Man; but we are in search now of something that is so.

It may readily occur to any one, that it would be better to attain a knowledge of it with a view to such concrete goods as are attainable and practical, because, with this as a kind of model in our hands, we shall the better know what things are good for us individually, and when we know them, we shall attain them.

Some plausibility, it is true, this argument possesses, but it is contradicted by the facts of the Arts and Sciences; for all these, though aiming at some good, and seeking that which is deficient, yet pretermit the knowledge of it: now it is not exactly probable that all artisans without exception should be ignorant of so great a help as this would be, and not even look after it; neither is it easy to see wherein a weaver or a carpenter will be profited in respect of his craft by knowing the very-good, or how a man will be the more apt to effect cures or to command an army for having seen the ἰδέα itself. For manifestly it is not health after this general and abstract fashion which is the subject of the physician's investigation, but the health of Man, or rather perhaps of this or that man; for he has to heal individuals.—Thus much on these points.

And now let us revert to the Good of which we are in search: what can it be? for manifestly it is different in different actions and arts: for it is different in the healing art and in the art military, and similarly in the rest. What then is the Chief Good in each? Is it not "that for the sake of which the other things are done?" and this in the healing art is health, and in the art military victory, and in that of house-building a house, and in any other thing something else; in short, in every action and moral choice the End, because in all cases men do everything else with a view to this. So that if there is some one End of all things which are and may be done, this must

other way inactive; but the working cannot so, for it will of necessity act, and act well. And as at the Olympic games it is not the finest and strongest men who are crowned, but they who enter the lists, for out of these the prize-men are selected; so too in life, of the honourable and the good, it is they who act who rightly win the prizes.

Their life too is in itself pleasant: for the feeling of pleasure is a mental sensation, and that is to each pleasant of which he is said to be fond: a horse, for instance, to him who is fond of horses, and a sight to him who is fond of sights: and so in like manner just acts to him who is fond of justice, and more generally the things in accordance with virtue to him who is fond of virtue. Now in the case of the multitude of men the things which they individually esteem pleasant clash, because they are not such by nature, whereas to the lovers of nobleness those things which are pleasant are such by nature: but the actions in accordance with virtue are of this kind, so that they are pleasant both to the individuals and also in themselves.

So then their life has no need of pleasure as a kind of additional appendage, but involves pleasure in itself. For, besides what I have just mentioned, a man is not a good man at all who feels no pleasure in noble actions, just as no one would call that man just who does not feel pleasure in acting justly, or liberal who does not in liberal actions, and similarly in the case of the other virtues which might be enumerated: and if this be so, then the actions in accordance with virtue must be in themselves pleasurable. Then again they are certainly good and noble, and each of these in the highest degree; if we are to take as right the judgment of the good man, for he judges as we have said.

Thus then Happiness is most excellent, most noble, and most pleasant, and these attributes are not separated as in the well-known Delian inscription—

"Most noble is that which is most just, but
best is health;
And naturally most pleasant is the obtaining one's desires."

For all these co-exist in the best acts of working: and we say that Happiness is these, or one, that is, the best of them.

Still it is quite plain that it does require the addition of external goods, as we have said: because without appliances it is impossible, or at all events not easy, to do noble actions: for friends, money, and political influence are in a manner instruments whereby many things are done: some things there are again a deficiency in which mars blessedness; good birth, for instance, or fine offspring, or even personal beauty: for he is not at all capable of Happiness who is very ugly, or is ill-born, or solitary and childless; and still less perhaps supposing him to have very bad children or friends, or to have lost good ones by death. As we have said already, the addition of prosperity of this kind does seem necessary to complete the idea of Happiness; hence some rank good fortune, and others virtue, with Happiness.

And hence to a question is raised, whether it is a thing that can be learned, or acquired by habituation or discipline of some other kind, or whether it comes in the way of divine dispensation, or even in the way of chance.

Now to be sure, if anything else is a gift of the Gods to men, it is probable that Happiness is a gift of theirs too, and specially because of all human goods it is the highest. But this, it may be, is a question belonging more properly to an investigation different from ours: and it is quite clear, that on the supposition of its not being sent from the Gods direct, but coming to us by reason of virtue and learning of a certain kind, or discipline, it is yet one of the most Godlike things; because the prize and End of virtue is manifestly somewhat most excellent, nay divine and blessed.

It will also on this supposition be widely participated, for it may through learning and diligence of a certain kind exist in all who have not been maimed of virtue.

And if it is better we should be happy thus than as a result of chance, this is in itself an argument that the case is so; because those things which are in the way of nature, and in like manner of art, and of every cause, and specially the best cause, are by nature in the best way possible: to leave then to chance what is greatest and most noble would be very much out of harmony with all these facts.

The question may be determined also by a reference to our definition of Happiness, that it is a working of the soul in the way of excellence or virtue of a certain kind: and of the other goods, some we must have to begin with, and those which are co-operative and useful are given by nature as instruments.

These considerations will harmonise also with what we said at the commencement: for we assumed the End of πολιτική to be most excellent: now this bestows most care on making the members of a community of a certain character; good that is and apt to do what is honourable.

With good reason then neither ox nor horse nor any other brute animal do we call happy, for none of them can partake in such working: and for this same reason a child is not happy either, because by reason of his tender age he cannot yet perform such actions: if the term is applied it is by way of anticipation.

For to constitute Happiness, there must be, as we have said, complete virtue and a complete life: for many changes and chances of all kinds arise during a life, and he who is most prosperous may become involved in great misfortunes in his old age, as in the heroic poems the tale is told of Priam: but the man who has experienced such fortune and died in wretchedness, no man calls happy.

Are we then to call no man happy while he lives, and, as Solon would have us, look to the end? And again, if we are to maintain this position, is a man then happy when he is dead? or is not this a complete absurdity, specially in us who say Happiness is a working of a certain kind?

If on the other hand we do not assert that the dead man is happy, and Solon does not mean this, but only that one would then be safe in pronouncing a man happy, as being thenceforward out of the reach of evils and misfortunes, this too admits of some dispute, since it is thought that the dead has somewhat both of good and evil (if, as we must allow, a man may have when alive but not aware of the circumstances), as honour and dishonour, and good and bad fortune of children and descendants generally.

Nor is this view again without its difficulties: for, after a man has lived in blessedness to old age and died accordingly, many changes may befall him in right of his descendants; some of them may be good and obtain positions in life accordant to their merits, others again quite the contrary: it is plain too that the descendants may at different intervals or grades stand in all manner of relations to the ancestors. Absurd indeed would be the position that even the dead man is to change about with them and become at one time happy and at another miserable. Absurd however it is on the other hand that the affairs of the descendants should in no degree and during no time affect the ancestors.

But we must revert to the point first raised, since the present question will be easily determined from that.

If then we are to look to the end and then pronounce the man blessed, not as being so but as having been so at some previous time, surely it is absurd that when he *is* happy the truth is not to be asserted of him, because we are unwilling to pronounce the living happy by reason of their liability to changes, and because, whereas we have conceived of happiness as something stable and no way easily changeable, the fact is that good and bad fortune are constantly circling about the same people: for it is quite plain, that if we are to depend upon the fortunes of men, we shall often have to call the same man happy, and a little while after miserable, thus representing our happy man

"Chameleon-like, and based on rottenness."

Is not this the solution? that to make our sentence dependent on the changes of fortune, is no way right: for not in them stands the well, or the ill, but though human life needs these as accessories (which we have allowed already), the workings in the way of virtue are what determine Happiness, and the contrary the contrary.

And, by the way, the question which has been here discussed, testifies incidentally to the truth of our account of Happiness. For to nothing does a stability of human results attach so much as it does to the workings in the way of virtue, since these are held to be more abiding even than the sciences: and of these last again the most precious are the most abiding, because the blessed live in them most and most continuously, which seems to be the reason why they are not forgotten. So then this stability which is sought will be in the happy man, and he will be such through life, since always, or most of all, he will be doing and contemplating the things which are in the way of virtue: and the various chances of life he will bear most nobly, and at all times and in all ways harmoniously, since he is the truly good man, or in the terms of our proverb "a faultless cube."

And whereas the incidents of chance are many, and differ in greatness and smallness, the small pieces of good or ill fortune evidently do not affect the balance of life, but the great and numerous, if happening for good, will make life more blessed (for it is their nature to contribute to ornament, and the using of them comes to be noble and excellent), but if for ill, they bruise as it were and maim the blessedness: for they bring in positive pain, and hinder many acts of working. But still, even in these, nobleness shines through when a man bears contentedly many and great mischances not from insensibility to pain but because he is noble and high-spirited.

And if, as we have said, the acts of working are what determine the character of life, no one of the blessed can ever become wretched, because he will never do those things which are hateful and mean. For the man who is truly good and sensible bears all fortunes, we presume, becomingly, and always does what is noblest under the circumstances, just as a good general employs to the best advantage the force he has with him; or a good shoemaker makes the handsomest shoe he can out of the leather which has been given him; and all other good artisans likewise. And if this be so, wretched never can the happy man come to be: I do not mean to say he will be blessed should he fall into fortunes like those of Priam.

Nor, in truth, is he shifting and easily changeable, for on the one hand from his happiness he will not be shaken easily nor by ordinary mischances, but if at all, by those which are great and numerous; and, on the other, after such mischances he cannot regain his happiness in a little time; but, if at all, in a long and complete period, during which he has made himself master of great and noble things. Why then should we not call happy the man who works in the way of perfect virtue, and is furnished with external goods sufficient for acting his part in the drama of life: and this during no ordinary period but such as constitutes a complete life as we have been describing it.

Or we must add, that not only is he to live so, but his death must be in keeping with such life, since the future is dark to us, and Happiness we assume to be in every way an end and complete. And, if this be so, we shall call them among the living blessed who have and will have the things specified, but blessed *as Men*.

On these points then let it suffice to have defined thus much.

—From the Ethics, Book I, of Aristotle, Greek (384–322 B.C.), translated by D. P. Chase.

Ecclesiastes

I

THE words of the Preacher, the son of David, king in Jerusalem.

Vanity of vanities, saith the Preacher, vanity of vanities; all is vanity.

What profit hath a man of all his labour which he taketh under the sun?

One generation passeth away, and another generation cometh: but the earth abideth for ever.

The sun also ariseth, and the sun goeth down, and hasteth to his place where he arose.

The wind goeth toward the south, and turneth about unto the north; it whirleth about continually, and the wind returneth again according to his circuits.

All the rivers run into the sea; yet the sea is not full: unto the place from whence the rivers come, thither they return again.

All things are full of labour; man cannot utter it: the eye is not satisfied with seeing, nor the ear filled with hearing.

The thing that hath been, it is that which shall be; and that which is done is that which shall be done: and there is no new thing under the sun.

Is there anything whereof it may be said, See, this is new? it hath been already of old time, which was before us.

There is no remembrance of former things; neither shall there be any remembrance of things that are to come with those that shall come after.

I the Preacher was king over Israel in Jerusalem.

And I gave my heart to seek and search out by wisdom concerning all things that are done under heaven: this sore travail hath God given to the sons of man to be exercised therewith.

I have seen all the works that are done

under the sun; and behold, all is vanity and vexation of spirit.

That which is crooked cannot be made straight: and that which is wanting cannot be numbered.

I communed with mine own heart, saying, Lo, I am come to great estate, and have gotten more wisdom than all they that have been before me in Jerusalem: yea, my heart had great experience of wisdom and knowledge.

And I gave my heart to know wisdom, and to know madness and folly: I perceived that this also is vexation of spirit.

For in much wisdom is much grief: and he that increaseth knowledge increaseth sorrow.

II

I said in mine heart, Go to now, I will prove thee with mirth; therefore enjoy pleasure: and behold, this also is vanity.

I said of laughter, It is mad: and of mirth, What doeth it?

I sought in mine heart to give myself unto wine, yet acquainting mine heart with wisdom; and to lay hold on folly, till I might see what was that good for the sons of men, which they should do under the heaven all the days of their life.

I made me great works; I builded me houses; I planted me vineyards;

I made me gardens and orchards, and I planted trees in them of all kind of fruits;

I made me pools of water, to water therewith the wood that bringeth forth trees;

I got me servants and maidens, and had servants born in my house; also I had great possessions of great and small cattle above all that were in Jerusalem before me;

I gathered me also silver and gold, and the peculiar treasure of kings, and of the provinces; I gat me men-singers and women-singers, and the delights of the sons of men, as musical instruments, and that of all sorts.

So I was great, and increased more than all that were before me in Jerusalem: also my wisdom remained with me.

And whatsoever mine eyes desired I kept not from them, I withheld not my heart from any joy; for my heart rejoiceth in all my labour: and this was my portion of all my labour.

Then I looked on all the works that my hands had wrought, and on the labour that I had laboured to do: and behold, all was vanity and vexation of spirit, and there was no profit under the sun.

And I turned myself to behold wisdom, and madness, and folly: for what can the man do that cometh after the king? even that which hath been already done.

Then I saw that wisdom excelleth folly, as far as light excelleth darkness.

The wise man's eyes are in his head; but the fool walketh in darkness: and I myself perceived also that one event happeneth to them all.

Then said I in my heart, As it happeneth to the fool, so it happeneth even to me; and why was I then more wise? Then I said in my heart, that this also is vanity.

For there is no remembrance of the wise more than of the fool for ever; seeing that which now is in the days to come shall all be forgotten. And how dieth the wise man? as the fool.

Therefore I hated life; because the work that is wrought under the sun is grievous unto me: for all is vanity, and vexation of spirit.

Yea, I hated all my labour which I had taken under the sun: because I should leave it unto the man that shall be after me.

And who knoweth whether he shall be a wise man or a fool? yet shall he have rule over all my labour wherein I have laboured, and wherein I have shewed myself wise under the sun. This is also vanity.

Therefore I went about to cause my heart to despair of all the labour which I took under the sun.

For there is a man whose labour is in wisdom, and in knowledge, and in equity; yet to a man that hath not laboured therein shall he leave it for his portion. This also is vanity and a great evil.

For what hath man of all his labour, and of the vexation of his heart, wherein he hath laboured under the sun?

For all his days are sorrows, and his travail grief; yea, his heart taketh not rest in the night. This is also vanity.

There is nothing better for a man than that he should eat and drink, and that he should make his soul enjoy good in his labour. This also I saw, that it was from the hand of God.

For who can eat, or who else can hasten hereunto more than I?

For God giveth to a man that is good in his sight, wisdom, and knowledge, and joy:

but to the sinner he giveth travail, to gather and to heap up, that he may give to him that is good before God. This also is vanity and vexation of spirit.

III

To every thing there is a season, and a time to every purpose under the heaven:

A time to be born, and a time to die; a time to plant, and a time to pluck up that which is planted;

A time to kill, and a time to heal; a time to break down, and a time to build up;

A time to weep, and a time to laugh; a time to mourn, and a time to dance;

A time to cast away stones, and a time to gather stones together; a time to embrace, and a time to refrain from embracing;

A time to get, and a time to lose; a time to keep, and a time to cast away;

A time to rend, and a time to sew; a time to keep silence, and a time to speak;

A time to love, and a time to hate; a time of war, and a time of peace.

What profit hath he that worketh in that wherein he laboreth?

I have seen the travail, which God hath given to the sons of men to be exercised in it.

He hath made everything beautiful in his time: also he hath set the world in their heart, so that no man can find out the work that God maketh from the beginning to the end. . . .

I know that whatsoever God doeth, it shall be forever: nothing can be put to it, nor anything taken from it, that men should fear before him.

That which hath been is now; and that which is to be hath already been; and God requireth that which is past. . . .

IV

So I returned, and considered all the oppressions that are done under the sun: and behold the tears of such were oppressed, and they had no comforter; and on the side of their oppressors there was power; but they had no comforter.

Wherefore I praised the dead which are already dead more than the living which are yet alive.

Yea, better is he than both they, which hath not yet been, who hath not seen the evil work that is done under the sun. . . .

Two are better than one; because they have a good reward for their labour.

For if they fall, the one will lift up his fellow: but woe to him that is alone when he falleth; for he hath not another to help him up.

Again, if two lie together, then they have heat: but how can one be warm alone?

And if one prevail against him, two shall withstand him; and a threefold cord is not quickly broken. . . .

V

. . . He that loveth silver shall not be satisfied with silver; nor he that loveth abundance with increase: this is also vanity.

When goods increase they are increased that eat them: and what good is there to the owners thereof, saving the beholding of them with their eyes?

The sleep of a labouring man is sweet, whether he eat little or much: but the abundance of the rich will not suffer him to sleep.

There is a sore evil which I have seen under the sun, namely, riches kept for the owners thereof to their hurt.

But those riches perish by evil travail: and he begetteth a son, and there is nothing in his hand.

As he came forth of his mother's womb, naked shall he return to go as he came, and shall take nothing of his labour, which he may carry away in his hand.

And this also is a sore evil, that in all points as he came, so shall he go: and what profit hath he that hath laboured for the wind?

All his days also he eateth in darkness, and he hath much sorrow and wrath with his sickness.

Behold that which I have seen: it is good and comely for one to eat and to drink, and to enjoy the good of all his labour that he taketh under the sun all the days of his life, which God hath given him: for it is his portion. . . .

VI

There is an evil which I have seen under the sun, and it is common among men:

A man to whom God hath given riches, wealth, and honour, so that he wanteth nothing for his soul of all that he desireth, yet God giveth him not power to eat thereof, but a stranger eateth it: this is vanity, and it is an evil disease.

If a man beget an hundred children, and

live many years, so that the days of his years be many, and his soul be not filled with good, and also that he have no burial; I say, that an untimely birth is better than he.

For he cometh in with vanity, and departeth in darkness, and his name shall be covered with darkness.

Moreover he hath not seen the sun, nor known any thing: this hath more rest than the other. . . .

VII

A good name is better than precious ointment; and the day of death than the day of one's birth.

It is better to go to the house of mourning, than to go to the house of feasting: for that is the end of all men; and the living will lay it to his heart.

Sorrow is better than laughter: for by the sadness of the countenance the heart is made better.

The heart of the wise is in the house of mourning; but the heart of fools is in the house of mirth.

It is better to hear the rebuke of the wise, than for a man to hear the song of fools.

For as the crackling of thorns under a pot, so is the laughter of the fool: this also is vanity. . . .

All things have I seen in the days of my vanity: there is a just man that perisheth in his righteousness, and there is a wicked man that prolongeth his life in his wickedness.

Be not righteous over much; neither make thyself over wise: why shouldest thou destroy thyself?

Be not over much wicked, neither be thou foolish: why shouldest thou die before thy time? . . .

I applied mine heart to know, and to search, and to seek out wisdom, and the reason of things, and to know the wickedness of folly, even of foolishness and madness.

And I find more bitter than death the woman whose heart is snares and nets, and her hands as bands: whoso pleaseth God shall escape from her: but the sinner shall be taken by her.

Behold, this have I found, saith the Preacher, counting one by one, to find out the account;

Which yet my soul seeketh, but I find not: one man among a thousand have I found; but a woman among all those have I not found.

Lo, this only have I found, that God hath made man upright; but they have sought out many inventions.

VIII

. . . There is no man that hath power over the spirit to retain the spirit: neither hath he power in the day of death: and there is no discharge in that war; neither shall wickedness deliver those that are given to it.

All this have I seen, and applied my heart unto every work that is done under the sun: there is a time wherein one man ruleth over another to his own hurt.

And so I saw the wicked buried, who had come and gone from the place of the holy, and they were forgotten in the city where they had so done: this is also vanity.

Because sentence against an evil work is not executed speedily, therefore the heart of the sons of men is fully set in them to do evil. . . .

Then I commended mirth, because a man hath no better thing under the sun, than to eat, and to drink, and to be merry.

IX

All things come alike to all: there is one event to the righteous and to the wicked; to the good, and to the clean, and to the unclean; to him that sacrificeth, and to him that sacrificeth not: as is the good, so is the sinner; and he that sweareth, as he that feareth an oath. . . .

Go thy way, eat thy bread with joy, and drink thy wine with a merry heart, for God now accepteth thy works.

Live joyfully with the wife whom thou lovest all the days of the life of thy vanity, which he hath given thee under the sun, all the days of thy vanity: for that is thy portion in this life, and in thy labour which thou takest under the sun.

Whatsoever thy hand findeth to do, do it with thy might; for there is no work, nor device, nor knowledge, nor wisdom, in the grave, whither thou goest.

I returned, and saw under the sun, that the race is not to the swift, nor the battle to the strong, neither yet bread to the wise, nor yet riches to men of understanding, nor yet favour to men of skill; but time and chance happeneth to them all.

For man also knoweth not his time: as the fishes that are taken in an evil net, and as the

23

These wise people, meditative,
ways possessed of strong powers
Nirvana, the highest happiness.

24

If a reflecting person has rouse
if he is not forgetful, if his deed
if he acts with consideration, if h
himself, and lives according to
his glory will increase.

25

By rousing himself, by reflect
straint and control, the wise man
for himself an island which no
overwhelm. . .

29

Reflecting among the thoughtl
among the sleepers, the wise ma
like a racer leaving behind the

III

THOUGHT

33

As a fletcher makes straight h
wise man makes straight his trem
unsteady thought, which is difficu
difficult to turn.

34

As a fish taken from his watery
thrown on the dry ground, our tho
bles all over in order to escape th
of Mara (the tempter).

35

It is good to tame the mind, w
ficult to hold in and flighty, rusl
ever it listeth; a tamed mind bri
ness.

36

Let the wise man guard his th
they are difficult to perceive, very
they rush wherever they list: tho
guarded bring happiness.

37

Those who bridle their mind w
els far, moves about alone, is
body, and hides in the chamb

birds that are caught in the snare; so are the sons of men snared in an evil time, when it falleth suddenly upon them.

This wisdom have I seen also under the sun, and it seemed great unto me:

There was a little city, and few men within it; and there came a great king against it, and besieged it, and built great bulwarks against it.

Now there was found in it a poor wise man, and he by his wisdom delivered the city; yet no man remembered that same poor man.

Then said I, Wisdom is better than strength: nevertheless the poor man's wisdom is despised, and his words are not heard. . . .

X

. . . He that diggeth a pit shall fall into it; and whoso breaketh an hedge, a serpent shall bite him.

Whoso removeth stones shall be hurt therewith; and he that cleaveth wood shall be endangered thereby.

If the iron be blunt, and he do not whet the edge, then must he put to more strength: but wisdom is profitable to direct.

Surely the serpent will bite without enchantment, and a babbler is no better.

The words of a wise man's mouth are gracious; but the lips of a fool will swallow up himself. . . .

XI

Cast thy bread upon the waters: for thou shalt find it after many days. Give a portion to seven, and also to eight; for thou knowest not what evil shall be upon the earth.

If the clouds be full of rain, they empty themselves upon the earth: and if the tree fall toward the south, or toward the north, in the place where the tree falleth, there it shall be.

He that observeth the wind shall not sow; and he that regardeth the clouds shall not reap.

Thou knowest not what is the way of the spirit, nor how the bones do grow in the womb of her that is with child.

In the morning sow thy seed, and in the evening withhold not thine hand: for thou knowest not whether shall prosper, either this or that, or whether they both shall be alike good.

Truly the light is sweet, and a pleasant thing it is for the eyes to behold the sun:

But if a man live many years, and rejoice in them all; yet let him remember the days of darkness; for they shall be many. All that cometh is vanity.

Rejoice, O young man, in thy youth; and let thy heart cheer thee in the days of thy youth, and walk in the ways of thine heart, and in the sight of thine eyes. Therefore remove sorrow from thy heart, and put away evil from thy flesh: for childhood and youth are vanity.

Remember now thy Creator in the days of thy youth, while the evil days come not, nor the years draw nigh, when thou shalt say, I have no pleasure in them;

While the sun, or the light, or the moon, or the stars, be not darkened, nor the clouds return after the rain:

In the day when the keepers of the house shall tremble, and the strong men shall bow themselves, and the grinders cease because they are few, and those that look out of the windows be darkened,

And the doors shall be shut in the streets, when the sound of the grinding is low, and he shall rise up at the voice of the bird, and all the daughters of music shall be brought low.

Also when they shall be afraid of that which is high, and fear shall be in the way, and the almond-tree shall flourish, and the grasshopper shall be a burden, and desire shall fail: because man goeth to his long home, and the mourners go about the streets:

Or ever the silver cord be loosed, or the golden bowl be broken, or the pitcher be broken at the fountain, or the wheel broken at the cistern.

Then shall the dust return to the earth as it was: and the spirit shall return unto God who gave it.

Vanity of vanities, saith the Preacher; all is vanity.

And moreover, because the preacher was wise, he still taught the people knowledge; yea, he gave good heed, and sought out, and set in order many proverbs. . . .

And further, by these, my son, be admonished: of making many books there is no end; and much study is a weariness of the flesh.

Let us hear the conclusion of the whole matter: Fear God, and keep his commandments: for this is the whole duty of man.

For God shall bring every w
ment, with every secret thing
good, or whether it be evil.

—From the Old Testament, Heb
Version.

~ ❁ ~

Buddhist Aphorisms
Dhammapad

I

THE TWIN-VERSI

1

ALL that we are is a result of
thought: it is founded on our
made up of our thoughts. If a
acts with an evil thought, pa
as the wheel follows the foot
draws the carriage.

2

All that we are is a result o
thought: it is founded on our
made up of our thoughts. If a
acts with a pure thought, ha
him, like a shadow that never

3

"He abused me, he beat m
me, he robbed me,"—hatred
harbor such thoughts will nev

4

"He abused me, he beat m
me, he robbed me,"—hatred
do not harbor such thoughts

5

For hatred does not cease b
time: hatred ceases by love;
rule.

6

And some do not know th
come to an end here; but ot
hence their quarrels cease.

7

He who lives looking for
his senses uncontrolled, imm
enjoyments, idle, and wea
tempter) will certainly overc
wind throws down a weak t

61

If a traveller does not meet with one who is his better, or his equal, let him firmly keep to his solitary journey; there is no companionship with a fool.

62

"These sons belong to me, and this wealth belongs to me"; with such thoughts a fool is tormented. He himself does not belong to himself; how much less his sons and wealth?

63

The fool who knows his own foolishness, is wise at least so far. But a fool who thinks himself wise, he is called a fool indeed.

64

If a fool be associated with a wise man even all his life, he will perceive the truth as little as a spoon perceives the taste of soup.

65

If an intelligent man be associated for one minute only with a wise man, he will soon perceive the truth, as the tongue perceives the taste of soup.

66

Fools of little understanding have themselves for their greatest enemies, for they do evil deeds which must bear bitter fruits.

67

That deed is not well done of which a man must repent, and the reward of which he receives crying and with a tearful face.

68

That deed is well done of which a man does not repent, and the reward of which he receives gladly and cheerfully.

69

As long as the evil deed done does not bear fruit, the fool thinks it is like honey; but when it ripens, then the fool suffers grief. . . .

VIII

THE THOUSANDS

100

Even though a speech be a thousand (of words), but made up of senseless words, one word of sense is better, which if a man hears he becomes quiet.

101

Even though a Gatha (poem) be a thousand, but is made up of senseless words, one word of a Gatha is better, which if a man hears he becomes quiet.

102

Though a man recite a hundred Gathas made up of senseless words, one word of the Law is better, which if a man hears he becomes quiet.

103

If one man conquer in battle a thousand times a thousand men, and if another conquer himself, he is the greatest of conquerors.

104, 105

One's own self conquered is better than all other people; not even a god, a Gandharva, not Mara with Brahman could change into defeat the victory of a man who has vanquished himself, and always lives under restraint.

106

If a man for a hundred years sacrifice month by month with a thousand, and if he but for one moment pay homage to a man whose soul is grounded in true knowledge, better is that homage than a sacrifice for a hundred years. . . .

X

PUNISHMENT

129

All men tremble at punishment, all men fear death; remember that you are like unto them, and do not kill, nor cause slaughter.

130

All men tremble at punishment, all men love life; remember that thou art like unto them, and do not kill, nor cause to slaughter.

131

He who, for his own sake, punishes or kills beings longing for happiness, will not find happiness after death.

132

He who, for his own sake, does not punish or kill beings longing for happiness, will find happiness after death.

133

Do not speak harshly to anybody; those who are spoken to will answer thee in the same way. Angry speech is painful: blows for blows will touch thee.

134

If like a trumpet trampled underfoot, thou utter not, then thou hast reached Nirvana; anger is not known in thee.

135

As a cowherd with his staff gathers his cows into the stable, so do Old Age and Death gather the life of man. . . .

145

Well-makers guide the water; fletchers bend the arrow; carpenters break a log of wood; wise people fashion themselves.

XI

OLD AGE

146

How is there laughter, how is there joy, as this world is always burning? Why do you not seek a light, ye who are surrounded by darkness?

147

Look at this dressed-up lump, covered with wounds, joined together, sickly, full of many thoughts, which has no strength, no hold!

148

This body is wasted, full of sickness, and frail; this heap of corruption breaks to pieces, the life in it is death.

149

Those white bones, like gourds thrown away in the autumn, what pleasure is there in looking at them?

150

After a frame has been made of the bones, it is covered with flesh and blood, and there dwell in it old age and death, pride and deceit.

151

The brilliant chariots of kings are destroyed, the body also approaches destruction, but the virtues of good people never approach destruction, thus do the good say to the good.

152

A man who has learnt little, grows old like an ox; his flesh grows, but his knowledge does not grow.

XVII

ANGER

221

Let a man leave anger, let him forsake pride, let him overcome all bondage! No sufferings befall the man who is not attached either body or soul, and who calls nothing his own.

222

He who holds back rising anger like a rolling chariot, him I call a real driver; other people are but holding the reins.

224

Speak the truth; do not yield to anger; give, if thou art asked, from the little thou hast; by those steps thou wilt go near the gods.

—From the Dhammapada or "Path of Virtue" (third century B.C.?), translated from the Pali by F. Max Müller.

~ ✿ ~

From the Encheiridion

EPICTETUS

I

OF THINGS some are in our power, and others are not. In our power are opinion, movement towards a thing, desire, aversion (turning from a thing); and in a word, whatever are our own acts: not in our power are the body, property, reputation, offices (magisterial power), and in a word, whatever are not our own acts. And the things in our power are by nature free, not subject to restraint nor hindrance: but the things not in our power are weak, slavish, subject to restraint, in the power of others. Remember then that if you think the things which are by nature slavish to be free, and the things which are in the power of others to be your own, you will be hindered, you will lament, you will be disturbed, you will blame both gods and men: but if you think that only which is your own to be your own, and if you think that what is another's, as it really is, belongs to another, no man will ever compel you, no man will hinder you, you will never blame any man, you will accuse no man, you will do nothing involuntarily, no man will harm you, you will have no enemy, for you will not suffer any harm.

If then you desire such great things, remember that you must not lay hold of them with a small effort; but you must leave alone some things entirely, and postpone others for the present. But if you wish for these things also, and power and wealth, perhaps you will not gain even these very things because you aim also at those former things: certainly you will fail in those things through which alone happiness and freedom are secured. Straightway then practice saying to every harsh appearance. You are in appearance, and in no manner what you appear to be. Then examine it by the rules which you possess, and by this first and chiefly, whether it relates to the things which are in our power or to the things which are not in our power: and if it relates to anything which is not in our power, be ready to say, that it does not concern you.

II

Men are disturbed not by the things which happen, but by the opinions about the things: for example, death is nothing terrible, for if it were it would have seemed so to Socrates; for the opinion about death, that it is terrible, is the terrible thing. When then we are impeded or disturbed or grieved, let us never blame others, but ourselves, that is, our opinions. It is the act of an ill-instructed man to blame others for his bad condition; it is the act of one who has begun to be instructed, to lay the blame on himself; and of one whose instruction is completed, neither to blame another, nor himself.

III

Seek not that the things which happen should happen as you wish; but wish the things which happen to be as they are, and you will have a tranquil flow of life.

IV

If you would have your children and your wife and your friends to live forever, you are silly; for you would have the things which are not in your power to be in your power, and the things which belong to others to be yours. So if you would have your slave to be free from faults, you are a fool; for you would have badness not to be badness, but something else. But if you wish not to fail in your desires, you are able to do that. Practice then this which you are able to do. He is the master of every man who has the power over the things, which another person wishes or does not wish, the power to confer them on him or to take them away. Whoever then wishes to be free, let him neither wish for anything nor avoid anything which depends on others: if he does not observe this rule, he must be a slave.

V

Remember that in life you ought to behave as at a banquet. Suppose that something is carried round and is opposite to you. Stretch out your hand and take a portion with decency. Suppose that it passes by you. Do not detain it. Suppose that it is not yet come to you. Do not send your desire forward to it, but wait till it is opposite to you. Do so with respect to children, so with respect to a wife, so with respect to magisterial offices, so with respect to wealth, and you will be some time a worthy partner of the banquets of the gods. But if you take none of the things which are set before you, and even despise them, then you will be not only a fellow-banqueter with the gods, but also a partner with them in power. For by acting thus Diogenes and Heracleitus and those like them were deservedly divine, and were so called.

VI

When you see a person weeping in sorrow either when a child goes abroad or when he is dead, or when the man has lost his property, take care that the appearance do not hurry you away with it, as if he were suffering in external things. But straightway make a distinction in your own mind, and be in readiness to say, it is not that which has happened that afflicts this man, for it does not afflict another, but it is the opinion about this thing which afflicts the man. So far as words then do not be unwilling to show him sympathy, and even if it happens so, to lament with him. But take care that you do not lament internally also.

VII

Remember that thou art an actor in a play of such a kind as the author may choose; if short, of a short one; if long, of a long one: if he wishes you to act the part of a poor man, see that you act the part naturally; if the part of a lame man, of a magistrate, of a private person, (do the same). For this is your duty, to act well the part that is given to you; but to select the part, belongs to another.

VIII

Remember that it is not he who reviles you or strikes you, who insults you, but it is your opinion about these things as being insulting. When then a man irritates you, you must know that it is your own opinion which has irritated you. Therefore especially try not to be carried away by the appearance. For if you once gain time and delay, you will more easily master yourself.

IX

Let death and exile and every thing which appears dreadful be daily before your eyes; but most of all death: and you will never think of anything mean nor will you desire anything extravagantly.

X

If you desire philosophy, prepare yourself from the beginning to be ridiculed, to expect that many will sneer at you, and say, He has all at once returned to us as a philosopher; and whence does he get this supercilious look for us? Do you not show a supercilious look; but hold on to the things which seem to you best as one appointed by God to this station. And remember that if you abide in the same principles, these men who first ridiculed will afterward admire you: but if you shall have been overpowered by them, you will bring on yourself double ridicule.

XI

Let not these thoughts afflict you, I shall live unhonored and be nobody nowhere. For if want of honor is an evil, you cannot be in evil through the means of another any more than you can be involved in anything base. Is it then your business to obtain the rank of a magistrate, or to be received at a banquet? By no means. How then can this be want of honor? And how will you be nobody nowhere, when you ought to be somebody in those things only which are in your power, in which indeed it is permitted to you to be a man of the greatest worth? But your friends will be without assistance! What do you mean by being without assistance? They will not receive money from you, nor will you make them Roman citizens. Who then told you that these are among the things which are in our power, and not in the power of others? And who can give to another what he has not himself? Acquire money then, your friends say, that we also may have something. If I can acquire money and also keep myself modest, and faithful and magnanimous, point out the way, and I will acquire it. But if you ask me to lose the things which are good and my own, in order that you may gain the things which are not good, see how unfair and silly you are. Besides, which would you rather have, money or a faithful and modest friend? For this end then rather help me to be such a man, and do not ask me to do this by which I shall lose that character. But my country, you say, as far as it depends on me, will be without my help. I ask again, what help do you mean? It will not have porticoes or baths through you. And what does this mean? For it is not furnished with shoes by means of a smith, nor with arms by means of a shoemaker. But it is enough if every man fully discharges the work that is his own: and if you provided it with another citizen faithful and modest, would you not be useful to it? Yes. Then you also cannot be useless to it. What place then, you say, shall I hold in the city? Whatever you can, if you maintain at the same time your fidelity and modesty. But if when you wish to be useful to the state, you shall lose these qualities, what profit could you be to it, if you were made shameless and faithless?

XII

Immediately prescribe some character and some form to yourself, which you shall observe both when you are alone and when you meet with men.

And let silence be the general rule, or let only what is necessary be said, and in few words. And rarely and when the occasion calls we shall say something; but about none of the common subjects, nor about gladiators, nor horse-races, nor about athletes, nor about eating or drinking, which are the usual subjects; and especially not about men, as blaming them or praising them, or comparing them. If then you are able, bring over by your conversation the conversation of your associates to that which is proper; but if you should happen to be confined to the company of strangers, be silent.

Let not your laughter be much, nor on many occasions, nor excessive.

Refuse altogether to take an oath, if it is possible; if it is not refuse as far as you are able.

Avoid banquets which are given by strangers, and by ignorant persons. But if ever there is occasion to join in them, let your attention be carefully fixed, that you slip not into the manners of the vulgar. For you must know, that if your companion be impure, he also who keeps company with him must become impure, though he should happen to be pure.

Take the things which relate to the body as far as the bare use, as food, drink, clothing, house, and slaves: but exclude everything which is for show or luxury. . . .

In company take care not to speak much and excessively about your own acts or dangers: for as it is pleasant to you to make mention of your dangers, it is not so pleasant to others to hear what has happened to you. Take care also not to provoke laughter; for this is a slippery way toward vulgar habits, and is also adapted to diminish the respect of your neighbors. It is a dangerous habit also to approach obscene talk. When then anything of this kind happens, if there is a good opportunity, rebuke the man who has proceeded to this talk: but if there is not an opportunity, by your silence at least, and blushing and expression of dissatisfaction by your countenance, show plainly that you are displeased at such talk.

XIII

If you have received the impression of any pleasure, guard yourself against being carried away by it; but let the thing wait for you, and allow yourself a certain delay on your own part. Then think of both times, of the time when you will enjoy the pleasure, and of the time after the enjoyment of the pleasure when you will repent and will reproach yourself. And set against these things how you will rejoice if you have abstained from the pleasure, and how you will commend yourself. But if it seem to you seasonable to undertake (do) the thing, take care that the charm of it, and the pleasure, and the attraction of it shall not conquer you: but set on the other side the consideration how much better it is to be conscious that you have gained this victory.

XIV

When you have decided that a thing ought to be done and are doing it, never avoid being seen doing it, though the many shall form an unfavorable opinion about it. For if it is not right to do it, avoid doing the thing; but if it is right, why are you afraid of those who shall find fault wrongly?

XV

It is mark of a mean capacity to spend much time on the things which concern the body, such as much exercise, much eating, much drinking, much easing of the body, much copulation. But these things should be done as subordinate things: and let all your care be directed to the mind.

XVI

When at a small cost you are supplied with everything for the body, do not be proud of this; nor, if you drink water, say on every occasion, I drink water. But consider first how much more frugal the poor are than we, and how much more enduring of labor. And if you ever wish to exercise yourself in labor and endurance, do it for yourself and not for others: do not embrace statutes. But if you are ever very thirsty, take a draught of cold water, and spit it out, and tell no man.

XVII

The condition and characteristic of an uninstructed person is this: he never expects from himself profit nor harm, but from externals. The condition and characteristic of a philosopher is this: he expects all advantage and all harm from himself. The signs of one who is making progress are these: he censures no man, he praises no man, he blames no man, he accuses no man, he says nothing about himself as if he were somebody or knew something; when he is impeded at all or hindered, he blames himself if a man praises him, he ridicules the praiser to himself: if a man censures him, he makes no defense: he goes about like weak persons, being careful not to move any of the things which are placed, before they are firmly fixed he removes all desire from himself, and he transfers aversion to those things only of the things within our power which are contrary to nature: he employs a moderate movement toward everything: whether he is considered foolish or ignorant, he cares not: and in a word he watches himself as if he were an enemy and lying in ambush.

—*From The Encheiridion of Epictetus, Greek (A.D. 60–?), translated by George Long.*

Meditations

MARCUS AURELIUS

1. BEGIN the morning by saying to thyself, I shall meet with the busybody, the ungrateful, arrogant, deceitful, envious, unsocial. All these things happen to them by reason of their ignorance of what is good and evil. But I who have seen the nature of the good that it is beautiful and of the bad that it is ugly, and the nature of him who does wrong, that it is akin to me, not (only) of the same blood or seed, but that it participates in (the same) intelligence and the same portion of the divinity, I can neither be injured by any of them, for no one can fix on me what is ugly, nor can I be angry with my kinsman, nor hate him. For we are made for co-operation, like feet, like hands, like eyelids, like the rows of the upper and lower teeth. To act against one another then is contrary to nature; and it is acting against one another to be vexed and to turn away.

2. Every moment think steadily as a Roman and a man to do what thou hast in hand with perfect and simple dignity, and feeling of affection, and freedom, and justice; and to give thyself relief from all other thoughts. And thou wilt give thyself relief, if thou doest every act of thy life as if it were the last, laying aside all carelessness and passionate aversion from the commands of reason, and all hypocrisy, and self-love, and discontent with the portion which has been given to thee. Thou seest how few the things are, the which if a man lays hold of, he is able to live a life which flows in quiet, and is like the existence of the gods; for the gods on their part will require nothing more from him who observes these things.

3. Of the human life the time is a point, and the substance is in a flux, and the perception dull, and the composition of the whole body subject to putrefaction, and the soul of a whirl, and fortune hard to divine, and face a thing devoid of judgment. And, to say all in a word, everything which belongs to the body is a stream, and what belongs to the soul is a dream and vapour, and life is a warfare and a stranger's sojourn, and after-fame is oblivion. What, then, is that which is able to conduct a man? One thing, and only one – philosophy. But this consists in keeping the daemon within a man free from violence and unharmed, superior to pains and pleasures, doing nothing without a purpose, nor yet falsely and with hypocrisy, not feeling the need of another man's doing or not doing anything; and besides, accepting all that happens, and all that is allotted, as coming from thence, wherever it is, from whence he himself came; and, finally, waiting for death with a cheerful mind, as being nothing else than a dissolution of the elements of which every living being is compounded. But if there is no harm to the elements themselves in each continually changing into another, why should a man have any apprehension about the change and dissolution of all the elements? For it is according to nature, and nothing is evil which is according to nature.

4. We ought to consider not only that our life is daily wasting away and a smaller part of it is left, but another thing also must be taken into the account, that if a man should live longer it is quite uncertain whether the understanding will still continue sufficient for the comprehension of things, and retain the power of contemplation which strives to acquire the knowledge of the divine and the human. For if he shall begin to fall into dotage, perspiration and nutrition and imagination and appetite, and whatever else there is of the kind, will not fail; but the powers of making use of ourselves, and filling up the measure of our duty, and clearly separating all appearances, and considering whether a man should now depart from life, and whatever else of the kind absolutely requires a disciplined reason, all this is already extinguished. We must make haste then, not only because we are daily nearer to death,

but also because the conception of things and the understanding of them cease first.

5. Do not waste the remainder of thy life in thoughts about others, when thou dost not refer thy thoughts to some object of common utility. For thou losest the opportunity of doing something else when thou hast such thoughts as these, What is such a person doing, and why, and what is he saying, and what is he thinking of, and what is he contriving, and whatever else of the kind makes us wander away from the observation of our own ruling power. We ought then to check in the series of our thoughts everything that is without a purpose and useless, but most of all the overcurious feeling and the malignant; and a man should use himself to think of those things only about which if one should suddenly ask, What hast thou now in thy thoughts? with perfect openness thou mightest immediately answer, This or That; so that from thy words it should be plain that everything in thee is simple and benevolent, and such as befits a social animal, one that cares not for thoughts about pleasure or sensual enjoyments at all, nor has any rivalry or envy and suspicion, or anything else for which thou wouldst blush if thou shouldst say that thou hadst it in thy mind. For the man who is such and no longer delays being among the number of the best, is like a priest and minister of the gods, using too the deity which is planted within him, which makes the man uncontaminated by pleasure, unharmed by any pain, untouched by any insult, feeling no wrong, a fighter in the noblest fight, one who cannot be overpowered by any passion, dyed deep with justice, accepting with all his soul everything which happens and is assigned to him as his portion; and not often, nor yet without necessity and for the general interest, imagining what another says, or does, or thinks. For it is only what belongs to himself that he makes the matter for his activity; and he constantly thinks of that which is allotted to himself out of the sum total of things, and he makes his own acts fair, and he is persuaded that his own portion is good. For the lot which is assigned to each man is carried along with him and carries him along with it. And he remembers also that every rational animal is his kinsman, and that to care for all men is according to man's nature; and a man should hold on to the opinion not of all but of those only who confessedly live according to nature. But as to those who live not so, he always bears in mind what kind of men they are both at home and from home, both by night and by day, and what they are, and with what men they live an impure life. Accordingly, he does not value at all the praise which comes from such men, since they are not even satisfied with themselves.

6. Labour not unwillingly, nor without regard to the common interest, nor without due consideration, nor with distraction; nor let studied ornament set off thy thoughts, and be not either a man of many words, or busy about too many things. And further, let the deity which is in thee be the guardian of a living being, manly and of ripe age, and engaged in matter political, and a Roman, and a ruler, who has taken his post like a man waiting for the signal which summons him from life, and ready to go, having need neither of oath nor of any man's testimony. Be cheerful also, and seek not external help nor the tranquillity which others give. A man then must stand erect, not be kept erect by others.

7. If thou findest in human life anything better than justice, truth, temperance, fortitude, and, in a word, anything better than thy own mind's self-satisfaction in the things which it enables thee to do according to right reason, and in the condition that is assigned to thee without thy own choice; if, I say, thou seest anything better than this, turn to it with all thy soul, and enjoy that which thou hast found to be the best. But if nothing appears to be better than the deity which is planted in thee, which has subjected to itself all thy appetites, and carefully examines all the impressions, and as Socrates said, has detached itself from the persuasions of sense, and has submitted itself to the gods, and cares for mankind; if thou findest everything else smaller and of less value than this, give place to nothing else, for if thou dost once diverge and incline to it, thou wilt no longer without distraction be able to give the preference to that good thing which is thy proper possession and thy own; for it is not right that anything of any other kind, such as praise from the many, or power, or enjoyment of pleasure, should come into competition with that which is rationally and politically (or, practically) good. All these things, even though they may seem to adapt themselves (to the

better things) in a small degree, obtain the superiority all at once, and carry us away. But do thou, I say, simply and freely choose the better, and hold to it. — But that which is useful is the better. — Well then, if it is only useful to thee as a rational being, keep to it; but if it is only useful to thee as an animal, say so, and maintain thy judgment without arrogance; only take care that thou makest the inquiry by a sure method. . . .

9. Let no act be done without a purpose, nor otherwise than according to the perfect principles of art.

10. Men seek retreats for themselves, houses in the country, seashores and mountains; and thou too art wont to desire such things very much. But this is altogether a mark of the most common sort of men, for it is in thy power whenever thou shalt choose to retire into thyself. For nowhere, either with more quiet or more freedom from trouble, does a man retire than into his own soul, particularly when he has within him such thoughts that by looking into them he is immediately in perfect tranquillity; and I affirm that tranquillity is nothing else then the good ordering of the mind. Constantly then give to thyself this retreat, and renew thyself; and let thy principles be brief and fundamental, which, as soon as thou shalt recur to them, will be sufficient to cleanse the soul completely, and to send thee back free from all discontent with the things to which thou returnest. . . .

11. This then remains: Remember to retire into this little territory of thy own, and, above all, do not distract or strain thyself, but be free, and look at things as a man, as a human being, as a citizen, as a mortal. But among the things readiest to thy hand to which thou shalt turn, let there be these, which are two. One is that things do not touch the soul, for they are external and remain immovable; but our perturbations come only from the opinion which is within. The other is that all these things, which thou seest, change immediately and will no longer be; and constantly bear in mind how many of these changes thou hast already witnessed. The universe is transformation: life is opinion.

12. If our intellectual part is common, the reason also, in respect of which we are rational beings, is common: if this is so, common also is the reason which commands us what to do, and what not to do; if this is so, there is a common law also; if this is so, we are fellow-citizens; if this is so, we are members of some political community; if this is so, the world is in a manner a state. For of what other common political community will any one say that the whole human race are members? And from thence, from this common political community comes also our very intellectual faculty and reasoning faculty and our capacity for laws; or whence do they come? For as my earthly part is a portion given to me from certain earth, and that which is watery from another element, and that which is hot and fiery from some peculiar source (for nothing comes out of that which is nothing, as nothing also returns to non-existence), so also the intellectual part comes from some source.

13. Death is such as generation is, a mystery of nature; a composition out of the same elements, and a decomposition into the same; and altogether not a thing of which any man should be ashamed, for it is not contrary to the nature of a reasonable animal, and not contrary to the reason of our constitution.

14. Occupy thyself with few things, says the philosopher, if thou wouldst be tranquil. — But consider if it would not be better to say, Do what is necessary, and whatever the reason of the animal which is naturally social requires, and as it requires. For this brings not only the tranquillity which comes from doing well, but also that which comes from doing few things. For the greatest part of what we say and do being unnecessary, if a man takes this away, he will have more leisure and less uneasiness. Accordingly on every occasion a man should ask himself, Is this one of the unnecessary things? Now a man should take away not only unnecessary acts but also unnecessary thoughts, for thus superfluous acts will not follow after.

15. Try how the life of the good man suits thee, the life of him who is satisfied with his portion out of the whole, and satisfied with his own just acts and benevolent disposition.

16. Hast thou seen those things? Look also at these. Do not disturb thyself. Make thyself all simplicity. Does any one do wrong? It is to himself that he does the wrong. Has anything happened to thee? Well, out of the universe from the beginning everything which happens has been apportioned and spun out to thee. In a word, thy life is short. Thou must turn to profit the

present by the aid of reason and justice. Be sober in thy relaxation. . . .

18. In the morning when thou risest unwillingly, let this thought be present — I am rising to the work of a human being. Why then am I dissatisfied if I am going to do the things for which I exist and for which I was brought into the world? Or have I been made for this, to lie in the bed-clothes and keep myself warm? — But this is more pleasant. — Dost thou exist then to take thy pleasure, and not at all for action or exertion? Dost thou not see the little plants, the little birds, the ants, the spiders, the bees working together to put in order their several parts of the universe? And art thou unwilling to do the work of a human being, and dost thou not make haste to do that which is according to thy nature? — But it is necessary to take rest also. — It is necessary: however, nature has fixed bounds to this too: she has fixed bounds both to eating and drinking, and yet thou goest beyond these bounds, beyond what is sufficient; yet in thy acts it is not so, but thou stoppest short of what thou canst do. So thou lovest not thyself, for if thou didst, thou wouldst love thy nature and her will. But those who love their several arts exhaust themselves in working at them unwashed and without food; but thou valuest thy own nature less than the turner values the turning art, or the dancer the dancing art, or the lover of money values his money, or the vainglorious man his little glory. And such men, when they have a violent affection to a thing, choose neither to eat nor to sleep rather than to perfect the things which they care for. But are the acts which concern society more vile in thy eyes and less worthy of thy labour?

19. How easy it is to repel and to wipe away every impression which is troublesome or unsuitable, and immediately to be in all tranquillity.

20. Judge every word and deed which are according to nature to be fit for thee; and be not diverted by the blame which follows from any people, nor by their words, but if a thing is good to be done or said, do not consider it unworthy of thee. For those persons have their peculiar leading principle and follow their peculiar movement; which things do not thou regard, but go straight on, following thy own nature and the common nature; and the way of both in one.

21. I go through the things which happen according to nature until I shall fall and rest, breathing out my breath into that element out of which I daily draw it in, and falling upon that earth out of which my father collected the seed, and my mother the blood, and my nurse the milk; out of which during so many years I have been supplied with food and drink; which bears me when I tread on it and abuse it for so many purposes. . . .

24. About what am I now employing my own soul? On every occasion I must ask myself this question, and inquire, what have I now in this part of me which they call the ruling principle? and whose soul have I now? that of a child, or of a young man, or of a feeble woman, or of a tyrant, or of a domestic animal, or of a wild beast.

25. What kind of things those are which appear good to the many, we may learn even from this. For if any man should conceive certain things really good, such as prudence, temperance, justice, fortitude, he would not after having first conceived these endure to listen to anything which should not be in harmony with what is really good. But if a man has first conceived as good the things which appear to the many to be good, he will listen and readily receive as very applicable that which was said by the comic writer. Thus even the many perceive the difference. For were it not so, this saying would not offend and would not be rejected (in the first case), while we receive it when it is said of wealth, and of the means which further luxury and fame, as said fitly and wittily. Go on then and ask if we should value and think those things to be good, to which after their first conception in the mind the words of the comic writer might be aptly applied — that he who has them, through pure abundance has not a place to ease himself in.

26. Such as are thy habitual thoughts, such also will be the character of thy mind; for the soul is dyed by the thoughts. Dye is then with a continuous series of such thoughts as these: for instance, that where a man can live, there he can also live well. But he must live in a palace — well then, he can also live well in a palace. And again, consider that for whatever purpose each thing has been constituted, for this it has been constituted, and toward this it is carried; and its end is in that toward which it is carried; and

where the end is, there also is the advantage and the good of each thing. Now the good for the reasonable animal is society; for that we are made for society has been shown above. . . .

27. To seek what is impossible is madness: and it is impossible that the bad should not do something of this kind.

28. Nothing happens to any man which he is not formed by nature to bear. The same things happen to another, and either because he does not see that they have happened or because he would show a great spirit he is firm and remains unharmed. It is a shame then that ignorance and conceit should be stronger than wisdom.

29. Things themselves touch not the soul, not in the least degree; nor have they admission to the soul, nor can they turn or move the soul; but the soul turns and moves itself alone, and whatever judgments it may think proper to make, such it makes for itself the things which present themselves to it.

30. In one respect man is the nearest thing to me, so far as I must do good to men and endure them. But so far as some men make themselves obstacles to my proper acts, man becomes to me one of the things which are indifferent, no less than the sun or wind or a wild beast. Now it is true that these may impede my action, but they are no impediments to my affects and disposition, which have the power of acting conditionally and changing: for the mind converts and changes every hindrance to its activity into an aid; and so that which is a hindrance is made a furtherance to an act; and that which is an obstacle on the road helps us on this road.

31. Reverence that which is best in the universe; and this is that which makes use of all things and directs all things. And in like manner also reverence that which is best in thyself; and this of the same kind as that. For in thyself also, that which makes use of everything else, in this, and thy life is directed by this.

32. That which does no harm to the state, does no harm in the citizens. In the case of every appearance of harm apply this rule: if the state is not harmed by this, neither am I harmed. But if the state is harmed, thou must not be angry with him who does harm to the state. Show him where his error is.

33. Often think of the rapidity with which things pass by and disappear, both the things which are and the things which are produced. For substance is like a river in a continual flow, and the activities of things are in constant change, and the causes work in infinite varieties; and there is hardly anything which stands still. And consider this which is near to thee, this boundless abyss of the past and of the future in which all things disappear. How then is he not a fool who is puffed up with such things or plagued about them or makes himself miserable? for they vex him only for a time, and a short time.

34. Think of the universal substance, of which thou hast a very small portion; and of universal time, of which a short and indivisible interval has been assigned to thee; and of that which is fixed by destiny, and how small a part of it thou art.

35. Does another do me wrong? Let him look to it. He has his own disposition, his own activity. I now have what the universal nature wills me to have; and I do what my nature now wills me to do.

36. Let the part of thy soul which leads and governs be undisturbed by the movements in the flesh, whether of pleasure or of pain; and let it not unite with them, but let it circumscribe itself and limit those affects to their parts. But when these affects rise up to the mind by virtue of that one, then thou must not strive to resist the sensation, for it is natural: but let not the ruling part of itself add to the sensation the opinion that it is either good or bad.

37. Live with the gods. And he does live with the gods who constantly shows to them that his own soul is satisfied with that which is assigned to him, and that it does all that the daemon wishes, which Zeus hath given to every man for his guardian and guide, a portion of himself. And this is every man's understanding and reason.

38. Thou canst pass thy life in an equable flow of happiness, if thou canst go by the right way, and think and act in the right way. These two things are common both to the soul of God and to the soul of man, and to the soul of every rational being, not to be hindered by another; and to hold good to consist in the disposition to justice and the practice of it, and in this to let thy desire find its termination.

39. If this is neither my own badness, nor

an effect of my own badness, and the common weal is not injured, why am I troubled about it? and what is the harm to the common weal? . . .

42. Let it make no difference to thee whether thou art cold or warm, if thou art doing thy duty; and whether thou art drowsy or satisfied with sleep; and whether ill-spoken of or praised; and whether dying or doing something else. For it is one of the acts of this life, this act by which we die; it is sufficient then in this act also to do well what we have in hand.

43. Look within. Let neither the peculiar quality of anything nor its value escape thee.

44. All existing things soon change, and they will either be reduced to vapor, if indeed all substance is one, or they will be dispersed.

45. The reason which governs knows what its own disposition is, and what it does, and on what material it works.

46. The best way of avenging thyself is not to become like the wrong doer.

47. Take pleasure in one thing and rest in it, in passing from one social act to another social act, thinking of God.

48. When thou hast been compelled by circumstances to be disturbed in a manner, quickly return to thyself and do not continue out of tune longer than the compulsion lasts; for thou wilt have more mastery over the harmony by continually recurring to it.

49. He who has seen present things has seen all, both everything which has taken place from all eternity and everything which will be for time without end; for all things are of one kin and of one form.

50. Frequently consider the connection of all things in the universe and their relation to one another. For in a manner all things are implicated with one another, and all in this way are friendly to one another, for one thing comes in order after another, and this is by virtue of the active movement and mutual conspiration and the unity of the substance.

51. Adapt thyself to the things with which thy lot has been cast; and the men among whom thou hast received thy portion, love them, but do it truly (sincerely).

52. Retire into thyself. The rational principle which rules has this nature, that it is content with itself when it does what is just, and so secure tranquillity. . . .

54. Direct thy attention to what is said. Let thy understanding enter into the things that are doing and the things which do them.

55. Adorn thyself with simplicity and modesty and with indifference towards the things which lie between virtue and vice. Love mankind. Follow God. The poet says that Law rules all. And it is enough to remember that Law rules all.

56. About death: whether it is a dispersion, or a resolution into atoms, or annihilation, it is either extinction or change.

57. About pain: the pain which is intolerable carries us off; but that which lasts a long time is tolerable; and the mind maintains its own tranquillity by retiring into itself, and the ruling faculty is not made worse. But the parts which are harmed by pain, let them, if they can, give their opinion about it.

58. About fame: look at the minds (of those who seek fame), observe what they are, and what kind of things they avoid, and what kind of things they pursue. And consider that as the heaps of sand piled on one another hide the former sands, so in life the events which go before are soon covered by those which come after.

59. From Plato: the man who has an elevated mind and takes a view of all time and of all substance, dost thou suppose it possible for him to think that human life is anything great? It is not possible, he said. Such a man then will think that death also is no evil. Certainly not.

60. From Antisthenes: It is royal to do good and to be abused.

61. It is a base thing for the countenance to be obedient and to regulate and compose itself as the mind commands, and for the mind not to be regulated and composed by itself.

62. It is not right to vex ourselves at things, for they care nought about it.

63. This is a fine saying of Plato: That he who is discoursing about men should look also at earthly things as if he viewed them from some higher place; should look at them in their assemblies, armies, agricultural labours, marriages, treaties, births, deaths, noise of the courts of justice, desert places, various nations of barbarians, feasts, lamentations, markets, a mixture of all things and an orderly combination of contraries.

64. It is in thy power to live free from all

compulsion in the greatest tranquillity of mind, even if all the world cry out against thee as much as they choose, and even if wild beasts tear in pieces the members of this kneaded matter which has grown around thee. For what hinders the mind in the midst of all this from maintaining itself in tranquillity, and in a just judgment of all surrounding things, and in a ready use of the objects which are presented to it, so that the judgment may say to the thing which falls under its observation: This thou art in substance (reality), though in men's opinion thou mayest appear to be of a different kind; and the use shall say to that which falls under the hand: Thou art the thing that I was seeking; for to me that which presents itself is always a material for virtue, both rational and political, and, in a word, for the exercise of art, which belongs to man or God. For everything which happens has a relationship either to God or man, and is neither new nor difficult to handle, but usual and apt matter to work on.

65. The perfection of moral character consists in this, in passing every day as the last, and in being neither violently excited nor torpid, nor playing the hypocrite.

66. The gods who are immortal are not vexed because during so long a time they must tolerate continually men such as they are and so many of them bad; and besides this, they also take care of them in all ways. But thou, who art destined to end so soon, art thou wearied of enduring the bad, and this too when thou art one of them?

67. It is a ridiculous thing for a man not to fly from his own badness, which is indeed possible, but to fly from other men's badness, which is impossible.

68. He who acts unjustly acts impiously. For since the universal nature has made rational animals for the sake of one another to help one another according to their deserts, but in no way to injure one another, he who transgresses her will, is clearly guilty of impiety towards the highest divinity. And he too who lies is guilty of impiety to the same divinity; for the universal nature is the nature of things that are; and things that are have a relation to all things that come into existence. And further, his universal nature is named truth, and is the prime cause of all things that are true. He then who lies intentionally is guilty of impiety inasmuch as he acts unjustly by deceiving; and he also who lies unintentionally, inasmuch as he is at variance with the universal nature, and inasmuch as he disturbs the order by fighting against the nature of the world; for he fights against it, who is moved of himself to that which is contrary to truth, for he had received powers from nature through the neglect of which he is not able now to distinguish falsehood from truth. And indeed he who pursues pleasure as good, and avoids pain as evil, is guilty of impiety. For of necessity such a man must often find fault with the universal nature, alleging that it assigns things to the bad and the good contrary to their deserts, because frequently the bad are in the enjoyment of pleasure and possess the things which procure things which cause pain. And further, he who is afraid of pain will sometimes also be afraid of some of the things which will happen in the world, and even this is impiety. And he who pursues pleasure will not abstain from injustice, and this is plainly impiety. Now, with respect to the things towards which the universal nature is equally affected – for it would not have made both, unless it was equally affected towards both – towards these they who wish to follow nature should be of the same mind with it, and equally affected. With respect to pain, then, and pleasure, or death and life, or honour and dishonour, which the universal nature employs equally, whoever is not equally affected is manifestly acting impiously. And I say that the universal nature employs them equally, instead of saying that they happen alike to those who are produced in continuous series and to those who come after them by virtue of a certain original movement of Providence, according to which it moved from a certain beginning to this ordering of things, having conceived certain principles of the things which were to be, and having determined powers productive of beings and of changes and of such like successions. . . .

70. Do not despise death, but be well content with it, since this too is one of those things which nature wills. For such as it is to be young and to grow old, and to increase and to reach maturity, and to have teeth and beard and gray hairs, and to beget, and to be pregnant, and to bring forth, and all the other natural operations which the seasons of thy life bring, such also is dissolution. This, then, is consistent with the character of a reflecting man, to be neither careless nor

impatient nor contemptuous with respect to death, but to wait for it as one of the operations of nature. As thou now waitest for the time when the child shall come out of thy wife's womb, so be ready for the time when thy soul shall fall out of this envelope. But if thou requirest also a vulgar kind of comfort which shall reach thy heart, thou wilt be made best reconciled to death by observing the objects from which thou art going to be removed, and the morals of those with whom thy soul will no longer be mingled. For it is no way right to be offended with men, but it is thy duty to care for them and to bear with them gently; and yet to remember that thy departure will be not from men who have the same principles as thyself. For this is the only thing, if there be any, which could draw us the contrary way and attach us to life, to be permitted to live with those who have the same principles as ourselves. But now thou seest how great is the trouble arising from the discordance of those who live together, so that thou mayest say, Come quick, O death, lest perchance I, too, should forget myself.

71. He who does wrong does wrong against himself. He who acts unjustly acts unjustly to himself, because he makes himself bad.

72. He often acts unjustly who does not do a certain thing; not only he who does a certain thing.

73. Thy present opinion founded on understanding, and thy present conduct directed to social good, and thy present disposition of contentment with everything which happens – that is enough.

74. Acquire the contemplative way of seeing how all things change into one another, and constantly attend to it, and exercise thyself about this part (of philosophy). For nothing is so much adapted to produce magnanimity. Such a man has put off the body, and as he sees that he must, no one knows how soon, go away from among men and leave everything here, he gives himself up entirely to just doing in all his actions, and in everything else that happens he resigns himself to the universal nature. But as to what any man shall say or think about him, or do against him, he never even thinks of it, being himself contented with these two things, with acting justly in what he now does, and being satisfied with what is assigned to him; and he lays aside all distracting and busy pursuits, and desires nothing else than to accomplish the straight course through the law, and by accomplishing the straight course to follow God.

75. What need is there of suspicious fear, since it is in thy power to inquire what ought to be done? And if thou seest clear, go by this way content, without turning back: but if thou dost not see clear, stop and take the best advisers. But if any other things oppose thee, go on according to thy powers with due consideration, keeping to that which appears to be just. For it is best to reach this object, and if thou dost fail, let thy failure be in attempting this. He who follows reason in all things is both tranquil and active at the same time, and also cheerful and collected.

76. Short is the little which remains to thee of life. Live as on a mountain. For it makes no difference whether a man lives there or here, if he lives everywhere in the world as in a state (political community). Let men see, let them know a real man who lives according to nature. If they cannot endure him, let them kill him. For that is better than to live thus (as men do).

77. No longer talk at all about the kind of man that a good man ought to be, but be such. . . .

81. Socrates used to say, What do you want? Souls of rational men or irrational? – Souls of rational men. – Of what rational men? – Sound or unsound? – Sound. – Why then do you not seek for them? – Because we have them. – Why then do you fight and quarrel?

82. What dost thou wish? to continue to exist? Well, dost thou wish to have sensation? movement? growth? and then again to cease to grow? to use thy speech? to think? What is there of all these things which seem to thee worth desiring? But if it is easy to set little value on all these things, turn to that which remains, which is to follow reason and God. But it is inconsistent with honouring reason and God to be troubled because by death a man will be deprived of the other things.

How small a part of the boundless and unfathomable time is assigned to every man? for it is very soon swallowed up in the eternal. And how small a part of the soul? and on what a small clod of the whole earth thou creepest? Reflecting on all this consider nothing to be great, except to act as thy nature leads thee, and to endure that which the common nature brings.

—*From the Meditations of the Emperor Marcus Aurelius Antoninus, Roman (121–180), translated from the Greek by George Long.*

The Gulistan

SA'DI

PREFACE

ONE NIGHT I was thinking upon my past time; reflecting with regret upon my prodigal use of life; boring the flinty mansion of my heart with the diamond of my tears; and repeating these verses [the verses of the original are set in italics in the translation] as applicable to the state of my affairs:

Every moment a breath is expiring of my life; when I curiously inspect it, I find that only a little is left. O man! fifty years of thy life are gone, and thou art still in a dream; perhaps thou mayest avail thyself of the remaining five days. Shame on him who departed, and had not finished his task; the call of march was beaten, and he had not made up his baggage; the fascinating drowsiness of the morning of departure arrests the traveller from setting out on his journey.—Every man that came, projected for himself a new house; he went and left his dwelling to another, and that other in like manner gratified his vanity; but none of them put a finishing hand to his building.—Set not thy affections on so fickle a mistress; a being so capricious merits not thy attachment. Since the good and bad are alike doomed to die, happy is he who carried off the prize of virtue! Let the means of future enjoyment precede thee to the grave; dispatch them before, for nobody can send them after thee; life is like snow, and the sun is burning hot; the vanities, O sir! of the present day soon melt away!—The four contending and refractory temperaments may chime harmoniously for some few days; but let one of them once get the upper hand and it will thrust the sweet soul from its dwelling; consequently a prudent and upright man sets not his heart on the life of this world.—Yes! thou hast gone empty-handed to market; I fear of thee that thou wilt not bring thy turban back; that man who can eat up his crop of unripe wheat must be content at harvest to glean his neighbour's field.—Listen with a willing ear to the admonition of Sa'di; such is the path, be resolute and follow it.

After pondering on this mystery I saw its policy, and said: "I will betake myself to the cell of retirement, withdraw my skirt from social enjoyment, erase from my tablets all vain compositions, and henceforth refrain from idle confabulations." *To have the tongue cut out and to be seated deaf and dumb in a corner were preferable to his condition who cannot govern his tongue.* At length one of my friends who had been the litter-companion of my travels and the chamber-chum of my studies entered my cell with his usual familiarity; but however much he indulged in pleasantry and mirth and spread abroad the carpet of social intercourse, I made him no return, nor raised my head from the knee of pious abstraction. Offended at my behaviour, he looked wistfully at me and said:

"Now that thou hast the faculty of speech, converse, O brother! with cheerfulness and joy, for to-morrow that the messenger of death shall present himself thou must of necessity restrain thy tongue." One of my comrades made him aware of events, saying: "Such a person has firmly resolved and fully determined to pass the remaining life in this world in contemplative devotion and to observe silence; do thou also, if thou art able, keep thine own counsel and take thyself aside." He replied and swore: "By our glorious faith and ancient friendship, I will neither breathe nor stir till he shall have answered me with his accustomed freedom and his usual frank manner; for it were savage to grate the hearts of friends, and it is easy to compromise on oath. Moreover, it is repugnant to good sense and an infringement on the policy of the wise that Ali's sword should rest in its scabbard and that Sa'di's tongue should cleave to his palate. *What, O wise man, is the tongue in the mouth? It is a key to the casket of the intellectual treasurer; so long as the lid remains shut how can any person say whether he be a dealer in gems or in pedlary?—Though in the estimation of the wise silence be mannerly, at the season of giving advice it were*

better to be explicit. Two circumstances cast a shade over the understanding—that of silence when we should speak, and that of speech when we should be silent."

In short, I could no longer reserve myself in answering him, nor see it generous to withhold being familiar, for he had ever been a most companionable and sincere friend.—*If forced into a combat, with him be the fight whom thou hast strength to cope with or legs to escape from.*

As a matter of necessity I spoke, and went joyfully abroad during the spring, when the cold of winter was meliorated and the auspicious season of the roses had arrived. *The leafy vestments of the trees resembled the holyday apparel of the orthodox or happy. On the 1st of Ardebihist, that charming month, the nightingales were carolling on their pulpits, the tree boughs, and the dew-fallen pearl on the damask rose rivalled the perspired drop on the cheek of our chiding mistress.*

I happened that night to fall into a nocturnal conversation in a garden with a friend, a lovely and refreshing spot, and its heart-gladdening groves intertwining overhead; its walks you might say were strewed with spangles of crystal, and clusters of fruit like the pleiades hung aloft from its boughs; *meadows, the water of whose rivulets meandered like the links of a chain; bowers, the melodies of whose aviaries were harmonious; those studded with flowers of various colours, and these loaded with fruits of divers kinds; while the zephyrs in the moving moonlight and shade of the trees were spreading a carpet of variegated hues.*

At dawn, when the thought of going home overcame a wish for sitting still, I remarked that my companion had filled his skirt with roses, hyacinths, spikenards, and sweet-basils, and was desirous of returning to the city. I said: "As you well know, the flower of the garden has no continuance, nor can we confide in the promise of the rose-bower; and philosophers have told us whatever is not lasting merits not our affection." He asked: "What is our alternative?" I replied: "For the gratification of beholders and recreation of spectators I can write such a Kitabi Gulistan, or book of a Flower-garden, as neither the rude storm of autumn shall be able to lay the hand of usurpation upon its leaves, nor the revolution of the season convert the serenity of its summer into the gloom of winter. *What can a basket of flowers avail thee? Pluck but one leaf from my Flower-garden; a rose can thus continue five or six days, but this rose-bower must bloom to all eternity!"*

So soon as I uttered these words he let the flowers drop from his lap and seized upon my skirt, saying: *"As the generous man promised, so he performed!"* That same day two chapters, one of them on the Accomplishments of Education, and the other on the Rules for Conversation, were recorded in my note-book in such a clothing as may come in practice with orators, and decorate the style of letter-writers. In short, roses yet continued to flourish in the garden when the book of the Gulistan was finished.

PURGATORY MAY BE PARADISE

A king was embarked along with a Persian slave on board a ship. The boy had never been at sea, nor experienced the inconvenience of a ship. He set up a weeping and wailing, and all his limbs were in a state of trepidation; and, however much they soothed him, he was not to be pacified. The king's pleasure-party was disconcerted by him; but they had no help. On board that ship there was a physician. He said to the king: "If you will order it, I can manage to silence him." The king replied: "It will be an act of great favour." The physician so directed that they threw the boy into the sea, and after he had plunged repeatedly, they seized him by the hair of the head and drew him close to the ship, when he clung with both hands by the rudder, and, scrambling upon the deck, slunk into a corner and sat down quiet. The king, pleased with what he saw, said: "What art is there in this?" The physician replied: "Originally he had not experienced the danger of being drowned, and undervalued the safety of being in a ship; in like manner as a person is aware of the preciousness of health when he is overtaken with the calamity of sickness. *A barley loaf of bread has, O epicure, no relish for thee. That is my mistress who appears so ugly to thy eye.—To the houris, or nymphs of paradise, purgatory would be a hell; ask the inmates of hell whether purgatory is not paradise.—There is a distinction between the man that folds his mistress in his arms and him whose two eyes are fixed on the door expecting her."*

THE WRESTLER

A person had become a master in the art of wrestling; he knew three hundred and sixty sleights in this art, and could exhibit a fresh trick for every day throughout the year. Perhaps owing to a liking that a corner of his heart took for the handsome person of one of his scholars, he taught him three hundred and fifty-nine of those feats, but he was putting off the last one, and under some pretence deferring it.

In short, the youth became such a proficient in the art and talent of wrestling that none of his contemporaries had ability to cope with him, till he at length had one day boasted before the reigning sovereign, saying: "To any superiority my master possesses over me, he is beholden to my reverence of his seniority, and in virtue of his tutorage; otherwise I am not inferior in power, and am his equal in skill." This want of respect displeased the king. He ordered a wrestling match to be held, and a spacious field to be fenced in for the occasion. The ministers of state, nobles of the court, and gallant men of the realm were assembled, and the ceremonials of the combat marshalled. Like a huge and lusty elephant, the youth rushed into the ring with such a crash that had a brazen mountain opposed him he would have moved it from its base. The master being aware that the youth was his superior in strength, engaged him in that strange feat of which he had kept him ignorant. The youth was unacquainted with its guard. Advancing, nevertheless, the master seized him with both hands, and, lifting him bodily from the ground, raised him above his head and flung him on the earth. The crowd set up a shout. The king ordered them to give the master an honorary dress and handsome largess, and the youth he addressed with reproach and asperity, saying: "You played the traitor with your own patron, and failed in your presumption of opposing him." He replied: "O sire! my master did not overcome me by strength and ability, but one cunning trick in the art of wrestling was left which he was reserved in teaching me, and by that little feat had today the upper hand of me." The master said: "I reserved myself for such a day as this. As the wise have told us, put not so much into a friend's power that, if hostilely disposed, he can do you an injury. Have you not heard what that man said who was treacherously dealt with by his own pupil: *'Either in fact there was no good faith in this world, or nobody has perhaps practised it in our days. No person learned the art of archery from me who did not in the end make me his butt.'*"

FROM SLAVERY TO SLAVERY

Having taken offence with the society of my friends at Damascus, I retired into the wilderness of the Holy Land, or Jerusalem, and sought the company of brutes till such time as I was made a prisoner by the Franks, and employed by them, along with some Jews, in digging earth in the ditches of Tripoli. At length one of the chiefs of Aleppo, between whom and me an intimacy had of old subsisted, happening to pass that way, recognized me, and said: "How is this? and how came you to be thus occupied?" I replied: "What can I say? *I was flying from mankind into the forests and mountains, for my resource was in God and in none else. Fancy to thyself what my condition must now be, when forced to associate with a tribe scarcely human?—To be linked in a chain with a company of acquaintance were pleasanter than to walk in a garden with strangers.*"

He took pity on my situation; and, having for ten dinars redeemed me from captivity with the Franks, carried me along with him to Aleppo. Here he had a daughter, and her he gave me in marriage, with a dower of a hundred dinars. Soon after this damsel turned out a termagant and vixen, and discovered such a perverse spirit and virulent tongue as quite unhinged all my domestic comfort. *A scolding wife in the dwelling of a peaceable man is his hell even in this world. Protect and guard us against a wicked inmate. Save us, O Lord, and preserve us from the fiery, or hell, torture.*

Having on one occasion given a liberty to the tongue of reproach, she was saying: "Are you not the fellow whom my father redeemed from the captivity of the Franks for ten dinars?" I replied: "Yes, I am that same he delivered from captivity for ten dinars, and enslaved me with you for a hundred!" *I have heard that a reverend and mighty man released a sheep from the paws and jaws of a wolf. That same night he was sticking a knife into its throat, when the spirit of the sheep reproached him, saying: "Thou didst deliver me from the clutches of a wolf, when I at length saw that thou didst prove a wolf to me thyself."*

BARE FEET ARE BETTER THAN NONE

I had never complained of the vicissitudes of fortune, nor murmured at the ordinances of heaven, excepting on one occasion, that my feet were bare, and I had not wherewithal to shoe them. In this desponding state I entered the metropolitan mosque at Cufah, and there I beheld a man that had no feet. I offered up praise and thanksgiving for God's goodness to myself, and submitted with patience to my want of shoes. *In the eye of one satiated with meat a roast fowl is less esteemed at his table than a salad; but to him who is stinted of food a boiled turnip will relish like a roast fowl.*

KING AND PEASANT

A king, attended by a select retinue, had, on a sporting excursion during the winter, got at a distance from any of his hunting seats, and the evening was closing fast, when they espied from afar a peasant's cottage. The king said: "Let us repair thither for the night, that we may shelter ourselves from the inclemency of the weather." One of the courtiers replied: "It would not become the dignity of the sovereign to take refuge in the cottage of a low peasant; we can pitch a tent here and kindle a fire." The peasant saw what was passing; he came forward with what refreshments he had at hand, and, laying them before the king, kissed the earth of subserviency, and said: "The lofty dignity of the king would not be lowered by this condescension; but these gentlemen did not choose that the condition of a peasant should be exalted." The king was pleased with this speech, and they passed the night at his cottage. In the morning he bestowed an honorary dress and handsome largess upon him. I have heard that the peasant was resting his hand for some paces upon the king's stirrup, and saying: *"The state and pomp of the sovereign suffered no degradation by his condescension in becoming a guest at the cottage of a peasant; but the corner of the peasant's cap rose to a level with the sun when the shadow of such a monarch as thou art fell upon his head."*

A POET'S WIT

A certain poet presented himself before the chief of a gang of robbers, and recited a kasidah, or elegy, in his praise. He ordered that they should strip off the poet's clothes, and thrust him from the village. The naked wretch was going away shivering in the cold, and the village dogs were barking at his heels. He stooped to pick up a stone, in order to shy at the dogs, but found the earth frost-bound, and was disappointed. He exclaimed: "What rogues these villagers are, for they let loose their dogs, and tie up their stones!" The chief robber saw and overheard him from a window. He smiled at his wit, and, calling him near, said: "O learned sir! ask me for a boon." He replied: "I ask for my own garments, if you will vouchsafe to give them. *I shall have enough of boons in your suffering me to depart. Mankind expect charity from others; I expect no charity from thee, only do me no injury."* The chief robber felt compassion for him. He ordered his clothes to be restored, and added to them a robe of fur and sum of money.

FOR GOD'S SAKE

A person with a harsh voice was reciting the Koran in a loud tone. A good and holy man went up to him, and asked: "What is your monthly stipend?" He answered: "Nothing." "Then," asked the other, "why give yourself so much trouble?" He said: "I am reading for the sake of God." The good and holy man replied: "For God's sake do not read, *for if thou chantest the Koran after this manner, thou must cast a shade over the glory of Islạm."*

MASTER AND SLAVE

They tell a story of a gentleman who had a slave singularly handsome; and her he regarded with an eye of fondness and affection. He observed to one of his friends: "What a pity that this slave, with the beauty and grace which she possesses, should be a termagant and vixen." He replied: "O brother, now you have made her your companion, expect not the service of a waiting woman; for where the lover and mistress come in play, the distinction of master and slave is done away." *When the gentleman begins to joke and toy with his angel-faced and handsome hand-maid, it should not surprise if she order like a master, and he bear the burthen of coquetry like a bondswoman. It becomes the bondswoman to be a water-carrier and brickmaker. Let her be a charmer and she becomes a boxer and bruiser.*

PARROT AND CROW

They shut up a parrot in the same cage with a crow. The parrot was affronted at his ugly look, and said: "What an odious visage is this, a hideous figure; what an accursed appearance, and ungracious demeanour! *Would to God, O raven of the desert! we were wide apart as the east is from the west. The serenity of his peaceful day would change into the gloom of night, who on issuing forth in the morning might cross thy aspect. An ill-conditioned wretch like thyself should be thy companion; but where could we find such another in the world?*"

But what is more strange, the crow was also out of all patience, and vexed to the soul at the society of the parrot. Bewailing his misfortune, he was railing at the revolutions of the skies; and, wringing the hands of chagrin, was lamenting his condition, and saying: "What an unpropitious fate is this; what ill-luck, and untoward fortune! Could they any way suit the dignity of me, who would in my day strut with my fellow-crows along the wall of a garden? *It were durance sufficient for a good and holy man that he should be made the companion of the wicked. What sin have I committed that my stars in retribution of it have linked me in the chain of companionship, and immured me in the dungeon of calamity, with a conceited blockhead, and good-for-nothing babbler? Nobody will approach the foot of a wall on which they have painted thy portrait; wert thou to get a residence in paradise, others would go in preference to hell.*"

I have introduced this parable to show that however much learned men despise the ignorant, these are a hundredfold more scornful of the learned. *A zahid, or holy man, fell in company with some wandering minstrels. One of them, a charmer of Balkh, said to him: "If thou art displeased with us, do not look sour, for thou art already sufficiently offensive. — An assemblage is formed of roses and tulips, and thou art stuck up amidst them like a withered stalk; like an opposing storm, and a chilling winter blast; like a ball of snow, or lump of ice."*

REMEMBERED BEAUTY

In my youth I recollect I was passing through a street, and caught a glimpse of a moon-like charmer during the dog-days, when their heat was drying up the moisture of the mouth, and the simoom melting the marrow of the bones. From the weakness of human nature I was unable to withstand the darting rays of a noon-tide sun, and took refuge under the shadow of a wall, hopeful that somebody would relieve me from the oppressive heat of summer, and quench the fire of my thirst with a draught of water. All at once I beheld a luminary in the shadowed portico of a mansion, so splendid an object that the tongue of eloquence falls short in summing up its loveliness; such as the day dawning upon a dark night, or the fountain of immortality issuing from chaos. She held in her hand a goblet of snow-cooled water, into which she dropt some sugar, and tempered it with spirit of wine; but I know not whether she scented it with attar, or sprinkled it with a few blossoms from her own rosy cheek. In short, I received the beverage from her idol-fair hand; and, having drunk it off, found myself restored to a new life. "*Such is not my parching thirst that it is to be quenched with the limpid element of water, were I to swallow it in oceans. Joy to that happy aspect whose eye can every morning contemplate such a countenance as thine. A person intoxicated with wine lies giddy and awake half the night; but if intoxicated with the Cup-bearer, the day of judgment must be his dawn or morning.*"

LAILA AND MAJNUN

To a certain king of Arabia they were relating the story of Laila and Majnun [classic lovers], and his insane state, saying: "Notwithstanding his knowledge and wisdom, he has turned his face towards the desert, and abandoned himself to distraction." The king ordered that they bring him into his presence; and he reproved him, and spoke, saying: "What have you seen unworthy in the noble nature of man that you should assume the manners of a brute, and forsake the enjoyment of human society?"

Majnun wept and answered: "*Many of my friends reproach me for my love of her, namely Laila. Alas! that they could one day see her, that my excuse might be manifest for me! Would to God that such as blame me could behold thy face, O thou ravisher of hearts! that at the sight of thee they might, from inadvertency, cut their own fingers in-*

stead of the orange in their hands. Then might the truth of the reality bear testimony against the semblance of fiction, what manner of person that was for whose sake you were upbraiding me."

The king resolved within himself to view in person the charms of Laila, that he might be able to judge what her form could be which had caused all this misery, and ordered her to be produced in his presence. Having searched through the Arab tribes, they discovered and presented her before the king in the courtyard of his seraglio. He viewed her figure, and beheld a person of a tawny complexion and feeble frame of body. She appeared to him in a contemptible light, inasmuch as the lowest menial in his harem, or seraglio, surpassed her in beauty and excelled her in elegance. Majnun, in his sagacity, penetrated what was passing in the royal mind, and said: "It would behove you, O king, to contemplate the charms of Laila through the wicket of a Majnun's eye, in order that the miracle of such a spectacle might be illustrated to you. *Thou canst have no fellow-feeling for my disorder; a companion to suit me must have the self-same malady, that I may sit by him the live-long day repeating my tale; for by rubbing two pieces of dry firewood one upon another they will burn all the brighter. Had that grove of verdant reeds heard the murmurings of love which in detail of my mistress's story have passed through my ear, it would somehow have sympathized in my pain. Tell it, O my friends, to such as are ignorant of love; would ye could be aware of what wrings me to the soul! The anguish of a wound is not known to the hale and sound; we must detail our aches only to a fellow-sufferer. It were idle to talk of a hornet to him who has never during his life smarted from its sting. Till thy condition may in some sort resemble mine, my state will seem to thee an idle fable. Compare not my pain with that of another man; he holds salt in his hand, but I hold it on a wounded limb.*"

MAY AND JANUARY

An old man was telling a story, saying: "I had married a young virgin, adorned the bridal chamber with flowers, seated myself with her in private, and riveted my heart and eyes upon her. Many a long night I would lie awake, and indulge in pleasantries and jests, in order to remove any coyness on her part, and encourage familiarity. One of those nights I was addressing her, and saying: 'Lofty fortune was your friend, and the eye of your prosperity broad awake, when you fell into the society of such an old gentleman as I am, being of mature judgment, well-bred, worldly experienced, inured to the vicissitudes of heat and cold, and practised in the goods and evils of life; who can appreciate the rights of good-fellowship, and fulfil the duties of loving attachment; and is kind and affable, sweet-spoken and cheerful. *I will treat thee with affection, as far as I can, and if thou dealest with me unkindly, I cannot be unkind in return. If, like a parrot, thy food be sugar, I will devote my sweet life for thy nourishment.* And you did not become the victim of a rude, conceited, rash, and headstrong youth, who one moment gratifies his lust, and the next has a fresh object; who every night shifts his abode, and every day changes his mistress. *Young men are lively and handsome, but they keep good faith with nobody. Expect not constancy from nightingales, who will every moment serenade a fresh rose.* Whereas my class of seniors regulate their lives by good breeding and sense, and are not deluded by youthful ignorance. *Court the society of a superior, and make much of the opportunity; for in the company of an equal thy good fortune must decline.*'"

The old man continued: "I spoke a great deal in this style, and thought that I had caught her heart in my snare, and made sure of her as my prey; when she suddenly drew a cold sigh from the bottom of a much afflicted bosom, and answered: 'All this speech which you have delivered has not, in the scale of my judgment, the weight of that one sentence which I have heard of my nurse: that it were better to plant a spear in a young maiden's side than to lay her by an old man in bed! *Much contention and strife will arise in that house where the wife shall get up dissatisfied with her husband. Unable to rise without the help of a staff, how can an old man stir the staff of life?*'"

In short, there being no prospect of concord, they agreed to separate. After the period prescribed by the law, they united her in wedlock with a young man of an ill-tempered and sullen disposition, and in very narrow circumstances, so that she endured much tyranny and violence, penury and hardship; yet she was thus offering up thanksgivings for the Almighty's goodness, and saying: "Praised be God that I have escaped from such hell-torment, and secured a blessing so permanent. *With all this violence and impetuosity of temper, I bear with thy caprice, because thou art lovely. It were better for me to burn with thee in hell-fire than to dwell in paradise with another. The smell of an onion from the mouth of the lovely is sweeter than a rose in the hand of the ugly.*"

FATHER AND SON

In the territory of Diarbekr, or Mesopotamia, I was the guest of an old man, who was very rich, and had a handsome son. One night he told a story, saying: "During my whole life I never had any child but this boy. And in this valley a certain tree is a place of pilgrimage, where people go to supplicate their wants; and many was the night that I have besought God at the foot of that tree before he would bestow upon me this boy." I have heard that the son was also whispering his companions, and saying: "How happy I should be if I could discover the site of that tree, in order that I might pray for the death of my father." The gentleman was rejoicing and saying: "What a sensible youth is my son!" and the boy was complaining and crying: "What a tedious old dotard is my father!" *Many years are passing over thy head, during which thou didst not visit thy father's tomb. What pious oblation didst thou make to the manes of a parent that thou shouldst expect so much from thy son?*

SCHOOLMASTERS

In the west of Africa I saw a schoolmaster of a sour aspect and bitter speech, crabbed, misanthropic, beggarly, and intemperate, insomuch that the sight of him would derange the ecstasies of the orthodox; and his manner of reading the Koran cast a gloom over the minds of the pious. A number of handsome boys and lovely virgins were subject to his despotic sway, who had neither the permission of a smile nor the option of a word, for this moment he would smite the silver cheek of one of them with his hand, and the next put the crystalline legs of another in the stocks. In short, their parents, I heard, were made aware of a part of his disloyal violence, and beat and drove him from his charge. And they made over his school to a peaceable creature, so pious, meek, simple, and good-natured that he never spoke till forced to do so, nor would he utter a word that could offend anybody. The children forgot that awe in which they had held their first master, and remarking the angelic disposition of their second master, they became one after another as wicked as devils; and relying on his clemency, they would so neglect their studies as to pass most part of their time at play, and break the tablets of their unfinished tasks over each other's heads. *When the schoolmaster relaxes in his discipline, the children will stop to play at marbles in the market-place.*

A fortnight after I passed by the gate of that mosque and saw the first schoolmaster, with whom they had been obliged to make friends, and to restore him to his place. I was in truth offended, and calling on God to witness, asked, saying: "Why have they again made a devil the preceptor of angels?" A facetious old gentleman, who had seen much of life, listened to me and replied: "Have you not heard what they have said: '*A king sent his son to school, and hung a tablet of silver round his neck. On the face of that tablet he had written in golden letters: The severity of the master is more useful than the indulgence of the father.*'"

EXPERIENCE

One year I was on a journey with some Syrians from Balkh, and the road was infested with robbers. One of our escort was a youth expert at wielding his shield and brandishing his spear, mighty as an elephant, and cased in armour, so strong that ten of the most powerful of us could not string his bow, or the ablest wrestler on the face of the earth throw him on his back. Yet, as you must know, he had been brought up in luxury and reared in a shade, was inexperienced of the world, and had never travelled. The thunder of the great war-drum had never rattled in his ears, nor had the lightning of the trooper's scimitar ever flashed across his eyes. *He had never fallen a captive into the hands of an enemy, nor been overwhelmed amidst a shower of their arrows.*

It happened that this young man and I

kept running on together; and any venerable ruin that might come in our way he would overthrow with the strength of his shoulder; and any huge tree that we might see he would wrench from its root with his lion-seizing wrist, and boastfully cry: *"Where is the elephant, that he may behold the shoulder and arm of warriors? Where the lion, that he may feel the wrist and gripe of heroes?"*

Such was our situation when two Hindus darted from behind a rock and prepared to cut us off, one of them holding a bludgeon in his hand, and the other having a mallet under his arm. I called to the young man: "Why do you stop? *Display whatever strength and courage thou hast, for the foe came on his own feet up to his grave.*" I perceived that the youth's bow and arrows had dropped from his hands, and that a tremor had fallen upon his limbs. *It is not he that can split a hair with a coat-of-mail-cleaving arrow that is able to withstand an assault from the formidable.* No alternative was left us but that of surrendering our arms, accoutrements, and clothes, and escaping with our lives. *"On an affair of importance employ a man experienced in business who can bring the fierce lion within the noose of his halter; though the youth be strong of arm and has the body of an elephant, in his encounter with a foe every limb will quake with fear. A man of experience is best qualified to explore a field of battle, as one of the learned is to expound a point of law."*

SAYINGS

No reliance can be placed on the friendship of kings, nor vain hope put in the melodious voice of boys; for that passes away like a vision, and this vanishes like a dream.

Bruise the serpent's head with the hand of an antagonist, that of two things you may make sure of one; for if the adversary succeed, you kill the reptile; and if this prevail, you get rid of a rival.

Every person thinks his own intellect perfect, and his own child handsome.

Whoever shall argue with one more learned than himself that others may take him for a wise man, only confirms them in his being a fool.

The idle cannot endure the industrious any more than the curs of the market-place, who, on meeting dogs employed for sporting, will snarl at and prevent them passing.

Let a gem fall into the mire, and it remains the same precious stone it was; and let dust be whirled up to heaven, and it retains its base origin.

A wise man is, like a vase in a druggist's shop, silent, but full of virtues; and the ignorant man resembles the drum of the warrior, being full of noise, and an empty babbler.

The sinner who spends and gives away is better than the devotee who begs and lays by.

The fisherman, unless it be his lot, catches no fish in the Tigris; and the fish, unless it be its fate, does not die on the dry land. *The wretched miser is prowling all over the world, he in quest of pelf, and death in quest of him.*

A scholar without diligence is a lover without money; a traveller without knowledge is a bird without wings; a theorist without practice is a tree without fruit; and a devotee without learning is a house without an entrance.

The object of sending the Koran down from heaven was that mankind might make it a manual of morals, and not that they should recite it by sections.

It is contrary to sound judgment, and repugnant to the maxims of the prudent, to take a medicine on conjecture, or to follow a road but in the track of the caravan.

To tell a falsehood is like the cut of a sabre; for though the wound may heal, the scar of it will remain.

A wise man, where he meets opposition, labours to get through it, and where he finds quiet he drops his anchor; for there safety is on one side, and here enjoyment in the middle of it.

The gamester wants three sixes, but he throws only three aces. *The pasture meadow is a thousand times richer than the common, but the horse has not his tether at command.*

—*From The Gulistan of Sa'di, Persian (c. 1184–1291), translated by James Ross.*

~ ✿ ~

Notes on Human Life

LEONARDO DA VINCI

SEEING that I cannot choose any subject of great utility or pleasure, because my predecessors have already taken as their own all useful and necessary themes, I will do like one who, because of his poverty, is the last to arrive at the fair, and not being able otherwise to provide himself, chooses all the things which others have already looked over and not taken, but refused as being of little value. With these despised and rejected wares — the leavings of many buyers — I will load my modest pack, and therewith take my course, distributing, not indeed amid the great cities, but among the mean hamlets, and taking such reward as befits the things I offer.

Thou, O God, dost sell unto us all good things at the price of labour.

The soul desires to dwell in the body because without the members of that body it can neither act nor feel.

In life beauty perishes, not in art.

Tears come from the heart not from the brain.

Vows begin when hope dies.

Behold now the hope and desire to go back to our own country, and to return to our former state, how like it is to the moth with the light! And the man who with perpetual longing ever looks forward with joy to each new spring and each new summer, and to the new months and the new years, deeming that the things he longs for are too slow in coming, does not perceive that he is longing for his own destruction. But this longing is the quintessence and spirit of the elements, which, finding itself imprisoned with the life of the human body, desires continually to return to its source. And I would have you to know that this very same longing is that quintessence inherent in nature, and that man is a type of the world.

In youth acquire that which may requite you for the deprivations of old age; and if you are mindful that old age has wisdom for its food, you will so exert yourself that your old age will not lack sustenance.

As a well-spent day brings happy sleep, so life well used brings happy death.

While I thought that I was learning how to live, I have been learning how to die.

Life well spent is long.

In rivers, the water that you touch is the last of what has passed and the first of that which comes: so with time present.

O Time, thou that consumest all things! O envious age, thou destroyest all things and devourest all things with the hard teeth of the years, little by little, in slow death! Helen, when she looked in her mirror and saw the withered wrinkles which old age had made in her face, wept, and wondered to herself why ever she had twice been carried away. O Time, thou that consumest all things! O envious age, whereby all things are consumed.

Just as eating contrary to the inclination is injurious to the health, so study without desire spoils the memory, and it retains nothing that it takes in.

The natural desire of good men is knowledge.

All our knowledge originates in opinions.

Whoever in discussion adduces authority uses not intellect but rather memory.

Science is the captain, practice the soldiers.

To devise is the work of the master, to execute the act of the servant.

There is no certainty where one can neither apply any of the mathematical sciences nor any of those which are based upon the mathematical sciences.

There is no result in nature without a cause; understand the cause and you will have no need of the experiment.

Nature never breaks her own law.

Every weight tends to fall towards the centre by the shortest way.

Experience is not at fault; it is only our judgment that is in error in promising itself from experience things which are not within her power.

Falsehood is so utterly vile that though it should praise the great works of God it offends against His divinity; truth is of such excellence that if it praise the meanest things they become ennobled.

The line that is straightest offers most resistance.

As courage endangers life even so fear preserves it.

Fear springs to life more quickly than anything else.

He who does not value life deserves it not.

He who takes the snake by the tail is afterwards bitten by it.

He who thinks little makes many mistakes.

No counsel is more trustworthy than that which is given upon ships in peril.

Patience serves as a protection against wrongs as clothes do against cold. For if you put on more clothes as the cold increases it will have no power to hurt you. So in like manner you must grow in patience when you meet with great wrongs, and they will then be powerless to vex your mind.

In the moment when virtue is born she gives birth to envy against her, and a body shall sooner exist without a shadow than virtue without envy.

Pleasure and Pain are represented as twins, as though they were joined together, for there is never the one without the other; and they turn their backs because they are contrary to each other.

Intellectual passion drives out sensuality.

You can have neither a greater nor a less dominion than that over yourself.

It is easier to resist at the beginning than at the end.

The water wears away the mountains and fills up the valleys, and if it had the power it would reduce the earth to a perfect sphere.

If a drop of water falls into the sea when it is calm, it must of necessity be that the whole surface of the sea is raised imperceptibly, seeing that water cannot be compressed within itself, like air.

The first picture was nothing but a line which surrounded the shadow of a man made by the sun upon a wall.

OF THE CRUELTY OF MAN

Creatures shall be seen upon the earth who will always be fighting one with another with very great losses and frequent deaths on either side. These shall set no bounds to their malice; by their fierce limbs a great number of the trees in the immense forests of the world shall be laid level with the ground; and when they have crammed themselves with food it shall gratify their desire to deal out death, affliction, labours, terrors, and banishment to every living thing. And by reason of their boundless pride they shall wish to rise towards heaven, but the excessive weight of their limbs shall hold them down. There shall be nothing remaining on the earth or under the earth or in the waters that shall not be pursued and molested or destroyed, and that which is in one country taken away to another; and their own bodies shall be made the tomb and the means of transit of all the living bodies which they have slain.

O Earth! what delays thee to open and hurl them headlong into the deep fissures of thy huge abysses and caverns, and no longer to display in the sight of heaven so savage and ruthless a monster?

—*From the Notebooks of Leonardo da Vinci, Italian (1452–1519), translated by Edward McCurdy.*

Social Intercourse

KAIBARA EKKEN

IN ASSOCIATING with others we should make love and respect our chief concern. If we lack these the gulf between ourselves and others becomes wide and the way of mankind cannot be practised. Between parents and children, brothers and sisters, husband and wife, hosts and guests, there must exist both love and respect. If we love our parents and yet lack respect our relation towards them becomes very much like that of brutes. In serving our master we must do so not only with fear, but also with respect and love.

Not only should we love intimate friends and respect honourable people, but also we should in a lesser degree love and respect the stranger at the wayside or even the beggar, for they, too, are children of Heaven and Earth. At any rate, never hate or despise them. The amount of our love and respect must vary according to their importance and degree of our intimacy. But there is no one to whom we are not bound to give at least a measure of love and respect.

When others are rude let us not blame them as long as they do not injure our honour. If we forgive discourtesy in others we do not lose the peace of our hearts. As an old saying has it: Gladness is the reward of patience.

Do not endeavour to teach others those things with which they are not gifted, but teach them those things for which they have talent. Never try to put others into your own private mould. Do not trust a man altogether just because he has proved himself efficient in one thing, for he may well be deficient in others. Do not, on the other hand, mistrust a man altogether because he has proved himself incapable in one thing, for he may well be capable in others. Do not scorn your neighbour because he cannot do some things as well as yourself, for there are others which he may do infinitely better.

A good physician uses the humblest herb for his medical purpose. A good carpenter does not throw away a crooked tree. A wise man finds some use in every man. No man in the world is absolutely useless, provided he be rightly employed.

Do not truckle before a man of high rank, nor exalt yourself when you stand before a man of humble position. Confucius reverenced great men, for he honoured the exalted position with which they were entrusted. Mencius looked down on even great men, for he did not yield to their power. We should make both of them our examples.

In associating with men we give presents. This is the courtesy with which men express their love and respect. Without this means we cannot express our feeling in love and respect. In olden days men used to offer the green stuff gathered in running water to the gods. Today, when we see our teacher for the first time, we present him with our entrance fee. These presents are the outward sign of our respect towards both gods and men, and must be well chosen. A poor man need not endeavour to present others with money, as an old man should not offer to others his physical strength.

In conversation we should reflect on our age and position as well as others' and use discretion in what we say. This is an important piece of etiquette. If we meet a man with whom we are not yet acquainted it is safer to give him even undue courtesy. To exalt ourselves before others is always most distasteful to them. In a company of men we should take seats suitable to our rank and position. To sit in a higher place than we are entitled to is ridiculous. To take a seat in a lower place than we should is not a great mistake, though not exactly in accordance with etiquette. To lower ourselves before others is amiable. Yet if you carry this to an extreme length it becomes an insult to others. For instance, in a company of men, if the older men or those who are in the highest position take lowly seats, what can young and humble men do?

If we find men with whom our hearts are in accord we become intimate friends though thousands of miles may separate us, while next-door neighbours remain total strangers if their hearts do not agree. In the world we have many acquaintances, yet those with whom we know our hearts agree are very rare. Even brothers do not know each other's hearts. Do not resent the fact when the world fails to know you.

There are men who are mentally deaf and dumb. With them we should not quarrel on questions of right and wrong. To quarrel with them is to show our ignorance.

The way of dealing with impossible men is to treat them most gently. To do a difficult task, do it leisurely; and to perform an urgent matter, do it calmly.

Do not bestow either rewards or punishments while you are in great joy or anger, but rather wait until your emotion has subsided, lest your award may be unjust. To give judgment according to one's mood is like doing so in proportion to a bribe.

We often encounter treacherous men who distress us with detestable deeds and words. When we are placed in such an adverse circumstance, we should try to suppress our anger and resentment and control our countenance. This is a chance to improve our character and to make an advance in learning. Let us not let the chance slip by without availing ourselves of it.

There are some things people do, the good or evil of which is quite apparent, while there are others, the right or wrong of which is obscure. Often those actions which we think right are really wrong, while those which we considered wrong are right. Therefore we should not praise or blame others rashly.

You may meet a man who speaks smoothly, who is talented in all things, and is very agreeable to you. Yet, if the pupils of his eyes are not right do not make a friendship with him, lest you may afterwards reap regret and remorse. Especially in choosing subjects is this important. Chikurei foresaw the treason of Anrokuzan by the latter's appearance. It is safest to employ honest men, even though they may not be the cleverest.

To know others is very difficult. A man who speaks well, whose manners are respectful, and who is gentle and obedient, often proves to be an unreliable person; a man of strict probity may often lack gentleness, yet is very faithful. They are the men to whom we can safely trust our children, house, and property when we are dead. Choose men who are both talented and faithful. But such men are rare. The next best thing is to select faithful men, though they may lack talent. Never use talented yet faithless men, for they will work you mischief.

Do good toward others, but do not expect it to be reciprocated. I am I, and he is he; let me do what is right. That his justice is injustice does not concern me.

—*From The Way of Contentment by Kaibara Ekken, Japanese (1629–1712), translated by Ken Hoshimo.*

Resolutions

JONATHAN EDWARDS

BEING sensible that I am unable to do anything without God's help, I do humbly entreat him by his grace, to enable me to keep these Resolutions, so far as they are agreeable to his will, for Christ's sake.

REMEMBER TO READ OVER THESE RESOLUTIONS ONCE A WEEK

1. *Resolved,* That *I will do whatsoever* I think to be most to the glory of God and my own good, profit and pleasure, in the whole of my duration; without any consideration of the time, whether now, or never so many myriads of ages hence. Resolved to do whatever I think to be my *duty,* and most for the good and advantage of mankind in general. Resolved, so to do whatever *difficulties* I meet with, how many soever, and how great soever.

2. *Resolved,* To be continually endeavouring to find out some *new contrivance,* and invention, to promote the forementioned things.

3. *Resolved,* If ever I shall fall and grow dull, so as to negect to keep any part of these Resolutions, to repent of all I can remember, when I come to myself again.

4. *Resolved,* Never *to do* any manner of thing, whether in soul or body, less or more, but what it tends to the glory of God, nor *be* nor *suffer* it, if I can possibly avoid it.

5. *Resolved,* Never to lose one moment of time, but to improve it in the most profitable way I possibly can.

6. *Resolved,* To live with all my might, while I do live.

7. *Resolved,* Never to do anything, which I should be afraid to do, if it were the last hour of my life.

8. *Resolved,* To act, in all respects, both speaking and doing, as if nobody had been so vile as I, and as if I had committed the same sins, or had the same infirmities or failings as others; and that I will let the knowledge of their failings promote nothing but shame in myself, and prove only an occasion of my confessing my own sins and misery to God. *Vid. July* 30.

9. *Resolved,* To think much, on all occasions, of my own dying, and of the common circumstances which attend death.

10. *Resolved,* When I feel pain, to think of the pains of Martyrdom, and of Hell.

11. *Resolved,* When I think of any Theorem in divinity to be solved, immediately to do what I can towards solving it, if circumstances do not hinder.

12. *Resolved,* If I take delight in it as a gratification of pride, or vanity, or on any such account, immediately to throw it by.

13. *Resolved,* To be endeavouring to find out fit objects of charity and liberality.

14. *Resolved,* Never to do anything out of Revenge.

15. *Resolved,* Never to suffer the least motions of anger towards irrational beings.

16. *Resolved,* Never to speak evil of anyone, so that it shall tend to his dishonour, more or less, upon no account except for some real good.

17. *Resolved,* That I will live so, as I shall wish I had done when I come to die.

18. *Resolved,* To live so, at all times, as I think is best in my most devout frames, and when I have the clearest notions of the things of the Gospel, and another world.

19. *Resolved,* Never to do anything, which I should be afraid to do, if I expected it would not be above an hour, before I should hear the last trump.

20. *Resolved,* To maintain the strictest temperance, in eating and drinking.

21. *Resolved,* Never to do anything, which, if I should see in another, I should count a just occasion to despise him for, or to think any way more meanly of him.

22. *Resolved,* To endeavour to obtain for myself as much happiness, in the other world, as I possibly can, with all the power, might, vigour, and vehemence, yea violence, I am capable of, or can bring myself to exert, in any way that can be thought of.

23. *Resolved,* Frequently to take some deliberate action, which seems most unlikely to be done, for the glory of God, and trace it back to the original intention, designs and ends of it; and if I find it not to be for God's

glory, to repute it as a breach of the fourth Resolution.

24. *Resolved,* Whenever I do any conspicuously evil action, to trace it back, till I come to the original cause; and then, both carefully endeavour to do so no more, and to fight and pray with all my might against the original of it.

25. *Resolved,* To examine carefully, and constantly, what that one thing in me is, which causes me in the least to doubt of the love of God; and to direct all my forces against it.

26. *Resolved,* To cast away such things, as I find do abate my assurance.

27. *Resolved,* Never wilfully to omit anything, except the omission be for the glory of God; and frequently to examine my omissions.

28. *Resolved,* To study the Scriptures so steadily, constantly and frequently, as that I may find, and plainly perceive myself to grow in the knowledge of the same.

29. *Resolved,* Never to count that a prayer, nor to let that pass as a prayer, nor that as a petition of a prayer, which is so made, that I cannot hope that God will answer it; nor that as a confession, which I cannot hope God will accept.

30. *Resolved,* To strive, every week, to be brought higher in Religion, and to a higher exercise of grace, than I was the week before.

31. *Resolved,* Never to say any thing at all against any body, but when it is perfectly agreeable to the highest degree of christian honour, and of love to mankind, agreeable to the lowest humility, and sense of my own faults and failings, and agreeable to the Golden Rule; often, when I have said any thing against any one, to bring it to, and try it strictly by the test of this Resolution.

32. *Resolved,* To be strictly and firmly faithful to my trust, that that, in Prov. xx, 6, *A faithful man who can find?* may not be partly fulfilled in me.

33. *Resolved,* To do, always, what I can towards making, maintaining and preserving peace, when it can be done without an over-balancing detriment in other respects. *Dec.* 26, 1722.

34. *Resolved,* In narrations, never to speak of any thing but the pure and simple verity.

35. *Resolved,* Whenever I do so much question whether I have done my duty, as that my quiet and calm is thereby disturbed, to set it down, and also how the question was resolved. *Dec.* 19, 1722.

36. *Resolved,* Never to speak evil of any, except I have some particular good call to it. *Dec.* 19, 1722.

37. *Resolved,* To enquire every night, as I am going to bed, Wherein I have been negligent, – What sin I have committed, – and wherein I have denied myself; – also, at the end of every week, month, and year. *Dec.* 22 *and* 26, 1722.

38. *Resolved,* Never to utter anything that is sportive, or matter of laughter, on a Lord's day. *Sabbath evening, Dec.* 23, 1722.

39. *Resolved,* Never to do anything, of which I so much as question the lawfulness, as that I intend, at the same time, to consider and examine afterwards, whether it be lawful or not; unless I as much question the lawfulness of the omission.

40. *Resolved,* To enquire every night, before I go to bed, whether I have acted in the best way I possibly could, with respect to eating and drinking. *Jan.* 7, 1723.

41. *Resolved,* To ask myself, at the end of every day, week, month and year, wherein I could possibly, in any respect, have done better, *Jan.* 11, 1723.

42. *Resolved,* Frequently to renew the dedication of myself to God, which was made at my baptism, which I solemnly renewed, when I was received into the communion of the church, and which I have solemnly re-made this 12th day of January, 1723.

43. *Resolved,* Never, henceforward, till I die, to act as if I were any way my own, but entirely and altogether God's; agreeably to what is to be found in Saturday, Jan. 12th. *Jan.* 12th, 1723.

44. *Resolved,* That no other end but religion, shall have any influence at all on any of my actions; and that no action shall be, in the least circumstance, any otherwise than the religious end will carry it. *Jan.* 12, 1723.

45. *Resolved,* Never to allow any pleasure or grief, joy or sorrow, nor any affection at all, nor any degree of affection, nor any circumstance relating to it, but what helps Religion. *Jan.* 12 and 13, 1723.

46. *Resolved,* Never to allow the least measure of any fretting or uneasiness at my father or mother. *Resolved,* To suffer no effects of it, so much as in the least alteration of speech, or motion of my eye; and to be

especially careful of it with respect to any of our family.

47. *Resolved,* To endeavour, to my utmost, to deny whatever is not most agreeable to a good and universally sweet and benevolent, quiet, peaceable, contented and easy, compassionate and generous, humble and meek, submissive and obliging, diligent and industrious, charitable and even, patient, moderate, forgiving and sincere, temper; and to do, at all times, what such a temper would lead me to; and to examine strictly, at the end of every week, whether I have so done. *Sabbath Morning, May* 5, 1723.

48. *Resolved,* Constantly, with the utmost niceness and diligence, and the strictest scrutiny, to be looking into the state of my soul, that I may know whether I have truly an interest in Christ or not; that when I come to die, I may not have any negligence respecting this, to repent of. *May* 26, 1723.

49. *Resolved,* That this shall never be, if I can help it.

50. *Resolved,* That I will act so, as I think I shall judge would have been best, and most prudent, when I come into the future world. *July* 5, 1723.

51. *Resolved,* That I will act so, in every respect, as I think I shall wish I had done, if I should at last be damned. *July* 8, 1723.

52. I frequently hear persons in old age, say how they would live, if they were to live their lives over again: *Resolved,* That I will live just so as I think I shall wish I had done, supposing I live to old age. *July* 8, 1723.

53. *Resolved,* To improve every opportunity, when I am in the best and happiest frame of mind, to cast and venture my soul on the Lord Jesus Christ, to trust and confide in him, and consecrate myself wholly to him; that from this I may have assurance of my safety, knowing that I confide in my Redeemer. *July* 8, 1723.

54. *Resolved,* Whenever I hear anything spoken in commendation of any person, if I think it would be praiseworthy in me, that I will endeavor to imitate it. *July* 8, 1723.

55. *Resolved,* To endeavour, to my utmost, so to act, as I can think I should do, if I had already seen the happiness of Heaven, and Hell torments. *July* 8, 1723.

56. *Resolved,* Never to give over, nor in the least to slacken, my fight with corruptions, however unsuccessful I may be.

57. *Resolved,* When I fear misfortunes and adversity, to examine whether I have done my duty, and resolve to do it, and let the event be just as Providence orders it. I will, as far as I can, be concerned about nothing but my duty, and my sin. *June* 9, *and July* 13, 1723.

58. *Resolved,* Not only to refrain from an air of dislike, fretfulness, and anger in conversation, but to exhibit an air of love, cheerfulness, and benignity. *May* 27, *and July* 13, 1723.

59. *Resolved,* When I am most conscious of provocations to ill-nature and anger, that I will strive most to feel and act good-naturedly; yea, at such times, to manifest good-nature, though I think that in other respects it would be disadvantageous, and so as would be imprudent at other times. *May* 12, *July* 11, *and July* 13, 1723.

60. *Resolved,* Whenever my feelings begin to appear in the least out of order, when I am conscious of the least uneasiness within, or the least irregularity without, I will then subject myself to the strictest examination. *July* 4, *and* 13, 1723.

61. *Resolved,* That I will not give way to that listlessness which I find unbends and relaxes my mind from being fully and fixedly set on religion, whatever excuse I may have for it — that what my listlessness inclines me to do, is best to be done, &c. *May* 21, *and July* 13, 1723.

62. *Resolved,* Never to do anything but my duty, and then according to Eph. vi, 6–8, to do it willingly and cheerfully, as unto the Lord, and not to man: knowing that whatever good thing any man doth, the same shall he receive of the Lord. *June* 25, *and July* 13, 1723.

63. On the supposition, that there never was to be but one individual in the world, at any one time, who was properly a complete christian, in all respects of a right stamp, having christianity always shining in its true lustre, and appearing excellent and lovely, from whatever part and under whatever character viewed: *Resolved,* To act just as I would do, if I strove with all my might to be that one, who should live in my time. *Jan.* 14, *and July* 13, 1723.

64. *Resolved,* When I find those *"groanings which cannot be uttered,"* of which the Apostle speaks, and those *"breakings of soul* for the longing it hath," of which the Psalmist speaks, Psalm cxix, 20, That I will pro-

mote them to the utmost of my power, and that I will not be weary of earnestly endeavouring to vent my desires, nor of the repetitions of such earnestness. *July* 23, *and August* 10, 1723.

65. *Resolved,* Very much to exercise myself in this, all my life long, viz. With the greatest openness, of which I am capable, to declare my ways to God, and lay my soul open to him, all my sins, temptations, difficulties, sorrows, fears, hopes, desires, and every thing, and every circumstance, according to Dr. Manton's sermon on the 119th Psalm. *July* 26, *and Aug.* 10, 1723.

66. *Resolved,* that I will endeavour always to keep a benign aspect, and air of acting and speaking in all places, and in all companies, except it should so happen that duty requires otherwise.

67. *Resolved,* After afflictions, to enquire, What am I the better for them; What good have I got by them; and, What I might have got by them.

68. *Resolved,* To confess frankly to myself all that which I find in myself, either infirmity or sin; and if it be what concerns religion, also to confess the whole case to God, and implore needed help. *July* 23, *and August* 10, 1723.

69. *Resolved,* Always to do that, which I shall wish I had done when I see others do it. *Aug.* 11, 1723.

70. Let there be something of benevolence, in all that I speak. *Aug.* 17, 1723.

—By Jonathan Edwards, American (1703–1758). From President Edwards' Seventy Resolutions.

~ ✲ ~

The Way to Wealth

BENJAMIN FRANKLIN

COURTEOUS READER: I have heard nothing gives an author so great pleasure as to find his works respectfully quoted by other learned authors. This pleasure I have seldom enjoyed. For though I have been, if I may say it without vanity, an eminent author of almanacs annually now for a full quarter of a century, my brother authors in the same way, for what reason I know not, have ever been very sparing in their applauses, and no other author has taken the least notice of me; so that did not my writings produce me some solid pudding, the great deficiency of praise would have quite discouraged me.

I concluded at length that the people were the best judges of my merit, for they buy my works; and besides, in my rambles, where I am not personally known I have frequently heard one or other of my adages repeated, with *as Poor Richard says* at the end of it. This gave me some satisfaction, as it showed not only that my instructions were regarded, but discovered likewise some respect for my authority; and I own that to encourage the practice of remembering and repeating those sentences, I have sometimes quoted myself with great gravity.

Judge, then, how much I must have been gratified by an incident I am going to relate to you. I stopped my horse lately where a great number of people were collected at a vendue of merchant's goods. The hour of sale not being come, they were conversing on the badness of the times; and one of the company called to a plain, clean old man with white locks; "Pray, Father Abraham, what think you of the times? Won't these heavy taxes quite ruin the country? How shall we ever be able to pay them? What would you advise us to?" Father Abraham stood up and replied: "If you would have my advice, I will give it to you in short; for 'a word to the wise is enough,' and 'many words won't fill a bushel,' as Poor Richard says." They all joined, desiring him to speak his mind, and gathering round him he proceeded as follows:

"Friends and neighbors, the taxes are indeed very heavy, and if those laid on by the government were the only ones we had to pay, we might the more easily discharge them; but we have many others, and much more grievous to some of us. We are taxed twice as much by our idleness, three times as much by our pride, and four times as much by our folly; and from these taxes the commissioners cannot ease or deliver us by allowing an abatement. However, let us hearken to good advice, and something may be done for us. 'God helps them that help themselves,' as Poor Richard says in his almanac of 1733.

"It would be thought a hard government that should tax its people one-tenth part of their time, to be employed in its service, but idleness taxes many of us much more, if we reckon all that is spent in absolute sloth or doing of nothing, with that which is spent in idle employments or amusements that amount to nothing. Sloth, by bringing on diseases, absolutely shortens life. 'Sloth, like rust, consumes faster than labor wears; while the used key is always bright,' as Poor Richard says. 'But dost thou love life? then do not squander time, for that's the stuff life is made of,' as Poor Richard says.

"How much more than is necessary do we spend in sleep? forgetting that 'the sleeping fox catches no poultry,' and that 'there will be sleeping enough in the grave,' as Poor Richard says. If time be of all things the most precious, 'wasting of time must be,' as Poor Richard says, 'the greatest prodigality;' since, as he elsewhere tells us, 'lost time is never found again,' and what we call 'time enough! always proves little enough.' Let us, then, up and be doing, and doing to the purpose; so by diligence shall we do more with less perplexity. 'Sloth makes all things difficult, but industry all things easy,' as Poor Richard says; and 'he that riseth late must trot all day, and shall scarce overtake his business at night; while laziness travels so slowly that poverty soon overtakes him,' as we read in Poor Richard; who adds; 'drive thy business! let not that drive thee!' and

'Early to bed and early to rise
Makes a man healthy, wealthy, and wise.'

"So what signifies wishing and hoping for better times? We may make these times better if we bestir ourselves. 'Industry need not wish,' as Poor Richard says, and 'he that lives on hope will die fasting.' 'There are no gains without pains; then help, hands! for I have no lands;' or, if I have, they are smartly taxed. And as Poor Richard likewise observes: 'he that hath a trade hath an estate, and he that hath a calling hath an office of profit and honour;' but then the trade must be worked at and the calling well followed, or neither the estate nor the office will enable us to pay our taxes. If we are industrious we shall never starve; for, as Poor Richard says, 'at the working-man's house hunger looks in, but dares not enter.' Nor will the bailiff or the constable enter, for 'industry pays debts, while despair increaseth them.'

"What though you have found no treasure, nor has any rich relation left you a legacy, 'diligence is the mother of good luck,' as Poor Richard says, and 'God gives all things to industry.'

'Then plow deep while sluggards sleep,
And you shall have corn to sell and to keep,'

says Poor Dick. Work while it is called to-day, for you know not how much you may be hindered to-morrow; which makes Poor Richard say; 'one to-day is worth two to-morrows;' and further, 'have you somewhat to do to-morrow? Do it to-day!'

"If you were a servant would you not be ashamed that a good master should catch you idle? Are you, then, your own master? 'Be ashamed to catch yourself idle,' as Poor Dick says. When there is so much to be done for yourself, your family, your country, and your gracious king, be up by peep of day! 'Let not the sun look down and say, "Inglorious here he lies!"' Handle your tools without mittens! remember that 'the cat in gloves catches no mice!' as Poor Richard says.

"'Tis true there is much to be done, and perhaps you are weak-handed; but stick to it steadily and you will see great effects; for 'constant dropping wears away stones;' and 'by diligence and patience the mouse ate in two the cable;' and 'little strokes fell great oaks;' as Poor Richard says in his almanac, the year I cannot just now remember.

"Methinks I hear some of you say; 'Must a man afford himself no leisure?' I will tell thee, my friend, what Poor Richard says: 'employ thy time well if thou meanest to gain leisure;' and 'since thou art not sure of a minute, throw not away an hour!' Leisure is time for doing something useful; this leisure the diligent man will obtain, but the lazy man never; so that, as Poor Richard says, 'a life of leisure and a life of laziness are two things.' Do you imagine that sloth will afford you more comfort than labor? No! for, as Poor Richard says, 'trouble springs from idleness and grievous toil from needless ease.' 'Many, without labor, would live by their wits only, but they'll break for want of stock' [means]; whereas industry gives comfort, and plenty, and respect. 'Fly pleasures and they'll follow you;' 'the diligent spinner has a large shift!' and

'Now I have a sheep and a cow,
Everybody bids me good-morrow.'

"All of which is well said by Poor Richard. But with our industry we must likewise be steady, settled, and careful, and oversee our own affairs with our own eyes and not trust too much to others; for, as Poor Richard says—

'I never saw an oft-removed tree
Nor yet an oft-removed family
That throve so well as those that settled be.'

"And again: 'three removes are as bad as a fire;' and again, 'keep thy shop and thy shop will keep thee;' and again, 'if you would have your business done, go; if not, send.' And again

'He that by the plow would thrive,
Himself must either hold or drive.'

"And again, 'the eye of the master will do more work than both his hands;' and again, 'want of care does us more damage than want of knowledge;' and again, 'not to oversee workmen is to leave them your purse open.'

"Trusting too much to others' care is the ruin of many; for, as the almanac says, 'in the affairs of this world men are saved, not by faith, but by the want of it;' but a man's own care is profitable; for, saith Poor Dick, 'learning is to the studious and riches to the careful;' as well as 'power to the bold' and 'heaven to the virtuous.' And further, 'if you would have a faithful servant and one that you like, serve yourself.'

"And again, he adviseth to circumspection and care, even in the smallest matters; because sometimes 'a little neglect may breed great mischief;' adding, 'for want of a nail the shoe was lost; for want of a shoe the horse was lost; and for want of a horse the rider was lost;' being overtaken and slain by the enemy; all for want of a little care about a horseshoe nail!

"So much for industry, my friends, and attention to one's own business; but to these we must add frugality if we would make our industry more certainly successful. 'A man may,' if he knows not how to save as he gets, 'keep his nose all his life to the grindstone and die not worth a groat at last.' 'A fat kitchen makes a lean will,' as Poor Richard says; and

'Many estates are spent in the getting,
Since women for tea forsook spinning and knitting,
And men for punch forsook hewing and splitting."

If you would be wealthy, says he in another almanac, 'think of saving as well as of getting. The Indies have not made Spain rich, because her outgoes are greater than her incomes.'

"Away, then, with your expensive follies, and you will not have so much cause to complain of hard times, heavy taxes, and chargeable families; for, as Poor Dick says,

'Women and wine, game and deceit,
Make the wealth small and the wants great.'

And further, 'what maintains one vice would bring up two children.' You may think, perhaps, that a little tea or a little punch now and then, a diet a little more costly, clothes a little finer, and a little more entertainment now and then, can be no great matter; but remember what Poor Richard says: 'many a little makes a mickle;' and further, 'beware of little expenses; a small leak will sink a great ship;' and again

'Who dainties love shall beggars prove;'

and moreover, 'fools make feasts and wise men eat them.'

"Here are you all got together at this vendue of fineries and knick-knacks. You call them goods; but if you do not take care they will prove evils to some of you. You expect they will be sold cheap, and perhaps they may for less than they cost; but if you have no occasion for them they must be dear to you. Remember what Poor Richard says: 'Buy what thou hast no need of, and ere long thou shalt sell thy necessaries.' And again, 'at a great pennyworth pause awhile.' He means that perhaps the cheapness is apparent only and not real; or the bargain by straitening thee in thy business may do thee more harm than good. For in another place he says: 'many have been ruined by buying good pennyworths.'

"Again, Poor Richard says, ''tis foolish to lay out money in a purchase of repentance;' and yet this folly is practiced every day at vendues for want of minding the almanac.

"'Wise men,' as Poor Richard says, 'learn by others' harms; fools scarcely by their own;' but *Felix quem faciunt aliena pericula cautum*. Many a one, for the sake of finery on the back, has gone with a hungry belly and half-starved their families. 'Silks and satins, scarlets and velvets,' as Poor Richard says, 'put out the kitchen fire.' These are not the necessaries of life; they can scarcely be called the conveniences; and yet, only because they look pretty, how many want to have them! The artificial wants of mankind thus become more numerous than the natural; and as Poor Dick says, 'for one poor person there are a hundred indigent.'

"By these and other extravagances the genteel are reduced to poverty and forced to borrow of those whom they formerly despised, but who, through industry and frugality, have maintained their standing; in which case it appears plainly that 'a plowman on his legs is higher than a gentleman on his knees,' as Poor Richard says. Perhaps they have had a small estate left them, which they knew not the getting of; they think, ''tis day and will never be night;' that 'a little to be spent out of so much is not worth minding' (a child and a fool, as Poor Richard says, imagine twenty shillings and twenty years can never be spent); but 'always taking out of the meal-tub, and never putting in, soon comes to the bottom.' Then, as Poor Dick says, 'when the well's dry they know the worth of water.' But this they might have known before if they had taken his advice. 'If you would know the value of money, go and try to borrow some;' for 'he that goes a-borrowing goes a-sorrowing,' and indeed so does he that lends to such people, when he goes to get it in again.

"Poor Dick further advises and says:

'Fond pride of dress is, sure, a very curse;
Ere fancy you consult, consult your purse.'

And again, 'pride is as loud a beggar as want and a great deal more saucy.' When you have bought one fine thing you must buy ten more, that your appearance may be all of a piece; but Poor Dick says: ''tis easier to suppress the first desire than to satisfy all that follow it.' And 'tis as truly folly for the poor to ape the rich as for the frog to swell in order to equal the ox.

'Great estates may venture more,
But little boats should keep near shore.'

"'Tis, however, a folly soon punished; for 'pride that dines on vanity sups on contempt,' as Poor Richard says. And in another place, 'pride breakfasted with plenty, dined with poverty, and supped with infamy.'

"And after all, of what use is this pride of appearance, for which so much is risked, so much is suffered? It cannot promote health or ease pain; it makes no increase of merit in the person; it creates envy; it hastens misfortune.

'What is a butterfly? At best
He's but a caterpillar drest,
The gaudy fop's his picture just,'

as Poor Richard says.

"But what madness must it be to run into debt for these superfluities! We are offered by the terms of this vendue six months' credit; and that, perhaps, has induced some of us to attend it, because we cannot spare the ready money and hope now to be fine without it. But ah! think what you do when you run in debt: you give to another power over your liberty. If you cannot pay at the time, you will be ashamed to see your creditor; you will be in fear when you speak to him; you will make poor, pitiful, sneaking excuses, and by degrees come to lose your veracity and sink into base, downright lying; for, as Poor Richard says, 'the second vice is lying, the first is running into debt;' and again, to the same purpose, 'lying rides upon debt's back;' whereas a free-born Englishman ought not to be ashamed or afraid to see or speak to any man living. But poverty often deprives a man of all spirit and virtue. ''Tis hard for an empty bag to stand upright!' as Poor Richard truly says. What would you think of that prince or the government who should issue an edict forbidding you to dress like a gentleman or gentlewoman, on pain of imprisonment or servitude? Would you not say that you are free, have a right to dress as you please, and that such an edict would be a breach of your privileges and such a government tyrannical? And yet you are about to put yourself under such tyranny when you run in debt for such dress! your creditor has authority, at his pleasure, to deprive you of your liberty by confining you in jail for life or to sell you for a servant if you should not be able to pay him. When you have got your bargain you may, perhaps, think little of payment; 'creditors,' Poor Richard tells us, 'have better memories than debtors;' and in another place says, 'creditors are a superstitious set, great observers of set days and times.' The day comes round before you are aware, and the demand is made before you are prepared to satisfy it; or, if you bear your debt in mind, the term which at first seemed so long will, as it lessens, appear extremely short.

Time will seem to have added wings to his heels as well as his shoulders. 'Those have a short Lent,' saith Poor Richard, 'who owe money to be paid at Easter.' Then since, as he says, 'the borrower is a slave to the lender and the debtor to the creditor,' disdain the chain, preserve your freedom, and maintain your independency. Be industrious and free; be frugal and free. At present, perhaps, you may think yourself in thriving circumstances, and that you can bear a little extravagance without injury; but

'For age and want, save while you may;
No morning sun lasts a whole day.'

"As Poor Richard says, gain may be temporary and uncertain; but ever while you live expense is constant and certain; and ''tis easier to build two chimneys than to keep one in fuel,' as Poor Richard says; so, 'rather go to bed supperless than rise in debt.'

'Get what you can, and what you get hold;
'Tis the stone that will turn all your lead
into gold,'

as Poor Richard says; and when you have got the philosopher's stone, sure you will no longer complain of bad times or the difficulty of paying taxes.

"This doctrine, my friends, is reason and wisdom; but, after all, do not depend too much upon your own industry and frugality and prudence, though excellent things, for they may all be blasted without the blessing of Heaven; and therefore ask that blessing humbly, and be not uncharitable to those that at present seem to want it, but comfort and help them. Remember Job suffered and was afterward prosperous.

"And now, to conclude, 'experience keeps a dear school, but fools will learn in no other, and scarce in that;' for it is true, 'we may give advice, but we cannot give conduct,' as Poor Richard says. However, remember this: 'they that won't be counseled can't be helped,' as Poor Richard says; and further, that 'if you will not hear reason she'll surely rap your knuckles.'"

Thus the old gentleman ended his harangue. The people heard it and approved the doctrine, and immediately practiced the contrary, just as if it had been a common sermon. For the vendue opened and they began to buy extravagantly, notwithstanding all his cautions and their own fear of taxes. I found the good man had thoroughly studied my almanacs and digested all I had dropped on those topics during the course of twenty-five years. The frequent mention he made of me must have tired any one else; but my vanity was wonderfully delighted with it, though I was conscious that not a tenth part of the wisdom was my own which he ascribed to me, but rather the gleanings that I had made of the sense of all ages and nations. However, I resolved to be the better for the echo of it, and though I had at first determined to buy stuff for a new coat, I went away resolved to wear my old one a little longer. Reader, if thou wilt do the same, thy profit will be as great as mine. I am, as ever, thine to serve thee,

RICHARD SAUNDERS.

—*From Poor Richard's Almanack, 1757, by Benjamin Franklin, American (1706–1790).*

The Evening Hours of a Hermit

JOHANN HEINRICH PESTALOZZI

MAN who is one and the same whether on a throne or in a cottage, what in his innermost nature is he? Why do not the wise tell us? Why do not the most highly endowed of the human race learn what man really is? Does the peasant make use of his ox without studying him? Does not the herdsman seek to familiarize himself with the nature of his sheep?

And you who make use of man and say that you protect and nurture him, do you bestow upon him the care that the peasant does upon his ox? Do you trouble yourselves about him as the herdsmen do about their sheep? Does your wisdom consist in a thorough understanding of your race and is your goodness the goodness of enlightened shepherds of the people?

What man is, what his needs are, what elevates and what degrades him, what invigorates and what weakens him, that is what it is necessary for the highest and for the humblest to know.

Men feel the need of this everywhere. Everywhere man is toiling and straining and struggling upward. Because of lack of this knowledge successive generations wither away with their lives unfulfilled and at the end of life the majority of mankind cry aloud that the completion of their course has not satisfied them. Their end is not the ripening of the perfect fruit which having completed the pre-destined course of development sinks to the rest of the winter.

Why does man grope after the truth without system or purpose? Why does he not try to discover the fundamental needs of his nature in order that he may base upon this the enjoyment and the blessedness of his life? Why does he not seek truth, which is peace and the enjoyment of life, truth which satisfies his innermost cravings, which develops his powers, gladdens his days and endows his life with happiness?

Man under the compulsion of his needs finds the road to this truth in his innermost being.

The infant, its hunger satisfied, learns in this way what his mother is to him. She calls forth love, the essence of gratitude, in him before he can utter the words, "duty" or "gratitude." The son who eats his father's bread and warms himself at his hearth finds by this path of nature his happiness in the duties of the child.

Man! if you seek the truth through this means provided by nature you will find it as you need it for your particular case and for your career.

Man! just as it is indispensable to your rest and peace, as it is thy guiding star in thy immediate affairs, just as it is the support on which thy life rests so it is to you an inestimable blessing.

You cannot in this course make use of all truths.

The circle of knowledge by which one in man's situation may be really benefitted is narrow, and this circle begins immediately around him, around his nearest relationships, extends thence outward and must at every extension regulate itself according to this centre of all the beneficent power of truth.

The pure feeling for truth develops in a limited field. Pure wisdom rests upon the firm basis of the knowledge of one's immediate relationships and of a capacity for management that has been trained in the handling of one's most intimate affairs.

This human wisdom which reveals itself in the necessities of our situation, strengthens and develops our effectiveness. The type of mind which it calls forth is simple and clear-sighted. Moulded under the powerful influence of contact with things as they are actually related to each other in real life it is easily directed to every side of truth. (It is easily led to deal with every aspect of truth.)

It manifests itself in a feeling of power and in the right application of this.

Sublime path of Nature, the truth to which thou leadest is power and deed, the source of development, the inspiration and the destiny of human nature.

Truly thou formest man not in a hasty, flashy growth, and the son of Nature is restricted, his speech is the expression and the outcome of complete knowledge of the subject. But if men exceed thy pace they work confusion within themselves and dissolve the peace and the equilibrium of their innermost natures.

They do this whenever, instead of rendering their minds obedient to truth and wisdom through first-hand knowledge of actual objects, they plunge into the thousandfold confusion of verbal instruction and opinions and make sound and speech instead of truth and actual objects the foundation of their mental structure and of the earliest cultivation of their powers.

This artificial procedure of the school which everywhere forges ahead of the quiet, orderly, slow procedure of Nature in the matter of speech gives man a superficial polish which conceals the lack of natural power within and gratifies times like ours.

The standpoint of actual life, the actual condition and circumstances of the individual man is the book of nature. In these the power and the method (*Ordnung*) of this wise guide are to be looked for, and every school education, which is not based upon the foundation of the natural education of man, leads astray.

Man! father of thy children, do not compel them to dissipate their powers on remote objects before they have acquired strength through exercising it on their immediate surroundings, and beware of severity and strain.

The power of Nature although it leads irresistibly to truth is not rigid and formal in its action; the song of the nightingale trills through the darkness and all nature rolls on in vitalizing freedom. Nowhere is there a suggestion of a restrictive routine.

Were there a rigid and compulsory procedure in the education of Nature, she also would develop one-sidedness and her truth would not gently and freely nourish the whole nature of man.

The repulsive, exhausting effort to attain the mere shadows of truth; the struggle for the mere tone and sound and verbal images of truth, where no interest attracts and delights and no application is possible; the misdirection of all the powers of the developing human being in the pursuit of the opinion of severe, and one-sided teachers and the thousand and one little arts of word-trafficking and of the latest fashion in teaching which are put forward to serve as a foundation for the education of man; all this is a laborious leading astray from the path of Nature.

In consequence of this harsh procedure truth becomes neither the gentle servant of mankind, nor the kindly sympathetic mother whose happiness and wisdom is the happiness and the need of her children.

Man loses the equilibrium of his strength, the power of his wisdom, if his mind is directed too one-sidedly and too powerfully toward one object. This is why the instructional procedure of Nature is never violent.

Nevertheless there is firmness in her training and in her arrangements there is the strict orderliness of the careful housekeeper.

Nor is the confusion resulting from a too eager pursuit of knowledge any nearer the course of Nature.

The man who hovers around and lightly tastes of every branch of knowledge and fails to develop strength through the quiet steady application of knowledge, he also deviates from the path of Nature, he loses that steady, clear, attentive glance, that calm, quiet feeling for truth receptive to real happiness.

Faltering and uncertain will be the course of those men who in the multiplicity of their knowledge find much occasion for talk, but who have sacrificed to it the quiet sense of pure human wisdom. Notwithstanding their noisy pride, their immediate surroundings are to them barren and obscure while those of the truly wise are lighted up by the light of intelligent understanding.

The education of man to truth is the education of his nature to that wisdom which brings calmness and serenity.

Where art thou, power of Nature, thou who dost really train and develop mankind? Even the dead and empty wastes of gloomy ignorance lead one astray from thy path. (As well as the noisy pride above mentioned.)

Want of acquaintanceship with thine own nature, O Man, will place greater restrictions upon thy knowledge than will thy necessities. Distortion of the first fundamental ideas of thy relationship to others; murderous, oppressive power of tyranny; withholding of all enjoyment of truth and blessedness; unnatural lack of a general rational understanding of the foremost and most essential needs and relationships of mankind; how thy gloomy shadow darkens the world!

Hence the fully developed power of mankind, this source of their mighty deeds and of their quiet enjoyment is no merely imaginary impulse and no deceptive illusion.

Satisfaction of the innermost needs of our being, pure power of our nature, thou blessing of our existence, thou art no dream! To seek and search for thee is the aim and destiny of mankind and my need and the yearning of my innermost soul is to seek thee, thou aim and destiny of mankind.

Where and how shall I find thee, Truth, who art my salvation and who exaltest me to the perfection of my nature?

In my inner nature is to be found the gateway to this truth. All mankind are fundamentally alike and for the satisfaction of their needs there is one and the same way. Hence the truth which will be discovered in our innermost being will apply to mankind at large and it will serve as a unifying influence to bring together those who by thousands are quarreling over mere externals.

The pure and beneficent powers of mankind are not the gifts of art or of accident. In our inner nature they lie bound up with our fundamental tendencies and capacities. Their development is the fundamental need of mankind. Therefore the path of nature which reveals it must be open and easy. It must be simple and capable of use by the rank and file of humanity for the education of man to true and tranquillizing wisdom.

Nature develops all the powers of mankind through exercise, and their growth results from use.

The procedure of Nature in the development of mankind is that of application and of making use of its knowledge, of its endowments and talents.

Hence it is the man of simple and upright character, who, since he with pure and humble application of his knowledge and with quiet industry uses and exercises every one of his capacities and talents, is educated by Nature to true human wisdom. On the other hand the man who destroys within himself this orderly process of Nature and weakens the sense of the conformity of his knowledge (to Nature) becomes incapable of the enjoyment of truth.

Actions that do violence to that inner feeling of justice, undermine our capacity for apprehending the truth, they confuse our clear sense of the lofty and noble simplicity of our fundamental ideas and of our fundamental feelings.

Hence all human wisdom rests upon the power of a good heart obedient to the truth, and all human blessedness upon this sense of simplicity and uprightness.

Education of mankind to this pure sense of simplicity and uprightness, thou art the fatherly care of mankind that the uncorrupted fundamental impulses of the heart protect the course of its mental and spiritual development and rightly guide it.

The general building-up of these inner powers of man's nature to pure human wisdom is the general aim of the education even of the humblest and lowest.

The exercise, application and use of his strength and wisdom in the particular situations and circumstances of mankind is vocational and class education. This must always be subordinate to the general aim of the education of man.

Wisdom and strength based upon simplicity and virtue is a blessing in every variety of circumstance in which human beings live, even in the lowest, just as it is an indispensable necessity at every height in the social scale.

Whoever is not a man, is not a man with his native capacities fully developed, lacks the foundation on which to base his preparation for a definite vocation and for his particular place in life — a defect for which no rank in society, however high, may serve as an excuse.

A wide gulf separates the ordinary father of a family and the prince, the poor man burdened with anxiety for his daily bread and the rich groaning with the burden of still heavier cares, the ignorant woman and the famous savant, the idle sluggard and the soaring genius whose influence is felt throughout the world.

Yet if the one in his lofty station is lacking in true humanity, dark clouds will gather about him while, in the humble cottages of the poor, cultivated humanity radiates pure, exalted and contented human greatness.

So in his lofty position a prince may seek wise and just laws for offenders against the law yet perhaps he may spend his money in vain. If he wishes to manifest, however, the truly paternal spirit in the council of war, in the hunt, in the management of his lands and of his household, he will educate judges and warders of the criminal classes to be wise, earnest and fatherly in spirit.

Otherwise the talk about enlightened laws is like the talk of the love of one's neighbor by those whose hearts are devoid of love.

So far are you, perhaps, O prince, from attaining the blessedness of the truth which you seek.

Meanwhile fathers in the dust beneath thy feet are acting wisely in dealing with foolish sons. Prince, learn in the tears of their night watches and in the toil and trouble of their daily life how to deal wisely with offenders and give thy right over life and death to men who seek wisdom by this path. O Prince, a truly cultivated humanity is a blessing to the world. Only through it does the might of enlightenment and of wisdom manifest itself. It alone makes laws a boon to mankind.

Man! thou thyself, the inner awareness of thy being and of thy powers is the first object of the creative, developing activity of Nature. But you do not live for yourself alone. Hence Nature fits you for external relationships and by means of these.

Just in proportion as these relationships are close at hand are they important for the moulding of thy character so as to adapt it to thy calling in life.

The power developed through interaction with the immediate environment is always the source of the wisdom and power of man in dealing with the more remote.

A fatherly spirit fits one for the position of ruler, a brotherly spirit for that of the citizen; both give rise to system and order in the home and in the state.

The domestic relationships of mankind are the earliest and the most excellent of the relationships of Nature.

Man labors at his vocation and bears the

burden of the state and government in order that he may enjoy his domestic happiness in peace.

Hence the training of the man for his calling and station in life must be subordinated to the aim of fitting him to appropriate the pure happiness of home life.

Hence the home is the place where the natural educational process runs its course.

Home! thou school of morals and of the state!

First thou art a child, a human being, only afterwards an apprentice of thy trade or profession.

The virtues of childhood should bear fruit in the period of apprenticeship and they should afford the earliest training of thy capacity for the enjoyment of all the blessings of thy life.

Whoever turns aside from this order of nature and gives precedence contrary to nature to class, vocational training, training for ruling or serving, leads mankind away from the enjoyment of the most natural blessings to a sea of dangers and difficulties.

Man must be trained to inner peace. Contentment with his lot and with attainable pleasures, patience, carefulness, faith in the love of the Father in the face of every hindrance, that is education to human wisdom.

Without inner peace man wanders on wild pathways. The eager urge to attain impossibly distant goals deprives him of all enjoyment of his immediate surroundings and of all the strength of the wise, patient and obedient nature.

If feeling is not suffused with inner peace its force enervates man in his inner being and afflicts him with sorrow and anguish under circumstances which the wise endure with smiling contentment.

Peace and quiet enjoyment are the first ends of human education and the greatest needs of the time. Man! thy knowledge and ambition must be subordinated to these higher aims. Otherwise envy and ambition will be a source of pain and unhappiness.

— *From the Evening Hours of a Hermit by Johann Heinrich Pestalozzi, Swiss (1746–1827), translated by Lewis Flint Anderson.*

Thoughts

JOSEPH JOUBERT

God is so great, and so vast, that to understand Him it is necessary to divide Him.

We always believe that God is like ourselves. The indulgent proclaim Him indulgent, the malignant preach Him as terrible.

Dare I say it? God may be easily known if only we do not force ourselves to define Him.

Earth is only comprehensible to those who have known heaven. Without the world of religion, the world of sense offers nothing but a desolating enigma.

The God of metaphysics is but an idea, but the God of religion, the Creator of heaven and earth, the sovereign Judge of actions and thoughts, is a force.

Would God have made human life merely to contemplate the flow of it, merely to watch the tossing, and tumbling, the play, and the variety — or merely to have the sight of ever-moving hands passing a torch from one to another? No; God does nothing but for eternity.

Heaven is for those who think upon it.

Piety is a sublime wisdom surpassing all other wisdom; a kind of genius, that gives wings to the mind. No one is wise who has not piety.

Piety is a kind of modesty. It makes us turn away our thoughts, as modesty makes us turn away our eyes, from all that is unlawful.

To think of God is an act.

Religion is the poetry of the heart; it has enchantments useful to our daily life; it gives us both happiness and virtue.

* Religion is neither a theology nor a theosophy; it is more than all this; it is a discipline, a law, a yoke, an indissoluble engagement.

One man finds in religion his literature and his science, another finds in it his joy and his duty.

To attain the regions of light we must pass through clouds. Some of us never emerge; others know how to pass beyond.

In our religious life, we should be simple, unconstrained, and cheerful; not dignified, grave, and calculating.

---

* Starred passages are Matthew Arnold's translation, in his essay on Joubert, *Essays in Criticism, First Series.*

* Why is even a bad preacher almost always heard by the pious with pleasure? Because he talks to them about what they love. But you who have to expound religion to the children of this world, you who have to speak to them of that which they loved once perhaps, or which they would be glad to love — remember that they do not love it yet, and to make them love it take heed to speak with power.

We see everything through ourselves. We are a medium always interposed between things and ourselves.

The mind is a fire, of which thought is the flame. Like flame it tends upwards. Men do their best to smother it by turning the point downwards.

Good sense is to know what we must do; intelligence, to know what we must think.

Imagination is the eye of the soul.

It is to imagination that the greatest truths are revealed; for instance, Providence, its course, its designs; they escape our judgment; imagination alone sees them.

Minds are measured by their stature; it were better worth while to measure them by their beauty.

A mind has still some strength, so long as it has strength to bewail its feebleness.

* The man of imagination without learning has wings and no feet.

We employ in the service of our passions the stuff that was given us for happiness.

All the passions seek what feeds them; fear loves the idea of danger.

Happiness is to feel one's soul good; there is really no other, and one may have this happiness even in sorrow; hence there are some griefs that are preferable to any joy, and that would be preferred by all who have felt them.

One element in all happiness is to feel that we have deserved it.

Those who love always have no leisure to pity themselves, or to be unhappy.

Those who watch with a malicious eye for the faults of their friends discover them with joy. He cannot be a friend who is never a dupe.

We must make ourselves beloved, for men are only just towards those whom they love.

Tenderness is the repose of passion.

Everything that multiplies the ties that unite man to man, makes him better and happier.

It is a happiness, and a great piece of good fortune, to be born good.

The wish to be independent of all men, and not to be under obligation to any one, is the sure sign of a soul without tenderness.

Proud natures love whom they serve.

Conceited people always seem to me, like dwarfs, to have the stature of a child, and the countenance of a man.

Everything wears out, even esteem, if we do not take care of it.

Think well of no young man whom old men do not find polite.

The beginning and the end of human life are the best of it, or at least the most worthy of our reverence; the one is the age of innocence, the other the age of reason.

What in youth is passion, in old age is vice.

To do well, we should forget our age when we are old, and not feel our youth too keenly when we are young.

There is nothing good in a man, but his young feelings and his old thoughts.

The evening of life comes bearing its own lamp.

Every year forms a knot in our nature, as it does in trees; some branch of intelligence develops, or decays and dries up.

Politeness smooths away wrinkles.

Life is a country that the old have seen, and lived in. Those who travel through it can only learn the way from them.

* Our life is woven wind.

How many people drink, eat, and are married; buy, sell, and build; make contracts and take care of their money; have friends and enemies, pleasures and pains; are born, grow, live, and die, — but still — asleep!

We are happy if we part from health to enter into wisdom.

Let us die good-tempered, if we can.

One should only choose for a wife a woman whom one would choose for a friend, were she a man.

To be an agreeable guest one needs only to enjoy oneself.

We should wear our velvet within, that is to say, show ourselves most amiable to those of our own house.

The aim of argument, or of discussion, should not be victory, but progress.

We may convince others by our own arguments, but they can only be persuaded by their own.

What can one put into a mind which is filled, and filled with itself?

A clever talk between two men is a unison; between a man and a woman it is harmony, a concord; we come away satisfied by the one, enchanted by the other.

In speaking of what is hateful, gentle natures always speak with reserve; they spare others and themselves.

Politeness is the blossom of our humanity. Whoever is not sufficiently polite, is not sufficiently humane.

Gravity is only the bark of the tree of wisdom; but it preserves it.

Wisdom is a science whereby we distinguish things that are good for the soul from those that are not. It is the science of sciences, because it alone knows their value, their exact importance, their true use, their dangers, and their purpose.

Wisdom is rest in the light. Happy are the minds lofty enough to be at ease in that radiance.

Whenever our judgments and our feelings lack patience, they also lack wisdom and virtue.

Never cut what you can unravel.

Everything may be learnt, even goodness.

There are some people who keep their morality in the piece; they never make themselves a coat of it.

When we act, we must follow the rules, and when we judge, we must allow for the exceptions.

Without duty, life is soft and boneless; it cannot hold itself together.

Our moments of light are moments of happiness. When light shines in the mind, it is fair weather there.

Time and truth are friends, although there are many moments hostile to truth.

The credulity that comes from the heart does no harm to the intelligence.

The worst quality in error is not its falseness, but its wilfulness, blindness, and passion.

Those who never retract love themselves better than truth.

Simple and sincere minds are never more than half mistaken.

In eager minds, where reasoning ends, poetry begins.

Nothing that does not carry us away is poetry. The lyre is, in some sort, a winged instrument.

There must be in a poem, not only the poetry of images, but also the poetry of ideas.

A poet should not traverse at a walk an interval that he can clear at a leap.

He who has no poetry in himself will find poetry in nothing.

Words light up, when the poet's finger touches them with its phosphorus.

All languages are rivers that run gold.

Before employing a fine phrase, make a place for it.

All fine speech is capable of more than one interpretation; when a beautiful phrase suggests a finer meaning than the author intended, it is well to adopt it.

Words should stand out from the paper; that is to say, should attach themselves easily to the attention and to the memory; they should be handy to quote, and to transplant.

Words, like glass, obscure when they do not aid vision.

Only a temperate style is classical.

Brevity adorned — the highest beauty of style.

We become correct by correcting.

The natural gift! — it is but the material that art must use, the silk that it must spin and smooth.

Genius begins great works; but labor alone finishes them.

We know nothing well till a long time after we have learnt it.

It is impossible to become very well-informed if we read only what is agreeable.

Young writers give their minds a great deal of exercise, and very little food.

The end of a work should always recall the beginning.

In literature how many people have a correct ear, and sing out of tune!

The best literary work does not intoxicate — it enchants!

National literature begins with fables, and finishes with novels.

We find little in a book but what we put there. But in great books, the mind finds room to put many things.

—*From the Thoughts of Joseph Joubert, French (1754–1824), translated by Katherine Lyttelton.*

Reflections and Maxims

JOHANN WOLFGANG VON GOETHE

I

MAN'S highest virtue always is as much as possible to rule external circumstances, and as little as possible to let himself be ruled by them. Life lies before us, as a huge quarry before the architect: he deserves not the name of architect except, out of this fortuitous mass, he can combine, with the greatest economy, suitableness and durability, some form, the pattern of which originated in his own soul. All things without us—nay, I may add, all things within us—are mere elements; but deep in the inmost shrine of our nature lies the creative force, which out of these can produce what they were meant to be, and which leaves us neither sleep nor rest, till in one way or another, without us or within us, this product has taken shape.

II

When I become acquainted with a man my first inquiry is: With what does he occupy himself, and how, and with what degree of perseverance? The answer regulates the interest which I take in that man for life.

III

Nothing more exposes us to madness than distinguishing ourselves from others, and nothing more contributes to maintain our common sense than living in the common way with multitudes of men.

IV

There is a politeness of the heart; this is closely allied to love. Those who possess this purest fountain of natural politeness find it easy to express the same in forms of outward propriety.

V

To preserve our place and our peace of mind with pleasure in the face of the decided superiority of another, our competitor in the same sphere of action, there is only one charm, and that is love.

VI

Fools and sensible men are equally innocuous. It is in the half fools and the half wise that the great danger lies.

VII

The formation of his character is not, as it ought to be, the chief concern with every man. Many wish merely to find a sort of recipe for comfort, directions for acquiring riches, or whatever good they aim at.

VIII

Honest, clear, and unselfish co-operation for the realization of the good and true, that lies between two extremes, is seldom to be met with. What we do meet with is obstinate adherence to an obsolete and soulless tradition on the one hand, and a rash lust for change on the other; retardation without reason and haste without safety.

IX

The battle between the old and the new, the persistent and the progressive, is always the same. All order is apt to stiffen into a lifeless formalism; to get rid of which, order is destroyed, and some time will elapse before people see that order must be recalled. Classicism and romanticism, monopolies of guilds and freedom of crafts, accumulation and division of land—under whatever name, it is always the same conflict, which, after fighting out its result in one direction, in due season creates a new conflict in the opposite direction. The great wisdom of governments would be so to regulate this conflict, that a balance might be established betwixt the two opposites, creating the new without the absolute loss of the old; but this is something that seems to go beyond the strength of men, and God, so far as we may judge, does not seem to wish it.

X

Nothing is more terrible than ignorance with spurs on.

XI

Man is entitled to believe in immortality; such belief is agreeable to his nature; and his instincts in this direction are confirmed by religious assurances. My belief in the immortality of the soul springs from the idea of activity; for when I persevere to the end in a course of restless activity, I have a sort of guarantee from Nature that, when the present form of my existence proves itself inadequate for the energizing of my spirit, she will provide another form more appropriate.

XII

A tendency to superstition is of the very essence of humanity; and, when we think we have completely extinguished it, we shall find it retreating into the strangest nooks and corners, that it may issue out thence on the first occasion it can do so with safety.

XIII

I am heartily sorry for those persons who are constantly talking of the perishable nature of things, and the nothingness of human life; for, for this very end we are here, to stamp the perishable with an imperishable worth; and this can be done only by taking a just estimate of both.

XIV

Freedom is an odd thing, and every man has enough of it, if he can only satisfy himself. What avails a superfluity of freedom which we cannot use? Look at this chamber and the next, in which, through the open door, you see my bed. Neither of them is large; and they are rendered still narrower by necessary furniture, books, manuscripts, and works of art; but they are enough for me. I have lived in them all the winter, scarcely entering my front rooms. What have I done with my spacious house, and the liberty of going from one room to another, when I have not found it requisite to make use of them?

If a man has freedom enough to live healthily, and work at his craft, he has enough; and so much all can easily obtain. Then all of us are only free under certain conditions, which we must fulfill. . . . Freedom consists not in refusing to recognize anything above us, but in respecting something which is above us; for, by respecting it, we raise ourselves to it, and by our very acknowledgment make manifest that we bear within ourselves what is higher, and are worthy to be on a level with it.

I have, on my journeys, often met merchants from the north of Germany, who fancied they were my equals, if they rudely seated themselves next to me at table. They were, by this method, nothing of the kind; but they would have been so, if they had known how to value and treat me.

XV

All great excellence in life or art, at its first recognition, brings with it a certain pain arising from the strongly felt inferiority of the spectator; only at a later period, when we take it into our own culture, and appropriate as much of it as our capacities allow, we learn to love and to esteem it. Mediocrity, on the other hand, may often give us unqualified pleasure; it does not disturb our self-satisfaction, but rather encourages us with the thought that we are as good as another.

XVI

Let me not be told that the actual world is destitute of a poetic interest. It is the great triumph of genius to make the common appear novel by opening our eyes to its beauty. Reality gives the motive, the hinging points, the kernel; but to create a beautiful living whole out of these rough materials — that is the work of the poet.

XVII

People are always talking about originality; but what do they mean? As soon as we are born, the world begins to work upon us, and this goes on to the end. And after all, what can we call our own except energy, strength, and will? If I could give an account of all that I owe to great predecessors and contemporaries, there would be but a small balance in my favor.

XVIII

I cannot but look upon it as one of the greatest misfortunes of our age, that it allows nothing to ripen quietly; that the next moment, so to speak, devours the preceding; that no time is allowed for digestion; and that we live from hand to mouth, without leisure to bring forth any finished product.

XIX

Altogether, the style of a writer is a faithful representative of his mind; therefore, if any man wishes to write a clear style, let him first be clear in his thoughts; and, if any would write in a noble style, let him first possess a noble soul, and live a noble life.

XX

Very few of our recent young poets write good *prose*. This is very easily explained. To write prose one must have something to say; but he who has nothing to say can still twirl verses and find rhymes, where one word suggests the other, and at last something comes out, which in fact is nothing, but which looks as if it were something.

XXI

He who attacks marriage, he who by word or deed sets himself to undermine this foundation of all moral society, must settle the matter with me; and if I don't bring him to reason, then I have nothing to do with him. Marriage is the beginning and the summit of all civilization. It makes the savage mild; and the most highly cultivated man has no better means of demonstrating his mildness. Marriage must be indissoluble, for it brings so much general happiness that any individual case of unhappiness that may be connected with it cannot come into account.

What do people mean when they talk about unhappiness? It is not so much unhappiness as impatience that from time to time possesses men, and then they choose to call themselves miserable. Let the moment of irritation but pass over, and people will find cause enough to think themselves happy that a state which has already existed so long still exists. For separation there can be no sufficient reason. In our present human condition there is so much of sorrow and joy interwoven, that it is beyond all calculation what obligations a married pair lie under to one another. It is an infinite debt which it requires an eternity to cancel. Disagreeable it may be, I admit, sometimes: that is just as it should be. Are we not really married to our conscience, of which we might often be willing to rid ourselves because it often annoys us more than any man or woman can possibly annoy one another?

—By Johann Wolfgang von Goethe, German (1749—1832) (selected from John Stuart Blackie's The Wisdom of Goethe).

~ ❁ ~

Panegyric of Birds

GIACOMO LEOPARDI

AMELIO, a lonely philosopher, was seated, reading, one spring morning in the shade of his country house. Being distracted by the songs of the birds in the fields, he gradually resigned himself to listening and thinking. At length he threw his book aside, and taking up a pen wrote as follows: —

Birds are naturally the most joyful creatures in the world. I do not say this because of the cheerful influence they always exercise over us; I mean that they themselves are more light-hearted and joyful than any other animal. For we see other animals ordinarily stolid and grave, and many even seem melancholy. They rarely give signs of joy, and when they do, these are but slight and of brief duration. In most of their enjoyments and pleasures they do not express any gratification. The green fields, extensive and charming landscapes, noble planets, pure and sweet atmosphere, if even a cause of pleasure to them, do not excite in them any joyful demonstrations; save that on the authority of Zenophon, hares are said to skip and frolic with delight when the moon's radiance is at its brightest.

Birds, on the other hand, show extreme joy, both in motion and appearance; and it is the sight of this evident disposition for enjoyment on their part that gladdens us as we watch them. And this appearance must not be regarded as unreal and deceptive. They sing to express the happiness they feel, and the happier they are, the more vigorously do they sing. And if, as it is said, they sing louder and more sweetly when in love than at other times, it is equally certain that other pleasures besides love incite them to sing. For we may notice they warble more on a quiet and peaceful day, than when the day is dark and uncertain. And in stormy weather, or when frightened, they are silent; but the storm passed, they reappear, singing and frolicking with one another. Again, they sing in the morning when they awake; being partly incited to this by a feeling of joy for the new day, and partly by the pleasure generally felt by every animal when refreshed and restored by sleep. They also delight in gay foliage, rich valleys, pure and sparkling water, and beautiful country. . . .

It is said that birds' voices are softer and sweeter, and their songs more refined, with us than among wild and uncivilized people. This being so, it would seem that birds are subject to the influence of the civilization with which they associate. Whether or not this be true, it is a remarkable instance of the providence of nature that they should have capacity for flight, as well as the gift of song, so that their voices might from a lofty situation reach a greater number of auditors. It is also providential that the air, which is the natural element of sound, should be inhabited by vocal and musical creatures.

Truly the singing of birds is a great solace and pleasure to us, and all other animals. This fact is not, I believe, so much due to the sweetness of the sounds, nor to their variety and harmony, as to the joyful signification of songs generally, and those of birds in particular. Birds laugh, as it were, to show their contentment and happiness. It may therefore be said that they partake in a degree of man's privilege of laughter, unpossessed by other animals. Now some people think that man may as well be termed a laughing animal, as an animal possessed of mind and reason; for laughter seems to them quite as much peculiar to man as reason. And it is certainly wonderful that man, the most wretched and miserable of all creatures, should have the faculty of laughter, which is wanting in other animals. Marvellous also is the use we make of this faculty! We see people suffering from some terrible calamity or mental distress, others who have lost all love of life, and regard every human thing as full of vanity, who are almost incapable of joy, and deprived of hope, laugh nevertheless. Indeed, the more such men realize the vanity of hope, and the misery of life, the fewer their expectations and pleasures, so much the more do they feel inclined to laugh. Now it is scarcely possible to explain or analyze the nature of laughter in general, and its connection with the human mind. Perhaps it may aptly be termed a species of momentary folly or delirium. For men can have no reasonable and just cause for laughter, because nothing really satisfies nor truly pleases them. It would be curious to discover and trace out the history of this faculty. There is no doubt that in man's primitive and wild state, it was expressed by a peculiar gravity of countenance, as in other animals, who show it even to the extent of melancholy. For this reason I imagine that laughter not only came into the world after tears, which cannot be questioned, but that a long time passed before it appeared. During that time, neither the mother greeted her child with a smile, nor did the child smilingly recognize her, as Virgil says. And the reason why, in the present day, among civilized people, children smile as soon as they are born, is explainable by virtue of example: they see others smile, therefore they also smile.

It is probable that laughter originated in drunkenness, another peculiarity of the human race. This vice is far from being confined to civilized nations, for we know that scarcely any people can be found that do not possess an intoxicating liquor of some kind, which they indulge in to excess. And this cannot be wondered at, when we remember that men, the most unhappy of all animals, are above all pleased with anything that easily alienates their minds, such as self-forgetfulness, or a suspension of their usual life; from which interruption and temporary diminution of the sense and knowledge of their peculiar evils they receive no slight benefit. And whereas savages have ordinarily a sad and grave countenance, yet, when in a state of drunkenness, they laugh immoderately, and talk and sing incessantly, contrary to their custom. But I will discuss this matter more in detail in a history of laughter which I think of composing. Having discovered its origin, I will trace its history and fortune to the present day, when it is more valued than at any previous time. It occupies among civilized nations a place, and fills an office somewhat similar to the parts formerly played by virtue, justice, honour, and the like, often indeed frightening and deterring men from the committal of evil.

But to return to the birds. From the effect their singing produces in me, I conclude that the sight and recognition of joy in others, of which we are not envious, gratifies and rejoices us. We may therefore be grateful to Nature for having ordained that the songs of birds, which are a demonstration of joy and a species of laughter, should be in public, differing from the private nature of the singing and laughter of men, who represent the rest of the world. And it is wisely decreed that the earth and air should be enlivened by creatures that seem to applaud universal life with the joyful harmony of their sweet voices, and thus incite other living beings to joy, by their continual, though false, testimony to the happiness of things.

It is reasonable that birds should be, and show themselves, more joyful than other creatures. For, as I have said, they are naturally better adapted for joy and happiness. In the first place, apparently, they are not subject to ennui. They change their position momentarily, and pass from country to country, however distant, and from the lowest regions of the air to the highest, quickly and with wonderful ease. Life to them is made up of an infinite variety of sights and experiences. Their bodies are in a continuous state of activity, and they themselves are full of vital power. All other animals, their wants being satisfied, love quietude and laziness; none, except fishes and certain flying insects, keep long in motion simply for amusement. The savage, for instance, except to supply his daily wants, which demand little and brief exertion, or when unable to hunt scarcely stirs a step. He loves idleness and tranquillity above everything, and passes nearly the whole day sitting in silence and indolence within his rude cabin, or at its opening, or in some rocky cave or place of shelter. Birds, on the contrary, very rarely stay long in one place. They fly backwards and forwards without any necessity, simply as a pastime, and often having gone several hundred miles away from the country they usually frequent, they return thither the same evening. And even for the short time they are in one place, their bodies are never still. Ever turning here and there, they are always either flocking together, pecking, or shaking themselves, or hopping about in their extraordinarily vivacious and active manner. In short, from the time a bird bursts its shell until it dies, save intervals of sleep, it is never still for a moment. From these considerations it may reasonably be affirmed that whereas the normal state of animals, including even man, is quietude, that of birds is motion.

We find also that birds are so endowed that their natural qualities harmonize with the exterior qualities and conditions of their life; this again makes them better adapted for happiness than other animals. They have remarkably acute powers of hearing, and a faculty of vision almost inconceivably perfect. Owing to this last they can discern simultaneously a vast extent of country, and are daily charmed by spectacles the most immense and varied. From these things it may be inferred that birds ought to possess an imagination, vivid and powerful in the highest degree. Not the ardent and stormy imagination of Dante or Tasso; for this is a disastrous endowment, and the cause of endless anxieties and sufferings. But a fertile, light, and childish fancy, such as is productive of joyful thoughts, sweet unrealities, and manifold pleasures. This is the noblest gift of Nature to living creatures. And birds have this faculty in a great measure for their own delight and benefit, without experiencing any of its hurtful and painful consequences. For their prolific imagination, as with children, combines, with their bodily vigour, to render them happy and contented, instead of being injurious, and productive of misery, as with most men. Thus, birds may be said to resemble children equally in their vivacity and restlessness, and the other attributes of their nature. If the advantages of childhood were common to other ages, and its evils not exceeded later in life, man might perhaps be better able to bear patiently the burden of existence.

To me it seems that the nature of birds, considered aright, is manifestly more perfect than that of other animals. For, in the first place, birds are superior to other animals in sight and hearing, which are the principal senses of life. In the second place, birds naturally prefer motion to rest, whereas other creatures have the contrary preference. And since activity is a more living thing than repose, birds may be said to have more life than other animals. It follows therefore that birds are physically, and in the exercise of their faculties, superior to other creatures.

Now, if life be better than its contrary, the fuller and more perfect the life, as with birds, the greater is the superiority of creatures possessing it, over less endowed animals.

We must not forget also that birds are adapted to bear great atmospheric changes. Often they rise instantaneously from the ground far up into the air, where the cold is extreme; and others in their travels fly through many different climates.

In short, just as Anacreon wished to be changed into a mirror that he might be continually regarded by the mistress of his heart, or into a robe that he might cover her, or balm to anoint her, or water to wash her, or bands that she might draw him to her bosom, or a pearl to be worn on her neck, or shoes that she might at least press him with her feet; so I should like temporarily to be transformed into a bird, in order to experience their contentment and joyfulness of life.

—*Giacomo Leopardi, Italian (1798–1837), translated by Charles Edwards.*

Self-Reliance

RALPH WALDO EMERSON

I READ the other day some verses written by an eminent painter which were original and not conventional. The soul always hears an admonition in such lines, let the subject be what it may. The sentiment they instil is of more value than any thought they may contain. To believe your own thought, to believe that what is true for you in your private heart is true for all men — that is genius. Speak your latent conviction, and it shall be the universal sense; for the inmost in due time becomes the outmost, and our first thought is rendered back to us by the trumpets of the Last Judgment. Familiar as the voice of the mind is to each, the highest merit we ascribe to Moses, Plato and Milton is that they set at naught books and traditions, and spoke not what men, but what *they* thought. A man should learn to detect and watch that gleam of light which flashes across his mind from within, more than the luster of the firmament of bards and sages. Yet he dismisses without notice his thought, because it is his. In every work of genius we recognize our own rejected thoughts; they come back to us with a certain alienated majesty. Great works of art have no more affecting lesson for us than this. They teach us to abide by our spontaneous impression with good-humored inflexibility then most when the whole cry of voices is on the other side. Else to-morrow a stranger will say with masterly good sense precisely what we have thought and felt all the time, and we shall be forced to take with shame our own opinion from another.

There is a time in every man's education when he arrives at the conviction that envy is ignorance; that imitation is suicide; that he must take himself for better for worse as his portion; that though the wide universe is full of good, no kernel of nourishing corn can come to him but through his toil bestowed on that plot of ground which is given to him to till. The power which resides in him is new in nature, and none but he knows what that is which he can do, nor does he know until he has tried. Not for nothing one face, one character, one fact, makes much impression on him and another none. This sculpture in the memory is not without preestablished harmony. The eye was placed where one ray should fall, that it might testify of that particular ray. We but half express ourselves, and are ashamed of that divine idea which each of us represents. It may be safely trusted as proportionate and of good issues, so it be faithfully imparted, but God will not have his work made manifest by cowards. A man is relieved and gay when he has put his heart into his work and done his best; but what he has said or done otherwise shall give him no peace. It is a deliverance which does not deliver. In the attempt his genius deserts him; no muse befriends; no invention, no hope.

Trust thyself: every heart vibrates to that iron string. Accept the place the divine providence has found for you, the society of your contemporaries, the connection of events. Great men have always done so, and confided themselves childlike to the genius of their age, betraying their perception that the absolutely trustworthy was seated at their heart, working through their hands, predominating in all their being. And we are now men, and must accept in the highest mind the same transcendent destiny; and not minors and invalids in a protected corner, not cowards fleeing before a revolution, but guides, redeemers, and benefactors, obeying the Almighty effort and advancing on Chaos and the Dark.

What pretty oracles nature yields us on this text in the face and behavior of children, babes, and even brutes! That divided and rebel mind, that distrust of a sentiment because our arithmetic has computed the strength and means opposed to our purpose, these have not. Their mind being whole, their eye is as yet unconquered, and when we look in their faces we are disconcerted. Infancy conforms to nobody; all conform to it; so that one babe commonly makes four or five out of the adults who prattle and play to it. So God has armed youth and puberty and manhood no less with its own piquancy and charm, and made it enviable and gracious and its claims not to be put by, if it will stand by itself. Do not think the youth has no force, because he cannot speak to you and me. Hark! in the next room his voice is sufficiently clear and emphatic. It seems he knows how to speak to his contemporaries. Bashful or bold then, he will know how to make us seniors very unnecessary.

The nonchalance of boys who are sure of a dinner, and would disdain as much as a lord to do or say aught to conciliate one, is the healthy attitude of human nature. A boy is in the parlor what the pit is in the playhouse; independent, irresponsible, looking out from his corner on such people and facts as pass by, he tries and sentences them on their merits, in the swift, summary way of boys, as good, bad, interesting, silly, eloquent, troublesome. He cumbers himself never about consequences, about interests; he gives an independent, genuine verdict. You must court him; he does not court you. But the man is as it were clapped into jail by his consciousness. As soon as he has once acted or spoken with *éclat* he is a committed person, watched by the sympathy or the hatred of hundreds, whose affections must now enter into his account. There is no Lethe for this. Ah, that he could pass again into his neutrality! Who can thus avoid all pledges and, having observed, observe again from the same unaffected, unbiased, unbribable, unaffrighted innocence — must always be formidable. He would utter opinions on all passing affairs, which being seen to be not private but necessary, would sink like darts into the ear of men and put them in fear.

These are the voices which we hear in solitude, but they grow faint and inaudible as we enter into the world. Society everywhere is in conspiracy against the manhood of every one of its members. Society is a joint-stock company, in which the members agree, for the better securing of his bread to each shareholder, to surrender the liberty and culture of the eater. The virtue in most request is conformity. Self-reliance is its aversion. It loves not realities and creators, but names and customs.

Whoso would be a man, must be a nonconformist. He who would gather immortal palms must not be hindered by the name of goodness, but must explore if it be goodness. Nothing is at last sacred but the integrity of your own mind. Absolve you to yourself, and you shall have the suffrage of the world. I remember an answer which when quite young I was prompted to make to a valued adviser who was wont to importune me with the dear old doctrines of the church. On my saying, "What have I to do with the sacredness of traditions, if I live wholly from within?" my friend suggested — "But these impulses may be from below, not from above." I replied, "They do not seem to me to be such; but if I am the Devil's child, I will live then from the Devil." No law can be sacred to me but that of my nature. Good and bad are but names very readily transferable to that or this; the only right is what is after my constitution; the only wrong what is against it. A man is to carry himself in the presence of all opposition as if everything were titular and ephemeral but he. I am ashamed to think how easily we capitulate to badges and names, to large societies and dead institutions. Every decent and well-spoken individual affects and sways me more than is right. I ought to go upright and vital, and speak the rude truth in all ways. If malice and vanity wear the coat of philanthropy, shall that pass? If an angry bigot assumes this bountiful cause of Abolition, and comes to me with his last news from Barbadoes, why should I not say to him, "Go love thy infant; love thy woodchopper; be good-natured and modest; have that grace; and never varnish your hard, uncharitable ambition with this incredible tenderness for black folk a thousand miles off. Thy love afar is spite at home." Rough and graceless would be such greeting, but truth is handsomer than the affectation of love. Your goodness must have some edge to it — else it is none. The doctrine of hatred must be preached, as the counteraction of the doctrine of love, when that pules and whines. I shun father and mother and wife and brother when my genius calls me. I would write on the lintels of the doorpost, *Whim*. I hope it is somewhat better than whim at last, but we cannot spend the day in explanation. Expect me not to show cause why I seek or why I exclude company. Then again, do not tell me, as a good man did today, of my obligation to put all poor men in good situations. Are they *my* poor? I tell thee, thou foolish philanthropist, that I grudge the dollar, the dime, the cent I give to such men as do not belong to me and to whom I do not belong. There is a class of persons to whom by all spiritual affinity I am bought and sold; for them I will go to prison if need be; but your miscellaneous popular charities; the education at college of fools; the building of meeting-houses to the vain end to which many now stand; alms to sots, and the thousand-fold Relief Societies; — though I confess with shame I sometimes succumb and give the dollar, it is a wicked dollar, which by and by I shall have the manhood to withhold.

Virtues are, in the popular estimate, rather the exception than the rule. There is the man *and* his virtues. Men do what is called a good action, as some piece of courage or charity, much as they would pay a fine in expiation of daily non-appearance on parade. Their works are done as an apology or extenuation of their living in the world — as invalids and the insane pay a high board. Their virtues are penances. I do not wish to expiate, but to live. My life is for itself and not for a spectacle. I much prefer that it should be of a lower strain, so it be genuine and equal, than that it should be glittering and unsteady. I wish it to be sound and sweet, and not to need diet and bleeding. I ask primary evidence that you are a man, and refuse this appeal from the man to his actions. I know that for myself it makes no difference whether I do or forbear those actions which are reckoned excellent. I cannot consent to pay for a privilege where I have intrinsic right. Few and mean as my gifts may be, I actually am, and do not need for my own assurance or the assurance of my fellows any secondary testimony.

What I must do is all that concerns me, not what the people think. This rule, equally arduous in actual and in intellectual life, may serve for the whole distinction between greatness and meanness. It is the harder because you will always find those who think they know what is your duty better than you know it. It is easy in the world to live after the world's opinion; it is easy in solitude to live after our own; but the great man is he who in the midst of the crowd keeps with perfect sweetness the independence of solitude.

The objection to conforming to usages that have become dead to you is that it scatters your force. It loses your time and blurs the impression of your character. If you maintain a dead church, contribute to a dead Bible-society, vote with a great party either for the government or against it, spread your table like base housekeepers — under all these screens I have difficulty to detect the precise man you are: and of course so much force is withdrawn from all your proper life. But do your work, and I shall know you. Do your work, and you shall reinforce yourself. A man must consider what a blind-man's-buff is this game of conformity. If I know your sect I anticipate your argument. I hear a preacher announce for his text and topic the expediency of one of the institutions of his church. Do I not know beforehand that not possibly can he say a new and spontaneous word? Do I not know that with all this ostentation of examining the grounds of the institution he will do no such thing? Do I not know that he is pledged to himself not to look but at one side, the permitted side, not as a man, but as a parish minister? He is a retained attorney, and these airs of the bench are the emptiest affectation. Well, most men have bound their eyes with one or another handkerchief, and attached themselves to some one of these communities of opinion. This conformity makes them not false in a few particulars, authors of a few lies, but false in all particulars. Their every truth is not quite true. Their two is not the real two, their four not the real four; so that every word they say chagrins us and we know not where to begin to set them right. Meantime Nature is not slow to equip us in the prison-uniform of the party to which we adhere. We come to wear one cut of face and figure, and acquire by degrees the gentlest asinine expression. There is a mortifying experience in particular, which does not fail to wreak itself also in the general history; I mean the "foolish face of praise," the forced smile which we put on in company where we do not feel at ease, in answer to conversation which does not interest us. The muscles, not spontaneously moved but moved by a low usurping wilfulness, grow tight about the outline of the face, with the most disagreeable sensation.

For nonconformity the world whips you with its displeasure. And therefore a man must know how to estimate a sour face. The by-standers look askance on him in the public street or in the friend's parlor. If this aversion had its origin in contempt and resistance like his own, he might well go home with a sad countenance; but the sour faces of the multitude, like their sweet faces, have no deep cause, but are put on and off as the wind blows and a newspaper directs. Yet is the discontent of the multitude more formidable than that of the senate and the college. It is easy enough for a firm man who knows the world to brook the rage of the cultivated classes. Their rage is decorous and prudent, for they are timid, as being very vulnerable themselves. But when to their feminine rage the indignation of the people is added, when the ignorant and the poor are aroused, when the unintelligent brute force that lies at the bottom of society is made to growl and mow, it needs the habit of magnanimity and religion to treat it godlike as a trifle of no concernment.

The other terror that scares us from self-trust is our consistency; a reverence for our past act or word because the eyes of others have no other data for computing our orbit than our past acts, and we are loth to disappoint them.

But why should you keep your head over your shoulder? Why drag about this corpse of your memory, lest you contradict somewhat you have stated in this or that public place? Suppose you should contradict yourself; what then? It seems to be a rule of wisdom never to rely on your memory alone, scarcely even in acts of pure memory, but to bring the past for judgment into the thousand-eyed present, and live ever in a new day. In your metaphysics you have denied personality to the Deity, yet when the devout motions of the soul come, yield to them heart and life, though they should clothe God with shape and color. Leave your theory, as Joseph his coat in the hand of the harlot, and flee.

A foolish consistency is the hobgoblin of little minds, adored by little statesmen and philosophers and divines. With consistency a great soul has simply nothing to do. He may as well concern himself with his shadow on the wall. Speak what you think now in hard words and to-morrow speak what to-morrow thinks in hard words again, though it contradict everything you said to-day.—"Ah, so you shall be sure to be misunderstood."—Is it so bad then to be misunderstood? Pythagoras was misunderstood, and Socrates and Jesus, and Luther, and Copernicus, and Galileo, and Newton, and every pure and wise spirit that ever took flesh. To be great is to be misunderstood. . . .

It is easy to see that a greater self-reliance must work a revolution in all the offices and relations of men; in their religion; in their education; in their pursuits; their modes of living; their association; in their property; in their speculative views.

1. In what prayers do men allow themselves! That which they call a holy office is not so much as brave and manly. Prayer looks abroad and asks for some foreign addition to come through some foreign virtue, and loses itself in endless mazes of natural and supernatural, and mediatorial and miraculous. Prayer that craves a particular commodity, anything less than all good, is vicious. Prayer is the contemplation of the facts of life from the highest point of view. It is the soliloquy of a beholding and jubilant soul. It is the spirit of God pronouncing his works good. But prayer as a means to effect a private end is meanness and theft. It supposes dualism and not unity in nature and consciousness. As soon as the man is at one with God, he will not beg. He will then see prayer in all action. The prayer of the farmer kneeling in his field to weed it, the prayer of the rower kneeling with the stroke of his oar, are true prayers heard throughout nature, though for cheap ends. Caratach, in Fletcher's *Bonduca*, when admonished to inquire the mind of the god Audate, replies—

His hidden meaning lies in our endeavors;
Our valors are our best gods.

Another sort of false prayers are our regrets. Discontent is the want of self-reliance: it is infirmity of will. Regret calamities if you can thereby help the sufferer; if not, attend your own work and already the evil begins to be repaired. Our sympathy is just as base. We come to them who weep foolishly and sit down and cry for company, instead of imparting to them truth and health in rough electric shocks, putting them once more in communication with their own reason. The secret of fortune is joy in our hands. Welcome evermore to gods and men is the self-helping man. For him all doors are flung wide; him all tongues greet, all honors crown, all eyes follow with desire. Our love goes out to him and embraces him because he did not need it. We solicitously and apologetically caress and celebrate him because he held on his way and scorned our disapprobation. The gods love him because men hated him. "To the persevering mortal," said Zoroaster, "the blessed Immortals are swift."

As men's prayers are a disease of the will, so are their creeds a disease of the intellect. They say with those foolish Israelites, "Let not God speak to us, lest we die. Speak thou, speak any man with us, and we will obey." Everywhere I am hindered of meeting God in my brother, because he has shut his own temple doors and recites fables merely of his brother's, or his brother's brother's God. Every new mind is a new classification. If it prove a mind of uncommon activity and power, a Locke, a Lavoisier, a Hutton, a Bentham, a Fourier, it imposes its classification on other men, and lo! a new system! In proportion to the depth of the thought, and so to the number of the objects it touches and brings within reach of the pupil, is his complacency. But chiefly is this apparent in creeds and churches, which are also classifications of some powerful mind acting on the elemental thought of duty and man's relation to the Highest. Such is Calvinism, Quakerism, Swedenborgism. The pupil takes the same delight in subordinating everything to the new terminology as a girl who has just learned botany in seeing a new earth and new seasons thereby. It will happen for a time that the pupil will find his intellectual power has grown by the study of his master's mind. But in all unbalanced minds the classification is idolized, passes for the end and not for a speedily exhaustible means, so that the walls of the system blend to their eye in the remote horizon with the walls of the universe; the luminaries of heaven seem to them hung on the arch their master built. They cannot imagine how you aliens have any right to see — how you can see; "It must be somehow that you stole the light from us." They do not yet perceive that light, unsystematic, indomitable, will break into any cabin, even into theirs. Let them chirp awhile and call it their own. If they are honest and do well, presently their neat new pinfold will be too strait and low, will crack, will lean, will rot and vanish, and the immortal light, all young and joyful, million-orbed, million-colored, will beam over the universe as on the first morning.

2. It is for want of self-culture that the superstition of Traveling, whose idols are Italy, England, Egypt, retains its fascination for all educated Americans. They who made England, Italy, or Greece venerable in the imagination, did so by sticking fast where they are like an axis of the earth. In manly hours we feel that duty is our place. The soul is no traveler; the wise man stays at home, and when his necessities, his duties, on any occasion call him from his house, or into foreign lands, he is at home still and shall make men sensible by the expression of his countenance that he goes, the missionary of wisdom and virtue, and visits cities and men like a sovereign and not like an interloper or a valet.

I have no churlish objection to the circumnavigation of the globe for the purposes of art, of study, and benevolence, so that the man is first domesticated, or does not go abroad with the hope of finding somewhat greater than he knows. He who travels to be amused, or to get somewhat which he does not carry, travels away from himself, and grows old even in youth among old things. In Thebes, in Palmyra, his will and mind have become old and dilapidated as they. He carries ruins to ruins.

Traveling is a fool's paradise. Our first journeys discover to us the indifference of places. At home I dream that at Naples, at Rome, I can be intoxicated with beauty and lose my sadness. I pack my trunk, embrace my friends, embark on the sea and at last wake up in Naples, and there beside me is the stern fact, the sad self, unrelenting, identical, that I fled from. I seek the Vatican and the palaces. I affect to be intoxicated with sights and suggestions, but I am not intoxicated. My giant goes with me wherever I go.

3. But the rage of traveling is a symptom of a deeper unsoundness affecting the whole intellectual action. The intellect is vagabond, and our system of education fosters restlessness. Our minds travel when our bodies are forced to stay at home. We imitate; and what is imitation but the traveling of the mind? Our houses are built with foreign taste; our shelves are garnished with foreign ornaments; our opinions, our tastes, our faculties lean, and follow the Past and the Distant. The soul created the arts wherever they have flourished. It was in his own mind that the artist sought his model. It was an application of his own thought to the thing to be done and the conditions to be observed. And why need we copy the Doric or the Gothic model? Beauty, convenience, grandeur of thought and quaint expression are as near to us as to any, and if the American artist will study with hope and love the precise thing to be done by him, considering the climate, the soil, the length of the day, the wants of the people, the habit and form of the government, he will create a

house in which all these will find themselves fitted, and taste and sentiment will be satisfied also.

Insist on yourself; never imitate. Your own gift you can present every moment with the cumulative force of a whole life's cultivation; but of the adopted talent of another you have only an extemporaneous half-possession. That which each can do best, none but his Maker can teach him. No man yet knows what it is, nor can, till that person has exhibited it. Where is the master who could have taught Shakspeare? Where is the master who could have instructed Franklin, or Washington, or Bacon, or Newton? Every great man is a unique. The Scipionism of Scipio is precisely that part he could not borrow. Shakspeare will never be made by the study of Shakspeare. Do that which is assigned you, and you cannot hope too much or dare too much. There is at this moment for you an utterance brave and grand as that of the colossal chisel of Phidias, or trowel of the Egyptians, or the pen of Moses or Dante, but different from all these. Not possibly will the soul, all rich, all eloquent, with thousand-cloven tongue, deign to repeat itself; but if you can hear what these patriarchs say, surely you can reply to them in the same pitch of voice; for the ear and the tongue are two organs of one nature. Abide in the simple and noble regions of thy life, obey thy heart, and thou shall reproduce the Foreworld again.

4. As our Religion, our Education, our Art look abroad, so does our spirit of society. All men plume themselves on the improvement of society, and no man improves.

Society never advances. It recedes as fast on one side as it gains on the other. It undergoes continual changes; it is barbarous, it is civilized, it is christianized, it is rich, it is scientific; but this change is not amelioration. For everything that is given something is taken. Society acquires new arts and loses old instincts. What a contrast between the well-clad, reading, writing, thinking American, with a watch, a pencil, and a bill of exchange in his pocket, and the naked New Zealander, whose property is a club, a spear, a mat, and an undivided twentieth of a shed to sleep under! But compare the health of the two men and you shall see that the white man has lost his aboriginal strength. If the traveller tell us truly, strike the savage with a broad-axe and in a day or two the flesh shall unite and heal as if you struck the blow into soft pitch, and the same blow shall send the white to his grave.

The civilized man has built a coach, but has lost the use of his feet. He is supported on crutches, but lacks so much support of muscle. He has a fine Geneva watch, but he fails of the skill to tell the hour by the sun. A Greenwich nautical almanac he has, and so being sure of the information when he wants it, the man in the street does not know a star in the sky. The solstice he does not observe; the equinox he knows as little; and the whole bright calendar of the year is without a dial in his mind. His note-books impair his memory; his libraries overload his wit; the insurance-office increases the number of accidents; and it may be a question whether machinery does not encumber; whether we have not lost by refinement some energy, by a Christianity, entrenched in establishments and forms, some vigor of wild virtue. For every Stoic was a Stoic; but in Christendom where is the Christian?

There is no more deviation in the moral standard than in the standard of height or bulk. No greater men are now than ever were. A singular equality may be observed between the great men of the first and of the last ages; nor can all the science, art, religion, and philosophy of the nineteenth century avail to educate greater men than Plutarch's heroes, three or four and twenty centuries ago. Not in time is the race progressive. Phocion, Socrates, Anaxagoras, Diogenes, are great men, but they leave no class. He who is really of their class will not be called by their name, but will be his own man, and in his turn the founder of a sect. The arts and inventions of each period are only its costume and do not invigorate men. The harm of the improved machinery may compensate its good. Hudson and Behring accomplished so much in their fishing-boats as to astonish Parry and Franklin, whose equipment exhausted the resources of science and art. Galileo, with an opera-glass, discovered a more splendid series of celestial phenomena than any one since. Columbus found the New World in an undecked boat. It is curious to see the periodical disuse and perishing of means and machinery which were introduced with loud laudation a few years or centuries before. The great genius returns to essential man. We reckoned the improvements of the art of war among the triumphs of science, and yet Napoleon conquered Europe by the bivouac, which consisted of falling back on naked valor and disencumbering it of all aids. The Emperor held it impossible to make a perfect army, says Las Casas, "without abolishing our arms, magazines, commissaries and carriages, until, in imitation of the Roman custom, the soldier should receive his supply of corn, grind it in his handmill and bake his bread himself."

Society is a wave. The wave moves onward, but the water of which it is composed does not. The same particle does not rise from the valley to the ridge. Its unity is only phenomenal. The persons who make up a nation to-day, next year die, and their experience dies with them.

And so the reliance of Property, including the reliance on governments which protect it, is the want of self-reliance. Men have looked away from themselves and at things so long that they have come to esteem the religious, learned, and civil institutions as guards of property, and they deprecate assaults on these, because they feel them to be assaults on property. They measure their esteem of each other by what each has, and not by what each is. But a cultivated man becomes ashamed of his property, out of new respect for his nature. Especially he hates what he has if he see that it is accidental — came to him by inheritance, or gift, or crime; then he feels that it is not having; it does not belong to him, has no root in him and merely lies there because no revolution or no robber takes it away. But that which a man is, does always by necessity acquire; and what the man acquires, is living property, which does not wait the back of rulers, or mobs, or revolutions, or fire, or storm, or bankruptcies, but perpetually renews itself wherever the man breathes. "Thy lot or portion of life," said the Caliph Ali, "is seeking after thee; therefore be at rest from seeking after it." Our dependence on these foreign goods leads us to our slavish respect for numbers. The political parties meet in numerous conventions; the greater the concourse and with each new uproar of announcement, The delegation from Essex! The Democrats from New Hampshire! The Whigs of Maine! the young patriot feels himself stronger than before by a new thousand of eyes and arms. In like manner the reformers summon conventions and vote and resolve in multitude. Not so O friends! will the God deign to enter and inhabit you, but by a method precisely the reverse. It is only as a man puts off all foreign support and stands alone that I see him to be strong and to prevail. He is weaker by every recruit to his banner. Is not a man better than a town? Ask nothing of men, and, in the endless mutation, thou only firm column must presently appear the upholder of all that surrounds thee. He who knows that power is inborn, that he is weak because he has looked for good out of him and elsewhere, and, so perceiving, throws himself unhesitatingly on his thought, instantly rights himself, stands in the erect position, commands his limbs, works miracles; just as a man who stands on his feet is stronger than a man who stands on his head.

So use all that is called Fortune. Most men gamble with her, and gain all, and lose all, as her wheel rolls. But do thou leave as unlawful these winnings, and deal with Cause and Effect, the chancellors of God. In the Will work and acquire, and thou hast chained the wheel of Chance, and shalt sit hereafter out of fear from her rotations. A political victory, a rise of rents, the recovery of your sick or the return of your absent friend, or some other favorable event raises your spirits, and you think good days are preparing for you. Do not believe it. Nothing can bring you peace but yourself. Nothing can bring you peace but the triumph of principles.

—*By Ralph Waldo Emerson, American (1803–1882).*

Labour

THOMAS CARLYLE

There is a perennial nobleness, and even sacredness, in work. Were he never so benighted, forgetful of his high calling, there is always hope in a man that actually and earnestly works: in Idleness alone is there perpetual despair. Work, never so Mammonish, mean, *is* in communication with Nature; the real desire to get Work done will itself lead one more and more to truth, to Nature's appointments and regulations, which are truth.

The latest Gospel in this world is, "Know thy work and do it." "Know thyself": long enough has that poor "self" of thine tormented thee; thou wilt never get to "know" it, I believe! Think it not thy business, this of knowing thyself; thou art an unknowable individual: know what thou canst work at; and work at it, like a Hercules! That will be thy better plan.

It has been written, "an endless significance lies in Work"; a man perfects himself by working. Foul jungles are cleared away, fair seedfields rise instead, and stately cities; and withal the man himself first ceases to be a jungle and foul unwholesome desert thereby. Consider how, even in the meanest sorts of Labour, the whole soul of a man is composed into a kind of real harmony, the instant he sets himself to work! Doubt, Desire, Sorrow, Remorse, Indignation, Despair itself, all these like hell-dogs lie beleaguering the soul of the poor day-worker, as of every man; but he bends himself with free valour against his task, and all these are stilled, all these shrink murmuring far off into their caves. The man is now a man. The blessed glow of Labour in him, is it not as purifying fire, wherein all poison is burnt up, and of sour smoke itself there is made bright blessed flame!

Destiny, on the whole, has no other way of cultivating us. A formless Chaos, once set it *revolving*, grows round and ever rounder; ranges itself, by mere force of gravity, into strata, spherical courses; is no longer a Chaos, but a round compacted World. What would become of the Earth, did she cease to revolve? In the poor old Earth, so long as she revolves, all inequalities, irregularities disperse themselves; all irregularities are incessantly becoming regular. Hast thou looked on the Potter's wheel – one of the venerablest objects; old as the Prophet Ezekiel and far older? Rude lumps of clay, how they spin themselves up, by mere quick whirling, into beautiful circular dishes. And fancy the most assiduous Potter, but without his wheel; reduced to make dishes or rather amorphous botches, by mere kneading and baking! Even such a Potter were Destiny, with a human soul that would rest and lie at ease, that would not work and spin! Of an idle unrevolving man the kindest Destiny, like the most assiduous Potter without wheel, can bake and knead nothing other than a botch: let her spend on him what expensive colouring, what gilding and enamelling she will, he is but a botch. Not a dish; no, a bulging, kneaded, crooked, shambling, squint-cornered, amorphous botch – a mere enamelled vessel of dishonour! Let the idle think of this.

Blessed is he who has found his work; let him ask no other blessedness. He has a work, a life-purpose; he has found it, and will follow it! How, as a free-flowing channel, dug and torn by noble force through the sour mud-swamp of one's existence, like an ever-deepening river there, it runs and flows; – draining off the sour festering water, gradually from the root of the remotest grass-blade; making, instead of pestilential swamp, a green fruitful meadow with its clear-flowing stream. How blessed for the meadow itself, let the stream and *its* value be great or small! Labour is Life: from the inmost heart of the Worker rises his god-given Force, the sacred celestial Life-essence breathed into him by Almighty God; from his inmost heart awakens him to all nobleness – to all knowledge, "self-knowledge" and much else, so soon as Work fitly begins. Knowledge? The knowledge that will hold good in working, cleave thou to that; for Nature herself accredits that, says "Yea" to that. Properly thou hast no other knowledge but what thou hast got by working: the rest is yet all a hypothesis of knowledge; a thing to be argued of in schools, a thing floating in the clouds, in endless logic-vortices, till we try it and fix it. "Doubt, of whatever kind, can be ended by Action alone."

And again, hast thou valued Patience, Courage, Perseverance, Openness to light; readiness to own thyself mistaken, to do better next time? All these, all virtues, in wrestling with the dim brute Powers of Fact, in ordering of thy fellows in such wrestle, there and elsewhere not at all, thou wilt continually learn. Set down a brave Sir Christopher in the middle of black ruined Stone-heaps, of foolish unarchitectural Bishops, red-tape Officials, idle Nell Gwyn Defenders of the Faith; and see whether he will ever raise a Paul's Cathedral out of all that, yea or no! Rough, rude, contradictory are all things and persons, from the mutinous masons and Irish hodmen, up to the idle Nell Gwyn Defenders, to blustering red-tape Officials, foolish unarchitectural Bishops. All these things and persons are there not for Christopher's sake and his Cathedral's; they are there for their own sake mainly! Christopher will have to conquer and constrain all these – if he be able. All these are against him. Equitable Nature herself, who carries her mathematics and architectonics not on the face of her, but deep in the hidden heart of her – Nature herself is but partially for him; will be wholly against him, if he constrain her not! His very money, where is it to come from? The pious munificence of England lies far-scattered, distant, unable to speak and say, "I am here"; – must be spoken to before it can speak. Pious munificence, and all help, is so silent, invisible, like the gods; impediment, contradictions manifold are so loud and near! O brave Sir Christopher, trust thou in those notwithstanding, and front all these; understand all these; by valiant patience, noble effort, insight, by man's-strength, vanquish and compel all these – and, on the whole, strike down victoriously the last top-stone of that Paul's Edifice; thy monument for certain centuries, the stamp "Great Man" impressed very legibly on Portland-stone there!

Yes, all manner of help, and pious response from Men or Nature, is always what we call silent; cannot speak or come to light, till it be seen, till it be spoken to. Every noble work is at first "impossible." In very truth, for every noble work the possibilities will lie diffused through Immensity; inarticulate, undiscoverable except to faith. Like Gideon thou shalt spread out thy fleece at the door of thy tent; see whether under the wide arch of Heaven there be any bounteous moisture, or none. Thy heart and life-purpose shall be as a miraculous Gideon's fleece, spread out in silent appeal to Heaven: and from the kind Immensities, what from the poor unkind Localities and town and country Parishes there never could, blessed dew-moisture to suffice thee shall have fallen!

Work is of a religious nature: – work is of a *brave* nature; which it is the aim of all religion to be. All work of man is as the swimmer's: a waste ocean threatens to devour him; if he front it not bravely, it will keep its word. By incessant wise defiance of it, lusty rebuke and buffet of it, behold how it loyally supports him, bears him as its conqueror along. "It is so," says Goethe, "with all things that man undertakes in this world."

Brave Sea-captain, Norse Sea-king – Columbus, my hero, royalest Sea-king of all! it is no friendly environment this of thine, in the waste deep waters; around thee mutinous discouraged souls, behind thee disgrace and ruin, before thee the unpenetrated veil of Night. Brother, these wild water-mountains, bounding from their deep bases (ten miles deep, I am told) are not entirely there on thy behalf! Meseems *they* have other work than floating thee forward: – and the huge Winds, that sweep from Ursa Major to the Tropics and Equators, dancing their giant-waltz through the kingdoms of Chaos and Immensity, they care little about filling rightly or filling wrongly the small shoulder-of-mutton sails in this cockle-skiff of thine! Thou art not among articulate-speaking friends, my brother; thou art among immeasurable dumb monsters, tumbling, howling wide as the world here. Secret, far off, invisible to all hearts but thine, there lies a help in them: see how thou wilt get at that. Patiently thou wilt wait till the mad Southwester spend itself, saving thyself by dextrous science of defence, the while: valiantly, with swift decision, wilt thou strike in, when the favouring East, the Possible, springs up. Mutiny of men thou wilt sternly repress; weakness, despondency, thou wilt cheerily encourage: thou wilt swallow down complaint, unreason, weariness, weakness of others and thyself; – how much wilt thou swallow down! There shall be a depth of Silence in thee, deeper than this Sea, which is but ten miles deep: a Silence unsoundable; known to God only. Thou shalt be a Great Man. Yes, my World-Soldier, thou of the World Marine-service – thou wilt have to be *greater* than this tumultuous unmeasured World here round thee is; thou, in thy strong soul, as with wrestler's arms, shalt embrace it, harness it down; and make it bear thee on – to new Americas, or whither God wills!

– From Past and Present, by Thomas Carlyle, English (1795–1881).

~ ✿ ~

A Talk Among Leisured People

LEO TOLSTOY

SOME guests assembled at a wealthy house one day happened to start a serious conversation about life.

They spoke of people present and absent,

but failed to find anyone who was satisfied with his life.

Not only could no one boast of happiness, but not a single person considered that he was living as a Christian should do. All confessed that they were living worldly lives concerned only for themselves and their families, none of them thinking of their neighbours, still less of God.

So said all the guests, and all agreed in blaming themselves for living godless and unchristian lives.

"Then why do we live so?" exclaimed a youth. "Why do we do what we ourselves disapprove of? Have we no power to change our way of life? We ourselves admit that we are ruined by our luxury, our effeminacy, our riches, and above all by our pride—our separation from our fellow-men. To be noble and rich we have to deprive ourselves of all that gives man joy. We crowd into towns, become effeminate, ruin our health, and in spite of all our amusements we die of ennui, and of regrets that our life is not what it should be.

"Why do we live so? Why do we spoil our lives and all the good that God gives us? I don't want to live in that old way! I will abandon the studies I have begun—they would only bring me to the same tormenting life of which we are all now complaining. I will renounce my property and go to the country and live among the poor. I will work with them, will learn to labour with my hands, and if my education is of any use to the poor I will share it with them, not through institutions and books but directly by living with them in a brotherly way.

"Yes, I have made up my mind," he added, looking inquiringly at his father, who was also present.

"Your wish is a worthy one," said his father, "but thoughtless and ill-considered. It seems so easy to you only because you do not know life. There are many things that seem to us good, but the execution of what is good is complicated and difficult. It is hard enough to walk well on a beaten track, but it is harder still to lay out a new one. New paths are made only by men who are thoroughly mature and have mastered all that is attainable by man. It seems to you easy to make new paths of life only because you do not yet understand life. It is an outcome of thoughtlessness and youthful pride. We old folk are needed to moderate your impulsiveness and guide you by our experience, and you young folk should obey us in order to profit by that experience. Your active life lies before you. You are now growing up and developing. Finish your education, make yourself thoroughly conversant with things, get on to your own feet, have firm convictions of your own, and then start a new life if you feel you have strength to do so. But for the present you should obey those who are guiding you for your own good, and not try to open up new paths of life."

The youth was silent and the older guests agreed with what the father had said.

"You are right," said a middle-aged married man, turning to the youth's father. "It is true that the lad, lacking experience of life, may blunder when seeking new paths of life and his decision cannot be a firm one. But you know we all agreed that our life is contrary to our conscience and does not give us happiness. So we cannot but recognize the justice of wishing to escape from it.

"The lad may mistake his fancy for a reasonable deduction, but I, who am no longer young, tell you for myself that as I listened to the talk this evening the same thought occurred to me. It is plain to me that the life I now live cannot give me peace of mind or happiness. Experience and reason alike show me that. Then what am I waiting for? We struggle from morning to night for our families, but it turns out that we and our families live ungodly lives and get more and more sunk in sins. We work for our families, but our families are no better off, because we are not doing the right thing for them. And so I often think that it would be better if I changed my whole way of life and did just what that young man proposed to do: ceased to bother about my wife and children and began to think about my soul. Not for nothing did Paul say: 'He that is married careth how he may please his wife, but he that is unmarried careth how he may please the Lord.'"

But before he had finished speaking his wife and all the women present began to attack him.

"You ought to have thought of that before," said an elderly woman. "You have put on the yoke, so you must draw your load. Like that, everyone will say he wishes to go off and save his soul when it seems hard to him to support and feed his family. That is false and cowardly. No! A man should be able to live in godly fashion with his family. Of course it would be easy enough to save your own soul all by yourself. But to behave like that would be to run contrary to Christ's teaching. God bade us love others; but in that way you would in His name offend others. No. A married man has his definite obligations and he must not shirk them. It's different when your family are already on their own feet. Then you may do as you please for yourself, but no one has a right to force his family."

But the man who had spoken did not agree. "I don't want to abandon my family," he said. "All I say is that my family should not be brought up in a worldly fashion, nor brought up to live for their own pleasure, as we have just been saying, but should be brought up from their early days to become accustomed to privation, to labour, to the service of others, and above all to live a brotherly life with all men. And for that we must relinquish our riches and distinctions."

"There is no need to upset others while you yourself do not live a godly life," exclaimed his wife irritably. "You yourself lived for your own pleasure when you were young, then why do you want to torment your children and your family? Let them grow up quietly, and later on let them do as they please without coercion from you!"

Her husband was silent, but an elderly man who was there spoke up for him.

"Let us admit," said he, "that a married man, having accustomed his family to a certain comfort, cannot suddenly deprive them of it. It is true that if you have begun to educate your children it is better to finish it than to break up everything – especially as the children when grown up will choose the path they consider best for themselves. I agree that for a family man it is difficult and even impossible to change his way of life without sinning. But for us old men it is what God commands. Let me say for myself: I am now living without any obligations, and to tell the truth, simply for my belly. I eat, drink, rest, and am disgusting and revolting even to myself. So it is time for me to give up such a life, to give away my property, and at least before I die to live for a while as God bids a Christian live."

But the others did not agree with the old man. His niece and godchild was present, to all of whose children he had stood sponsor and gave presents on holidays. His son was also there. They both protested.

"No," said the son. "You worked in your time, and it is time for you to rest and not trouble yourself. You have lived for sixty years with certain habits and must not change them now. You would only torment yourself in vain."

"Yes, yes," confirmed his niece. "You would be in want and out of sorts, and would grumble and sin more than ever. God is merciful and will forgive all sinners – to say nothing of such a kind old uncle as you!"

"Yes, and why should you?" added another old man of the same age. "You and I have perhaps only a couple of days to live, so why should we start new ways?"

"What a strange thing!" exclaimed one of the visitors who had hitherto been silent. "What a strange thing! We all say that it would be good to live as God bids us and that we are living badly and suffer in body and soul, but as soon as it comes to practice it turns out that the children must not be upset and must be brought up not in godly fashion but in the old way. Young folk must not run counter to their parents' will and must live not in a godly fashion but in the old way. A married man must not upset his wife and children and must live not in a godly way but as of old. And there is no need for old men to begin anything: they are not accustomed to it and have only a couple of days left to live. So it seems that none of us may live rightly: we may only talk about it."

— *Leo Tolstoy, Russian (1828–1910), translated by Aylmer Maude.*

PART NINETEEN

Wit and Epigram

MAN'S WIT when contained in the poetic atom beyond which lies no further reduction is called the epigram. Such a poem is, in a word, simply the briefest poem. It is true that mere brevity by no means obviously implies the existence of a literary genre, since all manner of styles and themes lend themselves to terseness. But in brevity itself lies a psychological factor more significant than any merely convenient classifications. All true poetry seeks succinctness and shuns diffusiveness, even though in some forms this preference becomes more apparent than in others. The brief poem itself is, therefore, of aesthetic and psychological importance in being the least unit or cell from which all more extensive poems must be constructed. It is an ideal germ of thought fashioned into an ideal sentence. In unique perfection such a work resembles an individual leaf or blade of grass. The Greek epigrammatist, Meleager, who made one of the earliest collections of such material, found, however, the inevitable image. To him the briefest poems seemed minute flowers, each with a light and fragrance of its own.

The brevity of such works springs from a variety of causes. Wit, for example, aims at quick utterance, hard substance and sharpness of point; a keen epigram will outlast a dull epic. Verse used for inscriptions is strictly confined to the limits of the actual space to be inscribed. An illumination may come to a poet in lightning-like manner and admit no more room for elaboration than the moment of its inception. The most succinct expression may seem the most vigorous, especially if an artist may feel that a little speech surrounded by a sphere of silence will fall most deeply upon the soul. Human tragedy has its brevities no less than the human comedy. Finally, a poet may believe that to say little but hint much best conveys the essence of his thought. He relies upon the sensibilities of his reader to fill in with colors drawn from his own heart the mere outline which the words afford.

All these points of view are widely familiar throughout the literary world, but the last has its chief home in the Far East. Since the dawn of Japanese poetry, at least as early as the eighth century of our own era, the prevailing form has been a brief epigram rigidly prescribed even in the number of its syllables. The haiku consists of three lines of five, seven and five syllables respectively. No literary tradition has ever been more austere. The Japanese poems are sometimes descriptions of nature, or sometimes minute scenes of vivid social drama. The utmost intensity of feeling is conveyed in archly drawn miniatures. They originally lent themselves to both singing and inscription; and they were frequently written on paintings to form an harmonious conjunction of the two arts.

Although the Chinese poets were, as a whole, less strict and mechanical than the Japanese in their observance of genre and convention, they, too, possessed theories of prosody and a comparable addiction to brevity. Indeed in all its forms the Japanese was merely a local refinement upon earlier Chinese inventions. The two literatures together provided Western men of letters at the beginning of the present century with a new and exciting corpus of epigrammatic verse from which to seek suggestion and inspiration. Accordingly, the history of the verse epigram as here exhibited runs to some extent a circular course. The oldest are those of the Orient. And the discovery of such poems by the Western World stimulated notable developments in the brief poem, especially in America and in the present century.

Yet we must avoid undue emphasis upon Oriental influences. While the recent popularity of Japanese and Chinese verse in translation, and the knowledge acquired chiefly in the previous century of the epigrammatic poetry of Persia and Arabia, have unquestionably influenced our poets, hardly any culture has been without demand for an art of the brief poem, and most have left memorable specimens to posterity. No poetic tradition has had more enduring vitality than that of the Greek Anthology, which enjoyed a vital existence from the seventh century B.C. to the eighth century A.D., and moreover never has been entirely forgotten by civilized Europe. The collection contains some ten thousand poems. With this body of verse in mind, any serious study of the history and development of the brief poem in Europe must begin.

The poems of this ancient anthology fall into several distinct categories. Many of the most famous are epitaphs to the dead, and a large proportion of the epitaphs read today originated not in books but shone on snow-white pentelic marble. No wonder, then, that the words are chiseled to the finest and most durable edge. A number of epitaphs may even be found for other than human beings, as one given here in memory of a valiant hunting dog. Implements and tools of common use, as mirrors, spears, oars, and ships, receive their brief memorials. Inscriptions are composed for all sorts of monuments and markers, notably at springs, groves and playing-fields. But these inscriptions comprise only a small proportion of the anthology. Some epigrams are philosophic maxims, others, like two here given in the sprightly versions of Humbert Wolfe, are barbed with satire. As the Japanese delight to paint and describe the smallest objects in nature, so insects and small birds attract the Greek poets in their lighter moods and assume their perfect place in the light verses. While graver authors, as Aeschylus and Plato, seem to encompass a whole world in a sublime quatrain, the Anacreontic poets reduce a world to a trinket. There is an exquisite epigram on a jewel, here given in the skillful translation of Thomas Stanley. Whatever the mood or theme, the gem-like Greek art is always masterly in its sharpness of line. Simonides, chief of the epigrammatists, best sums up their ideal:

> No breath of wind rose then
> To stir the leaves of the trees,
> Nor any quivering breeze
> To stay the sweet note of his song
> From travelling straight along
> To be fixed to the ears of men.

The Greek anthology is indeed fixed in the ears of men – as long as they have ears to hear. Always in some measure beloved, it was the most assiduously imitated during the neo-classical period, in England extending from the age of Elizabeth to that of Byron. Ben Jonson's most famous song, "Drink to me only with thine eyes," is, for instance, pieced together from the anthology, as the poem here given from Agathias Scholasticus reminds us. Byron especially valued and frequently imitated the great Palatine Anthology, as first made really popular in England by Robert Bland in 1805. As specimens given here exhibit, however, the anthology was well known and diligently followed by Robert Herrick, Alexander Pope and many others. Nor has its value to inspire original poetry in both England and America disappeared with the neo-classical spirit. Verse by Shelley, Landor and A. E. Housman attests its value in England, while the American poet E. A. Robinson gracefully translated and imitated its pages.

Space admits the citation here of only a few miscellaneous short poems from more recent continental literature. But some indication is given that a subtle art in brevity of utterance has never wholly deserted the Western World, from the Medieval period to our own times. Among the most artful short poems written in Europe during the last century are the briefest lyrics of Heine and Verlaine, both poets deriving much of their inspiration from popular, indigenous traditions extant for at least six centuries. The briefest poems by Goethe rank among the most prized possessions in all German literature.

In the United States an oriental influence made itself strongly felt as early as the noble epigrams of Emerson. The great transcendentalist responded most warmly to the philosophical epigrams of the Near East, especially those of Sa'di. At the beginning of the twentieth century a group of poets calling themselves "Imagists" responded chiefly to the aesthetic spell of the Japanese and Chinese short lyrics. The verse of Amy Lowell, Ezra Pound, John Gould Fletcher and Witter Bynner consciously emulating the oriental style – like the imitation of the Greek Anthology by "H. D." (Hilda Doolittle) – is of less lasting importance than the reflection of this fruitful vogue upon still more eminent and more indigenous writers. In such felicitous trifles as "Fog," Carl Sandburg has delighted countless readers with an art only indirectly inspired by the oriental vogue. Many years earlier Whitman and Emily Dickinson had composed short poems of extraordinary excellence in complete innocence of either the Greeks or the Orientals. The few extremely brief and recently written pieces by Robert Frost, unmannered, underivative, and unpedantic, witness that a major poet may still instinctively turn to a succinctness and brevity admired by discriminating lovers of poetry in all countries and in all times. Thus an American anthology is yearly amassed like a silent growth from coral shells, well worthy of its place beside the jewelled workmanship of older lands.

On a Quiet Night

I saw the moonlight before my couch,
And wondered if it were not the frost on the ground.
I raised my head and looked out on the mountain moon;
I bowed my head and thought of my far-off home.

—*From the Chinese of Li Po (701–762), translated by Shigeyoshi Obata.*

Burial Song

How swiftly it dries,
The dew on the garlic-leaf.
The dew that dries so fast
To-morrow will fall again.
But he whom we carry to the grave
Will never more return.

—*From the Chinese, anon., translated by Arthur Waley.*

Lao-Tzu

"Those who speak know nothing;
Those who know are silent."
These words, as I am told,
Were spoken by Lao-tzu.
If we are to believe that Lao-tzu
Was himself *one who knew,*
How comes it that he wrote a book
Of five thousand words?

—*From the Chinese of Po Chü-i (772–846 A.D.), translated by Arthur Waley.*

Five Japanese Haiku

THE AFTERGLOW

The summer grasses grow.
Of mighty warriors' splendid dreams
The afterglow.

—*Matsuo Basho (1644–1694).*

DUSK

A village where they ring
No bells! — Oh, what *do* they do
At dusk in spring?

—*ibid.*

WINTER

Mountains and plains,
All are taken by the snow —
Nothing remains!

—*Joso.*

QUIET

Come, and pass, and go:
One umbrella — only one — ;
Evening, and the snow.

—*Yaha.*

LONELINESS

No sky at all;
No earth at all; — And still
The snowflakes fall. . . .

—*Hanshin.*
Translations by Harold Gould Henderson.

Alas!

She, who could neither rest nor sleep
Ere round her she had scattered hyacinths and roses,
Now with the roses of her face death-strewn reposes,
And o'er her tomb wild brambles creep.

—*From the Persian of Sa'di (d. 1291), translated by L. Cranmer-Byng.*

Sparta

Spear-points of young men blossom there:
Clear-voiced the Muse's songs arise:
Justice is done in open air,
The help of gallant enterprise.

—*From the Greek of Terpander (fl. 676 B.C.), translated by C. M. Bowra.*

Evening

Thou, Hesper, bringest homeward all
That radiant dawn sped far and wide,
The sheep to fold, the goat to stall,
The children to their mother's side.

—*From the Greek of Sappho (fl. 600? B.C.), translated by Sir Rennell Rodd.*

A Small City on a Rock

This also said Phocylides:
 A tiny rock-built citadel
Is finer far, if ordered well,
 Than all your frantic Ninevehs.

—*From the Greek of Phocylides (fl. 544 B.C.), translated by C. M. Bowra.*

Lais' Mirror

Venus, take my votive glass:
 Since I am not what I was,
What from this day I shall be,
 Venus, let me never see.

—*From the Greek of Plato (429–347 B.C.), translated by Matthew Prior.*

On a Seal

Five oxen, grazing in a flowery mead,
A jasper seal, done to the life, doth hold;
The little herd away long since had fled,
Were't not enclos'd within a pale of gold.

—*From the Greek of Plato, translated by Thomas Stanley.*

A Swallow

Attic maid! with honey fed,
 Bear'st thou to thy callow brood
Yonder locust from the mead,
 Destined their delicious food?

Ye have kindred voices clear,
 Ye alike unfold the wing,
Migrate hither, sojourn here,
 Both attendant on the spring.

Ah! for pity drop the prize;
 Let it not with truth be said,
That a songster gasps and dies,
 That a songster may be fed.

—*From the Greek of Evenus (1st Cent. B.C.?), translated by William Cowper.*

Passing Away

The world is fleeting; all things pass away;
Or is it we that pass and they that stay?

—*From the Greek of Lucian (120–200 A.D.), translated by Walter Leaf.*

Reading Hesiod

I on Hesiod idly browsing,
 when I saw where Pyrrha trod,
 dumped the volume with a rousing
 "So much for old Hesiod!"

—*From the Greek of Marcus Argentarius (fl. 60? A.D.), translated by Humbert Wolfe.*

Leave a Kiss Within the Cup

I love not wine; yet if thou'ldst make
 A sad man merry, sip first sup,
 And when thou giv'st I'll take the cup:
If thy lip touch it, for thy sake
 No more may I be stiff and staid
 And the luscious jug evade:
The cup convoys thy kiss to me,
And tells the joy it had of thee.

—*From the Greek of Agathias Scholasticus (c. 536–582 A.D.), translated by J. M. Edmonds.*

At Thermopylæ

Tell them in Lakedaimon, passer-by,
That here obedient to their word we lie.

—*From the Greek of Simonides (556–467 B.C.), translated by various hands.*

The Athenian Dead

On Dirphys' wrinkled slope we fell;
 And here beside Euripus' drift
Our countrymen, to mark us well,
 Raised up this cairn, their gift.

A gift deserved; for youth is sweet,
 And youth we gave, nor turned away,
Though sharp the storm of battle beat
 That darkened all our day.

—*From the Greek of Simonides, translated by T. F. Higham.*

Lost at Sea

A strange land holds thy bones; the Euxine sea
Has brought thee, roving Cleisthenes, thy doom.
No honey-sweet returning was for thee,
Nor sight of thy sea-girdled Chian home.

—*From the Greek of Simonides, translated by Walter Leaf.*

~ ❁ ~

A Hound

Although beneath this grave-mound thy white bones now are lying,
Surely, my huntress Lycas, the wild things dread thee still.
The memory of thy worth tall Pelion keeps undying,
And the looming peak of Ossa, and Cithæron's lonely hill.

—*From the Greek of Simonides, translated by F. L. Lucus.*

~ ❁ ~

Star

Thou wert the morning-star among the living,
Ere thy fair light had fled;
Now, having died, thou art as Hesperus, giving
New splendour to the dead.

—*From the Greek of Plato (429–327 B.C.), translated by P. B. Shelley.*

~ ❁ ~

Heraclitus

They told me, Heraclitus, they told me you were dead;
They brought me bitter news to hear and bitter tears to shed.
I wept, as I remember'd, how often you and I
Had tired the sun with talking and sent him down the sky.

And now that thou art lying, my dear old Carian guest,
A handful of grey ashes, long, long ago at rest,
Still are thy pleasant voices, thy nightingales, awake,
For Death, he taketh all away, but them he cannot take.

—*From the Greek of Callimachus (310–c.240 B.C.), translated by William Cory.*

~ ❁ ~

Pass On

Tomb of a shipwrecked mariner am I,
But sail thou on, and never stay for me;
Yea, for when death to us was drawing nigh
The other ships were sailing on the sea.

—*From the Greek of Theodorides (fl. 240 B.C.), translated by W. H. D. Rouse.*

~ ❁ ~

A Dead Song-Writer

Eutychides is dead, and what is worse
(fly wretched shades!) he's coming with his verse.
And listen! they have burned upon his pyre
two tons of music, and a ton of lyre.
You're caught, poor ghosts. But what I want to know
is where in Hell, now he's in hell, to go.

—*From the Greek of Lucilius (fl. A.D. 60), translated by Humbert Wolfe.*

~ ❁ ~

A Bride

Bridegroom none but death alone
Has my Clearista won,
So to loose her virgin zone.

Yester eve the flutes blew sweet,
Bridegroom and the bride to greet,
And the bridal doors were beat.

Now at dawn they sound again,
But another sadder strain,
Hymen's song is hushed in pain;

And the torch that flared so gay,
Lighting up her bride's array,
Lit the dead her downward way.

—*From the Greek of Meleager (fl. 90 B.C.), translated by H. C. Beeching.*

~ ❁ ~

Persian Fopperies

Boy, I hate their empty shows,
  Persian garlands I detest,
Bring not me the late-blown rose
  Lingering after all the rest:

Plainer myrtle pleases me
  Thus outstretched beneath my vine,
Myrtle more becoming thee,
  Waiting with thy master's wine.

—*From the Latin of Horace (65–8 B.C.), translated by William Cowper.*

Bought Locks

The golden hair that Gulla wears
  Is hers: who would have thought it?
She swears 'tis hers, and true she swears,
  For I know where she bought it.

—*From the Latin of Martial (40–104), translated by Sir John Harington.*

On the Soul

Ah! gentle, fleeting, wavering sprite,
Friend and associate of this clay!
  To what unknown region borne,
Wilt thou now wing thy distant flight?
No more with wonted humor gay,
  But pallid, cheerless, and forlorn.

—*From the Latin of the Emperor Hadrian (76–138), translated by Lord Byron.*

To Anne

When thou art near to me, it seems
  As if the sun along the sky,
Though he awhile withheld his beams,
  Burst forth in glowing majesty:

But like a storm that lowers on high,
  Thy absence clouds the scene again;—
Alas! that from so sweet a joy
  Should spring regret so full of pain!

—*From the French of Clément Marot (1505–1544), translated by Louisa S. Costello.*

At My Father's Grave

Peace now and ever on this gravestone be,
The gentle peace of God! Ah yes, but they
Have laid a fine good man away;
And more than that to me

This man showered blessings on his son,
Like some kind star from out a better sphere.
And I can never pay him here
For all that he has done.

He fell asleep. They laid him with the stones.
May God console him with his soft sweet
  care,
And of eternal life may some faint air
Stir lightly in his bones,

Till great and glorious Jesus Christ, till He
Waken him like a friend. Ah yes, but they
Have laid a fine good man away;
And more than that to me.

—*From the German of Matthais Claudius (1740–1815), translated by Ralph Marcus.*

Wanderer's Night-Songs

I

Thou that from the heavens art,
Every pain and sorrow stillest,
And the doubly wretched heart
Doubly with refreshment fillest,

I am weary with contending!
Why this rapture and unrest?
Peace descending
Come, ah, come into my breast!

II

O'er all the hill-tops
Is quiet now,
In all the tree-tops
Hearest thou
Hardly a breath;
The birds are asleep in the trees:
Wait; soon like these
Thou too shalt rest.

—*From the German of Johann Wolfgang von Goethe (1749–1832), by H. W. Longfellow.*

With Inky Sails

With inky sails my pinnace drives
  Across the stormy sea;
You know how wretched I am, and yet
  So cruelly torture me.

Your heart is faithless as the wind,
  As fickle as heart may be;
With inky sails my pinnace drives
  Across the stormy sea.

— From the German of Heinrich Heine (1797–1856), translated by Sir Theodore Martin.

Song of Autumn

When a sighing begins
In the violins
Of the autumn-song,

My heart is drowned
In the slow sound
Languorous and long.

Pale as with pain,
Breath fails me when
The hour tolls deep.
My thoughts recover
The days that are over,
And I weep.

And I go
Where the winds know,
Broken and brief,
To and fro,
As the winds blow
A dead leaf.

— From the French of Paul Verlaine (1844–1896), translated by Arthur Symons.

Earth to Earth

Earth took from earth earth with woe;
Earth upon earth toward earth did go;
Earth laid earth with earthen throw;
Then earth had of earth earth enou'.

— Anon., English (c. 1250).

Even Such Is Time

Even such is Time that takes in trust
Our youth, our joys, our all we have,
And pays us but with earth and dust;
Who in the dark and silent grave,
When we have wandered all our ways,
Shuts up the story of our days;
But from this earth, this grave, this dust,
My God shall raise me up, I trust.

— Sir Walter Raleigh, English (1552–1618).

Sealed in Vain

Take, O take those lips away,
  That so sweetly were forsworn;
And those eyes, the break of day,
  Lights that do mislead the morn:
But my kisses bring again,
                Bring again;
Seals of love, but sealed in vain,
                Sealed in vain.

— William Shakespeare, English (1564–1616).

On the Countess of Pembroke

Underneath this sable hearse
Lies the subject of all verse:
Sidney's sister, Pembroke's mother:
Death, ere thou hast slain another
Fair, and learned, and good as she,
Time shall throw a dart at thee.

Marble piles let no man raise
To her name: in after days,
Some kind woman, born as she,
Reading this, like Niobe
Shall turn marble, and become
Both her mourner and her tomb.

— Ben Jonson, English (1573–1637), and William Browne, English (1591–1643).

On My First Son

Farewell, thou child of my right hand, and joy;
My sin was too much hope of thee, loved boy.
Seven years thou wert lent to me, and I thee pay,
Exacted by thy fate, on the just day.
O, could I lose all father now! for why
Will man lament the state he should envy—
To have so soon 'scaped world's and flesh's rage,
And, if no other misery, yet age?

Rest in soft peace; and, asked, say, "Here doth lie
Ben Jonson his best piece of poetry;
For whose sake henceforth all his vows be such
As what he loves may never like too much."

— *Ben Jonson, English (1573–1637).*

Upon the Death of Sir Albert Morton's Wife

He first deceased; she for a little tried
To live without him, liked it not, and died.

— *Sir Henry Wotton, English (1568–1639).*

To Dianeme

Sweet, be not proud of those two eyes,
Which star-like sparkle in their skies;
Nor be you proud that you can see
All hearts your captives, yours yet free;
Be you not proud of that rich hair,
Which wantons with the love-sick air;
Whenas that ruby which you wear,
Sunk from the tip of your soft ear,
Will last to be a precious stone
When all your world of beauty's gone.

— *Robert Herrick, English (1591–1674).*

Anacreontic

Born I was to be old,
And for to die here,
After that, in the mold
Long for to lie here.
But before that day comes,
Still I be bousing,
For I know in the tombs
There's no carousing.

— *Robert Herrick.*

On the Hon. Simon Harcourt

Only son of the Lord Chancellor Harcourt; at the Church of Stanton-Harcourt, in Oxfordshire, 1720

To this sad shrine, whoe'er thou art, draw near;
Here lies the friend most loved, the son most dear:
Who ne'er knew joy, but friendship might divide,
Or gave his father grief but when he died.
How vain is reason, eloquence how weak!
If *Pope* must tell what Harcourt cannot speak.
Oh, let thy once-loved friend inscribe thy stone,
And with a father's sorrows, mix his own!

— *Alexander Pope, English (1688–1744).*

Rose Aylmer

Ah, what avails the sceptered race,
Ah what the form divine!
What every virtue, every grace!
Rose Aylmer, all were thine.

Rose Aylmer, whom these wakeful eyes
May weep, but never see,
A night of memories and of sighs
I consecrate to thee.

— *Walter Savage Landor, English (1775–1864).*

With Rue My Heart Is Laden

With rue my heart is laden
For golden friends I had.
For many a rose-lipt maiden
And many a lightfoot lad.

By brooks too broad for leaping
The lightfoot boys are laid;
The rose-lipt girls are sleeping
In fields where roses fade.

— *Alfred Edward Housman, English (1850–1936).*

Concord Hymn

SUNG AT THE COMPLETION OF THE BATTLE MONUMENT, JULY 4, 1837

By the rude bridge that arched the flood,
Their flag to April's breeze unfurled,
Here once the embattled farmers stood,
And fired the shot heard round the world.

The foe long since in silence slept;
Alike the conqueror silent sleeps;

And Time the ruined bridge has swept
  Down the dark stream which seaward creeps.

On this green bank, by this soft stream,
  We set to-day a votive stone;
That memory may their dead redeem,
  When like our sires, our sons are gone.

Spirit, that made those heroes dare
  To die, and leave their children free,
Bid Time and Nature gently spare
  The shaft we raise to them and thee.

— *Ralph Waldo Emerson, American (1803–1882).*

A Farm Picture

Through the ample open door of the peaceful country barn,
A sunlit pasture field with cattle and horses feeding,
And haze and vista, and the far horizon fading away.

— *Walt Whitman, American (1819–1892).*

Epitaph for Lincoln

This dust was once the man,
Gentle, plain, just and resolute, under whose cautious hand,
Against the foulest crime in history known in any land or age,
Was saved the Union of these States.

— *Walt Whitman.*

To Make A Prairie

To make a prairie it takes a clover and one bee, —
And revery.
The revery alone will do
If bees are few.

— *Emily Dickinson, American (1830–1886).*

Fog

The fog comes
on little cat feet.

It sits looking
over harbor and city
on silent haunches
and then moves on.

— *Carl Sandburg, American (1878–).*

Fire and Ice

Some say the world will end in fire,
Some say in ice.
From what I've tasted of desire
I hold with those who favor fire.
But if it had to perish twice,
I think I know enough of hate
To say that for destruction ice
Is also great
And would suffice.

— *Robert Frost, American (1875–).*

PART TWENTY

Worlds of the Mind and Spirit

THE POET Robert Southwell once wrote: "Not where I breathe, but where I love, I live." Men live in many worlds of their own making or discovery. The material world which their bodies inhabit is only one. There are others, realms of the mind and spirit, which are their truer homes and in which they find satisfactions transcending those of the environment of sense. To deny the existence of these worlds, because an individual may not have discovered them, is to disclose a limitation of experience or an unwillingness to recognize the dimensions of other minds. A Chinese mystic once described intolerant realists who scoffed at the spiritual values he sought as summer insects that deny the existence of ice. In a universe filled with intangible values and unknown worlds, a wise and considered effort to understand the spiritual experiences of other men is better than indifference and unwarranted denial.

In the selections which follow many differing minds are represented, ranging from early mystics to Cardinal Newman's rationalization of his religious position, from Rousseau's "Savoyard Vicar's Creed" to Thoreau's clear summary of what he conceived as the Good Life on earth, and to Santayana's "Preface to a New Philosophy" of skepticism. All men ultimately believe in something. If it is only existence itself, it will eventually be expressed in conclusions about its meaning, its purpose, its value, and its source. And these conclusions inevitably shape the realms in which their minds and spirits most truly live.

The beliefs of mankind are not easily summarized. Furthermore it is not true that there are exclusively "Occidental" or "Oriental" modes of thought: in both hemispheres there are idealists and materialists, mystics and rationalists.

Science and rationalism have played so fundamental a role in the rise of the world's civilization, and the Industrial Revolution has so subverted ancestral modes of life and sense of values, that recent generations have lost their perspective. As the minds of men have been impressed by the multiplicity of things about them, they have sought for rational principles to explain, to organize, and to regulate the world; to harness the forces of nature for human use; and to train men who will accomplish these tasks with increasing efficiency. All such training is designed to conquer physical nature. It fails, however, to satisfy all man's wants, to answer all his questions about the nature of the universe, and to reconcile him to his highest moral concepts. Only philosophy and religion can achieve these ends.

In both ancient and contemporary literature therefore a peculiar note persists.

Some critics would label it "romantic," but it represents an effort to awaken belief in values or things which are invisible and often remain inconceivable to the earth-bound, to bridge the gap between the seen and the unseen, to heal the soul's blindness, and develop its sense of oneness with the Spirit of the universe. There are of course differing types of mysticism or idealism, just as there may be distinctions between the philosophies of individuals within a single school of thought. One type, represented in America by Emerson and some of his teachers in Greece and India, would see each individual as "part and parcel" of the Over-Soul of the universe, with all its infinite resources available to him, and suffering from want and error only as he fails to realize his kinship with the Divine. To this school also belong Thoreau and Tagore. Another type, stemming from Hebraic-Christian thought, emphasizes the separation of man by his carnal nature from the Divine, seeks the means of reconciliation, stresses the role of faith in bridging the gap between the finite and the Infinite; and awaits illumination from without through the grace of God. Many other minds never strive for citizenship in countries of such mystics and idealists. They are content to follow inherited creeds and modes of life; and they render great service to humanity by exemplifying a kindly tolerance and magnanimity toward those of differing views. Still others find their highest good merely in developing to the greatest perfection possible the talents nature gave them.

To enumerate all the worlds of the mind and spirit in which many types of men live most essentially and deeply, to survey their different concepts of the finite and Infinite, to explore or suggest the sources of their moral codes and aesthetic satisfactions, would require a library of books. The selections which follow will serve as a hint of what might be discovered in world literature in these areas of human experience.

The Image of the Cave

PLATO

AND now, I said, let me show in a figure how far our nature is enlightened or unenlightened: — Behold! human beings living in an underground den, which has a mouth open towards the light and reaching all along the den; here they have been from their childhood, and have their legs and necks chained so that they cannot move, and can only see before them, being prevented by the chains from turning round their heads. Above and behind them a fire is blazing at a distance, and between the fire and the prisoners there is a raised way; and you will see, if you look, a low wall built along the way, like the screen which marionette players have in front of them, over which they show the puppets.

I see.

And do you see, I said, men passing along the wall carrying all sorts of vessels, and statues and figures of animals made of wood and stone and various materials, which appear over the wall? Some of them are talking, others silent.

You have shown me a strange image, and they are strange prisoners.

Like ourselves, I replied; and they see only their own shadows, or the shadows of one another, which the fire throws on the opposite wall of the cave?

True, he said; how could they see anything but the shadows if they were never allowed to move their heads?

And of the objects which are being carried in like manner they would see only the shadows?

Yes, he said.

And if they were able to converse with one another, would they not suppose that they were naming what was actually before them?

Very true.

And suppose further that the prison had an echo which came from the other side, would they not be sure to fancy when one of the passersby spoke that the voice which they heard came from the passing shadow?

No question, he replied.

To them, I said, the truth would be literally nothing but the shadows of the images.

That is certain.

And now look again, and see what will naturally follow if the prisoners are released and disabused of their error. At first, when any of them is liberated and compelled suddenly to stand up and turn his neck round and walk and look towards the light, he will suffer sharp pains; the glare will distress him, and he will be unable to see the realities of which in his former state he had seen the shadows; and then conceive some one saying to him, that what he saw before was an illusion, but that now, when he is approaching nearer to being and his eye is turned towards more real existence, he has a clearer vision, — what will be his reply? And you may further imagine that his instructor is pointing to the objects as they pass and requiring him to name them, — will he not be perplexed? Will he not fancy that the shadows which he formerly saw are truer than the objects which are now shown to him?

Far truer.

And if he is compelled to look straight at the light, will he now have a pain in his eyes which will make him turn away to take refuge in the objects of vision which he can see, and which he will conceive to be in reality clearer than the things which are now being shown to him?

True, he said.

And suppose once more, that he is reluctantly dragged up a steep and rugged ascent, and held fast until he is forced into the presence of the sun himself, is he not likely to be pained and irritated? When he approaches the light his eyes will be dazzled, and he will not be able to see anything at all of what are now called realities.

Not all in a moment, he said.

He will require to grow accustomed to the sight of the upper world. And first he will see the shadows best, next the reflections of men and other objects in the water, and then the objects themselves; then he will gaze upon the light of the moon and the stars by night better than the sun or the light of the sun by day?

Certainly.

Last of all he will be able to see the sun, and not mere reflections of him in the water, but he will see him in his own proper place, and not in another; and he will contemplate him as he is.

Certainly.

He will then proceed to argue that this is he who gives the seasons and the years, and is the guardian of all that is in the visible world, and in a certain way the cause of all things which he and his fellows have been accustomed to behold?

Clearly, he said, he would first see the sun and then reason about him.

And when he remembered his old habitation, and the wisdom of the den and his fellow prisoners, do you not suppose that he would felicitate himself on the change, and pity them?

Certainly he would.

And if they were in the habit of conferring honours among themselves on those who were quickest to observe the passing shadows and to remark which of them went before, and which followed after, and which were together; and who were therefore best able to draw conclusions as to the future, do you think that he would care for such honours and glories, or envy the possessors of them? Would he not say with Homer, "Better to be the poor servant of a poor master," and to endure anything, rather than think as they do and live after their manner?

Yes, he said, I think that he would rather suffer anything than entertain these false notions and live in this miserable manner.

Imagine once more, I said, such an one coming suddenly out of the sun to be replaced in his old situation; would he not be certain to have his eyes full of darkness?

To be sure, he said.

And if there were a contest, and he had to compete in measuring the shadows with the prisoners who had never moved out of the den, while his sight was still weak, and before his eyes had become steady (and the time which would be needed to acquire this new habit of sight might be very considerable), would he not be ridiculous? Men would say of him that up he went and down he came without his eyes: and that it was better not even to think of ascending; and if any one tried to loose another and lead him up to the light, let them only catch the offender, and they would put him to death.

No question, he said.

This entire allegory, I said, you may now append, dear Glaucon, to the previous argument; the prison-house is the world of sight, the light of the fire is the sun, and you will not misapprehend me if you interpret the journey upwards to be the ascent of the soul into the intellectual world according to my poor belief, which, at your desire, I have expressed – whether rightly or wrongly God knows. But, whether true or false, my opinion is that in the world of knowledge the idea of good appears last of all, and is seen only with an effort; and, when seen, is also inferred to be the universal author of all things beautiful and right, parent of light and of the lord of light in this visible world, and the immediate source of reason and truth in the intellectual; and that this is the power upon which he who would act rationally either in public or private life must have his eye fixed.

I agree, he said, as far as I am able to understand you.

Moreover, I said, you must not wonder that those who attain to this beatific vision are unwilling to descend to human affairs; for their souls are ever hastening into the upper world where they desire to dwell; which desire of theirs is very natural, if our allegory may be trusted.

Yes, very natural.

And is there anything surprising in one who passes from divine contemplations to the evil state of man, misbehaving himself in a ridiculous manner; if, while his eyes are blinking and before he has become accustomed to the surrounding darkness, he is compelled to fight in courts of law, or in other places, about the images or the shadows of images of justice, and is endeavouring to meet the conceptions of those who have never yet seen absolute justice?

Anything but surprising, he said.

Any one who has common sense will remember that the bewilderments of the eyes are of two kinds, and arise from two causes, either from coming out of the light or from going into the light, which is true of the mind's eye, quite as much as of the bodily eye; and he who remembers this when he sees any one whose vision is perplexed and weak, will not be too ready to laugh; he will first ask whether that soul of man has come out of the brighter life, and is unable to see because unaccustomed to the dark, or having turned from darkness to the day is dazzled by excess of light. And he will count the one happy in his condition and state of being, and he will pity the other; or, if he have a mind to laugh at the soul which comes from below into the light, there will be more reason in this than in the laugh which greets him who returns from above out of the light into the den.

That, he said, is a very just distinction.

But then, if I am right, certain professors of education must be wrong when they say that they can put a knowledge into the soul which was not there before, like sight into blind eyes.

They undoubtedly say this, he replied.

Whereas, our argument shows that the power and capacity of learning exists in the soul already; and that just as the eye was unable to turn from darkness to light without the whole body, so too the instrument of knowledge can only by the movement of the whole soul be turned from the world of becoming into that of being, and learn by degrees to endure the sight of being, and of the brightest and best of being, or in other words, of the good.

Very true.

And must there not be some art which will effect conversion in the easiest and quickest manner; not implanting the faculty of sight, for that exists already, but has been turned in the wrong direction, and is looking away from the truth?

Yes, he said, such an art may be presumed.

And whereas the other so-called virtues of the soul seem to be akin to bodily qualities, for even when they are not originally innate they can be implanted later by habit and exercise, the virtue more than anything else contains a divine element which always remains, and by this conversion is rendered useful and profitable; or, on the other hand, hurtful and useless. Did you never observe the narrow intelligence flashing from the keen eye of a clever rogue – how eager he is, how clearly his paltry soul sees the way to his end; he is the reverse of blind, but his keen eye-sight is forced into the service of evil, and he is mischievous in proportion to his cleverness?

Very true, he said.

But what if there had been a circumcision of such natures in the days of their youth; and they had been severed from those sensual pleasures, such as eating and drinking, which, like leaden weights, were attached to them at their birth, and which drag them down and turn the vision of their souls upon the things that are below – if, I say, they had been released from these impediments and turned in the opposite direction, the very same faculty in them would have seen the truth as keenly as they see what their eyes are turned to now.

Very likely.

Yes, I said: and there is another thing which is likely, or rather a necessary inference from what has preceded, that neither the uneducated and uninformed of the truth, nor those who never make an end of their education, will be able ministers of State; not the former, because they have no single aim of duty which is the rule of all their actions, private as well as public; nor the latter, because they will not act at all except upon compulsion, fancying that they are already dwelling apart in the islands of the blest.

Very true, he replied.

Then, I said, the business of us who are the founders of the State will be to compel the best minds to attain that knowledge which we have already shown to be the greatest of all – they must continue to ascend until they arrive at the good; but when they have ascended and seen enough we must not allow them to do as they do now.

What do you mean?

I mean that they remain in the upper world: but this must not be allowed; they must be made to descend again among the prisoners in the den, and partake of their labours and honours, whether they are worth having or not.

But is not this unjust? he said; ought we to give them a worse life, when they might have a better?

You have again forgotten, my friend, I said, the intention of the legislator, who did not aim at making any one class in the State happy above the rest; the happiness was to be in the whole State, and he held the citizens together by persuasion and necessity, making them benefactors of the State, and therefore benefactors of one another; to this end he created them, not to please themselves, but to be his instruments in binding up the State.

True, he said, I had forgotten.

Observe, Glaucon, that there will be no injustice in compelling our philosophers to have a care and providence of others; we shall explain to them that in other States, men of their class are not obliged to share in the toils of politics; and this is reasonable, for they grow up at their own sweet will, and the government would rather not have them. Being self-taught, they cannot be expected to show any gratitude for a culture which they have never received. But we have brought you into the world to be rulers of the hive, kings of yourselves and of the other citizens, and have educated you far better and more perfectly than they have been educated, and you are better able to share in the double duty. Wherefore each of you, when his turn comes, must go down to the general underground abode, and get the habit of seeing in the dark. When you have acquired the habit, you will see ten thousand times better than the inhabitants of the den, and you will know what the several images are, and what they represent, because you have seen the beautiful and just and good in their truth. And thus our State, which is also yours, will be a reality, and not a dream only, and will be administered in a spirit unlike that of other States, in which men fight with one another about shadows only and are distracted in the struggle for power, which in their eyes is a great good. Whereas the truth is that the State in which the rulers are most reluctant to govern is always the best and most quietly governed, and the State in which they are most eager, the worst.

—From Book VII of the Republic of Plato (c. 427–347 B.C.), translated by Benjamin Jowett.

On the God Within Us

SENECA

To Lucilius:

You are doing an excellent thing, one which will be wholesome for you, if, as you write me, you are persisting in your effort to attain sound understanding; it is foolish to pray for this when you can acquire it from yourself. We do not need to uplift our hands towards heaven, or to beg the keeper of a temple to let us approach his idol's ear, as if in this way our prayers were more likely to be heard. God is near you, he is with you, he is within you. That is what I mean, Lucilius: a holy spirit indwells within us, one who marks our good and bad deeds, and is our guardian. As we treat this spirit, so are we treated by it. Indeed, no man can be good without the help of God. Can one rise superior to fortune unless God helps him to rise? He it is that gives noble and upright counsel. In each good man

"A god doth dwell, but what god know we not."

If ever you have come upon a grove that is full of ancient trees which have grown to an unusual height, shutting out a view of the sky by a veil of pleached and intertwining branches, then the loftiness of the forest, the seclusion of the spot, and your marvel at the thick unbroken shade in the midst of the open spaces, will prove to you the presence of deity. Or if a cave, made by the deep crumbling of the rocks, holds up a mountain on its arch, a place not built with hands but hollowed out into such spaciousness by natural causes, your soul will be deeply moved by a certain intimation of the existence of God. We worship the sources of mighty rivers; we erect altars at places where great streams burst suddenly from hidden sources; we adore springs of hot water as divine, and consecrate certain pools because of their dark waters or their immeasurable depth. If you see a man who is unterrified in the midst of dangers, untouched by desires, happy in adversity, peaceful amid the storm, who looks down upon men from a higher plane, and views the gods on a footing of equality, will not a feeling of reverence for him steal over you? Will you not say: "This quality is too great and too lofty to be regarded as resembling this petty body in which it dwells? A divine power has descended upon that man." When a soul rises superior to other souls, when it is under control, when it passes through every experience as if it were of small account, when it smiles at our fears and at our prayers, it is stirred by a force from heaven. A thing like this cannot stand upright unless it be propped by the divine. Therefore, a greater part of it abides in that place from whence it came down to earth. Just as the rays of the sun do indeed touch the earth but still abide at the source from which they are sent; even so the great and hallowed soul, which has come down in order that we may have a nearer knowledge of divinity, does indeed associate with us, but still cleaves to its origin; on that source it depends, thither it turns its gaze and strives to go, and it concerns itself with our doings only as a being superior to ourselves.

What, then, is such a soul? One which is resplendent with no external good, but only with its own. For what is more foolish than to praise in a man the qualities which come from without? And what is more insane than to marvel at characteristics which may at the next instant be passed on to someone else? A golden bit does not make a better horse. The lion with gilded mane, in process of being trained and forced by weariness to endure the decoration, is sent into the arena in quite a different way from the wild lion whose spirit is unbroken; the latter, indeed, bold in his attack, as nature wished him to be, impressive because of his wild appearance, — and it is his glory that none can look upon him without fear, — is favoured in preference to the other lion, that languid and gilded brute.

No man ought to glory except in that which is his own. We praise a vine if it makes the shoots teem with increase, if by its weight it bends to the ground the very poles which hold its fruit; would any man prefer to this vine one from which golden grapes and golden leaves hang down? In a vine the virtue peculiarly its own is fertility; in man also we should praise that which is his own. Suppose that he has a retinue of comely slaves and a beautiful house, that his farm is large and large his income; none of these things is in the man himself; they are all on the outside. Praise the quality in him which cannot be given or snatched away, that which is the peculiar property of the man. Do you ask what this is? It is soul, and reason brought to perfection in the soul. For man is a reasoning animal. Therefore, man's highest good is attained, if he has fulfilled the good for which nature designed him at birth. And what is it which this reason demands of him? The easiest thing in the world, — to live in accordance with his own nature. But this is turned into a hard task by the general madness of mankind; we push one another into vice. And how can a man be recalled to salvation, when he has none to restrain him, and all mankind to urge him on? Farewell.

—From the Epistles to Lucilius, XLI, of Seneca, Roman (54 B.C.?–39 A.D.), translated by Richard M. Gummere.

True Happiness

PLOTINUS

What is happiness?

If we base happiness upon life, drawing no distinction as to kinds of life, everything that lives will be capable of happiness. We could not deny it to the irrational whilst allowing it to the rational. But this word *life* embraces many forms which shade down from primal to secondary, and so on—life of animal and life of plant, each phase brighter or dimmer than the next; and so it evidently must be with the good of life.

Happiness demands fullness of life and exists, therefore, where nothing is lacking of all that belongs to the idea of life. Only one that lives fully will possess happiness, for he possesses the Supreme Good if, indeed, the Supreme Good is the authentically living, life in its greatest plenitude, life in which the good is present as something essential, not as something brought in from without. The perfect life, the true and essential life, is in the Intellectual Nature beyond this sphere—all other kinds are incomplete, are phantoms of life, imperfect, not pure, not more truly life than they are its contrary. Since all living things proceed from the one Principle but possess life in different degrees, this Principle must be the first life and the most complete.

If, then, the perfect life is within human reach, the man attaining it attains happiness; if not, happiness must be made over to the gods. But since we hold that happiness is for human beings too, we must consider how this is possible. The matter may be stated thus: Man, when he commands not merely the life of sensation but also Reason and Authentic Intellection, has realized the perfect life.

But are we to picture it as something foreign imported into his nature?

No: there exists no single human being that does not either potentially or effectively possess this thing which we hold to constitute happiness. While in some men it is present as a mere portion of their total being, there is, too, the man already in possession of true felicity, who is this perfection realized, who has passed over into actual identification with it. All else is now mere clothing about the man, not to be called part of him since it lies about him unsought, not his because not appropriated to himself by any act of the will. To the man in this state, he himself is the Good by what he has and is, and the Author and Principle of what he is and holds is the Supreme. The sign that this state has been achieved is that the man seeks nothing else. What could he be seeking? Certainly none of the less worthy things, and with the Best he is already one.

Once the man is adept, the means of happiness, the way to good, are within, for nothing is good that lies outside him. Anything he desires further than this he seeks as a necessity, and not for himself but for a subordinate, for the body bound to him, to which since it has life he must minister the needs of life, not needs, however, to the true man. He knows these (to be of the lower order), and what he gives he so gives as to leave his true life undiminished.

Adverse fortune does not shake his felicity; the life so founded is stable ever. Suppose death strikes at his household or friends; he knows what death is, as the victims, if they are among the wise, know too. And if death does bring him grief, it is not to him, the true man, but to that in him which stands apart from the Supreme,—that lower man in whose distress he takes no part.

If happiness did indeed require freedom from pain, sickness, misfortune, disaster, it would be utterly denied to anyone confronted by such trials; but if it lies in the acquiring of the Authentic Good, why turn away from this Term and look to means, imagining that to be happy a man must need a variety of things none of which enter into happiness? If our quest is of one term alone, that only can be elected which is ultimate and noblest, that which calls to the tenderest longings of the soul.

The quest and will of the soul are not pointed directly towards freedom from this sphere; the reason which disciplines away our concern about this life has no fundamental quarrel with things of this order; it merely resents their interference; essentially all the aspiration is not so much away from evil as towards the soul's highest and noblest: this attained, all is won and there is rest – and this is the veritably willed state of life. There can be no such thing as "willing" the acquirement of necessaries, if *will* is to be taken in its strict sense, and not misapplied to the mere recognition of need. Such things can never make part of our final object; our Term must be such that though these pleasanter conditions be absent and their contraries present, it shall remain intact.

In any case if the man that has attained felicity meets some turn of fortune that he would not have chosen, there is not the slightest lessening of his happiness for that. If there were, he would be veering and falling from felicity from day to day. What human thing is so great as not to be despised by one who has mounted above all we know here, and is bound no longer to anything below?

As for violent personal sufferings, he will carry them off as well as he can; if they overpass his endurance they will carry him off.

And so in all his pain he asks no pity; there is always the radiance in the inner soul of the man, untroubled like the light in a lantern when fierce gusts beat about it in a wild turmoil of wind and tempest. Neither ordinary experiences nor pains and sorrows, whether touching himself or others, pierce to the inner hold. It is virtue's use to raise the general level of nature towards the better and finer, above the mass of men. And the finer is to set at nought what terrifies the common mind.

We cannot be indolent; this is an arena for the powerful combatant holding his ground against the blows of fortune and knowing that, sore though they be, they are little to him, nothing dreadful, nursery terrors. It is precisely to meet the undesired when it appears that he has the virtue which gives him, to confront it, his passionless and unshakable soul.

Thus he is ever cheerful, and the order of his life untroubled; his state is fixedly happy and nothing whatever of all that is known as evil can set it awry. If anyone seeks for some other pleasure in the life of the adept, it is not the life of the adept that he is looking for. In him is the self-gathered which can never be robbed of the vision of the All-Good.

It would be absurd to think that happiness begins and ends with the living body; happiness is the possession of the good of life; it is centred therefore in Soul, is an act of Soul. The body must be lessened, reduced, that the veritable man may show forth, the man behind the appearances; while he will safeguard his bodily health, the tyranny of the body he will work down or wear away by inattention to its claims. He would be neither wise nor in the state of happiness if he had not quitted trifling with such things and become as it were another being, having confidence in his own nature, faith that evil can never touch him. In such a spirit he can be fearless through and through; where there is dread, there is not perfect virtue; the man is some sort of a half-being.

As for any involuntary fear rising in him and taking the judgment by surprise, the wise man will attack it and drive it out; he will, so to speak, calm the hurt and frightened child within him by reason or menace, as an infant might feel itself rebuked by a glance of severity.

This does not make the man unfriendly or harsh; giving freely to his intimates of all he has to give, he will be the best of friends by his very union with Divine Mind.

Plato rightly taught that he who is to be wise and possess happiness should draw his good from the Supreme, fixing his gaze on That, becoming like to That, living by That. He must care for no other Term than That; all else he will attend to only as he might change his residence, not in expectation of any increase to his settled felicity, but simply in a reasonable attention to the differing conditions surrounding him as he lives here or there.

He will give to the body all that he sees to be useful or possible, but he himself is of another order, and leaves it at nature's hour, although he himself is always the master to decide in its regard – the things he tends and bears with as the musician cares for his lyre as long as it can serve him: when the lyre fails him, he will change it or give it up, as having now another craft, one that needs no lyre; and then he will let it rest unregarded at his side while he sings on without accompaniment. But it was not idly that the instrument was given him in the beginning; he has found it useful until now, many a time.

THE INTELLECTUAL BEAUTY

One who has attained to the vision of the Intellectual Beauty and grasped the Beauty of the Authentic Intellect will be able also to understand the Father and Transcendent of that Divine Being. It concerns us, then, to try to see how the Beauty of the Divine Intellect and of the Intellectual Cosmos may be revealed to contemplation.

Suppose two blocks of stone lying side by side, one unpatterned, quite untouched by art, the other wrought into the statue of some god or man, Grace or Muse — a creation in which the sculptor's art has concentrated every loveliness.

Now the stone thus wrought by the artist's hand to beauty of form is beautiful not as stone — for so the crude block would be as pleasant — but in virtue of the form imposed on it by art. This form is in the designer before ever it enters the stone; he holds it not by his equipment of eyes and hands but by his participation in his art. The beauty, therefore, exists in a far higher state in the art; that original beauty is not transferred; what comes over is a derivative and a minor, and even that appears in the statue only in so far as the stone yielded to the art. Art, then, must itself be beautiful in a far higher and purer degree, since it is the seat and source of that beauty; in the degree in which the beauty is diffused by entering into matter it is so much the weaker than that concentrated in unity.

But let us leave the arts and consider those works produced by nature where the Maker has subdued the material and given the form He desired. Whence shone forth the beauty of Helen, battle-sought; or of all those women like in loveliness to Aphrodite, or of Aphrodite herself? In all of these is it not the Idea communicated to the produced from within the producer, just as in works of art it is communicated from the arts to their creations? Now we can surely not believe that, while the made thing and the Idea thus impressed upon matter are beautiful, yet the Idea not so alloyed but resting still with the Creator — the Idea primal, immaterial — is not Beauty. The Nature, then, which creates things so lovely must be of itself of a far earlier beauty. We, undisciplined in discernment of the inward, pursue the outer, not perceiving that it is by the inner we are stirred.

But that the thing we are pursuing is something other, and that the beauty is not in the concrete things is manifest from the beauty there is in the sciences, in pursuits and in Soul. It is precisely here that the greater beauty lies, perceived when you look to the wisdom in a man and delight in it, regarding not the face which may be hideous, but catching only at the inner comeliness. If you are still unmoved and cannot acknowledge beauty under such conditions, then looking to your own inner being you will find no beauty to delight you and it will be futile to seek the greater vision, for you will be questing it through the ugly and impure.

Thus there is in the Nature-Principle itself, an ideal archetype of the beauty found in material forms, and, of that archetype again, a still more beautiful archetype in Soul, source of that in nature. In the proficient soul this is brightest and of more advanced loveliness; adorning the soul and bringing to it a light which is Beauty primally, its immediate presence sets the soul reflecting upon the quality of this prior.

This prior is the Divine Intellect abiding ever, not fluctuating, since It takes nothing from outside Itself. There can be no representation of It except in the sense that we represent gold by some portion of gold, purified, if it be impure, insisting at the same time that this is not the total thing *gold*, but merely a particular bit of gold. In the same way we learn in this matter from the purified intellect in ourselves or from the gods and the greatness of the Intellect in them.

For assuredly the gods are august and beautiful in a beauty beyond our speech. Not through the loveliness of their corporeal forms — it is in virtue of Intellect that they are gods and as gods, beautiful. They do not veer between wisdom and folly in the immunity of Intellect, immutable and pure, they are wise always, all-knowing, taking cognizance of all that lies within the contemplation of Intellect. Those of them whose dwelling is in the heavens are ever in this meditation, since all leisure is theirs, and from afar they look, too, into that further heaven by a lifting of the head. For all There is heaven; earth is heaven and sea heaven, and animal and plant and man; all There is heavenly. And the gods traverse that region and all space in peace.

To "live at ease" is There; and to these divine Beings Verity is mother and nurse, essence and sustenance; all that is not of process but of authentic being they see, and themselves in all; for all is transparent, nothing dark, nothing impenetrable; every being is lucid to every other, light manifest to light. And each of them contains all within itself and sees all in every other, so that everywhere there is all, and each is all, and infinite the glory! Each of them is great: the small is great; the sun There is all the stars; and every star, again, is all the stars and sun; each is mirrored in every other. Perfect rest is There; and the Beauty is all beauty.

How could there be weariness There where the living is most noble? Life, pure, is never a burden. That very life is Wisdom, not a wisdom built up by reasonings but from the beginning complete, primal, underived, not something added to the Being, but its very essence. This is the authentic knowing. The greatness and the power of the Wisdom There we may know from this, that it embraces all the real Beings and has made all, and all follow it. If we have failed to understand, it is that we have thought of knowledge as a mass of theorems and an accumulation of propositions. But this is not a wisdom built up of theorems but one totality, not manifold detail reduced to a unity, but rather a unity working out into detail.

The true Wisdom, then, is Real Being, and Real Being is Wisdom; it is Wisdom that gives value to Real Being and Being is real in virtue of its origin in Wisdom.

This, then, is Beauty primally; it is entire and omnipresent as an entirety; and therefore in none of its parts or members lacking in beauty; beautiful thus beyond denial. That which is the first to manifest itself—Form and object of vision to the intellect—cannot but be lovely to see. Hence Plato represents the Creator as approving the work He has achieved; he makes us feel the lovable beauty of the autotype and of the Divine Idea by telling us that the beauty here is only the image of That. And indeed if the Divine did not exist, the transcendently beautiful, in a beauty beyond all thought, what could be lovelier than the things we see? Certainly no reproach can rightly be brought against this world save only that it is not That.

Let us, then, make a mental picture of our universe; each member shall remain distinctly apart; yet all is to form a complete unity so that whenever any one thing comes into view, for example, the surface of the orb over all, it shall bring immediately with it the vision of the sun and all the other stars with earth and sea and all living things as in a transparent globe in which you could see everything. Now picture mentally the gleaming representation of a sphere, holding all things of the universe in motion or repose. Keep this sphere before you, and imagine another, stripped of magnitude and spatial differences; cast out your inborn sense of matter, call on God, Maker of the sphere whose image you now hold, and pray Him to enter. And may He come bringing His own Universe with all the gods that dwell in it—He who is the one God and all the gods, one Power divine with many facets. For in the coming to be of all those the One has suffered no diminishing. He and all have one existence, while each again is distinct. The Divine is one all-power reaching out to infinity; and so great is God that His very members are infinites. What place can be named to which He does not reach?

Great, too, is this firmament of ours and all the powers constellated within it, but it would be greater still, unspeakably, but that there is inbound in it something of the petty power of body. The power in that other world has merely Being and beauty of Being. How could Beauty void of Being be? Or Being void of Beauty? Being is desirable because it is identical with Beauty, and Beauty is loved because it is Being. The false being here needs some imposed image of Beauty to insure its existence; it exists to the degree in which it has taken some share in the beauty of Idea; the more deeply it has drawn on this, the more perfect it is.

This is why Zeus, the oldest of the gods and their sovereign, advances first (in the *Phaedrus* myth) towards the vision of the Beautiful followed by the gods and demigods and such souls as are of strength to see. It shines forth upon them from some invisible place and, rising loftily over them, pours Its light upon all things, so that all gleams in Its radiance. It upholds some beings and they see; the lower are dazzled and turn away, unable to gaze upon that

Sun, the trouble falling more heavily on those most remote.

Of those looking upon It and able to see, all take something, but not all the same vision always; intently gazing, one sees the fount and principle of Justice, another is filled with the sight of Wisdom, the original of that quality as found sometimes among men, copied by them from the divine Virtue which, covering all the expanse of the Intellectual Realm, is the last to be seen by those who have known already many splendid visions.

This is the vision Zeus beholds, and it is for such of us also as share his love and appropriate our part of the Beauty There, the final object of all seeing, the entire Beauty upon all things; for It makes all things to shine and envelops those that have found their way Thither so that they too become beautiful; thus often those who are climbing heights where the soil has taken a yellow glow will themselves be bathed in it, borrowing the color from the ground whereon they move. The color flowering on that other Height is Beauty; or rather all There is color and beauty through and through, for the beauty is no mere bloom upon the surface.

To those that do not see entire, the immediate impression is alone taken into account; but those drunken with this wine, filled with the nectar, all their soul penetrated by this Beauty, cannot remain mere gazers; they hold the vision within themselves. All that one sees as a spectacle is still external; we must bring the vision within and see it as one with ourselves. Thus a man filled with a God holds his vision of the Divine Being within himself if he but have the strength.

Any one possessed by God has but to bring that Divine-within before his consciousness and at once he sees an image of himself lifted to a better beauty; now let him ignore that image, lovely though it be, and sink into a perfect self-identity, no such separation remaining; at once he forms a multiple unity with God silently present; in the degree of his power and will the two become one; should he turn back to the former duality, still he is pure and remains very near to God; he has but to look again and the same Presence is there. At the first stage, that of separation, a man is aware of self; but retreating inwards, he becomes possessor of all; he puts sense away behind him in dread of the separated life and becomes one with the Divine; if he plans to see in separation, he sets himself outside.

The novice must hold himself constantly under some image of the Divine Being and seek in the light of a clear conception; knowing thus, in a deep conviction, whither he is going, into what a sublimity he penetrates, he must give himself to the inner and, radiant with the Divine Intellections, be no longer the seer, but as that place has made him, the seen. To see the Divine as something external is to be outside of It; to become It is to be most truly in Beauty. There can be no vision unless in the sense of identification with the object.

We have told how this vision is to be procured: now what does it report? The vision has been of God in travail of a beautiful offspring, God engendering a universe within Himself in a painless labor and, rejoiced by what He has brought into being, proud of His children, keeping all closely by Him for the pleasure He has in His radiance and theirs.

This second cosmos at every point copies the archetype: it has life and being in copy, and has Beauty as springing from that diviner world.

Soul also has Beauty, but it is less beautiful than Intellect as being its image and taking increase of beauty by looking to that original. Since Soul then is so lovely in its own right, of what quality must that Prior be? And since its being is derived, what must that Power be from which Soul takes the double beauty, the borrowed and the inherent?

We ourselves possess Beauty when we are true to our own being; ugliness is in going over to another order; knowing ourselves, we are beautiful; in self-ignorance, we are ugly.

Thus Beauty is of the Divine and comes Thence only.

—*From the first and fifth Enneads of Plotinus, Egyptian (205?–270?), selected by Grace H. Turnbull from the translation from the Greek by Stephen Mackenna and B. S. Page.*

Of the Greatest Good

BOETHIUS

THEN, for a while looking steadfastly upon the ground, and, as it were, retiring herself to the most secret seat of her soul, she (Philosophy) began in this manner: "All men's thoughts, which are turmoiled with manifold cares, take indeed divers courses, but yet endeavor to attain the same end of happiness, which is that good which, being once obtained, nothing can be further desired. Which is the chiefest of all goods, and containeth in itself whatsoever is good, and if it wanted anything it could not be the chiefest, because there would something remain besides it which might be wished for. Wherefore, it is manifest that blessedness is an estate replenished with all that is good. This, as we said, all men endeavor to obtain by divers ways. For there is naturally ingrafted in men's minds an earnest desire of that which is truly good; but deceitful error withdraweth it to that which falsely seemeth such. So that some, esteeming it their greatest good to want nothing, labor by all means to abound with riches; others, deeming that to be good which is most deserving of honor, hunt after preferments, to be respected by their fellow-citizens. Others think it the greatest felicity to have great power and authority, and these will either reign themselves or at least procure to be with great princes. But they who think fame better than all these, make all speed possible to spread their names far and near, by achieving some worthy enterprise either in war or peace. Many measure good by joy and mirth, and their chiefest care is how they may abound with pleasure. Some interchange the ends and means of these things one with the other, wanting now riches for the sake of power and pleasure, now power for the sake of wealth and fame. At these and such other do men's actions and desires aim, as nobility and popularity, which make men esteemed; wife and children, which bring pleasure and delight. But friendship, that most sacred thing, is rather to be attributed to virtue than to fortune. Other things for the most part are desired either for power or pleasure. And it is an easy matter to reduce all corporal goods to the former heads. For strength and greatness give ability; beauty and swiftness, fame; and health yieldeth pleasure. By all which we manifestly seek for nothing else but happiness. For that which every man seeketh most after, is by him esteemed his greatest good. Which is all one with happiness. Wherefore he esteemeth that estate happy which he preferreth before all other.

And thus thou hast in a manner seen the form of human felicity – riches, honor, power, glory, pleasure. Which Epicurus only considering, consequently took pleasure for his chiefest good, because all the rest seemed to delight the mind. But I return to the careful thoughts of men, whose minds, though obscured, yet seek after the greatest good, but like a drunken man know not the way home. For seem they to err who endeavor to want nothing? But nothing can cause happiness so much as the plentiful possession of all that is good, needing the help of none, but is sufficient of itself. Or do they err who take that which is best to be likewise most worthy of respect? No. For it is no vile or contemptible thing which almost all men labor to obtain. Or is not power to be esteemed good? Why, then, is that to be accounted feeble and of no force, which manifestly surpasses all other things? Or is fame to be contemned? But it cannot be ignored that the most excellent is also most famous. For to what purpose should I say that happiness is not sad or melancholy, or subject to grief and trouble, when even in the smallest matters we desire that which we delight to have and enjoy? And these be the things which men desire to obtain, and to this end procure riches, dignities, kingdoms, glory, and pleasures, because by them they think to have sufficiency, respect, power, fame, delight, and joy. Wherefore that is good which men seek after by divers desires, in which the force of nature is easily descried, since though there be many and different opinions, yet they agree in choosing for their end that which is good. . . .

Dignities make him honorable and revered on whom they light. Have offices that force to plant virtues and expel vices in the minds of those who have them? But they are not wont to banish, but rather to make wickedness splendid. So that we many times complain because most wicked men obtain them. . . . We cannot for their honors account them worthy of respect whom we judge unworthy of the honors themselves. But if thou seest any man endued with wisdom, canst thou esteem him unworthy of that respect or wisdom which he hath? No, truly. For virtue hath a proper dignity of her own, which she presently endueth her possessors withal. Which since popular preferments cannot do, it is manifest that they have not the beauty which is proper to true dignity.

In which we are farther to consider that, if to be contemned of many make men abject, dignities make the wicked to be despised the more by laying them open to the view of the world. But the dignities go not scot-free, for wicked men do as much for them, defiling them with their own infection. And that thou mayst plainly see that true respect cannot be gotten by these painted dignities, let one that hath been often Consul go among barbarous nations; will that honor make those barbarous people respect him? And yet, if this were natural to dignities, they would never forsake their function in any nation whatsoever; as fire, wheresoever it be, always remaineth hot. But because not their own nature, but the deceitful opinion of men attributeth that to them, they forthwith come to nothing, being brought to them who esteem them not to be dignities.

And this for foreign nations. But do they always last among them where they had their beginning? The Praetorship, a great dignity in time past, is now an idle name, and an heavy burden of the Senate's fortune. If heretofore one had care of the people's provision, he was accounted a great man; now what is more abject than that office? For as we said before, that which hath no proper dignity belonging unto it sometime receiveth and sometime loseth his value at the users' discretion. Wherefore if dignities cannot make us respected, if they be easily defiled with the infection of the wicked, if their worth decays by changes of times, if diversities of nations make them contemptible, what beauty have they in themselves, or can they afford to others, worth desiring?

Though fierce and lustful Nero did adorn
Himself with purple robes, which pearls did
grace,
He did but gain a general hate and scorn.
Yet wickedly he officers most base
Over the reverend Senators did place.
Who would esteem of fading honors then
Which may be given thus by the wickedest
men?

But can kingdoms and the familiarity of kings make a man mighty? Why not, when their felicity lasteth always? But both former and present times are full of examples that many kings have changed their happiness with misery. O excellent power, which is not sufficient to uphold itself! And if this strength of kingdoms be the author of blessedness, doth it not diminish happiness and bring misery, when it is in any way defective? But though some empires extend themselves far, there will still remain many nations out of their dominions. Now, where the power endeth which maketh them happy, there entereth the contrary which maketh them miserable, so that all kings must needs have less happiness than misery. That Tyrant, knowing by experience the dangers of his estate, signified the fears incident to a kingdom, by the hanging of a drawn sword over a man's head. What power is this, then, which cannot expel nor avoid biting cares and pricking fears? They would willingly have lived securely, but could not, and yet they brag of their power. Thinketh thou him mighty whom thou seest desire that which he cannot do? Thinketh thou him mighty who dareth not go without his guard; who feareth others more than they fear him; who cannot seem mighty, except his servants please? For what should I speak of kings' followers, since I show that kingdoms themselves are so full of weakness? Whom the power of kings often standing, but many times falling, doth overthrow. Nero compelled Seneca, his familiar friend and master, to make choice of his own death. Antonius called Papinianus, who had been long a gallant courtier, to be cut in pieces with his soldiers' swords. Yet they would both have renounced their power, yea Seneca endeavored to deliver up his riches also to Nero, and to give himself to a contemplative life. But their very greatness drawing them to their destruction, neither of them could compass that which they desired. Wherefore what power is this that the possessors fear, which when thou wilt have, thou art not secure, and when thou wilt leave, thou canst not avoid? Are we the better for those friends which love us not for our virtue but for our prosperity? But whom prosperity maketh our friend, adversity will make our enemy. And what plague is able to hurt us more than a familiar enemy?

Who would be powerful, must
His own affections check,
Nor let foul reins of lust

Subdue his conquered neck.
For though the Indian land
Should tremble at thy beck,
And though thy dread command
Far Thule's isle obey,
Unless thou canst withstand
And boldly drive away
Black care and wretched moan,
Thy might is small or none.

As for glory, how deceitful it is oftentimes, and dishonest! For which cause the tragic poet deservedly exclaimeth: "O glory, glory, thou hast raised to honor and dignity myriads of worthless mortals!" For many have often been much spoken of through the false opinions of the common people. Than which what can be imagined more vile? For those who are falsely commended must needs blush at their own praises. Which glory though it be gotten by deserts, yet what adds it to a wise man's conscience who measureth his own good, not by popular rumors, but by his own certain knowledge? And if it seem a fair thing to have dilated our fame, consequently we must judge it a foul thing not to have it extended. But since, as I showed a little before, there must needs be many nations to which the fame of one man cannot arrive, it cometh to pass that he whom thou esteemeth glorious, in the greater part of the world seemeth to have no glory at all. And here now I think popular glory not worth speaking of, which neither proceedeth from judgment, nor ever hath any firmness. Likewise, who seeth not what a vain and idle thing it is to be called noble? Which forasmuch as belongeth to fame, is not our own. For nobility seemeth to be a certain praise proceeding from our parents' deserts. But if praising causeth fame, they must necessarily be famous who are praised. Wherefore the fame of others, if thou hast none of thine own, maketh not thee renowned. But if there be anything good in nobility, I judge it to be only this, that it imposeth a necessity upon those which are noble, not to suffer their nobility to degenerate from the virtue of their ancestors.

The general race of men from a like birth is
born.
All things one Father have, Who doth them
all adorn,
Who gave the sun his rays, and the pale
moon her horn,
The lofty heaven for stars, low earth for
mortals chose;
He souls fetched down from high in bodies
did enclose;
And thus from noble seed all men did first
compose.
Why brag you of your stock? Since none is
counted base,
If you consider God the author of your race,
But he that with foul vice doth his own birth
deface.

—*From Book III of the Consolation of Philosophy by Boethius (Anicius Manlius Severinus), Roman (480–524), translated by "I.T." and revised by H. F. Stewart.*

~ ❁ ~

Of the Royal Way of the Holy Cross

THOMAS À KEMPIS

To many this seems a hard saying: "Deny thyself, take up thy cross, and follow Jesus."

But it will be much harder to hear that last word: "Depart from me, ye cursed, into everlasting fire."

For they that at present willingly hear and follow the word of the cross shall not then be afraid of eternal condemnation.

This sign of the cross will be in heaven when the Lord shall come to judge.

Then all the servants of the cross, who in their lifetime have conformed themselves to Him that was crucified, shall come to Christ their judge with great confidence.

Why art thou then afraid to take up thy cross, which leads to a kingdom?

In the cross is salvation; in the cross is life; in the cross is protection from thy enemies.

In the cross is infusion of heavenly sweetness; in the cross is strength of mind; in the cross is joy of spirit.

In the cross is the height of virtue; in the cross is the perfection of sanctity.

There is no health in the soul nor hope of eternal life but in the cross.

Take up, therefore, thy cross and follow Jesus, and thou shalt go into life everlasting.

He is gone before thee carrying his own cross; and he died for thee upon the cross that thou mayst also bear thy cross and love to die on the cross.

Because if thou die with Him thou shalt also live with Him, and if thou art His companion in suffering thou shalt also partake in His glory.

Behold the cross is all and in dying to thyself all consists, and there is no other way to life and to true internal peace but the holy way of the cross and of daily mortification.

Go where thou wilt, seek what thou wilt, and thou shalt not find a higher way above, nor a safer way below than the way of the holy cross.

Dispose and order all things according as thou wilt, and as seems best to thee, and thou wilt still find something to suffer, either willingly or unwillingly, and so shalt thou still find the cross.

For either thou shalt feel pain in the body, or sustain in thy soul tribulation of spirit.

Sometimes thou shalt be left by God, other times thou shalt be afflicted by thy neighbor, and what is more, thou shalt often be a trouble to thyself.

Neither canst thou be delivered or eased by any remedy or comfort, but as long as it shall please God thou must bear it.

For God would have thee learn to suffer tribulation without comfort, and wholly submit thyself to Him, and to become more humble through tribulation.

No man hath so lively a feeling of the passion of Christ, as he who hath happened to suffer such like things.

The cross, therefor, is always ready and everywhere waits for thee.

Thou canst not escape it, whithersoever thou runnest; for whithersoever thou goest thou carriest thyself with thee and shalt always find thyself.

Turn thyself upwards, or turn thyself downwards; turn thyself without, or turn thyself within thee, and everywhere thou shalt find the cross.

And everywhere thou must of necessity have patience if thou desirest inward peace and wouldst merit an eternal crown.

If thou carry the cross willingly, it will carry thee and bring thee to thy desired end; to wit to that place where there will be an end of suffering, though here there will be no end.

If thou carry it unwillingly thou makest it a burden to thee and loadest thyself the more, and nevertheless thou must bear it.

If thou fling away one cross, without doubt thou shalt find another and perhaps a heavier.

Dost thou think to escape that which no mortal ever could avoid? What saint was there ever in the world without his cross and affliction?

Our Lord Jesus Christ Himself was not one hour of His Life without suffering: "It behooved Christ to suffer," saith He, "and rise again from the dead, and so enter into His glory."

And why dost thou pretend to seek another way than this royal way, which is the way of the holy cross?

The whole life of Christ was a cross and a martyrdom, and dost thou seek rest and joy?

Thou errest, thou errest, if thou seekest any other thing than to suffer tribulations; for this whole mortal life is full of miseries and beset on all sides with crosses.

And the higher a person is advanced in spirit the heavier crosses he shall often meet with, because the pain of his banishment increases in proportion to his love.

Yet this man, thus many ways afflicted, is not without some allay of comfort, because he is sensible of the great profit which he reaps by bearing the cross.

For whilst he willingly resigns himself to it, all the burden of tribulation is converted into an assured hope of comfort from God.

And the more the flesh is brought down by affliction the more the spirit is strengthened by inward grace.

And it sometimes gains such strength through affection to tribulation and adversity, by loving to be conformable to the cross of Christ, as not to be willing to be without suffering and affliction; and because it is confident that it is so much the more acceptable to God, as it shall be able to bear more and greater things for Him.

This is not man's power, but the grace of Christ, which can and does effect such great things in frail flesh, that what it naturally abhors and flies, even this, through fervor of spirit, it now embraces and loves.

To bear the cross, to love the cross, to chastise the body, and bring it under subjection; to fly honors, to be willing to suffer reproaches, to despise one's self and wish to be despised; to bear all adversities and losses, and to desire no prosperity in this world, are not according to man's natural inclination.

If thou look upon thyself, thou canst do nothing of this of thyself. But if thou confide in the Lord, strength will be given thee from heaven and the world and the flesh shall be made subject to thee.

Neither shalt thou fear thine enemy, the devil, if thou be armed with faith and signed with the cross of Christ.

Set thyself then like a good and faithful servant of Christ, to bear manfully the cross of thy Lord, crucified for the love of thee.

Prepare thyself to suffer many adversities and divers evils in this miserable life; for so it will be with thee wherever thou art, and so indeed wilt thou find it wheresoever thou mayst hide thyself.

It must be so, and there is no remedy against the tribulation of evil and sorrow but to bear them patiently.

Drink of the chalice of thy Lord lovingly if thou desire to be His friend and to have part with Him.

Leave consolations to God, to do with them as best pleaseth Him.

But prepare thyself to bear tribulations, and account them the greatest consolations; for the sufferings of this life bear no proportion to the glory to come, although thou alone couldst suffer them all.

When thou shalt arrive thus far, that tribulation becomes sweet and savory to thee for the love of Christ, then think that it is well with thee, for thou hast found a paradise upon earth.

As long as suffering appear grievous to thee and thou seek to fly from it, so long will it be ill with thee, and the tribulation from which thou fliest will everywhere follow thee.

If thou set thyself to what thou oughtst, that is to suffer and die to thyself, it will quickly be better with thee and thou shalt find peace.

Although thou shouldst have been rapt up to the third heaven with St. Paul, thou art not thereby assured that thou shalt suffer no adversity. "I" said Jesus, "will show him how great things he must suffer for My name."

To suffer therefore, is what waits for thee, if thou wilt love Jesus and constantly serve Him.

Would to God thou wert worthy to suffer something for the name of Jesus! how great a glory would be laid up for thee, how great joy would it be to all the saints of God and how great edification to thy neighbor.

All recommend patience, but alas! how few there are that desire to suffer.

With good reason oughtest thou willingly to suffer a little for Christ, since many suffer greater things for the world.

Know for certain that thou must lead a dying life and the more a man dies to himself the more he begins to live to God.

No man is fit to comprehend heavenly things who has not resigned himself to suffer adversities for Christ.

Nothing is more acceptable to God, nothing more wholesome for thee, in this world than to suffer willingly for Christ.

And if thou wert to choose, thou oughtst to wish rather to suffer adversities for Christ than to be delighted with many comforts, because thou wouldst thus be more like unto Christ and more conformable to all the saints.

For our merit and the advancement of our state consist, not in having many sweetnesses and consolations, but rather in bearing great afflictions and tribulations.

If indeed there had been anything better and more beneficial to man's salvation than suffering, Christ certainly would have showed it by word and example.

For He manfully exhorts both His disciples that followed Him and all that desire to follow Him to bear the cross, saying: "If any one will come after Me, let him deny himself and take up his cross and follow Me."

So that when we have read and searched all let this be the final conclusion, that "through many tribulations we must enter into the kingdom of God."

—From the Imitation of Christ by Thomas à Kempis, German (1380–1471), translated by the Right Reverend Richard Challoner.

~ ❁ ~

Discourse on Method

RENÉ DESCARTES

Good Sense is, of all things among men, the most equally distributed; for every one thinks himself so abundantly provided with it, that those even who are the most difficult to satisfy in everything else, do not usually desire a larger measure of this quality than they already possess. And in this it is not likely that all are mistaken: the conviction is rather to be held as testifying that the power of judging aright and of distinguishing Truth from Error, which is properly what is called Good Sense or Reason, is by nature equal in all men; and that the diversity of our opinions, consequently, does not arise from some being endowed with a larger share of Reason than others, but solely from this, that we conduct our thoughts along different ways, and do not fix our attention on the same objects. For to be possessed of a vigorous mind is not enough; the prime requisite is rightly to apply it. The greatest minds, as they are capable of the highest excellencies, are open likewise to the greatest aberrations; and those who travel very slowly may yet make far greater progress, provided they keep always to the straight road, than those who, while they run, forsake it.

For myself, I have never fancied my mind to be in any respect more perfect than those of the generality; on the contrary, I have often wished that I were equal to some others in promptitude of thought, or in clearness and distinctness of imagination, or in fullness and readiness of memory. And besides these, I know of no other qualities that contribute to the perfection of the mind; for as to the Reason or Sense, inasmuch as it is that alone which constitutes us men, and distinguishes us from the brutes, I am disposed to believe that it is to be found complete in each individual; and on this point to adopt the common opinion of philosophers, who say that the difference of greater and less holds only among the *accidents,* and not among the *forms* or *natures* of *individuals* of the same *species.*

I will not hesitate, however, to avow my belief that it has been my singular good fortune to have very early in life fallen in with certain tracks which have conducted me to considerations and maxims, of which I have formed a Method that gives me the means, as I think, of gradually augmenting my knowledge, and of raising it by little and little to the highest point which the mediocrity of my talents and the brief duration of my life will permit me to reach. For I have already reaped from it such fruits, that, although I have been accustomed to think lowly enough of myself, and although when I look with the eye of a philosopher at the varied courses and pursuits of mankind at large, I find scarcely one which does not appear vain and useless, I nevertheless derive the highest satisfaction from the progress I conceive myself to have already made in the search after truth, and cannot help entertaining such expectations of the future as to believe that if, among the occupations of men as men, there is any one really excellent and important, it is that which I have chosen.

After all, it is possible I may be mistaken; and it is but a little copper and glass, perhaps, that I take for gold and diamonds. I know how very liable we are to delusion in what relates to ourselves, and also how much the judgments of our friends are to be suspected when given in our favor. But I shall endeavor in this Discourse to describe the paths I have followed, and to delineate my life as in a picture, in order that each one may be able to judge of them for himself, and that in the general opinion entertained of them, as gathered from current report, I myself may have a new help toward instruction to be added to those I have been in the habit of employing.

My present design, then, is not to teach the Method which each ought to follow for the right conduct of his Reason, but solely to describe the way in which I have endeavored to conduct my own. They who set themselves to give precepts must of course regard themselves as possessed of greater skill than those to whom they prescribe; and if they err in the slightest particular, they subject themselves to censure. But as this Tract is put forth merely as a history, or, if you will, as a tale, in which, amid some examples worthy of imitation, there will be found, perhaps, as many more which it were advisable not to follow, I hope it will prove useful to some without being hurtful to any, and that my openness will find some favor with all.

From my childhood, I have been familiar with letters; and as I was given to believe that by their help a clear and certain knowledge of all that is useful in life might be acquired, I was ardently desirous of instruction. But as soon as I had finished the entire course of study, at the close of which it is customary to be admitted into the order of the learned, I completely changed my opinion. For I found myself involved in so many doubts and errors, that I was convinced I had advanced no farther in all my attempts at learning, than the discovery at every turn of my own ignorance. And yet I was studying in one of the most celebrated Schools in Europe, in which I thought there must be learned men, if such were anywhere to be found. I had been taught all that others learned there; and not contented with the sciences actually taught us, I had, in addition, read all the books that had fallen into my hands, treating of such branches as are esteemed the most curious and rare. I knew the judgment which others had formed of me; and I did not find that I was considered inferior to my fellows, although there were among them some who were already marked out to fill the places of our instructors. And, in fine, our age appeared to me as flourishing, and as fertile in powerful minds as any preceding one. I was thus led to take the liberty of judging of all other men by myself, and of concluding that there was no science in existence that was of such a nature as I had previously been given to believe.

I still continued, however, to hold in esteem the studies of the Schools. I was aware that the Languages taught in them are necessary to the understanding of the writings of the ancients; that the memorable deeds of History elevate it; and, if read with discretion, aid in forming the judgment; that the perusal of all excellent books is, as it were, to interview with the noblest men of past ages, who have written them, and even a studied interview, in which are discovered to us only their choicest thoughts; that Eloquence has incomparable force and beauty; that Poesy has its ravishing graces and delights; that in the Mathematics there are many refined discoveries eminently suited to gratify the inquisitive, as well as further all the arts and lessen the labor of man; that numerous highly useful precepts and exhortations to virtue are contained in treatises on Morals; that Theology points the path to heaven; that Philosophy affords the means of discoursing with an appearance of truth on all matters, and commands the admiration of the more simple; that Jurisprudence, Medicine, and the other Sciences, secure for their cultivators honors and riches; and, in fine, that it is useful to bestow some attention upon all, even upon those abounding the most in superstition and error, that we may be in a position to determine their real value, and guard against being deceived.

But I believed that I had already given sufficient time to Languages, and likewise to the reading of the writings of the ancients, to their Histories and Fables. For to hold converse with those of other ages and to travel, are almost the same thing. It is useful to know something of the manners of different nations, that we may be enabled to form a more correct judgment regarding our own, and be prevented from thinking that everything contrary to our customs is ridiculous and irrational, — a conclusion usually come to by those whose experience has been limited to their own country. On the other hand, when too much time is occupied in traveling, we become strangers to our native country; and the over-curious in the customs of the past are generally ignorant of those of the present. Besides, fictitious narratives lead us to imagine the possibility of many events that are impossible; and even the most faithful histories, if they do not wholly misrepresent matters, or exaggerate their importance to render the account of them more worthy of perusal, omit, at least, almost always the meanest and least striking of the attendant circumstances; hence it happens that the remainder does not represent the truth, and that such as regulate their conduct by examples drawn from this source, are apt to fall into the extravagances of the knight-errants of Romance, and to entertain projects that exceed their powers.

I esteemed Eloquence highly, and was in raptures with Poesy, but I thought that both were gifts of nature rather than fruits of study. Those in whom the faculty of Reason is predominant and who most skillfully dispose their thoughts with a view to render them clear and intelligible, are always the best able to persuade others of the truth of what they lay down, though they should speak only in the language of Lower Brittany, and be wholly ignorant of the rules of Rhetoric; and those whose minds are stored with the most agreeable fancies, and who can give expression to them with the greatest embellishment and harmony, are still the best poets, though unacquainted with the Art of Poetry.

I was especially delighted with the Mathematics, on account of the certitude and evidence of their reasonings: but I had not as yet a precise knowledge of their true use; and thinking that they but contributed to the advancement of the mechanical arts, I was astonished that foundations, so strong and solid, should have had no loftier superstructure reared on them. On the other hand, I compared the disquisitions of the ancient Moralists to very towering and magnificent palaces with no better foundation than sand and mud: they laud the virtues very highly, and exhibit them as estimable far above anything on earth; but they give us no adequate criterion of virtue, and frequently that which they designate with so fine a name is but apathy, or pride, or despair, or parricide.

I revered our Theology, and aspired as much as any one to reach heaven: but being given assuredly to understand that the way is not less open to the most ignorant than to the most learned, and that the revealed truths which lead to heaven are above our comprehension, I did not presume to subject them to the impotency of my Reason; and I thought that in order competently to undertake their examination, there was need of some special help from heaven, and of being more than man.

Of Philosophy I will say nothing, except that when I saw that it had been cultivated for many ages by the most distinguished men, and that yet there is not a single matter within its sphere which is not still in dispute, and nothing, therefore, which is above doubt, I did not presume to anticipate that my success would be greater in it than that of others; and further, when I considered the number of conflicting opinions touching a single matter that may be upheld by learned men, while there can be but one true, I reckoned as well-nigh false all that was only probable.

As to the other Sciences, inasmuch as these borrow their principles from Philosophy, I judged that no solid superstructures could be reared on foundations so infirm; and neither the honor nor the gain held out by them was sufficient to determine me to their cultivation: for I was not, thank Heaven, in a condition which compelled me to make merchandise of Science for the bettering of my fortune; and though I might not profess to scorn glory as a Cynic, I yet made very slight account of that honor which I hoped to acquire only through fictitious titles. And, in fine, of false Sciences I thought I knew the worth sufficiently to escape being deceived by the professions of an alchemist, the predictions of an astrologer, the impostures of a magician, or by the artifices and boasting of any of those who profess to know things of which they are ignorant.

For these reasons, as soon as my age permitted me to pass from under the control of my instructors, I entirely abandoned the study of letters, and resolved no longer to seek any other science than the knowledge of myself, or of the great book of the world. I spent the remainder of my youth in traveling, in visiting courts and armies, in holding intercourse with men of different dispositions and ranks, in collecting varied experience, in proving myself in the different situations into which fortune threw me, and, above all, in making such reflection on the matter of my experience as to secure my improvement. For it occurred to me that I should find much more truth in the reasonings of each individual with reference to the affairs in which he is personally interested, and the issue of which must presently punish him if he has judged amiss, than in those conducted by a man of letters in his study, regarding speculative matters that are of no practical moment, and followed by no consequences to himself, farther, perhaps, than that they foster his vanity the better the more remote they are from common sense; requiring, as they must in this case, the exercise of greater ingenuity and art to render them probable. In addition, I had always a most earnest desire to know how to distinguish the true from the false, in order that I might be able clearly to discriminate the right path in life, and proceed in it with confidence.

It is true that, while busied only in considering the manners of other men, I found here, too, scarce any ground for settled conviction, and remarked hardly less contradiction among them than in the opinions of the philosophers. So that the greatest advantage I derived from the study consisted in this, that, observing many things which, however extravagant and ridiculous to our apprehension, are yet by common consent received and approved by other great nations, I learned to entertain too decided a belief in regard to nothing of the truth of which I had been persuaded merely by example and custom; and thus I gradually extricated myself from many errors powerful enough to darken our Natural Intelligence, and incapacitate us in great measure from listening to Reason. But after I had been occupied several years in thus studying the book of the world, and in essaying to gather some experience, I at length resolved to make myself an object of study, and to employ all the powers of my mind in choosing the paths I ought to follow; an undertaking which was accompanied with greater success than it would have been had I never quitted my country or my books.

I was then in Germany, attracted thither by the wars in that country, which have not yet been brought to a termination; and as I was returning to the army from the coronation of the Emperor, the setting in of winter arrested me in a locality where, as I found no society to interest me, and was besides fortunately undisturbed by any cares or passions, I remained the whole day in seclusion, with full opportunity to occupy my attention with my own thoughts. Of these one of the very first that occurred to me was, that there is seldom so much perfection in works composed of many separate parts, upon which different hands have been employed, as in those completed by a single master. Thus it is observable that the buildings which a single architect has planned and executed, are generally more elegant and commodious than those which several have attempted to improve, by making old walls serve for purposes for which they were not originally built. Thus also, those ancient cities which, from being at first only villages, have become, in course of time, large towns, are usually but ill laid out compared with the regularly constructed towns which a professional architect has freely planned on an open plain; so that although the several buildings of the former may often equal or surpass in beauty those of the latter, yet when one observes their indiscriminate juxtaposition, there a large one and here a small, and the consequent crookedness and irregularity of the streets, one is disposed to allege that chance rather than any human will guided by reason, must have led to such an arrangement. And if we consider that nevertheless there have been at all times certain officers whose duty it was to see that private buildings contributed to public ornament, the difficulty of reaching high perfection with but the materials of others to operate on, will be readily acknowledged. In the same way I fancied that those nations which, starting from a semi-barbarous state and advancing to civilization by slow degrees, have had their laws successively determined, and, as it were, forced upon them simply by experience of the hurtfulness of particular crimes and disputes, would by this process come to be possessed of less perfect institutions than those which, from the commencement of their association as communities, have followed the appointments of some wise legislator. It is thus quite certain that the constitution of the true religion, the ordinances of which are derived from God, must be incomparably superior to that of every other. And, to speak of human affairs, I believe that the past pre-eminence of Sparta was due not to the goodness of each of its laws in particular, for many of these were very strange, and even opposed to good morals, but to the circumstance that, originated by a single individual, they all tended to a single end. In the same way I thought that the sciences contained in books (such of them at least as are made up of probable reasonings, without demonstrations), composed as they are of the opinions of many different individuals massed together, are farther removed from truth than the simple inferences which a man of good sense using his natural and unprejudiced judgment draws respecting the matters of his experience. And because we have all to pass through a state of infancy to manhood, and have been of necessity, for a length of time, governed by our desires and preceptors (whose dictates were frequently conflicting, while neither perhaps always counseled us for the best), I farther concluded that it is almost impossible that our judgments can be so correct or solid as they would have been, had our Reason been mature from the moment of our birth, and had we always been guided by it alone.

It is true, however, that it is not customary to pull down all the houses of a town with the single design of rebuilding them differently, and thereby rendering the streets more handsome; but it often happens that a private individual takes down his own with the view of erecting it anew, and that people are even sometimes constrained to this when their houses are in danger of falling from age, or when the foundations are insecure. With this before me by way of example, I was persuaded that it would indeed be preposterous for a private individual to think of reforming a state by fundamentally changing it throughout, and overturning it in order to set it up amended; and the same I thought was true of any similar project for reforming the body of the Sciences, or the order of teaching them established in the Schools: but as for the opinions which up to that time I had embraced, I thought that I could not do better than resolve at once to sweep them wholly away, that I might afterward be in a position to admit either others more correct, or even perhaps the same when they had undergone the scrutiny of Reason. I firmly believed that in this way I should much better succeed in the conduct of my life, than if I built only upon old foundations, and leaned upon principles which, in my youth, I had taken upon trust. For although I recognized various difficulties in this undertaking, these were not, however, without remedy, nor once to be compared with such as attend the slightest reformation in public affairs. Large bodies, if once overthrown, are with great difficulty set up again, or even kept erect when once seriously shaken, and the fall of such is always disastrous. Then if there are any imperfections in the constitutions of states (and that many such exist the diversity of constitutions is alone sufficient to assure us), custom has without doubt materially smoothed their inconveniences, and has even managed to steer altogether clear of, or insensibly corrected, a number which sagacity could not have provided against with equal effect; and, in fine, the defects are almost always more tolerable than the change necessary for their removal; in the same manner that highways which wind among mountains, by being much frequented, become gradually so smooth and commodious, that it is much better to follow them than to seek a straighter path by climbing over the tops of rocks and descending to the bottoms of precipices.

Hence it is that I cannot in any degree approve of those restless and busy meddlers who, called neither by birth nor fortune to take part in the management of public affairs, are yet always projecting reforms; and if I thought that this Tract contained aught which might justify the suspicion that I was a victim of such folly, I would by no means permit its publication. I have never contemplated anything higher than the reformation of my own opinions, and basing them on a foundation wholly my own. And although my own satisfaction with my work has led me to present here a draft of it, I do not by any means therefore recommend to everyone else to make a similar attempt. Those whom God has endowed with a larger measure of genius will entertain, perhaps, designs still more exalted; but for the many I am much afraid lest even the present undertaking be more than they can safely venture to imitate. The single design to strip oneself of all past beliefs is one that ought not to be taken by everyone. The majority of men is composed of two classes, for neither of which would this be at all a befitting resolution: in the *first* place, of those who with more than a due confidence in their own powers, are precipitate in their judgments and want the patience requisite for orderly and circumspect thinking; whence it happens, that if men of this class once take the liberty to doubt of their accustomed opinions, and quit the beaten highway, they will never be able to thread the byway that would lead them by a shorter course, and will lose themselves and continue to wander for life; in the *second* place, of those who, possessed of sufficient sense of modesty to determine that there are others who excel them in the power of discriminating between truth and error, and by whom they may be instructed, ought rather to content themselves with the opinions of such than trust for more correct to their own Reason.

For my own part, I should doubtless have belonged to the latter class, had I received instruction from but one master, or had I never known the diversities of opinion that from time immemorial have prevailed among men of the greatest learning. But I had become aware, even so early as during my college life, that no opinion, however absurd and incredible, can be imagined, which has not been maintained by some one of the philosophers; and afterward in the course of my travels I remarked that all those whose opinions are decidedly repugnant to ours are not on that account barbarians and savages, but on the contrary that many of these nations make an equally good, if not a better, use of their Reason than we do. I took into account also the very different character which a person brought up from infancy in France or Germany exhibits, from that which, with the same mind originally, this individual would have possessed had he lived always among the Chinese or with savages, and the circumstance that in dress itself the fashion which pleased us ten years ago, and which may again, perhaps, be received into favor before ten years have gone, appears to us at this moment extravagant and ridiculous. I was thus led to infer that the ground of our opinions is far more custom and example than any certain knowledge. And, finally, although such be the ground of our opinions, I remarked that a plurality of suffrages is no guarantee of truth where it is at all of difficult discovery, as in such cases it is much more likely that it will be found by one than by many. I could, however, select from the crowd no one whose opinions seemed worthy of preference, and thus I found myself constrained, as it were, to use my own Reason in the conduct of my life.

But like one walking alone and in the dark, I resolved to proceed slowly and with such circumspection, that if I did not advance far, I would at least guard against falling. I did not even choose to dismiss summarily any of the opinions that had crept into my belief without having been introduced by Reason, but first of all took sufficient time carefully to satisfy myself of the general nature of the task I was setting myself, and ascertain the true Method by which to arrive at the knowledge of whatever lay within the compass of my powers.

—*From The Method, Meditations and Philosophy of René Descartes, French (1596–1650), translated by John Veitch.*

~ ⚙ ~

Thoughts

BLAISE PASCAL

MAN BETWEEN THE INFINITIES

LET man then contemplate the whole of nature in her full and grand majesty, and turn his vision from the low objects which surround him. Let him gaze on that brilliant light, set like an eternal lamp to illumine the universe; let the earth appear to him a point in comparison with the vast circle described by the sun; and let him wonder at the fact that this vast circle is itself but a very fine point in comparison with that described by the stars in their revolution round the firmament. But if our view be arrested there, let our imagination pass beyond; it will sooner exhaust the power of conception than nature that of supplying material for conception. The whole visible world is only an imperceptible atom in the ample bosom of nature. No idea approaches it. We may enlarge our conceptions beyond all imaginable space; we only produce atoms in comparison with the reality of things. It is an infinite sphere, the centre of which is everywhere, the circumference nowhere. In short it is the greatest sensible mark of the almighty power of God, that imagination loses itself in that thought.

Returning to himself, let man consider what he is in comparison with all existence; let him regard himself as lost in this remote corner of nature; and from the little cell in which he finds himself lodged, I mean the universe, let him estimate at their true value the earth, kingdoms, cities, and himself. What is a man in the Infinite?

But to show him another prodigy equally astonishing, let him examine the most delicate things he knows. Let a mite be given him, with its minute body and parts incomparably more minute, limbs with their joints, veins in the limbs, blood in the veins, humours in the blood, drops in the humours, vapours in the drops. Dividing these last things again, let him exhaust his powers of conception, and let the last object at which he can arrive be now that of our discourse. Perhaps he will think that here is the smallest point in nature. I will let him see therein a new abyss. I will paint for him not only the visible universe, but all that he can conceive of nature's immensity in the womb of this abridged atom. Let him see therein an infinity of universes, each of which has its firmament, its planets, its earth, in the same proportion as in the visible world; in each earth animals, and in the last mites, in which he will find again all that the first had, finding still in these others the same thing without end and without cessation. Let him lose himself in wonders as amazing in their littleness as the others in their vastness. For who will not be astounded at the fact that our body, which a little while ago was imperceptible in the universe, itself imperceptible in the bosom of the whole, is now a colossus, a world, or rather a whole, in respect of the nothingness which we cannot reach? He who regards himself in this light will be afraid of himself, and observing himself sustained in the body given him by nature between those two abysses of the Infinite and Nothing, will tremble at the sight of these marvels; and I think that, as his curiosity changes into admiration, he will be more disposed to contemplate them in silence than to examine them with presumption.

For in fact what is man in nature? A Nothing in comparison with the Infinite, an All in comparison with the Nothing, a mean between nothing and everything. Since he is infinitely removed from comprehending the extremes, the end of things and their beginning are hopelessly hidden from him in an impenetrable secret; he is equally incapable of seeing the Nothing from which he was made, and the Infinite in which he is swallowed up.

What will he do then, but perceive the appearance of the middle of things, in an eternal despair of knowing either their beginning or their end. All things proceed from the Nothing, and are borne towards the Infinite. Who will follow these marvellous processes? The Author of these wonders understands them. None other can do so.

Through failure to contemplate these Infinites, men have rashly rushed into the examination of nature, as though they bore some proportion to her. It is strange that they have wished to understand the beginnings of things, and thence to arrive at the knowledge of the whole, with a presumption as infinite as their object. For surely this design cannot be formed without presumption or without a capacity infinite like nature.

If we are well informed, we understand that, as nature has graven her image and that of her Author on all things, they almost all partake of her double infinity. . . .

Of these two Infinites of science, that of greatness is the most palpable, and hence a few persons have pretended to know all things. "I will speak of the whole," said Democritus.

But the infinitely little is the least obvious. Philosophers have much oftener claimed to have reached it, and it is here they have all stumbled. This has given rise to such common titles as *First Principles, Principles of Philosophy,* and the like, as ostentatious in fact, though not in appearance, as that one which blinds us, *De omni scibili.*

We naturally believe ourselves far more capable of reaching the centre of things than of embracing their circumference. The visible extent of the world visibly exceeds us; but as we exceed little things, we think ourselves more capable of knowing them. And yet we need no less capacity for attaining the Nothing than the All. Infinite capacity is required for both, and it seems to me that whoever shall have understood the ultimate principles of being might also attain to the knowledge of the Infinite. The one depends on the other, and one leads to the other. These extremes meet and reunite by force of distance, and find each other in God, and in God alone.

Let us then take our compass; we are something, and we are not everything. The nature of our existence hides from us the knowledge of first beginnings which are born of the Nothing; and the littleness of our being conceals from us the sight of the Infinite.

Our intellect holds the same position in the world of thought as our body occupies in the expanse of nature.

Limited as we are in every way, this state which holds the mean between two extremes is present in all our impotence. Our senses perceive no extreme. Too much sound deafens us; too much light dazzles us; too great distance or proximity hinders our view. Too great length and too great brevity of discourse tend to obscurity; too much truth is paralysing (I know some who cannot understand that to take four from nothing leaves nothing.) First principles are too self-evident for us; too much pleasure disagrees with us. Too many concords are annoying in music; too many benefits irritate us; we wish to have the wherewithal to over-pay our debts. We feel neither extreme heat nor extreme cold. Excessive qualities are prejudicial to us and not perceptible by the senses; we do not feel but suffer them. Extreme youth and extreme age hinder the mind, as also too much and too little education. In short, extremes are for us as though they were not, and we are not within their notice. They escape us, or we them.

This is our true state; this is what makes us incapable of certain knowledge and of absolute ignorance. We sail within a vast sphere, ever drifting in uncertainty, driven from end to end. When we think to attach ourselves to any point and to fasten to it, it wavers and leaves us; and if we follow it, it eludes our grasp, slips past us, and vanishes for ever. Nothing stays for us. This is our natural condition, and yet most contrary to our inclination; we burn with desire to find solid ground and an ultimate sure foundation whereon to build a tower reaching to the Infinite. But our whole groundwork cracks, and the earth opens to abysses.

Let us therefore not look for certainty and stability. Our reason is always deceived by fickle shadows; nothing can fix the finite between the two Infinites, which both enclose and fly from it.

If this be well understood, I think that we shall remain at rest, each in the state wherein nature has placed him. As this sphere which has fallen to us as our lot is always distant from either extreme, what matters it that man should have a little more knowledge of the universe? If he has it, he but gets a little higher. Is he not always infinitely removed from the end, and is not the duration of our life equally removed from eternity, even if it lasts ten years longer?

In comparison with these Infinites all finites are equal, and I see no reason for fixing our imagination on one more than on another. The only comparison which we make of ourselves to the finite is painful to us. . . .

This is what I see and what troubles me. I look on all sides, and I see only darkness everywhere. Nature presents to me nothing which is not matter of doubt and concern. If I saw nothing there which revealed a Divinity, I would come to a negative conclusion; if I saw everywhere the signs of a Creator, I would remain peacefully in faith. But, seeing too much to deny and too little to be sure, I am in a state to be pitied; wherefore I have a hundred times wished that if a God maintains nature, she should testify to Him unequivocally, and that, if the signs she gives are deceptive, she should suppress them altogether; that she should say everything or nothing, that I might see which cause I ought to follow. Whereas in my present state, ignorant of what I am or of what I ought to do, I know neither my condition nor my duty. My heart inclines wholly to know where is the true good, in order to follow it; nothing would be too dear to me for eternity.

I envy those whom I see living in the faith with such carelessness, and who make such a bad use of a gift of which it seems to me I would make such a different use.

It is incomprehensible that God should exist, and it is incomprehensible that He should not exist; that the soul should be joined to the body, and that we should have no soul; that the world should be created, and that it should not be created, etc.; that original sin should be, and that it should not be. . . .

Our soul is cast into a body, where it finds number, time, dimension. Thereupon it reasons, and calls this nature, necessity, and can believe nothing else.

Unity joined to infinity adds nothing to it, no more than one foot to an infinite measure. The finite is annihilated in the presence of the infinite, and becomes a pure nothing. So our spirit before God, so our justice before divine justice. There is not so great a disproportion between our justice and that of God, as between unity and infinity.

The justice of God must be vast like His compassion. Now justice to the outcast is less vast, and ought less to offend our feelings than mercy towards the elect.

We know that there is an infinite, and are ignorant of its nature. As we know it to be false that numbers are finite, it is therefore true that there is an infinity in number. But we do not know what it is. It is false that it is even, it is false that it is odd; for the addition of a unit can make no change in its nature. Yet it is a number, and every number is odd or even (this is certainly true of every finite number). So we may well know that there is a God without knowing what He is. Is there not one substantial truth, seeing there are so many things which are not the truth itself? . . .

Let us now speak according to natural lights.

If there is a God, He is infinitely incomprehensible, since, having neither parts nor limits, He has no affinity to us. We are then incapable of knowing either what He is or if He is. This being so, who will dare to undertake the decision of the question? Not we, who have no affinity to Him.

Who then will blame Christians for not being able to give a reason for their belief, since they profess a religion for which they cannot give a reason? They declare, in expounding it to the world, that it is a foolishness, *stultitiam;* and then you complain that they do not prove it! If they proved it, they would not keep their word; it is in lacking proofs, that they are not lacking in sense. "Yes, but although this excuses those who offer it as such, and takes away from them the blame of putting it forward without reason, it does not excuse those who receive it." Let us then examine this point, and say, "God is, or He is not." But to which side shall we incline? Reason can decide nothing here. There is an infinite chaos which separated us. A game is being played at the extremity of this infinite distance where heads or tails will turn up. What will you wager? According to reason, you can do neither the one thing nor the other; according to reason, you can defend neither of the propositions.

Do not then reprove for error those who have made a choice; for you know nothing about it. "No, but I blame them for having made, not this choice, but a choice; for again both he who chooses heads and he who chooses tails are equally at fault, they are both in the wrong. The true course is not to wager at all."

Yes; but you must wager. It is not optional. You are embarked. Which will you choose then? Let us see. Since you must choose, let us see which interests you least. You have two things to lose, the true and the good; and two things to stake, your reason and your will, your knowledge and your happiness; and your nature has two things to shun, error and misery. Your reason is no more shocked in choosing one rather than the other, since you must of necessity choose. This is one point settled. But your happiness? Let us weigh the gain and the loss in wagering that God is. Let us estimate these two chances. If you gain, you gain all; if you lose, you lose nothing. Wager, then, without hesitation that He is. — "That is very fine. Yes, I must wager; but I may perhaps wager too much." — Let us see. Since there is an equal risk of gain and of loss, if you had only to gain two lives, instead of one, you might still wager. But if there were three lives to gain, you would have to play (since you are under the necessity of playing), and you would be imprudent, when you are forced to play, not to chance your life to gain three at a game where there is an equal risk of loss and gain. But there is an eternity of life and happiness. And this being so, if there were an infinity of chances, of which one only would be for you, you would still be right in wagering one to win two, and you would act stupidly, being obliged to play, by refusing to stake one life against three at a game in which out of an infinity of chances there is one for you, if there were an infinity of an infinitely happy life to gain. But there is here an infinity of an infinitely happy life to gain, a chance of gain against a finite number of chances of loss, and what you stake is finite. It is all divided; wherever the infinite is and there is not an infinity of chances of loss against that of gain, there is no time to hesitate, you must give all. And thus, when one is forced to play, he must renounce reason to preserve his life, rather than risk it for infinite gain, as likely to happen as the loss of nothingness.

For it is no use to say it is uncertain if we will gain, and it is certain that we risk, and that the infinite distance between the *certainty* of what is staked and the *uncertainty* of what will be gained, equals the finite good which is certainly staked against the uncertain infinite. It is not so, as every player stakes a certainty to gain an uncertainty, and yet he stakes a finite certainty to gain a finite uncertainty, without transgressing against reason. There is not an infinite distance between the certainty staked and the uncertainty of the gain; that is untrue. In truth, there is an infinity between the certainty of gain and the certainty of loss. But the uncertainty of the gain is proportioned to the certainty of the stake according to the proportion of the chances of gain and loss. Hence it comes that, if there are as many risks on one side as on the other, the course is to play even; and then the certainty of the stake is equal to the uncertainty of the gain, so far is it from fact that there is an infinite distance between them. And so our proposition is of infinite force, when there is the finite to stake in a game where there are equal risks of gain and of loss, and the infinite to gain. This is demonstrable; and if men are capable of any truths, this is one.

"I confess it, I admit it. But, still, is there no means of seeing the faces of the cards?" — Yes, Scripture and the rest, etc. "Yes, but I have my hands tied and my mouth closed; I am forced to wager, and am not free. I am not released, and am so made that I cannot believe. What, then, would you have me do?"

True. But at least learn your inability to believe, since reason brings you to this, and yet you cannot believe. Endeavour then to convince yourself, not by increase of proofs of God, but by the abatement of your passions. You would like to attain faith, and do not know the way; you would like to cure yourself of unbelief, and ask the remedy for it. Learn of those who have been bound like you, and who now stake all their possessions. These are people who know the way which you would follow, and who are cured of an ill of which you would be cured. Follow the way by which they began; by acting as if they believed, taking the holy water, having masses said, etc. Even this will naturally make you believe, and deaden your acuteness. — "But this is what I am afraid of." — And why? What have you to lose? . . .

If we must not act save on a certainty, we ought not to act on religion, for it is not certain. But how many things we do on an uncertainty, sea voyages, battles! I say then we must do nothing at all, for nothing is certain, and that there is more certainty in religion than there is as to whether we may see to-morrow; for it is not certain that we may see to-morrow, and it is certainly possible that we may not see it. We cannot say as much about religion. It is not certain that it is; but who will venture to say that it is certainly possible that it is not? Now when we work for to-morrow, and so on an uncertainty, we act reasonably. . . .

According to the doctrine of chance, you ought to put yourself to the trouble of searching for the truth; for if you die without worshipping the True Cause, you are lost. — "But," say you, "if He had wished me to worship Him, He would have left me signs of His will." — He has done so; but you neglect them. Seek them, therefore; it is well worth it.

—From the Pensées of Blaise Pascal, French (1623–1662), translated by William F. Trotter.

The Savoyard Vicar's Creed

JEAN JACQUES ROUSSEAU

ABOUT thirty years ago a young man, who had forsaken his own country and rambled into Italy, found himself reduced to a condition of great poverty and distress. He had been bred a Calvinist; but in consequence of his misconduct and of being unhappily a fugitive in a foreign country, without money or friends, he was induced to change his religion for the sake of subsistence. To this end he procured admittance into a *hospice* for catechumens, that is to say, a house established for the reception of proselytes. The instructions he here received concerning some controversial points excited doubts he had not before entertained, and first caused him to realize the evil of the step he had taken. He was taught strange dogmas, and was eye-witness to strange manners; and to these he saw himself a destined victim. He now sought to make his escape, but was prevented and more closely confined. If he complained, he was punished for complaining; and, lying at the mercy of his tyrannical oppressors, found himself a criminal because he could not without reluctance submit to be so. . . .

He would doubtless have been entirely ruined had it not been for the good offices of an honest ecclesiastic, who came to the hospital on some business, and with whom he found an opportunity for a private conference. The good priest was himself poor, and stood in need of every one's assistance; the oppressed proselyte, however, stood yet in greater need of him. The former did not hesitate, therefore, to favor his escape, even at the risk of making a powerful enemy.

Having escaped from vice only to return to indigence, this young adventurer struggled against his destiny without success. For a moment, indeed, he thought himself above it, and at the first prospect of good fortune, his former distresses and his protector were forgotten together. He was soon punished, however, for his ingratitude, as his groundless hopes vanished. . . . Having fallen into his former distress, and being not only in want of clothes and lodging, but even in danger of perishing with hunger, he recollected his former benefactor.

To him he returned, and was well received. . . . This good priest was naturally humane and compassionate. His own misfortunes had taught him to feel for those of others, nor had prosperity hardened his heart. In a word, the maxims of true wisdom and conscious virtue had confirmed the kindness of his natural disposition. He cordially embraced the young wanderer, provided for him a lodging, and shared with him the slender means of his own subsistence. Nor was this all; he went still farther, freely giving him both instruction and consolation, and also endeavoring to teach him the difficult art of supporting adversity with patience. Could you believe, ye sons of prejudice! that a priest, and a priest in Italy too, could be capable of this?

This honest ecclesiastic was a poor Savoyard, who having in his younger days incurred the displeasure of his bishop, was obliged to pass the mountains in order to seek that provision which was denied him in his own country. He was neither deficient in literature nor understanding; his talents, therefore, soon procured him a patron, who recommended him as tutor to a young man of quality. He preferred poverty, however, to dependence; and, being a stranger to the manners and behavior of the great, he remained but a short time in that situation. In quitting this service, however, he fortunately did not lose the esteem of his friend; and, as he behaved with great prudence and was universally beloved, he flattered himself that he should in time regain the good opinion of his bishop also, and be rewarded with some little benefice in the mountains, where he hoped to spend in tranquillity and peace the remainder of his days. This was the height of his ambition.

Interested by a natural affinity in favor of the young fugitive, he examined very carefully into his character and disposition. In this examination, he saw that his misfortunes had already debased his heart; — that the shame and contempt to which he had been exposed had depressed his ambition, and that his disappointed pride, converted into indignation, had deduced, from the injustice and cruelty of mankind, the depravity of human nature and the emptiness of virtue. He had observed religion made use of as a mask to self-interest, and its worship as a cloak to hypocrisy. He had seen the terms heaven and hell prostituted in the subtlety of vain disputes; and the joys of the one and the pains of the other being annexed to a mere repetition of words. He had observed the sublime and primitive idea of the Divinity disfigured by the fantastical imaginations of men; and, finding that in order to believe in God it was necessary to give up that understanding he hath bestowed on us, he held in disdain as well the sacred object of our idle reveries as those idle reveries themselves. Without knowing anything of natural causes, or giving himself any trouble to investigate them, he remained in a condition of the most stupid ignorance, mixed with profound contempt for those who pretended to greater knowledge than his own.

A neglect of all religious duties leads to a neglect of all moral obligations. The heart of this young vagabond had already made a great progress from one toward the other. Not that he was constitutionally vicious; but misfortune and incredulity, having stifled by degrees the propensities of his natural disposition, were hurrying him on to ruin, adding to the manners of a beggar the principles of an atheist.

But I will continue to speak no longer in the third person, which is indeed a superfluous caution; as you, my dear countrymen, are very sensible that the unhappy fugitive I have been speaking of is myself. I believe that I am now so far removed from the irregularities of my youth as to dare to avow them, and think that the hand which extricated me from them is too well deserving of my gratitude for me not to do it honor even at the expense of a little shame.

The most striking circumstance of all was to observe in the retired life of my worthy master virtue without hypocrisy and humanity without weakness. His conversation was always honest and simple, his conduct ever conformable to his discourse. I never found him troubling himself whether the persons he assisted went constantly to vespers — whether they went frequently to confession — or fasted on certain days of the week. Nor did I ever know him to impose on them any of those conditions without which a man might perish from want, and have no hope of relief from the devout.

Encouraged by these observations, so far was I from affecting in his presence the forward zeal of a new proselyte, that I took no pains to conceal my thoughts, nor did I ever remark his being scandalized at this freedom. Hence, I have sometimes said to myself, he certainly overlooks my indifference for the new mode of worship which I have embraced, in consideration of the disregard which he sees I have for that in which I was educated; as he finds my indifference is not partial to either. . . . As I lived with him in the greatest intimacy, I learned every day to respect him more and more; and as he had entirely won my heart by so many acts of kindness, I waited with an impatient curiosity to know the principles on which a life and conduct so singular and uniform could be founded.

It was some time, however, before this curiosity was satisfied, as he endeavored to cultivate those seeds of reason and goodness which he had endeavored to instill, before he would disclose himself to his disciple. The greatest difficulty he met with was to eradicate from my heart a proud misanthropy, a certain rancorous hatred which I bore to the wealthy and fortunate. . . .

Without directly attacking this pride, he yet strove to prevent it from degenerating into barbarity, and without diminishing my self-esteem, made me less disdainful of my neighbors. In withdrawing the gaudy veil of external appearances, and presenting to my view the real evils it concealed, he taught me to lament the failings of my fellow-creatures, to sympathize with their miseries, and to pity instead of envying them. Moved to compassion for human frailties from a deep sense of his own, he saw mankind everywhere the victims of either their own vices or of the vices of others, – he saw the poor groan beneath the yoke of the rich, and the rich beneath the tyranny of their own idle habits and prejudices.

"Believe me," said he, "our mistaken notions of things are so far from hiding our misfortunes from our view, that they augment those evils by rendering trifles of importance, and making us sensible of a thousand wants which we should never have known but for our prejudices. Peace of mind consists in a contempt for everything that may disturb it. The man who gives himself the greatest concern about life is he who enjoys it least; and he who aspires the most earnestly after happiness is always the one who is the most miserable."

"Alas!" cried I, with all the bitterness of discontent, "what a deplorable picture do you present of human life! If we may indulge ourselves in nothing, to what purpose were we born? If we must despise even happiness itself, who is there that can know what it is to be happy?"

"I know," replied the good priest, in a tone and manner that struck me.

"You!" said I, "so little favored by fortune! so poor! exiled! persecuted! can you be happy? And if you are, what have you done to purchase happiness?"

"My dear child," he replied, embracing me, "I will willingly tell you. As you have freely confessed to me, I will do the same to you. I will disclose to you all the sentiments of my heart. You shall see me, if not such as I really am, at least such as I believe myself to be: and when you have heard my whole *Profession of Faith* – when you know fully the situation of my heart – you will know why I think myself happy; and if you agree with me, what course you should pursue in order to become so likewise.

"But this profession is not to be made in a moment. It will require some time to disclose to you my thoughts on the situation of mankind and on the real value of human life. We will therefore take a suitable opportunity for a few hours' uninterrupted conversation on this subject."

As I expressed an earnest desire for such an opportunity, an appointment was made for the next morning. We rose at the break of day and prepared for the journey. Leaving the town, he led me to the top of a hill, at the foot of which ran the river Po, watering in its course the fertile vales. That immense chain of mountains, called the Alps, terminated the distant view. The rising sun cast its welcome rays over the gilded plains, and by projecting the long shadows of the trees, the houses, and adjacent hills, formed the most beautiful scene ever mortal eye beheld. One might have been almost tempted to think that nature had at this moment displayed all its grandeur and beauty as a subject for our conversation. Here it was that, after contemplating for a short time the surrounding objects in silence, my teacher and benefactor confided to me with impressive earnestness the principles and faith which governed his life and conduct.

"Expect from me neither learned declamations nor profound arguments. I am no great philosopher, and give myself but little trouble in regard to becoming such. Still I perceive sometimes the glimmering of good sense, and have always a regard for the truth. I will not enter into any disputation, or endeavor to refute you; but only lay down my own sentiments in simplicity of heart. Consult your own during this recital: this is all I require of you. If I am mistaken, it is undesignedly, which is sufficient to absolve me of all criminal error; and if I am right, reason, which is common to us both, shall decide. We are equally interested in listening to it, and why should not our views agree?

"I was born a poor peasant, destined by my situation to the business of husbandry. It was thought, however, much more advisable for me to learn to get my bread by the profession of a priest, and means were found to give me a proper education. In this, most certainly, neither my parents nor I consulted what was really good, true or useful for me to know; but only that I should learn what was necessary to my ordination. I learned, therefore, what was required of me to learn, — I said what was required of me to say, — and, accordingly, was made a priest. It was not long, however, before I perceived too plainly that, in laying myself under an obligation to be no longer a man, I had engaged for more than I could possibly perform. . . .

"I was in that state of doubt and uncertainty in which Descartes requires the mind to be involved, in order to enable it to investigate truth. This disposition of mind, however, is too disquieting to long continue, its duration being owing only to indolence or vice. My heart was not so corrupt as to seek fresh indulgence; and nothing preserves so well the habit of reflection as to be more content with ourselves than with our fortune.

"I reflected, therefore, on the unhappy lot of mortals floating always on the ocean of human opinions, without compass or rudder — left to the mercy of their tempestuous passions, with no other guide than an inexperienced pilot, ignorant of his course, as well as from whence he came, and whither he is going. I often said to myself: I love the truth — I seek, yet cannot find it. Let anyone show it to me and I will readily embrace it. Why doth it hide its charms from a heart formed to adore them?

"I have frequently experienced at times much greater evils; and yet no part of my life was ever so constantly disagreeable to me as that interval of scruples and anxiety. Running perpetually from one doubt and uncertainty to another, all that I could deduce from my long and painful meditations was incertitude, obscurity, and contradiction; as well with regard to my existence as to my duty. . . .

"What added further to my perplexity was, that as the authority of the church in which I was educated was decisive, and tolerated not the slightest doubt, in rejecting one point I thereby rejected in a manner all the others. The impossibility of admitting so many absurd decisions, threw doubt over those more reasonable. In being told I must believe all, I was prevented from believing anything, and I knew not what course to pursue.

"In this situation I consulted the philosophers. I turned over their books, and examined their several opinions. I found them vain, dogmatical and dictatorial — even in their pretended skepticism. Ignorant of nothing, yet proving nothing; but ridiculing one another instead. . . .

"I conceived that the weakness of the human understanding was the first cause of the prodigious variety I found in their sentiments, and that pride was the second. We have no standard with which to measure this immense machine; we cannot calculate its various relations; we neither know the first cause nor the final effects; we are ignorant even of ourselves; we neither know our own nature nor principle of action; nay, we hardly know whether man be a simple or compound being. Impenetrable mysteries surround us on every side; they extend beyond the region of sense; we imagine ourselves possessed of understanding to penetrate them, and we have only imagination. Every one strikes out a way of his own across this imaginary world; but no one knows whether it will lead him to the point he aims at. We are yet desirous to penetrate, to know, everything. The only thing we know not is to contentedly remain ignorant of what it is impossible for us to know. We had much rather determine at random, and believe the thing which is not, than to confess that none of us is capable of seeing the thing that is. Being ourselves but a part of that great whole, whose limits surpass our most extensive views, and concerning which its creator leaves us to make our idle conjectures, we are vain enough to decide what that whole is in itself, and what we are in relation to it. . . .

"The first fruit I gathered from these meditations was to learn to confine my enquiries to those things in which I was immediately interested; — to remain contented in a profound ignorance of the rest; and not to trouble myself so far as even to doubt about what it did not concern me to know. . . .

"Taking a retrospect, then, of the several opinions which had successively prevailed with me from my infancy, I found that, although none of them were so evident as to produce immediate conviction, they had nevertheless different degrees of probability, and that my innate sense of truth and falsehood leaned more or less to each. On this first observation, proceeding to compare impartially and without prejudice these different opinions with each other, I found that the first and most common was also the most simple and most rational; and that it wanted nothing more to secure universal suffrage, than the circumstance of having been the last proposed. . . .

"The love of truth then comprises all my philosophy; and my method of research being the simple and easy rule of common sense, which dispenses with the vain subtlety of argumentation, I re-examined by this principle all the knowledge of which I was possessed, resolved to admit as evident everything to which I could not in the sincerity of my heart refuse to assent, to admit also as true all that seemed to have a necessary connection with it, and to leave everything else as uncertain, without either rejecting or admitting, being determined not to trouble myself about clearing up any point which did not tend to utility in practice.

"You will find that my exposition treats of nothing more than natural religion. It is very strange that we should stand in need of any other! By what means can I find out such necessity? In what respect can I be culpable for serving God agreeably to the dictates of the understanding he hath given me, and the sentiments he hath implanted in my heart? What purity of morals, what system of faith useful to man or honorable to his Creator, can I deduce from any positive doctrines, that I cannot deduce equally as well from a good use of my natural faculties? Let any one show me what can be added, either for the glory of God, the good of society, or my own advantage, to the obligations we are laid under by nature. Let him show me what virtue can be produced from any new worship, which is not also the consequence of mine. The most sublime ideas of the Deity are inculcated by reason alone. Take a view of the works of nature, listen to the voice within, and then tell me what God hath omitted to say to your sight, your conscience, your understanding? Where are the men who can tell us more of him than he thus tells us of himself? Their revelations only debase the Deity, in ascribing to him human passions. So far from giving us enlightened notions of the Supreme Being, their particular tenets, in my opinion, give us the most obscure and confused ideas. To the inconceivable mysteries by which the Deity is hid from our view, they add the most absurd contradictions. They serve to make man proud, persecuting, and cruel. Instead of establishing peace on earth, they bring fire and sword. I ask myself what good purpose all this contention serves, without being able to resolve the question. Artificial religion presents to my view only the wickedness and miseries of mankind.

"I am told, indeed, that revelation is necessary to teach mankind the manner in which God should be served. As a proof of this, they bring the diversity of whimsical modes of worship which prevail in the world; and without remarking that this very diversity arises from the practice of adopting revelations. Ever since men have taken it into their heads to make the Deity speak, every people make him speak in their own way, and say what they like best. Had they listened only to what the Deity hath said in their hearts, there would have been but one religion on earth.

"It is necessary that the worship of God should be uniform; I would have it so: but is this a point so very important that the whole apparatus of divine power was necessary to establish it? Let us not confound the ceremonials of religion with religion itself. The worship of God demands that of the heart; and this, when it is sincere, is ever uniform."

—*From The Profession of Faith of a Savoyard Vicar, by Jean Jacques Rousseau, French (1712–1778), translated by Olive Schreiner.*

~ ❁ ~

On the Feeling of Immortality in Youth

WILLIAM HAZLITT

NO YOUNG man believes he shall ever die. It was a saying of my brother's, and a fine one. There is a feeling of Eternity in youth which makes us amends for everything. To be young is to be as one of the Immortals. One-half of time indeed is spent—the other half remains in store for us with all its countless treasures, for there is no line drawn, and we see no limit to our hopes and wishes. We make the coming age our own—

> The vast, the unbounded prospect lies
> before us.

Death, old age, are words without a meaning, a dream, a fiction, with which we have nothing to do. Others may have undergone, or may still undergo them — we "bear a charmed life," which laughs to scorn all such idle fancies. As, in setting out on a delightful journey, we strain our eager sight forward,

> Bidding the lovely scenes at distance hail,

and see no end to prospect after prospect, new objects presenting themselves as we advance, so in the outset of life we see no end to our desires nor to the opportunities of gratifying them. We have as yet found no obstacle, no disposition to flag, and it seems that we can go on so forever. We look round in a new world, full of life and motion, and ceaseless progress, and feel in ourselves all the vigor and spirit to keep pace with it, and do not foresee from any present signs how we shall be left behind in the race, decline into old age, and drop into the grave. It is the simplicity and, as it were, abstractedness of our feelings in youth that (so to speak) identifies us with nature and (our experience being weak and our passions strong) makes us fancy ourselves immortal like it. Our short-lived connection with being, we fondly flatter ourselves, is an indissoluble and lasting union. As infants smile and sleep, we are rocked in the cradle of our desires, and hushed into fancied security by the roar of the universe around us — we quaff the cup of life with eager thirst without draining it, and joy and hope seem ever mantling to the brim — objects press around us, filling the mind with their magnitude and with the throng of desires that wait upon them, so that there is no room for the thoughts of death. We are too much dazzled by the gorgeousness and novelty of the bright waking dream about us to discern the dim shadow lingering for us in the distance. Nor would the hold that life has taken of us permit us to detach our thoughts that way, even if we could. We are too much absorbed in present objects and pursuits. While the spirit of youth remains unimpaired, ere "the wine of life is drunk," we are like people intoxicated or in a fever, who are hurried away by the violence of their own sensations: it is only as present objects begin to pall upon the sense, as we have been disappointed in our favorite pursuits, cut off from our closest ties, that we by degrees become weaned from the world, that passion loosens its hold upon futurity, and that we begin to contemplate as in a glass darkly the possibility of parting with it for good. Till then, the example of others has no effect upon us. Casualties we avoid; the slow approaches of age we play at *hide and seek* with. Like the foolish fat scullion in Sterne, who hears that Master Bobby is dead, our only reflection is: "So am not I!" The idea of death, instead of staggering our confidence, only seems to strengthen and enhance our sense of the possession and enjoyment of life. Others may fall around us like leaves, or be mowed down by the scythe of Time like grass: these are but metaphors to the unreflecting, buoyant ears and overweening presumption of youth. It is not till we see the flowers of Love, Hope, and Joy withering around us, that we give up the flattering delusions that before led us on, and that the emptiness and dreariness of the prospect before us reconciles us hypothetically to the silence of the grave.

Life is indeed a strange gift, and its privileges are most mysterious. No wonder, when it is first granted to us, that our gratitude, our admiration, and our delight should prevent us from reflecting on our own nothingness, or from thinking it will ever be recalled. Our first and strongest impressions are borrowed from the mighty scene that is opened to us, and we unconsciously transfer its durability as well as its splendor to ourselves. So newly found, we cannot think of parting with it yet, or at least put off that consideration *sine die*. Like a rustic at a fair, we are full of amazement and rapture, and have no thought of going home, or that it will soon be night. We know our existence only by ourselves, and confound our knowledge with the objects of it. We and Nature are therefore one. Otherwise the illusion, the "feast of reason and the flow of soul" to which we are invited, is a mockery and a cruel insult. We do not go from a play till the last act is ended, and the lights are about to be extinguished. But the fairy face of Nature still shines on: shall we be called away before the curtain falls, or ere we have scarce had a glimpse of what is going on? Like children, our stepmother Nature holds us up to see the raree-show of the universe, and then, as if we were a burden to her to support, lets us fall down again. Yet what brave sublunary things does not this pageant present, like a ball or *fête* of the universe!

To see the golden sun, the azure sky, the outstretched ocean; to walk upon the green earth, and be lord of a thousand creatures; to look down yawning precipices or over distant sunny vales; to see the world spread out under one's feet on a map; to bring the stars near; to view the smallest insects through a microscope; to read history, and consider the revolutions of empire and the successions of generations; to hear of the glory of Tyre, of Sidon, of Babylon, and of Susa, and to say all these were before me and are now nothing; to say I exist in such a point of time, and in such a point of space; to be a spectator and a part of its ever-moving scene; to witness the change of season, of spring and autumn, of winter and summer; to feel hot and cold, pleasure and pain, beauty and deformity, right and wrong; to be sensible to the accidents of nature; to consider the mighty world of eye and ear; to listen to the stock-dove's notes amid the forest deep; to journey over moor and mountain; to hear the midnight sainted choir; to visit lighted halls, or the cathedral's gloom, or sit in crowded theatres and see life itself mocked; to study the works of art and refine the sense of beauty to agony; to worship fame, and to dream of immortality; to look upon the Vatican, and to read Shakespeare; to gather up the wisdom of the ancients, and to pry into the future; to listen to the trump of war, the shout of victory; to question history as to the movements of the human heart; to seek for truth; to plead the cause of humanity; to overlook the world as if time and nature poured their treasures at our feet—to be and to do all this, and then in a moment to be nothing—to have it all snatched from us as by a juggler's trick, or a phantasmagoria! There is something in this transition from all to nothing that shocks us and damps the enthusiasm of youth new flushed with hope and pleasure, and we cast the comfortless thought as far from us as we can. In the first enjoyment of the state of life we discard the fear of debts and duns, and never think of the final payment of our great debt to Nature. Art we know is long; life, we flatter ourselves, should be so too. We see no end of the difficulties and delays we have to encounter: perfection is slow of attainment, and we must have time to accomplish it in. The fame of the great names we look up to is immortal: and shall not we who contemplate it imbibe a portion of ethereal fire, the *divinæ particula auræ,* which nothing can extinguish? A wrinkle in Rembrandt or in Nature takes whole days to resolve itself into its component parts, its softenings and its sharpnesses; we refine upon our perfections, and unfold the intricacies of nature. What a prospect for the future! What a task have we not begun! And shall we be arrested in the middle of it? We do not count our time thus employed lost, or our pains thrown away; we do not flag or grow tired, but gain new vigor at our endless task. Shall Time, then, grudge us to finish what we have begun, and have formed a compact with Nature to do? Why not fill up the blank that is left us in this manner? I have looked for hours at a Rembrandt without being conscious of the flight of time, but with ever new wonder and delight, have thought that not only my own but another existence I could pass in the same manner. This rarefied, refined existence seemed to have no end, nor stint, nor principle of decay in it. The print would remain long after I who looked on it had become the prey of worms. The thing seems in itself out of all reason: health, strength, appetite are opposed to the idea of death, and we are not ready to credit it till we have found our illusions vanished, and our hopes grown cold. Objects in youth, from novelty, etc., are stamped upon the brain with such force and integrity that one thinks nothing can remove or obliterate them. They are riveted there, and appear to us an element of our nature. It must be a mere violence that destroys them, not a natural decay. In the very strength of this persuasion we seem to enjoy an age by anticipation. We melt down years into a single moment of intense sympathy, and by anticipating the fruits defy the ravages of time. If, then, a single moment of our lives is worth years, shall we set any limits to its total value and extent? Again, does it not happen that so secure do we think ourselves of an indefinite period of existence, that at times, when left to ourselves, and impatient of novelty, we feel annoyed at what seems to us the slow and creeping progress of time, and argue that if it always moves at this tedious snail's pace it will never come to an end? How ready are we to sacrifice any space of time which separates us from a favorite object, little thinking that before long we shall find it move too fast.

For my part, I started in life with the French Revolution, and I have lived, alas! to see the end of it. But I did not foresee this result. My sun arose with the first dawn of liberty, and I did not think how soon both must set. The new impulse to ardor given to men's minds imparted a congenial warmth and glow to mine; we were strong to run a race together, and I little dreamed that long before mine was set the sun of liberty would turn to blood, or set once more in the night of despotism. Since then, I confess, I have no longer felt myself young, for with that my hopes fell.

I have since turned my thoughts to gathering up some of the fragments of my early recollections, and putting them into a form to which I might occasionally revert. The future was barred to my progress, and I turned for consolation and encouragement to the past. It is thus that, while we find our personal and substantial identity vanishing from us, we strive to gain a reflected and vicarious one in our thoughts: we do not like to perish wholly, and wish to bequeath our names, at least, to posterity. As long as we can make our cherished thoughts and nearest interests live in the minds of others, we do not appear to have retired altogether from the stage. We still occupy the breasts of others, and exert an influence and power over them, and it is only our bodies that are reduced to dust and powder. Our favorite speculations still find encouragement, and we make as great a figure in the eye of the world, or perhaps a greater, than in our lifetime. The demands of our self-love are thus satisfied, and these are the most imperious and unremitting. Besides, if by our intellectual superiority we survive ourselves in this world, by our virtues and faith we may attain an interest in another, and a higher state of being, and may thus be recipients at the same time of men and of angels.

> E'en from the tomb the voice of Nature cries,
> E'en in our ashes live their wonted fires.

As we grow old, our sense of the value of time becomes vivid. Nothing else, indeed, seems of any consequence. We can never cease wondering that that which has ever been should cease to be. We find many things remain the same: why then should there be change in us? This adds a convulsive grasp of whatever is, a sense of a fallacious hollowness in all we see. Instead of the full, pulpy feeling of youth tasting existence and every object in it, all is flat and vapid — a whited sepulcher, fair without but full of ravening and all uncleanness within. The world is a witch that puts us off with false shows and appearances. The simplicity of youth, the confiding expectation, the boundless raptures, are gone: we only think of getting out of it as well as we can, and without any great mischance or annoyance. The flush of illusion, even the complacent retrospect of past joys and hopes, is over: if we can slip out of life without indignity, can escape with little bodily infirmity, and frame our minds to the calm and respectable composure of *still-life* before we return to physical nothingness, it is as much as we can expect. We do not die wholly at our deaths: we have moldered away gradually long before. Faculty after faculty, interest after interest, attachment after attachment disappear: we are torn from ourselves while living, year after year sees us no longer the same, and death only consigns the last fragment of what we were to the grave. That we should wear out to slow stages, and dwindle at last into nothing, is not wonderful, when even in our prime our strongest impressions leave little trace but for the moment, and we are the creatures of petty circumstance. How little effect is made on us in our best days by the books we have read, the scenes we have witnessed, the sensations we have gone through! Think only of the feelings we experienced in reading a fine romance (one of Sir Walter's, for instance); what beauty, what sublimity, what interest, what heart-rending emotions! You would suppose the feelings you then experienced would last forever, or subdue the mind to their own harmony and tone: while we are reading it seems as if nothing could ever put us out of our way, or trouble us: — the first splash of mud that we get on entering the street, the first twopence we are cheated out of, the feeling vanishes clean out of our minds, and we become the prey of petty and annoying circumstance. The mind soars to the lofty: it is at home in the groveling, the disagreeable, and the little. And yet we wonder that age should be feeble and querulous, — that the freshness of youth should fade away.

Both worlds would hardly satisfy the extravagance of our desires and of our presumption.

—*From the Essays of William Hazlitt, English (1778–1830).*

~ ⚙ ~

Where I Lived, and What I Lived For

HENRY DAVID THOREAU

WHEN first I took up my abode in the woods, that is, began to spend my nights as well as days there, which, by accident, was on Independence Day, on the 4th of July, 1845, my house was not finished for winter, but was merely a defence against the rain, without plastering or chimney, the walls being of rough weather-stained boards, with wide chinks, which made it cool at night. The upright white hewn studs and freshly planed door and window-casings gave it a clean and airy look, especially in the morning, when its timbers were saturated with dew, so that I fancied that by noon some sweet gum would exude from them. To my imagination it retained throughout the day more or less of this auroral character, reminding me of a certain house on a mountain which I had visited the year before. This was an airy, an unplastered cabin, fit to entertain a travelling god, and where a goddess might trail her garments. The winds which passed over my dwelling were such as sweep over the ridges of mountains, bearing the broken strains, or celestial parts only, of terrestrial music. The morning wind forever blows, the poem of creation is uninterrupted; but few are the ears that hear it. Olympus is but the outside of the earth everywhere.

The only house I had been the owner of before, if I except a boat, was a tent, which I used occasionally when making excursions in the summer, and this is still rolled up in my garret; but the boat, after passing from hand to hand, has gone down the stream of time. With this more substantial shelter about me, I had made some progress toward settling in the world. This frame, so slightly clad, was a sort of crystallization around me, and reacted on the builder. It was suggestive somewhat as a picture in outlines. I did not need to go out doors to take the air, for the atmosphere within had lost none of its freshness. It was not so much within doors as behind a door where I sat, even in the rainiest weather. The Harivansa says: "An abode without birds is like a meat without seasoning." Such was not my abode, for I found myself suddenly neighbour to the birds; not by having imprisoned one, but having caged myself near them. I was not only nearer to some of those which commonly frequent the garden and the orchard, but to those wilder and more thrilling songsters of the forest which never, or rarely, serenade a villager—the woodthrush, the veery, the scarlet tanager, the field-sparrow, the whippoorwill, and many others.

I was seated by the shore of a small pond, about a mile and a half south of the village of Concord and somewhat higher than it, in the midst of an extensive wood between that town and Lincoln, and about two miles south of that our only field known to fame, Concord battle ground; but I was so low in the woods that the opposite shore, half a mile off, like the rest, covered with wood, was my most distant horizon. For the first week, whenever I looked out on the pond, it impressed me like a tarn high up on the one side of a mountain, its bottom far above the surface of other lakes, and, as the sun arose, I saw it throwing off its nightly clothing of mist, and here and there, by degrees, its soft ripples or its smooth reflecting surface was revealed, while the mists, like ghosts, were stealthily withdrawing in every direction into the woods, as at the breaking up of some nocturnal conventicle. The very dew seemed to hang upon the trees later into the day than usual, as on the sides of mountains.

This small lake was of most value as a neighbour in the intervals of a gentle rainstorm in August, when, both air and water being perfectly still, but the sky overcast, mid-afternoon had all the serenity of evening, and the woodthrush sang around, and was heard from shore to shore. A lake like this is never smoother than at such a time; and the clear portion of the air above it being shallow and darkened by clouds, the water, full of light and reflections, becomes a lower heaven itself so much the more important. From a hill-top near by, where the wood had been recently cut off, there was a pleasing vista southward across the pond, through a wide indentation in the hills which form the shore there, where their opposite sides sloping toward each other suggested a stream flowing out in that direction through a wooded valley, but stream there was none. That way I looked between and over the near green hills to some distant and higher ones in the horizon, tinged with blue. Indeed, by standing on tiptoe I could catch a glimpse of some of the peaks of the still bluer and more distant mountain ranges in the north-west, those true-blue coins from heaven's own mint, and also of some portion of the village. But in other directions, even from this point, I could not see over or beyond the woods which surrounded me. It is well to have some water in your neighbourhood, to give buoyancy to and float the earth. One value even of the smallest well is, that when you look into it you see that earth is not continent but insular. This is as important as that it keeps butter cool. When I looked across the pond from this peak toward the Sudbury meadows, which in time of flood I distinguished elevated perhaps by a mirage in their seething valley, like a coin in a basin, all the earth beyond the pond appeared like a thin crust insulated and floated even by this small sheet of intervening water, and I was reminded that this on which I dwelt was but *dry land.*

Though the view from my door was still more contracted, I did not feel crowded or confined in the least. There was pasture enough for my imagination. The low shrub-oak plateau to which the opposite shore arose, stretched away toward the prairies of the West and the steppes of Tartary, affording ample room for all the roving families of men. "There are none happy in the world but beings who enjoy freely a vast horizon," said Damodara, when his herds required new and larger pastures.

Both place and time were changed, and I dwelt nearer to those parts of the universe and to those eras in history which had most attracted me. Where I lived was as far off as many a region viewed nightly by astronomers. We are wont to imagine rare and delectable places in some remote and more celestial corner of the system, behind the constellation of Cassiopeia's Chair, far from noise and disturbance. I discovered that my house actually had its site in such a withdrawn, but for ever new and unprofaned, part of the universe. If it were worth the while to settle in those parts near to the Pleiades or the Hyades, to Aldebaran or Altair, then I was really there, or at an equal remoteness from the life which I had left behind, dwindled and twinkling with as fine a ray to my nearest neighbour, and to be seen only in moonless nights by him. Such was that part of creation where I had squatted —

"There was a shepherd that did live,
And held his thoughts as high
As were the mounts whereon his flocks
Did hourly feed him by."

What should we think of the shepherd's life if his flocks always wandered to higher pastures than his thoughts?

Every morning was a cheerful invitation to make my life of equal simplicity, and I may say innocence, with Nature herself. I have been as sincere a worshipper of Aurora as the Greeks. I got up early and bathed in the pond: that was a religious exercise, and one of the best things which I did. They say that characters were engraven on the bathing tub of king Tching-thang to this effect: "Renew thyself completely each day; do it again, and again, and forever again." I can understand that. Morning brings back the heroic ages. I was as much affected by the faint hum of a mosquito making its invisible and unimaginable tour through my apartment at earliest dawn, when I was sitting with door and windows open, as I could be by any trumpet that ever sang of fame. It was Homer's requiem; itself an Iliad and Odyssey in the air, singing its own wrath and wanderings. There was something cosmical about it; a standing advertisement, till forbidden, of the everlasting vigour and fertility of the world. The morning, which is the most memorable season of the day, is the awakening hour. Then there is least somnolence in us; and for an hour, at least, some part of us awakes which slumbers all the rest of the day and night. Little is to be expected of that day, if it can be called a day, to which we are not awakened by our Genius, but by the mechanical nudgings of some servitor, are not awakened by our own newly-acquired force and aspirations from within, accompanied by the undulations of celestial music, instead of factory bells, and a fragrance filling the air — to a higher life than we fell asleep from; and thus the darkness bear its fruit, and prove itself to be good, no less than the light. That man who does not believe that each day contains an earlier, more sacred and auroral hour than he has yet profaned, has despaired of life, and is pursuing a descending and darkening way. After a partial cessation of his sensuous life, the soul of man, or its organs rather, are reinvigorated each day, and his Genius tries again what noble life it can make. All memorable events, I should say, transpire in morning time and in a morning atmosphere. The Vedas say: "All intelligences awake with the morning." Poetry and art, and the fairest and most memorable of the actions of men, date from such an hour. All poets and heroes, like Memnon, are the children of Aurora, and emit their music at sunrise. To him whose elastic and vigorous thought keeps pace with the sun, the day is a perpetual morning. It matters not what the clocks say, or the attitudes and labours of men. Morning is when I am awake and there is a dawn in me. Moral reform is the effort to throw off sleep. Why is it that men give so poor an account of their day if they have not been slumbering? They are not such poor calculators. If they had not been overcome with drowsiness they would have performed something. The millions are awake enough for physical labour; but only one in a million is awake enough for effective intellectual exertion, only one in a hundred millions to a poetic or divine life. To be awake is to be alive. I have never yet met a man who was quite awake. How could I have looked him in the face?

We must learn to reawaken and keep ourselves awake, not by mechanical aids, but by an infinite expectation of the dawn, which does not forsake us in our soundest sleep. I know of no more encouraging fact than the unquestionable ability of man to elevate his life by a conscious endeavour. It is something to be able to paint a particular picture, or to carve a statue, and so to make a few objects beautiful; but it is far more glorious to carve and paint the very atmosphere and medium through which we look, which morally we can do. To affect the quality of the day, that is the highest of arts. Every man is tasked to make his life, even in its details, worthy of the contemplation of his most elevated and critical hour. If we refused, or rather used up, such paltry information as we get, the oracles would distinctly inform us how this might be done.

I went to the woods because I wished to live deliberately, to front only the essential facts of life, and see if I could not learn what it had to teach, and not, when I came to die, discover that I had not lived. I did not wish to live what was not life, living is so dear; nor did I wish to practise resignation, unless it was quite necessary. I wanted to live deep and suck out all the marrow of life, to live so sturdily and Spartan-like as to put to rout all that was not life, to cut a broad swath and shave close, to drive life into a corner, and reduce it to its lowest terms, and, if it proved to be mean, why then to get the whole and genuine meanness of it, and publish its meanness to the world; or if it were sublime, to know it by experience, and be able to give a true account of it in my next excursion. For most men, it appears to me, are in a strange uncertainty about it, whether it is of the devil or of God, and have *somewhat hastily* concluded that it is the chief end of man here to "glorify God and enjoy Him forever."

Still we live meanly, like ants; though the fable tells us that we were long ago changed into men; like pygmies we fight with cranes; it is error upon error, and clout upon clout, and our best virtue has for its occasion a superfluous and evitable wretchedness. Our life is frittered away by detail. An honest man has hardly need to count more than his ten fingers, or in extreme cases he may add his ten toes, and lump the rest. Simplicity, simplicity, simplicity! I say, let your affairs be as two or three, and not a hundred or a thousand; instead of a million count half-a-dozen, and keep your accounts on your thumb-nail. In the midst of this chopping sea of civilized life, such are the clouds and storms and quicksands and thousand-and-one items to be allowed for, that a man has to live, if he would not founder and go to the bottom and not make his port at all, by dead reckoning, and he must be a great calculator indeed who succeeds. Simplify, simplify. Instead of three meals a-day, if it be necessary eat but one; instead of a hundred dishes, five; and reduce other things in proportion. Our life is like a German Confederacy, made up of petty states, with its boundary forever fluctuating, so that even a German cannot tell you how it is bounded at any moment. The nation itself, with all its so-called internal improvements, which, by the way, are all external and superficial, is just such an unwieldy and overgrown establishment, cluttered with furniture and tripped up by its own traps, ruined by luxury and heedless expense, by want of calculation and a worthy aim, as the million households in the land; and the only cure for it as for them is in a rigid economy, a stern and more than Spartan simplicity of life and elevation of purpose. It lives too fast. Men think that it is essential that the *Nation* have commerce, and export ice, and talk through a telegraph, and ride thirty miles an hour, without a doubt, whether *they* do or not; but whether we should live like baboons or like men, is a little uncertain. If we do not get out sleepers, and forge rails, and devote days and nights to the work, but go to tinkering upon our *lives* to improve *them,* who will build railroads? And if railroads are not built, how shall we get to heaven in season? But if we stay at home and mind our business, who will want railroads? We do not ride on the railroad; it rides upon us. Did you ever think what those sleepers are that underlie the railroad? Each one is a man, an Irishman or a Yankee man. The rails are laid on them, and they are covered with sand, and the cars run smoothly over them. They are sound sleepers, I assure you. And every few years a new lot is laid down and run over; so that, if some have the pleasure of riding on a rail, others have the misfortune to be ridden upon. And when they run over a man that is walking in his sleep, a supernumerary sleeper in the wrong position, and wake him up, they suddenly stop the cars, and make a hue and cry about it, as if this were an exception. I am glad to know that it takes a gang of men for every five miles to keep the sleepers down and level in their beds as it is, for this is a sign that they may sometime get up again.

Why should we live with such hurry and waste of life? We are determined to be starved before we are hungry. Men say that a stitch in time saves nine, and so they take a thousand stitches to-day to save nine to-morrow. As for *work,* we haven't any of any consequence. We have the Saint Vitus' dance, and cannot possibly keep our heads still. If I should only give a few pulls at the parish bell-rope, as for a fire, that is, without setting the bell, there is hardly a man on his farm in the outskirts of Concord, notwithstanding that press of engagements which was his excuse so many times this morning, nor a boy, nor a woman, I might almost say, but would forsake all and follow that sound, not mainly to save property from the flames, but, if we will confess the truth, much more to see it burn, since burn it must, and we, be it known, did not set it on fire — or to see it put out, and have a hand in it, if that is done as handsomely; yes, even if it were the parish church itself. Hardly a man takes a half-hour's nap after dinner, but when he wakes he holds up his head and asks "What's the news?" as if the rest of mankind had stood his sentinels. Some give directions to be waked every half-hour, doubtless for no other purpose; and then to pay for it, they tell what they have dreamed. After a night's sleep the news is as indispensable as the breakfast. "Pray, tell me anything new that has happened to a man anywhere on this globe" — and he reads it over his coffee and rolls, that a man has had his eyes gouged out this morning on the Wachito River; never dreaming the while that he lives in the dark unfathomed mammoth cave of this world, and has but the rudiment of an eye himself.

For my part, I could easily do without the post office. I think that there are very few important communications made through it. To speak critically, I never received more than one or two letters in my life — I wrote this some years ago — that were worth the postage. The penny-post is commonly an institution through which you seriously offer a man that penny for his thoughts which is so often safely offered in jest. And I am sure that I never read any memorable news in a newspaper. If we read of one man robbed, or murdered, or killed by accident, or one house burned, or one vessel wrecked, or one steam-boat blown-up or one cow run over on the Western Railroad, or one mad dog killed, or one lot of grass-hoppers in the winter — we never need read of another. One is enough. If you are acquainted with the principle, what do you care for a myriad instances and applications? To a philosopher all *news,* as it is called, is gossip, and they who edit and read it are old women over their tea. Yet not a few are greedy after this gossip. There was such a rush, as I hear, the other day at one of the offices to learn the foreign news by the last arrival, that several large squares of plate glass belonging to the establishment were broken by the pressure — news which I seriously think a ready wit might write a twelvemonth or twelve years beforehand with sufficient accuracy. As for

Spain, for instance, if you know how to throw in Don Carlos and the Infanta, and Don Pedro and Seville and Granada, from time to time in the right proportions — they may have changed the names a little since I saw the papers — and serve up a bull-fight when other entertainments fail, it will be true to the letter, and give us as good an idea of the exact state or ruin of things in Spain as the most succinct and lucid reports under this head in the newspapers; and as for England, almost the last significant scrap of news from that quarter was the Revolution of 1649; and if you have learned the history of her crops for an average year, you never need attend to that thing again, unless your speculations are of a merely pecuniary character. If one may judge who rarely looks into the newspapers, nothing new does ever happen in foreign parts, a French Revolution not excepted.

What news! how much more important to know what that is which was never old! "Kieou-he-yu (great dignitary of the state of Wei) sent a man to Khoung-tseu to know his news. Khoung-tseu caused the messenger to be seated near him, and questioned him in these terms: What is your master doing? The messenger answered with respect: My master desires to diminish the number of his faults, but he cannot come to the end of them. The messenger being gone, the philosopher remarked: What a worthy messenger! What a worthy messenger!" The preacher, instead of vexing the ears of drowsy farmers on their day of rest at the end of the week — for Sunday is the fit conclusion of an ill-spent week, and not the fresh and brave beginning of a new one — with this one other draggle-tail of a sermon, should shout with thundering voice: "Pause! Avast! Why so seeming fast, but deadly slow?"

Shams and delusions are esteemed for soundest truths, while reality is fabulous. If men would steadily observe realities only, and not allow themselves to be deluded, life, to compare it with such things as we know, would be like a fairy tale and the Arabian Nights' Entertainments. If we respected only what is inevitable and has a right to be, music and poetry would resound along the streets. When we are unhurried and wise, we perceive that only great and worthy things have any permanent and absolute existence — that petty fears and petty pleasures are but the shadow of the reality. This is always exhilarating and sublime. By closing the eyes and slumbering, and consenting to be deceived by shows, men establish and confirm their daily life of routine and habit everywhere, which still is built on purely illusory foundations. Children, who play life, discern its true law and relations more clearly than men, who fail to live it worthily, but who think that they are wiser by experience, that is, by failure. I have read in a Hindoo book, that "there was a king's son, who, being expelled in infancy from his native city, was brought up by a forester, and, growing up to maturity in that state, imagined himself to belong to the barbarous race with which he lived. One of his father's ministers having discovered him, revealed to him what he was, and the misconception of his character was removed, and he knew himself to be a prince. So soul," continues the Hindoo philosopher, "from the circumstances in which it is placed, mistakes its own character, until the truth is revealed to it by some holy teacher, and then it knows itself to be *Brahme*." I perceive that we inhabitants of New England live this mean life that we do because our vision does not penetrate the surface of things. We think that that *is* which *appears* to be. If a man should walk through this town and see only the reality, where, think you, would the Mill dam go to? If he should give us an account of the realities he beheld there, we should not recognize the place in his description. Look at a meeting-house, or a courthouse, or a jail, or a shop, or a dwelling-house, and say what that thing really is before a true gaze, and they would all go to pieces in your account of them. Men esteem truth remote, in the outskirts of the system, behind the farthest star, before Adam and after the last man. In eternity there is indeed something true and sublime. But all these times and places and occasions are now and here. God Himself culminates in the present moment, and will never be more divine in the lapse of all the ages. And we are enabled to apprehend at all what is sublime and noble only by the perpetual instilling and drenching of the reality that surrounds us. The universe constantly and obediently answers to our conceptions; whether we travel fast or slow, the track is laid for us. Let us spend our lives in conceiving then. The poet or the artist never yet had so fair and noble a design but some of his posterity at least could accomplish it.

Let us spend one day as deliberately as Nature, and not be thrown off the track by every nutshell and mosquito's wing that falls on the rails. Let us rise early and fast, or break fast, gently and without perturbation; let company come and let company go, let the bells ring and the children cry — determined to make a day of it. Why should we knock under and go with the stream? Let us not be upset and overwhelmed in that terrible rapid and whirlpool called a dinner, situated in the meridian shallows. Weather this danger and you are safe, for the rest of the way is down hill. With unrelaxed nerves, with morning vigour, sail by it, looking another way, tied to the mast like Ulysses. If the engine whistles, let it whistle till it is hoarse for its pains. If the bell rings, why should we run? We will consider what kind of music they are like. Let us settle ourselves, and work and wedge our feet downward through the mud and slush of opinion, and prejudice, and tradition, and delusion, and appearance, that alluvion which covers the globe, through Paris and London, through New York and Boston and Concord, through church and state, through poetry and philosophy and religion, till we come to a hard bottom and rocks in place, which we call *reality*, and say, This is, and no mistake; and then begin, having a *point d'appui*, below freshet and frost and fire, a place where you might found a wall or a state, or set a lamp-post safely, or perhaps a gauge, not a Nilometer, but a Realometer, that future ages might know how deep a freshet of shams and appearances had gathered from time to time. If you stand right fronting and face to face to a fact, you will see the sun glimmer on both its surfaces, as if it were a cimeter, and feel its sweet edge dividing you through the heart and marrow, and so you will happily conclude your mortal career. Be it life or death, we crave only reality. If we are really dying, let us hear the rattle in our throats and feel cold in the extremities; if we are alive, let us go about our business.

Time is but the stream I go a-fishing in. I drink at it; but while I drink I see the sandy bottom and detect how shallow it is. Its thin current slides away, but eternity remains. I would drink deeper; fish in the sky, whose bottom is pebbly with stars. I cannot count one. I know not the first letter of the alphabet. I have always been regretting that I was not as wise as the day I was born. The intellect is a cleaver; it discerns and rifts its way into the secret of things. I do not wish to be any more busy with my hands than is necessary. My head is hands and feet. I feel all my best faculties concentrated in it. My instinct tells me that my head is an organ for burrowing, as some creatures use their snout and forepaws, and with it I would mine and burrow my way through these hills. I think that the richest vein is somewhere hereabouts; so by the divining rod and thin rising vapours I judge; and here I will begin to mine.

— *From Walden, by Henry David Thoreau, American (1817–1862).*

~ ✲ ~

Solitude

MIGUEL DE UNAMUNO

It is my love for the multitude that makes me fly from them. In flying from them, I go on seeking them. Do not call me a misanthrope. Misanthropes seek society and intercourse with people; they need them in order to feed their hatred and disdain of them. Love can live upon memories and hopes; hate needs present realities.

Let me, then, fly from society and take refuge in the quiet of the country, seeking in the heart of it and within my own soul the company of people.

Men only feel themselves really brothers when they hear one another in the silence of things in the midst of solitude. The hushed moan of your neighbour which reaches you through the wall that separates you penetrates much more deeply into your heart than would all his laments if he told you them to your face. I shall never forget a night that I once spent at a watering-place, during the whole of which I was kept awake by a very faint intermittent moaning — a moaning that seemed to wish to stifle itself in order not to awaken those who were asleep, a discreet and gentle moaning that came to me from the neighbouring bedroom. That moaning, which came from I know not whom, had lost all personality; it produced upon me the illusion of coming out of the silence of the night itself, as if it were the silence or the night that lamented, and there was even a moment when I dreamt that that gentle lament rose to the surface from the depths of my own soul.

I left the following day without having sought to ascertain who was the sufferer or why he suffered. And I believe that I have never felt so much pity for any other man.

It is only solitude that dissolves that thick cloak of shame that isolates us from one another; only in solitude do we find ourselves; and in finding ourselves, we find in ourselves all our brothers in solitude. Solitude unites us, believe me, just as much as society separates us. And if we do not know how to love one another, it is because we do not know how to be alone.

It is only in solitude, when it has broken the thick crust of shame that separates us from one another and separates us all from God, that we have no secrets from God; only in solitude do we raise our heart to the Heart of the Universe; only in solitude does the redeeming hymn of supreme confession issue from our soul.

There is no other real dialogue than the dialogue that you hold with yourself, and you can hold this dialogue only when you are alone. In solitude and only in solitude can you know yourself as a neighbour; and so long as you do not know yourself as a neighbour, you can never hope to see in your neighbours other I's. If you want to learn to love others, withdraw into yourself.

I am accused of not caring about or being interested in the anxieties of men. It is just the contrary. I am convinced that there is no more than one anxiety, one and the same for all men, and never do I feel it or understand it more deeply than when I am alone. Each day I believe less and less in the social question, and in the political question, and in the aesthetic question, and in the moral question, and in the religious question, and in all the other questions that people have invented in order that they shall not have to face resolutely the only real question that exists — the human question, which is mine, yours, his, everyone's.

And as I know that you will say that I am playing with words and that you will ask me what I mean by this human question, I shall have to repeat it once again: The human question is the question of knowing what is to become of my consciousness, of yours, of his, of everyone's, after each one of us has died. So long as we are not facing this question, all that we are doing is simply making a noise so that we shall not hear it. And that is why we fear solitude so much and seek the company of one another.

The greatest thing that there is among men is a poet, a lyric poet, that is to say a real poet. A poet is a man who keeps no secrets from God in his heart, and who, in singing his griefs, his fears, his hopes and his memories, purifies and purges them from all falsehood. His songs are your songs are my songs.

Have you ever heard any deeper, any more intimate, any more enduring poetry than that of the Psalms? And the Psalms are meant for singing alone. I know that they are sung by crowds, assembled together under the same roof in religious services, but in singing them the crowd ceases to be a crowd. In singing the Psalms, each one withdraws into himself and the voices of others echo in his ears simply as the consonance and reinforcement of his own voice.

And I observe this difference between a crowd assembled to see a drama or to hear an orator: it is that the former is a real society, a company of living souls, in which each one exists and subsists by himself, while the other is a formless mass and each one of those who compose it no more than a fragment of the human herd.

I have never felt any desire to move a crowd, to exercise influence upon a mass of people — who lose their personality in being massed together — and on the other hand I have always felt a furious desire to perturb the heart of each individual man, to exercise an influence upon each one of my brothers in humanity. Whenever I have spoken in public I have almost always succeeded in employing a kind of lyrical oratory, and I have endeavoured to force upon myself the illusion that I was speaking to only one of my hearers, to any one, no matter which, to each one, not to all of them *en masse*.

We men are impenetrable. Spirits, like solid bodies, can only communicate with one another by the contact of surfaces, not by penetrating one another, still less by fusing together.

You have heard me say a thousand times that most spirits seem to me like crustaceans, with the bone outside and the flesh inside. And when in some book that I have forgotten I read what a painful and terrible thing it would be if the human spirit were to be incarnated in a crab and had to make use of the crab's senses, organs and members, I said to myself: "This is what actually happens; we are all unfortunate crabs, shut up in hard shells."

And the poet is he whose flesh emerges from the shell, whose soul oozes forth. And when, in our hours of anguish or joy, our soul oozes forth, we are all of us poets.

And that is why I believe that it is necessary to agitate the masses, to shake men and winnow them as in a sieve, to throw against one another, in order to see if in this way their shells will not break and their spirits flow forth, whether they will not mingle and unite with one another, and whether the real collective spirit, the soul of humanity, may not thus be welded together.

But the sad thing is, if we are to go by past experience, that all these mutual rubbings and clashings, far from breaking the shells, harden, thicken and enlarge them. They are like corns that grow larger and stronger with rubbing. Although perhaps it is that the clashes are not violent enough. And in any case it must be clashing, not rubbing. I do not like to rub against people but to clash against them; I do not like to approach people obliquely and glance off them at a tangent, but to meet them frontally, and if possible split them in two. It is the best service I can do them. And there is no better preparation for this task than solitude.

It is very sad that we have to communicate with one another by touching, at most by rubbing, through the medium of the hard shells that isolate us from one another. And I am convinced that this hard shell becomes weaker and more delicate, in solitude, until it changes into the most tenuous membrane which permits of the action of osmosis and exosmosis. And that is why I believe that it is solitude that makes men really sociable and human.

There are two kinds of union: one by removing differences, separating the elements that differentiate from those that unite, the other by fusion, bringing these differences into agreement. If we take away from the mind of each man that which is his own, that way of looking at things that is peculiar to him, everything that he takes care to hide for fear people should think him mad, we are left with that which he has in common with everyone else, and this common element gives us that wretched thing that is called common sense and which is nothing more than the abstract of the practical intelligence. But if we fuse into one the differing judgments of people, with all that they jealously preserve, and bring their caprices, their oddities, their singularities into agreement, we shall have human sense, which, in those who are rich in it, is not common but private sense.

The best that occurs to men is that which occurs to them when they are alone, that which they dare not confess, not only not to their neighbour but very often not even to themselves, that which they fly from, that which they imprison within themselves while it is in a state of pure thought and before it can flower into words. And the solitary is usually daring enough to express this, to allow it to flower, and so it comes about that he speaks that which others think in solitude by themselves and which nobody dares to publish. The solitary thinks everything aloud, and surprises others by saying that which they think beneath their breath, while they seek to deceive one another by pretending to make them believe that they are thinking something else, but without anybody believing them.

All this will help you to deduce for yourself in what way and to what extent solitude is the great school of sociability, and how right it is that we should sometimes withdraw ourselves from men in order that we may the better serve them.

—*Miguel de Unamuno, Spanish (1864–1936), translated by J. E. Crawford Flitch.*

Infallibility

JOHN HENRY NEWMAN

STARTING then with the being of a God (which, as I have said, is as certain to me as the certainty of my own existence, though when I try to put the grounds of that certainty into logical shape, I find a difficulty in doing so in mood and figure to my satisfaction), I look out of myself into the world of men, and there I see a sight which fills me with unspeakable distress. The world seems simply to give the lie to that great truth of which my whole being is so full; and the effect upon me is, in consequence, as a matter of necessity, as confusing as if it denied that I am in existence myself. If I looked into a mirror and did not see my face, I should have the sort of feeling which actually comes upon me when I look into this living busy world and see no reflexion of its Creator. This is, to me, one of the great difficulties of this absolute primary truth to which I referred just now. Were it not for this voice, speaking so clearly in my conscience and my heart, I should be an atheist, or a pantheist, or a polytheist when I looked into the world. I am speaking for myself only; and I am far from denying the real force of the arguments in proof of a God, drawn from the general facts of human society, but these do not warm me or enlighten me; they do not take away the winter of my desolation, or make the buds unfold and the leaves grow within me, and my moral being rejoice. The sight of the world is nothing else than the prophet's scroll, full of "lamentations, and mourning, and woe."

To consider the world in its length and breadth, its various history, the many races of man, their starts, their fortunes, their mutual alienation, their conflicts; and then their ways, habits, governments, forms of worship; their enterprises, their aimless courses, their random achievements and acquirements, the impotent conclusion of long-standing facts, the tokens so faint and broken of a superintending design, the blind evolution of what turn out to be great powers or truth, the progress of things as if from unreasoning elements not towards final causes, the greatness and littleness of man, his far-reaching aims, his short duration, the curtain hung over his futurity, the disappointments of life, the defeat of good, the success of evil, physical pain, mental anguish, the prevalence and intensity of sin, the pervading idolatries, the corruptions, the dreary hopeless irreligion, that condition of the whole race so fearfully yet exactly described in the Apostle's words: "having no hope and without God in the world"—all this is a vision to dizzy and appal; and inflicts upon the mind the sense of a profound mystery which is absolutely beyond human solution.

What shall be said to this heart-piercing, reason-bewildering fact? I can only answer that either there is no Creator or this living society of men is in a true sense discarded from His presence. Did I see a boy of good make and mind, with the tokens on him of a refined nature, cast upon the world without provision, unable to say whence he came, his birthplace or his family connections, I should conclude that there was some mystery connected with his history, and that he was one of whom, from one cause or other, his parents were ashamed. Thus only should I be able to account for the contrast between the promise and condition of his being. And so I argue about the world: *if* there be a God, *since* there is a God, the human race is implicated in some terrible aboriginal calamity. It is out of joint with the purposes of its Creator. This is a fact, a fact as true as the fact of its existence; and thus the doctrine of what is theologically called original sin becomes to me almost as certain as that the world exists and as the existence of God.

And now, supposing it were the blessed and loving will of the Creator to interfere in this anarchical condition of things, what are we to suppose would be the methods which might be necessarily or naturally involved in His object of mercy? Since the world is in so abnormal a state, surely it would be no surprise to me if the interposition were of necessity equally extraordinary—or what is called miraculous. But that subject does not directly come into the scope of my present remarks. Miracles as evidence involve an argument; and of course I am thinking of some means which does not immediately run into argument. I am rather asking what must be the face-to-face antagonist by which to withstand and baffle the fierce energy of passion and the all-corroding, all-dissolving scepticism of the intellect in religious inquiries? I have no intention at all to deny that truth is the real object of our reason, and that, if it does not attain to truth, either the premise or the process is in fault; but I am not speaking of right reason, but of reason as it acts in fact and concretely in fallen man. I know that even the unaided reason, when correctly exercised, leads to a belief in God, in the immortality of the soul, and in a future retribution; but I am considering it actually and historically; and in this point of view I do not think I am wrong in saying that its tendency is towards a simple unbelief in matters of religion. No truth, however sacred, can stand against it, in the long run; and hence it is that in the pagan world, when our Lord came, the last traces of the religious knowledge of former times were all but disappearing from those portions of the world in which the intellect had been active and had had a career.

And in these latter days, in like manner, outside the Catholic Church things are tending, with far greater rapidity than in that old time from the circumstance of the age, to atheism in one shape or other. What a scene, what a prospect, does the whole of Europe present at this day! and not only Europe, but every government and every civilisation through the world which is under the influence of the European mind! Especially, for it most concerns us, how sorrowful, in the view of religion, even taken in its most elementary, most attenuated form, is the spectacle presented to us by the educated intellect of England, France, and Germany! Lovers of their country and of their race, religious men, external to the Catholic Church, have attempted various expedients to arrest fierce wilful human nature in its onward course and to bring it into subjection. The necessity of some form of religion for the interests of humanity has been generally acknowledged; but where was the concrete representative of things invisible which would have the force and toughness necessary to be a breakwater against the deluge? Three centuries ago the establishment of religion, material, legal, and social, was generally adopted as the best expedient for the purpose, in those countries which separated from the Catholic Church; and for a long time it was successful; but now the crevices of those establishments are admitting the enemy. Thirty years ago, education was relied upon; ten years ago there was a hope that wars would cease for ever, under the influence of commercial enterprise and the reign of the useful and fine arts; but will any one venture to say that there is anything anywhere on this earth which will afford a fulcrum for us whereby to keep the earth from moving onwards?

The judgment which experience passes on establishments or education, as a means of maintaining religious truth in this anarchical world, must be extended even to Scripture, though Scripture be divine. Experience proves surely that the Bible does not answer a purpose for which it was never intended. It may be accidentally the means of the conversion of individuals; but a book, after all, cannot make a stand against the wild living intellect of man, and in this day it begins to testify, as regards its own structure and contents, to the power of that universal solvent which is so successfully acting upon religious establishments.

Supposing then it to be the Will of the Creator to interfere in human affairs, and to make provisions for retaining in the world a knowledge of Himself, so definite and distinct as to be proof against the energy of human scepticism, in such a case—I am far from saying that there was no other way—but there is nothing to surprise the mind, if He should think fit to introduce a power into the world invested with the prerogative of infallibility in religious matters. Such a provision would be a direct, immediate, active, and prompt means of withstanding the difficulty; it would be an instrument suited to the need; and when I find that this is the very claim of the Catholic Church, not only do I feel no difficulty in admitting the idea, but there is a fitness in it which recommends it to my mind. And thus I am brought to speak of the church's infallibility as a provision adapted by the mercy of the Creator to preserve religion in the world, and to restrain that freedom of thought which of course in itself is one of the greatest of our natural gifts, and to rescue it from its own suicidal excesses. And let it be observed that, neither here nor in what follows, shall I have occasion to speak directly of the revealed body of truths, but only as they bear upon the defence of natural religion. I say that a power possessed of infallibility in religious teaching is happily adapted to be a working instrument for smiting hard and throwing back the immense energy of the aggressive intellect: and in saying this, as in the other things that I have to say, it must still be recollected that I am all along bearing in mind my main purpose, which is a defence of myself.

I am defending myself here from a plausible charge brought against Catholics, as will be seen better as I proceed. The charge is this: that I, as a Catholic, not only make profession to hold doctrines which I cannot possibly believe in my heart, but that I also believe in the existence of a power on earth which at its own will imposes upon men any new set of *credenda*, when it pleases, by a claim to infallibility; in consequence, that my own thoughts are not my own property; that I cannot tell that to-morrow I may not have to give up what I hold to-day, and that the necessary effect of such a condition of mind must be a degrading bondage, or a bitter inward rebellion relieving itself in secret infidelity, or the necessity of ignoring the whole subject of religion in a sort of disgust, and of mechanically saying everything that the Church says and leaving to others the defence of it. As then I have above spoken of the relation of my mind towards the Catholic Creed, so now I shall speak of the attitude which it takes up in the view of the Church's infallibility.

And first, the initial doctrine of the infallible teacher must be an emphatic protest against the existing state of mankind. Man had rebelled against his Maker. It was this that caused the divine interposition: and the first act of the divinely accredited messenger must be to proclaim it. The Church must denounce rebellion as of all possible evils the greatest. She must have no terms with it; if she would be true to her Master, she must ban and anathematise it. This is the meaning of a statement which has furnished matter for one of those special accusations to which I am at present replying: I have, however, no fault at all to confess in regard to it; I have nothing to withdraw, and in consequence I here deliberately repeat it. I said: "The Catholic Church holds it better for the sun and moon to drop from heaven, for the earth to fail, and for all the many millions on it to die of starvation in extremest agony, as far as temporal affliction goes, than that one soul, I will not say should be lost, but should commit one single venial sin, should tell one wilful untruth, or should steal one poor farthing without excuse." I think the principle here enunciated to be the mere preamble in the formal credentials of the Catholic Church, as an Act of Parliament might begin with a "*Whereas.*" It is because of the intensity of the evil which has possession of mankind that a suitable antagonist has been provided against it; and the initial act of that divinely-commissioned power is of course to deliver her challenge and to defy the enemy. Such a preamble then gives a meaning to her position in the world and an interpretation to her whole course of teaching and action.

In like manner she has ever put forth, with most energetic distinctness, those other great elementary truths which either are an explanation of her mission or give a character to her work. She does not teach that human nature is irreclaimable, else wherefore should she be sent? not that it is to be shattered and reversed, but to be extricated, purified, and restored; not that it is a mere mass of evil, but that it has the promise of great things, and even now has a virtue and a praise proper to itself. But in the next place she knows and she preaches that such a restoration as she aims at effecting in it must be brought about, not simply through any outward provision of preaching and teaching, even though it be her own, but from a certain inward spiritual power of grace imparted directly from above, and which is in her keeping. She has it in charge to rescue human nature from its misery, but not simply by raising it upon its own level, but by lifting it up to a higher level than its own. She recognises in it real moral excellence though degraded, but she cannot set it free from earth except by exalting it towards heaven. It was for this end that a renovating grace was put into her hands, and therefore from the nature of the gift, as well as from the reasonableness of the case, she goes on, as a further point, to insist that all true conversion must begin with the first springs of thought, and to teach that each individual man must be in his own person one whole and perfect temple of God while he is also one of the living stones which build up a visible religious community. And thus the distinctions between nature and grace, and between outward and inward religion, become two further articles in what I have called the preamble of her divine commission.

Such truths as these she vigorously reiterates and pertinaciously inflicts upon mankind; as to such she observes no half-measures, no economical reserve, no delicacy or prudence. "Ye must be born again," is the simple, direct form of words which she uses after her Divine Master; "your whole nature must be reborn, your passions, and your affections, and your aims, and your conscience, and your will, must all be bathed in a new element, and reconsecrated to your Maker, and, the last not the least, your intellect." It was for repeating these points of her teaching in my own way that certain passages of one of my volumes have been brought into the general accusation which has been made against my religious opinions. The writer has said that I was demented if I believed, and unprincipled if I did not believe, in my statement that a lazy, ragged, filthy, story-telling woman, if chaste, sober, cheerful, and religious, had a prospect of heaven which was absolutely closed to an accomplished statesman, or lawyer, or noble, be he ever so just, upright, generous, honourable, and conscientious, unless he had also some portion of the divine Christian grace; yet I should have thought myself defended from criticism by the words which our Lord used to the chief priests: "The publicans and harlots go into the kingdom of God before you." And I was subjected again to the same alternative of imputations, for having ventured to say that consent to an unchaste wish was indefinitely more heinous than any lie viewed apart from its causes, its motives, and its consequences; though a lie, viewed under the limitation of these conditions, is a random utterance, an almost outward act, not directly from the heart, however disgraceful it may be, whereas we have the express words of our Lord to the doctrine that "whoso looketh on a woman to lust after her, hath committed adultery with her already in his heart." On the strength of these texts I have surely as much right to believe in these doctrines as to believe in the doctrine of original sin, or that there is a supernatural revelation, or that a Divine Person suffered, or that punishment is eternal.

Passing now from what I have called the preamble of that grant of power with which the Church is invested, to that power itself, Infallibility, I make two brief remarks: on the one hand, I am not here determining anything about the essential seat of that power, because that is a question doctrinal, not historical and practical; nor, on the other hand, am I extending the direct subject-matter over which that power has jurisdiction, beyond religious opinion: and now as to the power itself.

This power, viewed in its fullness, is as tremendous as the giant evil which has called for it. It claims, when brought into exercise in the legitimate manner, for otherwise of course it is but dormant, to have for itself a sure guidance into the very meaning of every portion of the divine message in detail which was committed by our Lord to His apostles. It claims to know its own limits, and to decide what it can determine absolutely and what it cannot. It claims, moreover, to have a hold upon statements not directly religious, so far as this, to determine whether they indirectly relate to religion, and, according to its own definitive judgment, to pronounce whether or not, in a particular case, they are consistent with revealed truth. It claims to decide magisterially, whether infallibly or not, that such and such statements are or are not prejudicial to the apostolic *depositum* of faith, in their spirit or in their consequences, and to allow them, or condemn and forbid them, accordingly. It claims to impose silence at will on any matters, or controversies, of doctrine, which on its own *ipse dixit* it pronounces to be dangerous, or inexpedient, or inopportune. It claims that whatever may be the judgment of Catholics upon such acts, these acts should be received by them with those outward marks of reverence, submission, and loyalty, which Englishmen, for instance, pay to the presence of their sovereign, without public criticism on them, as being in their matter inexpedient, or in their manner violent or harsh. And lastly, it claims to have the right of inflicting spiritual punishment, of cutting off from the ordinary channels of the divine life, and of simply excommunicating, those who refuse to submit themselves to its formal declarations. Such is the infallibility lodged in the Catholic Church, viewed in the concrete, as clothed and surrounded by the appendages of its high sovereignty: it is, to repeat what I said above, a super-eminent prodigious power sent upon earth to encounter and master a giant evil.

—*From Apologia pro Vita Sua, by John Henry Newman, English (1801–1890).*

~ ✿ ~

The Realization of the Infinite

RABINDRANATH TAGORE

THE Upanishads say: "Man becomes true if in this life he can apprehend God; if not, it is the greatest calamity for him."

But what is the nature of this attainment of God? It is quite evident that the infinite is not like one object among many, to be definitely classified and kept among our possessions, to be used as an ally specially favouring us in our politics, warfare, money-making, or in social competitions. We cannot put our God in the same list with our summer-houses, motor-cars, or our credit at the bank, as so many people seem to want to do.

We must try to understand the true character of the desire that a man has when his soul longs for his God. Does it consist of his wish to make an addition, however valuable, to his belongings? Emphatically no! It is an endlessly wearisome task, this continual adding to our stores. In fact, when the soul seeks God she seeks her final escape from this incessant gathering and heaping and never coming to an end. It is not an additional object that she seeks, but it is the *nityo 'nityānām,* the permanent in all that is impermanent, the *rasānām rasatamah,* the highest abiding joy unifying all enjoyments. Therefore when the Upanishads teach us to realise everything in Brahma, it is not to seek something extra, not to manufacture something new.

Know everything that there is in the universe as enveloped by God. Enjoy whatever is given by him and harbour not in your mind the greed for wealth which is not your own.

When you know that whatever there is is filled by him and whatever you have is his gift, then you realise the infinite in the finite, and the giver in the gifts. Then you know that all the facts of the reality have their only meaning in the manifestation of the one truth, and all your possessions have their only significance for you, not in themselves but in the relation they establish with the infinite.

So it cannot be said that we can find Brahma as we find other objects; there is no question of searching for him in one thing in preference to another, in one place instead of somewhere else. We do not have to run to the grocer's shop for our morning light; we open our eyes and there it is; so we need only give ourselves up to find that Brahma is everywhere.

This is the reason why Buddha admonished us to free ourselves from the confinement of the life of the self. If there were nothing else to take its place more positively perfect and satisfying, then such admonition would be absolutely unmeaning. No man can seriously consider the advice, much less have any enthusiasm for it, of surrendering everything one has for gaining nothing whatever.

So our daily worship of God is not really the process of gradual acquisition of him, but the daily process of surrendering ourselves, removing all obstacles to union and extending our consciousness of him in devotion and service, in goodness and in love.

The Upanishads say: *Be lost altogether in Brahma like an arrow that has completely penetrated its target.* Thus to be conscious of being absolutely enveloped by Brahma is not an act of mere concentration of mind. It must be the aim of the whole of our life. In all our thoughts and deeds we must be conscious of the infinite. Let the realisation of this truth become easier every day of our life, that *none could live or move if the energy of the all-pervading joy did not fill the sky.* In all our actions let us feel that impetus of the infinite energy and be glad.

It may be said that the infinite is beyond our attainment, so it is for us as if it were naught. Yes, if the word attainment implies any idea of possession, then it must be admitted that the infinite is unattainable. But we must keep in mind that the highest enjoyment of man is not in the having but in a getting, which is at the same time not getting. Our physical pleasures leave no margin for the unrealised. They, like the dead satellite of the earth, have but little atmosphere around them. When we take food and satisfy our hunger it is a complete act of possession. So long as the hunger is not satisfied it is a pleasure to eat. For then our enjoyment of eating touches at every point the infinite. But, when it attains completion, or in other words, when our desire for eating reaches the end of the stage of its non-realisation, it reaches the end of its pleasure. In all our intellectual pleasures the margin is broader, the limit is far off. In all our deeper love getting and non-getting run ever parallel. In one of our Vaishnava lyrics the lover says to his beloved: "I feel as if I have gazed upon the beauty of thy face from my birth, yet my eyes are hungry still: as if I have kept thee pressed to my heart for millions of years, yet my heart is not satisfied."

This makes it clear that it is really the infinite whom we seek in our pleasures. Our desire for being wealthy is not a desire for a particular sum of money but it is indefinite, and the most fleeting of our enjoyments are but the momentary touches of the eternal. The tragedy of human life consists in our vain attempts to stretch the limits of things which can never become unlimited, — to reach the infinite by absurdly adding to the rungs of the ladder of the finite.

It is evident from this that the real desire of our soul is to get beyond all our possessions. Surrounded by things she can touch and feel, she cries, "I am weary of getting; ah, where is he who is never to be got?"

We see everywhere in the history of man that the spirit of renunciation is the deepest reality of the human soul. When the soul says of anything, "I do not want it, for I am above it," she gives utterance to the highest truth that is in her. When a girl's life outgrows her doll, when she realises that in every respect she is more than her doll is, then she throws it away. By the very act of possession we know that we are greater than the things we possess. It is a perfect misery to be kept bound up with things lesser than ourselves. This it is that Maitreyī felt when her husband gave her his property on the eve of leaving home. She asked him, "Would these material things help one to attain the highest?"—or, in other words, "Are they more than my soul to me?" When her husband answered, "They will make you rich in worldly possessions," she said at once, "Then what am I to do with these?" It is only when a man truly realises what his possessions are that he has no more illusions about them; then he knows his soul is far above these things and he becomes free from their bondage. Thus man truly realises his soul by outgrowing his possessions, and man's progress in the path of eternal life is through a series of renunciations.

That we cannot absolutely possess the infinite being is not a mere intellectual proposition. It has to be experienced, and this experience is bliss. The bird, while taking its flight in the sky, experiences at every beat of its wings that the sky is boundless, that its wings can never carry it beyond. Therein lies its joy. In the cage the sky is limited; it may be quite enough for all the purposes of the bird's life, only it is not more than is necessary. The bird cannot rejoice within the limits of the necessary. It must feel that what it has is immeasurably more than it ever can want or comprehend, and then only can it be glad.

Thus our soul must soar in the infinite, and she must feel every moment that in the sense of not being able to come to the end of her attainment is her supreme joy, her final freedom.

Man's abiding happiness is not in getting anything but in giving himself up to what is greater than himself, to ideas which are larger than his individual life, the idea of his country, of humanity, of God. They make it easier for him to part with all that he has, not excepting his life. His existence is miserable and sordid till he finds some great idea which can truly claim his all, which can release him from all attachment to his belongings. Buddha and Jesus, and all our great prophets, represent such great ideas. They hold before us opportunities for surrendering our all. When they bring forth their divine alms-bowl we feel we cannot help giving, and we find that in giving is our truest joy and liberation, for it is uniting ourselves to that extent with the infinite.

Man is not complete; he is yet to be. In what he *is* he is small, and if we could conceive him stopping there for eternity we should have an idea of the most awful hell that man can imagine. In his *to be* he is infinite, there is his heaven, his deliverance. His *is* is occupied every moment with what it can get and have done with; his *to be* is hungering for something which is more than can be got, which he never can lose because he never has possessed.

The finite pole of our existence has its place in the world of necessity. There man goes about searching for food to live, clothing to get warmth. In this region—the region of nature—it is his function to get things. The natural man is occupied with enlarging his possessions.

But this act of getting is partial. It is limited to man's necessities. We can have a thing only to the extent of our requirements, just as a vessel can contain water only to the extent of its emptiness. Our relation to food is only in feeding, our relation to a house is only in habitation. We call it a benefit when a thing is fitted only to some particular want of ours. Thus to get is always to get partially, and it never can be otherwise. So this craving for acquisition belongs to our finite self.

But that side of our existence whose direction is towards the infinite seeks not wealth, but freedom and joy. There the reign of necessity ceases, and there our function is not to get but to be. To be what? To be one with Brahma. For the region of the infinite is the region of unity. Therefore the Upanishads say: *If man apprehends God he becomes true.* Here it is becoming, it is not having more. Words do not gather bulk when you know their meaning; they become true by being one with the idea.

Though the West has accepted as its teacher him who boldly proclaimed his oneness with his Father, and who exhorted his followers to be perfect as God, it has never been reconciled to this idea of our unity with the infinite being. It condemns, as a piece of blasphemy, any implication of man's becoming God. This is certainly not the idea that Christ preached, nor perhaps the idea of the Christian mystics, but this seems to be the idea that has become popular in the Christian West.

But the highest wisdom in the East holds that it is not the function of our soul to *gain* God, to utilise him for any special material purpose. All that we can aspire to is to become more and more one with God. In the region of nature, which is the region of diversity, we grow by acquisition; in the spiritual world, which is the region of unity, we grow by losing ourselves, by uniting. Gaining a thing, as we have said, is by its nature partial, it is limited only to a particular want; but *being* is complete, it belongs to our wholeness, it springs not from any necessity but from our affinity with the infinite, which is the principle of perfection that we have in our soul.

Yes, we must become Brahma. We must not shrink to avow this. Our existence is meaningless if we never can expect to realise the highest perfection that there is. If we have an aim and yet can never reach it, then it is no aim at all.

But can it then be said that there is no difference between Brahma and our individual soul? Of course the difference is obvious. Call it illusion or ignorance, or whatever name you may give it, it is there. You can offer explanations but you cannot explain it away. Even illusion is true as illusion.

Brahma is Brahma, he is the infinite ideal of perfection. But we are not what we truly are; we are ever to become true, ever to become Brahma. There is the eternal play of love in the relation between this being and the becoming; and in the depth of this mystery is the source of all truth and beauty that sustains the endless march of creation.

In the music of the rushing stream sounds the joyful assurance, "I shall become the sea." It is not a vain assumption; it is true humility, for it is the truth. The river has no other alternative. On both sides of its banks it has numerous fields and forests, villages and towns; it can serve them in various ways, cleanse them and feed them, carry their produce from place to place. But it can have only partial relations with these, and however long it may linger among them it remains separate; it never can become a town or a forest.

But it can and does become the sea. The lesser moving water has its affinity with the great motionless water of the ocean. It moves through the thousand objects on its onward course, and its motion finds its finality when it reaches the sea.

The river can become the sea, but she can never make the sea part and parcel of herself. If, by some chance, she has encircled some broad sheet of water and pretends that she has made the sea a part of herself, we at once know that it is not so, that her current is still seeking rest in the great ocean to which it can never set boundaries.

In the same manner, our soul can only become Brahma as the river can become the sea. Everything else she touches at one of her points, then leaves and moves on, but she never can leave Brahma and move beyond him. Once our soul realises her ultimate object of repose in Brahma, all her movements acquire a purpose. It is this ocean of infinite rest which gives significance to endless activities. It is this perfectness of being that lends to the imperfection of becoming that quality of beauty which finds its expression in all poetry, drama, and art.

There must be a complete idea that animates a poem. Every sentence of the poem touches that idea. When the reader realises that pervading idea, as he reads on, then the reading of the poem is full of joy to him. Then every part of the poem becomes radiantly significant by the light of the whole. But if the poem goes on interminably, never expressing the idea of the whole, only throwing off disconnected images, however beautiful, it becomes wearisome and unprofitable in the extreme. The progress of our soul is like a perfect poem. It has an infinite idea which once realised makes all movement full of meaning and joy. But if we detach its movements from that ultimate idea, if we do not see the infinite rest and only see the infinite motion, then existence appears to us a monstrous evil, impetuously rushing towards an unending aimlessness.

I remember in our childhood we had a teacher who used to make us learn by heart the whole book of Sanskrit grammar, which is written in symbols, without explaining their meaning to us. Day after day we went toiling on, but on towards what, we had not the least notion. So, as regards our lessons, we were in the position of the pessimist who only counts the breathless activities of the world, but cannot see the infinite repose of the perfection whence these activities are gaining their equilibrium every moment in absolute fitness and harmony. We lose all joy in thus contemplating existence, because we miss the truth. We see the gesticulations of the dancer, and we imagine these are directed by a ruthless tyranny of chance, while we are deaf to the eternal music of perfection, becoming one with it, dedicating to that melody at every step the multitudinous forms they go on creating.

And this is the truth of our soul, and this is her joy, that she must ever be growing into Brahma, that all her movements should be modulated by this ultimate idea, and all her creations should be given as offerings to the supreme spirit of perfection.

There is a remarkable saying in the Upanishads: *I think not that I know him well, or that I know him, or even that I know him not.*

By the process of knowledge we can never know the infinite being. But if he is altogether beyond our reach then he is absolutely nothing to us. The truth is that we know him not, yet we know him.

This has been explained in another saying of the Upanishads: *From Brahma words come back baffled, as well as the mind, but he who knows him by the joy of him is free from all fears.*

Knowledge is partial, because our intellect is an instrument, it is only a part of us, it can give us information about things which can be divided and analysed, and whose properties can be classified, part by part. But Brahma is perfect, and knowledge which is partial can never be a knowledge of him.

But he can be known by joy, by love. For joy is knowledge in its completeness, it is knowing by our whole being. Intellect sets us apart from the things to be known, but love knows its object by fusion. Such knowledge is immediate and admits no doubt. It is the same as knowing our own selves, only more so.

Therefore, as the Upanishads say, mind can never know Brahma, words can never describe him; he can only be known by our soul, by her joy in him, by her love. Or, in other words, we can only come into relation with him by union – union of our whole being. We must be one with our Father, we must be perfect as he is.

But how can that be? There can be no grade in infinite perfection. We cannot grow more and more into Brahma. He is the absolute one, and there can be no more or less in him.

Indeed, the realisation of the *paramātman,* the supreme soul, within our *antarātman,* our inner individual soul, is in a state of absolute completion. We cannot think of it as non-existent and depending on our limited powers for its gradual construction. If our relation with the divine were all a thing of our own making, how should we rely on it as true, and how should it lend us support?

Yes, we must know that within us we have that where space and time cease to rule and where the links of evolution are merged in unity. In that everlasting abode of the *ātman,* the soul, the revelation of the *paramātman,* the supreme soul, is already complete. Therefore the Upanishads say: *He who knows Brahman, the true, the all-conscious, and the infinite as hidden in the depths of the soul, which is the supreme sky (the inner sky of consciousness), enjoys all objects of desire in union with the all-knowing Brahman.*

The union is already accomplished. The *paramātman,* the supreme soul, has himself chosen this soul of ours as his bride and the marriage has been completed. The solemn *mantram* has been uttered: *Let thy heart be even as my heart is.* There is no room in this marriage for evolution to act the part of the master of ceremonies. The *eshah,* who cannot otherwise be described than as *This,* the nameless immediate presence, is ever here in our innermost being. "This *eshah,* or *This,* is the supreme end of the other this"; "this *This* is the supreme treasure of the other this"; "this *This* is the supreme dwelling of the other this"; "this *This* is the supreme joy of the other this." Because the marriage of supreme love has been accomplished in timeless time. And now goes on the endless *līlā*, the play of love. He who has been gained in eternity is now being pursued in time and space, in joys and sorrows, in this world and in the worlds beyond. When the soul-bride understands this well, her heart is blissful and at rest. She knows that she, like a river, has attained the ocean of her fulfilment at one end of her being, and at the other end she is ever attaining it; at one end it is eternal rest and completion, at the other it is incessant movement and change. When she knows both ends as inseparably connected, then she knows the world as her own household by the right of knowing the master of the world as her own lord. Then all her services becomes services of love, all the troubles and tribulations of life come to her as trials triumphantly borne to prove the strength of her love, smilingly to win the wager from her lover. But so long as she remains obstinately in the dark, lifts not her veil, does not recognise her lover, and only knows the world dissociated from him, she serves as a handmaid here, where by right she might reign as a queen; she sways in doubt, and weeps in sorrow and dejection. *She passes from starvation to starvation, from trouble to trouble, and from fear to fear.*

I can never forget that scrap of a song I once heard in the early dawn in the midst of the din of the crowd that had collected for a festival the night before: "Ferryman, take me across to the other shore!"

In the bustle of all our work there comes out this cry, "Take me across." The carter in India sings while driving his cart, "Take me across." The itinerant grocer deals out his goods to his customers and sings, "Take me across."

What is the meaning of this cry? We feel we have not reached our goal; and we know with all our striving and toiling we do not come to the end, we do not attain our object. Like a child dissatisfied with its dolls, our heart cries, "Not this, not this." But what is that other? Where is the further shore?

Is it something else than what we have? Is it somewhere else than where we are? Is it to take rest from all our works, to be relieved from all the responsibilities of life?

No, in the very heart of our activities we are seeking for our end. We are crying for the across, even where we stand. So, while our lips utter their prayer to be carried away, our busy hands are never idle.

In truth, thou ocean of joy, this shore and the other shore are one and the same in thee. When I call this my own, the other lies estranged; and missing the sense of that completeness which is in me, my heart incessantly cries out for the other. All my this, and that other, are waiting to be completely reconciled in thy love.

This "I" of mine toils hard, day and night, for a home which it knows as its own. Alas, there will be no end of its sufferings so long as it is not able to call this home thine. Till then it will struggle on, and its heart will ever cry, "Ferryman, lead me across." When this home of mine is made thine, that very moment is it taken across, even while its old walls enclose it. This "I" is restless. It is working for a gain which can never be assimilated with its spirit, which it never can hold and retain. In its efforts to clasp in its own arms that which is for all, it hurts others and is hurt in its turn, and cries, "Lead me across." But as soon as it is able to say, "All my work is thine," everything remains the same, only it is taken across.

Where can I meet thee unless in this mine home made thine? Where can I join thee unless in this my work transformed into thy work? If I leave my home I shall not reach thy home; if I cease my work I can never join thee in thy work. For thou dwellest in me and I in thee. Thou without me or I without thee are nothing.

Therefore, in the midst of our home and our work, the prayer rises, "Lead me across!" For here rolls the sea, and even here lies the other shore waiting to be reached—yes, here is this everlasting present, not distant, not anywhere else.

—*From Sadhana, by Rabindranath Tagore, East Indian (1861–1941).*

~ ✿ ~

Retrospect

Æ (GEORGE WILLIAM RUSSELL)

I HAD travelled all day and was tired, but I could not rest by the hearth in the cottage on the hill. My heart was beating with too great an excitement. After my year in the city I felt like a child who wickedly stays from home through a long day, and who returns frightened and penitent at nightfall, wondering whether it will be received with forgiveness by its mother. Would the Mother of us all receive me again as one of her children? Would the winds with wandering voices be as before the evangelists of her love? Or would I feel like an outcast amid the mountains, the dark valleys, and the shining lakes? I knew if benediction came how it would come. I would sit among the rocks with shut eyes, waiting humbly as one waits in the antechambers of the mighty, and if the invisible ones chose me as companion they would begin with a soft breathing of their intimacies, creeping on me with shadowy affection like children who steal nigh to the bowed head and suddenly whisper fondness in the ear before it has even heard a footfall. So I stole out of the cottage and over the dark ridges to the place of rocks, and sat down, and let the coolness of the night chill and still the fiery dust in the brain. I waited trembling for the faintest touch, the shyest breathing of the Everlasting within my soul, the sign of reception and forgiveness. I knew it would come. I could not so desire what was not my own, and what is our own we cannot lose. Desire is hidden identity. The darkness drew me heavenward. From the hill the plains beneath slipped away grown vast and vague, remote and still. I seemed alone with immensity, and there came at last that melting of the divine darkness into the life within me for which I prayed. Yes, I still belonged, however humbly, to the heavenly household. I was not outcast. Still, though by a thread fine as that by which a spider hangs from the rafters, my being was suspended from the habitations of eternity. I longed to throw my arms about the hills, to meet with kisses the lips of the seraph wind. I felt the gaiety of childhood springing up through weariness and age, for to come into contact with that which is eternally young is to have that childhood of the spirit it must attain ere it can be moulded by the Magician of the Beautiful and enter the House of Many Mansions.

I had not always this intimacy with nature. I never felt a light in childhood which faded in manhood into the common light of day, nor do I believe that childhood is any nearer than age to this being. If it were so what would the spirit have to hope for after youth was gone? I was not conscious in my boyhood of any heaven lying about me. I lived in the city, and the hills from which aid was to come to me were only a far flush of blue on the horizon. Yet I was drawn to them, and as years passed and legs grew longer I came nearer and nearer until at last one day I found myself on the green hillside. I came to play with other boys, but years were yet to pass before the familiar places grew strange once more and the mountains dense with fiery forms and awful as Sinai.

While the child is still in its mother's arms it is nourished by her, yet it does not know it is a mother which feeds it. It knows later in whose bosom it has lain. As the mother nourishes the body so the Mighty Mother nourishes the soul. Yet there are but few who pay reverence where reverence is due, and that is because this benign deity is like a mother who indulges the fancies of her children. With some she imparts life to their own thoughts. Others she endows with the vision of her own heart. Even of these last some love in silence, being afraid to speak of the majesty which smiled on them, and others deceived think with pride: "This vision is my own."

I was like these last for a long time. I was aged about sixteen or seventeen years, when I, the slackest and least ideal of boys, with my life already made dark by those desires of body and heart with which we so soon learn to taint our youth, became aware of a mysterious life quickening within my life. Looking back I know not of anything in friendship, anything I had read, to call this forth. It was, I thought, self-begotten. I began to be astonished with myself, for, walking along country roads, intense and passionate imaginations of another world, of an interior nature began to overpower me. They were like strangers who suddenly enter a house, who brush aside the doorkeeper, and who will not be denied. Soon I knew they were the rightful owners and heirs of the house of the body, and the doorkeeper was only one who was for a time in charge, who had neglected his duty, and who had pretended to ownership. The boy who existed before was an alien. He hid himself when the pilgrim of eternity took up his abode in the dwelling. Yet, whenever the true owner was absent, the sly creature reappeared and boasted himself as master once more.

That being from a distant country who took possession of the house began to speak in a language difficult to translate. I was tormented by limitations of understanding. Somewhere about me I knew there were comrades who were speaking to me, but I could not know what they said. As I walked in the evening down the lanes scented by the honeysuckle my senses were expectant of some unveiling about to take place, I felt that beings were looking in upon me out of the true home of man. They seemed to be saying to each other of us, "Soon they will awaken; soon they will come to us again," and for a moment I almost seemed to mix with their eternity. The tinted air glowed before me with intelligible significance like a face, a voice. The visible world became like a face, a voice. The visible world became like a tapestry blown and stirred by winds behind it. If it would but raise for an instant I knew I would be in Paradise. Every form on that tapestry appeared to be the work of gods. Every flower was a word, a thought. The grass was speech; the trees were speech; the waters were speech; the winds were speech. They were the Army of the Voice marching on to conquest and dominion over the spirit; and I listened with my whole being, and then these apparitions would fade away and I would be the mean and miserable boy once more. So might one have felt who had been servant of the prophet, and had seen him go up in the fiery chariot, and the world had no more light or certitude in it with that passing. I knew these visitations for what they were and named them truly in my fantasy, for writing then in the first verses of mine which still seem to me to be poetry, I said of the earth that we and all things were her dreams:

She is rapt in dreams divine.
As her clouds of beauty pass
On our glowing hearts they shine,
Mirrored there as in a glass.

Earth, whose dreams are we and they,
With her deep heart's gladness fills
All our human lips can say
Or the dawn-fired singer trills.

Yet such is human nature that I still felt vanity as if this vision was mine, and I acted like one who comes across the treasure-house of a king, and spends the treasure as if it were his own. We may indeed have a personal wisdom, but spiritual vision is not to speak of as ours any more than we can say at the rising of the sun: "This glory is mine." By the sudden uprising of such vanities in the midst of vision I was often outcast, and found myself in an instant like those warriors of Irish legend, who had come upon a lordly house and feasted there and slept, and when they woke they were on the barren hillside, and the Faed Fia was drawn about that lordly house. Yet though the imagination apprehended truly that this beauty was not mine, and hailed it by its heavenly name, for some years my heart was proud, for as the beauty sank into memory it seemed to become a personal possession, and I said "I imagined this" when I should humbly have said, "The curtain was a little lifted that I might see." But the day was to come when I could not deny the Mighty Mother the reverence due, when I was indeed to know by what being I had been nourished, and to be made sweet and mad as a lover with a consciousness of her intermingling spirit.

The sages of old found that at the close of intense meditation their being was drawn into union with that which they contemplated. All desire tends to bring about unity with the object adored, and this is no less true of spiritual and elemental than of bodily desire; and I, with my imagination more and more drawn to adore an ideal nature, was tending to that vital contact in which what at first was apprehended in fantasy would become the most real of all things. When that certitude came I felt as Dante might have felt after conceiving of Beatrice close at his side and in the Happy World, if, after believing it a dream, half hoping that it might hereafter be a reality, that beloved face before his imagination grew suddenly intense, vivid and splendidly shining, and he knew beyond all doubt that her spirit was truly in that form, and had descended to dwell in it, and would be with him forever more. So did I feel one warm summer day lying idly on the hillside, not then thinking of anything but the sunlight, and how sweet it was to drowse there, when, suddenly, I felt a fiery heart throb, and knew it was personal and intimate, and started with every sense dilated and intent, and turned inwards, and I heard first a music as of bells going away, away into that wondrous underland whither, as legend relates, the Danaan gods withdrew; and then the heart of the hills was opened to me, and I knew there was no hill for those who were there, and they were unconscious of the ponderous mountain piled above the palaces of light, and the winds were sparkling and diamond clear, yet full of colour as an opal, as they glittered through the valley, and I knew the Golden Age was all about me, and it was we who had been blind to it but that it had never passed away from the world.

— From The Candle of Vision, by Æ (George William Russell), Irish (1867–1935).

~ ⚙ ~

Preface to a New Philosophy

GEORGE SANTAYANA

HERE is one more system of philosophy. If the reader is tempted to smile, I can assure him that I smile with him, and that my system — to which this volume is a critical introduction — differs widely in spirit and pretensions from what usually goes by that name. In the first place, *my system is not mine, nor new.* I am merely attempting to express for the reader the principles to which he appeals when he smiles. There are convictions in the depths of his soul, beneath all his overt parrot beliefs, on which I would build our friendship. I have a great respect for orthodoxy; not for those orthodoxies which prevail in particular schools or nations, and which vary from age to age, but for a certain shrewd orthodoxy which the sentiment and practice of laymen maintain everywhere. I think that common sense, in a rough dogged way, is technically sounder than the special schools of philosophy, each of which squints and overlooks half the facts and half the difficulties in its eagerness to find in some detail the key to the whole. I am animated by distrust of all high guesses, and by sympathy with the old prejudices and workaday opinions of mankind: they are ill expressed, but they are well grounded. What novelty my version of things may possess is meant simply to obviate occasions for sophistry by giving to everyday beliefs a more accurate and circumspect form. I do not pretend to place myself at the heart of the universe nor at its origin, nor to draw its periphery. I would lay siege to the truth only as animal exploration and fancy may do so, first from one quarter and then from another, expecting the reality to be not simpler than my experience of it, but far more extensive and complex. I stand in philosophy exactly where I stand in daily life; I should not be honest otherwise. I accept the same miscellaneous witnesses, bow to the same obvious facts, make conjectures no less instinctively, and admit the same encircling ignorance.

My system, accordingly, is *no system of the universe.* The Realms of Being of which I speak are not parts of a cosmos, nor one great cosmos together: they are only kinds or categories of things which I find conspicuously different and worth distinguishing, at least in my own thoughts. I do not know how many things in the universe at large may fall under each of these classes, nor what other Realms of Being may not exist, to which I have no approach or which I have not happened to distinguish in my personal observation of the world. Logic, like language, is partly a free construction and partly a means of symbolising and harnessing in expression the existing diversities of things; and whilst some languages, given a man's constitution and habits, may seem more beautiful and convenient to him than others, it is a foolish heat in a patriot to insist that only his native language is intelligible or right. No language or logic is right in the sense of being identical with the facts it is used to express, but each may be right by being faithful to these facts, as a translation may be faithful. My endeavour is to think straight in such terms as are offered to me, to clear my mind of cant and free it from the cramp of artificial traditions; but I do not ask any one to think in my terms if he prefers others. Let him clean better, if he can, the windows of his soul, that the variety and beauty of the prospect may spread more brightly before him.

Moreover, my system, save in the mocking literary sense of the word, is *not metaphysical.* It contains much criticism of metaphysics, and some refinements in speculation, like the doctrine of essence, which are not familiar to the public; and I do not disclaim being metaphysical because I at all dislike dialectic or disdain immaterial things: indeed, it is of immaterial things, essence, truth, and spirit that I speak chiefly. But logic and mathematics and literary psychology (when frankly literary) are not metaphysical, although their subject-matter is immaterial, and their application to existing things is often questionable. Metaphysics, in the proper sense of the word, is dialectical physics, or an attempt to determine matters of fact by means of logical or moral or rhetorical constructions. It arises by a confusion of those Realms of Being which it is my special care to distinguish. It is neither physical speculation nor pure logic nor honest literature, but (as in the treatise of Aristotle first called by that name) a hybrid of the three, materialising ideal entities, turning harmonies into forces, and dissolving natural things into terms of discourse. Speculations about the natural world, such as those of the Ionian philosophers, are not metaphysics, but simply cosmology or natural philosophy. Now in natural philosophy I am a decided materialist—apparently the only one living; and I am well aware that idealists are fond of calling materialism, too, metaphysics, in rather an angry tone, so as to cast discredit upon it by assimilating it to their own systems. But my materialism, for all that, is not metaphysical. I do not profess to know what matter is in itself, and feel no confidence in the divination of those *esprits forts* who, leading a life of vice, thought the universe must be composed of nothing but dice and billiard-balls. I wait for the men of science to tell me what matter is, in so far as they can discover it, and am not at all surprised or troubled at the abstractness and vagueness of their ultimate conceptions: how should our notions of things so remote from the scale and scope of our senses be anything but schematic? But whatever matter may be, I call it matter boldly, as I call my acquaintances Smith and Jones without knowing their secrets: whatever it may be, it must present the aspects and undergo the motions of the gross objects that fill the world: and if belief in the existence of hidden parts and movements in nature be metaphysics, then the kitchen-maid is a metaphysician whenever she peels a potato.

My system, finally, though, of course, formed under the fire of contemporary discussions, is *no phase of any current movement.* I cannot take at all seriously the present flutter of the image-lovers against intelligence. I love images as much as they do, but images must be discounted in our waking life, when we come to business. I also appreciate the other reforms and rebellions that have made up the history of philosophy. I prize their sharp criticism of one another and their several discoveries; the trouble is that each in turn has denied or forgotten a much more important truth than it has asserted. The first philosophers, the original observers of life and nature, were the best; and I think only the Indians and the Greek naturalists, together with Spinoza, have been right on the chief issue, the relation of man and of his spirit to the universe. It is not unwillingness to be a disciple that prompts me to look beyond the modern scramble of philosophies: I should gladly learn of them all, if they had learned more of one another. Even as it is, I endeavour to retain the positive insight of each, reducing it to the scale of nature and keeping it in its place; thus I am a Platonist in logic and morals, and a transcendentalist in romantic soliloquy, when I choose to indulge in it. Nor is it necessary, in being teachable by any master, to become eclectic. All these vistas give glimpses of the same wood, and a fair and true map of it must be drawn to a single scale, by one method of projection, and in one style of calligraphy. All known truth can be rendered in any language, although the accent and poetry of each may be incommunicable; and as I am content to write in English, although it was not my mother-tongue, and although in speculative matters I have not much sympathy with the English mind, so I am content to follow the European tradition in philosophy, little as I respect its rhetorical metaphysics, its humanism, and its worldliness.

There is one point, indeed, in which I am truly sorry not to be able to profit by the guidance of my contemporaries. There is now a great ferment in natural and mathematical philosophy and the times seem ripe for a new system of nature, at once ingenuous and comprehensive, such as has not appeared since the earlier days of Greece. We may soon be all believing in an honest cosmology, comparable with that of Heraclitus, Pythagoras, or Democritus. I wish such scientific systems joy, and if I were competent to follow or to forecast their procedure, I should gladly avail myself of their results, which are bound to be no less picturesque than instructive. But what exists today is so tentative, obscure, and confused by bad philosophy, that there is no knowing what parts may be sound and what parts merely personal and scatter-brained. If I were a mathematician I should no doubt regale myself, if not the reader, with an electric or logistic system of the universe expressed in algebraic symbols. For good or ill, I am an ignorant man, almost a poet, and I can only spread a feast of what everybody knows. Fortunately exact science and the books of the learned are not necessary to establish my essential doctrine, nor can any of them claim a higher warrant than it has in itself: for it rests on public experience. It needs, to prove it, only the stars, the seasons, the swarm of animals, the spectacle of birth and death, of cities and wars. My philosophy is justified, and has been justified in all ages and countries by the facts before every man's eyes; and no great wit is requisite to discover it, only (what is rarer than wit) candour and courage. Learning does not liberate men from superstition when their souls are cowed or perplexed; and, without learning, clear eyes and honest reflection can discern the hang of the world, and distinguish the edge of truth from the might of imagination. In the past or in the future, my language and my borrowed knowledge would have been different, but under whatever sky I had been born, since it is the same sky, I should have had the same philosophy.

—*From the Preface to Scepticism and Animal Faith, by George Santayana, American (1863–).*

Gorgias' Farewell

JOSÉ E. RODÓ

THOSE seated at a table, laden with flowers and amphorae of wine, over which presides an old man, beautiful and serene as a god; who drink but show no sign of mirth; those who frequently rise to consult the height of the sun and at times let fall a tear — they are the disciples of Gorgias. Gorgias has taught a new philosophy in the city that cradled him. Its implications have stirred up suspicion and have alarmed the authorities. Gorgias is going to die. He has been allowed to choose a way of death and he has chosen that of Socrates. At sunset he is to drink the hemlock; he still has two hours to live and he passes them in sublime serenity as host at a melancholy feast where flowers caress the eyes of the guests. Their thought kindles the banquet with an intimate light and a mild wine gives inspiration for the last toast. Gorgias says to his disciples: "My life is a garland to which we are going to fasten the last rose."

This time the pleasure of gracefully philosophizing, which belongs to exquisite souls, is enhanced by an unusual unction. "Master," says one, "we shall never be able to forget either you or your doctrines." Another puts in, "We would rather die than deny a single word which has come from your lips." And enlarging upon this sentiment a third adds: "Let us pledge fidelity to every word he has uttered, to whatever is virtually contained in each of his words, faithful before men and in the depths of our conscience, always and invariably faithful." Gorgias asks the one who has spoken in this way, "Do you know, Lucius, what it is to swear falsely?" "I know," replies the youth, "but I firmly feel the profundity of our convictions and I believe that we ought to console you in your last hour with that promise which is sweetest to your soul."

Then Gorgias begins to speak in this manner: "Lucius, listen to an incident of my childhood. When I was a little boy, my mother took so much delight in my goodness, in my beauty, and above all, in the love which I bore her, that it pained her deeply to think that my childhood and all that happiness would have to pass. Thousands upon thousands of times I have heard her repeat: 'How much would I give that you never cease to be a child! . . .' Weeping, she anticipated the loss of my youthful happiness, of my candor, of that beauty which was like that of a flower or a bird, of that unique love, thanks to which only she existed on this earth for me. She was not resigned to the idea of the inevitable work of Time, that barbarous deity who would place his hand on such a fragile and divine good, who would destroy the delicate and graceful form and who would embitter the taste of life, bringing guilt where there was once unblemished innocence. She was even less reconciled to the image of a future but certain woman who perhaps would bring grief to my soul in payment for love. And she insisted on her pertinacious desire: 'How much would I give that you might never, never cease to be a child.' On a certain occasion, a woman from Thessaly, who pretended to be familiar with charms and enchantments, heard her and showed her a means of attaining that vehement desire, so unrealizable within the common bounds of Nature. Repeating certain magic incantations she was to place over my heart every day the warm and still-bleeding heart of a dove; this would serve as a sponge with which to eradicate each trace of time; and to rub my forehead with a wild iris, massaging it until the flower lost all of its moisture, thus keeping my thoughts clean and pure. Possessing this precious secret, my mother returned with the determination to carry out the instructions immediately. That night she had a dream. She dreamed that she had proceeded as she had been directed, that many years had passed but that I had kept my childhood intact and that she, herself favored with the gift of attaining an extreme old-age, was in constant ecstasy at the contemplation of my unaltered good-fortune: my untouched beauty, my unpolluted purity. . . . Then in her dream there came a day when she could find neither the iris flower nor the dove's heart. And on awakening and running to me the following morning, she saw instead of me an old man austere and dejected; everything about him indicated an endless anxiety; there was nothing noble or grand in his appearance and in his glance shone flashes of desperation and hatred. 'Evil woman!' she heard him cry, turning to her with an angry frown, 'you have robbed me of life because of a ferocious egoism, giving me a shameful happiness in exchange, which is the mask under which you hide from your own eyes your frightful crime. . . . You have converted my soul into a vile toy. You have sacrificed me to a foolish whim. You have deprived me of the action that ennobles, of the thought that illumines, of the love that creates. . . . Return to me what you have taken! But this is not the hour to return it to me because this very day is the one which Nature has set for the end of my life, which you have squandered in a miserable fiction, and now I'm going to die with only enough time to curse and despise you. . . .' My mother's dream ended there. From then on she stopped deploring the brevity of my childhood. If I were to accept the vow you propose, O Lucius, I would be forgetting the moral of my parable which is directed against the absolutism of a dogma made at one time for always; against the faith that does not permit us flight further than the horizon it revealed to us at first. My philosophy is not a religion that takes a man at the dawn of childhood and with the faith that it infuses in him, aims to take possession of his life, making his infancy eternal just as my mother wished to do before she was undeceived by her dream. I was to you a teacher of love. I have tried to give you a love for the truth, and not the truth, for that is infinite. Continue to seek and renew it like a fisherman who casts his net every day without expecting to exhaust the treasure of the sea. My philosophy has been a mother to your conscience, a mother to your reason. It does not close the circle of your thought. The truth that I have given you with it has cost you no effort, comparison, choice, verification or responsibility. A price you will have to pay as soon as you begin to really live and to seek your truth independently. Thus we do not gain a mother's love by our own merits: it is a present Nature gives us. But then another love takes its place, according to the natural order of life, the love of a sweetheart, and this time we must indeed gain it. Seek a new love, a new truth. Do not be concerned if this new truth leads you to be unfaithful to something you may have heard from my lips. Remain faithful to me, love my memory as far as it may be an evocation of myself, alive and real, an emanation of my person, a perfume of my soul in the affection that I have for you; but do not cherish my doctrine unless there is a brighter lantern for the search of truth. Ideas may become as much of a prison as the letter of the law. Ideas fly rapidly over laws and formulae; but there is something that goes even faster than they – it is the life-spirit that blows in the direction of Truth.". . .

Then after a brief pause he adds, "You, Leucippus, who are most saturated with my teaching, what do you think of all this? And now that my hour is near, now that the light fades and the noise of the world grows still – for whom shall we pour our libation? For whom this sparkling amber that remains in the bottom of the cups?". . .

"Let it be," says Leucippus, "for the one who after the first sun that you do not see will show us the truth, the light, the way; for the one who will remove the doubts that you leave in the shadow; for the one who will go beyond your last footprint, whose mind will dwell in a clearer and wider realm than yours. Let it be for all your disciples, if we have the right to that title, or for one of us, or for some foreign mentor who may captivate us with a book, a lecture or an example. If he shows us the error that you have mixed with the truth, if he makes one word of yours appear false, if he sees where you did not see, by these evidences we must understand that you are surpassed: Master, let us drink to him who will take your place in us, with honor!"

"To him," say Gorgias; and holding aloft his cup, hearing the executioner already approaching, while an august clarity dawns in his face, he repeats, "To the one who will take my place in you with honor!"

— *From Motives of Proteus, by José Enrique Rodó, Uruguayan (1872–1917), translated from the Spanish by Angel Flores.*

PART TWENTY-ONE

Man in Love

Not all men are gifted with imagination as shown in the metaphysical lyric, but no human emotion is more comprehensive than love. So comprehensive is it that the poet has played upon the theme with infinite variety, and no poetry exhibits more clearly the state of the civilization of which he sings, from the simplicity of the folk-song to the over-elaborate poems of a decadent culture. The subject assumes a new interest as one considers the diverse attitudes of individual authors, of distinct groups within a society, and especially of the historical periods.

The Orient exhibits quite as much diversity in outlook as Europe. The Japanese poets, for example, excel in the delicacy of their romantic sentiment; the Chinese, in the depth of their affection. Thus the Japanese poems often have the vivid images of Japanese prints, while those in Chinese possess the more inward and philosophical quality of the colorless but masterfully drawn Sung paintings. The love of man and woman as the accumulated emotion of long family life receives some of its most eloquent expressions at the hands of the Chinese, who combine their extreme ethical refinement with a refinement of more distinctively amorous experience. Love poetry, to conclude, in both Japan and China proves unsurpassed for poignancy of feeling, succinctness of expression, and a depth of natural humanity enhanced by traditional and aristocratic disciplines.

Indian, Persian, Arabic and Hebrew literatures possess an opulence and a warmth of sensuous imagery rarely discovered in literature of either the extreme Orient or of Europe. The art of the Near East glows with color and breathes intoxicating perfumes; with religious enthusiasm it offers the entire world known to the senses as sacrificial incense to the lover's experience. This opulence is manifested most powerfully, perhaps, in early stages of the Sanskrit, Arabic and Hebrew, reaching a height familiar to Christian readers in the biblical *Song of Songs.* Unsurpassed for a fusion of warmth with delicacy, and energy with wit, is the culminating lyric art of Hafiz, who flourished in Persia during the fourteenth century of our own era. After Hafiz, Mohammedan culture pursued a downward road.

In their view of love, as in their views of so many phases of human life, the Greeks became the foremost innovators. Not only do they record their feelings and perceptions with a clarity and a firmness scarcely equalled elsewhere; they have new experiences to record. Their high regard for individuality holds distinct significance for their refinements of the more impassioned imagination. For to the Greeks, love poetry no longer consists, as in most literature from India to Palestine, in the celebration of a standardized conception of physical beauty, but rests on an intuitive assumption of the individuality of the beloved. The entire personality, including body, mind and soul, becomes the object of passionate regard. The romantic relationship, in other words, shows an attraction both toward the person and toward the personality. Helen of Troy, for example, is in Greek eyes indubitably an active human being as well as the mere possessor of great sensuous and aesthetic charm. She is the first true heroine in European literature. Even in lyric poetry this fundamental attitude makes itself sharply felt.

The outlook of the mercurial Greeks toward love is often religious, often humorous, and often both. Moreover it is, like other Greek attitudes, highly skeptical, for love is appraised equally as a great blessing, a great nuisance, and a trifling entertainment. The scope of their view is expressed in the numerous mythological deities reflecting the varied aspects of love. Prominent in the Greek mind were the sober fertility myths, with their legends of Demeter and Persephone, Aphrodite and Adonis. Love might, then, be of the utmost dignity; or it might be lightened and relieved by the fancies of Cupid and the amoretti. No deity has, indeed, possessed more varied aspects than Eros himself. To Sappho and Euripides, as our citations will show, he is a mighty and an awful god; to Anacreon he commonly appears as a playful and a childish companion; to Theocritus he assumes both roles. And to Aristophanes, also, love becomes all things to all men, not to mention all women, inspiring in the greatest of comic dramatists either the most glowing of lyrical praise or the most obscene and untranslatable of laughter-provoking jests. The grave religion of beauty prevalent among the more high-minded of the Greeks and, paradoxically, their extremely frank practice of homosexuality, lend further variations to their unprecedented and most pragmatic explorations. Thus the Greeks bequeathed to Western culture an unforgettable and extraordinarily varied heritage of insights into the kingdom of Eros.

Roman poets enlarged upon the Greek themes without materially altering them or enriching the more fundamental conceptions. Horace and Catullus depict a society strongly colored by the amorous adventures of witty men and women who are all distinctly individualized. Ovid contributes grace and order to the lover's world; while the religion of natural love appears in its brightest guise in the hymn *Pervigilium Veneris,* or Vigil of Venus. All these contributions are represented in the following selections.

With the collapse of classical culture there still flourished a popular poetry in praise of a lusty and physical love, giving us frank and naive songs issuing from the youthful heart of the Middle Ages. Instances of such verse are given here from Latin, German, and Norman French. The realism of the great French poet, Villon, ultimately derives from this popular tradition. Meanwhile the rise of chivalry, the rebirth of Platonism and the popularity of various types of mysticism leaning upon the increasing veneration of the Blessed Virgin, gave rise, first in Italy and Provençe, and later throughout Europe, to a type of love poetry more congenial to ascetic or philosophical Christianity. The love and beauty of women became in one way or another a stepping stone to the love of the Christian God. This movement, we may assume, was indeed inspired to the greater glory of her Creator, since we can hardly suppose it to have been to woman's greater earthly comfort. The chief spokesmen for this new and exalted type of love poetry were in turn Guido Guinicelli, Dante and Petrarch.

If English poets from the Elizabethan to the present day have treated love less imaginatively than the Greeks, they have none the less presented it with a comparable diversity and realism. A glance at the following verses reveals how powerful and how diverse are the contributions of Wyatt, Sidney, Spenser, Shakespeare, Dryden, Burns, Keats and Byron. German poetry, always distinguished for the brief and popular lyric of sentiment, reached the culmination of its most typical vein in the songs of Heine. Occasionally the lyric poets of both Spain and South America proved in the nineteenth century still to command the key to a rare harmony between the heroic and the real. Meanwhile with much ingenuity the French explored both the lyric art and the darker recesses of the impassioned soul. Much of their verse, especially as written by the "Symbolists," hardly admits translation. Nevertheless, chiefly through the genius of Arthur Symons, the slight but exquisite studies of the moods of lovers by the great lyricist Paul Verlaine are in a measure accessible to the English reader. A large part of the Symbolist poetry is a harmony of half tones and tinted shadows, exquisite but correspondingly tenuous. Much of it also, following in the path of Baudelaire, becomes profound chiefly in its disillusionment.

American poets, either chilled by the Puritan tradition, or diverted to more strenuous fields, have as a whole hardly excelled in the poetry of Eros. Yet the love lyrics of Emily Dickinson have lasting power, and our more recent interpreters of the stronger emotions have made rapid progress in a variety of directions, usually building on spiritual foundations of the past. As our selections illustrate, Robinson Jeffers returns for inspiration to primitivism, and — perhaps most interestingly of all — the New Englander, Robert Frost, to a deep humanism curiously close to the earliest masters of the love theme in the ancient China of Confucian civilization.

The Wife

My husband is far, far away
At the wars.
I know not when he'll come back to me,
Nor where he may be this day.

'Tis sunset.
The fowls roost in the holes in the wall,
The sheep and cattle come in from the field;
But my husband is far, far away
At the wars.
Can my thoughts be of anything
Save of him?

My husband is far, far away
At the wars.
The days and months seem
Without end.

The fowls nestle sleepily on their high roosts,
The cattle and sheep are safe in their barns;
But my husband is far, far away
At the wars.
Heaven keep from him
Hunger and thirst!

— *From the Chinese of an unknown poet (before 206 B.C.), translated by Henry H. Hart.*

The Night of Sorrow

A lovely woman rolls up
The delicate bamboo blind.
She sits deep within,
Twitching her moth eyebrows.
Who may it be
That grieves her heart?

On her face one sees
Only the wet traces of tears.

—*From the Chinese of Li Po (701–762), translated by Shigeyoshi Obata.*

~ ❁ ~

The Beautiful Woman

I, who was the flower of my day among the beauties,
Now dwell alone in a deserted valley;
I, who was well born,
Live desolate in a country retreat.
In past times there was ruin and turmoil in the frontier passes;
My brothers met with destruction;
What availed such high officials their lofty rank
When they could not protect their own flesh and blood?
It is the way of the world to turn in loathing from adversity and decay.
The affairs of men flicker like a guttering candle.
My husband holds me in light esteem,
But his new mistress seems as beautiful as jade.
Even the morning glory has its passing hour.
The Mandarin duck and drake do not roost apart,
But wrapt in his new favourite's smiles
How can he hear his old love's sighs?
In the hills the spring water runs clear,
But on leaving the hills it becomes muddy.
My servant girl sells my pearls and returns
To pull the creepers to patch my thatched roof.
Her mistress plucks flowers, but not to stick in her hair;
The cypress needles slide through her listless fingers.
The weather is cold and my kingfisher-blue sleeves are thin;
As day draws to dusk I lean against the tall bamboos thinking of other days.

—*From the Chinese of Tu Fu (713–770), translated by Soame Jenyns.*

~ ❁ ~

Plucking the Rushes

Green rushes with red shoots,
Long leaves bending to the wind—
You and I in the same boat
Plucking rushes at the Five Lakes.
We started at dawn from the orchid-island:
We rested under the elms till noon.
You and I plucking rushes
Had not plucked a handful when night came!

—*From the Chinese, anon. (fourth century), translated by Arthur Waley.*

~ ❁ ~

Crossing the Mountain Alone

How will you manage
To cross alone
The autumn mountain,
Which was so hard to get across
Even when we went the two of us together?

—*From the Japanese of Princess Daihaku (eighth century), translated by Arthur Waley.*

~ ❁ ~

Pretext

By way of pretext
I said "I will go
And look at
The condition of the bamboo fence";
But it was really to see you!

—*From the Japanese of Yakamochi (d. 785), translated by Arthur Waley.*

~ ❁ ~

A Bright Night

Shall we make love
Indoors
On this night when the moon has begun to shine
Over the rushes
Of Inami Moor?

—*From the Japanese, anon., translated by Arthur Waley.*

~ ❁ ~

Love's Terror

You are like the lightning
Flashing near
To the clouds of the sky;
When I see you I am frightened;
When I do not see you, I am sad.

—*From the Japanese, anon., translated by Arthur Waley.*

~ ❁ ~

Whirlpool

They say there is
A still pool even in the middle of
The rushing whirlpool, —
Why is there none in the whirlpool of my
love?

— *From the Japanese, anon., translated by Arthur Waley.*

~ ❁ ~

From the Song of Songs

Behold, thou art fair, my love; behold, thou art fair; thou hast doves' eyes within thy locks: thy hair is as a flock of goats, that appear from mount Gilead.

Thy teeth are like a flock of sheep that are even shorn, which came up from the washing; whereof every one bear twins, and none is barren among them.

Thy lips are like a thread of scarlet, and thy speech is comely: thy temples are like a piece of a pomegranate within thy locks.

Thy neck is like the tower of David builded for an armory, whereon there hang a thousand bucklers, all shields of mighty men.

Thy two breasts are like two young roes that are twins, which feed among the lilies.

Until the day break, and the shadows flee away, I will get me to the mountains of myrrh, and to the hill of frankincense.

Thou art all fair, my love; there is no spot in thee.

Come with me from Lebanon, my spouse, with me from Lebanon: look from the top of Amana, from the top of Shenir and Hermon, from the lions' dens, from the mountains of the leopards.

Thou hast ravished my heart, my sister, my spouse; thou hast ravished my heart with one of thine eyes, with one chain of thy neck.

How fair is thy love, my sister, my spouse! how much better is thy love than wine! and the smell of thine ointments than all spices!

Thy lips, O my spouse, drop as the honeycomb: honey and milk are under thy tongue; and the smell of thy garments is like the smell of Lebanon.

A garden inclosed is my sister, my spouse; a spring shut up, a fountain sealed.

Thy plants are an orchard of pomegranates, with pleasant fruits; camphire, with spikenard,

Spikenard and saffron; calamus and cinnamon, with all trees of frankincense; myrrh and aloes, with all the chief spices:

A fountain of gardens, a well of living waters, and streams from Lebanon.

Awake, O north wind; and come, thou south; blow upon my garden, that the spices thereof may flow out. Let my beloved come into his garden, and eat his pleasant fruits.

— *From the King James Version of the Bible.*

~ ❁ ~

I Cease Not from Desire

I cease not from desire till my desire
Is satisfied; or let my mouth attain
My love's red mouth, or let my soul expire,
Sighed from those lips that sought her lips
in vain.
Others may find another love as fair;
Upon the threshold I have laid my head,
The dust shall cover me, still lying there,
When from my body life and love have fled.

My soul is on my lips ready to fly,
But grief beats in my heart and will not
cease,
Because not once, not once before I die,
Will her sweet lips give all my longing peace.
My breath is narrowed down to one long
sigh
For a red mouth that burns my thoughts like
fire:
When will that mouth draw near and make
reply
To one whose life is straitened with desire?

When I am dead, open my grave and see
The cloud of smoke that rises round thy feet:
In my dead heart the fire still burns for thee;
Yea, the smoke rises from my winding-sheet!
Ah, come, Beloved; for the meadows wait
Thy coming, and the thorn bears flowers instead
Of thorns, the cypress fruit, and desolate
Bare winter from before thy steps has fled.

Hoping within some garden ground to find
A red rose soft and sweet as thy soft cheek,
Through every meadow blows the western
wind,
Through every garden he is fain to seek.
Reveal thy face! that the whole world may
be
Bewildered by thy radiant loveliness;

The cry of man and woman comes to thee,
Open thy lips and comfort their distress!

Each curling lock of thy luxuriant hair
Breaks into barbed hooks to catch my heart,
My broken heart is wounded everywhere
With countless wounds from which the red drops start.
Yet when sad lovers meet and tell their sighs,
Not without praise shall Hafiz' name be said,
Not without tears, in those pale companies
Where joy has been forgot and hope has fled.

—*From the Persian of Hafiz (d. 1389), translated by Gertrude Lowthian Bell.*

To a Bride

Blest beyond earth's bliss, with heaven I deem him
Blest, the man that in thy presence near thee
Face to face may sit, and while thou speakest,
Listening may hear thee,

And thy sweet-voiced laughter:—In my bosom
The rapt heart so troubleth, wildly stirred:
Let me see thee, but a glimpse—and straightway
Utterance of word

Fails me; no voice comes; my tongue is palsied;
Thrilling fire through all my flesh hath run;
Mine eyes cannot see, mine ears make dinning
Noises that stun;

The sweat streameth down,—my whole frame seized with
Shivering,—and wan paleness o'er me spread,
Greener than the grass; I seem with faintness
Almost as dead.

—*From the Greek of Sappho (fl. 600? B.C.), translated by Walter Headlam.*

Wormwood

It is humiliating
the manner in which
you degrade yourself
now that you are gone from me.

Foolish girl, what
bucolic wench is this,
sour with sweat in countrified clothes,
who inflames you
although she does not know
how to lift her gown over her ankles
and is unlearned
in the first principles of passion?
Surely, it were better to give thyself free
to all comers for the asking
than to so perpetuate this travesty of our desire
with such an uncouth proselyte.

I cannot conceive of you, Mnasidice,
who are as fragile as a poppy plant,
and who of the maidens
have no rival in your art
opening to this slut
all chambers of the house
that formerly was mine,

And once again shall be.
But I tell you
until you return
my mind is like the foot of a madman
forever moving
without purpose or design
and fruitlessly.

—*From the Greek of the Sapphic Fragments, translated by Randolph Shaffer, Jr.*

At the Mid Hour of Night

Downward was the wheeling Bear
Driven by the Waggoner:
Men by powerful sleep opprest,
Gave their busy troubles rest:
Love, in this still depth of night,
Lately at my house did light;
Where perceiving all fast lockt,
At the door he boldly knockt.
"Who's that," said I, "that does keep
Such a noise, and breaks my sleep?"
"Ope," saith Love, "for pity hear;
'Tis a child, thou need'st not fear,
Wet and weary, from his way

Led by this dark night astray."
With compassion this I heard;
Light I struck; the door unbarr'd:
Where a little Boy appears,
Who wings, bow, and quiver bears;
Near the fire I made him stand,
With my own I chaft his hand;
And with kindly busy care
Wrung the chill drops from his hair:
When well warm'd he was, and dry,
"Now," saith he, "'tis time to try
If my bow no hurt did get,
For methinks the string is wet."
With that, drawing it, a dart
He let fly that pierc'd my heart:
Leaping then, and laughing said,
"Come, my friend, with me be glad;
For my Bow thou see'st is sound,
Since thy heart hath got a wound."

—*From the Greek; ascribed to Anacreon (c. 563–478 B.C.), translated by Thomas Stanley.*

Love

Love, under thy dominion unbending hearts bow low—
Gods' hearts, and hearts of mortals; when, flashing through thy portals
On glory-gleaming pinion, flits Eros to and fro,
Love, under thy dominion unbending hearts bow low.

Gold-glittering wings, wide-soaring, they rain down witchery:
O'er maddened hearts prevailing, o'er earth triumphant sailing,
O'er music of the roaring of spray-bemantled sea,
Gold-glittering wings wide-soaring, they rain down witchery.

He kindleth with his yearning all things of earth-born race:
The mountain's whelps he thrilleth, the ocean's brood he filleth;
Where'er the sun's eye burning down looketh on earth's face,
He kindleth with his yearning all things of earth-born race.

They bend—all, all are bending, Love-queen, beneath thy hand!
O crownéd brows, whom loyal vassals acclaim sole-royal,
By spells all-comprehending in sky and sea and land;
They bend—all, all are bending, Love-queen, beneath thy hand!

—*From the Greek of Euripides (480–406 B.C.), translated by Arthur S. Way.*

Love, the Vagrant

Love, I proclaim, the vagrant child,
Who, even now, at dawn of day,
Stole from his bed and flew away.
He's wont to weep, as though he smiled,
For ever prattling, swift, and daring;
Laughs with wide mouth and wrinkled nose;
Wing'd on the back, and always bearing
A quiver, rattling as he goes.
Unknown the author of his birth;
For Air, 'tis certain, ne'er begot
The saucy boy; and as for Earth
And Sea, both swear they own him not.
To all and every where a foe.
But you must look, and keep good watch,
Lest he should still around him throw
Fresh nets, unwary souls to catch.
Stay, while I am yet speaking, lo!
There, there he sits, like one forbidden;
And did you hope to 'scape me so—
In Lesbia's eyes, you truant, hidden.

—*From the Greek of Meleager (fl. 90 B.C.), translated by John Herman Merivale.*

Love Sleeping

Within the covert of a shady grove
We saw the little red-cheek'd god of Love:
He had nor bow nor quiver: these among
The neighboring trees upon a bow were hung.
Upon a bank of tender rosebuds laid,
He smiling slept; bees with their noise invade
His rest, and on his lips their honey made.

—*From the Greek of Plato (429–347 B.C.), translated by Thomas Stanley.*

Bridal Hymn

Thou of the hill Heliconian
Haunter, child of Urania,
Thou who lead'st with thy holiest
Hand the tender and tremulous
Bride to her lord, her loved one!

Bind thy temples with blossoming
Scented sprays of amaracus!
Come to us bearing the rose-coloured
Veil, with thy white feet glancing in
Sandals dyed like roses!

Hie thee hitherward, carolling
Marriage music and madrigals!
Hitherward, waving thy cedary
Torch, till the nuptial flame of it
Breaks in golden sparkles!

Haste, for Julia—Julia
This high day to her Manlius
Comes, as once the Idalian
Queen to the Phrygian arbiter
Came in the clefts of Ida!

Fair she blooms, as in bowery
Haunted thicket of Asia
Blooms some chosen and odorous
Myrtle, fed by Dryades
All night long with dew-drops.

Wherefore, leave thou the murmuring
Gorge of the Thespian waterfall,
Hymen! Leave thou the shadowy
Grottoes moist with the pouring of
Ice-cold clear Aganippe!

Leave them, and haste to her festival,
Hymen, calling the heart of her
Home to her new home, binding it
Close with love, as the wandering
Ivy enwinds the oak tree!

Ye too, ye with your virginal
Voices, who still are awaiting him,
Virgins, call to the god for her!
"Hymen" call ye in unison—
"Hymen, oh Hymenaeus!"

So shall the Deity, hearing you,
Lend an ear to us gladlier—
Gladlier the child of Urania
Haste to us, leading the heavenly
Love to an earthly hearth-stone!

Ah! of all the Celestials,
Whom, ah, whom does the passioning
Lover's heart, or the fatherly
Heart of a man's solicitude,
Yearn for more than Hymen?

Thee the father, with tremulous
Lips, invokes for his little ones.
Thee the maiden immaculate
Bares her breast to. The hearkening
Bridegroom awaits thy foot-fall!

Thou the maid from the motherly
Arms, and eyes that are dim for her,
Tak'st, and giv'st to the amorous
Arms, and the eyes that are fire for her,
Holy and tender Hymen!

All the desire of the amorous
Blood, without thee, in bitterness
End; but end in beatitude
Thou commanding. What heavenly
God can compare with this god!

Storied line and illustrious
Dies without Thee. The heir of it
Cannot be: but he flourishes,
Thou commanding. What heavenly
God can compare with this god?

Open your gates, for she comes to us.
See the torches! Their glittering
Hair is tossed! But thou tarriest!
Tarry not! Daylight goes from us.
Come to us, spousal virgin!

Ah, she halts; and her hesitant
Eyes, in vain, with her destiny
Plead, and the hour that is calling her.
Plead not! Daylight goes from us.
Come to us, spousal virgin!

Come, oh Julia, Julia!.
Weep not, loveliest! Lovelier
Eyes on the morrow awaiting them
Shall not shine to the rose-coloured
Sun as he comes from ocean.

Fair among women, and eminent,
Thou, as in garden of various
Hues, the flower of the hyacinth.
Tarry not! Daylight goes from us.
Come to us, spousal virgin!

Ah, she is coming, she comes to us—
Spousal maid; and our canticles

Reach her ear; and the heralding
Torches shake their tumultuous
  Hair on the deepening twilight!

Faint not, heart of the chosen one!
Thou no cruel adulterer
Seek'st, but a lord and a lover, who
Never in dreams shall rest upon
  Tenderer breast than thy breast.

Even as the vine its companioning
Elm-tree enrings, shall the heart of thee
Round the heart of the chosen one
Grow, and closely and closelier
  Wind and enwind its tendrils.

Ah, for the holy, ineffable
Purple couch of the bride-chamber!
Love for a banner is over it —
Couch of cedar and ivory —
  Couch with the feet of silver!

Ah, what joys shall the lord of thee
Know in the still overshadowing
Night! What joys in the languorous
Noon! But the daylight goes from us.
  Come to us, spousal virgin!

Lift your torches, ye torch-bearers!
Shake their flames: for the rose-coloured
Veil at last in the shine of them
Comes. Now shout ye in unison,
  "Hymen, oh Hymenaeus!"

Shout! But hist! They are calling thee,
Bridegroom! Hark, 'tis thy play-fellows,
Laughing a long good-bye to thee —
Thee who, a man, art casting thy
  Childish things behind thee.

Hark, they laugh "Have you done with them,
You — not you — with the vagabond
Loves, and the lips of yesterday?"
Let them laugh! Thou hast done with them.
  Thou hast cast them all behind thee.

Him then, Julia, trusting him,
Take, all thine. But, oh loveliest,
Heed thou this, that thy tenderness
Turn not chill, nor abandon him
  Lorn to an alien haven.

Lift, ye gates of the sanctuary,
Lift up your heads! Let the chosen one
Enter into her blessedness —
Enter the home that is hers — that is
  Hers, until all be ended!

Hers, all hers, till the brows of her
Nod with snow, and the luminous
Halls fade dim from the eyes of her,
As from the eyes of all of us
  All shall be one day fading!

Hymen, hither! Be near to her!
Bless the gates of the sanctuary!
Bless the threshold, as over it,
Lo, she is lifting her delicate
  Feet with their golden sandals!

Him too — Hymen, be near to him —
Him who within, on the Tyrian
Couch, is pale with expecting her.
Love for a banner is over him;
  Love, for a pavement, under!

Hymen, hither! To both of them
Near — be near — to the fiery
Heart that burns as a sacrifice —
Near to the heart that shall cast on it
  All its garnered sweetness!

Paranymph, boy of the bride-chamber,
Thou whose hand has been leading her,
Loose her, and say good-bye to her!
Loose her! Her hand may rest upon
  Hand of thine no longer.

Leave her; and ye draw nigh to her,
Sealed with the seal of widowhood,
Matrons faithful of memory!
Ye, with your solemn and consecrate
  Hands, lead in the virgin!

Lead her in, and call to him;
Call the bridegroom, and say to him,
"Take her, fair as the virginal
White wild rose, or the slumbering
  Cheek of the scarlet poppy!"

Bridegroom, take her, and tarry not!
Comelier art thou than the comeliest
Sons of men. To the arms of her
Haste thee, smelling of frankincense!
  Haste to the bridal kingdom!

Open the gates of the mystical
Kingdom. There in beatitude
Love has rest from its pilgrimage —
There, where the strong and the beautiful
  Mingle and meet together!

He shall number the numberless
Sands which the billow of Araby
Breaks on, number the million
Midnight stars, who shall number the
Joys of the bridal kingdom.

Realm of marvel and miracle!
Passioning heart to passioning
Heart is pressed, and the alien
World shut out; but the solitude
Brings to their loves a new love.

Ah, may a little Torquatulus
One day stretch from a motherly
Knee, to a sire that shall gaze at him,
Sweet, small hands, with the flower on his
Lips of baby laughter!

Baby face, may the Manlian
Far-descended illustrious
Spirit reign on the brows of it!
Baby face, may the spirit of
Julia shine in those eyes!

Muse of my song, we have done with you!
All that of earthly or heavenly
Joy for a man is possible,
This, for these, we have prophesied.
Muse of my song, be silent!

—*From the Latin of Catullus (84?–54? B.C.), translated by W. H. Mallock.*

Slowly, Slowly

The old man's fair-haired consort, whose dewy axle-tree
Brings morning to us mortals, now rises from the Sea.
I pray you, stay, Aurora; and to your Memnon's shade
A sacrifice—I vow it—shall every year be made.
'Tis now my love is by me, her lips are mine to kiss,
Her arms are twined about me—is any hour like this?
'Tis cool, and one is sleepy, and from their slender throats
The little feathered songsters pour forth their liquid notes.
Now prithy, Rosy Fingers, why take such parlous pains
To hurry? No one wants you! Then stay those dewy reins.
Ere you arrive, the sailor can watch his stars and keep
His course, nor wander blindly amid the vasty deep;
With you, the weary traveler must rise and hie away,
Must rise the cruel soldier and arm him for the fray;
The hind resumes his mattock and grubs the stubborn soil,
The slow and patient oxen begin their day of toil;
Schoolboys you cheat of slumber, to go at your commands
Where pedagogues are waiting to smack their tender hands;
You summon to the courthouse the bailsmen, where they taste
The pain of paying dearly for one word said in haste.
The lawyers find you hateful, i'faith, and always will;
You wake them every morning to new contention still.
That girls cease toiling sometimes, 'twere surely fair to ask;
But no, you rouse the spinners each to her daily task.
All else I might put up with; but who was ever known
To make the girls rise early, who had one of his own?
How oft I've prayed that Darkness refuse to give you place,
How oft, that Stars might brave you, nor flee before your face;
How oft, I've prayed some whirlwind an axle-tree might twist,
Or that a courser stumble and stick in some thick mist!
Why hurry, spiteful goddess? I see it now, alack,
Why Memnon was so swarthy—his mother's heart was black!
I wish poor old Tithonus had power to testify
To what he knows—'twould make you the scandal of the sky!
Your spouse is old and feeble; that's why you leave your bower
And mount your hateful chariot at such an early hour!
If Cephalus replaced him, you know you'd clasp him tight,
And cry out, "Pray, go slowly, ye coursers of the Night!"

Why pester me, a lover? Your spouse is all but dead;
But did I urge him on you, or ever bid you wed?
How oft, the while he slumbers, our sovereign Lady Moon —
And she more fair than you are — comes to Endymion.
Jove joined two nights in one; I dare swear the tale is true,
For Jove was then a lover — and tired of seeing you!
You'd know Aurora heard me — she turned so rosy red;
The day though came no later, in spite of all I said.

— From the Latin of Ovid (43 B.C.–18 A.D.), translated by Kirby Flower Smith.

Revenge

The gods have heard me, Lyce,
The gods have heard my prayer.
Now you who were so icy
Observe with cold despair
Your thin and snowy hair.

Your cheeks are lined and sunken;
Your smiles have turned to leers;
But still you sing a drunken
Appeal to Love who hears
With inattentive ears.

Young Chia with her fluty
Caressing voice compels.
Love lives upon her beauty;
Her cheeks, in which he dwells,
Are his fresh citadels.

He saw the battered ruin,
This old and twisted tree;
He marked the scars, and flew in
Haste that he might not see
Your torn senility.

No silks, no purple gauzes
Can hide the lines that last.
Time, with his iron laws, is
Implacable and fast.
You cannot cheat the past.

Where now are all your subtle
Disguises and your fair
Smile like a gleaming shuttle?
Your shining skin, your rare
Beauty half breathless — where?

Only excelled by Cinara,
Your loveliness ranked high.
You even seemed the winner, a
Victor as years went by,
And she was first to die.

But now — the young men lightly
Laugh at your wrinkled brow.
The torch that burned so brightly
Is only ashes now,
A charred and blackened bough.

— From the Latin of Horace (65–8 B.C.), translated by Louis Untermeyer.

The Vigil of Venus

Let those love now, who never loved before;
And those who always loved, now love the more.

The spring, the new, the warbling spring appears;
The youthful season of reviving years;
In spring the loves enkindle mutual heats,
The feather'd nation choose their tuneful mates,
The trees grow fruitful with descending rain,
And, drest in different greens, adorn the plain.
She comes; to-morrow beauty's empress roves
Through walks that winding run within the groves;
She twines the shooting myrtle into bowers,
And ties their meeting tops with wreaths of flowers;
Then, raised sublimely on her easy throne,
From nature's powerful dictates draws her own.

Let those love now, who never loved before;
And those who always loved, now love the more.

'Twas on that day which saw the teeming flood
Swell round, impregnate with celestial blood;

Wand'ring in circles stood the finny crew,
The rest was left a void expanse of blue;
Then parent ocean work'd with heaving throes,
And dripping wet the fair Dione rose.

Let those love now, who never loved before;
And those who always loved, now love the more.

She paints the purple year with varied show,
Tips the green gem, and makes the blossom glow.
She makes the turgid buds receive the breeze,
Expand to leaves and shade the naked trees.
When gath'ring damps the misty nights diffuse,
She sprinkles all the morn with balmy dews;
Bright trembling pearls depend at every spray,
And kept from falling, seem to fall away.
A glossy freshness hence the rose receives,
And blushes sweet through all her silken leaves;
(The drops descending through the silent night,
While stars serenely roll their golden light;)
Close till the morn her humid veil she holds;
Then deck'd with virgin pomp the flower unfolds.
Soon will the morning blush, ye maids, prepare;
In rosy garlands bind your flowing hair;
'Tis Venus' plant: the blood fair Venus shed,
O'er the gay beauty pour'd immortal red:
From love's soft kiss a sweet ambrosial smell
Was taught for ever on the leaves to dwell;
From gems, from flames, from orient rays of light,
The richest lustre makes her purple bright;
And she to-morrow weds; the sportive gale
Unties her zone; she bursts the verdant veil;
Through all her sweets the rifling lover flies,
And as he breathes, her glowing fires arise.

Let those love now, who never loved before;
And those who always loved, now love the more.

Now fair Dione to the myrtle grove
Sends the gay Nymphs, and sends her tender love.
And shall they venture? Is it safe to go,
While nymphs have hearts and Cupid wears a bow?
Yes, safely venture; 'tis his mother's will;
He walks unarm'd and undesiring ill;
His torch extinct, his quiver useless hung,
His arrows idle, and his bow unstrung.
And yet, ye nymphs, beware, his eyes have charms;
And love that's naked, still is love in arms.

Let those love now, who never loved before;
And those who always loved, now love the more.

From Venus' bower to Delia's lodge repairs
A virgin train complete with modest airs:
"Chaste Delia, grant our suit! oh shun the wood,
Nor stain this sacred lawn with savage blood.
Venus, O Delia, if she could persuade,
Would ask thy presence, might she ask a maid."
Here cheerful choirs for three auspicious nights
With songs prolong the pleasurable rites:
Her crowds in measures lightly decent move;
Or seek by pairs the covert of the grove,
Where meeting greens for arbours arch above,
And mingling flowerets strew the scenes of love.
Here dancing Ceres shakes her golden sheaves;
Here Bacchus revels, deckt with viny leaves;
Here wit's enchanting god, in laurel crown'd,
Wakes all the ravish'd hours with silver sound.
Ye fields, ye forests, own Dione's reign,
And Delia, huntress Delia, shun the plain.

Let those love now, who never loved before;
And those who always loved, now love the more.

Gay with the bloom of all her opening year,
The Queen at Hybla bids her throne appear,
And there presides; and there the fav'rite band,
Her smiling Graces, share the great command.
Now, beauteous Hybla! dress thy flowery beds
With all the pride the lavish season sheds;

Now all thy colours, all thy fragrance yield,
And rival Enna's aromatic field.
To fill the presence of the gentle court
From every quarter rural Nymphs resort,
From woods, from mountains, from these humble vales,
From waters curling with the wanton gales.
Pleased with the joyful train, the laughing Queen
In circles seats them round the bank of green;
And, "lovely girls," she whispers, "guard your hearts;
My boy, though stript of arms, abounds in arts."

Let those love now, who never loved before;
And those who always loved, now love the more.

Let tender grass in shaded alleys spread;
Let early flowers erect their painted head;
To-morrow's glory be to-morrow seen;
That day old Ether wedded Earth in green.
The vernal father bade the spring appear,
In clouds he coupled to produce the year;
The sap descending o'er her bosom ran,
And all the various sorts of soul began
By wheels unknown to sight, by secret veins
Distilling life; the fruitful goddess reigns
Through all the lovely realms of native day,
Through all the circled land and circling sea;
With fertile seed she fill'd the pervious earth,
And ever fix'd the mystic ways of birth.

Let those love now, who never loved before;
And those who always loved, now love the more.

'Twas she, the parent, to the Latian shore
Through various dangers Troy's remainder bore.
She won Lavinia for her warlike son,
And winning her, the Latian empire won.
She gave to Mars the maid whose honour'd womb
Swell'd with the founder of immortal Rome.
Decoy'd by shows the Sabine dames she led,
And taught our vigorous youth the means to wed.
Hence sprung the Romans, hence the race divine
Through which great Cæsar draws his Julian line.

Let those love now, who never loved before;
And those who always loved, now love the more.

In rural seats the soul of pleasure reigns;
The love of Beauty fills the rural scenes;
Ev'n Love (if fame the truth of Love declare)
Drew first the breathings of a rural air,
Some pleasing meadow pregnant Beauty prest,
She laid her infant on its bowery breast;
From nature's sweets he supp'd the fragrant dew,
He smiled, he kiss'd them, and by kissing grew.

Let those love now, who never loved before;
And those who always loved, now love the more.

Now bulls o'er stalks of broom extend their sides,
Secure of favours from their lowing brides.
Now stately rams their fleecy consorts lead,
Who bleating follow through the wand'ring shade.
And now the goddess bids the birds appear,
Raise all their music, and salute the year;
Then deep the swan begins, and deep the song
Runs o'er the water where he sails along;
While Philomela tunes a treble strain,
And from the poplar charms the list'ning plain.
We fancy love exprest at every note;
It melts, it warbles in her liquid throat.
Of barbarous Tereus she complains no more,
But sings for pleasure, as for grief before.
And still her graces rise, her airs extend,
And all is silence till the syren end.
How long in coming is my lovely spring?
And when shall I, and when the swallow sing?
Sweet Philomela, cease; – or here I sit,
And silent loose my rapturous hour of wit.
'Tis gone; the fit retires, the flames decay;
My tuneful Phœbus flies averse away.
His own Amyclæ thus, as stories run,
But once was silent, and that once undone.

Let those love now, who never loved before;
And those who always loved, now love the more.

— *From the Latin, anon. (third century), translated by Thomas Parnell.*

I Serve

I love a noble lady, the reason why is clear;
And ever since I 'gan to serve she groweth yet more dear:
And still as more I love her the lovelier she grows,
Crowned with a richer beauty than is the queenly rose.
And if for her sweet sake I died, but came to life again,
A second time my sighs would rise deep with the olden pain.

— *From the German of Sir Meinloh von Sevelingen (twelfth century), translated by Jethro Bithell.*

Matin-Song

The warder, from his watch-tower high,
Blares forth the baneful morning nigh.
"Arise, O comrade! Heart and heart,
That would be fain no more to part,
Are sundered soon!
Through the greenwood gleams the moon."

"O truelove, mark the words I say,
It is not nigh unto the day,
Through the rack shine moon and star,
Our joy the warder fain would mar;
I tell thee, sweet:
The midnight cannot be so fleet."

He pressed her closely to his breast,
He said: "Thou makest my heart blest!
The rapture of my heart art thou;
All my pain is vanished now.
I swear to thee:
So dear as thou is none to me."

What is this thing his fingers hold?
It is a ring of the good red gold.
"See, love, the red gold! Oft I swore,
I loved thee in my deep heart's core!
I did not lie:
For thee I'd lay me down and die!"

The nightingale sang from the spray,
As she had sung so many a day.
Now all the East was purpled o'er:
"Hearts that were fain to part no more,
Are parted soon.
Through the green wood gleams the moon."

— *Anon., from the German, c. 1500, translated by Jethro Bithell.*

"There Is a Lady Conquering"

There is a lady conquering with glances:
Happy the hour she was to me revealed!
A hard-embattled legion of my fancies
Against her sent, were forced and fain to yield.
And sure I know that ransom there is none.
Her excellence and beauty have done this,
And her red, laughing mouth that were so sweet to kiss.

And so my soul and senses serve and crave her,
Who is so sweet, and pure, and excellent;
And, lest I die of longing for her favour,
I dare to hope that she may yet relent,
And grant the greatest guerdon e'er I won.
Her excellence and beauty have done this,
And her red, laughing mouth that were so sweet to kiss.

— *From the German of Walther von der Vogelweide (c. 1170–c. 1230), translated by Jethro Bithell.*

His Own True Wife

Hidden lovers' woes
Thou wast wont to sing ere dawn arose:
Bitter parting after raptured meeting.
Whosoever love and lady's greeting
So received that he was torn
From her breast by fear of men,
Thou wouldst sing him counsel, when
Shone the star of morn.
Warder, sing it now no more, lay by thy bugle-horn!

He to whom is given
Not to be from love by morning riven —
Whom the watchers think not to beleaguer,
Hath no need to be alert and eager
To avert the peril rife
In the day: his rest is pure,

Nor a warder makes secure
His unhappy life.
Love so sweet bestows in all men's sight his
own true wife!

— From the German of Sir Wolfram von Eschenbach (c. 1170–c. 1220), translated by Jethro Bithell.

"Fair Is Her Body"

Fair is her body, bright her eye,
With smiles her mouth is kind to me;
Then, think no evil, this is she
Whom God hath made my only joy.

Between the earth and heaven high
There is no maid so fair as she;
The beauty of her sweet body
Doth ever fill my heart with joy.

He is a knave, nor do I lie,
Who loveth her not heartily;
The grace that shines from her body
Giveth to lovers all great joy.

— Medieval Norman Student Song, anon., translated by John Addington Symonds.

The Complaint of the Fair Armoress

I

Meseemeth I heard cry and groan
That sweet who was the armorer's maid;
For her young years she made sore moan,
And right upon this wise she said:
"Ah fierce old age with foul bald head,
To spoil fair things thou art over fain;
Who holdeth me? who? would God I were
dead!
Would God I were well dead and slain!

II

"Lo, thou hast broken the sweet yoke
That my high beauty held above
All priests and clerks and merchant-folk;
There was not one but for my love
Would give me gold and gold enough,
Though sorrow his very heart had riven,
To win from me such wage thereof
As now no thief would take if given.

III

"I was right chary of the same,
God wot it was my great folly,
For love of one sly knave of them,
Good store of that same sweet had he;
For all my subtle wiles, perdie,
God wot I loved him well enow;
Right evilly he handled me,
But he loved well my gold, I trow.

IV

"Though I gat bruises green and black,
I loved him never the less a jot;
Though he bound burdens on my back,
If he said, 'Kiss me, and heed it not,'
Right little pain I felt, God wot,
When that foul thief's mouth, found so
sweet,
Kissed me — Much good thereof I got!
I keep the sin and the shame of it.

V

"And he died thirty year agone.
I am old now, no sweet thing to see;
By God, though, when I think thereon,
And of that good glad time, woe's me,
And stare upon my changed body
Stark naked, that has been so sweet,
Lean, wizen, like a small dry tree,
I am nigh mad with the pain of it.

VI

"Where is my faultless forehead's white,
The lifted eyebrows, soft gold hair,
Eyes wide apart and keen of sight,
With subtle skill in the amorous air;
The straight nose, great nor small, but
fair,
The small carved ears of shapeliest growth,
Chin dimpling, color good to wear,
And sweet red splendid kissing mouth?

VII

'The shapely slender shoulders small,
Long arms, hands wrought in glorious
wise,
Round little breasts, the hips withal
High, full of flesh, not scant of size,
Fit for all amorous masteries;

. . . .

. . . .

VIII

"A writhled forehead, hair gone gray,
Fallen eyebrows, eyes gone blind and red,
Their laughs and looks all fled away,
Yea, all that smote men's hearts are fled;
The bowed nose, fallen from goodlihead;

Foul flapping ears like water-flags;
Peaked chin, and cheeks all waste and dead,
And lips that are two skinny rags:

IX

"Thus endeth all the beauty of us.
The arms made short, the hands made lean,
The shoulders bowed and ruinous,
The breasts, alack! all fallen in;
The flanks too, like the breasts, grown thin;
. . .
For the lank thighs, no thighs but skin,
They are speckled with spots like sausage-meat.

X

"So we make moan for the old sweet days,
Poor old light women, two or three
Squatting above the straw-fire's blaze,
The bosom crushed against the knee,
Like fagots on a heap we be,
Round fires soon lit, soon quenched and done;
And we were once so sweet, even we!
Thus fareth many and many an one."

—*From the French of François Villon (1431–1463), translated by Algernon Charles Swinburne.*

Of the Gentle Heart

Within the gentle heart Love shelters him
As birds within the green shade of the grove.
Before the gentle heart, in nature's scheme,
Love was not, nor the gentle heart ere Love.
For with the sun, at once,
So sprang the light immediately; nor was
Its birth before the sun's.
And Love hath his effect in gentleness
Of very self; even as
Within the middle fire the heat's excess.

The fire of Love comes to the gentle heart
Like as its virtue to a precious stone;
To which no star its influence can impart
Till it is made a pure thing by the sun:
For when the sun hath smit
From out its essence that which there was vile
The star endoweth it.
And so the heart created by God's breath
Pure, true, and clean from guile,
A woman, like a star, enamoreth.

In gentle heart Love for like reason is
For which the lamp's high flame is fanned and bow'd:
Clear, piercing bright, it shines for its own bliss;
Nor would it burn there else, it is so proud.
For evil natures meet
With Love as it were water met with fire,
As cold abhorring heat.
Through gentle heart Love doth a track divine,—
Like knowing like; the same
As diamond runs through iron in the mine.

The sun strikes full upon the mud all day:
It remains vile, nor the sun's worth is less.
"By race I am gentle," the proud man doth say:
He is the mud, the sun is gentleness.
Let no man predicate
That aught the name of gentleness should have,
Even in a king's estate,
Except the heart there be a gentle man's.
The star-beam lights the wave,—
Heaven holds the star and the star's radiance.

God, in the understanding of high Heaven,
Burns more than in our sight the living sun:
There to behold His Face unveiled is given;
And Heaven, whose will is homage paid to One
Fulfills the things which live
In God, from the beginning excellent.
So should my lady give
That truth which in her eyes is glorified,
On which her heart is bent,
To me whose service waiteth at her side.

My lady, God shall ask, "What daredst thou?"
(When my soul stands with all her acts review'd;)
"Thou passedst Heaven, into My sight, as now,
To make Me of vain love similitude.
To Me doth praise belong,

And to the Queen of all the realm of grace
Who slayeth fraud and wrong."
Then may I plead: "As though from Thee he came,
Love wore an angel's face:
Lord, if I loved her, count it not my shame."

—*From the Italian of Guido Guinicelli (thirteenth century), translated by D. G. Rossetti.*

"Ladies That Have Intelligence in Love"

Ladies that have intelligence in love,
Of mine own lady I would speak with you;
Not that I hope to count her praises through,
But telling what I may, to ease my mind.
And I declare that when I speak thereof,
Love sheds such perfect sweetness over me
That if my courage failed not, certainly
To him my listeners must be all resign'd.
Wherefore I will not speak in such large kind
That mine own speech should foil me, which were base;
But only will discourse of her high grace
In these poor words, the best that I can find,
With you alone, dear dames and damozels:
'Twere ill to speak thereof with any else.

An Angel, of his blessed knowledge, saith
To God: "Lord, in the world that Thou hast made,
A miracle in action is display'd,
By reason of a soul whose splendors fare
Even hither: and since Heaven requireth
Nought saving her, for her it prayeth Thee,
Thy Saints crying aloud continually."
Yet Pity still defends our earthly share
In that sweet soul; God answering thus the prayer:
"My well-belovèd, suffer that in peace
Your hope remain, while so My pleasure is,
There where one dwells who dreads the loss of her:
And who in Hell unto the doomed shall say,
'I have looked on that for which God's chosen pray.' "

My lady is desired in the high Heaven:
Wherefore, it now behoveth me to tell,
Saying: Let any maid that would be well
Esteemed keep with her: for as she goes by,
Into foul hearts a deathly chill is driven
By Love, that makes ill thought to perish there:
While any who endures to gaze on her
Must either be ennobled, or else die.
When one deserving to be raised so high
Is found, 'tis then her power attains its proof,
Making his heart strong for his soul's behoof
With the full strength of meek humility.
Also this virtue owns she, by God's will:
Who speaks with her can never come to ill.

Love saith concerning her: "How chanceth it
That flesh, which is of dust, should be thus pure?"
Then, gazing always, he makes oath: "Forsure,
This is a creature of God till now unknown."
She hath that paleness of the pearl that's fit
In a fair woman, so much and not more;
She is as high as Nature's skill can soar;
Beauty is tried by her comparison.
Whatever her sweet eyes are turned upon,
Spirits of love do issue thence in flame,
Which through their eyes who then may look on them
Pierce to the heart's deep chamber every one.
And in her smile Love's image you may see;
Whence none can gaze upon her steadfastly.

Dear Song, I know thou wilt hold gentle speech
With many ladies, when I send thee forth:
Wherefore (being mindful that thou hadst thy birth
From Love, and art a modest, simple child,)
Whomso thou meetest, say thou this to each:
"Give me good speed! To her I wend along
In whose much strength my weakness is made strong."

And if, i' the end, thou wouldst not be beguiled
Of all thy labor seek not the defiled
And common sort; but rather choose to be
Where man and woman dwell in courtesy.
So to the road thou shalt be reconciled,
And find the Lady, and with the lady, Love.
Commend thou me to each, as doth behove.

—From The New Life by Dante (1265–1321), translated from the Italian by Dante Gabriel Rossetti.

Who Wishes to Behold

Who wishes to behold the utmost might
Of Heaven and Nature, on her let him gaze,
Sole sun, not only in my partial lays,
But to the dark world, blind to virtue's light!
And let him haste to view; for death in spite
The guilty leaves, and on the virtuous preys;
For this loved angel heaven impatient stays;
And mortal charms are transient as they're bright!
Here shall he see, if timely he arrive,
Virtue and beauty, royalty of mind,
In one bless'd union join'd. Then shall he say
That vainly my weak rhymes to praise her strive,
Whose dazzling beams have struck my genius blind.—
He must for ever weep if he delay.

—From the Italian of Petrarch (1304–1374), translated by Lord Charlemont.

A Deathless Flower

Yes! hope may with my strong desire keep pace,
And I be undeluded, unbetrayed;
For if of our affections none finds grace
In sight of Heaven, then wherefore hath God made
The world which we inhabit? Better plea
Love cannot have than that in loving thee
Glory to that eternal Peace is paid,
Who such divinity to thee imparts
As hallows and makes pure all gentle hearts.
His hope is treacherous only whose love dies
With beauty, which is varying every hour;
But in chaste hearts, uninfluenced by the power
Of outward change, there blooms a deathless flower,
That breathes on earth the air of paradise.

—From the Italian of Michelangelo (1475–1564), translated by William Wordsworth.

A Supplication

Forget not yet the tried intent
Of such a truth as I have meant;
My great travail so gladly spent,
Forget not yet!

Forget not yet when first began
The weary life ye know, since whan
The suit, the service none tell can;
Forget not yet!

Forget not yet the great assays,
The cruel wrong, the scornful ways,
The painful patience in delays,
Forget not yet!

Forget not! O, forget not this,
How long ago hath been, and is
The mind that never meant amiss—
Forget not yet!

Forget not then thine own approved
The which so long hath thee so loved,
Whose steadfast faith yet never moved—
Forget not this!

—Sir Thomas Wyatt, English (1503–1542).

Song

"Who is it that, this dark night,
Underneath my window plaineth?"
"It is one, who from thy sight
Being, ah! exiled, disdaineth
Every other vulgar light."

"Why, alas! and are you he?
Be not yet those fancies changed?"
"Dear, when you find change in me,
Though from me you be estranged,
Let my change to ruin be."

"Well, in absence this will die;
Leave to see, and leave to wonder."
"Absence sure will help, if I
Can learn how myself to sunder
From what in my heart doth lie."

"But time will these thoughts remove;
Time doth work what no man knoweth."
"Time doth as the subject prove,
With time still the affection groweth
In the faithful turtle dove."

"What if you new beauties see?
Will they not stir new affections?"
"I will think they pictures be,
Image-like of saint's perfections,
Poorly counterfeiting thee."

"But your reason's purest light
Bids you leave such minds to nourish."
"Dear, do reason no such spite,
Never doth thy beauty flourish
More than in my reason's sight."

"But the wrongs love bears will make
Love at length leave undertaking."
"No, the more fools it do shake
In a ground of so firm making,
Deeper still they drive the stake."

"Peace, I think that some give ear;
Come no more lest I get anger."
"Bliss, I will my bliss forbear,
Fearing, sweet, you to endanger,
But my soul shall harbour there."

"Well, begone, begone I say,
Lest that Argus' eyes perceive you."
"O unjust Fortune's sway!
Which can make me thus to leave you
And from louts to run away!"

— *Sir Philip Sidney, English (1554–1586).*

Epithalamion

Ye learnèd sisters, which have oftentimes
Beene to me ayding, others to adorne,
Whom ye thought worthy of your gracefull
rymes,
That even the greatest did not greatly scorne
To heare theyr names sung in your simple
layes,
But joyèd in theyr praise;
And when ye list your owne mishaps to
mourne,
Which death, or love, or fortunes wreck did
rayse,
Your string could soone to sadder tenor
turne,
And teach the woods and waters to lament
Your doleful dreriment:
Now lay those sorrowfull complaints aside;
And, having all your heads with girlands
crownd,
Helpe me mine owne loves prayses to re-
sound;
Ne let the same of any be envide:
So Orpheus did for his owne bride;
So I unto my selfe alone will sing;
The woods shall to me answer, and my Eccho
ring.

Early, before the worlds light-giving lampe
His golden beame upon the hils doth spred,
Having disperst the nights uncheareful
dampe,
Doe ye awake; and, with fresh lusty-hed,
Go to the bowre of my belovèd love,
My truest turtle dove;
Bid her awake; for Hymen is awake,
And long since ready forth his maske to
move,
With his bright Tead that flames with many
a flake,
And many a bachelor to waite on him,
In theyr fresh garments trim.
Bid her awake therefore, and soone her
dight,
For lo! the wishèd day is come at last,
That shall, for all the paynes and sorrowes
past,
Pay to her usury of long delight:
And, whylest she doth her dight,
Doe ye to her of joy and solace sing,
That all the woods may answer, and your
eccho ring.

Bring with you all the Nymphes that you
can heare
Both of the rivers and the forrests greene,
And of the sea that neighbours to her neare:
Al with gay girlands goodly wel beseene.
And let them also with them bring in hand
Another gay girland
For my fayre love, of lillyes and of roses,
Bound truelove wize, with a blew silke
riband.
And let them make great store of bridale
poses,
And let them eeke bring store of other flow-
ers,
To deck the bridale bowers.
And let the ground whereas her foot shall
tread,

For feare the stones her tender foot should
wrong,
Be strewed with fragrant flowers all along,
And diapred lyke the discolored mead.
Which done, doe at her chamber dore awayt,
For she will waken strayt;
The whiles doe ye this song unto her sing,
The woods shall to you answer, and your
Eccho ring.

Ye Nymphes of Mulla, which with careful
heed
The silver scaly trouts doe tend full well,
And greedy pikes which use therein to feed;
(Those trouts and pikes all others doo ex-
cell;)
And ye likewise, which keepe the rushy
lake,
Where none doo fishes take;
Bynd up the locks the which hang scatterd
light,
And in his waters, which your mirror make,
Behold your faces as the christall bright,
That when you come whereas my love doth
lie,
No blemish she may spie.
And eke, ye lightfoot mayds, which keepe
the deere,
That on the hoary mountayne used to towre;
And the wylde wolves, which seeke them to
devoure,
With your steele darts doo chace from com-
ming neer;
Be also present heere,
To helpe to decke her, and to help to sing,
That all the woods may answer, and your
eccho ring.

Wake now, my love, awake! for it is time;
The Rosy Morne long since left Tithones
bed,
All ready to her silver coche to clyme;
And Phœbus gins to shew his glorious hed.
Hark! how the cheerefull birds do chaunt
theyre laies
And carroll of Loves praise.
The merry Larke hir mattins sings aloft;
The Thrush replyes; the Mavis descant
playes;
The Ouzell shrills; the Ruddock warbles
soft;
So goodly all agree, with sweet consent,
To this dayes merriment.
Ah! my deere love, why doe ye sleepe thus
long?
When meeter were that ye should now
awake,
T' awayt the comming of your joyous make,
And hearken to the birds love-learnèd song,
The deawy leaves among!
Nor they of joy and pleasance to you sing,
That all the woods them answer, and theyr
eccho ring.

My love is now awake out of her dreames,
And her fayre eyes, like stars that dimmèd
were
With darksome cloud, now shew theyr
goodly beams
More bright then Hesperus his head doth
rere.
Come now, ye damzels, daughters of de-
light,
Helpe quickly her to dight:
But first come ye fayre houres, which were
begot
In Joves sweet paradice of Day and Night;
Which doe the seasons of the yeare allot,
And al, that ever in this world is fayre,
Doe make and still repayre:
And ye three handmayds of the Cyprian
Queene,
The which doe still adorne her beauties
pride,
Helpe to addorne my beautifullest bride:
And, as ye her array, still throw betweene
Some graces to be seene;
And, as ye use to Venus, to her sing,
The whiles the woods shal answer, and your
eccho ring.

Now is my love all ready forth to come:
Let all the virgins therefore well awayt:
And ye fresh boyes, that tend upon her
groome,
Prepare your selves; for he is comming
strayt.
Set all your things in seemely good aray,
Fit for so joyfull day:
The joyfulst day that ever sunne did see.
Fair Sun! shew forth thy favourable ray,
And let thy lifull heat not fervent be,
For feare of burning her sunshyny face,
Her beauty to disgrace.
O fayrest Phœbus! father of the Muse!
If ever I did honour thee aright,
Or sing the thing that mote thy mind de-
light,
Doe not thy servants simple boone refuse;
But let this day, let this one day, be myne;
Let all the rest be thine.

Then I thy soverayne prayses loud wil sing,
That all the woods shal answer, and theyr
eccho ring.

Harke! how the Minstrils gin to shrill aloud
Their merry Musick that resounds from far,
The pipe, the tabor, and the trembling
Croud,
That well agree withouten breach or jar.
But, most of all, the damzels doe delite
When they their tymbrels smyte,
And thereunto doe daunce and carrol sweet,
That all the sences they doe ravish quite;
The whyles the boyes run up and downe the
street,
Crying aloud with strong confusèd noyce,
As if it were one voyce,
Hymen, iö Hymen, Hymen, they do shout;
That even to the heavens theyr shouting
shrill
Doth reach, and all the firmament doth fill;
To which the people standing all about,
As in approvance, doe thereto applaud,
And loud advaunce her laud;
And evermore they Hymen, Hymen sing,
That al the woods them answer, and theyr
eccho ring.

Loe! where she comes along with portly
pace,
Lyke Phœbe, from her chamber of the East,
Arysing forth to run her mighty race,
Clad all in white, that seemes a virgin best.
So well it her beseemes, that ye would weene
Some angell she had beene.
Her long loose yellow locks lyke golden
wyre,
Sprinckled with perle, and perling flowres
atweene,
Doe lyke a golden mantle her attyre;
And, being crownèd with a girland greene,
Seeme lyke some mayden Queene.
Her modest eyes, abashèd to behold
So many gazers as on her do stare,
Upon the lowly ground affixèd are;
Ne dare lift up her countenance too bold,
But blush to heare her prayses sung so loud,
So farre from being proud.
Nathlesse doe ye still loud her prayses sing,
That all the woods may answer, and your
eccho ring.

Tell me, ye merchants daughters, did ye see
So fayre a creature in your towne before;
So sweet, so lovely, and so mild as she,
Adornd with beautyes grace and vertues
store?
Her goodly eyes lyke Saphyres shining
bright,
Her forehead yvory white,
Her cheekes lyke apples which the sun hath
rudded,
Her lips lyke cherryes charming men to byte,
Her brest like to a bowle of creame uncrud-
ded,
Her paps lyke lyllies budded,
Her snowie neck lyke to a marble towre;
And all her body like a pallace fayre,
Ascending up, with many a stately stayre,
To honors seat and chastities sweet bowre.
Why stand ye still ye virgins in amaze,
Upon her so to gaze,
Whiles ye forget your former lay to sing,
To which the woods did answer, and your
eccho ring?

But if ye saw that which no eyes can see,
The inward beauty of her lively spright,
Garnisht with heavenly guifts of high de-
gree,
Much more then would ye wonder at that
sight,
And stand astonisht lyke to those which red
Medusaes mazeful hed.
There dwels sweet love, and constant chas-
tity,
Unspotted fayth, and comely womanhood,
Regard of honour, and mild modesty;
There vertue raynes as Queene in royal
throne,
And giveth lawes alone,
The which the base affections doe obay,
And yeeld theyr services unto her will;
Ne thought of thing uncomely ever may
Thereto approch to tempt her mind to ill.
Had ye once seene these her celestial threas-
ures,
And unrevealèd pleasures,
Then would ye wonder, and her prayses
sing,
That al the woods should answer, and your
echo ring.

Open the temple gates unto my love,
Open them wide that she may enter in,
And all the postes adorne as doth behove,
And all the pillours deck with girlands trim,
For to receyve this Saynt with honour dew,
That commeth in to you.
With trembling steps, and humble rever-
ence,

She commeth in, before th' Almighties view;
Of her ye virgins learne obedience,
When so ye come into those holy places,
To humble your proud faces:
Bring her up to th' high altar, that she may
The sacred ceremonies there partake,
The which do endlesse matrimony make;
And let the roring Organs loudly play
The praises of the Lord in lively notes;
The whiles, with hollow throates,
The Choristers the joyous Antheme sing,
That al the woods may answere, and their
 eccho ring.

Behold, whiles she before the altar stands,
Hearing the holy priest that to her speakes,
And blesseth her with his two happy hands,
How the red roses flush up in her cheekes,
And the pure snow, with goodly vermill
 stayne
Like crimsin dyde in grayne:
That even th' Angels, which continually
About the sacred Altare doe remaine,
Forget their service and about her fly,
Ofte peeping in her face, that seems more
 fayre,
The more they on it stare.
But her sad eyes, still fastened on the
 ground,
Are governèd with goodly modesty,
That suffers not one looke to glaunce awry,
Which may let in a little thought unsownd.
Why blush ye, love, to give to me your
 hand,
The pledge of all our band!
Sing, ye sweet Angels, Alleluya sing,
That all the woods may answere and your
 eccho ring.

Now al is done: bring home the bride againe;
Bring home the triumph of our victory:
Bring home with you the glory of her gaine;
With joyance bring her and with jollity.
Never had man more joyfull day then this,
Whom heaven would heape with blis,
Make feast therefore now all this live-long
 day;
This day for ever to me holy is.
Poure out the wine without restraint or
 stay,
Poure not by cups, but by the belly full,
Poure out to all that wull,
And sprinkle all the postes and wals with
 wine,
That they may sweat, and drunken be with-
 all.
Crowne ye God Bacchus with a coronall,
And Hymen also crowne with wreathes of
 vine;
And let the Graces daunce unto the rest,
For they can doo it best:
The whiles the maydens doe theyr carroll
 sing,
To which the woods shall answer, and theyr
 eccho ring.

Ring ye the bels, ye yong men of the towne,
And leave your wonted labors for this day:
This day is holy; doe ye write it downe,
That ye for ever it remember may.
This day the sunne is in his chiefest hight,
With Barnaby the bright,
From whence declining daily by degrees,
He somewhat loseth of his heat and light,
When once the Crab behind his back he
 sees.
But for this time it ill ordainèd was,
To chose the longest day in all the yeare,
And shortest night, when longest fitter
 weare:
Yet never day so long, but late would passe.
Ring ye the bels, to make it weare away,
And bonefiers make all day;
And daunce about them, and about them
 sing,
That all the woods may answer, and your
 eccho ring.

Ah! when will this long weary day have end,
And lende me leave to come unto my love?
How slowly do the houres theyr numbers
 spend?
How slowly does sad Time his feathers
 move?
Hast thee, O fayrest Planet, to thy home,
Within the Westerne fome:
Thy tyrèd steedes long since have need of
 rest.
Long though it be, at last I see it gloome,
And the bright evening-star with golden
 creast
Appeare out of the East.
Fayre childe of beauty! glorious lampe of
 love!
That all the host of heaven in rankes doost
 lead,
And guydest lovers through the nights sad
 dread,
How chearefully thou lookest from above,
And seemst to laugh atweene thy twinkling
 light,
As joying in the sight

Of these glad many, which for joy doe sing,
That all the woods them answer, and their echo ring!

Now ceasse, ye damsels, your delights forepast;
Enough it is that all the day was youres:
Now day is doen, and night is nighing fast,
Now bring the Bryde into the brydall boures.
The night is come, now soon her disaray,
And in her bed her lay;
Lay her in lillies and in violets,
And silken courteins over her display,
And odourd sheetes, and Arras coverlets.
Behold how goodly my faire love does ly,
In proud humility!
Like unto Maia, when as Jove her took
In Tempe, lying on the flowry gras,
Twixt sleepe and wake, after she weary was,
With bathing in the Acidalian brooke.
Now it is night, ye damsels may be gon,
And leave my love alone,
And leave likewise your former lay to sing:
The woods no more shall answere, nor your echo ring.

Now welcome, night! thou night so long expected,
That long daies labour doest at last defray,
And all my cares, which cruell Love collected,
Hast sumd in one, and cancellèd for aye:
Spread thy broad wing over my love and me,
That no man may us see;
And in thy sable mantle us enwrap,
From feare of perrill and foule horror free.
Let no false treason seeke us to entrap,
Nor any dread disquiet once annoy
The safety of our joy;
But let the night be calme, and quietsome,
Without tempestuous storms or sad afray:
Lyke as when Jove with fayre Alcmena lay,
When he begot the great Tirynthian groome:
Or lyke as when he with thy selfe did lie
And begot Majesty.
And let the mayds and yong men cease to sing;
Ne let the woods them answer nor theyr eccho ring.

Let no lamenting cryes, nor dolefull teares,
Be heard all night within, nor yet without:
Ne let false whispers, breeding hidden feares,
Breake gentle sleepe with misconceivèd dout.
Let no deluding dreames, nor dreadfull sights,
Make sudden sad affrights;
Ne let house-fyres, nor lightnings helpelesse harmes,
Ne let the Pouke, nor other evill sprights,
Ne let mischivous witches with theyr charmes,
Ne let hob Goblins, names whose sence we see not,
Fray us with things that be not:
Let not the shriech Oule nor the Storke be heard,
Nor the night Raven, that still deadly yels;
Nor damnèd ghosts, cald up with mighty spels,
Nor griesly vultures, make us once affeard:
Ne let th' unpleasant Quyre of Frogs still croking
Make us to wish theyr choking.
Let none of these theyr drery accents sing;
Ne let the woods them answer, nor theyr eccho ring.

But let stil Silence trew night-watches keepe,
That sacred Peace may in assurance rayne,
And tymely Sleep, when it is tyme to sleepe,
May poure his limbs forth on your pleasant playne;
The whiles an hundred little wingèd loves,
Like divers-fethered doves,
Shall fly and flutter round about your bed,
And in the secret darke, that none reproves,
Their prety stealthes shal worke, and snares shal spread
To filch away sweet snatches of delight,
Conceald through covert night.
Ye sonnes of Venus, play your sports at will!
For greedy pleasure, carelesse of your toyes,
Thinks more upon her paradise of joyes,
Then what ye do, albe it good or ill.
All night therefore attend your merry play,
For it will soone be day:
Now none doth hinder you, that say or sing;
Ne will the woods now answer, nor your Eccho ring.

Who is the same, which at my window peepes?
Or whose is that faire face that shines so bright?
Is it not Cinthia, she that never sleepes,
But walkes about high heaven al the night?
O! fayrest goddesse, do thou not envy

My love with me to spy:
For thou likewise didst love, though now unthought,
And for a fleece of wooll, which privily
The Latmian shepherd once unto thee brought
His pleasures with thee wrought.
Therefore to us be favorable now;
And sith of womens labours thou hast charge
And generation goodly dost enlarge,
Encline thy will t' effect our wishfull vow,
And the chast wombe informe with timely seed,
That may our comfort breed:
Till which we cease our hopefull hap to sing;
Ne let the woods us answere, nor our Eccho ring.

And thou, great Juno! which with awful might
The lawes of wedlock still dost patronize;
And the religion of the faith first plight
With sacred rites hast taught to solemnize;
And eeke for comfort often callèd art
Of women in their smart;
Eternally bind thou this lovely band,
And all thy blessings unto us impart.
And thou, glad Genius! in whose gentle hand
The bridale bowre and geniall bed remaine,
Without blemish or staine;
And the sweet pleasures of theyr loves delight
With secret ayde doest succor and supply,
Till they bring forth the fruitfull progeny;
Send us the timely fruit of this same night.
And thou, fayre Hebe! and thou, Hymen free!
Grant that it may so be.
Til which we cease your further prayse to sing;
Ne any woods shall answer, nor your Eccho ring.

And ye high heavens, the temple of the gods,
In which a thousand torches flaming bright
Doe burne, that to us wretched earthly clods
In dreadful darknesse lend desirèd light;
And all ye powers which in the same remayne,
More then we men can fayne!
Poure out your blessing on us plentiously,
And happy influence upon us raine,
That we may raise a large posterity,
Which from the earth, which they may long possesse
With lasting happinesse,
Up to your haughty pallaces may mount;
And, for the guerdon of theyr glorious merit,
May heavenly tabernacles there inherit,
Of blessèd Saints for to increase the count.
So let us rest, sweet love, in hope of this,
And cease till then our tymely joyes to sing:
The woods no more us answer, nor our eccho ring!

Song! made in lieu of many ornaments,
With which my love should duly have been dect,
Which cutting off through hasty accidents,
Ye would not stay your dew time to expect,
But promist both to recompens;
Be unto her a goodly ornament,
And for short time an endlesse moniment.

—*Edmund Spenser, English (1552–1599).*

∽ ✿ ∼

Five Sonnets by Shakespeare

I

Let those who are in favor with their stars
Of public honor and proud titles boast,
Whilst I, whom fortune of such triumph bars,
Unlook'd for joy in that I honor most.
Great princes' favorites their fair leaves spread
But as the marigold at the sun's eye;
And in themselves their pride lies burièd,
For at a frown they in their glory die.
The painful warrior famousèd for fight,
After a thousand victories once foil'd,
Is from the book of honor razèd quite,
And all the rest forgot for which he toil'd:
Then happy I, that love and am belov'd
Where I may not remove nor be remov'd.

II

When to the sessions of sweet silent thought
I summon up remembrance of things past,
I sigh the lack of many a thing I sought,
And with old woes new wail my dear time's waste:
Then can I drown an eye, unus'd to flow,
For precious friends hid in death's dateless night,
And weep afresh love's long-since cancel'd woe,

And moan th' expense of many a vanish'd sight:
Then can I grieve at grievances foregone,
And heavily from woe to woe tell o'er
The sad account of fore-bemoanèd moan,
Which I new pay as if not paid before.
But if the while I think on thee, dear friend,
All losses are restor'd, and sorrows end.

III

Being your slave, what should I do but tend
Upon the hours and times of your desire?
I have no precious time at all to spend,
Nor services to do, till you require.
Nor dare I chide the world-without-end hour
Whilst I, my sovereign, watch the clock for you,
Nor think the bitterness of absence sour
When you have bid your servant once adieu;
Nor dare I question with my jealous thought
Where you may be, or your affairs suppose,
But, like a sad slave, stay and think of naught
Save, where you are how happy you make those.
So true a fool is love, that in your will,
Though you do any thing, he thinks no ill.

IV

Then hate me when thou wilt; if ever, now;
Now, while the world is bent my deeds to cross,
Join with the spite of fortune, make me bow,
And do not drop in for an after-loss:
Ah, do not, when my heart hath scap'd this sorrow,
Come in the rearward of a conquer'd woe;
Give not a windy night a rainy morrow,
To linger out a purpos'd overthrow.
If thou wilt leave me, do not leave me last,
When other petty griefs have done their spite,
But in the onset come: so shall I taste
At first the very worst of fortune's might;
And other strains of woe, which now seem woe,
Compar'd with loss of thee will not seem so.

V

O, never say that I was false of heart,
Though absence seem'd my flame to qualify.
As easy might I from myself depart
As from my soul, which in thy breast doth lie:
That is my home of love: if I have rang'd,
Like him that travels, I return again;
Just to the time, not with the time exchang'd,—
So that myself bring water for my stain.
Never believe, though in my nature reign'd
All frailties that besiege all kinds of blood,
That it could so preposterously be stain'd,
To leave for nothing all thy sum of good;
For nothing this wide universe I call,
Save thou, my rose; in it thou art my all.

—*William Shakespeare, English (1564–1616).*

Song

From AMPHITRYON

Fair Iris I love, and hourly I die,
But not for a lip, nor a languishing eye:
She's fickle and false, and there we agree,
For I am as false and as fickle as she.
We neither believe what either can say;
And, neither believing, we neither betray.
'Tis civil to swear, and say things of course;
We mean not the taking for better or worse.
When present, we love; when absent, agree:
I think not of Iris, nor Iris of me.
The legend of love no couple can find,
So easy to part, or so equally join'd.

—*John Dryden, English (1631–1700).*

Farewell to Nancy

Ae fond kiss, and then we sever;
Ae farewell, and then for ever!
Deep in heart-wrung tears I 'll pledge thee,
Warring sighs and groans I 'll wage thee.

Who shall say that Fortune grieves him
While the star of hope she leaves him?
Me, nae cheerfu' twinkle lights me,
Dark despair around benights me.

I 'll ne'er blame my partial fancy;
Naething could resist my Nancy;
But to see her was to love her,
Love but her, and love for ever.

Had we never loved sae kindly,
Had we never loved sae blindly,

Never met—or never parted,
We had ne'er been broken-hearted.

Fare thee weel, thou first and fairest!
Fare thee weel, thou best and dearest!
Thine be ilka joy and treasure,
Peace, enjoyment, love, and pleasure!

Ae fond kiss, and then we sever!
Ae fareweel, alas, for ever!
Deep in heart-wrung tears I 'll pledge thee,
Warring sighs and groans, I 'll wage thee.

—*Robert Burns, Scottish (1759–1796).*

La Belle Dame Sans Merci

O what can ail thee, knight-at-arms,
  Alone and palely loitering?
The sedge has withered from the lake,
  And no birds sing.

O what can ail thee, knight-at-arms,
  So haggard and so woe-begone?
The squirrel's granary is full,
  And the harvest's done.

I see a lily on thy brow
  With anguish moist and fever dew,
And on thy cheek a fading rose
  Fast withereth too.

I met a lady in the meads,
  Full beautiful—a faery's child;
Her hair was long, her foot was light,
  And her eyes were wild.

I made a garland for her head,
  And bracelets too, and fragrant zone;
She looked at me as she did love,
  And made sweet moan.

I set her on my pacing steed,
  And nothing else saw all day long,
For sidelong would she bend, and sing
  A faery's song.

She found me roots of relish sweet,
  And honey wild, and manna dew,
And sure in language strange she said—
  "I love thee true!"

She took me to her elfin grot,
  And there she wept and sighed full sore,
And there I shut her wild wild eyes
  With kisses four.

And there she lullèd me asleep,
  And there I dreamed—ah! woe betide!
The latest dream I ever dreamed
  On the cold hill's side.

I saw pale kings and princes too,
  Pale warriors, death-pale were they all;
They cried—"La Belle Dame sans Merci
  Thee hath in thrall!"

I saw their starved lips in the gloam,
  With horrid warning gapèd wide,
And I awoke and found me here,
  On the cold hill's side.

And this is why I sojourn here,
  Alone and palely loitering,
Though the sedge is withered from the lake
  And no birds sing.

—*John Keats, English (1795–1821).*

She Walks in Beauty

She walks in beauty, like the night
  Of cloudless climes and starry skies;
And all that's best of dark and bright
  Meet in her aspect and her eyes:
Thus mellowed to that tender light
  Which heaven to gaudy day denies.

One shade the more, one ray the less,
  Had half impaired the nameless grace
Which waves in every raven tress,
  Or softly lightens o'er her face;
Where thoughts serenely sweet express
  How pure, how dear their dwelling-place.

And on that cheek, and o'er that brow,
  So soft, so calm, yet eloquent,
The smiles that win, the tints that glow,
  But tell of days in goodness spent,
A mind at peace with all below,
  A heart whose love is innocent!

—*George Gordon, Lord Byron, English (1788–1824).*

Sonatina

The princess is sad. What brings tears to her eyes?
From her strawberry mouth escape tremulous sighs,

And the smile that once played on her lips
is now gone.
The princess is pale in her chair of bright
gold;
The keys of her clavier are now mute and
cold;
In their vases, forgotten, the flowers have
grown wan.

The garden is filled with the peacock's
glory;
The duenna continues her tiresome story;
To the pranks of the clown all oblivious she
seems,
For the eyes of the princess, in the far eastern
sky,
Are following the flight of a vague dragonfly
That bears her away to the land of her
dreams.

Of the princes of Asia perhaps she is
dreaming;
Or of him who has paused, in silvery coach
gleaming,
To enjoy for a moment the light of her eyes.
Perhaps she is thinking of the king of the
Isles
Who with roses and diamonds would win
her bright smiles;
Or perhaps for the lord of rich pearls she
now sighs.

"Would I were," cries the princess with
lips rosy and sweet,
"A butterfly gay or a swallow fleet!
Had I only their wings, o'er the clouds I'd
take flight;
I would greet the fair lilies with verses of
May;
On sea-sweeping breezes I'd sail far away;
Or I'd climb to the sun on a ray of clear
light."

Of her distaff she's weary, she's tired of
the tower;
Tired, too, of her jester, of falcon and bower;
Of the white, placid swans that swim on the
lake.
The jasmins of the east, the dahlias of the
west,
The lilies of the north, they are sad and depressed;
For the flower of the court, they are sad, for
her sake.

The poor little princess with eyes of skyblue,
In her gems she's captive, in her gowns of
bright hue;
A prison for her is the palace renowned,
A magnificent palace, well guarded by
slaves,
A hundred black slaves with a hundred
sharp glaives,
A colossal dragoon and a vigilant hound.

"Oh would I were winged like the butterfly
glad!
(The princess is languid; the princess is sad)
Oh vision of roses, of ivory and gold!
To the land of a prince would I then wing
my flight,
(The princess is sad; the princess is white)
Who is fairer than dawn, with a beauty
untold."

Says the fairy godmother: "Hush, hush,
dear, your crying;
On a Pegasus fleet there comes to you flying,
From a faraway land, the victor of death;
With a hawk on his wrist, at his girdle a
sword,
One who loves you unseen, your cavalier
lord,
To kindle your lips with the warmth of his
breath!"

— *From the Spanish of Rubén Darío (1867–1916), translated by G. W. Umphrey and Laura Forsberg.*

~ ✲ ~

Beauty Rohtraut

What is the name of King Ringang's daughter?
Rohtraut, Beauty Rohtraut!
And what does she do the livelong day,
Since she dare not knit and spin alway?
O hunting and fishing is ever her play!
And, heigh! that her huntsman I might be!
I'd hunt and fish right merrily!
Be silent, heart!

And it chanced that, after this some time,
Rohtraut, Beauty Rohtraut!
The boy in the Castle has gained access,
And a horse he has got and a huntsman's
dress,
To hunt and to fish with the merry Princess;

And, O! that a king's son I might be!
Beauty Rohtraut I love so tenderly.
Hush! hush! my heart.

Under a gray old oak they sat,
Beauty, Beauty Rohtraut!
She laughs: "Why look you so slyly at me?
If you have heart enough, come, kiss me."
Cried the breathless boy, "Kiss thee?"
But he thinks kind fortune has favored my youth;
And thrice he has kissed Beauty Rohtraut's mouth.
Down! down! mad heart.

Then slowly and silently they rode home,—
Rohtraut, Beauty Rohtraut!
The boy was lost in his delight:
"And, wert thou Empress this very night,
I would not heed or feel the blight;
Ye thousand leaves of the wild wood wist
How Beauty Rohtraut's mouth I kiss'd.
Hush! hush! wild heart."

—*From the German of Eduard Mörike (1804–1875), translated by George Meredith.*

Two Songs by Heine

I

Immovable, unchanging,
The stars stand in the skies,
Upon each other gazing
With sad and loving eyes.

They speak throughout the ages
A speech so rich and grand;
But none of all the sages
That speech can understand.

But I that speech have mastered,
Can all its meaning trace;
What for my grammar served me
Was my beloved's face.

II

People have teased and vexed me,
Worried me early and late:
Some with the love they bore me,
Other some with their hate.

They drugged my glass with poison,
They poisoned the bread I ate:
Some with the love they bore me,
Other some with their hate.

But she, who has teased and vexed me,
And worried me far the most,—
She never hated me, never,
And her love I could never boast.

—*From the German of Heinrich Heine (1797–1856), translated by Sir Theodore Martin.*

The Dance by the Roadside

They danced by the roadside on Saturday night,
And the laughter resounded to left and to right,
With shouts of "Hip, hip!" and of "Hey!"
Nils Utterman, famed as a queer old freak,
Sat there and made his accordion squeak
With doodely, doodely, day!

There was Cottage Bess,—whose attractions are many,
She is pretty and slim, though she has n't a penny,
She's brimful of mischief and fun.
There was Christie,—the wild, independent young lassie!—
And Biddy of Finnthorpe, and Tilly, and Cassie,
And rollicking Meg o' the Run.

There was Pete o' the Ridge and Gus o' the Rise,—
Who are nimble at tossing a girl to the skies
And at catching her when she comes down.
There was Phil o' the Croft and Nick o' the Flume,
And Tommy the Soldier, and Jimmy the Groom,
And Karl-John of Taylortown.

They danced as with bodies of tow set afire,
All jumping like grasshoppers higher and higher,
And heel it rang sharp upon stone.
The coat-tails they fluttered, the aprons they flew,
And braids were a-flapping and skirts flung askew,
While the music would whimper and drone.

Then in birch, or in alder, or hazel thicket
There was whispering light as the chirp of a cricket

From the depths of the darkness near.
Over stock, over stone, there was flight and pursuing,
And under green boughs there was billing and cooing —
"If you want me, come have me right here!"

Over all lay the twinkling, star-lovely night;
In the wood-bordered bay a shimmery light
Fell soft on the waves as they broke.
A breeze, clover-laden, was borne from the meadow,
And a whiff from the firs and the pines that o'ershadow
The hills with their resinous cloak.

A fox lent his voice to the din of the crew,
And out of the brambles an owl cried "Oohoo!"
But they heard not, they heeded not, they.
"Oohoo!" from Goat Mountain the echo cried,
And to Utterman's doodling in turn replied
With a doodely, doodely, day!

— From the Swedish of Gustaf Fröding (1860–1911), translated by Charles Wharton Stork.

All, All

The Devil up my attic stair
Came tiptoeing a while ago
And trying to catch me unaware,
Said laughing, "I should like to know,

"Of all her many charms, what springs
Most often to your mind? Of all
The rose-coloured and shadowy things
Whereby her beauty may enthrall,

"Which is the sweetest?" — O my soul,
You answered the abhorred Guest:
"Her beauty is complete and whole.
No single part is loveliest.

"When she is near, I cannot say
What gives me such intense delight.
She dazzles like the break of day,
She comforts like the fall of night.

"My senses seem to merge in one;
The harmony that rules her being
Is all my knowledge — I have none
Of hearing, smelling, touching, seeing.

"No, no. I cannot make a choice
In this sublime bewilderment.
Perhaps the music of her scent!
Perhaps the perfume of her voice!"

— From the French of Charles Baudelaire (1821–1867), translated by George Dillon.

The Lake

Thus sailing, sailing on forevermore,
Still borne along, to winds and waves a prey,
Can we not, on life's sea without a shore,
Cast anchor for a day?

Dear lake! one little year has scarcely flown,
And near thy waves she longed once more to see,
Behold I sit alone upon this stone,
Where once she sat with me.

As now, thy restless waves were moaning through
The creviced rocks, where they their death did meet;
And flecks of foam from off thy billows blew
Over my dear one's feet.

One night we rowed in silence, — dost recall
That night? When under all the starry sky
Was heard alone the beat of oars that fall
In cadenced harmony.

When suddenly, upon the startled ear
Accents unknown to earth melodious break;
And with these mournful words, a voice most dear
Charms all the listening lake: —

"O Time, pause in thy flight! and you, propitious hours,
Pause on your rapid ways!
Let us enjoy the springtime of our powers,
The fairest of all days!

"So many wretched souls would speed your flight,
Urge on the lingering suns,
Take with their days the canker and the blight;
Forget the happy ones!

"But all in vain I try to stay its course;
Time slips away and flies.
I say to night, Pass slowly! and the dawn
Breaks on my startled eyes.

"Let us love, then, and love forevermore!
Enjoy life while we may;
Man has no port, nor has time any shore;
It flees, we pass away!"

She paused: our hearts speak through our ardent eyes,
Half-uttered phrases tremble on the air;
And in that ecstasy our spirits rise
Up to a world more fair.

And now we cease to speak; in sweet eclipse
Our senses lie, weighed down with all love's store;
Our hearts are beating, and our clinging lips
Murmur, "Forevermore!"

Great Heaven! can then these moments of delight,
When love all happiness upon us showers,
Vanish away as swiftly in their flight
As our unhappy hours?

Eternity, the Darkness, and the Past,
What have you done with all you've made your prey?
Answer us! will you render back at last
What you have snatched away?

O lake, O silent rocks, O verdurous green! —
You that time spares, or knows how to renew, —
Keep of this night, set in this lovely scene,
At least a memory true!

A memory in thy storms and thy repose,
O lake! and where thy smiling waters lave
The sunny shore, or where the dark fir grows,
And hangs above the wave.

In the soft breeze that sighs and then is gone,
In thy shores' song, by thy shores echoed still:
In the pale star whose silvery radiance shone
Above thy wooded hill!

That moaning winds, and reeds that clashing strike,
And perfumes that on balmy breezes moved,
With all we hear, we see, we breathe, alike
May say, "They loved!"

—*From the French of Alphonse Marie Louis Lamartine (1790–1869), translated by Katherine Hillard.*

Woman and Cat

They were at play, she and her cat,
And it was marvelous to mark
The white paw and the white hand pat
Each other in the deepening dark.

The stealthy little lady hid
Under her mittens' silken sheath
Her deadly agate nails that thrid
The silk-like dagger-points of death.

The cat purred primly and drew in
Her claws that were of steel filed thin:
The devil was in it all the same.
The devil was in it all the same.

And in the boudoir, while a shout
Of laughter in the air rang out,
Four sparks of phosphor shone like flame.

—*From the French of Paul Verlaine (1844–1896), translated by Arthur Symons.*

Cortège

A silver-vested monkey trips
And pirouettes before the face
Of one who twists a kerchief's lace
Between her well-gloved finger-tips.

A little negro, a red elf,
Carries her drooping train, and holds
At arm's length all the heavy folds,
Watching each fold displace itself.

The monkey never lets his eyes
Wander from the fair woman's breast.
White wonder that to be possessed
Would call a god out of the skies.

Sometimes the little negro seems
To lift his sumptuous burden up
Higher than need be, in the hope
Of seeing what all night he dreams.

She goes by corridor and stair,
Still to the insolent appeals

Of her familiar animals
Indifferent or unaware.

—From the French of Paul Verlaine (1844–1896), translated by Arthur Symons.

The Young Reaper

The sun in the heavens
Is high overhead,
And bakes with his rays
Our dear mother-earth.

He stifles a maid
At toil in the fields
That gloomily reaps
The rye in the ear.

The scorching field burns
And pities her not,
As shown by her pale
Disconsolate face.

Her head has drooped low,
Upon her soft breast;
The corn she has cut
Falls out of her hands.

It may be she reaps
In far-away thought,
Or glances aside
Forgetting her task.

Alas, her poor heart
Is downcast and aches,
Is sore in a way
It never has known.

A saint's day it was
When lately she walked
Alone in a wood
And raspberries picked;

And then it occurred
A stripling approached,
Who once had before
The maiden beheld.

Each other they faced,
Till, stopping, he sighed,
Admiringly saw,
Long looked in her eyes;

But passed and began
A song about love
Whose words did not cease,
Were heard from afar.

Oh, deep in the soul
Of one that is fair
Sweet music has come
And found a new home.

For her in the fields
Who's stifled and hot
'Tis wretched to reap
The rye in the ear.

—From the Russian of Alexis B. Koltsov (1808–1842), translated by C. Fillingham Coxwell.

Elysium

Elysium is as far as to
The very nearest room,
If in that room a friend await
Felicity or doom.

What fortitude the soul contains,
That it can so endure
The accent of a coming foot,
The opening of a door!

—Emily Dickinson, American (1830–1886).

Steelhead

The sky was cold December blue with great tumbling clouds, and the little river
Ran full but clear. A bare-legged girl in a red jersey was wading in it, holding a five-tined
Hay-fork at her head's height; suddenly she darted it down like a heron's beak and panting
Leaned on the shaft, looking down passionately, her gipsy-lean face, then stooped and dipping
One arm to the little breasts she drew up her catch, great hammered-silver steelhead with the tines through it
And the fingers of her left hand hooked in its gills, her slender body
Rocked with its writhing. She took it to the near bank
And was dropping it behind a log when someone said

Quietly "I guess I've got you, Vina." Who gasped and looked up
At a young horseman half hidden in the willow bushes,
She'd been too intent to notice him, and said "My God,
I thought it was the game-warden." "Worse," he said smiling, "This river's ours.
You can't get near it without crossing our fences.
Besides that you mustn't spear 'em, and . . . three, four, you little bitch,
That's the fifth fish." She answered with her gipsy face, "Take half o' them, honey. I loved the fun."
He looked up and down her taper legs, red with cold, and said fiercely, "Your fun.
To kill them and leave them rotting." "Honey, let me have one o' them," she answered,
"You take the rest." He shook his blond head. "You'll have to pay a terrible fine." She answered laughing,
"Don't worry: you wouldn't tell on me." He dismounted and tied the bridle to a bough, saying "Nobody would.
I know a lovely place deep in the willows, full of warm grass, safe as a house,
Where you can pay it." Her body seemed to grow narrower suddenly, both hands at her throat, and the cold thighs
Pressed close together while she stared at his face, it was beautiful, long heavy-lidded eyes like a girl's,
"I can't do that, honey . . . I," she said shivering, "your wife would kill me." He hardened his eyes and said
"Let that alone." "Oh," she answered; the little red hands came down from her breast and faintly
Reached toward him, her head lifting, he saw the artery on the lit side of her throat flutter like a bird
And said "You'll be sick with cold, Vina," flung off his coat
And folded her in it with his warmth in it and carried her
To that island in the willows.

He warmed her bruised feet in his hands;
She paid her fine for spearing fish, and another
For taking more than the legal limit, and would willingly
Have paid a third for trespassing; he sighed and said,
"You'll owe me that. I'm afraid somebody might come looking for me,
Or my colt break his bridle." She moaned like a dove, "Oh Oh Oh Oh,
You are beautiful, Hugh." They returned to the stream-bank. There
While Vina put on her shoes – they were like a small boy's, all stubbed and shapeless – young Flodden strung the five fish
On a willow rod through the red gills and slung them
To his saddle-horn. He led the horse and walked with Vina, going part way home with her.

Toward the canyon sea-mouth
The water spread wide and shoal, fingering through many channels down a broad flood-bed, and a mob of sea-gulls
Screamed at each other. Vina said, "That's a horrible thing."
"What?" "What the birds do. They're worse than I am."
When Flodden returned alone he rode down and watched them.
He saw that one of the thousand steelhead
Which irresistible nature herded up stream to the spawning-gravel in the mountain, the river headwaters,
Had wandered into a shallow finger of the current, and was forced over on his flank, sculling uneasily
In three inches of water: instantly a gaunt herring-gull hovered and dropped, to gouge the exposed
Eye with her beak; the great fish writhing, flopping over in his anguish, another gull's beak
Took the other eye. Their prey was then at their mercy, writhing blind, soon stranded, and the screaming mob
Covered him.

Young Flodden rode into them and drove them up; he found the torn stealhead
Still slowly and ceremoniously striking the sand with his tail and a bloody eye-socket, under the
Pavilion of wings. They cast a cold shadow in the air, a fleeting sense of fortune's iniquities: why should
Hugh Flodden be young and happy, mounted on a good horse,
And have had another girl besides his dear wife, while others have to endure blindness and death,

Pain and disease, misery, old age, God knows
what worse?

— *Robinson Jeffers, American (1887–).*

∽ ✪ ∾

To Earthward

Love at the lips was touch
As sweet as I could bear;
And once that seemed too much;
I lived on air

That crossed me from sweet things,
The flow of — was it musk
From hidden grapevine springs
Down hill at dusk?

I had the swirl and ache
From sprays of honeysuckle
That when they're gathered shake
Dew on the knuckle.

I craved strong sweets, but those
Seemed strong when I was young;
The petal of the rose
It was that stung.

Now no joy but lacks salt
That is not dashed with pain
And weariness and fault;
I crave the stain

Of tears, the aftermark
Of almost too much love,
The sweet of bitter bark
And burning clove.

When stiff and sore and scarred
I take away my hand
From leaning on it hard
In grass and sand,

The hurt is not enough:
I long for weight and strength
To feel the earth as rough
To all my length.

— *Robert Frost, American (1875–).*

PART TWENTY-TWO

The Stream of Story Telling

IN THE BEGINNING stories were not written with pen and ink. They were told by mothers to their children, by hunters to their friends, by priests to their followers, by professional minstrels for the pleasure of guests, and by later purveyors for the entertainment of patrons. At first, furthermore, stories were mere scraps of narrative, disjointed anecdotes devoid of the now familiar emphasis on setting and character, and the author's insights into their motives. Primitive men very slowly developed the art of story telling as they narrated their experiences on a hunt for food, or boasters told of their exploits to admiring minds, as parents invented plausible stories with alarming details to dissuade children from fire, or battle grimed couriers with high spirits announced the details of victory over a dreaded enemy. Man's interest in the experiences of his fellows has led to the development of an art that is older than recorded history, and as infinitely varied.

Probably in no branch of literature did the invention of printing effect greater changes than in the art of narration. As the earliest story-tellers discovered their audiences, they sensed the spell which could be worked by the adding of details, figures of speech, or allusions. Increasing in confidence and skill, they developed all the niceties of oral delivery. With the invention of printing, however, story-telling entered upon its modern developments. The narrator's audience was no longer the folk in a castle's banqueting hall, but the world; no longer a patron's circle of intimate friends, but all men who could buy and read books. And as newspapers and periodicals later came from printing presses, the artists who sought audiences through them were obliged to rely on more than the charm of voice and personality. Mistakes could not be corrected until revised printings. It was no longer possible to remedy a defect in a story, or to improve it, with each day's telling. What was put on paper remained for the eye of all posterity to read. This stern fact, together with the incalculable extension of the story-teller's audience, inspired the development of narrative techniques which would never have been devised if the art had remained in the purely oral tradition. With books on the history of the art and its methods the world is filled.

It will be sufficient to remind the reader that some stories are designed to represent not contemporary life, but contemporary ideals; that others reveal many skirmishes and campaigns on the border line between the discursive essay with its anecdotes and the fiction designed to censure social follies; that *contes* or philosophic tales, picaresque novels and saints' legends, are all part of the history of story-telling.

How a story is developed and the purpose for which it is told depend on the character of the occasion and the motives of the narrator. Washington Irving once stated his purposes: "For my part, I consider a story merely as a frame on which to stretch the materials; it is the play of thought, and sentiment, and language, the weaving in of characters, lightly, yet expressively delineated; the familiar and faithful expression of scenes in common life; and the half-concealed vein of humor that is often playing through the whole, — these are among what I aim at, and upon which I felicitate myself in proportion as I think I succeed." In these words Irving reveals himself the heir of eighteenth century English essayists. Had he lived in other times and countries, he doubtless would have set himself different goals and tested his work by different standards.

The stream of story telling thus has its fountain head in the dawn of man's desire to record his personal experiences or those of his tribe; it flows through many centuries and countries, from which tributaries have added their accretions of changing taste and varied preferences; and in the novels and short stories of the present time, it reveals every facet of modern life in naturalistic or romantic and other styles. No preface to a collection of tales from world literature can hope to do more than remind the reader that the world is filled with many types of human beings and that the literary history of every great people is marked by many epochs and artistic movements: fortunately the best stories of the world are their own excuse for being and can be enjoyed without gloss.

Anpu and Bata

The Tale of the Two Brothers

(EGYPTIAN)

ONCE there were two brethren, of one mother and one father; Anpu was the name of the elder, and Bata was the name of the younger. Now, as for Anpu he had a house, and he had a wife. But his little brother was to him as it were a son; he it was who made for him his clothes; he it was who followed behind his oxen to the fields; he it was who did the plowing; he it was who harvested the corn; he it was who did for him all the matters that were in the field. Behold, his younger brother grew to be an excellent worker, there was not his equal in the whole land; behold, the spirit of a god was in him.

Now after this the younger brother followed his oxen in his daily manner; and every evening he turned again to the house, laden with all the herbs of the field, with milk and with wood, and with all things of the field. And he put them down before his elder brother, who was sitting with his wife; and he drank and ate, and he lay down in his stable with the cattle. And at the dawn of day he took bread which he had baked, and laid it before his elder brother; and he took with him his bread to the field, and he drave his cattle to pasture in the fields. And as he walked behind his cattle, they said to him, "Good is the herbage which is in that place"; and he listened to all that they said, and he took them to the good place which they desired. And the cattle which were before him became exceeding excellent, and they multiplied greatly.

Now at the time of plowing his elder brother said unto him, "Let us make ready for ourselves a goodly yoke of oxen for plowing, for the land has come out from the water, it is fit for plowing. Moreover, do thou come to the field with corn, for we will begin the plowing in the morrow morning." Thus said he to him; and his younger brother did all things as his elder brother had spoken unto him to do them.

And when the morn was come, they went to the fields with their things; and their hearts were pleased exceedingly with their task in the beginning of their work. And it came to pass after this that as they were in the field they stopped for corn, and he sent his younger brother, saying, "Haste thou, bring to us corn from the farm." And the younger brother found the wife of his elder brother, as she was sitting tiring her hair. He said to her: "Get up, and give to me corn, that I may run to the field, for my elder brother hastened me; do not delay." She said to him: "Go, open the bin, and thou shalt take to thyself according to thy will, that I may not drop my locks of hair while I dress them."

The youth went into the stable; he took a large measure, for he desired to take much corn; he loaded it with wheat and barley; and he went out carrying it. She said to him, "How much of the corn that is wanted, is that which is on thy shoulder?" He said to her: "Three bushels of barley, and two of wheat, in all five; these are what are upon my shoulder": thus said he to her. And she conversed with him, saying, "There is great strength in thee, for I see thy might every day." And her heart knew him with the knowledge of youth. And she arose and came to him, and conversed with him, saying, "Come, stay with me, and it shall be well for thee, and I will make for thee beautiful garments." Then the youth became like a panther of the south with fury at the evil speech which she had made to him; and she feared greatly. And he spake unto her, saying, "Behold thou art to me as a mother, thy husband is to me as a father, for he who is elder than I has brought me up. What is this wickedness that thou hast said to me? Say it not to me again. For I will not tell it to any man, for I will not let it be uttered by the mouth of any man." He lifted up his burden, and he went to the field and came to his elder brother; and they took up their work, to labor at their task.

Now afterward, at eventime, his elder brother was returning to his house; and the younger brother was following after his oxen, and he loaded himself with all the things of the field; and he brought his oxen before him, to make them lie down in their stable which was in the farm. And behold the wife of the elder brother was afraid for the words which she had said. She took a parcel of fat, she became like one who is evilly beaten, desiring to say to her husband, "It is thy younger brother who has done this wrong." Her husband returned in the even, as was his wont of every day; he came unto his house; he found his wife ill of violence; she did not give him water upon his hands as he used to have, she did not make a light before him, his house was in darkness, and she was lying very sick. Her husband said to her, "Who has spoken with thee?" Behold she said, "No one has spoken with me except thy younger brother. When he came to take for thee corn he found me sitting alone; he said to me, 'Come, let us stay together, tie up thy hair.' Thus spake he to me. I did not listen to him, but thus spake I to him: 'Behold, am I not thy mother, is not thy elder brother to thee as a father?' And he feared, and he beat me to stop me from making report to thee, and if thou lettest him live I shall die. Now behold he is coming in the evening; and I complain of these wicked words, for he would have done this even in daylight."

And the elder brother became as a panther of the south; he sharpened his knife; he took it in his hand; he stood behind the door of his stable to slay his younger brother as he came in the evening to bring his cattle into the stable.

Now the sun went down, and he loaded himself with herbs in his daily manner. He came, and his foremost cow entered the stable, and she said to her keeper, "Behold thou thy elder brother standing before thee with his knife to slay thee; flee from before him." He heard what his first cow had said; and the next entering, she also said likewise. He looked beneath the door of the stable; he saw the feet of his elder brother; he was standing behind the door, and his knife was in his hand. He cast down his load to the ground, and betook himself to flee swiftly; and his elder brother pursued after him with his knife. Then the younger brother cried out unto Ra Harakhti, saying, "My good Lord! Thou art he who divides the evil from the good." And Ra stood and heard all his cry; and Ra made a wide water between him and his elder brother, and it was full of crocodiles; and the one brother was on one bank, and the other on the other bank; and the elder brother smote twice on his hands at not slaying him. Thus did he. And the younger brother called to the elder on the bank, saying: "Stand still until the dawn of day; and when Ra ariseth, I shall judge with thee before him, and he discerneth between the good and the evil. For I shall not be with thee any more forever; I shall not be in the place in which thou art; I shall go to the valley of the acacia."

Now when the land was lightened, and the next day appeared, Ra Harakhti arose, and one looked unto the other. And the youth spake with his elder brother, saying: "Wherefore camest thou after me to slay me in craftiness, when thou didst not hear the words of my mouth? For I am thy brother in truth, and thou art to me as a father, and thy wife even as a mother: is it not so? Verily, when I was sent to bring for us corn, thy wife said to me, 'Come, stay with me'; for behold this has been turned over unto thee into another wise." And he caused him to understand of all that happened with him and his wife. And he swore an oath by Ra Harakhti, saying, "Thy coming to slay me by deceit with thy knife was an abomination." Then the youth took a knife, and cut off his flesh, and cast it into the water, and the fish swallowed it. He failed; he became faint; and his elder brother cursed his own heart greatly; he stood weeping for him afar off; he knew not how to pass over to where his younger brother was, because of the crocodiles. And the younger brother called unto him, saying, "Whereas thou hast devised an evil thing, wilt thou not also devise a good thing, even like that which I would do unto thee? When thou goest to thy house thou must look to thy cattle, for I shall not stay in the place where thou art; I am going to the valley of the acacia. And now as to what thou shalt do for me; it is even that thou shalt come to seek after me, if thou perceivest a matter, namely, that there are things happening unto me. And this is what shall come to pass, that I shall draw out my soul, and I shall put it upon the top of the flowers of the acacia, and when the acacia is cut down, and it falls to the ground, and thou comest to seek for it, if thou searchest for it seven years do not let thy heart be wearied. For thou wilt find it, and thou must put it in a cup of cold water, and expect that I shall live again, that I may make answer to what has been done wrong. And thou shalt know of this, that is to say, that things are happening to me, when one shall give to thee a cup of beer in thy hand, and it shall be troubled; stay not then, for verily it shall come to pass with thee."

And the youth went to the valley of the acacia; and his elder brother went unto his house; his hand was laid on his head, and he cast dust on his head; he came to his house, and he slew his wife, he cast her to the dogs, and he sat in mourning for his younger brother.

Now many days after these things, the younger brother was in the valley of the acacia; there was none with him; he spent his time in hunting the beasts of the desert, and he came back in the even to lie down under the acacia, which bore his soul upon the topmost flower. And after this he built himself a tower with his own hands, in the valley of the acacia; it was full of all good things, that he might provide for himself a home.

And he went out from his tower, and he met the Nine Gods, who were walking forth to look upon the whole land. The Nine Gods talked one with another, and they said unto him: "Ho! Bata, bull of the Nine Gods, art thou remaining alone? Thou hast left thy village for the wife of Anpu, thy elder brother. Behold his wife is slain. Thou hast given him an answer to all that was transgressed against thee." And their hearts were vexed for him exceedingly. And Ra Harakhti said to Khnumu, "Behold, frame thou a woman for Bata, that he may not remain alive alone." And Khnumu made for him a mate to dwell with him. She was more beautiful in her limbs than any woman who is in the whole land. The essence of every god was in her. The seven Hathors came to see her: they said with one mouth, "She will die a sharp death."

And Bata loved her very exceedingly, and she dwelt in his house; he passed his time in hunting the beasts of the desert, and brought and laid them before her. He said, "Go not outside, lest the sea seize thee; for I cannot rescue thee from it, for I am a woman like thee; my soul is placed on the head of the flower of the acacia; and if another find it, I must fight with him." And he opened unto her his heart in all its nature.

Now after these things Bata went to hunt in his daily manner. And the young girl went to walk under the acacia which was by the side of her house. Then the sea saw her, and cast its waves up after her. She betook herself to flee from before it. She entered her house. And the sea called unto the acacia, saying, "Oh, would that I could seize her!"

And the acacia brought a lock from her hair, and the sea carried it to Egypt, and dropped it in the place of the fullers of Pharaoh's linen. The smell of the lock of hair entered into the clothes of Pharaoh; and they were wroth with the fullers of Pharaoh, saying, "The smell of ointment is in the clothes of Pharaoh." And the people were rebuked every day, they knew not what they should do. And the chief fuller of Pharaoh walked by the bank, and his heart was very evil within him after the daily quarrel with him. He stood still, he stood upon the sand opposite to the lock of hair, which was in the water, and he made one enter into the water and bring it to him; and there was found in it a smell, exceeding sweet. He took it to Pharaoh; and they brought the scribes and the wise men, and they said unto Pharaoh, "This lock of hair belongs to a daughter of Ra Harakhti: the essence of every god is in her, and it is a tribute to thee from another land. Let messengers go to every strange land to seek her: and as for the messenger who shall go to the valley of the acacia, let many men go with him to bring her." Then said his Majesty, "Excellent exceedingly is what has been said to us"; and they sent them. And many days after these things the people who were sent to strange lands came to give report unto the King: but there came not those who went to the valley of the acacia, for Bata had slain them, but let one of them return to give a report to the King. His Majesty sent many men and soldiers, as well as horsemen, to bring her back. And there was a woman among them, and to her had been given in her hand beautiful ornaments of a woman. And the girl came back with her, and they rejoiced over her in the whole land.

And his Majesty loved her exceedingly, and raised her to high estate; and he spake unto her that she should tell him concerning her husband. And she said, "Let the acacia be cut down, and let one chop it up." And they sent men and soldiers with their weapons to cut down the acacia; and they came to the acacia, and they cut the flower upon which was the soul of Bata, and he fell dead suddenly.

And when the next day came, and the earth was lightened, the acacia was cut down. And Anpu, the elder brother of Bata, entered his house, and washed his hands; and one gave him a cup of beer, and it became troubled; and one gave him another of wine, and the smell of it was evil. Then he took his staff, and his sandals, and likewise his clothes, with his weapons of war; and he betook himself forth to the valley of the acacia. He entered the tower of his younger brother, and he found him lying upon his mat; he was dead. And he wept when he saw his younger brother verily lying dead. And he went out to seek the soul of his younger brother under the acacia tree, under which his younger brother lay in the evening. He spent three years in seeking for it, but found it not. And when he began the fourth year, he desired in his heart to return into Egypt; he said "I will go tomorrow morn": thus spake he in his heart.

Now when the land lightened, and the next day appeared, he was walking under the acacia; he was spending his time in seeking it. And he returned in the evening, and labored at seeking it again. He found a seed. He returned with it. Behold this was the soul of his younger brother. He brought a cup of cold water, and he cast the seed into it: and he sat down, as he was wont. Now when the night came his soul sucked up the water; Bata shuddered in all his limbs, and he looked on his elder brother; his soul was in the cup. Then Anpu took the cup of cold water, in which the soul of his younger brother was; Bata drank it, his soul stood again in its place, and he became as he had been. They embraced each other, and they conversed together.

And Bata said to his elder brother, "Behold I am to become as a great bull, which bears every good mark; no one knoweth its history, and thou must sit upon my back. When the sun arises I shall be in the place where my wife is, that I may return answer to her; and thou must take me to the place where the King is. For all good things shall be done for thee; for one shall lade thee with silver and gold, because thou bringest me to Pharaoh, for I become a great marvel, and they shall rejoice for me in all the land. And thou shalt go to thy village."

And when the land was lightened, and the next day appeared, Bata became in the form which he had told to his elder brother. And Anpu sat upon his back until the dawn. He came to the place where the King was, and they made his Majesty to know of him; he saw him, and he was exceeding joyful with him. He made for him great offerings, saying, "This is a great wonder which has come to pass." There were rejoicings over him in the whole land. They presented unto him silver and gold for his elder brother, who went and stayed in his village. They gave to the bull many men and many things, and Pharaoh loved him exceedingly above all that is in this land.

And after many days after these things, the bull entered the purified place; he stood in the place where the princess was; he began to speak with her, saying, "Behold, I am alive indeed." And she said to him, "And, pray, who art thou?" He said to her, "I am Bata. I perceived when thou causedst that they should destroy the acacia of Pharaoh, which was my abode, that I might not be suffered to live. Behold, I am alive indeed, I am as an ox." Then the princess feared exceedingly for the words that her husband had spoken to her. And he went out from the purified place.

And his Majesty was sitting, making a good day with her: she was at the table of his Majesty, and the King was exceeding pleased with her. And she said to his Majesty, "Swear to me by God, saying, 'What thou shalt say, I will obey it for thy sake.'" He hearkened unto all that she said, even this. "Let me eat of the liver of the ox, because he is fit for naught." Thus spake she to him. And the King was exceeding sad at her words, the heart of Pharaoh grieved him greatly. And after the land was lightened, and the next day appeared, they proclaimed a great feast with offerings to the ox. And the King sent one of the chief butchers of his Majesty, to cause the ox to be sacrificed. And when he was sacrificed, as he was upon the shoulders of the people, he shook his neck, and he threw two drops of blood over against the two doors of his Majesty. The one fell upon the one side, on the great door of Pharaoh, and the other upon the other door. They grew as two great Persea trees, and each of them was excellent.

And one went to tell unto his Majesty, "Two great Persea trees have grown, as a great marvel of his Majesty, in the night by the side of the great gate of his Majesty." And there was rejoicing for them in all the land, and there were offerings made to them.

And when the days were multiplied after these things, his Majesty was adorned with the blue crown, with garlands of flowers on his neck, and he was upon the chariot of pale gold, and he went out from the palace to behold the Persea trees: the princess also was going out with horses behind his Majesty. And his Majesty sat beneath one of the Persea trees, and it spake thus with his wife: "Oh, thou deceitful one, I am Bata, I am alive, though I have been evilly entreated. I knew who caused the acacia to be cut down by Pharaoh at my dwelling. I then became an ox, and thou causedst that I should be killed."

And many days after these things the princess stood at the table of Pharaoh, and the King was pleased with her. And she said to his Majesty, "Swear to me by God, saying, 'That which the princess shall say to me I will obey it for her.'" And he hearkened unto all she said. And he commanded, "Let these two Persea trees be cut down, and let them be made into goodly planks." And he hearkened unto all she said. And after this his Majesty sent skillful craftsmen, and they cut down the Persea trees of Pharaoh; and the princess, the royal wife, was standing looking on, and they did all that was in her heart unto the trees. But a chip flew up, and it entered into the mouth of the princess; she swallowed it, and after many days she bore a son. And one went to tell his Majesty, "There is born to thee a son." And they brought him, and gave to him a nurse and servants; and there were rejoicings in the whole land. And the King sat making a merry day, as they were about the naming of him, and his Majesty loved him exceedingly at that moment, and the King raised him to be the royal son of Kush.

Now after the days had multiplied after these things, his Majesty made him heir of all the land. And many days after that, when he had fulfilled many years as heir, his Majesty flew up to heaven. And the heir said, "Let my great nobles of his Majesty be brought before me, that I may make them to know all that has happened to me." And they brought also before him his wife, and he judged with her before him, and they agreed with him. They brought to him his elder brother; he made him hereditary prince in all his land. He was thirty years King of Egypt, and he died, and his elder brother stood in his place on the day of burial.

Excellently finished in peace, for the ka of the scribe of the treasury Kagabu, of the treasury of Pharaoh, and for the scribe Hora, and the scribe Meremapt. Written by the scribe Anena, the owner of this roll. He who speaks against this roll, may Tahuti smite him.

— From an Egyptian papyrus (c. 1300 B.C.), translated by Francis Llewellyn Griffith, edited by Sir W. M. Flinders Petrie.

~ ⚙ ~

A Fickle Widow

(CHINESE)

At a distance from the capital, and in the peaceful retirement of the country there dwelt many centuries ago a philosopher named Chwang, who led a pleasurable existence in the society of his third wife, and in the study of the doctrines of his great master, Lao-tsze. Like many philosophers, Chwang had not been fortunate in his early married life. His first wife died young; his second he found it necessary to divorce, on account of misconduct; but in the companionship of the Lady T'ien he enjoyed a degree of happiness which had previously been denied him. Being a philosopher, however, he found it essential to his peace that he should occasionally exchange his domestic surroundings for the hillsides and mountain solitudes. On one such expedition he came unexpectedly on a newly made grave at the side of which was seated a young woman dressed in mourning, who was gently fanning the new mound. So strange a circumstance was evidently one into which a philosopher should inquire. He therefore approached the lady, and in gentle accents said, "May I ask what you are doing?"

"Well," replied the lady, "the fact is that this grave contains my husband. And, stupid man, just before he died he made me promise that I would not marry again until the soil above his grave should be dry. I watched it for some days, but it got dry so very slowly that I am fanning it to hasten the process." So saying she looked up into Chwang's face with so frank and engaging a glance that the philosopher at once decided to enlist himself in her service.

"Your wrists are not strong enough for such work," he said. "Let me relieve you at it."

"By all means," replied the lady briskly. "Here is the fan, and I shall owe you an everlasting debt of gratitude if you will fan it dry as quickly as possible."

Without more ado, Chwang set to work, and by the exercise of his magical powers he extracted every drop of moisture from the grave with a few waves of the fan. The lady was delighted with his success, and with the sunniest smile said, "How can I thank you sufficiently for your kindness! As a small mark of my gratitude, let me present you with this embroidered fan which I had in reserve; and as a token of my esteem, I really must ask you to accept one of my silver hairpins." With these words she presented the philosopher with the fan, and drawing out one of her ornamented hairpins, she offered it for his acceptance. The philosopher took the fan, but, possibly having the fear of Lady T'ien before his eyes, he declined the pin. The incident made him thoughtful, and as he seated himself again in his thatched hall, he sighed deeply.

"Why are you sighing?" inquired the Lady T'ien, who happened to enter at that moment, "and where does the fan come from which you hold in your hand?"

Thus invited, Chwang related all that had passed at the tomb. As he proceeded with the tale, Lady T'ien's countenance fell, and when he had concluded she broke forth indignantly, inveighing against the young widow, who she vowed was a disgrace to her sex. So soon as she had exhausted her vituperations, Chwang quietly repeated the proverb, "Knowing men's faces is not like knowing their hearts."

Interpreting this use of the saying as implying some doubts as to the value of her protestations, Lady T'ien exclaimed:

"How dare you condemn all women as though they were all formed in the same mold with this shameless widow? I wonder you are not afraid of calling down a judgment on yourself for such an injustice to me, and others like me."

"What need is there of all this violence?" rejoined her husband. "Now, tell me, if I were to die, would you, possessed as you are of youth and beauty, be content to remain a widow for five, or even three years?"

"A faithful minister does not serve two princes, and a virtuous woman never thinks of a second husband," sententiously replied the lady. "If fate were to decree that you should die, it would not be a question of three years or of five years, for never, so long as life lasted, would I dream of a second marriage."

"It is hard to say, it is hard to say," replied Chwang.

"Do you think," rejoined his wife, "that women are like men, destitute of virtue and devoid of justice? When one wife is dead you look out for another, you divorce this one and take that one; but we women are for one saddle to one horse. Why do you say these things to annoy me?"

With these words she seized the fan and tore it to shreds.

"Calm yourself," said her husband; "I only hope, if occasion offers, you will act up to your protestations."

Not many days after this Chwang fell dangerously ill, and as the symptoms increased in severity, he thus addressed his wife:

"I feel that my end is approaching, and that it is time I should bid you farewell. How unfortunate that you destroyed that fan the other day! You would have found it useful for drying my tomb."

"Pray, my husband, do not at such a moment suggest suspicions of me. Have I not studied the 'Book of Rites,' and have I not learned from it to follow one husband, and one only? If you doubt my sincerity, I will die in your presence to prove to you that what I say, I say in all faithfulness."

"I desire no more," replied Chwang; and then, as weakness overcame him, he added faintly, "I die. My eyes grow dim."

With these words he sank back motionless and breathless.

Having assured herself that her husband was dead, the Lady T'ien broke out into loud lamentations, and embraced the corpse again and again. For days and nights she wept and fasted, and constantly dwelt in her thoughts on the virtues and wisdom of the deceased. As was customary, on the death of so learned a man as Chwang, the neighbors all came to offer their condolences and to volunteer their assistance. Just as the last of these had retired, there arrived at the door a young and elegant scholar, whose face was like a picture, and whose lips looked as though they had been smeared with vermillion. He was dressed in a violet silk robe, and wore a black cap, an embroidered girdle, and scarlet shoes. His servant announced that he was a Prince of the Kingdom of Tsoo, and he himself added by way of explanation:

"Some years ago I communicated to Chwang my desire to become his disciple. In furtherance of this purpose I came hither, and now, to my inexpressible regret, I find on my arrival that my master is dead."

To evince his respectful sorrow, the Prince at once exchanged his colored clothing for mourning garments, and prostrating himself before the coffin, struck his forehead four times on the ground, and sobbed forth, "Oh, learned Chwang, I am indeed unfortunate in not having been permitted to receive your instructions face to face. But to show my regard and affection for your memory, I will here remain and mourn for you a hundred days."

With these words he prostrated himself again four times, while he watered the earth with his tears. When more composed, he begged to be allowed to pay his respects to Lady T'ien, who, however, thrice declined to see him, and only at last consented when it was pointed out to her that, according to the most recondite authorities, the wives of deceased instructors should not refuse to see their husband's disciples.

After then receiving the Prince's compliments with downcast eyes, the Lady T'ien ventured just to cast one glance at her guest, and was so struck by his beauty and the grace of his figure, that a sentiment of more than interest suffused her heart. She begged him to take up his abode in her house, and when dinner was prepared, she blended her sighs with his. As a token of her esteem, so soon as the repast was ended, she brought him the copies of "The Classic of Nan-hwa," and the "Sûtra of Reason and of Virtue," which her husband had been in the habit of using, and presented them to the Prince. He, on his part, in fulfilment of his desire of mourning for his master, daily knelt and lamented by the side of the coffin, and thither also the Lady T'ien repaired to breathe her sighs. These constant meetings provoked short conversations, and the glances, which on these occasions were exchanged between them, gradually betook less of condolence and more of affection, as time went on. It was plain that already the Prince was half enamored, while the lady was deeply in love. Being desirous of learning some particulars about her engaging guest, she one evening summoned his servant to her apartment, and having plied him with wine, inquired from him whether his master was married.

"My master," replied the servant, "has never yet been married."

"What qualities does he look for in the fortunate woman he will choose for his wife?" inquired the lady.

"My master says," replied the servant, who had taken quite as much wine as was good for him, "that if he could obtain a renowned beauty like yourself, madam, his heart's desire would be fulfilled."

"Did he really say so? Are you sure you are telling me the truth?" eagerly asked the lady.

"Is it likely that an old man like me would tell you a lie?" replied the servant.

"If it be so, will you then act as a go-between, and arrange a match between us?"

"My master has already spoken to me of the matter, and would desire the alliance above all things, if it were not for the respect due from a disciple to a deceased master, and for the animadversions to which such a marriage would give rise."

"But as a matter of fact," said the Lady T'ien, "the Prince was never my husband's disciple; and as to our neighbors about here, they are too few and insignificant to make their animadversions worth a thought."

The objections having thus been overcome, the servant undertook to negotiate with his master, and promised to bring word of the result at any hour of the day or night at which he might have anything to communicate.

So soon as the man was gone, the Lady T'ien gave way to excited impatience. She went backwards and forwards to the chamber of death, that she might pass the door of the Prince's room, and even listened at his window, hoping to hear him discussing with his servant the proposed alliance. All, however, was still until she approached the coffin, when she heard an unmistakable sound of hard breathing. Shocked and terrified, she exclaimed, "Can it be possible that the dead has come to life again!"

A light, however, relieved her apprehensions by discovering the form of the Prince's servant lying in a drunken sleep on a couch by the corpse. At any other time such disrespect to the deceased would have drawn from her a torrent of angry rebukes, but on this occasion she thought it best to say nothing, and on the next morning she accosted the defaulter without any reference to his escapade of the night before. To her eager inquiries the servant answered that his master was satisfied on the points she had combated on the preceding evening, but that there were still three unpropitious circumstances which made him hesitate.

"What are they?" asked the lady.

"First," answered the man, "my master says that the presence of the coffin in the saloon makes it difficult to conduct marriage festivities in accordance with usage; secondly, that the illustrious Chwang having so deeply loved his wife, and that affection having been so tenderly returned by her in recognition of his great qualities, he fears that a second husband would probably not be held entitled to a like share of affection; and thirdly, that not having brought his luggage, he has neither the money nor the clothes necessary to play the part of a bridegroom."

"These circumstances need form no obstacle to our marriage," replied the lady. "As to the first objection, I can easily have the coffin removed into a shed at the back of the house; then as to the second, though my husband was a great Taoist authority, he was not by any means a very moral man. After his first wife's death he married a second, whom he divorced, and just before his own decease, he flirted outrageously with a widow whom he found fanning her husband's grave on the hill yonder. Why, then, should your master, young, handsome, and a prince, doubt the quality of my affection? Then as to the third objection, your master need not trouble himself about the expenses connected with our marriage; I will provide them. At this moment I have twenty taels of silver in my room, and these I will readily give him to provide himself clothes withal. Go back, then, and tell the Prince what I say, and remind that there is no time like the present, and that there could be no more felicitous evening for our marriage than that of to-day."

Carrying the twenty taels of silver in his hand, the servant returned to his master, and presently brought back word to the lady that the Prince was convinced by her arguments, and ready for the ceremony.

On receipt of this joyful news, Lady T'ien exchanged her mourning for wedding garments, painted her cheeks, reddened her lips, and ordered some villagers to carry Chwang's coffin into a hut at the back of the house, and to prepare for the wedding. She herself arranged the lights and candles in the hall, and when the time arrived stood ready to receive the Prince, who presently entered, wearing the insignia of his official rank, and dressed in a gayly embroidered tunic. Bright as a polished gem and a gold setting, the two stood beneath the nuptial torch, radiant with beauty and love. At the conclusion of the ceremony, with every demonstration of affection, the Prince led his bride by the hand into the nuptial chamber. Suddenly, as they were about to retire to rest, the Prince was seized with violent convulsions. His face became distorted, his eyebrows stood on end, and he fell to the ground, beating his breast with his hands.

The Lady T'ien, frantic with grief, embraced him, rubbed his chest, and when these remedies failed to revive him, called in his old servant.

"Has your master ever had any fits like this before?" she hurriedly inquired.

"Often," replied the man, "and no medicine ever alleviates his sufferings; in fact, there is only one thing that does."

"Oh, what is that?" asked the lady.

"The brains of a man, boiled in wine," answered the servant. "In Tsoo, when he has these attacks, the king, his father, beheads a malefactor and takes his brains to form the decoction; but how is it possible here to obtain such a remedy?"

"Will the brains of a man who has died a natural death do?" asked the lady.

"Yes, if forty-nine days have not elapsed since the death."

"My former husband's would do then. He has only been dead twenty days. Nothing will be easier than to open the coffin and take them out."

"But would you be willing to do it?"

"I and the Prince are now husband and wife. A wife with her body serves her husband, and should I refuse to do this for him out of regard for a corpse, which is fast becoming dust?"

So saying, she told the servant to look after his master, and seizing a hatchet, went straight to the hut to which the corpse had been removed. Having arranged the light conveniently, she tucked up her sleeves, clenched her teeth, and with both hands brought down the hatchet on the coffin-lid. Blow after blow fell upon the wood, and at the thirty-first stroke the plank yielded, and the head of the coffin was forced open. Panting with her exertions, she cast a glance on the corpse preparatory to her further grim office, when, to her inexpressible horror, Chwang sighed twice, opened his eyes, and sat up. With a piercing shriek she shrank backwards, and dropped the hatchet from her palsied hands.

"My dear wife," said the philosopher, "help me to rise."

Afraid to do anything else but obey, she assisted him out of the coffin and offered him support, while he led the way, lamp in hand, to her chamber. Remembering the sight that would there meet his eyes, the wretched woman trembled as they approached the door. What was her relief, however, to find that the Prince and his servant had disappeared. Taking advantage of this circumstance, she assumed every woman's wile, and in softest accents, said, "Ever since your death you have been in my thoughts day and night. Just now, hearing a noise in your coffin, and remembering how, in the tales of old, souls are said to return to their bodies, the hope occurred to me that it might be so in your case, and I took a hatchet to open your coffin. Thank Heaven and Earth my felicity is complete; you are once more by my side."

"Many thanks, madam," said Chwang, "for your deep consideration. But may I ask why you are dressed in such gay clothing."

"When I went to open your coffin, I had, as I say, a secret presentiment of my good fortune, and I dared not receive you back to life in mourning attire."

"Oh," replied her husband, "but there is one other circumstance which I should like to have explained. Why was not my coffin placed in the saloon, but tossed into a ruined barn?"

To this question Lady T'ien's woman's wit failed to supply an answer. Chwang looked at the cups and wine which formed the relics of the marriage feast, but made no other remark thereon, except to tell his wife to warm him some wine. This she did, employing all her most engaging wiles to win a smile from her husband; but he steadily rejected her advances, and presently, pointing with his finger over her shoulder, he said, "Look at those two men behind you."

She turned with an instinctive knowledge that she would see the Prince and his servant in the courtyard, and so she did. Horrified at the sight, she turned her eyes towards her husband, but he was not there. Again looking towards the courtyard she found that the Prince and his servant had now disappeared, and that Chwang was once more at her side. Perceiving then the true state of the case, that the Prince and his servant were but Chwang's other self, which he by his magical power was able to project into separate existences, she saw that all attempts at concealment were vain; and taking her girdle from her waist, she tied it to a beam and hung herself on the spot.

So soon as life was extinct Chwang put his frail wife into the coffin from which he had lately emerged, and setting fire to his house, burnt it with its contents to ashes. The only things saved from the flames were the "Sûtra of Reason and of Virtue," and "The Classic of Nan-hwa," which were found by some neighbors, and carefully treasured.

As to Chwang, it is said that he set out as on a journey towards the West. What his ultimate destination was is not known, but one thing is certain, and that is, that he remained a widower for the rest of his life.

—*From the Marvelous Tales, Chinese (fifteenth century or earlier), translated by A. K. Douglas.*

~ ✿ ~

Cupid and Psyche

APULEIUS

In a certain city lived a king and queen who had three daughters exceeding fair. But the beauty of the elder sisters, though pleasant to behold, yet passed not the measure of human praise, while such was the loveliness of the youngest that men's speech was too poor to commend it worthily and could express it not at all. Many of the citizens and of strangers, whom the fame of this excellent vision had gathered thither, confounded by that matchless beauty, could but kiss the fingertips of their right hands at sight of her, as in adoration to the goddess Venus herself. And soon a rumor passed through the country that she whom the blue deep had borne, forbearing her divine dignity, was even then moving among men, or that by some fresh germination from the stars, not the sea now, but the earth, had put forth a new Venus, endued with the flower of virginity.

This belief, with the fame of the maiden's loveliness, went daily further into distant lands, so that many people were drawn together to behold that glorious model of the age. Men sailed no longer to Paphos, to Cnidos or Cythera, to the presence of the goddess Venus: her sacred rites were neglected, her images stood uncrowned, the cold ashes were left to disfigure her forsaken altars. It was to a maiden that men's prayers were offered, to a human countenance they looked, in propitiating so great a godhead: when the girl went forth in the morning they strewed flowers on her way, and the victims proper to that unseen goddess were presented as she passed along. This conveyance of divine worship to a mortal kindled meantime the anger of the true Venus. "Lo! now, the ancient parent of nature," she cried, "the fountain of all elements! Behold me, Venus, benign mother of the world, sharing my honors with a mortal maiden, while my name, built up in heaven, is profaned by the mean things of earth! Shall a perishable woman bear my image about with her? In vain did the shepherd of Ida prefer me! Yet shall she have little joy, whosoever she be, of her usurped and unlawful loveliness!" Thereupon she called to her that winged, bold boy, of evil ways, who wanders armed by night through men's houses, spoiling their marriages; and stirring yet more by her speech his inborn wantonness, she led him to the city, and showed him Psyche as she walked.

"I pray thee," she said, "give thy mother a full revenge. Let this maid become the slave of an unworthy love." Then, embracing him closely, she departed to the shore and took her throne upon the crest of the wave. And lo! at her unuttered will, her ocean-servants are in waiting: the daughters of Nereus are there singing their song, and Portunus, and Salacia, and the tiny charioteer of the dolphin, with a host of Tritons leaping through the billows. And one blows softly through his sounding sea-shell, another spreads a silken web against the sun, a third presents the mirror to the eyes of his mistress, while the others swim side by side below, drawing her chariot. Such was the escort of Venus as she went upon the sea.

Psyche meantime, aware of her loveliness, had no fruit thereof. All people regarded and admired, but none sought her in marriage. It was but as on the finished work of the craftsman that they gazed upon that divine likeness. Her sisters, less fair than she, were happily wedded. She, even as a widow, sitting at home, wept over her desolation, hating in her heart the beauty in which all men were pleased.

And the king, supposing the gods were angry, inquired of the oracle of Apollo, and Apollo answered him thus: "Let the damsel be placed on the top of a certain mountain, adorned as for the bed of marriage, and of death. Look not for a son-in-law of mortal birth; but for that evil serpent-thing, by reason of whom even the gods tremble and the shadows of Styx are afraid."

So the king returned home and made known the oracle to his wife. For many days she lamented, but at last the fulfillment of the divine precept is urgent upon her, and the company make ready to conduct the maiden to her deadly bridal. And now the nuptial torch gathers dark smoke and ashes: the pleasant sound of the pipe is changed into a cry: the marriage hymn concludes in a sorrowful wailing: below her yellow wedding-veil the bride shook away her tears; insomuch that the whole city was afflicted together at the ill-luck of the stricken house.

But the mandate of the god impelled the hapless Psyche to her fate, and, these solemnities being ended, the funeral of the living soul goes forth, all the people following. Psyche, bitterly weeping, assists not at her marriage but at her own obsequies, and while the parents hesitate to accomplish a thing so unholy the daughter cries to them: "Wherefore torment your luckless age by long weeping? This was the prize of my extraordinary beauty! When all people celebrated us with divine honors, and in one voice named the New Venus, it was then ye should have wept for me as one dead. Now at last I understand that that one name of Venus has been my ruin. Lead me and set me upon the appointed place. I am in haste to submit to that well-omened marriage, to behold that goodly spouse. Why delay the coming of him who was born for the destruction of the whole world?"

She was silent, and with firm step went on the way. And they proceeded to the appointed place on a steep mountain, and left there the maiden alone, and took their way homewards dejectedly. The wretched parents, in their close-shut house, yielded themselves to perpetual night; while to Psyche, fearful and trembling and weeping sore upon the mountain-top, comes the gentle Zephyrus. He lifts her mildly, and, with vesture afloat on either side, bears her by his own soft breathing over the windings of the hills, and sets her lightly among the flowers in the bosom of a valley below.

Psyche, in those delicate grassy places, lying sweetly on her dewy bed, rested from the agitation of her soul and arose in peace. And lo! a grove of mighty trees, with a fount of water, clear as glass, in the midst; and hard by the water, a dwelling-place, built not by human hands but by some divine cunning. One recognized, even at the entering, the delightful hostelry of a god. Golden pillars sustained the roof, arched most curiously in cedar-wood and ivory. The walls were hidden under wrought silver,—all tame and woodland creatures leaping forward to the visitor's gaze. Wonderful indeed was the craftsman, divine or half-divine, who by the subtlety of his art had breathed so wild a soul into the silver! The very pavement was distinct with pictures in goodly stones. In the glow of its precious metal the house is its own daylight, having no need of the sun. Well might it seem a place fashioned for the conversation of gods with men!

Psyche, drawn forward by the delight of it, came near, and, her courage growing, stood within the doorway. One by one, she admired the beautiful things she saw; and, most wonderful of all! no lock, no chain, nor living guardian protected that great treasure-house. But as she gazed there came a voice,—a voice, as it were, unclothed by bodily vesture. "Mistress!" it said, "all these things are thine. Lie down, and relieve thy weariness, and rise again for the bath when thou wilt. We thy servants, whose voice thou hearest, will be beforehand with our service, and a royal feast shall be ready."

And Psyche understood that some divine care was providing, and, refreshed with sleep and the bath, sat down to the feast. Still she saw no one: only she heard words falling here and there, and had voices alone to serve her. And the feast being ended, one entered the chamber and sang to her unseen, while another struck the chords of a harp, invisible with him who played on it. Afterwards the sound of a company singing together came to her, but still so that none was present to sight, yet it appeared that a great multitude of singers was there.

And the hour of evening inviting her, she climbed into the bed; and as the night was far advanced, behold a sound of a certain clemency approaches her. Then, fearing for her maidenhood in so great solitude, she trembled, and more than any evil she knew dreaded that she knew not. And now the husband, that unknown husband, drew near, and ascended the couch, and made her his wife; and lo! before the rise of dawn he had departed hastily. And the attendant voices ministered to the needs of the newly married. And so it happened with her for a long season. And as nature has willed, this new thing, by continual use, became a delight to her: the sound of the voice grew to be her solace in that condition of loneliness and uncertainty.

One night the bridegroom spoke thus to his beloved, "O Psyche, most pleasant bride! Fortune is grown stern with us, and threatens thee with mortal peril. Thy sisters, troubled at the report of thy death and seeking some trace of thee, will come to the mountain's top. But if by chance their cries reach thee, answer not, neither look forth at all, lest thou bring sorrow upon me and destruction upon thyself." Then Psyche promised that she would do according to his will. But the bridegroom was fled away again with the night. And all that day she spent in tears, repeating that she was now dead indeed, shut up in that golden prison, powerless to console her sisters sorrowing after her, or to see their faces; and so went to rest weeping.

And after a while came the bridegroom again, and embracing her as she wept, complained, "Was this thy promise, my Psyche? What have I to hope from thee? Even in the arms of thy husband thou ceasest not from pain. Do now as thou wilt. Indulge thine own desire, though it seeks what will ruin thee. Yet wilt thou remember my warning, repentant too late." Then, protesting that she is like to die, she obtains from him that he suffer her to see her sisters, and present to them moreover what gifts she would of golden ornaments; but therewith he ofttimes advised her never at any time yielding to pernicious counsel, to inquire concerning his bodily form, lest she fall, through unholy curiosity, from so great a height of fortune, nor feel ever his embrace again. "I would die a hundred times," she said, cheerfully at last, "rather than be deprived of thy most sweet usage. I love thee as my own soul, beyond comparison even with Love himself. Only bid thy servant Zephyrus bring hither my sisters, as he brought me. My honeycomb! My Husband! Thy Psyche's breath of life!" So he promised; and ere the light appeared, vanished from the hands of his bride.

And the sisters, coming to the place where Psyche was abandoned, wept loudly among the rocks, and called upon her by name, so that the sound came down to her, and running out of the palace distraught, she cried, "Wherefore afflict your souls with lamentation? I whom you mourn am here." Then, summoning Zephyrus, she reminded him of her husband's bidding; and he bare them down with a gentle blast. "Enter now," she said, "into my house, and relieve your sorrow in the company of Psyche your sister."

And Psyche displayed to them all the treasures of the golden house, and its great family of ministering voices, nursing in them the malice which was already at their hearts. And at last one of them asks curiously who the lord of that celestial array may be, and what manner of man her husband. And Psyche answered dissemblingly, "A young man, handsome and mannerly, with a goodly beard. For the most part he hunts upon the mountains." And lest the secret should slip from her in the way of further speech, loading her sisters with gold and gems, she commanded Zephyrus to bear them away.

And they returned home, on fire with envy. "See now the injustice of fortune!" cried one. "We, the elder children, are given like servants to be the wives of strangers, while the youngest is possessed of so great riches, who scarcely knows how to use them. You saw, sister! what a hoard of wealth lies in the house; what glittering gowns; what splendor of precious gems, besides all that gold trodden under foot. If she indeed has, as she said, a bridegroom so goodly then no one in all the world is happier. And it may be that this husband, being of divine nature, will make her too a goddess. Nay, so in truth it is. It was even thus she bore herself. Already she looks aloft and breathes divinity, who, though but a woman, has voices for her handmaidens, and can command the winds." "Think," answered the other, "how arrogantly she dealt with us, grudging us these trifling gifts out of all that store, and when our company became a burden, causing us to be hissed and driven away from her through the air! But I am no woman if she keep her hold on this great fortune; and if the insult done us has touched thee too, take we counsel together. Meanwhile let us hold our peace, and know nought of her, alive or dead. For they are not truly happy of whose happiness other folk are unaware."

And the bridegroom, whom still she knows not, warns her thus a second time, as he talks with her by night: "Seest thou what peril besets thee? Those cunning wolves have made ready for thee their snares, of which the sum is that they persuade thee to search into the fashion of my countenance, the seeing of which, as I have told thee often, will be the seeing of it no more forever. But do thou neither listen nor make answer to ought regarding thy husband. Besides, we have sown also the seed of our race. Even now this bosom grows with a child to be born to us, a child, if thou but keep our secret, of divine quality; if thou profane it, subject to death." And Psyche was glad at the tidings, rejoicing in that solace of a divine seed, and in the glory of that pledge of love to be, and the dignity of the name of mother. Anxiously she notes the increase of the days, the waning months. And again, as he tarries briefly beside her, the bridegroom repeats his warning: "Even now the sword is drawn with which thy sisters seek thy life. Have pity on thyself, sweet wife, and upon our child, and see not those evil women again." But the sisters make their way into the palace once more, crying to her in wily tones, "O Psyche! and thou too wilt be a mother! How great will be the joy at home! Happy indeed shall we be to have the nursing of the golden child. Truly if he be answerable to the beauty of his parents, it will be a birth of Cupid himself."

So, little by little, they stole upon the heart of their sister. She, meanwhile, bids the lyre to sound for their delight, and the playing is heard: she bids the pipes to move, the quire to sing, and the music and the singing come invisibly, soothing the mind of the listener with sweetest modulation. Yet not even thereby was their malice put to sleep: once more they seek to know what manner of husband she has, and whence that seed. And Psyche, simple over-much, forgetful of her first story, answers, "My husband comes from a far country, trading for great sums. He is already of middle age, with whitening locks." And therewith she dismisses them again.

And returning home upon the soft breath of Zephyrus one cried to the other, "What shall be said of so ugly a lie? He who was a young man with goodly beard is now in middle life. It must be that she told a false tale: else is she in very truth ignorant of what manner of man he is. Howsoever it be, let us destroy her quickly. For if she indeed knows not, be sure that her bridegroom is one of the gods: it is a god she bears in her womb. And let that be far from us! If she be called the mother of a god, then will life be more than I can bear."

So, full of rage against her, they returned to Psyche, and said to her craftily, "Thou livest in an ignorant bliss, all incurious of thy real danger. It is a deadly serpent, as we certainly know, that comes to sleep at thy side. Remember the words of the oracle, which declared thee destined to a cruel beast. There are those who have seen it at nightfall, coming back from its feeding. In no long time, they say, it will end its blandishments. It but waits for the babe to be formed in thee, that it may devour thee by so much the richer. If indeed the solitude of this musical place, or it may be the loathsome commerce of a hidden love, delight thee, we at least in sisterly piety have done our part." And at last the unhappy Psyche, simple and frail of soul, carried away by the terror of their words, losing memory of her husband's precepts and her own promise, brought upon herself a great calamity. Trembling and turning pale, she answers them, "And they who tell those things, it may be, speak the truth. For in very deed never have I seen the face of my husband, nor know I at all what manner of man he is. Always he frights me diligently from the sight of him, threatening some great evil should I too curiously look upon his face. Do ye, if ye can help your sister in her great peril, stand by her now."

Her sisters answered her, "The way of safety we have well considered, and will teach thee. Take a sharp knife, and hide it in that part of the couch where thou art wont to lie: take also a lamp filled with oil, and set it privily behind the curtain. And when he shall have drawn up his coils into the accustomed place, and thou hearest him breathe in sleep, slip then from his side and discover the lamp, and, knife in hand, put forth thy strength, and strike off the serpent's head." And so they departed in haste.

And Psyche left alone (alone but for the furies which beset her) is tossed up and down in her distress, like a wave of the sea; and though her will is firm, yet, in the moment of putting hand to the deed, she falters, and is torn asunder by various apprehensions of the great calamity upon her. She hastens and anon delays, now full of distrust, and now of angry courage: under one bodily form she loathes the monster and loves the bridegroom. But twilight ushers in the night; and at length in haste she makes ready for the terrible deed. Darkness came, and the bridegroom; and he first falls into a deep sleep.

And she, erewhile of no strength, the hard purpose of destiny assisting her, is confirmed in force. With lamp plucked forth, knife in hand, she put by her sex; and lo! as the secrets of the bed became manifest, the sweetest and most gentle of all creatures, Love himself, reclined there, in his own proper loveliness! At sight of him the very flame of the lamp kindled more gladly! But Psyche was afraid of the vision, and, faint of soul, trembled back upon her knees, and would have hidden the steel in her own bosom. But the knife slipped from her hand; and now, undone, yet ofttimes looking upon the beauty of that divine countenance, she lives again. She sees the locks of that golden head, pleasant with the unction of the gods, shed down in graceful entanglement behind and before, about the ruddy cheeks and white throat. The pinions of the winged god, yet fresh with the dew, are spotless upon his shoulders, the delicate plumage wavering over them as they lie at rest. Smooth he was, and touched with light, worthy of Venus his mother. At the foot of the couch lay his bow and arrows, the instruments of his power, propitious to men.

And Psyche, gazing hungrily thereon, draws an arrow from the quiver, and trying the point upon the thumb, tremulous still, drave in the barb, so that a drop of blood came forth. Thus fell she, by her own act, and unaware, into the love of Love. Falling upon the bridegroom, with indrawn breath, in a hurry of kisses from eager and open lips, she shuddered as she thought how brief that sleep might be. And it chanced that a drop of burning oil fell from the lamp upon the god's shoulder. Ah! maladroit minister of love, thus to wound him from whom all fire comes; though 'twas a lover, I trow, first devised thee, to have the fruit of his desire even in the darkness! At the touch of the fire the god started up, and beholding the overthrow of her faith, quietly took flight from her embraces.

And Psyche, as he rose upon the wing, laid hold on him with her two hands, hanging upon him in his passage through the air, till she sinks to the earth through weariness. And as she lay there, the divine lover, tarrying still, lighted upon a cypress tree which grew near, and, from the top of it, spake thus to her, in great emotion. "Foolish one! unmindful of the command of Venus, my mother, who had devoted thee to one of base degree, I fled to thee in his stead. Now know I that this was vainly done. Into mine own flesh pierced mine arrow, and I made thee my wife, only that I might seem a monster beside thee—that thou shouldst seek to wound the head wherein lay the eyes so full of love to thee! Again and again, I thought to put thee on thy guard concerning these things, and warned thee in loving-kindness. Now I would but punish thee by my flight hence." And therewith he winged his way into the deep sky.

Psyche, prostrate upon the earth, and following far as sight might reach the flight of the bridegroom, wept and lamented; and when the breadth of space had parted him wholly from her, cast herself down from the bank of a river which was nigh. But the stream, turning gentle in honor of the god, put her forth again unhurt upon its margin. And as it happened, Pan, the rustic god, was sitting just then by the waterside. Hard by, his flock of goats browsed at will. And the shaggy god called her, wounded and outworn, kindly to him and said, "I am but a rustic herdsman, pretty maiden, yet wise, by favor of my great age and long experience; and if I guess truly by those faltering steps, by thy sorrowful eyes and continual sighing, thou laborest with excess of love. Listen then to me, and seek not death again, in the stream or otherwise. Put aside thy woe, and turn thy prayers to Cupid. He is in truth a delicate youth: win him by the delicacy of thy service."

So the shepherd-god spoke, and Psyche, answering nothing, but with a reverence to this serviceable deity, went on her way. And while she, in her search after Cupid, wandered through many lands, he was lying in the chamber of his mother, heart-sick. And the white bird which floats over the waves plunged in haste into the sea, and approaching Venus, as she bathed, made known to her that her son lies afflicted with some grievous hurt, doubtful of life. And Venus cried, angrily, "My son, then, has a mistress! And it is Psyche, who witched away my beauty and was the rival of my godhead, whom he loves!"

Therewith she issued from the sea, and returning to her golden chamber, found there the lad, sick, as she had heard, and cried from the doorway, "Well done, truly! to trample thy mother's precepts under foot, to spare my enemy that cross of an unworthy love; nay, unite her to thyself, child as thou art, that I might have a daughter-in-law who hates me! I will make thee repent of thy sport, and the savor of thy marriage bitter. There is one who shall chasten this body of thine, put out thy torch and unstring thy bow. Not till she has plucked forth that hair, into which so oft these hands have smoothed the golden light, and sheared away thy wings, shall I feel the injury done me avenged." And with this she hastened in anger from the doors.

And Ceres and Juno met her, and sought to know the meaning of her troubled countenance. "Ye come in season," she cried; "I pray you, find for me Psyche. It must needs be that ye have heard the disgrace of my house." And they, ignorant of what was done, would have soothed her anger, saying, "What fault, Mistress, hath thy son committed, that thou wouldst destroy the girl he loves? Knowest thou not that he is now of age? Because he wears his years so lightly must he seem to thee ever but a child? Wilt thou forever thus pry into the pastimes of thy son, always accusing his wantonness, and blaming in him those delicate wiles which are all thine own?" Thus, in secret fear of the boy's bow, did they seek to please him with their gracious patronage. But Venus, angry at their light taking of her wrongs, turned her back upon them, and with hasty steps made her way once more to the sea.

Meanwhile Psyche, tossed in soul, wandering hither and thither, rested not night or day in the pursuit of her husband, desiring, if she might not soothe his anger by the endearments of a wife, at the least to propitiate him with the prayers of a handmaid. And seeing a certain temple on the top of a high mountain, she said, "Who knows whether yonder place be not the abode of my lord?" Thither, therefore, she turned her steps, hastening now the more because desire and hope pressed her on, weary as she was with the labors of the way, and so, painfully measuring out the highest ridges of the mountain, drew near to the sacred couches. She sees ears of wheat, in heaps or twisted into chaplets; ears of barley also, with sickles and all the instruments of harvest, lying there in disorder, thrown at random from the hands of the laborers in the great heat. These she curiously sets apart, one by one, duly ordering them; for she said within herself, "I may not neglect the shrines, nor the holy service, of any god there be, but must rather win by supplication the kindly mercy of them all."

And Ceres found her bending sadly upon her task, and cried aloud, "Alas, Psyche! Venus, in the furiousness of her anger, tracks thy footsteps through the world, seeking for thee to pay her the utmost penalty; and thou, thinking of anything rather than thine own safety, hast taken on thee the care of what belongs to me!" Then Psyche fell down at her feet, and sweeping the floor with her hair, washing the footsteps of the goddess in her tears, besought her mercy, with many prayers: "By the gladdening rites of harvest, by the lighted lamps and mystic marches of the marriage and mysterious invention of thy daughter Proserpine, and by all beside that the holy place of Attica veils in silence, minister, I pray thee, to the sorrowful heart of Psyche! Suffer me to hide myself but for a few days among the heaps of corn, till time have softened the anger of the goddess, and my strength, outworn in my long travail, be recovered by a little rest."

But Ceres answered her, "Truly thy tears move me, and I would fain help thee; only I dare not incur the ill-will of my kinswoman. Depart hence as quickly as may be." And Psyche, repelled against hope, afflicted now with twofold sorrow, making her way back again, beheld among the half-lighted woods of the valley below a sanctuary builded with cunning art. And that she might lose no way of hope, howsoever doubtful, she drew near to the sacred doors. She sees there gifts of price, and garments fixed upon the doorposts and to the branches of the trees, wrought with letters of gold which told the name of the goddess to whom they were dedicated, with thanksgiving for that she had done. So, with bent knee and hands laid about the glowing altar, she prayed, saying, "Sister and spouse of Jupiter! be thou to these my desperate fortunes Juno the Auspicious! I know that thou dost willingly help those in travail with child; deliver me from the peril that is upon me." And as she prayed thus, Juno in the majesty of her godhead was straightway present, and answered, "Would that I might incline favorably to thee: but against the will of Venus, whom I have ever loved as a daughter, I may not, for very shame, grant thy prayer."

And Psyche, dismayed by this new shipwreck of her hope, communed thus with herself, "Whither, from the midst of the snares that beset me, shall I take my way once more? In what dark solitude shall I hide me from the all-seeing eye of Venus? What if I put on at length a man's courage, and yielding myself unto her as my mistress, soften by a humility not yet too late the fierceness of her purpose? Who knows but that I may find him also whom my soul seeketh after, in the abode of his mother?"

And Venus, renouncing all earthly aid in her search, prepared to return to heaven. She ordered the chariot to be made ready, wrought for her by Vulcan as a marriage-gift, with a cunning of hand which had left his work so much the richer by the weight of gold it lost under his tool. From the multitude which housed the bed-chamber of their mistress, white doves came forth, and with joyful motions bent their painted necks beneath the yoke. Behind it, with playful riot, the sparrows sped onward, and other birds sweet of song, making known by their soft notes the approach of the goddess. Eagle and cruel hawk alarmed not the quireful family of Venus. And the clouds broke away, as the uttermost ether opened to receive her, daughter and goddess, with great joy.

And Venus passed straightway to the house of Jupiter to beg from him the service of Mercury, the god of speech. And Jupiter refused not her prayer. And Venus and Mercury descended from heaven together; and as they went, the former said to the latter, "Thou knowest, my brother of Arcady, that never at any time have I done anything without thy help; for how long time, moreover, I have sought a certain maiden in vain. And now nought remains but that by thy heraldry, I proclaim a reward for whomsoever shall find her. Do thou my bidding quickly." And therewith she conveyed to him a little scrip, in the which was written the name of Psyche, with other things; and so returned home.

And Mercury failed not in his office; but departing into all lands, proclaimed that whosoever delivered up to Venus the fugitive girl should receive from herself seven kisses — one thereof full of the inmost honey of her throat. With that the doubt of Psyche was ended. And now, as she came near to the doors of Venus, one of the household, whose name was Use-and-Wont, ran out to her, crying, "Hast thou learned, Wicked Maid! now at last! that thou hast a mistress?" and seizing her roughly by the hair, drew her into the presence of Venus. And when Venus saw her, she cried out, saying, "Thou hast deigned, then, to make thy salutations to thy mother-in-law. Now will I in turn treat thee as becometh a dutiful daughter-in-law."

And she took barley and millet and poppyseed, every kind of grain and seed, and mixed them together, and laughed, and said to her: "Methinks so plain a maiden can earn lovers only by industrious ministry: now will I also make trial of thy service. Sort me this heap of seed, the one kind from the others, grain by grain; and get thy task done before the evening." And Psyche, stunned by the cruelty of her bidding, was silent, and moved not her hand to the inextricable heap. And there came forth a little ant, which had understanding of the difficulty of her task, and took pity upon the consort of the god of Love; and he ran deftly hither and thither, and called together the whole army of his fellows. "Have pity," he cried, "nimble scholars of the Earth, Mother of all things! — have pity upon the wife of Love, and hasten to help her in her perilous effort." Then, one upon the other, the hosts of the insect people hurried together; and they sorted asunder the whole heap of seed, separating every grain after its kind, and so departed quickly out of sight.

And at nightfall Venus returned, and seeing that task finished with so wonderful diligence, she cried, "The work is not thine, thou naughty maid, but his in whose eyes thou hast found favor." And calling her again in the morning, "See now the grove," she said, "beyond yonder torrent. Certain sheep feed there, whose fleeces shine with gold. Fetch me straightway a lock of that precious stuff, having gotten it as thou mayst."

And Psyche went forth willingly, not to obey the command of Venus, but even to seek a rest from her labor in the depths of the river. But from the river, the green reed, lowly mother of music, spake to her: "O Psyche! pollute not these waters by self-destruction, nor approach that terrible flock; for, as the heat groweth, they wax fierce. Lie down under yon planetree, till the quiet of the river's breath have soothed them. Thereafter thou mayst shake down the fleecy gold from the trees of the grove, for it holdeth by the leaves."

And Psyche, instructed thus by the simple reed, in the humanity of its heart, filled her bosom with the soft golden stuff, and returned to Venus. But the goddess smiled bitterly, and said to her, "Well know I who was the author of this thing also. I will make further trial of thy discretion, and the boldness of thy heart. Seest thou the utmost peak of yonder steep mountain? The dark stream which flows down thence waters the Stygian fields, and swells the flood of Cocytus. Bring me now, in this little urn, a draught from its innermost source." And therewith she put into her hands a vessel of wrought crystal.

And Psyche set forth in haste on her way to the mountain, looking there at last to find the end of her hapless life. But when she came to the region which borders on the cliff that was shown to her, she understood the deadly nature of her task. From a great rock, steep and slippery, a horrible river of water poured forth, falling straightway by a channel exceeding narrow into the unseen gulf below. And lo! creeping from the rocks on either hand, angry serpents, with their long necks and sleepless eyes. The very waters found a voice and bade her depart, in smothered cries of, "Depart hence!" and, "What doest thou here? Look around thee!" and, "Destruction is upon thee!" And then sense left her, in the immensity of her peril, as one changed to stone.

Yet not even then did the distress of this innocent soul escape the steady eye of a gentle providence. For the bird of Jupiter spread his wings and took flight to her, and asked her, "Didst thou think, simple one, even thou! that thou couldst steal one drop of that relentless stream, the holy river of Styx, terrible even to the gods? But give me thine urn." And the bird took the urn, and filled it at the source, and returned to her quickly from among the teeth of the serpents, bringing with him of the waters, all unwilling—nay! warning him to depart away and not molest them.

And she, receiving the urn with great joy, ran back quickly that she might deliver it to Venus, and yet again satisfied not the angry goddess. "My child!" she said, "in this one thing further must thou serve me. Take now this tiny casket, and get thee down even unto hell, and deliver it to Proserpine. Tell her that Venus would have of her beauty so much at least as may suffice for but one day's use, that beauty she possessed erewhile being forworn and spoiled, through her tendance upon the sick-bed of her son; and be not slow in returning."

And Psyche perceived there the last ebbing of her fortune—that she was now thrust openly upon death, who must go down, of her own motion, to Hades and the Shades. And straightway she climbed to the top of an exceeding high tower, thinking within herself, "I will cast myself down thence: so shall I descend most quickly into the kingdom of the dead." And the tower again broke forth into speech: "Wretched Maid! Wretched Maid! Wilt thou destroy thyself? If the breath quit thy body, then wilt thou indeed go down into Hades, but by no means return hither. Listen to me. Among the pathless wilds not far from this place lies a certain mountain, and therein one of hell's vent-holes. Through the breach a rough way lies open, following which thou wilt come, by straight course, to the castle of Orcus. And thou must not go empty-handed. Take in each hand a morsel of barley-bread, soaked in hydromel; and in thy mouth two pieces of money. And when thou shalt be now well onward in the way of death, then wilt thou overtake a lame ass laden with wood, and a lame driver, who will pray thee reach him certain cords to fasten the burden which is falling from the ass; but be thou cautious to pass on in silence. And soon as thou comest to the river of the dead, Charon, in that crazy bark he has, will put thee over upon the further side.

"There is greed even among the dead; and thou shalt deliver to him, for the ferrying, one of those two pieces of money, in such wise that he take it with his hand from between thy lips. And as thou passest over the stream, a dead old man, rising on the water, will put up to thee his moldering hands, and pray thee draw him into the ferry-boat. But beware thou yield not to unlawful pity.

"When thou shalt be come over, and art upon the causeway, certain aged women, spinning, will cry to thee to lend thy hand to their work; and beware again that thou take no part therein; for this also is the snare of Venus, whereby she would cause thee to cast away one at least of those cakes thou bearest in thy hands. And think not that a slight matter; for the loss of either one of them will be to thee the losing of the light of day. For a watch-dog exceeding fierce lies ever before the threshold of that lonely house of Proserpine. Close his mouth with one of thy cakes; so shalt thou pass by him, and enter straightway into the presence of Proserpine herself. Then do thou deliver thy message, and taking what she shall give thee, return back again; offering the watch-dog the other cake, and to the ferryman that other piece of money thou hast in thy mouth. After this manner mayst thou return again beneath the stars. But withal, I charge thee, think not to look into, nor open, the casket thou bearest, with that treasure of the beauty of the divine countenance hidden therein."

So spake the stones of the tower; and Psyche delayed not, but proceeding diligently after the manner enjoined, entered into the house of Proserpine, at whose feet she sat down humbly, and would have neither the delicate couch nor that divine food the goddess offered her, but did straightway the business of Venus. And Proserpine filled the casket secretly, and shut the lid, and delivered it to Psyche, who fled therewith from Hades with new strength. But coming back into the light of day, even as she hasted now to the ending of her service, she was seized by a rash curiosity. "Lo! now," she said within herself, "my simpleness! who bearing in my hands the divine loveliness, heed not to touch myself with a particle at least therefrom, that I may please the more, by the favor of it, my fair one, my beloved." Even as she spoke, she lifted the lid; and behold! within, neither beauty, nor anything beside, save sleep only, the sleep of the dead, which took hold upon her, filling all her members with its drowsy vapor, so that she lay down in the way and moved not, as in the slumber of death.

And Cupid being healed of his wound, because he would endure no longer the absence of her he loved, gliding through the narrow window of the chamber where he was holden, his pinions being now repaired by a little rest, fled forth swiftly upon them, and coming to the place where Psyche was, shook that sleep away from her, and set him in his prison again, awakening her with the innocent point of his arrow: "Lo! thine old error again," he said, "which had like once more to have destroyed thee! But do thou now what is lacking of the command to my mother: the rest shall be my care." With these words, the lover rose upon the air; and being consumed inwardly with the greatness of his love, penetrated with vehement wing into the highest place of heaven, to lay his cause before the father of the gods. And the father of the gods took his hand in his, and kissed his face, and said to him, "At no time, my son, hast thou regarded me with due honor. Often hast thou vexed my bosom, wherein lies the disposition of the stars, with those busy darts of thine. Nevertheless, because thou hast grown up between these mine hands, I will accomplish thy desire." And straightway he bade Mercury call the gods together; and, the council-chamber being filled, sitting upon a high throne, "Ye gods," he said, "all ye whose names are in the white book of the Muses, ye know yonder lad. It seems good to me that his youthful heats should by some means be restrained. And that all occasion may be taken from him, I would even confine him in the bonds of marriage. He has chosen and embraced a mortal maiden. Let him have fruit of his love, and possess her forever."

Thereupon he bade Mercury produce Psyche in heaven; and holding out to her his ambrosial cup, "Take it," he said, "and live forever; nor shall Cupid ever depart from thee." And the gods sat down together to the marriage-feast. On the first couch lay the bridegroom, and Psyche in his bosom. His rustic serving-boy bare the wine to Jupiter; and Bacchus to the rest. The Seasons crimsoned all things with their roses. Apollo sang to the lyre, while a little Pan prattled on his reeds, and Venus danced very sweetly to the soft music. Thus—with due rites—did Psyche pass into the power of

Cupid; and from them was born the daughter whom men call Voluptas.

—*From the Metamorphoses, or the Golden Ass, of Lucius Apuleius, Roman (second century), translated by Walter Pater in Marius the Epicurean.*

~ ✿ ~

The Story of Malchus

ST. JEROME

THOSE who are going to fight a sea-battle prepare for it beforehand in a harbour on calm water. They turn the tiller, ply the oars, make ready the hooks and grappling irons. They draw up the soldiers on the deck and train them to stand steady on a slippery surface with one foot in the air. And then they feel no fear in the real encounter, since they have gained experience in their sham fights. So I, who have long held my peace—for silence was laid upon me by one who found my words a punishment—now desire some previous practice on a small work, so that I may wipe the rust from my tongue before I approach the wider field of history. For, if God grants me life and if my critics will allow me peace now that I have fled to the seclusion of a monastery, I propose to write a history of the church of Christ from the coming of our Saviour down to our own days, that is, from the apostles to the dregs of this present age. I shall describe by what means and by whose agency the church came into existence, and how, as it gained strength, it grew by persecution and was crowned with martyrdom, and then, coming to the Christian emperors, increased in power and wealth but decreased in virtue. But of this elsewhere. Now to the matter in hand.

Maronia is a little village about thirty miles from Antioch the capital of Syria. When as a young man I was living in that country, after having had several owners and patrons the hamlet had passed into the hands of my friend the Bishop of Evagrius, whose name I now give to show the source of my information. Well, at that time an old man was living there called Malchus, a name which in Syriac means "king," a Syrian by birth and speech, in fact a genuine son of the soil. His house companion was an old woman very decrepit who seemed to be at death's door. The pair were devotedly pious and so haunted the church door that you might have thought them the Zacharias and Elizabeth of the Gospel except for the fact that they had no John. I made careful inquiries of the villagers as to what was the bond between them; was it marriage, kinship or, a spiritual union? All with one accord replied that they were righteous folk well pleasing to God, and added further some strange details about them. Attracted by their story I approached the man and, inquiring eagerly about the truth of what I heard, learnt the following facts.

My son, the old man said, I was my parents' only child and used to farm a piece of ground at Nisibis. As I was the sole representative of our line and the family heir, my people tried to force me into marriage, but I told them that I would rather be a monk. The mere fact that at last I ran away from home and parents will prove to you what threats were used by my father and what persuasions by my mother to make me betray my chastity. I could not go eastwards, since Persia was close by and the Roman soldiers were on guard; and so I turned my steps to the west, taking with me a little store of provisions just sufficient to ward off destitution. To cut a long tale short, I came at last to the desert of Chalcis between Immae and Beroa to the south. There I found some monks under whose direction I placed myself, earning a livelihood by manual labour and curbing the wantonness of the flesh by fasting; but after some years a longing came over me to return to my native place. I had heard that my father was dead, and I thought that I would comfort my widowed mother as long as she lived, and then sell my little property and give one-third to the poor, one-third to the monastery, and—why blush to confess my lack of faith?—keep one-third to supply myself with comforts.

My abbot cried out that it was a temptation of the devil, and that under pretext of a good deed some snare of the old enemy lay concealed. This is a case, he said, of the dog returning to his vomit; many monks had been deceived in this fashion, for the devil never showed himself openly. He set before me many examples from the Scriptures; among others how at the beginnnig he overthrew Adam and Eve by giving them the hope of becoming gods. Finally, when arguments proved useless, he fell upon his knees and begged me not to forsake him to my own destruction, nor look back after putting my hand to the plough. Alas, alas! I won a fatal victory and disregarded his advice; for I thought that he was seeking, not my salvation, but his own comfort. He followed me from the monastery as though he were walking at my funeral, and when at last he bade me farewell he said: "I see that you are branded as a son of Satan. I ask not your reasons. I do not accept your excuses. The sheep that leaves the fold is at once exposed to the jaws of the wolf."

As you go from Beroa to Edessa there is a piece of lonely country near the high road, across which the Saracens who have no fixed abode are continually roaming in all directions. Through fear of them travellers in that district usually assemble in a party so that by mutual assistance they may escape impending danger. In my company there were about seventy persons, men, women, and children, old and young. Suddenly the Ishmaelites attacked us, riding on horses and camels. Their long hair was bound with fillets, their bodies were half naked, their cloaks trailed behind them, and they wore loose boots. They had slung their quivers over their shoulders and, carrying their bows unstrung, they brandished long spears; for they had come not to fight, but to plunder. We were seized, divided, and carried off in different directions. I, meanwhile, repenting too late of my plans and very far now from entering into possession of my inheritance, was assigned as slave to a master together with one other woman captive. We were led off, or, rather, carried high on camels' backs, through a desert waste, expecting every moment to fall and hanging rather than sitting in our place. Our only food was half-raw meat, our drink camel's milk.

At length we crossed a wide river and came to the interior of the desert, where we were bidden to make obeisance to our master's wife and children and bow our heads humbly to them, as is the custom with that people. There like a prison captive I changed my dress; that is, I learned to go about naked. For the excessive heat rendered any covering but a loin cloth unbearable. Some sheep were given me to feed; and when I came to compare troubles I found that I had at least one advantage; I seldom saw my masters or my fellow-slaves. I thought that I was in somewhat the same case as that holy man Jacob, and I remembered the life of Moses; for both of these had once been shepherds in the desert. My food was fresh cheese and milk; I prayed continually and sung the psalms I had learned in the monastery. My captivity was a pleasure to me, and I rendered grateful thanks to God's judgment, inasmuch as I had found in the desert that monk whom I was on the point of losing in my own country.

But how true is it that with the devil safety is impossible! How manifold and ineffable are his snares! Hid though I was, his malice found me out. My master, seeing that his flock was growing and finding no dishonesty in me — for I knew that the apostle bade us serve our masters as faithfully as we serve God — wished to reward me and thus secure my fidelity. Accordingly, he gave me the slave woman who had previously been taken captive with me. I refused to take her and said I was a Christian and that it was not lawful for me to have a woman for wife whose husband was still alive; for her husband had been taken prisoner with us and carried off by another owner. At this my master went mad with anger and, drawing his sword, came furiously at me. Indeed, if I had not at once stretched out my hand and taken possession of the woman he would have killed me on the spot.

Soon night came on, for me all too early, a night darker than its wont. I led my new bride into a tumbledown cave, with grief as bridesmaid, both of us shrinking from one another although we did not confess it. Then truly I realized that I was a slave, and flinging myself upon the ground began to lament the monk that I had ceased to be. "Was it for this misery that my life was spared?" I cried. "Have my sins brought me to this, that I who have lived a virgin should in my old age take a wife? What avails it me to have scorned parents, country, and estate for the Lord's sake, if now I do the thing which I scorned them to avoid. Unless indeed it is because I regretted my native land that I now have these troubles to bear! What are we to do, my soul? Die, or conquer? Wait for the hand of God, or stab ourselves with our own sword? Do thou turn the blade upon thyself: the soul's death is more to be feared than the body's. Chastity even if preserved has its own martyrdom. Let the witness to Christ lie unburied in the desert: I will be both persecutor and martyr."

So speaking, I drew my sword, which gleamed still in the darkness, and turning its point towards me said: "Farewell, unhappy woman; take me as a martyr rather than as a husband." At that she threw herself at my feet and cried: "I pray you by Jesus Christ and by the dread compulsion of this hour, do not shed your blood and make me a criminal. If you are resolved on death, turn your sword against me first. Let that be our union. Even if my husband came back to me I should cling to the chastity which I have learned in captivity. I would die rather than lose it now. Why kill yourself to prevent a union with me? I should kill myself if you insisted on our mating. Take me, therefore, as your partner in chastity, and love the bond of the spirit more than you could ever love the bond of the flesh. Let our masters fancy that you are my husband, but let Christ know you for my brother. We shall easily convince people of our marriage when they see us so loving." I confess I was astonished: I had admired the woman's virtue before, but I loved her as a wife still more. Yet I never looked upon her naked body; I never touched her flesh; I feared to lose in peace that which I had kept in battle. In this strange wedlock many days passed. Our marriage had increased our master's liking for us, and he had no fear that we should run away. Indeed, I was sometimes absent for a whole month, a faithful shepherd in the wilderness.

A long time passed, and as I sat alone one day in the desert with nothing in sight save earth and sky, I began quietly to turn things over in my mind. Among other things I called back to memory the monks with whom I had lived, and especially the look of the father who had taught me, detained me, and lost me. While busied with these thoughts I suddenly noticed a crowd of ants swarming over a narrow pathway. You could see that the loads they carried were larger than themselves. Some with their mandibles were dragging grass seed along; others were throwing the earth out of pits they had made and banking it up to prevent an overflow of water. One party, mindful of the winter's approach, were cutting off the tips of the grain they had brought in, so that the damp might not turn their store into grass. Another company with mournful ceremonies were carrying out the bodies of their dead comrades. And, what is especially strange in such a host, those who were coming out did not hinder those who were going in; nay rather, if they saw anyone sink beneath the weight of his load, they would put their shoulders to it and assist him. To be brief, that day gave me a delightful entertainment.

The result of it was that I remembered how Solomon sends us to the shrewdness of the ant and by its example rouses our sluggish wits. I began to be weary of captivity and to regret the monastery cells, and long to take pattern by these ants who work for the community, and, since nothing belongs to anyone, all things belong to all. When I returned to my lodging my wife met me, and my looks could not disguise the sadness that I felt. She asked why I was so depressed. I told her the reasons and urged her to escape. She made no objection. I begged her to say nothing. She gave me her word. We spoke all the time in whispers, wavering between hope and fear. I had in my flock two particularly large he-goats: these I killed, made their skins into leather bottles, and prepared their flesh as food on our way. In the early evening, when our masters thought we had retired to rest, we set off, taking with us the skins and portions of the meat. When we reached the river, which was ten miles off, we inflated the skins and getting astride them trusted ourselves to the water, rowing slowly with our feet for oars, so that the stream should carry us down to a point on the further bank much below that at which we had embarked, and so our pursuers would lose track of us. In the crossing, however, part of our meat became sodden with water, and part was carried away, so that we had scarcely three days' food to depend on. We drank till we could drink no more, in preparation for the thirst that we knew would come upon us, and then hurried away, looking continually behind us, and moving more by night than by day for fear of an ambush of the roaming Saracens and also because of the sun's excessive heat. Even now I shudder when I recall our misery; and though my mind is at ease every part of my body is trembling.

On the fourth day of our flight we saw in the dim distance two men on camels riding quickly towards us. I foreboded trouble at once, the sun turned dark before my eyes, and I thought that my master would certainly put us to death. We realized that our footsteps in the sand had betrayed us; but at the height of our fear we suddenly saw on our right a cavern extending far underground. We entered it in deadly fear of venomous beasts – for vipers, basilisks, scorpions, and such like are wont to frequent these dark places out of the heat of the sun – and stopping just inside its mouth took refuge in a pit on the left, not going any further in lest we should come upon destruction while flying from it. We thought to ourselves: "If the Lord helps us in our trouble, we are saved. If he heeds us not because of our sins, we have a grave here." Suddenly we saw our master and one of his slaves standing in front of the cave quite close to us. Our footsteps had again betrayed us, and they had discovered our hiding-place. What do you imagine were our feelings, what our terror? Ah, how much more cruel is the expectation of death than death itself! Even now my tongue stammers with the terror and distress which then I knew.

I fancy that I hear my master calling and am afraid to mutter.

Well, he sent the slave to drag us from the cavern, while he himself holding the camels waited for us to come out with his sword ready. The man came in for about five or six feet, and we in our hiding place saw his back though he did not see us, for the nature of the eye is such that people coming into the dark from sunlight find themselves quite blinded. His voice echoed through the cave: "Come out, you rogues; come out and die; why are you standing there? Why do you delay? Come out; your master calls and patiently awaits you." He was still speaking when lo! in the dark we saw a lioness spring upon the fellow, grip him by the throat, and drag him all bloody into the inner cave. Good Jesus! How great then was our terror and our joy! We beheld our enemy perish while our owner stood in ignorance of his fate.

Soon, however, the master himself, impatient of delay and suspecting that one man was no match for two, rushed furiously angry into the cave. Sword in hand he fiercely upbraided his slave's slowness; but before he could reach our hiding place he, too, was seized by the wild beast. Who would ever have thought that before our very eyes a brute would fight for us? Our first fears were thus dispelled, but we had still facing us the prospect of a death like theirs, although we preferred the rage of the lioness to the anger of the man. We trembled in our retreat and not daring to move awaited the issue, only protected by our consciousness of chastity as by a wall. Early in the morning the lioness, afraid of a trap and aware that she had been seen, took up her cub in her teeth and carried it away, leaving us in possession. We did not have enough confidence to come out at once; and even after a long wait whenever we thought of leaving we pictured to ourselves the horror of meeting her again.

Well, we got rid of our fright at last, and at the end of the day, towards evening we sallied forth and saw the camels – called dromedaries because of their excessive speed – quietly chewing the cud. We got on their backs and after recruiting our strength with the fresh provisions started to cross the desert. On the tenth day we arrived at a Roman camp, and being presented to the tribune told him the whole story. He sent us on to Sabianus, general in command of Mesopotamia, and we there sold the camels.

My dear old abbot by this time was sleeping in the Lord; I therefore came back here and joined the monks for a time, handing over my companion to the care of the virgins; for though I loved her as a sister, I could not trust myself with her as a sister.

I was quite a young man and Malchus was old when he related all this to me. I in my old age have now repeated it to you, a story of chastity for the chaste. I exhort you, virgins, to guard your chastity. Tell this tale to those that come after, so that they may know that even in the midst of swords and deserts and wild beasts virtue is never made a captive, and that he who has surrendered himself to Christ may be slain but cannot be conquered.

—*Saint Jerome (Eusebius Sophronius Hieronymus) (c. 340–420), translated from the Latin by F. A. Wright.*

The Story of Griselda

BOCCACCIO

THERE was in olden days a certain Marquis of Saluzzo, Gualtieri by name, a young man, but head of the house, who, having neither wife nor child, passed his time in nought else but in hawking and hunting, and of taking a wife and begetting children had no thought; wherein he should have been accounted very wise. But his vassals, brooking it ill, did oftentimes entreat him to take a wife, that he might not die without an heir, and they be left without a lord; offering to find him one of such a pattern, and of such parentage, that he might marry with good hope, and be well content with the sequel. To whom, "My friends," replied Gualtieri, "you enforce me to that which I had resolved never to do, seeing how hard it is to find a wife whose ways accord well with one's own, and how plentiful is the supply of such as run counter thereto, and how grievous a life he leads who chances upon a lady that matches ill with him. And to say that you think to know the daughters by the qualities of their fathers and mothers, and thereby — so you would argue — to provide me with a wife to my liking, is but folly; for I wot not how you may penetrate the secrets of their mothers so as to know their fathers; and granted that you do know them, daughters oftentimes resemble neither of their parents. However, as you are minded to rivet these fetters upon me, I am content that so it be; and that I may have no cause to reproach any but myself, should it turn out ill, I am resolved that my wife shall be of my own choosing. But of this rest assured, that, no matter whom I choose, if she receive not from you the honor due to a lady, you shall prove to your great cost how sorely I resent being thus constrained by your importunity to take a wife against my will."

The worthy men replied that they were well content, so only he would marry without more ado. And Gualtieri, who had long noted with approval the mien of a poor girl that dwelt on a farm hard by his house, and found her fair enough, deemed that with her he might pass a tolerably happy life. Wherefore he sought no further, but forthwith resolved to marry her; and having sent for her father, who was a very poor man, he contracted with him to take her to wife. Which done, Gualtieri assembled all the friends he had in those parts, and, "My friends," quoth he, "you were and are minded that I should take a wife, and rather to comply with your wishes than for any desire that I had to marry, I have made up my mind to do so. You remember the promise you gave me, to wit, that, whomsoever I should take, you would pay her the honor due to a lady, which promise I now require you to keep, the time being come when I am to keep mine. I have found hard by here a maiden after mine own heart, whom I purpose to take to wife, and to bring hither to my house in the course of a few days. Wherefore bethink you how you may make the nuptial feast splendid, and welcome her with all honor, that I may confess myself satisfied with your observance of your promise, as you will be with my observance of mine."

The worthy men, one and all, answered with alacrity that they were well content, and that, whoever she might be, they would entreat her as a lady, and pay her all due honor as such. After which, they all addressed them to make goodly and grand and gladsome celebration of the event, as did also Gualtieri. He arranged for a wedding most stately and fair, and bade thereto a goodly number of his friends and kinsfolk, and great gentlemen, and others, of the neighborhood; and therewithal he caused many a fine and costly robe to be cut and fashioned to the figure of a girl who seemed to him of the like proportions as the girl that he proposed to wed; and laid in store, besides, of girdles and rings, with a costly and beautiful crown, and all the other paraphernalia of a bride.

The day that he appointed for the wedding being come, about half tierce he got him to horse with as many as had come to do him honor, and having made all needful dispositions, "Gentlemen," quoth he, "'tis time to go bring home the bride." And so away he rode with his company to the village; where, being come to the house of the girl's father, they found her returning from the spring with a bucket of water, making all the haste she could that she might afterwards go with the other woman to see Gualtieri's bride come by; whom Gualtieri no sooner saw than he called her by her name, to wit, Griselda, and asked her where her father was. To whom she modestly made answer, "My lord, he is in the house."

Whereupon Gualtieri dismounted, and having bidden the rest await him without, entered the cottage alone, and meeting her father, whose name was Giannucolo, "I am come," quoth he, "to wed Griselda, but first of all there are some matters I would learn from her own lips in thy presence."

He then asked her, whether, if he took her to wife, she would study to comply with his wishes, and be not wroth, no matter what he might say or do, and be obedient, with not a few other questions of a like sort; to all which she answered, "Aye."

Whereupon Gualtieri took her by the hand, led her forth, and before the eyes of all his company, and as many other folk as were there, caused her to strip naked, and let bring the garments that he had had fashioned for her, and had her forthwith arrayed therein, and upon her unkempt head let set a crown; and then, while all wondered, "Gentlemen," quoth he, "this is she whom I purpose to make my wife, so she be minded to have me for husband."

Then, she standing abashed and astonished, he turned to her, saying, "Griselda, wilt thou have me for thy husband?"

To whom, "Aye, my lord," answered she.

"And I will have thee to wife," said he, and married her before them all. And having set her upon a palfrey, he brought her home with pomp.

The wedding was fair and stately, and had he married a daughter of the King of France, the feast could not have been more splendid. It seemed as if, with the change of her garb, the bride had acquired a new dignity of mind and mien. She was, as we have said, fair of form and feature; and therewithal she was now grown so engaging and gracious and debonair, that she showed no longer as the shepherdess and daughter of Giannucolo, but as the daughter of some noble lord, insomuch that she caused as many as had known her before to marvel. Moreover, she was so obedient and devoted to her husband that he deemed himself the happiest and luckiest man in the world. And likewise so gracious and kindly was she to her husband's vassals that there was none of them but loved her more dearly than himself, and was zealous to do her honor and prayed for her welfare and prosperity and aggrandizement, and instead of, as erstwhile, saying that Gualtieri had done foolishly to take her to wife, now averred that he had not his like in the world for wisdom and discernment, for that, save to him, her noble qualities would ever have remained hidden under her sorry apparel and the garb of the peasant girl. And in short she so comported herself as in no long time to bring it to pass that, not only in the marquisate, but far and wide besides, her virtues and her admirable conversation were matter of common talk, and, if aught had been said to the disadvantage of her husband when he married her, the judgment was now altogether to the contrary effect.

She had not been long with Gualtieri before she conceived; and in due time she was delivered of a girl, whereat Gualtieri made great cheer. But, soon after, a strange humor took possession of him, to wit, to put her patience to the proof by prolonged and intolerable hard usage; wherefore he began by afflicting her with his gibes, putting on a vexed air, and telling her that his vassals were most sorely dissatisfied with her by reason of her base condition, and all the more so since they saw that she was a mother, and that they did nought but most ruefully murmur at the birth of a daughter. Whereto Griselda, without the least change of countenance or sign of discomposure, made answer, "My lord, do with me as thou mayest deem best for thine own honor and comfort, for well I wot that I am of less account than they, and unworthy of this honorable estate to which of thy courtesy thou hast advanced me." By which answer Gualtieri was well pleased, witting that she was in no degree puffed up with pride by his or any other's honorable entreatment of her.

A while afterwards, having in general terms given his wife to understand that the vassals could not endure her daughter, he sent her a message by a servant. So the servant came, and "Madame," quoth he with a dolorous mien, "so I value my life, I must needs do my lord's bidding. He has bidden me to take your daughter and —" He said no more, but the lady by what she heard, and read in his face, and remembered of her husband's words, understood that he was bidden to put the child to death.

Whereupon she presently took the child from the cradle, and having kissed and blessed her, albeit she was very sore at heart, she changed not countenance, but placed it in the servant's arms, saying, "See that thou leave nought undone that my lord and thine has charged thee to do, but leave her nought so that the beasts and the birds devour her, unless he have so bidden thee." So the servant took the child, and told Gualtieri what the lady had said; and Gualtieri, marveling at her constancy, sent him with the child to Bologna, to one of his kinswomen, whom he besought to rear and educate the child with all care, but never to let it be known whose child she was.

Soon after it befell that the lady again conceived, and in due time was delivered of a son, whereat Gualtieri was overjoyed. But, not content with what he had done, he now even more poignantly afflicted the lady; and one day with a ruffled mien, "Wife," quoth he, "since thou gavest birth to this boy, I may on no wise live in peace with my vassals, so bitterly do they reproach me that a grandson of Giannucolo is to succeed me as their lord; and therefore I fear that, so I be not minded to be sent a-packing hence, I must even do herein as I did before, and in the end put thee away, and take another wife."

The lady heard him patiently, and answered only, "My lord, study how thou mayest content thee and best please thyself, and waste no thought upon me; for there is nought I desire save in so far as I know that 'tis thy pleasure."

Not many days after, Gualtieri, in like manner as he had sent for the daughter, sent for the son, and having made a show of putting him to death, provided for his, as for the girl's nurture, at Bologna. Whereat the lady showed no more discomposure of countenance or speech than at the loss of her daughter, which Gualtieri found passing strange, and inly affirmed that there was never another woman in the world that would have so done. And but that he had marked that she was most tenderly affectionate towards her children, while 'twas well pleasing to him, he had supposed that she was tired of them; whereas he knew that 'twas of her discretion that she so did. His vassals, who believed that he had put the children to death, held him mightily to blame for his cruelty, and felt the utmost compassion for the lady. She, however, said never aught to the ladies that condoled with her on the death of her children, but that the pleasure of him that had begotten them was her pleasure likewise.

Years not a few had passed since the girl's birth, when Gualtieri at length deemed the time come to put his wife's patience to the final proof. Accordingly, in the presence of a great company of his vassals he declared that on no wise might he longer brook to have Griselda to wife, that he confessed that in taking her he had done a sorry thing and the act of a stripling, and that he therefore meant to do what he could to procure the Pope's dispensation to put Griselda away, and take another wife; for which cause being much upbraided by many worthy men, he made no other answer but only that needs must it so be. Whereof the lady being apprised, and now deeming that she must look to go back to her father's house, and perchance tend the sheep, as she had aforetime, and see him, to whom she was utterly devoted, engrossed by another woman, did inly bewail herself right sorely; but still with the same composed mien with which she had borne Fortune's former buffets, she set herself to endure this last outrage.

Nor was it long before Gualtieri by counterfeit letters, which he caused to be sent to him from Rome, made his vassals believe that the Pope had thereby given him a dispensation to put Griselda away, and take another wife. Wherefore, having caused her to be brought before him, he said to her in the presence of not a few, "Wife, by license granted me by the Pope, I am now free to put thee away, and take another wife; and, for that my forebears have always been great gentlemen and lords of these parts, whereas thine have ever been husbandmen, I purpose that thou go back to Giannucolo's house with the dowry that thou broughtest me; whereupon I shall bring home a lady that I have found, and who is meet to be my wife."

'Twas not without travail most grievous that the lady, as she heard this announcement, got the better of her woman's nature, and suppressing her tears, made answer, "My lord, I ever knew that my low degree was on no wise congruous with your nobility, and acknowledged that the rank I had with you was of your and God's bestowal, nor did I ever make as if it were mine by gift, or so esteem it, but still accounted it as a loan. 'Tis your pleasure to recall it, and therefore it should be, and is, my pleasure to render it up to you. So, here is your ring, with which you espoused me; take it back. You bid me take with me the dowry that I brought you; which to do will require neither paymaster on your part nor purse nor pack-horse on mine; for I am not unmindful that naked was I when you first had me. And if you deem it seemly that the body in which I have borne children, by you begotten, be beheld of all, naked will I depart; but yet, I pray you, be pleased, in guerdon of the virginity that I brought you and take not away, to suffer me to bear hence upon my back a single shift — I crave no more — beside my dowry."

There was nought of which Gualtieri was so fain as to weep; but yet setting his face as a flint, he made answer, "I allow thee a shift to thy back; so get thee hence." All that stood by besought him to give her a robe, that she, who had been his wife for thirteen years and more, might not be seen to quit his house in so sorry and shameful a plight, having nought on her but a shift. But their entreaties went for nothing; the lady in her shift, and barefoot and bareheaded, having bade them adieu, departed the house, and went back to her father amid the tears and lamentations of all that saw her. Giannucolo, who had ever deemed it a thing incredible that Gualtieri should keep his daughter to wife, and had looked for this to happen every day, and had kept the clothes that she had put off on the morning that Gualtieri had wedded her, now brought them to her; and she, having resumed them, applied herself to the petty drudgery of her father's house, as she had been wont, enduring with fortitude this cruel visitation of adverse Fortune.

Now no sooner had Gualtieri dismissed Griselda, than he gave his vassals to understand that he had taken to wife a daughter of one of the Counts of Panago. He accordingly made great preparations as for the nuptials, during which he sent for Griselda. To whom, being come, quoth he, "I am bringing hither my new bride, and in this her first home-coming I purpose to show her honor; and thou knowest that women I have none in the house that know how to set chambers in due order, or attend to the many other matters that so joyful an event requires; wherefore do thou, that understandest these things better than another, see to all that needs be done, and bid hither such ladies as thou mayest see fit, and receive them, as if thou wert the lady of the house, and then, when the nuptials are ended, thou mayest go back to thy cottage."

Albeit each of these words pierced Griselda's heart like a knife, for that, in resigning her good fortune, she had not been able to renounce the love she bore Gualtieri, nevertheless, "My lord," she made answer, "I am ready and prompt to do your pleasure." And so, clad in her sorry garments of coarse romagnole, she entered the house, which, but a little before, she had quitted in her shift, and addressed her to sweep the chambers, and arrange arras and cushions in the halls, and make ready the kitchen, and set her hand to everything, as if she had been a paltry serving-wench; nor did she rest until she had brought all into such meet and seemly trim as the occasion demanded. This done, she invited in Gualtieri's name all the ladies of those parts to be present at his nuptials, and awaited the event. The day being come, still wearing her sorry weeds, but in heart and soul and mien the lady, she received the ladies as they came, and gave each a gladsome greeting.

Now Gualtieri, as we said, had caused his children to be carefully nurtured and brought up by a kinswoman of his at Bologna, which kinswoman was married into the family of the Counts of Panago; and, the girl being now twelve years old, and the loveliest creature that ever was seen, and the boy being about six years old, he had sent word to his kinswoman's husband at Bologna, praying him to be pleased to come with this girl and boy of his to Saluzzo, and to see that he brought a goodly and honorable company with him, and to give all to understand that he brought the girl to him to wife, and on no wise to disclose to any who she really was.

The gentleman did as the Marquis bade him, and within a few days of his setting forth arrived at Saluzzo about breakfast-time with the girl, and her brother, and a noble company, and found all the folk of those parts, and much people besides, gathered there in expectation of Gualtieri's new bride; who, being received by the ladies, was no sooner come into the hall where the tables were set than Griselda advanced to meet her, saying with hearty cheer, "Welcome, my lady!"

So the ladies, who had with much insistence, but in vain, besought Gualtieri, either to let Griselda keep in another room, or at any rate to furnish her with one of the robes that had been hers, that she might not present herself in such a sorry guise before the strangers, sat down to table; and the service being begun, the eyes of all were set on the girl, and everyone said that Gualtieri had made a good exchange, and Griselda joined with the rest in greatly commending her, and also her little brother.

And now Gualtieri, sated at last with all that he had seen of his wife's patience, marking that this new and strange turn made not the least alteration in her demeanor, and being well assured that 'twas not due to apathy, for he knew her to be of excellent understanding, deemed it time to relieve her of the suffering which he judged her to dissemble under a resolute front; and so, having called her to him in presence of them all, he said with a smile, "And what thinkest thou of our bride?"

"My lord," replied Griselda, "I think mighty well of her; and if she be but as discreet as she is fair – and so I deem her – I make no doubt but you may reckon to lead with her a life of incomparable felicity; but with all earnestness I entreat you, that you spare her those tribulations which you did once inflict upon another that was yours, for I scarce think she would be able to bear them as well because she is younger, as for that she has been delicately nurtured, whereas that other had known no respite of hardship since she was but a little child."

Marking that she made no doubt but that the girl was to be his wife, and yet spoke never a whit the less sweetly, Gualtieri caused her to sit down beside him, and, "Griselda," said he, " 'tis now time that thou see the reward of thy long patience; and those who have deemed me cruel and unjust and insensate should know that what I did was done of purpose aforethought, for that I was minded to give both thee and them a lesson, that thou mightest learn to be a wife, and they in like manner might learn how to take and keep a wife, and that I might beget me perpetual peace with thee for the rest of my life; whereof being in great fear, when I came to take a wife, lest I should be disappointed, I, therefore, to put the matter to the proof, did – and how sorely thou knowest – harass and afflict thee. And since I never knew thee either by deed, or by word to deviate from my will, I now, deeming myself to have of thee that assurance of happiness which I desired, am minded to restore to thee at once all that, step by step, I took from thee, and by extremity of joy to compensate the tribulations that I inflicted on thee. Receive, then, this girl, whom thou supposest to be my bride, and her brother, with glad heart, as thy children and mine. These are they, whom by thee and many another it has long been supposed that I did ruthlessly to death, and I am thy husband, that loves thee more dearly than aught else, deeming that other there is none that has the like good cause to be well content with his wife."

Which said, he embraced and kissed her; and then, while she wept for joy, they rose and hied them there where sat the daughter all astonished to hear the news, whom, as also her brother, they tenderly embraced, and explained to them, and many others that stood by, the whole mystery. Whereat the ladies, transported with delight, rose from table and betook them with Griselda to a chamber, and, with better omen, divested her of her sorry garb, and arrayed her in one of her own robes of state; and so, in guise of a lady (howbeit in her rags she had showed as no less) they led her back into the hall. Wondrous was the cheer which there they made with the children; and all overjoyed at the event, they reveled and made merry amain, and prolonged the festivities for several days, and very discreet they pronounced Gualtieri, albeit they censured as intolerably harsh the probation to which he had subjected Griselda, and most discreet beyond all compare they accounted Griselda.

Some days after, the Count of Panago returned to Bologna, and Gualtieri took Giannucolo from his husbandry, and established him in honor as his father-in-law, wherein to his great solace he lived for the rest of his days. Gualtieri himself, having mated his daughter with a husband of high degree, lived long and happily thereafter with Griselda, to whom he ever paid all honor.

Now what shall we say in this case but that even into the cots of the poor the heavens let fall at times spirits divine, as into the palaces of kings, souls that are fitter to tend hogs than to exercise lordship over men? Who but Griselda had been able, with a countenance not only tearless, but cheerful, to endure the hard and unheard-of trials to which Gualtieri subjected her? Who perhaps might have deemed himself to have made no bad investment, had he chanced upon one who, having been turned out of his house in her shift, had found means so to dust the pelisse of another as to get herself thereby a fine robe.

EPILOGUE

So ended Dioneo's story, whereof the ladies, diversely inclining, one to censure where another found matter for commendation, had discoursed not a little, when the king, having glanced at the sky, and marked that the sun was now low, insomuch that 'twas nigh the vesper hour, still keeping his seat, thus began, "Exquisite my ladies, as, methinks, you wot, 'tis not only in minding them of the past and apprehending the present that the wit of mortals consists; but by one means or the other to be able to foresee the future. Tomorrow, as you know, 'twill be fifteen days since, in quest of recreation and for the conservation of our health and life, we, shunning the dismal and dolorous and afflicting spectacles that have ceased not in our city since this season of pestilence began, took our departure from Florence. Wherein, to my thinking, we have done nought that was not seemly; for, if I have duly used my powers of observation, albeit some gay stories, and of a kind to stimulate concupiscence, have here been told, and we have daily known no lack of dainty dishes and good wine, nor yet of music and song, things one and all apt to incite weak minds to that which is not seemly, neither on your part, nor on ours, have I marked deed or word, or aught of any kind, that called for reprehension; but, by what I have seen and heard, seemliness and the sweet intimacy of brothers and sisters have ever reigned among us. Which, assuredly, for the honor and advantage which you and I have had thereof, is most grateful to me. Wherefore, lest too long continuance in this way of life might beget some occasion of weariness, and that no man may be able to misconstrue our too long abidance here, and as we have all of us had our day's share of the honor which still remains in me, I should deem it meet, so you be of like mind, that we now go back whence we came: and that the rather than that our company, the bruit whereof has already reached divers others that are in our neighborhood, might be so increased that all our pleasure would be destroyed. And so, if my counsel meet with your approval, I will keep the crown I have received of you until our departure, which I purpose shall be tomorrow morning. Should you decide otherwise, I have already determined whom to crown for the ensuing day."

Much debate ensued among the ladies and young men; but in the end they approved the king's proposal as expedient and seemly, and resolved to do even as he had said. The king, therefore, summoned the seneschal; and having conferred with him of the order he was to observe on the morrow, he dismissed the company until supper-time. So, the king being risen, the ladies and the rest likewise rose, and betook them, as they were wont, to their several diversions. Supper-time being come, they supped with exceeding great delight. Which done, they addressed them to song and music and dancing; and, while Lauretta was leading a dance, the king bade Fiammetta give them a song; whereupon Fiammetta right debonairly sang.

Several other songs followed; and it being then nigh upon midnight, all, as the king was pleased to order, betook them to rest. With the first light of the new day they rose, and, the seneschal having already conveyed thence all their chattels, they, following the lead of their discreet king, hied them back to Florence; and in Santa Maria Novella, whence they had set forth, the three young men took leave of the seven ladies, and departed to find other diversions elsewhere, while the ladies in due time repaired to their homes.

—*From the Decameron by Giovanni Boccaccio, Italian (1467?–1524?), translated by J. M. Rigg.*

~ ❂ ~

How Guzmán Excited the Compassion of My Lord Cardinal

MATEO ALEMÁN

Having roused myself early one fine morning, according to custom, I went and seated myself at the door of a cardinal, concerning whom I had heard an excellent character, being one of the most charitably disposed in Rome. I had taken the trouble of getting one of my legs swelled, on which, notwithstanding what had passed, was to be seen a new ulcer, one that might set at defiance the most penetrating eye or probe of a surgeon. I had not this time omitted to have my face as pale as death; and thus, filling the air with horrible lamentations while I was asking alms, I moved the souls of the different domestics who came in and out to take pity upon me; they gave me something; but I was yet only beating up for game — it was their master I wanted. He at length made his appearance — I redoubled my cries and groans — I writhed in anguish; and then

I accosted him in these terms: "O most noble Christian; thou friend of Christ and his afflicted ones! have pity upon me, a poor wretched sinner — Behold me cut down in the flower of my days — may your excellency be touched with my extreme misery, for the sake of the sufferings of our dear Redeemer." The cardinal, who was really a pious man, stopped and, after looking at me earnestly, turned to his attendants. "In the name of Christ, take this unhappy being, and bear him into my own apartments! let the rags that cover him be exchanged for fine linen; put him into a good bed — nay, into my own — and I will go into another room. I will tend on him; for in him do I verily see what must have been the sufferings of our Saviour." He was obeyed; and, O charity! how didst thou shame those lordly prelates who think Heaven in debt to them, if they do but look down on some poor wretch: while my good cardinal, not content with what he had done, ordered two surgeons to attend, recommending them to do all in their power to ease my agony, and to examine and cure my leg; after which they should be well recompensed. He then, bidding me be of good cheer, left me, to pursue his affairs; and the surgeons, to make the best of my case. They declared at once that it was useless, and that gangrene had already commenced. So seriously did they pronounce this, that, though I knew the effect was solely produced by staining my leg with a certain herb, I almost felt alarmed for the consequence. They then took out their case of instruments, called for a cauldron of hot water, for some fine linen, and a poultice. While these were in preparation, they questioned me as to the origin of my disease, how long I had had it, etc., etc. — moreover, whether I drank wine, and what was my usual diet? To these, and to a hundred such interrogatories, I replied not a word; so great was my alarm at the terrific processes that appeared to be going on, in order to restore me to my pristine health and soundness. I was infinitely perplexed, not knowing to what saint to have recourse; for I was apprehensive there might not be a single one in heaven inclined to interfere in behalf of so thorough-paced a rascal. . . . The surgeons ranked high in their profession; and, after having curiously turned round my leg about twenty times, retired into another room to discuss the result of their observations. I remained in a state of horror not to be described; for it had got into my head that they would decide upon amputation; to learn which I crept softly towards the door to listen, fully resolved to reveal the imposture in so dreadful an alternative. "Sir," said one, "we may consult here for ever, to little purport; he has got St. Anthony's fire." "No such thing," replied the other, "he has no more fire in his leg than I have in my hand: we might easily remove it in a couple of days." "You cannot be serious," said the first speaker. "By St. Comus, I know something of ulcers; and here, I maintain it, we have a gangrene." "No, no, friend," replied the second, "we have no ulcer — we have a rogue to deal with — nothing is the matter with him. I know the whole history of his ulcer, and how it was made. It is by no means very rare; for I know the herbs with which the impostor has prepared it, and the ingenious method in which they have been applied." The other seemed quite confounded by this assertion; but, ashamed of owning himself a dupe, he persisted in his former opinion: on which a pretty warm colloquy would have ensued, had not the more ingenious of the two had the sense to recommend first to examine the leg, and to end the dispute afterwards. "Look a little deeper into the matter," said he, "and you will see the fellow's knavery." "With all my heart. I will confess that you are right, when I see there is no ulcer, or rather gangrene." "That is not enough," replied his colleague. "In acknowledging your error, you must also admit I am entitled to at least a third more fees than yourself." "By no means," retorted the other. "I have eyes to detect imposture as well as you; and I am of the opinion we ought to divide the good cardinal's fees fairly between us." The dispute now waxed warm, and rather than give up his point, each declared that he would make the cardinal acquainted with the whole business.

In this dilemma I did not hesitate a moment — there was no time to lose — escape was impossible, I rushed into the presence of the faculty, and threw myself at their feet. With well-dissembled grief, I thus addressed them: "Alas! my dear sirs, take pity upon an unfortunate fellow-creature. Think, gentlemen, *homo sum; nihil humani, etc.* (I am a man! nothing that touches man is foreign to me): I am mortal like yourselves — you know the hard-heartedness of the great, and how the poor and forlorn are compelled to assume the most horrible shapes in order to soften their hardness: and in doing this what risks and sufferings do we not encounter, and all for so small a remuneration. Besides, what advantage will you get by exposing such a poor miserable sinner? You will certainly lose your fees, which you need not do if you will let us understand each other. You may rely on my discretion; the fear of consequence will keep me silent, and we may each benefit in our respective professions."

Upon this the men of physic again consulted, and at length came to the resolution of pocketing their fees, *secundum artem* (according to the practice). Being all of one mind, we now begged to be ushered into the presence of the cardinal, and the surgeons then ordered me to be placed upon a couch, at the side of which they made an immense display of chirurgical instruments, dressings, &., again consulted, and after wrapping my leg in a great number of bandages, they desired that I might be put into a warm bed. His excellency, meanwhile, was full of anxiety to learn the state of my health, and whether there were any hopes of recovery? "My lord," replied one of the surgeons, "the patient is in a deplorable condition, gangrene has already begun; still, with time and care, there is a chance that he might recover, please God, but it will be a long affair." "And he is fortunate," said his coadjutor, "in having fallen into our hands; another day, and he was lost forever; but no doubt Providence must have directed him to the door of your excellency."

This account seemed to please the cardinal; it gave him occasion to display the truest Christian charity, and he desired that neither time nor skill might be spared in the endeavor to restore me to health. He also directed that I should be supplied with everything; and the surgeons on their part pledged themselves to do all that art could effect, and each of them to pay me a visit at least twice in the day; it being necessary to detect the slightest change that might occur in my present condition. They then withdrew, not a little to my consolation; for I could not but regard them while present in the light of two executioners, who might fall upon me at any moment, or publish my imposition to the world. So far from this, however, they made me keep my apartment for three months, which to me seemed like so many ages, so difficult is it to give up the habit of gambling—or begging, with the tone of freedom they seem to include. In vain was I daintily lodged and fed, like his excellency himself; the *ennui* I felt was intolerable. I was incessantly beseeching the doctors to take pity on me, and bring the farce to a close, until they were at length compelled to yield to my importunity.

They left off dressing my leg, and, on its being reduced to its natural size, they acquainted the good cardinal with the fact, who was in raptures with the performance, under his auspices, of so great a cure. He rewarded them handsomely, and came in to congratulate me on the miraculous event; and having acquitted myself well in his frequent visits to me, in regard both to my opinions and my principles, he imbibed a real kindness for me; and to give me a further proof of it, he gave me the situation of one of his confidential attendants—a species of honor I was too deeply sensible of to be able to refuse.

—*From Guzmán de Alfarache, by Mateo Alemán, Spanish (1547?–1610?), translated by James Mabbe.*

The Casting of the Perseus

BENVENUTO CELLINI

As I HAD been particularly successful in casting my Medusa, I made a model of my Perseus in wax, and flattered myself that I should have the same success in casting the latter in bronze, as I had had with the former. Upon its appearing to such advantage, and looking so beautiful in wax, the duke, whether somebody else put it into his head, or whether it was a notion of his own, as he came to my house oftener than usual, once took occasion to say to me, "Benvenuto, this statue cannot be cast in bronze; it is not in the power of your art to compass it." Hearing him express himself in that manner, I discovered great vexation, and said, "My lord, I know that your excellency places very little confidence in me, and that you have but too good an opinion of those who speak ill of me; or else you do not understand things of this nature." Scarce did he suffer me to utter these words, when he answered, "I profess to understand them, and

I do understand them perfectly." I replied, "You may understand them as a prince, but not as an artist; for if you had that skill in these matters, which you think you have, you would believe me upon account of the fine bronze head which I cast for your excellency, and which was sent to the Elbe; as also for having restored the beautiful figure of Ganymede, a work that gave me infinite trouble, insomuch that it would have been easier for me to have made a new one; likewise for having cast the Medusa, which stands here before your excellency, a performance of immense difficulty, in which I have done what no other man has done before me in this most laborious art. Consider, my lord, I have constructed a new sort of a furnace, in a manner unknown to other artists; for besides many other particulars and curious inventions to be seen in it, I have made two issues for the bronze; for otherwise that difficult and distorted figure could never come out, and it was only by means of my skill and invention that it came out as well as it did: and do not imagine that every common artist could have done as much. Know likewise, my lord, that all the great and difficult undertakings that I have been employed in by the renowned King Francis, were attended with admirable success, purely on account of that king's generous encouragement of my labors, in providing me with everything I wanted, and allowing me as many hands as I required. At certain times I had under me above forty journeymen, all of my own choosing; and this was the reason that I finished so many undertakings in so short a time. Therefore, my lord, take my advice, and afford me the assistance I want, for I have great hopes of producing a work that will please you; whereas, if your excellency discourages me, and does not supply me with the necessary helps, it is impossible that either I or any man living can produce any thing worth notice."

The duke scarcely had patience to hear me out, but sometimes turned one way, sometimes another; and I was quite in despair when I recollected the circumstances in which I had lived in France. At last he all on a sudden said, "Tell me, Benvenuto, how is it possible that this fine head of Medusa, which Perseus holds aloft in his hand, should ever come out cleverly?" I immediately answered, "It is clear, my lord, that you are no connoisseur in statuary, as your excellency boasts yourself; for if you had any skill in the art, you would not be afraid of that fine head not coming out, but would express your apprehensions concerning that right foot, which is at such a distance below." The duke, half angry, addressing himself to some noblemen who were with him, said, "I really believe it is a practice of Benvenuto's to contradict and oppose everything he hears advanced"; then turning to me, as it were in derision, in which he was imitated by all present, he expressed himself thus: "I am willing to have patience to hear what reason you can allege, that can possibly induce me to believe what you affirm." I answered, "I will give your excellency a reason so satisfactory, that you will be able to conceive the full force of it." I thereupon began in these terms: "You know, my lord, that the nature of fire is to fly upwards; I therefore assure you that the head of Medusa will come out perfectly well. But as it is not the property of fire to descend, and it is necessary to force it down six cubits by art, hence, I affirm that it is impossible that yon foot should ever come out; but it will be an easy matter for me to make a new one." The duke thereupon said, "Why did you not think of contriving to make that foot come out as well as the head?" "I must then," answered I, "have made the furnace much bigger, to be able to cast a piece of brass as thick as my leg, and with that weight of hot metal I should have made it come out by force; whereas, my brass, which goes down to the feet six cubits, as I mentioned before, is not above two inches thick. Therefore, it was not worth your notice, for it can soon be rectified; but when my mold is something more than half full, I have good hopes that from that half upwards, the fire mounting, by its natural property, the heads of Perseus and Medusa will come out admirably; and this you may depend upon." When I had laid before the duke all these reasons, with many more, which I for the sake of brevity omit, he shook his head, and departed.

I now took courage, resolving to depend on myself, and banished all those thoughts which from time to time occasioned me great inquietude, and made me sorely repent my ever having quitted France, with a view of assisting six poor nieces at Florence; which good intention proved the source and origin of all the misfortunes that afterwards befell me. However, I still flattered myself that if I could but finish my statue of Perseus, all my labors would be converted to delight, and meet with a glorious and happy reward. Thus, having recovered my vigor of mind, I exerted all my strength of body and of purse, though indeed I had but little money left, and began to purchase several loads of pinewood from the pine-grove of the Serristori, hard by Monte Lupo; and whilst I was waiting for it, I covered my Perseus with the earth which I had prepared several months beforehand, that it might have its proper seasoning. After I had made its coat of earth, covered it well, and bound it properly with irons, I began by means of a slow fire to draw off the wax, which melted away by many vent-holes; for the more of these are made, the better the molds are filled: and when I had entirely stripped off the wax, I made a sort of fence round my Perseus, that it, round the mold above-mentioned, of bricks, piling them one upon another, and leaving several vacuities for the fire to exhale at. I next began gradually to put on the wood, and kept a constant fire for two days and two nights, till, the wax being quite off, and the mold well baked, I began to dig a hole to bury my mold in, and observed all those fine methods of proceeding that are prescribed by our art. When I had completely dug my hole, I took my mold, and by means of levers and strong cables directed it with care, and suspended it a cubit above the level of the furnace, so that it hung exactly in the middle of the hole. I then let it gently down to the very bottom of the furnace, and placed it with all the care and exactness I possibly could. After I had finished this part of my task, I began to make a covering of the very earth I had taken off, and in proportion as I raised the earth, I made vents for it, which are a sort of tubes of baked earth, generally used for conduits, and other things of a similar nature. As soon as I saw that I had placed it properly, and that this manner of covering it, by putting on these small tubes in their proper places, was likely to answer, as also that my journeymen thoroughly understood my plan, which was very different from that of all other masters, and I was sure that I could depend upon them, I turned my thoughts to my furnace. I had caused it to be filled with several pieces of brass and bronze, and heaped them upon one another in the manner taught us by our art, taking particular care to leave a passage for the flames, that the metal might the sooner assume its color and dissolve into a fluid. Thus, I with great alacrity, excited my men to lay on the pinewood, which, because of the oiliness of the resinous matter that oozes from the pinetree, and that my furnace was admirably well made, burned at such a rate, that I was continually obliged to run to and fro, which greatly fatigued me. I, however, bore the hardship; but to add to my misfortune, the shop took fire, and we were all very much afraid that the roof would fall in and crush us. From another quarter, that is, from the garden, the sky poured in so much rain and wind, that it cooled my furnace.

Thus did I continue to struggle with these cross accidents for several hours, and exerted myself to such a degree that my constitution, though robust, could no longer bear such severe hardship, and I was suddenly attacked by a most violent intermitting fever: in short, I was so ill that I found myself under a necessity of lying down upon my bed. This gave me great concern, but it was unavoidable. I thereupon addressed myself to my assistants, who were about ten in number, consisting of masters who melted bronze, helpers, men from the country, and the journeymen that worked in the shop, amongst whom was Bernardino Manellini di Mugello, who had lived with me several years. After having recommended it to them all to take proper care of my business, I said to Bernardino, "My friend, be careful to observe the method which I have shown you, and use all possible expedition, for the metal will soon be ready. You cannot mistake: these two worthy men here will quickly make the tubes; with two such directors you can certainly contrive to pour out the hot metal by means of the mandriani or iron crooks; and I have no doubt but my mold will be filled completely. I find myself extremely ill, and really believe that in a few hours this severe disorder will put an end to my life." Thus I left them in great sorrow, and went to bed. I then ordered the maids to carry victuals and drink into the shop for all the men, and told them I did not expect to live till the next morning. They encouraged me notwithstanding, assuring me that my disorder would not last, as it was only the effect of over-fatigue. In this manner did I continue for two hours in a violent fever, which I every moment perceived to increase; and I was incessantly crying out, "I am dying, I am dying."

My housekeeper, whose name was Mona Fiore da Castel del Rio, was one of the most sensible and affectionate women in the world: she rebuked me for giving way to vain fears, and at the same time attended me with the greatest kindness and care imaginable: however, seeing me so very ill, and terrified to such a degree, she could not contain herself, but shed a flood of tears, which she endeavored to conceal from me. Whilst we were both in this deep affliction, I perceived a man enter the room, who in his person appeared to be as crooked and distorted as a great S, and began to express himself in these terms, with a tone of voice as dismal and melancholy as those who exhort and pray with persons who are going to be executed: "Alas! poor Benvenuto, your work is spoiled, and the misfortune admits of no remedy."

No sooner had I heard the words uttered by this messenger of evil, but I cried out so loud that my voice might be heard to the skies, and got out of bed. I began immediately to dress, and giving plenty of kicks and cuffs to the maidservants and the boy as they offered to help me on with my clothes, I complained bitterly in these terms: "O you envious and treacherous wretches, this is a piece of villainy contrived on purpose; but I swear by the living God that I will sift it to the bottom, and before I die, give such proofs who I am as shall not fail to astonish the whole world." Having huddled on my clothes, I went with a mind boding evil to the shop, where I found all those whom I had left so alert, and in such high spirits, standing in the utmost confusion and astonishment. I thereupon addressed them thus: "Listen all of you to what I am going to say; and since you either would not or could not follow the method I pointed out, obey me now that I am present: my work is before us, and let none of you offer to oppose or contradict me, for such cases as this require activity and not counsel." Hereupon one Alessandro Lastricati had the assurance to say to me, "Look you, Benvenuto, you have undertaken a work which our art cannot compass, and which is not to be effected by human power."

Hearing these words I turned round in such a passion, and seemed so bent upon mischief, that both he and all the rest unanimously cried out to me, "Give you orders, and we will all second you in whatever you command: we will assist you as long as we have breath in our bodies." These kind and affectionate words they uttered, as I firmly believe, in a persuasion that I was upon the point of expiring. I went directly to examine the furnace, and saw all the metal in it concreted. I thereupon ordered two of the helpers to step over the way to Capretta, a butcher, for a load of young oak, which had been above a year drying, and been offered me by Maria Ginevera, wife to the said Capretta.

Upon his bringing me the first bundles of it, I began to fill the grate. This sort of oak makes a brisker fire than any other wood whatever; but the wood of elder-trees and pine-trees is used in casting artillery, because it makes a mild and gentle fire. As soon as the concreted metal felt the power of this violent fire, it began to brighten and glitter. In another quarter I made them hurry the tubes with all possible expedition, and sent some of them to the roof of the house to take care of the fire, which through the great violence of the wind had acquired new force; and towards the garden I had caused some tables with pieces of tapestry and old clothes to be placed, in order to shelter me from the rain. As soon as I had applied the proper remedy to each evil, I with a loud voice cried out to my men to bestir themselves and lend a helping hand; so that when they saw that the concreted metal began to melt again, the whole body obeyed me with such zeal and alacrity, that every man did the work of three. Then I caused a mass of pewter weighing about sixty pounds to be thrown upon the metal in the furnace, which with the other helps, as the brisk wood fire, and stirring it sometimes with iron, and sometimes with long poles, soon became completely dissolved. Finding that, contrary to the opinion of my ignorant assistants, I had effected what seemed as difficult as to raise the dead, I recovered my vigor to such a degree, that I no longer perceived whether I had any fever, nor had I the least apprehension of death. Suddenly a loud noise was heard, and a glittering of fire flashed before our eyes, as if it had been the darting of a thunderbolt. Upon the appearance of this extraordinary phenomenon, terror seized on all present, and on none more than myself.

This tremendous noise being over, we began to stare at each other, and perceived that the cover of the furnace had burst and flown off, so that the bronze began to run.

I immediately caused the mouths of my mold to be opened; but finding that the metal did not run with its usual velocity, and apprehending that the cause of it was that the fusibility of the metal was injured by the violence of the fire, I ordered all my dishes and porringers, which were in number about two hundred, to be placed one by one before my tubes, and part of them to be thrown into the furnace; upon which all present perceived that my bronze was completely dissolved, and that my mold was filling; they now with joy and alacrity assisted and obeyed me. I for my part was sometimes in one place, sometimes in another, giving my directions and assisting my men, before whom I offered up this prayer: "O God, I address myself to thee, who, of thy divine power, didst rise from the dead, and ascend in glory to heaven. I acknowledge in gratitude this mercy that my mold has been filled: I fall prostrate before thee, and with my whole heart return thanks to thy divine majesty." My prayer being over, I took a plate of meat which stood upon a little bench, and ate with a great appetite. I then drank with all my journeymen and assistants, and went joyful and in good health to bed; for there were still two hours of night; and I rested as well as if I had been troubled with no manner of disorder.

My good housekeeper, without my having given any orders, had provided a young capon for my dinner. When I arose, which was not till about noon, she accosted me in high spirits, and said merrily, "Is this the man that thought himself dying? It is my firm belief that the cuffs and kicks which you gave us last night, when you were quite frantic and possessed, frightened away your fever, which, apprehending lest you should fall upon it in the same manner, took to flight." So my whole poor family, having got over such panics and hardships, without delay procured earthen vessels to supply the place of the pewter dishes and porringers, and we all dined together very cheerfully; indeed, I do not remember having ever in my life eaten a meal with greater satisfaction, or with a better appetite. After dinner, all those who had assisted me in my work came and congratulated me upon what had happened, returned thanks to the Divine Being, for having interposed so mercifully in our behalf, and declared that they had in theory and practice learnt such things as were judged impossible by other masters. I thereupon thought it allowable to boast a little of my knowledge and skill in this fine art, and, pulling out my purse, satisfied all my workmen for their labor.

My mortal enemy, Pierre Francesco Ricci, the duke's steward, was very eager to know how the affair had turned out; so that the two whom I suspected of being the cause of my metal's concreting in the manner above related, told him that I was not a man, but rather a downright devil, for I had compassed that which was not in the power of art to effect; with many other surprising things which would have been too much even for the infernal powers. As they greatly exaggerated what had passed, perhaps with a view of excusing themselves, the steward wrote to the duke, who was then at Pisa, an account still more pompous, and more replete with the marvelous than that which the workingmen had given him.

Having left my work to cool during two days after it was cast, I began gradually to uncover it. I first of all found the Medusa's head, which had come out admirably by the assistance of the vents, as I had observed to the duke that the property of fire was to fly upwards. I proceeded to uncover the rest, and found that the other head, I mean that of Perseus, was likewise come out perfectly well. This occasioned me still greater surprise, because, as it is seen in the statue, it is much lower than that of Medusa, the mouth of that figure being placed over the head and shoulders of Perseus. I found that where the head of Perseus ends, all the bronze was exhausted which I had in my furnace. This surprised me very much, that there should not be any thing over and above what is necessary in casting. My astonishment, indeed, was raised to such a degree, that I looked upon it as a miracle immediately wrought by the Almighty. I went on uncovering it with great success, and found every part turn out to admiration, till I reached the foot of the right leg, which supports the figure, where I found the heel come out: so proceeding to examine it, and thinking that the whole was filled up, in one respect I was glad, in another sorry, because I had told the duke it would not have that effect. Continuing, however, to uncover it, I found that not only the toes were wanting, but part of the foot itself, so that there was almost one half deficient. This occasioned me some new trouble; but I was not displeased at it, because I could thereby convince the duke that I understood my business thoroughly; and though there had come out a great deal more of that foot than I thought there would, the reason was, that in consequence of the several accidents that had happened, it was heated much more than it could have been in the regular course of business; especially as the pewter plates had been thrown into the furnace, a thing never done before.

I was highly pleased that my work had succeeded so well, and went to Pisa to pay my respects to the duke, who received me in the most gracious manner imaginable. The duchess vied with him in kindness to me; and though the steward had written them an account of the affair, it appeared to them much more wonderful and extraordinary when I related it myself. Upon my speaking to him of the foot of Perseus, which had not come out (a circumstance of which I had apprised his excellency), I perceived that he was filled with the utmost astonishment, and told the affair to the duchess in the same terms that I had before related to him. Finding that these great personages were become so favorable to me, I availed myself of the opportunity to request the duke's permission to go to Rome: he granted it in the most obliging terms, and desired me to return speedily, in order to finish my statue of Perseus. He at the same time gave me letters of recommendation to his ambassador Averardo Serristori. This happened in the beginning of the pontificate of Pope Julio de Monti.

—*From the Autobiography of Benvenuto Cellini, Italian (1507–1571), translated by Thomas Roscoe.*

Don Quixote

MIGUEL DE CERVANTES

Chapter I

WHICH TREATS OF THE CONDITION AND PURSUITS OF THE FAMOUS DON QUIXOTE DE LA MANCHA

In a village of la Mancha, the name of which I have no desire to recollect, there lived, not long ago, one of those gentlemen who usually keep a lance upon a rack, an old buckler, a lean horse, and a coursing greyhound. Soup, composed of somewhat more beef than mutton, salmagundy at night, lentils on Fridays, and a pigeon, by way of addition, on Sundays, consumed three-fourths of his income; the remainder of it supplied him with a cloak of fine cloth, velvet breeches, with slippers of the same for holidays, and a suit of the best homespun, in which he adorned himself on week days. His establishment consisted of a housekeeper above forty, a niece not quite twenty, and a lad who served him both in the field and at home, who could saddle the horse or handle the pruning hook. The age of our gentleman bordered upon fifty years; he was of a strong constitution, spare-bodied, of a meager visage, a very early riser, and a lover of the chase. Some pretend to say that he had the surname of Quixada, or Quesada, for on this point his historians differ: but, from very plausible conjectures, we may conclude that his name was Quixada. That is, however, of little importance to our history: let it suffice that in relating it, we swerve not a jot from the truth.

Be it known, then, that the above-mentioned gentleman, in his leisure moments, which composed the greater part of the year, applied himself with so much ardor and relish to the perusal of books of chivalry, that he almost wholly neglected the exercise of the chase, and even the regulation of his domestic affairs; indeed, so extravagant was his zeal in this pursuit that he sold many acres of arable land to purchase books of knight-errantry: collecting as many as he could possibly obtain. Among these, there were none he admired so much as those written by the famous Feliciano de Silva, whose brilliant prose and intricate style were, in his opinion, infinitely precious; especially those amorous speeches and challenges in which they so abound; such as: "the reason of unreasonable treatment of my reason so enfeebles my reason that with reason I complain of your beauty." And again: "the high heavens that, with your divinity, divinely fortify you with the stars, rendering you meritorious of the merit merited by your greatness." These and similar rhapsodies distracted the poor gentleman; for he labored to comprehend and unravel their meaning, which was more than Aristotle himself could do, were he to rise from the dead expressly for that purpose. He was not quite satisfied as to the wounds which Don Belianis gave and received; for he could not help thinking that, however skillful the professors who healed them, his face and whole body must infallibly have been covered with seams and scars. Nevertheless, he commended his author for concluding his book with the promise of that interminable adventure; and he often felt an inclination to seize the pen himself and conclude it, literally as it is there promised: this he would doubtless have done, and with success, had he not been diverted from it by meditations of greater moment, on which his mind was incessantly employed.

He often debated with the curate of the village, a man of learning, and a graduate of Siguenza, which of the two was the best knight, Palmerin of England, or Amadis de Gaul; but master Nicholas, barber of the same place, declared that none ever equaled the knight of the sun; if, indeed, anyone could be compared to him, it was Don Galaor, brother of Amadis de Gaul, for he had a genius suited to everything: he was no effeminate knight, no whimperer, like his brother; and in point of courage, he was by no means his inferior. In short, he became so infatuated with this kind of study that he passed whole days and nights over these books: and thus, with little sleeping and much reading, his brains were dried up and his intellects deranged. His imagination was full of all that he had read; of enchantments, contests, battles, challenges, wounds, blandishments, amours, tortures, and impossible absurdities; and so firmly was he persuaded of the truth of the whole tissue of visionary fiction that, in his mind, no history in the world was more authentic. The Cid Ruy Diaz, he asserted, was a very good knight, but not to be compared with the knight of the flaming sword, who, with a single backstroke, cleft asunder two fierce and monstrous giants. He was better pleased with Bernardo del Carpio, because, at Roncesvalles, he slew Roland the enchanted, by availing himself of the stratagem employed by Hercules upon Anteus, whom he squeezed to death within his arms. He spoke very favorably of the giant Morganti, for, although of that monstrous brood who are always proud and insolent, he alone was courteous and well-bred. Above all, he admired Rinaldo de Montalvan, particularly when he saw him sallying forth from his castle to plunder all he encountered; and when, moreover, he seized upon that image of Mahomet, which according to history, was of massive gold. But he would have given his housekeeper, and even his niece into the bargain, for a fair opportunity of kicking the traitor, Ganelon.

In fine, his judgment being completely obscured, he was seized with one of the strangest fancies that ever entered the head of a madman; this was a persuasion that it behooved him, as well for the advancement of his glory as the service of his country, to become a knight-errant, and traverse the world, armed and mounted, in quest of adventures, and to practice all that had been performed by the knights-errant, of whom he had read; redressing every species of grievance, and exposing himself to dangers which, being surmounted, might secure to him eternal glory and renown. The poor gentleman imagined himself at least crowned Emperor of Trapisonda, by the valor of his arm: and thus indulging in these agreeable meditations, and borne away by the extraordinary pleasure he found in them, he hastened to put his designs into execution.

The first thing he did was to scour up some rusty armor, which belonged to his great-grandfather, and had lain many years neglected in a corner. These he cleaned and adjusted as well as he could, but he found one grand defect; the helmet was incomplete; having only the morion: this deficiency, however, he ingeniously supplied, by making a kind of vizor of pasteboard, which, being fixed to the morion, gave the appearance of an entire helmet. True it is that, in order to prove its strength, he drew his sword and gave it two strokes, the first of which instantly demolished the labor of a week; but not altogether approving of the facility with which it was destroyed, and in order to secure himself against a similar misfortune, he made another vizor, which, having fenced in the inside with small bars of iron, he felt assured of its strength, and without making any more experiments, held it to be a most excellent helmet.

In the next place, he visited his steed; and although this animal had more blemishes than the horse of Gonela, which "tantum pellis et ossa fuit," yet, in his eyes, neither the Bucephalus of Alexander, nor the

Cid's Babieca, could be compared with him. Four days was he deliberating upon what name he should give him; for, as he said to himself, it would be very improper that a horse so excellent, appertaining to a knight so famous, should be without an appropriate name: he therefore endeavored to find one that should express what he had been before he belonged to a knight-errant, and also what he now was: nothing could, indeed, be more reasonable than that, when the master changed his state, the horse should likewise change his name and assume one, pompous and high-sounding as became the new order he now professed. So after having devised, altered, lengthened, curtailed, rejected, and again framed in his imagination a variety of names, he finally determined upon Rozinante, a name, in his opinion, lofty, sonorous, and full of meaning; importing that he had been only a *Rozin,* a drudge-horse, *before* his present condition, and that now he was *before* all the *Rozins* in the world.

Having given his horse a name so much to his satisfaction, he resolved to fix upon one for himself. This consideration employed him eight more days, which at length he determined to call himself Don Quixote; whence some of the historians of this most true history have concluded that his name was certainly Quixada, and not Quesada, as others would have it. Then recollecting that the valorous Amadis, not content with the simple appellation of Amadis, added thereto the name of his kingdom, and native country, in order to render it famous, styling himself Amadis de Gaul; so he, like a good knight, also added the name of his province, and called himself Don Quixote de la Mancha; whereby, in his opinion, he fully proclaimed his lineage and country, which, at the same time, he honored, by taking its name.

His armor being now furbished, his helmet made perfect, his horse and himself provided with names, he found nothing wanting but a lady to be in love with: for a knight-errant without the tender passion was a tree without leaves and fruit — a body without a soul. If, said he, for my sins, or rather, through my good fortune, I encounter some giant — an ordinary occurrence to knights-errant — and overthrow him at the first onset, or cleave him in twain, or, in short, vanquish him and force him to surrender, must I not have some lady, to whom I may send him, as a present? that when he enters into the presence of my charming mistress, he may throw himself upon his knees before her, and in a submissive, humble voice, say: "Madam, in me you behold the giant Caraculiambro, lord of the island Malendrania, who, being vanquished in single combat by the never-enough-to-be-praised Don Quixote de la Mancha, am by him commanded to present myself before you, to be disposed of according to the will and pleasure of your highness." How happy was our good knight after this harangue! How much more so when he found a mistress! It is said that, in a neighboring village, a good-looking peasant girl resided, of whom he had formerly been enamored, although it does not appear that she ever knew or cared about it; and this was the lady whom he chose to nominate mistress of his heart. He then sought a name for her, which, without entirely departing from her own, should incline and approach towards that of a princess, or great lady, and determined upon Dulcinea del Toboso (for she was a native of that village), a name, he thought, harmonious, uncommon, and expressive — like all the others which he had adopted.

Chapter II

WHICH TREATS OF THE FIRST SALLY THAT DON QUIXOTE MADE FROM HIS NATIVE ABODE

These arrangements being made, he would no longer defer the execution of his project, which he hastened from a consideration of what the world suffered by his delay: so many were the grievances he intended to redress, the wrongs to rectify, errors to amend, abuses to reform, and debts to discharge! Therefore, without communicating his intentions to any individual, and wholly unobserved, one morning before day, being one of the most sultry in the month of July, he armed himself cap-a-pie, mounted Rozinante, placed the helmet on his head, braced on his target, took his lance, and, through the private gate of his back yard, issued forth into the open plain, in a transport of joy to think he had met with no obstacles to the commencement of his honorable enterprise. But scarcely had he found himself on the plain when he was assailed by a recollection so terrible as almost to make him abandon the undertaking: for it just then occurred to him, that he was not yet a knight; therefore, in conformity to the laws of chivalry, he neither could nor ought to enter the lists against any of that order; and, even if he had been actually dubbed, he should, as a new knight, have worn white armor, without any device on his shield, until he had gained one by force of arms. These considerations made him irresolute whether to proceed; but frenzy prevailing over reason, he determined to get himself made a knight by the first one he should meet, like many others, of whom he had read. As to white armor, he resolved, when he had an opportunity, to scour his own, so that it should be whiter than ermine. Having now composed his mind, he proceeded, taking whatever road his horse pleased; for therein, he believed, consisted the true spirit of adventure.

Our new adventurer, thus pursuing his way, conversed within himself, saying: "Who doubts but that in future times, when the true history of my famous achievements is brought to light, the sage who records them will, in this manner, describe my first sally! 'Scarcely had ruddy Phœbus extended over the face of this wide and spacious earth the golden filaments of his beautiful hair, and scarcely had the little painted birds, with their forked tongues, hailed, in soft and mellifluous harmony, the approach of the rosy harbinger of morn, who, leaving the soft couch of her jealous consort, had just disclosed herself to mortals through the gates and balconies of the Manchegan horizon, when the renowned knight, Don Quixote de la Mancha, quitting the slothful down, mounted Rozinante, his famous steed, and proceeded over the ancient memorable plain of Montiel (which was indeed the truth).' O happy era, happy age," he continued, "when my glorious deeds shall be revealed to the world; deeds worthy of being engraven on brass, sculptured in marble, and recorded by the pencil; and thou, O sage enchanter, whosoever thou mayest be, destined to chronicle this extraordinary history! forget not, I beseech thee, my good Rozinante, the inseparable companion of all my toils!" Then again, as if really enamored, he exclaimed, "O Dulcinea, my princess! sovereign of this captive heart! greatly do you wrong me by a cruel adherence to your decree, forbidding me to appear in the presence of your beauty! Deign, O lady, to think on this enslaved heart, which, for love of you, endures so many pangs!"

In this wild strain he continued, imitating the style of his books as nearly as he could, and proceeding slowly on, while the sun arose with such intense heat that it was enough to dissolve his brains, if any had been left. He traveled almost the whole of that day without encountering any thing worthy of recital, which caused him much vexation, for he was impatient for an opportunity to prove the valor of his powerful arm.

Some author says his first adventure was that of the straits of Lapice; others affirm it to have been that of the wind-mills; but, from what I have been able to ascertain of this matter, and have found written in the annals of La Mancha, the fact is that he traveled all that day, and as night approached, both he and his horse were wearied and dying of hunger; and in this state, as he looked around him, in hopes of discovering some castle, or shepherd's cot, where he might repose and find refreshment, he descried, not far from the road, an inn, which to him was a star conducting him to the portals, if not the palaces, of his redemption. He made all the haste he could, and reached it at night-fall. There chanced to stand at the door two young women, ladies of pleasure (as they are called), on their journey to Seville, in the company of some carriers who rested there that night. Now as every thing that our adventurer saw and conceived was, by his imagination, molded to what he had read, so, in his eyes, the inn appeared to be a castle, with its four turrets, and pinnacles of shining silver, together with its draw-bridge, deep moat, and all the appurtenances with which such castles are usually described. When he had advanced within a short distance of it, he checked Rozinante, expecting some dwarf would mount the battlements, to announce, by sound of trumpet, the arrival of a knight-errant at the castle; but finding them tardy, and Rozinante impatient for the stable, he approached the inn-door, and there saw the two strolling girls, who to him appeared to be beautiful damsels or lovely dames, enjoying themselves before the gate of their castle.

It happened that just at this time a swineherd collecting his hogs (I make no apology, for so they are called) from an adjoining stubble field, blew the horn which assembles them together, and instantly Don Quixote was satisfied, for he imagined it was a dwarf who had given the signal of his arrival. With extraordinary satisfaction, therefore, he went up to the inn; upon which the ladies, being startled at the sight of a man armed in that manner, with lance and buckler, were retreating into the house; but Don Quixote, perceiving their alarm, raised his pasteboard vizor, thereby partly discovering his meager dusty visage and, with gentle demeanor and placid voice, thus addressed them: "Fly not, ladies, nor fear any discourtesy, for it would be wholly inconsistent with the order of knighthood which I profess to offer insult to any person, much less to virgins of that exalted rank which your appearance indicates." The girls stared at him, and were endeavoring to find out his face, which was almost concealed by the sorry vizor; but hearing themselves called virgins, a thing so much out of the way of their profession, they could not forbear laughing, and to such a degree that Don Quixote was displeased, and said to them: "Modesty well becomes beauty, and excessive laughter, proceeding from a slight cause, is folly; but I say not this to humble or distress you, for my part is no other than to do you service." This language, so unintelligible to the ladies, added to the uncouth figure of our knight, increased their laughter; consequently he grew more indignant, and would have proceeded further, but for the timely appearance of the inn-keeper, a very corpulent, and therefore a very pacific, man, who, upon seeing so ludicrous an object, armed, and with accouterments so ill-sorted as were the bridle, lance, buckler, and corslet, felt disposed to join the damsels in demonstrations of mirth; but, in truth, apprehending some danger from a form thus strongly fortified, he resolved to behave with civility, and therefore said, "If, Sir Knight, you are seeking for a lodging, you will here find, excepting a bed (for there are none in this inn) every thing in abundance." Don Quixote, perceiving the humility of the governor of the fortress, for such to him appeared the inn-keeper, answered: "For me, Señor Castellano, any thing will suffice: since arms are my ornaments, warfare my repose." The host thought he called him Castellano, because he took him for a sound Castilian, whereas he was an Andalusian, of the coast of St. Lucar, as great a thief as Cacus, and not less mischievous than a collegian or a page: and he replied, "If so, your worship's beds must be hard rocks, and your sleep continual watching; and, that being the case, you may dismount with a certainty of finding here sufficient cause for keeping awake the whole year, much more a single night." So saying, he laid hold of Don Quixote's stirrup, who alighted with much difficulty and pain, for he had fasted the whole of the day. He then desired the host to take especial care of his steed, for it was the finest creature that ever fed; the inn-keeper examined him, but thought him not so good by half as his master had represented him. Having led the horse to the stable, he returned to receive the orders of his guest, whom the damsels, being now reconciled to him, were disarming; they had taken off the back and breastplates, but endeavored in vain to disengage the gorget, or take off the counterfeit beaver, which he had fastened with green ribbons, in such a manner that they could not be untied, and he would upon no account allow them to be cut; therefore he remained all that night with his helmet on, making the strangest and most ridiculous figure imaginable.

While these light girls, whom he still conceived to be persons of quality and ladies of the castle, were disarming him, he said to them with infinite grace, "Never before was Knight so honored by ladies as Don Quixote, after his departure from his native village! damsels attended upon him; princesses took charge of his steed! O Rozinante, – for that, ladies, is the name of my horse, and Don Quixote de la Mancha my own; although it was not my intention to have discovered myself, until deeds, performed in your service, should have proclaimed me; but impelled to make so just an application of the ancient romance of Lanzarote, to my present situation, I have thus prematurely disclosed my name: yet the time shall come when your ladyships may command, and I obey; when the valor of my arm shall make manifest the desire I have to serve you." The girls, unaccustomed to such rhetorical flourishes, made no reply, but asked him whether he would please to eat anything. "I shall willingly take some food," answered Don Quixote, "for I apprehend it would be of much service to me." That day happened to be Friday, and there was nothing in the house but some fish, of that kind which in Castile is called Abadexo, in Andalusia, Bacallao, in some parts Curadillo, and in others Truchuela. They asked if his worship would like some truchuela, for they had no other fish to offer him. "If there be many troutlings," replied Don Quixote, "they will supply the place of one trout; for it is the same to me whether I receive eight single rials or one piece of eight. Moreover, these troutlings may be preferable, as veal is better than beef, and kid superior to goat; be that as it may, let it come immediately, for the toil and weight of arms cannot be sustained by the body unless the interior be supplied with aliments." For the benefit of the cool air, they placed the table at the door of the inn, and the landlord produced some of his ill-soaked, and worse-cooked, bacallao, with bread as foul and black as the Knight's armor: but it was a spectacle highly risible to see him eat; for his hands being engaged in holding his helmet on, and raising the beaver, he could not feed himself, therefore one of the ladies performed this office for him; but to drink would have been utterly impossible had not the inn-keeper bored a reed, and, placing one end into his mouth, at the other poured in the wine; and all this he patiently endured rather than cut the lacings of his helmet.

In the mean time there came to the inn a sow-gelder, who, as soon as he arrived, blew his pipe of reeds four or five times, which finally convinced Don Quixote that he was now in some famous castle, where he was regaled with music; that the poor jack was trout, the bread of the purest white, the strolling wenches ladies of distinction, and the inn-keeper governor of the castle; consequently he remained satisfied with his enterprise and first sally, though it troubled him to reflect that he was not yet a knight, being persuaded that he could not lawfully engage in any adventure until he had been invested with the order of knighthood.

Chapter III

IN WHICH IS DESCRIBED THE DIVERTING CEREMONY OF KNIGHTING DON QUIXOTE

Tormented by this idea, he abruptly finished his scanty meal, called the inn-keeper, and, shutting himself up with him in the stable, he fell on his knees before him, and said, "Never will I rise from this place, valorous knight, until your courtesy shall vouchsafe to grant a boon which it is my intention to request: a boon that will redound to your glory and to the benefit of all mankind." The inn-keeper, seeing his guest at his feet, and hearing such language, stood confounded, and stared at him, without knowing what to do or say; he entreated him to rise, but in vain, until he had promised to grant the boon he requested. "I expected no less, signor, from your great magnificence," replied Don Quixote; "know, therefore, that the boon I have demanded, and which your liberality has conceded, is that, on the morrow, you will confer upon me the honor of knighthood. This night I will watch my arms in the chapel of your castle, in order that, in the morning, my earnest desire may be fulfilled, and I may with propriety traverse the four quarters of the world, in quest of adventures, for the relief of the distressed; conformable to the duties of chivalry and of knights-errant, who, like myself, are devoted to such pursuits."

The host, who, as we have said, was a shrewd fellow, and had entertained some doubts respecting the wits of his guest, was now confirmed in his suspicions; and, to make sport for the night, determined to follow his humor. He told him therefore that his desire was very reasonable, and that such pursuits were natural and suitable to knights so illustrious as he appeared to be, and as his gallant demeanor fully testified; that he had himself in the days of his youth followed that honorable profession, and traveled over various parts of the world in search of adventures; failing not to visit the suburbs of Malaga, the isles of Riaran, the compass of Seville, the market place of Segovia, the olive field of Valencia, the rondilla of Granada, the coast of St. Lucar, the fountain of Cordova, the taverns of Toledo, and divers other parts, where he had exercised the agility of his heels and the dexterity of his hands; committing sundry wrongs, soliciting widows, seducing damsels, cheating youths; in short, making himself known to most of the tribunals in Spain; and that finally he had retired to this castle, where he lived upon his own revenue and that of others; entertaining therein all knights-errant of every quality and degree, solely for the great affection he bore them, and that they might share their fortune with him, in return for his good will. He further told him that in his castle there was no chapel wherein he could watch his armor, for it had been pulled down, in order to be rebuilt; but that, in cases of necessity, he knew it might be done wherever he pleased: therefore he might watch it that night in a court of the castle, and the following morning, if it pleased God, the requisite ceremonies should be performed, and he should be dubbed so effectually that the world would not be able to produce a more perfect knight. He then enquired if he had any money about him? Don Quixote told him he had none: having never read in their histories that knights-errant provided themselves with money. The inn-keeper assured him he was mistaken, for, admitting that it was not mentioned in their history, the authors deeming it unnecessary to specify things so obviously requisite as money and clean shirts, yet was it not, therefore, to be inferred that they had none; but, on the contrary, he might consider it as an established fact that all the knights-errant, of whose history so many volumes are filled, carried their purses well provided against accidents; that they were also supplied with shirts, and a small casket full of ointments, to heal the wounds they might receive; for, in plains and deserts, where they fought and were wounded, no aid was near, unless they had some sage enchanter for their friend, who could give them immediate assistance, by conveying in a cloud through the air some damsel or dwarf, with a vial of water, possessed of such virtue that, upon tasting a single drop of it, they should instantly become as sound as if they had received no injury. But when the knights of former times were without such a friend, they always took care that their esquires should be provided with money, and such necessary articles as lint and salves; and when they had no esquires, which very rarely happened, they carried these things themselves, upon the crupper of their horse, in wallets so small as to be scarcely visible, that they might seem to be something of more importance: for, except in such cases, the custom of carrying wallets was not tolerated among knights-errant. He therefore advised, though, as his godson (which he was soon to be), he might command him, never henceforth to travel without money and the aforesaid provisions; and he would find them serviceable when he least expected it. Don Quixote promised to follow his advice with punctuality; and an order was now given for performing the watch of the armor, in a large yard adjoining the inn. Don Quixote, having collected it together, placed it on a cistern which was close to a well; then, bracing on his target and grasping his lance, with graceful demeanor, he paced to and fro, before the pile, beginning his parade as soon as it was dark.

The inn-keeper informed all who were in the inn of the frenzy of his guest, the watching of his armor, and of the intended knighting. They were surprised at so singular a kind of madness, and went out to observe him at a distance. They perceived him sometimes quietly pacing along, and sometimes leaning upon his lance with his eyes fixed upon his armor, for a considerable time. It was now night, but the moon shone with a splendor which might vie even with that whence it was borrowed; so that every motion of our new knight might be distinctly seen.

At this time, it happened that one of the carriers wanted to give his mules some water; for which purpose it was necessary to remove Don Quixote's armor from the cistern, who, seeing him advance, exclaimed with a loud voice, "O thou, whosoever thou art, rash knight! who approachest the armor of the most valiant adventurer that ever girded sword, beware of what thou dost, and touch it not, unless thou wouldst yield thy life as the forfeit of thy temerity." The carrier heeded not this admonition (though better would it have been for him if he had) but, seizing hold of the straps, he threw the armor some distance from him, which Don Quixote perceiving, he raised his eyes to heaven, and addressing his thoughts, apparently, to his lady Dulcinea, said: "Assist me, O lady, to avenge this first insult offered to your vassal's breast; nor let your favor and protection fail me in this my first perilous encounter!" Having uttered these and similar ejaculations, he let slip his target, and, raising his lance with both hands, he gave the carrier such a stroke upon the head that he fell to the ground in so grievous a plight that, had the stroke been repeated, there would have been no need of a surgeon. This done, he replaced his armor, and continued his parade with the same tranquillity as before.

Soon after another carrier, not knowing what had passed, for the first yet lay stunned, came out with the same intention of watering his mules; and, as he approached to take away the armor from the cistern, Don Quixote, without saying a word or imploring any protection, again let slip his target, raised his lance, and, with no less effect than before, smote the head of the second carrier. The noise brought out all the people in the inn, and the landlord among the rest; upon which Don Quixote braced on his target, and, laying his hand upon his sword, said: "O lady of beauty! strength and vigor of my enfeebled heart! Now is the time for thee to turn thy illustrious eyes upon this thy captive knight, whom so mighty an encounter awaits!" This address had, he conceived, animated him with so much courage that, were all the carriers in the world to have assailed him, he would not have retreated one step.

The comrades of the wounded, upon discovering the situation of their friends, began at a distance to discharge a shower of stones upon Don Quixote, who sheltered himself as well as he could with his target, without daring to quit the cistern, because he would not abandon his armor. The innkeeper called aloud to them, begging they would desist, for he had already told them he was insane, and that, as a madman, he would be acquitted, though he were to kill them all. Don Quixote, in a voice still louder, called them infamous traitors, and the lord of the castle a cowardly, base-born knight, for allowing knight-errant to be treated in that manner; declaring that, had he received the order of knighthood, he would have made him sensible of his perfidy. "But as for you, ye vile and worthless rabble, I utterly despise ye! Advance! Come on, molest me as far as ye are able, for quickly shall ye receive the reward of your folly and insolence!" This he uttered with so much spirit and intrepidity that the assailants were struck with terror; which, in addition to the landlord's persuasions, made them cease their attack; he then permitted the wounded to be carried off, and, with the same gravity and composure, resumed the watch of his armor.

The host, not relishing these pranks of his guest, determined to put an end to them, before any further mischief ensued, by immediately investing him with the luckless order of chivalry; approaching him, therefore, he disclaimed any concurrence, on his part, in the insolent conduct of those low people, who were, he observed, well chastised for their presumption. He repeated to him that there was no chapel in the castle, nor was it by any means necessary for what remained to be done; that the stroke of knighting consisted in blows on the neck and shoulders, according to the ceremonial of the order, which might be effectually performed in the middle of a field; that the duty of watching his armor he had now completely fulfilled, for he had watched more than four hours, though only two were required. All this Don Quixote believed, and said that he was there ready to obey him, requesting him, at the same time, to perform the deed as soon as possible; because, should he be assaulted again when he found himself knighted, he was resolved not to leave one person alive in the castle, excepting those whom, out of request, he might be induced to spare.

The constable, thus warned and alarmed, immediately brought forth a book in which he kept his account of the straw and oats he furnished to the carriers, and, attended by a boy, who carried an end of candle, and the two damsels beforementioned, went towards Don Quixote, whom he commanded to kneel down; he then began reading in his manual, as if it were some devout prayer, in the course of which he raised his hand and gave him a good blow on the neck, and, after that, a handsome stroke over the shoulders, with his own sword, still muttering between his teeth, as if in prayer. This being done, he commanded one of the ladies to gird on his sword, an office she performed with much alacrity, as well as discretion, no small portion of which was necessary to avoid bursting with laughter at every part of the ceremony; but indeed the prowess they had seen displayed by the new knight kept their mirth within bounds. At girding on the sword, the good lady said: "God grant you may be a fortunate knight, and successful in battle." Don Quixote enquired her name, that he might thenceforward know to whom he was indebted for the favor received, as it was his intentions to bestow upon her some share of the honor he should acquire by the valor of his arm. She replied, with much humility, that her name was Tolosa, and that she was the daughter of a cobbler at Toledo, who lived at the stalls of Sanchobienaya; and that, wherever she was, she would serve and honor him as her lord.

Don Quixote, in reply, requested her, for his sake, to do him the favor henceforth to add to her name the title of Don, and call herself Donna Tolosa, which she promised to do. The other girl now buckled on his spur, and with her he held nearly the same conference as with the lady of the sword; having enquired her name, she told him it was Molinera, and that she was daughter to an honest miller of Antiquera; he then requested her likewise to assume the Don, and style herself Donna Molinera, renewing his proffers of service and thanks.

These never-till-then-seen ceremonies being thus speedily performed, Don Quixote was impatient to find himself on horseback, in quest of adventures: he therefore instantly saddled Rozinante, mounted him, and, embracing his host, made his acknowledgments for the favor he had conferred, by knighting him, in terms so extraordinary that it would be in vain to attempt to repeat them. The host, in order to get rid of him the sooner, replied with no less flourish, but with more brevity; and, without making any demand for his lodging, wished him a good journey.

Chapter VIII

OF THE VALOROUS DON QUIXOTE'S SUCCESS IN THE DREADFUL AND NEVER-BEFORE-IMAGINED ADVENTURE OF THE WIND-MILLS; WITH OTHER EVENTS WORTHY TO BE RECORDED

As they were thus discoursing, they came in sight of thirty or forty wind-mills, which are in that plain; and, as soon as Don Quixote espied them, he said to his squire: "Fortune disposes our affairs better than we ourselves could have desired: look yonder, friend Sancho Panza, where thou mayest discover somewhat more than thirty monstrous giants, whom I intend to encounter and slay; and with their spoils we will begin to enrich ourselves: for it is lawful war, and doing God good service to remove so wicked a generation from off the face of the earth." "What giants?" said Sancho Panza. "Those thou seest yonder," answered his master, "with their long arms; for some are wont to have them almost of the length of two leagues." "Look, sir," answered Sancho, "those, which appear yonder are not giants, but wind-mills; and what seem to be arms are the sails, which, whirled about by the wind, make the mill-stone go." "It is very evident," answered Don Quixote, "that thou art not versed in the business of adventures: they are giants: and, if thou art afraid, get thee aside and pray, whilst I engage with them in fierce and unequal combat." So saying, he clapped spurs to his steed, notwithstanding the cries his squire sent after him, assuring him that they were certainly wind-mills, and not giants. But he was so fully possessed that they were giants that he neither heard the outcries of his squire Sancho, nor yet discerned what they were, though he was very near them, but went on crying out aloud: "Fly not, ye cowards and vile caitiffs; for it is a single knight who assaults you." The wind now rising a little, the great sails began to move: upon which Don Quixote called out: "Although ye should move more arms than the giant Briareus, ye shall pay for it."

Then recommending himself devoutly to his lady Dulcinea, beseeching her to succor him in the present danger, being well covered with his buckler, and setting his lance in the rest, he rushed on as fast as Rozinante could gallop, and attacked the first mill before him; when, running his lance into the sail, the wind whirled it about with so much violence that it broke the lance to shivers, dragging horse and rider after it, and tumbling them over and over on the plain, in very evil plight. Sancho Panza hastened to his assistance, as fast as the ass could carry him; and when he came up to his master, he found him unable to stir, so violent was the blow which he and Rozinante had received in their fall. "God save me!" quoth Sancho, "did I not warn you to have a care of what you did, for that they were nothing but wind-mills? And nobody could mistake them, but one that had the like in his head." "Peace, friend Sancho," answered Don Quixote: "for matters of war are, of all others, most subject to continual change. Now I verily believe, and it is most certainly the fact, that the sage Freston, who stole away my chamber and books, has metamorphosed those giants into wind-mills, on purpose to deprive me of the glory of vanquishing them, so great is the enmity he bears me! But his wicked arts will finally avail but little against the goodness of my sword." "God grant it!" answered Sancho Panza; then helping him to rise, he mounted him again upon his steed, which was almost disjointed.

Conversing upon the late adventure, they followed the road that led to the pass of Lapice; because there, Don Quixote said, they could not fail to meet with many and various adventures, as it was much frequented. He was, however, concerned at the loss of his lance; and, speaking of it to his squire, he said: "I remember to have read that a certain Spanish knight, called Diego Perez de Vargas, having broken his sword in fight, tore off a huge branch or limb from an oak, and performed such wonders with it that day, and dashed out the brains of so many Moors, that he was surnamed Machuca; and, from that day forward, he and his descendants bore the names of Vargas and Machuca. I now speak of this, because from the first oak we meet, I mean to tear a limb, at least as good as that; with which I purpose and resolve to perform such feats that thou shalt deem thyself most fortunate in having been thought worthy to behold them, and to be an eye-witness of things which will scarcely be credited." "God's will be done!" quoth Sancho; "I believe all just as you say, sir. But, pray set yourself more upright in your saddle: for you seem to me to ride sideleg, owing, perhaps, to bruises received by your fall." "It is certainly so," said Don Quixote; "and, if I do not complain of pain, it is because knights-errant are not allowed to complain of any wound whatever, even though their entrails should issue from it." "If so, I have nothing more to say;" quoth Sancho; "but God knows I should be glad to hear your worship complain when anything ails you. As for myself, I must complain of the least pain I feel, unless this business of not complaining extend also to the squires of knights-errant." Don Quixote could not forbear smiling at the simplicity of his squire, and told him he might complain whenever and as much as he pleased, either with or without cause, having never yet read any thing to the contrary in the laws of chivalry.

Sancho put him in mind that it was time to dine. His master answered that at present he had no need of food, but that he might eat whenever he thought proper. With this license, Sancho adjusted himself as well as he could upon his beast; and, taking out the contents of his wallet, he jogged on behind his master, very leisurely, eating, and ever anon raising the bottle to his mouth, with so much relish that the best fed victualer of Malaga might have envied him. And whilst he went on in this manner, repeating his draughts, he thought no more of the promises his master had made him; nor did he think it any toil, but rather a recreation, to go in quest of adventures, however perilous they might be. In fine, they passed that night under the shelter of some trees; and from one of them the knight tore a withered branch, to serve him in some sort as a lance, after fixing upon it the iron head of the one that had been broken. All that night Don Quixote slept not, but ruminated on his lady Dulcinea; comfortably to the practice of knights-errant, who, as their histories told him, were wont to pass many successive nights in woods and deserts, without closing their eyes, indulging the sweet remembrance of their mistresses. Not so did Sancho spend the night; for, his stomach being full, and not of succory water, he made but one sleep of it; and, had not his master roused him, neither the beams of the sun, that darted full in his face, nor the melody of the birds, which, in great numbers, cheerfully saluted the approach of the new day, could have awaked him. At his uprising he applied again to his bottle, and found it much lighter than the evening before; which grieved him to the heart, for he did not think they were in the way soon to remedy that defect. Don Quixote would not yet break his fast; resolving, as we have said, still to subsist upon savory remembrances.

They now turned again into the road they had entered upon the day before, leading to the pass of Lapice, which they discovered about three in the afternoon. "Here, friend Sancho," said Don Quixote upon seeing it, "we may plunge our arms up to the elbows in what are termed adventures. But attend to this caution, that, even shouldst thou see me in the greatest peril in the world, thou must not lay hand to thy sword to defend me, unless thou perceivest that my assailants are vulgar and low people; in that case thou mayest assist me: but should they be knights, it is no wise agreeable to the laws of chivalry that thou shouldst interfere, until thou art thyself dubbed a knight." "Your worship," answered Sancho, "shall be obeyed most punctually therein, and the rather as I am naturally very peaceable, and an enemy to thrusting myself into brawls and squabbles; but, for all that, as to what regards the defense of my own person, I shall make no great account of those same laws, since both divine and human law allows every man to defend himself against whoever would wrong him." "That I grant," answered Don Quixote; "but with respect to giving me aid against knights, thou must refrain and keep within bounds thy natural impetuosity." "I say, I will do so," answered Sancho; "and I will observe this precept as religiously as the Lord's-day."

As they were thus discoursing, there appeared on the road two monks of the order of St. Benedict, mounted upon dromedaries; for the mules whereon they rode were not much less. They wore traveling masks, and carried umbrellas. Behind them came a coach, accompanied by four or five men on horseback, and two muleteers on foot. Within the coach, as it afterwards appeared, was a Biscaine lady on her way to join her husband at Seville, who was there waiting to embark for India, where he was appointed to a very honorable post. The monks were not in her company, but were only traveling the same road. Scarcely had Don Quixote espied them, when he said to his squire: "Either I am deceived, or this will prove the most famous adventure that ever happened; for those blacks figures that appear yonder must undoubtedly be enchanters, who are carrying off, in that coach, some princess, whom they have stolen; which wrong I am bound to use my utmost endeavors to redress." "This may prove a worse business than the wind-mills," said Sancho: "pray, sir, take notice that those are Benedictine monks, and the coach must belong to some travelers. Hearken to my advice, sir; have a care what you do, and let not the devil deceive you." "I have already told thee, Sancho," answered Don Quixote, "that thou knowest little concerning adventures: what I say is true, as thou wilt presently see." So saying, he advanced forward, and planted himself in the midst of the highway, by which the monks were to pass; and when they were so near that he supposed they could hear what he said, he cried out, with a loud voice: "Diabolical and monstrous race! Either instantly release the high-born princesses whom ye are carrying away perforce in that coach, or prepare for instant death, as the just chastisement of your wicked deeds." The monks stopped their mules, and stood amazed, as much at the figure of Don Quixote, as at his expressions; to which they answered: "Signor cavalier, we are neither diabolical nor monstrous, but monks of the Benedictine order, traveling on our own business, and entirely ignorant whether any princesses are carried away in that coach, by force, or not." "No fair speeches to me: for I know ye, treacherous scoundrels!" said Don Quixote: and, without waiting for a reply, he clapped spurs to Rozinante, and, with his lance couched, ran at the foremost monk, with such fury and resolution that, if he had not slid down from his mule, he would certainly have been thrown to the ground, and wounded too, if not killed outright. The second monk, on observing how his comrade was treated, clapped spurs to the sides of his good mule, and began to scour along the plain, lighter than the wind itself.

Sancho Panza, seeing the monk on the ground, leaped nimbly from his ass, and running up to him, began to disrobe him. While he was thus employed, the two lackeys came up and asked him why he was stripping their master. Sancho told them that they were his lawful perequisites, being the spoils of the battle, which his Lord Don Quixote had just won. The lackeys, who did not understand the jest, nor what was meant by spoils or battles, seeing that Don Quixote was at a distance, speaking with those in the coach, fell upon Sancho, threw him down, and, besides leaving him not a hair in his beard, gave him a hearty kicking, and left him stretched on the ground, deprived of sense and motion. Without losing a moment, the monk now got upon his mule again, trembling, terrified, and pale as death; and was no sooner mounted than he spurred after his companion, who stood at some distance, to observe the issue of this strange encounter: but, being unwilling to wait, they pursued their way, crossing themselves as often as if the devil had been at their heels. In the meantime Don Quixote, as it hath been already mentioned, addressing the lady in the coach, "Your beauteous ladyship may now," said he, "dispose of your person as pleaseth you best; for the pride of your ravishers lies humbled in the dust, overthrown by my invincible arm; and, that you may be at no trouble to learn the name of your deliverer, know that I am called Don Quixote de la Mancha, knight-errant and adventurer, and captive to the peerless and beauteous Dulcinea del Toboso; and, in requital of the benefit you have received at my hands, all that I desire is that you would return to Toboso, and, in my name, present yourselves before that lady, and tell her what I have done to obtain your liberty."

All that Don Quixote said was overheard by a certain squire, who accompanied the coach, a Biscainer, who, finding he would not let it proceed, but talked of their immediately returning to Toboso, flew at Don Quixote, and, taking hold of his lance, addressed him, in bad Castilian and worse Biscaine, after this manner: "Cavalier, begone! and the devil go with thee! I swear, by the God that made me, if thou dost not quit the coach, thou forfeitest thy life, as I am a Biscainer."

Don Quixote understood him very well, and with great calmness answered: "If thou wert a gentleman, as thou art not, I would before now have chastised thy folly and presumption, thou pitiful slave." "I no gentleman!" said the Biscainer; "I swear by the great God, thou lyest, as I am a Christian; if thou wilt throw away thy lance, and draw thy sword, thou shalt see how soon the cat will get into the water: Biscainer by land, gentleman by sea, gentleman for the devil and thou lyest! Now what hast thou to say?" "Thou shalt see that presently, as said Agrages," answered Don Quixote; then, throwing down his lance, he drew his sword, grasped his buckler, and set upon the Biscainer, with a resolution to take his life. The Biscainer, seeing him come on in that manner, would fain have alighted, knowing that his mule, a wretched hackney, was not to be trusted, but he had only time to draw his sword. Fortunately for him he was so near the coach as to be able to snatch from it a cushion, that served him for a shield; whereupon, they immediately fell to, as if they had been mortal enemies. The rest of the company would have made peace between them, but it was impossible; for the Biscainer swore, in his jargon, that, if they would not let him finish the combat, he would murder his mistress, or whoever attempted to prevent him. The lady of the coach, amazed and affrighted at what she saw, ordered the coachman to remove a little out of the way, and sat at a distance, beholding the rigorous conflict; in the progress of which, the Biscainer gave Don Quixote so mighty a stroke on one of his shoulders, and above his buckler, that, had it not been for his armor, he had cleft him down to the girdle. Don Quixote, feeling the weight of that unmeasurable blow, cried out aloud, saying: "O lady of my soul! Dulcinea, flower of all beauty! Succor this thy knight, who, to satisfy thy great goodness, exposes himself to this perilous extremity!" This invocation, the drawing his sword, the covering himself well with his buckler, and rushing with fury on the Biscainer, was the work of an instant — resolving to venture all on the fortune of a single blow. The Biscainer, perceiving his determination, resolved to do the same, and therefore waited for him, covering himself well with his cushion; but he was unable to turn his mule either to the right, or the left, for, being already jaded, and unaccustomed to such sport, the creature would not move a step.

Don Quixote, as we before said, now advanced against the wary Biscainer, with his uplifted sword, fully determined to cleave him asunder; and the Biscainer awaited him, with his sword also raised, and guarded by his cushion. All the bystanders were in fearful suspense as to the event of those prodigious blows with which they threatened each other; and the lady of the coach and her attendants were making a thousand vows, and promises of offerings, to all the images and places of devotion in Spain, that God might deliver them and their squire from this great peril. But the misfortune is that the author of the history, at that very crisis, leaves the combat unfinished, pleading, in excuse, that he could find no more written of the exploits of Don Quixote than what he has already related. It is true, indeed, that the second undertaker of this work could not believe that so curious a history should have been consigned to oblivion; or that the wits of La Mancha should have so little curiosity as not to preserve in their archives, or cabinets, some memorials of this famous knight; and, under that persuasion, he did not despair of finding the conclusion of this delectable history; which, through the favor of heaven, actually came to pass, and in the manner that shall be faithfully recounted in the following chapter.

— *From Don Quixote, by Miguel de Cervantes Saavedra, Spanish (1547–1616), translated by Peter Motteux.*

Memnon the Philosopher, or Human Wisdom

VOLTAIRE

MEMNON one day took it into his head to become a great philosopher. Said he to himself, "To be a perfect philosopher and to be perfectly happy, I have nothing to do but to divest myself entirely of passions; and nothing is more easy, as everybody knows. In the first place, I will never be in love; for, when I see a beautiful woman, I will say to myself, — these cheeks will one day grow sallow and wrinkled, these eyes be encircled with vermilion, that bosom become lean and emaciated, that head bald and palsied. Now I have only to consider her at present in imagination, as she will afterwards appear in reality; and certainly a fair face will never turn my head.

"In the second place, I will always be temperate. It will be in vain to tempt me with good cheer, with delicious wines, or the charms of society. I will have only to figure to myself the consequences of excess, — an aching head, a loathing stomach, the loss of reason, of health, and of time: I will then eat only to supply the waste of nature; my health will be always equal, my ideas pure and luminous. All this is so easy that there is no merit in accomplishing it.

"But," says Memnon, "I must think a little of how I am to regulate my fortune: why, my desires are moderate, my wealth is securely placed with the Receiver General of the finances of Nineveh. I have wherewithal to live independent; and that is the greatest of blessings. I shall never be under the cruel necessity of dancing attendance at court. I will never envy anyone, and nobody will envy me. Still, all this is easy. I have friends, and I will preserve them, for we shall never have any difference. I will never take amiss anything they may say or do; and they will behave in the same way to me. There is no difficulty in all this."

Having thus laid his little plan of philosophy in his closet, Memnon put his head out of the window. He saw two women walking under the plane-trees near his house. The one was old, and appeared quite at her ease. The other was young, handsome, and seemingly much agitated. She sighed, she wept, and seemed on that account still more beautiful. Our philosopher was touched, not, to be sure, with the lady (he was too much determined not to feel any uneasiness of that kind) but with the distress he saw her in. He came downstairs and accosted the young Ninevite, in the design of consoling her with philosophy. That lovely person related to him, with an air of great simplicity, and in the most affecting manner, the injuries she sustained from an imaginary uncle, with what art he had deprived her of some imaginary property, and of the violence which she pretended to dread from him.

"You appear to me," said she, "a man of such wisdom that if you will condescend to come to my house and examine into my affairs, I am persuaded you will be able to draw me from the cruel embarrassment I am at present involved in."

Memnon did not hesitate to follow her, to examine her affairs philosophically and to give her sound counsel.

The afflicted lady led him into a perfumed chamber, and politely made him sit down with her on a large sofa, where they both placed themselves opposite to each other in the attitude of conversation; the one eager in telling her story, the other listening with devout attention. The lady spoke with downcast eyes, whence there sometimes fell a tear, and which, as she now and then ventured to raise them, always met those of the sage Memnon. Their discourse was full of tenderness, which redoubled as often as their eyes met. Memnon took her affairs exceedingly to heart, and felt himself every instant more and more inclined to oblige a person so virtuous and so unhappy. By degrees, in the warmth of their conversation, they drew nearer. Memnon counseled her with great wisdom and gave her the most tender advice.

At this interesting moment, as may be easily imagined, who should come in but the uncle.

He was armed from head to foot, and the first thing he said was, that he would immediately sacrifice, as was just, the sage Memnon and his niece.

The latter, who made her escape, knew that he was well enough disposed to pardon, provided a good round sum were offered him. Memnon was obliged to purchase his safety with all he had about him. In those days people were happy in getting so easily quit. America was not then discovered, and distressed ladies were not nearly as dangerous as they are now.

Memnon, covered with shame and confusion, got home to his own house.

There he found a card inviting him to dinner with some of his intimate friends.

"If I remain at home alone," said he, "I shall have my mind so occupied with this vexatious adventure that I shall not be able to eat a bit, and I shall bring upon myself some disease. It will therefore be prudent in me to go to my intimate friends, and partake with them of a frugal repast. I shall forget in the sweets of their society, the folly I have this morning been guilty of."

Accordingly, he attends the meeting; he is discovered to be uneasy at something, and he is urged to drink and banish care.

"A little wine, drunk in moderation, comforts the heart of god and man": so reasoned Memnon the philosopher, and he becomes intoxicated. After the repast, play is proposed.

"A little play with one's intimate friends is a harmless pastime." He plays and loses all that is in his purse, and four times as much on his word. A dispute arises on some circumstances in the game, and the disputants grow warm. One of his intimate friends throws a dice box at his head, and strikes out one of his eyes. The philosopher Memnon is carried home to his house, drunk and penniless, with the loss of an eye.

He sleeps out his debauch, and when his head becomes clear, he sends his servant to the Receiver General of the finances of Nineveh, to draw a little money to pay his debts of honor to his intimate friends. The servant returns and informs him that the Receiver General had that morning been declared a fraudulent bankrupt, and that by this means an hundred families are reduced to poverty and despair. Memnon, almost beside himself, puts a plaster on his eye and a petition in his pocket, and goes to court to solicit justice from the king against the bankrupt. In the saloon he meets a number of ladies, all in the highest spirits, and sailing with hoops four-and-twenty feet in circumference. One of them eyed him askance, and cried aloud, "Ah! What a horrid monster!"

Another, who was better acquainted with him, thus accosts him: "Good-morrow, Mr. Memnon. I hope you are well, Mr. Memnon. La! Mr. Memnon, how did you lose your eye?" and, turning upon her heel, she tripped away without waiting for an answer.

Memnon hid himself in a corner and waited for the moment when he could throw himself at the feet of the monarch. That moment at last arrived. Three times he kissed the earth, and presented his petition. His gracious majesty received him very favorably, and referred the paper to one of his satraps. The satrap takes Memnon aside, and says to him with a haughty air and a satirical grin,

"Hark ye, you fellow with the one eye, you must be a comical dog indeed, to address yourself to the king rather than to me; and still more so, to dare to demand justice against an honest bankrupt, whom I honor with my protection, and who is nephew to the waiting-maid of my mistress. Proceed no further in this business, my good friend, if you wish to preserve the eye you have left."

Memnon, having thus, in his closet, resolved to renounce women, the excess of the table, play and quarreling, but especially having determined never to go to court, had been in the short space of four-and-twenty hours, duped and robbed by a gentle dame, had got drunk, had gamed, had been engaged in a quarrel, had got his eye knocked out, and had been at court where he was sneered at and insulted.

Petrified with astonishment, and his heart broken with grief, Memnon returns homeward in despair. As he is about to enter his house, he is repulsed by a number of officers who are carrying off his furniture for the benefit of his creditors: he falls down almost lifeless under a plane tree. There he finds the fair dame of the morning, who was walking with her dear uncle; and both set up a loud laugh on seeing Memnon with his plaster. The night approached, and Memnon made his bed on some straw near the walls of his house. Here the ague seized him, and he fell asleep in one of the fits, when a celestial spirit appeared to him in a dream.

It was resplendent with light: it had six beautiful wings, but neither head nor feet nor tail, and could be likened to nothing.

"What art thou?" said Memnon.

"Thy good genius," replied the spirit.

"Restore to me then my eye, my health,

my fortune, my reason," said Memnon; and he related how he had lost them all in one day.

"These are adventures which never happen to us in the world we inhabit," said the spirit.

"And what world do you inhabit?" said the man of affliction.

"My native country," replied the other, "is five hundred millions of leagues distant from the sun, in a little star near Sirius, which you see from hence."

"Charming country!" said Memnon. "And are there indeed no jades to dupe a poor devil, no intimate friends that win his money, and knock out an eye for him, no fraudulent bankrupts, no satraps that make a jest of you while they refuse you justice?"

"No," said the inhabitant of the star, "we have nothing of the kind; we are never duped by women, because we have none among us; never commit excesses at table, because we neither eat nor drink; we have no bankrupts, because with us there is neither silver nor gold; our eyes cannot be knocked out because we have not bodies in the form of yours; and satraps never do us injustice because in our world we are all equal."

"Pray, my lord," then said Memnon, "without women and without eating how do you spend your time?"

"In watching," said the genius, "over the other worlds that are entrusted to us; and I am now come to give you consolation."

"Alas!" replied Memnon, "why did you not come yesterday to hinder me from committing so many indiscretions?"

"I was with your elder brother Hassan," said the celestial being. "He is still more to be pitied than you are. His Most Gracious Majesty, the Sultan of the Indies, in whose court he has the honor to serve, has caused both his eyes to be put out for some small indiscretion; and he is now in a dungeon, his hands and feet loaded with chains."

"'Tis a happy thing truly," said Memnon, "to have a good genius in one's family, when out of two brothers one is blind in an eye, the other blind of both: one stretched upon straw, the other in a dungeon."

"Your fate will soon change," said the spirit of the star. "It is true you will never recover your eye, but, except that, you may be sufficiently happy if you never again take it into your head to be a perfect philosopher."

"Is it then impossible?" said Memnon.

"As impossible as to be perfectly wise, perfectly strong, perfectly powerful, perfectly happy. We ourselves are very far from it. There is a world indeed where all of this takes place; but in the hundred thousand millions of worlds dispersed over the regions of space, everything goes on by degrees. There is less philosophy, and less enjoyment, in the second than in the first, less in the third than in the second, and so forth till the last in the scale, where all are completely fools."

"I am afraid," said Memnon, "that our little terraqueous globe here is the madhouse of those hundred thousand millions of worlds of which Your Lordship does me the honor to speak."

"Not quite," said the spirit, "but very nearly: everything must be in its proper place."

"But are those poets and philosophers wrong, then, who tell us that everything is for the best?"

"No, they are right, when we consider things in relation to the gradation to the whole universe."

"Oh! I shall never believe it till I recover my eye again," said poor Memnon.

—*From the Romances, Tales, and Smaller Pieces of Voltaire (French, 1694–1778), translated by Peter Eckler.*

~✲~

The Latin Boy. A Tale from Montenegro

SIMO MATAVULJ

On St. Peter's Day, towards sunset, the serdar Jovan Knezevic betook himself to his large threshing-floor, which lay behind his house. He was a small, dark man, with a rosy face and a beard which had slightly turned gray. He had donned festive attire. Over his green dolama he had flung his toka, while two silver-mounted pistols and a long knife were thrust into his belt. With his chibuk flung across his shoulders, he was stamping and tripping about on the threshing-floor. From time to time he came to a standstill and then turned once more around his shadow, in which he examined the end of the blade that projected from his belt at the upper part of his thigh.

Suddenly someone of the community called out:

"Serdar, we have come to have a chat with you for an hour or so."

"You are welcome!" he replied and sat down on one of the two round stones which lay on top of each other in the middle of the threshing floor, where the threshing animals were tethered.

While he was filling his pipe, four men came up, all without vests. They sat down on the paving which lies beneath the stone enclosure of the threshing-floor.

"What a heat!" exclaimed the oldest among the arrivals. He had a huge moustache, and with his sleeve he wiped the sweat from his forehead.

The three other fellows were also panting, and they too were wiping the sweat away, which was oozing from them as if they had come up at the double, although they had really been walking quite slowly.

The serdar adjusted the tinder on the flint, and as he lighted his pipe, he exclaimed:

"Yes, a heat such as we have every year about this time."

"And you, cousin, have put on your jacket into the bargain. . . . It is a marvel that you do not melt beneath it!" added one of the younger men.

The serdar frowned, and his eyebrows were drawn together; he seemed to have become angry at this remark. He blew some clouds of smoke into the air, and then, turning to the speaker, he exclaimed:

"I have been used to that from my childhood, and have kept it up to this very day. You could go about even without trousers, if you wished, but we old Montenegrins do not consider what is most pleasant, but what is more becoming. Melt? As if I were made of sugar! What braggarts the youth of today are, and how feeble they have grown. . . ."

The little fellow flushed as if glowing coals had been scattered over him. His comrades looked at him with reproachful glances. But the one with the big moustache exclaimed soothingly:

"Do not chide him, serdar, it is no great matter. He did not mean to affront you. Go, Lale, ask pardon of your cousin!"

Lale kissed Jovan's hand. The latter gave a kindly smile and fondled his head. This was his answer; he was gracious in a trice, — a true "old Montenegrin."

The serdar had not a big family. Besides his wife he had only a grandson named Ivan, and a daughter, Dunja. She was a girl as sturdy as her father, but she was taller than he. She had great dark eyes and splendid long hair. The lads often crept secretly into the serdar's courtyard, to watch the girl as she was combing her hair. The plaits came down below her waist. And when she ran barefoot in her chemise across the courtyard, the ground fairly shook beneath her tread. Little Ivan was scarcely two months old when his father fell in battle at the time of Dervish Pasha. His mother died soon afterwards.

In this fashion it had come about that the serdar's house, which was once so famous, had remained almost without male successors. Now all the old man's hopes were centred upon the five-year-old boy and a good husband for his daughter, if God willed it so.

Silence continued on all sides. The younger men were waiting for the serdar to speak, but he was gazing abstractedly at the light of his pipe.

Suddenly steps were heard in the distance. About twenty more members of the family now came up. They greeted each other and sat down, some on the flagstones, the others with their feet crossed upon the enclosure of the threshing-floor.

As there were also some older men among the new-comers, the conversation resumed its course. The serdar himself was now in the best of humours. He began to banter first one and then the other, in turn. This pleased them all very much, for he was a wit, the like of whom could not be found far and wide. He had just overwhelmed a distant relative with the whole power of his wit, when someone among those present exclaimed:

"Stop, stop, wedding guests are coming to us!"

Everyone turned round and general laughter ensued. About twenty of the more distant townsfolk were approaching as wedding guests, one after another. But that was as much as to say that they were coming to pay a visit to a chieftain. The serdar again stared angrily in front of him, for he was vexed with the man who had mocked at the arrivals by the name in question.

"Let them come, and make room for the people!" he cried, and rose up from his seat. The others present also rose up on one side when the first guests had advanced closer.

"Just look, by God, the little Latin boy is among them too, and not among the last ones, either!" exclaimed the same waggish lad who had given them all the name of wedding guests.

"Do not speak so, my children!" the serdar suddenly burst forth. "If he is among them, it is fitting for him to be among them. Surely you know whose son he is?"

"By God, he is a handsome lad, too," exclaimed the man with the big moustache, "and we only tease him because we like him. . . . But we will stop doing it."

"Welcome!" exclaimed the serdar. "Come, brothers, and the best of thanks for your visit!"

They all embraced and then sat down. About forty of them were now sitting down together on the threshing-floor. Dunja, her mother, and little Ivan watched the company from the threshold of the kitchen door. Women were leaning against the enclosure, and even little children stopped in their play for a moment, to feast their eyes on the sight of the grown-ups.

As long as man could remember, the assembly of the people had been held on the same spot where the serdar's threshing-floor was now. Jovan's father, the serdar Mícun, had paved the place with flag-stones and provided it with an enclosure, and such an assembly-place was not to be found far and near.

After each had questioned the other as to how it fared with him, his family and his distant relatives, the serdar turned to the "little Latin boy."

He had been given the nickname of "Latin" because his face was fair and tender, – just like a Latin boy. But his real name was Luka Lipovac. He was the orphan son of the famous hero Kosta Lipovac.

He was sitting directly opposite the serdar.

"Well, how fares it with you, Luka?"

"Well, God be thanked!" replied the latter, blushing slightly.

"And tell me, pray, do these lads tease you, at all?"

"A little," answered Luka with a forced laugh.

"But from to-day onwards they have no more right to do so!" observed one of the Knezevic family.

"Oh, why from to-day onwards?" came a shout from several sides.

"Because early to-day he surpassed all in stone-throwing, with the exception of Kicun!"

"Is it possible?" exclaimed the serdar in astonishment.

"Yes, by God, it is!" cried several with one accord.

"Then come hither, that I may embrace you!"

And the serdar gave the youth a kiss upon the forehead. The latter was so abashed at this, that he did not know what he should do with his hands. He drew them across his upper lip, upon which, however, not even the down of a moustache was so far to be observed; at the same time his eyes were beaming with clear fire, and he was splendid to look upon in his beauty.

The rest of the people were not altogether pleased with this, and someone called out: "First of all we must make sure whether we were contending in sober earnest, or whether it was only in play."

"Don't make any pretence," cried the others. "There were close on thirty of us lads who saw it. Each one of you did his level best to beat him, but he beat you all, Kicun alone excepted."

There was a silence after these words. The older men thought it would be best to broach another subject. Then one of the Lipova men stood up and cried:

"You would hardly believe, serdar, all the things that Luka does in order to appear more of a man. The whole livelong day he roves about in this heat, and why? To get a brown tan! But he cannot succeed. It is true that he will not admit it, but finds an excuse of one sort or another; but I know only too well what makes him do it. We laugh at him. The young women envy him for his milky face. Besides that, he rarely practises stone-throwing, jumping, and running. . . ."

"That is all to his credit," the serdar interrupted him. "A stalwart lad! He will take after his heroic father. Like father like son!"

"May God grant it," cried some of the Lipova men.

"And now we will moisten our dry throats," cried the serdar.

"There is no need! Not on our account, pray!" was the cry on all sides.

"But we shall, though . . . Dunja, bring the jug and the gusla, do you hear?"

All were now silent.

The girl brought a jug and a glass; little Milan took the gusla in his arms. The girl stood aloof in a shy and shamefaced manner. She would not venture among so many men, and wished to hand the jug with the brandy over to a female relative who stood closest to her.

But the young men shouted: "Either you alone shall serve us, or nobody shall do it."

And the serdar cried sternly:

"Serve us, my child!"

In order to give her time to gain her composure, they took little Ivan amongst them, and fondled him and asked him questions. Dunja, red as a rose, now went from one to the other, handing the jug first to those older in years and pedigree. Each one drank the serdar's health, and each one's eyes strayed towards the beautiful girl as he did so.

When the young Latin boy's turn came . . . (I know you will not credit it) . . . all were silent, he alone raised his voice and cried aloud:

"And even though it were poison, I would drink it from your hand!"

All stood mute with amazement. Who was it dared to say such a thing in the presence of her father? The bashful little Latin boy! However could such a daring notion have entered his mind? Heaven alone knew. Certain it was that these words had passed his lips merely by the way. He, however, seemed to have observed nothing; he emptied his glass and was about to hand it back to the girl, but she had escaped. It was in vain that the serdar called her back. She had already vanished in the house.

Not until then did the Latin boy look round about him in bewilderment.

"You seem to look upon our Dunja with favour," was the sullen remark of a relative who was the same age as Dunja.

The Latin boy felt as if someone had boxed his ears. He answered in the same tone: "And why should I not look upon her with favour?"

"Because she could thrust you into her girdle and then climb this hill at full speed; do you understand me!"

"She might do that with you, but not with me; do you understand me?" cried the Latin boy.

The people feared that the quarrel might take an ugly turn, and began to pacify the two. The serdar turned the whole thing into a joke. But there was one who cried: "Calm down, both of you. Such a buxom girl as that could overcome the two of you, if she wanted!"

"That she could not!" exclaimed the Latin boy, and stood up.

"We can easily make sure. We will call the girl in, and you shall match yourself against her, to see who is the stronger," cried the other.

Noise and laughter now arose.

"Stop now, you young scamps, we will now hear the serdar play on the gusla!" shouted the older men. But the younger ones were fairly bursting with laughter as they saw how haughtily the Latin boy bore himself. Some shouted:

"Call Dunja here. . . . Call Dunja! The serdar will allow it. Why should he not? That is no disgrace, God forbid. . . . Will you, Luka? Say so and then you will see!"

He beckoned with his hand as a sign that they should keep quiet. Then he cried:

"I will!"

When they saw that the serdar was laughing, full ten of them leaped into the house to fetch Dunja. She struggled, she waved her powerful arms, and pushed several of the men a couple of yards away from her. But the rascals fell upon her and at last managed to get her out.

"Do not let me, father!" she exclaimed with a ringing laugh.

"You must!" cried her father, also laughing. "You must, and why not, since we desire it? Bear yourself firmly, my darling. You are the daughter of Jovan Knezevic!"

The girl now grew serious, looked her father straight in the eyes, and then, rolling up her sleeves, she said:

"Let him come, then!"

The young Latin boy now drew his weapons from his girdle, threw them to the ground with his cap, and ran up to the girl who was awaiting him on the free space in the threshing-floor.

They clutched each other by the arms.

She lifted him up in the air like a feather, but he stood alertly on his feet again.

"Now you lift her up!" his kinsmen shouted to him.

"Dunja, our champion!" shouted the Knezevic men to the girl.

This Luka would not do, but let her have the mastery. Again the girl lifted him up to the right, then again to the left. But each time he regained his foothold as alertly as a roebuck.

"He is artful," cried some. "He is waiting till she is tired, and then he will begin!"

"On, on. Dunja!" cried all her kinsmen with one accord.

"Come, Luka, our champion. Do not disgrace us;" cried the Lipova men.

"Stop, Dunja!"

"Stop, Luka!"

"Stop, stop!"

He pressed her to him as hard as he could, with the intention of letting her go, or else to confuse her. But at the same moment she sprang alertly sideways, waved her arms and fell to the ground on top of him.

You can imagine what now took place. Such din and laughter arose, that not a word could be understood. The Lipova men made the best of a bad bargain and joined in the laughter. Dunja's relatives embraced and kissed one another. But the Latin boy, pale in the face, walked up to the assembly and eyed them narrowly in turn. The serdar was afraid that it might lead to something awkward, and so he took up the gusla and drew the bow once or twice across the strings. In an instant there was complete silence, for everybody understood what the old man's object was in so doing.

"You sit down with us as well, Luka! Do not be vexed, for it was only a joke!" spoke the serdar to him in a fatherly tone.

"I will obey you, serdar, but I only ask your leave for one word more."

"Good, what is it?" asked the serdar, giving him an encouraging glance.

"Brother!" began the Latin boy, "a girl has overcome me, has she not?"

"Truly!" exclaimed several through their teeth.

"But I tell you it was not so. Rather was it the girl's blood by which I was overcome. If anyone does not believe it, I am at his service!"

"Come, Luka, stop your foolish talk!" cried his kinsmen.

"I have said nothing. I only ask whether there is one among you who would venture to enter the lists with me now, although I have been overcome by a girl?"

"Stop, that is folly!"

"Whichever one of you Knezevic men pleases, and there are real heroes among you, I am sure."

"I accept the challenge," cried Kicun, angrily, "but from the knee upwards!"

"Have no fear, we shall strive together like men."

They seized one another.

Kicun was the strongest lad among the Gradjani.

"Don't break him in two, Kicun," jeered the kinsmen of the latter.

And, by Heaven, Kicun did not spare the young Latin boy, he strained every muscle, in his endeavour to throw him to the ground. They swayed to and fro, they scuffled, until the Latin boy suddenly lifted Kicun up and threw him sideways to the ground.

"Was there no foul play about it?" asked the serdar, sternly.

"No, by God, serdar, what is true, is true. He has thrown me like a hero, and all honour to him!"

"If that is so, kiss him!"

"I will and gladly."

"And you others will also?"

"Very gladly."

"Listen to me, then. Whoever from this time onward calls this lad the little Latin boy will pay a fine of 50 florins, in addition I will lay about his back with this chibuk, as true as I live. But you, my dear boy, come to me."

And embracing Luka, he said to him:

"Do you know that your father was my dearest friend?"

"I know it, and I am glad of it."

"Do you know that among the townsfolk there was no better fellow than your father? And . . . and therefore"—he cleared his throat—"brother, even though it is against the Montenegrin custom, you must not take it amiss if I now do . . . say something that was not known hitherto. . . . Listen, Luka, will you have my Dunja for your wife?"

"Yes!" he exclaimed, beside himself with delight.

"Then send your uncle to me to-morrow with the betrothal ring."

"Good luck!" said all in agreement.

"Only you must not reproach me later with having forced her upon you. Do not quarrel with her and do not put your strength against her as you have against Kicun!"

The Lipova men thereupon fired off their

rifles in token of their joy. The whole neighbourhood hastened up; in a thrice a great ring was formed and the kolo began. The festivities came to an end only with the approach of night.

At the Assumption of the Blessed Virgin, Dunja and Luka were wedded.

By Simo Mutavulj, Montenegrin, translated by Paul Selver.

The Pope's Mule

ALPHONSE DAUDET

OF ALL the pretty sayings, proverbs, adages, with which our Provençal peasantry decorate their discourse, I know of none more picturesque, or more peculiar than this:—for fifteen leagues around my mill, when they speak of a spiteful and vindictive man, they say: "That fellow! distrust him! he's like the Pope's mule who kept her kick for seven years."

I tried for a long time to find out whence that proverb came, what that Pope's mule was, and why she kept her kick for seven years. No one could give me any information on the subject, not even Francet Mamaï, my old fife-player, though he knows his Provençal legends to the tips of his fingers. Francet thought, as I did, that there must be some ancient chronicle of Avignon behind it, but he had never heard of it otherwise than as a proverb.

"You won't find it anywhere except in the Grasshoppers' Library," said the old man, laughing.

The idea struck me as a good one; and as the Grasshoppers' Library is close at my door, I shut myself up there for over a week.

It is a wonderful library, admirably stocked, open to poets night and day, and served by little librarians with cymbals who make music for you all the time. I spent some delightful days there, and after a week of researches (on my back) I ended by discovering what I wanted, namely: the story of the mule and that famous kick which she kept for seven years. The tale is pretty, though rather naïve, and I shall try to tell it to you just as I read it yesterday in a manuscript coloured by the weather, smelling of good dried lavender and tied with the Virgin's threads—as they call gossamer in these parts.

Whoso did not see Avignon in the days of the Popes has seen nothing. For gayety, life, animation, the excitement of festivals, never was a town like it. From morning till night there was nothing but processions, pilgrimages, streets strewn with flowers, draped with tapestries, cardinals arriving by the Rhone, banners in the breeze, galleys dressed in flags, the Pope's soldiers chanting Latin on the squares, and the tinkling rattle of the begging friars; while from garret to cellar of houses that pressed, humming, round the great papal palace like bees around their hive, came the tick-tack of lace-looms, the to-and-fro of shuttles weaving the gold thread of chasubles, the tap-tap of the goldsmith's chasing-tools tapping on the chalices, the tuning of choir-instruments at the lute-makers, the songs of the spinners at their work; and above all this rose the sound of bells, and always the echo of certain tambourines coming from away down there on the bridge of Avignon. Because, with us, when the people are happy they must dance—they must dance; and as in those days the streets were too narrow for the *farandole,* fifes and tambourines posted themselves on the bridge of Avignon in the fresh breeze of the Rhone, and day and night folks danced, they danced. Ah! the happy times! the happy town! Halberds that did not wound, prisons where the wine was put to cool; no hunger, no war. That's how the Popes of the Comtat governed their people; and that's why their people so deeply regretted them.

There was one Pope especially, a good old man called Boniface. Ah! that one, many were the tears shed in Avignon when he was dead. He was so amiable, so affable a prince! He laughed so merrily on the back of his mule! And when you passed him, were you only a poor little gatherer of madder-roots, or the grand provost of the town, he gave you his benediction so politely! A real Pope of Yvetot, but a Yvetot of Provence, with something delicate in his laugh, a sprig of sweet marjoram in his cardinal's cap, and never a Jeanneton,—the only Jeanneton he was ever known to have, that good Father, was his vineyard, his own little vineyard which he planted himself, three leagues from Avignon, among the myrtles of Château-Neuf.

Every Sunday, after vespers, the good man paid court to his vineyard; and when he was up there, sitting in the blessed sun, his mule near him, his cardinals stretched out beneath the grapevines, he would order a flask of the wine of his own growth to be opened, — that beautiful wine, the colour of rubies, which is now called the *Chateau-Neuf des Papes*, and he sipped it with sips, gazing at his vineyard tenderly. Then, the flask empty, the day fading, he rode back joyously to town, the Chapter following; and when he crossed the bridge of Avignon through the tambourines and the *farandoles*, his mule, set going by the music, paced along in a skipping little amble, while he himself beat time to the dance with his cap, which greatly scandalized the cardinals but made the people say: "Ah! the good prince! Ah! the kind Pope!"

What the Pope loved best in the world, next to his vineyard of Château-Neuf, was his mule. The good man doted on that animal. Every evening before he went to bed he went to see if the stable was locked, if nothing was lacking in the manger; and never did he rise from table without seeing with his own eyes the preparation of a great bowl of wine in the French fashion with sugar and spice, which he took to his mule himself, in spite of the remarks of his cardinals. It must be said that the animal was worth the trouble. She was a handsome black mule, with reddish points, sure-footed, hide shining, back broad and full, carrying proudly her thin little head decked out with pompons and ribbons, silver bells and streamers; gentle as an angel withal, innocent eyes, and two long ears, always shaking, which gave her the look of a downright good fellow. All Avignon respected her, and when she passed through the streets there were no civilities that the people did not pay her; for every one knew there was no better way to stand well at court, and that the Pope's mule, for all her innocent look, had led more than one man to fortune, — witness Tistet Védène and his amazing adventure.

This Tistet Védène was, in point of fact, an impudent young rogue, whom his father, Guy Védène, the goldsmith, had been forced to turn out of his house, because he would not work and only debauched the apprentices. For six months Tistet dragged his jacket through all the gutters of Avignon, but principally those near the papal palace; for the rascal had a notion in his head about the Pope's mule, and you shall now see what mischief was in it.

One day when his Holiness was riding all alone beneath the ramparts, behold our Tistet approaching him and saying, with his hands clasped in admiration: —

"Ah! *mon Dieu*, Holy Father, what a fine mule you are riding! Just let me look at her. Ah! Pope, what a mule! The Emperor of Germany hasn't her equal."

And he stroked her and spoke to her softly as if to a pretty young lady: —

"Come here, my treasure, my jewel, my pearl —"

And the good Pope, quite touched, said to himself: —

"What a nice young fellow; how kind he is to my mule!"

And the next day what do you think happened? Tistet Védène changed his yellow jacket for a handsome lace alb, a purple silk hood, shoes with buckles; and he entered the household of the Pope, where no one had ever yet been admitted but sons of nobles and nephews of cardinals. That's what intriguing means! But Tistet was not satisfied with that.

Once in the Pope's service, the rascal continued the game he had played so successfully. Insolent to every one, he showed attentions and kindness to none but the mule, and he was always to be met with in the courtyards of the palace with a handful of oats, or a bunch of clover, shaking its pink blooms at the window of the Holy Father as if to say: "Hein! who's that for, hey?" Time and again this happened, so that, at last, the good Pope, who felt himself getting old, left to Tistet the care of looking after the stable and of carrying to the mule his bowl of wine, — which did not cause the cardinals to laugh.

Nor the mule either. For now, at the hour her wine was due she beheld half a dozen little pages of the household slipping hastily into the hay with their hoods and their laces; and then, soon after, a good warm smell of caramel and spices pervaded the stable, and Tistet Védène appeared bearing carefully the bowl of hot wine. Then the poor animal's martyrdom began.

That fragrant wine she loved, which kept her warm and gave her wings, they had the cruelty to bring it into her stall and let her smell of it; then, when her nostrils were full of the perfume, away! and the beautiful rosy liquor went down the throats of those young scamps! And not only did they steal her wine, but they were like devils, those young fellows, after they had drunk it. One pulled her ears, another her tail. Quiquet jumped on her back, Béluguet put his hat on her head, and not one of the rascals ever thought that with one good kick of her hind-legs the worthy animal could send them all to the polar star, and farther still if she chose. But no! you are not the Pope's mule for nothing — that mule of benedictions and plenary indulgences. The lads might do what they liked, she was never angry with them; it was only Tistet Védène whom she hated. He, indeed! when she felt him behind her, her hoofs itched; and reason enough too. That good-for-nothing Tistet played her such villainous tricks. He had such cruel ideas and inventions after drinking.

One day he took it into his head to make her go with him into the belfry, high up, very high up, to the peak of the palace! What I am telling you is no tale; two hundred thousand Provençal men and women saw it. Imagine the terror of that unfortunate mule, when, after turning for an hour, blindly, round a corkscrew staircase and climbing I don't know how many steps, she found herself all of a sudden on a platform blazing with light, while a thousand feet below her she saw a diminutive Avignon, the booths in the market no bigger than nuts, the Pope's soldiers moving about their barrack like little red ants, and down there, bright as a silver thread, a microscopic little bridge on which they were dancing, dancing. Ah! poor beast! what a panic! At the cry she gave, all the windows of the palace shook.

"What's the matter? what are they doing to my mule?" cried the good Pope, rushing out upon his balcony.

Tistet Védène was already in the courtyard pretending to weep and tear his hair.

"Ah! great Holy Father, what's the matter, indeed! *Mon Dieu!* what will become of us? There's your mule gone up to the belfry."

"All alone?"

"Yes, great Holy Father, all alone. Look up there, high up. Don't you see the tips of her ears pointing out — like two swallows?"

"Mercy!" cried the poor Pope, raising his eyes. "Why, she must have gone mad! She'll kill herself! Come down, come down, you luckless thing!"

Pécaïre! she wanted nothing so much as to come down; but how? which way? The stairs? not to be thought of; they can be mounted, those things; but as for going down! why, they are enough to break one's legs a hundred times. The poor mule was in despair, and while circling round and round the platform with her big eyes full of vertigo she thought of Tistet Védène.

"Ah! bandit, if I only escape — what a kick to-morrow morning!"

That idea of a kick put some courage into her heart; without it she never could have held good. . . . At last, they managed to save her; but 'twas quite a serious affair. They had to get her down with a derrick, ropes, and a sling. You can fancy what humiliation it was for a Pope's mule to see herself suspended at that height, her four hoofs swimming in the void like a cockchafer hanging to a string. And all Avignon looking at her!

The unfortunate beast could not sleep at night. She fancied she was still turning round and round that cursèd platform while the town laughed below, and again she thought of the infamous Tistet and the fine kick of her heels she would let fly at him next day. Ah! friends, what a kick! the dust of it would be seen as far as Pampérigouste.

Now, while this notable reception was being made ready for him in the Pope's stable what do you think Tistet Védène was about? He was descending the Rhone on a papal galley, singing as he went his way to the Court of Naples with a troop of young nobles whom the town of Avignon sent every year to Queen Jeanne to practise diplomacy and fine manners. Tistet Védène was not noble; but the Pope was bent on rewarding him for the care he had given to his mule, and especially for the activity he displayed in saving her from her perilous situation.

The mule was the disappointed party on the morrow!

"Ah! the bandit! he suspected something," she thought, shaking her silver bells. "No matter for that, scoundrel; you'll find it when you get back, that kick; I'll keep it for you!"

And she kept it for him.

After Tistet's departure the Pope's mule returned to her tranquil way of life and her usual proceedings. No more Quiquet, no more Béluguet in the stable. The good old days of the spiced wine came back, and with them good-humour, long siestas, and the little gavotte step as she crossed the bridge of Avignon. Nevertheless, since her adventure a certain coldness was shown to her in the town. Whisperings were heard as she passed, old people shook their heads, children laughed and pointed to the belfry. The good Pope himself no longer had quite the same confidence in his friend, and when he let himself go into a nice little nap on her back of a Sunday, returning from his vineyard, he always had this thought latent in his mind: "What if I should wake up there on the platform!" The mule felt this, and she suffered, but said nothing; only, whenever the name of Tistet Védène was uttered in her hearing, her long ears quivered, and she struck the iron of her shoes hard upon the pavement with a little snort.

Seven years went by. Then, at the end of those seven years, Tistet Védène returned from the Court of Naples. His time was not yet finished over there, but he had heard that the Pope's head mustard-bearer had died suddenly at Avignon, and as the place seemed a good one, he hurried back in haste to solicit it.

When this intriguing Védène entered the palace the Holy Father did not recognize him, he had grown so tall and so stout. It must also be said that the good Pope himself had grown older, and could not see much without spectacles.

Tistet was not abashed.

"What, great Holy Father! you don't remember me? It is I, Tistet Védène."

"Védène?"

"Why, yes, you know the one that took the wine to your mule."

"Ah! yes, yes, — I remember. A good little fellow, that Tistet Védène! And now, what do you want of me?"

"Oh!" very little, great Holy Father. I came to ask — By the bye, have you still got her, that mule of yours? Is she well? Ah! good! I came to ask you for the place of the chief mustard-bearer who lately died."

"Mustard-bearer, you! Why you are too young. How old are you?"

"Twenty-two, illustrious pontiff; just five years older than your mule. Ah! palm of God, what a fine beast she is! If you only knew how I love her, that mule, — how I pined for her in Italy! Won't you let me see her?"

"Yes, my son, you shall see her," said the worthy Pope, quite touched. "And as you love her so much I must have you live near her. Therefore, from this day I attach you to my person as chief mustard-bearer. My cardinals will cry out, but no matter! I'm used to that. Come and see me to-morrow, after vespers, and you shall receive the insignia of your rank in presence of the whole Chapter, and then I will show you the mule and you shall go to the vineyard with us, hey! hey!"

I need not tell you if Tistet Védène was content when he left the palace, and with what impatience he awaited the ceremony of the morrow. And yet there was one more impatient and more content than he: it was the mule. After Védène's return, until vespers on the following day that terrible animal never ceased to stuff herself with oats, and practise her heels on the wall behind her. She, too, was preparing for the ceremony.

Well, on the morrow, when vespers were said, Tistet Védène made his entry into the papal courtyard. All the grand clergy were there; the cardinals in their red robes, the devil's advocate in black velvet, the convent abbots in their small mitres, the wardens of Saint-Agrico, the violet hoods of the Pope's household, the lower clergy also, the Pope's guard in full uniform, the three penitential brotherhoods, the hermits of Mont-Ventoux, with their sullen faces, and the little clerk who walks behind them with a bell, the flagellating friars naked to the waist, the ruddy sextons in judge's gowns, all, all, down to the givers of holy water, and the man who lights and him who puts out the candles — not one was missing. Ah! 'twas a fine ordination! Bells, fire-crackers, sunshine, music, and always those frantic tambourines leading the *farandole* over there, on the bridge.

When Védène appeared in the midst of this great assembly, his fine bearing and handsome face sent a murmur of admiration through the crowd. He was truly a magnificent Provençal; but of the blond type, with thick hair curling at the tips, and a dainty little beard that looked like slivers of fine metal fallen from the chisel of his father, the goldsmith. The rumour ran that the fingers of Queen Jeanne had sometimes played in the curls of that golden beard; and, in truth, the Sieur de Védène had the self-glorifying air and the abstracted look of men that queens have loved. On this day, in order to do honour to his native town, he had substituted for his Neapolitan clothes a tunic edged with pink, *à la Provençale*, and in his hood there quivered a tall feather of the Camargue ibis.

As soon as he entered the new official bowed with a gallant air, and approached the high portico where the Pope was waiting to give him the insignias of his rank, namely, a wooden spoon and a saffron coat. The mule was at the foot of the steps, saddled and bridled, all ready to go to the vineyard; as he passed beside her, Tistet Védène smiled pleasantly, and stopped to give her a friendly pat or two on the back, glancing, as he did so, out of the corner of his eye to see if the Pope noticed it. The position was just right, — the mule let fly her heels.

"There, take it, villain! Seven years have I kept it for thee!"

And she gave him so terrible a kick, — so terrible that even at Pampérigouste the smoke was seen, a whirlwind of blond dust, in which flew the feather of an ibis, and that was all that remained of the unfortunate Tistet Védène!

Mule kicks are not usually so destructive; but this was a papal mule; and then, just think! she had kept it for him for seven years. There is no finer example of ecclesiastical rancour.

—*From Letters from My Mill, by Alphonse Daudet, French (1840–1897), translated by Katharine Prescott Wormley.*

~ ❁ ~

The Christmas Tree and the Wedding

FEODOR DOSTOIEVSKY

THE other day I saw a wedding. . . . But no! I would rather tell you about a Christmas tree. The wedding was superb. I liked it immensely. But the other incident was still finer. I don't know why it is that the sight of the wedding reminded me of the Christmas tree. This is the way it happened:

Exactly five years ago, on New Year's Eve, I was invited to a children's ball by a man high up in the business world, who had his connections, his circle of acquaintances, and his intrigues. So it seemed as though the children's ball was merely a pretext for the parents to come together and discuss matters of interest to themselves, quite innocently and casually.

I was an outsider, and, as I had no special matters to air, I was able to spend the evening independently of the others. There was another gentleman present who like myself had just stumbled upon this affair of domestic bliss. He was the first to attract my attention. His appearance was not that of a man of birth or high family. He was tall, rather thin, very serious, and well dressed. Apparently he had no heart for the family festivities. The instant he went off into a corner by himself the smile disappeared from his face, and his thick dark brows knitted into a frown. He knew no one except the host and showed every sign of being bored to death, though bravely sustaining the rôle of thorough enjoyment to the end. Later I learned that he was a provincial, had come to the capital on some important, brain-racking business, had brought a letter of recommendation to our host, and our host had taken him under his protection, not at all *con amore*. It was merely out of politeness that he had invited him to the children's ball.

They did not play cards with him, they did not offer him cigars. No one entered into conversation with him. Possibly they recognized the bird by its feathers from a distance. Thus, my gentleman, not knowing what to do with his hands, was compelled to spend the evening stroking his whiskers. His whiskers were really fine, but he stroked them so assiduously that one got the feeling that the whiskers had come into the world first and afterwards the man in order to stroke them.

There was another guest who interested me. But he was of quite a different order. He was a personage. They called him Julian Mastakovich. At first glance one could tell he was an honored guest and stood in the same relation to the host as the host to the gentleman of the whiskers. The host and hostess said no end of amiable things to him, were most attentive, wining him, hovering over him, bringing guests up to be introduced, but never leading him to any one else. I noticed tears glisten in our host's eyes when Julian Mastakovich remarked that he had rarely spent such a pleasant evening. Somehow I began to feel uncomfortable in this personage's presence. So, after amusing myself with the children, five of whom, remarkably well-fed young persons, were our host's, I went into a little sitting-room, entirely unoccupied, and seated myself at the end that was a conservatory and took up half the room.

The children were charming. They absolutely refused to resemble their elders, notwithstanding the efforts of mothers and governesses. In a jiffy they had denuded the Christmas tree down to the very last sweet and had already succeeded in breaking half of their playthings before they even found out which belonged to whom.

One of them was a particularly handsome little lad, dark-eyed, curly-haired, who stubbornly persisted in aiming at me with his wooden gun. But the child that attracted the greatest attention was his sister, a girl of about eleven, lovely as a Cupid. She was quiet and thoughtful, with large, full, dreamy eyes. The children had somehow offended her, and she left them and walked into the same room that I had withdrawn into. There she seated herself with her doll in a corner.

"Her father is an immensely wealthy business man," the guests informed each other in tones of awe. "Three hundred thousand rubles set aside for her dowry already."

As I turned to look at the group from which I heard this news item issuing, my glance met Julian Mastakovich's. He stood listening to the insipid chatter in an attitude of concentrated attention, with his hands behind his back and his head inclined to one side.

All the while I was quite lost in admiration of the shrewdness our host displayed in the dispensing of the gifts. The little maid of the many-rubled dowry received the handsomest doll, and the rest of the gifts were graded in value according to the diminishing scale of the parents' stations in life. The last child, a tiny chap of ten, thin, red-haired, freckled, came into possession of a small book of nature stories without illustrations or even head and tail pieces. He was the governess's child. She was a poor widow, and her little boy, clad in a sorry-looking little nankeen jacket, looked thoroughly crushed and intimidated. He took the book of nature stories and circled slowly about the children's toys. He would have given anything to play with them. But he did not dare to. You could tell he already knew his place.

I like to observe children. It is fascinating to watch the individuality in them struggling for self-assertion. I could see that the other children's things had tremendous charm for the red-haired boy, especially a toy theater, in which he was so anxious to take a part that he resolved to fawn upon the other children. He smiled and began to play with them. His one and only apple he handed over to a puffy urchin whose pockets were already crammed with sweets, and he even carried another youngster pickaback — all simply that he might be allowed to stay with the theater.

But in a few moments an impudent young person fell on him and gave him a pummeling. He did not dare even to cry. The governess came and told him to leave off interfering with the other children's games, and he crept away to the same room the little girl and I were in. She let him sit down beside her, and the two set themselves busily to dressing the expensive doll.

Almost half an hour passed, and I was nearly dozing off, as I sat there in the conservatory half listening to the chatter of the red-haired boy and the dowered beauty, when Julian Mastakovich entered suddenly. He had slipped out of the drawing-room under cover of a noisy scene among the children. From my secluded corner it had not escaped my notice that a few moments before he had been eagerly conversing with the rich girl's father, to whom he had only just been introduced.

He stood still for a while reflecting and mumbling to himself, as if counting something on his fingers.

"Three hundred — three hundred — eleven — twelve — thirteen — sixteen — in five years! Let's say four per cent — five times twelve — sixty, and on these sixty ——. Let us assume that in five years it will amount to — well, four hundred. Hm — hm! But the shrewd old fox isn't likely to be satisfied with four per cent. He gets eight or even ten, perhaps. Let's suppose five hundred, five hundred thousand, at least, that's sure. Anything above that for pocket money — hm —"

He blew his nose and was about to leave the room when he spied the girl and stood still. I, behind the plants, escaped his notice. He seemed to me to be quivering with excitement. It must have been his calculations that upset him so. He rubbed his hands and danced from place to place, and kept getting more and more excited. Finally, however, he conquered his emotions and came to a standstill. He cast a determined look at the future bride and wanted to move toward her, but glanced about first. Then, as if with a guilty conscience, he stepped over to the child on tip-toe, smiling, and bent down and kissed her head.

His coming was so unexpected that she uttered a shriek of alarm.

"What are you doing here, dear child?" he whispered, looking around and pinching her cheek.

"We're playing."

"What, with him?" said Julian Mastakovich with a look askance at the governess's child. "You should go into the drawing-room, my lad," he said to him.

The boy remained silent and looked up at the man with wide-open eyes. Julian Mastakovich glanced round again cautiously and bent down over the girl.

"What have you got, a doll, my dear?"

"Yes, sir." The child quailed a little, and her brow wrinkled.

"A doll? And do you know, my dear, what dolls are made of?"

"No, sir," she said weakly, and lowered her head.

"Out of rags, my dear. You, boy, you go back to the drawing-room, to the children," said Julian Mastakovich, looking at the boy sternly.

The two children frowned. They caught hold of each other and would not part.

"And do you know why they gave you the doll?" asked Julian Mastakovich, dropping his voice lower and lower.

"No."

"Because you were a good, very good little girl the whole week."

Saying which, Julian Mastakovich was seized with a paroxysm of agitation. He looked round and said in a tone faint, almost inaudible with excitement and impatience:

"If I come to visit your parents will you love me, my dear?"

He tried to kiss the sweet little creature, but the red-haired boy saw that she was on the verge of tears, and he caught her hand and sobbed out loud in sympathy. That enraged the man.

"Go away! Go away! Go back to the other room, to your playmates."

"I don't want him to. I don't want him to! You go away!" cried the girl. "Let him alone! Let him alone!" She was almost weeping.

There was a sound of footsteps in the doorway. Julian Mastakovich started and straightened up his respectable body. The red-haired boy was even more alarmed. He let go the girl's hand, sidled along the wall, and escaped through the drawing-room into the dining-room.

Not to attract attention, Julian Mastakovich also made for the dining-room. He was red as a lobster. The sight of himself in a mirror seemed to embarrass him. Presumably he was annoyed at his own ardor and impatience. Without due respect to his importance and dignity, his calculations had lured and pricked him to the greedy eagerness of a boy, who makes straight for his object – though this was not as yet an object; it only would be so in five years' time. I followed the worthy man into the dining-room, where I witnessed a remarkable play.

Julian Mastakovich, all flushed with vexation, venom in his look, began to threaten the red-haired boy. The red-haired boy retreated farther and farther until there was no place left for him to retreat to, and he did not know where to turn in his fright.

"Get out of here! What are you doing here? Get out, I say, you good-for-nothing! Stealing fruit, are you? Oh, so, stealing fruit! Get out, you freckle face, go to your likes!"

The frightened child, as a last desperate resort, crawled quickly under the table. His persecutor, completely infuriated, pulled out his large linen handkerchief and used it as a lash to drive the boy out of his position.

Here I must remark that Julian Mastakovich was a somewhat corpulent man, heavy, well-fed, puffy-cheeked, with a paunch and ankles as round as nuts. He perspired and puffed and panted. So strong was his dislike (or was it jealousy?) of the child that he actually began to carry on like a madman.

I laughed heartily. Julian Mastakovich turned. He was utterly confused and for a moment, apparently, quite oblivious of his immense importance. At that moment our host appeared in the doorway opposite. The boy crawled out from under the table and wiped his knees and elbows. Julian Mastakovich hastened to carry his handkerchief, which he had been dangling by the corner, to his nose. Our host looked at the three of us rather suspiciously. But, like a man who knows the world and can readily adjust himself, he seized upon the opportunity to lay hold of his very valuable guest and get what he wanted out of him.

"Here's the boy I was talking to you about," he said, indicating the red-haired child. "I took the liberty of presuming on your goodness in his behalf."

"Oh," replied Julian Mastakovich, still not quite master of himself.

"He's my governess's son," our host continued in a beseeching tone. "She's a poor creature, the widow of an honest official. That's why, if it were possible for you—"

"Impossible, impossible!" Julian Mastakovich cried hastily. "You must excuse me, Philip Alexeyevich, I really cannot. I've made inquiries. There are no vacancies, and there is a waiting list of ten who have a greater right—I'm sorry."

"Too bad," said our host. "He's a quiet, unobtrusive child."

"A very naughty little rascal, I should say," said Julian Mastakovich, wryly. "Go away, boy. Why are you here still? Be off with you to the other children."

Unable to control himself, he gave me a sidelong glance. Nor could I control myself. I laughed straight in his face. He turned away and asked our host, in tones quite audible to me, who that odd young fellow was. They whispered to each other and left the room, disregarding me.

I shook with laughter. Then I, too, went to the drawing-room. There the great man, already surrounded by the fathers and mothers and the host and the hostess, had begun to talk eagerly with a lady to whom he had just been introduced. The lady held the rich little girl's hand. Julian Mastakovich went into fulsome praise of her. He waxed ecstatic over the dear child's beauty, her talents, her grace, her excellent breeding, plainly laying himself out to flatter the mother, who listened scarcely able to restrain tears of joy, while the father showed his delight by a gratified smile.

The joy was contagious. Everybody shared in it. Even the children were obliged to stop playing so as not to disturb the conversation. The atmosphere was surcharged with awe. I heard the mother of the important little girl, touched to her profoundest depths, ask Julian Mastakovich in the choicest language of courtesy, whether he would honor them by coming to see them. I heard Julian Mastakovich accept the invitation with unfeigned enthusiasm. Then the guests scattered decorously to different parts of the room, and I heard them, with veneration in their tones, extol the business man, the business man's wife, the business man's daughter, and, especially, Julian Mastakovich.

"Is he married?" I asked out loud of an acquaintance of mine standing beside Julian Mastakovich.

Julian Mastakovich gave me a venomous look.

"No," answered my acquaintance, profoundly shocked by my—intentional—indiscretion.

Not long ago I passed the Church of ——. I was struck by the concourse of people gathered there to witness a wedding. It was a dreary day. A drizzling rain was beginning to come down. I made my way through the throng into the church. The bridegroom was a round, well-fed, pot-bellied little man, very much dressed up. He ran and fussed about and gave orders and arranged things. Finally word was passed that the bride was coming. I pushed through the crowd, and I beheld a marvelous beauty whose first spring was scarcely commencing. But the beauty was pale and sad. She looked distracted. It seemed to me even that her eyes were red from recent weeping. The classic severity of every line of her face imparted a peculiar significance and solemnity to her beauty. But through that severity and solemnity, through the sadness, shone the innocence of a child. There was something inexpressibly naïve, unsettled and young in her features, which, without words, seemed to plead for mercy.

They said she was just sixteen years old. I looked at the bridegroom carefully. Suddenly I recognized Julian Mastakovich, whom I had not seen again in all those five years. Then I looked at the bride again—. Good God! I made my way, as quickly as I could, out of the church. I heard gossiping in the crowd about the bride's wealth—about her dowry of five hundred thousand rubles—so and so much for pocket money.

"Then his calculations were correct," I thought, as I pressed out into the street.

—*By Feodor Dostoievsky, Russian (1821–1881), translated anonymously.*

The Taking of Lungtungpen

RUDYARD KIPLING

MY FRIEND Private Mulvaney told me this, sitting on the parapet of the road to Dagshai, when we were hunting butterflies together. He had theories about the Army, and coloured clay pipes perfectly. He said that the young soldier is the best to work with, "on account av the surpassing innocinse av the child."

"Now, listen!" said Mulvaney, throwing himself full length on the wall in the sun. "I'm a born scutt av the barrick-room! The Army's mate an' dhrink to me, bekaze I'm wan av the few that can't quit ut. I've put in sivinteen years, an' the pipeclay's in the marrow av me. Av I cud have kept out av wan big dhrink a month, I wud have been a Hon'ry Lift'nint by this time—a nuisance to my betthers, a laughin'-shtock to my equils, an' a curse to meself. Bein' fwhat I am, I'm Privit Mulvaney, wid no good-conduc' pay an' a devourin' thirst. Always barrin' me little frind Bobs Bahadur, I know as much about the Army as most men."

I said something here.

"Wolseley be shot! Betune you an' me an' that butterfly net, he's a ramblin', incoherint sort av a divil, wid wan oi on the Quane an' the Coort, an' the other on his blessed silf—everlastin'ly playing Saysar an' Alexandrier rowled into a lump. Now Bobs is a sinsible little man. Wid Bobs an' a few three-year-olds, I'd swape any army av the earth into a towel, an' throw it away aftherwards. Faith, I'm not jokin'! 'Tis the bhoys—the raw bhoys—that don't know fwhat a bullut manes, an' wudn't care av they did—that dhu the work. They're crammed wid bull-mate till they fairly *ramps* wid good livin'; and thin, av they don't fight, they blow each other's hids off. 'Tis the trut' I'm tellin' you. They shud be kept on water an' rice in the hot weather; but there'd be a mut'ny av 'twas done.

"Did ye iver hear how Privit Mulvaney tuk the town av Lungtungpen? I thought not! 'Twas the Lift'nint got the credit; but 'twas me planned the schame. A little before I was inviladed from Burma, me an' four-an'-twenty young wans undher a Lift'nint Brazenose, was ruinin' our dijeshins thryin' to catch dacoits. An' such double-ended divils I niver knew! 'Tis only a *dah* an' a Snider that makes a dacoit. Widout thim, he's a paceful cultivator, an' felony for to shoot. We hunted, an' we hunted, an' tuk fever an' elephints now an' again; but no dacoits. Evenshually, we *puckarowed* wan man. 'Trate him tinderly,' sez the Lift'nint. So I tuk him away into the jungle, wid the Burmese Interprut'r an' my clanin'-rod. Sez I to the man, 'My paceful squireen,' sez I, 'you shquot on your hunkers an' dimonstrate to *my* frind here, where *your* frinds are whin they're at home?' Wid that I introjuced him to the clanin'-rod, an' he comminst to jabber; the Interprut'r interprutin' in betweens, an' me helpin' the Intilligince Department wid my clanin'-rod whin the man misremimbered.

"Prisintly, I learn that, acrost the river, about nine miles away, was a town just dhrippin' wid dahs, an' bohs an' arrows, an' dacoits, an' elephints, an' *jingles*. 'Good!' sez I, 'this office will now close!'

"That night, I went to the Lift'nint an' communicates my information. I never thought much of Lift'nint Brazenose till that night. He was shtiff wid books an' the-ouries, an' all manner av thrimmin's no manner av use. 'Town did ye say?' sez he. 'Accordin' to the the-ouries av War, we shud wait for reinforcemints.'—'Faith!' thinks I, 'we'd betther dig our graves thin;' for the nearest throops was up to their shtocks in the marshes out Mimbu way. 'But,' says the Lift'nint, 'since 'tis a speshil case, I'll make an excepshin. We'll visit this Lungtungpen to-night.'

"The bhoys was fairly woild wid deloight whin I tould 'em; an', by this an' that, they wint through the jungle like buck-rabbits. About midnight we come to the sthrame which I had clane forgot to minshin to my orficer. I was on ahead, wid four bhoys, an' I thought that the Lift'nint might want to the-ourise. 'Shtrip bhoys!' sez I. 'Shtrip to the buff, and shwim in where glory waits!'—'But I *can't* shwim!' sez two av thim. 'To think I should live to hear that from a bhoy wid a board-school edukashin!' sez I. 'Take a lump av thimber, an' me an' Conolly here will ferry ye over, ye young ladies!'

"We got an ould tree-trunk, an' pushed off wid the kits an' the rifles on it. The night was chokin' dhark, an' just as we was fairly embarked, I heard the Lift'nint behind av me callin' out. 'There's a bit av a *nullah* here, Sorr,' sez I, 'but I can feel the bottom already.' So I cud, for I was not a yard from the bank.

" 'Bit av a *nullah!* Bit av an eshtuary!' sez the Lift'nint. 'Go on, ye mad Irishman! Shtrip bhoys!' I heard him laugh; an' the bhoys begun sthrippin' an' rollin' a log into the wather to put their kits on. So me an' Conolly shtruck out through the warm wather wid our log, an' the rest come on behind.

"That shtrame was miles woide! Orth'ris, on the rear-rank log, whispers we had got into the Thames below Sheerness by mistake. 'Kape on shwimmin', ye little blayguard,' sez I, 'an' don't go pokin' your dirty jokes at the Irriwaddy.'—'Silince, men!' sings out the Lift'nint. So we shwum on into the black dhark, wid our chests on the logs, trustin' in the Saints an' the luck av the British Army.

"Evenshually, we hit ground—a bit av sand—an' a man. I put my heel on the back av him. He skreeched an' ran.

" '*Now* we've done it!' sez Lift'nint Brazenose. 'Where the Divil *is* Lungtungpen?' There was about a minute and a half to wait. The bhoys laid a hould av their rifles an' some thried to put their belts on; we was marchin' with fixed baynits av coorse. Thin we knew where Lungtungpen was; for we had hit the river-wall av it in the dhark, an' the whole town blazed wid thim messin' *jingles* an' Sniders like a cat's back on a frosty night. They was firin' all ways at wanst; but over our hids into the sthrame.

" 'Have you got your rifles?' sez Brazenose. 'Got 'em!' sez Orth'ris. 'I've got that thief Mulvaney's for all my back-pay, an' she'll kick my heart sick wid that blunderin' long shtock av hers.'—'Go on!' yells Brazenose, whippin' his sword out. 'Go on an' take the town! An' the Lord have mercy on our sowls!'

"Thin the bhoys gave wan divastatin' howl, an' pranced into the dhark, feelin' for the town, an' blindin' an' stiffin' like Cavalry Ridin' Masters whin the grass pricked their bare legs. I hammered wid the butt at some bamboo-thing that felt wake, an' the rest come an' hammered contagious, while the *jingles* was jingling, an' feroshus yells from inside was shplittin' our ears. We was too close under the wall for thim to hurt us.

"Evenshually, the thing, whatever ut was, bruk; an' the six-an'-twenty av us tumbled, wan after the other, nakid as we were borrun, into the town of Lungtungpen. There was a *melly* av a sumpshus kind for a whoile; but whether they tuk us, all white an' wet, for a new breed av divil, or a new kind av dacoit, I don't know. They ran as though we was both, an' we wint into thim, baynit an' butt, shriekin' wid laughin'. There was torches in the shtreets, an' I saw little Orth'ris rubbin' his showlther ivry time he loosed my long-shtock Martini; an' Brazenose walkin' into the gang wid his sword, like Diarmid av the Gowlden Collar—barring he hadn't a stitch av clothin' on him. We diskivered elephints wid dacoits under their bellies, an', what wid wan thing an' another, we was busy till mornin' takin' possession av the town of Lungtungpen.

"Thin we halted an' formed up, the wimmen howlin' in the houses an' Lift'nint Brazenose blushin' pink in the light av the mornin' sun. 'Twas the most ondasint p'rade I iver tuk a hand in. Foive-and-twenty privits an' a orficer av the Line in review ordher, an' not as much as wud dust a fife betune 'em all in the way of clothin'! Eight av us had their belts an' pouches on; but the rest had gone in wid a handful av cartridges an' the skin God gave thim. *They* was as nakid as Vanus.

" 'Number off from the right!' sez the Lift'nint. 'Odd numbers fall out to dress; even numbers pathrol the town till relieved by the dressing party.' Let me tell you, pathrollin' a town wid nothing on is an ex*pay*rience. I pathrolled for tin minutes, an' begad, before 'twas over, I blushed. The women laughed so. I niver blushed before or since; but I blushed all over my carkiss thin. Orth'ris didn't pathrol. He sez only, 'Portsmith Barricks an' the 'Ard av a Sunday!' Thin he lay down an' rowled any ways wid laughin'.

"Whin we was all dhressed, we counted the dead—sivinty-foive dacoits, besides wounded. We tuk five elephints, a hunder' an' sivinty Sniders, two hunder' dahs, and a lot av other burglarious thruck. Not a man av us was hurt—excep' maybe the Lift'nint, an' he from the shock to his dasincy.

"The Headman av Lungtungpen, who surrinder'd himself, asked the Interprut'r—'Av the English fight like that wid their clo'es off, what in the wurruld do they do wid their clo'es on?' Orth'ris began rowlin' his eyes an' crackin' his fingers an' dancin' a step-dance for to impress the Headman.

He ran to his house; an' we spint the rest av the day carryin' the Lift'nint on our showlthers round the town, an' playin' wid the Burmese babies – fat, little, brown little divils, as pretty as picturs.

"Whin I was inviladed for the dysent'ry to India, I sez to the Lift'nint, 'Sorr,' sez I, 'you've the makin's in you av a great man; but, av you'll let an ould sodger spake, you're too fond of the-ourisin'.' He shuk hands wid me and sez, 'Hit high, hit low, there's no plasin' you, Mulvaney. You've seen me waltzin' through Lungtungpen like a Red Injin widout the war-paint, an' you say I'm too fond av the-ourisin'?' – 'Sorr,' sez I, for I loved the bhoy, 'I wud waltz wid you in that condishin through *Hell*, an' so wud the rest av the men!' Thin I wint downshtrame in the flat an' left him my blessin'. May the Saints carry ut where ut shud go, for he was a fine upstandin' young orficer.

"To reshume. Fwhat I've said jist shows the use av three-year-olds. Wud fifty seasoned sodgers have taken Lungtungpen in the dhark that way? No! They'd know the risk av fever and chill. Let alone the shootin'. Two hundher' might have done ut. But the three-year-olds know little an' care less; an' where there's no fear, there's no danger. Catch thim young, feed thim high, an' by the honour av that great, little man Bobs, behind a good orficer, 'tisn't only dacoits they'd smash wid their clo'es off – 'tis Continental Ar-r-r-mies! They tuk Lungtungpen nakid; an' they'd take St. Pethersburg in their dhrawers! Begad, they would that!

"Here's your pipe, Sorr. Shmoke her tinderly wid honey-dew, afther letting the reek av the Canteen plug die away. But 'tis no good, thanks to you all the same, fillin' my pouch wid your chopped hay. Canteen baccy's like the Army. It shpoils a man's taste for moilder things."

So saying, Mulvaney took up his butterfly-net, and returned to barracks.

—*From Plain Tales from the Hills, by Rudyard Kipling, English (1865–1936).*

The Hero

GABRIELE D'ANNUNZIO

Already the huge standards of Saint Gonselvo had appeared on the square and were swaying heavily in the breeze. Those who bore them in their hands were men of herculean stature, red in the face and with their necks swollen from effort; and they were playing with them.

After the victory over the Radusani the people of Mascalico celebrated the feast of September with greater magnificence than ever. A marvellous passion for religion held all souls. The entire country sacrificed the recent richness of the corn to the glory of the Patron Saint. Upon the streets from one window to another the women had stretched their nuptial coverlets. The men had wreathed with vines the doorways and heaped up the thresholds with flowers. As the wind blew along the streets there was everywhere an immense and dazzling undulation which intoxicated the crowd.

From the church the procession proceeded to wind in and out and to lengthen out as far as the square. Before the altar, where Saint Pantaleone had fallen, eight men, privileged souls, were awaiting the moment for the lifting of the statue of Saint Gonselvo; their names were: Giovanni Curo, l'Ummalido, Mattala, Vencenzio Guanno, Rocco di Cenzo, Benedetto Galante, Biagio di Clisci, Giovanni Senzapaura. They stood in silence, conscious of the dignity of their work, but with their brains slightly confused. They seemed very strong; had the burning eye of the fanatic, and wore in their ears, like women, two circles of gold. From time to time they tested their biceps and wrists as if to calculate their vigour; or smiled furtively at one another.

The statue of the Patron Saint was enormous, very heavy, made of hollow bronze, blackish, with the head and hands of silver.

Mattala cried:

"Ready!"

The people, everywhere, struggled to see. The windows of the church roared at every gust of the wind. The nave was fumigated with incense and resin. The sounds of instruments were heard now and then. A kind of religious fever seized the eight men, in the centre of that turbulence. They extended their arms to be ready.

Mattala cried:

"One! Two! Three!"

Simultaneously the men made the effort to raise the statue to the altar. But its weight was overpowering, and the figure swayed to the left. The men had not yet succeeded in getting a firm grip around the base. They bent their backs in their endeavour to resist. Biago di Clisci and Giovanni Curo, the least strong, lost their hold. L'Ummalido gave a cry.

"Take care! Take care!" vociferated the spectators on seeing the Patron Saint so imperilled. From the square came a resounding crash that drowned all voices.

L'Ummalido had fallen on his knees with his right arm beneath the bronze. Thus kneeling, he held his two large eyes, full of terror and pain, fixed on his hand which he could not free, while his mouth twisted but no longer spoke. Drops of blood sprinkled the altar.

His companions, all together, made a second effort to raise the weight. The operation was difficult. L'Ummalido, in a spasm of pain, twisted his mouth. The women spectators shuddered.

At length the statue was lifted and L'Ummalido withdrew his hand, crushed and bleeding and formless. "Go home, now! Go home!" the people cried, while pushing him toward the door of the church.

A woman removed her apron and offered it to him for a bandage. L'Ummalido refused it. He did not speak, but watched a group of men who were gesticulating and disputing around the statue.

"It is my turn!"

"No! – no! It's my turn!"

"No! let me!"

Cicco Ponno, Mattia Scafarolo and Tommaso di Clisci were contending for the place left vacant by L'Ummalido.

He approached the disputants. Holding his bruised hand at his side, and with the other opening a path, he said simply:

"The position is mine."

And he placed his left shoulder as a prop for the Patron Saint. He stifled down his pain, gritting his teeth, with fierce willpower.

Mattala asked him:

"What are you trying to do?"

He answered:

"What Saint Gonselvo wishes me to do."

And he began to walk with the others. Dumbfounded the people watched him pass. From time to time, someone, on seeing the wound which was bleeding and growing black, asked him:

"L'Umma', what is the matter?"

He did not answer. He moved forward gravely, measuring his steps by the rhythm of the music, with his mind a little hazy, beneath the vast coverlets that flapped in the wind and amongst the swelling crowd.

At a street corner he suddenly fell. The Saint stopped an instant and swayed, in the centre of a momentary confusion, then continued its progress. Mattia Scafarola supplied the vacant place. Two relations gathered up the swooning man and carried him to a nearby house.

Anna di Cenzo, who was an old woman, expert at healing wounds, looked at the formless and bloody member, and then shaking her head, said:

"What can I do with it?"

Her little skill was able to do nothing. L'Ummalido controlled his feelings and said nothing. He sat down and tranquilly contemplated his wound. The hand hung limp, forever useless, with the bones ground to powder.

Two or three aged farmers came to look at it. Each, with a gesture or a word, expressed the same thought.

L'Ummalido asked:

"Who carried the Saint in my place?"

They answered:

"Mattia Scafarola."

Again he asked:

"What are they doing now?"

They answered:

"They are singing the vespers."

The farmers bid him goodbye and left for vespers. A great chiming came from the mother church.

One of the relations placed near the wound a bucket of cold water, saying:

"Every little while put your hand in it. We must go. Let us go and listen to the vespers."

L'Ummalido remained alone. The chiming increased, while changing its metre. The light of day began to wane. An olive tree, blown by the wind, beat its branches against the low window.

L'Ummalido began to bathe his hand little by little. As the blood and concretions fell away, the injury appeared even greater. L'Ummalido mused:

"It is entirely useless. It is lost. Saint Gonselvo, I offer it up to you."

He took a knife and went out. The streets were deserted. All of the devotees were in the church. Above the houses sped, like fugitive herds of cattle, the violet clouds of a September sunset.

In the church the united multitude sang in measured intervals as if in chorus to the music of the instruments. An intense heat emanated from the human bodies and the burning tapers. The silver head of Saint Gonselvo scintillated from on high like a light house. L'Ummalido entered. To the stupefaction of all, he walked up to the altar and said, in a clear voice, while holding the knife in his left hand:

"Saint Gonselvo, I offer it up to you."

And he began to cut around the right wrist, gently, in full sight of the horrified people. The shapeless hand became detached little by little amidst the blood. It swung an instant suspended by the last filaments. Then it fell into a basin of copper which held the money offerings at the feet of the Patron Saint.

L'Ummalido then raised the bloody stump and repeated in a clear voice:

"Saint Gonselvo, I offer it up to you."

—*Translated from the Italian of Gabriele D'Annunzio (1863–1938), by Rafael Mantellini.*

Chivalry

RICARDO FERNÁNDEZ-GUARDIA

ONE night in the month of July four horsemen, well mounted, emerged from an hacienda in Uruca and rode hurriedly along the highway to the joining of the road to San Antonio de Belén, where they stopped.

"Here we must separate," said one of them. "May you have good luck, Ramón," he added, searching in the darkness for his friend's hand.

"Adiós, Salvador, adiós,' replied the one spoken to, in a voice trembling with emotion. The two men, without letting go of each other's hands, drew together until their stirrups touched, and embraced warmly.

"Adiós, adiós"—"Good luck."

After a last embrace, long and affectionate, both started off in different directions, each escorted by one of the two horsemen who had just witnessed the sad scene of farewell. Those who followed the highroad did not get very far. At the Ciruelas river they fell into the hands of a picket of soldiers who carried them prisoners to the Alajuela Barracks. The other two fugitives, for fugitives they were, kept on, with better fortune, along the San Antonio road. The darkness did not permit them to see where they were going, so that the travelers had to trust to the instinct of their horses to avoid the bad places or to get out of them. Luckily it did not rain, which would have been one more hindrance to the rapid march that the critical situation in which Salvador Moreno found himself necessitated, for he was being eagerly searched for on account of his share in the attack made the night before on the Cuartel Principal in San José. The revolutionary uprising had failed through the fault of those who were to have brought men from the neighboring towns, with the intention of arming them when the Cuartel had surrendered, and of laying siege to the other ones. Not one of them appeared at the critical moment, and the few valiant ones who had surprised the garrison asleep at two o'clock in the morning had to abandon at daybreak the conquest which had cost them so much blood.

Salvador did not answer the questions which from time to time his companion asked him. Absorbed in his thoughts he lived over again the happenings of last night's bloody drama; the meeting in the house of one of the conspirators, the irritating wait for those who did not come, the fear of a betrayal, the doubts and hesitations of the last hour, finally the moment of marching, the gate of the Cuartel opened by the hand of a traitor, the hand-to-hand fight with the guard, the gallantry of the officers meeting death at their posts. But more than all there harassed him the vision of a young lieutenant running up hurriedly, saber in hand, to aid his comrades, whom he had laid low by a shot at barely arm's length. In vain he tried to make himself believe that it was a legitimate act of warfare. An internal voice cried out in the tribunal of his conscience against the blood that had been shed. Salvador Moreno was a high-strung, refined man to whom the brutality of force was repugnant. At the same time his indomitable and lofty spirit could not bend itself to the political despotism which is killing us like a shameful chronic sore. In the conspiracy he had seen the shaking off of the heavy yoke, the dignity of his country avenged, and the triumph of liberty. To gain all that, the sacrifice of his life had not seemed too much. Now his sorrow was very great, his patriotic illusions had disappeared like the visions of a beautiful dream when one awakens, and his heart was throbbing with wrath against those who through their cowardice had caused the daring attempt to fail. With keen regret he thought of his comrades uselessly sacrificed, of the agony of a brave young fellow whom he had carried out of the Cuartel in his arms, mortally wounded. Clear and exact the events of the combat went marching through his mind, some of which were atrocious, worthy of savages, others irresistibly comical, like that of the boastful fellow who withdrew from the gate of the Cuartel to go in search of his revolver which he pretended to have forgotten; and always persistent and sad, the vision of the lieutenant falling without a cry, his hand at his breast. Afterwards the despair at the failure, the retreat at daybreak through the deserted streets of the capital, the interminable hours of anguish, hidden with Ramón Solares under some sacks in the country house of a friend, listening to the voices of those who were searching for them. Finally the sheltering night, the hurried flight, the gloomy future, forbidding as the wrath of the enraged dictator. In order to aid their escape the fugitives had agreed to follow different roads; Salvador Moreno chose the one to Puntarenas, passing through San Antonio de Belén, and the plains of Carmen. Ramón Solares preferred the San Carlos route, with the idea of seeking refuge in Nicaragua by land, where the two friends were to meet if Salvador should succeed in escaping the vigilance of the authorities of the port.

Both were accompanied by trusty retainers who knew the country and were of proved courage. It was Fate that decided in this case, and we have already seen that she declared in favor of Salvador Moreno, who without meeting a soul, arrived at the highroad to Puntarenas at one o'clock in the morning, while his friend, chained in his prison, offered prayers that he might succeed in escaping from those who pursued him. At three o'clock he passed through Atenas and at six in the morning he and his companion arrived at the gates of San Mateo. But now the horses could endure no more. It was part of the fugitive's plan to pass the day hidden in a friendly and secure house on the plains of Surubres, although now this was not possible, on account of the fatigue of the horses and the danger of the young conspirator's being recognized in passing through the village, in spite of the fact that he was wearing the costume of a countryman. It was necessary then to decide on something.

"Don Salvador," said the guide, "three hundred yards from here there lives an acquaintance of mine, who is a man you can trust. If you like we can dismount here, so that we shan't have to pass through San Mateo in the daytime."

"Very well, let us go there."

The two men spurred their horses and a few minutes afterwards arrived at a house situated a short distance from the road. Through the unbarred gate they entered, saluted by the barking of three thin, mangy dogs. At this disturbance an old and corpulent countryman came out on the veranda.

"Buenos días, 'Nor José," said the guide.

"Buenos días, Pedro," replied the old man. "How goes it?"

"Well; and how are you? How are the girls getting on?"

"Very well, thank you. Why don't you get off a while and rest?" added the old fellow.

The horseman dismounted and Salvador dropped, half dead with fatigue, on the settle that stood on the veranda. While he was stretching his aching legs, 'Nor José and Pedro unsaddled the horses and the latter confided to the old man that his companion was fleeing the country. Hurriedly he told him a story which he made up as he went on; something about a quarrel in which machetes had been flourished in the air. The old man did not insist on the details, promising to keep quiet about the unlooked for guests in his house.

Pedro went to take the horses to the pasture and Salvador accepted with pleasure the coffee which the youngest daughter of 'Nor José served him. The old man was proud of having for a son-in-law the *jefe politico* of San Mateo, who had married his oldest daughter, a handsome girl, so people said. Noticing that his guest was getting sleepy he conducted him to a cot bed that he might rest.

Five minutes afterwards the fugitive was sleeping like a log. The night came on without Salvador's awakening from the deep slumber into which he had fallen, his bones aching and his nerves being unstrung by the fatigue and emotions he had endured.

Pedro had improved the time by bathing the horses in the neighboring river and giving them a good feed of corn. This task ended, he took a nap for a couple of hours, which was sufficient to restore to his muscles the necessary energy; and as it was not two o'clock in the afternoon, he shared the frugal dinner of his host.

On hearing the church bells of San Mateo tolling "Las Animas" he resolved to awaken Salvador, which was not an easy thing to do. For all that he shook him, it was impossible to overcome the stupor which held him fast. Finally he opened his eyes, looking about in a dazed way without comprehending, until Pedro's voice insisting on the urgency of taking the road made him remember the reality of the situation. Salvador got up with difficulty; each movement that he made aroused a dormant pain in his body, which was agitated by a painful, feverish sensation. A little glass of cognac produced the necessary reaction, and the odor of supper already served began to remind him that he had been fasting for many hours.

While Salvador was devouring a chicken, which at Pedro's request the daughter of 'Nor José had cooked, the latter, seated on a bench, observed him closely. Naturally keen, he had scented the fact that beneath the short jacket was hidden a person who was not accustomed to wear it. The attentiveness of Pedro to Salvador, the respect with which he talked to him, were indications that this man belonged to a higher class of society than his garb would imply. This was evident; but looking well into the matter, what difference did it make to him that the stranger was who he was?

A five-dollar bill which Salvador put in his hand completely confirmed the old man's suspicions. In a little while Pedro entered to give notice that the horses were ready and Salvador, in bidding farewell, warmly squeezed the hand of his chance host, who almost fell over himself in his salutations and wishes for a safe journey. They were already going out to the veranda, when a boy came running up with the news that 'Nor José's oldest daughter was very ill. About to give birth to a child she had suffered a fall with bad consequences.

The old man was very much alarmed and Salvador tried to calm him, advising him to call a doctor.

"We have no doctor here," replied 'Nor José, much distressed, "and while one is coming from Alajuela the girl may die."

Salvador, who was a warm-hearted fellow, did not hesitate a moment.

"Let us go and see her," he said. "I am a doctor."

The old man, surprised and pleased, did not know what to say.

"May God pay you, señor, may God pay you!" he finally murmured with tears in his eyes. Pedro, plainly anxious, improved the moment when the countryman went to get his hat and call his daughter, to whisper in Salvador's ear that the sick woman was no less than the wife of the *jefe politico*, who must already have had orders to capture him.

"No matter, Pedro. It is my duty not to allow this poor woman to die. Let us go at once."

The old man, who returned hurriedly, heard these last words. "May God pay you, señor," he said again in a low voice. Pedro took the old man behind him on the crupper and Salvador the girl. After fifteen minutes of fast riding, the four stopped in front of the *jefe politico's* office.

The house was full of gossipers of the neighborhood, who had come in armed with infallible remedies which they were anxious to apply to the sufferer. The friends of the *jefe politico*, gathered together in the dining-room about a bottle of white rum, told discreetly, for the comfort of the official, of similar cases which finally had ended happily.

The arrival of her father and sister called forth a groan from the sick one, who in her rôle of a first-time mother considered herself as good as dead.

"Enter, enter, doctor!" exclaimed the old man, politely addressing the fugitive, whom nobody in the midst of the general confusion had as yet noticed. Judging by his costume, those present took him for one of those country quacks who live on the ignorance and avarice of the country people. Salvador examined the sick woman carefully and was convinced that, although the case was a serious one, it would not be difficult to save her. Without loss of time he took such measures as the circumstances demanded, and from that moment he thought only of the life of the little human creature which depended on his care. In vain Pedro reminded him many times of the great peril he was incurring in that house; nothing could make him withdraw.

'Nor José and the *jefe politico,* feeling more at ease after hearing the doctor's opinion, went to join the circle of friends, who had already given a good account of the first bottle of rum. When the second was opened, tongues began to get loosened, and the conversation acquired an animation which it lacked at the beginning.

Incidentally they talked of the revolution which had just taken place, and 'Nor José, who, on account of the isolation in which he lived, was ignorant of it all, made them tell him what had happened, listening to the story with anxiety. On learning that it was the Cuartel Principal which had been attacked, he asked his son-in-law whether he had news of Rafael, his son, who was one of the garrison.

"I don't know anything about him," replied the *jefe politico.* "I suppose that there is no news, since they have not sent me any word. Nevertheless in order to feel easy I am going to telegraph to San José."

When the despatch was written it was sent to the telegraph office.

Salvador did not leave his patient, encouraging her with cheering words to bear her pains with fortitude. Pedro, ill at ease, was watching the street, near the horses which were dozing with their heads low down.

At ten o'clock at night a long telegram came for the *jefe politico.* As he was reading it his hands trembled slightly. Suddenly a violent exclamation broke from his lips.

On hearing it, the people present got up as though to ask the cause, but the *jefe politico* without speaking a word conducted his father-in-law to a neighboring room. There, without any preamble, he told him that his son had been killed in the attack of the night before, and that Doctor Salvador Moreno was supposed to have been his slayer, and that he was then trying to escape from the country.

The poor old man, falling limp into a chair, wept bitterly over the death of his son. After a while he aroused himself with an expression of unspeakable wrath and the tears dried up in his eyes, which now shone like red-hot coals. "Salvador Moreno," he murmured in a hoarse voice. "I won't forget that name."

"I have heard it," said the *jefe politico.* "I believe it is that of a young doctor recently come back from Europe."

One of the women neighbors interrupted the conversation with the glad news of the birth of a strong and healthy man-child. Both were going in to see it, but it was not yet time for them to enter.

Pedro, always uneasy, had hardly heard the news when he went in search of 'Nor José to ask him to remind his companion of the urgency of starting.

"Tell Don Salvador that it is already very late and that I am waiting for him," he said forgetting to use the assumed name. On hearing this name the old man became petrified. Then he exclaimed with fury:

"Don Salvador! Don Salvador Moreno! That's the doctor's name, isn't it so?"

"Yes. Did he tell you?"

Without replying, 'Nor José went to a corner of the room where a machete was leaning against the wall. He drew it from its scabbard and with an expression of unheard-of ferocity went toward the apartment of his daughter.

At that moment, the door opened. Upon the bed lay the mother, very pale, but her eyes and lips were smiling. With his sleeves rolled up and absorbed in his task, Salvador was bathing the new born child in a wash basin. On seeing this the angry father felt a surge of generous feeling invade his heart. That man was the slayer of his Rafael; that was the terrible truth; but that same man who had shed the blood of his son had just saved another bit of his soul at the risk of his liberty and perhaps of his very life. He stood looking at the peaceful scene; the happy mother, the anxious and busy neighbors, and the doctor, very earnest, coddling the child, whose cries seemed to ask pardon for the savior of its mother.

The old man drew back slowly, letting go of the machete. After a moment of hesitation, he passed his rough hand across his face and drawing near to the fugitive said in a hoarse and trembling voice:

"Don Salvador, I beg you to go soon, because you are in great danger in this house."

—*From Costa Rican Tales, by Ricardo Fernández-Guardía, Costa Rican (1867–   ), translated from the Spanish by Gray Casement.*

~ ✿ ~

A New-Year's Eve Confession

HERMANN SUDERMANN

THANKS be to God, dear lady, that I may once more sit beside you for a peaceful chat. The holiday tumult is past, and you have a little leisure for me again.

Oh, this Christmas season! I believe that it was invented by some evil demon expressly to annoy us poor bachelors, to show us the more clearly all the desolation of our homeless existence. For others a source of joy, it is for us a torture. Of course, I know, we are not all entirely lonely—for us also the joy of making others happy may blossom, that joy upon which rests the whole secret of the blessed holiday mood. But the pleasure of joining in the happiness of others is tainted for us by a touch of self-irony partly, and also by that bitter longing to which—in contrast to homesickness—I would give the name of "marriage sickness."

Why didn't I come to pour out my heart to you? you ask, you pitying soul, you—you that can give of your sympathy in the same rich measure that others of your sex save for their dainty malices. There's a reason. You remember what Speidel says in his delightful *Lonely Sparrows*, which you sent me the day after Christmas, with a true perception of my state of mind? "The bachelor by instinct," he says, "does not desire comfort. Once he is unhappy, he wishes to have the full enjoyment of his unhappiness."

Besides the "lonely sparrow" whom Speidel portrays, there is another sort of bachelor, the so-called "friend of the family." By this I do not mean those professional wreckers of homes, in whose eyes the serpent glitters as they settle down comfortably at the hospitable hearthstone. I mean the good uncle, papa's former school friend, who rocks the baby on his knee while he reads the magazine essays to mamma, carefully omitting all the doubtful portions.

I know men who give up their entire lives to the service of some family whose friendship they have won—men who live on without desire by the side of a beautiful woman whom in their hearts they secretly adore.

You doubt me? Oh, it is the words "without desire" that disturb you? You are right, perhaps. In the depth of even the tamest heart some wild desire lies, but—understand me here—it lies bound in chains.

As an instance I would like to tell you about a conversation which took place day before yesterday, on New Year's Eve, between two old, two very old, gentlemen. It is my secret how I came to know of this conversation, and I ask you not to let it go any further. May I begin, then?

Picture to yourself, as a setting for my story, a high-ceilinged room, old-fashioned in furnishings, lighted by a green-shaded, impertinently bright hanging-lamp of the sort our parents had in use before the era of petroleum. The cone of light that goes out from the flame falls upon a round, white-clothed table, upon which stands the various ingredients for a New-Year's punch, while several drops of oil show out broadly in the center of the table.

My two old gentlemen sat half in the shadow of the green lamp-shade, moldering ruins both, from long-past days, bowed and trembling, gazing before them with the dull glance of the dimming eyes of age. One, the host, is evidently an old officer, as you would recognize at once from his carefully wound cravat, his pointed, sharply cut mustache, and his martial eyebrows. He sits holding the handle of his roller-chair like a crutch tightly clasped in both hands. He is motionless except for his jaws, which move up and down ceaselessly with the motion of chewing. The other, who sits near him on the sofa, a tall, spare figure, his narrow shoulders crowned by the high-domed head of a thinker, draws occasional thin puffs of smoke from a long pipe which is just about to go out. Among the myriad wrinkles of his smooth-shaven, dried-up face, framed in a wreath of snow-white curls, there lurked a quiet, gentle smile, a smile which the peace of resignation alone can bring to the face of age.

The two were silent. In the perfect stillness of the room the soft bubbling of the burning oil mingled with the soft bubbling of the tobacco juice. Then, from the darkness of the background, the hanging clock began to announce hoarsely the eleventh hour. "This is the hour when she would begin to make the punch," said the man with the domed forehead. His voice was soft, with a slight vibration.

"Yes, this is the time," repeated the other. The sound of his speech was hard, as if the rattle of command still lingered in it.

"I did not think it would be so desolate without her," said the first speaker again.

The host nodded, his jaws moving.

"She made the New-Year's punch for us four-and-forty times," continued his friend.

"Yes, it's as long as that since we moved to Berlin, and you became our friend," said the old soldier.

"Last year at this time we were all so jolly together," said the other. "She sat in the armchair there, knitting socks for Paul's eldest. She worked busily, saying she must finish it by twelve o'clock. And she did finish it. Then we drank our punch and spoke quite calmly of death. And two months later they carried her away. As you know, I have written a fat book on the 'Immortality of the Idea.' You never cared much about it—I don't care for it myself now that your wife is dead. The entire Idea of the Universe means nothing to me now."

"Yes, she was a good wife," said the husband of the dead woman; "she cared for me well. When I had to go out for service at five o'clock in the morning, she was always up before me to look after my coffee. Of course she had her faults. When she got into philosophizing with you—h'm."

"You never understood her," murmured the other, the corners of his mouth trembling in controlled resentment. But the glance that rested long on his friend's face was gentle and sad, as if a secret guilt pressed upon his soul.

After a renewed pause, he began:

"Franz, there is something I want to tell you, something that has long troubled me, something that I do not want to carry with me to my grave."

"Well, fire away," said the host, taking up the long pipe that stood beside his chair.

"There was once—something—between your wife and me."

The host let his pipe fall back again, and stared at his friend with wide-opened eyes.

"No jokes, please, doctor," he said finally.

"It is bitter earnest, Franz," replied the other. "I have carried it about with me these forty years, but now it is high time to have it out with you."

"Do you mean to say that the dead woman was untrue to me?" cried the husband angrily.

"For shame, Franz," said his friend with a soft, sad smile.

The old soldier murmured something and lit his pipe.

"No, she was as pure as God's angels," continued the other. "It is you and I who are the guilty ones. Listen to me. It is now forty-three years ago; you had just been ordered here as captain to Berlin, and I was teaching at the University. You were a gay bird then, as you know."

"H'm," remarked the host, raising his trembling old hand to his mustache.

"There was a beautiful actress with great black eyes and little white teeth—do you remember?"

"*Do* I? Bianca was her name," answered the other as a faded smile flashed over his weather-beaten, self-indulgent face. "Those little white teeth could bite, I can tell you."

"You deceived your wife, and she suspected it. But she said nothing and suffered in silence. She was the first woman who had come into my life since my mother's death. She came into it like a shining star, and I gazed up to her in adoration as one might adore a star. I found the courage to ask her about her trouble. She smiled and said that she was not feeling quite strong yet—you remember it was shortly after the birth of your Paul. Then came New Year's Eve—forty-three years ago to-night. I came in at eight o'clock as usual. She sat over her embroidery and I read aloud to her while we waited for you. One hour after another passed and still you did not come. I saw that she grew more and more uneasy, and began to tremble. I trembled with her. I knew where you were, and I feared you might forget the hour of midnight in the arms of that woman. She had dropped her work, I read no longer. A terrible silence weighed upon us. Then I saw a tear gather under her eyelid and drop slowly down upon the embroidery in her lap. I sprang up to go out and look for you. I felt myself capable of tearing you away from that woman by force. But at the same moment she sprang up also from her seat—this very same place where I am sitting now.

"'Where are you going?' she cried, terror in every feature. 'I am going to fetch Franz,' I said. And then she screamed aloud: 'For God's sake, *you* stay with me at least—don't *you* forsake me also.'

"And she hurried to me, laid both hands on my shoulders and buried her tear-bedewed face on my breast. I trembled in every fiber, no woman had ever stood so near me before. But I controlled myself, and soothed and comforted her – she was so sadly in need of comfort. You came in soon after. You did not notice my emotion, your cheeks were burning, your eyes heavy with the fatigue of love. Since that evening a change had come over me, a change that frightened me. When I had felt her soft arms around my neck, when I had felt the fragrance of her hair, the shining star fell from its heaven, and – a woman stood before me, beautiful, breathing love. I called myself a villain, a betrayer, and to soothe my conscience somewhat I set about separating you from your mistress. Fortunately I had some money at my disposal. She was satisfied with the sum I offered her, and – "

"The devil!" exclaimed the old soldier in surprise; "then you were the cause of that touching farewell letter that Bianca sent me – in which she declared that she must give me up – although her heart would break?"

"Yes, I was the cause of it," said his friend. "But listen, there is more to tell. I had thought to purchase peace with that money, but the peace did not come. The wild thoughts ran riot all the more madly in my brain. I buried myself in my work – it was just about that time that I was working out the plan of my book on the 'Immortality of the Idea' – but still could not find peace. And thus the year passed and New-Year's Eve came round again. Again we sat together here, she and I. You were at home this time, but you lay sleeping on the sofa in the next room. A merry Casino dinner had tired you. And as I sat beside her, and my eyes rested on her pale face, then memory came over me with irresistible power. Once more I would feel her head on my breast, once more I would kiss her – and then – the end, if need be. Our eyes met for an instant; I seemed to see a secret understanding, an answer in her glance. I could control myself no longer; I fell at her feet and buried my burning face in her lap.

"I lay there motionless for two seconds perhaps, then I felt her soft hand rest cool upon my head, and her voice, soft and gentle, spoke the words: 'Be brave, dear friend; yes, be brave – do not deceive the man sleeping so trustfully in the next room.' I sprang up and gazed about, bewildered. She took a book from the table and handed it to me. I understood, opened it at random, and began to read aloud. I do not know what it was I read, the letters danced before my eyes. But the storm within my soul began to abate, and when twelve o'clock struck, and you came in sleepily for the New-Year's wishes, it was as if that moment of sin lay far, far behind me, in days that had long passed.

"Since that day I have been calmer. I knew that she did not return my love, and that I had only pity to hope from her. Years passed, your children grew up and married, we three grew old together. You gave up your wild life, forgot the other women, and lived for one alone, as I did. It was not possible that I should ever cease to love her, but my love took on another shape; earthly desires faded, and a bond of the spirit grew up between us. You have often laughed when you heard us philosophizing together. But if you had known how close were our souls at such moments you would have been very jealous. And now she is dead, and before the next New-Year's Eve comes round we two may follow her. It is, therefore, high time that I rid myself of this secret and say to you, 'Franz, I sinned against you once, forgive me.' "

He held out an imploring hand toward his friend; but the other answered, grumbling: "Nonsense. There is nothing to forgive. What you told me there, I knew it long ago. She confessed it herself forty years ago. And now I will tell you why I ran after other women until I was an old man – because she told me then that you were the one and only love of her life."

The friend stared at him without speaking, and the hoarse clock began to strike – midnight.

— *By Hermann Sudermann, German (1857–1928), translated by Grace I. Colbron.*

The Eclipse

SELMA LAGERLÖF

THERE were Stina of Ridgecôte and Lina of Birdsong and Kajsa of Littlemarsh and Maja of Skypeak and Beda of Finn-darkness and Elin, the new wife on the old soldier's place, and two or three other peasant women besides – all of them lived at the far end of the parish, below Storhöjden, in a region so wild and rocky none of the big farm owners had bothered to lay hands on it.

One had her cabin set up on a shelf of rock, another had hers put up at the edge of a bog, while a third had one that stood at the crest of a hill so steep it was a toilsome climb getting to it. If by chance any of the others had a cottage built on more favorable ground, you may be sure it lay so close to the mountain as to shut out the sun from autumn fair time clear up to Annunciation Day.

They each cultivated a little potato patch close by the cabin, though under serious difficulties. To be sure, there were many kinds of soil there at the foot of the mountain, but it was hard work to make the patches of land yield anything. In some places they had to clear away so much stone from their fields, it would have built a cowhouse on a manorial estate; in some they had dug ditches as deep as graves, and in others they had brought their earth in sacks and spread it on the bare rocks. Where the soil was not so poor, they were forever fighting the tough thistle and pigweed which sprang up in such profusion you would have thought the whole potato land had been prepared for their benefit.

All the livelong day the women were alone in their cabins; for even where one had a husband and children, the man went off to his work every morning and the children went to school. A few among the older women had grown sons and daughters, but they had gone to America. And some there were with little children, who were always around, of course; but these could hardly be regarded as company.

Being so much alone, it was really necessary that they should meet sometimes over the coffee cups. Not that they got on so very well together, nor had any great love for each other; but some liked to keep posted on what the others were doing, and some grew despondent living like that, in the shadow of the mountain, unless they met people now and then. And there were those, too, who needed to unburden their hearts, and talk about the last letter from America, and those who were naturally talkative and jocular, and who longed for opportunity to make use of these happy God-given talents.

Nor was it any trouble at all to prepare for a little party. Coffee-pot and coffee cups they all had of course, and cream could be got at the manor, if one had no cow of one's own to milk; fancy biscuits and small cakes one could, at a pinch, get the dairyman's driver to fetch from the municipal bakery, and country merchants who sold coffee and sugar were to be found everywhere. So, to get up a coffee party was the easiest thing imaginable. The difficulty lay in finding an occasion.

For Stina of Ridgecôte, Lina of Birdsong, Kajsa of Littlemarsh, Maja of Skypeak, Beda of Finn-darkness, and Elin, the new wife at the old soldier's, were all agreed that it would never do for them to celebrate in the midst of the common everyday life. Were they to be that wasteful of the precious hours which never return, they might get a bad name. And to hold coffee parties on Sundays or great Holy Days was out of the question; for then the married women had husband and children at home, which was quite company enough. As for the rest—some liked to attend church, some wished to visit relatives, while a few preferred to spend the day at home, in perfect peace and stillness, that they might really feel it was a Holy Day.

Therefore they were all the more eager to take advantage of every possible opportunity. Most of them gave parties on their name-days, though some celebrated the great event when the wee little one cut its first tooth, or when it took its first steps. For those who received money-letters from America that was always a convenient excuse, and it was also in order to invite all the women of the neighborhood to come and help tack a quilt or stretch a web just off the loom.

All the same, there were not nearly as many occasions to meet as were needed. One year one of the women was at her wit's end. It was her turn to give a party, and she had no objection to carrying out what was expected of her; but she could not seem to hit upon anything to celebrate. Her own name-day she could not celebrate, being named Beda, as Beda has been stricken out of the almanac. Nor could she celebrate that of any member of her family, for all her dear ones were resting in the churchyard. She was very old, and the quilt she slept under would probably outlast her. She had a cat of which she was very fond. Truth to tell, it drank coffee just as well as she did; but she could hardly bring herself to hold a party for a cat!

Pondering, she searched her almanac again and again, for there she felt she must surely find the solution of her problem.

She began at the beginning, with "The Royal House" and "Signs and Forecasts," and read on, right through to "Markets and Postal Transmittances for 1912," without finding anything.

As she was reading the book for the seventh time, her glance rested on "Eclipses." She noted that that year, which was the year of our Lord nineteen-hundred twelve, on April seventeenth there would be a solar eclipse. It would begin at twenty minutes past high noon and end at 2.40 o'clock, and would cover nine-tenths of the sun's disk.

This she had read before, many times, without attaching any significance to it; but now, all at once, it became dazzlingly clear to her.

"Now I have it!" she exclaimed.

But it was only for a second or two that she felt confident; and then she put the thought away, fearing that the other women would just laugh at her.

The next few days, however, the idea that had come to her when reading her almanac kept recurring to her mind, until at last she began to wonder whether she hadn't better venture. For when she thought about it, what friend had she in all the world she loved better than the Sun? Where her hut lay not a ray of sunlight penetrated her room the whole winter long. She counted the days until the Sun would come back to her in the spring. The Sun was the only one she longed for, the only one who was always friendly and gracious to her and of whom she could never see enough.

She looked her years, and felt them, too. Her hands shook as if she were in a perpetual chill and when she saw herself in the looking-glass, she appeared so pale and washed out, as if she had been lying out to bleach. It was only when she stood in a strong, warm, down-pouring sunshine that she felt like a live human being and not a walking corpse.

The more she thought about it, the more she felt there was no day in the whole year she would rather celebrate than the one when her friend the Sun battled against darkness, and after a glorious conquest, came forth with new splendor and majesty.

The seventeenth of April was not far away, but there was ample time to make ready for a party. So, on the day of the eclipse Stina, Lina, Kajsa, Maja, and the other women all sat drinking coffee with Beda at Finn-darkness. They drank their second and their third cups, and chatted about everything imaginable. For one thing, they said they couldn't for the life of them understand why Beda should be giving a party.

Meanwhile, the eclipse was under way. But they took little notice of it. Only for a moment, when the sky turned blackish gray, when all nature seemed under a leaden pall, and there came driving a howling wind with sounds as of the Trumpet of Doom and the lamentations of Judgment Day—only then did they pause and feel a bit awed. But here they each had a fresh cup of coffee, and the feeling soon passed.

When all was over, and the Sun stood out in the heavens so beamingly happy—it seemed to them it had not shone with such brilliancy and power the whole year—they saw old Beda go over to the window, and stand with folded hands. Looking out toward the sunlit slope, she sang in her quavering voice:

"Thy shining sun goes up again,
I thank Thee, O my Lord!
With new-found courage, strength and hope,
I raise a song of joy."

Thin and transparent, old Beda stood there in the light of the window, and as she sang the sunbeams danced about her, as if wanting to give her, also, of their life and strength and color.

When she had finished the old hymn-verse she turned and looked at her guests, as if in apology.

"You see," she said, "I haven't any better friend than the Sun, and I wanted to give her a party on the day of her eclipse. I felt that we should come together to greet her, when she came out of her darkness."

Now they understood what old Beda meant, and their hearts were touched. They began to speak well of the Sun. "She was kind to rich and poor alike, and when she came peeping into the hut on a winter's day, she was as comforting as a glowing fire on the hearth. Just the sight of her smiling face made life worth living, whatever the troubles one had to bear."

The women went back to their homes after the party, happy and content. They somehow felt richer and more secure in the thought that they had a good, faithful friend in the Sun.

— By Selma Lagerlöf, Swedish (1858–1940), translated by Velma Swanston Howard.

~ ❁ ~

Banasiowa

MARIA KONOPNICKA

IT WAS a still, broiling afternoon, and everything in the Lyczaków Park at Lwów seemed to be steeped in the intense, glaring radiance of the molten atmosphere.

Without whirr and life a swarm of tiny flies hung listlessly in front of me in the gossamer golden-green mesh net of beams which filtered through the boughs of a shady lime tree; over a lawn near by, white butterflies were flapping and wheeling low, dipping deep in the grass; the glare from the gravel on the paths which met round the benches was dazzling, and the air was heavy with a multiplicity of perfumes, as though it were charged with incense. All this had followed suddenly upon a fresh, dew-drenched dawn, and by now the sun had risen high in the heavens, and, like a white-hot globe, was blazing down upon the panting, sweltering earth. The park was empty. The early-morning comers had already gone, and those in search of shade and coolness had not yet arrived. The heat seemed intensified in the utter stillness, and the distant chirping of grasshoppers sounded like invisible sparks crackling as they fed the mid-day blaze.

Suddenly I heard behind me the quick tap, tap of a stick. I looked round. A little and deeply-bowed old woman was drawing near to my bench with short, quick steps. Her white cap shone in the sunlight with the sheen of silver, and silver-like were the white kerchief fastened crosswise over her coarse bodice, and the broad apron she wore. One arm was burdened with a basket. The other was stiffly stretched out and held a short stick with which she made her regular taps. She used it to support her legs and it may have been of service to her eyes also.

I could hear her quick, laboured breathing while she was still a long way off. She was obviously in a hurry to reach the bench and rest there, laying her basket on it. The strain of urging her shrunken legs faster made her steps more and more uneven and crooked; she kept her head so bent that I could not catch sight of her face. And she undoubtedly did not see me. Not until my shadow was full on her did she come to a sudden stop, straighten herself a little and raise her face. What a net of wrinkles it was! The life which had spun the threads of that net must have been long, very long; it must have been, too, a life of ceaseless toil. A life which made her begin her labours at dawn by the flicker of a candle stump and finish them half blindly as the cocks crew midnight. Life must have wrested all the fibres out of her breast for its own grey spindle; it must have torn and worried at the thread, torn it again and worried it again, without smoothing the knots away, but hurrying, hurrying, hurrying. . . .

She stopped a moment as though bewildered and blinking her little grey eyes. Then she set off again, came up to the bench and, leaning against it her basket half filled with gingerbreads, she took one deep breath after another.

"It is very hot," I remarked, just to say something.

"Christ Jesus save us, that it is," she replied, and with her scraggy hand she wiped the sweat away from her wafer-pale face. "What a terrible hot day to be sure."

"Would you not like to sit down a bit?"

"Sitting down, lady, is it? I'd as soon lean here. It's hard, you see, for old folks like us to sit down and to stand up. You get a crick in your back straight away."

"How old do you reckon to be?"

"And why should I reckon my age, begging your pardon, lady? Christ Jesus does that without me. . . . But I'll be eighty or thereabouts, ay, eighty, and maybe more. It is hard to cast up from memory, but the people in our parish will know. . . . There are documents with it in. . . ."

"So you are not from here?"

"From here, lady? I should think not. I come from Wadowice, a village it was, though now it is called an 'urban district,' and the ways are all different. But the people there still know me. Banasiowa, that's who I am, and everybody, big and little, knows who Banasiowa is."

"And you have moved into Lwów then?"

"Me move into Lwów, lady? Why, what has it to offer me? Well enough for the young ones to rush and gad about the world, but it doesn't suit folk of my age. You see, lady, I have the children here, or rightly a daughter who is married to a nail-maker in a factory. Ay, she is so. So when I felt the hand of the Lord on me and that I was going to be taken, I came over to them to die. Death comes easier when you are with your own people. God grant me an easy passage, and may straw at least be laid down on the floor and the soul helped out of the sinful body."

"And are you comfortable at your children's?"

"Ay, that I am. Nothing comes amiss to old folk, they take good and bad as they come. But things did not turn out for me just as I had reckoned."

"And how didn't they turn out right?"

"Well, it was that dying, lady. I came over to the children to die, and here I am going on living. Like a bubble I look, breathe on me and I'll burst, but the life in me is tough, God help me. From the very start there was no trouble, thanks be to God. I was entered in the books, nicely and properly; my son-in-law would be off to his work in the factory and my daughter bustled about doing the housework, while I would sit by the fireside, plucking the feathers which I had brought with me to make into a pillow. And I'd say my prayers and wait for the last summons. I waited one month, and I waited two, but nothing happened, until I began to fidget with all the waiting. But one Sunday the house watchman came in and said: 'I say, Peter'—that is the name, you know, my son-in-law was baptised—'you'd better see about a lodging permit for your mother now she's staying with you.' My son-in-law thought a minute and said: 'Will that come to a great deal?' So the watchman says: 'Sixpence a quarter.' So Peter treated him to some tobacco and off he went. When he had gone I said to Peter: 'What's the use of a lodging permit for me when I have come here to die, not to live? I may draw my last breath any time, for I am dreadfully weak inside.' And my daughter breaks in with: 'That's right enough. Why let it cost you all that, and Mamma here today and gone tomorrow?' That is how we all reckoned it out among ourselves—quiet and cosy like. And just then, lady, there came upon me such mortal pains and aches that every bone in my body felt like moaning and cracking like any leaf in the wind, and things went all black before my eyes just as if someone was showering down soot. And what with the cricks in my back, too, I couldn't lift my head up, that I couldn't, not if there had been three dawns in the sky. So I saw clear enough that I wasn't long for this world. But what does sinful man know? The first quarter passed, then the second, and still nothing. I eat my bit of food, take my nap on the floor by the fireplace, and go on living. Ay, that I do. Till I marvel at it myself. I began to wonder if Christ Jesus Himself had not put His holy foot down on my number and stamped me out of those to be taken. And one day my son-in-law comes back from his work with the watchman standing behind him in the doorway. ''Fore God, Peter,' says he, 'what about that mother of yours? You said she'd come to die, but there she is living her third quarter with her lodging ticket still unpaid. The fine will have grown to be twice as much now. The other tenants are thinking of trying on the same dodge, and so the inspector has ordered me to keep an eye on the lot down in the basement. If he were to find out, it would be the worse for me and for you. Come to some settlement over the job one way or the other, or it will mount up to more than ten shillings.' That put Peter in a quandary. He threw his cap on the table, and standing there in the middle of the room he scratched his head. My daughter goes all red in the face and says: 'Mamma, God forgive her, has got her reckoning wrong. She came here to die, but there's no dying about it. But there, people haven't any sense as they get on in years. And where is this ten shillings to come from? And that's not the end of it either.' But Peter says to her: 'Easy, Fanny, don't grumble, for you can't tell yet what may be in store for yourself!' For he is that kindhearted, lady, that he wouldn't kill a fly. Well then, the upshot of it all was that he gave the watchman ninepence to keep for the time, well, for the time when . . . the door creaks and death is at hand. And it fair wrenched my heart to see him give that ninepence.

Fanny, too, flared up and dashed the pot under the table so hard that it nearly broke into smithereens, but she said not a word. And no wonder she acted the like. What a heap of money, what a waste! It wouldn't have been so bad even if it had been spent on food and drink, but to throw it away for nothing just like that!"

She drew a deep breath and wiped away the drops of sweat which had gathered on her forehead.

"Grudge me my bit of food, that they never did, and may the Lord God punish me if ever I say different. Though I didn't do them much hurt by the bit of food I ate. I scraped up the bits left in the dish, and that would be all. Why should a withered old stick like me eat the young folk out of hearth and home? Every age has its own ways. Nothing matters the same to the old ones, even if they feel half starved; they haven't to rush off to work; but the young folk, they must be ready to do what's asked of them any and every time. They were never niggardly with me, neither of them; but that money thrown away!"

She stopped and shook her grey head.

"And after that?"

"Well, the second winter came, and nothing. The watchman was bribed a bit, and everything was quiet. And it was all the while in my head that things had not turned out for me as I had expected. People's imaginations, fools' consolations. . . . Before I had finished plucking the feathers, the idea came into my head and I said to myself: 'It'll do for her; let them have at least the bit of pillow when I'm gone'; but when I finished it. . . . And at the close of the winter I began again to have the crick in my back and a cough comes along to make things worse – a sort of asthma – so I said to Fanny: 'Well, it'll be the end now because the cough stops me from breathing.' But she says: 'For all the harm a cough will do you, Ma, you might as well try to stop a dog from barking by throwing a stick at it.' You see, it irked her, begging your pardon, lady, that bribing of the watchman. So without a word to Christ Jesus I began to fast two days before the feast of the Transfiguration of Our Lord. You see, by now I felt ashamed in the presence of people. Everybody in the basements knew that I had come to die, and they'd all be astonished at seeing me. . . . But there! At first, my son-in-law would not let me fast. 'What are you at, mother, tempting the Lord God? What must come, will come. Now that winter is drawing to an end, the old folks mostly die, and that will happen to you without any need to fast. . . .' But I didn't let myself be talked over."

"And was it any good?"

"Any good? By the third week I was so wasted that I could not sweep the room out, no, not even swallow water down. Death has come for me, I thought, and at once I felt easier in mind. I had a thorough good wash, put on a clean shift, sat down by the threshold, said my prayers and waited. White puffs of cloud were passing in the sky, and the sun was getting up and the sparrows were chirping, and all creation felt spring was at hand. And just then the bells began to ring out over the town. So I said to myself: 'Grant me, O Lord, everlasting peace, and may eternal brightness shine upon me for ever and ever, Amen!' And my eyes began to close of themselves and a sweetness came over me like when you are falling into a doze.

"But there was somebody coming, stamping his boots. I looked up and saw the watchman. He had a paper in his hand and was summoning me to the office of the police station, about the lodging ticket. . . . I thought the earth had opened up in front of me. Peter wasn't at home, my daughter was washing, so there wasn't any talking to be done with her just then, so I went into the living-room, and I stopped stock still in the middle of it, with no one to advise me.

"If Peter had been at home he would have kept the watchman quiet with something or other for a time at any rate, and then by the evening the whole thing might have blown over. Yes, but Peter wasn't there. While I was standing and thinking it out, in comes my daughter with a pot of boiling water for the wash-tub. She banged up against me and said: 'Why stand in the way, mother, like a picture of misery? This isn't the time for gossiping. If they've sent for you from the police office, go there. You ought to have thought of ways and means before and not show off your cleverness just now – and at the wrong time, too.' 'Yes,' I said, 'you are right.' So I put my shawl on and set off. Our Holy Lord Jesus marked out my way for me. There I was, holding on to the walls like a drunkard, with stars dancing before my eyes, and I felt that hot and cold all over just as if I was being drenched and scalded at the same time. But I got there. Yes, and when I was inside I looked round and saw the gentlemen sitting at their tables; one was very fine and smart, and there was another all in black; ay, and there'd be a third, too. I made my curtsey and began to go through it all. But they just waved their hands — 'Not here, not here,' they said. So I passed on. But the young fellow told me it wasn't there either. So they sent me from room to room until my last bit of strength was gone. But at last one of them, a thin, lanky man, took pity on me and pointed with his finger to another room where the chief was sitting. I stopped at the entrance and my legs were like jelly under me. The gentleman turned round, and at once said: 'Well, what's the matter?' So I told him the whole story from the beginning. He listened and then said once more: 'What's the matter?' So I went through it all over again from the beginning, and I told him how I had come to my children to die, how I had not taken out a lodging card because it was all the same for an old woman whether death came today or tomorrow, and I told that our Holy Lord Jesus had forgotten about me, and how I was still living and how they had sent for me.

"Then the chief rang the bell. And then another gentleman came in, all in buttons. And then it really began; they started questioning me once more all from the beginning, and when they had done with their questions the chief said: 'Now, my good woman, we shall want ten and six from you.' When I heard that, I nearly collapsed. Ten shillings! Christ Jesus! That was the very sum that I had given Peter to put aside for my burial when I went to their house. . . . And a faintness came over me all of a sudden and I leant against the wall as though I were dead. I did not know whether I was on my head or my heels or flying through the air. I could not see properly, and my ears were thudding and beating like a hammer. The gentlemen rushed up to me, the one in the buttons flew for water and the other wanted to put me into the armchair. . . . I saw that he was a kindhearted gentleman, so I plumped down at his feet and said: 'Beg pardon, Sir, kind Sir. Wherever am I to turn to get so much money? How can I pay, a poor old woman like me? Kind Sir, look at me! Skin and bone I am, like a withered and mouldy stump of wood, with nothing to draw my last breath from. And I'm not keeping anybody in the world from a place. I lie on my wisp of straw in front of the stove, I drink a drop of water, I pick at my food like any sparrow. . . . I don't do the air any harm either, for I can hardly draw breath, and I haven't even a ray of sunshine, for I stay in the basements where the sun is not to be seen. . . . I know, honoured Sir, that I ought to have died long since. But what can I do if the life within me is tough? Take mercy on me, honoured Sir! Pardon me. And to be sure, I look for death ever so, every day and every hour. . . . I have already paid for my lodging to the Lord Jesus; praised be His Holy Name. Thirteen children I've had, and seven I've buried — like little white flowers they were; two of my sons were taken from me for the army, they were young and innocent, all roses and cream. One of my lads was drowned in the river, one of the daughters ran away to the town, and my youngest was burnt while he was at his uncle's, as it might be a sparrow in the eaves. The Lord God has made me pay for the lodging by child-bearing and grief and hard work and hunger and bloody tears, and those mounds of yellow sand.' "

She stopped, and down her dried-up face flowed big tears, chasing and rubbing each other out, all golden in the clear sunlight. The fleshless lips trembled with unspoken words and the old head shook helplessly. In truth God had already exacted from this human creature the uttermost farthing in return for her lodging.

"And then?" I asked gently, when she had quieted down a little.

"Well, I had to pay. Ten shillings, lady — like ice they were. Ay, and Peter gave me sixpence of his own to make up the count. What was for the funeral, it all went. May the Lord God in Heaven not remember it against them. But there, they were innocent, the poor things, it was the law — their orders."

"And now you are peddling?"

"Peddle, lady? What have I to peddle? I sold the pillow; they gave me eighteenpence for it. So that meant right away sixpence for a new lodging ticket, for the next quarter, and I began to save every farthing I had left, to avoid being fined again. What with the life in me being so tough, I may have to pay for this year, too.". . .

She stared in front of her with her sparse, grey eyebrows lifted right up, and she wagged her head as though in great wonder at the world and its arrangement.

—*Maria Konopnicka, Polish (1842?–1916?), translated by N. B. Jopson.*

PART TWENTY-THREE

The Happy Life

MUCH POETRY WOOS "honey sweet melancholy." Tragedy is often regarded by too sober critics as a "higher" art than comedy; and the imaginative mind itself seems prone, like Hamlet, to a dark sobriety. Especially in the literary age that has now definitely passed, when the novel has so often followed in the doomed footsteps of Dostoevski and American poetry felt the strong influence of such gloomy and powerful writers as T. S. Eliot, Robinson Jeffers and E. A. Robinson, tragic thought may for intervals have seemed supreme. Nevertheless the broader view of historical and comparative literature reminds us that the resilient human spirit has always looked to our happiness as well as to our misfortunes. The salvation or felicity of the individual is a common theme of metaphysical or amorous poetry; the pride and well being of the state a familiar subject in formal odes and, by implication, in political satire. But some of the most lasting forms of human happiness are fruits of neither romantic passion, subjective meditation nor political action. They spring more simply from our common social relations with family, friends and neighbors. There is a distinct vein of writing which, neglecting political grandeurs and meditative sublimities, has celebrated, from the remote past to the present day, the happy, normal, social life of private men and women. Optimism has, to be sure, sometimes proved a quicksand to art more fatal than the blackest gulf of pessimism. Authors endowed merely with good intentions and lacking either vivid experiences or creative powers, have produced a literature of domestic or social beatitude. The sentimental school of the last century most clearly betrays this weakness. Still, poetry has never entirely forgotten the simpler joys. The high thinkers have not always worsted the good livers. The wise person, even if fallen on evil times, will not lose track of the latter and their long ray of genial sunlight.

The immediately following pages are wholly dedicated to this tradition. In them we perceive how similar have been these homely and refreshing springs of the enjoyment of living, flowing from the earliest age of China to our own day. As the poets remind us, we love to practice sociability along with our children and our friends. We like the plain pleasures that such life affords: leisure for talk and song, for play and art, for eating and drinking. It has been the conclusion of the sages that the most enduring happiness arises from these private sources, instead of from burdensome responsibilities and strenuous heroics. One does not need to be a sybarite to believe so; in fact the simplicity and purity of true joy has been the classical theme of moralists in both the Occident and the Orient. The hearthstone, the playground, the garden and the tavern have, we are told, yielded serener pleasures than the office, the senate or the field of battle.

To state these platitudes is to summarize thousands of true poems produced, in Doctor Johnson's words, from China to Peru. T'ao Ch'ien, Euripides, Horace, Claudianus, Shakespeare, Béranger, Dehmel, Whitman and Carl Sandburg, we may observe, say substantially the same thing. Here is a type of literature and of human thought so elemental and direct as to be virtually common to all peoples.

Yet certain cultures have a special relish or aptitude for the enjoyment of living. The Chinese and the Japanese of their classical periods possessed such happy powers. In the Near East, Omar pursued a like science of contentment, to be followed by Sa'di, Attar and Hafiz, all equally perfect in theory and practice. A high sense for the enjoyment of life is reflected in Homer's *Odyssey,* although often the Greeks seem too restless and unreposeful a people to relish mere contentment. The Romans of the early Empire, however, shared the gift, as shown by famous passages from Horace, Ovid, and Martial. No deeper or quieter joy may be found than in some of the Latin poets of their Golden Age. Herein lies a great part of their abiding charm.

Each age and nation interprets such happiness in accordance with its own light. Among the Spanish and the Russians the mood often seems a bit more strenuous and more transient than with more restrained peoples. The tavern songs and glees of the German Minnesingers have a gusto and a violence of joy missing in the more sober and domestic German lyrics of the last century. We find a deeper and a quieter conviction in the poetry of Richard Dehmel, who died in 1920. For centuries the French have cultivated the good life as led with one's family or intimate friends. Even their most imposing political achievements have often seemed bulwarks to defend their humbler and more local shrines of happiness. We have a long line of spokesmen for an earthly felicity, including poets of old Provençe, and Du Bellay, Ronsard, La Fontaine, Béranger, Mistral and Paul Fort. Especially in the age of the Medici, Italy resounded with some of the world's sunniest and happiest verses. But probably the greatest outburst of robust and open hearted joyousness known to the Christian world occurred in England from the times of Elizabeth to those of Charles Second. Even the Puritan Milton, author of *L'Allegro,* believed in the joy of life. To the English poets, almost without exception men of some classical learning, the examples of the Romans held a peculiar fascination and gave their own utterances body and form. Shakespeare, Jonson, Dekker, Campion, Herrick, Greene and numerous others belong to England's most manly and mirthful age. It is hoped that the few specimens possible to give here in illustration of this great period will indicate the solid grounds on which it is regarded as a new golden age in poetry and in the spirit of man. Since this period British verse has never lost a power to depict the most sincere and human types of joy. Burns in this respect seems a belated Elizabethan; and even among the lyrics of W. H. Davies and William Butler Yeats are to be found rousing expressions of delight.

The American contribution lacks the intimacy with a great tradition grasped by the neo-classical Elizabethans, but boasts instead the racy tang of a new soil. Our most indigenous poets, furthest in spirit from the centers of the book trade and the classical libraries and nearest the hearts of the people, exhibit our best understanding of this ancient theme. Walt Whitman and his heir, Carl Sandburg, best illustrate the sane core of happiness that, if not life itself, is always life's surest support.

"From Break of Day"

From break of day
Till sunset glow
I toil.
I dig my well,
I plow my field,
And earn my food
And drink.
What care I
Who rules the land
If I am left in peace?

—From the Chinese of an unknown poet (2500 B.C.?), translated by Henry H. Hart.

Success

I ask you, my friend,
What ought a man want
But to sit with his wine
In the sun?

My neighbors all come to talk over the news,
And to settle the problems of state.
I've no taxes to pay
On my house or my field.
I'm lucky, you say?
So I am!
My three sons?
Married, all of them;
Fine wives they've got,
And from the best families, too!

My daughters?
I've five of them, all wed.
Good husbands I found for them,
And every one rich!

So I sit in the sun
With my jug of old wine,
And I'd not change with the lords of the land!

—From the Chinese of Wang Chi (T'ang Dynasty, 618–905), translated by Henry H. Hart.

The Arrival of a Guest

It is springtime, to the south and north of my cottage the floods are out.
All I see is a crowd of seagulls that visit me day by day.
The petal-strewn path is not yet swept for a guest;
For you, the first, I open my thatched door to-day.
The market is far away, I can but give you vegetable dishes with no second choice.
My family is too poor for a good goblet of wine, there are only old spirits.
Are you willing to drink with my old neighbour across the way?
He is only separated by that wattle hedge and I will call him over here to help us finish off the wine that is left.

—From the Chinese of Tu Fu (eighth century), translated by Soame Jenyns.

"Shady, Shady"

Shady, shady the wood in front of the Hall:
At midsummer full of calm shadows.
The south wind follows summer's train:
With its eddying puffs it blows open my coat.
I am free from ties and can live a life of retirement.
When I rise from sleep, I play with books and harp.
The lettuce in the garden still grows moist:
Of last year's grain there is always plenty left.
Self-support should maintain strict limits:
More than enough is not what I want.
I grind millet and make good wine:
When the wine is heated, I pour it out for myself.
My little children are playing at my side,
Learning to talk, they babble unformed sounds.
These things have made me happy again
And I forget my lost cap of office.
Distant, distant I gaze at the white clouds:
With a deep yearning I think of the Sages of Antiquity.

—From the Chinese of T'ao Ch'ien, translated by Arthur Waley.

Rubáiyát

I

Wake! For the Sun, who scattered into flight
The Stars before him from the Field of Night,

Drives Night along with them from Heaven, and strikes
The Sultàn's Turret with a Shaft of Light.

II

Before the phantom of False morning died,
Methought a Voice within the Tavern cried,
"When all the Temple is prepared within,
Why nods the drowsy Worshiper outside?"

III

And, as the Cock crew, those who stood before
The Tavern shouted – "Open then the Door!
You know how little while we have to stay,
And, once departed, may return no more."

IV

Now the New Year reviving old Desires,
The thoughtful Soul to Solitude retires,
Where the WHITE HAND OF MOSES on the Bough
Puts out, and Jesus from the Ground suspires.

V

Iram indeed is gone with all his Rose,
And Jamshyd's Seven-ringed Cup where no one knows;
But still a Ruby kindles in the Vine,
And many a Garden by the Water blows.

VI

And David's lips are lockt; but in divine
High-piping Pehlevì, with "Wine! Wine! Wine!
Red Wine!" – the Nightingale cries to the Rose
That sallow cheek of hers to incarnadine.

VII

Come, fill the Cup, and in the fire of Spring
Your Winter-garment of Repentance fling:
The Bird of Time has but a little way
To flutter – and the Bird is on the Wing.

VIII

Whether at Naishápúr or Babylon,
Whether the Cup with sweet or bitter run,
The Wine of Life keeps oozing drop by drop,
The Leaves of Life keep falling one by one.

XI

With me along the strip of Herbage strown
That just divides the desert from the sown,
Where name of Slave and Sultán is forgot –
And Peace to Mahmúd on his golden Throne!

XII

A Book of Verses underneath the Bough,
A Jug of Wine, a Loaf of Bread – and Thou
Beside me singing in the Wilderness –
Oh, Wilderness were Paradise enow!

XIII

Some for the Glories of This World; and some
Sigh for the Prophet's Paradise to come;
Ah, take the Cash, and let the Credit go,
Nor heed the rumble of a distant Drum!

XIV

Look to the blowing Rose about us – "Lo,
Laughing," she says, "into the world I blow,
At once the silken tassel of my Purse
Tear, and its Treasure on the Garden throw."

XV

And those who husbanded the Golden Grain,
And those who flung it to the winds like Rain,
Alike to no such aureate Earth are turned
As, buried once, Men want dug up again.

XVI

The Worldly Hope men set their Hearts upon
Turns Ashes – or it prospers; and anon,
Like Snow upon the Desert's dusty Face,
Lighting a little hour or two – is gone.

XVII

Think, in this battered Caravanserai
Whose Portals are alternate Night and Day,
How Sultán after Sultán with his Pomp
Abode his destined Hour, and went his way.

XVIII

They say the Lion and the Lizard keep
The Courts where Jamshyd gloried and drank deep:
And Bahrám, that great Hunter – the Wild Ass
Stamps o'er his Head, but cannot break his Sleep.

XIX

I sometimes think that never blows so red
The Rose as where some buried Cæsar bled;
That every Hyacinth the Garden wears
Dropt in her Lap from some once lovely Head.

XX

And this reviving Herb whose tender Green
Fledges the River-Lip on which we lean —
Ah, lean upon it lightly! for who knows
From what once lovely Lip it springs unseen!

XXI

Ah, my Belovèd, fill the Cup that clears
To-day of past Regrets and future Fears:
To-morrow! — Why, To-morrow I may be
Myself with Yesterday's Seven thousand Years.

XXII

For some we loved, the loveliest and the best
That from his Vintage rolling Time hath prest,
Have drunk their Cup a Round or two before
And one by one crept silently to rest,

XXIII

And we, that now make merry in the Room
They left, and Summer dresses in new bloom,
Ourselves must we beneath the Couch of Earth
Descend — ourselves to make a Couch — for whom?

XXIV

Ah, make the most of what we yet may spend,
Before we too into the Dust descend;
Dust into Dust, and under Dust to lie,
Sans Wine, sans Song, sans Singer, and — sans End!

XXV

Alike for those who for To-day prepare,
And those that after some To-morrow stare,
A Muezzin from the Tower of Darkness cries,
"Fools! your Reward is neither Here nor There."

XXVI

Why, all the Saints and Sages who discussed
Of the Two Worlds so wisely — they are thrust
Like foolish Prophets forth; their Words to Scorn
Are scattered, and their Mouths are stopt with Dust.

XXVII

Myself when young did eagerly frequent
Doctor and Saint, and heard great argument
About it and about: but evermore
Came out by the same door where in I went.

XXVIII

With them the seed of Wisdom did I sow,
And with mine own hand wrought to make it grow;
And this was all the Harvest that I reaped —
"I came like Water, and like Wind I go."

XXIX

Into this Universe, and *Why* not knowing
Nor *Whence*, like Water willy-nilly flowing;
And out of it, as Wind along the Waste,
I know not *Whither*, willy-nilly blowing.

XXX

What, without asking, hither hurried *Whence?*
And, without asking, *Whither* hurried hence?
Oh, many a Cup of this forbidden Wine
Must drown the memory of that insolence!

XXXI

Up from Earth's Center through the Seventh Gate
I rose, and on the Throne of Saturn sate,
And many a Knot unraveled by the Road;
But not the Master-knot of Human Fate.

XXXII

There was the Door to which I found no Key;
There was the Veil through which I might not see:
Some little talk awhile of Me and Thee
There was — and then no more of Thee and Me.

XXXIII

Earth could not answer; nor the Seas that mourn
In flowing Purple, of their Lord forlorn;
Nor rolling Heaven, with all his Signs revealed
And hidden by the sleeve of Night and Morn.

XXXV

Then to the Lip of this poor earthen Urn
I leaned, the Secret of my Life to learn:
And Lip to Lip it murmured—"While you live,
Drink!—for, once dead, you never shall return."

XLI

Perplext no more with Human or Divine
To-morrow's tangle to the winds resign,
And lose your fingers in the tresses of
The Cypress-slender Minister of Wine.

XLII

And if the Wine you drink, the Lip you press,
End in what All begins and ends in—Yes;
Think then you are TO-DAY what YESTERDAY
You were—TO-MORROW you shall not be less.

XLIII

So when the Angel of the darker Drink
At last shall find you by the river-brink,
And, offering his Cup, invite your Soul
Forth to your Lips to quaff—you shall not shrink.

XLVI

And fear not lest Existence closing your
Account and mine, should know the like no more;
The Eternal Sákí from that Bowl has poured
Millions of Bubbles like us, and will pour.

XLVII

When You and I behind the Veil are past,
Oh, but the long, long while the World shall last,
Which of our Coming and Departure heeds
As the Sea's self should heed a pebble-cast.

XLVIII

A Moment's Halt—a momentary taste
Of BEING from the Well amid the Waste—
And Lo!—the phantom Caravan has reached
The NOTHING it set out from—Oh, make haste!

LVIII

And lately, by the Tavern Door agape,
Came shining through the Dusk an Angel Shape
Bearing a Vessel on his Shoulder; and
He bid me taste of it; and 't was—the Grape!

LIX

The Grape that can with Logic absolute
The Two-and-Seventy jarring Sects confute:
The sovereign Alchemist that in a trice
Life's leaden metal into Gold transmute:

LXIII

Oh, threats of Hell and Hopes of Paradise!
One thing at least is certain—*This* Life flies;
One thing is certain and the rest is Lies;
The Flower that once has blown for ever dies.

LXIV

Strange, is it not? that of the myriads who
Before us passed the door of Darkness through,
Not one returns to tell us of the Road,
Which to discover we must travel too.

LXV

The Revelations of Devout and Learned
Who rose before us, and as Prophets burned,
Are all but Stories, which, awoke from Sleep
They told their comrades, and to Sleep returned.

LXVI

I sent my Soul through the Invisible,
Some letter of that After-life to spell:
And by and by my Soul returned to me,
And answered "I Myself am Heaven and Hell:"

LXVII

Heaven but the Vision of fulfilled Desire,
And Hell the Shadow from a Soul on fire,
Cast on the Darkness into which Ourselves,
So late emerged from shall so soon expire.

LXVIII

We are no other than a moving row
Of Magic Shadow-shapes that come and go
Round with the Sun-illumined Lantern held
In Midnight by the Master of the Show;

LXIX

But helpless Pieces of the Game He plays
Upon this Chequer-board of Nights and Days;
Hither and thither moves, and checks, and slays,
And one by one back in the Closet lays.

LXX

The Ball no question makes of Ayes and Noes,
But Here or There as strikes the Player goes;
And He that tossed you down into the Field,
He knows about it all — HE knows — HE knows!

LXXI

The Moving Finger writes; and, having writ,
Moves on: nor all your Piety nor Wit
Shall lure it back to cancel half a Line,
Nor all your Tears wash out a Word of it.

LXXII

And that inverted Bowl they call the Sky,
Whereunder crawling cooped we live and die,
Lift not your hands to *It* for help — for It
As impotently moves as you or I.

LXXIII

With Earth's first Clay They did the Last Man knead,
And there of the Last Harvest sowed the Seed:
And the first Morning of Creation wrote
What the Last Dawn of Reckoning shall read.

LXXIV

YESTERDAY *This* Day's Madness did prepare;
TO-MORROW's Silence, Triumph, or Despair:
Drink! for you know not whence you came, nor why:
Drink! for you know not why you go, nor where.

LXXX

Oh Thou, who didst with pitfall and with gin
Beset the Road I was to wander in,
Thou wilt not with Predestined Evil round
Enmesh, and then impute my Fall to Sin!

LXXXI

Oh Thou, who Man of baser Earth didst make,
And even with Paradise devise the Snake:
For all the Sin wherewith the Face of Man
Is blackened — Man's forgiveness give — and take!

C

Yon rising Moon that looks for us again —
How oft hereafter will she wax and wane;
How oft hereafter rising look for us
Through this same Garden — and for *one* in vain!

CI

And when like her, Oh Saki, you shall pass
Among the Guests Star-scattered on the Grass,
And in your joyous errand reach the spot
Where I made One — turn down an empty Glass!

— *From the Persian of Omar Khayyám (d. 1123), translated by Edward Fitzgerald.*

Children

Lady, the sunlit hour is beautiful,
And beautiful, when winds blow soft, the sea,
And Earth in her spring flower, and affluent streams.
Of many beauties I could tell the praise,
But none there is beams on the eye so bright
As when the childless, heart-sore with desire,
See children like young buds about their house.

— *From the Greek of Euripides (480–406 B.C.), translated by T. F. Higham.*

Baucis and Philemon

FROM THE METAMORPHOSES

Heaven's power is infinite: earth, air, and sea,
The manufactur'd mass, the making power obey:
By proof to clear your doubt; in Phrygian ground
Two neighboring trees, with walls encompass'd round,
Stand on a moderate rise, with wonder shown;
One a hard oak, a softer linden one:
I saw the place, and them, by Pittheus sent
To Phrygian realms, my grandsire's government.
Not far from thence is seen a lake, the haunt
Of coots, and of the fishing cormorant:
Here Jove with Hermes came; but in disguise
Of mortal men conceal'd their deities;
One laid aside his thunder, one his rod,
And many toilsome steps together trod:
For harbor at a thousand doors they knock'd;
Not one of all the thousand but was lock'd.
At last a hospitable house they found,
A homely shed; the roof, not far from ground,
Was thatch'd, with reeds and straw together bound.
There Baucis and Philemon lived, and there
Had lived long married, and a happy pair:
Now old in love, though little was their store,
Inured to want, their poverty they bore,
Nor aim'd at wealth, professing to be poor.
For master or for servant here to call
Were all alike, where only two were all.
Command was none, where equal love was paid,
Or rather both commanded, both obey'd.
From lofty roofs the gods repulsed before,
Now stooping, enter'd through the little door:
The man (their hearty welcome first express'd)
A common settle drew for either guest,
Inviting each his weary limbs to rest.
But ere they sat, officious Baucis lays
Two cushions stuff'd with straw, the seat to raise;
Coarse, but the best she had; then rakes the load
Of ashes from the hearth, and spreads abroad
The living coals; and, lest they should expire,
With leaves and bark she feeds her infant fire.
It smokes; and then with trembling breath she blows,
Till in a cheerful blaze the flames arose.
With brushwood and with chips she strengthens these
And adds at last the boughs of rotten trees.
The fire thus form'd, she sets the kettle on
(Like burnish'd gold the little seether shone;)
Next took the coleworts which her husband got
From his own ground (a small, well-water'd spot;)
She stripp'd the stalks of all their leaves; the best
She cull'd, and them with handy care she dress'd.
High o'er the hearth a chine of bacon hung;
Good old Philemon seized it with a prong,
And from the sooty rafter drew it down,
Then cut a slice, but scarce enough for one;
Yet a large portion of a little store,
Which for their sakes alone he wish'd were more.
This in the pot he plunged without delay,
To tame the flesh, and drain the salt away.
The time between, before the fire they sat,
And shorten'd the delay by pleasing chat.
A beam there was, on which a beechen pail
Hung by the handle, on a driven nail:
This fill'd with water, gently warmed, they set
Before their guests; in this they bathed their feet,
And after with clean towels dried their sweat.
This done, the host produced the genial bed,
Sallow the feet, the borders, and the stead,
Which with no costly coverlet they spread,
But coarse old garments; yet such robes as these
They laid alone at feasts on holydays.
The good old housewife, tucking up her gown
The table sets; the invited gods lie down.
The trivet-table of a foot was lame,
A blot which prudent Baucis overcame,
Who thrust beneath the limping leg a sherd;
So was the mended board exactly rear'd:

Then rubb'd it o'er with newly-gather'd mint,
A wholesome herb, that breathed a grateful scent.
Pallas began the feast, where first was seen
The party-color'd olive, black and green:
Autumnal cornels next in order serv'd,
In lees of wine well pickled and preserved.
A garden salad was the third supply,
Of endive, radishes, and succory:
Then curds and cream, the flower of country fare,
And new-laid eggs, which Baucis' busy care
Turn'd by a gentle fire, and roasted rare.
All these in earthenware were served to board,
And, next in place, an earthen pitcher stored
With liquor of the best the cottage could afford.
This was the table's ornament and pride,
With figures wrought: like pages at his side
Stood beechen bowls; and these were shining clean,
Varnish'd with wax without, and lined within.
By this the boiling kettle had prepared,
And to the table sent the smoking lard;
On which with eager appetite they dine,
A sav'ry bit, that serv'd to relish wine;
The wine itself was suiting to the rest,
Still working in the must, and lately press'd.
The second course succeeds like that before,
Plums, apples, nuts; and of their wintry store
Dry figs, and grapes, and wrinkled dates were set
In canisters, to enlarge the little treat:
All these a milkwhite honey-comb surround,
Which in the midst a country banquet crown'd:
But the kind hosts their entertainment grace
With hearty welcome, and an open face:
In all they did, you might discern with ease
A willing mind, and a desire to please.
  Meanwhile the beechen bowls went round, and still,
Though often emptied, were observed to fill:
Fill'd without hands, and, of their own accord,
Ran without feet, and danced about the board.
Devotion seiz'd the pair, to see the feast
With wine, and of no common grape, increased;
And up they held their hands, and fell to pray'r,
Excusing, as they could, their country fare.
  One goose they had ('twas all they could allow,)
A wakeful sentry, and on duty now,
Whom to the gods for sacrifice they vow:
Her with malicious zeal the couple view'd;
She ran for life, and limping they pursued:
Full well the fowl perceived their bad intent,
And would not make her master's compliment;
But persecuted, to the powers she flies,
And close between the legs of Jove she lies:
He with a gracious ear the suppliant heard,
And saved her life; then what he was declared,
And own'd the god. "The neighborhood," said he,
"Shall justly perish for impiety:
You stand alone exempted: but obey
With speed, and follow where we lead the way:
Leave these accursed, and to the mountain's height
Ascend, nor once look backward in your flight."
  They haste, and what their tardy feet denied,
The trusty staff (their better leg) supplied.
An arrow's flight they wanted to the top,
And there secure, but spent with travel, stop;
They turn their now no more forbidden eyes;
Lost in a lake the floated level lies:
A watery desert covers all the plains,
Their cot alone, as in an isle, remains.
Wondering, with weeping eyes, while they deplore
Their neighbors' fate, and country now no more;
Their little shed, scarce large enough for two,
Seems, from the ground increased, in height and bulk to grow.
A stately temple shoots within the skies,
The crotches of their cot in columns rise;
The pavement polish'd marble they behold,
The gates with sculpture graced, the spires and tiles of gold.
  Then thus the sire of gods, with looks serene:
"Speak thy desire, thou only just of men;
And thou, O woman, only worthy found
To be with such a man in marriage bound."

Awhile they whisper; then, to Jove address'd,
Philemon thus prefers their joint request:
"We crave to serve before your sacred shrine,
And offer at your altar rites divine:
And since not any action of our life
Has been polluted with domestic strife,
We beg one hour of death, that neither she
With widow's tears may live to bury me,
Nor weeping I, with wither'd arms, may bear
My breathless Baucis to the sepulchre."
The godheads sign their suit. They run their race,
In the same tenor, all the appointed space:
Then, when their hour was come, while they relate
These past adventures at the temple gate,
Old Baucis is by old Philemon seen
Sprouting with sudden leaves of sprightly green:
Old Baucis look'd where old Philemon stood,
And saw his lengthen'd arms a sprouting wood:
New roots their fasten'd feet begin to bind,
Their bodies stiffen in a rising rind:
Then, ere the bark above their shoulders grew,
They give and take at once their last adieu.
"At once farewell, O faithful spouse," they said;
At once the encroaching rinds their closing lips invade.
E'en yet, an ancient Tyanæan shows
A spreading oak, that near a linden grows;
The neighborhood confirm the prodigy,
Grave men, not vain of tongue, or like to lie.
I saw myself the garlands of their boughs,
And tablets hung for gifts of granted vows;
And offering fresher up, with pious prayer,
"The good," said I, "are God's peculiar care,
And such as honor Heaven, shall heavenly honor share."

—*From the Metamorphoses of Ovid (43 B.C.–18 A.D.), translated from the Latin by John Dryden.*

Revery of a Business Man

How happy in his low degree,
How rich in humble poverty is he
Who leads a quiet country life,
Discharged of business, void of strife,
And from the griping scrivener free!
Thus, ere the seeds of vice were sown,
Lived men in better ages born,
Who plowed with oxen of their own
Their small paternal field of corn.
Nor trumpets summon him to war,
Nor drums disturb his morning sleep,
Nor knows he merchants' gainful care,
Nor fears the dangers of the deep.
The clamors of contentious law,
And court and state he wisely shuns;
Nor bribed with hopes, nor dared with awe,
To servile salutations runs;
But either to the clasping vine
Does the supporting poplar wed,
Or with his pruning hook disjoin
Unbearing branches from their head,
And grafts more happy in their stead;
Or climbing to a hilly steep,
He views his buds in vales afar,
Or shears his overburdened sheep,
Or mead for cooling drink prepares;
Or virgin honey in the jars;
Or, in the now declining year,
When beauteous Autumn rears his head,
He joys to pull the ripened pear
And clustering grapes with purple spread.
Sometimes beneath an ancient oak,
Or on the matted grass he lies:
No god of sleep he need invoke;
The stream that o'er the pebble flies
With gentle slumber crowns his eyes.
The wind that whistles through the sprays
Maintains the concert of the song,
And hidden birds with native lays
The golden sleep prolong.
But when the blast of winter blows,
And hoary frost invests the year,
Into the naked woods he goes
And seeks the tusky boar to rear
With well-mouthed hounds and pointed spear!
Or spreads his subtle nets from sight,
With twinkling glasses, to betray
The larks that in the meshes light;
Or makes the fearful bear the prey.
Amidst his harmless, easy joys,
No anxious care invades his health,
Nor love his peace of mind destroys,
Nor wicked avarice of wealth.
But if a chaste and pleasing wife,
To ease the business of his life,
Divides with him his household care,
Such as the Sabine matrons were,
Such as the swift Apulian's bride,
Sunburnt and swarthy though she be
Will fire for winter nights provide,

And, without noise, will oversee
His children and his family,
And order all things till he come,
Sweaty and overlabored, home.
If she in pens his flocks will fold,
And then produce her dairy store,
With wine to drive away the cold,
And unbought dainties for the poor;
Not oysters of the Lucrine lake
My sober appetite would wish,
Nor turbot, or the foreign fish
That rolling tempests overtake,
And hither waft the costly dish.
Not heathpolt, or the rarer bird,
Which Phasis or Ionia yields
More pleasing morsels would afford
Than the fat olives of my fields;
Than shards and mallows for the pot,
That keep the loosened body sound,
Or than the lamb that falls by lot
To the just guardian of my ground.
Amidst these feasts of happy swains
The jolly shepherd smiles to see
His flock returning from the plains;
The farmer is as pleased as he
To view his oxen, sweating smoke,
Bear on their necks the loosened yoke:
To look upon his menial crew
That sit around his cheerful hearth,
And bodies spent in toil renew
With wholesome food and country mirth.
This Alphaeus said within himself.
Resolved to leave the wicked town,
And live retired upon his own,
He called his money in.
But the prevailing love of pelf
Soon split him on the former shelf:
He put it out again!

—From the Latin of Horace (65–8 B.C.), translated by John Dryden.

The Means to Attain Happy Life

The things that make a life to please
(Sweetest Martial), they are these:
Estate inherited, not got:
A thankful field, hearth always hot:
City seldom, law-suits never:
Equal friends agreeing ever:
Health of body, peace of mind:
Sleeps that till the morning bind:
Wise simplicity, plain fare:
Not drunken nights, yet loos'd from care:
A sober, not a sullen spouse:
Clean strength, not such as his that plows;
Wish only what thou art, to be;
Death neither wish, nor fear to see.

—From the Latin of Martial (40–104), translated by Sir Richard Fanshawe.

The Old Man of Verona

Happy the man, who his whole time doth bound
Within th' inclosure of his little ground.
Happy the man whom the same humble place,
The hereditary cottage of his race,
From his first rising infancy has known,
And by degrees sees gently bending down,
With natural propension, to that earth
Which both preserved his life, and gave him birth.
Him no false distant lights, by fortune set,
Could ever into foolish wanderings get.
He never dangers either saw or feared:
The dreadful storms at sea he never heard.
He never heard the shrill alarms of war,
Or the worse noises of the lawyers' bar.
No change of consuls marks to him the year;
The change of seasons is his calendar.
The cold and heat, winter and summer shows;
Autumn by fruits, and spring by flowers, he knows.
He measures time by landmarks, and has found
For the whole day the dial of his ground.
A neighboring wood, born with himself, he sees,
And loves his old contemporary trees.
He has only heard of near Verona's name,
And knows it, like the Indies, but by fame.
Does with a like concernment notice take
Of the Red sea, and of Benacus' lake.
Thus health and strength he to a third age enjoys,
And sees a long posterity of boys.
About the spacious world let others roam,
The voyage, life, is longest made at home.

—From the Latin of Claudius Claudianus (c. 400), translated by Abraham Cowley.

Gaudeamus Igitur[1]

Let us live then and be glad
While young life's before us!
After youthful pastime had,
After old age hard and sad,
Earth will slumber o'er us.

Where are they who in this world,
Ere we kept, were keeping?
Go ye to the gods above;
Go to hell; inquire thereof:
They are not; they're sleeping.

Brief is life, and brevity
Briefly shall be ended:
Death comes like a whirlwind strong,
Bears us with his blast along;
None shall be defended.

Live this university,
Men that learning nourish;
Live each member of the same,
Long live all that bear its name;
Let them ever flourish!

Live the commonwealth also,
And the men that guide it!
Live our town in strength and health,
Founders, patrons, by whose wealth
We are here provided!

Live all girls! A health to you,
Melting maids and beauteous!
Live the wives and women too,
Gentle, loving, tender, true,
Good, industrious, duteous!

Perish cares that pule and pine!
Perish envious blamers!
Die the Devil, thine and mine!
Die the starch-neck Philistine!
Scoffers and defamers!

—*Anonymous medieval Latin student song, translated by John Addington Symonds.*

Winter-Time

Winter, we are by thy might
Into houses driven
From the wood and hill,
Where thine icy blizzards bite.
Lark, thou art forgiven
That thy song grows still;
War upon thee rime and snow,
All thy trilling chilling;
And the clover, too, must go.
May to praise I'm willing,
But winter is my foe!
Dance and laugh as youth befits,
Though the trees are smitten
Till return of spring.
See! To spice the cheer my wits
Freshly here have written
Words for all to sing,
Lest encumbered skies should bar
Natural pleasure-seeking.
Warm thy room is, Engelmar,
While on moorlands shrieking
The sprites of winter are!

—*From the German of Sir Neidhart von Reuental (c. 1210–c. 1245), translated by Jethro Bithell.*

The Life Removed

How tranquil is the life
Of him who, shunning the vain world's uproar,
May follow, free from strife,
The hidden path, of yore
Chosen by the few who conned true wisdom's lore!

For he, with thoughts aloof,
By proud men's great estate is not oppressed,
Nor marvels at the roof
Of gold, built to attest
The Moor's skill and on jasper pillars rest.

He heeds not though fame raise
His name, afar on wings of rumour flung,
He cares not for the praise
Of cunning flatterer's tongue,
Nor for what truth sincere would leave unsung.

What boots it my content
That the vain voice of fame should favour me,
If in its service spent
I find myself to be
Vexed by dull care and gnawing misery?

O hill, O stream, O field,
O solitary refuge of delight,
Since my bark now must yield
To the storm, your solace bright
I seek and flee this sea's tempestuous might.

[1] So Let us rejoice.

Sleep broken by no fear
Be mine, and a day clear, serene, and free,
Shunning the look severe,
Lofty exceedingly,
Of him whom gold exalts or ancestry.

Me may the birds awake
With their sweet, unpremeditated song,
And those dark cares forsake
That e'er to him belong
Who lives not in his independence strong!

I to myself would live,
To enjoy the blessings that to Heaven I owe,
Alone, contemplative,
And freely love forgo,
Nor hope, fear, hatred, jealousy e'er know.

Upon the bare hillside
An orchard I have made with my own hand,
That in the sweet Springtide
All in fair flower doth stand
And promise sure of fruit shows through the
land.

And, as though swift it strove
To see and to increase that loveliness,
From the clear ridge above
A stream pure, weariless,
Hurrying to reach that ground doth onward
press;

And straightway in repose
Its course it winds there tree and tree be-
tween,
And ever as it goes
The earth decks with new green
And with gay wealth of flowers spreads the
scene.

The air in gentle breeze
A myriad scents for my delight distils,
It moves among the trees
With a soft sound that fills
The mind, and thought of gold or sceptre
kills.

Treasure and gold be theirs
Who to a frail bark would entrust their life:
I envy not the cares
Of those whose fears are rife
When the North wind with the South wind
is at strife.

In the storm's strain the mast
Groans, and clear day is turned to eyeless
night,
While to the skies aghast
Rise wild cries of affright
And they enrich the sea in their despite.

But me may still suffice,
Rich only in meek peace, a humble fare;
And the wrought artifice
Be his of gold plate rare
Who dreads not o'er the raging sea to fare.

And while in misery
Others are pledged to fierce ambition's
throng,
Afire insatiably
For power that stays not long,
May I in pleasant shade recite my song;

Yea, lying in the shade,
My brow with ivy and bay immortal
crowned,
My ear attentive made
To the soft, tuneful sound
Of zither touched by fingers' skill profound.

—*From the Spanish of Luis de León (1527–1591), translated by Aubrey F. G. Bell.*

Let Me Go Warm

Let me go warm and merry still;
And let the world laugh, an it will.

Let others muse on earthly things,—
The fall of thrones, the fate of kings,
And those whose fame the world doth fill;
Whilst muffins sit enthroned in trays,
And orange-punch in winter sways
The merry scepter of my days;—
And let the world laugh, an it will.

He that the royal purple wears
From golden plate a thousand cares
Doth swallow as a gilded pill:
On feasts like these I turn my back,
Whilst puddings in my roasting-jack
Beside the chimney hiss and crack;—
And let the world laugh, an it will.

And when the wintry tempest blows,
And January's sleets and snows
Are spread o'er every vale and hill,
With one to tell a merry tale
O'er roasted nuts and humming ale,
I sit, and care not for the gale;—
And let the world laugh, an it will.

Let merchants traverse seas and lands,
For silver mines and golden sands;
Whilst I beside some shadowy rill,
Just where its bubbling fountain swells,
Do sit and gather stones and shells,
And hear the tale the blackbird tells;—
And let the world laugh, an it will.

For Hero's sake the Grecian lover
The stormy Hellespont swam over:
I cross, without the fear of ill,
The wooden bridge that slow bestrides
The Madrigal's enchanting sides,
Or barefoot wade through Yepes' tides;—
And let the world laugh, an it will.

But since the Fates so cruel prove,
That Pyramus should die of love,
And love should gentle Thisbe kill;
My Thisbe be an apple-tart,
The sword I plunge into her heart
The tooth that bites the crust apart;—
And let the world laugh, an it will.

—*From the Spanish of Luis de Gongora (1561–1627), translated by H. W. Longfellow.*

Youth Is Sweet and Well

Youth is sweet and well
But doth speed away!
Let who will be gay,
To-morrow, none can tell.
Bacchus and his Fair,
Contented with their fate,
Chase both time and care,
Loving soon and late;
High and low estate
With the nymphs at play;
Let who will be gay,
To-morrow, none can tell.
Laughing satyrs all
Set a hundred snares,
Lovelorn dryads fall
In them unawares:
Glad with wine, in pairs
They dance the hours away:
Let who will be gay,
To-morrow, none can tell.
Not unwillingly
Were these nymphs deceived:
From Love do but flee
Graceless hearts aggrieved:
Deceivers and deceived
Together wend their way.
Let who will be gay,
To-morrow, none can tell.
Fat Silenus nears
On an ass astride:
Full of wine and years,
Come and see him ride:
He lolls from side to side
But gleefully alway:
Let who will be gay,
To-morrow, none can tell.
Midas following,
Turneth all to gold:
What can treasure bring
To a heart that's cold?
And what joy unfold
For who thirsteth, pray?
Let who will be gay,
To-morrow, none can tell.
Ears be very bold,
Count not on to-morrow:
Let both young and old,
Lads and lassies, borrow
Joy and banish sorrow,
Doleful thoughts and grey:
Let who will be gay,
To-morrow, none can tell.
Lads and lassies all,
Love and Bacchus hail!
Dance and song befall!
Pain and sadness fail!
Tender hearts prevail,
Happen then what may!
Let who will be gay,
To-morrow, none can tell.
Youth is sweet and well
But doth speed away.
. . . .

—*From the Italian of Lorenzo de' Medici (1448–1492), translated by Lorna de' Lucchi.*

With Dreams of Wealth and Fame

With dreams of wealth and fame
Why in my soul breed strife,
Since Atropos even now
Severs my thread of life?
Since now the pilot dread
For me bends to his oar
There, where it has been said
We may return no more?
The hours that still remain,
So blithe, so fain to flee,
Sweetly and gaily pass
In rural liberty;

From Ceres corn we see,
And Bacchus wine doth bear,
And lovely Chastity
Winds blossoms in her hair.
I know deemed fortunate
Is he who owns a chest
Wherein, through Plutus, do
Uncounted treasures rest;
But with a heart of grief
Full oftentimes appear
The great ones, bowed beneath
The frozen hand of fear.
I will not knock on harsh,
Illustrious doors; I'll tread
Naked indeed, but free,
The kingdom of the dead!
For wealth or potency,
With false and coward deed,
This venal century
Will never see me plead!
O placid hill serene,
My sweet Eüpili
With gently rising slopes
Embracing tenderly;
Beauty entranceth me
By nature squandered here,
Though I an exile be,
Contented I draw near.
That peace scarce known to men,
Upon your shadowy breast
I find, come back again
To your beloved rest;
Sorrow and care I see
In flight precipitate,
The pride of tyranny
Eager to agitate.
How they must be inspired
To envy me, flower crowned,
In this rusticity
Unto no slavery bound;
As Phoebus used to wile,
Shepherd in Thessaly,
So too will I, and smile
To my harp's melody.
Hymns from my suppliant breast
I'll lift up to the skies,
So that afar from us
The cruel whirlwinds rise,
So that we do not see
The bitter wrath of war,
And our fields trampled be
By foeman's steed no more.
Thee, toiler diligent,
Who wilt direct the vine
In furrows new, and then
It with lithe willows twine,
Who to thy sterile part
Of country wilt bestow
Fecundity with art
Thy fathers did not know;
Thee, blissful, in my hymns
I'll show posterity,
And down the centuries
'Twill still be told of thee;
And under the wan grass,
In sorrow to revere
Thy quiet bones, will pass
Thy children's children here.
To me may it be given
To end, O meadows blest,
These happy days of mine
In your transcendent rest;
He hath, indeed, true fame
If a regretful breath
Still call upon his name
After the day of death.

—*From the Italian of Giuseppe Parini (1729–1799), translated by Lorna de' Lucchi.*

Content

Sweet are the thoughts that savour of content;
The quiet mind is richer than a crown;
Sweet are the nights in careless slumber spent;
The poor estate scorns fortune's angry frown:
Such sweet content, such minds, such sleep, such bliss,
Beggars enjoy, when princes oft do miss.

The homely house that harbours quiet rest;
The cottage that affords no pride nor care;
The mean that 'grees with country music best;
The sweet consort of mirth and music's fare;
Obscuréd life sets down a type of bliss:
A mind content both crown and kingdom is.

—*Robert Greene, English (c. 1560–1592).*

Under the Greenwood Tree

Under the greenwood tree
Who loves to lie with me,
And turn his merry note
Unto the sweet birds' throat,

Come hither, come hither, come hither:
Here shall he see
No enemy
But winter and rough weather.

Who doth ambition shun
And loves to live i' the sun,
Seeking the food he eats
And pleased with what he gets,
Come hither, come hither, come hither:
Here shall he see
No enemy
But winter and rough weather.

—*William Shakespeare, English (1564–1616).*

The Happy Heart

Art thou poor, yet hast thou golden slumbers?
O sweet content!
Art thou rich, yet is thy mind perplex'd?
O punishment!
Dost thou laugh to see how fools are vex'd
To add to golden numbers, golden numbers?
O sweet content! O sweet, O sweet content!
Work apace, apace, apace, apace;
Honest labour bears a lovely face;
Then hey nonny nonny, hey nonny nonny!

Canst drink the waters of the crispéd spring?
O sweet content!
Swimm'st thou in wealth, yet sink'st in thine own tears?
O punishment!
Then he that patiently want's burden bears
No burden bears, but is a king, a king!
O sweet content! O sweet, O sweet content!
Work apace, apace, apace, apace;
Honest labour bears a lovely face;
Then hey nonny nonny, hey nonny nonny!

—*Thomas Dekker, English (fl. 1600).*

"Now Winter Nights . . ."

Now winter nights enlarge
The number of their hours,
And clouds their storms discharge
Upon the airy towers.
Let now the chimneys blaze,
And cups o'erflow with wine;
Let well-tuned words amaze
With harmony divine.
Now yellow waxen lights
Shall wait on honey love,
While youthful revels, masques and courtly sights
Sleep's leaden spells remove.

This time doth well dispense
With lovers' long discourse;
Much speech hath some defence,
Though beauty no remorse.
All do not all things well;
Some measures comely tread,
Some knotted riddles tell,
Some poems smoothly read.
The summer hath his joys
And winter his delights;
Though love and all his pleasures are but toys,
They shorten tedious nights.

—*Thomas Campion, English (1567–1619).*

A Thanksgiving to God, for His House

Lord, Thou hast given me a cell
Wherein to dwell,
A little house, whose humble roof
Is weather-proof;
Under the spars of which I lie
Both soft, and dry;
Where Thou my chamber for to ward
Hast set a guard
Of harmless thoughts, to watch and keep
Me, while I sleep.
Low is my porch, as is my fate,
Both void of state;
And yet the threshold of my door
Is worn by th' poor,
Who thither come, and freely get
Good words, or meat:
Like as my parlour, so my hall
And kitchen's small:
A little buttery, and therein
A little bin,
Which keeps my little loaf of bread
Unchipp'd, unflead:
Some brittle sticks of thorn or briar
Make me a fire,
Close by whose living coal I sit,
And glow like it.
Lord, I confess too, when I dine,
The pulse is thine,
And all those other bits, that be

There plac'd by thee;
The worts, the purslain, and the mess
Of water-cress,
Which of Thy kindness Thou has sent;
And my content
Makes those, and my beloved beet,
To be more sweet.
'Tis Thou that crown'st my glittering hearth
With guiltless mirth;
And giv'st me wassail bowls to drink,
Spic'd to the brink.
Lord, 'tis Thy plenty-dropping hand,
That soils my land;
And giv'st me, for my bushel sown,
Twice ten for one:
Thou mak'st my teeming hen to lay
Her egg each day:
Besides my healthful ewes to bear
Me twins each year:
The while the conduits of my kine
Run cream, (for wine.)
All these, and better Thou dost send
Me, to this end,
That I should render, for my part,
A thankful heart;
Which, fir'd with incense, I resign,
As wholly Thine;
But the acceptance, that must be,
My Christ, by Thee.

—*Robert Herrick, English (1591–1674).*

~ ✿ ~

L'Allegro

Hence, loathéd Melancholy,
Of Cerberus and blackest Midnight born
In Stygian cave forlorn
'Mongst horrid shapes, and shrieks, and sights unholy!
Find out some uncouth cell
Where brooding Darkness spreads his jealous wings
And the night-raven sings;
There under ebon shades, and low-brow'd rocks
As ragged as thy locks,
In dark Cimmerian desert ever dwell.

But come, thou Goddess fair and free,
In heaven yclept Euphrosyne,
And by men, heart-easing Mirth,
Whom lovely Venus at a birth
With two sister Graces more
To ivy-crownéd Bacchus bore;
Or whether (as some sager sing)
The frolic wind that breathes the spring
Zephyr, with Aurora playing,
As he met her once a-Maying—
There on beds of violets blue
And fresh-blown roses wash'd in dew
Fill'd her with thee, a daughter fair,
So buxom, blithe, and debonair.
Haste thee, Nymph, and bring with thee
Jest, and youthful jollity,
Quips, and cranks, and wanton wiles,
Nods, and becks, and wreathéd smiles
Such as hang on Hebe's cheek,
And love to live in dimple sleek;
Sport that wrinkled Care derides,
And Laughter holding both his sides:—
Come, and trip it as you go
On the light fantastic toe;
And in thy right hand lead with thee
The mountain-nymph, sweet Liberty;
And if I give thee honour due
Mirth, admit me of thy crew,
To live with her, and live with thee
In unreprovéd pleasures free;
To hear the lark begin his flight
And singing startle the dull night
From his watch-tower in the skies,
Till the dappled dawn doth rise;
Then to come, in spite of sorrow,
And at my window bid good-morrow
Through the sweetbriar, or the vine,
Or the twisted eglantine:
While the cock with lively din
Scatters the rear of darkness thin,
And to the stack, or the barn-door,
Stoutly struts his dames before:
Oft listening how the hounds and horn
Cheerly rouse the slumbering morn,
From the side of some hoar hill,
Through the high wood echoing shrill:
Sometime walking, not unseen,
By hedge-row elms, on hillocks green,
Right against the eastern gate
Where the great Sun begins his state
Robed in flames and amber light,
The clouds in thousand liveries dight;
While the ploughman, near at hand,
Whistles o'er the furrow'd land,
And the milkmaid singeth blithe,
And the mower whets his scythe,
And every shepherd tells his tale
Under the hawthorn in the dale.
Straight mine eye hath caught new pleasures
Whilst the landscape round it measures;
Russet lawns, and fallows gray,

Where the nibbling flocks do stray;
Mountains, on whose barren breast
The labouring clouds do often rest;
Meadows trim with daisies pied,
Shallow brooks, and rivers wide;
Towers and battlements it sees
Bosom'd high in tufted trees,
Where perhaps some Beauty lies,
The Cynosure of neighbouring eyes.
Hard by, a cottage chimney smokes
From betwixt two aged oaks,
Where Corydon and Thyrsis, met,
Are at their savoury dinner set
Of herbs, and other country messes
Which the neat-handed Phillis dresses;
And then in haste her bower she leaves
With Thestylis to bind the sheaves;
Or, if the earlier season lead,
To the tann'd haycock in the mead.
Sometimes with secure delight
The upland hamlets will invite,
When the merry bells ring round,
And the jocund rebecks sound
To many a youth and many a maid,
Dancing in the chequer'd shade;
And young and old come forth to play
On a sun-shine holyday,
Till the live-long day-light fail:
Then to the spicy nut-brown ale,
With stories told of many a feat,
How Faery Mab the junkets eat: —
She was pinch'd, and pull'd, she said;
And he, by Friar's lantern led;
Tells how the drudging Goblin sweat
To earn his cream-bowl duly set,
When in one night, ere glimpse of morn,
His shadowy flail hath thresh'd the corn
That ten day-labourers could not end;
Then lies him down the lubber fiend,
And, stretch'd out all the chimney's length,
Basks at the fire his hairy strength;
And crop-full out of doors he flings,
Ere the first cock his matin rings.
Thus done the tales, to bed they creep,
By whispering winds soon lull'd asleep.
Tower'd cities please us then
And the busy hum of men,
Where throngs of knights and barons bold,
In weeds of peace, high triumphs hold,
With store of ladies, whose bright eyes
Rain influence, and judge the prize
Of wit or arms, while both contend
To win her grace, whom all commend.
There let Hymen oft appear
In saffron robe, with taper clear,
And pomp, and feast, and revelry,
With mask, and antique pageantry;
Such sights as youthful poets dream
On summer eves by haunted stream.
Then to the well-trod stage anon,
If Jonson's learned sock be on,
Or sweetest Shakespeare, Fancy's child,
Warble his native wood-notes wild.
And ever against eating cares
Lap me in soft Lydian airs
Married to immortal verse,
Such as the meeting soul may pierce
In notes, with many a winding bout
Of linkéd sweetness long drawn out,
With wanton heed and giddy cunning,
The melting voice through mazes running,
Untwisting all the chains that tie
The hidden soul of harmony;
That Orpheus' self may heave his head
From golden slumber, on a bed
Of heap'd Elysian flowers, and hear
Such strains as would have won the ear
Of Pluto, to have quite set free
His half-regain'd Eurydice.
These delights if thou canst give,
Mirth, with thee I mean to live.

— *John Milton, English (1608–1674).*

Nurse's Song

When the voices of children are heard on the green
And laughing is heard on the hill,
My heart is at rest within my breast
And everything else is still.

"Then come home, my children, the sun is gone down
And the dews of night arise;
Come, come, leave off play, and let us away
Till the morning appears in the skies."

"No, no, let us play, for it is yet day
And we cannot go to sleep;
Besides, in the sky the little birds fly
And the hills are all covered with sheep."

"Well, well, go and play till the light fades away
And then go home to bed."
The little ones leapèd and shouted and laughed
And all the hills echoèd.

— *William Blake, English (1757–1827).*

Leisure

What is this life if, full of care,
We have no time to stand and stare.

No time to stand beneath the boughs
And stare as long as sheep or cows.

No time to see, when woods we pass,
Where squirrels hide their nuts in grass.

No time to see, in broad daylight,
Streams full of stars, like stars at night.

No time to turn at Beauty's glance,
And watch her feet, how they can dance.

No time to wait till her mouth can
Enrich that smile her eyes began.

A poor life this if, full of care,
We have no time to stand and stare.

— *William Henry Davies, English (1870–1940).*

From A Prayer for My Daughter

I have walked and prayed for this young child an hour
And heard the sea-wind scream upon the tower,
And under the arches of the bridge, and scream
In the elms above the flooded stream;
Imagining in excited reverie
That the future years had come,
Dancing to a frenzied drum
Out of the murderous innocence of the sea.

May she be granted beauty and yet not
Beauty to make a stranger's eye distraught,
Or hers before a looking-glass, for such,
Being made beautiful overmuch,
Consider beauty a sufficient end,
Lose natural kindness and maybe
The heart-revealing intimacy
That chooses right, and never find a friend.

. . . .

In courtesy I'd have her chiefly learned;
Hearts are not had as a gift but hearts are earned
By those that are not entirely beautiful;
Yet many, that have played the fool
For beauty's very self, has charm made wise,
And many a poor man that has roved,
Loved and thought himself beloved,
From a glad kindness cannot take his eyes.

. . . .

My mind, because the minds that I have loved,
The sort of beauty that I have approved,
Prosper but little, has dried up of late,
Yet knows that to be choked with hate
May well be of all evil chances chief.
If there's no hatred in a mind
Assault and battery of the wind
Can never tear the linnet from the leaf.

An intellectual hatred is the worst,
So let her think opinions are accursed.
Have I not seen the loveliest woman born
Out of the mouth of Plenty's horn,
Because of her opinionated mind
Barter that horn and every good
By quiet natures understood
For an old bellows full of angry wind?

. . . .

And may her bridegroom bring her to a house
Where all's accustomed, ceremonious;
For arrogance and hatred are the wares
Peddled in the thoroughfares.
How but in custom and in ceremony
Are innocence and beauty born?
Ceremony's a name for the rich horn,
And custom for the spreading laurel tree.

— *William Butler Yeats, Irish (1865–1939).*

The Happy Ulysses

Happy who like Ulysses, or that lord
That raped the fleece, returning full and sage,
With usage and the world's wide reason stored,
With his own kin can wait the end of age.
When shall I see, when shall I see, God knows!
My little village smoke; or pass the door,
The old dear door of that unhappy house,
That is to me a kingdom and much more?
Mightier to me the house my fathers made,
Than your audacious heads, O Halls of Rome;
More than immortal marbles undecayed,
The thin sad slates that cover up my home;
More than your Tiber is my Loire to me,

Than Palatine my little Lyré there;
And more than all the winds of all the sea,
The quiet kindness of the Angevin air.

—*From the French of Joachim du Bellay (1525–1560), translated by G. K. Chesterton.*

The Summer's Revel

Oh! but my mind is weary!
Long I have conned the dreary
Tomes of Aratus.
Surely 'tis time to play now!
Ho! to the fields away now!
Shall we not live to-day now?
What though dull fools berate us!

What is the use of learning
When it but brings new yearning
Problems to tease us?
When, or at eve or morning,
Soon, without a warning,
Pleadings and pity scorning,
Orcus the dull shall seize us.

Corydon, lead the way, and
Find where good wines to pay, and
Coll me a flagon!
Then in vine-trellised bowers,
Bedded on thick-strewn flowers,
Hours upon idle hours
Sweetly shall haste or lag on.

Artichokes bring me, mellow
Apricotes, melons yellow,
Cream, and strawberries.
These have the sweetest savor
Eaten in forest cave, or
Lying by brooks that rave or
Streamlet that singing tarries.

Now in my youth's fresh buoyance
Laughter shall wait on joyance,
Wine shall flow fast now;
Lest, when my life grows colder,
Sickness, by age made bolder,
Say, as he taps my shoulder:
"Come, friend—you've drunk your last now!"

—*From the French of Pierre de Ronsard (1524–1585), translated by Curtis Hidden Page.*

The King of Yvetot

There flourished once a potentate,
Whom history doesn't name;
He rose at ten, retired at eight,
And snored unknown to fame!
A night-cap for his crown he wore,
A common cotton thing,
Which Jeanette to his bedside bore,
This jolly little king!
Ho, ho, ho, ho! Ha, ha, ha, ha!
This jolly little king!

With four diurnal banquets he
His appetite allayed,
And on a jackass leisurely
His royal progress made.
No cumbrous state his steps would clog,
Fear to the winds he'd fling;
His single escort was a dog,
This jolly little king!
Ho, ho, ho, ho! Ha, ha, ha, ha!
This jolly little king!

He owned to only one excess,—
He doted on his glass,—
But when a king gives happiness,
Why that, you see, will pass!
On every bottle, small or great,
For which he used to ring,
He laid a tax inordinate,
This jolly little king!
Ho, ho, ho, ho! Ha, ha, ha, ha!
This jolly little king!

Such crowds of pretty girls he found
Occasion to admire,
It gave his subjects double ground
For greeting him as Sire!
To shoot for cocoanuts he manned
His army every spring,
But all conscription sternly banned
This jolly little king!
Ho, ho, ho, ho! Ha, ha, ha, ha!
This jolly little king!

He eyed no neighboring domain
With envy or with greed,
And, like a pattern sovereign,
Took Pleasure for his creed!
Yet, it was not, if aright I ween,
Until his life took wing,
His subjects saw that he had been
A jolly little king.
Ho, ho, ho, ho! Ha, ha, ha, ha!
This jolly little king!

This worthy monarch, readers mine,
  You even now may see,
Embellishing a tavern-sign
  Well known to you and me!
There, when the fête-day bottle flows,
  Their bumpers they will bring,
And toast beneath his very nose
  This jolly little king.
Ho, ho, ho, ho! Ha, ha, ha, ha!
  This jolly little king!

—*From the French of Pierre Jean de Béranger (1780–1857), translated by William Toynbee.*

From Ballad of the Bells

Ah! what joy, the bagpipe and the flute touch our hearts in their accordant round, here come the lads and all the lasses to't, and all the old folks at the music's sound.

Gay, gay, let us marry today, trumpets, ribbons of scarlet and blue; gay, gay, let us marry today, and this jolly young couple too!

What happiness when from the festive church great bell and chimes search folk from every part; three hundred peals for the eyes of the bride, and one great clang for the bridegroom's heart.

Gay, gay, let us marry today, trumpets, ribbons of scarlet and blue; gay, gay, let us marry today, and this jolly young couple too!

At length the ringing quiets us. What pain when our own bells are through! Old folk, let tears on your prayer books rain, who can tell, soon the ringing will be for you.

Gay, gay, let us marry today, trumpets, ribbons of scarlet and blue; gay, gay, let us marry today, and this jolly young couple too!

And then they're done, the bells are still. Come dance that their days be glorious. Long live the pair of the festival! Oh, what joy when it's not for us!

Gay, gay, let us marry today, trumpets, ribbons of scarlet and blue; gay, gay, let us marry today, and this jolly young couple too!

What happiness, the bagpipe and the flute rejuvenate the oldsters for the round; see how the lasses and lads are dancing to't! Ah, what joy at the music's sound!

—*From the French of Paul Fort (1872–), translated by Joseph T. Shipley.*

Evening in May

Now in the Mayday twilight
O'er the bright skies pearl-coloured clouds float through the emerald spaces,
While on the shore the wavelets
Lightly take hands, rise and subside, dance like enamoured naiads.

Never a sail is seen there;
But with gay song swallows afar fleetly wing o'er the waters,
Stretched in long lines of shadow:
Sharp and acute odours of tar come on the freshening breezes.

Ah! and the happy children,
Whom the sun first smiled on, whom first burned the malignant south wind,
Down the long sands are racing;
Laughter and shouts mingle afar as of a band of seagulls.

Vesper of Maytime ending!
Now in my heart sweetly the rhymes buzz like a swarming beehive;
Vesper, to thee made sacred,
Bend to my yoke, quivering still, leaping, the sapphic verses,

Bend to my yoke, quiescent!
Beautiful girls, sunburnt and bright, magical songs are singing—
Now that the lunar crescent
Rises o'er hills Samnite afar, set the loud echoes ringing!

—*From the Italian of Gabriele d'Annunzio (1864–1938), translated by G. A. Greene.*

The Laborer

We have a bed, and a baby too,
My wife!
We have work besides, we have work for two,
And we have the sun, and the wind, and the rain,
And we only need one little thing more,
To be as free as the birds that soar:
Only time.

When we go through the fields on the Sunday morn,
My child,
And far and away o'er the bending corn,

We see the swarming swallows flash,
Then we only need a bit of a dress,
To have the birds' bright loveliness:
Only time.

The storm is gathering black as jet,
Feel the poor.
Only a little eternity yet;
We need nothing else, my wife, my child,
Except all things through us that thrive,
To be bold as the birds through the air that drive:
Only time!

— From the German of Richard Dehmel (1863–1920), translated by Jethro Bithell.

∽ ❂ ∼

Winter Evening

(TO HIS OLD NURSE)

The Heaven's angry face is scowling
High o'er the swiftly whirling snow;
We hear a fearful creature howling,
And now a wailing child in woe.

Ere long a curious noise arises
Within the thatched and sloping roof,
Or a strange knocking us surprises,
Although from guests we live aloof.

Here in our dwelling old and roomy,
Delapidated, sad and dark;
Companion, nurse, old woman gloomy,
Why sit you silent, naught remark?

The storm, its dismal rage disclosing,
Perhaps has left you ill and tired?
Or at the spinning wheel you're dozing,
Because no more to toil required?

Come let us drink, before we slumber,
You kindest friend of early days;
We, that have troubles without number,
Should pass the jug, our spirits raise.

Sing me about the tomtit's sorrow
Who lives beyond the foaming seas;
Sing me about the maiden's morrow
After she fled from home and ease.

The heavens' angry face is scowling
High o'er the swiftly whirling snow,
We hear a fearful creature howling,
And now a wailing child in woe.

Come let us drink, before we slumber,
You kindest friend of early days:
We, that have troubles without number,
Should pass the jug, our spirits raise!

— From the Russian of A. S. Pushkin (1799–1837), translated by Fillingham Coxwell.

∽ ❂ ∼

Country Girl, Don't Stay Away . . .

Country girl, don't stay away from the market,
you with the blond hair — cauliflower in mustard —
and those eyes, those eyes where wickedness makes its nest! . . .

Who wouldn't run to watch you crossing the square!
Even the village priest, that frank and simple soul,
when you appear shakes off his lazy languor! . . .

You are an eclogue! . . . and you sing, without singing, the seeds,
the furrows, the mills, the bubbling streams
where leaves float their yellow sadness. . . .

What do you care if that crass, that potbellied banker,
and that spinster there — old and very ugly —
do not buy from you (slaves to their useless wealth!)

your pinks and lilies — lovely flower of your village. . . .
To the devil with them! To the garlic and
tomato with them! Let them eat rice and turtle-meat!

For you, country girl with your hat and skirt,
you, debonaire and sweet, riding by on your donkey,
give the wings and trills of a goldfinch to a crow!

The wings and trills! . . . And you take away the rose
of your face! . . . And you take away your malicious glance,
and your sweet smile which has said to me the thing
that to a glutton suggests the half-open pomegranate! . . .

—From the Spanish of the Colombian Luis Carlos López (1880–), translated by Donald Devenish Walsh.

There Was a Child Went Forth

There was a child went forth every day,
And the first object he look'd upon, that object he became,
And that object became part of him for the day or a certain part of the day,
Or for many years or stretching cycles of years.

The early lilacs became part of this child,
And grass and white and red morning-glories, and white and red clover, and the song of the phœbe-bird,
And the Third-month lambs and the sow's pink-faint litter, and the mare's foal and cow's calf,
And the noisy brood of the barnyard or by the mire of the pond-side,
And the fish suspending themselves so curiously below there, and the beautiful curious liquid,
And the water-plants with their graceful flat heads, all became part of him.

The field-sprouts of Fourth-month and Fifth-month became part of him,
Winter-grain sprouts and those of the light-yellow corn, and the esculent roots of the garden,
And the apple-trees cover'd with blossoms and the fruit afterward, and wood-berries, and the commonest weeds by the road,
And the old drunkard staggering home from the outhouse of the tavern whence he had lately risen,
And the schoolmistress that pass'd on her way to the school,
And the friendly boys that pass'd, and the quarrelsome boys,
And the tidy and fresh-cheek'd girls, and the barefoot negro boy and girl,
And all the changes of city and country wherever he went.

His own parents, he that had father'd him and she that had conceiv'd him in her womb and birth'd him,
They gave this child more of themselves than that,
They gave him afterward every day, they became part of him.

The mother at home quietly placing the dishes on the supper-table,
The mother with mild words, clean her cap and gown, a wholesome odor falling off her person and clothes as she walks by,
The father, strong, self-sufficient, manly, mean, anger'd, unjust,
The blow, the quick loud word, the tight bargain, the crafty lure,
The family usages, the language, the company, the furniture, the yearning and swelling heart,
Affection that will not be gainsay'd, the sense of what is real, the thought if after all it should prove unreal,
The doubts of day-time and the doubts of night-time, the curious whether and how,
Whether that which appears so is so, or is it all flashes and specks?
Men and women crowding fast in the streets, if they are not flashes and specks what are they?
The streets themselves and the façades of houses, and goods in the windows,
Vehicles, teams, the heavy-plank'd wharves, the huge crossing at the ferries,
The village on the highland seen from afar at sunset, the river between,
Shadows, aureola and mist, the light falling on roofs and gables of white or brown two miles off,
The schooner near by sleepily dropping down the tide, the little boat slack-tow'd astern,
The hurrying tumbling waves, quick-broken crests, slapping,
The strata of color'd clouds, the long bar of maroon-tint away solitary by itself, the spread of purity it lies motionless in,
The horizon's edge, the flying sea-crow, the fragrance of salt marsh and shore mud,

These became part of that child who went
forth every day, and who now goes,
and will always go forth every day.

— Walt Whitman, American (1819–1892).

~ ❂ ~

The Picnic Boat

Sunday night and the park policemen tell
each other it is dark as a stack of black
cats on Lake Michigan.
A big picnic boat comes home to Chicago
from the peach farms of Saugatuck.
Hundreds of electric bulbs break the night's
darkness, a flock of red and yellow birds
with wings at a standstill.
Running along the deck railings are festoons
and leaping in curves are loops of light
from prow and stern to the tall smokestacks.
Over the hoarse crunch of waves at my pier
comes a hoarse answer in the rhythmic
oompa of the brasses playing a Polish
folk-song for the home-comers.

— Carl Sandburg, American (1878–).

~ ❂ ~

Happiness

I asked professors who teach the meaning
of life to tell me what is happiness.
And I went to famous executives who boss
the work of thousands of men.
They all shook their heads and gave me a
smile as though I was trying to fool
with them.
And then one Sunday afternoon I wandered
out along the Desplaines River
And saw a crowd of Hungarians under the
trees with their women and children
and a keg of beer and an accordion.

— Carl Sandburg.

~ ❂ ~

Fish Crier

I know a Jew fish crier down on Maxwell
Street, with a voice like a north wind
blowing over corn stubble in January.
He dangles herring before prospective customers evincing a joy identical with
that of Pavlova dancing.
His face is that of a man terribly glad to be
selling fish, terribly glad God made
fish, and customers to whom he may
call his wares from a pushcart.

— Carl Sandburg.

PART TWENTY-FOUR

Voices of the Forum

~ ❂ ~

THE ORATIONS which are usually delivered on commemorative occasions, the witty speeches sometimes given for the amusement of festive groups, and even the routine addresses at our congresses and the sermons of our churches may frequently show felicities of phrase and flashes of wit that make them pleasing and worthy of print. But they do not have as honored a place in world literature as other forms of expression is probably to be explained by the fact that they were not uttered with travail of soul and communicated in times of moral or political crisis. In no other department of social intercourse can it be more appropriately said that great occasions produced great eloquence than in the history of great orations. The national crises in which the selections which follow were given to the world vary greatly: they range from periods of moral stress in the pastoral centuries of Israel's early history to the tumultuous years of a World Depression and the Second World War. They range also from funeral orations for national heroes to stirring defences of religious freedom, from persuasive pleading for political support to compelling expositions of national policy, and from a poised leader's calming of national hysteria at a time of financial panic to the raising of a race for a last struggle against an implacable foe. This is a literature which represents national experience at its best.

No fact stands out more clearly in the records of the world's great orations than that the finest monuments are the product of progressive and freedom-loving peoples. The forums where leaders of a nation meet in public debate, or speak to their assembled followers, or have the opportunity to defend themselves against unjust charges, are rarely to be found in countries under despotic rule. Where free speech is encouraged, or prophets can arise in indignation to remind a people of their failures, there may be heard "jeremiads" which put men to shame and rallying-calls which nerve them for any calamity which may befall. And, as in Luther's example, a brief address may mark a change in the history of ecclesiastical empire no less than political. The records of the voices of the forum are not a negligible part of world literature.

The future of the oration as a means of communication between great leaders of a nation and their followers, even between international statesmen and their colleagues, is but at its beginning. If we have outgrown the circumlocutory style and rotund periods of earlier generations, we still have an ear for words which startle the imagination, phrases which stir the blood, and sentences which convince the mind.

The Hebrew Prophets

JEREMIAH

Chapter VII

A CALL FOR TRUE REPENTANCE

The word that came to Jeremiah from the Lord, saying,

Stand in the gate of the Lord's house, and proclaim there this word, and say, Hear the word of the Lord, all ye of Judah, that enter in at these gates to worship the Lord.

Thus saith the Lord of hosts, the God of Israel, Amend your ways and your doings, and I will cause you to dwell in this place.

Trust ye not in lying words, saying, The temple of the Lord, The temple of the Lord, The temple of the Lord, are these.

For if ye thoroughly amend your ways and your doings; if ye thoroughly execute judgment between a man and his neighbor;

If ye oppress not the stranger, the fatherless, and the widow, and shed not innocent blood in this place, neither walk after other gods to your hurt:

Then will I cause you to dwell in this place, in the land that I gave to your fathers, for ever and ever.

Behold, ye trust in lying words, that cannot profit.

Will ye steal, murder, and commit adultery, and swear falsely, and burn incense unto Baal, and walk after other gods whom ye know not;

And come and stand before me in this house, which is called by my name, and say, We are delivered to do all these abominations?

Is this house, which is called by my name, become a den of robbers in your eyes? Behold, even I have seen it, saith the Lord.

But go ye now unto my place which was in Shiloh, where I set my name at first, and see what I did to it for the wickedness of my people Israel.

And now, because ye have done all these works, saith the Lord, and I spake unto you, rising up early and speaking, but ye heard not; and I called you, but ye answered not;

Therefore will I do unto this house, which is called by my name, wherein ye trust, and unto the place which I gave to you and your fathers, as I have done to Shiloh.

And I will cast you out of my sight, as I have cast out all your brethren, even the whole seed of Ephraim.

Therefore pray not thou for this people, neither lift up cry nor prayer for them, neither make intercession to me: for I will not hear thee.

Seest thou not what they do in the cities of Judah and in the streets of Jerusalem?

The children gather wood, and the fathers kindle the fire, and the women knead their dough, to make cakes to the queen of heaven, and to pour out drink offerings unto other gods, that they may provoke me to anger.

Do they provoke me to anger? saith the Lord: do they not provoke themselves to the confusion of their own faces?

Therefore thus saith the Lord God; Behold, mine anger and my fury shall be poured out upon this place, upon man, and upon beast, and upon the trees of the field, and upon the fruit of the ground; and it shall burn, and shall not be quenched.

Chapter VIII

PEACE! AND THERE IS NO PEACE

At that time, saith the Lord, they shall bring out the bones of the kings of Judah, and the bones of his princes, and the bones of the priests, and the bones of the prophets, and the bones of the inhabitants of Jerusalem, out of their graves:

And they shall spread them before the sun, and the moon, and all the host of heaven, whom they have loved, and whom they have served, and after whom they have walked, and whom they have sought, and whom they have worshipped: they shall not be gathered, nor be buried; they shall be for dung upon the face of the earth.

And death shall be chosen rather than life by all the residue of them that remain of this evil family, which remain in all the places whither I have driven them, saith the Lord of hosts.

Moreover thou shalt say unto them, Thus saith the Lord; Shall they fall, and not arise? shall he turn away, and not return?

Why then is this people of Jerusalem slidden back by a perpetual backsliding? they hold fast deceit, and they refuse to return.

I hearkened and heard, but they spake not aright: no man repented of his wickedness, saying, What have I done? every one turned to his course, as the horse rusheth into the battle.

Yea, the stork in the heaven knoweth her appointed times; and the turtle and the crane and the swallow observe the time of their coming; but my people know not the judgment of the Lord.

How do you say, We are wise, and the law of the Lord is with us? Lo, certainly in vain he made it; the pen of the scribes is in vain.

The wise men are ashamed, they are dismayed and taken: lo, they have rejected the word of the Lord; and what wisdom is in them?

Therefore will I give their wives unto others, and their fields to them that shall inherit them: for every one from the least even unto the greatest is given to covetousness, from the prophet even unto the priest every one dealeth falsely.

For they have healed the hurt of the daughter of my people slightly, saying, Peace, peace; where there is no peace.

Were they ashamed when they had committed abomination? nay, they were not at all ashamed, neither could they blush: therefore shall they fall among them that fall: in the time of their visitation they shall be cast down, saith the Lord.

I will surely consume them, saith the Lord: there shall be no grapes on the vine, nor figs on the fig tree, and the leaf shall fade; and the things that I have given them shall pass away from them.

Why do we sit still? assemble yourselves, and let us enter into the defenced cities, and let us be silent there; for the Lord our God hath put us to silence, and given us water of gall to drink, because we have sinned against the Lord.

We looked for peace, but no good came; and for a time of health, and behold trouble!

The snorting of his horses was heard from Dan; the whole land trembled at the sound of the neighing of his strong ones; for they are come, and have devoured the land, and all that is in it; the city, and those that dwell therein.

For behold, I will send serpents, cockatrices, among you, which will not be charmed, and they shall bite you, saith the Lord.

When I would comfort myself against sorrow, my heart is faint within me.

Behold the voice of the cry of the daughter of my people because of them that dwell in a far country: Is not the Lord in Zion? is not her king in her? Why have they provoked me to anger with their graven images and strange vanities?

The harvest is past, the summer is ended, and we are not saved.

For the hurt of the daughter of my people am I hurt; I am black; astonishment hath taken hold on me.

Is there no balm in Gilead; is there no physician there? why then is not the health of the daughter of my people recovered?

Chapter XVIII

THE POTTER AND THE CLAY

The word which came to Jeremiah from the Lord, saying,

Arise, and go down to the potter's house, and there I will cause thee to hear my words.

Then I went down to the potter's house, and, behold, he wrought a work on the wheels.

And the vessel that he made of the clay was marred in the hand of the potter: so he made it again another vessel, as seemed good to the potter to make it.

Then the word of the Lord came to me, saying,

O house of Israel, cannot I do with you as this potter? saith the Lord. Behold, as the clay is in the potter's hand, so are ye in mine hand, O house of Israel.

At what instant I shall speak concerning a nation, and concerning a kingdom, to pluck up, and to pull down, and to destroy it;

If that nation against whom I have pronounced, turn from their evil, I will repent of the evil that I thought to do unto them.

And at what instant I shall speak concerning a nation, and concerning a kingdom, to build and to plant it; if it do evil in my sight, that it obey not my voice, then I will repent of the good, wherewith I said I would benefit them.

Now therefore go to, speak to the men of Judah, and to the inhabitants of Jerusalem, saying, Thus saith the Lord; Behold, I frame evil against you, and devise a device against you; return ye now every one from his evil way, and make your ways and your doings good.

Ezekiel

Chapter XXXIV

UNFAITHFUL SHEPHERDS

And the word of the Lord came unto me, saying,

Son of man, prophesy against the shepherds of Israel, prophesy, and say unto them, Thus saith the Lord God unto the shepherds; Woe be to the shepherds of Israel that do feed themselves! should not the shepherds feed the flocks?

Ye eat the fat, and ye clothe you with the wool, ye kill them that are fed: but ye feed not the flock.

The diseased have ye not strengthened, neither have ye healed that which was sick, neither have ye bound up that which was broken, neither have ye brought again that which was driven away, neither have ye sought that which was lost; but with force and with cruelty have ye ruled them.

And they were scattered, because there is no shepherd: and they became meat to all the beasts of the field, when they were scattered.

My sheep wandered through all the mountains, and upon every high hill: yea, my flock was scattered upon all the face of the earth, and none did search or seek after them.

Therefore, ye shepherds, hear the word of the Lord;

As I live, saith the Lord God, surely because my flock became a prey, and my flock became meat to every beast of the field, because there was no shepherd, neither did my shepherds search for my flock, but the shepherds fed themselves, and fed not my flock;

Therefore, O ye shepherds, hear the word of the Lord;

Thus saith the Lord God; Behold, I am against the shepherds; and I will require my flock at their hand, and cause them to cease from feeding the flock; neither shall the shepherds feed themselves any more; for I will deliver my flock from their mouth, that they may not be meat for them.

For thus saith the Lord God; Behold, I, even I, will both search my sheep, and seek them out.

As a shepherd seeketh out his flock in the day that he is among his sheep that are scattered; so will I seek out my sheep, and will deliver them out of all places where they have been scattered in the cloudy and dark day.

And I will bring them out from the people, and gather them from the countries, and will bring them to their own land, and feed them upon the mountains of Israel by the rivers, and in all the inhabited places of the country.

I will feed them in a good pasture, and upon the high mountains of Israel shall their fold be: there shall they lie in a good fold, and in a fat pasture shall they feed upon the mountains of Israel.

I will feed my flock, and I will cause them to lie down, saith the Lord God.

I will seek that which was lost, and bring again that which was driven away, and will bind up that which was broken, and will strengthen that which was sick: but I will destroy the fat and the strong; I will feed them with judgment.

And as for you, O my flock, thus saith the Lord God; Behold, I judge between cattle and cattle, between the rams and the he-goats.

Seemeth it a small thing unto you to have eaten up the good pasture, but ye must tread down with your feet the residue of your pastures? and to have drunk of the deep waters, but ye must foul the residue with your feet?

And as for my flock, they eat that which ye have trodden with your feet; and they drink that which ye have fouled with your feet.

Therefore thus saith the Lord God unto them; Behold I, even I, will judge between the fat cattle and the lean cattle.

Because ye have thrust with side and with shoulder, and pushed all the diseased with your horns, till ye have scattered them abroad;

Therefore I will save my flock, and they shall no more be a prey; and I will judge between cattle and cattle.

And I will set up one shepherd over them, and he shall feed them, even my servant David; he shall feed them, and he shall be their shepherd.

And I the Lord will be their God, and my servant David a prince among them; I the Lord have spoken it.

And I will make with them a covenant of peace, and will cause the evil beasts to cease out of the land: and they shall dwell safely in the wilderness, and sleep in the woods.

And I will make them and the places round about my hill a blessing; and I will cause the shower to come down in his season; there shall be showers of blessing.

And the tree of the field shall yield her fruit, and the earth shall yield her increase, and they shall be safe in their land, and shall know that I am the Lord, when I have broken the bands of their yoke, and delivered them out of the hand of those that served themselves of them.

And they shall no more be a prey to the heathen, neither shall the beasts of the land devour them; but they shall dwell safely, and none shall make them afraid.

—*From the Old Testament, the King James Version.*

The Funeral Oration of Pericles

THUCYDIDES

IN THE same winter the Athenians gave a funeral at the public cost to those who had first fallen in this war. It was a custom of their ancestors, and the manner of it is as follows. Three days before the ceremony, the bones of the dead are laid out in a tent which has been erected; and their friends bring to their relatives such offerings as they please. In the funeral procession cypress coffins are borne in cars, one for each tribe; the bones of the deceased being placed in the coffin of their tribe. Among these is carried one empty bier decked for the missing, that is, for those whose bodies could not be recovered. Any citizen or stranger who pleases, joins in the procession: and the female relatives are there to wail at the burial. The dead are laid in the public sepulcher in the beautiful suburb of the city, in which those who fall in war are always buried; with the exception of those slain at Marathon, who for their singular and extraordinary valor were interred on the spot where they fell. After the bodies have been laid in the earth, a man chosen by the state, of approved wisdom and eminent reputation, pronounces over them an appropriate panegyric; after which all retire. Such is the manner of the burying; and throughout the whole of the war, whenever the occasion arose, the established custom was observed. Meanwhile these were the first that had fallen, and Pericles, son of Xanthippus, was chosen to pronounce their eulogium. When the proper time arrived, he advanced from the sepulcher to an elevated platform in order to be heard by as many of the crowd as possible, and spoke as follows:

"Most of my predecessors in this place have commended him who made this speech part of the law, telling us that it is well that it should be delivered at the burial of those who fall in battle. For myself, I should have thought that the worth which had displayed itself in deeds, would be sufficiently rewarded by honors also shown by deeds; such as you now see in this funeral prepared at the people's cost. And I could have wished that the reputations of many brave men were not to be imperilled in the mouth of a single individual, to stand or fall according as he spoke well or ill. For it is hard to speak properly upon a subject where it is even difficult to convince your hearers that you are speaking the truth. On the one hand, the friend who is familiar with every fact of the story, may think that some point has not been set forth with that fulness which he wishes and knows it to deserve; on the other, he who is a stranger to the matter may be led by envy to suspect exaggeration if he hears anything above his own nature. For men can endure to hear others praised only so long as they can severally persuade themselves of their own ability to equal the actions recounted: when this point is passed, envy comes in and with it incredulity. However, since our ancestors have stamped this custom with their approval, it becomes my duty to obey the law and to try to satisfy your several wishes and opinions as best I may.

"I shall begin with our ancestors: it is both just and proper that they should have the honor of the first mention on an occasion like the present. They dwelt in the country without break in the succession from generation to generation, and handed it down free to the present time by their valor. And if our more remote ancestors deserve praise, much more to our own fathers, who added to their inheritance the empire which we now possess, and spared no pains to be able to leave their acquisitions to us of the present generation. Lastly, there are few parts of our dominions that have not been augmented by those of us here, who are still more or less in the vigor of life; while the mother country has been furnished by us with everything that can enable her to depend on her own resources whether for war or for peace. That part of our history which tells of the military achievements which gave us our several possessions, or of the ready valor with which either we or our fathers stemmed the tide of Hellenic or foreign aggression, is a theme too familiar to my hearers for me to dilate on, and I shall therefore pass it by. But what was the road by which we reached our position, what the form of government under which our greatness grew, what the national habits out of which it sprang; these are questions which I may try to solve before I proceed to my panegyric upon these men; since I think this to be a subject upon which on the present occasion a speaker may properly dwell, and to which the whole assemblage, whether citizens or foreigners, may listen with advantage.

"Our constitution does not copy the laws of neighboring states; we are rather a pattern to others than imitators ourselves. Its administration favors the many instead of the few; this is why it is called a democracy. If we look to the laws, they afford equal justice to all in their private differences; if to social standing, advancement in public life falls to reputation for capacity, class considerations not being allowed to interfere with merit; nor again does poverty bar the way; if a man is able to serve the state, he is not hindered by the obscurity of his condition. The freedom which we enjoy in our government extends also to our ordinary life. There, far from exercising a jealous surveillance over each other, we do not feel called upon to be angry with our neighbor for doing what he likes, or even to indulge in those injurious looks which cannot fail to be offensive, although they inflict no positive penalty. But all this ease in our private relations does not make us lawless as citizens. Against this fear is our chief safeguard, teaching us to obey the magistrates and the laws, particularly such as regard the protection of the injured, whether they are actually on the statute book, or belong to that code which, although unwritten, yet cannot be broken without acknowledged disgrace.

"Further, we provide plenty of means for the mind to refresh itself from business. We celebrate games and sacrifices all the year round, and the elegance of our private establishments forms a daily source of pleasure and helps to banish the spleen; while the magnitude of our city draws the produce of the world into our harbor, so that to the Athenian the fruits of other countries are as familiar a luxury as those of his own.

"If we turn to our military policy, there also we differ from our antagonists. We throw open our city to the world, and never by alien acts exclude foreigners from any opportunity of learning or observing, although the eyes of an enemy may occasionally profit by our liberality; trusting less in system and policy than to the native spirit of our citizens; while in education, where our rivals from their very cradles by a painful discipline seek after manliness, at Athens we live exactly as we please, and yet are just as ready to encounter every legitimate danger. In proof of this it may be noticed that the Lacedæmonians do not invade our country alone, but bring with them all their confederates; while we Athenians advance unsupported into the territory of a neighbor, and fighting upon a foreign soil usually vanquish with ease men who are defending their homes. Our united force was never yet encountered by any enemy, because we have at once to attend to our marine and to despatch our citizens by land upon a hundred different services; so that, wherever they engage with some such fraction of our strength, a success against a detachment is magnified into a victory over the nation, and a defeat into a reverse suffered at the hands of our entire people. And yet if with habits not of labor but of ease, and courage not of art but of nature, we are still willing to encounter danger, we have the double advantage of escaping the experience of hardships in anticipation and of facing them in the hour of need as fearlessly as those who are never free from them.

"Nor are these the only points in which our city is worthy of admiration. We cultivate refinement without extravagance and knowledge without effeminacy; wealth we employ more for use than for show, and place the real disgrace of poverty not in owning to the fact but in declining the struggle against it. Our public men have, besides politics, their private affairs to attend to, and our ordinary citizens, though occupied with the pursuits of industry, are still fair judges of public matters; for, unlike any other nation, regarding him who takes no part in these duties not as unambitious but as useless, we Athenians are able to judge at all events if we cannot originate, and instead of looking on discussion as a stumbling-block in the way of action, we think it an indispensable preliminary to any wise action at all. Again, in our enterprises we present the singular spectacle of daring and deliberation, each carried to its highest point, and both united in the same persons; although usually decision is the fruit of ignorance, hesitation of reflection. But the palm of courage will surely be adjudged most justly to those who best know the difference between hardship and pleasure and yet are never tempted to shrink from danger. In generosity we are equally singular, acquiring our friends by conferring not by receiving favors. Yet, of course, the doer of the favor is the firmer friend of the two, in order by continued kindness to keep the recipient in his debt; while the debtor feels less keenly from the very consciousness that the return he makes will be a payment, not a free gift. And it is only the Athenians who, fearless of consequences, confer their benefits not from calculations of expediency, but in the confidence of liberality.

"In short, I say that as a city we are the school of Hellas; while I doubt if the world can produce a man, who where he has only himself to depend upon, is equal to so many emergencies, and graced by so happy a versatility as the Athenian. And that this is no mere boast thrown out for the occasion, but plain matter of fact, the power of the state acquired by these habits proves. For Athens alone of her contemporaries is found when tested to be greater than her reputation, and alone gives no occasion to her assailants to blush at the antagonist by whom they have been worsted, or to her subjects to question her title by merit to rule. Rather, the admiration of the present and succeeding ages will be ours, since we have not left our power without witness, but have shown it by mighty proofs; and far from needing a Homer for our panegyrist, or other of his craft whose verses might charm for the moment only for the impression which they gave to melt at the touch of fact, we have forced every sea and land to be the highway of our daring, and everywhere, whether for evil or for good, have left imperishable monuments behind us. Such is the Athens for which these men, in the assertion of their resolve not to lose her, nobly fought and died; and well may every one of their survivors be ready to suffer in her cause.

"Indeed if I have dwelt at some length upon the character of our country, it has been to show that our stake in the struggle is not the same as theirs who have no such blessings to lose, and also that the panegyric of the men over whom I am now speaking might be by definite proofs established. That panegyric is now in a great measure complete; for the Athens that I have celebrated is only what the heroism of these and their like have made her, men whose fame, unlike that of most Hellenes, will be found to be only commensurate with their deserts. And if a test of worth be wanted, it is to be found in their closing scene, and this not only in the cases in which it set the final seal upon their merit, but also in those in which it gave the first intimation of their having any. For there is justice in the claim that steadfastness in his country's battles should be as a cloak to cover a man's other imperfections; since the good action has blotted out the bad, and his merit as a citizen more than out-weighed his demerits as an individual. But none of these allowed either wealth with its prospect of future enjoyment to unnerve his spirit, or poverty with its hope of a day of freedom and riches to tempt him to shrink from danger. No, holding that vengeance upon their enemies was more to be desired than any personal blessings, and reckoning this to be the most glorious of hazards, they joyfully determined to accept the risk, to make sure of their vengeance and to let their wishes wait; and while committing to hope the uncertainty of final success, in the business before them they thought fit to act boldly and trust in themselves. Thus choosing to die resisting, rather than to live submitting, they fled only from dishonor, but met danger face to face, and after one brief moment, while at the summit of their fortune, escaped, not from their fear, but from their glory.

"So died these men as became Athenians. You, their survivors, must determine to have as unfaltering a resolution in the field, though you may pray that it may have a happier issue. And not contented with ideas derived only from words of the advantages which are bound up with the defence of your country, though these would furnish a valuable text to a speaker even before an audience so alive to them as the present, you must yourselves realize the power of Athens, and feed your eyes upon her from day to day, till love of her fills your hearts; and then when all her greatness shall break upon you, you must reflect that it was by courage, sense of duty, and a keen feeling of honor in action that men were enabled to win all this, and that no personal failure in an enterprise could make them consent to deprive their country of their valor, but they laid it at her feet as the most glorious contribution that they could offer. For this offering of their lives made in common by them all they each of them individually received that renown which never grows old, and for a sepulcher, not so much that in which their bones have been deposited, but that noblest of shrines wherein their glory is laid up to be eternally remembered upon every occasion on which deed or story shall call for its commemoration. For heroes have the whole earth for their tomb; and in lands far from their own, where the column with its epitaph declares it, there is enshrined in every breast a record unwritten with no tablet to preserve it, except that of the heart. These take as your model, and judging happiness to be the fruit of freedom and freedom of valor, never decline the dangers of war. For it is not the miserable that would most justly be unsparing of their lives; these have nothing to hope for: it is rather they to whom continued life may bring reverses as yet unknown, and to whom a fall, if it came, would be most tremendous in its consequences. And surely, to a man of spirit, the degradation of cowardice must be immeasurably more grievous than the unfelt death which strikes him in the midst of his strength and patriotism!

"Comfort, therefore, not condolence, is what I have to offer to the parents of the dead who may be here. Numberless are the chances to which, as they know, the life of man is subject; but fortunate indeed are they who draw for their lot a death so glorious as that which has caused your mourning, and to whom life has been so exactly measured as to terminate in the happiness in which it has been passed. Still I know that this is a hard saying, especially when those are in question of whom you will constantly be reminded by seeing in the homes of others blessings of which once you also boasted: for grief is felt not so much for the want of what we have never known, as for the loss of that to which we have been long accustomed. Yet you who are still of an age to beget children must bear up in the hope of having others in their stead; not only will they help you to forget those whom you have lost, but will be to the state at once a reinforcement and a security; for never can a fair or just policy be expected of the citizen who does not, like his fellows, bring to the decision the interests and apprehensions of a father. While those of you who have passed your prime must congratulate yourselves with the thought that the best part of your life was fortunate, and that the brief span that remains will be cheered by the fame of the departed. For it is only the love of honor that never grows old; and honor it is, not gain, as some would have it, that rejoices the heart of age and helplessness.

"Turning to the sons or brothers of the dead, I see an arduous struggle before you. When a man is gone, all are wont to praise him, and should your merit be ever so transcendent, you will still find it difficult not merely to overtake, but even to approach their renown. The living have envy to contend with, while those who are no longer in our path are honored with a good-will into which rivalry does not enter. On the other hand, if I must say anything on the subject of female excellence to those of you who will now be in widowhood, it will be all comprised in this brief exhortation. Great will be your glory in not falling short of your natural character; and greatest will be hers who is least talked of among the men whether for good or for bad.

"My task is now finished. I have performed it to the best of my ability, and in word, at least, the requirements of the law are now satisfied. If deeds be in question, those who are here interred have received part of their honors already, and for the rest, their children will be brought up till manhood at the public expense: the state thus offers a valuable prize, as the garland of victory in this race of valor, for the reward both of those who have fallen and their survivors. And where the rewards for merit are greatest, there are found the best citizens.

"And now that you have brought to a close your lamentations for your relatives, you may depart."

—*From the History of the Peloponnesian War, by Thucydides (471?–400? B.C.), translated from the Greek by Richard Crawley*

Why Another Crusade?

You can not but know that we live in a period of chastisement and ruin; the enemy of mankind has caused the breath of corruption to fly over all regions; we behold nothing but unpunished wickedness. The laws of men or the laws of religion have no longer sufficient power to check depravity of manners and the triumph of the wicked. The demon of heresy has taken possession of the chair of truth, and God has sent forth His malediction upon His sanctuary.

Oh, ye who listen to me! hasten then to appease the anger of Heaven, but no longer implore His goodness by vain complaints; clothe not yourselves in sackcloth, but cover yourselves with your impenetrable bucklers; the din of arms, the dangers, the labors, the fatigues of war are the penances that God now imposes upon you. Hasten then to expiate your sins by victories over the infidels, and let the deliverance of holy places be the reward of your repentance.

If it were announced to you that the enemy had invaded your cities, your castles, your lands; had ravished your wives and your daughters, and profaned your temples, which among you would not fly to arms? Well, then, all these calamities, and calamities still greater, have fallen upon your brethren, upon the family of Jesus Christ, which is yours. Why do you hesitate to repair so many evils — to revenge so many outrages? Will you allow the infidels to contemplate in peace the ravages they have committed on Christian people? Remembering that their triumph will be a subject for grief to all ages, and an eternal opprobrium upon the generation that has endured it. Yes, the living God has charged me to announce to you that He will punish them who shall not have defended Him against His enemies.

Fly then to arms; let a holy rage animate you in the fight, and let the Christian world resound with these words of the prophet, "Cursed be he who does not stain his sword with blood!" If the Lord calls you to the defense of His heritage think not that His hand has lost its power. Could He not send twelve legions of angels or breathe one word and all His enemies would crumble away into dust? But God has considered the sons of men, to open for them the road to His mercy. His goodness has caused to dawn for you a day of safety by calling on you to avenge His glory and His name.

Christian warriors, He who gave His life for you, today demands yours in return. These are combats worthy of you, combats in which it is glorious to conquer and advantageous to die. Illustrious knights, generous defenders of the Cross, remember the examples of your fathers who conquered Jerusalem, and whose names are inscribed in Heaven; abandon then the things that perish, to gather unfading palms, and conquer a kingdom which has no end.

— St. Bernard, French (1091–1153), translated by W. Robson from the French of J. F. Michaud.

Address to the Diet at Worms

(Delivered April 18, 1521)

Most Serene Emperor, Illustrious Princes, Gracious Lords: —

In obedience to your commands given me yesterday, I stand here, beseeching you, as God is merciful, so to deign mercifully to listen to this cause, which is, as I believe, the cause of justice and of truth. And if through inexperience I should fail to apply to any his proper title, or offend in any way against the manners of courts, I entreat you to pardon me as one not conversant with courts, but rather with the cells of monks, and claiming no other merit than that of having spoken and written with that simplicity of mind which regards nothing but the glory of God and the pure instruction of the people of Christ.

Two questions have been proposed to me: Whether I acknowledge the books which are published in my name, and whether I am determined to defend or disposed to recall them. To the first of these I have given a direct answer, in which I shall ever persist that those books are mine and published by me, except so far as they may have been altered or interpolated by the craft or officiousness of rivals. To the other I am now about to reply; and I must first entreat your Majesty and your Highnesses to deign to consider that my books are not all of the same description. For there are some in which I have treated the piety of faith and morals with simplicity so evangelical that my very adversaries confess them to be profitable and harmless and deserving the perusal of a Christian. Even the Pope's bull, fierce and cruel as it is, admits some of my books to be innocent, though even these, with a monstrous perversity of judgment, it includes in the same sentence. If, then, I should think of retracting these, should I not stand alone in my condemnation of that truth which is acknowledged by the unanimous confession of all, whether friends or foes?

The second species of my publications is that in which I have inveighed against the papacy and the doctrine of the papists, as of men who by their iniquitous tenets and examples have desolated the Christian world, both with spiritual and temporal calamities. No man can deny or dissemble this. The sufferings and complaints of all mankind are my witnesses, that, through the laws of the Pope and the doctrines of men, the consciences of the faithful have been ensnared, tortured, and torn in pieces, while, at the same time, their property and substance have been devoured by an incredible tyranny, and are still devoured without end and by degrading means, and that too, most of all, in this noble nation of Germany. Yet it is with them a perpetual statute, that the laws and doctrines of the Pope be held erroneous and reprobate when they are contrary to the Gospel and the opinions of the Fathers.

If, then, I shall retract these books, I shall do no other than add strength to tyranny and throw open doors to this great impiety, which will then stride forth more widely and licentiously than it has dared hitherto; so that the reign of iniquity will proceed with entire impunity, and, notwithstanding its intolerable oppression upon the suffering vulgar, be still further fortified and established; especially when it shall be proclaimed that I have been driven to this act by the authority of your serene Majesty and the whole Roman Empire. What a cloak, blessed Lord, should I then become for wickedness and despotism!

In a third description of my writings are those which I have published against individuals, against the defenders of the Roman tyranny and the subverters of the piety taught by men. Against these I do freely confess that I have written with more bitterness than was becoming either my religion or my profession; for, indeed, I lay no claim to any special sanctity, and argue not respecting my own life, but respecting the doctrine of Christ. Yet even these writings it is impossible for me to retract, seeing that through such retraction despotism and impiety would reign under my patronage, and rage with more than their former ferocity against the people of God.

Yet since I am but man and not God, it would not become me to go further in defense of my tracts than my Lord Jesus went in defense of his doctrine; who, when he was interrogated before Annas, and received a blow from one of the officers, answered: "If I have spoken evil, bear witness of the evil; but if well, why smitest thou me?" If then the Lord himself, who knew his own infallibility, did not disdain to require arguments against his doctrine even from a person of low condition, how much rather ought I, who am the dregs of the earth and the very slave of error, to inquire and search if there be any to bear witness against my doctrine! Wherefore, I entreat you, by the mercies of God, that if there be any one of any condition who has that ability, let him overpower me by the sacred writings, prophetical and evangelical. And for my own part, as soon as I shall be better instructed I will retract my errors and be the first to cast my books into the flames.

It must now, I think, be manifest that I have sufficiently examined and weighed, not only the dangers, but the parties and dissensions excited in the world by means of my doctrine, of which I was yesterday so gravely admonished. But I must avow that to me it is of all others the most delightful spectacle to see parties and dissensions growing up on account of the word of God, for such is the progress of God's word, such its ends and object. "Think not I am come to send peace on earth. I came not to send peace, but a sword. For I am come to set a man at variance against his father, and the daughter against her mother, and the daughter-in-law against her mother-in-law; and a man's foes shall be those of his own household."

Moreover we should reflect that our God is wonderful and terrible in his counsels; so that his work which is now the object of so much solicitude, if we should found it in the condemnation of the word of God, may be turned by his providence into a deluge of intolerable calamity; and the reign of this young and excellent prince (in whom is our hope after God), not only should begin, but should continue and close under the most glowing auspices.

I could show more abundantly by reference to scriptural examples — to those of Pharaoh, the King of Babylon, the kings of Israel — that they have brought about their own destruction by those very counsels of worldly wisdom, which seemed to promise them peace and stability. For it is he who taketh the wise in their craftiness and removeth the mountains, and they know not, and overturneth them in his anger. So that it is the work of God to fear God. Yet I say not these things as if the great personages here present stood at all in need of my admonitions, but only because it was a service which I owed to my native Germany, and it was my duty to discharge it. And thus I commend myself to your serene Majesty and all the princes, humbly beseeching you not to allow the malice of my enemies to render me odious to you without a cause. I have done.

No sooner had he ceased than the orator reminded him in a tone of reproach, that they were not assembled to discuss matters which had long ago been decided by the council, but that a simple answer was required of him to a simple question — whether he would retract or not?

Then Luther:

Since your most serene Majesty and the princes require a simple answer, I will give it thus: Unless I shall be convinced by proofs from Scripture or by evident reason, — for I believe neither in Popes nor councils, since they have frequently both erred and contradicted themselves, — I cannot choose but adhere to the word of God, which has possession of my conscience; nor can I possibly, nor will I ever make any recantation, since it is neither safe nor honest to act contrary to conscience! Here I stand; I cannot do otherwise; so help me God! Amen.

— *Martin Luther, German (1483–1546), translated by George Waddington.*

~ ✿ ~

Speech in the Virginia Convention of Delegates

PATRICK HENRY

March 23, 1775

No man thinks more highly than I do of the patriotism, as well as abilities, of the very worthy gentlemen who have just addressed the house. But different men often see the same subjects in different lights; and, therefore, I hope it will not be thought disrespectful to those gentlemen, if, entertaining as I do, opinions of a character very opposite to theirs, I shall speak forth my sentiments freely, and without reserve. This is no time for ceremony. The question before the house is one of awful moment to this country. For my own part, I consider it as nothing less than a question of freedom or slavery. And in proportion to the magnitude of the subject, ought to be the freedom of the debate. It is only in this way that we can hope to arrive at truth, and fulfil the great responsibility which we hold to God and our country. Should I keep back my opinions at such a time, through fear of giving offence, I should consider myself as guilty of treason towards my country, and of an act of disloyalty toward the majesty of Heaven, which I revere above all earthly kings.

Mr. President, it is natural to man to indulge in the illusions of hope. We are apt to shut our eyes against a painful truth and listen to the song of the syren, till she transforms us into beasts. Is this the part of wise men, engaged in a great and arduous struggle for liberty? Are we disposed to be of the number of those, who having eyes, see not, and having ears, hear not, the things which so nearly concern their temporal salvation? For my part, whatever anguish of spirit it may cost, I am willing to know the whole truth; to know the worst, and to provide for it.

I have but one lamp by which my feet are guided; and that is the lamp of experience. I know of no way of judging of the future but by the past. And judging by the past, I wish to know what there has been in the conduct of the British ministry for the last ten years, to justify those hopes with which gentlemen have been pleased to solace themselves and the house? Is it that insidious smile with which our petition has been lately received? Trust it not, sir; it will prove a snare to your feet. Suffer not yourselves to be betrayed with a kiss. Ask yourselves how this gracious reception of our petition comports with those warlike preparations which cover our waters and darken our land. Are fleets and armies necessary to a work of love and reconciliation? Have we shown ourselves so unwilling to be reconciled, that force must be called in to win back our love? Let us not deceive ourselves, sir. These are the implements of war and subjugation, the last arguments to which kings resort.

I ask gentlemen, sir, what means this martial array, if its purpose be not to force us to submission? Can gentlemen assign any other possible motive for it? Has Great Britain any enemy in this quarter of the world, to call for all this accumulation of navies and armies? No, sir, she has none. They are meant for us; they can be meant for no other. They are sent over to bind and rivet upon us those chains, which the British ministry have been so long forging. And what have we to oppose to them? Shall we try argument? Sir, we have been trying that for the last ten years. Have we any thing new to offer upon the subject? Nothing. We have held the subject up in every light of which it is capable; but it has been all in vain. Shall we resort to entreaty and humble supplication? What terms shall we find, which have not been already exhausted? Let us not, I beseech you, sir, deceive ourselves longer. Sir, we have done every thing that could be done, to avert the storm which is now coming on. We have petitioned, we have remonstrated, we have supplicated, we have prostrated ourselves before the throne, and have implored its interposition to arrest the tyrannical hands of the ministry and parliament. Our petitions have been slighted; our remonstrances have produced additional violence and insult; our supplications have been disregarded; and we have been spurned, with contempt, from the foot of the throne. In vain, after these things, may we indulge the fond hope of peace and reconciliation. There is no longer any room for hope. If we wish to be free, if we mean to preserve inviolate those inestimable privileges for which we have been so long contending, if we mean not basely to abandon the noble struggle in which we have been so long engaged, and which we have pledged ourselves never to abandon, until the glorious object of our contest shall be obtained, we must fight!—I repeat it, sir, we must fight!! An appeal to arms and to the God of Hosts is all that is left us!

They tell us, sir, that we are weak, unable to cope with so formidable an adversary. But when shall we be stronger? Will it be the next week or the next year? Will it be when we are totally disarmed, and when a British guard shall be stationed in every house? Shall we gather strength by irresolution and inaction? Shall we acquire the means of effectual resistance by lying supinely on our backs, and hugging the delusive phantom of hope, until our enemies shall have bound us hand and foot? Sir, we are not weak, if we make a proper use of those means which the God of nature hath placed in our power. Three millions of people, armed in the holy cause of liberty, and in such a country as that which we possess, are invincible by any force which our enemy can send against us. Besides, sir, we shall not fight our battles alone. There is a just God who presides over the destinies of nations, and who will raise up friends to fight our battles for us. The battle, sir, is not to the strong alone; it is to the vigilant, the active, the brave. Besides, sir, we have no election. If we were base enough to desire it, it is now too late to retire from the contest. There is no retreat, but in submission and slavery! Our chains are forged. Their clanking may be heard on the plains of Boston! The war is inevitable —and let it come!! I repeat it, sir, let it come!!!

It is in vain, sir, to extenuate the matter. Gentlemen may cry, peace, peace—but there is no peace. The war is actually begun! The next gale that sweeps from the north will bring to our ears the clash of resounding arms! Our brethren are already in the field! Why stand we here idle? What is it that gentlemen wish? What would they have? Is life so dear, or peace so sweet, as to be purchased at the price of chains and slavery? Forbid it, Almighty God! I know not what course others may take; but as for me, give me liberty, or give me death!

—*Patrick Henry, American* (*1736–1799*).

Address to the French National Assembly

LAMARTINE

Delivered May 7, 1848

Citizen-Representatives of the People: —

At the moment of your entrance on the exercise of your sovereignty—at the moment of our resigning into your hands the special powers with which the Revolution provisionally invested us—we wish, in the first place, to render you an account of the situation in which we found ourselves, and in which you also find the nation.

A revolution burst forth on the twenty-fourth of February. The people overthrew the throne. They swore upon its ruins thenceforth to reign alone, and entirely by themselves. They charged us to provide temporarily for the necessity of the interregnum which they had to traverse to reach, without disorder or anarchy, their unanimous and final power. Our first thought was to abridge this interregnum by immediately convoking the national representation, in which alone reside right and force. Simply citizens, without any other summons than public peril, without any other title than our devotedness, trembling to accept, hastening to restore the deposit of national destinies, we have had but one ambition,—that of resigning the dictatorship to the bosom of popular sovereignty.

The throne overturned, the dynasty crumbling of itself, we did not proclaim the Republic; it proclaimed itself, by the voice of an entire people;—we did nothing but register the cry of the nation.

Our first thought, as well as the first requirement of the country, after the proclamation of the Republic, was the re-establishment of order and security in Paris. In this labor,—which would have been more difficult and more meritorious at another time and in another country,—we were aided by the concurrence of the citizens. While holding in one hand the musket which had just given the death-blow to royalty, this magnanimous people with the other raised up the vanquished and the wounded of the opposite party. They protected the life and property of the inhabitants. They preserved the public monuments. Each citizen of Paris was at once the soldier of liberty and the voluntary magistrate of order. History has recorded the innumerable acts of heroism, of probity, and disinterestedness, which have characterized these first days of the Republic. Till this time the people had sometimes been flattered by allusions to their virtues; posterity, which is no flatterer, will find all these expressions beneath the dignity of the people of Paris in this crisis.

It was they who inspired us with the first decree destined to give its true signification to victory,—the decree of the abolition of the penalty of death in political cases. They suggested, adopted, and ratified it, by the acclamation of two hundred thousand voices, on the square and quay of the Hôtel de Ville. Not a single exclamation of anger protested against it. France and Europe understood that God had his inspirations in the mass, and that a revolution inaugurated by grandeur of soul would be pure as an idea, magnanimous as a sentiment, and holy as a virtue.

The red flag, presented for a moment,—not as a symbol of menace and disorder, but as a temporary flag of victory,—was laid aside by the combatants themselves, to cover the Republic with that tricolored flag which had shaded its cradle, and led the glory of our arms over every continent and every ocean.

After having established the authority of government in Paris, it was necessary to make the Republic recognized in the departments, the colonies, in Algeria, and the army. The telegraphic news and couriers were enough. France, her colonies and armies, recognized their own idea in the idea of the Republic. There was no resistance from a single hand or voice, nor from one free heart in France, to the installation of the new government.

Our second thought was for the exterior. Europe awaited, in doubt, the first word from France. This first word was the abolition, in fact and right, of the reactionary treaties of 1815; the restoration of liberty to our foreign policy; the declaration of peace to the territories; of sympathy to nations; of justice, loyalty, and moderation, to governments. France, in this manifesto, laid aside her ambition, but did not lay aside her ideas. She permitted her principle to shine out. This was all her warfare. The special report of the minister of foreign affairs will show you the fruits of this noonday system of diplomacy, and the legitimate and great fruits it must yield to the influences of France.

This policy required the minister of war to employ measures in harmony with the system of armed negotiation. He energetically re-established a discipline scarcely shaken, and honorably recalled to Paris the army, removed temporarily from our walls, that the people might have an opportunity of arming themselves. The people, henceforth invincible, did not delay summoning with loud cries their brethren of the army, not only as the safeguard, but as the ornament, of the capital. In Paris the army was only an honorary garrison, designed to prove to our brave soldiers that the capital of the country belongs to all her children.

We decreed moreover, the formation of four armies of observation: the army of the Alps, the army of the Rhine, the army of the north, and the army of the Pyrenees.

Our navy – confided to the hands of the same minister, as a second army of France – was rallied under its commanders, in a discipline governed by a confidence in its vigilance. The fleet of Toulon sailed to display our colors to nations friendly to France on the shores of the Mediterranean.

The army of Algiers had neither an hour nor a thought of hesitation. The Republic and the country were united in their view by a feeling of the same duty. A leader, whose republican name, sentiments, and talents, were at once pledges for the army and the revolution, General Cavaignac, received the command of Algeria.

The corruption which had penetrated the holiest institutions compelled the minister of war to adopt expurgations demanded by the public voice. It was necessary promptly to separate justice from policy. The minister made the separation with pain, but with inflexibility.

In proclaiming the Republic, the cry of France had not only proclaimed a form of government, but a principle. This principle was practical democracy, equality in rights, fraternity in institutions. The revolutions accomplished by the people ought, according to us, to be organized for the profit of the people, by a series of fraternal and guardian institutions, proper to confer regularly on all the conditions of individual dignity, instruction, intelligence, wages, morality, the elements of labor, competence, aid, and advancement to property, which would suppress the servile name of proletary, and would elevate the laborer to the level of the rights, duties, and well-being of the firstborn of prosperity; to raise up and enrich the one, without debasing and degrading the other; to preserve property, and render it more prolific and sacred, by multiplying it and dividing it in the hands of the greatest number; distributing the taxes in such a manner as to make the burden fall heaviest on the strongest, by easing and succoring the weakest; to create by the state the labor which might accidentally fail, from the fact of the timidity of capital, so that there should not be a laborer in France whose bread and wages should fail him; and, finally, to study with the workmen themselves the practical and true phenomena of association, and the yet problematical theories of systems, and to seek conscientiously their applications, and to ascertain their errors; – such was the idea of the provisional government, in all the decrees; whose execution or examination it confided to the minister of finance, the minister of public works, and to the commissioner of the Luxembourg, – the laboratory of ideas, the preparatory and statistical congress of labor and employment, enlightened by studious and intelligent delegates from all the laborious professions, presided over by two members of the Government itself.

The sudden fall of the monarchy, the disorder of the finances, the momentary displacement of an immense mass of factory laborers, the shocks which these masses of unoccupied arms might have given society, if their reason, their patience, and their practical resignation, had not been a miracle of popular reason, and the admiration of the world; the recoverable debt of nearly a thousand millions, which the fallen Government had accumulated on the first two months of the Republic; the industrial and commercial crisis universal on the continent and in England, coinciding with the political crisis in Paris; the enormous accumulation of railway shares and other fictitious property thrown into the hands of agents and bankers by the panic of capital; finally, the imagination of the country, which is carried beyond the truth at moments of political convulsion and social terror, – had exhausted active capital, caused the disappearance of specie, and suspended free and voluntary labor, the only labor sufficient for thirty-five millions of men. It was necessary to supply it temporarily, or be false to all the principles, all the precautions, and all the necessities of the Republic that can be relieved. The minister of finance will tell you how this prostration of labor and credit was provided for, while waiting for the moment now reached, when the restoration of confidence to men's minds would restore capital to the hands of manufacturers, and wages to labor; when your wisdom and national power will be equal to all difficulties.

The ministry of public instruction and worship, confided to the same hand, was for the Government a manifestation of intention, and for the country a presage of the new position which the Republic wished and ought to assume, under the twofold necessity of national enlightenment, and a more real independence of equal and free worship before conscience and the law.

The ministry of agriculture and commerce, a ministry foreign from its nature to politics, could only prepare with zeal, and sketch with sagacity, the new institutions summoned to fertilize the first of useful arts. It extended the hand of state over the suffering interests of commerce, which you alone can raise up by making them secure.

Such were our different and incessant cares. Thanks to that Providence, which has never more clearly manifested its intervention in the cause of nations and the human mind; thanks to the people themselves, who have never better shown the treasures of reason, civil virtue, generosity, patience, and morality, — the true civilization which fifty years of imperfect liberty have elaborated in their hearts, — we succeeded in accomplishing, very imperfectly without doubt, but yet not unhappily, a part of the immense and perilous task with which events had burthened us.

We have founded the Republic, a government declared impossible in France on any other conditions than foreign war, civil war, anarchy, prisons and the scaffold. We have displayed a Republic, happily compatible with European peace, with internal security, with voluntary order, with individual liberty, with the sweetness and amenity of manners of a nation for whom hatred is a punishment, and harmony a national instinct.

We have promulgated the great principles of equality, fraternity, and unity, which must, in their daily development in our laws, enacted by all and for all, accomplish the unity of the people by the unity of representation.

We have rendered the right of citizenship universal, by rendering the right of election universal; and universal suffrage has responded to us.

We have armed the entire people in the National Guard, and the entire people have answered us by devoting the arms we confided to it to the unanimous defense of the nation, order, and law.

We have gone through the interregnum with no other executive force than the entirely unarmed moral authority, whose right the nation voluntarily recognized in us; and these people consented to suffer themselves to be governed by our words, our counsels, and their own generous inspirations.

We have passed more than two months of crisis, of cessation of labor, of misery, of elements of political agitation, of social sufferings and passions, accumulated in countless masses in a capital with a population of a million and a half, without property having been violated, without anger menacing a single life, without one repression, one proscription, one political imprisonment, without one drop of blood shed in our name, saddening the government in Paris. We can descend from this long dictatorship to the public square, and mingle with the people without one citizen being able to ask: "What hast thou done with a citizen?"

Before summoning the National Assembly to Paris, we completely assured its security and independence by arming and organizing the National Guard, and giving you an entire armed people for your protection. There is no longer a possibility of faction in a Republic where there is no longer a division between enfranchised and disfranchised citizens, between armed and unarmed citizens. All have their rights, all have their army. In such a State insurrection is no longer the extreme right of resistance to oppression; it would be a crime. He who separates himself from the people is no longer of the people. This is the unanimity we have created; perpetuate it, for it is the common safety.

Citizen-representatives! our work is accomplished; yours now begins. Even the presentation of a plan of government, or a project of constitution, on our part, would have been a rash prolongation of power, or an infringement on your sovereignty. We disappear the moment you rise to receive the Republic from the hands of the people. We will only permit ourselves a single counsel and a single wish, in the name of our citizenship, and not as members of the provisional government. This wish, citizens, France utters with us; it is the voice of circumstance. Do not waste time, that precious element of human crises. After having absorbed the sovereignty in yourselves, do not suffer a new interregnum to clog the wheels of the country. Let not a commission of Government, springing from your body, allow power to fluctuate a single instant longer, precariously and provisionally, in a country which has need of power and security. Let a committee on a constitution, emanating from your suffrages, report, without delay, for your deliberation and vote, the simple, brief, and democratic mechanism of a constitution, whose organic and secondary laws you can afterwards discuss at your leisure.

In the meanwhile, as members of the Government, we restore to you our powers.

We also confidently submit all our acts to your judgment, only we pray you to take into consideration the period and the difficulties. Our conscience reproaches us with nothing intentionally wrong. Providence has favored our efforts. Grant an amnesty to our involuntary dictatorship. We ask but to return to the ranks of good citizens.

Only may history record with indulgence, beneath and at a great distance from the great deeds achieved by France, the story of these three months, passed in the void between a fallen Monarchy and a Republic to be enthroned; and may it, instead of the obscure and forgotten names of men who devoted themselves to the common safety, inscribe on its pages two names only: the name of the people, who saved everything, and the name of God, who blessed everything, in the foundation of the Republic.

—*From History of the Revolution of 1848, by Alphonse Marie Louis Lamartine, French (1790–1869).*

Inaugural Address

JEFFERSON DAVIS

Gentlemen of the Congress of the Confederate States of America, Friends, and Fellow-Citizens: Called to the difficult and responsible station of Chief Magistrate of the Provisional Government which you have instituted, I approach the discharge of the duties assigned to me with humble distrust of my abilities, but with a sustaining confidence in the wisdom of those who are to guide and aid me in the administration of public affairs, and an abiding faith in the virtue and patriotism of the people. Looking forward to the speedy establishment of a permanent government to take the place of this, which by its greater moral and physical power will be better able to combat with many difficulties that arise from the conflicting interests of separate nations, I enter upon the duties of the office to which I have been chosen with the hope that the beginning of our career, as a Confederacy, may not be obstructed by hostile opposition to our enjoyment of the separate existence and independence we have asserted, and which, with the blessing of Providence, we intend to maintain.

Our present political position has been achieved in a manner unprecedented in the history of nations. It illustrates the American idea that governments rest on the consent of the governed, and that it is the right of the people to alter or abolish them at will whenever they become destructive of the ends for which they were established. The declared purpose of the compact of the Union from which we have withdrawn was to "establish justice, insure domestic tranquillity, provide for the common defense, promote the general welfare, and secure the blessings of liberty to ourselves and our posterity"; and when, in the judgment of the sovereign States composing this Confederacy, it has been perverted from the purposes for which it was ordained, and ceased to answer the ends for which it was established, a peaceful appeal to the ballot box declared that, so far as they are concerned, the Government created by that compact should cease to exist. In this they merely asserted the right which the Declaration of Independence of July 4, 1776, defined to be "inalienable." Of the time and occasion of its exercise they as sovereigns were the final judges, each for itself. The impartial and enlightened verdict of mankind will vindicate the rectitude of our conduct; and He who knows the hearts of men will judge of the sincerity with which we have labored to preserve the Government of our fathers in its spirit.

The right solemnly proclaimed at the birth of the United States, and which has been solemnly affirmed and reaffirmed in the Bills of Rights of the States subsequently admitted into the Union of 1789, undeniably recognizes in the people the power to resume the authority delegated for the purposes of government. Thus the sovereign States here represented have proceeded to form this Confederacy; and it is by abuse of language that their act has been denominated a revolution. They formed a new alliance, but within each State its government has remained; so that the rights of person and property have not been disturbed. The agent through which they communicated with foreign nations is changed, but this does not necessarily interrupt their international relations. Sustained by the consciousness that the transition from the former Union to the present Confederacy has not proceeded from a disregard on our part of just obligations, or any failure to perform every constitutional duty, moved by no interest or passion to invade the rights of others, anxious to cultivate peace and commerce with all nations, if we may not hope to avoid war, we may at least expect that posterity will acquit us of having needlessly engaged in it. Doubly justified by the absence of wrong on our part, and by wanton aggression on the part of others, there can be no cause to doubt that the courage and patriotism of the people of the Confederate States will be found equal to any measure of defense which their honour and security may require.

An agricultural people, whose chief interest is the export of commodities required in every manufacturing country, our true policy is peace, and the freest trade which our necessities will permit. It is alike our interest and that of all those to whom we would sell, and from whom we would buy, that there should be the fewest practicable restrictions upon the interchange of these commodities. There can, however, be but little rivalry between ours and any manufacturing or navigating community, such as the Northeastern States of the American Union. It must follow, therefore, that mutual interest will invite to good will and kind offices on both parts. If, however, passion or lust of dominion should cloud the judgment or inflame the ambition of those States, we must prepare to meet the emergency and maintain by the final arbitrament of the sword, the position which we have assumed among the nations of the earth.

We have entered upon the career of independence, and it must be inflexibly pursued. Through many years of controversy with our late associates of the Northern States, we have vainly endeavored to secure tranquillity and obtain respect for the rights to which we were entitled. As a necessity, not a choice, we have resorted to the remedy of separation, and henceforth our energies must be directed to the conduct of our own affairs, and the perpetuity of the Confederacy which we have formed. If a just perception of mutual interest shall permit us peaceably to pursue our separate political career, my most earnest desire will have been fulfilled. But if this be denied to us, and the integrity of our territory and jurisdiction be assailed, it will but remain for us with firm resolve to appeal to arms and invoke the blessing of Providence on a just cause.

As a consequence of our new condition and relations, and with a view to meet anticipated wants, it will be necessary to provide for the speedy and efficient organization of branches of the Executive department having special charge of foreign intercourse, finance, military affairs, and the postal service. For purposes of defense, the Confederate States may, under ordinary circumstances, rely mainly upon the militia; but it is deemed advisable, in the present condition of affairs, that there should be a well-instructed and disciplined army, more numerous than would usually be required on a peace establishment. I also suggest that, for the protection of our harbors and commerce on the high seas, a navy adapted to those objects will be required. But this, as well as other subjects appropriate to our necessities, have doubtless engaged the attention of Congress.

With a Constitution differing only from that of our fathers in so far as it is explanatory of their well-known intent, freed from sectional conflicts, which have interfered with the pursuit of the general welfare, it is not unreasonable to expect that States from which we have recently parted may seek to unite their fortunes to ours under the Government which we have instituted. For this your Constitution makes adequate provision; but beyond this, if I mistake not the judgment and will of the people, a reunion with the States from which we have separated is neither practicable nor desirable. To increase the power, develop the resources, and promote the happiness of the Confederacy, it is requisite that there should be so much of homogeneity that the welfare of every portion shall be the aim of the whole. When this does not exist, antagonisms are engendered which must and should result in separation.

Actuated solely by the desire to preserve our own rights, and promote our own welfare, the separation by the Confederate States has been marked by no aggression upon others, and followed by no domestic convulsion. Our industrial pursuits have received no check, the cultivation of our fields has progressed as heretofore, and, even should we be involved in war, there would be no considerable diminution in the production of the staples which have constituted our exports, and in which the commercial world has an interest scarcely less than our own. This common interest of the producer and consumer can only be interrupted by exterior force which would obstruct the transmission of our staples to foreign markets — a course of conduct which would be as unjust, as it would be detrimental, to manufacturing and commercial interests abroad.

Should reason guide the action of the Government from which we have separated, a policy so detrimental to the civilized world, the Northern States included, could not be dictated by even the strongest desire to inflict injury upon us; but, if the contrary should prove true, a terrible responsibility will rest upon it, and the suffering of millions will bear testimony to the folly and wickedness of our aggressors. In the meantime there will remain to us, besides the ordinary means before suggested, the well-known resources for retaliation upon the commerce of an enemy.

Experience in public stations, of subordinate grade to this which your kindness has conferred, has taught me that toil and care and disappointment are the price of official elevation. You will see many errors to forgive, many deficiencies to tolerate; but you shall not find in me either want of zeal or fidelity to the cause that is to me the highest in hope, and of most enduring affection. Your generosity has bestowed upon me an undeserved distinction, one which I neither sought nor desired. Upon the continuance of that sentiment, and upon your wisdom and patriotism, I rely to direct and support me in the performance of the duties required at my hands.

We have changed the constituent parts, but not the system of government. The Constitution framed by our fathers is that of these Confederate States. In their exposition of it, and in the judicial construction it has received, we have a light which reveals its true meaning.

Thus instructed as to the true meaning and just interpretation of that instrument, and ever remembering that all offices are but trusts held for the people, and that powers delegated are to be strictly construed, I will hope by due diligence in the performance of my duties, though I may disappoint your expectations, yet to retain, when retiring, something of the good will and confidence which welcome my entrance into office.

It is joyous in the midst of perilous times to look around upon a people united in heart, where one purpose of high resolve animates and actuates the whole; where the sacrifices to be made are not weighed in the balance against honor and right and liberty and equality. Obstacles may retard, but they cannot long prevent, the progress of a movement sanctified by its justice and sustained by a virtuous people. Reverently let us invoke the God of our fathers to guide and protect us in our efforts to perpetuate the principles which by his blessing they were able to vindicate, establish, and transmit to their posterity. With the continuance of his favor ever gratefully acknowledged, we may hopefully look forward to success, to peace, and to prosperity.

— *By Jefferson Davis, American (1808–1899).*

Address at Gettysburg

ABRAHAM LINCOLN

FOURSCORE and seven years ago our fathers brought forth on this continent a new nation, conceived in liberty, and dedicated to the proposition that all men are created equal. Now, we are engaged in a great civil war, testing whether that nation, or any nation so conceived and so dedicated, can long endure. We are met on a great battle field of that war. We have come to dedicate a portion of that field as a final resting-place for those who here gave their lives that that nation might live. It is altogether fitting and proper that we should do this. But, in a larger sense, we cannot dedicate, we cannot consecrate, we cannot hallow this ground. The brave men, living and dead, who struggled here, have consecrated it, far above our poor power to add or to detract. The world will little note nor long remember what we say here, but it can never forget what they did here. It is for us, the living, rather, to be dedicated here to the unfinished work which they who fought here have thus far so nobly advanced. It is rather for us to be here dedicated to the great task remaining before us; that from these honored dead we take increased devotion to that cause for which they gave the last full measure of devotion; that we here highly resolve that these dead shall not have died in vain; that this nation, under God, shall have a new birth of freedom; and that government of the people, by the people, for the people, shall not perish from the earth.

∽ ✿ ∼

Second Inaugural Address

ABRAHAM LINCOLN

FELLOW-COUNTRYMEN: — At this second appearing to take the oath of the presidential office, there is less occasion for an extended address than there was at the first. Then a statement, somewhat in detail, of a course to be pursued, seemed fitting and proper. Now, at the expiration of four years, during which public declarations have been constantly called forth on every point and phase of the great contest which still absorbs the attention and engrosses the energies of the nation, little that is new can be presented. The progress of our arms, upon which all else chiefly depends, is as well known to the public as to myself; and it is, I trust, reasonably satisfactory and encouraging to all. With high hope for the future, no prediction in regard to it is ventured.

On the occasion corresponding to this four years ago, all thoughts were anxiously directed to an impending civil war. All dreaded it — all sought to avert it. While the inaugural address was being delivered from this place, devoted altogether to saving the Union without war, insurgent agents were in the city seeking to destroy it without war — seeking to dissolve the Union, and divide effects, by negotiation. Both parties deprecated war; but one of them would make war rather than let the nation survive; and the other would accept war rather than let it perish. And the war came.

One-eighth of the whole population were colored slaves, not distributed generally over the Union, but localized in the Southern part of it. These slaves constituted a peculiar and powerful interest. All knew that this interest was, somehow, the cause of the war. To strengthen, perpetuate, and extend this interest was the object for which the insurgents would rend the Union, even by war; while the government claimed no right to do more than to restrict the territorial enlargement of it.

Neither party expected for the war the magnitude or the duration which it has already attained. Neither anticipated that the cause of the conflict might cease with, or even before, the conflict itself should cease. Each looked for an easier triumph, and a result less fundamental and astounding. Both read the same Bible, and pray to the same God; and each invokes his aid against the other. It may seem strange that any men should dare to ask a just God's assistance in wringing their bread from the sweat of other men's faces; but let us judge not, that we be not judged. The prayers of both could not be answered — that of neither has been answered fully.

The Almighty has his own purposes. "Woe unto the world because of offenses! for it must needs be that offenses come: but woe to that man by whom the offense cometh." If we shall suppose that American slavery is one of those offenses which, in the providence of God, must needs come, but which, having continued through his appointed time, he now wills to remove, and that he gives to both North and South this terrible war, as the woe due to those by whom the offense came, shall we discern therein any departure from those divine attributes which the believers in a living God always ascribe to him? Fondly do we hope —fervently do we pray—that this mighty scourge of war may speedily pass away. Yet, if God wills that it shall continue until all the wealth piled by the bondman's two hundred and fifty years of unrequited toil shall be sunk, and until every drop of blood drawn with the lash shall be paid by another drawn with the sword, as was said three thousand years ago, so still it must be said, "The judgments of the Lord are true and righteous altogether."

With malice toward none; with charity for all; with firmness in the right, as God gives us to see the right, let us strive on to finish the work we are in; to bind up the nation's wounds; to care for him who shall have borne the battle, and for his widow, and his orphan—to do all which may achieve and cherish a just and lasting peace among ourselves, and with all nations.

—*By Abraham Lincoln, American (1809–1865).*

To the Italian Working-Men

GIUSEPPE MAZZINI

I WANT to speak to you of your duties. I want to speak to you, as my heart dictates to me, of the most sacred things which we know—of God, of Humanity, of the Fatherland, of the Family. Listen to me with love, even as I shall speak to you with love. My words are words of conviction matured by long years of sorrow and of observation and of study. The duties which I am going to point out to you I strive and shall strive as long as I live to fulfil, to the utmost of my power. I may make mistakes, but my heart is true. I may deceive myself, but I will not deceive you. Hear me therefore as a brother; judge freely among yourselves, whether it seems to you that I speak the truth; abandon me if you think that I preach what is false; but follow me and do according to my teaching if you find me an apostle of truth. To be mistaken is a misfortune to be pitied; but to know the truth and not to conform one's actions to it is a crime which Heaven and Earth condemn.

Why do I speak to you of your *duties* before speaking to you of your *rights*? Why in a society in which all, voluntarily or involuntarily, oppress you, in which the exercise of all the rights which belong to man is constantly denied you, in which misery is your lot, and what is called happiness is for other classes of men, why do I speak to you of self-sacrifice, and not of conquest; of virtue, moral improvement, education, and not of material *well-being*? This is a question which I must answer before going further, because here precisely lies the difference between our school and many others which are being preached to-day in Europe; because, moreover, it is a question which rises readily in the indignant mind of the suffering working-man.

We are poor, enslaved, unhappy; speak to us of better material conditions, of liberty, of happiness. Tell us if we are doomed to suffer for ever, or if we too may enjoy in our turn. Preach duty to our masters, to the classes above us which treat us like machines, and monopolize the blessings which belong to all. To us speak of rights; speak of the means of vindicating them; speak of our strength. Wait till we have a recognized existence; then you shall speak to us of duties and of sacrifice. This is what many of our working-men say, and follow teachers and associations which respond to their desires. They forget one thing only, and that is, that the doctrine which they invoke has been preached for the last fifty years without producing the slightest material improvement in the condition of the working-people.

For the last fifty years whatever has been done for the cause of progress and of good against absolute governments and hereditary aristocracies has been done in the name of the Rights of Man; in the name of liberty as the means, and of *well-being* as the object of existence. All the acts of the French Revolution and of the revolutions which followed and imitated it were consequences of a Declaration of the Rights of Man. All the works of the philosophers who prepared it were based upon a theory of liberty, and upon the need of making known to every individual his own rights. All the revolutionary schools preached that man is born for happiness, that he has the right to seek it by all the means in his power, that no one has the right to impede him in this search, and that he has the right of overthrowing all the obstacles which he may encounter in his path. And the obstacles were overthrown; liberty was conquered. It endured for years in many countries; in some it still endures. Has the condition of the people improved? Have the millions who live by the daily labour of their hands gained the least fraction of the well-being hoped for and promised to them?

No; the condition of the people has not improved; rather it has grown and grows worse in nearly every country, and especially here where I write the price of the necessaries of life has gone on continually rising, the wages of the working-man in many branches of industry falling, and the population multiplying. In nearly every country the lot of workers has become more uncertain, more precarious, and the labour crises which condemn thousands of working-men to idleness for a time have become more frequent. The yearly increase of emigration from one country to another, and from Europe to other parts of the world, and the evergrowing number of beneficent institutions, the increase of poor rates and provisions for the destitute, are enough to prove this. The latter prove also that public attention is waking more and more to the ills of the people; but their inability to lessen those ills to any visible extent points to a no less continual increase of poverty among the classes which they endeavour to help.

And nevertheless, in these last fifty years, the sources of social wealth and the sum of material blessings have steadily increased. Production has doubled. Commerce, amid continual crises, inevitable in the utter absence of organization, has acquired a greater force of activity and a wider sphere for its operations. Communication has almost everywhere been made secure and rapid, and the price of commodities has fallen in consequence of the diminished cost of transport. And, on the other hand, the idea of rights inherent in human nature is to-day generally accepted; accepted in word and, hypocritically, even by those who seek to evade it in deed. Why, then, has the condition of the people not improved? Why is the consumption of products, instead of being divided equally among all the members of the social body in Europe, concentrated in the hands of a small number of men forming a new aristocracy? Why has the new impulse given to industry and commerce produced, not the well-being of the many, but the luxury of the few?

The answer is clear to those who will look a little closely into things. Men are creatures of education, and act only according to the principle of education given to them. The men who have promoted revolutions hitherto have based them upon the idea of the rights belonging to the individual; the revolutions conquered liberty – individual liberty, liberty of teaching, liberty of belief, liberty of trade, liberty in everything and for everybody. But of what use was the recognition of their rights to those who had no means of exercising them? What did liberty of teaching mean to those who had neither time nor means to profit by it, or liberty of trade to those who had nothing to trade with, neither capital nor credit? In all the countries where these principles were proclaimed society was composed of a small number of individuals who possessed the land, the credit, the capital, and of vast multitudes of men who had nothing but their own hands and were forced to give the labour of them to the former class, on any terms, in order to live, and forced to spend the whole day in material and monotonous toil. For these, constrained to battle with hunger, what was liberty but an illusion and a bitter irony? To make it anything else it would have been necessary for the men of the well-to-do classes to consent to reduce the hours of labour, to increase the remuneration, to institute free and uniform education for the masses, to make the instruments of labour accessible to all, and to provide a bonus fund for the working-man endowed with capacity and good intentions. But why should they do it? Was not *well-being* the supreme object in life? Were not material blessings desirable before all other things? Why should they lessen their own enjoyment for the advantage of others? Let those who could, help themselves. When society has secured to everybody who can use them the free exercise of the rights belonging to human nature, it does all that is required of it. If there be any one who is unable from the fatality of his own circumstances to exercise any of these rights, he must resign himself and not blame others.

It was natural that they should say thus, and thus, in fact, they did say. And this attitude of mind towards the poor in the classes privileged by fortune soon became the attitude of every individual towards every other. Each man looked after his own rights and the improvement of his own condition without seeking to provide for others; and when his rights clashed with those of others, there was war; not a war of blood, but of gold and of cunning; a war less manly than the other, but equally destructive; cruel war, in which those who had the means and were strong relentlessly crushed the weak or the unskilled. In this continual warfare, men were educated in egoism and in greed for material welfare exclusively. Liberty of belief destroyed all community of faith. Liberty of education produced moral anarchy. Men without a common tie, without unity of religious belief and of aim, and whose sole vocation was enjoyment, sought every one his own road, not heeding if in pursuing it they were trampling upon the heads of their brothers — brothers in name and enemies in fact. To this we are come to-day, thanks to the theory of *rights*.

Certainly rights exist; but where the rights of an individual come into conflict with those of another, how can we hope to reconcile and harmonize them, without appealing to something superior to all rights? And where the rights of an individual, or of many individuals, clash with the rights of the Country, to what tribunal are we to appeal? If the right to *well-being*, to the greatest possible well-being, belongs to every living person, who will solve the difficulty between the working-man and the manufacturer? If the right to existence is the first and inviolable right of every man, who shall demand the sacrifice of that existence for the benefit of other men? Will you demand it in the name of Country, of Society, of the multitude of your brothers? What is Country, in the opinion of those of whom I speak, but the place in which our individual rights are most secure? What is Society but a collection of men who have agreed to bring the strength of the many in support of the rights of each? And after having taught the individual for fifty years that Society is established for the purpose of *assuring to him the exercise of his rights*, would you ask him to sacrifice them all to Society, to submit himself, if need be, to continuous toil, to prison, to exile, for the sake of improving it? After having preached to him everywhere that the object of life is *well-being*, would you all at once bid him give up well-being and life itself to free his country from the foreigner, or to procure better conditions for a class which is not his own? After having talked to him for years of *material* interests, how can you maintain that, finding wealth and power in his reach, he ought not to stretch out his hand to grasp them, even to the injury of his brothers?

Italian Working-men, this is not a chance thought of my mind, without a foundation in fact. It is history, the history of our own times, a history the pages of which drip with blood, the blood of the people. Ask all the men who transformed the revolution of 1830 into a mere substitution of one set of persons for another, and, for example, made the bodies of your French comrades, who were killed fighting in the Three Days, into stepping-stones to raise themselves to power; all their doctrines, before 1830, were founded on the old theory of the *rights* of man, not upon a belief in his *duties*. You call them to-day traitors and apostates, and yet they were only consistent with their own doctrine. They fought with sincerity against the government of Charles X because that Government was directly hostile to the classes from which they sprang, and violated and endeavoured to suppress their rights. They fought in the name of the well-being which they did not possess as much of as they thought they ought to have. Some were persecuted for freedom of thought; others, men of powerful mind, saw themselves neglected, shut out from offices occupied by men of capacity inferior to their own. Then the wrongs of the people angered them also. Then they wrote boldly and in good faith about the rights which belong to every man. Afterwards, when their own political and intellectual rights had been secured, when the path to office was opened to them, when they had conquered the *well-being* which they sought, they forgot the people, forgot that the millions, inferior to them in education and in aspirations, were seeking the exercise of other rights and the achievement of *well-being* of another sort, and they set their minds at rest and troubled no longer about anybody but themselves. Why call them traitors? Why not rather call their doctrine treacherous?

There lived and wrote at that time in

France a man whom you ought never to forget, more powerful in mind than all of them put together. He was our opponent then; but he believed in Duty; in the duty of sacrificing the whole existence to the common good, to the pursuit and triumph of Truth. He studied the men and the circumstances of the time deeply, and did not allow himself to be led astray by applause, or to be discouraged by disappointment. When he had tried one way and failed, he tried yet another for the amelioration of the masses. And when the course of events had shown him that there was one power alone capable of achieving it, when the people had proved themselves in the field of action more virtuous and more believing than all those who had pretended to deal with their cause, he, Lamennais, author of the *Words of a Believer,* which you have all read, became the best apostle of the cause in which we are brothers. There you see in him, and in the men of whom I have been speaking, the difference between the men of *rights* and those of *duty.* To the first the acquisition of their individual rights, by withdrawing stimulus, proves a sufficient check to further effort; the work of the second only ceases here on earth with life.

And among the peoples who are completely enslaved, where the conflict has very different dangers, where every step made towards a better state of things is signed with the blood of a martyr, where the operations against injustice in high places are necessarily secret and lack the consolation of publicity and of praise, what obligation, what stimulus to constancy can maintain upon the path of progress men who degrade the holy social war which we carry on to a mere battle for their *rights?* I speak, be it understood, of the generality and not of the exceptions to be met with in all schools of thought. When the hot blood and the impulse of reaction against tyranny which naturally draw youth into the conflict have calmed down, what can prevent these men, after a few years of effort, after the disappointments inevitable in any such enterprise, from growing weary? Why should they not prefer any sort of repose to an unquiet existence, agitated by continual struggles and danger, and liable to end any day in imprisonment, or the scaffold, or exile? It is the too common story of most of the Italians of to-day, imbued as they are with the old French ideas; a very sad story, but how can it be altered except by changing the principle with which they start as their guide? How and in whose name are they to be convinced that danger and disappointment ought to make them stronger, that they have got to fight not for a few years, but for their whole lives? Who shall say to a man, *Go on struggling for your rights,* when to struggle for them costs him dearer than to abandon them?

And even in a society constituted on a juster basis than our own, who shall convince a believer in the theory of *rights* solely that he has to work for the common purpose and devote himself to the development of the social *idea?* Suppose he should rebel; suppose he should feel himself strong and should say to you: *I break the social compact; my inclinations, my faculties, call me elsewhere; I have a sacred and inviolable right to develop them, and I choose to be at war with everybody:* What answer can you give him while he keeps to his theory of rights? What right have you, because you are a majority, to compel his obedience to laws which do not accord with his desires and with his individual aspirations? What right have you to punish him if he violates them? Rights belong equally to every individual; the fact of living together in a community does not create a single one. Society has greater strength, not more rights, than the individual. How, then, are you going to prove to the individual that he must merge his will in the will of those who are his brothers, whether in the Country or in the wider fellowship of Humanity? By means of the executioner, of the prison? Societies existing up till now have used such means. But that is war, and we want peace; that is tyrannical repression, and we want education.

Education, we have said; and this is the great word which sums up our whole doctrine. The vital question agitating our century is a question of education. What we have to do is not to establish a new order of things by violence. An order of things so established is always tyrannical even when it is better than the old. *We have to overthrow by force the brute force which opposes itself to-day to every attempt at improvement,* and then propose for the approval of the nation, free to express its will, what we believe to be the best order of things and by every possible means educate men to develop it and act in conformity with it. The theory of *rights* enables us to rise and overthrow obstacles, but not to found a strong and lasting accord between all the elements which compose the nation. With the theory of happiness, of *well-being,* as the primary aim of existence we shall only form egoistic men, worshippers of the material, who will carry the old passions into the new order of things and corrupt it in a few months. We have therefore to find a principle of education superior to any such theory, which shall guide men to better things, teach them constancy in self-sacrifice and link them with their fellow men without making them dependent on the ideas of a single man or on the strength of all. And this principle is Duty. We must convince men that they, sons of one only God, must obey one only law, here on earth; that each one of them must live, not for himself, but for others; that the object of their life is not to be more or less happy, but to make themselves and others better; that to fight against injustice and error for the benefit of their brothers is not only a *right,* but a *duty;* a duty not to be neglected without sin, — the duty of their whole life.

Italian Working-men, my Brothers! understand me fully. When I say that the knowledge of their *rights* is not enough to enable men to effect any appreciable or lasting improvement, I do not ask you to renounce these rights; I only say that they cannot exist except as a consequence of duties fulfilled, and that one must begin with the latter in order to arrive at the former. And when I say that by proposing *happiness, well-being,* or *material* interest as the aim of existence, we run the risk of producing egoists, I do not mean that you should never strive after these things. I say that material interests pursued alone, and not as a means, but as an end, lead always to this most disastrous result. When under the Emperors, the old Romans asked for nothing but *bread* and *amusements,* they became the most abject race conceivable, and after submitting to the stupid and ferocious tyranny of the Emperors they basely fell into slavery to the invading Barbarians. In France and elsewhere the enemies of all social progress have sown corruption and tried to divert men's minds from ideas of change by furthering the development of *material* activity. And shall we help the enemy with our own hands? Material improvement is essential, and we shall strive to win it for ourselves; but not because the one thing necessary for man is to be well fed and housed, but rather because you cannot have a sense of your own dignity or any moral development while you are engaged, as at the present day, in a continual duel with want. You work ten or twelve hours a day: how can you find *time* to educate yourselves? The uncertainty of your employment and the frequent interruptions in it cause you to alternate between too much work and periods of idleness: how are you to acquire habits of order, regularity, and assiduity? The scantiness of your earnings does away with any hope of saving enough to be useful some day to your children, or to your own old age: how are you to educate yourselves into habits of economy? Many of you are compelled by poverty to separate your children, we will not say from the careful bringing-up — what sort of bringing-up can the poor wives of working-men give their children? — but from the love and the watchful eye of their mothers, and to send them out, for the sake of a few halfpence, to unwholesome labour in factories: how, in such conditions, can family affection unfold itself and be ennobled? You have not the rights of citizens, nor any participation, by election or by vote, in the laws which regulate your actions and your life: how should you feel the pride of citizenship or have any zeal for the State, or sincere affection for the laws? Justice is not dealt out to you with the same equal hand as to the other classes: whence, then, are you to learn respect and love for justice? Society treats you without a shadow of sympathy: whence are you to learn sympathy with society? You need, then, a change in your material conditions to enable you to develop morally; you need to work less so as to have some hours of your day to devote to the improvement of your minds; you need a sufficient remuneration of your labour to put you in a position to accumulate savings, and so set your minds at rest about the future, and to purify yourselves above all of every sentiment of *retaliation,* every impulse of revenge, every thought of injustice towards those who have been unjust to you. You must strive, then, for this change, and you will obtain it, but you must strive for it as a *means,* not as an *end;* strive for it from a sense of *duty,* not only as a *right;* strive for it in order to make yourselves better, not only to make yourselves *materially* happy. If not, what difference would there be between you and your tyrants? They are tyrants precisely because they do not think of anything but *well-being,* pleasure and power.

To make yourselves better; this must be the aim of your life. You cannot make yourselves permanently less unhappy except by improving yourselves. Tyrants will arise by the thousand among you, if you fight only in the name of material interests, or of a particular organization. A change of social organization makes little difference if you and the other classes keep the passions and the egoism of to-day; organizations are like certain plants which yield poison or remedies according to the way in which they are administered. Good men make bad organizations good, and bad men make good organizations bad. You have got to improve the classes which, voluntarily or involuntarily, oppress you to-day, and convince them of their duties; but you will never succeed in this unless you begin by making yourselves better as far as possible.

When therefore you hear men who preach the necessity of a social transformation telling you that they can accomplish it by invoking your *rights* only, be grateful to them for their good intentions, but distrustful of the outcome. The ills of the poor man are known, in part at least, to the well-to-do classes; *known* but not *felt.* In the general indifference born of the absence of a common faith; in the egoism, inevitably resulting from the continual preaching through so many years of the doctrine of material *well-being,* those who do not suffer have grown accustomed little by little to consider these ills as a sad necessity of the social order and to leave the trouble of remedying them to the generations to come. The difficulty is not to convince them, but to shake them out of inertia and to induce them, when they are convinced, to *act,* to associate themselves, to unite with you in brotherly fellowship for the purpose of creating such a social organization as shall put an end, as far as the conditions of humanity allow, to your ills and to their own fears. Now, this is a work of faith, of faith in the mission which God has given to the human creature here upon earth; of faith in the responsibility weighing upon all those who do not fulfil that mission, and in the duty which bids every one work continually, and with self-sacrifice, for the cause of Truth. All possible theories of rights and of material *well-being* can only lead you to attempts which, so long as they remain isolated and dependent on your strength only, will not succeed, but can only bring about the worst of social crimes, a civil war between class and class.

Italian Working-men, my Brothers! When Christ came and changed the face of the world, He did not speak of rights to the rich, who had no need to conquer them; nor to the poor, who would perhaps have abused them, in imitation of the rich. He did not speak of utility or of self-interest to a people whom utility and self-interest had corrupted. He spoke of Duty, He spoke of Love, of Sacrifice, of Faith: *He said that they only should be first among all who had done good to all by their work.* And these thoughts, breathed into the ear of a society which had no longer any spark of life, reanimated it, conquered the millions, conquered the world, and caused the education of the human race to progress a degree. Italian Working-men! we live in an epoch like Christ's. We live in the midst of a society rotten as that of the Roman Empire, and feel in our souls the need of reviving and transforming it, of associating all its members and its workers in one single faith, under one single law, and for one purpose; the free and progressive development of all the faculties which God has planted in His creatures. We seek the reign of God upon earth as in heaven, or better, that the earth shall be a preparation for heaven, and society an endeavour towards a progressive approach to the Divine Idea.

But every act of Christ's represented the faith which He preached, and round Him there were apostles who embodied in their acts the faith which they had accepted. Be such as they, and you will conquer. Preach Duty to the men of the classes above you, and fulfil, as far as possible, your own duties; preach virtue, sacrifice, love; and be yourselves virtuous and prompt to self-sacrifice and love. Declare with courage your needs and your ideas; but without wrath, without vindictiveness, without threats. The most powerful threat, if there are any who need threats, is firm, not angry, speech. While you propagate among your companions the conception of their future destinies, the conception of a nation which will give them a name, education, work, and fair wages, together with the self-respect and vocation of men, while you kindle their spirit for the inevitable struggle for which they must prepare themselves, so that they may conquer all this in spite of all the forces of our evil government and of the foreigner, strive to instruct yourselves, to grow better, and to educate yourselves to the full knowledge and to the practice of your duties. This is an impossible task for the masses in a great part of Italy; no plan of popular education could be realized among us without a change in the material condition of the people, and without a political revolution; they who deceive themselves into hoping for it, and preach it as an indispensable preparation for any attempt at emancipation, preach a gospel of inertia, nothing else. But the few among you whose circumstances are somewhat better, and to whom a sojourn in foreign lands has afforded more liberal means of education, can do it, and therefore ought to do it. And these few, once imbued with the true principles upon which the education of a people depends, will be enough to spread them among the thousands as a guide for their path and a protection from the fallacies and the false doctrines which will come to waylay them.

—*From The Duties of Man by Giuseppe Mazzini, Italian (1805–1872), translated by Thomas Okey.*

Fascism and the Corporations

BENITO MUSSOLINI

[THE following address was made by Mussolini after he had read the resolution of the National Council of Corporations as follows:

"The National Council of Corporations defines the Corporations as the instrument, guided by the State, for realizing the integrated, organic, and unified regulation of the productive energies of the Italian people, in order to promote its wealth, political power, and welfare;

"It affirms that the number of Corporations to be constituted according to the chief branches of production must be adapted as closely as possible to the real necessities of the national economy;

"It determines that the Chief of Staff of the Corporations should include representatives of the administration of the State, of the Party, of capital, of labor, and of technology;

"It assigns to the Corporations the specific tasks of compulsory arbitration and consultation in dealing with the most important problems, and the enactment, by means of the National Council, of laws regulating the economic life of the nation;

"It refers to the Grand Council of Fascism the decisions of a political and constitutional nature necessary for the further development of the Corporations, in view of the consequences of their effective organization and practical operation."]

The applause with which my statements were received yesterday makes me question this morning whether or not it is necessary to make a speech explaining a document which appealed directly to your intelligence, interpreted your convictions, and aroused your revolutionary sentiments. However it may interest you to know along what lines of reasoning and thought I arrived at the conclusions which I formulated last evening.

But first of all I want to congratulate this Assembly and express my delight over the discussions that have taken place. Only the feeble-minded need be astonished to see differences arise and discussions occur among us. Such things are inevitable, I might say necessary. Harmony is harmony, not cacophony. On the other hand, in the discussion of a problem as delicate as this one, it is perfectly logical and inevitable that each should bring to it not only his own background of beliefs, not only his own state of mind, but also his own personal temperament. The most abstract philosopher, the most transcendental metaphysician can not totally ignore or set aside his personal temperament.

You will remember how on October 16 of the Tenth Year, before the thousands of Party officers gathered in the Piazza Venezia at Rome for the celebration of the tenth anniversary, I asked: Is this crisis that has tortured us for four years—we have now lived through one month of the fifth—is this crisis *in* our system or *of* it? A grave question, a question which can not be answered immediately. To answer it, it is necessary to reflect, to reflect long and to arm oneself with facts. Today I reply: The crisis has penetrated the system so profoundly that it has become a crisis *of* the system. It is no longer a mere lesion, it is a constitutional disease. Today we can assert that the capitalistic method of production has been superseded, and with it the theory of liberal economics that illustrated and defended it.

I want to trace for you in broad outline the history of capitalism in the last century, which might be called the century of capitalism. But first of all, what is capitalism? We do not need to confuse capitalism and the bourgeoisie. The bourgeoisie is something else. It is a mode of being that may be great or petty, heroic or philistine. Capitalism, on the contrary, is a particular type of production, it is a system of industrial production. In its perfect expression capitalism is a system of mass production for mass consumption, by mass finances, that is, by issuing incorporated capital, both national and international. Capitalism is therefore industrial and has not shown great importance in the field of agriculture.

I would distinguish three periods in the history of capitalism: the dynamic period, the static period, and the decadent period. The dynamic period extends from 1830 to 1870. It coincides with the introduction of the power-loom and the appearance of the steam-engine, the rise of the factory. The factory is the typical manifestation of industrial capitalism. This is the period of big margins, and hence the law of free competition and the struggle of all against all had full play. The fallen and the dead are picked up by the Red Cross. In this period, too, there are crises, but they are clinical crises, not long or universal. Capitalism still has enough vitality and strength to recover brilliantly. This is the period in which Luigi Filippo cries: "Get rich." Cities spring up. Berlin, which had 100 thousand inhabitants at the beginning of the century, reaches a million; Paris from 560 thousand at the time of the French Revolution also reaches nearly a million. Similarly London and the cities across the Atlantic. In this first period of the life of capitalism selection really operates.

And there are also wars. These wars can not be compared with the World War through which we have lived. They are short wars. The Italian war of 1848–49 lasted four months during the first year, four days during the second; the war of 1859 lasted a few weeks. The same may be said of the war in 1866. The Prussian war did not last longer. The war of the Dukes in 1864 against Denmark lasted a few days; that of 1866 against Austria, which was a consequence of the former, lasted a few days and ended at Sadowa. Even that of 1870, which included the tragic day of Sedan, did not last more than two seasons. These wars, I dare say, in one sense stimulated the economic life of the countries, so that it is true that hardly eight years afterward, in 1878, France had already sufficiently recovered to organize the World's Fair, an event which made Bismark do some thinking. What took place in America we should perhaps not call heroic. That is a word we must reserve for affairs of a strictly military nature; but the conquest of the Far West was certainly difficult and exacting and had the risks and the losses of a great conquest.

This dynamic period of capitalism lasted from the appearance of the steam-engine to the opening of the Suez Canal. Forty years. During these forty years the State was an onlooker, took no part, and the theorists of liberalism said to it: You have only one duty — to see that your existence should not even be suspected in the realm of economics. The better the government, the less it concerns itself with the problems of the economic system. Hence the economic system in all its manifestations was limited only by the penal code and the code of commerce.

But after 1870 this period changes. No longer the struggle for existence, free competition, survival of the strongest. We notice the first symptoms of weariness and decline in the capitalistic world. The era of cartels, of syndicates, of consortiums, of "trusts." Certainly I need not elaborate for you the differences there are in these four institutions. The differences are hardly conspicuous. They are like the differences between imposts and taxes. Economists have not yet defined them. But the taxpayer at the cashier's window realizes that it is useless to argue about them, for both imposts and taxes have to be paid.

It is not true, as one Italian economist of the liberal school has said, that the economic system of trusts, cartels, and syndicates is the result of the War, for the coal trust in Germany, founded at Dortmund, dates from 1879. In 1905, ten years before the World War broke out, there were 62 metal trusts in Germany. There was a potash trust in 1904; a sugar trust in 1903; 10 trusts in the glass industry. Roughly in this period from 500 to 700 trusts divided among them the control of industry and commerce in Germany. In France in 1877 the industrial organization of Longwy was founded, to deal with the metal industry; in 1888, that of petroleum; in 1881 all the insurance companies had already united. The iron trust in Austria dates from 1873; and shortly after the national trusts, international ones developed. The syndicate of bottle-makers dates from 1907. That of the manufacturers of glass and mirrors, which included French, English, Austrian, and Italian, dates from 1909. The manufacturers of railroad rails formed an international cartel in 1904. The zinc syndicate was born in 1899. I spare you the annoyance of hearing about all the chemical, textile, marine, and other syndicates that were formed in this historical period. The nitrate trust between the English and Chileans came in 1901. I have here the whole list of the national and international trusts, which I shall not inflict on you. It may be said that there was no section of the economic life of the countries of Europe and America in which this characteristic power of capitalism did not take shape.

But what is the consequence? The end of free competition. Margins having become restricted, capitalistic enterprise found it better to agree, to unite, to organize, for the division of the market and sharing of the profits. Even the law of supply and demand ceased to be a dogma, since through the cartels and trusts it was possible to control both supply and demand; finally this capitalistic economic system, organized and syndicated, turned to the State and what did they ask? Protective tariff. Free trade, which is only a larger aspect of the doctrine of economic liberalism, free trade received a deathblow. Among the nations that first raised almost insurmountable barriers was America. And on this side, even England has renounced now for some years all that which hitherto seemed traditional in her political, economic and moral life and has undertaken an increasingly stringent policy of protection.

Then came the War. After the War and as a consequence of it, capitalistic enterprise was inflated. The size of businesses passed from millions to billions. The so-called vertical constructions, or holding companies, seen at a distance, give an idea of the monstrosity of this tower of Babel. Enterprise on such a scale surpasses human ability: first it was spirit that dominated matter, now matter controls and subjugates spirit. What was physiology has become pathology; everything is abnormal. Two persons — since in all human affairs representative men loom on the horizon — two persons can be identified as representative of this situation: Kreuger, the Swedish match manufacturer, and Insull, the American manipulator. For the sake of the brutal truth that it is our Fascist habit to tell, we must add that in Italy, too, there have been specimens of this species; but on the whole they have not attained the same dizzy heights.

Having arrived at this point, super-capitalism draws its inspiration and its justification from a Utopian dream, the dream of unlimited consumption. The ideal of super-capitalism would be the standardization of human life from the cradle to the grave. Super-capitalism would like to have all babies born uniform in size so that cradles could be standardized; they want all children to like the same toys; they want all men to wear the same livery, all to read the same books, all to have the same tastes in the movies, all, in short, to become a so-called utilitarian machine. This is not a caprice, but it is the logic of events, for only in this way can super-capitalism project its plans. When did capitalistic enterprise cease to be an economic fact? When its dimensions made of it a social fact.

And this is precisely the moment in which capitalistic enterprise, finding itself in difficulty, pitched itself straight into the arms of the State, and this is the moment in which State intervention was born and since when it has become more and more necessary. And those who had ignored it, now sought it frantically. We have reached the point where if in all the nations of Europe the State should go to sleep for twenty-four hours, that interval would be enough to precipitate disaster. There is no longer any economic field in which the State can not interfere. If, purely hypothetically, we wanted to give way to this current capitalism, we should fly into State capitalism, which is nothing else but State socialism up-side down; we should arrive in one way or another at the exercise of national economy!

This is the crisis of the capitalistic system taken in its universal significance. But for us there is a specific crisis which we face particularly as Italians and Europeans. It is a European crisis, typically European. Europe is no longer the continent that directs human civilization. To this dramatic conclusion men must come who think for themselves and for others. There was a time when Europe was the political, spiritual, and economic leader of the world. Spiritually by means of all that the spirit of Europe had produced throughout the centuries. Economically because it was the only continent completely industrialized. But, across the Atlantic, a great industrial and capitalistic enterprise has developed. In the Far East is Japan which, having made a contact with Europe through the war of 1905, is encroaching on the big markets of the West. Here is the political problem. I talk of politics here because this Assembly, too, is strictly political. Europe can still try to regain the leadership of universal civilization if she finds a "minimum" of political unity. We must carry on as heretofore. Europe's political goal can not be achieved unless certain grave injustices are first rectified.

We have come to an extremely serious point in this situation: the League of Nations has lost everything that gave it political significance or historical importance. Even the country that invented it has failed to join it. Russia, the United States, Japan, and Germany are absent. This League of Nations was founded on one of those principles that sound very beautiful at first but when considered and analyzed and taken apart reveal their absurdity. What other diplomatic means exist that can re-establish contacts among the nations? Locarno? Locarno is another matter. Locarno has nothing to do with disarmament; that is no way out. A great silence has reigned of late concerning the Four Power Pact. Nobody talks of it, but everybody thinks about it. It is precisely for this reason that we do not intend to start over again or to speed up a situation that is bound to mature logically and inevitably.

Let us ask ourselves now: Is Italy a capitalistic nation? You have never asked this question? If by capitalism one means that totality of manners, customs, and technical progress now common to all the nations, it can be said that Italy, too, is capitalistic. But if we go into the subject and examine the situation from a statistical point of view, that is, from the mass of different economic groups of our population, we have the facts in the case which will permit us to say that Italy is not a capitalistic nation in the current meaning of that word.

April 21, 1931, there were 2,943,000 farmers on their own land; 858,000 tenant-farmers. There were 1,631,000 share-croppers; and the other farmers, farm-hands, and agricultural day-laborers numbered 2,475,000. The total of the population directly and immediately dependent on agriculture is 7,900,000. There are 523,000 industrialists; 841,000 merchants; 724,000 artisans, dependent or independent; 4,283,000 wage earners; 849,000 domestic servants and porters; the armed forces of the state number 541,000, including, of course, the police force. In the professions and liberal arts there are 553,000; public and private office employees, 905,000. The total in this and the above groups is 17,000,000. There are few landed proprietors and large landowners in Italy — 201,000; 1,945,000 students; 11,244,000 housewives. Then there is the item called other non-professional occupations — 1,295,000 — an item which can be interpreted in various ways.

You see at once from this picture that the economic life of Italy is varied, complex, and can not be defined according to one pattern. Furthermore the industrialists, who make up the imposing number of 523,000, almost all operate either small or medium-sized concerns. The small concern may go from a minimum of 50 employees to a maximum of 500. From 500 to five or six thousand is the medium-sized industry; above that is big industry, and only here and there does Italian industry overflow into super-capitalism.

This survey demonstrates also how wrong Karl Marx was, who, following his own apocalyptic schemes, pretended that human society could be divided into two classes neatly distinguished from each other and eternally irreconcilable. Italy, in my opinion, must remain a nation of mixed economy, with a strong agriculture, which is the base of all, inasmuch as it is true that what little revival of industry there has been of late has been due, according to the unanimous opinion of those who have studied the matter, to the respectable yields of agriculture in these years. A healthy small or medium-sized industry, a bank that does not engage in speculation, a commerce that performs its irreplaceable duty of distributing merchandise to consumers rapidly and reasonably.

In my statements presented last evening, the Corporation is defined as we understand it and intend to create it, and its purposes too are defined. I said the Corporation was created in view of the development of the wealth, the political power, and the welfare of the Italian people. These three elements interact. Political power creates wealth, and wealth in its turn reinforces political power.

I want to call your attention to what I said was the aim of the Corporation, the welfare of the Italian people. It is necessary that at any given time these institutions which we have created should be felt and recognized directly by the masses as instruments through which they can raise their standard of living. It is necessary that at a given time the workman and the farm-laborer should be able to say to himself: if today my status is improved, I owe it to the institutions which the Fascist Revolution has created. In all societies there is inevitable poverty. There is a group of persons who live on the margin of society; special institutions deal with them. However, that which should trouble us is the poverty of strong and honest men who are earnestly looking for work in vain. We must see to it that Italian workmen, in whom we are interested as Italians, workmen, and Fascists, feel that we are not creating institutions only to give form to our doctrines, but we are creating institutions that must sometime show positive, concrete, practical, and tangible results.

I shall not pause to discuss the work of arbitration that the Corporations may undertake, and I see no obstacle to the exercise of their advisory function. It is already a fact that every time the Government has to take over important responsibilities, it calls in the interested parties. If tomorrow this practice should become compulsory in the settlement of disputes, I do not see anything wrong in it, because everything that brings the citizen in contact with the State, everything that introduces the citizen into the workings of the State, is useful to the social and national aims of Fascism.

Our State is not an absolute state, and still less absolutistic, alien to men and armed only with inflexible laws, as laws must be. Our State is an organic state, human, desirous of sticking close to the realities of life. The bureaucracy itself is not today, and wants to be still less tomorrow, a membrane separating the State's business from the interests and concrete and actual needs of the Italian people. I am absolutely certain that the Italian bureaucracy, which is admirable, the Italian bureaucracy, just as it has done so far, will in the future work with the Corporations whenever that is necessary for the most successful solution of their problems.

But the point that struck this Assembly most forcefully is the intention of giving legislative powers to the National Council of Corporations. Some people, being ahead of time, have already talked about the end of the present Chamber of Deputies. Let us explain. The present Chamber of Deputies, when this legislative session is over, must be dissolved. Then, since there is not enough time in these months to create the new corporative institutions, the new Chamber will be selected in the same manner as in 1929. But some time or other the Chamber must decide its own destiny. Are there Fascists running around crying over this prospect? In any case they know we shall not dry their tears.

It is perfectly conceivable that a National Council of Corporations might replace the present Chamber of Deputies *in toto.* I have never liked the Chamber of Deputies. At bottom this Chamber of Deputies is an anachronism, even in its name. It is an institution that we found and that is foreign to our Fascist mentality and feelings. The Chamber presupposes a world we have destroyed; presupposes several parties which often and gladly rock the boat. On the day when we destroyed the other parties, the Chamber of Deputies lost its significance. Almost without exception our Fascist Deputies have been men of the highest calibre, and we must remember that they must have had very healthy blood indeed not to have succumbed to melancholy, breathing that atmosphere of the past. All this will come presently, but we need not rush it. It is important to establish the principle, because inevitable consequences follow from it.

On January 13, 1923, when the Grand Council was created, superficial thinkers may have thought, only one more institute. On the contrary. On that day we buried political liberalism. With the Militia, the armed guard of the Party and the Revolution, with the establishment of the Grand Council, the supreme organ of the Revolution, we dealt the death-blow to the whole theory and practice of liberalism; we definitely set out on the road of revolution.

Today we are burying economic liberalism. The corporation will function on economic ground as the Grand Council and the Militia function on political ground. Corporatism is economics disciplined and therefore controlled, for discipline without control is unthinkable. Corporatism supersedes socialism and supersedes liberalism; it creates a new synthesis.

One fact is symptomatic — a fact we have perhaps thought too little about: that the decline of capitalism coincides with the decline of socialism. All the socialist parties in Europe are in fragments. I am not speaking only of Italy and Germany, but also of the other countries. Evidently these two phenomena — I do not claim that they are necessarily connected logically — were nevertheless historically simultaneous. This is why the corporative economy takes its rise at the very juncture in history when those two concurrent phenomena, capitalism and socialism, have given all they can give. From each we inherit what was vital in it. We have rejected the theory of the economic man, the liberal theory, and we go up in the air every time we hear anybody talk of labor as a commodity. The economic man does not exist; the whole man exists, being political, economic, and religious, saint and soldier.

Today we are taking a decisive new step in the path of the Revolution. Justly did Deputy Tassinari say that in order for a revolution to be great, to make a profound impression in the lives of the people, it must be social. If you look deeply, you will see that the French Revolution was eminently social in that it demolished all that was left of the Middle Ages from road tolls to *"corvées"*; social in that it provoked a vast change of the whole feudal system in France and created those millions of landowners who have been and are the sane and solid strength of that country. Otherwise anybody could think he had made a revolution. Revolution is a serious matter, not just a palace conspiracy, and still less merely a change of Ministries or the victory of one party over another. It is laughable to read that there was a revolution in 1876 when the Left came into power.

Finally we must ask ourselves this question: Can Corporatism be applied in other countries? We must ask this question because it will be raised in all the other countries where people study and make an effort to understand us. There is no doubt that, given the general crisis of capitalism, some of the solutions of Corporatism will become imperative everywhere. But to carry on a complete, full, integral, revolutionary Corporatism three conditions are necessary. A single party which flanks economic discipline with political discipline and which is over and above conflicting interests, binding all together in a common faith. This is not enough. After a single party you have to have a totalitarian state, that is, a state that absorbs within itself, in order to transform and invigorate them, all the energy, all the interests, all the hopes of a people. This is still not enough. The third and last and most important condition: there must be a time of the highest moral vigor.

We live in this time of high moral vigor. This is why, step by step, we give strength and consistency to all our dreams, translating all our doctrine into fact. How can it be denied that this our Fascist period is one of the highest moral vigor? Nobody can deny it. These are the times when arms have been crowned with victory, when human institutions are being regenerated, when lands are being redeemed and cities founded.

— *By Benito Mussolini, Italian (1883–1945). Address to the General Assembly of the National Council of Corporations, November 14, 1933.*

~ ✿ ~

In the Name of the People

FRANKLIN DELANO ROOSEVELT

THIS is a day of national consecration, and I am certain that my fellow Americans expect that on my induction into the Presidency I will address them with a candor and a decision which the present situation of our people impels. This is pre-eminently the time to speak the truth, the whole truth, frankly and boldly. Nor need we shrink from honestly facing conditions in our country today. This great nation will endure, as it has endured, and it will revive and will prosper.

So first of all let me assert my firm belief that the only thing we have to fear is fear itself—nameless, unreasoning, unjustified terror, which paralyzes needed effort to convert retreat into triumph.

In every dark hour of our national life leadership of frankness and vigor has met with that understanding and support of the people themselves which is essential to victory, and I am convinced that you will again give that support to leadership in these critical days. In such a spirit we face our common difficulties. They concern, thank God, material things. Values have sunk to fantastic levels; our factories are without orders; taxes have risen; our ability to pay has fallen; government of all kinds is faced by serious curtailment of income; the means of exchange are frozen; the withered leaves of our industrial enterprise lie on every side. Farmers find no markets for their produce, and the savings of many years in thousands of families are gone. More important, a host of unemployed citizens face the grim problem of existence, and an equally great number toil with little return.

Only a foolish optimist can deny the dark realities of the moment. We are stricken by no plague of locusts compared with the perils which our forefathers conquered because they believed and were not afraid. Nature still affords her bounty, but the generous use of it languishes in the very sight of supply. This is primarily because the rulers of the exchange of mankind's goods have failed through their own stubbornness and their own incompetence, have admitted their failure, and have abdicated.

The practices of unscrupulous money-changers stand indicted in the court of public opinion, rejected by the hearts and the minds of men. True, they have tried; but, faced by the failure of credit, they have proposed only lending more money. Stripped of the lure of profit by which to induce our people to follow them they have resorted to exhortations, pleading tearfully for restored confidence. They only know the rules of a generation of self-seekers. They have no vision, and where there is no vision the people perish.

The money-changers having fled from their high seats in the temple of our civilization, we may now restore that temple to the ancient truths. The measure of the restoration lies in the extent to which we apply social values more noble than mere monetary profit. Happiness lies not in the mere possession of money; it lies in the joy of achievement, the thrill of creative effort. The dark days will be worth all they cost if they teach us that our true destiny is not to be ministered unto, but to minister to ourselves and our fellow-men.

Recognition of the falsity of material wealth as the standard of success goes hand in hand with the abandonment of the false belief that public office and high political position are to be valued only by standards of pride of place and personal profit; and there must be an end to a conduct in banking and business that too often has given to a sacred trust the likeness of callous and selfish wrongdoing. But restoration calls not for changes in ethics alone; the nation is asking for action, and action now.

Our greatest primary task is to put the people to work. This is no unsolvable problem if we face it wisely and courageously. It can be accomplished in part by direct recruiting by the Government itself, treating the task as we would an emergency of war; but at the same time we can accomplish greatly needed projects to stimulate and organize the use of our national resources.

Hand in hand with that we must frankly recognize the over-balance of population in industrial centers, and endeavor on a national scale by redistribution to encourage the settlement on the land of those best fitted for the land. The task can be helped by definite efforts to raise the values of agricultural products, thus increasing the power to purchase the output of the cities; by preventing realistically the tragedy of growing loss through foreclosure on small homes and farms; by the unifying of relief activities that to-day are often scattered and uneconomic; by insistence that the Federal, the State and the local governments act forthwith on the demands that their costs be drastically reduced; by national planning for, and supervision of, all forms of transportation, communication and other public utilities. There are many ways by which the task can be helped, but it can never be helped merely by talking about it. We must act and act quickly.

Finally we require two safeguards against a return of the evils of the old order. There must be strict supervision of all banking and credit investments. There must be an end to speculation with other people's money. There must be provision for an adequate but sound currency. These, my friends, are the lines of attack. I shall urge on the new Congress in a special session detailed measures and I shall seek the immediate assistance of the forty-eight states. Through this programme we shall address ourselves to our national task of putting our house in order and of making our income balance our outgoings.

Our international trade relations, though vastly important, are, in point of time and necessity, secondary to the establishment of a sound national economy. I favor as a practical policy the putting of first things first. I shall spare no effort to restore world trade by international economic adjustment, but the emergency at home cannot wait on that accomplishment. In the field of world policy I would dedicate the nation to the policy of the good neighbor, who resolutely respects himself and, because he does so, respects the rights of others; the neighbor who respects obligations and respects the sanctity of his agreements with his neighbors in the world.

If I read the temper of our people correctly we now realize as never before our interdependence on each other, that we cannot merely take, but must give as well; that if we are to go forward we must go as a trained and loyal army willing to accept sacrifices for the sake of common discipline. We are, I know, ready and willing to submit our lives and our property to such discipline, because it makes possible a leadership which aims at the larger good, and because without it no progress can be made and no leadership becomes effective. This leadership I propose to offer with the pledge that its purposes shall be binding upon us all as a sacred obligation, with a united duty heretofore invoked only in times of armed strife. With this pledge taken I assume unhesitatingly the leadership of this great army of our people in action dedicated to a disciplined attack upon our main difficulties. This image is feasible under the form of government we have inherited from our ancestors.

Our Constitution is so simple, so practical, that it is possible always to meet extraordinary needs by changes in emphasis and arrangement without loss of essential form. That is why our constitutional system has proved itself the most superbly enduring political mechanism the world has ever seen. It has met every stress of a vast expansion of territory, of foreign wars, of bitter international strife, of world difficulties, and it is fully adequate to meet the unprecedented issues before us.

It is to be hoped that the normal balance of the Executive and Legislative authority may be adequate to meet the task, but it may be that the unprecedented situation and the need for undelayed action may call for a temporary departure. I am prepared to recommend measures that a stricken nation may require. These measures, or such other measures as Congress out of its experience and wisdom may build, I shall seek within my constitutional authority to bring to speedy adoption.

But in the event that Congress shall fail to take one or other of these courses, and in the event of a critical national emergency, I shall not evade the clear course of duty. I shall ask Congress for the one remaining instrument to meet such a crisis — namely, a broad executive power to wage war against the emergency as great as the power that would be given to me if we were in fact invaded by a foreign foe.

We do not mistrust the future of essential democracy. The people of the United States have not failed. In their need they have registered a mandate that they want vigorous action. For the trust reposed in me I will return the courage and devotion that befit the time. We face the arduous days that lie before us in the warm courage of national unity, with the clear satisfaction that comes from the stern performance of duty by old and young alike. We may add the assurance of a rounded and permanent national life. Our people have asked for discipline and direction in leadership. They have made me the present instrument of their wishes. In the spirit of the gift I take it. In this dedication, in this dedication of a nation, we humbly ask the blessing of God. May He protect each and every one of us. May He guide me in the days to come.

— *From the inaugural address, March 4, 1933, of Franklin Delano Roosevelt, American (1882–1945).*

Dunkirk

WINSTON CHURCHILL

FROM the moment that the French defenses at Sedan and on the Meuse were broken at the end of the second week of May, only a rapid retreat to Amiens and the south could have saved the British and French Armies who had entered Belgium at the appeal of the Belgian King; but this strategic fact was not immediately realized. The French High Command hoped they would be able to close the gap, and the Armies of the north were under their orders. Moreover, a retirement of this kind would have involved almost certainly the destruction of the fine Belgian Army of over 20 divisions and the abandonment of the whole of Belgium. Therefore, when the force and scope of the German penetration were realized and when a new French Generalissimo, General Weygand, assumed command in place of General Gamelin, an effort was made by the French and British Armies in Belgium to keep on holding the right hand of the Belgians and to give their own right hand to a newly created French Army which was to have advanced across the Somme in great strength to grasp it.

However, the German eruption swept like a sharp scythe around the right and rear of the Armies of the north. Eight or nine armored divisions, each of about four hundred armored vehicles of different kinds, but carefully assorted to be complementary and divisible into small self-contained units, cut off all communications between us and the main French Armies. It severed our own communications for food and ammunition, which ran first to Amiens and afterwards through Abbeville, and it shore its way up the coast to Boulogne and Calais, and almost to Dunkirk. Behind this armored and mechanized onslaught came a number of German divisions in lorries, and behind them again plodded comparatively slowly the dull brute mass of the ordinary German Army and German people, always so ready to be led to the trampling down in other lands of liberties and comforts which they have never known in their own.

I have said this armored scythe-stroke almost reached Dunkirk — almost but not quite. Boulogne and Calais were the scenes of desperate fighting. The Guards defended Boulogne for a while and were then withdrawn by orders from this country. The Rifle Brigade, the 60th Rifles, and the Queen Victoria's Rifles, with a battalion of British tanks and 1,000 Frenchmen, in all about four thousand strong, defended Calais to the last. The British Brigadier was given an hour to surrender. He spurned the offer, and four days of intense street fighting passed before silence reigned over Calais, which marked the end of a memorable resistance. Only 30 unwounded survivors were brought off by the Navy, and we do not know the fate of their comrades. Their sacrifice, however, was not in vain. At least two armored divisions, which otherwise would have been turned against the British Expeditionary Force, had to be sent to overcome them. They have added another page to the glories of the light divisions, and the time gained enabled the Graveline water lines to be flooded and to be held by the French troops.

Thus it was that the port of Dunkirk was kept open. When it was found impossible for the Armies of the north to reopen their communications to Amiens with the main French Armies, only one choice remained. It seemed, indeed, forlorn. The Belgian, British and French Armies were almost surrounded. Their sole line of retreat was to a single port and to its neighboring beaches. They were pressed on every side by heavy attacks and far outnumbered in the air.

When, a week ago today, I asked the House to fix this afternoon as the occasion for a statement, I feared it would be my hard lot to announce the greatest military disaster in our long history. I thought — and some good judges agreed with me — that perhaps 20,000 or 30,000 men might be reembarked. But it certainly seemed that the whole of the French First Army and the whole of the British Expeditionary Force north of the Amiens-Abbeville gap would be broken up in the open field or else would have to capitulate for lack of food and ammunition. These were the hard and heavy tidings for which I called upon the House and the nation to prepare themselves a week ago. The whole root and core and brain of the British Army, on which and around which we were to build, and are to build, the great British Armies in the later years of the war, seemed about to perish upon the field or to be led into an ignominious and starving captivity.

That was the prospect a week ago. But another blow which might well have proved final was yet to fall upon us. The King of the Belgians had called upon us to come to his aid. Had not this Ruler and his Government severed themselves from the Allies, who rescued their country from extinction in the late war, and had they not sought refuge in what has proved to be a fatal neutrality, the French and British Armies might well at the outset have saved not only Belgium but perhaps even Poland. Yet at the last moment, when Belgium was already invaded, King Leopold called upon us to come to his aid, and even at the last moment we came. He and his brave, efficient Army, nearly half a million strong, guarded our left flank and thus kept open our only line of retreat to the sea. Suddenly, without prior consultation, with the least possible notice, without the advice of his Ministers and upon his own personal act, he sent a plenipotentiary to the German Command, surrendered his Army, and exposed our whole flank and means of retreat.

I asked the House a week ago to suspend its judgment because the facts were not clear, but I do not feel that any reason now exists why we should not form our own opinions upon this pitiful episode. The surrender of the Belgian Army compelled the British at the shortest notice to cover a flank to the sea more than 30 miles in length. Otherwise all would have been cut off, and all would have shared the fate to which King Leopold had condemned the finest Army his country had ever formed. So in doing this and in exposing his flank, as anyone who followed the operations on the map will see, contact was lost between the British and two out of the three corps forming the First French Army, who were still farther from the coast than we were, and it seemed impossible that any large number of Allied troops could reach the coast.

The enemy attacked on all sides with great strength and fierceness, and their main power, the power of their far more numerous Air Force, was thrown into the battle or else concentrated upon Dunkirk and the beaches. Pressing in upon the narrow exit, both from the east and from the west, the enemy began to fire with cannon upon the beaches by which alone the shipping could approach or depart. They sowed magnetic mines in the channels and seas; they sent repeated waves of hostile aircraft, sometimes more than a hundred strong in one formation, to cast their bombs upon the single pier that remained and upon the sand dunes upon which the troops had their eyes for shelter. Their U-boats, one of which was sunk, and their motor launches took their toll of the vast traffic which now began. For four or five days an intense struggle reigned. All their armored divisions – or what was left of them – together with great masses of infantry and artillery, hurled themselves in vain upon the ever-narrowing, ever-contracting appendix within which the British and French Armies fought.

Meanwhile, the Royal Navy, with the willing help of countless merchant seamen, strained every nerve to embark the British and Allied troops; 220 light warships and 650 other vessels were engaged. They had to operate upon the difficult coast, often in adverse weather, under an almost ceaseless hail of bombs and an increasing concentration of artillery fire. Nor were the seas, as I have said, themselves free from mines and torpedoes. It was in conditions such as these that our men carried on, with little or no rest, for days and nights on end, making trip after trip across the dangerous waters, bringing with them always men whom they had rescued. The numbers they have brought back are the measure of their devotion and their courage. The hospital ships, which brought off many thousands of British and French wounded, being so plainly marked were a special target for Nazi bombs; but the men and women on board them never faltered in their duty.

Meanwhile, the Royal Air Force, which had already been intervening in the battle, so far as its range would allow, from home bases, now used part of its main metropolitan fighter strength, and struck at the German bombers and at the fighters which in large numbers protected them. This struggle was protracted and fierce. Suddenly the scene cleared, the crash and thunder has for the moment – but only for the moment – died away. A miracle of deliverance, achieved by valor, by perseverance, by perfect discipline, by faultless service, by resource, by skill, by unconquerable fidelity, is manifest to us all. The enemy was hurled back by the retreating British and French troops. He was so roughly handled that he did not hurry their departure seriously. The

Royal Air Force engaged the main strength of the German Air Force, and inflicted upon them losses of at least four to one; and the Navy, using nearly 1,000 ships of all kinds, carried over 335,000 men, French and British, out of the jaws of death and shame, to their native land and to the tasks which lie immediately ahead. We must be very careful not to assign to this deliverance the attributes of a victory. Wars are not won by evacuations. But there was a victory inside this deliverance, which should be noted. It was gained by the Air Force. Many of our soldiers coming back have not seen the Air Force at work; they saw only the bombers which escaped its protective attack. They underrate its achievements. I have heard much talk of this; that is why I go out of my way to say this. I will tell you about it.

This was a great trial of strength between the British and German Air Forces. Can you conceive a greater objective for the Germans in the air than to make evacuation from these beaches impossible, and to sink all these ships which were displayed, almost to the extent of thousands? Could there have been an objective of greater military importance and significance for the whole purpose of the war than this? They tried hard, and they were beaten back; they were frustrated in their task. We got the Army away; and they have paid fourfold for any losses which they have inflicted. Very large formations of German aeroplanes — and we know that they are a very brave race — have turned on several occasions from the attack of one-quarter of their number of the Royal Air Force, and have dispersed in different directions. Twelve aeroplanes have been hunted by two. One aeroplane was driven into the water and cast away by the mere charge of a British aeroplane, which had no more ammunition. All of our types — the Hurricane, the Spitfire and the new Defiant — and all our pilots have been vindicated as superior to what they have at present to face.

When we consider how much greater would be our advantage in defending the air above this Island against an overseas attack, I must say that I find in these facts a sure basis upon which practical and reassuring thought may rest. I will pay my tribute to these young airmen. The great French Army was very largely, for the time being, cast back and disturbed by the onrush of a few thousands of armored vehicles. May it not also be that the cause of civilization itself will be defended by the skill and devotion of a few thousand airmen? There never has been, I suppose, in all the world, in all the history of war, such an opportunity for youth. The Knights of the Round Table, the Crusaders, all fall back into the past — not only distant but prosaic; these young men, going forth every morn to guard their native land and all that we stand for, holding in their hands these instruments of colossal and shattering power, of whom it may be said that

"Every morn brought forth a noble chance
And every chance brought forth a noble
knight,"

deserve our gratitude, as do all of the brave men who, in so many ways and on so many occasions, are ready, and continue ready, to give life and all for their native land.

I return to the Army. In the long series of very fierce battles, now on this front, now on that, fighting on three fronts at once, battles fought by two or three divisions against an equal or somewhat larger number of the enemy, and fought fiercely on some of the old grounds that so many of us knew so well — in these battles our losses in men have exceeded 30,000 killed, wounded and missing. I take occasion to express the sympathy of the House to all who have suffered bereavement or who are still anxious. The President of the Board of Trade is not here today. His son has been killed, and many in the House have felt the pangs of affliction in the sharpest form. But I will say this about the missing: We have had a large number of wounded come home safely to this country, but I would say about the missing that there may be very many reported missing who will come back home, some day, in one way or another. In the confusion of this fight it is inevitable that many have been left in positions where honor required no further resistance from them.

Against this loss of over 30,000 men, we can set a far heavier loss certainly inflicted upon the enemy. But our losses in material are enormous. We have perhaps lost one-third of the men we lost in the opening days of the battle of 21st March, 1918, but we have lost nearly as many guns — nearly one thousand — and all our transport, all the armored vehicles that were with the Army in the north. This loss will impose a further delay on the expansion of our military strength. That expansion had not been proceeding as fast as we had hoped. The best of all we had to give had gone to the British Expeditionary Force, and although they had not the numbers of tanks and some articles of equipment which were desirable, they were a very well and finely equipped Army. They had the first-fruits of all that our industry had to give, and that is gone. And now here is this further delay. How long it will be, how long it will last, depends upon the exertions which we make in this Island. An effort the like of which has never been seen in our records is now being made. Work is proceeding everywhere, night and day, Sundays and week days. Capital and Labor have cast aside their interests, rights, and customs and put them into the common stock. Already the flow of munitions has leaped forward. There is no reason why we should not in a few months overtake the sudden and serious loss that has come upon us, without retarding the development of our general program.

Nevertheless, our thankfulness at the escape of our Army and so many men, whose loved ones have passed through an agonizing week, must not blind us to the fact that what has happened in France and Belgium is a colossal military disaster. The French Army has been weakened, the Belgian Army has been lost, a large part of those fortified lines upon which so much faith had been reposed is gone, many valuable mining districts and factories have passed into the enemy's possession, the whole of the Channel ports are in his hands, with all the tragic consequences that follow from that, and we must expect another blow to be struck almost immediately at us or at France. We are told that Herr Hitler has a plan for invading the British Isles. This has often been thought of before. When Napoleon lay at Boulogne for a year with his flat-bottomed boats and his Grand Army, he was told by someone, "There are bitter weeds in England." There are certainly a great many more of them since the British Expeditionary Force returned.

The whole question of home defense against invasion is, of course, powerfully affected by the fact that we have for the time being in this Island incomparably more powerful military forces than we have ever had at any moment in this war or the last. But this will not continue. We shall not be content with a defensive war. We have our duty to our Ally. We have to reconstitute and build up the British Expeditionary Force once again, under its gallant Commander-in-Chief, Lord Gort. All this is in train; but in the interval we must put our defenses in this Island into such a high state of organization that the fewest possible numbers will be required to give effective security and that the largest possible potential of offensive effort may be realized. On this we are now engaged. It will be very convenient, if it be the desire of the House, to enter upon this subject in a secret Session. Not that the Government would necessarily be able to reveal in very great detail military secrets, but we like to have our discussions free, without the restraint imposed by the fact that they will be read the next day by the enemy; and the Government would benefit by views freely expressed in all parts of the House by Members with their knowledge of so many different parts of the country. I understand that some request is to be made upon this subject, which will be readily acceded to by His Majesty's Government.

We have found it necessary to take measures of increasing stringency, not only against enemy aliens and suspicious characters of other nationalities, but also against British subjects who may become a danger or a nuisance should the war be transported to the United Kingdom. I know there are a great many people affected by the orders which we have made who are the passionate enemies of Nazi Germany. I am very sorry for them, but we cannot, at the present time and under the present stress, draw all the distinctions which we should like to do. If parachute landings were attempted and fierce fighting attendant upon them followed, these unfortunate people would be far better out of the way, for their own sakes as well as for ours. There is, however, another class, for which I feel not the slightest sympathy. Parliament has given us the powers to put down Fifth Column activities with a strong hand, and we shall use those powers, subject to the supervision and correction of the House, without the slightest hesitation until we are satisfied, and more than satisfied, that this malignancy in our midst has been effectively stamped out.

Turning once again, and this time more

generally, to the question of invasion, I would observe that there has never been a period in all these long centuries of which we boast when an absolute guarantee against invasion, still less against serious raids, could have been given to our people. In the days of Napoleon the same wind which would have carried his transports across the Channel might have driven away the blockading fleet. There was always the chance, and it is that chance which has excited and befooled the imaginations of many Continental tyrants. Many are the tales that are told. We are assured that novel methods will be adopted, and when we see the originality of malice, the ingenuity of aggression, which our enemy displays, we may certainly prepare ourselves for every kind of novel stratagem and every kind of brutal and treacherous maneuver. I think that no idea is so outlandish that it should not be considered and viewed with a searching, but at the same time, I hope, with a steady eye. We must never forget the solid assurances of sea power and those which belong to air power if it can be locally exercised.

I have myself, full confidence that if all do their duty, if nothing is neglected, and if the best arrangements are made, as they are being made, we shall prove ourselves once again able to defend our Island home, to ride out the storm of war, and to outlive the menace of tyranny, if necessary for years, if necessary alone. At any rate, that is what we are going to try to do. That is the resolve of His Majesty's Government—every man of them. That is the will of Parliament and the nation. The British Empire and the French Republic, linked together in their cause and in their need, will defend to the death their native soil, aiding each other like good comrades to the utmost of their strength. Even though large tracts of Europe and many old and famous States have fallen or may fall into the grip of the Gestapo and all the odious apparatus of Nazi rule, we shall not flag or fail. We shall go on to the end, we shall fight in France, we shall fight on the seas and oceans, we shall fight with growing confidence and growing strength in the air, we shall defend our Island, whatever the cost may be, we shall fight on the beaches, we shall fight on the landing grounds, we shall fight in the fields and in the streets, we shall fight in the hills; we shall never surrender, and even if, which I do not for a moment believe, this Island or a large part of it were subjugated and starving, then our Empire beyond the seas, armed and guarded by the British Fleet, would carry on the struggle, until, in God's good time, the New World, with all its power and might, steps forth to the rescue and the liberation of the old.

—*Address to the House of Commons, June 4, 1940 by Winston Churchill, English (1874–).*

PART TWENTY-FIVE

Man at Work

NEITHER LOFTY THOUGHT, political rivalry, nor social recreations consume the greater part of human energy. In our world all but the drones feel, to use Shakespeare's phrase, "the penalty of Adam." In less poetic language, men are toilers. We must labor to feed, clothe and sustain ourselves against the obstacles of a "stepmother nature." Work is nature's discipline, which, if properly observed, results in physical and mental well being. To be more explicit, it may either decline to brutal slavery or be refined to an austere pleasure. But whatever aspect labor takes, both natural and social law requires that man labor for his bread and that this labor become the daily rule of his existence.

Although the arts are our most refined recreations, they necessarily feel the pressure of this laborious world. As image of life, art becomes also the mirror of our toil. It is not enough that it should report our social diversions, personal ecstasies or winged dreams. A sane and healthy art is also dedicated to the story of man as a worker: to the celebration of his proud achievements, to the tragedy of his brute oppressions, and to whatever incidental delights flower along his hard path. Men sing at their work to lighten the burden or deal critically with the problems which their labor raises. Here is, in fact, one of the oldest functions of literature. If it has occasionally been slighted in slothful or decadent times, this in no way invalidates the truth that as a spiritual function of man it is coeternal with him and worthy of his lasting regard.

While all primitive poetry and all literary remains contain specimens of such art, it suffices here to begin with three substantial quotations giving a rounded picture of the heritage left us by the earliest European civilizations. These notable pages constitute a triangulation of the ancient mind, showing its sturdy foundations and its ripest developments in a humanistic philosophy and an aesthetic culture.

Hesiod, virtually contemporary with Homer, is a poet of the seventh century B.C. who wrote didactic verse in an epic style. Most beloved of his poems by the ancient world was his "Works and Days." The entire piece sketches the fundamentals of labor in an agrarian culture. It falls into three parts, of which the first is introductory and the last, dealing with "days," is a farmer's almanac or calendar. The core of the poem is Book Two, from which selections are taken here. Hesiod's book of over twenty-five hundred years ago for the most part proves as lucid and vigorous as it was when composed. It reveals a people clear of head and strong of hand engaged in peaceful labors, proud of their toil and appreciative of its fruits. On such a firm basis was built the first historically important culture of Europe. Hesiod's poetry has the energy and primitivism of all the earliest Greek art.

Over six centuries later the Roman poet Lucretius synthesized the philosophy of worldliness which Hesiod put into such homely practice. It is the thesis of the *De Rerum Natura,* or poem on the nature of things, that mankind should depend only upon himself, his own intelligence and his knowledge of nature's laws. Lucretius repudiates supernatural religion, holding that man has no contact with the gods and the gods no concern for man, that death is absolute and the hereafter an erroneous and, indeed, a pernicious fable. Knowing little or nothing of the beginning or the end of the world, man should not concern himself with them, but with the practical problems of his present days. Whatever glory man earns, Lucretius believes to be man's own. Following this line of thought, in an important section of his poem, quoted without abridgement here, he traces human progress from brutishness to civilization, always emphasizing the ingenuity and labor which have earned us our hard won gains. The theme is, indeed, a common one in classical literature, since all the ancients still felt themselves close to the first major achievements of mankind and correspondingly gloried in their rise from barbarism. Aeschylus, for example, so treats the myth of Prometheus, the giver of fire and all inventions to man, and Sophocles sees in the founding of Athens the establishment of the practical arts. The philosophy of Lucretius, however, best summarizes the long-practiced dialectical materialism of the ancient world.

Only a generation after Lucretius, Virgil represents in his verse the highest organization and refinement of which the Latin world was to prove capable. In his martial epic, the *Aeneid,* he followed Homer, the poet of war; in his *Eclogues* he followed the purely recreative verses of Theocritus; while in his *Georgics* he gave the refined Roman version of the primitive Hesiod. The *Georgics,* then, represent the solid, agrarian foundations of the Roman economy. With Roman genius for organization, Virgil's work describes in four books agriculture, arboriculture, animal husbandry and bee culture. So closely does he follow Hesiod in many passages of his own first book, that to quote the two authors together would lead often to mere repetition. The fourth book, however, marks most clearly the progress between the first and the last creative stages of ancient civilization. The strenuousness of Hesiod has departed, giving place in Virgil to the celebration of lighter toils relieved by intelligence and yielding the taste of honey. Hesiod depicts the peasant farmer, Virgil the gentleman farmer. Nothing is decadent in Virgil's book. He promulgates the soundest rules for the raising of vegetables, fruits, animals and bees. But he describes man, as Lucretius also celebrates him, as the happy master of nature, living peacefully and in a high state of refinement, with classical balance extracting delight from toil and relieving toil by delight.

Here, then, lies the three-fold heritage of the enlightened classical world, in its sane foundations, its speculative principles, and its cultural refinements. Although didactic verse in imitation of Virgil has been produced almost continuously throughout the Christian era, and the essential meaning of Lucretius and even of Hesiod was not lost upon the Renaissance, the relatively static nature of argrarian culture and the very gradual advances of commercialism begot no vital changes in this sphere of literature for many centuries. There is no real evolution. The English eighteenth-century poet James Thomson, for example, is considerably closer to Virgil than Virgil to Hesiod. Songs and poems of labor are numerous but not as a whole fresh or remarkable until the entire character of man's life undergoes through the industrial revolution a change at least as great as that from the earliest known modes of life to the dawn of Greek civilization as evinced by Hesiod and Homer. Suddenly we find a new vitality and meaning in the type of poetry which Hesiod, Lucretius and even Virgil produced. In this respect we live in an age which may not too fancifully be denominated the second coming of Prometheus. Far more astonishing than ever and more stimulating to the imagination are the new engines which we produce. Moreover, the grave human problems created by the rise of new machines and a new laboring class constitute the chief social issues of our day. The conception of progress, which from Lucretius to Darwin tended to lapse into disuse, rises with vastly increased force. Vital poetry cannot help reflecting these changes; it cannot escape its obligations of supplying vision and inspiration to man as he faces this new world.

From both Europe and America we have selected for this section of our book a few poems epitomizing the continuity between the ancient, agrarian world and our own times. Harvest songs from the Germany of Ludwig Hölty, from the Provençe of Frédéric Mistral, and from South America, hint at the subtle changes passing over the agrarian world even without more than the barest prophetic touch with the new era. Whittier in North America turned toward the laborer with deep and most commendable concern but without serious understanding of his approaching problems. More recently the awareness of the importance of tools by the conservative pastoral poet, Robert Frost, though his tools are relatively old fashioned, shows an approach to the new mind even in orthodox literary forms.

The full consciousness of the machine world and its meanings for human labor and life shows to best advantage in the recent literature of Belgium, Russia, England and America. The great Belgian poet Verhaeren, writing in French, but often with a Teutonic mysticism, possessed an imagination profoundly haunted by the machine and its workmen. His crepuscular art is charged with a spiritual apprehensiveness, like the gray of twilight before dawn. This dawn breaks most luridly over Russia, a land desperately endeavoring at once to industrialize itself at a forced pace, and to solve the human problems implicit in all industrialization. Unhappily the German spirit has recently proved weaker than the powerful German hand, with the result that no literary or poetic expression of the machine age has issued from its authors in any way comparable to the genius shown in its industries themselves. English poets grapple more effectively with the issues involved, as may be seen by selections from the work of Stephen Spender and Day-Lewis.

In America, a land singularly proud of its tools and machines, there exists a vigorous tradition nearly a century old. The pride of the pioneers who conquered the forests and prairies, and of the men who first laid a network of railroads across a great continent, found ideal expression in Walt Whitman. His *Song of the Broad Axe* attests his insight into new works and days. Nevertheless Whitman understood outdoor labor much better than factory labor, which is more representative of the present age. It must not be forgotten that his mind was oriented at least a hundred years ago. He wrote, in other words, of the broad axe of the pioneer and of the old fashioned ferry-boat. Thus Hart Crane in his *The Bridge* more clearly envisages the new-world problems affecting nerves, mind and moral consciousness. In his chief poem he fancies himself, as he crosses Brooklyn Bridge, meditating on Whitman, who had celebrated the primitive ferry over the same stream. He querulously asks how Whitman's "open road" has changed through such inventions as the airplane. In the part of Crane's poem given here he writes of the menacing progress in naval and air warfare. He pries into the very nerve-center of this sudden and unpredictable advance: the great electric dynamo. But Crane is hardly more than a sensitive and amazed child, now terrified and now exalted by the strange, new scene. More truly at home in this world, more widely informed of it and more imaginatively in command of it, is such a representative American poet as Carl Sandburg, likewise, as previously observed, an heir of Whitman. In such pieces as *Smoke and Steel,* too long for inclusion here, and in his still longer work, *The People, Yes,* Sandburg gives powerful images of labor, the products of labor and the hopes of labor which comprise the very heart of our contemporary world. Such a poet as Sandburg may, then, be described as heir not only of Whitman but of Hesiod, Lucretius and Virgil. Here the oldest and the newest ways meet as if in a circle, and in their meeting infallibly lead toward new visions of mankind.

Works and Days

HESIOD

When, Atlas-born, the Pleiad stars arise
Before the sun above the dawning skies,
'Tis time to reap; and when at sunrise now
They sink beneath the west, 'tis time to
 plough.
Know too they set, immerged into the sun,
While forty days entire their circle run,
And with the lapse of the revolving year,
When sharpen'd is the sickle, reappear.
Law of the fields, and known to every swain,
Who turns the fallow soil beside the main;
Or who, remote from billowy ocean's gales,
Tills the rich glebe of inland-winding vales.
 Sow naked, husbandman! and naked
 plough,
And naked reap, if, timely to thy vow,
Thou wouldst that Ceres load thy harvest
 field,
And fruits their increase, each in season,
 yield;
Lest thou to strangers' doors, a beggar, trail
Thy steps, with longing need, and nought
 prevail;
E'en as to me thou camest: but hope no
 more
That I shall give, or lend thee of my store.
O foolish Perses! be the labors thine,
Which the good gods to earthly man assign;
Lest with thy spouse, thy babes, thou food
 demand,
And meet denial at each neighbor's hand:
If twice, nay thrice, thou speed, the grievous
 pray'r
Will fail at last, and all thy words are air.
I bid thee muse on what concerns thy peace,
Escape from hunger, and from debt release.
 A house, a ploughing steer, a maid be
 thine,
Not wife, but purchased slave, to tend thy
 kine.
Within, let all fit implements abound,
Lest with refused intreaty wandering round
Thy wants still press, the season glide away,
And thou with scanted labor mourn the day.
Thy task defer not till the morn arise,
Or the third sun th' unfinish'd work surprise.
The sluggish man shall ne'er his garner fill,
Nor he that still delays, and lingers still;
Zeal speeds the work; the loiterer at his cost
Wrestles with damage, and his pains are
 lost. . . .
 Mark yearly when among the clouds on
 high
Thou hear'st the shrill crane's migratory cry;
Of ploughing-time the sign and wintry rains:
Care gnaws his heart who destitute remains
Of the fit yoke; for then the season falls
To feed thy horned steers within their stalls.
Easy to speak the word, "Beseech thee,
 friend!
Thy waggon and thy yoke of oxen lend:"
Easy the prompt refusal; "Nay, but I
Have need of oxen, and their work is nigh."
Rich in his own conceit, he then, too late,

May think to rear the waggon's timber'd weight;
Fool! nor yet knows the complicated frame
A hundred season'd blocks may fitly claim;
These let thy timely care provide before,
And pile beneath thy roof the ready store.
Improve the season: to the plough apply
Both thou and thine, and toil in wet and dry:
Haste to the field with break of glimmering morn,
That so thy grounds may wave with thickening corn.
In spring upturn the glebe; nor spare the toil
In summer days to break afresh the soil:
It shall not mock thy hopes: then freely sow
The fallow field, whilst light the mould below:
The fallow field bids mutter'd curses flee,
And gathers happy children round thy knee.
Jove subterrene, chaste Ceres claim thy vow,
When grasping first the handle of thy plough,
O'er thy broad oxen's backs thy quickening hand
With lifted stroke lets fall the goading wand;
Whilst, yoked and harness'd by the fastening thong,
They slowly drag the draught-pole's length along:
So shall the sacred gifts of earth appear,
And ripe luxuriance clothe the plenteous ear.
A boy should tread thy steps, with rake o'erlay
The buried seed, and scare the birds away:
(Good is the apt economy of things,
While evil management its mischief brings:)
So, if aërial Jove thy cares befriend,
And crown thy tillage with a prosperous end,
Shall the rich ear in fulness of its grain
Nod on the stalk, and bend it to the plain.
So shalt thou sweep the spider's films away,
That round thy hollow bins lie hid from day;
I ween, rejoicing in the foodful stores
Obtain'd at last, and laid within thy doors;
For plenteousness shall glad thee through the year,
Till the white blossoms of the spring appear:
Nor thou on other's heaps a gazer be;
But others owe their borrow'd store to thee. . . .
Beware the January month: beware
Those hurtful days, that keenly piercing air
Which flays the steers; when wide o'er fell and flood
Ice in its curdled masses nips the blood.
From Thracia, nurse of steeds, comes rushing forth,
O'er the broad sea, the whirlwind of the north,
And moves it with his breath; earth roars through all
Its woodlands; oaks of towering foliage fall,
And thick branch'd pines, as in his fitful swell
He sweeps the hollows of the mountain dell:
He stoops to earth; the crash is heard around,
The boundless forest rolls the roar of sound.
Now shrink the beasts, and shuddering as they run,
The gust, low crouch'd, with cowering bodies, shun.
Thick is the hairy coat, the shaggy skin,
But that all-chilling breath shall pierce within:
Not his rough hide can then the ox avail;
The long-hair'd goat defenceless feels the gale:
Yet vain the north wind's rushing strength to wound
The flock, with thickening fleeces fenced around.
The old man bends him double in the blast,
Whose harmless breath the tender virgin pass'd:
Home-keeping she with her own mother dwells,
Yet innocent of Venus' golden spells,
And bathing her soft limbs, and with smooth balm
Anointing, in the shelter and the calm
Of that her secret chamber, nightly so
Seeks her safe couch, while wintry tempests blow.
Now gnaws the boneless polypus his feet,
Starved midst bleak rocks, his desolate retreat:
For now no more the sun's refracted ray
Through seas transparent lights him to his prey;
O'er the swarth Ethiop rolls his bright career,
And slowly gilds the Grecian hemisphere.
And now the horn'd and unhorn'd kind,
Whose lair is in the wood, sore famish'd grind
Their sounding jaws, and frozen and quaking fly

Where oaks the mountain dells imbranch on high;
They seek to couch in thickets of the glen,
Or lurk deep shelter'd in the rocky den.
Like aged men, who, propp'd on crutches, tread
Tottering with broken strength and stooping head,
So move the beasts of earth, and creeping low,
Shun the white flakes, and dread the drifting snow.
 I warn thee now the season's rigor meet
With soft-napp'd cloak, and tunic to the feet;
Wrap in the cloak thy body, tempest-proof,
If on scant warp thou weave a plenteous woof;
Lest o'er thy every limb each bristling hair
Should rouse and shiver to the searching air.
Shoes from the hide of a blow-slaughter'd ox
Bind round thy feet, lined thick with woollen socks;
And kid-skins with the bull's tough sinew sew,
And 'gainst the rain-storm o'er thy shoulders throw;
Upon thy head a cap close-felted wear,
Lest thine ears trickle from the drizzling air.
 Bleak is the morn, when blows the north from high;
Oft when the dawnlight paints the starry sky,
A misty cloud suspended hovers o'er
Heaven's bless'd earth, and wafts its wheaten store,
Drain'd from the living streams: aloft in air
The whirling winds the buoyant vapor bear,
Resolved at eve in rain or gusty cold,
As by the north the troubled rack is roll'd.
Preventing this, the labor of the day
Accomplish'd, homeward bend thy hastening way,
Lest the dark cloud, with whelming rush depress'd,
Drench thy chill'd limbs, and soak thy dripping vest.
This winter month with prudent caution fear,
Severe to flocks, nor less to men severe:
Feed thy keen husbandman with larger bread;
With half their provender thy steers be fed:
Them rest assists; the night's protracted length
Recruits their vigor, and supplies their strength.
This rule observe, while still the various earth
Gives every fruit and kindly seedling birth:
Still to the toil proportionate the cheer,
The day to night, and equalize the year.
 When from the wintry tropic of the sun
Full sixty days their finish'd round have run,
Lo! then the sacred deep Arcturus leave,
First whole apparent on the verge of eve.
Through the grey dawn the swallow lifts her wing,
Morn-plaining bird, the harbinger of spring.
Anticipate the time: the care be thine
An earlier day to prune the shooting vine.
When the house-bearing snail is slowly found
To shun the Pleiad heats that scorch the ground,
And climb the plant's tall stem, insist no more
To dress the vine, but give the vineyard o'er.
Whet the keen sickle, hasten every swain,
From shady booths, from morning sleep refrain;
Now, in the fervor of the harvest-day,
When the strong sun dissolves the frame away;
Now haste afield; now bind thy sheafy corn,
And earn thy food by rising with the morn.
Lo! the third portion of thy labor's cares
The early morn anticipating shares;
In early morn the labor swiftly wastes;
In early morn the speeded journey hastes;
The time, when many a traveller tracks the plain,
And the yoked oxen bend them to the wain. . . . .
 But if thy breast with nautical desire
The perilous deep's uncertain gains inspire;
When, chased by strong Orion down the heaven,
Sink the seven stars in gloomy ocean driven;
Then varying winds in gustful eddies rave;
Let not a vessel tempt the blackening wave:
But heedful care to this my caution yield,
As, as I bid thee, labor safe the field.
Hale on firm land the ship, with stones made fast
Against the force of humid-blowing blast.
Draw from its keel the peg, lest rotting rain
Suck'd in the hollow of the hold remain:

Within thy house the tackling order'd be,
And furl thy vessel's wings that skimm'd the sea:
The well-framed rudder in the smoke suspend,
And calm and navigable seas attend.
Then launch the rapid bark; fit cargo load;
And freighted rich, repass the liquid road. . . .

When from the summer tropic fifty days
Have roll'd, when summer's time of toil decays,
Then is the season fair to spread the sail,
Nor then thy ship shall founder in the gale;
Nor the deep drown thy men; unless the power
Who shakes the shores have will'd their mortal hour;
Or heaven's eternal king require their breath,
Whose hands the issues hold of life and death,
Of evil and of good; but now the seas
Are dangerless, and clear the calmy breeze.
But rapidly retrace the homeward way,
Nor the new-wine month wait with rash delay;
The shower of autumn, winter hastening fast,
And the strong breathings of the southern blast,
That, ruffling ocean, drags a rush of rain,
And in impervious billows heaves the main.
Men, too, may sail in spring; when first the crow
Prints her light footsteps on the sands below,
And to man's eyes, so few and rare between,
The fig-tree's top puts forth its leaves of green;
This vernal voyage practicable seems,
And pervious are the boundless ocean streams.
I praise it not; for thou, with anxious mind,
Must hasty snatch th' occasion of the wind.
The drear event may baffle all thy care;
Yet thus, e'en thus, will human folly dare.
Of wretched mortals, lo! the soul is gain;
But death is dreadful midst the whelming main.
These counsels lay to heart; and, warn'd by me,
Trust not thy whole precarious wealth to sea,
Toss'd in the hollow keel; leave most behind,
And with a smaller freight intrust the wind.
Grievous, when one frail plank conveys thy all,
Should some mishap midst ocean's waves befall:
Grievous, as when thy sheaves o'erload the wain,
And the crash'd axle spoils the scatter'd grain.
Observe the seasonable times to sail:
Th' occasion well observed will most avail.

—From the Greek of Hesiod (fl. eighth century, B.C.), translated by C. A. Elton (abridged).

Of Human Progress

FROM THE FIFTH BOOK OF LUCRETIUS' OF THE NATURE OF THINGS

But mortal man
Was then far hardier in the old champaign,
As well he should be, since a hardier earth
Had him begotten; builded too was he
Of bigger and more solid bones within,
And knit with stalwart sinews through the flesh,
Nor easily seized by either heat or cold,
Or alien food or any ail or irk.
And whilst so many lustrums of the sun
Rolled on across the sky, men led a life
After the roving habit of wild beasts.
Not then were sturdy guiders of curved ploughs,
And none knew then to work the fields with iron,
Or plant young shoots in holes of delvèd loam,
Or lop with hookèd knives from off high trees
The boughs of yester-year. What sun and rains
To them had given, what earth of own accord
Created then, was boon enough to glad
Their simple hearts. Mid acorn-laden oaks
Would they refresh their bodies for the nonce;
And the wild berries of the arbute-tree,
Which now thou seest to ripen purple-red
In winter time, the old telluric soil
Would bear then more abundant and more big.
And many coarse foods, too, in long ago
The blooming freshness of the rank young world

Produced, enough for those poor wretches there.
And rivers and springs would summon them of old
To slake the thirst, as now from the great hills
The water's down-rush calls aloud and far
The thirsty generations of the wild.
So, too, they sought the grottos of the Nymphs—
The woodland haunts discovered as they ranged—
From forth of which they knew that gliding rills
With gush and splash abounding laved the rocks,
The dripping rocks, and trickled from above
Over the verdant moss; and here and there
Welled up and burst across the open flats.
As yet they knew not to enkindle fire
Against the cold, nor hairy pelts to use
And clothe their bodies with the spoils of beasts;
But huddled in groves, and mountain-caves, and woods,
And 'mongst the thickets hid their squalid backs,
When driven to flee the lashings of the winds
And the big rains. Nor could they then regard
The general good, nor did they know to use
In common any customs, any laws:
Whatever of booty fortune unto each
Had proffered, each alone would bear away,
By instinct trained for self to thrive and live.
And Venus in the forests then would link
The lovers' bodies; for the woman yielded
Either from mutual flame, or from the man's
Impetuous fury and insatiate lust,
Or from a bribe—as acorn-nuts, choice pears,
Or the wild berries of the arbute-tree.
And trusting wondrous strength of hands and legs,
They'd chase the forest-wanderers, the beasts;
And many they'd conquer, but some few they fled,
A-skulk into their hiding-places.
And by the time of night
O'ertaken, they would throw, like bristly boars,
Their wildman's limbs naked upon the earth,
Rolling themselves in leaves and fronded boughs.
Nor would they call with lamentations loud
Around the fields for daylight and the sun,
Quaking and wand'ring in shadows of the night;
But, silent and buried in a sleep, they'd wait
Until the sun with rosy flambeau brought
The glory to the sky. From childhood wont
Ever to see the dark and day begot
In times alternate, never might they be
Wildered by wild misgiving, lest a night
Eternal should possess the lands, with light
Of sun withdrawn forever. But their care
Was rather that the clans of savage beasts
Would often make their sleep-time horrible
For those poor wretches; and, from home y-driven,
They'd flee their rocky shelters at approach
Of boar, the spumy-lipped, or lion strong,
And in the midnight yield with terror up
To those fierce guests their beds of out-spread leaves.
And yet in those days not much more than now
Would generations of mortality
Leave the sweet light of fading life behind.
Indeed, in those days here and there a man,
More oftener snatched upon, and gulped by fangs,
Afforded the beasts a food that roared alive,
Echoing through groves and hills and forest-trees,
Even as he viewed his living flesh entombed
Within a living grave; whilst those whom flight
Had saved, with bone and body bitten, shrieked,
Pressing their quivering palms to loathsome sores,
With horrible voices for eternal death—
Until, forlorn of help, and witless what
Might medicine their wounds, the writhing pangs
Took them from life. But not in those far times
Would one lone day give over unto doom
A soldiery in thousands marching on
Beneath the battle-banners, nor would then
The ramping breakers of the main seas dash
Whole argosies and crews upon the rocks.
But ocean uprisen would often rave in vain,
Without all end or outcome, and give up
Its empty menacings as lightly too;
Nor soft seductions of a sérene sea
Could lure by laughing billows any man
Out to disaster: for the science bold
Of ship-sailing lay dark in those far times.

Again, 'twas *then* that lack of food gave o'er
Men's fainting limbs to dissolution: now
'Tis plenty overwhelms. Unwary, they
Oft for themselves themselves would then outpour
The poison; now, with nicer art, themselves
They give the drafts to others. Afterwards,
When huts they had procured and pelts and fire,
And when the woman, joined unto the man,
Withdrew with him into one dwelling place,
. . . and when they saw an offspring born
From out themselves, then first the human race
Began to soften. For 'twas now that fire
Rendered their shivering frames less staunch to bear,
Under the canopy of sky, the cold;
And Love reduced their shaggy hardiness;
And children, with the prattle and the kiss,
Soon broke the parents' haughty temper down.
Then, too, did neighbours 'gin to league as friends,
Eager to wrong no more or suffer wrong,
And urged for children and the womankind
Mercy, of fathers, whilst with cries and gestures
They stammered hints how meet it was that all
Should have compassion on the weak. And still,
Though concord not in every wise could then
Begotten be, a good, a goodly part
Kept faith inviolate — or else mankind
Long since had been unutterably cut off,
And propagation never could have brought
The species down the ages.
Lest, perchance,
Concerning these affairs thou ponderest
In silent meditation, let me say
'Twas lightning brought primevally to earth
The fire for mortals, and from thence hath spread
O'er all the lands the flames of heat. For thus
Even now we see so many objects, touched
By the celestial flames, to flash aglow,
When thunderbolt has dowered them with heat.
Yet also when a many-branchèd tree,
Beaten by winds, writhes swaying to and fro,
Pressing 'gainst branches of a neighbour tree,
There by the power of mighty rub and rub
Is fire engendered; and at times out-flares
The scorching heat of flame, when boughs do chafe
Against the trunks. And of these causes, either
May well have given to mortal men the fire.
Next, food to cook and soften in the flame
The sun instructed, since so oft they saw
How objects mellowed, when subdued by warmth
And by the raining blows of fiery beams,
Through all the fields.
And more and more each day
Would men more strong in sense, more wise in heart,
Teach them to change their earlier mode and life
By fire and new devices. Kings began
Cities to found and citadels to set,
As strongholds and asylums for themselves,
And flocks and fields to portion for each man
After the beauty, strength, and sense of each —
For beauty then imported much, and strength
Had its own rights supreme. Thereafter, wealth
Discovered was, and gold was brought to light,
Which soon of honour stripped both strong and fair;
For men, however beautiful in form
Or valorous, will follow in the main
The rich man's party. Yet were man to steer
His life by sounder reasoning, he'd own
Abounding riches, if with mind content
He lived by thrift; for never, as I guess,
Is there a lack of little in the world.
But men wished glory for themselves and power
Even that their fortunes on foundations firm
Might rest forever, and that they themselves,
The opulent, might pass a quiet life —
In vain, in vain; since, in the strife to climb
On to the heights of honour, men do make
Their pathway terrible; and even when once
They reach them, envy like the thunderbolt
At times will smite, O hurling headlong down
To murkiest Tartarus, in scorn; for, lo,

All summits, all regions loftier than the rest,
Smoke, blasted as by envy's thunderbolts;
So better far in quiet to obey,
Than to desire chief mastery of affairs
And ownership of empires. Be it so;
And let the weary sweat their life-blood out
All to no end, battling in hate along
The narrow path of man's ambition;
Since all their wisdom is from others' lips,
And all they seek is known from what they've heard
And less from what they've thought. Nor is this folly
Greater to-day, nor greater soon to be,
Than 'twas of old. . . .

Now for the rest: copper and gold and iron
Discovered were, and with them silver's weight
And power of lead, when with prodigious heat
The conflagrations burned the forest trees
Among the mighty mountains, by a bolt
Of lightning from the sky, or else because
Men, warring in the woodlands, on their foes
Had hurlèd fire to frighten and dismay,
Or yet because, by goodness of the soil
Invited, men desired to clear rich fields
And turn the countryside to pasture-lands,
Or slay the wild and thrive upon the spoils.
(For hunting by pit-fall and by fire arose
Before the art of hedging the covert round
With net or stirring it with dogs of chase.)
Howso the fact, and from what cause so-ever
The flamy heat with awful crack and roar
Had there devourèd to their deepest roots
The forest trees and baked the earth with fire,
Then from the boiling veins began to ooze
Out rivulets of silver and of gold,
Of lead and copper too, collecting soon
Into the hollow places of the ground.
And when men saw the coolèd lumps anon
To shine with splendour-sheen upon the ground,
Much taken with that lustrous smooth delight,
They 'gan to pry them out, and saw how each
Had got a shape like to its earthy mould.
Then would it enter their heads how these same lumps,
If melted by heat, could into any form
Or figure of things be run, and how, again,
If hammered out, they could be nicely drawn
To sharpest point or finest edge, and thus
Yield to the forgers tools and give them power
To chop the forest down, to hew the logs,
To shave the beams and planks, besides to bore
And punch and drill. And men began such work
At first as much with tools of silver and gold
As with the impetuous strength of the stout copper;
But vainly—since their over-mastered power
Would soon give way, unable to endure,
Like copper, such hard labour. In those days
Copper it was that was the thing of price;
And gold lay useless, blunted with dull edge.
Now lies the copper low, and gold hath come
Unto the loftiest honours. Thus it is
That rolling ages change the times of things:
What erst was of a price, becomes at last
A discard of no honour; whilst another
Succeeds to glory, issuing from contempt,
And day by day is sought for more and more,
And, when 'tis found, doth flower in men's praise,
Object of wondrous honour.

Now, Memmius,
How nature of iron discovered was, thou mayst
Of thine own self divine. Man's ancient arms
Were hands, and nails and teeth, stones too and boughs—
Breakage of forest trees—and flame and fire,
As soon as known. Thereafter force of iron
And copper discovered was; and copper's use
Was known ere iron's, since more tractable
Its nature is and its abundance more.
With copper men to work the soil began,
With copper to rouse the hurly waves of war,
To straw the monstrous wounds, and seize away
Another's flocks and fields. For unto them,
Thus armèd, all things naked of defence
Readily yielded. Then by slow degrees
The sword of iron succeeded, and the shape
Of brazen sickle into scorn was turned:
With iron to cleave the soil of earth they 'gan,

And the contentions of uncertain war
Were rendered equal. . . .
  Now, clothes of roughly inter-plaited strands
Were earlier than loom-wove coverings;
The loom-wove later than man's iron is,
Since iron is needful in the weaving art,
Nor by no other means can there be wrought
Such polished tools — the treadles, spindles, shuttles,
And sounding yarn-beams. And nature forced the men,
Before the woman kind, to work the wool:
For all the male kind far excels in skill,
And cleverer is by much — until at last
The rugged farmer folk jeered at such tasks,
And so were eager soon to give them o'er
To women's hands, and in more hardy toil
To harden arms and hands.
                    But nature herself,
Mother of things, was the first seed-sower
And primal grafter; since the berries and acorns,
Dropping from off the trees, would there beneath
Put forth in season swarms of little shoots;
Hence too men's fondness for ingrafting slips
Upon the boughs and setting out in holes
The young shrubs o'er the fields. Then would they try
Ever new modes of tilling their loved crofts,
And mark they would how earth improved the taste
Of the wild fruits by fond and fostering care.
And day by day they'd force the woods to move
Still higher up the mountain, and to yield
The place below for tilth, that there they might,
On plains and uplands, have their meadow-plats,
Cisterns and runnels, crops of standing grain,
And happy vineyards, and that all along
O'er hillocks, intervales, and plains might run
The silvery-green belt of olive-trees,
Marking the plotted landscape; even as now
Thou seest so marked with varied loveliness
All the terrain which men adorn and plant
With rows of goodly fruit-trees and hedge round
With thriving shrubberies sown.
                    But by the mouth
To imitate the liquid notes of birds
Was earlier far 'mongst men than power to make,
By measured song, melodious verse and give
Delight to ears. And whistlings of the wind
Athrough the hollows of the reeds first taught
The peasantry to blow into the stalks
Of hollow hemlock-herb. Then bit by bit
They learned sweet plainings, such as pipe out-pours,
Beaten by finger-tips of singing men,
When heard through unpathed groves and forest deeps
And woodsy meadows, through the untrod haunts
Of shepherd folk and spots divinely still.
Thus time draws forward each and every-thing
Little by little unto the midst of men,
And reason uplifts it to the shores of light.
These tunes would soothe and glad the minds of mortals
When sated with food, — for songs are wel-come then.
And often, lounging with friends in the soft grass
Beside a river of water, underneath
A big tree's branches, merrily they'd refresh
Their frames, with no vast outlay — most of all
If the weather were smiling and the times of the year
Were painting the green of the grass around with flowers.
Then jokes, then talk, then peals of jollity
Would circle round; for then the rustic muse
Was in her glory; then would antic Mirth
Prompt them to garland head and shoulders about
With chaplets of intertwinèd flowers and leaves,
And to dance onward, out of tune, with limbs
Clownishly swaying, and with clownish foot
To beat our mother earth — from whence arose
Laughter and peals of jollity, for, lo,
Such frolic acts were in their glory then,
Being more new and strange. And wakeful men
Found solaces for their unsleeping hours
In drawing forth variety of notes,
In modulating melodies, in running
With puckered lips along the tunèd reeds,
Whence, even in our day do the watchmen guard

These old traditions, and have learnèd well
To keep true measure. And yet they no whit
Do get a larger fruit of gladsomeness
Than got the woodland aborigines
In olden times. For *what* we have at hand—
If theretofore naught sweeter we have known—
That chiefly pleases and seems best of all;
But then some later, likely better, find
Destroys its worth and changes our desires
Regarding good of yesterday.
And thus
Began the loathing of the acorn; thus
Abandoned were those beds with grasses strewn
And with the leaves beladen. Thus, again,
Fell into new contempt the pelts of beasts—
Erstwhile a robe of honour, which, I guess,
Aroused in those days envy so malign
That the first wearer went to woeful death
By ambuscades,—and yet that hairy prize,
Rent into rags by greedy foemen there
And splashed by blood, was ruined utterly
Beyond all use or vantage. Thus of old
'Twas pelts, and of to-day 'tis purple and gold
That cark men's lives with cares and weary with war.
Wherefore, methinks, resides the greater blame
With us vain men to-day: for cold would rack,
Without their pelts, the naked sons of earth;
But us it nothing hurts to do without
The purple vestment, broiderèd with gold
And with imposing figures, if we still
Make shift with some mean garment of the Plebs.
So man in vain futilities toils on
Forever and wastes in idle cares his years—
Because, of very truth, he hath not learnt
What the true end of getting is, nor yet
At all how far true pleasure may increase.
And 'tis desire for better and for more
Hath carried by degrees mortality
Out onward to the deep, and rousèd up
From the far bottom mighty waves of war.
But sun and moon, those watchmen of the world,
With their own lanterns traversing around
The mighty, the revolving vault, have taught
Unto mankind that seasons of the years
Return again, and that the Thing takes place
After a fixèd plan and order fixed.
Already would they pass their life, hedged round
By the strong towers; and cultivate an earth
All portioned out and boundaried; already
Would the sea flower with sail-wingèd ships;
Already men had, under treaty pacts,
Confederates and allies, when poets began
To hand heroic actions down in verse;
Nor long ere this had letters been devised—
Hence is our age unable to look back
On what has gone before, except where reason
Shows us a footprint.
Sailings on the seas,
Tillings of fields, walls, laws, and arms, and roads,
Dress and the like, all prizes, all delights
Of finer life, poems, pictures, chiselled shapes
Of polished sculptures—all these arts were learned
By practice and the mind's experience,
As men walked forward step by eager step.
Thus time draws forward each and every-thing
Little by little into the midst of men,
And reason uplifts it to the shores of light.
For one thing after other did men see
Grow clear by intellect, till with their arts
They've now achieved the súpreme pinnacle.

—*From the Latin of Lucretius, Roman (c. 96–c. 55 B.C.), translated by William Ellery Leonard.*

The Honey-Farm

FROM THE FOURTH BOOK OF VIRGIL'S GEORGICS

The gifts of heav'n my foll'wing song pursues,
Aërial honey, and ambrosial dews.
Maecenas, read this other part, that sings
Embattled squadrons, and advent'rous kings:
A mighty pomp, tho' made of little things.
Their arms, their arts, their manners, I disclose,
And how they war, and whence the people rose:
Slight is the subject, but the praise not small,
If Heav'n assist, and Phoebus hear my call.
First, for thy bees a quiet station find,
And lodge 'em under covert of the wind,

(For winds, when homeward they return, will drive
The loaded carriers from their ev'ning hive,)
Far from the cows' and goats' insulting crew,
That trample down the flow'rs, and brush the dew.
The painted lizard, and the birds of prey,
Foes of the frugal kind, be far away;
The titmouse, and the peckers' hungry brood,
And Progne, with her bosom stain'd in blood;
These rob the trading citizens, and bear
The trembling captives thro' the liquid air,
And for their callow young a cruel feast prepare.
But near a living stream their mansion place,
Edg'd round with moss and tufts of matted grass;
And plant (the winds' impetuous rage to stop)
Wild olive trees, or palms, before the busy shop;
That, when the youthful prince, with proud alarm,
Calls out the vent'rous colony to swarm;
When first their way thro' yielding air they wing,
New to the pleasures of their native spring,
The banks of brooks may make a cool retreat
For the raw soldiers from the scalding heat,
And neighb'ring trees with friendly shade invite
The troops, unus'd to long laborious flight.
Then o'er the running stream, or standing lake,
A passage for thy weary people make;
With osier floats the standing water strow;
Of massy stones make bridges, if it flow;
That basking in the sun thy bees may lie,
And, resting there, their flaggy pinions dry,
When, late returning home, the laden host
By raging winds is wreck'd upon the coast.
Wild thyme and sav'ry set around their cell,
Sweet to the taste, and fragrant to the smell;
Set rows of rosemary with flow'ring stem,
And let the purple vi'lets drink the stream.
Whether thou build the palace of thy bees
With twisted osiers, or with barks of trees,
Make but a narrow mouth; for, as the cold
Congeals into a lump the liquid gold,
So 'tis again dissolv'd by summer's heat,
And the sweet labors both extremes defeat.
And therefore, not in vain, th' industrious kind
With dauby wax and flow'rs the chinks have lin'd
And, with their stores of gather'd glue, contrive
To stop the vents and crannies of their hive.
Not birdlime, or Idaean pitch, produce
A more tenacious mass of clammy juice.
Nor bees are lodg'd in hives alone, but found
In chambers of their own, beneath the ground;
Their vaulted roofs are hung in pumices,
And in the rotten trunks of hollow trees.
But plaister thou the chinky hives with clay,
And leafy branches o'er their lodgings lay:
Nor place them where too deep a water flows,
Or where the yew, their pois'nous neighbor grows;
Nor roast red crabs, t' offend the niceness of their nose;
Nor near the steaming stench of muddy ground;
Nor hollow rocks that render back the sound,
And doubled images of voice rebound.
For what remains, when golden suns appear,
And under earth have driv'n the winter year,
The winged nation wanders thro' the skies,
And o'er the plains and shady forest flies;
Then, stooping on the meads and leafy bow'rs,
They skim the floods, and sip the purple flow'rs.
Exalted hence, and drunk with secret joy,
Their young succession all their cares employ:
They breed, they brood, instruct, and educate,
And make provision for the future state;
They work their waxen lodgings in their hives,
And labor honey to sustain their lives.
But when thou seest a swarming cloud arise,
That sweeps aloft, and darkens all the skies,
The motions of their hasty flight attend;
And know, to floods or woods their airy march they bend.
Then melfoil beat, and honeysuckles pound;
With these alluring savors strew the ground,
And mix with tinkling brass the cymbals' droning sound.
Straight to their ancient cells, recall'd from air,
The reconcil'd deserters will repair.

But if intestine broils alarm the hive,
(For two pretenders oft for empire strive,)
The vulgar in divided factions jar;
And murm'ring sounds proclaim the civil war.
Inflam'd with ire, and trembling with disdain,
Scarce can their limbs their mighty souls contain.
With shouts the cowards' courage they excite,
And martial clangors call 'em out to fight;
With hoarse alarms the hollow camp rebounds,
That imitates the trumpets' angry sounds;
Then to their common standard they repair;
The nimble horsemen scour the fields of air;
In form of battle drawn, they issue forth,
And ev'ry knight is proud to prove his worth.
Press'd for their country's honor, and their king's,
On their sharp beaks they whet their pointed stings,
And exercise their arms, and tremble with their wings. . . .
Yet all those dreadful deeds, this deadly fray,
A cast of scatter'd dust will soon allay,
And undecided leave the fortune of the day.
When both the chiefs are sunder'd from the fight,
Then to the lawful king restore his right;
And let the wasteful prodigal be slain,
That he who best deserves alone may reign. . . .
The better brood, unlike the bastard crew,
Are mark'd with royal streaks of shining hue;
Glitt'ring and ardent, tho' in body less:
From these, at pointed seasons, hope to press
Huge heavy honeycombs, of golden juice,
Not only sweet, but pure, and fit for use,
T' allay the strength and hardness of the wine,
And with old Bacchus new metheglin join. . . .
Now, when thou hast decreed to seize their stores,
And by prerogative to break their doors,
With sprinkled water first the city choke,
And then pursue the citizens with smoke.
Two honey harvests fall in ev'ry year:
First, when the pleasing Pleiades appear,
And, springing upward, spurn the briny seas;
Again, when their affrighted choir surveys
The wat'ry Scorpion mend his pace behind,
With a black train of storms, and winter wind,
They plunge into the deep, and safe protection find.
Prone to revenge, the bees, a wrathful race,
When once provok'd, assault th' aggressor's face,
And thro' the purple veins a passage find;
There fix their stings, and leave their souls behind.
But if a pinching winter thou foresee,
And wouldst preserve thy famish'd family;
With fragrant thyme the city fumigate,
And break the waxen walls to save the state.
For lurking lizards often lodge, by stealth,
Within the suburbs, and purloin their wealth;
And worms, that shun the light, a dark retreat
Have found in combs, and undermin'd the seat;
Or lazy drones, without their share of pain,
In winter quarters free, devour the gain;
Or wasps infest the camp with loud alarms,
And mix in battle with unequal arms;
Or secret moths are there in silence fed;
Or spiders in the vault their snary webs have spread.
The more oppress'd by foes, or famine-pin'd,
The more increase thy care to save the sinking kind;
With greens and flow'rs recruit their empty hives,
And seek fresh forage to sustain their lives.
But, since they share with man one common fate,
In health and sickness, and in turns of state;
Observe the symptoms when they fall away,
And languish with insensible decay.
They change their hue; with haggard eyes they stare;
Lean are their looks, and shagged is their hair;
And crowds of dead, that never must return
To their lov'd hives, in decent pomp are borne:
Their friends attend the hearse; the next relations mourn.
The sick for air before the portal gasp,
Their feeble legs within each other clasp,
Or idle in their empty hives remain,
Benumb'd with cold, and listless of their gain.
Soft whispers then, and broken sounds are heard,

As when the woods by gentle winds are stirr'd;
Such stifled noise as the close furnace hides,
Or dying murmurs of departing tides.
This when thou seest, galbanean odors use,
And honey in the sickly hive infuse.
Thro' reeden pipes convey the golden flood,
T' invite the people to their wonted food.
Mix it with thicken'd juice of sodden wines,
And raisins from the grapes of Psythian vines:
To these add pounded galls, and roses dry,
And, with Cecropian thyme, strong-scented centaury.

—From the Latin of Virgil (70–19 B.C.), translated by John Dryden (abridged).

Ballad of Poor Chimney Sweeps

Men talk of those the fields that till;
Of those that sift out chaff from corn;
Of him that has, will he or nill,
A wife that scoldeth night and morn, —
As folk hard driven and forlorn:
Of men that often use the sea;
Of monks that of poor convents be;
Of those behind the ass that go:
But, when all things consider we,
Poor chimneysweeps have toil eno'.

To govern boys and girls with skill,
God wot, 's no labour lightly borne:
Nor to serve ladies at Love's will;
Or do knight suit at sound of horn,
Helmet and harness always worn,
And follow arms courageously:
To joust and tilt with spears, perdie,
And quintain play, is hard, I know;
But, when all things consider we,
Poor chimneysweeps have toil eno'.

God wot, they suffer little ill
By whom wheat's reaped and meadows shorn;
Or those that thresh grain for the mill
Or plead the Parliament beforne;
To borrow money's little scorn;
Tinkers and carters have to dree
But little hardship, seemeth me;
Nor does Lent irk us much, I trow:
But, when all things consider we,
Poor chimneysweeps have toil eno'.

—From the French of François Villon (1431–1463), translated by John Payne.

Hymn to the Winds

(The winds are invoked by the winnowers of corn)

To you, who troop so fleet,
That with winged wandering feet,
Through the wide world pass,
And with soft murmuring
Toss the green shades of spring
In woods and grass,
Lily and violet
I give, and blossoms wet,
Roses and dew;
This branch of blushing roses,
Whose fresh bud uncloses;
Wind-flowers too.

Ah, winnow with sweet breath,
Winnow the holt and heath
Round this retreat;
Where all the golden morn
We fan the gold o' the corn,
In the sun's heat.

—From the French of Joachim du Bellay (1525–1560), translated by Andrew Lang.

Harvest Song

Sickles sound;
On the ground
Fast the ripe ears fall;
Every maiden's bonnet
Has blue blossoms on it;
Joy is over all.

Sickles ring,
Maidens sing
To the sickle's sound;
Till the moon is beaming,
And the stubble gleaming,
Harvest songs go round.

All are springing,
All are singing,
Every lisping thing.
Man and master meet;
From one dish they eat;
Each is now a king.

Hans and Michael
Whet the sickle,
Piping merrily.
Now they mow; each maiden
Soon with sheaves is laden,
Busy as a bee.

Now the blisses,
And the kisses!
Now the wit doth flow
Till the beer is out;
Then, with song and shout,
Home they go, yo ho!

— *From the German of Ludwig Hölty (1748–1776), translated by Charles T. Brooks.*

~ ❂ ~

The Ox

I love thee, pious ox, through whom my heart
To a sweet sense of peace and vigour yields;
Majestic, like a monument thou art,
Gazing out over the far fruitful fields!
Thou joinest, well-content beneath the yoke,
Thy strength unto man's nimble toil; he cries
And pricks thee, but thou turnest to his stroke
The slow response of thine all-patient eyes.
From the moist dusk of thy wide nostrils flows
Thy spirit's breath, and like a happy prayer
Thy lowing dies upon the tranquil air;
Serene and mild, each green orb gravely shows,
As in a mirror, without bound or stain,
The heavenly silence of the verdant plain.

— *From the Italian of Giosuè Carducci (1835–1907), translated by Lorna de' Lucchi.*

Brazil

In this hour of pure sunlight
still palms
shining rocks
flashes
gleams
scintillations

I hear the vast song of Brazil!
I hear the thundering steeds of Iguassú pounding the naked rocks, prancing in the wet air, trampling with watery feet the morning of spume and green trills;
I hear thy solemn melody, thy barbaric and solemn melody, Amazon, the melody of thy lazy flood, heavy as oil, that swells greater and ever greater, licking the mud of banks, gnawing roots, dragging along islands, goring the listless ocean like a bull infuriated with rods, darts, branches and leaves;
I hear the earth crackling in the hot north-east wind, earth that heaves beneath the bare bronze foot of the outlaw, earth that turns to dust and whirls in silent clouds through the streets of Joazeiro and falls to powder on the dry plains of Crato;
I hear the chirping of jungles — trills, pipings, peepings, quavers, whistles, whirrings, tapping of beaks, deep tones that hum like taut wires, clearly vibrating drums, throats that creak, wings that click and flicker, cries like the cricket's whispers, dreamy calls, long languid calls — jungles beneath the sky!
I hear the streams laughing, dashing the flanks of greedy golden carp, disturbing the bearded catfish in their oozy holes and hiding places beneath submerged stones;
I hear the millstones grinding sugar cane, the gurgle of sweet juice flowing into vats, the clank of pails among rubber trees;
and axes opening paths,
and saws cutting timber,
and packs of hounds named Wind-cutters, Iron-breakers, Flashes and Sharks holding at bay the red leopards and the jaguars,
and mangroves leafing in the sun,
and peccaries snapping their jaws at alligators asleep in the tepid mud of bayous . . .
I hear all Brazil singing, humming, calling, shouting!
Hammocks swaying,
whistles blowing,
factories grinding, pounding, panting, screaming, howling and snoring,
cylinders exploding,
cranes revolving,
wheels turning,
rails trembling,
noises of foothills and plateaux, cattlebells, neighings, cowboy songs, and lowings,
chiming of bells, bursting of rockets, Ouro-Preto, Baia, Congonhas, Sabara,
clamour of stock-exchanges shrieking numbers like parrots,
tumult of streets that seethe beneath sky-scrapers,
voices of all the races that the wind of the seaports tosses into the jungle!

In this hour of pure sunlight I hear Brazil.
All thy conversations, tawny homeland, wander in the air . . .
the talk of planters among coffee bushes,
the talk of miners in gold mines,
the talk of workmen in furnaces where steel is made,
the talk of diamond hunters shaking sieves,
the talk of colonels on the verandas of country houses . . .

But what I hear, above all, in this hour of pure sunlight
still palms
shining rocks
flashes
gleams
scintillations
is the song of thy cradles, Brazil, of all thy cradles, in which there sleeps, mouth dripping with milk, dusky trusting,
the man of tomorrow!

—*From the Portuguese of the Brazilian Ronald de Carvalho (1893–1935), translated by Dudley Poore.*

Reaping the Barley

On a bull's hollow horn
Juan blew the message that the barley was ready.

In their clay huts
the seven families
poured the sun-juice
into brown jars.

The hill squatted in the field
wrapped in a plaid poncho.

Red, green, yellow dresses
began to climb the road.

Amid a riot of colours
the glowing barley sheaves went down with a swish,
decimated by the sickles.

Tomasa weighed the ripeness of the sky
in the scales of her sunflower arms.

The slow swing of the field
molded the shape of her waist.

Men and women of the seven families,
seated in the tender noon-day gold,
drank sun-juice
from the clay jars.

—*From the Spanish of the Ecuadorean Jorge Carrera Andrade (1903–), translated by Muna Lee de Muñoz Marin.*

The Cocooning

FROM THE MIRÈIO

When the crop is fair in the olive-yard,
And the earthen jars are ready
For the golden oil from the barrels poured,
And the big cart rocks unsteady
With its tower of gathered sheaves, and strains
And groans on its way through fields and lanes:

When brawny and bare as an old athlete
Comes Bacchus the dance a-leading,
And the laborers all, with juice-dyed feet,
The vintage of Crau are treading,
And the good wine pours from the brimful presses,
And the ruby foam in the vats increases;

When under the leaves of the Spanish broom
The clear silk-worms are holden,
An artist each, in a tiny loom,
Weaving a web of golden,
Fine, frail cells out of sunlight spun,
Where they creep and sleep by the million, —

Glad is Provence on a day like that,
'Tis the time of jest and laughter:
The Ferigoulet and the Baume Muscat
They quaff, and they sing thereafter.
And lads and lasses, their toils between,
Dance to the tinkling tambourine.

—*From the French of Frédéric Mistral (1830–1914), translated by Harriet Waters Preston.*

The Mill

Deep in grey dusk the mill turns faltering,
Under a sombre, melancholy sky,
It turns and turns; its earth-hued wheel drifts by
Endlessly feeble and heavy and lingering.

Since dawn its arms in plaintive gesture rise
Heavenward and fall in turn: behold them
there
Drooping again deep through the blacken-
ing air
And utter silence of a world that dies.

Over the hamlets a cold day foredone
Slumbers; the clouds are weary of voyaging,
To the black woods the massive shadows
cling,
To an horizon dead the roads run on.

Some beechen huts, upon the roadway's
hem,
Squat in a wretched circle; on their wall
And window a feeble blotch of light lets fall
A copper lamp hanging in one of them.

And in the empty vast of plain and skies
These poor, pinched hovels fix their glances
vain
From under lids of broken window-pane
On the old mill that turns and turns and
dies.

—From the French of the Belgian poet Emile Verhaeren (1855–1916), translated by Ludwig Lewisohn.

We Grow Out of Iron

Look! I stand among work-benches, ham-
mers, furnaces, forges, and among hun-
dreds of comrades.
Overhead – hammered iron space.
On either side – beams and girders.
They rise to a height of seventy feet.
They arch right and left.
They meet in the cupola and with giant
shoulders support the whole iron struc-
ture.
They thrust upward, they are sturdy, they
are strong.
They demand yet greater strength.
I look at them and grow straight.
Fresh iron blood pours into my veins.
I have grown taller.
I am growing shoulders of steel and arms
immeasurably strong.
I am one with the iron building.
I have risen.
My shoulders are forcing the rafters, the up-
per beams, the roof.
My feet remain on the ground, but my head
is above the building.
I choke with the inhuman effort, but al-
ready I am shouting: "Let me speak,
comrades, let me speak!"
An iron echo drowns my words, the whole
structure shakes with impatience. And
I have risen yet higher, I am on a level
with the chimneys.
I shall not tell a story or make a speech, I
shall only shout my iron word:
"We will conquer!"

—From the Russian of Alexey Gastev (1882–), translated by Babette Deutsch and Avrahm Yarmolinsky.

The Charcoal-Burner's Son

My father he's at the kiln away,
My mother sits at her spinning;
But wait, I'll too be a man some day,
And a sweetheart I'll then be winning.
So dark it is far off in the forest.

At dawn I am up and off with the sun—
Hurrah! when the sun's a-shimmer.
To father then with his food I run;
Soon follows the twilight's glimmer.
So dark it is far off in the forest.

I roam the green foot-path fearlessly
As I haste through the woods alone there.
But darkly the pines look down on me,
And long mountain shadows are thrown
there.
So dark it is far off in the forest.

Tralala! As glad as a bird in flight
I'll sing as the path I follow.
But harsh the reply from the mountain
height,
And the woods are heavy and hollow.
So dark it is far off in the forest.

If I were but with my old father, though!
Hark! the bear is growling with hunger.
And the bear is the mightiest fellow, I know,
And spares neither older nor younger.
So dark it is far off in the forest.

The shadows come down so thick, so thick,
As if curtains were drawn together.
There's rustle and rattle of stone and stick,
And trolls are walking the heather.
So dark it is far off in the forest.

There's one! There are two! In their net they'll take
Me, alas! – how the firs are waving.
They beckon. O God, do not Thou forsake!
By flight my life I'd be saving.
So dark it is far off in the forest.

. . . . .

The hours went by, the daylight was gone,
The way it grew ever more wild now,
There's whisp'ring and rustling o'er stick and o'er stone
As over the heath runs the child now.
So dark it is far off in the forest.

With rosy-red cheek and heart beating fast
To his father's kiln swiftly fleeing,
He fell. "My dear son, oh, welcome at last!"
" 'T is trolls, aye and worse I've been seeing.
So dark it is far off in the forest."

"My son, it is long here I've had to dwell,
But God has preserved me from evil.
Whoever knows his Our Father well
Fears neither for troll nor for devil,
Though dark it is far off in the forest."

—From the Swedish of Erik Gustaf Geijer (1783–1847), translated by Charles Wharton Stork.

Factory Street in Daylight

Only walls. No grass, nor glass;
The street flings out its mottled bars
Of gray façades. No tramway jars.
The pavement shimmers moist and hard as brass.

A man slips by; his icy eye
Bites cold and deep into your soul.
His steps strike fire where black walls scowl,
His breath, a frosty cloud against the sky.

No prison cell packs thought in ice
As does this walk between high walls
Which stare but at themselves. God's curse appalls.

He in this street delights to strike
At rich and virtuous alike
By putting time within a vise.

—From the German of Paul Zech (1881–), translated by Thomas Riley.

The Worked-Out Mine

On summer nights when moonbeams flow
And glisten o'er the high, white tips,
And winds make lamentation low,
As through the ribs of shattered ships,
And steal about the broken brace
Where pendant timbers swing and moan,
And flitting bats give aimless chase,
Who dares to seek the mine alone?

The shrinking bush with sable rims
A skeleton forlorn and bowed,
With pipe-clay white about its limbs
And at its feet a tattered shroud;
And ghostly figures lurk and groan,
Shrill whispers sound from ghostly lips,
And ghostly footsteps start the stone
That clatters sharply down the tips.

The engine-house is dark and still,
The life that raged within has fled;
Like open graves the boilers chill
That once with glowing fires were red;
Above the shaft in measured space
A rotted rope swings to and fro,
Whilst o'er the plat and on the brace
The silent shadows come and go.

And there below, in chambers dread
Where darkness like a fungus clings,
Are lingering still the old mine's dead –
Bend o'er and hear their whisperings!
Up from the blackness sobs and sighs
Are flung with moans and muttered fears,
A low lament that never dies,
And ceaseless sound of falling tears.

My ears intent have heard *their* grief –
The fitful tones of Carter's tongue,
The strong man crushed beneath the reef,
The groans of Panton, Praer, and Young,
And "Trucker Bill" of Number Five,
Along the ruined workings roll;
For deep in every shoot and drive
This mine secretes a shackled soul.

Ah! woful mine, where wives have wept,
And mothers prayed in anxious pain,
And long, distracting vigil kept,
You yawn for victims now in vain!
Still to that god, whose shrine you were,
Is homage done in wild device;
Men hate you as the sepulchre
That stores their bloody sacrifice.

—Edward Dyson, Australian.

The Man and the Machine

By right of fires that smelted ore
Which he had tended years before,
The man whose hands were on the wheel
Could trace his kinship through her steel,
Between his body warped and bent
In every bone and ligament,
And this "eight-cylinder" stream-lined,
The finest model yet designed.
He felt his lesioned pulses strum
Against the rhythm of her hum,
And found his nerves and sinews knot
With sharper spasm as she climbed
The steeper grades, so neatly timed
From petrol tank to piston shot—
This creature with the panther grace,
This man with slag upon his face.

—*Edwin John Pratt, Canadian (1883–).*

The Sleepers

As I walked down the waterside
This silent morning, wet and dark;
Before the cocks in farmyards crowed,
Before the dogs began to bark;
Before the hour of five was struck
By old Westminster's mighty clock:

As I walked down the waterside
This morning, in the cold damp air,
I saw a hundred women and men
Huddled in rags and sleeping there:
These people have no work, thought I,
And long before their time they die.

That moment, on the waterside,
A lighted car came at a bound;
I looked inside, and saw a score
Of pale and weary men that frowned;
Each man sat in a huddled heap,
Carried to work while fast asleep.

Ten cars rushed down the waterside,
Like lighted coffins in the dark;
With twenty dead men in each car,
That must be brought alive by work:
These people work too hard, thought I,
And long before their time they die.

—*William Henry Davies, English (1870–1940).*

Let Us Be Off!

Let us be off! Our steam
Is deafening the dome.
The needle in the gauge
Points to a long-banked rage,
And trembles there to show
What a pressure's below.
Valve cannot vent the strain
Nor iron ribs refrain
That furnace in the heart.
Come on, make haste and start
Coupling-rod and wheel
Welded of patient steel,
Piston that will not stir
Beyond the cylinder
To take in its stride
A teeming countryside.

A countryside that gleams
In the sun's weeping beams;
Where wind-pump, byre and barrow
Are mellowed to mild sorrow,
Agony and sweat
Grown over with regret.
What golden vesper hours
Halo the old grey towers,
What honeyed bells in valleys
Embalm our faiths and follies!
Here are young daffodils
Wind-wanton, and the hills
Have made their peace with heaven.
Oh lovely the heart's haven,
Meadows of endless May,
A spirit's holiday!

Traveller, take care,
Pick no flowers there!

—*Cecil Day Lewis, English (1904–).*

The Landscape Near an Aerodrome

More beautiful and soft than any moth
With burring furred antennae feeling its huge path
Through dusk, the air-liner with shut-off engines
Glides over suburbs and the sleeves set trailing tall
To point the wind. Gently, broadly, she falls,
Scarcely disturbing charted currents of air.

Lulled by descent, the travelers across sea
And across feminine land indulging its easy
 limbs
In miles of softness, now let their eyes
 trained by watching
Penetrate through dusk the outskirts of this
 town
Here where industry shows a fraying edge.
Here they may see what is being done.

Beyond the winking masthead light
And the landing-ground, they observe the
 outposts
Of work: chimneys like lank black fingers
Or figures frightening and mad: and squat
 buildings
With their strange air behind trees, like
 women's faces
Shattered by grief. Here where few houses
Moan with faint light behind their blinds
They remark the unhomely sense of com-
 plaint, like a dog
Shut out and shivering at the foreign moon.

In the last sweep of love, they pass over
 fields
Behind the aerodrome, where boys play all
 day
Hacking dead grass: whose cries, like wild
 birds,
Settle upon the nearest roofs
But soon are hid under the loud city.

Then, as they land, they hear the tolling
 bell
Reaching across the landscape of hysteria
To where, larger than all the charcoaled
 batteries
And imaged towers against that dying sky,
Religion stands, the church blocking the sun.

—*Stephen Spender, English (1909–).*

The Lumbermen

Wildly round our woodland quarters
 Sad-voiced Autumn grieves;
Thickly down these swelling waters
 Float his fallen leaves.
Through the tall and naked timber,
 Column-like and old,
Gleam the sunsets of November,
 From their skies of gold.

O'er us, to the southland heading,
 Screams the gray wild-goose;
On the night-frost sounds the treading
 Of the brindled moose.
Noiseless creeping, while we're sleeping,
 Frost his task-work plies;
Soon, his icy bridges heaping,
 Shall our log-piles rise.

When, with sounds of smothered thunder,
 On some night of rain,
Lake and river break asunder
 Winter's weakened chain,
Down the wild March flood shall bear them
 To the saw-mill's wheel,
Or where Steam, the slave, shall tear them
 With his teeth of steel.

Be it starlight, be it moonlight,
 In these vales below,
When the earliest beams of sunlight
 Streak the mountain's snow,
Crisps the hoar-frost, keen and early,
 To our hurrying feet,
And the forest echoes clearly
 All our blows repeat.

Where the crystal Ambijejis
 Stretches broad and clear,
And Millnoket's pine-black ridges
 Hide the browsing deer:
Where, through lakes and wide morasses,
 Or through rocky walls,
Swift and strong, Penobscot passes
 White with foamy falls;

Where, through clouds, are glimpses given
 Of Katahdin's sides,—
Rock and forest piled to heaven,
 Torn and ploughed by slides!
Far below, the Indian trapping,
 In the sunshine warm;
Far above, the snow-cloud wrapping
 Half the peak in storm!

Where are mossy carpets better
 Than the Persian weaves,
And than Eastern perfumes sweeter
 Seem the fading leaves;
And a music wild and solemn,
 From the pine-tree's height,
Rolls its vast and sea-like volume
 On the wind of night;

Make we here our camp of winter;
 And, through sleet and snow,
Pitchy knot and beechen splinter
 On our hearth shall glow.

Here, with mirth to lighten duty,
  We shall lack alone
Woman's smile and girlhood's beauty,
  Childhood's lisping tone.

But their hearth is brighter burning
  For our toil to-day;
And the welcome of returning
  Shall our loss repay,
When, like seamen from the waters,
  From the woods we come,
Greeting sisters, wives, and daughters,
  Angels of our home!

Not for us the measured ringing
  From the village spire,
Not for us the Sabbath singing
  Of the sweet-voiced choir;
Ours the old, majestic temple,
  Where God's brightness shines
Down the dome so grand and ample,
  Propped by lofty pines!

Through each branch-enwoven skylight,
  Speaks He in the breeze,
As of old beneath the twilight
  Of lost Eden's trees!
For His ear, the inward feeling
  Needs no outward tongue;
He can see the spirit kneeling
  While the axe is swung.

Heeding truth alone, and turning
  From the false and dim,
Lamp of toil or altar burning
  Are alike to Him.
Strike then, comrades! Trade is waiting
  On our rugged toil;
Far ships waiting for the freighting
  Of our woodland spoil!

Ships whose traffic links these highlands,
  Bleak and cold, of ours,
With the citron-planted islands
  Of a clime of flowers;
To our frosts the tribute bringing
  Of eternal heats;
In our lap of winter flinging
  Tropic fruits and sweets.

Cheerly, on the axe of labor,
  Let the sunbeams dance,
Better than the flash of sabre
  Or the gleam of lance!
Strike! With every blow is given
  Freer sun and sky,
And the long-hid earth to heaven
  Looks, with wondering eye!

Loud behind us grow the murmurs
  Of the age to come;
Clang the smiths, and tread of farmers,
  Bearing harvest home!
Here her virgin lap with treasures
  Shall the green earth fill;
Waving wheat and golden maize-ears
  Crown each beechen hill.

Keep who will the city's alleys,
  Take the smooth-shorn plain;
Give to us the cedarn valleys,
  Rocks and hills of Maine!
In our North-land, wild and woody,
  Let us still have part;
Rugged nurse and mother sturdy,
  Hold us to thy heart!

Oh, our free hearts beat the warmer
  For thy breath of snow;
And our tread is all the firmer
  For thy rocks below.
Freedom, hand in hand with labor,
  Walketh strong and brave;
On the forehead of his neighbor
  No man writeth Slave!

Lo, the day breaks! old Katahdin's
  Pine-trees show its fires,
While from these dim forest gardens
  Rise their blackened spires.
Up my comrades! up and doing!
  Manhood's rugged play
Still renewing, bravely hewing
  Through the world our way!

—*John Greenleaf Whittier, American (1807–1892).*

~ ⚙ ~

Song of the Broad-Axe

1

Weapon shapely, naked, wan,
Head from the mother's bowels drawn,
Wooded flesh and metal bone, limb only one and lip only one,
Gray-blue leaf by red-heat grown, helve produced from a little seed sown,
Resting the grass amid and upon,
To be lean'd and to lean on.

Strong shapes and attributes of strong shapes, masculine trades, sights and sounds,

Long varied train of an emblem, dabs of music,
Fingers of the organist skipping staccato over the keys of the great organ.

2

Welcome are all earth's lands, each for its kind,
Welcome are lands of pine and oak,
Welcome are lands of the lemon and fig,
Welcome are lands of gold,
Welcome are lands of wheat and maize, welcome those of the grape,
Welcome are lands of sugar and rice,
Welcome the cotton-lands, welcome those of the white potato and sweet potato,
Welcome are mountains, flats, sands, forests, prairies,
Welcome the rich borders of rivers, table-lands, openings,
Welcome the measureless grazing-lands, welcome the teeming soil of orchards, flax, honey, hemp;
Welcome just as much the other more hard-faced lands,
Lands rich as lands of gold or wheat and fruit lands,
Lands of mines, lands of the manly and rugged ores,
Lands of coal, copper, lead, tin, zinc,
Lands of iron – lands of the make of the axe.

3

The log at the wood-pile, the axe supported by it,
The sylvan hut, the vine over the doorway, the space clear'd for a garden,
The irregular tapping of rain down on the leaves after the storm is lull'd,
The wailing and moaning at intervals, the thought of the sea,
The thought of ships struck in the storm and put on their beam ends, and the cutting away of masts,
The sentiment of the huge timbers of old-fashion'd houses and barns,
The remember'd print or narrative, the voyage at a venture of men, families, goods,
The disembarkation, the founding of a new city,
The voyage of those who sought a New England and found it, the outset anywhere,
The settlements of the Arkansas, Colorado, Ottawa, Willamette,
The slow progress, the scant fare, the axe, rifle, saddle-bags;
The beauty of all adventurous and daring persons,
The beauty of wood-boys and wood-men with their clear untrimm'd faces,
The beauty of independence, departure, actions that rely on themselves,
The American contempt for statutes and ceremonies, the boundless impatience of restraint,
The loose drift of character, the inkling through random types, the solidification;
The butcher in the slaughter-house, the hands aboard schooners and sloops, the raftsman, the pioneer,
Lumbermen in their winter camp, daybreak in the woods, stripes of snow on the limbs of trees, the occasional snapping,
The glad clear sound of one's own voice, the merry song, the natural life of the woods, the strong day's work,
The blazing fire at night, the sweet taste of supper, the talk, the bed of hemlock-boughs and the bear-skin;
The house-builder at work in cities or anywhere,
The preparatory jointing, squaring, sawing, mortising,
The hoist-up of beams, the push of them in their places, laying them regular,
Setting the studs by their tenons in the mortises according as they were prepared,
The blows of mallets and hammers, the attitudes of the men, their curv'd limbs,
Bending, standing, astride the beams, driving in pins, holding on by posts and braces,
The hook'd arm over the plate, the other arm wielding the axe,
The floor-men forcing the planks close to be nail'd,
Their postures bringing their weapons downward on the bearers,
The echoes resounding through the vacant building;
The huge storehouse carried up in the city well under way,
The six framing-men, two in the middle and two at each end, carefully bearing on their shoulders a heavy stick for a cross-beam,
The crowded line of masons with trowels in their right hands rapidly laying the long side-wall, two hundred feet from front to rear,

The flexible rise and fall of backs, the continual click of the trowels striking the bricks,
The bricks one after another each laid so workmanlike in its place, and set with a knock of the trowel-handle,
The piles of materials, the mortar on the mortar-boards, and the steady replenishing by the hod-men;
Spar-makers in the spar-yard, the swarming row of well-grown apprentices,
The swing of their axes on the square-hew'd log shaping it toward the shape of a mast,
The brisk short crackle of the steel driven slantingly into the pine,
The butter-color'd chips flying off in great flakes and slivers,
The limber motion of brawny young arms and hips in easy costumes,
The constructor of wharves, bridges, piers, bulk-heads, floats, stays against the sea;
The city fireman, the fire that suddenly bursts forth in the close-pack'd square,
The arriving engines, the hoarse shouts, the nimble stepping and daring,
The strong command through the fire-trumpets, the falling in line, the rise and fall of the arms forcing the water,
The slender, spasmic, blue-white jets, the bringing to bear of the hooks and ladders and their execution,
The crash and cut away of connecting woodwork, or through floors if the fire smoulders under them,
The crowd with their lit faces watching, the glare and dense shadows;
The forger at his forge-furnace and the user of iron after him,
The maker of the axe large and small, and the welder and temperer,
The chooser breathing his breath on the cold steel and trying the edge with thumb,
The one who clean-shapes the handle and sets it firmly in the socket;
The shadowy processions of the portraits of the past users also,
The primal patient mechanics, the architects and engineers,
The far-off Assyrian edifice and Mizra edifice,
The Roman lictors preceding the consuls,
The antique European warrior with his axe in combat,
The uplifted arm, the clatter of blows on the helmeted head,
The death-howl, the limpsy tumbling body, the rush of friend and foe thither,
The siege of revolted lieges determin'd for liberty,
The summons to surrender, the battering at castle gates, the truce and parley,
The sack of an old city in its time,
The bursting in of mercenaries and bigots tumultuously and disorderly,
Roar, flames, blood, drunkenness, madness,
Goods freely rifled from houses and temples, screams of women in the gripe of brigands,
Craft and thievery of camp-followers, men running, old persons despairing,
The hell of war, the cruelties of creeds,
The list of all executive deeds and words just or unjust,
The power of personality just or unjust.

4

Muscle and pluck forever!
What invigorates life invigorates death,
And the dead advance as much as the living advance,
And the future is no more uncertain than the present,
For the roughness of the earth and of man encloses as much as the delicatesse of the earth and of man,
And nothing endures but personal qualities.

What do you think endures?
Do you think a great city endures?
Or a teaming manufacturing state? or a prepared constitution? or the best built steamships?
Or hotels of granite and iron? or any chef-d'oeuvres of engineering, forts, armaments?

Away! these are not to be cherish'd for themselves,
They fill their hour, the dancers dance, the musicians play for them,
The show passes, all does well enough of course,
All does very well till one flash of defiance.

A great city is that which has the greatest men and women,
If it be a few ragged huts it is still the greatest city in the whole world.

5

The place where a great city stands is not the place of stretch'd wharves, docks, manufactures, deposits of produce merely,
Nor the place of ceaseless salutes of new-comers or the anchor-lifters of the departing,
Nor the place of the tallest and costliest buildings or shops selling goods from the rest of the earth,
Nor the place of the best libraries and schools, nor the place where money is plentiest,
Nor the place of the most numerous population.

Where the city stands with the brawniest breed of orators and bards,
Where the city stands that is belov'd by these, and loves them in return and understands them,
Where no monuments exist to heroes but in the common words and deeds,
Where thrift is in its place, and prudence is in its place,
Where men and women think lightly of the laws,
Where the slave ceases, and the master of slaves ceases,
Where the populace rise at once against the never-ending audacity of elected persons,
Where fierce men and women pour forth as the sea to the whistle of death pours its sweeping and unript waves,
Where outside authority enters always after the precedence of inside authority,
Where the citizen is always the head and ideal, and President, Mayor, Governor, and what not, are agents for pay,
Where children are taught to be laws to themselves, and to depend on themselves,
Where equanimity is illustrated in affairs,
Where speculations on the soul are encouraged,
Where women walk in public processions in the streets the same as the men;
Where they enter the public assembly and take places the same as the men;
Where the city of the faithfulest friends stands,
Where the city of the cleanliness of the sexes stands,
Where the city of the healthiest fathers stands,
Where the city of the best-bodied mothers stands,
There the great city stands.

6

How beggarly appear arguments before a defiant deed!
How the floridness of the materials of cities shrivels before a man's or woman's look!

All waits or goes by default till a strong being appears;
A strong being is the proof of the race and of the ability of the universe,
When he or she appears materials are overaw'd,
The dispute on the soul stops,
The old customs and phrases are confronted, turn'd back, or laid away.

What is your money-making now? what can it do now?
What is your respectability now?
What are your theology, tuition, society, traditions, statute-books, now?
Where are your jibes of being now?
Where are your cavils about the soul now?

7

A sterile landscape covers the ore, there is as good as the best for all the forbidding appearance,
There is the mine, there are the miners,
The forge-furnace is there, the melt is accomplish'd, the hammers-men are at hand with their tongs and hammers,
What always served and always serves is at hand.

Than this nothing has better served, it has served all,
Served the fluent-tongued and subtle-sensed Greek, and long ere the Greek,
Served in building the buildings that last longer than any,
Served the Hebrew, the Persian, the most ancient Hindustanee,
Served the mound-raiser on the Mississippi, served those whose relics remain in Central America,
Served Albic temples in woods or on plains, with unhewn pillars and the druids,

Served the artificial clefts, vast, high, silent, on the snow-cover'd hills of Scandinavia,
Served those who time out of mind made on the granite walls rough sketches of the sun, moon, stars, ships, ocean waves,
Served the paths of the irruptions of the Goths, served the pastoral tribes and nomads,
Served the long distant Kelt, served the hardy pirates of the Baltic,
Served before any of those the venerable and harmless men of Ethiopia,
Served the making of helms for the galleys of pleasure and the making of those for war,
Served all great works on land and all great works on the sea,
For the medieval ages and before the medieval ages,
Served not the living only then as now, but served the dead.

8

I see the European headsman,
He stands mask'd, clothed in red, with huge legs and strong naked arms,
And leans on a ponderous axe.

(Whom have you slaughter'd lately European headsman?
Whose is that blood upon you so wet and sticky?)

I see the clear sunsets of the martyrs,
I see from the scaffolds the descending ghosts,
Ghosts of dead lords, uncrown'd ladies, impeach'd ministers, rejected kings,
Rivals, traitors, poisoners, disgraced chieftains and the rest.

I see those who in any land have died for the good cause,
The seed is spare, nevertheless the crop shall never run out,
(Mind you O foreign kings, O priests, the crop shall never run out.)

I see the blood wash'd entirely away from the axe,
Both blade and helve are clean,
They spirt no more the blood of European nobles, they clasp no more the necks of queens.

I see the headsman withdraw and become useless,
I see the scaffold untrodden and mouldy, I see no longer any axe upon it,
I see the mighty and friendly emblem of the power of my own race, the newest, largest race.

(America! I do not vaunt my love for you,
I have what I have.)

The axe leaps!
The solid forest gives fluid utterances,
They tumble forth, they rise and form,
Hut, tent, landing, survey,
Flail, plough, pick, crowbar, spade,
Shingle, rail, prop, wainscot, jamb, lath, panel, gable,
Citadel, ceiling, saloon, academy, organ, exhibition-house, library,
Cornice, trellis, pilaster, balcony, window, turret, porch,
Hoe, rake, pitchfork, pencil, wagon, staff, saw, jack-plane, mallet, wedge, rounce,
Chair, tub, hoop, table, wicket, vane, sash, floor,
Work-box, chest, string'd instrument, boat, frame, and what not,
Capitols of States, and capitol of the nation of States,
Long stately rows in avenues, hospitals for orphans or for the poor or sick,
Manhattan steamboats and clippers taking the measure of all seas.

The shapes arise!
Shapes of the using of axes anyhow, and the users and all that neighbors them,
Cutters down of wood and haulers of it to the Penobscot or Kennebec,
Dwellers in cabins among the Californian mountains or by the little lakes, or on the Columbia,
Dwellers south on the banks of the Gila or Rio Grande, friendly gatherings, the characters and fun,
Dwellers along the St. Lawrence, or north in Kanada, or down by the Yellowstone, dwellers on coasts and off coasts,
Seal-fishers, whalers, arctic seamen breaking passages through the ice.

The shapes arise!
Shapes of factories, arsenals, foundries, markets,

Shapes of the two-threaded tracks of railroads,
Shapes of the sleepers of bridges, vast frameworks, girders, arches,
Shapes of the fleets of barges, tows, lake and canal craft, river craft,
Ship-yards and dry-docks along the Eastern and Western seas, and in many a bay and by-place,
The live-oak kelsons, the pine planks, the spars, the hackmatack-roots for knees,
The ships themselves on their ways, the tiers of scaffolds, the workmen busy outside and inside,
The tools lying around, the great auger and little auger, the adze, bolt, square, gouge, and bead-plane.

10

The shapes arise!
The shape measur'd, saw'd, jack'd, join'd, stain'd,
The coffin-shape for the dead to lie within in his shroud,
The shape got out in posts, in the bedstead posts, in the posts of the bride's bed,
The shape of the little trough, the shape of the rockers beneath, the shape of the babe's cradle,
The shape of the floor-planks, the floor-planks for dancer's feet,
The shape of the planks of the family home, the home of the friendly parents and children,
The shape of the roof of the home of the happy young man and woman, the roof over the well-married young man and woman,
The roof over the supper joyously cook'd by the chaste wife, and joyously eaten by the chaste husband, content after his day's work.

The shapes arise!
The shape of the prisoner's place in the court-room, and of him or her seated in the place.
The shape of the liquor-bar lean'd against by the young rum-drinker and the old rum-drinker,
The shape of the shamed and angry stairs trod by sneaking footsteps,
The shape of the sly settee, and the adulterous unwholesome couple,
The shape of the gambling-board with its devilish winnings and losings,
The shape of the step-ladder for the convicted and sentenced murderer, the murderer with haggard face and pinion'd arms,
The sheriff at hand with his deputies, the silent and white-lipp'd crowd, the dangling of the rope.

The shapes arise!
Shapes of doors giving many exits and entrances,
The door passing the dissever'd friend flush'd and in haste,
The door that admits good news and bad news,
The door whence the son left home confident and puff'd up,
The door he enter'd again from a long and scandalous absence, diseased, broken down, without innocence, without means.

11

Her shape arises,
She less guarded than ever, yet more guarded than ever,
The gross and soil'd she moves among do not make her gross and soil'd,
She knows the thoughts as she passes, nothing is conceal'd from her,
She is none the less considerate or friendly therefor,
She is the best belov'd, it is without exception, she has no reason to fear and she does not fear,
Oaths, quarrels, hiccupp'd songs, smutty expressions are idle to her as she passes,
She is silent, she is possess'd of herself, they do not offend her,
She receives them as the laws of Nature receive them, she is strong,
She too is a law of Nature — there is no law stronger than she is.

12

The main shapes arise!
Shapes of Democracy total, result of centuries,
Shapes ever projecting other shapes,
Shapes of turbulent manly cities,
Shapes of the friends and home-givers of the whole earth,
Shapes bracing the earth and braced with the whole earth.

— *Walt Whitman, American (1819–1892).*

The Man With the Hoe[1]

(Written after seeing Millet's world-famous painting)

Bowed by the weight of centuries he leans
Upon his hoe and gazes on the ground,
The emptiness of ages in his face,
And on his back the burden of the world.
Who made him dead to rapture and despair,
A thing that grieves not and that never hopes,
Stolid and stunned, a brother to the ox?
Who loosened and let down this brutal jaw?
Whose was the hand that slanted back this brow?
Whose breath blew out the light within this brain?

Is this the Thing the Lord God made and gave
To have dominion over sea and land;
To trace the stars and search the heavens for power;
To feel the passion of Eternity?
Is this the dream He dreamed who shaped the suns
And marked their ways upon the ancient deep?
Down all the caverns of Hell to their last gulf
There is no shape more terrible than this —
More tongued with censure of the world's blind greed —
More filled with signs and portents for the soul —
More packt with danger to the universe.

What gulfs between him and the seraphim!
Slave of the wheel of labor, what to him
Are Plato and the swing of Pleiades?
What the long reaches of the peaks of song,
The rift of dawn, the reddening of the rose?
Through this dread shape the suffering ages look;
Time's tragedy is in that aching stoop;
Through this dread shape humanity betrayed,
Plundered, profaned, and disinherited,
Cries protest to the Judges of the World,
A protest that is also prophecy.

O masters, lords and rulers in all lands,
Is this the handiwork you give to God,
This monstrous thing distorted and soul-quenched?
How will you ever straighten up this shape;
Touch it again with immortality;
Give back the upward looking and the light;
Rebuild in it the music and the dream;
Make right the immemorial infamies,
Perfidious wrongs, immedicable woes?

O masters, lords and rulers in all lands,
How will the Future reckon with this man?
How answer his brute question in that hour
When whirlwinds of rebellion shake all shores?
How will it be with kingdoms and with kings —
With those who shaped him to the thing he is —
When this dumb terror shall rise to judge the world,
After the silence of the centuries?

— *Edwin Markham, American* (1852–1940).

[1] Revised version, 1920. Copyright by Edwin Markham.

After Apple-Picking

My long two-pointed ladder's sticking through a tree
Toward heaven still,
And there's a barrel that I didn't fill
Beside it, and there may be two or three
Apples I didn't pick upon some bough.
But I am done with apple-picking now.
Essence of winter sleep is on the night,
The scent of apples: I am drowsing off.
I cannot rub the strangeness from my sight
I got from looking through a pane of glass
I skimmed this morning from the drinking trough
And held against the world of hoary grass.
It melted, and I let it fall and break.
But I was well
Upon my way to sleep before it fell,
And I could tell
What form my dreaming was about to take.
Magnified apples appear and disappear,
Stem-end and blossom-end,
And every fleck of russet showing clear.
My instep arch not only keeps the ache,
It keeps the pressure of a ladder-round.
I feel the ladder sway as the boughs bend.
And I keep hearing from the cellar bin
The rumbling sound
Of load on load of apples coming in.
For I have had too much

Of apple-picking: I am overtired
Of the great harvest I myself desired.
There were ten thousand fruit to touch,
Cherish in hand, lift down, and not let fall.
For all
That struck the earth,
No matter if not bruised or spiked with stubble,
Went surely to the cider-apple heap
As of no worth.
One can see what will trouble
This sleep of mine, whatever sleep it is.
Were he not gone,
The woodchuck could say whether it's like his
Long sleep, as I describe its coming on,
Or just some human sleep.

—*Robert Frost, American (1875–).*

Cape Hatteras

FROM THE BRIDGE

The nasal whine of power whips a new universe . . .
Where spouting pillars spoor the evening sky,
Under the looming stacks of the gigantic power house
Stars prick the eyes with sharp ammoniac proverbs,
New verities, new inklings in the velvet hummed
Of dynamos, where hearing's leash is strummed . . .
Power's script,—wound, bobbin-bound, refined—
Is stropped to the slap of belts on booming spools, spurred
Into the bulging bouillon, harnessed jelly of the stars.
Towards what? The forked crash of split thunder parts
Our hearing momentwise; but fast in whirling armatures,
As bright as frogs' eyes, giggling in the girth
Of steely gizzards—axle-bound, confined
In coiled precision, bunched in mutual glee
The bearings glint,—O murmurless and shined
In oilrinsed circles of blind ecstasy!

Stars scribble on our eyes the frosty sagas,
The gleaming cantos of unvanquished space . . .
O sinewy silver biplane, nudging the wind's withers!
There, from Kill Devils Hill at Kitty Hawk
Two brothers in their twinship left the dune;
Warping the gale, the Wright windwrestlers veered
Capeward, then blading the wind's flank, banked and spun
What ciphers risen from prophetic script,
What marathons new-set between the stars!
The soul, by naphtha fledged into new reaches,
Already knows the closer clasp of Mars,—
New latitudes, unknotting, soon give place
To what fierce schedules, rife of doom apace!

Behold the dragon's covy—amphibian, ubiquitous
To hedge the seaboard, wrap the headland, ride
The blue's cloud-templed districts unto ether . . .
While Iliads glimmer through eyes raised in pride
Hell's belt springs wider into heaven's plumed side.
O bright circumferences, heights employed to fly
War's fiery kennel masked in downy offings,—
This tournament of space, the threshed and chiselled height,
Is baited by marauding circles, bludgeon flail
Of raucous grenades whose screaming petals carve us
Wounds that we wrap with theorems sharp as hail!

Wheeled swiftly, wings emerge from larval-silver hangars.
Taut motors surge, space-gnawing, into flight;
Through sparkling visibility, outspread, unsleeping,
Wings clip the last peripheries of light . . .
Tellurian wind-sleuths on dawn patrol,
Each plane a hurtling javelin of winged ordnance,
Bristle the heights above a screeching gale to hover;
Surely no eye that Sunward Escadrille can cover!
There, meaningful, fledged as the Pleiades
With razor sheen they zoom each rapid helix!

Up-chartered choristers of their own speeding
They, cavalcade on escapade, shear Cumulus —
Lay siege and hurdle Cirrus down the skies!
While Cetus-like, O thou Dirigible, enormous Lounger
Of pendulous auroral beaches, — satellited wide
By convoy planes, moonferrets that rejoin thee
On fleeing balconies as thou dost glide,
— Hast splintered space!

Low, shadowed of the Cape,
Regard the moving turrets! From grey decks
See scouting griffons rise through gaseous crepe
Hung low . . . until a conch of thunder answers
Cloud-belfries, banging, while searchlights, like fencers,
Slit the sky's pancreas of foaming anthracite
Toward thee, O Corsair of the typhoon, — pilot, hear!
Thine eyes bicarbonated white by speed, O Skygak, see
How from thy path above the levin's lance
Thou sowest doom thou hast nor time nor chance
To reckon — as thy stilly eyes partake
What alcohol of space. . . ! Remember, Falcon-Ace,
Thou hast there in thy wrist a Sanskrit charge
To conjugate infinity's dim marge —
Anew. . . !

But first, here at this height receive
The benediction of the shell's deep, sure reprieve!
Lead-perforated fuselage, escutcheoned wings
Lift agonized quittance, tilting from the invisible brink
Now eagle-bright, now
quarry-hid, twist-
ing, sink with
Enormous repercussive list-
ings down
Giddily spiralled
gauntlets, upturned, unlooping
In guerrilla sleights, trapped in combustion gyr-
Ing, dance the curdled depth
down whizzing
Zodiacs, dashed
(Now nearing fast the Cape!)
down gravitation's
vortex into crashed
. . . dispersion . . . mashed and shapeless debris. . . .
By Hatteras bunched the beached heap of high bravery!

— *Hart Crane, American (1899–1932).*

Classic Scene

A power-house
in the shape of
a red brick chair
90 feet high

on the seat of which
sit the figures
of two metal
stacks — aluminum —

commanding an area
of squalid shacks
side by side —
from one of which

buff smoke
streams while under
a grey sky
the other remains

passive today —

— *William Carlos Williams, American (1883–).*

Five Towns on the B. and O.

By day . . . tireless smokestacks . . . hungry smoky shanties hanging to the slopes . . . crooning: We get by, that's all.
By night . . . all lit up . . . fire-gold bars, fire-gold flues . . . and the shanties shaking in clumsy shadows . . . almost the hills shaking . . . all crooning:
By God, we're going to find out or know why.

— *Carl Sandburg, American (1878–).*

PART TWENTY-SIX

The Utopian Dream

THE WORD *utopia,* coined from the Greek and meaning literally "nowhere," was used by Sir Thomas More in 1516 to describe an ideal commonwealth that presumably existed on a far-distant island. Since the publication of More's *Utopia* numerous writers have appropriated the term and applied it indiscriminately to any literary work which seeks to conjure up a society or state free from human imperfections. As a literary *genre,* utopian fiction was launched in Western literature by Plato, notably by his *Republic,* which became the general model for subsequent utopian works through many centuries. Plato, it may however be noted, was motivated chiefly by an authoritarian desire to buttress with as rational terms as possible the social and political system in which he lived. More and his fellow humanists of the Renaissance, and most subsequent utopian writers, viewed objectively the current social norms and institutions of their day, drew upon their travels and increasingly available knowledge of comparative civilization, and sought the constitutions and forms of government most ideally suited to their country in troubled times.

Utopian literature may fairly be called a literature of wishful thinking. But to dismiss it for that reason is to ignore its force and usefulness. Many symbols of the first utopian dreams have been institutionalized in human society. Indeed the utopian element in the thought of every generation is the underlying thread which knits together the common interests of differing classes in a society. As did the ancient Hebrew prophets, the greater utopian writers are unanimous in announcing that collective social evils are not to be exorcised by magic, and that human progress is marked by the willingness of men to shoulder individual responsibility. Utopian literature is therefore, at its best, ethical criticism of society.

The three selections which conclude this book will be found self-explanatory. Studied with care, they also will reward the reader with an insight into the continuing and basic social problems of his generation. Hawthorne's satire on the reformers of his day suggests the great ado which men raise over reform in some inconsequential departments of life, while they neglect the most fundamental issues. James's comments on war are far from outmoded. And H. G. Wells, in the role of both prophet and critic, suggests that today there is a race between the education of man and suicide for all that is best in him; that the task of keeping human intelligence sympathetically in pace with the broadening responsibilities of all men is one no honest mind can shirk. The havoc which can be wrought in human life by science-implemented war has compelled our generation to consider anew the greatest utopian dream of all – a federation of the world and the brotherhood of man.

Earth's Holocaust

NATHANIEL HAWTHORNE

Once upon a time — but whether in the time past or time to come is a matter of little or no moment — this wide world had become so overburdened with an accumulation of worn-out trumpery that the inhabitants determined to rid themselves of it by a general bonfire. The site fixed upon at the representation of the insurance companies, and as being as central a spot as any other on the globe, was one of the broadest prairies of the West, where no human habitation would be endangered by the flames, and where a vast assemblage of spectators might commodiously admire the show. Having a taste for sights of this kind, and imagining, likewise, that the illumination of the bonfire might reveal some profundity of moral truth heretofore hidden in mist or darkness, I made it convenient to journey thither and be present. At my arrival, although the heap of condemned rubbish was as yet comparatively small, the torch had already been applied. Amid that boundless plain, in the dusk of the evening, like a far-off star alone in the firmament, there was merely visible one tremulous gleam, whence none could have anticipated so fierce a blaze as was destined to ensue. With every moment, however, there came foot travellers, women holding up their aprons, men on horseback, wheelbarrows, lumbering baggage wagons, and other vehicles great and small, and from far and near, laden with articles that were judged fit for nothing but to be burned.

"What materials have been used to kindle the flame?" inquired I of a bystander; for I was desirous of knowing the whole process of the affair from beginning to end.

The person whom I addressed was a grave man, fifty years old or thereabout, who had evidently come thither as a looker-on. He struck me immediately as having weighed for himself the true value of life and its circumstances, and therefore as feeling little personal interest in whatever judgment the world might form of them. Before answering my question, he looked me in the face by the kindling light of the fire.

"O, some very dry combustibles," replied he, "and extremely suitable to the purpose — no other, in fact, than yesterday's newspapers, last month's magazines, and last year's withered leaves. Here now comes some antiquated trash that will take fire like a handful of shavings."

As he spoke some rough-looking men advanced to the verge of the bonfire, and threw in, as it appeared, all the rubbish of the herald's office — the blazonry of coat armor, the crests and devices of illustrious families, pedigrees that extended back, like lines of light, into the mist of the dark ages, together with stars, garters, and embroidered collars, each of which, as paltry a bauble as it might appear to the uninstructed eye, had once possessed vast significance, and was still, in truth, reckoned among the most precious of moral or material facts by the worshippers of the gorgeous past. Mingled with this confused heap, which was tossed into the flames by armfuls at once, were innumerable badges of knighthood, comprising those of all the European sovereignties, and Napoleon's decoration of the Legion of Honor, the ribbons of which were entangled with those of the ancient order of St. Louis. There, too, were the medals of our own Society of Cincinnati, by means of which, as history tells us, an order of hereditary knights came near being constituted out of the king quellers of the revolution. And besides, there were the patents of nobility of German counts and barons, Spanish grandees, and English peers, from the worm-eaten instruments signed by William the Conqueror down to the brand-new parchment of the latest lord who has received his honors from the fair hand of Victoria.

At sight of the dense volumes of smoke, mingled with vivid jets of flame, that gushed and eddied forth from this immense pile of earthly distinctions, the multitude of plebeian spectators set up a joyous shout, and clapped their hands with an emphasis that made the welkin echo. That was their moment of triumph, achieved, after long ages, over creatures of the same clay and the same spiritual infirmities, who had dared to assume the privileges due only to Heaven's better workmanship. But now there rushed towards the blazing heap a gray-haired man, of stately presence, wearing a coat from the breast of which a star, or other badge of rank, seemed to have been forcibly wrenched away. He had not the tokens of intellectual power in his face; but still there was the demeanor, the habitual and almost native dignity, of one who had been born to the idea of his own social superiority, and had never felt it questioned till that moment.

"People," cried he, gazing at the ruin of what was dearest to his eyes with grief and wonder, but nevertheless with a degree of stateliness, — "people, what have you done? This fire is consuming all that marked your advance from barbarism, or that could have prevented your relapse thither. We, the men of the privileged orders, were those who kept alive from age to age the old chivalrous spirit; the gentle and generous thought; the higher, the purer, the more refined and delicate life. With the nobles, too, you cast off the poet, the painter, the sculptor — all the beautiful arts; for we were their patrons, and created the atmosphere in which they flourish. In abolishing the majestic distinctions of rank, society loses not only its grace, but its steadfastness" —

More he would doubtless have spoken; but here there arose an outcry, sportive, contemptuous, and indignant, that altogether drowned the appeal of the fallen nobleman, insomuch that, casting one look of despair at his own half-burned pedigree, he shrunk back into the crowd, glad to shelter himself under his new-found insignificance.

"Let him thank his stars that we have not flung him into the same fire!" shouted a rude figure, spurning the embers with his foot. "And henceforth let no man dare to show a piece of musty parchment as his warrant for lording it over his fellows. If he have strength of arm, well and good; it is one species of superiority. If he have wit, wisdom, courage, force of character, let these attributes do for him what they may; but from this day forward no mortal must hope for place and consideration by reckoning up the mouldy bones of his ancestors. That nonsense is done away."

"And in good time," remarked the grave observer by my side, in a low voice, however, "if no worse nonsense comes in its place; but, at all events, this species of nonsense has fairly lived out its life."

There was little space to muse or moralize over the embers of this time-honored rubbish; for, before it was half burned out, there came another multitude from beyond the sea, bearing the purple robes of royalty, and the crowns, globes, and sceptres of emperors and kings. All these had been condemned as useless baubles, playthings at best, fit only for the infancy of the world, or rods to govern and chastise it in its nonage, but with which universal manhood at its full-grown stature could no longer brook to be insulted. Into such contempt had these regal insignia now fallen that the gilded crown and tinselled robes of the player king from Drury Lane Theatre had been thrown in among the rest, doubtless as a mockery of his brother monarchs on the great stage of the world. It was a strange sight to discern the crown jewels of England glowing and flashing in the midst of the fire. Some of them had been delivered down from the time of the Saxon princes; others were purchased with vast revenues, or perchance ravished from the dead brows of the native potentates of Hindostan; and the whole now blazed with a dazzling lustre, as if a star had fallen in that spot and been shattered into fragments. The splendor of the ruined monarchy had no reflection save in those inestimable precious stones. But enough on this subject. It were but tedious to describe how the Emperor of Austria's mantle was converted to tinder, and how the posts and pillars of the French throne became a heap of coals, which it was impossible to distinguish from those of any other wood. Let me add, however, that I noticed one of the exiled Poles stirring up the bonfire with the Czar of Russia's sceptre, which he afterwards flung into the flames.

"The smell of singed garments is quite intolerable here," observed my new acquaintance, as the breeze enveloped us in the smoke of a royal wardrobe. "Let us get to windward and see what they are doing on the other side of the bonfire."

We accordingly passed around, and were just in time to witness the arrival of a vast procession of Washingtonians, — as the votaries of temperance call themselves nowadays, — accompanied by thousands of the Irish disciples of Father Matthew, with that great apostle at their head. They brought a rich contribution to the bonfire — being nothing less than all the hogsheads and barrels of liquor in the world, which they rolled before them across the prairie.

"Now, my children," cried Father Matthew, when they reached the verge of the fire, "one shove more, and the work is done. And now let us stand off, and see Satan deal with his own liquor."

Accordingly, having placed their wooden

vessels within reach of the flames, the procession stood off at a safe distance, and soon beheld them burst into a blaze that reached the clouds and threatened to set the sky itself on fire. And well it might; for here was the whole world's stock of spirituous liquors, which, instead of kindling a frenzied light in the eyes of individual topers as of yore, soared upwards with a bewildering gleam that startled all mankind. It was the aggregate of that fierce fire which would otherwise have scorched the hearts of millions. Meantime numberless bottles of precious wine were flung into the blaze, which lapped up the contents as if it loved them, and grew, like other drunkards, the merrier and fiercer for what it quaffed. Never again will the insatiable thirst of the fire fiend be so pampered. Here were the treasures of famous bon vivants – liquors that had been tossed on the ocean, and mellowed in the sun, and hoarded long in the recesses of the earth – the pale, the gold, the ruddy juice of whatever vineyards were most delicate – the entire vintage of Tokay – all mingling in one stream with the vile fluids of the common pothouse, and contributing to heighten the selfsame blaze. And while it rose in a gigantic spire that seemed to wave against the arch of the firmament and combine itself with the light of stars, the multitude gave a shout as if the broad earth were exulting in its deliverance from the curse of ages.

But the joy was not universal. Many deemed that human life would be gloomier than ever when that brief illumination should sink down. While the reformers were at work, I overheard muttered expostulations from several respectable gentlemen with red noses and wearing gouty shoes; and a ragged worthy, whose face looked like a hearth where the fire is burned out, now expressed his discontent more openly and boldly.

"What is this world good for," said the last toper, "now that we can never be jolly any more? What is to comfort the poor man in sorrow and perplexity? How is he to keep his heart warm against the cold winds of this cheerless earth? And what do you propose to give him in exchange for the solace that you take away? How are old friends to sit together by the fireside without a cheerful glass between them? A plague upon your reformation! It is a sad world, a cold world, a selfish world, a low world, not worth an honest fellow's living in, now that good fellowship is gone forever!"

This harangue excited great mirth among the bystanders; but, preposterous as was the sentiment, I could not help commiserating the forlorn condition of the last toper, whose boon companions had dwindled away from his side, leaving the poor fellow without a soul to countenance him in sipping his liquor, nor indeed any liquor to sip. Not that this was quite the true state of the case; for I had observed him at a critical moment filch a bottle of fourth-proof brandy that fell beside the bonfire and hide it in his pocket.

The spirituous and fermented liquors being thus disposed of, the zeal of the reformers next induced them to replenish the fire with all the boxes of tea and bags of coffee in the world. And now came the planters of Virginia, bringing their crops and tobacco. These, being cast upon the heap of inutility, aggregated it to the size of a mountain, and incensed the atmosphere with such potent fragrance that methought we should never draw pure breath again. The present sacrifice seemed to startle the lovers of the weed more than any that they had hitherto witnessed.

"Well, they've put my pipe out," said an old gentleman, flinging it into the flames in a pet. "What is this world coming to? Everything rich and racy – all the spice of life – is to be condemned as useless. Now that they have kindled the bonfire, if these nonsensical reformers would fling themselves into it, all would be well enough!"

"Be patient," responded a stanch conservative; "it will come to that in the end. They will first fling us in, and finally themselves."

From the general and systematic measures of reform I now turned to consider the individual contributions to this memorable bonfire. In many instances these were of a very amusing character. One poor fellow threw in his empty purse, and another a bundle of counterfeit or insolvable banknotes. Fashionable ladies threw in their last season's bonnets, together with heaps of ribbons, yellow lace, and much other half-worn milliner's ware, all of which proved even more evanescent in the fire than it had been in the fashion. A multitude of lovers of both sexes – discarded maids or bachelors and couples mutually weary of one another – tossed in bundles of perfumed letters and enamored sonnets. A hack politician, being deprived of bread by the loss of office, threw in his teeth, which happened to be false ones. The Rev. Sydney Smith — having voyaged across the Atlantic for that sole purpose — came up to the bonfire with a bitter grin and threw in certain repudiated bonds, fortified though they were with the broad seal of a sovereign state. A little boy of five years old, in the premature manliness of the present epoch, threw in his playthings; a college graduate his diploma; an apothecary, ruined by the spread of homoeopathy, his whole stock of drugs and medicines; a physician his library; a parson his old sermons; and a fine gentleman of the old school his code of manners, which he had formerly written down for the benefit of the next generation. A widow, resolving on a second marriage, slyly threw in her dead husband's miniature. A young man, jilted by his mistress, would willingly have flung his own desperate heart into the flames, but could find no means to wrench it out of his bosom. An American author, whose works were neglected by the public, threw his pen and paper into the bonfire, and betook himself to some less discouraging occupation. It somewhat startled me to overhear a number of ladies, highly respectable in appearance, proposing to fling their gowns and petticoats into the flames, and assume the garb, together with the manners, duties, offices, and responsibilities, of the opposite sex.

What favor was accorded to this scheme I am unable to say, my attention being suddenly drawn to a poor, deceived, and half-delirious girl, who, exclaiming that she was the most worthless thing alive or dead, attempted to cast herself into the fire amid all that wrecked and broken trumpery of the world. A good man, however, ran to her rescue.

"Patience, my poor girl!" said he, as he drew her back from the fierce embrace of the destroying angel. "Be patient, and abide Heaven's will. So long as you possess a living soul, all may be restored to its first freshness. These things of matter and creations of human fantasy are fit for nothing but to be burned when once they have had their day; but your day is eternity!"

"Yes," said the wretched girl, whose frenzy seemed now to have sunk down into deep despondency, — "yes, and the sunshine is blotted out of it!"

It was now rumored among the spectators that all the weapons and munitions of war were to be thrown into the bonfire, with the exception of the world's stock of gunpowder, which, as the safest mode of disposing of it, had already been drowned in the sea. This intelligence seemed to awaken great diversity of opinion. The hopeful philanthropist esteemed it a token that the millennium was already come; while persons of another stamp, in whose view mankind was a breed of bulldogs, prophesied that all the old stoutness, fervor, nobleness, generosity, and magnanimity of the race would disappear, — these qualities, as they affirmed, requiring blood for their nourishment. They comforted themselves, however, in the belief that the proposed abolition of war was impracticable for any length of time together.

Be that as it might, numberless great guns, whose thunder had long been the voice of battle, — the artillery of the Armada, the battering trains of Marlborough, and the adverse cannon of Napoleon and Wellington, — were trundled into the midst of the fire. By the continual addition of dry combustibles, it had now waxed so intense that neither brass nor iron could withstand it. It was wonderful to behold how these terrible instruments of slaughter melted away like playthings of wax. Then the armies of the earth wheeled around the mighty furnace, with their military music playing triumphant marches, and flung in their muskets and swords. The standard-bearers, likewise, cast one look upward at their banners, all tattered with shot holes and inscribed with the names of victorious fields; and, giving them a last flourish on the breeze, they lowered them into the flame, which snatched them upward in its rush towards the clouds. This ceremony being over, the world was left without a single weapon in its hands, — except possibly a few old king's arms and rusty swords, and other trophies of the Revolution in some of our state armories. And now the drums were beaten and the trumpets brayed all together, as a prelude to the proclamation of universal and eternal peace and the announcement that glory was no longer to be won by blood, but that it would henceforth be the contention of the human race to work out the greatest mutual good, and that beneficence, in the future annals of the earth, would claim the praise of valor.

The blessed tidings were accordingly promulgated, and caused infinite rejoicings among those who had stood aghast at the horror and absurdity of war.

But I saw a grim smile pass over the seared visage of a stately old commander, — by his warworn figure and rich military dress, he might have been one of Napoleon's famous marshals, — who, with the rest of the world's soldiery, had just flung away the sword that had been familiar to his right hand for half a century.

"Ay! ay!" grumbled he. "Let them proclaim what they please; but, in the end, we shall find that all this foolery has only made more work for the armorers and cannon founders."

"Why, sir," exclaimed I, in astonishment, "do you imagine that the human race will ever so far return on the steps of its past madness as to weld another sword or cast another cannon?"

"There will be no need," observed, with a sneer, one who neither felt benevolence nor had faith in it. "When Cain wished to slay his brother, he was at no loss for a weapon."

"We shall see," replied the veteran commander. "If I am mistaken, so much the better; but in my opinion, without pretending to philosophize about the matter, the necessity of war lies far deeper than these honest gentlemen suppose. What! is there a field for all the petty disputes of individuals? and shall there be no great law court for the settlement of national difficulties? The battlefield is the only court where such suits can be tried."

"You forget, general," rejoined I, "that, in this advanced stage of civilization, Reason and Philanthropy combined will constitute just such a tribunal as is requisite."

"Ah, I had forgotten that, indeed!" said the old warrior, as he limped away.

The fire was now to be replenished with materials that had hitherto been considered of even greater importance to the well being of society than the warlike munitions which we had already seen consumed. A body of reformers had travelled all over the earth in quest of the machinery by which the different nations were accustomed to inflict the punishment of death. A shudder passed through the multitude as these ghastly emblems were dragged forward. Even the flames seemed at first to shrink away, displaying the shape and murderous contrivance of each in a full blaze of light, which of itself was sufficient to convince mankind of the long and deadly error of human law. Those old implements of cruelty; those horrible monsters of mechanism; those inventions which seemed to demand something worse than man's natural heart to contrive, and which had lurked in the dusky nooks of ancient prisons, the subject of terror-stricken legend, — were now brought forth to view. Headsmen's axes, with the rust of noble and royal blood upon them, and a vast collection of halters that had choked the breath of plebeian victims, were thrown in together. A shout greeted the arrival of the guillotine, which was thrust forward on the same wheels that had borne it from one to another of the blood-stained streets of Paris. But the loudest roar of applause went up, telling the distant sky of the triumph of the earth's redemption, when the gallows made its appearance. An ill-looking fellow, however, rushed forward, and, putting himself in the path of the reformers, bellowed hoarsely, and fought with brute fury to stay their progress.

It was little matter of surprise, perhaps, that the executioner should thus do his best to vindicate and uphold the machinery by which he himself had his livelihood and worthier individuals their death; but it deserved special note that men of a far different sphere — even of that consecrated class in whose guardianship the world is apt to trust its benevolence — were found to take the hangman's view of the question.

"Stay, my brethren!" cried one of them. "You are misled by a false philanthropy, — you know not what you do. The gallows is a heaven-ordained instrument. Bear it back, then, reverently, and set it up in its old place, else the world will fall to speedy ruin and desolation!"

"Onward! onward!" shouted a leader in the reform. "Into the flames with the accursed instrument of man's blood policy! How can human law inculcate benevolence and love while it persists in setting up the gallows as its chief symbol? One heave more, good friends, and the world will be redeemed from its greatest error."

A thousand hands, that nevertheless loathed the touch, now lent their assistance, and thrust the ominous burden far, far into the centre of the raging furnace. There its fatal and abhorred image was beheld, first black, then a red coal, then ashes.

"That was well done!" exclaimed I.

"Yes, it was well done," replied, but with less enthusiasm than I expected, the thoughtful observer who was still at my side; "well done, if the world be good enough for the measure. Death, however, is an idea that cannot easily be dispensed with in any condition between the primal innocence and that other purity and perfection which perchance we are destined to attain after travelling round the full circle; but, at all events, it is well that the experiment should now be tried."

"Too cold! too cold!" impatiently exclaimed the young and ardent leader in this triumph. "Let the heart have its voice here as well as the intellect. And as for ripeness, and as for progress, let mankind always do the highest, kindest, noblest thing, that, at any given period, it has attained the perception of; and surely that thing cannot be wrong nor wrongly timed."

I know not whether it were the excitement of the scene, or whether the good people around the bonfire were really growing more enlightened every instant; but they now proceeded to measures in the full length of which I was hardly prepared to keep them company. For instance, some threw their marriage certificates into the flames, and declared themselves candidates for a higher, holier, and more comprehensive union than that which had subsisted from the birth of time under the form of the connubial tie. Others hastened to the vaults of banks and to the coffers of the rich, — all of which were open to the first comer on this fated occasion, — and brought entire bales of paper money to enliven the blaze, and tons of coin to be melted down by its intensity. Henceforth, they said, universal benevolence, uncoined and exhaustless, was to be the golden currency of the world. At this intelligence the bankers and speculators in the stocks grew pale, and a pickpocket, who had reaped a rich harvest among the crowd, fell down in a deadly fainting fit. A few men of business burned their day-books and ledgers, the notes and obligations of their creditors, and all other evidences of debts due to themselves; while perhaps a somewhat larger number satisfied their zeal for reform with the sacrifice of any uncomfortable recollection of their own indebtment. There was then a cry that the period was arrived when the title deeds of landed property should be given to the flames, and the whole soil of the earth revert to the public, from whom it had been wrongfully abstracted and most unequally distributed among individuals. Another party demanded that all written constitutions, set forms of government, legislative acts, statute-books, and everything else on which human invention had endeavored to stamp its arbitrary laws, should at once be destroyed, leaving the consummated world as free as the man first created.

Whether any ultimate action was taken with regard to these propositions is beyond my knowledge; for, just then, some matters were in progress that concerned my sympathies more nearly.

"See! see! What heaps of books and pamphlets!" cried a fellow, who did not seem to be a lover of literature. "Now we shall have a glorious blaze!"

"That's just the thing!" said a modern philosopher. "Now we shall get rid of the weight of dead men's thought, which has hitherto pressed so heavily on the living intellect that it has been incompetent to any effectual self-exertion. Well done, my lads! Into the fire with them! Now you are enlightening the world indeed!"

"But what is to become of the trade?" cried a frantic bookseller.

"O, by all means, let them accompany their merchandise," coolly observed an author. "It will be a noble funeral pile!"

The truth was, that the human race had now reached a stage of progress so far beyond what the wisest and wittiest men of former ages had ever dreamed of that it would have been a manifest absurdity to allow the earth to be any longer encumbered with their poor achievements in the literary line. Accordingly a thorough and searching investigation had swept the booksellers' shops, hawkers' stands, public and private libraries, and even the little bookshelf by the country fireside, and had brought the world's entire mass of printed paper, bound or in sheets, to swell the already mountain bulk of our illustrious bonfire. Thick, heavy folios, containing the labors of lexicographers, commentators and encyclopaedists, were flung in, and falling among the embers with a leaden thump, smouldered away to ashes like rotten wood. The small, richly gilt French tomes of the last age, with the hundred volumes of Voltaire among them, went off in a brilliant shower of sparkles and little jets of flame; while the current literature of the same nation burned red and blue, and threw an infernal light over the visages of the spectators, converting them all to the aspect of party-colored fiends. A collection of German stories emitted a scent of brimstone. The English standard authors made excellent fuel, generally exhibiting the properties of sound oak logs. Milton's works, in particular, sent up a powerful blaze, gradually reddening into a coal, which promised to endure longer than almost any other material of the pile. From Shakespeare there gushed a flame of such marvellous splendor that men shaded their eyes as against the sun's meridian glory; nor even when the works of his own elucidators were flung upon him did he cease to flash forth a dazzling radiance from beneath the ponderous heap. It is my belief that he is blazing as fervidly as ever. . . .

I felt particular interest in watching the combustion of American authors, and scrupulously noted by my watch the precise number of moments that changed most of them from shabbily printed books to indistinguishable ashes. It would be invidious, however, if not perilous, to betray these awful secrets; so that I shall content myself with observing that it was not invariably the writer most frequent in the public mouth that made the most splendid appearance in the bonfire. I especially remember that a great deal of excellent inflammability was exhibited in a thin volume of poems by Ellery Channing; although, to speak the truth, there were certain portions that hissed and spluttered in a very disagreeable fashion. A curious phenomenon occurred in reference to several writers, native as well as foreign. Their books, though of highly respectable figure, instead of bursting into blaze, or even smouldering out their substance in smoke, suddenly melted away in a manner that proved them to be ice.

If it be no lack of modesty to mention my own works, it must here be confessed that I looked for them with fatherly interest, but in vain. Too probably they were changed to vapor by the first action of the heat; at best, I can only hope that, in their quiet way, they contributed a glimmering spark or two to the splendor of the evening.

"Alas! and woe is me!" thus bemoaned himself a heavy-looking gentleman in green spectacles. "The world is utterly ruined, and there is nothing to live for any longer. The business of my life is snatched from me. Not a volume to be had for love or money!"

"This," remarked the sedate observer beside me, "is a bookworm — one of those men who are born to gnaw dead thoughts. His clothes, you see, are covered with the dust of libraries. He has no inward fountain of ideas; and, in good earnest, now that the old stock is abolished, I do not see what is to become of the poor fellow. Have you no word of comfort for him?"

"My dear sir," said I to the desperate bookworm, "is not Nature better than a book? Is not the human heart deeper than any system of philosophy? Is not life replete with more instruction than past observers have found it possible to write down in maxims? Be of good cheer. The great book of Time is still spread wide open before us; and, if we read it aright, it will be to us a volume of eternal truth."

"O, my books, my books, — my precious printed books!" reiterated the forlorn bookworm. "My only reality was a bound volume; and now they will not leave me even a shadowy pamphlet!"

In fact, the last remnant of the literature of all the ages was now descending upon the blazing heap in the shape of a cloud of pamphlets from the press of the New World. These likewise were consumed in the twinkling of an eye, leaving the earth, for the first time since the days of Cadmus, free from the plague of letters — an enviable field for the authors of the next generation.

"Well, and does anything remain to be done?" inquired I somewhat anxiously. "Unless we set fire to the earth itself, and then leap boldly off into infinite space, I know not that we can carry reform to any farther point."

"You are vastly mistaken, my good friend," said the observer. "Believe me, the fire will not be allowed to settle down without the addition of fuel that will startle many persons who have lent a willing hand thus far."

Nevertheless there appeared to be a relaxation of effort for a little time, during which, probably, the leaders of the movement were considering what should be done next. In the interval, a philosopher threw his theory into the flames, — a sacrifice which, by those who knew how to estimate it, was pronounced the most remarkable that had yet been made. The combustion, however, was by no means brilliant. Some indefatigable people, scorning to take a moment's ease, now employed themselves in collecting all the withered leaves and fallen boughs of the forest, and thereby recruited the bonfire to a greater height than ever. But this was mere by-play.

"Here comes the fresh fuel that I spoke of," said my companion.

To my astonishment, the persons who now advanced into the vacant space around the mountain fire bore surplices and other priestly garments, mitres, crosiers, and a confusion of Popish and Protestant emblems, with which it seemed their purpose to consummate the great act of faith. Crosses from the spires of old cathedrals were cast upon the heap with as little remorse as if the reverence of centuries, passing in long array beneath the lofty towers, had not looked up to them as the holiest of symbols. The font in which infants were consecrated to God, the sacramental vessels whence piety received the hallowed draught, were given to the same destruction. Perhaps it most nearly touched my heart to see among these devoted relics fragments of the humble communion-tables and undecorated pulpits which I recognized as having been torn from the meeting-houses of New England. Those simple edifices might have been permitted to retain all of the sacred embellishment that their Puritan founders had bestowed, even though the mighty structure of St. Peter's had sent its spoils to the fire of this terrible sacrifice. Yet I felt that these were but the externals of religion, and might most safely be relinquished by spirits that best knew their deep significance.

"All is well," said I, cheerfully. "The wood-paths shall be the aisles of our cathedral, — the firmament itself shall be its ceiling. What needs an earthly roof between the Deity and his worshippers? Our faith can well afford to lose all the drapery that even the holiest men have thrown around it, and be only the more sublime in its simplicity."

"True," said my companion; "but will they pause here?"

The doubt implied in his question was well founded. In the general destruction of books already described, a holy volume, that stood apart from the catalogue of human literature, and yet, in one tense, was at its head, had been spared. But the Titan of innovation, — angel or fiend, double in his nature, and capable of deeds befitting both characters, — at first shaking down only the old and rotten shapes of things, had now, as it appeared, laid his terrible hand upon the main pillars which supported the whole edifice of our moral and spiritual state. The inhabitants of the earth had grown too enlightened to define their faith within a form of words, or to limit the spiritual by any analogy to our material existence. Truths which the heavens trembled at were now but a fable of the world's infancy. Therefore, as the final sacrifice of human error, what else remained to be thrown upon the embers of that awful pile except the book which, though a celestial revelation to past ages, was but a voice from a lower sphere as regarded the present race of man? It was done! Upon the blazing heap of falsehood and wornout truth — things that the earth had never needed, or had ceased to need, or had grown childishly weary of — fell the ponderous church Bible, the great old volume that had lain so long on the cushion of the pulpit, and whence the pastor's solemn voice had given holy utterance on so many a Sabbath day. There likewise fell the family Bible, which the long-buried patriarch had to read to his children, — in prosperity or sorrow, by the fireside and in the summer shade of trees,—and had bequeathed downward as the heirloom of generations. There fell the bosom Bible, the little volume that had been the soul's friend of some sorely tried child of dust, who thence took courage, whether his trial were for life or death, steadfastly confronting both in the strong assurance of immortality.

All these were flung into the fierce and riotous blaze; and then a mighty wind came roaring across the plain with a desolate howl, as if it were the angry lamentation of the earth for the loss of heaven's sunshine, — and it shook the gigantic pyramid of flame and scattered the cinders of half-consumed abominations around upon the spectators.

"This is terrible!" said I, feeling that my cheeks grew pale, and seeing a like change in the visages about me.

"Be of good courage yet," answered the man with whom I had so often spoken. He continued to gaze steadily at the spectacle with a singular calmness, as if it concerned him merely as an observer. "Be of good courage, nor yet exult too much; for there is far less both of good and evil in the effect of this bonfire than the world might be willing to believe."

"How can that be?" exclaimed I impatiently. "Has it not consumed everything? Has it not swallowed up or melted down every human or divine appendage of our mortal state that had substance enough to be acted on by fire? Will there be anything left us to-morrow morning better or worse than a heap of embers and ashes?"

"Assuredly there will," said my grave friend. "Come hither to-morrow morning, or whenever the combustible portion of the pile shall be quite burned out, and you will find among the ashes everything really valuable that you have seen cast into the flames. Trust me, the world of to-morrow will again enrich itself with the gold and diamonds which have been cast off by the world of to-day. Not a truth is destroyed nor buried so deep among the ashes but it will be raked up at last."

This was a strange assurance. Yet I felt inclined to credit it, the more especially as I beheld among the wallowing flames a copy of the Holy Scriptures, the pages of which, instead of being blackened into tinder, only assumed a more dazzling whiteness as the fingermarks of human imperfection were purified away. Certain marginal notes and commentaries, it is true, yielded to the intensity of the fiery test, but without detriment to the smallest syllable that had flamed from the pen of inspiration.

"Yes; there is the proof of what you say," answered I, turning to the observer; "but if only what is evil can feel the action of the fire, then, surely, the conflagration has been of inestimable utility. Yet, if I understand aright, you intimate a doubt whether the world's expectation of benefit would be realized by it."

"Listen to the talk of these worthies," said he, pointing to a group in front of the blazing pile; "possibly they may teach you something useful without intending it."

The persons whom he indicated consisted of that brutal and most earthly figure who had stood forth so furiously in defence of the gallows, — the hangman, in short, — together with the last thief and the last murderer, all three of whom were clustered about the last toper. The latter was literally passing the brandy bottle, which he had rescued from the general destruction of wines and spirits. This little convivial party seemed at the lowest pitch of despondency, as considering that the purified world must needs be utterly unlike the sphere that they had hitherto known, and therefore but a strange and desolate abode for gentlemen of their kidney.

"The best counsel for all of us is," remarked the hangman, "that, as soon as we have finished the last drop of liquor, I help you, my three friends, to a comfortable end upon the nearest tree, and then hang myself on the same bough. This is no world for us any longer."

"Poh, poh, my good fellows!" said a dark-complexioned personage, who now joined the group, — his complexion was indeed fearfully dark, and his eyes glowed with a redder light than that of the bonfire; "be not so cast down, my dear friends; you shall see good days yet. There's one thing that these wiseacres have forgotten to throw into the fire, and without which all the rest of the conflagration is just nothing at all; yes, though they had burned the earth itself to a cinder."

"And what may that be?" eagerly demanded the last murderer.

"What but the human heart itself?" said the dark-visaged stranger, with a portentous grin. "And, unless they hit upon some method of purifying that foul cavern, forth from it will reissue all the shapes of wrong and misery — the same old shapes or worse ones — which they have taken such a vast deal of trouble to consume to ashes. I have stood by this livelong night and laughed in my sleeve at the whole business. O, take my word for it, it will be the old world yet!"

This brief conversation supplied me with a theme for lengthened thought. How sad a truth, if true it were, that man's age-long endeavor for perfection had served only to render him the mockery of the evil principle, from the fatal circumstance of an error at the very root of the matter! The heart, the heart, — there was the little yet boundless sphere wherein existed the original wrong of which the crime and misery of this outward world were merely types. Purify that inward sphere, and the many shapes of evil that haunt the outward, and which now seem almost our only realities, will turn to shadowy phantoms and vanish of their own accord; but if we go no deeper than the intellect, and strive, with merely that feeble instrument, to discern and rectify what is wrong, our whole accomplishment will be a dream, so unsubstantial that it matters little whether the bonfire, which I have so faithfully described, were what we choose to call a real event and a flame that would scorch the finger, or only a phosphoric radiance and a parable of my own brain.

— From Mosses from an Old Manse, by Nathaniel Hawthorne, American (1804–1864).

The Moral Equivalent of War

WILLIAM JAMES

THE war against war is going to be no holiday excursion or camping party. The military feelings are too deeply grounded to abdicate their place among our ideals until better substitutes are offered than the glory and shame that come to nations as well as to individuals from the ups and downs of politics and the vicissitudes of trade. There is something highly paradoxical in the modern man's relation to war. Ask all our millions, north and south, whether they would vote now (were such a thing possible) to have our war for the Union expunged from history, and the record of a peaceful transition to the present time substituted for that of its marches and battles, and probably hardly a handful of eccentrics would say yes. Those ancestors, those efforts, those memories and legends, are the most ideal part of what we now own together, a sacred spiritual possession worth more than all the blood poured out. Yet ask those same people whether they would be willing in cold blood to start another civil war now to gain another similar possession, and not one man or woman would vote for the proposition. In modern eyes, precious though wars may be, they must not be waged solely for the sake of the ideal harvest. Only when forced upon one, only when an enemy's injustice leaves us no alternative, is a war now thought permissible.

It was not thus in ancient times. The earlier men were hunting men, and to hunt a neighboring tribe, kill the males, loot the village and possess the females, was the most profitable, as well as the most exciting, way of living. Thus were the more martial tribes selected, and in chiefs and peoples a pure pugnacity and love of glory came to mingle with the more fundamental appetite for plunder.

Modern war is so expensive that we feel trade to be a better avenue to plunder; but modern man inherits all the innate pugnacity and all the love of glory of his ancestors. Showing war's irrationality and horror is of no effect upon him. The horrors make the fascination. War is the *strong* life; it is life *in extremis;* war-taxes are the only ones men never hesitate to pay, as the budgets of all nations show us.

History is a bath of blood. The Iliad is one long recital of how Diomedes and Ajax, Sarpedon and Hector *killed.* No detail of the wounds they made is spared us, and the Greek mind fed upon the story. Greek history is a panorama of jingoism and imperialism – war for war's sake, all the citizens being warriors. It is horrible reading, because of the irrationality of it all – save for the purpose of making "history" – and the history is that of the utter ruin of a civilization in intellectual respects perhaps the highest the earth has ever seen.

Those wars were purely piratical. Pride, gold, women, slaves, excitement, were their only motives. In the Peloponnesian war, for example, the Athenians ask the inhabitants of Melos (the island where the "Venus of Milo" was found), hitherto neutral, to own their lordship. The envoys meet, and hold a debate which Thucydides gives in full, and which, for sweet reasonableness of form, would have satisfied Matthew Arnold. "The powerful exact what they can," said the Athenians, "and the weak grant what they must." When the Meleans say that sooner than be slaves they will appeal to the gods, the Athenians reply: "Of the gods we believe and of men we know that, by a law of their nature, wherever they can rule they will. This law was not made by us, and we are not the first to have acted upon it; we did but inherit it, and we know that you and all mankind, if you were as strong as we are, would do as we do. So much for the gods; we have told you why we expect to stand as high in their good opinion as you." Well, the Meleans still refused, and their town was taken. "The Athenians," Thucydides quietly says, "thereupon put to death all who were of military age and made slaves of the women and children. They then colonized the island, sending thither five hundred settlers of their own."

Alexander's career was piracy pure and simple, nothing but an orgy of power and plunder, made romantic by the character of the hero. There was no rational principle in it, and the moment he died his generals and governors attacked one another. The cruelty of those times is incredible. When Rome finally conquered Greece, Paulus Æmilius was told by the Roman Senate to reward his soldiers for their toil by "giving" them the old kingdom of Epirus. They sacked seventy cities and carried off a hundred and fifty thousand inhabitants as slaves. How many they killed I know not; but in Etolia they killed all the senators, five hundred and fifty in number. Brutus was "the noblest Roman of them all," but to reanimate his soldiers on the eve of Philippi he similarly promises to give them the cities of Sparta and Thessalonica to ravage, if they win the fight.

Such was the gory nurse that trained societies to cohesiveness. We inherit the warlike type; and for most of the capacities of heroism that the human race is full of we have to thank this cruel history. Dead men tell no tales, and if there were any tribes of other type than this they have left no survivors. Our ancestors have bred pugnacity into our bone and marrow, and thousands of years of peace won't breed it out of us. The popular imagination fairly fattens on the thought of wars. Let public opinion once reach a certain fighting pitch, and no ruler can withstand it. In the Boer war both governments began with bluff but couldn't stay there; the military tension was too much for them. In 1898 our people had read the word "war" in letters three inches high for three months in every newspaper. The pliant politician McKinley was swept away by their eagerness, and our squalid war with Spain became a necessity.

At the present day, civilized opinion is a curious mental mixture. The military instincts and ideals are as strong as ever, but are confronted by reflective criticisms which sorely curb their ancient freedom. Innumerable writers are showing up the bestial side of military service. Pure loot and mastery seem no longer morally avowable motives, and pretexts must be found for attributing them solely to the enemy. England and we, our army and navy authorities repeat without ceasing, arm solely for "peace," Germany and Japan it is who are bent on loot and glory. "Peace" in military mouths today is a synonym for "war expected." The word has become a pure provocative, and no government wishing peace sincerely should allow it ever to be printed in a newspaper. Every up-to-date dictionary should say that "peace" and "war" mean the same thing, now *in posse*, now *in actu*. It may even reasonably be said that the intensely sharp competitive *preparation* for war by the nations *is the real war*, permanent, unceasing; and that the battles are only a sort of public verification of the mastery gained during the "peace"-interval.

It is plain that on this subject civilized man has developed a sort of double personality. If we take European nations, no legitimate interest of any one of them would seem to justify the tremendous destructions which a war to compass it would necessarily entail. It would seem as though common sense and reason ought to find a way to reach agreement in every conflict of honest interests. I myself think it our bounden duty to believe in such international rationality as possible. But, as things stand, I see how desperately hard it is to bring the peace-party and the war-party together, and I believe that the difficulty is due to certain deficiencies in the program of pacificism which set the militarist imagination strongly, and to a certain extent justifiably, against it. In the whole discussion both sides are on imaginative and sentimental ground. It is but one utopia against another, and everything one says must be abstract and hypothetical. Subject to this criticism and caution, I will try to characterize in abstract strokes the opposite imaginative forces, and point out what to my own very fallible mind seems the best utopian hypothesis, the most promising line of conciliation.

In my remarks, pacifist though I am, I will refuse to speak of the bestial side of the war-*régime* (already done justice to by many writers) and consider only the higher aspects of militaristic sentiment. Patriotism no one thinks discreditable; nor does anyone deny that war is the romance of history. But inordinate ambitions are the soul of every patriotism, and the possibility of violent death the soul of all romance. The militarily patriotic and romantic-minded everywhere, and especially the professional military class, refuse to admit for a moment that war may be a transitory phenomenon in social evolution. The notion of a sheep's paradise like that revolts, they say, our higher imagination. Where then would be the steeps of life? If war had ever stopped, we should have to re-invent it, on this view, to redeem life from flat degeneration.

Reflective apologists for war at the present day all take it religiously. It is a sort of sacrament. Its profits are to the vanquished as well as to the victor; and quite apart from any question of profit, it is an absolute good, we are told, for it is human nature at its highest dynamic. Its "horrors" are a cheap price to pay for rescue from the only alternative supposed, of a world of clerks and teachers, of co-education and zoophily, of "consumer's leagues" and "associated charities," of industrialism unlimited, and feminism unabashed. No scorn, no hardness, no valor any more! Fie upon such a cattleyard of a planet!

So far as the central essence of this feeling goes, no healthy-minded person, it seems to me, can help to some degree partaking of it. Militarism is the great preserver of our ideals of hardihood, and human life with no use for hardihood would be contemptible. Without risks or prizes for the darer, history would be insipid indeed; and there is a type of military character which everyone feels that the race should never cease to breed, for everyone is sensitive to its superiority. The duty is incumbent on mankind, of keeping military characters in stock — of keeping them, if not for use, then as ends in themselves and as pure pieces of perfection, — so that Roosevelt's weaklings and mollycoddles may not end by making everything else disappear from the face of nature.

This natural sort of feeling forms, I think, the innermost soul of army-writings. Without any exception known to me, militarist authors take a highly mystical view of their subject, and regard war as a biological or sociological necessity, uncontrolled by ordinary psychological checks and motives. When the time of development is ripe the war must come, reason or no reason, for the justifications pleaded are invariably fictitious. War is, in short, a permanent human *obligation.* General Homer Lea, in his recent book *The Valor of Ignorance,* plants himself squarely on this ground. Readiness for war is for him the essence of nationality, and ability in it the supreme measure of the health of nations.

Nations, General Lea says, are never stationary — they must necessarily expand or shrink, according to their vitality or decrepitude. Japan now is culminating; and by the fatal law in question it is impossible that her statesmen should not long since have entered, with extraordinary foresight, upon a vast policy of conquest — the game in which the first moves were her wars with China and Russia and her treaty with England, and of which the final objective is the capture of the Philippines, the Hawaiian Islands, Alaska, and the whole of our coast west of the Sierra Passes. This will give Japan what her ineluctable vocation as a state absolutely forces her to claim, the possession of the entire Pacific Ocean; and to oppose these deep designs we Americans have, according to our author, nothing but our conceit, our ignorance, our commmercialism, our corruption, and our feminism. General Lea makes a minute technical comparison of the military strength which we at present could oppose to the strength of Japan, and concludes that the islands, Alaska, Oregon, and Southern California, would fall almost without resistance, that San Francisco must surrender in a fortnight to a Japanese investment, that in three or four months the war would be over, and our republic, unable to regain what it had heedlessly neglected to protect sufficiently, would then "disintegrate," until perhaps some Cæsar should arise to weld us again into a nation.

A dismal forecast indeed! Yet not unplausible, if the mentality of Japan's statesmen be of the Cæsarian type of which history shows so many examples, and which is all that General Lea seems able to imagine. But there is no reason to think that women can no longer be the mothers of Napoleonic or Alexandrian characters; and if these come in Japan and find their opportunity, just such surprises as *The Valor of Ignorance* paints may lurk in ambush for us. Ignorant as we still are of the innermost recesses of Japanese mentality, we may be foolhardy to disregard such possibilities.

Other militarists are more complex and more moral in their considerations. The *Philosophie des Krieges,* by S. R. Steinmetz, is a good example. War, according to this author, is an ordeal instituted by God, who weighs the nations in its balance. It is the essential form of the State, and the only function in which peoples can employ all their powers at once and convergently. No victory is possible save as the resultant of a totality of virtues, no defeat for which some vice or weakness is not responsible. Fidelity, cohesiveness, tenacity, heroism, conscience, education, inventiveness, economy, wealth, physical health and vigor—there isn't a moral or intellectual point of superiority that doesn't tell, when God holds his assizes and hurls the peoples upon one another. *Die Weltgeschichte ist das Weltgericht;* and Dr. Steinmetz does not believe that in the long run chance and luck play any part in apportioning the issues.

The virtues that prevail, it must be noted, are virtues anyhow, superiorities that count in peaceful as well as in military competition; but the strain on them, being infinitely intenser in the latter case, makes war infinitely more searching as a trial. No ordeal is comparable to its winnowings. Its dread hammer is the welder of men into cohesive states, and nowhere but in such states can human nature adequately develop its capacity. The only alternative is "degeneration."

Dr. Steinmetz is a conscientious thinker, and his book, short as it is, takes much into account. Its upshot can, it seems to me, be summed up in Simon Patten's word, that mankind was nursed in pain and fear, and that the transition to a "pleasure-economy" may be fatal to a being wielding no powers of defence against its disintegrative influences. If we speak of the *fear of emancipation from the fear-régime,* we put the whole situation into a single phrase; fear regarding ourselves now taking the place of the ancient fear of the enemy.

Turn the fear over as I will in my mind, it all seems to lead back to two unwillingnesses of the imagination, one æsthetic, and the other moral; unwillingness, first to envisage a future in which army-life, with its many elements of charm, shall be forever impossible, and in which the destinies of peoples shall nevermore be decided quickly, thrillingly, and tragically, by force, but only gradually and insipidly by "evolution"; and, secondly, unwillingness to see the supreme theater of human strenuousness closed, and the splendid military aptitudes of men doomed to keep always in a state of latency and never show themselves in action. These insistent unwillingnesses, no less than other æsthetic and ethical insistencies, have, it seems to me, to be listened to and respected. One cannot meet them effectively by mere counter-insistency on war's expensiveness and horror. The horror makes the thrill; and when the question is of getting the extremest and supremest out of human nature, talk of expense sounds ignominious. The weakness of so much merely negative criticism is evident—pacificism makes no converts from the military party. The military party denies neither the bestiality nor the horror, nor the expense; it only says that these things tell but half the story. It only says that war is *worth* them; that, taking human nature as a whole, its wars are its best protection against its weaker and more cowardly self, and that mankind cannot *afford* to adopt a peace-economy.

Pacifists ought to enter more deeply into the æsthetical and ethical point of view of their opponents. Do that first in any controversy, says J. J. Chapman, *then move the point,* and your opponent will follow. So long as antimilitarists propose no substitute for war's disciplinary function, no *moral equivalent* of war, analogous, as one might say, to the mechanical equivalent of heat, so long they fail to realize the full inwardness of the situation. And as a rule they do fail. The duties, penalties, and sanctions pictured in the utopias they paint are all too weak and tame to touch the military-minded. Tolstoi's pacificism is the only exception to this rule, for it is profoundly pessimistic as regards all this world's values, and makes the fear of the Lord furnish the moral spur provided elsewhere by the fear of the enemy. But our socialistic peace-advocates all believe absolutely in this world's values; and instead of the fear of the Lord and the fear of the enemy, the only fear they reckon with is the fear of poverty if one be lazy. This weakness pervades all the socialistic literature with which I am acquainted. Even in Lowes Dickinson's exquisite dialogue, high wages and short hours are the only forces invoked for overcoming man's distaste for repulsive kinds of labor. Meanwhile men at large still live as they always have lived, under a pain-and-fear economy—for those of us who live in an ease-economy are but an island in the stormy ocean—and the whole atmosphere of present-day utopian literature tastes mawkish and dishwatery to people who still keep a sense for life's more bitter flavors. It suggests, in truth, ubiquitous inferiority.

Inferiority is always with us, and merciless scorn of it is the keynote of the military temper. "Dogs, would you live forever?" shouted Frederick the Great. "Yes," say our utopians, "let us live forever, and raise our level gradually." The best thing about our "inferiors" today is that they are as tough as nails, and physically and morally almost as insensitive. Utopianism would see them soft and squeamish, while militarism would keep their callousness, but transfigure it into a meritorious characteristic, needed by "the service," and redeemed by that from the suspicion of inferiority. All the qualities of a man acquire dignity when he knows that the service of the collectivity that owns him needs them. If proud of the collectivity, his own pride rises in proportion. No collectivity is like an army for nourishing such pride; but it has to be confessed that the only sentiment which the image of pacific cosmopolitan industrialism is capable of arousing in countless worthy breasts is shame at the idea of belonging to *such* a collectivity. It is obvious that the United States of America as they exist today impress a mind like General Lea's as so much human blubber. Where is the sharpness and precipitousness, the contempt for life, whether one's own, or another's? Where is the savage "yes" and "no," the unconditional duty? Where is the conscription? Where is the blood-tax? Where is anything that one feels honored by belonging to?

Having said thus much in preparation, I will now confess my own utopia. I devoutly believe in the reign of peace and in the gradual advent of some sort of a socialistic equilibrium. The fatalistic view of the war-function is to me nonsense, for I know that war-making is due to definite motives and subject to prudential checks and reasonable criticisms, just like any other form of enterprise. And when whole nations are the armies, and the science of destruction vies in intellectual refinement with the sciences of production, I see that war becomes absurd and impossible from its own monstrosity. Extravagant ambitions will have to be replaced by reasonable claims, and nations must make common cause against them. I see no reason why all this should not apply to yellow as well as to white countries, and I look forward to a future when acts of war shall be formally outlawed as between civilized peoples.

All these beliefs of mine put me squarely into the antimilitarist party. But I do not believe that peace either ought to be or will be permanent on this globe, unless the states pacifically organized preserve some of the old elements of army-discipline. A permanently successful peace-economy cannot be a simple pleasure-economy. In the more or less socialistic future towards which mankind seems drifting we must still subject ourselves collectively to those severities which answer to our real position upon this only partly hospitable globe. We must make new energies and hardihoods continue the manliness to which the military mind so faithfully clings. Martial virtues must be the enduring cement; intrepidity, contempt of softness, surrender of private interest, obedience to command, must still remain the rock upon which states are built – unless, indeed, we wish for dangerous reactions against commonwealths fit only for contempt, and liable to invite attack whenever a center of crystallization for military-minded enterprise gets formed anywhere in their neighborhood.

The war-party is assuredly right in affirming and reaffirming that the martial virtues, although originally gained by the race through war, are absolute and permanent human goods. Patriotic pride and ambition in their military form are, after all, only specifications of a more general competitive passion. They are its first form, but that is no reason for supposing them to be its last form. Men now are proud of belonging to a conquering nation, and without a murmur they lay down their persons and their wealth, if by so doing they may fend off subjection. But who can be sure that *other aspects of one's country* may not, with time and education and suggestion enough, come to be regarded with similarly effective feelings of pride and shame? Why should men not some day feel that it is worth a blood-tax to belong to a collectivity superior in *any* ideal respect? Why should they not blush with indignant shame if the community that owns them is vile in any way whatsoever? Individuals, daily more numerous, now feel this civic passion. It is only a question of blowing on the spark till the whole population gets incandescent, and on the ruins of the old morals of military honor, a stable system of morals of civic honor builds itself up. What the whole community comes to believe in grasps the individual as in a vise. The war-function has grasped us so far; but constructive interests may some day seem no less imperative, and impose on the individual a hardly lighter burden.

Let me illustrate my idea more concretely. There is nothing to make one indignant in the mere fact that life is hard, that men should toil and suffer pain. The planetary conditions once for all are such, and we can stand it. But that so many men, by mere accidents of birth and opportunity, should have a life of *nothing else* but toil and pain and hardness and inferiority imposed upon them, should have *no* vacations, while others natively no more deserving never get any taste of this campaigning life at all — *this* is capable of arousing indignation in reflective minds. It may end by seeming shameful to all of us that some of us have nothing but campaigning, and others nothing but unmanly ease. If now — and this is my idea — there were, instead of military conscription a conscription of the whole youthful population to form for a certain number of years a part of the army enlisted against *Nature*, the injustice would tend to be evened out, and numerous other goods to the commonwealth would follow. The military ideals of hardihood and discipline would be wrought into the growing fiber of the people; no one would remain blind as the luxurious classes now are blind, to man's relations to the globe he lives on, and to the permanently sour and hard foundations of his higher life. To coal and iron mines, to freight trains, to fishing fleets in December, to dish-washing, clothes-washing, and window-washing, to road-building and tunnel-making, to foundries and stokeholes, and to the frames of skyscrapers, would our gilded youths be drafted off, according to their choice, to get the childishness knocked out of them, and to come back into society with healthier sympathies and soberer ideas. They would have paid their blood-tax, done their own part in the immemorial human warfare against nature; they would tread the earth more proudly, the women would value them more highly, they would be better fathers and teachers of the following generation.

Such a conscription, with the state of public opinion that would have required it, and the many moral fruits it would bear, would preserve in the midst of a pacific civilization the manly virtues which the military party is so afraid of seeing disappear in peace. We should get toughness without callousness, authority with as little criminal cruelty as possible, and painful work done cheerily because the duty is temporary, and threatens not, as now, to degrade the whole remainder of one's life. I spoke of the "moral equivalent" of war. So far, war has been the only force that can discipline a whole community, and until an equivalent discipline is organized, I believe that war must have its way. But I have no serious doubt that the ordinary prides and shames of social man, once developed to a certain intensity, are capable of organizing such a moral equivalent as I have sketched, or some other just as effective for preserving manliness of type. It is but a question of time, of skillful propagandism, and of opinion-making men seizing historic opportunities.

The martial type of character can be bred without war. Strenuous honor and disinterestedness abound elsewhere. Priests and medical men are in a fashion educated to it, and we should all feel some degree of it imperative if we were conscious of our work as an obligatory service to the state. We should be *owned*, as soldiers are by the army, and our pride would rise accordingly. We could be poor, then, without humiliation, as army officers now are. The only thing needed henceforward is to inflame the civic temper as past history has inflamed the military temper. H. G. Wells, as usual, sees the center of the situation. "In many ways," he says, "military organization is the most peaceful of activities. When the contemporary man steps from the street of clamorous, insincere advertisement, push, adulteration, underselling, and intermittent employment into the barrackyard, he steps on to a higher social plane, into an atmosphere of service and cooperation and of infinitely more honorable emulations. Here at least men are not flung out of employment to degenerate because there is no immediate work for them to do. They are fed and drilled and trained for better services. Here at least a man is supposed to win promotion by self-forgetfulness and not by self-seeking. And besides the feeble and irregular endowment of research by commercialism, its little short-sighted snatches at profit by innovation and scientific economy, see how remarkable is the steady and rapid development of method and appliances in naval and military affairs! Nothing is more striking than to compare the progress of civil conveniences which has been left almost entirely to the trader, to the progress in military apparatus during the last few decades. The house-appliances of today, for example, are little better than they were fifty years ago. A house of today is still almost as ill-ventilated, badly heated by wasteful fires, clumsily arranged and furnished as the house of 1858. Houses a couple of hundred years old are still satisfactory places of residence, so little have our standards risen. But the rifle or battleship of fifty years ago was beyond all comparison inferior to those we possess; in power, in speed, in convenience alike. No one has a use now for such superannuated things."

Wells adds that he thinks that the conceptions of order and discipline, the tradition of service and devotion, of physical fitness, unstinted exertion, and universal responsibility, which universal military duty is now teaching European nations, will remain a permanent acquisition, when the last ammunition has been used in the fireworks that celebrate the final peace. I believe as he does. It would be simply preposterous if the only force that could work ideals of honor and standards of efficiency into English or American natures should be the fear of being killed by the Germans or the Japanese. Great indeed is Fear; but it is not, as our military enthusiasts believe and try to make us believe, the only stimulus known for awakening the higher ranges of men's spiritual energy. The amount of alteration in public opinion which my utopia postulates is vastly less than the difference between the mentality of those black warriors who pursued Stanley's party on the Congo with their cannibal war-cry of "Meat! Meat!" and that of the "general-staff" of any civilized nation. History has seen the latter interval bridged over: the former one can be bridged over much more easily.

—*William James, American (1842–1910).*

Earth, Air and Mind

H. G. WELLS

Our world is changing with an ever-increasing violence. An old world dies about us. A new world struggles into existence. But it is not developing the brain and the sensitiveness and delicacy necessary for its new life. That is the essence of what I have in mind when I say that the time is ripe for a very extensive revision and modernization of the intellectual organization of mankind.

It is, so to speak, a matter of current observation that in a century and a half there has been an enormous increase in the speed and facility of communication between men in every part of the world. Two hundred years ago Oliver Goldsmith said that if every time a man fired a gun in England, someone was killed in China, we should never hear of it and no one would bother very much about it. All that is changed. We should hear about that murdered Chinaman almost at once. Today we can go all round the world in the time it took a man to travel from New York to Washington in 1800, we can speak to anyone anywhere as soon as the proper connections have been made and in a little while we shall be able to look one another in the face from the ends of the earth. In a very few years now we shall be able to fly in the stratosphere across the Atlantic in a few hours with a cargo of passengers, or bombs or other commodities. There has in fact been a complete revolution in our relation to distances.

And the practical consequences of these immense approximations are only now beginning to be realized. Everybody knows these facts now, but round about 1900 we were only beginning to take notice of this abolition of distance. Even in 1919 the good gentlemen who settled the world forever at Versailles had not observed this strange new thing in human affairs. They had not observed that it was no longer possible to live in little horse-and-foot communities because of this change of scale. We know better now. Now the consequences of this change of scale force themselves upon our attention everywhere. Often in the rudest fashion.

Our interests and our activities interpenetrate more and more. We are all consciously or unconsciously adapting ourselves to a single common world. For a time, North

America and the great sprawl of Russia and Siberia, are for obvious reasons feeling less restricted than, let us say, Japan or Germany, but, as my glancing allusion to the stratosphere was intended to remind you, this relative isolation of yours is also a diminishing isolation. The abolition of distance is making novel political and economic arrangements more and more imperative if the populations of the earth are not to grind against each other to their mutual destruction.

That imperative expansion of the scale of the community in which we have to live is the first truism I want to recall to you and bring into the foreground of our discussion. The second truism is the immense increase in our available power that has been going on. I do not know if any precise estimate of the physical energy at the disposal of mankind now and at any previous age, has ever been made, but the disproportion between what we have and what our great-grandparents had, is stupendous and continually increasing. I am told that two or three power stations in the United States are today pouring out more energy night and day than could be produced by the sustained muscular effort of the entire United States population; and that the Roman empire at its mightiest could not — even by one vast unanimous thrust, not a single soul doing anything but push and push — have kept the street and road transport of New York State moving as it moves today. You are almost sick of being told it, in this form or that, over and over again. But we all know about this sort of thing. Man was slower and feebler beyond comparison a century ago than he is today. He has become a new animal incredibly swift and strong — except in his head. We all know — in theory at least — how this increase of power affects the nature of war.

None of our new powers in this world of increasing power, has been so rapidly applied as our powers of mutual injury. A child of five with a bomb no bigger than my hand, can kill as many men in a moment as any paladin of antiquity hacking and hewing and bashing through a long and tiring battle. Both these two realities, these two portentous realities, the change of scale in human affairs and the monstrous increase of destructive power, haunt every intelligent mind today. One needs an exceptional stupidity even to question the urgency we are under to establish some effective World Pax, before gathering disaster overwhelms us. The problem of reshaping human affairs on a world scale, this World Problem, is drawing together an ever increasing multitude of minds. It is becoming the common solicitude of all sane and civilized men. We must do it — or knock ourselves to pieces.

I think it would be profitable if a group of history students were to trace how this World Problem has dawned upon the popular mind from, let us say, 1900 up to the present time. To begin with it was hardly felt to be important. Our apprehension of what it really amounts to has grown in breadth and subtlety during all these past seven-and-thirty years. We have been learning hard in the past third of a century. And particularly since 1919. In 1900 the general sense of the historical process, of what was going on in the world, was altogether shallower than ours today. People were extraordinarily ignorant of the operating causes of political events. It was quite possible then for them to agree that war was not at all a nice or desirable thing and that it ought to be put an end to, and to imagine that setting up a nice little international court at The Hague to which states could bring their grievances and get a decision without going to the trouble and expense of hostilities would end this obsolescent scandal. Then we should have peace forever — and everything else would go on as before. But now even the boy picking cotton or working the elevator, knows that nothing will go as before. The fear of change has reached them.

You will recall that Andrew Carnegie set aside quite a respectable fraction of his savings to buy us world peace forever and have done with it. The Great War was an enlightening disappointment to this earlier school of peacemakers, and it released a relatively immense flow of thought about the World Problem. But even at Versailles the people most immediately powerful were still evidently under the impression that world peace was simply a legal and political business. They thought the Great War had happened, but they were busy politicians, and had not remarked that vastly greater things were happening. They did not realize even that elementary point about the unsuitable size of contemporary states to which I recall your attention — much less did they think about the new economic stresses that were revolutionizing every material circumstance of life. They saw the issue as a simple affair upon the lines of old-fashioned history. So far as their ideas went it was just Carthage and Rome over again. The Central Powers were naughty naughty nations and had to be punished. Their greatest novelty was the League of Nations, which indeed was all very well as a gesture and an experiment, but which as an irremovable and irreplaceable reality in the path of world adjustment has proved anything but a blessing. It had been a brilliant idea in the reign of Francis I of France. Still we have to recognize that in 1919 the Geneva League was about as far as anyone's realization of the gravity of the World Problem had gone. It is our common quality to be wise after the event and still quite unprepared for the next change ahead. It is an almost universal human failing to believe that now we know everything, that nothing more than we know *can* be known about human relations, and that in our limitless wisdom we can fix up our descendants forever more, by constitutions, treaties, boundaries, and leagues. So my poor generation built this insufficient league. For a time a number of well-meaning people *did* consider that the League of Nations settled the World Problem for good and all, and that they need not bother their heads about it any more. There were, we felt, no further grounds for anxiety, and we all sat down within our nice little national boundaries to resume business according to the old ways, securing each of us the largest possible share of the good things the new Era of Peace and Prosperity was to bring—at least to the good countries to whom victory had been accorded. When later the history of our own times comes to be written, I imagine this period between 1919 and 1929 will be called the Fatuous Twenties.

We all know better now. Now that we are living in what no doubt the historian will some day call the Frightened Thirties. Versailles was no settlement. There is still no settlement. The World Problem still pursues us. And it seems now vastly nearer, uglier and more formidable than it ever did before. It emerges through all our settlements like a dangerous rhinoceros coming through a reed fence. Our mood changes now from one in which offhand legal solutions were acceptable, to an almost feverish abundance of mental activity. From saying, "There is the Hague Court and what more do you want?" or "There is the League of Nations, what more *can* you want?" or "There is the *British Peace Ballot* and please don't bother me further," we are beginning to apprehend something of the full complexity of the situation that faces mankind, that is to say all of us, as a living species. Our minds are beginning to grasp the vastness of these grim imperatives. That change of scale, that enhancement of power has altered the fundamental conditions of human life—of our lives. The traditions of the old world, the comparatively easy traditions in which we have grown up and by which we have shaped our lives, are bankrupt. They are outworn. They are outgrown. They are too decayed for much more patching. They are as untrustworthy and dangerous as a very old car whose engine has become explosive, which has lost its brake lining and has a loose steering wheel. What I am saying now is gradually becoming as plain in men's minds as the roundness of the earth. New World or nothing. We have to make a new world for ourselves or we shall suffer and perish amidst the downfall of the decaying old. This is a business of fundamentals in which we are all called upon to take part, and through which the lives of all of us are bound to be changed essentially and irrevocably.

With this realization of the true immensity and penetration of the World Problem we are passing out of the period of panaceas—of simple solutions. As we grow wiser we realize more and more that the World Problem is not a thing like a locked door for which it is only necessary to find a single key. It is infinitely more complex. It is a battle all along the line and every man is a combatant or a deserter. Popular discussion is thick with competing simple remedies, these one-thing-needful proposals, each of which has its factor of truth and each of which in itself is entirely inadequate. Consider some of them. Arbitration, League of Nations, I have spoken of. World Socialism? The socialist very rightly points out the evils and destructive stresses that arise from the free play of the acquisitive impulse in production and business affairs, but his solution, which is to take the control of things out of the hands of the acquisitive in order to put it into the hands of the inexperienced, plainly leaves the bulk of the world's troubles unsolved. The communist and fascist have theorized about and experimented with the seizure and concentration of power, but they produce no sound schemes for its beneficial use. Seizing power by itself is a gangster's game. You can do nothing with power except plunder and destroy – unless you know exactly what to do with it. People tell us that Christianity, the Spirit of Christianity, holds a key to all our difficulties. Christianity, they say, has never yet been tried. We have all heard *that*. The trouble is that Christianity in all its various forms never does try. Ask it to work out practical problems and it immediately floats off into otherworldliness. Plainly there is much that is wrong in our property-money arrangements, but there again prescriptions for a certain juggling with currency and credit, seem unlikely in themselves to solve the World Problem. A multitude of suggestions are bandied about with increasing passion. In comparison with any preceding age, we are in a state of extreme mental fermentation. This is, I suggest, an inevitable phase in the development of our apprehension of the real magnitude and complexity of the World Problem which faces us. Except for the faddists and fanatics we all feel a sort of despairing inadequacy amidst this wild storm of suggestions and rash beginnings. We want to know more, we want digested facts to go upon. Our minds are not equipped for the job.

We are ships in uncharted seas. We are big-game hunters without weapons of precision. To mark the point we have reached, I repeat, our minds are not equipped for the job.

This present uproar of incomplete ideas was as inevitable as the Imperialist Optimism of 1900, the Futile Amazement of the Great War, and the self-complacency of the Fatuous Twenties. These were all phases, in the march of our race through disillusionment to understanding. After the phase of panaceas there comes now, I hope, a phase of intelligent coordination of creative movements, a balanced treatment of our complex difficulties. We are going to think again. We are all beginning to realize that the World Problem, the universal world problem of adapting our life to its new scale and its new powers, has to be approached on a broad front, along many paths and in many fashions.

At the start I stressed our spreading realization of the possibility of a great catastrophe in world affairs. One immediate consequence of our full realization of what this World Problem before us means is dismay. We lose heart. We feel that anyhow we cannot adjust that much. We throw up the sponge. We say, let us go on as long as possible anyhow, and after us, let what will happen. A considerable and a growing number of people are persuaded that a drift towards a monstrously destructive war cycle which may practically obliterate our present civilization is inevitable. I have, I suppose, puzzled over such possibilities rather more than most people. I do not agree with that inevitability of another great war. But I agree with its possibility. I think such a collapse so possible that I have played with it imaginatively in a book or so and a film. It is so much a possibility that it is wholesome to bear it constantly in mind. But all the same I do not believe that world disaster is unavoidable.

It is extraordinarily difficult to estimate the relative strength of the driving forces in human affairs today. We are not dealing with measurable quantities. We are easily the prey of our moods, and our latest vivid impression is sure to count for far too much. Values in my own mind, I find, shift about from hour to hour. I guess it is about the same with most people. Just as in a battle, so here, our moods are factors in the situation. When we feel depressed, the world is going to the devil and we meet defeat halfway; when we are elated, the world is all right and we win. And I think that most of us are inclined to overestimate the menace of violence, the threats of nationalist aggression and the suppression of free discussion in many parts of the world at the present time. I admit the darkness and grimness on the face of things. Indisputably vehement *state-ism* now dominates affairs over large regions of the civilized world. Everywhere liberty is threatened or outraged. Here again, I merely repeat what the whole intelligent world is saying.

Well. . . .

I do not want to seem smug amidst such immunities as we English-speaking people still enjoy, nevertheless I must confess I think it possible to overrate the intensity and staying power of this present nationalist phase. I think that the present vehemence of nationalism in the world may be due not to the strength of these tyrannies but to their weakness. This change of scale, this increment of power that has come into human affairs, has strained every boundary, every institution and every tradition in the world. It is an age of confusion, an age of gangster opportunity. After the gangsters the vigilantes. Both the dying old and the vamped-up new are on the defensive. They build up their barriers and increase their repression because they feel the broad flood of change towards a vastly greater new order is rising. Every old government, every hasty new government that has leapt into power, is made crazy by the threat of a wider and greater order, and its struggle to survive becomes desperate. It tries still to carry on — to deny that it is an experiment — even if it survives, crippled and monstrous. The dogmatic Russian Revolution has not held power for a score of years and yet it, too, is now as much on the defensive as any other upstart dictatorship. A lot of what looks to us now like triumphant reaction may in the end prove to be no more than doomed, dwarfed and decaying dogmas and traditions at bay. None of the utterances of these militant figures that most threaten the peace of the world today have the serene assurance of men conscious that they are creating something that marches with the ruling forces of life. For the most part they are shouts — screams — of defiance. They scold and rant and threaten. That is the rebel note and not the note of mastery.

We hear very much about the suppression of thought in the world. Is there really — even at the present time—in spite of all this current violence, any real diminution of creative thought in the world — as compared with 1800 or 1850 — or 1900 or 1914 or 1924? You have to remember that the suppression of free discussion in such countries as Germany, Italy, and Russia does not mean an end to original thought in these countries. Thought like gunpowder, may be all the more effective for being confined. I know that beneath the surface Germany is thinking intensely, and Russia is thinking more clearly if less discursively than ever before. Maybe we overestimate the value of that idle and safe, slack, go-as-you-please discussion that we English-speaking folk enjoy under our democratic regime. The concentration camps of today may prove after all to be the austere training grounds of a new freedom.

Let us glance for a moment at the chief forces that are driving against all that would keep the world in its ancient tradition of small national governments, warring and planning perpetually against each other, of a perpetual struggle not only of nations but individuals for a mere cramped possessiveness.

Consider now the drives toward release, abundance, one World Pax, one world control of violence, that are going on today. They seem to me very much like those forces that drove the United States to the Pacific coast and then prevented the break-up of the Union. No doubt, many a heart failed in the covered wagons as they toiled westward, face to face with the Red Indian and every sort of lawless violence. Yet the drive persisted and prevailed. The vigilantes prepared the way for the reign of law. The railway, the telegraph and so on followed the covered wagon and knitted this new-scale community of America together. In the middle nineteenth century all Europe thought that the United States must break up into a lawless confusion. The railway, the printing press, saved that. The greater unity conquered because of its immense appeal to common sense in the face of the new conditions. And because it was able to appeal to common sense through these media.

The United States could spread gigantically and still keep a common mind. And today I believe in many ways, in a variety of fashions and using many weapons and devices, the vigilantes of World Peace, under the stimulus of still wider necessities, are finding themselves and each other and getting together to ride.

That is to say their minds are getting together.

One great line of development must be towards a common control of the air. The great spans of the Atlantic and Pacific may prevent this from beginning as a world-wide air control, but that I think is just a passing phase of the problem. I submit to you that a state of affairs in which vast populations are under an ever increasing threat of aerial bombardment with explosives, incendiary bombs and poison gas at barely an hour's notice, is intolerable to human reason. Maybe there will be terrible wars first. Quite possibly not. It may after all prove unnecessary to have very many great cities destroyed and very many millions of people burnt, suffocated, blown limb from limb, before men see what stares them in the face and accept the obvious. Men are, after all, partly reasonable creatures — they have at least spasmodic moral impulses. There is already in action a movement for World Air Control. But you can't have a thing like that by itself. Who or what will control the air?

This is a political question. None of us quite know the answer, but the answer has to be found, and hundreds of thousands of the best brains on earth are busy at the riddle of that adjustment. We can rule out any of the pat, ready-made answers of yesterday, League of Nations or what not. Nonetheless that implacable necessity for world air control insists upon something, something with at least the authority of a world federal government in these matters, and that trails with it, you will find, a revelation of other vast collateral necessities. I cannot now develop these at any great length. But in the end I believe we are led to the conviction that the elemental forces of human progress, the stars in their courses, are fighting to evoke at least this much world community as involves a control of communications throughout the whole world, a common federal protection of everyone in the world from private, sectarian or national violence, a common federal protection of the natural resources of the planet from national, class or individual appropriation, and a world system of money and credit. The obstinacy of man is great but the forces that grip him are greater and in the end, after I know not what wars, struggles and afflictions, this is the road along which he will go. He has to see it first — and then he will do it, I am as sure of the ultimate necessity of this federal world state — and at the backs of your minds at least, I believe most of you are too — as I am sure that, whatever clouds may obscure it, the sun will rise tomorrow.

And now having recapitulated and brought together this general conception of human progress towards unity which is forming in most of our minds, as an answer to the ever more insistent World Problem, I come to the discussion of one particular aspect of this march towards a world community, the necessity it brings with it, for a correlated educational expansion. This has not so far been given anything like the attention it may demand in the near future. We have been gradually brought to the pitch of imagining and framing our preliminary ideas of a federal world control of such things as communications, health, money, economic adjustments, and the suppression of crime. In all these material things we have begun to foresee the possibility of a world-wide network being woven between all men about the earth. So much of the World Peace has been brought into the range of — what shall I call it? — the general imagination. But I do not think we have yet given sufficient attention to the prior necessity, of linking together its mental organizations into a much closer accord than obtains at the present time. All these ideas of unifying mankind's affairs depend ultimately for their realization on mankind having a unified mind for the job. The want of such effective mental unification is the key to most of our present frustrations. While men's minds are still confused, their social and political relations will remain in confusion, however great the forces that are grinding them against each other and however tragic and monstrous the consequences.

Now I know of no general history of human education and discussion in existence. We have nowadays — in what is called the New History — books which trace for us in rough outline the growth in size and complexity of organized human communities. But so far no one has attempted to trace the stages through which *teaching* has developed, how schools began, how discussions grew, how knowledge was acquired and spread, how the human intelligence kept pace with its broadening responsibilities. We know that in the small tribal community and even in the city states of — for example — Greece, there was hardly any need for reading or writing. The youngsters were instructed and initiated by their elders. They could walk all over the small territory of their community and *see* and *hear,* how it was fed, guarded, governed. The bright young men gathered for oral instruction in the porch or the academy. With the growth of communities into states and kingdoms we know that the medicine man was replaced by an organized priesthood; we know that scribes appeared, written records. There must have been schools for the priests and scribes but we know very little about it. We know something of the effect of the early writings, the Bible particularly, in consolidating and preserving the Jewish tradition

— giving it such a start-off that for a long time it dominated the subsequent development of the Gentile world; and we know that the survival and spread of Christianity is largely due to its resort to written records to supplement the oral teaching of disciples with which it began. But the growing thirst for medical, theological and general knowledge that appeared in the Middle Ages and which led to these remarkable gatherings of hungry minds, the universities, has still to be explained and described. That appearance and that swarming of scholars would make an extraordinary story. After the lecture room, the book; after that the newspaper, universal education, the cinema, the radio. No one has yet appeared to make an orderly story of the developments of information and instruction that have occurred in the past hundred years. Age by age the world's Knowledge Apparatus has grown up. Unpremeditated. Without a plan. But enlarging the possible areas of political cooperation at every stage in its growth.

It is a very interesting thing indeed to ask oneself certain questions. How did I come to know what I know about the world and myself? What ought I to know? If I want to know about this or that, where can I get the clearest, best and latest information? And where did these other people about me get their ideas about things? Which are sometimes so different from mine. Why do we differ so widely? Surely about a great number of things upon which we differ there is in existence exact knowledge? So that we ought not to differ in these things. This is true not merely about small matters [illegible] pute but about vitally important things co[illegible]cerning our business, our money, our political outlook, our health, the general conduct of our lives.

We are guessing, when we might know.

The facts are there, but we don't know them completely. We are inadequately informed. We blunder about in our ignorance and this great ruthless world in which we live, beats upon us and punishes our ignorance like a sin. Not only in our mass-ruled democracies but in the countries where dogmas and dictators rule, tremendous decisions are constantly being made affecting human happiness, root and branch, in complete disregard of realities that are known.

You see we are beginning to realize not only that the formal political structures of the world and many of the methods of our economic life are out-of-date and out-of-scale, but also another thing that hampers us hopelessly in every endeavor we make to adjust life to its new conditions: our World Knowledge Apparatus is not up to our necessities. We are neither collecting, arranging nor digesting what knowledge we have at all adequately, and our schools, our instruments of distribution are old-fashioned and ineffective.

We are not being told enough, we are not being told properly, and that is one main reason why we are all at sixes and sevens in our collective life.

— H. G. Wells, English (1866–1946).

Appendix

Topics for Discussion

PART ONE: Man and His Cultural Heritages

1. In what ways do the ideas of Kaibara Ekken's essay on books transcend the time and place of their origin? Can any traces of Ekken's nationality be discerned in the essay?

2. Why does poetry offer ideal material for the anthologist?

3. In what way does nature-imagery constitute a part of the language of Japanese poetry, as described by Ki no Tsurayuki? What authors writing in English also cultivate this field?

4. Is Stevenson's view of culture romantic? Is it authoritarian? What merits or defects can be found in his point of view?

5. How does Gilbert Murray describe the role of imaginative literature in the growth of the mind?

6. What are some of the distinctive properties which John Addington Symonds ascribes to individual arts? How should other arts than those which he discusses, such as the radio and screen, be described? What are the chief aesthetic principles and cultural values which different arts share in common?

7. What are some of the chief principles of social history laid down by Hippolyte Taine? Does his philosophy of history and culture tend more to unite or to divide the major groupings of men? What relations does Taine bear to the rise of modern nationalism?

8. Who is the "Ariel" of whom Rodó writes?

9. What are some of the outstanding aspects of the idealism expressed in Rodó's essay? Can such idealistic concepts be used as groundwork for evil as well as for good?

10. Is Rodó an "aesthete"? How does the spirit of his work contrast with that of the selection in Part Five of this book from Confucius?

PART TWO: Geneses: The Origins of Man and Life

1. What strong elements of democracy as this word is understood today can be found in the Protagoras myth by Plato?

2. Does Plato picture the political life as a form of liberal education?

3. Why does Plato refer to the Athenians in this account of man's social life? What in general is known of the contribution of ancient Athens to the public life?

4. Why is the selection chosen here from the Upanishads considered one of the outstanding passages in the world's literature?

5. How does the selection from the Upanishads illustrate metaphysical thought?

6. May we call the first three chapters of the Book of Genesis a poem?

7. To what cravings of the human mind and spirit have these chapters given satisfaction?

8. What formal artistry, if any, can be detected in them?

9. What debt did Milton or Michelangelo owe to the Book of Genesis?

10. What intellectual creations of the twentieth century approach nearest to this book?

11. What foreshadowings of modern scientific theories are found in the imaginary cosmology of the prose Edda by Snorri Sturluson?

12. What theological significance have the pictures of the supreme and good "Manito" and of the secondary and evil Manito as described in the *Walam Olum*, the American Indian legend?

13. Do the tribal traditions depicted in the *Walam Olum* chiefly concern the origin of men or their subsequent history?

14. How shall we criticize the relation of patriotism and religion as exhibited in the myth of the Mikado and the Sun Goddess?

PART THREE: The People's Story

1. What human values seem most persistent in epic poetry from its earliest known beginnings – in such a work as *Gilgamesh*, for example – to the present day?

2. Why have the Homeric poems fascinated the Western World?

3. Of what human values unknown to Homer was Virgil aware?

4. How does the view of life represented by *The Song of Roland* differ from that of the Greeks or Romans?

5. What differences do you discern between the spirit of the *Nibelungenlied* and the epics springing from Latin or Mediterranean countries?

6. What powerful use of irony is made in the *Nibelungenlied?*

7. What are some of the characteristics of Camoëns' imagination? What indications does Camoëns afford of the influence of the Oriental peoples on the culture of sixteenth-century Europe in general and on the Spanish peninsula in particular?

8. In what ways does Milton chiefly resemble the major epic poets before him? How does Puritanism make itself felt in his poem? How do you yourself account for the pleasure which you derive from his work?

9. Accepting Benét's picture of John Brown as substantially true to life, what are the soundest arguments to be given both for and against Brown?

PART FOUR: Myths, Fables, and Allied Forms

1. What good stories, such as *The Ass in the Lion's Skin,* do we readily think of which admirably illustrate a point?

2. What quality is there in stories such as this attractive to both young and old?

3. What outstanding contrasts distinguish the witty animal stories in Aesop's *Fables* from folklore such as *The Star Family,* a legend of the Shawnee Indians? Which type of fable is more attractive to children?

4. For what features in his stories besides dialect was Joel Chandler Harris indebted to the imagination of the Negroes of the South?

5. How are animal fables reflected in the art of the centuries?

6. Does one find in Adolf Dygasiński's story any analogues to political life? Might a Polish writer of strong imagination be likely to be singularly sensitive to this type of irony?

7. The story entitled "Chinese Cinderella" at once suggests the world-wide currency of certain themes in folklore. What is the social and cultural significance of this use of common property in the imagination? In what respects have men overridden national boundaries in their aesthetic life?

8. The story of the Canadian, Charles G. D. Roberts, represents an outlook often called naturalistic. This suggests the question whether nature seems to us today more wonderful than folklore?

9. Conceding Roberts' story to be naturalism in literature, one may still debate whether it stands closer to art or to science. May it share in the thinking of both domains, and still be justified in its own right? What may be inferred from this as to the compartmentalizing of knowledge and thought?

10. Granting that through its moral or didactic spirit Björnson's tale is related to many of the preceding fables, what literary element is here encountered in this group of selections for the first time?

11. May we infer from this and other selections from Scandinavian literature in this book that that literature excels in tragedy? Do any explanations suggest themselves?

12. By reading the stories of Björnson and Cankar side by side, one naturally considers the distinctions between tragedy and pathos. What are some of these distinctions? Are both of these literary achievements legitimate? Are they or are they not of equal value?

13. Of the two stories, *Mujo the Drunkard,* and *The Quest Begins,* which appears to be the more sophisticated in the sense of being artificially concocted and emotionally diluted?

PART FIVE: Scriptures of Some Living Religions

1. May we say that in Buddhism divinity is conceived as a state of the human mind?

2. In what respect does Buddhism assume a different evaluation of passivity and active will from that preached by Christianity?

3. How far can we comprehend the motives for "the great retirement" as attained by Sidhattha, the Future Buddha?

4. From the sermon by Buddha entitled "Questions Which Tend Not To Edification," what may be inferred as to the Buddhistic view of rationalism in theology?

5. How can the teaching contained in the passage entitled, "The Middle Doctrine" be said to define a cyclical view of existence?

6. What democratic principles are found in the teaching of Confucius?

7. What is the role of the family in Confucius's system of the state?

8. What inferences are drawn from Confucius's statement, "Benevolence is the characteristic element of humanity, and the great exercise of it is in loving relations"?

9. What role in the human spirit does Confucius assign to tranquillity?

10. What are Confucius's views of aggression and ostentation?

11. How shall we distinguish between the moral tranquillity praised by Confucius and the mystical tranquillity praised by Lao Tze?

12. What did Lao Tze think of ceremonies? of rationalism? Does his thought bear any resemblance to Western anarchism?

13. What, broadly speaking, does Lao Tze mean by the "Tao"?

14. What in general terms are the relations between the teachings of Judaism and Christianity, and of Judaism and Mohammedanism?

15. What in general has been the contribution of the Jews to the world's religious thought?

16. What are some leading characteristics of Jewish religious poetry?

17. Of the three religions, Judaism, Mohammedanism and Christianity, which appears the most idealistic?

18. Whence, historically speaking, does the idealistic element in Christian philosophy chiefly derive?

19. How can one account for the irony that the conduct of the Christian world more nearly resembles the teachings of Mohammed than those of Christ?

20. What, in brief, has been the role of Mohammedanism in history, and what is its geographical and ethnological role today?

21. Since one of the major problems of religion is the conception of the relation of the human and the divine, the question naturally arises, how is this problem treated by Buddhism, Confucianism, Christianity and Mohammedanism?

22. What are the different conceptions of "heaven" in the four faiths?

PART SIX: The Creative Imagination

1. What evidence do the Chinese poems in this section offer that the Chinese themselves are a highly imaginative people?

2. Why is St. Francis's *Canticle of the Sun* so widely and highly prized? How does it compare with Ikhnaton's hymn?

3. In what ways does the metaphysical insight of the Spanish appear remarkable?

4. What type of experience does Leopardi describe in *The Infinite?*

5. How does the mythology of Goethe's *Prometheus* compare with that of Hölderlin's *Hyperion's Song of Fate?*

6. What kinds of insight are expressed by Rilke?

7. Why has the type of poetry written by Baudelaire sometimes been called "imagism"?

8. Christopher Smart's contemporaries regarded his *Song to David* as "a melancholy example of enthusiasm." Do you?

9. What is the meaning of Blake's *Tiger?* What would be meant in saying that in his *Auguries of Innocence* he is both an idealist and an aesthete?

10. How would you describe in prose the experience lying behind Wordsworth's poem *On the Intimations of Immortality?*

11. How does Björnson's *Child in the Soul* differ from Wordsworth's poem? Do any racial traits appear in Björnson's lyric?

12. What basic concept do *Quia Amore Langueo* and Francis Thompson's celebrated *Hound of Heaven* share in common?

13. How is Emily Dickinson more "modern" than Wordsworth?

14. What is the irony in Aiken's *Morning Song of Senlin?*

15. What evidence do the poems by Archibald MacLeish and Wallace Stevens give of the attitude of the metaphysical mind toward nature and art?

PART SEVEN: The Unfolding Universe

1. What principles in argumentation are suggested by Cosmas Indicopleustes' defense of the Ptolomaic System? Are there writers today who in any respect resemble him?

2. How does the more philosophical approach to nature in our selection from Copernicus compare with the more experimental approach in the selections from Leeuwenhoek, Linnaeus and Pasteur?

3. How does Bacon's point of view contrast with that of his predecessors?

4. Has the greater contribution to mankind been made by the microscope or the telescope?

5. What typical and important applications of botany have been made by Dutchmen, Russians, Germans and Americans?

6. What relation exists in Darwin's thinking between science, philosophy and religion? Is there also an aesthetic element in Darwin's thought? Is he a man of letters as well as a man of science?

7. Was Darwin's optimism typical of his century? What relation exists between such optimism and his own scientific thought?

8. Have Darwin's theories lent themselves at times to a pessimistic or a cynical outlook on life?

9. Should the physicist today accept ethical responsibilities for his learning and discoveries?

10. What scientists beside Pasteur have left an impression of ethical inspiration as well as of the power of learning in the material world?

11. May we find a kinship with the poetical imagination in the astronomical speculations of Emanuel Kant as summarized by Edwin P. Hubble? Do Kant's methods in science more nearly resemble those of Copernicus or Pasteur?

12. Which seems the more abstract science: astronomy or bacteriology? Which leans the more heavily upon mathematics?

13. What branches of modern science are the most affected by the Einstein theory?

14. How do the conclusions of modern astronomy affect our view of modern life? Do they have influences, direct or indirect, on religion?

15. Was the abstract art of the Egyptians influenced by the comparatively advanced state of Egyptian astronomy? Does abstract art today owe a debt to our new mathematical or astronomical science as indicated by Professor Hubble?

PART EIGHT: TRAVEL AND EXPLORATION

1. Do we meet people whose travel has contributed to their education, and others for whom travel has been an idle luxury and merely a source of vanity and pride?

2. What may travel give us which books — not even books of travel — cannot afford?

3. What roles have art and photography played in enriching our knowledge of the peoples of the world?

4. How does Marco Polo compare with the travelling salesmen of modern times? Is there evidence that business men have aided the cause of friendliness among the peoples of the world? Has business competition contributed more to peace or to war?

5. In what respect may provincialism be regarded as a virtue and when does it become an evil?

6. What explains the great success of Wendell Willkie's book, *One World*?

7. How shall we contrast the spirit of such widely different travellers as Marco Polo, Cortez, and Marcus Ehrenpreis?

8. What have been some of the different roles of missionaries in travel considered as a social art? Have missionaries been willing to learn as well as to teach?

9. What importance is to be attached to the exchange of foreign students?

10. What have been some of the most important scientific expeditions?

11. How does the typical philosophy of archeologists and ethnologists differ from that of patriotic politicians or jingoistic admirals?

12. Can any significance be inferred from the common practice of referring to "my country" and "our world"?

13. What new phases have overtaken geographical study and exploration within the last few generations?

14. What different kinds of idealism are exhibited in the travel literature of Marco Polo, Saka, Linnaeus, Captain Scott, Langdon Warner, and Marcus Ehrenpreis?

15. Is Marcus Ehrenpreis in any way justified in his attitude towards the East?

16. What significance can be foreseen in the vastly accelerated means of travel in the world of the airplane?

PART NINE: Social Satire

1. Is Theocritus's description of life in the idyl here given true also of life today?

2. How does the first Satire given here from Horace compare with the poem by John Gay?

3. How does the second Satire given here from Horace compare with the poem by Alexander Pope?

4. How does the thought in the third Satire from Horace compare with the poem by Robert Browning?

5. Do you know shoppers resembling the man described by Martial?

6. Why should the contrasted claims of nature and religion have struck the medieval poet, Jean de Meun, so forcibly?

7. How does Villon's *Lesser Testament* differ from Latin satire?

8. What did the sense of humor mean for Chaucer?

9. What view of mankind do you find expressed in Langland's poem?

10. Can you suggest why the Spanish satires are so intense?

11. What is typically French in the poems by La Fontaine?

12. Do you note a medieval inheritance in the poem given here from Baudelaire?

13. What marks of irony do you find in the poem by Heine?

14. Do you find anything typically Russian in the poems by Lermontov and Blok?

15. What was Emerson's meaning when he wrote:

    Things are in the saddle
    And ride mankind.

16. What are some of the implications of the poem by Carl Sandburg?

PART TEN: Foundations of the State

1. What estimate is to be placed upon the high-mindedness of the selection from Plato?

2. Why does the modern reader find himself so sympathetic with the objective and realistic discussion of democracy selected here from Aristotle's *Politics?*

3. Does Cicero's essay appear as brilliant as the passages taken from Plato and Aristotle? Does Cicero appear to speak for as ripe a culture as the Greeks? Does he show a shrewd knowledge of practical politics?

4. How shall we appraise Mencius's doctrine of benevolence?

5. Does Machiavelli argue correctly in urging a distinction between political and private ethics?

6. To what extent does Machiavelli's argument reflect the life of Renaissance Italy?

7. Is there a parallel between the despotism reflected in Machiavelli's *Prince* and Sari Mehmed Pasha's *Illustrious Grand Vezir?*

8. What are the outstanding features of political life as reflected in the treatise on the Grand Vezir?

9. What value today has Milton's view of political liberty?

10. What are the outstanding distinctions between the English Bill of Rights and the French Declaration of the Rights of Man and of Citizens?

11. To what extent did Rousseau's conception of the Social Contract contain seeds of revolutionary action?

12. What distinctions may be drawn between Rousseau's dialectic and Paine's simpler argument? For whom was Paine writing? Did his writing affect the course of history?

13. How does the *Declaration of Rights* by Shelley and Godwin reflect the character of its authors?

14. What estimates does Nietzsche place on the civilizations of ancient Greece, Renaissance Italy, and nineteenth-century Europe? What, in general, is his view of Christianity?

15. What appear to be the strongest and weakest points in Nietzsche's argument?

16. What parts of his teaching gave support to Hitler's Germany?

17. What debt did he owe to the nineteenth-century doctrine of evolution?

18. Does Karl Marx offer a searching analysis of history? Has he proved a good prophet? To what extent do his views appear objective, and to what extent do they seem biased by the passions of partisanship and prejudice?

PART ELEVEN: Political Satire

1. What political complaints of Po Chü-i apply also to our world today?

2. What testimony have Italian or Spanish poets on the historical misgovernment of their countries?

3. What, in brief, was Victor Hugo's role in French politics?

4. From selections given in various parts of this book from Emile Verhaeren, how would you characterize his thought?

5. In the poems before us, what is Johan Runeberg's view of war?

6. What are Byron's views of militarism and of military heroism? What major wars occurred during his life-time?

7. How true to life is the poem by de la Montagne?

8. What is the political background of Yeats's poem?

9. Is Freneau's picture of European colonization ethically or historically justified?

10. What circumstances occasioned the writing of Whittier's *Massachusetts to Virginia?*

11. How is Archibald MacLeish's poem faithful to the ideals of American democracy?

PART TWELVE: The Critical Intellect

1. Judging from the specimen of his poetry here given, would you consider Pindar as a reflective poet?

2. How does the ode from Aeschylus illustrate his concentrated power?

3. Sophocles' ode to Colonus, a locality on the outskirts of Athens, is regarded by classical scholars as one of the most perfect expressions of the Greek spirit. Why?

4. From the ode from Euripides' *Hecuba* what do you judge to be this poet's views on war?

5. What critical ideas do you discern beneath the dazzle of Aristophanes' fancy?

6. What do you think Aristophanes would have thought of Horace, if he could have known him?

7. What ethical theory is expressed in Tasso's ode?

8. What views of nature, science, war and peace are expressed in Leopardi's ode?

9. Do you discern any qualities which you suspect to be characteristically Dutch in the ode by Vondel?

10. Does the view of life in Schiller's ode give the preference to reason or to feeling?

11. Why can we say that Gautier's ode exhibits, even when read in translation, a disciplined and controlled style?

12. What criticism of life is contained in the choral scene from Hardy's *Dynasts?*

13. What element of cynicism appears in the ode by Phelps Putnam?

14. What ideals does John Crowe Ransom hold forth to the American South?

PART THIRTEEN: Great Episodes and Characters in History

1. Is history best considered as a branch of the arts, the sciences, or of speculative philosophy?

2. What are the outstanding qualities of Greek civilization as exhibited in the selections from Herodotus and Plato?

3. What public characters have most nearly resembled Socrates in giving their lives for freedom of thought?

4. How shall we analyze the charges against Socrates? Are ideas similar to those of his "good and patriotic" accusers current today?

5. What was Socrates' conception of the role of philosophy in human living? What were his views of religion? What of the relation of life and death?

6. How does the death of Jesus, as described in the apocryphal gospel, compare with that of Socrates?

7. How does Caesar as depicted by Mommsen differ from Socrates or Jesus? How does Caesar compare with other of the world's outstanding statesmen?

8. Is Froude an impartial historian? In what sense is impartiality a virtue in an historian?

9. What exploits can most justly be compared to the voyage of Columbus?

10. What explains the immense role played in public opinion by the fall of the Bastile? What were Marmontel's own feelings in the presence of this event?

11. Is it necessary at times that injustices of a minor scope be committed in the interests of some larger justice? Do ethical values change in time of revolution? in times of war?

12. What were some of the major factors leading up to the battle of Saratoga which strengthened the Americans and weakened the British?

13. Does a rational sense of values give preference to victories of war or peace? What are the views on this subject in the public opinion of the Western World, in the ethical teachings of Christianity, and in those of Confucius?

14. How does the adventure of the scientist, as instanced in Madame Curie, compare with adventure in other fields of human activity?

PART FOURTEEN: Contacts of Races

1. What are the familiar conflicts of personal and racial loyalty depicted in *The Book of Ruth*?

2. Are there likenesses between the political problems of Palestine as depicted by Anatole France in his story of Pontius Pilate and Palestinian problems following the Second World War?

3. What does Anatole France represent as Pilate's prejudices concerning the Jews? What is a prejudice?

4. What racial problem lies at the bottom of the story of Aucassin and Nicolete? What, in broad outlines, have been the relations of Moslem and Christian in the Mediterranean countries?

5. What are some of the relations between religion and race where prejudices are concerned? How is this illustrated in Kristov's picture from Balkan life?

6. What are some of the ironical inconsistencies of the Jews as described in Raisin's story from the Yiddish? How common is this humorous self-criticism?

7. What elements of condescension are to be found in Kipling's picture of British rule in India?

8. Is imperialism implicit in Mille's story, *Victory?* Is socialism or patriotism also indicated?

9. What aspects of Japanese manners or psychology are exhibited in *The Pier?*

10. How does *The Pier* dramatically depict feelings which all races share?

11. Do subordinate races wish romantic praise or plain equality? How is this problem illustrated in the romantic sketch by Lafcadio Hearn? How is it illustrated in the life of American Negroes? How is it illustrated in the social life of the sexes?

12. What are the marks of Hearn's keen understanding of the Indian mythology?

13. What are the outstanding qualities of Hearn's style?

14. Is the intolerance exhibited by the revolutionists as portrayed in Pearl Buck's story common among revolutionists in general? What explanation can be found for this attitude?

15. What are some of the grossest examples of racial animosity in the world today?

16. What are the chief factors prompting such animosities?

17. Are such antagonisms often excuses for antagonisms arising from other sources?

18. What are the best means, public and private, for combatting racial antagonisms?

PART FIFTEEN: Man Against Fate

1. What do you understand to be the nature of tragedy?

2. What are some distinguishing features of tragedy on the stage as distinguished from tragic materials in novels, lyrics, histories, and other literary forms?

3. What is Aeschylus's view of the relation between pride and impiety?

4. What do tension, conflict and climax mean for tragedy?

5. What "anterior action" is implied by Aeschylus's *Agamemnon?*

6. Study the Greek play in respect to its concentration of action. What are its limits as to time and place?

7. If you have read Shakespeare's *Hamlet,* compare it with this play by Aeschylus.

8. If you have read Ibsen's *Ghosts,* compare it to this play.

9. Compare the play of Synge with that of Aeschylus.

10. Compare the play by Moody with that of Aeschylus.

11. What do you consider the psychological or moral function of tragedy?

12. How does reading a play differ from seeing it?

13. What motion pictures come the closest to the old tragedies?

PART SIXTEEN: Comedy of Manners

1. What are some special advantages enjoyed by the stage in presenting an emotional or a pathetic subject matter?

2. Among terms commonly used in discussion of comedy and always standing in need of further definition are: humor, burlesque, farce, caricature, whimsy, nonsense, clowning, extravaganza, satire, and mirth.

3. How shall we define the term, "comedy of manners"?

4. From quotations from Aristophanes given in this book what can be inferred concerning this father of Greek comedy?

5. What are some of the characteristics of a Japanese "Noh" play?

6. What is the usual role of pantomime or action in "low" comedy?

7. Does the comic spirit appear to be an inviting subject for philosophical speculation, and if so, why?

8. How should we describe the psychological or moral functions of comedy?

9. What do you know of the comic spirit in Shakespeare, Jonathan Swift, Lewis Carroll, Mark Twain?

10. What types of comedy do the motion pictures share with the comedies included in this volume?

11. What do these plays show of the national humor of Italy, Russia, and Hungary?

12. How should we characterize the national humor of the Irish, the French, the German, the Chinese, or the Negro?

13. What are some characteristic features of humor in America?

14. Who are your own favorite comic actors, and why?

PART SEVENTEEN: Man in Bereavement

1. What do we learn from Bion's poem regarding the religious cult of Adonis?

2. What was the debt of Moschus as a poet to Bion?

3. How does Boccaccio, the Italian Humanist, weave together in his *Olympia* his heritage of classical poetry and Christian religion?

4. How does the thought and feeling in Villon's *Ballad of the Gibbet* differ from that in the classical and neo-classical elegies?

5. Manrique's *Coplas* was composed when the modern world was evolving from the medieval world. What characteristics of each epoch are to be found in his poem? Judging from this specimen, what seem some of the strongest elements in Spanish thought?

6. Comparing Milton's *Lycidas* with the classical elegies and with Boccaccio's poem, what appear to be the contributions of Milton's Puritan culture?

7. What does Shelley's *Adonais* share with Milton, with Bion and with Moschus?

8. Why have great masses of men preferred Gray's elegy to all others?

9. Is the retrospective attitude in de Musset's poem typical of the poetry of the last century as you know it? Is this attitude significant to you?

10. What do you consider "modern" in the art of José Asunçion Silva?

11. What symbolical significance have the star, the lilac, and the bird in Whitman's elegy? What symbolical significance has Lincoln?

PART EIGHTEEN: The Conduct of Life

1. What role is played by idealism in Aristotle's system of ethics?

2. What is the prevailing religious mood in the chapters chosen from *Ecclesiastes*?

3. In the Buddhist aphorisms from the *Dhammapada,* what is signified by "contemplation"?

4. On what basis does Epictetus build his moving doctrine of self-sufficiency and personal serenity?

5. How explain the impression of moral grandeur produced by Marcus Aurelius's account of human duties and responsibilities?

6. What is the relation in Sa'di's thinking between mystical contemplation and sensuous pleasures? between gravity and humor? How shall we account for the impression of urbanity and ripe culture which his writing conveys?

7. What ideals in education are implied in Leonardo's aphorism: "study without desire spoils the memory, and it retains nothing that it takes in."

8. How do Japanese ideals of courtesy as expressed by Ekken differ from European ideals of chivalry? Do Ekken's precepts seem more applicable to a feudal or a democratic society?

9. What elements of spiritual strength in Jonathan Edwards' writings have the most lasting significance?

10. What merits has Franklin's *Way to Wealth* considered from the point of view of its ethics? of its style?

11. What likenesses exist between Pestalozzi's conception of sound family relations and the social philosophy of Confucius and Mencius?

12. Which seem the outstanding aphorisms of Joubert?

13. What classical qualities appear in the selection from Goethe?

14. What romantic qualities enliven Leopardi's exquisite essay on birds?

15. What are some of the strong and weak features of Emerson's doctrine of self-reliance? In what respect is his thought typically American? or typically democratic?

16. How shall we analyze and appraise Carlyle's eloquence?

17. Does Tolstoy's *Talk Among Leisured People* show chiefly moral courage, obstinacy, or foolhardiness?

PART NINETEEN: Wit and Wisdom

1. What in general accounts for the long success of the Japanese haiku?
2. What can be said of the formal perfection of the Greek epigram?
3. What is the spirit of the epitaphs of Simonides?
4. What in their epitaphs do the Greeks and Romans tell us of their attitudes towards death?
5. What is the distinction of the wit of Martial?
6. How do the short poems by Verlaine compare with those from the Chinese and Japanese?
7. In what instances do the English epigrams resemble those of the Greeks or Romans?
8. If you have a marked preference for the poems given here from either Whitman or Emily Dickinson, how do you account for your own taste?
9. Which of the poems in this section are also philosophical maxims?
10. What are a few of the familiar quotations which you know from any poems whatsoever?

PART TWENTY: Worlds of the Mind and Spirit

1. How does Plato's *Image of the Cave* illustrate his idealism? What are some of the meanings commonly given to this word?
2. What are the outstanding features in Plato's dialectical method?
3. Can Seneca be regarded as a transitional figure between the ancient Greeks and the Christians? How does he differ from each?
4. Why is the passage on intellectual beauty from Plotinus widely regarded as one of the great expressions of religious insight?
5. Can any relation be traced between the philosophies of Boethius and Thomas à Kempis?
6. What does the conception of God as a sufferer signify for Thomas?
7. How does it come about that the scientific and the religious imagination fall into such acute relationships in Pascal's mind?
8. What are the outstanding qualities of Pascal's imagination? of his style? Is he a poet? Do we today regard him chiefly as a scientist or as a mystic?

9. Is Rousseau, a writer of Swiss origins, international in his outlook?

10. What did Rousseau contribute to deism? what to naturalism? In what respects is his Vicar a romantic?

11. On the evidence of the selection from Hazlitt, why should this author be regarded as a leading master in the English essay and in English prose?

12. What were some of the values which Thoreau sought by living in the woods? Do creative artists frequently go into retirement to produce their major works?

13. Does Thoreau belong more to America or to the world? What were his views of each?

14. How shall we contrast the thought of Miguel de Unamuno and Karl Marx?

15. How shall we contrast Cardinal Newman and his contemporary, Thoreau?

16. How shall we contrast the romantic individualism of Thoreau and Unamuno with the popularization of the Asiatic religious philosophy by Tagore?

17. In what sense can Russell's essay, *Retrospect*, be called mystical?

18. How shall we appraise George Russell as a convincing reporter of mystical experience?

19. What relationship does George Santayana discern between philosophy and common sense? Is he patronizing to the common man? is he urbanely arrogant towards contemporary philosophers?

20. What does Rodó's *Gorgias' Farewell* gain and lose by its freedom from dogmatism?

PART TWENTY–ONE: Man in Love

1. What aspects of love appear stressed by the Chinese poets? by the Japanese?

2. What is, summarily speaking, the picture of love as afforded by Greek mythology?

3. How does the attitude toward love as expressed in Latin poetry appear to differ from that expressed in Greek?

4. What characteristics seem typical of medieval German folk-songs on love?

5. What chiefly constitutes the chivalrous ideal of love as shown by medieval French and German lyrics?

6. Why is Villon's *Complaint of the Fair Armoress* a poem in keeping with Christian teaching?

7. What are the primary ideas of Italian neo-platonic love poetry as written by Guinicelli, Dante, and Michelangelo?

8. How do Shakespeare's sonnets differ in their point of view from those given here from the Italian?

9. Does Rubén Dario's *Sonatina* impress you as a poem true to life?

10. What are outstanding differences in the lyrics from Heine and Verlaine?

11. How do Jeffers and Frost differ in the relative importance which they ascribe to the physical and the humane aspects of love?

12. What poems in this section would in your opinion constitute the best songs? Why?

PART TWENTY–TWO: The Stream of Story Telling

1. On the evidence of the Egyptian story, *Anpu and Bata,* what aspects of human behavior appear from primitive times to the present to have changed the least? what aspects the most?

2. What inexhaustible source of humor is used by the writer of the Chinese story, *A Fickle Widow?*

3. What is there in the story of Psyche's divided heart and will which has led thinkers to regard this mythological tale as an allegory of the human soul?

4. What features of St. Jerome's legend of Malchus, quite apart from its religious connotations, make it a good story?

5. What social relations between the sexes are indicated by Boccaccio's tale of Griselda?

6. What are some memorable tales of roguery, new or old, which might reasonably be compared to that told by Mateo Alemán?

7. What characteristics of his own personality are revealed, consciously or unconsciously, by Cellini in the story from his autobiography?

8. From Cervantes' story of Don Quixote does it appear that its author was a partisan of idealism, of materialism, or, perhaps, impartial between the two?

9. What appear the chief distinctions between the humor of the Balkan folktale, as exemplified in Simo Mutavulj's story, *The Latin Boy,* and the humor of the Western European short story, as exemplified in Alphonse Daudet's *The Pope's Mule?*

10. In what respect is Dostoievsky's story, *The Christmas Tree and the Wedding,* a criticism of Russian society of the last century?

11. What were Kipling's motives in writing such a story as *The Taking of Lungtungpen?*

12. Does the chief incident as told in D'Annunzio's story, *The Hero,* impress us as being primarily heroic or brutal?

13. How shall we appraise the ethics represented in Ricardo Fernandez-Guardia's story, *Chivalry?*

14. How is a sophisticated irony of the essence of Sudermann's story, *A New-Year's Eve Confession?*

15. How does the story here selected from the Scandinavian writer, Selma Lagerlöf, reflect the region of her birth? Is it readily intelligible elsewhere?

16. What is the social philosophy implicit in the story *Banasiowa,* by Maria Konopnika?

PART TWENTY-THREE: The Happy Life

1. What do you consider to be the philosophy of Omar's *Rubaiyat?*

2. What is the economic background indicated in the poems given here from Ovid, Horace, Martial, and Claudianus?

3. What traces do you find of the thought and art of these Latin poems in the selections given here from Spanish, Italian, French, Dutch, and English?

4. How may one describe the general temper of the English poems given here from Shakespeare to Milton?

5. How is the Italian landscape characterized by D'Annunzio?

6. What do you find typical of the Germanic spirit in the poetry of Richard Dehmel?

7. What homely wisdom is expressed in W. H. Davies's poem, *Leisure?*

8. How is the democratic viewpoint expressed in Whitman's poem, *There Was a Child Went Forth?*

9. What do you regard as the most typically American in the poems by Carl Sandburg?

PART TWENTY-FOUR: Voices of the Forum

1. In view of Patrick Henry's quotation from Jeremiah, "Peace, peace, but there is no peace," what can be inferred of the influence of the Bible upon our literature?

2. What are some of the abiding truths in the words of Ezekiel when these are considered as a plea for social and political regeneration and reform?

3. What can be said of the lasting significance of Pericles' definitions of freedom and democracy?

4. How shall we account for the extraordinary eloquence and passion of Saint Bernard's words urging the Crusade?

5. How shall we account for the more restrained eloquence of Luther at the Diet of Worms? Which American President in the conclusion of a speech urging war on Germany quoted Luther's closing words?

6. How shall we analyze the effectiveness of Patrick Henry's celebrated address?

7. What are the basic principles of French democracy as outlined by Lamartine?

8. Shall we consider Jefferson Davis's inaugural high-minded, patriotic, heroic, and effective? What important factor in American politics of the Civil War period is mentioned many times by Lincoln in his two addresses and overlooked in Davis's speech?

9. What does Lincoln mean by "freedom" in his address at Gettysburg?

10. Why is the last paragraph in Lincoln's Second Inaugural cherished as one of the finest utterances in American history?

11. What does Mazzini's discussion of duties versus privileges signify in the evolution of the idea of democracy?

12. Are the ideas of freedom and democracy older than the nineteenth-century liberal tradition?

13. What place does the role of American democracy hold in the total drama of world democracy?

14. Is there some truth in Mussolini's analysis of economic history?

15. Is his analysis of Socialism sound?

16. What elements of fascism as described by Mussolini are the most offensive to the democratic mind?

17. What enabled Mussolini to underestimate freedom and democracy?

18. How shall we contrast the politics of the different fascist countries? of the different totalitarian countries?

19. What are the fundamental ideas in Franklin Roosevelt's First Inaugural?

20. What are the chief structural and rhetorical features of Churchill's great address? of the incomparable first paragraph in his address?

PART TWENTY-FIVE: Man at Work

1. In what respect is the community depicted in Hesiod's *Works and Days* a typically primitive society, and in what ways does this early Greek society seem to you remarkable?

2. What were the historical conditions enabling Lucretius to write his eloquent passage on the theme of human progress?

3. How does Virgil describe the gentleman farmer?

4. What are some of the outstanding characteristics of popular poetry as exhibited in the above selections from French and German folk-songs?

5. What are some typical examples of poetry pleading the workman's cause?

6. How valid is the attack on industrialism as represented here by Paul Zech?

7. Do such poems as those by Gastev, E. J. Pratt, Spender, Crane, and William Carlos Williams really help to interpret man's intimate relation with modern machinery?

8. How do poems dealing with modern machinery compare with poems dealing with old-fashioned tools as written by Whittier, Whitman and Robert Frost?

9. What does Carl Sandburg's *Five Towns on the B. and O.* contribute to our grasp of the world we live in?

10. How does Sandburg's work compare as poetry with the work of older poets, as Hesiod, Du Bellay, Carducci, or Mistral?

11. Do the descriptions of aviation by Stephen Spender and Hart Crane seem genuinely poetic? How revealing are they?

PART TWENTY-SIX: The Utopian Dream

1. Is fatalism a feature of Hawthorne's thought? Whence could he have derived such a point of view?

2. What attitude does Hawthorne imply toward institutionalism? What course, if any, does he favor?

3. Is the thought of William James indebted to Calvinism? to Puritanism? to evolutionism?

4. Is his psychological analysis of modern war a sufficient analysis of the general problem of war?

5. Is James a shrewd judge of human nature?

6. How does he, as a thinker, compare with his antagonist, General Lea?

7. Is James's freedom of thought and criticism indicative of American ideals?

8. Are civilized men as pugnacious as James declares them to be?

9. How do James's ideas on war compare with Confucius's?

10. Since James wrote, what changes have occurred in the character of war?

11. In what respect does the essay by H. G. Wells sum up the fundamental ideas of this book?

12. How does H. G. Wells's view of the great modern problem of militarism contrast with views advanced by Hawthorne and James?

13. What new aspects has the problem of world brotherhood in the Atomic Age?

Index of Authors

AESCHYLUS (525–456 B.C.): The first and most austere of the Greek tragic playwrights whose work survives. An ardent patriot, he fought by land at Marathon and by sea at Salamis. He died in Sicily. Of some ninety plays, seven remain: *The Suppliants, The Persians, The Seven Against Thebes, Prometheus Bound, Agamemnon, The Libation Pourers,* and *The Eumenides.* These works are unsurpassed in their severe beauty. Later playwrights excel him in subtlety of characterization and fluidity of movement; none outdoes him in poetic sublimity. He records the Greek religious myths with an energy and a piety approached only by Pindar. There are many translations; those by E. H. Plumptre, S. Blackie, and G. M. Cookson may be read to advantage.

AESOP: This is the name of an author belonging rather to legend than to sober history. The works ascribed to him are witty fables, largely moral tales of animals, later given their best-known forms in ancient literature by Babrius, Phaedrus and Planudes Maximus. The common story is that Aesop was a sharp-tongued slave, as ugly in his face as shrewd in his wit. He is said to have flourished in the sixth century B.C. By far the larger number of the so-called fables of Aesop derive from oriental originals. Different versions of the tales have spread to all the European languages, finding their most celebrated modern forms in the fables of La Fontaine.

AGATHIAS SCHOLASTICUS (c. 536–582): A distinctly late member of the poets of the Greek Anthology, now best known for this beautiful little poem, which inspired Ben Jonson's famous song: "Drink to me only with thine eyes."

AIKEN, CONRAD (1889–): American poet and prose writer, born in Savannah, Georgia, a versatile and prolific author especially inspired by modern psychology and gifted with metaphysical imagination. Much of his best work is contained in *Selected Poems* (1929); but *John Deth and Other Poems* (1930), *Preludes for Memnon* (1931), *Time in the Rock* (1936), and *Brownstone Eclogues* (1943) are also notable. In *The Melody of Chaos* Houston Peterson has written an able study of his work.

ALEMÁN, MATEO (1547–c. 1610): This Spanish physician and novelist is known chiefly as author of the famous tale of roguery, *Guzman of Affarache.* He was born in Seville and is said to have died in Mexico. His masterpiece was promptly translated into Italian, French and English, and imitated in many lands, with special success by the French novelist Le Sage in his *Gil Blas.*

ANACREON (c. 563–478 B.C.): This Greek lyric poet was born at Teos, an Ionian town in Asia Minor. He lived at Samos and at Athens, in the latter meeting the poet Simonides. Legend reports that he died in his eighty-sixth year, choked by the stone of a dried grape. Love, wine and conviviality are subjects of most of his verse. Many gay songs written by his followers passed under his name, forming a small anthology now known as the Anacreontic verses. These were popular not only in antiquity, but in the Renaissance, and have many times been imitated and translated, into English, for example, by Spenser, Cowley and Thomas Moore. The poems have enjoyed great favor in France.

ANDRADE, JORGE CARRERA (1903–): This Ecuadorian poet was editor of a literary review at fifteen. Later active as journalist and diplomat, he has lived in France, Germany, Spain and Japan, and since 1940, has been Consul General in San Francisco. While his verse bears evidence of his cosmopolitan outlook, it also expresses the native Andean culture of his own country. In such a lyric as *Reaping the Barley,* he plunges us into the world of the Indians. Like Emily Dickinson, he can sketch much in little and be at the same time humorous, fanciful and metaphysical, as appears in his brief lyric, *The Perfect Life.* Andrade is a modern with the wisdom of ancient man behind him. He has been admired by the American poet, William Carlos Williams.

ANDREYEV, LEONID (1871–1919): This leading Russian author, born in Orel, lived much of his life near Moscow. He was of a neurotic character. During his early life he aided revolution against the Czar and suffered imprisonment. He was a zealous patriot during the First World War, but died in bitter opposition to Bolshevism. His works gained immense popularity. His best-known play is *He Who Gets Slapped,* but many others have been successful, and he has few rivals in the writing of short plays. He is equally known for his short stories, among which are *The Red Laugh, The Abyss, Lazarus,* and *The Seven Who Were Hanged.* He admirably expresses the intense, volatile and brooding Slavic temperament, which he sometimes accepts, and sometimes, as in the play given here, *An Incident,* subjects to ironic scrutiny. There is a collection of his plays in translation with an introduction by V. V. Brusyanin.

AN-NAWAWI (fl. 13th Cent.): A Damascene scholar, lawyer and traditionalist. In the six hundred years since the Hegira, various scholars had sifted and collected the mass of Moslem traditions, the most notable collection being one of more than seven thousand by Bukhari, on which Moslem canon law is largely based. Drawing from this and other sources, an-Nawawi selected these forty-two for a collection which has been very widely popular throughout the Moslem world, and is still reprinted. See *The Moslem World,* April, 1939.

ANNUNZIO, GABRIELE D' (1863–1938): This Italian poet, novelist and dramatist is author of many works notable for their high eloquence and unrestrained emotionalism. From 1910 to 1914 he lived in France, from which country he returned to urge Italy's participation in the First World War, in which he later served as an aviator. Disappointed in his ambitions for an imperialistic Italy, with a small group of followers he occupied Fiume for two years, in defiance of the Paris Conference. Among his novels are *The Child of Pleasure* and *The Flame of Life* (in which he depicts his relations with the great actress, Eleonora Duse). His plays, chiefly romantic tragedies, include *The Dead City* and *Francesca da Rimini.* Many of his lyrics are of great beauty. See F. Nardelli and A. Livingston, *Gabriel the Archangel.*

APULEIUS, LUCIUS (2nd Cent.): This Latin satirical novelist is known as author of *Metamorphoses,* or *The Golden Ass.* He studied in Carthage and Athens, and lived in various parts of Asia and Italy. Considerable is known of his eventful life. His chief book is a compound of satire, fancy, humor, and idealism. Its most famous episode tells the romantic story of the love of Cupid and Psyche, a story commonly regarded as a myth of the soul seeking perfection. The lively accounts of magic contain gibes at priestly superstition. The work has been translated into many languages and imitated by such diverse writers as Boccaccio, Cervantes, Le Sage, Fielding, and Smollett.

ARISTOPHANES (448?–380? B.C.): The only comic dramatist surviving from the great period of Athenian culture, and doubtless by far the chief. His eleven extant plays include *The Knights, The Clouds, The Peace, Lysistrata, The Birds* and *The Frogs.* They contain a discussion of general ideas, social, political and personal satire, literary and dramatic burlesque and the mirth and profanity appropriate to the festival of the wine-god, Dionysus. Under this god's patronage the dramatist was able to produce his daring works. His unequalled fancy is both earthy and ethereal, his style ranges from coarse puns to lofty poetry, his choruses from familiar verse to exalted hymns. Never have such bold paradoxes produced such exquisite artistic unity. He has inspired many poets but been rivaled or imitated in his own manner by none. See the edition by L. E. Rogers in the Loeb Classical Library.

ARISTOTLE (384–322 B.C.): This Greek philosopher probably did more than any other single man to formulate the speculative life of the Western World. Although a pupil of Plato, he frequently differed from Plato's conclusions and added new fields of thought and knowledge. He proved master of whatever subject he examined at length, with the result that not only Greek and Roman thought, but Arabian, Jewish and Christian thinkers virtually till modern times have been his followers, and in some fields his ideas are still found highly convincing. The Scholastic system of the Middle Ages was founded upon him. He has left treatises on logic, metaphysics, physics, astronomy, zoology, biology, psychology, politics, ethics, rhetoric and the aesthetics of poetry. He was born in Macedonia, where he was teacher to Alexander the Great. Much of his life he passed in Athens. See the study by A. E. Taylor.

BACON, FRANCIS (1561–1626): This English philosopher was son of the Elizabethan statesman, Sir Nicholas Bacon. He himself rose rapidly in favor under both Elizabeth and James I, until in 1618 he became Lord Chancellor. He was deprived of this office on the charge of accepting bribes. A man of tremendous intellectual energy and imagination, he discerned all that was most forward looking in the thought of his age, and cloaked his thoughts in an eloquence unsurpassed in English prose. His earliest work, his *Essays*, contains shrewd and worldly moralizing. Far weightier are his later books, in which he champions the new science and defines its methods and aims. His *New Atlantis* depicts a scientist's Utopia. *The Advancement of Learning* sketches the whole field of learning. In the *Novum Organum* he deals at length with the inductive method of the new sciences, which he opposes to the *a priori* method of medieval scholasticism. Although he was regarded by thinkers of succeeding generations as a major leader in the advance of science, he himself made no important discoveries. But he marshalled those who came after him. See the study of R. W. Church.

BASHO, MATSUO (1643–1694): This Japanese poet did more than any other writer to refine the Japanese short poem and win it a lasting popularity. Basho belonged to a Samurai family in the province of Ise. He became both a Zen Buddhist and a Taoist. He achieved fame not only in verse but in painting.

BAUDELAIRE, CHARLES (1821–1867): This French poet, born in Paris, devoted himself to his writing and to the cultivation of various vices which he deemed aids to his art. In youth he travelled in the East; all his life he pursued the exotic. In 1856 he translated Poe's *Tales*. The following year appeared his *Les Fleurs du Mal* (*Flowers of Evil*), one of the greatest collections of French lyrics. In gorgeous imagery these poems express a bitter revolt against scientific determinism. With mystic fervor the poet pursued a world of imagination stretching beyond the doors of death. Haunted by Christian thinking, he sought his salvation through devotion to Satan. In addition to his metaphysical poetry, he discovered a new vein in his tender and terrible poems, in prose and verse, describing the impoverished life within the great cities. His influence has been increasingly felt throughout the world. See the translations of his poems by George Dillon and Edna St. Vincent Millay.

BELLAY, JOACHIM DU (1524–1560): This French poet was, next to Ronsard, the leader in the group of seven reformers in French literature known as the *Pléiade*. This group presented a somewhat sober and academic view of the meaning of the Renaissance, or the new age, in France. They combined French patriotism and the French spirit with the canons of the new neo-classicism. Du Bellay voiced their views in his critical essay, *Défense et Illustration de la Langue Française* (1549). The following year he published a collection of lyrics much indebted to Petrarch. He travelled in Italy. When he died he had been designated archbishop of Bordeaux. He translated a part of Virgil's *Aeneid*. His finest original works are sonnets on Rome and a collection of poems, *Les Regrets*. His work shows strict form, powerful imagination and a refined melancholy.

BENÉT, STEPHEN VINCENT (1898–1943): American poet and prose writer. His residence in many parts of the United States helped him to develop national themes on an epic scale. Uniting verse and history, he wrote *John Brown's Body* (1928), and *Western Star* (1943). Many of his essays and stories deal with American ideals. Best known of his short stories is *The Devil and Daniel Webster*. A selected edition of his verse and prose appeared in 1942.

BÉRANGER, PIERRE JEAN DE (1780–1857): This French lyric poet enjoyed prosperity and ease or disfavor and imprisonment according to the political state of France; his strong republicanism favoring him under a republican government and hurting him under an autocratic one. His fame is based upon his many songs, expressing the hedonism, materialism and republicanism of the French middle classes. He is both a national and a patriotic poet, but, as in the case of Holty in Germany or Kipling in England, there is enough of a world-wide appeal in his verses to give them wide and lasting interest. His best-known poem, *The King of Yvetot,* given in this book, contains a gentle rebuke of the undemocratic government of Napoleon I.

BERNARD OF CLAIRVAUX, SAINT (1091–1153): This French ecclesiastic and political leader was an abbot of the Cistercian order, which he did much to advance. By his mystic zeal he acquired an extraordinary influence over Pope, Emperor, and people. His fiery preaching did much to lead Europe into the ill-fated and unscrupulous Second Crusade (1146). Vigorously opposed to the rising intellectualism of his age, he secured the condemnation of the philosopher Abelard. He was, however, capable of notable and dramatic acts of charity, as on the occasion in which he prevented a pogrom against the Jews at Mainz. He is author of many treatises, sermons and hymns, largely inspired by his mysticism. Dante depicts him as particularly devoted to the Virgin Mary. See the studies by R. S. Storrs and S. J. Eales.

BION (c. 120 B.C.): This Greek pastoral poet lived in Sicily, where he is said to have died of poison. His death is lamented in a fine elegy by Moschus. This elegy and Bion's own *Dirge of Adonis* have become models for elegiac poetry throughout the western world, and are followed closely by Milton and Shelley. In addition to his great ritualistic poem on Adonis, Bion left a number of short and elegant lyrics.

BJÖRNSON, BJÖRNSTJERNE (1832–1910): This leading Norwegian poet, novelist and dramatist, has at the same time won international acclaim and succeeded in giving notable expression to many dominant qualities of the Norwegian people. He succeeded his friend, Ibsen, as director of the chief theatre at Bergen. In 1903 he received the Nobel prize for literature. He edited a collection of Norwegian ballads. His own work includes his epic poem, *Arnljot Gelline,* the novels *Synnöve Solbakken* and *The Fishermaiden,* and the dramas *The Bankrupt* and *Beyond Human Power.* He shows great power in depicting the peasant life, both from a romantic and a realistic point of view. He is author of the Norwegian national hymn. As a political thinker he became increasingly devoted to liberal ideas.

BLAKE, WILLIAM (1757–1827): English poet, painter and mystic. He received a thorough training in the art schools of London, but grew up in violent opposition to the prevailing materialism of "the Age of Reason." He explored many media as an artist, engraving and printing his own books. *Songs of Innocence* and *Songs of Experience,* produced in the general manner of children's books, rank among the most exquisite booklets of modern times. Blake not only accepted the most extreme of the romantic doctrines of the French Revolution, but composed a metaphysical system of his own, based on his worship of art, and couched in a highly obscure and elaborate personal symbolism. His long poems, as *Milton, Jerusalem,* and *The Marriage of Heaven and Hell,* are magnificent but often unintelligible. It is by his aphorisms, lyrics and brilliant passages, that he is best known. See *William Blake,* by S. Foster Damon.

BLOK, ALEXANDER ALEXANDROVICH (1880–1921): One of the chief Russian poets of the twentieth century. He attended the University of Petersburg, where his grandfather was rector. Much of his poetry belongs to the symbolist school. His early verse is both sensuous and mystical. His restless and inventive mind turned to children's verse and elusive and symbolical poetic drama. An abstract conception of beauty haunted him, no less than a devoted patriotism and love for Russia's medieval past. He also possessed strong religious inclinations. The Russian Revolution he greeted with prophetic enthusiasm. His masterpiece, *The Twelve,* which epitomizes his thought and art, is said to have been written in a single day, during January, 1918, in the midst of the tumults in the capital. It has been translated into many languages.

BOCCACCIO, GIOVANNI (1313–1375): This Italian poet and novelist was born in Paris of an Italian father and French mother. He lived almost all his life in Italy, at times in Florence, where his father was a banker, but more often in other cities. His extensive writing in both Latin and Italian shows a great breadth of vision, which makes it difficult to assign his work strictly to a medieval or a Renaissance tradition. His chief work, the *Decameron*, is a collection of a hundred tales, variously derived from the classics, oriental sources, folklore and medieval legend, narrated with high skill. Many have a licentious tone. The book was a mine for later poets and playwrights, as Chaucer and Shakespeare. Boccaccio's *Teseida* is the basis for Chaucer's *Knight's Tale* and his *Filostrata* for Chaucer's *Troilus and Criseyde*. See translation of the *Decameron* by Edward Hutton. Also the life by T. C. Chubb.

BOETHIUS ANICIUS (480–524): This Roman statesman and philosopher was one of the last of the scholars in the ancient world to study the Greeks. He was appointed advisor in the court of Theodoric, the seat of whose government was in Rome. Later he was imprisoned and put to death with torture. While in confinement he wrote his *Consolation of Philosophy*, a highly idealistic treatise many times translated, as by King Alfred, Chaucer and Queen Elizabeth. He has been thought to have been a Christian.

BROWNE, WILLIAM (1591–1643?): Only in a few instances did this British author achieve the distinction shown in the brief poem taken from him in this book. Usually a graceful but not a powerful writer, he follows the general patterns of the Renaissance pastoral. His best work appears in *Britannia's Pastorals* and *The Shepherd's Pipe*. These contain some graceful descriptions of the Devonshire countryside.

BROWNING, ROBERT (1812–1889): An English poet well representing the eclectic tastes of the nineteenth century: he versified the liberal ideas of his own times in poems for the most part with historical settings. In 1846 he married the poet Elizabeth Barrett, with whom he lived chiefly in Italy. He preserved an indefatigably cheerful view of life and of the world. Many of his poems have classical or Italian backgrounds. His longest work is *The Ring and the Book*. But more widely read are his *Men and Women, Dramatic Lyrics* and other works in which he develops his favorite form, the short dramatic monologue. He is also author of numerous stories and plays in verse. Of recent years he has been increasingly admired for a humor and an irony approximating the grotesque, as exhibited in the lively selection included in this book. See W. C. DeVane, *A Browning Handbook*.

BUCK, PEARL SYDENSTRICKER (1892–): This American author was born in West Virginia. For twenty years she taught in universities in China. Translator from the Chinese and author of many novels, short stories, and essays, she received the Nobel award in literature in 1938. Her best known novel is *The Good Earth* (1931). Few Americans have done so much to acquaint their fellow-countrymen with the thought and social conditions of the Far East.

BUDDHA (died c. 483 B.C.): The founder of Buddhism was, by tradition, a prince of the family of Gautama, who bore himself the name, Siddhartha. The name Buddha, which means the enlightened one, was given him only after he received the vision of the true way of life. He is said to have been brought up in the luxury of his ancestral palace, removed from all knowledge of suffering. On his escape he discovered the evils of the world and meditated upon them while leading a life of severe asceticism. Much of the sacred literature of India deals with the philosophy which he evolved, namely, Buddhism. Among its leading ideals are compassion and contemplation. This religion has spread to all parts of the Far East and profoundly affected the art, architecture and habits of thought of the Orient. See the studies by T. W. Rhys Davids, T. Stcherbatsky and A. B. Keith.

BURNS, ROBERT (1759–1796): The best-known Scottish poet was born on a farm in Ayrshire. Although he had only an elementary education, he became by no means ill read, and knew by heart hundreds of the traditional songs and ballads of his native country. Farming was not profitable in Ayrshire, and for Burns, who loved equally poetry and conviviality, it was disastrous. To raise money to emigrate to Jamaica he published at Kilmarnock, in 1786, *Poems, Chiefly in the Scottish Dialect.* It was a great success. He remained in Scotland, married his early love, Jean Armour, but died after a brief period of errors and misfortunes. He is probably the greatest spokesman of the folk spirit, a more powerful poet, for example, than Koltzov in Russia, Fröding in Sweden or Whittier in America. Convivial, satirical and tender, he is typically represented by such poems as *Tam o'Shanter, The Jolly Beggars, Holy Willie's Prayer, A Man's a Man for a' That* and *Ae Fond Kiss.* See biographical and critical studies by C. Carswell, J. L. Ferguson, and F. B. Snyder.

Byron, George Gordon, Lord Byron (1788–1824): An English poet who has exercised a wide influence over the literature of England, Europe and America. His career as a radical in the House of Lords was cut short by social scandals which brought on his divorce and caused him to leave England in 1816. For seven years he lived in Italy, and died while aiding the armies of Greece in their revolt against the Turks. His poems include a philosophical travel-diary, *Childe Harold;* political satire, such as *The Vision of Judgment;* romantic drama, such as *Manfred;* and his brilliant comment on the manners of various countries of Europe, *Don Juan.* Among his literary masters he acknowledged the Englishman Pope, the Italian Tasso, the Spaniard Quevedo, and the German Goethe. He denounced war, oppression and tyranny and championed republicanism. His fine irony and satire deeply influenced Russian writers, notably Pushkin and Lermontov. His letters and diaries are of outstanding interest. See the critical study by W. J. Calvert and the lives by John Drinkwater, André Maurois and Peter Quennell.

Callimachus (310–c. 240 b.c.): This poet and scholar was curator of the greatest of ancient libraries, that at Alexandria in Egypt. Among his learned works was a catalogue of books, with scholarly discussions of their genuine or spurious nature. He composed learned poems dealing with the founders and traditions of the chief ancient cities. His elegies were much imitated by the Latins, notably by Catullus. But he is best known for sixty-four epigrams, or poems in the Greek Anthology, where he takes the leading role in Alexandrian times. His work is graceful and unimpassioned.

Camoëns, Luis Vaz de (1524?–1579?): The chief Portuguese poet was born in Lisbon, the son of a sea captain, about the time of the death of the great explorer Vasco da Gama, to whom he was related, and with whom his grandfather had sailed to India. The poet lost an eye in a naval engagement. For sixteen years he lived in India, where he wrote much of his great patriotic epic, the *Lusiad,* celebrating the exploits of da Gama. His life ended tragically. Out of favor at court, old and enfeebled, he was denied his wish to accompany the Portuguese army to Africa. This army met a defeat from which Portugal never recovered. Camoëns' last written words are a letter in which he concludes: "It was not enough that I should die in my fatherland; I am dying with it." Author of many lyrics and satires, he is known chiefly for his *Lusiad,* one of the most deeply patriotic of all epics and one of the most typical expressions of the classical Renaissance in Europe. See Richard Burton, *Camoëns, His Life and His Lusiads.*

Campanella, Tommaso (1568–1639): This Italian monk, philosopher and poet possessed a powerful imagination and a dangerous degree of originality. His early philosophical writings attacked the Aristotelian tradition. While imprisoned for twenty-seven years, he wrote his Utopian book, *The City of the Sun* (translated by T. W. Halliday in *Ideal Commonwealths,* Morley's *Universal Library*). After his release he fled to France, where he was aided by Richelieu and pensioned by Louis XIII. His fine sonnets have been translated by J. A. Symonds in a volume with those of Michelangelo. The sonnet included in this book illustrates the boldness of his political thinking.

Campbell, Wilfred (1860–1919): This poet lived in childhood and youth in the beautiful Georgian Bay region in western Ontario, Canada. He studied at the Harvard Divinity School, and was for a few years a minister in Massachusetts and Canada. A disposition to heterodoxy induced him to leave the ministry. During his most productive years as a writer he held a minor post in the Canadian government in Toronto. He worked extensively for newspapers and magazines, writing a number of successful short stories. In the latter part of his life, as with many of his fellow-Canadians of Scotch descent, his loyalty to the British Empire became a leading emotion. Largely through his poetry he gained a high role in Canadian literature. His verse has much native freshness, although it represents as a whole the intellectual and emotional life of the Anglo-Saxon world in the late nineteenth century. There is a life by Carl Klinck.

Campion, Thomas (1567–1619): An English song writer. By profession a physician, he devoted his real genius to the writing of songs and masques, and became both a musician and a critic of music and poetry. He composed four books of *Ayres*. His training, temperament and association with the English Court helped to make him a more refined lyricist than the popular playwrights of the times. He is generally regarded today as the finest craftsman among the host of song writers contemporary with Shakespeare. An enthusiastic student of the Italian and classical backgrounds of his art, he sought to persuade English poets to follow the verse patterns of the ancients. Among his best lyrics are free renderings of Horace. See the study by M. M. Kastendieck.

Carducci, Giosué (1835–1907): This Italian poet served for many years as professor of literature in the University of Bologna. He was also an essayist, an editor and an Italian senator. His political views changed from radicalism to conservatism. In poetry he may be associated with the Parnassian school in France, led by Leconte de Lisle, and the neoclassical Victorians in England led by Matthew Arnold. He attempted a bold revival of classical verse forms in Italian and on the whole preferred the ancient to the Christian philosophy of life. His paganism appears in his *Odi barbare* and *Hymn to Satan*. The firm naturalism and high vigor of his poetry helped its recognition as an important contribution to modern literature. He was awarded the Nobel Prize in 1906. See studies by Orlo Williams and John Baily.

Carlyle, Thomas (1795–1881): This British author was born in the village of Ecclefechan, Scotland. In 1834 he moved to London. He became a spokesman for social order, for a relief from the brutalities of the new industrialized society, and for leadership by the hand of strong individuals. Against the rationalism and materialism of the rising liberals he presented a vigorous but unsystematic criticism of his own. A violent style aided in his great popularity. Some of his earliest writing consists of translations from the German, especially from Goethe. Among his chief books are *Sartor Resartus, Heroes and Hero Worship, Past and Present* and his historical works, *The French Revolution, Cromwell* and *Frederick the Great*. See the life by Emery Neff, and his study, *Carlyle and Mill*.

Carvalho, Ronald de (1893–1935): This outstanding Brazilian poet was a student of law, philosophy and sociology. He was active in Brazilian diplomatic service. His writings appeared in France and North America as well as in Brazil. They are distinguished by the raciness and vigor with which they reflect contemporary Brazilian life. Since Brazil is today what North America was a century ago, perhaps the first pioneering country in the world, her writers have shown a remarkable similarity to Walt Whitman, spokesman for the pioneering age in the United States. Many Brazilian poets have deliberately imitated the great American. Carvalho was one of the most successful. His prose has been quite as warmly admired as his poetry.

Catullus, Caius Valerius (84?–54? b.c.): This Roman lyric poet was born in Verona, moving to Rome when about twenty. His vain attempt to gain a fortune by serving as praetor in Bithynia cost him dearly but aided his knowledge of the Greek poets, whom he imitated. His last few years he lived as a man of pleasure in Rome. His poems are in turn delicate and coarse; most are amatory, others satirical, almost all personal. Among his best-known lyrics is an elegy on his brother, a mock elegy on the death of Lesbia's sparrow, a poem on the legend of Attis, and several marriage hymns, or epithalamiums, one of which is given in this volume. His works are equally remarkable for their artistic integrity and their moral laxity. See K. P. Harrington,

Catullus, and the translation by Horace Gregory.

CELLINI, BENVENUTO (1500–1571): This Italian artist and author was born in Florence, where at fifteen he was apprenticed to a goldsmith. He was forced to leave the city after a duel. His art as goldsmith, sculptor and decorator he practiced in many cities and courts, especially in Rome and Paris, and finally in his native Florence. As a craftsman in miniatures he had no rival during his lifetime. He is best remembered for his autobiography, which tells the story of an adventurous and highly unscrupulous life. His narrative boasts of many escapades and hairbreadth escapes. He claims that in the siege of Rome he killed both the French general and the Prince of Orange. The book gives a lurid but highly entertaining description of a colorful age. It recounts its author's relations with many famous people, including, for example, Michelangelo. See the study by T. Longueville.

CERVANTES SAAVEDRA, MIGUEL DE (1547–1616): This celebrated Spanish writer came of ancient Castilian stock. Fighting against the Turks at the battle of Lepanto, 1571, he lost his left hand. Four years later he was captured by pirates and held for five years a captive, suffering many painful adventures, until his ransom. His literary work dates chiefly from his return to Spain. It includes poems, plays and a pastoral novel, *Galatea;* but only his fantastic, satiric, philosophical and romantic novel, *Don Quixote,* has won him great and lasting fame. The hero of this novel, Don Quixote, represents the idealistic side of man, noble but impractical; his servant, Sancho Panza, represents the materialistic side, somewhat ignoble but thoroughly sane. The ethics of the book rise from exquisite irony and humor. It expresses outstanding characteristics of the Spanish character; and in its intense humanity it perfectly fuses the spirit of comedy and tragedy. His mind was sufficiently broad to embrace the best and most vital qualities of both the medieval and the modern world. See the life by J. Fitzmaurice-Kelly.

CHAUCER, GEOFFREY (c. 1340–1400): The chief figure in English literature before Shakespeare was son of a London vintner. From youth he served at court, going from time to time on diplomatic or military missions. During his later years he was comptroller of customs, director of public works and member of Parliament. His poetry, rich in the knowledge of character and men, reflects his role as a man of affairs. Among his earliest work is an incomplete translation of the French *Romance of the Rose.* Influence of Boccaccio, Dante and Italian literature is to be seen in the allegorical *House of Fame* and the fine romantic novel in verse, *Troilus and Criseyde.* He retells a number of classical stories, chiefly Ovidean, in his *Legend of Good Women.* But his greatest work is *The Canterbury Tales,* a collection of highly diverse stories with much delightfully humorous characterization, some satire and some strong touches of pathos. The best edition is that by F. N. Robinson. There is a prose translation by J. S. P. Tatlock and Percy Mackaye.

CHOCANO, JOSÉ (1875–1934): This notable Peruvian poet is known as one of the boldest champions of the indigenous element in New World literature. He demanded that this literature should express a somewhat different world from that of Europe and the European authors. Hence such a native theme as seen in his ode given in this book. For his activities in behalf of democracy and radicalism he was thrown into prison. Both as artist and thinker he has been a leader in the remarkable revival of letters in modern South America. It will be observed, however, that the ode given in this anthology is no less indebted to classical tradition than to the life of the South American Indian.

CHUANG TZE (4th Cent. B.C.): This Chinese sage was a follower of Lao-Tsu, but represented an even more violent divorce from reason and institutionalism. Like Lao Tsu, he founded his system upon Nature; but the Nature of Chuang Tze is violently romantic. He is a god-intoxicated man, whose wild humor and divine madness stand wholly apart from the sober and ethical system of Confucius and even from the philosophical quietism of Buddhism and early Taoism.

CHURCHILL, RT. HON. WINSTON (1872–): One of the greatest of British Prime Ministers. As a young man Churchill served in the British Army and was a war correspondent. From 1900 he led a parliamentary career. During the First World War he was in turn First Lord of the Admiralty, Minister of Munitions, and Minister of War. He became Prime Minister and Minister of Defence in 1940, holding these posts till after the conclusion of the Second World War in 1945. Author of many books, including a life of his ancestor, the Duke of Marlborough, and a history of the First World War. A Conservative in British politics, a leader of incomparable enterprise and courage in time of war, he has become an outstanding figure in the modern world. His speeches rank among the most moving in the English tongue. He is at the same time one of the most typical and outstanding of Englishmen. His defeat in the general election in 1945 indicated, however, a tendency of the British people toward a social and political thinking more progressive than his.

Cicero, Marcus Tullius (106–43 b.c.): This Roman philosopher, orator and statesman became consul in 63 b.c. At this time as leader of the senatorial party, he attacked Catiline, as he later attacked Caesar and Antony, throwing in his lot with Pompey. He was murdered at the instigation of Antony, after having held a large number of important political offices. His oratory was his strongest political weapon. Posterity has on the whole prized more highly his literary and speculative activities. His voluminous works include letters of unique importance for the social historian, familiar essays, and treatises on oratory, rhetoric, morals, politics, philosophy and religion. No author gives a broader image of the ancient world. He summarized his Greek predecessors and passed on works of inestimable value to the Middle Ages and the Renaissance. See the study by Strachan-Davidson.

Claudianus, Claudius (c. 400): This Roman poet was born in Alexandria, coming to Rome in 395. His patron was the Vandal, Stilicho, whose fall in 408 he may not have survived. The chief poet of his times, he also represented his age in cultural decadence. With little essentially new to contribute, he leaned heavily on the older Greeks and Romans, embellishing their themes with glittering rhetoric. His best long poem is on the story of Proserpina. In addition he wrote marriage hymns, eulogies, satires, historical poems in the epic style, and epigrams. The best known of his works is the epigram upon the contented old farmer, given in this book.

Claudius, Matthias (1740–1815): This German poet was a native of Holstein. He received a minor post as auditor from Crown Prince Frederick of Denmark. His literary work included translating and periodical editing. His sane and cheerful verse acquired considerable popularity and well expresses a slightly provincial, Nordic temper. Several of his lyrics are well known as songs. The tender elegy on his father easily stands among his finest works.

Confucius (551–478 b.c.): The greatest of Chinese philosophers left writings upon which are based the ideals of the Chinese people to the present day. He was himself somewhat unsuccessful as a courtier, and was banished from the court through the intrigues of his enemies. Yet for much of his life he was active in an advisory capacity in political affairs. His latter years he devoted wholly to writing and study. His system does not deny the gods, but turns aside from a consideration of them. He views the laws of human society as founded upon the laws of nature. Nature's laws underlie the family as the family underlies the state. Personal relationships are all important, as those of sovereign and subject, father and son, elder and younger brother, husband and wife, and friend and friend. Human welfare lies in tranquillity. Ceremony, convention and ancestor worship are altogether essential. However much a part of Chinese life the views of Confucius have become, his teachings have in large measure a universal appeal, and as an essayist on manners and morals he has probably never been equaled. Confucianism contrasts in China with the more imaginative and poetic outlook of Taoism. See R. K. Douglas, *Confucianism and Taoism* and the studies by A. Loomis and E. H. Parker.

Copernicus, Nikolaus (1473–1543): This Polish astronomer was born at Thorn, a Prussian town on the Vistula. He studied at Cracow and later, for eight years, in Italy, after which he returned to his native country to the life of a priest and scholar. He delayed the publication of his great work on astronomy, *Concerning the Revolutions of the Celestial Spheres,* through fears that it might be held unorthodox; and it is said that the printed book came first to his hands only a few hours before his death. Whereas the earlier, or Ptolomaic, system of astronomy described the earth as the center of the universe, his system regarded the sun as center, thus altering and simplifying the entire method of astronomical calculation. He became the founder of modern astronomy. The more philosophical implications of his system had vast and incalculable consequences.

COSMAS INDICOPLEUSTES (fl. 6th Cent.): This merchant-traveler, who later became a monk, was probably born in Alexandria, Egypt. His last name, signifying Indian navigator, he received by virtue of his travels to the East. He wrote in Greek a geographical work, *Christian Topography,* highly erroneous and reactionary in its theory of the earth, but not without value in its own time in the light of its descriptions of many lands, and especially of the animals of India and Ceylon. His work, in short, was preposterous as science but by no means contemptible as a book of travel.

CRANE, HART (1899–1932): A gifted American poet. The writing of poetry was the center of Crane's highly bohemian, emotional and tragically brief life. *Collected Poems* (1933) contains, along with work of uneven merit, his masterpiece, *The Bridge,* an essentially religious, symbolic and highly idealistic poem dedicated to Whitman's mystical conception of the destiny of America. In its incisive style and its assimilation of mechanistic as well as naturalistic imagery, it has proved a distinctly forward-looking work.

CREASY, SIR EDWARD SHEPHERD (1812–1878): This English historian is chiefly known as author of a highly popular historical work, *Fifteen Decisive Battles of the World.* He wrote also on English military and constitutional history, and on the history of the Ottoman Turks. He was a lawyer, a professor, and the chief justice of Ceylon.

CURIE, EVE (1904–): This French author and journalist is the daughter of Pierre and Marie Curie, the discoverers of radium. Her best-known book is a life of her mother. In 1941 she started on a trip around the world, reporting for English and American papers on the progress of the Second World War. This led to her book, *Journey Among Warriors,* marked by a spirit of high courage and a warm love of freedom and democracy.

DANA, RICHARD HENRY (1815–1882): This American author and lawyer is best known for his sea-story, *Two Years Before the Mast* (1840). After his sophomore year at Harvard College, he shipped as a common sailor on a sailing vessel which went around Cape Horn to California. His avowed motive in the trip was to cure eye-trouble, but its chief result was his vivid account of what the common sailor endured in the days of the greatest of sailing ships. The book has become a classic of its kind, and has been widely imitated and several times translated. Later in life Dana became a distinguished lawyer. His chief publications of this period deal with laws for the protection of seamen. He also took part in politics, assisted in founding the Free Soil Party, organized to combat the spread of slavery, and supported the Republican Party under Lincoln. See the life by C. F. Adams.

DANTE ALIGHIERI (1265–1321): The most celebrated of Italian poets was born in Florence. A political leader in the city, he was expelled in 1302 when a hostile faction took control. He died and was buried at Ravenna. In prose he wrote a treatise *On Monarchy,* and another on the use of the Italian language. He is author of a discursive work, *Convito* (*Symposium*), and an allegorical work on ideals of love, *La Vita Nuova* (*The New Life*). But his masterpiece is *The Divine Comedy,* a great philosophical poem epitomizing the culture of the Christian Middle Ages. In it, however, he stands much in debt to the classics, for Virgil is his acknowledged master in poetry and morals, and much of his philosophy comes, as he acknowledges, by way of the Arabians. Both *The New Life* and *The Divine Comedy* are translated by C. E. Norton; an admirable verse translation of *The Divine Comedy* is that by J. B. Fletcher. See also the prose version with notes by Carlyle-Wicksteed (Modern Library), the biography and Dante dictionary by P. Toynbee, and the study by E. G. Gardner.

DARÍO, RUBÉN (1867–1916): This poet, born in León, Nicaragua, is regarded as the leading poet of Spanish America during his lifetime, and perhaps in its entire literary history. He lived as a journalist in several countries of South America, later moving to Madrid. He returned to Nicaragua not long before his death. His influence has been internationally felt. A boldness and vigor of thought and language have commended him to an age outgrowing the clichés of expression and banalities of sentiment often prevailing in the generation before him. Darió helped to bring literature into increasingly vital contact with a changing world. His poetry has indubitable inspiration. The poem given here is addressed to Theodore Roosevelt as an aggressor in Central America.

DARWIN, CHARLES ROBERT (1809–1882): This English naturalist began his serious investigations during a five years' cruise chiefly through the South Pacific, which he described in his *Voyage of a Naturalist On H. M. S. Beagle.* He was indebted to geologists who early in the nineteenth century contended for the great antiquity of the world. Darwin came to believe that in the course of ages the survival of the fittest in each species had through the laws of heredity caused modifications in the species and in time caused new species to arise. Similar views were shared by several scientists of the times, notably A. R. Wallace. But Darwin's *Origin of Species* (1859) proved by far the most formidable expression of this theory. Although many of Darwin's speculations have since been seriously questioned by scientists, his dynamic view of the origins of life has had profound influence over both science and philosophy. His friend, T. H. Huxley, led in the bitter controversy between the new science and the conservative interpretation of the Bible. Since Darwin, humanity and the universe have appeared in an increasingly fluid state. His theory first encouraged an optimistic belief in progress, which in more recent years has been much undermined. His chief discussion of the meaning of his theories for human life is his *Descent of Man.* Many of his shorter works of a purely naturalistic character, as his studies of coral or of earthworms, have charm and value for the general reader. See G. A. Dorsey, *The Evolution of Charles Darwin.*

DAUDET, ALPHONSE (1840–1897): This French novelist was born in Provence, southern France. About the lovely land of his birth he wrote a number of tales, most successfully in his charming volume, *Letters from My Mill.* Another volume rich in humor and local color, *Tartarin de Tarascon,* met with much success. More ambitious are his novels *Sapho* and *The Nabob.* Many of his stories are realistic pictures of life and manners in nineteenth-century Paris. He has also written a revealing autobiography describing his own childhood. As stylist and story-teller he has had few superiors.

DAVIES, WILLIAM HENRY (1870–1940): This English lyric poet, born in a tavern, was in youth a cattleman, berry-picker and vagabond. He lost his right leg in hopping a freight train. The story of his early life appears in *The Autobiography of a Super-Tramp* (1906). As Davies grew, he learnt a great deal about artless living and artful poetry. His small volumes of lyrics are gathered into *Collected Poems* (1935). The subjects of these lyrics are often racy and proletarian; their technique is imitated from such neo-classical poets as Robert Herrick (q. v.). He is generally cheerful, but well aware of human suffering. His critics find his art at times rather too thin, but the vitality and attractiveness of much of his work cannot easily be denied.

DAVIS, JEFFERSON (1808–1889): The President of the Confederate States of America was born in Kentucky, moving as a boy to Mississippi, his future home. In 1828 he graduated from West Point and served in both the Black Hawk and Mexican Wars. He was Secretary of War under President Pierce and was several times elected Senator from Mississippi. As President of the Confederacy he served with skill and devotion, yet encountered much opposition and failed to win the unqualified devotion bestowed upon General Lee and other Confederate leaders. It is unfair to compare him with Lincoln. He proved an able spokesman for his cause. Throughout his life he was an imperialist, and, had American politics admitted, he would have much increased the American slave-owning territories by further acquisitions in Latin America. See the lives by W. E. Dodd and A. Tate.

DEHMEL, RICHARD (1863–1920): This German poet was at an early age a student of philosophy, sociology and natural science. He worked briefly as a newspaper editor. He was secretary of the Union of German Fire Insurance Companies from 1887–1895. During the First World War he fought as a volunteer. Among his many books are children's stories, an epic, a verse novel, a war diary, plays, and, above all, his collection of powerful lyrics. The last are often on erotic, often on political and social themes. Whatever he wrote is characterized by an extraordinary energy of thought, feeling and expression.

DEKKER, THOMAS (1570?–1641?): This popular dramatist of the time of Shakespeare wrote for the theatre and for the reading public with an almost equal measure of carelessness and genius. Little is known of him personally, except that he was for several years imprisoned for debt. His best plays are *The Shoemaker's Holiday, Old Fortunatus* and *The Honest Whore*. His racy prose pamphlets abound in pathos and realism, with sympathy for the poor and hatred of their oppressors. They vividly describe the ravages of the plague in London. His *Gull's Hornbook* gives a brisk commentary on city manners. Like all literary Englishmen of his times, Dekker admired the Italians, but he also understood much of the life, thought and culture of Protestant Germany. Among the somewhat pagan-minded Elizabethan playwrights, Dekker is the most Christian-hearted. His songs are the epitome of his genius.

DESCARTES, RENÉ (1596–1650): This French scientist and philosopher received Jesuit schooling, traveled in Germany, in 1628 retired to Holland, and died shortly after his arrival on a visit to Sweden. Many fields of science and philosophy are enriched by his work. He originated the Cartesian coordinates, and made important contributions to the study of curves, to analytical geometry, and algebra. He also wrote on both physiology and psychology, and his materialistic outlook closely associated the two sciences. Much of his philosophical and metaphysical system he evolved from his mathematics. In his analysis of nature he dismissed all authority from religion or predetermined doctrines, and started with the assumption that man can employ reason from the outset of a philosophical system, demonstrating the existence of God and all the ensuing propositions. To the orthodox religious of his own day he appeared a skeptic and non-believer. His prestige among the chief philosophers of the eighteenth century was immense; but the opposition long continued from conservative sources. Descartes was one of the many geniuses in mathematics who studied music. One of his earliest works is his *Compendium of Music*. His most celebrated essay is his *Discourse on Method*. See the studies by E. S. Haldane and C. Adam.

DÍAZ DEL CASTILLO, BERNAL (born c. 1492): This Spanish soldier served as one of the Conquistadors under Cortés in the conquest of Mexico. As a result of his adventures, he wrote *The True History of the Conquest of New Spain*. This is easily the most attractive document dealing with the early history of the New World. It has become a major source for subsequent accounts of its subject, as W. H. Prescott's *Conquest of Mexico*, and the epic poem, *Conquistador*, by Archibald MacLeish. See also R. B. Cunninghame Graham, *Bernal Diaz del Castillo*.

DICKINSON, EMILY (1830–1886): An America poet born in Amherst, Massachusetts, where she lived and died. She never married and passed an outwardly uneventful life, of which her charming letters afford the best record. Throughout her life she wrote short poems in a crisp, new idiom which she well knew to be too unconventional to admit of popular publication. The poems have been published from manuscript since her death; the last and fullest edition being that of 1937, supplemented by *Bolts of Memory: New Poems*, 1945. Her reputation has grown steadily, until she has come to be regarded as one of the greatest of lyric poets, the foremost among women of modern times. She voices deep feeling in a few, vibrant words and images. Her art has been much imitated; but her independence of mind has often concealed her likeness to other great metaphysical poets, a likeness clarified in this anthology. The best study of her life is *This Was a Poet*, by George F. Whicher. See also, *Introduction to Emily Dickinson*, by H. W. Wells, and *Ancestors' Brocades*, by M. T. Bingham.

Donne, John (1573–1631): English poet and divine. Early in life Donne acquired great learning, especially in theology. After a roving youthful career, he became an Anglican minister and later as Dean of St. Paul's, London, one of England's greatest preachers. His lyrics range from bitter realism to impassioned devotion. Great vigor and originality made him a leader in Elizabethan times, and though neglected for many years, he has become a leading inspiration to English and American writers of the twentieth century. See George Williamson, *The Donne Tradition.*

Dostoievsky, Feodor Mikhailovich (1821–1881): This Russian novelist best represents the introspective element in Russian literature. His life abounded in misfortunes. He early suffered from epilepsy. His revolutionary activities against the regime of the Czar caused him to be sentenced to penal servitude in Siberia, from which he was released after six years. His growing mysticism alienated him from the revolutionary movement. Among his chief books are *The Brothers Karamazov; Crime and Punishment; The House of the Dead; The Idiot; Memoirs from Underground;* and *Poor Folk.* His stories reveal a profound psychological understanding of abnormal and criminal types, a deep sympathy with the poor and the oppressed, and a faith in long-suffering innocence. His influence is strongly felt in all civilized countries. See the studies by E. H. Carr, J. Meier-Graefe and A. Yarmolinsky.

Dryden, John (1631–1700): English poet, playwright, translator and critic and leader in English letters during the latter part of the seventeenth century. In his earliest poetry he praised the Protector, Cromwell, but shortly eulogized the new monarch, Charles II. Under James II he became a Catholic. He passed most of his life in London, where he composed panegyrics in verse for the Court, and heroic plays for a courtly audience. He also wrote satires against political and religious factions opposed to the Court. On the accession of William and Mary he retired from his more active career, devoting himself largely to translation and literary criticism. Falling just short of the most powerful creative imagination, he achieved a noble, distinguished and vigorous style. He seasoned sententiousness with humor. A love of music aided him in writing admirable songs. Dryden was a master of comparative literature, rendering into the language of his own day many of the chief Greek, Latin and Italian poets, as well as the Middle-English Chaucer. See Mark Van Doren, *John Dryden.*

Du Bois, William E. Burghardt (1868–): This American educator, editor and writer was born in Great Barrington, Mass., of Negro ancestry. He received his higher education at Fiske University and at Harvard. Among his principal achievements has been the founding of the Pan-African Congress. He is author of numerous books dealing with the social problem of the Negro, both in the United States and in the world.

Edwards, Jonathan (1703–1758): This American theologian and philosopher was for twenty-three years minister to a large congregation in Northampton, Massachusetts. Disputes with his congregation caused him to remove to a small church at Stockbridge, in what was then a wild section of the state. Here he lived virtually till his death and here produced his major work, the *Freedom of Will.* This book is a contribution to the Calvinistic doctrine of absolute predestination. It is chiefly esteemed for metaphysical subtlety. Other of his works defining sin and virtue have almost equal value in theology. His powers as a preacher were unsurpassed, both because of his eloquence and the high sincerity of his religious convictions. See the studies by O. E. Winslow, H. B. Parkes and A. C. McGiffert, Jr.

Eeden, Frederik Willem Van (1860–1932): This important Dutch author has written stories and plays ranging from tales for children to romantic tragedies. *Little Johannes* was translated into English in 1895 with an introductory essay by the English critic, Andrew Lang. His tragicomedy, *Ysbrand,* was translated and produced in America in 1910. In the latter years of his life he became sympathetic with socialism and communism. He was a poet as well as dramatist and writer of fiction. Moreover, he published notable studies in painting, and wrote essays on authors of many lands, as Thoreau, Ruskin, and Tagore.

Ehrenpreis, Marcus (1869–): This Swedish scholar has written important books on historical and philosophical subjects, chiefly on comparative religion and mysticism, including the kabala; also two books of travel, *The Land Between Orient and Occident: a Jew's Travels in Spain* (1928) and *The Soul of the East* (1927; translated into English 1928), from which our selection is taken. This book recounts a journey through the Balkans to Athens, Egypt, and Palestine, with special attention to the rapidly developing new city of Tel-Aviv and the hope of a Jewish national state. It is full of enlightened observation of details of life, and illuminated by his regard for the integrity of historical cultures and his insight into the spiritual values of Oriental mysticism.

Emerson, Ralph Waldo (1803–1882): This leading American thinker, essayist and poet, unsurpassed by his countrymen of the nineteenth century for stimulating and provocative writing, was born in Boston, Massachusetts, and resided for most of his life in near-by Concord. Though prepared to be, like his father, a Unitarian minister, and for a few years pastor of a Boston church, he retired after a difference with his parishioners regarding the Lord's Supper, continuing through life to preach occasionally. But his real pulpit was the lecture platform; here he could speak freely his own idealistic thoughts, stimulated by the philosophy of Coleridge, the visions of Swedenborg, and his life-long friendship with Carlyle. He dealt with religion, nature, government, ethics, education and virtually all phases of life, generally from a fresh and typically American point of view, but borrowing ideas at will from English, European and Asiatic thought and from both moderns and ancients. His first book was *Nature* (1836). This, and his *Ode Inscribed to W. H. Channing*, well illustrate his idealism. Other notable books are *Representative Men; Conduct of Life; Society and Solitude;* and *Letters and Social Aims. His Journals*, however, give the best evidence of his high intellectual vitality; their twelve volumes are filled with shrewd observations and inspiring thoughts, phrased with such finality that we frequently find them used word for word as the best remembered passages in his essays. Emerson lays down general principles by which a humane, democratic society may be made coexistent with the freedom and self-reliance typical of the American character. See Bliss Perry, *Emerson Today*.

Epictetus (a.d. 60–?): This leader of the Stoic school of philosophy was born in Phrygia. He was a slave, though freed during his lifetime. After living some years in Rome, he was banished by the Emperor Domitian, who disliked his philosophy. Thenceforth he lived in Nicopolis, Epirus. Although no writing is known certainly to proceed from his own hand, the book by his pupil, Arrian, is confidently viewed as in substance his. Personal rectitude and calm endurance are the foundations of his austere ethical doctrine. This is based on the belief that God directs the events of the universe; that men are the sons of God and are of kindred nature; and that their highest duty is to discipline their wills to the acceptance of His. These views are expressed in a most dignified, simple and unaffected language, which has helped to render the book one of the most popular of ethical treatises. The Stoic philosophy appealed strongly to the Christian Middle Ages and the Renaissance. Its influence may be seen, for example, in the ethical sentiments of Shakespeare. See the volumes on Stoicism by R. D. Hicks and E. V. Arnold.

Euripides (480–406 b.c.): This playwright, last of the great tragic poets of Greece, according to tradition was born in Salamis on the day of the Grecian naval victory near that island; but there are various other alleged dates, all of them, like the supposed facts of his life, legendary. Aristophanes says his mother was an herb-seller and that he was twice unhappily married. He studied painting, oratory and philosophy. Forced to leave Athens, he lived the last years of his life in Macedonia. He was author of some eighty plays, about a quarter of which survive, along with many brief fragments of others. Among the surviving plays are *Medea; Alcestis; Hippolytus; Electra; The Trojan Women; Iphigenia in Tauris; Orestes;* and *The Bacchae.* All his works are tragedies or tragi-comedies, except *The Cyclops*, (beautifully translated by Shelley), a comic fantasy, or Satyr Play. He is celebrated for his skepticism in religion and morals, his irony and sophistication, his gifts in dramatic story-telling, romancing, psychology and characterization. Pathos, tenderness, pacifism and a preoccupation with women are also notable qualities. Compared with Aeschylus and Sophocles, he represents the rapid social decline of Athens. He has certainly been the most widely read and imitated of all ancient dramatists, though possibly not the most generally admired. Gilbert Murray has translated the plays into romantic verse. There are prose translations by Moses Hadas and J. H. McLean. See the studies by Paul Decharme, J. P. Mahaffy and Gilbert Murray.

FERNANDEZ-GUARDIA, RICARDO (1867–): This Costa Rican author stands among the major writers of Latin America. His short stories were translated into English in 1904, his *History of the Discovery and Conquest of Costa Rica* in 1913. He has contributed important studies in early Latin American history. His father, Don Leon Fernández, was the leading Costa Rican author of the last century. Both materially aided the cause of liberalism and democracy.

FILICAJA, VINCENZO DA (1642–1707): This Italian poet held a number of political posts, including those of Governor of Pisa and Volterra. His verses reveal the successful man of the world and leader in public affairs. They are for the most part formal and dignified works in the strictest neo-classical manner. His heroic odes, by which he first acquired fame, celebrate the delivery of Vienna from the Turks in 1683. His best-known lines are an expression of lofty pathos lamenting the misfortunes of Italy. They are thus a high mark in the development of a melancholy theme common in Italian literature from Dante to Leopardi. Byron made them still more famous by incorporating an English version into his *Childe Harold*.

FOMBONA-PACHANO, JACINTO (1901–): During his early years this Venezuelan poet studied political science and held a number of positions in local government. His early poems were fresh and attractive but hardly serious. A second stage in his work appeared with his residence in Washington while serving in the Venezuelan Embassy. His poetry published since the Second World War deals most imaginatively and forcefully with world conditions. Few poets in the United States have written so thoughtfully, forcefully and imaginatively on Lincoln as this visitor from Latin America. *A Warning for Abraham Lincoln* is of interest in its statement of the spiritual relationship of Lincoln to Whitman and of both to the gravest issues of the twentieth century. Fombona-Pachano is a spokesman for the highest ideals of international democracy.

FORT, PAUL (1872–): This French poet, born in Rheims, at the age of eighteen founded a theatre in protest against the naturalistic stage, and in support of a poetic and symbolic drama. In this theatre were performed plays by Shelley, Verlaine, Maeterlinck and Mallarmé. After the theatrical phase of his career, he turned his great energies largely to poetry, producing in rapid succession numerous volumes of poems which he denominated ballades. Printed as prose, these were actually in free verse. Their buoyancy and vitality at once won them wide favor, though the more subjective or decadent school of writers was inclined to view them as banal and vulgar. He is thus one of the challenging figures in modern literature. See *Six French Poets*, by Amy Lowell.

FRANCE, ANATOLE (pseud. of *Jacques Anatole Thibault*) (1844–1924): This French novelist and social critic voices the ideas of nineteenth-century liberalism with the wit and irony traditional in French satire from the Middle Ages and the Renaissance to his own day. His first work of importance is *The Crime of Sylvester Bonnard*. His defense of the novelist Zola in the anti-semitic agitation over Dreyfus showed him allied with the forces of humanitarianism and enlightenment as against social and religious prejudice and oppression. His peculiar genius appears in works equally remarkable for the audacity of their imagination and the power of their social criticism: *Penguin Island* and *The Revolt of the Angels*. France observes with what superfluous cruelty mankind torments itself. See the studies by B. Cerf and W. L. George.

FRANCIS, SAINT OR SAINT FRANCIS OF ASSISI (1182–1226): Francis was born in Assisi, Italy, the son of a merchant. After brief experience as a soldier, he underwent a religious conversion and made a pilgrimage to

Rome. With permission of the Pope, he organized his order of Franciscan friars. He traveled widely in Europe and to the Holy Land and preached before the Sultan. Wounds received in his hands and feet, known as the stigmata, resembled the wounds of Christ. He and his order showed great devotion to the poor, and attempted an almost literal imitation of Christ's life. Francis' love of nature is celebrated in the story that he preached to the birds. He breathed a new warmth, tenderness and sincerity into Christianity, deeply influencing both lyric poetry and the fine arts. The lives of the Saint by Thomas of Celano and St. Bonaventura are less widely known than *The Little Flowers of St. Francis,* or anecdotes regarding him. He himself wrote little, but is generally credited with the fine *Hymn to the Sun.*

Franklin, Benjamin (1706–1790): This American statesman, scientist, and author was born in Boston, Massachusetts, where he commenced his career as printer and editor. At seventeen he moved to Philadelphia, which became his American home for the rest of his life, though he lived many years, divided among several visits, in England and France. In each of these countries he represented the American Revolutionary Government. He signed the Declaration of Independence and helped to negotiate the peace with England. His political career was happily concluded with his conciliatory policy at the Constitutional Convention of 1787. He was remarkably successful in promoting civic, philanthropic and educational reforms. He became equally well known for his many contributions to science and to practical inventions. He was, for example, a pioneer experimenter in electricity and the inventor of the Franklin stove. His writings comprise essays and articles reflecting his varied scientific, political and humanitarian interests. His magazine editing and his *Poor Richard's Almanac* won him wide recognition. But posterity prizes most his *Autobiography,* the record of a man at once a representative and a pre-eminent American. See the life by Carl Van Doren.

Freneau, Philip (1752–1832): Born of a Huguenot family in New Jersey,. Freneau graduated from Princeton in 1771. At various times teacher, lawyer and sea captain, he finally turned to journalism as his profession. His capture by the British during the Revolutionary War is described in *The British Prison Ship.* He edited several periodicals, chiefly in New York and Philadelphia, supporting the democratic and republican policies of Jefferson. His verse, at times merely propaganda for the issues of the moment, in some instances rises to considerable power. Eloquent champion of American political idealism, he attacked the imperialistic oppression of subject peoples in such poems as *Discovery.* Many of his poems, such as *The New England Sabbath-Day Chase,* are brisk satires on manners. In both his satirical and his lyrical and elegiac poetry, he follows the neo-classical standards of his times as far as his rugged and independent American mind allows. See the biography of Freneau by L. G. Leary.

Fröding, Gustaf (1860–1911): This leading Swedish poet is chiefly known for his faithful and sincere expression of the emotional life of the Swedish peasants. Unlike Burns, he had a university training. For a time he made journalism a profession. But this occupation he soon left, and passed most of his life in a highly bohemian manner. His lyrics, rich in irony and humor, stand among the most prized in Scandinavian literature.

Frost, Robert (1875–): This leading American poet has lived most of his life in New England, expressing in his verse the sturdy individualism traditional to this section of the country. Without the social outlook of Carl Sandburg, he is a sterner judge of his own art. In *North of Boston* (1914) he gives us racy poems rich in the dialect and temper of rural New England; in his later volumes a lyrical tone has been heard with increasing frequency and distinction. His poems are tender, thoughtful, often humorous, and almost always artistically satisfying. See Richard Thornton, *Recognition of Robert Frost.*

Froude, James Anthony (1818–1894): This English historian is author of a large number of works chiefly relating to England. He lived the life of a scholar, teacher and lecturer, traveling in connection with his profession to the United States and in many parts of the British Empire. His major work is *The History of England from the Fall of Wolsey to the Defeat of the Spanish Armada.* He wrote extensively on the history of British seafaring and on Ireland. His Protestant and Conservative point of view, and his extreme patriotism, often biased his statement of historical fact. Many of his attitudes were formed in his friendly association with Thomas Carlyle. Like Carlyle, he believed that historical writing should possess literary value, and he was not less successful than his master in realizing this ideal. See the life by H. Paul.

GASTEV, ALEXEY KAPITONIVICH (1882–): This poet, representative of modern Russia, lived a life of and for the proletariat. His manual trade was that of locksmith. In 1918 he published his only book of poems. Taking an active part in the revolutionary movement, he gave up literary work to organize the Central Institute of Labor in Moscow. His art and his social ideal are epitomized in the poem here given, *We Grow Out of Iron.*

GAUTIER, THÉOPHILE (1811–1872): This French poet, novelist and critic lived and wrote in Paris, except when away on his numerous travels to gather material for more books. He wrote extensively for papers and reviews. His works include poems, novels, short stories, travel books, and much literary criticism. As a young man he became a somewhat superficial champion of freedom, expressed in a famous scarlet waistcoat. His hedonistic ethics appears in his novel, *Mademoiselle de Maupin.* A love of the exotic is seen in romances dealing with the Middle Ages. His poems sacrifice feeling and thought to a remarkable precision of form. A few are strongly symbolical, as a celebrated panegyric on white. His love for the abstract in poetry has exerted a strong influence on modern theory and practice in both literature and the arts. See L. B. Dillingham, *Creative Imagination of Théophile Gautier.*

GAY, JOHN (1685–1732): English poet and playwright, celebrated for his wit. He lived a life marked by conviviality and idleness, enriched by friendships with Swift, Pope and other leaders in literature and politics. Varying between moods of cynicism, moralizing and trifling, his own words inscribed on his monument in Westminster Abbey sum up much:

> Life is a jest, and all things show it;
> I thought so once, and now I know it.

His most popular work is the political farce-satire, *The Beggar's Opera,* often revived in modern times. His poetry is more clever than profound. As shown in the selection given in this book, he deliberately follows the worldliness and urbanity of Horace. For a study of his life, see O. Sherwin, *Mr Gay,* and of his background, W. H. Irving, *John Gay's London.*

GEIJER, ERIK GUSTAF (1783–1847): This Swedish poet was also an historian and professor of history. His researches were closely related to his poetry, since he belonged to what was called the "Gothic Society" and, like Walter Scott in England, did much to stimulate the study of the legends and folklore in his own country.

GIBBON, EDWARD (1737–1794): This great English historian, on a visit to Rome in 1759, conceived the plan of writing a history of the downfall of the Roman Empire. The writing of this work became thenceforth the major task of his life. Its volumes were published from 1776 to 1788. It gives an account of European history through a period of thirteen centuries. The central theme is the decline of the pagan civilization of Rome and the rise of the ruder civilization of the Christian Middle Ages. Gibbon was no partisan of Christianity, and his suave irony enriches his balanced and artificial prose. He is generally held the foremost of English historians, especially when his work is considered from a literary point of view. Equally notable for literary merit is his brief autobiography, where dignified reticence combines with grace and charm. His letters are also of much interest.

GILBERT, SIR WILLIAM SCHWENK (1836–1911): An English humorist, playwright and poet who discovered new varieties of farce and satire peculiarly expressive of the British mind. He first achieved fame as author of *The Bab Ballads,* where nonsense mingles with gibes at British foibles. In 1871 he began a collaboration with Arthur Sullivan, a musical composer well grounded in the traditions of English song. Their comic operas were given under the direction of Richard D'Oyly Carte at the Savoy Theatre, built especially for this purpose. Among them are *H.M.S. Pinafore* (1878); *Pirates of Penzance* (1879); *Patience* (1881); *Iolanthe* (1882); *The Mikado* (1885); and *The Gondoliers* (1889). They contain much literary and political satire: only the Church and Crown are spared. The British Navy, the House of Lords, the bar, and the poet laureate contribute to fun quite Aristophanic, save for its purity. In our selection from *Patience*, Oscar Wilde and his aestheticism are ridiculed. See the study by Hesketh Pearson.

Giusti, Giuseppe (1809–1850): This political poet and satirist, a leader in nineteenth-century Italian literature, was trained as a lawyer. He resided chiefly in Florence. Here he studied Dante and, in the more serious of his poems, attempted to emulate the political and moral satire of the *Divine Comedy*. Many of his verses, including racy and dialectical poems, were circulated in manuscript to avoid the Austrian censor, and first published only after the Revolution of 1848. One of his best-known satires depicts the down-at-heel condition of "the Italian boot," another is an ironical funeral oration on the Emperor Francis I. Several of his short poems are translated in W. D. Howells, *Modern Italian Poets*. The poem in this book shows the irony of social relationships between the citizens of a conquered country and their conquerors.

Godwin, William (1756–1836): This English novelist and political philosopher as a young man retired from the Presbyterian ministry and became a non-Christian, a complete materialist, anarchist and social radical. His ideas receive their best expression in his *Enquiry Concerning Political Justice*. They underlie his problem novel, *The Adventures of Caleb Williams*. Slightly less doctrinaire is his romance, *Saint Leon*. Besides these works he composed several volumes of history, essays and fiction. He was husband of the great leader in the social and legal emancipation of women, Mary Wollstonecraft, and father-in-law of the poet Shelley, who was one of his most ardent followers. Some of his thought remains challenging, even though his extravagance and inconsistency often become absurd. See H. N. Brailford, *Shelley, Godwin, and Their Circle*.

Goethe, Johann Wolfgang von (1749–1832): Germany's outstanding author was born in Frankfurt-am-Main. The romantic episodes of his youth are recorded in various of his autobiographical writings. From his friend Herder he gained many of his ideas and much of the direction of his literary studies. He was a still closer friend of Schiller. Travel in Italy reinforced his strong love of classical ideals, which grew on him throughout life. His early work, such as the play, *Götz von Berlichingen*, and the novel *The Sorrows of Werther*, are tempestuous and romantic. After 1775 he lived chiefly in Weimar. His plays of this period include *Egmont*, *Iphigenia in Tauris* and *Torquato Tasso*. Among his chief prose works are *Wilhelm Meister's Apprenticeship*, *Wilhelm Meister's Travels*, and his philosophical autobiography, *From My Life: Truth and Poetry*. His masterpiece is *Faust*, a poetic drama in two parts. Both parts are strongly philosophical and idealistic. The earlier section is marked by its metaphysical poetry and its love story. The later section, completed shortly before his death, is characterized by a more classical tone and a stronger social consciousness. It reveals his increasing interest in natural science, in politics and in public welfare. Throughout his life he composed lyrics and short poems of high excellence. See G. Lowes Dickinson, *Goethe and Faust*. Among the translations of *Faust* are those by Bayard Taylor and John Anster.

Góngora y Argote, Luis de (1561–1627): This Spanish poet was born and died at Cordova and there led most of his life. In youth he studied law and at forty-five took holy orders. During his lifetime his poems circulated only in manuscript, but shortly thereafter editions began to appear and his great literary influence to increase. His early poems are relatively simple in style, and for the most part racy and satiric in tone. Later he cultivated a difficult and ornate style, akin aesthetically to Spanish baroque art. He became a more conscious and artificial stylist, and at the same time his work gained a metaphysical subtlety and depth. It promoted a school of poets, often much inferior to their master, known as the Góngorists, and aided movements for stylistic reform and sophistication in other nations, notably the Euphuists under John Lyly in England, and the Marinists under Marini in Italy and France. See E. Churton, *Góngora, an Historical and Critical Essay, with Translations.*

GRAY, THOMAS (1716–1771): At Eton school this English poet formed friendships with two boys, Horace Walpole and Richard West, who were later to make names for themselves as intellectuals and to mean much in Gray's outwardly uneventful life. After touring Europe in their company, he became a teacher at Cambridge and later professor of modern history. Literary studies both in the classics and in Celtic and medieval fields much affected his poetry. He wrote many striking letters and some essays, but few poems. These are the products of a scrupulous craftsmanship. Several are odes in the classical manner. His *Elegy in a Country Churchyard*, unlike some of his other lyrics, is anything but pedantic. The mood is easily grasped, while the delicate refinement of the style is hardly wasted upon even the least-educated reader. See the life of Gray by Edmund Gosse.

GREENE, ROBERT (c. 1560–1592): English poet, playwright and novelist and a predecessor of Shakespeare, he did much to initiate the great Elizabethan cultural movement by mating the classical Renaissance to the national temper. After study and travel, he supported himself as a miscellaneous writer in London, where he died, dissipated and impoverished but undismayed. He utilized the Greek pastoral romances in such prose tales as *Menaphon* and *Pandosto*, the latter dramatized by Shakespeare in *The Winter's Tale*. He wrote a number of confessional pamphlets in a realistic style, but in a highly penitential and Puritanical spirit. The best of his romantic comedies is *The Honorable History of Friar Bacon and Friar Bungay* (1592). His lyrics have sprightliness and charm. They also show a kinship with the revival of English music under Italian inspiration. See Gwyn Jones, *Garland of Bays.*

GUILLEN, JORGE (1893–): This Spanish poet was born in Valladolid. As a young man he studied in Switzerland, France and Spain and after his student days taught in a large number of colleges and universities, ranging from Rumania, Austria, France, Spain and England, to the United States. His researches have been chiefly in Spanish literature. He has published a translation into Spanish from the French of Valéry. His poetry is thus based upon a wide historical and cosmopolitan foundation. It is, in the manner of much contemporary verse, usually terse, symbolical, metaphysical and, to the average reader, somewhat obscure. Yet it is of great power, and holds much promise. For translations and a critical study, see F. A. Pleak, *The Poetry of Jorge Guillen.*

GUINICELLI, GUIDO (c. 1240–1276): This Italian poet was born in Bologna, became a lawyer and died a political exile. Only a few of his poems survive, the most notable being a song, or canzone, *The Gentle Heart.* He is said by Dante to be the father of Italian poetry. Less figuratively, he appears to have aided in turning Italian verse from the manner of the troubadours to that of the school of philosophical idealists including Guido Cavalcanti, Dante and Petrarch.

HADRIAN (76–138): This Roman emperor ruled at the height of the imperial power and the ripest years of Roman culture preceding its decline. He is eminent both in peace and war. Especially noteworthy from the cultural standpoint is his munificent patronage of the arts. Many arches and public buildings were erected under his sovereignty. Being himself a connoisseur, he ornamented his own villa with countless works of art, largely of Greek origin or inspiration. Yet he felt the cool shadow of approaching decadence. He experienced the ennui of the collector and imitator who lacks creative genius and whose over-ripe society lacks such genius. In one of the most famous of epigrams he gives elegant expression to this refined pessimism. The poem has been many times translated into the modern European languages. The American poet Philip Freneau has a version of it. Perhaps the best known in English is that by Byron. See the biography by B. W. Henderson.

HAFIZ (d. 1389): This leading Persian poet was born and lived at Shiraz. At the Persian

Court he became a distinguished teacher of religion and literature. Thoroughly versed in the Koran and the mystical philosophy of the Sufists, he nevertheless encountered considerable hostility from the priests, who questioned his orthodoxy. The *Divan*, or collection of his poems, contains his famous odes. These appear to be chiefly love songs, although allegorical and mystical interpretations have often been given them. They have been widely known in both East and West, and have been of influence on Goethe, Emerson and many leaders of Western thought. See the translation, biography and commentary by H. W. Clarke and the translation by Gertrude Bell.

Hardy, Thomas (1840–1928): This English novelist and poet lived throughout his life near Dorchester in southwest England, celebrating this region under the name of Wessex in many of his books. Among his chief novels are *The Return of the Native* (1878), *Tess of the D'Urbervilles* (1891) and *Jude the Obscure* (1908). His masterpiece is *The Dynasts* (1908), an epic-drama on the wars with Napoleon. This work is not only memorable for its faithful presentation of history, but for its expression of the author's philosophy, projected in allegorical characters such as The Spirit of the Pities, The Spirit Sinister and The Spirit of the Years. These characters speak in poetry modeled after the Greek choral odes. In addition to his novels and epic drama he wrote many lyrics, likewise characterized by tenderness, frankness and a somber view of life. See the studies by E. C. Blunden, H. C. Duffin, A. S. McDowall, W. R. Rutland, H. M. Tomlinson and C. J. Weber.

Harris, Joel Chandler (1848–1908): This American author lived in Atlanta, Georgia, where he was editor of *The Constitution.* He is known chiefly for his *Nights with Uncle Remus* and later volumes of children's tales with a Negro setting dealing largely with the adventures of Br'er Fox and Br'er Rabbit. See the life by J. C. Harris.

Hawthorne, Nathaniel (1804–1864): This American author lived a quiet life devoted chiefly to his writing. He was born at Salem, Massachusetts, where he served for several years as surveyor of the port. He studied at Bowdoin College, resided in Boston, Concord and in western Massachusetts, and spent seven years abroad, where he served at the American consulate in Liverpool. His stories are marked by subtle and detached criticism, often to the disadvantage of the prevalent Puritan modes of thought. His masterpiece is *The Scarlet Letter*. Other notable novels are *The House of the Seven Gables, The Blithedale Romance* and *The Marble Faun.* Some of his best work is in his short stories, collected in *Twice-Told Tales,* and *Mosses from an Old Manse.* The tales are often comments on the Puritan conscience. His *Note-Books* contain much of his shrewdest criticism of society. See the study by N. Arvin.

Hazlitt, William (1778–1830): This leading English essayist and critic displays the highest versatility in his many writings, which have in common little but the singular vigor of their author's manly style. He expressed the ideas of the younger, romantic age with the firm, straightforward energy of the prose of the English Augustan eighteenth century. As a young man he discarded theology and painting for literature. For several years he supported himself by lecturing and periodical writing. A radical in politics, he greatly admired Napoleon. Much of his criticism dealt with Shakespeare and the Elizabethan age. Notable among his books are: *The Spirit of the Age; Views of the English Stage; Lectures on The English Comic Writers; Characters of Shakespeare's Plays;* and his volume of familiar essays, *Table Talk.* See the studies by H. Pearson, P. P. Howe and A. Birrell.

Hearn, Lafcadio (1850–1904): This author may perhaps be termed American, but in fact his history encompasses much of the globe. He was born of Irish-Greek parentage in one of the Ionian Islands, and as a youth was educated in France and England. In 1869 he came to America, where he meagerly supported himself by journalism and the writing of books in a somewhat precious or over-elegant style, with French, Negro or oriental backgrounds. In 1890 he went to Japan, where he became a Japanese citizen and lived for the remainder of his life. He married a Japanese woman and taught in a Japanese university. His works show a remarkably wide and exquisite appreciation of the literature and culture of Japan. Hearn is a man of letters rather than a great artist; he has left no single work of outstanding value; but almost all his critical appreciations of literature, both oriental and occidental, and his translations from the French and Japanese are of high value. He remains a masterful craftsman and a valuable interpreter of East to West and West to East. See his voluminous collected works, the biography and fascinating letters compiled by Elizabeth Bisland, Noguchi, *Lafcadio Hearn in Japan,* and Tinker, *Lafcadio Hearn's American Days.*

Heine, Heinrich (1797–1856): This German poet, a Jew, was born in Düsseldorf. His political radicalism compelled him to leave Germany, and after 1831 he lived in Paris, where his last years were further embittered by illness. He is best known for his many brief lyrics, rich in sentiment, wit and irony, and a unique blending of artfulness and simplicity. They contain some of the most famous of songs. His longer poems abound in the most savage satire. His prose works are scarcely inferior to his verse. Among the former are his *Harz Journey* and *Travel Pictures.* The songs have been translated by Louis Untermeyer and Humbert Wolfe. See Ludwig Masure, *Heine* and A. Vallentin, *Poet in Exile.*

Henry, Patrick (1736–1799): This American statesman and orator is one of the major figures in the years which witnessed the foundation of the United States. He was born in rural Virginia and privately educated. He entered public life through the law. His love for freedom and democracy prompted him in famous speeches to urge American independence and the Revolutionary War. A love for the liberties of the individual led him to oppose the union of the States; but the same love led him to frame much of the Bill of Rights, the most democratic part of the Constitution. He declined Washington's offers to make him Chief Justice of the Supreme Court and Secretary of State, preferring his quiet life on his Virginia estate. See Tyler, *Patrick Henry.*

Herodotus (c. 484–425 b.c.): The first of the great Greek historians was born at Halicarnassus, Asia Minor. He traveled extensively throughout the Near East. In 443 b.c. he assisted in the founding in Italy of the Athenian colony at Thurii. Here he is believed to have written his *History.* This work describes the history, customs and traditions of the peoples whom the author had visited and proceeds to an account of the wars between Greece and Persia. The work is full of shrewd observations, fascinating comments on men and geography and stories told with much humanity and often much humor. Its style is so ingratiating that it long has been considered among the most eminently readable books in the world. See J. B. Bury, *Ancient Greek Historians,* and the translation by George Rawlinson.

Herrick, Robert (1591–1674): This English poet was born in London and as a youth apprenticed to his uncle, the jeweler to the king. A love of learning induced him to become a clergyman. After 1629 he was vicar at Dean Prior, except for a period in which the Puritans expelled him from his parish. His jewel-like poems of prevailingly royalist sentiment were published in 1648 as *Hesperides.* Herrick modeled his poems on the pastoral verse of the Greeks and Romans and on the Latin satirists and epigrammatists. He was well acquainted with Anacreon and the Greek Anthology. Accepting the art patterns and philosophy of the ancients, he created a wonderfully clear and simple English style and achieved a charm, delicacy and humor altogether his own. Many of his highly lyrical poems were put to music by the chief composers of his own times.

Hesiod (fl. 8th Cent. b.c.): One of the earliest of all Greek poets known to us, Hesiod lived in Boeotia, and apparently he and his brother, Perses, with whom he quarreled, were farmers and shepherds. He has left two long poems, *Works and Days,* a versified treatise on farming; and *Theogony,* or a miscellany on the origin of the world and the myths of the gods. There is also a fragment possibly his describing the shield of Hercules. His style is rude, digressive and literal, but with force, feeling, sincerity and a strong rustic flavor. In *Works and Days* we see a vigorous, clear-headed peasant people; in *Theogony* we glimpse their harsh and even brutal mythology. Hesiod is quite without the refinement of Homer, who inherited much from the rich Cretan civilization. There are translations of *Works and Days* by the Elizabethan poet George Chapman and by C. A. Elton and A. W. Mair.

HÖLDERLIN, JOHANN CHRISTIAN FRIEDRICH (1770–1843): This German poet became early in life a friend of Hegel, Schelling and Schiller. After attending the University at Tübingen, he became a private tutor in the house of Schiller's friend, Charlotte von Kalb. From 1806 his mind failed him and he sank into insanity. He expressed the common German fusion of the classical and the romantic. Chief among his works are a romance, *Hyperion, or the Hermit in Greece;* an incomplete drama, *Empedocles;* able translations from Sophocles; and, above all, his lyric poems. See the volume of translations by Frederic Prokosch.

HÖLTY, LUDWIG HEINRICH CHRISTOPH (1748–1776): This German poet, though not of a commanding genius, has written some of the most popular of German songs and lyrics. His work represents the people rather than the intellectuals. It is often sentimental, sometimes joyous, sometimes romantically melancholy. The note of patriotism is conspicuous. Such work is pleasing in itself and affords a valuable key to the Germanic character. There is also just enough of the universal in it to challenge wide sympathy.

HOMER (c. 900 B.C.): The father of Greek poetry, about whom nothing is certainly known. During the revival of classical studies at the close of the Middle Ages, he was universally assumed to be author of the two epics, the *Iliad* and the *Odyssey*, and of many hymns and shorter poems. Later scholars denied him the hymns and fragments; many believe the *Odyssey* a considerably later poem than the *Iliad;* and some even hold the *Iliad* to have developed by accretion rather than to be primarily by a single hand. But general opinion favors the existence of a great epic poet of this name, who lived in Asia Minor, and to whose genius we are chiefly indebted for the two epics. These poems were the bible of Greek culture. They are notable for their mythology, but even the gods are profoundly human and the stories as a whole are characterized by their brilliance, vigor and humanity. See Gilbert Murray, *Rise of the Greek Epic*.

HOPKINS, GERARD MANLEY (1844–1889): This English poet was educated at Oxford where he became a Roman Catholic. He was ordained a Jesuit priest in 1877. In 1884 he became professor of Greek at the Royal University, Dublin, where he also studied and taught versification. His highly original lyrics – original for succinct phrase and strong image, brilliant rhetoric and metrical virtuosity – remained unpublished till 1918, when his friend, the poet laureate, Robert Bridges, deemed the public prepared to receive such revolutionary work. At least the more educated public was prepared, and Hopkins is now regarded as one of the greatest of literary innovators, along with Emily Dickinson, Rimbaud and Rilke. In substance his poetry is both metaphysical and religious. See a biography by G. F. Lahey, and E. E. Phare, *The Poetry of Gerard Manley Hopkins.*

HORACE (QUINTUS HORATIUS FLACCUS) (65–8 B.C.): This Roman poet studied in Rome and Athens. In Rome he met Virgil, who introduced him to the munificent patron of letters, Maecenas. The latter gave him a country estate, the Sabine Farm, which Horace celebrates in his lyrics. He wrote collections of satires, odes and epistles, as well as an epistolary essay on verse known as *The Art of Poetry.* His poetry lacks grandeur, enthusiasm, subjectivity and the liveliest imagination, but remains unsurpassed as an artful reflection of the surface of society. No ancient poet has been more widely read and imitated. His theory and practice provided a basis for Boileau in France and Pope in England. See translations by Louis Untermeyer and A. F. Murison.

HOUSMAN, A. E. (1859–1936): English poet and classical scholar. Throughout most of his life a professor of Latin, he assimilated perhaps more fully than any other Englishman of his age the classical conception of form. His poetry is somewhat narrow in its scope, using humble rural life for its setting and dwelling on a limited range of experiences and ideas. A realism, devoid, however, of a broad or lively inquiry into life, unites with a pervasive pessimism. How remarkably close he comes to the mood of the classical elegy and epitaph may be seen by comparing his poems given in this book with the classical selections in the section *Wit and Epigram.* See the study by Grant Richards.

HUBBLE, EDWIN POWELL (1889–): This American astronomer graduated from the University of Chicago, was a Rhodes Scholar at Oxford, worked at the Yerkes Observatory in Wisconsin and, after 1919, at the Mount Wilson Observatory in California. He is widely known for his studies of diffuse nebulae.

HUGO, VICTOR MARIE (1802–1885): This French novelist, poet and playwright is the leading figure among the French romanticists. His political opinions caused his exile to Guernsey, where he wrote savage satires against the regime of Louis Napoleon, represented by two poems in this book. He returned to France in triumph after the re-establishment of republican rule. His great novels include *Notre Dame de Paris; Les Miserables; Travailleurs de la mer* (*Toilers of the Sea*); and *Quatre-vingt-treize* (*Ninety-Three*). His admiration for Shakespeare led him to a type of romantic drama represented by *Cromwell* and *Hernani.* His poetry has unsurpassed eloquence and sonority, but is sometimes deemed, with much of his prose, slightly affected and over-rhetorical. His poems on children are universally admired. In England Swinburne proved his closest follower and warmest admirer. See the life by Matthew Josephson.

IKHNATON, AMENHOTEP IV (c. 1375–1357 B.C.): This Egyptian pharaoh held new religious ideas and instigated sweeping religious reforms. His worship of the sun, Aton, as the sole God is the initial chapter in the history of monotheism in the Mediterranean cultures. His zeal in religion, with his distaste for the earlier cult of the god Amon, brought him into a struggle with a conservative priesthood, and divided and weakened his kingdom politically. His spiritual leadership, however, stimulated art and poetry, especially in the direction of a new naturalism. His *Hymn to the Sun* resembles many later Jewish and Christian hymns, as well as several of the psalms and the canticle by St. Francis. See J. H. Breasted, *History of Egypt.*

JAMES, WILLIAM (1842–1910): This American philosopher was the son of a Swedenborgian theologian. For thirty-five years he taught at Harvard University, chiefly in the fields of psychology and philosophy. Here he advocated an outlook which he termed pragmatism. Behind this view stood the skepticism typical of liberal New Englanders. The highest truth becomes the highest expediency. Reality must be discerned through experience, and ideas organized to accord with our actual experiences and needs. The emphasis in his teaching is moral, ethical and practical, and hospitable to scientific progress. Among his chief books are *Principles of Psychology; The Will to Believe; Varieties of Religious Experience; Pragmatism; A Pluralistic Universe;* and *The Meaning of Truth.* His place in American life and thought is revealed in his fascinating *Letters.* See the study by H. M. Kallen.

JAMI (1414–1492): This Persian poet associated himself with the dervish teaching and the religious Sufi philosophy. To Western eyes his position often seems ambiguous between sensualism and asceticism. He wrote *Baharistan* (*Abode of Spring*), a collection of short stories and parables. Among his many poems is the *Haft Aurang* (*The Seven Thrones*), which includes the allegory, *Salaman and Absal,* brilliantly translated by Edward Fitzgerald. From this work is taken the lyric, with its amusing fable, given in this book. His parables and imagery suggest to us poetic passages of the Bible.

JEAN DE MEUN (c. 1250–c. 1305): This French poet, best known for his love of satire, is the continuator of *The Romance of the Rose,* a long poem of which Guillaume de Lorris had left only the first part (4670 verses). Jean de Meun added some 20,000 verses, bringing the work to its conclusion. The poem as a whole deals with love and the place of woman, two favorite subjects for medieval authors. The first part treats the theme chivalrously and idealistically, the second part satirically and realistically. Many philosophical subjects, such as the true interpretation of Nature, long suspected by the schoolmen to be feminine and evil, are introduced. A specimen is given in this book. There is also much social satire, especially against the monks. Jean opposes the celibacy of the clergy, distrusts magic and doubts the divine right of kings. He is the father of French social satire. See the translation by F. S. Ellis.

Jeffers, Robinson (1887–): One of the most powerful and philosophical of American writers, equally successful in lyrics and narrative verse. *Selected Poems* (1937) gives a generous representation of his work, but *Cawdor* (1928); *Dear Judas* (1929); and *Be Angry at the Sun* (1943), are also impressive. He has gathered ideas freely from history, metaphysics, psychology and the natural sciences, and has been influenced by Lucretius, Schopenhauer and Nietzsche. There is much pessimism but also much nobility in his thinking. Aloof, but sensitive and noble, he is in many respects the American Leopardi. See the study by L. C. Powell.

Jensen, Johannes Vilhelm (1873–): This poet and novelist stands among the foremost writers of modern Denmark. His novels deal realistically with many aspects of Danish life, including the historical and even the pre-historical. He is admired for his fidelity to the manners and landscape of his native country and for his imaginative style in both verse and prose.

Jerome, Saint (c. 340–420): This Father of the Church was born in Dalmatia, studied in Rome, and journeyed into Syria. Here he experienced a vision which persuaded him to lead an ascetic and saintly life. He returned to Rome, and thence traveled to Bethlehem, where he lived in a monastery for thirty-four years. He made the translation of the Bible into Latin known as the Vulgate, the version authorized by the Catholic Church. He conducted many vehement theological controversies. Over a hundred of his letters survive, all of much interest, especially those to St. Augustine. A selection of the letters is translated by F. A. Wright. See E. K. Rand, *Founders of the Middle Ages.*

Jiménez, Juan Ramón (1881–): This poet stands among the leading figures in modern Spanish literature. His work possesses the subjectivity, succinctness and symbolical subtley typical of literary taste in the Western World during the last three or four decades. His influence has been widely felt throughout Spanish speaking lands.

Jonson, Ben (1573?–1637): English playwright, poet and man of letters. Jonson lived and died in London, where for over thirty years he remained the central figure in its literary life. Like his friend Shakespeare, he reconciled the humanist movement with the British genius, but he was more the scholar than Shakespeare. His plays such as *Every Man in His Humor* (1598); *Volpone* (1606); and *The Alchemist* (1610), are celebrated for vigorous social satire. *Discoveries* shows him to much advantage as a moralist and literary critic. His poems were widely imitated. All his work leans heavily upon the materialistic spirit and forceful language of the Latin poets. His epigrams, for example, resemble Martial; his odes, Pindar or Horace. See E. C. Dunn, *Ben Jonson's Art.*

Joubert, Joseph (1754–1824): This French philosopher and moralist lived for the most part a retired life, restricted by poor health, but for brief periods was associated with the College of Toulouse and the University of Paris. Although none of his writings were published during his lifetime, he exercised a considerable influence through his brilliant conversation and his many friendships. A volume of his essays was posthumously published, edited by Chateaubriand and reviewed enthusiastically by Sainte-Beuve. The best study of him in English is to be found in Matthew Arnold's *Essays in Criticism.*

Juvenal (Decimus Junius Juvenalis) (c. 60–c. 140): This Roman satirist held various civil and military offices of minor importance and at one time visited Egypt. His objective satire tells us little of himself but much of Rome. His heightened style and intense indignation have sometimes been suspected of insincerity; but the general effect of his work is powerful in the extreme. His righteous anger is commonly contrasted with the urbane humor of Horace. Savage attacks on worldly life made him peculiarly attractive to Christian moralists and for many centuries he exercised an immense literary influence. English translations abound from

Tudor to modern times. Among the best are renderings of a few of the satires by John Dryden; a comprehensive translation by William Gifford; and the free adaptations by Dr. Johnson entitled *London* and *Vanity of Human Wishes*. See the study by Edward Walford.

KAIBARA EKKEN (1629–1713): This Japanese essayist and poet is author of more than a hundred works, including ethical treatises, studies of Chinese classics, and books on botany, travel and language. His style is simple and direct; partly because of his homely wisdom and his serious and educational aims, he has become one of the most influential of Japanese authors.

KEATS, JOHN (1795–1821): The most fastidious craftsman among the English romantic poets, Keats possessed a rare sense for poetic form. Although he often writes of nature much as his contemporaries were accustomed to do, most of his poems continue in the tradition of the amorous pastoral as cultivated by the later Greeks and the poets of the Renaissance. Keats, for example, was much influenced by the Italian Boccaccio, some of whose works he knew through translation by Dryden. Keats is celebrated for a colorful, musical and rich style, notable in his odes, as *Ode to a Nightingale, Ode on a Grecian Urn* and *Ode on Melancholy*. His fragmentary epic, *Hyperion*, is his finest long poem. His sonnets contain some of his best work. His poetry was little esteemed during his lifetime. He died in Rome, where he had gone for his health. Of recent years he has been increasingly appreciated. See Amy Lowell's *John Keats*.

KIPLING, RUDYARD (1865–1936): This English poet, novelist and short-story writer was born in Bombay, India. Although educated in England, he returned to India as a journalist. In 1902 his marriage to an American led him to live for a few years in Brattleboro, Vermont. His latter years he passed in England. In 1907 he received the Nobel Prize. He is buried in Westminster Abbey. His early poems and stories are his best. These deal largely with army life in India and Africa, and with oriental scenes and fantasies. He possessed an extraordinary ear for language, especially for dialect and slang. His children's stories and rhymes, his tales of adventure and his rapid strokes of characterization show him to be a master. Many of his lyrics are well known as songs. He appreciated the viewpoint of the common man, often revealing special fondness for the Scotch. With advancing years his mind hardened, he became increasingly moralistic, imperialistic and didactic and his old age failed to bear out the promise of a youth of almost Shakespearean richness. His strength declined into mere obstinacy. Among his works are *Barrack Room Ballads; The Jungle Book; The Just So Stories; Kim; Plain Tales from the Hills; Stalky and Co.;* and *The Light That Failed*. See the studies by W. M. Hart, G. L. Palmer, and R. T. Hopkins.

KOLTZOV, ALEXEY VASILYEVICH (1808–1842): This lyric poet has been described as a Russian Burns. He was a cattle driver and a man of the people. Contacts during the latter part of his life with the literary world merely diluted his art. His best work always derives from the folksong. The larger number of his racy, rustic poems have been set to music by leading Russian composers.

LA FONTAINE, JEAN DE (1621–1695): This French poet and fabulist was born at Château-Thierry, where his father was inspector of streams and forests. His early writing came to the attention of the French Minister, Fouquet, who lent him his patronage. After Fouquet's fall the poet was patronized by a number of ladies of the Court. He wrote a collection of racy verse stories largely based on Italian sources, a poem on Cupid and Psyche, an epic and a number of plays, but by his *Fables* alone is he commonly known. These borrow extensively from Aesop, European folklore and ultimately from oriental sources. They inspired many followers, notably John Gay in England. La Fontaine proves singularly happy in catching the wit and good sense of the neo-classical French ideal, for which only one spokesman surpasses him, his friend, Molière. See the translations by Eliazur Wright and Walter Thornbury.

LAGERLÖF, SELMA (1858–1940): One of the leaders of recent Swedish literature, she has travelled widely, written of many lands, and given unsurpassed descriptions of her own.

In 1909 she won the Nobel award for literature. Her novels and short stories have been translated into many languages. Among her books are: *The Outcast, Harvest, Jerusalem, The Ring of the Löwenskölds,* and *Gösta Berling's Saga.*

Lamartine, Alphonse Marie Louis de (1790–1869): This French poet, prose writer and statesman began his active career in the diplomatic service under the French Monarchy restored after the Revolution. As time advanced he himself acquired republican and radical ideas. In the Revolution of 1848 he was a leader, later an apologist for its failure. His prose includes romances, short stories, autobiographical books and numerous works in history. His poetry consists of elegies, love poems, nature poems, genre pieces, romances, imitations of Byron and an unfinished epic. He is regarded as a founder of the romantic school in French verse, and known especially for poems of love and nature marked by a slightly specious melancholy. See the life by H. R. Whitehouse.

Landor, Walter Savage (1775–1864): From youth he possessed a fiery and independent temperament, so that his life is a story of equally warm quarrels and friendships. His large estate shrank in his hands. He lived for many years in Bath, but for longer periods in Italy. His voluminous works include a long poem, *Gebir;* a verse drama, *Count Julian;* his *Imaginary Conversations,* imagined dialogues between historical persons; and many short poems and epigrams, often in the manner of the Greek Anthology. Landor is eclectic rather than deeply creative. His prose often paraphrases or enlarges upon earlier literature, while his shorter poems, though admirable in style, lack the highest type of originality. He comprehended the past more readily than the present. Yet he incontestably possessed nobility of mind. See the life by Elwin Malcolm.

Langland, William: This name is commonly assigned to the author of the great English allegorical poem, *Piers Plowman,* although nothing beyond conjecture can be ascertained regarding either the author's name or life. He was possibly a poor priest living in and about London. The poem exists in three versions extending from approximately 1362 to approximately 1395. As an allegory of the Christian life it resembles Dante's *Divine Comedy,* but it is a racy, homespun version of Dante's learned and polished poem. Its impassioned social satire has seldom been surpassed and it contains many passages of deep religious feeling. It is written in long lines with consonantal alliteration. A transcription into modern English has been made by H. W. Wells. See also the study by J. Jusserand.

Leeuwenhoek, Anthony van (1632–1723): This Dutch naturalist was born in Delft. He is said to have first experimented with lenses for the purpose of examining cloth, while he was apprenticed to a draper. A man of no formal education, he became one of the foremost scientists of his times. Through his improvements in the microscope he opened up many new fields of study. He discovered the red corpuscles of the blood, and was the first to see bacteria, protozoa, infusoria and rotifers. His descriptive studies in anatomy ranged from insects to man. He had able pupils and his work had a wide and rapid influence.

León, Luis Ponce de (1527–1591): This Spanish poet and mystic was a professor of theology at Salamanca. He was imprisoned for rendering the *Song of Songs* into Spanish for the benefit of a nun. In four years he was was released and continued his studies. His humanistic bent is shown by translations into Spanish from Pindar, Euripides, Virgil, Horace, Tibullus and Seneca. In addition to theological commentaries on *Job*, the *Song of Songs* and the names applied to Christ, he is author of many lyrics both secular and religious. His finest verse is strongly metaphysical and mystical. He has had a deep influence upon Spanish literature and even upon poets and writers in other lands. See the study of his life and work by Aubrey Bell (1925).

Leonardo da Vinci (1454–1519): This Italian artist, scientist and thinker was born in Florence. The vast scope of his activities is often noted as typical of his own humanistic age and foreign to our own times of narrow specialization. He worked for long periods in both Florence and Milan and died in France. Although best known today for his painting and magnificent draftsmanship, he was extremely active in architecture, civil engineering and experimental science. His notebooks, some of them only recently published, best reveal his inquisitive, daring and versatile mind. For Leonardo as an author, see J. P. Richter; for his art, see B. Berenson, *The Drawings of the Florentine Painters;* for his life, see D. Merezhkovsky.

Leopardi, Giacomo (1798–1837): This leading Italian poet was throughout his life a severe invalid and an indefatigable and brilliant scholar, especially of the classics and of Italian. He lived much of the time in enforced retirement and in the austere shadow of ancient family tradition. He became a distinguished philologist; his letters are of great literary value, as also are a collection of reflective prose, *Pensieri,* and essays on moral themes. His few poems are unsurpassed in Italian literature for depth of thought and feeling, sincerity and formal perfection. Many are odes, some in rhymed stanzas, others in a chaste and controlled free verse. Their timeless splendor epitomizes much of the best of both classical and modern thought. Their most characteristic mood is heroic pessimism. The poems have been translated by G. L. Bickersteth, J. Morrison and R. C. Trevelyan.

Lermontov, Mikhail Yurevich (1818–1841): During his brief and stormy life this Russian poet was twice sent to the Caucasus by the Czar's government; the first time for writing a eulogy on Pushkin at the death of that poet. He was more subjective than Pushkin, but resembled him in his gallantries and a fatal fascination for dueling. Russian folklore inspires *Song of the Merchant Kalashnikoff.* His powers of ironic criticism appear in *Hero of Our Times,* a prose novel, while his most impassioned work is, perhaps, *The Demon.* Like Pushkin, he both resembles Byron and expresses the indigenous Russian culture. There are English translations of his chief works.

Lewis, Cecil Day (1904–): This English poet was born in Ireland and educated at Oxford. A collection of his early work appeared in *Poems 1929–1933.* In 1935 appeared *A Time to Dance.* His critical views he has expressed in *A Hope for Poetry.* With his heart eager for a new and saner social system, he has written considerable poetry more notable for spirit and energy than for form or definition. Nevertheless his keen sense for the realities of industrial life has led to some refreshing lyrics, such as the poem given in this book. *Selected Poems* appeared in 1940.

Li Po or Li Tai Po (701–762): One of the leading Chinese poets. Tradition reports him to have led a gay and dissolute life at Court, from which he was expelled. His writings deal with the good things of life and with the pathos of human destiny. Love, friendship, wine, nature and simple village living are treated with a vividness which time and translation have by no means effaced. Many of his poems are rendered into English by Arthur Waley.

Lincoln, Abraham (1809–1865): The sixteenth President of the United States was born in a pioneer's cabin in Kentucky. His family moved to Indiana and to Illinois. His schooling amounted to only a few months; his rather wide reading and knowledge he acquired at much hardship through personal enterprise. After working at many small-town jobs, and traveling through much of the Middle West, he became a lawyer and politician. His debates in the open air with his rival Douglas on the slavery issue form one of the most remarkable chapters in the history of democracy. Lincoln saw the slave issue in the light of world-wide problems of the freedom of man. His own life taught him to esteem the American doctrine of Thomas Jefferson, and at an early age he dedicated himself to the great principle "that government of the people, by the people and for the people shall not perish from the earth." He found himself in 1861 as President of the United States engaged in a war which he conceived as fought upon this principle as well as in the cause of the preservation of the Union. It is not because Lincoln was a Unionist but because he was the greatest democrat thus far produced by the New World that he is daily invoked in the twentieth century as the embodiment of America's social ideal. Lincoln delivered many great addresses in the purest and most unaffected English. Of these his address at Gettysburg and his Second Inaugural are regarded as the masterpieces. He was killed by the assassin John Wilkes Booth while attending Ford's Theatre in Washington, April 14, 1865. See the long biography by Carl Sandburg and the briefer study by Lord Charnwood.

LINNAEUS (KARL VON LINNÉ) (1707–1778): This most celebrated of botanists was born in Rashult, Sweden. From childhood he brushed aside all obstacles to his devoted study of plants. The first of his many botanical expeditions was to Lapland. For a number of years he lived with fellow-botanists in the Netherlands. The latter part of his life he was professor at the University of Upsala in his native land. Here he received wide recognition for his remarkable labors. He is chiefly known for his thorough and accurate classification and description of plants, which he was the first to divide into genus and species. Few men have possessed the power to observe so many aspects of nature or to order their observations so systematically. He is not only father of modern botany, but has exercised an indirect influence on all branches of natural science. See the life by T. M. Fries.

LÓPEZ, LUIS CARLOS (1880–): This Colombian poet was once the Colombian consul in Baltimore. He uses a terse, free form of the sonnet, which, contrary to the sentimentality which the sonnet has so often conveyed, he employs for purposes of social satire. In this respect he resembles the American, Merrill Moore, whose *Joe Greene* may be compared with López's *Tropic Siesta.* López is not always satirical; his natural gusto and joy of life is often delightful, as in *Country Girl, Don't Stay Away.* His influence has been widely felt throughout Latin America.

LUCIAN (120–200 A.D.): One of the last of the great Greek authors in the classical tradition. In youth he was apprenticed to a sculptor; later he became a lawyer. He lived in various parts of the Near East, especially at Antioch and in Egypt. His works establish him as one of the world's foremost humorists. A skeptic in an age of social and moral decline, he made a jest of the gods and studied the follies of his fellow-men, all in an entirely urbane and good-natured spirit, at times making fun of himself. His best-known work is *Dialogues of the Dead,* imitated by Landor in his *Imaginary Conversations* and by many others. Almost as good are his *Dialogues of the Gods.* The philosophical systems of antiquity served to amuse him. Skeptics of all later ages have turned to him as a friend, notably the rationalist, Erasmus. The item in this book is one of the few poems ascribed to him. His major works are translated by F. G. Fowler.

LUCILIUS, CAIUS (fl. 60): A Greek poet known for epigrams which take their place in the Greek Anthology, or collection of short poems. He belongs to the later, or Alexandrian, phase of this lyric tradition, where grace and wit supplant strength and depth of feeling.

LUCRETIUS (TITUS LUCRETIUS CARUS) (c. 96– c. 55 B.C.): This major Roman poet is known by a single poem, *On the Nature of Things,* while his personal life remains in obscurity. The story of his madness as the result of a love potion and of his suicide is told by St. Jerome, but has no real authority. His masterpiece is a philosophical poem giving us our clearest views of the materialistic philosophy of Epicurus and Democritus. The world and the soul are described as produced by atoms and the gods as wholly disinterested in human affairs. Man has no immortality, but has capacity for social progress based upon his intelligent study of nature and society. These views, shocking to religious sensibilities, have commended his poem to rationalists both in ancient and modern times. It is the product of a rebellious, fervent, noble spirit, with passages of unsurpassed power. See J. Masson, *Lucretius, Epicurean and Poet,* and translations by H. A. J. Munro and W. E. Leonard.

LUTHER, MARTIN (1483–1546): This German theologian and leader of the Protestant Christianity was born in Eisleben, Saxony, his father being a miner. His early education included the neo-classical studies of the humanists. Religious conviction led him to become an Augustinian friar. But the same zeal for religion led him into violent opposition to many of the practices and teachings of the Church, especially the use of indulgences. He found the Church materialistic, hypocritical and corrupt and was inclined to see all its evils embodied in the papacy, for which he found no warrant in the Bible. The political interests of many of the German princes also conflicted with the papacy; and Luther and the princes made common cause; he to purify the Church, they to establish their political liberties. In 1517 he nailed to the door of a church in Wittenberg his charges against indulgences. Two years later he affiliated the cause of the reformed faith with a patriotic German nationalism. His own marriage confirmed his opposition to celibacy of the clergy and the monastic institutions. He was excommunicated and ordered to be burnt, but instead he burnt the papal order itself. The princes and the rising sentiment of the people protected him, and he died peacefully, exhausted by his strenuous labors. He wrote many tracts and controversial essays, marked often by vehemence and coarseness. He aided in the writing of catechisms and a revised liturgy. Of his many stirring hymns, the most famous is: "A Mighty Fortress is Our God." Perhaps his greatest literary work is his vigorous translation of the Bible into German. He left the world with a new religion and Europe with a legacy of fierce religious wars. See the studies by Preserved Smith and A. C. McGiffert.

Machiavelli, Niccolò di Bernardo (1469–1527): This Italian historian, statesman and man of letters was born in Florence, where he lived for almost all his life, holding various political offices, which brought him into contact with the devious ways of Renaissance statecraft in the petty Italian city-states. When the return of the Medici to power put him out of office, he turned to imaginative literature and produced poems and a few notable comedies. But his major works are on history and statecraft. He composed a history of Florence, a commentary upon Livy and a treatise on the art of war. He left also a number of diplomatic papers. More important are his *Discourses* and his masterpiece, *The Prince*. These are realistic and somewhat cynical studies in political policy, often advocating expediency at the expense of personal honor. He believed that Italy could be saved from foreign oppression and internal faction only by a ruthless and unscrupulous ruler, such as Cesare Borgia, whom he idealized. He has scandalized idealists, encouraged the unscrupulous and instructed all serious students of political science. His name was perpetuated by Elizabethan dramatists as the "Machiavel," the type of archvillain if not of the devil. See the studies by P. Villari and M. Praz.

MacLeish, Archibald (1892–): American poet and author, born in Glencoe, Illinois, soldier, lawyer, publicist, and director of the Library of Congress. In World War I, he was in the army in France; in the last war, he was assistant to the director of war information, later assistant secretary of state in charge of public and cultural relations. He is the author of essays on political subjects, of radio plays and several volumes of verse. His longest poem is *Conquistador* (1932), an epic narrative of the Spanish conquest of Mexico, based on the first-hand account of Bernal Diaz, a selection from which is in this book. His *Frescoes for Mr. Rockefeller's City*, also represented, is a poem-sequence satirizing the unrestricted exploitation of the railroad-building era. *Poems, 1924–1943* contains most of his best work.

Manrique, Gómez (1415–1491): This poet was of a noble Spanish family. He participated in the civil wars which evidenced the disunity of Spain, but resulted at last in Spanish consolidation. He promoted the marriage of Ferdinand and Isabella; politically he was a moderate, and protected the converted Jews of Toledo against persecution. His verse is notable at times for pathos, at times for vigorous satire. He also wrote didactic verse, a Passion play, and court interludes, and is the earliest known Spanish dramatist. It is in his capacity as satirist in a medieval tradition that he is represented in this book.

Manrique, Jorge (1440–1479): This celebrated Spanish poet was son of Rodrigo, Grand-Master of Santiago, one of Spain's best-known soldiers. The poet fought with his father in behalf of the claims of Alfonso and Isabel of Castile. He was killed in battle. His best-known poem is an elegiac ballad in memory of Rodrigo. This piece, in a somewhat abridged form, appears in this volume as translated by the American poet, H. W. Longfellow. It may be read as a typical example of the native vein of the elegy in Spanish poetry, uniting pathos with realism.

MARCUS ARGENTARIUS (fl. 60 A.D.): A notable member of the poets of the Greek Anthology, well representing the sophisticated wit and delicate artistry achieved by Greek verse of this period. As we see from one of his best-remembered trifles, old Hesiod to him appeared a bit too sober.

MARCUS AURELIUS (121–180): This Roman emperor and stoic philosopher is equally honored by historians for the wisdom and integrity of his government and by readers of ethics for the nobility of his brief volume, *Meditations*. This unique work continues the stoical tradition as founded by Epictetus, but with a difference. We may see a reason for this difference in the circumstances of the two men, one an emperor, the other a slave. To the more personal virtues of honor and fortitude Aurelius adds a fuller awareness of human obligation and social responsibility. See the studies by G. H. Rendall and H. P. Sedgwick.

MARÍN, LUIS MUÑOZ (1898–): This Puerto Rican poet is son of Luis Muñoz Rivera, considered the liberator of his country. He has edited a Spanish West Indian Review. Leader of the Popular Democratic Party and President of the Senate of Puerto Rico, he has written extensively, both verse and prose, in Spanish and in English. Much of his work has been published in the United States. His deep devotion to the cause of the common man, especially in his impoverished island, appears in the highly imaginative poem given in this volume. The English translation is by his wife.

MARKHAM, EDWIN (1852–1940): This American poet was born in Oregon, the son of pioneer parents. As a young man he turned from farming to school teaching. Throughout his long life he has written many poems of a social content, *Lincoln, and Other Poems* (1901), and *The Shoes of Happiness* (1914), being typical volumes. Democracy and social justice were the leading ideals of his life; their best known expression is his poem given in this book, *The Man With the Hoe,* suggested by Millet's famous painting.

MARMONTEL, JEAN FRANÇOIS (1723–1799): This French author and critic began his literary career under the encouragement of Voltaire. His works have a didactic tendency; they are critiques of books and men. He contributed many articles, generally in the field of literature, to that great compilation of learning, the *Encyclopedie*. He also wrote moralizing tales, novels and plays and fascinating memoirs. His work as a whole made him a powerful and representative figure of the French Enlightenment.

MAROT, CLÉMENT (1496?–1544): This French poet was alternately in favor and disfavor with the French court, as he was free of the suspicion of Protestant leanings or suffering under such a charge. He joined Calvin in Geneva, only to quarrel with him. Marot possessed the brilliant craftsmanship, the hard, brittle wit and cool realism typical of his age, behind which there stood a strong piety. His translation of the Psalms became famous. His influence spread to England, where he helped to inspire Spenser to write a notable elegy. Marot excels in light verse, fables and epistles. He composed rondeaux, ballads and epigrams, the latter in competent imitation of Martial and other Latin poets.

MARTIAL, VALERIUS (c. 40–c. 104): The master of the Latin epigram, or short poem, was born in Bilbilis, Spain, where he died, although he lived and wrote at Rome. His poems in flattery of the emperors Titus and Domitian won him considerable wealth and place. Altogether he left some 1500 epigrams, many of only two lines. Among them are some extremely coarse and bitter pieces, reflecting the loose living of the Roman plutocracy. His pages give an unrivaled image of Roman manners. There are specimens of great urbanity and wit. He afforded a model for writers in both ancient and modern times, and in Italy, Spain, France, Germany and England. His popularity rose to its height in the Renaissance. He was assiduously imitated by Ben Jonson. See the translations by P. Nixon.

MARVELL, ANDREW (1621–1678): English poet and statesman. A fastidious Puritan of impeccable taste and unimpeachable character, he has left an enviable name in English literature and history. He is remembered as friend and protector of Milton and champion of political liberty and personal integrity in the corrupt court of Charles II. His political writings and satires are, however, less admired than his lyrical verse. Without Milton's power, he has an almost equal share in Horatian grace and an even greater gift for the metaphysical thinking and the neo-platonic idealism characteristic of poetry in the seventeenth century. See the life by A. Birrell and the study by M. C. Bradbrook and M. G. Lloyd.

Marx, Karl (1818–1883): This German political and social philosopher was born of Jewish parents in Trier, Prussia. After engaging in radical propaganda in Germany and France, he found refuge in England. Here he wrote and studied, serving as reporter for the *New York Tribune*. His *Communist Manifesto*, written with Paul Engels (1848), is the simplest expression of his political and economic beliefs, while *Capital* is his major work. Communism holds that capitalism is doomed, that the proletariat must seize power by force and control all means of production and that each individual should give according to his means and take according to his needs. This political creed is accepted as the ideal of the present Soviet Union, although the Soviets hold that at present they have at best attained not communism but an advanced stage of socialism. See *Communism* by Harold J. Laski and the study by E. and C. Paul.

Mazzini, Giuseppe (1805–1872): This Italian revolutionist and radical was early exiled from his country because of his schemes for the unification and republicanization of Italy. He lived in France, in Switzerland and chiefly in England, laying the plans for political and social revolution. The uprisings in 1848 enabled him to return to Italy, where for a few months he was one of the national leaders in Rome. The failure of this revolution drove him again into exile. Other plots proved for the time being no more successful. Not a great statesman, nor a practical executive, he was an important political essayist and thinker, inclining in his latter years to an advanced socialism. His unwillingness to compromise with political realities distinguishes him from the more successful Garibaldi and Cavour. See the lives by B. King and G. O. Griffith.

Medici, Lorenzo de' (1449–1492): This Italian prince and poet was ruler of Florence from 1469, when his father died, till his own assassination. One of the chief patrons of arts and letters, he founded the Greek Academy at Florence and the University of Pisa and made superb collections of manuscripts and objects of art. He well earned the name of Lorenzo the Magnificent. Among his literary followers were Politian, Pico della Mirandola, Ficino and Pulci; among the artists at his court were Botticelli, Signorelli, Ghirlandaio, Filippino Lippi, Verrocchio and Pollaiuolo. His own poetry commonly follows the ancient pastoral tradition, but in a strong and racy native idiom. None of his lyrics is more admired than the popular song included in this book. See studies by W. Roscoe, E. Armstrong and S. Brinton.

Meinloh von Sevelingen, Sir (12th Cent.): This Germany lyrical poet of the Middle Ages is a typical member of the Minnesingers, whose chivalrous songs followed the strictly prescribed lyrical patterns of their group. He lived in Bavaria, in the neighborhood of Ulm. See Jethro Bithell, *The Minnesingers*.

Meleager (fl. 90 b.c.): Of the personal life of this Greek poet little is known. His great service consisted in making an anthology of short poems by forty-one poets, known as the Garland of Meleager, which became the basis of the far larger Palatine Anthology. Meleager's collection included poets of several centuries. He prefaced it by a poem likening each poet to a particular flower. Meleager's own epigrams are unsurpassed in delicacy and charm.

Mencius (c. 371–288 b.c.): This Chinese sage was born over a century after the death of the still greater Confucius, whom he acknowledged as his master. His voluminous writings deal with the widest fields of human affairs, treating philosophy, ethics, politics, history, and literature. In his teaching he is both humane and democratic, believing in the essential goodness of human nature, corrupted by evil environment, and in the obligation of the state to serve the interests of the many rather than the material advantages of the few. His writings have been widely admired by Western thinkers, as, for example, by Emerson.

Michelangelo Buonarroti (1475–1564): Italian painter, sculptor, architect and poet, and one of the outstanding figures of his age. He is best known for his achievements in the fine arts. Many of the chief masterpieces of his sculpture are in Florence, the city of his birth, but his genius in painting, sculpture and architecture was revealed on a still greater scale by works in Rome and especially in the Vatican. He displayed, however, in sketches and unfinished pieces of sculpture perhaps as strong genius as in his designs for the vast edifice of St. Peter's. Much of his poetry, as the sonnet given here, is inspired by the ideas and emotions of Italian neo-platonism. Whatever medium he used, and no matter how small the space he allowed himself, he achieved the heroic. See the studies by C. H. Wilson and A. Condivi.

Mille, Pierre (1864–): This French man of letters went on expeditions to explore the Congo, West Africa, British India, and Indo-China. He was a war correspondent for French journals in both the war between the Turks and Greeks in 1897 and in the World War, 1914–1918. Among his notable stories are *The Monarch* and *Barnavaux and Some Women*. As a writer of fiction he is notable for his powerful imagination, and for the vivid scenes which he is enabled to paint as result of his wide travels among the varied races of mankind. He has often been likened to Kipling.

Milton, John (1608–1674): English poet and political writer. Son of a distinguished musician, as a young man Milton wished to make poetry the end of his studies, and wrote both religious and philosophical poetry and some verse, like *L'Allegro*, wholly unpretentious and charming. He followed, in general, the Renaissance patterns as formulated in Italy. With the English Civil Wars and the triumph of Cromwell, he turned to political propaganda for the Puritan cause. His prose essay, *Areopagitica* (1644), is one of the noblest pleas for freedom of opinion and the press. After the failure of the Puritan party, he returned to poetry, composing masterpieces that combined the stern idealism of the Puritan mind with the aesthetic warmth and distinction of the Renaissance: *Paradise Lost* (1667); *Paradise Regained* (1671); and *Samson Agonistes* (1671).

Mistral, Frédéric (1830–1914): This poet is the best-known author writing in the language of Provence, or south-central France. This language of the people he did much to revive as a language also for literature. His masterpiece is *Mirèio*, a pastoral and narrative poem, rich in its pictures of the work, life and legends of the folk. His *Calendau* is a work of broadly similar nature. His *Nerto* is a story laid in the days of Avignon's greatest splendor, when this city was the seat of the Popes. In addition to his stories, he wrote notable songs and compiled an exhaustive dictionary of his native dialect. In 1904 he was awarded the Nobel Prize. His works are more familiar to the world in French translation than in their original form. An attempt at translation into English has been made by Harriet Preston.

Mohammed (c. 570–632): The founder of the Islam faith was born in Mecca, Arabia, of a wealthy and notable family. He lived a worldly life till his fortieth year, when he received a religious call to preach the true faith in God. He received many subsequent revelations, as recorded in the Islamic bible, the Koran. When his enemies drove him out of Mecca he established a religious colony at Medina. Military victories aided his cause and helped in his triumphant return to Mecca. He accepted much of the Jewish and Christian theology, although in practice he showed hostility to the Jews. He taught a fervent monotheism, with many ceremonial usages, as fasting and pilgrimage. His religion rapidly spread over southern Asia, northern Africa and the two southern extremities of Europe, the Balkans and Spain. See the studies by C. S. Hurgronje, D. S. Marglionth and A. N. Wollaston.

Molnár, Ferenc (1878–): This Hungarian playwright and novelist is a man of abounding wit, versatility and imagination, dominated by a romantic tenderness and an almost unlimited zest for life. Although his plays and novels range from the tragic to the farcical, he is most at home in a sophisticated comedy. Trained for the law, he shifted his attention to journalism, and at an early date turned to composing music, writing stories and writing and directing of plays. His somber novel, *The Hungry*, is memorable. Among his numerous plays successfully produced in many countries, including the United States, are *Liliom, The Guardsman,* and *The Devil.*

MOMMSEN, THEODOR (1817–1903): This eminent German historian was for many years professor of ancient history at Berlin. He took an active part in German political life on the side of liberalism. He is celebrated for his grasp of Roman law, for his monumental studies in Roman inscriptions, and above all, for his eloquent and masterly history of Rome.

MOODY, WILLIAM VAUGHAN (1860–1910). This American poet and playwright was born in Indiana, educated in New England, and later became professor in the University of Chicago. He wrote an important play, *The Great Divide,* and a number of lyrics distinguished by delicacy of language and power of social vision. His poem "Gloucester Moors" is best known. He composed three philosophical and poetic tragedies, *The Masque of Judgment, The Fire-Bringer,* and the unfinished *Death of Eve.*

MOORE, MERRILL (1903–): American poet, born in Columbia, Tennessee. Distinguished, in addition to his literary work, for achievements as a psychiatrist both in civil life and with the American Army in the South Pacific. Dr. Moore's volume, *M, A Thousand Autobiographical Sonnets,* is an extremely lively and imaginative panorama of American life.

MORI OGWAI (1862–1922): This major Japanese author studied in Germany from 1884 to 1888. On returning to Japan he became a physician, but achieved his chief fame in literature. His prolific work comprises many poems, plays, novels, works of criticism, and translations, the last especially from German philosophical writers.

MORIKE, EDUARD FRIEDRICH (1804–1875): This German poet was first a clergyman in Tübingen and later a professor of literature at Stuttgart. He belonged to the Swabian school of idyllic poets. He achieved great distinction in his lyrics, many of which are still highly popular in Germany. A large number have been set to music, especially by Hugo Wolf. His best prose is a short story, *Mozart's Trip to Prague.*

MOSCHUS (fl. 2nd Cent. B.C.): A Greek lyric poet living in Syracuse, in Sicily. No biographical information regarding him has come down to us. He is generally regarded as author of the elegy on the death of his fellow-poet, Bion. Both Bion and Moschus are followers of Theocritus. The elegy is well known, and imitated by many authors, including Shelley.

MURRAY, GILBERT (1866–): This British classical scholar was born in Australia. From 1908 to 1936 he was Regius Professor of Greek at Oxford. He has made many eloquent translations from the Greek poets and dramatists, and written notable essays on ancient literature and culture. See his *History of Ancient Greek Literature* and *The Classical Tradition in Poetry.*

MUSSET, ALFRED DE (1810–1857): This poet, novelist and playwright is one of the important figures of his age in French literature. An affair in his early twenties with the chief woman of letters of the times, George Sand, gained him notoriety. His later years were much occupied with the writing of plays and in disputes concerning theories of the drama. His stories, as *Mimi Pinson,* helped to advance realism in fiction. But he is chiefly known for his poetry, written largely in his early years, often in a somewhat sentimental and melancholy vein, but of a true and moving eloquence. See the life by H. D. Sedgwick.

MUSSOLINI, BENITO (1883–1945): Italian statesman, dictator and originator of fascism. As a young man he engaged in socialistic journalism. During the First World War he served as private and corporal in the Italian army, from which he was discharged on account of wounds. He turned abruptly against the radical parties in Italy — the socialists and communists — and organized fascism as a revolutionary patriotic movement, half military and half political. Fascists adopted the black shirt uniform. In 1922 he and his supporters marched on Rome, where the weak government yielded control. After some difficulty, peace was established with the Vatican. Democratic and parliamentary rule on the earlier scheme was abolished; the chief preceding labor movements were savagely quelled; political freedom infringed; labor and capital alike reorganized and centrally controlled; and a military and imperialistic policy pursued. Under his leadership in 1935 Italy invaded Ethiopia, in defiance of the League of Nations. In 1936 it aided the fascist rebels in Spain. In 1939 it abruptly invaded Albania. In 1940 it attacked France after that country had been crushed by Germany. Shortly thereafter it attempted to invade Greece. In 1943 he and his fascist government, weakened in power by an unpopular and unsuccessful war, were suddenly overthrown. A fluent orator, he made many statements of his political and social system, one of which is given in this book. He was killed by a mob in Milan, April 29, 1945.

NEIDHART VON REUENTAL, SIR (c. 1210–c. 1245): This German poet of the Middle Ages, while accepting some of the conventions of the more decorous or courtly lyric, is best known for the new and vigorous infusion of a homely realism which he successfully employed. His songs often deal with peasant life, and are based upon folk dances. They have both irony and good humor. The simplest themes of love and death, summer and winter, and natural conviviality characterize his verses. See Jethro Bithell, *The Minnesingers*.

NEWMAN, JOHN HENRY, CARDINAL (1801–1890): This English churchman studied at Oxford and there took an active part in the revival of religion known as the Oxford Movement, aimed to arouse religious zeal and to combat the rising materialism and skepticism of the age. Newman found in Catholicism the full satisfaction of his religious needs. His new faith he upheld in many writings and in many disputes, notably with the Protestant spokesman, Charles Kingsley. Among his major books dealing with his belief are his *Apologia Pro Vita Sua* and his *Grammar of Assent*. A man of great culture and refinement, he possessed deep interest in education, which he conceived as moral and spiritual rather than factual and practical. Thus he wrote his *Idea of a University*. He also wrote hymns and other poems. See the studies by W. P. Ward, G. G. Atkins, S. L. May and J. J. Reilly.

NIETZSCHE, FRIEDRICH WILHELM (1844–1900): This German philosopher and essayist was for many years professor of philology at Basel. Especially in youth he was devoted to music. His service in the German army helped to form his philosophical apologies for overmastering power. He was himself of a quarrelsome nature and over-excitement and disease led to madness in his last years. He wrote several highly important books in a poetic prose and with a spirit deeply significant for modern German thought. Indeed he is often considered as a prophet of the Nazi doctrines. Among his chief books are *The Birth of Tragedy; Human, All Too Human; Joyful Wisdom; The Will To Power;* and the brilliant *Thus Spake Zarathustra*. He attacks the Christian ideals as weak and slavish and advocates instead an aristocratic, masterful, domineering spirit in both the individual and the state. Pity, humanitarianism, tolerance, democracy and all the leading views of nineteenth-century liberals he violently scorns. He champions "the Superman." See the studies by Georg Brandes and A. H. J. Knight.

NOVO, SALVADOR (1904–): This leading Mexican poet has been professor of Italian, Comparative Literature and Drama, Secretary of Foreign Affairs and Mexican delegate to the Second Pan-American Conference. Like so many poets in Spanish, he combines wit and irony with emotion. His work has been translated into several languages. The clever lyric given in this book has been especially popular, for it not only represents its author's art, but is a delightfully ironical comment upon the Latin American sense of values.

OMAR KHAYYAM (d. 1123): This Persian poet and mathematician was born at Nishapur. Khayyam, the name also of his father, signifies tent maker, a possible reference to his father's profession. Omar wrote an important algebra and made valuable contributions to a new and more accurate calendar, based on his astronomical studies. He is best known, however, for his *Rubaiyat*, a philosophical poem. The precise meaning and the authenticity of many verses remain in doubt, but in its general purpose the poem undoubtedly praises a life of pleasure, retirement and sensuous satisfaction, and casts doubts upon religious orthodoxy and human reason. The poem is most familiar through the free but glowing condensation by Edward Fitzgerald.

OVID (PUBLIUS OVIDIUS NASO) (43 B.C.–18A.D.): This poet lived in Rome from boyhood till the Emperor Augustus banished him to Tomi on the Black Sea. Here he died. His chief work, the *Metamorphoses,* deals with magic transformations recorded in mythology. An allied work, *Fasti* (*Calendar*), describes the rituals and legends associated with Roman holidays from January to June. His shorter poems include *The Art of Love* and *Love's Cure;* a series of love lyrics; and numerous epistles in verse. One collection consists of imaginary letters written by heroines to their lovers. Another group comprises letters written by Ovid in exile. Also in exile he composed a series of short poems, *Tristia* (*Sorrow*). He has been more highly valued for the subject matter than for the refinement of his art. Hence his great popularity in all periods. See the translation by Brookes More and the study by Alfred Church.

PAINE, THOMAS (1737–1809): This American political writer was born in England, the son of a Quaker farmer. In 1774 he came to America, where he met Franklin and engaged in journalistic propaganda. His *Common Sense* helped to promote the Declaration of Independence. His pamphlets greatly aided the Revolutionary cause. While visiting England he published *The Rights of Man,* a defense of the French Revolution. He fled to France but was there imprisoned by the Jacobins. Partly while in prison he wrote *The Age of Reason,* an argument against the revelation of the Christian religion. He returned to the United States in 1802. Throughout his audacious career he made increasing numbers of enemies; yet he has always had his warm admirers and his influence both in America and abroad has been considerable. See the edition and life by M. D. Conway, and selections with critical introduction by H. H. Clark (American Writers Series).

PARINI, GIUSEPPE (1729–1799): This representative Italian poet of the eighteenth century became a priest in 1754, but this did not deter him from holding political office when France under Napoleon severed the Italian subjugation to Austria. His odes often have the traditional Arcadian manner which in some degree marks the poem given in this book. His longer poem, *The Day,* is a mock heroic work telling how the parasitical courtier will pass his time in the morning, noon, evening and night. Like all Parini's work, it follows broad lines of literary convention known throughout the European world (cf. Thomas Dekker's *Gull's Hornbook* and John Gay's *Trivia*). Parini well represents the cosmopolitan tradition.

PASCAL, BLAISE (1623–1662): This French mathematician and philosopher is celebrated for his discoveries in pure science and his eloquent writings on metaphysics, mysticism and religion. His scientific researches were conducted continuously from extremely early years. He established the theory of probabilities, invented the arithmetical triangle, analyzed the cycloid and contributed to the progress of calculus. The principle of pressure, or Pascal's law, is among his chief contributions to physics. His religious life became intense with his conversion in 1653. He was influenced by Jansenism, and frequented the convent at Port Royal. Against the Jesuits he wrote his suave, ironical and devastating *Provincial Letters.* His *Thoughts,* however, contain his own beliefs expressed in their most eloquent and appealing form. He asserts the need of an inner and religious life, without which no life of reason or action, however brilliant, can in his eyes be truly satisfying. See the studies by S. H. N. St. Cyres and by R. H. Soltau.

PASTEUR, LOUIS (1822–1895): This French chemist taught science in a number of institutions of higher learning in France. The Pasteur Institute in Paris was established in 1886. He is the founder of modern stereochemistry. Through his discoveries in the field of vaccination he made contributions of the greatest importance in the lives of animals and man. His work led to the discovery of pasteurization of milk. He solved the problem of the most virulent silkworm disease. Among his discoveries is a vaccination against hydrophobia. His studies contributed greatly to antiseptic surgery. Few men have conferred more definite blessings upon mankind. See the lives by Vallery-Radot and S. J. Holmes.

PAUL, SAINT (d. 67?): This Christian saint was the first organizing genius of the Christian Church and its chief early author on theology. His missionary work firmly established the Christian churches throughout the eastern Mediterranean, while his writings came to be regarded as the foremost commentary upon the sayings of Christ which are recorded in the narrative Gospels. Paul is equally administrator and philosopher. He was born in Tarsus, the son of a tent maker, and had the Jewish name of Saul. His conservatism made him at first a bitter enemy of the Christians; under his leadership St. Stephen, the first Christian martyr, was killed. While Paul was traveling to Damascus he saw a vision of Jesus which converted him to the new religion. Under his guidance Christianity definitely broke away from Judaism. He made three or more voyages from city to city, establishing Christian churches and delivering missionary sermons. Some of his most brilliant efforts were in Corinth and Athens. When tried for sedition in Jerusalem, he pleaded his rights as a Roman citizen and went to Rome. Here several years later he underwent martyrdom, according to tradition, in the company of St. Peter. His life is recounted in *The Acts of the Apostles*, while his own extant works are a number of Epistles generally addressed to the Christian communities in various cities, as Rome, Corinth, Ephesus, etc., these Epistles forming an important part of the New Testament. Their doctrine is mystical, with emphasis upon faith and salvation through Christ. See the studies by T. R. Glover, F. J. F. Jackson, B. W. Robinson, A. Schweitzer, and E. Baumann.

PESTALOZZI, JOHANN HEINRICH (1746–1827): This Swiss educational reformer devoted himself to the problems of education chiefly in the latter part of his life. Stimulated by Rousseau, he utilized whatever he found sound in his predecessor and discarded his extravagances. He attempted to relate education more closely than hitherto to environment and to the mind of the child. This led him to consider education in the home and to advocate manual training and a program of social activity as well as routine learning. He believed that the child learns from practice as well as from books. He gathered about him many teachers and came into contact with the growing systems of popular education, which he directly and indirectly did much to shape. He saw in education the chief hope for society. Among his works are a novel on education, *Leonard and Gertrude*, and an exposition of his views, *How Gertrude Teaches her Children*. See the studies by J. A. Green and W. H. Monroe.

PETRARCH, OR FRANCESCO PETRARCA (1304–1374): This Italian poet and leader of the humanists lived much of his scholarly life in France, notably at Vaucluse, near Avignon, which was then the seat of the Papacy. He traveled widely and died at Arquà, near Padua. A worshipper of the classics, he uncovered several lost manuscripts, especially of Cicero. His letters reveal much of his character and times. Notable also in his prose is a subjective treatise *On Solitude*. In Latin he composed a pompous epic, *Africa*. In Italian he wrote his best-known works, his odes and sonnets, chiefly to his ideal mistress, Laura, and a series of didactic poems called *Triumphs*. Petrarch was a sensitive, inquisitive and highly individualistic man and an author gifted with eloquence, subtlety, tenderness and pathos. He, with his friend Boccaccio, greatly stimulated classical scholarship; but it is chiefly on the model of Petrarch that subsequent poets and prose writers cultivated the vein of love-sick melancholy. For a biographical appraisal see J. H. Robinson and H. Reeve. The poems are translated by C. B. Cayley, J. Auslander and H. L. Peabody.

PHAEDRUS: A Latin poet of the first century A.D., author of a large collection of fables said to be derived from the Greek of Aesop, of the sixth century B.C. Phaedrus's work was in turn freely translated into Greek and turned into Latin again during the Middle Ages. Indirectly he has been the source of much of the fable-writing of Europe, including that of the French poet, La Fontaine. Phaedrus himself is said to have been of Macedonian origin, and to have been in the service of the Emperor Augustus.

PHOCYLIDES (fl. 544 B.C.): A Greek poet born in Ionia. His verse is chiefly of a didactic nature. Only eighteen specimens survive. These are brief, vigorous and pithy.

PINDAR (522–448 B.C.): The foremost of Greek lyric poets, Pindar lived in Thebes but traveled throughout Greece and to Sicily to attend the choral performance of his odes. Many of his religious hymns and other pieces are missing, but forty-four odes celebrating victories in the Greek athletic games survive entire, together with many fragments. These odes make small mention of the victors themselves, celebrating the events obliquely by retelling the legends of the city and family of the victor. As a result, the odes give an unsurpassed image of the Greek mind. Their reflection of a virile culture is implemented by their extremely heightened and difficult style. In his youth Pindar was advised "to sow with the hand and not with the whole sack," but he followed this advice only in part. His odes have been imitated throughout all Europe. They are translated by E. Myers and C. J. Billson. See the study by F. D. Morice.

PIRANDELLO, LUIGI (1867–1936): This most widely known of Italian playwrights in recent times was professor of Italian literature at the Normal College for Women in Rome, 1897–1921. Especially in his earlier years he wrote novels, read largely in Italy; but his plays attracted international attention. His first and most widely-played drama is *Six Characters in Search of an Author*. Later plays include *Henry IV; Right You Are If You Think You Are; Each in His Own Way;* and *As You Desire Me*, all translated into English. His one-act plays, including his masterpiece in miniature, *The Jar,* may be read in English in a collection edited by Arthur Livingston. His work possesses great subtlety, wit and charm. Metaphysical and aesthetic problems which have fascinated intellectuals throughout the contemporary world are treated imaginatively. The scenes are commonly of Sicilian peasant life; the substance is philosophical. He won the Nobel Prize in 1934. There are studies of his art and thought by W. Starkie and F. Passini.

PLATO (429–347 B.C.): This Greek philosopher lived most of his life in Athens, where he founded his Academy, or school of philosophy. He was a pupil of Socrates, who is the central figure in most of his dialogues; he in turn was master of Aristotle. The dialogues are imaginary conversations between men in search of wisdom. Among them are *The Republic,* on the ideal state; *The Symposium,* on love; *Phaedo,* on immortality; *Theaetetus,* on knowledge; *Gorgias,* on ethics; *Parmenides,* on metaphysics; *Protagoras,* on virtue; *Ion,* on poetry; and *Crito* and the *Apology,* on the life and death of Socrates. The scientific interests of Plato were developed further by Aristotle, the mystical elements by Plotinus and the neo-platonists. His idealism attracted Christian thinkers. The beauty of his dialogues and their praise of beauty have made Plato a favorite philosopher among artists and art lovers. See translations by B. Jowett, *The Dialogues of Plato* and F. J. E. Woodbridge, *The Son of Apollo.*

PLOTINUS (205?–270?): This Egyptian philosopher of the Neo-Platonic school travelled extensively in the ancient world, eventually settling in Rome, where he became a popular teacher and leader of a movement in mystical thought. A man of deep learning, he was even more one of deep and spiritual imagination. In both life and doctrine he became an ascetic. His style is singularly eloquent; his metaphysics are subtle; and his powerful fancy at times violently divorces him from the material world. In ideas he proved an important link between the idealistic philosophers of ancient Greece and the early theologians of the Christian Church. His writings have had a prolonged influence. See Grace Turnbull, *The Essence of Plotinus.*

PO-CHÜI (772–846): This well-known Chinese poet represents the classical tradition in Chinese literature, politics and morality. In his life he held political office and was inspired by what would in the idiom of our own day be called a strong social conscience. This brings much of his verse peculiarly close to us. His poetry, often of a satirical nature, chastised war-makers, corrupt politicians and all who trouble the serener course of human life. Some critics deem his work too didactic; and he undeniably lacks the flair of Tu Fu and Li Po. But in his more sober field he has complete mastery. His sturdy poetry lasts well and withstands translation and transportation. See the study of his work and numerous translations by Arthur Waley.

Polo, Marco (1254–1324): This celebrated Venetian traveler belonged to a most adventurous family. His father and uncle made a trip across Central Asia to China, starting in 1255. They returned in 1269. In 1271 they turned Eastward again, now with the young Marco. The three lived in China for seventeen years. They were well received and highly honored. For three years Marco was governor of a province. In 1295 they returned to Venice. The following year Marco was taken prisoner by the Genoese. While in captivity he dictated his memoirs in French. They immediately became popular in many tongues. Statements in them once suspected as exaggerated are now believed faithful. It is perhaps the most remarkable of all books of travel.

Pope, Alexander (1688–1744): Residing in and about London, this English poet led an outwardly quiet life marked chiefly by friendships and quarrels typical of the literary profession. The later years he passed on his estate at Twickenham by the Thames. Poor health nursed an irritable disposition. Wholly discarding the romantic narrative, popular in Europe for many centuries, he turned to a witty, critical and satirical type of verse, sharpening his wit by a perfection of the rhymed couplet. Among his chief poems are *An Essay on Criticism* (1711); *The Rape of the Lock* (1714); *An Essay on Man* (1733); *The Dunciad* (1728–43); and *Moral Essays* (1735). His last poems were free paraphrases of Horace and reminders that throughout his life he stood close to the Horatian spirit. He admired contemporary French literature and was himself admired by the French. His celebrated translation of Homer is too much marked by his own character and that of his times. See the lives by R. K. Root, George Sherburn and Leslie Stephen and the critical studies by Geoffrey Tillotson and Edith Sitwell.

Pratt, Edwin John (1883–): This leading Canadian poet is author of several volumes of verse, including *Brébeuf and His Brethren* and *Dunkirk.* He has served as editor of *The Canadian Poetry Magazine* and is widely recognized as a notable spokesman for the literary and spiritual life of Canada at the present time. *Collected Poems* appeared in 1945.

Prescott, William Hickling (1796–1859): This American historian heroically surmounted the obstacle of failing eyesight which amounted in time to virtual blindness but never curbed his unfailing energies. His chief works deal with Spain and South America during the sixteenth century. His first and last volumes, which concern Spain, *The Reign of Ferdinand and Isabella* and *Philip II,* are today less often read than his stories of the conquest of Mexico and Peru. The daring and savagery of the Spanish Conquistadors and the glamour and mystery of the Indian cultures afforded an ideal theme for his brilliant pen. Subject and style united to make these books literary classics. See the lives by G. Ticknor and H. T. Peck.

Pushkin, Alexander Sergeyevich (1799–1837): This Russian poet and prose writer, commonly regarded as the chief of his countrymen in poetry, was son of a noble Russian father and a mother inheriting Negro blood. His life was marked by exile and persecution at the hands of the Czar's government and by various gallantries ending with a duel in defense of his wife's honor. To his Russian nurse he owed much of his love for Russian folklore, but he enjoyed a cosmopolitan education, knew French and English and admired and imitated Byron, whose republicanism attracted him. He also represents the Asiatic phase of Russian culture. Among his long poems are *Ruslan and Ludmilla,* a fairy tale; *Eugene Oniegin,* a realistic novel in verse; and *The Prisoner of the Caucasus.* He deals with Russian history in *Boris Godunov.* His finest prose story is *The Queen of Spades.* See Mirsky's *Pushkin* and Turner's *Translations from Pushkin.* For selected works in translation, see the edition in The Modern Library.

Putnam, Phelps (1894–): This American poet was born in Boston, Massachusetts. He is author of two books of verse, *Trinc* (1927) and *The Five Seasons* (1933). While not a major poet, he has written some interesting pieces of a reflective character. His *Hymn to Chance,* reproduced here, affords interesting comparisons with earlier poems in the tradition of the classical ode.

Quevedo y Villegas, Francisco Gómez de (1580–1645): This Spanish novelist and poet lived an uncommonly eventful life in both

Italy and Spain. He early became widely read in several languages and many fields. A cripple and short-sighted, he nevertheless fought many duels. His addiction to satire together with the changing fortunes of his different patrons caused him to pass between heights of prosperity and years of imprisonment. His *Life and Adventures of Buscon* is one of the first and most important of the Spanish picaresque novels, or tales of roguery. His highly imaginative *Visions* are also sharply satiric, in the savage manner of Juvenal. He became an important figure in European literature. To his memory Byron dedicated a fine satire, *The Vision of Judgment.* His spirit lived again in the Spanish painter and satirist, Goya. See translations by Roger L'Estrange with the life by Charles Duff.

RALEIGH, SIR WALTER (1552–1618): English soldier, navigator and author. He sent out the first colonizing expeditions to Virginia, which paved the way for the later successful settlements. He made two voyages to South America, describing one in his *Discovery of Guiana.* Most of his military expeditions were against the Spaniards. When at home he cultivated science, free thinking and literature. His *History of the World* he wrote while a political prisoner, charged with conspiracy against the English king, James I. Much of his poetry has been lost, and since much was also circulated anonymously, it is difficult to form a sound estimate of his poetic powers. Yet from a few pieces, such as those given in this book, it is evident that he found able expression for his forceful, imaginative and trenchant mind. See the poems edited by A. M. C. Latham, prose selections edited by G. E. Hadow and the life by Irvin W. Anthony.

RANSOM, JOHN CROWE (1888–): American poet, essayist and teacher. Formerly a Rhodes Scholar from Tennessee, he is at present professor at Kenyon College in Ohio and editor of *The Kenyon Review.* His poems are collected in *Chills and Fever* (1924) and *Two Gentlemen in Bonds* (1927). Many of his lyrics, such as the one reprinted here, deal with the culture of his native South. Although in this poem he is entirely serious, the literary ideals which he most commonly pursues are wit, irony and grace.

RILKE, RAINER MARIA (1875–1926): This important poet was born in Prague and wrote chiefly in German, but strikingly represents the cosmopolitan nature of modern culture. He lived in all the chief countries of Europe, knew their languages and in several cases made translations. He was an art scholar, acting for several years as secretary in Paris to the sculptor, Rodin. His prose contains much art criticism. His many volumes of poetry range from tender lyrics showing deep sympathy with Czech peasant life to austere and difficult flights of the metaphysical imagination. Many of his metaphysical poems show understanding of oriental philosophy and religion; many are new interpretations of Catholic thought. There are translations by Jessie Lemont, M. D. H. Norton, J. B. Leishman and Stephen Spender, and others, and a life by E. M. Butler.

RIMBAUD, ARTHUR (1854–1891): A leading forerunner of the decadent movement in modern French poetry. This astonishing poet composed his verses between his sixteenth and nineteenth year. The poems combine the unbridled imagination of dreams and childhood with the most bitter disillusionment of age and misfortune. They prove equally remarkable for their creative genius and their intense morbidity. Rimbaud is a symbolist, the heir of Mallarmé and the inspirer of T. S. Eliot. His metaphysical imagination is haunted by the tyranny of time. He himself scorned his poetry and devoted the few remaining years of his life to travel and engineering. The poems were published through his friends. Their international influence has been increasingly felt. See the translations by Delmore Schwartz.

ROBERTS, CHARLES GEORGE DOUGLAS (1860–1943): This Canadian author is recognized as a leader in a number of branches of literature: as poet, historian, novelist, short-story writer and especially as a writer of nature stories for children. His *History of Canada* appeared in 1897. His work is strongly indigenous, and even his childrens' tales give vivid images of the Canadian landscape. He is a devoted observer of bird and beast. See the life by J. Cappon.

ROBINSON, EDWIN ARLINGTON (1869–1935): American poet, born at Head Tide, Maine and one of the foremost American writers of the early twentieth century. Although he wrote many lyrics and reflective poems, the larger part of his work consists of short stories, or novels in verse. A few, as *Tristram*, deal with exotic themes, but most of the verse tales are psychological studies with contemporary settings. Notable among these are the tragic *Roman Bartholow* (1923); *The Man Who Died Twice* (1924); *Cavender's House* (1929); *The Glory of the Nightingales* (1930); *Matthias at the Door* (1931); *King Jasper* (1935); and the fanciful but profound *Amaranth* (1934). See Herman Hagedorn, *Edwin Arlington Robinson* and the study by Charles Cestre. A collected edition of his poems appeared in 1937.

Rodó, José Enrique (1872–1917): This Uruguayan essayist enjoyed throughout his active life a high reputation in all Latin America. As an editor and a university professor he made his views felt in both politics and literature. *Ariel* is his best-known essay; other volumes translated into English are *Motives of Proteus* and *The Road to Paros*. He is admirably representative of many aspects of Latin America, as may be seen in one respect in the warmth of his poetic prose. His position is that of the liberal and eclectic. His outlook is cosmopolitan, though on the whole chiefly indebted to the thought of nineteenth-century France. He is a democrat with reservations; he seeks for change, but loves much of the past. Although some of his thinking may today be suspect as loose and romantic, his important role in South American literature seems assured.

Ronsard, Pierre de (1524–1585): This French poet, known in his own day as "prince of poets," deserted a military or diplomatic career for literary studies because of deafness. He was held in much honor not only in the French court but by admirers who read his works throughout Europe. With six associates he shared in the Plèiade, a group of reformers who sought at once to classicize French poetry and to assert its national importance and dignity. He wrote skillfully in all literary forms except the drama, which he did not essay. His epic, the *Franciade*, is his most ambitious work, but his odes, songs and sonnets are his most fully accomplished compositions, rich and sonorous in expression and by no means weak in thought and feeling. See translations by C. H. Page and a biographical and critical study by Morris Bishop.

Roosevelt, Franklin Delano (1882–1945): The thirty-second President of the United States was born at Hyde Park, New York, and graduated from Harvard College and Columbia University Law School. He was Assistant Secretary of the Navy 1913–1920, Governor of New York 1929–1933, and President 1933–1945. He led the nation in time of two national crises, the greatest of its economic depressions and the Second World War. His sponsorship of legislation strengthening the federal government, his humanitarian policies, and his vigorous leadership made him popular in his own country; his championship of democracy throughout the world made his name more widely known and beloved than that of any of his countrymen. His sudden death occurred just before the conclusion of the Second World War. Many of his addresses have marked literary distinction.

Rousseau, Jean Jacques (1712–1778): This French philosopher and novelist was born in Geneva of a Huguenot family. His earlier years were marked by romantic affairs with his patronesses. He supported himself in part as musician and copyist of music. By degrees his literary reputation rose to great heights. Among his chief books are the highly sentimental novel, *La Nouvelle Héloïse;* his study of "progressive education," *Émile;* and his great work on political justice, *The Social Contract*. His novel set fashions in romantic fiction for over a century and contained ideas on nature and spirit of great importance. His educational theory is still felt throughout the entire democratic world. Finally, his social theory aided in the overthrow of monarchy and the rise of the republican and democratic movements in Europe and America. His brilliance both as writer and thinker now seems highly vulnerable, but his influence was incalculable in his own times and remains considerable today. See the study by E. H. Wright.

Runeberg, Johan Ludvig (1804–1877): This Swedish poet was of Finnish birth. He was a journalist and a teacher. In verse he composed in an epic vein, frequently celebrating the war with Russia. Among his shorter pieces are ballads, idyls and hymns.

Russell, George William (1867–1935): This Irish poet, painter and mystic took a leading role in the literary and social revival in Ireland which occurred during his lifetime. A truly great man in a small country, he made his influence felt upon all sides, and by a magnetic personality achieved almost as much as by his writings. He played a considerable part in agricultural and economic reforms, as well as in art and the theatre, scholarship and religion. Much of his prose and verse shows his understanding not only of the mystical literature of the West, but of the deeper mysticism of the East. His plays, essays and treatises have great interest; but the volume by which he will be most often remembered is his *Collected Poems.* A number of Russell's books were published under the initials Æ.

Sa'di (d. 1291): This major Persian poet and moralist was born at Shiraz. He passed his early years in Baghdad. Later he visited India, Abyssinia and the Holy Land. In the last of these he was captured by Crusaders, but in time ransomed. He visited Mecca as a pilgrim and died in his native city. His masterpiece, the *Gulistan* (*Rose Garden*), is a didactic work dealing with public and private life and the pleasures and duties of mankind. It is in prose interspersed with verse. Similar in general, but graver in tone, is his poem, *Bustan.* Many of his aphorisms have become popular quotations in Persia and have found their way into Western literature. Sa'di was translated into French as early as 1634. He has frequently been rendered into English, notably by Sir Edwin Arnold. Goethe, Emerson and others have esteemed and paraphrased his work.

Sandburg, Carl (1878–): American poet and biographer, born in Galesburg, Illinois. As a young man he fought in the Spanish-American War and worked at miscellaneous jobs in all parts of this country. His life of Lincoln is one of the foremost American biographies, equally accurate, complete and sympathetic. A singer of folk-songs, he has collected American popular lyrics in *The American Songbag.* His *Rootabaga Stories* rank high in the imaginative literature for children. No poet since Whitman gives so lively a panoramic view of America. His best short poems appear in *Chicago Poems* (1916); *Corn Huskers* (1918); *Smoke and Steel* (1920); and *Slabs of the Sun-burnt West* (1923); while an epic scope is achieved in *The People, Yes* (1936). See the study by K. W. Detzer.

Santayana, George (1863–): This philosopher and essayist of international fame was born in Madrid, Spain, coming as a child to the United States. He studied at Harvard, later studied for two years in Berlin and then returned to Harvard, where he taught philosophy for twenty-two years. Since 1912 he has lived in England and in various parts of Europe. He has written and translated many poems and is author of notable fiction. Some of his best informal essays are in *Soliloquies in England.* Among his more philosophical volumes are *Three Philosophical Poets; Character and Opinion in the United States; Egotism in German Philosophy; Skepticism and Animal Faith; Platonism and the Spiritual Life; Realms of Essence;* and *The Realm of Matter.* He is largely eclectic in his thinking; but without doubt is one of the foremost literary masters in the field of modern philosophy.

Sappho (fl. 600 b.c.): The most celebrated of the Greek lyric poets before the rise of Athens, Sappho lived in Mitylene on the island of Lesbos. There is no historical basis for a number of legends regarding her, as that she committed suicide by leaping from the Leucadian rock. She lived intimately with the other chief lyric poet of her times, Alcaeus. About her she gathered a school of poets. Only one or two complete poems certainly hers survive, although we have a large number of fine fragments and of lyrics written by her followers and commonly associated with her name. Her poetry treats love in many phases and with great intensity, though not always without an ironical humor. See the volume of Sappho in the Loeb Classical Library, the edition by H. T. Wharton and the study by A. E. P. Weigall.

Schiller, Johann Christoph Friedrich von (1759–1805): A German poet, dramatist and critic. He vacillated in youth between church, army, medicine and law. Resisting all pressure to the contrary, he finally persisted in a career of letters, which led him eventually to Weimar and a friendship with Goethe. At this period he studied and wrote history. Hence he came to compose some of his finest historical dramas, notably three on Wallenstein. These were followed by similar plays, *The Maid of Orleans* and *Maria Stuart.* These mature works exhibit the restraining influences of classical study, differing from his early and much more romantic plays, *The Robbers, Fiesco* and *Intrigue and Love.* He is author of many odes and lyrics of a somewhat didactic character, as his *Hymn to Joy,* set to music in Beethoven's Ninth Symphony, and the famous *Song of the Bell.* A Life of Schiller was written by Thomas Carlyle. See also the life by E. Kühnemann.

Scott, Robert Falcon (1868–1912): This British antarctic explorer is one of the heroes in British naval tradition and one of the ablest writers on travel in the cause of science. His first trip (1901) he describes in *The Voyage of the "Discovery."* The story of his second voyage (1910) is told in *Scott's Last Expedition,* which contains diaries and correspondence. On this epic journey many unforeseen obstacles beset the well-prepared explorers. They reached the South Pole, Jan. 18, 1912, to find evidence that the great Norwegian explorer, Roald Amundsen, had arrived there a little over a month before. On the return trip by sled the wounded Captain Oates walked out at night into a storm and died so as not to retard his companions. Nevertheless, all died in a blizzard a few days later. Their bodies, and complete scientific records of the expedition, were recovered a considerable time afterwards. See also the books on Scott by S. L. Gwynn and Martin Lindsay.

Seneca, Lucius Annaeus (c. 3 b.c.–65 a.d.): This Roman philosopher, dramatist and statesman was born in Corduba, Spain, coming to Rome as a child. He early acquired skill in oratory and philosophy, and was thus made tutor to the prince, Nero. During Nero's childhood Seneca was, with Nero's military guardian, a major force in the Roman government; but as Nero grew older and betrayed the guardians of his youth, he turned upon Seneca, forcing him to commit suicide. He is author of many sententious treatises on such themes as anger, consolation, constancy, providence, tranquility and the brevity of life. To him are ascribed ten somewhat turgid tragedies, intended rather for reading than for the stage. Throughout the Christian Middle Ages and the Renaissance Seneca was honored as one of the chief spokesmen for the Stoic philosophy.

Shakespeare, William (1564–1616): The foremost English poet and dramatist was born at Stratford-on-Avon. He presumably went to the local grammar school. In 1582 he married Anne Hathaway. From 1592 he is known to have been engaged in the writing, acting and producing of plays in London. His chief theatre was the Globe (built 1599). Among his great plays are *A Midsummer Night's Dream* (1594); *Romeo and Juliet* (1594); *The Merchant of Venice* (1595); *Henry IV* (1597–8); *As You Like It* (1599); *Twelfth Night* (1601); *Hamlet* (1602); *Othello* (1604); *King Lear* (1605); *Macbeth* (1606); *Antony and Cleopatra* (1608); and *The Tempest* (1611). His chief non-dramatic poems are *Venus and Adonis* (1593), *The Rape of Lucrece* (1594) and *Sonnets* (1609). The last five years of his life he seems to have passed in retirement at Stratford. His work strikingly exhibits the reasonableness of considering literature in its world-wide significance. He himself borrowed from whatever cultures were known to him. Several of his plays, notably *Julius Caesar, Antony and Cleopatra* and *Coriolanus,* are dramatizations of the Greek biographer, Plutarch. *The Comedy of Errors* derives from the *Menaechmi* of the Latin comic poet, Plautus. Many plays, as *Othello,* dramatize Italian novels. *Hamlet* derives ultimately from chronicles of Danish history. Stories in *The Merchant of Venice* and *Cymbeline* go back to Asiatic tales. His Sonnets are bold variations on themes commenced by the Italian, Petrarch. As Shakespeare appropriated from all available sources, the entire civilized world has read and enjoyed his plays, finding in them the most vivid images of our common human nature. Important criticism of Shakespeare may be read in the German of Goethe, the French of Hugo, or the Italian of Croce. For the background of his plays, see *Shakespeare's England,* edited by Walter Raleigh. The most comprehensive scholarly study is E. K. Chambers's *William Shakespeare.* A less exhaustive summary is the life by J. Q. Adams. For a guidebook, see *Facts About Shakespeare* by W. A. Neilson and A. H. Thorndike. For literary criticism, see *William Shakespeare* by Mark Van Doren, *Shakespeare Criticism* edited by A. Bradby, and *Shakespeare Criticism* edited by D. N. Smith. For the dramatic background, see H. W. Wells' *Elizabethan and Jacobean Drama.*

SHELLEY, PERCY BYSSHE (1792–1822): English poet of the Romantic period. Rebellion against the tyrannies of British school life began a career of idealistic combat in behalf of human freedom. He was expelled from Oxford for anti-Christian and atheistical views. He attempted to arouse Irishmen and British laborers to revolt. Political and marital difficulties induced him to reside in Italy, where, after living for five years, he was drowned in the loss of a small sailboat. His poetry has a unique music and fanciful imagery, much idealistic thinking and a somewhat rarefied emotional excitement. Plato and Greek poetry proved his chief literary inspirations, as may be seen in *Adonais* and his verse drama, *Prometheus Unbound.* He was also influenced by the poetical classics of Italy, Germany and Spain. A strong lyrical vein predominates, no matter what form of poetry he writes. See the lives by W. E. Peck and N. I. White and the essay by Francis Thompson.

SIDNEY, SIR PHILIP (1554–1586): English author, statesman and soldier, and the most widely admired of Queen Elizabeth's courtiers. After the usual education in England, he traveled extensively on the continent, usually on diplomatic missions. As a soldier in the Netherlands, defending the Hollanders against Spain, he was killed in the battle of Zutphen. His acknowledged skill in all the accomplishments of a courtier did not spare him enemies and much of his writing was probably done in periods of enforced retirement. He wrote essays on politics and literary criticism, a romantic pastoral novel, *The Arcadia,* in imitation of Greek and Italian models, and some sonnets and songs. The best of these are in a collection, *Astrophel and Stella,* these being the assumed names of the two lovers. Sidney followed in the paths of Petrarch and Sannazaro in Italy, and Ronsard and du Bellay in France. See the lives by A. H. Bill and Mona Wilson and the study by K. O. Myrick.

SILVA, JOSÉ ASUNCIÓN (1860–1896): This poet was born at Bogotá, Colombia. Misfortunes saddened his brief life, which he ended by his own hand. In many of his moods he perpetuated the decadent emotionalism of the Romantic School; yet in the vigor of his imagination and boldness of his experiments with poetic language he sided against the old, romantic sentimentalists and with a rising school of more strongly aesthetic writers. In a number of his poems he followed the lead of Poe. His best-known lyric, *Nocturne,* is to be read in this volume.

SILVA, MIGUEL OTERO (1908–): This Venezuelan poet was exiled from his country during the regime of the dictator Gomez. His poetry, as *Crossroads,* given in this book, shows his sympathy with a proletarian revolution. It is in temper both romantic and dramatic.

SIMONIDES (556–467 B.C.): One of the masters of Greek lyric poetry, he was born in Ceos, and made music and poetry his profession. Most of his life he lived at Athens, and much of his art he employed to celebrate the Greek struggles against the Persians. No poet has, perhaps, ever equaled him in tributes to military valor. He composed verses on Marathon, Thermopylae, Artemisium and Salamis, the chief battles in the war. His latter years he passed in Syracuse in Sicily. He is said to have been the first man to receive money for literary work. This brought much rebuke upon him, especially from Pindar. He excels all classical poets in the epitaph, being the epigram or inscription for the dead. The simplicity and sweetness of his style, not unlike that of Sophocles, attracted much attention among his contemporaries. His influence on later writers of epitaphs and elegies has been incalculable.

SMART, CHRISTOPHER (1722–1772): After a brilliant university career, he attempted to support himself by his pen in London, with no great success. His misfortunes were followed by insanity. Most of his poems, including his translations, are in the rationalistic vein of the poetry of Alexander Pope, the prevailing style during his own lifetime. But during his period of emotional excitement and instability, he wrote *Song to David*, one of the finest mystical and devotional poems ever composed in England. It remained virtually unknown, or was regarded as giving "melancholy proofs of the estrangement of Smart's mind," until Robert Browning, in 1887, praised it highly, after which its worth has been widely acknowledged. It should be compared with other hymns of praise, as that by Abelard.

SNORRI STURLUSON (1179–1241): An Icelandic historian. He became president of the legislative assembly and supreme court of Iceland. After many changes of political fortune, he was killed in a feud. He is author of the great Prose Edda, of a collection of sagas dealing with the Norwegian kings, and of a life of Saint Olaf. By virtue of his able retelling of old stories, he became one of the outstanding figures in medieval literature.

SOPHOCLES (495–406 B.C.): This Greek tragic poet was born at Colonus, a village about a mile from Athens, which he celebrated in the ode given in this book. At sixteen he composed an ode in celebration of the Athenian victory at Salamis. Thereafter he served Athens in both civil and military posts. As in the case of Aeschylus, out of many times their number only seven tragedies survive: *Oedipus the King; Oedipus at Colonius; Antigone; Ajax; Electra; Trachinae;* and *Philoctetes*. His work is less austere than that of Aeschylus, less romantic than that of Euripides. His plays give more scope than those of Aeschylus to the characters, less to the lyric chorus. They excel in proportion, grace, pathos and humanity. Persons in Aeschylus seem beyond humanity, persons in Euripides often pettier than humanity. No playwright has so closely measured the just and fitting proportions of human nature. See translations by R. C. Jebb, E. H. Plumptre, J. T. Sheppard and J. S. Phillimore.

SPENDER, STEPHEN (1909–): This leader among a group of young English writers including W. H. Auden, C. Day Lewis and Louis MacNeice, was born near London, of mixed German, Jewish and English origins. He has written stories, as *The Backward Son* (1940); literary criticism, *The Destructive Element* (1935) and *Life and the Poet* (1942); a powerful verse play on the Nazi intolerance, *Trial of a Judge* (1938); translations, as that of Rilke (1943) and the Spaniard Lorca; and several small volumes of verse, much of which is contained in *Ruins and Visions* (1942). In a nervous idiom characteristic of his times he expresses the pathos and confusion, the hopes and doubts of the age. Occasionally obscure and personal, the poetry is often highly sensitive. His grasp of the new social climate created by the machine age is indicated in the lyric selected in this volume.

SPENSER, EDMUND (1552–1599): This prominent Elizabethan poet was probably born in London; he attended Cambridge University, and lived the latter part of his life in Ireland. The chief of the humanist poets associated with the court of Queen Elizabeth, he became spokesman for British imperialism and British Protestantism. His chief work, *The Faerie Queene,* is a brilliant verse-treatise in allegorical imagery on religion, government, ethics, and courtly education. It is written in the eloquent and graceful "Spenserian stanza." Author of many amorous poems in the fashion of the times, he composed an epithalamium, or marriage hymn, on the model of the hymn, here given, by Catullus. Much of his idealism, warmth of imagery and colorful style he learned from Tasso, while in Ariosto he discovered a model for his urbane wit and facile romancing. See the handbook by H. S. V. Jones and the study by W. L. Renwick.

STEVENS, WALLACE (1879–): American poet and business man, living in Hartford, Connecticut. Most of his more attractive poems appear in his first volume, *Harmonium* (1923), one of the most brilliant and fastidious books of verse as yet published in America. French symbolists had a considerable influence upon him. Much of his later poetry deals in an esoteric fashion with ideas in aesthetics. Stevens is clever and humorous. His subtleties not only limit his audience but may often restrict his significance. He is a bold experimenter in his art and a bold explorer in his thinking.

STEVENSON, ROBERT LOUIS (1850–1894): This British author was born in Edinburgh. He traveled widely for his health, living in California, the Adirondacks and the South Seas. He died in Samoa. The best known of his poems are those for children, *A Child's Garden of Verses.* He perfected the informal essay. His short stories are much admired for their artistry. Several of his longer works, as *Treasure Island,* appeal strongly to children. His typical books are romances of adventure, such as *Kidnapped, The Wrecker* and *The Master of Ballantrae.* One of his most imaginative tales is *Dr. Jekyll and Mr. Hyde.* Among several charming travel books are *An Inland Voyage* and *Travels With a Donkey.* See the biographies by W. Raleigh, J. A. Stewart and G. Balfour.

SUDERMANN, HERMANN (1857–1928): This German novelist and dramatist was born in East Prussia. An ethical criticism runs strongly throughout his works, but his ethics are generally subversive to conservative standards and akin to the advanced individualism of Ibsen and Nietzsche. His masterpiece as a playwright is the highly successful *Magda.* The best known of his novels is *Dame Care;* another notable book, *Song of Songs.* The story of his early life may be read in his *Book of My Youth.*

SWIFT, JONATHAN (1667–1745): An English author of both prose and verse, born in Dublin, Ireland. He lived part of his life in England, where he was highly active in political affairs in London, and part in Dublin, where he was Dean of St. Patrick's Cathedral. He had close friendships with two women: Esther Johnson, whom he addressed as Stella and to whom he wrote a fascinating *Journal,* and Esther Vanhomrigh, whom he addressed as Vanessa. Illness, physical and mental, made tragic the last years of his life. His works include *The Battle of the Books,* a defense of ancient as against modern writers; *The Tale of a Tub,* a satire on Christian sectarianism; *Gulliver's Travels,* a comprehensive satire veiled as a childlike fancy; and many bitter and ironic pamphlets, such as his *Drapier Letters, Argument against the Abolishing of Christianity* and *A Modest Proposal.* His poems are equally forthright in style and ironic in conception. He is one of the chief masters of vigorous, direct English. There are notable books on him by Leslie Stephen, Carl Van Doren and S. L. Gwynn.

SYMONDS, JOHN ADDINGTON (1840–1893): This English author, who was for most of his life an invalid, devoted himself with great energy to literary studies, especially in the fields of Greek and the Italian Renaissance. His chief books are *Studies of the Greek Poets* and *The Renaissance in Italy.* He did much translating and editing and wrote lives of Shelley, Sir Philip Sidney, Ben Jonson, Michelangelo and Whitman.

SYNGE, JOHN MILLINGTON (1871–1909): This Irish playwright took a leading part in the powerful revival of literature in Ireland which occurred at the beginning of the present century. He studied music in Germany and literature in Paris, where he was persuaded by his friend Yeats to return to Ireland and base his creative efforts on the spirit of the Irish people. His life in a primitive peasant community he describes in *The Aran Islands.* His plays were written during his last six years. *The Playboy of the Western World* is rich in vitality, irony and poetic feeling. Similar, though less brilliant, are *The Shadow of the Glen* and *The Well of the Saints.* His masterpiece in tragedy, reprinted in this volume, is his brief *Riders to the Sea.* The plays were given fine performances at the newly organized Abbey Theatre in Dublin. They contain some of the most moving and poetic passages in modern English prose; the tragic gravity of *Riders to the Sea* has often been described as Greek. A warm and discerning appreciation of Synge has been written by W. B. Yeats.

TAGORE, SIR RABINDRANATH (1861–): This Indian poet, essayist and mystic has done much to interpret the thought of India to the Western World. His complete mastery of the English language has been one of his chief assets in establishing this transmission of ideas. As a youth he went from Calcutta to study in England. He has founded an important school for Indian studies which is called Visva-Bharati. Much of his life he has spent in travel, making many friends among leading intellectuals of the West and lecturing to many audiences. Among his works are musical compositions, and poems, plays, stories and essays. Some of his notable works in

English versions are *Sādhanā: The Realization of Life; Reminiscences; Personality; Nationalism; Sakuntala; Greater India;* and *The Religion of Man.*

TAINE, HIPPOLYTE ADOLPHE (1828–1893): This French historian, critic and philosopher gave forceful expression to many of the leading views of his age. A follower of Comte and a supporter of positivism, he developed materialistic conceptions which connected physiology with psychology and thus encouraged the realistic school of fiction led by Zola and Flaubert. A staunch believer in race and in the social importance of geography, he held somewhat doctrinaire views of literature, most strikingly expressed in his brilliant but biased *History of English Literature.* He stands among the founders of the study of comparative literature. His sociological views evolved into strong anti-democratic opinions, expressed in his interpretations of the French Revolution.

TASSO, TORQUATO (1544–1595): An Italian poet of the late Renaissance. He was son of another narrative and romantic poet, Bernardo Tasso. During much of his life he suffered from mental derangement, considering himself persecuted by numerous persons, notably by his patron, the Duke d'Este. He was in the service of several Italian courts. Arrangements made to crown him poet laureate in Rome were frustrated by his death. His philosophical and critical prose is of much less value than his poetry. This consists of songs, odes and sonnets on love, religion and politics, a poem on the creation of the world, a pastoral drama, *Aminta* and his masterpiece, the epic *Jerusalem Delivered,* telling of the crusade of Godfrey of Bouillon. Late in life he revised this poem in the interests of religious orthodoxy, but his revision impaired its merits. The best translation is by Edward Fairfax.

TASSONI, ALESSANDRO (1565–1635): This Italian poet and critic was secretary to various prelates and princes in his native land. His literary criticism includes a commentary on the poems of Petrarch. His temperament, like that of his land and times, inclined him to gaiety and trifling. Hence his major work, *The Rape of the Bucket,* the first celebrated specimen of mock heroic humor in modern times and the model in France for Boileau's *Lutrin* and in England for Pope's *Rape of the Lock.* The brief poem given in this volume gives a fair example of his skillful craftsmanship and light-hearted charm. His satire is thoroughly enlightened and urbane.

TERPANDER (fl. 676 B.C.): A Greek poet and musician, born on the island of Lesbos. He added three strings to the lyre, which formerly had only four, thus laying the foundation of the octave in Western music. His music school was celebrated throughout the Grecian world and he is commonly spoken of as father of music. Only a few brief poems by him have come down to us.

THEOCRITUS (c. 316–c. 260 B.C.): This Greek bucolic or pastoral poet after studying his art in Alexandria, Egypt, resided in Syracuse, Sicily. Here he cultivated a type of short idyllic poem, purporting to describe the life of shepherds. That his poems are less artificial and sophisticated than the pastorals of Virgil and other of his followers, does not mean that they are themselves for the most part naturalistic. He, too, is above all elegant. His idyl on city life, given in this volume, offers final evidence of his urbanity. His shepherds are artificial universalizings of men and women confronted by love and death, pleasure and pain. Theocritus is the chief master of the Alexandrian school of poetry. Partly through Virgil, his influence became widespread in Europe, especially during the Renaissance. He is father of all pastoral verse. See the translation by Andrew Lang.

THEODORIDES (fl. 240 B.C.): A Greek poet known for delicate and tender lyrics now found within the Greek Anthology, or collection of short poems. Little of his work survives.

THOMAS À KEMPIS (1379?–1471): This German monk, author of *The Imitation of Christ,* was born at Kempen, in northwest Germany. His early education brought him under the influence of a religious order, the Brothers of the Common Life. In 1413 he became an Augustinian monk, living in a convent in the Netherlands. Here he wrote many devotional books, of which by far the chief, *The Imitation of Christ,* has only in recent years been positively ascertained as his. This book, of an orthodox, though highly mystical character, has had few rivals in popularity among the entire literature of Christian piety.

THOMPSON, FRANCIS (1859–1907): This English poet is known for splendid eloquence, a warmth of color and a mystic fervor often suggesting the poetry of Renaissance Spain, with which, however, he had no direct contact other than his ardent Catholicism. Some of his poetic values he derived from Victor Hugo, whom he greatly admired. After years of distinctly bohemian living, he found shelter with friends, notably the poet, Alice Meynell. The imagery of his nature poems is sumptuous and glowing. His mystical poems are brilliant, but at times vague in meaning and specious in their eloquence. His best-known lyric, *The Hound of Heaven,* may be compared with *Quia Amore Langueo,* given in this book. Probably none of his work, however, surpasses in sincerity the briefer lyric given here. See the life by Everard Meynell and the study by R. L. Mégroz.

THOREAU, HENRY DAVID (1817–1862): This American essayist, born in Concord, Massachusetts, more than any other writer of his times successfully detached himself from the provinciality of his environment and subjected life and society to fundamental criticism. An uncompromising idealist, he analyzed the ills of war, slavery, industry, commercialism and materialism. Like his friend Emerson, he enriched his mind by studies in the classics of both Europe and Asia. His books published during his lifetime are *A Week on the Concord and Merrimack Rivers* (1849) and *Walden* (1854). His *Journals* are of great interest. He has attracted much attention abroad; being admired, for example, by Tolstoy and Gandhi. *Thoreau* by H. S. Canby, is an able study of his life and thought.

THUCYDIDES (d. c. 400 B.C.): This great Greek historian has left only a single work, his *History of the Peloponnesian War,* depicting the struggle between the rival leagues of Athens and Sparta. An Athenian general, he was exiled for twenty years because of the failure of a military expedition of which he was one of the commanders. His history describes only what pertains to the war, but treats this theme with thoroughness and brilliant criticism. Opinions, motives and policies of the various leaders are stated and analyzed with masterly skill, so that it has always been regarded as one of the most valuable of books on statecraft, diplomacy and the political problems of war and peace. It philosophically examines the rival systems of Athenian democracy and Spartan autocracy. Its restrained eloquence affords a model for historical and literary writing. See J. B. Bury, *Ancient Greek Historians.*

TOLSTOY, LEO NIKOLAYEVICH (1828–1910): This Russian novelist and thinker was born of a noble family whose traditions he ultimately renounced. His own works contain much that is autobiographical. *Childhood, Boyhood* and *Youth* reflect his earliest years; *The Cossacks* and *Sebastopol* contain reminiscences of his army life; and his tales and novels are indebted to his gay years in upper-class society and to his life of devotion among the peasants. He denounced the ways of modern, civilized man, turning instead to an ideal derived from primitive Christianity. His attempt to put his beliefs into practice strained his family relationships. Some of his most notable work was in the field of educational reform. His chief novels are *War and Peace, Anna Karenina* and *Resurrection.* His life and writings have made a world-wide impression, evidence of which are studies by Maxim Gorky, D. S. Merezhkovsky, Romain Rolland, Constance Garnett and H. J. A. Fausset.

TSURAYUKI, KI NO (d. 946): This major figure in classical Japanese literature was a court noble who held many political offices. About 922 he edited a celebrated collection of poems, the *Kokinshiu,* with a preface on the nature of poetry, the preface translated in this book. He was himself a notable poet. Among his prose works is a remarkable travel-diary, the *Tosa Nikki,* giving an account of Japanese manners in the Middle Ages.

TU FU (713–770): Since this great Chinese poet writes much of himself, and even in his lifetime enjoyed great popularity, there is a considerable amount of data on his life. He experienced brief periods of favor with the government, alternated with longer periods of exile, wandering and disgrace. His many poems are rich in historical allusion. They are remarkable for the breadth and often for the simplicity of their humanity. He deals freely with nature, the common aspects of daily life, work, the family, the pleasures of peace and the ravages and tragedy of war. Admirable translations have been made by Arthur Waley, Florence Ayscough and, in collaboration, by E. W. Underwood and C. H. Chu.

Tyutchev, Fyodor Ivanovich (1803–1873): This Russian poet was a radical in literature, but a reactionary in his political views and conduct. During the central years of his life he served in the Russian consulate at Munich, while during his last twenty years he acted as censor. He believed in Orthodox Russia and the cause of the united Slavs. His poems, few in number, have recently come into high esteem. They show him at once a realist and a metaphysician. His sincere and deeply imaginative art is well represented by the lyric given in this volume. He reveals that inwardness in the nineteenth-century Slavic character peculiarly fascinating to the world at large.

Unamuno, Miguel de (1864–1936): A Spanish author and statesman of Basque descent. He taught Greek and became rector of the University of Salamanca, from which post he was removed on account of liberal opinions. Because of opposition to the dictator, Primo de Rivera, he was exiled to the Canary Islands. He aided the revolution which overthrew the monarchy and founded the republic (1931), holding a cabinet post in the new government. His writings include poems, novels and critical essays all imbued with fresh interpretations of the traditional mysticism and idealism of Spain. The chief books as translated into English are *The Life of Don Quixote and Sancho Panza; The Tragic Sense of Life; Essays and Soliloquies;* and *The Agony of Christianity.*

Vaughan, Henry (1622–1695): This English poet reached maturity during the troubled period of the English Civil Wars, in which he was of the royalist party. He associated himself with the Cavalier poets. Later he lived a retired life as a Welsh country doctor. His poetry is generally introspective, mystical, somber and religious, reflecting a tragic life and the tragic misfortunes of the English Church. The poem given here glances at the ruthless military rule of the English dictator, Cromwell, as it appeared to the Anglicans, who regarded Cromwell as usurper and not as Lord Protector.

Verhaeren, Émile (1855–1916): A leading Belgian poet and dramatist, writing extensively of Flemish life, in French. He lived and traveled in various parts of Europe and resided for some time in London. He has written in both a realistic and a symbolistic manner. His poems are difficult to translate, and many have not been attempted. His plays, as *The Dawn* and *The Cloister,* are translated more readily; similarly his short stories and his war book, *Belgium's Agony.* He has written three sequences of love poems and a larger number of volumes somber in tone dealing with the ills of city life and of modern industrial society. His view is stern, but in the end refreshing. See the biographical studies by Stefan Zweig and P. M. Jones; also A. F. Corell, *Contribution of Verhaeren to Modern French Lyric Poetry.*

Verlaine, Paul (1844–1896): This French lyric poet lived a notoriously bohemian life. While traveling with his fellow-poet, Rimbaud, he shot him and was imprisoned for two years. The unhappy story of his life is lightened only by his art. He possesses an uninhibited expressiveness similar to that of Villon. His highly personal lyrics combine an intimate realism with a most effective symbolism, and a colloquial style with a pure magic of phrase and sound. They range from the morally shocking to the fervently religious. Behind the naïve exterior of his lyric manner stands a mind subtle, sophisticated and decadent, appearing clearly in his literary criticism. There are translations by Arthur Symons, Ernest Dowson and Wilfred Thorley, and critical studies by Stefan Zweig and H. G. Nicolson.

Villon (b. François de Montcorbier) (1431–1463?): This French poet was born in Paris, studied at the Sorbonne and, after his student days, lived a checkered life. He was several times arrested on charges of theft and murder. His desperate career of vagabondage forms the basis for his highly personal, sincere and intense lyric poems. Many of these describe the more sordid social conditions of the times. A few are expressions of piety and repentance. He wrote many lyrics in the ballade form. The direct outpouring of his feelings and the biting realism of his style have helped to make him one of the most widely read of all French poets. See translations by John Payne.

VIRGIL (70–19 B.C.): The chief Latin epic poet was born near Mantua and lived several years on his father's farm. His literary education was primarily in Greek poetry and philosophy. His first work was *Eclogues,* pastorals in imitation of Theocritus. In 30 B.C. he completed his *Georgics,* poetical essays on agriculture. The epic, *Aeneid,* written in the latter years of his life, takes suggestions from the *Iliad* and *Odyssey,* but aims by historical and legendary reference to enhance the glory of imperial Rome under Augustus. Virgil has less fire than Homer, but excels in pathos, dignity and a highly conscious and an impeccable craftsmanship. He has profoundly influenced the poetry of Europe, not only in Roman times, but notably from Dante to Tennyson. See Tenney Frank, *Vergil: A Biography,* and D. L. Durling, *Georgic Tradition in English Poetry.*

VOLTAIRE, FRANÇOIS MARIE AROUET DE (1694–1778): This French philosopher, poet and critic was born in Paris. From his youth he became celebrated for his conversation and wit and lived throughout his life in the company of enlightened intellectuals. He was a leader of the Encyclopédists, who were organizing human knowledge, especially in scientific fields. After imprisonment in France caused by his political liberalism, he resided two years in England, whose more tolerant and liberal customs attracted him. For two years also he lived at the court of Frederick the Great. He finally found sanctuary near Geneva. His voluminous works include epic and tragic poetry, histories, and essays on a great variety of subjects. *Candide,* a fantastic novel, is often held his literary masterpiece. It ridicules fanaticism and intolerance, and advises man to "cultivate his garden." In wit and irony exercised in behalf of human dignity and rights, Voltaire has seldom been surpassed. Not an original thinker, he has nevertheless exercised an incalculable influence on mankind. See the lives by John Morley and Georg Brandes.

VONDEL, JOOST VAN DEN (1587–1679): The foremost Dutch poet and dramatist was born in Cologne but lived chiefly in Amsterdam, where he held a minor government post and became a convert to Catholicism. He wrote many serious plays, some on classical themes, some on biblical subjects, but all in the neoclassical manner. A few of his plays deal with modern history. His masterpiece, *Lucifer,* parallels the work of his contemporary, Milton, in *Paradise Lost.* He composed many lyrics strikingly typical of Dutch thought and taste, political ideas and domestic life. See the study by A. J. Barnouw.

WALTHER VON DER VOGELWEIDE (c. 1170–1230): This medieval German lyric poet, or minnesinger, lived for the first part of his life chiefly in Vienna, but later wandered over much of central Europe, and died in Würzburg. Some of his fine songs are amatory, but many are political and satirical. For the Emperor Frederick II he wrote a group of songs urging the prosecution of a crusade. His denunciation of social evils rings with startling sincerity. Churchmen and laymen alike came under his fearless attack. He is often considered the most brilliant of German poets before Goethe.

WARNER, LANGDON (1881–): This American archaeologist is one of the most active students in the Far-Eastern field. He has made many trips to various parts of Asia, working for several of the chief scholarly foundations in the United States. He was for a while director of the American School of Archaeology in Peking under the auspices of the Smithsonian Institution. He has also served as curator of art in the Boston Art Museum and the Fogg Museum, Cambridge, Massachusetts, and has taught at Harvard University.

WELLS, HERBERT GEORGE (1866–1946): This novelist and sociologist was the son of a professional cricketer. His life is best told in his own spirited *Experiment in Autobiography.* He has a wonderful gift of zest, humor and optimism. Some of his books, as his early *Time Machine,* are remarkable for their lively fancy. Wells was equally concerned with past and future. Among his early books, also, are prophetic stories such as *The War of the Worlds* and *The War in the Air.* His social and economic criticism, often enlivened by much humor, may be seen in the novels *Tono Bungay, The History of Mr. Polly* and *The New Machiavelli.* His socialism appears vividly in *New Worlds for Old.* A broader panorama of his social philosophy is afforded by his *Outline of History.* His notable views on education appear in *Peter and Joan.* Wells is the most popular modern heir of the English nineteenth-century liberal tradition. See the studies by J. D. Beresford, V. Brooks and S. Dark.

WHITMAN, WALT (1819–1892): This leading American poet was born at Westhills, Long Island. He was educated by his varied experiences with life rather than by schooling. After doing odd jobs, he turned to printing, newspaper reporting and editing. This led to experiments in prose and verse, at first unpromising but in time resulting in poetry of major importance. He lived for a while in New Orleans and traveled with an observant eye through most of the then existent States of the Union. During the Civil War he was a hospital attendant in and about Washington, D. C. Illness confined him throughout his later years to his home in Camden, New Jersey. He attempted to fashion a new art and a new faith from the gospel of American democracy. He unquestionably achieved new forms of art, of which free verse was only a phase, and projected a powerful image of American life. His influence has been widely felt upon literature both in America and abroad. (Compare, for example, his *Song of the Broad-Axe* with Ronald de Carvalho's *Brazil.*) Our selections reveal important aspects of his work. His grasp of American ideals of labor appears in the aforementioned poem; his deep love of Lincoln may be seen in his elegy on the martyred president; his characteristic optimism, materialism and naïveté in *There Was a Child Went Forth;* his no less characteristic mysticism in *When I Heard the Learned Astronomer;* and his gift for painting memorable vignettes in his artful epigrams. *Song of Myself,* a longer poem than any given here, best summarizes all his qualities as poet and thinker. See biographies by Bliss Perry and Emory Holloway and the studies by B. de Selincourt, H. I. Fausset and N. Arvin.

WHITTIER, JOHN GREENLEAF (1807–1892): An American poet known chiefly for his power in expressing the thoughts and feelings of the common man, especially in New England. Of a Quaker family, he was born and lived much of his life near Haverhill, Massachusetts. He early associated himself with the abolitionist movement, subject of much of his verse. The reading of Burns first turned him to poetry. Undistinguished and imitative in his earliest work, he soon gained strength. In his political poetry, as *Massachusetts to Virginia,* the sternness of the abolitionist is often the more powerful in its modification by the restraint of the Quaker. Among his popular poems are ballads such as *Barbara Frietchie, Skipper Ireson's Ride* and *Telling the Bees.* His masterpiece is the farm idyl, *Snow-Bound.* He was a sincere democrat, interested in many social causes, as pacifism, toleration and the labor movement. There are lives by G. R. Carpenter, Bliss Perry and A. Mordell.

WILLIAMS, WILLIAM CARLOS (1883–   ): This American poet, by profession a physician, is best known for his lyrics and novels, both being reflections of modern urban life. As a poet, he is an impressionist, attempting to say much with the use of only a few vivid words and images. Thus he is usually abrupt, sometimes obscure, but often forceful. His collected poems appeared in 1941.

WOLFRAM VON ESCHENBACH (c. 1170–c. 1220): A leader among poets of medieval Germany, he was born at Eschenbach, Bavaria, but lived chiefly in Thuringia, where he met Walther von der Vogelweide. He tells us that he could neither read nor write. Nevertheless he created masterpieces of German literature. His first group of lyrics, *Dawn-Songs,* are based on Provençal models and are conventional but spirited love songs. Later he wrote *Parzival,* a romance on the Holy Grail, containing, however, criticism of chivalry and court life. His *Willehalm* includes scenes of home and family life against a background of history and philosophy. Wolfram's style combines an intimate touch and a moral idealism typical of German literature at its best.

WORDSWORTH, WILLIAM (1770–1850): This English poet, the chief spokesman for the romantic interpretation of nature, was born in the mountainous district of northern England and throughout his life cultivated a warm devotion for the scenes of his childhood. He first welcomed and then repudiated the French Revolution. His long poem, *The Prelude,* affords an introspective record of the crucial experiences of his life. His lyrics, especially those published in *Lyrical Ballads* (1798), a volume written in collaboration with Coleridge, have proved his most popular and influential works. These poems helped to turn the course of English poetry from stylistic formalities and rationalism to coloquial informality and warmth of feeling, if not to sentimentality. By temperament quiet and pensive, he cultivated a contemplative mysticism which, joined with his romantic reverence for nature and childhood, produced the great *Ode on Intimations of Immortality.* See the studies by G. M. Harper, R. D. Havens, C. H. Herford and W. Raleigh.

WOTTON, SIR HENRY (1568–1639): This English diplomat and poet was for nearly twenty years ambassador to Venice. He enjoyed many friendships with leading thinkers and men of action, gaining a high reputation as a student and a wit. He is known to have written only a few poems, all brief, but of a highly refined and polished character. He excelled in courtly epigram and eloquent compliment.

WYATT, SIR THOMAS (1503–1542): This English poet and statesman lived a brief but active life in the court of Henry VIII. He was twice imprisoned, once because of relations with Anne Boleyn, first the king's mistress, then his queen, and, second, when his patron, Lord Cromwell, was beheaded. Wyatt led important diplomatic missions. He was prompted to poetry by a strong, native sense for sincere, realistic expression and by a love for the chief poets of Renaissance Italy and ancient Rome. He imitated both Petrarch and Horace. His imitations of Petrarch often seem quaint in their stiff formality, as though the Englishman moved awkwardly in an Italian dress; but his simpler songs are unsurpassable for lyric sincerity and his satires contain some of the most attractive English paraphrases of Horace.

YEATS, WILLIAM BUTLER (1865–1939): Irish poet and playwright. Leader in Irish literary life for nearly fifty years, he devoted much of his energy to stimulating interest in Celtic folklore and to the revival of the Dublin theatre. The collected edition of his poems contains much that for nervous energy probably has been unequaled in modern English poetry. His ideas often seem disturbingly reactionary, but because of the breadth of his vision and his poetic fusion of thought and feeling he attains great distinction. Warmth of heart and catholicity of soul make him a major poet. Consult his autobiography. See also the biography by J. M. Hone and the studies by Louis MacNiece and J. P. O'Donnell.

ZECH, PAUL (1881–): This German poet was born in Briesen (in the later Polish Corridor) of Westphalian peasant stock. He began writing of the forest and of nature; then under pressure of the mechanized world of the city developed a social-religious philosophy. He edited a magazine of verse and wrote short stories. As he grew older, he became increasingly a pacifist.

Nationalities Represented

~ ❁ ~

American (u.s.a.)
Aiken, Benét, Buck, Crane, Dana, Davis, Dickinson, DuBois, Emerson, Edwards, Franklin, Freneau, Frost, Harris, Hawthorne, Hearn, Henry (P.), Hubble, James (W.), Jeffers, Lincoln, MacLeish, Markham, Moody, Moore, Paine, Prescott, Putnam, Ransom, Roosevelt (F. D.), Sandburg, Santayana, Stevens, Thoreau, Warner, Whitman, Whittier, Williams
Anon. (*American Indian*), *The Walam Olum, The Star Sisters*

Arabic
The Koran

Australian
Dyson

Babylonian
Anon. (*from ancient tablets*), *Gilgamesh*

Belgian
De la Montagne, Verhaeren

Brazilian
Carvalho

Bulgarian
Kristov

Canadian
Campbell, Pratt, Roberts

Chinese
Ch' ēn Tzu-ang, Cheng Hsaio, Chih-Ming, Chuang-Tze, Confucius, Fu Hsüan, Hsi Pei Lan, Li Po, Mencuis, Po-Chüi, Su Tung-Po, Tao-Chi'en, Tu Fu, Wang Chi
Anon., A Fickle Widow, Chinese Cinderella, Burial Song, From Break of Day, On a Quiet Night, Plucking the Rushes, The Wife

Colombian
Lopez, Silva

Costa Rican
Fernandez-Guardia

Danish
Jensen

Dutch
Van den Vondel, Van Eden, Van Leeuwenhoek

Ecuadorean
Andrade

Egyptian
Cosmas Indicopleustes, Ikhnaton, Plotinus
Anon., Anpu and Bata

English
Bacon, Blake, Browne, Browning, Byron, Campion, Carlyle, Chaucer, Churchill, Creasy, Darwin, Davies, Dekker, Donne, Dryden, Froude, Gay, Gilbert, Godwin, Gray, Greene, Hardy, Hazlitt, Herrick, Hopkins, Housman, Jonson, Keats, Kipling, Landor, Langland, Lewis, Marvell, Milton, Murray, Newman, Pope, Raleigh, Scott (R. F.), Shakespeare, Shelley, Sidney, Smart, Spender, Spenser, Stevenson, Swift, Symonds, Thompson, Vaughan, Wells, Wordsworth, Wotton, Wyatt
Anon., Earth to Earth, Quia Amore Langueo

French
Baudelaire, du Bellay, Béranger, Saint Bernard, Curie (E.), Daudet, Descartes, Fort, France (Anatole), Gautier, Hugo, Jean de Meun, Joubert, La Fontaine, Lamartine, Marmontel, Marot, Mille, Mistral, de Musset, Pascal, Pasteur, Rimbaud, Ronsard, Rousseau, Taine, Verlaine, Villon, Voltaire
Anon., Aucassin and Nicolete, Fair is Her Body

German
Dehmel, Goethe, Heine, Hölderlin, Hölty, Luther, Marx, Matthias Claudius, Sir

Meinloh von Sevelingen, Mommsen, Mörike, Sir Neidhart von Reuental, Nietzsche, Rilke, Schiller, Sudermann, Thomas à Kempis, Walther von der Vogelweide, Sir Wolfram von Eschenbach, Zech
Anon., Matin Song, Song of the Nibelungs

GREEK
Aeschylus, Aesop, Agathias Scholasticus, Anacreon, Aristophanes, Aristotle, Bion, Callimachus, Epictetus, Euripides, Evenus, Herodotus, Hesiod, Homer, Lucian, Lucilius, Marcus Argentarius, Meleager, Moschus, Phocylades, Pindar, Plato, Sappho, Simonides, Sophocles, Terpander, Theocritus, Theodorides, Thucydides

HEBREW
The Bible

HINDU
Buddha, Tagore
The Bhagavad Gita, The Dhammapada, The Jataka, The Hitopadesa, The Panchatrata, The Upanishads

HUNGARIAN
Molnár

ICELANDIC
Snorri Sturluson

IRISH
Æ (Russell), Synge, Yeats

ITALIAN
Boccaccio, Campanella, Carduccio, Cellini, D'Annunzio, Dante, Filicaja, St. Francis of Assisi, Giusti, Guinicelli, Leonardo da Vinci, Leopardi, Lorenzo de' Medici, Machiavelli, Marco Polo, Mazzini, Michelangelo, Mussolini, Parini, Petrarch, Pirandello, Tasso, Tassoni

JAPANESE
Basho, Princess Daihaku, Hanshin, Joso, Kaibara Ekken, Mori Ogwai, Motokiyo, Saki, Tsurayuki, Yaha, Yakamochi
Anon., The Sun Goddess and the Mikado, A Bright Night, Love's Terror, Whirlpool

LATIN
Apuleius, Boethius, Catullus, Cicero, Claudianus, Hadrian, Horace, Saint Jerome, Juvenal, Lucretius, Marcus Aurelius, Martial, Ovid, Phaedrus, Seneca, Virgil

MEXICAN
Novo

MONTENEGRIN
Matavulj

NICARAGUAN
Darío

NORWEGIAN
Björnson

PERSIAN
Hafiz, Jami, Omar Khayyám, Sa'di

PERUVIAN
Chocano

POLISH
Copernicus, Dygasínski, Konopnicka

PORTUGUESE
Camoëns

PUERTO-RICAN
Marín

RUSSIAN
Andreyev, Blok, Dostoyevsky, Gastev, Koltsov, Lermontov, Pushkin, Raisin, Tolstoy, Tyutchev

SCOTTISH
Burns

SERB
Karadžić

SLOVENE
Cankar

SPANISH
Alemán, Bernal Díaz, Cervantes, Guillen, Jiménez, Luis de Góngora, Luis de León, Gómez Manrique, Jorge Manrique, Quevedo, Unamuno

SWEDISH
Ehrenpreis, Fröding, Geijer, Lagerlöf, Linnaeus, Runeberg

SWISS
Pestalozzi

SYRIAN
An-Nawawi

TURKISH
Sari Mehmed Pasha

URUGUAYAN
Rodó

VENEZUELAN
Fombona-Pachano, Silva

Acknowledgments

The editors and publishers of World Literature: an Anthology of Human Experience *acknowledge with thanks permission granted by the following authors, literary agents or executors, journals, and publishing houses for the use of copyrighted selections listed after their names.*

George Allen and Unwin, Ltd.: for "The Order of Rank," from Nietzsche's *The Will to Power,* translated by Anthony M. Ludovici, edited by Dr. Oscar Levy; for "Troy," a chorus from Gilbert Murray's translation of the *Troades* of Euripides; and for "Literature as Revelation," from Gilbert Murray's *Essays and Addresses.*

The American-Scandinavian Foundation: for Jensen's "At Memphis Station," from Damon and Hillyer's *A Book of Danish Verse;* for Selma Lagerlöf's "The Eclipse," translated by Velma S. Howard, from the *American Scandinavian Review,* December 1922; for selections from Snorri Sturluson's *The Prose Edda,* translated by Gilchrist Brodeur; for Fröding's "The Dance by the Roadside," Runeberg's "The Soldier Boy," and Geiger's "The Charcoal Burner's Son," all from Charles Wharton Stork's *Anthology of Swedish Lyrics;* and for "The Child in Our Soul," from Björnstjerne Björnson: *Poems and Songs,* translated by A. H. Palmer.

Angus and Robertson, Ltd.: for Edward Dyson's "The Worked-Out Mine."

D. Appleton-Century Company, Inc.: for "Tagasako," from W. G. Aston's *History of Japanese Literature.*

Ernest Benn, Ltd.: for translations by Humbert Wolfe in *Others Abide* of "Reading Hesiod" by Marcus Argentarius and "A Dead Song-Writer" by Lucilius.

Brandt and Brandt: for a selection from *John Brown's Body* by Stephen Vincent Benét, published by Farrar and Rinehart, copyright, 1927, 1928 by Stephen Vincent Benét; for four poems, "All, All," "Dawn," "The King of the Rainy Country," and "The Albatross," from Baudelaire's *Flowers of Evil,* translated by George Dillon and Edna St. Vincent Millay, published by Harper and Brothers, copyright, 1936, by George Dillon and Edna St. Vincent Millay.

University of California Press: for six poems translated from the Chinese: Wang Chi's "Success," Chih Ming's "Facing Death," Hsi P'ei Lan's "The Morning Bell of Fang Ta," and three anonymous poems, "The Hundred Names," "The Wife," and "Success," from Henry H. Hart's *The Hundred Names,* published by the University of California Press, copyright, 1933.

Jonathan Cape, Ltd.: for "Leisure" and "The Sleepers," from *Collected Poems* by W. H. Davies, published by Jonathan Cape.

The Clarendon Press: for Tsurayuki's "Japanese Poetry," from F. V. Dickins's *Primitive and Medieval Japanese Texts;* for six poems, "Pretext," "Crossing the Mountain Alone," "A Bright Night," "Love's Terror," "Whirlpool," and "The Wake," from Arthur Waley's *Japanese Poetry;* for Simonides' "The Athenian Dead," from Higham and Bowra's *From the Greek;* for Terpander's "Sparta," Phocylades' "A Small City on a Rock," Simonides' "At Thermopylae," and Euripides' "The Children," from Higham and Bowra's *Oxford Book of Greek Verse in Translation;* for Luis de Leon's "Avarice," from A. G. F. Bell's *Luis de Leon* and Bell's translation of his "The Life Removed" in *The Oxford Book of Spanish Verse* (No. 77).

Columbia University Press: for Hölderlin's "Song of Fate," reprinted from Neff's *A Revolution in European Poetry 1660–1900,* by permission of Columbia University Press.

C. W. Daniel Company, Ltd.: for Pushkin's "Winter Evening" and Koltsov's "The Young Reaper," from Coxwell's *Russian Poems* (1929).

Peter Davies, Ltd. and J. M. Edmonds: for Agathias Scholasticus' "I love not wine," from J. M. Edmonds, *Some Greek Love Poems* (1929), published by Peter Davies, Ltd.

J. M. Dent & Sons, Ltd.: for a selection from *The Song of Roland,* translated by René Hague, published (1937) by Faber and Faber, Ltd.

Dodd, Mead & Company, Inc.: for passages from *Joubert: a Selection from His Thoughts,* translated by Katharine Lyttelton, with a Preface by Mrs. Humphrey Ward; for "The Procurator of Judea," from *Mother of Pearl* by Anatole France; for "The Pier," by Mori Ogwai, from Paulowina's *Seven Stories by Japanese Writers;* for Arthur Symons' translation of Paul Verlaine's "Woman and Cat"; for Du Bellay's "Happy who like Ulysses, or that Lord," from *The Collected Poems of G. K. Chesterton;* for a selection from *Scott's Last Expedition;* all the foregoing reprinted by permission of Dodd, Mead & Company, Inc.

Doubleday & Company, Inc.: for "The Discovery of Radium," from Eve Curie's *Madame Curie,* copyright, 1937, by Doubleday, Doran & Company, Inc.; for "The Road to the West," Chapter III of *The Long Road to Old China,* by Langdon Warner, copyright, 1926, by Doubleday, Doran & Company, Inc.; for "The Hero," by Gabriele D'Annunzio, from *Tales of My Native Town,* copyright, 1920, by Doubleday, Doran & Company, Inc.

E. P. Dutton & Company, Inc.: for Kaibara Ekken's "On Books" and "Social Intercourse," both from *The Way of Contentment* (Wisdom of the East series), translated by Ken Hoshimo; for selections from *The Pensées of Blaise Pascal,* translated by William F. Trotter; for passages from *The Song of the Niblungs* by Margaret Armour, Everyman's Library; for "The Story of Griselda," from *The Decameron* of Boccaccio, translated by J. M. Rigg; for "Chinese Cinderella," from Wolfram Eberhard, *Chinese Fairy Tales and Folk Tales;* for three poems, "The Beautiful Women," "Peasant Life," and "The Arrival of a Guest," from Soame Jenyns, *Selections from the 300 Poems of the T'ang Dynasty;* for four poems, "The Night of Sorrow," "On a Quiet Night," "Three with the Moon and His Shadow," and "The Nefarious War," from Li Po, *Works,* translated by Shigeyoshi Obata, copyright 1922, E. P. Dutton & Company, Inc.; for "Of Human Progress," from Lucretius, *Of the Nature of Things* (Book V), translated by William Ellery Leonard, Everyman's Library; for "To the Italian Workingmen," from *The Duties of Man* by Guiseppe Mazzini, translated by Thomas Okey; for a selection from *The Romance of the Rose* by Jean de Meun, translated by F. S. Ellis; for "The Jar," from *The One Act Plays of Pirandello* by Luigi Pirandello, edited by Arthur Livingston, copyright 1928, E. P. Dutton & Company, Inc.; for "The Dove and the Crow," from *Ancient Indian Fables and Stories: Panchatantra* by Stanley P. Rice; for scattered passages from *The Koran,* translated by J. M. Rodwell; for Theodorides' "Pass On," from *An Echo of Greek Song* by W. H. D. Rouse; for Verlaine's "Cortège" and "Song of Autumn," from *The Symbolist Movement in French Poetry* by Arthur Symons, copyright 1919, renewed 1936, E. P. Dutton & Company, Inc.; for "The Funeral Oration of Pericles" from *The History of the Peloponnesian War* of Thucydides, translated by R. Crawley, Everyman's Library; for Saint Jerome's "The Story of Malchus," from *Fathers of the Church* by F. A. Wright: all the above published and copyright by E. P. Dutton & Company, Inc.

Max Eastman: for his translations of Lermontov's "A Thought" and Pushkin's "Message to Siberia," both from *Kinds of Love* by Max Eastman, published by Charles Scribner's Sons.

Greenberg, Publisher: for a part of Paul Fort's "Ballad of the Bells," from *Modern French Poetry* by Joseph T. Shipley.

The Hakluyt Society, London: for "The Medieval Christian World," from *The Christian Topography* of Cosmas Indicopleustes, translated by J. W. McCrindle, published by The Hakluyt Society.

Harcourt, Brace & Company, Inc.: for "Clean Curtains" and "Five Towns on the B & O," from *Smoke and Steel* by Carl Sandburg, copyright, 1920, by Harcourt, Brace & Company, Inc.; for "Joe Greene," from *M: One Thousand Autobiographical Sonnets* by Merrill Moore, copyright, 1938, by Harcourt, Brace & Company, Inc.; for Horace's "Revenge," from *Including Horace* by Louis Untermeyer, copyright, 1919, by Harcourt, Brace & Company, Inc.; for a chapter from *Dark Princess* by W. E. B. DuBois, copyright, 1928, by Harcourt, Brace & Company, Inc.

Lucien Harris: for "Brother Rabbitt's Money Mint," from *Uncle Remus and His Friends* by Joel Chandler Harris, published by Houghton Mifflin Company.

Harvard University Press: for "Duties of the Individual to the State," from Cicero: *Offices,* translated by Walter Miller (Loeb Classical Library); for "Of the Greatest Good," passages from H. F. Stewart and E. K. Rand (translators),

Boethius (Loeb Classical Library), Consolation of Philosophy, Book III; for R. M. Gummere (translator), *Seneca* (Loeb Classical Library), Epistles to Lucilius, XLI; for A. S. Way (translator), *Euripides: Works* (Loeb Classical Library), IV, p. 261, Chorus from Hippolytus; for B. B. Rogers (translator), *Aristophanes, Works* (Loeb Classical Library), II: The Birds: Chorus — "Ye men who are daily existing"; for H. C. Warren (translator), *Buddhism in Translation: The Jataka Story,* The Great Retirement; The Attainment of Buddhaship; Questions Which Tend Not to Edification; and from the *Samyutta-Nikaya,* The Middle Doctrine; for F. C. Conybeare (translator), *Philostratus: The Life of Apollonius of Tyana,* Bk. II, Ch. 5 (selection).

WILLIAM HEINEMANN, LTD.: for "I cease not from desire," from Gertrude Bell: *Poems From the Divan of Hafiz,* published by William Heinemann, Ltd.

MAJOR HAROLD GOULD HENDERSON: for five haiku, "The Afterglow," "Dusk," "Winter," "Quiet," and "Loneliness," from *The Bamboo Broom* by Harold G. Henderson, published by Houghton Mifflin Company.

THE HISPANIC SOCIETY OF AMERICA: for Manrique's "On the Bad Government of Toledo," Luis de Leon's "The Night Serene," Quevedo's "Letrilla," Unamuno's "Domestic Scenes," Silva's "Nocturne," Dario's "To Roosevelt," and Chocano's "Sylvan Ode," all from Thomas Walsh: *Hispanic Anthology.*

HENRY HOLT & COMPANY: for "After Apple-Picking," "Fire and Ice," and "To Earthward," from *Collected Poems, 1939,* by Robert Frost; for "With rue my heart is laden," from *A Shropshire Lad* by A. E. Housman; for "The Picnic Boat," "Happiness," "Fish Crier," and "Fog," from *Chicago Poems* by Carl Sandburg.

HOUGHTON MIFFLIN COMPANY: The selections listed below used by permission of Houghton Mifflin Company: for "In the Twilight of the Gods," from Lafcadio Hearn, *Out of the East* (*Works,* 1922: Vol. VII, 423–32); for "You, Andrew Marvell" and "Burying Ground by the Ties" ("Frescoes," iii), from Archibald MacLeish, *Poems, 1924–1933;* for two selections from José Enrique Rodó, *Ariel,* translated by F. J. Stimson; for "The Death of Eve," from William Vaughn Moody, *Poems and Poetic Dramas,* Vol. I. Also to Houghton Mifflin Company as authorized publishers of the following works out of copyright: Björnstjerne Björnson: "The Father," from *The Bridal March;* Thomas Carlyle: "Labour," from *Past and Present;* H. W. Emerson: *Self Reliance,* and four poems, "Brahma," "Concord Hymn," "Hamatreya," and "Ode Inscribed to W. H. Channing"; Nathaniel Hawthorne: "Earth's Holocaust," from *Mosses from an Old Manse;* Jean François Marmontel: "The Fall of the Bastile," from *Memoirs of a Father* (Houghton and Osgood, 1878); Longfellow: translations of Dante's *Divine Comedy* (Purgatorio, vi), "Political Chaos in Italy"; Goethe's "Wanderer's Night Songs"; Gongora's "Let Me Go Warm"; Manrique's "Ode on the Death of his Father" (in part); Marot's "Friar Lubin"; Thoreau: from *Poems,* "All Things Are Current Found"; from *Walden,* the chapter "Where I Lived and What I Lived For"; Whittier: *Poems,* "The Lumbermen," "Massachusetts to Virginia."

THE JEWISH PUBLICATION SOCIETY OF AMERICA: for Abraham Raisin's story "Late," in *Yiddish Tales,* translated by Helena Frank, reprinted with the permission of the copyright owners, The Jewish Publication Society of America.

THE JOHNS HOPKINS PRESS: for "The Old Man's Fair-haired Consort," from Ovid (*Elegies,* I, 14), translated by Kirby Flower Smith in his *Martial the Epigrammatist and Other Essays* (1920), published by the Johns Hopkins Press.

KEGAN PAUL, TRENCH, TRUBNER & COMPANY, LTD.: for "Panegyric of Birds," from Leopardi's *Essays and Discourses,* translated by Charles Edwards; for "The Latin Boy, a Tale from Montenegro," translated by Paul Selver, in *Modern Slavonic Literature;* both published by Kegan Paul, Trench, Trubner & Company, Ltd.

KELLY & WALSH, LTD.: for a selection from *Chuang Tze, Mystic, Moralist, and Social Reformer* by H. A. Giles.

ALFRED A. KNOPF, INC.: all the following reprinted by permission of. "Antique Harvesters," from *Two Gentlemen in Bonds* by John Crowe Ransom, copyright, 1927, by Alfred A. Knopf, Inc.; "Peter Quince at the Clavier," from *Harmonium* by Wallace Stevens, copyright, 1923, 1931, by Alfred A. Knopf, Inc.; "Solitude," from *Essays and Soliloquies* by Miguel de Unamuno, copyright, 1924, by Alfred A. Knopf, Inc.; "Burial Song," "Satire on Paying Calls," "Woman," "Shady, Shady," "Plucking the Rushes," "The Business Men," "On the Birth of His Son," "Lao-Tzu," "The Flower-Market," and "The Charcoal Seller," from *170 Chinese Poems* by Arthur Waley, copyright, 1919, 1947, by Alfred A. Knopf, Inc., Arthur Waley: "The Man and the Machine," from *Collected Poems* by Edwin J. Pratt, copyright, 1945, by Edwin J. Pratt.

John Lane, The Bodley Head, Ltd.: for D'Annunzio's "Evening in May" translated by G. A. Greene, in his *Italian Lyrists of Today*, 1898; for Leopardi's "To Italy," translated by Romilda Rendel, in *Anthology of Italian Lyrics*, 1925; for "Victory," from Pierre Mille: *Under the Tricolor*, translated by Berangere Drillen, 1915; for Meleager's "A Bride," translated by John Beeching, in his *In a Garden*, 1895; all published by John Lane, The Bodley Head, Ltd.

Miss Jessie Lemont: for her translation of Rilke's "Silent Hour," first printed in Van Doren's *Anthology of World Poetry*, 1929.

Little, Brown & Company: for "The Pope's Mule," from Alphonse Daudet: *Letters from My Mill* (*Works*, Vol. XIX), translated by Katherine P. Wormley; for three poems, "To Make a Prairie," "Elysium is as far as to," and "Behind Me Dips Eternity," from *The Poems of Emily Dickinson*, edited by Martha Dickinson Bianchi and Alfred Leete Hanson.

Liveright Publishing Corporation: for a passage from Hart Crane's "The Bridge," in *Collected Poems*, 1933.

David Lloyd: for "Father Andrea," from *The First Wife and Other Stories* by Pearl S. Buck, copyright, 1929, 1933, by Pearl S. Buck, published by The John Day Company; by arrangement with the author's agent, David Lloyd, 49 East 34th Street, New York 16, N. Y.

Longmans, Green & Company: for six poems from Jethro Bithell: *The Minnesingers*, Vol. 1 (1909): "I Serve," "There Is a Lady Conquering," "Awake! The Day Is Coming Now," "His Own True Wife," "Wintertime," and "Matin Song"; for William James: "The Moral Equivalent of War," from *Memories and Studies*, 1911; for Sappho's "Evening," translated by Sir Rennell Rodd in *Love, Worship, and Death*, 1916; for Villon's "Ballad of the Gibbet," translated by Andrew Lang in *Ballads and Lyrics of Old France* (*Poetical Works*, Vol. II).

Robert M. McBride & Company: for Lucian's "Passing Away" and Simonides' "Lost at Sea," translated by Walter Leaf in his *Little Poems from the Greek*, 1922, published by Robert M. McBride & Company.

McGraw-Hill Book Company, Inc.: for "The Evening Hours of a Hermit" by Pestalozzi, translated by Lewis Flint Anderson in his *Pestalozzi* (McGraw-Hill Educational Classics), 1931.

The Macmillan Company: for Apuleius' tale of Cupid and Psyche, from Walter Pater: *Marius the Epicurean;* for "The Overworld," from Thomas Hardy: *The Dynasts, Part III;* for a translation of Quevedo's sonnet "I saw the ramparts of my native land," from John Masefield: *Collected Poems;* for "Retrospect," from George E. Russell (Æ): *The Candle of Vision;* for "The Realization of the Infinite," from Rabindranath Tagore: *Sadhana;* for "The First Pythian Ode," from Arthur S. Way, translator: *The Odes of Pindar;* for "A Prayer for My Daughter" (with omissions), and "An Irish Airman Foresees His Death," from William Butler Yeats: *Collected Poems*, 1933, all reprinted with permission of The Macmillan Company, publishers. For "The Protagoras Myth," from J. A. Stewart: *The Myths of Plato*, published by Macmillan & Company, London, and reprinted by permission of The Macmillan Company; for "The Infinite" and "The Broom," from Leopardi: *Translations from Leopardi*, translated by R. C. Trevelyan; for Simonides' "A Hound," from F. L. Lucas: *Poems*, 1935, and for Sophocles, Chorus from "Oedipus at Colonus," and Sappho, "To a Bride," from Walter Headlam; *A Book of Greek Verse*, published by the Cambridge University Press, England, and reprinted by permission of The Macmillan Company.

Virgil Markham; for Edwin Markham: "The Man with the Hoe," reprinted by permission.

Methuen & Company, Ltd.: for "Anpu and Bata," from Sir W. M. Flinders Petrie: *Egyptian Tales Translated from the Papyri*, by permission of Methuen & Company, Ltd.

The Moslem World: for Eric F. F. Bishop: "The Forty-Two Traditions of An-Nawawi," from *The Moslem World* for April, 1939.

John Murray: for Sa'di's "Alas!", from L. Cranmer-Byng: *Rose-Garden of Sa'di.*

New Directions: for "Tract" and "Classic Scene," from William Carlos Williams: *Complete Collected Poems;* for nine poems, Andrade's "Reaping the Barley" and "The Perfect Life," Carvalho's "Brazil," Fombona-Pochano's "A Warning for Abraham Lincoln," Lopez' "Country Girl, Don't Stay Away" and "Tropic Siesta," Marin's "Pamphlet," Novo's "The Departed Friend," and Silva's "Crossroads," all from Dudley Fitts: *Anthology of Latin-American Poetry.*

Paul Nixon: for Martial's "Unchanged," from Paul Nixon: *A Roman Wit.*

OXFORD UNIVERSITY PRESS (NEW YORK): for "The Starlit Night," from Gerard Manley Hopkins: *Poems,* 2nd Edition, copyright, 1937; for selections from Plotinus, from Grace H. Turnbull: *Essence: Extracts from the Six Enneads,* copyright, 1934. By permission of Oxford University Press, New York.

OXFORD UNIVERSITY PRESS (LONDON): for "The Quarrel," from Homer's *Iliad,* translated by Sir William Marris, 1934; for Boccaccio's "Olympia" (abridged), from Sir Israel Gollancz: *The Pearl;* for "A Talk among Leisured People," from Leo Tolstoy: *Works,* Vol. xv, translated by Alymer Maude, 1934. By permission of Oxford University Press, London.

CURTIS HIDDEN PAGE: for the translation of "The Summer's Revel," in his *Songs and Sonnets of Pierre de Ronsard.*

L. C. PAGE & COMPANY: for "The Young Ravens that Call upon Him," reprinted from Charles G. D. Roberts: *Earth's Enigmas,* by permission of the publisher, L. C. Page & Company.

EDMOND PAUKER, agent for Ferenc Molnár: for "Still Life," from *All the Plays of Molnár,* translated by Sanford J. Greenburger.

POET LORE: for Andreyev's "An Incident," translated by Leo Pasvolsky, (*Poet Lore* 1916); St. Francis' "Canticle of the Sun," translated by Eleanor L. Turnbull (1938); the Sapphic Fragment "Wormwood," translated by Randolph Shaffer, Jr. (1940); Jimenez's "What Becomes of a Strain of Music," translated by John Crow (1940); Du Bellay's sonnet "If of our life the span be not a day," translated by Eleanor L. Turnbull; and Dario's "Sonatina," translated by G. W. Humphrey and Laura Forsberg (1939).

PRINCETON UNIVERSITY PRESS: for "Twelve by the Clock," from Frances Avery Pleak: *Poems of Jorge Guillen;* for "The Illustrious Grand Vezir," from Walter Livingston Wright, Jr., Translator: *Ottoman Statecraft, the Book of Counsel for Vezirs and Governors, by Sari Mehmed Pasha.*

G. P. PUTNAM'S SONS: for the Dunkirk speech from Winston Churchill: *Blood, Sweat, and Tears,* copyright, 1941, by G. P. Putnam's Sons; for selections from *The Writings of Thomas Paine,* edited by Moncure D. Conway, reprinted by courtesy of G. P. Putnam's Sons.

RANDOM HOUSE, INC.: for Dostoyevsky's story "The Christmas Tree and the Wedding," translated by Thomas Selzer, from the Modern Library anthology *Best Russian Short Stories,* copyright, 1925, by Modern Library, Inc.; for "Landscape Near an Airdrome," from Stephen Spender: *Poems,* copyright, 1934, by Modern Library, Inc.; for "Steelhead," from Robinson Jeffers, copyright, 1938, by Robinson Jeffers: *Selected Poems;* for a selection from "The Magnetic Mountain," Part One, 5, from C. Day Lewis: *Collected Poems, 1929–1933,* copyright, 1946, by C. D. Lewis.

GEORGE ROUTLEDGE & SONS, LTD.: for selections from Chapter IX and Chapter XXIV of Bernal Diaz del Castillo: *The Discovery and Conquest of Mexico* (Broadway Travelers Series), translated by A. P. Maudsley, George Routledge & Sons, Ltd., publishers.

THE RYERSON PRESS: for "Stella Flammarum (to Halley's Comet)," from *The Collected Poems of William Wilfred Campbell.* By permission of the Ryerson Press.

CHARLES SCRIBNER'S SONS: for "Morning Song of Senlin," from "Senlin: a Biography," in Conrad Aiken: *Selected Poems,* 1931; for "The Defeat of the Armada," from James Anthony Froude: *English Seamen in the Sixteenth Century;* for Ikhnaton's "Hymn to the Sun," from James K. Breasted: *History of the Ancient Egyptians;* for selected passages from *The Travels of Marco Polo,* translated by Henry Yule; for "Hymn to Chance," from Phelps Putnam: *The Five Seasons;* for two translations, Alfred de Musset's "Souvenir" and Theophile Gautier's "Art," from George Santayana: *The Hermit of Carmel.*

Also, by courtesy of Charles Scribner's Sons as authorized publishers, Emil Verhaeren's "The Fishermen," translated by Jethro Bithell in *Anthology of Contemporary Belgian Poetry* (Scott Library); V. A. de la Montagne's "Congress, 1878," in Bithell's *Contemporary Flemish Poetry;* Arthur Rimbaud's "Waifs and Strays," in Bithell's *Anthology of Contemporary French Poetry;* Richard Dehmel's "The Laborer," in Bithell's *Contemporary German Poetry;* "Notes on Human Life," from *The Notebooks of Leonardo Da Vinci,* translated by Edward McCurdy; Heinrich Heine's "With Inky Sails," from his *Songs and Ballads,* translated by Sir Theodore Martin; "Preface to a New Philosophy," from George Santayana: *Scepticism and Animal Faith;* Morike's "Beauty Rothraut," from George Meredith: *Poetical Works;* for "The King of Yvetot," from William Toynbee: *Pierre Jean de Béranger;* for "The Provinces of the Several Arts," from J. A. Symonds: *Essays Speculative and Suggestive.*

SHEED AND WARD: for "Two Confessions, Envy and Wrath," from William Langland: *Piers Plowman*, newly rendered into modern English by Henry W. Wells (1945).

THE SLAVONIC AND EAST EUROPEAN REVIEW AND PROFESSOR S. H. CROSS: for Cyril Kristov's "Baba Meglena" (Slavonic Rev., Vol. IX), A. Dygasinski's "The Just Hare," translated by D. F. Tait (Vol. IX), Maria Konopnika's "Banasiowa," translated by N. B. Jopson (Vol. X), Vuk Karadzic's "Mujo the Drunkard," translated by N. B. Jopson (Vol. X), and Ivan Cankar's "Children and Old People," translated by A. J. Klanear and G. R. Noyes (Vol. XIII).

D. V. VAN NOSTRAND COMPANY, INC.: for Mussolini's "Address to the General Assembly of the National Council of Corporations, Nov. 14, 1933," from Herbert W. Schneider: *Source Book on European Governments: Sec. III,* Documents on the Fascist Government of Italy.

THE VIKING PRESS, INC.: for Emil Verhaeren's "The Mill," "November," and "The Poor," from Ludwig Lewisohn: *Poets of Modern France;* copyright, 1946, by Ludwig Lewisohn; for an excerpt from William Ellery Leonard: *Gilgamesh, Epic of Old Babylonia;* for "On the Way to Myself," from Marcus Ehrenpreis: *The Soul of the East,* translated from the Swedish by Alfhild Huebsch; all reprinted by permission of The Viking Press, Inc., New York.

MRS. HAYWARD WALLIS: for "The New Idea of the Universe," from Charles Glen Wallis's translation of Copernicus: *De Revolutionibus Orbium Coelestium,* copyright, 1939, by Charles Glen Wallis.

THE LATE H. G. WELLS: for his article "Air, Earth, and Mind," from the *Survey-Graphic,* December, 1937.

YALE UNIVERSITY PRESS: for selections from Edwin Hubble: *The Realm of the Nebulae,* published by the Yale University Press, 1936.

AVRAHM YARMOLINSKY AND BABETTE DEUTSCH: for Pushkin's "With Freedom's Seed," Lermontov's "A Sail," Tyutchev's "Silentium," Blok's "Russia," and Gastev's "We Grow Out of Iron," from their *Modern Russian Poetry.*

Index

~ ❁ ~

Authors' names are set in roman capitals; titles of selections, their more important sources, and of the parts of this book are set in italic; the first lines of poems in roman type.

A far sail shimmers, white and lonely, 395
A lovely woman rolls up, 795
A Man's a Man for A' That, 396
A power-house, 998
A rainy country this, that I am monarch of, —, 393
A silver-vested monkey trips, 822
A strange land holds thy bones; the Euxine sea, 730
A village where they ring, 728
A youthful mouse, not up to trap, 303
Address at Gettysburg, Lincoln, 949
Address to the Diet at Worms, Luther, 939
Address to the French National Assembly, 1848, Lamartine, 943
Adonais, 639
"Æ" (GEORGE WILLIAM RUSSELL), 784, 1085
Ae fond kiss, and then we sever, 817
Aeneid, The, 68
AESCHYLUS, 409, 553, 1045
AESOP, 95, 1045
After Apple-Picking, 996
Afterglow, The, 728
Agamemnon, 553
AGATHIAS SCHOLASTICUS, 729, 1045
Ah! gentle, fleeting, wavering sprite, 731
Ah, what avails the sceptered race, 733
Ah! what joy, the bagpipe and the flute, 927
AIKEN, CONRAD, 190, 1045
Alas! 728
Albatross, The, 175
ALEMÁN, MATEO, 855, 1045
All, All, 821
All things are current found, 189
All things are doubly fair, 421
All things he saw, even to the ends of the earth, 60
Although beneath this grave-mound thy white bones now are lying, 730
Am I alone, 315
An old charcoal seller, 383
ANACREON, 798, 1045
Anacreontic, 733
And did those feet in ancient time, 182
And dost thou faithlessly abandon me? 420
And here face down beneath the sun, 189
ANDRADA, JORGE CARRERA, 172, 985, 1045
ANDREYEV, LEONID, 599, 1046
AN-NAWAWI, 159, 1046
Anno 1829, 306
ANNUNZIO, GABRIELE D', 891, 927, 1046
Another age ground down by civil strife! 384
Anpu and Bata: The Tale of the Two Brothers, 828
Antique Harvesters, 426
Apochryphal New Testament, 449
Apologia Pro Vita Sua, 775
Apology and Death of Socrates, 435
APULEIUS, 837, 1046
Ariel, 30
ARISTOPHANES, 411, 1046
ARISTOTLE, 327, 656, 1046
Arms and the heroes signalised in fame, 77
Around the Horn, 260
Arrival of a Guest, The, 909
Art, 421
Art thou poor, yet hast thou golden slumbers? 922
As I walked down the waterside, 988
Ass in the Lion's Skin, 92
At first, in that place, at all times, above the earth, 48
At Memphis Station, 174
At My Father's Grave, 731

At the Mid Hour of Night, 798
At Thermopylæ, 729
Athenian Dead, The, 729
Attainment of Buddhaship, 126
Attic maid! with honey fed, 729
Aucassin and Nicolete, 505
Auguries of Innocence, 182
Autobiography of Benvenuto Cellini, 857
Avarice, 300
Avenge, O Lord, thy slaughtered saints, whose bones, 396
"Awake! The Day Is Coming Now," 386
Ayee! Ai! This is heavy earth on our shoulders, 404

Baba Meglena, 519
Babylon and Sion (*Goa and Lisbon*), 300
BACON, FRANCIS, 208, 1047
Ballad of Poor Chimneysweeps, 983
Ballad of the Bells, 927
Ballade of the Gibbet, 633
Banasiowa, 902
BASHO, MATSUO, 728, 1047
Baucis and Philemon, 914
BAUDELAIRE, CHARLES, 175, 304, 393, 821, 1047
Be silent, hidden, and conceal, 177
Beautiful Woman, The, 796
Beauty Rothraut, 819
Behind me dips eternity, 189
Behold, thou art fair, my love, 797
Being your slave what should I do but tend, 817
BELLAY, JOACHIM DU, 175, 925, 983, 1047
BENÉT, STEPHEN VINCENT, 84, 1047
Benevolence, 335
Bewildered Arab, The, 168
BÉRANGER, PIERRE JEAN DE, 926, 1048
BERNARD OF CLAIRVAUX, SAINT, 939, 1048
Bhagavad Gita, The, 119
Bible, The: Old Testament, 39, 142, 145, 496, 663, 797, 932; *New Testament*, 146, 149, 153
Bion, 625, 1048
BJÖRNSON, BJÖRNSTJERNE, 106, 186, 304, 1048
Black in the fog and in the snow, 304
Blacken thy heavens, Jove, 173
BLAKE, WILLIAM, 182, 312, 313, 924, 1048
Blest beyond earth's bliss, with heaven I deem him, 798
BLOK, ALEXANDER, 306, 1048
BOCCACCIO, GIOVANNI, 630, 849, 1049
BOETHIUS, 745, 1049
Bold Satirist, The, 287
Book of Ruth, 496
Books Which Have Influenced Me, 8
Born I was to be old, 733
Bought Locks, 731
Bowed by the weight of centuries he leans, 996
Boy and the Schoolmaster, The, 302
Boy, I hate their empty shows, 731
Brahma, 188
Brahmanism and Buddhism, 116
Brazil, 984
Bridal Hymn, 800
Bride, A, 730
Bridegroom none but death alone, 730
Bridge, The, 997
Bright Night, A, 796
Broom, The, 414
Brother Rabbit's Money Mint, 97
Brothers and men that shall after us be, 633
BROWNE, WILLIAM, 732, 1049
BROWNING, ROBERT, 313, 1049
BUCK, PEARL S., 537, 1049
BUDDHA, 129, 1049
Buddhism, see *Brahmanism and Buddhism*
Buddhist Aphorisms, 668
Bulkeley, Hunt, Willard, Hosmer, Meriam, Flint, 188
Burial Song, 728
BURNS, ROBERT, 313, 396, 817, 1049
Burying Ground by the Ties, 404
Business Men, 168
Business men boast of their skill and cunning, 168
But mortal man was then far hardier in the old champaign, 975
By day . . . tireless smokestacks . . . hungry shanties, 998
By right of fires that smelted ore, 988
By the rude bridge that arched the flood, 733
By way of pretext, 796
BYRON, GEORGE GORDON, LORD, 397, 818, 1050

CALLIMACHUS, 730, 1050
CAMOËNS, LUIS VAZ DE, 77, 300, 1050
CAMPANELLA, TOMMASO, 386, 1050
CAMPBELL, WILLIAM WILFRED, 187, 1050

CAMPION, THOMAS, 922, 1051
Candle of Vision, The, 784
CANKAR, IVAN, 108
Canterbury Tales (Prologue to), 297
Canticle of the Sun, 170
Cape Hatteras, 997
Captain, I have seen, 391
CARDUCCI, GIOSUÈ, 984, 1051
CARLYLE, THOMAS, 719, 1051
CARVALHO, RONALD DE, 984, 1051
Casting of the Perseus, The, 857
CATULLUS, 800, 1051
CELLINI, BENVENUTO, 857, 1052
CERVANTES SAAVEDRA, MIGUEL DE, 862, 1052
Character of Caesar, The, 454
Charcoal-Burner's Son, The, 986
Charcoal-Seller, The, 383
CHAUCER, GEOFFREY, 297, 1052
CH'ĒN TZU-ANG, 168
CH'ENG HSIAO, 282
CHIH MING, 168
Child in Our Soul, The, 186
Children, 913
Children and Old People, 108
Chinese Cinderella, The, 101
Chivalry, 893
CHOCANO, JOSÉ SANTOS, 417, 1052
Chorus from Hellas, 423
Chorus of Batavian Women, 418
Chorus of Birds, 411
Chorus of the Furies, 409
Christian Topography, 195
Christianity, see *Judaism and Christianity*
Christmas Tree and the Wedding, The, 885
CHUANG-TZE, 138, 1052
CHURCHILL, WINSTON, 964, 1052
CICERO, 331, 1053
Classic Scene, 998
CLAUDIANUS, CLAUDIUS, 917, 1053
CLAUDIUS, MATTHIAS, 731, 1053
Clean Curtains, 319
Cockerel, the Cat, and the Young Mouse, The, 303
Cocooning, The, 985
Columbus Sets Sail, 465
Come, and pass, and go, 728
Comedy of Manners, 595–622
Common Sense, 357
Communist Manifesto, 366
Complaint of the Fair Armoress, The, 807
Concord Hymn, 733
Conduct of a Successful Ruler, The, 337
Conduct of Life, The, 655–723
Confucianism and Taoism, 132
CONFUCIUS, 132, 1053
Congress: 1878, 393
Consolation of Philosophy, The, 745
Contacts of Races, 495–548
COPERNICUS, NIKOLAUS, 200, 1053
Cortège, 822
Content, 921
COSMAS INDICOPLEUSTES, 195, 1054
Country girl, don't stay away from the market, 928
Country Mouse and the Town Mouse, 95
CRANE, HART, 997, 1054
CREASY, SIR EDWARD S., 475, 1054
Creation, The, 39
Creative Design, 221
Creative Imagination, 165–191
Critical Intellect, The, 405–427
Crossing the Mountain Alone, 796
Crossroads, 391
Cupid and Psyche, 837
CURIE, EVE, 485, 1054

DAIHAKU, PRINCESS, 796
DANA, RICHARD HENRY, JR., 260, 1054
Dance by the Roadside, The, 820
DANTE ALIGHIERI, 384, 809, 1054
DARÍO, RUBÉN, 390, 818, 1055
Dark Princess, The, 543
DARWIN, CHARLES R., 217, 1055
DAUDET, ALPHONSE, 881, 1055
DAVIES, WILLIAM, 925, 988, 1055
DAVIS, JEFFERSON, 946, 1055
Dawn, 304
Dead Song-Writer, A, 730
Dear to me always was this lonely hill, 173
Death of Eve, The, 582
Death of Roland, The, 71
Death of Turnus, The, 68
Deathless Flower, A, 810
Decameron, The, 849
Declaration of Rights, 364
Declaration of the Rights of Man and of Citizens (French, 1789), 363
Deep in grey dusk the mill turns faltering, 985
Deep in the Siberian mine, 396
Defeat of the Armada, The, 459
DEHMEL, RICHARD, 927, 1056

DEKKER, THOMAS, 922, 1056
Departed Friend, The, 301
DESCARTES, RENÉ, 750, 1056
Dhammapada, The, 668
Diary of a Pilgrim to Ise, 248
DIAZ DEL CASTILLO, BERNAL, 251, 1056
DICKINSON, EMILY, 189, 734, 823, 1056
Discourse on Method, 750
Discovery, 400
Discovery of Radium, The, 485
Divine Comedy, The (*Purgatorio, VI*), 384
Doctrine of the Mean, The, 132
Domestic Scenes, 172
Don Juan, 397
Don Quixote, 862
DONNE, JOHN, 178, 1057
DOSTOIEVSKY, FEODOR M., 885, 1057
Dove and the Crow, The, 92
Downward was the wheeling Bear, 798
Drop of Dew, A, 179
DRYDEN, JOHN, 817, 1057
DU BOIS, WILLIAM E. BURGHARDT, 543, 1057
Dunkirk, 964
Dusk, 728
Duties of the Individual to the State, 331
DYGASIŃSKI, ADOLF, 99
Dynasts, The, 423
DYSON, EDWARD, 987

Earth, Air and Mind, 1015
Earth to Earth, 732
Earth took from earth earth with woe, 732
Earth's Holocaust, 1000
Ecclesiastes, 663
Eclipse, The, 899
EDWARDS, JONATHAN, 694, 1057
EEDEN, FREDERIK WILLEM VAN, 109, 1057
EHRENPREIS, MARCUS, 276, 1057
Elegy Written In a Country Church-yard, 645
Elysium is as far as to, 823
EMERSON, RALPH WALDO, 188, 317, 713, 733, 1058
Encheiridion, The, 671
Enfant Perdu, 394
English Bill of Rights, The, 351
Enneads, The, 741
Envy, 296
EPICTETUS, 671, 1058
Epistle to Dr. Arbuthnot, 307
Epistles to Lucilius (*XLI*), 739
Epitaph of Bion, 627
Epitaph for Lincoln, 734
Epithalamion, 811
Eternal Self, The, 119
EURIPIDES, 410, 799, 913, 1058
Eutychides is dead, and what is worse, 730
Even such is Time that takes in trust, 732
Evening, 728
Evening Hours of a Hermit, The, 701
Evening in May, 927
EVENUS, 729
Exploration of Space, The, 229
Ezekiel, 934

Facing Death, 168
Facism and the Corporations, 956
Factory Street in Daylight, 987
Fair Iris I love, and hourly I die, 817
Fair is her body, bright her eye, 807
Fall of Siegfried, The, 74
Fall of the Bastile, The, 470
Fallen Angels, The, 80
Families, when a child is born, 383
Farewell, thou child of my right hand, and joy, 732
Farewell to Nancy, 817
Farm Picture, A, 734
Father, The, 106
Father Andrea, 537
FERNÁNDEZ-GUARDIA, RICARDO, 893, 1059
Fickle Widow, A, 833
FILICAJA, VINCENZO DA, 386, 1059
Fire and Ice, 734
First Inaugural Address (*F. D. Roosevelt*), 961
First Pythian Ode of Pindar, The, 407
Fish Crier, 930
Fishermen, The, 305
Five Japanese Haiku, 728
Five oxen, grazing in a flowery mead, 729
Five Sonnets by Shakespeare, 816
Five Towns on the B. and O., 998
Flower Market, The, 383
Fog, 734
FOMBONA-PACHANO, JACINTO, 391, 1059
For hours without stopping, 290
Forget not yet the tried intent, 810
FORT, PAUL, 927, 1059
Forty-Two Traditions of An-Nawawi, The, 159

Foundations of the State, 321–380
FRANCE, ANATOLE, 499, 1059
FRANCIS OF ASSISI, SAINT, 170, 1059
FRANKLIN, BENJAMIN, 697, 1060
FRENEAU, PHILIP, 315, 400, 1060
Friar Lubin, 302
FRÖDING, GUSTAF, 820, 1060
From break of day, 909
From the solitary desert, 168
FROST, ROBERT, 734, 825, 996, 1060
FROUDE, JAMES ANTHONY, 459, 1060
FU HSÜAN, 283
Funeral Oration of Pericles, The, 935
Future and Past, 30

GASTEV, ALEXEY K., 986, 1061
Gaudeamus Igitur, 918
GAUTIER, THÉOPHILE, 421, 1061
GAY, JOHN, 311, 1061
GEIJER, ERIK GUSTAF, 986, 1061
Geneses: The Origins of Man and Life, 35–55
Genesis (*Old Testament*), 39
Georgics, The, Book IV, 980
GILBERT, W. S., 315, 1061
Gilgamesh, 60
GIUSTI, GUISEPPE, 388, 1068
Go, Soul, the body's guest, 307
GODWIN, WILLIAM, 364, 1062
GOETHE, JOHANN WOLFGANG VON, 173, 708, 731, 1062
Golden Age, The, 413
GÓNGORA Y ARGOTE, LUIS DE, 919, 1062
Gorgias' Farewell, 789
Government by Philosophers, 322
GRAY, THOMAS, 645, 1063
Great Episodes and Characters in History, 429–493
Great Retirement, The, 124
Green rushes with red shoots, 796
GREENE, ROBERT, 921, 1063
Grove of Colonus, The, 410
GUILLEN, JORGE, 172, 1063
GUINICELLI, GUIDO, 808, 1063
Gulistan, The, 683
Guzman de Alfarache, 855

Ha! whaur ye gaun, ye crowlin ferlie? 313
Had I but plenty of money, money enough and to spare, 313
HADRIAN, THE EMPEROR, 731, 1063
HAFIZ, 797, 1063
Half-awake and half-dozing, 174
Hamatreya, 188
HANSHIN, 728
Happiness, 930
Happy Heart, The, 922
Happy Life, The, 907–930
Happy the man, who his whole time doth bound, 917
Happy Ulysses, The, 925
Happy who like Ulysses, or that lord, 925
HARDY, THOMAS, 423, 1064
HARRIS, JOEL CHANDLER, 97, 1064
Harvest Song, 983
HAWTHORNE, NATHANIEL, 1000, 1064
HAZLITT, WILLIAM, 764, 1064
He first deceased; she for a little tried, 733
HEARN, LAFCADIO, 534, 1064
Heaven's power is infinite: earth, air, and sea, 914
Hebrew Prophets, The, 932
HEINE, HEINRICH, 306, 394, 732, 820, 1065
Hence, loathéd Melancholy, 923
HENRY, PATRICK, 941, 1065
HERACLITUS, 730
Here on the arid shoulder, 414
Here, where fecundity of Babel frames, 300
Hero, The, 891
HERODOTUS, 430, 1065
HERRICK, ROBERT, 733, 922, 1065
HESIOD, 972, 1065
Hidden lovers' woes, 806
His Chance in Life, 524
His Own True Wife, 806
History of Literature, The, 23
Hitopadesa, The, 94
HÖLDERLIN, FRIEDRICH, 173, 1066
HÖLTY, LUDWIG, 983, 1066
HOMER, 63, 1066
Honey-Farm, The, 980
HOPKINS, GERARD MANLEY, 187, 1066
HORACE, 285, 287, 288, 384, 412, 731, 803, 916, 1066
Horrors of Civil War, 384
Hound, A, 730
HOUSMAN, ALFRED EDWARD, 733, 1066
How Guzman Excited the Compassion of My Lord Cardinal, 855
How happy in his low degree, 916
How sad it is to be a woman! 283
How shall we summon you? 425

How swiftly it dries, 728
How tranquil is the life, 918
How will you manage, 796
Hsi P'ei Lan, 168
Hubble, Edwin P., 229, 1067
Hugo, Victor, 392, 393, 1067
Hymn to Chance, 425
Hymn to Christ, 178
Hymn to the Sun, 169
Hymn to the Winds, 983

I ask you, my friend, 909
I asked professors who teach the meaning of life, 930
I cease not from desire till my desire, 797
I crave an amplier, worthier sphere, 306
I gaze with grief upon our generation, 306
I have broken the rainbow, 390
I have walked and prayed for this young child an hour, 925
I know a Jew fish crier, 930
I know that I shall meet my fate, 400
I love a noble lady, 806
I love not wine; yet if thou'ldst make, 729
I love thee, pious ox, through whom my heart, 984
I on Hesiod idly browsing, 729
I said: All now complete! 172
I saw eternity, the other night, 178
I saw the moonlight before my couch, 728
I saw the ramparts of my native land, 389
I Serve, 806
I wander through each chartered street, 312
I weep, but with no bitterness I weep, 647
I weep for Adonais—he is dead! 639
I, who was the flower of my day among the beauties, 796
I will teach you my townspeople, 318
If I err not, the sylvan spirits rejoice, 630
If of our life the span be not a day, 175
If the red slayer think he slays, 188
Ikhnaton (Amenhotep IV), 169, 1067
Iliad, The, 63
Illustrious Grand Vezir, The, 344
Image of the Cave, The, 736
Imitation of Christ, The, 748
Immovable, unchanging, 820
In a valley of this restless mind, 177
In Freedom's War, of "Thirty Years" and more, 394
In Salamis, filled with the foaming, 410
In the east of the city, 168
In the Name of the People, 961
In the Royal City spring is almost over, 385
In the Twilight of the Gods, 534
In this hour of pure sunlight, 984
In what torn ship soever I embark, 178
Inaugural Address of Jefferson Davis, 946
Incident, An, 599
Indignation, 393
Infallibility, 775
Infinite, The, 173
Inoculation for Hydrophobia, 224
Intellectual Beauty, The, 743
Intimations of Immortality from Recollections of Early Childhood, 184
Irish Airman Foresees His Death, An, 400
Is Praxinoa at home? Dear Gorgo, yes! 283
Is there for honest poverty, 396
Isaiah, 145
It is humiliating, 798
It is morning, Senlin says, and in the morning, 190
It is springtime, to the south and north of my cottage the floods are out, 909
Italia! Oh Italia! thou who hast, 386
Italy, 386

Jackal, The, 94
James, William, 1009, 1067
Jami, 168, 1067
Japanese Poetry, 5
Jar, The, 603
Jataka Collections, The, 92, 124, 126
Jean de Meun, 293, 1067
Jeffers, Robinson, 823, 1068
Jensen, Johannes V., 174, 1068
Jeremiah, 932
Jerome, Saint, 846, 1068
Jiménez, Juan Ramón, 171, 1068
Joe Greene, 318
Joe Greene was a tom-cat, he had learned his manners, 318
John Brown, 84
Jonson, Ben, 732, 1068
Jonson, Ben, and Browne, William, 732, 1049, 1068
Joso, 728
Joubert, Joseph, 705, 1068
Journey to Brundusium, 285
Journey to Exeter, A, 311
Judaism and Christianity, 142

Just as my fingers on these keys, 191
Just Hare, The, 99
JUVENAL, 290, 1068

KAIBARA EKKEN, 5, 692, 1069
KARADŽIĆ, VUK, 105
KEATS, JOHN, 422, 818, 1069
King of the Rainy Country, The, 393
King of Yvetot, The, 926
Kingdom of God, The, 186
KIPLING, RUDYARD, 524, 889, 1069
KOLTZOV, ALEXEY V., 823, 1069
KONOPNICKA, MARIA, 902
Koran, The, 154
KRISTOV, CYRIL, 519

La Belle Dame Sans Merci, 818
LA FONTAINE, JEAN DE, 302, 303, 1069
Laborer, The, 927
Labour, 719
Ladies that have intelligence in love, 809
Lady, the sunlit hour is beautiful, 913
LAGERLÖF, SELMA, 899, 1069
Lais' Mirror, 729
Lake, The, 821
L'Allegro, 923
LAMARTINE, ALPHONSE MARIE LOUIS, 821, 943, 1070
Lament for Adonis, 625
LANDOR, WALTER SAVAGE, 733, 1070
Landscape Near an Aerodrome, The, 988
LANGLAND, WILLIAM, 296, 1070
Lao-Tzu, 728
Last March, The, 266
Last year we fought by the head-stream of the So-kan, 382
Late, 522
Latin Boy, The, 876
Leave a Kiss within the Cup, 729
LEEUWENHOEK, ANTHONY VAN, 210, 1070
Leisure, 925
LEÓN, LUIS PONCE DE, 170, 300, 918, 1070
LEONARDO DA VINCI, 690, 1070
LEOPARDI, GIACOMO, 173, 386, 414, 710, 1071
LERMONTOV, MIKHAIL YURYEVICH, 306, 395, 1071
Lesser Testament, The, 294
Let me go warm and merry still, 919
Let those love now, who never loved before, 803
Let those who are in favor with their stars, 816
Let us be off! Our steam, 988
Let us live then and be glad, 918
Letrilla: The Lord of Dollars, 301
LEWIS, CECIL DAY, 988, 1071
LI PO, 168, 382, 728, 795, 1071
Lie, The, 307
Life and Letters of Charles Darwin, 221
Life Removed, The, 918
LINCOLN, ABRAHAM, 949, 1071
LINNAEUS, 214, 256, 1072
Literature as Revelation, 11
London, 312
Loneliness, 728
Long Old Road in China, The, 272
Look at the stars! look, look up at the skies! 187
Look! I stand among work-benches, 986
Look round the habitable world, how few, 290
Look, sisters, look! 409
LÓPEZ, LUIS CARLOS, 390, 928, 1072
Lord, Thou hast given me a cell, 922
Lost at Sea, 730
Love, 799
Love at the lips was touch, 825
Love I proclaim, the vagrant child, 799
Love Sleeping, 799
Love the Vagrant, 799
Love, under thy dominion unbending hearts bow low, 799
Love's Terror, 796
Lucian, 729, 1072
LUCILIUS, 730, 1072
LUCRETIUS, 975, 1072
Lumbermen, The, 989
Lusiad, The, 77
LUTHER, MARTIN, 939, 1072
Lycidas, 637

MACHIAVELLI, NICCOLO, 337, 1073
MACLEISH, ARCHIBALD, 189, 404, 1073
Man Against Fate, 549–593
Man and His Cultural Heritages, 3–34
Man and the Machine, The, 988
Man at Work, 969–998
Man in Bereavement, 623–654
Man in Love, 793–825
Man With the Hoe, The, 996
MANRIQUE, GÓMEZ, 389, 1073

Manrique, Jorge, 633, 1073
Marcus Argentarius, 729, 1074
Marcus Aurelius, 675, 1074
Marín, Luis Muñoz, 390, 1074
Markham, Edwin, 996, 1074
Marmontel, Jean François, 470, 1074
Marot, Clément, 302, 731, 1074
Martial, 290, 731, 916, 1074
Marvell, Andrew, 179, 1074
Marx, Karl Heinrich, 366, 1075
Massachusetts to Virginia, 402
Matavulj, Simo, 876
Matin-Song, 806
Mazzini, Giuseppe, 950, 1075
Means to Attain a Happy Life, The, 916
Medici, Lorenzo de', 920, 1075
Medieval Christian World, 195
Meditations, 675
Meinloh von Sevelingen, Sir, 806, 1075
Meleager, 730, 799, 1075
Memnon the Philosopher, or Human Wisdom, 874
Men of England, wherefore plough, 400
Men talk of those the fields that till, 983
Mencius, 335, 1075
Meseemeth I heard cry and groan, 807
Message to Siberia, 396
Metamorphoses, (Ovid), 914
Metamorphoses, or the Golden Ass, (Apuleius), 837
Method of Inductive Science, The, 208
Michelangelo, 810, 1076
Middle Doctrine, The, 131
Mill, The, 985
Mille, Pierre, 527, 1076
Milton, John, 80, 347, 396, 637, 923, 1076
Mirèio, The, 985
Mistral, Frédéric, 985, 1076
Mohammed, 154, 1076
Mohammedanism, 154
Molnár, Ferenc, 613, 1076
Mommsen, Theodor, 454, 1077
Montagne, de la, Victor Alexis, 393
Moody, William Vaughn, 582, 1077
Moore, Merrill, 318, 1077
Moral Equivalent of War, The, 1009
More beautiful and soft than any moth, 988
Mori Ogwai, 532, 1077
Mörike, Eduard F., 819, 1077
Morning Bell of Fang T'a, 168
Morning Song from "Senlin," 190
Moschus, 627, 1077
Motives of Proteus, 789
Motokiyo, 597
Mountains and plains, 728
Mournfully answer my groan, dark vales and Dorian water, 627
Mujo the Drunkard, 105
Murray, Gilbert, 11, 1077
Musset, Alfred de, 647, 1077
Mussolini, Benito, 956, 1077
My ceiling shows not brave, 412
My existence in the world has been, 168
My father he's at the kiln away, 986
My father was a soldier young, the finest you might see, 395
My heart aches, and a drowsy numbness pains, 422
My husband is far, far away, 795
My long two-pointed ladder's sticking through a tree, 996
Myths, Fables, and Allied Forms, 91–113

Napoleon writes me, 301
Nature of Democracy, The, 327
Nefarious War, The, 382
Neidhart von Reuental, Sir, 918, 1078
New Life, The, 809
New neighbors came to the corner house, 319
New-Year's Eve Confession, A, 897
Newman, John Henry, 775, 1078
Nibelungenlied, The, 74
Nietzsche, Friedrich, 376, 1078
Night of Sorrow, The, 795
Night Serene, The, 170
No sky at all, 728
Nocturne, 650
Notes on Human Life, 690
November, 176
Novo, Salvador, 301, 1078
Novum Organum, 208
Now in the Mayday twilight, 927
Now Turnus rolls aloof o'er empty plains, 68
Now winter nights enlarge, 922
Now Wrath awoke with white eyes staring, 296
Nurse's Song, 924

O Golden Lyre, who art Phoebus' treasure, 407
O Italy, I see the lonely towers, 386
O, let the soul her slumbers break, 633
O Love! O Glory! what are ye who fly, 397

O lovely age of gold! 413
O Most High, Omnipotent, Good Lord, 170
O never say that I was false of heart, 817
O servant of God's holiest charge, 180
O what can ail thee, knight-at-arms, 818
O world invisible, we view thee, 186
Observations on Animalculae, 210
Ode Inscribed to W. H. Channing, 317
Ode on the Death of His Father, 633
Ode to a Nightingale, 422
O'er all the hill-tops, 731
Of Human Progress, 975
Of man's first disobedience, and the fruit, 80
Of the Gentle Heart, 808
Of the Greatest Good, 745
Of the Nature of Things, 975
Of the Royal Way of the Holy Cross, 748
Oh! but my mind is weary! 926
Old Man of Verona, The, 917
Olympia, 630
OMAR KHAYYÁM, 909, 1078
On a bull's hollow horn, 985
On a fine Sunday morning I mounted my steed, 315
On a Quiet Night, 728
On a Seal, 729
On Books, 5
On Dirphys' wrinkled slope we fell, 729
On My First Son, 732
On summer nights when moonbeams flow, 987
On the Bad Government of Toledo, 389
On the Birth of his Son, 383
On the Countess of Pembroke, 732
On the Death of Dr. Swift, 310
On the Feeling of Immortality in Youth, 764
On the God Within Us, 739
On the Hon. Simon Harcourt, 733
On the Late Massacre in Piedmont, 396
On the Soul, 731
On the Way to Myself, 276
One night, 650
Only walls. No grass, nor glass, 987
Order of Rank, The, 376
Origin of Government, 347
Origin of Species, The, 217
Ours was a happy lot, 418
Outside the barracks now the bugle called, and woke, 304
Over kings and priests and scholars, 301
Overworld, The, 423
OVID, 802, 914, 1079
Ox, The, 984
Oyster and the Litigants, The, 303

PAINE, THOMAS, 357, 1079
Pamphlet, 390
Panchatantra, The, 92
Panegyric of Birds, 710
Paradise Lost, 80
PARINI, GIUSEPPE, 920, 1079
PASCAL, BLAISE, 756, 1079
Pass On, 730
Passage to India, 77
Passing Away, 729
PASTEUR, LOUIS, 224, 1079
PAUL, SAINT, 153, 1080
Peace now and ever on this gravestone be, 731
People, The, 386
People have teased and vexed me, 820
People's Story, The, 57–90
Perfect Life, The, 172
Persian Fopperies, 731
PESTALOZZI, JOHANN HEINRICH, 701, 1080
Peter Quince at the Clavier, 191
PETRARCH, 810, 1080
PHAEDRUS, 95, 1080
Philosophy of Chuang-Tze, The, 138
PHOCYLIDES, 729, 1080
Picnic Boat, The, 930
Pier, The, 532
PINDAR, 407, 1081
PIRANDELLO, LUIGI, 603, 1081
PLATO, 36, 322, 435, 729, 730, 736, 799, 1081
PLOTINUS, 741, 743, 1081
Plucking the Rushes, 796
PO CHÜ-I, 383, 728, 1081
Political Chaos in Italy, 384
Political Satire, 381–404
Politics, The, (Aristotle), 327
POLO, MARCO, 236, 1082
Poor, The, 393
POPE, ALEXANDER, 307, 733, 1082
Pope's Mule, The, 881
Portugal's ships in vain, 300
PRATT, EDWIN JOHN, 988, 1082
Prayer for My Daughter, A, 925
Preface to a New Philosophy, 787
PRESCOTT, WILLIAM H., 465, 1082
Pretext, 796

Prince, The, 337
Procurator of Judea, The, 499
Prologue to the Canterbury Tales, 297
Prometheus, 173
Prose Edda, The, 42
Protagoras Myth, The, 36
Provinces of the Several Arts, The, 17
Psalms of David, The, 142
PUSHKIN, ALEXANDER, 395, 396, 928, 1082
PUTNAM, PHELPS, 425, 1082

Quarrel, The, 63
Quest Begins, The, 109
Questions Which Tend Not to Edification, 129
QUEVEDO Y VILLEGAS, FRANCISCO DE, 301, 389, 1082
Quia Amore Langueo, 177
Quiet, 728

Rabbit: timid brother! My teacher and philosopher! 172
RAISIN, ABRAHAM, 522
RALEIGH, SIR WALTER, 307, 732, 1083
RANSOM, JOHN CROWE, 426, 1083
Reading Hesiod, 729
Realization of the Infinite, The, 779
Realm of the Nebulae, The, 229
Reaping the Barley, 985
Recitation and Song, from "Patience," 315
Reflections and Maxims of Goethe, 708
Relations, 302
Relations mine (if any still remain), 302
Republic, The, 322, 736
Resolutions of Jonathan Edwards, 694
Retrospect, 784
Revenge, 803
Revery of a Business Man, 916
Revolutions of the Celestial Spheres, The, 200
Riders to the Sea, 577
Rights of Man, The, 357
RILKE, RAINER MARIA, 174, 1083
RIMBAUD, ARTHUR, 304, 1083
Road to the West, The, 272
ROBERTS, CHARLES G. D., 104, 1083
RODÓ, JOSÉ, ENRIQUE, 30, 789, 1084
Romance of the Rose, 293
RONSARD, PIERRE DE, 926, 1084
ROOSEVELT, FRANKLIN DELANO, 961, 1084
Rose Aylmer, 733
ROUSSEAU, JEAN JACQUES, 352, 760, 1084
Rubaiyat of Omar Khayyám, The, 909
RUNEBERG, JOHAN LUDVIG, 395, 1084
RUSSELL, GEORGE WILLIAM ("Æ"), 784, 1085
Russia, 306

Sabbath-Day Chace, 315
Sadhana, 779
SA'DI, 683, 728, 1085
Sail, A, 395
SAKA, 248
SANDBURG, CARL, 319, 734, 930, 998, 1085
SANTAYANA, GEORGE, 787, 1085
SAPPHO, 728, 798, 1085
SARI MEHMED PASHA, 344
Satire on Paying Calls, 282
Savoyard Vicar's Creed, The, 760
Scepticism and Animal Faith, 787
SCHILLER, FRIEDRICH VON, 420, 1085
SCOTT, CAPTAIN ROBERT F., 266, 1086
Scriptures of Some Living Religions, 115–163
Sealed in Vain, 732
Second Inaugural Address, (Lincoln), 949
See how the orient dew, 179
Self Reliance, 713
SENECA, 739, 1086
Sex of Plants, The, 214
Shady, shady the wood in front of the Hall, 909
SHAKESPEARE, WILLIAM, 732, 816, 921, 1086
Shall we make love, 796
She walks in beauty like the night, 818
She, who could neither rest nor sleep, 728
SHELLEY, PERCY BYSSHE, 400, 423, 639, 1087
SHELLEY, P. B., and GODWIN, WILLIAM, 364
Shipwreck of Simonides, The, 95
Shut, shut the door, good John! fatigued, I said, 307
Sickles sound, 983
SIDNEY, SIR PHILIP, 810, 1087
Siege of Ismail, 397
Silent Hour, 174
Silentium, 177
SILVA, JOSÉ ASUNCIÓN, 650, 1087
SILVA, MIGUEL OTERO, 391, 1087
SIMONIDES, 729, 730, 1087
Sing, Goddess, of Achilles, Peleus' son, 63
Six thousand years in these dull regions pass'd, 400

Sleepers, The, 988
Slowly, Slowly, 802
Small City on a Rock, A, 729
SMART, CHRISTOPHER, 180, 1087
SNORRI STURLUSON, 42, 1088
Social Contract, The, 352
Social Intercourse, 692
Social Satire, 279–319
Soldier Boy, The, 395
Solitude, 773
Some say the world will end in fire, 734
Some Sayings and Discourses of Jesus, 146
Sometimes, to entertain themselves, the men of the crew, 175
Sonatina, 818
Song, 810
Song from Amphitryon, 817
Song from Milton, 182
Song of Autumn, 732
Song of Fate, 173
Song of Roland, The, 71
Song of Songs, The, 797
Song of the Broad-Axe, 990
Song of the Nibelungs, 74
Song to David, 180
Song to the Men of England, 400
Sonnet: Death Warnings, 389
Sonnet: "If of our life," 175
SOPHOCLES, 410, 1088
Soul of the East, The, 276
Sound, sound forever, clarions of thought! 392
Souvenir, 647
Spaniards in Mexico, The, 251
Sparta, 728
Spear-points of young men blossom there, 728
Speech in the Virginia Convention, 941
SPENDER, STEPHEN, 988, 1088
SPENSER, EDMUND, 811, 1088
Star, 730
Star Family, or the Celestial Sisters, The, 96
Starlit Night, The, 187
Steelhead, 823
Stella Flammarum (to Halley's Comet), 187
STEVENS, WALLACE, 191, 1088
STEVENSON, ROBERT LOUIS, 8, 1089
Still Life, 613
Story of Griselda, The, 849
Story of Malchus, The, 846
Story of Svetaketu, The, 116
Strange wanderer out of the deeps, 187
Stranger, where thy feet now rest, 410
Stream of Story Telling, The, 827–906
SU TUNG-P'O, 383
Success, 909
SUDERMANN, HERMANN, 897, 1089
Sultry Sunday, noon, 390
Summer's Revel, The, 926
Summum Bonum, 656
Sun Goddess and the Mikado, The, 52
Sunday night and the park policemen tell each other, 930
Supplication, A, 810
Swallow, A, 729
Sweet are the thoughts that savour of content, 921
Sweet, be not proud of those two eyes, 733
SWIFT, JONATHAN, 310, 1089
Sylvan Ode, 417
SYMONDS, JOHN ADDINGTON, 17, 1089
SYNGE, JOHN MILLINGTON, 577, 1089
Syracusan Women, The, 283

TAGORE, SIR RABINDRANATH, 779, 1089
TAINE, HIPPOLYTE, 23, 1090
Takasago, 597
Take, O take those lips away, 732
Taking of Lungtungpen, The, 889
Talk Among Leisured People, A, 721
T'AO CH'IEN, 909
TASSO, TORQUATO, 413, 1090
TASSONI, ALESSANDRO, 302, 1090
Tawny are the leaves turned, but they still hold, 426
Teaching of Mohammed, The, 154
Tell them in Lakedaimon, passer-by, 729
Tenth Satire of Juvenal, The, 290
Tenure of Kings and Magistrates, 347
Terpander, 728, 1090
Thanksgiving to God, for His House, A, 922
The blast from Freedom's Northern hills, upon its Southern way, 402
The Curfew tolls the knell of parting day, 645
The Devil up my attic stair, 821
The fog comes, 734
The gifts of heav'n my foll'wing song pursues, 980
The gods have heard me, Lyce, 803
The golden hair that Gulla wears, 731
The Heaven's angry face is scowling, 928

The highways run in figure of the rood, 176
The nasal whine of power whips a new universe, 997
The old man's fair-haired consort, whose dewy axle-tree, 802
The people is a beast of muddy brain, 386
The princess is sad. What brings tears to her eyes? 818
The sky was cold December blue, 823
The summer grasses grow, 728
The sun in the heavens, 823
The things that make a life to please, 916
The time is not remote when I, 310
The warder, from his watch-tower high, 806
The world is fleeting; all things pass away, 729
The world's great age begins anew, 423
Then hate me when thou wilt; if ever, now, 817
THEOCRITUS, 283, 1090
THEODORIDES, 730, 1090
Theory of Evolution, The, 217
There are, to whom too poignant I appear, 287
There flourished once a potentate, 926
There is a lady conquering with glances, 806
There was a child went forth every day, 929
There was a time when meadow, grove and stream, 184
Thermopylae, 430
They danced by the roadside on Saturday night, 820
They reached the Maryland bridge of Harper's Ferry, 84
They say there is, 797
They sit at the green baize table, 393
They told me, Heraclitus, they told me you were dead, 730
They were at play, she and her cat, 822
This also said Phocylides, 729
This dust was once the man, 734
This fourteen six and fiftieth year, 294
This was of old my wishes' utmost bound, 288
THOMAS À KEMPIS, 748, 1090
THOMPSON, FRANCIS, 186, 1091
THOREAU, HENRY DAVID, 189, 768, 1091
Those who speak know nothing, 728
Thou, Hesper, bringest homeward all, 728
Thou of the hill Heliconian, 800
Thou that from the heavens art, 731
Thou wert the morning-star among the living, 730
Thou who loved Juvenal, and filed, 393
Though loath to grieve, 317
Thought, A, 306
Thoughts of Joubert, 705
Thoughts of Pascal, 756
Three with the Moon and His Shadow, 168
Through the ample open door of the peaceful country barn, 734
THUCYDIDES, 935, 1091
Thus doth the Great Foresightless mechanize, 424
Thus sailing, sailing on forevermore, 821
Thy dawning is beautiful in the horizon of heaven, 169
Tiger, The, 182
'Tis only with the Bible or with Walt Whitman's verse, 390
To a Bride, 798
To a Louse on Seeing One on a Lady's Bonnet in Church, 313
To Anne, 731
To Dianeme, 733
To Earthward, 825
To gallop off to town post-haste, 302
To Italy, 386
To Make a Prairie, 734
To Roosevelt, 390
To see a world in a grain of sand, 182
To sin, unshamed, to lose, unthinking, 306
To the Italian Working-Men, 950
To this sad shrine, whoe'er thou art! draw near, 733
To you, who troop so fleet, 983
TOLSTOY, COUNT LEO, 721, 1091
Tomb of a shipwrecked mariner am I, 730
Tour in Lapland, A, 256
Toward God in heaven spacious, 186
Town and the Country Mouse, The, 288
Tract, 318
Travel and Exploration, 235–278
Travels of Marco Polo, 236
Trial of Jesus, The, 449
Tropic Siesta, 390
Troy, 410
True Happiness, 741
Trumpets of the Mind, The, 392
TSURAKUYI, KI NO, 5, 168, 1091
TU FU, 796, 909, 1091
'Twas a long journey lay before us, 285

Twelve by the Clock, 172
Two Confessions, 296
Two pilgrims on the sand espied, 303
Two Songs by Heine, 820
Two Years Before the Mast, 260
Tyger, tyger: burning bright, 182
TYUTCHEV, FYODOR I., 177, 1092

UNAMUNO, MIGUEL DE, 172, 773, 1092
Unchanged, 290
Under the greenwood tree, 921
Underneath this sable hearse, 732
Unfolding Universe, The, 193–233
Universal Self, The, 37
Unreal! 168
Unrealities, The, 420
Up at a Villa – Down in the City, 313
Up from the sea a flaky, dank, 305
Upanishads, The, 37, 116
Upon the Death of Sir Albert Morton's Wife, 733
Utopian Dream, The, 999–1021

Vanity of Riches, 412
VAUGHAN, HENRY, 178, 1092
Venus, take my votive glass, 729
VERHAEREN, EMIL, 176, 305, 393, 985, 1092
VERLAINE, PAUL, 732, 822, 1092
Victory, 527
Victory of the Americans Over Burgoyne at Saratoga, 475
Vigil of Venus, The, 803
VILLON, FRANÇOIS, 294, 633, 807, 983, 1092
VIRGIL, 68, 980, 1093
Voices of the Forum, 931–968
VOLTAIRE, FRANÇOIS MARIE AROUET DE, 874, 1093
VONDEL, JOOST VAN DEN, 418, 1093

Waifs and Strays, 304
Wail, wail, Ah for Adonis! He is lost to us, lovely Adonis! 625
Wake, The, 168
Wake! For the Sun, who scattered into flight, 909
Walam Olum, The, 48
Walden, 768
WALTHER VON DER VOGELWEIDE, 386, 806, 1093
Wanderer's Night-Songs, 731
WANG CHI, 909
WARNER, LANGDON, 272, 1093
Warning for Abraham Lincoln, A, 391
Way of Contentment, The, 5
Way to Wealth, The, 697
We Grow Out of Iron, 986
We have a bed, and a baby too, 927
We were shut off from the street, 391
Weapon shapely, naked, wan, 990
WELLS, H. G., 1015, 1093
What becomes of a strain of music, 171
What is the name of King Ringang's daughter? 819
What is this life if, full of care, 925
When a sighing begins, 732
When, Atlas born, the Pleiad stars arise, 972
When I contemplate o'er me, 170
When I heard the learn'd Astronomer, 188
When I was young, throughout the hot season, 282
When Lilacs Last in the Dooryard Bloomed, 651
When mighty Rome was conqueror, 389
When shades of night have come, 172
When that sweet April showers with downward shoot, 297
When the crop is fair in the olive-yard, 985
When the voices of children are heard on the green, 924
When thou art near to me, it seems, 731
When to the sessions of sweet silent thought, 816
Where I Lived and What I Lived For, 768
While you, my lord, bid stately piles ascend, 311
Whirlpool, 797
WHITMAN, WALT, 188, 651, 734, 929, 990, 1094
WHITTIER, JOHN GREENLEAF, 402, 989, 1094
"Who is it that, this dark night," 810
Who wishes to behold the utmost might, 810
Whoever weeps somewhere out in the world, 174
Why Another Crusade? 939
Wife, The, 795
Wildly round our woodland quarters, 989
Will to Power, The, 376
WILLIAMS, WILLIAM CARLOS, 318, 998, 1094
Winter, 728
Winter Evening, 928
Winter-Time, 918
Winter, we are by thy might, 918
Wise counsel is not always wise, 302

Wit and Epigram, 725–734
With a jar of wine I sit by the flowering trees, 168
With an heavy heart Envy asked pardon, 296
With dreams of wealth and fame, 920
With freedom's seed the desert sowing, 395
With hearts of poor men it is so, 393
With inky sails my pinnace drives, 732
With rue my heart is laden, 733
Within the covert of a shady grove, 799
Within the gentle heart Love shelters him, 808
Wolfram von Eschenbach, Sir, 806, 1094
Woman, 283
Woman and Cat, 822
Woods of my fathers, sovereign deity, 417
Wordsworth, William, 184, 1095
Worked-out Mine, The, 987
Works and Days, 972
World, The, 178
Worlds of the Mind and Spirit, 735–791
Wormwood, 798
Wotton, Sir Henry, 733, 1095
Wrath, 296
Wyatt, Sir Thomas, 810, 1095

Yaha, 728
Yakamochi, 796
Ye learnèd sisters, which have oftentimes, 811
Ye men who are dimly existing below, 411
Yeats, William Butler, 400, 925, 1095
Yes! hope may with my strong desires keep pace, 810
Yet once more, O ye laurels, and once more, 637
Yonder there behold! a soul that stationed, 384
You, Andrew Marvell, 189
You are like the lightning, 796
You walk up there in the light, 173
Young Ravens That Call Upon Him, The, 104
Young Reaper, The, 823
Your Excellency, who eyes me with disfavour, 388
Youth is sweet and well, 920

Zech, Paul, 987, 1095
Zeuxis, the painter, strove in vain, 293